Street by Str[...]

LONDON

C000071825

7th edition April 2012

Original edition printed May 2001

Published by AA Publishing (a trading name of AA Media Limited, whose registered office is Fanum House, Basing View, Basingstoke, Hampshire RG21 4EA. Registered number 06112600).

Produced by the Mapping Services Department of The Automobile Association. (A04695)

A CIP Catalogue record for this book is available from the British Library.

Printed by Oriental Press in Dubai

Ref: ML038u

Key to map pages ii–iii
Key to map symbols iv–1
Enlarged map pages 2–19
Main map pages 20–217
Index – towns & villages 218
Index – streets 220–308
Index – featured places 308–332
Acknowledgements 332

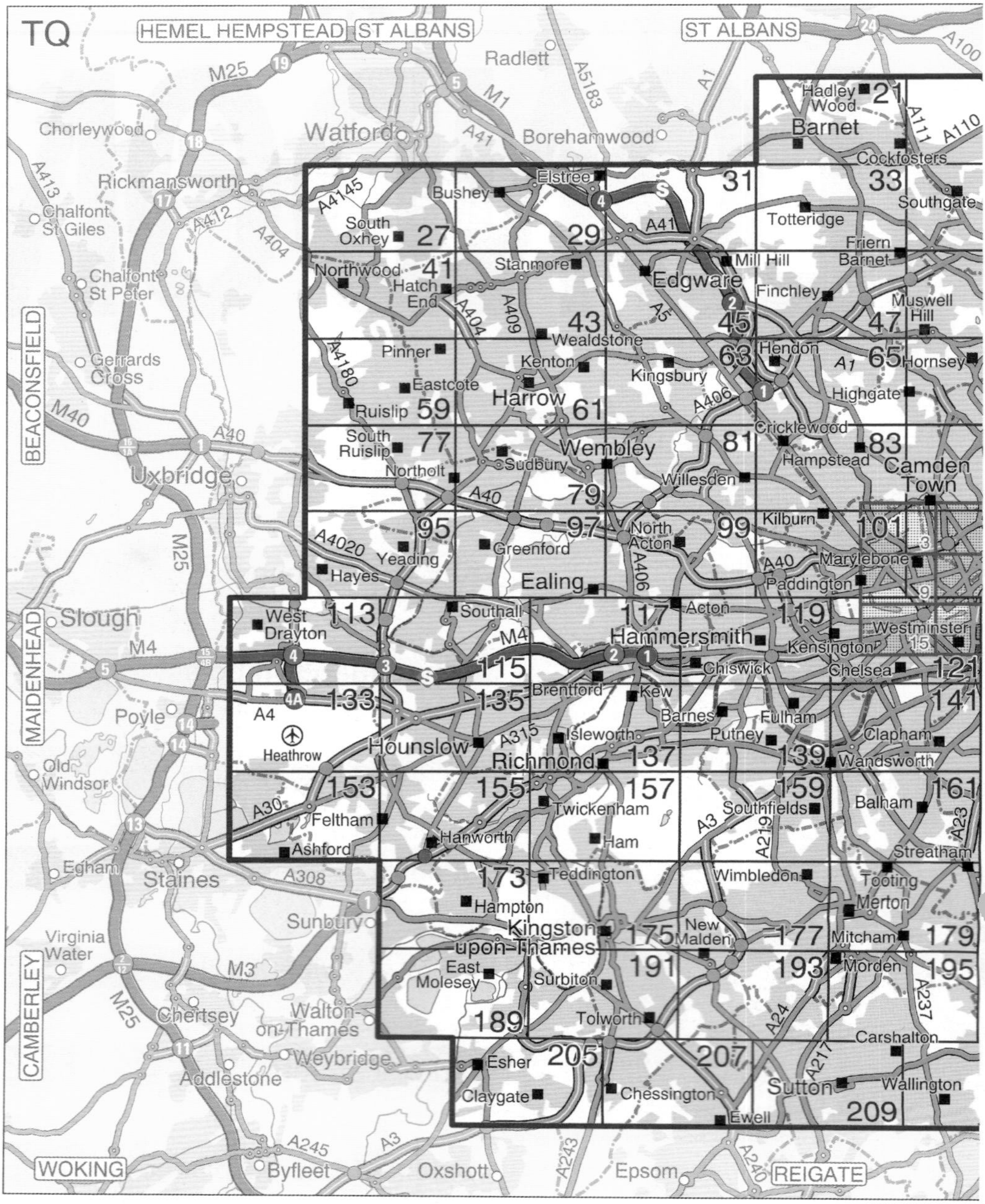

TQ
HEMEL HEMPSTEAD
ST ALBANS
Radlett
A5183
A1
ST ALBANS
A100
M25
M1
Chorleywood
Watford
A41
Borehamwood
Hadley Wood 21
Barnet
A111
A110
Cockfosters
A413
Rickmansworth
A4145
Bushey
Elstree
31
33
Southgate
Chalfont St Giles
A412
A404
South Oxhey 27
29
A41
Totteridge
Chalfont St Peter
Northwood 41
Hatch End
Stanmore
Edgware
Mill Hill
Finchley
Friern Barnet
Muswell Hill
A404
A409
43
A5
45
47
Wealdstone
BEACONSFIELD
Gerrards Cross
A4180
Pinner
Kenton
Kingsbury
63
Hendon
A1
65
Hornsey
Eastcote
Harrow
A406
Highgate
M40
Ruislip 59
61
Cricklewood
A40
South Ruislip 77
Wembley
81
83
Camden Town
Sudbury
Hampstead
Uxbridge
Northolt
Willesden
A40
79
M25
95
97
99
Kilburn
101
A4020
Yeading
Greenford
North Acton
A406
A40
Marylebone
Hayes
Ealing
Paddington
MAIDENHEAD
Slough
West Drayton 113
Southall
117
Acton
119
Westminster
M4
M4
Hammersmith
Kensington
115
Chiswick
Chelsea
121
A4
133
135
Brentford
Kew
141
Poyle
Barnes
Fulham
Heathrow
Hounslow
A315
Isleworth
Putney
Clapham
Old Windsor
Richmond
137
139
Wandsworth
153
155
157
159
161
A30
Feltham
Twickenham
A3
Southfields
Balham
Ashford
Hanworth
Ham
A219
A23
Egham
Streatham
Staines
A308
173
Teddington
Wimbledon
Tooting
Sunbury
Hampton
Merton
Virginia Water
Kingston upon Thames
175
New Malden
177
Mitcham
179
M3
East Molesey
191
193
Morden
195
CAMBERLEY
M25
Chertsey
Walton-on-Thames
Surbiton
A24
A237
189
Tolworth
A217
Carshalton
Weybridge
Esher 205
207
Addlestone
Sutton
Wallington
Claygate
Chessington
Ewell
209
A245
A3
A243
A240
WOKING
Byfleet
Oxshott
Epsom
REIGATE

Scale of enlarged map pages 1:10,000

6.3 inches to 1 mile

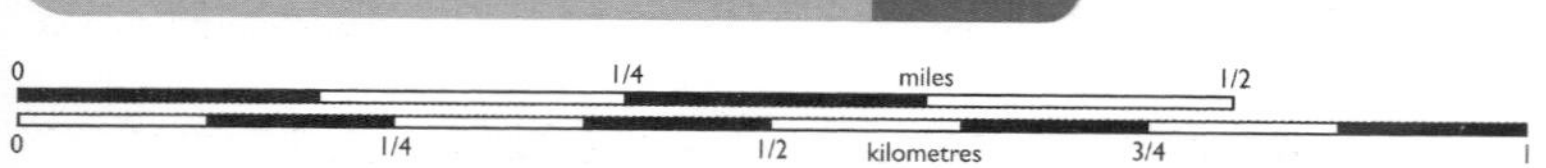

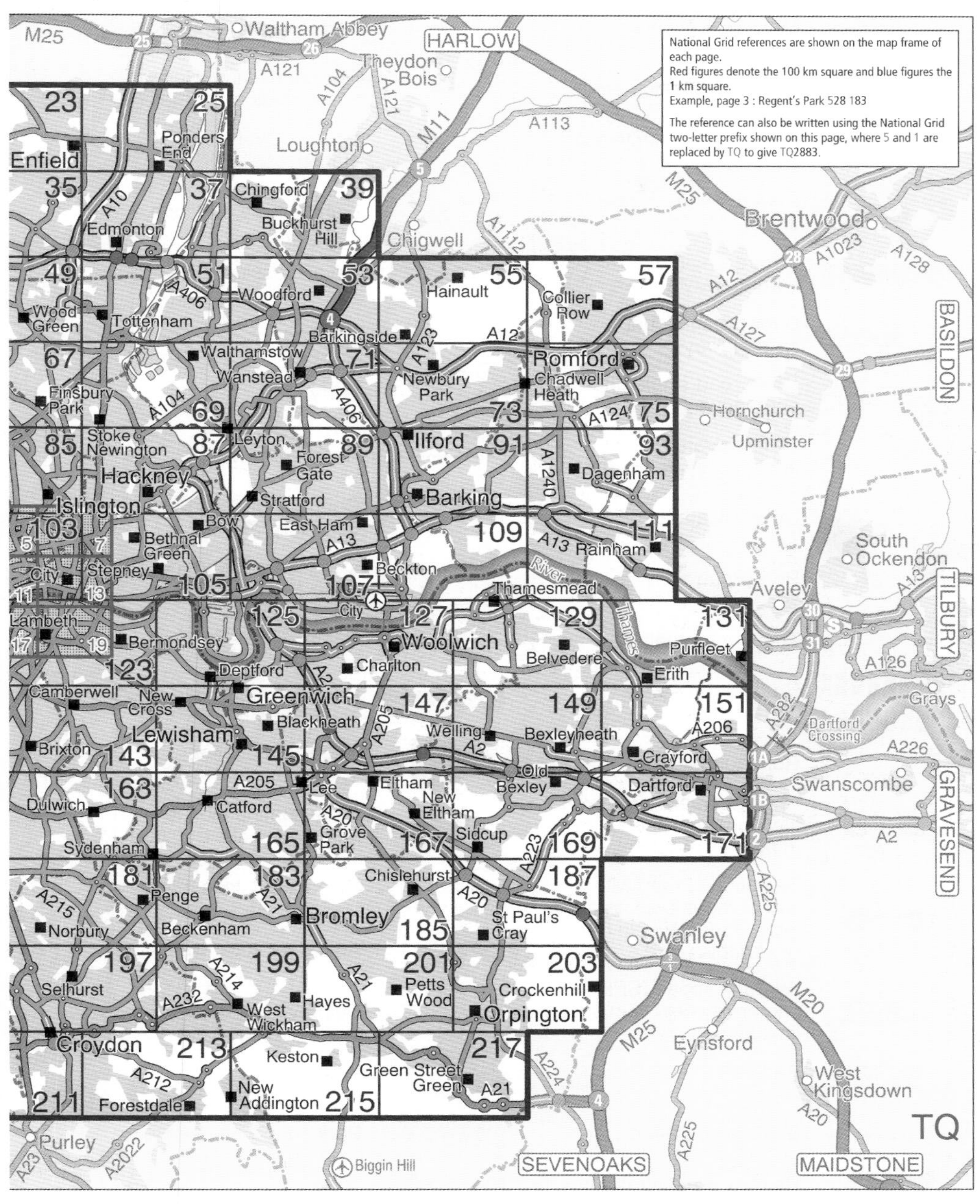

3.6 inches to 1 mile

Scale of main map pages **1:17,500**

0 1/2 miles 1

0 1/2 1 kilometres 1 1/2

Junction 9	Motorway & junction		Underground station
Services	Motorway service area		Docklands Light Railway (DLR) station
	Primary road single/dual carriageway		London Overground station
Services	Primary road service area		Light railway & station
	A road single/dual carriageway	LC	Level crossing
	B road single/dual carriageway		Tramway
	Other road single/dual carriageway		Ferry route
	Minor/private road, access may be restricted		Airport runway
	One-way street		County, administrative boundary
	Pedestrian area		Congestion Charging Zone *
	Track or footpath		Olympic Park Boundary
	Road under construction		Low Emission Zone (LEZ) (visit **theaa.com** for further information)
	Road tunnel	17	Page continuation 1:17,500
30 V	Speed camera site (fixed location) with speed limit in mph or variable	3	Page continuation to enlarged scale 1:10,000
40 V	Selection of road with two or more fixed camera sites; speed limit in mph or variable		River/canal, lake, pier
50 50	Average speed (SPECS™) camera system with speed limit in mph		Aqueduct, lock, weir
P P+	Parking, Park & Ride		Beach
	Bus/coach station		Woodland
	Railway & main railway station		Park
	Railway & minor railway station		Cemetery
			Built-up area

* The AA central London Congestion Charging map is also available

	Industrial/business building
	Leisure building
	Retail building
	Other building
	City wall
A&E	Hospital with 24-hour A&E department
PO	Post Office, public library
	Tourist Information Centre, seasonal
	Petrol station, 24 hour Major suppliers only
	Church/chapel
	Public toilets, with facilities for the less able
PH	Public house AA recommended
	Restaurant AA inspected
Madeira Hotel	Hotel AA inspected
	Theatre or performing arts centre, cinema
	Golf course
	Camping AA inspected
	Caravan site AA inspected
	Camping & caravan site AA inspected
	Theme park
	Abbey, cathedral or priory
	Castle
	Historic house or building
Wakehurst Place (NT)	National Trust property
M	Museum or art gallery
	Roman antiquity
	Ancient site, battlefield or monument
	Industrial interest
	Garden
	Garden Centre Garden Centre Association Member
	Garden Centre Wyevale Garden Centre
	Arboretum
	Farm or animal centre
	Zoological or wildlife collection
	Bird collection
	Nature reserve
	Aquarium
V	Visitor or heritage centre
	Country park
	Cave
	Windmill
	Distillery, brewery or vineyard

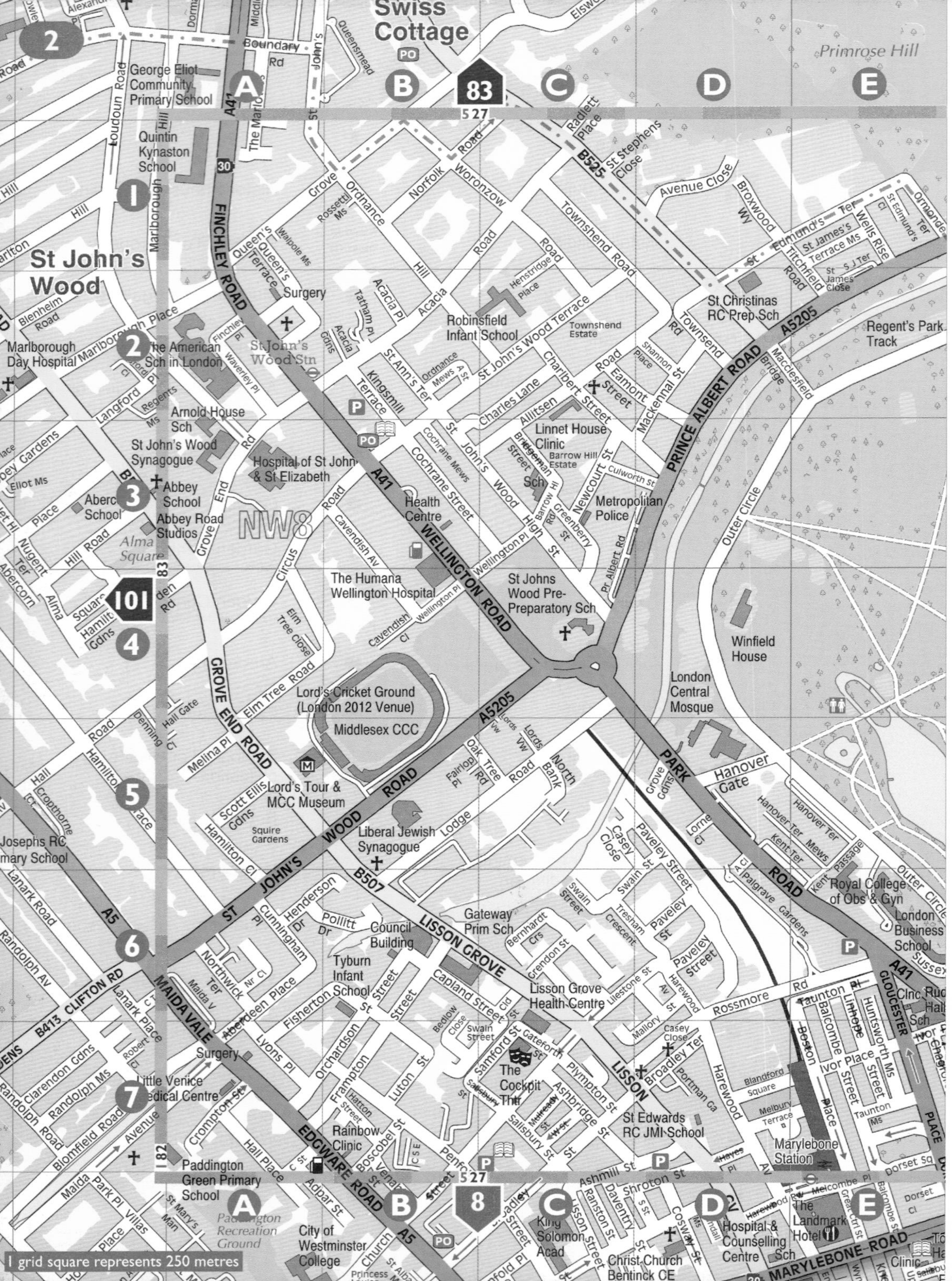
2
Swiss Cottage
Primrose Hill
A
B
C
D
E
83
527
Boundary Rd
George Eliot Community Primary School
Quintin Kynaston School
Loudoun Road
Marlborough Hill
FINCHLEY ROAD
A41
The Marlowes
St John's
Queensmead
Radlett Place
St Stephens Close
B525
Avenue Close
Broxwood Wy
St Edmund's Ter
St James's Terrace Ms
Wells Rise
Ormonde Ter
Townshend Road
Woronzow Road
Norfolk Road
Ordnance Hill
Grove
Rossetti Ms
Queen's Terrace
Walpole Ms
Acacia Road
Acacia Pl
Tatham Pl
Surgery
St John's Wood
Blenheim Road
Marlborough Day Hospital
Marlborough Place
The American Sch in London
St John's Wood Stn
Robinsfield Infant School
Henstridge Place
Townshend Estate
St John's Wood Terrace
St Christinas RC Prep Sch
A5205
Regent's Park Track
PRINCE ALBERT ROAD
Macclesfield Bridge
Langford Pl
Regents Ms
Arnold House Sch
St John's Wood Synagogue
Abbey Gardens
Elliot Ms
Abbey School
Abercorn School
Abbey Road Studios
Hospital of St John & St Elizabeth
Kingsmill Terrace
St Ann's Ter
Ordnance Mews
Charles Lane
Allitsen Road
Charlbert Street
Eamont Street
Mackennal St
Shannon Place
Linnet House Clinic
Barrow Hill Estate
Culworth St
Newcourt St
Cochrane Mews
Cochrane Street
St John's Wood High St
Bridgeman Street
Greenberry St
Metropolitan Police
Health Centre
WELLINGTON ROAD
NW8
Alma Square
Hill Road
Nugent Ter
Abercorn Pl
101
Hamilton Gdns
Grove End Road
Circus Road
Cavendish Av
The Humana Wellington Hospital
Wellington Pl
St Johns Wood Pre-Preparatory Sch
Pr Albert Rd
Outer Circle
Winfield House
Elm Tree Close
Cavendish Cl
Elm Tree Road
Lord's Cricket Ground (London 2012 Venue)
Middlesex CCC
London Central Mosque
Hall Gate
Denning Cl
Hall Road
Hamilton Terrace
Melina Pl
GROVE END ROAD
Lord's Tour & MCC Museum
Lords Vw
Oak Tree Rd
Fairlop Pl
North Bank
Hanover Gate
PARK ROAD
Hanover Ter Mews
Hanover Ter
Kent Ter
Kent Passage
Scott Ellis Gdns
Squire Gardens
ST JOHN'S WOOD ROAD
Liberal Jewish Synagogue
Lodge Road
Casey Close
Paveley Street
Grove Gdns
Lorne Cl
Royal College of Obs & Gyn
London Business School
Sussex
Cropthorne Ct
Josephs RC Primary School
Lanark Road
Hamilton Cl
B507
Henderson Dr
Pollitt Dr
Council Building
Gateway Prim Sch
Swain Street
Tresham Crescent
Palgrave Gardens
Bernhardt Crs
Grendon St
A5
Randolph Av
Cunningham Pl
LISSON GROVE
6
CLIFTON RD
B413
Lanark Place
MAIDA VALE
Northwick Ter
Maida V
Nr Cl
Aberdeen Place
Tyburn Infant School
Fisherton St
Capland Street
Lisson Grove Health Centre
Lilestone St
Harewood Av
Rossmore Rd
Taunton Pl
Balcombe Street
Linhope Street
Huntsworth Ms
GLOUCESTER PLACE
Clarendon Gdns
Randolph Ms
Robert Cl
Surgery
Lyons Pl
Orchardson St
Bedlow Close
Swain Street
Samford St
Gateforth St
The Cockpit Thtr
Mallory St
Casey Close
Broadley Ter
Ivor Place
Boston Place
Little Venice Medical Centre
Crompton St
Frampton Street
Hatton Street
Luton St
Plympton St
Ashbridge St
Salisbury St
Portman Ga
Blandford Square
Melbury Terrace
Taunton Ms
Randolph Road
Blomfield Road
Avenue
Rainbow Clinic
Boscobel St
St Edwards RC JMI School
Harewood Av
Marylebone Station
Dorset Sq
182
Paddington Green Primary School
Hall Place
Adpar St
EDGWARE ROAD
Ashmill St
Shroton St
Hayes Pl
Melcombe Pl
Balcombe St
Dorset Cl
8
Paddington Recreation Ground
City of Westminster College
Maida Park Pl Villas
St Mary's Man
Church St
King Solomon Acad
Lisson Street
Ranston St
Daventry St
Cosway St
Hospital & Counselling Centre
The Landmark Hotel
MARYLEBONE ROAD
Christ Church Bentinck CE
Clinic
1 grid square represents 250 metres

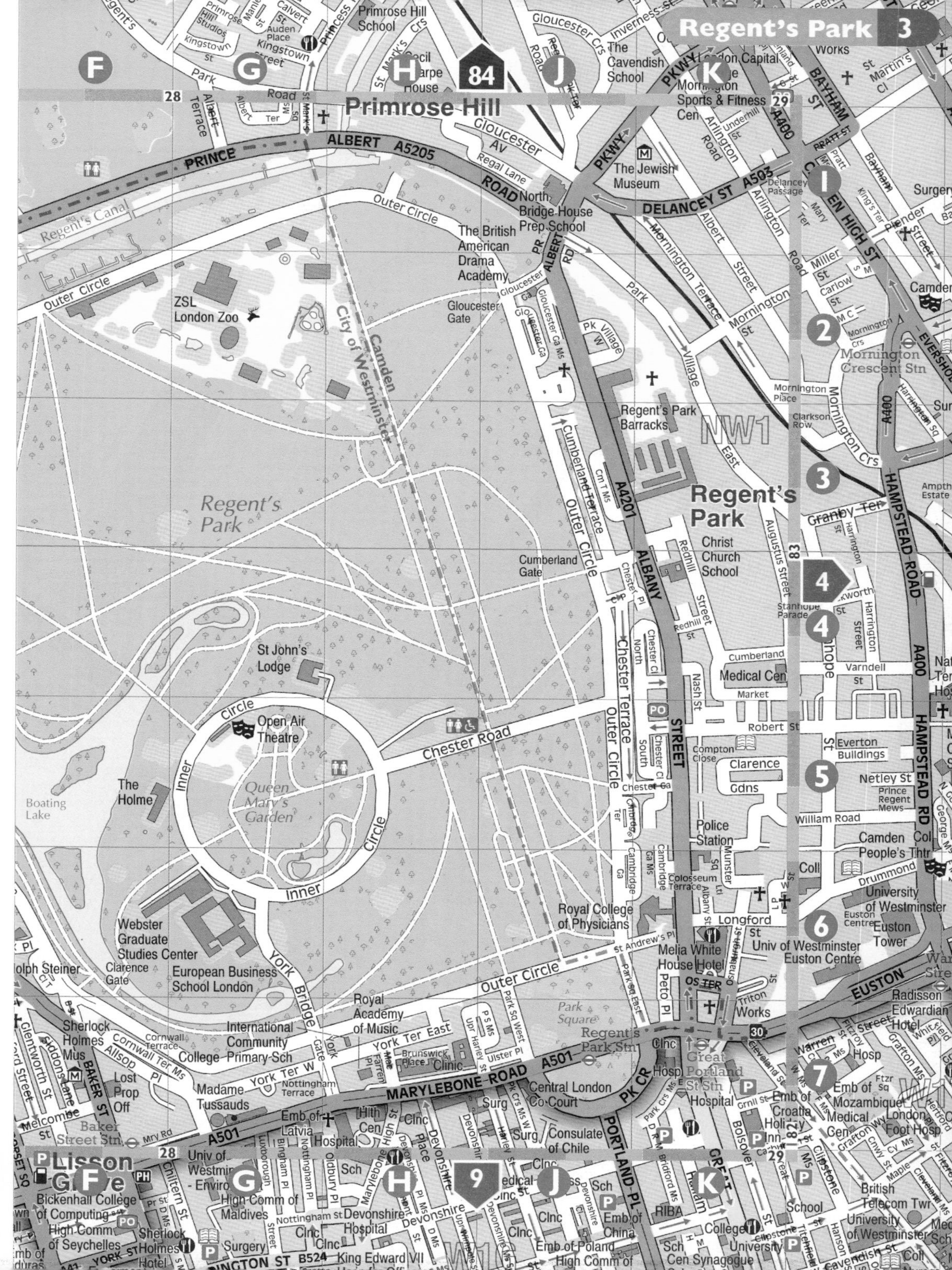
Primrose Hill
Regent's Park
Regent's Park
ZSL London Zoo
Open Air Theatre
Queen Mary's Garden
Boating Lake
The Holme
St John's Lodge
Webster Graduate Studies Center
European Business School London
Royal Academy of Music
Royal College of Physicians
The British American Drama Academy
The Jewish Museum
North Bridge House Prep School
Regent's Park Barracks
Christ Church School
Madame Tussauds
Sherlock Holmes Mus
Mornington Crescent Stn
Regent's Park Stn
Great Portland St Stn
Baker Street Stn
Euston Tower
University of Westminster
Camden People's Thtr
PRINCE ALBERT ROAD A5205
MARYLEBONE ROAD A501
ALBANY STREET A4201
HAMPSTEAD ROAD A400
Outer Circle
Inner Circle
Chester Road
Cumberland Gate
Gloucester Gate
Clarence Gate
York Bridge
Park Square
NW1

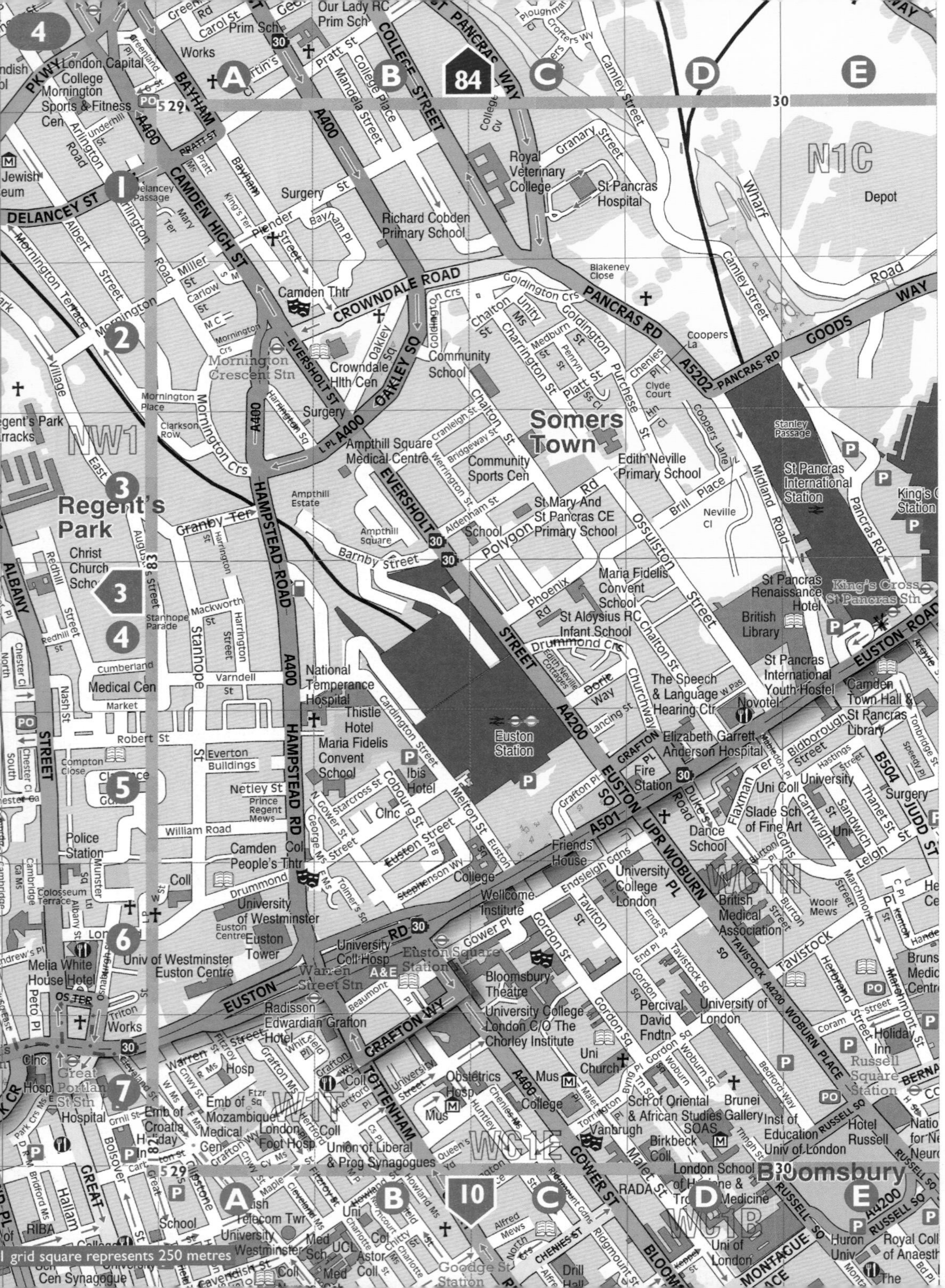

1 grid square represents 250 metres

Pentonville
FINSBURY
St Pancras
Clerkenwell
PENTONVILLE ROAD
KING'S CROSS ROAD
GRAY'S INN RD
CALEDONIAN RD
YORK WAY
FARRINGDON ROAD
ROSEBERY AVENUE
CLERKENWELL ROAD
CITY ROAD
UPPER STREET
ST JOHN STREET
GRAY'S INN ROAD
THEOBALD'S ROAD
GUILFORD STREET
COPENHAGEN ST
WHARFDALE ROAD
The London Canal Museum
Kingsway College
Royal National Throat Nose & Ear Hosp
Sadler's Wells Theatre
Angel Station
Mount Pleasant (Postal Sorting Office)
The Foundling Museum
Coram's Fields Playground
Great Ormond St Hospital for Children
The Charles Dickens Mus
Farringdon Station
The Business Design Centre
N1 Shopping Centre
Finsbury Health Cen
Clerkenwell Parochial CE Prim Sch
Eastman Dental Hosp
Holiday Inn
Travelodge
Magistrates Court
Police Stn
WC1X
WC1N
WC1R
EC1R
EC1M
N1

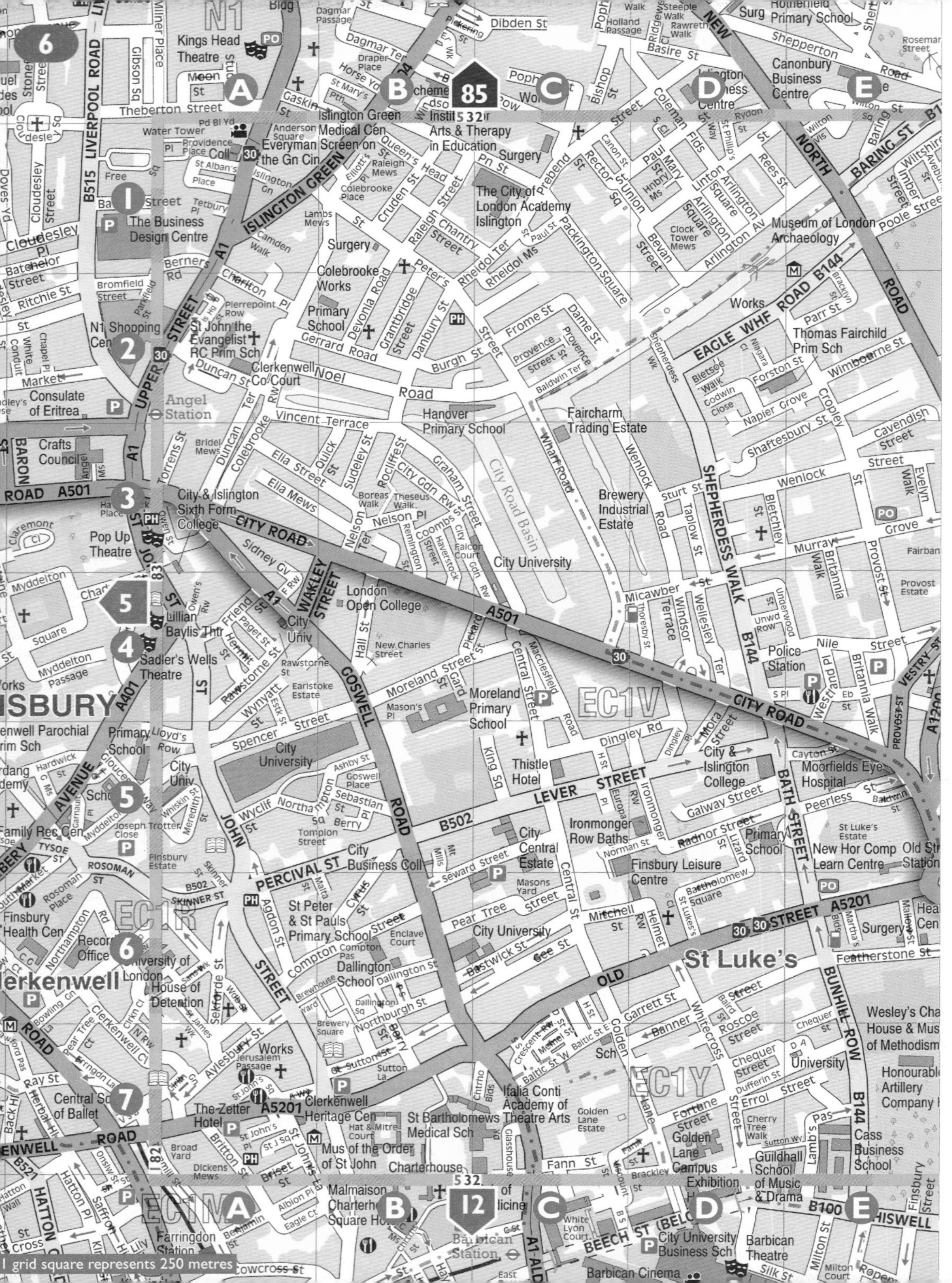
6
N1
Kings Head Theatre
Islington Green Medical Cen
Everyman Screen on the Gn Cin
Institute for Arts & Therapy in Education
The City of London Academy Islington
The Business Design Centre
LIVERPOOL ROAD
ISLINGTON GREEN
UPPER STREET
N1 Shopping Cen
Angel Station
Consulate of Eritrea
Crafts Council
St John the Evangelist RC Prim Sch
Clerkenwell Co Court
Colebrooke Works
Primary School
Hanover Primary School
Museum of London Archaeology
Thomas Fairchild Prim Sch
Canonbury Business Centre
Faircharm Trading Estate
Brewery Industrial Estate
City & Islington Sixth Form College
CITY ROAD
City Road Basin
City University
London Open College
Pop Up Theatre
Lillian Baylis Thtr
Sadler's Wells Theatre
FINSBURY
Moreland Primary School
EC1V
Police Station
SHEPHERDESS WALK
Thistle Hotel
City & Islington College
Moorfields Eye Hospital
LEVER STREET
Ironmonger Row Baths
Finsbury Leisure Centre
New Hor Comp Learn Centre
City Central Estate
City Business Coll
PERCIVAL ST
St Peter & St Pauls Primary School
City University
Dallington School
GOSWELL ROAD
JOHN STREET
ST JOHN STREET
EC1R
Finsbury Health Cen
Record Office
University of London
House of Detention
Clerkenwell
St Luke's
OLD STREET
Wesley's Chapel House & Museum of Methodism
Honourable Artillery Company
EC1Y
University
BUNHILL ROW
Golden Lane Estate
Golden Lane Campus
Guildhall School of Music & Drama
Cass Business School
Italia Conti Academy of Theatre Arts
St Bartholomews Medical Sch
Clerkenwell Heritage Cen
The Zetter Hotel
Mus of the Order of St John
Charterhouse
Central School of Ballet
CLERKENWELL ROAD
EC1M
Farringdon Station
Barbican Station
Barbican Theatre
Barbican Cinema
City University Business Sch
BEECH ST
Malmaison Charterhouse Square Hotel
85
12
5
1 grid square represents 250 metres

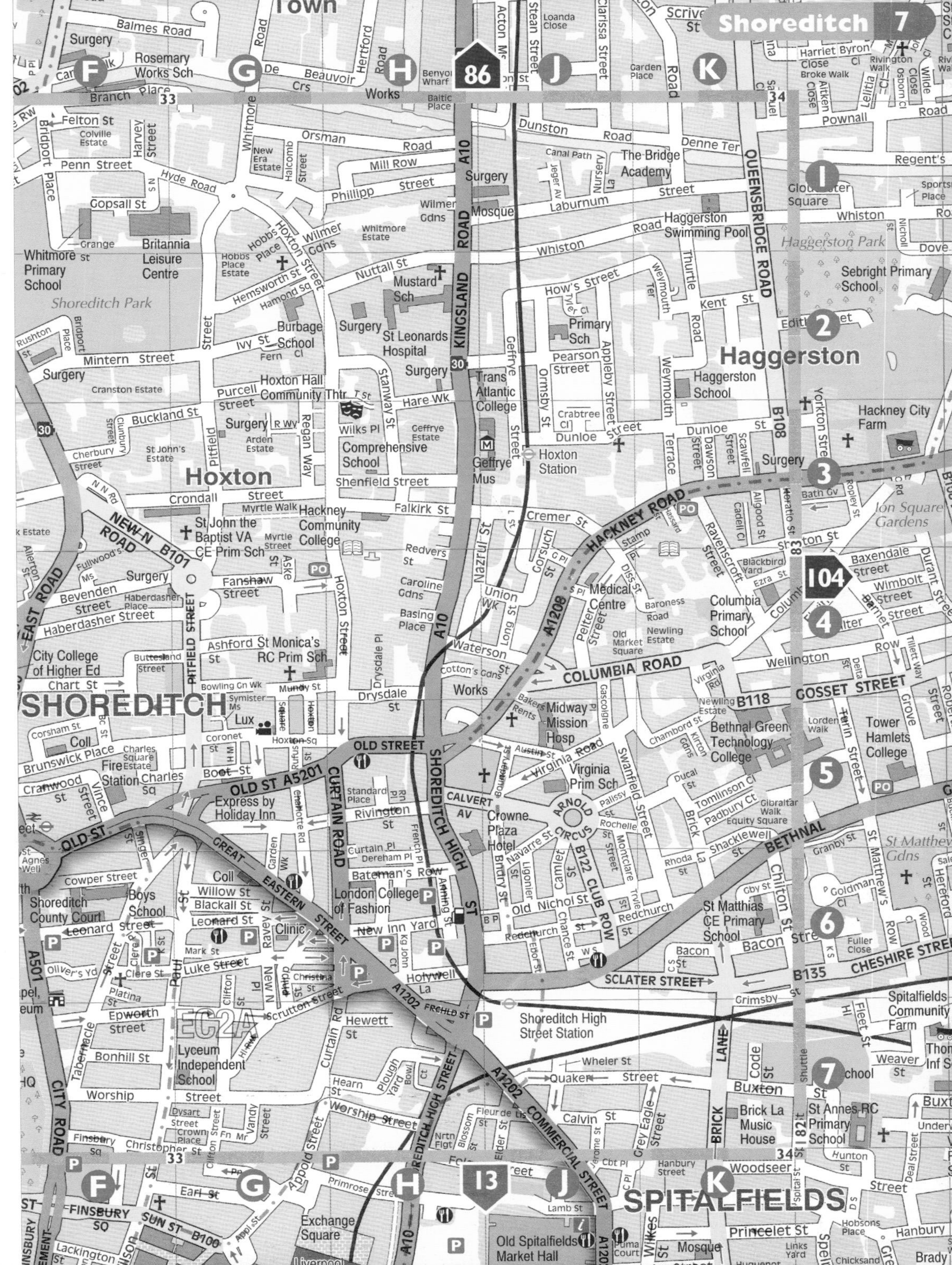
Town
Balmes Road
Surgery
Rosemary Works Sch
De Beauvoir Crs
Hertford Road
Benyon Wharf
86
Acton Ms
Stean Street
Loanda Close
Clarissa Street
Garden Place
Harriet Byron Cl
Broke Walk
Rivington Walk
Branch Place
33
Works
Baltic Place
34
Felton St
Colville Estate
Bridport Place
Harvey Street
Whitmore Road
New Era Estate
Halcomb Street
Orsman Road
Mill Row
Dunston Road
Canal Path
Denne Ter
The Bridge Academy
Queensbridge Road
Pownall Road
Regent's
Penn Street
Hyde Road
Phillipp Street
Surgery
Kingsland Road
A10
Jeger Av
Nursery La
Laburnum Street
Gloucester Square
Sportsman Place
Copsall St
Wilmer Gdns
Mosque
Haggerston Swimming Pool
Whiston Road
Grange St
Britannia Leisure Centre
Hobbs Place Estate
Whitmore Estate
Haggerston Park
Nicholl St
Dove Row
Whitmore Primary School
Hoxton Street
Nuttall St
Mustard Sch
Thurtle Road
How's Street
Tyler Cl
Weymouth Ter
Sebright Primary School
Hemsworth St
Hamond Sq
Shoreditch Park
Kent St
Edith St
Rushton St
Burbage School
Surgery
St Leonards Hospital
Geffrye Street
Primary Sch
Appleby Street
Haggerston
Ivy St
Fern Cl
Mintern Street
Pearson Street
Surgery
Stanway St
30
Trans Atlantic College
Ormsby St
Weymouth Terrace
Haggerston School
Hoxton Hall Community Thtr
Cranston Estate
Purcell Street
Hare Wk
Crabtree Cl
Hackney City Farm
Yorkton Street
Buckland St
Clunbury Street
Surgery
R Wy
Regan Way
Wilks Pl
Geffrye Estate
Dunloe Street
Dawson Street
Scawfell Street
B108
St John's Estate
Pitfield Street
Arden Estate
Comprehensive School
Geffrye Mus
Hoxton Station
Surgery
Cherbury Street
Hoxton
Shenfield Street
Horatio St
Cadell Cl
Allgood St
Bath Gv
Ropley St
Ion Square Gardens
N N Rd
Crondall Street
Myrtle Walk
Falkirk St
Hackney Road
PO
Cremer St
Hackney Community College
Nazrul St
Gorsuch St
Stamp Pl
Ravenscroft Street
St John the Baptist VA CE Prim Sch
Myrtle Street
Redvers St
Diss St
Blackbird Yard
Baxendale Street
New North Road
B101
Fullwood's Ms
Surgery
Aske St
Hoxton Street
Caroline Gdns
Union Wk
Ezra St
104
Durant Street
Bevenden Street
Fanshaw Street
Medical Centre
Baroness Road
Columbia Primary School
Wimbolt Street
Haberdasher Place
Basing Place
A1208
Newling Estate
4
East Road
Haberdasher Street
Long St
Pelter Street
Old Market Square
Ashford St
St Monica's RC Prim Sch
Drysdale Pl
Waterson St
Columbia Road
Wellington Row
Delta St
Tillett Way
City College of Higher Ed
Buttesland Street
Chart St
Bowling Gn Wk
Mundy St
Drysdale St
Cotton's Gdns
Works
Virginia Rd
Gosset Street
Shoreditch
Symister Ms
Lux
Hoxton Sq
Bakers Rents
Midway Mission Hosp
Gascoigne Pl
Chambord St
B118
Bethnal Green Technology College
Lorden Walk
Tower Hamlets College
Corsham St
Coll
Coronet St
Old Street
Austin St
Virginia Road
Virginia Prim Sch
Swanfield Street
Kirton Gdns
Ducal St
Turin Street
Grove
Brunswick Place
Charles Square Estate
Fire Station
Charles Sq
Boot St
Curtain Road
Shoreditch High St
Boundary St
Tomlinson Cl
5
Cranwood St
Vince Street
Old St A5201
Express by Holiday Inn
Standard Place
Calvert Av
Crowne Plaza Hotel
Arnold Circus
Palissy St
Padbury Ct
Gibraltar Walk
Equity Square
Old St
Rivington St
Charlotte Rd
Rochelle St
Shacklewell St
Bethnal
St Matthew's Gdns
St Agnes Well
Great Eastern Street
Garden Wk
Curtain Pl
French Pl
Dereham Pl
Navarre St
Ligonier St
Camlet St
B122 Club Row
Montclare Street
Rhoda St
Granby St
St Matthew's Row
Goldman Cl
Cowper Street
Bateman's Row
Brick La
Gby St
Hereford
Shoreditch County Court
Boys School
Willow St
Blackall St
Leonard St
London College of Fashion
Anning St
Old Nichol St
Chance St
Redchurch St
Chilton St
St Matthias CE Primary School
6
Leonard Street
Clinic
Ravey St
New Inn Yard
Kg John Ct
B P
Fuller Close
Wood Close
Mark St
Clere St
Paul St
Luke Street
Christina St
Holywell La
Bacon St
Bacon Street
Cheshire Street
A501
Oliver's Yd
Platina St
Clifton St
New North Pl
Scrutton Street
A1202
Sclater Street
B135
Grimsby St
Spitalfields Community Farm
EC2A
Epworth Street
Hewett St
Frchld St
Shoreditch High Street Station
Fleet St
Tabernacle St
Lyceum Independent School
Curtain Rd
Plough Yard
Bowl Ct
Brick Lane
Code St
Shuttle St
7
School
Weaver St
Bonhill St
Hearn St
Wheler St
Quaker Street
Buxton St
City Road
Worship Street
Dysart Street
Crown Place
Fn Mr
Vandy Street
Worship Street
Shoreditch High Street
Commercial Street
Fleur de Lis St
Calvin St
Grey Eagle Street
Brick La Music House
St Annes RC Primary School
Underwood
Finsbury Sq
Christopher St
Clifton Street
Nrtn Flgt
Blossom St
Elder St
Jerome St
Cbt Pl
Hanbury Street
Woodseer
Hunton St
Deal Street
82
Earl St
Appold Street
Primrose St
13
Lamb St
Spitalfields
Spital St
Finsbury Sq
Sun St
B100
Appl St
Exchange Square
Old Spitalfields Market Hall
Puma Court
Wilkes St
Mosque
Princelet St
Links Yard
Hobsons Place
Hanbury St
Lackington St
Liverpool
Fournier Street
Huguenot
Chicksand Estate
Brady

Little Venice Medical Centre
Randolph Road
Blomfield Road
Maida Avenue
Crompton St
Paddington Green Primary School
Rainbow Clinic
The Cockpit Thtr
Salisbury St
Ashbridge St
Plympton St
LISSON
St Edwards RC JMI Scho
Harewood
Blandford Square
Melbury Terrace
Marylebone Station
Ivor Place
Taunton
Dorset Sq
EDGWARE ROAD
A5
2
527
Frampton
Luton
Hatton Street
Boscobel
Venables St
Penfold Street
Adpar St
Paddington Recreation Ground
St Mary's Man
Park Pl Villas
Howley Place
John Aird Ct
City of Westminster College
Church
Princess Louise Close
St Alban's Ms
Paddington Gn
Newcastle Pl
Police Stn
St Mary's Ter
St Mary's Sq
Hogan
Porteus Rd
Gilpin Close
Broadley Street
King Solomon Acad
Lisson Street
Ashmill St
Ranston St
Daventry St
Shroton St
Cosway St
Bendall Ms
Penfold St
Corlett
Bell St
Burne St
Christ Church Bentinck CE Prim Sch
Hospital & Counselling Centre
The Landmark Hotel
Harewood Rw
Melcombe Pl
Balcombe St
Dorset Cl
Gloucester Pl
Great Ctrl St
MARYLEBONE ROAD
MARYLEBONE FLYOVER
HARROW RD FLYOVER
A40
30
Marylebone Mag Ct
Hosp
Prim Sch
Enford St
Wyndham St
Knox St
Clinic
Upr Montagu St
Edgware Road Stn
CHAPEL ST
A501
OLD MARYLEBONE RD
Harcourt St
Homer Street
Homer Row
York St
Tarrant Place
Crawford St
School
Medical Cen
Surg High Comm of Tonga
Seymour Leisure Cen
Shouldham St
Molyneux St
Cato Street
Brendon St
Crawford Pl
Watson's Ms
Bryanston Pl
Montagu Pl
Emb of Switzerland
Hosp
Bryanston Square
Seymour Place
Bryanston Ms W
Brown St
Harrowby St
University
Sch
Nutford Pl
Marriott Hotel
George Street
West London Synagogue
Clenston Mews
Wythburn Pl
Berkeley
Upper
Gt C Ms
A5204
Seymour St
Harbet Road
Hermitage St
North Wharf Road
Council Building
PADDINGTON
A4205
Business Centre
Sale Place
Junction Ms
A4209
Paddington Basin
South Wharf Road
STREET
PRAED
Medical School
A&E
St Marys Hospital
Fleming Lab Museum
Michael's St
School
Clnc St
Rainsford St
Surgery
The Water Gardens
Bouverie Pl
Norfolk Pl
Star St
Sthwck Ms
Sssx Gdns
GARDENS
The Quadrangle
Norfolk Crs
Cambridge Sq
Southwick St
Park W Pl
EDGWARE ROAD
B Pl
Paddington Station
Winsland St
Winsland Ms
London St
Eastbourne Ms
Westbourne Ter
CLEVELAND TER
BISHOP'S BRIDGE ROAD
Sheldon Sq
Kingdom Street
Hotel
ROAD
A4205
EASTBOURNE TERRACE
London Ms
Praed Ms
Norfolk Square
Norfolk Sq
Norfolk Sq Ms
Days Inn
Radnor Mews
Radnor Place
Somers Crs
Hyde Pk Crs
Oxford Sq
Porchester Pl
Portsea Pl
Portsea Mews
Connaught St
Connaught House Sch
101
Chilworth St
Chilworth Mew
Gloucester Ms
Gloucester Ms West
Upbrook Ms
Devonshire Ter
Gloucester Ter
Conduit Pl
Conduit Mews
Spring St
Hotel Indigo
Tlbt Sq
Hotel
University
CRAVEN ROAD
B410
SUSSEX
Sussex Gardens
Sussex Place
Gloucester Sq
Southwick Pl
Hyde Pk Sq Ms
Hyde Park Sq
Connaught Street
Kendal St
Archery Cl
Connaught Sq
Albion Street
Albion Ms
Albion Cl
Connaught Cl
Hyde Pk St
Clarendon Pl
Strathearn Pl
St Georges Fields
Surg
Frederick Close
Stanhope Pl
Hyde Park Place
Craven Hl Ms
Craven Hl
Craven Ter
Craven Hl Gdns
Wstbrn Ter
Westbourne Crs
Westbourne Crescent Mews
Brook Ms N
Terrace
Bathurst Mews
Bathurst St
Clifton Pl
Sussex Sq
Hyde Pk Gdns Ms
Hyde Park Gardens
Stanhope Terrace
Brook St
Hyde Pk Gdns
Sussex Ms W
St James & St Michaels CE Prim Sch
London Toy & Model Mus
Emb of Costa Rica
Elms Ms
Lancaster Gate
Lancaster Court
Bayswater Rd
LANCASTER TER
WESTBOURNE ST
Lancaster Hotel
High Comm of Sri Lanka
BAYSWATER ROAD
A402
North Carriage Drive
Albion Gate
Clarendon Gate
Victoria Gate
Westbourne Gate
Stanhope Gate
Buses Only
Lancaster Gate Station
Marlborough Gate
Thistle Hotel
A402
30
BAYSWATER ROAD
Lancaster Gate
W2
West Carriage Drive
Speke's Monument
Peter Pan Statue
Kensington Gardens
Hyde Park
Physical Energy Statue
527
14
Norwegian/British Monument
Hyde Park (London 2012 Site)
Serpentine Road
Diana Princess of Wales Memorial Fountain
Serpentine
A
B
C
D
E
1
2
3
4
5
6
7
grid square represents 250 metres

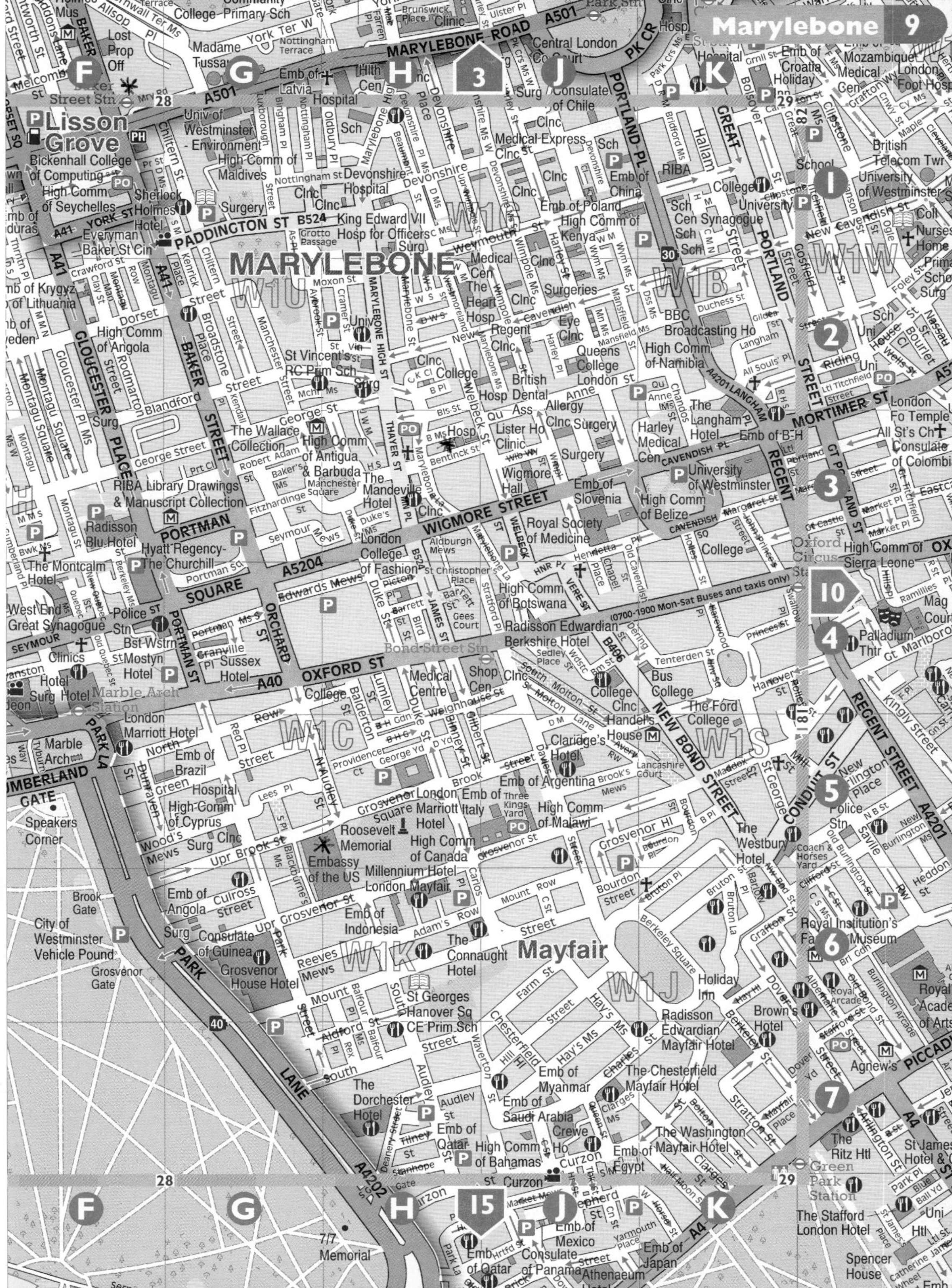

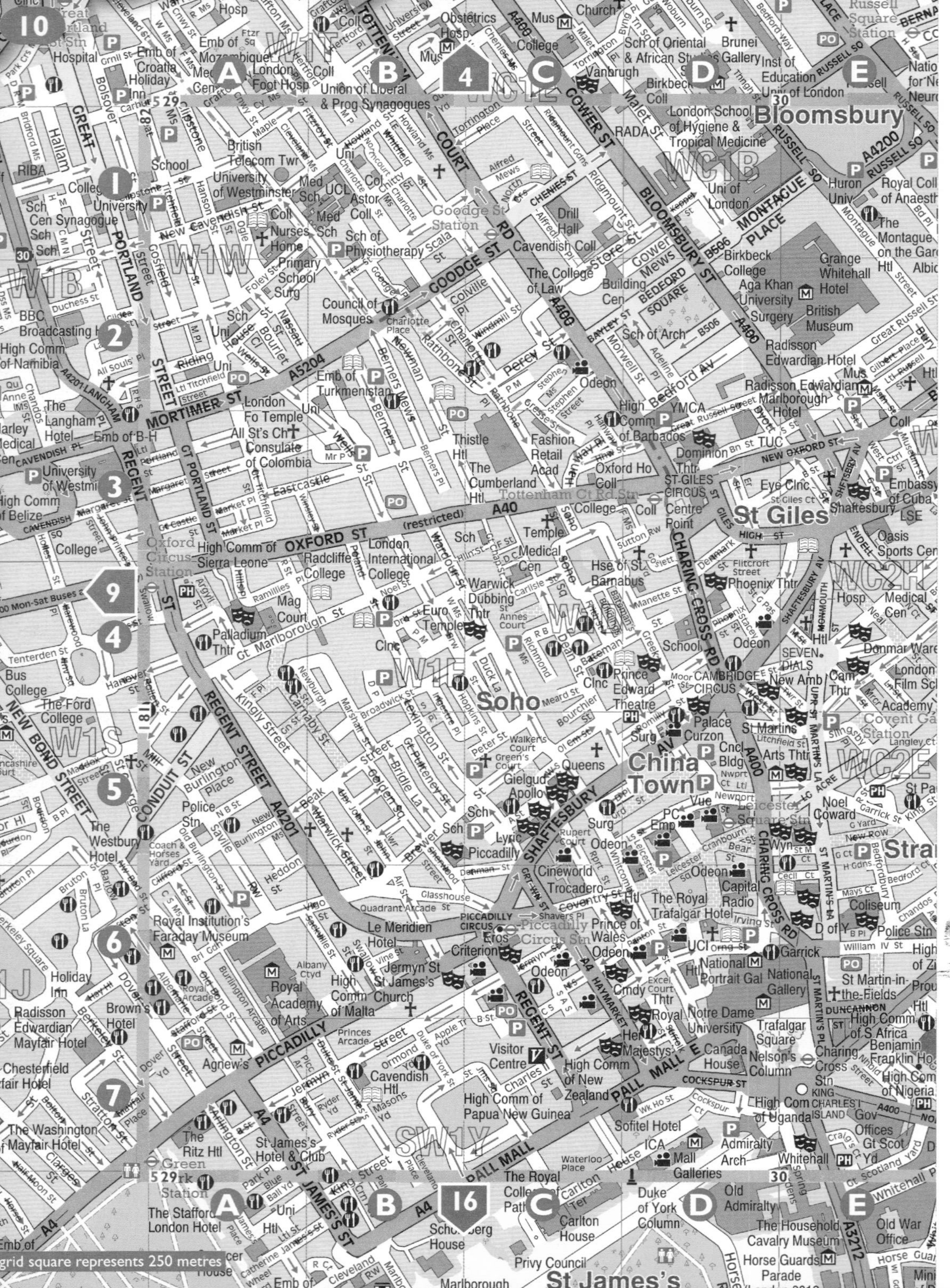

10
4
A
B
C
D
E
Bloomsbury
Great Portland St Stn
Hospital
Emb of Mozambique
Emb of Croatia
Holiday Inn
Obstetrics Hosp
Mus
College
Church
Sch of Oriental & African Studies
Brunei Gallery
Inst of Education Univ of London
Russell Square Station
Vanbrugh
Birkbeck Coll
Union of Liberal & Prog Synagogues
London Foot Hosp
London School of Hygiene & Tropical Medicine
RADA
TOTTENHAM COURT RD
GOWER ST
Malet St
RUSSELL SQ
A4200
British Telecom Twr
University of Westminster
Med Sch
UCL
Astor Coll
Uni of London
MONTAGUE PLACE
Royal Coll of Anaesth
Huron Univ
The Montague on the Gardens Htl
BLOOMSBURY ST
Goodge St Station
Drill Hall
Cavendish Coll
The College of Law
Building Cen
Birkbeck College
Aga Khan University
Surgery
Grange Whitehall Hotel
British Museum
BEDFORD SQUARE
Sch of Arch
Bedford Av
GOODGE ST
Council of Mosques
Charlotte Place
Nurses Home
Primary School
Surg
Sch of Physiotherapy
W1W
W1B
WC1B
WC1E
PORTLAND PLACE
GREAT PORTLAND STREET
RIBA
University
Sch
Cen Synagogue
BBC Broadcasting House
High Comm of Namibia
All Souls'
A4201 LANGHAM
The Langham Hotel
Emb of B-H
Harley Medical Cen
University of Westminster
High Comm of Belize
CAVENDISH SQ
College
MORTIMER ST
A5204
London Fo Temple
All St's Ch
Consulate of Colombia
Emb of Turkmenistan
Berners Mews
Thistle Htl
The Cumberland Htl
Fashion Retail Acad
Odeon
High Comm of Barbados
YMCA
Radisson Edwardian Hotel
Radisson Edwardian Marlborough Hotel
Great Russell St
Dominion Thtr
TUC
NEW OXFORD ST
Oxford Ho Coll
ST GILES CIRCUS
Centre Point
Tottenham Ct Rd Stn
St Giles
Shaftesbury
Embassy of Cuba
LSE
Oasis Sports Cen
Eye Clnc
OXFORD ST
A40
(restricted)
Oxford Circus Station
High Comm of Sierra Leone
Radcliffe College
London International College
Temple
Medical Cen
Hse of St Barnabus
Phoenix Thtr
WC2H
Hosp
Medical Cen
9
1900 Mon-Sat Buses
Mag Court
Euro Temple
Warwick Dubbing Thtr
Gt Marlborough St
Palladium Thtr
W1D
W1F
W1S
W1J
Soho
CHARING CROSS RD
School
Odeon
SEVEN DIALS
Donmar Warehouse
London Film Sch
Cam Thtr
Academy
Covent Garden Station
Prince Edward Theatre
CAMBRIDGE CIRCUS
New Amb
St Martins
Arts Thtr
Palace
Curzon
Cncl Bldg
China Town
Vue
Leicester Square Stn
Wyn
Noel Coward
Tenterden St
Bus College
The Ford College
NEW BOND STREET
CONDUIT ST
REGENT STREET A4201
New Burlington Place
Police Stn
Kingly Street
Carnaby St
Broadwick St
Lexington St
Gt Pulteney St
Golden Sq
Bridle La
Beak St
Brewer St
Warwick Street
Walker's Court
Green's Court
Queens
Gielgud
Apollo
Lyric
Piccadilly
SHAFTESBURY AV
Rupert Court
Surg
Odeon
Emp
PC
Cineworld
Trocadero
Odeon
Capital Radio
The Royal Trafalgar Hotel
Stra
The Westbury Hotel
Bruton St
Berkeley Square
Royal Institution's Faraday Museum
Heddon St
Quadrant Arcade
Classhouse St
Le Meridien Hotel
PICCADILLY CIRCUS
Piccadilly Circus Stn
Eros
Criterion
Prince of Wales
Odeon
UCI
National Portrait Gal
Garrick
D of Y
Coliseum
Police Stn
William IV St
Holiday Inn
Radisson Edwardian Mayfair Hotel
Brown's Hotel
Royal Academy of Arts
Albany Ctyd
High Comm of Malta
Jermyn St
St James's Church
Odeon
Cmdy
Royal
Excel Court Thtr
National Gallery
St Martin-in-the-Fields
HAYMARKET
REGENT ST
Her Majestys
Notre Dame University
Trafalgar Square
Nelson's Column
Canada House
Charing Cross Stn
High Comm of S Africa
Benjamin Franklin Ho
High Comm of Nigeria
DUNCANNON ST
The Chesterfield Mayfair Hotel
PICCADILLY
Princes Arcade
Agnew's
Cavendish Htl
Visitor Centre
High Comm of New Zealand
High Comm of Papua New Guinea
PALL MALL
COCKSPUR ST
High Com of Uganda
KING CHARLES I ISLAND
A400
Gov Offices Gt Scot Yd
The Washington Mayfair Hotel
The Ritz Htl
St James's Hotel & Club
Sofitel Hotel
ICA
Mall Galleries
Admiralty Arch
Whitehall
Green Park Station
The Stafford London Hotel
ST JAMES'S ST
King Street
16
A4
The Royal College of Path
Carlton House
Duke of York Column
Old Admiralty
The Household Cavalry Museum
Old War Office
Horse Guards Parade
A3212
Schomberg House
Privy Council
St James's
Marlborough
Emb of
Waterloo Place
grid square represents 250 metres

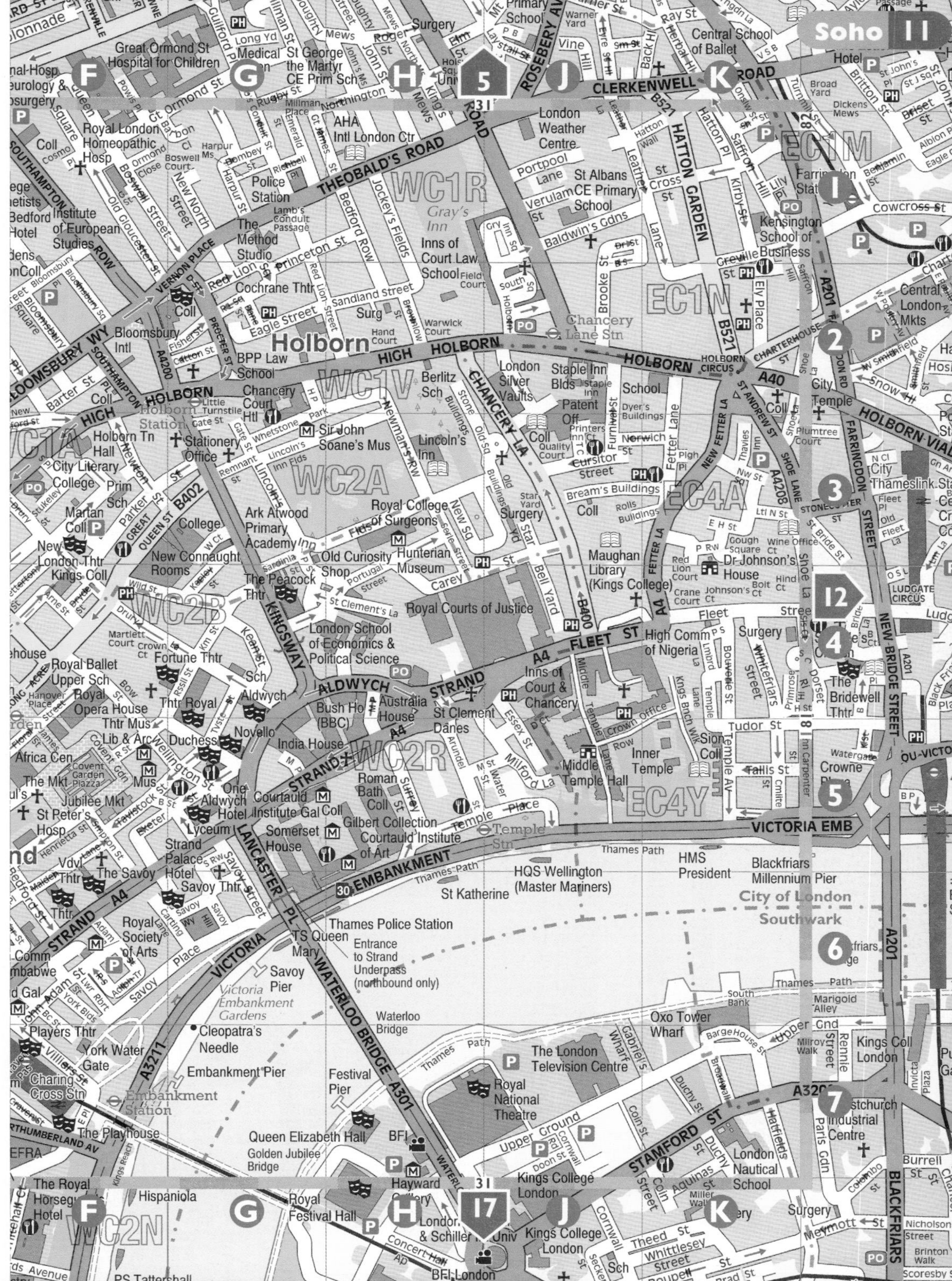
F
G
H
5
J
K
1
2
3
4
5
6
7
12
17
Great Ormond St Hospital for Children
St George the Martyr CE Prim Sch
Surgery
Central School of Ballet
CLERKENWELL ROAD
THEOBALD'S ROAD
Royal London Homeopathic Hosp
AHA Intl London Ctr
London Weather Centre
Police Station
WC1R
Gray's Inn
Inns of Court Law School
EC1M
EC1N
Kensington School of Business
Cowcross St
HATTON GARDEN
Institute of European Studies
The Method Studio
Cochrane Thtr
Holborn
HIGH HOLBORN
Bloomsbury Intl
BPP Law School
Chancery Lane Stn
HOLBORN
HOLBORN CIRCUS
HOLBORN VIAD
Central London Mkts
City Temple
WC1V
Chancery Court Htl
Berlitz Sch
London Silver Vaults
Staple Inn Blds
Patent Off
Holborn Stn
Holborn Tn Hall
Stationery Office
Sir John Soane's Mus
Lincoln's Inn
City Literary College
WC2A
Royal College of Surgeons
Ark Atwood Primary Academy
Hunterian Museum
Old Curiosity Shop
EC4A
City Thameslink Stat
Maughan Library (Kings College)
Dr Johnson's House
New Connaught Rooms
New London Thtr
The Peacock Thtr
Royal Courts of Justice
WC2B
KINGSWAY
London School of Economics & Political Science
FLEET ST
High Comm of Nigeria
LUDGATE CIRCUS
NEW BRIDGE STREET
FARRINGDON STREET
Royal Ballet Upper Sch
Fortune Thtr
Royal Opera House
Thtr Royal
Aldwych
ALDWYCH
STRAND
Bush Ho (BBC)
Australia House
St Clement Danes
Inns of Court & Chancery
The Bridewell Thtr
India House
WC2R
Novello
Duchess
Covent Garden Piazza
Jubilee Mkt
Africa Cen
Middle Temple Hall
Inner Temple
Crowne Plaza
Roman Bath
Courtauld Institute Gal
One Aldwych Hotel
Lyceum
Somerset House
Gilbert Collection
Courtauld Institute of Art
Temple Stn
EC4Y
VICTORIA EMB
Strand Palace Hotel
The Savoy
Savoy Thtr
EMBANKMENT
HQS Wellington (Master Mariners)
St Katherine
HMS President
Blackfriars Millennium Pier
City of London
Southwark
Royal Society of Arts
Thames Police Station
TS Queen Mary
Entrance to Strand Underpass (northbound only)
Savoy Pier
Victoria Embankment Gardens
Waterloo Bridge
WATERLOO BRIDGE
VICTORIA
Players Thtr
York Water Gate
Cleopatra's Needle
Embankment Pier
Charing Cross Stn
Embankment Station
Oxo Tower Wharf
The London Television Centre
Kings Coll London
Royal National Theatre
Festival Pier
The Playhouse
Queen Elizabeth Hall
Golden Jubilee Bridge
BFI
Christchurch Industrial Centre
STAMFORD ST
London Nautical School
The Royal Horseguards Hotel
Hispaniola
Royal Festival Hall
Hayward Gallery
London & Schiller Int Univ
Kings College London
BLACKFRIARS
WC2N
PS Tattershall
BFI London IMAX Cinema

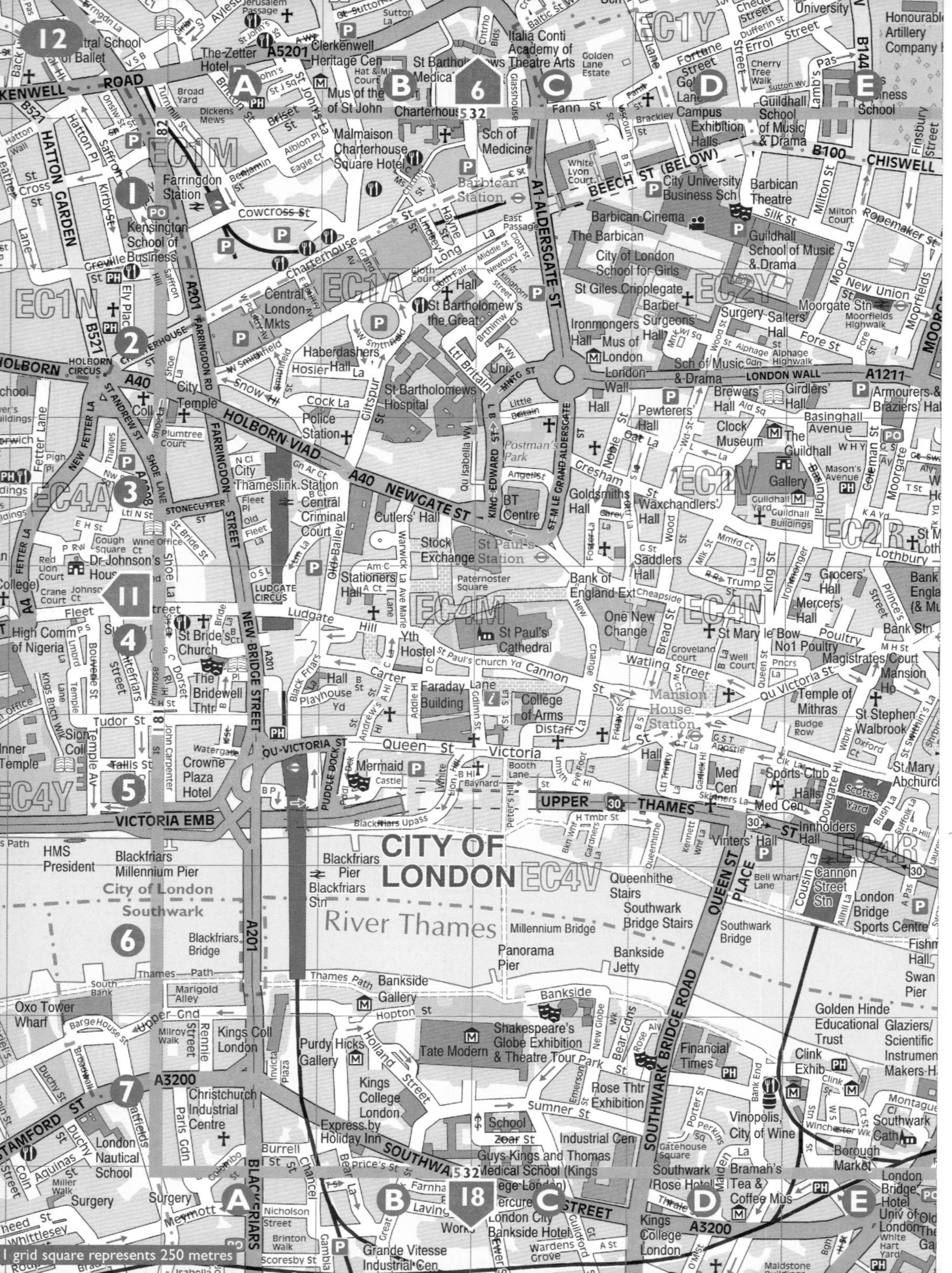
12
6
11
18
A
B
C
D
E
1
2
3
4
5
6
7
EC1M
EC1N
EC1A
EC1Y
EC2Y
EC2V
EC2R
EC4A
EC4M
EC4N
EC4Y
EC4V
EC4R
CITY OF LONDON
River Thames
City of London
Southwark
Clerkenwell Rd
Farringdon Station
Barbican Station
St Paul's Station
Mansion House Station
Blackfriars Stn
Cannon Street Stn
Bank Stn
Moorgate Stn
Holborn Circus
Ludgate Circus
Holborn Viad
Newgate St
Farringdon Rd
Farringdon Street
New Bridge Street
Victoria Emb
Upper Thames St
Queen Victoria St
Southwark Bridge Road
Queen St Place
London Wall
Aldersgate St
Beech St (Below)
Chiswell St
Charterhouse St
Fleet St
Shoe Lane
Fetter Lane
New Fetter La
Hatton Garden
Stamford St
Southwark St
Blackfriars Bridge
Millennium Bridge
Southwark Bridge
Central London Mkts
St Bartholomews Hospital
St Bartholomew's the Great
Central Criminal Court
Stationers Hall
St Paul's Cathedral
Paternoster Square
One New Change
Bank of England Ext
The Guildhall
Guildhall School of Music & Drama
The Barbican
Barbican Theatre
Barbican Cinema
City of London School for Girls
St Giles Cripplegate
Mus of London
Clock Museum
Dr Johnson's House
St Bride's Church
The Bridewell Thtr
Crowne Plaza Hotel
Mermaid Castle
College of Arms
Faraday Building
BT Centre
Postman's Park
Tate Modern
Shakespeare's Globe Exhibition & Theatre Tour
Bankside Gallery
Kings Coll London
Oxo Tower Wharf
HMS President
Blackfriars Millennium Pier
Panorama Pier
Bankside Jetty
Financial Times
Vinopolis, City of Wine
Southwark Cath
Borough Market
Golden Hinde Educational Trust
Clink Exhib
Rose Thtr Exhibition
Temple of Mithras
1 grid square represents 250 metres

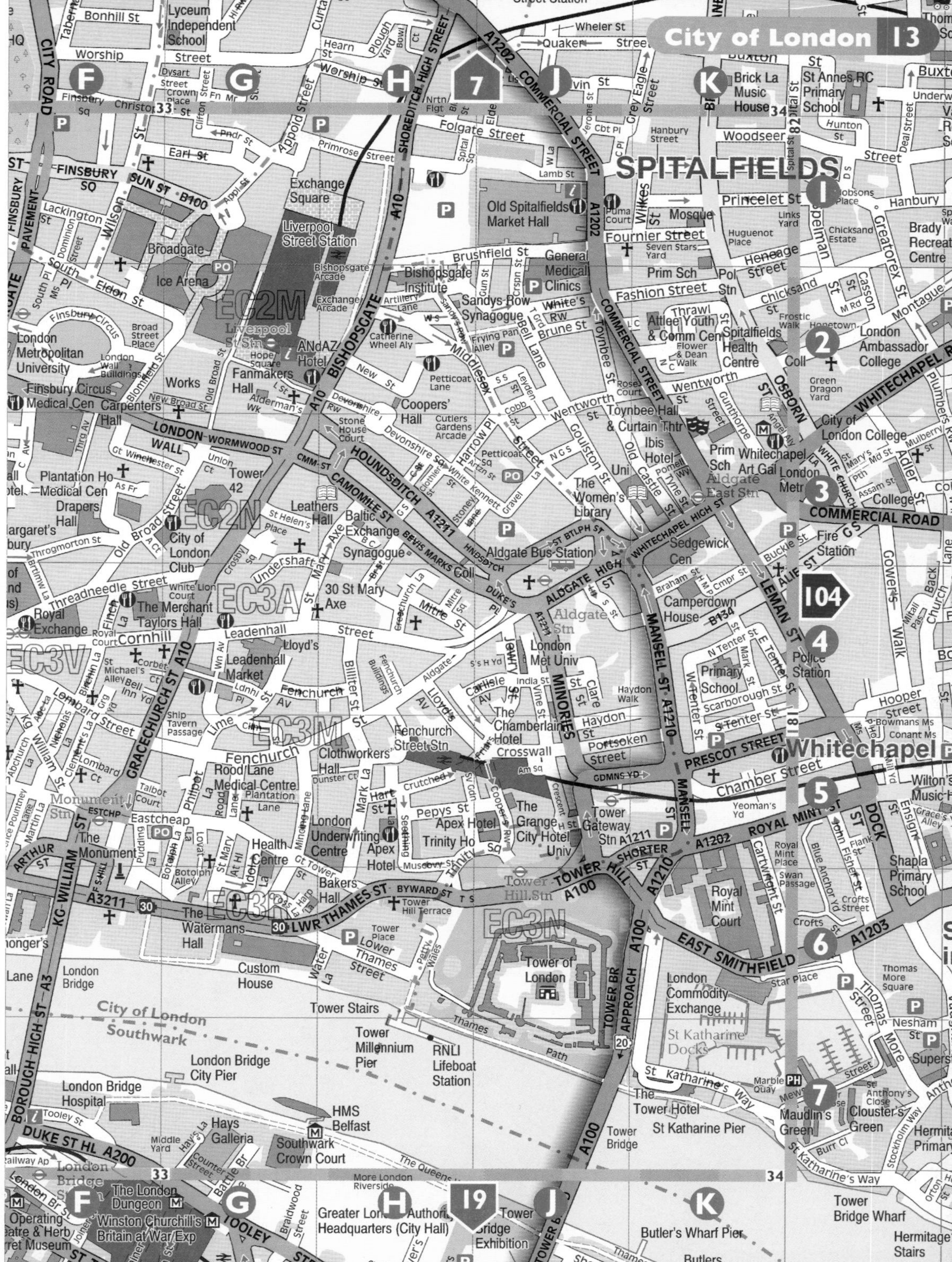
SPITALFIELDS
Whitechapel
City of London
Southwark
Liverpool Street Station
Exchange Square
Broadgate
Ice Arena
Finsbury Circus
London Metropolitan University
Old Spitalfields Market Hall
Bishopsgate Institute
Sandys Row Synagogue
Petticoat Lane
Middlesex Street
Houndsditch
Bishopsgate
Commercial Street
Commercial Road
Whitechapel High St
Aldgate High St
Aldgate Bus Station
Aldgate Stn
Aldgate East Stn
Toynbee Hall & Curtain Thtr
The Women's Library
Whitechapel Art Gal
London College
Minories
Mansell St
Leman St
Prescot Street
Royal Mint St
East Smithfield
Tower Hill
Tower Gateway Stn
Tower Hill Stn
Tower of London
Tower Bridge Approach
Tower Bridge
St Katharine Docks
St Katharine's Way
The Tower Hotel
St Katharine Pier
London Commodity Exchange
Royal Mint Court
Fenchurch Street Stn
Fenchurch St
Leadenhall Street
Leadenhall Market
Lloyd's
Cornhill
Royal Exchange
Threadneedle Street
London Wall
Tower 42
Baltic Exchange
30 St Mary Axe
Gracechurch St
Lombard Street
King William St
Monument Stn
The Monument
Eastcheap
Lower Thames Street
Custom House
Tower Stairs
Tower Millennium Pier
RNLI Lifeboat Station
London Bridge City Pier
London Bridge Hospital
HMS Belfast
Hays Galleria
Southwark Crown Court
Tooley Street
The London Dungeon
Winston Churchill's Britain at War Exp
Greater London Authority Headquarters (City Hall)
Tower Bridge Exhibition
Butler's Wharf Pier
Borough High St A3
Duke St Hl A200
Thames Path
EC2M
EC2N
EC3A
EC3V
EC3M
EC3R
EC3N
7
19
104
33
34

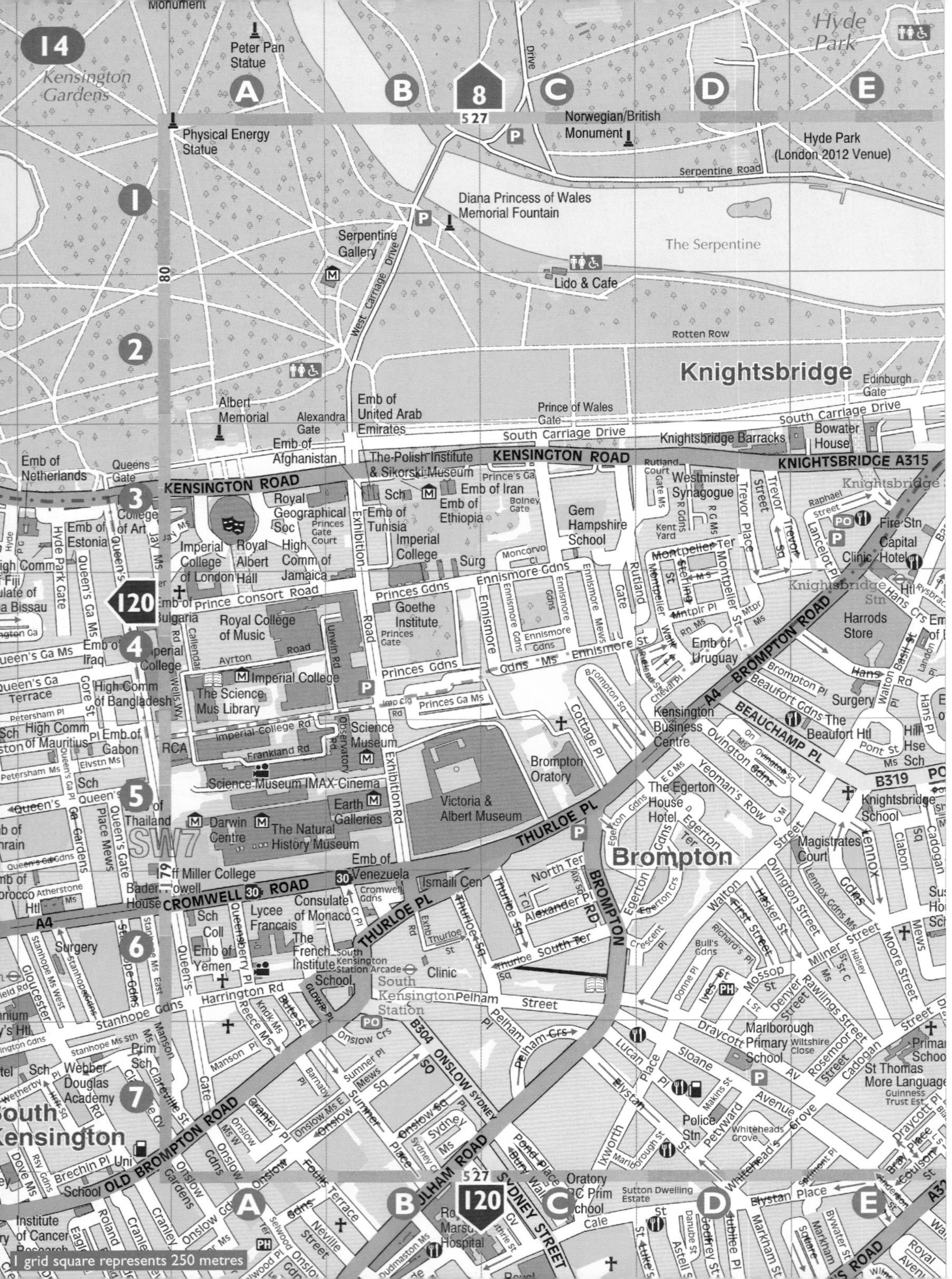

14
Kensington Gardens
Peter Pan Statue
Monument
A
B
8
C
D
E
Hyde Park
527
Physical Energy Statue
Norwegian/British Monument
Hyde Park (London 2012 Venue)
Serpentine Road
1
Diana Princess of Wales Memorial Fountain
Serpentine Gallery
The Serpentine
West Carriage Drive
Lido & Cafe
80
2
Rotten Row
Knightsbridge
Edinburgh Gate
Albert Memorial
Alexandra Gate
Emb of United Arab Emirates
Prince of Wales Gate
South Carriage Drive
Knightsbridge Barracks
Bowater House
Emb of Afghanistan
The Polish Institute & Sikorski Museum
KENSINGTON ROAD
KNIGHTSBRIDGE A315
Emb of Netherlands
Queens Gate
3
Royal Geographical Soc
Emb of Iran
Emb of Tunisia
Emb of Ethiopia
Westminster Synagogue
Gem Hampshire School
Knightsbridge
Fire Stn
Capital Hotel
Clinic
Royal College of Art
Emb of Estonia
Imperial College of London
Royal Albert Hall
High Comm of Jamaica
Imperial College
Surg
Exhibition Road
Ennismore Gdns
Montpelier Ter
Knightsbridge Stn
Harrods Store
High Comm of Fiji
Hyde Park Gate
Queen's Ga Ms
120
Emb of Bulgaria
Prince Consort Road
Princes Gdns
Goethe Institute
Royal College of Music
Emb of Uruguay
BROMPTON ROAD
A4
4
Emb of Iraq
Imperial College
Princes Gdns
Ennismore St
Queen's Ga Terrace
High Comm of Bangladesh
The Science Mus Library
Imperial College
Princes Ga Ms
Kensington Business Centre
BEAUCHAMP PL
The Beaufort Htl
Surgery
High Comm of Mauritius
Emb of Gabon
RCA
Imperial College Rd
Frankland Rd
Science Museum
Brompton Oratory
Hill Hse Sch
Science Museum IMAX Cinema
Victoria & Albert Museum
The Egerton House Hotel
B319
Knightsbridge School
5
Emb of Thailand
Earth Galleries
Darwin Centre
The Natural History Museum
THURLOE PL
Brompton
Magistrates Court
SW7
Emb of Venezuela
Ismaili Cen
Cromwell Gdns
North Ter
BROMPTON RD
CROMWELL ROAD
Consulate of Monaco
Lycee Francais
Sch Coll
A4
Surgery
6
Emb of Yemen
The French Institute
South Kensington School
South Kensington Station Arcade
Clinic
Thurloe Sq
South Ter
Pelham Street
South Kensington Station
Harrington Rd
Stanhope Gdns
Draycott
Marlborough Primary School
Primary School
St Thomas More Language
Guinness Trust Est
Webber Douglas Academy
7
Sloane Avenue
Police Stn
South Kensington
Old Brompton Road
ONSLOW SQ
FULHAM ROAD
Oratory RC Prim School
Sutton Dwelling Estate
Elystan Place
SYDNEY STREET
Institute of Cancer Research
Royal Marsden Hospital
1 grid square represents 250 metres

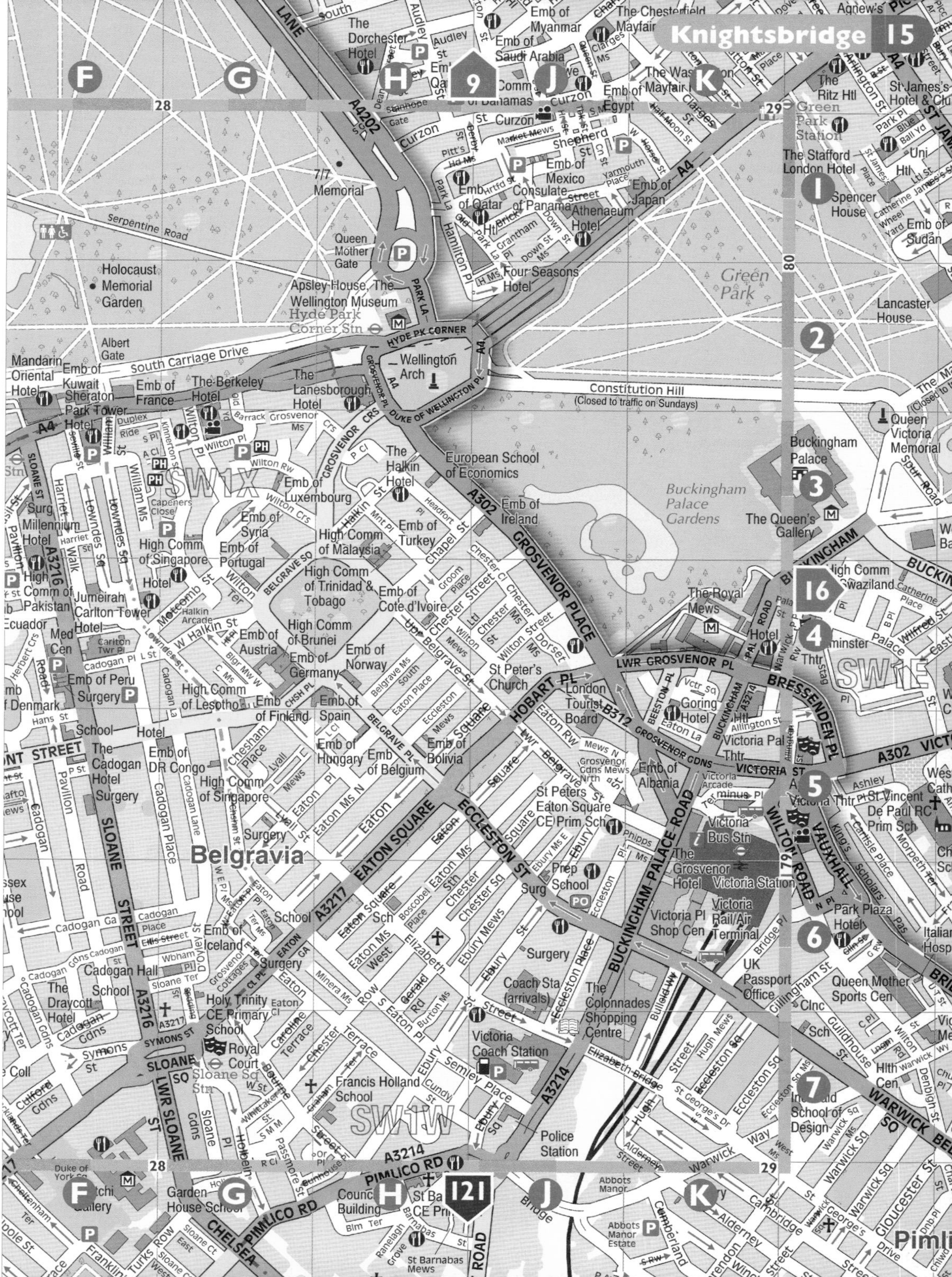
The Dorchester Hotel
Emb of Myanmar
The Chesterfield Mayfair
Emb of Saudi Arabia
Comm of Bahamas
Curzon
The Washington Mayfair
Emb of Egypt
The Ritz Htl
St James's Hotel & Club
Green Park Station
The Stafford London Hotel
Spencer House
Emb of Sudan
Emb of Mexico
Consulate of Panama
Emb of Qatar
Emb of Japan
Athenaeum Hotel
Four Seasons Hotel
7/7 Memorial
Serpentine Road
Queen Mother Gate
Holocaust Memorial Garden
Apsley House, The Wellington Museum
Hyde Park Corner Stn
HYDE PK CORNER
Green Park
Lancaster House
Albert Gate
South Carriage Drive
Wellington Arch
Constitution Hill
(Closed to traffic on Sundays)
Mandarin Oriental Hotel
Emb of Kuwait
Sheraton Park Tower Hotel
Emb of France
The Berkeley Hotel
The Lanesborough Hotel
DUKE OF WELLINGTON PL
Queen Victoria Memorial
Buckingham Palace
Buckingham Palace Gardens
The Queen's Gallery
European School of Economics
The Halkin Hotel
Emb of Luxembourg
SW1X
Emb of Syria
High Comm of Malaysia
Emb of Turkey
Emb of Ireland
A302 GROSVENOR PLACE
Emb of Portugal
High Comm of Singapore
High Comm of Trinidad & Tobago
Emb of Cote d'Ivoire
High Comm Swaziland
The Royal Mews
Jumeirah Carlton Tower Hotel
High Comm of Pakistan
Emb of Austria
High Comm of Brunei
Emb of Germany
Emb of Norway
LWR GROSVENOR PL
BRESSENDEN PL
SW1E
Emb of Peru
High Comm of Lesotho
Emb of Finland
Emb of Spain
St Peter's Church
London Tourist Board
Goring Hotel
Victoria Pal Thtr
Emb of Albania
VICTORIA ST
Emb of DR Congo
Emb of Hungary
Emb of Belgium
Emb of Bolivia
The Cadogan Hotel
High Comm of Singapore
St Peters Eaton Square CE Prim Sch
Victoria Bus Stn
Victoria Thtr
St Vincent De Paul RC Prim Sch
Belgravia
EATON SQUARE
ECCLESTON ST
BUCKINGHAM PALACE ROAD
VAUXHALL BRIDGE ROAD
The Grosvenor Hotel
Victoria Station
Victoria Rail/Air Terminal
Victoria Pl Shop Cen
Park Plaza Hotel
Emb of Iceland
Cadogan Hall
Holy Trinity CE Primary School
Coach Sta (arrivals)
The Colonnades Shopping Centre
UK Passport Office
Queen Mother Sports Cen
The Draycott Hotel
SLOANE STREET
SLOANE SQ
Royal Court
Sloane Sq Stn
Victoria Coach Station
Francis Holland School
SW1W
Police Station
Imperial School of Design
WARWICK SQ
PIMLICO RD
Garden House School
Abbots Manor
Abbots Manor Estate
St Barnabas Mews
Pimlico

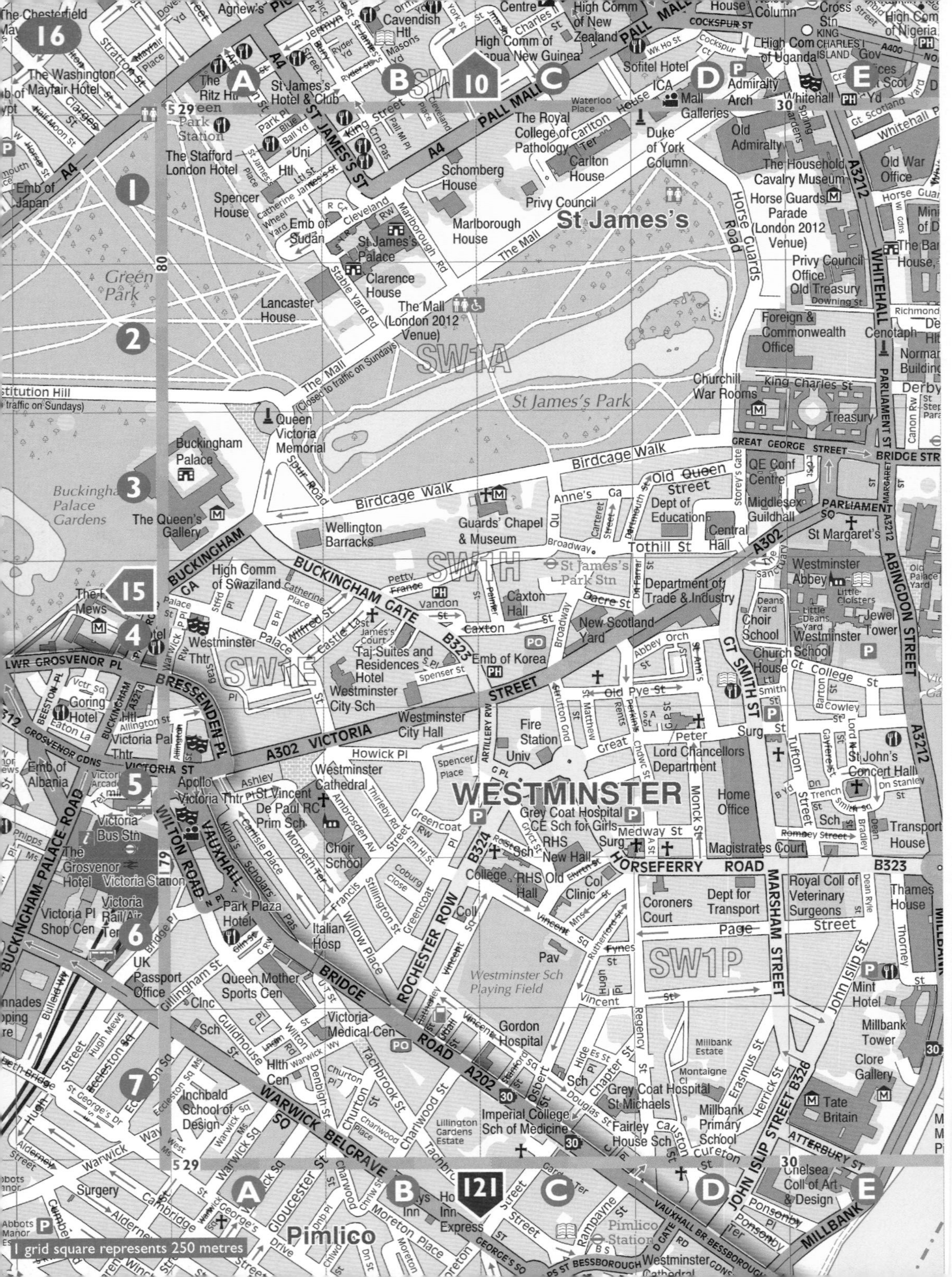

16
10
15
121
A
B
C
D
E
1
2
3
4
5
6
7
The Chesterfield
The Washington Mayfair Hotel
The Ritz Htl
St James's Hotel & Club
Cavendish Htl
High Comm of Papua New Guinea
High Comm of New Zealand
High Comm of Nigeria
High Com of Uganda
Sofitel Hotel
ICA
Mall Galleries
Admiralty Arch
Whitehall
Gov Offices
Green Park Station
The Stafford London Hotel
Uni Htl
Emb of Japan
Spencer House
Emb of Sudan
St James's Palace
Clarence House
Lancaster House
Schomberg House
Marlborough House
The Royal College of Pathology
Carlton House
Duke of York Column
Privy Council
St James's
Old Admiralty
The Household Cavalry Museum
Horse Guards Parade (London 2012 Venue)
Privy Council Office
Old Treasury
Old War Office
Horse Guards Road
The Mall
The Mall (London 2012 Venue)
The Mall (Closed to traffic on Sundays)
Green Park
SW1A
St James's Park
Constitution Hill
Foreign & Commonwealth Office
Cenotaph
Churchill War Rooms
King Charles St
Treasury
Norman Building
Queen Victoria Memorial
Buckingham Palace
Buckingham Palace Gardens
The Queen's Gallery
Birdcage Walk
Spur Road
GREAT GEORGE STREET
BRIDGE STREET
PARLIAMENT ST
WHITEHALL
QE Conf Centre
Middlesex Guildhall
Dept of Education
Central Hall
Old Queen Street
Anne's Ga
Guards' Chapel & Museum
Wellington Barracks
Tothill St
St Margaret's
PARLIAMENT SQ
Westminster Abbey
Little Cloisters
Jewel Tower
ABINGDON STREET
SW1H
St James's Park Stn
High Comm of Swaziland
BUCKINGHAM GATE
Petty France
Caxton Hall
Department of Trade & Industry
New Scotland Yard
Choir School
Westminster School
The Royal Mews
Westminster Thtr
Taj Suites and Residences Hotel
Emb of Korea
Westminster City Sch
Westminster City Hall
SW1E
LWR GROSVENOR PL
BRESSENDEN PL
Goring Hotel
Victoria Pal Thtr
VICTORIA ST
A302 VICTORIA STREET
Emb of Albania
Apollo Victoria Thtr
Old Pye St
Fire Station
Univ
Great Peter St
Lord Chancellors Department
GT SMITH ST
Church House
St John's Concert Hall
WESTMINSTER
Home Office
Grey Coat Hospital CE Sch for Girls
RHS New Hall
Westminster Cathedral
St Vincent De Paul RC Prim Sch
Choir School
Victoria Bus Stn
The Grosvenor Hotel
Victoria Station
Victoria Pl Shop Cen
Victoria Rail/Air Ter
BUCKINGHAM PALACE ROAD
WILTON ROAD
VAUXHALL BRIDGE ROAD
Park Plaza Hotel
Italian Hosp
ROCHESTER ROW
HORSEFERRY ROAD
Magistrates Court
Transport House
Coroners Court
Dept for Transport
Royal Coll of Veterinary Surgeons
Thames House
MARSHAM STREET
Page Street
SW1P
Westminster Sch Playing Field
UK Passport Office
Queen Mother Sports Cen
Victoria Medical Cen
Gordon Hospital
Mint Hotel
Millbank Tower
Clore Gallery
Tate Britain
MILLBANK
JOHN ISLIP STREET
Millbank Estate
Grey Coat Hospital St Michaels
Millbank Primary School
Fairley House Sch
Imperial College Sch of Medicine
Lillington Gardens Estate
Inchbald School of Design
WARWICK SQ
BELGRAVE RD
ATTERBURY ST
Chelsea Coll of Art & Design
Pimlico
Pimlico Station
VAUXHALL BR
Westminster Gdns
Surgery
1 grid square represents 250 metres

Charing Cross Stn
Embankment Pier
Embankment Station
Festival Pier
Television Centre
Royal National Theatre
Gallery
Playhouse
Queen Elizabeth Hall
Golden Jubilee Bridge
Upper Ground
Stamford St
Industrial Centre
London Nautical School
Paris Gdn
Hatfields
Colin St
DEFRA
The Royal Horseguards Hotel
Hispaniola
WC2N
Royal Festival Hall
Hayward Gallery
Waterloo Rd
Kings College London
Aquinas St
Miller Walk
Surgery
Cornwall Rd
Coin Street
Burrell St
Chancel St
Colombo St
Blackfriars
Nicholson Street
Brinton Walk
London City Coll & Schiller Int Univ
Concert Hall Ap
Theed St
Whittlesey Street
Meymott St
Avenue
PS Tattershall Castle
BFI London IMAX Cinema
Secker St
Sch
Roupell St
Brad St
Isabella St
Joan Street
Scoresby St
Southwark Station
Gambia St
Ministry of Defence
Banqueting House Whitehall
Jubilee Gardens
Belvedere Road
Shell Centre
Mepham St
Exton St
Alaska St
Sandell St
Wootton Street
Greet St
Waterloo East Stn
B300
A3211
A3200
York Road
Waterloo Station
Mepham St
Waterloo Rd
Young Vic Theatre
The Cut
Southwark College
Burrows Ms
Nelson Sq
London Eye Millennium Pier
London Eye
London Marriott Hotel
Chicheley Street
Department of Health
Norman Shaw (MP's Offices)
Victoria Emb
The Movieum of London
County Hall
Dali Universe
Forum Magnum Square
Leake Street
Holmes Ter
Pear Pl
Mitre Rd
Ufford St
Chaplin Close
Surrey Row
Pocock St
Friars Primary Foundation School
Undary Rw
Valentine Place
Works
Westminster Pier
Portcullis House
Westminster Station
Sealife London Aquarium
Park Plaza Hotel
Addington St
Spur Road
Old Vic Theatre
Webber Street
Coral St
Baron's Place
Westminster Bridge Rd
Westminster Bridge Park Plaza Hotel
Marsh
Launcelot St
Johanna Primary School
Webber Row
Big Ben
Westminster Bridge
Florence Nightingale Museum
Lower Marsh
Grindal St
Waterloo Health Centre
Murphy Street
Baylis Road
Frazier St
Morley St
Cooper Cl
Dodson St
Waterloo Road
Lancaster
Davidge St
Milcote St
South Bank University
St George's Circus
Palace of Westminster Houses of Parliament
A&E
Upper Marsh
Westminster Br Rd
A23
Creenham Cl
Pearman Street
Gerridge St
Emery
Lambeth North Stn
St Thomas' Hospital
Royal Street
Lane
Newnham Ter
Westminster Br Rd
A302
Metropolitan Hosp
Rotary St
A201
Borough
Lambeth
Morley College
St George's Cathedral
Girls School
South Bank Univ
Victoria Tower Gardens
United Medical & Dental Schools
Thames Path
City of Westminster
Lambeth
Lambeth Palace Road
Centaur St
Virgil St
Carlisle
Hercules Rd
McAuley Cl
Police Stn
Oakey Lane
King Edward Wk
Churchill Clinic
Mead Row
Cosser Street
Gladstone St
Colnbrook St
St George's Road
Sch
Garden Rw
A302
Archbishop's Park
Council Building
Geraldine Mary Harmsworth Park
Morton Place
Days Hotel
Road
A3036
Sidford Place
Lambeth
Imperial War Museum
Lambeth Palace
Surgery
Kennington
West Sq
Newington
The Garden Museum
Fairley House Junior School
A3203
Harmsworth Mews
IWM Annexe
Brook Drive
Southwark
Lambeth
Austral St
Orient St
Hayles St
Hedger St
Lamlash St
Elliott's Rw
A3203
Lambeth Bridge
Novotel
Norfolk Row
Pratt Walk
Sail Street
Bedlam Mews
Hornbeam Cl
Walnut Tree Walk
Walcot Sq
Walcot Sq
Juxon St
Ingram Cl
Old Paradise St
Saperton Walk
Fitzalan
Walnut Tree Walk Primary School
St Mary's Wk
Sullivan Rd
Polperro Ms
Castlebrook Cl
Brook Drive
L Rd
Fire Brigade HQ
Lambeth High Street
Bishop's Ter
St Mary's Gdns
Oakden St
Monkton St
Nightingale Ms
Gilbert Rd
Heralds Pl
Renfrew Road
Dugard Way
Dante Rd
Holyoak Rd
Grg Mthrs Rd
Whitgift Street
Dragon Road
Lollard Street
Saunders St
Street
Distin St
Works
Newport Street
Gibson Road
Wincott St
The Michael Tippett School
London College of FE
Park Plaza Hotel
Simnc Pl
Black Prince
Lollard St
Archbishop Sumners CE Prim Sch
Knights
Salamanca Plaza on the River Hotel
Street
Road
Lilac Pl
S Cl
Beaufoy Walk
Ethelred Estate
SE11
Reedworth Street
K Rd
Hinley Clinic
Cotton Gardens Estate
A3204
Kennington Park Road
Millbank Millennium Pier
Albert Embankment
Randall Road
Randall Rw
Lillian Baylis School
Road
Marylee Way
Chester Way
Opal St
Citadel Pl
Walk
Street
Surgery
St Thomas Childrens Day Hospital
Denny St
Denny Cres
Kennington Lane
Cottington St
Othello Cl
Thames Path
Tinworth Street
Vauxhall
Graphite Square
Jonathan Street
Orsett St
Sancroft
Street
Tavy Close
Seaton Close
White Hart Street
Alberta
Works
Morgan St
Tyers
Wickham St
Burn Street
Court
Lambeth County
Kennington
Glasshouse
A23
Road
Kennington
A301
A201
B300
A3203

18
17
12
122
532
A
B
C
D
E
1
2
3
4
5
6
7
STAMFORD ST
A3200
Christchurch Industrial Centre
Kings College London
Express by Holiday Inn
Gallery
Sumner St
Rose Thtr Exhibition
SOUTHWARK ST
Times
Exhib
Clink St
Makers-Hall
Vinopolis, City of Wine
Southwark Cath
Borough Market
Montague Cl
Winchester Sq
London Nautical School
Hatfields
Paris Gdn
Burrell St
Chancel St
Bear La
Price's St
SOUTHWARK STREET
School
Zoar St
Industrial Cen
Guys Kings and Thomas Medical School (Kings College London)
Gatehouse Square
Southwark Rose Hotel
Bramah's Tea & Coffee Mus
London Bridge Hotel
Univ of London
White Hart Yard
Talbot Yard
Coin St
Duchy St
Aquinas St
Miller Walk
Surgery
Meymott St
Nicholson Street
Farnham Pl
Lavington St
Works
Mercure London City Bankside Hotel
Thrale St
A3200
Kings College London
Maidstone Buildings Mews
Theed St
Whittlesey Street
Roupell St
Brad St
Waterloo East Stn
Wootton Street
Isabella St
Joan Street
Brinton Walk
Scoresby St
Gambia St
Grande Vitesse Industrial Cen
Ewer St
Wardens Grove
Guildford St
A St
O'Meara St
Southwark Station
UNION STREET
B300
London Ctr of Cntpy Music
Mayall Cl
A300
A3
York Clinic
Young Vic Theatre
THE CUT
Southwark College
Burrows Ms
Nelson Sq
Works
Copperfield St
Loman Street
Pepper St
Fire Brigade Mus
Ayres Street
Cathedral Sch of St Saviour & St Mary Overy
Newcomen St
Mermaid Ct
Chapel Court
Davies's Coll
Mitre Rd
Surrey Row
Crown Court at the Borough
Quilp St
Mint St
MARSHALSEA RD
Saint Josephs RC Prim Sch
Tabard Garden Estate
Baden Place
Plantain Pl
Southwark Coroners Court
Old Vic Theatre
Webber St
Ufford St
Chaplin Close
Valentine Place
Boundary Rw
Pocock St
Friars Primary Foundation School
Rushworth St
Glasshill Street
Sawyer St
Sturge St
Tdle St
Lant St
Sudrey St
Toulmin St
School
Pickwick Street
Sanctuary St
BOROUGH HIGH ST
Borough Stn
London Christian School
Empire Sq
B300
A301
Coral St
Baron's Place
Webber Row
Works
Webber Street
A201
BLACKFRIARS ROAD
Boyfield Street
Silex St
PO
Great Suffolk St
Collinson Street
Collinson Walk
The Borough
Sterry St
Pilgrimage Street
Globe St
Cole St
Swan St
Trinity St
WATERLOO ROAD
Cooper Cl
Frazier St
Morley St
Pearman St
Gerridge St
Dodson St
South Bank University
ST GEORGE'S CIRCUS
Milcote St
Davidge St
Lancaster Street
Kg James St
Mathieson Court
Scovell Rd
McCoid Way
Borough Square
Police Stn
Surgery
BOROUGH ROAD
South Bank University
Church Sq
Becket St
GREAT DOVER ST
WESTMINSTER BR RD
A3202
Metropolitan Hospital
Kell St
Rotary St
London South Bank University
SOUTHWARK BRIDGE RD
NEWINGTON CSWY
Inner London Sessions Ho (Crown Court)
SE1
Merrick Sq
Brockham St
Dickens Sq
Morley College
St George's Cathedral
Girls School
A207
Thomas Doyle St
South Bank University
Keyworth St
Gaunt St
Avonmouth St
Newington Gardens
HARPER RD
Oakey Lane
Churchill Clinic
Gladstone St
Eden College
Tiverton St
Alderney Mews
Spurgeon St
Chettle Close
ROAD
Council Building
Sch
Colnbrook St
GARDEN RW
A302
LONDON ROAD
Ontario St
Elephant & Castle Stn
Bath Terrace
Tarn St
Falmouth Rd
B240
Burbage Close
Globe Academy Lower Sch
Deverell St
Geraldine Mary Harmsworth
Imperial War Museum
Newington
Geraldine St
West St
GEORGE'S RD
Gaywood St
Princess St
Newington Court Business Cen
Rockingham St
Arch Street
Meadow Rw
South Bank University
County Street
Theobald St
KENNINGTON ROAD
Harmsworth Mews
West Sq
IWM Annexe
A201
NEW KENT ROAD
Brook Drive
Southwark
Lambeth
London College of Communication
Elephant & Castle Shopping Centre
Elephant & Castle Stn
Austral St
Orient St
Hayles St
Metropolitan Tabernacle
Castle Industrial Est
Rodney Pl
Balfour St
Bytr Mws
Walcot Sq
Hedger St
Lamlash St
Elliott's Rw
Oswin St
Elephant Rd
Heygate Estate
Munton Road
Victory Primary School
John Maurice Cl
Henshaw Street
Bishop's Ter
St Mary's Gdns
St Mary's Wk
Castlebrook Cl
Brook Drive
L Rd
Churchyard Rw
Elephant & Castle Leisure Cen
Deacon Way
Victory Place
Oakden St
Monkton St
Nightingale Ms
Gilbert Rd
Renfrew Road
Dugard Way
Dante Rd
NEWINGTON BUTTS
Draper Estate
Wollaston Close
WALWORTH ROAD
Heygate Street
Brandon St
Rodney Road
Chatham St
Salisbury Cl
Wincott St
The Michael Tippett School
Howell Wk
Hampton St
Hampton St
Marlborough Close
Robert Dashwood Way
The Cumming Museum
Wansey St
Larcom St
Content St
Wadding St
Stead St
Archbishop Sumners CE Prim Sch
Knights Walk
Cotton Gardens Estate
London College of FE
A3204
Newington Industrial Estate
Walworth Town Hall
Surg
Charleston St
Cotham St
Brandon St
Nursery Row
English Ma Primary Sc
Reedworth Street
Hinley Clinic
Chester Way
Wesley Close
Crampton Primary School
Canterbury Place
Peacock St
John Smith House
Primary School
Walcorde Avenue
Browning Street
Morecambe Street
Orb St
A23
KENNINGTON LANE
Cottington St
Othello Cl
KENNINGTON PARK ROAD
Penton Pl
Iliffe St
Crampton St
Police Station
King and Queen St
Tavy Close
Seaton Close
Alberta Street
Alberta Estate
Thrush St
Manor Place
Occupation Road
Surgery
PO
Robert Browning Primary School
Pilton Place
Blackwood St
Surgery
Tibetan
Kennington
Lambeth County
1 grid square represents 250 metres

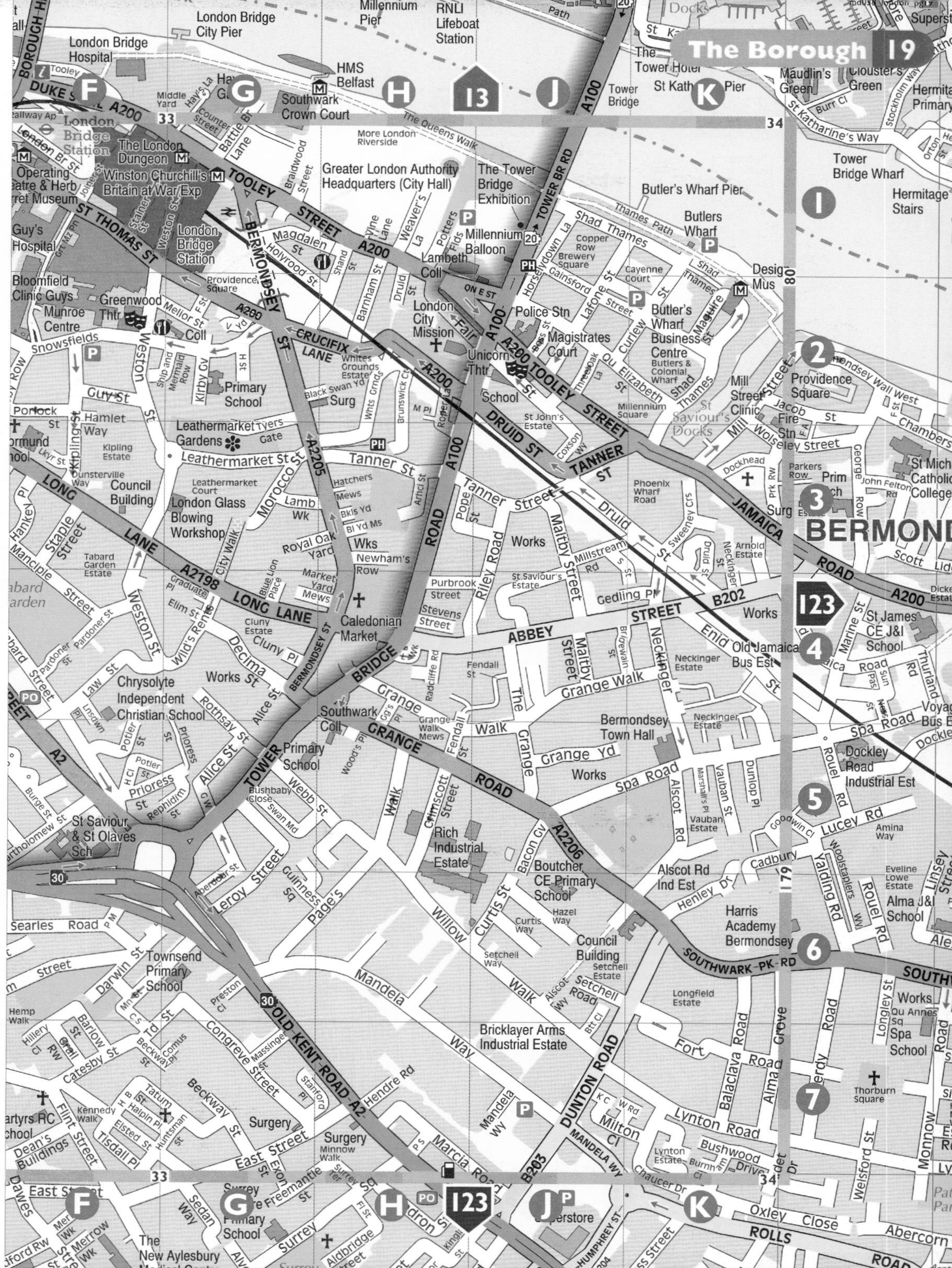

London Bridge City Pier
Millennium Pier
RNLI Lifeboat Station
London Bridge Hospital
HMS Belfast
Southwark Crown Court
The Tower Hotel
Tower Bridge
St Katharine's Way
London Bridge Station
The London Dungeon
Winston Churchill's Britain at War Exp
Operating Theatre & Herb Garret Museum
Greater London Authority Headquarters (City Hall)
The Tower Bridge Exhibition
Millennium Balloon
Butler's Wharf Pier
Tower Bridge Wharf
Hermitage Stairs
Guy's Hospital
TOOLEY STREET
ST THOMAS ST
BERMONDSEY ST
CRUCIFIX LANE
Bloomfield Clinic Guys
Greenwood Thtr
Munroe Centre
Police Stn
Magistrates Court
Butler's Wharf Business Centre
Design Mus
Providence Square
London City Mission
Unicorn Thtr
Primary School
Leathermarket Gardens
Leathermarket St
Tanner St
DRUID ST
JAMAICA ROAD
BERMOND
Council Building
London Glass Blowing Workshop
LONG LANE
Tabard Garden Estate
Caledonian Market
ABBEY STREET
Neckinger Estate
Old Jamaica Bus Est
Grange Walk
Bermondsey Town Hall
Dockley Road Industrial Est
Chrysolyte Independent Christian School
GRANGE ROAD
TOWER BRIDGE ROAD
Spa Road
Lucey Rd
St Saviour & St Olaves Sch
Rich Industrial Estate
Boutcher CE Primary School
Alscot Rd Ind Est
Harris Academy Bermondsey
SOUTHWARK PK RD
Townsend Primary School
Mandela Way
Council Building
Bricklayer Arms Industrial Estate
OLD KENT ROAD A2
DUNTON ROAD
Lynton Road
Longfield Estate
Thorburn Square
The New Aylesbury Medical Centre
ROLLS ROAD
Superstore

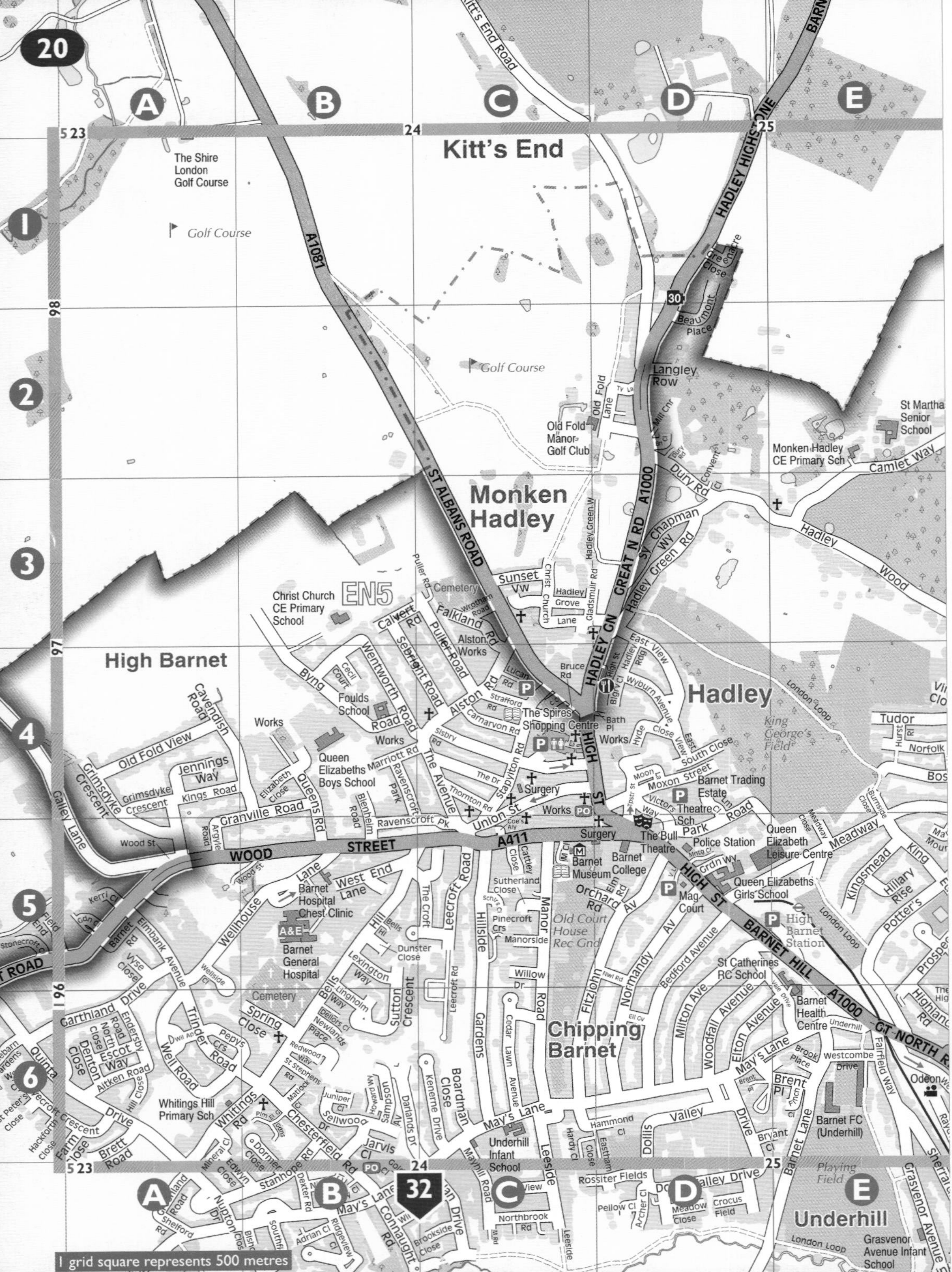
Kitt's End
Kitt's End Road
The Shire London Golf Course
Golf Course
A1081
ST ALBANS ROAD
HADLEY HIGHSTONE
Gree Close
Beaumont Place
Langley Row
Old Fold Lane
Old Fold Manor Golf Club
Mill Cnr
Dury Rd
Convent Cl
St Martha Senior School
Monken Hadley CE Primary Sch
Camlet Way
Hadley Wood
Monken Hadley
Hadley Green W
GREAT N RD
A1000
Chapman Wy
Hadley Green Rd
Sunset Vw
Christ Church Lane
Hadley Grove
Gladsmuir Rd
Cemetery
EN5
Christ Church CE Primary School
Puller Rd
Calvert Rd
Falkland Rd
Wrotham Road
Alston Works
HADLEY GN
East View
High Barnet
Byng Rd
Cecil Court
Wentworth Road
Sebright Road
Lucan Rd
Bruce Rd
Hadley
London Loop
King George's Field
Tudor
Norfolk
Foulds School
Alston Rd
Strafford Rd
Carnarvon Rd
The Spires Shopping Centre
Bath Pl
Works
Hyde Close
Wyburn Avenue
South Close
Cavendish Road
Old Fold View
Jennings Way
Grimsdyke Crescent
Grimsdyke Crescent
Kings Road
Elizabeth Close
Queens Rd
Queen Elizabeths Boys School
Marriott Rd
Ravenscroft Park
The Avenue
Stapylton Rd
The Dr
Thornton Rd
Surgery
Moon La
Moxon Street
Barnet Trading Estate
Victors Way
Theatre Sch
Park Road
Queen Elizabeth Leisure Centre
Meadway
Galley Lane
Granville Road
Argyle Road
Blenheim Road
Ravenscroft Pk
Union St
Coe's Aly
HIGH ST
Wood St
WOOD STREET
A411
Surgery
The Bull Theatre
Police Station
Barnet Museum
Barnet College
Cattley Close
Leecroft Road
West End Lane
Barnet Hospital Chest Clinic
Wellhouse Lane
Sutherland Close
Orchard Rd
Elm Rd
Mag Court
Grdn Wy
Queen Elizabeths Girls School
High Barnet Station
Kingsmead
Hillary Rise
Potter's
King
Kerri Cl
Field End
Elmbank Avenue
Barnet Rd
A&E
Barnet General Hospital
The Croft
Bells Hill
Dunster Close
Lexington Way
Hillside Gardens
Pinecroft Crs
Manorside
Manor Road
Old Court House Rec Gnd
Fitzjohn Av
Normandy Av
Bedford Avenue
BARNET HILL
St Catherines RC School
A1000
GT NORTH RD
Stonecroft Cl
Vyse Close
Wellside Cl
Cemetery
Lingholm Way
Sutton Crescent
Leecroft Rd
Willow Dr
Milton Ave
Woodfall Avenue
Elton Avenue
Barnet Health Centre
Underhill
Highlands Rd
Garthland Drive
Endersby Road
Trinder Road
Pepys Crs
Spring Close
Newlands Place
Redwood Way
St Stephens Rd
Boardman Close
Cedar Lawn Avenue
Chipping Barnet
Ell Cv
May's Lane
Brook Place
Westcombe Drive
Fairfield Way
Odeon
North Close
Escot Way
Well Road
Denton Close
Aitken Road
Hill Close
Quinta Drive
Whitings Hill Primary Sch
Whitings Rd
Chesterfield Rd
Juniper Cl
Sellwood Dr
Sampson Av
Darlands Dr
Kenerne Drive
May's Lane
Underhill Infant School
Hardy Cl
Hammond Cl
Eastham Close
Dollis Valley Drive
Brent Pl
Bryant Cl
Barnet Lane
Barnet FC (Underhill)
St Peter's Close
Hackforth Close
Farm Close
Brett Road
Edwyn Close
Dormer Close
Stanhope Rd
Jarvis Cl
Mayhill Road
Leeside
Rossiter Fields
Dollis Valley Drive
Playing Field
Underhill
Shelford Rd
Nunton Clo
Dexter Rd
Ridgeview Rd
Adrian Cl
May's Lane
Connaught Rd
Brookside Close
Northbrook Rd
Pellow Cl
Archer Cl
Meadow Close
Crocus Field
London Loop
Grasvenor Avenue
Grasvenor Avenue Infant School
A B C D E
1 2 3 4 5 6
5 23
24
25
98
97
96
1 grid square represents 500 metres

32

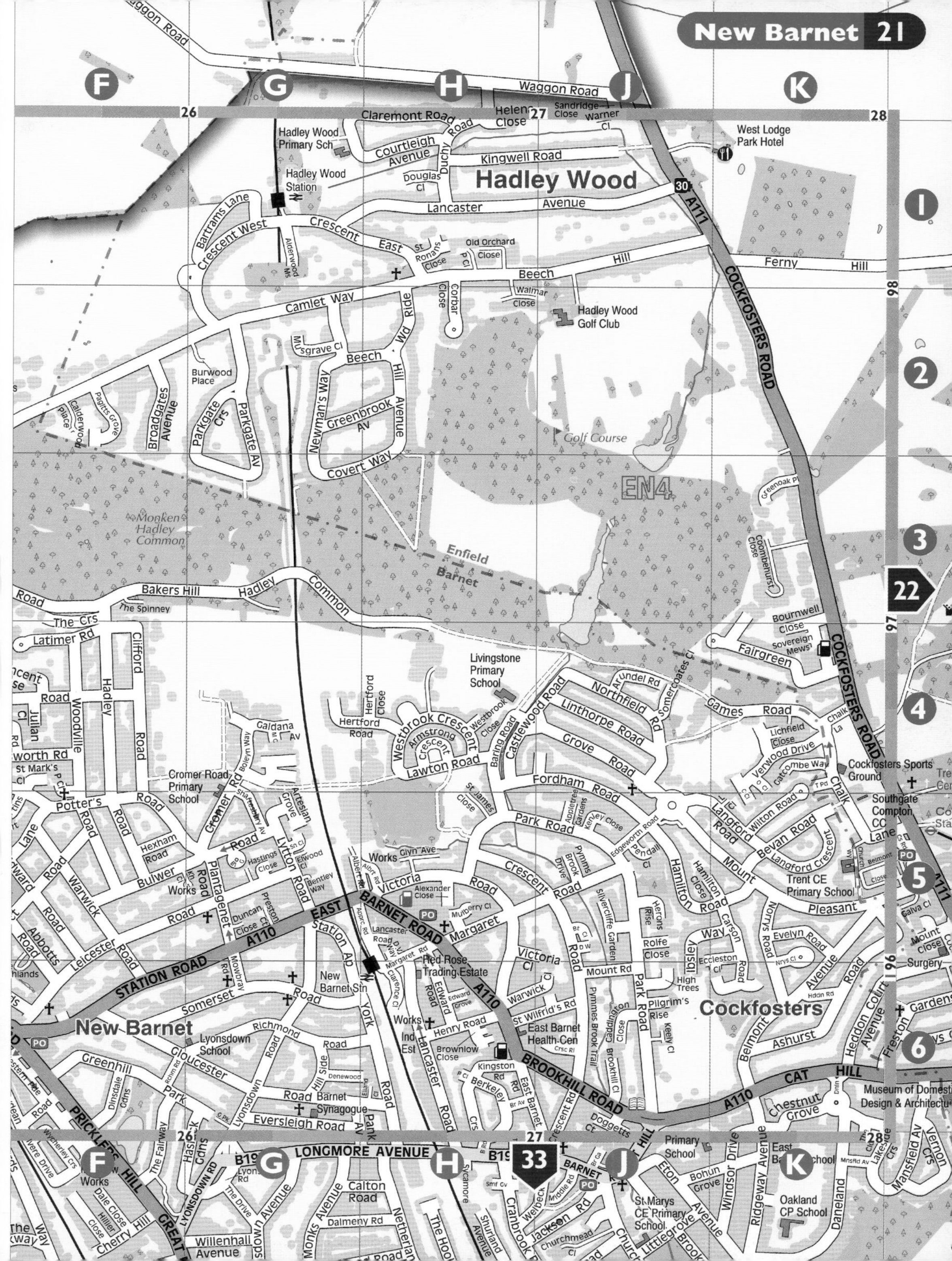

New Barnet 21
F
G
H
J
K
26
27
28
Waggon Road
Claremont Road
Helena Close
Sandridge Close
Warner Cl
Hadley Wood Primary Sch
Courtleigh Avenue
Duchy Road
Kingwell Road
West Lodge Park Hotel
Hadley Wood Station
Douglas Cl
Hadley Wood
30
A111
Lancaster Avenue
Bartrams Lane
Crescent West
Alderwood Ms
Crescent East
St Ronans Close
P Cl
Old Orchard Close
Beech Hill
Ferny Hill
Camlet Way
Corbar Close
Walmar Close
Hadley Wood Golf Club
COCKFOSTERS ROAD
Musgrave Cl
Beech Hill
Wd Ride
Burwood Place
Broadgates Avenue
Parkgate Crs
Parkgate Av
Newman's Way
Greenbrook Av
Hill Avenue
Calderwood Place
Pagitts Grove
Covert Way
Golf Course
EN4
Greenoak Pl
Monken Hadley Common
Enfield
Barnet
Coombehurst Close
Road
Bakers Hill
Hadley Common
The Spinney
The Crs
Latimer Rd
Clifford Road
Hadley Road
Woodville Road
Julian Cl
St Mark's Cl
Bournwell Close
Sovereign Mews
Fairgreen
Livingstone Primary School
Arundel Rd
Northfield Rd
Somercoates Cl
Linthorpe Road
Castlewood Road
Games Road
Hertford Close
Hertford Road
Westbrook Crescent
Armstrong Crescent
Westbrook Close
Baring Road
Grove Road
Lichfield Close
Verwood Drive
Chalk La
Galdana Av
Boleyn Way
Lawton Road
Catcombe Way
Cockfosters Sports Ground
Cromer Road Primary School
Cromer Rd
Potter's Road
St James Close
Fordham Road
Southgate Compton CC
Chalk Lane
Wilton Road
Langford Road
Artesian Grove
Appletree Gardens
Kenley Close
Edgeworth Road
Hexham Road
Lytton Road
Park Road
Pendall Cl
Bevan Road
Langford Crescent
Mount Pleasant
Hastings Close
Elwood Cl
Bentley Way
Works
Glyn Ave
Pymms Brook Drive
Hamilton Road
Hamilton Close
Belmont Close
Bulwer Road
Plantagenet Road
Warwick Road
Albert Rd
Victoria Road
Alexander Close
Crescent Road
Trent CE Primary School
Preston Cl
Duncan Close
EAST BARNET ROAD
PO
Mulberry Cl
Silvercliffe Gardens
Herons Rise
Isbley Way
Carson Road
Norrys Road
Evelyn Road
Galva Cl
Leicester Road
Abbotts Road
A110
Station Ap
Lancaster Road
Margaret Road
Rolfe Close
Eccleston Cl
Mount Close
STATION ROAD
Mowbray Rd
New Barnet Stn
Red Rose Trading Estate
Victoria Cl
Mount Rd
High Trees
Avenue Road
Surgery
96
97
98
Somerset Road
Edward Road
Edward Grove
Warwick Cl
Pymmes Brook Trail
Pilgrim's Rise
Cockfosters
Hadn Rd
Gardens
New Barnet
Clarence Cl
York Road
St Wilfrid's Rd
Caddington Close
Keely Cl
Lyonsdown School
Richmond Road
Works
Ind Est
Henry Road
Brownlow Close
East Barnet Health Cen
Crsc Rl
Brookhill Cl
Belmont Avenue
Ashurst Road
Heddon Court Avenue
Freston Gardens
Greenhill Park
Gloucester Road
Kingston Rd
BROOKHILL ROAD
CAT HILL
Museum of Domestic Design & Architecture
Dinsdale Gdns
Lyonsdown Road
Hill Side
Denewood
Barnet Synagogue
Berkeley Crs
Br Av
East Barnet Road
Chestnut Grove
Eversleigh Road
Pank Av
Doggetts Ct
A110
PRICKLERS HILL
Hasluck Gdns
The Fairway
Wycherley Crs
Belvedere Drive
Works
Dale Close
Hillier Close
Cherry Hill
B19
LONGMORE AVENUE
B19
33
BARNET
Primary School
East Barnet School
Mnsfld Av
Lakeside Crs
Vernon Crs
Mansfield Av
LYONSDOWN RD
Lyonsdown Avenue
The Drive
Calton Road
Monks Avenue
Dalmeny Rd
Netherlands Road
The Hook
Sycamore
Shurland Avenue
Cranbrook
Welbeck
Middle Rd
Jackson Rd
Churchmead
Church
Bohun Grove
St Marys CE Primary School
Littlegrove
Eton Avenue
Brook
Windsor Drive
Ridgeway Avenue
Oakland CP School
Daneland
GREAT
Willenhall Avenue
The Way

London Loop
A
B
C
D
E
A1005
THE RI
528
29
30
Park Farm
London Loop
Ferny Hill
Hadley Road
Hill
Hadley Rd
98
1
2
3
21
97
London Loop
Middlesex University (Trent Park Campus)
Trent Country Park
Snakes Lane
Golf Course
4
COCKFOSTERS ROAD
Cockfosters Sports Ground
Trent Park Cemetery
Southgate Compton CC
Cockfosters Station
Chalk Lane
ENFIELD RD
40
A110
Trent Park Golf Club
5
A111
Norfolk Close
West Close
East Close
Galva Cl
Mount Close
Cockfosters Road
Gloucester Gardens
Kent Drive
Westpole Avenue
Oakwood Station
Southgate School
Way
Sussex
Oakwood Medical Cen
Lakeside
Greystoke Gdns
Lowther Drive
Culgaith Gardens
Merryhills Drive
Lonsdale Drive
South Lodge Drive
Grosvenor Gdns
Prince George Av
Brantwood Gardens
Clifton Gardens
Belgrave Gdns
96
Surgery
Freston Gardens
Leys Gdns
6
HILL
A110 BRAMLEY ROAD
Priory Close
Chase Road
Reservoir Road
Lakenheath
Sheringham Av
Merrivale
South Lodge Drive
South Ldg Dr
Overton Road Dr
Prince George Avenue
Museum of Domestic Design & Architecture
Chicken Shed Theatre
Homestead Paddock
De Bohun Primary School
Vita et Pax School
Tregenna Cl
Wolverton Wy
Ashmead
528
29
30
A
B
C
D
E
Salcombe Preparatory School (Infants)
34
Mansfield Av
Vernon Crs
Middlesex University (Cat Hill Campus)
CHASE SIDE
Green
The Fairway
Cowper Gardens
Linden Close
Saxon Wy
Sheringham Avenue
Oakwood
Oakwood Park
Daneland
Oak Hill Theological
1 grid square represents 500 metres

EN2
Clay Hill
Golf Club
F
G
H
J
K
31
32
33
THE RIDGEWAY
A1005
The Kings Oak Private Hospital
Royal Chace Hotel
Chase Farm Hospital
A&E
Oak Avenue
Mount View
High Oaks
Spring Court Rd
Ridge Crest
Harefield Cl
Hunters Way
Shooters Rd
Albuhera Close
Comreddy Close
Lavender Hill
London Loop
Cook's Hole Road
Cemetery
Cedar Road
Lime Tree Walk
Blossom Lane
Lavender Gdns
Rendlesham Road
Tudor Crs
Phipps Hatch Lane
Ps Hh La
Cedar Park Road
Brodie Road
Gloucester Road
Browning Road
Park Nook Gardens
Elm Gardens
Hillside Crescent
Morley Hill
Birkbeck Road
Woodbine Grove
Myrtle Grove
Kilvinton Drive
Lavender Primary School
Enfield Ch School
Chantry Close
Ripley Road
Wetherby Road
Brigadier Hill
Glenville Avenue
Merton Rd
Sterling Rd
Brigadier Avenue
Burlington Rd
Woodlands Rd
White House Lane
Primary School
Hawthorn Grove
Acacia Rd
Lavender Rd
Rosemary Av
Primrose Avenue
Baker Street
Lancaster Road
Farorna Walk
Farmlands
Hardy Way
Fairview Road
Jaycroft
Hansart Way
St Johns Senior School
Acorn Close
Avalon Cl
Drapers Road
Harris Close
John
Lee View
Hedge Hill
Gordon Hill Station
Bankside Cl
Gordon Hill
Youngmans Close
Kirkland Drive
Laurel Bank Road
Lea Rd
Lynn St
Drake Street
Armfield Road
Kynaston Road
Weardale Gardens
Playing Field
Gater Care Centre
Farr Road
The Drive
Sports Grnd
Bell Road
Batley Road
Chase Side Crescent
Heene Road
College Road
Holtwhite's Hill
Gooch Drive
Padstow Rd
Comfort Hotel
Chasewood Av
Perry Mead
Banbury
Monks Road
Black Fan Close
Sports Ground
Holtwhite Avenue
Halifax Road
Gordon Road
St Georges RC Primary School
Manor Road
Cheviot Cl
Crofton Way
Dunraven Drive
Audley Road
Rowantree Road
Byculla Road
Bn Ct
Abbotts Crs
Trinity Street
Chase Side Primary School
Nunns Rd
Cavell Drive
North London Nuffield Hospital
Uplands Park Road
Canford Cl
The Grove
Chase Ridings
Robson Cl
Chase Green Avenue
Monks Close
Christchurch Cl
Conical Corner
Chase Side
Chase Side Avenue
Parsonage Gardens
Parsonage Lane
Riverside Gdns
Monastery Gardens
Baker Street
Primary School
Ridgemount Gardens
Colonels Walk
Posterns Green
Culloden Road
Temple Grove
Glebe Avenue
Byculla Avenue
Elizabeth
Byculla Road
Chase Court Gardens
Florence Dr
West Bank
Chase Gdns
Enfield Town
Enfield Grammar Lower
Police Station
Sports Grnd
Portcullis Lodge Rd
Enfield County School
Civic Cen
Surgery
Slades Gardens
Windmill Gardens
Park Way
The Glade
Grafton Road
Trentwood Side
Elmer Close
Enfield Rd
SLADES HILL
30
Taunton Drive
Slades Close
Slades Rise
Hunting Ga Cl
A110 WINDMILL HILL
Merryhills Clinic
Foxmead Cl
Linkside Gardens
Links Side
Linkside Close
Bincote Road
Costwold Way
Old Park View
Millers Green Close
Windcroft Close
Old Park Road
Calshot Wy
Waverley Road
Badgers Close
Gladbeck Way
Enfield Chase Station
Shirley Road
Chase Green Avenue
Gentleman's Row
Little Park Gdns
Enfield Grammar Sch Upper
Church Lane
Silver St
St Andrew's Rd
River Front
CHURCH STREET
A110
GENOTIN RD
Enfield Town Stn
Palace Gardens Shopping Centre
CECIL RD
Town Park
School
Merryhills Primary School
Glenbrook N
Glenbrook S
World's End
Enfield Golf Club
Crescent Road
The Coppice
Old Park Rd South
The Glen
Firbank Cl
Old Park Avenue
ENFIELD
Raleigh Rd
Sydney Rd
Essex Road
London Rd
Chalkwell
Lyndhurst Gdns
Golf Course
Chiltern Dene
Lane
World's End
Roundhill Dr
Rushey Hill
Grange Park Primary School
Old Pk Gv
New River
Tiptree Dr
Park Crs
Walsingham Road
Ridings Av
Tresilian Av
Fleming Dr
Hanbury Dr
Treves Cl
Firs Sq
Highlands Av
Newsholme Dr
Uplands Way
Onslow Gardens
Langham Gdns
Cheyne Wk
Cranleigh Gdns
Chine
Ridings
Whitethorn Gardens
Uvedale Road
Amwell
LONDON ROAD
A105 PARK AVENUE
Castleleigh Ct
Private Rd
Grange Park
Grange Park Station
Bush Hill Park Golf Club
Carrs Lane
Bush Hill
Ringmer Pl
Walnut Gv
Regency Ct
Mortimer Dr
Chaseville Park Road
Vera Avenue
Cadogan Gdns
Green
Brook Pk Cl
The
35
Chaseville Clinic
Maplin Cl
Drake Road
Maxim
Bazile Rd
Viga Road
Landra Gardens
Merridene
Nestor Av
Preparatory School
Old Park
Golf Course
Quakers Walk
The Orchard
Orchard
Faversham Av
Stringbourne Av
Eversley Park Road
Eversley Close
Eversley Crescent
The Birches
Holly Hill
Willow Walk
Brookside
Wade's Hill
Lane
Hadley Close
Hadley Wy
Deepdene
Hartland
Elmscott Gdns
Village Rd
6
5
4
3
2
I
24
98
97
96

24
23
36
Forty Hill
Enfield
Ponders End
Bush Hill Park
EN1
Enfield Playing Fields
Forty Hall
Forty Hill CE Primary Sch
Enfield Crematorium
Worcesters Primary School
Lavender Primary School
Enfield County School
Chace Community School
Adath Yisroel Cemetery
Queen Elizabeth Stadium
David Lloyd Sports Centre
Russet House School
Carterhatch Infant School
Suffolks Primary School
George Spicer Primary School
Kingsmead School
Cineworld
Superstore
Works
Northgate Business Centre
Haslemere Business Centre
Martinbridge Industrial Estate
Great Cambridge Industrial Est
Middlesex University (Enfield Campus)
College of Haringey, & North E
Waverley School
Cemetery
Enfield Business Centre
Bush Hill Park
Recreation Ground
Enfield Town Stn
Southbury Station
Bush Hill Park Stn
Bush Hill Park Primary School
Bush Hill Park Medical Cen
Enfield CC
Martindale Ind Estate
Lincoln Road Clnc
GREAT CAMBRIDGE ROAD
SOUTHBURY ROAD
HERTFORD ROAD
LONDON ROAD
A105 PARK AVENUE
NAGS HEAD
A10
A110
A1010
Forty Hill
Goat Lane
Hoe Lane
Carterhatch Lane
Lincoln Road
Donkey Lane
Tenniswood Road
Baker Street
Myddelton Avenue
Russell Road
Willow Road
Crown Road
Baird Road
Queensway
Main Av
1 grid square represents 500 metres

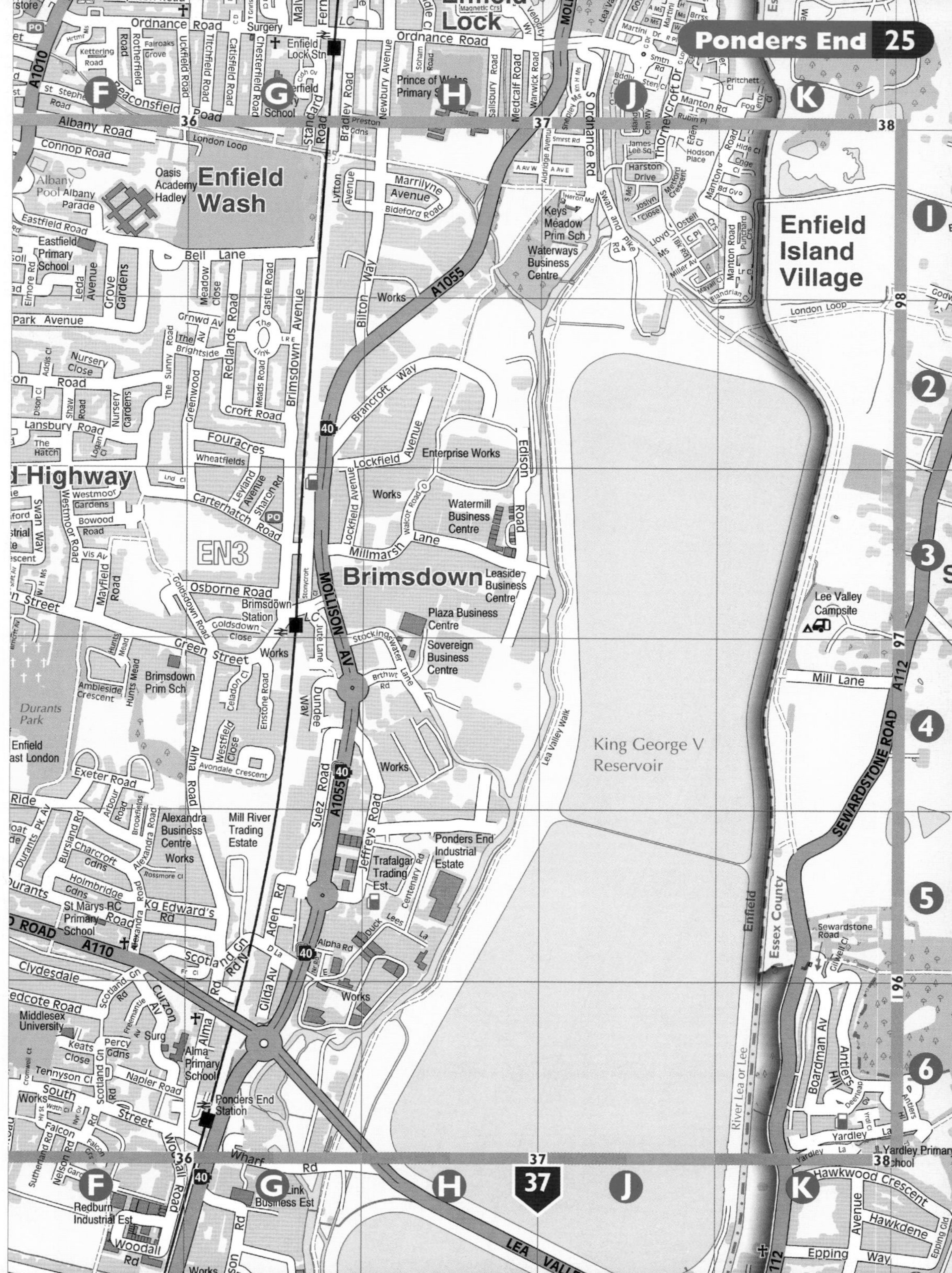
Enfield Lock
Enfield Wash
Enfield Island Village
Brimsdown
EN3
King George V Reservoir
Lee Valley Campsite
Ordnance Road
Albany Road
Connop Road
Bell Lane
Park Avenue
Lansbury Road
Fouracres
Carterhatch Road
Osborne Road
Green Street
Millmarsh Lane
Lockfield Avenue
Brancroft Way
Bilton Way
Mollison Av
A1055
A110
A112
A1010
Sewardstone Road
Mill Lane
Lea Valley Walk
River Lea or Lee
Enfield
Essex County
Exeter Road
Alma Road
Suez Road
Jeffreys Road
Wharf Rd
Woodall Road
South Street
Ponders End Station
Brimsdown Station
Enfield Lock Stn
Enterprise Works
Watermill Business Centre
Leaside Business Centre
Plaza Business Centre
Sovereign Business Centre
Mill River Trading Estate
Alexandra Business Centre
Ponders End Industrial Estate
Trafalgar Trading Est
Redburn Industrial Est
Link Business Est
Waterways Business Centre
Keys Meadow Prim Sch
Brimsdown Prim Sch
Alma Primary School
Eastfield Primary School
Oasis Academy Hadley
St Marys RC Primary School
Middlesex University
Yardley Primary School
Durants Park
Albany Pool
Hawkwood Crescent
Epping Way
Manton Road
Thorneycroft Dr
S Ordnance Rd
Swan and Pike Rd
London Loop

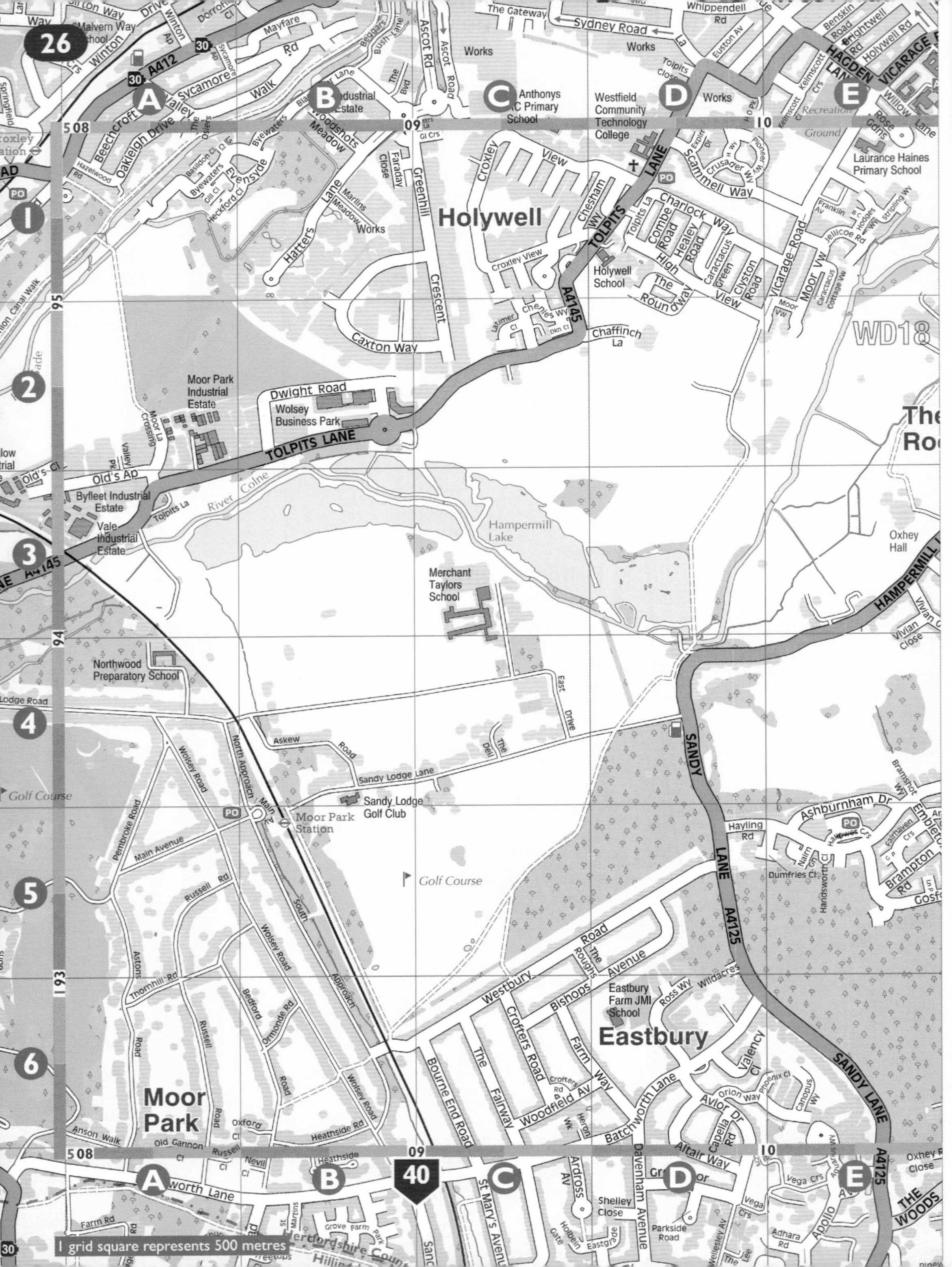

26
Winton Way
Malvern Way School
Winton Crs
Winton Dr
Dorrofield Cl
Mayfare
Sycamore Rd
Beggars Bush Lane
Ascot Rd
Ascot Road
The Gateway
Sydney Road
Whippendell Rd
Works
A412
30
Sycamore Walk
Valley Walk
Beechcroft
Oakleigh Drive
Hazelwood Rd
The Osiers
Byewaters
Basildon Cl
Evensyde
Gill Cl
Heckford Cl
Woodshots Meadow
Industrial Estate
The Bvd
St Anthonys RC Primary School
Westfield Community Technology College
Tolpits Close
Euston Av
Works
Benskin Road
Brightwell Rd
Holywell Rd
HAGDEN LANE
VICARAGE RD
Kelmscott Crs
Recreation Ground
Rose Gdns
Willow Lane
Laurance Haines Primary School
508
09
10
Croxley Station
PO
Greenhill Crescent
Faraday Close
Marlins Meadow
Hatters Lane
Works
Croxley View
Holywell
Chesham Wy
TOLPITS LANE
Scammell Way
Crusader Wy
Pioneer Wy
Tolpits La
Charlock Way
Combe Road
Healey Road
High View
Caractacus Green
Clyston Road
Vicarage Road
Moor Vw
Franklin Av
Hodges Wy
Stripling Wy
Jellicoe Rd
Caractacus Cottage Vw
Holywell School
The Roundway
A4145
Chenies Wy
Latimer Cl
Chaffinch La
Caxton Way
WD18
95
Moor Park Industrial Estate
Dwight Road
Wolsey Business Park
Moor La Crossing
Valley Pk
TOLPITS LANE
Old's Cl
Old's Ap
Byfleet Industrial Estate
Vale Industrial Estate
Tolpits La
River Colne
Hampermill Lake
Oxhey Hall
HAMPERMILL LANE
Vivian Close
Merchant Taylors School
94
Northwood Preparatory School
Lodge Road
East Drive
The Dell
Askew Road
Sandy Lodge Lane
Sandy Lodge Golf Club
Moor Park Station
North Approach
Main Av
Wolsey Road
Pembroke Road
Main Avenue
Russell Rd
Golf Course
Golf Course
SANDY LANE
A4125
Bramshot Wy
Ashburnham Dr
Hayling Rd
Nairn Gn
Handsworth Cl
Dumfries Cl
Brampton Rd
Embleton
Gosforth
South Approach
193
Astons Road
Thornhill Rd
Russell Road
Bedford Road
Ormonde Rd
Wolsey Road
Westbury Road
The Roughs
Bishops Avenue
Eastbury Farm JMI School
Ross Wy
Wildacres
Eastbury
Valency Cl
Crofters Road
Crofters Rd
Farm Way
The Fairway
Bourne End Road
Woodfield Av
Heron Wk
Batchworth Lane
Avior Dr
Orion Way
Phoenix Cl
Canopus Wy
Capella Rd
Altair Way
SANDY LANE
Moor Park
Oxford Cl
Heathside Rd
Wolsey Road
Anson Walk
Old Gannon Cl
Russell Cl
Nevil Cl
Heathside
508
09
10
A4125
Oxhey Ridge Close
Vega Crs
THE WOODS
Apollo Av
Adhara Rd
Vega Crs
Parkside Road
Davenham Avenue
Shelley Close
Ardross Av
Holbein Gate
Eastgrade
Wellesley Av
St Mary's Avenue
Grove Farm Park
Hertfordshire County
40
Farm Rd
Worth Lane
1 grid square represents 500 metres
30

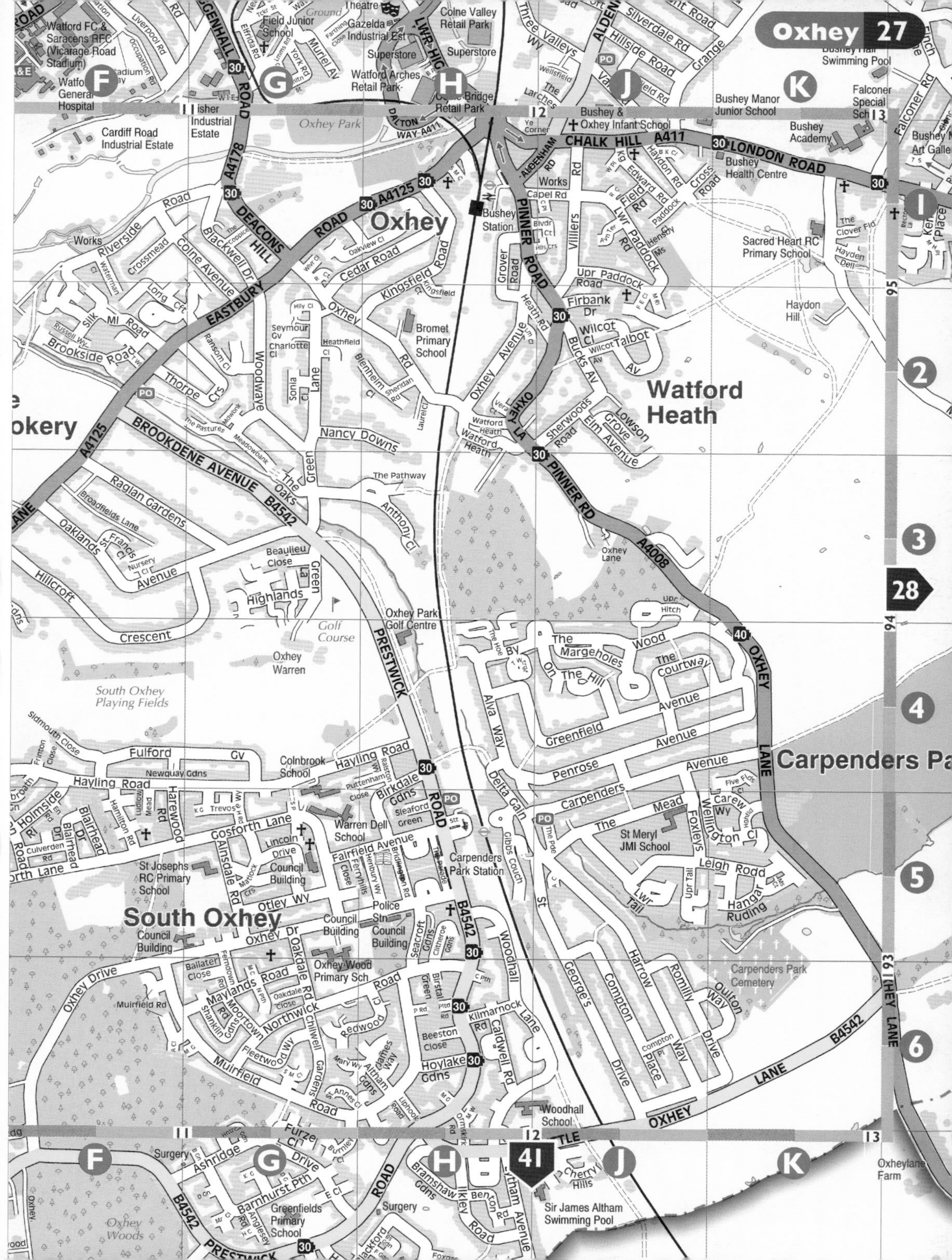
Watford FC & Saracens RFC (Vicarage Road Stadium)
Watford General Hospital
Colne Valley Retail Park
Gazelda Industrial Est
Superstore
Watford Arches Retail Park
Colne Bridge Retail Park
Bushey Hall Swimming Pool
Silverdale Rd
Hillside Road
Three Valleys Wy
Falconer Special Sch
Bushey Manor Junior School
Bushey & Oxhey Infant School
Bushey Academy
Bushey Health Centre
Fisher Industrial Estate
Oxhey Park
Cardiff Road Industrial Estate
DALTON WAY A411
CHALK HILL A411
LONDON ROAD
ALDENHAM RD
Capel Rd
Works
Falconer Rd
A4178
DEACONS HILL
A4125
Oxhey
Bushey Station
Villiers Rd
Edward Rd
Haydon Rd
Cross Road
Paddock Rd
Field Rd
Lwr Paddock Rd
Hensley Ms
Sacred Heart RC Primary School
The Clover Fld
Hayden Dell
Haydon Hill
Riverside Road
Crossmead
Colne Avenue
Blackwell Dr
Works
EASTBURY ROAD
Cedar Road
Oakview Cl
Kingsfield Road
Kingsfield Ct
Grover Road
PINNER ROAD
Upr Paddock Road
Firbank Dr
Heath Rd
Wilcot Cl
Talbot Rd
Talbot Av
Wilcot Av
Bucks Av
Silk Mill Road
Russell Wy
Brookside Road
Seymour Gv
Charlotte Cl
Heathfield Cl
Oxhey Rd
Blenheim Cl
Sheridan Rd
Bromet Primary School
Oxhey Avenue
Watford Heath
Woodwaye
Thorpe Crs
Ransom Cl
Sonia Cl
Lane
Laurel Cl
OXHEY LA
Sherwoods Road
Grove
Elm Avenue
Lowson
The Pastures
Meadowbank
Nancy Downs
Watford Heath
Rookery
A4125
BROOKDENE AVENUE B4542
The Oaks
Green
The Pathway
Raglan Gardens
Broadfields Lane
Oaklands
St Francis Cl
Nursery Cl
Avenue
Hillcroft
Crescent
Beaulieu Close
Green La
Highlands
Anthony Cl
Oxhey Lane
A4008
PINNER RD
Upr Hitch
Golf Course
Oxhey Park Golf Centre
PRESTWICK
Oxhey Warren
South Oxhey Playing Fields
The Hoe
By The Wood
The Margeholes
The Hill
The Courtway
Avenue
Greenfield Avenue
Alva Way
OXHEY LANE
Carpenders Park
Penrose Avenue
Carpenders Avenue
Delta Gain
Sidmouth Close
Frinton Close
Fulford Gv
Colnbrook School
Hayling Road
Newquay Gdns
Hayling Road
Harewood Rd
Holmside Rd
Blairhead Dr
Hamilton Rd
Trevose
Puttenham Close
Ralston
Birkdale Gdns
Sleaford Green
Warren Dell School
Gosforth Lane
Culverden Rd
Ainsdale Rd
Lincoln Drive
Council Building
Fairfield Avenue
Ferryhills Close
Bridlington Rd
The Parade
Carpenders Park Station
Gibbs Couch
The Pde
The Mead
St Meryl JMI School
Foxleys
Wellington Cl
Carew Wy
Five Flds Cl
Leigh Road
St Josephs RC Primary School
Matlock Crs
Otley Wy
Police Stn
Council Building
Lwr Tail
Upr Tail
Hangar Ruding
South Oxhey
Council Building
Oxhey Dr
Oakdale Rd
Oxhey Wood Primary Sch
Seacroft Gdns
Clitheroe Gdns
B4542
Woodhall Lane
St Georges Drive
Compton Drive
Harrow Way
Romilly Drive
Oulton Way
Carpenders Park Cemetery
Oxhey Drive
Ballater Close
Ferndown Close
Maylands Road
Oakdale Close
Moortown Rd
Northwick Road
Muirfield Rd
Shanklin Gdns
Fleetwood Wy
Chilwell Gardens
Redwood
Birstal Green
Beeston Close
Kilmarnock Rd
Caldwell Rd
Compton Place
Compton Pl
OXHEY LANE B4542
Muirfield Road
Mary Wy
Altham Gdns
James Way
St Annes Cl
Hoylake Gdns
Liphook Road
Ormskirk Rd
Woodhall School
Furze Cl
Burnley Cl
Surgery
Ashridge Drive
Barnhurst Pth
E Cl
Greenfields Primary School
Anglesey
Oxhey Woods
B4542
PRESTWICK ROAD
Surgery
Bramshaw Gdns
Ilkley Road
Benton Rd
Altham Avenue
Cherry Hills
Sir James Altham Swimming Pool
Oxheylane Farm
F
G
H
J
K
I
2
3
4
5
6
11
12
13
93
94
95
28
41
30

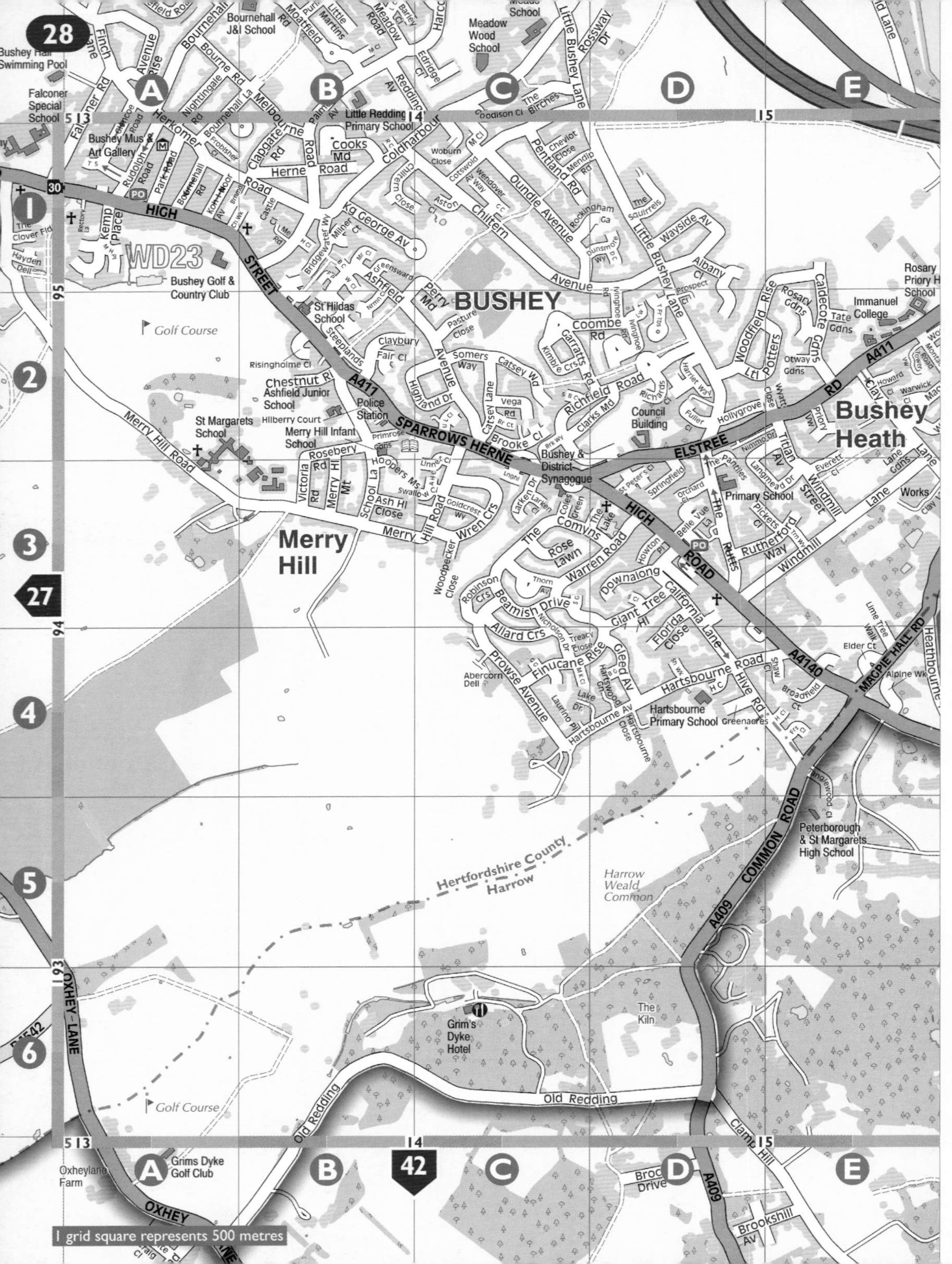
28
Bushey Hall Swimming Pool
Falconer Special School
Bournehall J&I School
Meadow Wood School
Little Redding Primary School
Bushey Mus & Art Gallery
WD23
Bushey Golf & Country Club
Golf Course
St Hildas School
BUSHEY
Risingholme Cl
Chestnut Ri
Ashfield Junior School
Police Station
Hilberry Court
Merry Hill Infant School
St Margarets School
Council Building
Bushey & District Synagogue
Primary School
Bushey Heath
Rosary Priory H School
Immanuel College
Merry Hill
27
HIGH STREET
A411
SPARROWS HERNE
ELSTREE RD
HIGH ROAD
A4140
MAGPIE HALL RD
Merry Hill Road
Merry Hill Rd
Hartsbourne Primary School
Abercorn Dell
Peterborough & St Margarets High School
Hertfordshire County
Harrow
Harrow Weald Common
A409
COMMON ROAD
Grim's Dyke Hotel
The Kiln
Old Redding
OXHEY LANE
Golf Course
Grims Dyke Golf Club
Oxheylane Farm
Brookshill
Clamp Hill
42
1 grid square represents 500 metres

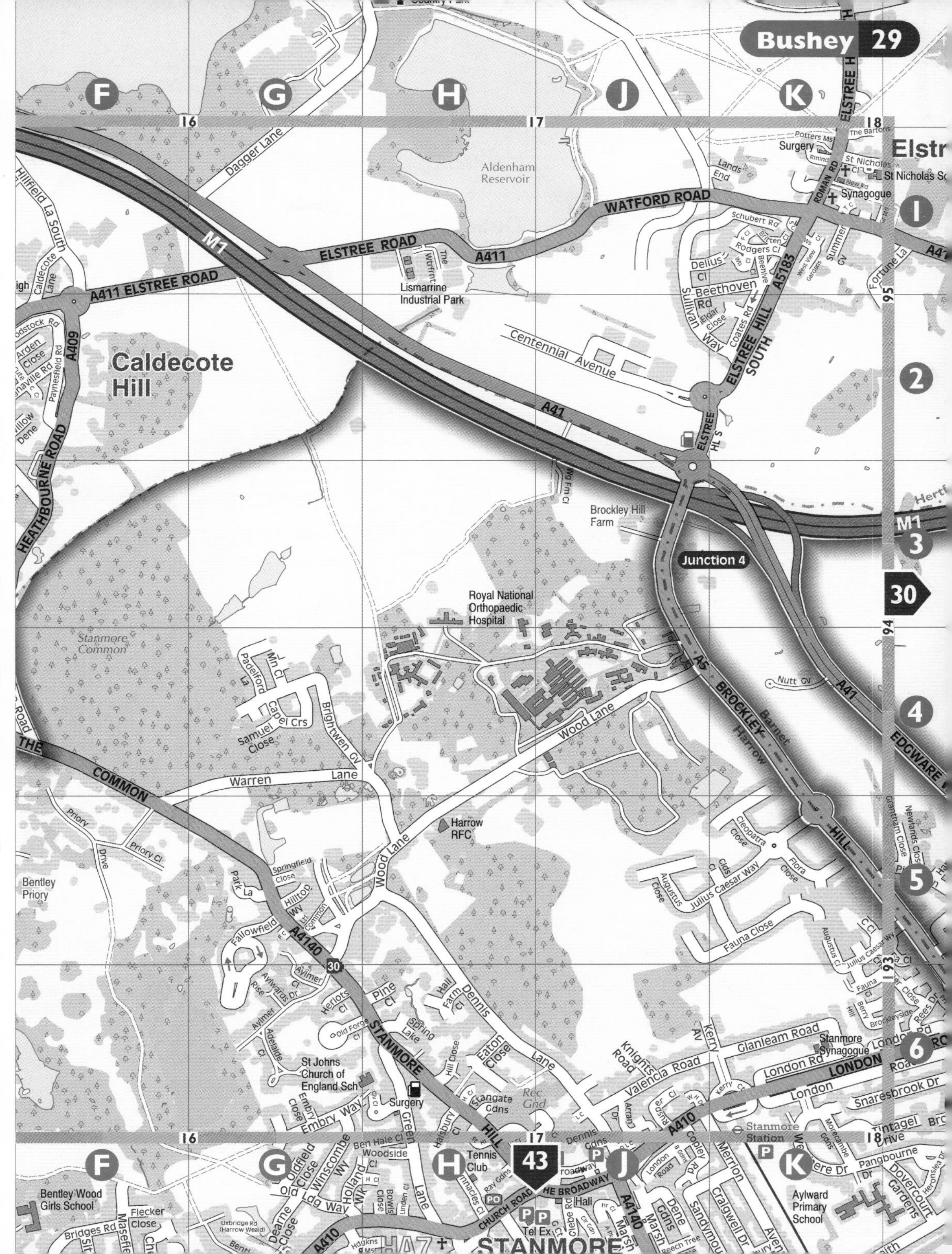

Caldecote Hill
Aldenham Reservoir
Lismarrine Industrial Park
ELSTREE ROAD
A411 ELSTREE ROAD
WATFORD ROAD
A411
M1
A41
Dagger Lane
HEATHBOURNE ROAD
A409
Centennial Avenue
ELSTREE HILL SOUTH
A5183
ROMAN RD
Surgery
Synagogue
St Nicholas Sc
Junction 4
Brockley Hill Farm
Royal National Orthopaedic Hospital
Stanmore Common
Wood Lane
Warren Lane
Brightwen Gv
Samuel Close
Capel Crs
Padelford La
THE COMMON
A5 BROCKLEY HILL
Barnet
Harrow
EDGWARE
Nutt Gv
Harrow RFC
Bentley Priory
Priory Drive
Priory Cl
A4140
STANMORE HILL
Julius Caesar Way
Cleopatra Close
Flora Close
Augustus Close
Fauna Close
Glanleam Road
Stanmore Synagogue
London Rd
LONDON RD
Valencia Road
Knights Road
Kerry Av
Stanmore Station
A410
St Johns Church of England Sch
Surgery
Tennis Club
Rec Gnd
Dennis Lane
Eaton Close
Stangate Gdns
Spring Lake
Pine Cl
Aylmer Dr
Fallowfield
Hilltop Wy
Springfield Close
Park La
Embry Way
Bentley Wood Girls School
Flecker Close
Bridges Rd
Aylward Primary School
Pangbourne Dr
Dovercourt Gardens
Snaresbrook Dr
Tintagel Drive
CHURCH ROAD
THE BROADWAY
Tel Ex
Hall
STANMORE
Elstr
30
43
F G H J K
1 2 3 4 5 6
16 17 18
93 94 95

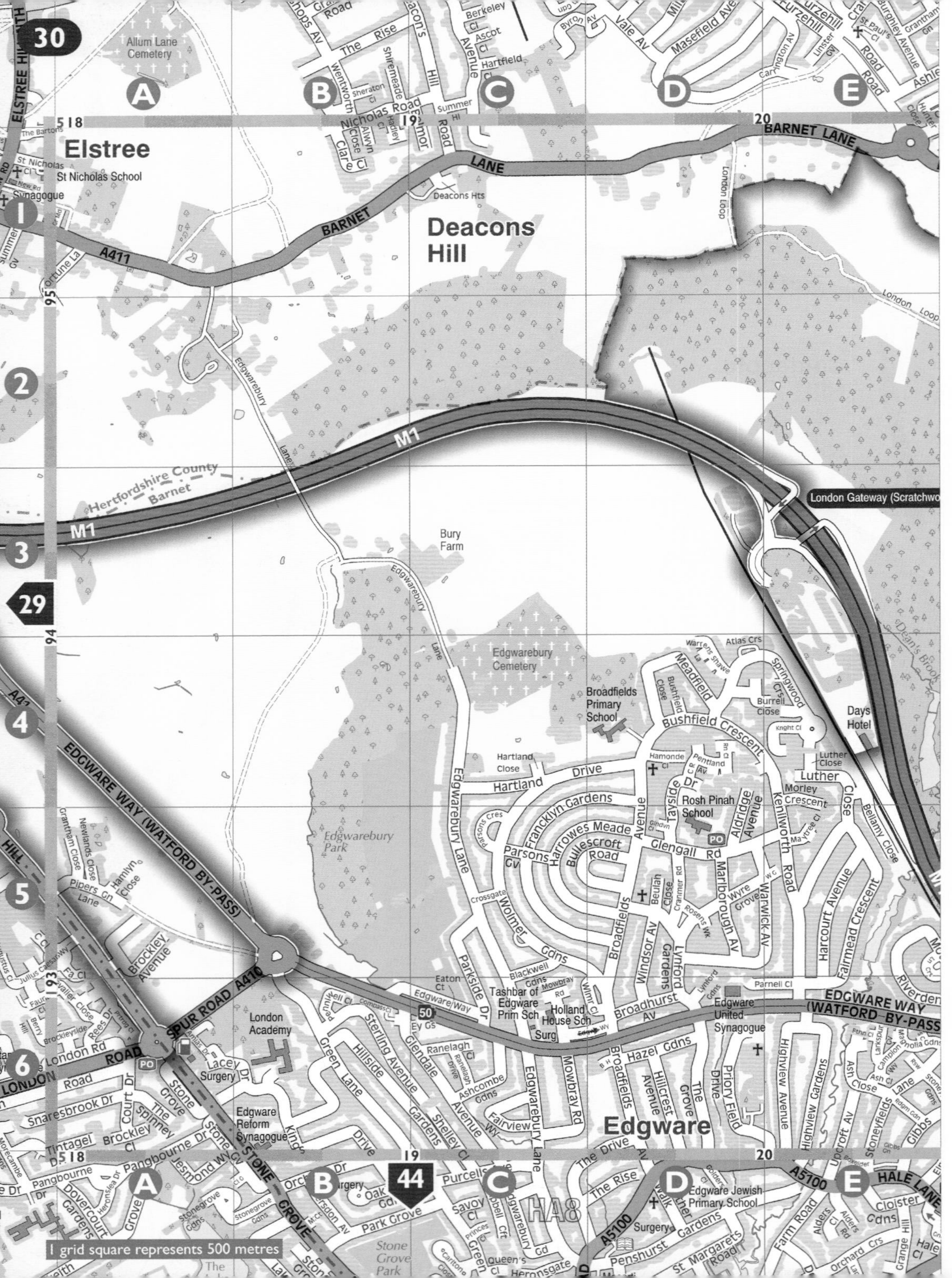
Elstree
Deacons Hill
Edgware
Allum Lane Cemetery
St Nicholas School
Synagogue
BARNET LANE
A411
M1
Hertfordshire County
Barnet
London Gateway (Scratchwo
Bury Farm
Edgwarebury Lane
Edgwarebury Cemetery
Broadfields Primary School
Rosh Pinah School
Edgwarebury Park
Days Hotel
EDGWARE WAY (WATFORD BY-PASS)
SPUR ROAD A410
London Academy
Tashbar of Edgware Prim Sch
Holland House Sch
Edgware United Synagogue
Edgware Reform Synagogue
Edgware Jewish Primary School
Stone Grove Park
HALE LANE
A5100
HA8
London Loop
Dean's Brook
29
44
1 grid square represents 500 metres

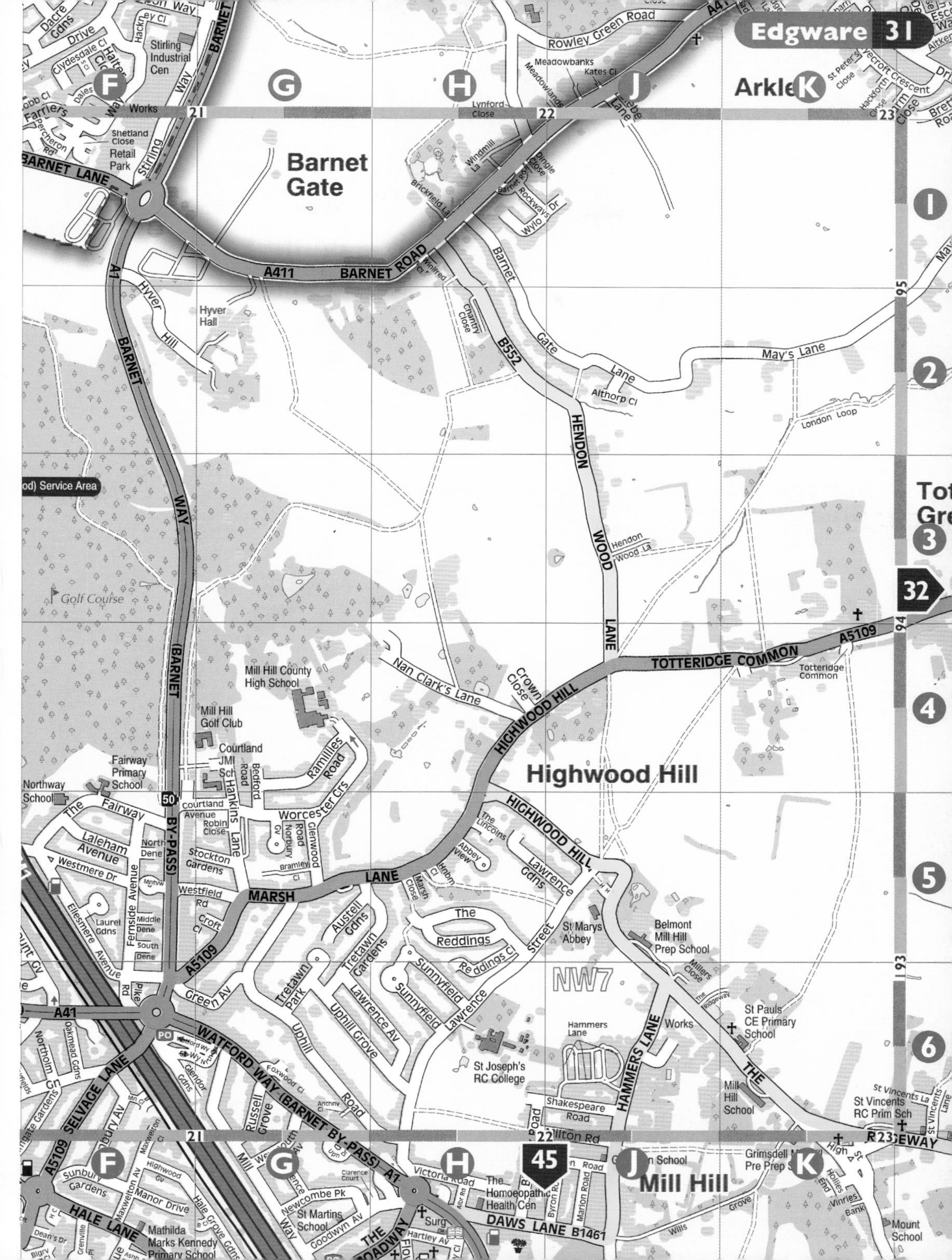
Edgware 31
Barnet Gate
Arkley
Highwood Hill
Mill Hill
A411 BARNET ROAD
BARNET LANE
A1 BARNET WAY
(BARNET BY-PASS)
B552 HENDON WOOD LANE
Barnet Gate Lane
May's Lane
London Loop
TOTTERIDGE COMMON
A5109
Totteridge Common
HIGHWOOD HILL
Nan Clark's Lane
Crown Close
MARSH LANE
WATFORD WAY (BARNET BY-PASS) A1
HAMMERS LANE
THE RIDGEWAY
DAWS LANE B1461
SELVAGE LANE
HALE LANE
Rowley Green Road
Stirling Industrial Cen
Shetland Close
Retail Park
Hyver Hall
Hyver Hill
Chantry Close
Althorp Cl
Hendon Wood La
Golf Course
Mill Hill County High School
Mill Hill Golf Club
Courtland JMI Sch
Fairway Primary School
Northway School
The Fairway
Laleham Avenue
Westmere Dr
Stockton Gardens
Westfield Rd
Croft Cl
Worcester Crs
Ramillies Road
Bedford Road
Hankins Lane
The Reddings
Reddings Cl
Lawrence Gdns
Lawrence Street
Sunnyfield
Uphill Grove
Tretawn Gardens
Tretawn Park
Austell Gdns
Green Av
St Marys Abbey
Belmont Mill Hill Prep School
NW7
St Pauls CE Primary School
St Joseph's RC College
Shakespeare Road
Mill Hill School
St Vincents RC Prim Sch
Grimsdell Mill Hill Pre Prep School
The Homoeopathic Health Cen
Victoria Road
Newcombe Pk
St Martins School
Goodwyn Av
THE BROADWAY
Sunbury Gardens
Manor Drive
Mathilda Marks Kennedy Primary School
Mount School
Marion Road
Byron Rd
Hale Grove Gdns
Millers Close
Works
Service Area
F
G
H
J
K
1
2
3
4
5
6
21
22
23
32
45
93
94
95

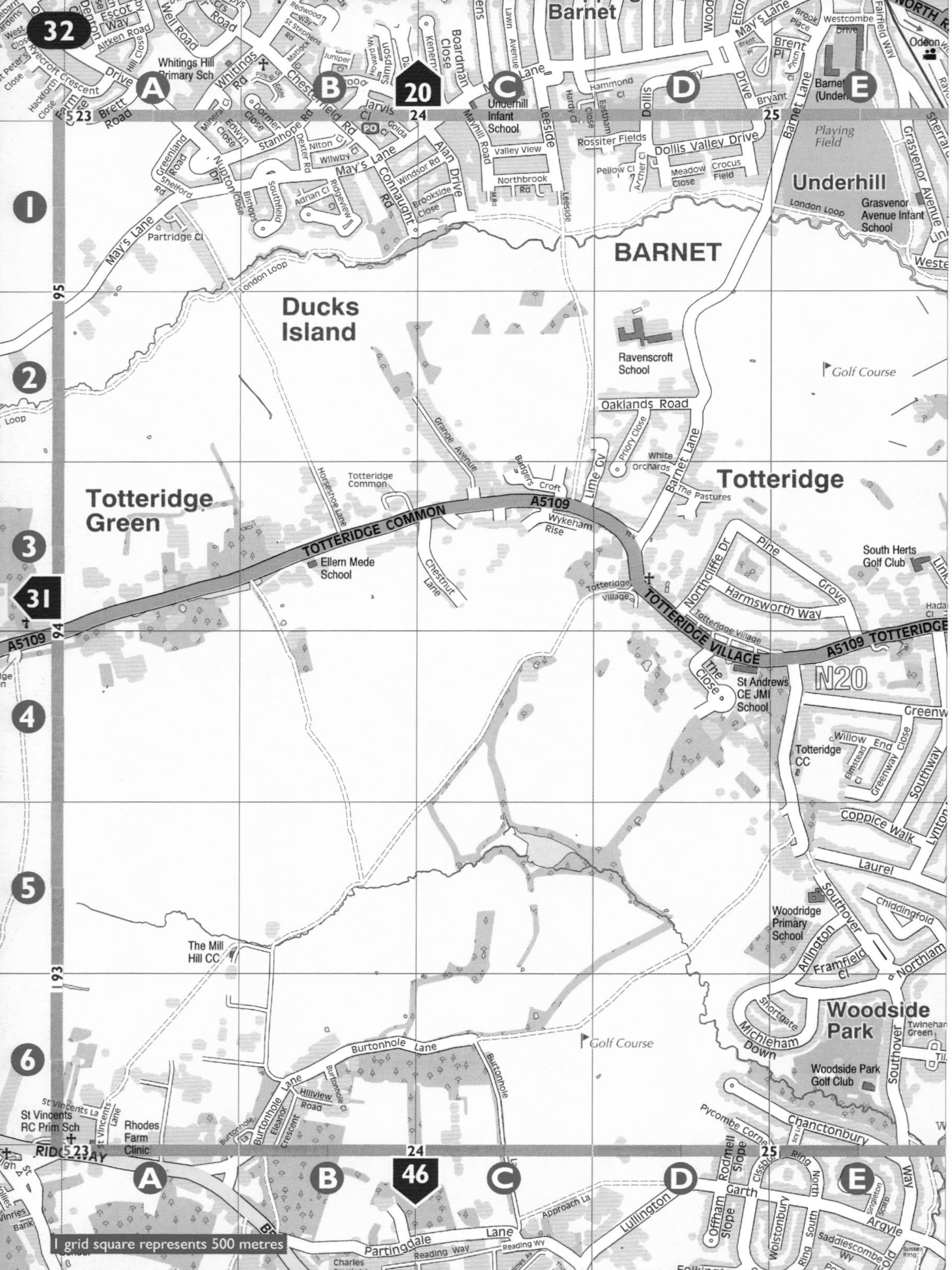
Barnet
BARNET
Ducks Island
Totteridge Green
Totteridge
Underhill
Woodside Park
N20
TOTTERIDGE COMMON
TOTTERIDGE VILLAGE
A5109
Whitings Hill Primary Sch
Underhill Infant School
Ravenscroft School
Ellern Mede School
St Andrews CE JMI School
Woodridge Primary School
Grasvenor Avenue Infant School
South Herts Golf Club
Woodside Park Golf Club
Golf Course
The Mill Hill CC
Totteridge CC
St Vincents RC Prim Sch
Rhodes Farm Clinic
Totteridge Common
Oaklands Road
Barnet Lane
Dollis Valley Drive
Rossiter Fields
Burtonhole Lane
Partingdale Lane
May's Lane
London Loop
Playing Field
1 grid square represents 500 metres

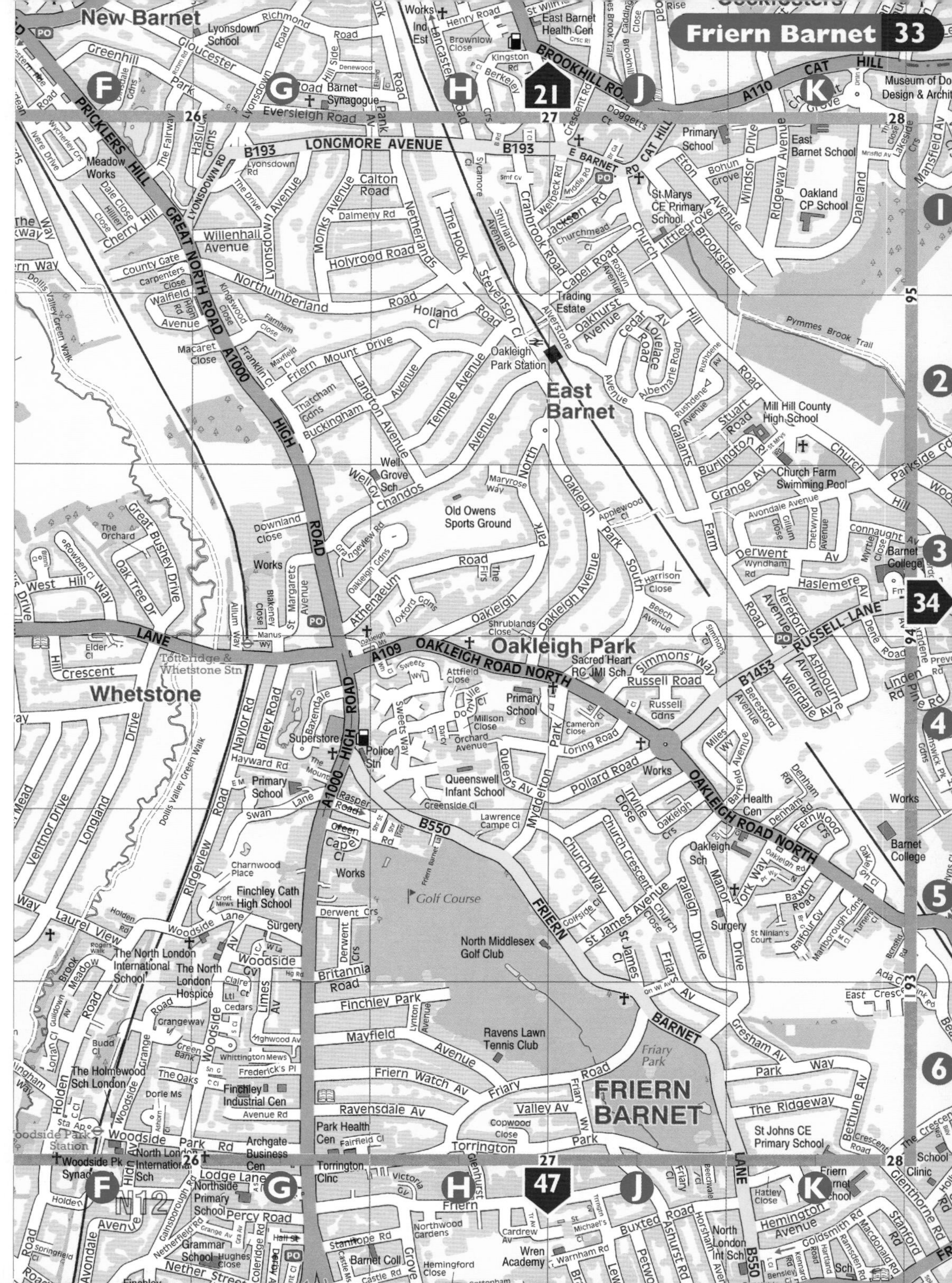

Friern Barnet 33
New Barnet
Lyonsdown School
Richmond Road
Gloucester Road
Greenhill Park
Barnet Synagogue
Eversleigh Road
Henry Road
Brownlow Close
Kingston Rd
Berkeley Crs
East Barnet Health Cen
BROOKHILL ROAD
CAT HILL
A110
Museum of Domestic Design & Architecture
21
PRICKLERS HILL
Meadow Works
LONGMORE AVENUE
B193
Lyonsdown Rd
Calton Road
Dalmeny Rd
Monks Avenue
Netherlands Road
The Hook
Cranbrook Road
Welbeck Rd
Jackson Rd
Capel Road
Primary School
Bohun Grove
Windsor Drive
Ridgeway Avenue
East Barnet School
Oakland CP School
Daneland
Mansfield Av
St Marys CE Primary School
Littlegrove
Brookside
GREAT NORTH ROAD
LYONSDOWN RD
Lyonsdown Avenue
Willenhall Avenue
Holyrood Road
Cherry Hill
County Gate
Carpenters Close
Walfield Avenue
Northumberland Road
Holland Cl
Stevenson Cl
Trading Estate
Oakhurst Avenue
Cedar Av
Lovelace Road
Albemarle Road
Rushdene Avenue
Pymmes Brook Trail
Dollis Valley Green Walk
Macaret Close
A1000
Farnham Close
Friern Mount Drive
Oakleigh Park Station
East Barnet
Thatcham Gdns
Buckingham Avenue
Langton Avenue
Temple Avenue
HIGH ROAD
Mill Hill County High School
Stuart Road
Burlington Ri
Gallants Farm Road
Church Hill
Church Farm Swimming Pool
Parkside Gdns
Well Grove Sch
Well Cl
Chandos Avenue
Maryrose Way
Old Owens Sports Ground
Oakleigh Park North
Oakleigh Park South
Applewood Cl
Grange Av
Avondale Avenue
Gillum Close
Chetwynd Avenue
Connaught Av
Barnet College
Derwent Av
Wyndham Rd
Haslemere Av
Great Bushey Drive
The Orchard
Oak Tree Dr
West Hill Way
Downland Close
Grangeview Rd
Oakleigh Gdns
Works
Athenaeum Road
Oxford Gdns
Oakleigh Road
The Firs
Harrison Close
Beech Avenue
Hereford Avenue
RUSSELL LANE
Dene Road
34
Allum Way
Blakeney Close
St Margarets Avenue
Manus Wy
LANE
Elder Cl
Hill Crescent
Totteridge & Whetstone Stn
Whetstone
A109
OAKLEIGH ROAD NORTH
Oakleigh Park
Shrublands Close
Sacred Heart RC JMI Sch
Simmons' Way
Russell Road
Russell Gdns
B1453
Beresford Avenue
Ashbourne Avenue
Weirdale Av
Linden Rd
Attfield Close
Primary School
Naylor Rd
Birley Road
Baxendale
Superstore
Police Stn
Sweets Way
Millson Close
Orchard Avenue
Cameron Close
Loring Road
Pollard Road
Miles Wy
Barfield Avenue
Denham Rd
Hayward Rd
The Mount
Queens Av
Myddelton Park
Queenswell Infant School
Irvine Close
Oakleigh Crs
Health Cen
Fernwood Crs
Barnet College
Swan Lane
Rasper Road
Green Rd
Cape Cl
Greenside Cl
B550
Lawrence Campe Cl
Church Way
Church Crescent
Oakleigh Sch
Manor Drive
York Way
Oakleigh Rd
Bawtry Road
Ventnor Drive
Longland Drive
Ridgeview Road
Charnwood Place
Works
Golf Course
FRIERN
Raleigh Drive
Surgery
St Ninian's Court
Balfour Gv
Marlborough Gdns
Croft Mews
Finchley Cath High School
Holden Rd
Laurel View
Woodside Lane
Surgery
Derwent Crs
Golfside Cl
St James Avenue
St James Cl
Friars Av
North Middlesex Golf Club
East Crescent
The North London International School
The North London Hospice
Claire Ct
Woodside Gv
Britannia Road
Brook Meadow Road
Limes Av
Finchley Park
Lynton Avenue
BARNET
Gresham Av
Grangeway
Cedars
Highwood Av
Mayfield Avenue
Ravens Lawn Tennis Club
Friary Park
Budd Cl
Green Bank
Whittington Mews
Frederick's Pl
Friern Watch Av
Friary Road
Park Way
6
The Holmewood Sch London
The Oaks
Dorle Ms
Finchley Industrial Cen
Avenue Rd
Ravensdale Av
Valley Av
FRIERN BARNET
The Ridgeway
Bethune Av
Woodside Park Station
Sta Ap
Woodside Park Rd
Archgate Business Cen
Park Health Cen
Fairfield Cl
Copwood Close
Torrington Park
St Johns CE Primary School
Crescent Road
The Crescent
Woodside Pk Synag
North London International Sch
Lodge Lane
Torrington Clnc
Victoria Gv
Glenhurst
47
Friary Cl
Beechvale
LANE
Friern Barnet School
Clinic
Glenthorne Rd
Northside Primary School
Percy Road
Hatley Close
Hemington Avenue
Stanford Rd
N12
Avondale Avenue
Gainsborough Rd
Netherfield Rd
Grammar School
Hughes Close
Coleridge Rd
Stanhope Rd
Barnet Coll
Northwood Gardens
Cardrew Av
St Michael's Cl
Wren Academy
Warnham Rd
Buxted Road
Ashurst Rd
Horsham Av
North London Int Sch
B550
Goldsmith Rd
Macdonald Rd
Nether Street
Castle Rd
Hemingford Close
Cottonham
Finchley
F
G
H
J
K
1
2
3
4
5
26
27
28
93
94
95

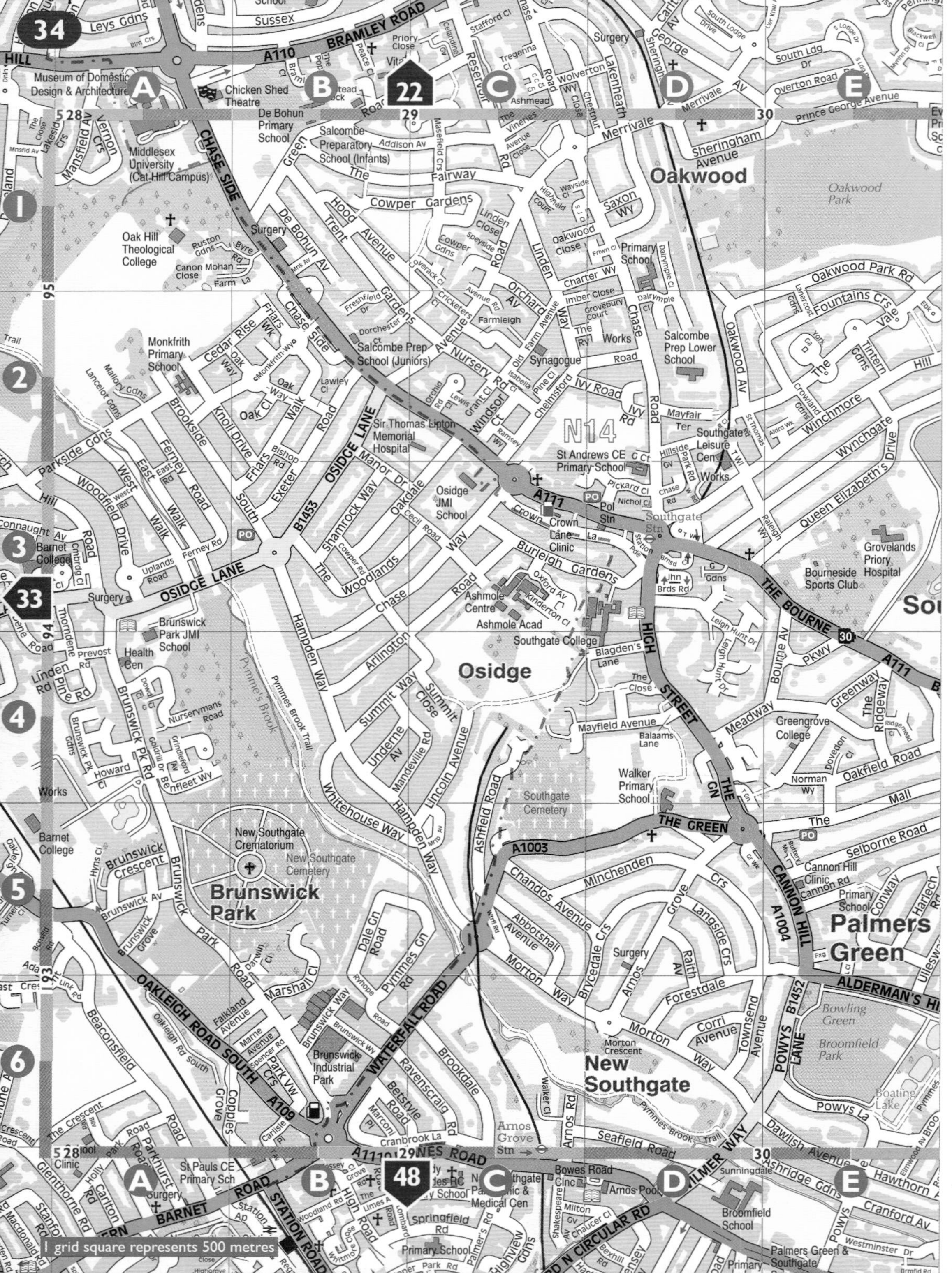

34
22
33
48
A
B
C
D
E
1
2
3
4
5
6
528
29
30
95
94
93
BRAMLEY ROAD
A110
Leys Gdns
Sussex
School
Museum of Domestic Design & Architecture
Chicken Shed Theatre
De Bohun Primary School
Salcombe Preparatory School (Infants)
Middlesex University (Cat Hill Campus)
Oak Hill Theological College
Canon Mohan Close
Monkfrith Primary School
Salcombe Prep School (Juniors)
Sir Thomas Lipton Memorial Hospital
Osidge JMI School
Crown Lane Clinic
St Andrews CE Primary School
Southgate Leisure Cen
Southgate Stn
Salcombe Prep Lower School
Primary School
Synagogue
Surgery
Works
Oakwood
Oakwood Park
Oakwood Park Rd
Fountains Crs
Prince George Avenue
Sheringham Avenue
Merrivale
Overton Road
South Lodge Drive
CHASE SIDE
Chase Side
Cowper Gardens
The Fairway
Hood Avenue
Trent Gardens
De Bohun Av
Nursery Rd
Orchard Av
Farmleigh
Charter Wy
Chelmsford
Ivy Road
Mayfair Ter
N14
A111
THE BOURNE
Queen Elizabeth's Drive
Wynchgate
Winchmore Hill
Grovelands Priory Hospital
Bourneside Sports Club
OSIDGE LANE
B1453
Osidge
Brookside
Ferney Road
Knoll Drive
Friars Walk
Uplands Road
Parkside Gdns
Woodfield Drive
Connaught Av
Barnet College
Brunswick Park JMI School
Health Cen
Nurserymans Road
Prevost Rd
Linden Rd
Pine Rd
Howard Cl
Benfleet Wy
Works
Ashmole Centre
Ashmole Acad
Southgate College
Burleigh Gardens
Hampden Way
Arlington
Summit Way
Summit Close
Underne Av
Mandeville Rd
Lincoln Avenue
Whitehouse Way
Pymmes Brook Trail
Pymme's Brook
HIGH STREET
Blagden's Lane
The Close
Mayfield Avenue
Balaams Lane
Walker Primary School
Greengrove College
Meadway
Greenway
The Ridgeway
Oakfield Road
Norman Wy
The Mall
THE GREEN
THE GN
A1003
A1004
CANNON HILL
Selborne Road
Cannon Hill Clinic
Primary School
Palmers Green
ALDERMAN'S HILL
Bowling Green
Broomfield Park
Boating Lake
Powys La
POWYS LANE
B1452
Southgate Cemetery
New Southgate Crematorium
New Southgate Cemetery
Brunswick Park
Brunswick Crescent
Brunswick Park Road
Ashfield Road
Chandos Avenue
Minchenden Crs
Abbotshall Avenue
Morton Way
Brycedale Crs
Langside Crs
Forestdale
Corri Avenue
Townsend Avenue
Morton Crescent
New Southgate
Dale Gn Road
Pymmes Gn Rd
Brunswick Way
Brunswick Industrial Park
WATERFALL ROAD
OAKLEIGH ROAD SOUTH
A109
Beaconsfield
Marshall Cl
Falkland Avenue
Marne Avenue
Park Vw Crs
Coppies Grove
Ravenscraig Rd
Brookdale
Betstyle Road
Cranbrook La
Arnos Grove Stn
Arnos Rd
Walker Cl
Seafield Road
Dawlish Avenue
Ashridge Gdns
Hawthorn Av
Cranford Av
Westminster Dr
WILMER WAY
Sunningdale
Broomfield School
Palmers Green & Southgate Synagogue
N CIRCULAR RD
Bowes Road Clinc
Arnos Pool
Springfield Rd
Primary School
Upper Park Rd
St Pauls CE Primary Sch
Surgery
BARNET ROAD
STATION ROAD
Station Ap
Clinic
The Crescent
Parkhurst Road
Glenthorne Rd
1 grid square represents 500 metres

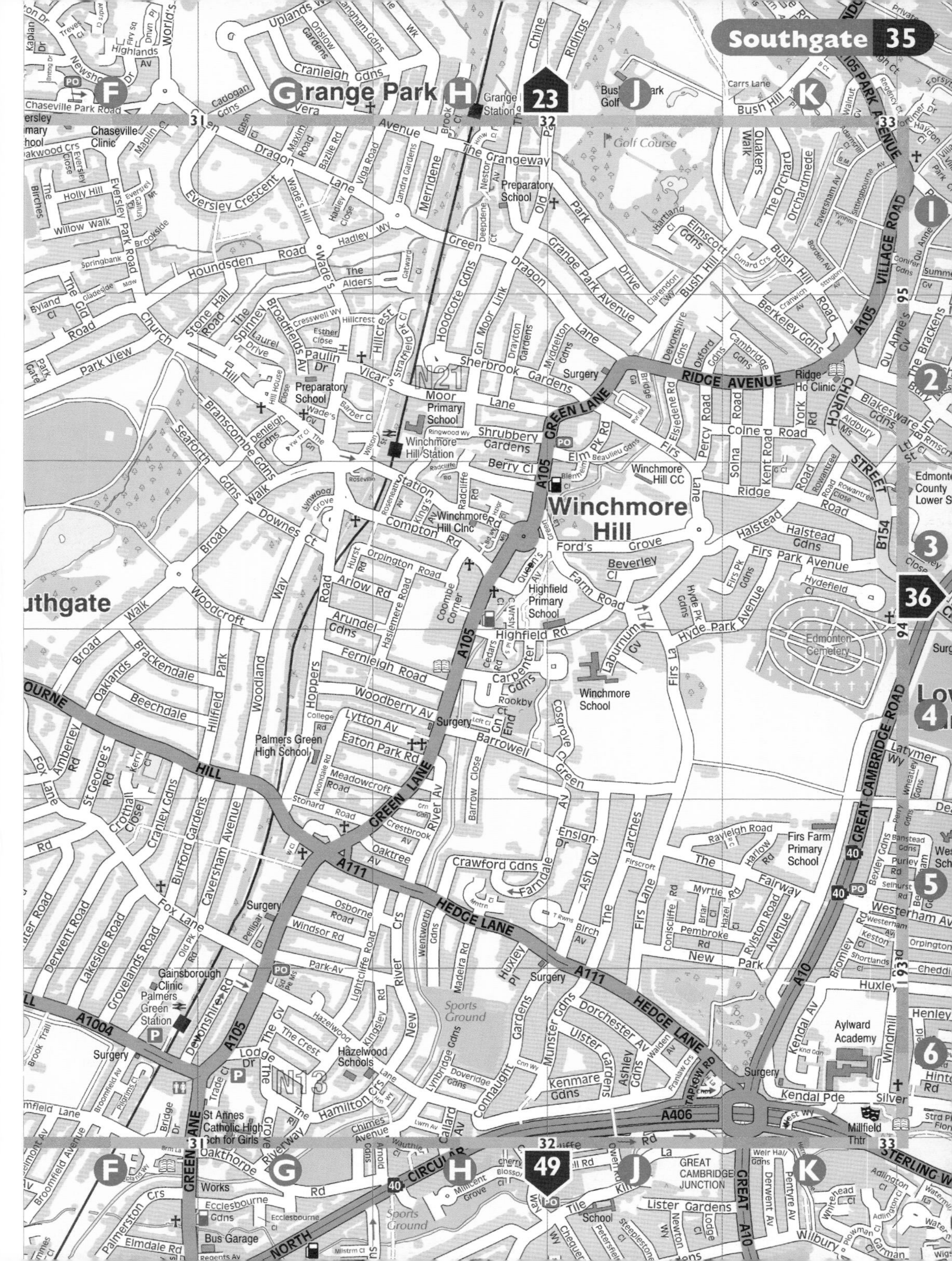

Grange Park
Winchmore Hill
Southgate
N21
N13
Grange Park Station
Winchmore Hill Station
Palmers Green Station
Bush Hill Park Golf Course
Golf Course
Edmonton Cemetery
Sports Ground
Chaseville Clinic
Preparatory School
Moor Primary School
Winchmore Hill Clnc
Winchmore Hill CC
Highfield Primary School
Winchmore School
Palmers Green High School
Firs Farm Primary School
Aylward Academy
Hazelwood Schools
St Annes Catholic High Sch for Girls
Gainsborough Clinic
Ridge Ho Clinic
Edmonton County Lower S
Millfield Thtr
Bus Garage
Works
School
Surgery
GREAT CAMBRIDGE JUNCTION
Chaseville Park Road
Cranleigh Gdns
Uplands Wy
Onslow Gardens
Langham Gdns
Vera Avenue
Dragon Lane
The Grangeway
Eversley Crescent
Eversley Park Road
Houndsden Road
Church Hill
Park View
Old Park Ridings
Grange Park Avenue
Bush Hill
Green Dragon Lane
Sherbrook Gardens
Vicar's Moor Lane
Shrubbery Gardens
Berry Cl
Ridge Avenue
Green Lane
Firs Lane
Station Rd
Compton Rd
Ford's Grove
Farm Road
Highfield Rd
Fernleigh Road
Woodberry Av
Lytton Av
Eaton Park Rd
Barrowell Green
Broad Walk
Woodcroft
Bourne Hill
Fox Lane
Hedge Lane
Village Road
Church Street
Great Cambridge Road
Park Avenue
Firs Park Avenue
Hyde Park Avenue
Halstead Gdns
The Fairway
New Park Avenue
Westerham Av
Kendal Pde
Silver St
North Circular
Sterling Way
A105
A111
A406
A10
A1004
B154
A105 PARK AVENUE
23
36
49
31
32
33
94
95
F
G
H
J
K
1
2
3
4
5
6

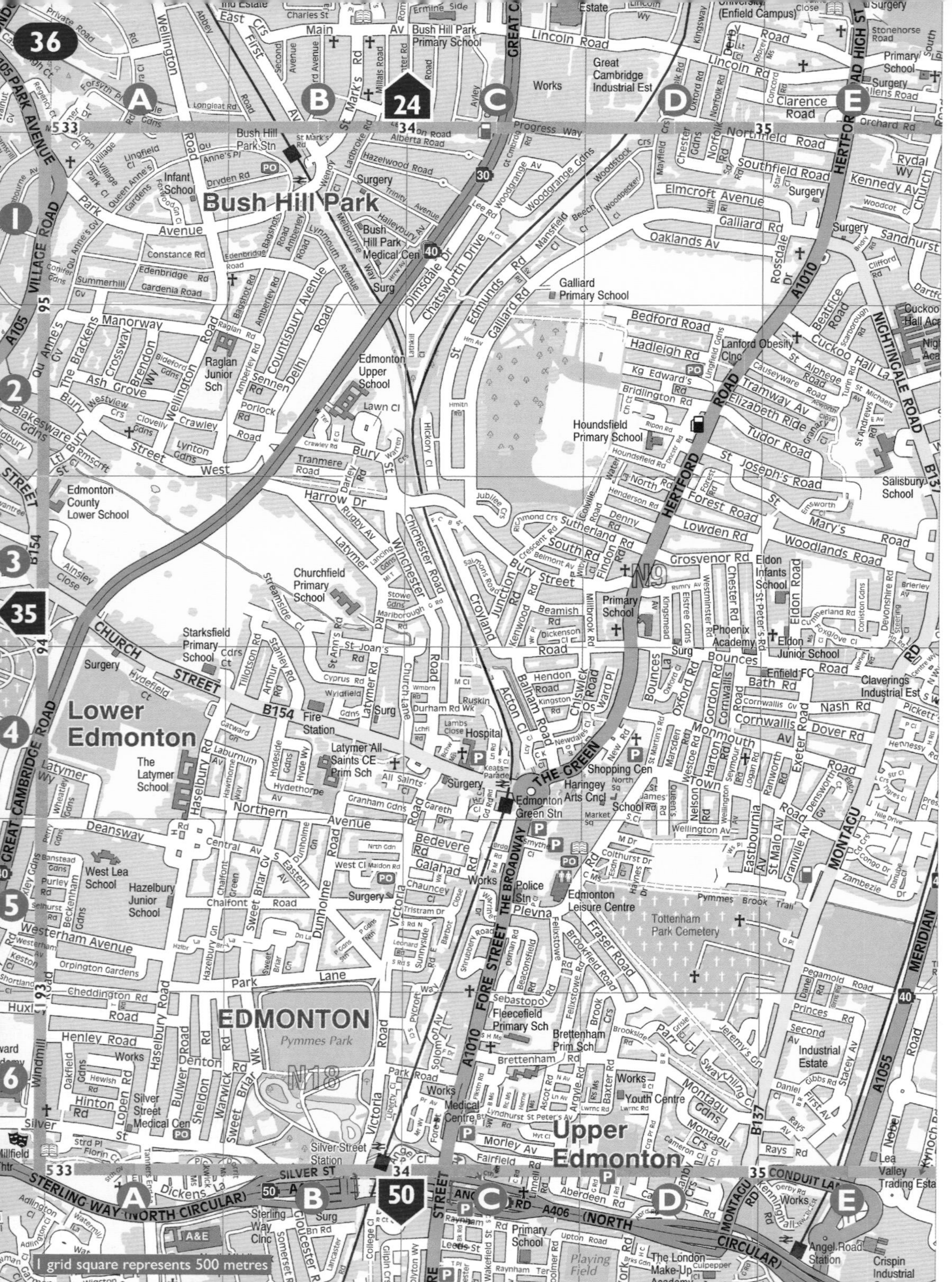
36
24
35
50
A
B
C
D
E
1
2
3
4
5
6
533
34
35
Bush Hill Park
Bush Hill Park Stn
Bush Hill Park Primary School
Bush Hill Park Medical Cen
Infant School
Great Cambridge Industrial Est
Works
University (Enfield Campus)
Lincoln Road
Lincoln Rd
Clarence Road
Orchard Rd
Progress Way
Northfield Road
Southfield Road
Elmcroft Avenue
Galliard Rd
Oaklands Av
Kennedy Av
Sandhurst
Galliard Primary School
Bedford Road
Hadleigh Rd
Lanford Obesity Clnc
Kg Edward's Rd
Bridlington Rd
Houndsfield Primary School
Cuckoo Hall La
Elizabeth Ride
Tudor Road
St Joseph's Road
Forest Road
St Mary's Road
Woodlands Road
Lowden Rd
Grosvenor Rd
Eldon Infants School
Eldon Junior School
Phoenix Academy
Salisbury School
NIGHTINGALE ROAD
HERTFORD ROAD
HERTFORD ROAD HIGH ST
A1010
B137
Enfield FC
Claverings Industrial Est
Nash Rd
Dover Rd
Cornwallis Av
Monmouth Road
MONTAGU ROAD
MERIDIAN
A1055
Pymmes Brook Trail
Tottenham Park Cemetery
Pegamold Road
Princes Rd
Industrial Estate
Lea Valley Trading Esta
Angel Road Station
Crispin Industrial
Upper Edmonton
Youth Centre
Montagu Gdns
Brettenham Prim Sch
Fleecefield Primary Sch
Edmonton Leisure Centre
Police Stn
Edmonton Green Stn
THE GREEN
Shopping Cen
Haringey Arts Cncl
THE BROADWAY
FORE STREET
Plevna
Fraser Road
Hospital
Keats Parade
Latymer All Saints CE Prim Sch
Fire Station
B154
CHURCH STREET
Starksfield Primary School
Churchfield Primary School
Edmonton Upper School
Chichester Road
Winchester Road
Harrow Dr
Bury Street
Raglan Junior Sch
Manorway
Edmonton County Lower School
Lower Edmonton
The Latymer School
Northern Avenue
Deansway
West Lea School
Hazelbury Junior School
Westerham Avenue
Orpington Gardens
Cheddington Rd
Henley Road
EDMONTON
Pymmes Park
N9
N18
Park Lane
Silver Street Medical Cen
Silver Street Station
Medical Centre
Millfield Thtr
SILVER ST
STERLING WAY (NORTH CIRCULAR)
A406 (NORTH CIRCULAR)
Sterling Way Clnc
A&E
Primary School
Playing Field
The London Make-Up Academy
GREAT CAMBRIDGE ROAD
VILLAGE ROAD
A105 PARK AVENUE
Windmill
Surgery
1 grid square represents 500 metres

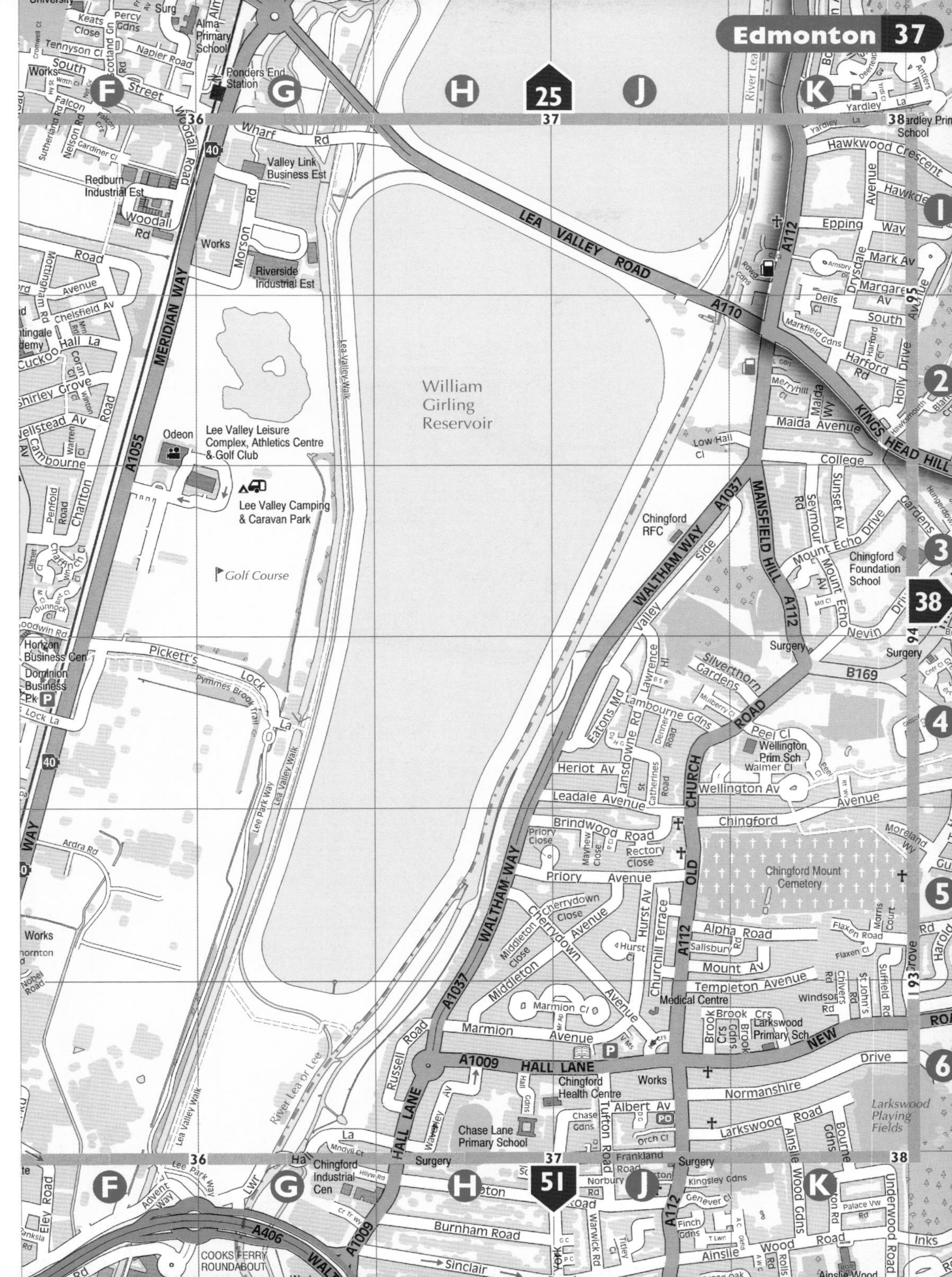
Keats Close
Percy Gdns
Surg
Alma Primary School
Tennyson Cl
Scotland Gn
Napier Road
Works
South Street
Ponders End Station
F
G
H
25
J
K
Yardley La
Yardley Prim School
Falcon Rd
Falcon Crs
Sutherland Rd
Nelson Rd
Gardiner Cl
Woodall Road
36
37
38
Wharf Rd
Valley Link Business Est
Redburn Industrial Est
Woodall Rd
Hawkwood Crescent
LEA VALLEY ROAD
Epping Way
Works
Morson Rd
Riverside Industrial Est
Road
Mottingham Rd
Avenue
Chelsfield Av
Mark Av
Margaret Av
Dells Cl
South
A110
A112
Drysdale Avenue
Markfield Gdns
Harford Rd
Holly Drive
Cuckoo Hall La
Coran Cl
Shirley Grove
Wellstead Av
Cambourne Av
Warren Cl
MERIDIAN WAY
A1055
William Girling Reservoir
Lea Valley Walk
Merryhill Cl
Maida Wy
Maida Avenue
KINGS HEAD HILL
Odeon
Lee Valley Leisure Complex, Athletics Centre & Golf Club
Lee Valley Camping & Caravan Park
Low Hall Cl
College
Sunset Av
Seymour Rd
Gardens
Penfold Rd
Charlton
Golf Course
Chingford RFC
WALTHAM WAY
A1037
MANSFIELD HILL
Mount Echo Drive
Chingford Foundation School
Mount Echo Av
38
Nevin Dri
Surgery
B169
Horizon Business Cen
Dominion Business Pk
Pickett's Lock La
Pymmes Brook Trail
Valley Side
Lawrence Hl
Silverthorn Gardens
Lambourne Gdns
Eatons Md
Lansdowne Rd
Dennis Road
Peel Cl
Wellington Prim Sch
Walmer Cl
Heriot Av
St Catherines Road
Wellington Av
Leadale Avenue
Avenue
Chingford
CHURCH ROAD
OLD
Brindwood Road
Priory Close
Mayhew Close
Rectory Close
Moreland Wy
Chingford Mount Cemetery
Priory Avenue
Lee Park Way
Ardra Rd
Cherrydown Close
Cherrydown Avenue
Middleton Close
Hurst Av
Hurst Cl
Churchill Terrace
Alpha Road
Salisbury Rd
Flaxen Road
Flaxen Cl
Morris Court
Mount Av
Templeton Avenue
Middleton Avenue
Medical Centre
Windsor Rd
Chivers Rd
St John's Rd
Suffield Rd
Grove
Harold Rd
Marmion Cl
Brook Crs
Larkswood Primary Sch
Marmion Avenue
Russell Road
NEW ROAD
A1009
HALL LANE
Drive
Works
Normanshire
Works
Nobel Road
Chingford Health Centre
Albert Av
Waverley Av
Hall Gdns
Chase Gdns
Tufton Road
Larkswood Road
Ainslie Wood Gdns
Bourne Gdns
Larkswood Playing Fields
Chase Lane Primary School
River Lea Or Lee
Orch Cl
Frankland Road
Surgery
Chingford Industrial Cen
51
Norbury Rd
Kingsley Gdns
Genever Cl
Eley Road
Advent Way
A406
Burnham Road
Finch Gdns
Palace Vw Rd
Underwood Road
COOKS FERRY ROUNDABOUT
Sinclair
York
Warwick Rd
Ainslie Wood Rd
Inks
Ainslie Wood
A1009
1
2
3
4
5
6
94
95
193

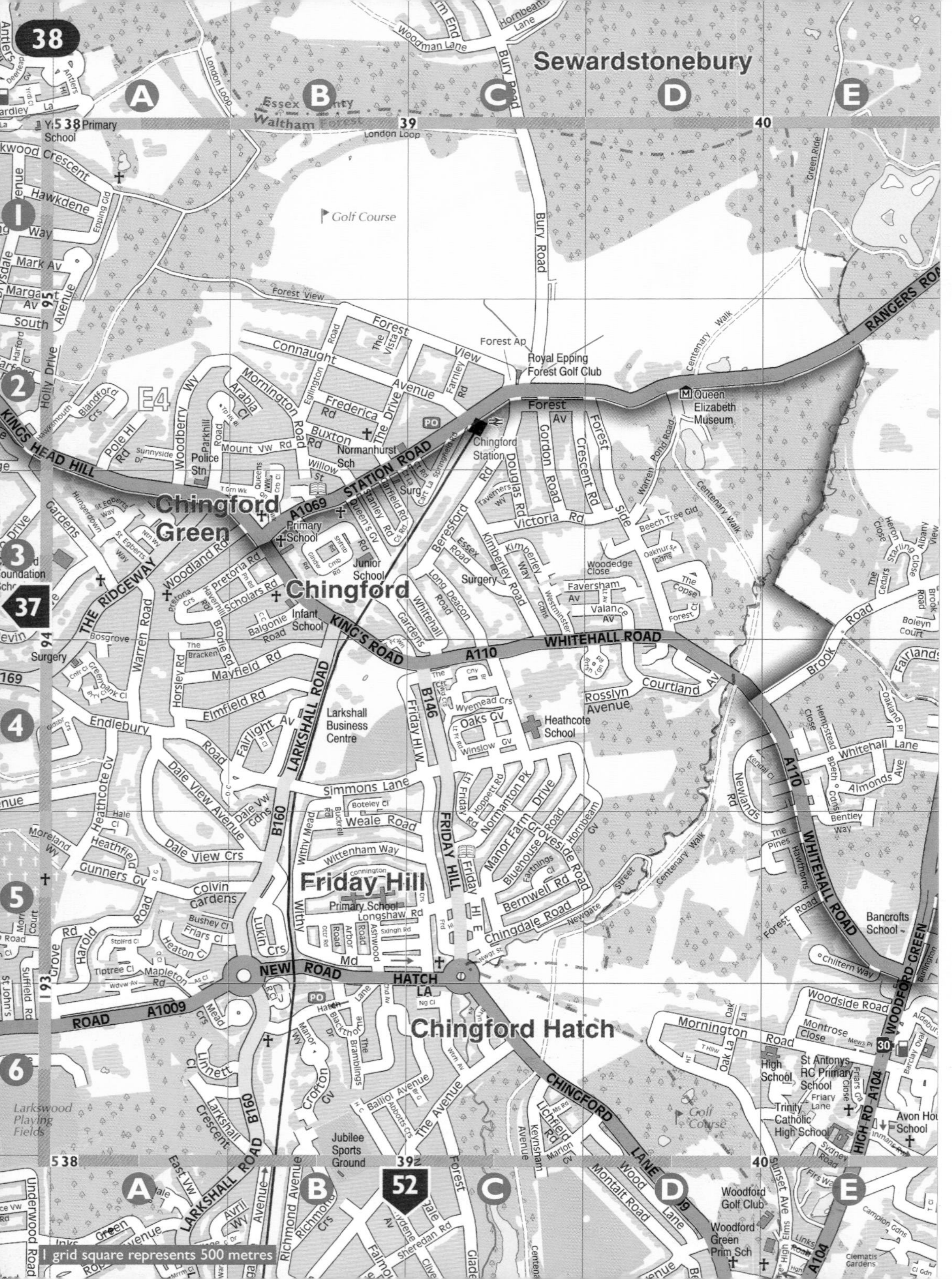
38
Sewardstonebury
A
B
C
D
E
Essex County
Waltham Forest
39
40
Golf Course
Bury Road
London Loop
Woodman Lane
Hornbeam Lane
Forest View
Forest Ap
Royal Epping Forest Golf Club
Queen Elizabeth Museum
Rangers Road
Centenary Walk
Green Ride
Connaught Avenue
Forest View
The Drive
Frederica Rd
Mornington Road
Buxton Rd
Normanhurst Sch
Chingford Station
Station Road
A1069
Kings Head Hill
Chingford Green
Chingford
Police Stn
Mount Vw Rd
Woodberry Wy
Arabia Cl
Parkhill Road
Pole Hill Rd
Blandford Crs
Holly Drive
E4
Primary School
Junior School
Infant School
Woodland Rd
Pretoria Rd
Scholars Rd
Balgonie Road
The Ridgeway
Warren Road
Forest Av
Gordon Road
Crescent Rd
Forest Side
Douglas Rd
Victoria Rd
Beresford Rd
Essex Road
Kimberley Road
Kimberley Way
Surgery
Faversham Av
Valance Av
Woodedge Close
Beech Tree Gld
The Copse
Whitehall Road
A110
King's Road
Long Deacon Road
Whitehall Gardens
Mayfield Rd
Elmfield Rd
Horsley Rd
Endlebury Road
Larkshall Road
Larkshall Business Centre
Friday Hill W
B146
Wyemead Crs
Oaks Gv
Winslow Gv
Heathcote School
Rosslyn Avenue
Courtland Av
Brook Road
Boleyn Court
Fairlands
Whitehall Lane
Almonds Ave
Bentley Way
Newlands Rd
The Pines
Hawthorns
Whitehall Road
Bancrofts School
Chiltern Way
Woodford Green
Simmons Lane
Weale Road
Wittenham Way
Dale View Avenue
Dale View Crs
Heathcote Gv
Heathfield
Gunners Gv
Colvin Gardens
Friday Hill
Primary School
Longshaw Rd
Friday Hill
Normanton Pk
Manor Farm Drive
Groveside Road
Bluehouse Road
Hornbeam Gv
Bernwell Rd
Chingdale Road
Newgate Street
B160
New Road
Hatch La
A1009
Road
Chingford Hatch
Chingford Lane
Mornington Road
Woodside Road
Montrose Close
High School
St Antonys RC Primary School
Trinity Catholic High School
Avon House School
High Rd A104
Golf Course
Larkswood Playing Fields
Jubilee Sports Ground
Balliol Avenue
The Avenue
Crofton Gv
Linnett Cl
Larkshall Crescent
Lichfield Rd
Keynsham Avenue
Montalt Road
Wood Lane
Woodford Golf Club
Woodford Green Prim Sch
Sunset Ave
Richmond Avenue
Larkshall Road
52
37
Surgery
Bosgrove
1
2
3
4
5
6
95
94
93
1 grid square represents 500 metres

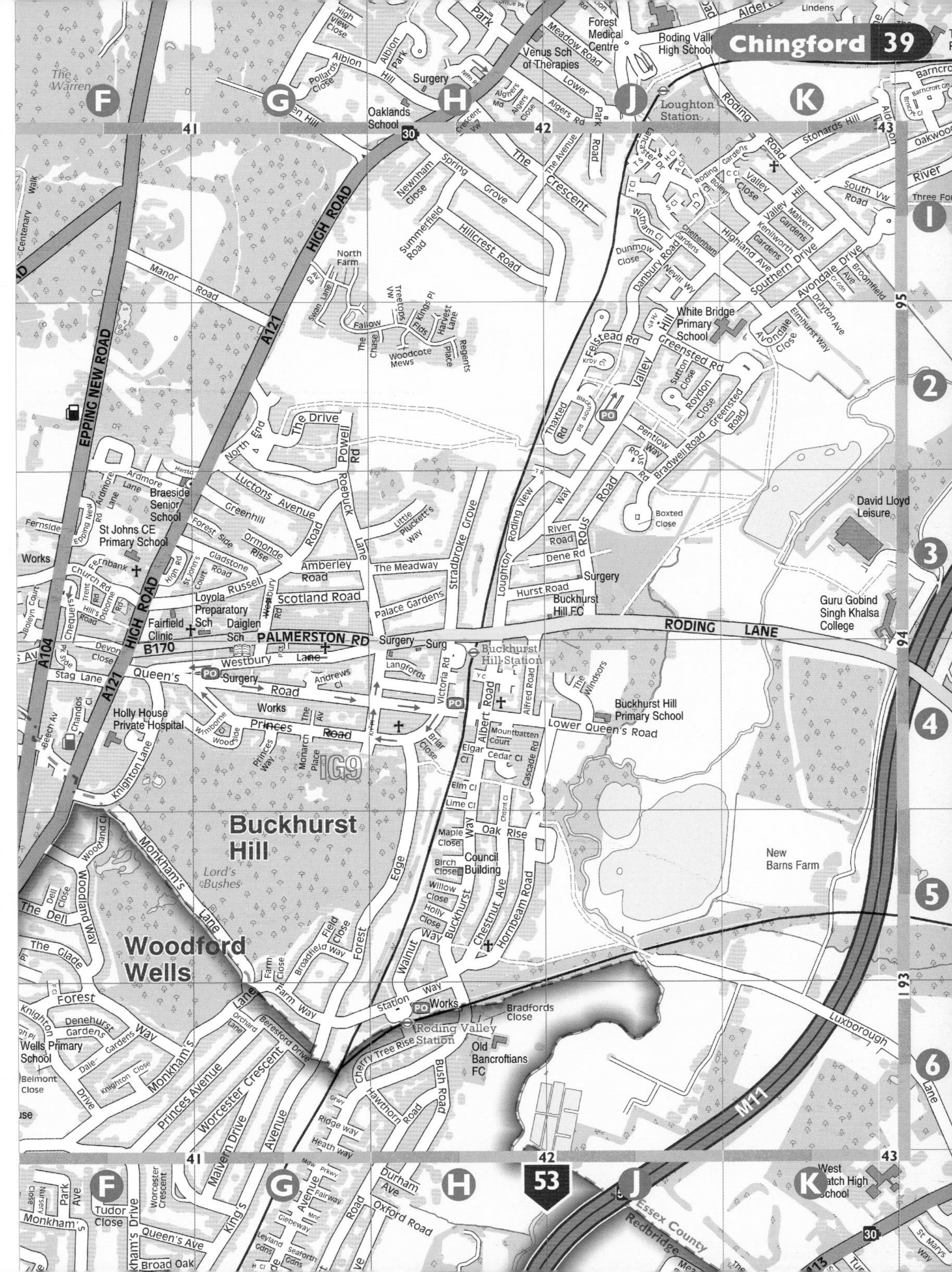

Chingford 39
53
Buckhurst Hill
Woodford Wells
Loughton Station
Buckhurst Hill Station
Roding Valley Station
Roding Valley High School
Forest Medical Centre
Venus Sch of Therapies
Oaklands School
White Bridge Primary School
Braeside Senior School
St Johns CE Primary School
Loyola Preparatory Sch
Fairfield Clinic
Daiglen Sch
Holly House Private Hospital
Buckhurst Hill Primary School
Buckhurst Hill FC
David Lloyd Leisure
Guru Gobind Singh Khalsa College
New Barns Farm
Council Building
Old Bancroftians FC
Wells Primary School
West Hatch High School
North Farm
Lord's Bushes
The Warren
HIGH ROAD
A121
A104
B170
EPPING NEW ROAD
PALMERSTON RD
RODING LANE
M11
Manor Road
Queen's Road
Princes Road
Lower Queen's Road
Forest Edge
Monkham's Lane
Luxborough Lane
Roding View
Loughton Way
Stradbroke Grove
Hillcrest Road
Spring Grove
The Crescent
Valley Hill
Southern Drive
Greensted Rd
Bradwell Road
Rous Road
Hurst Road
Albert Road
Hornbeam Road
Chestnut Ave
Buckhurst Way
Station Way
Farm Way
Cherry Tree Rise
Hawthorn Road
Bush Road
Princes Avenue
Worcester Crescent
Malvern Drive
Durham Ave
Oxford Road
Essex County
Redbridge
IG9
Surgery
Works
PO

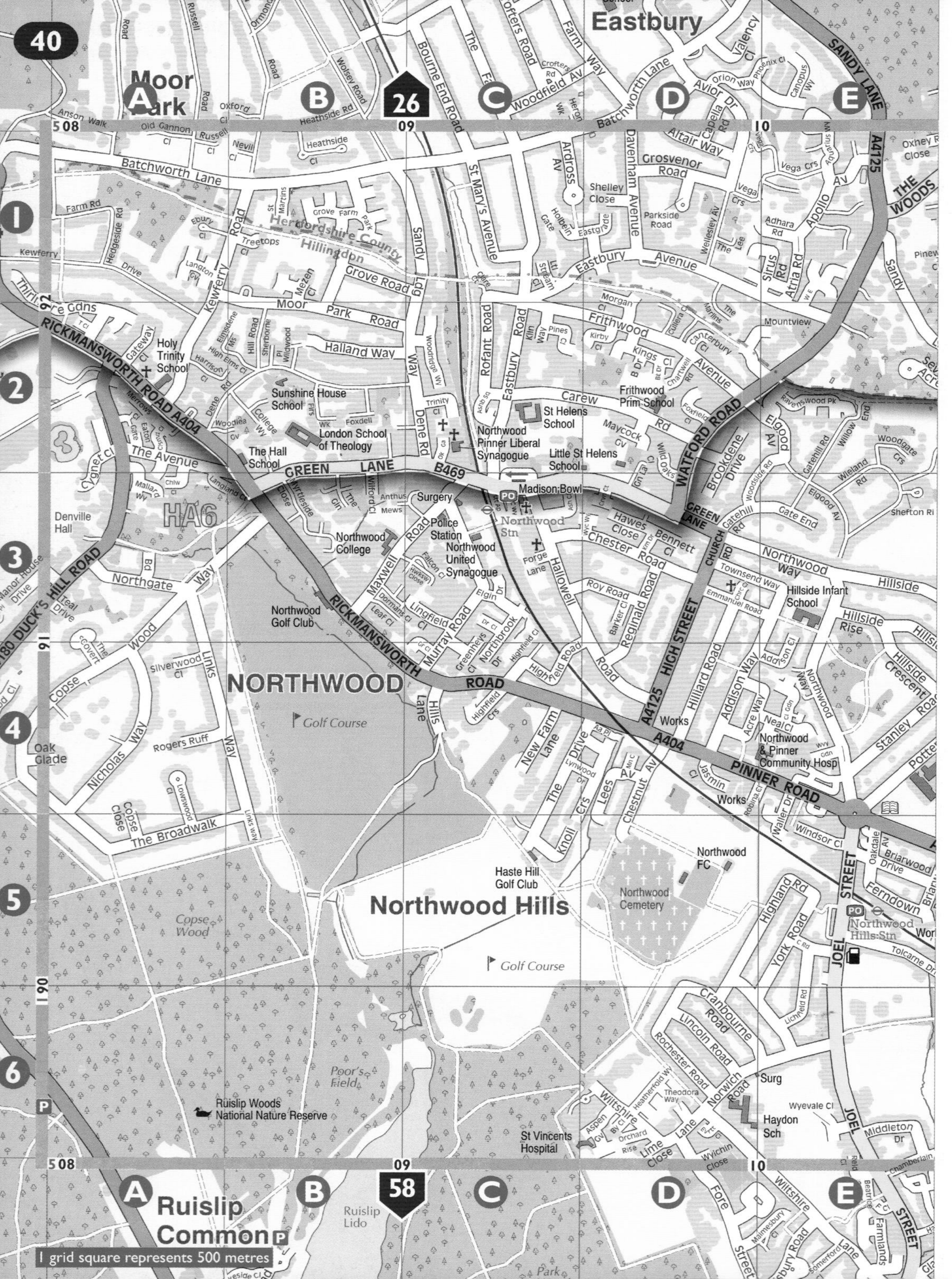
Moor Park
Eastbury
26
A
B
C
D
E
508
09
10
Batchworth Lane
Hertfordshire County
Hillingdon
Moor Park Road
Grove Road
Halland Way
Sandy Lodge Way
St Mary's Avenue
Eastbury Avenue
Grosvenor Road
Davenham Avenue
Frithwood Avenue
Shelley Close
Parkside Road
Mountview
Sandy Lane
A4125
The Woods
RICKMANSWORTH ROAD A404
Holy Trinity School
Sunshine House School
London School of Theology
The Hall School
GREEN LANE B469
Northwood Pinner Liberal Synagogue
St Helens School
Little St Helens School
Frithwood Prim School
Carew Rd
WATFORD ROAD
Madison Bowl
Surgery
Northwood Stn
Police Station
Northwood United Synagogue
Northwood College
HA6
Denville Hall
The Avenue
Northgate
Chester Road
Hawes Close
Bennett Cl
CHURCH RD
Northwood Way
Hillside
Hillside Infant School
Hillside Rise
Hillside Crescent
A180 DUCK'S HILL ROAD
Northwood Golf Club
RICKMANSWORTH ROAD
NORTHWOOD
Golf Course
Hallowell Road
Reginald Road
A4125 HIGH STREET
Hillard Road
Addison Way
Works
Northwood & Pinner Community Hosp
A404
PINNER ROAD
Copse Wood Way
Nicholas Way
Rogers Ruff
Links Way
Silverwood Cl
Oak Glade
Copse Close
The Broadwalk
New Farm Lane
The Drive
Lees Av
Chestnut Av
Knoll Crs
Haste Hill Golf Club
Northwood Hills
Northwood FC
Northwood Cemetery
Copse Wood
Golf Course
Highland Rd
York Road
JOEL STREET
Northwood Hills Stn
Ferndown
Tolcarne Dr
Windsor Cl
Briarwood Drive
Stanley Road
Cranbourne Road
Lincoln Road
Rochester Road
Norwich Road
Surg
Haydon Sch
Wyevale Cl
Middleton Dr
Poor's Field
Ruislip Woods National Nature Reserve
St Vincents Hospital
Wiltshire Lane
Lime Close
Fore Street
58
Ruislip Common
Ruislip Lido
1 grid square represents 500 metres
1
2
3
4
5
6
92
91
190

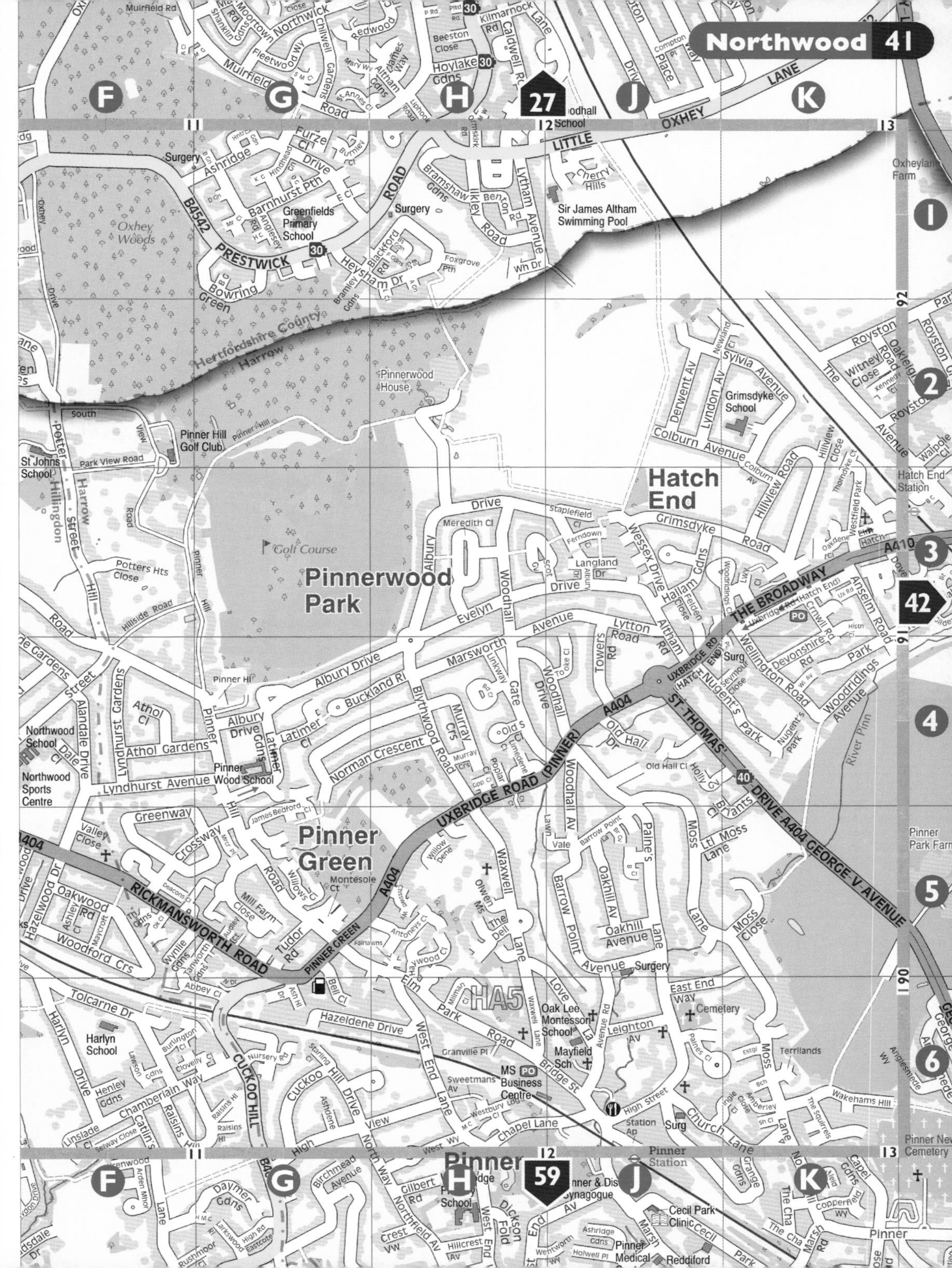

Hatch End
Pinnerwood Park
Pinner Green
Pinner
Oxhey Woods
Hertfordshire County
Harrow
Pinnerwood House
Pinner Hill Golf Club
Golf Course
Greenfields Primary School
Grimsdyke School
Sir James Altham Swimming Pool
St Johns School
Northwood School
Northwood Sports Centre
Pinner Wood School
Harlyn School
Hatch End Station
Pinner Station
Oxheylane Farm
Pinner Park Farm
Pinner New Cemetery
Cemetery
Oak Lee Montessori School
Mayfield Sch
MS Business Centre
Cecil Park Clinic
UXBRIDGE ROAD (PINNER)
RICKMANSWORTH ROAD
ST THOMAS' DRIVE A404 GEORGE V AVENUE
THE BROADWAY
OXHEY LANE
PRESTWICK ROAD
CUCKOO HILL
HA5
27
42
59

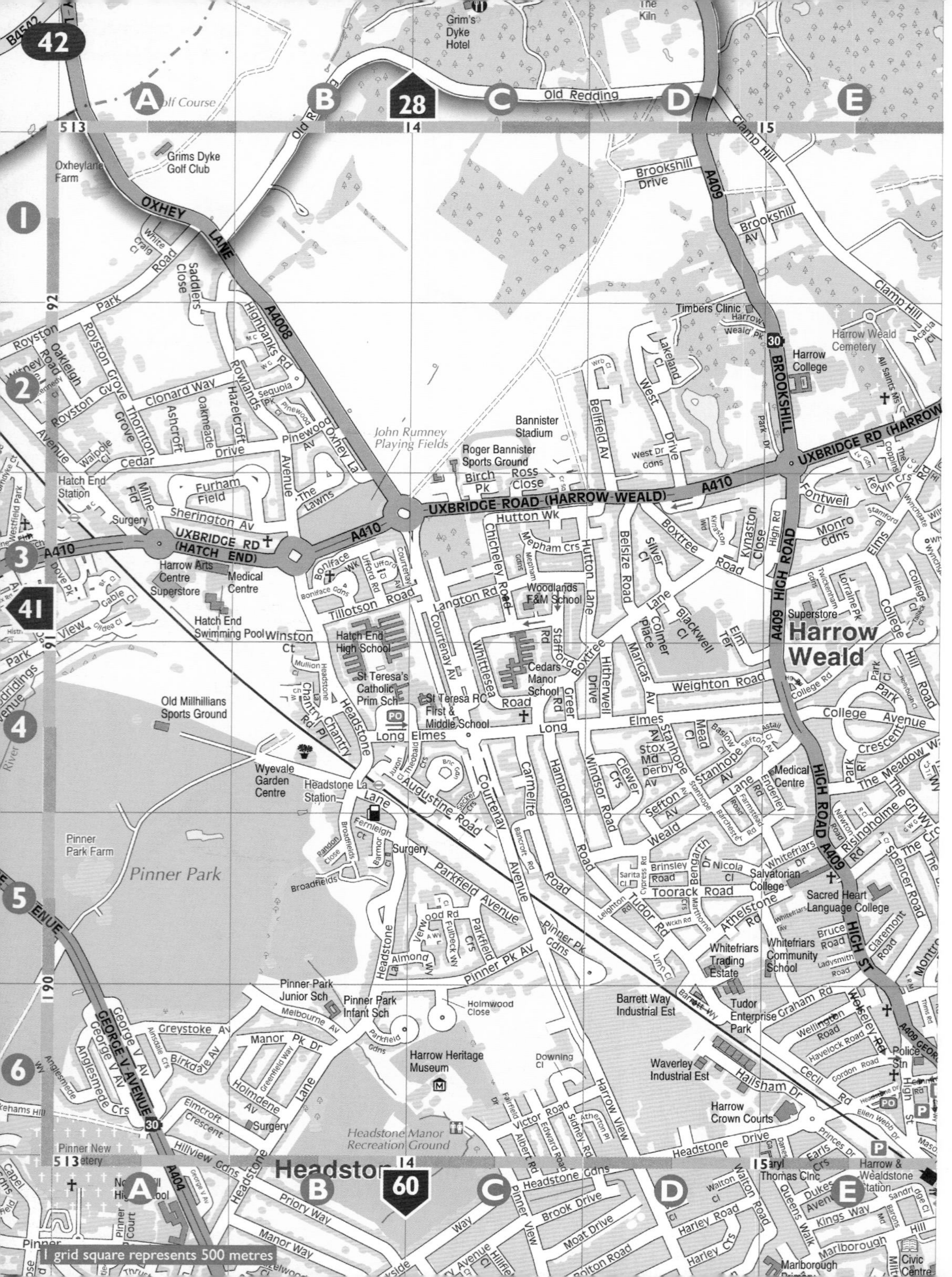

42
28
41
60
30
Grim's Dyke Hotel
The Kiln
Old Redding
Clamp Hill
Grims Dyke Golf Club
Oxheylane Farm
Brookshill Drive
Brookshill Av
Oxhey Lane
A4008
A409
Timbers Clinic
Harrow Weald Pk
Harrow Weald Cemetery
Harrow College
Brookshill
John Rumney Playing Fields
Bannister Stadium
Roger Bannister Sports Ground
Uxbridge Road (Harrow Weald)
A410
Uxbridge Rd (Hatch End)
Hatch End Station
Harrow Arts Centre
Superstore
Medical Centre
Hatch End Swimming Pool
Hatch End High School
St Teresa's Catholic Prim Sch
St Teresa RC First & Middle School
Woodlands F&M School
Cedars Manor School
Harrow Weald
High Road
Old Millhillians Sports Ground
Wyevale Garden Centre
Headstone La Station
Pinner Park Farm
Pinner Park
Medical Centre
Salvatorian College
Sacred Heart Language College
Whitefriars Trading Estate
Whitefriars Community School
Barrett Way Industrial Est
Tudor Enterprise Park
Waverley Industrial Est
Harrow Crown Courts
Police Stn
Pinner Park Junior Sch
Pinner Park Infant Sch
Harrow Heritage Museum
Headstone Manor Recreation Ground
George V Avenue
A404
Headstone
Pinner New Cemetery
Harrow & Wealdstone Station
Civic Centre
1 grid square represents 500 metres

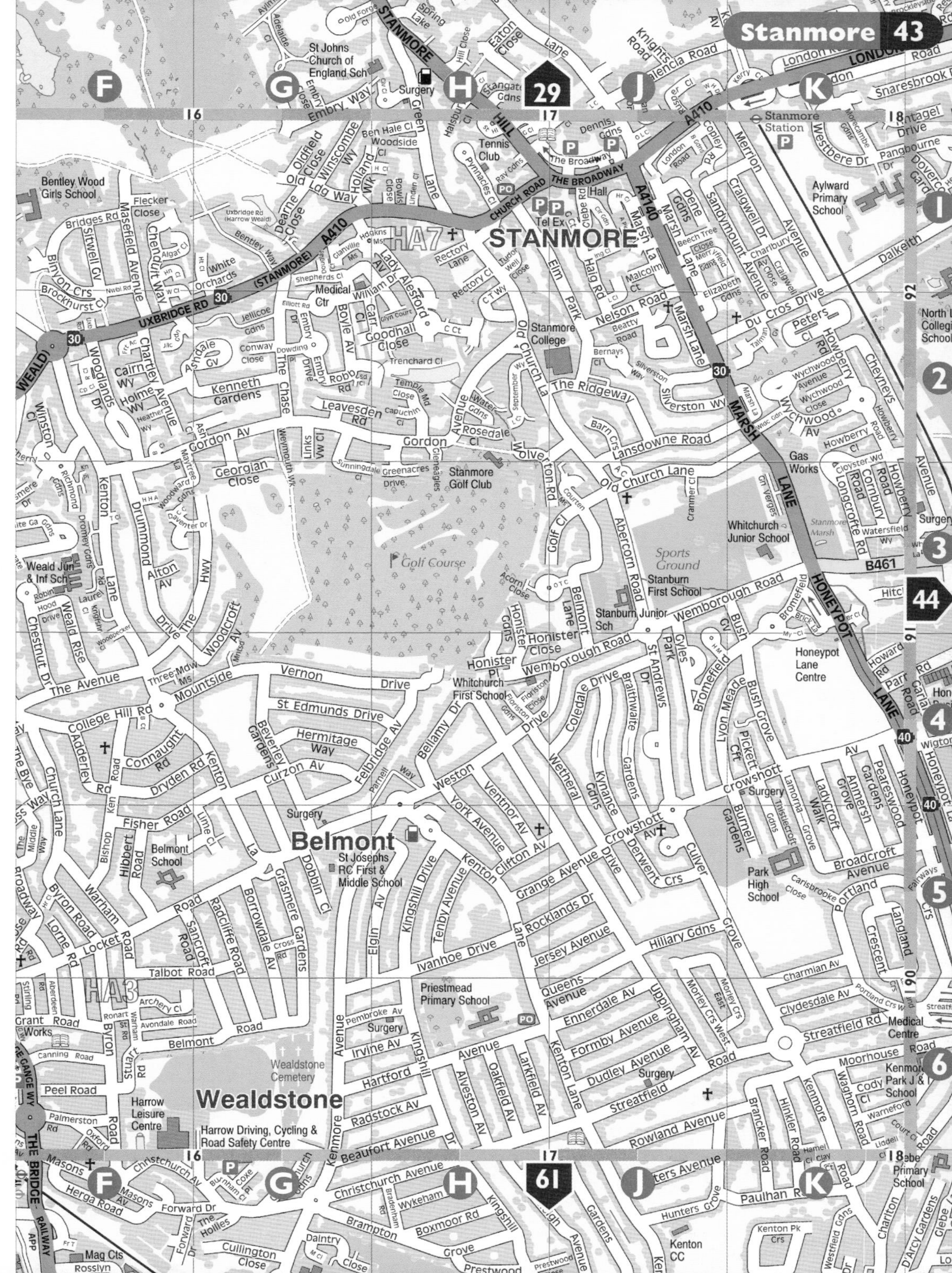
STANMORE
Belmont
Wealdstone
HA7
HA3
29
44
61
F
G
H
J
K
16
17
18
92
91
90
St Johns Church of England Sch
Surgery
Bentley Wood Girls School
Tennis Club
Stanmore Station
Aylward Primary School
North London Collegiate School
Medical Ctr
Stanmore College
Stanmore Golf Club
Golf Course
Gas Works
Whitchurch Junior School
Sports Ground
Stanburn First School
Stanburn Junior Sch
Weald Jun & Inf Sch
Whitchurch First School
Honeypot Lane Centre
Belmont School
St Josephs RC First & Middle School
Park High School
Priestmead Primary School
Wealdstone Cemetery
Harrow Leisure Centre
Harrow Driving, Cycling & Road Safety Centre
Kenmore Park J & I School
Medical Centre
Kenton CC
Mag Cts
UXBRIDGE RD
CHURCH ROAD
THE BROADWAY
STANMORE HILL
MARSH LANE
HONEYPOT LANE
Uxbridge Rd (Harrow Weald)
London Road
Old Church Lane
Wemborough Road
Kenton Lane
Kenton Road
The Avenue
Gordon Av
Du Cros Drive
Streatfield Rd
Christchurch Avenue
Beaufort Avenue
Rowland Avenue
Kingshill Drive
Belmont Lane
Elm Park
Marsh Lane
Canning Road
Peel Road
Palmerston Rd
Masons Av
Herga Road
Forward Dr
Cullington Close
Prestwood
A410
A4140
B461
30
40

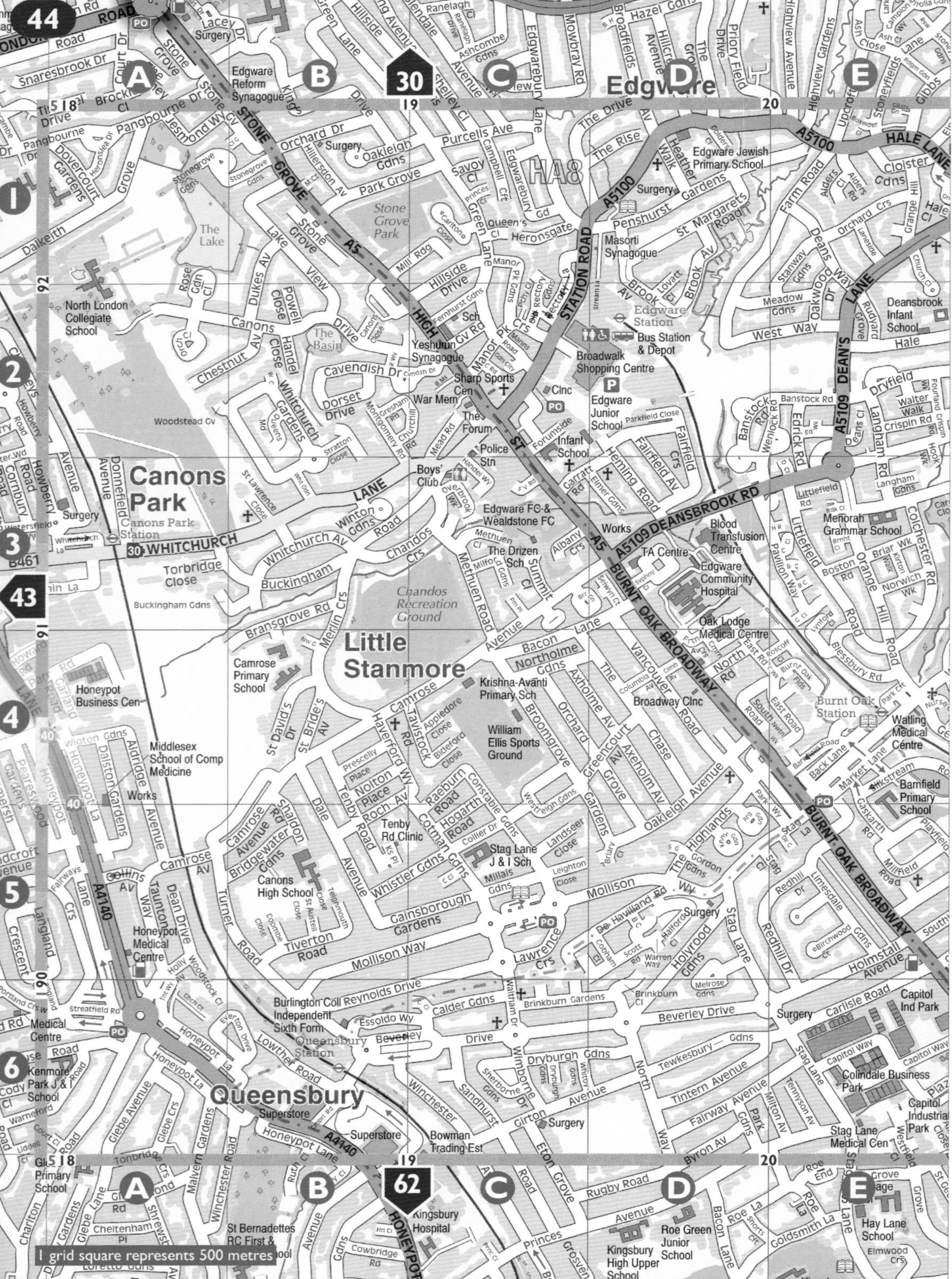

44
30
43
62
A
B
C
D
E
1
2
3
4
5
6
18
19
20
92
91
90
Edgware
Canons Park
Little Stanmore
Queensbury
HA8
LONDON ROAD
Snaresbrook Dr
Academy
Lacey Dr
Surgery
Stone Grove
Edgware Reform Synagogue
Green Lane
Hillside Drive
Glendale Avenue
Ranelagh Cl
Ashcombe Gdns
Edgwarebury Lane
Mowbray Rd
Broadfields Av
Hazel Gdns
Hillcrest Avenue
The Grove
Priory Field Drive
Synagogue
Highview Avenue
Highview Gardens
Ash Close
Stoneyfields Lane
Upcroft
Gibbs
The Drive
The Rise
A5100
HALE LANE
Edgware Jewish Primary School
Heather Walk
Pangbourne Dr
Dovercourt Gardens
Jesmond Wy
Stonegrove Gdns
STONE GROVE
Orchard Dr
Oakleigh Gdns
Purcells Ave
Savoy Cl
Park Grove
Stone Grove Park
Queen's Cl
Heronsgate
Penshurst Gardens
St Margarets Road
Masorti Synagogue
Farm Road
Alders Cl
Orchard Crs
Cloister Gdns
Grange Hill
Hale Cl
Dalkeith Grove
The Lake
North London Collegiate School
Lake View
Dukes Av
Powell Close
Rose Gdn Cl
A5
HIGH ST
Mill Rdg
Hillside Drive
Manor Pk Gdns
Rectory La
STATION ROAD
Edgware Station
Bus Station & Depot
Broadwalk Shopping Centre
Brook Av
Lovatt Cl
Stanway Gdns
Oakwood Dr
Deans Way
Meadow Gdns
West Way
Hale
DEAN'S LANE
A5109
Rudyard Grove
Deansbrook Infant School
Canons Drive
The Basin
Chestnut Av
Handel Close
Yeshurun Synagogue
Manor Pk Crs
Cavendish Dr
Dorset Drive
Sharp Sports Cen
War Mem
Whitchurch Gardens
Montgomery Rd
Churchill Rd
Mead Rd
The Forum
Clnc
Edgware Junior School
Parkfield Close
Forumside
Infant School
Heming Road
Fairfield Av
Fairfield Crs
Banstock Rd
Edrick Rd
Dryfield
Walter Walk
Crispin Rd
Langham Rd
Woodstead Gv
Police Stn
Boys' Club
Garratt Rd
Elmer Gdns
Littlefield Rd
Menorah Grammar School
Colchester Rd
St Lawrence Close
WHITCHURCH LANE
Winton Gdns
Edgware FC & Wealdstone FC
Works
A5109 DEANSBROOK RD
Blood Transfusion Centre
Canons Park Station
Whitchurch Av
Chandos Crs
Methuen Cl
The Drizen Sch
Summit Cl
Albany Crs
TA Centre
Edgware Community Hospital
Pavilion Way
Boston Rd
Orange Hill Road
Briar Wk
Norwich Wk
B461
Torbridge Close
Buckingham Road
Chandos Recreation Ground
Methuen Road
Buckingham Gdns
Bransgrove Rd
Merlin Crs
Avenue
Bacon Lane
BURNT OAK BROADWAY
Oak Lodge Medical Centre
Blessbury Rd
Camrose Primary School
Northolme Gdns
Krishna-Avanti Primary Sch
Axholme Av
The Chase
Vancouver Road
North Rd
East Rd
Broadway Clnc
Burnt Oak Station
Watling Medical Centre
Honeypot Business Cen
Camrose Avenue
William Ellis Sports Ground
Broomgrove Gdns
Orchard Gdns
Greencourt Av
Axeholm Av
Oakleigh Avenue
Barnfield Road
Back Lane
Market Lane
Silkstream
Barnfield Primary School
Middlesex School of Comp Medicine
Works
Aldridge Avenue
Dalston Gardens
Honeypot Lane
St David's Dr
St Bride's Av
Haverford Wy
Tavistock Rd
Appledore Close
Bideford Close
Prescelly Place
Nolton Place
Roch Av
Tenby Road
Dale Avenue
Raeburn Road
Hogarth Road
Constable Gdns
Tenby Rd Clinic
Cotman Gdns
Landseer Close
Gardens
Grove
The Highlands
Stag Cl
Gaskarth Rd
Playfield
Millfield Road
Camrose Av
Collins Av
Taunton Way
Dean Drive
Canons High School
Bridgewater Gdns
Whistler Gdns
Stag Lane J & I Sch
Millais Gdns
Leighton Close
Mollison Wy
Gordon Gdns
Surgery
Redhill Dr
Linkscale Gdns
A4140
Fairways
Langland Crs
Honeypot Medical Centre
Turner Road
Tiverton Road
Gainsborough Gardens
Lawrence Crs
De Havilland Rd
Holyrood Gdns
Stag Lane
Redhill Dr
Holmstall Avenue
Mollison Way
Woodstock Cl
Reynolds Drive
Brinkburn Gardens
Brinkburn Cl
Capitol Ind Park
Carlisle Road
Medical Centre
Burlington Coll Independent Sixth Form
Calder Gdns
Beverley Drive
Streatfield Rd
Honeypot La
Queensbury Station
Essoldo Wy
Beverley Drive
Waltham Dr
Surgery
Colindale Business Park
Capitol Way
Kenmore Park J & I School
Lowther Road
Winchester Road
Sandhurst Rd
Wimborne Dr
Dryburgh Gdns
North Way
Tewkesbury Gdns
Tintern Avenue
Fairway Avenue
Milton Av
Tennyson Av
Capitol Industrial Park
Glebe Avenue
Glebe Crs
Malvern Gardens
Superstore
Honeypot Lane
Superstore
Bowman Trading Est
Girton Avenue
Surgery
Park Gdns
Stag Lane Medical Cen
Byron Av
Tonbridge Crs
Winchester Road
Rugby Road
Roe Green Junior School
Kingsbury Hospital
HONEYPOT
Chalton
Glebe Lane
Cheltenham Pl
St Bernadettes RC First & ...ool
Cowbridge Rd
Princes Avenue
Grosvenor
Kingsbury High Upper School
Bacon Lane
Roe La
Goldsmith La
Hay Lane School
Elmwood Crs
Kingsbury
1 grid square represents 500 metres

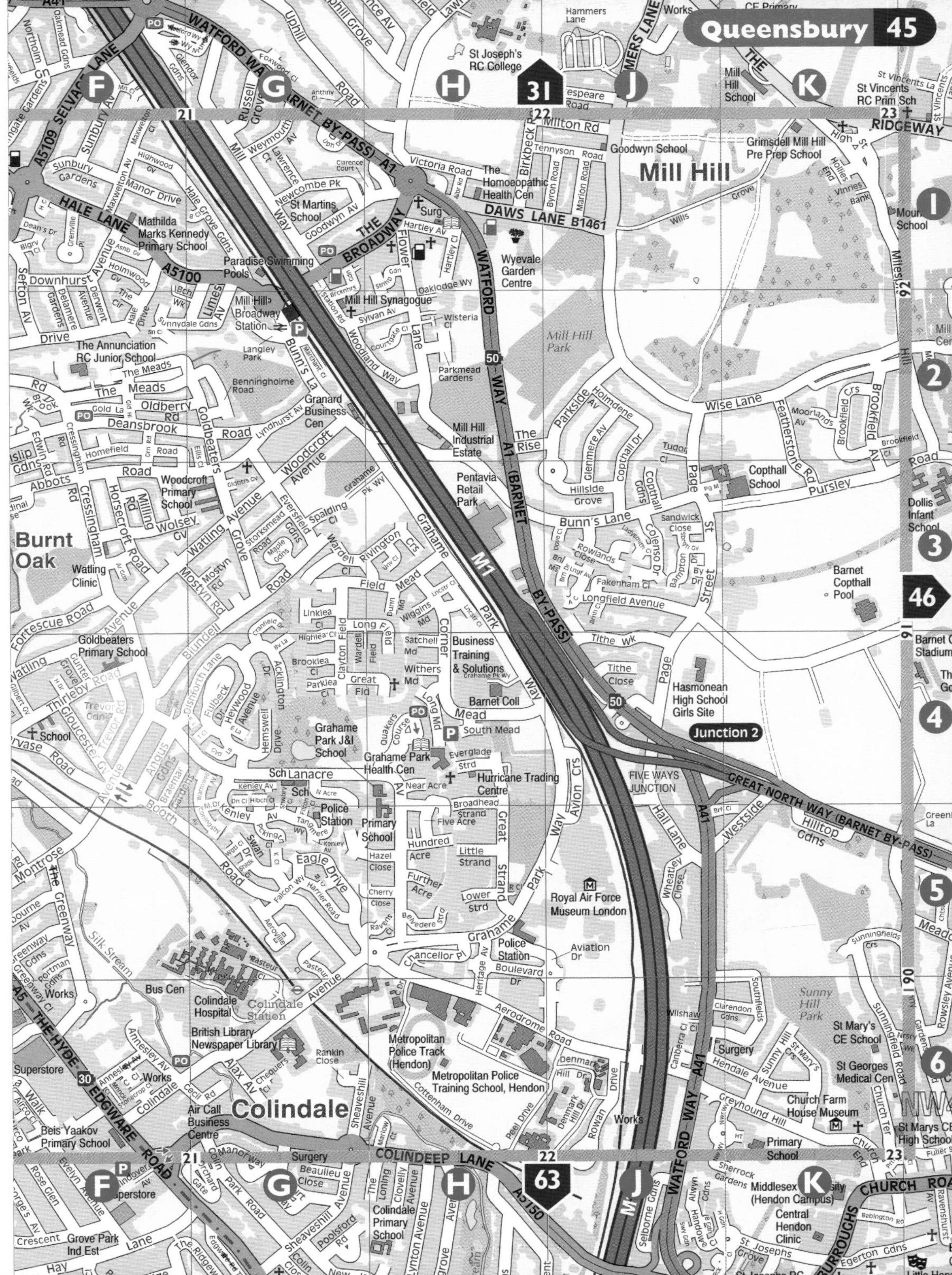

Mill Hill
Burnt Oak
Colindale
St Joseph's RC College
Mill Hill School
St Vincents RC Prim Sch
Grimsdell Mill Hill Pre Prep School
Goodwyn School
The Homoeopathic Health Cen
Mathilda Marks Kennedy Primary School
Paradise Swimming Pools
Wyevale Garden Centre
Mill Hill Synagogue
Mill Hill Broadway Station
The Annunciation RC Junior School
Mill Hill Park
Granard Business Cen
Mill Hill Industrial Estate
Pentavia Retail Park
Copthall School
Dollis Infant School
Woodcroft Primary School
Watling Clinic
Barnet Copthall Pool
Goldbeaters Primary School
Business Training & Solutions
Barnet Coll
Hasmonean High School Girls Site
Junction 2
Grahame Park J&I School
Grahame Park Health Cen
Hurricane Trading Centre
FIVE WAYS JUNCTION
Police Station
Primary School
Royal Air Force Museum London
Sunny Hill Park
Colindale Hospital
Colindale Station
Bus Cen
British Library Newspaper Library
Metropolitan Police Track (Hendon)
Metropolitan Police Training School, Hendon
Air Call Business Centre
Beis Yaakov Primary School
St Mary's CE School
St Georges Medical Cen
Church Farm House Museum
St Marys CE High School
Middlesex University (Hendon Campus)
Central Hendon Clinic
Colindale Primary School
Grove Park Ind Est
WATFORD WAY
BARNET BY-PASS
GREAT NORTH WAY (BARNET BY-PASS)
DAWS LANE B1461
HALE LANE
SELVAGE LANE
THE BROADWAY
COLINDEEP LANE
EDGWARE ROAD
THE HYDE
CHURCH ROAD
BURROUGHS
RIDGEWAY
M1
A1
A41
A5100
A5109
A5150
A5
31
46
63

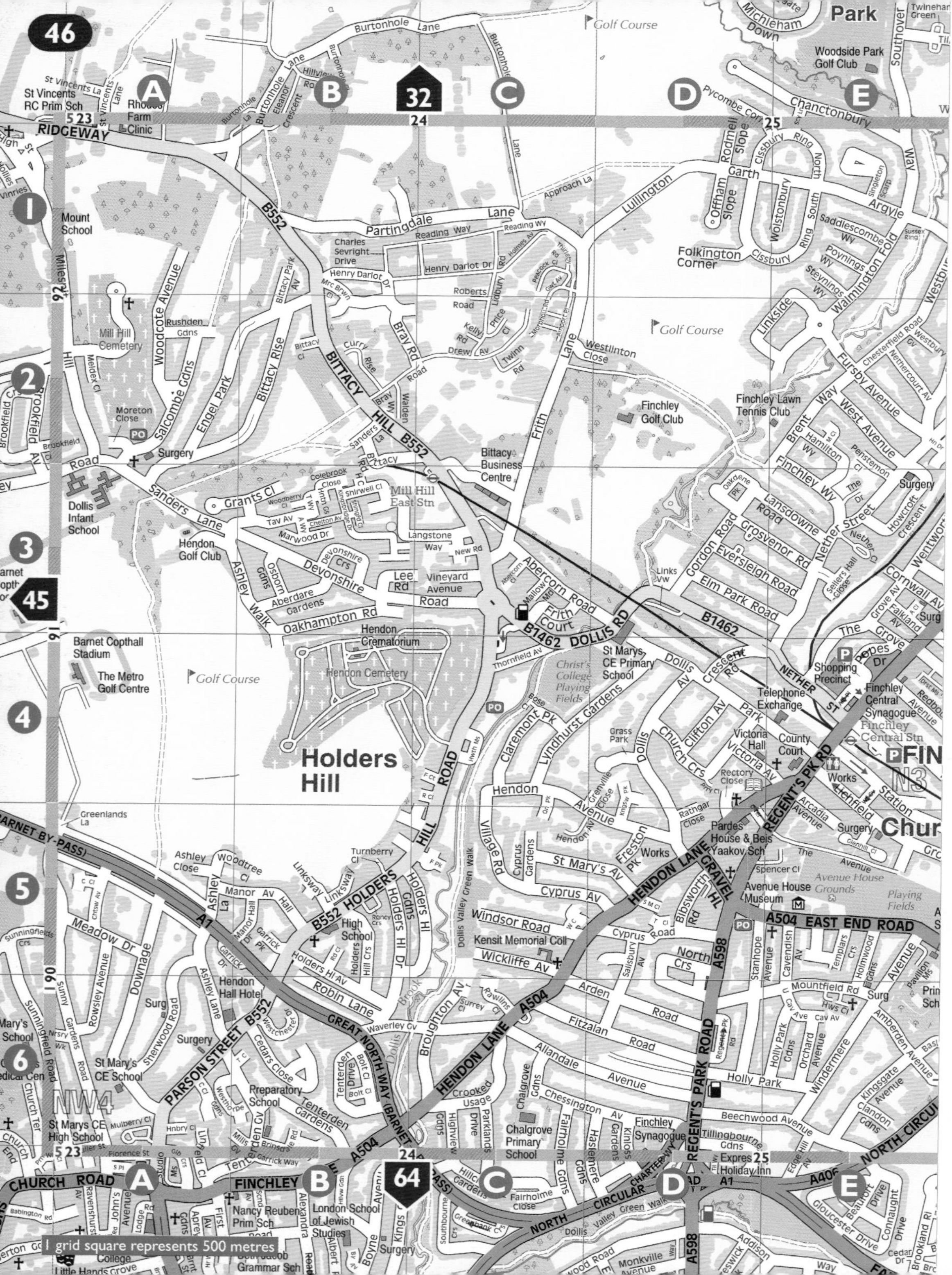

32
45
64
A
B
C
D
E
1
2
3
4
5
6
Park
Golf Course
Burtonhole Lane
Burtonhole Lane
Hillview Rd
Eleanor Crescent
St Vincents La
St Vincents Lane
St Vincents RC Prim Sch
Rhodes Farm Clinic
RIDGEWAY
Michleham Down
Woodside Park Golf Club
Southover
Twinehams Green
Pycombe Corner
Chanctonbury
Rodmell Slope
Cissbury Ring North
Garth
Lullington
Approach La
Offham Slope
Wolstonbury
Cissbury Ring South
Argyle
Saddlescombe Wy
Poynings Wy
Steynings Wy
Walmington Fold
Folkington Corner
Mount School
Milespit Hill
B552
Partingdale Lane
Reading Way
Charles Sevright Drive
Henry Darlot Dr
Henry Darlot Dr
Roberts Road
Lidbury Rd
Price Cl
Kelly Rd
Drew Av
Twinn Rd
Bray Rd
Curry Rise
Bittacy Cl
Bittacy Park Av
Bittacy Rise
Woodcote Avenue
Rushden Gdns
Mill Hill Cemetery
Meldex Cl
Salcombe Gdns
Engel Park
Moreton Close
Surgery
Brookfield Av
Brookfield Cres
Road
BITTACY HILL B552
Walden
Bray Wy
Golf Course
Frith Lane
Westlinton Close
Finchley Golf Club
Linkside
Chesterfield Road
Fursby Avenue
Finchley Lawn Tennis Club
Brent Way
West Avenue
Hamilton Wy
Finchley Wy
Surgery
Bittacy Business Centre
Sanders La
Sanders Lane
Grants Cl
Colebrook Close
Shirwell Cl
Mill Hill East Stn
Tav Av
Marwood Dr
Langstone Way
New Rd
Dollis Infant School
Hendon Golf Club
Ashley Walk
Osborn Gdns
Devonshire Crs
Devonshire Road
Lee Rd
Vineyard Avenue
Aberdare Gardens
Oakhampton Rd
Abercorn Road
Frith Court
B1462 DOLLIS RD
Links Vw
Gordon Road
Lansdowne Road
Grosvenor Rd
Eversleigh Road
Elm Park Road
B1462
Nether Street
Howcroft Crescent
Cornwall Av
The Grove
Barnet Copthall Stadium
The Metro Golf Centre
Golf Course
Hendon Crematorium
Hendon Cemetery
Thornfield Av
Christ's College Playing Fields
St Marys CE Primary School
Dollis Av
Crescent Rd
NETHER ST
Shopping Precinct
Finchley Central Synagogue
Finchley Central Stn
Telephone Exchange
County Court
Holders Hill
HOLDERS HILL ROAD
Claremont Pk
Lyndhurst Gardens
Grass Park
Dollis Pk
Church Crs
Clifton Av
Victoria Hall
Victoria Av
Rectory Close
REGENT'S PK RD
Works
Lichfield
Station
Arcadia Avenue
FIN
N3
Chur
Greenlands La
BARNET BY-PASS
Hendon Avenue
Village Rd
Cyprus Gardens
Freston Pk
Works
Rathgar Close
Pardes House & Beis Yaakov Sch
Surgery
The Avenue
Avenue House Grounds
Avenue House Museum
Playing Fields
Ashley Close
Woodtree Cl
Turnberry Cl
Linksway
B552 HOLDERS
Holders Hill Gdns
Holders Hill Dr
High School
Manor Av
Meadow Dr
Downage
Rowsley Avenue
Sunningfields Crs
Sunny Gardens Road
Sunningfield Road
St Mary's Av
Cyprus Av
HENDON LANE
GRAVEL HL
Bibsworth Rd
Windsor Road
Cyprus Road
Kensit Memorial Coll
Wickliffe Av
Salisbury Av
North Crs
A598
A504 EAST END ROAD
Stanhope Avenue
Cavendish Avenue
Templars Crs
Holmwood Gdns
Avenue
Pavilion Ms
Prim Sch
Mountfield Rd
Surg
Ashley Lane
Hendon Hall Hotel
Sherwood Road
Surg
Robin Lane
Holders Hl Av
GREAT NORTH WAY
A1
Dollis Brook
Dollis Valley Green Walk
Broughton Av
Surrey Ms
Rawlins Cl
A504
Arden Road
Fitzalan Road
Allandale Avenue
Holly Park Gdns
Orchard Avenue
Windermere Avenue
Amberden Avenue
Kingsgate Avenue
Clandon Gdns
Surgery
PARSON STREET B552
Westchester Dr
Cedars Close
Waverley Gv
St Mary's CE School
Preparatory School
Tenterden Gardens
Tenterden Drive
Bolt Cl
HENDON LANE
GREAT NORTH WAY (BARNET
Crooked Usage
Highview Gdns
Drive
Parklands
Chalgrove Gdns
Chessington Av
Holly Park
Chalgrove Primary School
Fairholme Gdns
Haslemere Gardens
Kinloss Gardens
Finchley Synagogue
REGENT'S PARK ROAD
Beechwood Avenue
Tillingbourne Gdns
Expres Holiday Inn
NORTH CIRCULAR
NW4
St Marys CE High School
Mulberry Cl
Church Ter
Church End
Mary's School
edical Cen
CHURCH ROAD
FINCHLEY
A504
Florence St
Carrick Way
Studio Ms
Lodge Rd
Ravenshurst Av
Babington Rd
Nancy Reuben Prim Sch
London School of Jewish Studies
Alexandra
Kings
Boyne Avenue
Surgery
Hillcrest Gardens
Fairholme Close
NORTH CIRCULAR
CHARTER WY
Dollis Valley Green Walk
Southbourne
Addison
A598
A1
A406
NORTH CIRCULAR
Beaufort Drive
Gloucester Drive
Connaught Drive
Brookland Ri
Monkville Avenue
Wood Road
Grammar Sch
Little Hands Grove
College
1 grid square represents 500 metres

Finchley 47
FRIERN BARNET
North Finchley
Colney Hatch
East Finchley
Fortis Green
CHLEY
ch End
N12
N2
33
48
65
F
G
H
J
K
26
27
28
1
2
3
4
5
6
Mayfield Avenue
Ravens Lawn Tennis Club
Friary Park
Friern Watch Av
Friary Road
Ravensdale Av
Copwood Close
The Ridgeway
St Johns CE Primary School
Bethune Av
The Crescent
School Clinic
Torrington Park
Park Health Cen
Fairfield Cl
Torrington Clnc
Victoria Gv
Glenhurst Rd
Friern Park
Friern Barnet Lane
Friern Barnet School
Hatley Close
Hemington Avenue
Goldsmith Rd
Macdonald Rd
Stanford Rd
Glenthorne Rd
Holly Park Rd
Woodside Park Station
Woodside Pk Synagogue
Woodside Av
Woodside Grange Rd
Holden Rd
Holden Road
The Holmewood Sch London
Dorie Ms
The Oaks
Green Bank
Whittington Mews
Frederick's Pl
Highwood Av
Finchley Industrial Cen
Archgate Business Cen
North London International Sch
Lodge Lane
Northside Primary School
Percy Road
Gainsborough Rd
Netherfield Rd
Grange Av
Coleridge Rd
Derby Av
Grammar School
Hughes Close
Nether Street
Hall St
Regent Cl
Stanhope Rd
Barnet Coll
Castle Rd
Castle Ms
Lambert Wy
Lambert Rd
Grove Road
Northwood Gardens
Hemingford Close
Cottonham Cl
Fenstanton Av
Bxwrth Cl
Cardrew Av
Wren Academy
Warnham Rd
St Michael's Cl
Hilton Ave
Bramber Road
Lewes Road
Buxted Road
Petworth Road
Ashurst Rd
Horsham Avenue
North London Int Sch
B550
Constable Cl
Bensley Cl
Kemnal Rd
Hartland Rd
Ramsden Rd
Sch
Hillside Av
Shapwick Close
Radstock Cl
Avondale Avenue
Springfield Cl
Finchley Progressive Synagogue
Birkbeck Rd
Dale Gv
Artsdepot
Hutton Gv
Alexandra Grove
Court House Road
Hillcourt Av
KINGSWAY
WOODHOUSE ROAD
A1003
Woodhouse College
Woodgrange Av
Churchfield Av
Superstore
Rsmn Av
Ch Wy
Short Wy
Woodhouse Rd
Lyndhurst Av
Ferncroft Av
Woodleigh Av
Thurlestone Av
COLNEY HATCH LANE
Dudrich Cl
Asher Loftus Wy
Pickering Gdns
Hollickwood Av
Ingleway
Schoolway
Crossway
Garthway
Crescentway
Summerside JMI School
The Compton School
Compton Sports Centre
Fallowfields Dr
Summerfield Av
Thistley Cl
Newstead Wy
Agnesfield Cl
Pond Cl
B550
Firs Av
Poplar
Larch Cl
Nether St
Moss Hall Grove
Moss Hall Crescent
Thyra Gv
Grove
LANE
Christchurch Avenue
Woodberry Grove
Woodberry Way
West Finchley Stn
Morasha Jewish Primary School
Essex Park
Montrose Crs
Fallow Ct Av
Eton Av
Kenver Av
Addington Drive
Sandringham Gdns
HIGH ROAD
A1000
Summers Road
Sunny Wy
Legion Way
Coppetts Cl
Finchley Reform Synagogue
Granville Road
BALLARDS
Brownlow Road
Gruneisen Road
Seymour Road
Surg
Police Stn
Etchingham Park Road
Chislehurst Avenue
Holdenhurst Avenue
Finchley Memorial Hospital
High Road
Leisure Wy
David Lloyd Leisure
Wingate & Finchley FC
Finchley Lido Leisure Centre
N CIRCULAR RD
A406
50
Victoria Park
A598
The Ridgeway
St Paul's Way
Willow Way
Parkside
Long Lane
Claverley Gv
Millers Yd
Princes Av
Dukes Av
Vines Av
Oakfield Rd
Park Crs
Woodlands Avenue
Queen's Av
Bow Lane
Clifton Road
Our Lady of Lourdes RC Prim Sch
Crowder Cl
Vue Cinema
TA Centre
Glebelands Cl
ROAD
Old Farm Rd
Stable Wk
Surgery
Glebe Rd
Dickens Av
Park Vw Rd
Park Av
Manorside Primary School
Tudor Prim Sch
Strawberry Vale
Nursery
St Martin's Rd
Lankaster Gdns
Boundary Rd
St Pancras & Islington Cemetery
Islington Crematorium
Greenfields Special School
Gilson Pl
Coppetts Wood Hospital
Coppetts Wood Primary Sch
Coppetts Rd
Osier Crs
Marriot Road
Barrenger Road
Steeds Road
Hill Road
Everington Rd
Coldfall Wood
Coldfall Avenue
Nelson Mand
Hallwick
Hervey Cl
Strathmore Gdns
Vineyard Gv
Squires Lane
Queen's Road
Montpelier Road
Avondale Road
Cromwell Road
Abingdon Road
Long Lane
Nursery Avenue
CIRCULAR
NORTH CIRCULAR
Tarling Rd
Brrwd Cl
Lewis Gdns
Exit Rd
Sylvester Rd
Font Hills
The Mead
Simms Gdns
Tarling Rd
Road
Rosemary Av
Squires La
Surgery
View
Manor View
Dudley Rd
Briarfield Av
Primrose Cl
Lucas Gdns
Lane
Blackdown Cl
Taunton Dr
Brendon Gv
Oak Lane
Challoner Cl
Central Av
Chandos Road
New Oak Rd
New Trinity Rd
William Cl
Creighton Avenue
Fortismere School
Eastwood Road
Akiva School
The Jewish Museum
Finchley CC
Tangle Tree Cl
Bishop Douglass RC School
Brighton Rd
E End Rd
Moat Crescent
St Mary's Green
Clare Cl
Juliana Cl
Helen Cl
Christs College School
Hamilton Road
Brackenbury Road
Sedgemere Av
Elm Gdns
Manor Pk Road
Hobbs Gn
Trinity Rd
Church Lane
Elmfield Road
King St
Leopold Road
Leslie Road
Park Gate
Creigton Avenue
School
Hertford Road
Bedford Road
Huntingdon Road
Leicester Rd
Lincoln Road
Durham Road
Church Vale
Beech Drive
Ringwood Av
Twyford Avenue
Burlington Road
Muswell Synagogue
Fortis Green Health Clinic
Police Station
FORTIS GREEN
A504
Clissold Rd
Midhurst Av
Collingwood Av
St Marylebone Crematorium
Denison Close
EAST END ROAD
Christs College Finchley
East Finchley Cemetery
Holyoake Walk
Ossulton Way
Neale Close
Heath View
Oak Lodge School
Trinity Av
Talbot Av
Homefield Rd
Stanley Rd
Oakridge Dr
Park Road
Market Pl
Chapel Ct
Kitchener Rd
Beresford Rd
Finchley Youth Theatre
Primary School
Prospect
PO
Surgery
Dnry Cl
Martin Prim School
Med Cen
Phoenix
Park Hall Rd
Summerlee Avenue
Springcroft Avenue
Western Road
Eastern Road
Lynmouth Rd
Lauradale Road
Southern Road
Baronsmere Road
Summerlee Gardens
Cherry Tree Road
Shakespeare Gdns
Greenfield Dr
Brookland Junior School
Brookland Rise
Brookland Hill
Way
Ludlow Way
Maya Rd
Pulham Av
Elmshurst Crescent
Heath View
The Leys
Howard Walk
Abbots Gdns
Cedar Drive
The Institute Hampstead Garden Suburb
East Finchley
Hill Top
Brim Hill
Eastholm
Brompton Gv
Ingram Road
Road
Teth Prim Sch

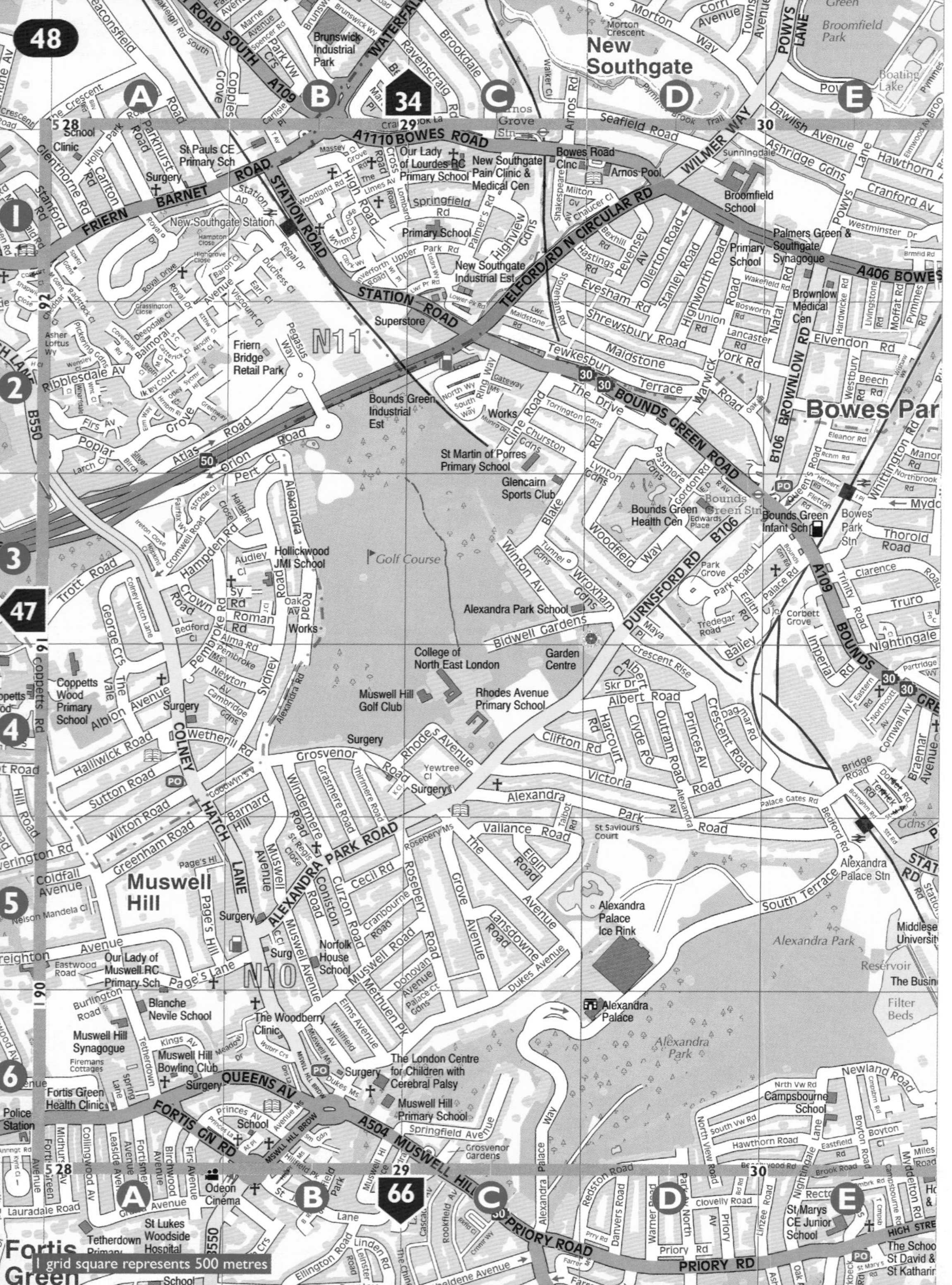

New Southgate
Bowes Park
Muswell Hill
Fortis Green
N11
N10
A1110 BOWES ROAD
FRIERN BARNET ROAD
STATION ROAD
TELFORD RD N CIRCULAR RD
BOUNDS GREEN ROAD
DURNSFORD RD
COLNEY HATCH LANE
ALEXANDRA PARK ROAD
QUEENS AV
A504 MUSWELL HILL
PRIORY ROAD
FORTIS GN RD
WILMER WAY
A406 BOWES
BROWNLOW RD
Friern Bridge Retail Park
Bounds Green Industrial Est
New Southgate Industrial Est
Golf Course
Muswell Hill Golf Club
College of North East London
Alexandra Park School
Alexandra Palace
Alexandra Palace Ice Rink
Alexandra Park
Alexandra Palace Stn
Bowes Park Stn
Bounds Green Stn
New Southgate Station
Broomfield Park
Coppetts Wood Primary School
Hollickwood JMI School
Rhodes Avenue Primary School
St Martin of Porres Primary School
Glencairn Sports Club
Bounds Green Health Cen
Bounds Green Infant Sch
Broomfield School
Palmers Green & Southgate Synagogue
Brownlow Medical Cen
Our Lady of Lourdes RC Primary School
New Southgate Pain Clinic & Medical Cen
St Pauls CE Primary Sch
Arnos Pool
Bowes Road Clnc
Superstore
Garden Centre
Norfolk House School
Our Lady of Muswell RC Primary Sch
Blanche Nevile School
Muswell Hill Synagogue
Muswell Hill Bowling Club
Fortis Green Health Clinic
Police Station
The Woodberry Clinic
The London Centre for Children with Cerebral Palsy
Muswell Hill Primary School
Odeon Cinema
St Lukes Woodside Hospital
Campsbourne School
St Marys CE Junior School
Middlesex University
Filter Beds
Reservoir
1 grid square represents 500 metres

34
47
66

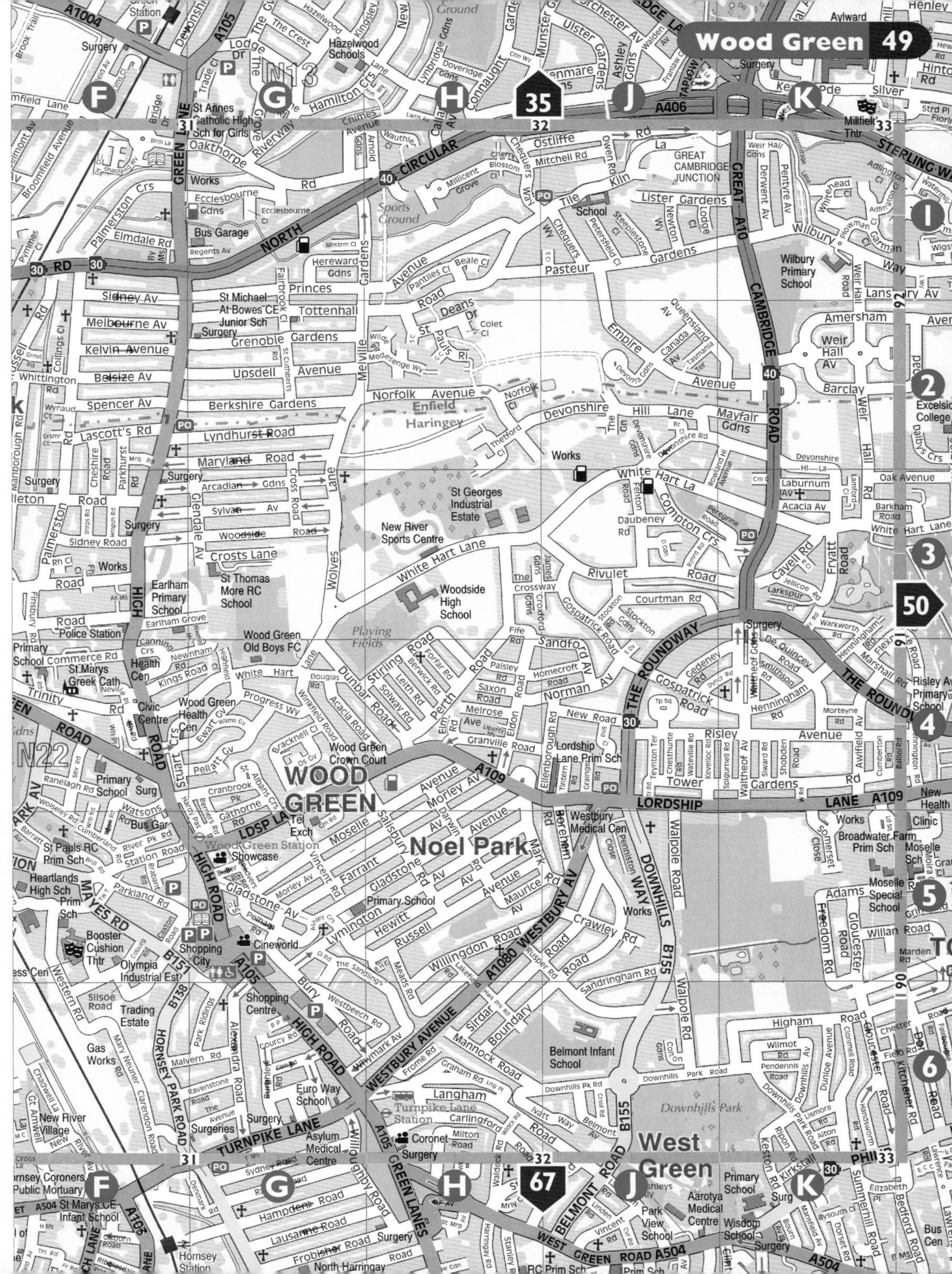

Wood Green 49
WOOD GREEN
Noel Park
West Green
Downhills Park
GREAT CAMBRIDGE JUNCTION
NORTH CIRCULAR RD
GREAT CAMBRIDGE ROAD
THE ROUNDWAY
LORDSHIP LANE A109
HIGH ROAD
GREEN LANE
WESTBURY AVENUE
TURNPIKE LANE
WEST GREEN ROAD A504
HORNSEY PARK ROAD
Wood Green Station
Turnpike Lane Station
Hornsey Station
St Georges Industrial Estate
New River Sports Centre
Woodside High School
Wood Green Crown Court
Shopping City
Olympia Industrial Est
Belmont Infant School
Wilbury Primary School
Excelsior College
Broadwater Farm Prim Sch
Moselle Special School
Enfield
Haringey
N13
N22
35
50
67

50
36
49
68
A
B
C
D
E
1
2
3
4
5
6
533
34
35
92
91
90
Upper Edmonton
TOTTENHAM
Tottenham Hale
N18
N17
Pymmes Park
Henley Road
Silver Street Medical Cen
Silver Street Station
Millfield Thtr
Hinton Rd
Bulwer Rd
Denton Rd
Sheldon Rd
Warwick Rd
Sweet Briar Wk
Victoria Rd
Park Road
Works
Medical Centre
Brettenham Prim Sch
Brettenham Rd
Baxter Rd
Youth Centre
Montagu Gdns
Montagu Crs
Industrial Estate
Gibbs Rd
First Av
Rays Rd
Lea Valley Trading Esta
SILVER ST
STERLING WAY (NORTH CIRCULAR)
A406
Dickens La
Fairfield Rd
ANGEL RD
(NORTH CIRCULAR)
Aberdeen Rd
Cavendish Rd
CONDUIT LANE
MONTAGU RD
Angel Road Station
Crispin Industrial Cen
Sterling Way Clnc
A&E
North Middlesex Hospital
Somerset Rd
Gloucester Rd
Surg
Bn Rd
College Cl
Gilpin Crs
Colyton Wy
FORE STREET
Raynham Rd
Leeds St
Primary School
Upton Road
Playing Field
Raynham Ter
Seaton St
Sandal Rd
The London Make-Up Academy
Culpepper
Leopold Rd
Yorkshire Gdns
Ladysmith Rd
Alston Rd
Albany Rd
Kimberley Road
Dyson's Rd
Gas Works
Superstore
Glover Dr
MERIDIAN WAY
Bridport Road
Wigston Cl
Tiverton Rd
Lansbury Av
Avenue
Shaftesbury Road
Joyce Av
School
County Court
Cowper Rd
Alpha Rd
Claremont St
Stockton Road
Leyburn Road
Middleham Road
Works
Commercial Rd
Parkstone Av
Branksome Av
Hawthorne Rd
Pretoria Rd N
Langhedge Lane
Grove St
Snell's Pk
Clive Av
Nutfield Cl
Langhedge Lane Industrial Est
Surgery
Excelsior College
Frontier Works
Hebden Ter
Durban Rd
Academia Way
College Rd
Peacock Est
Gibson Business Centre
Sunrise School
Brantwood Road
Coniston Rd
Grange Rd
Tariff Road
Leeside Road
Triumph Trading Est
Hotspur Industrial Est
West Road
Lake Business Cen
The Royal London Est
Northumberland Park Industrial Est
Leeside Trading Est
Leeside Works
Oak Avenue
Allington Av
Haringey Sixth Form Centre
Peacock Industrial Est
The Gibson Business Cen
Northumberland Pk
Northumberland Pk Comm Sch
Elm Lea Trading Est
White Hart Lane Station
White Hart Lane
Creighton Road
Barkham Road
Wingate Trading Est
Bill Nicholson Wy
Worcester Av
Paxton Road
Farningham Road
Waverley Rd
Haynes Cl
Heybourne Rd
Garman Rd
Mowlem Trading Est
Sedge Rd
Penshurst Rd
Tenterden Rd
Beaufoy Rd
Whitehall St
Tottenham Hotspur FC (White Hart Lane)
St Pauls & All Hallows CE Jun Sch
Inf Sch
Lea Valley Primary School
Willoughby Lane
Park Av Rd
LC
Unicorn Works
Tottenham Cemetery
Orchard Pl
Sch
Church Rd
Park Lane
Surgery
Marsh La
Marigold Road
Northumberland Park Station
Church Rd
Lancasterian Prim Sch
King's Road
Sports Cen
Bromley Rd
Argyle Road
Vicarage Rd
Sutherland Rd
St Paul's Road
Manor Road
Chalgrove Rd
Asplins Rd
Surgery
Foyle Road
Risley Avenue Primary School
THE ROUNDWAY
Bruce Castle Park
Ruskin Rd
Cedar Road
Pembury Rd
Bruce Castle Rd
Birkbeck Road
School
Campbell Road
Hampden Road
Hampden La
Baronet Rd
Shelbourne Road
Bruce Castle Museum
A10
LORDSHIP LANE
A109
Lansdowne Road
Tilson Rd
Wycombe Road
Glendish Rd
Primary School
Halefield Rd
WATERMEAD WAY
Waltham Forest
Haringey
Magistrates Court
New Health Centre
Clinic
Broadwater Farm Prim Sch
Moselle Sch
Surgery
Elsden Rd
Newlyn Rd
Kenmare Dr
Rheola Cl
Kemble Rd
Stirling Road
Siddons Rd
Spencer Rd
Poynton Road
Rosebery Ind Park
Rosebery Av
Lockwood Reservoir
Linley Rd
Mount Pleasant Rd
Broadwater Rd
Whitley Rd
Elmhurst Rd
BRUCE GROVE
HIGH ROAD
A1010
Pembury Rd
Mulberry Primary School
Ind Est
Parkhurst Rd
Sherringham Av
Seymour Av
Thackeray Avenue
Hanbury Rd
Havelock Rd
Lea Valley Walk
Moselle Special School
Grant Cl
Drayton Rd
Chandos Rd
The Avenue
Woodside Gdns
Assunah Sch
Reform Rw
Dowsett Road
Griffin Rd
Willan Road
Bruce Grove Stn
Carew Road
Mafeking Rd
Buller Rd
Park View Road
Gloucester Road
Marden Rd
Sperling Rd
School
Reed Rd
Ladysmith Rd
Kimberley Rd
School
Milmead Industrial Cen
St Loy's Rd
Steele Road
Eve Rd
Fire Station
Forster Rd
Stoneleigh Rd
Holcombe Road
Mitchley Rd
Junction Rd
Down Lane Recreation Ground
Ashley Road
Chester Rd
Dongola Road
Kitchener Rd
Morrison Av
Napier Rd
Ranelagh Road
Greyhound Rd
Winchelsea Road
Flxs Rd
Retail Park
Scales Road
Circular Rd
Devon Rd
Dawlish Rd
Police Station
Chesnut Rd
Lockwood Ind Park
Tottenham Hale Station
Mill Mead Rd
Loxwood Rd
North London College
Hamilton Cl
Sch
THE HALE
HALE ROAD
Walt Colle
Ferry Lan Industrial
Handsworth Rd
LANE
PHILIP
Stowe Place
Jansons Rd
Bus Garage
MONUMENT WAY
Clinic
A503
FERRY LANE
Fairweather Cl
Tottenham Gn Leisure Cen
Town Hall
Town Hall AP Rd
HIGH RD
Ill Road
Sringfield Rd
Health Centre
Tynemouth Road
BROAD
Tottenham Hale Retail Park
Reedham Cl
Erskine Crs
Bream Cl
Jarrow Rd
Fountayne Business Centre
FOREST ROAD
Summerhill Road
Bedford Rd
Lawrence Rd
Elizabeth Pl
Bus Cen
Works
Field Road
North East London
1 grid square represents 500 metres

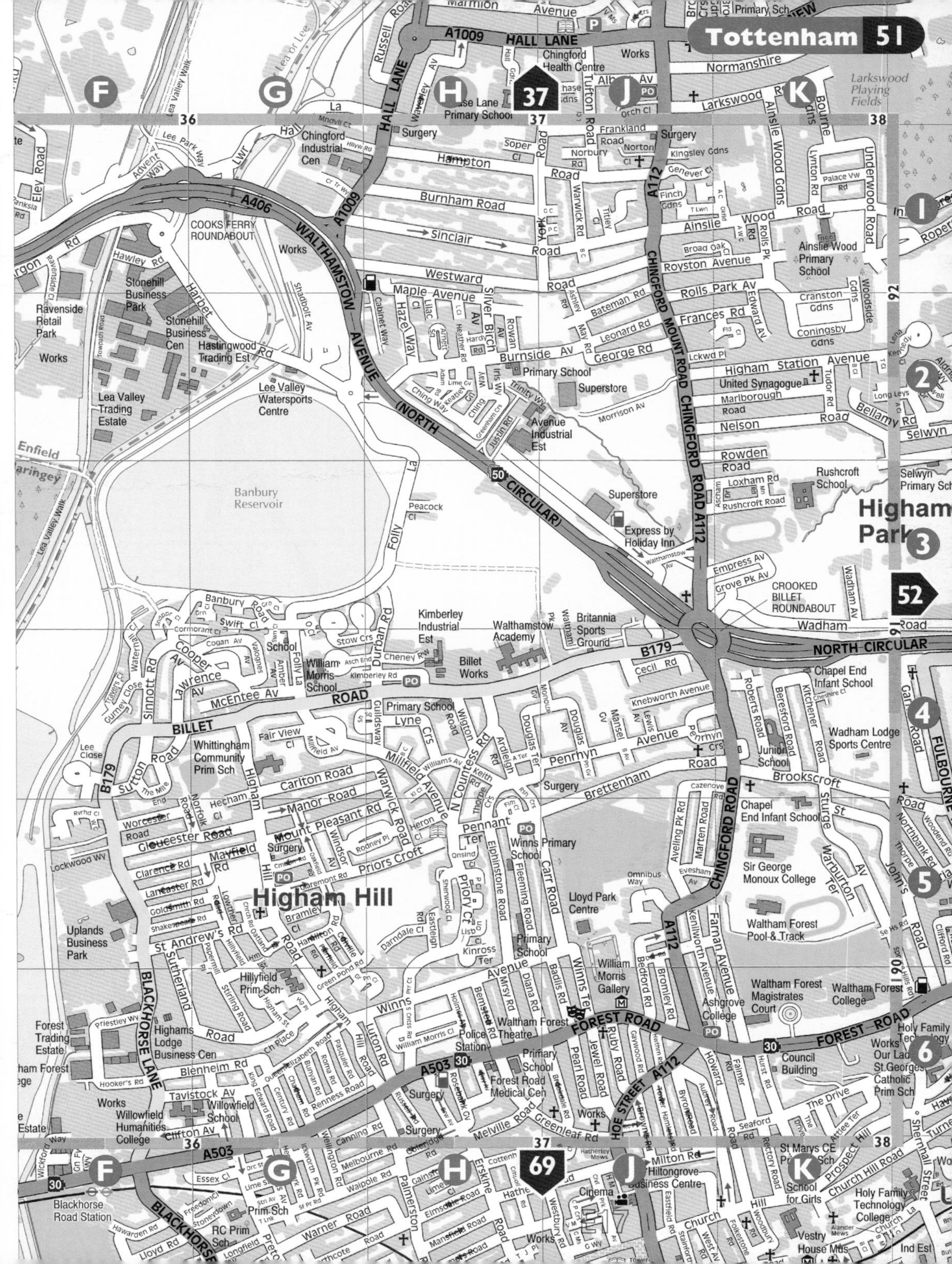
Tottenham 51
37
F
G
H
J
K
36
37
38
Larkswood Playing Fields
Hall Lane
A1009
Chingford Health Centre
Works
Normanshire
Larkswood Rd
Chingford Industrial Cen
Surgery
Hampton
Burnham Road
Sinclair Road
A406
Cooks Ferry Roundabout
Walthamstow Avenue (North Circular)
Westward Road
Maple Avenue
Hazel Way
Silver Birch Av
Royston Avenue
Rolls Park Av
Frances Rd
Ainslie Wood Road
Ainslie Wood Primary School
Chingford Mount Road A112
Chingford Road A112
Stonehill Business Park
Stonehill Business Cen
Hastingwood Trading Est
Ravenside Retail Park
Lea Valley Trading Estate
Lea Valley Watersports Centre
Banbury Reservoir
Enfield
Haringey
Lea Valley Walk
Peacock Cl
Folly La
George Rd
Burnside Av
Primary School
Superstore
Avenue Industrial Est
Higham Station Avenue
United Synagogue
Marlborough Road
Nelson Road
Rowden Road
Loxham Rd
Rushcroft Road
Rushcroft School
Higham Park
Selwyn Primary Sch
Express by Holiday Inn
Empress Av
Grove Pk Av
Crooked Billet Roundabout
52
Wadham Road
North Circular
Kimberley Industrial Est
Walthamstow Academy
Britannia Sports Ground
Billet Works
B179
Billet Road
William Morris School
Chapel End Infant School
Wadham Lodge Sports Centre
Fulbourne Road
Knebworth Avenue
Penrhyn Avenue
Brettenham Road
Brookscroft Road
Junior School
Whittingham Community Prim Sch
Higham Hill
Carlton Road
Manor Road
Mount Pleasant Rd
Warwick Road
Millfield Avenue
N Countess Rd
Gloucester Road
Worcester Road
Priors Croft
Winns Primary School
Lloyd Park Centre
Sir George Monoux College
Waltham Forest Pool & Track
Uplands Business Park
Hillyfield Prim Sch
Higham Hill Road
Blackhorse Lane
Sutherland Road
Forest Trading Estate
Highams Lodge Business Cen
Winns Avenue
William Morris Gallery
Waltham Forest Theatre
Police Station
Forest Road
Waltham Forest Magistrates Court
Waltham Forest College
Ashgrove College
Council Building
Holy Family Technology College
St Georges Catholic Prim Sch
A503
Blenheim Rd
Tavistock Av
Willowfield School
Willowfield Humanities College
Forest Road Medical Cen
Hoe Street A112
Melville Road
Greenleaf Rd
St Marys CE Prim Sch
School for Girls
Blackhorse Road Station
69
Hiltongrove Business Centre
Cinema
Church Hill Road
Vestry House Mus
Ind Est
Higham Hill
90
91
92
1
2
3
4
5
6

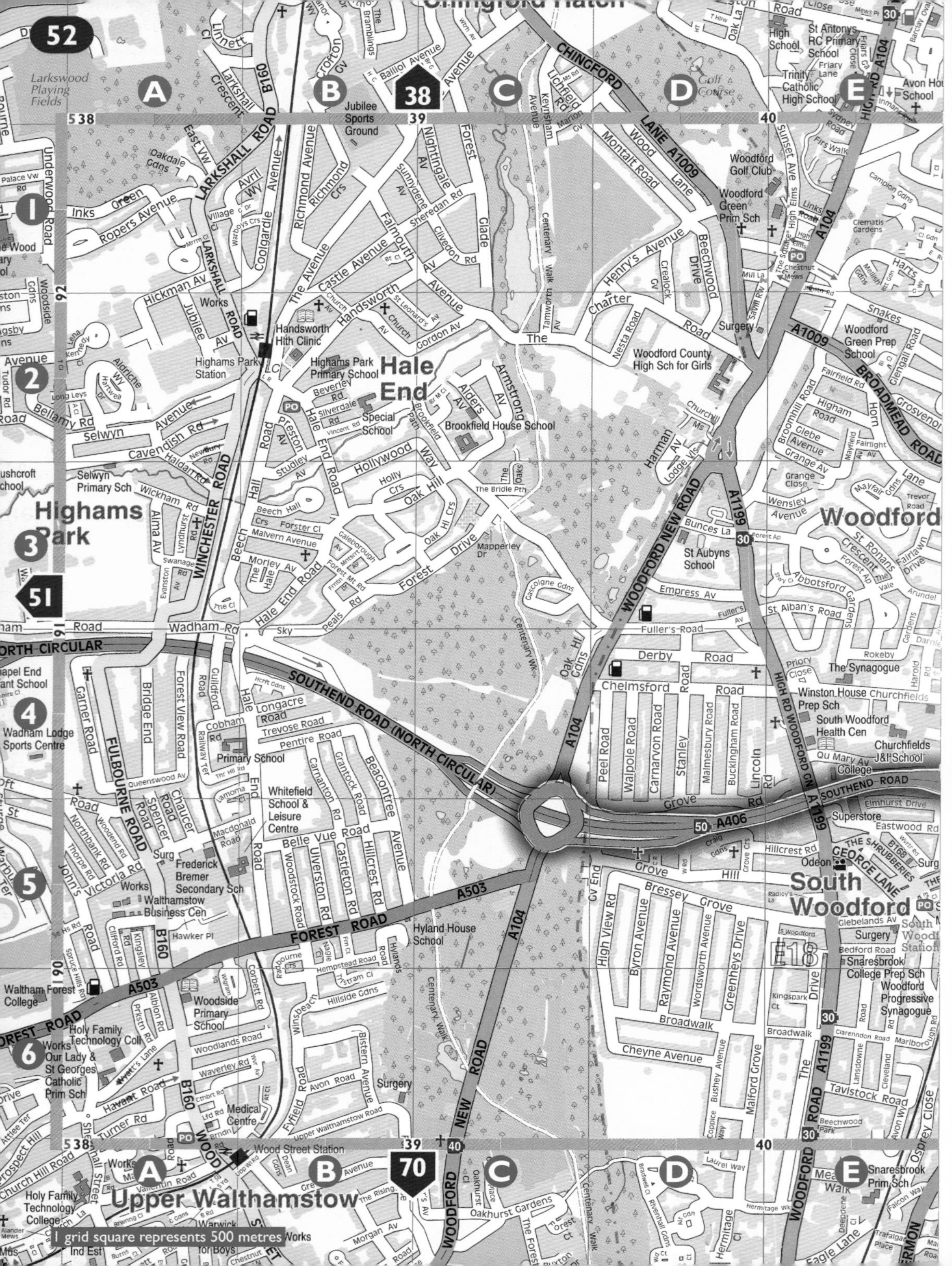

Chingford Hatch
Larkswood Playing Fields
Jubilee Sports Ground
38
A
B
C
D
E
1
2
3
4
5
6
Golf Course
St Antonys RC Primary School
High School
Trinity Catholic High School
Avon House School
Woodford Golf Club
Woodford Green Prim Sch
CHINGFORD LANE A1009
LARKSHALL ROAD
B160
Larkshall Crescent
East Vw
Oakdale Gdns
Avril Wy
Coolgardie Avenue
Richmond Avenue
Richmond Crs
Nightingale Av
Sunnydene Av
Forest Glade
Falmouth Av
Sheredan Rd
Clivedon Rd
Castle Avenue
The Avenue
Handsworth Avenue
Gordon Av
St Leonard's Av
Church Av
Inks Green
Ropers Avenue
Hickman Av
Jubilee Av
Works
Handsworth Hlth Clinic
Highams Park Station
Highams Park Primary School
Hale End
Brookfield House School
Special School
Beverley Rd
Silverdale Rd
Vincent Rd
Preston Av
Hale End Road
Hollywood Way
Holly Crs
Oak Hill
Oak Hl Crs
The Bridle Pth
The Oaks
Armstrong Av
Alders Av
Montalt Road
Wood Lane
Henry's Avenue
Crealock Gv
Beechwood Drive
The Charter Road
Nesta Road
Woodford County High Sch for Girls
Surgery
Churchill Ms
Harman Av
Lodge Vls
WOODFORD NEW ROAD
A1199
A104
A1009
BROADMEAD ROAD
Snakes
Woodford Green Prep School
Fairfield Rd
Broomhill Road
Higham Road
Glebe Avenue
Grange Av
Grange Close
Wensley Avenue
Woodford
St Ronans Crescent
Abbotsford Gardens
Bunces La
St Aubyns School
Empress Av
Fuller's Av
Fuller's Road
St Alban's Road
Derby Road
Chelmsford Road
Priory Close
The Synagogue
Winston House Prep Sch
South Woodford Health Cen
Churchfields J&I School
Qu Mary Av College
SOUTHEND ROAD
A406
Superstore
Eastwood Rd
Elmhurst Drive
Hillcrest Rd
Odeon
GEORGE LANE
THE SHRUBBERIES
South Woodford
E18
Glebelands Av
Surgery
Bedford Road
Snaresbrook College Prep Sch
Woodford Progressive Synagogue
Clarendon Road
Tavistock Road
Osprey Close
Lansdowne Road
Cleveland Road
Beechwood Park
HIGH RD WOODFORD GN
WOODFORD ROAD
The Drive
Kingspark Ct
Broadwalk
Cheyne Avenue
Malford Grove
Bushey Avenue
Greenheys Drive
Wordsworth Avenue
Raymond Avenue
Byron Avenue
High View Rd
Bressey Grove
Grove Hill
Peel Road
Walpole Road
Carnarvon Road
Stanley Road
Malmesbury Road
Buckingham Road
Lincoln Rd
Grove Rd
Oak Hl Gdns
Centenary Walk
Highams Park
Selwyn Primary Sch
Wickham Rd
Alma Av
Lyndhurst Rd
Swanage Rd
Evanston Av
WINCHESTER ROAD
Beech Hall Crs
Forster Cl
Malvern Avenue
Morley Av
The Hale
Forest Mt Rd
Forest Drive
Mapperley Dr
Peals Rd
Gascoigne Gdns
Wadham Rd
Sky
NORTH CIRCULAR
SOUTHEND ROAD (NORTH CIRCULAR)
Wadham Lodge Sports Centre
Garner Road
Bridge End
Forest View Road
Guildford Road
Longacre Road
Trevose Road
Pentire Road
Cobham Rd
Primary School
Carnanton Rd
Grantock Road
Beacontree Avenue
Whitefield School & Leisure Centre
FULBOURNE ROAD
Spencer Road
Chaucer Road
Queenswood Av
Macdonald Road
Belle Vue Road
Woodstock Road
Ulverston Rd
Castleton Rd
Hillcrest Rd
Frederick Bremer Secondary Sch
Walthamstow Business Cen
Victoria Rd
Surg
Hawker Pl
Hyland House School
A503
FOREST ROAD
Hempstead Road
Hillside Gdns
Waltham Forest College
Woodside Primary School
Holly Family Technology Coll
Our Lady & St Georges Catholic Prim Sch
Woodlands Road
Waverley Rd
Havant Road
Turner Rd
Medical Centre
Avon Road
Bisterne Avenue
Fyfield Road
Upper Walthamstow Road
Surgery
NEW ROAD
Wood Street Station
70
Upper Walthamstow
Holy Family Technology College
Sheriall Street
Church Hill Road
Prospect Hill
Warwick Works for Boys
Morgan Av
Oakhurst Gardens
Laurel Way
Hermitage Ct
Snaresbrook Prim Sch
Eagle Lane
51
1 grid square represents 500 metres

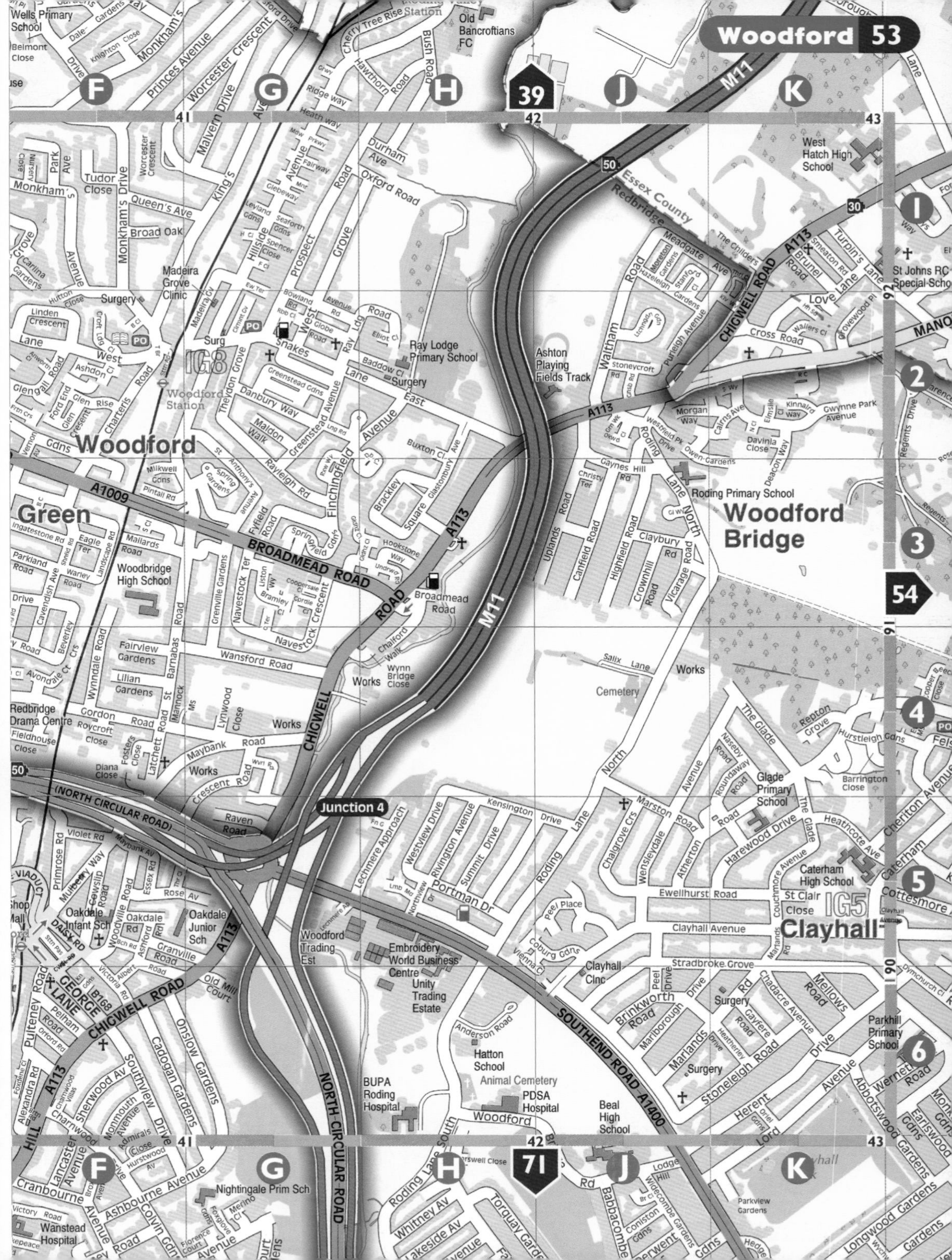

Wells Primary School
Belmont Close
Monkham's
Princes Avenue
Worcester Crescent
Cherry Tree Rise
Bush Road
Old Bancroftians FC
Hawthorn Road
Ridge way
Heath way
Durham Ave
Oxford Road
Malvern Drive
Worcester Crescent
Tudor Close
Monkham's Drive
Queen's Ave
Broad Oak
King's
Prospect
Grove
Essex County
Redbridge
M11
West Hatch High School
A113
Meadgate Ave
Chigwell Road
Brunel Road
Turpin's Lane
Love Lane
Cross Road
St Johns RC Special School
Madeira Grove Clinic
Surgery
Linden Crescent
West
Snakes
Lane
Ray Lodge Primary School
Surgery
Woodford Station
Danbury Way
Maldon Walk
Greenstead Avenue
Lane East
Ashton Playing Fields Track
Waltham Road
Purleigh Avenue
Stoneycroft Rd
Morgan Way
Gwynne Park Avenue
Davinia Close
Deacon Way
Woodford Green
A1009
Broadmead Road
Rayleigh Rd
Finchingfield Avenue
Buxton Cl
Brackley Square
Hookstone Way
Gaynes Hill Rd
Christy Ter
Roding Primary School
Woodford Bridge
Uplands Road
Canfield Road
Highfield Road
Claybury Rd
Crownhill Road
Vicarage Road
Ingatestone Rd
Eagle Ter
Mallards Road
Woodbridge High School
Parkland Road
Warley Road
Cavendish Ave
Navestock Ter
Navestock Crescent
Broadmead Road
Chalford Walk
Wynn Bridge Close
Works
Salix Lane
Works
Cemetery
Fairview Gardens
Lilian Gardens
Wynndale Road
Wansford Road
St Barnabas Road
Lynwood Close
Redbridge Drama Centre
Fieldhouse Close
Gordon Road
Roycroft Close
Works
Maybank Road
Latchett Road
Works
Crescent Road
Diana Close
Chigwell Road
North
Lane
The Glade
Repton Grove
Hurstleigh Gdns
Barrington Close
Glade Primary School
Cheriton Avenue
(North Circular Road)
Raven Road
Junction 4
Kensington Drive
Marston Road
Violet Rd
Primrose Road
Rose Av
Westview Drive
Rivington Avenue
Summit Drive
Roding Lane
Lechmere Approach
Portman Dr
Harewood Drive
Heathcote Ave
Caterham High School
Caterham
Oakdale Infant Sch
Oakdale Junior Sch
Ewellhurst Road
St Clair Close
IG5
Cottesmore
Clayhall
Clayhall Avenue
Woodford Trading Est
Embroidery World Business Centre
Unity Trading Estate
Peel Place
Coburg Gdns
Clayhall Clnc
Stradbroke Grove
Mellows Road
Granville Road
Old Mill Court
George Lane
Chigwell Road
Pulteney Road
Pelham Road
A113
Brinkworth Road
Marlborough Drive
Surgery
Gayfere Road
Chadacre Avenue
Parkhill Primary School
Anderson Road
Hatton School
Animal Cemetery
Southend Road A1400
Marlands Road
Stoneleigh Road
Surgery
Avenue
Abbotswood Gardens
BUPA Roding Hospital
PDSA Hospital
Woodford
Beal High School
Herent Drive
Lord Avenue
Alexandra Rd
Sherwood Av
Southview Drive
Cadogan Gardens
Onslow Gardens
North Circular Road
Roding Lane South
Earlswood Gdns
Charnwood
Lancaster Avenue
Monmouth Avenue
Admirals Close
Hurstwood Av
Ashbourne Avenue
Nightingale Prim Sch
Whitney Av
Lakeside Av
Torquay Gardens
Babbacombe Gardens
Widecombe Gardens
Coniston Gdns
Parkview Gardens
Longwood Gardens
Cranbourne Avenue
Victory Road
Wanstead Hospital
Colvin Gdns
Florence Court
F
G
H
J
K
39
41
42
43
50
30
92
91
90
1
2
3
4
5
6
54
71
IG8

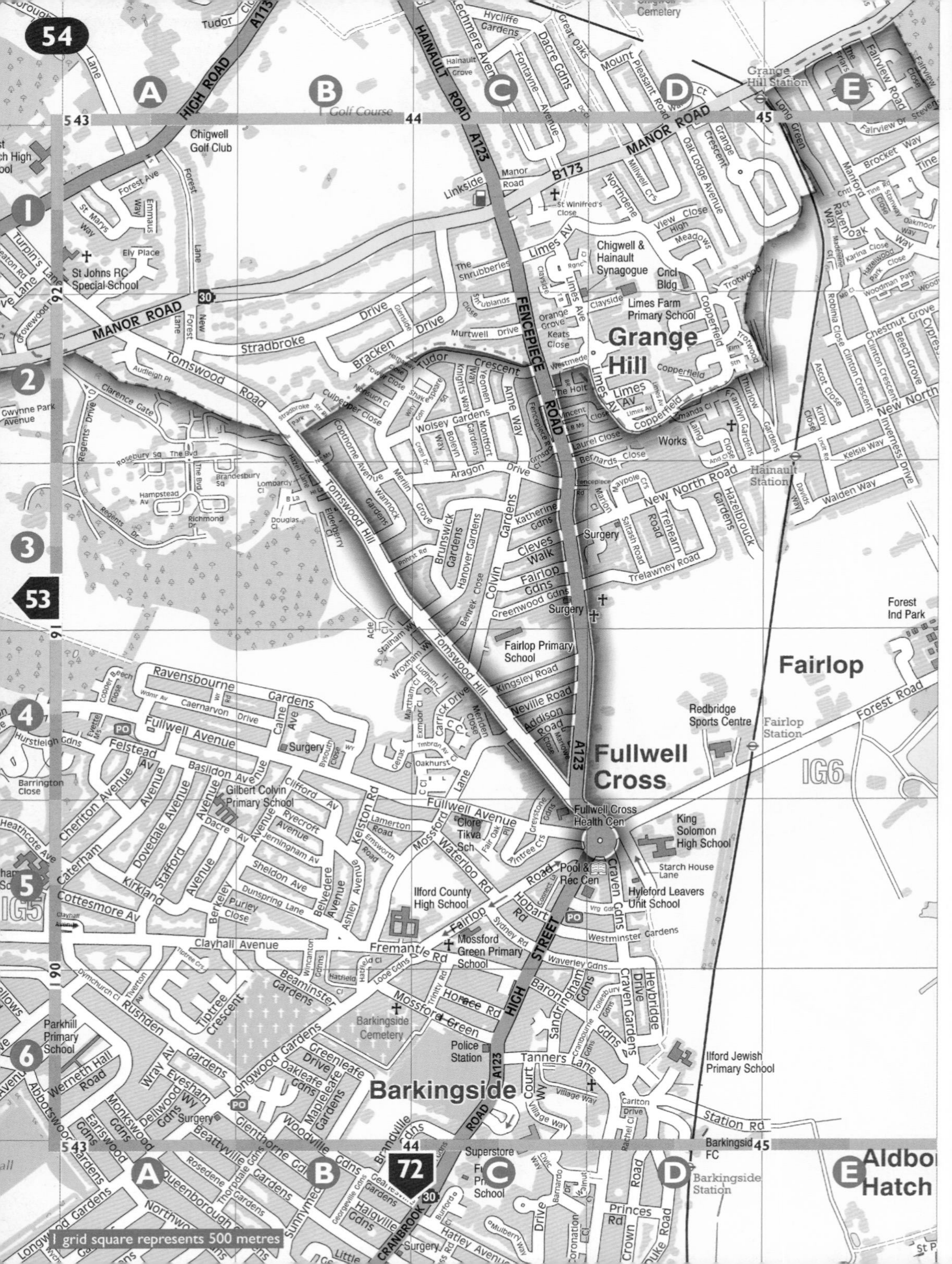
54
A
B
C
D
E
1
2
3
4
5
6
53
72
43
44
45
92
91
90
HIGH ROAD
A113
HAINAULT ROAD
A123
MANOR ROAD
B173
FENCEPIECE ROAD
HIGH STREET
CRANBROOK ROAD
Golf Course
Chigwell Golf Club
Grange Hill Station
Hainault Station
Fairlop Station
Barkingside Station
Grange Hill
Fairlop
Fullwell Cross
Barkingside
Aldborough Hatch
IG5
IG6
St Johns RC Special School
Chigwell & Hainault Synagogue
Cncl Bldg
Limes Farm Primary School
Works
Surgery
Fairlop Primary School
Forest Ind Park
Redbridge Sports Centre
Fullwell Cross Health Cen
King Solomon High School
Starch House Lane
Pool & Rec Cen
Hyleford Leavers Unit School
Ilford County High School
Mossford Green Primary School
Gilbert Colvin Primary School
Clore Tikva Sch
Barkingside Cemetery
Police Station
Ilford Jewish Primary School
Parkhill Primary School
Barkingside FC
Superstore
Tomswood Road
Tomswood Hill
Stradbroke Drive
Bracken Drive
Tudor Crescent
Forest Road
New North Road
Fullwell Avenue
Clayhall Avenue
Fremantle Rd
Mossford Green
Tanners Lane
Station Rd
Ravensbourne Gardens
Craven Gdns
Westminster Gardens
Horace Rd
Waterloo Rd
Manford Way
Hainault Grove
Lechmere Ave
Fontayne Avenue
Dacre Gdns
Limes Av
Copperfield
Trelawney Road
Colvin Gardens
Kingsley Road
Neville Road
Addison Road
Felstead Av
Cheriton Avenue
Dovedale Avenue
Kirkland
Stafford Avenue
Cottesmore Av
Longwood Gardens
Beattyville Gdns
Glenthorne Gdns
Abbotswood Gardens
Werneth Hall Road
Rushden Gardens
Tiptree Crescent
Princes Rd
Crown Road
1 grid square represents 500 metres

Hainault
Romford Road
A1112
Forest Road
Hainault Road
Painters Road
Billet Road
Eastern Avenue
A12
Manford Way
New North Road
Huntsman Road
Forest Park Cemetery & Crematorium
Hainault Business Park
Hog Hill
Hainault Forest Golf Complex
Roebuck Road Trading Estate
Burnside Industrial Estate
Hainault Forest High School & The Learning Centre
Coppice Primary School
Manford Prim Sch
Manford Way Health Cen.
John Bramston Primary School
Bracken Industrial Estate
LPR Sports Club
Fairlop Waters
Hainault Works
Hainault Farm
Seven Kings Water
Red House Farm
Redbridge
Barking and Dagenham
Little Heath
Little Heath School
St James Gardens
Kennylands Road
Elmbridge Road
Fowler Road
Works
Surgery

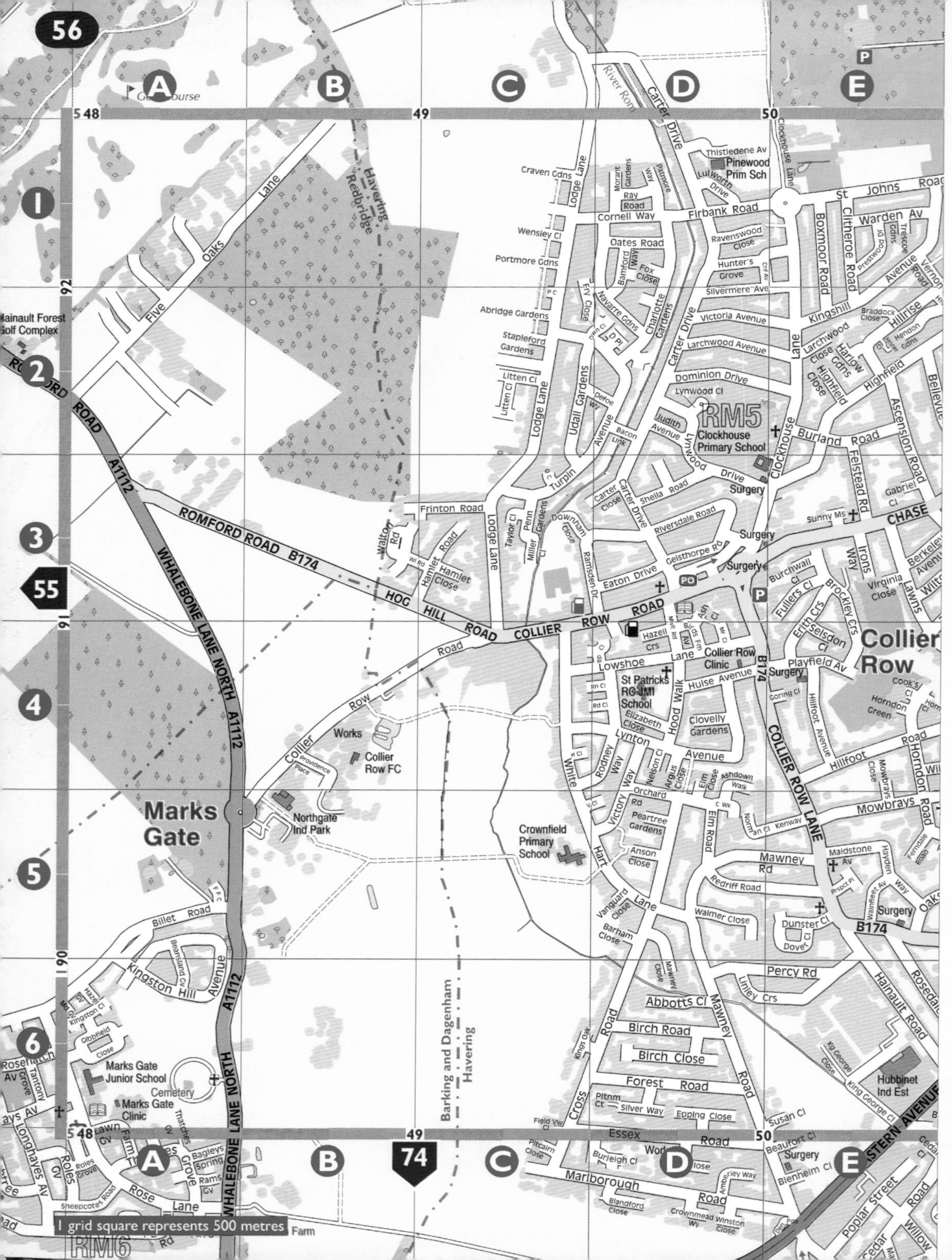

56
A
B
C
D
E
548
49
50
92
91
90
1
2
3
4
5
6
55
74
Golf Course
Hainault Forest Golf Complex
Five Oaks Lane
Havering
Redbridge
ROMFORD ROAD
A1112
ROMFORD ROAD B174
WHALEBONE LANE NORTH A1112
HOG HILL ROAD
COLLIER ROW ROAD
Collier Row Road
Marks Gate
River Rom
Carter Drive
Thistledene Av
Pinewood Prim Sch
Lulworth Drive
Clockhouse Lane
St Johns Road
Craven Gdns
Lodge Lane
Morant Gardens
Way
Patmore
Ray Road
Cornell Way
Firbank Road
Wensley Cl
Oates Road
Ravenswood Close
Portmore Gdns
Bamford Way
Fox Close
Hunter's Grove
Silvermere Ave
Fry Close
Navarre Gdns
Charlotte Gardens
Abridge Gardens
Victoria Avenue
Stapleford Gardens
Larchwood Avenue
Dominion Drive
Litten Cl
Udall Gardens
Defoe Wy
Lynwood Cl
RM5
Clockhouse Primary School
Judith Avenue
Bacon Link
Turpin Avenue
Lynwood Drive
Clockhouse Lane
Surgery
Boxmoor Road
Clitheroe Road
Warden Av
Prestwood Dr
Trescoe Gdns
Avenue
Vernon Road
Kingshill
Braddock Close
Hillrise
Larchwood Close
Harlow Gdns
Hendon Gdns
Highfield Close
Highfield
Bellevue
Ascension Road
Burland Road
Felstead Rd
Gabriel Cl
Sunny Ms
CHASE
Frinton Road
Walton Rd
Hamlet Road
Hamlet Close
Taylor Cl
Penn Gardens
Miller Cl
Downham Close
Ramsden Dr
Carter Close
Carter Drive
Sheila Road
Riversdale Road
Gelsthorpe Rd
Eaton Drive
PO
Burchwall Cl
Fullers Cl
Irons Way
Berkeley Avenue
Virginia Close
Lawns
Brockley Crs
Erith Crs
Selsdon Cl
Collier Row
Hazell Crs
Birds Fm Av
Mr Cl
Ash Cl
Lowshoe Lane
Collier Row Clinic
Playfield Av
Cook's Cl
Horndon Green
St Patricks RC JMI School
Hulse Avenue
B174
Goring Cl
Hillfoot Avenue
Hood Walk
Elizabeth Close
Clovelly Gardens
COLLIER ROW LANE
Hillfoot Road
Horndon Road
Lynton Avenue
Works
Collier Row FC
Providence Place
Rodney Way
Nelson Cl
Argus Close
Elm Close
Ashdown Walk
Mowbrays Close
Mowbrays Road
White Hart Lane
Orchard Rd
Victory Way
Peartree Gardens
Norman Cl
Kenway
C Wk
Northgate Ind Park
Crownfield Primary School
Anson Close
Elm Road
Mawney Rd
Maidstone Av
Hayden Way
Ferndale Road
Redriff Road
Prspct Pl
Wainfleet Av
Oaks
Billet Road
Vanguard Close
Walmer Close
Dunster Cl
Dove Cl
Barham Close
Lane
Beansland Gv
Kingston Hill Avenue
Percy Rd
Linley Crs
Rosedale
Mawney Close
Abbotts Cl
Mawney Road
Hainault Road
Hazel Gv
Kingston Cl
Gibbfield Close
Kings Oak
Birch Road
Birch Close
Kg George Close
King George Cl
Hubbinet Ind Est
Rosehatch Av
Tantony Grove
Marks Gate Junior School
Cemetery
Forest Road
Cross Road
Pitman Ct
Silver Way
Epping Close
Marks Gate Clinic
Thatches Gv
Field Vw Cl
Susan Cl
Barking and Dagenham
Havering
Essex Road
Lawn Farm Gv
Bagleys Spring
Rams Gv
Roles Grove
Longhayes Av
Pitcairn Close
Burleigh Cl
Word Close
Beaufort Cl
Surgery
EASTERN AVENUE
Cedar Cl
Rose Lane
Sheepcotes Road
Marlborough Road
Amberley Way
Blenheim Cl
Poplar Street
Road
Blandford Close
Crownmead Wy
Winston Close
Cedar
Willow
Farm
Rd
RM6
1 grid square represents 500 metres

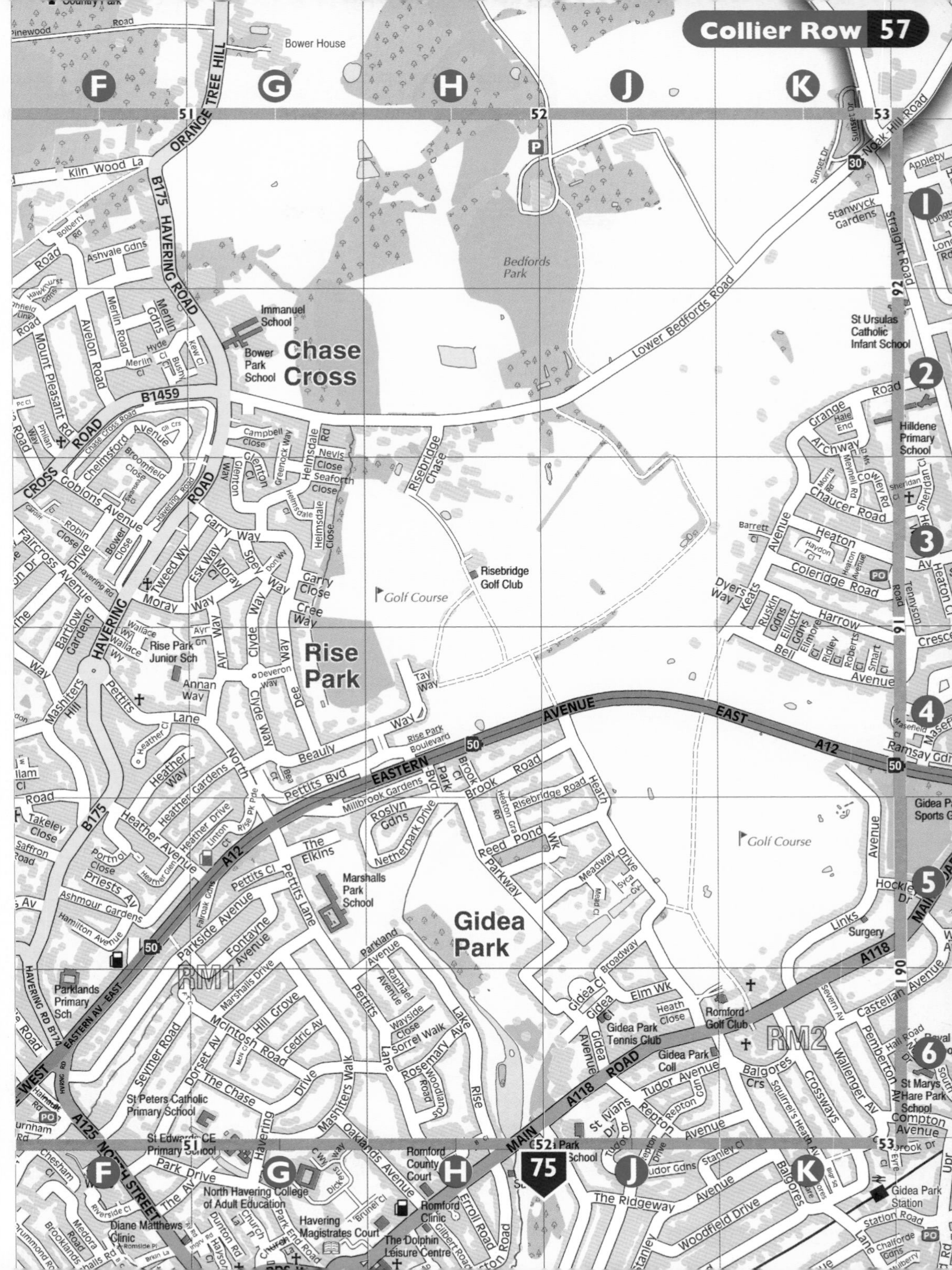
Chase Cross
Rise Park
Gidea Park
Bedfords Park
Bower House
Immanuel School
Bower Park School
Rise Park Junior Sch
Risebridge Golf Club
Golf Course
Marshalls Park School
Parklands Primary Sch
St Peters Catholic Primary School
St Edwards CE Primary School
North Havering College of Adult Education
Havering Magistrates Court
Romford County Court
Romford Clinic
The Dolphin Leisure Centre
Diane Matthews Clinic
Gidea Park Tennis Club
Romford Golf Club
Gidea Park Coll
St Ursulas Catholic Infant School
Hilldene Primary School
St Marys Hare Park School
Gidea Park Station
Surgery
ORANGE TREE HILL
B175 HAVERING ROAD
Lower Bedfords Road
Noak Hill Road
Straight Road
EASTERN AVENUE EAST
A12
MAIN ROAD A118
A125 NORTH STREET
RM1
RM2
75

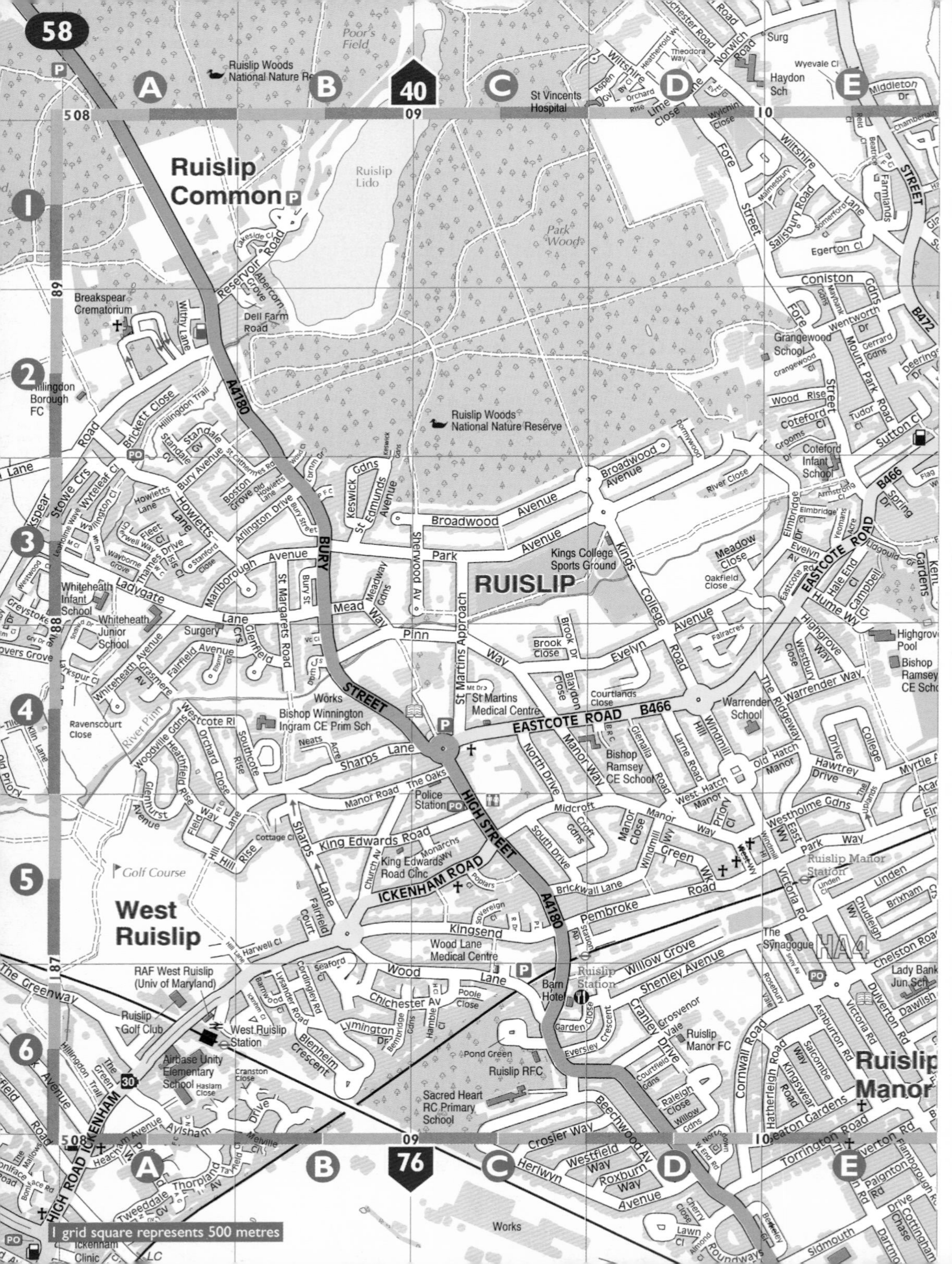
Ruislip Common
Ruislip Lido
Ruislip Woods National Nature Reserve
Park Wood
RUISLIP
West Ruislip
Ruislip Manor
Breakspear Crematorium
Hillingdon Borough FC
Kings College Sports Ground
Whiteheath Infant School
Whiteheath Junior School
Bishop Winnington Ingram CE Prim Sch
St Martins Medical Centre
Bishop Ramsey CE School
Warrender School
Police Station
King Edwards Road Clnc
Wood Lane Medical Centre
RAF West Ruislip (Univ of Maryland)
Ruislip Golf Club
West Ruislip Station
Ruislip Station
Ruislip Manor Station
Airbase Unity Elementary School
Sacred Heart RC Primary School
Ruislip RFC
Ruislip Manor FC
Highgrove Pool
Grangewood School
Coteford Infant School
Haydon Sch
St Vincents Hospital
The Synagogue
Lady Bank Jun Sch
Golf Course
A4180
B466
B472
EASTCOTE ROAD
HIGH STREET
BURY STREET
ICKENHAM ROAD
HIGH ROAD ICKENHAM
HA4
40
76
1 grid square represents 500 metres

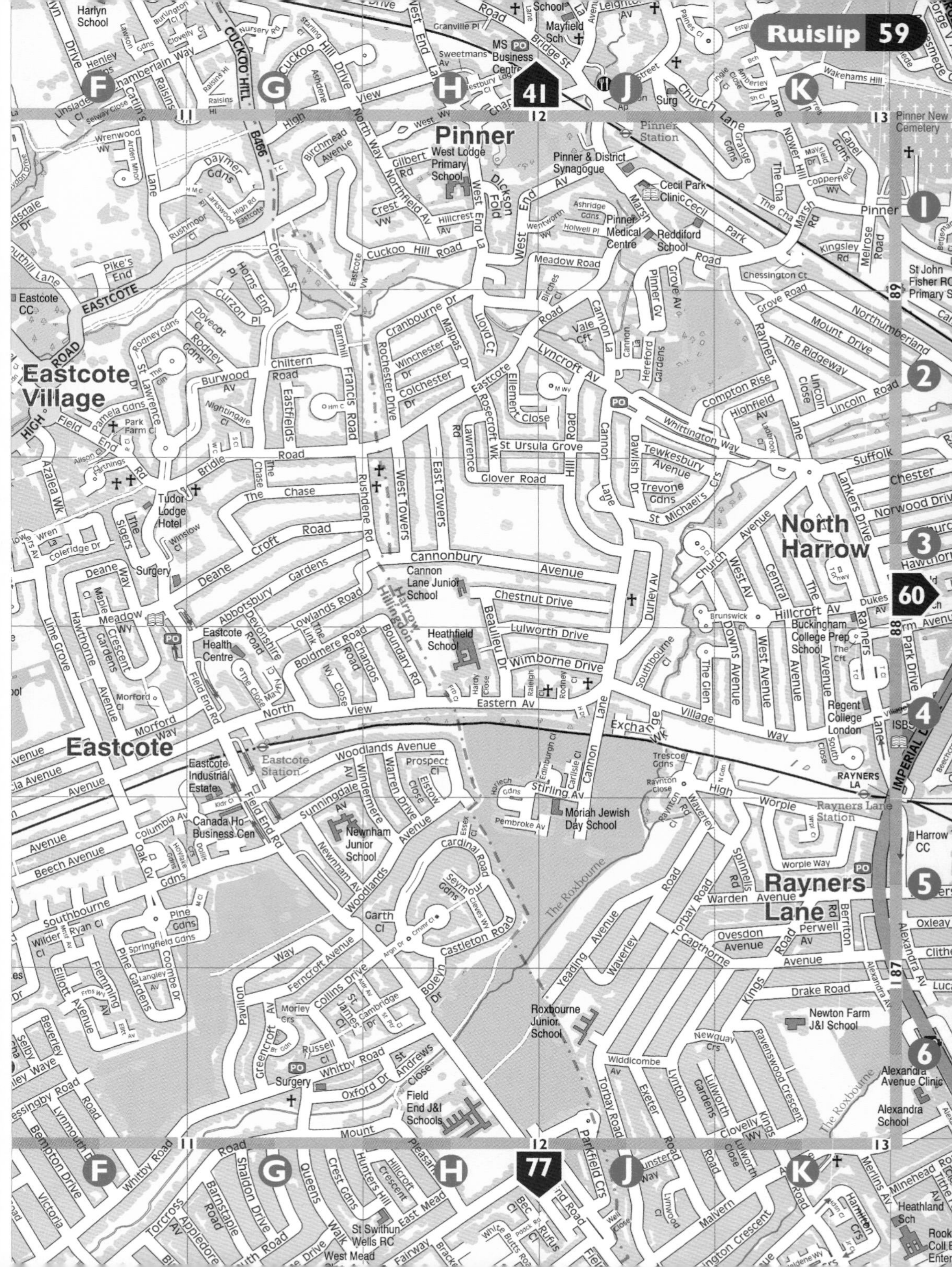
Pinner
Eastcote Village
Eastcote
North Harrow
Rayners Lane
Pinner Station
Eastcote Station
Rayners Lane Station
41
60
77
Cannon Lane Junior School
Heathfield School
Newnham Junior School
Roxbourne Junior School
Field End J&I Schools
Moriah Jewish Day School
Newton Farm J&I School
West Lodge Primary School
Pinner & District Synagogue
Cecil Park Clinic
Pinner Medical Centre
Reddiford School
Tudor Lodge Hotel
Eastcote Health Centre
Eastcote Industrial Estate
Canada Ho Business Cen
Buckingham College Prep School
Regent College London
Alexandra Avenue Clinic
Alexandra School
St John Fisher RC Primary Sc
St Swithun Wells RC
Pinner New Cemetery
Harlyn School
Mayfield Sch
Heathland Sch
Cuckoo Hill Road
Eastcote Road
Cannonbury Avenue
Village Way
Imperial Drive
Field End Rd
Cannon Lane

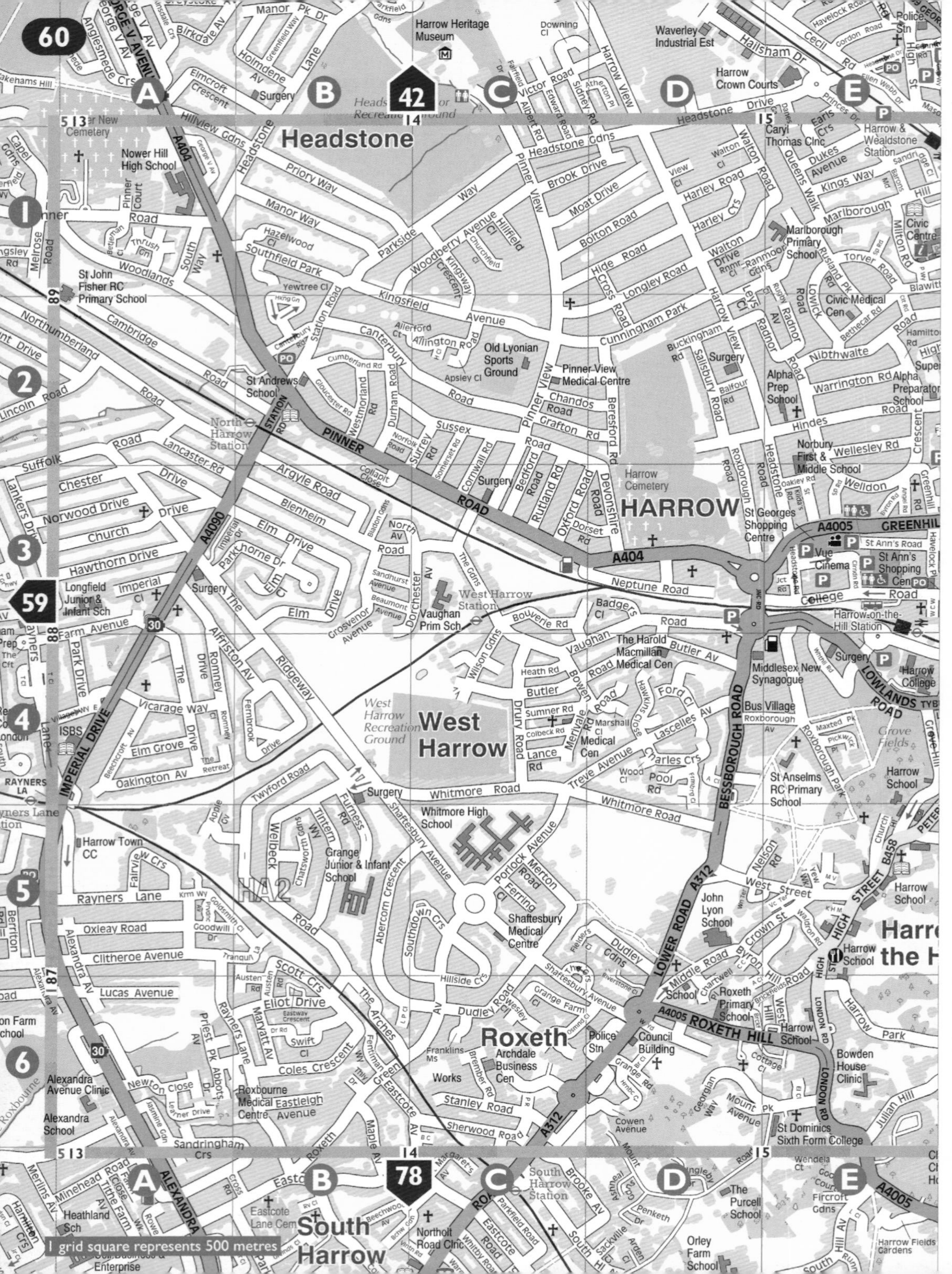
Headstone
HARROW
West Harrow
Roxeth
South Harrow
Harrow on the Hill
Harrow Heritage Museum
Waverley Industrial Est
Harrow Crown Courts
Harrow & Wealdstone Station
Civic Centre
Nower Hill High School
St John Fisher RC Primary School
St Andrews School
North Harrow Station
Old Lyonian Sports Ground
Pinner View Medical Centre
Marlborough Primary School
Civic Medical Cen
Alpha Prep School
Alpha Preparatory School
Norbury First & Middle School
Harrow Cemetery
St Georges Shopping Centre
St Ann's Shopping Cen
Vue Cinema
Harrow-on-the-Hill Station
West Harrow Station
Vaughan Prim Sch
The Harold Macmillan Medical Cen
Middlesex New Synagogue
Harrow College
Bus Village
West Harrow Recreation Ground
Marshall Cl Medical Cen
St Anselms RC Primary School
Harrow School
Longfield Junior & Infant Sch
Whitmore High School
Grange Junior & Infant School
Shaftesbury Medical Centre
John Lyon School
Harrow Town CC
HA2
Roxeth Primary School
Council Building
Police Stn
Archdale Business Cen
Works
Roxbourne Medical Centre
Alexandra Avenue Clinic
Alexandra School
Bowden House Clinic
St Dominics Sixth Form College
South Harrow Station
The Purcell School
Orley Farm School
Heathland Sch
Eastcote Lane Cem
Northolt Road Clnc
Rayners Lane Station
A404
A4090
A4005
A312
B458
PINNER ROAD
IMPERIAL DRIVE
ALEXANDRA AVENUE
BESSBOROUGH ROAD
LOWER ROAD
ROXETH HILL
LOWLANDS ROAD
GREENHILL
HIGH STREET
LONDON RD
Headstone Drive
Headstone Lane
Station Road
Pinner View
Whitmore Road
Shaftesbury Avenue
Rayners Lane
Eastcote Avenue
Northolt Road
42
59
78
1
2
3
4
5
6
A
B
C
D
E
1 grid square represents 500 metres

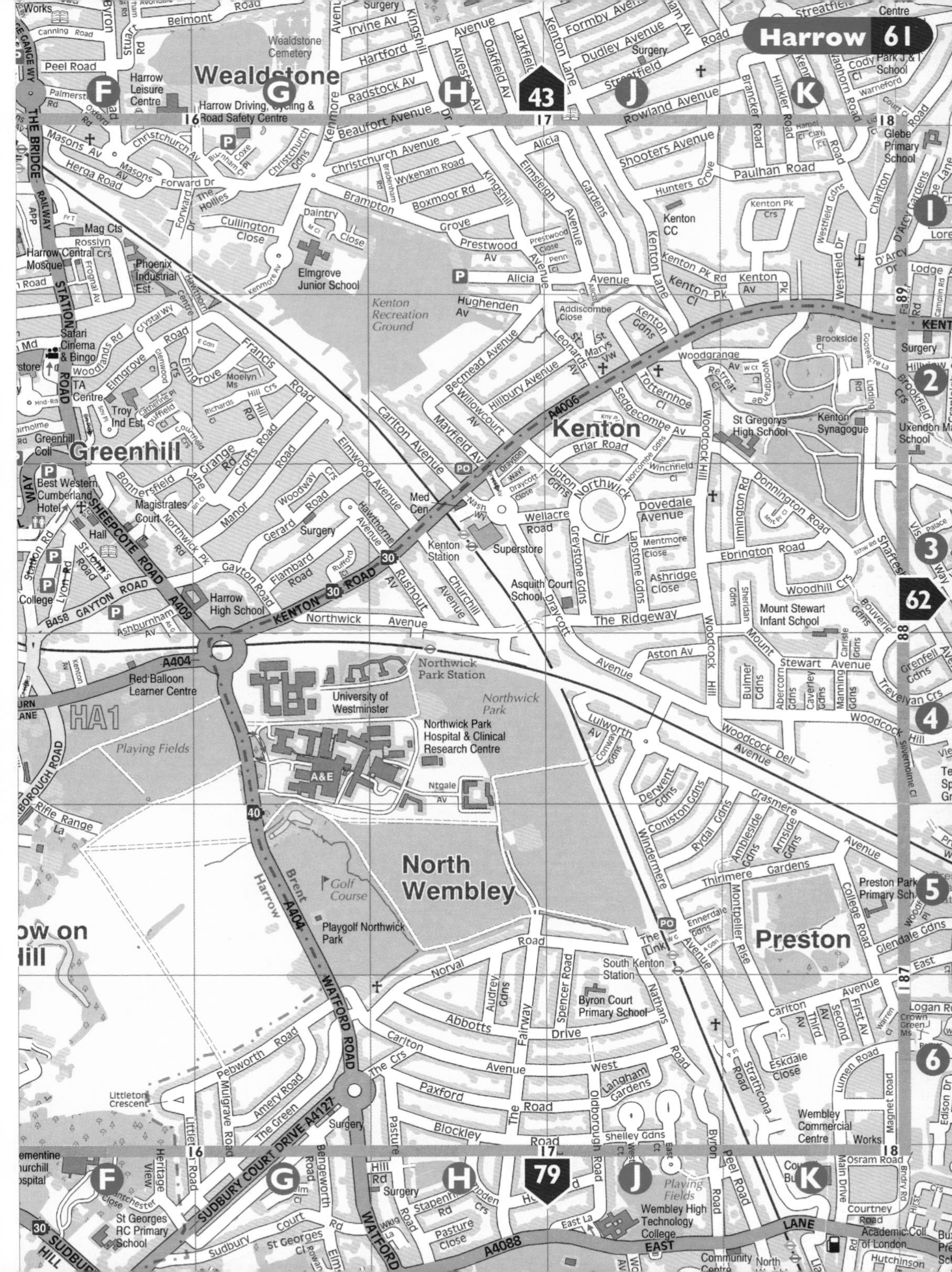
Wealdstone
Wealdstone Cemetery
Harrow Leisure Centre
Harrow Driving, Cycling & Road Safety Centre
Kenton
Kenton Recreation Ground
Elmgrove Junior School
Greenhill
Harrow Central Mosque
Phoenix Industrial Est
Safari Cinema & Bingo
Troy Ind Est
Best Western Cumberland Hotel
Magistrates Court
Harrow High School
Kenton Station
Superstore
Asquith Court School
Northwick Park Station
University of Westminster
Northwick Park Hospital & Clinical Research Centre
Northwick Park
Playing Fields
HA1
Red Balloon Learner Centre
North Wembley
Golf Course
Playgolf Northwick Park
South Kenton Station
Byron Court Primary School
Preston
Preston Park Primary School
Wembley Commercial Centre
Wembley High Technology College
St Georges RC Primary School
St Gregorys High School
Kenton Synagogue
Mount Stewart Infant School
Uxendon Manor School
Glebe Primary School
Kenton CC
KENTON ROAD
A4006
A404
A409
A4088
A4127
WATFORD ROAD
SHEEPCOTE ROAD
STATION ROAD
SUDBURY COURT DRIVE
EAST LANE
The Ridgeway
Woodcock Hill
Northwick Avenue
Preston Road
Kenton Lane
Norval Road
Abbotts Drive
Carlton Avenue West
Littleton Crescent
Rifle Range La
43
62
79
16
17
18

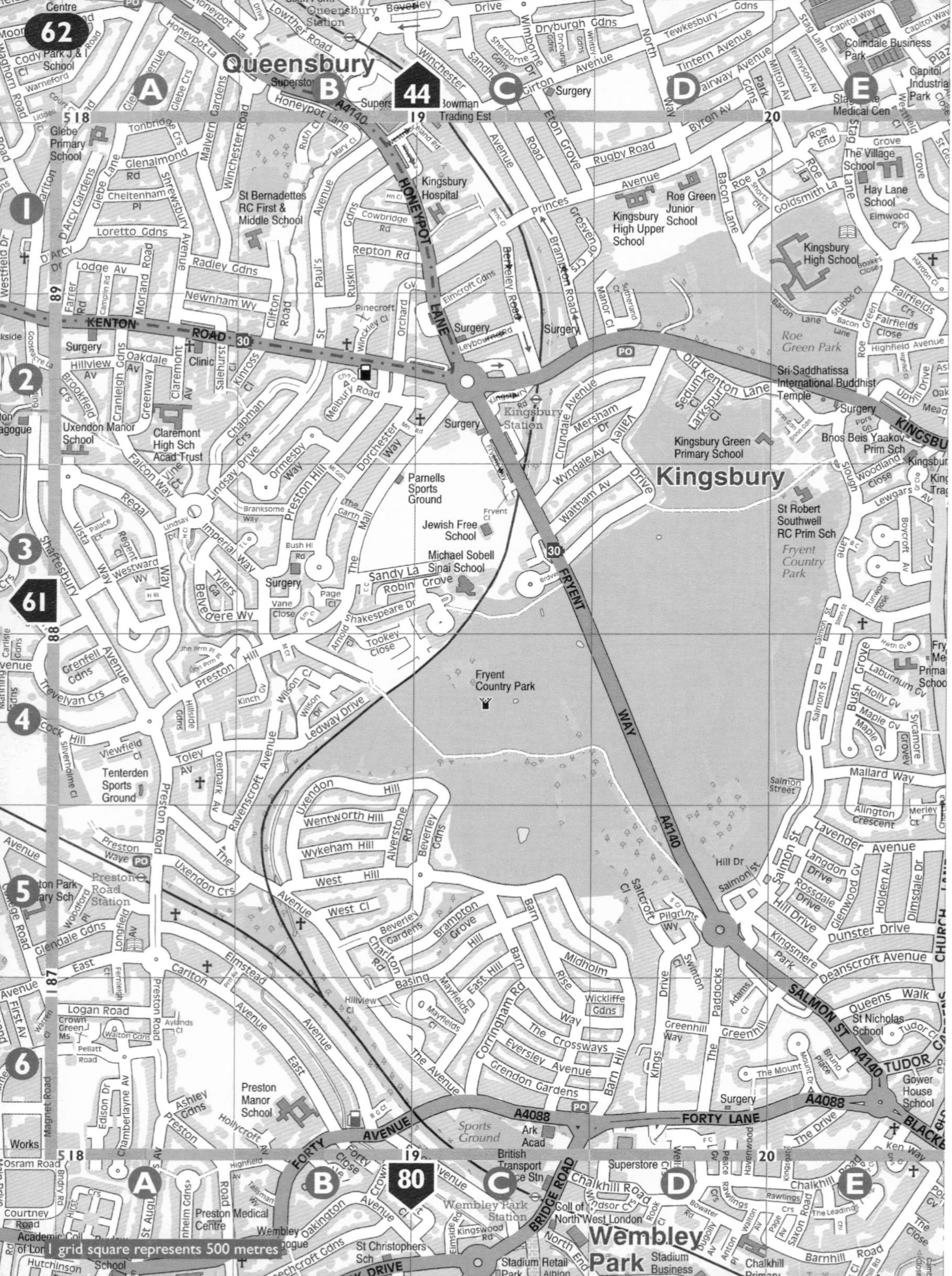
62
44
61
80
Queensbury
Queensbury Station
Kingsbury
Kingsbury Station
Wembley Park
Wembley Park Station
A B C D E
1 2 3 4 5 6
518
19
20
89
88
187
Honeypot Lane
Honeypot La
A4140
HONEYPOT LANE
Kenton Road
KENTON ROAD
FRYENT WAY
A4088
FORTY LANE
FORTY AVENUE
SALMON ST
TUDOR
BRIDGE ROAD
CHURCH LANE
KINGSBURY
BLACKBIRD
Bowman Trading Est
Colindale Business Park
Capitol Industrial Park
Capitol Way
Stag Lane
Stag Lane Medical Cen
Glebe Primary School
Cody Park J & I School
St Bernadettes RC First & Middle School
Kingsbury Hospital
Kingsbury High Upper School
Roe Green Junior School
The Village School
Hay Lane School
Kingsbury High School
Roe Green Park
Sri Saddhatissa International Buddhist Temple
Kingsbury Green Primary School
Bnos Beis Yaakov Prim Sch
St Robert Southwell RC Prim Sch
Fryent Country Park
Uxendon Manor School
Claremont High Sch Acad Trust
Clinic
Surgery
Parnells Sports Ground
Jewish Free School
Michael Sobell Sinai School
Tenterden Sports Ground
Preston Road Station
Preston Manor School
Sports Ground
Ark Acad
British Transport Police Stn
Coll of North West London
Superstore
Gower House School
St Nicholas School
Preston Medical Centre
Wembley Synagogue
St Christophers Sch
Stadium Retail Park
Stadium Business
Chalkhill Primary
Academic Coll of Lon
Works
Magnet Road
Osram Road
Courtney Road
Hutchinson
Preston Road
Preston Waye
Uxendon Crs
Uxendon Hill
Wentworth Hill
Wykeham Hill
West Hill
Beverley Gdns
Alverstone Rd
Barn Hill
Barn Rise
Eversley Avenue
Grendon Gardens
The Crossways
Corringham Rd
Mayfields
East Hill
Basing
Charlton Rd
Brampton Grove
Carlton
Elmstead Avenue
East Lane
Glendale Gdns
Logan Road
Ashley Gdns
Hollycroft Av
Preston Hill
Ledway Drive
Wilson Dr
Sandy La
Robin Grove
Shakespeare Dr
Tookey Close
The Mall
The Garth
Preston Hill
Dorchester Way
Ormesby Way
Lindsay Drive
Imperial Way
Belvedere Wy
Tylers Ga
Regal Way
Vista Way
Westward Wy
Shaftesbury
Falcon Way
Chapman Crs
Kinross Cl
Salehurst Cl
Claremont Av
Greenway
Cranleigh Gdns
Oakdale Av
Hillview Av
Brookfield Crs
Newnham Wy
Lodge Av
Farrer Rd
Morland Road
Radley Gdns
Loretto Gdns
Cheltenham Pl
Glenalmond Rd
Tonbridge Crs
Malvern Gardens
Winchester Road
Shrewsbury Avenue
Glebe Lane
D'Arcy Gardens
Westfield Dr
Repton Rd
Cowbridge Rd
Ruskin Gdns
Paul's Avenue
Orchard Gv
Elmcroft Gdns
Berkeley Road
Brampton Road
Grosvenor Crs
Manor Cl
Sutherland Ct
Princes Avenue
Rugby Road
Eton Grove
Byron Av
Fairway Avenue
Tintern Avenue
Tewkesbury Gdns
Dryburgh Gdns
Wimborne Dr
Girton Avenue
Winchester Drive
North Way
Park Gdns
Milton Av
Tennyson Av
Bacon Lane
Roe Green
Goldsmith La
Fairfields Crs
Highfield Avenue
Uphill Drive
Old Kenton Lane
Sedum Cl
Larkspur Cl
Mersham Dr
Crundale Avenue
Valley Drive
Wyndale Av
Waltham Av
Slough Lane
Woodland Close
Lewgars Av
Boycroft Av
Salmon St
Bush Grove
Laburnum Gv
Holly Gv
Maple Gv
Sycamore Grove
Mallard Way
Alington Crescent
Lavender Avenue
Langdon Drive
Rossdale Drive
Glenwood Gv
Holden Av
Dimsdale Dr
Dunster Drive
Kingsmere Park
Deanscroft Avenue
Queens Walk
Tudor Cl
Bruno Place
The Mount
Hill Drive
Saltcroft Cl
Pilgrims Wy
Swinton Cl
Paddocks
Adams Cl
Greenhill Way
Kings Drive
The Paddocks
Wickliffe Gdns
Midholm
The Avenue
The Drive
Ken Way
Chalkhill Road
Rawlings Crs
Saxon Road
Barnhill Road
Windsor Crs
Rook Cl
Bowater Rd
Oakington Avenue
Crown Cl
Forty Close
Kingswood Rd
North End Rd
Wembley
1 grid square represents 500 metres

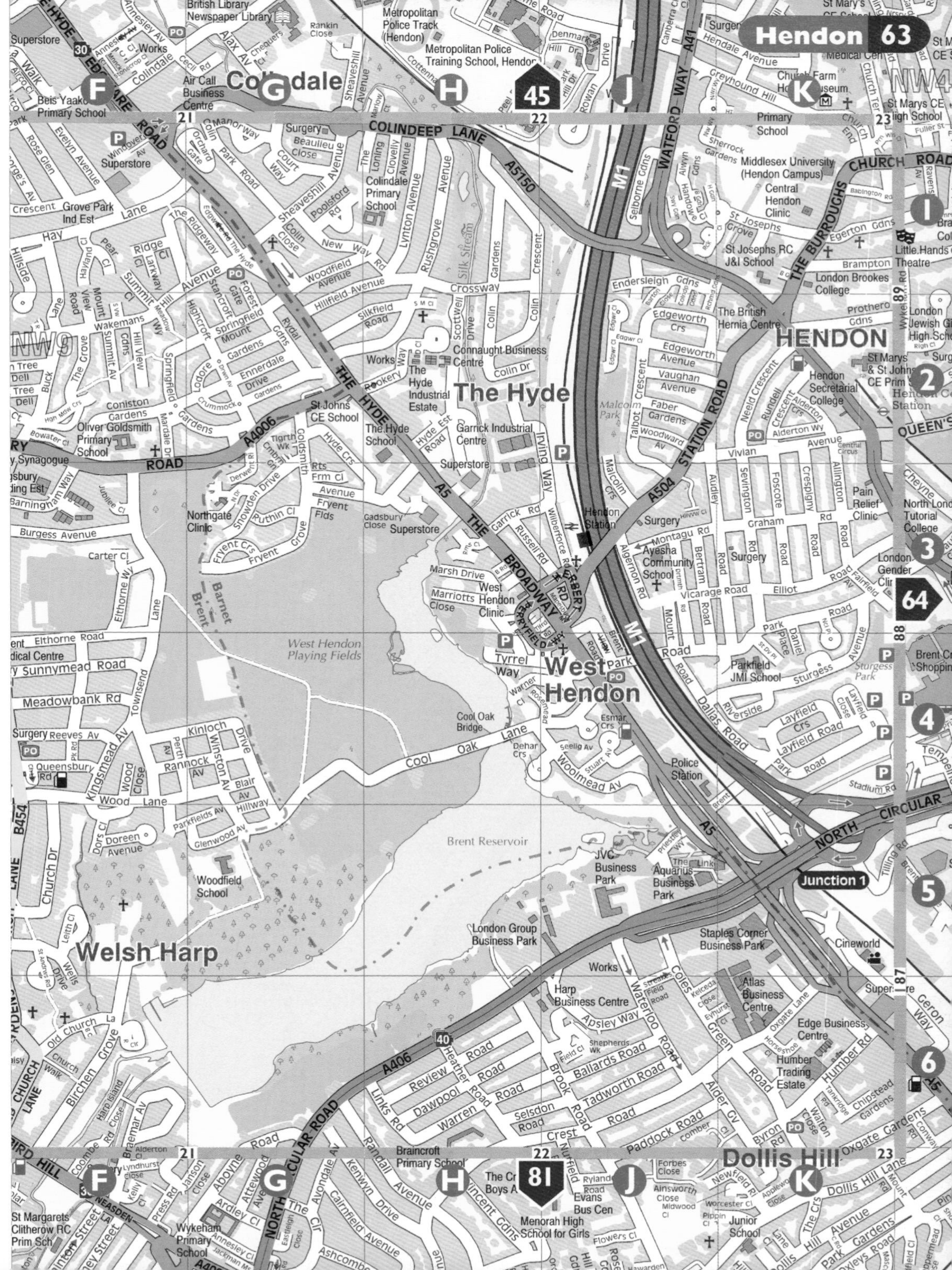

British Library
Newspaper Library
Metropolitan
Police Track
(Hendon)
Metropolitan Police
Training School, Hendon
Rankin Close
Superstore
Works
Colindale
Air Call
Business
Centre
Beis Yaakov
Primary School
45
Colindeep Lane
A5150
Watford Way
A41
M1
Hendale Avenue
Greyhound Hill
Church Farm
House Museum
St Marys CE
High School
NW4
Primary
School
Sherrock
Gardens
Middlesex University
(Hendon Campus)
Central
Hendon
Clinic
Church Road
The Burroughs
Brampton
London Brookes
College
Little Hands
Theatre
Edge Hill Rd
Woodfield Avenue
Hillfield Avenue
Crossway
Silk Stream
Rushgrove Avenue
Lynton Avenue
Colindale
Primary
School
Sheaveshill Avenue
Poolsford Rd
Grove Park
Ind Est
Hay Lane
Summit Way
Edgware Road
The Hyde
NW9
Wakemans Hill
Springfield Mount
Highcroft
Ennerdale Drive
Coniston
Gardens
Oliver Goldsmith
Primary
School
Kingsbury Road
A4006
Synagogue
St Johns
CE School
The Hyde
School
Works
The
Hyde
Industrial
Estate
The Hyde
Connaught Business
Centre
Colin Dr
Garrick Industrial
Centre
Superstore
Irving Way
Malcolm
Park
Endersleigh Gdns
Edgeworth
Crs
Edgeworth
Avenue
Vaughan
Avenue
Faber
Gardens
Woodward
Av
The British
Hernia Centre
HENDON
Hendon
Secretarial
College
St Marys
& St Johns
CE Prim
Hendon Central
Station
Queen's Road
London
Jewish Girls
High School
Prothero
Gdns
Station Road
A504
Hendon
Station
Vivian Avenue
Central
Circus
Alderton Wy
Audley
Sevington
Foscote
Crespigny
Allington
Pain
Relief
Clinic
North London
Tutorial
College
Graham Rd
Surgery
Montagu Rd
Ayesha
Community
School
Bertram
Surgery
Vicarage Road
Elliot Road
London
Gender
Clinic
64
A5
The Broadway
Garrick
Russell Rd
Wilberforce Rd
Herbert Rd
Perryfield Way
Marsh Drive
Marriotts
Close
West
Hendon
Clinic
West Hendon Playing Fields
Barnet
Brent
Northgate
Clinic
Snowden Drive
Fryent Crs
Fryent Grove
Gadsbury
Close
Superstore
Burgess Avenue
Carter Cl
Elthorne Way
Elthorne Road
Medical Centre
Sunnymead Road
Meadowbank Rd
Townsend Lane
Surgery
Reeves Av
Kinloch Drive
Winston Av
Rannock Av
Queensbury Rd
Kingsmead Av
Wood Close
Wood Lane
B454
Tyrrel
Way
West
Hendon
Park
Cool Oak
Bridge
Cool Oak Lane
Woolmead Av
Esmar
Crs
Police
Station
Dallas Road
Parkfield
JMI School
Sturgess Avenue
Sturgess
Park
Riverside
Layfield
Crs
Layfield Road
Park Road
Stadium Rd
Brent Cross
Shopping
North Circular
Junction 1
Brent Reservoir
JVC
Business
Park
Aquarius
Business
Park
Doreen
Avenue
Parkfields Av
Glenwood Av
Hillway
Woodfield
School
Church Dr
Welsh Harp
London Group
Business Park
Staples Corner
Business Park
Cineworld
Works
Harp
Business Centre
Apsley Way
Waterloo Road
Coles Green
Atlas
Business
Centre
Oxgate Lane
Edge Business
Centre
Humber
Trading
Estate
Humber Rd
Geron Way
Old Church La
Church Walk
Birchen Grove
Church Lane
Harp Island Close
Braemar Av
40
A406
North Circular Road
Review Road
Heather Road
Dawpool Road
Warren Road
Links Rd
Ballards Road
Tadworth Road
Selsdon Road
Brook Road
Crest Road
Paddock Road
Alder Gv
Byron Rd
Walton Close
Oxgate Gardens
Chipstead Gardens
Dollis Hill
Braincroft
Primary School
Neasden Lane
Coombe Rd
Press Rd
Janson Close
Aboyne
Attewood Av
Ardley Cl
Wykeham
Primary
School
St Margarets
Clitherow RC
Prim Sch
Kenwyn Drive
Randall Avenue
Cairnfield Avenue
Avondale Av
Ashcombe
81
Menorah High
School for Girls
Evans
Bus Cen
Ainsworth
Close
Forbes
Close
Newfield Ri
Worcester Cl
Junior
School
Dollis Hill Lane
Hill Avenue
Park Gardens
21
22
23
89
88
87
F
G
H
J
K
1
2
3
4
5
6

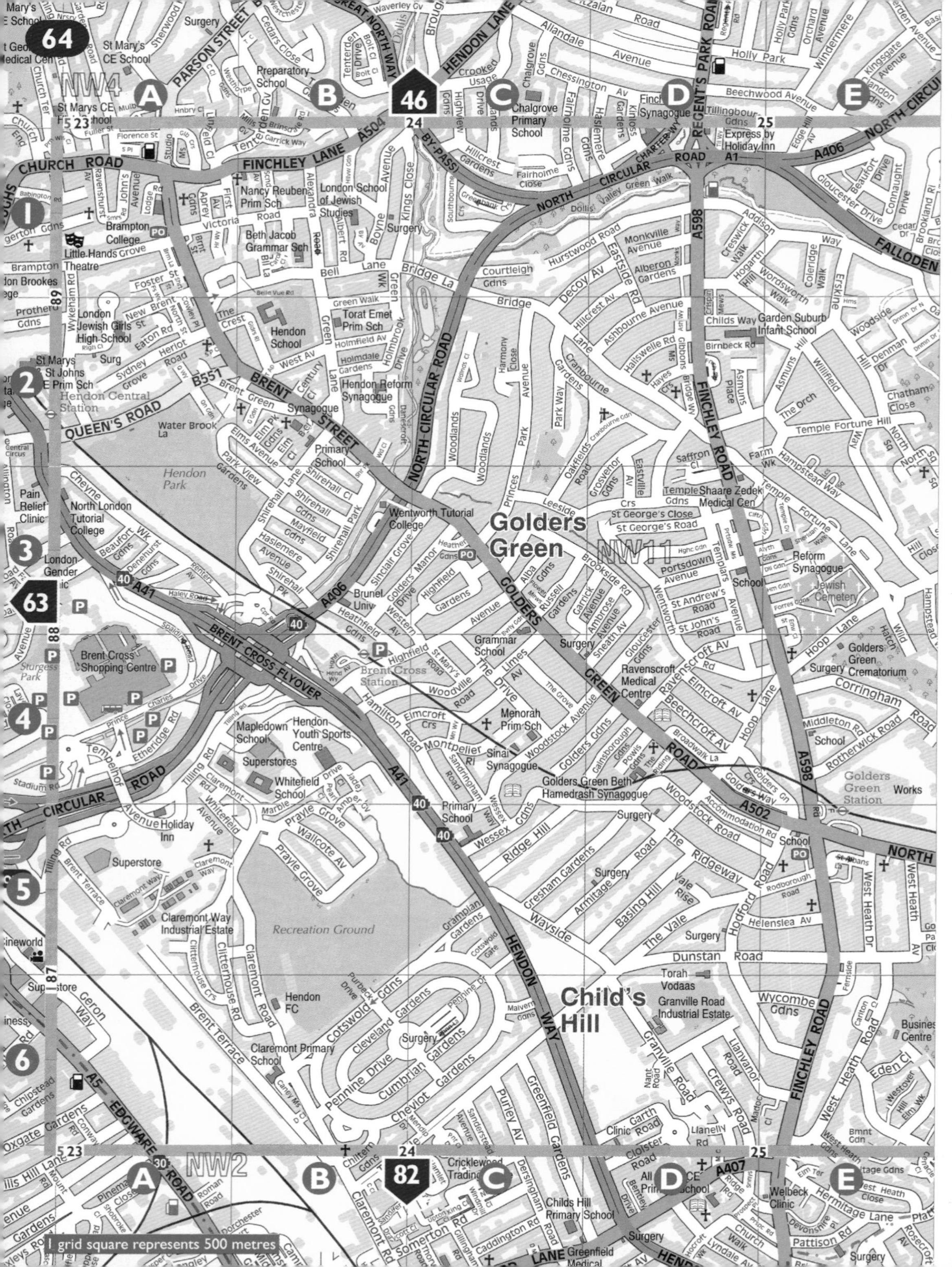
64
46
63
82
NW4
NW11
NW2
A
B
C
D
E
1
2
3
4
5
6
23
24
25
89
88
87
Golders Green
Child's Hill
Parson Street
Hendon Lane
Great North Way
Waverley Gv
Dollis
Allandale Avenue
Fitzalan Road
Holly Park
Orchard Avenue
Windermere
Kingsgate Avenue
Beechwood Avenue
Chessington Av
Regent's Park Road
Tillingbourne Gdns
Express by Holiday Inn
Finchley Synagogue
Chalgrove Primary School
Chalgrove Gdns
Fairholme Gdns
Haslemere Gdns
Kinloss Gardens
Hillcrest Gardens
Fairholme Close
St Mary's CE School
St Marys CE High School
Preparatory School
Surgery
Crooked Usage
Church Road
Church End
Church Ter
Finchley Lane
Florence St
Tenterden Gv
Studio Ms
Lodge Rd
St John's Avenue
Ravenshurst Av
Babington Rd
Nancy Reuben Prim Sch
London School of Jewish Studies
Alexandra Road
Bell Lane
Kings Close
Boyne Avenue
Beth Jacob Grammar Sch
Victoria Road
Brampton College
Brampton Grove
Little Hands Theatre
Brampton Gdns
Egerton Gdns
Hendon Brookes College
Wykeham Rd
Prothero Gdns
Foster St
New Brent St
North St
Cowley Pl
The Crest
Hendon School
London Jewish Girls High School
Eaton Rd
Heriot Road
Sydney Grove
Surg
West Av
Holmfield Av
Holmdale Gardens
Holmbrook Drive
Green Lane
Green Walk
Torat Emet Prim Sch
Hendon Reform Synagogue
Synagogue
Century Cl
St Marys & St Johns CE Prim Sch
Hendon Central Station
Queen's Road
Brent Street
Brent Green
B551
Water Brook La
Elms Avenue
Park View Gardens
Hendon Park
Shirehall Lane
Shirehall Cl
Shirehall Gdns
Shirehall Park
Mayfield Gdns
Haslemere Avenue
Primary School
Bridge La
Courtleigh Gdns
Bridge Lane
North Circular Road
Dollis Valley Green Walk
Hurstwood Road
Monkville Avenue
Eastside Rd
Alberon Gardens
Decoy Av
Hillcrest Av
Ashbourne Avenue
Childs Way
Garden Suburb Infant School
Birnbeck Rd
Hallswelle Rd
Hayes Crs
Bridge Wy
Gibbons Ms
Finchley Road
A598
A1
A406
Falloden Way
Addison Way
Creswick Walk
Hogarth Hill
Wordsworth Walk
Coleridge Walk
Erskine
Woodside
Denman Dr
Asmuns Hill
Asmuns Place
Willifield Way
The Orch
Chatham Close
Temple Fortune Hill
Temple Fortune Lane
Hampstead Way
Farm Wk
Gloucester Drive
Beaufort Drive
Connaught Drive
Brookland Ri
Cedar Dr
Saffron Cl
Temple Gdns
Shaare Zedek Medical Cen
Harmony Close
Woodlands
Princes Park Avenue
Park Way
Cranbourne Gardens
Oakfields Road
Grosvenor Gdns
Eastville Av
Leeside Crs
St George's Close
St George's Road
Portsdown Avenue
St Andrew's Road
St John's Road
Templars Avenue
Wentworth Road
School
Reform Synagogue
Jewish Cemetery
Golders Green Crematorium
Hoop Lane
Wild Hatch
Hampstead Way
Sinclair Grove
Golders Manor Drive
Highfield Gardens
Heather Gdns
Wentworth Tutorial College
Brunel Univ
Western Av
Heathfield Gdns
Alba Gdns
Russell Gardens
Garrick Avenue
Ambrose Avenue
Sneath Av
Brookside Rd
Golders Green Road
Grammar School
Gloucester Gdns
Ravenscroft Av
Ravenscroft Medical Centre
Elmcroft Av
Beechcroft Av
Broadwalk La
Hoop Lane
Corringham Road
Middleton Rd
Rotherwick Road
Golders Green Station
Works
A502
North End
Pain Relief Clinic
North London Tutorial College
Cheyne Walk
Beaufort Gdns
Denehurst Gdns
Renters Av
London Gender Clinic
A41
Haley Road
Brent Cross Flyover
Brent Cross Shopping Centre
Sturgess Park
Prince Charles Drive
Tempelhof Av
Etheridge Rd
Stadium Rd
Highfield Av
St Mary's Rd
Brent Cross Station
Woodville Road
Hamilton Road
Elmcroft Crs
The Drive
Limes Av
The Grove
Woodstock Avenue
Menorah Prim Sch
Montpelier Ri
Sandringham Road
Sinai Synagogue
Golders Gdns
Gainsborough Gdns
Golders Green Beth Hamedrash Synagogue
The Riding
Mapledown School
Hendon Youth Sports Centre
Superstores
Whitefield School
Tilling Rd
Claremont Rd
Whitefield Avenue
Holiday Inn
Prayle Grove
Wallcote Av
Amber Gv
Marble Dr
Hendon Way
Primary School
Wessex Gdns
Ridge Hill
Woodstock Road
Accommodation Rd
The Ridgeway
Hodford Road
Rodborough Road
Helenslea Av
West Heath Dr
West Heath Av
Gresham Gardens
Armitage Road
Basing Hill
Vale Rise
The Vale
Wayside
Dunstan Road
Superstore
Claremont Way
Claremont Way Industrial Estate
Brent Terrace
Recreation Ground
Grampian Gardens
Cotswold Gate
Clitterhouse Crs
Clitterhouse Rd
Claremont Road
Hendon FC
Cineworld
Superstore
Geron Way
Purbeck Drive
Cotswold Gdns
Cleveland Gardens
Pennine Dr
Pennine Drive
Cumbrian Gardens
Cheviot Gardens
Claremont Primary School
Malvern Gdns
Torah Vodaas
Granville Road Industrial Estate
Granville Road
Llanvanor Road
Crewys Road
Wycombe Gdns
Carlton Road
Business Centre
West Heath Road
Eden Cl
Westover Hill
A5
Edgware Road
Chipstead Gardens
Oxgate Gardens
Conway
Sanderstead Avenue
Purley Av
Greenfield Gardens
Dersingham Road
Childs Hill Primary School
Cricklewood Trading
Garth Road
Clinic
Cloister Road
Llanelly Rd
All Saints CE Prim School
A407
Welbeck Clinic
Hermitage Lane
Pattison Rd
Devonshire
Rosecroft Av
Claremont Rd
Somerton Rd
Caddington Rd
Lane
Greenfield Medical
Hendon
Pinemartin Close
Roman Road
Mount Rd
Dorchester
Surgery
Church Walk
Lyndale
1 grid square represents 500 metres

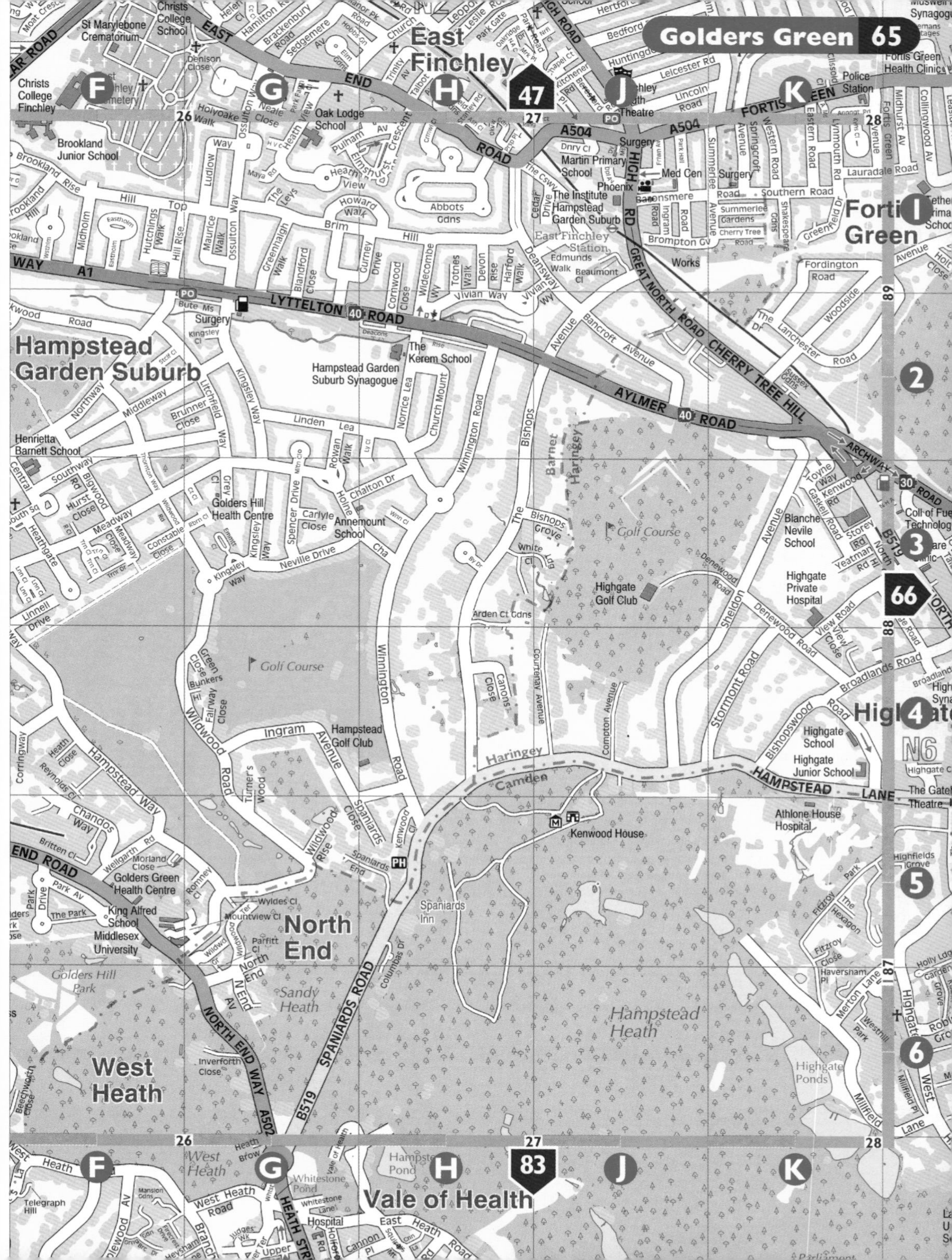
East Finchley
Hampstead Garden Suburb
Fortis Green
North End
West Heath
Vale of Health
Hampstead Heath
Sandy Heath
Golders Hill Park
St Marylebone Crematorium
Christs College School
Christs College Finchley
Brookland Junior School
Oak Lodge School
Martin Primary School
The Institute Hampstead Garden Suburb
East Finchley Station
The Kerem School
Hampstead Garden Suburb Synagogue
Henrietta Barnett School
Golders Hill Health Centre
Annemount School
Highgate Golf Club
Golf Course
Hampstead Golf Club
Kenwood House
Spaniards Inn
Blanche Nevile School
Highgate Private Hospital
Highgate School
Highgate Junior School
Athlone House Hospital
Golders Green Health Centre
King Alfred School
Middlesex University
Highgate Ponds
Hampstead Pond
Whitestone Pond
Telegraph Hill
Police Station
Fortis Green Health Clinic
Phoenix
Med Cen
Surgery
Works
EAST END ROAD
FORTIS GREEN
A504
HIGH ROAD
GREAT NORTH ROAD
CHERRY TREE HILL
LYTTELTON ROAD
AYLMER ROAD
ARCHWAY ROAD
A1
B519
HAMPSTEAD LANE
SPANIARDS ROAD
NORTH END WAY
A502
NORTH END ROAD
WEST HEATH ROAD
Hampstead Way
Winnington Road
Bishops Avenue
Wildwood Road
Ingram Avenue
Kingsley Way
Meadway
Northway
Sheldon Avenue
Stormont Road
Bishopswood Road
Broadlands Road
Denewood Road
Compton Avenue
Courtenay Avenue
Haringey
Camden
Barnet
N6
47
83
66
26
27
28
F
G
H
J
K
2
3
4
5
6
89
88
87

1 grid square represents 500 metres

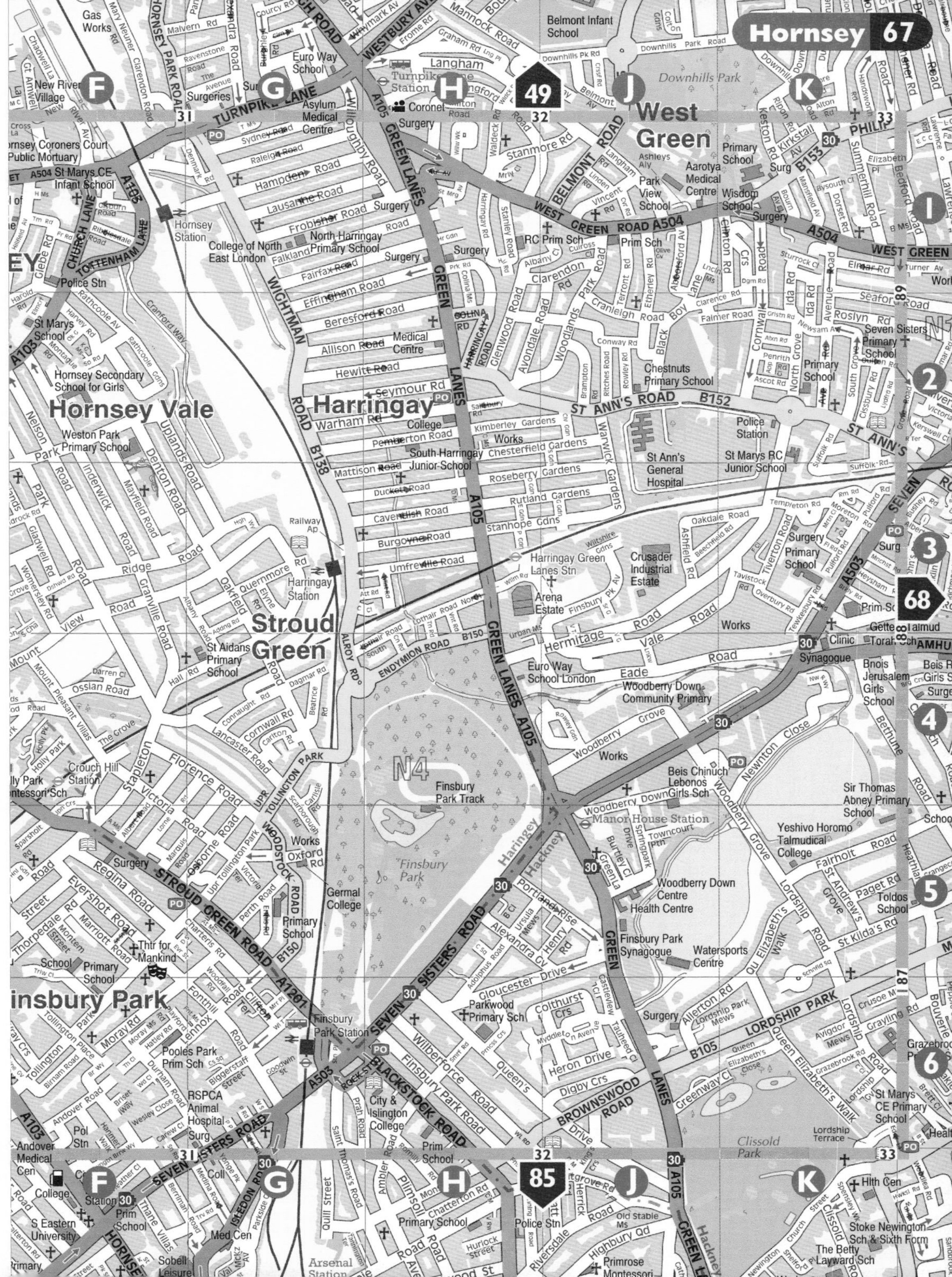

Gas Works
Belmont Infant School
Downhills Park
West Green
Turnpike Lane
Turnpike Lane Station
Coronet
Asylum Medical Centre
Euro Way School
New River Village
Surgeries
Hornsey Coroners Court
Public Mortuary
St Marys CE Infant School
Hornsey Station
College of North East London
North Harringay Primary School
Green Lanes
West Green Road A504
Belmont Road
Park View School
Aarotya Medical Centre
Wisdom School
Primary School
RC Prim Sch
Philip Lane
Police Stn
St Marys School
Hornsey Secondary School for Girls
Hornsey Vale
Weston Park Primary School
Harringay
Wightman Road
Medical Centre
College
Works
South Harringay Junior School
St Ann's Road B152
Chestnuts Primary School
Seven Sisters Primary School
Police Station
St Ann's General Hospital
St Marys RC Junior School
Harringay Station
Harringay Green Lanes Stn
Crusader Industrial Estate
Arena Estate
Stroud Green
St Aidans Primary School
Endymion Road
Hermitage Road
Vale Road
Euro Way School London
Woodberry Down Community Primary
Eade Road
Gette Talmud Torah Sch
Synagogue
Clinic
Bnois Jerusalem Girls School
Beis Ro Girls Sc
Woodberry Grove
N4
Finsbury Park Track
Finsbury Park
Beis Chinuch Lebonos Girls Sch
Manor House Station
Sir Thomas Abney Primary School
Yeshivo Horomo Talmudical College
Crouch Hill Station
Stroud Green Road
Seven Sisters Road
Germal College
Woodberry Down Centre
Health Centre
Finsbury Park Synagogue
Watersports Centre
Toldos School
Thtr for Mankind
Primary School
Finsbury Park
Parkwood Primary Sch
Finsbury Park Station
Lordship Park
Grazebrook Prim Sch
Pooles Park Prim Sch
RSPCA Animal Hospital
City & Islington College
Blackstock Road
Brownswood Road
St Marys CE Primary School
Lordship Terrace
Clissold Park
Andover Medical Cen
Pol Stn
College
S Eastern University
Prim School
Med Cen
Sobell Leisure
Arsenal Station
Primary School
Police Stn
Primrose Montessori
Hlth Cen
Stoke Newington Sch & Sixth Form
The Betty Layward Sch
Hackney
Haringey
49
68
85

68
50
67
86
A
B
C
D
E
1
2
3
4
5
6
33
34
35
88
87
89
Tottenham Hale
Retail Park
Scales Road
Police Station
Chesnut Rd
North London College
Hamilton Cl
Lockwood Ind Park
Tottenham Hale Station
Lea Valley
Ferry Lane Industrial
Bus Garage
Monument Way
Clinic
Primary School
Antill Road
Tottenham Hale Retail Park
A503
FERRY LANE
FOREST ROAD
PHILIP LANE
Stowe Place
Fairweather Cl
Clyde Road
Tottenham Grn Leisure Cen
Town Hall
Bedford Road
Lawrence Rd
Summerhill Rd
Elizabeth Pl
Bus Cen
Works
Beaconsfield Road
Grove Park Road
College Of Haringey, Enfield & North East London
Talbot Road
Health Centre
Tynemouth Road
HIGH ROAD
BROAD LANE
Fountayne Business Centre
Reedham Cl
Erskine Crs
Jarrow Road
Bream Cl
Ferry Lane Primary School
Yarmouth Crs
Armadale Cl
Kessock Cl
WEST GREEN ROAD
Turner Av
Pelham Rd
Portland Rd
High Cross Centre
Markfield Road
Seven Sisters Station
Seaford Road
Roslyn Rd
Seven Sisters Primary School
N15
South Tottenham
Southey Road
Greenfield Rd
Culvert Road
Victoria Crs
Stonebridge Rd
Ashby Rd
Stamford Rd
Constable Crs
Wakefield Rd
Rangemoor Rd
Herbert Rd
Newton Rd
Colless Rd
City of London Business College
SEVEN SISTERS ROAD
ST ANN'S ROAD
Superstore
South Tottenham Stn
South Tottenham District Synagogue
Crowland Road
Crowland Primary School
City of London Business College
Ferndale Road
Lealand Road
Elm Park Av
Wargrave Av
Lemsford Cl
Grovelands Rd
Plevna Crs
SEVEN SISTERS ROAD
Gladesmore Road
Fairview Rd
Wellington Av
Springfield Community Prim Sch
Warwick Reservoir
Copper Mills Works
Coppermill Lane
Waterside
B152
Wargrave Av
Norfolk Av
Clifton Gdns
Castlewood Road
Leadale Road
Maple Close
Saw Mill Wy
Rostrevor Av
Craven Park Road
Olinda Road
Moundfield Road
St John's Rd
Franklin St
Richmond Rd
Eastbourne Rd
Daleview Road
Primary School
Surg
Vartry Rd
Stamford Hill Stn
Gers Talmud Torah Sch
Clinic
AMHURST PARK
Ravensdale Road
Leabourne Road
Bobov Foundation Sch
Yesodey Hatorah Jewish Boys School
Bnois Jerusalem Girls School
Beis Rochel d'Satmar Girls School
Surgery
Denver Rd
Cranwich Road
Durley Road
West Bank
Egerton Rd
Yesodey Hatorah Sch for Girls Senior Site
Lubavitch Boys Prim Sch
Clapton Common
Craven Wk
Ashtead Road
Lingwood Road
Talmud Torah Machzikei Hadass Sch
Spring Hill
Walthamstow Marsh Nature Reserve
Springfield Park
Lea Valley Walk
Bethune Road
Skinners Academy Hackney
Northfield Rd
Lubavitch House Sch (Sen Girls)
Stamford Hill
A107
CLAPTON COMMON
The Bobov Foundation Sch for Girls
East Bank
Glaserton Rd
Wilderton Rd
Beth Hamedrash Skver Synagogue
Portland Av
Braydon Rd
Sir Thomas Abney Primary School
School
Dunsmure Road
Holmleigh Primary School
Holmleigh Rd
Darenth Road
Kyverdale Road
Firsby Rd
Walsham Cl
Tyssen Street
Tyssen Primary School
Upper Clapton
Hawkwood Mount
Spring Lane
Springfield
Springfield Gardens
Holmbury View
High Hill Ferry
Harrington Hill
Waltham Marshes
Heathland Road
Grangecourt Rd
St Andrew's Ms
Toldos School
Leatherhead Cl
Lynmouth Road
Oldhill Street
Forburg Road
Chardmore Road
Tayyibah Girls School
Jessam Ave
Mount Pleasant Lane
Prim Sch
Leaside Road
Ziam Trading Estate
St Kilda's Rd
MANOR ROAD
Royal Close
Reizel Cl
Lampard Gv
Oldhill Medical Centre
Beis Malka Girls Sch
Filey Avenue
Gilda Crs
Moresby Road
Our Ladys Convent High Sch
Healy Medical Cen
Yetev Lev Day School for Boys
Warwick Grove
Beis Trana Girls Sch
Knightland Road
Synagogue
Theydon Road
Riverside Close
Hackney
Waltham Forest
Abney Park Cemetery
N16
Listria Park
B105
A10
STAMFORD HILL
Stoke Newington Station
Boys School
Cazenove Road
Satmer Trust Sch
George Downing Estate
Fountayne Road Health Centre
Fountayne Road
Osbaldeston Road
Geldeston Rd
Knightland Rd
Sach Road
Mount Pleasant Hill
Primary School
Lordship Rd
Grayling Rd
Bouverie Road
Grazebrook Primary School
STOKE NEWINGTON
Fire Station
Alkham Road
Durlston Rd
Cncl Bldg
Rossington St
UPPER CLAPTON ROAD
Clapton Stn
Southwold Road
E5
St Marys CE Primary School
Surg
RECTORY ROAD
B111
NORTHWOLD ROAD
Primary School
Narford Rd
Gunton Road
Health Cen
STOKE NEWINGTON CH ST
Prim Sch
Dumont Rd
Brooke Road
Reighton Road
Evering Road
Ickburgh Road
Cleveleys Road
Casimir Road
Hlth Cen
Kynaston Rd
Oldfield Rd
Lavers Rd
Manley Ct
HIGH ST
Surgery
Rectory Road Station
West Hackney Synagogue
Ickburgh School
Works
Prout Rd
Clapton Synagogue
B Six Sixth Form College
Walsingham Road
St Scholasticas RC Prim
Kenninghall Road
Benthal Primary
Cotesbach Rd
Thornby Rd
Chatsworth Road
Stoke Newington Sch & Sixth Form
1 grid square represents 500 metres

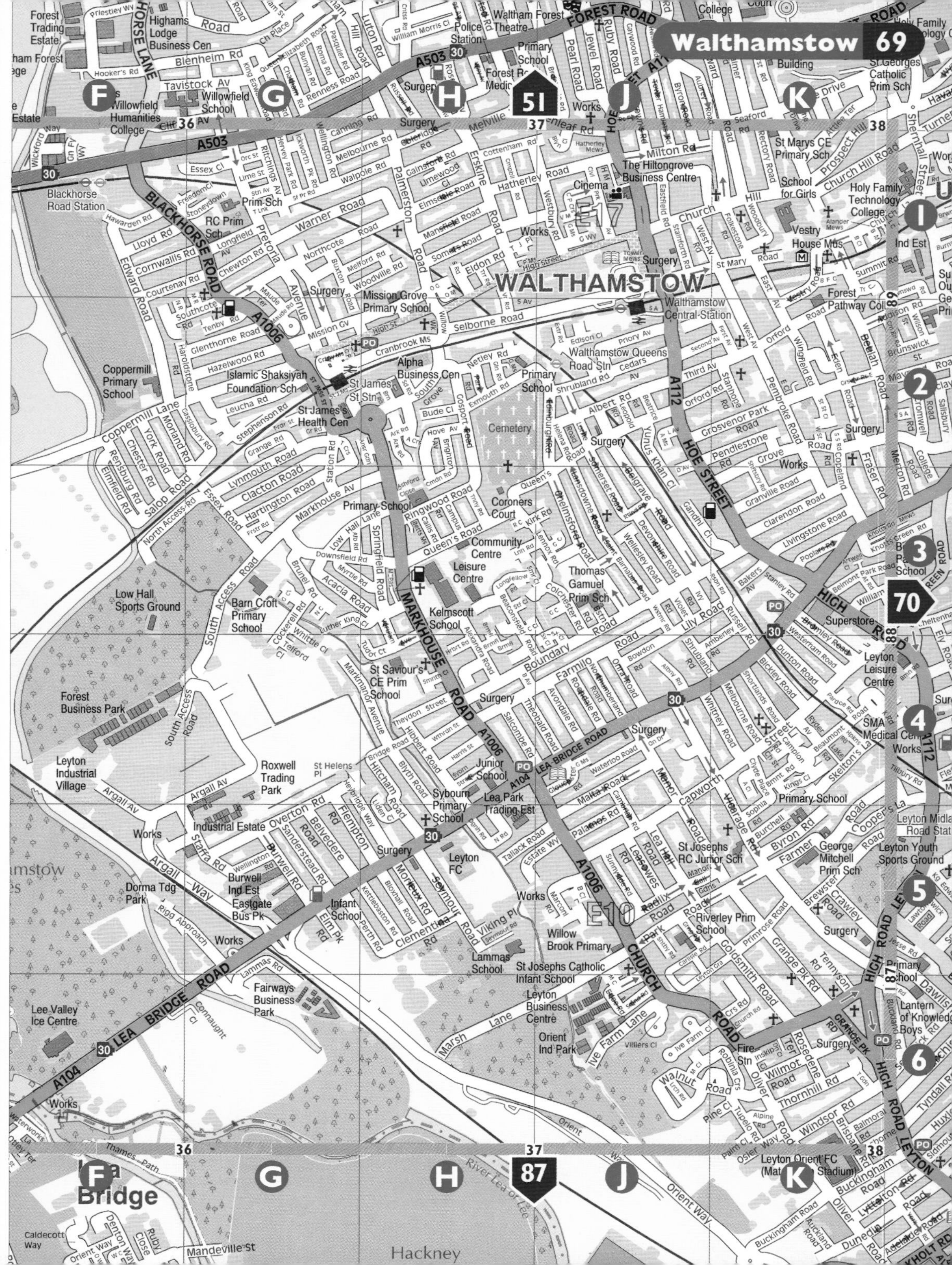

Walthamstow
69
51
70
87
F
G
H
J
K
1
2
3
4
5
6
36
37
38
88
89
WALTHAMSTOW
E17
E10
FOREST ROAD
BLACKHORSE ROAD
HORSE LANE
HOE STREET
MARKHOUSE ROAD
LEA BRIDGE ROAD
CHURCH ROAD
HIGH ROAD LEYTON
HIGH ROAD
A503
A1006
A104
A112
Forest Trading Estate
Highams Lodge Business Cen
Blenheim Rd
Tavistock Av
Willowfield School
Willowfield Humanities College
Police Station
Waltham Forest Theatre
Primary School
Forest Rd Medic
Surgery
Works
College
St Georges Catholic Prim Sch
Building
Blackhorse Road Station
Prim Sch
RC Prim Sch
The Hiltongrove Business Centre
Cinema
St Marys CE Primary Sch
School for Girls
Holy Family Technology College
Vestry House Mus
Ind Est
Walthamstow Central Station
Walthamstow Queens Road Stn
Forest Pathway Coll
Mission Grove Primary School
Coppermill Primary School
Islamic Shaksiyah Foundation Sch
St James St Stn
St James's Health Cen
Alpha Business Cen
Cemetery
Coroners Court
Community Centre
Leisure Centre
Thomas Gamuel Prim Sch
Kelmscott School
Low Hall Sports Ground
Barn Croft Primary School
Forest Business Park
Leyton Industrial Village
Roxwell Trading Park
St Saviour's CE Prim School
Superstore
Leyton Leisure Centre
SMA Medical Cen
Junior School
Sybourn Primary School
Lea Park Trading Est
Industrial Estate
Dorma Tdg Park
Burwell Ind Est
Eastgate Bus Pk
Infant School
Leyton FC
St Josephs RC Junior Sch
George Mitchell Prim Sch
Leyton Midland Road Stat
Leyton Youth Sports Ground
Riverley Prim School
Willow Brook Primary
Lammas School
St Josephs Catholic Infant School
Leyton Business Centre
Orient Ind Park
Fairways Business Park
Lee Valley Ice Centre
Fire Stn
Lantern of Knowledge Boys
Leyton Orient FC (Matchroom Stadium)
Lea Bridge
Hackney
River Lea or Lee
Orient Way
Thames Path
Mandeville St
Caldecott Way
Denton Way
Ruby Close
Buckingham Road

70
52
69
88
A
B
C
D
E
1
2
3
4
5
6
538
39
40
Upper Walthamstow
Leytonstone
LEYTON
E11
Holy Family Technology Coll
St Georges Catholic Prim Sch
Primary School
Woodlands Road
Waverley Rd
Havant Road
Turner Road
Medical Centre
Upper Walthamstow Road
Avon Road
Bisterne Avenue
Fyfield Road
NEW ROAD
Broadwalk
Cheyne Avenue
Bushey Avenue
Malford Grove
The Drive
Tavistock Road
Wood Street Station
Marlowe
Works
Valentin Road
Church Hill Road
Prospect Hill
Holy Family Technology College
Greenway Avenue
The Risings
Forest Rise
St Peter's Av
WOODFORD ROAD
Oakhurst Gardens
The Forest
Centenary Walk
Laurel Way
Meadow Walk
Snaresbrook Prim Sch
WOODFORD ROAD
Hermitage Cl
Riverhall Gdns
Warwick School for Boys
WOOD STREET
Works
Ind Est
Morgan Av
Salters Road
Foresters Drive
Lucerne Gv
Woodside Pk Av
Buxton Dr
Snaresbrook Road
Eagle Lane
HERMON
Malcolm Way
Sylvan Road
Wellington Road
Summit Rd
Barrett
Greville Rd
Brooke Rd
Surgery
Our Lady & St Georges Catholic Prim Sch
Forest Pathway Cl
Addison Rd
Brunswick St
Beulah Road
Oliver Rd
Ferndale Av
Chestnut Av South
St Helens Catholic Infant School
Raglan Rd
Maynard Road
Barclay Road
Cromwell
Salisbury
Shernhall Street
Eastern
Western Rd
LEA BRIDGE ROAD
A104
Halford Road
Eatington Road
Fulready Rd
Snaresbrook Crown Court
HOLLYBUSH HILL
The Rise
Hollybush Close
Forest Close
Snaresbrook Station
Wellesley
Wanstead CE Primary School
NEW WANSTEAD
A113
A1199
Surgery
Copeland
Fraser Rd
Merton Rd
College Rd
Carnarvon Rd
Liverpool Rd
Peterborough
W End Av
A114
WHIPPS CROSS ROAD
A&E
Ambulance Rd
Whipps Cross Hospital
Back Road
Margaret Road
Bridge Road
Hospital Road
Ellesmere Close
Selworthy Cl
Church Path
Surgery
Wanstead Place
Police Station
Spratt Hall Road
Surgery
East Row
Greg Cl
Matlock
Nottingham Road
Essex
Leyton VI Form College
Barclay Primary School
James Lane
Leytonstone Business & Enterprise Specialist Sch
Forest Glade
Fladgate Road
Maple Road
Dyson Road
Preston Road
Belmont Park School
Belmont Park Road
LEYTON GREEN ROAD
Epsom Road
Griggs Road
Chesterfield Road
Canterbury
Sandringham Road
Forest Drive East
Colworth
Poppleton
Road
Surgery
Chadwick Road
Teesdale
Ashbridge
Surgery
Addison Road
Dangan Road
Chaucer Rd
Gordon Road
Chestnut Dr
Our Lady of Lourdes RC Prim Sch
Convent School
Highstone Avenue
Cambridge Park Road
Cambridge Road
A12
Leyton Leisure Centre
Cheltenham Road
Ely Road
Colchester
Cromer Road
Hainault Rd
Wadley Rd
Lytton Road
Percy Road
Esther Road
Corbicum
Holly Rd
Selsdon Road
Woodcote Road
Felstead Road
Surgery
Abbotts Park Road
Lyndhurst Dr
Leigh
Forest Drive West
Gwyn Jones Primary School
Essex Road S
Woodriffe Road
Road
Kingswood Rd
Superstore
Hanbury Dr
A11
GMA Medical Cen
Works
A112
Fletcher Lane
James Lane
Forest
Fairlop
Wallwood
King's Road
Queen's Road
Allum Medical Centre
Bus Cen
Browning Road
Beacontree Road
Bushwood
BUSH ROAD A114
BLAKE HALL ROAD
GAINSBOROUGH RD
A106
50
Midland Road
Hainault Road
Hawbridge Road
Clarendon Road
Leyton Midland Road Station
The Sidings
Cavendish
Bulwer Rd
Leytonstone Stn
Kirkdale Rd
Superstore
Leytonstone Mosque
Hartley Rd
Coopers La
Leyton Youth Sports Ground
George Mitchell Prim Sch
Belgrave Rd
Grosvenor Rd
Norlington
Scarborough Rd
Chelmsford
The Synagogue
Church Lane
College
Harvey Road
Surg
Leyspring Rd
Woodville
Police Cadet School
Norlington Sch
Pretoria Road
Southwest Road
Drayton Rd
GROVE GN RD
Primary School
Harold Rd
Vernon
Leytonstone Rd
Barclay Road
Mornington Rd
Stanmore Road
Leybourne Road
Michael Road
Bushwood
Lister Road
Bushwood
Belgrave Road
Windsor Road
Richmond Way
Road
HIGH ROAD LEYTON
Scott's Road
Morley Road
Claude Road
Police Station
Albert Road
Jersey Rd
Twickenham Rd
Connaught School for Girls
Connaught Rd
Madeira Rd
Leytonstone High Road Stn
Davies Lane
Davies Lane Primary School
Ferndale Road
Malvern Road
Montague Road
Centenary Walk
Primary School
Surgery
Dawlish
Noor Ul Islam Primary School
Newport School
Newport
Rhodesia
Kimberley Rd
Thornton Rd
Richmond
Oakdale Road
Pearcroft Road
Central
Ashville
Lantern of Knowledge Boys
Buckland Rd
Sedgwick Rd
Murchison Road
FRANCIS ROAD
Surgery
Elm Road
Norman Road
Granleigh Rd
Park Gv Road
Melford Rd
Mayville Rd
Southwell Gv Rd
Trinity Cl
Health Cen
Lancaster Rd
Cookes Close
Police Station
Lansdowne Rd
Tyndall Road
Huxley Road
St Mary's Road
Leyton Pk Rd
Grove Green Road
GROVE GREEN ROAD
A106
B161
Marchant Rd
Lincoln St
Cobden Road
Cecil Road
Acacia Road
Briscoe Cl
House
Balmoral Rd
Brisbane Rd
Osborne Rd
Buckingham Road
St George's Road
A106 WARREN ROAD
GROVE GREEN RD
A12
Cath
Mayville J&P Sch
Beachcroft
Surgery
B161
Lake
CENTRE ROAD
Acacia Bus Cen
CATHALL RD
Cemetery
Hollydown Way
Pear Rd
Apple Rd
Melon Rd
Corn Way
Buxton School
Terling Cl
Primary School
Matcham Rd
Chichester
Oliver Road
Lyttelton Road
Dunedin
1 grid square represents 500 metres

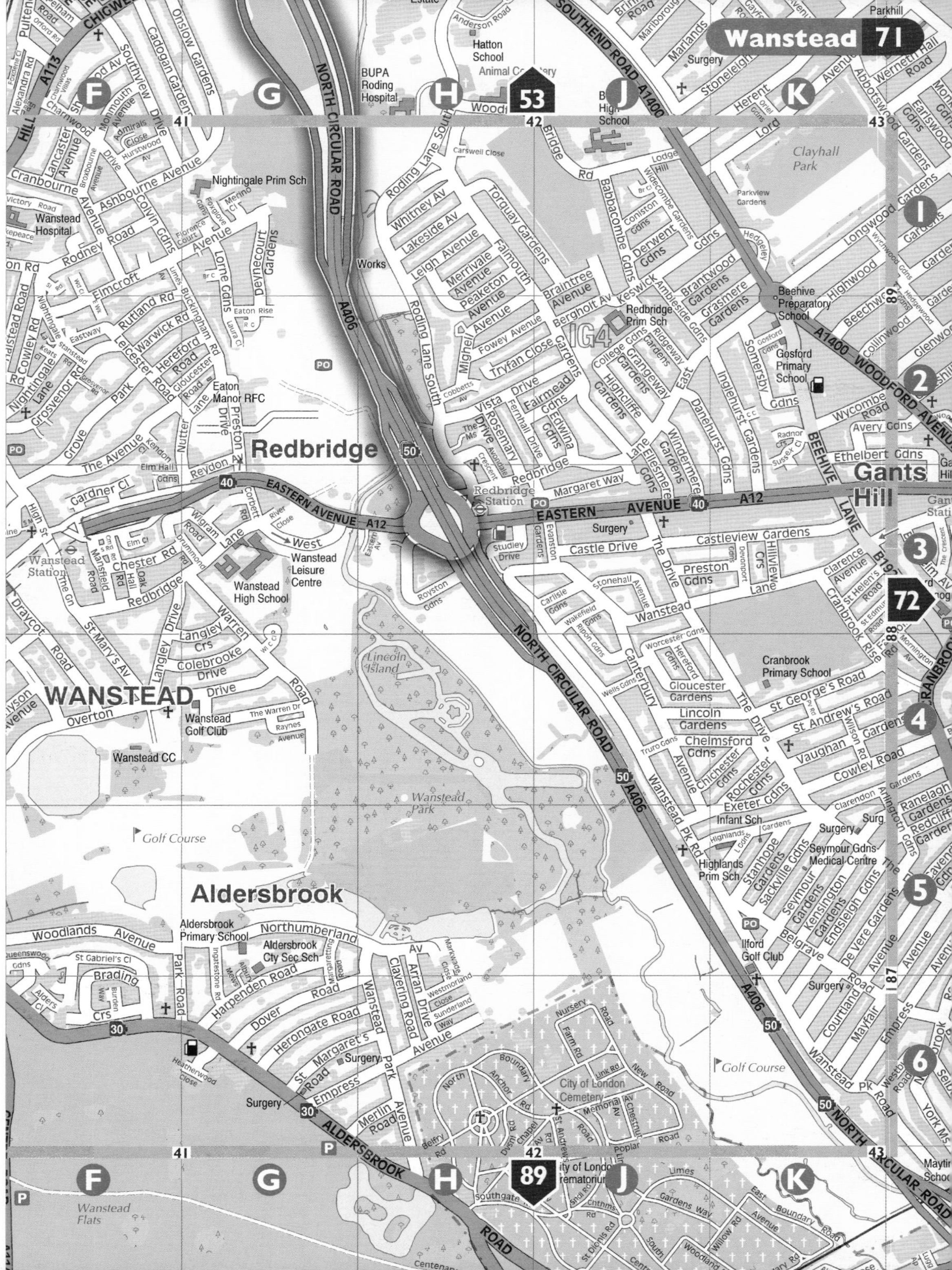
Redbridge
WANSTEAD
Aldersbrook
Gants Hill
Wanstead Park
City of London Cemetery
Wanstead Flats
NORTH CIRCULAR ROAD
EASTERN AVENUE
ALDERSBROOK ROAD
Wanstead High School
Wanstead Leisure Centre
Wanstead Golf Club
Redbridge Station
Cranbrook Primary School
Ilford Golf Club
Clayhall Park
53
72
89

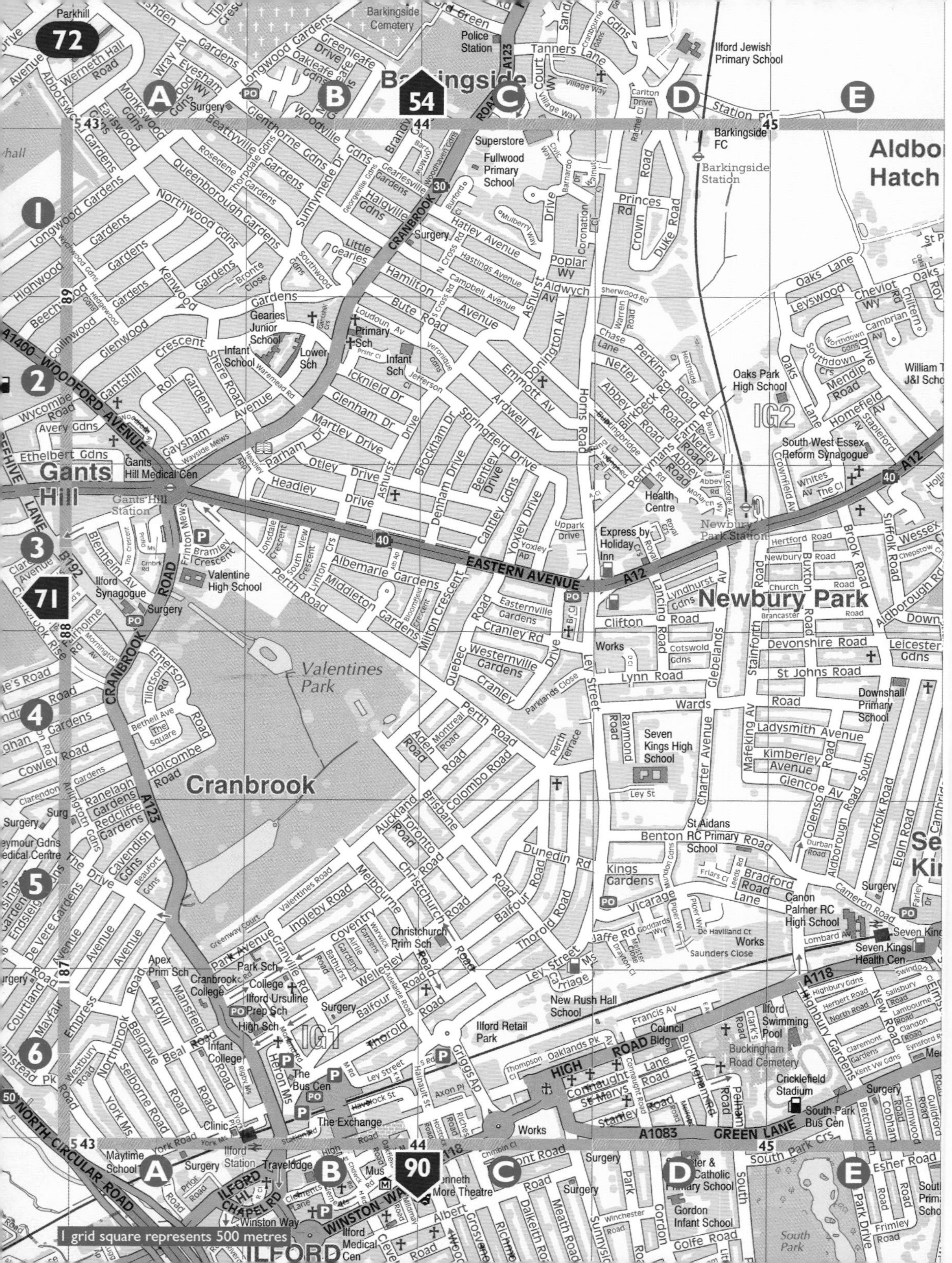

72
Parkhill
Barkingside Cemetery
Police Station
Ilford Jewish Primary School
Barkingside
54
Tanners Lane
Village Way
Station Rd
Barkingside FC
Barkingside Station
Aldborough Hatch
Superstore
Fullwood Primary School
Princes Rd
Crown Road
Duke Road
Coronation
Poplar Wy
Aldwych Av
Oaks Lane
Leyswood
Cheviot Wy
Cambrian
Chiltern
Southdown Crs
Mendip Road
Oaks Park High School
IG2
William T J&I Sch
Homefield Av
Stapleford
South-West Essex Reform Synagogue
A12
40
Whites Av
The Cl
Crownfield Av
Newbury Park Station
Health Centre
Perrymans Farm Rd
Netley Road
Abbey Road
Birkbeck Rd
Perkins Road
Chase Lane
Horns Road
Donington Av
Emmott Av
Ardwell Av
Springfield Drive
Bentley Drive
Brockham Dr
Denham Drive
Cantley Gdns
Yoxley Drive
Uppark Drive
Express by Holiday Inn
EASTERN AVENUE
Newbury Park
Hertford Road
Newbury Road
Church Road
Brook Road
Suffolk Road
Wessex
Aldborough Rd
Devonshire Road
St Johns Road
Leicester Gdns
Downshall Primary School
Ladysmith Avenue
Kimberley Avenue
Glencoe Av
Mafeking Av
Stainforth Road
Buxton Road
Lynn Road
Wards Road
Glebelands Av
Cotswold Gdns
Clifton Road
Lancing Road
Lyndhurst Gdns
Works
Seven Kings High School
Ley St
Charter Avenue
Raymond Road
St Aidans RC Primary School
Benton Road
Kings Gardens
Bradford Road
Vicarage Lane
Canon Palmer RC High School
Cameron Road
Seven Kings
Seven Kings Health Cen
Saunders Close
New Rush Hall School
Ley Street
Ilford Retail Park
Francis Av
Council Bldg
Ilford Swimming Pool
Buckingham Road Cemetery
Highbury Gardens
New Road
Cricklefield Stadium
South Park Bus Cen
A118
A1083
GREEN LANE
HIGH ROAD
Connaught Road
Oaklands Pk Av
South Park Crs
Esher Road
South Park
Park Drive
Frimley Road
Gordon Infant School
Golfe Road
Surgery
Winchester Road
Gordon Road
Meath Road
Dalkeith Road
90
Kenneth More Theatre
WINSTON WAY
ILFORD
Ilford Medical Cen
Winston Way
CHAPEL RD
ILFORD HILL
Ilford Station
Travelodge
Mus
Maytime School
York Road
NORTH CIRCULAR ROAD
Clinic
The Exchange
The Bus Cen
Ley Street
Hainault St
Havelock St
Axon Pl
Griggs Ap
Works
Thorold Road
Balfour Road
IG1
Ilford Ursuline Prep Sch
High Sch
Heron Ms
Infant College
Cranbrook College
Park Sch
College
Apex Prim Sch
Park Avenue
Granville Rd
Christchurch Prim Sch
Christchurch Road
Coventry Road
Wellesley Road
Melbourne Road
Ingleby Road
Valentines Road
Toronto Road
Auckland Road
Brisbane Road
Colombo Road
Aden Road
Montreal Road
Perth Road
Perth Terrace
Dunedin Rd
Thorold Road
Balfour Road
Jaffe Rd
Cranbrook
Valentines Park
A123
CRANBROOK ROAD
Holcombe Road
The Square
Bethell Ave
Tillotson Rd
Emerson Road
Cowley Road
Ranelagh Gardens
Redcliffe Gardens
Cavendish Gdns
Beaufort Gdns
The Drive
De Vere Gardens
Endsleigh Gardens
Empress Avenue
Mayfair Avenue
Courtland Road
Northbrook Road
Belgrave Road
Argyll Road
Mansfield Road
Selborne Road
York Ms
Westbury Road
Beal Road
Ilford Synagogue
Valentine High School
Bramley Crescent
Frinton Mews
Gants Hill Station
Gants Hill
Gants Hill Medical Cen
Ethelbert Gdns
Avery Gdns
Wycombe Road
A1400 WOODFORD AVENUE
71
B192
Blenheim Av
Perth Road
Middleton Gardens
Milton Crescent
Albemarle Gardens
Lynton Crs
South View Crescent
Lonsdale Crescent
Headley Drive
Otley Drive
Parham Dr
Martley Drive
Glenham Dr
Icknield Dr
Gaysham Avenue
Wayside Mews
Roll Gardens
Shere Road
Crescent Gardens
Infant School
Geariess Junior School
Lower Sch
Primary Sch
Infant Sch
Loudoun Av
Bute Road
Hamilton Avenue
Hatley Avenue
Campbell Avenue
Hastings Avenue
Little Gearies
Surgery
Haigville Gdns
Gearlesville Gardens
Sunnymede Dr
Gearlesville Gdns
Glenthorne Gdns
Woodville Gdns
Queenborough Gardens
Northwood Gdns
Kenwood Gardens
Glenwood Gardens
Collinwood Gardens
Beechwood Gardens
Highwood Gardens
Longwood Gardens
Beattyville Gardens
Rosedene
Thorndale Gdns
Earlswood Gdns
Monkswood Gdns
Abbotswood Gardens
Werneth Hall Road
Evesham Wy
Wray Av
Longwood Gardens
Greenleafe Drive
Oakleafe Gdns
Surgery
1
2
3
4
5
6
A
B
C
D
E
5 43
44
45
89
88
87
1 grid square represents 500 metres

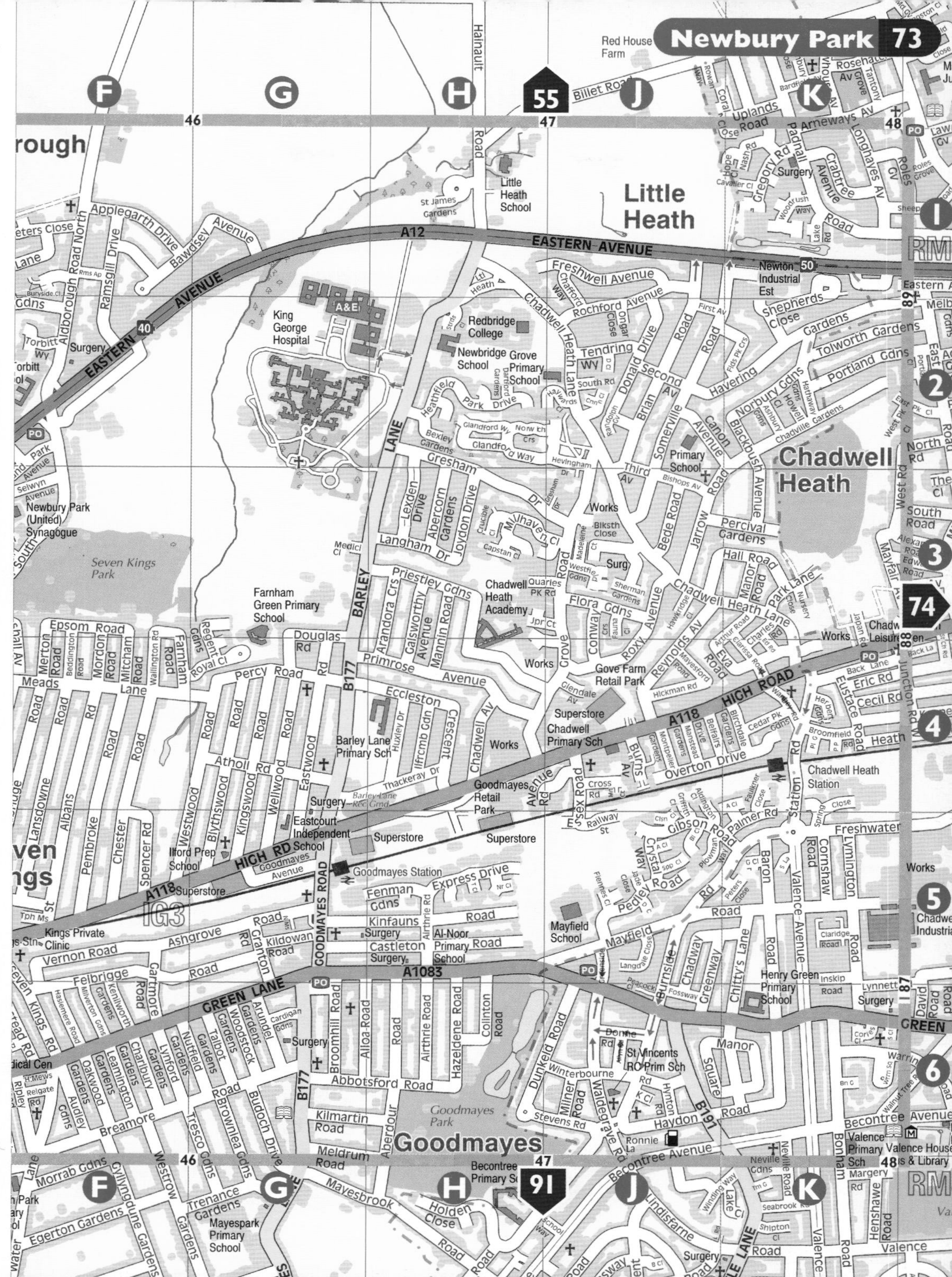
Little Heath
Chadwell Heath
Goodmayes
King George Hospital
A&E
Seven Kings Park
EASTERN AVENUE
A12
A118
HIGH ROAD
A1083
GREEN LANE
BARLEY LANE
B177
GOODMAYES ROAD
B191
Redbridge College
Newbridge School
Grove Primary School
Little Heath School
Chadwell Heath Academy
Farnham Green Primary School
Barley Lane Primary Sch
Eastcourt Independent School
Ilford Prep School
Goodmayes Station
Chadwell Heath Station
Goodmayes Retail Park
Gove Farm Retail Park
Chadwell Primary Sch
Mayfield School
Henry Green Primary School
St Vincents RC Prim Sch
Al-Noor Primary School
Goodmayes Park
Becontree Primary Sch
Mayespark Primary School
Valence Primary Sch
Valence House & Library
Newbury Park (United) Synagogue
Kings Private Clinic
Newton Industrial Est
Red House Farm
IG3
RM6
55
74
91
46
47
48
F
G
H
J
K
1
2
3
4
5
6

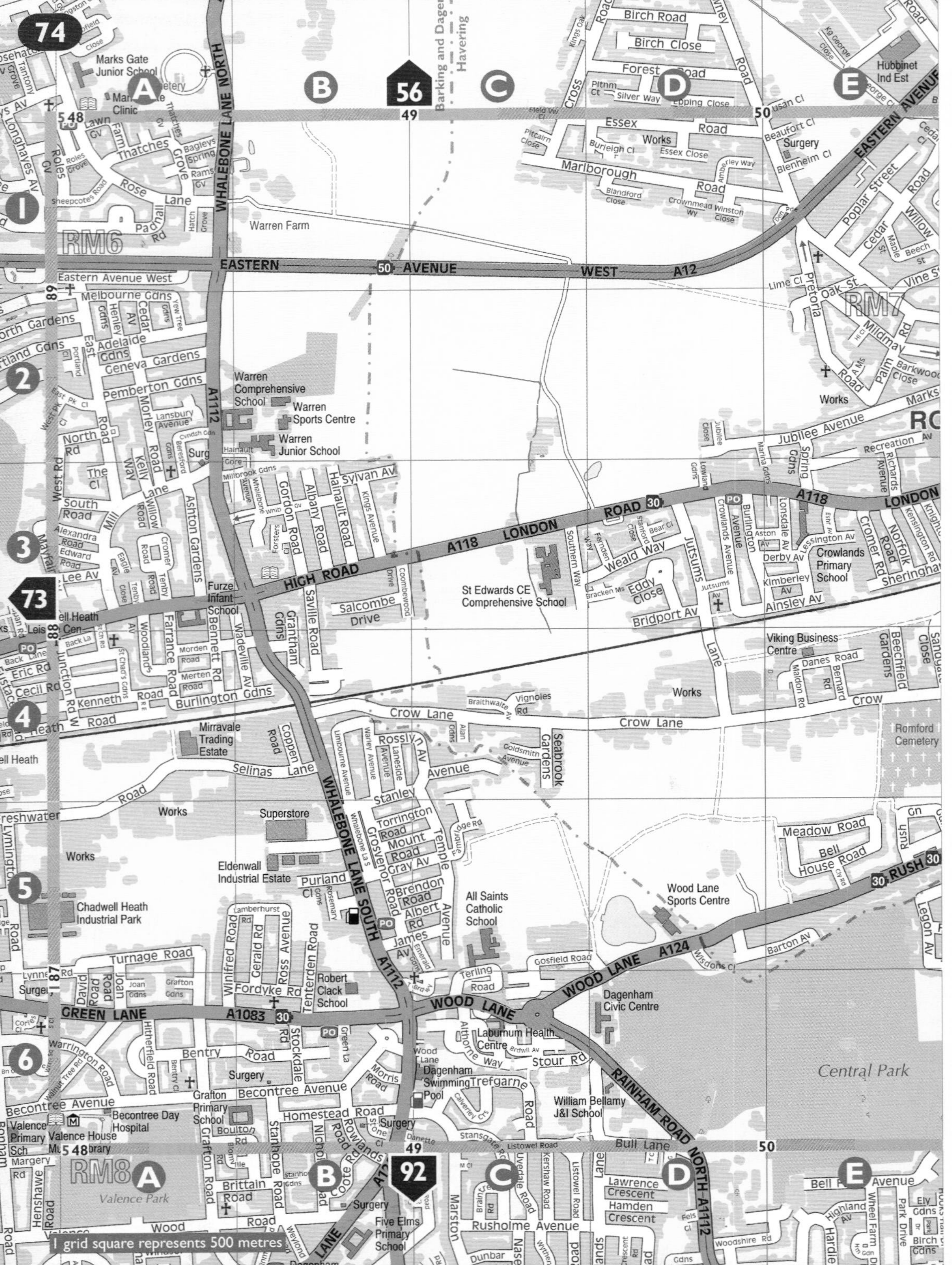
74
56
73
92
A
B
C
D
E
1
2
3
4
5
6
RM6
RM7
RM8
Eastern Avenue West
A12
A118 London Road
High Road
A1112
Whalebone Lane North
Whalebone Lane South
Wood Lane
A124
Green Lane
A1083
Rainham Road North A1112
Crow Lane
Bull Lane
Marks Gate Junior School
Warren Farm
Warren Comprehensive School
Warren Sports Centre
Warren Junior School
Furze Infant School
St Edwards CE Comprehensive School
Crowlands Primary School
Viking Business Centre
Romford Cemetery
Mirravale Trading Estate
Superstore
Eldenwall Industrial Estate
Chadwell Heath Industrial Park
All Saints Catholic School
Wood Lane Sports Centre
Robert Clack School
Dagenham Civic Centre
Laburnum Health Centre
Dagenham Swimming Pool
William Bellamy J&I School
Grafton Primary School
Becontree Day Hospital
Valence House
Valence Park
Five Elms Primary School
Central Park
Hubbinet Ind Est
1 grid square represents 500 metres

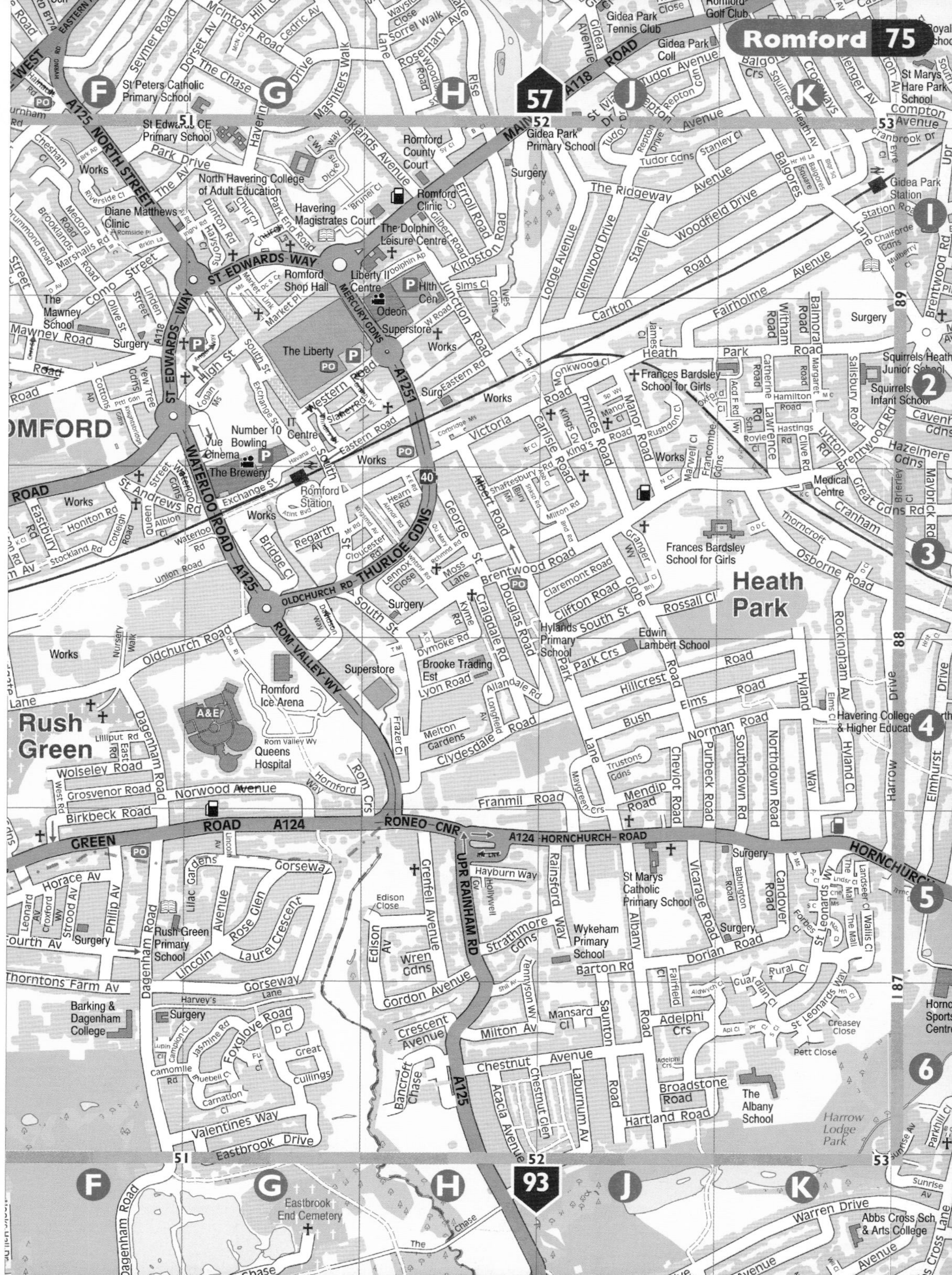

ROMFORD
Rush Green
Heath Park
North Street
St Edwards Way
Waterloo Road
Thurloe Gdns
Rom Valley Wy
Oldchurch Road
Upr Rainham Rd
Roneo Cnr
A124 Hornchurch Road
Main Road
Eastern Road
Victoria Road
Brentwood Road
Heath Park Road
Balgores Lane
Carlton Road
Gidea Park Station
Romford Station
The Liberty
Liberty II Centre
Romford Shop Hall
Odeon
The Brewery
Vue Cinema
Number 10 Bowling
The Dolphin Leisure Centre
Havering Magistrates Court
Romford County Court
Romford Clinic
North Havering College of Adult Education
St Peters Catholic Primary School
St Edwards CE Primary School
Gidea Park Primary School
Gidea Park Tennis Club
Gidea Park Coll
Frances Bardsley School for Girls
Squirrels Heath Junior School
Squirrels Infant School
Hylands Primary School
Edwin Lambert School
Havering College of Further & Higher Education
Romford Ice Arena
Queens Hospital
A&E
Rush Green Primary School
Barking & Dagenham College
St Marys Catholic Primary School
Wykeham Primary School
The Albany School
Harrow Lodge Park
Eastbrook End Cemetery
Abbs Cross Sch. & Arts College
Brooke Trading Est
The Mawney School
Diane Matthews Clinic
Medical Centre
Superstore
Surgery
Works
57
93
F G H J K
1 2 3 4 5 6
51 52 53
87 88 89

Ruislip Golf Club
West Ruislip Station
Airbase Unity Elementary School
Pond Green
Ruislip RFC
Ruislip Manor FC
Ruislip Manor
Sacred Heart Primary School
58
Works
Ruislip Gardens
Ruislip Gardens Primary School
Ruislip High School
Ruislip Gardens Station
Ickenham Clinic
Compass Theatre
Ickenham Station
Glebe Primary School
Ickenham Manor
UB10
Hillingdon Trail
Northolt Aerodrome
A40
WESTERN AVENUE A437
A4180
North Hillingdon
Gutteridge Wood
Ryefield Primary School
Dog Rose Ramble
Old Abbotstonians RFC
94
Works
Charrville Primary School
Swakeleys School for Girls
1 grid square represents 500 metres

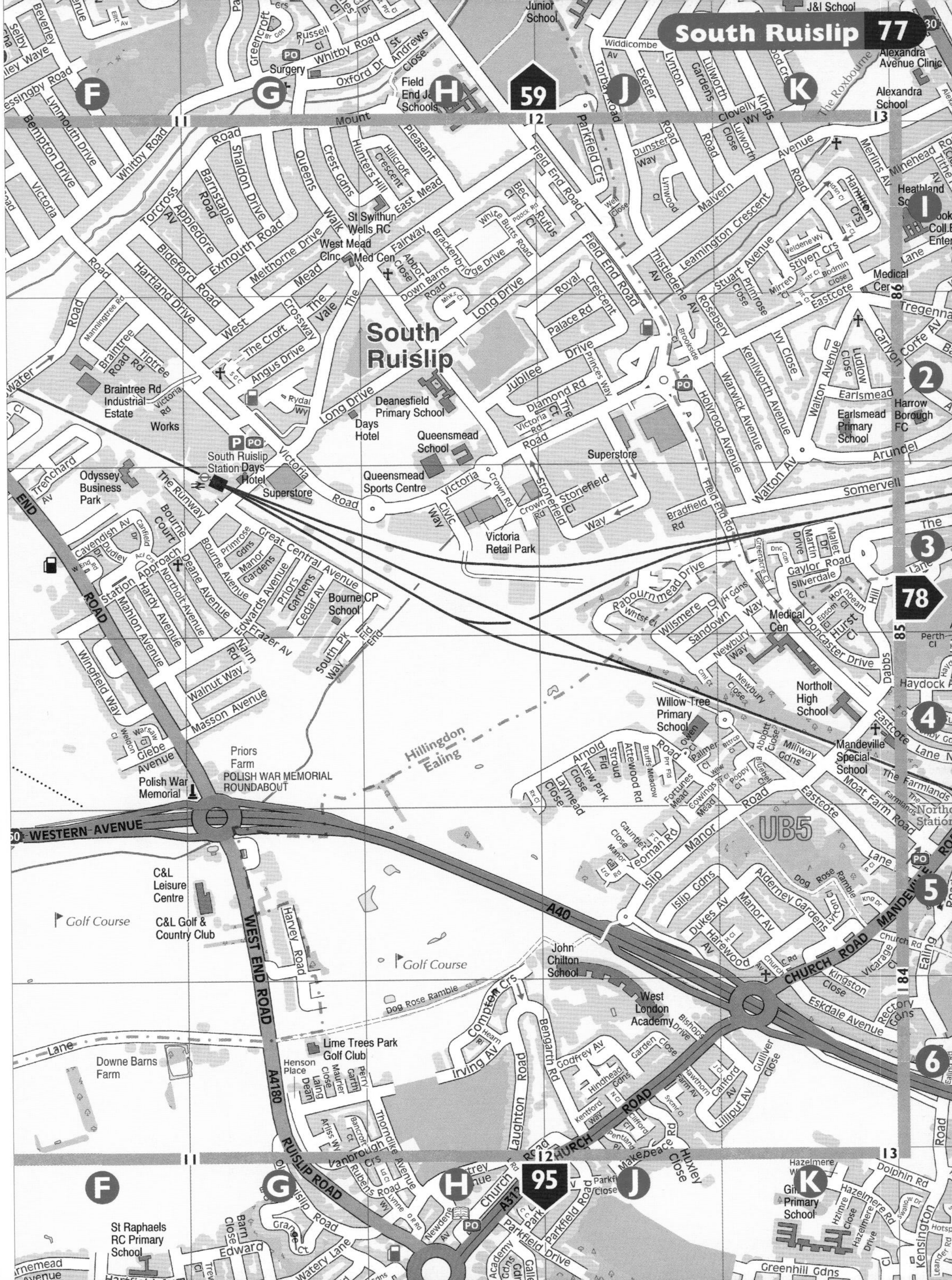
South Ruislip
South Ruislip Station
Deanesfield Primary School
Queensmead School
Queensmead Sports Centre
Victoria Retail Park
Odyssey Business Park
Braintree Rd Industrial Estate
Bourne CP School
Willow Tree Primary School
Northolt High School
Mandeville Special School
Earlsmead Primary School
Harrow Borough FC
John Chilton School
West London Academy
Lime Trees Park Golf Club
C&L Leisure Centre
C&L Golf & Country Club
Golf Course
Downe Barns Farm
Priors Farm
POLISH WAR MEMORIAL ROUNDABOUT
Polish War Memorial
St Raphaels RC Primary School
Field End J&I Schools
St Swithun Wells RC
West Mead Clnc
Days Hotel
Superstore
WESTERN AVENUE
A40
WEST END ROAD
A4180
RUISLIP ROAD
CHURCH ROAD
MANDEVILLE ROAD
Hillingdon
Ealing
UB5
Dog Rose Ramble
59
78
95

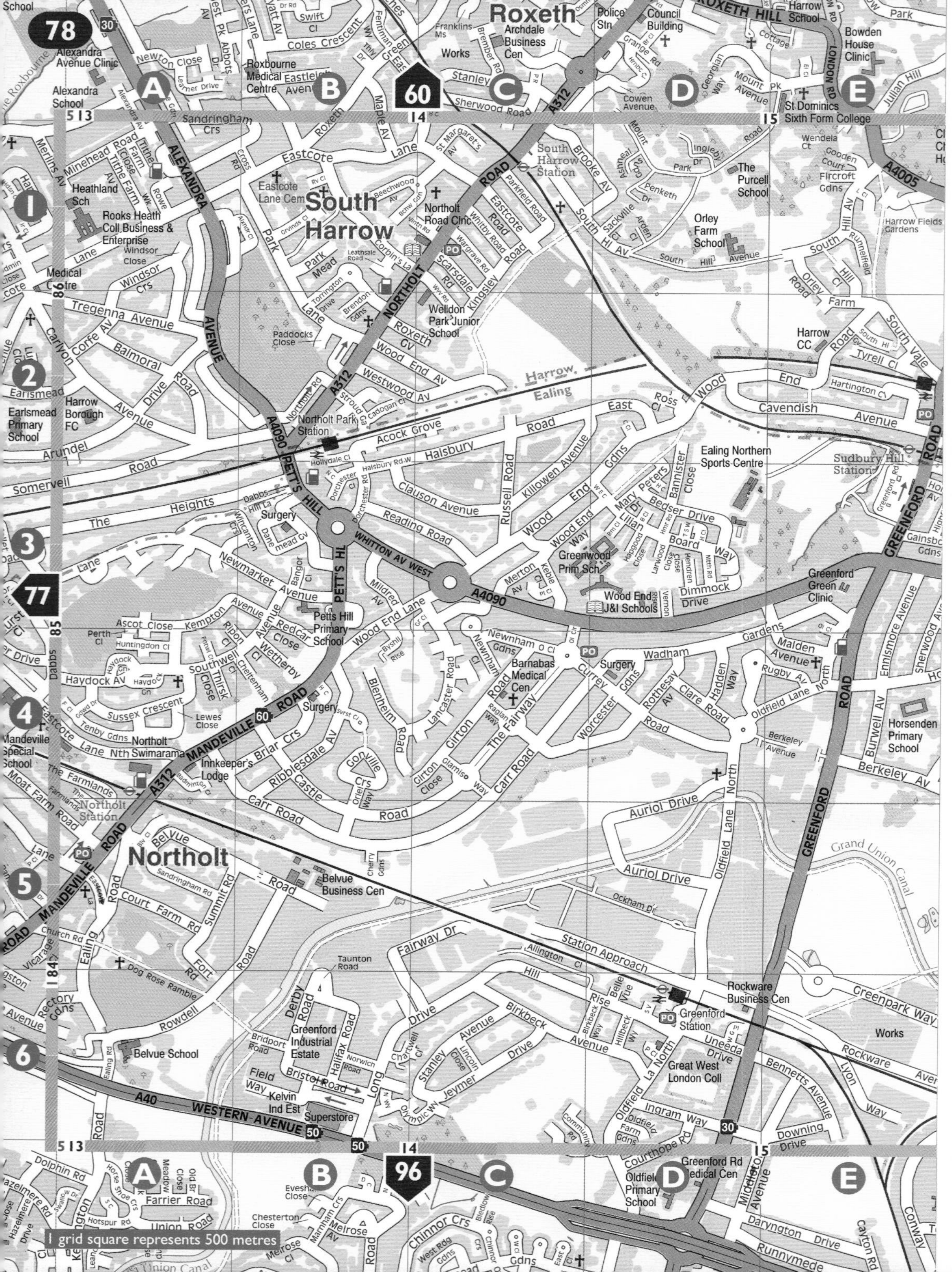

78
77
60
96
A
B
C
D
E
1
2
3
4
5
6
513
14
15
86
85
184
School
Alexandra Avenue Clinic
Alexandra School
Newton Close
Learner Drive
Swift Cl
Coles Crescent
Roxbourne Medical Centre
Eastleigh Avenue
Roxeth
Franklins Ms
Archdale Business Cen
Works
Brember Rd
Stanley
Sherwood Road
Police Stn
Council Building
Roxeth Hill
Harrow School
London Rd
Grange Rd
Cottage Cl
Bowden House Clinic
Julian Hill
Georgian Way
Mount Pk Avenue
St Dominics Sixth Form College
Cowen Avenue
Sandringham Crs
Minehead Road
Farm Cl
Tithe Farm Close
Tithe
Heathland Sch
Rooks Heath Coll Business & Enterprise
Windsor Close
Alexandra Avenue
Cross Rd
Eastcote Lane
Eastcote Lane Cem
South Harrow
Beechwood Av
Northolt Road Clinic
St Margaret's Av
Parkfield Road
Eastcote Road
Whitby Road
Wargrave Rd
Kingsley Road
Scarsdale Rd
Corbin's La
Leathsale Road
Park Mead
Torrington Drive
Brendon Gdns
Welldon Park Junior School
Roxeth Gv
Paddocks Close
Wood End Av
Westwood Av
Stroud Ga
Cadogan Cl
South Harrow Station
Brooke Av
South Hl Av
Sackville Cl
Arden Cl
Ashneal Gdns
Mount Road
Ingleby Dr
Park Dr
Penketh Dr
The Purcell School
Orley Farm School
South Hill Avenue
Wendela Ct
Gooden Court
Fircroft Gdns
A4005
Harrow Fields Gardens
South Hill Av
Runnelfield
Orley Farm Road
Harrow CC
South Vale
Tyrell Cl
Hartington Cl
Cavendish Avenue
Medical Centre
Tregenna Avenue
Windsor Crs
Corfe Av
Balmoral Road
Carlyon
Drive
Avenue
Earlsmead
Earlsmead Primary School
Harrow Borough FC
Arundel Road
Somervell
Harrow
Ealing
Northolt Park Station
A4090
Acock Grove
Halsbury Rd W
Halsbury Road
East Road
Ross Cl
Wood End
Ealing Northern Sports Centre
Bannister Close
Sudbury Hill Station
Greenford Road
Hollydale Cl
Dorchester Rd
Clauson Avenue
Russell Road
Killowen Avenue
Wood End Gdns
Mary Peters Dr
Lilian Dr
Bedser Drive
Board Way
The Heights
Dabbs Hill La
Surgery
Danemead Gv
Pett's Hill
Reading Road
Wood End Way
Greenwood Prim Sch
Whitton Av West
Newmarket Avenue
Bangor Cl
Mildred Av
Merton Av
Keble Cl
Dimmock Drive
Wood End J&I Schools
Vernon
Greenford Green Clinic
Gainsborough Gdns
Lane
Pett's Hill Primary School
Wood End Lane
Ascot Close
Kempton Avenue
Perth Cl
Huntingdon Cl
Ripon Cl
Redcar Close
Wetherby
Southwell Cl
Thirsk Close
Cheltenham
Haydock Av
Haydock Gn
Sussex Crescent
Lewes Close
Tenby Gdns
Northolt Swimarama
Eastcote Lane Nth
Mandeville Special School
Mandeville Road
A312
Innkeeper's Lodge
Briar Crs
Ribblesdale Av
Castle Road
Gonville Crs
Blenheim Road
Lancaster Road
Newnham Gdns
Newnham Cl
Barnabas Medical Cen
Girton Road
Girton Close
The Fairway
Carr Road
Currey
Worcester Gdns
Rothesay Av
Surgery
Wadham Gardens
Malden Avenue
Rugby Av
Clare Road
Hadden Way
Oldfield Lane North
Berkeley Avenue
Ennismore Avenue
Sherwood Avenue
Burwell Av
Horsenden Primary School
Berkeley Av
The Farmlands
Moat Farm Road
Northolt Station
Belvue
Northolt
Sandringham Rd
Summit Rd
Road
Belvue Business Cen
Cherry Gdns
Auriol Drive
Oldfield Lane North
Grand Union Canal
Court Farm Rd
Church Rd
Vicarage
Ealing Road
Fort Rd
Dog Rose Ramble
Rectory Gdns
Rowdell
Belvue School
Ealing Rd
Ockham Dr
Fairway Dr
Allington Cl
Station Approach
Taunton Road
Derby Road
Greenford Industrial Estate
Halifax Road
Bridport Road
Norwich Road
Hill
Rise
Belle Vue
Birkbeck Avenue
Birkbeck Way
Hillbeck Wy
Greenford Station
Rockware Business Cen
Greenpark Way
Works
Rockware Avenue
Uneeda Drive
Great West London Coll
Bennetts Avenue
Lyon Way
Stanley Avenue
Lincoln Close
Drive
Chartwell Ct
Jeymer
Field Way
Bristol Road
Kelvin Ind Est
Superstore
A40 Western Avenue
Long
Olympic Wy
Community
Oldfield La North
Oldfield Farm Gdns
Ingram Way
Courthope Rd
Downing Drive
Greenford Rd Medical Cen
Oldfield Primary School
Middleton Avenue
Darwin Drive
Carlton Rd
Conway
Dolphin Rd
Hazelmere Rd
Horse Shoe Crs
Meadow Close
Old Br Close
Farrier Road
Union Road
Hotspur Rd
Evesham Close
Chesterton Close
Marnham Crs
Melrose Av
Melrose Cl
Chinnor Crs
Bledlow Rise
Oxford Gdns
Runnymede
1 grid square represents 500 metres

Sudbury
Perivale
HA0
Barham Park
Golf Course
Horsenden Hill Golf Club
Sudbury Golf Club
Vale Farm Sports Centre
Wembley FC
Sudbury Court Sports Club
Wembley High Technology College
Sudbury & Harrow Road Station
Sudbury Town Station
Sudbury Hill Harrow Station
North Wembley Station
Alperton Station
Perivale Station
Perivale Industrial Park
Phoenix Trading Est
Athlon Industrial Estate
Alperton Sports Ground
Barham Primary School
Sudbury Primary School
St Georges RC Primary School
Wembley Hospital
Police Station
Fire Station
Ambulance Station
Health Centre
Grand Union Canal
HARROW ROAD
WATFORD ROAD
BRIDGEWATER ROAD
WHITTON AVENUE EAST
SUDBURY COURT DRIVE A4127
EAST LANE
EALING ROAD
61
80
97

62
79
98
A
B
C
D
E
1
2
3
4
5
6
518
19
20
Preston Manor School
FORTY AVENUE
FORTY LANE
A4088
A4140 TUDOR
Gower House School
Sports Ground
Ark Acad
British Transport Police Stn
Superstore
Chalkhill Road
Wembley Park Station
Coll of North West London
Wembley Park
BRIDGE ROAD
Preston Medical Centre
Wembley Synagogue
Buxlow Preparatory School
St Christophers Sch
WEMBLEY PARK DRIVE
HA9
The Gables
Stadium Retail Park
Studios
Stadium Business Cen
Chalkhill Primary School
Wembley Park Business Cen
Wembley Stadium Industrial Estate
Wembley Primary School
Surgery
Wembley Stadium Ind Estate
Quality Hotel
EMPIRE WAY
Olympic Retail Park
Olympic Ind Est
Metro Trading Cen
MSP Business Cen
Works
Hannah Close
King Edward VII Park
WEMBLEY
PARK LANE
A4089
Bingo Hall
Wembley Arena (London 2012 Venue)
Market Area
Olympic Trading Estate
Cannon Trading Est
Towers Business Park
Hallmark Trading Estate
Conference Centre
Stadium Way
Exhibition Halls
Wembley Stadium (London 2012 Venue)
Metro Trading Cen
GREAT CENTRAL WAY
Park Lane Primary School
Royal Route
Pop In Business Cen
Adams Bridge Bus Cen
Stadium Industrial Est
Ibis London Wembley
SOUTH WAY
B4557
WEMBLEY HILL ROAD
B4565
Wembley Stadium Station
Tokyngton Community Centre
HIGH ROAD
Oakington Manor Drive
Oakington Manor School
Wembley Central Station
Copland Specialist Science Coll
St Josephs RC J&I School
Regal International Coll
HARROW RD
Tudor Court North
Tudor Court South
St Raphaels Way Medical Cen
Central Square Shopping Centre
Mosque
Playing Fields
Elsley Primary School
Surgery
Tokyngton
Hazeldene Medical Cen
A404
River Brent
EALING ROAD
Stonebridge Park Station
BRENTFIELD
Bridge Park Business & Leisure Centre
The One Stanley Medical Centre
Alperton Community School
Lyon Park Infant School
Alperton Community Sch
Stanley Works
Our Lady of Lourdes RC Prim Sch
The Princess Royal Distribution Centre
Alperton Station
Abbey Industrial Estate
Northfields Industrial Estate
The Stonebridge Primary School (London Welsh School)
Alperton
CIRCULAR ROAD
Works
Townsend Industrial Estate
Water Road
Premier Park Road
Mill Trading Estate
Grand Union Industrial Estate
Grand Union Canal Walk
Willenfield Road
Bus Park
West Twyford
Queensbury Road
1 grid square represents 500 metres

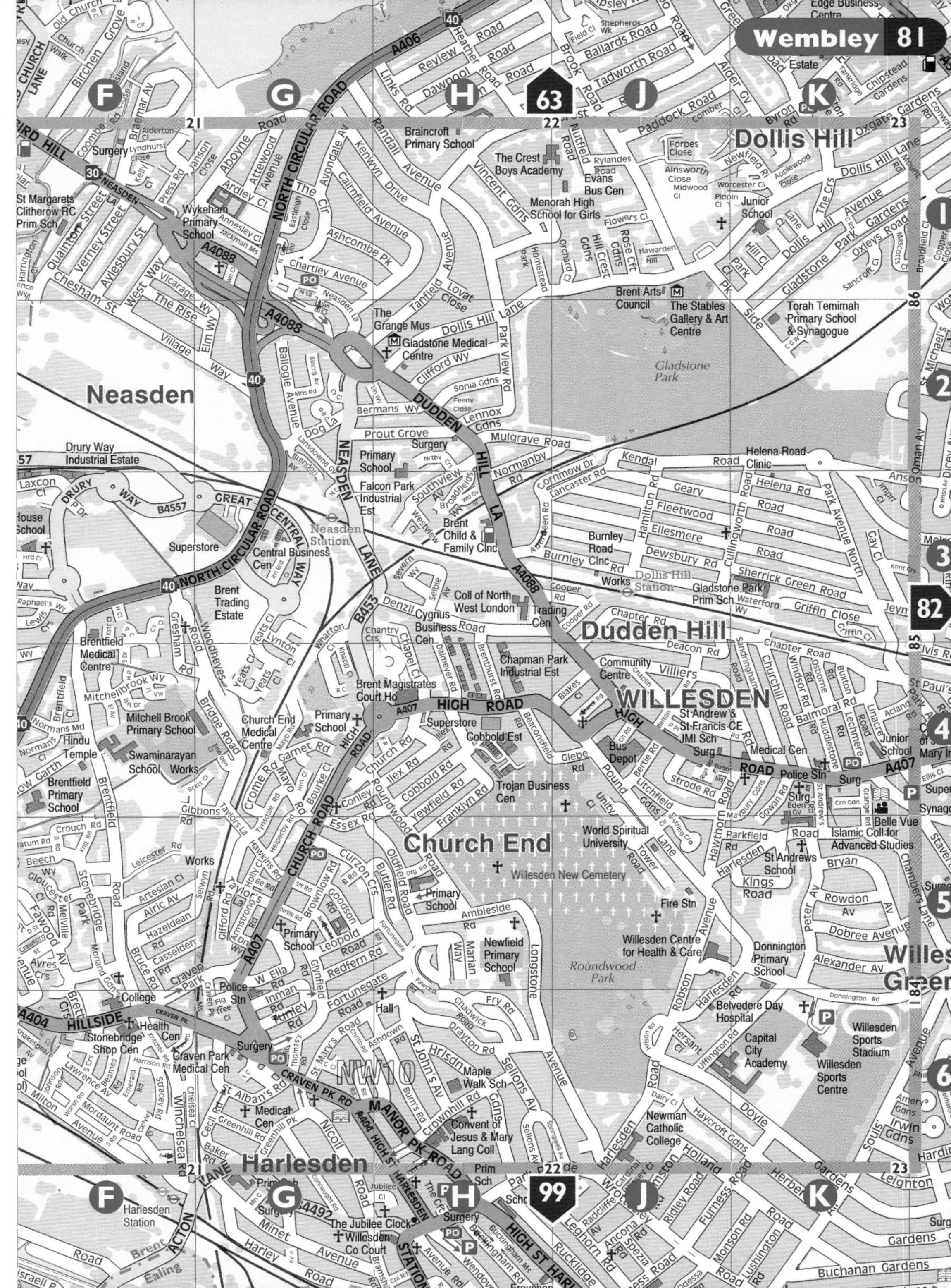
Dollis Hill
Neasden
Dudden Hill
WILLESDEN
Church End
Harlesden
NW10
Gladstone Park
Roundwood Park
Willesden New Cemetery
NORTH CIRCULAR ROAD
DUDDEN HILL LA
HIGH ROAD
CHURCH ROAD
NEASDEN LANE
CRAVEN PK RD
MANOR PK ROAD
HILLSIDE
Neasden Station
Dollis Hill Station
Harlesden Station
Brent Trading Estate
Chapman Park Industrial Est
Drury Way Industrial Estate
Capital City Academy
Willesden Sports Stadium
Willesden Sports Centre
The Crest Boys Academy
Menorah High School for Girls
Brent Magistrates Court Ho
Coll of North West London
Gladstone Park Prim Sch
Newfield Primary School
Donnington Primary School
Belvedere Day Hospital
Willesden Centre for Health & Care
The Stables Gallery & Art Centre
Torah Temimah Primary School & Synagogue
Swaminarayan School
Mitchell Brook Primary School
Brentfield Primary School
Newman Catholic College
Convent of Jesus & Mary Lang Coll
The Jubilee Clock
63
82
99

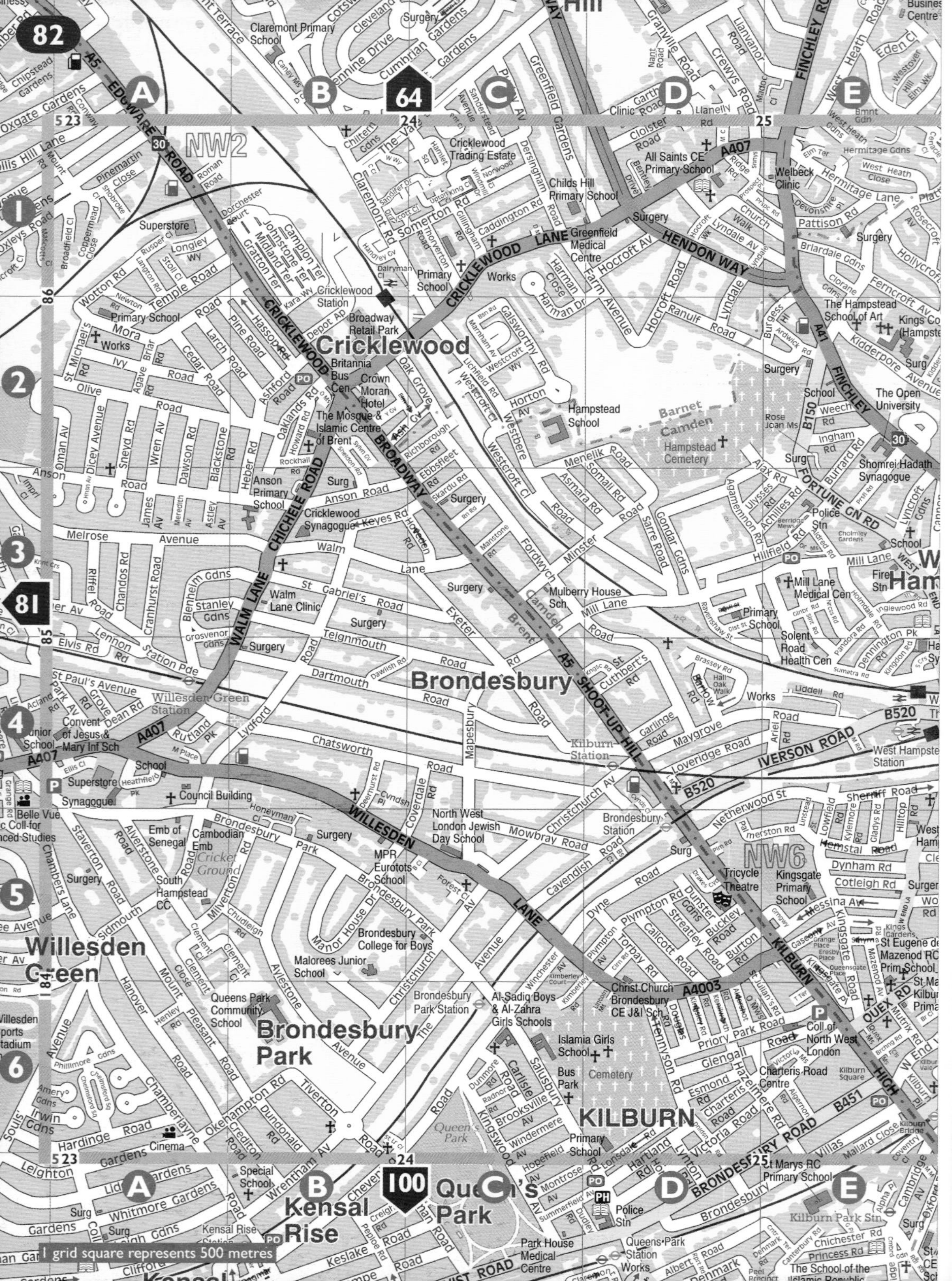

82
64
81
100
A
B
C
D
E
1
2
3
4
5
6
523
24
25
86
85
84
NW2
NW6
Cricklewood
Brondesbury
Willesden Green
Brondesbury Park
KILBURN
Kensal Rise
Queen's Park
EDGWARE ROAD
CRICKLEWOOD BROADWAY
CRICKLEWOOD LANE
HENDON WAY
FINCHLEY ROAD
FORTUNE GN RD
SHOOT-UP HILL
KILBURN HIGH ROAD
WILLESDEN LANE
WALM LANE
CHICHELE ROAD
IVERSON ROAD
BRONDESBURY ROAD
QUEX RD
A5
A41
A407
A4003
B520
B451
B150
Oxgate Gardens
Chipstead Gardens
Claremont Primary School
Cleveland Gardens
Pennine Drive
Cumbrian Gardens
Surgery
Cricklewood Trading Estate
Childs Hill Primary School
Greenfield Medical Centre
All Saints CE Primary School
Welbeck Clinic
Hermitage Lane
West Heath Close
Pattison Rd
Superstore
Temple Road
Cricklewood Station
Broadway Retail Park
Britannia Bus Cen
Crown Moran Hotel
The Mosque & Islamic Centre of Brent
Hampstead School
Hampstead Cemetery
Barnet
Camden
The Hampstead School of Art
The Open University
Shomrei Hadath Synagogue
Kidderpore Avenue
Anson Primary School
Cricklewood Synagogue
Melrose Avenue
Walm Lane Clinic
Mulberry House Sch
Mill Lane
Mill Lane Medical Cen
Police Stn
Fire Stn
Primary School
Solent Road Health Cen
Willesden Green Station
Convent of Jesus & Mary Inf Sch
Kilburn Station
West Hampstead Station
Council Building
Synagogue
Belle Vue
Emb of Senegal
Cambodian Emb
Cricket Ground
South Hampstead CC
North West London Jewish Day School
MPR Eurotots School
Brondesbury Station
Tricycle Theatre
Kingsgate Primary School
Brondesbury College for Boys
Malorees Junior School
Queens Park Community School
Brondesbury Park Station
Al-Sadiq Boys & Al-Zahra Girls Schools
Islamia Girls School
Christ Church Brondesbury CE J&I Sch
Coll of North West London
Charteris Road Centre
St Eugene de Mazenod RC Prim School
Cemetery
Bus Park
Willesden Sports Stadium
Cinema
Special School
St Marys RC Primary School
Police Stn
Kilburn Park Stn
Park House Medical Centre
Queens Park Station
Works
The School of the Islamic Republic
1 grid square represents 500 metres

West Heath
Hampstead Heath
Vale of Health
HAMPSTEAD
Parliament Hill
Parliament Hill Fields Athletics Track
Highgate Ponds
Hampstead Pond
Whitestone Pond
Telegraph Hill
West Hampstead
South Hampstead
Swiss Cottage
Maitland Park
Primrose Hill
St John's Wood
NW3
65
84
101
F
G
H
J
K
I
2
3
4
5
6
26
27
28
86
85
84
NORTH END WAY
SPANIARDS RD
HEATH STREET
Heath Road
West Heath Road
Branch Hill
Redington Road
Templewood Av
Frognal
Frognal Lane
FINCHLEY ROAD
Arkwright Rd
Fitzjohn's Avenue
Maresfield Gdns
Netherhall Gardens
Lyndhurst Road
Rosslyn Hill
A502 HAVERSTOCK HILL
Belsize Park
Belsize Av
Belsize Lane
Belsize Rd
Belsize Sq
Belsize Park Gardens
Lancaster Grove
Eton Av
Eton Road
Fellows Road
Adelaide Road
ADELAIDE RD
HILGROVE ROAD
BELSIZE ROAD
Boundary Road
Abbey Road
Springfield Road
Greville Place
Carlton Hill
Kilburn Priory
Aberdare Gardens
Goldhurst Ter
Canfield Gardens
Compayne Gardens
Broadhurst Gardens
Greencroft Gardens
Fairfax Rd
Harben Rd
Winchester Rd
Avenue Road
Queen's Grove
Norfolk Road
Woronzow Road
Townshend Road
Prince Albert Road
Elsworthy Road
Primrose Hill Rd
King Henry's Road
Englands La
Downside Crs
Agincourt Rd
Fleet Rd
Constantine Rd
Mansfield Road
Nassington Rd
Parliament Hill
Tanza Road
Pond St
Keats Gv
Downshire Hill
Willow Road
Flask Wk
Well Walk
Christchurch Hill
East Heath Road
Church Row
Gayton Rd
Willoughby Rd
Pilgrim's La
Thurlow Road
Wedderburn Rd
Akenside Rd
Ornan Road
Glenilla Road
Howitt Rd
Upper Park Rd
Parkhill Rd
Lawn Road
Fawley Rd
Lithos Rd
Fenton House (NT)
2 Willow Road (NT)
Keats House
Hampstead Stn
Hampstead Heath Stn
Belsize Park Stn
Finchley Road & Frognal Station
West Hampstead Thameslink Station
West Hampstead Station
Finchley Road Station
Swiss Cottage Stn
South Hampstead Station
Kilburn High Road Station
St John's Wood Stn
Chalk Farm Station
Royal Free Hospital School of Medicine
University College School
St Margarets School
Freud Mus
The Portman Clinic
Tavistock Clinic
Central School of Speech & Drama
Hampstead Theatre
Leisure Centre
Odeon
Vue Cinema 02 Centre
London Marriott Hotel
Swiss Cottage School
Jack Taylor School
Ben Uri Gallery London Jewish Mus of Art
Abbey Medical Centre
Quintin Kynaston School Tech Coll
The American School in London
Regent's Park
Regent's Canal
Hampstead Coll of Fine Arts
South Hampstead High Sch
Phoenix School
The Hall School
Hereward House Sch
Trevor Roberts School
Sarum Hall School
St Christophers School
Rosary RC Primary School
Everyman Belsize Park
South Hampstead Synagogue
Belsize Square Synagogue
St Pauls CE Primary School
St Christinas RC Prep Sch
George Eliot Community Prim Sch
Naima Jewish Preparatory School
The Village School
St Dominics RC Primary School
L'Ile Aux Enfants
Council Building
Primrose Hill

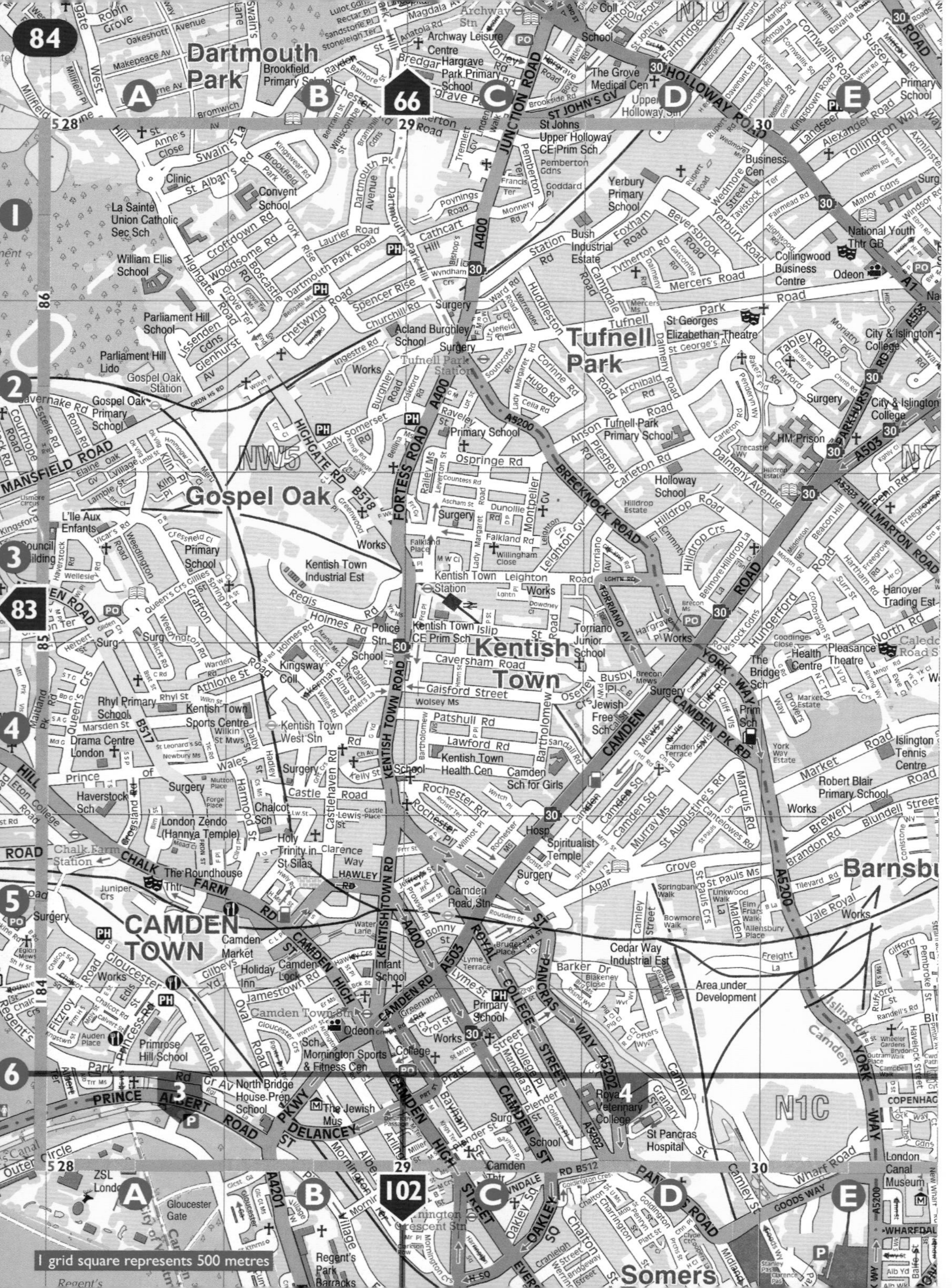

84
Dartmouth Park
Tufnell Park
Gospel Oak
Kentish Town
CAMDEN TOWN
Barnsbury
Somers Town
NW5
N19
N7
N1C
66
83
102
A
B
C
D
E
1
2
3
4
5
6
JUNCTION ROAD
HOLLOWAY ROAD
ST JOHN'S GV
FORTESS ROAD
HIGHGATE RD
MANSFIELD ROAD
BRECKNOCK ROAD
CAMDEN ROAD
YORK WAY
KENTISH TOWN ROAD
CHALK FARM RD
PRINCE ALBERT ROAD
PARKHURST RD
HILLMARTON ROAD
CAMDEN HIGH ST
ROYAL COLLEGE ST
PANCRAS WAY
CAMDEN PK RD
DELANCEY ST
PKWY
GOODS WAY
Archway Leisure Centre
Hargrave Park Primary School
Brookfield Primary School
La Sainte Union Catholic Sec Sch
William Ellis School
Parliament Hill School
Parliament Hill Lido
Gospel Oak Station
Gospel Oak Primary School
Acland Burghley School
Tufnell Park Station
St Georges Elizabethan Theatre
City & Islington College
HM Prison
Holloway School
Anson Tufnell Park Primary School
Kentish Town Industrial Est
Kentish Town CE Prim Sch
Kentish Town Health Cen
Camden Sch for Girls
Kentish Town West Stn
Kentish Town Sports Centre
Drama Centre London
Rhyl Primary School
Haverstock Sch
London Zendo (Hannya Temple)
Holy Trinity in St Silas
The Roundhouse Thtr
Chalk Farm Station
Camden Market
Holiday Inn
Camden Lock
Camden Town Stn
Odeon
Mornington Sports & Fitness Cen
Primrose Hill School
North Bridge House Prep School
The Jewish Mus
Royal Veterinary College
St Pancras Hospital
Cedar Way Industrial Est
Area under Development
London Canal Museum
ZSL London
Gloucester Gate
Regent's Park Barracks
Mornington Crescent Stn
Camden Road Stn
Spiritualist Temple
Robert Blair Primary School
Islington Tennis Centre
Pleasance Theatre
Hanover Trading Est
Torriano Junior School
Jewish Free Sch
Yerbury Primary School
National Youth Thtr GB
Collingwood Business Centre
St Johns Upper Holloway CE Prim Sch
Bush Industrial Estate
The Grove Medical Cen
Upper Holloway Stn
Archway Stn
1 grid square represents 500 metres

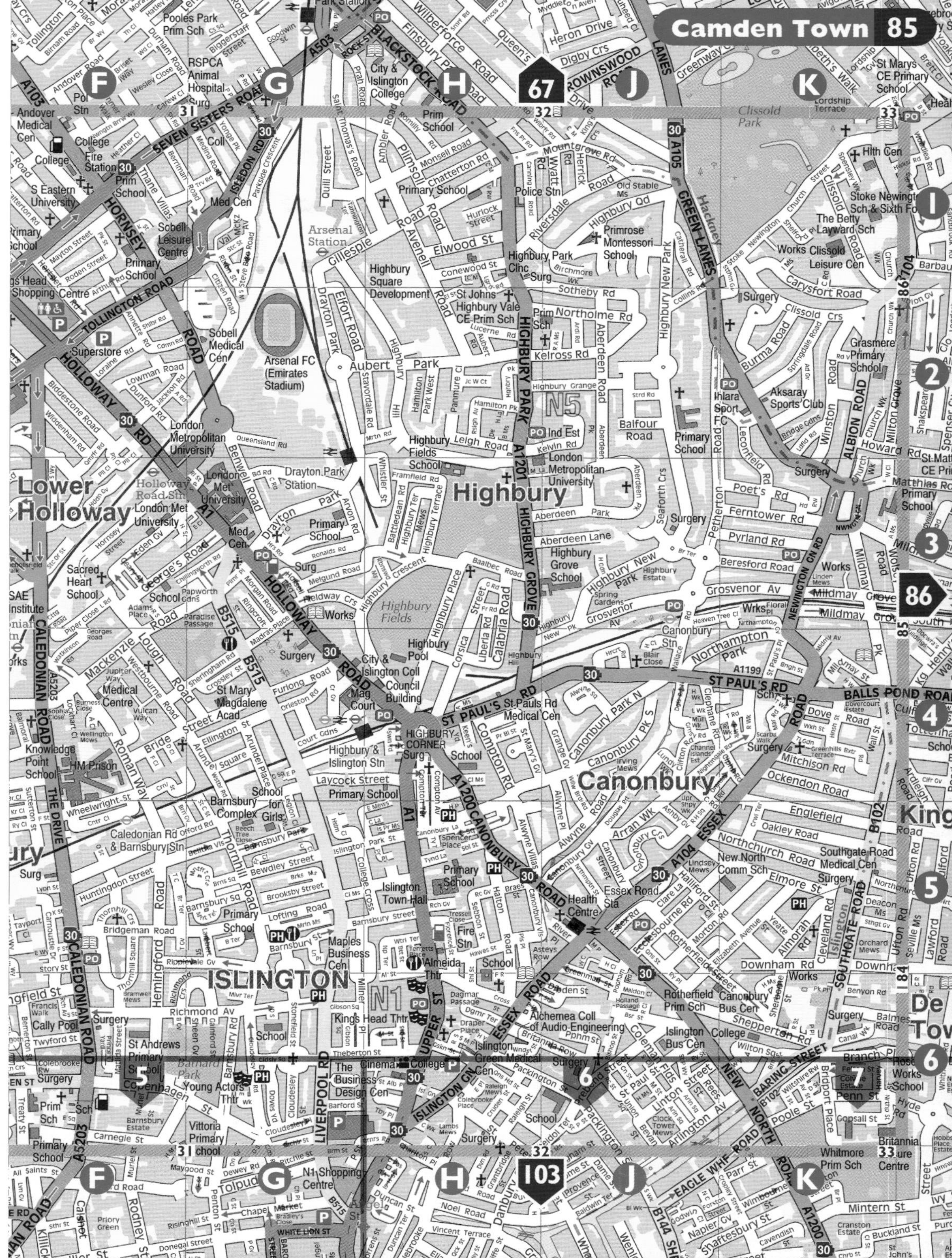

67
86
103
Lower Holloway
Highbury
Canonbury
ISLINGTON
N5
N1
Arsenal FC (Emirates Stadium)
Arsenal Station
Highbury Fields
Clissold Park
Hackney
Highbury & Islington Stn
HIGHBURY CORNER
Canonbury Stn
Drayton Park Station
Holloway Road Stn
Finsbury Park Station
Caledonian Rd & Barnsbury Stn
Essex Road Sta
HM Prison
Islington Town Hall
London Metropolitan University
City & Islington College
Sobell Leisure Centre
Clissold Leisure Cen
Almeida Thtr
Kings Head Thtr
N1 Shopping Centre
SEVEN SISTERS ROAD
HOLLOWAY ROAD
HORNSEY ROAD
TOLLINGTON ROAD
BLACKSTOCK ROAD
HIGHBURY PARK
HIGHBURY GROVE
GREEN LANES
ST PAUL'S RD
BALLS POND ROAD
CALEDONIAN ROAD
THE DRIVE
UPPER ST
LIVERPOOL RD
ESSEX ROAD
CANONBURY ROAD
NEW NORTH ROAD
NEWINGTON GN RD
SOUTHGATE ROAD
ALBION ROAD
BARING STREET
EAGLE WHF ROAD
ROWNSWOOD ROAD
Highbury New Park
Aberdeen Park
Grosvenor Av
Mildmay Grove
Northampton Park
Canonbury Park N
Canonbury Pk S
Ockendon Road
Englefield
Northchurch Road
Downham Rd
Shepperton Rd
Packington St
Barnsbury St
Richmond Av
Copenhagen St
Carnegie St

86
STOKE NEWINGTON
68
A
B
C
D
E
1
2
3
4
5
6
7
85
104
34
35
533
NORTHWOLD ROAD
UPPER CLAPTON ROAD
Mount Pleasant Hill
Southwold Road
Gunton Road
Cleveleys Road
Casimir Road
Clapton Synagogue
Ickburgh Road
Ickburgh School
Reighton Road
Evering Road
Narford Rd
Brooke Road
Jenner Rd
Rectory Road Station
West Hackney Synagogue
Surgery
Fire Station
St Marys CE Primary School
Health Cen
Hlth Cen
Newington Sixth Form
Dumont Rd
Kynaston Rd
Lavers Rd
Dynevor Rd
Oldfield Road
Harcombe Rd
Sandbrook Rd
Barbauld Road
Yorkshire Cl
Victorian Gv
Police Station
STOKE NEWINGTON HIGH ST
STOKE NEWINGTON ROAD
KINGSLAND HIGH ST
KINGSLAND ROAD
A10 MANSE RD
EVERING RD
Benthal Primary School
St Scholasticas RC Prim School
Kenninghall Road
Primary School
B Six Sixth Form College
Nightingale Prim Sch
Della Pth
Downs Road
Downsview School
Shacklewell
Hackney Downs
Mossbourne Community Academy
CRICKETFIELD RD
PEMBURY RD A104
LOWER CLAPTON ROAD
Clarence Road
Millfields Primary School
Athena Medical Centre
Portico City Learning Cen
College
Kings Hall Leisure Centre
Health Cen
URSWICK RD
LWR CLAPTON RD
Police Station
Coroners Court
Sutton House
The City Acad-Hackney
Beatty Rd
Walford Road Synagogue
Mosque
Brighton Rd
Allen Rd
Palatine Av
Palatine Rd
Horizon School
Pr George Road
Belgrade Road
Prs May Rd
Howard Rd
St Matthias CE Prim Sch
Matthias Rd
Primary School
Pellerin Rd
Elton Pl
Arundel Gv
Mildmay Road
Crossway
Boleyn Rd
Qu Margaret's Gv
North
South
St Judes & St Pauls CE Prim Sch
Dalston Kingsland Stn
Foulden Rd
Farleigh Road
Amhurst Rd
Sydner Rd
Shacklewell Rd
Somerford Gv
West Hackney Synagogue
Works
School
The Petchey Academy
Independent Place
Arcola St
Downs Park Road
Cecilia Road
Andre Street
Amhurst Road
Sandringham Road
Montague Rd
Hackney Downs Stn
Brook Comm Prim Sch
DALSTON LANE
A107
AMHURST RD
Marcon Place
Shellness Rd
Hindrey Rd
Kingsland Shopping Cen
Ridley Road
Primary School
Colvestone
Cncl Bldg
BALLS POND ROAD
A104
DALSTON LA
A1207 GRAHAM ROAD
Navarino Rd
Greenwood Rd
Fassett Sq
Hackney Central Stn
MORNING LANE
Superstore
Hackney Empire Variety Thr
Town Hall
Mus
HACKNEY
Darnley Road
Brenthouse Road
Elsdale Street Health Cen
Wilton Way
Culford Ms
Tottenham Road
School
Buckingham Rd
Eagle Mews
Works
Stamford Rd
Kingsland
Dalston Junction Station
E London Christian Choir Sch
Dalston
Forest Road
Richmond Road
Queensbridge Sports Cen
Lenthall Rd
Gayhurst Road
Mapledene Road
Lavender Grove
Middleton Road
QUEENSBRIDGE ROAD
Queensbridge Primary Sch
Albion Drive
Primary School
London Fields Lido
London Fields
London Fields Stn
London Flds East Side
Lansdowne Drive
MARE ST
MARE STREET
Hackney Business Cen
Cordwainers College
Orchard J&I School
WELL ST
A106
Surgery
Tudor Road
Kg Edward's Rd
VICTORIA PARK ROAD
South Hackney
Metropolitan Business Centre
Haggerston Station
Hertford Road
Culford Road
De Beauvoir Road
SOUTHGATE RD
Downham Road
De Beauvoir Town
Shrubland Road
St Pauls with St Michaels CE Prim Sch
Brownlow Road
Pownall Road
Regent's Row
Ada St
Andrews Road
Primary School
Bocking St
Beck Rd
Bush Rd
Ash Grove
Works
Northiam St
School
Orsman Road
Mill Row
Phillipp St
Mosque
Rosemary Works School
The Bridge Academy
Dunston Rd
Haggerston Swimming Pool
Whiston Rd
Whiston Road
Dove Row
Nuttall St
Britannia Leis Centre
Haggerston
Primary School
How's Street
Hackney City Farm
Teale Street
Pritchard's Rd
Emma St
Peterley Bus Cen
Parmiter Ind Cen
Primary School
BISHOP'S WAY
St Elizabeths RC Prim Sch
London Chest Hosp
Cambridge Heath Stn
College
Coate St
Days Hotel
Mosque
A1208
Hoxton
Museum
Mintern St
Purcell St
Hare Walk
Kingsland
Geffrye St
Ormsby St
Thurtle Road
Kent St
1 grid square represents 500 metres

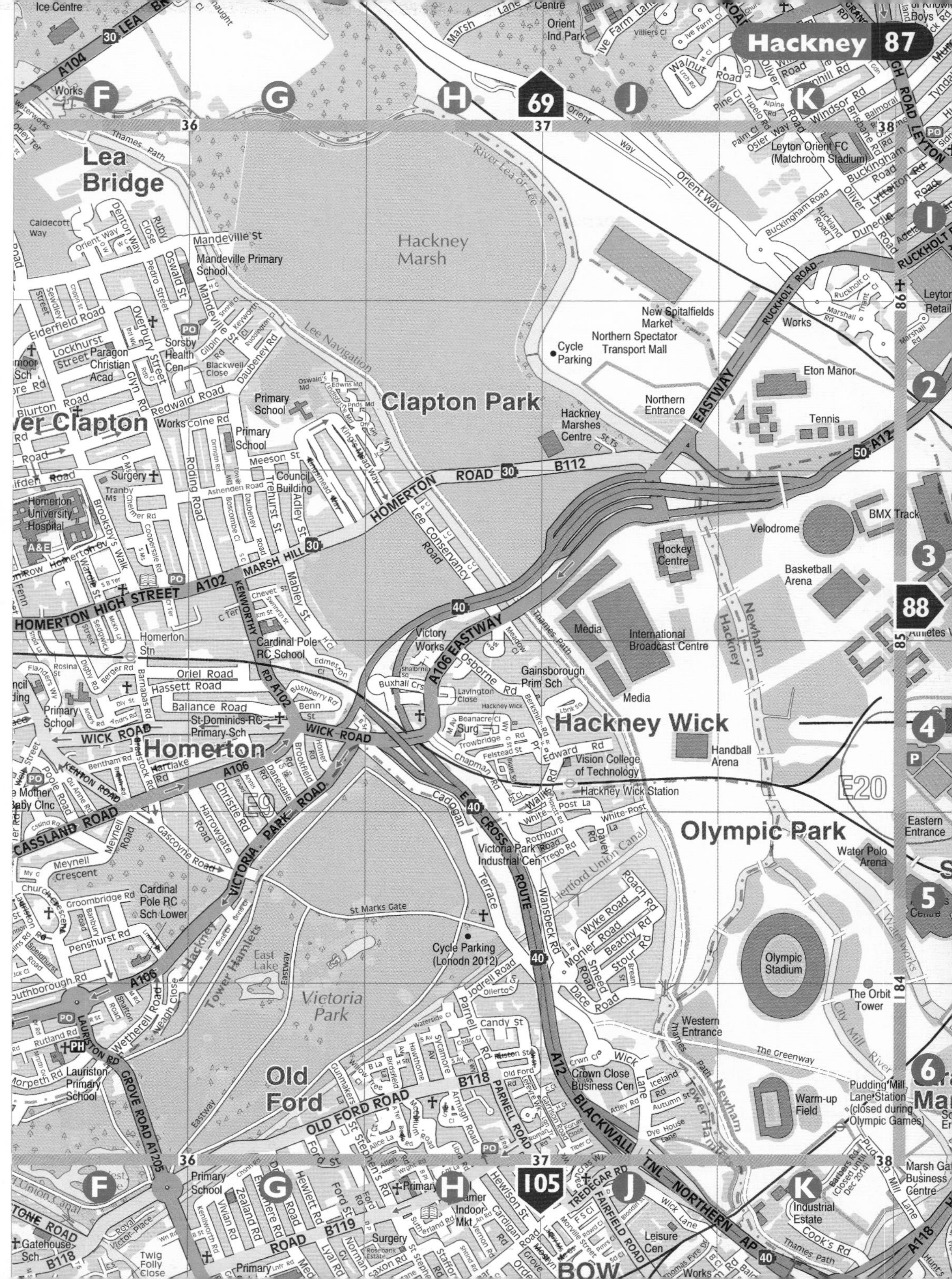

Lea Bridge
Hackney Marsh
Clapton Park
Homerton
Hackney Wick
Olympic Park
Old Ford
Victoria Park
BOW
E9
E20
Leyton Orient FC (Matchroom Stadium)
New Spitalfields Market
Northern Spectator Transport Mall
Cycle Parking
Eton Manor
Northern Entrance
Tennis
Hackney Marshes Centre
Mandeville Primary School
Sorsby Health Cen
Paragon Christian Acad
Homerton University Hospital
A&E
Velodrome
BMX Track
Hockey Centre
Basketball Arena
Media
International Broadcast Centre
Gainsborough Prim Sch
Handball Arena
Vision College of Technology
Hackney Wick Station
Homerton Stn
Cardinal Pole RC School
Cardinal Pole RC Sch Lower
St Dominics RC Primary Sch
Victory Works
Victoria Park Industrial Cen
Eastern Entrance
Water Polo Arena
Olympic Stadium
The Orbit Tower
Western Entrance
Warm-up Field
Pudding Mill Lane Station (closed during Olympic Games)
Crown Close Business Cen
Cycle Parking (Lonodn 2012)
East Lake
The Greenway
Lauriston Primary School
Marsh Gate Business Centre
Industrial Estate
Leisure Cen
Roman Indoor Mkt
HOMERTON HIGH STREET
A102
MARSH HILL
HOMERTON ROAD
B112
A12
EASTWAY
A106 EASTWAY
RUCKHOLT ROAD
WICK ROAD
VICTORIA PARK ROAD
CASSLAND ROAD
KENTON ROAD
KENWORTHY RD A102
EAST CROSS ROUTE
A12 BLACKWALL TNL NORTHERN AP
OLD FORD ROAD
B118
PARNELL ROAD
GROVE ROAD A1205
LAURISTON RD
Orient Way
River Lea or Lee
Lee Navigation
Hertford Union Canal
Thames Path
Lee Conservancy Road
Wansbeck Rd
Wick Lane
Tower Hamlets
Hackney
Newham
F
G
H
J
K
69
88
105
36
37
38
84
85
86
2
3
4
5
6

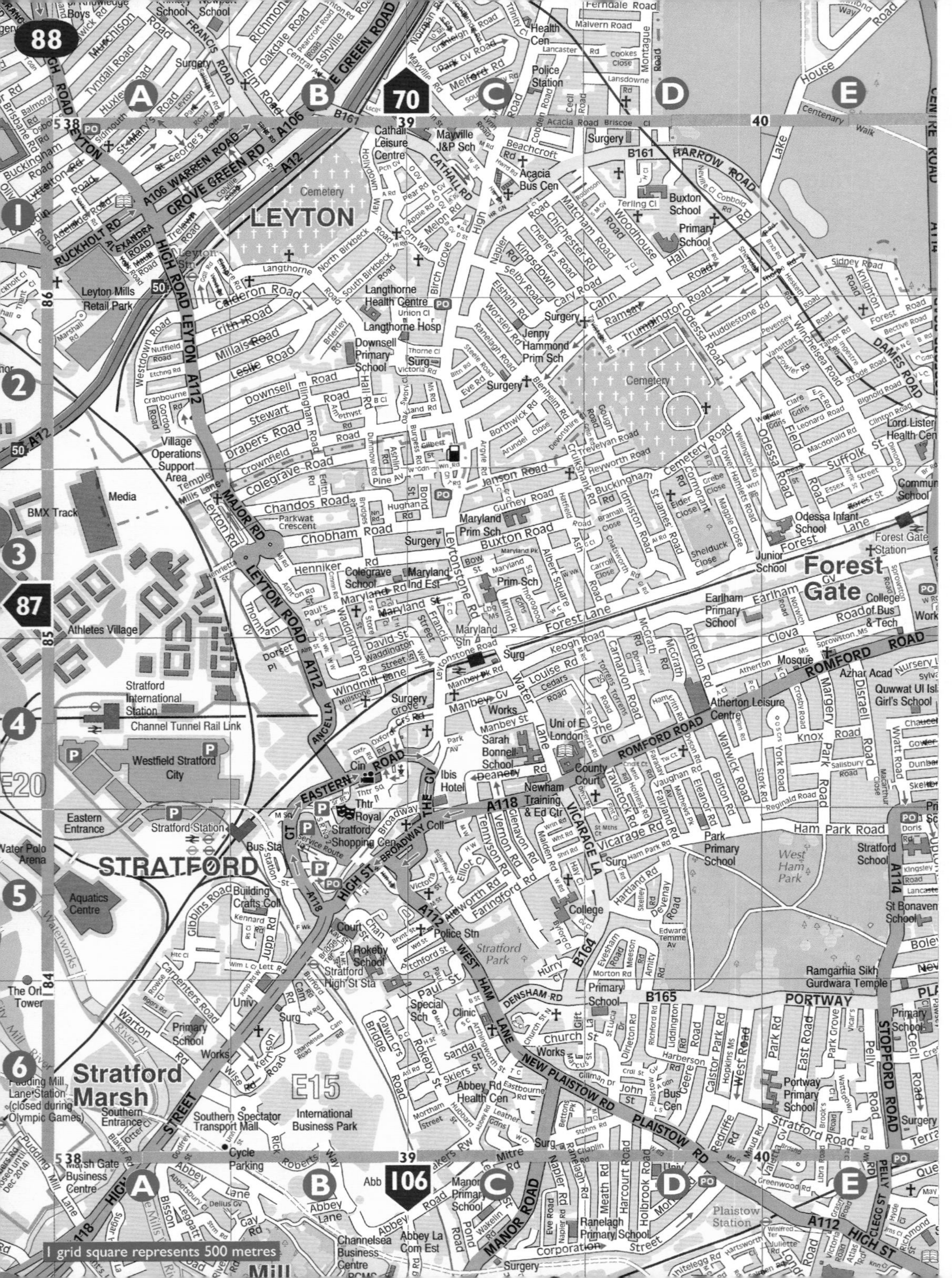
88
70
87
106
A
B
C
D
E
1
2
3
4
5
6
38
39
40
86
85
84
LEYTON
STRATFORD
Forest Gate
Stratford Marsh
E20
E15
HIGH ROAD LEYTON
A112
A106 WARREN ROAD
GROVE GREEN RD
A12
A106
B161
RUCKHOLT RD
LEYTON ROAD
MAJOR RD
ANCELL LA
EASTERN ROAD
HIGH ST
BROADWAY
THE GV
A118
WEST HAM LANE
NEW PLAISTOW RD
PLAISTOW RD
MANOR ROAD
ROMFORD ROAD
VICARAGE LA
B164
B165
DENSHAM RD
PORTWAY
STOPFORD ROAD
HARROW ROAD
DAMES ROAD
A114
HIGH ST
STREET
Cemetery
Leyton Mills Retail Park
Village Operations Support Area
Media
BMX Track
Athletes Village
Stratford International Station
Channel Tunnel Rail Link
Westfield Stratford City
Eastern Entrance
Stratford Station
Water Polo Arena
Aquatics Centre
Southern Spectator Transport Mall
Southern Entrance
Cycle Parking
Pudding Mill Lane Station (closed during Olympic Games)
The Orbit Tower
Marsh Gate Business Centre
International Business Park
Channelsea Business Centre
Abbey La Com Est
Manor Primary School
Ranelagh Primary School
Plaistow Station
Stratford Park
West Ham Park
Ham Park Road
Park Primary School
Portway Primary School
Ramgarhia Sikh Gurdwara Temple
Stratford School
St Bonaventure's School
Atherton Leisure Centre
Uni of E London
County Court
Newham Training & Ed Ctr
Sarah Bonnell School
Ibis Hotel
Stratford Shopping Cen
Thtr Royal
Coll
Police Stn
Rokeby School
Stratford High St Sta
Building Crafts Coll
Langthorne Health Centre
Langthorne Hosp
Downsell Primary School
Jenny Hammond Prim Sch
Maryland Prim Sch
Colegrave School
Maryland Ind Est
Maryland Stn
Odessa Infant School
Junior School
Earlham Primary School
College of Bus & Tech
Forest Gate Station
Lord Lister Health Cen
Buxton School
Primary School
Acacia Bus Cen
Mayville J&P Sch
Cathall Leisure Centre
Health Cen
Police Station
Mosque
Azhar Acad
Quwwat Ul Islam Girl's School
Abbey Rd Health Cen
Special Sch
Clinic
Bus Cen
Surgery
1 grid square represents 500 metres

Stratford 89
71
90
107
F
G
H
J
K
I
2
3
4
5
6
Wanstead Flats
Aldersbrook Road
Forest Drive
A116
A117
A118
A124
B165
B167
B109
Centenary Walk
City of London Cemetery
City of London Crematorium
Manor Park Crematorium
Manor Park Cemetery
Manor Park Station
Manor Park
Woodgrange Park Cemetery
Woodgrange Park Stn
Plashet Jewish Cemetery
Plashet
Plashet Park
Upton
Upton Park
Upton Park Station
East Ham Stn
Wanstead Park Stn
Romford Road
Ilford Rd
Romford Rd
North Circular Road
Woodgrange Rd
Woodford Road
Upton La
Green Street
High St North
Station Rd
Rabbits Rd
Forest View Road
Carlyle Road
Durham Road
Clarence Road
Sebert Road
Hampton Road
Osborne Road
Claremont Road
Windsor Road
Richmond Road
Balmoral Road
Capel Road
Tylney Road
Lorne Road
Cranmer Road
Godwin Road
Latimer Road
Ridley Road
Sherrard Road
Halley Road
Monega Road
Strone Road
Shrewsbury Road
Katherine Road
Plashet Grove
Plashet Road
Barking Road
Ron Leighton Way
East Avenue
Browning Rd
Church Rd
Little Ilford Lane
Dersingham Avenue
Sheringham Avenue
Shakespeare Crescent
Southend Road
Burges Road
Lathom Road
Clements Road
Caulfield Road
Caledon Road
Skeffington Road
Kempton Road
Stamford Road
Oakfield Road
Wakefield St
Milton Avenue
Heigham Road
Elizabeth Road
Victoria Avenue
Grangewood Street
Lincoln Road
Kensington Avenue
Gladstone Avenue
Sibley Grove
Sheridan Road
Morris Av
Chesterford Rd
Rectory Rd
Essex Primary School
Little Ilford School
Dersingham Primary School
St Winefrides Cath Prim Sch
Sheringham Junior School
London Sri Murugan Temple
Dashmesh Darbar Sikh Temple
Ravandos Sikh Temple
Sir John Heron Prim Sch
London Christian Learning Cen Prim Sch
Avenue Primary School
Monega Primary School
Katherine Road Medical Centre
Health Cen
Iman Zakaria Academy
Police Station
Woodgrange Infant School
Godwin Junior Sch
Kubrick Business Estate
St Angela's Ursuline Sch
St Bonaventures Sixth Form Centre
Elmhurst Primary School
Plashet Road Medical Centre
Upton Cross Primary School
Shrewsbury Road Health Centre
East Ham Memorial Hospl
Grangewood Independent Sch
Cleves Primary School
Lathom Junior School
Altmore Infant School
Hartley Prim School
East Ham Leisure Cen
Newham College of FE
West Ham United FC (Upton Park)
Newham Medical Centre
Plaistow Prim Sch
Southern Rd Prim School
Plaistow Hosp
St Michaels RC Primary School
Lister Community School
Primary School
Surgery
Works
Mosque
The Warren

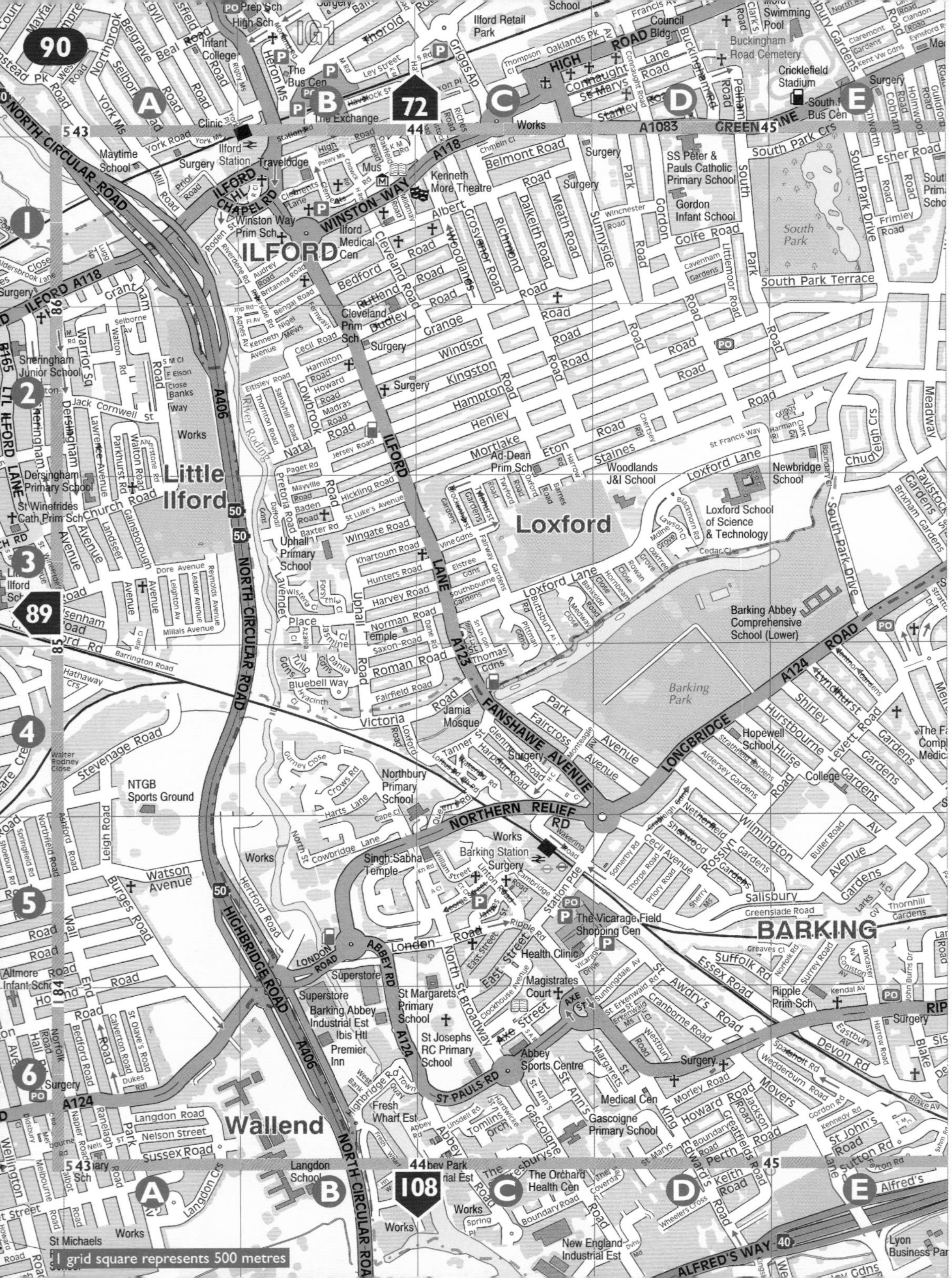
ILFORD
Little Ilford
Loxford
BARKING
Wallend
1 grid square represents 500 metres

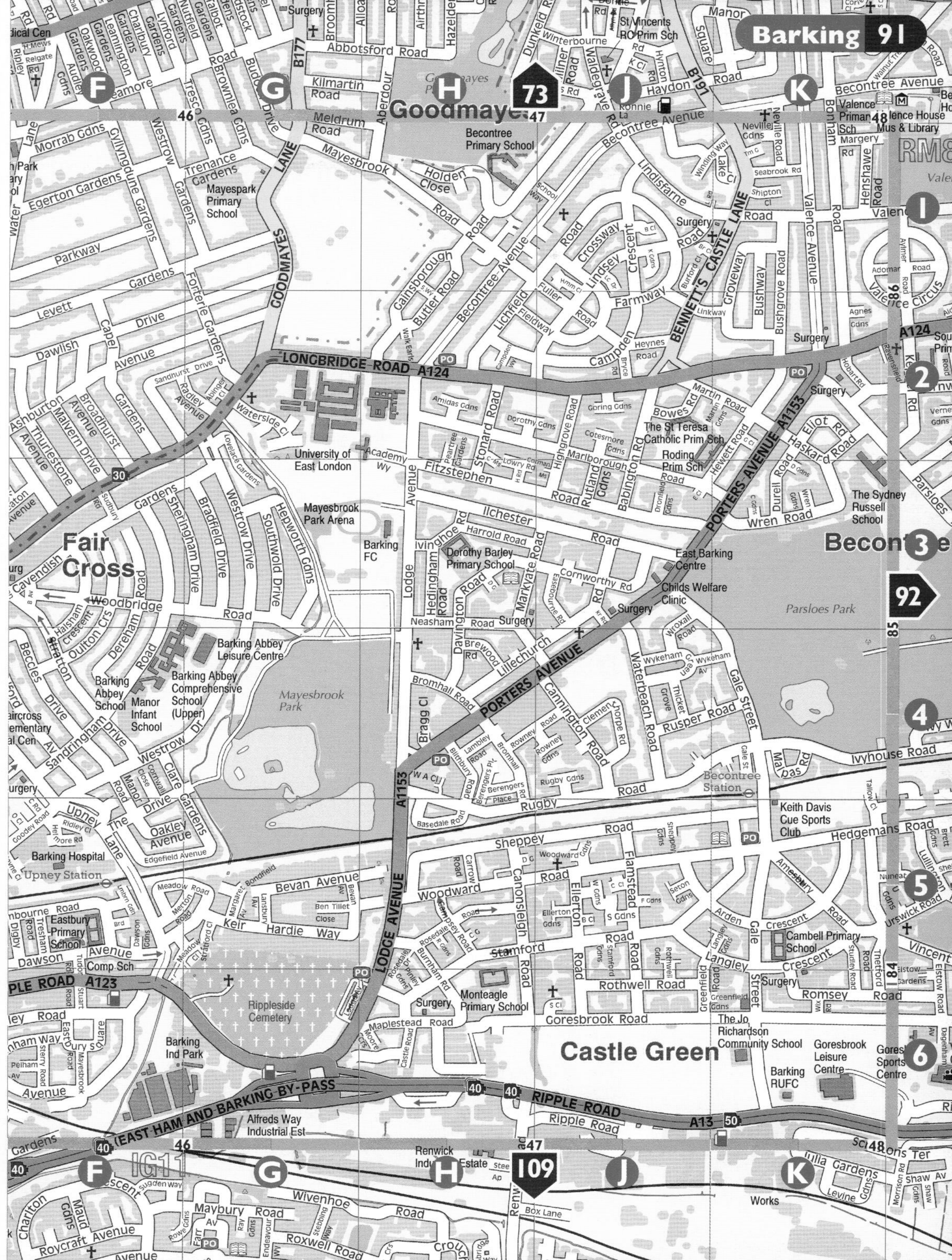

Barking 91
Goodmayes
Fair Cross
Becontree
Castle Green
73
92
109
RM8
IG11
F
G
H
J
K
1
2
3
4
5
6
46
47
48
84
85
86
LONGBRIDGE ROAD A124
PORTERS AVENUE A1153
PORTERS AVENUE
LODGE AVENUE
A1153
GOODMAYES LANE
BENNETT'S CASTLE LANE
EAST HAM AND BARKING BY-PASS
RIPPLE ROAD
A13
RIPPLE ROAD A123
A124
B177
B191
Becontree Avenue
Abbotsford Road
Kilmartin Road
Meldrum Road
Mayesbrook Road
Haydon Road
Winterbourne Rd
St Vincents RC Prim Sch
Becontree Primary School
Mayespark Primary School
Morrab Gdns
Egerton Gardens
Parkway
Levett Gardens
Capel Avenue
Drive
Dawlish
Ashburton Avenue
Thurlestone Avenue
Malvern Drive
Broadhurst Gardens
Forterie Gardens
Westrow Gardens
Trenance Gardens
Gyllyngdune Gardens
Holden Close
Gainsborough Road
Butler Road
Lichfield Road
Fieldway
Fuller Road
Lindsey Road
Crescent
Crossway
Farmway
Campden Crescent
Heynes Road
Lindisfarne Road
Groveway
Bushway
Bushgrove Road
Valence Avenue
Henshawe Road
Valence Circus
Valence House Mus & Library
Valence Primary Sch
Surgery
University of East London
Academy Wy
Fitzstephen Road
Stonard Road
Highgrove Road
Dorothy Gdns
Goring Gdns
Cotesmore Gdns
Marlborough Road
Rutland Gdns
Babington Rd
Bowes Rd
Martin Road
The St Teresa Catholic Prim Sch
Roding Prim Sch
Hewett Road
Eliot Rd
Haskard Road
The Sydney Russell School
Parsloes Park
Parsloes
Wren Road
Durell Road
Ilchester Road
Harrold Road
Ivinghoe Rd
Dorothy Barley Primary School
Markyate Road
Cornworthy Rd
East Barking Centre
Childs Welfare Clinic
Mayesbrook Park Arena
Barking FC
Mayesbrook Park
Hepworth Gdns
Southwold Drive
Westrow Drive
Bradfield Drive
Sheringham Drive
Woodbridge Road
Dereham Road
Oulton Crs
Halsham Crescent
Stratton Drive
Beccles Drive
Sandringham Drive
Westrow Dr
Barking Abbey Leisure Centre
Barking Abbey School
Manor Infant School
Barking Abbey Comprehensive School (Upper)
Manor Road
Clare Gardens
Oakley Avenue
Upney Lane
Barking Hospital
Upney Station
Edgefield Avenue
Neasham Road
Hedingham Road
Davington Road
Brewood Rd
Lillechurch Road
Bromhall Road
Bragg Cl
Cannington Road
Waterbeach Road
Wykeham Av
Wroxall Road
Grove
Thicket
Rusper Road
Gale Street
Malbas Rd
Ivyhouse Road
Becontree Station
Rugby Road
Rugby Gdns
Rowney Road
Basedale Road
Berengers Place
Keith Davis Cue Sports Club
Hedgemans Road
Sheppey Road
Woodward Road
Canonsleigh Road
Ellerton Road
Flamstead Road
Amesbury Road
Arden Crescent
Langley Crescent
Cambell Primary School
Stamford Road
Rothwell Road
Romsey Road
Goresbrook Road
Monteagle Primary School
Rippleside Cemetery
Maplestead Road
Bevan Avenue
Ben Tillet Close
Keir Hardie Way
Eastbury Primary School
Dawson Avenue
Comp Sch
Eastbury Square
Barking Ind Park
Alfreds Way Industrial Est
Renwick Industrial Estate
The Jo Richardson Community School
Goresbrook Leisure Centre
Barking RUFC
Gores Sports Centre
Julia Gardens
Works
Wivenhoe Road
Maybury Road
Roycraft Avenue
Roxwell Road
Box Lane
Vincent
Urswick Road
Fair Cross

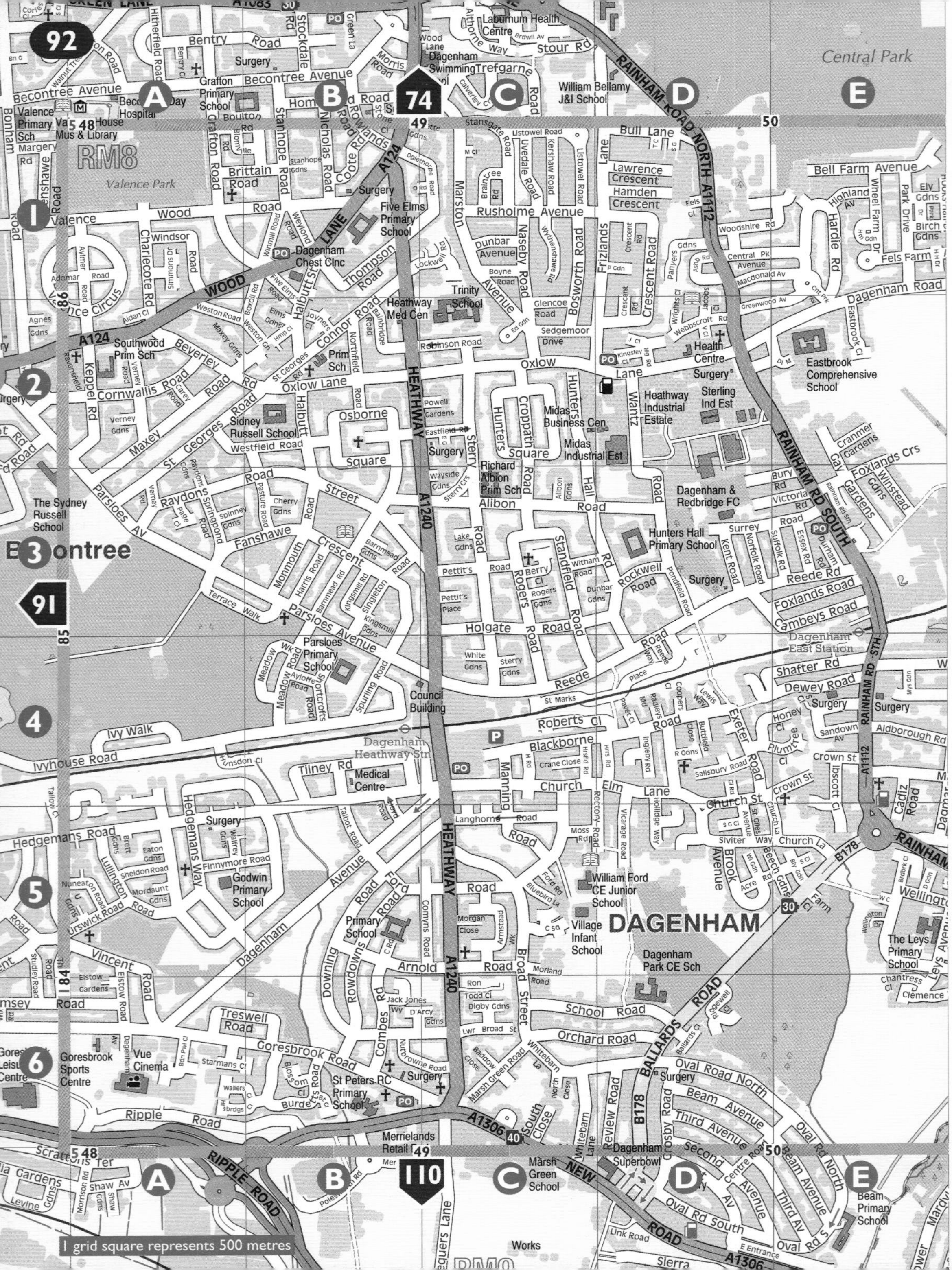
92
74
91
110
Central Park
Valence Park
RM8
Becontree
DAGENHAM
Dagenham East Station
Dagenham Heathway Stn
Dagenham & Redbridge FC
Eastbrook Comprehensive School
Hunters Hall Primary School
Parsloes Primary School
William Ford CE Junior School
Village Infant School
Dagenham Park CE Sch
Goresbrook Sports Centre
Vue Cinema
St Peters RC Primary School
Godwin Primary School
Five Elms Primary School
Trinity School
Sydney Russell School
The Sydney Russell School
Richard Alibon Prim Sch
Heathway Industrial Estate
Sterling Ind Est
Midas Business Cen
Midas Industrial Est
Council Building
Medical Centre
Merrielands Retail
Dagenham Superbowl
Marsh Green School
Beam Primary School
The Leys Primary School
HEATHWAY
A1240
RAINHAM ROAD NORTH A1112
RAINHAM RD SOUTH
BALLARDS ROAD
RIPPLE ROAD
NEW ROAD
A1306
1 grid square represents 500 metres

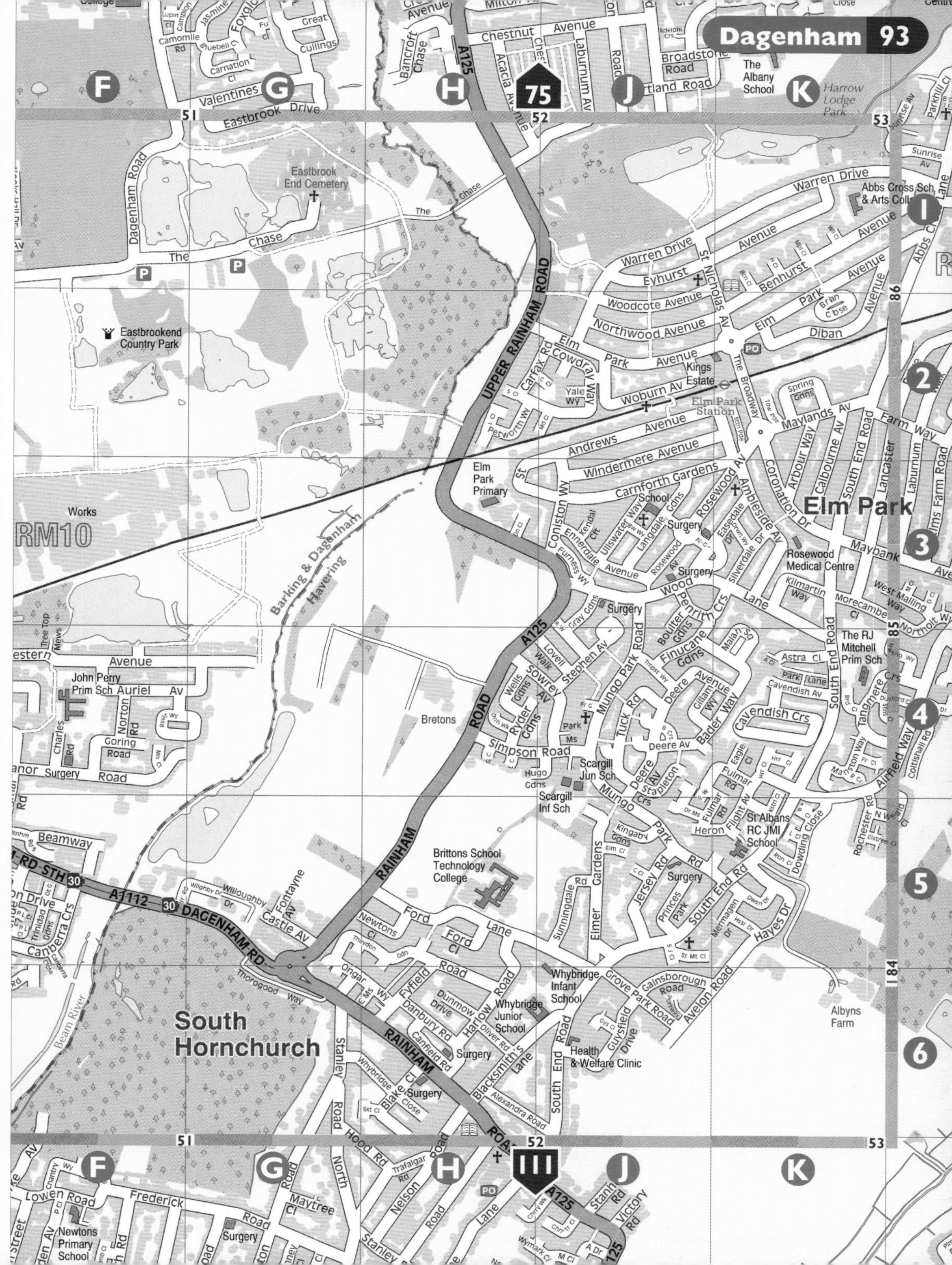

75
111
Chestnut Avenue
Laburnum Av
Broadstone Road
The Albany School
Harrow Lodge Park
Valentines
Eastbrook Drive
Eastbrook End Cemetery
The Chase
Dagenham Road
Eastbrookend Country Park
Upper Rainham Road
A125
Warren Drive
Abbs Cross Sch & Arts Coll
Eyhurst Av
Benhurst Av
St Nicholas Av
Woodcote Avenue
Northwood Avenue
Elm Park Avenue
Diban
Kings Estate
Woburn Av
Elm Park Station
The Broadway
Maylands Av
Farm Way
St Andrews Avenue
Windermere Avenue
Carnforth Gardens
Elm Park Primary
Coronation Dr
Arbour Way
Calbourne Av
South End Road
Lancaster
Elm Park
Works
RM10
Barking & Dagenham
Havering
Coniston Wy
Rosewood Av
Ambleside Av
Rosewood Medical Centre
Maybank Ave
Kilmartin Way
Morecambe Cl
West Malling Way
Northolt Wy
Wood Lane
Penrith Crs
Surgery
Mungo Park Road
The RJ Mitchell Prim Sch
Cavendish Crs
Tangmere Crs
Airfield Way
Western Avenue
John Perry Prim Sch
Auriel Av
Bretons
Simpson Road
Scargill Jun Sch
Scargill Inf Sch
Deere Av
Bader Way
St Albans RC JMI School
Dowding Close
Beamway
Rainham Road
A1112
Dagenham Rd
Brittons School Technology College
Ford Lane
Castle Av
Fortayne Av
Canberra Crs
Willoughby Dr
Sunningdale Rd
Elmer Gardens
Jersey Rd
Princes Park
South End Rd
Hayes Dr
South Hornchurch
Beam River
Thorogood Way
Fyfield Road
Dunmow Drive
Harlow Road
Whybridge Infant School
Whybridge Junior School
Gainsborough Road
Avelon Road
Grove Park Road
Guysfield Drive
Health & Welfare Clinic
Blacksmith's Lane
Albyns Farm
Stanley Road
Blake Cl
Alexandra Road
Hood Rd
Trafalgar Rd
Nelson Road
North Road
Frederick Road
Lowen Road
Newtons Primary School
Maytree Cl
Victory Rd
51
52
53
84
85
86
F
G
H
J
K
1
2
3
4
5
6

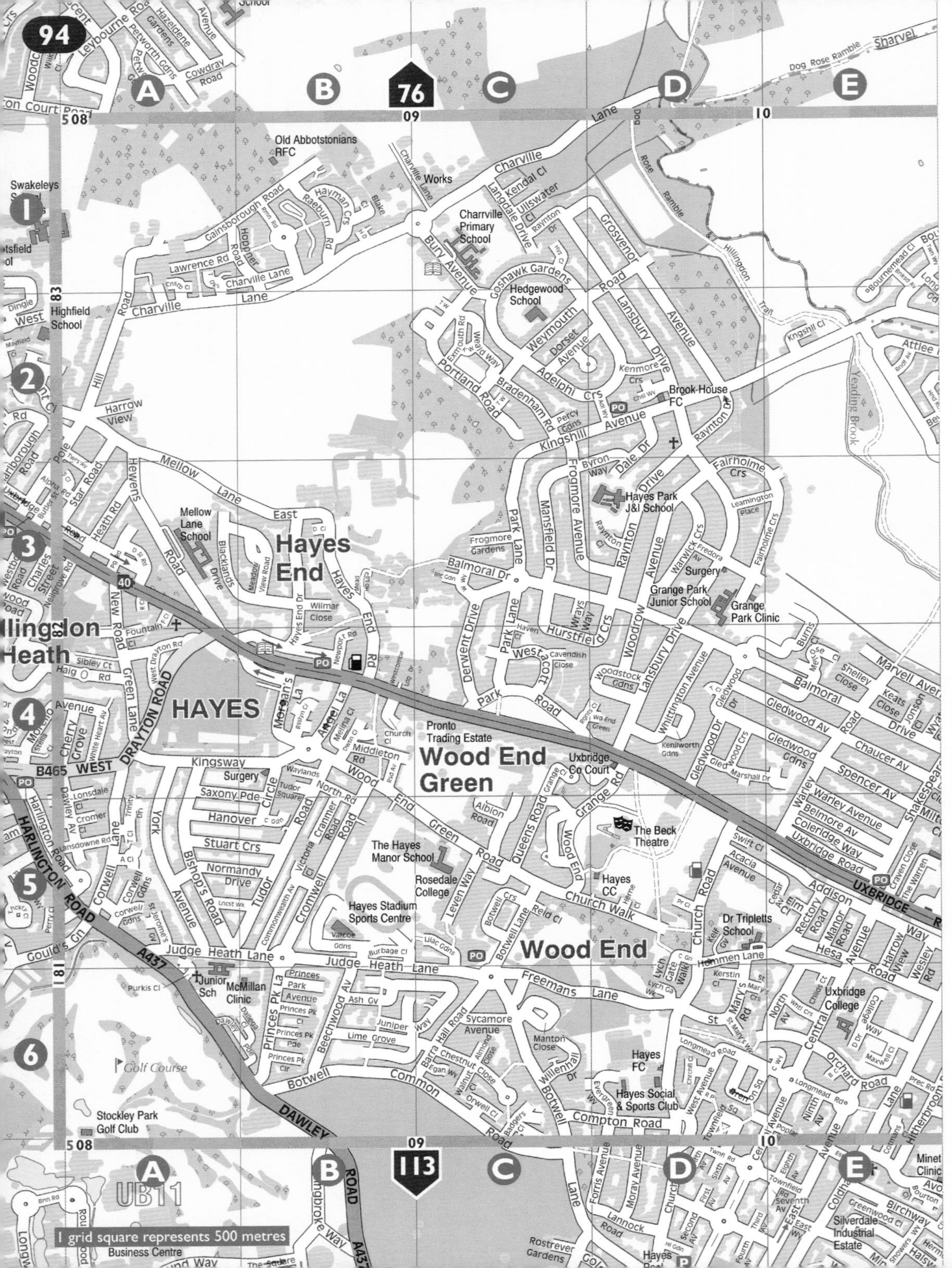
94
76
113
A
B
C
D
E
1
2
3
4
5
6
508
09
10
83
82
81
Dog Rose Ramble
Sharvel
Charville Lane
Old Abbotstonians RFC
Works
Swakeleys School
Highfield School
Gainsborough Road
Hayman Crs
Raeburn Rd
Hoppner Road
Lawrence Rd
Charville Lane
Charrville Primary School
Bury Avenue
Langdale Drive
Kendal Cl
Ullswater Cl
Raynton Dr
Grosvenor Road
Goshawk Gardens
Hedgewood School
Weymouth Road
Dorset Avenue
Lansbury Drive
Avenue
Hillingdon Trail
Bournemead Cl
Kingshill Cl
Attlee
Yeading Brook
Exmouth Rd
Weald Way
Portland Road
Bradenham Rd
Adelphi Crs
Kenmore Crs
Brook House FC
Raynton Dr
Percy Gdns
Kingshill Avenue
Byron Way
Dale Dr
Fairholme Crs
Leamington Place
Hayes Park J&I School
Frogmore Gardens
Park Lane
Mansfield Dr
Frogmore Avenue
Raynton Cl
Raynton Drive
Woodrow Avenue
Warwick Crs
Fredora Av
Surgery
Grange Park Junior School
Grange Park Clinic
Fairholme Crs
Balmoral Dr
Derwent Drive
Wrays Way
Hurstfield Crs
Lansbury Drive
Burns
Harrow View
Mellow Lane
East
Mellow Lane School
Hayes End
Blacklands Drive
Meadow View Road
Hayes End Dr
Hayes End Rd
Wilmar Close
Star Road
Heath Rd
Hewens Road
New Road
Hillingdon Heath
Fountain Cl
Sibley Ct
Haig Rd
Green Lane
West Drayton Road
Newport Rd
Westcombe
West Acott
Cavendish Close
Woodstock Gdns
Whittington Avenue
Gledwood Dr
Balmoral
Shelley Close
Keats Close
Marvell Ave
Gledwood Av
Road
Drive
HAYES
Morgan's La
Angel La
Melina Cl
Church Cl
Pronto Trading Estate
Wood End Green
Middleton Rd
Kingsway
Surgery
Saxony Pde
Hanover
Circle
Tudor Square
Wood End Green Road
Uxbridge Co Court
Grange Rd
Kenilworth Gdns
Gledwood Crs
Gledwood Gdns
Marshall Dr
Chaucer Av
Spencer Av
Warley Avenue
Belmore Av
Coleridge Way
Uxbridge Road
B465
WEST
DRAYTON ROAD
Harlington Road
Lonsdale
Cromer
Dawley Av
Lansdowne Rd
Stuart Crs
Normandy Drive
Bishop's Road
Tudor
Victoria Road
Cranmer Road
Albion Road
Queens Road
Wood End
The Beck Theatre
Swift Cl
Acacia Avenue
The Hayes Manor School
Rosedale College
Leven Way
Hayes CC
Church Walk
Church Road
Addison
Cedar
Elm
Rectory Road
Manor Road
UXBRIDGE
York Avenue
Corwell
Corwell Gdns
Commonwealth Av
Cromwell
Hayes Stadium Sports Centre
Botwell Crs
Botwell Lane
Reid Cl
Dr Tripletts School
Hesa Road
Harrow View
Wesley Rd
HARLINGTON ROAD
Gould's Gn
Judge Heath Lane
Varcoe Gdns
Burbage Cl
Lilac Gdns
Wood End
Hemmen Lane
Kerstin Cl
St Mary's Rd
Uxbridge College
A437
Purkis Cl
Junior Sch
McMillan Clinic
Princes Park Avenue
Princes Pk Cl
Princes Pk Pde
Princes Pk Cir
Beechwood Av
Ash Gv
Juniper Way
Lime Grove
Barra Hall Road
Sycamore Avenue
Freemans Lane
Manton Close
Hayes FC
Central Avenue
Orchard Road
College Way
Golf Course
Chestnut Close
Walnut Cl
Willenhall Dr
Hayes Social & Sports Club
West Avenue
Longmead Road
Stockley Park Golf Club
Botwell Common Road
DAWLEY
Compton Road
Botwell
Townfield Sq
North Av
Lane
UB11
ROAD
Moray Avenue
Forris Avenue
Lannock Road
Second Av
First Av
Sixth Av
Seventh Av
Eighth Av
Coldharbour
Greenwood Cl
Birchway
Silverdale Industrial Estate
Minet Clinic
Rostrever Gardens
1 grid square represents 500 metres
Business Centre
The Square

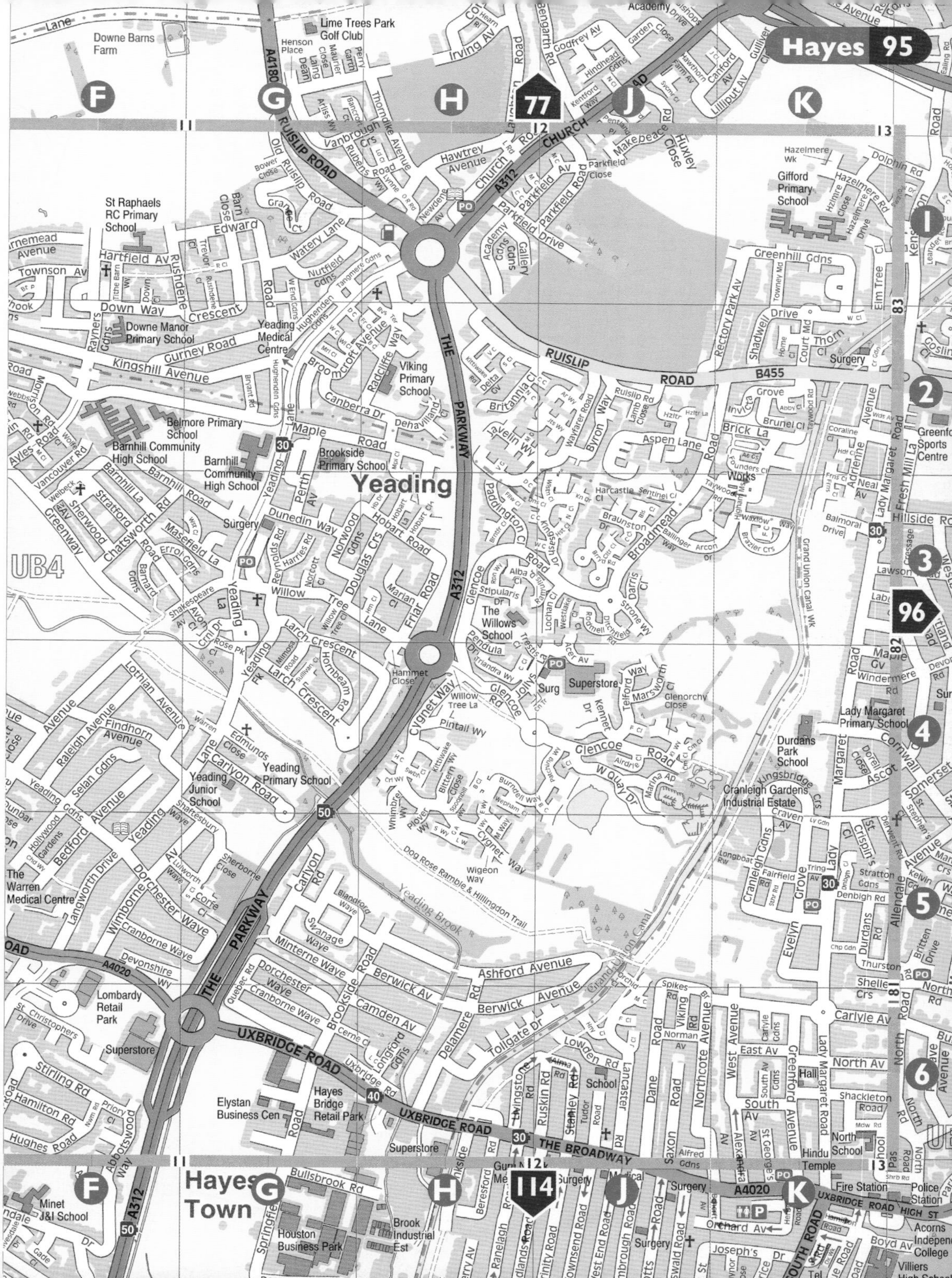
Yeading
UB4
Hayes Town
THE PARKWAY
A312
RUISLIP ROAD
UXBRIDGE ROAD
THE BROADWAY
CHURCH ROAD
Downe Barns Farm
Lime Trees Park Golf Club
St Raphaels RC Primary School
Downe Manor Primary School
Yeading Medical Centre
Viking Primary School
Belmore Primary School
Barnhill Community High School
Brookside Primary School
Gifford Primary School
Greenford Sports Centre
The Willows School
Superstore
Lady Margaret Primary School
Durdans Park School
Cranleigh Gardens Industrial Estate
Yeading Primary School
Yeading Junior School
The Warren Medical Centre
Lombardy Retail Park
Elystan Business Cen
Hayes Bridge Retail Park
Minet J&I School
Houston Business Park
Brook Industrial Est
Acorns Independent College
Grand Union Canal
Yeading Brook
Dog Rose Ramble & Hillingdon Trail
Kingshill Avenue
Gurney Road
Ashford Avenue
Berwick Avenue
Glencoe Road
Broadmead
Lady Margaret Road
North Road
A4020
B455
A4180
77
96
114

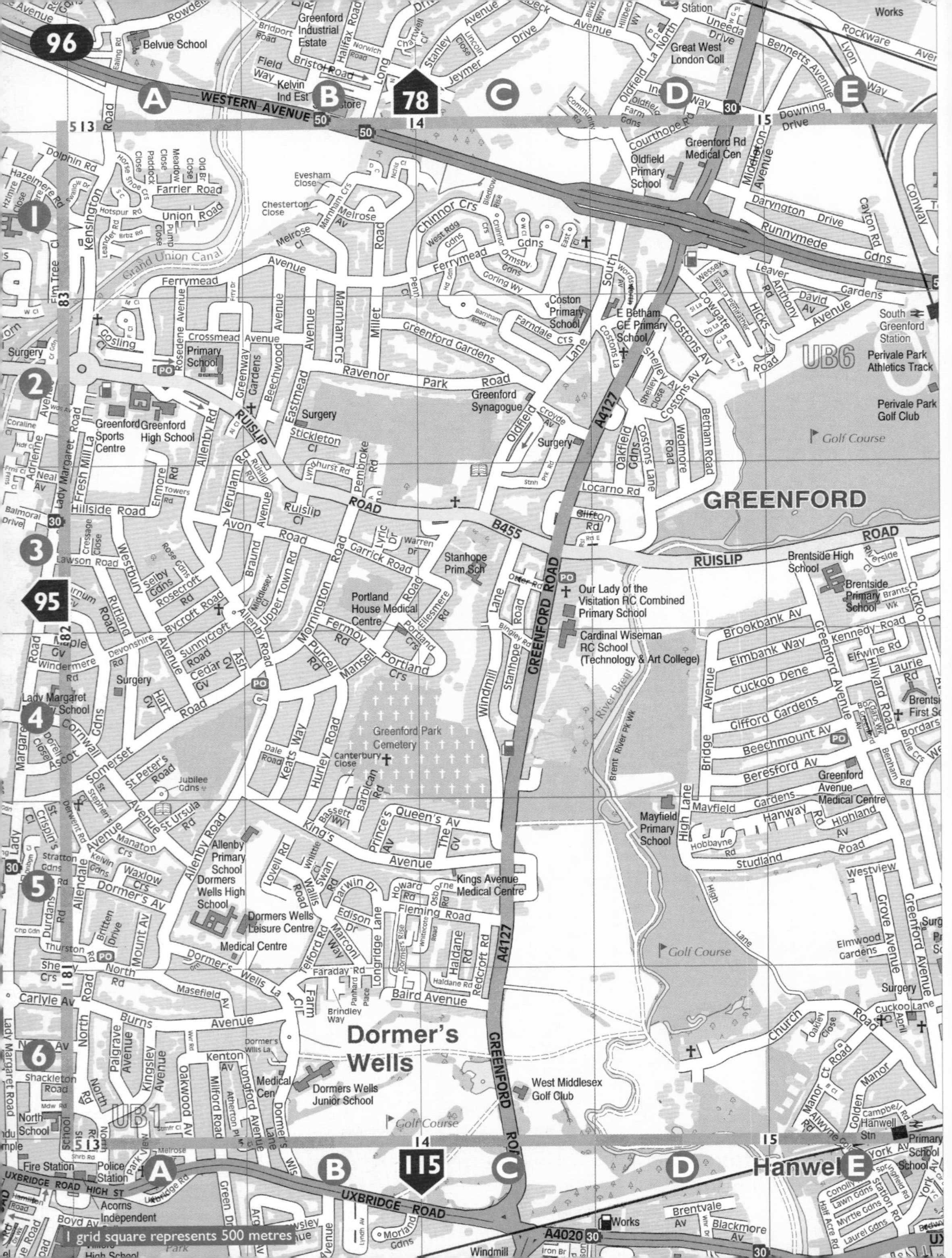
96
78
95
115
A
B
C
D
E
1
2
3
4
5
6
513
14
15
GREENFORD
Dormer's Wells
Hanwell
UB6
UB1
WESTERN AVENUE
RUISLIP ROAD
B455
GREENFORD ROAD
A4127
UXBRIDGE ROAD
HIGH ST
A4020
Belvue School
Greenford Industrial Estate
Kelvin Ind Est
Great West London Coll
Station
Works
Rockware Avenue
Bennetts Avenue
Lyon Way
Downing Drive
Oldfield Primary School
Greenford Rd Medical Cen
Middleton Avenue
Conway
Daryngton Drive
Runnymede Gdns
Cayton Rd
Leaver Gardens
Anthony Rd
David Av
Hicks Av
South Greenford Station
Perivale Park Athletics Track
Perivale Park Golf Club
Golf Course
Grand Union Canal
Dolphin Rd
Hazelmere Rd
Farrier Road
Union Road
Kensington Road
Elm Tree Cl
Ferrymead Avenue
Chinnor Crs
Melrose Av
Marnham Crs
Evesham Close
Chesterton Close
Coston Primary School
E Betham CE Primary School
Costons Lane
Costons Av
Cowgate Rd
Greenford Gardens
Ravenor Park Road
Greenford Synagogue
Crossmead Avenue
Primary School
Surgery
Greenford Sports Centre
Greenford High School
Fresh Mill La
Lady Margaret Road
Allenby Rd
Stickleton Cl
Pembroke Rd
Eastmead Avenue
Beechwood Avenue
Greenway Gardens
Oldfield Lane
Oakfield Gdns
Wedmore Road
Betham Road
Locarno Rd
Clifton Rd
Hillside Road
Lawson Road
Westbury Avenue
Rutland Road
Verulam Rd
Avon Road
Braund Avenue
Upper Town Rd
Garrick Road
Stanhope Prim Sch
Our Lady of the Visitation RC Combined Primary School
Cardinal Wiseman RC School (Technology & Art College)
Brentside High School
Brentside Primary School
Brookbank Av
Elmbank Way
Cuckoo Dene
Gifford Gardens
Beechmount Av
Beresford Av
Greenford Avenue
Greenford Avenue Medical Centre
Hillyard Road
Kennedy Road
Elfwine Rd
Bordars Rd
Mayfield Primary School
Mayfield Gardens
Hanway Rd
Highland Av
Studland Road
Westview
Grove Avenue
Elmwood Gardens
River Brent
Brent River Pk Wk
Portland House Medical Centre
Mornington Road
Fermoy Rd
Portland Crs
Purcell Rd
Mansell Rd
Greenford Park Cemetery
Canterbury Close
Keats Way
Hurley Road
Barbican Rd
Queen's Av
King's Avenue
Windmill Lane
Stanhope Road
Bycroft Road
Rosecroft Rd
Selby Gdns
Sunnycroft Road
Cedar Gv
Maple Gv
Windermere Rd
Devonshire Rd
Cornwall Gdns
Somerset Road
Ascot Close
St Peter's Road
Jubilee Gdns
St Ursula Rd
Allenby Primary School
Dormers Wells High School
Dormers Wells Leisure Centre
Medical Centre
Kings Avenue Medical Centre
Darwin Dr
Fleming Road
Edison Dr
Marconi Way
Telford Rd
Longridge Lane
Haldane Rd
Redcroft Rd
Faraday Rd
Baird Avenue
Brindley Way
Dormer's Wells La
Masefield Av
Burns Avenue
Carlyle Av
North Road
Palgrave Avenue
Kingsley Avenue
Oakwood Av
Milford Road
Longford Avenue
Kenton Av
Dormers Wells Junior School
West Middlesex Golf Club
Church Road
Manor Ct Road
Golden Manor
Hanwell Stn
Primary School
York Av
Station Rd
Brentvale Av
Blackmore Av
Shackleton Road
North School
Fire Station
Police Station
Acorns Independent
Boyd Av
Morland Gdns
Windmill
1 grid square represents 500 metres

Perivale
79
98
116
F
G
H
J
K
16
17
18
Bilton Road
Horsenden Lane
Buckingham Av
Ceci Manning Cl
Doris Ashby Cl
Sunley Gdns
Selborne Gdns
Perivale Industrial Park
Works
Phoenix Trading Est
Grand Union
Eden Close
Superstore
Glacier Way
Capital Business Centre
Woodhouse Cl
Woodhouse Av
Selborne School
Thames Avenue
Medway Drive
Hodder Drive
Barmouth Avenue
Rhyl Rd
Scorton Av
Colwyn Av
Perivale Station
Perivale Ind Park
Chilham Cl
Tavistock Av
Rockford Av
Bideford Av
Wadsworth Road
Fleetway Business Park
Sheraton Business Cen
Silicon Business Cen
Wadsworth Business Cen
Perivale New Business Cen
Perimeade Road
Athlon Rd
Athlon Industrial Estate
Federal Rd
Fairfield Dr
Sarsfield Road
Aintree Road
Alperton Sports Ground
Pleasant Way
Primrose Way
Manor Farm Rd
Primary School
Lily Gdns
May Gardens
ALPERTON LANE
B456
Nagi Business Centre
Marsh Road
Works
Ealing Central Sports Ground
Welland Gdns
Dawlish Avenue
Superstore
Crescent
B456 TEIGNMOUTH GDNS
A40 WESTERN AVENUE
Rydal Coniston Avenue
Thirlmere Av
St John Fisher School
Works
A40
40
Haymill Close
Haymill Cl
Stockdove Way
Ribchester Av
Wyresdale Crs
ARGYLE ROAD
Wicket Road
Perivale Lane
Ealing Golf Club
Golf Course
River Brent
Brent River Pk Wk
Gurnell Leisure Centre
EAST
Gurnell Gv
B455
Brentside Close
Argyle Close
Avalon Road
Crossway
Downside Crescent
Royle Crs
Avalon Cl
Meadvale Road
Harrow Vw
Selby Road
Barnfield Road
Lindfield Rd
North Vw
Holyoake Walk
Denison Rd
Ludlow Road
Neville Rd
Brunner Rd
Brentham Way
Fowler's Walk
Kingfield Rd
Mulgrave Road
Brunswick Road
Lynwood Road
Ainsdale Rd
Perivale Gdns
Bellevue Rd
Woodbury Pk Rd
Curzon Road
Pitshanger Lane
Princes Gdns
Mount Pleasant Rd
Woodfield Rd
Woodfield Crs
St Gregorys RC Primary School
Brentcot Cl
Primary School
Glencairn Dr
Albert Rd
Castlebar Mews
Queen's Gdns
Queen's Walk
Buckingham Cl
Pd Cl
Lanark Close
Avenue
Helena Rd
Upfield Road
Greatdown Road
Harp
Copley
Castlebar School
Castle Bar Park Station
Castlebar Special School
Vallis Way
SCOTCH COMMON
KENT GARDENS
Castlebar
Claremont Road
Fosse Way
Bruton Way
Hathaway Gdns
B452
Kent Avenue
Templewood
The Md
The Dene
Victoria Rd
Park
Eaton Rise
Mount Road
Montpelier Primary School
Montpelier
Aston House Sch
St Benedicts School
Park Hill
Kings Road
Hillcroft Crs
Queen's
Templeman Road
Alcott Close
Crs
Close
Cavendish Avenue
Robinson's Cl
Cleveland Road
CASTLEBAR HILL
The Knoll
Montpelier Av
Notting Hill & Ealing High Sch
The Firs
School
Ealing Abbey
Ealing Abbey Scriptorium
Marchwood Crs
Elmcroft Close
Kings Av
Pk
Charles Rd
Rosemount Rd
Surg
Hollingbourne Gdns
Ravensbourne Gdns
North Avenue
Sherborne Gdns
Wimborne Gdns
St Stephen's Rd
Cavendish Special School
Littlejohn Road
Stephenson Rd
Browning Av
Homefarm Road
Framfield Road
Dryden Av
Springhallow School
Kingsley Av
Highview Road
ARGYLE ROAD
Rosebery Gdns
Lynton Av
Colebrooke Av
The Avenue
Egerton Gardens
Bradley Gdns
Montague Rd
White Ledges
Mortimer Road
Amherst Avenue
Amherst Rd
Charlbury Gv
Blakesley Av
Eaton Rise
CASTLEBAR ROAD
B455
Aston House School
Mount Pk Crs
Durston House School
Mount Pk
Harvington School
Haven Green Clnc
HAVEN GN
Mountfield Rd
Haven
Copley Cl
Browning Av
Middle School
Drayton Manor High School
Drayton Br
Drayton Green Station
Cowper Road
Shakespeare Road
Milton Road
Allingham Cl
Tennyson Road
Park Rd
Berners Dr
Grafton Cl
Ealing Liberal Synagogue
Courtfield Gdns
Ealing College Upper School
Sutherland Avenue
Avenue House School
Waldeck Rd
Arlington Road
Albany Road
Denbigh Road
Saint Leonard's Road
Sports Ground
Carlton Road
Carlton Gdns
Longfield Av
W5
Arcadia Shopping Centre
Springbridge Rd
Madeley's Road
Ealing Broadway Stn
Sports Cen
Sutherland Rd
Primary School
Drayton Gv
Drayton Gdns
Drayton Green
W13
Langham Gardens
Gordon Road
EALING
Town Hall
Christ Church CE Junior School
THE BROADWAY
Ealing Broadway Centre
Windsor Road
Oxford Rd
Western Rd
Grove Rd
Manor Av
Drayton Road
West Ealing Station
DRAYTON GREEN ROAD
West Ealing Business Centre
Works
Cemetery
Felix Road
Endsleigh Rd
Tewkesbury Rd
Eccleston Rd
Alexandria Rd
Bedford Rd
Kirchen Rd
St Johns Primary School
Hastings Road
Hartington Road
Broughton Road
Craven Avenue
Craven Road
Bowling Club
Ealing Civic Centre
University
Fire Station
Denmark Rd
Arden Rd
College
Police Station
Clifton Ldg Sch
Cineworld
Uni
The Questors Theatre
NEW BROADWAY
BOND ST
HIGH STREET
UXBRIDGE ROAD
Church
Holly Pk
West Ealing
Mag Ct
Witham Rd
Broomfield Rd
Lane
Pitshanger Manor Mus
Ealing & W London College
Telephone Exchange
University
Walpole Park
Ealing Film Studios
EALING GN
School
University
Balmain Close
Ealing & Grange
Acton Synagogue
Webster Gdns
Park Pl
Shirley Gdns
Nightingale Rd
Azalea
Singapore Road
BROADWAY A4020
Canberra Rd
Leeland Terrace
Snooker Club
St Johns Ambulance Station
Gordon House Hlth Cen
Culmington
Somerset Rd
Churchfield Rd
Hlth Cen
Surg
UXBRIDGE ROAD
Michael Gaynor Cl
Grosvenor
B452
Alperton Station
Alperton
A4005
Brindley
Rosemount
Cromwell Road
Alp
Super
83
82
81
I
2
3
4
5
6
Clarendon
West
Croft
Regal
Woodville Rd
Harrie
Surg
Kenilworth

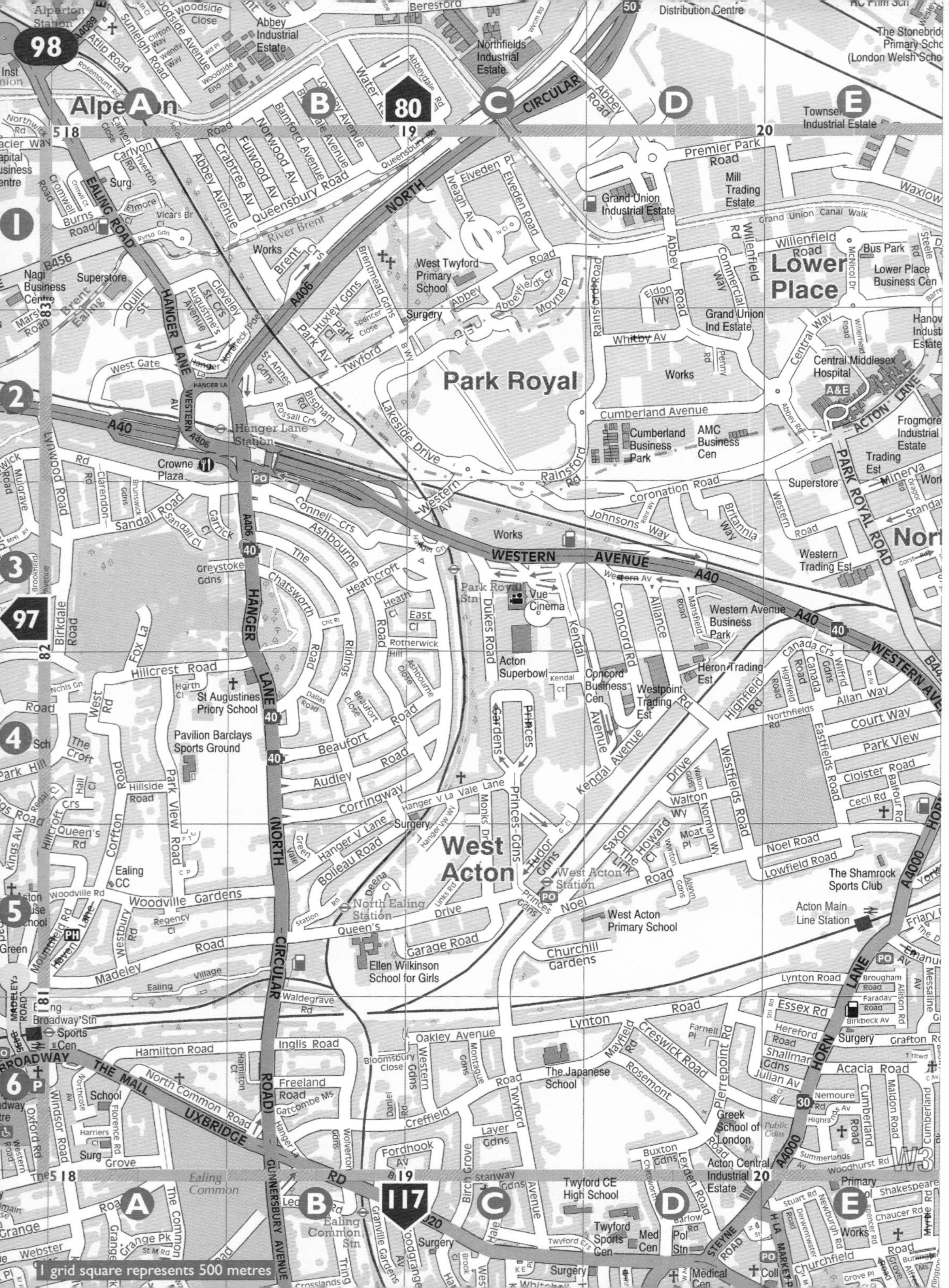

1 grid square represents 500 metres

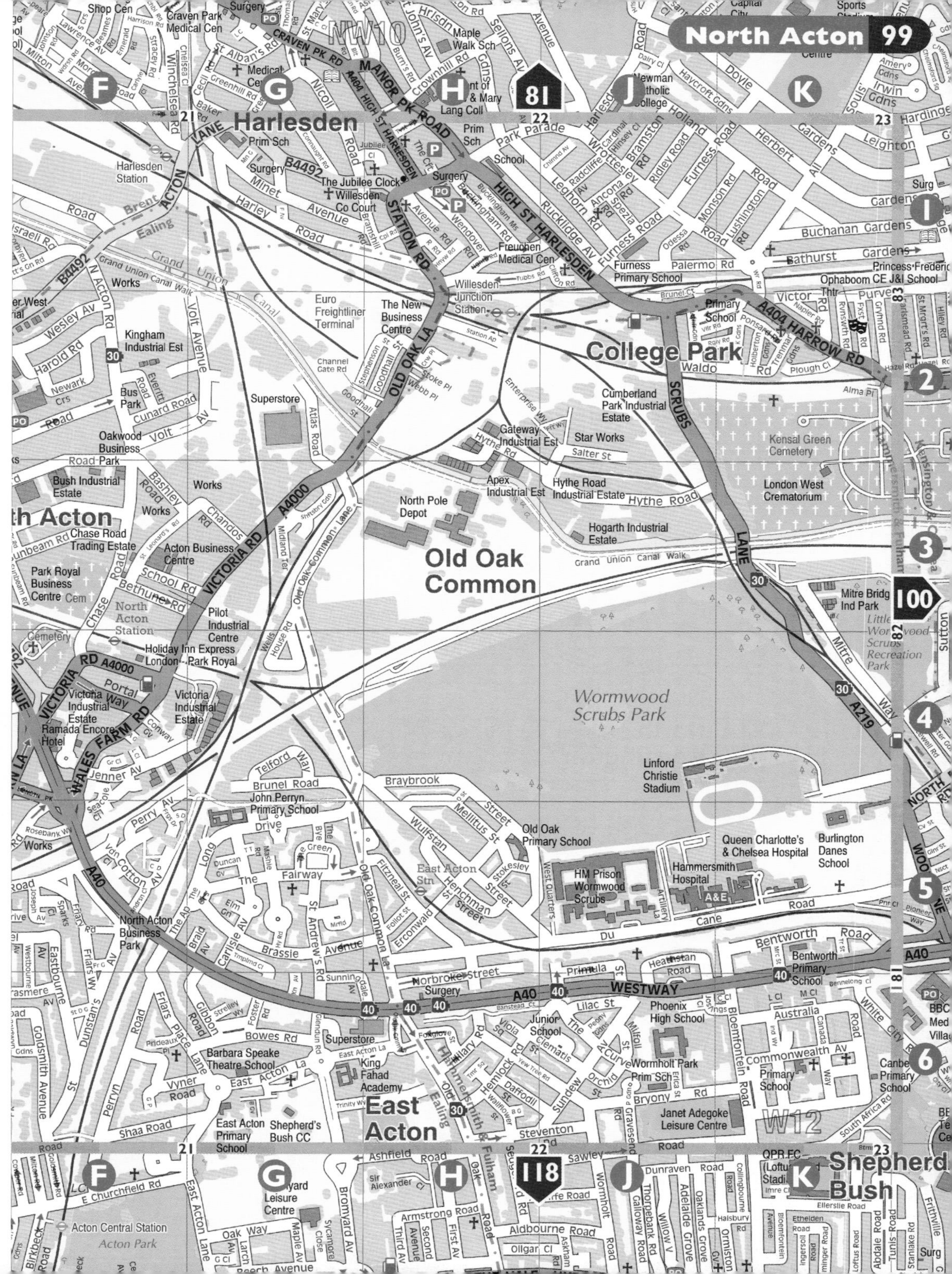
Harlesden
College Park
Old Oak Common
North Acton
East Acton
Shepherd's Bush
Wormwood Scrubs Park
Kensal Green Cemetery
London West Crematorium
Linford Christie Stadium
Queen Charlotte's & Chelsea Hospital
Hammersmith Hospital
HM Prison Wormwood Scrubs
Burlington Danes School
Old Oak Primary School
North Pole Depot
Willesden Junction Station
Harlesden Station
North Acton Station
East Acton Stn
Euro Freightliner Terminal
The New Business Centre
Cumberland Park Industrial Estate
Gateway Industrial Est
Star Works
Apex Industrial Est
Hythe Road Industrial Estate
Hogarth Industrial Estate
Mitre Bridg Ind Park
Little Wormwood Scrubs Recreation Park
Kingham Industrial Est
Bush Industrial Estate
Chase Road Trading Estate
Acton Business Centre
Park Royal Business Centre
Pilot Industrial Centre
Holiday Inn Express London - Park Royal
Victoria Industrial Estate
Ramada Encore Hotel
North Acton Business Park
John Perryn Primary School
Barbara Speake Theatre School
King Fahad Academy
East Acton Primary School
Shepherd's Bush CC
Phoenix High School
Wormholt Park Prim Sch
Janet Adegoke Leisure Centre
Bentworth Primary School
Furness Primary School
Ophaboom CE J&I School
The Jubilee Clock
Willesden Co Court
Freuchen Medical Cen
Grand Union Canal Walk
VICTORIA RD A4000
OLD OAK LA
SCRUBS LANE
A40 WESTWAY
Du Cane Road
HIGH ST HARLESDEN
A404 HARROW RD
NW10
W12
Acton Central Station
Acton Park
81
100
118
F G H J K
1 2 3 4 5 6
21 22 23
81 82 83

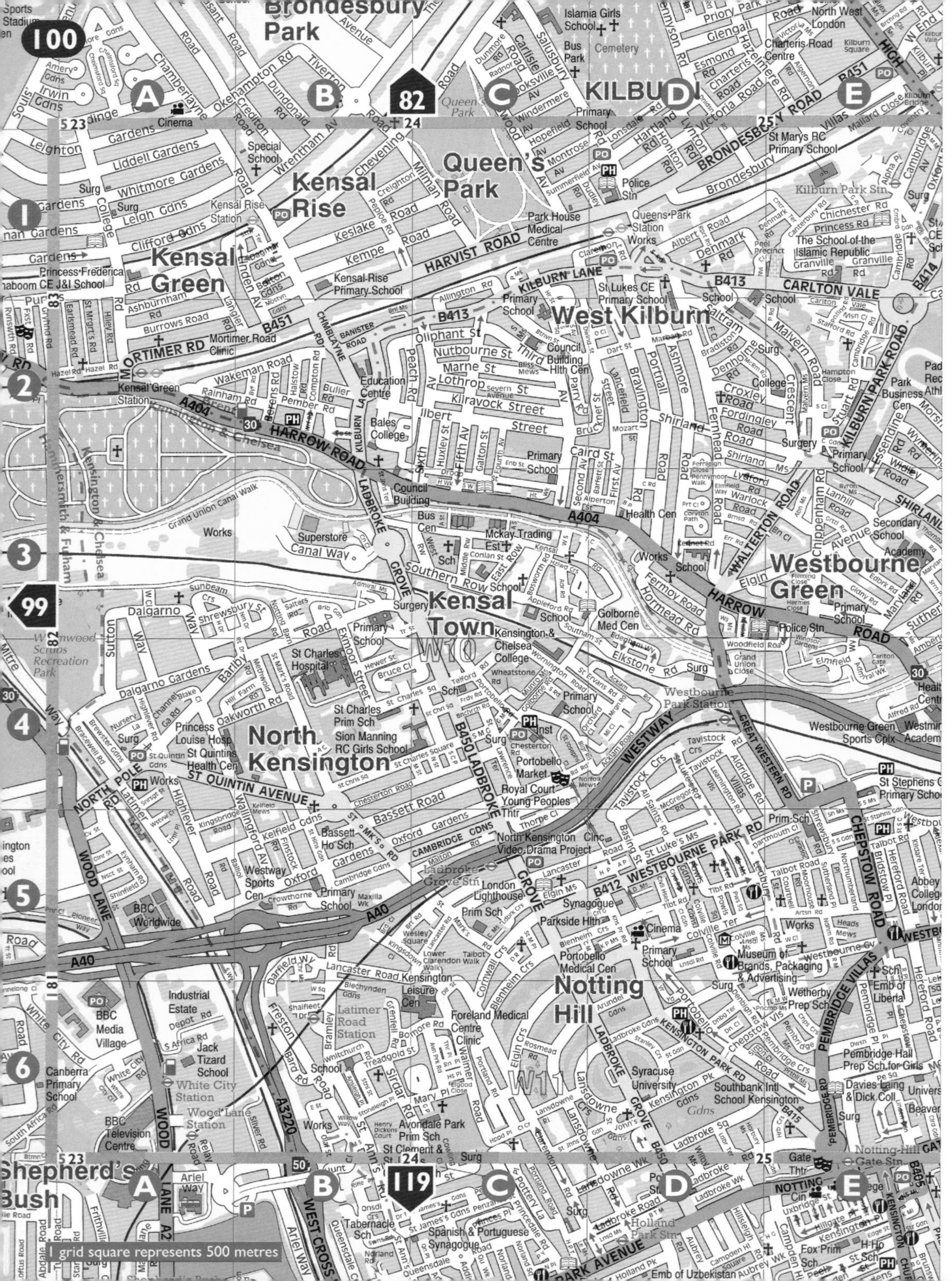

100
82
99
119
A
B
C
D
E
1
2
3
4
5
6
523
24
25
83
82
81
Brondesbury Park
Kensal Rise
Queen's Park
KILBURN
Kensal Green
West Kilburn
Kensal Town
Westbourne Green
North Kensington
Notting Hill
Shepherd's Bush
W10
W11
HARVIST ROAD
KILBURN LANE
CARLTON VALE
HARROW ROAD
MORTIMER RD
BRONDESBURY ROAD
KILBURN PARK ROAD
LADBROKE GROVE
WESTWAY
GREAT WESTERN RD
ST QUINTIN AVENUE
NORTH POLE RD
WOOD LANE
CAMBRIDGE GDNS
WESTBOURNE PARK RD
CHEPSTOW ROAD
PEMBRIDGE VILLAS
KENSINGTON PARK RD
WALTERTON ROAD
WEST CROSS
A404
A40
A3220
B413
B451
B450
B412
B415
Kensal Green Station
Kensal Rise Station
Queens Park Station
Kilburn Park Stn
Westbourne Park Station
Ladbroke Grove Stn
White City Station
Wood Lane Station
Holland Park Stn
Notting Hill Gate Stn
Kensington & Chelsea
Grand Union Canal Walk
Wormwood Scrubs Recreation Park
St Charles Hospital
Princess Louise Hosp
St Quintins Health Cen
Portobello Market
Royal Court Young Peoples Thtr
Kensington & Chelsea College
Westbourne Green Sports Cplx
BBC Worldwide
BBC Media Village
BBC Television Centre
Museum of Brands, Packaging & Advertising
Syracuse University
Kensington Leisure Cen
Latimer Road Station
Superstore
Works
Cemetery
1 grid square represents 500 metres

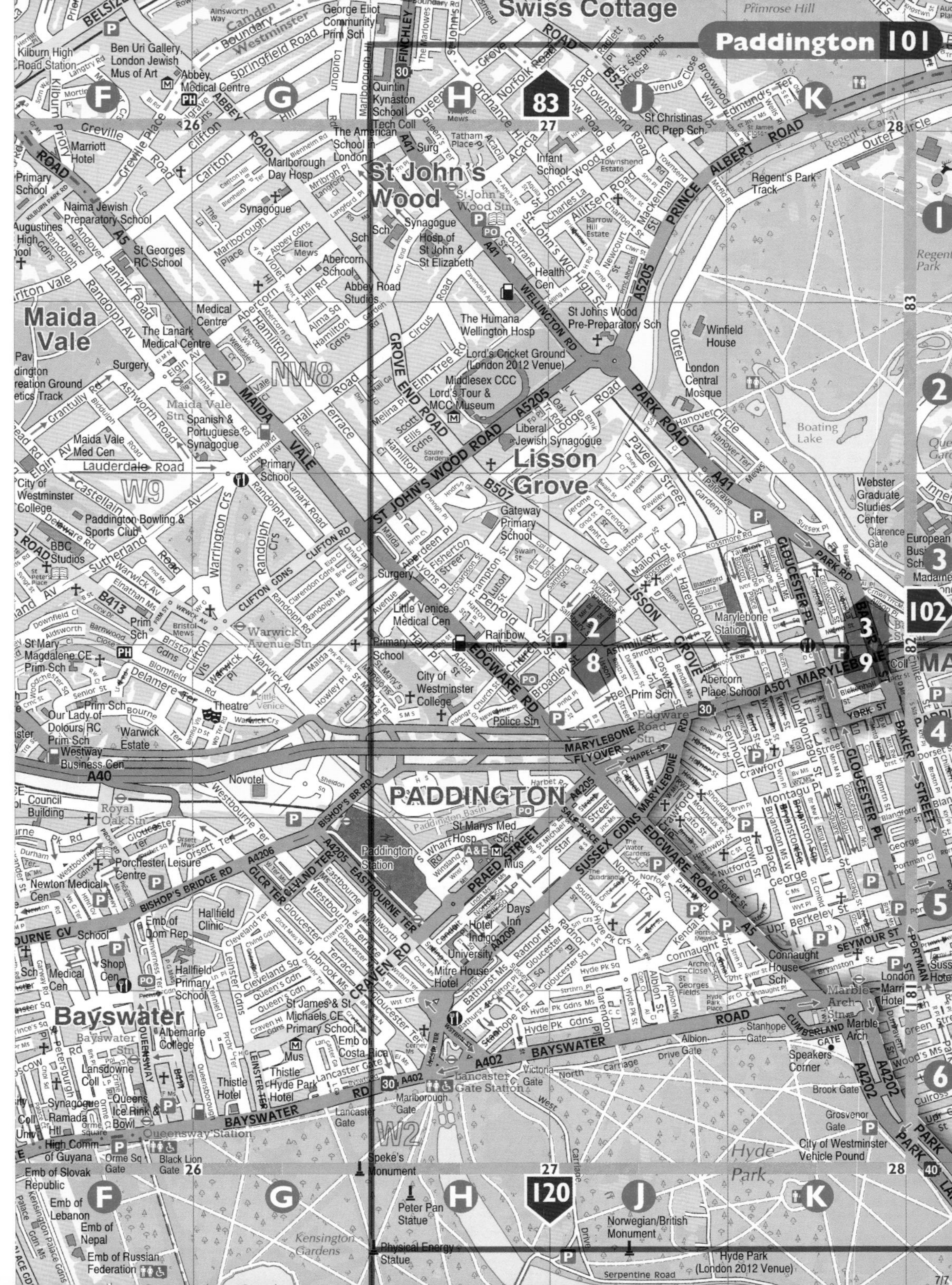
Swiss Cottage
Primrose Hill
St John's Wood
Maida Vale
Lisson Grove
PADDINGTON
Bayswater
NW8
W9
W2
Kilburn High Road Station
Ben Uri Gallery, London Jewish Mus of Art
Abbey Medical Centre
George Eliot Community Prim Sch
Quintin Kynaston School Tech Coll
The American School in London
St Christinas RC Prep Sch
Marriott Hotel
Marlborough Day Hosp
Synagogue
Naima Jewish Preparatory School
St Georges RC School
Hosp of St John & St Elizabeth
Abercorn School
Abbey Road Studios
St John's Wood Stn
Health Cen
St Johns Wood Pre-Preparatory Sch
Winfield House
London Central Mosque
Regent's Park Track
Regent's Park
Boating Lake
The Humana Wellington Hosp
Lord's Cricket Ground (London 2012 Venue)
Middlesex CCC Lord's Tour & MCC Museum
Liberal Jewish Synagogue
The Lanark Medical Centre
Medical Centre
Maida Vale Stn
Spanish & Portuguese Synagogue
Maida Vale Med Cen
City of Westminster College
Paddington Bowling & Sports Club
BBC Studios
Gateway Primary School
Webster Graduate Studies Center
European Business School
Marylebone Station
Little Venice Medical Cen
Rainbow Clinic
Warwick Avenue Stn
St Mary Magdalene CE Prim Sch
Our Lady of Dolours RC Prim Sch
Warwick Estate
Westway Business Cen
Theatre
Little Venice
Police Stn
Abercorn Place School
Edgware Road Stn
Bell Street Prim Sch
Novotel
Council Building
Royal Oak Stn
Porchester Leisure Centre
Newton Medical Cen
Hallfield Clinic
Emb of Dom Rep
Paddington Station
Paddington Basin
St Marys Med Sch
St Marys Hosp
A&E
Mus
Days Inn Hotel
Hotel Indigo
University
Mitre House Hotel
Hallfield Primary School
Shop Cen
Medical Cen
Albemarle College
St James & St Michaels CE Primary School
Emb of Costa Rica
Thistle Hyde Park Hotel
Thistle Hotel
Lansdowne Coll
Queens Ice Rink & Bowl
Ramada Htl
Queensway Station
High Comm of Guyana
Black Lion Gate
Orme Sq Gate
Lancaster Gate Station
Marlborough Gate
Lancaster Gate
Victoria Gate
Albion Gate
Stanhope Gate
Speakers Corner
Brook Gate
Grosvenor Gate
City of Westminster Vehicle Pound
Hyde Park
Hyde Park (London 2012 Venue)
Kensington Gardens
Speke's Monument
Peter Pan Statue
Physical Energy Statue
Norwegian/British Monument
Emb of Slovak Republic
Emb of Lebanon
Emb of Nepal
Emb of Russian Federation
Connaught House Sch
Marble Arch Stn
Marble Arch
London Marriott Hotel
Madame Tussauds
MARYLEBONE FLYOVER
EDGWARE RD
BAYSWATER RD
PRAED STREET
MAIDA VALE
ST JOHN'S WOOD ROAD
PARK ROAD
PRINCE ALBERT ROAD
WELLINGTON RD
GROVE END ROAD
SUSSEX GDNS
CRAVEN RD
BISHOP'S BRIDGE RD
GLOUCESTER PL
BAKER STREET
PORTMAN ST
SEYMOUR ST
A40
A41
A5
A5205
A402
A4202
A501 MARYLEBONE
83
102
120
F G H J K
26 27 28
2 3 4 5 6

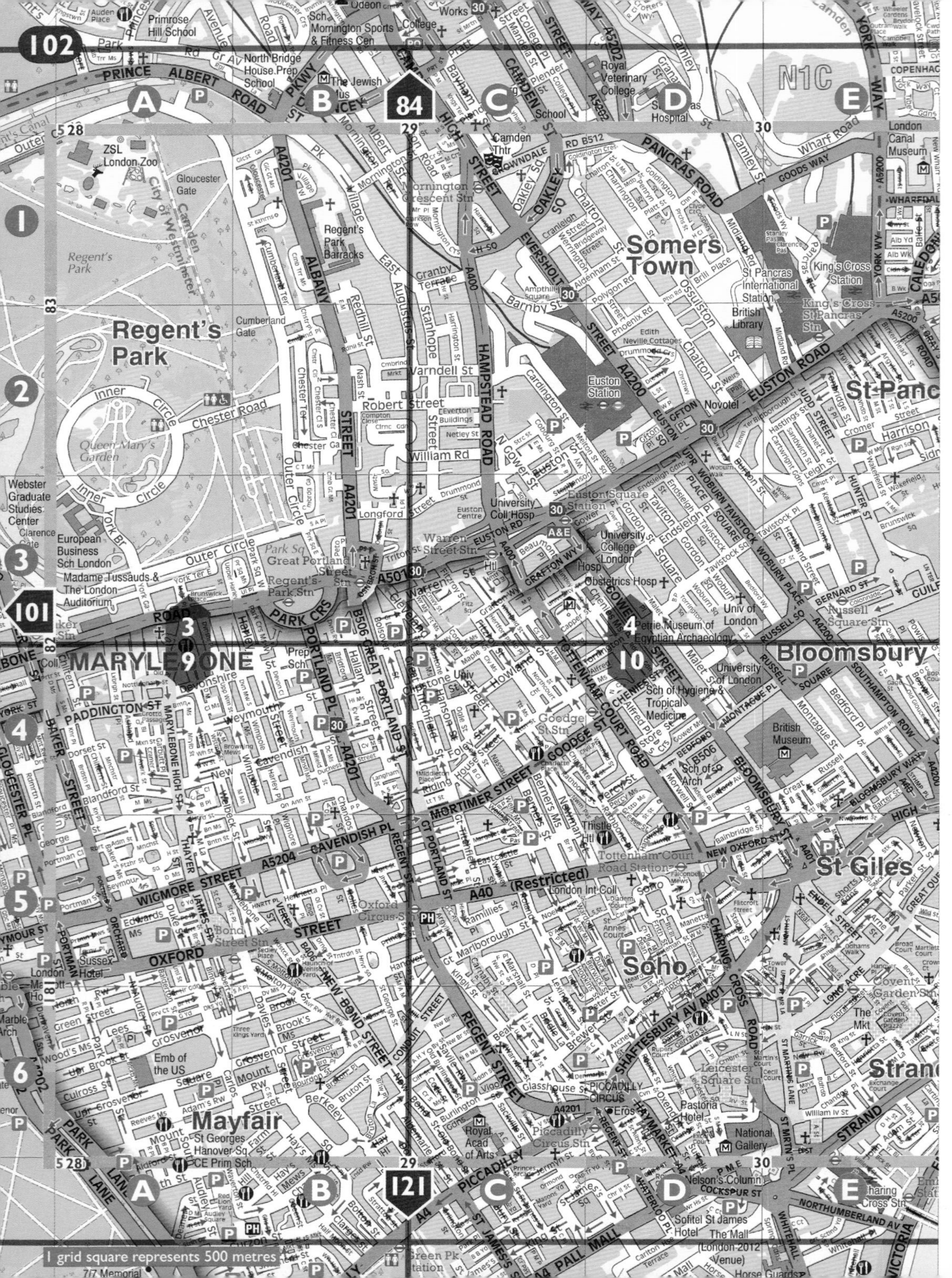
102
84
101
121
A
B
C
D
E
1
2
3
4
5
6
28
29
30
83
82
81
N1C
Primrose Hill School
North Bridge House Prep School
The Jewish Mus
Mornington Sports & Fitness Cen
College
Works
Royal Veterinary College
Hospital
PRINCE ALBERT ROAD
ZSL London Zoo
Gloucester Gate
Regent's Park
Cumberland Gate
Inner Circle
Chester Road
Queen Mary's Garden
Outer Circle
Regent's Park Barracks
ALBANY STREET
A4201
Camden Thtr
Mornington Crescent Stn
HAMPSTEAD ROAD
EVERSHOLT STREET
Somers Town
PANCRAS ROAD
London Canal Museum
Wharf Road
GOODS WAY
King's Cross Station
St Pancras International Station
King's Cross St Pancras Stn
British Library
Euston Station
EUSTON ROAD
Novotel
St Pancras
Harrison St
Webster Graduate Studies Center
European Business Sch London
Madame Tussauds & The London Auditorium
Park Sq
Great Portland Street Stn
Regent's Park Stn
Warren Street Stn
Euston Square Station
University Coll Hosp
University College London
Obstetrics Hosp
Univ of London
Petrie Museum of Egyptian Archaeology
Russell Square Stn
MARYLEBONE
Bloomsbury
University of London
Sch of Hygiene & Tropical Medicine
British Museum
BAKER STREET
PADDINGTON ST
MARYLEBONE HIGH ST
Goodge St Stn
TOTTENHAM COURT ROAD
GOWER STREET
BLOOMSBURY ST
SOUTHAMPTON ROW
NEW OXFORD ST
HIGH
St Giles
MORTIMER STREET
CAVENDISH PL
A5204
WIGMORE STREET
A40 (Restricted)
London Int Coll
Tottenham Court Road Station
Soho
Oxford Circus Stn
OXFORD STREET
Bond Street Stn
Sussex Hotel
London Marriott Ho
Marble Arch
REGENT STREET
NEW BOND STREET
Emb of the US
Grosvenor Square
Mayfair
St Georges Hanover Sq CE Prim Sch
CHARING CROSS ROAD
SHAFTESBURY AV A401
Covent Garden Stn
The Mkt
LONG ACRE
Strand
Leicester Square Stn
PICCADILLY CIRCUS
Piccadilly Circus Stn
Royal Acad of Arts
PICCADILLY
National Gallery
Nelson's Column
COCKSPUR ST
Charing Cross Stn
NORTHUMBERLAND AV
STRAND
Sofitel St James Hotel
The Mall (London 2012 Venue)
PALL MALL
PARK LANE
Green Pk Station
7/7 Memorial
Horse Guards
1 grid square represents 500 metres

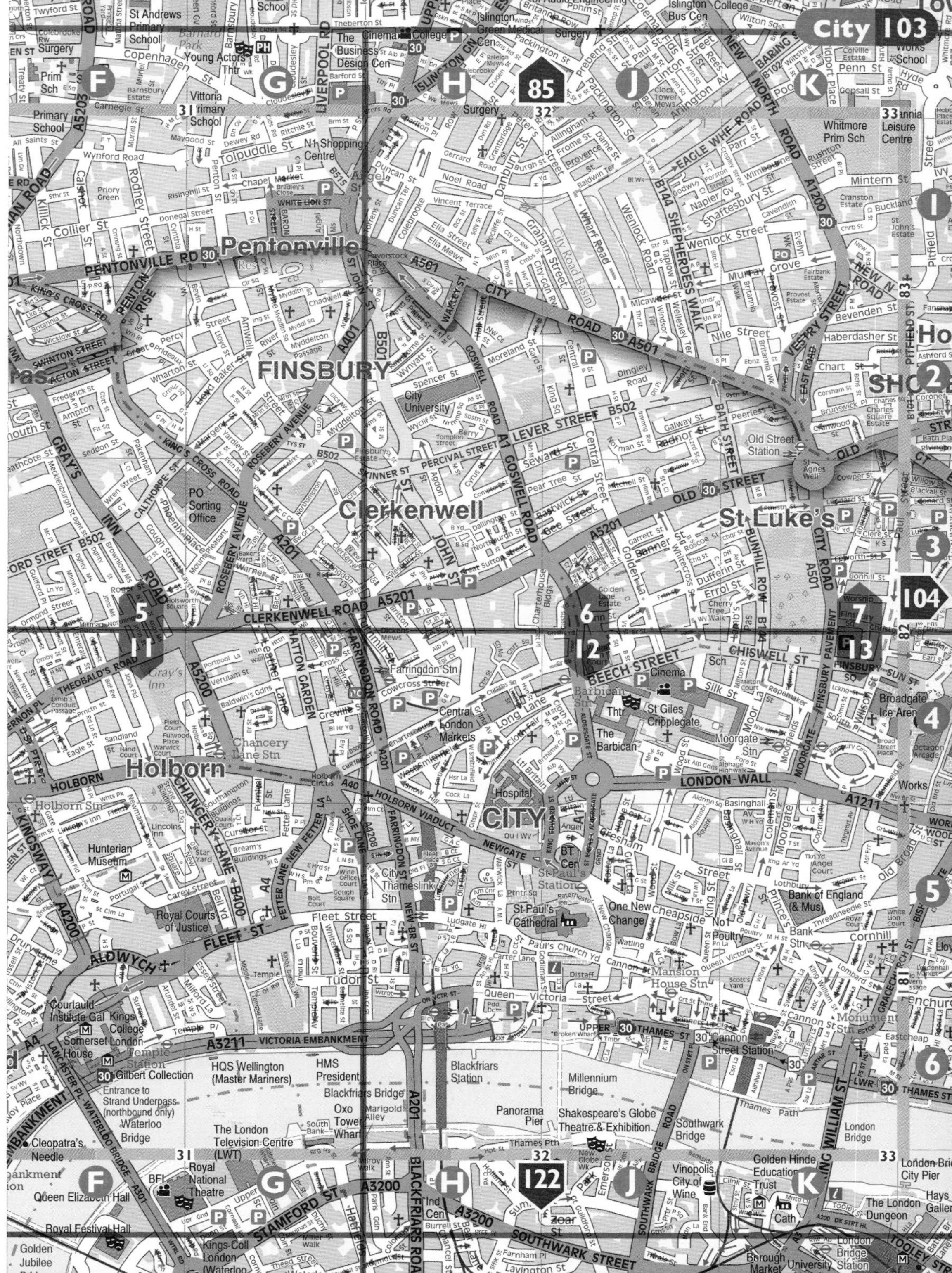

Pentonville
FINSBURY
Clerkenwell
St Luke's
Holborn
CITY
PENTONVILLE RD
CITY ROAD
A501
GOSWELL ROAD
CLERKENWELL ROAD
A5201
OLD STREET
KING'S CROSS ROAD
ROSEBERY AVENUE
FARRINGDON ROAD
HATTON GARDEN
CHANCERY LANE
KINGSWAY
ALDWYCH
FLEET ST
HOLBORN VIADUCT
NEWGATE ST
LONDON WALL
CHISWELL ST
BEECH STREET
FINSBURY PAVEMENT
MOORGATE
VICTORIA EMBANKMENT
A3211
THAMES ST
SOUTHWARK STREET
STAMFORD ST
BLACKFRIARS ROAD
SOUTHWARK BRIDGE ROAD
KING WILLIAM ST
GRACECHURCH ST
City University
PO Sorting Office
Farringdon Stn
Barbican Stn
The Barbican
St Giles Cripplegate
St Paul's Cathedral
Bank of England (& Mus)
Royal Courts of Justice
Hunterian Museum
Chancery Lane Stn
Holborn Stn
Old Street Station
Blackfriars Station
Cannon Street Station
Mansion House Stn
Millennium Bridge
Shakespeare's Globe Theatre & Exhibition
Southwark Bridge
London Bridge
Blackfriars Bridge
Waterloo Bridge
Royal National Theatre
Royal Festival Hall
Queen Elizabeth Hall
Somerset House
Cleopatra's Needle
HMS President
HQS Wellington (Master Mariners)
Oxo Tower Wharf
The London Television Centre (LWT)
Vinopolis City of Wine
Golden Hinde Educational Trust
The London Dungeon
Borough Market
85
104
122
F G H J K
31 32 33
1 2 3 4 5 6

104
86
103
123
A
B
C
D
E
1
2
3
4
5
6
533
34
35
Haggerston
Hoxton
SHOREDITCH
BETHNAL
GREEN
Spitalfields
Whitechapel
St George
in the East
Shadwell
Wapping
South
Hackney
E2
E1
E1W
VICTORIA PARK
Orsman Road
Mill Row
Regent's Row
Dunston Rd
Pownall Road
Whiston Rd
Andrews Road
Mare Street
Kingsland
Hackney Road
A1208
Old Ford Road
Old Bethnal Green Rd
Columbia Road
Gosset Street
B118
Bethnal Green Road
A1209
Cambridge Heath Road
A107
Shoreditch High St
Great Eastern Street
Old St
Curtain Road
Calvert Av
Arnold Circus
Club Row
Brick Lane
Cheshire Street
B135
Sclater St
Dunbridge St
Quaker St
Commercial Street
A1202
Bishopsgate
A10
Wormwood St
Houndsditch
Bevis Marks
Duke's Pl
Minories
Mansell Street
Leman Street
Alie St
Prescot St
Royal Mint St
Whitechapel Road
New Rd
Commercial Road
A13
Cannon St Rd
Cable Street
The Highway
A1203
A11 Mile End Rd
E Smithfield
Thames St
Fenchurch St
Leadenhall St
Eastcheap
Liverpool Street Station
Broadgate Ice Arena
Old Spitalfields Market Hall
Shoreditch High Street Stn
Hoxton Station
Geffrye Museum
Hackney City Farm
Spitalfields Community Farm
Bethnal Green Stn
Whitechapel Stn
Aldgate East Stn
Aldgate Stn
Fenchurch St Stn
Tower Gateway Stn
Tower Hill Stn
Tower of London
Royal Mint Court
Shadwell Stn
Mile End & Bow Business Cen
St Bartholomews & The Royal London Hospital
East London Central Synagogue
E London Mosque
News International
Tobacco Dock
Tower Bridge
London Bridge City Pier
Hays Galleria
The London Dungeon
Winston Churchill's Britain at War Experience
The Tower Hotel Tower Bridge
The Tower Bridge Exhibition
River Thames
1 grid square represents 500 metres

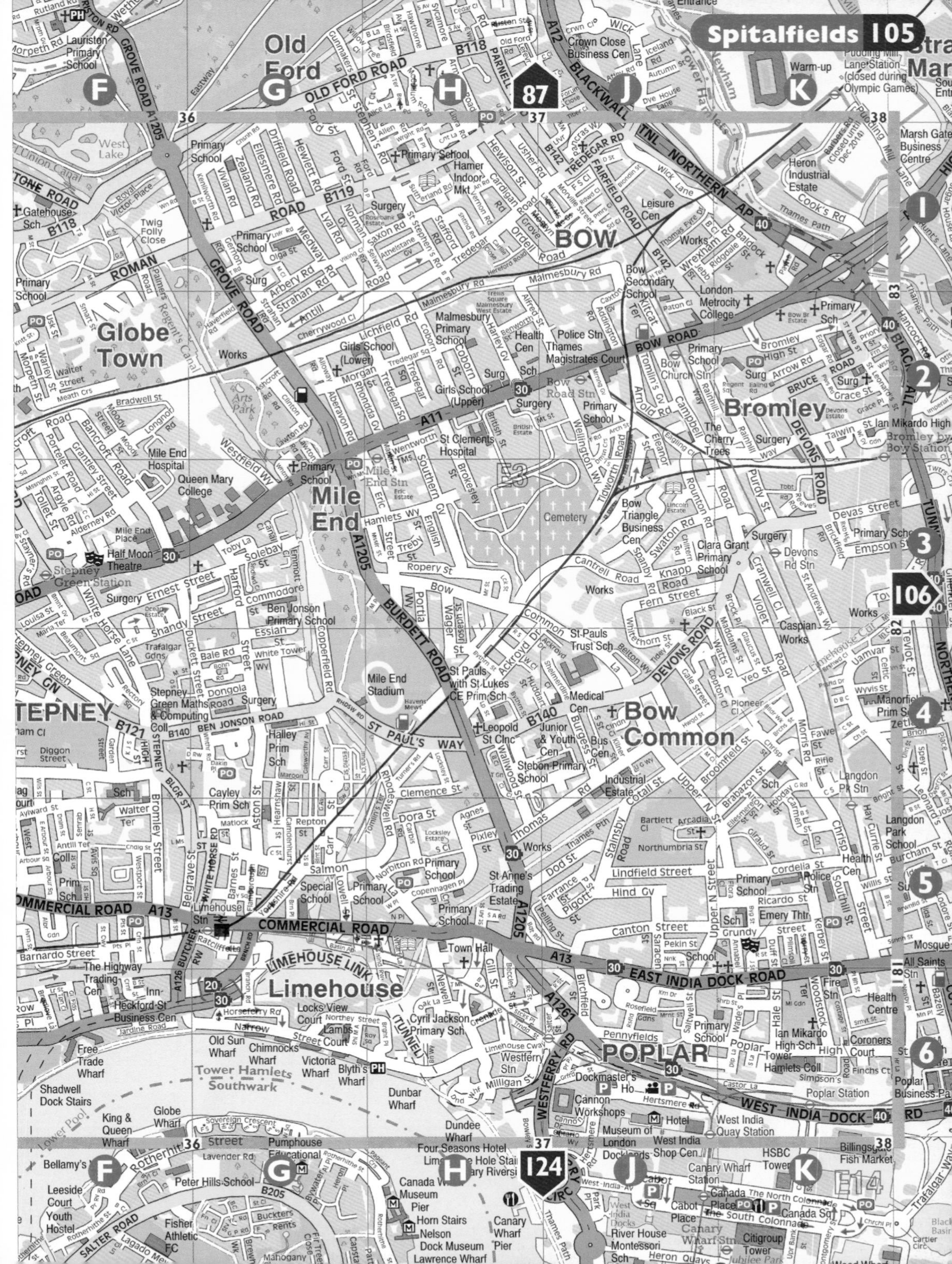
Old Ford
Bow
Globe Town
Mile End
Bromley
Bow Common
Stepney
Limehouse
Poplar
Old Ford Road
Grove Road
Roman Road
Bow Road
Mile End Road
Burdett Road
Commercial Road
East India Dock Road
West India Dock Road
Limehouse Link
Mile End Hospital
Queen Mary College
Mile End Stadium
Cemetery
Tower Hamlets
Southwark
87
106
124
F
G
H
J
K
2
3
4
5
6

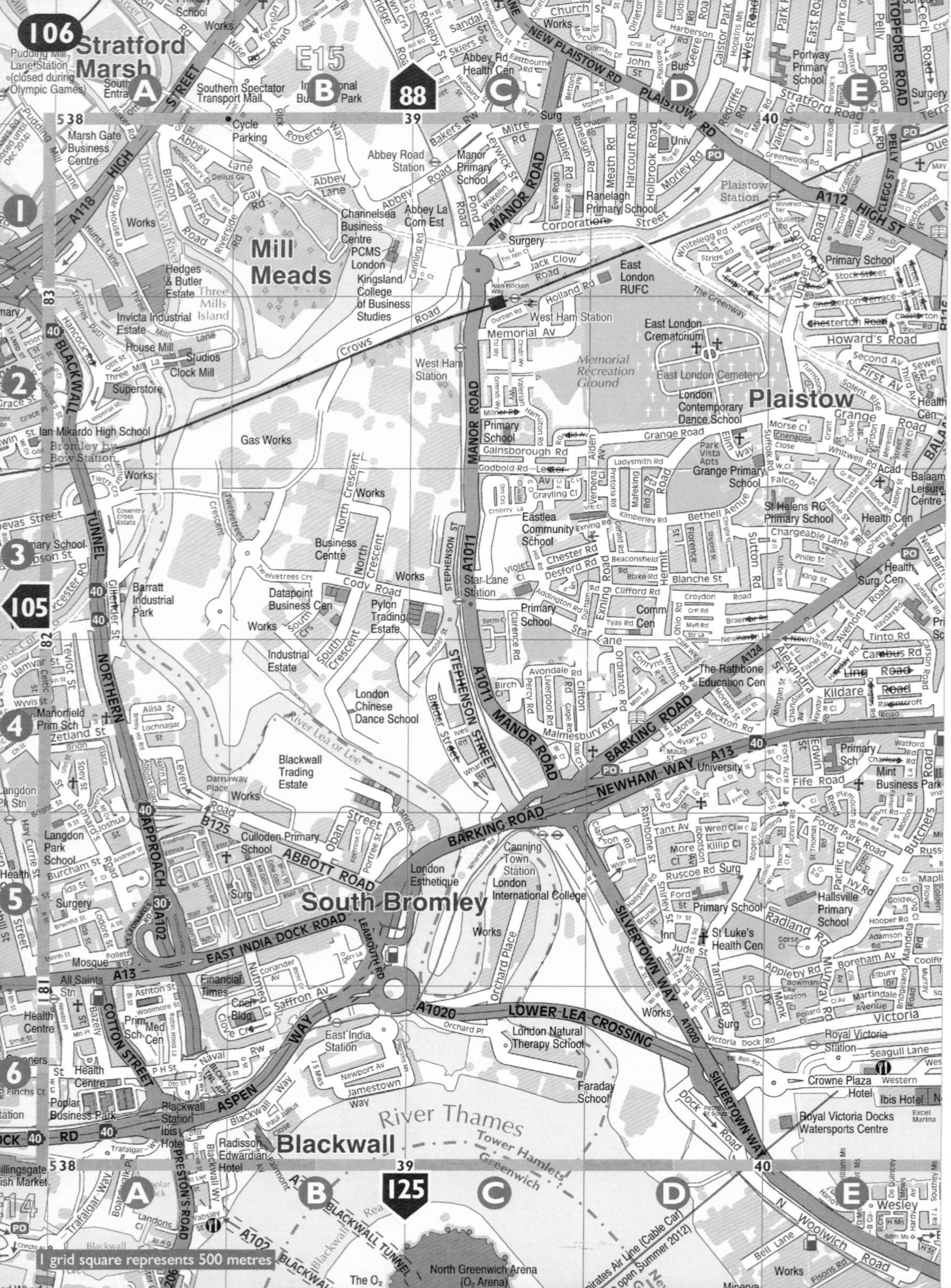

106
Stratford Marsh
Pudding Mill Lane Station (closed during Olympic Games)
E15
88
Southern Spectator Transport Mall
Abbey Rd Health Cen
New Plaistow Rd
Portway Primary School
Stratford Road
Topford Road
Cycle Parking
Marsh Gate Business Centre
Abbey Road Station
Manor Primary School
Manor Road
Ranelagh Primary School
Corporation Street
Plaistow Station
A112 High St
Mill Meads
Channelsea Business Centre
PCMS London
Kingsland College of Business Studies
Abbey La Com Est
Surgery
Jack Clow Road
East London RUFC
Hedges & Butler Estate
Three Mills Island
Invicta Industrial Estate
House Mill
Studios
Clock Mill
Superstore
West Ham Station
Memorial Av
East London Crematorium
The Greenway
Memorial Recreation Ground
East London Cemetery
London Contemporary Dance School
Plaistow
Grange Road
Chesterton Road
Howard's Road
Second Av
First Av
Crows Road
Ian Mikardo High School
Bromley by Bow Station
Gas Works
Primary School
Gainsborough Rd
Godbold Rd
Grange Primary School
Balaam Leisure Centre
St Helens RC Primary School
Health Cen
Devas Street
Works
North Crescent
Business Centre
Eastlea Community School
Chester Rd
Desford Rd
Blanche St
Bethell Avenue
Barratt Industrial Park
105
Twelvetrees Crs
Cody Road
Datapoint Business Cen
Pylon Trading Estate
Star Lane Station
A1011
Stephenson Street
Clifford Rd
Star Lane
Industrial Estate
South Crescent
Northern Approach
Blackwall Tunnel
The Rathbone Education Cen
Manorfield Prim Sch
London Chinese Dance School
Avondale Rd
River Lea or Lee
Blackwall Trading Estate
Barking Road
Newham Way
A13
University
Fife Road
Mint Business Park
Langdon Pk Stn
Langdon Park School
Culloden Primary School
Abbott Road
London Esthetique
Canning Town Station
London International College
South Bromley
Ford Primary School
St Luke's Health Cen
Hallsville Primary School
Radland Rd
Silvertown Way
East India Dock Road
Mosque
All Saints Stn
A13
Financial Times
Saffron Av
Orchard Place
Lower Lea Crossing
A1020
Boreham Av
Victoria Dock Rd
Royal Victoria Station
Seagull Lane
Cotton Street
East India Station
London Natural Therapy School
Faraday School
Crowne Plaza Hotel
Ibis Hotel
Royal Victoria Docks Watersports Centre
Health Centre
Poplar Business Park
Blackwall Station
Aspen Way
Ibis Hotel
Radisson Edwardian Hotel
River Thames
Blackwall
Tower Hamlets
Greenwich
Billingsgate Fish Market
E14
125
Blackwall Tunnel
A102
Preston's Road
N Woolwich Road
Wesley
Emirates Air Line (Cable Car) (to open Summer 2012)
North Greenwich Arena (O_2 Arena)
The O_2
1 grid square represents 500 metres

Upton Park
East Ham
Canning Town
Beckton
Custom House
E13
E16
West Ham United FC (Upton Park)
Newham General Hospital
Newham Leisure Centre
East Ham Industrial Est
Central Park
East Ham Jewish Cemetery
Beckton District Park
Royal Victoria Dock
Royal Albert Dock
ExCeL London (London 2012 Venue)
London City Airport
BARKING ROAD A124
NEWHAM WAY A13
PRINCE REGENT LANE
ROYAL ALBERT WAY A1020
CONNAUGHT BR
HIGH STREET SOUTH A117
CENTRAL PK ROAD B167
89
108
126

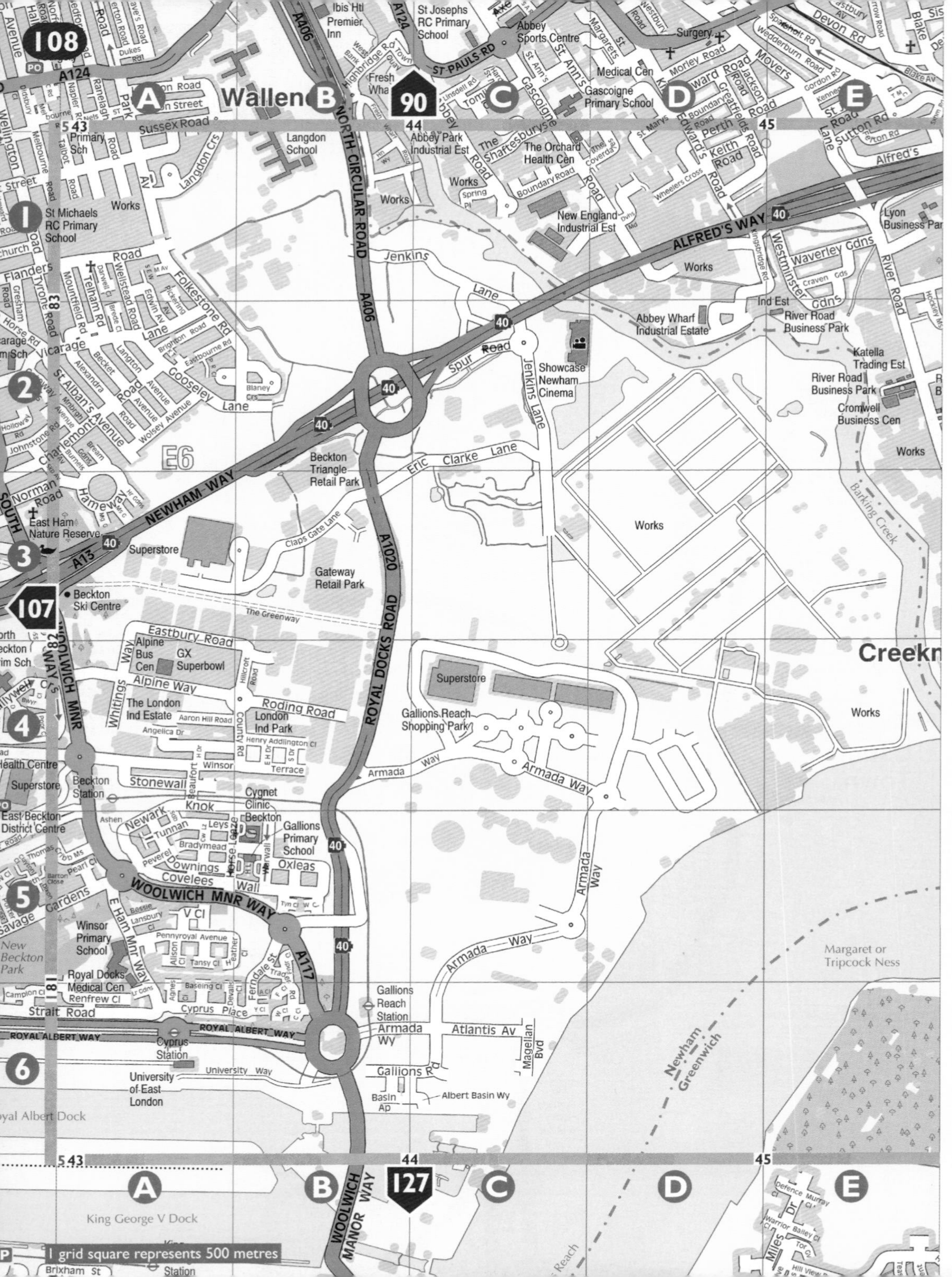

108
90
107
127
A
B
C
D
E
1
2
3
4
5
6
543
44
45
A124
A406
A1020
A117
A13
40
Wallend
NORTH CIRCULAR ROAD
ROYAL DOCKS ROAD
ALFRED'S WAY
NEWHAM WAY
WOOLWICH MNR WAY
WOOLWICH MANOR WAY
ROYAL ALBERT WAY
E6
St Pauls Rd
Ibis Htl
Premier Inn
St Josephs RC Primary School
Abbey Sports Centre
Surgery
Medical Cen
Gascoigne Primary School
Morley Road
Devon Rd
Sussex Road
Primary Sch
Langdon School
Langdon Crs
Abbey Park Industrial Est
The Shaftesburys
The Orchard Health Cen
Boundary Road
Perth Road
Keith Road
Greatfields Road
Movers Lane
Works
New England Industrial Est
Wheelers Cross
Lyon Business Park
St Michaels RC Primary School
Jenkins Lane
Westminster Gdns
Waverley Gdns
River Road
Kingsbridge Rd
Ind Est
Abbey Wharf Industrial Estate
River Road Business Park
Katella Trading Est
Cromwell Business Cen
Showcase Newham Cinema
Spur Road
Folkestone Rd
Tyrone Road
Flanders Road
Vicarage Lane
St Alban's Avenue
Gooseley Lane
Wolsey Avenue
Charlemont Road
Norman Road
Hameway
East Ham Nature Reserve
Beckton Triangle Retail Park
Eric Clarke Lane
Barking Creek
Superstore
Claps Gate Lane
Gateway Retail Park
Beckton Ski Centre
The Greenway
Eastbury Road
Alpine Bus Cen
GX Superbowl
Alpine Way
Whitings Way
The London Ind Estate
Roding Road
London Ind Park
Aaron Hill Road
Angelica Dr
Henry Addington Cl
County Rd
Winsor Terrace
Stonewall
Beaufort
Creekmouth
Gallions Reach Shopping Park
Armada Way
Health Centre
Beckton Station
East Beckton District Centre
Cygnet Clinic Beckton
Gallions Primary School
Knok
Newark
Tunnan
Leys
Bradymead
Peverel
Downings
Oxleas
Covelees
Wall
Horse Leaze
Savage Gardens
Winsor Primary School
New Beckton Park
Royal Docks Medical Cen
Renfrew Cl
Pennyroyal Avenue
V Cl
Tansy Cl
Ferndale St
E Ham Mnr Way
Strait Road
Cyprus Place
Cyprus Station
Gallions Reach Station
Armada Wy
Atlantis Av
Magellan Blvd
Gallions R
Basin Ap
Albert Basin Wy
University Way
University of East London
Royal Albert Dock
King George V Dock
Margaret or Tripcock Ness
Newham
Greenwich
Defence Cl
Murray Cl
Warrior Cl
Bailey Cl
Miles Dr
Hill View
Brixham St
Station
1 grid square represents 500 metres

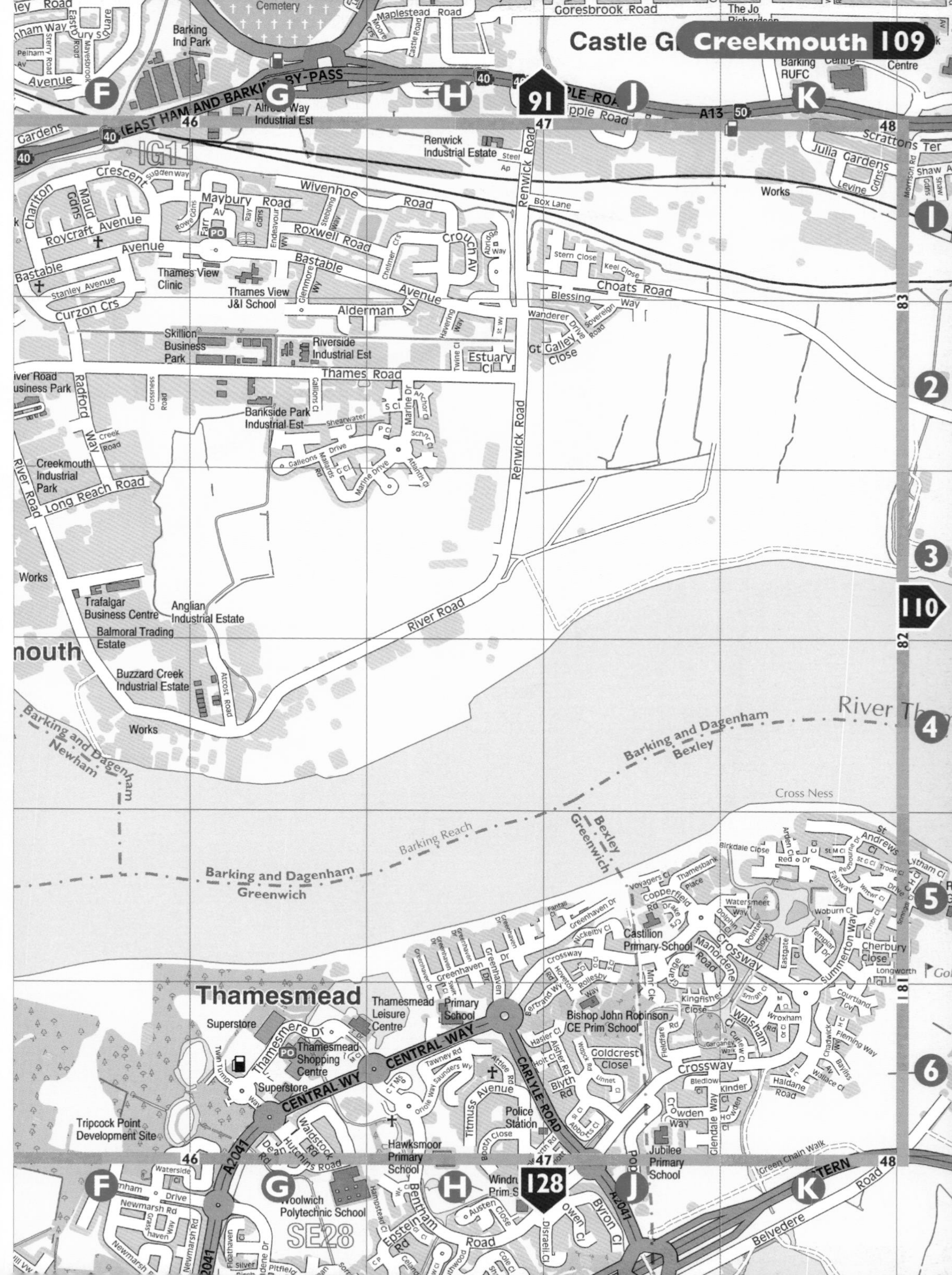
Castle Green
Barking Ind Park
Cemetery
Goresbrook Road
Maplestead Road
Castle Road
Barking RUFC
EAST HAM AND BARKING BY-PASS
Alfreds Way Industrial Est
A13
Renwick Industrial Estate
Renwick Road
IG11
Scrattons Ter
Julia Gardens
Levine Gdns
Works
Crescent
Sugden Way
Wivenhoe Road
Maybury Road
Charlton
Maud Gdns
Roycraft Avenue
Roxwell Road
Crouch Av
Box Lane
Bastable Avenue
Thames View Clinic
Thames View J&I School
Stern Close
Keel Close
Choats Road
Blessing Way
Stanley Avenue
Curzon Crs
Alderman Av
Wanderer Drive
Sovereign Road
Gt Galley Close
Skillion Business Park
Riverside Industrial Est
Estuary Cl
Thames Road
River Road Business Park
Radford Way
Creek Road
Bankside Park Industrial Est
Shearwater Cl
Marine Dr
Galleons Drive
Marine Drive
Creekmouth Industrial Park
Long Reach Road
River Road
Works
Trafalgar Business Centre
Anglian Industrial Estate
Balmoral Trading Estate
Creekmouth
Buzzard Creek Industrial Estate
Atcost Road
Works
River Thames
Barking and Dagenham
Newham
Barking and Dagenham
Bexley
Cross Ness
Barking Reach
Bexley
Greenwich
Barking and Dagenham
Greenwich
Thamesbank Place
Birkdale Close
St Andrews Cl
Copperfield Rd
Watersmeet Way
Castilion Primary School
Crossway
Manordene Road
Woburn Cl
Cherbury Close
Summerton Way
Greenhaven Dr
Thamesmead
Thamesmead Leisure Centre
Primary School
Superstore
Thamesmere Dr
Thamesmead Shopping Centre
Bishop John Robinson CE Prim School
Kingfisher Close
Walsham Cl
Wroxham Rd
Courtland Gv
Fleming Way
CENTRAL WAY
CENTRAL WY
CARLYLE ROAD
Goldcrest Close
Crossway
Haldane Road
Tripcock Point Development Site
Superstore
Titmuss Avenue
Police Station
Blyth Rd
Crowden Way
Glendale Way
Kinder Cl
Jubilee Primary School
Green Chain Walk
Waldstock Rd
Hutchins Road
Hawksmoor Primary School
Woolwich Polytechnic School
Windrush Prim Sch
SE28
Newmarsh Rd
Bentham Road
Byron Cl
Belvedere Road
Austen Close
Owen Cl
Disraeli Cl
A2041
F G H J K
1 2 3 4 5 6
46 47 48
83 82 81
91 110 128

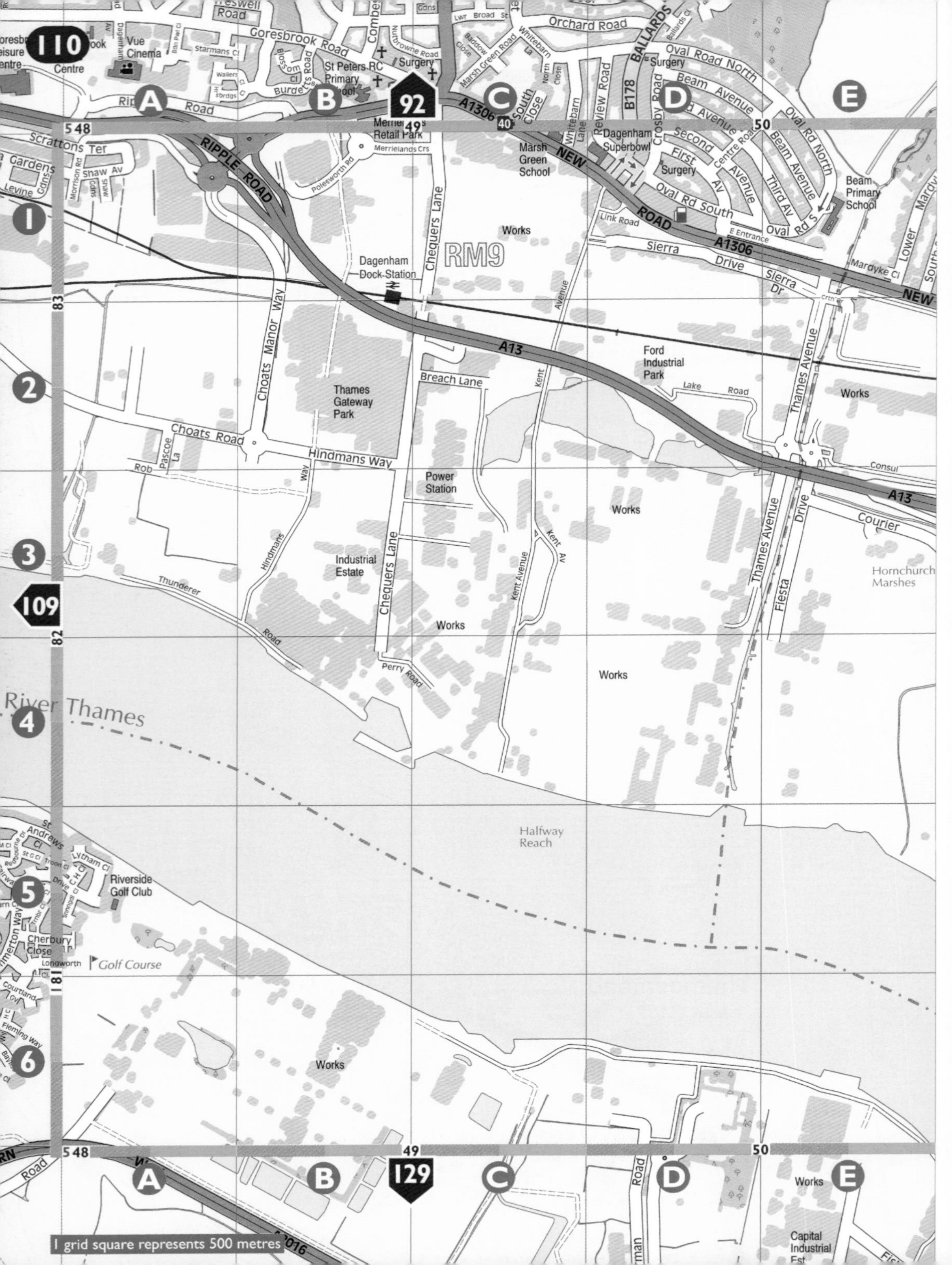

110
92
109
129
RM9
A13
A1306
B178
RIPPLE ROAD
NEW ROAD
Goresbrook Road
Orchard Road
Oval Road North
Dagenham Dock Station
Chequers Lane
Thames Gateway Park
Choats Road
Choats Manor Way
Hindmans Way
Breach Lane
Power Station
Industrial Estate
Thunderer Road
Perry Road
Kent Avenue
Ford Industrial Park
Thames Avenue
Fiesta Drive
Sierra Drive
Works
Marsh Green School
Dagenham Superbowl
Beam Primary School
Hornchurch Marshes
River Thames
Halfway Reach
Riverside Golf Club
Golf Course
Capital Industrial Est
1 grid square represents 500 metres

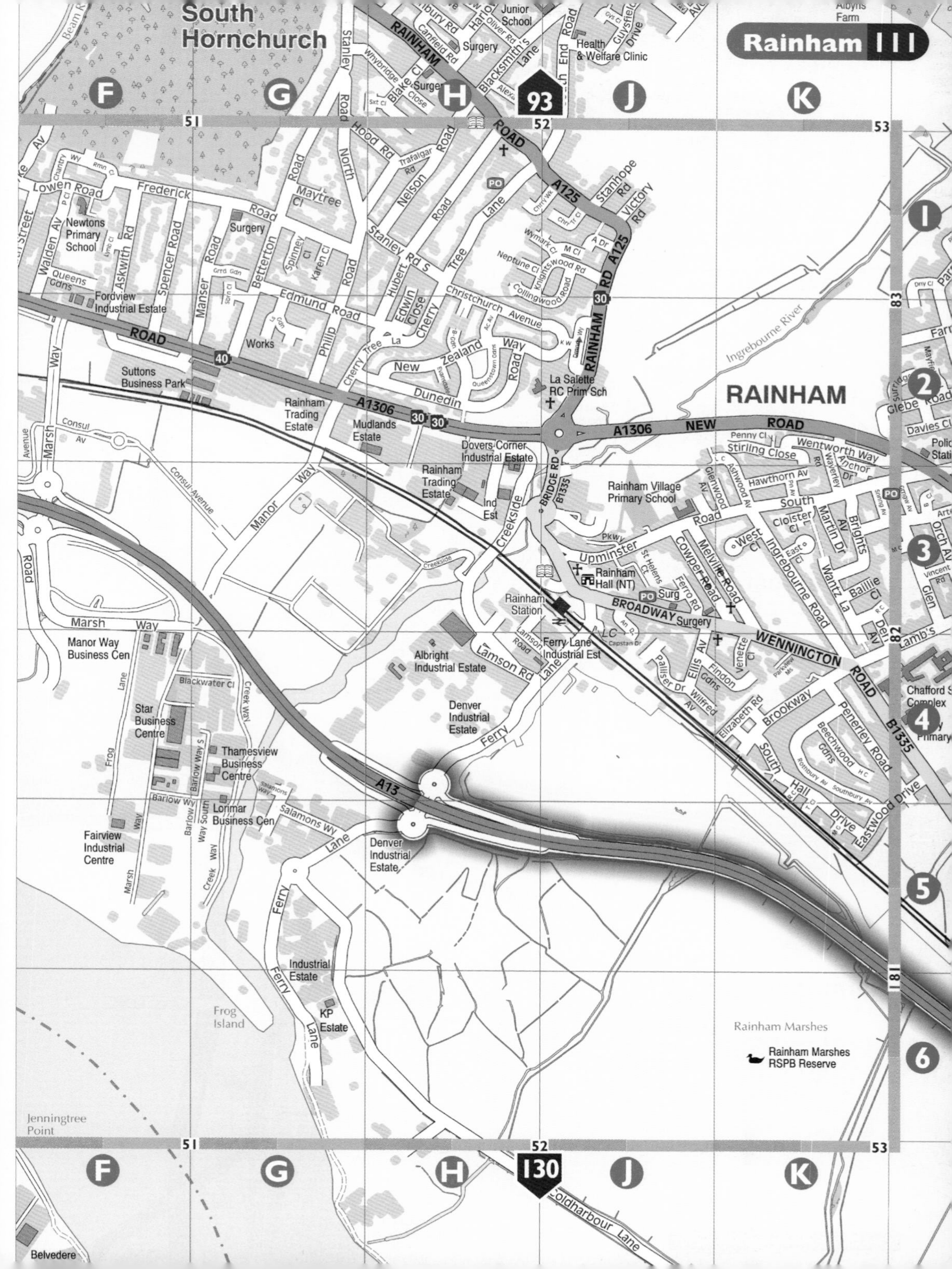
South Hornchurch
RAINHAM
Rainham Marshes
Rainham Marshes RSPB Reserve
Frog Island
Jenningtree Point
Belvedere
Ingrebourne River
Newtons Primary School
Fordview Industrial Estate
Suttons Business Park
Rainham Trading Estate
Mudlands Estate
Dovers Corner Industrial Estate
La Salette RC Prim Sch
Rainham Village Primary School
Rainham Hall (NT)
Rainham Station
Ferry Lane Industrial Est
Albright Industrial Estate
Denver Industrial Estate
Manor Way Business Cen
Star Business Centre
Thamesview Business Centre
Lorimar Business Cen
Fairview Industrial Centre
Industrial Estate
KP Estate
Chafford Sports Complex
Health & Welfare Clinic
Junior School
Surgery
A1306 NEW ROAD
RAINHAM ROAD A125
BROADWAY
WENNINGTON ROAD B1335
BRIDGE RD B1335
A13
Coldharbour Lane
Ferry Lane
Marsh Way
Manor Way
Consul Avenue
Upminster Road
Ingrebourne Road
Lamson Road
Salamons Way
Barlow Way
Creek Way
Frog Lane
Lowen Road
Frederick Road
Edmund Road
Christchurch Avenue
New Zealand Way
Dunedin
Cherry Tree Lane
Stanley Road North
Melville Road
Cowper Road
Brookway
Penerley Road
Eastwood Drive
Wentworth Way
Stirling Close
Hawthorn Av
Glebe Road
93
130
51
52
53
F
G
H
J
K
1
2
3
4
5
6
83
82
81

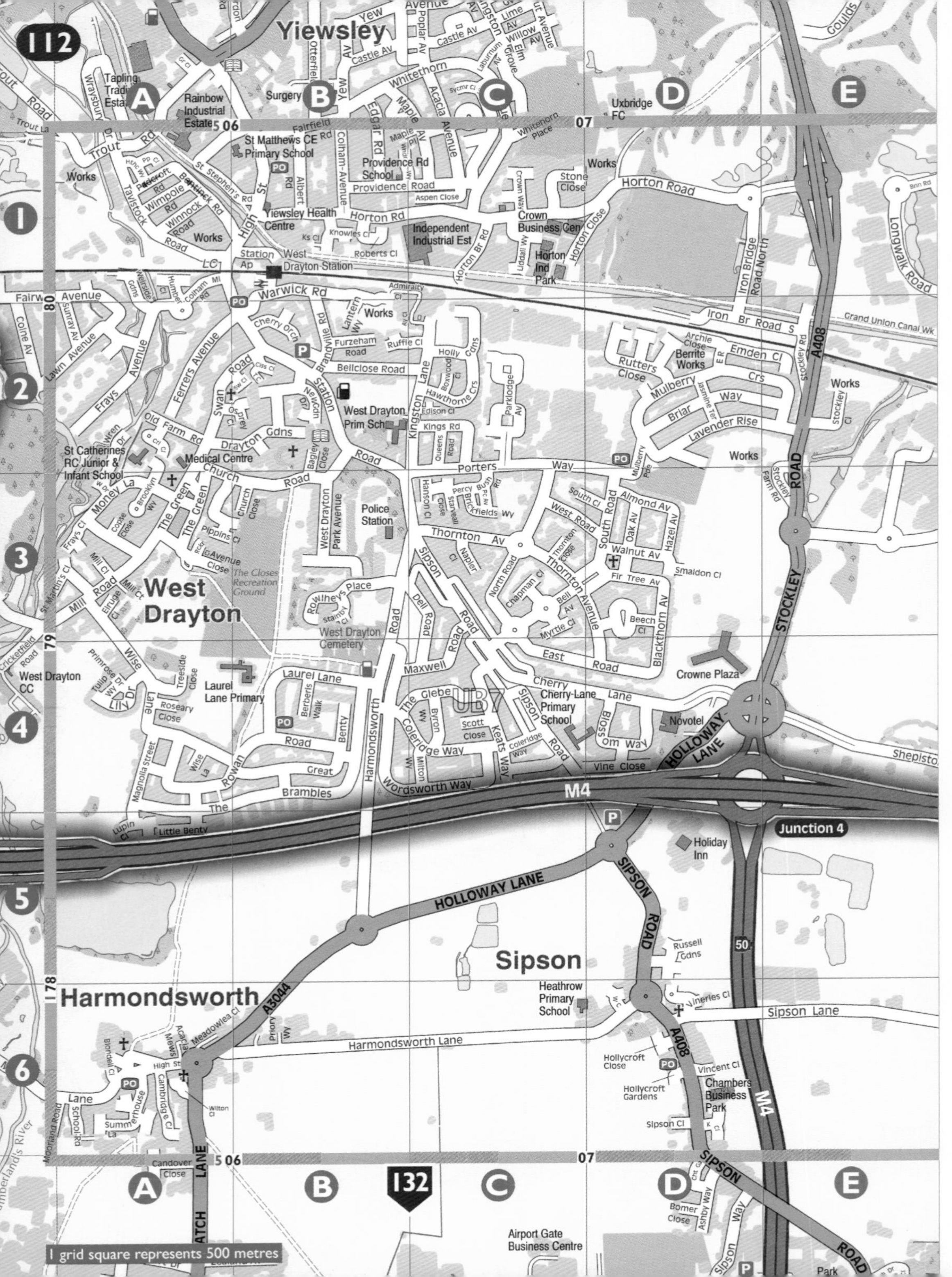
112
Yiewsley
Tapling Trading Estate
Rainbow Industrial Estate
Surgery
St Matthews CE Primary School
Providence Rd School
Yiewsley Health Centre
Independent Industrial Est
Crown Business Cen
Horton Ind Park
Uxbridge FC
Works
Horton Road
Horton Rd
Providence Road
West Drayton Station
Warwick Rd
Iron Bridge Road North
Iron Br Road S
Grand Union Canal Wk
Berrite Works
Longwalk Road
A408
Stockley Road
West Drayton Prim Sch
St Catherines RC Junior & Infant School
Medical Centre
Police Station
Porters Way
Church Road
Thornton Av
Station Road
Kingston Lane
Ferrers Avenue
Lawn Avenue
The Closes Recreation Ground
West Drayton
West Drayton Cemetery
West Drayton CC
Laurel Lane Primary
Cherry-Lane Primary School
Crowne Plaza
Novotel
Holloway Lane
UB7
Harmondsworth Road
Wordsworth Way
M4
Junction 4
Holiday Inn
Sipson Road
Sipson
Heathrow Primary School
Sipson Lane
Harmondsworth
A3044
Harmondsworth Lane
Chambers Business Park
Hatch Lane
Airport Gate Business Centre
132
1 grid square represents 500 metres

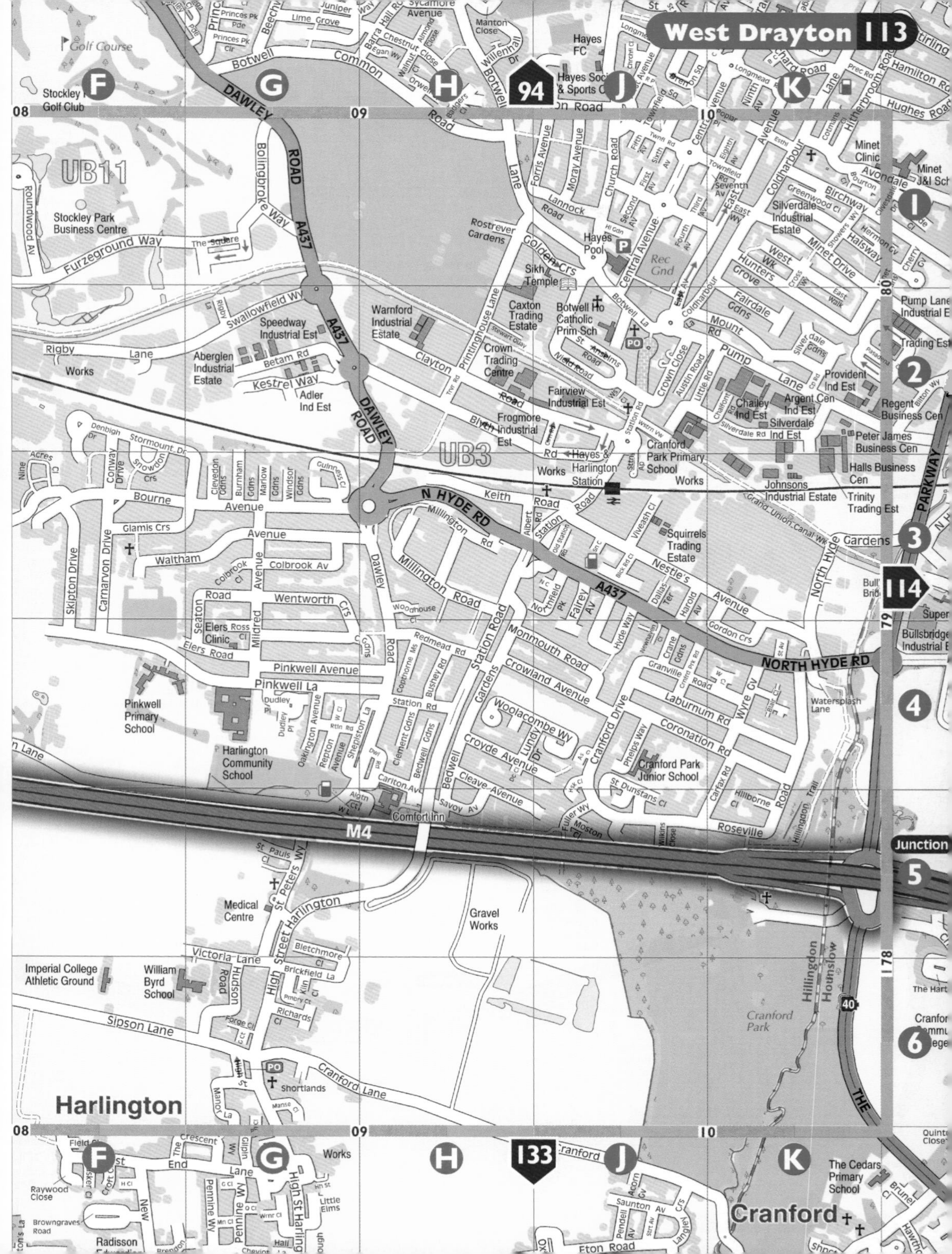
West Drayton 113
94
114
133
F
G
H
J
K
1
2
3
4
5
6
08
09
10
80
79
178
UB11
UB3
Golf Course
Stockley Park Golf Club
Stockley Park Business Centre
Furzeground Way
The Square
Bolingbroke Way
Roundwood Av
Swallowfield Wy
Speedway Industrial Est
Rigby Lane
Works
Aberglen Industrial Estate
Betam Rd
Kestrel Way
Adler Ind Est
DAWLEY ROAD
A437
Botwell Common Road
Princes Pk Pde
Princes Pk Cir
Lime Grove
Juniper Way
Chestnut Close
Walnut Close
Almond Close
Sycamore Avenue
Manton Close
Willenhall Dr
Botwell Lane
Hayes FC
Hayes Social & Sports Club
Forris Avenue
Moray Avenue
Church Road
Central Avenue
Lannock Road
Rostrever Gardens
Golden Crs
Hayes Pool
Rec Gnd
Sikh Temple
Caxton Trading Estate
Botwell Ho Catholic Prim Sch
St Anselms Road
Nield Road
Crown Close
Austin Road
Warnford Industrial Estate
Printinghouse Lane
Clayton Road
Crown Trading Centre
Fairview Industrial Est
Frogmore Industrial Est
Blyth Rd
Hayes & Harlington Station
Cranford Park Primary School
Station Rd
Coldharbour Lane
Pump Lane
Mount Rd
Fairdale Gdns
West Wk
Hunters Grove
Silverdale Industrial Estate
Minet Drive
Birchway
Avondale
Minet Clinic
Minet J&I Sch
Hitherbroom Road
Hamilton Rd
Hughes Road
Pump Lane Industrial Est
Trading Est
Provident Ind Est
Argent Cen
Chailey Ind Est
Silverdale Ind Est
Regent Business Cen
Peter James Business Cen
Halls Business Cen
Johnsons Industrial Estate
Trinity Trading Est
PARKWAY
Grand Union Canal Wk
North Hyde Gardens
Squirrels Trading Estate
Viveash Cl
Nestle's Avenue
N HYDE RD
NORTH HYDE RD
Keith Road
Millington Rd
Millington Road
Denbigh Dr
Stormount Dr
Snowdon Crs
Nine Acres Cl
Conway Drive
Bourne Avenue
Glamis Crs
Avenue
Waltham Avenue
Colbrook Cl
Colbrook Av
Clevedon Gdns
Burnham Gdns
Marlow Gdns
Windsor Gdns
Guinness Cl
Skipton Drive
Carnarvon Drive
Seaton Road
Mildred Avenue
Wentworth Crs
Woodhouse Cl
Elers Clinic
Elers Road
Ross Cl
Pinkwell Avenue
Pinkwell La
Pinkwell Primary School
Harlington Community School
Dudley Pl
Oakington Avenue
Repton Avenue
Shepiston La
Station Rd
Clement Gdns
Bedwell Gdns
Bedwell Gardens
Station Road
Redmead Rd
Copthorne Ms
Bushey Rd
Dawley Road
Monmouth Road
Crowland Avenue
Woolacombe Wy
Croyde Avenue
Lundy Dr
Cleave Avenue
Savoy Av
Carlton Av
Comfort Inn
Northfield Pk
Fairey Av
Hyde Way
Dallas Ter
Harold Av
Gordon Crs
Crane Gdns
Granville Road
Laburnum Rd
Wyre Gv
Coronation Rd
Cranford Drive
Phelps Way
Cranford Park Junior School
St Dunstans Cl
Fuller Wy
Moston Cl
Carfax Rd
Hillborne Cl
Roseville
Waterspash Lane
Hillingdon Trail
Bullsbridge Industrial Est
Junction 5
M4
St Pauls Cl
St Peters Wy
Medical Centre
High Street Harlington
Gravel Works
Bletchmore Cl
Brickfield La
Kiln Cl
Victoria Lane
Hudson Road
Richards Cl
Forge Cl
Imperial College Athletic Ground
William Byrd School
Sipson Lane
Cranford Lane
Shortlands
Manor La
Harlington
Cranford Park
Hillingdon
Hounslow
40
THE
The Hart
Field Cl
The Crescent
Gladin Wy
Works
Raywood Close
Browngraves Road
Radisson
Pennine Wy
Little Elms
Acorn Gv
Saunton Av
Pendell Av
Langley Crs
Cranford
The Cedars Primary School
Brunel Cl
Eton Road
Quinta Close

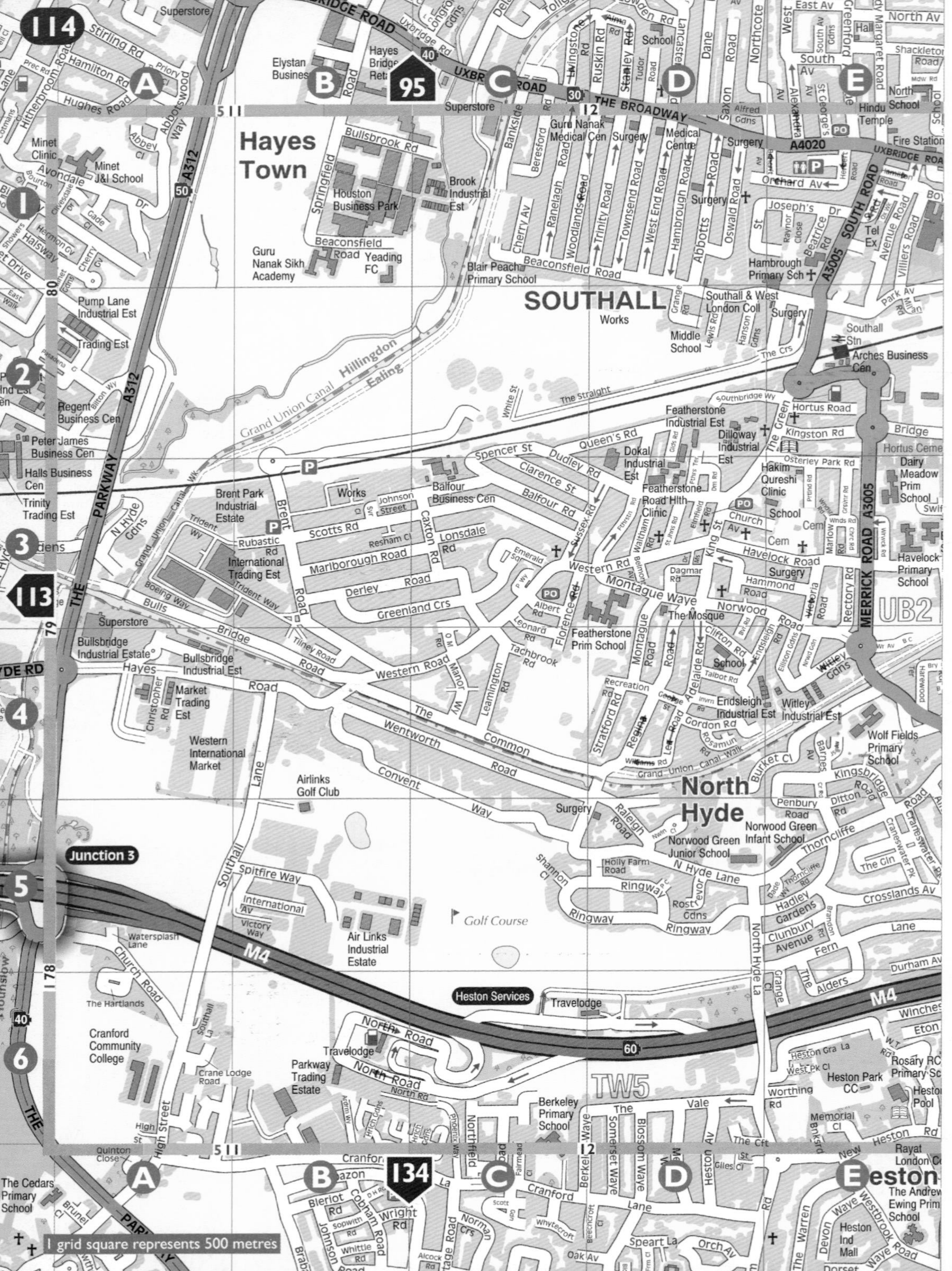
114
95
113
134
A
B
C
D
E
A
B
C
D
E
1
2
3
4
5
6
5 11
12
80
79
178
UXBRIDGE ROAD
UXBRIDGE ROAD
THE BROADWAY
A4020
Hayes Town
SOUTHALL
North Hyde
UB2
TW5
Superstore
Stirling Rd
Hamilton Rd
Hughes Road
Hitherbroon Road
Prec Rd
Priory
Abbotswood Way
Abbey Cl
Minet Clinic
Minet J&I School
Avondale Dr
Gade Cl
Halsway
Cherry Cl
Pump Lane Industrial Est
Trading Est
Regent Business Cen
Peter James Business Cen
Halls Business Cen
Trinity Trading Est
Superstore
Bullsbridge Industrial Estate
Bullsbridge Industrial Est
HYDE RD
Hayes Road
Christopher Rd
Market Trading Est
Western International Market
Junction 3
Watersplash Lane
Church Road
The Hartlands
Cranford Community College
Crane Lodge Road
High Street
High St
Quinton Close
The Cedars Primary School
Brunel Cl
Hounslow
THE PARKWAY
A312
50
40
Elystan Business
Hayes Bridge Retail
Bullsbridge Rd
Springfield Road
Houston Business Park
Brook Industrial Est
Beaconsfield Road
Guru Nanak Sikh Academy
Yeading FC
Blair Peach Primary School
Grand Union Canal
Hillingdon
Ealing
Brent Park Industrial Estate
Brent Road
Trident Wy
Rubastic Rd
International Trading Est
Works
Johnson Street
Balfour Business Cen
Scotts Rd
Resham Cl
Caxton Rd
Lonsdale Rd
Marlborough Road
Derley Road
Greenland Crs
Boeing Way
Bulls Bridge Road
Tilney Road
Western Road
Manor Wy
Leamington Rd
Tachbrook Rd
The Common
Wentworth Road
Convent Way
Airlinks Golf Club
Southall Lane
Spitfire Way
International Av
Victory Way
Air Links Industrial Estate
Golf Course
M4
Heston Services
Travelodge
North Road
Travelodge
Parkway Trading Estate
North Road
60
Northfield Road
Berkeley Primary School
The Vale
Somerset Waye
Blossom Waye
Heston Av
The Cft
Giles Cl
Cranford Lane
Bleriot Rd
Cobham Road
Wright Rd
Johnson Road
Whittle Rd
Norman Crs
Whytecroft
Speart La
Oak Av
Orch Av
Superstore
Bankside
Beresford Road
Guru Nanak Medical Cen
Surgery
Medical Centre
Ranelagh Road
Woodlands Road
Trinity Road
Townsend Road
West End Road
Hambrough Road
Abbotts Road
Oswald Road
Cherry Av
Beaconsfield Road
Ruskin Rd
Stanley Rd
Tudor Road
Lancaster Rd
Dane Road
Saxon Road
Northcote Av
Lowden Rd
School
Alfred Gdns
Surgery
Works
Grange Rd
Southall & West London Coll
Middle School
Lewis Rd
Hanson Gdns
The Crs
Surgery
Southall Stn
Arches Business Cen
The Straight
White St
Southbridge Wy
Featherstone Industrial Est
Dilloway Industrial Est
The Green
Hortus Road
Kingston Rd
Bridge
Queen's Rd
Spencer St
Dudley Rd
Clarence St
Balfour Rd
Dokal Industrial Est
Featherstone Road Hlth Clinic
Sussex Rd
Waltham Rd
Hakim Qureshi Clinic
School
Church Av
Cem
Havelock Road
Surgery
Hammond Road
Norwood Road
Western Rd
Emerald Sq
Albert Rd
Leonard Rd
Florence Rd
Featherstone Prim School
Montague Waye
Montague Road
The Mosque
Dagmar Rd
King St
Clifton Rd
Endsleigh Rd
Adelaide Rd
School
Talbot Rd
Recreation Rd
Stratford Rd
Regina Rd
Lea Road
Gordon Rd
Rosamun Rd
Williams Rd
Endsleigh Industrial Est
Witley Industrial Est
Witley Gdns
Grand Union Canal Walk
Burket Cl
Surgery
Raleigh Road
Norwood Green Junior School
Norwood Green Infant School
Holly Farm Road
Shannon Cl
N Hyde Lane
Ringway
Ringway
Ringway
Rost Gdns
North Hyde La
Grange Cl
Penbury Road
Ditton Rd
Kingsbridge Road
Thorncliffe
Hadley Gardens
Clunbury Avenue
Fern Lane
Crosslands Av
The Gln
Cranesw ater Pk
Durham Av
The Alders
Wolf Fields Primary School
Barnes Av
Rectory Rd
Victoria Road
Ellison Gdns
Marlow
Havelock Primary School
Dairy Meadow Prim School
Osterley Park Rd
Hortus Cem
MERRICK ROAD A3005
SOUTH ROAD A3005
Orchard Av
Joseph's Dr
Raynor Close
Beatrice Rd
Hambrough Primary Sch
Tel Ex
Avenue Road
Villiers Road
Park Av
Fire Station
Hindu Temple
North School
Shackleton Road
North Av
East Av
West
South Av
Greenford
Margaret Road
Alexandra Av
St George's
PO
Hall
Heston Gra La
West Pk Cl
Heston Park CC
Worthing Rd
Memorial Cl
Heston Rd
Rosary RC Primary Sc
Heston Pool
Rayat London Co
Heston
The Andrew Ewing Prim School
Westbrook Road
Devon Wave
Heston Ind Mall
Dorset Waye
The Warren
New Heston Rd
Winches
Eton
1 grid square represents 500 metres

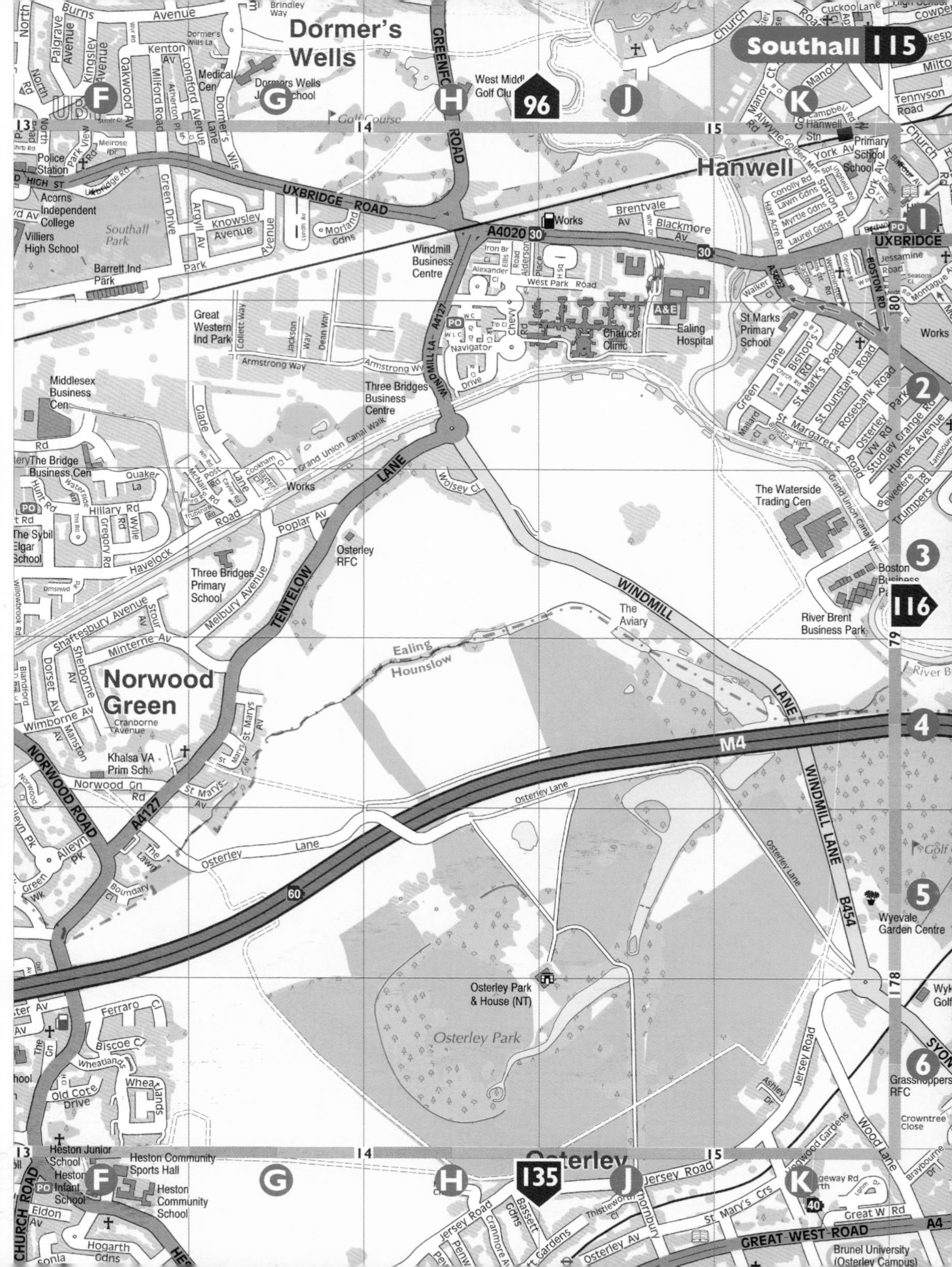

Southall 115
Dormer's Wells
Dormers Wells
Medical Cen
West Middl Golf Clu
96
Golf Course
Hanwell
Hanwell Stn
Primary School
Police Station
Acorns Independent College
Villiers High School
Southall Park
Barrett Ind Park
UXBRIDGE ROAD
HIGH ST
A4020
30
Works
Windmill Business Centre
Brentvale Av
Blackmore Av
West Park Road
UXBRIDGE
Great Western Ind Park
Armstrong Way
Navigator Drive
Chaucer Clinic
A&E
Ealing Hospital
St Marks Primary School
Middlesex Business Cen
Three Bridges Business Centre
Grand Union Canal Walk
The Bridge Business Cen
Quaker La
Hillary Rd
Havelock Road
Poplar Av
Osterley RFC
The Sybil Elgar School
Three Bridges Primary School
Melbury Avenue
Shaftesbury Avenue
Minterne Av
TENTELOW LANE
WINDMILL LA A4127
GREENFORD ROAD
WINDMILL LANE
The Aviary
The Waterside Trading Cen
Boston Business Pa
116
River Brent Business Park
Ealing
Hounslow
Norwood Green
Cranborne Avenue
Wimborne Av
Khalsa VA Prim Sch
Norwood Gn Rd
NORWOOD ROAD
A4127
M4
Osterley Lane
60
B454
Golf
Wyevale Garden Centre
Osterley Park & House (NT)
Osterley Park
Grasshoppers RFC
Crowntree Close
Jersey Road
Wood Lane
Heston Junior School
Heston Community Sports Hall
Heston Infant School
Heston Community School
Osterley
135
Jersey Road
Thornbury
Great W Rd
GREAT WEST ROAD
A4
Brunel University (Osterley Campus)
CHURCH ROAD
Hogarth Gdns
Old Cote Drive
Wheatlands
Biscoe Cl
Ferraro Cl
F G H J K
2 3 4 5 6
13 14 15
179 178 180

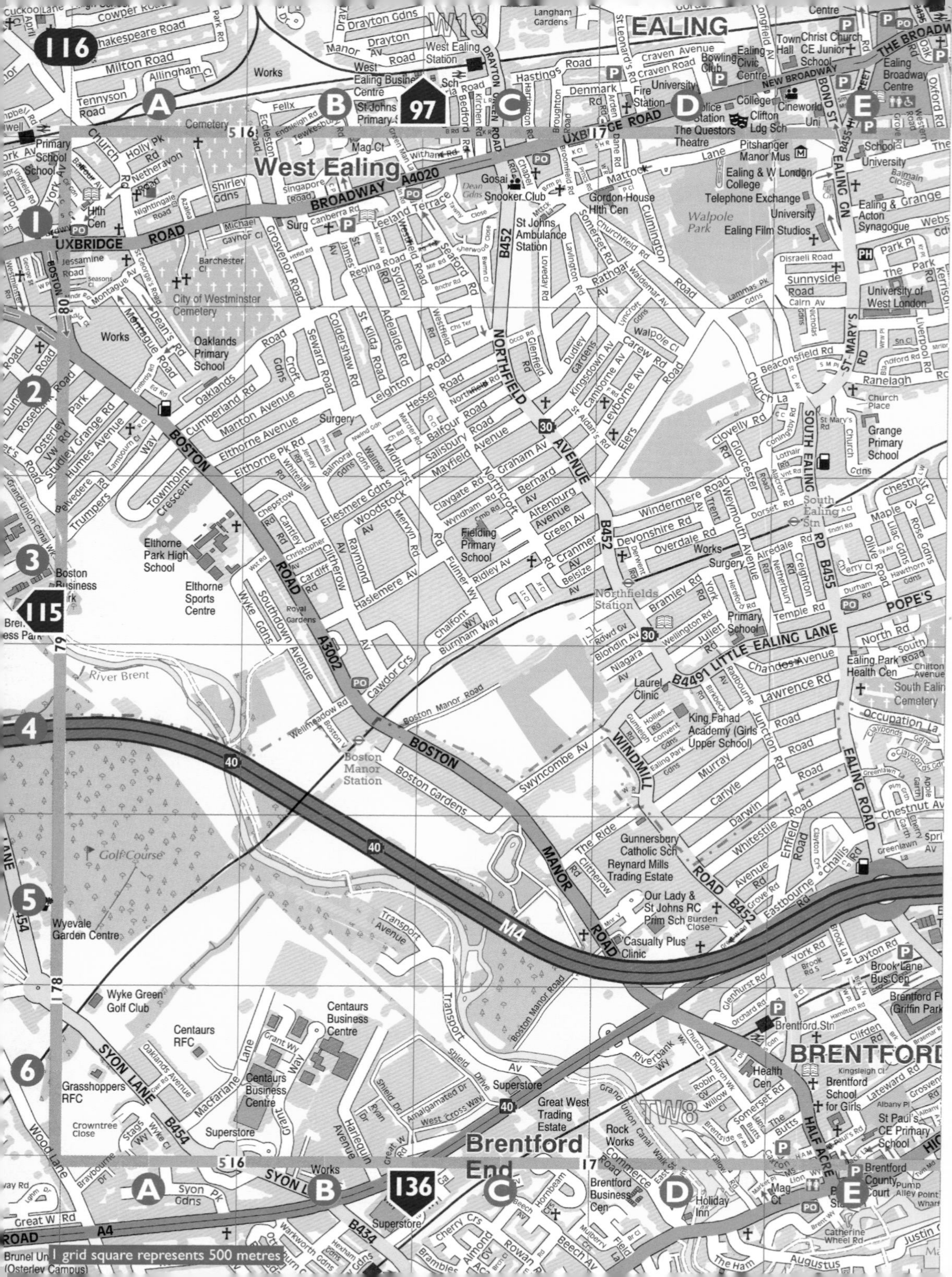
116
97
115
136
A
B
C
D
E
1
2
3
4
5
6
516
17
80
79
78
EALING
W13
West Ealing
Brentford End
BRENTFORD
TW8
Cowper Road
Shakespeare Road
Milton Road
Allingham Cl
Tennyson Road
Drayton Gdns
Drayton Av
Manor Road
West Ealing Station
West Ealing Business Centre
Works
Langham Gardens
Hastings Road
Denmark Rd
Craven Avenue
Craven Road
St Leonard's Rd
Ealing Civic Centre
Bowling Club
Town Hall
Christ Church CE Junior School
THE BROADWAY
NEW BROADWAY
Ealing Broadway Centre
Cineworld
Fire Station
Police Station
University
College
Clifton Ldg Sch
The Questors Theatre
Uni
Pitshanger Manor Mus
Felix
St Johns Primary S
Cemetery
Eccleston Road
Tewkesbury Rd
Mag Ct
Witham Rd
UXBRIDGE ROAD
BROADWAY A4020
Primary School
Holly Pk Rd
Netheravon Road
Shirley Gdns
Singapore Road
Leeland Terrace
Gosai Snooker Club
Gordon House Hlth Cen
Mattock Lane
Ealing & W London College
Telephone Exchange
University
Ealing Film Studios
Walpole Park
Ealing & Acton Synagogue
Hlth Cen
Surg
Canberra Rd
Michael Gaynor Cl
Barchester Cl
Jessamine Road
Grosvenor Road
St Johns Ambulance Station
Churchfield Rd
Culmington Road
Somerset Rd
Loveday Rd
Lavington Rd
Rathgar Av
Waldemar Av
Regina Road
Sydney Rd
Westfield Road
Seaford Rd
Disraeli Road
Sunnyside Road
Calrn Av
Park Pl
The Park
University of West London
Montague Av
City of Westminster Cemetery
Works
Oaklands Primary School
Oaklands Rd
Cumberland Rd
Manton Avenue
Croft Gdns
Seward Road
Coldershaw Rd
St Kilda Road
Adelaide Rd
Leighton Rd
Hessel Road
NORTHFIELD AVENUE
B452
Glenfield Rd
Dudley Gardens
Kingsdown Av
Camborne Av
Leyborne Av
Carew Rd
Walpole Cl
Lammas Pk Gdns
Church La
Beaconsfield Rd
ST MARY'S RD
Ranelagh
Church Place
Grange Primary School
SOUTH EALING RD
Clovelly Rd
Gloucester Rd
St Mary's Rd
Church Gdns
Montague Road
Dean's Rd
Rosebank Road
Osterley Park Vw Rd
Studley Grange Rd
Humes Avenue
Belvedere Rd
Trumpers
Grand Union Canal Wk
BOSTON ROAD
A3002
Townholm Crescent
Elthorne Avenue
Elthorne Pk Rd
Surgery
Balfour Road
Salisbury Road
Mayfield Avenue
Graham Av
Bernard Av
Altenburg Avenue
Green Av
Cranmer Av
Elers Rd
Midhurst Rd
Walmer Gdns
Balmoral Gdns
Erlesmere Gdns
Woodstock Av
Mervyn Rd
Claygate Rd
Wyndham Rd
Northcroft Rd
Fielding Primary School
Ridley Av
Beisize Av
Windermere Road
Devonshire Rd
Overdale Rd
Dorset Rd
Works
Surgery
Airedale Rd
Weymouth Avenue
Netherbury Rd
Creighton Rd
South Ealing Stn
Chestnut Gv
Maple Gv
Rose Gdns
Lilac Gdns
Olive Road
Hawthorn Gdns
Durham Rd
POPE'S
Temple Rd
North Rd
South Road
Elthorne Park High School
Elthorne Sports Centre
Boston Business Park
Chepstow Rd
Cantley Rd
Cardiff Rd
Clitherow Av
Raymond Rd
Haslemere Av
Fulmer Wy
Chalfont Wy
Burnham Way
Southdown Avenue
Wyke Gdns
Royal Gardens
Northfields Station
Bramley Rd
York Rd
Primary School
Wellington Rd
Jullien Rd
Blondin Av
Niagara Av
LITTLE EALING LANE
B4491
Chandos Avenue
Lawrence Rd
Ealing Park Health Cen
South Ealing Cemetery
Occupation La
River Brent
Cawdor Crs
Boston Manor Road
Boston Manor Station
BOSTON MANOR ROAD
Boston Gardens
Swyncombe Av
Laurel Clinic
King Fahad Academy (Girls Upper School)
WINDMILL ROAD
Murray
Carlyle
Darwin
Whitestile Road
Enfield Road
Junction Rd
EALING ROAD
Chestnut Av
Greenlawn
40
M4
Golf Course
The Ride
Clitherow Rd
Gunnersbury Catholic Sch
Reynard Mills Trading Estate
Our Lady & St Johns RC Prim Sch
Burden Close
Casualty Plus Clinic
Eastbourne Rd
Grove Rd
Transport Avenue
Wyevale Garden Centre
Wyke Green Golf Club
Centaurs RFC
Centaurs Business Centre
Grasshoppers RFC
SYON LANE
B454
Oaklands Avenue
Macfarlane Lane
Grant Way
Superstore
Crowntree Close
Wood Lane
Harlequin Avenue
Shield Drive
Amalgamated Dr
West Cross Way
Great West Trading Estate
Boston Manor Road
Riverbank Wy
Glenhurst Rd
Orchard Rd
Brentford Stn
Church Wk
Health Cen
Robin Gv
Willow
Somerset Rd
The Butts
HALF ACRE
Brentford School for Girls
St Paul's CE Primary School
Brook Lane Bus Cen
Brentford FC (Griffin Park)
Clifden Rd
York Rd
Brook La N
Layton Rd
Lateward Rd
Rock Works
Commerce Road
Grand Union Canal Walk
Brentford Business Cen
Holiday Inn
Mag Ct
Brentford County Court
Catherine Wheel Rd
Syon Pk Gdns
SYON L
Works
Superstore
B434
Great W Rd
A4
ROAD
Cherry Crs
Almond
Rowan Rd
Brambles
Hornbeam
Beech Av
Warkworth Gdns
Hexham Gdns
The Ham
Augustus
Brunel Un (Osterley Campus)
1 grid square represents 500 metres

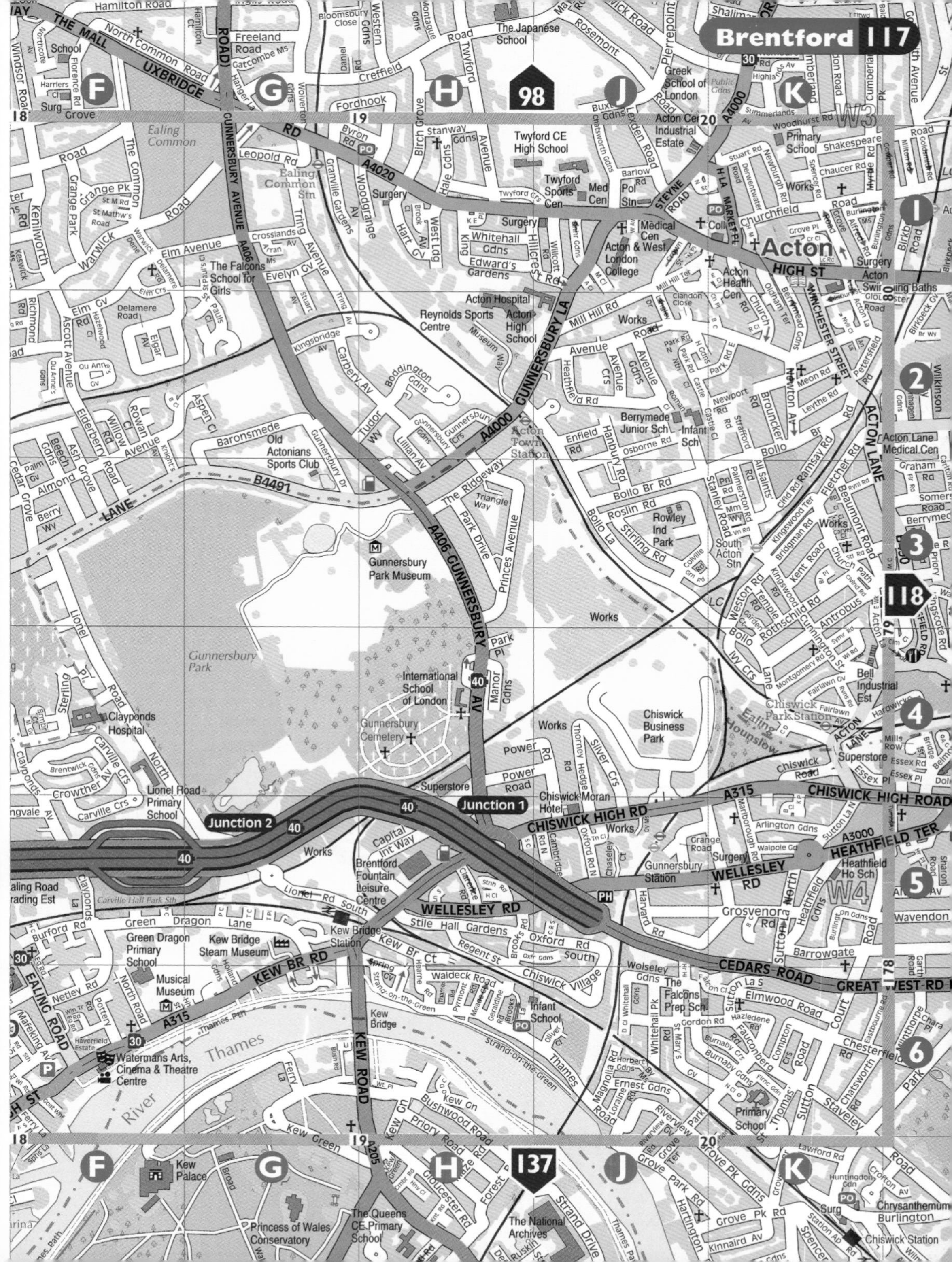

Brentford 117
98
118
137
F
G
H
J
K
18
19
20
2
3
4
5
6
Acton
W3
W4
Ealing Common
Gunnersbury Park
Gunnersbury Park Museum
Gunnersbury Cemetery
International School of London
The Japanese School
Greek School of London
Twyford CE High School
Twyford Sports Cen
Ealing Common Stn
Acton Hospital
Acton High School
Reynolds Sports Centre
Acton & West London College
Acton Health Cen
Acton Town Station
South Acton Stn
Berrymede Junior Sch
Infant Sch
Old Actonians Sports Club
The Falcons School for Girls
Rowley Ind Park
Chiswick Business Park
Chiswick Park Station
Bell Industrial Est
Acton Lane Medical Cen
Claypondss Hospital
Lionel Road Primary School
Junction 1
Junction 2
Superstore
Chiswick Moran Hotel
Gunnersbury Station
Heathfield Ho Sch
Brentford Fountain Leisure Centre
Kew Bridge Station
Kew Bridge Steam Museum
Green Dragon Primary School
Musical Museum
Waterman's Arts, Cinema & Theatre Centre
The Falcons Prep Sch
Infant School
Primary School
Kew Palace
Princess of Wales Conservatory
The Queens CE Primary School
The National Archives
Chiswick Station
River Thames
UXBRIDGE RD
A4020
GUNNERSBURY AVENUE
A406
GUNNERSBURY LA
A4000
B4491
CHISWICK HIGH RD
A315
WELLESLEY RD
CEDARS ROAD
GREAT WEST RD
HEATHFIELD TER
A3000
KEW BR RD
KEW ROAD
EALING ROAD
ACTON LANE
HIGH ST
STEYNE ROAD
Strand-on-the-Green
Kew Green

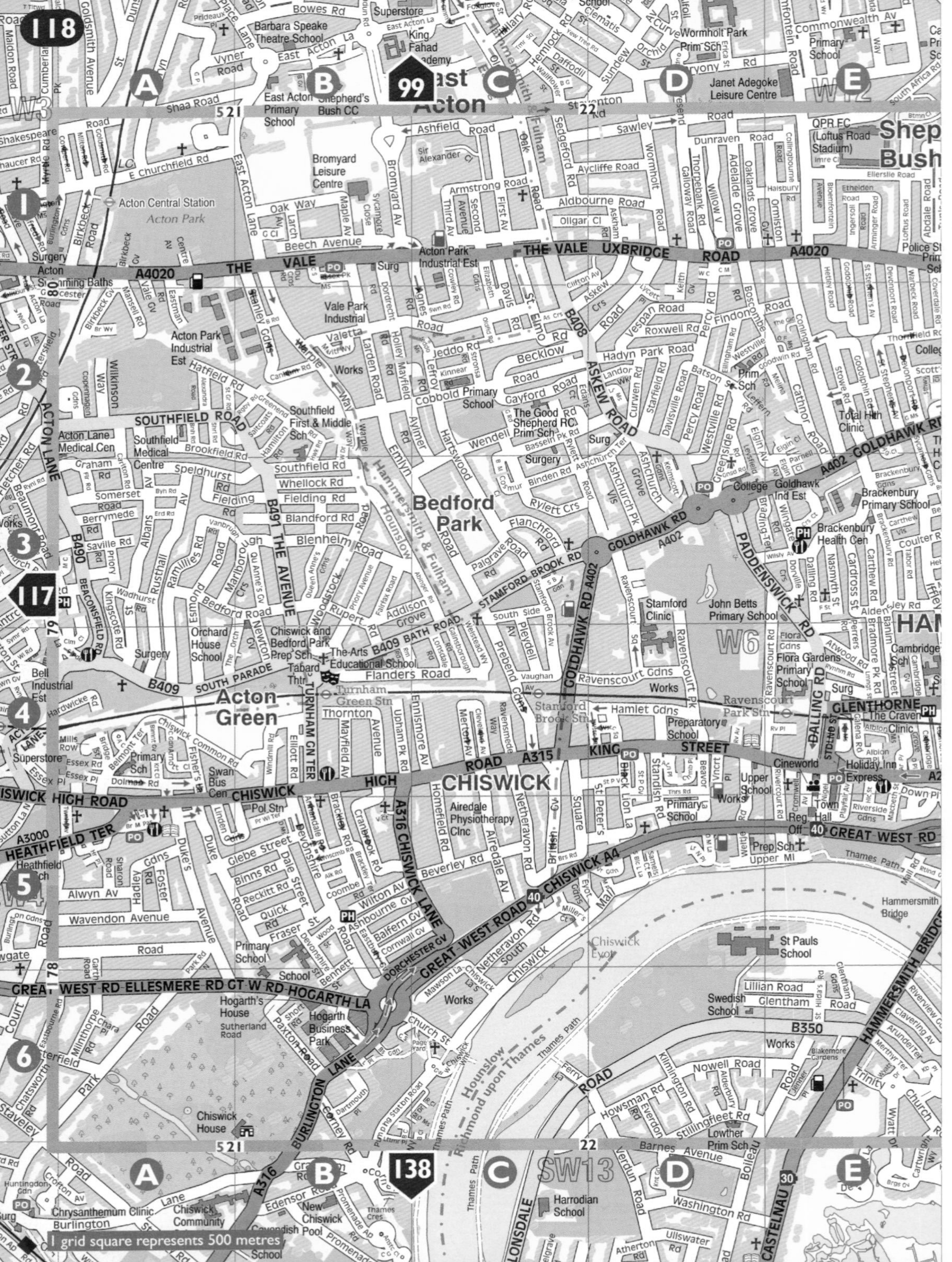
118
99
117
138
A
B
C
D
E
1
2
3
4
5
6
521
22
W3
W12
W6
SW13
East Acton
Shepherd's Bush
Bedford Park
Acton Green
CHISWICK
Barbara Speake Theatre School
King Fahad Academy
Superstore
East Acton Primary School
Shepherd's Bush CC
Wormholt Park Prim Sch
Janet Adegoke Leisure Centre
Primary School
QPR FC (Loftus Road Stadium)
Bromyard Leisure Centre
Acton Central Station
Acton Park
Acton Park Industrial Est
Acton Swimming Baths
Vale Park Industrial
Works
Surgery
Acton Lane Medical Cen
Southfield Medical Centre
Southfield First & Middle Sch
Cobbold Primary School
The Good Shepherd RC Prim Sch
Prim Sch
Total Hlth Clinic
College
Goldhawk Ind Est
Brackenbury Primary School
Brackenbury Health Cen
Stamford Clinic
John Betts Primary School
Flora Gardens Primary School
Cambridge Sch
Orchard House School
Chiswick and Bedford Park Prep Sch
The Arts Educational School
Tabard Thtr
Turnham Green Stn
Stamford Brook Stn
Ravenscourt Park Stn
Preparatory School
Upper School
Primary School
Cineworld
Holiday Inn Express
The Craven Clinic
Town Hall
Reg Off
Prep Sch
Bell Industrial Est
Superstore
Primary Sch
Swan Bus Cen
Pol Stn
Airedale Physiotherapy Clnc
Heathfield Ch
Hogarth's House
Hogarth Business Park
Chiswick Eyot
St Pauls School
Swedish School
Lowther Prim Sch
Harrodian School
Chiswick House
Chrysanthemum Clinic
Chiswick Community School
New Chiswick Pool
Hammersmith Bridge
Hounslow
Richmond upon Thames
Thames Path
THE VALE
UXBRIDGE ROAD
A4020
GOLDHAWK RD
A402
ASKEW ROAD
B408
ACTON LANE
SOUTHFIELD ROAD
B491 THE AVENUE
B409 BATH ROAD
STAMFORD BROOK RD
GOLDHAWK RD A402
PADDENSWICK RD
DALLING RD
GLENTHORNE RD
KING STREET
A315
CHISWICK HIGH ROAD
HEATHFIELD TER
A3000
A316 CHISWICK LANE
GREAT WEST RD ELLESMERE RD GT W RD HOGARTH LA
GREAT WEST ROAD
CHISWICK A4
BURLINGTON LANE
A316
HAMMERSMITH BRIDGE
B350
CASTELNAU
LONSDALE
BEACONSFIELD RD
B490
I grid square represents 500 metres

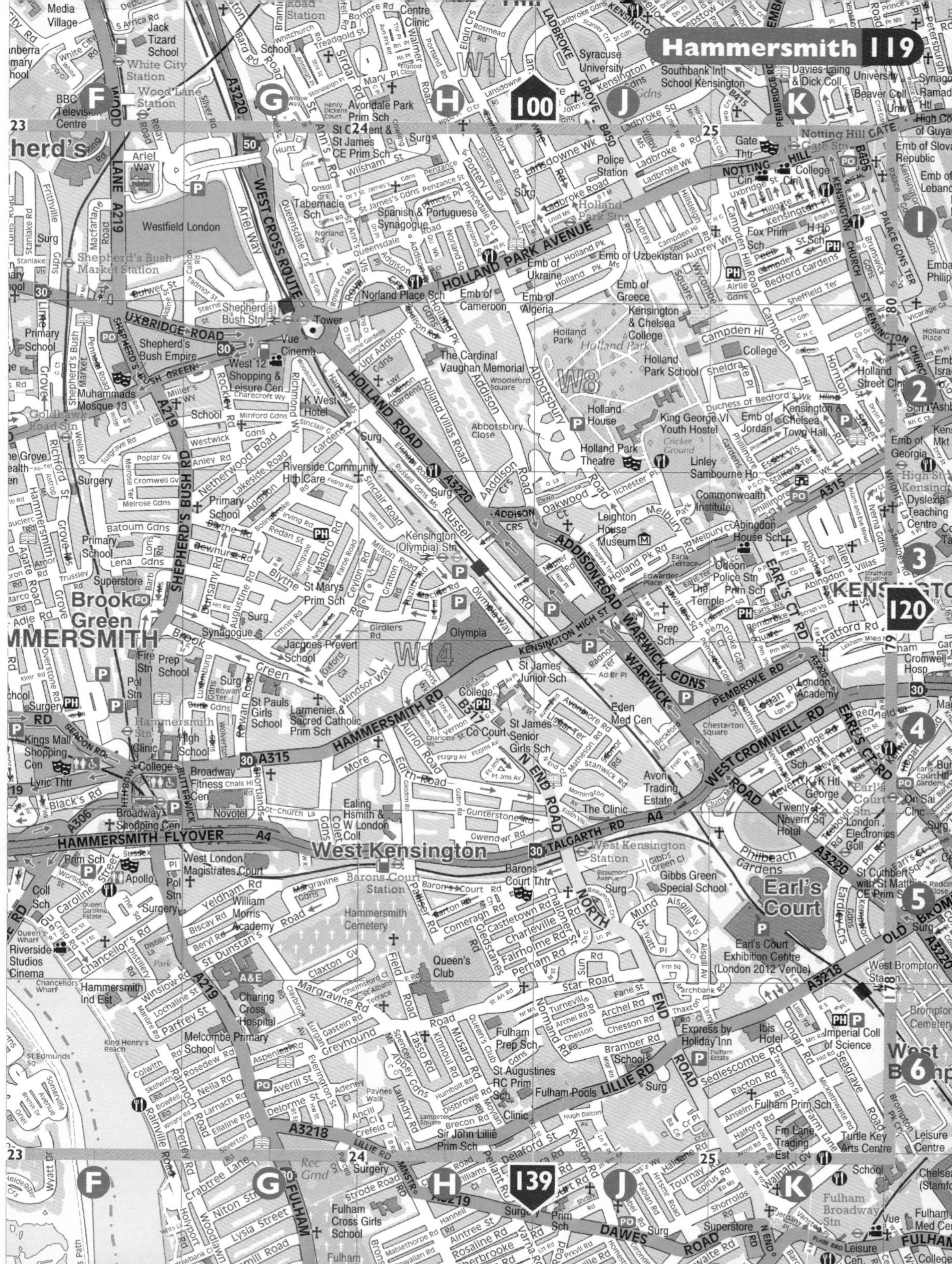
Media Village
Jack Tizard School
White City Station
Wood Lane Station
BBC Television Centre
Avondale Park Prim Sch
Syracuse University
Southbank Intl School Kensington
Davies Laing & Dick Coll
Notting Hill Gate Stn
Westfield London
Shepherd's Bush Market Station
Shepherd's Bush Stn
Tower
Vue Cinema
Shepherd's Bush Empire
West 12 Shopping & Leisure Cen
WEST CROSS ROUTE
HOLLAND PARK AVENUE
UXBRIDGE ROAD
Holland Park Stn
Norland Place Sch
Emb of Ukraine
Emb of Uzbekistan
Emb of Algeria
Emb of Greece
Emb of Cameroon
Kensington & Chelsea College
Holland Park
Holland Park School
Holland House
King George VI Youth Hostel
Holland Park Theatre
Linley Sambourne Ho
Commonwealth Institute
Leighton House Museum
Kensington & Chelsea Town Hall
The Cardinal Vaughan Memorial
HOLLAND ROAD
Abbotsbury Close
Riverside Community Hlth Care
Kensington (Olympia) Stn
Olympia
W14
W8
W11
KENSINGTON HIGH ST
ADDISON ROAD
WARWICK GDNS
PEMBROKE RD
WEST CROMWELL RD
EARL'S CT RD
Brook Green
HAMMERSMITH
Muhammads Mosque 13
Goldhawk Road Stn
Jacques Prevert School
St Pauls Girls School
Larmenier & Sacred Catholic Prim Sch
HAMMERSMITH RD
St James Junior Sch
St James Senior Girls Sch
Eden Med Cen
Avon Trading Estate
Chesterton Square
London Academy
Cromwell Hosp
Hammersmith Stn
Kings Mall Shopping Cen
Lyric Thtr
Broadway Shopping Cen
Novotel
HAMMERSMITH FLYOVER
TALGARTH RD
West Kensington
West Kensington Station
Barons Court Station
Barons Court Thtr
Ealing Hsmith & W London Coll
West London Magistrates Court
William Morris Academy
Hammersmith Cemetery
Queen's Club
Gibbs Green Special School
Earl's Court
Earl's Court Exhibition Centre (London 2012 Venue)
Earl's Court Stn
London Electronics Coll
Philbeach Gardens
Riverside Studios Cinema
Charing Cross Hospital
Hammersmith Ind Est
Melcombe Primary School
Fulham Prep Sch
St Augustines RC Prim Sch
Fulham Pools
LILLIE RD
Sir John Lillie Prim Sch
Express by Holiday Inn
Ibis Hotel
Imperial Coll of Science
West Brompton Station
Brompton Cemetery
Fulham Prim Sch
Fm Lane Trading Est
Turtle Key Arts Centre
Fulham Cross Girls School
Fulham Broadway Stn
DAWES ROAD
FULHAM
100
120
139

101
119
140
8
14
A
B
C
D
E
1
2
3
4
5
6
BAYSWATER RD
A402
Lancaster Gate Station
Queensway Station
Hyde Park
Speakers Corner
Victoria Gate
City of Westminster Vehicle Pound
Speke's Monument
Peter Pan Statue
Kensington Gardens
Physical Energy Statue
Round Pond
Norwegian/British Monument
Hyde Park (London 2012 Venue)
Serpentine Road
The Serpentine
Diana Princess of Wales Memorial Fountain
Serpentine Gallery
Kensington Palace State Apartments & Royal Ceremonial Dress Collection
Rotten Row
SW7
Knightsbridge
Albert Memorial
Alexandra Gate
Prince of Wales Gate
Edinburgh Gate
Albert Gate
South Carriage Drive
KENSINGTON ROAD
A315
KNIGHTSBRIDGE
Royal Albert Hall
Royal Geographical Society
Imperial Coll of London
Royal College of Music
Science Mus
Victoria & Albert Mus
The Natural History Mus
Earth Galleries
Brompton Oratory
Harrods Store
Brompton
KENSINGTON
High St Kensington Stn
Gloucester Road Stn
CROMWELL RD A4
Cromwell Hosp
South Kensington Stn
Pelham Street
BROMPTON RD
A4 BROMPTON RD
THURLOE PL
SLOANE STREET
PONT ST
BEAUCHAMP PL
Earl's Court Stn
BROMPTON ROAD
South Kensington
Royal Marsden Hosp
Royal Brompton Hospital
FULHAM ROAD
KING'S ROAD
Chelsea Old Town Hall
Chelsea Cinema
Chelsea Leisure Cen
National Army Mus
Chelsea Physic Garden
ROYAL HOSPITAL ROAD
CHELSEA EMBANKMENT
A3212
Cadogan Pier
Albert Bridge
Battersea Bridge
Kensington & Chelsea
Wandsworth
Carlyle's Ho (NT)
Saatchi Gallery
Duke of York Sq
West Brompton Stn
Brompton Cemetery
West Brompton
SW10
REDCLIFFE GDNS
FINBOROUGH RD
OLD BROMPTON RD
A3220
A3218
Chelsea & Westminster Hospital
Fulham Broadway Stn
FULHAM ROAD
Chelsea FC (Stamford Bridge)
Millennium & Copthorne Hotels at Chelsea FC
Worlds End Place
Kensington Wharf
Albert Bridge Gate
Peace Pagoda
Ransomes Dock Bus Cen
ALBERT
A3031
A3217
1 grid square represents 500 metres

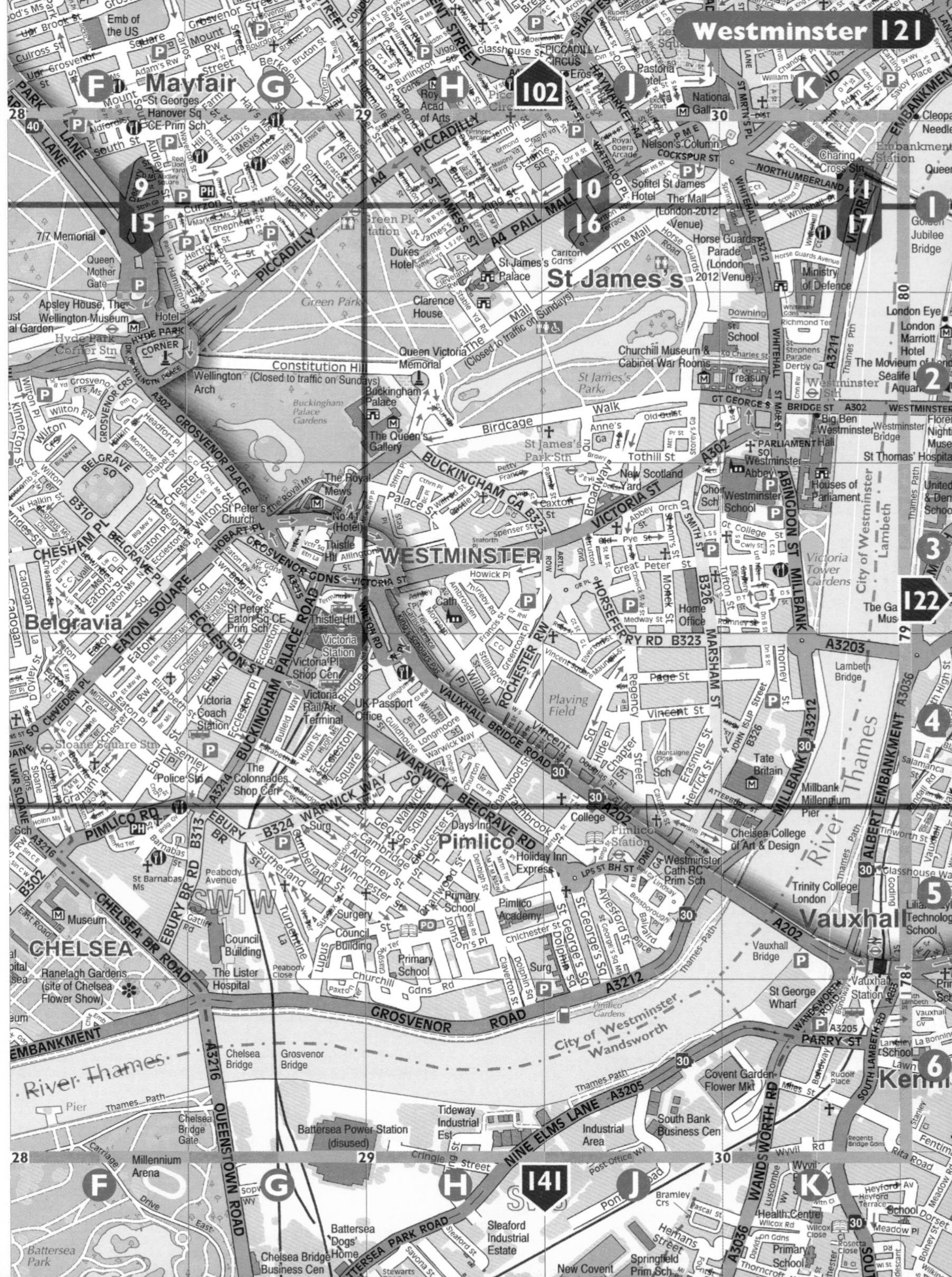
Mayfair
St James's
WESTMINSTER
Belgravia
Pimlico
Vauxhall
CHELSEA
Green Park
St James's Park
River Thames
Buckingham Palace
Victoria Station
Houses of Parliament
Westminster Abbey
Tate Britain
Battersea Power Station (disused)
Ranelagh Gardens (site of Chelsea Flower Show)
102
122
141

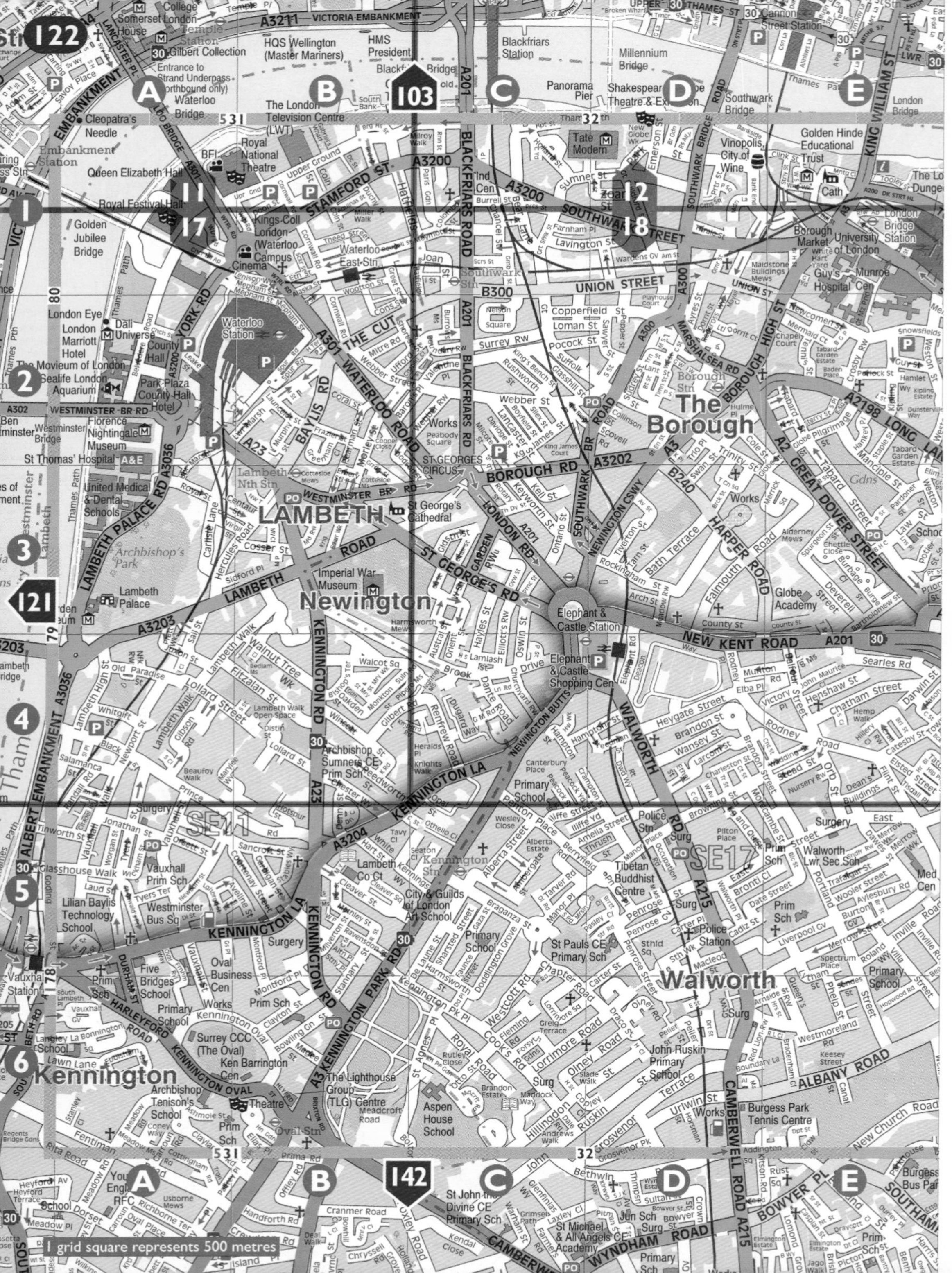
122
103
121
142
A
B
C
D
E
1
2
3
4
5
6
VICTORIA EMBANKMENT
Somerset House
Gilbert Collection
HQS Wellington (Master Mariners)
HMS President
Blackfriars Station
Millennium Bridge
Panorama Pier
Shakespeare's Globe Theatre & Exhibition
Southwark Bridge
London Bridge
Cleopatra's Needle
Waterloo Bridge
The London Television Centre (LWT)
Embankment Station
Royal National Theatre
BFI
Queen Elizabeth Hall
Royal Festival Hall
Golden Jubilee Bridge
Tate Modern
Vinopolis, City of Wine
Golden Hinde Educational Trust
Cath
The London Dungeon
London Bridge Station
Borough Market
University of London
Guy's Hospital
Kings Coll London (Waterloo Campus)
Waterloo East Stn
Cinema
STAMFORD ST
SOUTHWARK STREET
UNION STREET
BLACKFRIARS ROAD
SOUTHWARK BRIDGE ROAD
Southwark Stn
London Eye
London Marriott Hotel
Dali Universe
County Hall
Waterloo Station
The Movieum of London
Sealife London Aquarium
Park Plaza County Hall Hotel
WESTMINSTER BR RD
Westminster Bridge
Florence Nightingale Museum
St Thomas' Hospital
A&E
United Medical & Dental Schools
THE CUT
WATERLOO ROAD
BAYLIS RD
YORK RD
MARSHALSEA RD
BOROUGH HIGH ST
LONG LANE
The Borough
Borough Stn
Peabody Square
ST GEORGES CIRCUS
BOROUGH RD
Lambeth Nth Stn
LAMBETH
St George's Cathedral
WESTMINSTER BR RD
LAMBETH PALACE RD
Archbishop's Park
Lambeth Palace
LAMBETH ROAD
ST GEORGE'S RD
Imperial War Museum
Newington
LONDON RD
Elephant & Castle Station
Elephant & Castle Shopping Cen
NEWINGTON CSWY
HARPER ROAD
GREAT DOVER STREET
Globe Academy
NEW KENT ROAD
Bath Terrace
KENNINGTON RD
NEWINGTON BUTTS
KENNINGTON LA
WALWORTH RD
Archbishop Sumners CE Prim Sch
ALBERT EMBANKMENT
SE11
SE17
Lambeth Walk
Vauxhall Prim Sch
Lilian Baylis Technology School
Westminster Bus Sq
Lambeth Co Ct
City & Guilds of London Art School
Kennington Stn
Tibetan Buddhist Centre
Walworth Lwr Sec Sch
Police Stn
St Pauls CE Primary Sch
Walworth
Vauxhall Station
Five Bridges School
Oval Business Cen
HARLEYFORD ROAD
KENNINGTON OVAL
KENNINGTON PARK RD
Surrey CCC (The Oval)
Ken Barrington Cen
Kennington
Archbishop Tenison's School
Theatre
Oval Stn
The Lighthouse Group (TLG) Centre
Aspen House School
John Ruskin Primary School
CAMBERWELL ROAD A215
ALBANY ROAD
Burgess Park Tennis Centre
Young England RFC
St John the Divine CE Primary Sch
St Michael & All Angels CE Academy
WYNDHAM ROAD
BOWYER PL
Burgess Bus Park
531
32
80
79
1 grid square represents 500 metres

Lambeth 123
Shadwell
St George in the East
104
Wapping
BERMONDSEY
River Thames
Tower of London
Tower Bridge
Tower Stairs
London Bridge City Pier
Hays Galleria
HMS Belfast
Winston Churchill's Britain at War Experience
GLA HQ (City Hall)
The Tower Bridge Exhibition
Design Museum
Butlers & Colonial Wharf
Millennium Square
The Tower Hotel
St Katharine Docks
Royal Mint Court
THE HIGHWAY A1203
Wapping Lane
Wapping High Street
Wapping Station
Wapping Wharf
Tower Bridge Wharf
Capital Wharf
Aberdeen Wharf
Police Station
Chambers Wharf
Cherry Garden Pier
Kings Stairs
Church Stairs
Brunel Engine House
Rotherhithe
Rotherhithe Tunnel
Rotherhithe Street
Tower Hamlets
Southwark
JAMAICA ROAD
JAMAICA RD A200
TOOLEY STREET
TOWER BRIDGE RD
A2206 GRANGE ROAD
B202 ABBEY STREET
A2206 SOUTHWARK PARK RD
RAYMOUTH ROAD
ROTHERHITHE NEW RD
LOWER ROAD A200
OLD KENT ROAD
ALBANY ROAD
ROLLS ROAD B204
CATLIN ST
A2208
DUNTON ROAD
TRAFALGAR AV
B215
WILLOWBROOK RD
PECKHAM PK ROAD
B216
Drummond Road
Southwark Park Road
SE16
Southwark Park
Southwark College
Harris Academy Bermondsey
St Michaels Catholic Coll
City of London Academy
Canada Water Station
Canada Water Retail Park
Seven Islands Leisure Cen
Dock Offices
Southwark Park Primary School
Southwark Park Sports Centre
Cavendish School
Bermondsey Trading Est
Admiral Hyson Industrial Est
South Bermondsey Station
Lewisham Lions Centre
Millwall FC (The New Den)
Surrey Canal
Orion Business Cen
Canterbury Ind Est
Enterprise Ind Est
Sandgate Trading Estate
Kent Park Industrial Estate
Rich Industrial Estate
Pilgrims Way J&I School
Livesey Museum for Children
St Francis RC Primary School
Haymerle Sch
Horizon Ind Est
Six Bridges Trading Est
Cantium Retail Park
Council Building
Phoenix Prim Sch
Burgess Park
Burgess Park Lake
Cobourg Prim Sch
New Peckham Mosque
Winchcombe Business Cen
Gloucester Prim Sch
Damilola Taylor Cen
Surrey Sq Prim Sch
Discovery Business Park
Voyager Business Est
Dockley Road Ind Est
John Dixon Clnc
Bermondsey Stn
Health Cen
Civic Cen
Albion Prim Sch
City Bus Cen
Great Jubilee Wharf
New Crane Wharf
St Peters CE Primary School
Hermitage Primary School
John Orwell Sports Cen
Infants School
13
19
124
143
33
34
35
F
G
H
J
K
1
2
3
4
5
6

124
105
123
144
A
B
C
D
E
1
2
3
4
5
6
536
37
80
79
78
POPLAR
Rotherhithe
Canary Wharf
Millwall
DEPTFORD
E14
SE8
Tower Hamlets
Southwark
Lewisham
River Thames
Limehouse Reach
Surrey Docks
Greenland Dock
Millwall Docks
Free Trade Wharf
Shadwell Dock Stairs
Old Sun Wharf
Chimnocks Wharf
Victoria Wharf
Blyth's Wharf
Dunbar Wharf
Dundee Wharf
King & Queen Wharf
Globe Wharf
Pumphouse Educational Mus
Four Seasons Hotel
Limehouse Hole Stairs
Canary Riverside
Canada Wharf Museum
Pier
Horn Stairs
Nelson Dock Museum
Lawrence Wharf
Canary Wharf Pier
Westferry Stn
Westferry Circ
Museum of London Docklands
West India Quay Station
West India Shop Cen
Canary Wharf Station
Cabot Sq
Cabot Place
Canada Place
The North Colonnade
The South Colonnade
Canada Sq
Citigroup Tower
Heron Quays Station
Heron Quays
River House Montessori Sch
Lutomer House Business Centre
Wood Wharf
HSBC Tower
Billingsgate Fish Market
West India Dock
Bellamy's Wharf
Leeside Court
Youth Hostel
Peter Hills School
Salter Road
Fisher Athletic FC
Bacon's College
Redriff Prim Sch
Surrey Docks Health Cen
St Johns RC Primary School
Alfred Salter Prim Sch
Mulberry Business Cen
Quebec Industrial Estate
Durands Wharf
Trinity Business Cen
Surrey Docks Farm
West India Pier
Millennium Harbour
Marsh Wall
Byng Street
South Quay Plaza
South Quay Sta
Poplar Business Park
Guardian Newspapers
Barkantine Clinic
Seven Mills Primary Sch
Enterprise Business Park
New Caledonian Wharf
Helsinki Sq
New Atlas Wharf
Tiller Road
Tiller Cen (Swimming Baths)
Crossharbour Station
Glengall Bridge
Canada Water Station
Associated Newspapers Off
Hollywood Bowl
Canada Water Retail Park
Dock Offices
Odeon Cinema
Surrey Quays Leisure Park
Surrey Quays Shopping Centre
Redriff Rd
Finland Street
Rainbow Quay
Greenland Pier
Primary School
Old Bellgate Wharf
Tiller Leisure Cen
Daily Telegraph
Docklands Sailing & Watersports Centre
Surrey Docks Watersports Centre
Howland Quay
Rope Street
South Lock
Surrey Quays Station
Greenland Quay
Plough Way
Lower Road
Rotherhithe New Rd
Med Cen
Hawkstone Estate
Millwall FC (The New Den)
Arden Crs
The Space Arts Centre Cinema
Medical Cen
Spindrift Avenue
Westferry Road
Grove St
Woodcroft Ms
Works
Cannon Wharf Bus Cen
Grove Medical Cen
Pepys Estate
Diploma Works
Pepys Park
Deptford Park Primary School
Victoria Wharf Industrial Estate
Deptford Park
Deptford Park Business Cen
Convoy's Wharf
Landing Stage
Borthwick Wharf
Trinity Estate
Phoenix Court
Burrells Wharf
Fire Station
Morecambe St
Gemini Business Estate
Orion Business Cen
Deptford Bus Cen
Silwood Estate Regeneration Area
Trundley's Road
Grinstead Road
Comelle Ho Trading Est
Deptford Trading Est
Evelyn St
Canal Road
Juno Way
Lewisham Business Cen
Elizabeth Trading Est
Bridge House Meadows
Juno Way Ind Est
Industrial Estate
Canterbury Ind Est
Folkestone Gardens
Parkside Business Est
The Kingfisher Medical Cen
Arklow Trading Est
Kings Langley College of Management
Primary School
Hlth Cen
Goldsmiths University
Creek Road
The Wallace Cen
Bellerbys College
Millennium Quay
Greenwich Reach
Deptford Creek
Sanford Street
Deptford Stn
Giffin Bus Cen
Cncl Bldg
Albany Cen & Theatre
Laban Centre
Faircharm Trading Est
Novotel
Arts Centre
New Cross Sports Arena
Health Cen
Deptford Church Street
1 grid square represents 500 metres

Blackwall
River Thames
Tower Hamlets
Greenwich
Newham
Blackwall Reach
Bugsby's Reach
BLACKWALL TUNNEL
A102
North Greenwich Arena
(O₂ Arena)
(London 2012 Venue)
The O₂
Emirates Air Line (Cable Car)
(due to open Summer 2012)
North Greenwich Pier
North Greenwich Station
Ravensbourne
London Soccerdome
Tunnel Avenue Trading Est
Delta Wharf
Millennium Way
Edmund Halley Way
West Parkside
East Parkside
John Harrison Wy
Gas Works
Millennium Prim Sch
BUGSBY'S WAY
Greenwich Odeon
Brocklebank Industrial Estate
Angerstein Business Park
Superstore
WOOLWICH ROAD
Westcombe Park Station
Lawrence Trading Estate
Maritime Mus
BLACKWALL LANE
A2203
East Greenwich Christ Church CE Prim Sch
The Heart of Greenwich Development
A206
TRAFALGAR ROAD
GREENWICH
University of Greenwich
Trinity Hospital
Lovell's Wharf
Meridian Prim Sch
Old Royal Naval College
Trinity College of Music
Cutty Sark Clipper Ship
Gypsy Moth IV
Cutty Sark Station
Greenwich Pier
National Maritime Museum
The Queens House
Greenwich Park
(London 2012 Venue)
Maze Hill Station
Arches Leisure Cen
ROMNEY ROAD
CREEK ROAD
Greenwich Theatre & Art Gallery
The Fan Museum
Flamsteed House Museum
Old Royal Observatory
Blackheath High Senior School
Invicta Primary School
Greenwich Steiner Sch
John Roan Sch
Cubitt Town
ISLE OF DOGS
Mudchute Park
Mudchute City Farm
Island Gardens Station
George Greens School
MANCHESTER ROAD
Cubitt Town Infant School
Millennium Wharf
Island Clinic
Pumping Station
Wood Wharf Business Park
PRESTON'S ROAD
A1206
Blackwall Station
Radisson Edwardian Hotel
Poplar Business Park
ASPEN
Royal Victoria Docks Watersports Centre
West Silvertown Station
Greenshields Industrial Est
Minerva Works
N Woolwich Road
SILVERTOWN WAY
Faraday School
East India Station
London Natural Therapy School
Ibis Hotel
Novotel
106
126
145
F G H J K
1 2 3 4 5 6
38 39 40

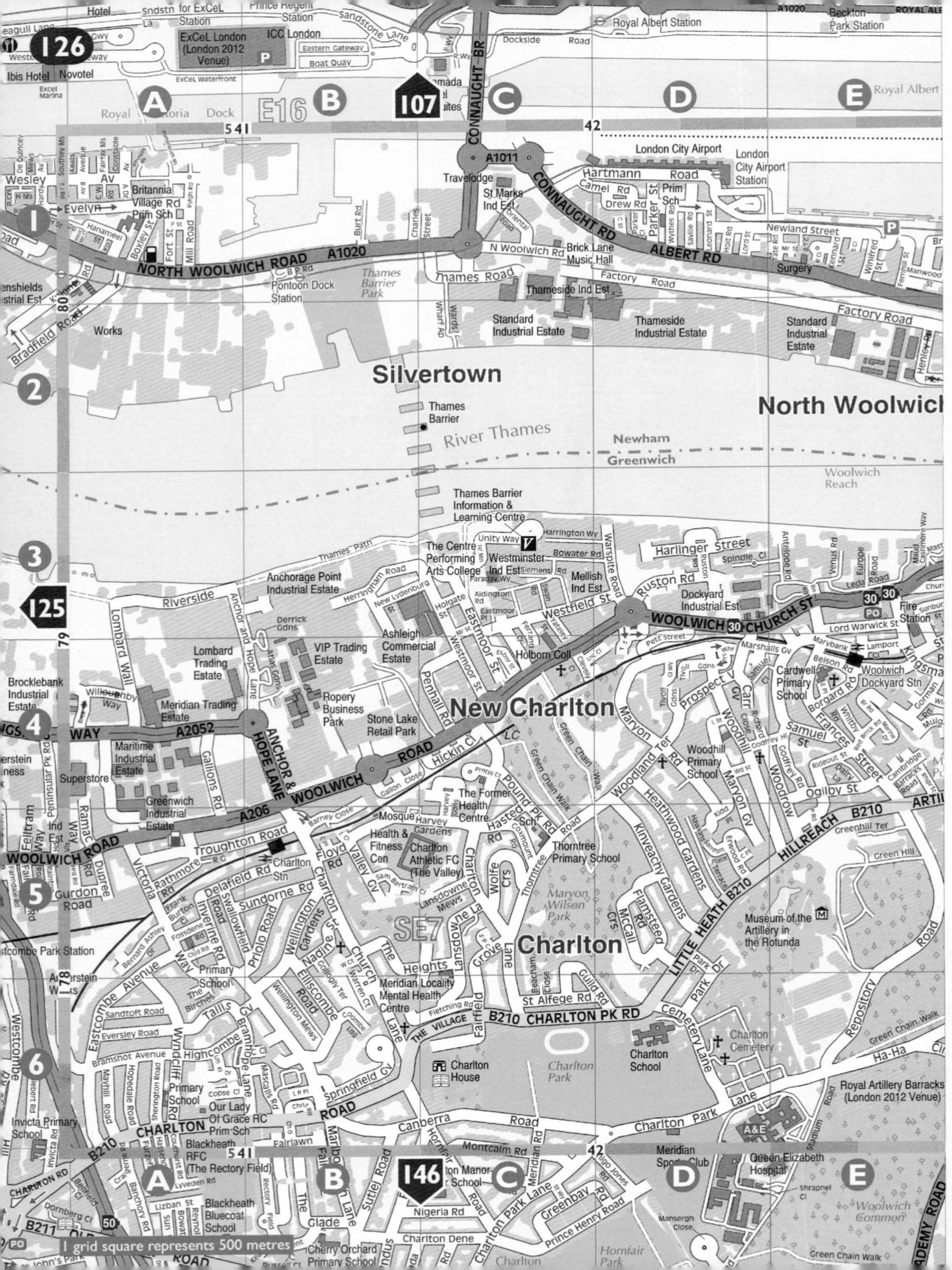
126
107
125
146
Silvertown
North Woolwich
New Charlton
Charlton
River Thames
Thames Barrier
Newham
Greenwich
E16
SE7
NORTH WOOLWICH ROAD A1020
CONNAUGHT BR
CONNAUGHT RD
ALBERT RD
A1011
London City Airport
London City Airport Station
Pontoon Dock Station
Thames Barrier Park
Thames Barrier Information & Learning Centre
WOOLWICH CHURCH ST
WOOLWICH ROAD
A206
A2052
ANCHOR & HOPE LANE
Charlton Stn
Charlton Athletic FC (The Valley)
Maryon Wilson Park
Charlton Park
Charlton House
Charlton Cemetery
Charlton School
B210 CHARLTON PK RD
LITTLE HEATH B210
HILLREACH B210
Woolwich Dockyard Stn
Museum of the Artillery in the Rotunda
Royal Artillery Barracks (London 2012 Venue)
Queen Elizabeth Hospital
Woolwich Common
ExCeL London (London 2012 Venue)
Royal Victoria Dock
Royal Albert Station
Westcombe Park Station
1 grid square represents 500 metres

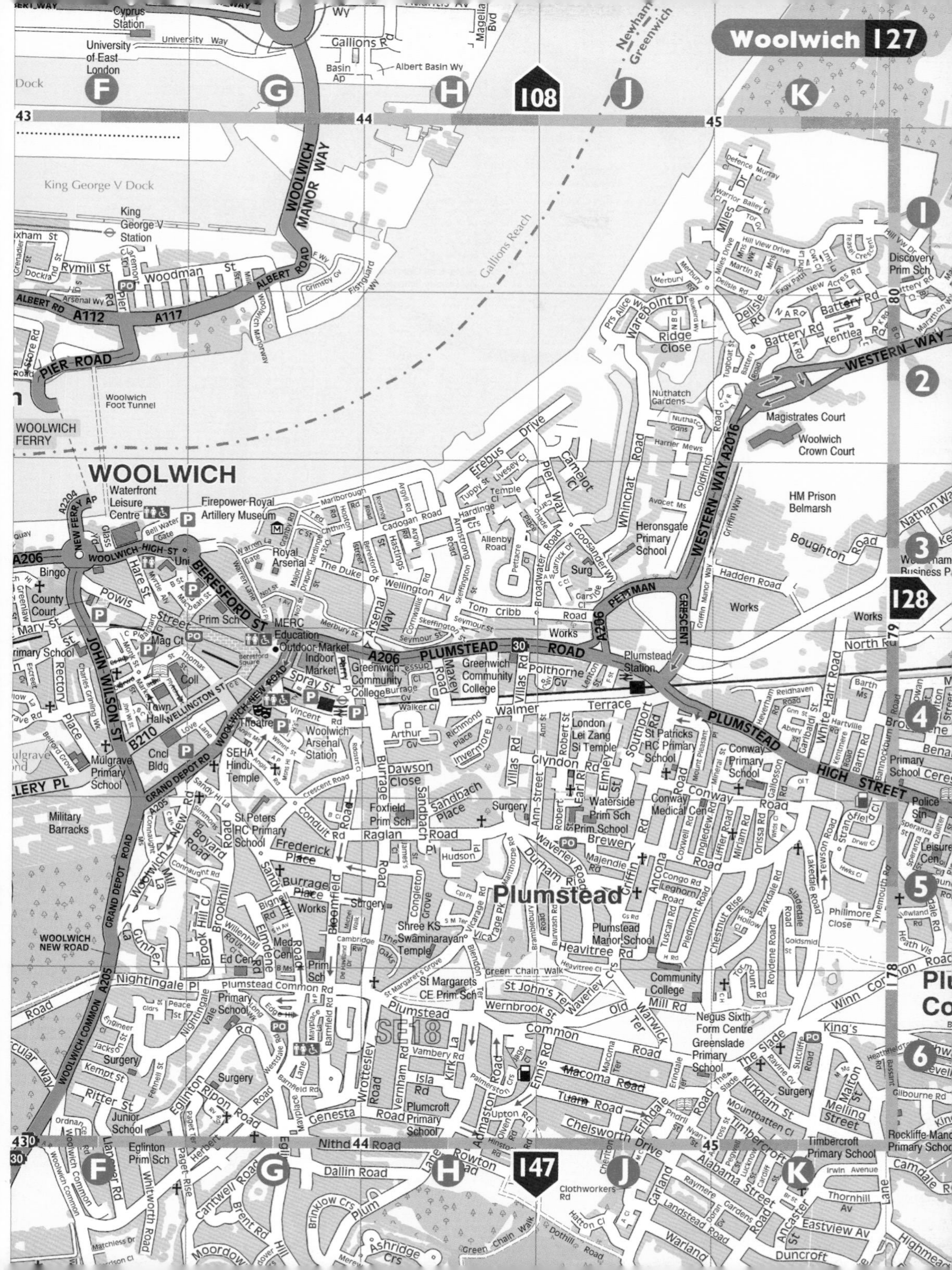

Woolwich 127
108
128
147
F
G
H
J
K
43
44
45
80
79
78
Newham
Greenwich
Cyprus Station
University of East London
University Way
Gallions Rd
Basin Ap
Albert Basin Wy
Magellan Blvd
King George V Dock
King George V Station
WOOLWICH MANOR WAY
ALBERT ROAD
ALBERT RD
A112
A117
Rymill St
Woodman St
Pier Rd
Arsenal Wy
Grimsby Gv
Fishguard Wy
Woolwich Manorway
PIER ROAD
Woolwich Foot Tunnel
WOOLWICH FERRY
Gallions Reach
WOOLWICH
Waterfront Leisure Centre
Firepower Royal Artillery Museum
NEW FERRY AP
A2204
A206
WOOLWICH HIGH ST
Bingo
County Court
Powis Street
Hare St
BERESFORD ST
Royal Arsenal
Prim Sch
Mag Ct
MERC Education
Outdoor Market
Indoor Market
JOHN WILSON ST
Rectory Place
Primary School
Coll
Town Hall
WELLINGTON ST
B210
Cncl Bldg
WOOLWICH NEW ROAD
Theatre
Spray St
Woolwich Arsenal Station
Vincent Rd
SEHA Hindu Temple
Mulgrave Primary School
Mulgrave Pond
GRAND DEPOT RD
GRAND DEPOT ROAD
Military Barracks
WOOLWICH NEW ROAD
A205
WOOLWICH COMMON
Woolwich Common
A206 PLUMSTEAD ROAD
Greenwich Community College
The Duke of Wellington Av
Arsenal Way
Tom Cribb Road
Cadogan Road
Erebus Drive
Camelot Cl
Pier Way
Whinchat Road
Allenby Road
Broadwater Road
Goosander Wy
Surg
Heronsgate Primary School
WESTERN WAY A2016
Magistrates Court
Woolwich Crown Court
HM Prison Belmarsh
Nuthatch Gardens
Harrier Mews
Avocet Ms
Griffin Way
Ridge Close
Warepoint Dr
Defence Cl
Murray Cl
Miles Dr
Hill View Drive
Battery Rd
Kentlea Rd
New Acres Rd
Discovery Prim Sch
WESTERN WAY
Boughton Road
Hadden Road
Griffin Manor Way
PETTMAN CRESCENT
Works
North Rd
Plumstead Station
Polthorne Gv
Maxey Road
Walmer Terrace
Arthur Gv
Richmond Place
Invermore Pl
Villas Rd
London Lei Zang Si Temple
St Patricks RC Primary School
Southport Rd
PLUMSTEAD HIGH STREET
Conway Primary School
White Hart Road
Barth Rd
Bannockburn Road
Primary School
Police Stn
Leisure Cen
Dawson Close
Burrage Road
Sandbach Place
Foxfield Prim Sch
Glyndon Rd
Waterside Prim Sch
Prim School
Conway Medical Cen
Conway Road
Brewery Rd
Raglan Road
Frederick Place
Burrage Place
Surgery
Conduit Rd
Crescent Road
Boyard Road
St Peters RC Primary School
Sandy Hill Rd
Woolwich Mill La
Connaught Rd
Brookhill Road
Brook Hill Cl
Gunner La
Willenhall Rd
Elmdene Rd
Med Cen
Ed Cen
Bloomfield Road
Works
Congleton Grove
Shree KS Swaminarayan Temple
The Oaks
Plumstead
Durham Ri
Waverley Road
Vicarage Rd
Plumstead Manor School
Heavitree Rd
Tuscan Rd
Piedmont Road
Chestnut Rise
Parkdale Rd
Slade Road
Lakedale Road
Phillmore Close
Nightingale Pl
Plumstead Common Rd
Primary School
St Margarets CE Prim Sch
Green Chain Walk
St John's Ter
Wernbrook St
Waverley Cres
Warwick Ter
Mill Rd
Community College
Negus Sixth Form Centre
Greenslade Primary School
Winn Common Road
King's
The Slade
Ravine Gv
Sutcliffe Road
Kirkham St
Melling Street
Malton St
SE18
Plumstead Common Road
Vambery Rd
Isla Rd
Wrottesley Road
Vernham Rd
Kirk La
Admaston Road
Ennis Rd
Macoma Road
Macoma Ter
Tuam Road
Chelsworth Drive
Erindale
Mountbatten Cl
Timbercroft La
Timbercroft Primary School
Rockliffe Manor Primary School
Camdale Rd
Plumcroft Primary School
Genesta Road
Upton Rd
Kempt St
Ritter St
Surgery
Junior School
Eglinton Prim Sch
Eglinton Hill
Ripon Road
Nithdale Road
Rowton Road
Dallin Road
Cantwell Road
Brent Rd
Whitworth Road
Llanover Rd
Paget Rise
Herbert Rd
Plum Lane
Brinklow Crs
Ashridge Crs
Moordown
Clothworkers Rd
Hatton Cl
Dothill Road
Garland Road
Alabama Street
Raymere Gardens
Landstead Road
Warland Road
Ancaster St
Thornhill Av
Eastview Av
Duncroft
Irwin Avenue
Highmead
Matchless Dr

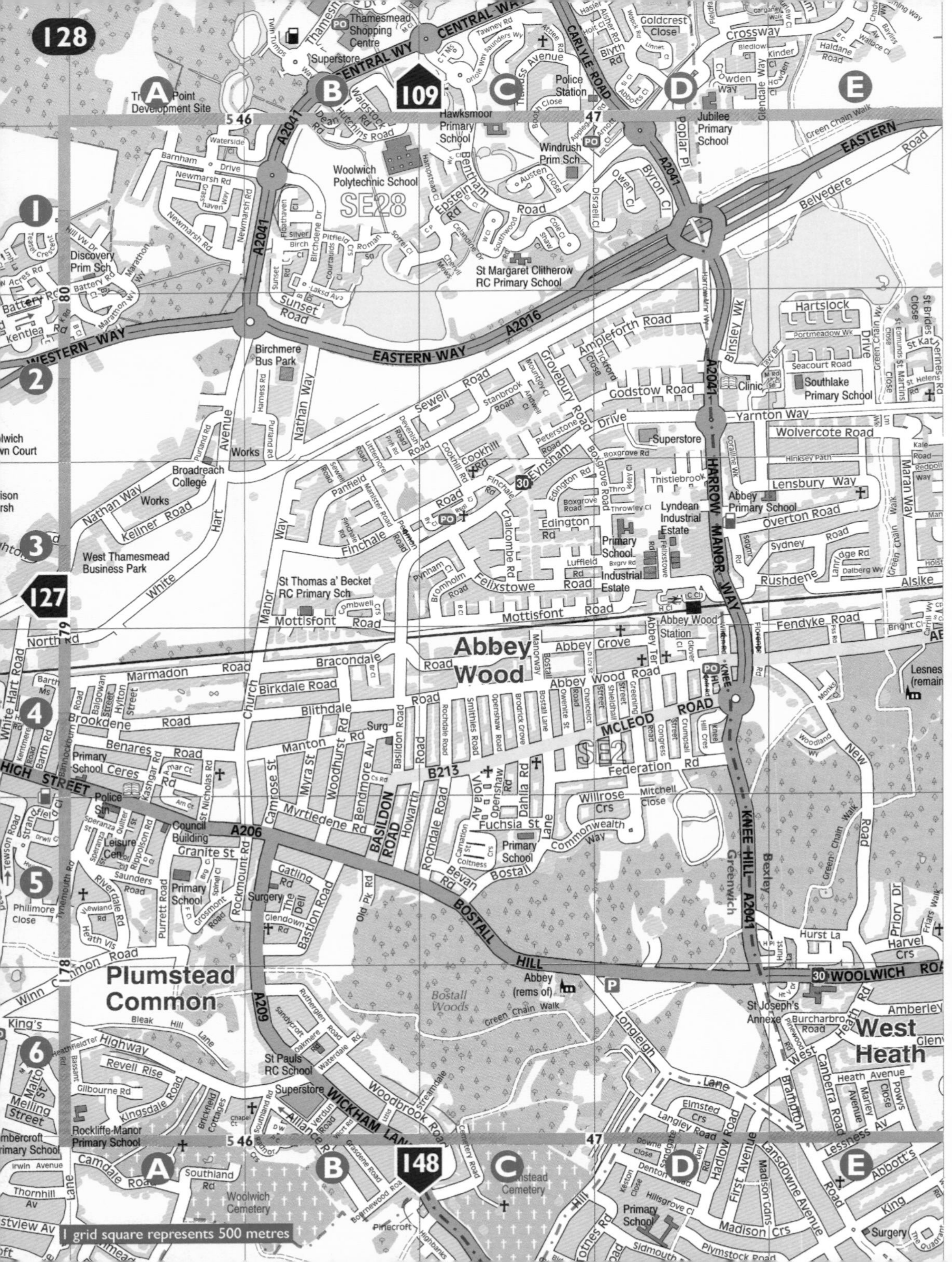

128
109
127
148
A
B
C
D
E
1
2
3
4
5
6
80
79
78
5 46
47
SE28
SE2
Thamesmead Shopping Centre
Superstore
Central Wy
Trust Point Development Site
Hawksmoor Primary School
Police Station
Carlyle Road
Goldcrest Close
Crossway
Jubilee Primary School
Woolwich Polytechnic School
Windrush Prim Sch
Barnham Drive
Newmarsh Rd
Discovery Prim Sch
Battery Rd
Marathon Wy
Western Way
Eastern Way
A2016
A2041
Sunset Road
St Margaret Clitherow RC Primary School
Birchmere Bus Park
Nathan Way
Ampleforth Road
Godstow Road
Hartslock
Portmeadow Wk
Seacourt Road
Southlake Primary School
Clinic
Yarnton Way
Wolvercote Road
Lensbury Way
Abbey Primary School
Overton Road
Harrow Manor Way
Superstore
Thistlebrook
Lyndean Industrial Estate
Sewell Road
Grovebury Road
Eynsham Drive
Broadreach College
Works
West Thamesmead Business Park
Nathan Way
Kellner Road
White Hart Avenue
Finchale Road
Chalcombe Rd
Edington Rd
Primary School
Industrial Estate
Felixstowe Road
Rushdene
St Thomas a' Becket RC Primary Sch
Mottisfont Road
Abbey Wood Station
Fendyke Road
North Rd
Abbey Wood
Abbey Grove
Abbey Wood Road
Bracondale Road
Marmadon Road
Birkdale Road
Blithdale Road
Brookdene Road
Benares Road
McLeod Road
Federation Rd
B213
Manton Rd
Woodhurst Rd
Basildon Road
High Street
Police Stn
Council Building
A206
Leisure Cen
Granite St
Primary School
Myrtledene Rd
Willrose Crs
Mitchell Close
Commonwealth Way
Fuchsia St
Primary School
Bostall Hill
Knee Hill A2041
Green Chain Walk
Lesnes Abbey (remains)
New Road
Hurst La
Harvel Crs
Woolwich Road
Surgery
Gatling Rd
The Dell
Bastion Road
Plumstead Common
A209
Abbey (rems of)
Bostall Woods
Longleigh Lane
St Joseph's Annexe
West Heath
Amberley
Burcharbro Road
Heath Avenue
Canberra Road
Bleak Hill Lane
Highway
Revell Rise
Kingsdale Road
St Pauls RC School
Superstore
Wickham Lane
Woodbrook Road
Elmsted Crs
Langley Road
Hadlow Road
First Avenue
Lansdowne Avenue
Brampton
Lessness Av
Rockliffe Manor Primary School
Camdale Road
Southland Rd
Woolwich Cemetery
Plumstead Cemetery
Primary School
Madison Crs
Surgery
Abbott's
King
1 grid square represents 500 metres

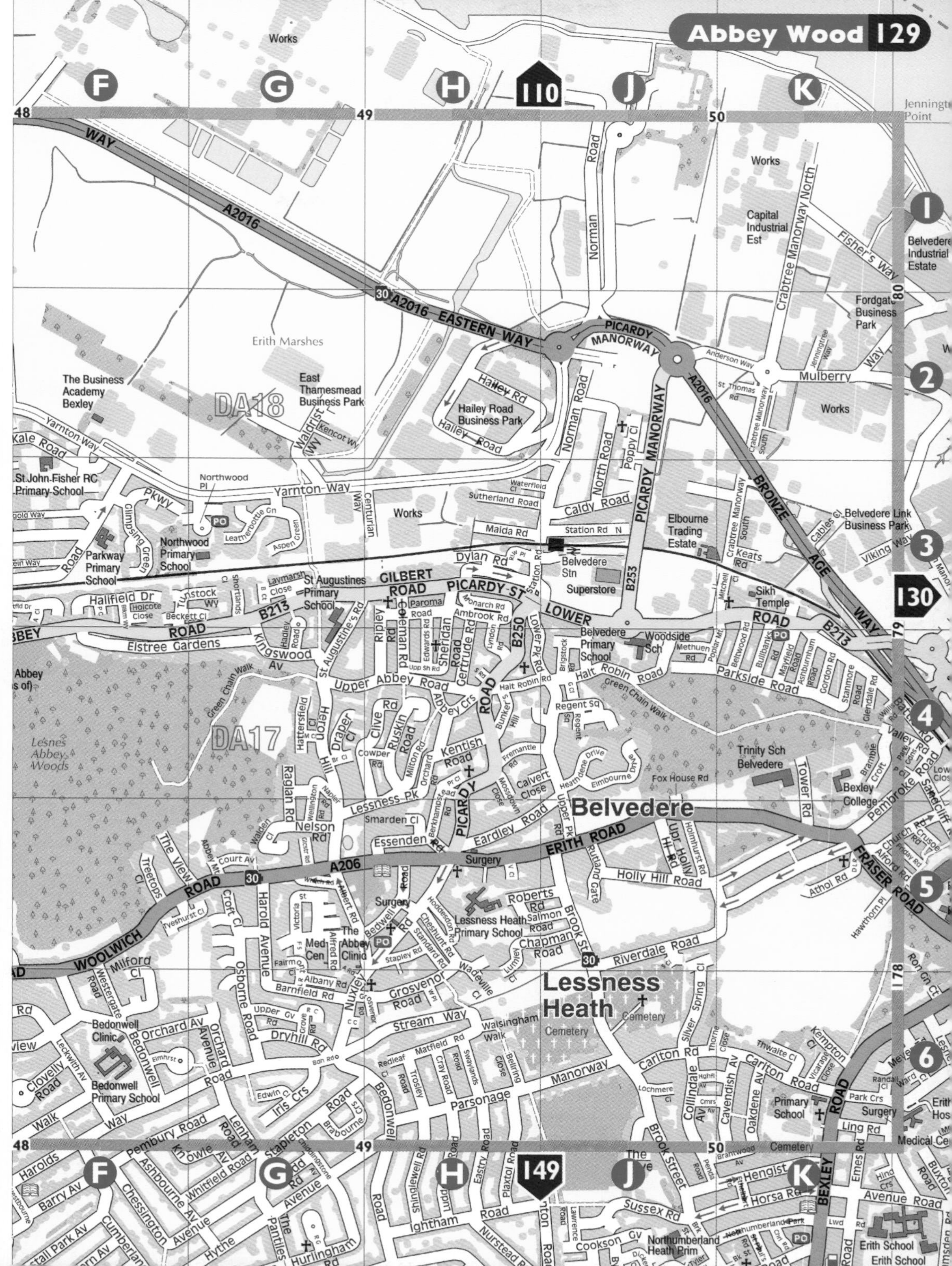
Works
F
G
H
110
J
K
Works
Capital Industrial Est
Belvedere Industrial Estate
Fordgate Business Park
Erith Marshes
The Business Academy Bexley
East Thamesmead Business Park
DA18
Hailey Road Business Park
EASTERN WAY
A2016
PICARDY MANORWAY
BRONZE AGE WAY
St John Fisher RC Primary School
Northwood Primary School
Parkway Primary School
Works
Elbourne Trading Estate
Belvedere Link Business Park
Belvedere Stn
Superstore
St Augustines Primary School
GILBERT ROAD
PICARDY ST
LOWER ROAD
Belvedere Primary School
Woodside Sch
Sikh Temple
Lesnes Abbey Woods
DA17
Trinity Sch Belvedere
Bexley College
Belvedere
ERITH ROAD
FRASER ROAD
WOOLWICH ROAD
A206
Lessness Heath Primary School
The Abbey Clinic
Med Cen
Lessness Heath
Cemetery
Bedonwell Clinic
Bedonwell Primary School
Primary School
Erith School
Northumberland Heath Prim
130
149
BEXLEY ROAD

130
111
129
150
Rainham Marshes
Rainham Marshes RSPB Reserve
Jenningtree Point
Belvedere Industrial Estate
Fisher's Way
Fordgate Business Park
Works
Belvedere Link Business Park
Viking Way
Church Manorway
Erith Reach
Coldharbour Lane
Coldharbour
Erith Rands
Havering
Bexley
Lower Rd
Corinthian Manorway
Galleon Close
West Street
Battle Rd
Valley Rd
Pembroke Road
Bexley College
Sandcliff Road
A2016
FRASER ROAD
Europa Trading Estate
Hamlet International Industrial Estate
Erith Station
Ind Park
Erith
Erith Playhouse
Erith High St
Library & Mus
Wharfside Cl
Superstore
Pier Road
Health Cen
Business Centre
James Watt Way
Wheatley Ter Road
Crescent Road
Manor Road
A206
A220
Christchurch Av
Park Crescent
Arran Close
Debrabant Close
Christ Church CE VA Prim Sch
Lesney Park Road
Erith & District Hosp
Surgery
Medical Cen
Avenue Road
QUEENS ROAD
Victoria Road
Compton Pl
Alexandra Rd
Frobisher Rd
Manford Industrial Estate
Ray Lamb Way
Reddy Road
David Ives (Erith) Stadium
Erith Leisure Centre
SOUTH ROAD
DA8
Larner Rd
Waterhead Close
Festival Close
Ind Est
Arthur St
Bilton Road
Church Trading Estate
Slade Green Primary School
Canada Rd
Jenningtree Rd
Erith School
551
52
1 grid square represents 500 metres

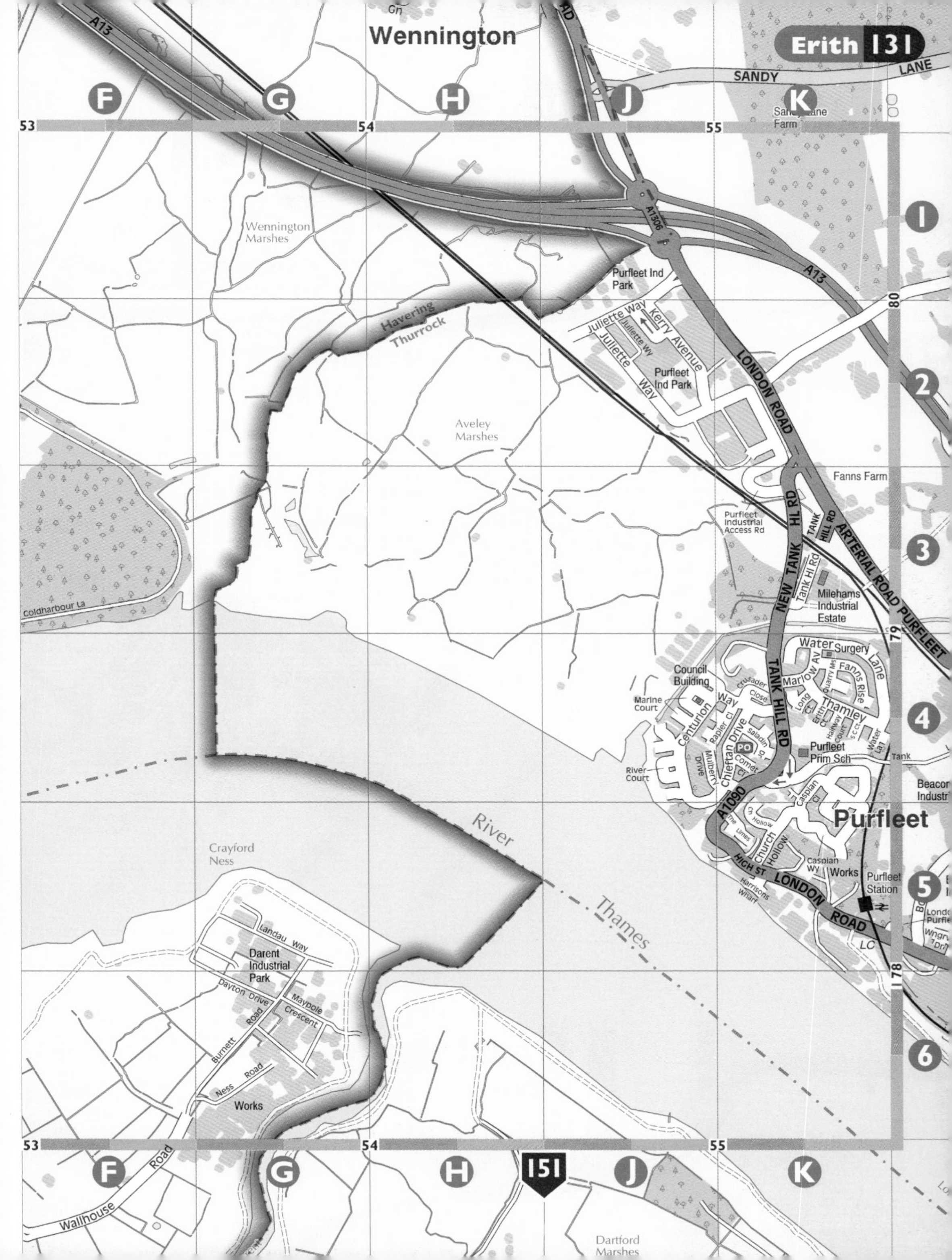
Wennington
A13
SANDY
LANE
F
G
H
J
K
53
54
55
Sandy Lane Farm
A1306
Wennington Marshes
Purfleet Ind Park
Havering
Thurrock
Juliette Way
Juliette Wy
Kerry Avenue
LONDON ROAD
Purfleet Ind Park
Aveley Marshes
Fanns Farm
Purfleet Industrial Access Rd
NEW TANK HL RD
TANK HILL RD
ARTERIAL ROAD PURFLEET
Tank Hl Rd
Milehams Industrial Estate
Coldharbour La
80
79
78
Water Lane
Surgery
Council Building
Crusader Close
Marlow Av
Fanns Rise
Thamley
Marine Court
Centurion Way
Rapier Cl
Saladin
Long Ct
Erith Ct
Halfway Court
Chieftan Drive
Mulberry Drive
Comet Cl
Purfleet Prim Sch
River Court
A1090
Caspian Cl
The Limes
Church Hollow
Purfleet
Caspian Wy
Works
Purfleet Station
HIGH ST
LONDON ROAD
Harrisons Wharf
LC
River
Thames
Crayford Ness
Landau Way
Darent Industrial Park
Dayton Drive
Maypole Crescent
Burnett Road
Ness Road
Works
Wallhouse Road
Dartford Marshes
1
2
3
4
5
6

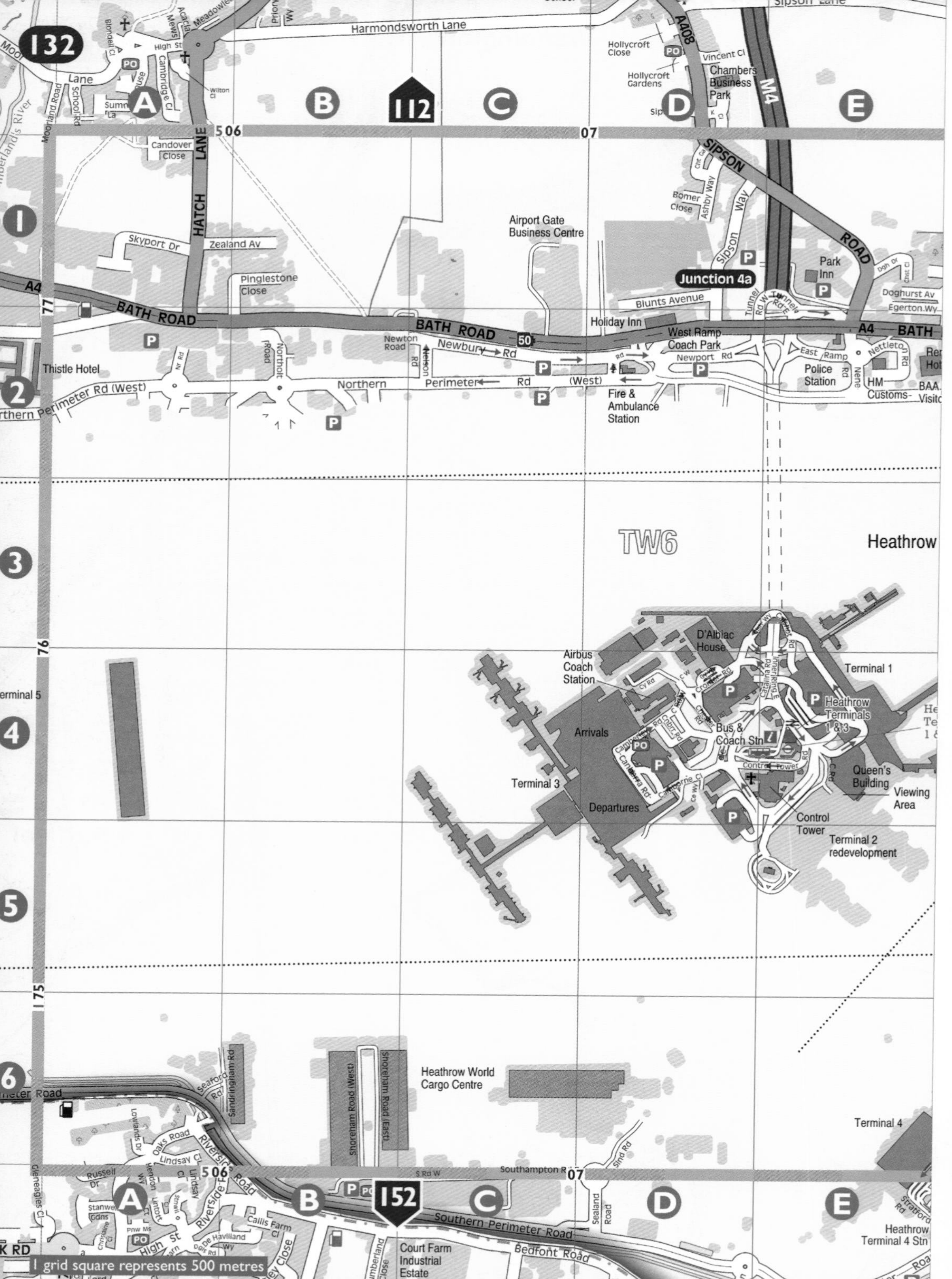

132
112
152
A
B
C
D
E
1
2
3
4
5
6
06
07
77
76
75
Harmondsworth Lane
Sipson Lane
High St
Cambridge Cl
School Rd
Moorland Road
Lane
Candover Close
HATCH LANE
Hollycroft Close
Hollycroft Gardens
Vincent Cl
Chambers Business Park
A408
M4
SIPSON
ROAD
Bomer Close
Ashby Way
Sipson Way
Airport Gate Business Centre
Skyport Dr
Zealand Av
Pinglestone Close
Junction 4a
Park Inn
Blunts Avenue
Holiday Inn
Doghurst Av
Egerton Wy
A4
BATH ROAD
BATH
50
Newton Road
Newbury Rd
West Ramp Coach Park
Newport Rd
East Ramp
Police Station
Nettleton Rd
Nene Rd
HM Customs
Thistle Hotel
Northern Perimeter Rd (West)
Northern Perimeter Rd (West)
Northolt Road
Fire & Ambulance Station
TW6
Heathrow
Terminal 5
D'Albiac House
Airbus Coach Station
Terminal 1
Heathrow Terminals 1 & 3
Arrivals
Bus & Coach Stn
Terminal 3
Departures
Queen's Building
Viewing Area
Control Tower
Terminal 2 redevelopment
Heathrow World Cargo Centre
Shoreham Road (West)
Shoreham Road (East)
Sandringham Rd
Seaford Rd
Perimeter Road
Oaks Road
Lindsay Cl
Riverside Road
Terminal 4
Southampton Rd
Sind Rd
Russell Dr
Stanwell Gdns
High St
Calls Farm
De Havilland Wy
Southern Perimeter Road
Sealand Road
Bedfont Road
Court Farm Industrial Estate
Heathrow Terminal 4 Stn
Stratford Rd
Gleneagles Cl
1 grid square represents 500 metres

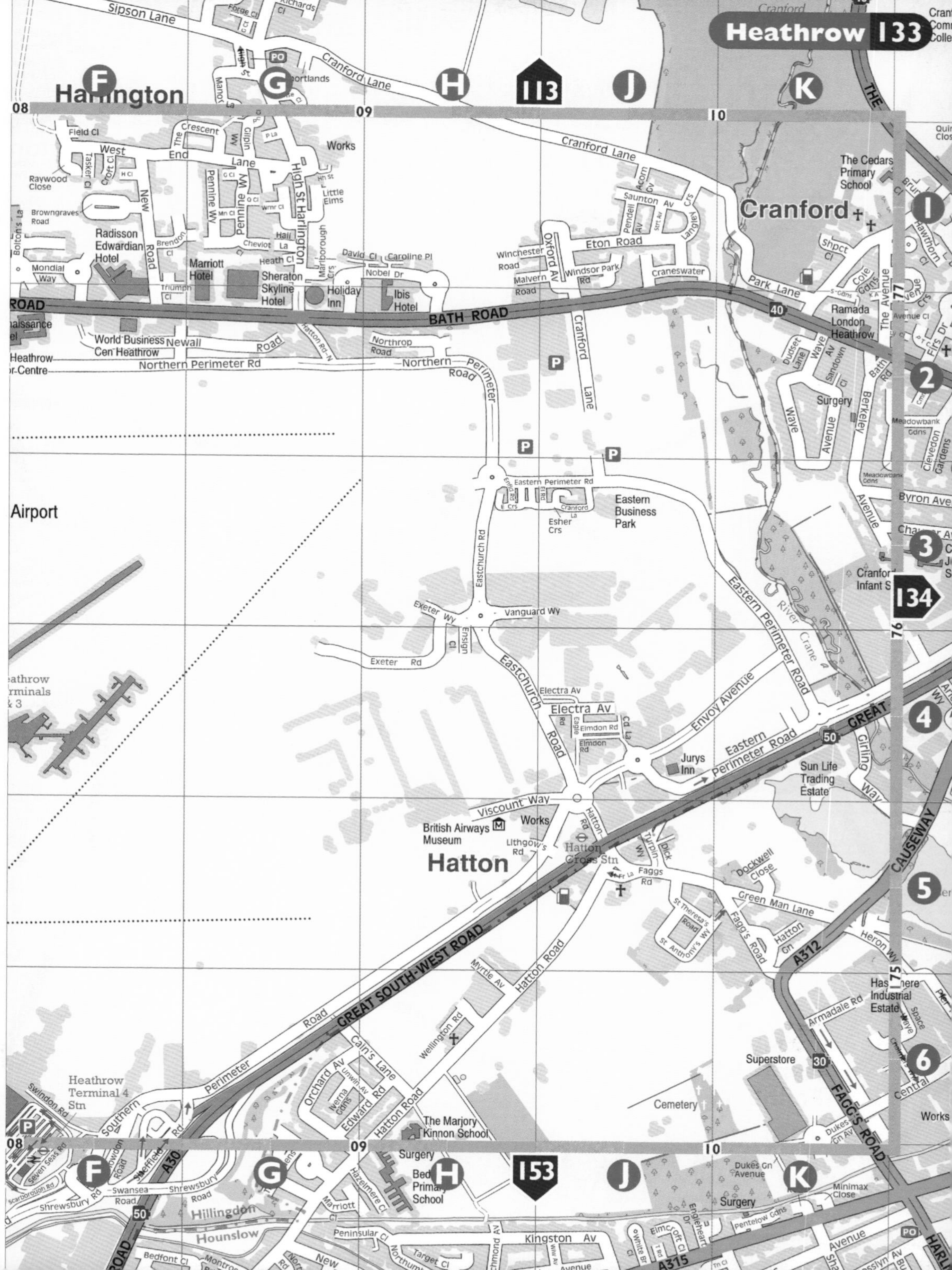

Harlington
Cranford
Hatton
Airport
Sipson Lane
Cranford Lane
Bath Road
Northern Perimeter Rd
Eastern Perimeter Rd
Eastchurch Rd
Eastchurch Road
Vanguard Wy
Exeter Rd
Electra Av
Envoy Avenue
Eastern Perimeter Road
Viscount Way
Great South-West Road
Hatton Road
Faggs Rd
Green Man Lane
Fagg's Road
Causeway
Southern Perimeter Rd
Radisson Edwardian Hotel
Marriott Hotel
Sheraton Skyline Hotel
Holiday Inn
Ibis Hotel
World Business Cen Heathrow
Eastern Business Park
Jurys Inn
British Airways Museum
Hatton Cross Stn
Sun Life Trading Estate
Hatton Industrial Estate
Superstore
Cemetery
Works
The Cedars Primary School
Ramada London Heathrow
Cranford Infant S
Heathrow Terminal 4 Stn
The Marjory Kinnon School
Bedfont Primary School
Surgery
River Crane
Hillingdon
Hounslow
Kingston Av
113
134
153

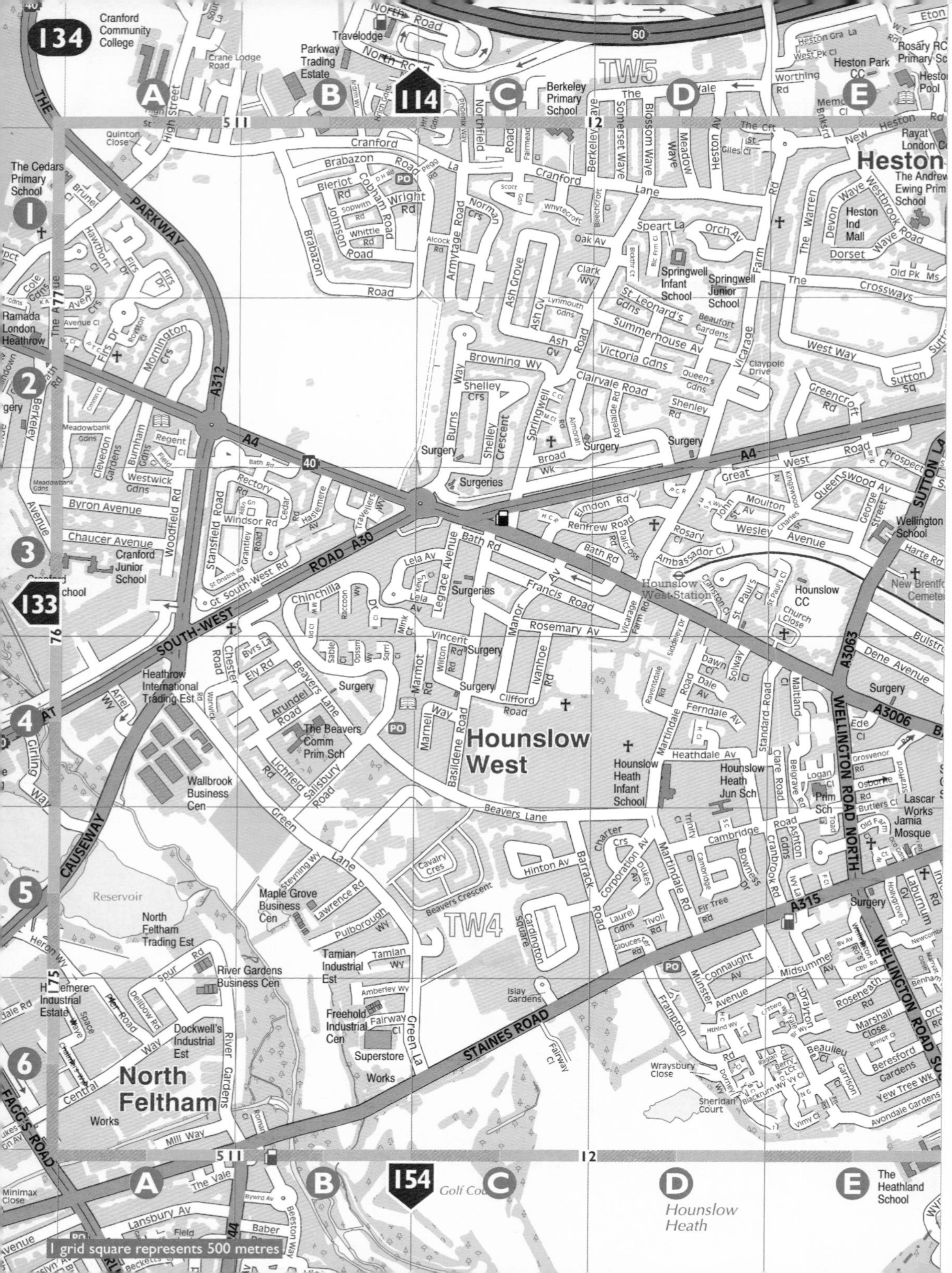
134
133
114
154
Cranford Community College
Parkway Trading Estate
Travelodge
TW5
TW4
Heston
Hounslow West
North Feltham
Berkeley Primary School
The Cedars Primary School
Ramada London Heathrow
Cranford Junior School
Springwell Infant School
Springwell Junior School
Heston Ind Mall
Wellington School
Hounslow West Station
Hounslow CC
Heathrow International Trading Est
The Beavers Comm Prim Sch
Wallbrook Business Cen
Hounslow Heath Infant School
Hounslow Heath Jun Sch
Reservoir
North Feltham Trading Est
Maple Grove Business Cen
Tamian Industrial Est
River Gardens Business Cen
Dockwell's Industrial Est
Freehold Industrial Cen
Superstore
Works
Lascar Works
Jamia Mosque
Hounslow Heath
The Heathland School
PARKWAY
SOUTH-WEST ROAD A30
A4
A312
A3063
A3006
A315
STAINES ROAD
WELLINGTON ROAD NORTH
CAUSEWAY
FAGG'S ROAD
Beavers Lane
Cranford Lane
Great West Road
Bath Rd
1 grid square represents 500 metres

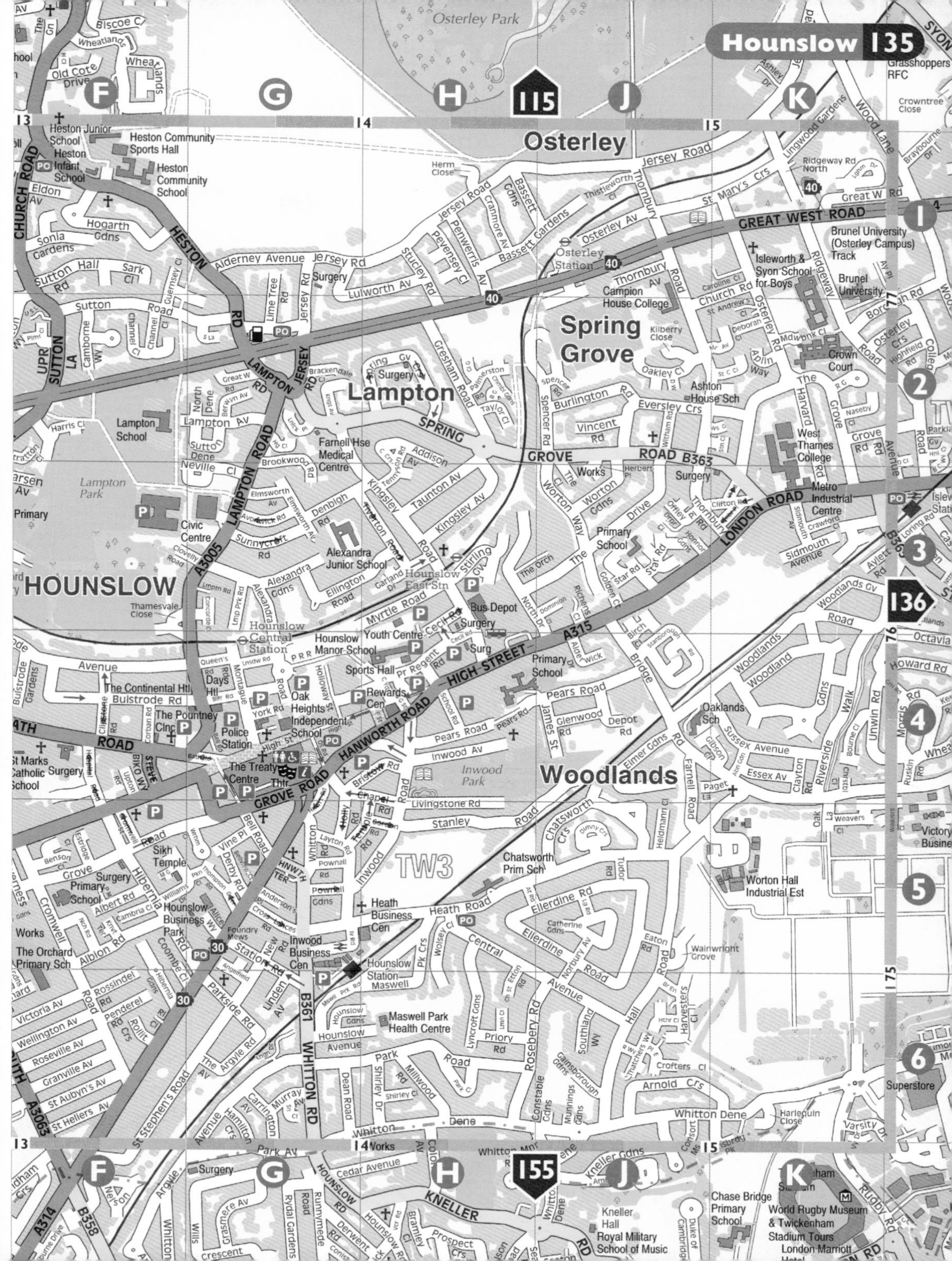

Hounslow 135
Osterley Park
115
Osterley
Spring Grove
Lampton
HOUNSLOW
Woodlands
TW3
136
155
GREAT WEST ROAD
LONDON ROAD
HIGH STREET A315
HANWORTH ROAD
GROVE ROAD
LAMPTON ROAD A3005
HESTON RD
SPRING GROVE ROAD B363
WHITTON RD B361
KNELLER RD
Jersey Road
Osterley Station
Hounslow East Stn
Hounslow Central Station
Hounslow Station
Lampton Park
Inwood Park
Civic Centre
Bus Depot
Police Station
The Treaty Centre
Heston Community Sports Hall
Heston Community School
Heston Junior School
Heston Infant School
Lampton School
Alexandra Junior School
Farnell Hse Medical Centre
Hounslow Manor School
Youth Centre
Sports Hall
Oak Heights Independent School
Rewards Cen
Isleworth & Syon School for Boys
Brunel University (Osterley Campus) Track
Brunel University
Campion House College
Ashton House Sch
West Thames College
Metro Industrial Centre
Crown Court
Oaklands Sch
Chatsworth Prim Sch
Worton Hall Industrial Est
Heath Business Cen
Inwood Business Cen
Hounslow Business Park
Maswell Park Health Centre
Sikh Temple
The Orchard Primary Sch
St Marks Catholic School
The Continental Htl
Days Htl
The Pountney Clnc
Grasshoppers RFC
Superstore
Chase Bridge Primary School
Kneller Hall Royal Military School of Music
World Rugby Museum & Twickenham Stadium Tours
London Marriott

136
116
135
156
A
B
C
D
E
1
2
3
4
5
6
BRENTFORD
Brentford End
ISLEWORTH
St Margarets
TW7
TW8
SYON LANE
SYON LA
Centaurs RFC
Grasshoppers RFC
Centaurs Business Centre
Superstore
Crowntree Close
Great West Trading Estate
Rock Works
Brentford Business Cen
Holiday Inn
Health Cen
Brentford School for Girls
St Paul's CE Primary School
Brentford County Court
Police Station
HALF ACRE
Great W Rd
A4
B454
B434
Brunel University (Osterley Campus) Track
Brunel University
Crown Court
Roxborough Av
Harewood Road
Northumberland Av
Wood Lane
Syon Lane Station
The Green School
SPUR ROAD
LONDON ROAD
A315
A310
Marlborough Primary School
Butterfly House
Syon House
Wyevale Garden Centre
Thames Path
Brentwaters Business Park
Augustus Close
The Ham
Brent Lea
Catherine Wheel Rd
Works
Lodge Cl
Busch Close
Park Road
Syon Park
Hounslow
Richmond upon Thames
Boathouse
Queen Charlotte's Cottage
Isleworth Station
Isleworth Town Primary School
Smallberry Green Primary School
Isleworth Cem
W Middlesex University Hosp
A&E
Amhurst Gardens
Linkfield
Smallberry Av
Mandeville Rd
Castle Road
ST JOHN'S ROAD
TWICKENHAM RD
Snowy Fielder Waye
Mill Plat
North St
Octavia Road
Howard Rd
Brewery Mews Bus Centre
Convent School
The Blue Sch
Prim Sch
SOUTH STEET
Clock Tower Rd
Works
Surgery
Worton Rd
Wheatley Road
Morris Rd
Victory Business Cen
Isleworth Recreation Centre
RICHMOND ROAD
Lion Whf Rd
Herons Place
Bridge Wharf Road
Old Deer Park
Golf Course
Royal Mid-Surrey Golf Club
The Falcon P Sch for Boys
Richmond FC
Pools on the Park
Community College
Richmond Magistrates Court
Park Lane
Richmond Lock
Richmond Theatre
Richmond Green
Green Med Cen
Clinic
Film House
Museum
Odeon
Richmond Bridge
BRIDGE ST
HILL RISE
Waterside Business Cen
Railshead Road
University
Brantwood Av
Cleveland Rd
Percy Rd
Talbot Rd
Primary School
Worple Road
Napier Road
Chestnut Gv
Lynton Cl
A3004
ST MARGARET'S RD
Kilmorey Rd
Ranelagh Drive
Twickenham Bridge
A316 TWICKENHAM ROAD
Rambert Sch of Ballet & Contemporary Dance
St Peter's Road
St George's Rd
Dawes Av
Woodstock Av
Northcote Av
Gordon Av
Allsa Av
Netherton Rd
Orchard Rd
Halliburton Road
Surgery
Crane Avenue
Mogden Lane
Beaumont Place
Ivybridge Retail Park
Superstore
THE AVENUE
Heathcote Rd
Riverdale Gdns
Summerwood Road
Twickenham Park Health Cen
Bingham Hotel
Works
Surgery
Trading Est
Primary School
Moormead
St Margaret's
ST MARGARET'S RD
1 grid square represents 500 metres

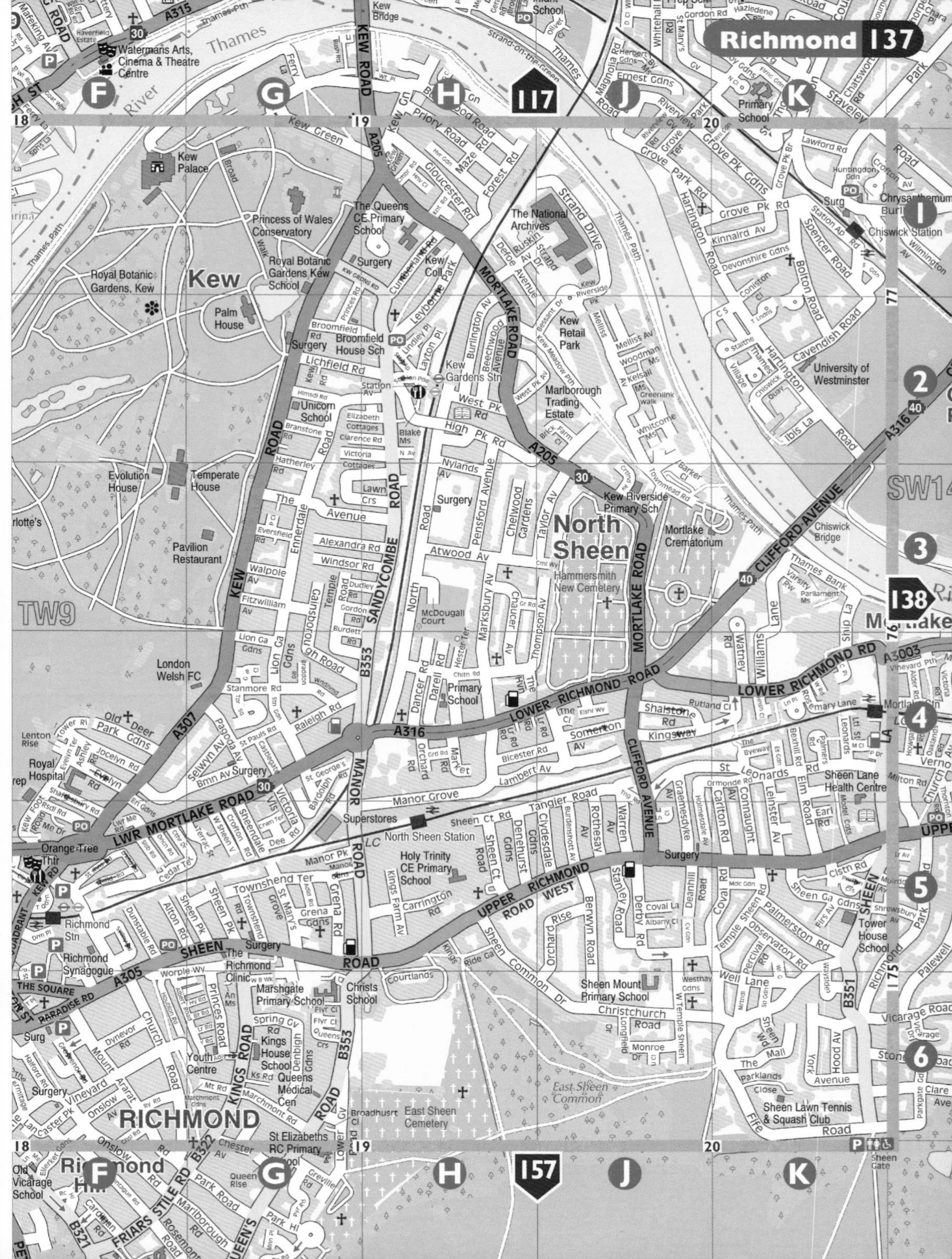

Richmond 137
117
138
157
F
G
H
J
K
18
19
20
2
3
4
5
6
76
77
175
Thames
River
Kew Bridge
Strand-on-the-Green
Watermans Arts, Cinema & Theatre Centre
Haverfield Estate
Mafeking Av
A315
Thames Pth
Ferry La
Kew Green
Kew Palace
Broad Walk
Princess of Wales Conservatory
Royal Botanic Gardens, Kew
Kew
Royal Botanic Gardens Kew School
Palm House
Evolution House
Temperate House
Pavilion Restaurant
TW9
London Welsh FC
KEW ROAD
A307
A205
Priory Road
Maze Rd
Gloucester Rd
Forest Rd
Ernest Gdns
Magnolia Rd
Riverview Gv
Grove Park Rd
Grove Pk Gdns
Grove Pk Rd
Hartington Road
Kinnaird Av
Devonshire Gdns
Bolton Road
Spencer Road
Cavendish Road
Chiswick Station
Staveley
Lawford Rd
Huntingdon Gdn
Chrysanthemum
Wilmington Av
University of Westminster
Ibis La
The Queens CE Primary School
Surgery
Kew Coll
Cumberland Rd
Leyborne Park
MORTLAKE ROAD
The National Archives
Strand Drive
Ruskin Av
Defoe Avenue
Thames Path
Kew Retail Park
Bessant Dr
Riverside
Melliss Av
Woodmans Ms
Kelsall Ms
Greenlink Walk
Whitcombe Ms
Kew Meadow Pth
Broomfield Rd
Broomfield House Sch
Lichfield Rd
Kew Gardens Stn
Station Av
Station Pde
Lindley Pl
Layton Pl
Burlington Av
Beechwood Avenue
West Pk Av
West Pk Rd
High Pk Rd
Marlborough Trading Estate
Brick Farm Cl
Unicorn School
Elizabeth Cottages
Clarence Rd
Victoria Cottages
Blake Ms
Branstone Rd
Hatherley Rd
The Avenue
Lawn Crs
SANDYCOMBE ROAD
Nylands Av
Pensford Avenue
Chelwood Gardens
Taylor Av
North Sheen
Kew Riverside Primary Sch
Townmead Rd
Barker Cl
Mortlake Crematorium
Hammersmith New Cemetery
Eversfield Rd
Ennerdale Rd
Alexandra Rd
Windsor Rd
Atwood Av
Walpole Av
Fitzwilliam Av
Temple Road
Dudley Rd
Gordon Rd
Burdett Rd
Gainsborough Road
North Road
McDougall Court
Marksbury Av
Chaucer Av
Thompson Av
Lion Ga Gdns
Lion Gdns
B353
Dancer Rd
Darell Rd
Hester Ter
Primary School
The Hvn
Stanmore Rd
Raleigh Rd
Old Deer Park Gdns
Lenton Rise
Tower Ri
Jocelyn Rd
Evelyn Rd
Royal Hospital
Pagoda Av
Selwyn Av
St Pauls Rd
Bmn Av
A316
LOWER RICHMOND ROAD
Orchard Rd
Market
Manor Grove
MANOR ROAD
Bicester Rd
Lambert Av
Somerton Av
Shalstone Rd
Kingsway
Rutland Cl
CLIFFORD AVENUE
A316
40
Chiswick Bridge
Thames Bank
Varsity Rw
Parliament Ms
SW14
Mortlake
Watney Rd
Williams Lane
Ship La
LOWER RICHMOND RD
A3003
Vineyard Pth
Mortlake
Sheen Lane Health Centre
St Leonards
Ormonde Rd
Bexhill Rd
Elm Road
Palmers Rd
Leonards
Leinster Av
Connaught
Carlton Rd
Graemesdyke
Earl Rd
Milton Rd
LWR MORTLAKE ROAD
30
Victoria Vls
Sheendale
Crofton
Superstores
North Sheen Station
LC
Sheen Ct Rd
Tangier Road
Denehurst Gdns
Clydesdale Gdns
Rothesay Av
Warren Av
Orange Tree Thtr
Kew Foot Road
Cedar Ter
Manor Pk
Holy Trinity CE Primary School
Kings Farm Av
Carrington Rd
Sheen Ct
Sheen Road
Surgery
UPPER RICHMOND ROAD WEST
Stanley Road
Derby Rd
Deanhill Road
Coval Rd
Coval La
Albany Cl
Temple Sheen Rd
Palmerston Rd
Observatory Rd
Sheen Ga Gdns
SHEEN LA
Tower House School
Richmond Park
B351
Townshend Ter
Townshend Rd
Grove Rd
St Mary's
Grena Gdns
Grena Rd
Dunstable Rd
Alton Rd
Sheen Pk
Richmond Stn
Richmond Synagogue
SHEEN ROAD
The Richmond Clinic
THE SQUARE
A305
PARADISE RD
Worple Wy
Marshgate Primary School
Christs School
Courtlands
Ride Ga
Sheen Common Dr
Orchard Rise
Berwyn Road
Sheen Mount Primary School
Westhay Gdns
Well Lane
Percival Rd
Christchurch Road
Longfield Dr
Monroe Dr
W Temple Sheen
Vicarage Road
The Mall
Parklands
Close
York Avenue
Hood Av
Sheen Lawn Tennis & Squash Club
Fife Road
Clare
Parkgate Gdns
Palewell
Princes Road
Spring Gv
Kings House School
Queens Medical Cen
Denbigh Gdns
Queens Crs
Dynevor Rd
Mount Ararat
Church Road
Youth Centre
Mt Rd
KINGS ROAD
Marchmont Rd
Vineyard
Onslow
Surgery
RICHMOND
East Sheen Common
East Sheen Cemetery
Broadhurst Cl
Lower Gv Rd
Chester Av
B322
St Elizabeths RC Primary School
Richmond Hill
Old Vicarage School
Queen Rise
Park Road
Greville Rd
Park Hl
Marlborough Rd
Rosemont Road
FRIARS STILE RD
B321
Sheen Gate

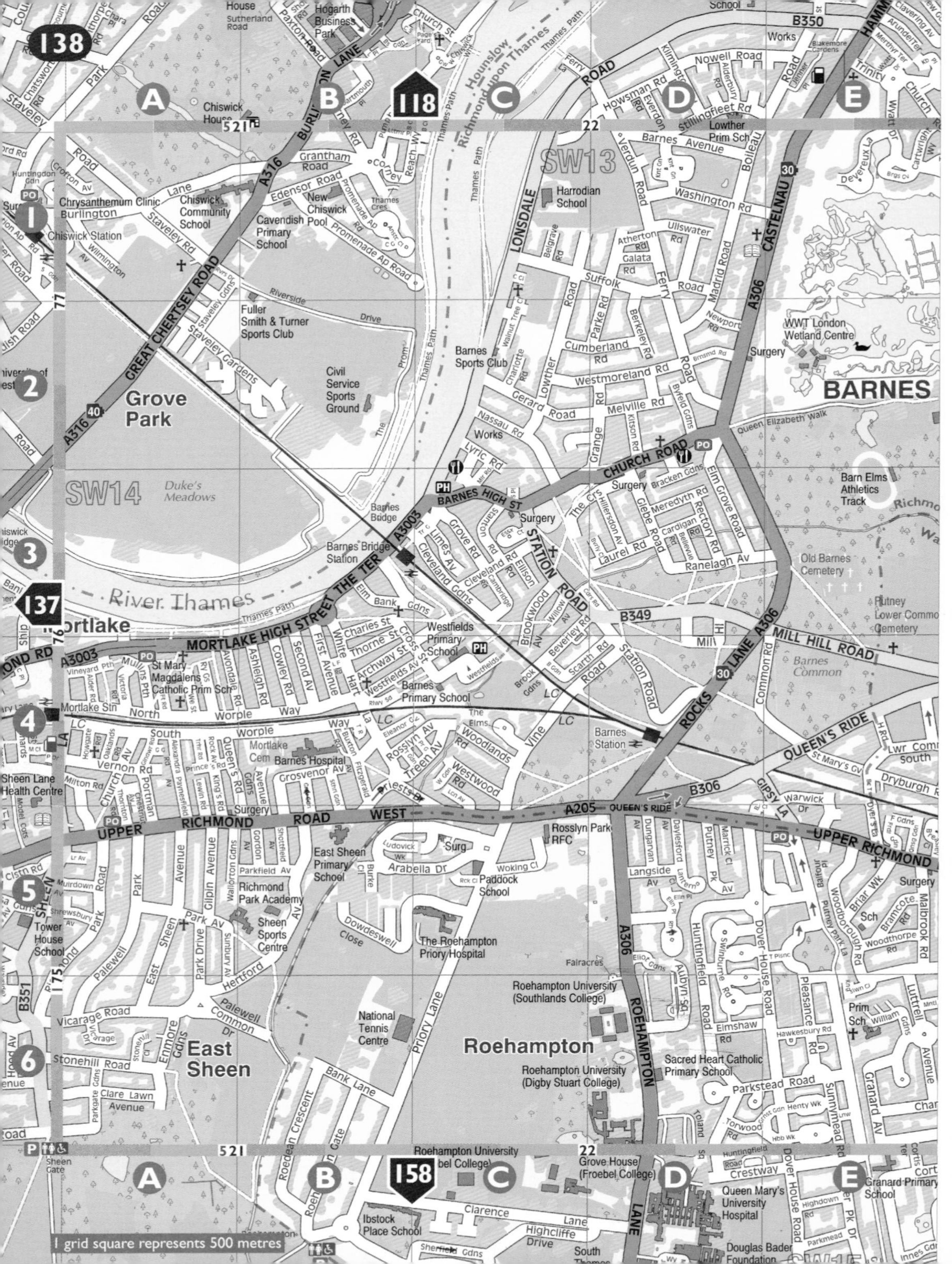

138
118
137
158
A
B
C
D
E
1
2
3
4
5
6
521
22
77
76
75
Hogarth Business Park
Sutherland Road
Paxton Road
Burlington Lane
Church St
Chiswick House
Staveley Rd
Park Rd
Chatsworth Rd
Grantham Road
Corney Reach Way
Edensor Road
New Chiswick Pool
Promenade Ap Road
Thames Cres
Chrysanthemum Clinic
Burlington Lane
Chiswick Community School
Cavendish Primary School
Chiswick Station
Wilmington Av
Crofton Av
Great Chertsey Road
A316
Staveley Gdns
Staveley Gardens
Riverside Drive
Fuller Smith & Turner Sports Club
Civil Service Sports Ground
The Prom
Thames Path
Grove Park
SW14
Duke's Meadows
River Thames
Hounslow
Richmond upon Thames
B350
Nowell Road
Howsman Rd
Stillingfleet Rd
Lowther Prim Sch
Barnes Avenue
Verdun Road
Boileau Rd
SW13
Harrodian School
Lonsdale Road
Washington Rd
Castelnau
A306
Belgrave Rd
Atherton Rd
Galata Rd
Ullswater Rd
Ferry Road
Madrid Road
Suffolk Road
Parke Rd
Berkeley Rd
Newport Rd
Cumberland Rd
Westmoreland Rd
Lowther Road
Walnut Tree Cl
Charlotte Rd
Barnes Sports Club
Gerard Road
Melville Rd
Kitson Rd
Byfeld Gdns
Grange Rd
Nassau Rd
Works
Lyric Rd
WWT London Wetland Centre
Surgery
BARNES
Queen Elizabeth Walk
Barn Elms Athletics Track
Church Road
Barnes High St
A3003
Barnes Bridge
Barnes Bridge Station
The Ter
Mortlake High Street
Surgery
Bracken Gdns
Meredyth Rd
Elm Grove Road
Rectory Rd
Cardigan Rd
Glebe Road
Laurel Rd
Ranelagh Av
Hillersdon Av
The Crs
Station Road
Grove Rd
Limes Av
Cleveland Gdns
Cleveland Rd
Ellison Rd
Stanton Rd
Old Barnes Cemetery
Putney Lower Common Cemetery
B349
Mill Hill Road
Rocks Lane
Barnes Common
Common Rd
Mortlake
Elm Bank Gdns
Charles St
Thorne St
Cross St
Archway St
White Hart La
Westfields Av
Westfields Primary School
Barnes Primary School
Brookwood Av
Willow Av
Beverley Rd
Scarth Rd
Station Road
Vine Rd
Brook Gdns
St Mary Magdalens Catholic Prim Sch
Vineyard Pth
Mullins Pth
Avondale Rd
Ashleigh Rd
Cowley Rd
Second Av
First Avenue
Mortlake Stn
North Worple Way
South Worple Way
Barnes Station
Queen's Ride
Lwr Comm South
St Mary's Gv
Dryburgh Rd
Sheen La
Oaklands Av
Vernon Rd
Mortlake Cem
Barnes Hospital
Rosslyn Av
Treen Av
Westwood Rd
Woodlands Rd
The Elms
Milton Rd
Church Av
Portman Av
Queen's Rd
King's Rd
Grosvenor Av
Priests Br
Sheen Lane Health Centre
Upper Richmond Road West
A205
B306
Gipsy La
Warwick Dr
Rosslyn Park RFC
Upper Richmond Rd
Surgery
Ludovick Wk
Surg
Arabella Dr
Woking Cl
Paddock School
East Sheen Primary School
Burke Cl
Parkfield Av
Richmond Park Academy
Sheen Sports Centre
Langside Av
Dungarvan Av
Daylesford Av
Putney Pk Av
Briar Wk
Bramcote Rd
Malbrook Rd
Woodthorpe Rd
Sheen Park
Tower House School
Palewell Park
East Sheen Av
Park Drive
Gilpin Avenue
Hertford Av
Dowdeswell Close
The Roehampton Priory Hospital
Fairacres
Roehampton University (Southlands College)
Huntingfield Road
Swinburne Rd
Dover House Road
Pleasance Rd
Woodborough Rd
Putney Park La
Luttrell Avenue
Prim Sch
B351
Vicarage Road
Palewell Common Dr
National Tennis Centre
Priory Lane
Roehampton
Elmshaw Rd
Hawkesbury Rd
Roehampton Lane
East Sheen
Stonehill Road
Enmore Gdns
Clare Lawn Avenue
Parkgate Gdns
Bank Lane
Roehampton University (Digby Stuart College)
Sacred Heart Catholic Primary School
Parkstead Road
Sunnymead Rd
Granard Av
Torwood Rd
Henty Wk
Roedean Crescent
Roehampton Gate
Roehampton University (Froebel College)
Grove House (Froebel College)
Crestway
Dover House Road
Granard Primary School
Queen Mary's University Hospital
Highdown Rd
Parkmead
Clarence Lane
Highcliffe Drive
Ibstock Place School
Sherfield Gdns
Douglas Bader Foundation
Sheen Gate
1 grid square represents 500 metres

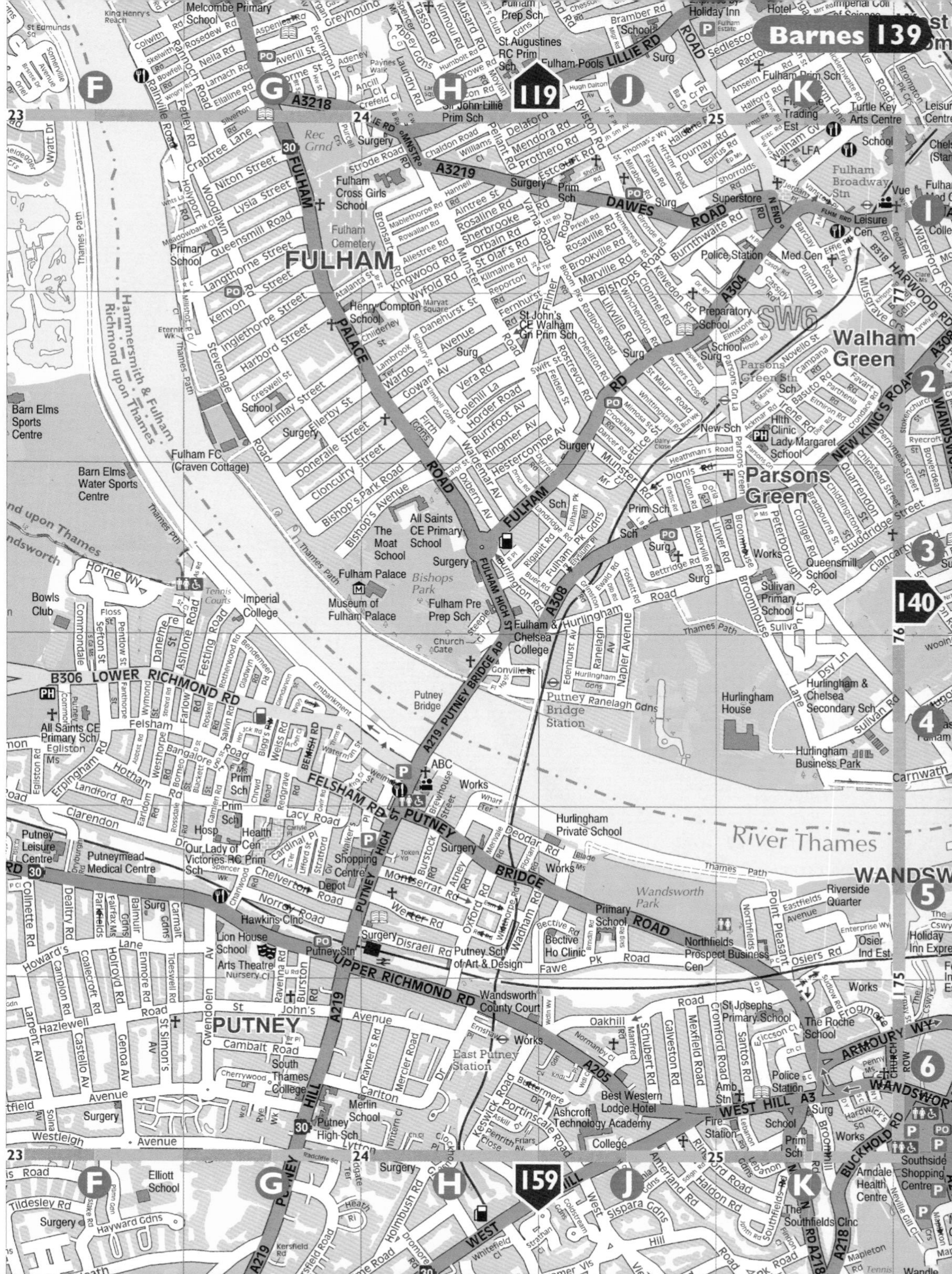
FULHAM
PUTNEY
Walham Green
Parsons Green
SW6
WANDSWORTH
River Thames
Hammersmith & Fulham
Richmond upon Thames
Thames Path
F
G
H
J
K
119
140
159
23
24
25
2
3
4
5
6
A3218
A3219
A304
A308
A219
A205
A3
A218
B306 LOWER RICHMOND RD
FULHAM PALACE ROAD
FULHAM RD
FULHAM HIGH ST
PUTNEY BRIDGE AP
PUTNEY HIGH ST
PUTNEY BRIDGE ROAD
UPPER RICHMOND RD
WEST HILL
NEW KING'S ROAD
DAWES ROAD
LILLIE RD
HARWOOD RD
ARMOURY WY
BUCKHOLD RD
FELSHAM RD
Fulham Cemetery
Fulham Cross Girls School
Henry Compton School
Fulham FC (Craven Cottage)
Barn Elms Sports Centre
Barn Elms Water Sports Centre
Bowls Club
Imperial College
Fulham Palace
Museum of Fulham Palace
Bishops Park
Fulham Pre Prep Sch
The Moat School
All Saints CE Primary School
Fulham & Chelsea College
Putney Bridge
Putney Bridge Station
Hurlingham House
Hurlingham & Chelsea Secondary Sch
Hurlingham Business Park
Hurlingham Private School
Sulivan Primary School
Queensmill School
St John's CE Walham Gn Prim Sch
Fulham Broadway Stn
Police Station
Putney Leisure Centre
Putneymead Medical Centre
Our Lady of Victories RC Prim Sch
Lion House School
Arts Theatre
Putney Stn
Putney Sch of Art & Design
Wandsworth County Court
East Putney Station
South Thames College
Merlin School
Putney High Sch
Ashcroft Technology Academy
Best Western Lodge Hotel
St Josephs Primary School
The Roche School
Wandsworth Park
Northfields Prospect Business Cen
Southside Shopping Centre
Arndale Health Centre
The Southfields Clinc
Elliott School
Melcombe Primary School
St Augustines RC Prim Sch
Sir John Lillie Prim Sch
Fulham Prim Sch
Turtle Key Arts Centre
Leisure Cen
Riverside Quarter
Osier Ind Est
Holiday Inn Express

140
West Brompton
SW10
120
139
160
A
B
C
D
E
1
2
3
4
5
6
526
27
77
76
175
Emb of Guatemala
Prim Sch
Hospital
A&E
Park Walk Prim Sch
Beaufort St
Frederick Hugh House
Carlyle's Ho (NT)
Chelsea Physic Garden
Chelsea
Kensington & Chelsea
Wandsworth
Cadogan Pier
Cheyne Cen
Cheyne Wk
Turtle Key Arts Centre
Leisure Centre
Chelsea FC (Stamford Bridge)
Millennium & Copthorne Hotels at Chelsea FC
College
Parayhouse School
Worlds End Place
Fulham Broadway Stn
Vue
Fulham Med Cen
Fulham Road
King's Rd
King's Road
Gunter Gv
Lots Rd
Kensington Wharf
Chelsea Wharf
Chelsea Group of Children
The Heatherley Sch of Fine Art
Harwood Rd
Walham Green
New King's Road
Sands End
Design Ctr
Imperial Wharf Station
Wyndham Grand London Hotel
Jurys Inn Chelsea
Wood Lane School
Chelsea College of Art & Design
Imperial Road
Townmead Road
Wandsworth Bridge Road
Battersea Reach
Hotel Verta
Atlas Transport Est
Trading Estate
Townmead Business Cen
Superstore
Works
Consulate of Burkina Faso
Coral Row
Carnwath Road Industrial Estate
Wandsworth Bridge
Thomas's Fulham
Albert Bridge
Battersea Bridge
Ransomes Dock
Ransomes Dock Bus Cen
Albert Bridge Road
Albert Bridge Gate
Battersea Bridge Rd
Battersea
Peace Pagoda
Bolingbroke Primary School
Westbridge Coll
Westbridge Rd
Battersea Church Rd
Vicarage Crs
Thomas's Preparatory School
Salesian Coll
L'Ecole De Battersea
Bridge Lane Thtr
Prince of Wales Dr
Med Cen
Grace Thtr at the Latchmere
Latchmere Leisure Cen
Latchmere Road
SW11
Battersea Park Sch
Reform Street
York Road
Lombard Rd
Lombard Bus Cen
Heliport Ind Est
Westland Heliport
Library & Community Centre
Thames Christian College
Falcon Rd
Fire Station
Infant School
Christ Church CE Primary School
Cranleigh Ms
Ingrave Street
Battersea Sports Cen
Clapham Junction Station
Superstore
Falcon Business Cen
Police Station & Magistrates Court
Lavender Hill
Elspeth Rd
High View Primary School
St John's Hl
Wandsworth
Swandon Wy
Wandsworth Town Stn
Holiday Inn Express
Ferrier Industrial Estate
Charterhouse Works
St John's Hospital Day Cen
Surgery
Ambulance Station
Battersea Rise
St Mary's Cemetery
Northcote Rd
Spencer Park
Emanuel School
Bolingbroke Hospital
Dolphin School
Wandsworth Common N Side
Huguenot Pl
Woodwell St
East Hl
Wandsworth High St
Town Hall
Cncl Building
Primary School
Fairfield St
Armoury Wy
Buckhold Rd
Southside Shopping Centre
Arndale Health Centre
Superstore
Med Cen
JMI School
Heathfield Rd
Lombard Business Park
Thomas's Clapham Prim Sch
Cobham Cl
Broomwood Rd
Northcote Lodge
1 grid square represents 500 metres

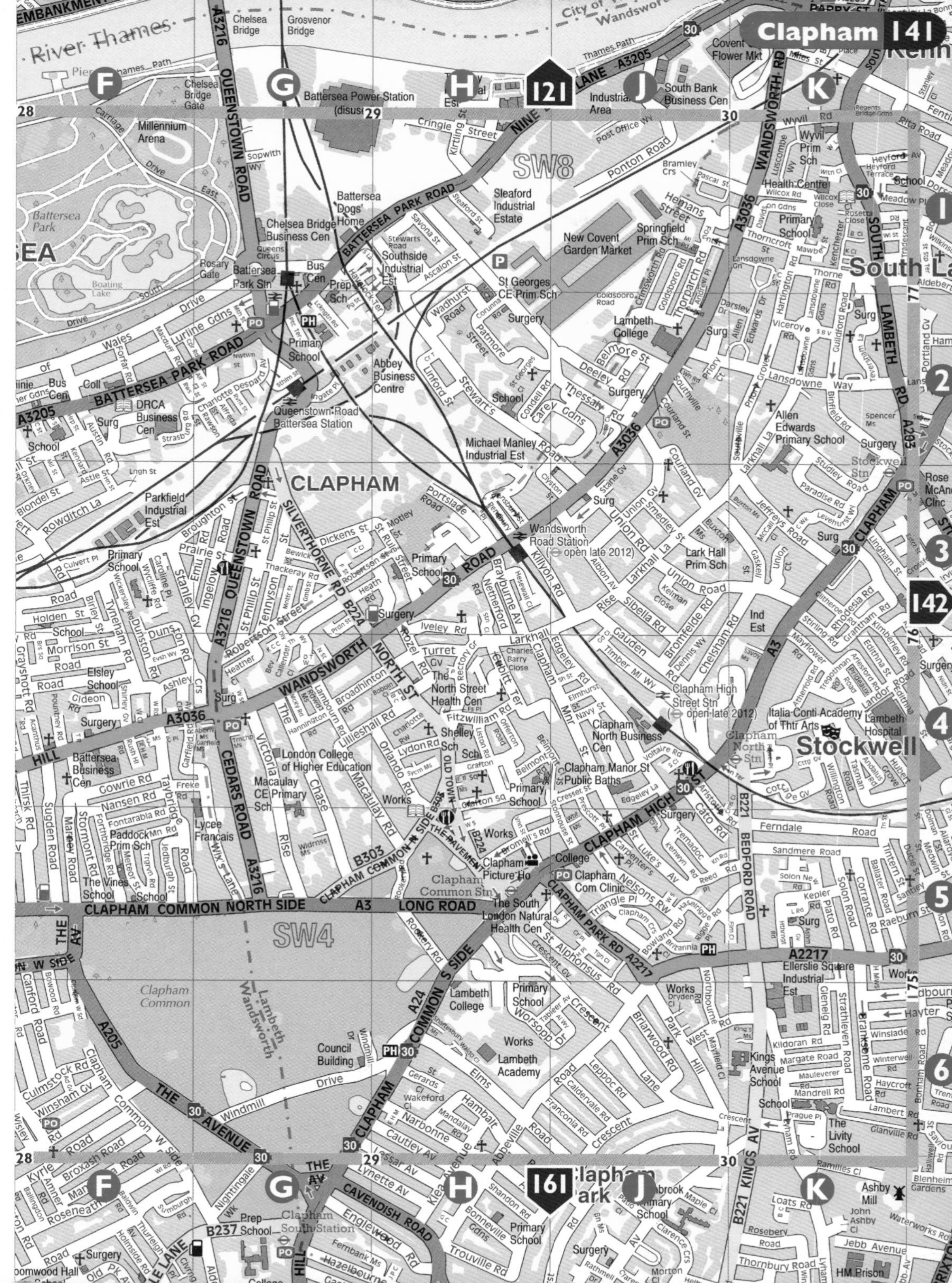
River Thames
Chelsea Bridge
Grosvenor Bridge
City of Wandsworth
Battersea Park
Millennium Arena
Battersea Power Station (disused)
Chelsea Bridge Gate
Queenstown Road
Nine Elms Lane
Industrial Area
South Bank Business Cen
Covent Garden Flower Mkt
Wandsworth Rd
SW8
Ponton Road
Battersea 'Dogs' Home
Chelsea Bridge Business Cen
Battersea Park Road
Sleaford Industrial Estate
New Covent Garden Market
Springfield Prim Sch
Battersea Park Stn
Southside Industrial Est
St Georges CE Prim Sch
Lambeth College
Abbey Business Centre
Queenstown Road Battersea Station
DRCA Business Cen
Michael Manley Industrial Est
CLAPHAM
Parkfield Industrial Est
Wandsworth Road Station (open late 2012)
Silverthorne Rd
Lark Hall Prim Sch
Union Road
Allen Edwards Primary School
Stockwell Stn
South Lambeth Rd
Wyvil Prim Sch
Clapham Road
Wandsworth Road
A3036
Queenstown Road A3216
The North Street Health Cen
London College of Higher Education
Macaulay CE Primary Sch
Clapham Manor St Public Baths
Clapham North Business Cen
Clapham High Street Stn (open late 2012)
Italia Conti Academy of Thtr Arts
Lambeth Hospital
Stockwell
Clapham North Stn
Cedars Road
Lycee Francais
Paddock Prim Sch
The Vines School
Battersea Business Cen
Clapham Picture Ho
Clapham Common Stn
Clapham Com Clinic
The South London Natural Health Cen
Clapham High St
Clapham Common North Side
A3 Long Road
SW4
Clapham Common
Lambeth
Wandsworth
Clapham Park Rd A2217
Bedford Road B221
Ellerslie Square Industrial Est
Clapham Common S Side A24
Lambeth College
Primary School
Council Building
Lambeth Academy
Kings Avenue School
The Livity School
The Avenue
Windmill Drive
Cavendish Road
Clapham South Station
Clapham Park
Ashby Mill
HM Prison
Kings Av B221
121
142
161
F G H J K
28 29 30
1 2 3 4 5 6

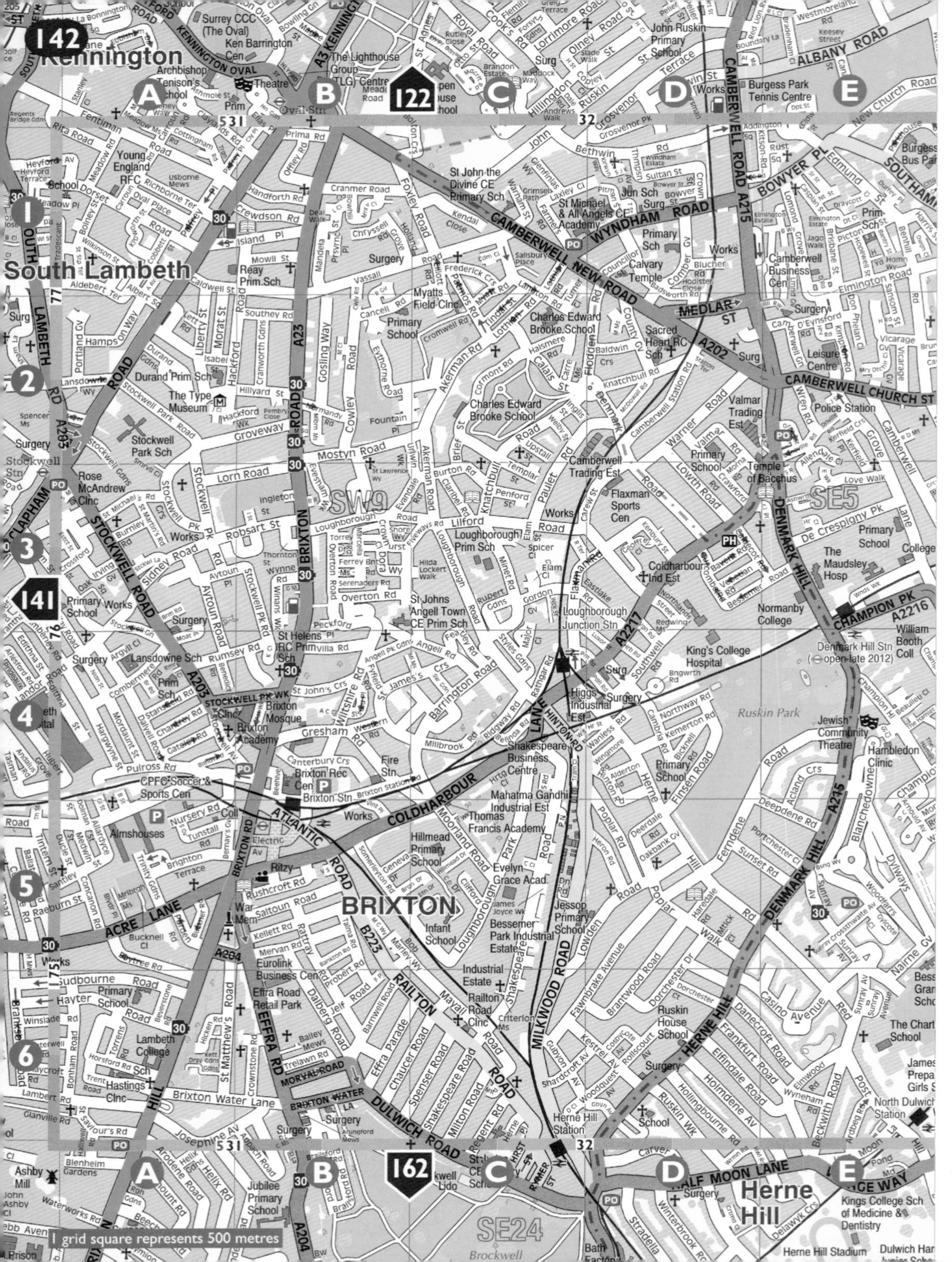
142
Kennington
South Lambeth
Brixton
Herne Hill
SW9
SE5
SE24
122
141
162
Surrey CCC (The Oval)
Ken Barrington Cen
Kennington Oval
Archbishop Tenison's School
Theatre
Oval Stn
Fentiman Road
Rita Road
Young England RFC
Dorset Road
Handforth Rd
Crewdson Rd
Island Pl
Mowll St
Reay Prim Sch
Vassall Road
Myatts Field Clnc
Southey Rd
Cranmer Road
Foxley Road
St John the Divine CE Primary Sch
Camberwell New Road
Wyndham Road
St Michael & All Angels CE Academy
Primary Sch
Calvary Temple
Works
Medlar St
Sacred Heart RC Sch
Charles Edward Brooke School
Camberwell Station Rd
Camberwell Church St
John Ruskin Primary School
Burgess Park Tennis Centre
Albany Road
Bowyer Pl
Camberwell Business Cen
Elmington Road
Leisure Centre
Police Station
Camberwell Road A215
Durand Prim Sch
The Type Museum
Stockwell Park Road
Stockwell Park Sch
Groveway
Stockwell Stn
Rose McAndrew Clnc
Clapham Road
Stockwell Road
Lambeth Road
Mostyn Road
Lorn Road
Robsart St
Loughborough Road
Loughborough Prim Sch
Cowley Road
Fountain Pl
Akerman Road
Camberwell Trading Est
Flaxman Sports Cen
Valmar Trading Est
Primary School
Temple of Bacchus
Denmark Hill
De Crespigny Pk
The Maudsley Hosp
Normanby College
Champion Pk
William Booth Coll
Denmark Hill Stn (open late 2012)
King's College Hospital
Coldharbour Ind Est
Loughborough Junction Stn
St Johns Angell Town CE Prim Sch
Overton Rd
Sidney Road
Aytoun Road
Lansdowne Sch
St Helens RC Prim Sch
Barrington Road
Higgs Industrial Est
Ruskin Park
Jewish Community Theatre
Hambledon Clinic
Brixton Mosque
Brixton Academy
Stockwell Pk Wk
Gresham Rd
Millbrook Rd
Shakespeare Business Centre
Fire Stn
Canterbury Crs
Brixton Rec Cen
Brixton Stn
CPFC Soccer & Sports Cen
Nursery Rd
Almshouses
Coldharbour Lane
Atlantic Road
Mahatma Gandhi Industrial Est
Thomas Francis Academy
Hillmead Primary School
Evelyn Grace Acad
Brixton Road
Acre Lane
Ritzy
Rushcroft Rd
Saltoun Road
War Mem
Kellett Rd
Infant School
Bessemer Park Industrial Estate
Jessop Primary School
Milkwood Road
Fawnbrake Avenue
Brantwood Road
Ruskin House School
Herne Hill
Eurolink Business Cen
Effra Road Retail Park
Railton Road
Industrial Estate
Railton Road Clnc
Sudbourne Road
Hayter Road
Primary School
Lambeth College
Hastings Clnc
Brixton Water Lane
Effra Rd
Dulwich Road
Morval Road
Surgery
Herne Hill Station
Half Moon Lane
Ashby Mill
Jubilee Primary School
Brockwell Lido
Kings College Sch of Medicine & Dentistry
North Dulwich Station
Herne Hill Stadium
The Charter School
Casino Avenue
1 grid square represents 500 metres

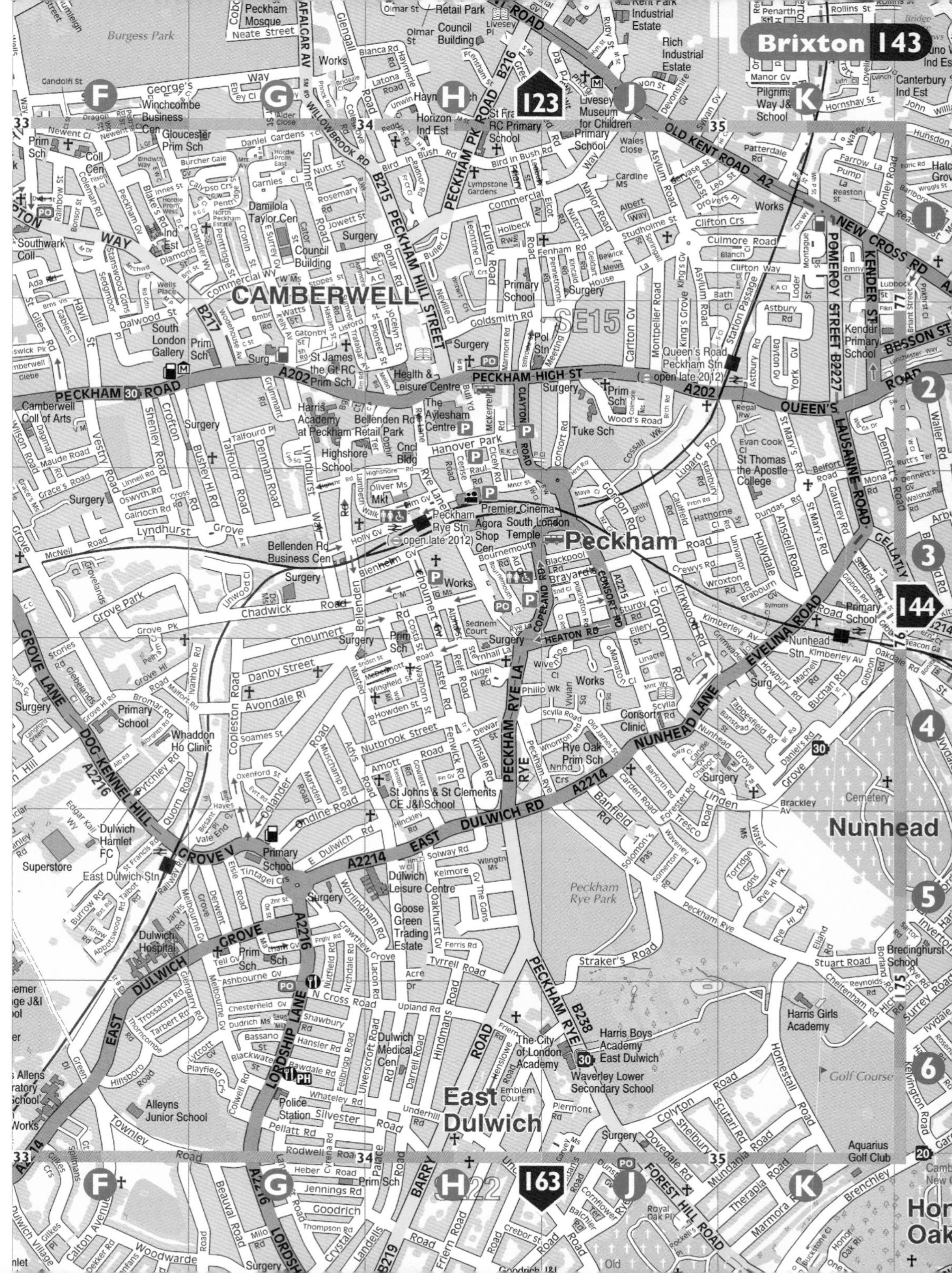

Brixton 143
123
163
144
CAMBERWELL
Peckham
Nunhead
East Dulwich
SE15
SE22
Burgess Park
Peckham Rye Park
Golf Course
Cemetery
PECKHAM ROAD
PECKHAM HIGH ST
QUEEN'S ROAD
OLD KENT ROAD A2
NEW CROSS RD
EAST DULWICH RD
DOG KENNEL HILL
GROVE LANE
LORDSHIP LANE
PECKHAM RYE
PECKHAM HILL STREET
PECKHAM PK ROAD
RYE LANE
EVELINA ROAD
NUNHEAD LANE
LAUSANNE ROAD
POMEROY STREET B2227
KENDER ST
GELLATLY
BESSON ST
CLAYTON ROAD
COPELAND RD
CONSORT RD
HEATON RD
WILLOWBROOK RD
EAST DULWICH GROVE
FOREST HILL ROAD
BARRY ROAD
A202
A2214
A2216
A2215
B215
B216
B217
B238
B219
Peckham Mosque
Council Building
Livesey Museum for Children
Winchcombe Business Cen
Gloucester Prim Sch
Horizon Ind Est
Damilola Taylor Cen
Southwark Coll
South London Gallery
Camberwell Coll of Arts
Health & Leisure Centre
The Aylesham Centre
Harris Academy at Peckham
Bellenden Rd Retail Park
Highshore School
Peckham Rye Stn
Premier Cinema
South London Temple
Agora Shop Cen
Bellenden Rd Business Cen
Queen's Road Peckham Stn
Tuke Sch
St Thomas the Apostle College
Nunhead Stn
Kender Primary School
Whaddon Ho Clinic
Dulwich Hamlet FC
Superstore
East Dulwich Stn
Dulwich Hospital
Dulwich Leisure Centre
Goose Green Trading Estate
Dulwich Medical Cen
The City of London Academy
Harris Boys Academy East Dulwich
Waverley Lower Secondary School
Harris Girls Academy
Bredinghurst School
Aquarius Golf Club
Alleyns Junior School
Police Station
Rye Oak Prim Sch
St Johns & St Clements CE J&I School
Consort Clinic
Rich Industrial Estate
Pilgrims Way J& School
Canterbury Ind Est

144
124
143
164
A
B
C
D
E
1
2
3
4
5
6
536
37
77
76
75
20
30
DEPTFORD
SE14
SE4
New Cross Gate
New Cross
St Johns
Ladywell
Brockley
Honor Oak
Honor Oak Park
Nunhead
NEW CROSS RD
NEW CROSS RD A2
DEPTFORD BROADWAY
BLACKHEATH RD A2
GREENWICH HIGH ROAD
CREEK ROAD
DEPTFORD CHURCH STREET
A2209
BROOKMILL RD
LEWISHAM WAY
LOAMPIT HILL
THURSTON RD
A2210
B2142 DRAKEFELL ROAD
BROCKLEY ROAD
B218
B236
ADELAIDE AV
LADYWELL ROAD
LEWISHAM HIGH ST
A21
MALPAS ROAD
FLORENCE ROAD
AMERSHAM RD
PARKFIELD RD
EDWARD ST
PAGNELL ST
SANFORD STREET
B207
KENDER ST
BESSON ST
GELLATLY RD
LAUSANNE ROAD
Juno Way Ind Est
Canterbury Ind Est
Industrial Estate
Lewisham Business Cen
Elizabeth Trading Est
Parkside Business Est
The Kingfisher Medical Cen
College of Management
Goldsmiths University
Laban Centre
Greenwich Cen Business Park
Faircharm Trading Est
Trading Est
Novotel
Arts Centre
Albany Cen & Theatre
Giffin Bus Cen
Deptford Stn
New Cross Stn
New Cross Gate Stn
New Cross Sports Arena
Hatcham Temple Grove Sch
Hatcham Mews Business Cen
Superstore
Goldsmiths University of London
Haberdashers Askes Hatcham Coll
Haberdashers Askes Hatcham College
St James Hatcham CE School
Edmund Waller Primary School
Kender Primary School
Lewisham College
Deptford Bridge Station
Greenwich Coroners Office
St Johns Stn
Elverson Road Stn
Thurston Industrial Est
Lewisham Bridge Primary School
Brockley Cross Business Cen
Crossways Sixth Form
Brockley Stn
Meadowgate Sch
Police Stn
St Marys Magdalens Catholic Prim Sch
Prendergast Hilly Fields College
Hilly Fields Medical Centre
Ladywell Cemetery
Ladywell Stn
Coroners Office
Register Office
University Hospital
Watergate School
Ivydale Primary School
Bredinghurst School
Honor Oak Health Centre
Honor Oak Crematorium
Crofton Park Station
Aquarius Golf Club
Camberwell New Cem
Crofton Leisure Centre
Ladywell Arena
Cemetery
1 grid square represents 500 metres

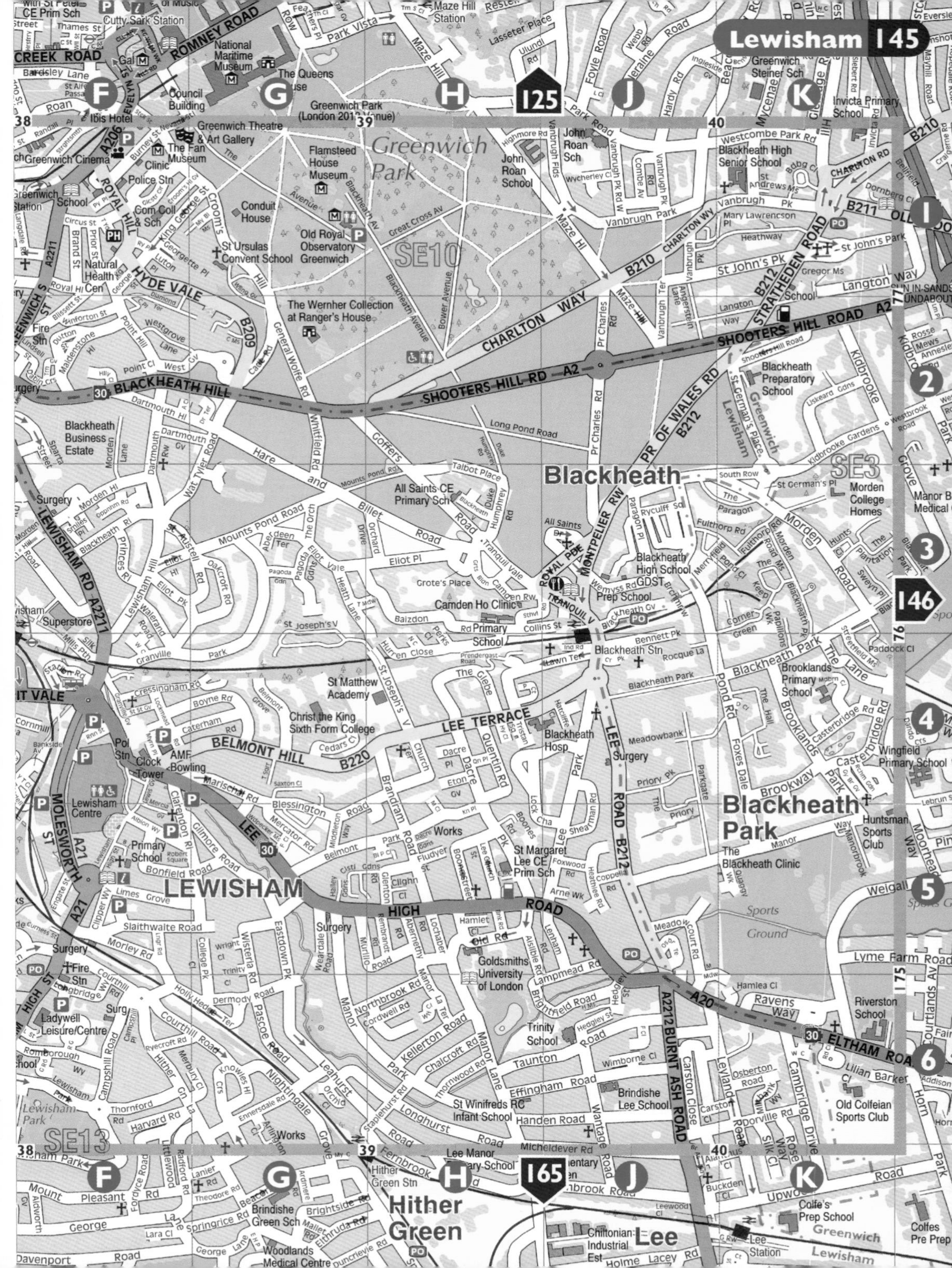
Lewisham
145
125
146
165
F
G
H
J
K
38
39
40
2
3
4
5
6
75
76
77
CREEK ROAD
ROMNEY ROAD
Cutty Sark Station
National Maritime Museum
The Queens House
Maze Hill Station
Park Vista
Lasseter Place
Greenwich Steiner Sch
Invicta Primary School
Ibis Hotel
Council Building
Greenwich Park (London 2012 Venue)
Greenwich Theatre & Art Gallery
The Fan Museum
Greenwich Cinema
Clinic
Police Stn
Greenwich Station
School
Flamsteed House Museum
Greenwich Park
John Roan Sch
John Roan School
Westcombe Park Rd
Blackheath High Senior School
Vanbrugh Park
Conduit House
Old Royal Observatory Greenwich
St Ursulas Convent School
SE10
Natural Health Cen
HYDE VALE
The Wernher Collection at Ranger's House
CHARLTON WAY
SHOOTERS HILL ROAD
STRATHEDEN ROAD
St John's Pk
Blackheath Preparatory School
BLACKHEATH HILL
SHOOTERS HILL RD
A2
Long Pond Road
PR OF WALES RD
Blackheath Business Estate
Hare and Billet Road
All Saints CE Primary Sch
Blackheath
SE3
Morden College Homes
Manor Brook Medical Cen
LEWISHAM RD A2211
Blackheath High School GDST
Prep School
Camden Ho Clinic
Primary School
Blackheath Stn
Superstore
Granville Park
Brooklands Primary School
St Matthew Academy
Christ the King Sixth Form College
LEE TERRACE
BELMONT HILL
Blackheath Hosp
Surgery
Wingfield Primary School
AMF Bowling
Clock Tower
Lewisham Centre
MOLESWORTH ST
Blackheath Park
Huntsman Sports Club
The Blackheath Clinic
Primary School
LEWISHAM
St Margaret Lee CE Prim Sch
LEE HIGH ROAD
Sports Ground
Goldsmiths University of London
Lyme Farm Road
Riverston School
Ladywell Leisure Centre
Trinity School
ELTHAM ROAD
Brindishe Lee School
Old Colfeian Sports Club
St Winifreds RC Infant School
BURNT ASH ROAD
SE13
Lewisham Park
Works
Brindishe Green Sch
Hither Green Stn
Hither Green
Chiltonian Industrial Est
Lee
Lee Station
Colfe's Prep School
Colfes Pre Prep
Woodlands Medical Centre

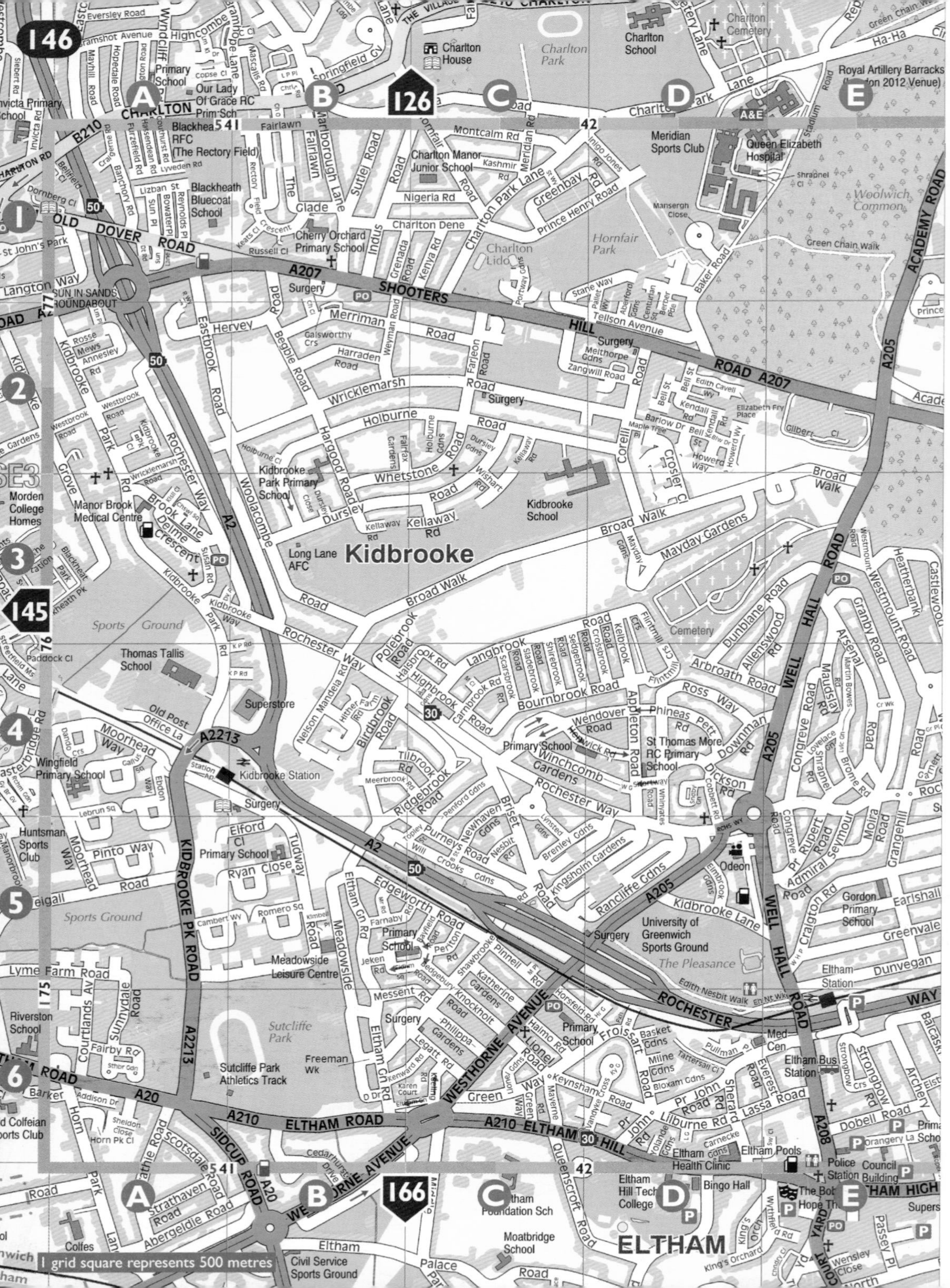

146
126
145
166
A
B
C
D
E
1
2
3
4
5
6
Kidbrooke
ELTHAM
SE3
Charlton House
Charlton Park
Charlton School
Charlton Cemetery
Royal Artillery Barracks (London 2012 Venue)
Queen Elizabeth Hospital
Meridian Sports Club
Woolwich Common
Charlton Manor Junior School
Blackheath RFC (The Rectory Field)
Blackheath Bluecoat School
Cherry Orchard Primary School
Hornfair Park
Charlton Lido
OLD DOVER ROAD
SUN IN SANDS ROUNDABOUT
A207
SHOOTERS HILL ROAD
ACADEMY ROAD
A205
WELL HALL ROAD
Kidbrooke Park Primary School
Kidbrooke School
Long Lane AFC
Morden College Homes
Manor Brook Medical Centre
Thomas Tallis School
Superstore
Kidbrooke Station
Wingfield Primary School
Huntsman Sports Club
Cemetery
St Thomas More RC Primary School
Odeon
University of Greenwich Sports Ground
The Pleasance
Gordon Primary School
Eltham Station
Meadowside Leisure Centre
Sutcliffe Park
Sutcliffe Park Athletics Track
Riverston School
Old Colfeian Sports Club
KIDBROOKE PK ROAD
A2213
A2
ROCHESTER WAY
A20
A210 ELTHAM ROAD
A210 ELTHAM HILL
SIDCUP ROAD
WESTHORNE AVENUE
Eltham Bus Station
Eltham Pools
Eltham Health Clinic
Police Station
Council Building
Bingo Hall
Eltham Hill Tech College
Moatbridge School
Civil Service Sports Ground
Colfes
1 grid square represents 500 metres

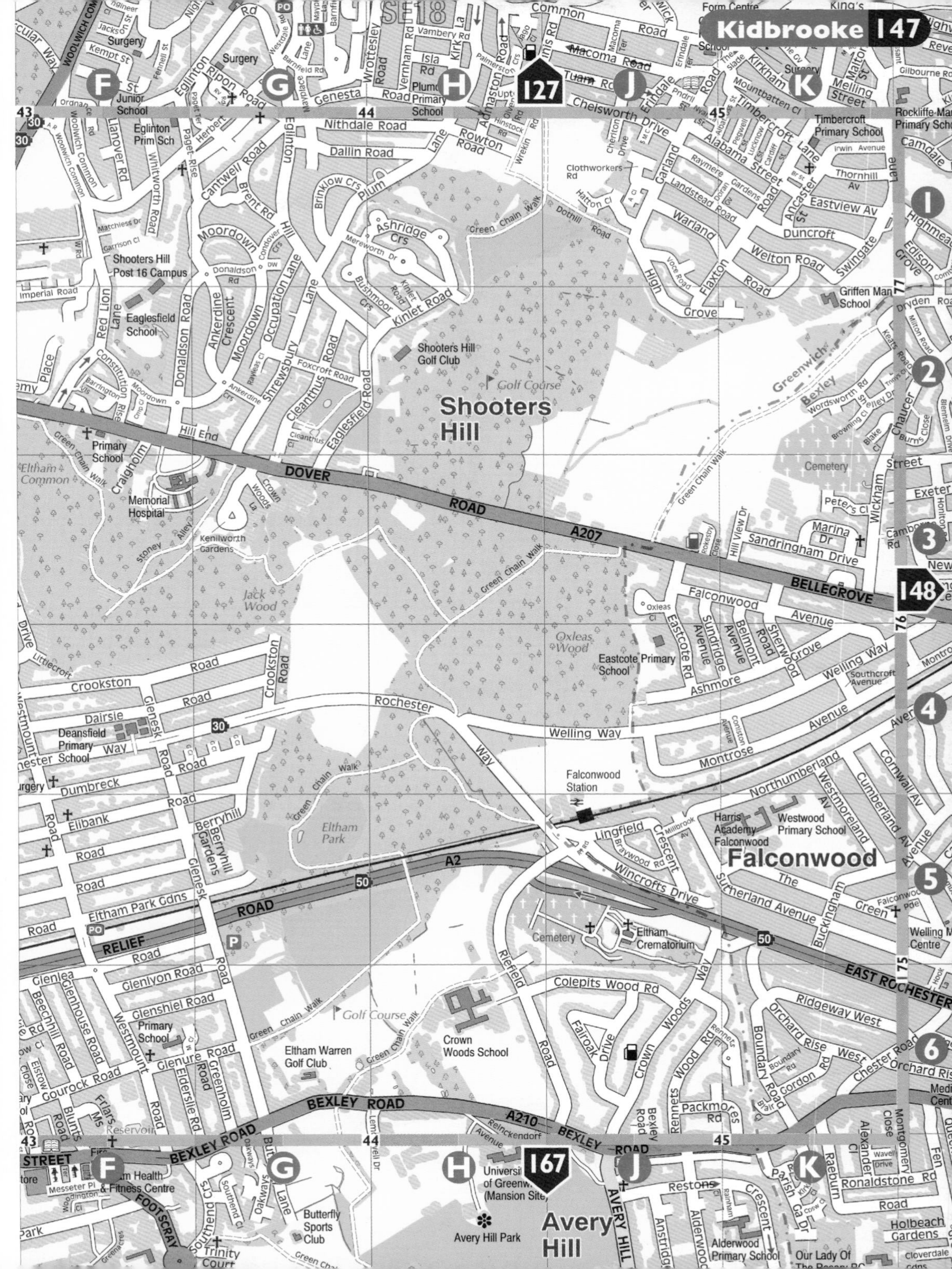
Shooters Hill
Falconwood
Avery Hill
SE18
Dover Road
A207
Bellegrove
A2
Rochester Way
Relief Road
East Rochester Way
Bexley Road
A210
Shooters Hill Golf Club
Golf Course
Jack Wood
Oxleas Wood
Eltham Common
Eltham Park
Eltham Warren Golf Club
Eltham Crematorium
Cemetery
Falconwood Station
Memorial Hospital
Shooters Hill Post 16 Campus
Eaglesfield School
Eglinton Prim Sch
Junior School
Primary School
Eastcote Primary School
Deansfield Primary School
Harris Academy Falconwood
Westwood Primary School
Crown Woods School
Timbercroft Primary School
Griffen Manor School
Alderwood Primary School
Butterfly Sports Club
University of Greenwich (Mansion Site)
Avery Hill Park
Green Chain Walk
127
148
167
43
44
45
77
76
75
1
2
3
4
5
6
F
G
H
J
K

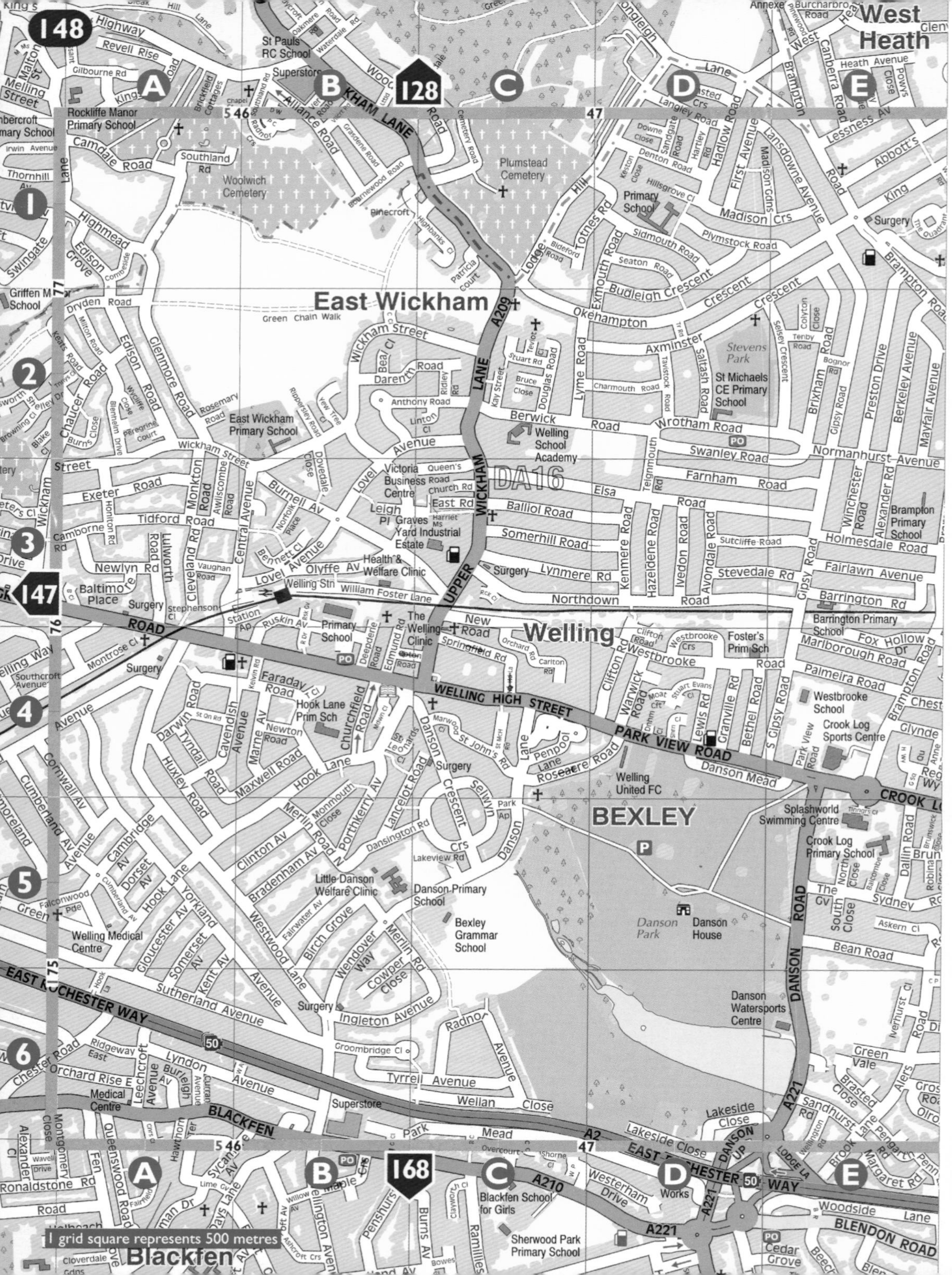

148
128
147
168
A
B
C
D
E
1
2
3
4
5
6
546
47
77
76
75
West Heath
East Wickham
Welling
BEXLEY
DA16
Blackfen
Rockliffe Manor Primary School
St Pauls RC School
Superstore
Woolwich Cemetery
Plumstead Cemetery
Pinecroft
Patricia Court
Green Chain Walk
East Wickham Primary School
Welling School Academy
Victoria Business Centre
Graves Yard Industrial Estate
Health & Welfare Clinic
Surgery
Welling Stn
The Welling Clinic
Primary School
Hook Lane Prim Sch
Westbrooke School
Crook Log Sports Centre
Welling United FC
Splashworld Swimming Centre
Crook Log Primary School
Stevens Park
St Michaels CE Primary School
Brampton Primary School
Barrington Primary School
Foster's Prim Sch
Little Danson Welfare Clinic
Danson Primary School
Bexley Grammar School
Danson Park
Danson House
Danson Watersports Centre
Welling Medical Centre
Medical Centre
Blackfen School for Girls
Sherwood Park Primary School
Griffen Manor School
Works
Highway
Revell Rise
Gilbourne Rd
Camdale Road
Southland Rd
Highmead
Edison Grove
Dryden Road
Edison Road
Glenmore Road
Wickham Lane
Upper Wickham Lane
Wickham Street
Exeter Road
Tidford Road
Newlyn Rd
Baltimore Place
Lovel Avenue
Olyffe Av
William Foster Lane
Welling High Street
Park View Road
Okehampton Crescent
Budleigh Crescent
Axminster Crescent
Berwick Road
Wrotham Road
Swanley Road
Farnham Road
Elsa Road
Balliol Road
Somerhill Road
Lynmere Rd
Northdown Road
Barrington Rd
Normanhurst Avenue
Holmesdale Road
Fairlawn Avenue
Stevedale Rd
Sutcliffe Road
Marlborough Road
Palmeira Road
Fox Hollow Dr
Brampton Road
Crook Log
Danson Road
Danson Mead
Danson Lane
Danson Crescent
Hook Lane
Maxwell Road
Cavendish Avenue
Huxley Road
Cornwall Av
Cumberland Av
Westwood Lane
Yorkland Avenue
Sutherland Avenue
Ingleton Avenue
Tyrrell Avenue
Wellan Close
East Rochester Way
Blackfen Road
Park Mead
Lakeside Close
Westerham Drive
Blendon Road
Woodside Lane
Ronaldstone Rd
Queenswood Road
Wellington Avenue
Penshurst
Burns Av
Ramillies
Green Vale
Bean Road
Askern Cl
Sydney Rd
Lansdowne Avenue
Madison Crs
Plymstock Road
Sidmouth Road
Exmouth Road
Totnes Rd
Lyme Road
Saltash Road
Preston Drive
Berkeley Avenue
Mayfair Avenue
Lessness Av
Abbott's
King
Langley Road
Denton Road
First Avenue
Hadlow Road
A209
A221
A210
A2
50
1 grid square represents 500 metres

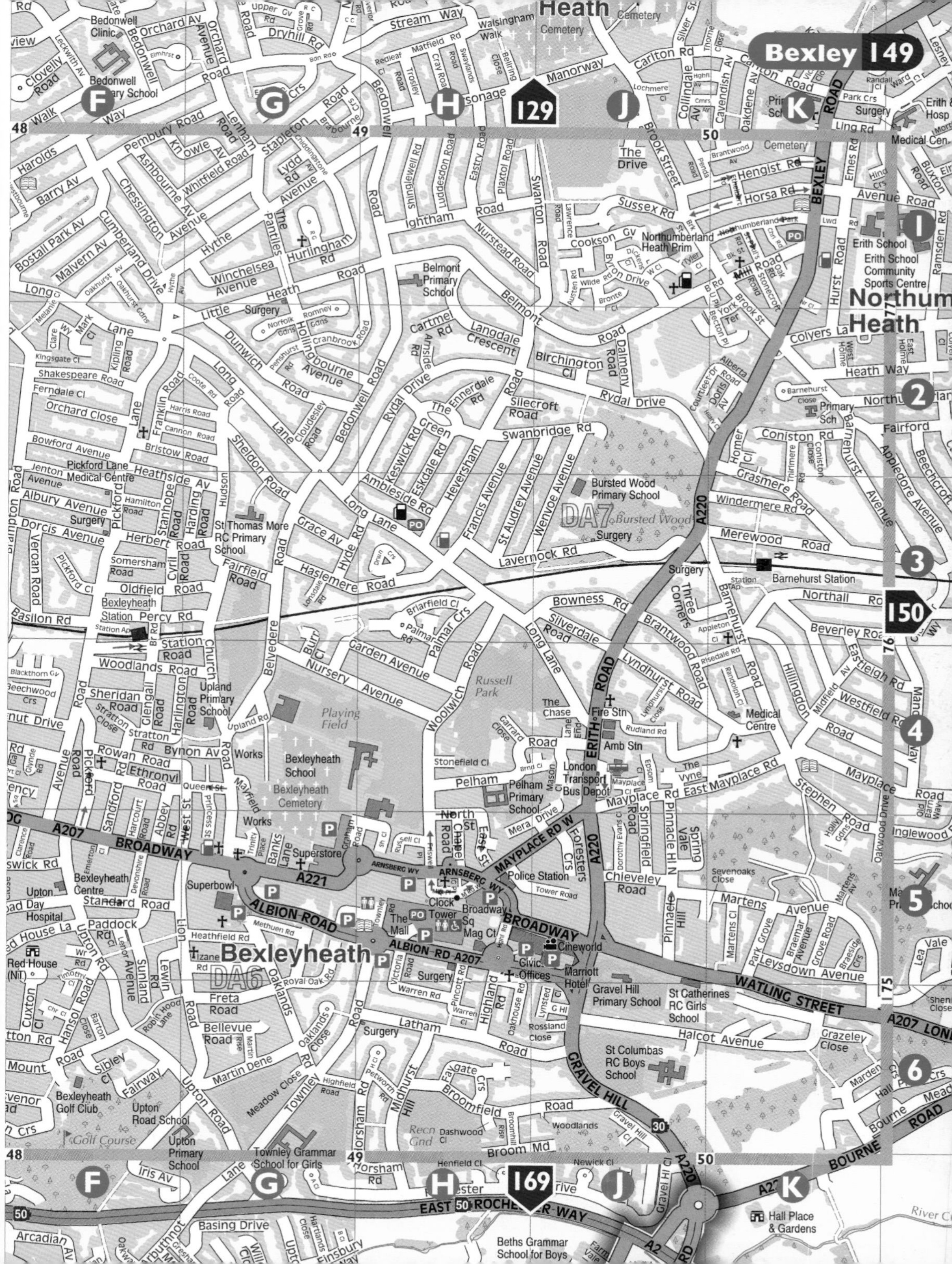
Bexleyheath
Northumberland Heath
Heath
DA6
DA7
129
150
169
Bedonwell Clinic
Bedonwell Primary School
Belmont Primary School
Northumberland Heath Prim
Erith School
Erith School Community Sports Centre
Bursted Wood Primary School
Barnehurst Station
Bexleyheath Station
St Thomas More RC Primary School
Upland Primary School
Bexleyheath School
Bexleyheath Cemetery
Russell Park
Pelham Primary School
London Transport Bus Depot
Police Station
Bexleyheath Centre
Upton Day Hospital
Red House (NT)
Civic Offices
Marriott Hotel
Cineworld
Gravel Hill Primary School
St Catherines RC Girls School
St Columbas RC Boys School
Bexleyheath Golf Club
Upton Road School
Upton Primary School
Townley Grammar School for Girls
Beths Grammar School for Boys
Hall Place & Gardens
BROADWAY
ALBION ROAD
WATLING STREET
GRAVEL HILL
ERITH ROAD
EAST ROCHESTER WAY
BOURNE ROAD
A207
A220
A221
A2
Long Lane
Pickford Lane
Brook Street
Mayplace Road East
Barnehurst Road
Upton Road
Belvedere Road

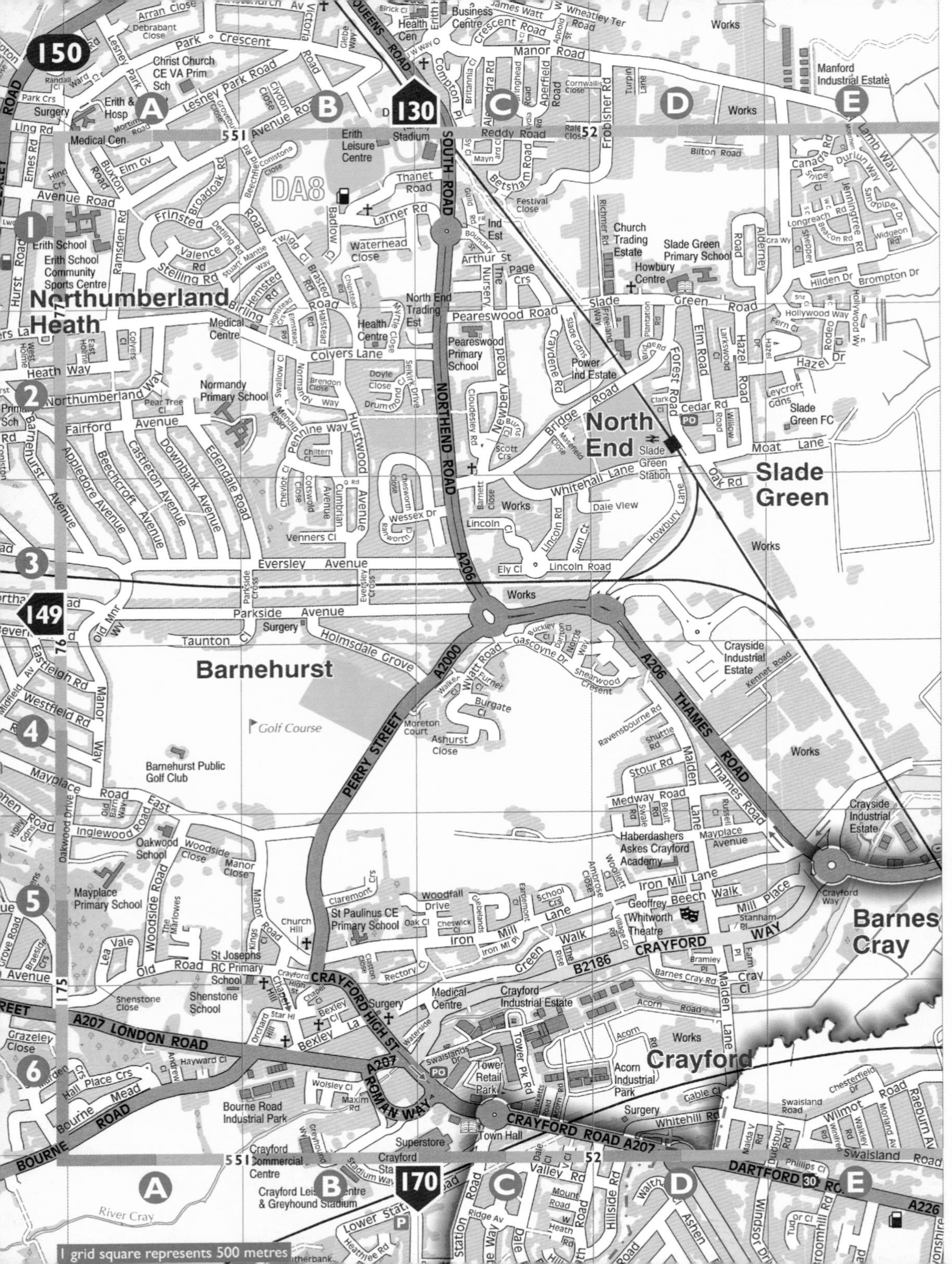

150
130
149
170
A
B
C
D
E
1
2
3
4
5
6
551
52
DA8
Northumberland Heath
Barnehurst
North End
Slade Green
Crayford
Barnes Cray
Park Crescent
Lesney Park Road
Christ Church CE VA Prim Sch
Erith & District Hosp
Surgery
Medical Cen
Avenue Road
Erith School
Erith School Community Sports Centre
Erith Leisure Centre
Stadium
Business Centre
Crescent Road
Manor Road
Wheatley Ter Road
Health Cen
Reddy Road
Frobisher Rd
Bilton Road
Works
Manford Industrial Estate
Lamb Way
SOUTH ROAD
QUEENS ROAD
Thanet Road
Larner Rd
Waterhead Close
Frinsted Road
Valence Rd
Stelling Rd
Brasted Rd
Arthur St
Page Crs
Ind Est
Betsham Road
Festival Close
Church Trading Estate
Slade Green Primary School
Howbury Centre
Slade Green Road
Peareswood Road
Peareswood Primary School
North End Trading Est
Health Centre
Medical Centre
Colyers Lane
Northumberland Way
Heath Way
Normandy Primary School
Fairford Avenue
Pennine Way
Hurstwood Avenue
NORTHEND ROAD
A206
Power Ind Estate
Bridge Road
Forest Road
Elm Road
Hazel Road
Hazel Dr
Moat Lane
Oak Rd
Slade Green Station
Whitehall Lane
Dale View
Howbury Lane
Slade Green FC
Cedar Rd
Lincoln Road
Eversley Avenue
Parkside Avenue
Taunton Cl
Holmsdale Grove
Gascoyne Dr
Shearwood Crescent
Crayside Industrial Estate
Kennet Road
THAMES ROAD
A2000
PERRY STREET
Golf Course
Barnehurst Public Golf Club
Mayplace Road East
Inglewood Road
Oakwood School
Mayplace Primary School
Woodside Road
Manor Road
Old Road
St Josephs RC Primary School
Shenstone School
St Paulinus CE Primary School
Woodfall Drive
Iron Mill Lane
Geoffrey Whitworth Theatre
Haberdashers Askes Crayford Academy
Mayplace Avenue
Maiden Lane
Medway Road
Stour Rd
CRAYFORD WAY
B2186
CRAYFORD HIGH ST
A207 LONDON ROAD
ROMAN WAY
Crayford Industrial Estate
Acorn Industrial Park
Tower Retail Park
Town Hall
CRAYFORD ROAD A207
Superstore
Bourne Road Industrial Park
Crayford Commercial Centre
Crayford Leisure Centre & Greyhound Stadium
BOURNE ROAD
River Cray
DARTFORD RD
A226
Swaisland Road
Crayford Way
1 grid square represents 500 metres

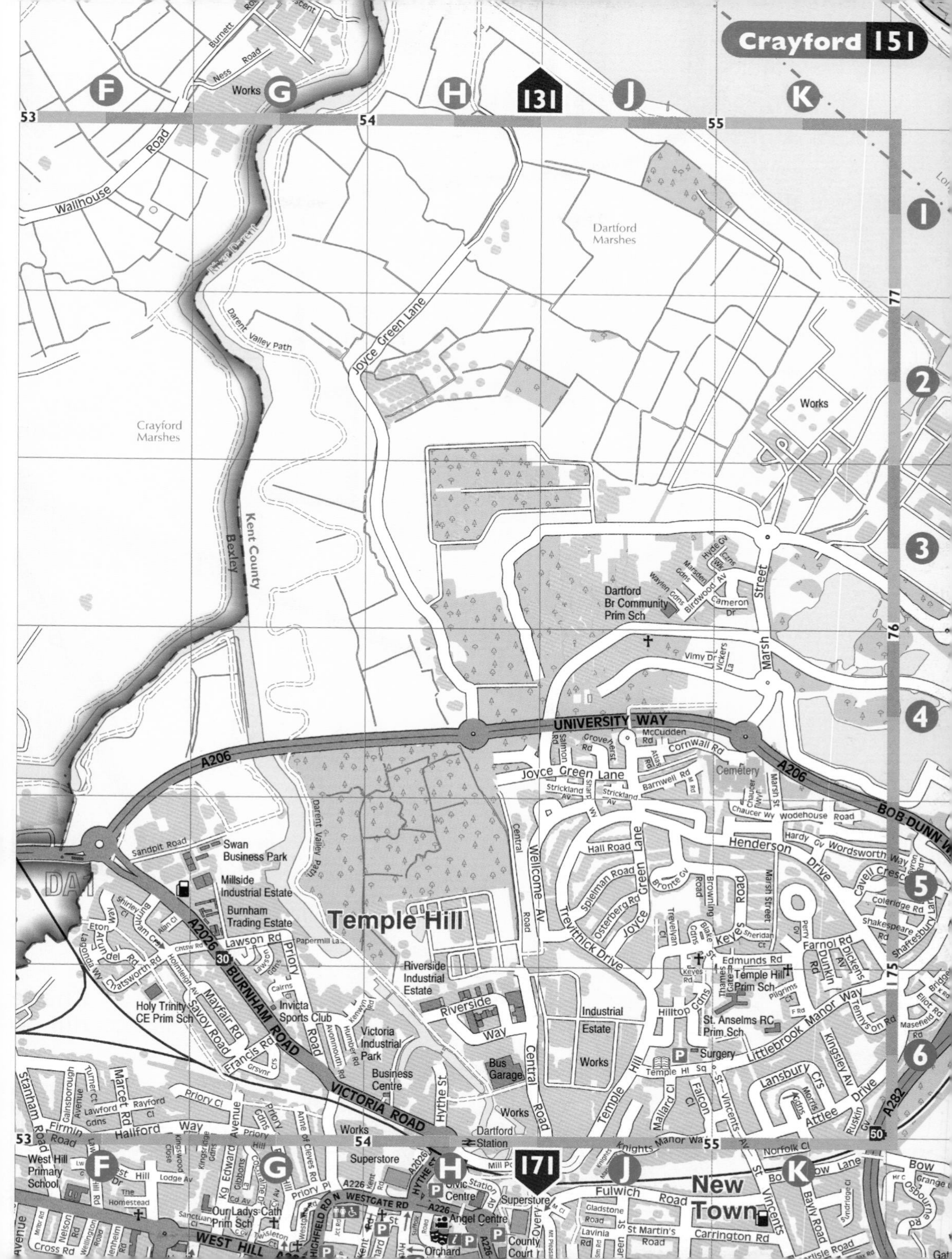

Crayford 151
131
171
F
G
H
J
K
53
54
55
1
2
3
4
5
6
75
76
77
50
Burnett Road
Ness Road
Works
Wallhouse Road
River Darent
Darent Valley Path
Joyce Green Lane
Dartford Marshes
Crayford Marshes
Kent County
Bexley
Works
Dartford Br Community Prim Sch
Hyde Gv
Marsden Gdns
Waylen Gdns
Birdwood Av
Cameron Dr
Marsh Street
Vimy Dr
Vickers La
UNIVERSITY WAY
A206
McCudden Rd
Salmon Rd
Grovehurst
Cornwall Rd
Atlas Rd
Joyce Green Lane
Barnwell Rd
Cemetery
Strickland Av
Sharp Wy
Chaucer Wy
Wodehouse Road
BOB DUNN WAY
Sandpit Road
Swan Business Park
Millside Industrial Estate
Burnham Trading Estate
Temple Hill
Central Road
Welcome Av
Hall Road
Henderson Drive
Hardy Gv
Wordsworth Way
Spielman Road
Bronte Gv
Browning Road
Osterberg Rd
Trevithick Drive
Trevelyan Cl
Keyes Road
Sheridan Ct
Cavell Cres
Coleridge Rd
Shakespeare Rd
Shaftesbury La
Farnol Rd
Dunkin Rd
Dickens Av
Edmunds Rd
Temple Hill Prim Sch
Pilgrims Ct
Thames Gate
Lawson Rd
Papermill La
Priory Road
Riverside Industrial Estate
Riverside Way
Industrial Estate
Works
Hilltop Gdns
St. Anselms RC Prim Sch
Littlebrook Manor Way
Tennyson Rd
Kingsley Av
Masefield Rd
Bridge
Eliot Rd
A2026
BURNHAM ROAD
Holmleigh Av
Chatsworth Rd
Lagonda Wy
Arundel Rd
Eton Way
Shirley Cl
Burnham Cres
Alan Cl
Holy Trinity CE Prim Sch
Savoy Road
Mayfair Rd
Francis Rd
Invicta Sports Club
Avonmouth Rd
Humber Rd
Kenwyn Rd
Victoria Industrial Park
Business Centre
Bus Garage
Surgery
Temple Hl Sq
St Vincents Av
Mallard Cl
Falcon Cl
Temple Hill
Lansbury Crs
Morris Gdns
Attlee Drive
Ruskin Gv
A282
VICTORIA ROAD
Hythe St
Works
Dartford Station
Stanham Road
Gainsborough Avenue
Turner Ct
Marcet Rd
Lawford Gdns
Rayford Cl
Priory Cl
Firmin Road
Hallford Way
Priory Gdns
Anne of Cleves Rd
Knights Manor Way
Norfolk Cl
West Hill Primary School
Superstore
Mill Pond
Civic Centre
Station Ap
Superstore
Fulwich Road
New Town
Bow Lane
Gladstone Road
Lavinia Rd
St Martin's Road
Carrington Rd
Bayly Road
Osbourne Rd
WESTGATE RD
HIGHFIELD RD N
A226
Our Ladys Cath Prim Sch
Angel Centre
County Court
Orchard
WEST HILL
Cross Rd
Nelson Road

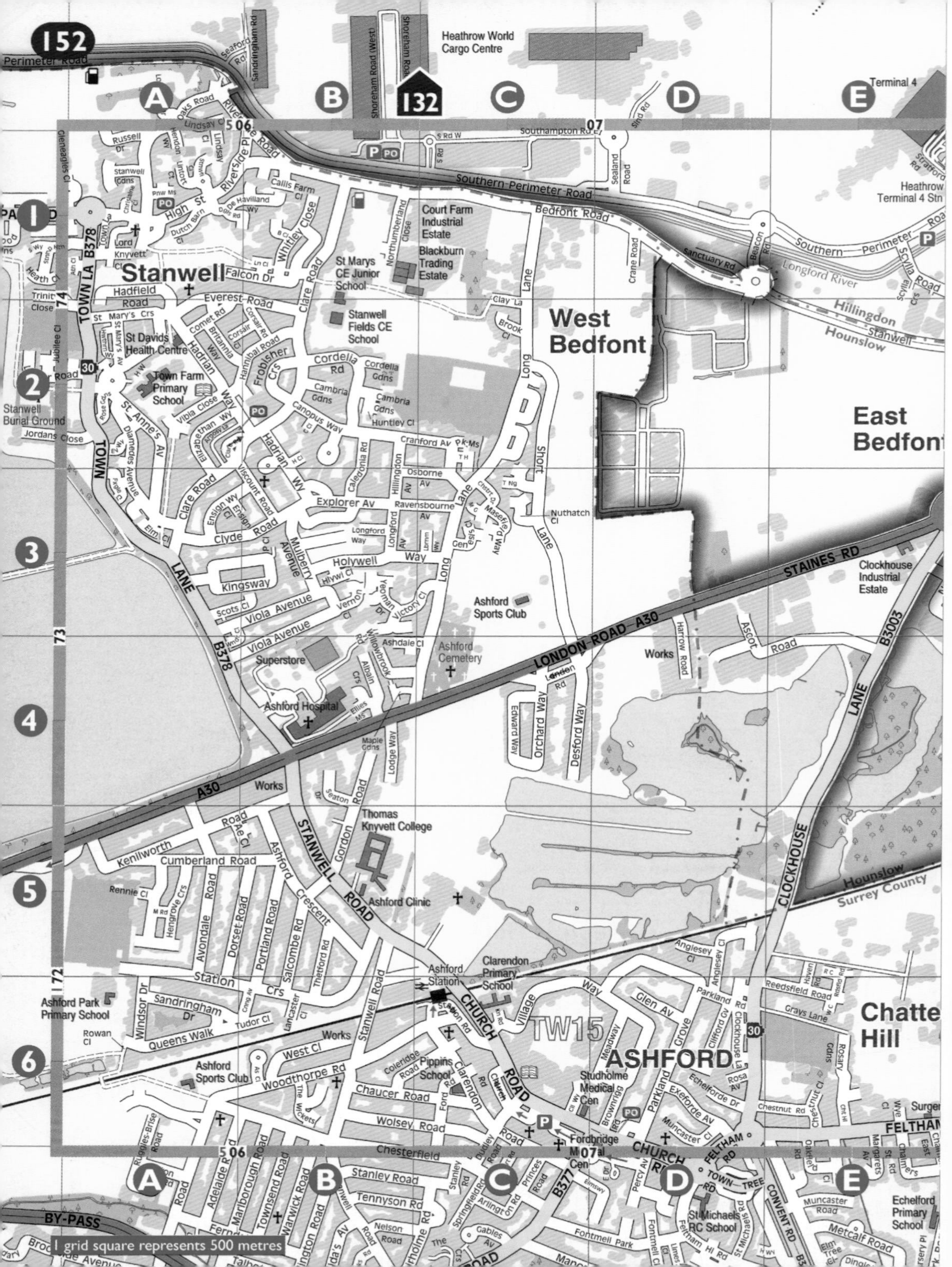
152
132
Heathrow World Cargo Centre
Terminal 4
Heathrow Terminal 4 Stn
Southern Perimeter Road
Bedfont Road
Court Farm Industrial Estate
Blackburn Trading Estate
St Marys CE Junior School
Stanwell Fields CE School
Stanwell
West Bedfont
East Bedfont
St Davids Health Centre
Town Farm Primary School
Stanwell Burial Ground
Longford River
Hillingdon
Stanwell
Hounslow
STAINES RD
Clockhouse Industrial Estate
LONDON ROAD A30
Ashford Sports Club
Ashford Cemetery
Superstore
Ashford Hospital
Works
Thomas Knyvett College
Ashford Clinic
Surrey County
CLOCKHOUSE LANE
STANWELL ROAD
Clarendon Primary School
Ashford Station
CHURCH ROAD
TW15
ASHFORD
Ashford Park Primary School
Ashford Sports Club
Pippins School
Studholme Medical Cen
Fordbridge Medical Cen
St Michaels RC School
Echelford Primary School
Chattern Hill
FELTHAM RD
BY-PASS
1 grid square represents 500 metres

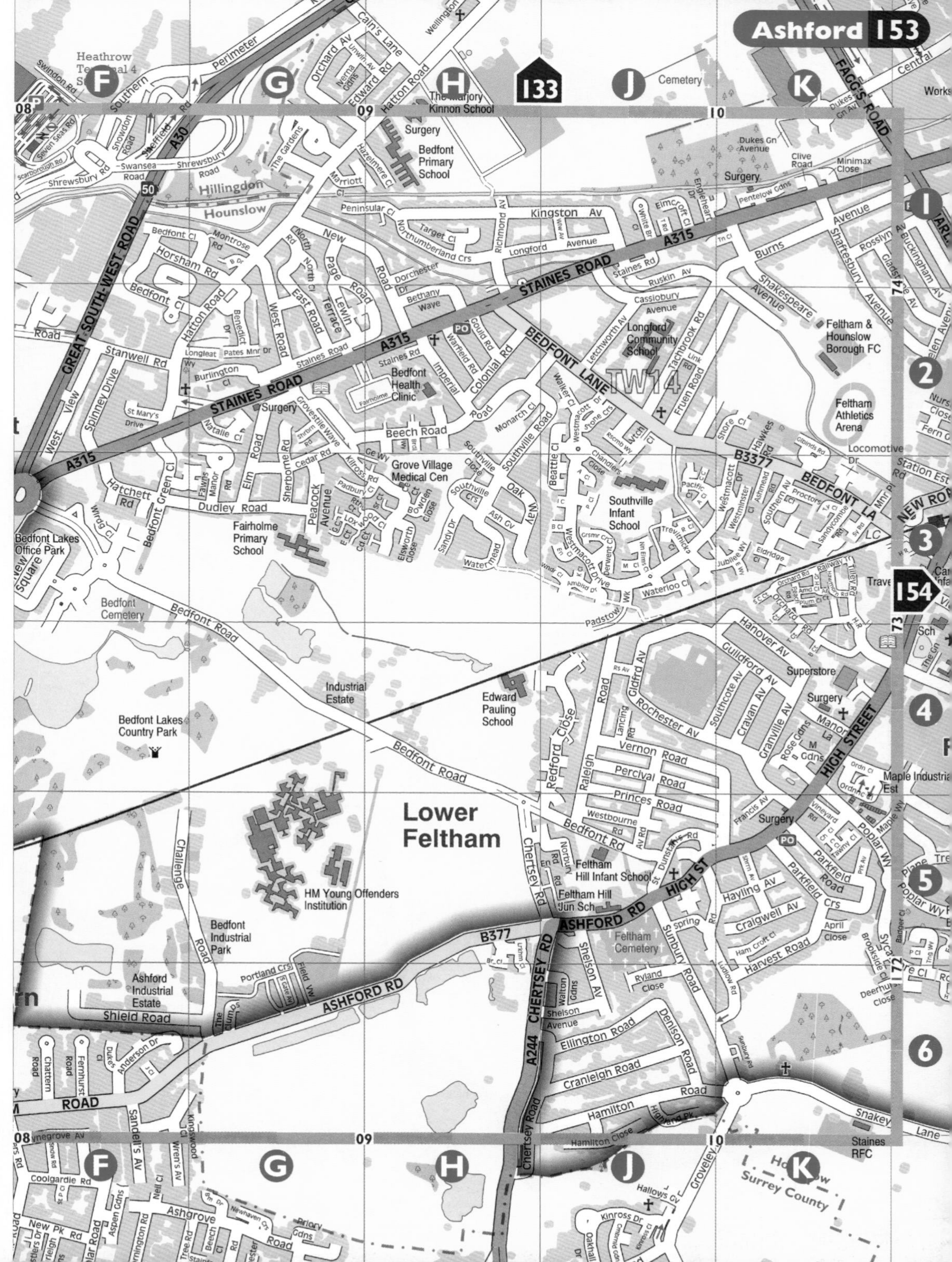
Heathrow
Cain's Lane
Wellington
Orchard Av
Unwin Av
Edward Rd
Hatton Road
The Marjory Kinnon School
133
Cemetery
FAGG'S ROAD
Central
Works
Swindon Rd
Southern
Perimeter
Seven Seas Rd
Snowdon Road
Sheffield Rd
A30
Scarborough Rd
Swansea Road
Shrewsbury Rd
Shrewsbury Road
The Gardens
Hazelmere Cl
Marriott Cl
Surgery
Bedfont Primary School
Dukes Gn Avenue
Clive Road
Minimax Close
Surgery
Pentelow Gdns
Engleheart Dr
Elmcroft Cl
Hillingdon
Hounslow
50
Peninsular Cl
Kingston Av
Target Cl
Richmond Av
Northumberland Crs
Longford Avenue
A315
Avenue
Rosslyn Av
Buckingham Av
Burns
Shaftesbury Avenue
Shakespeare Avenue
Bedfont Cl
Montrose Rd
Horsham Rd
New Road
North Rd
North Cl
Page Road
Lewin Terrace
East Road
West Road
Hatton Road
Benedict Dr
Bedfont Cl
Dorchester Dr
Bethany Wave
STAINES ROAD
Staines Rd
Ruskin Av
Cassiobury Avenue
Letchworth Av
Longford Community School
Tachbrook Rd
Link Rd
Fruen Road
Feltham & Hounslow Borough FC
GREAT SOUTH-WEST ROAD
Road
Stanwell Rd
Longleat Wy
Pates Mnr Dr
Staines Road
Staines Rd
Warfield Rd
Gould Rd
Imperial Road
Colonial Rd
BEDFONT LANE
TW14
Burlington Cl
Bedfont Health Clinic
Fairholme
Walker Cl
Westmacott Dr
Stone Crs
Feltham Athletics Arena
West View
Spinney Drive
St Mary's Drive
STAINES ROAD
Surgery
Grovestile Wave
Natalie Cl
Beech Road
Monarch Cl
Southville Road
Locomotive Dr
Elm Road
Sherborne Rd
Cedar Rd
Kilross Rd
Grove Village Medical Cen
Southville Close
Southville Crs
Oak Way
Beattie Cl
Chandlers Close
Shore Cl
Hawkes Rd
B3377
Station Est Rd
BEDFONT LA
NEW ROAD
A315
Hatchett Rd
Bedfont Green Cl
Fawns Manor Rd
Dudley Road
Peacock Avenue
Padbury Cl
Bowden Close
Elsworth Close
Ash Gv
Sandy Dr
Watermead
Southville Infant School
Westmacott Dr
Westminster Cl
Ashmead Rd
Southern Av
Proctors Cl
Sandycombe Rd
Pacific Cl
Trevithick Cl
Derwent Cl
Westmacott Drive
Jubilee Wy
Eldridge Cl
Waterloo Cl
Padstow Wk
Orchard Rd
Railway Ter
Tilley Rd
Bedfont Lakes Office Park
New Square
Fairholme Primary School
Bedfont Cemetery
Bedfont Road
Travel
154
Hanover Av
Guildford Av
Orchard Rd
Sch
Industrial Estate
Edward Pauling School
Rochester Av
Southcote Av
Cravan Av
Granville Av
Superstore
Surgery
Manor La
Bedfont Lakes Country Park
Redford Close
Raleigh Road
Lancing Rd
Vernon Road
Percival Road
Princes Road
Rose Gdns
HIGH STREET
Maple Industrial Est
Bedfont Road
Lower Feltham
Westbourne Rd
Bedfont Rd
Chertsey Rd
Norbury Rd
Francis Av
Surgery
Vineyard Rd
Tawny Cl
Poplar Wy
Parkfield Road
Challenge Road
HM Young Offenders Institution
Feltham Hill Infant School
Feltham Hill Jun Sch
St Dunstan's Rd
HIGH ST
Hayling Av
Craigwell Av
Parkfield Crs
April Close
Poplar Wy
Bedfont Industrial Park
B377
ASHFORD RD
CHERTSEY RD
Shelson Av
Feltham Cemetery
Spring Rd
Sunbury Road
Ham Croft Cl
Harvest Road
Brookside Cl
Badger Cl
Ashford Industrial Estate
Portland Crs
Field Vw
Walton Gdns
Ryland Close
Ludlow Rd
Deerhurst Close
Shield Road
The Clumps
ASHFORD RD
Shelson Avenue
Ellington Road
Denison Road
Chattern Road
Fernhurst Road
Dukes
Anderson Dr
A244
Cranleigh Road
ROAD
Sandell's Av
Kingswood Cl
Chertsey Road
Hamilton
Road
Highland Pk
Snakey Lane
Wynegrove Av
Hamilton Close
Staines RFC
08
09
10
F
G
H
J
K
1
2
3
4
5
6
71
72
73
74
Coolgardie Rd
Snow Rd
Neil Cl
Wren's Av
Ashgrove
Newhaven Crs
Priory Gdns
Road
New Pk Rd
Aspen Gdns
Tree Rd
Beech
Hallows Gv
Groveley
Kinross Dr
Hounslow
Surrey County

154
North Feltham
Works
Dockwell's Industrial Est
Superstore
Works
STAINES ROAD
134
Golf Course
Hounslow Heath
The Heathland School
HARLINGTON ROAD WEST
HOUNSLOW ROAD
HARLINGTON ROAD EAST
Sparrow Farm Infant School
Sparrow Farm Junior School
Feltham & Hounslow Borough FC
Feltham Athletics Arena
Feltham Station
NEW ROAD
HANWORTH ROAD
Cardinal Rd Infant Sch
Junior School
Cineworld
St Lawrence Business Cen
Feltham Superbowl
Feltham Community College
153
FELTHAM
UXBRIDGE ROAD
Feltham Airparcs Leisure Centre
Hounslow Cemetery
Mill Farm Business Park
South West Middlesex Crematorium
Crane Park Island
Maple Industrial Est
Felthambrook Industrial Estate
Five Ways Business Cen
TW13
Hanworth Park
Hanworth
Oriel Primary School
Hanworth Trading Est
Hampton Fm Industrial Est
HAMPTON ROAD WEST
Apex Retail Park
TWICKENHAM ROAD
Superstore
Staines RFC
172
Richmond House
1 grid square represents 500 metres

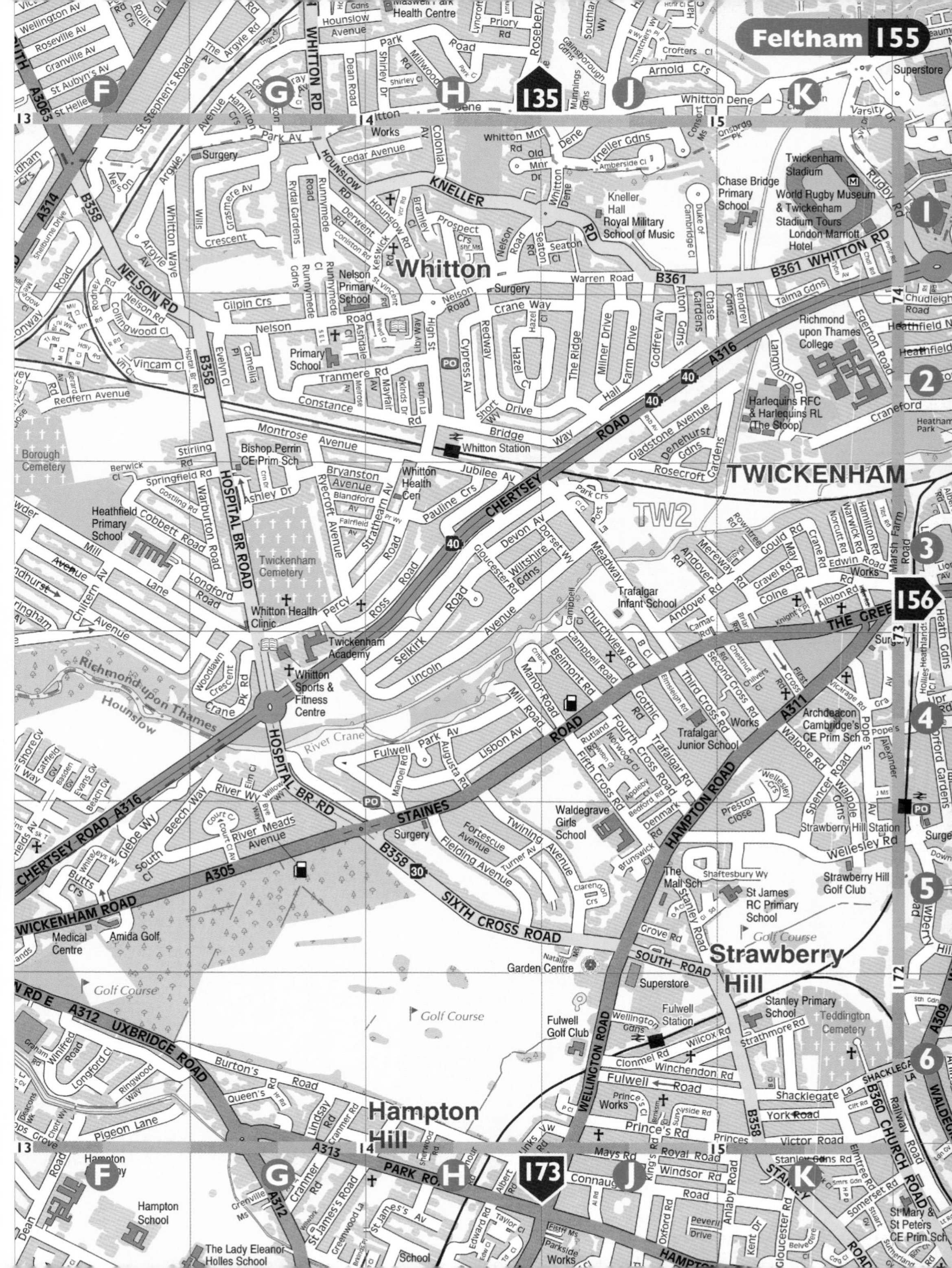

Feltham 155
135
156
173
Whitton
TWICKENHAM
TW2
Strawberry Hill
Hampton Hill
Hounslow Avenue
Maswell Park Health Centre
Priory Rd
Park Road
Whitton Rd
Dean Road
Arnold Crs
Crofters Cl
Whitton Dene
Superstore
Varsity Dr
Twickenham Stadium
World Rugby Museum & Twickenham Stadium Tours
London Marriott Hotel
Chase Bridge Primary School
Kneller Hall
Royal Military School of Music
Kneller Gdns
Amberside Cl
Kneller Rd
Whitton Rd
B361 Whitton Rd
Warren Road
Rugby Rd
Chudleigh Road
Heathfield N
Richmond upon Thames College
Egerton Road
Harlequins RFC & Harlequins RL (The Stoop)
Craneford
Heatham Park
St Aubyn's Av
Roseville Av
Granville Av
Wellington Av
St Stephen's Road
Hamilton Crs
Park Av
Cedar Avenue
Hounslow Rd
Colonial Av
Surgery
Grasmere Av
Wills Crescent
Rydal Gardens
Runnymede Road
Runnymede Gdns
Derwent Rd
Coniston Rd
Bramley Cl
Prospect Crs
Nelson Road
Seaton Cl
Argyle Av
Whitton Way
Nelson Rd
B358
Cilpin Crs
Nelson Primary School
Crane Way
Hazel Cl
The Ridge
Milner Drive
Hall Farm Drive
Godfrey Av
Alton Gdns
Chase Gardens
Kendrey Gdns
Talma Gdns
Langhorn Dr
Collingwood Cl
Vincam Cl
Evelyn Cl
Camellia Pl
Primary School
Tranmere Rd
Constance Rd
Mayfair Av
Cypress Av
Redway
Short Wy
Hazel Drive
Bridge Way
Hall Way
A316
Chertsey Road
Redfern Avenue
Borough Cemetery
Montrose Avenue
Stirling Rd
Berwick Cl
Springfield Rd
Bishop Perrin CE Prim Sch
Ashley Dr
Bryanston Avenue
Blandford Av
Fairfield Av
Ryecroft Avenue
Strathearn Av
Whitton Health Cen
Pauline Crs
Jubilee Av
Whitton Station
Gladstone Avenue
Denehurst Gdns
Rosecroft Gardens
Heathfield Primary School
Cobbett Road
Warburton Road
Hospital Br Road
Twickenham Cemetery
Mill Avenue
Longford Road
Chiltern Av
Lane
Whitton Health Clinic
Percy Road
Ross Road
Gloucester Rd
Devon Av
Wiltshire Gdns
Dorset Wy
Meadway
Park Crs
Post La
Andover Rd
Mereway Rd
Gould Rd
May Rd
Crane Rd
Edwin Road
Works
Marsh Farm Road
Trafalgar Infant School
Colne Rd
Albion Rd
The Green
Heath Gdns
Twickenham Academy
Whitton Sports & Fitness Centre
Selkirk Road
Lincoln Avenue
Churchview Rd
Campbell Rd
Belmont Rd
Manor Road
Gothic Rd
Third Cross Rd
Second Cross Rd
Chestnut Rd
Chilvers Rd
First Cross Rd
Vicarage Rd
Archdeacon Cambridge's CE Prim Sch
Pope's Av
Richmond-upon-Thames
Hounslow
Woodlawn Crescent
Crane Pk Rd
River Crane
Fulwell Park Av
Augusta Rd
Lisbon Av
Mill Road
Rutland Cl
Norwood Cl
Fourth Cross Road
Fifth Cross Rd
Trafalgar Rd
Trafalgar Junior School
A311
Hampton Road
Walpole Rd
Spencer Road
Walpole Gdns
Staines Road
PO
River Wy
Beech Way
Glebe Wy
Court Cl
River Meads Avenue
Surgery
Fortescue Avenue
Fielding Avenue
Twining Avenue
Turner Av
Waldegrave Girls School
Denmark Rd
Brunswick Cl
Preston Close
Wellesley Crs
Strawberry Hill Station
Wellesley Rd
Chertsey Road A316
A305
Twickenham Road
Butts Crs
B358
Sixth Cross Road
Clarendon Crs
The Mall Sch
Shaftesbury Wy
Stanley Road
St James RC Primary School
Strawberry Hill Golf Club
Medical Centre
Amida Golf
Grove Rd
Golf Course
South Road
Garden Centre
Superstore
Stanley Primary School
Teddington Cemetery
A312
Uxbridge Road
Golf Course
Fulwell Golf Club
Wellington Road
Wellington Gdns
Fulwell Station
Wilcox Rd
Strathmore Rd
Clonmel Rd
Winchendon Rd
Fulwell Road
Shacklegate La
B360 Church Road
Railway Road
A309
Winifred Road
Longford Cl
Ringwood Way
Burton's Road
Queen's Rd
Lindsay Rd
Cranmer Rd
Works
Prince's Rd
York Road
Victor Road
Pigeon Lane
A313
Park Rd
Mays Rd
Royal Road
Windsor Rd
Stanley Gdns Rd
Hampton School
Grenville Ms
St James's Rd
St James's Av
Greenwood La
Edward Rd
Albert Rd
Taylor Cl
Connaught Road
Oxford Rd
Peveril Drive
Anlaby Road
Kent Dr
Gloucester Rd
Somerset Rd
St Mary & St Peters CE Prim Sch
The Lady Eleanor Holles School
Parkside Works
School

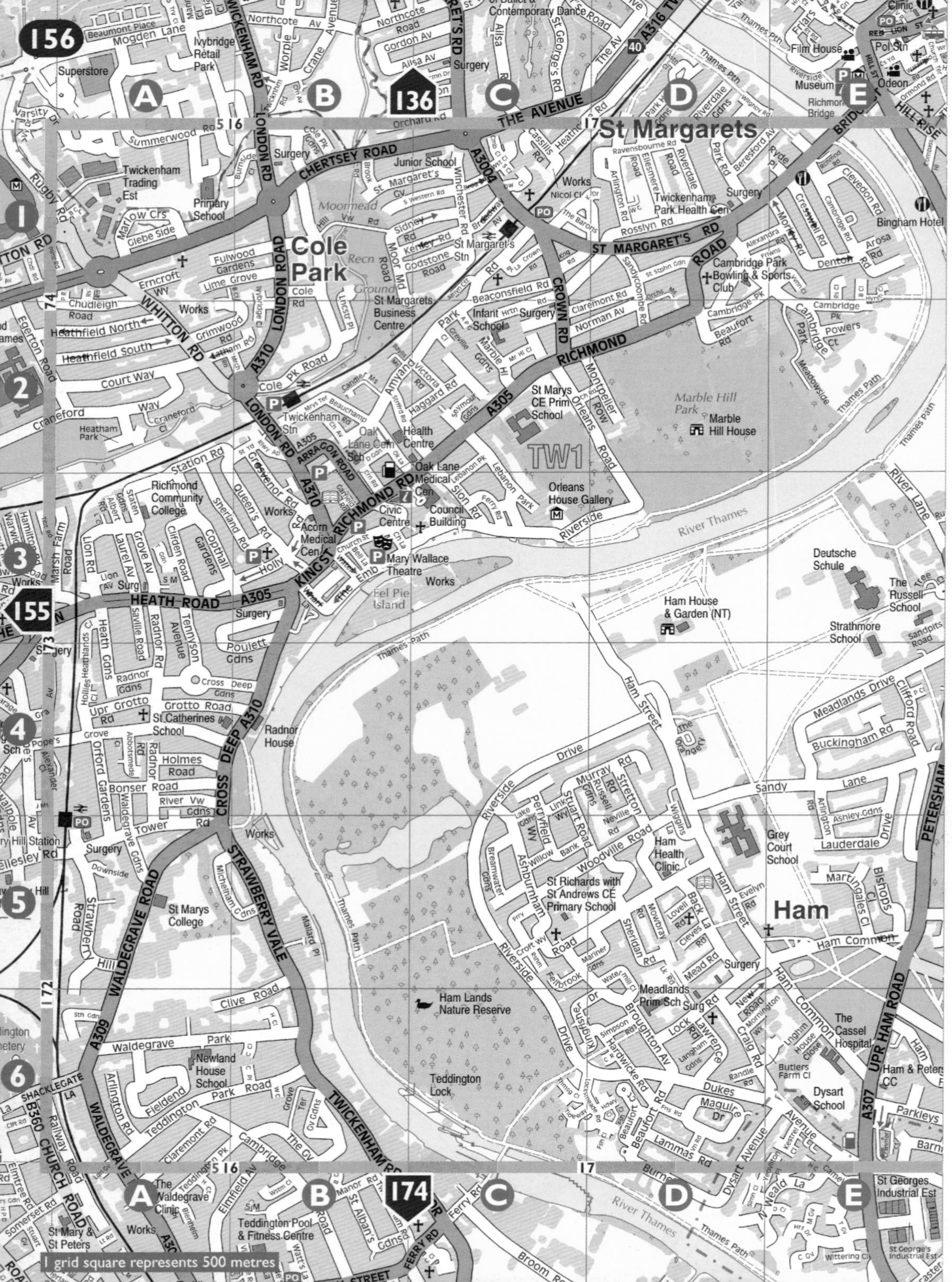

156
136
155
174
A
B
C
D
E
1
2
3
4
5
6
St Margarets
Cole Park
Ham
TW1
Mogden Lane
Beaumont Place
Ivybridge Retail Park
Superstore
Northcote Av
Northcote Road
Gordon Av
Ailsa Av
Surgery
The Avenue
A316
St George's Rd
Chertsey Road
Twickenham Trading Est
Primary School
Junior School
Marlow Crs
Glebe Side
Summerwood Rd
Rugby Rd
Whitton Rd
London Road
A310
A3004
Moormead
Recn Ground
St Margaret's Stn
St Margaret's Rd
Twickenham Park Health Cen
Ravensbourne Rd
Arlington Road
Riverdale Road
Park Rd
Beresford Av
Rosslyn Rd
Works
Nicol Cl
PO
Fulwood Gardens
Lime Grove
Erncroft Wy
Chudleigh Road
Heathfield North
Heathfield South
Court Way
Craneford Way
Heatham Park
Egerton Road
Cole Pk Road
Twickenham Stn
St Margarets Business Centre
Infant School
Beaconsfield Rd
Crown Rd
Claremont Rd
Norman Av
Richmond Road
A305
Cambridge Park Bowling & Sports Club
Cambridge Park
Beaufort Rd
Powers Ct
Meadowside
Thames Path
Marble Hill Park
Marble Hill House
St Marys CE Prim School
Montpelier Row
Orleans Road
Orleans House Gallery
Riverside
River Thames
Lebanon Park
Sion Rd
Ferry Rd
Oak Lane Medical Cen
Health Centre
Council Building
Civic Centre
Haggard Rd
Arragon Road
Station Rd
Richmond Community College
Grosvenor Rd
Queen's Rd
Sheriand Rd
Copthall Gardens
Clifden Road
Grove Av
Laurel Av
Lion Rd
Marsh Farm Road
Hamilton Rd
Acorn Medical Cen
Kingst
Holly
Mary Wallace Theatre
Eel Pie Island
Heath Road
Surgery
Poulett Gdns
Tennyson Avenue
Radnor Rd
Saville Road
Heath Gdns
Radnor Gdns
Cross Deep Gdns
Grotto Road
Upr Grotto Rd
St Catherines School
Radnor House
Cross Deep
Holmes Road
Bonser Road
River Vw Gdns
Tower Rd
Orford Gardens
Waldegrave Gdns
Strawberry Hill Station
Downside
Strawberry Hill
Strawberry Vale
Michelham Gdns
St Marys College
Waldegrave Road
A309
Clive Road
Waldegrave Park
Newland House School
Arlington Rd
Fieldend
Teddington Park Road
Claremont Rd
Cambridge
The Gv
Twickenham Rd
Shacklegate La
B360
Church Road
Railway Rd
The Waldegrave Clinic
Teddington Pool & Fitness Centre
St Mary & St Peters
Elmfield Av
St Alban's Gdns
Manor Rd
Ferry Rd
Deutsche Schule
The Russell School
Ham House & Garden (NT)
Strathmore School
Sandpits Road
River Lane
Ham Street
The Orangery
Meadlands Drive
Clifford Road
Buckingham Rd
Sandy Lane
Riverside Drive
Murray Rd
Stretton Rd
Russell Gdns
Stuart Road
Neville Rd
Perryfield Wy
Woodville Road
Ham Health Clinic
Grey Court School
Ashley Gdns
Lauderdale Drive
Martingales Cl
Bishops Cl
Petersham
St Richards with St Andrews CE Primary School
Ashburnham Road
Breamwater Gdns
Willow Bank
Evelyn Rd
Back La
Ham Common
Mowbray Rd
Sheridan Rd
Lovell Rd
Cleves Rd
Mead Rd
Surgery
Meadlands Prim Sch
Surg
New Road
Lock Rd
Lawrence Rd
Craig Rd
Mariner Gdns
Fellbrook
Broughton Av
Hardwicke Rd
Simpson Rd
Kingfisher Dr
Ham Lands Nature Reserve
Teddington Lock
Thames Path
Mallard Pl
The Cassel Hospital
Butlers Farm Cl
House Close
Dysart School
Dukes Avenue
Maguire Dr
Beaufort Rd
Lammas Rd
Dysart Avenue
Upr Ham Road
A307
Ham & Petersham CC
Parkleys
St Georges Industrial Est
Wittering Cl
Broom Rd
Bingham Hotel
Clevedon Rd
Cambridge Rd
Denton Rd
Arosa Rd
Film House
Museum
Odeon
Richmond Bridge
Hill Rise
Pol Stn
Clinic
1 grid square represents 500 metres

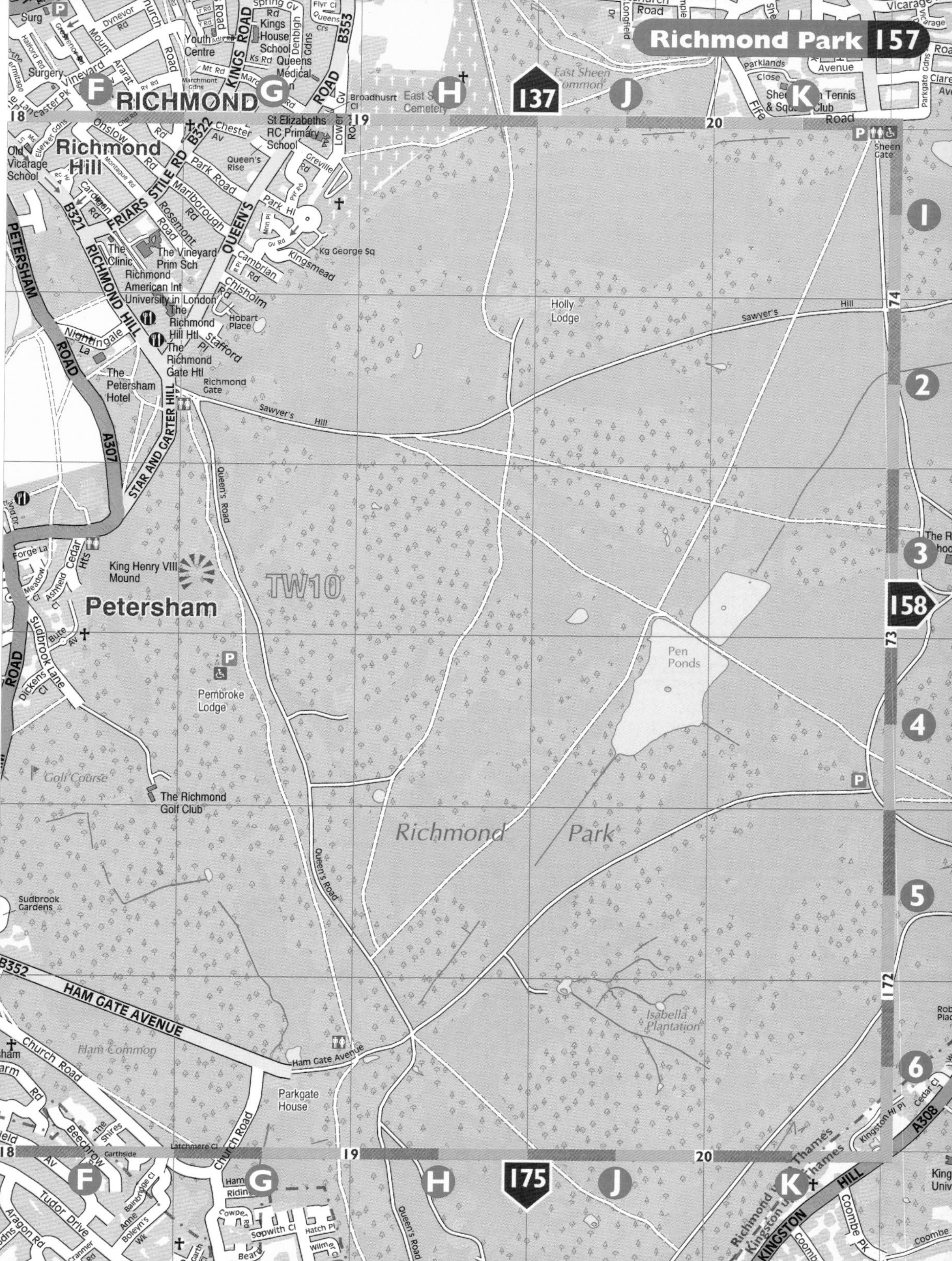
RICHMOND
Richmond Hill
Petersham
Richmond Park
TW10
Pen Ponds
Holly Lodge
Pembroke Lodge
King Henry VIII Mound
Isabella Plantation
Ham Common
Golf Course
The Richmond Golf Club
Sudbrook Gardens
Parkgate House
Sheen Gate
Richmond Gate
Sawyer's Hill
Queen's Road
HAM GATE AVENUE
Ham Gate Avenue
PETERSHAM ROAD
A307
B352
STAR AND GARTER HILL
RICHMOND HILL
FRIARS STILE RD
QUEEN'S ROAD
KINGS ROAD
KINGSTON HILL
A308
East Sheen Common
East Sheen Cemetery
St Elizabeths RC Primary School
Old Vicarage School
The Vineyard Prim Sch
Richmond American Int University in London
The Richmond Hill Htl
The Richmond Gate Htl
The Petersham Hotel
Sheen Lawn Tennis & Squash Club
Kg George Sq
Kingsmead
Church Road
Tudor Drive
Beechrow
Latchmere Cl
Coombe Pk
137
158
175
F G H J K
1 2 3 4 5 6
18 19 20
74 73 172

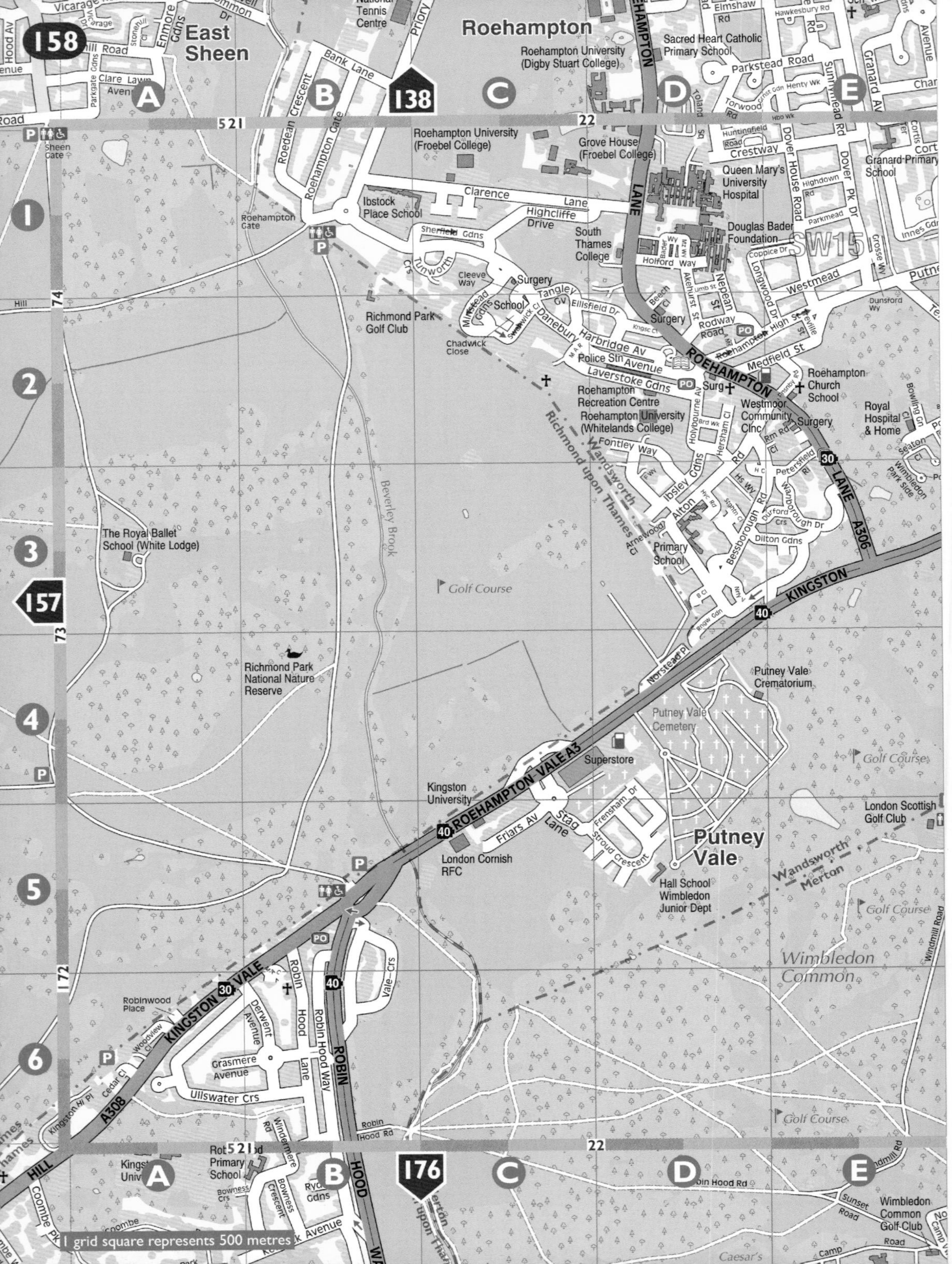

158
138
157
176
A
B
C
D
E
1
2
3
4
5
6
521
22
74
73
172
East Sheen
Roehampton
National Tennis Centre
Vicarage Rd
Enmore Gdns
Hill Road
Clare Lawn Avenue
Parkgate Gdns
Sheen Gate
Bank Lane
Priory
Roedean Crescent
Roehampton Gate
Roehampton University (Digby Stuart College)
Roehampton University (Froebel College)
Grove House (Froebel College)
Sacred Heart Catholic Primary School
Elmshaw Rd
Hawkesbury Rd
Parkstead Road
Sunnymead Rd
Granard Av
Avenue
Torwood Rd
Henty Wk
Huntingfield Road
Crestway
Dover House Road
Dover Pk Dr
Granard Primary School
Queen Mary's University Hospital
Highdown Rd
Parkmead
Innes Gdns
Douglas Bader Foundation
SW15
Clarence Lane
Ibstock Place School
Highcliffe Drive
Roehampton Gate
South Thames College
Holford Way
Coppice Dr
Longwood Dr
Westmead
Grosse Wy
Putney
Sherfield Gdns
Tunworth Crs
Cleeve Way
Surgery
Tangley Gv
Ellisfield Dr
Beech Cl
Nepean St
Akehurst St
Umb St
Rodway Road
Roehampton High St
Dunsford Wy
Minstead Gdns
School
Danebury Av
Harbridge Av
Chadwick Close
Richmond Park Golf Club
Police Stn
Avenue
Medfield St
ROEHAMPTON LANE
Laverstoke Gdns
Roehampton Recreation Centre
Roehampton University (Whitelands College)
Surg
Westmoor Community Clnc
Surgery
Roehampton Church School
Royal Hospital & Home
Bowling Gn Cl
Fontley Way
Holybourne Av
Hersham Cl
Brd Wk
Rm Rd
Petersfield Rl
Wanborough Dr
Ibsley Gdns
Alton Rd
Bessborough Rd
Dilton Gdns
Dufford Crs
Wimbledon Park Side
Seaton Cl
Richmond upon Thames
Wandsworth
Arnewood Cl
Primary School
A306
LANE
KINGSTON
30
40
Beverley Brook
Golf Course
The Royal Ballet School (White Lodge)
Richmond Park National Nature Reserve
Hill
Norstead Pl
Putney Vale Crematorium
Putney Vale Cemetery
Superstore
ROEHAMPTON VALE A3
Kingston University
Friars Av
Stag Lane
Frensham Dr
Stroud Crescent
London Cornish RFC
Putney Vale
Hall School Wimbledon Junior Dept
London Scottish Golf Club
Wandsworth
Merton
Wimbledon Common
Windmill Road
KINGSTON VALE
Robinwood Place
Woodview Cl
Cedar Cl
Derwent Avenue
Robin Hood Lane
Robin Hood Way
ROBIN HOOD WAY
Vale Crs
Grasmere Avenue
Ullswater Crs
Kingston Hl Pl
A308
HILL
Robin Hood Rd
Windermere Rd
Bowness Crescent
Bowness Crs
Primary School
Coombe Pk
Coombe
Sunset Road
Camp Road
Wimbledon Common Golf Club
Caesar's
1 grid square represents 500 metres

Cambalt Road
South Thames College
East Putney Station
Putney High Sch
Merlin School
Best Western
West Hill
Fire Station
Wandsworth
Elliott School
Putney Heath
Royal Hospital for Neuro-Disability
Prospect House Sch
Ronald Rose Primary Sch
West Hill
Wandle Recreation Centre
Southside Shopping Centre
Arndale Health Centre
Wandsworth Trading Estate
Merton Road Industrial Estate
Riverside Business Centre
Tibbet's Ride
A219
A3
A218
Merton Road
Granville Road
Primary School
Girdwood Rd
Skeena Hill
Saint Cecilias CE Sch
John Paul II RC School
Our Lady Queen of Heaven RC Prim Sch
Tudor Lodge Health Cen
Grammar School
Sheringdale Primary School
Southmead Primary School
Southfields Station
Southfields
Southfields Community College
Theatre of the Dispossessed
Linden Lodge School
Albemarle Primary Sch
Wimbledon Park Side
Wimbledon Park
Wimbledon Park Athletics Track
Boating Lake
Wimbledon Park Golf Club
Wimbledon Park Station
Wimbledon Park Primary School
Gresham Way Ind Est
Durnsford Road
Synagogue
Queensmere Road
Windmill
Windmill Road
Apostolic Nuncio
Parkside Hospital
Embassy of The Holy See
Wimbledon (London 2012 Venue)
The All England Lawn Tennis & Croquet Club
Wimbledon Lawn Tennis Museum
Church Road
Golf Course
Buddhapadipa Temple
SW19
Parkside
Ricards Lodge High School
Wimbledon
Primary School
The Study Preparatory School
The Causeway
Camp Road
Leopold Rd
Gap Road
139
160
177

160
140
159
178
A
B
C
D
E
1
2
3
4
5
6
26
27
WANDSWORTH HIGH ST
HUGUENOT PL
N SIDE WANDSWORTH COMMON
ARMOURY WY
BUCKHOLD RD
GARRATT LANE
TRINITY ROAD
WINDMILL RD
SPENCER PARK
BOLINGBROKE GROVE
BELLEVUE RD
ST JAMES'S DRIVE
EARLSFIELD ROAD
BURNTWOOD LANE
DURNSFORD ROAD
UPPER TOOTING ROAD
TOOTING HIGH ST
GAP ROAD
PLOUGH LANE
SUMMERSTOWN
Southside Shopping Centre
Arndale Health Centre
Wandle Recreation Centre
Sergeant Industrial Est
SW18
Wandsworth Trading Estate
King George's Park
Brocklebank Health Cen
Council Building
Merton Road Industrial Estate
Riverside Business Centre
Southfields Community College
Earlsfield
Earlsfield Station
Wandsworth Cemetery
HM Prison
Wandsworth Common
Wandsworth Common Station
Emanuel School
Lombard Business Park
Highfield School
Beatrix Potter Primary School
Haslemere Industrial Est
Rufus Business Centre
Wimbledon Park Primary School
Gresham Way Industrial Estate
Wimbledon Stadium Business Cen
Central London Golf Club
Burntwood School
Summerstown
Golf Course
Springfield Hospital
Ernest Bevin College
Upper Tooting
Nightingale School
Adult College
St Walter & St John Sports Ground
Upper Tooting Independent High School
Finton House Sch
Streatham Cemetery
SW17
Wimbledon Stadium
Lambeth Crematorium
Smallwood Primary School
Broadwater Primary School
Tooting Leisure Centre
Wimbledon (Gap Road) Cemetery
St Georges University of London
St Georges Hospital
South Wimbledon
Lambeth Cemetery
Tooting Graveney
Haydons Road Station
TOOTING
Balham Girls Preparatory Sec Sch
Ensham Sec Sch
1 grid square represents 500 metres

Balham 161
141
162
179
Clapham Park
Streatham Hill
Streatham Park
Furzedown
STREATHAM
Balham
SW12
Tooting Bec Common
Tooting Bec Athletics Track
THE AVENUE
CLAPHAM
CAVENDISH ROAD
A205 POYNDERS ROAD
ATKINS ROAD
STREATHAM PL
KINGS AVENUE
B221 KINGS AV
THORNTON AV
NIGHTINGALE LANE
A24 BALHAM HILL
BALHAM HIGH RD
BEDFORD HILL
B242
TOOTING BEC ROAD
A214
CHURCH LANE
CARRAD'S ROAD
STREATHAM HIGH RD
STREATHAM HILL
A23
STERNHOLD AV
TOOTING BEC GDNS
AMBLESIDE AV
MITCHAM LANE
Balham Station
Clapham South Station
Streatham Hill Station
Streatham Stn
Tooting Bec Stn
Lambeth Academy
College
Balham Mosque
Al-Risaala School
La Retraite RC Girls School
St Bedes RC Infant Sch
The White House Preparatory Sch
Telferscot Primary School
Richard Atkins Prim Sch
Aspen House Secondary & Primary Sch
HM Prison
Ashby Mill
Glenbrook Primary School
Broomwood Hall Upper School
Holy Ghost RC Primary School
Hornsby House School
Chrysalis Thtr
Trinity St Marys Primary School
Balham Leisure Centre
Balham Health Cen
Battersea Tutorial College
St. Anselms RC Prim Sch
Waldorf School of SW London
Streatham & Clapham High Sch
Mortimer School
Bowling Club
Lambeth College
Leisure Centre
Beechwood School
Broomwood Hall Lower Sch
Odeon
Refuge Temple
Police Stn
Bethel Temple
St Leonards CE Primary School
Streatham Swimming Pool
Streatham Ice Rink
Natural Therapy Clinic
Radha Krishna Temple
Zennor Rd Ind Est
Lido
The Livity School
Wandsworth
Lambeth

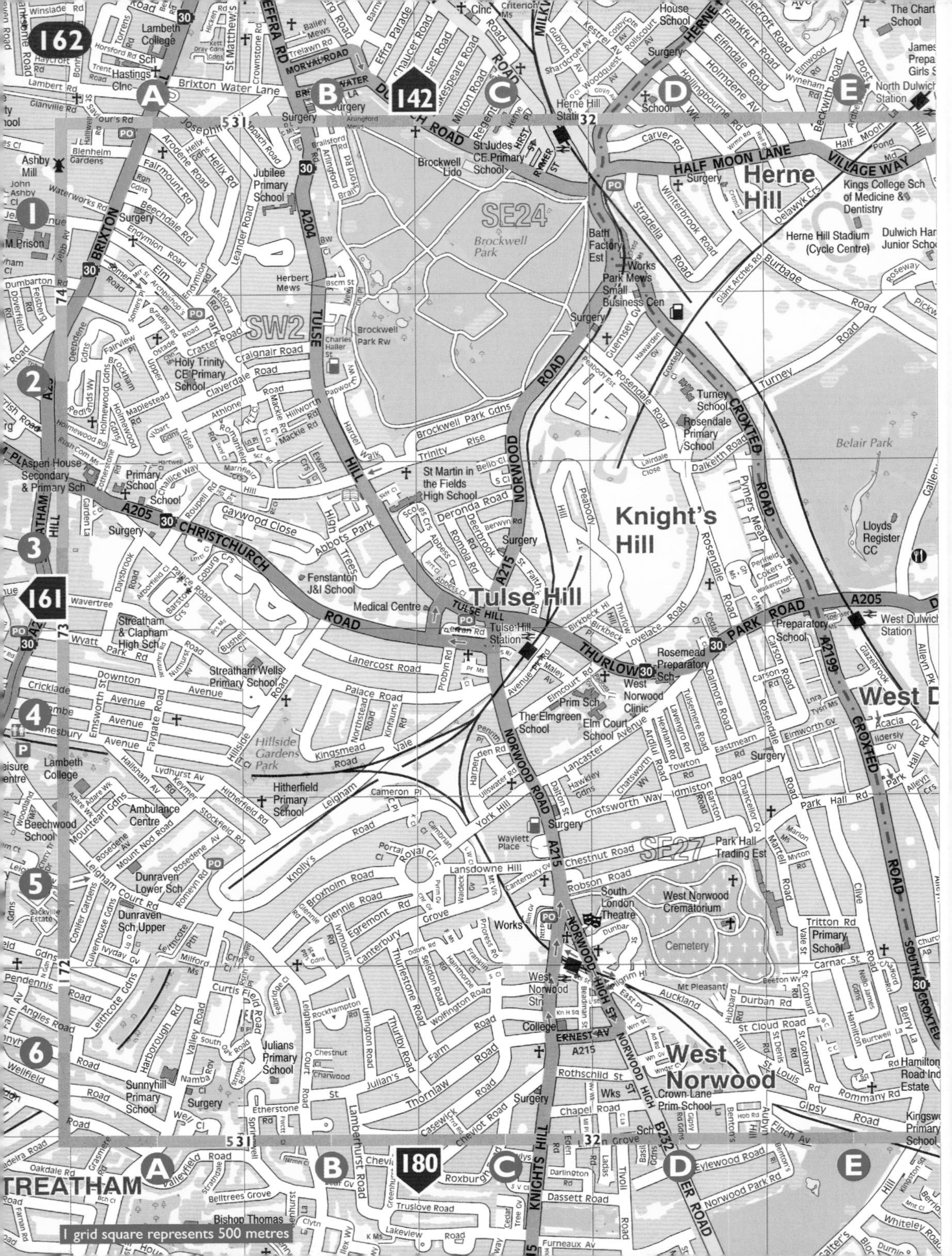
162
142
161
180
A
B
C
D
E
1
2
3
4
5
6
531
532
73
74
72
Lambeth College
Hastings Clnc
Brixton Water Lane
Effra Parade
Chaucer Road
Shakespeare Road
Milton Road
Dulwich Road
Morval Road
Trelawn Rd
Bailey Mews
Herne Hill Station
Half Moon Lane
Village Way
Herne Hill
Carver Rd
Winterbrook Road
Stradella Road
Kings College Sch of Medicine & Dentistry
Herne Hill Stadium (Cycle Centre)
Dulwich Hamlet Junior School
North Dulwich Station
SE24
Brockwell Park
Brockwell Lido
St Judes CE Primary School
Jubilee Primary School
Ashby Mill
H.M.Prison
Brixton Hill
Fairmount Rd
Beechdale Rd
Endymion Road
Leander Road
Herbert Mews
SW2
Tulse Hill
A204
Brockwell Park Rw
Charles Haller St
Craster Road
Craignair Road
Holy Trinity CE Primary School
Claverdale Road
Brockwell Park Gdns
Trinity Rise
St Martin in the Fields High School
Bath Factory Est
Works
Park Mews Small Business Cen
Norwood Road
Rosendale Road
Turney Road
Turney School
Rosendale Primary School
Croxted Road
Belair Park
Burbage Road
Knight's Hill
Lloyds Register CC
Peabody Hill
Dalkeith Road
Pymers Mead
Aspen House Secondary & Primary Sch
Primary School
A205 Christchurch Road
Gaywood Close
Abbots Park
Deronda Road
Fenstanton J&I School
Medical Centre
Tulse Hill
Tulse Hill Station
A215
Thurlow Park Road
Rosemead Preparatory Sch
West Norwood Clinic
West Dulwich Station
Preparatory School
A2199
Streatham & Clapham High Sch
Streatham Wells Primary School
Lanercost Road
Palace Road
Kingsmead Road
Hillside Gardens Park
Prim Sch
The Elmgreen School
Elm Court School
Lancaster Avenue
Chatsworth Way
Park Hall Rd
West Dulwich
Lambeth College
Ambulance Centre
Beechwood School
Hitherfield Primary School
Leigham Vale
York Hill
Waylett Place
SE27
Chestnut Road
Park Hall Trading Est
Robson Road
South London Theatre
West Norwood Crematorium
Cemetery
Tritton Rd
Primary School
Knolly's Road
Royal Circ
Lansdowne Hill
Dunraven Lower Sch
Dunraven Sch Upper
Leigham Court Rd
Broxholm Road
Glennie Road
Egremont Rd
Canterbury Grove
Works
West Norwood Station
Norwood High St
Auckland Hill
Durban Rd
St Cloud Road
College
Ernest Av
Julians Primary School
Sunnyhill Primary School
Surgery
Curtis Field Road
Thurlestone Road
Wolfington Road
Rothschild St
West Norwood
Crown Lane Prim School
Gipsy Road
Hamilton Road Ind Estate
Kingswood Primary School
Knights Hill
Chapel Road
Eylewood Road
Norwood Park Rd
Streatham
Belltrees Grove
Truslove Road
Dassett Road
Lakeview Road
Furneaux Av
Bishop Thomas
Valleyfield Road
1 grid square represents 500 metres

143
164
181
East Dulwich
SE22
Dulwich Village
Dulwich
SE21
Upper Sydenham
SE26
Dulwich Park
Golf Course
Southwark Sports Ground
Marlborough CC
Dulwich & Sydenham Hill Golf Club
Dulwich College
Dulwich College Track
Dulwich Picture Gallery
Dulwich Village CE Infant School
Alleyns Junior School
Dulwich Coll Pre Prep Sch
Kingsdale School
Langbourne Primary School
Sydenham Hill Station
Tollgate
Constable Walk
The City of London Academy
Harris Boys Academy East Dulwich
Waverley Lower Secondary School
Dulwich Medical Cen
St Anthonys RC Primary School
Goodrich J&I School
Old Cemetery
St Francesca Cabrini Primary School
Fairlawn Prim Sch
Horniman Primary School
The Horniman Museum & Gardens
Streamline Mews
Aquarius Golf Club
Forest Hill Station
Forest Hill Pools
Holy Trinity CE Prim Sch
Sydenham Girls Sch
Forest Hill Industrial Est
Forest Hill Business Cen
Malham Rd Industrial
Police Station
Willow Business Park
St Bartholomews CE Primary School
Infant School
Sydenham High School
Sydenham High Senior School
Sydenham Station
Gipsy Hill Station
Works
Surgery
DULWICH COMMON
LORDSHIP LANE A205
LORDSHIP LANE
A2216
B219
LONDON ROAD
DARTMOUTH ROAD
KIRKDALE A2216
FOREST HILL ROAD
HONOR OAK PARK
WESTWOOD HILL A212
CRYSTAL PALACE PARK
DULWICH WOOD PARK
COLLEGE RD A2199
A212
A213
A2214
Sydenham Hill
Crescent Wood Road
Peckarmans Wood
College Road
Hunts Slip Road
Grange Lane
Court Lane
Calton Avenue
Woodwarde Road
Wood Vale
Langton Rise
Underhill Road
Overhill Road
Melford Rd
Belvoir Rd
Honor Oak Road
Kirkdale
Sydenham Park Road
Longton Grove
Wells Park Road
Taylor's Lane
33
34
35
F
G
H
J
K
2
3
4
5
6
72
73
74

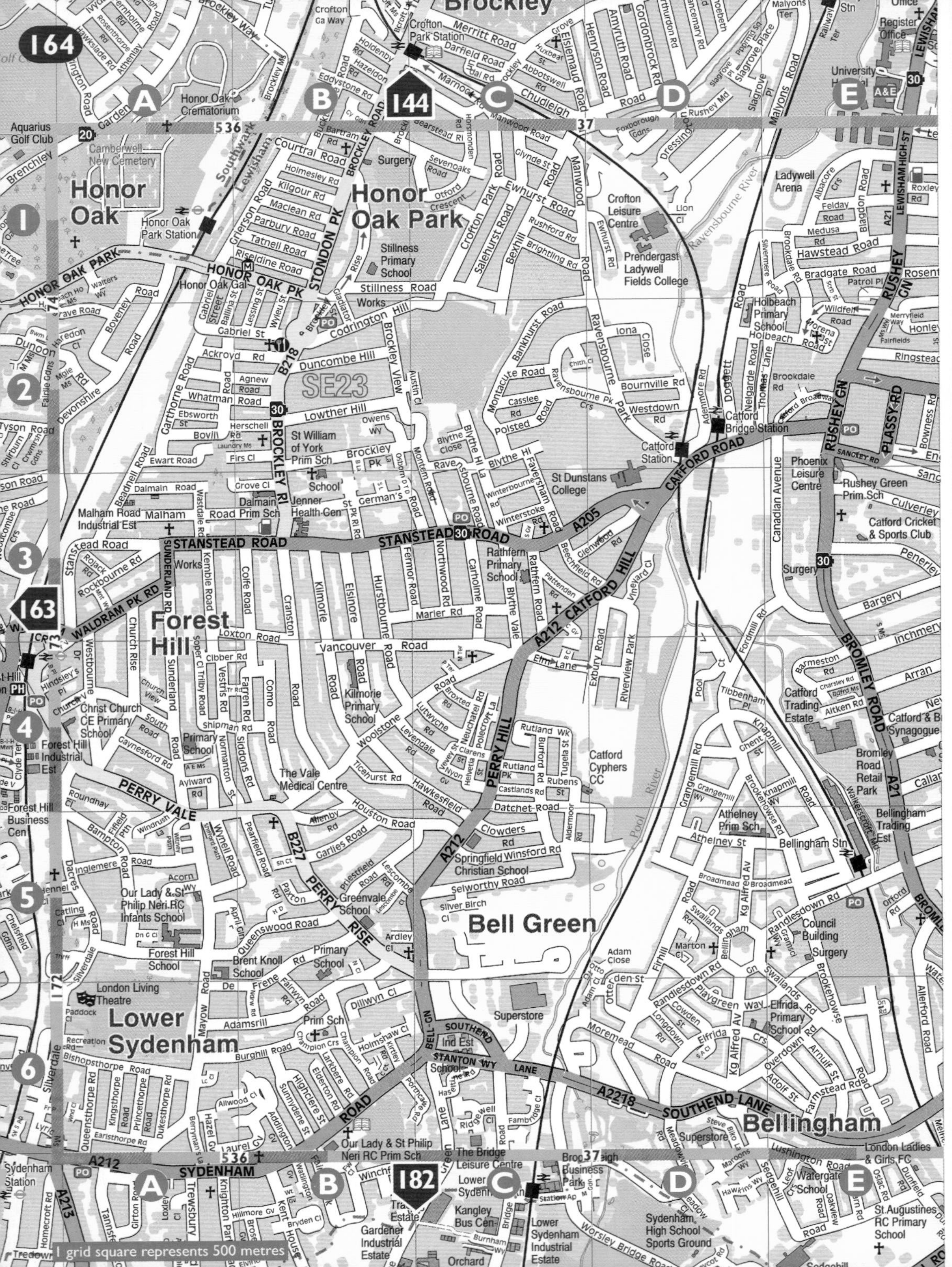

164
144
163
182
A
B
C
D
E
1
2
3
4
5
6
Brockley
Honor Oak
Honor Oak Park
Forest Hill
Lower Sydenham
Bell Green
Bellingham
SE23
Honor Oak Crematorium
Aquarius Golf Club
Camberwell New Cemetery
Honor Oak Park Station
Crofton Park Station
Crofton Leisure Centre
Prendergast Ladywell Fields College
Ladywell Arena
University Hospital
Register Office
Stillness Primary School
St William of York Prim Sch
Jenner Health Cen
Malham Road Industrial Est
Dalmain Road Prim Sch
St Dunstans College
Catford Station
Catford Bridge Station
Phoenix Leisure Centre
Rushey Green Prim Sch
Catford Cricket & Sports Club
Rathfern Primary School
Kilmorie Primary School
Christ Church CE Primary School
Forest Hill Industrial Est
Forest Hill Business Cen
The Vale Medical Centre
Springfield Christian School
Greenvale School
Our Lady & St Philip Neri RC Infants School
Forest Hill School
Brent Knoll School
London Living Theatre
Catford Cyphers CC
Catford Trading Estate
Catford & Bromley Synagogue
Bromley Road Retail Park
Bellingham Trading Est
Bellingham Stn
Athelney Prim Sch
Council Building
Surgery
Elfrida Primary School
Superstore
Ind Est
Our Lady & St Philip Neri RC Prim Sch
The Bridge Leisure Centre
Lower Sydenham
Kangley Bus Cen
Gardener Industrial Estate
Lower Sydenham Industrial Estate
Sydenham High School Sports Ground
Watergate School
St Augustines RC Primary School
London Ladies & Girls FC
Sydenham Station
Business Park
Honor Oak Park
Stanstead Road
Catford Road
Catford Hill
Perry Hill
Perry Vale
Perry Rise
Brockley Ri
Stondon Pk
Sunderland Rd
Waldram Pk Rd
Southend Lane
Bromley Road
Rushey Gn
Lewisham High St
Sydenham
A205
A212
A21
A2218
A213
B218
B227
536
37
20
30
Ravensbourne River
Pool River
1 grid square represents 500 metres

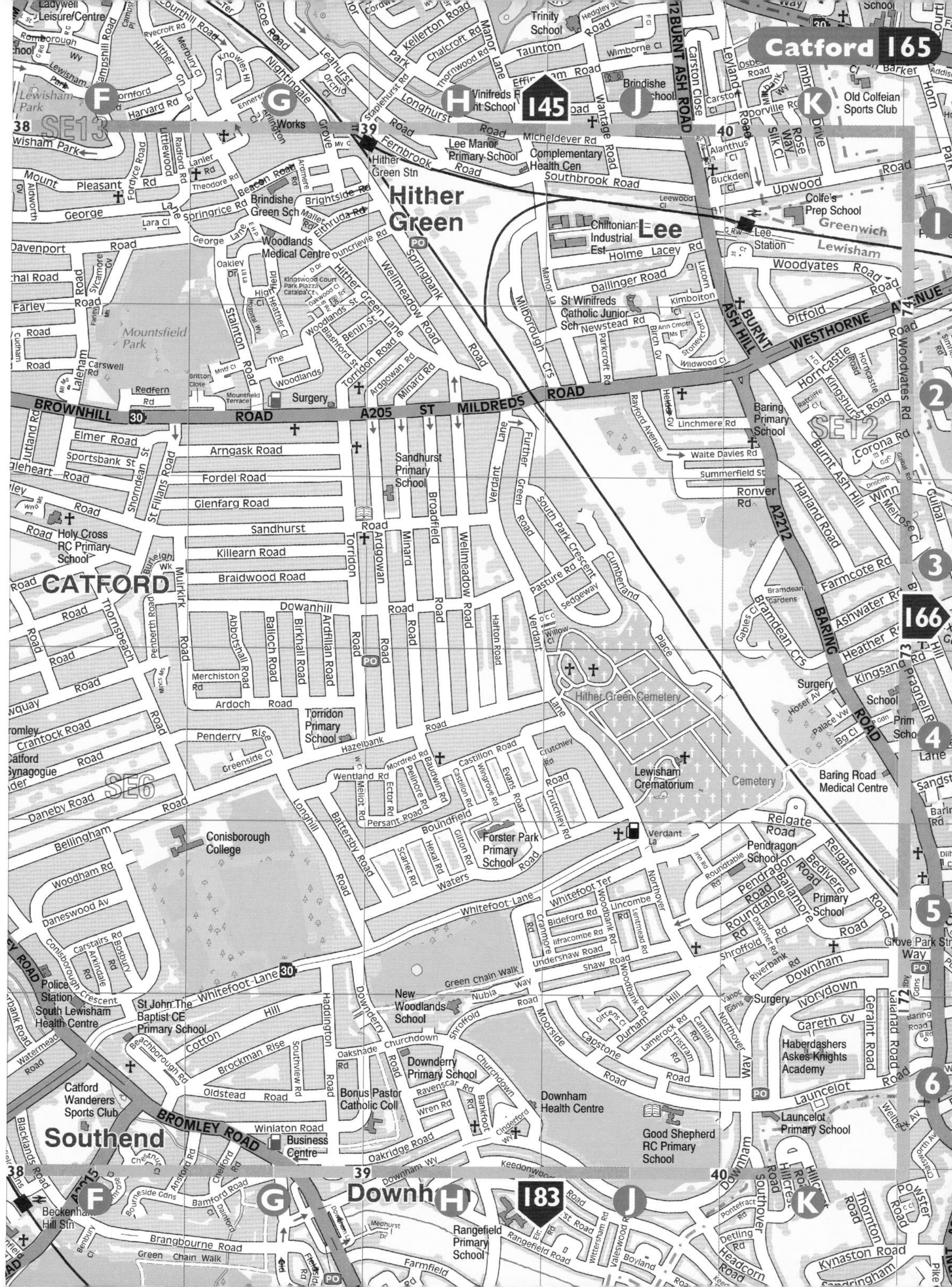
Hither Green
Lee
CATFORD
Southend
SE13
SE12
SE6
145
166
183
Lewisham Park
Mountsfield Park
Hither Green Cemetery
Lewisham Crematorium
Conisborough College
Sandhurst Primary School
Torridon Primary School
Forster Park Primary School
Holy Cross RC Primary School
Baring Primary School
Pendragon School
New Woodlands School
Downderry Primary School
Bonus Pastor Catholic Coll
Downham Health Centre
Good Shepherd RC Primary School
Launcelot Primary School
Haberdashers Askes Knights Academy
Catford Wanderers Sports Club
Police Station
South Lewisham Health Centre
St John The Baptist CE Primary School
Lee Station
Hither Green Stn
Grove Park Stn
Beckenham Hill Stn
Colfe's Prep School
Old Colfeian Sports Club
Brindishe Green Sch
Woodlands Medical Centre
Chiltonian Industrial Est
St Winifreds Catholic Junior Sch
Lee Manor Primary School
Complementary Health Cen
Baring Road Medical Centre
Rangefield Primary School
BROWNHILL ROAD
A205 ST MILDREDS ROAD
WESTHORNE AVENUE
BURNT ASH HILL
BARING ROAD
A2212
BROMLEY ROAD
Whitefoot Lane
Green Chain Walk
Downham
Catford Synagogue

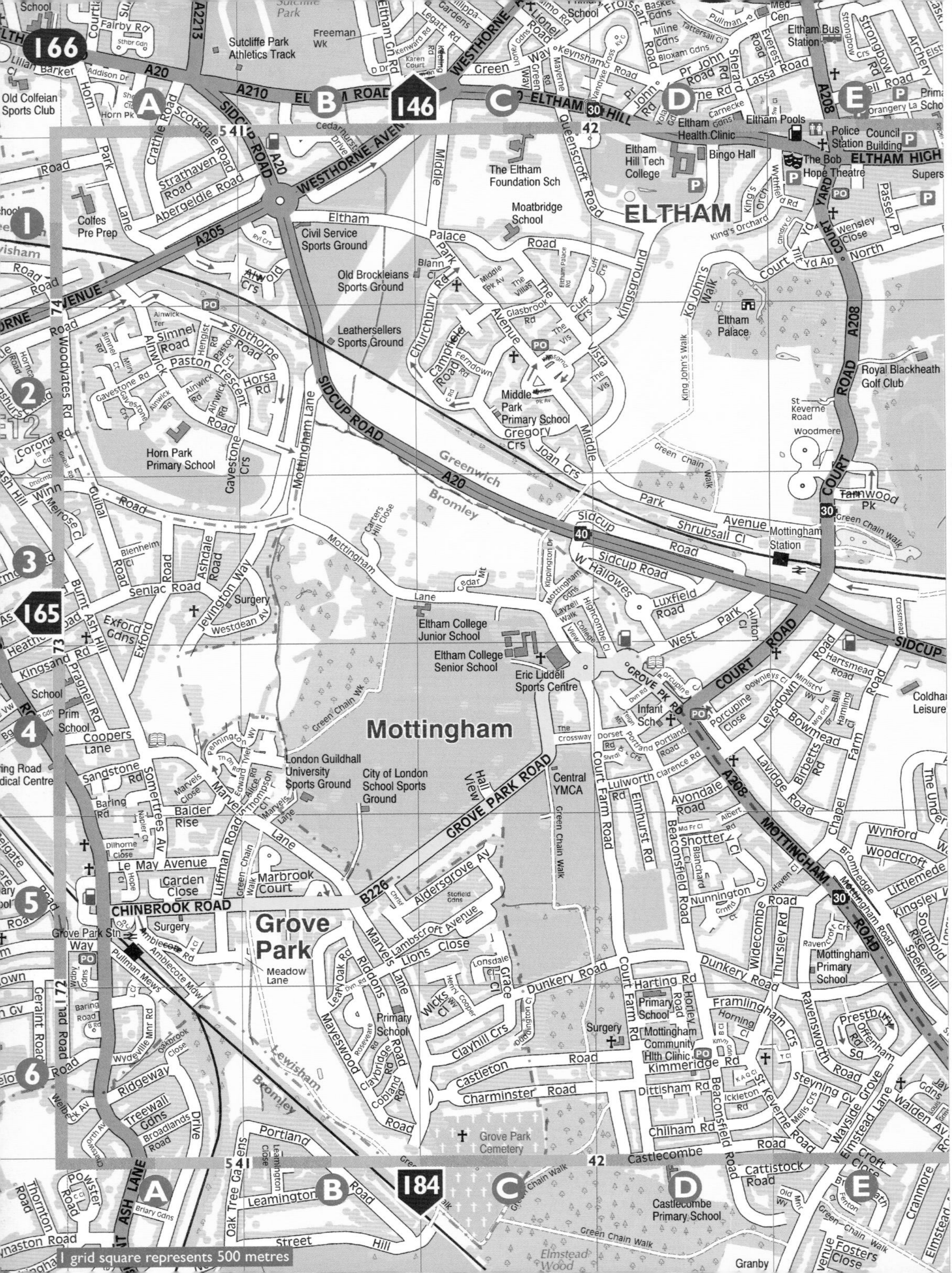

166
146
165
184
A
B
C
D
E
1
2
3
4
5
6
541
42
74
73
72
30
40
A20
A210
A205
A208
A2213
B226
ELTHAM
Mottingham
Grove Park
ELTHAM ROAD
ELTHAM HILL
ELTHAM HIGH
WESTHORNE AVENUE
SIDCUP ROAD
COURT ROAD
MOTTINGHAM ROAD
GROVE PARK ROAD
CHINBROOK ROAD
GROVE PK RD
BURNT ASH LANE
Sutcliffe Park Athletics Track
Old Colfeian Sports Club
Colfes Pre Prep
Civil Service Sports Ground
Old Brockleians Sports Ground
Leathersellers Sports Ground
The Eltham Foundation Sch
Moatbridge School
Eltham Hill Tech College
Eltham Health Clinic
Bingo Hall
Eltham Bus Station
Eltham Pools
Police Station
Council Building
The Bob Hope Theatre
Eltham Palace
Royal Blackheath Golf Club
Horn Park Primary School
Middle Park Primary School
Mottingham Station
Eltham College Junior School
Eltham College Senior School
Eric Liddell Sports Centre
London Guildhall University Sports Ground
City of London School Sports Ground
Central YMCA
Infant Sch
Mottingham Primary School
Mottingham Community Hlth Clinic
Primary School
Surgery
Grove Park Stn
Grove Park Cemetery
Castlecombe Primary School
Green Chain Walk
Greenwich
Bromley
Lewisham
Elmstead Wood
Woodvates Rd
Burnt Ash Hill
Mottingham Lane
Court Farm Road
Beaconsfield Road
Dunkery Road
Castleton Road
Charminster Road
Castlecombe Road
Kimmeridge Rd
Marvels Lane
Riddons Road
Lambscroft Avenue
Aldersgrove Av
Luffman Road
Somertrees Av
Senlac Road
Jevington Way
Guibal Road
Paston Crescent
Sibthorpe Road
Simnel Road
Alnwick Road
Gavestone Crs
Eltham Palace Road
Middle Park Avenue
Kingsground
Sidcup Road
West Park
Luxfield Road
Shrubsall Cl
Park Avenue
Tarnwood Pk
Dunkery Road
Framlingham Crs
Ravensworth Road
Wayside Grove
Elmstead Lane
Chapel Farm Road
Leysdown Road
Porcupine Close
Bowmead
Lavidge Road
Avondale Road
Shotter Cl
Nunnington Cl
Widecombe Road
Thursley Rd
Ridgeway
Treewall Gdns
Broadlands Road
Pullman Mews
Ambleoote Rd
Meadow Lane
Portland
Leamington
Oak Tree Gardens
Briary Gdns
Powster Road
Thornton Road
Castleton Road
Chilham Rd
Dittisham Rd
St Keverne Road
Steyning Gv
Prestbury Sq
1 grid square represents 500 metres

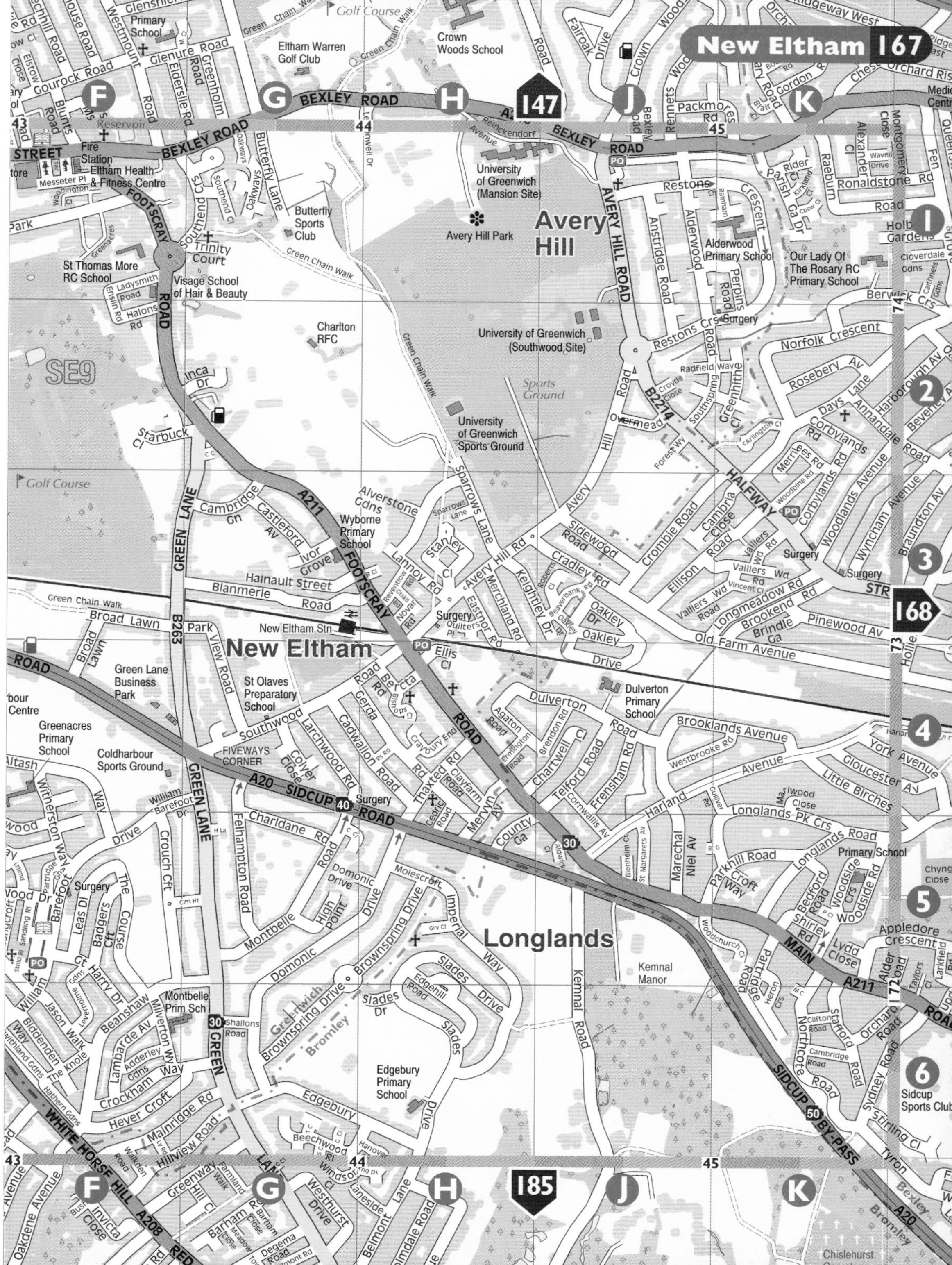

New Eltham
Avery Hill
Longlands
SE9
BEXLEY ROAD
FOOTSCRAY ROAD
A211
GREEN LANE
B263
A20 SIDCUP ROAD
SIDCUP BY-PASS
AVERY HILL ROAD
B2214
HALFWAY STREET
WHITE HORSE HILL
A208
MAIN ROAD
Eltham Warren Golf Club
Crown Woods School
Golf Course
University of Greenwich (Mansion Site)
Avery Hill Park
Butterfly Sports Club
St Thomas More RC School
Visage School of Hair & Beauty
Trinity Court
Charlton RFC
University of Greenwich (Southwood Site)
Sports Ground
University of Greenwich Sports Ground
Alderwood Primary School
Our Lady Of The Rosary RC Primary School
Surgery
Wyborne Primary School
New Eltham Stn
Green Lane Business Park
St Olaves Preparatory School
Greenacres Primary School
Coldharbour Sports Ground
Dulverton Primary School
FIVEWAYS CORNER
Montbelle Prim Sch
Edgebury Primary School
Kemnal Manor
Sidcup Sports Club
Chislehurst Cemetery
Fire Station
Eltham Health & Fitness Centre
Reservoir
Green Chain Walk
Primary School
Greenwich
Bromley
Bexley
147
168
185
F
G
H
J
K
43
44
45
1
2
3
4
5
6
72
73
74

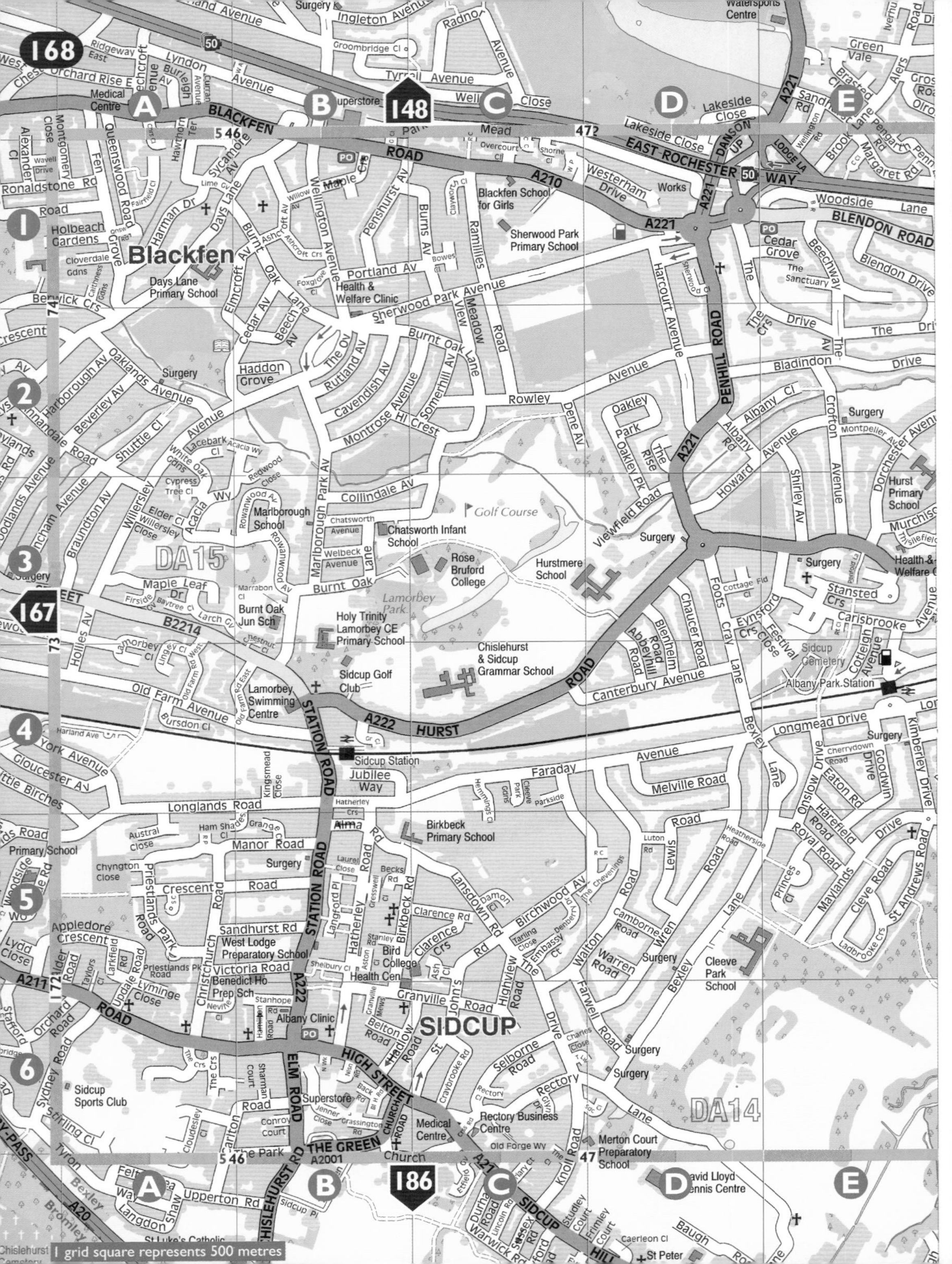

168
148
167
186
A
B
C
D
E
1
2
3
4
5
6
Blackfen
SIDCUP
DA15
DA14
BLACKFEN ROAD
A210
A221
EAST ROCHESTER WAY
DANSON UP
BLENDON ROAD
PENHILL ROAD
A222 HURST ROAD
B2214
STATION ROAD
ELM ROAD
HIGH STREET
CHISLEHURST RD
THE GREEN
A2001
SIDCUP HILL
A211
A20
Bexley Bromley
Sherwood Park Avenue
Burnt Oak Lane
Rowley Avenue
Longlands Road
Faraday Avenue
Old Farm Avenue
Canterbury Avenue
Longmead Drive
Days Lane Primary School
Blackfen School for Girls
Sherwood Park Primary School
Health & Welfare Clinic
Marlborough School
Chatsworth Infant School
Rose Bruford College
Hurstmere School
Burnt Oak Jun Sch
Holy Trinity Lamorbey CE Primary School
Chislehurst & Sidcup Grammar School
Sidcup Golf Club
Lamorbey Swimming Centre
Golf Course
Lamorbey Park
Sidcup Station
Albany Park Station
Sidcup Cemetery
Hurst Primary School
Birkbeck Primary School
West Lodge Preparatory School
Benedict Ho Prep Sch
Bird College
Health Cen
Albany Clinic
Sidcup Sports Club
Medical Centre
Rectory Business Centre
Merton Court Preparatory School
Cleeve Park School
David Lloyd Tennis Centre
Watersports Centre
Surgery
Superstore
Works
546
472
47
50
1 grid square represents 500 metres

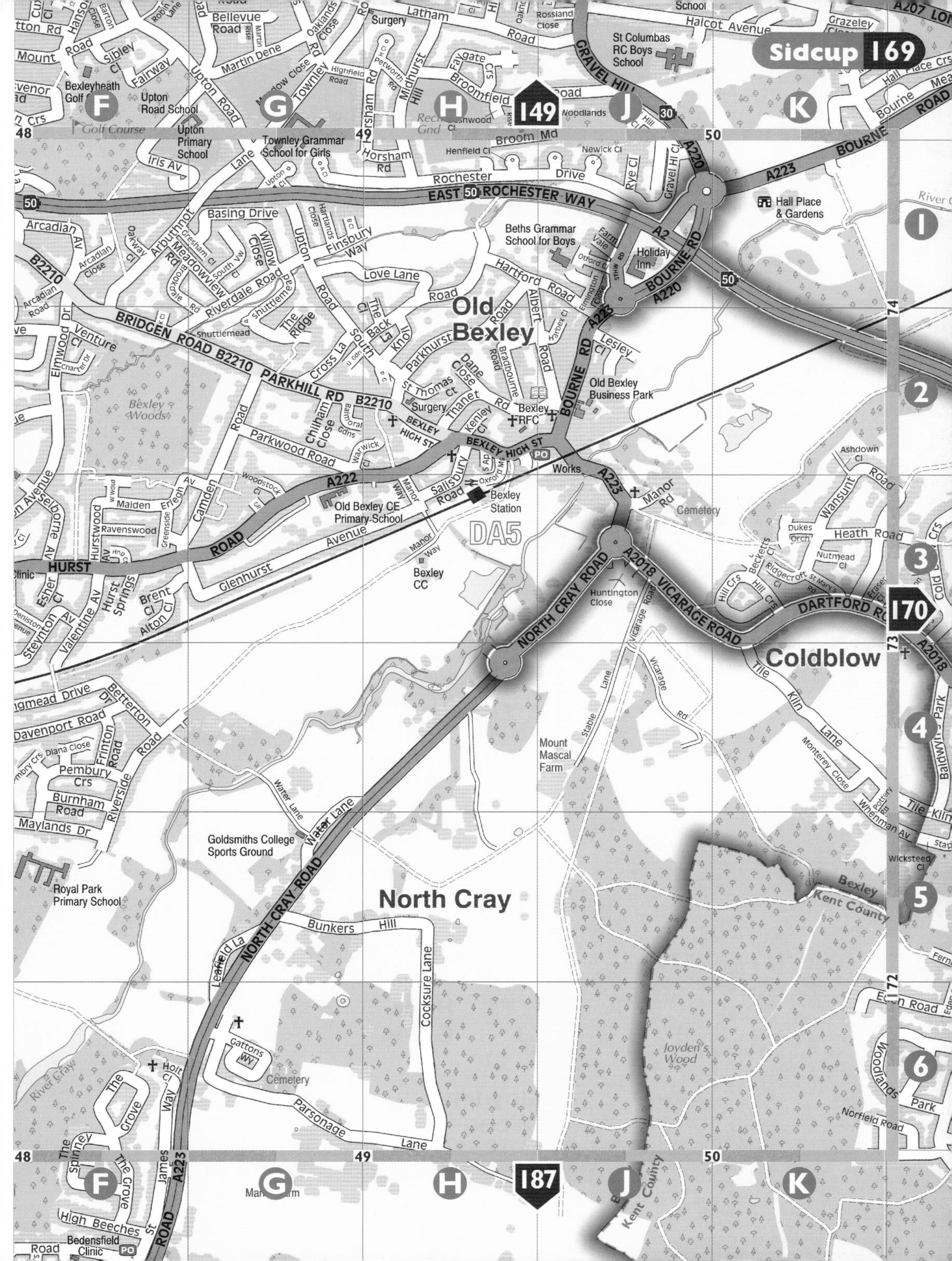
Old Bexley
North Cray
Coldblow
DA5
Bexley Station
Old Bexley CE Primary School
Bexley CC
Goldsmiths College Sports Ground
Royal Park Primary School
Mount Mascal Farm
Cemetery
Joyden's Wood
Hall Place & Gardens
Beths Grammar School for Boys
Holiday Inn
Old Bexley Business Park
Bexley RFC
Townley Grammar School for Girls
Upton Primary School
Upton Road School
Bexleyheath Golf
Golf Course
Bexley Woods
St Columbas RC Boys School
Surgery
Works
Huntington Close
Bexley
Kent County
EAST ROCHESTER WAY
BRIDGEN ROAD B2210
PARKHILL RD B2210
BEXLEY HIGH ST
BOURNE RD
NORTH CRAY ROAD
A2018 VICARAGE ROAD
DARTFORD RD
GRAVEL HILL
A223
A222
A220
A2
Bunkers Hill
Cocksure Lane
Parsonage Lane
Water Lane
Tile Kiln Lane
Heath Road
Manor Rd
Hartford Road
Love Lane
Albert Road
Parkwood Road
Glenhurst Avenue
Salisbury Road
Rochester Drive
Broomfield
Bedensfield Clinic
High Beeches
The Grove
The Spinney
149
170
187
48
49
50
F
G
H
J
K
1
2
3
4
5
6
74
73
72

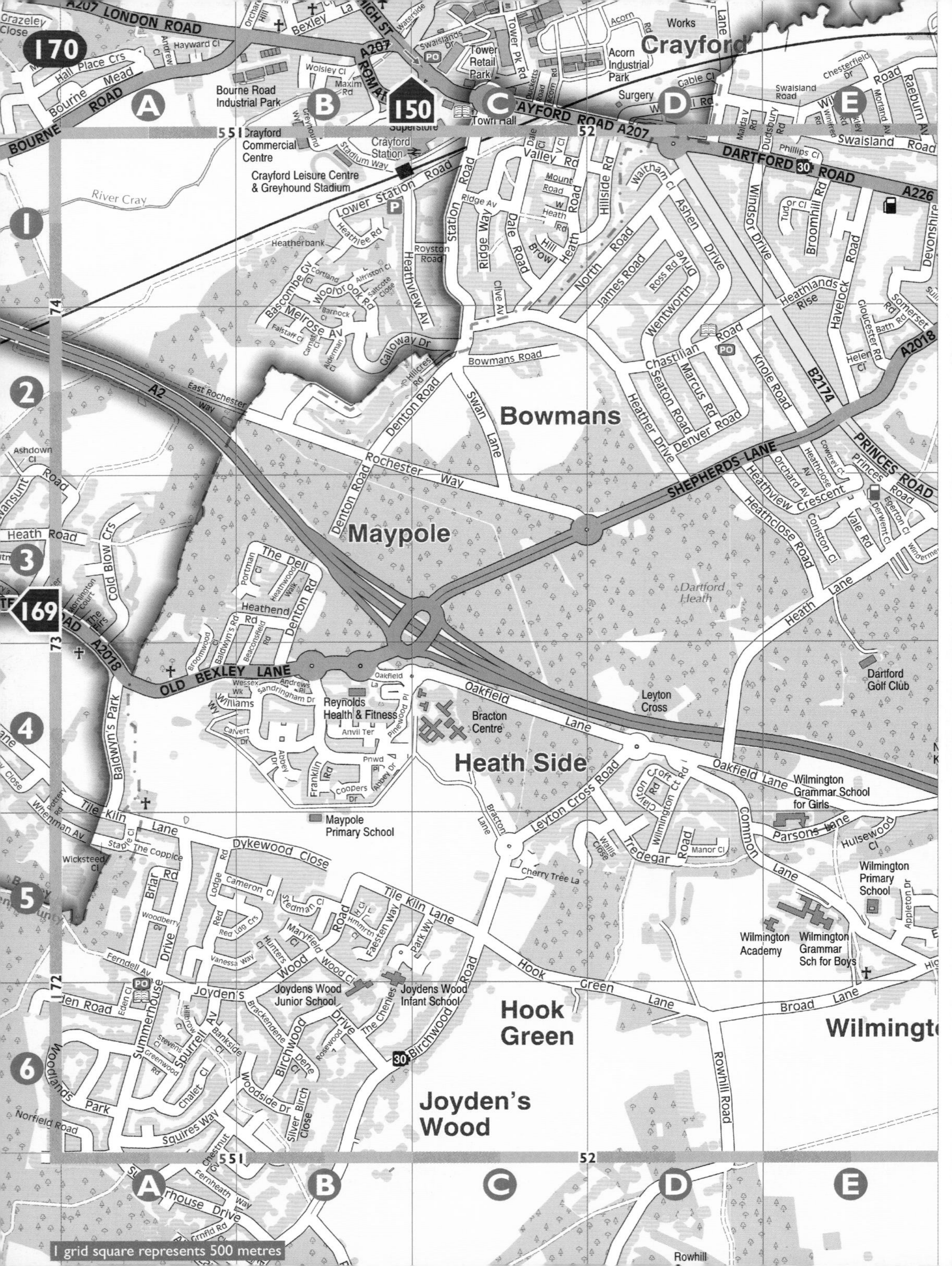
170
150
169
A
B
C
D
E
1
2
3
4
5
6
551
52
74
73
72
A207 LONDON ROAD
Grazeley Close
Hall Place Crs
Bourne Mead
Bourne Road
Hayward Cl
Andrew Cl
Bexley La
HIGH ST
Waterside
Wolsey Cl
Maxim Rd
Bourne Road Industrial Park
Greyhound Wy
Superstore
Swaislands Dr
Tower Retail Park
Tower Pk Rd
Acorn Industrial Park
Acorn Rd
Works
Crayford
Cable Cl
Surgery
Town Hall
CRAYFORD ROAD A207
Crayford Commercial Centre
Crayford Station
Stadium Way
Crayford Leisure Centre & Greyhound Stadium
River Cray
Lower Station Road
Heathfield Rd
Heatherbank
Cortland Cl
Woolbrook Rd
Alfriston Cl
Saltcote Close
Barnock Cl
Bascombe Gv
Melrose Av
Falstaff Cl
Carnet Cl
Alderman Cl
Galloway Dr
Royston Road
Heathview Av
Station Road
Ridge Av
Ridge Way
Dale Road
Valley Rd
Mount Road
Heath Road
Hill Brow
Hillside Rd
Clive Av
North Road
James Road
Waltham Cl
Ashen Drive
Ross Rd
Wentworth Drive
Chastilian Road
Seaton Road
Marcus Rd
Denver Road
Heather Drive
Knole Road
Windsor Drive
DARTFORD ROAD
A226
Swaisland Road
Chesterfield Dr
Raeburn Av
Morland Av
Dudsbury Rd
Maida V Rd
Phillips Cl
Tudor Cl
Broomhill Rd
Havelock Road
Devonshire
Heathlands Rise
Gloucester Rd
Bath Rd
Somerset
Helen Cl
A2018
B2174
PRINCES ROAD
SHEPHERDS LANE
Orchard Av
Heathclose Av
Cowdrey Cl
Princes Road
Heathview Crescent
Heathclose Road
Coniston Cl
Vale Rd
Derwent Cl
Egerton Cl
Windermere
Bowmans
Bowmans Road
Swan Lane
Hillcrest Rd
Denton Road
A2
East Rochester Way
Rochester Way
Maypole
Ashdown Cl
Road
Heath Road
Cold Blow Crs
The Dell
Portman Cl
Heathwood Walk
Denton Rd
Heathend Rd
Baldwyn's Rd
Beaconsfield Rd
Broomwood Rd
The Firs
A2018
OLD BEXLEY LANE
Wessex Wk
Andrews Pl
Sandringham Dr
Williams Wy
Calvert Dr
Abbey Dr
Franklin Rd
Coopers Dr
Anvil Ter
Pinewood Pl
Oakfield La
Reynolds Health & Fitness
Bracton Centre
Dartford Heath
Oakfield Lane
Leyton Cross
Heath Side
Heath Lane
Dartford Golf Club
Leyton Cross Road
Bracton Lane
Clayton Croft Rd
Wilmington Ct Rd
Walls Close
Tredegar Road
Manor Cl
Common Lane
Wilmington Grammar School for Girls
Parsons Lane
Hulsewood Cl
Wilmington Primary School
Appleton Dr
Baldwyn's Park
Tile Kiln Lane
Maypole Primary School
Whenman Av
Staple Cl
The Coppice
Dykewood Close
Wickstead Cl
Briar Rd
Lodge Rd
Cameron Cl
Stedman Cl
Woodberry Gv
Red Lodge Crs
Maryfield Cl
Hunters Ct
Vanessa Way
Ferndell Av
Summerhouse Drive
Wood Road
Faesten Way
Park Wy
Wood Cl
Tile Kiln Lane
Cherry Tree La
Hook Green Lane
Birchwood Road
Wilmington Academy
Wilmington Grammar Sch for Boys
Joydens Wood Junior School
Joydens Wood Infant School
Joyden's
Eden Road
Eden Cl
Hillbrow Cl
Spurrell Av
Bankside Cl
Brackendene
Birchwood Dene Cl
Drive
The Chenies
Rosewood
Hook Green
Broad Lane
Wilmington
Rowhill Road
Woodlands Park
Stevens Cl
Greenwood Rd
Chalet Cl
Woodside Dr
Silver Birch Close
Joyden's Wood
Norfield Road
Squires Way
Chestnut Gv
Fernheath Way
Summerhouse Drive
Crnfld Rd
Rowhill
1 grid square represents 500 metres

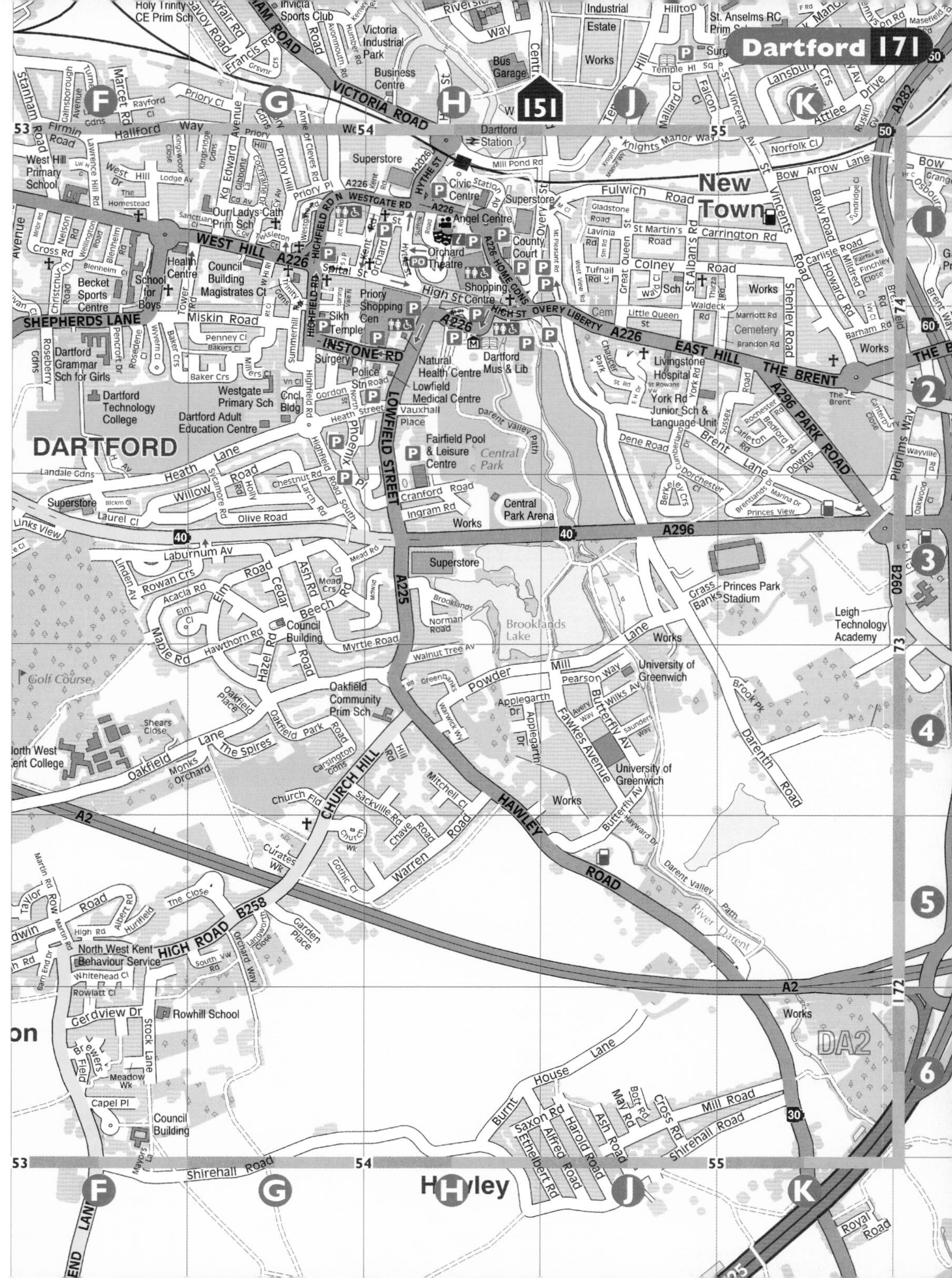
Dartford
171
151
DARTFORD
New Town
Hawley
DA2
Victoria Road
West Hill
Shepherds Lane
Instone Rd
Lowfield Street
Highfield Rd
Spital St
Hythe St
Westgate Rd
High St
Overy Liberty
East Hill
The Brent
Park Road
Fulwich Road
St Vincents Road
Shenley Road
Carrington Rd
Colney Road
Heath Lane
Heath Street
Willow Road
Olive Road
Laurel Cl
Links View
Laburnum Av
Rowan Crs
Acacia Rd
Elm Road
Cedar Road
Ash Rd
Beech Rd
Maple Rd
Hawthorn Rd
Hazel Rd
Myrtle Road
Walnut Tree Av
Powder Mill Lane
Oakfield Lane
Oakfield Place
Oakfield Park Road
The Spires
Monks Orchard
Church Hill
Hawley Road
Warren Road
High Road
Dene Road
Brent Lane
Darenth Road
Brook Pk
Pilgrims Way
Dartford Station
Superstore
Civic Centre
Angel Centre
Orchard Theatre
County Court
Shopping Centre
Priory Shopping Cen
Sikh Temple
Police Stn
Surgery
Natural Health Centre
Lowfield Medical Centre
Dartford Mus & Lib
Fairfield Pool & Leisure Centre
Central Park
Central Park Arena
Council Building
Magistrates Ct
Becket Sports Centre
School for Boys
Health Centre
Dartford Grammar Sch for Girls
Dartford Technology College
Westgate Primary Sch
Dartford Adult Education Centre
West Hill Primary School
Our Ladys Cath Prim Sch
Livingstone Hospital
York Rd Junior Sch & Language Unit
Cemetery
Princes Park Stadium
Leigh Technology Academy
University of Greenwich
Brooklands Lake
Oakfield Community Prim Sch
North West Kent College
North West Kent Behaviour Service
Rowhill School
Golf Course
Business Centre
Victoria Industrial Park
Industrial Estate
Bus Garage
Works
River Darent
Darent Valley Path
A2
A225
A226
A296
A282
B258
B260
Burnt House Lane
Mill Road
Shirehall Road
Stock Lane
F
G
H
J
K
53
54
55
1
2
3
4
5
6
72
73
74

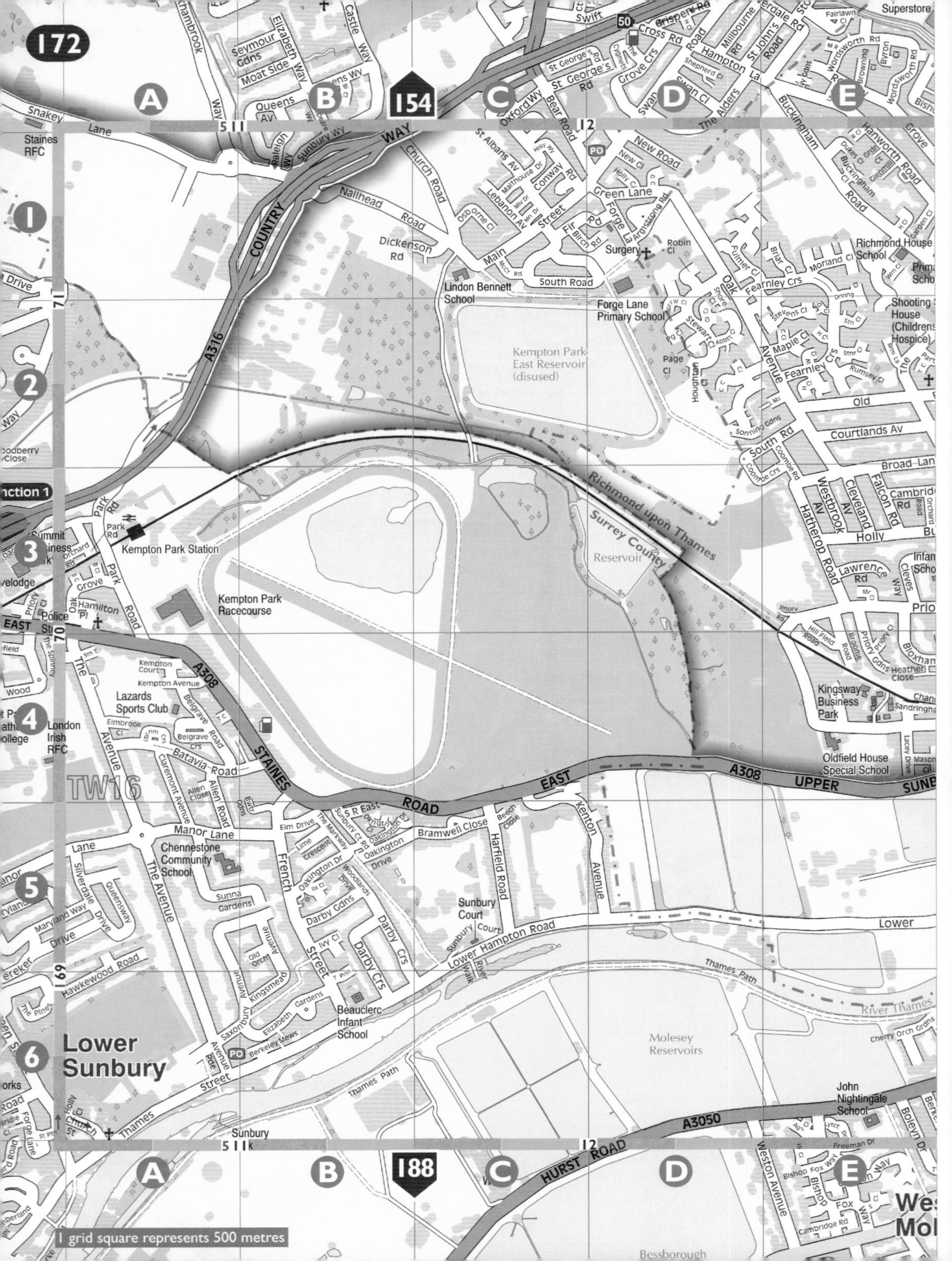
154
188
A
B
C
D
E
1
2
3
4
5
6
Staines RFC
Snakey Lane
Kempton Park Station
Kempton Park Racecourse
Kempton Park East Reservoir (disused)
Surrey County Reservoir
Richmond upon Thames
Lindon Bennett School
Forge Lane Primary School
Richmond House School
Shooting Star House (Childrens Hospice)
Lazards Sports Club
London Irish RFC
Chennestone Community School
Beauclerc Infant School
Kingsway Business Park
Oldfield House Special School
John Nightingale School
Molesey Reservoirs
Lower Sunbury
TW16
Sunbury Court
River Thames
Thames Path
A316
A308
A3050
COUNTRY WAY
STAINES ROAD EAST
UPPER SUNBURY
HURST ROAD
Nailhead Road
Church Road
Main Street
Green Lane
South Road
Oak Avenue
Fearnley Crs
Courtlands Av
Hatherop Road
Park Road
French Street
The Avenue
Manor Lane
Batavia Road
Lower Hampton Road
Harfield Road
Kenton Avenue
Hawkewood Road
Surgery
Superstore
Summit Business Park
Police Stn
Sunbury
1 grid square represents 500 metres

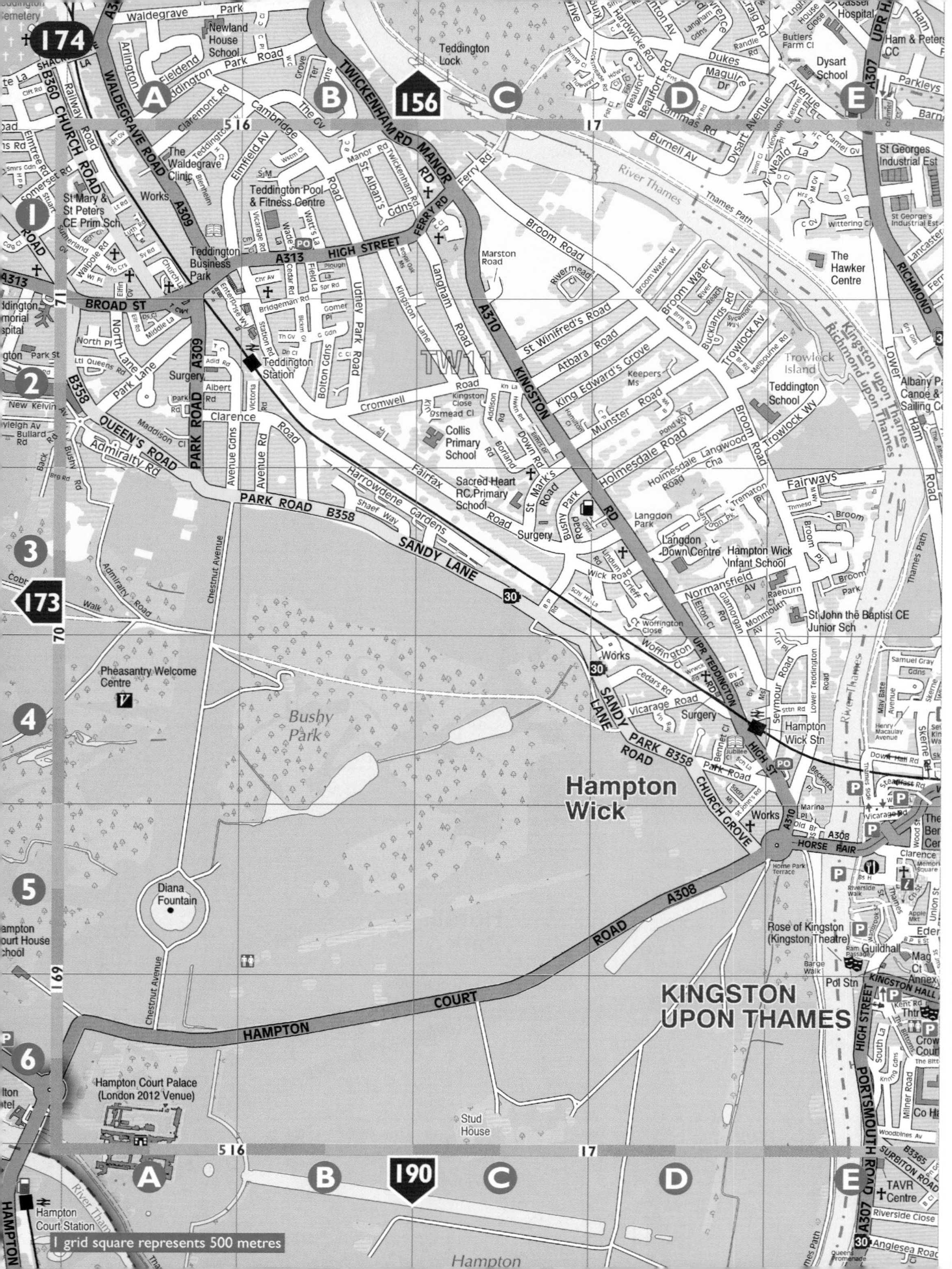

174
156
173
190
A
B
C
D
E
1
2
3
4
5
6
516
17
71
70
69
TW11
Teddington Lock
River Thames
Teddington
Bushy Park
Hampton Wick
KINGSTON UPON THAMES
Pheasantry Welcome Centre
Diana Fountain
Hampton Court Palace (London 2012 Venue)
Stud House
Teddington Station
Hampton Wick Stn
Hampton Court Station
Trowlock Island
Teddington School
Collis Primary School
Sacred Heart RC Primary School
Langdon Down Centre
Hampton Wick Infant School
St John the Baptist CE Junior Sch
Teddington Pool & Fitness Centre
The Waldegrave Clinic
Newland House School
St Mary & St Peters CE Prim Sch
Teddington Business Park
Dysart School
St Georges Industrial Est
The Hawker Centre
Rose of Kingston (Kingston Theatre)
Guildhall
HAMPTON COURT ROAD A308
PARK ROAD B358
SANDY LANE
KINGSTON RD A310
HIGH STREET A313
BROAD ST
PARK ROAD A309
WALDEGRAVE ROAD A309
B360 CHURCH ROAD
QUEEN'S ROAD
TWICKENHAM RD
MANOR RD
FERRY RD
Broom Road
Thames Path
Kingston upon Thames
Richmond upon Thames
PORTSMOUTH ROAD A307
HIGH STREET
HORSE FAIR
Chestnut Avenue
1 grid square represents 500 metres

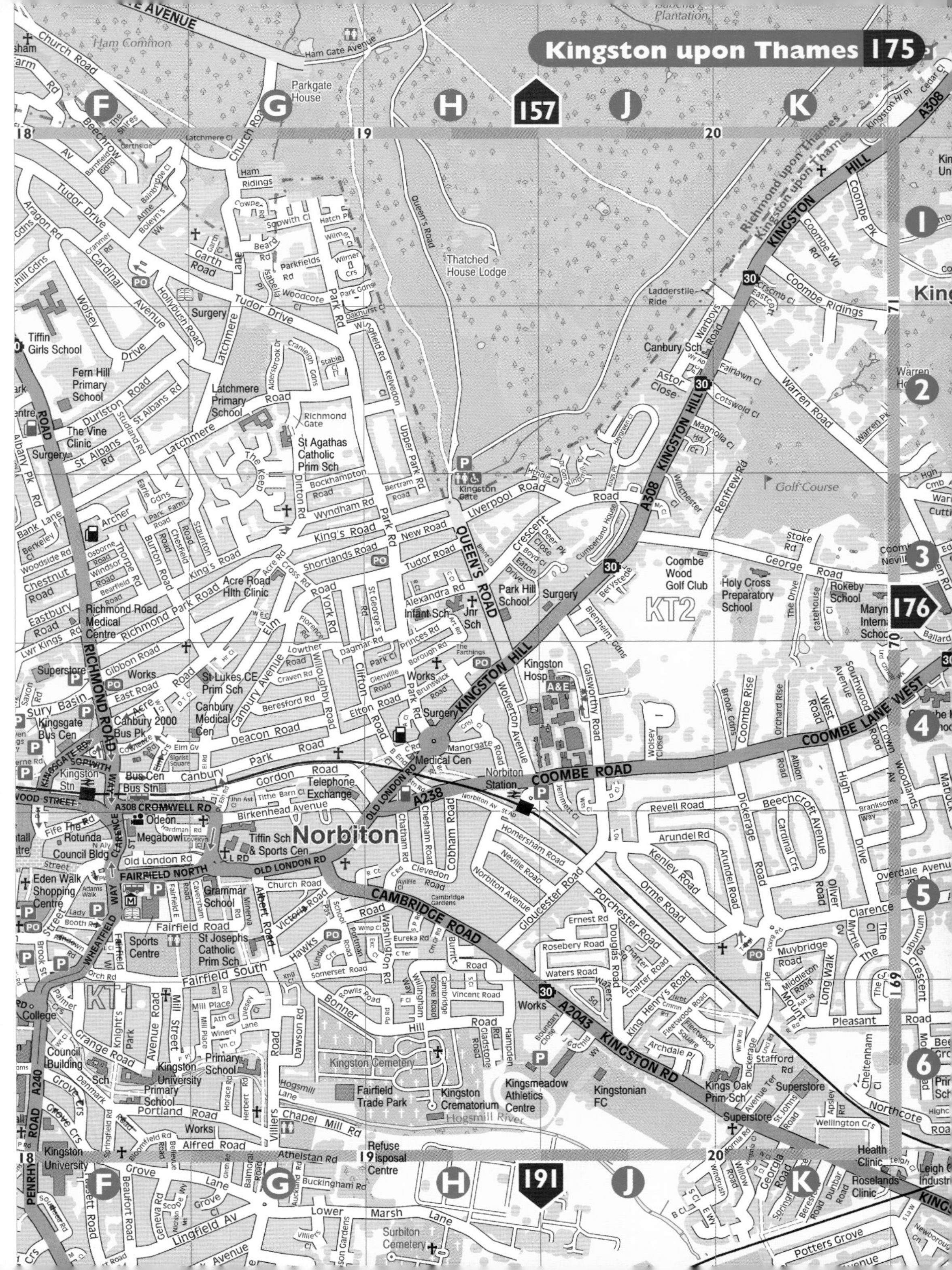

Ham Common
Church Road
Parkgate House
Thatched House Lodge
Queen's Road
Tiffin Girls School
Fern Hill Primary School
Latchmere Primary School
St Agathas Catholic Prim Sch
Richmond Gate
Kingston Gate
Canbury Sch
Coombe Wood Golf Club
Holy Cross Preparatory School
Rokeby School
Park Hill School
KT2
Kingston Hill
Richmond Road
Kingston Hosp
Norbiton
Norbiton Station
Coombe Road
Coombe Lane West
Cambridge Road
Kingston Rd
Tiffin Sch & Sports Cen
Grammar School
Eden Walk Shopping Centre
Sports Centre
St Josephs Catholic Prim Sch
KT1
Kingston University
Kingston Cemetery
Kingston Crematorium
Fairfield Trade Park
Kingsmeadow Athletics Centre
Kingstonian FC
Hogsmill River
Refuse Disposal Centre
Surbiton Cemetery
Kings Oak Prim Sch
Superstore
Health Clinic
Roselands Clinic
Golf Course
157
191
176

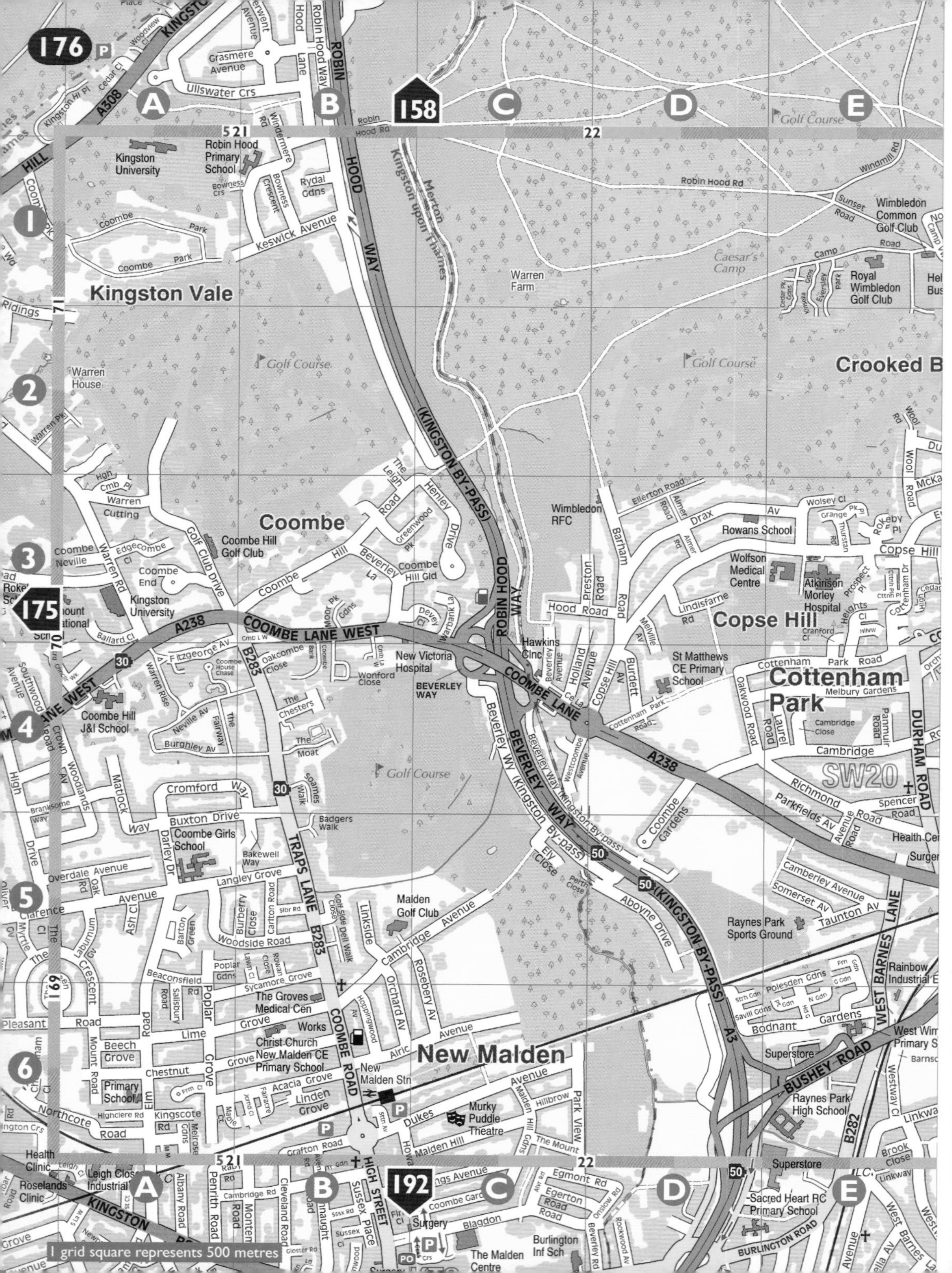
176
158
175
192
A
B
C
D
E
1
2
3
4
5
6
Kingston Vale
Coombe
Copse Hill
Cottenham Park
New Malden
Crooked B
Kingston University
Robin Hood Primary School
Wimbledon Common Golf Club
Royal Wimbledon Golf Club
Caesar's Camp
Warren Farm
Warren House
Golf Course
Coombe Hill Golf Club
Wimbledon RFC
Rowans School
Wolfson Medical Centre
Atkinson Morley Hospital
New Victoria Hospital
St Matthews CE Primary School
Coombe Hill J&I School
Coombe Girls School
Malden Golf Club
The Groves Medical Cen
Christ Church New Malden CE Primary School
New Malden Stn
Murky Puddle Theatre
Raynes Park Sports Ground
Raynes Park High School
Rainbow Industrial E
Superstore
Sacred Heart RC Primary School
Burlington Inf Sch
The Malden Centre
Health Clinic
Roselands Clinic
Leigh Close Industrial
Surgery
ROBIN HOOD WAY
(KINGSTON BY-PASS)
COOMBE LANE WEST
COOMBE LANE
BEVERLEY WAY
TRAPS LANE
COOMBE ROAD
HIGH STREET
BUSHEY ROAD
DURHAM ROAD
WEST BARNES LANE
BURLINGTON ROAD
KINGSTON
A238
A3
A308
B283
B282
SW20
Robin Hood Rd
Ullswater Crs
Grasmere Avenue
Keswick Avenue
Coombe Park
Windmill Rd
Sunset Road
Camp Road
Drax Av
Hood Road
Cottenham Park Road
Cambridge Road
Richmond Road
Parkfields Av
Camberley Avenue
Somerset Av
Taunton Av
Bodnant Gardens
Polesden Gdns
Cromford Way
Buxton Drive
Langley Grove
Woodside Road
Sycamore Grove
Lime Grove
Chestnut Grove
Northcote Road
Kingscote Rd
Dukes Av
Malden Hill
Grafton Road
Egmont Rd
Egerton Road
Blagdon
Coombe Gardens
Aboyne Drive
Ely Close
Warren Cutting
Golf Club Drive
Warren Rd
Beverley Avenue
Holland Avenue
Preston Road
Barham Road
Burdett Av
Lindisfarne Rd
Ellerton Road
Wolsey Cl
Copse Hill
Cambridge Close
Melbury Gardens
Laurel Road
Oakwood Road
Panmure Road
Overdale Avenue
Oak Avenue
Beaconsfield Rd
Poplar Grove
Elm Road
Mount Road
Beech Grove
Acacia Grove
Linden Grove
Rosebery Av
Orchard Av
Linkside
Cambridge Avenue
Alric Avenue
Park View
The Mount
Hillbrow
Albany Road
Penrith Road
Cleveland Road
Sussex Place
1 grid square represents 500 metres
521
22
71
70
69

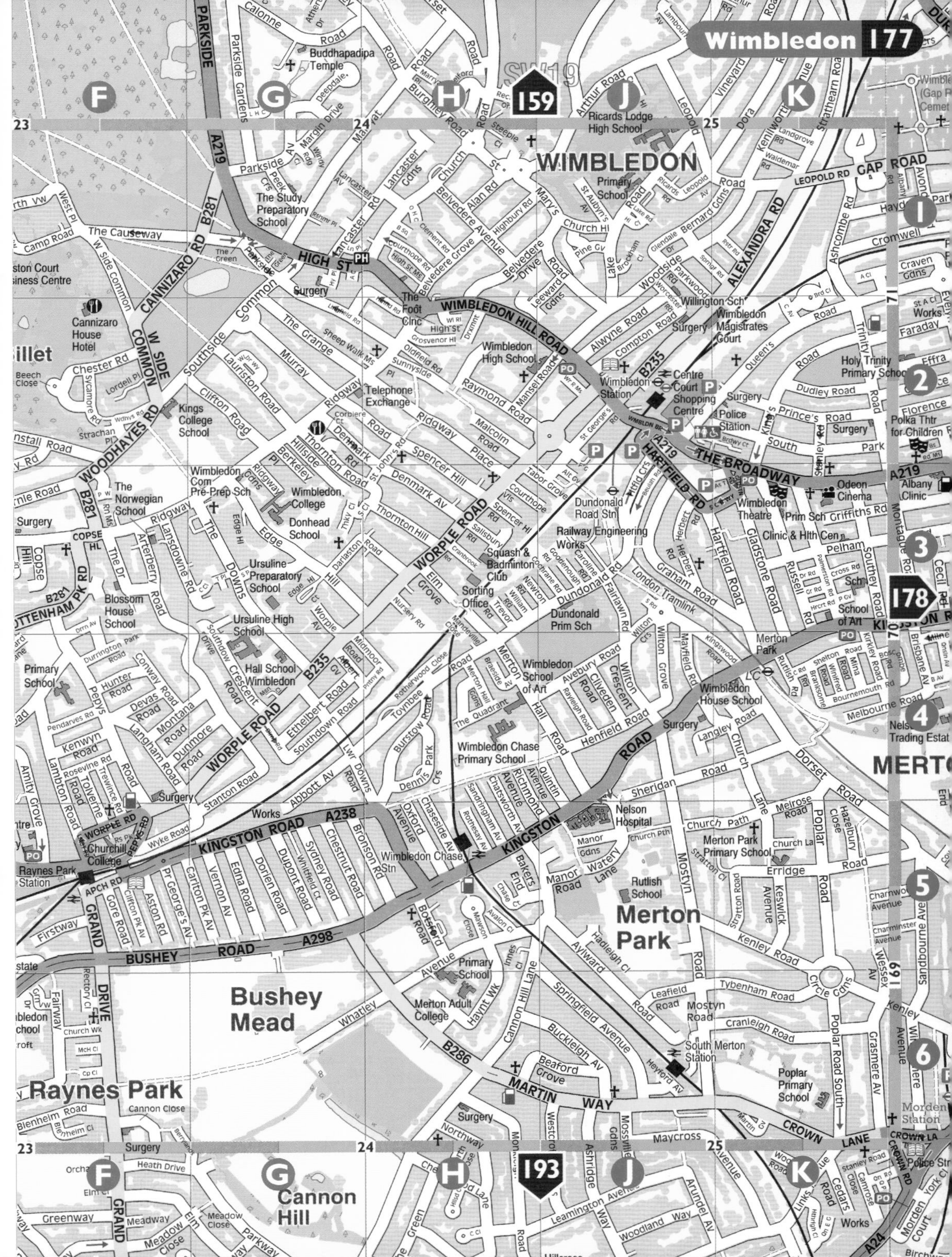
WIMBLEDON
Merton Park
Bushey Mead
Raynes Park
Cannon Hill
MERTON
159
178
193
F G H J K
23 24 25
Wimbledon Station
Centre Court Shopping Centre
Wimbledon Magistrates Court
Ricards Lodge High School
Kings College School
Wimbledon College
Wimbledon High School
Ursuline High School
Ursuline Preparatory School
Hall School Wimbledon
Wimbledon Chase Primary School
Wimbledon Chase Stn
Nelson Hospital
Merton Park Primary School
Rutlish School
South Merton Station
Merton Adult College
Raynes Park Station
Cannizaro House Hotel
The Norwegian School
Blossom House School
Donhead School
Wimbledon Theatre
Odeon Cinema
Polka Thtr for Children
Dundonald Road Stn
Dundonald Prim Sch
Wimbledon School of Art
Wimbledon House School
Squash & Badminton Club
Telephone Exchange
Sorting Office
Railway Engineering Works
Buddhapadipa Temple
The Study Preparatory School
Holy Trinity Primary School
Merton Park
Poplar Primary School
Churchill College
WORPLE ROAD
KINGSTON ROAD
WIMBLEDON HILL ROAD
THE BROADWAY
MARTIN WAY
BUSHEY ROAD
ALEXANDRA RD
HARTFIELD RD
CANNIZARO RD
WOODHAYES RD
W SIDE COMMON
PARKSIDE
HIGH ST
CROWN LANE
LEOPOLD RD GAP ROAD
A219
A238
A298
B235
B281
B286
A24

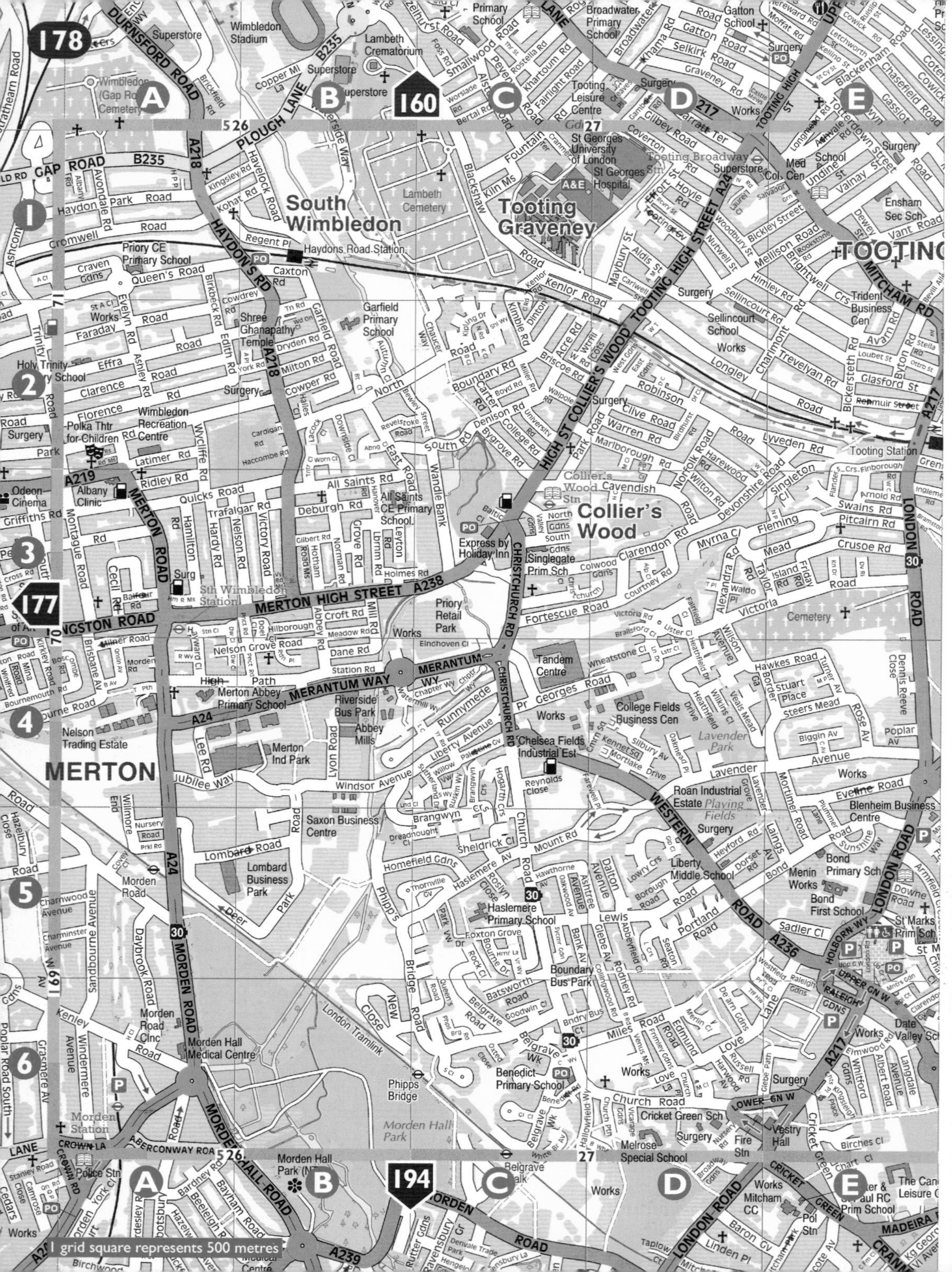
178
160
177
194
A
B
C
D
E
1
2
3
4
5
6
526
27
DURNSFORD ROAD
Superstore
Wimbledon Stadium
Lambeth Crematorium
Primary School
Broadwater Primary School
Gatton School
Surgery
Wimbledon (Gap Rd) Cemetery
PLOUGH LANE
B235
A218
GAP ROAD
Copper Mill La
Smallwood Road
Gatton Road
Selkirk Road
Graveney Rd
Tooting Leisure Centre
Fairlight Road
Khartoum Rd
Gilbey Road
Garratt Ter
A217
TOOTING HIGH ST
Blackenham Rd
Chasefield Road
Totterdown Street
Haydon Park Road
Havelock Road
Kingsley Rd
Kohat Rd
South Wimbledon
Lambeth Cemetery
Blackshaw
Kiln Ms
Fountain
St Georges University of London
St Georges Hospital
A&E
Tooting Graveney
Tooting Broadway
Superstore
Med Cen
School
Undine St
Valnay St
Ensham Sec Sch
Surgery
TOOTING
Cromwell Road
Regent Pl
Haydons Road Station
Priory CE Primary School
Craven Gdns
Queen's Road
Caxton Rd
HAYDON'S RD
Kenlor Road
Maybury St
Aldis St
TOOTING HIGH STREET
Woodbury St
Bickley Street
Mellison Road
Rookstone
Brightwell Crs
Himley Rd
Sellincourt Rd
Sellincourt School
Surgery
Trident Business Cen
MITCHAM RD
Faraday Road
Evelyn Rd
Works
Cowdrey Rd
Shree Ghanapathy Temple
Garfield Primary School
Garfield Road
Dryden Rd
Milton Rd
Cowper Rd
Chaucer Way
Kimble Rd
Dinton Rd
Acre Rd
Briscoe Rd
HIGH ST COLLIER'S WOOD
Longley
Charlmont Rd
Trevelyan Rd
Avarn Rd
Glasford St
Holy Trinity Primary School
Effra Road
Ashley Rd
Clarence Road
Florence Road
Surgery
Boundary Rd
North Road
Robinson Road
Clive Road
Warren Rd
Lyveden Rd
Tooting Station
Rennie Street
A217
Polka Thtr for Children
Wimbledon Recreation Centre
Wycliffe Rd
Cardigan Rd
Haccombe Rd
Latimer Rd
Ridley Rd
Denison Rd
College Rd
Bygrove Rd
South Rd
East Road
Park Road
Marlborough Rd
Norfolk Road
Harewood Rd
Wilton Rd
Devonshire Road
Singleton Cl
Finborough Rd
Arnold Rd
Swains Rd
Pitcairn Rd
Crusoe Rd
LONDON ROAD
A219
Odeon Cinema
Albany Clinic
MERTON ROAD
Quicks Road
Trafalgar Rd
Hamilton Rd
Hardy Rd
Nelson Rd
Victory Road
All Saints Rd
Deburgh Rd
All Saints CE Primary School
Grove Rd
Leyton Rd
Wandle Bank
Baltic Cl
Express by Holiday Inn
CHRISTCHURCH RD
Collier's Wood Stn
Cavendish
North Gdns
South Gdns
Collier's Wood
Valley Gdns
Clarendon Rd
Myrna Cl
Fleming Mead
Montague Road
Griffiths Rd
Cecil Rd
Balfour Rd
Surg
Sth Wimbledon Station
Holmes Rd
MERTON HIGH STREET
A238
Singlegate Prim Sch
Colwood Gdns
Christchurch
Courtney Rd
Alexandra Rd
Taylor Rd
Waldo Pl
Island Rd
Friday Rd
Road
Victoria
Cemetery
KINGSTON ROAD
Hilborough
Croft Rd
Mill Rd
Priory Retail Park
Fortescue Road
Victoria Rd
Lister Cl
Brisbane Av
Milner Road
Nelson Grove Road
Meadow Rd
Dane Rd
Works
Eindhoven Cl
Wilson Avenue
Station Rd
MERANTUM WAY
MERANTUM WY
Tandem Centre
Wheatstone Cl
Hawkes Road
Turner Av
Dennis Reeve Close
Bournemouth Rd
High Path
Merton Abbey Primary School
Chapter Wy
Riverside Bus Park
Abbey Mills
Pr Georges Road
College Fields Business Cen
Works
Stuart Place
Steers Mead
Rose Av
Poplar Av
A24
Nelson Trading Estate
MERTON
Lee Rd
Merton Ind Park
Lyon Road
Runnymede
Liberty Avenue
Chelsea Fields Industrial Est
Kennet Sq
Mortlake Drive
Silbury Av
Lavender Park
Biggin Av
Avenue
Works
Jubilee Way
Windsor Avenue
Reynolds Close
Hogarth Crs
Lavender Grove
Mortimer Road
Eveline Road
Blenheim Business Centre
Hazelbury Close
Willmore End
Nursery Road
Saxon Business Centre
Brangwyn Crs
Church Road
Roan Industrial Estate
Playing Fields
WESTERN ROAD
Surgery
Road
Sunshine Way
LONDON ROAD
Lombard Road
Lombard Business Park
Morden Road
Sheldrick Cl
Mount Rd
Heyford Rd
Dorset Rd
Liberty Middle School
Bond Primary Sch
Menin Works
Charnwood Avenue
A24
Deer Park
Homefield Gdns
Haslemere Av
Roslyn Close
Hawthorne Av
Dalton Avenue
Ashtree Avenue
Lowry Crs
Borough Road
Portland Road
Bond Road
Bond First School
Downe Road
St Marks Prim Sch
Sandbourne Avenue
Charminster Avenue
30
MORDEN ROAD
Daybrook Road
Phipp's Bridge Road
Haslemere Primary School
Foxton Grove
Bourne Dr
Rock Cl
Lewis Road
Glebe Av
Abbotsfield Cl
Seaton Rd
Sadler Cl
A236
HOLBORN WY
UPPER GN W
RALEIGH GDNS
Kenley Road
Windermere Avenue
Grasmere Av
Poplar Road South
Morden Road Clnc
Morden Hall Medical Centre
New Close
Belgrave Road
Batsworth Road
Goodwin Cl
Boundary Bus Park
Bank Av
Rodney Rd
Miles Road
Edmund Rd
Love Lane
London Tramlink
Phipps Bridge
Benedict Primary School
Belgrave Wk
Works
Russell Rd
Surgery
Harwood Rd
A217
Elmwood Rd
Albert Road
Whitford Gdns
Langdale Avenue
Date Valley Sch
Morden Station
Morden Hall Park
Church Road
Cricket Green Sch
LOWER GN W
Vestry Hall
Fire Stn
Surgery
Melrose Special School
Birches Cl
Cricket Green
CROWN LA
ABERCONWAY ROAD
LANE
Police Stn
Morden Hall Park (NT)
MORDEN HALL ROAD
Belgrave Walk
Works
Works Mitcham CC
LONDON ROAD
CRICKET GREEN
Pol Stn
Chart Cl
The Canons Leisure C
MADEIRA
A239
MORDEN ROAD
Baron Gv
Linden Pl
Cedars
Camrose Close
Stanley Road
Works
Bardney Rd
Bayham Road
Ravensbury
Denvale Trade Park
Rutter Gdns
1 grid square represents 500 metres

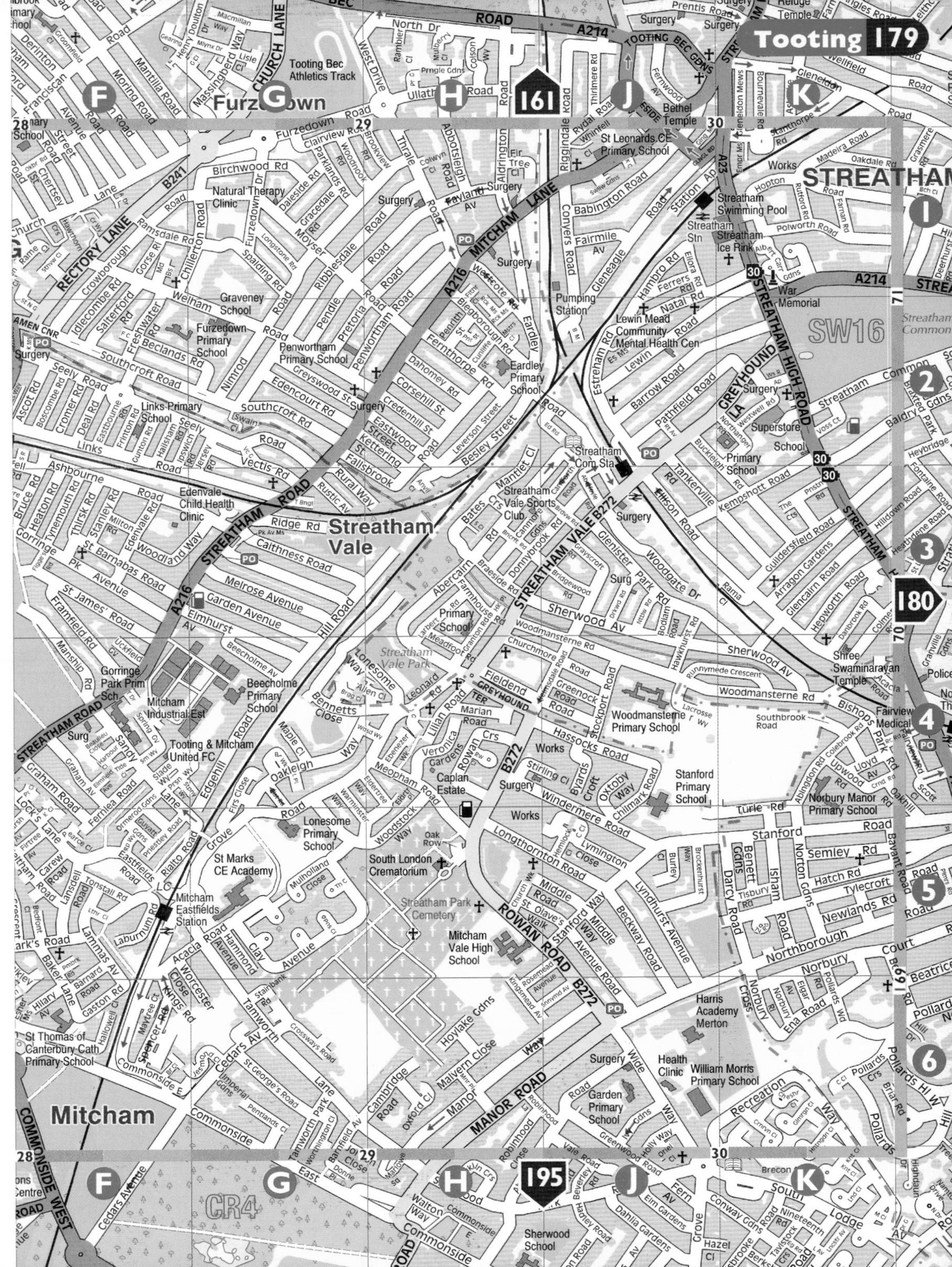
Furzedown
Tooting Bec Athletics Track
Streatham
Streatham Vale
Mitcham
SW16
CR4
Streatham Common
Mitcham Lane
Streatham Road
Streatham High Road
Streatham Vale
Rowan Road
Manor Road
Commonside West
Rectory Lane
Church Lane
Greyhound La
Streatham Stn
Streatham Com Sta
Mitcham Eastfields Station
Streatham Park Cemetery
South London Crematorium
Streatham Vale Park
Mitcham Industrial Est
Tooting & Mitcham United FC
Caplan Estate
Woodmansterne Primary School
Stanford Primary School
Norbury Manor Primary School
Harris Academy Merton
William Morris Primary School
Mitcham Vale High School
St Marks CE Academy
Lonesome Primary School
Beecholme Primary School
Gorringe Park Prim Sch.
Furzedown Primary School
Graveney School
Links Primary School
Penwortham Primary School
Eardley Primary School
St Leonards CE Primary School
Streatham Swimming Pool
Streatham Ice Rink
War Memorial
Lewin Mead Community Mental Health Cen
Edenvale Child Health Clinic
Shree Swaminarayan Temple
Fairview Medical
Sherwood School
St Thomas of Canterbury Cath Primary School
Garden Primary School
Health Clinic
Pumping Station
Natural Therapy Clinic
A214
A216
A23
B241
B272
161
180
195
28
29
30
F
G
H
J
K
1
2
3
4
5
6
69
70
71

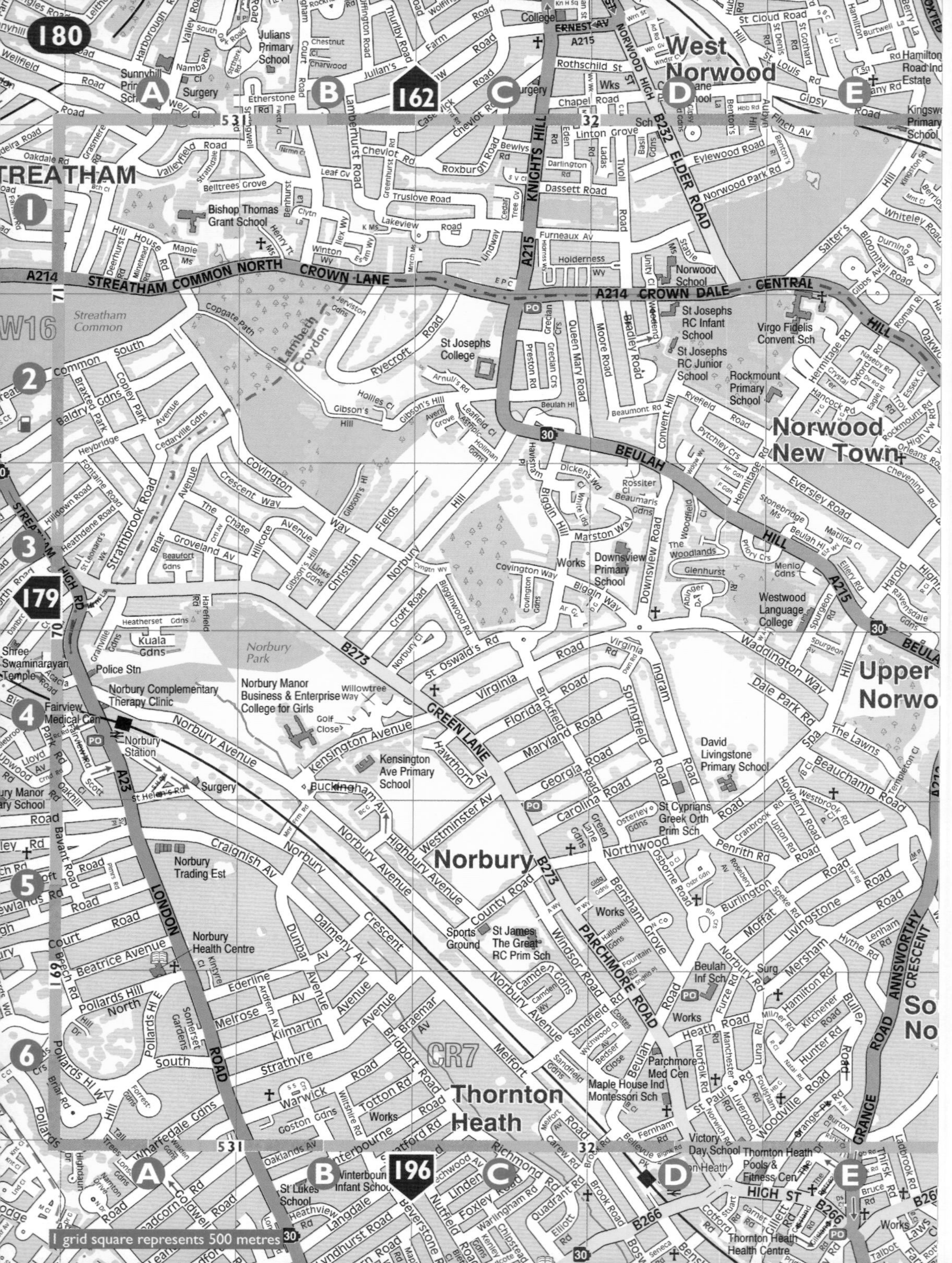

180
162
179
196
West Norwood
STREATHAM
Norwood New Town
Upper Norwood
Norbury
Thornton Heath
Streatham Common
Norbury Park
SW16
CR7
STREATHAM COMMON NORTH
CROWN LANE
CROWN DALE
CENTRAL HILL
BEULAH HILL
KNIGHTS HILL
ELDER ROAD
NORWOOD HIGH ST
GREEN LANE
LONDON ROAD
PARCHMORE ROAD
GRANGE ROAD
ANNSWORTHY CRESCENT
STREATHAM HIGH RD
HIGH ST
A214
A215
A23
B273
B232
B266
Julians Primary School
Bishop Thomas Grant School
Norwood School
St Josephs RC Infant School
St Josephs RC Junior School
St Josephs College
Virgo Fidelis Convent Sch
Rockmount Primary School
Downsview Primary School
Westwood Language College
David Livingstone Primary School
Norbury Manor Business & Enterprise College for Girls
Kensington Ave Primary School
St Cyprians Greek Orth Prim Sch
St James The Great RC Prim Sch
Beulah Inf Sch
Parchmore Med Cen
Maple House Ind Montessori Sch
Victory Day School
Thornton Heath Pools & Fitness Cen
Thornton Heath Health Centre
Norbury Health Centre
Norbury Trading Est
Norbury Station
Police Stn
Norbury Complementary Therapy Clinic
Fairview Medical Cen
Shree Swaminarayan Temple
St Lukes School
Winterbourne Infant School
Kingswood Primary School
Hamilton Road Ind Estate
Sports Ground
531
32
1 grid square represents 500 metres

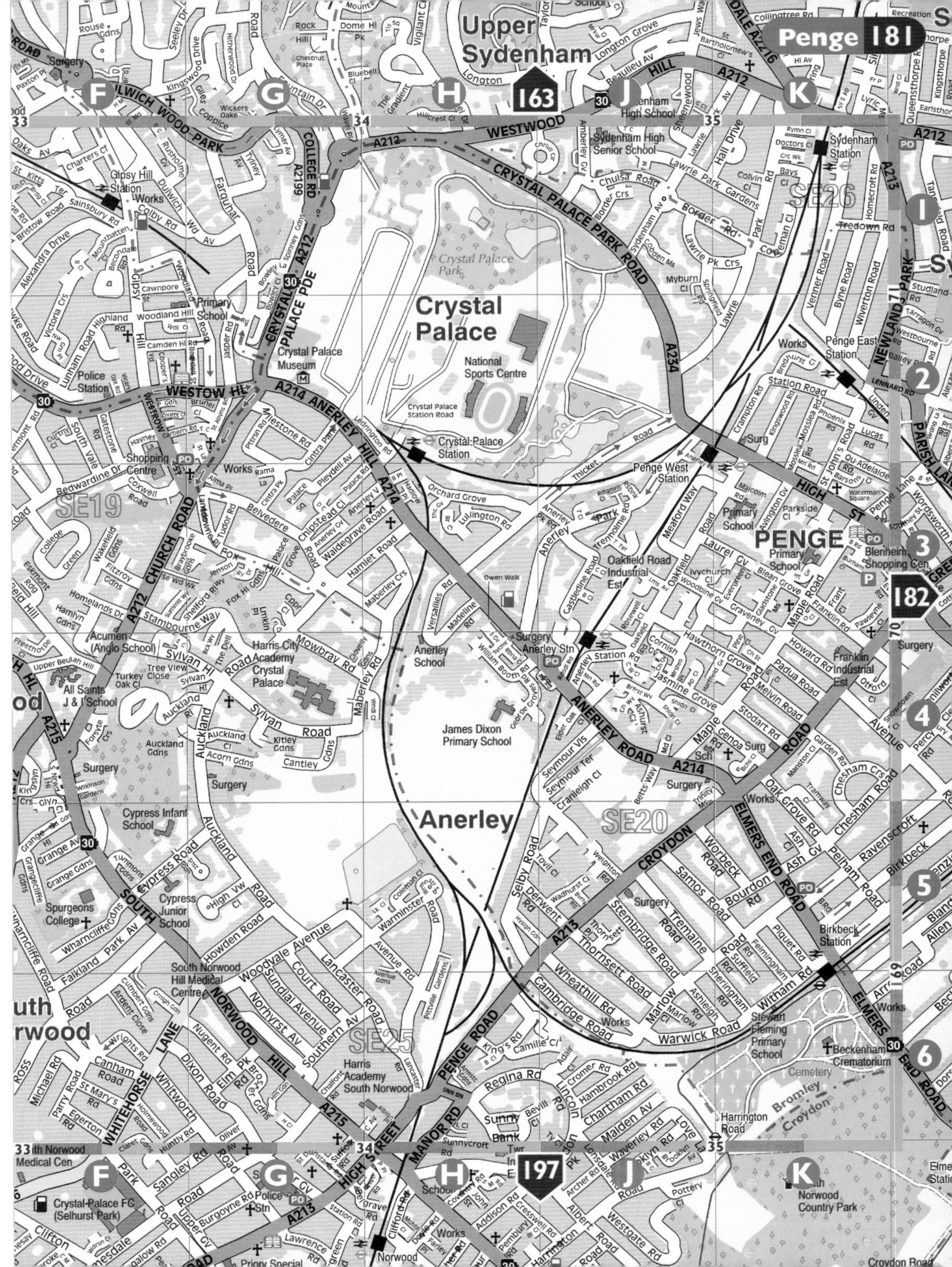
Upper Sydenham
Crystal Palace
Crystal Palace Park
National Sports Centre
Crystal Palace Museum
Crystal Palace Station
Penge West Station
PENGE
Anerley
Anerley Station
Penge East Station
Sydenham Station
Birkbeck Station
Gipsy Hill Station
SE19
SE20
SE25
SE26
South Norwood
Crystal Palace FC (Selhurst Park)
South Norwood Country Park
Beckenham Crematorium
Harris Academy South Norwood
James Dixon Primary School
Harris City Academy Crystal Palace
Spurgeons College
Cypress Infant School
Cypress Junior School
Stewart Fleming Primary School
Sydenham High Senior School
CRYSTAL PALACE PARK ROAD
ANERLEY ROAD
CROYDON ROAD
ELMERS END ROAD
HIGH ST
CHURCH ROAD
SOUTH NORWOOD HILL
PENGE ROAD
WESTOW HL
WESTWOOD HILL
163
182
197

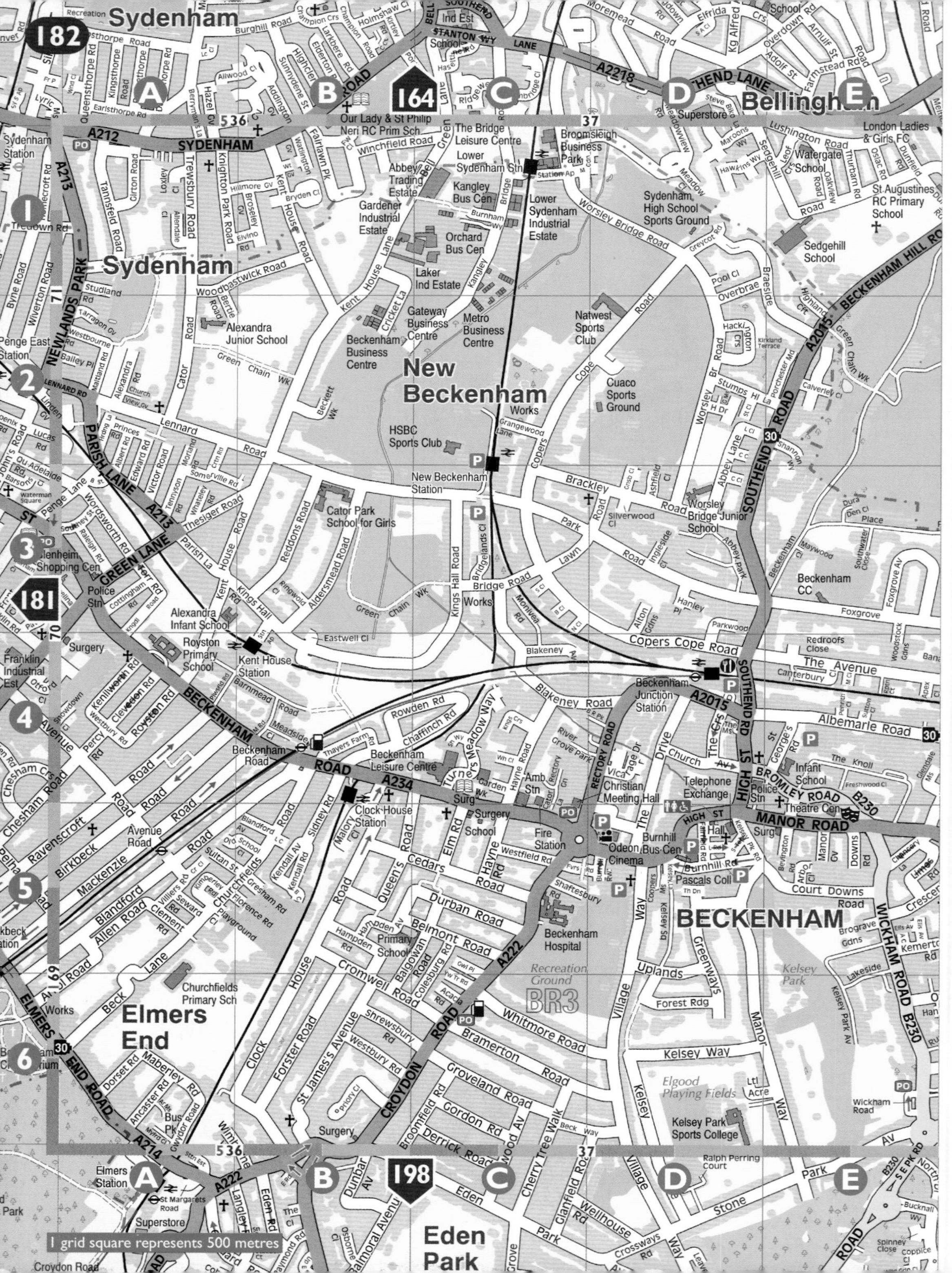
182
Sydenham
164
Bellingham
181
New Beckenham
BECKENHAM
Elmers End
Eden Park
198
BR3
1 grid square represents 500 metres

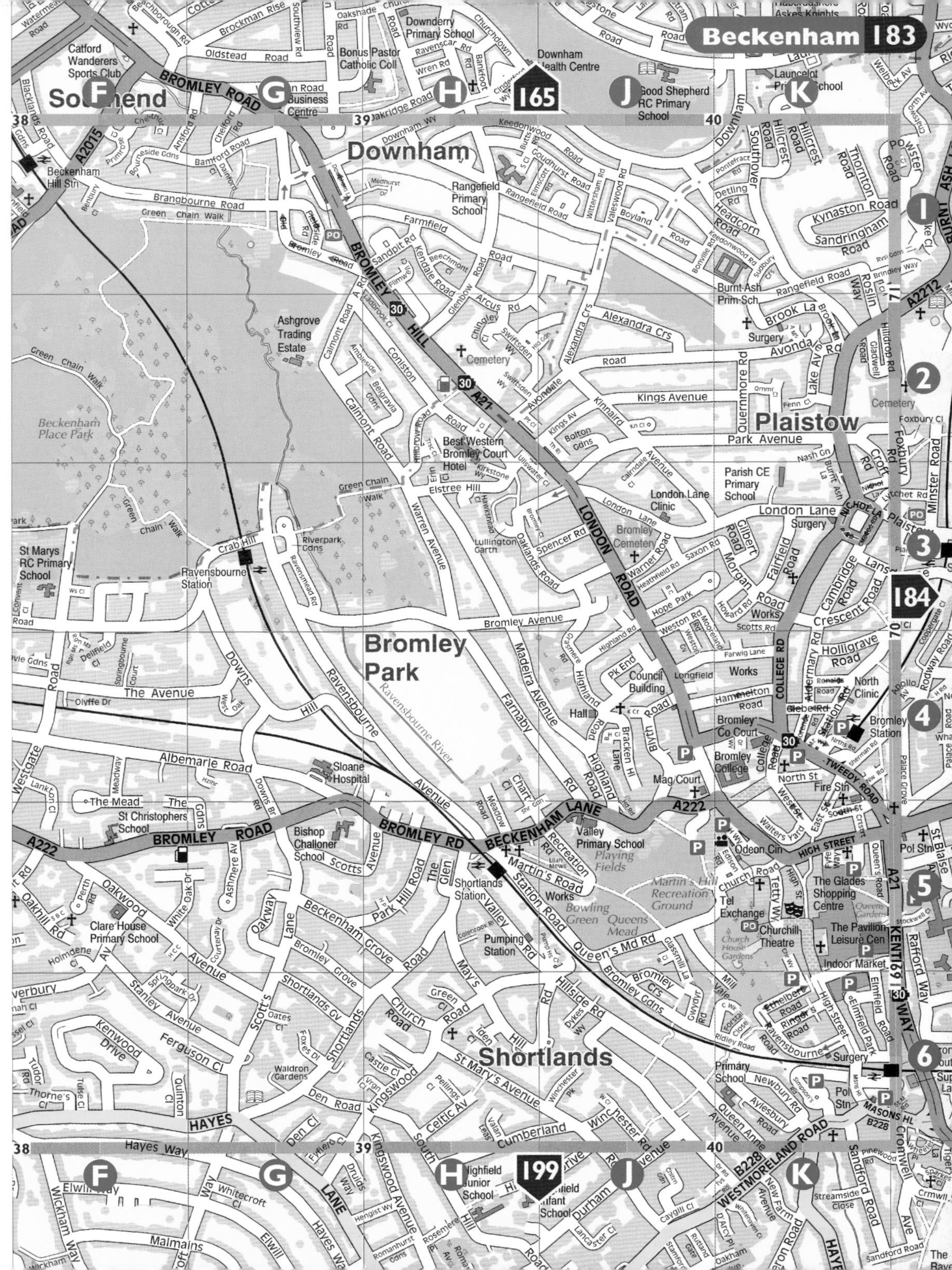

Beckenham 183
Southend
Catford Wanderers Sports Club
Downderry Primary School
Bonus Pastor Catholic Coll
Downham Health Centre
165
Good Shepherd RC Primary School
Launcelot Primary School
BROMLEY ROAD
Downham
Beckenham Hill Stn
Brangbourne Road
Green Chain Walk
Rangefield Primary School
Rangefield Road
Bromley Road
Farmfield
BROMLEY HILL
A21
Ashgrove Trading Estate
Cemetery
Alexandra Crs
Avondale Road
Kings Avenue
Plaistow
Park Avenue
Burnt Ash Prim Sch
Surgery
Kynaston Road
Sandringham Road
Rangefield Road
Brook La
A2212
BURNT ASH
Beckenham Place Park
Calmont Road
Coniston
Best Western Bromley Court Hotel
Elstree Hill
Green Chain Walk
Parish CE Primary School
London Lane Clinic
London Lane
LONDON ROAD
Bromley Cemetery
Spencer Rd
Lullington Garth
Oaklands Road
Crab Hill
Riverpark Gdns
Ravensbourne Station
St Marys RC Primary School
Ravensmead Rd
Warren Avenue
Bromley Avenue
Bromley Park
Ravensbourne River
Madeira Avenue
Farnaby
Highland Road
Council Building
Hall
COLLEGE RD
Crescent Road
Cambridge Road
Holligrave Road
North Clinic
Bromley Co Court
Bromley College
Bromley Station
TWEEDY ROAD
Mag Court
Fire Stn
184
The Avenue
Olyffe Dr
Downs Hill
Ravensbourne Avenue
Albemarle Road
Sloane Hospital
The Mead
St Christophers School
A222
BROMLEY ROAD
BROMLEY RD
BECKENHAM LANE
Bishop Challoner School
Valley Primary School
Playing Fields
Odeon Cin
HIGH STREET
Pol Stn
Shortlands Station
Martin's Road
Station Road
Martin's Hill Recreation Ground
Bowling Green
Queens Mead
Tel Exchange
Churchill Theatre
The Glades Shopping Centre
The Pavilion Leisure Cen
Indoor Market
A21
KENTISH WAY
Oakwood Avenue
Clare House Primary School
Beckenham Grove
Park Hill Road
The Glen
Pumping Station
Queen's Md Rd
Bromley Gdns
Bromley Crs
Ravensbourne Road
Surgery
Ferguson Cl
Kenwood Drive
Stanley Avenue
Scott's Lane
Shortlands
Shortlands Gv
Church Road
St Mary's Avenue
Waldron Gardens
Hillside Rd
Primary School
Newbury Rd
Aylesbury Road
Queen Anne Avenue
Pol Stn
MASONS HL
B228
Cromwell
HAYES LANE
Hayes Way
Den Road
Kingswood
Celtic Av
Cumberland
Winchester Rd
WESTMORELAND ROAD
B228
Elwill Way
Whitecroft Cl
Malmains
Wickham Way
Kingswood Avenue
Highfield Junior School
Highfield Infant School
199
Durham Rd
New Farm Avenue
Streamside Close
Sandford Road
Sandford Road
38
39
40
F
G
H
J
K
I
2
3
4
5
6

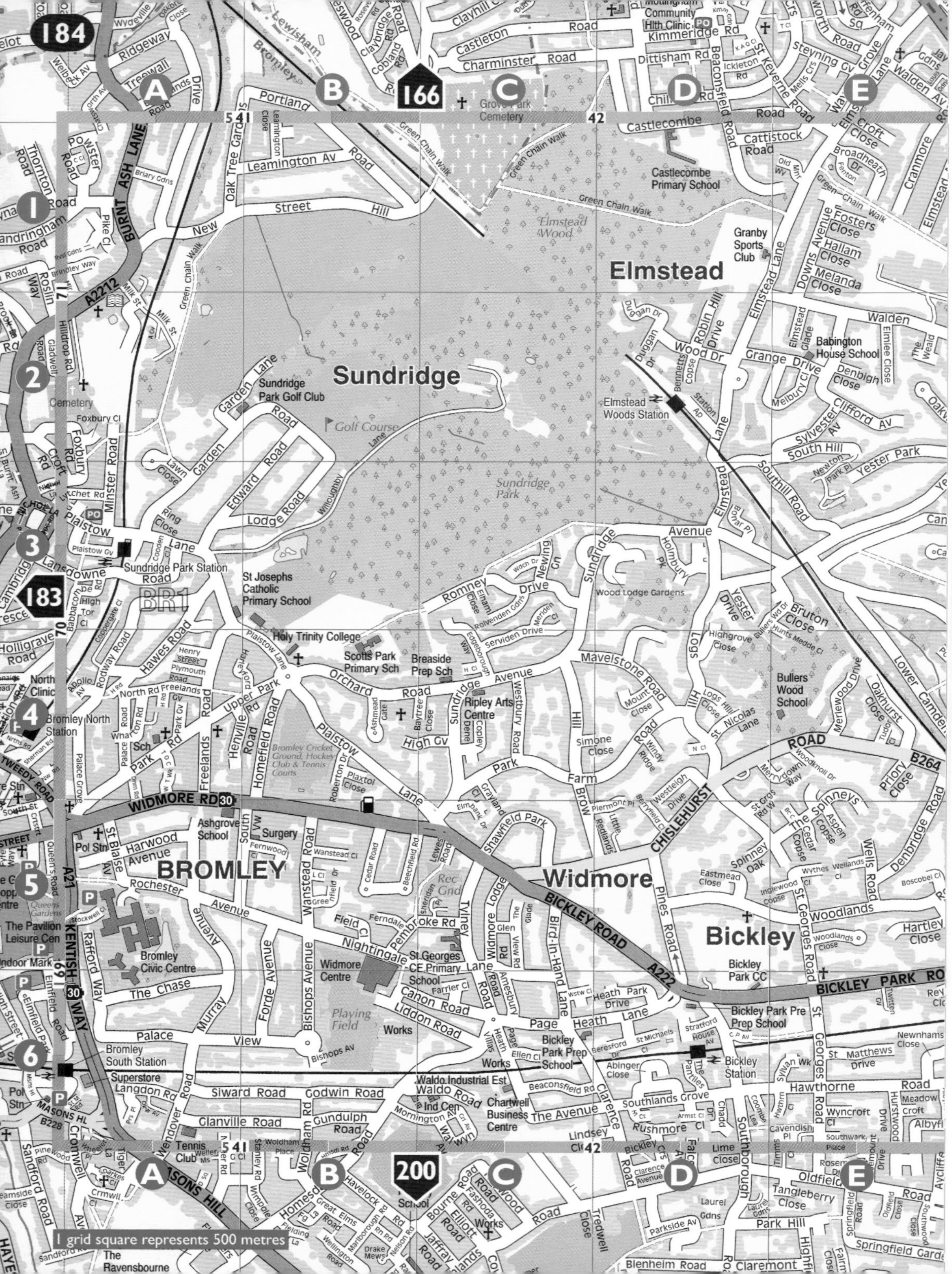
184
166
183
200
A
B
C
D
E
1
2
3
4
5
6
Sundridge
Elmstead
BROMLEY
Widmore
Bickley
Sundridge Park Golf Club
Golf Course
Elmstead Wood
Sundridge Park
Grove Park Cemetery
Castlecombe Primary School
Granby Sports Club
Elmstead Woods Station
Babington House School
Sundridge Park Station
St Josephs Catholic Primary School
Holy Trinity College
Scotts Park Primary Sch
Breaside Prep Sch
Ripley Arts Centre
Wood Lodge Gardens
Bullers Wood School
Bromley North Station
Bromley Cricket Ground, Hockey Club & Tennis Courts
Ashgrove School
Surgery
Rec Gnd
Bromley Civic Centre
The Pavilion Leisure Cen
Widmore Centre
St.Georges CE Primary School
Playing Field
Works
Bickley Park CC
Bickley Park Pre Prep School
Bickley Park Prep School
Bickley Station
Bromley South Station
Superstore
Waldo Industrial Est
Chartwell Business Centre
Tennis Club
Cemetery
Green Chain Walk
BURNT ASH LANE
A2212
WIDMORE RD
BICKLEY ROAD
A222
BICKLEY PARK ROAD
CHISLEHURST ROAD
B264
KENTISH WAY
A21
MASONS HILL
B228
Plaistow Lane
Sundridge Avenue
Orchard Road
Mavelstone Road
Elmstead Lane
Southhill Road
Garden Road
Edward Road
Lodge Road
Minster Road
Hawes Road
Upper Park Road
Homefield Road
Freelands Road
Bishops Avenue
Nightingale Lane
Rochester Avenue
Harwood Avenue
Palace View
Siward Road
Godwin Road
Clanville Road
Page Heath Lane
Bird-In-Hand Lane
Pines Road
St Georges Road
Woodlands Road
Hawthorne Road
Southborough Road
New Street Hill
Leamington Av
Portland Road
Castlecombe Road
Charminster Road
Grange Drive
Wood Dr
Robin Hill Drive
Romney Drive
Farm Brow
Park Farm Road
Widmore Lodge Road
Canon Road
Liddon Road
Waldo Road
Southlands Grove
Rushmore Cl
Park Hill
Blenheim Road
Bourne Road
Murray Avenue
Forde Avenue
Rafford Way
The Chase
Wendover Road
Cromwell
Sandford Road
1 grid square represents 500 metres
The Ravensbourne

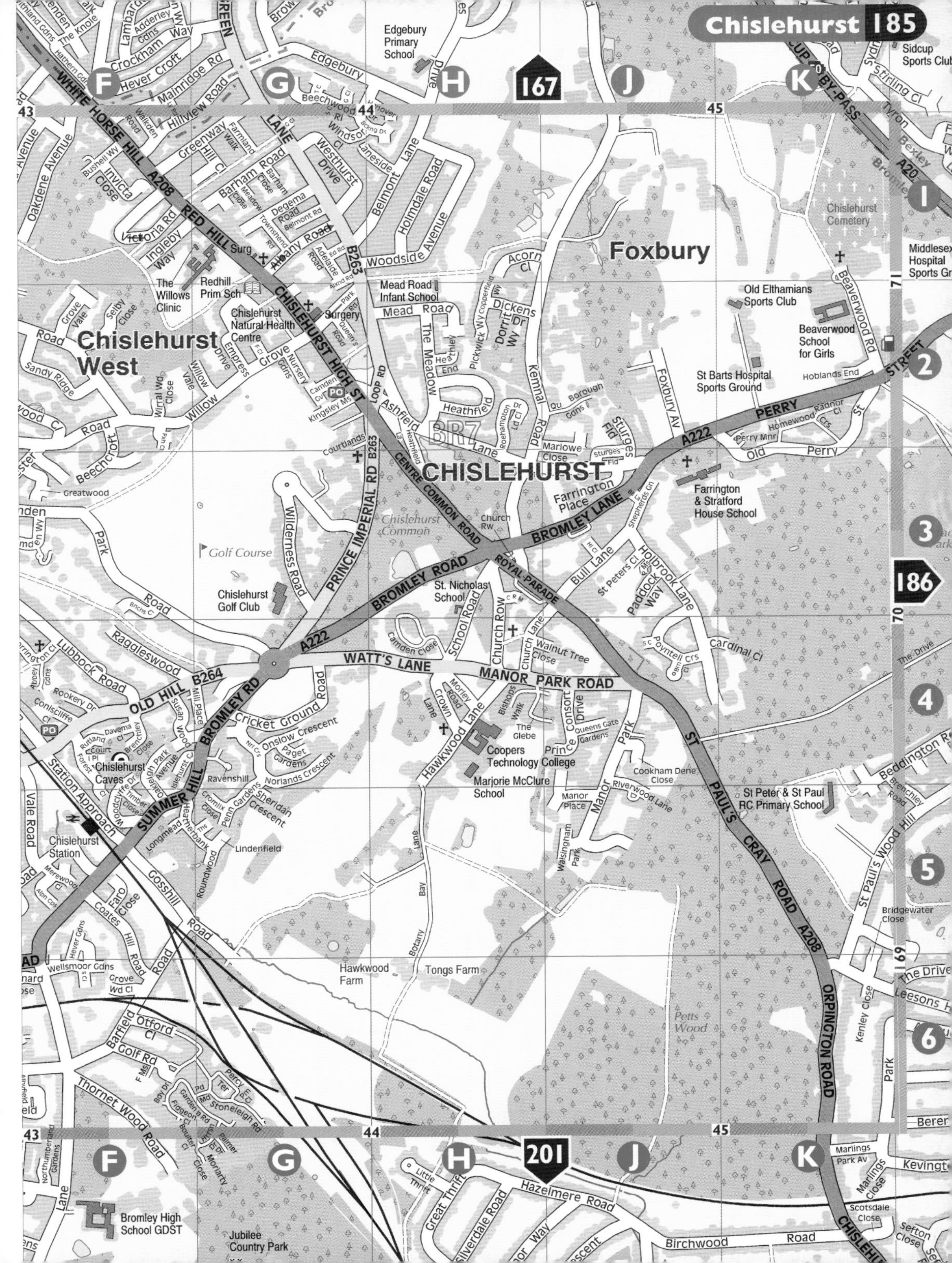

167
186
201
F
G
H
J
K
I
2
3
4
5
6
43
44
45
71
70
69
Foxbury
Chislehurst West
CHISLEHURST
BR7
Edgebury Primary School
Sidcup Sports Club
Chislehurst Cemetery
Middlesex Hospital Sports Gr
Old Elthamians Sports Club
Beaverwood School for Girls
St Barts Hospital Sports Ground
Farrington & Stratford House School
Mead Road Infant School
The Willows Clinic
Redhill Prim Sch
Chislehurst Natural Health Centre
Surgery
Chislehurst Common
Golf Course
Chislehurst Golf Club
St. Nicholas School
Coopers Technology College
Marjorie McClure School
St Peter & St Paul RC Primary School
Chislehurst Caves
Chislehurst Station
Hawkwood Farm
Tongs Farm
Petts Wood
Bromley High School GDST
Jubilee Country Park
WHITE HORSE HILL
A208
RED HILL
CHISLEHURST HIGH ST
B263
PRINCE IMPERIAL RD
CENTRE COMMON ROAD
BROMLEY LANE
BROMLEY ROAD
A222
ROYAL PARADE
PERRY STREET
WATT'S LANE
MANOR PARK ROAD
OLD HILL
B264
BROMLEY RD
SUMMER HILL
ST PAUL'S CRAY ROAD
ORPINGTON ROAD
Edgebury
Belmont Lane
Holmdale Road
Woodside Avenue
Westhurst Drive
Kemnal Road
Foxbury Av
Beaverwood Rd
Hoblands End
Mead Road
The Meadow
Heathfield
Ashfield
Lane
Loop Rd
Dickens Dr
Dorrit Wy
Pickwick Wy
Acorn Cl
Marlowe Close
Sturges Fld
Farrington Place
Homewood Crs
Perry Mnr
Old Perry St
Wilderness Road
Camden Close
School Road
Church Row
Church Lane
Walnut Tree Close
Bull Lane
St Peters Cl
Holbrook Lane
Paddock Way
Poyntell Crs
Cardinal Cl
Crown Lane
Morley Road
Hawkwood Lane
Bishops Walk
The Glebe
Consort Drive
Queens Gate Gardens
Prince Consort Drive
Cookham Dene Close
Manor Park
Riverwood Lane
Manor Place
Walsingham Park
Botany Bay Lane
Beddington Rd
Brenchley Road
St Paul's Wood Hill
Bridgewater Close
Kenley Close
The Drive
Leesons H
Park
Berer
Marlings Park Av
Marlings Close
Scotsdale Close
Sefton Close
Kevingt
Birchwood Road
Hazelmere Road
Great Thrift
Little Thrift
Silverdale Road
Cricket Ground Road
Onslow Crescent
Paget Gardens
Norlands Crescent
Ravenshill
Sheridan Crescent
Penn Gardens
Cromlix Close
Heatherbank
Longmead
Lindenfield
Roundwood
Gosshill Road
Station Approach
Vale Road
Faro Close
Coates Hill Road
Wellsmoor Gdns
Grove Wd Cl
Hever Gdns
Otford Cl
Barfield
Golf Rd
Thornet Wood Road
Stoneleigh Rd
Percy Rd
Pd
Ter
Bdy Dr
Garden Rd
Fidgeon
Boulter Close
Palmer Cl
Moriarty Close
Northumberland Gardens
Lane
Summer Wood
Susan Wood
Mill Place
Lubbock Road
Rookery Dr
Coniscliffe Cl
Raggleswood
Road
Park
Beechcroft
Greatwood
Sandy Ridge
Willow Vale
Willow Grove
Wirral Wd Close
Empress Drive
Nursery Gdns
Camden Gv
Kingsley Ms
Courtlands
Grove Vale
Selby Close
Ingleby Way
Victoria Rd
Invicta Close
Bushell Wy
Oakdene Avenue
Walkden Road
Hillview Road
Mainridge Rd
Hever Croft
Crockham Way
Adderley Gdns
The Knole
Greenway
Hill Cl
Farmland Walk
Barham Road
Barham Close
Meadow Close
Degema Road
Belmont Rd
Townshend Rd
Albany Road
Adelaide Road
Surg
Beechwood Ri
Windsor Cl
Laneside
Queen's Road
Davema Cl
Brenchley Close
Rutland Court
Forest Cl
Woodclyffe Dr
Oakleigh Park Avenue
Islehurst Cl
Timber Close
Merewood Cl

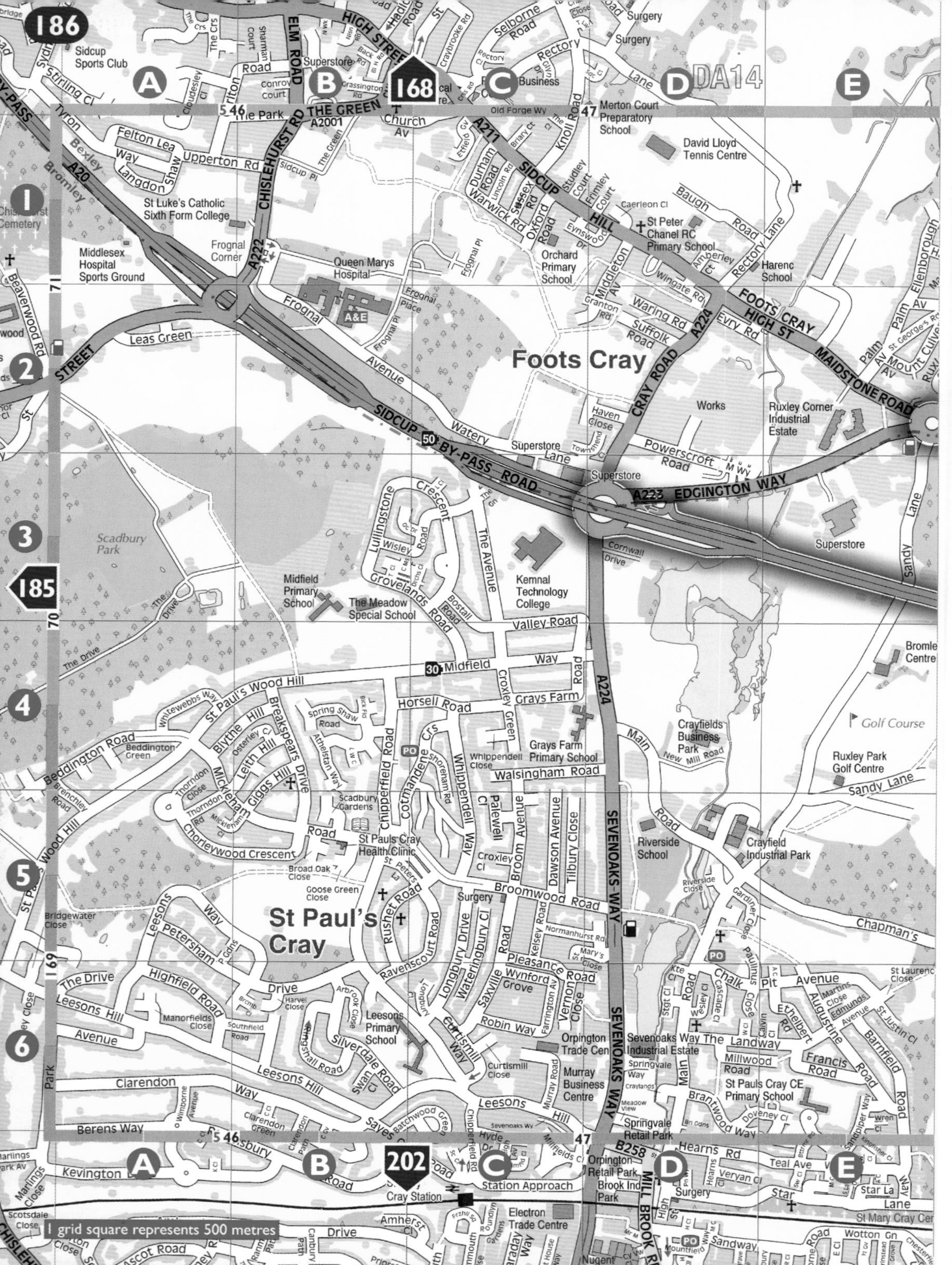
186
168
185
202
A
B
C
D
E
1
2
3
4
5
6
DA14
546
47
71
70
69
1 grid square represents 500 metres
Foots Cray
St Paul's Cray
Sidcup Sports Club
Stirling Cl
Tyron
The Crs
Cloudesley Cl
Sharman Court
Conroy Court
Road
ELM ROAD
HIGH STREET
Superstore
Grassington Rd
Craybrooke Rd
Selborne Road
Rectory Lane
Surgery
Business
The Park
THE GREEN
A2001
CHISLEHURST RD
Church Av
Old Forge Wy
Merton Court Preparatory School
David Lloyd Tennis Centre
Felton Lea
Way
Langdon Shaw
Upperton Rd
Sidcup Pl
The Green
A20
Bexley
Bromley
BY-PASS
St Luke's Catholic Sixth Form College
Chislehurst Cemetery
Middlesex Hospital Sports Ground
Beaverwood Rd
Frognal Corner
A222
Queen Marys Hospital
A&E
Frognal Place
Frognal Pl
Frognal
Durham Road
Lincoln Rd
Sussex Rd
Warwick Rd
Oxford Road
SIDCUP HILL
A211
Knoll Road
Studley Court
Frimley Court
Eynswood Dr
Caerleon Cl
Baugh Road
St Peter Chanel RC Primary School
Orchard Primary School
Middleton Av
Amberley Ct
Rectory Lane
Harenc School
Wingate Rd
Granton Rd
Waring Rd
Suffolk Road
Evry Rd
A224
FOOTS CRAY HIGH ST
MAIDSTONE ROAD
Palm Av
Mount Culver
St George's Rd
Ellenborough
Leas Green
STREET
Avenue
CRAY ROAD
Works
Ruxley Corner Industrial Estate
SIDCUP BY-PASS ROAD
50
Watery Lane
Superstore
Haven Close
Townshend
Powerscroft Road
M Wy
A223 EDGINGTON WAY
Superstore
Sandy Lane
Scadbury Park
Lullingstone Crescent
Wisley Road
Grovelands Road
Bostall Road
The Avenue
Kemnal Technology College
Cornwall Drive
Midfield Primary School
The Meadow Special School
Valley Road
The Drive
The Drive
Midfield Way
30
Bromley Centre
St Paul's Wood Hill
Whitewebbs Way
Breakspears Drive
Spring Shaw Road
Horsell Road
Croxley Green
Grays Farm Road
Grays Farm Primary School
Golf Course
Crayfields Business Park
Main Road
New Mill Road
Beddington Road
Beddington Green
Blythe Hill
Osterley Cl
Leith Hill
Athelstan Way
Chipperfield Road
Cotmandene Crs
Shoreham Rd
Whippendell Way
Whippendell Close
Walsingham Road
Ruxley Park Golf Centre
Sandy Lane
Brenchley Road
Thorndon Close
Mickleham
Giggs Hill
Scadbury Gardens
Palewell Cl
Broom Avenue
Dawson Avenue
Tilbury Close
SEVENOAKS WAY
Chorleywood Crescent
Road
St Pauls Cray Health Clinic
Croxley Cl
Riverside School
Crayfield Industrial Park
Broad Oak Close
Goose Green Close
St Peters
Broomwood Road
Riverside Close
Gardiner Close
Surgery
Chapman's
Bridgewater Close
Leesons Way
Rushet Road
Ravenscourt Road
Longbury Drive
Wateringbury Cl
Kelsey Road
Normanhurst Rd
Mary's Close
Petersham
Pleasance Road
Wynford Grove
PO
Paulinus Close
Chalk Pit Avenue
St Laurence Close
The Drive
Highfield Road
Drive
Harvel Close
Arbrook Close
Saxville Road
Farrington Av
Vernon Close
Wesley Cl
Cascade Cl
Ethelbert Rd
Augustine Road
Martins Close
Edmunds Avenue
St Justin Cl
Barnfield Road
Leesons Hill
Manorfields Close
Southfield Road
Leesons Primary School
Robin Way
Curtismill Way
Sevenoaks Way The Landway Industrial Estate
Orpington Trade Cen
Avenue
Ringshall Road
Silverdale Road
Swan Cl
Springvale Way
Millwood Road
Francis Road
Clarendon Way
Leesons Hill
Curtismill Close
Murray Road
Murray Business Centre
Craylands
Meadow View
Main Road
St Pauls Cray CE Primary School
Brantwood Way
Park
Wimborne Avenue
Clarendon Green
Clarendon Path
Sayes Court
Batchwood Green
Chipperfield Road
Leesons Hill
Sevenoaks Wy
Springvale Retail Park
Doveney Cl
Sandpiper Way
Wren Cl
Berens Way
Hyde
Millfields Cl
B258
Hearns Rd
Kingfisher Cl
Marlings Park Av
Kevington
Marlings Close
Station Approach
Orpington Retail Park
Brook Ind Park
Veryan Cl
Teal Ave
Star La
Lane
Star
MILL BROOK RD
Cray Station
Surgery
High St
Scotsdale Close
CHISLEHURST
Amherst Cl
Drive
Electron Trade Centre
St Mary Cray Cem
Ascot Road
Sandway
Wotton Gn
Mountfield Way
Nugent

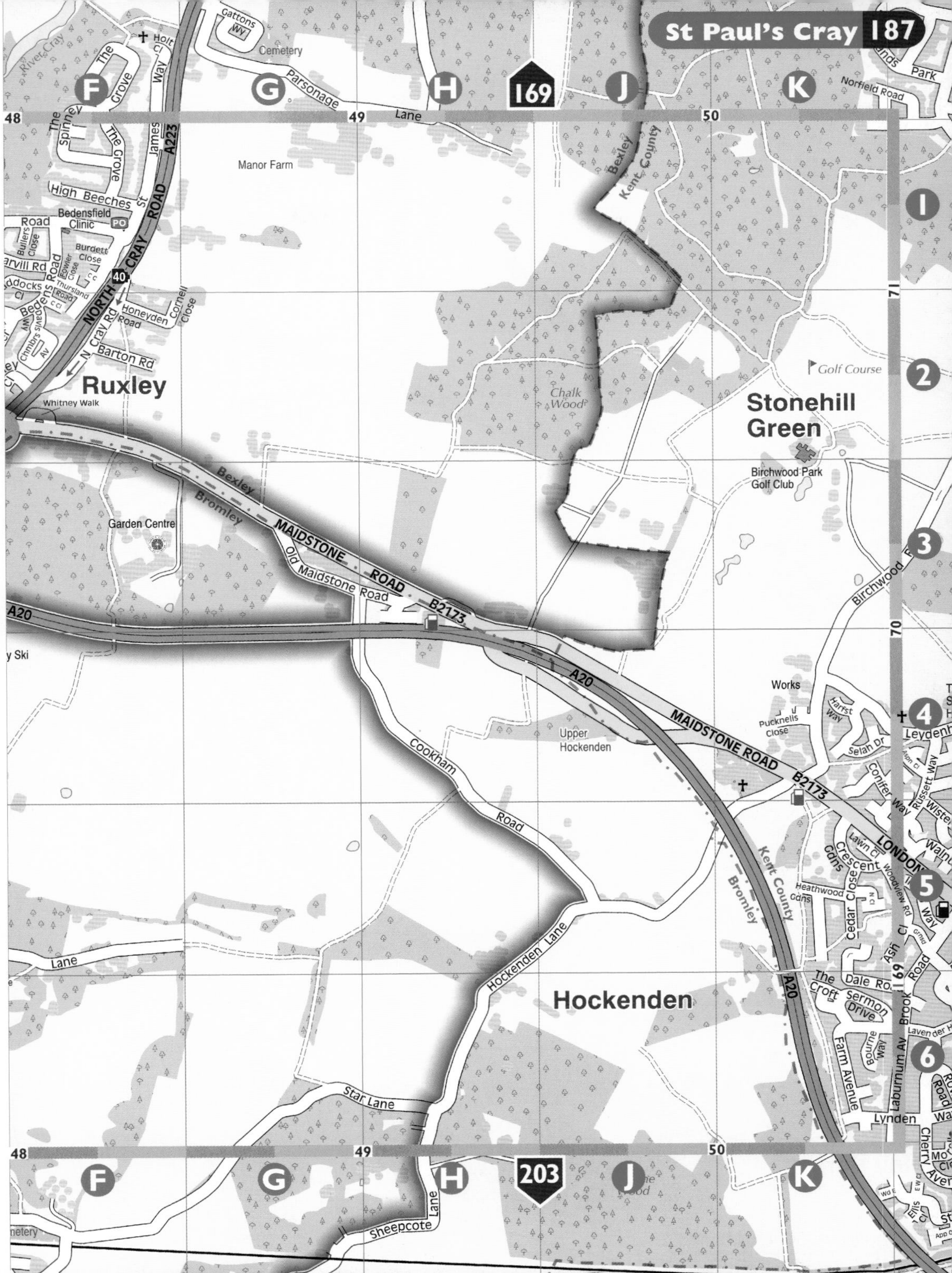
Ruxley
Stonehill Green
Hockenden
Upper Hockenden
Manor Farm
Cemetery
Chalk Wood
Birchwood Park Golf Club
Golf Course
Garden Centre
Works
Bedensfield Clinic
Whitney Walk
Parsonage Lane
NORTH CRAY ROAD
A223
MAIDSTONE ROAD
B2173
Old Maidstone Road
A20
Cookham Road
Hockenden Lane
Star Lane
Sheepcote Lane
Birchwood Road
LONDON
Kent County
Bexley
Bromley
High Beeches
The Grove
The Spinney
James St
Holt Cl
Gattons Wy
Honeyden Road
Cornell Close
Barton Rd
N Cray Rd
Burdett Close
Bullers Close
Pucknells Close
Harfst Way
Selah Dr
Conifer Way
Russett Way
Crescent Gdns
Heathwood Gdns
Cedar Close
Woodview Rd
The Croft
Dale Rd
Sermon Drive
Farm Avenue
Bourne Way
Laburnum Av
Brook Road
Ash Cl
Lynden Way
Cherry Avenue
Norfield Road
169
203

Lower Sunbury
172
Molesey Reservoirs
Bessborough Reservoir
Knight Reservoir
Queen Elizabeth II Reservoir
Sand & Gravel Works
Walton Casuals FC
Elmbridge Leisure Centre
River Thames
HURST ROAD
TERRACE ROAD
WALTON ROAD
B369
A3050
Waterside Drive
Grovelands School
Walton Business Centre
Field Common
Fieldcommon Lane
Molesey Road
Molesey Avenue
Monks Avenue
Central Avenue
Pool Road
Weston Avenue
Cottimore Lane
Cottimore Avenue
Sidney Road
Vanbrugh Drive
Braycourt Avenue
Swansmere School
Ambleside Junior School
Ambleside Avenue
King George Avenue
Rydens Road
Walton Park
Severn Drive
Hersham Road
Crutchfield Lane
Kings Road
Cromwell Road
Health Centre
Walton Community Hospital
Westward Prep School
Danesfield Manor School
Council Building
Walton Swimming Pool
WALTON-ON-THAMES
Rydens
North Weylands Industrial Est
Esher RFC
Hersham Trading Estate
Lyon Road
Ashley Park
Adelaide Road
Stoke Rd
Lindley Road
Works
1 grid square represents 500 metres

East Molesey
Lower Green
Island Barn Reservoir
Walton Road
Hampton Court Way
Esher Road
Ember Lane
Station Road
Portsmouth Road
Kingston Road
Embercourt Road
Hurst Road
Bridge Rd
Weston Green
Sandown Park Racecourse
Sandown Grandstand & Exhibition Centre
Esher Station
Thames Ditton & Esher Golf Club
Imber Court Trading Estate
Metropolitan Police FC
Molesey Hospital
Esher College
Littleworth Common
River Mole Business Park
Sandown Industrial Park
KT8
173
190
204

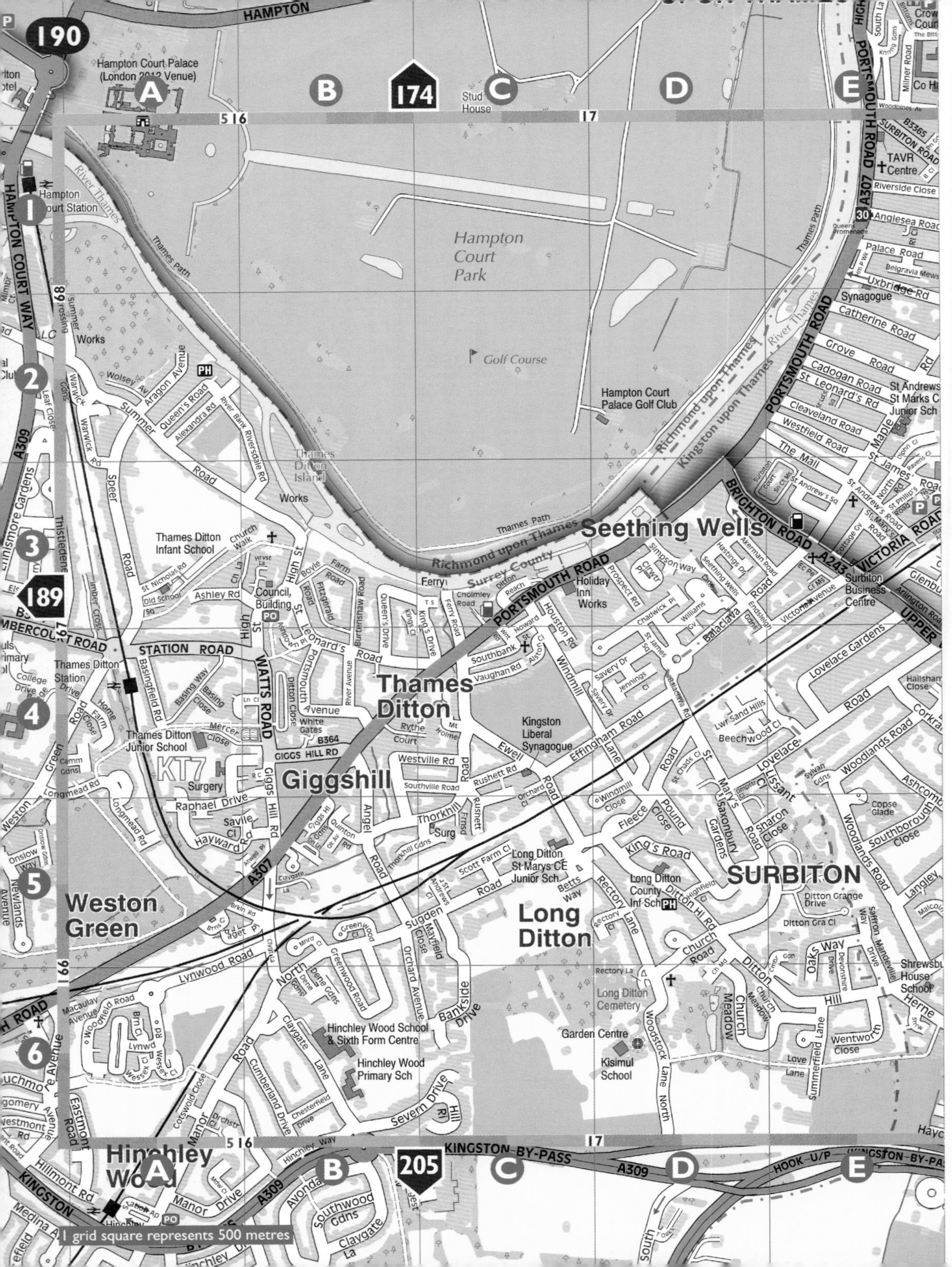
190
174
189
205
A
B
C
D
E
1
2
3
4
5
6
516
17
HAMPTON
Hampton Court Palace
(London 2012 Venue)
Stud House
Hampton Court Station
HAMPTON COURT WAY
River Thames
Thames Path
Hampton Court Park
Golf Course
Hampton Court Palace Golf Club
Thames Ditton Island
Works
Richmond upon Thames
Kingston upon Thames
Surrey County
Seething Wells
PORTSMOUTH ROAD
A307
HIGH ST
TAVR Centre
Riverside Close
Anglesea Road
Palace Road
Belgravia Mews
Uxbridge Rd
Synagogue
Catherine Road
Grove Road
Cadogan Road
St Leonard's Rd
Cleaveland Road
Westfield Road
The Mall
St James Road
St Andrews & St Marks CE Junior Sch
BRIGHTON ROAD
A243
VICTORIA ROAD
Surbiton Business Centre
UPPER
Thames Ditton Infant School
Church Walk
Summer Road
Aragon Avenue
Queen's Road
Alexandra Rd
River Bank
Riverside Rd
Warwick Rd
Speer Road
Imber Cross
Council Building
Ashley Rd
St Leonard's Road
Holiday Inn Works
Prospect Rd
Simpson Way
Houston Rd
Ferry
Ferry Road
Queen's Drive
King's Drive
Southbank
Vaughan Rd
IMBERCOURT ROAD
STATION ROAD
Thames Ditton Station
WATTS ROAD
Basingfield Rd
Thames Ditton
Portsmouth Avenue
River Avenue
Ditton Close
Windmill Lane
Savery Dr
Jennings Cl
Effingham Road
Balaclava Rd
Lovelace Gardens
Lovelace Road
Woodlands Road
Thames Ditton Junior School
Mercer Close
Giggs Hill Rd
KT7
Giggshill
Westville Rd
Southville Road
Rushett Rd
Kingston Liberal Synagogue
Ewell Road
Weston Green
Longmead Rd
Surgery
Raphael Drive
Savile Cl
Hayward Rd
Thorkhill Road
Angel Road
Long Ditton St Marys CE Junior Sch
Long Ditton County Inf Sch
Long Ditton
Scott Farm Cl
Fleece Road
King's Road
Pound Close
St Mary's Road
Saxonbury Gardens
Sharon Close
SURBITON
Ditton Grange Drive
Ditton Hill Rd
Rectory Lane
Church Road
Long Ditton Cemetery
Garden Centre
Kisimul School
Woodstock Lane North
Meadow Church
Summerfield Lane
Wentworth Close
Love Lane
Oaks Way
Hill
Shrewsbury House School
Sugden Road
Mayfield Close
Orchard Avenue
Greenwood Road
Bankside Drive
Lynwood Road
Macaulay Avenue
Woodfield Road
Weston Avenue
Hinchley Wood School & Sixth Form Centre
Hinchley Wood Primary Sch
Claygate Lane
Cumberland Drive
Severn Drive
Manor Road
Manor Drive
Hinchley Wood
Hillmont Rd
Southwood Gdns
KINGSTON BY-PASS
A309
HOOK U/P
Eastmont Road
1 grid square represents 500 metres

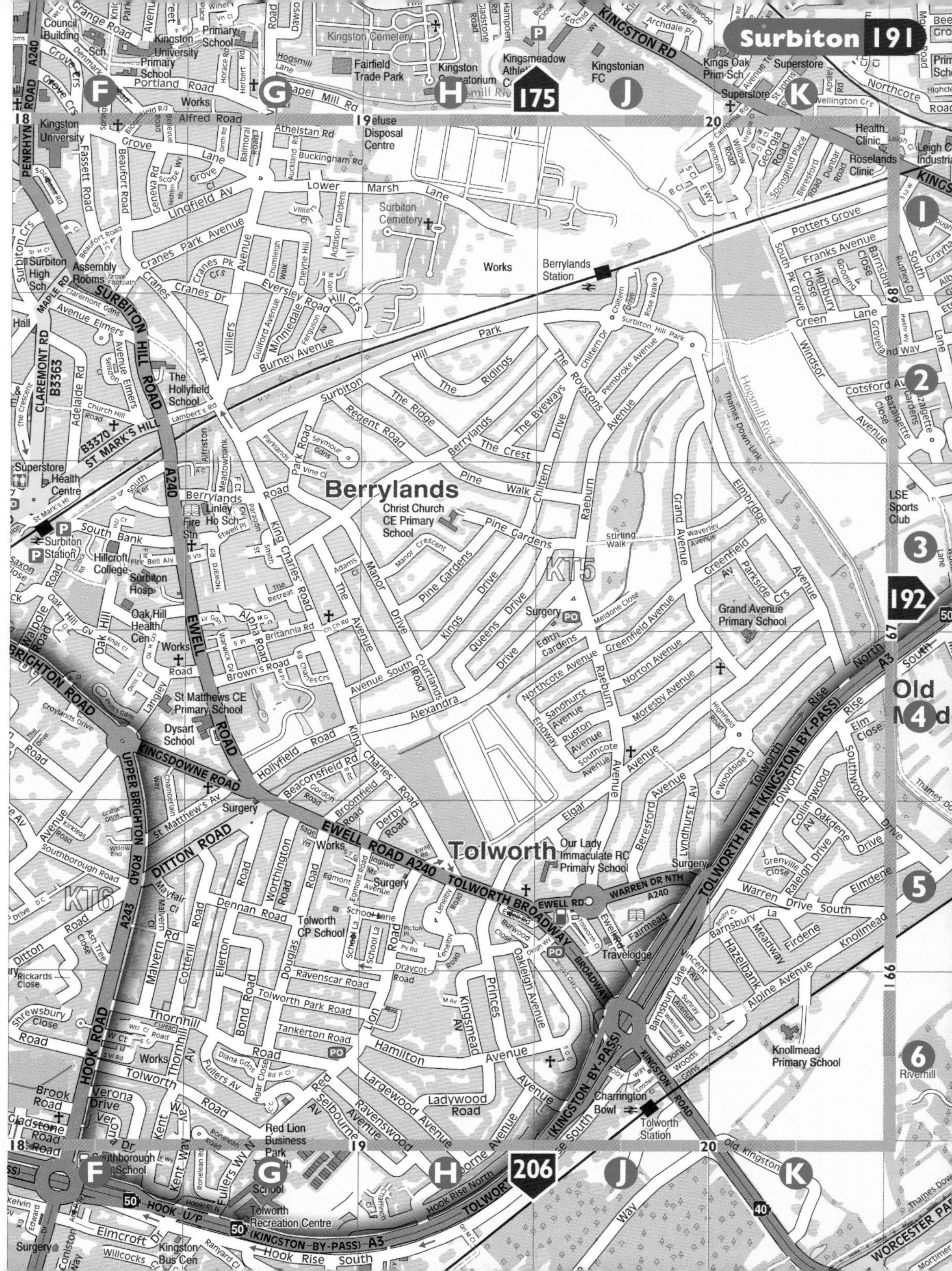
Surbiton
191
Berrylands
Tolworth
KT5
KT6
175
192
206
F
G
H
J
K
1
2
3
4
5
6
18
19
20
Kingston Cemetery
Fairfield Trade Park
Kingston Crematorium
Kingsmeadow Athletics Centre
Kingstonian FC
Kings Oak Prim Sch
Superstore
KINGSTON RD
Northcote Road
Kingston University
Council Building
Kingston University Primary School
Portland Road
Alfred Road
Refuse Disposal Centre
Athelstan Rd
Buckingham Rd
Lower Marsh Lane
Surbiton Cemetery
Works
Berrylands Station
Health Clinic
Roselands Clinic
Leigh Cl Industrial
Potters Grove
Franks Avenue
Green Lane
Windsor Avenue
Hogsmill River
Thames Down Link
LSE Sports Club
Surbiton High Sch
Assembly Rooms
Cranes Park Avenue
Eversley Road
Burney Avenue
Surbiton Hill Park
The Ridings
The Ridge
The Crest
The Byeways
The Roystons
Pembroke Avenue
Regent Road
Pine Walk
Chiltern Drive
Raeburn Avenue
Grand Avenue
Elmbridge Avenue
Christ Church CE Primary School
Pine Gardens
Manor Drive
Kings Drive
Queens Drive
Greenfield Avenue
Grand Avenue Primary School
Norton Avenue
Moresby Avenue
Northcote Avenue
Alexandra Drive
Surgery
SURBITON HILL ROAD
A240
EWELL ROAD
The Hollyfield School
ST MARK'S HILL
B3370
Surbiton Station
Hillcroft College
Surbiton Hosp
Oak Hill Health Cen
St Matthews CE Primary School
Dysart School
BRIGHTON ROAD
UPPER BRIGHTON ROAD
KINGSDOWNE ROAD
DITTON ROAD
Hollyfield Road
King Charles' Road
EWELL ROAD A240
TOLWORTH BROADWAY
Our Lady Immaculate RC Primary School
WARREN DR NTH
TOLWORTH RI N (KINGSTON BY-PASS)
Tolworth Rise
Old Malden
Collingwood Av
Oakdene Drive
Raleigh Drive
Warren Drive South
Elmdene
Knollmead
Alpine Avenue
Knollmead Primary School
Riverhill
Travelodge
Fairmead
Tolworth CP School
Dennan Road
Ravenscar Road
Tolworth Park Road
Tankerton Road
Hamilton Avenue
Largewood Avenue
Ladywood Road
Ravenswood Avenue
Selbourne Avenue
Charrington Bowl
Tolworth Station
KINGSTON BY-PASS
KINGSTON ROAD
HOOK ROAD
A243
Ditton Road
Shrewsbury Close
Thornhill Road
Tolworth Road
Verona Drive
Brook Road
Red Lion Business Park
Southborough School
Tolworth Recreation Centre
HOOK U/P
(KINGSTON BY-PASS) A3
Hook Rise North
Hook Rise South
Kingston Bus Cen
Elmcroft Dr
Willcocks Cl
WORCESTER PARK

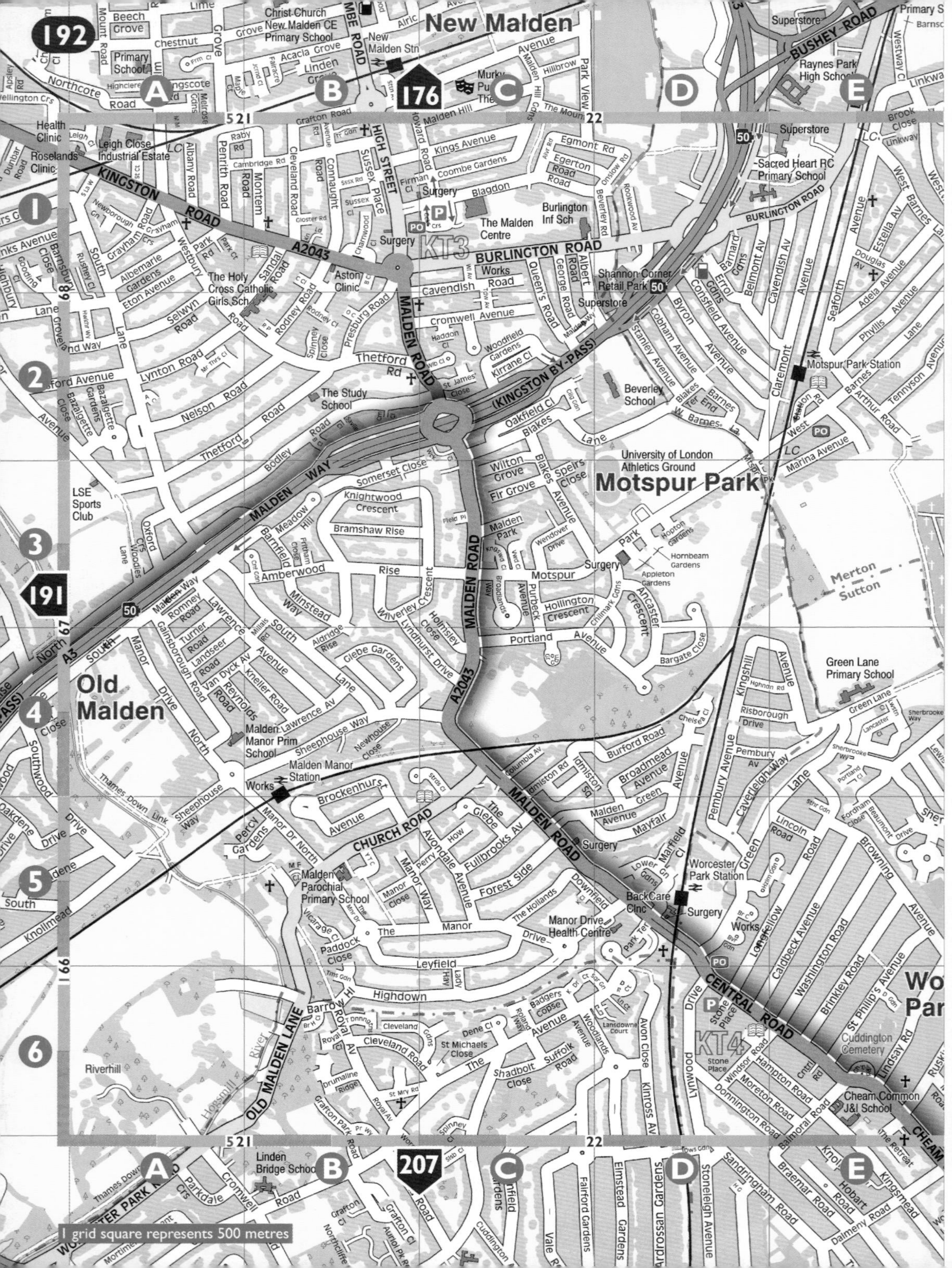
192
176
191
207
New Malden
Motspur Park
Old Malden
KT3
KT4
A
B
C
D
E
1
2
3
4
5
6
521
22
68
67
66
Christ Church New Malden CE Primary School
New Malden Stn
Primary School
Health Clinic
Roselands Clinic
Leigh Close Industrial Estate
KINGSTON ROAD
A2043
HIGH STREET
MALDEN ROAD
BURLINGTON ROAD
The Malden Centre
Burlington Inf Sch
Aston Clinic
The Holy Cross Catholic Girls Sch
Surgery
Superstore
Shannon Corner Retail Park
Raynes Park High School
BUSHEY ROAD
Sacred Heart RC Primary School
KINGSTON BY-PASS
MALDEN WAY
A3
The Study School
Beverley School
University of London Athletics Ground
Motspur Park Station
LSE Sports Club
Malden Manor Prim School
Malden Manor Station
CHURCH ROAD
Malden Parochial Primary School
Manor Drive Health Centre
Worcester Park Station
BackCare Clnc
CENTRAL ROAD
Green Lane Primary School
Cuddington Cemetery
Cheam Common J&I School
Merton
Sutton
OLD MALDEN LANE
Riverhill
Hogsmill River
Linden Bridge School
1 grid square represents 500 metres

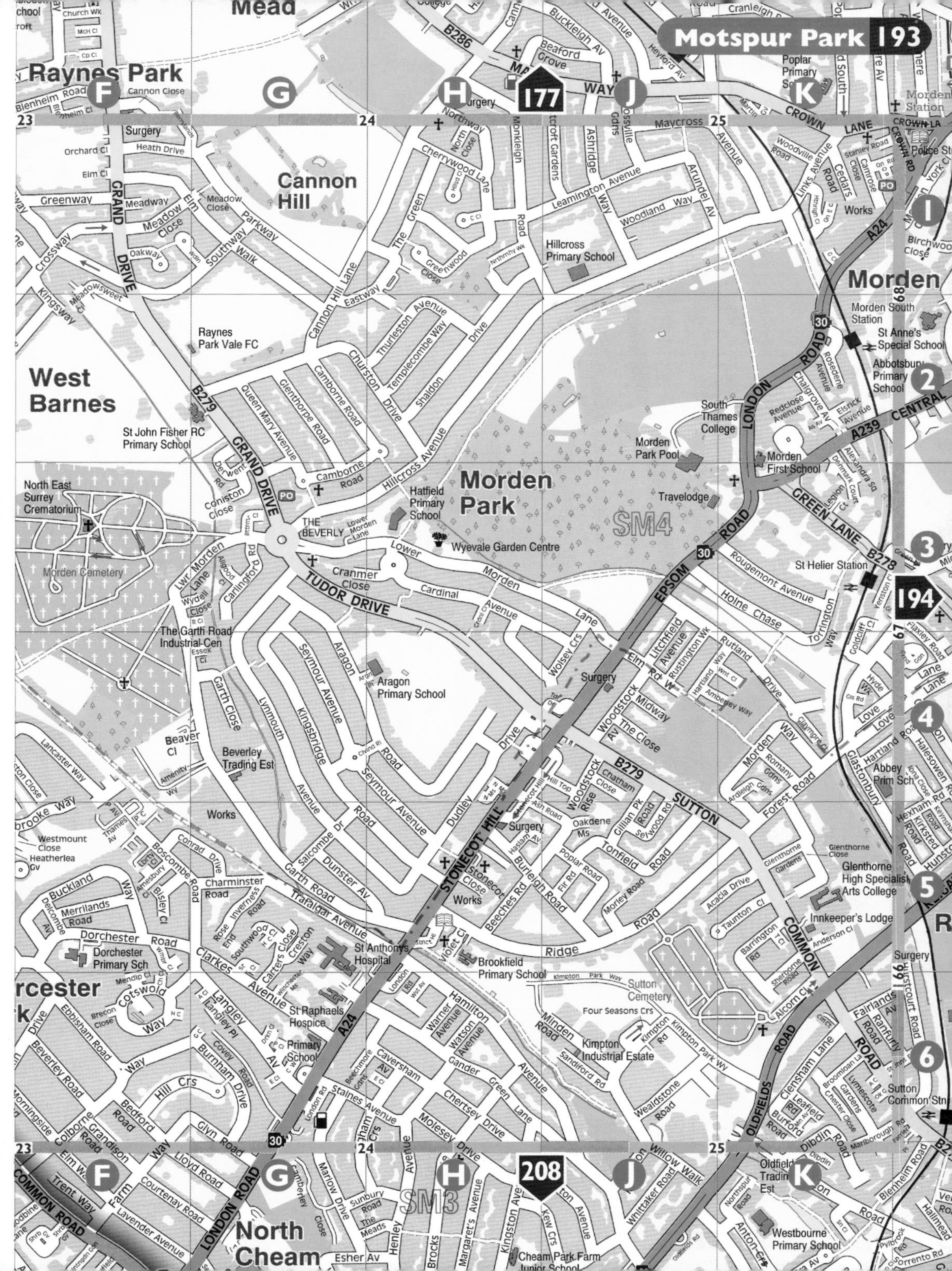
Raynes Park
Cannon Hill
West Barnes
Morden
Morden Park
North Cheam
SM4
SM3
Morden Cemetery
North East Surrey Crematorium
Raynes Park Vale FC
St John Fisher RC Primary School
Hillcross Primary School
Hatfield Primary School
Wyevale Garden Centre
South Thames College
Morden Park Pool
Travelodge
Morden South Station
St Anne's Special School
Abbotsbury Primary School
Morden First School
St Helier Station
Aragon Primary School
The Garth Road Industrial Cen
Beverley Trading Est
Abbey Prim Sch
Glenthorne High Specialist Arts College
Innkeeper's Lodge
Brookfield Primary School
St Anthony's Hospital
St Raphaels Hospice
Dorchester Primary Sch
Sutton Cemetery
Kimpton Industrial Estate
Sutton Common Stn
Oldfield Trading Est
Westbourne Primary School
Cheam Park Farm Junior School
Grand Drive
Tudor Drive
London Road
Epsom Road
Stonecot Hill
Sutton Common Road
Green Lane
Crown Lane
Central Road
Lower Morden Lane
Hillcross Avenue
Ridge Road
Oldfields Road
177
194
208
A24
A239
B278
B279
B286

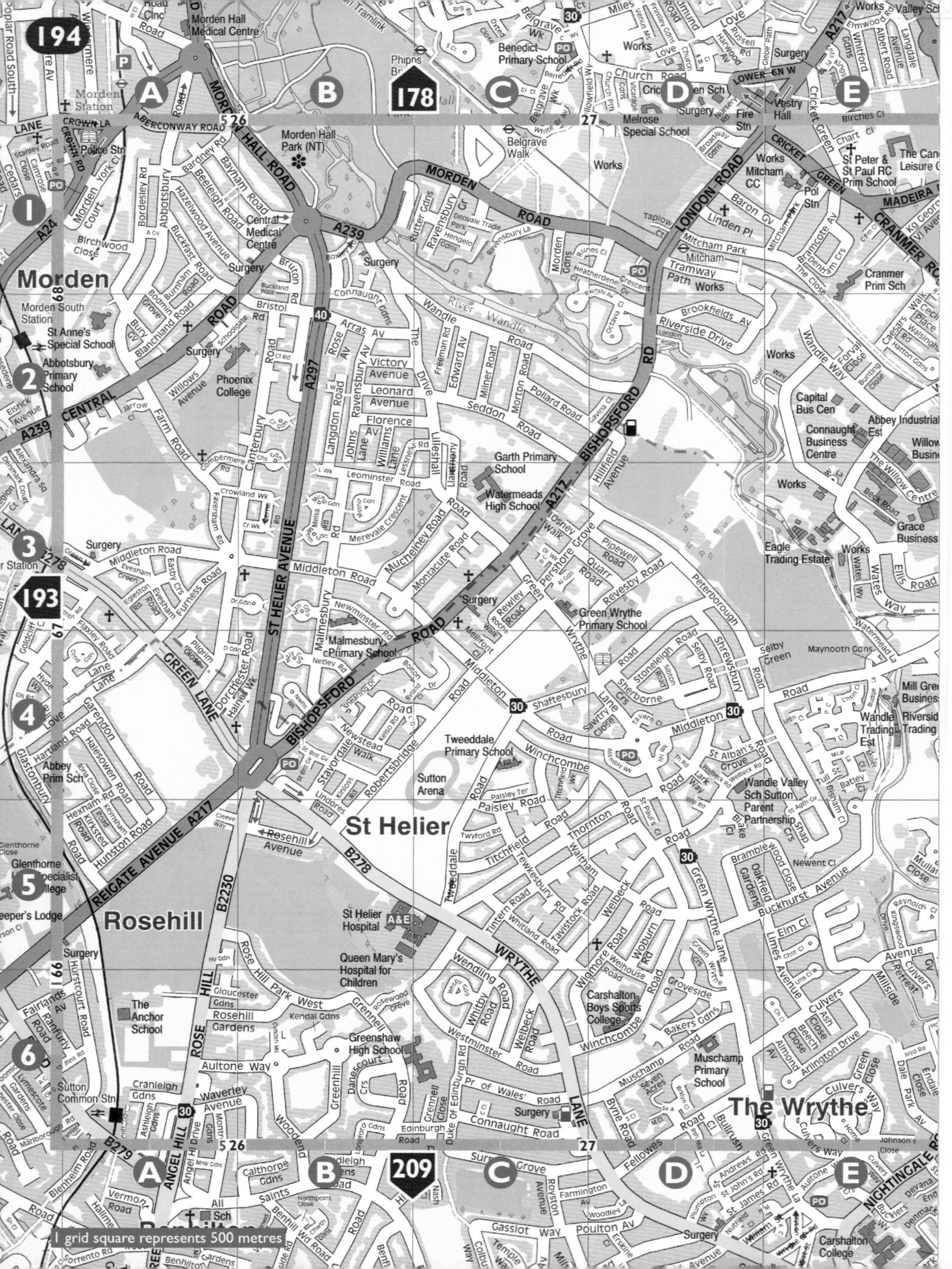
194
178
193
209
A
B
C
D
E
1
2
3
4
5
6
526
27
Morden
St Helier
Rosehill
The Wrythe
Morden Station
Morden South Station
Morden Hall Medical Centre
Morden Hall Park (NT)
Police Stn
Central Medical Centre
Surgery
St Anne's Special School
Abbotsbury Primary School
Phoenix College
Benedict Primary School
Melrose Special School
Belgrave Walk
Mitcham CC
St Peter & St Paul RC Prim School
Pol Stn
Cranmer Prim Sch
Vestry Hall
Fire Stn
Works
Capital Bus Cen
Abbey Industrial Est
Connaught Business Centre
Eagle Trading Estate
Garth Primary School
Watermeads High School
Green Wrythe Primary School
Malmesbury Primary School
Tweeddale Primary School
Sutton Arena
Wandle Valley Sch Sutton Parent Partnership
Wandle Trading Est
Abbey Prim Sch
Glenthorne Specialist College
St Helier Hospital
A&E
Queen Mary's Hospital for Children
The Anchor School
Greenshaw High School
Carshalton Boys Sports College
Muschamp Primary School
Carshalton College
Sutton Common Stn
MORDEN HALL ROAD
MORDEN ROAD
LONDON ROAD
BISHOPSFORD ROAD
ST HELIER AVENUE
CENTRAL ROAD
REIGATE AVENUE
GREEN LANE
WRYTHE LANE
ROSE HILL
ANGEL HILL
CRICKET GREEN
CRANMER ROAD
MADEIRA ROAD
LOWER GN W
A239
A297
A217
A24
B278
B279
B2230
River Wandle
Middleton Road
Tramway Path
Tramlink
1 grid square represents 500 metres

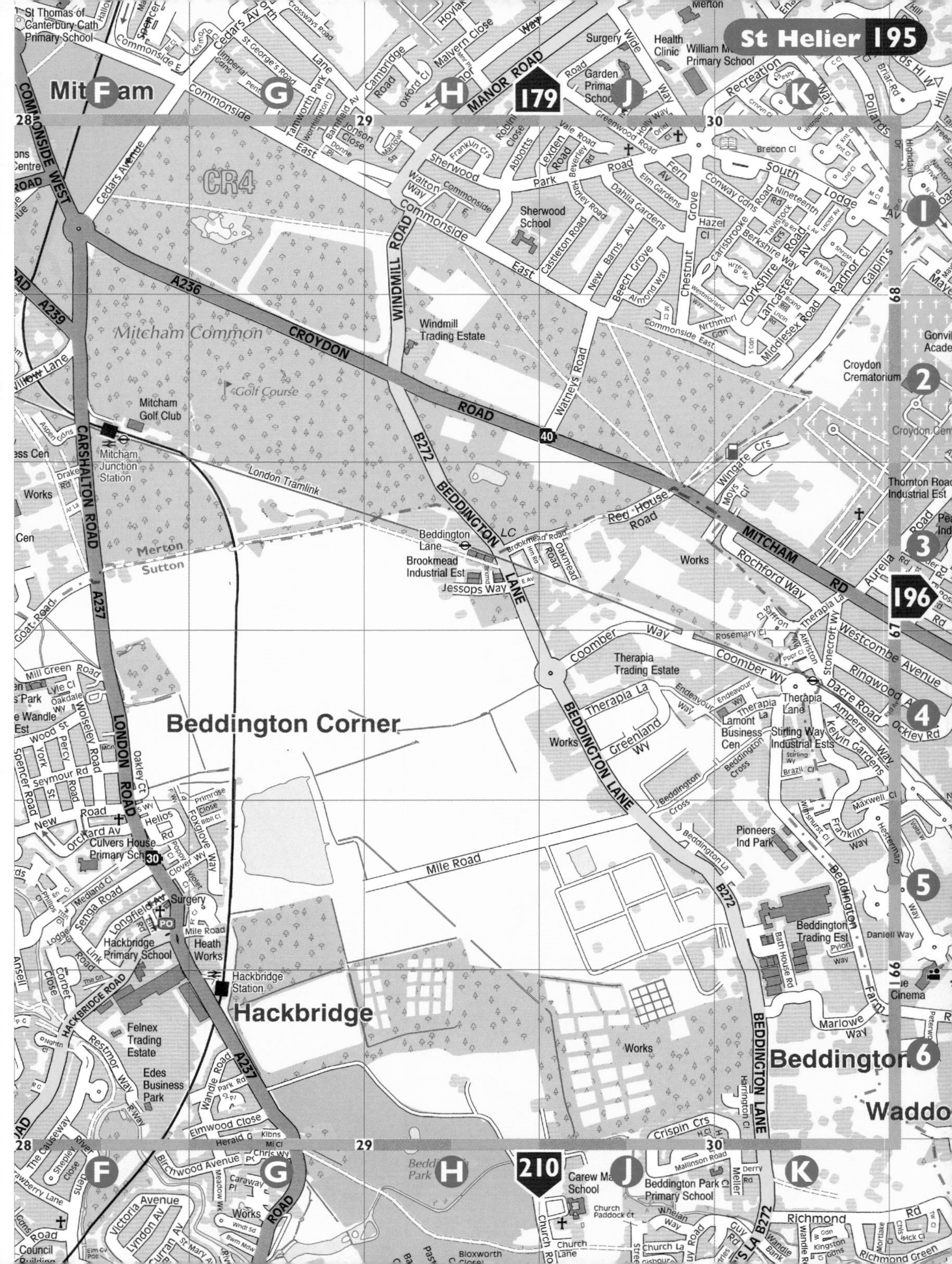
Mitcham
Mitcham Common
Golf Course
Mitcham Golf Club
Mitcham Junction Station
London Tramlink
Windmill Trading Estate
Sherwood School
Croydon Crematorium
Thornton Road Industrial Est
Beddington Lane
Brookmead Industrial Est
Therapia Trading Estate
Therapia Lane
Lamont Business Cen
Stirling Way Industrial Ests
Pioneers Ind Park
Beddington Trading Est
Beddington Corner
Hackbridge
Hackbridge Station
Hackbridge Primary School
Culvers House Primary Sch
Felnex Trading Estate
Edes Business Park
Beddington
Beddington Park Primary School
CROYDON ROAD
MITCHAM RD
CARSHALTON ROAD
LONDON ROAD
BEDDINGTON LANE
WINDMILL ROAD
HACKBRIDGE ROAD
Mile Road
Merton
Sutton
Works
179
196
210

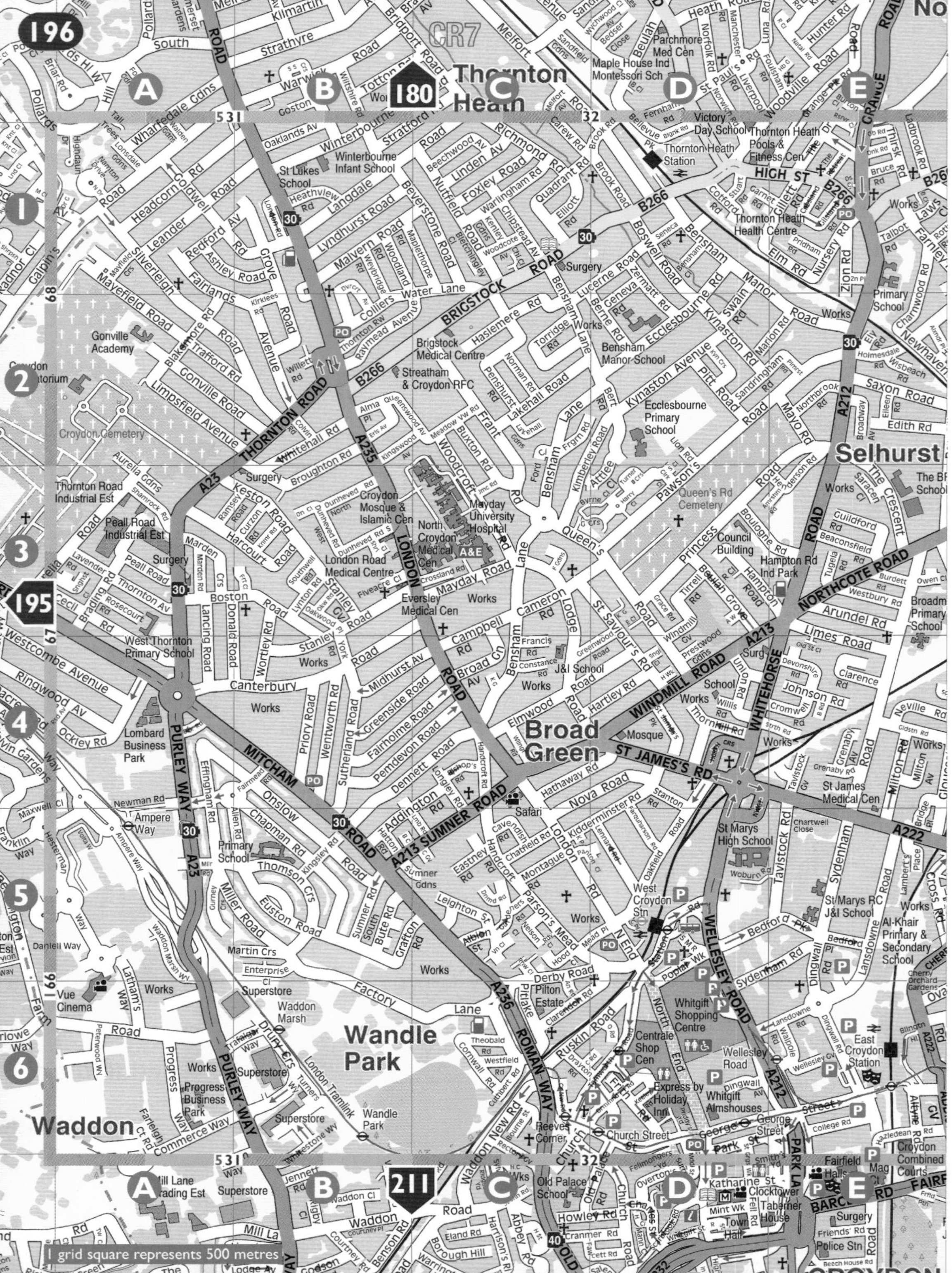
196
180
195
211
A
B
C
D
E
1
2
3
4
5
6
CR7
Thornton Heath
Thornton Heath Station
Thornton Heath Pools & Fitness Cen
Thornton Heath Health Centre
Victory Day School
Parchmore Med Cen
Maple House Ind Montessori Sch
HIGH ST
B266
BRIGSTOCK ROAD
THORNTON ROAD
A23
A235
LONDON ROAD
Winterbourne Infant School
St Lukes School
Gonville Academy
Croydon Crematorium
Croydon Cemetery
Brigstock Medical Centre
Streatham & Croydon RFC
Bensham Manor School
Ecclesbourne Primary School
Selhurst
Queen's Rd Cemetery
Council Building
Hampton Rd Ind Park
NORTHCOTE ROAD
WHITEHORSE ROAD
A212
Thornton Road Industrial Est
Peall Road Industrial Est
Croydon Mosque & Islamic Cen
Mayday University Hospital
North Croydon Medical Cen
London Road Medical Centre
Eversley Medical Cen
West Thornton Primary School
Lombard Business Park
Broad Green
WINDMILL ROAD
A213
ST JAMES'S RD
St James Medical Cen
A222
St Marys High School
MITCHAM ROAD
PURLEY WAY
A213 SUMNER ROAD
Safari
J&I School
Mosque
Ampere Way
Primary School
West Croydon Stn
St Marys RC J&I School
Al-Khair Primary & Secondary School
Whitgift Shopping Centre
WELLESLEY ROAD
Wellesley Road
Centrale Shop Cen
Express by Holiday Inn
Whitgift Almshouses
East Croydon Station
Vue Cinema
Superstore
Waddon Marsh
Wandle Park
Progress Business Park
Waddon
ROMAN WAY
A236
Reeves Corner
Church Street
George Street
Old Palace School
Katharine St
Clocktower
Taberner House
Town Hall
Fairfield Halls
Croydon Combined Courts
Police Stn
Mill Lane Trading Est
1 grid square represents 500 metres
CROYDON

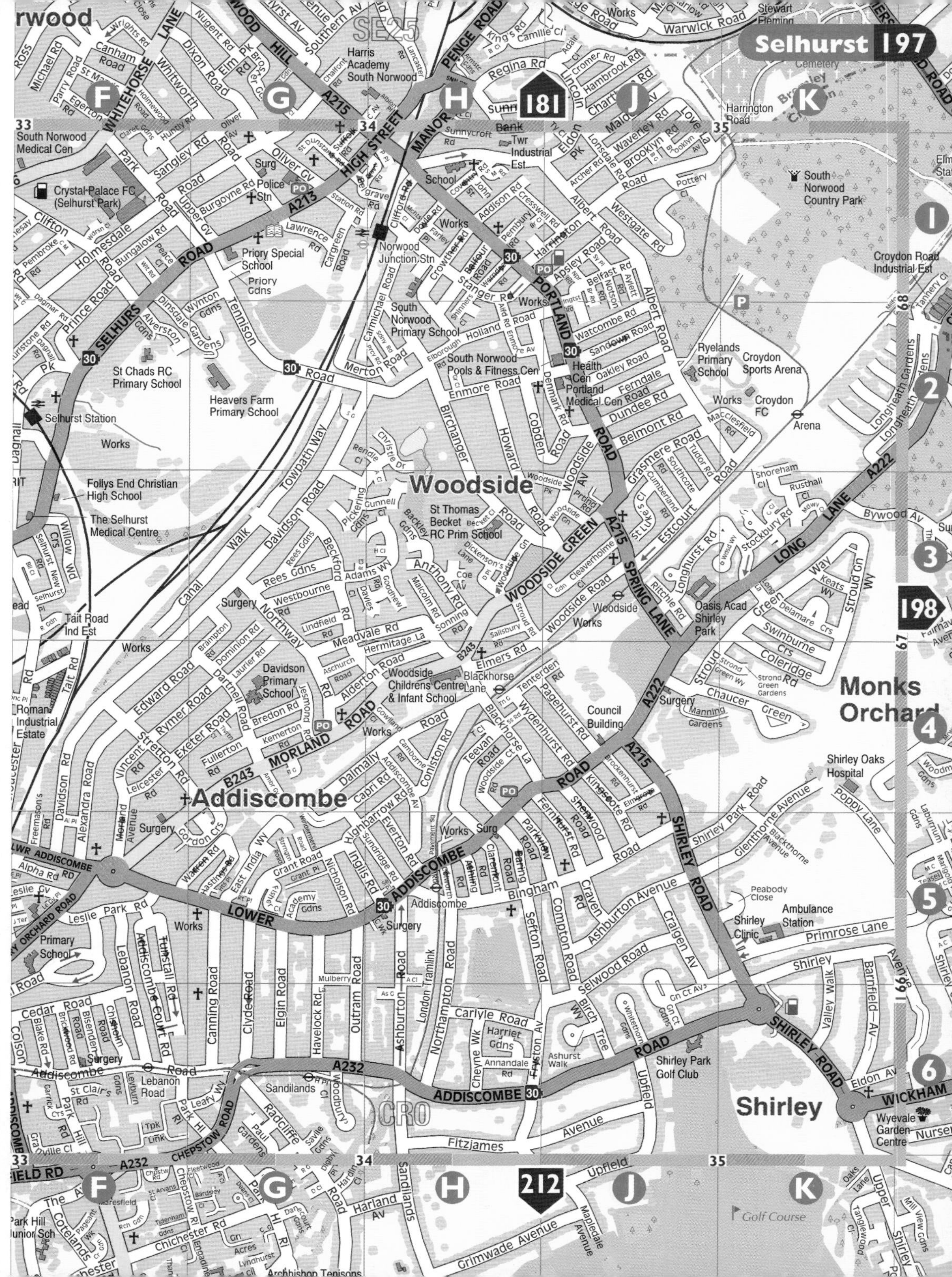

Selhurst 197
181
198
212
SE25
CR0
Woodside
Addiscombe
Shirley
Monks Orchard
South Norwood Medical Cen
Crystal Palace FC (Selhurst Park)
Harris Academy South Norwood
Police Stn
Priory Special School
Priory Gdns
Norwood Junction Stn
South Norwood Primary School
South Norwood Pools & Fitness Cen
Health Cen
Portland Medical Cen
St Chads RC Primary School
Heavers Farm Primary School
Selhurst Station
Follys End Christian High School
The Selhurst Medical Centre
Tait Road Ind Est
Roman Industrial Estate
St Thomas Becket RC Prim School
Davidson Primary School
Woodside Childrens Centre & Infant School
Blackhorse Lane
Council Building
Oasis Acad Shirley Park
South Norwood Country Park
Croydon Road Industrial Est
Ryelands Primary School
Croydon Sports Arena
Croydon FC
Arena
Shirley Oaks Hospital
Peabody Close
Ambulance Station
Shirley Clinic
Shirley Park Golf Club
Wyevale Garden Centre
Harrington Road
Golf Course
Sandilands
Lebanon Road
Primary School
Park Hill Junior Sch
Archbishop Tenisons
Stewart Fleming
Cemetery
SELHURST ROAD
HIGH STREET
PENGE ROAD
PORTLAND ROAD
WOODSIDE GREEN
SPRING LANE
LONG LANE
SHIRLEY ROAD
LOWER ADDISCOMBE ROAD
ADDISCOMBE ROAD
MORLAND ROAD
CHEPSTOW ROAD
WICKHAM
A215
A213
A222
A232
B243
F
G
H
J
K
1
2
3
4
5
6
33
34
35
66
67
68

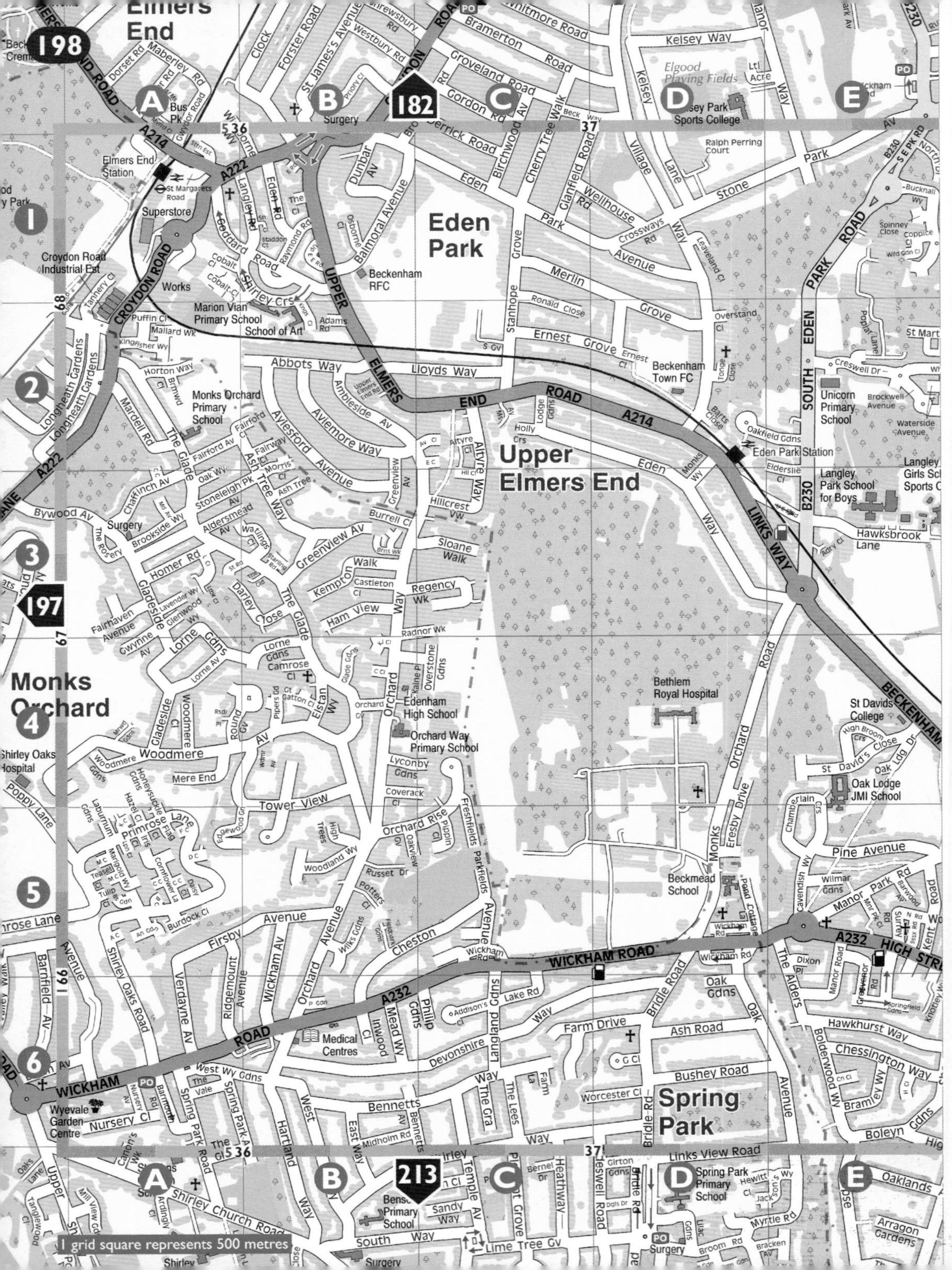

198
182
197
213
Elmers End
A
B
C
D
E
1
2
3
4
5
6
36
37
68
67
66
Maberley Rd
Dorset Rd
Bus Pk
Clock
Forster Road
St James's Avenue
Westbury Rd
Shrewsbury Rd
Bramerton
Road
Whitmore Road
Groveland Road
Gordon Rd
Kelsey Way
Elgood Playing Fields
Ltl Acre
Kelsey Park Sports College
Ralph Perring Court
Surgery
Derrick Road
Birchwood Av
Cherry Tree Walk
Glanfield Road
Village
Lane
Park
Stone
Way
A214
A222
Elmers End Station
St Margarets Road
Superstore
Langley Rd
Eden Rd
Dunbar Av
Balmoral Avenue
Osborne Cl
Eden Park
Wellhouse Rd
Crossways Rd
Avenue
Leaveland Cl
Beckenham RFC
Croydon Road Industrial Est
CROYDON ROAD
Goddard Road
Raymond Rd
Staddon Cl
Cobalt Cl
Shirley Crs
Works
Marion Vian Primary School
School of Art
Adams Rd
UPPER
ELMERS
END
ROAD
Merlin
Grove
Ronald Close
Stanhope Grove
Ernest Grove
Ernest Cl
Overstand Cl
Beckenham Town FC
Tonge Close
Tannery Cl
Puffin Cl
Mallard Wk
Kingfisher Wy
Abbots Way
Lloyds Way
Upper Elmers End Rd
Horton Way
Longheath Gardens
Mardell Rd
Monks Orchard Primary School
Fairford Av
Fairford Cl
Fairway Cl
Aylesford Avenue
Ambleside Av
Aviemore Way
Altyre Way
Holly Crs
Lodge Gdns
Upper Elmers End
Eden
Monks Wy
Barts Close
Oakfield Gdns
Eden Park Station
Eldersile Cl
SOUTH EDEN PARK ROAD
B230
Bucknall Wy
Spinney Close
Coppice
Wild Gdn Cl
Creswell Dr
Unicorn Primary School
Brockwell Avenue
Waterside Avenue
Langley Park School for Boys
Langley Girls School
Hawksbrook Lane
LINKS WAY
A222
The Glade
Oak Wy
Chaffinch Av
Stoneleigh Pk Av
Ash Tree Way
Morris Cl
Greenview Av
Burrell Cl
Hillcrest Vw
Sloane Walk
Bywood Av
Surgery
Brookside Wy
Aldersmead Av
Watlings Cl
Greenview Av
Homer Rd
Kempton Walk
Castleton Cl
Regency Wk
Darley Close
Gladeside
Lavender Wy
Glenwood Wy
Ham View
Fairhaven Avenue
Gwynne Av
Lorne Gdns
Radnor Wk
Overstone Gdns
Camrose Cl
Glade Gdns
Orchard Way
Monks Orchard
Woodmere Cl
Pipers Gdns
Gatton Cl
Elstan Wy
Edenham High School
Orchard Way Primary School
Bethlem Royal Hospital
Orchard Road
Monks Orchard Road
St Davids College
High Broom Crs
St David's Close
Oak Lodge JMI School
Oak Lodge Dr
BECKENHAM
Shirley Oaks Hospital
Woodmere
Woodmere Gdns
Round Gv
Mere End
Lyconby Gdns
Coverack Cl
Poppy Lane
Laburnum Gdns
Honeysuckle Gdns
Primrose Lane
Tower View
Orchard Rise
Pippin Cl
Freshfields
High Trees
Woodland Wy
Oakview Gv
Eresby Drive
Chamberlain Crs
Pine Avenue
Teasel Cl
Tulip Cl
Daisy
Burdock Cl
Russet Dr
Potters Cl
Parkfields
Avenue
Beckmead School
Cavendish Wy
Wilmar Gdns
Manor Park Rd
Barnfield Av
Firsby Avenue
Shirley Oaks Road
Verdayne Av
Ridgemount Avenue
Wickham Av
Orchard Avenue
Wilks Gdns
Cheston
Wickham Rd
WICKHAM ROAD
Bridle Road
Oak Gdns
Oak Avenue
The Alders
Dixon Pl
Manor Road
A232
HIGH STREET
Kent Road
Springfield Gdns
Mead Wy
Philip Gdns
Inwood
Addison's Cl
Lake Rd
Langland Gdns
Devonshire Way
Farm Drive
Ash Road
Hawkhurst Way
Bolderwood Wy
Chessington Way
Medical Centres
ROAD
WICKHAM
Wyevale Garden Centre
Nursery Cl
The Vale
West Wy Gdns
Spring Park Road
Bennetts Way
The Glade
The Lees
Farm La
Bushey Road
Worcester Cl
Spring Park
Bramley Way
Boleyn Gdns
Hartland Way
West Way
East Way
Midholm Rd
Links View Road
Shirley Church Road
Ardingly Cl
Upper Shirley Road
Tanglewood Cl
Bensham Primary School
Sandy Way
Temple Av
Lime Tree Gv
South Way
Heathway
Girton Gdns
Bridle Rd
Spring Park Primary School
Hewitts Rd
Jackson's Wy
Myrtle Rd
Bracken Av
Oaklands
Arragon Gardens
Broom Rd
Surgery
1 grid square represents 500 metres

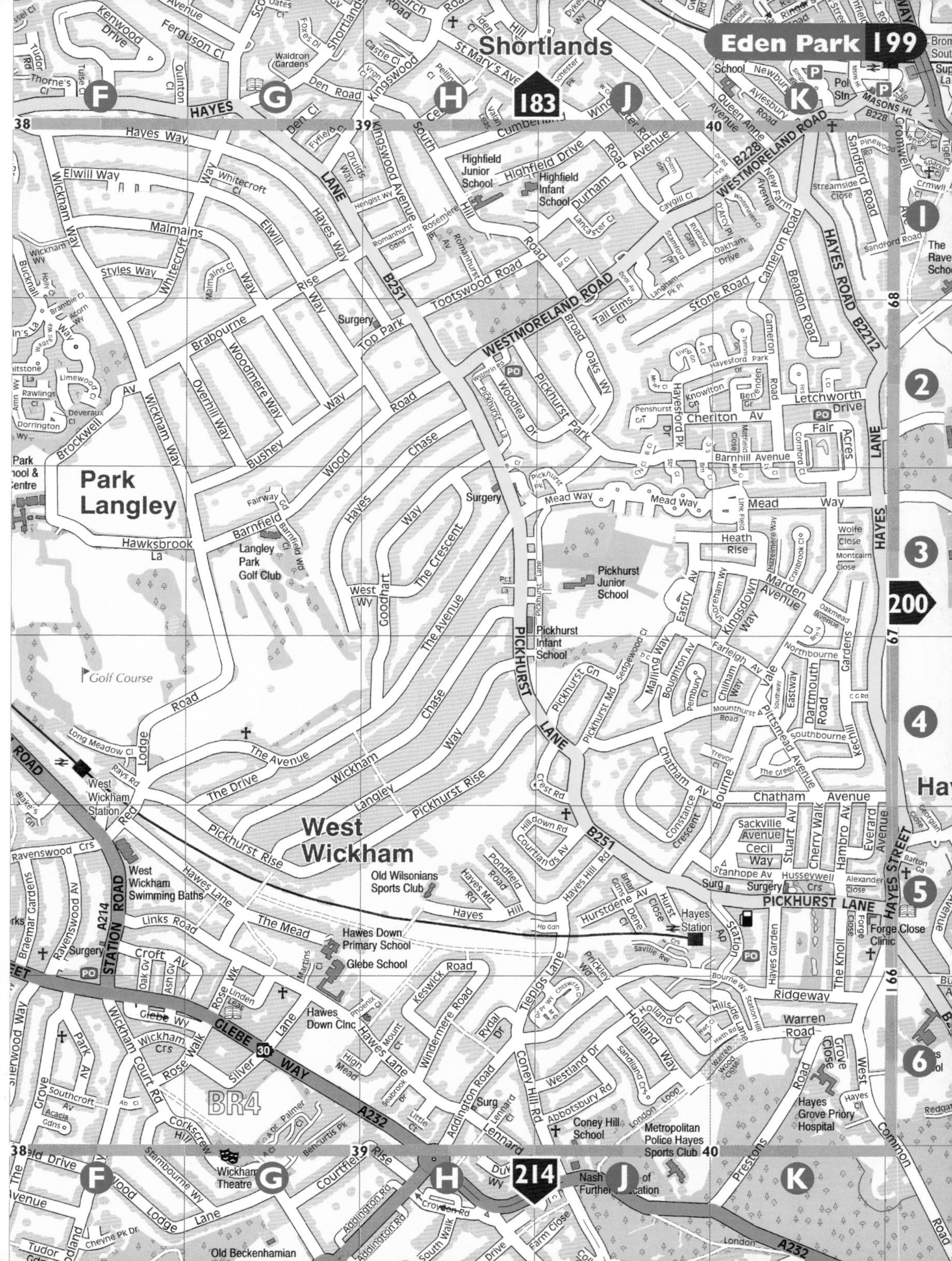
Shortlands
183
Park Langley
West Wickham
Langley Park Golf Club
Golf Course
Pickhurst Junior School
Pickhurst Infant School
Highfield Junior School
Highfield Infant School
West Wickham Station
West Wickham Swimming Baths
Old Wilsonians Sports Club
Hawes Down Primary School
Glebe School
Hayes Station
Coney Hill School
Metropolitan Police Hayes Sports Club
Hayes Grove Priory Hospital
Wickham Theatre
BR4
WESTMORELAND ROAD
HAYES ROAD
PICKHURST LANE
HAYES STREET
GLEBE WAY
STATION ROAD
200
214
F
G
H
J
K
2
3
4
5
6
38
39
40
66
67
68

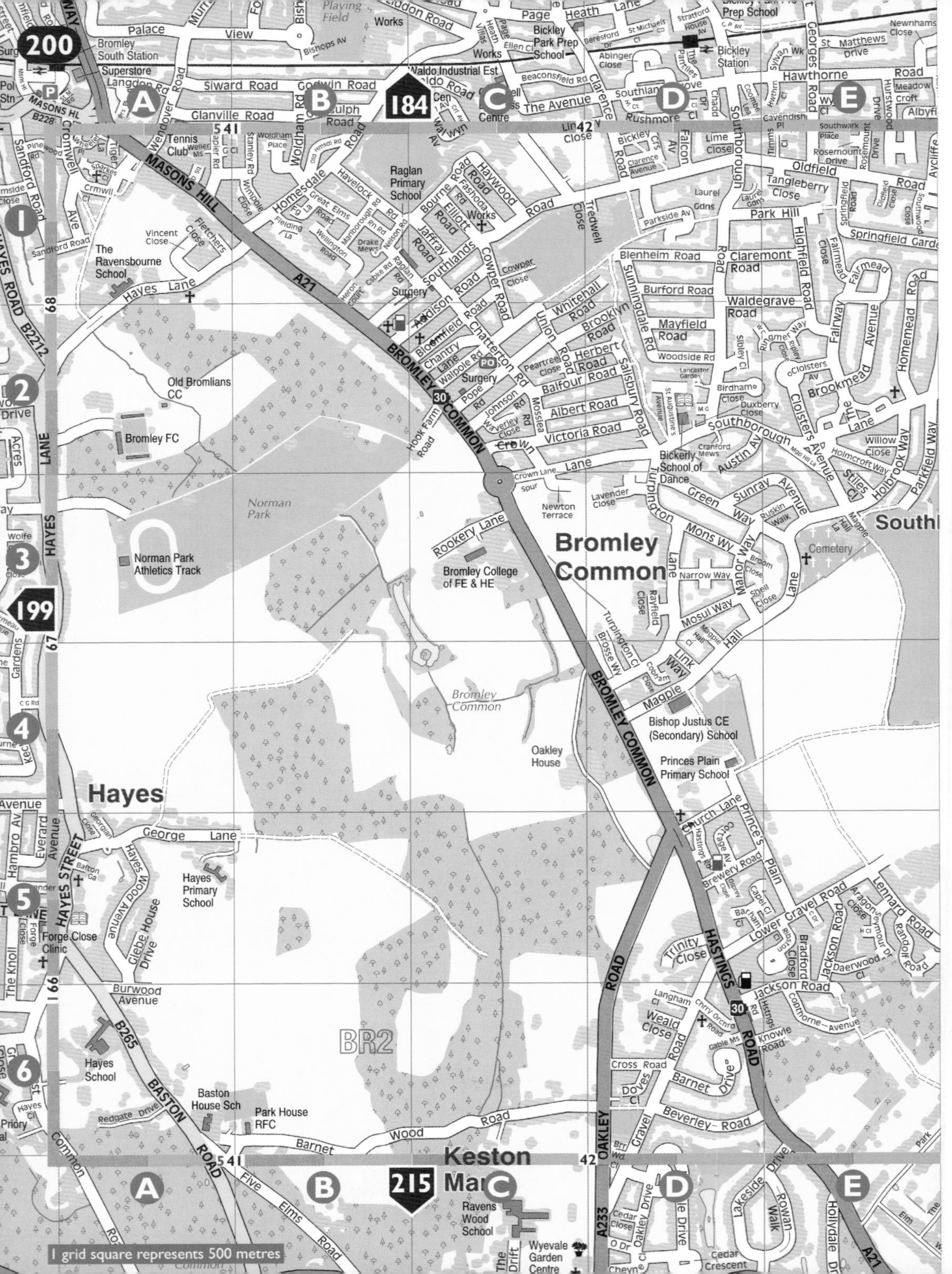

200
184
199
215
Bromley South Station
Superstore
Palace View
Siward Road
Godwin Road
Glanville Road
Langdon Rd
Wendover Road
Masons Hill
MASONS HL
B228
Waldo Industrial Est
Waldo Road
Works
Playing Field
Bishops Av
Page Heath Lane
Bickley Park Prep School
Stratford House Av
Bickley Station
St Michaels Cl
Beresford Dr
Abinger Close
Beaconsfield Rd
The Avenue
Clarence Road
Southlands Grove
Rushmore Cl
St Matthews Drive
Newnhams Close
Hawthorne Road
Meadow Croft
Albyfield
Sylvan Wk
St Georges Road
Southborough Lane
Cavendish Pl
Southwark Place
Rosemount Drive
Tangleberry Close
Oldfield Road
Park Hill
Springfield Gardens
Laurel Gdns
Lime Close
Bickley Crs
Clarence Avenue
Falcon Av
Tredwell Close
Parkside Av
Tennis Club
Woldham Place
Woldham Road
Stanley Rd
Homesdale Road
Havelock Rd
Great Elms Road
Marlborough Rd
Wellington Road
Fielding La
Drake Mews
Nelson Rd
Raglan Primary School
Raglan Rd
Jaffray Road
Elliott Road
Bourne Road
Fashoda Rd
Haywood Road
Southlands Road
Cowper Road
Cowper Close
Addison Road
Bloomfield Road
Chatterton Rd
Whitehall Road
Brooklyn Road
Union Road
Herbert Road
Balfour Road
Albert Road
Victoria Road
Salisbury Road
Sunningdale Rd
Blenheim Road
Claremont Road
Burford Road
Waldegrave Road
Mayfield Road
Woodside Rd
Highfield Road
Fairmead
Fairway
Homemead Road
Brookmead
Cloisters Av
Cloisters Avenue
Ringmer Way
Ripley Close
The Lane
Willow Close
Holmcroft Way
Holbrook Way
Parkfield Way
Stiles Cl
Sibley Cl
Lancaster Gardens
Birdham Close
Duxberry Close
St Augustines Avenue
Cranford Mews
Austin Av
Southborough
Bickerly School of Dance
Green Way
Sunray Avenue
Ruskin Walk
Mons Wy
Narrow Way
Manor Way
Broom Close
Shell Close
Mosul Way
Magpie Hall Lane
Link Way
Cobram Close
Turpington Cl
Brosse Wy
Rayfield Close
Turpington Lane
Lavender Close
Newton Terrace
Crown Lane
Crown Lane Spur
Cemetery
Southborough
Vincent Close
Fletchers Close
The Ravensbourne School
Hayes Lane
Sandford Road
Cromwell Ave
Surgery
Heron Court
Chantry Lane
Walpole Rd
Pope Rd
Johnson Rd
Waverley Close
Mosslea Rd
Peartree Close
Hook Farm Road
A21
BROMLEY COMMON
Old Bromlians CC
Bromley FC
Norman Park
Norman Park Athletics Track
Rookery Lane
Bromley College of FE & HE
Bromley Common
Magpie Hall
Bishop Justus CE (Secondary) School
Princes Plain Primary School
Oakley House
Church Lane
Prince's Plain
Cottage Av
Brewery Road
Hastings Rd
Capel Cl
Barham Cl
Lower Gravel Road
Lennard Road
Aragon Close
Randolph Road
Jackson Road
Bradford Close
Daerwood Cl
Trinity Close
Copthorne Avenue
Knowle Road
Gable Ms
Langham Cl
Weald Close
Chrry Orchrd Road
Barnet Drive
Cross Road
Doves Cl
Gravel Road
Beverley Road
HASTINGS ROAD
OAKLEY ROAD
A233
Hayes
HAYES ROAD
B2212
HAYES LANE
HAYES STREET
George Lane
Georgian Close
Hayes Wood Avenue
Glebe House Drive
Hayes Primary School
Bafton Ga
Forge Close
Forge Close Clinic
The Knoll
Hambro Av
Everard Avenue
Burwood Avenue
B265
Hayes School
BASTON ROAD
Baston House Sch
Park House RFC
Redgate Drive
Hayes Cl
Priory
Barnet Wood Road
BR2
Keston
Five Elms Road
Ravens Wood School
The Drift
Wyevale Garden Centre
Oakley Drive
Cedar Close
Cedar Crescent
Lakeside Drive
Rowan Walk
Hollydale Drive
Elm
Park
Common
Acres
Wolfe
Gardens
Avenue
541
42
68
67
66
A
B
C
D
E
1
2
3
4
5
6
30
1 grid square represents 500 metres

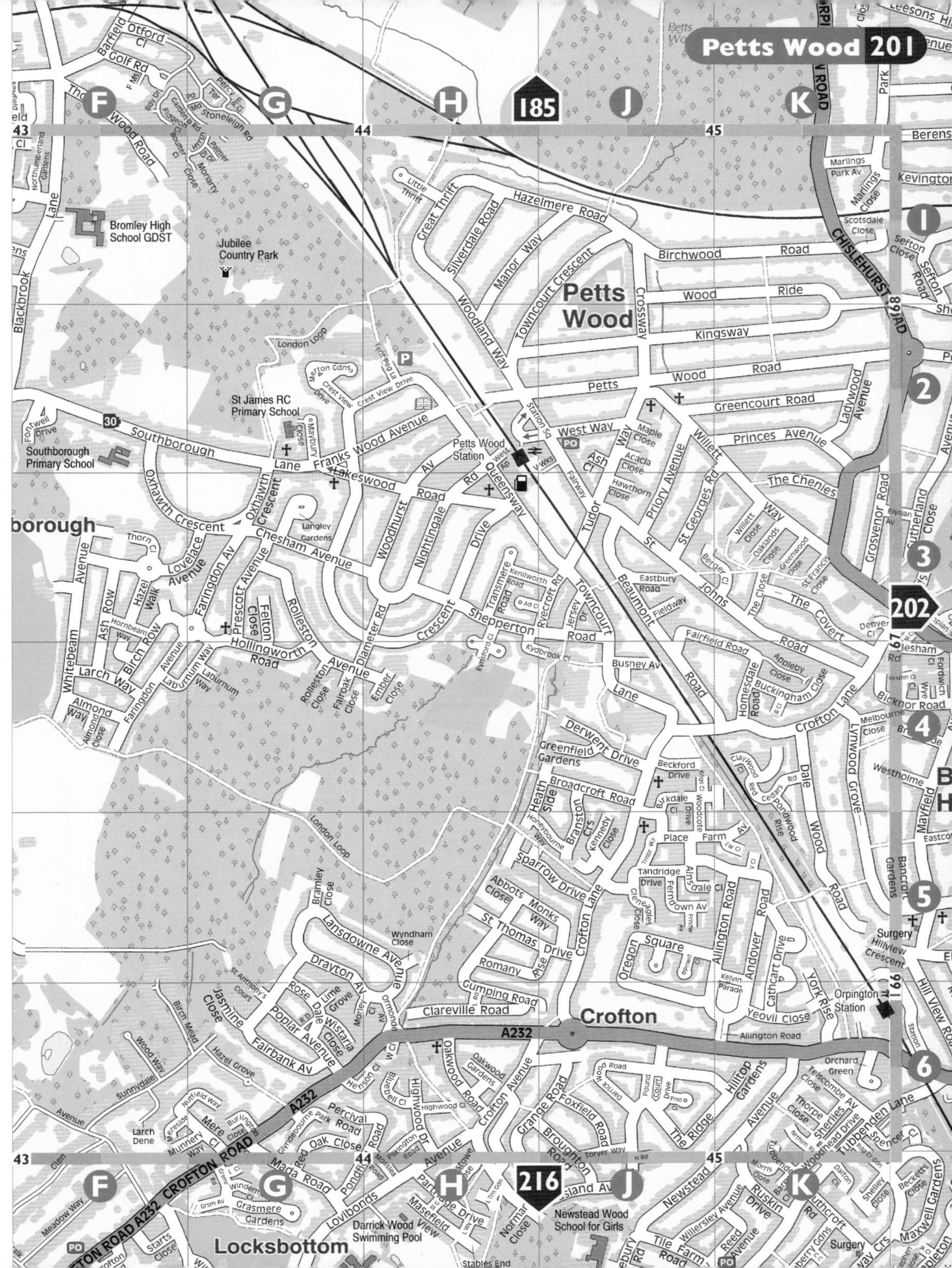
Petts Wood
Crofton
Locksbottom
Jubilee Country Park
Bromley High School GDST
St James RC Primary School
Southborough Primary School
Petts Wood Station
Orpington Station
Newstead Wood School for Girls
Darrick Wood Swimming Pool
Southborough Lane
Petts Wood Road
Birchwood Road
Hazelmere Road
Kingsway
Crofton Road
Crofton Lane
A232
185
202
216

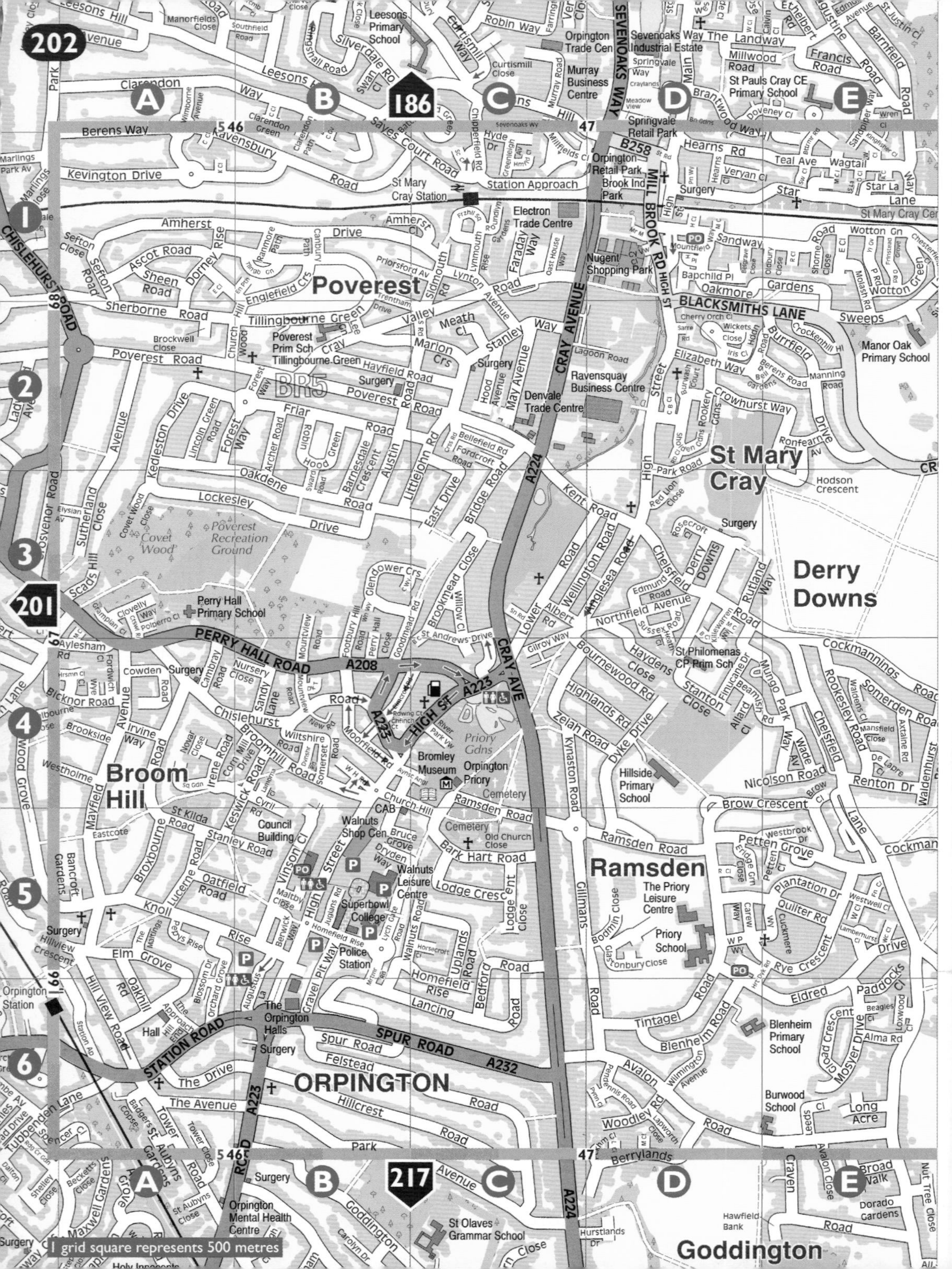
202
186
201
217
A
B
C
D
E
1
2
3
4
5
6
Leesons Hill
Manorfields Close
Southfield Road
Leesons Primary School
Silverdale Rd
Ringshall Road
Swan Cl
Curtismill Way
Curtismill Close
Robin Way
Orpington Trade Cen
Murray Business Centre
Murray Road
SEVENOAKS WAY
Sevenoaks Way The Industrial Estate
Springvale Way
Landway
Millwood Road
Francis Road
Barnfield Road
St Pauls Cray CE Primary School
Brantwood Way
Doveney Cl
Clarendon Way
Leesons Hill
Berens Way
Clarendon Green
Clarendon Path
Ravensbury Road
Sayes Court Road
Chipperfield Rd
Hyde Dr
Greenleigh Av
Millfields Cl
Springvale Retail Park
B258
Orpington Retail Park
Brook Ind Park
MILL BROOK RD
Hearns Rd
Veryan Cl
Teal Ave
Wagtail Way
Star La
Star Lane
Surgery
Marlings Park Av
Marlings Close
Kevington Drive
St Mary Cray Station
Station Approach
St Mary Cray Cer
CHISLEHURST ROAD
A208
Amherst Drive
Amherst Cl
Electron Trade Centre
Sefton Close
Sefton Road
Ascot Road
Sheen Road
Dorney Rise
Ranmore Path
Canbury Path
Priorsford Av
Sidmouth Rd
Lynmouth Rise
Faraday Way
Oast House Way
Nugent Shopping Park
HIGH ST
Sandway
Mountfield Way
Bapchild Pl
Oakmore Gardens
Wotton Gn
Wotton Green
Shorne Close
Poverest
Englefield Crs
Trentham Drive
Lynton Avenue
Sherborne Road
Tillingbourne Green
BLACKSMITHS LANE
Cherry Orch Cl
Wickets Close
Sweeps Lane
Crockenhill Rd
Burrfield Dr
Manor Oak Primary School
Brockwell Close
Poverest Prim Sch
Tillingbourne Green
Cray Valley Rd
Meath Cl
Marion Crs
Stanley Way
Lagoon Road
Poverest Road
Church Hill Wood
Forest Way
Hayfield Road
Surgery
BR5
CRAY AVENUE
Ravensquay Business Centre
Elizabeth Way
Berens Road
Manning Road
Crowhurst Way
Kedleston Drive
Lincoln Green Road
Friar Road
Archer Road
Robin Hood Green
Hood Avenue
May Avenue
Denvale Trade Centre
Rookery Gdns
Ronfearn Av
Barnesdale Crescent
Austin Road
Littlejohn Rd
Bellefield Rd
Fordcroft Road
A224
Park Road
St Mary Cray
Hodson Crescent
Oakdene Road
Lockesley Drive
East Drive
Bridge Road
Kent Road
Red Lion Close
Grosvenor Road
Sutherland Close
Elysian Av
Covet Wood Close
Poverest Recreation Ground
Covet Wood
Rosecroft Cl
Surgery
Derry Downs
Scads Hill
Glendower Crs
Brookmead Close
Willow Cl
Lower Road
Wellington Road
Anglesea Road
Chelsfield Road
Rutland Way
Clovelly Way
Perry Hall Primary School
Polperro Cl
Edmund Road
Northfield Avenue
Sussex Road
Killewarren Way
Aylesham Rd
Footbury Hill Road
Perry Hall Close
Goodmead Rd
St Andrews Drive
Albert Rd
Gilroy Way
PERRY HALL ROAD
A208
Bournewood Rd
Haydens Close
St Philomenas CP Prim Sch
Cockmannings Road
Cowden Road
Nursery Close
Sandy Lane
Mountview Road
Mountview
CRAY AVE
A223
HIGH ST
Highlands Rd
Stanton Close
Finucane Dr
Beamish Rd
Mungo Park Way
Somerden Road
Bicknor Road
Avenue
Chislehurst Road
Allard Cl
Rookesley Road
Brookside
Irvine Way
Wiltshire Road
Moorfield Rd
River Park Vw
Priory Gdns
Zelah Road
Dyke Drive
Mansfield Close
Axtaine Rd
Westholme
Wood Grove
Broom Hill
Broomhill Road
Somerset Road
Bromley Museum
Orpington Priory
Hillside Primary School
Wade Av
De Lapre Cl
Nicolson Road
Renton Dr
Waldenhurst Rd
Mayfield
Irene Road
Corn Mill Drive
Keswick Road
Cyril Rd
Church Hill
CAB
Cemetery
Ramsden Road
Brow Crescent
Brow Cl
Eastcote
St Kilda Road
Stanley Road
Council Building
Walnuts Shop Cen
Bruce Grove
Cemetery
Old Church Close
Kynaston Road
Ramsden Road
Westbrook Dr
Petten Grove
Cockman
Bancroft Gardens
Broxbourne Road
Lucerne Road
Oatfield Road
Vinson Cl
High Street
Dryden Way
Walnuts Leisure Centre
Bark Hart Road
Lodge Crescent
Ramsden
The Priory Leisure Centre
Petten Cl
Plantation Dr
Westwell Cl
Quilter Rd
Surgery
Knoll Rise
Maltby Close
Superbowl College
Lodge Close
Gillmans Road
Bodmin Close
Priory School
Cuckmere Way
Lamberhurst Cl
Drive
Hillview Crescent
Elm Grove
The Mailings
Pepys Rise
Berwick Way
Homefield Rise
Police Station
Lych Gate Rd
Walnuts Road
Horsecroft Cl
Uplands Road
Bedford Road
Glastonbury Close
Rye Crescent
Paddocks Cl
Eldred Drive
Beagles Cl
Lowood Cl
Orpington Station
Hill View Road
Oakhill Rd
Blossom Dr
Orchard Grove
Augustus La
Gravel Pit Way
Homefield Rise
Lancing Road
Tintagel Road
Blenheim Road
Blenheim Primary School
Cloonmore Crescent
Mosyer Drive
Alma Rd
Hall
The Approach
STATION ROAD
The Orpington Halls
Surgery
Spur Road
SPUR ROAD
A232
Avalon Road
Wilmington Avenue
Felstead Road
The Drive
ORPINGTON
Pendennis Road
Burwood School
Long Acre
The Avenue
Hillcrest Road
Woodley Rd
Lapworth Close
Tubbenden Lane
Spencer Cl
Tower Road
Tower Close
St Aubyns Gardens
Badgers Copse
A223
Park Avenue
Berrylands
Craven Road
Avalon Close
Broad Walk
Nut Tree Close
Dalton Cl
Shelley Close
Becketts Close
Maxwell Gardens
Grove
St Aubyns Close
Orpington Mental Health Centre
Surgery
Goddington Lane
Carolyn Dr
St Olaves Grammar School
Close
Hurstlands Dr
Hawfield Bank
Dorado Gardens
Goddington
Holy Innocents
Surgery
1 grid square represents 500 metres

F
G
H
187
J
K
48
49
50
Star Lane
Sheepcote Lane
Bourne Wood
Sheepcote Farm
Bromley
Kent County
Shawcroft School
CROCKENHILL ROAD
Kevingtown
B258
Crouch Farm
Crockenhill
Crockenhill Primary School
Broadway
Bransell Close
CRAY ROAD B258
MAIN RD
GREEN COURT
Church Road
Waldens Road
Tylers Green Road
Darns Hill
Old Chapel Road
Tudor Court
Stones Cross
Ct Road
Furness Swanley
Woodmount
East Hall Road
Lane
Lone Barn
Gorse Road
Daltons Road
Crown Wood
Skeet Hill Lane
Kibbs Lane
Lynden
Laburnum
Avenue
Cherry Avenue
Lavender H
68
67
66
1
2
3
4
5
6

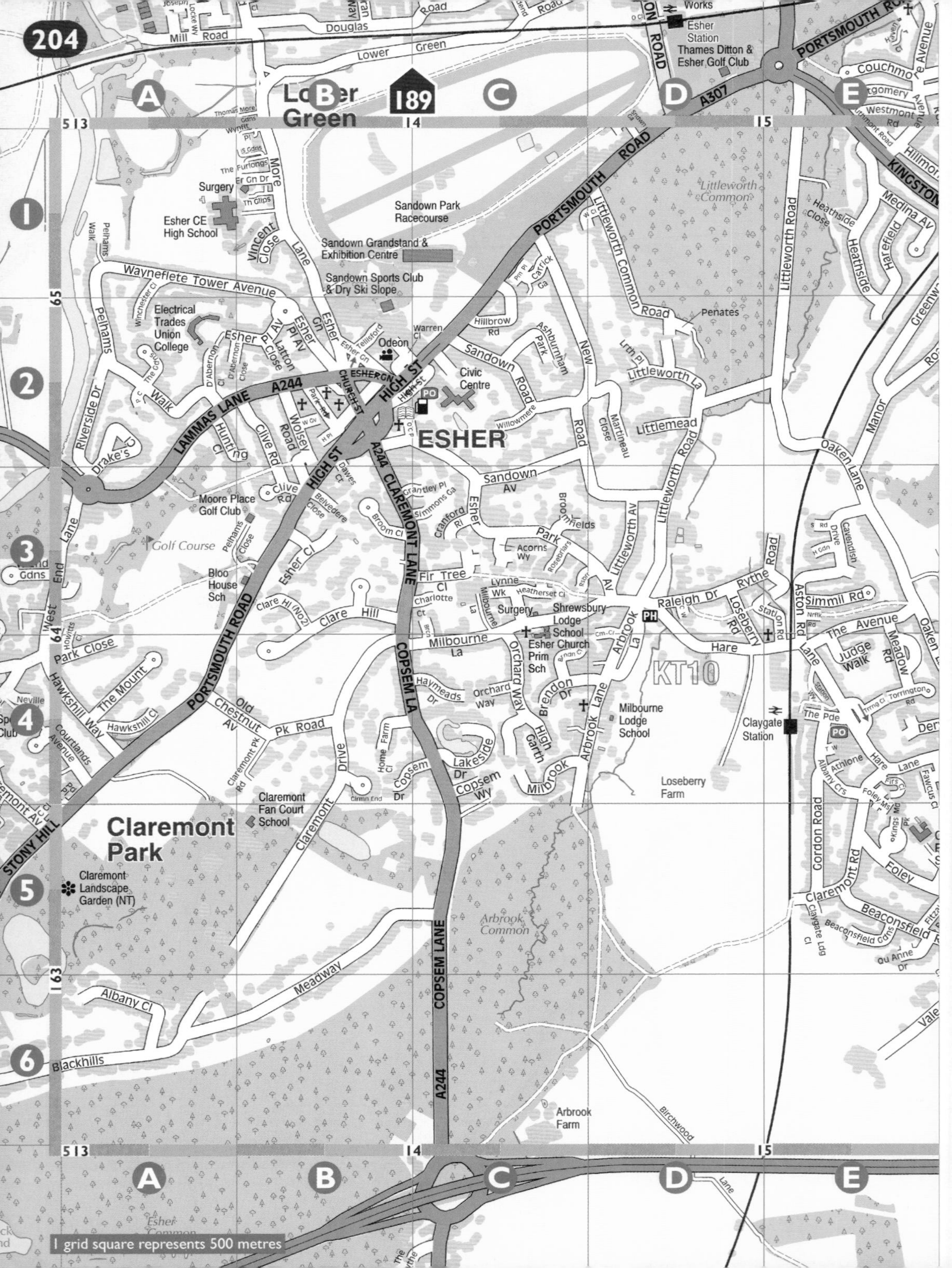

189
ESHER
Lower Green
Sandown Park Racecourse
Sandown Grandstand & Exhibition Centre
Sandown Sports Club & Dry Ski Slope
Esher CE High School
Surgery
Electrical Trades Union College
Odeon
Civic Centre
Moore Place Golf Club
Golf Course
Bloo House Sch
Claremont Park
Claremont Landscape Garden (NT)
Claremont Fan Court School
Shrewsbury Lodge School
Esher Church Prim Sch
Milbourne Lodge School
Claygate Station
Loseberry Farm
Arbrook Common
Arbrook Farm
Littleworth Common
Penates
Esher Station
Thames Ditton & Esher Golf Club
KT10
PORTSMOUTH ROAD
A307
A244
LAMMAS LANE
HIGH ST
CLAREMONT LANE
COPSEM LANE
STONY HILL
KINGSTON
Esher Common

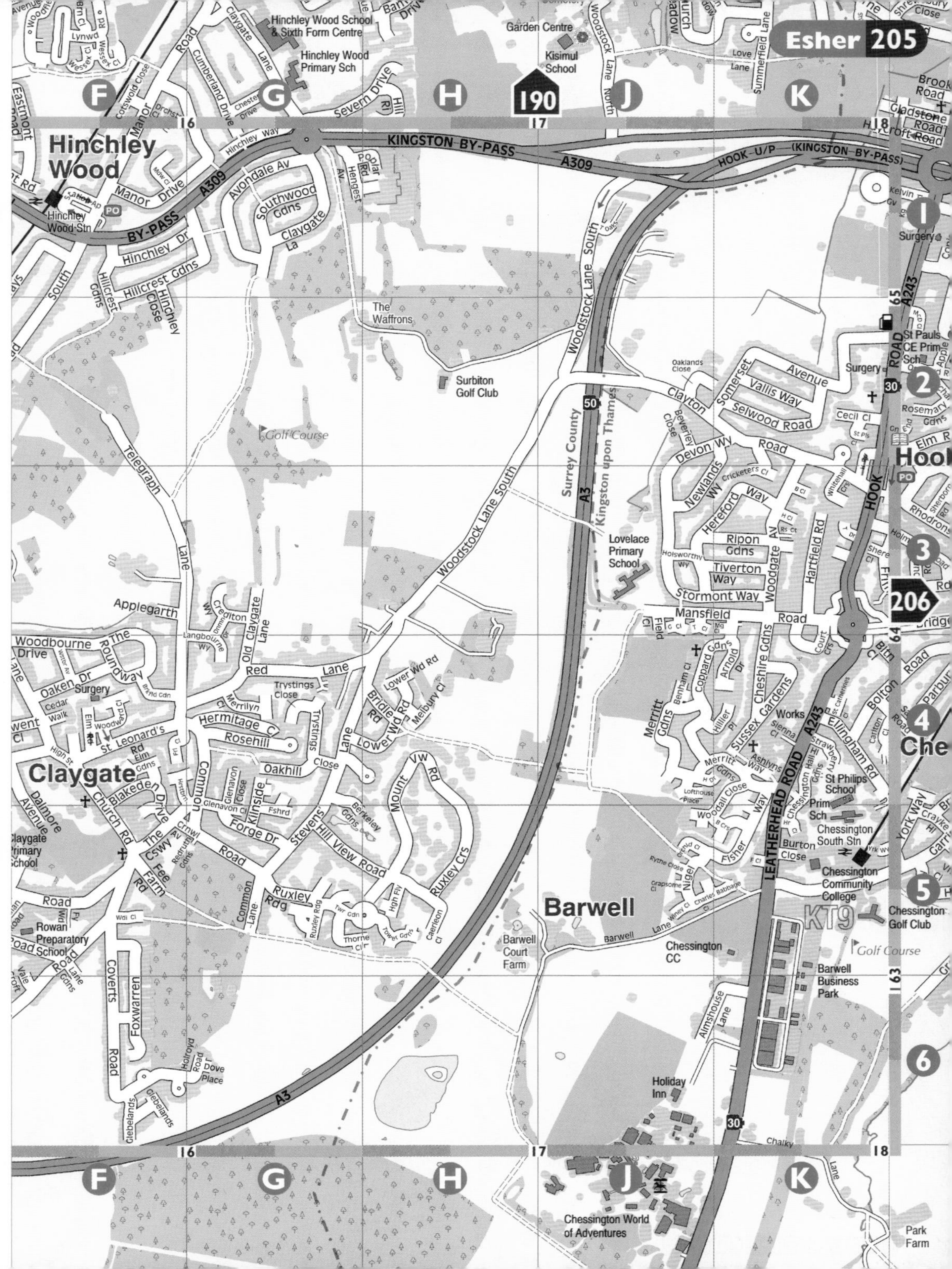

Hinchley Wood
Claygate
Barwell
Hook
KINGSTON BY-PASS
A309
HOOK U/P (KINGSTON BY-PASS)
A3
A243
LEATHERHEAD ROAD
HOOK ROAD
Surrey County
Kingston upon Thames
Hinchley Wood School & Sixth Form Centre
Hinchley Wood Primary Sch
Garden Centre
Kisimul School
Hinchley Wood Stn
The Waffrons
Surbiton Golf Club
Golf Course
Lovelace Primary School
St Pauls CE Prim Sch
St Philips School
Prim Sch
Chessington South Stn
Chessington Community College
Chessington Golf Club
Barwell Business Park
Chessington CC
Barwell Court Farm
Holiday Inn
Chessington World of Adventures
Park Farm
Claygate Primary School
Rowan Preparatory School
KT9
Telegraph Lane
Woodstock Lane South
Woodstock Lane North
Red Lane
Common Road
Church Rd
Coverts Road
Foxwarren
Hermitage Cl
Rosehill
Oakhill
Forge Dr
Hill View Road
Ruxley Rdg
Ruxley Crs
Mount Vw Rd
Stevens Lane
Trystings Close
Bridle Rd
Lower Wd Rd
Melbury Cl
Applegarth
Woodbourne Drive
The Roundway
Oaken Dr
Cedar Walk
St Leonard's Rd
Blakeden Drive
Dalmore Avenue
Fee Farm Rd
Holroyd Road
Dove Place
Glebelands
Barwell Lane
Almshouse Lane
Chalky Lane
Clayton Road
Mansfield Road
Stormont Way
Tiverton Way
Ripon Gdns
Hereford Way
Newlands Wy
Devon Wy
Somerset Avenue
Vallis Way
Selwood Road
Woodgate Av
Hartfield Rd
Cheshire Gdns
Sussex Gardens
Merritt Gdns
Coppard Gdns
Arnold Dr
Fisher Way
Woodgavil Close
Ellingham Rd
Bolton Road
Chessington Hall Gdns
Burton Close
Manor Drive
Avondale Av
Southwood Gdns
Claygate La
Hinchley Dr
Hillcrest Gdns
Hinchley Close
Cumberland Drive
Claygate Lane
Severn Drive
Love Lane
Summerfield Lane
Gladstone Road
Brook Road
Poplar Rd
Hengest Av
190
206
F G H J K
16 17 18
1 2 3 4 5 6
63 64 65

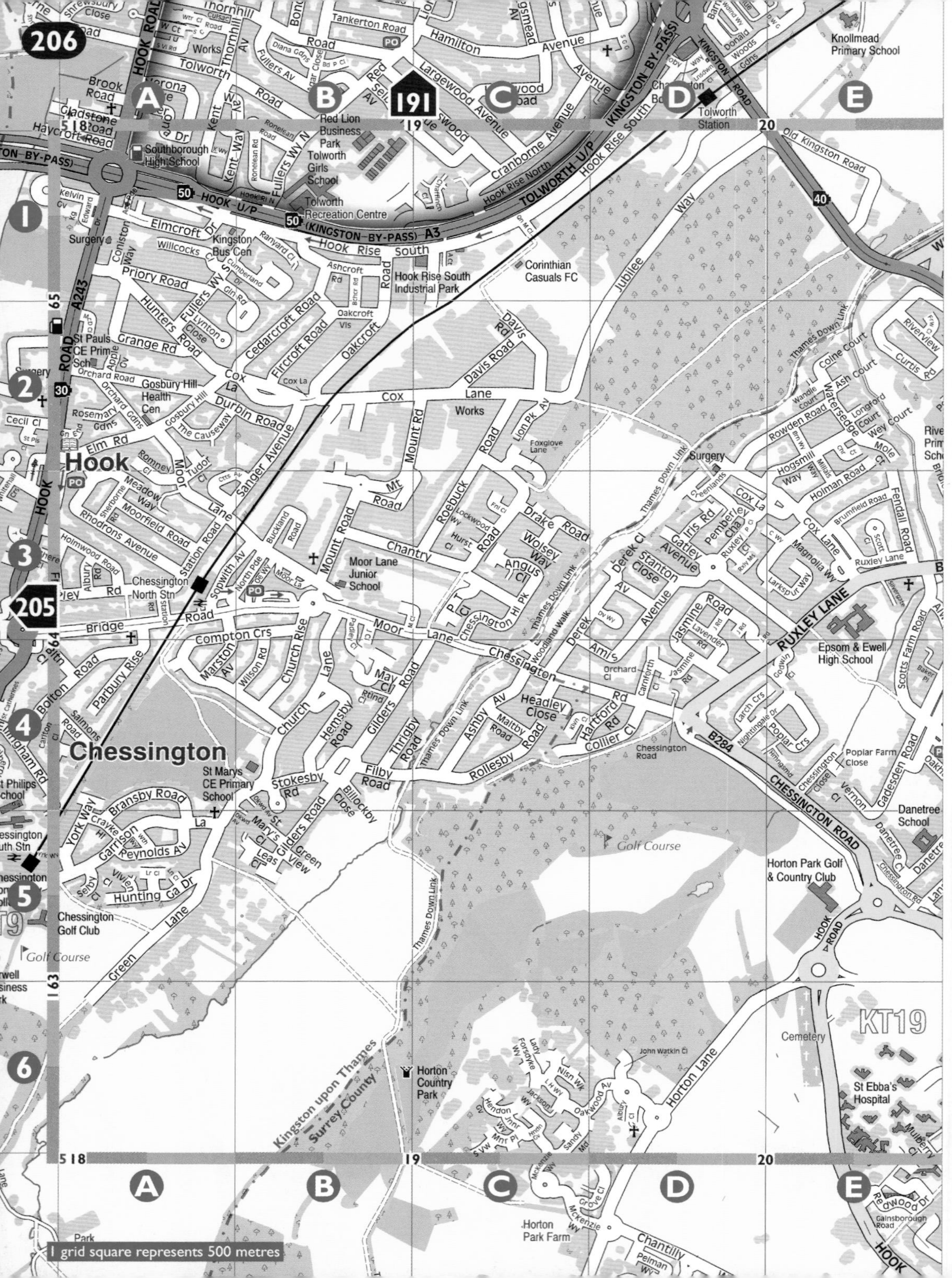

206
191
205
Hook
Chessington
Tolworth Station
Chessington North Stn
Chessington South Stn
Knollmead Primary School
Southborough High School
Red Lion Business Park
Tolworth Girls School
Tolworth Recreation Centre
Kingston Bus Cen
Hook Rise South Industrial Park
Corinthian Casuals FC
St Pauls CE Prim Sch
Gosbury Hill Health Cen
Moor Lane Junior School
Epsom & Ewell High School
St Marys CE Primary School
St Philips School
Chessington Golf Club
Golf Course
Horton Park Golf & Country Club
Danetree School
Horton Country Park
Horton Park Farm
Cemetery
St Ebba's Hospital
KT19
TOLWORTH U/P
HOOK U/P
(KINGSTON-BY-PASS) A3
KINGSTON ROAD
HOOK ROAD
A243
RUXLEY LANE
CHESSINGTON ROAD
B284
Thames Down Link
Kingston upon Thames
Surrey County
1 grid square represents 500 metres

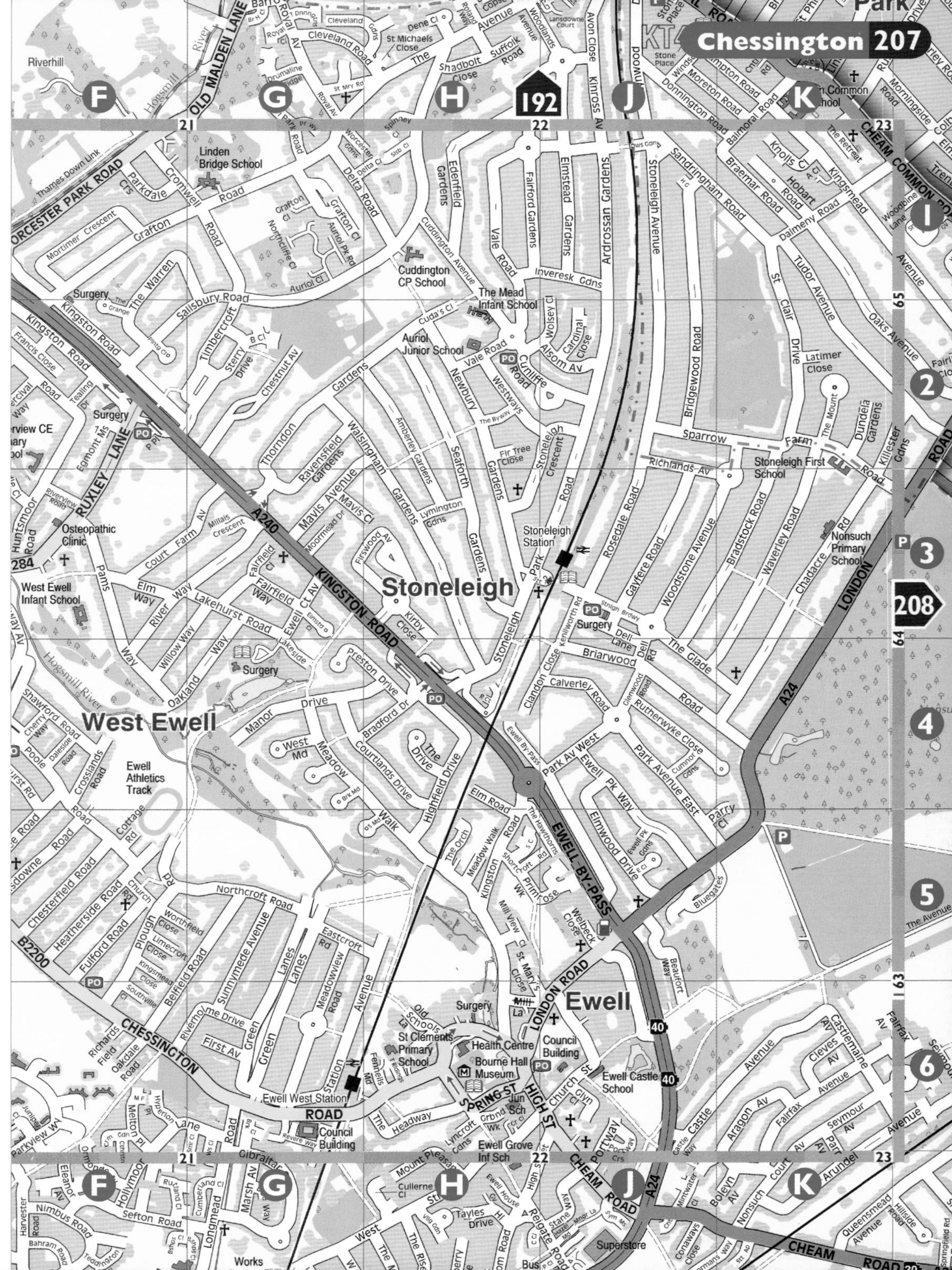
Stoneleigh
West Ewell
Ewell
KINGSTON ROAD
A240
EWELL BY-PASS
LONDON ROAD
A24
CHESSINGTON ROAD
CHEAM ROAD
CHEAM COMMON ROAD
RUXLEY LANE
OLD MALDEN LANE
WORCESTER PARK ROAD
B2200
Linden Bridge School
Cuddington CP School
The Mead Infant School
Auriol Junior School
Stoneleigh Station
Stoneleigh First School
Nonsuch Primary School
West Ewell Infant School
Osteopathic Clinic
Ewell Athletics Track
St Clements Primary School
Health Centre
Bourne Hall Museum
Council Building
Ewell Castle School
Ewell West Station
Ewell Grove Inf Sch
Superstore
Surgery
Hogsmill River
Riverhill
Sparrow Farm Road
Stoneleigh Avenue
Sandringham Road
Ardrossan Gardens
Salisbury Road
Grafton Road
Cromwell Road
Northcroft Road
Spring St
High St
The Glade
Briarwood Road
Park Avenue East
Park Av West
Ewell Pk Way
Elmwood Drive
Preston Drive
Manor Drive
Highfield Drive
Courtlands Drive
Lakehurst Road
Chestnut Av
Court Farm Av
Mavis Avenue
Walsingham Gardens
Seaforth Gardens
Newbury Gardens
Tudor Avenue
St Clair Drive
Bridgewood Road
Rosedale Road
Woodstone Avenue
Bradstock Road
Waverley Road
Chadacre Rd
F
G
H
J
K
I
2
3
4
5
6
21
22
23
63
64
65
192
208

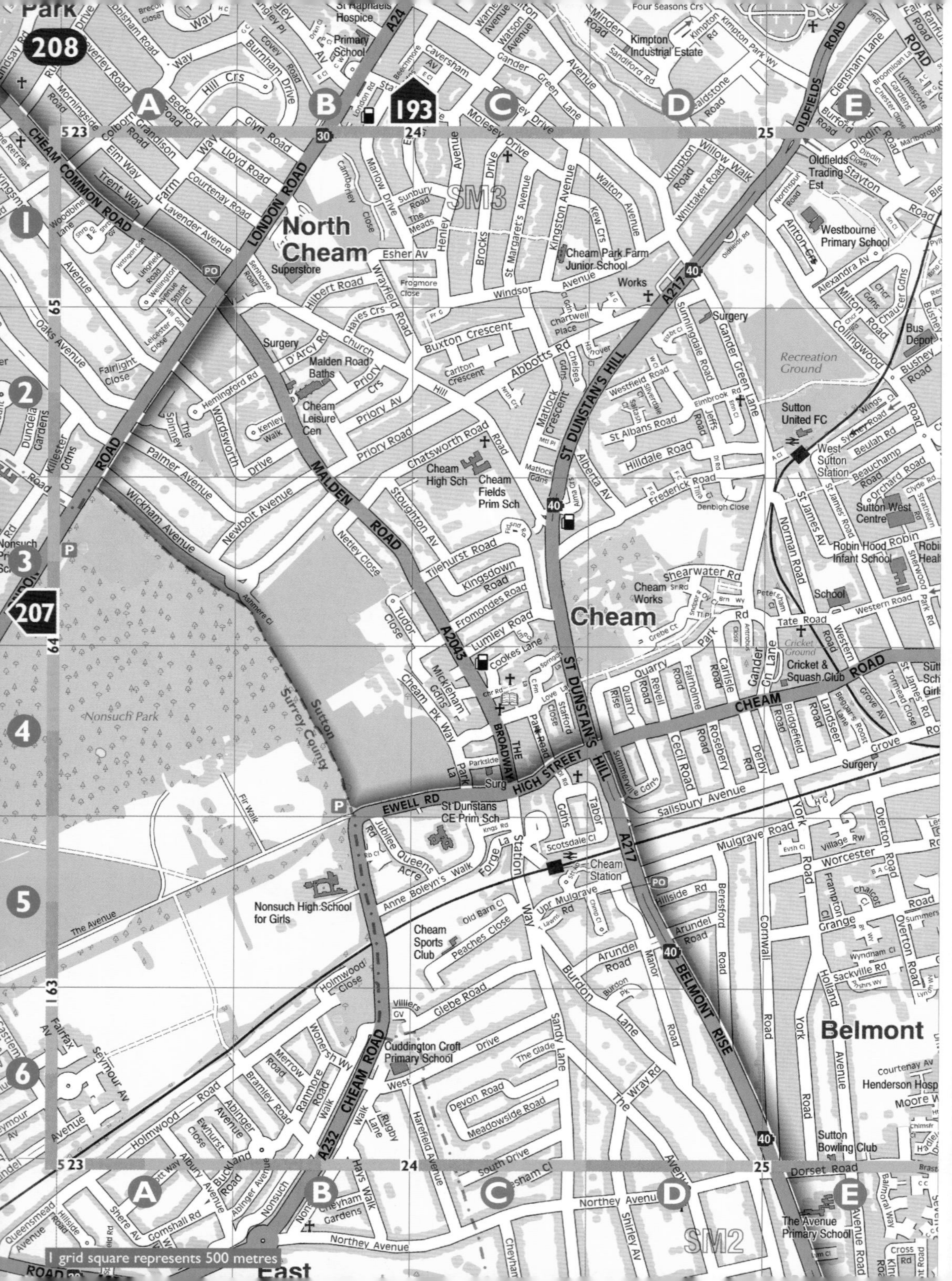
208
193
207
A
B
C
D
E
1
2
3
4
5
6
23
24
25
64
65
63
SM3
SM2
North Cheam
Cheam
Belmont
Nonsuch Park
St Raphaels Hospice
Primary School
Four Seasons Crs
Kimpton Industrial Estate
Kimpton Park Wy
Minden Road
Sandiford Rd
Caversham Av
Gander Green Lane
Oldfields Road
Clensham Lane
Oldfields Trading Est
Westbourne Primary School
Alexandra Av
Bus Depot
Recreation Ground
Sutton United FC
West Sutton Station
Sutton West Centre
Robin Hood Infant School
School
Tate Road
Western Road
Cricket Ground
Cricket & Squash Club
Cheam Road
Surgery
Salisbury Avenue
Mulgrave Road
Worcester Road
Overton Road
Grange Road
Cheam Common Road
London Road
Lavender Avenue
Courtenay Road
Lloyd Road
Farm Way
Trent Way
Elm Way
Grandison Road
Glyn Road
Burnham Drive
Hill Crs
Bedford Road
Morningside Road
Colborne Way
Superstore
Esher Av
Hilbert Road
Wrayfield Road
Windsor Avenue
Cheam Park Farm Junior School
Works
Kingston Avenue
Walton Avenue
Kew Crs
Brocks Drive
Henley Avenue
Molesey Drive
Sunbury Road
The Meads
Marlow Drive
Camberley Close
Surgery
D'Arcy Rd
Malden Road Baths
Cheam Leisure Cen
Church Hill Road
Priory Crs
Priory Av
Priory Road
Hemingford Rd
Kenley Walk
Wordsworth Drive
The Spinney
Palmer Avenue
Newbolt Avenue
Wickham Avenue
Fairlight Close
Oaks Avenue
Dundela Gardens
Killester Gdns
Chatsworth Road
Cheam High Sch
Cheam Fields Prim Sch
Stoughton Av
Netley Close
Tilehurst Road
Kingsdown Road
Fromondes Road
Lumley Road
Tudor Close
Malden Road
A2043
Cookes Lane
Mickleham Gdns
Cheam Pk Way
The Broadway
High Street
Park Road
Stafford Close
Buxton Crescent
Carlton Crescent
Abbotts Rd
Chartwell Place
Matlock Crescent
St Dunstan's Hill
A217
Alberta Av
Westfield Road
St Albans Road
Hilldale Road
Frederick Road
Denbigh Close
Sunningdale Road
Elmbrook Rd
Jeffs Road
Shearwater Rd
Cheam Works
Park Rd
Quarry Rise
Quarry Road
Revell Road
Fairholme Road
Carlisle Road
Gander Gn Lane
Cecil Road
Rosebery Road
Derby Rd
Bridgefield Road
Landseer Road
Grove Av
Norman Road
St James Av
Beauchamp Road
Beulah Rd
Orchard Road
Sydney Road
Nonsuch Park
Surrey County
Sutton
Ashmere Cl
Ewell Rd
Park La
Parkside
Surg
St Dunstans CE Prim Sch
Jubilee Rd
Queens Acre
Anne Boleyn's Walk
Forge La
Station Way
Scotsdale Cl
Cheam Station
Tabor Gdns
Summerville Gdns
Nonsuch High School for Girls
The Avenue
Flr Walk
Cheam Sports Club
Peaches Close
Old Barn Cl
Upr Mulgrave Rd
Hillside Rd
Beresford Road
Arundel Road
Burdon Lane
Manor Road
Belmont Rise
Cornwall Road
York Road
Holland Avenue
Frampton Cl
Sackville Rd
Wyndham Cl
Courtenay Av
Henderson Hosp
Moore W
Sutton Bowling Club
Dorset Road
The Avenue Primary School
Avenue Road
Balmoral Way
Holmwood Close
Glebe Road
Villiers Gv
Cuddington Croft Primary School
West Drive
The Glade
Sandy Lane
The Wray Rd
Devon Road
Meadowside Road
Harefield Avenue
South Drive
Rugby Lane
Hays Walk
Cheam Road
A232
Cheyham Gardens
Northey Avenue
Shirley Av
Ranmore Road
Wonersh Wy
Merrow Road
Bramley Road
Abinger Avenue
Ewhurst Close
Holmwood Road
Albury Avenue
Buckland Road
Gomshall Rd
Shere Av
Hillside Road
Queensmead Avenue
Nonsuch
Seymour Av
Fairfax Av
1 grid square represents 500 metres

Benhilton
Carshalton
SUTTON
The Wrythe
Carshalton Beeches
Carshalton on the Hill
SM1
SM5
194
210
Anchor School
Rosehill Gardens
Kendal Gdns
Greenshaw High School
College
Winchcombe
Bakers Gdns
Muschamp Primary School
Aultone Way
Cranleigh
Sutton Common Stn
Waverley Avenue
Westminster Road
Pr of Wales' Road
Connaught Road
Edinburgh Road
Surrey Grove
Royston Avenue
Chudleigh Gardens
Calthorpe Gdns
Angel Hill
B279
Vermont Road
Hallmead Road
All Saints Road
Benhill Wd Road
Benhill Avenue
Benhilton Gardens
Gassiot Way
Poulton Av
Farmington Av
Temple Way
Paget Av
Milton Road
Brookfield Avenue
Carshalton High School for Girls
Carshalton AFC
Rec Grnd
Carshalton College
Council Building
Oakhill Road
Erskine Road
Byron Gdns
Mead Crescent
War Mem Sports Ground
Playing Field
Junior Sch
Carshalton Station
North Street
West Street
B277
B278
Nightingale Road
Vale Road
Gas Works
Burnell Rd
Brunswick Road
Cressingham Gv
Thicket Road
Benhill Recreation Ground
Florian Av
Orchard Way
Kingsley Av
Milton Avenue
Browning Av
Coleridge Av
Shirley Av
Colston Avenue
St Marys Infant School
Sycamore Close
West St Lane
Council Building
Westcroft Leisure C
Lewis Clinic
St Nicholas Way
Throwley Way
Elm Grove
Constance Road
Westmead Road
Rossdale
Highfield Road
Ringstead Road
Carshalton Grove
Sutton Grove
Surgery
Manor La
Palmerston Business Cen
Myrtle Road
Lower Road
Waterloo Rd
Grammar School
Prim Sch
Vernon Rd
Upr Vernon Road
Bramley Rd
Croft Rd
Alma Road
Shorts Road
St Marys RC Infant School
St Philomenas Catholic High School
Pound St
High Street
Cemetery
Carshalton Pk
St Nicholas Centre
Times Square Shopping Centre
Greyhound Road
Sports Club
Superbowl
Health Cen
Manor Park
Carshalton Road
A232
Works
Gauntlett Road
King's Lane
Alpine View
Fairview Road
Harrow Road
Oxford Road
Cambridge Road
Wales Av
Walnut Close
Beynon Rd
The Park
Carshalton War Memorial Hospital
Civic Cen
Secombe Centre
Police Stn
Hall
Hill Rd
Mulgrave Road
Albert Rd
The Warren
Hawthorn Rd
Warren Park Road
Banstead Road
Bankside Close
Park Hill
Deroy Close
Salisbury Road
Cedar Cl
Ashcombe
Sutton High School for Girls
Sutton High Junior School
Sutton Station
Cumnor Road
Rutherford
Eaton Road
Hillcroome Road
Langley Road
Wellesley Road
Grove Rd
Downside Road
Hill Road
Blakehall Road
Gordon Road
Carshalton Beeches Station
Sussex Road
Stanley Park
Cedar Gdns
Cadogan Court
Conway Drive
Stanley Road
Brighton Road
Sutton Court
Cavendish Road
Langley Park
Albion Road
Mayfield Road
Ridgway
Willis Av
Waverley Way
Barrow Hedges Way
Crichton Road
Woodfield Av
Anglesey Gdns
Park Vw Cl
Stanley Park Prim Sch
Christchurch Park
Devonshire Primary School
Walnut Ms
Mitre Cl
The Farm Road
Upland Road
Kayemoor Rd
Prior Avenue
Farm Close
Farmdale Road
Central Way
Beeches Avenue
Stanley Park Road
Oaks Way
Fir Tree Grove
Tapestry Cl
Camborne Road
Effingham Cl
Devonshire Avenue
Devonshire Rd
Chalgrove Road
Staplehurst Road
Kings Av
Gaynesford Rd
Audley Pl
Ventnor Rd
Egmont Road
High St
B2230
Crossways
The Byway
Harbury Road
Barrow Hedges Primary School
Princes Av
Barrow Avenue
Fountain Drive
Courtney Crs
Overton Grange School
Chipstead Cl
The Downsway
The Gallop
The Causeway
Ingleton Road
Fullerton Road
The Close
East Drive
Dingwall Road
Stanley Square
Cranfield Rd
Chelsea
Sinclair Drive
Hulverston Cl
Heath Drive
Bassett Close
Cheviot Close
Beeches Walk
Woodmansterne Road
Fountain Dr
Damson Wy
Roman Rd
Kenny Dr
Homeland Dr
Autumn Dr
Hulverston Close
The Highway
The Linkway
Wellfield Gdns
The Warren
Rawson Wk
Chiltern Road
South Way
West Way
Sutton General Hospital
Cotswold Road
House School
Woodbury Drive
West Drive
Oakhurst Rise
Woodmansterne
Belmont Station
Royal Marsden Hospital
Baron
F
G
H
J
K
1
2
3
4
5
6
26
27
28
63
64
65

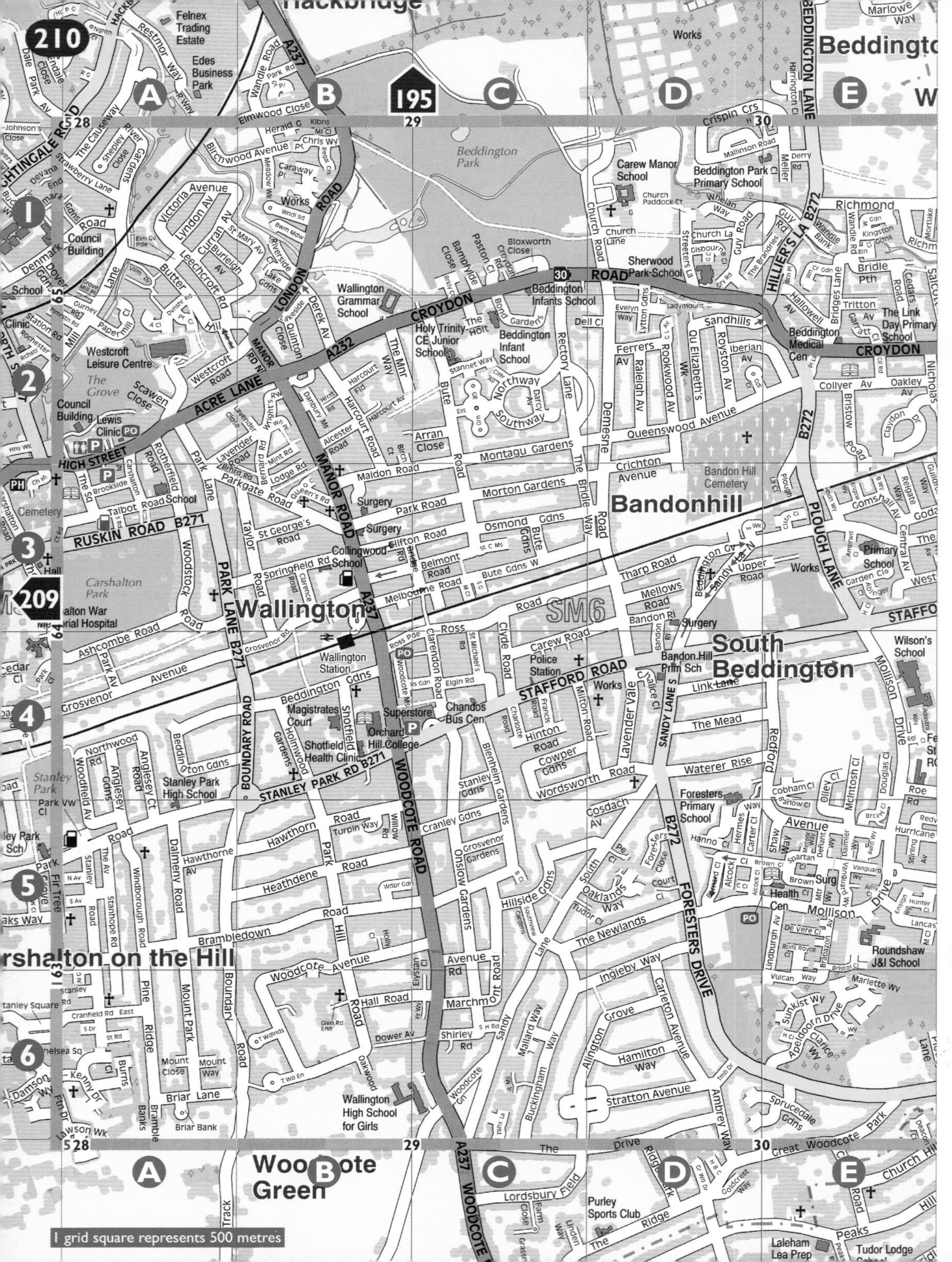

210
195
209
Hackbridge
Beddington
Beddington Park
Bandonhill
SM6
Wallington
South Beddington
Carshalton on the Hill
Woodcote Green
Carshalton Park
Stanley Park
The Grove
Bandon Hill Cemetery
LONDON ROAD
MANOR ROAD
WOODCOTE ROAD
CROYDON ROAD
ACRE LANE
HIGH STREET
RUSKIN ROAD B271
PARK LANE B271
BOUNDARY ROAD
STANLEY PARK RD B271
STAFFORD ROAD
SANDY LANE S
FORESTERS DRIVE
PLOUGH LANE
BEDDINGTON LANE
HILLIER'S LA B272
Carew Manor School
Beddington Park Primary School
Sherwood Park School
Wallington Grammar School
Holy Trinity CE Junior School
Beddington Infants School
Beddington Infant School
Westcroft Leisure Centre
Council Building
Collingwood School
Wallington Station
Magistrates Court
Orchard Hill College
Shotfield Health Clinic
Stanley Park High School
Bandon Hill Prim Sch
Foresters Primary School
Wilson's School
Roundshaw J&I School
Wallington High School for Girls
Purley Sports Club
Laleham Lea Prep
Tudor Lodge
Chandos Bus Cen
Felnex Trading Estate
Edes Business Park
1 grid square represents 500 metres

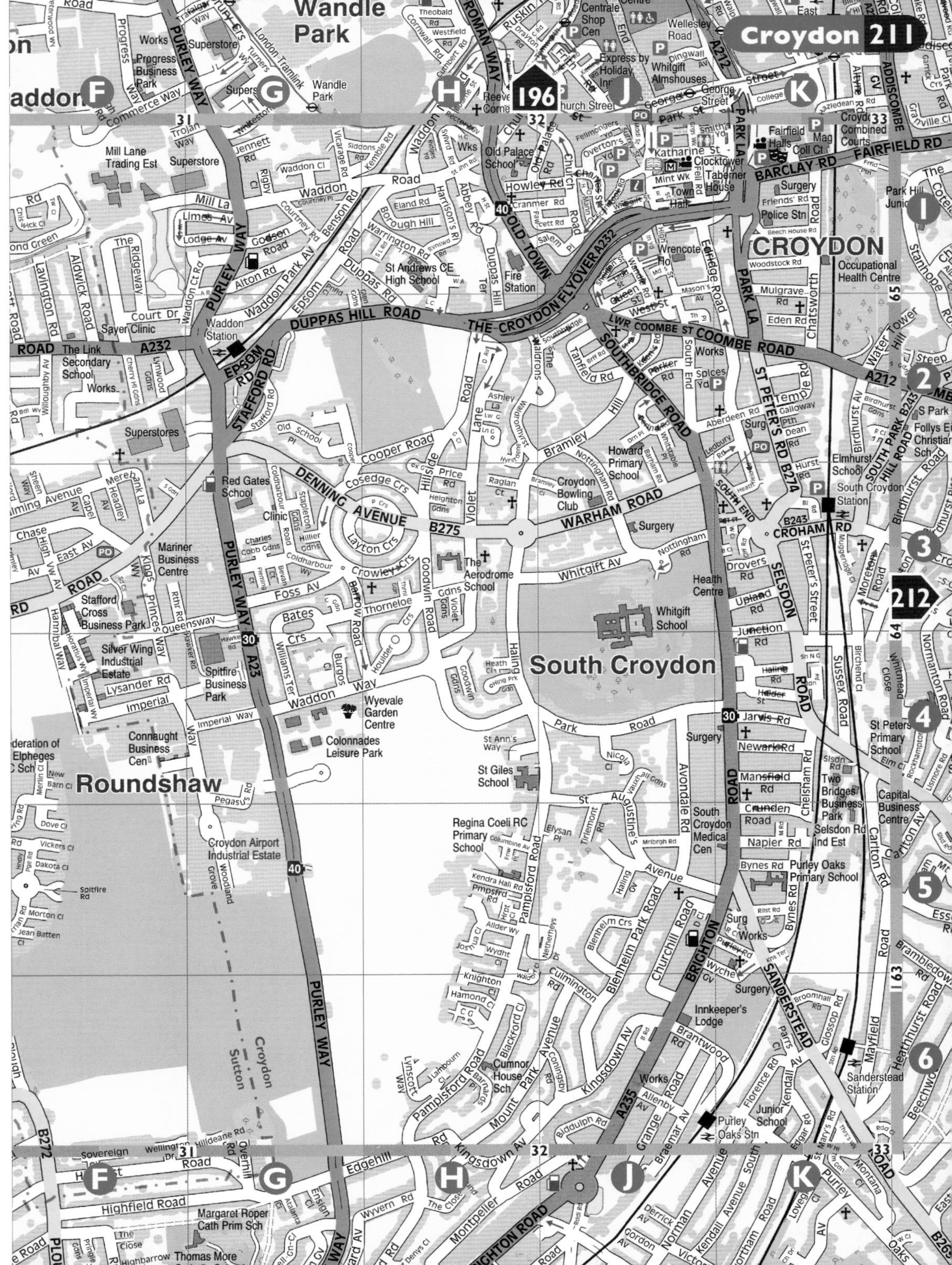
Wandle Park
Waddon
Croydon
South Croydon
Roundshaw
Purley Way
Duppas Hill Road
The Croydon Flyover A232
Coombe Road
Southbridge Road
Brighton Road
Denning Avenue
Warham Road
Waddon Way
Imperial Way
Park Lane
Selsdon Road
Sanderstead Road
196
212
Croydon Airport Industrial Estate
Whitgift School
Wyevale Garden Centre
Colonnades Leisure Park
Purley Oaks Stn
Sanderstead Station
South Croydon Station
Waddon Station
Fairfield Halls
Croydon Combined Courts
Croydon Sutton

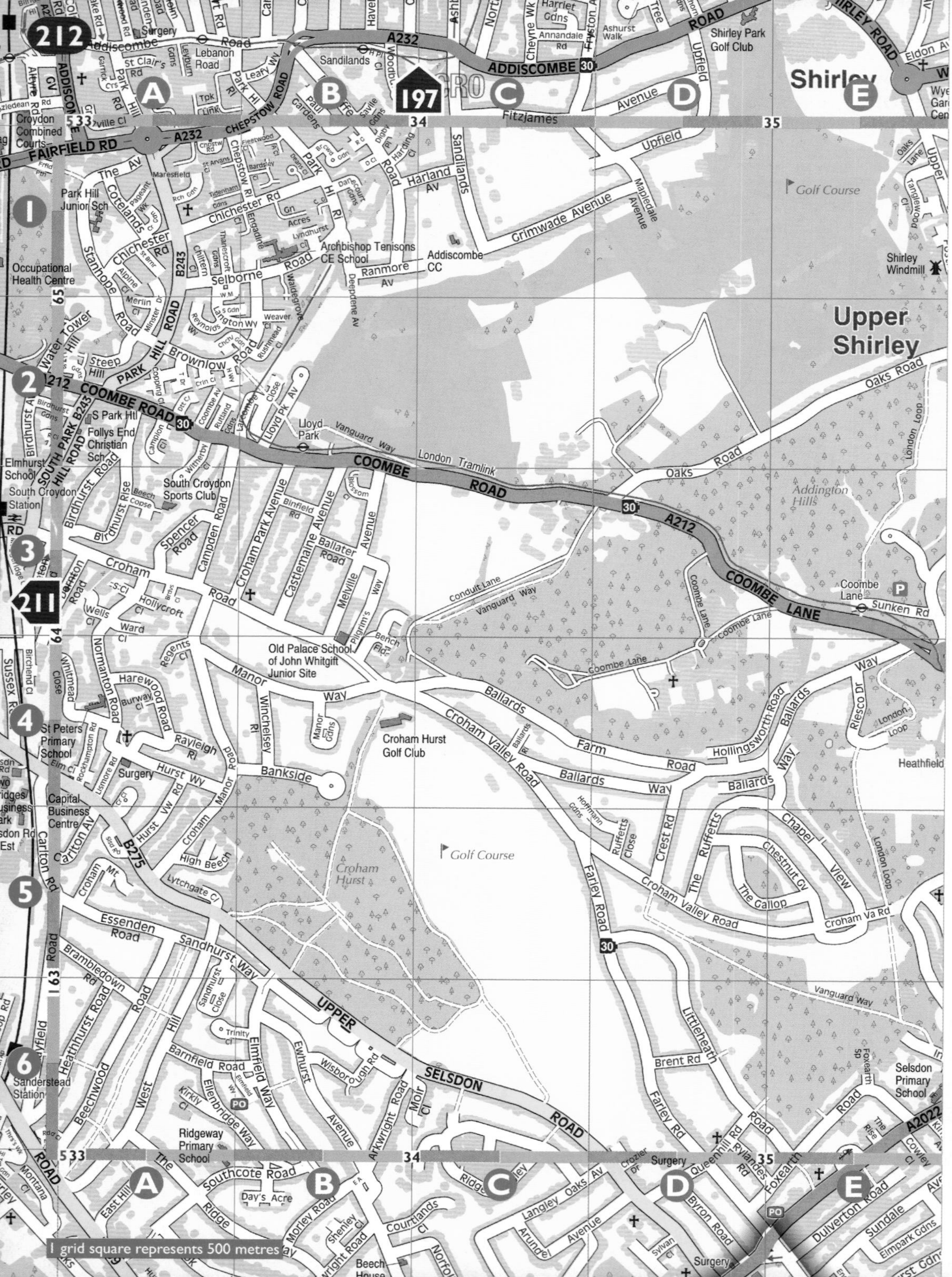

212
197
211
Addiscombe Road
A232
ADDISCOMBE ROAD
Shirley Park Golf Club
Shirley
Sandilands
Lebanon Road
Leybourne
Park Hill
Chepstow Road
Fairfield Rd
Croydon Combined Courts
Fitzjames Avenue
Upfield
Golf Course
Shirley Windmill
Park Hill Junior Sch
The Avenue
Coteland
Chichester Rd
Archbishop Tenisons CE School
Addiscombe CC
Ranmore Av
Grimwade Avenue
Mapledale Avenue
Harland Av
Selborne Road
Occupational Health Centre
Stanhope Road
Water Tower
Park Hill Road
Brownlow Road
Upper Shirley
Oaks Road
A212 COOMBE ROAD
S Park Htl
Follys End Christian Sch
Lloyd Park
Vanguard Way
London Tramlink
COOMBE ROAD
Elmhurst School
South Croydon Station
South Park Hill Road
Birdhurst Road
South Croydon Sports Club
Spencer Road
Campden Road
Croham Park Avenue
Castlemaine Avenue
Ballater Road
Melville Avenue
Addington Hills
London Loop
COOMBE LANE
Coombe Lane
Sunken Rd
Croham Road
Conduit Lane
Old Palace School of John Whitgift Junior Site
Manor Way
Ballards Farm Road
Croham Valley Road
Hollingsworth Road
Riesco Dr
Heathfield
Normanton Road
Harewood Road
Rayleigh Ri
Croham Hurst Golf Club
Bankside
St Peters Primary School
Surgery
Capital Business Centre
Carlton Rd
Croham Manor Road
High Beech
Golf Course
Croham Hurst
Ballards Way
Crest Rd
The Ruffetts
Chapel View
Chestnut Gv
The Gallop
Croham Va Rd
Farley Road
Lytchgate Cl
Essenden Road
Sandhurst Way
UPPER SELSDON ROAD
Brambledown Rd
Heathhurst Road
Beechwood Road
West Hill
Barnfield Road
Ellenbridge Way
Elmfield Way
Ewhurst Avenue
Arkwright Road
Littleheath
Brent Rd
Selsdon Primary School
Foxearth Rd
A2022
Sanderstead Station
Ridgeway Primary School
Southcote Road
Day's Acre
Morley Road
Courtlands Cl
Langley Oaks Av
Queenhill Rd
Rylandes Rd
Byron Road
Dulverton Road
Sundale
Beech House
Surgery
1 grid square represents 500 metres

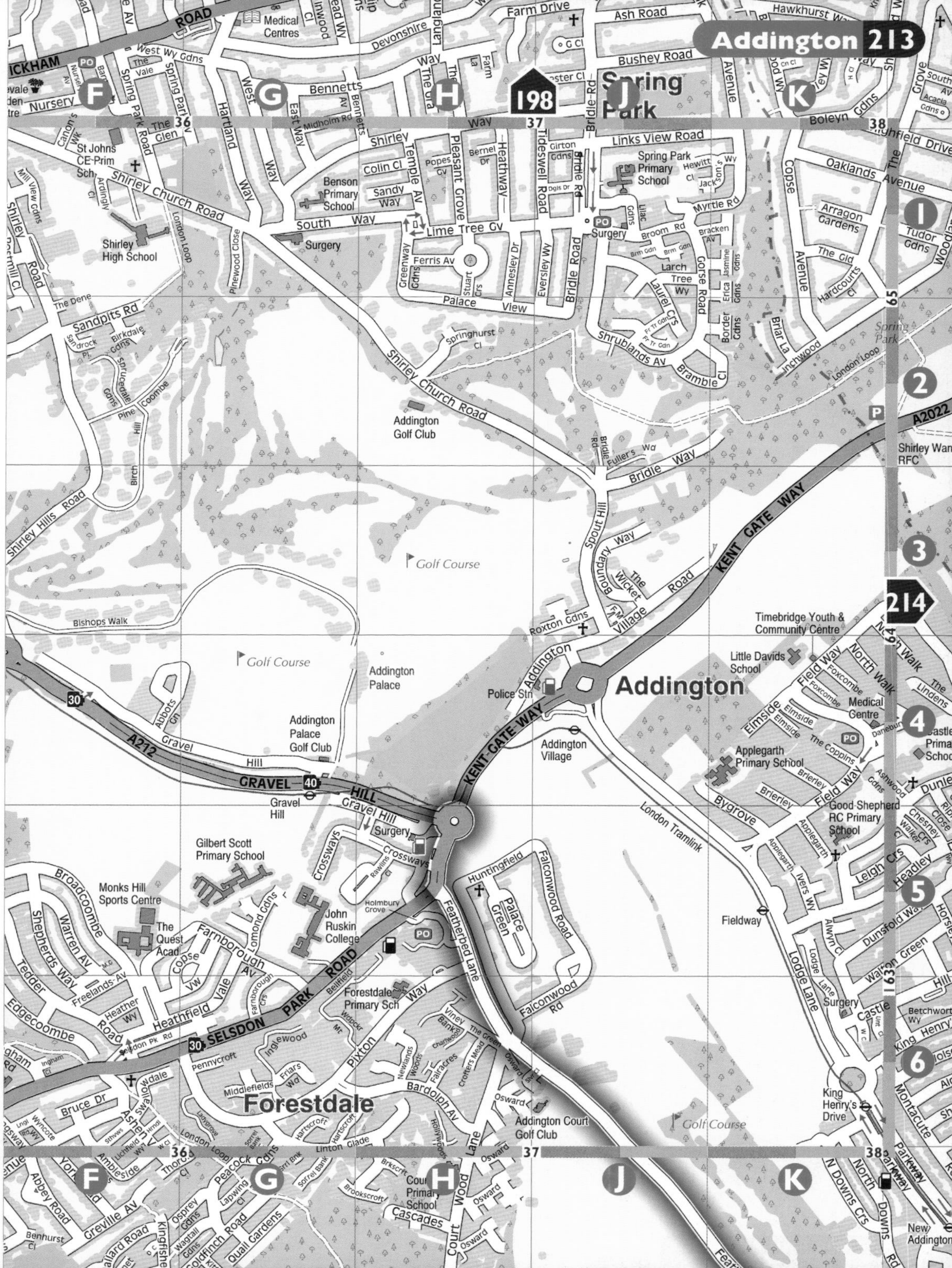
Addington
Spring Park
Forestdale
Shirley Church Road
Kent Gate Way
Gravel Hill
Selsdon Park Road
Addington Golf Club
Addington Palace
Addington Palace Golf Club
Addington Court Golf Club
Golf Course
Shirley High School
Spring Park Primary School
Benson Primary School
Gilbert Scott Primary School
John Ruskin College
Applegarth Primary School
Good Shepherd RC Primary School
Little Davids School
Timebridge Youth & Community Centre
Forestdale Primary Sch
Addington Village
Fieldway
King Henry's Drive
Gravel Hill
London Tramlink
London Loop
198
214

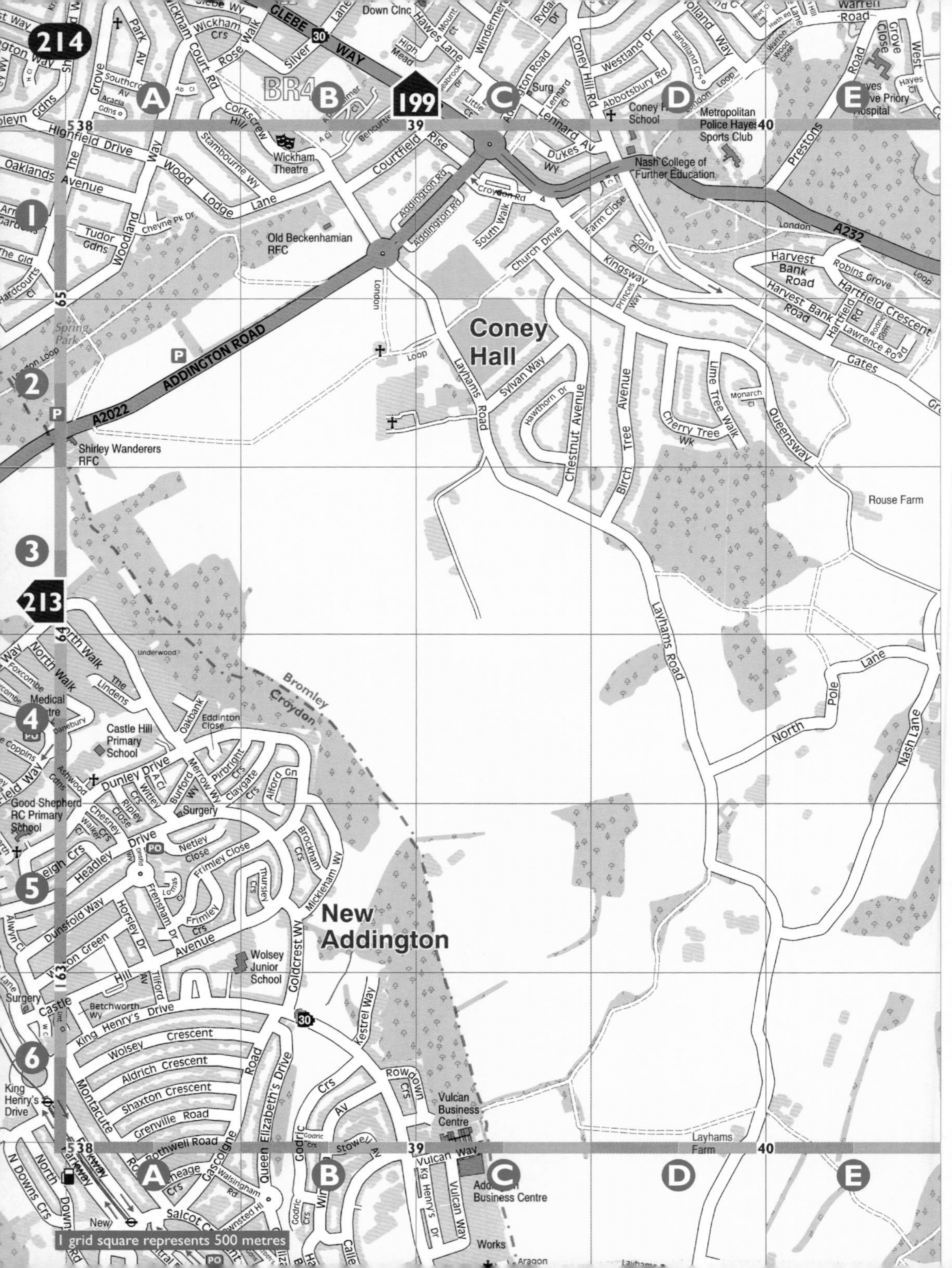

214
199
213
BR4
Glebe Way
Down Clnc
Hawes Lane
High Mead
Windermere
Coney Hill Rd
Westland Dr
Abbotsbury Rd
Warren Road
Grove Close
Hayes Grove Priory Hospital
Wickham Crs
Rose Walk
Wickham Court Rd
Park Av
Grove
Southcroft Av
Acacia Gdns
Boleyn Gdns
Highfield Drive
Oaklands Avenue
Corkscrew Hill
Stambourne Wy
Wickham Theatre
Courtfield Rise
Addington Rd
Surg
Lennard Av
Dukes Wy
Coney Hill School
Metropolitan Police Hayes Sports Club
Nash College of Further Education
Prestons Road
A232
Wood Lodge Lane
Woodland Way
Cheyne Pk Dr
Tudor Gdns
Old Beckenhamian RFC
Croydon Rd
South Walk
Church Drive
Farm Close
Colin Cl
Kingsway
Harvest Bank Road
Robins Grove
Hartfield Crescent
Hartfield Rd
Lawrence Road
Gates
Hardcourts Cl
Spring Park
London Loop
Addington Road
A2022
Shirley Wanderers RFC
Coney Hall
Princes Way
Sylvan Way
Layhams Road
Hawthorn Dr
Chestnut Avenue
Birch Tree Avenue
Lime Tree Walk
Cherry Tree Wk
Monarch Cl
Queensway
Rouse Farm
North Pole Lane
Nash Lane
North Walk
Foxcombe
The Lindens
Underwood
Bromley
Croydon
Medical Centre
Danebury
Castle Hill Primary School
Oakbank
Eddinton Close
Dunley Drive
Merrow Wy
Pirbright Crs
Claygate Crs
Alford Gn
Burford Wy
Ashwood Gdns
Ripley Close
Chesney Crs
Walker Cl
Good Shepherd RC Primary School
Surgery
Headley Drive
Netley Close
Frimley Close
Brockham Crs
Micklenham Wy
Thursley Crs
Frensham Dr
Frimley Crs
Dunsfold Way
Horsley Dr
New Addington
Avenue
Wolsey Junior School
Goldcrest Wy
Kestrel Way
Castle Hill Av
Tilford Av
Betchworth Wy
King Henry's Drive
Wolsey Crescent
Aldrich Crescent
Shaxton Crescent
Grenville Road
Rothwell Road
Montacute Road
Gascoigne Road
Queen Elizabeth's Drive
Rowdown Crs
Vulcan Business Centre
Vulcan Way
Addington Business Centre
Stowell Av
Godric Crs
Layhams Farm
King Henry's Drive
North Downs Crs
Salcot Crescent
Walsingham Rd
Works
Aragon
1 grid square represents 500 metres

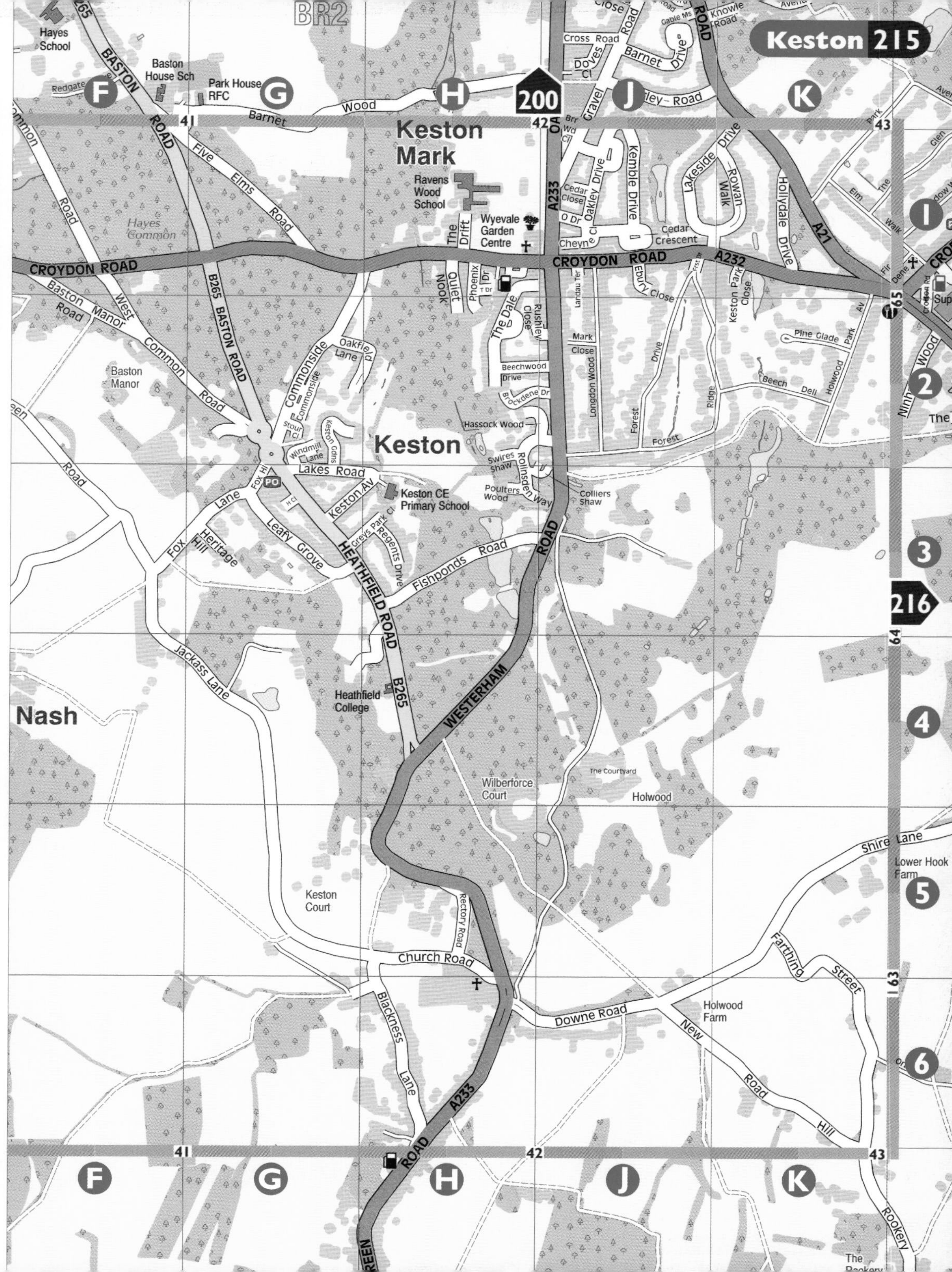

Keston 215
BR2
Hayes School
Baston House Sch
Park House RFC
Redgate
Barnet Wood
Keston Mark
Ravens Wood School
Wyevale Garden Centre
The Drift
Cross Road
Doves Cl
Barnet Drive
Gable Ms
Knowle Road
Gravel Road
Kemble Drive
Cedar Close
Oakley Drive
Lakeside Drive
Rowan Walk
Hollydale Drive
Cedar Crescent
Cheyne Cl
A233
A21
A232
CROYDON ROAD
Hayes Common
Five Elms Road
West Common Road
Baston Manor Road
B265 BASTON ROAD
Baston Manor
Commonside
Oakfield Lane
Quiet Nook
Phoenix Dr
The Dale
Rushley Close
Mark Close
Beechwood Drive
Brockdene Dr
Longdon Wood
Ebury Close
Keston Park Close
Forest Drive
Ridge
Pine Glade
Beech Dell
Holwood Park Av
Ninhams Wood
Hassock Wood
Keston
Windmill Lane
Keston Gdns
Lakes Road
Keston Av
Keston CE Primary School
Swires Shaw
Rollinsden Way
Poulters Wood
Colliers Shaw
Fox Hill
Fox Lane
Heritage Hill
Leafy Grove
Greys Park Cl
Regents Drive
Fishponds Road
HEATHFIELD ROAD
WESTERHAM ROAD
Heathfield College
Jackass Lane
Nash
The Courtyard
Wilberforce Court
Holwood
Shire Lane
Lower Hook Farm
Keston Court
Rectory Road
Church Road
Blackness Lane
Downe Road
New Road Hill
Holwood Farm
Farthing Street
Rookery
The Rookery
A233 ROAD
200
216
41
42
43
63
64
65
F
G
H
J
K
I
2
3
4
5
6

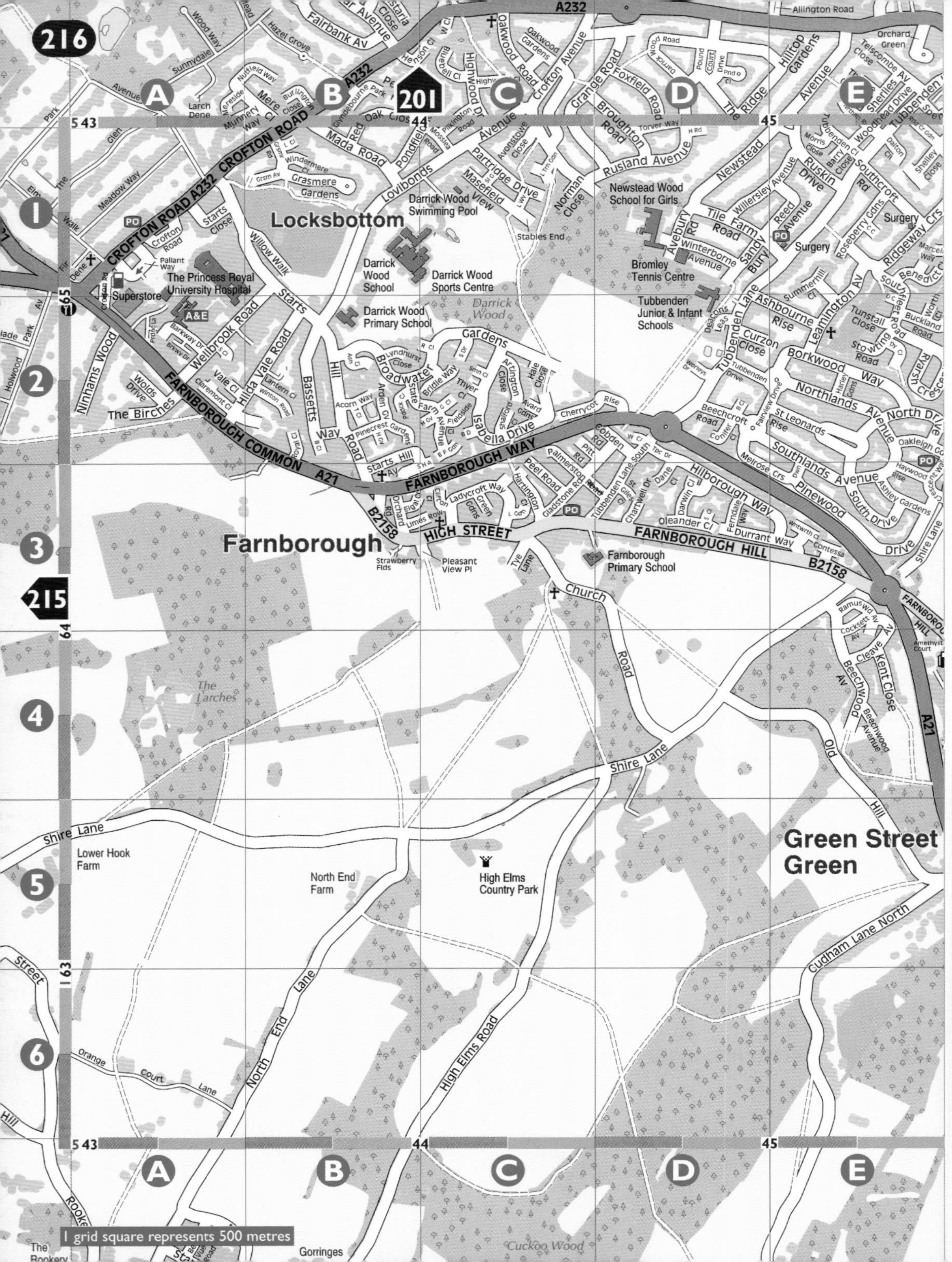
201
215
A
B
C
D
E
1
2
3
4
5
6
5 43
44
45
65
64
63
A232
Allington Road
Orchard Green
Fairbank Av
Hazel Grove
Wood Way
Sunnydale
Avenue
Larch Dene
Mere Cl
Munnery Way
Mada Road
Red Oak Close
Pondfield Road
Highwood Dr
Oakwood Gardens
Oakwood Road
Crofton Avenue
Grange Road
Foxfield Road
Broughton Road
Torver Way
The Ridge
Hilltop Gardens
Avenue
Tubbenden Drive
Woodhead Drive
Southcroft Rd
CROFTON ROAD A232 CROFTON ROAD
Meadow Way
Grasmere Gardens
Windermere Cl
Lovibonds Avenue
Partridge Drive
Masefield View
Avonstowe Close
Norman Close
Rusland Avenue
Newstead
Newstead Wood School for Girls
Willersley Avenue
Ruskin Drive
Tile Farm Road
Reed Avenue
Surgery
Darrick Wood Swimming Pool
Locksbottom
Stables End
Crofton Road
Starts Close
Willow Walk
PO
Pallant Way
The Princess Royal University Hospital
Superstore
A&E
Darrick Wood School
Darrick Wood Sports Centre
Darrick Wood
Darrick Wood Primary School
Starts Hill
Avebury Rd
Winterborne Avenue
Bromley Tennis Centre
Sandy Bury
Tubbenden Junior & Infant Schools
Ashbourne Rise
Leamington Av
Tunstall Close
Stowting Road
Buckland Road
Roseberry Gdns
Ridgeway Crs
Benedict Dr
Southfleet Road
Wellbrook Road
Hilda Vale Road
Ninhams Wood
Holwood
Woldis Drive
The Birches
Vale Cl
Claremont Cl
Lantern Cl
Winton Road
Bassetts Way
Broadwater Gardens
Lyndhurst Close
Bridle Way
Thyer Cl
Artington Close
Hale Close
Acorn Way
Arden Gv
State Farm Avenue
Pinecrest Gardens
Isabella Drive
Cherrycot Rise
Curzon Close
Tubbenden Lane
Borkwood Way
Northlands Avenue
North Drive
Beechcroft Road
St Leonards Rise
Southlands Avenue
Oakleigh Gdns
Haywood Rise
Ashley Gardens
Pinewood Drive
South Drive
FARNBOROUGH COMMON A21
FARNBOROUGH WAY
Royal Cl
Starts Hill Av
Cobden Rd
Pitt Rd
Palmerston Road
Peel Road
Hartington Cl
Gladstone Road
Tubbenden Lane South
Chartwell Dr
Dane Cl
Darwin Cl
Hilborough Way
Oleander Cl
Ferndale Way
Durrant Way
Contessa
Ladycroft Way
Green Gdns
Clifton Rd
Orchard Rd
Limes Row
B2158
HIGH STREET
FARNBOROUGH HILL
Farnborough
Strawberry Flds
Pleasant View Pl
Tye Lane
Farnborough Primary School
Church Road
Ramus Wd Av
Cocksett Av
Cleave Av
Kent Close
Beechwood Av
Beechwood Avenue
Amethyst Court
A21
The Larches
Shire Lane
Old Hill
Lower Hook Farm
North End Farm
High Elms Country Park
Green Street Green
Cudham Lane North
Street
Orange Court Lane
North End Lane
High Elms Road
Hill
Rookery
The Rookery
Gorringes
Cuckoo Wood
1 grid square represents 500 metres

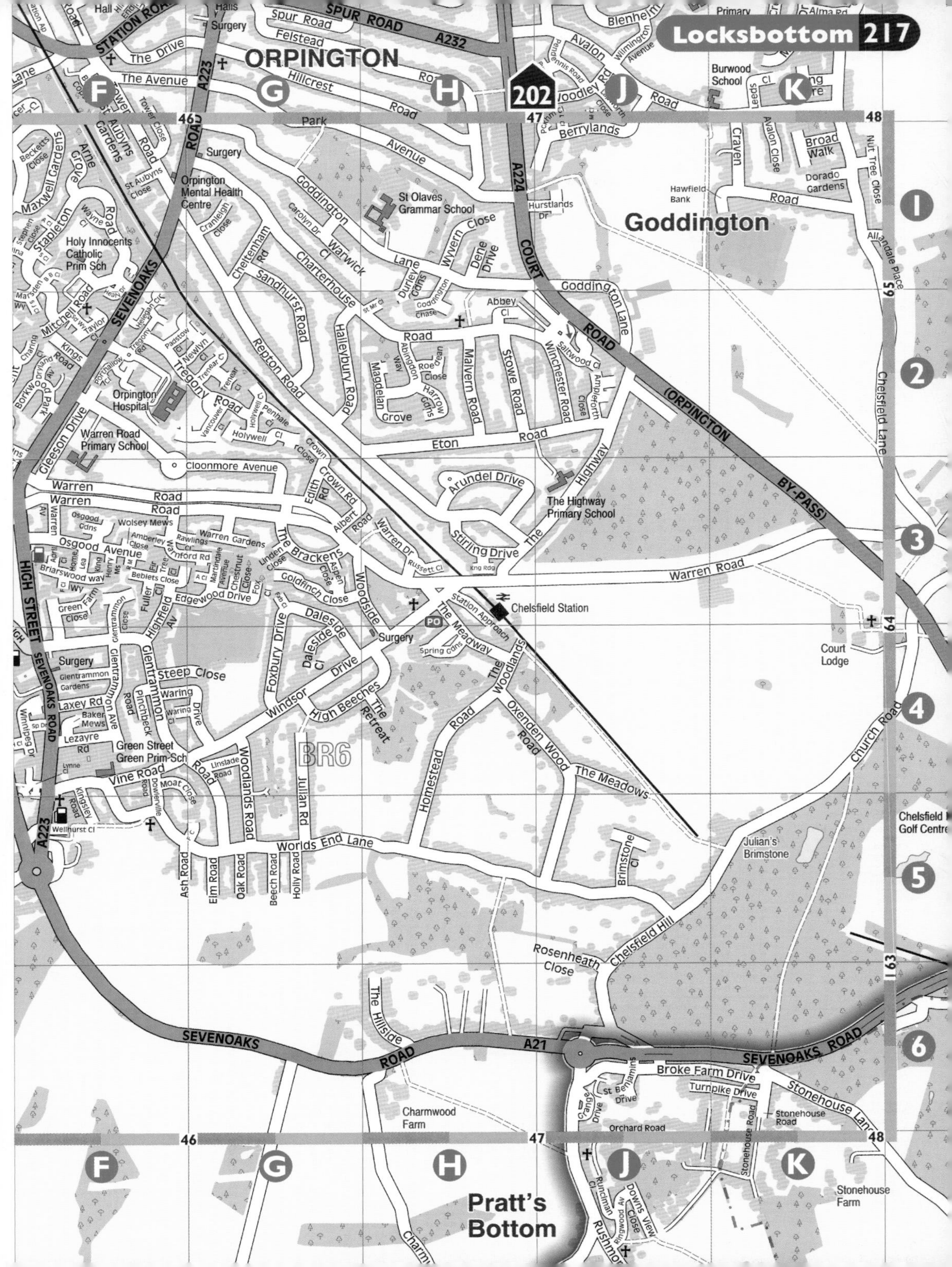
ORPINGTON
Goddington
Pratt's Bottom
Spur Road
A232
Station Road
The Drive
The Avenue
Hillcrest Road
Felstead
Avalon
Blenheim
Wilmington Avenue
Woodley Rd
Berrylands
Park Avenue
Goddington Lane
St Olaves Grammar School
Orpington Mental Health Centre
Holy Innocents Catholic Prim Sch
Orpington Hospital
Warren Road Primary School
Cloonmore Avenue
Warren Road
Osgood Avenue
Eton Road
Arundel Drive
The Highway Primary School
Stirling Drive
The Highway
Chelsfield Station
Station Approach
The Meadway
Surgery
Windsor Drive
High Beeches
The Retreat
BR6
Homestead Road
Oxenden Wood Road
The Woodlands
The Meadows
Worlds End Lane
Julian's Brimstone
Brimstone Cl
Chelsfield Hill
Rosenheath Close
Church Road
Court Lodge
Chelsfield Lane
Chelsfield Golf Centre
Court Road (Orpington By-Pass)
A224
A223
High Street
Sevenoaks Road
A21
Broke Farm Drive
Turnpike Drive
Stonehouse Lane
Stonehouse Road
Orchard Road
Charmwood Farm
Stonehouse Farm
The Hillside
Green Street Green Prim Sch
Vine Road
Woodlands Road
Julian Rd
Ash Road
Elm Road
Oak Road
Beech Road
Holly Road
Foxbury Drive
Daleside
Woodside
Goldfinch Close
Edgewood Drive
Highfield Av
Glentrammon Road
Steep Close
Laxey Rd
Lezayre Rd
Tregony Road
Repton Road
Sandhurst Road
Haileybury Road
Malvern Road
Stowe Road
Winchester Road
Charterhouse Road
Cheltenham Rd
Warwick Cl
Wyvern Close
Dene Drive
Hurstlands Dr
Hawfield Bank
Dorado Gardens
Broad Walk
Burwood School
Nut Tree Close
Allandale Place
Craven Road
Avalon Close
Mitchell Road
Maxwell Gardens
Arne Grove
Gleeson Drive
Kings Road
Crown Rd
Edith Rd
Albert Road
The Brackens
Warren Dr
Russett Cl
Magdelan Grove
Harrow Gdns
202
F G H J K
46 47 48
1 2 3 4 5 6
65 64 63

Abbey Wood 128 C4
Acton 117 K1
Acton Green 118 A4
Addington 213 J4
Addiscombe 197 G4
Aldborough Hatch 72 E1
Aldersbrook 71 G5
Alperton 80 A6
Anerley 181 H5
Ashford 152 D6
Avery Hill 167 H1
Balham 160 E2
Bandonhill 210 D3
Barking 90 D5
Barkingside 54 B6
Barnehurst 150 A4
Barnes 138 E2
Barnes Cray 150 E5
Barnet 32 D1
Barnet Gate 31 G1
Barnsbury 84 E5
Barwell 205 J5
Battersea 140 E1
Bayswater 101 F6
Beckenham 182 D5
Beckton 107 K5
Becontree 91 K3
Beddington 195 K6
Beddington Corner 195 F4
Bedford Park 118 C3
Belgravia 15 G6
Bell Green 164 C5
Bellingham 164 D6
Belmont 208 E6
Belmont 43 G5
Belvedere 129 J5
Benhilton 209 F1
Berrylands 191 G3
Bethnal Green 104 D2
Bexley 148 D5
Bexleyheath 149 G5
Bickley 184 D5
Blackfen 168 A1
Blackheath 145 J3
Blackheath Park 145 K5
Blackwall 106 B6
Bloomsbury 10 D1
The Borough 18 D3
Bow 105 J1
Bow Common 105 J4
Bowes Park 48 E2
Bowmans 170 C2
Brentford 116 E6
Brentford End 116 C6
Brimsdown 25 G3
Brixton 142 B5
Broad Green 196 C4
Brockley 144 C6
Bromley 184 A5
Bromley 105 K2
Bromley Common 200 C3
Bromley Park 183 H4
Brompton 14 C5
Brondesbury 82 C4
Brondesbury Park 82 B6
Brook Green 119 F3
Broom Hill 202 A4
Brunswick Park 34 A5
Buckhurst Hill 39 G5
Burnt Oak 45 F3
Bushey 28 C2
Bushey Heath 28 E2
Bushey Mead 177 G6
Bush Hill Park 36 A1
Caldecote Hill 29 F2
Camberwell 143 G2
Camden Town 84 A5
Canary Wharf 124 D1
Canning Town 107 F4
Cannon Hill 193 G1
Canonbury 85 J4
Canons Park 44 A3
Carpenders Park 27 K4
Carshalton 209 J2
Carshalton Beeches 209 J6
Carshalton on the Hill 209 K5
Castle Green 91 J6
Catford 165 F3
Chadwell Heath 73 K2
Charlton 126 C5
Chase Cross 57 G2
Chattern Hill 152 E6
Cheam 208 C3
Chelsea 121 F5
Chessington 206 A4
Child's Hill 64 C6
China Town 10 D5
Chingford 38 B3
Chingford Green 38 A3
Chingford Hatch 38 C6
Chipping Barnet 20 C6
Chislehurst 185 H3
Chislehurst West 185 F2
Chiswick 118 C4
Church End 46 E5
Church End 81 H5
City of London 12 B5
Clapham 141 G3
Clapham Park 161 J1
Clapton Park 87 H2
Claremont Park 204 A5
Claygate 205 F4
Clayhall 53 K5
Clerkenwell 5 J6
Cockfosters 21 J6
Coldblow 169 K4
Coldharbour 130 D4
Cole Park 156 B1
Colindale 45 G6
College Park 99 J2
Collier Row 56 E4
Collier's Wood 178 C3
Colney Hatch 47 K2
Coney Hall 214 C2
Coombe 176 B3
Copse Hill 176 D3
Cottenham Park 176 E4
Cranbrook 72 A4
Cranford 133 K1
Cranley Gardens 66 A1
Crayford 150 D6
Creekmouth 108 E4
Cricklewood 82 B2
Crockenhill 203 K3
Crofton 201 J6
Crooked Billet 176 E2
Crouch End 66 C3
Croydon 211 K1
Crystal Palace 181 H2
Cubitt Town 125 F4
Custom House 107 J6
Dagenham 92 D5
Dalston 86 B5
Dartford 171 F2
Dartmouth Park 66 A6
Deacons Hill 30 C1
De Beauvoir Town 86 A6
Deptford 124 C6
Derry Downs 202 E3
Dollis Hill 81 K1
Dormer's Wells 96 B6
Downham 183 G1
Ducks Island 32 B2
Dudden Hill 81 J3
Dulwich 163 G4
Dulwich Village 163 F2
Ealing 97 J6
Earl's Court 119 K5
Earlsfield 160 B3
East Acton 99 H6
East Barnet 33 H2
East Bedfont 152 E2
Eastbury 26 D6
Eastcote 59 F4
Eastcote Village 59 F2
East Dulwich 143 H6
East Finchley 47 H6
East Ham 107 J1
East Molesey 189 H2
East Sheen 138 A6
East Wickham 148 B2
Eden Park 198 C1
Edgware 30 D6
Edmonton 36 A6
Elmers End 182 A6
Elm Park 93 K3
Elmstead 184 D1
Elstree 30 A1
Eltham 166 D1
Enfield 23 J5
Enfield Highway 24 E3
Enfield Island Village 25 K1
Enfield Town 23 K4
Enfield Wash 25 G1
Erith 130 C5
Esher 204 C2
Ewell 207 J6
Fair Cross 91 F3
Fairlop 54 E4
Falconwood 147 K5
Farnborough 216 A3
Feltham 154 A4
Field Common 188 E4
Finchley 46 E4
Finsbury 5 J4
Finsbury Park 66 E6
Foots Cray 186 C2
Forestdale 213 G6
Forest Gate 88 E3
Forest Hill 164 A3
Fortis Green 65 K1
Forty Hill 24 B2
Foxbury 185 J1
Friday Hill 38 B5
Friern Barnet 33 J6
Fulham 139 G1
Fullwell Cross 54 D4
Furzedown 161 G6
Gants Hill 71 K3
Gidea Park 57 H5
Giggshill 190 B4
Globe Town 105 F2
Goddington 217 J1
Golders Green 64 C3
Goodmayes 73 H6
Gospel Oak 84 A3
Grange Hill 54 D2
Grange Park 23 G6
Greenford 96 D3
Greenhill 61 F2
Green Street Green 216 E5
Greenwich 125 G5
Grove Park 138 A2
Grove Park 166 B5
Hackbridge 195 G6
Hackney 86 E4
Hackney Wick 87 J4
Hadley 20 D4
Hadley Wood 21 H1
Haggerston 7 K2
Hainault 55 F3
Hale End 52 B2
Ham 156 E5
Hammersmith 118 E4
Hampstead 83 H2
Hampstead Garden Suburb 65 F2
Hampton 173 G4
Hampton Hill 155 H6
Hampton Wick 174 C4
Hanwell 115 J1
Hanworth 154 C5
Harlesden 99 G1
Harlington 113 F6
Harmondsworth 112 A6
Harringay 67 G2
Harrow 60 D3
Harrow on the Hill 60 E5
Harrow Weald 42 E3
Hatch End 41 J3
Hatton 133 H5
Hayes 94 A4
Hayes 200 A4
Hayes End 94 B3
Hayes Town 114 B1
Headstone 60 B1
Heath Park 75 K3
Heath Side 170 C4
Hendon 63 K2
Herne Hill 162 D1
Heston 134 E1
Higham Hill 51 G5
Highams Park 51 K3
High Barnet 20 A4
Highbury 85 H3
Highgate 65 K4
Highwood Hill 31 H4
Hinchley Wood 205 F1
Hither Green 165 H1
Hockenden 187 J6
Holborn 11 G2
Holders Hill 46 B4
Holywell 26 C1
Homerton 87 F4
Honor Oak 164 A1
Honor Oak Park 164 B1
Hook 206 A3
Hook Green 170 C6
Hornsey 66 E1
Hornsey Vale 67 F2
Hounslow 135 F3
Hounslow West 134 C4
Hoxton 7 G3
Hurst Park 173 H5
The Hyde 63 H2
Ilford 90 B1
Isle of Dogs 125 F4
Isleworth 136 C4
Islington 85 G6
Joyden's Wood 170 C6
Kennington 121 K6
Kensal Green 100 A1
Kensal Rise 100 B1
Kensal Town 100 C3
Kensington 119 K3
Kentish Town 84 C4
Kenton 61 J2
Keston 215 H2
Keston Mark 215 H1
Kevingtown 203 G3
Kew 137 G1
Kidbrooke 146 B3
Kilburn 82 C6
Kingsbury 62 D3
Kingsland 86 A5
Kingston upon Thames 174 D6
Kingston Vale 176 A1
Kitt's End 20 C1
Knightsbridge 14 D2
Knight's Hill 162 D3
Ladywell 144 D5
Lambeth 17 J4
Lampton 135 G2
Lea Bridge 87 F1
Lee 165 J1
Lessness Heath 129 J6
Lewisham 145 F5
Leyton 88 B1
Leytonstone 70 D5
Limehouse 105 G6
Lisson Grove 9 F1
Little Heath 73 J1
Little Ilford 90 A3
Little Stanmore 44 B4
Locksbottom 216 B1
Long Ditton 190 C5
Longlands 167 H5
Lower Clapton 86 E2
Lower Edmonton 36 A4
Lower Feltham 153 H5
Lower Green 189 G6
Lower Holloway 85 F3
Lower Place 98 E1
Lower Sydenham 164 A6
Loxford 90 C3
Maida Vale 101 F2
Maitland Park 83 K4
Manor Park 89 J2
Marks Gate 56 A5
Marylebone 9 G2
Mayfair 9 J6
Maypole 170 B3
Merry Hill 28 B3
Merton 177 K4
Merton Park 177 J5
Mile End 105 G3
Mill Hill 45 J1
Mill Meads 106 B1
Millwall 124 E3
Mitcham 179 F6
Monken Hadley 20 C3
Monks Orchard 197 K4
Moor Park 26 A6
Morden 193 K1
Morden Park 193 H3
Mortlake 137 K3
Motspur Park 192 D3
Mottingham 166 B4
Muswell Hill 48 A5
Nash 215 F4
Neasden 81 F2
New Addington 214 B5
New Barnet 21 F6
New Beckenham 182 B2
Newbury Park 72 D3
New Charlton 126 C4
New Cross 144 B3
New Cross Gate 144 B2
New Eltham 167 G4
Newington 17 K5
New Malden 176 C6
New Southgate 34 C6
New Town 171 J1
Noel Park 49 H5
Norbiton 175 G5
Norbury 180 C5
North Acton 98 E3
North Cheam 208 B1
North Cray 169 H5
North End 150 C2
North End 65 G5
North Feltham 134 A6
North Finchley 47 G2
North Harrow 59 K3
North Hyde 114 D4
North Kensington 100 B4
Northolt 78 A5
North Sheen 137 J3
Northumberland Heath 149 K1
North Wembley 61 H5
Northwood 40 A4
Northwood Hills 40 B5
North Woolwich 126 D2
Norwood Green 115 F4
Norwood New Town 180 E2
Notting Hill 100 C6
Nunhead 143 K5
Oakleigh Park 33 H4
Oakwood 34 D1
Old Bexley 169 H2
Old Ford 87 G6
Old Malden 192 A4
Old Oak Common 99 H3
Olympic Park 87 J5
Orpington 202 B6
Osidge 34 C4
Osterley 135 H1
Oxhey 27 H1
Paddington 8 A2
Palmers Green 34 E5
Park Langley 199 F3
Park Royal 98 C2
Parsons Green 139 K3
Peckham 143 J3
Penge 181 K3
Pentonville 5 H2
Perivale 79 J6
Petersham 157 F3
Petts Wood 201 J1
Pimlico 121 H5
Pinner 59 H1
Pinner Green 41 G5
Pinnerwood Park 41 G3
Plaistow 106 D2
Plaistow 183 K2
Plashet 89 H4
Plumstead 127 H5
Plumstead Common 128 A6
Ponders End 24 E6
Poplar 105 J6
Poverest 202 B1
Preston 61 K5
Primrose Hill 3 H1
Purfleet 131 K5
Putney 139 G6
Putney Heath 159 F2
Putney Vale 158 D5
Queensbury 44 A6
Queen's Park 100 C1
Rainham 111 K2
Ramsden 202 D5
Rayners Lane 59 K5
Raynes Park 177 F6
Redbridge 71 G2
Regent's Park 3 K3
Richmond 137 F6
Richmond Hill 157 F1
Rise Park 57 G4
Roehampton 138 C6
Romford 74 E2
The Rookery 26 E2
Rosehill 194 A5
Rotherhithe 124 A3
Roundshaw 211 F4
Roxeth 60 C6
Ruislip 58 C3
Ruislip Common 58 A1
Ruislip Gardens 76 C1
Ruislip Manor 58 E6
Rush Green 75 F4
Ruxley 187 F2
Rydens 188 B6
St George in the East 104 C6
St Giles 10 D3
St Helier 194 B5
St James's 16 C1
St Johns 144 D3
St John's Wood 101 G1
St Luke's 6 D6
St Margarets 156 D1
St Mary Cray 202 D2
St Pancras 5 F5
St Paul's Cray 186 B5
Sands End 140 B2
Seething Wells 190 C3
Selhurst 196 E2
Seven Kings 72 E5
Shacklewell 86 C2
Shadwell 104 E6
Shepherd's Bush 118 E1
Shirley 197 K6
Shooters Hill 147 H2
Shoreditch 7 F5
Shortlands 183 H6
Sidcup 168 C6
Silvertown 126 B2
Sipson 112 C5
Slade Green 150 D3
Soho 10 C4
Somers Town 4 C3
Southall 114 C2
South Beddington 210 D4
Southborough 200 E3
South Bromley 106 B5
South Croydon 211 H4
Southend 165 F6
Southfields 159 K3
Southgate 34 E3
South Hackney 86 E6
South Hampstead 83 F5
South Harrow 78 B1
South Hornchurch 93 F6
South Kensington 120 B5
South Lambeth 141 K1
South Norwood 180 E6
South Oxhey 27 F5
South Ruislip 77 H2
South Tottenham 68 A2
South Wimbledon 178 B1
South Woodford 52 E5
Spitalfields 13 J1
Spring Grove 135 J2
Spring Park 198 D6
Stamford Hill 68 B4
Stanmore 43 H1
Stanwell 152 A1
Stepney 104 E4
Stockwell 141 K4
Stoke Newington 68 B6
Stonehill Green 187 K2
Stoneleigh 207 H3
Strand 10 E5
Stratford 88 A5
Stratford Marsh 88 A6
Strawberry Hill 155 J5
Streatham 179 K1
Streatham Hill 161 K3
Streatham Park 161 H6
Streatham Vale 179 G3
Stroud Green 67 G3
Sudbury 79 F3
Summerstown 160 C4
Sundridge 184 B2
Surbiton 190 D5
Sutton 209 G3
Swiss Cottage 83 H6
Sydenham 182 A1
Teddington 173 J2
Temple Hill 151 G5
Thames Ditton 190 B4
Thamesmead 109 G6
Thornton Heath 180 C6
Tokyngton 80 D4
Tolworth 191 H5
Tooting 178 E1
Tooting Graveney 178 C1
Tottenham 50 A5
Tottenham Hale 50 B6
Totteridge 32 D3
Totteridge Green 32 A3
Tufnell Park 84 C2
Tulse Hill 162 C3
Twickenham 155 K3
Underhill 32 E1
Upper Clapton 68 C5
Upper Edmonton 36 C6
Upper Elmers End 198 C2
Upper Holloway 66 C5
Upper Norwood 180 E4
Upper Shirley 212 E2
Upper Sydenham 163 H6
Upper Tooting 160 D5
Upper Walthamstow 70 A1
Upton 89 F5
Upton Park 89 G6
Vale of Health 83 H1
Vauxhall 121 K5
Waddon 195 K6
Walham Green 139 K2
Wallend 90 A6
Wallington 210 A3
Walthamstow 69 H1
Walworth 122 D6
Wandle Park 196 B6
Wandsworth 139 K5
Wanstead 71 F4
Wapping 123 J1
Watford Heath 27 J2
Wealdstone 43 G6
Welling 148 C4
Welsh Harp 63 F5
Wembley 80 A2
Wembley Park 80 C1
West Acton 98 C5
West Barnes 193 F2
West Bedfont 152 C2
Westbourne Green 100 E3
West Brompton 120 A6
West Drayton 112 A3
West Dulwich 162 E4
West Ealing 116 B1
West Ewell 207 F4
West Green 49 J6
West Hampstead 82 E3
West Harrow 60 C4
West Heath 128 E6
West Heath 65 F6
West Hendon 63 J4
West Hill 159 H2
West Kensington 119 G5
West Kilburn 100 C2
Westminster 16 B5
West Molesey 188 E1
West Norwood 162 D6
Weston Green 189 K5
West Ruislip 58 A5
West Wickham 199 G5
Whetstone 33 F4
Whitechapel 13 K5
Whitton 155 H1
Widmore 184 C5
Willesden 81 J4
Willesden Green 81 K5
Wilmington 170 E6
Wimbledon 177 H1
Winchmore Hill 35 J3
Wood End 94 C5
Wood End Green 94 C4
Woodford 53 F2
Woodford Bridge 53 K3
Woodford Green 52 E3
Woodford Wells 39 F5
Wood Green 49 G4
Woodlands 135 J4
Woodside 197 H3
Woodside Park 32 E6
Woolwich 127 F3
Worcester Park 192 E6
World's End 23 G5
The Wrythe 194 D6
Yeading 95 G3

USING THE STREET INDEX

Street names are listed alphabetically. Each street name is followed by its postal town or area locality, the Postcode District, the page number, and the reference to the square in which the name is found.

Standard index entries are shown as follows:

1 Av *WOOL/PLUM* SE18..............**127** G3

Street names and selected addresses not shown on the map due to scale restrictions are shown in the index with an asterisk:

Abbeville Ms *CLAP* SW4 * **141** J6

Entries in red indicate streets located within the London Congestion Zone. Refer to the map pages for the location of the Zone boundary.

GENERAL ABBREVIATIONS

ACC	ACCESS
ALY	ALLEY
AP	APPROACH
AR	ARCADE
ASS	ASSOCIATION
AV	AVENUE
BCH	BEACH
BLDS	BUILDINGS
BND	BEND
BNK	BANK
BR	BRIDGE
BRK	BROOK
BTM	BOTTOM
BUS	BUSINESS
BVD	BOULEVARD
BY	BYPASS
CATH	CATHEDRAL
CEM	CEMETERY
CEN	CENTRE
CFT	CROFT
CH	CHURCH
CHA	CHASE
CHYD	CHURCHYARD
CIR	CIRCLE
CIRC	CIRCUS
CL	CLOSE
CLFS	CLIFFS
CMP	CAMP
CNR	CORNER
CO	COUNTY
COLL	COLLEGE
COM	COMMON
COMM	COMMISSION
CON	CONVENT
COT	COTTAGE
COTS	COTTAGES
CP	CAPE
CPS	COPSE
CR	CREEK
CREM	CREMATORIUM
CRS	CRESCENT
CSWY	CAUSEWAY
CT	COURT
CTRL	CENTRAL
CTS	COURTS
CTYD	COURTYARD
CUTT	CUTTINGS
CV	COVE
CYN	CANYON
DEPT	DEPARTMENT
DL	DALE
DM	DAM
DR	DRIVE
DRO	DROVE
DRY	DRIVEWAY
DWGS	DWELLINGS
E	EAST
EMB	EMBANKMENT
EMBY	EMBASSY
ESP	ESPLANADE
EST	ESTATE
EX	EXCHANGE
EXPY	EXPRESSWAY
EXT	EXTENSION
F/O	FLYOVER
FC	FOOTBALL CLUB
FK	FORK
FLD	FIELD
FLDS	FIELDS
FLS	FALLS
FM	FARM
FT	FORT
FTS	FLATS
FWY	FREEWAY
FY	FERRY
GA	GATE
GAL	GALLERY
GDN	GARDEN
GDNS	GARDENS
GLD	GLADE
GLN	GLEN
GN	GREEN
GND	GROUND
GRA	GRANGE
GRG	GARAGE
GT	GREAT
GTWY	GATEWAY
GV	GROVE
HGR	HIGHER
HL	HILL
HLS	HILLS
HO	HOUSE
HOL	HOLLOW
HOSP	HOSPITAL
HRB	HARBOUR
HTH	HEATH
HTS	HEIGHTS
HVN	HAVEN
HWY	HIGHWAY
IMP	IMPERIAL
IN	INLET
IND EST	INDUSTRIAL ESTATE
INF	INFIRMARY
INFO	INFORMATION
INT	INTERCHANGE
IS	ISLAND
JCT	JUNCTION
JTY	JETTY
KG	KING
KNL	KNOLL
L	LAKE
LA	LANE
LDG	LODGE
LGT	LIGHT
LK	LOCK
LKS	LAKES
LNDG	LANDING
LTL	LITTLE
LWR	LOWER
MAG	MAGISTRATES'
MAN	MANSIONS
MD	MEAD
MDW	MEADOWS
MEM	MEMORIAL
MI	MILL
MKT	MARKET
MKTS	MARKETS
ML	MALL
MNR	MANOR
MS	MEWS
MSN	MISSION
MT	MOUNT
MTN	MOUNTAIN
MTS	MOUNTAINS
MUS	MUSEUM
MWY	MOTORWAY
N	NORTH
NE	NORTH EAST
NW	NORTH WEST
O/P	OVERPASS
OFF	OFFICE
ORCH	ORCHARD
OV	OVAL
PAL	PALACE
PAS	PASSAGE
PAV	PAVILION
PDE	PARADE
PH	PUBLIC HOUSE
PK	PARK
PKWY	PARKWAY
PL	PLACE
PLN	PLAIN
PLNS	PLAINS
PLZ	PLAZA
POL	POLICE STATION
PR	PRINCE
PREC	PRECINCT
PREP	PREPARATORY
PRIM	PRIMARY
PROM	PROMENADE
PRS	PRINCESS
PRT	PORT
PT	POINT
PTH	PATH
PZ	PIAZZA
QD	QUADRANT
QU	QUEEN
QY	QUAY
R	RIVER
RBT	ROUNDABOUT
RD	ROAD
RDG	RIDGE
REP	REPUBLIC
RES	RESERVOIR
RFC	RUGBY FOOTBALL CLUB
RI	RISE
RP	RAMP
RW	ROW
S	SOUTH
SCH	SCHOOL
SE	SOUTH EAST
SER	SERVICE AREA
SH	SHORE
SHOP	SHOPPING
SKWY	SKYWAY
SMT	SUMMIT
SOC	SOCIETY
SP	SPUR
SPR	SPRING
SQ	SQUARE
ST	STREET
STN	STATION
STR	STREAM
STRD	STRAND
SW	SOUTH WEST
TDG	TRADING
TER	TERRACE
THWY	THROUGHWAY
TNL	TUNNEL
TOLL	TOLLWAY
TPK	TURNPIKE
TR	TRACK
TRL	TRAIL
TWR	TOWER
U/P	UNDERPASS
UNI	UNIVERSITY
UPR	UPPER
V	VALE
VA	VALLEY
VIAD	VIADUCT
VIL	VILLA
VIS	VISTA
VLG	VILLAGE
VLS	VILLAS
VW	VIEW
W	WEST
WD	WOOD
WHF	WHARF
WK	WALK
WKS	WALKS
WLS	WELLS
WY	WAY
YD	YARD
YHA	YOUTH HOSTEL

POSTCODE TOWNS AND AREA ABBREVIATIONS

ABR/ST	Abridge/Stapleford Abbotts
ABYW	Abbey Wood
ACT	Acton
ALP/SUD	Alperton/Sudbury
ARCH	Archway
ASHF	Ashford (Surrey)
BAL	Balham
BANK	Bank
BAR	Barnet
BARB	Barbican
BARK	Barking
BARK/HLT	Barkingside/Hainault
BARN	Barnes
BAY/PAD	Bayswater/Paddington
BCTR	Becontree
BECK	Beckenham
BELMT	Belmont
BELV	Belvedere
BERM/RHTH	Bermondsey/ Rotherhithe
BETH	Bethnal Green
BFN/LL	Blackfen/Longlands
BGVA	Belgravia
BKHH	Buckhurst Hill
BKHTH/KID	Blackheath/Kidbrooke
BLKFR	Blackfriars
BMLY	Bromley
BMSBY	Bloomsbury
BORE	Borehamwood
BOW	Bow
BROCKY	Brockley
BRXN/ST	Brixton north/Stockwell
BRXS/STRHM	Brixton south/ Streatham Hill
BRYLDS	Berrylands
BTFD	Brentford
BTSEA	Battersea
BUSH	Bushey
BXLY	Bexley
BXLYHN	Bexleyheath north
BXLYHS	Bexleyheath south
CAMTN	Camden Town
CAN/RD	Canning Town/Royal Docks
CANST	Cannon Street station
CAR	Carshalton
CAT	Catford
CAVSQ/HST	Cavendish Square/ Harley Street
CDALE/KGS	Colindale/Kingsbury
CEND/HSY/T	Crouch End/Hornsey/ Turnpike Lane
CHARL	Charlton
CHCR	Charing Cross
CHDH	Chadwell Heath
CHEAM	Cheam
CHEL	Chelsea
CHIG	Chigwell
CHING	Chingford
CHSGTN	Chessington
CHST	Chislehurst
CHSWK	Chiswick
CITYW	City of London west
CLAP	Clapham
CLAY	Clayhall
CLKNW	Clerkenwell
CLPT	Clapton
CMBW	Camberwell
CONDST	Conduit Street
COVGDN	Covent Garden
CRICK	Cricklewood
CROY/NA	Croydon/ New Addington
CRW	Collier Row
DAGE	Dagenham east
DAGW	Dagenham west
DART	Dartford
DEN/HRF	Denham/Harefield
DEPT	Deptford
DUL	Dulwich
E/WMO/HCT	East & West Molesey/ Hampton Court
EA	Ealing
EBAR	East Barnet
EBED/NFELT	East Bedfont/ North Feltham
ECT	Earl's Court
ED	Edmonton
EDGW	Edgware
EDUL	East Dulwich
EFNCH	East Finchley
EHAM	East Ham
ELTH/MOT	Eltham/Mottingham
EMB	Embankment
EMPK	Emerson Park
EN	Enfield
ENC/FH	Enfield Chase/ Forty Hill
ERITH	Erith
ERITHM	Erith Marshes
ESH/CLAY	Esher/Claygate
EW	Ewell
FARR	Farringdon
FBAR/BDGN	Friern Barnet/ Bounds Green
FELT	Feltham
FENCHST	Fenchurch Street
FITZ	Fitzrovia
FLST/FETLN	Fleet Street/ Fetter Lane
FNCH	Finchley
FSBYE	Finsbury east
FSBYPK	Finsbury Park
FSBYW	Finsbury west
FSTGT	Forest Gate
FSTH	Forest Hill
FUL/PGN	Fulham/Parsons Green
GDMY/SEVK	Goodmayes/ Seven Kings
GFD/PVL	Greenford/Perivale
GINN	Gray's Inn
GLDGN	Golders Green
GNTH/NBYPK	Gants Hill/ Newbury Park
GNWCH	Greenwich
GPK	Gidea Park
GTPST	Great Portland Street
GWRST	Gower Street
HACK	Hackney
HAMP	Hampstead
HARH	Harold Hill
HAYES	Hayes
HBRY	Highbury
HCH	Hornchurch
HCIRC	Holborn Circus
HDN	Hendon
HDTCH	Houndsditch
HEST	Heston
HGDN/ICK	Hillingdon/Ickenham
HGT	Highgate
HHOL	High Holborn
HMSMTH	Hammersmith
HNHL	Herne Hill
HNWL	Hanwell
HOL/ALD	Holborn/Aldwych
HOLWY	Holloway
HOM	Homerton
HOR/WEW	Horton/West Ewell
HPTN	Hampton
HRW	Harrow
HSLW	Hounslow
HSLWW	Hounslow west
HTHAIR	Heathrow Airport
HYS/HAR	Hayes/Harlington
IL	Ilford
IS	Islington
ISLW	Isleworth
KCROSS	King's Cross
KENS	Kensington
KIL/WHAMP	Kilburn/ West Hampstead
KTBR	Knightsbridge
KTN/HRWW/WS	Kenton/Harrow Weald/Wealdstone
KTTN	Kentish Town
KUT/HW	Kingston upon Thames/ Hampton Wick
KUTN/CMB	Kingston upon Thames north/Coombe
LBTH	Lambeth
LEE/GVPK	Lee/Grove Park
LEW	Lewisham
LEY	Leyton
LINN	Lincoln's Inn
LOTH	Lothbury
LOU	Loughton
LSQ/SEVD	Leicester Square/ Seven Dials
LVPST	Liverpool Street
MANHO	Mansion House
MBLAR	Marble Arch
MHST	Marylebone High Street
MLHL	Mill Hill
MNPK	Manor Park
MON	Monument
MORT/ESHN	Mortlake/East Sheen
MRDN	Morden
MTCM	Mitcham
MUSWH	Muswell Hill
MV/WKIL	Maida Vale/ West Kilburn
MYFR/PICC	Mayfair/Piccadilly
MYFR/PKLN	Mayfair/Park Lane
NFNCH/WDSPK	North Finchley/ Woodside Park
NKENS	North Kensington
NOXST/BSQ	New Oxford Street/ Bloomsbury Square
NRWD	Norwood
NTGHL	Notting Hill
NTHLT	Northolt
NTHWD	Northwood
NWCR	New Cross
NWDGN	Norwood Green
NWMAL	New Malden
OBST	Old Broad Street
OLYMPICPK	Olympic Park
ORP	Orpington
OXHEY	Oxhey
OXSTW	Oxford Street west
PECK	Peckham
PEND	Ponders End
PGE/AN	Penge/Anerley
PIM	Pimlico
PIN	Pinner
PLMGR	Palmers Green
PLSTW	Plaistow
POP/IOD	Poplar/Isle of Dogs
PUR	Purfleet
PUR/KEN	Purley/Kenley
PUT/ROE	Putney/Roehampton
RAIN	Rainham (Gt Lon)
RCH/KEW	Richmond/Kew
RCHPK/HAM	Richmond Park/Ham
RDART	Rural Dartford
REDBR	Redbridge
REGST	Regent Street
RKW/CH/CXG	Rickmansworth/ Chorleywood/ Croxley Green
ROM	Romford
ROMW/RG	Romford west/ Rush Green
RSEV	Rural Sevenoaks
RSLP	Ruislip
RSQ	Russell Square
RYLN/HDSTN	Rayners Lane/ Headstone
RYNPK	Raynes Park
SAND/SEL	Sanderstead/Selsdon
SCUP	Sidcup
SDTCH	Shoreditch
SEVS/STOTM	Seven Sisters/South Tottenham
SHB	Shepherd's Bush
SKENS	South Kensington
SNWD	South Norwood
SOCK/AV	South Ockendon/ Aveley
SOHO/CST	Soho/Carnaby Street
SOHO/SHAV	Soho/ Shaftesbury Avenue
SRTFD	Stratford
STAN	Stanmore
STBT	St Bart's
STHGT/OAK	Southgate/Oakwood
STHL	Southall
STHWK	Southwark
STJS	St James's
STJSPK	St James's Park
STJWD	St John's Wood
STKPK	Stockley Park
STLK	St Luke's
STMC/STPC	St Mary Cray/ St Paul's Cray
STNW/STAM	Stoke Newington/ Stamford Hill
STP	St Paul's
STPAN	St Pancras
STRHM/NOR	Streatham/Norbury
STWL/WRAY	Stanwell/Wraysbury
SUN	Sunbury
SURB	Surbiton
SUT	Sutton
SWFD	South Woodford
SWLY	Swanley
SYD	Sydenham
TEDD	Teddington
THDIT	Thames Ditton
THHTH	Thornton Heath
THMD	Thamesmead
TOOT	Tooting
TOTM	Tottenham
TPL/STR	Temple/Strand
TRDG/WHET	Totteridge/Whetstone
TWK	Twickenham
TWRH	Tower Hill
UED	Upper Edmonton
UX/CGN	Uxbridge/Colham Green
VX/NE	Vauxhall/Nine Elms
WALTH	Walthamstow

WALW Walworth
WAN Wanstead
WAND/EARL Wandsworth/Earlsfield
WAP Wapping
WAT Watford
WATW Watford west
WBLY Wembley
WBPTN West Brompton
WCHMH Winchmore Hill
WCHPL Whitechapel
WDGN Wood Green
WDR/YW West Drayton/Yiewsley
WEA West Ealing
WELL Welling
WEST Westminster
WESTW Westminster west
WFD Woodford
WHALL Whitehall
WHTN Whitton
WIM/MER Wimbledon/Merton
WKENS West Kensington
WLGTN Wallington
WLSDN Willesden
WNWD West Norwood
WOOL/PLUM Woolwich/Plumstead
WOT/HER Walton-on-Thames/Hersham
WPK Worcester Park
WWKM West Wickham
YEAD Yeading

Index - streets

1

1 Av *WOOL/PLUM* SE18 127 G3

A

Aaron Hill Rd *EHAM* E6 108 A4
Abberley Ms *BTSEA* SW11 141 G4
Abbess Cl *BRXS/STRHM* SW2 162 C3
Abbeville Ms *CLAP* SW4 * 141 J6
Abbeville Rd *CEND/HSY/T* N8 66 D1
CLAP SW4 161 H1
Abbey Av *ALP/SUD* HA0 98 A1
Abbey Cl *HYS/HAR* UB3 114 A1
NTHLT UB5 95 K2
ORP BR6 217 H2
PIN HA5 41 F6
ROM RM1 75 H3
Abbey Crs *BELV* DA17 129 H4
Abbeydale Rd *ALP/SUD* HA0 80 B6
Abbey Dr *RDART* DA2 170 B4
TOOT SW17 179 F1
Abbeyfield Cl *MTCM* CR4 178 D5
Abbeyfield Est
BERM/RHTH SE16 123 K4
Abbeyfield Rd
BERM/RHTH SE16 123 K4
Abbeyfields Cl *WLSDN* NW10 98 C2
Abbey Gdns *CHST* BR7 185 F4
HMSMTH W6 119 H6
STHWK SE1 123 H4
STJWD NW8 101 G1
Abbey Gv *ABYW* SE2 128 C4
Abbeyhill Rd *BFN/LL* DA15 168 D3
Abbey La *BECK* BR3 182 D3
SRTFD E15 106 A1
Abbey Ms *ISLW* TW7 136 C2
WALTH E17 69 J2
Abbey Mt *BELV* DA17 129 G5
Abbey Orchard St
WEST SW1P 16 D4
Abbey Pk *BECK* BR3 182 D3
Abbey Pl *DART* DA1 * 151 G6
Abbey Rd *BARK* IG11 90 B6
BELV DA17 128 E4
BXLYHN DA7 149 F5
CROY/NA CR0 211 H1
EN EN1 24 A6
GNTH/NBYPK IG2 72 D2
SRTFD E15 88 C6
STJWD NW8 83 G6
WIM/MER SW19 178 B3
WLSDN NW10 98 D1
Abbey St *PLSTW* E13 106 E3
STHWK SE1 19 J4
Abbey Ter *ABYW* SE2 128 D3
Abbey Vw *MLHL* NW7 31 H5
Abbey Wk *E/WMO/HCT* KT8 173 G6
Abbey Wood Rd *ABYW* SE2 128 C4
Abbot Cl *RSLP* HA4 77 H1
Abbotsbury Cl *SRTFD* E15 106 A1
WKENS W14 119 H2
Abbotsbury Gdns *PIN* HA5 59 G3
Abbotsbury Ms *PECK* SE15 143 K4
Abbotsbury Rd *MRDN* SM4 194 A1
WKENS W14 119 H2
WWKM BR4 199 J6
Abbots Cl *STMC/STPC* BR5 201 H5
Abbots Dr *RYLN/HDSTN* HA2 60 A6
Abbotsford Av
SEVS/STOTM N15 67 J1
Abbotsford Gdns *WFD* IG8 52 E3
Abbotsford Rd
GDMY/SEVK IG3 73 G6
Abbots Gdns *EFNCH* N2 65 H1
Abbots Gn *CROY/NA* CR0 213 F4
Abbotshade Rd
BERM/RHTH SE16 * 124 A1
Abbotshall Av
STHGT/OAK N14 34 C5
Abbotshall Rd *CAT* SE6 165 G3
Abbotsleigh Cl *BELMT* SM2 209 F5
Abbotsleigh Rd
STRHM/NOR SW16 161 H6
Abbots Mnr *PIM* SW1V * 121 G5
Abbotsmede Cl *TWK* TW1 156 A4
Abbots Pk *BRXS/STRHM* SW2 162 B3
Abbot's Pl *KIL/WHAMP* NW6 83 F6
Abbots Rd *EDGW* HA8 45 F3
EHAM E6 89 H6
Abbots Ter *CEND/HSY/T* N8 66 E3
Abbotstone Rd
PUT/ROE SW15 139 F4
Abbot St *HACK* E8 86 B4
Abbots Wk *KENS* W8 * 120 A3
Abbots Wy *BECK* BR3 198 B2
Abbotswell Rd *BROCKY* SE4 144 C6
Abbotswood Cl *BELV* DA17 129 F3
Abbotswood Gdns *CLAY* IG5 53 K6
Abbotswood Rd *EDUL* SE22 143 F5
STRHM/NOR SW16 161 J5
Abbotswood Wy
HYS/HAR UB3 114 A1
Abbott Av *RYNPK* SW20 177 G5
Abbott Cl *HPTN* TW12 172 D2
NTHLT UB5 77 K4
Abbott Rd *POP/IOD* E14 106 A4
Abbotts Cl *IS* N1 * 85 J5
ROMW/RG RM7 56 D6
THMD SE28 109 J6
Abbotts Crs *CHING* E4 38 B6
ENC/FH EN2 23 H3
Abbotts Dr *ALP/SUD* HA0 61 H6
Abbotts Md
RCHPK/HAM TW10 * 156 D6
Abbotts Park Rd *LEY* E10 70 A4
Abbotts Rd *BAR* EN5 21 F5
CHEAM SM3 208 C2
MTCM CR4 195 H1
STHL UB1 114 D1
Abbott's Wk *BXLYHN* DA7 148 E1
Abchurch La *MANHO* EC4N 13 F5
Abdale Rd *SHB* W12 118 E1
Aberavon Rd *BOW* E3 105 G2
Abercairn Rd
STRHM/NOR SW16 179 H3
Aberconway Rd *MRDN* SM4 178 A6
Abercorn Cl *MLHL* NW7 46 C3
STJWD NW8 101 G2
Abercorn Crs
RYLN/HDSTN HA2 60 B5
Abercorn Dell *BUSH* WD23 28 C4
Abercorn Gdns *CHDH* RM6 73 H3
KTN/HRWW/WS HA3 61 K4
Abercorn Gv *RSLP* HA4 58 B1
Abercorn Ms
RCHPK/HAM TW10 137 G6
Abercorn Pl *STJWD* NW8 101 G2
Abercorn Rd *MLHL* NW7 46 C3
STAN HA7 43 J3
Abercorn Wk *STJWD* NW8 101 G2
Abercorn Wy *STHWK* SE1 123 H5
Abercrombie Dr *EN* EN1 24 C2
Abercrombie St *BTSEA* SW11 140 D3
Aberdare Cl *WWKM* BR4 199 F6
Aberdare Gdns
KIL/WHAMP NW6 83 F5
MLHL NW7 46 B3
Aberdare Rd *PEND* EN3 24 E5
Aberdeen Cots *STAN* HA7 * 43 J3
Aberdeen La *HBRY* N5 85 H3
Aberdeen Pde *UED* N18 * 50 D1
Aberdeen Pk *HBRY* N5 85 H3
Aberdeen Pl *BAY/PAD* W2 2 A7
Aberdeen Rd *CROY/NA* CR0 211 J2
HBRY N5 85 J2
KTN/HRWW/WS HA3 43 F5
UED N18 50 C1
WLSDN NW10 81 H3
Aberdeen Ter *BKHTH/KID* SE3 145 G3
Aberdour Rd *GDMY/SEVK* IG3 91 H1
Aberdour St *STHWK* SE1 19 G6
Aberfeldy St *POP/IOD* E14 106 A5
Aberford Gdns
WOOL/PLUM SE18 146 D2
Aberfoyle Rd
STRHM/NOR SW16 179 J3
Abergeldie Rd *LEE/GVPK* SE12 166 A1
Abernethy Rd *LEW* SE13 145 H5
Abersham Rd *HACK* E8 86 B3
Abery St *WOOL/PLUM* SE18 127 K4
Abingdon Cl *STHWK* SE1 123 G5
WIM/MER SW19 178 B2
WPK KT4 207 K1
Abingdon Rd *FNCH* N3 47 G5
KENS W8 119 K3
STRHM/NOR SW16 179 K4
Abingdon St *WEST* SW1P 16 E3
Abingdon Vls *KENS* W8 119 K3
Abingdon Wy *ORP* BR6 217 H2
Abinger Av *BELMT* SM2 208 A6
Abinger Cl *BMLY* BR1 184 D6
CROY/NA CR0 214 A4
GDMY/SEVK IG3 91 G2
WLGTN SM6 210 E3
Abinger Dr *NRWD* SE19 180 D3
Abinger Gdns *ISLW* TW7 135 K5
Abinger Gv *DEPT* SE8 124 C6
Abinger Ms *MV/WKIL* W9 100 E3
Abinger Rd *CHSWK* W4 118 C3
Ablett St *BERM/RHTH* SE16 123 K5
Abney Park Ter
STNW/STAM N16 * 68 B6
Aboyne Dr *RYNPK* SW20 176 D5
Aboyne Rd *TOOT* SW17 160 B5
WLSDN NW10 81 G1
Abraham Cl *OXHEY* WD19 27 F6
Abridge Gdns *CRW* RM5 56 C2
Abridge Wy *BARK* IG11 109 H1
Abyssinia Cl *BTSEA* SW11 140 D5
Abyssinia Rd *BTSEA* SW11 * 140 D5
Acacia Av *BTFD* TW8 136 C1
HCH RM12 75 H6
HYS/HAR UB3 94 D5
RSLP HA4 58 E5
TOTM N17 49 K3
WBLY HA9 80 A3
Acacia Cl *DEPT* SE8 124 B4
STAN HA7 42 E2
STMC/STPC BR5 201 J2
Acacia Dr *CHEAM* SM3 193 J5
Acacia Gdns *STJWD* NW8 2 B2
WWKM BR4 199 F6
Acacia Gv *DUL* SE21 162 E4
NWMAL KT3 176 B6
Acacia Ms *WDR/YW* UB7 112 A6
Acacia Pl *STJWD* NW8 2 B2
Acacia Rd *ACT* W3 98 E6
BECK BR3 182 C6
DART DA1 171 F3
ENC/FH EN2 23 K2
HPTN TW12 173 F2
MTCM CR4 179 F5
STJWD NW8 2 B2
STRHM/NOR SW16 179 K4
WALTH E17 69 G3
WAN E11 70 C6
WDGN N22 49 G4
The Acacias *EBAR* EN4 * 21 H6
Acacia Wy *BFN/LL* DA15 168 A2
Academia Wy *TOTM* N17 50 A2
Academy Fields Rd *GPK* RM2 75 K2
Academy Gdns *CROY/NA* CR0 197 G5
NTHLT UB5 95 H1
Academy Pl *ISLW* TW7 135 K1
WOOL/PLUM SE18 146 E2
Academy Rd
WOOL/PLUM SE18 146 E1
Academy Wy *BCTR* RM8 91 H2
Acanthus Dr *STHWK* SE1 123 H5
Acanthus Rd *BTSEA* SW11 141 F4
Accommodation Rd
GLDGN NW11 64 D4
Ace Pde *CHSGTN* KT9 206 A1
Acer Av *YEAD* UB4 95 J3
Acer Rd *HACK* E8 86 B4
Acfold Rd *FUL/PGN* SW6 140 A2
Achilles Cl *STHWK* SE1 123 H5
Achilles Rd *KIL/WHAMP* NW6 82 E3
Achilles St *NWCR* SE14 144 B1
Acklam Rd *NKENS* W10 100 D4
Acklington Dr
CDALE/KGS NW9 45 G4
Ackmar Rd *FUL/PGN* SW6 139 K2
Ackroyd Dr *BOW* E3 105 H4
Ackroyd Rd *FSTH* SE23 164 A2
Acland Cl *WOOL/PLUM* SE18 147 J1
Acland Crs *CMBW* SE5 142 E5
Acland Rd *CRICK* NW2 81 K4
Acle Cl *BARK/HLT* IG6 54 B4
Acock Gv *NTHLT* UB5 78 B2
Acol Crs *RSLP* HA4 77 F3
Acol Rd *KIL/WHAMP* NW6 83 F5
Acorn Cl *CHING* E4 51 K1
CHST BR7 185 H1
ENC/FH EN2 23 G2
HPTN TW12 173 G2
STAN HA7 43 H3
Acorn Gdns *ACT* W3 99 F4
NRWD SE19 181 G4
Acorn Gv *HYS/HAR* UB3 133 J1
RSLP HA4 76 D2
Acorn Pde *PECK* SE15 * 143 J1
Acorn Rd *DART* DA1 150 C6
Acorns Wy *ESH/CLAY* KT10 204 C3
Acorn Wy *BECK* BR3 199 F2
FSTH SE23 164 A5
ORP BR6 216 B2
Acre Dr *EDUL* SE22 143 H5
Acre La *BRXS/STRHM* SW2 142 A5
CAR SM5 210 A2
Acre Rd *DAGE* RM10 92 D5
KUTN/CMB KT2 175 F4
WIM/MER SW19 178 C2
Acre Wy *NTHWD* HA6 40 D4
Acris St *WAND/EARL* SW18 140 B6
Acton Cl *ED* N9 36 C4
Acton Hill Ms *ACT* W3 * 117 J1
Acton La *CHSWK* W4 117 K3
WLSDN NW10 98 E2
Acton Ms *HACK* E8 86 B6
Acton St *FSBYW* WC1X 5 G5
Acuba Rd *WAND/EARL* SW18 160 A4
Acworth Cl *ED* N9 36 E2
Acworth Pl *DART* DA1 * 171 F1
Ada Cl *FBAR/BDGN* N11 33 K5
Ada Gdns *POP/IOD* E14 106 B5
SRTFD E15 88 D6
Adair Cl *SNWD* SE25 181 J6
Adair Rd *NKENS* W10 100 C3
Adam Cl *CAT* SE6 164 C6
FSTH SE23 163 K4
Adam & Eve Ms *KENS* W8 119 K3
Adam Rd *CHING* E4 51 H2
Adams Cl *BRYLDS* KT5 191 G3
FNCH N3 46 E3
WBLY HA9 62 D6
Adams Ct *OBST* EC2N 13 F3
Adams Ms *TOOT* SW17 160 E4
WDGN N22 49 F3
Adamson Rd *CAN/RD* E16 106 E5
HAMP NW3 83 H5
Adamson Wy *BECK* BR3 199 F2
Adams Pl *HOLWY* N7 85 F3
Adamsrill Cl *EN* EN1 35 K1
Adamsrill Rd *SYD* SE26 164 A6
Adams Rd *BECK* BR3 198 B2
TOTM N17 49 K5
Adam's Rw *MYFR/PKLN* W1K 9 H6
Adams Sq *BXLYHS* DA6 149 F4
Adam St *CHCR* WC2N 11 F6
Adams Wk *KUT/HW* KT1 175 F5
Adams Wy *CROY/NA* CR0 197 G3
Adam Wk *FUL/PGN* SW6 * 139 F1
Ada Pl *BETH* E2 86 C6
Adare Wk *STRHM/NOR* SW16 161 K4
Ada Rd *ALP/SUD* HA0 * 79 J1
CMBW SE5 143 F1
Adastra Wy *WLGTN* SM6 210 E4
Ada St *HACK* E8 86 D6
Adderley Gdns
ELTH/MOT SE9 167 F6
Adderley Gv *BTSEA* SW11 141 F6
Adderley Rd
KTN/HRWW/WS HA3 43 F4
Adderley St *POP/IOD* E14 106 A5
Addington Dr
NFNCH/WDSPK N12 47 H2
Addington Gv *SYD* SE26 164 B6
Addington Rd *BOW* E3 105 J2
CAN/RD E16 106 C3
CROY/NA CR0 196 B5
FSBYPK N4 67 G4
WWKM BR4 214 A2
Addington Sq *CMBW* SE5 142 D1
Addington St *STHWK* SE1 17 H3
Addington Village Rd
CROY/NA CR0 213 H4
Addis Cl *PEND* EN3 25 F2
Addiscombe Av *CROY/NA* CR0 197 H4
Addiscombe Cl
KTN/HRWW/WS HA3 61 J2
Addiscombe Court Rd
CROY/NA CR0 197 F5
Addiscombe Gv *CROY/NA* CR0 196 E6
Addiscombe Rd *CROY/NA* CR0 197 F6
Addison Av *HSLW* TW3 135 H2
NTGHL W11 119 H1
STHGT/OAK N14 34 B1
Addison Bridge Pl
WKENS W14 119 J4
Addison Cl *NTHWD* HA6 40 E4
STMC/STPC BR5 201 H3
Addison Crs *WKENS* W14 119 H3
Addison Dr *LEE/GVPK* SE12 146 A6
Addison Gdns *BRYLDS* KT5 191 G1
WKENS W14 119 G3
Addison Gv *CHSWK* W4 118 B3
Addison Pl *NTGHL* W11 119 H1
Addison Rd *BARK/HLT* IG6 54 C4
HAYES BR2 200 C2
PEND EN3 24 E2
SNWD SE25 197 H1
TEDD TW11 174 C2
WALTH E17 69 K5
WAN E11 70 E3
WKENS W14 119 H2
Addison's Cl *CROY/NA* CR0 198 C6
Addison Ter *CHSWK* W4 * 117 K4
Addison Wy *GLDGN* NW11 64 D1
HYS/HAR UB3 94 E5
NTHWD HA6 40 D4
Addle Hl *BLKFR* EC4V 12 B5
Addle St *CITYW* EC2V * 12 D3
Adecroft Wy *E/WMO/HCT* KT8 173 H6
Adela Av *NWMAL* KT3 192 E2
Adelaide Av *BROCKY* SE4 144 D5
Adelaide Cl *EN* EN1 24 A1
STAN HA7 29 G6
Adelaide Ct *HNWL* W7 116 A2
Adelaide Gdns *CHDH* RM6 74 A2
Adelaide Gv *SHB* W12 118 D1
Adelaide Rd *CHST* BR7 185 G1
HAMP NW3 83 K5
HEST TW5 134 D2
IL IG1 72 B6
LEY E10 88 A1
NWDGN UB2 114 D4
PUT/ROE SW15 139 K6
RCH/KEW TW9 137 G5
STJWD NW8 83 H5
SURB KT6 191 F2
TEDD TW11 174 A2
WEA W13 116 B2
Adelaide St *CHCR* WC2N * 10 E6
Adelaide Ter *BTFD* TW8 * 116 E5
Adela St *NKENS* W10 100 C3
Adelina Gv *WCHPL* E1 104 E4
Adelina Ms *BAL* SW12 161 J3
Adeline Pl *RSQ* WC1B 10 D2
Adeliza Cl *BARK* IG11 90 C5
Adelphi Crs *HCH* RM12 75 J6
YEAD UB4 94 C2
Adelphi Ter *CHCR* WC2N 11 F6
Adelphi Wy *YEAD* UB4 94 D2
Adeney Cl *HMSMTH* W6 119 G6
Aden Gv *STNW/STAM* N16 85 K2
Adenmore Rd *CAT* SE6 164 D2
Aden Rd *IL* IG1 72 B4
PEND EN3 25 G5
Adhara Rd *NTHWD* HA6 40 E1
Adie Rd *HMSMTH* W6 119 F3
Adine Rd *PLSTW* E13 106 E3
Adler St *WCHPL* E1 104 C4
Adley St *CLPT* E5 87 G3
Adlington Cl *UED* N18 49 K1
Admaston Rd
WOOL/PLUM SE18 147 H1
Admiral Cl *STMC/STPC* BR5 202 E1
Admiral Ms *NKENS* W10 100 B3
Admiral Pl *BERM/RHTH* SE16 124 B1
Admirals Cl *SWFD* E18 71 F1
Admiral Seymour Rd
ELTH/MOT SE9 146 E5
Admiral's Ga *GNWCH* SE10 144 E2
Admiral Sq *WBPTN* SW10 * 140 B2
Admiral St *DEPT* SE8 144 D2
Admiral's Wk *HAMP* NW3 83 G1
Admirals Wy *POP/IOD* E14 124 D2
Admiralty Cl *DEPT* SE8 * 144 D2
WDR/YW UB7 112 B1
Admiralty Rd *TEDD* TW11 174 A2
Admiralty Wy *TEDD* TW11 * 174 A2
Admiral Wk *MV/WKIL* W9 100 E4
Adnams Wk *RAIN* RM13 93 J3
Adolf St *CAT* SE6 164 D6
Adolphus Rd *FSBYPK* N4 67 H6
Adolphus St *DEPT* SE8 144 C1
Adomar Rd *BCTR* RM8 91 K1
Adpar St *BAY/PAD* W2 8 A1
Adrian Cl *BAR* EN5 32 B1
Adrian Ms *WBPTN* SW10 120 A6
Adrienne Av *STHL* UB1 95 K3
Advance Rd *WNWD* SE27 162 D6
Advent Wy *UED* N18 51 F1
Adys Lawn *CRICK* NW2 * 81 K4
Adys Rd *PECK* SE15 143 G4
Aerodrome Rd
CDALE/KGS NW9 45 H6
Aerodrome Wy *HEST* TW5 114 B6
Aeroville *CDALE/KGS* NW9 45 G5
Affleck St *IS* N1 * 5 H3
Afghan Rd *BTSEA* SW11 140 D3
Aftab Ter *WCHPL* E1 * 104 D3
Agamemnon Rd
KIL/WHAMP NW6 82 D3
Agar Cl *SURB* KT6 191 G6
Agar Gv *CAMTN* NW1 84 D5
Agar St *CHCR* WC2N 10 E6
Agate Cl *CAN/RD* E16 107 H5
Agate Rd *HMSMTH* W6 119 F3
Agatha Cl *WAP* E1W 123 J1
Agaton Rd *ELTH/MOT* SE9 167 H4
Agave Rd *CRICK* NW2 82 A2
Agdon St *FSBYE* EC1V 6 A6
Agincourt Rd *HAMP* NW3 83 K2
Agister Rd *CHIG* IG7 55 G1
Agnes Av *IL* IG1 90 A2
Agnes Cl *EHAM* E6 108 A6
Agnesfield Cl
NFNCH/WDSPK N12 47 J2
Agnes Gdns *BCTR* RM8 91 K2
Agnes Riley Gdns *CLAP* SW4 * 161 H2
Agnes Rd *ACT* W3 118 C2
Agnes St *POP/IOD* E14 105 H5
Agnew Rd *FSTH* SE23 164 B2
Agricola Pl *EN* EN1 24 B6
Aidan Cl *BCTR* RM8 92 A2
Ailsa Av *TWK* TW1 136 B6
Ailsa Rd *TWK* TW1 136 C6
Ailsa St *POP/IOD* E14 106 A4
Ainger Rd *HAMP* NW3 83 K5
Ainsdale Cl *ORP* BR6 201 J5
Ainsdale Crs *PIN* HA5 42 A6
Ainsdale Dr *STHWK* SE1 123 H5
Ainsdale Rd *EA* W5 97 K3
OXHEY WD19 27 G5
Ainsley Av *ROMW/RG* RM7 74 E3
Ainsley Cl *ED* N9 36 A3
Ainsley St *BETH* E2 104 D2
Ainslie Wood Crs *CHING* E4 51 K1
Ainslie Wood Gdns *CHING* E4 37 K6
Ainslie Wood Rd *CHING* E4 51 J1
Ainsty St *BERM/RHTH* SE16 * 123 K2
Ainsworth Cl *CMBW* SE5 * 143 F3
CRICK NW2 81 J1
Ainsworth Rd *CROY/NA* CR0 196 C5
HOM E9 86 E5
Ainsworth Wy *STJWD* NW8 83 G6
Aintree Av *EHAM* E6 89 J6
Aintree Crs *BARK/HLT* IG6 54 C5
Aintree Rd *GFD/PVL* UB6 97 H1
Aintree St *FUL/PGN* SW6 139 H1
Airco Cl *CDALE/KGS* NW9 44 E6
Airdrie Cl *IS* N1 * 85 F5
YEAD UB4 95 J4
Airedale Av *CHSWK* W4 118 C5
Airedale Av South
CHSWK W4 * 118 C5
Airedale Rd *BAL* SW12 160 E2
EA W5 116 D3
Airfield Wy *HCH* RM12 93 K4
Airlie Gdns *IL* IG1 72 B5
KENS W8 119 K1
Air St *REGST* W1B 10 B6
Airthrie Rd *GDMY/SEVK* IG3 73 H5
Aisgill Av *WKENS* W14 119 J5
Aisher Rd *THMD* SE28 109 J6
Aislibie Rd *LEE/GVPK* SE12 145 H5
Aiten Pl *HMSMTH* W6 118 D4
Aitken Cl *HACK* E8 86 C6
MTCM CR4 194 E4
Aitken Rd *BAR* EN5 20 A6
CAT SE6 164 E4
Aitman Dr *BTFD* TW8 * 117 H5
Ajax Av *CDALE/KGS* NW9 45 G6
Ajax Rd *KIL/WHAMP* NW6 82 D2
Akabusi Cl *CROY/NA* CR0 197 H3
Akehurst St *PUT/ROE* SW15 158 D1
Akenside Rd *HAMP* NW3 83 H3
Akerman Rd *BRXN/ST* SW9 142 C2
SURB KT6 190 D3
Alabama St *WOOL/PLUM* SE18 147 J1
Alacross Rd *EA* W5 116 D2
Alan Cl *DART* DA1 151 F5
Alandale Dr *PIN* HA5 41 F4
Alander Ms *WALTH* E17 69 K1
Alan Dr *BAR* EN5 32 C1
Alan Gdns *ROMW/RG* RM7 74 C4
Alan Hocken Wy *SRTFD* E15 106 C1
Alan Rd *WIM/MER* SW19 177 H1
Alanthus Cl *LEE/GVPK* SE12 165 J1
Alaska St *STHWK* SE1 17 J1
Alba Cl *YEAD* UB4 95 H3
Albacore Crs *LEW* SE13 164 E1
Alba Gdns *GLDGN* NW11 64 C3
Albain Crs *ASHF* TW15 152 B4
Albany Cl *BUSH* WD23 28 D1
BXLY DA5 168 D2
ESH/CLAY KT10 204 A6
MORT/ESHN SW14 137 J5
SEVS/STOTM N15 67 H1
Albany Cots *HNWL* W7 * 115 K1
Albany Ctyd *MYFR/PICC* W1J 10 A6

Albany Crs EDGW HA8 44 C3
ESH/CLAY KT10 204 E4
Albany Ms BMLY BR1 183 K2
CMBW SE5 122 D6
IS N1 85 G5
KUTN/CMB KT2 * 174 E2
SUT SM1 209 F3
Albany Pde BTFD TW8 * 117 F6
PEND EN3 25 F1
Albany Pk PEND EN3 * 25 F1
Albany Park Av PEND EN3 24 E2
Albany Park Rd
KUTN/CMB KT2 174 E2
Albany Pl BTFD TW8 116 E6
Albany Rd BELV DA17 129 G6
BTFD TW8 116 E6
BXLY DA5 168 D2
CHDH RM6 74 B3
CHST BR7 185 G1
CMBW SE5 123 F6
FSBYPK N4 67 F3
HCH RM12 75 J5
LEY E10 69 J4
MNPK E12 89 H2
NWMAL KT3 192 A1
RCHPK/HAM TW10 * 137 G6
UED N18 50 D1
WALTH E17 69 G3
WALW SE17 122 E6
WEA W13 97 H6
WIM/MER SW19 178 A1
Albany Rw EFNCH N2 * 65 J1
Albany St CAMTN NW1 3 K4
Albany Ter
RCHPK/HAM TW10 * 137 G6
The Albany KUTN/CMB KT2 174 E2
Albany Vw BKHH IG9 38 E3
Alba Pl NTGHL W11 100 D5
Albatross Cl EHAM E6 107 K3
Albatross St
WOOL/PLUM SE18 147 K1
Albemarle Ap
GNTH/NBYPK IG2 72 B3
Albemarle Av WHTN TW2 154 E3
Albemarle Gdns
GNTH/NBYPK IG2 72 B3
NWMAL KT3 192 A1
Albemarle Pk BECK BR3 * 182 E4
STAN HA7 43 J1
Albemarle Rd BECK BR3 182 E4
EBAR EN4 33 J2
Albemarle St CONDST W1S 10 A6
Albemarle Wy FSBYE EC1V 6 A7
Alberon Gdns GLDGN NW11 64 D1
Alberta Av SUT SM1 208 C2
Alberta Est WALW SE17 122 C5
Alberta Rd EN EN1 36 B1
ERITH DA8 149 K2
Alberta St WALW SE17 122 C5
Albert Av CHING E4 37 J6
VX/NE SW8 142 A1
Albert Basin Wy CAN/RD E16 108 C6
Albert Br BTSEA SW11 140 D1
Albert Bridge Ga BTSEA SW11 140 E1
Albert Bridge Rd BTSEA SW11 140 D1
Albert Carr Gdns
STRHM/NOR SW16 179 K1
Albert Cl HOM E9 86 D6
WDGN N22 48 D4
Albert Cots WCHPL E1 * 104 C4
Albert Crs CHING E4 37 J6
Albert Dr WIM/MER SW19 159 H4
Albert Emb STHWK SE1 121 K5
Albert Gdns WCHPL E1 105 F5
Albert Ga KTBR SW1X 15 F2
Albert Gv RYNPK SW20 177 G4
Albert Ms BROCKY SE4 * 144 C5
FSBYPK N4 67 F5
KENS W8 120 B3
POP/IOD E14 * 105 G6
Albert Pl FNCH N3 46 E4
KENS W8 120 A2
Albert Rd BCTR RM8 74 B5
BELV DA17 129 G5
BKHH IG9 39 H4
BXLY DA5 169 H1
CAN/RD E16 126 D1
EA W5 97 H3
EBAR EN4 21 G5
ELTH/MOT SE9 166 D5
FSBYPK N4 67 F5
HAYES BR2 200 C2
HDN NW4 64 B1
HPTN TW12 173 H1
HSLW TW3 135 F5
HYS/HAR UB3 113 H3
IL IG1 90 C1
KIL/WHAMP NW6 100 D1
KUT/HW KT1 175 G5
LEY E10 70 A6
MLHL NW7 45 H1
MTCM CR4 178 E6
NWDGN UB2 114 C3
NWMAL KT3 192 C1
ORP BR6 217 G3
PGE/AN SE20 182 A3
RCHPK/HAM TW10 137 F6
RDART DA2 171 F5
ROM RM1 75 H3
RYLN/HDSTN HA2 42 C6
SEVS/STOTM N15 68 A3
SNWD SE25 197 J1
STMC/STPC BR5 202 C3
SUT SM1 209 H3
SWFD E18 53 F6
TEDD TW11 174 A2
TWK TW1 156 A3
WALTH E17 69 J2
WDGN N22 48 D4
WDR/YW UB7 112 B1
Albert Sq SRTFD E15 88 C3
VX/NE SW8 142 A1
Albert St CAMTN NW1 3 K1
NFNCH/WDSPK N12 47 G1
Albert Ter CAMTN NW1 84 A6
EA W5 * 97 H3
WLSDN NW10 * 81 F6
Albert Wy PECK SE15 143 J1
Albion Av MUSWH N10 48 A4
VX/NE SW8 141 J3
Albion Cl BAY/PAD W2 8 D5
ROMW/RG RM7 75 F3
Albion Dr HACK E8 86 B5
Albion Est BERM/RHTH SE16 * 123 K2
Albion Ga BAY/PAD W2 8 D5
Albion Gv STNW/STAM N16 86 A2
Albion Ms BAY/PAD W2 8 D4
HMSMTH W6 118 E4
IS N1 * 85 G6
Albion Pl FARR EC1M 12 A1
HMSMTH W6 118 E4
SNWD SE25 181 H6
Albion Riverside BTSEA SW11 140 D1
Albion Rd BELMT SM2 209 H4
BXLYHS DA6 149 G5
HSLW TW3 135 F5
HYS/HAR UB3 94 C5
KUTN/CMB KT2 175 K4
STNW/STAM N16 85 K3
TOTM N17 50 B5
WALTH E17 52 A6
WHTN TW2 155 K3
Albion Sq HACK E8 86 B5
Albion St BAY/PAD W2 8 D4
BERM/RHTH SE16 123 K2
CROY/NA CR0 196 C5
Albion Ter CHING E4 * 25 K5
HACK E8 86 B5
Albion Villas Rd SYD SE26 163 K5
Albion Wk IS N1 5 F3
Albion Wy LEW SE13 145 F5
STBT EC1A 12 C2
WBLY HA9 80 C1
Albion Yd IS N1 5 F3
Albrighton Rd EDUL SE22 143 F4
Albuhera Cl ENC/FH EN2 23 G2
Albury Av BELMT SM2 208 A6
BXLYHN DA7 149 F3
ISLW TW7 136 A1
Albury Cl HOR/WEW KT19 206 D6
HPTN TW12 173 F2
Albury Dr PIN HA5 41 G4
Albury Ms MNPK E12 71 G5
Albury Rd CHSGTN KT9 206 A3
Albury St DEPT SE8 124 D6
Albyfield BMLY BR1 184 E6
Albyn Rd DEPT SE8 144 D2
Alcester Crs CLPT E5 68 D6
Alcester Rd WLGTN SM6 210 B2
Alcock Cl WLGTN SM6 210 D5
Alcock Rd HEST TW5 134 C1
Alconbury Rd CLPT E5 68 C6
Alcorn Cl CHEAM SM3 193 K6
Alcott Cl HNWL W7 97 F4
Alcuin Ct STAN HA7 43 J3
Aldborough Rd DAGE RM10 92 E4
Aldborough Rd North
GNTH/NBYPK IG2 73 F2
Aldborough Rd South
GDMY/SEVK IG3 72 E5
Aldbourne Rd SHB W12 118 C1
Aldbridge St WALW SE17 123 F5
Aldburgh Ms MHST W1U 9 H3
Aldbury Av WBLY HA9 80 D5
Aldbury Ms ED N9 35 K2
Aldebert Ter VX/NE SW8 142 A1
Aldeburgh Pl WFD IG8 38 E6
Aldeburgh St GNWCH SE10 125 K5
Alden Av SRTFD E15 106 D2
Aldenham Rd OXHEY WD19 27 H1
Aldenham St CAMTN NW1 4 B3
Alden Md PIN HA5 * 42 A3
Aldensley Rd HMSMTH W6 118 E3
Alderbrook Rd BAL SW12 161 G1
Alderbury Rd BARN SW13 118 D6
Alder Cl PECK SE15 123 G6
Alder Gv CRICK NW2 63 J6
Alderholt Wy PECK SE15 * 143 F1
Alderman Av BARK IG11 109 G2
Aldermanbury CITYW EC2V * 12 D3
Aldermanbury Sq
CITYW EC2V 12 D2
Alderman Cl DART DA1 170 B2
Alderman Judge Ml
KUT/HW KT1 * 175 F5
Alderman's Hl PLMGR N13 34 E6
Alderman's Wk LVPST EC2M 13 G2
Aldermary Rd BMLY BR1 183 K4
Aldermoor Rd CAT SE6 164 C5
Alderney Av HEST TW5 135 G1
Alderney Gdns NTHLT UB5 77 K5
Alderney Ms STHWK SE1 18 E4
Alderney Rd ERITH DA8 150 D1
WCHPL E1 105 F3
Alderney St PIM SW1V 15 J7
Alder Rd MORT/ESHN SW14 138 A4
SCUP DA14 167 K5
Alders Av WFD IG8 52 C2
Aldersbrook Av EN EN1 24 A3
Aldersbrook Dr
KUTN/CMB KT2 175 G2
Aldersbrook La MNPK E12 89 K1
Aldersbrook Rd MNPK E12 71 G6
Alders Cl EA W5 116 E3
EDGW HA8 44 E1
WAN E11 71 F6
Aldersey Gdns BARK IG11 90 D4
Aldersford Cl BROCKY SE4 144 A5
Aldersgate St CITYW EC2V 12 C3
Aldersgrove E/WMO/HCT KT8 189 J2
Aldersgrove Av
ELTH/MOT SE9 166 B5
Aldershot Rd
KIL/WHAMP NW6 82 D6
Aldershot Ter
WOOL/PLUM SE18 * 147 F1
Aldersmead Av CROY/NA CR0 198 A3
Aldersmead Rd BECK BR3 182 B3
Alderson Pl NWDGN UB2 115 H1
Alderson St NKENS W10 100 C3
Alders Rd EDGW HA8 44 E1
The Alders FELT TW13 172 D1
HEST TW5 114 E6
STRHM/NOR SW16 * 161 H6
WCHMH N21 35 G1
WWKM BR4 198 E5
Alderton Cl WLSDN NW10 81 F1
Alderton Crs HDN NW4 63 K2
Alderton Rd CROY/NA CR0 197 G4
HNHL SE24 142 D4
Alderton Wy HDN NW4 63 K2
Alderville Rd FUL/PGN SW6 139 J3
Alderwick Dr HSLW TW3 135 J4
Alderwood Ms EBAR EN4 21 G1
Alderwood Rd ELTH/MOT SE9 167 J1
Aldford St MYFR/PKLN W1K 9 G7
Aldgate FENCHST EC3M 13 H4
Aldgate Barrs WCHPL E1 * 13 K3
Aldgate High St TWRH EC3N 13 J4
Aldine St SHB W12 119 F2
Aldingham Gdns HCH RM12 93 J3
Aldington Cl CHDH RM6 73 J4
Aldington Rd CHARL SE7 126 C3
Aldis Ms TOOT SW17 178 D1
Aldis St TOOT SW17 178 D1
Aldred Rd KIL/WHAMP NW6 82 E3
Aldren Rd TOOT SW17 160 B5
Aldrich Crs CROY/NA CR0 214 A6
Aldriche Wy CHING E4 52 A2
Aldrich Gdns CHEAM SM3 208 D1
Aldrich Ter WAND/EARL SW18 160 B4
Aldridge Av EDGW HA8 30 D5
PEND EN3 25 J1
RSLP HA4 59 G6
STAN HA7 44 A4
Aldridge Ri NWMAL KT3 192 B4
Aldridge Road Vls NTGHL W11 100 D4
Aldridge Wk STHGT/OAK N14 34 E2
Aldrington Rd
STRHM/NOR SW16 179 H1
Aldsworth Cl MV/WKIL W9 101 F3
Aldwick Cl ELTH/MOT SE9 167 J5
Aldwick Rd CROY/NA CR0 211 F1
Aldworth Gv LEW SE13 165 F1
Aldworth Rd SRTFD E15 88 C5
Aldwych HOL/ALD WC2B 11 G4
Aldwych Av BARK/HLT IG6 72 C1
Aldwych Cl HCH RM12 75 J6
Alers Rd BXLYHS DA6 148 E6
Alesia Cl WDGN N22 48 E3
Alestan Beck Rd CAN/RD E16 107 H5
Alexander Av WLSDN NW10 81 K5
Alexander Cl BFN/LL DA15 147 K6
EBAR EN4 21 H5
HAYES BR2 199 K5
NWDGN UB2 115 H1
WHTN TW2 155 K4
Alexander Evans Ms
FSTH SE23 164 A4
Alexander Ms BAY/PAD W2 101 F5
Alexander Pl SKENS SW7 14 C6
Alexander Rd ARCH N19 84 E1
BXLYHN DA7 148 E3
CHST BR7 185 G2
Alexander Sq CHEL SW3 14 C6
Alexander St BAY/PAD W2 100 E5
Alexander Ter ABYW SE2 * 128 C5
Alexandra DEPT SE8 124 C6
Alexandra Av BTSEA SW11 * 141 F2
RYLN/HDSTN HA2 59 K5
STHL UB1 95 K6
SUT SM1 208 E1
WDGN N22 48 D4
Alexandra Cl
RYLN/HDSTN HA2 78 A1
Alexandra Cots NWCR SE14 144 C2
Alexandra Crs BMLY BR1 183 J2
Alexandra Dr BRYLDS KT5 191 H4
NRWD SE19 181 F1
Alexandra Gdns CAR SM5 210 A6
HSLW TW3 135 G3
MUSWH N10 66 B1
Alexandra Ga SKENS SW7 14 A2
Alexandra Gv FSBYPK N4 67 H5
NFNCH/WDSPK N12 47 F1
Alexandra Ms EFNCH N2 47 K6
Alexandra Palace Wy
CEND/HSY/T N8 66 C1
MUSWH N10 48 C6
Alexandra Pde
RYLN/HDSTN HA2 * 78 B2
Alexandra Park Rd
MUSWH N10 48 B5
Alexandra Pl CROY/NA CR0 197 F5
SNWD SE25 196 E2
STJWD NW8 83 G6
Alexandra Rd BTFD TW8 * 116 E6
CEND/HSY/T N8 49 G6
CHDH RM6 73 K3
CHSWK W4 118 A2
CROY/NA CR0 197 F5
ED N9 * 36 D2
EHAM E6 108 A2
ERITH DA8 130 C6
HDN NW4 64 B1
HSLW TW3 135 G3
KUTN/CMB KT2 175 H3
LEY E10 88 A1
MORT/ESHN SW14 138 A4
MTCM CR4 178 D3
MUSWH N10 48 B4
PEND EN3 25 F5
PGE/AN SE20 182 A2
RAIN RM13 93 H6
RCH/KEW TW9 137 G3
ROM RM1 75 H3
SEVS/STOTM N15 67 K2
STJWD NW8 83 G5
SWFD E18 53 F6
THDIT KT7 190 A2
TWK TW1 156 D1
WALTH E17 69 H3
WIM/MER SW19 177 K1
Alexandra Sq MRDN SM4 193 K2
Alexandra St CAN/RD E16 106 E4
NWCR SE14 144 B1
Alexandria Rd WEA W13 97 G6
Alexis St BERM/RHTH SE16 123 H4
Alfearn Rd CLPT E5 86 E2
Alford Gn CROY/NA CR0 214 B4
Alford Pl IS N1 * 6 D3
Alford Rd ERITH DA8 129 K5
Alfoxton Av SEVS/STOTM N15 67 H1
Alfreda St BTSEA SW11 141 G2
Alfred Cl CHSWK W4 118 A4
Alfred Gdns STHL UB1 95 J6
Alfred Ms GWRST WC1E 10 C1
Alfred Pl GWRST WC1E 10 C1
Alfred Rd ACT W3 117 K1
BAY/PAD W2 100 E4
BELV DA17 129 G5
BKHH IG9 39 H4
FELT TW13 154 B3
KUT/HW KT1 175 F6
RDART DA2 171 J6
SNWD SE25 197 H2
SRTFD E15 88 D3
SUT SM1 209 G3
Alfred's Gdns BARK IG11 108 E1
Alfred St BOW E3 105 H2
Alfred's Way (East Ham
& Barking By-Pass)
BARK IG11 108 D1
Alfred Vls WALTH E17 * 70 A1
Alfreton Cl WIM/MER SW19 159 G5
Alfriston BRYLDS KT5 191 G3
Alfriston Av CROY/NA CR0 195 K4
RYLN/HDSTN HA2 60 A3
Alfriston Cl BRYLDS KT5 191 G3
DART DA1 170 B1
Alfriston Rd BTSEA SW11 140 E6
Algar Cl STAN HA7 43 F1
Algar Rd ISLW TW7 136 B4
Algarve Rd WAND/EARL SW18 160 A3
Algernon Rd HDN NW4 63 J3
KIL/WHAMP NW6 82 E6
LEW SE13 144 E4
Algiers Rd LEW SE13 144 D5
Alguin Ct STAN HA7 * 43 J2
Alibon Gdns DAGE RM10 92 C3
Alibon Rd DAGE RM10 92 C3
Alice La BOW E3 87 H6
Alice St STHWK SE1 19 G5
Alice Thompson Cl
LEE/GVPK SE12 166 B4
Alice Walker Cl HNHL SE24 * 142 C5
Alice Wy HSLW TW3 135 G5
Alicia Av KTN/HRWW/WS HA3 61 H1
Alicia Cl KTN/HRWW/WS HA3 61 J1
Alicia Gdns
KTN/HRWW/WS HA3 61 H1
Alie St WCHPL E1 13 K4
Alington Crs CDALE/KGS NW9 62 E5
Alington Gv WLGTN SM6 210 D6
Alison Cl CROY/NA CR0 198 A5
EHAM E6 108 A5
PIN HA5 59 F3
Aliwal Ms BTSEA SW11 * 140 D5
Aliwal Rd BTSEA SW11 140 D5
Alkerden Rd CHSWK W4 118 B5
Alkham Rd STNW/STAM N16 68 B6
Allan Barclay Cl
SEVS/STOTM N15 68 B3
Allan Cl NWMAL KT3 192 A2
Allandale Av FNCH N3 46 C6
Allandale Pl ORP BR6 217 K1
Allandale Rd EMPK RM11 75 H4
Allan Wy ACT W3 98 E4
Allard Cl STMC/STPC BR5 202 D4
Allard Crs BUSH WD23 28 C4
Allardyce St CLAP SW4 142 A5
Allbrook Cl TEDD TW11 173 K1
Allcot Cl EBED/NFELT TW14 153 J3
Allcroft Rd KTTN NW5 84 A4
Allder Wy SAND/SEL CR2 211 H5
Allenby Av SAND/SEL CR2 211 J6
Allenby Cl GFD/PVL UB6 96 A2
Allenby Rd FSTH SE23 164 B5
STHL UB1 96 A5
WOOL/PLUM SE18 127 H3
Allen Cl MTCM CR4 179 G4
SUN TW16 172 A4
Allendale Av STHL UB1 96 A5
Allendale Cl CMBW SE5 142 E3
SYD SE26 182 A1
Allendale Rd GFD/PVL UB6 79 H4
Allen Edwards Dr VX/NE SW8 141 K2
Allen Rd BECK BR3 182 A5
BOW E3 105 H1
CROY/NA CR0 196 A4
STNW/STAM N16 86 A2
SUN TW16 172 A4
Allensbury Pl CAMTN NW1 84 D5
Allens Rd PEND EN3 24 E6
Allen St KENS W8 119 K3
Allenswood Rd
ELTH/MOT SE9 146 D4
Allerford Ct HRW HA1 60 B2
Allerford Rd CAT SE6 164 E6
Allerton Rd STNW/STAM N16 67 J6
Allerton St IS N1 7 F3
Allestree Rd FUL/PGN SW6 139 H1
Alleyn Crs DUL SE21 162 E4
Alleyndale Rd BCTR RM8 73 J6
Alleyn Pk DUL SE21 162 E4
NWDGN UB2 114 E5
Alleyn Rd DUL SE21 162 E5
Allfarthing La
WAND/EARL SW18 160 B1
Allgood Cl MRDN SM4 193 G3
Allgood St BETH E2 7 K3
Allhallows La CANST EC4R 12 E6
Allhallows Rd EHAM E6 107 J5
All Hallows Rd TOTM N17 50 A4
Alliance Cl ALP/SUD HA0 79 K2
HSLWW TW4 134 E6
Alliance Rd ACT W3 98 D3
PLSTW E13 107 G3
WOOL/PLUM SE18 128 B6
Allied Wy ACT W3 * 118 B2
Allingham Cl HNWL W7 97 F6
Allington Av TOTM N17 50 A2
Allington Cl GFD/PVL UB6 78 C5
WIM/MER SW19 177 G1
Allington Rd HDN NW4 63 K2
NKENS W10 100 C2
ORP BR6 201 K5
RYLN/HDSTN HA2 60 C2
Allington St BGVA SW1W 15 K5
WESTW SW1E 16 A5
Allison Cl GNWCH SE10 145 F2
Allison Gv DUL SE21 163 F3
Allison Rd ACT W3 98 E5
CEND/HSY/T N8 67 G2
Allitsen Rd STJWD NW8 2 C3
Allnutt Wy CLAP SW4 141 J6
Alloa Rd DEPT SE8 124 A5
GDMY/SEVK IG3 73 H6
Allonby Gdns WBLY HA9 61 J5
Alloway Rd BOW E3 105 G2
Allport Ms WCHPL E1 * 104 E4
All Saints' Cl ED N9 36 B4
All Saints Dr BKHTH/KID SE3 145 J3
All Saints Ms STAN HA7 42 E2
All Saints Pas
WAND/EARL SW18 * 139 K6
All Saints Rd SUT SM1 209 F1
WIM/MER SW19 178 B3
All Saints' Rd ACT W3 117 K3
NTGHL W11 100 D4
All Saints St IS N1 5 G2
Allsop Pl CAMTN NW1 3 F7
All Souls' Av WLSDN NW10 99 K1
All Souls' Pl REGST W1B 9 K2
Allum Wy TRDG/WHET N20 33 G3
Allwood Cl SYD SE26 164 A6
Alma Av CHING E4 52 A3
Almack Rd CLPT E5 86 E2
Alma Cl MUSWH N10 * 48 B4
Alma Ct RYLN/HDSTN HA2 * 60 D6
Alma Crs SUT SM1 208 C3
Alma Gv STHWK SE1 19 K7
Alma Pl NRWD SE19 181 G3
THHTH CR7 196 B2
WLSDN NW10 99 K2
Alma Rd BFN/LL DA15 168 B5
CAR SM5 209 J3
ESH/CLAY KT10 189 K5
MUSWH N10 48 A3
PEND EN3 25 G6
STHL UB1 95 J6
STMC/STPC BR5 202 E6
WAND/EARL SW18 140 B6
Alma Rw
KTN/HRWW/WS HA3 * 42 D4
Alma Sq STJWD NW8 101 G2
Alma St KTTN NW5 84 B4
SRTFD E15 88 B4
Alma Ter BOW E3 87 H6
KENS W8 * 119 K3
WAND/EARL SW18 160 C2
Almeida St IS N1 85 H6
Almeric Rd BTSEA SW11 140 E5
Almer Rd RYNPK SW20 176 D3
Almington St FSBYPK N4 * 66 E5
Almond Av CAR SM5 194 E6
EA W5 117 F3
WDR/YW UB7 112 D3
Almond Cl FELT TW13 153 K3
HAYES BR2 201 F4
HYS/HAR UB3 94 C6
PECK SE15 143 H3
RSLP HA4 76 D1
Almond Gv BTFD TW8 136 C1
Almond Rd BERM/RHTH SE16 123 J4
TOTM N17 50 C3
Almonds Av BKHH IG9 38 E4
Almond Wy HAYES BR2 201 F4
MTCM CR4 195 J2
RYLN/HDSTN HA2 42 B5
Almorah Rd HEST TW5 134 C2
IS N1 85 K5
Almshouse La CHSGTN KT9 205 J6
Alnwick Gv MRDN SM4 194 A1
Alnwick Rd CAN/RD E16 107 G5
LEE/GVPK SE12 166 A2
Alnwick Ter LEE/GVPK SE12 166 A2
Alperton La ALP/SUD HA0 97 K2
Alperton St NKENS W10 100 C3
Alphabet Gdns CAR SM5 194 C3
Alpha Cl CAMTN NW1 2 D6
Alpha Est HYS/HAR UB3 * 113 H2
Alpha Gv POP/IOD E14 124 D2
Alpha Pl CHEL SW3 120 D6
KIL/WHAMP NW6 100 E1
MRDN SM4 * 193 G4
Alpha Rd BRYLDS KT5 191 G3
CHING E4 37 J5
CROY/NA CR0 197 F5
NWCR SE14 144 C2
PEND EN3 25 G5
TEDD TW11 173 J1
UED N18 50 C2
Alpha St PECK SE15 143 H3
Alphea Cl WIM/MER SW19 178 D3
Alpine Av BRYLDS KT5 191 K6
Alpine Cl CROY/NA CR0 212 A1
Alpine Copse BMLY BR1 185 F5
Alpine Gv HOM E9 86 E5
Alpine Rd BERM/RHTH SE16 123 K4
LEY E10 69 K6
Alpine Vw CAR SM5 209 J3
Alpine Wk BUSH WD23 28 E4
Alpine Wy EHAM E6 108 A4
Alric Av NWMAL KT3 176 B6
WLSDN NW10 81 F5
Alroy Rd FSBYPK N4 67 G4
Alsace Rd WALW SE17 123 F5
Alscot Rd STHWK SE1 19 K5
Alscot Wy STHWK SE1 19 J6
Alsike Rd ERITHM DA18 128 E3
Alsom Av WPK KT4 207 H2
Alston Cl SURB KT6 190 C4
Alston Rd BAR EN5 20 C4
TOOT SW17 160 C6
UED N18 50 D1
Altair Cl TOTM N17 50 B2
Altair Wy NTHWD HA6 40 D1
Altash Wy ELTH/MOT SE9 166 E4
Altenburg Av WEA W13 116 C3
Altenburg Gdns BTSEA SW11 140 E5
Alt Gv WIM/MER SW19 177 J3
Altham Ct RYLN/HDSTN HA2 * 42 B4
Altham Gdns OXHEY WD19 27 H6
Altham Rd PIN HA5 41 J3
Althea St FUL/PGN SW6 140 A3
Althorne Gdns SWFD E18 70 D1
Althorne Wy DAGE RM10 74 C6
Althorp Cl BAR EN5 31 J2
Althorpe Rd HRW HA1 * 60 C2
Althorp Rd TOOT SW17 160 E3
Altmore Av EHAM E6 89 K5
Alton Av STAN HA7 43 F3
Alton Cl BXLY DA5 169 F3
ISLW TW7 136 A3
Alton Gdns BECK BR3 182 D3
WHTN TW2 155 J1
Alton Rd CROY/NA CR0 211 G1
PUT/ROE SW15 158 D3
RCH/KEW TW9 137 F5

TOTM N17 49 K6
Alton St POP/IOD E14 105 K4
Altyre Cl BECK BR3 198 C2
Altyre Rd CROY/NA CR0 196 E6
Altyre Wy BECK BR3 198 C2
Alvanley Gdns
KIL/WHAMP NW6 83 F3
Alva Wy OXHEY WD19 27 H4
Alverstone Av EBAR EN4 33 H2
WAND/EARL SW18 159 K4
Alverstone Gdns
ELTH/MOT SE9 167 G3
Alverstone Rd CRICK NW2 82 A5
MNPK E12 90 A2
NWMAL KT3 192 C1
WBLY HA9 62 B5
Alverston Gdns SNWD SE25 197 F2
Alverton St DEPT SE8 124 C5
Alveston Av
KTN/HRWW/WS HA3 43 H6
Alveston Sq SWFD E18 * 52 E5
Alvey St WALW SE17 123 F5
Alvia Gdns SUT SM1 209 G2
Alvington Crs HACK E8 86 B3
Alway Av HOR/WEW KT19 206 E3
Alwold Crs LEE/GVPK SE12 166 B1
Alwyn Av CHSWK W4 118 A5
Alwyn Cl BORE WD6 30 B1
CROY/NA CR0 213 K5
Alwyne La IS N1 * 85 H5
Alwyne Pl IS N1 85 J4
Alwyne Rd HNWL W7 96 E6
IS N1 85 J5
WIM/MER SW19 177 J2
Alwyne Sq IS N1 85 J4
Alwyne Vls IS N1 85 H5
Alwyn Gdns ACT W3 98 D5
HDN NW4 63 J1
Alyn Bank CEND/HSY/T N8 * 66 D3
Alyth Gdns GLDGN NW11 64 D3
Amalgamated Dr BTFD TW8 116 B6
Amanda Cl CHIG IG7 54 D2
Amanda Ms ROMW/RG RM7 74 E2
Amar Ct WOOL/PLUM SE18 128 A4
Amardeep Ct
WOOL/PLUM SE18 128 A5
Amazon St WCHPL E1 104 D5
Ambassador Cl HSLW TW3 134 D3
Ambassador Gdns EHAM E6 107 K4
Ambassador Sq POP/IOD E14 124 E4
Amber Av WALTH E17 51 G4
Amberden Av FNCH N3 46 E6
Ambergate St WALW SE17 122 C5
Amber Gv CRICK NW2 64 B5
Amberley Cl ORP BR6 217 F3
PIN HA5 41 K6
Amberley Ct SCUP DA14 186 D1
Amberley Gdns
HOR/WEW KT19 207 H2
Amberley Gv CROY/NA CR0 197 G4
SYD SE26 163 J6
Amberley Rd ABYW SE2 128 E6
BKHH IG9 39 G3
EN EN1 36 B2
LEY E10 69 J4
MV/WKIL W9 100 E4
PLMGR N13 35 F4
Amberley Wy HSLWW TW4 134 B6
MRDN SM4 193 J4
ROMW/RG RM7 74 D1
Amberside Cl ISLW TW7 155 J1
Amber St SRTFD E15 * 88 B4
Amberwood Cl WLGTN SM6 210 E3
Amberwood Ri NWMAL KT3 192 B3
Amblecote Cl LEE/GVPK SE12 166 A5
Amblecote Mdw
LEE/GVPK SE12 166 A5
Amblecote Mdws
LEE/GVPK SE12 * 166 A5
Amblecote Rd LEE/GVPK SE12 166 A5
Ambler Rd FSBYPK N4 85 H1
Ambleside BMLY BR1 183 G2
Ambleside Av BECK BR3 198 B2
HCH RM12 93 K3
STRHM/NOR SW16 161 J6
WOT/HER KT12 188 B5
Ambleside Cl HOM E9 86 E3
LEY E10 69 K4
SEVS/STOTM N15 50 B6
Ambleside Crs PEND EN3 25 F4
Ambleside Dr
EBED/NFELT TW14 153 J3
Ambleside Gdns BELMT SM2 209 G4
REDBR IG4 71 J1
WBLY HA9 61 K5
Ambleside Rd BXLYHN DA7 149 H3
WLSDN NW10 81 H5
Ambrey Wy WLGTN SM6 210 D6
Ambrook Rd BELV DA17 129 H3
Ambrosden Av WEST SW1P 16 B5
Ambrose Av GLDGN NW11 64 D3
Ambrose Cl DART DA1 150 C5
ORP BR6 217 F1
Ambrose St BERM/RHTH SE16 123 J4
Ambulance Rd WAN E11 70 B2
Amelia Cl ACT W3 117 J1
Amelia St WALW SE17 122 C5
Amen Cnr STP EC4M 12 B4
TOOT SW17 179 F2
Amen Ct STP EC4M 12 B4
Amenity Wy MRDN SM4 193 F4
America Sq TWRH EC3N 13 J5
America St STHWK SE1 18 C1
Amerland Rd PUT/ROE SW15 159 J1
Amersham Av UED N18 49 K2
Amersham Gv NWCR SE14 144 C1
Amersham Rd CROY/NA CR0 196 D3
NWCR SE14 144 C2
Amersham V NWCR SE14 144 C1
Amery Gdns WLSDN NW10 81 K6
Amery Rd HRW HA1 61 G6
Amesbury Av
BRXS/STRHM SW2 161 K4
Amesbury Cl WPK KT4 193 F5
Amesbury Dr CHING E4 37 K1
Amesbury Rd BMLY BR1 184 C6
DAGW RM9 91 K5
FELT TW13 154 C4
Ames Cots POP/IOD E14 * 105 G4
Amethyst Ct ORP BR6 216 E4
Amethyst Rd SRTFD E15 88 B2
Amherst Av WEA W13 97 J5
Amherst Cl STMC/STPC BR5 202 B1
Amherst Dr STMC/STPC BR5 202 A1
Amherst Gdns WEA W13 * 97 J5
Amherst Rd WEA W13 97 J5
Amhurst Gdns ISLW TW7 136 A2
Amhurst Pde
STNW/STAM N16 * 68 B4
Amhurst Pk STNW/STAM N16 68 A4
Amhurst Rd STNW/STAM N16 86 B2
Amhurst Ter STNW/STAM N16 86 C2
Amias Dr EDGW HA8 30 A6
Amidas Gdns BCTR RM8 91 H2
Amiel St WCHPL E1 104 E3
Amies St BTSEA SW11 140 E4
Amina Wy BERM/RHTH SE16 123 H3
Amis Av HOR/WEW KT19 206 C4
Amity Gv RYNPK SW20 177 F4
Amity Rd SRTFD E15 88 D5
Ammanford Gn
CDALE/KGS NW9 * 63 G3
Amner Rd BTSEA SW11 161 F1
Amor Rd HMSMTH W6 119 F3
Amott Rd PECK SE15 143 H4
Ampere Wy CROY/NA CR0 195 K4
Ampleforth Cl ORP BR6 217 J2
Ampleforth Rd ABYW SE2 128 C2
Amport Pl MLHL NW7 46 C2
Ampthill Est CAMTN NW1 4 A3
Ampthill Sq CAMTN NW1 4 B3
Ampton St FSBYW WC1X 5 G5
Amroth Cl FSTH SE23 163 J3
Amroth Gn CDALE/KGS NW9 * 63 G3
Amsterdam Rd POP/IOD E14 125 F3
Amwell Cl ENC/FH EN2 23 K6
Amwell St CLKNW EC1R 5 J4
Amyand Cots TWK TW1 156 C1
Amyand Park Gdns TWK TW1 156 C2
Amyand Park Rd TWK TW1 156 B2
Amy Cl WLGTN SM6 210 E5
Amyruth Rd BROCKY SE4 144 D6
Amy Warne Cl EHAM E6 107 J4
Anatola Rd ARCH N19 66 B6
Ancaster Crs NWMAL KT3 192 D3
Ancaster Ms BECK BR3 182 A6
Ancaster Rd BECK BR3 182 A6
Ancaster St
WOOL/PLUM SE18 147 K1
Anchorage Cl WIM/MER SW19 177 K1
Anchor Cl BARK IG11 109 H2
Anchor Dr RAIN RM13 111 K2
Anchor & Hope La CHARL SE7 126 A3
Anchor Rd MNPK E12 71 H6
Anchor St BERM/RHTH SE16 123 J4
Anchor Ter WCHPL E1 * 104 E3
Anchor Yd FSBYE EC1V * 6 D6
Ancill Cl HMSMTH W6 119 G6
Ancona Rd WLSDN NW10 99 J1
WOOL/PLUM SE18 127 J5
Andace Park Gdns
BMLY BR1 * 184 B4
Andalus Rd BRXN/ST SW9 141 K4
Ander Cl ALP/SUD HA0 79 K2
Anderson Cl ACT W3 99 F5
CHEAM SM3 193 K5
WCHMH N21 23 F6
Anderson Dr ASHF TW15 153 F6
Anderson Rd HOM E9 87 F4
WFD IG8 53 H6
Anderson's Pl HSLW TW3 135 G5
Anderson Sq IS N1 6 A1
Anderson St CHEL SW3 120 E5
Anderson Wy BELV DA17 129 J2
Andover Av CAN/RD E16 107 H5
Andover Cl EBED/NFELT TW14 153 J3
GFD/PVL UB6 96 B3
Andover Pl KIL/WHAMP NW6 101 F1
Andover Rd HOLWY N7 67 F6
ORP BR6 201 K5
WHTN TW2 155 J3
Andover Ter HMSMTH W6 * 118 E4
Andre St HACK E8 86 C3
Andrew Borde St
LSQ/SEVD WC2H * 10 D3
Andrew Cl BARK/HLT IG6 54 D3
DART DA1 150 A6
Andrewes Gdns EHAM E6 107 J5
Andrew Pl VX/NE SW8 141 J2
Andrews Cl BKHH IG9 39 G4
HRW HA1 60 D4
STMC/STPC BR5 186 E6
WPK KT4 193 G6
Andrews Pl RDART DA2 170 B4
Andrews Rd BETH E2 86 D6
Andrew St POP/IOD E14 106 A5
Andrews Wk WALW SE17 122 C6
Andwell Cl ABYW SE2 128 C2
Anerley Gv NRWD SE19 181 G3
Anerley Hl NRWD SE19 181 G2
Anerley Pk PGE/AN SE20 181 J2
Anerley Park Rd PGE/AN SE20 181 J3
Anerley Rd PGE/AN SE20 181 H4
Anerley Station Rd
PGE/AN SE20 181 J4
Anerley V NRWD SE19 181 G3
Anfield Cl BAL SW12 161 H2
Angela Carter Cl
BRXN/ST SW9 142 B4
Angel Alley WCHPL E1 13 K2
Angel Cl HPTN TW12 173 H1
UED N18 50 B1
Angel Corner Pde UED N18 * 50 C1
Angelfield HSLW TW3 135 G5
Angel Hl SUT SM1 209 F1
Angel Hill Dr SUT SM1 209 F1
Angelica Dr EHAM E6 108 A4
Angelica Gdns CROY/NA CR0 198 A5
Angel La HYS/HAR UB3 94 B4
SRTFD E15 88 B4
Angell Park Gdns
BRXN/ST SW9 142 B4
Angell Rd BRXN/ST SW9 142 C4
Angell Town Est
BRXN/ST SW9 * 142 B3
Angel Ms IS N1 5 K3
PUT/ROE SW15 158 D2
WCHPL E1 104 D6
Angel Pas CANST EC4R 12 E6
Angel Rd HRW HA1 60 E3
THDIT KT7 190 B5
Angel Rd (North Circular)
UED N18 50 C1
Angel Sq FSBYE EC1V * 6 A3
Angel St STBT EC1A 12 C3
Angel Wk HMSMTH W6 119 F4
Angel Wy ROM RM1 75 G2
Angerstein La BKHTH/KID SE3 145 J1
Anglers La KTTN NW5 84 B4
Anglers Reach SURB KT6 * 190 E2
Anglesea Ms
WOOL/PLUM SE18 127 G4
Anglesea Rd KUT/HW KT1 190 E1
STMC/STPC BR5 202 D3
WOOL/PLUM SE18 127 G4
Anglesey Cl ASHF TW15 152 D5
Anglesey Court Rd CAR SM5 210 A4
Anglesey Dr RAIN RM13 111 J3
Anglesey Gdns CAR SM5 210 A4
Anglesey Rd OXHEY WD19 41 G1
PEND EN3 24 D5
Anglesmede Crs PIN HA5 42 A6
Anglesmede Wy PIN HA5 41 K6
Angles Rd STRHM/NOR SW16 161 K6
Anglia Cl TOTM N17 50 D3
Anglian Rd WAN E11 88 B1
Anglo Rd BOW E3 105 H1
Angus Cl CHSGTN KT9 206 C3
Angus Dr RSLP HA4 77 G2
Angus Gdns CDALE/KGS NW9 45 F4
Angus Rd PLSTW E13 107 G2
Angus St NWCR SE14 144 B1
Anhalt Rd BTSEA SW11 140 D1
Ankerdine Crs
WOOL/PLUM SE18 147 G2
Anlaby Rd TEDD TW11 173 K1
Anley Rd HMSMTH W6 119 G2
Anmersh Gv STAN HA7 43 K4
Annabel Cl POP/IOD E14 105 K5
Anna Cl HACK E8 86 B6
Annandale Gv
HGDN/ICK UB10 76 A1
Annandale Rd BFN/LL DA15 167 K2
CHSWK W4 118 B4
CROY/NA CR0 197 H6
GNWCH SE10 125 J5
Anna Neagle Cl FSTGT E7 88 E2
Annan Wy ROM RM1 57 F4
Anne Boleyn's Wk
CHEAM SM3 208 B5
KUTN/CMB KT2 175 F1
Anne Case Ms NWMAL KT3 * 176 A6
Anne Compton Ms
LEE/GVPK SE12 165 J2
Anne of Cleves Rd DART DA1 151 G6
Annesley Av CDALE/KGS NW9 45 F6
Annesley Cl WLSDN NW10 81 G1
Annesley Dr CROY/NA CR0 213 H1
Annesley Rd BKHTH/KID SE3 146 A2
Annesmere Gdns
BKHTH/KID SE3 146 C4
Anne St PLSTW E13 106 E3
Annette Cl
KTN/HRWW/WS HA3 42 E5
Annette Rd HOLWY N7 85 F2
Anne Wy BARK/HLT IG6 54 C2
Annie Besant Cl BOW E3 * 87 H6
Anning St WCHPL E1 7 H6
Annington Rd EFNCH N2 47 K6
Annis Rd HOM E9 87 G4
Ann La WBPTN SW10 140 C1
Ann Moss Wy
BERM/RHTH SE16 123 K3
Ann's Cl KTBR SW1X 15 F3
Ann St WOOL/PLUM SE18 127 J4
Annsworthy Av THHTH CR7 180 E6
Annsworthy Crs SNWD SE25 180 E6
Ansar Gdns WALTH E17 69 G2
Ansdell Rd PECK SE15 143 K3
Ansdell St KENS W8 120 A3
Ansdell Ter KENS W8 120 A3
Ansell Gv CAR SM5 194 E5
Ansell Rd TOOT SW17 160 D5
Anselm Cl CROY/NA CR0 212 B1
Anselm Rd FUL/PGN SW6 119 K6
PIN HA5 41 K3
Ansford Rd BMLY BR1 183 F1
Ansleigh Pl NTGHL W11 100 B6
Anson Cl ROMW/RG RM7 56 D5
Anson Rd ARCH N19 84 C2
CRICK NW2 81 K3
Anson Wk NTHWD HA6 26 A6
Anstead Dr RAIN RM13 111 J1
Anstey Rd PECK SE15 143 H4
Anstice Cl CHSWK W4 138 B1
Anstridge Rd ELTH/MOT SE9 167 J1
Antelope Rd
WOOL/PLUM SE18 126 E3
Anthony Cl MLHL NW7 31 G6
OXHEY WD19 27 H3
Anthony Rd GFD/PVL UB6 96 E1
SNWD SE25 197 H3
WELL DA16 148 B2
Anthony's Cl WAP E1W 123 H1
Anthony St WCHPL E1 104 D5
Anthus Ms NTHWD HA6 40 B3
Antill Rd BOW E3 105 G2
SEVS/STOTM N15 68 C1
Antill Ter WCHPL E1 105 F5
Antlers Hl CHING E4 25 K6
Anton Crs SUT SM1 208 E1
Antoneys Cl PIN HA5 41 H5
Anton Pl WBLY HA9 80 D1
Anton St HACK E8 86 C3
Antrim Rd HAMP NW3 83 K4
Antrobus Cl SUT SM1 208 D3
Antrobus Rd CHSWK W4 117 K4
Anvil Cl STRHM/NOR SW16 179 H3
Anvil Ter RDART DA2 170 B4
Anworth Cl WFD IG8 53 F2
Aostle Wy THHTH CR7 180 C5
Apeldoorn Dr WLGTN SM6 210 E6
Aperfield Rd ERITH DA8 130 C6
Apex Cl BECK BR3 182 E4
Apex Pde MLHL NW7 * 31 F6
Aplin Wy ISLW TW7 135 K2
Apollo Av BMLY BR1 184 A4
NTHWD HA6 40 E1
Apollo Cl HCH RM12 75 K6
Apollo Pl WAN E11 88 C1
WBPTN SW10 * 140 C1
Apollo Wy ERITH DA8 130 A4
THMD SE28 127 J3
Apothecary St BLKFR EC4V * 12 A4
Appach Rd BRXS/STRHM SW2 142 B6
Apple Blossom Ct
VX/NE SW8 * 141 J1
Appleby Cl CHING E4 52 A2
SEVS/STOTM N15 67 K2
STMC/STPC BR5 201 K4
UX/CGN UB8 94 A5
WHTN TW2 155 J4
Appleby Gdns
EBED/NFELT TW14 * 153 J3
Appleby Rd CAN/RD E16 106 E5
HACK E8 86 C5
Appleby St BETH E2 7 J2
Appledore Av BXLYHN DA7 149 K2
RSLP HA4 77 F1
Appledore Cl EDGW HA8 44 C4
HAYES BR2 199 J2
TOOT SW17 160 E4
Appledore Crs SCUP DA14 167 K5
Appledore Wy MLHL NW7 46 B3
Appleford Rd NKENS W10 100 C3
Apple Garth BTFD TW8 116 E4
Applegarth CROY/NA CR0 213 K5
ESH/CLAY KT10 205 F3
Applegarth Dr DART DA1 171 H4
GNTH/NBYPK IG2 73 F1
Applegarth Rd THMD SE28 128 C1
WKENS W14 * 119 G3
Apple Gv CHSGTN KT9 206 A2
EN EN1 24 A4
RYLN/HDSTN HA2 60 A5
Apple Ldg ALP/SUD HA0 * 79 J1
Apple Market KUT/HW KT1 174 E5
Apple Rd WAN E11 88 C1
Appleton Cl BXLYHN DA7 149 J3
Appleton Dr RDART DA2 170 E5
Appleton Gdns NWMAL KT3 192 D3
Appleton Rd ELTH/MOT SE9 146 D4
Appletree Cl PGE/AN SE20 181 J4
Appletree Gdns EBAR EN4 21 J5
Apple Tree Yd STJS SW1Y 10 B7
Applewood Cl CRICK NW2 81 K1
TRDG/WHET N20 33 J3
Applewood Dr PLSTW E13 107 F3
Appold St ERITH DA8 130 C6
SDTCH EC2A 13 G1
Apprentice Gdns NTHLT UB5 95 K2
Apprentice Wy CLPT E5 86 D2
Approach La MLHL NW7 46 C1
Approach Rd BETH E2 104 E1
E/WMO/HCT KT8 189 F2
EBAR EN4 21 G5
RYNPK SW20 177 F5
The Approach ACT W3 99 F5
EN EN1 24 D3
HDN NW4 64 B2
ORP BR6 202 A6
Aprey Gdns HDN NW4 64 A1
April Cl FELT TW13 153 K5
HNWL W7 96 E6
ORP BR6 217 F3
April Gln FSTH SE23 164 A5
April St HACK E8 86 B2
Apsley Cl HRW HA1 60 C2
Apsley Rd NWMAL KT3 175 K6
SNWD SE25 197 J1
Apsley Wy CRICK NW2 63 J6
MYFR/PICC W1J * 15 J1
Aquarius TWK TW1 * 156 C3
Aquarius Wy NTHWD HA6 40 E1
Aquila St STJWD NW8 2 B2
Aquinas St STHWK SE1 17 K1
Arabella Dr PUT/ROE SW15 138 B5
Arabia Cl CHING E4 38 A2
Arabin Rd BROCKY SE4 144 B5
Aragon Av EW KT17 207 K6
THDIT KT7 190 A2
Aragon Cl ENC/FH EN2 23 F1
HAYES BR2 200 E5
LOU IG10 39 J1
Aragon Dr BARK/HLT IG6 54 C3
RSLP HA4 59 H5
Aragon Pl MRDN SM4 193 G4
Aragon Rd KUTN/CMB KT2 175 F1
MRDN SM4 193 G4
Arandora Crs CHDH RM6 73 H4
Arbery Rd BOW E3 105 G2
Arbor Cl BECK BR3 182 E5
Arborfield Cl
BRXS/STRHM SW2 162 A3
Arbor Rd CHING E4 38 B5
Arbour Rd PEND EN3 25 F5
Arbour Sq WCHPL E1 105 F5
Arbour Wy HCH RM12 93 K3
Arbroath Gn OXHEY WD19 26 E5
Arbroath Rd ELTH/MOT SE9 146 D4
Arbrook Cl STMC/STPC BR5 186 B6
Arbrook La ESH/CLAY KT10 204 D4
Arbuthnot La BXLY DA5 169 F1
Arbuthnot Rd NWCR SE14 144 A3
Arbutus St HACK E8 86 A6
Arcade Chambers
ELTH/MOT SE9 * 167 F1
Arcade Pde CHSGTN KT9 * 206 A2
The Arcade ELTH/MOT SE9 * 167 F1
LVPST EC2M * 13 G2
WALTH E17 * 69 J1
Arcadia Av FNCH N3 46 E4
Arcadia Cl CAR SM5 210 A2
Arcadian Av BXLY DA5 169 F1
Arcadian Cl BXLY DA5 169 F1
Arcadian Gdns WDGN N22 49 G3
Arcadian Pl WAND/EARL SW18 159 H2
Arcadian Rd BXLY DA5 169 F2
Arcadia St POP/IOD E14 105 J5
Archangel St
BERM/RHTH SE16 124 A2
Archbishop's Pl
BRXS/STRHM SW2 162 A1
Archdale Pl NWMAL KT3 175 J6
Archdale Rd EDUL SE22 143 G6
Archel Rd WKENS W14 119 J6
Archer Cl BAR EN5 32 D1
KUTN/CMB KT2 175 F3
Archer Ct FELT TW13 153 K3
Archer Ms HPTN TW12 173 H2
Archer Rd SNWD SE25 197 J1
STMC/STPC BR5 202 B3
Archers Dr PEND EN3 24 E3
Archer Sq NWCR SE14 124 B6
Archer St SOHO/SHAV W1D 10 C5
Archery Cl BAY/PAD W2 8 D4
KTN/HRWW/WS HA3 43 F6
Archery Rd ELTH/MOT SE9 146 E6
The Arches CHCR WC2N * 11 F7
RYLN/HDSTN HA2 60 B6
Archibald Rd HOLWY N7 84 D2
Archibold St BOW E3 105 J2
Archie Cl WDR/YW UB7 112 D2
Arch St STHWK SE1 18 C5
Archway HARH RM3 57 K2
Archway Cl ARCH N19 * 66 C6
NKENS W10 100 B4
WIM/MER SW19 160 A6
WLGTN SM6 * 210 E1
Archway Rd ARCH N19 66 C5
HGT N6 65 K2
Archway St BARN SW13 138 B4
Arcola St HACK E8 86 B3
Arcon Dr NTHLT UB5 95 J3
Arctic St KTTN NW5 84 B3
Arcus Rd BMLY BR1 183 H2
Ardbeg Rd HNHL SE24 162 E1
Arden Cl BUSH WD23 29 F2
HRW HA1 78 D1
THMD SE28 109 K5
WHTN TW2 154 E2
Arden Court Gdns EFNCH N2 65 H3
Arden Crs DAGW RM9 91 K5
POP/IOD E14 124 D4
Arden Est IS N1 7 G3
Arden Gv ORP BR6 216 B2
Arden Mhor PIN HA5 59 F1
Arden Rd FNCH N3 46 C6
WEA W13 97 J6
Ardent Cl SNWD SE25 181 F6
Ardfern Av STRHM/NOR SW16 180 B6
Ardfillan Rd CAT SE6 165 G3
Ardgowan Rd CAT SE6 165 H2
Ardilaun Rd HBRY N5 85 J2
Ardingly Cl CROY/NA CR0 213 F1
Ardleigh Gdns CHEAM SM3 193 K5
Ardleigh Rd IS N1 85 K4
WALTH E17 51 H4
Ardleigh Ter WALTH E17 51 H4
Ardley Cl CAT SE6 164 B5
WLSDN NW10 81 G1
Ardlui Rd WNWD SE27 162 D4
Ardmay Gdns SURB KT6 * 191 F2
Ardmere Rd LEW SE13 165 G1
Ardmore La BKHH IG9 39 F3
Ardmore Pl BKHH IG9 * 39 F2
Ardoch Rd CAT SE6 165 G4
Ardra Rd ED N9 37 F5
Ardrossan Gdns WPK KT4 207 J1
Ardross Av NTHWD HA6 40 C1
Ardshiel Cl PUT/ROE SW15 139 G4
Ardwell Av BARK/HLT IG6 72 C2
Ardwell Rd BRXS/STRHM SW2 161 K4
Ardwick Rd CRICK NW2 82 E2
Arena Est FSBYPK N4 * 67 H3
Argall Av LEY E10 69 F4
Argall Wy LEY E10 69 F5
Argenta Wy WLSDN NW10 80 D5
Argent Ct SURB KT6 * 191 H6
SURB KT6 206 C1
Argon Ms FUL/PGN SW6 139 K1
Argon Rd UED N18 50 E1
Argosy La STWL/WRAY TW19 152 A2
Argus Cl ROMW/RG RM7 56 D4
Argus Wy NTHLT UB5 95 J2
Argyle Av HSLW TW3 155 F1
Argyle Cl WEA W13 97 G3
Argyle Cnr WEA W13 * 97 H6
Argyle Pl HMSMTH W6 118 E4
Argyle Rd BAR EN5 20 A5
CAN/RD E16 107 F5
GFD/PVL UB6 97 F2
HSLW TW3 135 G6
IL IG1 72 A6
NFNCH/WDSPK N12 46 E1
RYLN/HDSTN HA2 60 B3
SRTFD E15 88 C2
TOTM N17 50 C4
UED N18 36 C6
WCHPL E1 105 F3
WEA W13 97 G5
Argyle Sq STPAN WC1H 5 F4
Argyle St KCROSS N1C 4 E4
STPAN WC1H 5 F5
Argyle Wk STPAN WC1H * 4 E5
Argyle Wy BERM/RHTH SE16 123 H5
Argyll Av STHL UB1 115 G1
Argyll Cl BRXN/ST SW9 142 A4
Argyll Gdns EDGW HA8 44 D5
Argyll Rd KENS W8 119 K2
WOOL/PLUM SE18 127 H3
Argyll St SOHO/SHAV W1D 10 A4
Arhchie St STHWK SE1 19 H3
Arica Rd BROCKY SE4 144 B5
Ariel Rd KIL/WHAMP NW6 82 E4
Ariel Wy HSLWW TW4 134 A4
SHB W12 119 F1
Aristotle Rd CLAP SW4 141 J4
Arkell Gv NRWD SE19 180 C3
Arkindale Rd CAT SE6 165 F5
Arkley Crs WALTH E17 69 H2
Arkley Rd WALTH E17 69 H2
Arklow Rd NWCR SE14 124 C6
Arkwright Rd HAMP NW3 83 G3
Arlesford Rd BRXN/ST SW9 141 K4
Arlingford Rd
BRXS/STRHM SW2 162 B1
Arlington NFNCH/WDSPK N12 32 E5
Arlington Av IS N1 6 D1
Arlington Cl BFN/LL DA15 167 K2
LEW SE13 145 G6
SUT SM1 193 K6
TWK TW1 * 156 D1
Arlington Ct HYS/HAR UB3 113 G5
Arlington Dr CAR SM5 194 E6
RSLP HA4 58 B3
Arlington Gdns CHSWK W4 117 K5
IL IG1 71 K4
Arlington Pde
BRXS/STRHM SW2 * 142 A5

Arlington Rd CAMTN NW1 3 K1
RCHPK/HAM TW10 156 E4
STHGT/OAK N14 34 B4
SURB KT6 190 E3
TEDD TW11 156 A6
TWK TW1 156 D1
WEA W13 97 H5
WFD IG8 52 E4
Arlington Sq IS N1 6 D1
Arlington St MYFR/PICC W1J 10 A7
Arlington Wy CLKNW EC1R 5 K4
Arliss Wy NTHLT UB5 77 G6
Arlow Rd WCHMH N21 35 G3
Armadale Cl TOTM N17 68 D1
Armadale Rd
EBED/NFELT TW14 133 K6
FUL/PGN SW6 139 K1
Armada St DEPT SE8 124 D6
Armada Wy CAN/RD E16 108 B6
Armagh Rd BOW E3 87 H6
Armfield Cl E/WMO/HCT KT8 188 E2
Armfield Crs MTCM CR4 178 E5
Armfield Rd ENC/FH EN2 23 K2
Arminger Rd SHB W12 118 E1
Armistice Gdns SNWD SE25 181 H6
Armitage Rd GLDGN NW11 64 C5
GNWCH SE10 125 J4
Armour Cl HOLWY N7 85 F4
Armoury Rd DEPT SE8 144 E3
Armoury Wy
WAND/EARL SW18 139 K6
Armstead Wk DAGE RM10 92 C5
Armstrong Av WFD IG8 52 C2
Armstrong Cl BCTR RM8 73 K4
BMLY BR1 184 D6
EHAM E6 107 K5
RSLP HA4 58 E3
Armstrong Crs EBAR EN4 21 H4
Armstrong Rd ACT W3 118 C1
FELT TW13 172 D1
WLSDN NW10 81 G5
WOOL/PLUM SE18 127 H3
Armstrong Wy NWDGN UB2 115 G2
Armytage Rd HEST TW5 134 C1
Arnal Crs WAND/EARL SW18 159 H2
Arncliffe Cl FBAR/BDGN N11 48 A2
Arne Gv ORP BR6 217 F1
Arne St LSQ/SEVD WC2H 11 F4
Arnett Sq CHING E4 51 H2
Arne Wk LEW SE13 145 J5
Arneways Av CHDH RM6 73 K1
Arneway St WEST SW1P 16 D5
Arnewood Cl PUT/ROE SW15 158 D3
Arney's La MTCM CR4 195 F3
Arngask Rd CAT SE6 165 G2
Arnheim Pl POP/IOD E14 124 D3
Arnison Rd E/WMO/HCT KT8 189 J1
Arnold Av East PEND EN3 25 J1
Arnold Av West PEND EN3 25 H1
Arnold Circ BETH E2 7 J5
Arnold Cl KTN/HRWW/WS HA3 62 B4
Arnold Crs ISLW TW7 135 J6
Arnold Dr CHSGTN KT9 205 K4
Arnold Est STHWK SE1 19 K3
Arnold Gdns PLMGR N13 49 H1
Arnold Rd BOW E3 105 J2
DAGW RM9 92 B5
NTHLT UB5 77 J4
SEVS/STOTM N15 50 B6
TOOT SW17 178 E3
Arnold Ter STAN HA7 * 43 F1
Arnos Gv STHGT/OAK N14 34 D6
Arnos Rd FBAR/BDGN N11 48 C1
Arnott Cl CHSWK W4 118 A4
THMD SE28 128 D1
Arnould Av CMBW SE5 142 E5
Arnsberg Wy BXLYHN DA7 149 H5
Arnside Gdns WBLY HA9 61 K5
Arnside Rd BXLYHN DA7 149 H2
Arnside St WALW SE17 122 D6
Arnulf St CAT SE6 164 E6
Arnull's Rd STRHM/NOR SW16 180 C2
Arodene Rd
BRXS/STRHM SW2 162 A1
Arosa Rd TWK TW1 156 E1
Arragon Gdns
STRHM/NOR SW16 179 K3
WWKM BR4 213 K1
Arragon Rd EHAM E6 89 H6
TWK TW1 156 B2
WAND/EARL SW18 159 K3
Arran Cl ERITH DA8 130 A6
WLGTN SM6 210 C2
Arran Dr MNPK E12 71 H5
STAN HA7 29 J6
Arran Gn OXHEY WD19 * 27 H6
Arran Ms EA W5 117 G1
Arran Rd CAT SE6 164 E4
Arran Wk IS N1 85 J5
Arran Wy ESH/CLAY KT10 189 G6
Arras Av MRDN SM4 194 B2
Arrol Rd BECK BR3 181 K6
Arrow Rd BOW E3 105 K2
Arrowsmith Rd CHIG IG7 55 F1
Arsenal Rd ELTH/MOT SE9 146 E3
Arsenal Wy CAN/RD E16 127 F2
Artemis Pl WAND/EARL SW18 159 J2
Arterberry Rd RYNPK SW20 177 F3
Arterial Rd Purfleet
SOCK/AV RM15 131 K3
Artesian Cl ROM RM1 75 H3
WLSDN NW10 81 F5
Artesian Gv BAR EN5 21 G5
Artesian Houses
BAY/PAD W2 * 100 E5
Artesian Rd BAY/PAD W2 100 E5
Arthingworth St SRTFD E15 88 C6
Arthurdon Rd BROCKY SE4 144 D6
Arthur Gv WOOL/PLUM SE18 127 H4
Arthur Rd CHDH RM6 73 J4
ED N9 36 B4
EHAM E6 107 K1
HOLWY N7 85 F2
KUTN/CMB KT2 175 H3
NWMAL KT3 192 E2
WIM/MER SW19 159 K5
Arthur St CANST EC4R 13 F6
ERITH DA8 150 C1
Artichoke Hl WAP E1W 104 D6
Artichoke Pl CMBW SE5 * 142 E2
Artillery Cl GNTH/NBYPK IG2 72 C3
Artillery La LVPST EC2M 13 H2
SHB W12 99 J5
Artillery Pas WCHPL E1 * 13 H2
Artillery Pl WOOL/PLUM SE18 126 E5
Artillery Rw WEST SW1P 16 C5
Artington Cl ORP BR6 216 C2
Artisan Cl EHAM E6 108 B6
Artizan St WCHPL E1 13 H3
Artwell Cl LEY E10 69 K3
Arundel Av MRDN SM4 193 J1
Arundel Cl BTSEA SW11 140 D6
BXLY DA5 169 G1
CROY/NA CR0 * 211 H1
HPTN TW12 173 G1
SRTFD E15 88 C2
Arundel Dr ORP BR6 217 H3
RYLN/HDSTN HA2 77 K2
WFD IG8 52 E3
Arundel Gdns EDGW HA8 45 F3
GDMY/SEVK IG3 73 G6
NTGHL W11 100 D6
WCHMH N21 35 G3
Arundel Gv IS N1 86 A3
Arundel Pl HOLWY N7 85 G4
Arundel Rd BELMT SM2 208 D5
CROY/NA CR0 196 E3
DART DA1 151 F5
EBAR EN4 21 J4
HSLWW TW4 134 B4
KUT/HW KT1 175 J5
Arundel Sq HOLWY N7 85 G4
Arundel St TPL/STR WC2R 11 H5
Arundel Ter BARN SW13 118 E6
Arungford Ms
BRXS/STRHM SW2 142 B6
Arvon Rd HBRY N5 85 G3
Asbaston Ter IL IG1 90 C3
Ascalon St VX/NE SW8 141 H1
Ascension Rd CRW RM5 56 E2
Ascham Dr CHING E4 51 K3
Ascham End WALTH E17 51 G4
Ascham St KTTN NW5 84 C3
Aschurch Rd CROY/NA CR0 197 G4
Ascot Cl BARK/HLT IG6 54 E2
NTHLT UB5 78 A3
Ascot Gdns STHL UB1 95 K4
Ascot Ms WLGTN SM6 210 C6
Ascot Pde CLAP SW4 * 141 K5
Ascot Rd EBED/NFELT TW14 152 D3
EHAM E6 107 K2
SEVS/STOTM N15 67 K2
STMC/STPC BR5 202 A1
TOOT SW17 179 F2
UED N18 36 C6
Ascott Av EA W5 117 F2
Ascott Ct PIN HA5 * 58 E1
Ashanti Ms HACK E8 * 86 D4
Ashbourne Sq NTHWD HA6 40 C2
Ashbourne Av BXLYHN DA7 149 F1
GLDGN NW11 64 D2
RYLN/HDSTN HA2 * 60 D6
SWFD E18 71 F1
TRDG/WHET N20 33 K4
Ashbourne Cl EA W5 98 B4
NFNCH/WDSPK N12 33 F6
Ashbourne Gv CHSWK W4 118 B5
EDUL SE22 143 G6
MLHL NW7 45 F1
Ashbourne Pde EA W5 * 98 B3
GLDGN NW11 * 64 D1
Ashbourne Ri ORP BR6 216 D2
Ashbourne Rd EA W5 98 B3
MTCM CR4 179 F2
Ashbourne Ter
WIM/MER SW19 177 K3
Ashbourne Wy GLDGN NW11 64 D2
Ashbridge Rd WAN E11 70 C4
Ashbridge St STJWD NW8 2 C7
Ashbrook EDGW HA8 * 44 B2
Ashbrook Rd ARCH N19 66 D6
DAGE RM10 92 D1
Ashburn Gdns SKENS SW7 120 B4
Ashburnham Av HRW HA1 61 F4
Ashburnham Cl EFNCH N2 47 H6
OXHEY WD19 * 26 E5
Ashburnham Dr OXHEY WD19 26 E5
Ashburnham Gdns HRW HA1 61 F3
Ashburnham Gv GNWCH SE10 144 E1
Ashburnham Pk
ESH/CLAY KT10 204 C2
Ashburnham Pl GNWCH SE10 144 E1
Ashburnham Retreat
GNWCH SE10 144 E1
Ashburnham Rd BELV DA17 129 K4
RCHPK/HAM TW10 156 C5
WBPTN SW10 * 140 B1
WLSDN NW10 100 A2
Ashburn Pl SKENS SW7 120 B4
Ashburton Av CROY/NA CR0 197 J5
GDMY/SEVK IG3 91 F2
Ashburton Cl CROY/NA CR0 197 H5
Ashburton Gdns
CROY/NA CR0 197 H6
Ashburton Rd CAN/RD E16 106 E5
CROY/NA CR0 197 H6
RSLP HA4 58 E6
Ashbury Gdns CHDH RM6 73 K2
Ashbury Pl WIM/MER SW19 178 B2
Ashbury Rd BTSEA SW11 140 E4
Ashby Av CHSGTN KT9 206 C4
Ashby Cl WWKM BR4 214 B1
Ashby Gv IS N1 85 J5
Ashby Ms BROCKY SE4 144 C4
Ashby Rd BROCKY SE4 144 C3
SEVS/STOTM N15 68 C2
Ashby St FSBYE EC1V 6 B5
Ashby Wk CROY/NA CR0 196 D3
Ashby Wy WDR/YW UB7 132 D1
Ashchurch Gv SHB W12 118 D3
Ashchurch Park Vls SHB W12 118 D3
Ashchurch Ter SHB W12 118 C3
Ash Cl CAR SM5 194 E6
CRW RM5 56 D3
EDGW HA8 30 E6
NWMAL KT3 176 A5
PGE/AN SE20 181 K5
SCUP DA14 168 C5
STAN HA7 43 G2
STMC/STPC BR5 201 J2
SWLY BR8 187 K5
Ashcombe Av SURB KT6 190 E4
Ashcombe Cl ASHF TW15 152 A5
Ashcombe Gdns EDGW HA8 30 C6
Ashcombe Pk CRICK NW2 81 G1
Ashcombe Rd CAR SM5 210 A4
WIM/MER SW19 177 K1
Ashcombe Sq NWMAL KT3 175 K6
Ashcombe St FUL/PGN SW6 * 140 A3
Ash Ct HOR/WEW KT19 206 E2
Ashcroft PIN HA5 42 A2
Ashcroft Av BFN/LL DA15 168 B1
Ashcroft Crs BFN/LL DA15 168 B1
Ashcroft Rd BOW E3 105 G2
CHSGTN KT9 206 B1
Ashdale Cl STWL/WRAY TW19 152 B4
WHTN TW2 155 G2
Ashdale Gv STAN HA7 43 F2
Ashdale Rd LEE/GVPK SE12 166 A3
Ashdene PIN HA5 41 G6
Ashdon Cl WFD IG8 53 F2
Ashdown WEA W13 * 97 H4
Ashdown Cl BECK BR3 182 E5
BXLY DA5 169 K2
Ashdown Crs KTTN NW5 * 84 A3
Ashdown Pl THDIT KT7 190 B3
Ashdown Rd KUT/HW KT1 175 F5
PEND EN3 24 E4
WLSDN NW10 81 G6
Ashdown Wk ROMW/RG RM7 56 D4
Ashdown Wy TOOT SW17 161 F4
Ashen EHAM E6 108 A5
Ashenden Rd CLPT E5 87 G3
Ashen Dr DART DA1 170 D1
Ashen Gv WIM/MER SW19 159 K5
Ashen V SAND/SEL CR2 213 F6
Asher Loftus Wy
FBAR/BDGN N11 47 K2
Asher Wy WAP E1W 123 H1
Ashfield Av BUSH WD23 28 B1
FELT TW13 154 A3
Ashfield Cl BECK BR3 182 D3
RCHPK/HAM TW10 157 F3
Ashfield Ct EA W5 * 98 A6
Ashfield La CHST BR7 185 H2
Ashfield Rd ACT W3 118 C1
FSBYPK N4 67 J3
STHGT/OAK N14 34 C5
Ashfield St WCHPL E1 104 D4
Ashfield Yd WCHPL E1 * 104 E4
Ashford Av CEND/HSY/T N8 66 E1
YEAD UB4 95 H5
Ashford Cl ASHF TW15 152 B6
WALTH E17 69 H3
Ashford Crs ASHF TW15 152 B5
PEND EN3 24 E3
Ashford Gn OXHEY WD19 41 H1
Ashford Ms TOTM N17 50 C4
Ashford Rd CRICK NW2 82 B2
EHAM E6 89 K4
FELT TW13 153 G6
SWFD E18 53 F5
Ashford St IS N1 7 G4
Ash Gv ALP/SUD HA0 79 G2
CRICK NW2 82 B2
EA W5 117 F2
EBED/NFELT TW14 153 H3
EN EN1 36 A2
HACK E8 86 D6
HEST TW5 134 C2
HYS/HAR UB3 94 B6
MUSWH N10 66 B1
PGE/AN SE20 181 K5
PLMGR N13 35 J5
STHL UB1 96 A4
WWKM BR4 199 F5
Ashgrove Rd BMLY BR1 183 G2
GDMY/SEVK IG3 73 F5
Ash Hill Cl BUSH WD23 28 B3
Ash Hill Dr PIN HA5 41 G6
Ashingdon Cl CHING E4 38 A6
Ashington Rd FUL/PGN SW6 * 139 J3
Ashlake Rd STRHM/NOR SW16 161 K6
Ashland Pl MHST W1U 9 G1
Ashlar Pl WOOL/PLUM SE18 127 G4
Ashleigh Gdns SUT SM1 194 A6
Ashleigh Rd
MORT/ESHN SW14 138 B4
PGE/AN SE20 181 J6
Ashley Av BARK/HLT IG6 54 B5
MRDN SM4 193 K2
Ashley Cl HDN NW4 46 A5
PIN HA5 41 F5
Ashley Crs BTSEA SW11 141 F4
WDGN N22 49 G5
Ashley Dr ISLW TW7 115 K6
WHTN TW2 155 G3
Ashley Gdns ORP BR6 216 E3
PLMGR N13 35 J6
RCHPK/HAM TW10 156 E5
WBLY HA9 62 A6
Ashley La CROY/NA CR0 211 H2
HDN NW4 46 A5
Ashley Pl WESTW SW1E 16 A5
Ashley Rd ARCH N19 66 E5
CHING E4 51 J1
FSTGT E7 89 G5
HPTN TW12 173 F4
PEND EN3 24 E3
RCH/KEW TW9 137 F4
THDIT KT7 190 A3
THHTH CR7 196 A1
TOTM N17 50 C6
WIM/MER SW19 178 A2
Ashleys Aly SEVS/STOTM N15 67 J1
Ashley Wk MLHL NW7 46 A3
Ashling Rd CROY/NA CR0 197 H5
Ashlin Rd SRTFD E15 88 B2
Ashlone Rd PUT/ROE SW15 139 G3
Ashlyns Wy CHSGTN KT9 205 K4
Ashmead STHGT/OAK N14 22 C6
Ashmead Ga BMLY BR1 184 B4
Ashmead Ms BROCKY SE4 144 D3
Ashmead Rd DEPT SE8 144 D3
EBED/NFELT TW14 153 K3
Ashmere Av BECK BR3 183 G5
Ashmere Cl CHEAM SM3 208 B3
Ashmere Gv
BRXS/STRHM SW2 141 K5
Ash Ms KTTN NW5 * 84 C3
Ashmill St STJWD NW8 8 C1
Ashmole St VX/NE SW8 122 A6
Ashmore Cl PECK SE15 143 G1
Ashmore Gv WELL DA16 147 J4
Ashmore Rd MV/WKIL W9 100 D2
Ashmount Rd
SEVS/STOTM N15 68 B2
Ashmount Ter EA W5 * 116 E4
Ashmour Gdns ROM RM1 57 F5
Ashneal Gdns HRW HA1 78 D1
Ashness Gdns GFD/PVL UB6 79 H4
Ashness Rd BTSEA SW11 140 E6
Ashridge Cl
KTN/HRWW/WS HA3 61 J3
Ashridge Crs
WOOL/PLUM SE18 147 H1
Ashridge Dr OXHEY WD19 41 G1
Ashridge Gdns PIN HA5 59 J1
PLMGR N13 48 E1
Ashridge Wy MRDN SM4 193 J1
Ash Rd CHEAM SM3 193 H5
CROY/NA CR0 198 D6
DART DA1 171 G3
ORP BR6 217 G5
RDART DA2 171 J6
SRTFD E15 88 C3
Ash Rw HAYES BR2 201 F3
Ashstead Rd STNW/STAM N16 68 C4
Ashton Cl SUT SM1 208 E2
Ashton Gdns CHDH RM6 74 A3
HSLWW TW4 134 E5
Ashton Rd SRTFD E15 88 B3
Ashton St POP/IOD E14 106 A6
Ashtree Av MTCM CR4 178 C5
Ash Tree Cl CROY/NA CR0 198 B3
Ashtree Cl ORP BR6 216 B2
Ash Tree Cl SURB KT6 191 F5
Ash Tree Dell CDALE/KGS NW9 62 E2
Ash Tree Wy CROY/NA CR0 198 B2
Ashurst Cl DART DA1 150 C4
NTHWD HA6 40 C3
PGE/AN SE20 181 J4
Ashurst Dr BARK/HLT IG6 72 C2
GNTH/NBYPK IG2 72 B3
Ashurst Gdns
BRXS/STRHM SW2 * 162 B3
Ashurst Rd EBAR EN4 21 K6
NFNCH/WDSPK N12 47 J1
Ashurst Wk CROY/NA CR0 197 J6
Ashvale Gdns CRW RM5 57 F1
Ashvale Rd TOOT SW17 178 E1
Ashville Rd WAN E11 70 B6
Ash Wk ALP/SUD HA0 79 J2
Ashwater Rd LEE/GVPK SE12 165 K3
Ashwell Cl EHAM E6 107 K5
Ashwin St HACK E8 86 B4
Ashwood Av RAIN RM13 111 K2
Ashwood Gdns CROY/NA CR0 213 K4
HYS/HAR UB3 113 J4
Ashwood Rd CHING E4 38 B5
Ashworth Cl CMBW SE5 142 E3
Ashworth Rd MV/WKIL W9 101 F2
Askern Cl BXLYHS DA6 148 E5
Aske St IS N1 7 G4
Askew Crs SHB W12 118 C2
Askew Rd NTHWD HA6 26 B4
SHB W12 118 C2
Askew Vls PLMGR N13 * 35 H5
Askham Rd SHB W12 118 D1
Askill Dr PUT/ROE SW15 139 H6
Askwith Rd RAIN RM13 111 F1
Asland Rd SRTFD E15 88 B6
Aslett St WAND/EARL SW18 160 A2
Asmara Rd CRICK NW2 82 C3
Asmuns Hl GLDGN NW11 64 E2
Asmuns Pl GLDGN NW11 64 D2
Aspen Cl EA W5 * 117 G2
ORP BR6 217 G3
WDR/YW UB7 112 C1
Aspen Copse BMLY BR1 184 E5
Aspen Ct HACK E8 * 86 C4
Aspen Dr ALP/SUD HA0 79 G1
Aspen Gdns MTCM CR4 195 F2
Aspen Gn ERITH DA18 129 G3
Aspen Gv PIN HA5 40 D6
Aspen La NTHLT UB5 95 J2
Aspenlea Rd HMSMTH W6 119 G6
Aspen Wy FELT TW13 154 A5
POP/IOD E14 106 A6
Aspern Gv HAMP NW3 83 J3
Aspinall Rd BROCKY SE4 144 A4
NWCR SE14 144 A4
Aspinden Rd
BERM/RHTH SE16 123 J4
Aspley Rd WAND/EARL SW18 140 A6
Asplins Rd TOTM N17 50 C4
Asplins Vls TOTM N17 * 50 C4
Asprey Ms BECK BR3 198 C2
Asquith Cl BCTR RM8 73 J5
Assam St WCHPL E1 104 C5
Assata Ms IS N1 85 H4
Assembly Pas WCHPL E1 104 E4
Assembly Wk CAR SM5 194 D4
Astall Cl KTN/HRWW/WS HA3 42 D4
Astbury Rd PECK SE15 143 K2
Astell St CHEL SW3 120 D5
Asteys Rw IS N1 * 85 H5
Astle St BTSEA SW11 141 F3
Astley Av CRICK NW2 82 A3
Aston Av KTN/HRWW/WS HA3 61 J4
Aston Cl BUSH WD23 28 C1
SCUP DA14 168 B5
Aston Gn HSLWW TW4 134 B3
Aston Pl STRHM/NOR SW16 180 C2
Aston Rd EA W5 97 K5
ESH/CLAY KT10 204 E3
RYNPK SW20 177 F5
Astons Rd NTHWD HA6 26 A5
Aston St POP/IOD E14 105 G5
Aston Ter BAL SW12 * 161 G1
Astonville St
WAND/EARL SW18 159 K3
Astor Av ROMW/RG RM7 74 D3
Astor Cl KUTN/CMB KT2 175 J2
Astoria Pde ASHF TW15 * 152 D6
STRHM/NOR SW16 * 161 K5
Astoria Wk BRXN/ST SW9 142 B4
Astra Cl HCH RM12 93 K4
Astrop Ms HMSMTH W6 119 F3
Astrop Ter HMSMTH W6 119 F3
Astwood Ms SKENS SW7 120 A4
Asylum Rd PECK SE15 143 J1
Atalanta St FUL/PGN SW6 139 G2
Atbara Rd TEDD TW11 174 C2
Atcham Rd HSLW TW3 135 H5
Atcost Rd BARK IG11 109 G4
Atheldene Rd
WAND/EARL SW18 160 A3
Athelney St CAT SE6 164 D5
Athelstane Gv BOW E3 105 H1
Athelstane Ms FSBYPK N4 67 G5
Athelstan Gdns
KIL/WHAMP NW6 * 82 C5
Athelstan Rd KUT/HW KT1 191 G1
Athelstan Wy STMC/STPC BR5 186 B4
Athelstone Rd
KTN/HRWW/WS HA3 42 D5
Athena Cl KUT/HW KT1 175 G6
RYLN/HDSTN HA2 60 D6
Athenaeum Pl MUSWH N10 48 B6
Athenaeum Rd
TRDG/WHET N20 33 G3
Athena Pl NTHWD HA6 40 D4
Athenlay Rd PECK SE15 144 A6
Athens Gdns MV/WKIL W9 * 100 E3
Atherden Rd CLPT E5 86 E2
Atherfold Rd BRXN/ST SW9 141 K4
Atherley Wy HSLWW TW4 154 E2
Atherstone Ms SKENS SW7 * 120 B4
Atherton Cl
STWL/WRAY TW19 152 A1
Atherton Dr WIM/MER SW19 159 G6
Atherton Hts ALP/SUD HA0 79 J4
Atherton Ms FSTGT E7 88 D4
Atherton Pl RYLN/HDSTN HA2 42 C6
STHL UB1 96 A6
Atherton Rd BARN SW13 138 D1
CLAY IG5 53 J5
FSTGT E7 88 D3
Atherton St BTSEA SW11 140 D3
Athlone ESH/CLAY KT10 204 E4
Athlone Cl CLPT E5 86 D3
Athlone Ct WALTH E17 52 B6
Athlone Rd BRXS/STRHM SW2 162 A2
Athlone St KTTN NW5 84 A4
Athlon Rd ALP/SUD HA0 97 K1
Athol Cl PIN HA5 41 F4
Athole Gdns EN EN1 24 A6
Athol Gdns PIN HA5 41 F4
Atholl Rd GDMY/SEVK IG3 73 G4
Athol Rd ERITH DA8 129 K5
Athol Sq POP/IOD E14 106 A5
Atkins Dr WWKM BR4 199 G6
Atkinson Cl ORP BR6 217 G3
Atkinson Rd CAN/RD E16 107 G4
Atkins Rd BAL SW12 161 H2
LEY E10 69 K3
Atlanta Bvd ROM RM1 75 G3
Atlantic Rd BRXN/ST SW9 142 B5
Atlantis Av CAN/RD E16 108 C6
Atlantis Cl BARK IG11 109 H2
Atlas Crs EDGW HA8 30 D4
Atlas Gdns CHARL SE7 126 B4
Atlas Ms HACK E8 86 B4
Atlas Rd DART DA1 151 J4
FBAR/BDGN N11 48 A2
PLSTW E13 106 E1
WBLY HA9 80 E2
WLSDN NW10 99 G2
Atley Rd BOW E3 87 J6
Atlip Rd ALP/SUD HA0 80 A6
Atney Rd PUT/ROE SW15 139 H5
Atria Rd NTHWD HA6 40 E1
Attenborough Cl
OXHEY WD19 27 J5
Atterbury Rd FSBYPK N4 67 G3
Atterbury St WEST SW1P 16 D7
Attewood Av WLSDN NW10 81 G1
Attewood Rd NTHLT UB5 77 J4
Attfield Cl TRDG/WHET N20 33 H4
Attlee Cl THHTH CR7 196 D3
YEAD UB4 * 95 F2
Attlee Dr DART DA1 151 K6
Attlee Rd THMD SE28 109 H6
YEAD UB4 94 E2
Attlee Ter WALTH E17 69 K1
Attneave St FSBYW WC1X 5 J6
Atwell Pl THDIT KT7 190 B5
Atwell Rd PECK SE15 * 143 H3
Atwood Av RCH/KEW TW9 137 H3
Atwood Rd HMSMTH W6 118 E4
Aubert Pk HBRY N5 85 G2
Aubert Rd HBRY N5 85 H2
Aubrey Pl STJWD NW8 101 G1
Aubrey Rd CEND/HSY/T N8 * 66 E2
NTGHL W11 119 J1
WALTH E17 51 J6
Aubrey Wk KENS W8 119 J1
Auburn Cl NWCR SE14 144 B1
Aubyn Hl WNWD SE27 162 D6
Aubyn Sq PUT/ROE SW15 138 D5
Auckland Av RAIN RM13 111 H2
Auckland Cl NRWD SE19 181 G4
Auckland Gdns NRWD SE19 181 F4
Auckland Hl WNWD SE27 162 D6
Auckland Ri NRWD SE19 181 F4
Auckland Rd BTSEA SW11 140 D5
IL IG1 72 B5
KUT/HW KT1 191 G1
LEY E10 87 K1
NRWD SE19 181 G4
Auckland St LBTH SE11 122 A5
Aucuba Vls WELL DA16 * 148 C4
Audax CDALE/KGS NW9 * 45 H5
Auden Pl CAMTN NW1 84 A6
CHEAM SM3 * 208 A2
Audleigh Pl CHIG IG7 54 A2
Audley Cl BTSEA SW11 141 F4
MUSWH N10 48 B3
Audley Ct PIN HA5 41 G5
WAN E11 70 D1
Audley Dr CAN/RD E16 126 A1
Audley Gdns GDMY/SEVK IG3 73 F6
Audley Pl BELMT SM2 209 F5
Audley Rd EA W5 98 B4
ENC/FH EN2 23 H3
HDN NW4 63 J3
RCHPK/HAM TW10 137 G6
Audley Sq MYFR/PKLN W1K * 9 H7
Audley St MYFR/PKLN W1K 9 H7

Audrey Cl BECK BR3 198 E3
Audrey Gdns ALP/SUD HA0 61 H6
Audrey Rd IL IG1 90 B1
Audrey St BETH E2 104 C1
Audric Cl KUTN/CMB KT2 175 H4
Augurs La PLSTW E13 107 F2
Augusta Cl E/WMO/HCT KT8 172 E6
Augusta Rd WHTN TW2 155 H4
Augustine Rd HMSMTH W6 119 G3
KTN/HRWW/WS HA3 42 B4
STMC/STPC BR5 186 E6
Augustus Cl BTFD TW8 136 E1
SHB W12 118 E2
STAN HA7 29 J5
Augustus La ORP BR6 202 B6
Augustus Rd WIM/MER SW19 159 G3
Augustus St CAMTN NW1 3 K3
Aultone Wy CAR SM5 209 K1
SUT SM1 194 A6
Aulton Pl LBTH SE11 122 B5
Aurelia Gdns CROY/NA CR0 196 A2
Aurelia Rd CROY/NA CR0 195 K3
Auriel Av DAGE RM10 93 F4
Auriga Ms IS N1 85 K3
Auriol Cl WPK KT4 207 G1
Auriol Dr GFD/PVL UB6 78 D5
Auriol Park Rd WPK KT4 207 G1
Auriol Rd WKENS W14 119 H4
Austell Gdns MLHL NW7 31 G5
Austen Cl THMD SE28 128 C1
Austen Rd ERITH DA8 149 J1
RYLN/HDSTN HA2 60 B6
Austin Av HAYES BR2 200 D3
Austin Cl FSTH SE23 164 B2
TWK TW1 136 D6
Austin Friars OBST EC2N 13 F3
Austin Friars Sq OBST EC2N * 13 F3
Austin Rd BTSEA SW11 141 F2
HYS/HAR UB3 113 J2
STMC/STPC BR5 202 B3
Austins La HGDN/ICK UB10 76 A1
Austin St BETH E2 7 J5
Austral Cl BFN/LL DA15 168 A5
Australia Rd SHB W12 99 K6
Austral St LBTH SE11 18 A6
Austyn Gdns BRYLDS KT5 * 191 J5
Autumn Cl EN EN1 24 D3
WIM/MER SW19 178 B2
Autumn Dr BELMT SM2 209 F6
Autumn Gv BMLY BR1 184 A2
Autumn St BOW E3 87 J6
Avalon Cl ENC/FH EN2 23 G3
ORP BR6 202 E6
RYNPK SW20 177 H5
WEA W13 97 G4
Avalon Rd FUL/PGN SW6 140 A2
ORP BR6 202 D6
WEA W13 97 G3
Avard Gdns ORP BR6 216 C2
Avarn Rd TOOT SW17 178 E2
Avebury Pk SURB KT6 * 190 E3
Avebury Rd ORP BR6 216 D1
WAN E11 70 B5
WIM/MER SW19 177 J4
Avebury St IS N1 6 E1
Aveley Cl ERITH DA8 130 C6
Aveley Rd ROM RM1 75 F1
Aveline St LBTH SE11 122 A5
Aveling Park Rd WALTH E17 51 J5
Avelon Rd CRW RM5 57 F2
RAIN RM13 93 J6
Ave Marie La STP EC4M 12 B4
Avenell Rd HBRY N5 85 H1
Avening Rd WAND/EARL SW18 159 K2
Avening Ter
WAND/EARL SW18 159 K1
Avenons Rd PLSTW E13 106 E4
Avenue Cl HEST TW5 134 A2
STHGT/OAK N14 34 C1
STJWD NW8 2 D1
WDR/YW UB7 112 A3
Avenue Crs ACT W3 117 J2
HEST TW5 134 A2
Avenue Elmers SURB KT6 191 F2
Avenue Gdns ACT W3 117 J2
HEST TW5 * 133 K1
MORT/ESHN SW14 138 B4
SNWD SE25 181 H6
TEDD TW11 174 A3
Avenue Ga LOU IG10 39 G1
Avenue Ms MUSWH N10 48 B6
Avenue Pde SUN TW16 172 A6
WCHMH N21 * 35 K2
Avenue Park Rd WNWD SE27 162 C4
Avenue Rd ACT W3 117 J2
BTFD TW8 116 D5
BXLYHN DA7 149 F4
CHDH RM6 73 H4
ERITH DA8 130 B6
ERITH DA8 149 K1
FELT TW13 153 J5
FSTGT E7 89 F2
HCT N6 66 C4
HPTN TW12 173 G4
ISLW TW7 135 K2
KUT/HW KT1 175 F6
NFNCH/WDSPK N12 33 G6
NWMAL KT3 176 B6
PGE/AN SE20 181 K4
PIN HA5 41 J6
RYNPK SW20 176 E5
SEVS/STOTM N15 67 K2
SNWD SE25 181 H5
STHGT/OAK N14 34 C1
STHL UB1 114 E1
STJWD NW8 83 H5
STRHM/NOR SW16 179 J5
TEDD TW11 174 B3
WFD IG8 53 G2
WLGTN SM6 210 C5
WLSDN NW10 99 H1
Avenue South BRYLDS KT5 191 G4
Avenue Ter NWMAL KT3 175 K6
OXHEY WD19 27 J1
The Avenue BAR EN5 20 C4
BECK BR3 182 E4
BELMT SM2 208 D6
BKHH IG9 39 G4
BMLY BR1 184 C6
BRYLDS KT5 191 G3
BXLY DA5 168 E2
CAR SM5 210 A5
CEND/HSY/T N8 49 G6
CHING E4 52 B2
CHSWK W4 118 B3
CLAP SW4 141 F6
CROY/NA CR0 212 A1
ESH/CLAY KT10 204 E4
EW KT17 208 A5
FBAR/BDGN N11 48 B1
FNCH N3 46 E5
GNWCH SE10 145 G1
HEST TW5 133 K2
HPTN TW12 172 E2
HSLW TW3 135 G6
KIL/WHAMP NW6 82 C5
KTN/HRWW/WS HA3 43 F4
LOU IG10 39 J1
MUSWH N10 48 C5
NTHWD HA6 40 A2
ORP BR6 202 A6
PIN HA5 41 K2
PIN HA5 59 K3
RCH/KEW TW9 137 G3
ROM RM1 75 F1
STMC/STPC BR5 186 C3
SUN TW16 172 A5
TOTM N17 50 A5
TWK TW1 136 D6
WAN E11 71 F3
WBLY HA9 62 A5
WEA W13 97 H6
WPK KT4 192 C6
WWKM BR4 199 G4
Averil Gv STRHM/NOR SW16 180 C2
Averill St HMSMTH W6 119 G6
Avern Gdns E/WMO/HCT KT8 189 G1
Avern Rd E/WMO/HCT KT8 189 G1
Avery Farm Rw BGVA SW1W * 15 J7
Avery Gdns GNTH/NBYPK IG2 71 K2
Avery Hill Rd ELTH/MOT SE9 167 H3
Avery Rw MYFR/PKLN W1K 9 J5
Avery Wy DART DA1 171 J4
Aviary Cl CAN/RD E16 106 D4
Aviation Dr CDALE/KGS NW9 45 J5
Aviemore Cl BECK BR3 198 C2
Aviemore Wy BECK BR3 198 B2
Avigdor Ms STNW/STAM N16 67 K6
Avignon Rd BROCKY SE4 144 A4
Avington Gv PGE/AN SE20 181 K3
Avington Wy PECK SE15 * 143 G1
Avion Crs CDALE/KGS NW9 45 J5
Avior Dr NTHWD HA6 26 D6
Avis Sq WCHPL E1 105 F5
Avoca Rd TOOT SW17 161 F6
Avocet Cl STHWK SE1 123 H5
Avocet Ms THMD SE28 127 J3
Avon Cl SUT SM1 209 G2
WPK KT4 192 D6
YEAD UB4 95 G3
Avon Ct PIN HA5 * 42 A3
Avondale Av CRICK NW2 81 G1
EBAR EN4 33 K3
ESH/CLAY KT10 205 G1
NFNCH/WDSPK N12 47 F1
WPK KT4 192 C5
Avondale Cl LOU IG10 39 K2
Avondale Ct SWFD E18 53 F4
Avondale Crs PEND EN3 25 G4
REDBR IG4 71 H2
Avondale Dr HYS/HAR UB3 113 K1
LOU IG10 39 K1
Avondale Gdns HSLWW TW4 134 E6
Avondale Park Gdns
NTGHL W11 * 100 C6
Avondale Park Rd
NTGHL W11 100 C6
Avondale Pavement
STHWK SE1 * 123 H5
Avondale Ri PECK SE15 143 G4
Avondale Rd ASHF TW15 152 A5
BMLY BR1 183 H2
CAN/RD E16 106 C4
ELTH/MOT SE9 166 D4
FNCH N3 47 G4
KTN/HRWW/WS HA3 43 F6
MORT/ESHN SW14 138 A4
PLMGR N13 35 G4
SAND/SEL CR2 211 J4
SEVS/STOTM N15 67 H2
WALTH E17 69 J4
WELL DA16 148 D3
WIM/MER SW19 178 A1
Avondale Sq STHWK SE1 123 H5
Avonley Rd NWCR SE14 143 K1
Avonmore Gdns
WKENS W14 * 119 J4
Avonmore Pl WKENS W14 119 H4
Avonmore Rd WKENS W14 119 J4
Avonmouth Rd DART DA1 151 G6
Avonmouth St STHWK SE1 18 C4
Avon Rd BROCKY SE4 144 D4
GFD/PVL UB6 96 A3
WALTH E17 52 B6
Avonstowe Cl ORP BR6 216 C1
Avon Wy SWFD E18 70 E1
Avonwick Rd HSLW TW3 135 G3
Avril Wy CHING E4 52 A1
Avro Wy WLGTN SM6 210 E5
Awberry Ct WATW WD18 * 26 B1
Awlfield Av TOTM N17 49 K4
Awliscombe Rd WELL DA16 148 A3
Axe St BARK IG11 90 C6
Axholme Av EDGW HA8 44 C4
Axis Ct GNWCH SE10 125 H6
Axminster Crs WELL DA16 148 D2
Axminster Rd HOLWY N7 84 E1
Axon Pl IL IG1 72 C6
Axtaine Rd STMC/STPC BR5 202 E4
Aybrook St MHST W1U 9 G2
Aycliff Ct KUT/HW KT1 * 175 H5
Aycliffe Cl BMLY BR1 200 E1
Aycliffe Rd SHB W12 118 C1
Aylands Cl WBLY HA9 62 A6
Aylesbury Cl FSTGT E7 88 D4
Aylesbury Rd HAYES BR2 183 K6
WALW SE17 122 E5
Aylesbury St CLKNW EC1R 6 A7
WLSDN NW10 81 F1
Aylesford Av BECK BR3 198 B2
Aylesford St PIM SW1V 121 J5
Aylesham Cl MLHL NW7 45 J3
Aylesham Rd ORP BR6 201 K4
Ayles Rd YEAD UB4 95 F2
Aylestone Av
KIL/WHAMP NW6 82 B5
Aylett Rd ISLW TW7 135 K3
SNWD SE25 197 J1
Ayley Cft EN EN1 24 C6
Ayliffe Cl KUT/HW KT1 175 H5
Aylmer Cl STAN HA7 29 G6
Aylmer Dr STAN HA7 29 G6
Aylmer Pde EFNCH N2 * 65 K2
Aylmer Rd BCTR RM8 92 A1
EFNCH N2 65 J2
SHB W12 118 B2
WAN E11 70 D4
Ayloffe Rd DAGW RM9 92 B4
Aylsham Dr HGDN/ICK UB10 58 A6
Aylton Est BERM/RHTH SE16 * 123 K2
Aylward Rd FSTH SE23 164 A4
RYNPK SW20 177 J5
Aylwards Ri STAN HA7 29 G6
Aylward St WCHPL E1 105 F5
Aynhoe Rd WKENS W14 119 G4
Aynscombe Angle ORP BR6 202 B4
Ayres Cl PLSTW E13 106 E2
Ayres Crs WLSDN NW10 81 F5
Ayres St STHWK SE1 18 D2
Ayr Gn ROM RM1 57 G4
Ayrsome Rd STNW/STAM N16 86 A1
Ayrton Rd SKENS SW7 14 A4
Ayr Wy ROM RM1 57 G4
Aysgarth Rd DUL SE21 162 E1
Aytoun Pl BRXN/ST SW9 142 A3
Aytoun Rd BRXN/ST SW9 142 A3
Azalea Cl HNWL W7 116 A1
IL IG1 90 B3
Azalea Ct WFD IG8 * 52 C3
Azalea Wk PIN HA5 59 F3
Azania Ms KTTN NW5 84 B3
Azenby Rd PECK SE15 143 G3
Azof St GNWCH SE10 125 H4

B

Baalbec Rd HBRY N5 85 H3
Babbacombe Cl CHSGTN KT9 205 K3
Babbacombe Gdns
REDBR IG4 71 J1
Babbacombe Rd BMLY BR1 184 A4
Baber Bridge Pde
EBED/NFELT TW14 * 154 B1
Baber Dr EBED/NFELT TW14 154 B1
Babington Ri WBLY HA9 80 C4
Babington Rd BCTR RM8 91 J3
HCH RM12 75 K5
HDN NW4 63 K1
STRHM/NOR SW16 179 J1
Babmaes St STJS SW1Y 10 C7
Bache's St IS N1 7 F5
Back Church La WCHPL E1 104 C6
Back Hl CLKNW EC1R 5 K7
Back La BTFD TW8 136 E1
BXLY DA5 169 H2
CEND/HSY/T N8 66 E2
CHDH RM6 73 K4
EDGW HA8 44 E4
HAMP NW3 83 G2
RCHPK/HAM TW10 156 D5
Backley Gdns CROY/NA CR0 197 H3
Back Rd SCUP DA14 168 B6
TEDD TW11 173 K3
WALTH E17 70 A1
WAN E11 70 B3
Bacon Gv STHWK SE1 19 J6
Bacon La CDALE/KGS NW9 62 D1
EDGW HA8 44 C4
Bacon Link CRW RM5 56 D2
Bacon's La HCT N6 66 A5
Bacon St BETH E2 7 K6
WCHPL E1 7 K6
Bacton St BETH E2 104 E2
Baddow Cl DAGE RM10 92 C6
WFD IG8 53 H2
Baden Pl STHWK SE1 18 E2
Baden Powell Cl DAGW RM9 92 A6
SURB KT6 191 G6
Baden Rd CEND/HSY/T N8 66 D1
IL IG1 90 B3
Bader Wy PUT/ROE SW15 158 D1
RAIN RM13 93 J4
Badger Cl FELT TW13 154 A5
GNTH/NBYPK IG2 72 C3
HSLWW TW4 134 B4
Badgers Cl ENC/FH EN2 23 H4
HRW HA1 60 D3
HYS/HAR UB3 113 H1
Badgers Copse ORP BR6 202 A6
WPK KT4 192 C6
Badgers Ct WPK KT4 * 192 C6
Badgers Cft ELTH/MOT SE9 167 F5
TRDG/WHET N20 32 C2
Badgers Wk NWMAL KT3 176 B5
Badlis Rd WALTH E17 51 J5
Badlow Cl ERITH DA8 150 B1
Badminton Cl HRW HA1 * 60 E1
NTHLT UB5 78 A4
Badminton Ms CAN/RD E16 125 K1
Badminton Rd BAL SW12 161 F1
Badsworth Rd CMBW SE5 142 D1
Bafton Ga HAYES BR2 200 A5
Bagley Cl WDR/YW UB7 112 B2
Bagley House
WOOL/PLUM SE18 * 146 D1
Bagley's La FUL/PGN SW6 140 A2
Bagleys Spring CHDH RM6 74 A1
Bagshot Ct
WOOL/PLUM SE18 * 147 F2
Bagshot Rd EN EN1 36 B1
Bagshot St WALW SE17 123 F5
Baildon St DEPT SE8 144 C1
Bailey Cl FBAR/BDGN N11 48 D4
THMD SE28 127 K1
Bailey Cots POP/IOD E14 * 105 G4
Bailey Crs CHSGTN KT9 205 K5
Bailey House
WOOL/PLUM SE18 * 146 D1
Bailey Ms BRXS/STRHM SW2 142 B6
CHSWK W4 117 J6
Bailey Pl SYD SE26 181 K2
Baillie Cl RAIN RM13 111 K3
Bainbridge Cl
RCHPK/HAM TW10 175 F1
Bainbridge Rd DAGW RM9 92 B2
Bainbridge St
NOXST/BSQ WC1A 10 D3
Baines Cl SAND/SEL CR2 211 K3
Baird Av STHL UB1 96 B6
Baird Cl BUSH WD23 28 B1
CDALE/KGS NW9 62 E3
LEY E10 69 J5
Baird Gdns NRWD SE19 163 F6
Baird Memorial Cots
STHGT/OAK N14 * 34 D4
Baird Rd EN EN1 24 D4
Baird St STLK EC1Y 6 D6
Baizdon Rd BKHTH/KID SE3 145 H3
Baker Crs DART DA1 171 F2
Baker La MTCM CR4 179 F5
Baker Ms ORP BR6 217 F4
Baker Pl HOR/WEW KT19 206 E4
Baker Rd WLSDN NW10 81 G6
WOOL/PLUM SE18 146 D1
Bakers Av WALTH E17 69 K3
Bakers Cl DART DA1 171 G2
Bakers End RYNPK SW20 177 H5
Bakers Fld HOLWY N7 84 D2
Bakers Gdns CAR SM5 194 D6
Bakers Hl BAR EN5 21 F3
CLPT E5 68 D5
Baker's Ms MHST W1U 9 G3
Bakers Rents BETH E2 7 J4
Bakers Rw SRTFD E15 106 C1
Baker's Rw CLKNW EC1R 5 J7
Baker St CAMTN NW1 3 F7
EN EN1 23 K3
EN EN1 24 A1
MHST W1U 9 G2
Baker's Yd CLKNW EC1R 5 J7
Bakery Cl BRXN/ST SW9 * 142 A1
Bakewell Wy NWMAL KT3 176 B5
Balaams La STHGT/OAK N14 34 D4
Balaam St PLSTW E13 106 E2
Balaclava Rd STHWK SE1 19 K7
SURB KT6 190 D4
Bala Gn CDALE/KGS NW9 * 63 G3
Balcaskie Rd ELTH/MOT SE9 146 E6
Balchier Rd EDUL SE22 163 J1
Balcombe Cl BXLYHS DA6 148 E5
Balcombe St CAMTN NW1 2 E6
Balcorne St HOM E9 86 E5
Balder Ri LEE/GVPK SE12 166 A4
Balderton St OXSTW W1C 9 H4
Baldock St BOW E3 105 K1
Baldry Gdns
STRHM/NOR SW16 179 K2
Baldwin Crs CMBW SE5 142 D2
Baldwin Gdns HSLW TW3 135 H2
Baldwin Rd BTSEA SW11 161 F1
Baldwin's Gdns FSBYW WC1X 11 J1
Baldwin St FSBYE EC1V 6 E5
Baldwin Ter IS N1 6 C2
Baldwyn Gdns ACT W3 98 E6
Baldwyn's Pk BXLY DA5 170 A4
Baldwyn's Rd BXLY DA5 170 A4
Bale Rd WCHPL E1 105 G4
Bales Ter ED N9 * 36 B5
Balfern Gv CHSWK W4 118 B5
Balfern St BTSEA SW11 140 D3
Balfe St IS N1 5 F3
Balfour Av HNWL W7 116 A1
Balfour Gv TRDG/WHET N20 33 K5
Balfour Ms ED N9 36 C5
MYFR/PKLN W1K 9 H7
Balfour Pl MYFR/PKLN W1K 9 H7
PUT/ROE SW15 138 E5
Balfour Rd ACT W3 98 E4
CAR SM5 209 K5
HAYES BR2 200 C2
HBRY N5 85 J2
HRW HA1 60 D2
HSLW TW3 135 G4
IL IG1 72 B6
NWDGN UB2 114 C3
SNWD SE25 197 H1
WEA W13 116 C2
WIM/MER SW19 178 A3
Balfour St STHWK SE1 18 E6
Balgonie Rd CHING E4 38 B3
Balgores Crs GPK RM2 57 K6
Balgores La GPK RM2 75 K1
Balgores Sq GPK RM2 75 K1
Balgowan Cl NWMAL KT3 192 B1
Balgowan Rd BECK BR3 182 B6
Balgowan St
WOOL/PLUM SE18 128 A4
Balham Gv BAL SW12 161 F2
Balham High Rd BAL SW12 161 G3
Balham Hl BAL SW12 161 G2
Balham New Rd BAL SW12 161 G2
Balham Park Rd BAL SW12 160 E3
Balham Rd ED N9 36 C4
Balham Station Rd BAL SW12 161 F3
Balkan Wk WAP E1W * 104 D6
Balladier Wk POP/IOD E14 105 K4
Ballamore Rd BMLY BR1 165 K5
Ballance Rd HOM E9 87 F4
Ballantine St
WAND/EARL SW18 140 B5
Ballantyne Cl ELTH/MOT SE9 166 D6
Ballard Cl KUTN/CMB KT2 176 A3
Ballards Cl DAGE RM10 92 D6
Ballards Farm Rd
SAND/SEL CR2 212 C4
Ballards La FNCH N3 47 F3
Ballards Ms EDGW HA8 44 C2
Ballards Ri SAND/SEL CR2 212 C4
Ballards Rd CRICK NW2 63 J6
DAGE RM10 92 D6
Ballards Wy SAND/SEL CR2 212 C4
Ballast Quay GNWCH SE10 125 G5
Ballater Cl OXHEY WD19 27 G6
Ballater Rd BRXS/STRHM SW2 141 K5
SAND/SEL CR2 212 B3
Ballina St FSTH SE23 164 A2
Ballingdon Rd BTSEA SW11 161 F1
Ballinger Wy NTHLT UB5 95 J3
Balliol Av CHING E4 38 B6
Balliol Rd NKENS W10 100 A5
TOTM N17 50 A4
WELL DA16 148 C3
Balloch Rd CAT SE6 165 G3
Ballogie Av WLSDN NW10 81 G2
Ballow Cl CMBW SE5 * 142 E1
Ball's Pond Pl IS N1 * 85 K4
Balls Pond Rd IS N1 85 K4
Balmain Cl EA W5 116 E1
Balmer Rd BOW E3 105 H1
Balmes Rd IS N1 85 K6
Balmoral Av BECK BR3 198 B1
FBAR/BDGN N11 48 A2
Balmoral Cl PUT/ROE SW15 * 159 G1
Balmoral Crs E/WMO/HCT KT8 173 F6
Balmoral Dr STHL UB1 95 K3
YEAD UB4 94 C3
Balmoral Gdns BXLY DA5 169 G2
WEA W13 116 B3
Balmoral Gv HOLWY N7 85 F4
Balmoral Ms SHB W12 118 C3
Balmoral Rd CRICK NW2 81 K4
FSTGT E7 89 G2
GPK RM2 75 K1
KUT/HW KT1 191 G1
LEY E10 69 K6
RYLN/HDSTN HA2 78 A2
WPK KT4 207 K1
Balmore Crs EBAR EN4 22 A6
Balmore St ARCH N19 66 B6
Balmuir Gdns PUT/ROE SW15 139 F5
Balnacraig Av WLSDN NW10 81 G2
Balniel Ga PIM SW1V 121 J5
Baltic Cl WIM/MER SW19 178 C3
Baltic St East STLK EC1Y 6 C7
Baltic St West FARR EC1M 6 C7
Baltimore Pl WELL DA16 148 A3
Balvaird Pl PIM SW1V 121 J5
Balvernie Gv
WAND/EARL SW18 159 J2
Bamber Rd PECK SE15 143 G2
Bamborough Gdns SHB W12 119 F2
Bamford Av ALP/SUD HA0 80 B6
Bamford Rd BMLY BR1 183 G1
Bamford Wy CRW RM5 56 D1
Bampfylde Cl WLGTN SM6 210 C1
Bampton Dr MLHL NW7 45 J3
Bampton Rd FSTH SE23 164 A5
Banavie Gdns BECK BR3 182 E4
Banbury Cl ENC/FH EN2 23 H2
Banbury Ct BELMT SM2 * 208 E5
COVGDN WC2E * 10 E5
Banbury Rd HOM E9 87 F5
WALTH E17 51 G3
Banbury St BTSEA SW11 * 140 D3
Banchory Rd BKHTH/KID SE3 146 A1
Bancroft Av EFNCH N2 65 J2
Bancroft Cha HCH RM12 75 H6
Bancroft Ct NTHLT UB5 77 G6
Bancroft Gdns
KTN/HRWW/WS HA3 42 C4
ORP BR6 202 A5
Bancroft Rd
KTN/HRWW/WS HA3 42 C5
WCHPL E1 104 E3
Bandon Ri WLGTN SM6 210 D3
Banfield Rd PECK SE15 143 J4
Bangalore St PUT/ROE SW15 139 F4
Bangor Cl NTHLT UB5 78 B3
Banim St HMSMTH W6 118 E3
Banister Rd NKENS W10 100 B2
Bank Av MTCM CR4 178 C5
Bank Blds CHING E4 * 52 B2
Bank End STHWK SE1 12 D7
Bankfoot Rd BMLY BR1 165 H6
Bankhurst Rd CAT SE6 164 C2
Bank La KUTN/CMB KT2 175 F3
PUT/ROE SW15 138 B6
Bank Ms SUT SM1 209 G4
Banksia Rd UED N18 50 E1
Bankside ENC/FH EN2 23 H2
SAND/SEL CR2 212 B4
STHL UB1 114 C1
STHWK SE1 12 C6
Bankside Av LEW SE13 145 F4
NTHLT UB5 94 E1
Bankside Cl BXLY DA5 170 A6
CAR SM5 209 J3
ISLW TW7 136 A5
Bankside Dr THDIT KT7 190 C6
Bankside Rd IL IG1 90 C3
Banks La BXLYHS DA6 149 G5
Banks Wy MNPK E12 90 A2
Banksyard HEST TW5 114 E6
The Bank HCT N6 66 B5
Bankton Rd
BRXS/STRHM SW2 142 B5
Bankwell Rd LEW SE13 145 H5
Banner St STLK EC1Y 6 D7
Banning St GNWCH SE10 125 H5
Bannister Cl
BRXS/STRHM SW2 162 B3
GFD/PVL UB6 78 D3
Bannister Gdns
STMC/STPC BR5 186 D6
Bannockburn Rd
WOOL/PLUM SE18 127 K4
Bannow Cl HOR/WEW KT19 207 G2
Banstead Ct SHB W12 99 H6
Banstead Gdns ED N9 35 K5
Banstead Rd CAR SM5 209 H5
Banstead St PECK SE15 143 K4
Banstead Wy WLGTN SM6 210 E3
Banstock Rd EDGW HA8 44 D2
Banting Dr WCHMH N21 23 F6
Banton Cl EN EN1 24 D3
Bantry St CMBW SE5 142 E1
Banwell Rd BXLY DA5 168 E1
Banyard Rd BERM/RHTH SE16 123 J3
Bapchild Pl STMC/STPC BR5 202 D1
Baptist Gdns KTTN NW5 84 A4
Barandon Wk NTGHL W11 * 100 B6
Barbara Castle Cl
FUL/PGN SW6 119 J6
Barbara Hucklesbury Cl
WDGN N22 49 H5
Barbauld Rd STNW/STAM N16 86 A1

Barber Cl WCHMH N21 35 G2
Barbers Rd SRTFD E15 105 K1
Barbican Rd GFD/PVL UB6 96 B5
Barb Ms HMSMTH W6 119 F3
Barbon Cl BMSBY WC1N 11 F1
Barbot Cl ED N9 36 C5
Barchard St
WAND/EARL SW18 140 A6
Barchester Cl HNWL W7 116 A1
Barchester Rd
KTN/HRWW/WS HA3 42 D4
Barchester St POP/IOD E14 105 K4
Barclay Cl FUL/PGN SW6 * 139 K1
WATW WD18 26 E1
Barclay Ov WFD IG8 38 E6
Barclay Rd CROY/NA CR0 211 K1
FUL/PGN SW6 139 K1
PLSTW E13 107 G3
UED N18 49 K2
WALTH E17 70 A2
WAN E11 70 D5
Barcombe Av
BRXS/STRHM SW2 161 K4
Barcombe Cl STMC/STPC BR5 186 B6
Barden St WOOL/PLUM SE18 147 K1
Bardfield Av CHDH RM6 55 K6
Bardney Rd MRDN SM4 194 A1
Bardolph Av CROY/NA CR0 213 H6
Bardolph Rd HOLWY N7 84 E2
RCH/KEW TW9 137 G5
Bard Rd NKENS W10 100 B6
Bardsey Pl WCHPL E1 104 E3
Bardsey Wk IS N1 * 85 J4
Bardsley Cl CROY/NA CR0 212 B1
Bardsley La GNWCH SE10 125 F6
Barfett St NKENS W10 100 D3
Barfield Av TRDG/WHET N20 33 K4
Barfield Rd BMLY BR1 185 F6
WAN E11 * 70 D5
Barford Cl HDN NW4 45 J5
Barford St IS N1 5 K1
Barforth Rd PECK SE15 143 J4
Barfreston Wy PGE/AN SE20 181 J4
Bargate Cl NWMAL KT3 192 D4
WOOL/PLUM SE18 128 A5
Barge House St STHWK SE1 11 K7
Barge La BOW E3 87 H6
Bargery Rd CAT SE6 164 E3
Barge Wk KUT/HW KT1 174 E5
Bargrove Cl PGE/AN SE20 181 H3
Bargrove Crs CAT SE6 164 C4
Barham Cl ALP/SUD HA0 79 H4
CHST BR7 185 G1
HAYES BR2 200 D5
ROMW/RG RM7 56 D5
Barham Ct ALP/SUD HA0 79 J4
Barham Rd CHST BR7 185 G1
DART DA1 171 K2
RYNPK SW20 176 D3
SAND/SEL CR2 211 J2
Baring Cl LEE/GVPK SE12 165 K4
Baring Rd CROY/NA CR0 197 H5
EBAR EN4 21 H4
LEE/GVPK SE12 166 A6
Baring St IS N1 6 E1
Barker Cl NTHWD HA6 40 D3
NWMAL KT3 191 J1
RCH/KEW TW9 137 J3
Barker Dr CAMTN NW1 84 C5
Barker St WBPTN SW10 120 B6
Barker Wk STRHM/NOR SW16 161 J5
Barkham Rd TOTM N17 49 K3
Bark Hart Rd ORP BR6 202 C5
Barking Rd CAN/RD E16 106 D4
EHAM E6 107 H1
PLSTW E13 107 F3
POP/IOD E14 106 C5
Bark Pl BAY/PAD W2 101 F6
Barkston Gdns ECT SW5 120 A4
Barkway Dr ORP BR6 216 A2
Barkwood Cl ROMW/RG RM7 74 E2
Barkworth Rd
BERM/RHTH SE16 123 J5
Barlborough St NWCR SE14 144 A1
Barlby Gdns NKENS W10 100 B3
Barlby Rd NKENS W10 100 A4
Barley Cl ALP/SUD HA0 79 K2
Barleycorn Wy POP/IOD E14 105 H6
Barley La GDMY/SEVK IG3 73 G3
Barley Mow Pas CHSWK W4 118 A5
Barlow Cl WLGTN SM6 210 E4
Barlow Dr BKHTH/KID SE3 146 D2
Barlow Pl MYFR/PICC W1J 9 K6
Barlow Rd ACT W3 117 J1
HPTN TW12 173 F3
KIL/WHAMP NW6 82 D4
Barlow St WALW SE17 19 F6
Barlow Wy RAIN RM13 111 F5
Barlow Wy South RAIN RM13 111 F5
Barmeston Rd CAT SE6 164 E4
Barmor Cl RYLN/HDSTN HA2 42 B5
Barmouth Av GFD/PVL UB6 97 F1
Barmouth Rd CROY/NA CR0 198 A6
WAND/EARL SW18 160 B1
Barnabas Rd HOM E9 87 F4
Barnaby Cl RYLN/HDSTN HA2 60 C6
Barnaby Pl SKENS SW7 14 A7
Barnard Cl CHST BR7 185 J4
SUN TW16 172 A3
WLGTN SM6 210 D5
WOOL/PLUM SE18 127 F4
Barnard Gdns NWMAL KT3 192 D1
YEAD UB4 95 F3
Barnard Hl MUSWH N10 48 B5
Barnard Ms BTSEA SW11 140 D5
Barnardo Dr BARK/HLT IG6 72 C1
Barnardo Gdns WCHPL E1 * 105 F5
Barnardo St WCHPL E1 105 F5
Barnard Rd BTSEA SW11 140 D5
EN EN1 24 D3
MTCM CR4 179 F6
Barnards Pl SAND/SEL CR2 211 H6
Barnby Sq SRTFD E15 * 88 C6
Barnby St CAMTN NW1 4 B3
SRTFD E15 88 C6
Barn Cl KTTN NW5 * 84 D3
NTHLT UB5 95 G1
Barn Crs STAN HA7 43 J2
Barneby Cl WHTN TW2 155 K3
Barnehurst Av BXLYHN DA7 149 K2
Barnehurst Cl ERITH DA8 149 K2
Barnehurst Rd BXLYHN DA7 149 K3
Barn End Dr RDART DA2 171 F6
Barnes Aly HPTN TW12 173 H5
Barnes Av BARN SW13 138 D1
NWDGN UB2 114 E4
Barnes Br CHSWK W4 138 B3
Barnes Cl MNPK E12 89 H2
Barnes Cray Rd DART DA1 150 D5
Barnesdale Crs
STMC/STPC BR5 202 B3
Barnes End NWMAL KT3 192 D2
Barnes High St BARN SW13 138 C3
Barnes Rd IL IG1 90 C3
UED N18 36 E6
Barnes St POP/IOD E14 105 G5
Barnes Ter DEPT SE8 124 C5
Barnet Dr HAYES BR2 200 D6
Barnet Gate La BAR EN5 31 H1
Barnet Gv BETH E2 104 C2
Barnet Hl BAR EN5 20 D5
Barnet La BORE WD6 30 B1
TRDG/WHET N20 32 D3
Barnet Rd BAR EN5 31 G1
Barnett Cl ERITH DA8 150 C3
Barnetts Ct
RYLN/HDSTN HA2 * 78 B1
Barnett St WCHPL E1 104 D5
Barnet Way (Barnet By-Pass)
MLHL NW7 31 F2
Barnet Wood Rd HAYES BR2 200 B6
Barney Cl CHARL SE7 126 B5
Barn Fld HAMP NW3 * 83 K3
Barnfield NWMAL KT3 192 B3
Barnfield Av CROY/NA CR0 197 K5
KUTN/CMB KT2 156 E6
MTCM CR4 195 G1
Barnfield Cl FSBYPK N4 66 E4
SWLY BR8 203 K4
TOOT SW17 160 B5
Barnfield Gdns
KUTN/CMB KT2 175 F1
WOOL/PLUM SE18 * 127 G6
Barnfield Pl POP/IOD E14 124 D4
Barnfield Rd BELV DA17 129 G6
EA W5 97 J3
EDGW HA8 44 E4
SAND/SEL CR2 212 A6
STMC/STPC BR5 186 E6
WOOL/PLUM SE18 127 G6
Barnfield Wood Cl BECK BR3 199 G3
Barnfield Wood Rd BECK BR3 199 G3
Barnham Dr THMD SE28 128 A1
Barnham Rd GFD/PVL UB6 96 C2
Barnham St STHWK SE1 19 H2
Barnhill PIN HA5 59 G2
Barn Hl WBLY HA9 62 D6
Barnhill Av HAYES BR2 199 K2
Barnhill La YEAD UB4 95 F2
Barnhill Rd WBLY HA9 80 E1
YEAD UB4 95 F3
Barnhurst Pth OXHEY WD19 41 G1
Barningham Wy
CDALE/KGS NW9 62 E3
Barnlea Cl FELT TW13 154 D4
Barnmead Gdns DAGW RM9 92 B3
Barnmead Rd BECK BR3 182 A4
DAGW RM9 92 B3
Barnock Cl DART DA1 170 B2
Barn Ri WBLY HA9 62 C5
Barnsbury Cl NWMAL KT3 191 K1
Barnsbury Crs BRYLDS KT5 191 K5
Barnsbury Est IS N1 5 H1
Barnsbury Gv HOLWY N7 85 F5
Barnsbury La BRYLDS KT5 191 J6
Barnsbury Pk IS N1 85 G5
Barnsbury Rd IS N1 5 J1
Barnsbury Sq IS N1 85 G5
Barnsbury St IS N1 85 G5
Barnsbury Ter IS N1 85 F5
Barnscroft RYNPK SW20 176 E6
Barnsdale Av POP/IOD E14 124 E4
Barnsdale Rd MV/WKIL W9 100 D3
Barnsley St WCHPL E1 104 D3
Barnstaple La LEW SE13 145 F5
Barnstaple Rd RSLP HA4 77 G1
Barnston Wk IS N1 * 85 J6
Barn St STNW/STAM N16 68 A6
Barn Wy WBLY HA9 62 C5
Barnwell Rd
BRXS/STRHM SW2 142 B6
DART DA1 151 J4
Barnwood Cl MV/WKIL W9 101 F3
RSLP HA4 58 B6
Baron Cl FBAR/BDGN N11 48 A1
Baroness Rd BETH E2 7 K4
Baronet Gv TOTM N17 50 C4
Baronet Rd TOTM N17 50 C4
Baron Gdns BARK/HLT IG6 54 C6
Baron Gv MTCM CR4 194 D1
Baron Rd BCTR RM8 73 K5
Barons Cl IS N1 * 5 J2
Barons Court Rd
WKENS W14 * 119 H5
Baron's Court Rd WKENS W14 119 H5
Baronsfield Rd TWK TW1 * 156 C1
Barons Ga EBAR EN4 33 J1
Barons Keep WKENS W14 * 119 H5
Barons Md HRW HA1 60 E1
Baronsmead Rd BARN SW13 138 D2
Baronsmede EA W5 117 G2
Baronsmere Ct BAR EN5 * 20 C5
Baronsmere Rd EFNCH N2 65 J1
Baron's Pl STHWK SE1 17 K3
The Barons TWK TW1 156 C1
Baron St IS N1 5 K3
Baron's Wk CROY/NA CR0 198 B3
Barque Ms DEPT SE8 124 D6
Barrack Rd HSLWW TW4 134 C5
Barra Hall Rd HYS/HAR UB3 94 C6
Barratt Av WDGN N22 49 F5
Barratt Wy
KTN/HRWW/WS HA3 42 D6
Barrenger Rd MUSWH N10 47 K3
Barrett Cl HARH RM3 57 K3
Barrett Rd WALTH E17 70 A1
Barrett's Green Rd
WLSDN NW10 98 E1
Barrett's Gv STNW/STAM N16 86 A3
Barrett St MHST W1U 9 H4
Barrhill Rd BRXS/STRHM SW2 161 K4
Barriedale NWCR SE14 144 B2
Barrier Point Rd CAN/RD E16 126 B1
Barringer Sq TOOT SW17 161 F6
Barrington Cl CLAY IG5 53 K4
KTTN NW5 84 A3
Barrington Rd BRXN/ST SW9 142 C4
BXLYHN DA7 148 E3
CEND/HSY/T N8 66 D2
CHEAM SM3 193 K5
MNPK E12 90 A4
Barrington Vls
WOOL/PLUM SE18 147 F2
Barrington Wk NRWD SE19 * 181 F2
Barrow Av CAR SM5 209 K5
Barrow Cl WCHMH N21 35 H5
Barrowdene Cl PIN HA5 41 J5
Barrowell Gn WCHMH N21 35 H4
Barrowgate Rd CHSWK W4 117 K5
Barrow Hedges Cl CAR SM5 209 J5
Barrow Hedges Wy CAR SM5 209 J5
Barrow Hl WPK KT4 192 B6
Barrow Hill Cl WPK KT4 192 B6
Barrow Hill Est STJWD NW8 2 C3
Barrow Hill Rd STJWD NW8 2 C3
Barrow Point Av PIN HA5 41 J5
Barrow Point La PIN HA5 41 J5
Barrow Rd CROY/NA CR0 211 G3
STRHM/NOR SW16 179 J2
Barrs Rd WLSDN NW10 81 F5
Barry Av BXLYHN DA7 149 F1
SEVS/STOTM N15 68 B3
Barry Cl ORP BR6 216 E1
Barry Pde EDUL SE22 * 143 H5
Barry Rd EDUL SE22 163 H1
EHAM E6 107 J5
WLSDN NW10 80 E5
Barry Ter ASHF TW15 * 152 C4
Barset Rd PECK SE15 143 K4
Barsons Cl PGE/AN SE20 181 K3
Barston Rd WNWD SE27 162 D4
Barstow Crs
BRXS/STRHM SW2 162 A3
Barter St NOXST/BSQ WC1A 11 F2
Barth Ms WOOL/PLUM SE18 127 K4
Bartholomew Cl STBT EC1A 12 C2
WAND/EARL SW18 140 B5
Bartholomew La OBST EC2N 13 F3
Bartholomew Rd KTTN NW5 84 C4
Bartholomew Sq FSBYE EC1V 6 D6
Bartholomew St STHWK SE1 18 E5
Bartholomew Vls KTTN NW5 84 C4
Barth Rd WOOL/PLUM SE18 127 K4
Bartle Av EHAM E6 107 J1
Bartle Rd NTGHL W11 100 B5
Bartlett Cl POP/IOD E14 105 J5
Bartlett Ct FLST/FETLN EC4A * 11 K3
Bartlett St SAND/SEL CR2 211 K3
Bartlow Gdns CRW RM5 57 F4
Barton Av ROMW/RG RM7 74 E5
Barton Cl BXLYHS DA6 149 F6
EHAM E6 107 K5
HDN NW4 63 J2
HOM E9 86 E3
PECK SE15 143 J4
Barton Gn NWMAL KT3 176 A5
Barton Mdw BARK/HLT IG6 72 B1
Barton Rd HCH RM12 75 J5
SCUP DA14 187 F2
WKENS W14 119 H5
The Bartons BORE WD6 29 K1
Barton St WEST SW1P 16 E5
Bartram Rd BROCKY SE4 144 B6
Bartrams La EBAR EN4 21 G1
Bartrip St HOM E9 87 G4
Barts Cl BECK BR3 198 D2
Barwell Ct CHSGTN KT9 * 205 J5
Barwell La CHSGTN KT9 205 J5
Barwick Rd FSTGT E7 89 F2
Barwood Av WWKM BR4 198 E5
Bascombe Gv DART DA1 170 B2
Bascome St
BRXS/STRHM SW2 162 B1
Basden Gv FELT TW13 155 F4
Basedale Rd DAGW RM9 91 H5
Baseing Cl EHAM E6 108 A6
Basevi Wy DEPT SE8 124 D6
Bashley Rd WLSDN NW10 99 F3
Basil Av EHAM E6 107 J2
Basildene Rd HSLWW TW4 134 C4
Basildon Av CLAY IG5 54 A4
Basildon Cl BELMT SM2 209 F6
WATW WD18 26 A1
Basildon Rd ABYW SE2 128 B4
Basil Gdns CROY/NA CR0 198 A5
WNWD SE27 180 D1
Basilon Rd BXLYHN DA7 149 F3
Basil St CHEL SW3 14 E3
Basin Ap CAN/RD E16 108 B6
POP/IOD E14 105 G5
Basing Cl THDIT KT7 190 A4
Basing Ct PECK SE15 143 G2
Basingdon Wy CMBW SE5 142 E5
Basing Dr BXLY DA5 169 G1
Basingfield Rd THDIT KT7 190 A4
Basinghall Av CITYW EC2V 12 E3
Basinghall Gdns BELMT SM2 209 F6
Basinghall St CITYW EC2V 12 E3
Basing Hl GLDGN NW11 64 D5
WBLY HA9 62 B6
Basing Pl BETH E2 7 H4
Basing St NTGHL W11 100 D5
Basing Wy FNCH N3 46 E6
THDIT KT7 190 A4
Basire St IS N1 85 J6
Baskerville Gdns
WLSDN NW10 81 G2
Baskerville Rd
WAND/EARL SW18 160 D2
Basket Gdns ELTH/MOT SE9 146 D6
Baslow Cl
KTN/HRWW/WS HA3 42 D4
Baslow Wk CLPT E5 87 F2
Basnett Rd BTSEA SW11 * 141 F4
Bassano St EDUL SE22 143 G6
Bassant Rd WOOL/PLUM SE18 128 A6
Bassein Park Rd SHB W12 118 C2
Bassett Cl BELMT SM2 209 F6
Bassett Gdns ISLW TW7 135 H1
Bassett Rd NKENS W10 100 B5
Bassetts Cl ORP BR6 216 B2
Bassett St KTTN NW5 84 A4
Bassetts Wy ORP BR6 216 B2
Bassett Wy GFD/PVL UB6 96 B5
Bassingham Rd ALP/SUD HA0 79 K4
WAND/EARL SW18 160 B2
Basswood Cl PECK SE15 143 J4
Bastable Av BARK IG11 109 F1
Bastion Rd ABYW SE2 128 B5
Baston Manor Rd WWKM BR4 215 F1
Baston Rd HAYES BR2 200 A6
HAYES BR2 215 G2
Bastwick St FSBYE EC1V 6 B6
Basuto Rd FUL/PGN SW6 139 K2
Batavia Ms NWCR SE14 144 B1
Batavia Rd NWCR SE14 144 B1
SUN TW16 172 A4
Batchelor St IS N1 5 J2
Batchwood Gn
STMC/STPC BR5 202 B1
Batchworth La NTHWD HA6 40 A1
Bateman Cl BARK IG11 90 C4
Bateman Ms CLAP SW4 161 J1
Bateman Rd CHING E4 51 J2
Bateman's Blds
SOHO/SHAV W1D 10 C4
Batemans Cnr CHSWK W4 * 118 A5
Bateman's Rw SDTCH EC2A 7 H6
Bateman St SOHO/SHAV W1D 10 C4
Bates Crs CROY/NA CR0 211 G3
STRHM/NOR SW16 179 H3
Bate St POP/IOD E14 105 H6
Bath Cl PECK SE15 143 J1
Bathgate Rd WIM/MER SW19 159 G5
Bath Gv BETH E2 104 C1
Bath House Rd CROY/NA CR0 195 K5
Bath Pas KUT/HW KT1 174 E5
Bath Pl BAR EN5 20 D4
SDTCH EC2A * 7 G5
Bath Rd CHSWK W4 118 B4
DART DA1 170 E2
ED N9 36 D4
FSTGT E7 89 H4
HTHAIR TW6 133 H2
WDR/YW UB7 132 A2
Baths Ap FUL/PGN SW6 * 139 J1
Bath St FSBYE EC1V 6 D5
Bath Ter STHWK SE1 18 C5
Bathurst Av WIM/MER SW19 178 A4
Bathurst Gdns WLSDN NW10 99 K1
Bathurst Ms BAY/PAD W2 8 B5
Bathurst Rd IL IG1 72 B5
Bathurst St BAY/PAD W2 8 B5
Bathway WOOL/PLUM SE18 127 F4
Batley Cl MTCM CR4 194 E4
Batley Pl STNW/STAM N16 86 B1
Batley Rd ENC/FH EN2 23 J2
STNW/STAM N16 86 B1
Batman Cl SHB W12 118 E1
Batoum Gdns HMSMTH W6 119 F3
Batson St SHB W12 118 D2
Batsworth Rd MTCM CR4 178 C6
Batten Cl EHAM E6 107 K5
Batten Cots POP/IOD E14 * 105 G4
Batten St BTSEA SW11 140 D4
Battersby Rd CAT SE6 165 G4
Battersea Br WBPTN SW10 140 C1
Battersea Bridge Rd
BTSEA SW11 140 D1
Battersea Church Rd
BTSEA SW11 140 C2
Battersea High St
BTSEA SW11 140 C3
Battersea Park Rd
BTSEA SW11 141 F2
Battersea Ri BTSEA SW11 140 D6
Battersea Sq BTSEA SW11 * 140 D1
Battery Rd THMD SE28 127 K2
Battishill St IS N1 85 H5
Battle Bridge La STHWK SE1 19 G1
Battle Cl WIM/MER SW19 178 B2
Battledean Rd HBRY N5 85 H3
Battle Rd ERITH DA8 129 K4
Batty St WCHPL E1 104 C5
Baudwin Rd CAT SE6 165 H4
Baugh Rd SCUP DA14 186 D1
The Baulk WAND/EARL SW18 159 K2
Bavant Rd STRHM/NOR SW16 179 K5
Bavaria Rd ARCH N19 66 E6
Bavent Rd CMBW SE5 142 D3
Bawdale Rd EDUL SE22 143 G6
Bawdsey Av GNTH/NBYPK IG2 73 F1
Bawtree Rd NWCR SE14 144 B1
Bawtry Rd TRDG/WHET N20 33 K5
Baxendale TRDG/WHET N20 33 G4
Baxendale St BETH E2 104 C2
Baxter Cl NWDGN UB2 115 G3
Baxter Rd CAN/RD E16 107 G5
IL IG1 90 B3
IS N1 85 K4
UED N18 36 D6
Bay Ct EA W5 * 117 F3
Baycroft Cl PIN HA5 * 41 G6
Bayfield Rd ELTH/MOT SE9 146 C5
Bayford Ms HACK E8 * 86 D5
Bayford Rd WLSDN NW10 100 B2
Bayford St HACK E8 86 D5
Baygrove Ms KUT/HW KT1 174 D4
Bayham Pl CAMTN NW1 4 A1
Bayham Rd CHSWK W4 118 A3
MRDN SM4 194 A1
WEA W13 97 H6
Bayham St CAMTN NW1 4 A1
Bayhurst Dr NTHWD HA6 40 D2
Bayleaf Cl HPTN TW12 173 J1
Bayley St FITZ W1T 10 C2
Baylis Ms TWK TW1 156 B2
Baylis Rd STHWK SE1 17 J4
Bayliss Av THMD SE28 109 K6
Bayliss Cl ENC/FH EN2 22 E6
Bayly Rd DART DA1 171 K1
Bayne Cl EHAM E6 107 K5
Baynes Cl EN EN1 24 C2
Baynes Ms HAMP NW3 83 H4
Baynes St CAMTN NW1 84 C5
Baynham Cl BXLY DA5 169 G1
Bayonne Rd HMSMTH W6 119 H6
Bays Cl SYD SE26 181 K1
Bayshill Ri NTHLT UB5 78 B4
Bayston Rd STNW/STAM N16 86 B1
Bayswater Rd BAY/PAD W2 101 G6
Baythorne St BOW E3 105 H4
Baytree Cl BFN/LL DA15 168 A3
BMLY BR1 184 C4
Baytree Ms STHWK SE1 18 E6
Baytree Rd BRXS/STRHM SW2 142 A5
Bazalgette Cl NWMAL KT3 191 K2
Bazalgette Gdns NWMAL KT3 192 A2
Bazely St POP/IOD E14 106 A6
Bazile Rd WCHMH N21 35 G1
Beacham Cl CHARL SE7 126 C6
Beachborough Rd BMLY BR1 165 F6
Beachcroft Rd WAN E11 88 C1
Beach Gv FELT TW13 155 F5
Beachy Rd BOW E3 87 J5
Beacon Ga NWCR SE14 144 A4
Beacon Hl HOLWY N7 84 E3
Beacon Pl CROY/NA CR0 210 E1
Beacon Rd ERITH DA8 150 E1
HTHAIR TW6 152 D1
LEW SE13 165 G1
Beaconsfield Cl
BKHTH/KID SE3 125 K6
CHSWK W4 117 K5
Beaconsfield Cots
TRDG/WHET N20 * 32 E5
Beaconsfield Gdns
ESH/CLAY KT10 204 E5
Beaconsfield Rd
BKHTH/KID SE3 125 K6
BMLY BR1 184 C6
BXLY DA5 170 B4
CAN/RD E16 106 D3
CHSWK W4 118 A3
CROY/NA CR0 196 E3
EA W5 116 D2
ED N9 36 C5
ELTH/MOT SE9 166 D6
ESH/CLAY KT10 204 E5
FBAR/BDGN N11 34 A6
LEY E10 * 88 A1
NWMAL KT3 176 A5
SEVS/STOTM N15 68 A1
STHL UB1 114 C1
SURB KT6 191 G4
TRDG/WHET N20 33 K5
TWK TW1 156 C1
WALTH E17 69 H3
WALW SE17 122 E6
WLSDN NW10 81 H4
YEAD UB4 114 B1
Beaconsfield Terrace Rd
WKENS W14 119 H3
Beaconsfield Wk
FUL/PGN SW6 139 J2
Beacontree Av WALTH E17 52 B4
Beacontree Rd WAN E11 70 D4
Beadlow Cl CAR SM5 194 C3
Beadman Pl WNWD SE27 * 162 C6
Beadman St WNWD SE27 162 C6
Beadnell Rd FSTH SE23 164 A3
Beadon Rd HAYES BR2 199 K1
HMSMTH W6 119 F4
Beaford Gv RYNPK SW20 177 H6
Beagle Cl FELT TW13 154 A6
Beagles Cl STMC/STPC BR5 202 E6
Beak St REGST W1B 10 A5
Beal Cl WELL DA16 148 B2
Beale Cl PLMGR N13 49 H1
Beale Pl BOW E3 105 H1
Beale Rd BOW E3 87 H6
Beal Rd IL IG1 72 A6
Beam Av DAGE RM10 92 D6
Beames Rd WLSDN NW10 81 F6
Beaminster Gdns
BARK/HLT IG6 54 B6
Beamish Dr BUSH WD23 28 C3
Beamish Rd ED N9 36 C3
STMC/STPC BR5 202 D4
Beamway DAGE RM10 93 F5
Beanacre Cl HOM E9 87 H4
Bean Rd BXLYHS DA6 148 E5
Beanshaw ELTH/MOT SE9 167 F6
Beansland Gv CHDH RM6 56 A5
Bear Aly FLST/FETLN EC4A * 12 A3
Bear Cl ROMW/RG RM7 74 D3
Beardell St NRWD SE19 181 G2
Beardow Gv
STHGT/OAK N14 * 34 C1
Beard Rd KUTN/CMB KT2 175 G1
Beardsfield PLSTW E13 88 E6
Beard's Hl HPTN TW12 173 F4
Beard's Hill Cl HPTN TW12 173 F4
Beardsley Wy ACT W3 118 A2
Bearfield Rd KUTN/CMB KT2 175 F3
Bear Gdns STHWK SE1 12 C7
Bear La STHWK SE1 12 B7
Bear Rd FELT TW13 154 C6
Bearstead Ri BROCKY SE4 144 C6
Bearstead Ter BECK BR3 * 182 D4
Bear St LSQ/SEVD WC2H 10 D5
Beatrice Av
STRHM/NOR SW16 180 A6
WBLY HA9 80 A3
Beatrice Cl PIN HA5 58 E1
PLSTW E13 106 E3
Beatrice Pl KENS W8 120 A3
Beatrice Rd ED N9 36 E2
FSBYPK N4 67 G4
RCHPK/HAM TW10 137 G6
STHL UB1 114 E1
STHWK SE1 123 H4
WALTH E17 69 J2
Beattie Cl EBED/NFELT TW14 153 J2
Beattock Ri MUSWH N10 66 B1
Beatty Rd STAN HA7 43 J2
STNW/STAM N16 86 A2
Beatty St CAMTN NW1 * 4 A2
Beattyville Gdns CLAY IG5 54 A6
Beauchamp Cl CHSWK W4 117 K3
Beauchamp Pl CHEL SW3 14 D4
Beauchamp Rd BTSEA SW11 140 D5
E/WMO/HCT KT8 189 G2
FSTGT E7 89 F5
NRWD SE19 180 E4
SUT SM1 208 E3
TWK TW1 156 B2
Beauchamp St HCIRC EC1N 11 J2
Beauchamp Ter BARN SW13 138 E4
Beauclerc Rd HMSMTH W6 118 E3
Beauclerk Cl FELT TW13 154 A3

Beaufort *EHAM* E6 108 A4
Beaufort Av
KTN/HRWW/WS HA3 61 G1
Beaufort Cl *CHING* E4 51 K2
EA W5 98 B4
PUT/ROE SW15 159 F3
ROMW/RG RM7 74 E1
Beaufort Ct
RCHPK/HAM TW10 156 D6
Beaufort Dr *GLDGN* NW11 64 E1
Beaufort Gdns *CHEL* SW3 14 D4
HDN NW4 64 A3
HEST TW5 134 D2
IL IG1 72 A5
STRHM/NOR SW16 180 A3
Beaufort Rd *EA* W5 98 B4
KUT/HW KT1 191 F1
RCHPK/HAM TW10 156 D6
RSLP HA4 * 58 B6
TWK TW1 156 D2
Beaufort St *CHEL* SW3 120 C6
Beaufort Wy *EW* KT17 207 J5
Beaufoy Rd *TOTM* N17 50 A3
Beaufoy Wk *LBTH* SE11 17 H7
Beaulieu Av *CAN/RD* E16 126 A1
SYD SE26 163 J6
Beaulieu Cl *CDALE/KGS* NW9 63 G1
CMBW SE5 142 E4
HSLWW TW4 134 E6
MTCM CR4 179 F4
OXHEY WD19 27 G3
TWK TW1 156 E1
Beaulieu Dr *PIN* HA5 59 H3
Beaulieu Gdns *WCHMH* N21 35 J2
Beaulieu Pl *CHSWK* W4 117 K3
Beauly Ct *ROM* RM1 57 G4
Beauly Wy *ROM* RM1 57 G4
Beaumaris Gdns *NRWD* SE19 180 D3
Beaumaris Gn
CDALE/KGS NW9 * 63 G3
Beaumont Av *ALP/SUD* HA0 79 J3
RCH/KEW TW9 137 G4
RYLN/HDSTN HA2 60 B3
WKENS W14 119 J5
Beaumont Cl *EFNCH* N2 65 J1
KUTN/CMB KT2 175 H3
Beaumont Ct *ALP/SUD* HA0 79 J2
Beaumont Crs *RAIN* RM13 93 J4
WKENS W14 119 J5
Beaumont Dr *WPK* KT4 192 E5
Beaumont Gdns *HAMP* NW3 64 E6
Beaumont Gv *WCHPL* E1 105 F3
Beaumont Ms *MHST* W1U * 9 H1
PIN HA5 * 41 J6
Beaumont Pl *BAR* EN5 20 D2
FITZ W1T 4 B6
ISLW TW7 136 A6
Beaumont Ri *ARCH* N19 66 D5
Beaumont Rd *CHSWK* W4 117 K3
LEY E10 69 K4
NRWD SE19 180 D2
PLSTW E13 107 F2
STMC/STPC BR5 201 J3
WIM/MER SW19 159 H2
Beaumont Sq *WCHPL* E1 105 F4
Beaumont St *CAVSQ/HST* W1G 9 H1
Beaumont Ter *LEW* SE13 * 165 H2
Beaumont Wk *HAMP* NW3 83 K5
Beauvais Ter *NTHLT* UB5 95 H2
Beauval Rd *EDUL* SE22 163 G1
Beaverbank Rd
ELTH/MOT SE9 167 J3
Beaver Cl *HPTN* TW12 173 G4
MRDN SM4 193 F4
PGE/AN SE20 * 181 H3
Beaver Rd *BARK/HLT* IG6 55 J1
Beavers Crs *HSLWW* TW4 134 C5
Beavers La *HSLWW* TW4 134 B4
Beaverwood Rd *CHST* BR7 185 K1
Beavor La *HMSMTH* W6 118 D4
Bebbington Rd
WOOL/PLUM SE18 * 127 K4
Beblets Cl *ORP* BR6 217 F3
Beccles Dr *BARK* IG11 91 F4
Beccles St *POP/IOD* E14 105 H5
Bec Cl *RSLP* HA4 77 H1
Beck Cl *GNWCH* SE10 144 E2
LEW SE13 144 E2
Beckenham Gdns *ED* N9 36 A5
Beckenham Gv *HAYES* BR2 183 G5
Beckenham Hill Rd *BECK* BR3 182 E2
Beckenham La *HAYES* BR2 183 H5
Beckenham Place Pk
BECK BR3 182 E3
Beckenham Rd *BECK* BR3 198 E4
PGE/AN SE20 182 A4
Becket Av *EHAM* E6 108 A2
Becket Cl *SNWD* SE25 197 H3
WIM/MER SW19 * 178 A4
Becket Fold *HRW* HA1 * 61 F2
Becket Rd *UED* N18 36 E6
Becket St *STHWK* SE1 18 E4
Beckett Cl *BELV* DA17 129 F3
STRHM/NOR SW16 161 J4
WLSDN NW10 81 F4
Becketts Cl *BXLY* DA5 169 K3
EBED/NFELT TW14 154 A1
ORP BR6 217 F1
Becketts Pl *KUT/HW* KT1 174 E4
Beckett Wk *BECK* BR3 182 B2
Beckford Cl *WKENS* W14 119 J4
Beckford Dr *STMC/STPC* BR5 201 J4
Beckford Pl *WALW* SE17 * 122 D5
Beckford Rd *CROY/NA* CR0 197 G3
Beck La *BECK* BR3 182 A6
Becklow Rd *SHB* W12 118 C2
Beck River Pk *BECK* BR3 182 C4
Beck Rd *HACK* E8 86 D6
MTCM CR4 194 E3
Becks Rd *SCUP* DA14 168 B5
Beckton Rd *CAN/RD* E16 106 D4
Beck Wy *BECK* BR3 182 C6
Beckway Rd
STRHM/NOR SW16 179 J5
Beckway St *WALW* SE17 19 F7
Beckwith Rd *HNHL* SE24 162 E1
Beclands Rd *TOOT* SW17 179 F2
Becmead Av
KTN/HRWW/WS HA3 61 H2
STRHM/NOR SW16 161 J6
Becondale Rd *NRWD* SE19 181 F1
Becontree Av *BCTR* RM8 91 H2
Bective Rd *FSTGT* E7 88 E2
PUT/ROE SW15 139 H5
Becton Pl *ERITH* DA8 149 J2
Bedale Rd *ENC/FH* EN2 23 J1
Bedale St *STHWK* SE1 * 18 E1
Beddington Cross
CROY/NA CR0 195 J5
Beddington Farm Rd
CROY/NA CR0 195 K5
Beddington Gdns *WLGTN* SM6 210 B4
Beddington Gn
STMC/STPC BR5 186 A4
Beddington Gv *WLGTN* SM6 210 D3
Beddington La *CROY/NA* CR0 195 H3
Beddington Rd
GDMY/SEVK IG3 73 F2
STMC/STPC BR5 185 K4
Beddington Ter
CROY/NA CR0 * 196 A4
Bede Cl *PIN* HA5 41 H4
Bedens Rd *SCUP* DA14 187 F2
Bede Rd *CHDH* RM6 73 J3
Bedevere Rd *ED* N9 36 C5
Bedfont Cl *EBED/NFELT* TW14 153 F1
MTCM CR4 179 F5
Bedfont Green Cl
EBED/NFELT TW14 153 F3
Bedfont La *EBED/NFELT* TW14 153 K3
Bedfont Rd
EBED/NFELT TW14 153 F3
STWL/WRAY TW19 152 C1
Bedford Av *BAR* EN5 20 D6
RSQ WC1B 10 D2
YEAD UB4 95 F5
Bedfordbury *CHCR* WC2N 10 E5
Bedford Cl *CHSWK* W4 118 B6
MUSWH N10 48 A3
Bedford Cnr *CHSWK* W4 * 118 B4
Bedford Ct *CHCR* WC2N 10 E6
Bedford Gdns *KENS* W8 119 K1
Bedford Hl *BAL* SW12 161 G4
Bedford Ms *CAT* SE6 164 E4
SEVS/STOTM N15 67 K1
Bedford Pk *CROY/NA* CR0 196 D5
Bedford Pl *CROY/NA* CR0 196 E5
RSQ WC1B 10 E1
Bedford Rd *BFN/LL* DA15 167 K5
CEND/HSY/T N8 66 D3
CHSWK W4 118 A3
CLAP SW4 141 K5
DART DA1 171 G3
ED N9 36 D2
EFNCH N2 47 J6
EHAM E6 90 A6
HRW HA1 60 C3
IL IG1 90 B1
MLHL NW7 31 G4
NTHWD HA6 26 B6
ORP BR6 202 C6
RSLP HA4 76 D2
SEVS/STOTM N15 67 K1
SWFD E18 52 E5
WALTH E17 51 J5
WDGN N22 48 E4
WEA W13 97 H6
WHTN TW2 155 J5
WPK KT4 193 F6
Bedford Rw *GINN* WC1R 11 H1
Bedford Sq *RSQ* WC1B 10 D2
Bedford St *COVGDN* WC2E 10 E5
Bedford Vls *KUT/HW* KT1 * 175 G5
Bedford Wy *STPAN* WC1H 4 D7
Bedgebury Gdns
WIM/MER SW19 159 H4
Bedgebury Rd *ELTH/MOT* SE9 146 C5
Bedivere Rd *BMLY* BR1 165 K5
Bedlam Ms *LBTH* SE11 17 H6
Bedlow Cl *STJWD* NW8 2 B7
Bedlow Wy *CROY/NA* CR0 211 F2
Bedonwell Rd *BXLYHN* DA7 149 G2
Bedser Cl *LBTH* SE11 * 122 A6
THHTH CR7 180 D6
Bedser Dr *GFD/PVL* UB6 78 D3
Bedster Gdns
E/WMO/HCT KT8 173 G5
Bedwardine Rd *NRWD* SE19 181 F3
Bedwell Gdns *HYS/HAR* UB3 113 H4
Bedwell Rd *BELV* DA17 129 H5
TOTM N17 50 A4
Beeby Rd *CAN/RD* E16 107 F4
Beech Av *ACT* W3 118 B1
BFN/LL DA15 168 B2
BKHH IG9 39 F4
BTFD TW8 136 C1
RSLP HA4 59 F5
TRDG/WHET N20 33 J3
Beech Cl *CAR* SM5 194 E6
DEPT SE8 124 C6
ED N9 36 C1
HCH RM12 93 K1
PUT/ROE SW15 158 D2
SUN TW16 172 C5
WDR/YW UB7 112 D3
WIM/MER SW19 177 F2
Beech Copse *BMLY* BR1 184 E5
SAND/SEL CR2 212 A3
Beech Ct *ELTH/MOT* SE9 * 166 D1
Beechcroft *CHST* BR7 185 F3
Beechcroft Av *BXLYHN* DA7 150 A2
GLDGN NW11 64 D4
NWMAL KT3 175 K4
RKW/CH/CXG WD3 26 A1
RYLN/HDSTN HA2 60 A4
STHL UB1 114 E1
Beechcroft Cl *HEST* TW5 134 D1
ORP BR6 216 D2
STRHM/NOR SW16 180 A1
Beechcroft Gdns *WBLY* HA9 80 B1
Beechcroft Rd *CHSGTN* KT9 206 B2
MORT/ESHN SW14 * 137 K4
ORP BR6 216 D2
SWFD E18 53 F5
TOOT SW17 160 E5
Beechdale *WCHMH* N21 35 F4
Beechdale Rd
BRXS/STRHM SW2 162 A1
Beech Dell *HAYES* BR2 215 K2
Beech Dr *EFNCH* N2 47 K6
Beechen Cliff Wy *ISLW* TW7 136 A2
Beechengrove *PIN* HA5 41 K6
Beechen Pl *FSTH* SE23 163 K4
Beeches Av *CAR* SM5 209 J5
Beeches Cl *PGE/AN* SE20 181 K4
Beeches Rd *CHEAM* SM3 193 H5
TOOT SW17 160 D5
The Beeches *CHING* E4 * 38 B3
HNWL W7 * 116 A2
Beeches Wk *BELMT* SM2 209 H6
Beechfield Gdns
ROMW/RG RM7 74 E4
Beechfield Rd *BMLY* BR1 184 B5
CAT SE6 164 C3
ERITH DA8 150 B1
FSBYPK N4 67 J3
Beech Gdns *DAGE* RM10 92 D5
EA W5 117 F2
Beech Gv *BARK/HLT* IG6 54 E2
MTCM CR4 195 J2
NWMAL KT3 176 A6
Beech Hall Crs *CHING* E4 52 B3
Beech Hall Rd *CHING* E4 52 A3
Beech Hl *EBAR* EN4 21 H1
Beech Hill Av *EBAR* EN4 21 G2
Beechhill Rd *ELTH/MOT* SE9 147 F6
Beech House Rd
CROY/NA CR0 211 K1
Beech Lawns
NFNCH/WDSPK N12 * 47 H1
Beechmont Cl *BMLY* BR1 183 H1
Beechmore Gdns *CHEAM* SM3 193 G6
Beechmore Rd *BTSEA* SW11 140 E2
Beechmount Av *HNWL* W7 96 D4
Beecholme Av *MTCM* CR4 179 G4
Beecholme Est *CLPT* E5 * 86 E1
Beech Rd *DART* DA1 171 G3
EBED/NFELT TW14 153 H2
FBAR/BDGN N11 48 E2
ORP BR6 217 G5
STRHM/NOR SW16 179 K5
Beechrow *KUTN/CMB* KT2 157 F6
Beech St *ROMW/RG* RM7 74 E1
Beech Street (Below)
BARB EC2Y 12 C1
Beech Tree Cl *IS* N1 85 G5
STAN HA7 43 J1
Beech Tree Gld *CHING* E4 38 D3
Beech Tree Pl *SUT* SM1 209 F3
Beechvale Cl
NFNCH/WDSPK N12 47 J1
Beech Wk *DART* DA1 150 D5
MLHL NW7 45 F1
Beechway *BXLY* DA5 168 E1
Beech Wy *WHTN* TW2 155 F5
WLSDN NW10 81 F5
Beechwood Av *FNCH* N3 46 D6
GFD/PVL UB6 96 B2
HYS/HAR UB3 94 B6
ORP BR6 216 E4
RCH/KEW TW9 137 H2
RSLP HA4 58 D6
RYLN/HDSTN HA2 78 B1
THHTH CR7 196 C1
Beechwood Cl *EFNCH* N2 * 65 K1
MLHL NW7 45 G1
SURB KT6 190 D4
Beechwood Crs *BXLYHN* DA7 148 E4
Beechwood Dr *HAYES* BR2 215 H2
WFD IG8 52 D1
Beechwood Gdns *CLAY* IG5 71 K2
RAIN RM13 111 K4
RYLN/HDSTN HA2 78 B1
Beechwood Gv *ACT* W3 99 G6
Beechwood Ms *ED* N9 36 C4
Beechwood Pk *SWFD* E18 52 E6
Beechwood Ri *CHST* BR7 167 G6
Beechwood Rd
CEND/HSY/T N8 66 D1
HACK E8 86 B4
SAND/SEL CR2 212 A6
Beechworth Cl *HAMP* NW3 65 F6
Beecot La *WOT/HER* KT12 188 B6
Beecroft La *BROCKY* SE4 144 B6
Beecroft Ms *BROCKY* SE4 144 B6
Beecroft Rd *BROCKY* SE4 144 B6
Beehive Cl *BORE* WD6 29 K1
HACK E8 86 B5
Beehive La *REDBR* IG4 71 K2
Beehive Pl *BRXN/ST* SW9 142 B4
Beeken Dene *ORP* BR6 216 C2
Beeleigh Rd *MRDN* SM4 194 A1
Beeston Cl *HACK* E8 86 C3
OXHEY WD19 27 H6
Beeston Pl *BGVA* SW1W 15 K5
Beeston Rd *EBAR* EN4 33 H1
Beeston Wy
EBED/NFELT TW14 154 B1
Beethoven Rd *BORE* WD6 29 J2
Beethoven St *NKENS* W10 100 C2
Beeton Cl *PIN* HA5 42 A3
Beeton Wy *WNWD* SE27 162 D6
Begbie Rd *BKHTH/KID* SE3 146 B2
Beggar's Roost La *SUT* SM1 208 E4
Begonia Cl *EHAM* E6 107 J4
Begonia Pl *HPTN* TW12 173 F2
Beira St *BAL* SW12 161 G2
Bekesbourne St
POP/IOD E14 * 105 G5
Belcroft Cl *BMLY* BR1 183 J3
Beldham Gdns
E/WMO/HCT KT8 173 G6
Belfairs Dr *CHDH* RM6 73 J4
Belfairs Gdn *OXHEY* WD19 41 H1
Belfairs Gn *OXHEY* WD19 41 H1
Belfast Rd *SNWD* SE25 197 J1
STNW/STAM N16 68 B6
Belfield Rd *HOR/WEW* KT19 207 F6
Belford Gv *WOOL/PLUM* SE18 127 F4
Belfort Rd *PECK* SE15 143 K3
Belfry Cl *BERM/RHTH* SE16 * 123 J5
Belfry Rd *MNPK* E12 89 H1
Belgrade Rd *HPTN* TW12 173 G4
STNW/STAM N16 86 A2
Belgrave Cl *ACT* W3 117 K2
MLHL NW7 45 F1
STHGT/OAK N14 22 C6
STMC/STPC BR5 202 D1
Belgrave Crs *SUN* TW16 172 A4
Belgrave Gdns *STAN* HA7 43 J1
STHGT/OAK N14 22 D6
STJWD NW8 83 F6
Belgrave Ms South
KTBR SW1X 15 H4
Belgrave Ms West *KTBR* SW1X 15 G4
Belgrave Pl *KTBR* SW1X 15 H5
Belgrave Rd *BARN* SW13 138 C1
HSLWW TW4 134 E4
IL IG1 71 K5
LEY E10 70 A5
MTCM CR4 178 C6
PIM SW1V 16 A7
PLSTW E13 107 G3
SNWD SE25 197 G1
SUN TW16 172 A4
WALTH E17 69 J3
WAN E11 70 E5
Belgrave Sq *KTBR* SW1X 15 G4
Belgrave St *WCHPL* E1 105 F4
Belgrave Wk *MTCM* CR4 178 C6
Belgravia Cl *BAR* EN5 20 D4
Belgravia Gdns *BMLY* BR1 183 H2
Belgravia Ms *KUT/HW* KT1 190 E1
Belgrove St *KCROSS* N1C 4 E4
Belinda Rd *BRXN/ST* SW9 142 C4
Belitha Vls *IS* N1 85 G5
Bellamaine Cl *THMD* SE28 128 A2
Bellamy Cl *EDGW* HA8 30 E5
POP/IOD E14 124 D2
WKENS W14 119 J5
Bellamy Dr *STAN* HA7 43 H4
Bellamy Rd *CHING* E4 51 K2
ENC/FH EN2 * 23 K3
Bellamy St *BAL* SW12 161 G2
Bel La *FELT* TW13 154 D5
Bellarmine Cl *THMD* SE28 128 A1
Bellasis Av *BRXS/STRHM* SW2 161 K3
Bell Av *HARH* RM3 57 K4
WDR/YW UB7 112 C3
Bell Cl *PIN* HA5 41 G6
RSLP HA4 76 D1
Bellclose Rd *WDR/YW* UB7 112 B2
Bell Dr *WAND/EARL* SW18 159 H2
Bellefield Rd *STMC/STPC* BR5 202 C2
Bellefields Rd *BRXN/ST* SW9 142 A4
Bellegrove Cl *WELL* DA16 148 A3
Bellegrove Rd *WELL* DA16 147 K3
Bellenden Rd *PECK* SE15 143 G3
Belle Staines Pleasaunce
CHING E4 37 J4
Belleville Rd *BTSEA* SW11 140 D6
Belle Vue *GFD/PVL* UB6 78 D6
Belle Vue La *BUSH* WD23 28 D3
Bellevue Pk *THHTH* CR7 180 D6
Bellevue Pl *WCHPL* E1 * 104 E3
Belle Vue Rd *HDN* NW4 64 B1
WALTH E17 52 B5
Bellevue Rd *BARN* SW13 138 D3
BXLYHS DA6 149 G6
CRW RM5 56 E2
FBAR/BDGN N11 34 A6
KUT/HW KT1 175 F6
TOOT SW17 160 E2
WEA W13 97 H3
Bellew St *TOOT* SW17 160 B5
Bell Farm Av *DAGE* RM10 92 E1
Bellfield *CROY/NA* CR0 213 G6
Bellfield Av
KTN/HRWW/WS HA3 42 D2
Bellfield Cl *BKHTH/KID* SE3 146 A1
Bell Gdns *LEY* E10 * 69 J5
STMC/STPC BR5 202 D2
Bellgate Ms *KTTN* NW5 84 B2
Bell Gn *SYD* SE26 164 C6
Bell Green La *SYD* SE26 182 C1
Bell House Rd *ROMW/RG* RM7 74 E5
Bellina Ms *KTTN* NW5 84 B2
Bellingham Gn *CAT* SE6 164 D5
Bellingham Rd *CAT* SE6 165 F5
Bell Inn Yd *BANK* EC3V 13 F4
Bell La *CAN/RD* E16 125 J1
HDN NW4 64 B1
PEND EN3 25 F1
TWK TW1 156 B3
WBLY HA9 * 61 K6
WCHPL E1 13 J2
Bell Meadow *NRWD* SE19 163 F6
Bello Cl *HNHL* SE24 162 C3
Bellot St *GNWCH* SE10 125 H5
Bell Pde *HSLW* TW3 * 135 G5
WWKM BR4 * 199 F6
Bellring Cl *BELV* DA17 129 H6
Bell Rd *E/WMO/HCT* KT8 189 J2
EN EN1 23 K2
HSLW TW3 135 G4
Bells Hl *BAR* EN5 20 B5
Bell St *BAY/PAD* W2 8 C1
WOOL/PLUM SE18 146 D2
Belltrees Gv
STRHM/NOR SW16 180 A1
Bellview Ct *HSLW* TW3 135 G5
Bell Water Ga
WOOL/PLUM SE18 127 F3
Bell Wharf La *CANST* EC4R 12 D6
Bellwood Rd *PECK* SE15 144 A5
Bell Yd *LINN* WC2A 11 J4
Bell Yard Ms *STHWK* SE1 19 H3
Belmont Av *ALP/SUD* HA0 80 B6
EBAR EN4 21 K6
ED N9 36 C3
NWDGN UB2 114 D3
NWMAL KT3 192 D2
PLMGR N13 48 E1
TOTM N17 49 J6
WELL DA16 147 K3
Belmont Cir
KTN/HRWW/WS HA3 * 43 H4
Belmont Cl *CHING* E4 52 B1
CLAP SW4 141 H4
EBAR EN4 21 K5
TRDG/WHET N20 33 F3
WFD IG8 39 F6
Belmont Gv *CHSWK* W4 118 A4
LEW SE13 145 G4
Belmont Hl *LEW* SE13 145 G4
Belmont La *CHST* BR7 185 H1
STAN HA7 43 J3
Belmont Pde *CHST* BR7 * 185 G1
GLDGN NW11 * 64 D2
Belmont Pk *LEW* SE13 145 G5
Belmont Park Cl *LEW* SE13 145 H5
Belmont Park Rd *LEY* E10 69 K3
Belmont Ri *BELMT* SM2 208 D5
Belmont Rd *BECK* BR3 182 B5
CHST BR7 185 G1
CLAP SW4 141 H4
ERITH DA8 149 H1
IL IG1 90 C1
KTN/HRWW/WS HA3 43 F6
SEVS/STOTM N15 67 J1
SNWD SE25 197 J2
WHTN TW2 155 J4
WLGTN SM6 210 C3
Belmont St *CAMTN* NW1 84 A5
Belmont Ter *CHSWK* W4 118 A4
Belmore Av *YEAD* UB4 94 E5
Belmore La *HOLWY* N7 84 D3
Belmore St *VX/NE* SW8 141 J2
Beloe Cl *PUT/ROE* SW15 138 D5
Belsham St *HOM* E9 86 E4
Belsize Av *HAMP* NW3 83 H4
PLMGR N13 49 F2
WEA W13 116 C3
Belsize Court Gdns
HAMP NW3 83 H3
Belsize Crs *HAMP* NW3 83 H3
Belsize Gdns *SUT* SM1 209 F2
Belsize Gv *HAMP* NW3 83 J4
Belsize La *HAMP* NW3 83 H4
Belsize Ms *HAMP* NW3 * 83 H4
Belsize Pk *HAMP* NW3 83 H4
Belsize Park Gdns *HAMP* NW3 83 H4
Belsize Park Ms *HAMP* NW3 83 H4
Belsize Pl *HAMP* NW3 83 H3
Belsize Rd *KIL/WHAMP* NW6 83 F6
KTN/HRWW/WS HA3 42 D3
Belsize Sq *HAMP* NW3 83 H4
Belsize Ter *HAMP* NW3 83 H4
Belson Rd *WOOL/PLUM* SE18 126 E4
Beltane Dr *WIM/MER* SW19 159 G5
Belthorn Crs *BAL* SW12 161 H2
Belton Rd *FSTGT* E7 89 F5
SCUP DA14 168 B6
TOTM N17 50 A6
WAN E11 88 C2
WLSDN NW10 81 J4
Belton Wy *BOW* E3 105 J4
Beltran Rd *FUL/PGN* SW6 140 A3
Beltwood Rd *BELV* DA17 129 K4
Belvedere Av *CLAY* IG5 54 B5
WIM/MER SW19 177 H1
Belvedere Blds *STHWK* SE1 18 B3
Belvedere Cl *ESH/CLAY* KT10 204 B3
TEDD TW11 173 K1
Belvedere Ct *BELV* DA17 129 G3
OXHEY WD19 27 H1
Belvedere Dr *WIM/MER* SW19 177 H1
Belvedere Gdns
E/WMO/HCT KT8 188 E2
Belvedere Gv *WIM/MER* SW19 177 H1
Belvedere Ms *PECK* SE15 143 K4
Belvedere Pl
BRXS/STRHM SW2 142 A5
Belvedere Rd *ABYW* SE2 128 E1
BXLYHN DA7 149 G4
HNWL W7 115 K3
LEY E10 69 G5
NRWD SE19 181 G3
STHWK SE1 17 G2
Belvedere Sq *WIM/MER* SW19 177 H1
Belvedere Strd
CDALE/KGS NW9 45 H5
The Belvedere *WBPTN* SW10 * 140 B2
Belvedere Wy
KTN/HRWW/WS HA3 62 A3
Belvoir Rd *EDUL* SE22 163 H2
Belvue Cl *NTHLT* UB5 78 A5
Belvue Rd *NTHLT* UB5 78 A5
Bembridge Cl
KIL/WHAMP NW6 82 C5
Bembridge Gdns *RSLP* HA4 58 B6
Bemerton St *IS* N1 85 F6
Bemish Rd *PUT/ROE* SW15 139 G4
Bempton Dr *RSLP* HA4 59 F6
Bemsted Rd *WALTH* E17 51 H6
Benares Rd *WOOL/PLUM* SE18 128 A4
Benbow Rd *HMSMTH* W6 118 E3
Benbow St *DEPT* SE8 124 D6
Benbury Cl *BMLY* BR1 183 F1
Bench Fld *SAND/SEL* CR2 212 B4
The Bench
RCHPK/HAM TW10 * 156 D5
Bencroft Rd
STRHM/NOR SW16 179 H3
Bencurtis Pk *WWKM* BR4 214 B1
Bendall Ms *CAMTN* NW1 8 D1
Bendemeer Rd
PUT/ROE SW15 139 G4
Bendish Rd *EHAM* E6 89 J5
Bendmore Av *ABYW* SE2 128 B5
Bendon Va
WAND/EARL SW18 160 A2
Benedict Cl *ORP* BR6 216 E1
Benedict Dr
EBED/NFELT TW14 153 G2
Benedict Rd *BRXN/ST* SW9 142 A4
MTCM CR4 178 C6
Benedict Wy *EFNCH* N2 * 47 G6
Benedict Whf *MTCM* CR4 178 D6
Benenden Gn *HAYES* BR2 199 K2
Benett Gdns
STRHM/NOR SW16 179 K5
Benfleet Cl *SUT* SM1 209 G1
Benfleet Wy *FBAR/BDGN* N11 34 A4
Bengal Rd *IL* IG1 90 B2
Bengarth Dr
KTN/HRWW/WS HA3 42 D5
Bengarth Rd *NTHLT* UB5 77 H6
Bengeworth Rd *CMBW* SE5 142 D4
HRW HA1 61 G6
Ben Hale Cl *STAN* HA7 43 G1
Benham Cl *CHSGTN* KT9 205 J4
Benham Gdns *HSLWW* TW4 134 E6
Benham Rd *HNWL* W7 96 E4
Benhill Av *SUT* SM1 209 F2
Benhill Rd *CMBW* SE5 142 E1
SUT SM1 209 H1
Benhill Wood Rd *SUT* SM1 209 G2
Benhilton Gdns *SUT* SM1 209 F1
Benhurst Av *HCH* RM12 93 K2

Benhurst La
STRHM/NOR SW16 180 B1
Benin St LEW SE13 165 G2
Benjafield Cl UED N18 36 D6
Benjamin Cl EMPK RM11 75 J3
HACK E8 86 C6
Benjamin Ms BAL SW12 161 H2
Benjamin St FARR EC1M 12 A1
Ben Jonson Rd WCHPL E1 105 G4
Benledi St POP/IOD E14 106 B5
Bennelong Cl SHB W12 99 K6
Bennerley Rd BTSEA SW11 140 D6
Bennet Cl KUT/HW KT1 174 D4
Bennetsfield Rd STKPK UB11 112 E1
Bennet's Hl BLKFR EC4V 12 B5
Bennett Cl HSLWW TW4 134 D6
NTHWD HA6 40 D3
WELL DA16 148 B3
Bennett Gv LEW SE13 144 E2
Bennett Pk BKHTH/KID SE3 145 J4
Bennett Rd BRXN/ST SW9 142 B3
CHDH RM6 74 A3
PLSTW E13 107 G3
STNW/STAM N16 86 A2
Bennetts Av CROY/NA CR0 198 B6
GFD/PVL UB6 78 E6
Bennett's Castle La BCTR RM8 91 J2
Bennetts Cl MTCM CR4 179 G4
TOTM N17 50 B2
Bennetts Copse CHST BR7 184 D2
Bennett St CHSWK W4 118 B6
WHALL SW1A 10 A7
Bennetts Wy CROY/NA CR0 198 B6
Bennett's Yd WEST SW1P 16 D5
Benningholme Rd EDGW HA8 45 G2
Bennington Rd TOTM N17 50 A4
WFD IG8 * 52 C3
Benn St HOM E9 87 G4
Benrek Cl BARK/HLT IG6 54 C3
Bensbury Cl PUT/ROE SW15 158 E2
Bensham Cl THHTH CR7 196 D1
Bensham Gv THHTH CR7 180 D5
Bensham La CROY/NA CR0 196 C4
THHTH CR7 196 C3
Bensham Manor Rd
THHTH CR7 196 D1
Bensley Cl FBAR/BDGN N11 47 K1
Ben Smith Wy
BERM/RHTH SE16 123 H3
Benson Av PLSTW E13 107 G1
Benson Cl HSLW TW3 135 F5
Benson Quay WAP E1W 104 E6
Benson Rd CROY/NA CR0 211 G1
FSTH SE23 163 K3
Benthal Rd STNW/STAM N16 68 B6
Bentham Rd HOM E9 87 F4
THMD SE28 128 C1
Ben Tillet Cl BARK IG11 91 G5
CAN/RD E16 126 E1
Bentinck Ms MHST W1U 9 H3
Bentinck Rd WDR/YW UB7 112 A1
Bentinck St MHST W1U 9 H3
Bentley Cl WIM/MER SW19 159 K5
Bentley Dr CRICK NW2 82 D1
GNTH/NBYPK IG2 72 C3
Bentley Ms EN EN1 35 K1
Bentley Rd IS N1 86 A4
Bentley Wy BAR EN5 21 G5
STAN HA7 43 G1
WFD IG8 38 E5
Benton Rd IL IG1 72 D5
OXHEY WD19 41 H1
Benton's La WNWD SE27 162 D6
Benton's Ri WNWD SE27 180 E1
Bentry Cl BCTR RM8 74 A6
Bentry Rd BCTR RM8 74 A6
Bentworth Rd SHB W12 99 K5
Benwell Rd HOLWY N7 85 G2
Benwick Cl BERM/RHTH SE16 123 J4
Benwood Ct SUT SM1 209 G1
Benworth St BOW E3 105 H2
Benyon Rd IS N1 85 K6
Benyon Whf IS N1 86 A6
Berberis Wk WDR/YW UB7 112 B4
Berber Pde WOOL/PLUM SE18 146 D2
Berber Rd BTSEA SW11 * 140 E6
Bercta Rd ELTH/MOT SE9 167 H4
Berengers Pl DAGW RM9 91 H4
Berenger Wk WBPTN SW10 * 140 C1
Berens Rd STMC/STPC BR5 202 D2
WLSDN NW10 100 B2
Berens Wy CHST BR7 202 A1
Beresford Av ALP/SUD HA0 80 C6
BRYLDS KT5 191 J5
HNWL W7 96 D4
TRDG/WHET N20 33 K4
TWK TW1 156 D1
Beresford Dr BMLY BR1 184 C6
WFD IG8 39 G6
Beresford Gdns CHDH RM6 74 A2
EN EN1 24 A5
HSLWW TW4 134 E6
Beresford Rd BELMT SM2 208 D5
CEND/HSY/T N8 67 G2
CHING E4 38 C3
EFNCH N2 47 J6
HBRY N5 85 K3
HRW HA1 60 D2
KUTN/CMB KT2 175 G4
NWMAL KT3 191 K1
STHL UB1 95 H6
WALTH E17 51 K4
Beresford Sq
WOOL/PLUM SE18 127 G4
Beresford St
WOOL/PLUM SE18 127 G3
Beresford Ter HBRY N5 85 J3
Berestede Rd HMSMTH W6 118 C5
Bere St WAP E1W 105 F6
Berger Cl STMC/STPC BR5 201 J3
Berger Rd HOM E9 87 F4
Berghem Ms WKENS W14 119 G3
Bergholt Av REDBR IG4 71 J2
Bergholt Crs STNW/STAM N16 68 A4
Bergholt Ms CAMTN NW1 84 C5
Bering Sq POP/IOD E14 124 D5
Bering Wk CAN/RD E16 107 H5
Berisford Ms
WAND/EARL SW18 160 B1
Berkeley Av BXLYHN DA7 148 E2
CLAY IG5 54 A5
CRW RM5 56 E3
GFD/PVL UB6 78 E4
HSLWW TW4 133 K2
Berkeley Cl KUTN/CMB KT2 175 F3
RSLP HA4 76 D1
STMC/STPC BR5 201 K4
Berkeley Ct WLGTN SM6 210 C1
Berkeley Crs DART DA1 171 J3
EBAR EN4 21 H6
Berkeley Dr E/WMO/HCT KT8 172 E6
Berkeley Gdns ESH/CLAY KT10 205 G5
KENS W8 119 K1
WCHMH N21 35 K2
Berkeley Ms MBLAR W1H 9 F3
SUN TW16 172 B6
Berkeley Pl WIM/MER SW19 177 G2
Berkeley Rd BARN SW13 138 D2
CDALE/KGS NW9 62 C1
CEND/HSY/T N8 66 D2
HGDN/ICK UB10 76 A5
MNPK E12 89 J3
SEVS/STOTM N15 67 K3
Berkeley Sq MYFR/PICC W1J 9 K6
The Berkeleys SNWD SE25 * 197 H1
Berkeley St MYFR/PICC W1J 9 K6
Berkeley Waye HEST TW5 134 D1
Berkhampstead Rd
BELV DA17 129 H5
Berkhamsted Av WBLY HA9 80 B4
Berkley Cl WHTN TW2 * 155 K5
Berkley Rd CAMTN NW1 83 K5
Berkshire Gdns PLMGR N13 49 G2
UED N18 50 D1
Berkshire Rd HOM E9 87 H4
Berkshire Wy MTCM CR4 195 K1
Bermans Wy WLSDN NW10 81 G2
Bermondsey Sq STHWK SE1 * 19 H4
Bermondsey St STHWK SE1 19 G4
Bermondsey Wall East
BERM/RHTH SE16 123 H2
Bermondsey Wall West
STHWK SE1 123 H2
Bernal Cl THMD SE28 109 K6
Bernard Ashley Dr CHARL SE7 126 A5
Bernard Av WEA W13 116 C3
Bernard Cassidy St
CAN/RD E16 106 D4
Bernard Gdns
WIM/MER SW19 177 J1
Bernard Rd ROMW/RG RM7 74 E4
SEVS/STOTM N15 68 B2
WLGTN SM6 210 A3
Bernards Cl BARK/HLT IG6 54 C3
Bernard St BMSBY WC1N 4 E7
Bernays Cl STAN HA7 43 J2
Bernay's Gv BRXN/ST SW9 142 A5
Bernel Dr CROY/NA CR0 213 H1
Berne Rd THHTH CR7 196 C2
Berners Dr WEA W13 97 G6
Berners Ms FITZ W1T 10 B2
Berners Pl FITZ W1T 10 B3
Berners Rd IS N1 6 A1
WDGN N22 49 G4
Berners St FITZ W1T 10 B2
Berner Ter WCHPL E1 * 104 C5
Berney Rd CROY/NA CR0 196 E4
Bernhardt Crs STJWD NW8 2 C6
Bernhart Cl EDGW HA8 44 E3
Bernwell Rd CHING E4 38 C5
Berridge Gn EDGW HA8 44 C3
Berridge Ms KIL/WHAMP NW6 82 E3
Berridge Rd NRWD SE19 180 E1
Berriman Rd HOLWY N7 85 F1
Berriton Rd RYLN/HDSTN HA2 59 K5
Berrybank Cl CHING E4 38 A4
Berry Cl DAGE RM10 92 C3
WCHMH N21 35 H3
Berry Cots POP/IOD E14 * 105 G5
Berry Ct HSLWW TW4 134 E6
Berrydale Rd YEAD UB4 95 J3
Berryfield Cl BMLY BR1 184 D4
Berry Field Cl WALTH E17 69 K1
Berryfield Rd WALW SE17 122 C5
Berryhill ELTH/MOT SE9 147 G5
Berry Hl STAN HA7 29 K6
Berryhill Gdns ELTH/MOT SE9 147 G5
Berrylands BRYLDS KT5 191 H2
ORP BR6 217 J1
RYNPK SW20 177 F6
Berrylands Rd BRYLDS KT5 191 G3
Berry La DUL SE21 162 E6
Berryman Cl BCTR RM8 91 J1
Berryman's La SYD SE26 164 A6
Berrymead Gdns ACT W3 117 K1
Berrymede Rd CHSWK W4 118 A3
Berry Pl FSBYE EC1V 6 B5
Berry St FSBYE EC1V 6 B7
Berry Wy EA W5 117 F3
Bertal Rd TOOT SW17 160 C6
Berthons Gdns WALTH E17 * 70 B2
Berthon St DEPT SE8 144 D1
Bertie Rd SYD SE26 182 A2
WLSDN NW10 81 J4
Bertram Rd EN EN1 24 C5
HDN NW4 63 J3
KUTN/CMB KT2 175 H3
Bertram St KTTN NW5 84 B1
Bertrand St LEW SE13 144 E4
Bertrand Wy THMD SE28 109 H6
Bert Rd THHTH CR7 196 D2
Bert Wy EN EN1 24 B5
Berwick Av YEAD UB4 95 H5
Berwick Cl STAN HA7 43 F2
WHTN TW2 155 F3
Berwick Crs BFN/LL DA15 167 K1
Berwick Gdns SUT SM1 209 G1
Berwick Rd CAN/RD E16 107 F5
WDGN N22 49 H4
WELL DA16 148 C2
Berwick St SOHO/CST W1F 10 B4
Berwick Wy ORP BR6 202 B5
Berwyn Av HSLW TW3 135 G2
Berwyn Rd HNHL SE24 162 C3
RCHPK/HAM TW10 137 J5
Beryl Av EHAM E6 107 J4
Beryl Rd HMSMTH W6 119 G5
Berystede KUTN/CMB KT2 175 J3
Besant Cl CRICK NW2 * 82 C1
Besant Pl EDUL SE22 143 G4
Besant Rd CRICK NW2 82 C2
Besant Wy WLSDN NW10 80 E3
Besley St STRHM/NOR SW16 179 H2
Bessant Dr RCH/KEW TW9 137 J2
Bessborough Pl PIM SW1V 121 J5
Bessborough Rd HRW HA1 60 D5
PUT/ROE SW15 158 D3
Bessborough St PIM SW1V 121 J5
Bessemer Pl GNWCH SE10 125 J3
Bessemer Rd CMBW SE5 142 D3
Bessie Lansbury Cl EHAM E6 108 A5
Bessingby Rd RSLP HA4 58 E6
Besson St NWCR SE14 143 K2
Bessy St BETH E2 * 104 E2
Best Ter SWLY BR8 * 203 K2
Bestwood St DEPT SE8 124 A4
Beswick Ms KIL/WHAMP NW6 83 F3
Betam Rd HYS/HAR UB3 113 G2
Betchworth Cl SUT SM1 209 H3
Betchworth Rd
GDMY/SEVK IG3 72 E6
Betchworth Wy
CROY/NA CR0 214 A6
Betham Rd GFD/PVL UB6 96 D2
Bethany Waye
EBED/NFELT TW14 153 H2
Bethecar Rd HRW HA1 60 E2
Bethel Cl HDN NW4 64 B2
Bethell Av CAN/RD E16 106 D3
IL IG1 72 A4
Bethel Rd WELL DA16 148 D4
Bethersden Cl BECK BR3 182 C3
Bethnal Green Rd BETH E2 7 K6
Bethune Av FBAR/BDGN N11 33 K6
Bethune Rd STNW/STAM N16 67 K4
WLSDN NW10 99 F3
Bethwin Rd CMBW SE5 142 C1
Betjeman Cl
RYLN/HDSTN HA2 60 A1
Betjeman Ct WDR/YW UB7 * 112 A1
Betony Cl CROY/NA CR0 198 A5
Betoyne Av CHING E4 38 C6
Betsham Rd ERITH DA8 150 C1
Betstyle Rd FBAR/BDGN N11 34 B6
Betterton Dr SCUP DA14 169 F4
Betterton Rd RAIN RM13 111 G1
Betterton St LSQ/SEVD WC2H 10 E4
Bettons Pk SRTFD E15 88 C6
Bettridge Rd FUL/PGN SW6 139 J3
Betts Cl BECK BR3 182 B5
Betts Ms WALTH E17 69 H3
Betts Rd CAN/RD E16 107 F5
Betts St WAP E1W 104 D6
Betts Wy PGE/AN SE20 181 J5
SURB KT6 190 C5
Beulah Av THHTH CR7 * 180 D5
Beulah Cl EDGW HA8 30 D5
Beulah Crs THHTH CR7 180 D5
Beulah Gv CROY/NA CR0 196 D3
Beulah Hl NRWD SE19 180 C2
Beulah Rd SUT SM1 208 E2
THHTH CR7 180 D6
WALTH E17 69 K2
WIM/MER SW19 177 J3
Beult Rd DART DA1 150 D4
Bevan Av BARK IG11 91 G5
Bevan Ct CROY/NA CR0 211 G3
Bevan Rd ABYW SE2 128 C5
EBAR EN4 21 K5
Bevan St IS N1 6 D1
Bev Callender Cl VX/NE SW8 141 G4
Bevenden St IS N1 7 F4
Beveridge Rd WLSDN NW10 81 G5
Beverley Av BFN/LL DA15 168 A2
HSLWW TW4 134 E5
RYNPK SW20 176 C4
Beverley Cl BARN SW13 138 D3
BTSEA SW11 140 C5
CHSGTN KT9 205 J2
WCHMH N21 35 J3
Beverley Ct BROCKY SE4 144 C4
Beverley Crs WFD IG8 53 F4
Beverley Dr EDGW HA8 44 B6
Beverley Gdns BARN SW13 138 C4
GLDGN NW11 64 C4
STAN HA7 43 G4
WBLY HA9 62 B5
WPK KT4 192 D5
Beverley La KUTN/CMB KT2 176 B3
Beverley Rd BARN SW13 138 C4
BXLYHN DA7 149 K3
CHING E4 52 B2
CHSWK W4 118 C5
DAGW RM9 92 A2
EHAM E6 107 H2
HAYES BR2 200 D6
KUT/HW KT1 174 D4
MTCM CR4 195 J1
NWDGN UB2 114 D4
NWMAL KT3 192 D1
PGE/AN SE20 181 J5
RSLP HA4 59 F6
WPK KT4 193 F6
Beverley Wy RYNPK SW20 176 C4
Beverley Way (Kingston
By-Pass) NWMAL KT3 176 C5
Beversbrook Rd ARCH N19 84 D1
Beverstone Rd
BRXS/STRHM SW2 142 A6
THHTH CR7 196 B1
Beverston Ms MBLAR W1H 8 E2
Bevill Allen Cl TOOT SW17 178 E2
Bevill Cl SNWD SE25 181 H6
Bevin Cl BERM/RHTH SE16 124 B1
Bevington Rd BECK BR3 182 E5
NKENS W10 * 100 C4
Bevington St
BERM/RHTH SE16 123 H2
Bevin Rd YEAD UB4 94 E2
Bevin Sq TOOT SW17 160 E5
Bevin Wy FSBYW WC1X 5 J3
Bevis Marks HDTCH EC3A 13 H3
Bewcastle Gdns ENC/FH EN2 22 E5
Bewdley St IS N1 85 G5
Bewick Ms PECK SE15 143 J1
Bewick St VX/NE SW8 141 G3
Bewley St WCHPL E1 104 D6
WIM/MER SW19 178 B2
Bewlys Rd WNWD SE27 180 C1
Bexhill Cl FELT TW13 154 D4
Bexhill Rd BROCKY SE4 164 C1
FBAR/BDGN N11 48 D1
MORT/ESHN SW14 137 K4
Bexley Cl DART DA1 150 B6
Bexley Gdns CHDH RM6 73 H2
ED N9 35 K5
Bexley High St BXLY DA5 169 H2
Bexley La DART DA1 150 B6
SCUP DA14 168 D6
Bexley Rd ELTH/MOT SE9 167 F1
ERITH DA8 149 K1
Beynon Rd CAR SM5 209 K3
Bianca Rd PECK SE15 123 G6
Bibsworth Rd FNCH N3 46 D5
Bibury Cl PECK SE15 123 F6
Bicester Rd RCH/KEW TW9 137 H4
Bickenhall St MHST W1U 9 F1
Bickersteth Rd TOOT SW17 178 E2
Bickerton Rd ARCH N19 66 B6
Bickles Yd STHWK SE1 19 H3
Bickley Crs BMLY BR1 200 D1
Bickley Park Rd BMLY BR1 184 E6
Bickley Rd BMLY BR1 184 C5
LEY E10 69 K4
Bickley St TOOT SW17 178 D1
Bicknell Rd CMBW SE5 142 D4
Bicknoller Rd EN EN1 24 B2
Bicknor Rd ORP BR6 201 K4
Bidborough Cl HAYES BR2 199 J2
Bidborough St STPAN WC1H 4 E5
Biddenden Wy ELTH/MOT SE9 167 F6
Bidder St CAN/RD E16 106 C4
Biddestone Rd HOLWY N7 85 F2
Biddulph Rd MV/WKIL W9 101 F2
SAND/SEL CR2 211 J6
Bideford Av GFD/PVL UB6 97 H2
Bideford Cl EDGW HA8 44 C4
FELT TW13 154 E5
Bideford Gdns EN EN1 36 A2
Bideford Rd BMLY BR1 165 J5
PEND EN3 25 H1
RSLP HA4 77 F1
WELL DA16 148 C1
Bidwell Gdns FBAR/BDGN N11 48 C4
Bidwell St PECK SE15 * 143 J2
Biggerstaff Rd SRTFD E15 88 A6
Biggerstaff St FSBYPK N4 67 G6
Biggin Av MTCM CR4 178 E4
Biggin Hl NRWD SE19 180 C3
Biggin Wy NRWD SE19 180 C3
Bigginwood Rd
STRHM/NOR SW16 180 C3
Bigg's Rw PUT/ROE SW15 139 G4
Biggs Sq HOM E9 87 H4
Big Hl CLPT E5 68 D5
Bigland St WCHPL E1 104 D5
Bignell Rd WOOL/PLUM SE18 127 G5
Bignold Rd FSTGT E7 88 E2
Bigwood Rd GLDGN NW11 65 F3
Billet Rd CHDH RM6 55 J6
WALTH E17 51 F4
Billets Hart Cl HNWL W7 115 K2
Bill Hamling Cl ELTH/MOT SE9 166 E4
Billingford Cl BROCKY SE4 144 A5
Billing Pl WBPTN SW10 * 140 A1
Billing Rd WBPTN SW10 140 A1
Billings Cl DAGW RM9 91 J5
Billing St WBPTN SW10 * 140 A1
Billington Hl CROY/NA CR0 196 E6
Billington Rd NWCR SE14 144 A1
Billiter Sq FENCHST EC3M * 13 H4
Billiter St FENCHST EC3M 13 H4
Bill Nicholson Wy TOTM N17 50 B3
Billockby Cl CHSGTN KT9 206 B4
Billson St POP/IOD E14 125 F4
Bilton Rd ERITH DA8 150 D1
GFD/PVL UB6 79 H6
Bilton Wy HYS/HAR UB3 114 A2
PEND EN3 25 H2
Bina Gdns ECT SW5 120 B4
Bincote Rd ENC/FH EN2 23 F4
Binden Rd SHB W12 118 C3
Binfield Rd CLAP SW4 141 K2
SAND/SEL CR2 212 B3
Bingfield St IS N1 84 E6
Bingham Ct IS N1 * 85 H5
Bingham Pl MHST W1U 9 G1
Bingham Rd CROY/NA CR0 197 H5
Bingham St IS N1 85 K4
Bingley Rd CAN/RD E16 107 G5
GFD/PVL UB6 96 C3
Binney St MYFR/PKLN W1K 9 H5
Binns Rd CHSWK W4 118 B5
Binsey Wk ABYW SE2 128 D2
Binstead Cl YEAD UB4 95 J4
Binyon Crs STAN HA7 43 F1
Birbetts Rd ELTH/MOT SE9 166 E4
Birchanger Rd SNWD SE25 197 H2
Birch Av PLMGR N13 35 J5
Birch Cl BKHH IG9 39 H5
BTFD TW8 136 C1
CAN/RD E16 106 C4
HSLW TW3 135 J4
ROMW/RG RM7 56 D6
TEDD TW11 174 B1
Birch Ct WLGTN SM6 210 B2
Birchdale Gdns CHDH RM6 73 K4
Birchdale Rd FSTGT E7 89 G3
Birchdene Dr THMD SE28 128 B1
Birchen Cl CDALE/KGS NW9 63 F6
Birchend Cl SAND/SEL CR2 211 K4
Birchen Gv CDALE/KGS NW9 63 F6
Birches Cl MTCM CR4 178 E6
PIN HA5 59 J2
The Birches CHARL SE7 126 A6
CMBW SE5 * 143 F4
HSLWW TW4 * 154 E2
ORP BR6 216 A2
WCHMH N21 35 F1
Birchfield St POP/IOD E14 105 J6
Birch Gdns DAGE RM10 92 E1
Birch Gv ACT W3 117 H1
LEE/GVPK SE12 165 J2
WAN E11 88 C1
WELL DA16 148 B5
Birch Hl CROY/NA CR0 213 F3
Birchington Cl BXLYHN DA7 149 J2
Birchington Rd BRYLDS KT5 191 G4
CEND/HSY/T N8 66 D3
KIL/WHAMP NW6 82 E6
Birchin La BANK EC3V 13 F4
Birchlands Av BAL SW12 160 E2
Birch Md ORP BR6 201 F6
Birchmead Av PIN HA5 59 G1
Birchmere Rw
BKHTH/KID SE3 145 J3
Birchmore Wk HBRY N5 85 J1
Birch Pk KTN/HRWW/WS HA3 42 C3
Birch Rd FELT TW13 172 C1
ROMW/RG RM7 56 D6
Birch Rw HAYES BR2 201 F4
Birch Tree Av WWKM BR4 214 D3
Birch Tree Wy CROY/NA CR0 197 J6
Birch Wk MTCM CR4 179 G4
Birchway HYS/HAR UB3 113 K1
Birchwood Av BECK BR3 198 C1
MUSWH N10 48 A6
SCUP DA14 168 C5
WLGTN SM6 210 A1
Birchwood Cl MRDN SM4 194 A1
Birchwood Ct EDGW HA8 44 E5
Birchwood Dr HAMP NW3 83 F1
RDART DA2 170 B6
Birchwood Gv HPTN TW12 173 F2
Birchwood La ESH/CLAY KT10 204 D6
Birchwood Rd RDART DA2 170 B6
STMC/STPC BR5 201 J1
SWLY BR8 187 K3
TOOT SW17 179 G1
Birchwood Ter SWLY BR8 * 187 K4
Birdbrook Cl DAGE RM10 92 E5
Birdbrook Rd BKHTH/KID SE3 146 B4
Birdcage Wk STJSPK SW1H 16 C3
WESTW SW1E 16 B3
Birdham Cl BMLY BR1 200 D2
Birdhurst Av SAND/SEL CR2 211 K2
Birdhurst Gdns SAND/SEL CR2 211 K2
Birdhurst Ri SAND/SEL CR2 212 A3
Birdhurst Rd SAND/SEL CR2 212 A3
WAND/EARL SW18 140 B5
WIM/MER SW19 178 D2
Bird In Bush Rd PECK SE15 143 H1
Bird-In-Hand La BMLY BR1 184 C5
Bird-In-Hand Ms FSTH SE23 163 K4
Bird-In-Hand Pas FSTH SE23 163 K4
Birds Farm Av CRW RM5 56 D4
Birdsfield La BOW E3 87 H6
Bird St MHST W1U 9 H4
Bird Wk WHTN TW2 154 E3
Birdwood Av DART DA1 151 J3
LEW SE13 165 G1
Birdwood Cl TEDD TW11 155 K6
Birkbeck Av ACT W3 98 E6
GFD/PVL UB6 78 C6
Birkbeck Gv ACT W3 118 A1
Birkbeck Hl DUL SE21 162 C4
Birkbeck Ms ACT W3 * 99 F6
HACK E8 86 B3
Birkbeck Pl DUL SE21 162 C3
Birkbeck Rd ACT W3 118 A1
BECK BR3 181 K5
CEND/HSY/T N8 66 E1
EA W5 116 D4
ENC/FH EN2 23 K1
GNTH/NBYPK IG2 72 D2
HACK E8 86 B3
MLHL NW7 45 H1
NFNCH/WDSPK N12 47 G1
ROMW/RG RM7 75 F5
SCUP DA14 168 B5
TOTM N17 50 B4
WIM/MER SW19 178 A1
Birkbeck St BETH E2 104 D2
Birkbeck Wy GFD/PVL UB6 78 D6
Birkdale Av PIN HA5 42 A6
Birkdale Cl
BERM/RHTH SE16 * 123 J5
ORP BR6 201 J4
THMD SE28 109 J5
Birkdale Gdns CROY/NA CR0 213 F2
OXHEY WD19 27 H5
Birkdale Rd ABYW SE2 128 B4
EA W5 98 A3
Birkenhead Av
KUTN/CMB KT2 175 G5
Birkenhead St KCROSS N1C 5 F4
Birkhall Rd CAT SE6 165 G3
Birkwood Cl BAL SW12 161 J2
Birley Rd TRDG/WHET N20 33 G4
Birley St BTSEA SW11 141 F3
Birling Rd ERITH DA8 150 A1
Birnam Rd FSBYPK N4 67 F6
Birnbeck Rd GLDGN NW11 64 D2
Birse Crs WLSDN NW10 81 G2
Birstal Gn OXHEY WD19 27 H6
Birstall Rd SEVS/STOTM N15 68 A2
Biscay Rd HMSMTH W6 119 G5
Biscoe Cl HEST TW5 115 F6
Biscoe Wy LEW SE13 * 145 G5
Bisenden Rd CROY/NA CR0 197 F6
Bisham Cl CAR SM5 194 E4
Bisham Gdns HGT N6 66 A5
Bishop Butt Cl ORP BR6 217 F1
Bishop Fox Wy
E/WMO/HCT KT8 188 E1
Bishop Ken Rd
KTN/HRWW/WS HA3 43 F5
Bishop King's Rd WKENS W14 119 H4
Bishop Ramsey Cl RSLP HA4 58 D4
Bishop Rd STHGT/OAK N14 34 B2
Bishops Av BMLY BR1 184 B6
CHDH RM6 73 J3
NTHWD HA6 26 C6
PLSTW E13 89 F6
Bishop's Av FUL/PGN SW6 139 G3
The Bishops Av EFNCH N2 65 H3
Bishop's Bridge Rd
BAY/PAD W2 101 F5
Bishops Cl BAR EN5 32 B1
CHSWK W4 117 K5
ELTH/MOT SE9 167 H4
EN EN1 24 D3
RCHPK/HAM TW10 156 E5
SUT SM1 208 E1
Bishop's Cl ARCH N19 84 C1
WALTH E17 69 K1
Bishop's Ct STP EC4M 12 A3
Bishops Dr EBED/NFELT TW14 153 G1
NTHLT UB5 77 J6
Bishopsford Rd MRDN SM4 194 B4

Bishopsgate LVPST EC2M 13 H2
Bishopsgate Ar LVPST EC2M 13 G2
Bishops Gn BMLY BR1 * 184 B4
Bishops Gv EFNCH N2 65 H3
HPTN TW12 154 E6
Bishop's Hall KUT/HW KT1 174 E5
Bishops Md CMBW SE5 * 142 D1
Bishops Park Rd
STRHM/NOR SW16 179 K4
Bishop's Park Rd
FUL/PGN SW6 139 G3
Bishop's Pl SUT SM1 209 G3
Bishops Rd FUL/PGN SW6 139 J2
HGT N6 66 A3
Bishop's Rd CROY/NA CR0 196 C4
HNWL W7 115 K2
HYS/HAR UB3 94 A5
Bishop's Ter LBTH SE11 17 K6
Bishopsthorpe Rd SYD SE26 164 A6
Bishops Wk CHST BR7 185 H4
CROY/NA CR0 213 F3
Bishop's Wy BETH E2 104 E1
Bishopswood Rd HGT N6 65 K4
Bishop Wilfred Wood Cl
PECK SE15 143 H3
Bisley Cl WPK KT4 193 F5
Bispham Rd WLSDN NW10 98 B2
Bisson Rd SRTFD E15 106 A1
Bistern Av WALTH E17 52 B6
Bittacy Cl MLHL NW7 46 B2
Bittacy Hl MLHL NW7 46 B2
Bittacy Park Av MLHL NW7 46 B1
Bittacy Ri MLHL NW7 46 B2
Bittacy Rd MLHL NW7 46 B2
Bittern Cl YEAD UB4 95 H4
Bittern Pl WDGN N22 * 49 F5
Bittern St STHWK SE1 18 C2
Bittoms Ct KUT/HW KT1 * 174 E6
The Bittoms KUT/HW KT1 174 E6
Bixley Cl NWDGN UB2 114 E4
Blackall St SDTCH EC2A 7 G6
Blackberry Farm Cl HEST TW5 134 D1
Blackberry Fld
STMC/STPC BR5 186 B4
Blackbird Hl WBLY HA9 62 E6
Blackbird Yd BETH E2 7 K4
Blackborne Rd DAGE RM10 92 C4
Black Boy La
SEVS/STOTM N15 67 J2
Blackbrook La HAYES BR2 201 F2
Blackburne's Ms
MYFR/PKLN W1K 9 G5
Blackburn Rd
KIL/WHAMP NW6 83 F4
Blackbush Av CHDH RM6 73 K2
Blackbush Cl BELMT SM2 209 F5
Blackdown Cl EFNCH N2 47 G5
Blackdown Ter
WOOL/PLUM SE18 * 146 E2
Blackenham Rd TOOT SW17 160 E6
Blackett St PUT/ROE SW15 139 G4
Black Fan Cl ENC/FH EN2 23 J2
Blackfen Pde BFN/LL DA15 * 168 B1
Blackfen Rd BFN/LL DA15 148 A6
Blackford Cl SAND/SEL CR2 211 H6
Blackford Rd OXHEY WD19 41 H1
Blackfriars Br STHWK SE1 12 A6
Black Friars La BLKFR EC4V 12 A4
Blackfriars Pas BLKFR EC4V 12 A5
Blackfriars Rd STHWK SE1 12 A7
Blackfriars U/P BLKFR EC4V 12 B5
Blackheath Av GNWCH SE10 145 G1
Blackheath Gv
BKHTH/KID SE3 145 J3
Blackheath Hl GNWCH SE10 145 F2
Blackheath Pk
BKHTH/KID SE3 145 J4
Blackheath Ri LEW SE13 145 F3
Blackheath Rd GNWCH SE10 144 E2
Blackheath V BKHTH/KID SE3 145 H3
Black Horse Ct STHWK SE1 * 19 F5
Blackhorse La CROY/NA CR0 197 H4
WALTH E17 51 F6
Black Horse Pde PIN HA5 * 59 F2
Blackhorse Rd DEPT SE8 124 B6
Black Horse Rd SCUP DA14 168 B6
Blackhorse Rd WALTH E17 69 F1
Blacklands Dr YEAD UB4 94 A3
Blacklands Rd CAT SE6 165 F6
Blacklands Ter CHEL SW3 14 E7
Black Lion Ga BAY/PAD W2 101 F6
Black Lion La HMSMTH W6 118 D4
Blackmans Cl DART DA1 171 F3
Blackmans Yd WCHPL E1 * 7 K6
Blackmore Av STHL UB1 115 J1
Blackmore Dr WLSDN NW10 80 D5
Blackmore Rd BKHH IG9 39 J2
Blackmore's Gv TEDD TW11 174 B2
Blackness Cots HAYES BR2 * 215 H6
Blackness La HAYES BR2 215 H6
Blackpool Gdns YEAD UB4 94 C3
Blackpool Rd PECK SE15 143 J3
Black Prince Rd LBTH SE11 17 G7
Black Rod Cl HYS/HAR UB3 113 J3
Blackrurn Wy HSLWW TW4 134 D6
Blackshaw Rd TOOT SW17 178 C1
Blacksmith Cl CHDH RM6 73 J3
Blacksmiths La
STMC/STPC BR5 202 D2
Blacksmith's La RAIN RM13 93 H6
Black's Rd HMSMTH W6 119 F5
Blackstock Rd FSBYPK N4 67 H6
Blackstone Est HACK E8 86 C5
Blackstone Rd CRICK NW2 82 A3
Black Swan Yd STHWK SE1 19 G2
Blackthorn Av WDR/YW UB7 112 D4
Blackthorn Ct HEST TW5 134 D1
Blackthorne Av CROY/NA CR0 197 K5
Blackthorne Dr CHING E4 38 B6
Blackthorn Gv BXLYHN DA7 149 F4
Blackthorn Rd IL IG1 90 D3
Blackthorn St BOW E3 105 J3
Blacktree Ms BRXN/ST SW9 * 142 B4
Blackwall La GNWCH SE10 125 H5
Blackwall Tnl POP/IOD E14 125 G1
Blackwall Tunnel Ap
POP/IOD E14 106 A6
Blackwall Tunnel Northern Ap
BOW E3 87 J6
BOW E3 106 A2
Blackwall Wy POP/IOD E14 106 A6
Blackwater Cl FSTGT E7 88 D2
RAIN RM13 111 F4
Blackwater St EDUL SE22 143 G6
Blackwell Cl CLPT E5 87 G2
KTN/HRWW/WS HA3 42 D3
WCHMH N21 22 E6
Blackwell Dr OXHEY WD19 27 G1
Blackwell Gdns EDGW HA8 30 C6
Blackwood St WALW SE17 122 E5
Blade Ms PUT/ROE SW15 139 J5
Bladindon Dr BXLY DA5 168 E2
Bladon Gdns
RYLN/HDSTN HA2 60 B3
Blagden's La STHGT/OAK N14 34 D4
Blagdon Rd CAT SE6 164 E1
NWMAL KT3 192 C1
Blagdon Wk TEDD TW11 174 D2
Blagrove Rd NKENS W10 100 C4
Blair Av CDALE/KGS NW9 63 G4
ESH/CLAY KT10 189 H6
Blair Cl BFN/LL DA15 147 K6
HYS/HAR UB3 113 K4
IS N1 85 J4
Blairderry Rd
BRXS/STRHM SW2 161 K4
Blairhead Dr OXHEY WD19 27 F5
Blair St POP/IOD E14 106 A5
Blake Av BARK IG11 90 E6
Blake Cl CAR SM5 194 D5
NKENS W10 100 A4
RAIN RM13 93 H6
WELL DA16 147 K2
YEAD UB4 94 B1
Blakeden Dr ESH/CLAY KT10 205 F5
Blake Gdns DART DA1 151 J5
FUL/PGN SW6 139 K2
Blakehall Rd CAR SM5 209 K4
Blake Hall Rd WAN E11 70 E5
Blake Ms RCH/KEW TW9 137 H2
Blakemore Gdns BARN SW13 118 E6
Blakemore Rd
STRHM/NOR SW16 161 K5
THHTH CR7 196 A2
Blakemore Wy BELV DA17 129 F3
Blakeney Av BECK BR3 182 C4
Blakeney Cl CAMTN NW1 4 C2
HACK E8 86 C3
TRDG/WHET N20 33 G3
Blakeney Rd BECK BR3 182 C4
Blaker Ct CHARL SE7 * 146 B1
Blake Rd CAN/RD E16 106 D3
CROY/NA CR0 197 F6
FBAR/BDGN N11 48 C3
MTCM CR4 178 D6
Blaker Rd SRTFD E15 88 A6
Blakes Av NWMAL KT3 192 C2
Blakes Cl WLSDN NW10 81 J4
Blake's Gn WWKM BR4 199 F4
Blakes La NWMAL KT3 192 C2
Blakesley Av EA W5 97 J5
Blakes Rd PECK SE15 * 143 F1
Blake's Rd PECK SE15 143 F1
Blakes Ter NWMAL KT3 192 D2
Blakesware Gdns ED N9 35 K2
Blakewood Cl FELT TW13 154 B6
Blanchard Cl ELTH/MOT SE9 166 D5
Blanchard Gv PEND EN3 25 J1
Blanchard Wy HACK E8 * 86 C4
Blanch Cl PECK SE15 143 K1
Blanchedowne CMBW SE5 142 E5
Blanche St CAN/RD E16 106 D3
Blanchland Rd MRDN SM4 194 A2
Blandfield Rd BAL SW12 161 F1
Blandford Av BECK BR3 182 B5
WHTN TW2 155 G3
Blandford Cl CROY/NA CR0 210 E1
EFNCH N2 65 G2
ROMW/RG RM7 74 D1
Blandford Crs CHING E4 38 A2
Blandford Rd BECK BR3 182 A5
CHSWK W4 118 B3
EA W5 116 E2
NWDGN UB2 115 F4
TEDD TW11 173 J1
Blandford Sq CAMTN NW1 2 D7
Blandford St MHST W1U 9 F3
Blandford Waye YEAD UB4 95 G5
Bland St ELTH/MOT SE9 146 C5
Blaney Crs EHAM E6 108 B2
Blanmerle Rd ELTH/MOT SE9 167 G3
Blann Cl ELTH/MOT SE9 166 C1
Blantyre St WBPTN SW10 140 C1
Blantyre Wk WBPTN SW10 * 140 C1
Blashford St LEW SE13 165 G2
Blawith Rd HRW HA1 60 E1
Blaydon Cl RSLP HA4 58 C4
TOTM N17 * 50 D3
Blaydon Wk TOTM N17 50 D3
Bleak Hill La
WOOL/PLUM SE18 128 A6
Blean Gv PGE/AN SE20 181 K3
Bleasdale Av GFD/PVL UB6 97 G1
Blechynden Gdns NKENS W10 100 B6
Blechynden St NKENS W10 * 100 B6
Bledlow Cl THMD SE28 109 J6
Bledlow Ri GFD/PVL UB6 96 C1
Bleeding Heart Yd
HCIRC EC1N * 11 K2
Blegborough Rd
STRHM/NOR SW16 179 H2
Blendon Dr BXLY DA5 168 E1
Blendon Rd BXLY DA5 168 E1
Blendon Ter
WOOL/PLUM SE18 127 H5
Blendworth Wy PECK SE15 143 F1
Blenheim CDALE/KGS NW9 * 45 H5
Blenheim Av
GNTH/NBYPK IG2 72 A3
Blenheim Cl DART DA1 171 F1
GFD/PVL UB6 * 96 D1
LEE/GVPK SE12 166 A3
OXHEY WD19 27 G2
ROMW/RG RM7 74 E1
RYNPK SW20 177 F6
WCHMH N21 35 J3
WLGTN SM6 210 C5
Blenheim Ct BFN/LL DA15 167 J5
WFD IG8 53 F3
Blenheim Crs NTGHL W11 100 C5
RSLP HA4 58 B6
SAND/SEL CR2 211 J5
Blenheim Dr WELL DA16 148 A2
Blenheim Gdns
BRXS/STRHM SW2 162 A1
CRICK NW2 82 A3
KUTN/CMB KT2 175 J3
WBLY HA9 80 A1
WLGTN SM6 210 C4
Blenheim Gv PECK SE15 143 G3
Blenheim Park Rd
SAND/SEL CR2 211 J6
Blenheim Pas STJWD NW8 101 G1
Blenheim Pl TEDD TW11 174 A1
Blenheim Ri
SEVS/STOTM N15 * 68 B1
Blenheim Rd BAR EN5 20 A3
BFN/LL DA15 168 D3
BMLY BR1 200 D1
CHSWK W4 118 B3
DART DA1 171 F1
EHAM E6 107 H2
NTHLT UB5 78 B4
ORP BR6 202 D6
PGE/AN SE20 181 K3
RYLN/HDSTN HA2 60 B3
RYNPK SW20 177 F6
STJWD NW8 101 G1
SUT SM1 208 E1
WALTH E17 51 F6
WAN E11 88 C2
Blenheim St CONDST W1S 9 J4
Blenheim Ter STJWD NW8 101 G1
Blenheim Wy ISLW TW7 136 B2
Blenhiem Ct ARCH N19 66 E6
Blenkarne Rd BTSEA SW11 160 E1
Bleriot Rd HEST TW5 134 B1
Blessbury Rd EDGW HA8 44 E4
Blessington Rd LEW SE13 145 G5
Blessing Wy BARK IG11 109 J1
Bletchingley Cl THHTH CR7 196 C1
Bletchley St IS N1 6 D3
Bletchmore Cl HYS/HAR UB3 113 G5
Bletsoe Wk IS N1 6 D2
Blincoe Cl WIM/MER SW19 159 G4
Blissett St GNWCH SE10 145 F2
Bliss Ms NKENS W10 100 C2
Blisworth Cl YEAD UB4 95 J3
Blithbury Rd DAGW RM9 91 H4
Blithdale Rd ABYW SE2 128 B4
Blithfield St KENS W8 120 A3
Blockley Rd ALP/SUD HA0 61 H6
Bloemfontein Av SHB W12 118 E1
Bloemfontein Rd SHB W12 99 K6
Blomfield Rd MV/WKIL W9 101 F4
Blomfield St LVPST EC2M 13 F2
Blomfield Vls BAY/PAD W2 101 F4
Blomville Rd BCTR RM8 74 A6
Blondell Cl WDR/YW UB7 112 A6
Blondel St BTSEA SW11 141 F3
Blondin Av EA W5 116 D4
Blondin St BOW E3 105 J1
Bloomfield Crs
GNTH/NBYPK IG2 72 B3
Bloomfield Pl
MYFR/PKLN W1K 9 K5
Bloomfield Rd HAYES BR2 200 C2
HGT N6 66 A3
KUT/HW KT1 191 F1
WOOL/PLUM SE18 127 G5
Bloomfield Ter BGVA SW1W 121 F5
Bloom Gv WNWD SE27 162 C5
Bloomhall Rd NRWD SE19 180 E1
Bloom Park Rd FUL/PGN SW6 139 J1
Bloomsbury Cl EA W5 98 B6
Bloomsbury Pl
NOXST/BSQ WC1A 11 F2
Bloomsbury Sq
NOXST/BSQ WC1A 11 F2
Bloomsbury St GWRST WC1E 10 D1
Bloomsbury Wy
NOXST/BSQ WC1A 10 E2
Blore Cl VX/NE SW8 141 J2
Blossom Cl DAGW RM9 92 B6
EA W5 117 F2
SAND/SEL CR2 212 B3
Blossom Dr ORP BR6 202 A6
Blossom La ENC/FH EN2 23 J2
Blossom St WCHPL E1 7 H7
Blossom Wy WDR/YW UB7 112 D4
Blossom Waye HEST TW5 114 D6
Blount St POP/IOD E14 105 G5
Bloxam Gdns ELTH/MOT SE9 146 D6
Bloxhall Rd LEY E10 69 H5
Bloxham Crs HPTN TW12 172 E4
Bloxworth Cl WLGTN SM6 210 C1
Blucher Rd CMBW SE5 142 D1
Blue Anchor La
BERM/RHTH SE16 123 H4
Blue Anchor Yd WCHPL E1 104 C6
Blue Ball Yd WHALL SW1A 16 A1
Bluebell Av MNPK E12 89 H3
Bluebell Cl HOM E9 86 E6
NTHLT UB5 77 K4
ORP BR6 201 H6
ROMW/RG RM7 75 G6
SYD SE26 163 G6
WLGTN SM6 195 G5
Bluebell Wy IL IG1 90 B4
Blueberry Cl WFD IG8 52 E2
Bluebird La DAGE RM10 92 C5
Bluebird Wy THMD SE28 127 J2
Bluefield Cl HPTN TW12 173 F1
Bluegates EW KT17 207 J5
Bluehouse Rd CHING E4 38 C5
Blue Lion Pl STHWK SE1 19 G4
Blue Riband Est
CROY/NA CR0 * 196 C6
Blundell Cl HACK E8 86 C2
Blundell Rd EDGW HA8 45 F4
Blundell St HOLWY N7 84 E5
Blunden Cl BCTR RM8 73 J5
Blunt Rd SAND/SEL CR2 211 K3
Blunts Av WDR/YW UB7 132 D1
Blunts Rd ELTH/MOT SE9 147 F6
Blurton Rd CLPT E5 87 F2
Blyth Cl TWK TW1 156 A1
Blythe Cl CAT SE6 164 C2
Blythe Hl CAT SE6 164 C2
STMC/STPC BR5 186 A4
Blythe Hill La CAT SE6 164 C2
Blythe Hill Pl FSTH SE23 * 164 B2
Blythe Ms WKENS W14 * 119 G3
Blythe Rd WKENS W14 119 G3
Blythe St BETH E2 * 104 D2
Blytheswood Pl
STRHM/NOR SW16 162 A6
Blythe V CAT SE6 164 C3
Blyth Rd BMLY BR1 183 J4
HYS/HAR UB3 113 H2
THMD SE28 109 J6
WALTH E17 69 H4
Blyth's Whf POP/IOD E14 * 105 G6
Blythswood Rd
GDMY/SEVK IG3 73 G5
Blythwood Rd FSBYPK N4 66 E4
PIN HA5 41 H4
Boadicea St IS N1 5 G1
Boakes Cl CDALE/KGS NW9 62 E1
Boardman Av CHING E4 25 K6
Boardman Cl BAR EN5 20 C6
Boardwalk Pl POP/IOD E14 125 F1
Boathouse Wk PECK SE15 143 G1
RCH/KEW TW9 136 E2
Boat Lifter Wy
BERM/RHTH SE16 124 B4
Boat Quay CAN/RD E16 107 G6
Bob Anker Cl PLSTW E13 106 E2
Bobbin Cl CLAP SW4 141 H4
Bob Dunn Wy DART DA1 151 K5
Bob Marley Wy HNHL SE24 142 B5
Bockhampton Rd
KUTN/CMB KT2 175 G3
Bocking St HACK E8 86 D6
Boddicott Cl WIM/MER SW19 159 H4
Boddington Gdns ACT W3 117 H2
Bodiam Cl EN EN1 23 K3
Bodiam Rd STRHM/NOR SW16 179 J4
Bodiam Wy WLSDN NW10 98 B2
Bodicea Ms HSLWW TW4 154 E1
Bodley Cl NWMAL KT3 192 B2
Bodley Rd NWMAL KT3 192 B3
Bodmin Cl RYLN/HDSTN HA2 77 K1
STMC/STPC BR5 202 D5
Bodmin Gv MRDN SM4 194 A1
Bodmin St WAND/EARL SW18 159 K3
Bodnant Gdns RYNPK SW20 176 D6
Bodney Rd CLPT E5 86 D3
Boeing Wy NWDGN UB2 114 A3
Bofors House CHARL SE7 * 146 D1
Bognor Gdns OXHEY WD19 41 G1
Bognor Rd WELL DA16 148 E2
Bohemia Pl HACK E8 86 E4
HOM E9 * 86 E4
Bohn Rd WCHPL E1 105 G4
Bohun Gv EBAR EN4 33 J1
Boileau Rd BARN SW13 138 D1
EA W5 98 B5
Bolberry Rd CRW RM5 57 F1
Bolden St DEPT SE8 144 E3
Boldero Pl STJWD NW8 * 2 C7
Bolderwood Wy WWKM BR4 198 E6
Boldmere Rd PIN HA5 59 G4
Boleyn Av EN EN1 24 D2
Boleyn Cl LOU IG10 39 J1
WALTH E17 69 J1
Boleyn Ct BKHH IG9 38 E3
Boleyn Dr E/WMO/HCT KT8 172 E6
RSLP HA4 59 H6
Boleyn Gdns DAGE RM10 92 E5
WWKM BR4 198 E6
Boleyn Rd EHAM E6 107 H1
FSTGT E7 88 E5
STNW/STAM N16 86 A3
Boleyn Wy BAR EN5 21 G4
BARK/HLT IG6 54 C2
Bolina Rd BERM/RHTH SE16 123 K5
Bolingbroke Gv BTSEA SW11 140 D6
Bolingbroke Rd WKENS W14 119 G3
Bolingbroke Wk
BTSEA SW11 * 140 C1
Bolingbroke Wy
HYS/HAR UB3 113 G1
Bollo Bridge Rd ACT W3 117 J3
Bollo La ACT W3 117 J3
Bolney Ga SKENS SW7 14 C3
Bolney St VX/NE SW8 142 A1
Bolsover St GTPST W1W 3 K7
Bolstead Rd MTCM CR4 179 G4
Bolster Gv WDGN N22 * 48 D4
Bolt Ct FLST/FETLN EC4A 11 K4
Boltmore Cl HDN NW4 46 B6
Bolton Cl CHSGTN KT9 205 K4
Bolton Crs LBTH SE11 122 B6
Bolton Dr MRDN SM4 194 B4
Bolton Gdns BMLY BR1 183 J2
ECT SW5 120 A5
TEDD TW11 174 B2
WLSDN NW10 100 B1
Bolton Gardens Ms
WBPTN SW10 120 A5
Bolton Pl IS N1 * 85 H5
Bolton Rd CHSGTN KT9 205 K4
CHSWK W4 137 K1
HRW HA1 60 C1
SRTFD E15 88 D4
STJWD NW8 83 F6
UED N18 50 B1
WLSDN NW10 81 G6
Bolton's La HYS/HAR UB3 133 F1
Boltons Pl ECT SW5 120 B5
The Boltons ALP/SUD HA0 79 F2
WBPTN SW10 * 120 B5
WFD IG8 * 38 E6
Bolton St MYFR/PICC W1J 9 K7
Bombay St BERM/RHTH SE16 123 J4
Bomer Cl WDR/YW UB7 132 D1
Bomore Rd NTGHL W11 100 B6
Bonar Pl CHST BR7 184 D3
Bonar Rd PECK SE15 143 H1
Bonchester Cl CHST BR7 185 F3
Bonchurch Cl BELMT SM2 209 F5
Bonchurch Rd NKENS W10 100 C4
WEA W13 116 C1
Bondfield Av YEAD UB4 94 E2
Bond Gdns WLGTN SM6 210 C2
Bond Rd MTCM CR4 178 E5
SURB KT6 191 G6
Bond St EA W5 97 K6
SRTFD E15 88 C3
Bondway VX/NE SW8 121 K6
Boneta Rd WOOL/PLUM SE18 126 E3
Bonfield Rd LEW SE13 145 F5
Bonham Gdns BCTR RM8 73 K6
Bonham Rd BCTR RM8 73 K6
BRXS/STRHM SW2 142 A6
Bonheur Rd CHSWK W4 118 A2
Bonhill St SDTCH EC2A 7 F7
Boniface Gdns
KTN/HRWW/WS HA3 42 B3
Boniface Wk
KTN/HRWW/WS HA3 42 B3
Bonita Ms PECK SE15 144 A4
Bonner Hill Rd KUT/HW KT1 175 G6
Bonner Rd BETH E2 104 E1
Bonnersfield Cl HRW HA1 61 G3
Bonnersfield La HRW HA1 61 F3
Bonner St BETH E2 * 104 E1
Bonneville Gdns CLAP SW4 161 H1
Bonnington Sq VX/NE SW8 122 A6
Bonny St CAMTN NW1 84 C5
Bonser Rd TWK TW1 156 A4
Bonsor St CMBW SE5 143 F1
Bonville Gdns HDN NW4 63 J1
Bonville Rd BMLY BR1 183 J1
Booker Cl POP/IOD E14 105 H4
Booker Rd UED N18 50 C1
Boones Rd LEW SE13 145 H5
Boone St LEW SE13 145 H5
Boord St GNWCH SE10 125 H3
Boothby Rd ARCH N19 66 D6
Booth Cl HOM E9 86 D6
THMD SE28 128 C1
Booth La BLKFR EC4V 12 C5
Booth Rd CDALE/KGS NW9 45 F4
CROY/NA CR0 * 196 C6
Boot Pde EDGW HA8 * 44 C2
Boot St FSBYE EC1V 7 G5
Bordars Rd HNWL W7 96 E4
Bordars Wk HNWL W7 96 E4
Borden Av EN EN1 35 K1
Border Crs SYD SE26 181 J1
Border Gdns CROY/NA CR0 213 K2
Border Ga MTCM CR4 178 D4
Border Rd SYD SE26 181 J1
Bordesley Rd MRDN SM4 194 A1
Bordon Wk PUT/ROE SW15 158 D2
Boreas Wk IS N1 6 B3
Boreham Av CAN/RD E16 106 E5
Boreham Cl WAN E11 70 A5
Boreham Rd WDGN N22 49 J4
Borgard House CHARL SE7 * 146 D1
Borgard Rd
WOOL/PLUM SE18 126 E4
Borkwood Pk ORP BR6 217 F2
Borkwood Wy ORP BR6 216 E2
Borland Rd PECK SE15 143 K5
TEDD TW11 174 C2
Borneo St PUT/ROE SW15 139 F4
Borough High St STHWK SE1 18 D3
Borough Hl CROY/NA CR0 211 H1
Borough Rd ISLW TW7 135 K2
KUTN/CMB KT2 175 H4
MTCM CR4 178 D5
STHWK SE1 18 A4
Borough Sq STHWK SE1 18 C3
Borrett Cl WALW SE17 122 D5
Borrodaile Rd
WAND/EARL SW18 160 A1
Borrowdale Av
KTN/HRWW/WS HA3 43 G5
Borrowdale Cl EFNCH N2 47 G5
REDBR IG4 71 J1
Borthwick Ms WAN E11 * 88 C2
Borthwick Rd
CDALE/KGS NW9 63 H3
SRTFD E15 88 C2
Borthwick St DEPT SE8 124 D5
Borwick Av WALTH E17 51 H6
Bosbury Rd CAT SE6 165 F5
Boscastle Rd KTTN NW5 84 B1
Boscobel Cl BMLY BR1 184 E5
Boscobel Pl BGVA SW1W 15 H6
Boscobel St BAY/PAD W2 8 B1
Boscombe Av LEY E10 70 B4
Boscombe Cl CLPT E5 87 G3
Boscombe Rd SHB W12 118 D2
TOOT SW17 179 F2
WIM/MER SW19 177 K4
WPK KT4 193 F5
Bose Cl FNCH N3 46 C4
Bosgrove CHING E4 38 A3
Boss St STHWK SE1 19 J2
Bostall Heath ABYW SE2 * 128 D5
Bostall Hl ABYW SE2 128 C5
Bostall La ABYW SE2 128 C5
Bostall Manorway ABYW SE2 128 C4
Bostall Park Av BXLYHN DA7 149 F1
Bostall Rd STMC/STPC BR5 186 C3
Boston Gdns BTFD TW8 116 B4
CHSWK W4 118 B6
Boston Gv RSLP HA4 58 A3
Boston Manor Rd BTFD TW8 116 B4
Boston Pde HNWL W7 * 116 B4
Boston Park Rd BTFD TW8 * 116 D6
Boston Pl CAMTN NW1 2 E7
Boston Rd CROY/NA CR0 196 A3
EDGW HA8 44 E3
EHAM E6 107 J2
HNWL W7 115 K1
WALTH E17 69 J3
Bostonthorpe Rd HNWL W7 * 115 K2
Boston V HNWL W7 116 B4
Boswell Cl STMC/STPC BR5 202 D3
Boswell Ct BMSBY WC1N 11 F1
Boswell Rd THHTH CR7 196 D1
Boswell St BMSBY WC1N 11 F1
Bosworth Cl WALTH E17 51 H4
Bosworth Rd BAR EN5 20 E4
DAGE RM10 92 C2
FBAR/BDGN N11 48 D2
NKENS W10 100 C3
Botany Bay La CHST BR7 185 H5
Botany Cl EBAR EN4 21 J5
Botany Ter PUR RM19 * 131 K5
Boteley Cl CHING E4 38 B4
Botham Cl EDGW HA8 44 E3
Botha Rd PLSTW E13 107 F4
Bothwell Cl CAN/RD E16 106 E4
Bothwell St HMSMTH W6 119 G6

Botolph Aly MON EC3R 13 C6
Botolph La MON EC3R 13 C6
Botsford Rd RYNPK SW20 177 H5
Bottonscroft Cl THHTH CR7 180 D6
Bott Rd RDART DA2 171 J6
Bott's Ms BAY/PAD W2 100 E5
Botwell Common Rd
HYS/HAR UB3 94 B6
Botwell Crs HYS/HAR UB3 94 C5
Botwell La HYS/HAR UB3 113 J2
Boucher Cl TEDD TW11 174 A1
Boughton Av HAYES BR2 199 J4
Boughton Rd THMD SE28 127 K3
Boulcott St WCHPL E1 105 F5
Boulevard Dr
CDALE/KGS NW9 45 H5
The Boulevard FUL/PGN SW6 140 B3
WFD IG8 54 A2
Boulogne Rd CROY/NA CR0 196 D3
Boulter Cl BMLY BR1 185 F6
Boulter Gdns RAIN RM13 93 J4
Boulton Rd BCTR RM8 74 A6
Boultwood Rd EHAM E6 107 K5
Bounces La ED N9 36 D4
Bounces Rd ED N9 36 D4
Boundaries Rd BAL SW12 160 E4
FELT TW13 154 B3
Boundary Av WALTH E17 69 H4
Boundary Business Ct
MTCM CR4 178 C6
Boundary Cl BAR EN5 20 D2
GDMY/SEVK IG3 90 E2
KUT/HW KT1 175 H6
NWDGN UB2 115 F5
Boundary La CMBW SE5 122 D6
PLSTW E13 107 H2
Boundary Ms STJWD NW8 83 G6
Boundary Pass WCHPL E1 7 J6
Boundary Rd BARK IG11 108 C1
BFN/LL DA15 147 K6
CAR SM5 210 A6
ED N9 36 E1
EFNCH N2 47 H4
PIN HA5 59 H3
PLSTW E13 107 G1
ROM RM1 75 J3
WALTH E17 69 H4
WBLY HA9 80 A1
WDGN N22 49 H6
WIM/MER SW19 178 C2
WLGTN SM6 210 B4
Boundary Rw STHWK SE1 18 A2
Boundary St BETH E2 7 J5
ERITH DA8 150 C1
Boundary Wy CROY/NA CR0 213 J3
Boundfield Rd CAT SE6 165 H5
Bounds Green Rd
FBAR/BDGN N11 48 D2
Bourchier St SOHO/SHAV W1D 10 C5
Bourdon Pl MYFR/PKLN W1K 9 K5
Bourdon Rd PGE/AN SE20 181 K5
Bourdon St MYFR/PKLN W1K 9 J6
Bourke Cl CLAP SW4 161 K1
WLSDN NW10 81 G4
Bourlet Cl GTPST W1W 10 A2
Bourn Av EBAR EN4 21 H6
SEVS/STOTM N15 67 K1
Bournbrook Rd
BKHTH/KID SE3 146 C4
Bourne Av HYS/HAR UB3 113 F3
RSLP HA4 77 G3
STHGT/OAK N14 34 E4
Bourne Cl ISLW TW7 135 K4
THDIT KT7 190 A6
Bourne Ct RSLP HA4 77 F3
Bourne Dr MTCM CR4 178 C6
Bourne End Rd NTHWD HA6 26 C6
Bourne Est HCIRC EC1N * 11 J1
Bourne Gdns CHING E4 37 K6
Bournehall BUSH WD23 * 28 A1
Bournehall La BUSH WD23 28 A1
Bournehall Rd BUSH WD23 28 A1
Bourne Hl PLMGR N13 34 E4
Bourne Hill Cl PLMGR N13 * 35 F4
Bournemead BUSH WD23 28 A1
Bourne Md BXLY DA5 149 K6
Bournemead Av NTHLT UB5 94 E1
Bournemead Cl NTHLT UB5 94 E2
Bournemouth Cl PECK SE15 143 H3
Bournemouth Rd PECK SE15 143 H3
WIM/MER SW19 177 K4
Bourne Pde BXLY DA5 * 169 J2
Bourne Rd BXLY DA5 169 J1
CEND/HSY/T N8 66 E3
HAYES BR2 200 C1
WAN E11 88 D1
Bourneside Crs
STHGT/OAK N14 34 D3
Bourneside Gdns CAT SE6 183 F1
Bourne St BGVA SW1W 15 G7
CROY/NA CR0 196 C6
Bourne Ter BAY/PAD W2 101 F4
The Bourne STHGT/OAK N14 34 D3
Bourne V HAYES BR2 199 K5
Bournevale Rd
STRHM/NOR SW16 161 K6
Bourne Vw GFD/PVL UB6 79 F4
Bourne Wy HAYES BR2 199 K6
HOR/WEW KT19 206 E2
SUT SM1 208 D3
SWLY BR8 187 K6
Bournewood Rd
STMC/STPC BR5 202 C4
WOOL/PLUM SE18 148 B1
Bournville Rd CAT SE6 164 D2
Bournwell Cl EBAR EN4 21 K3
Bourton Cl HYS/HAR UB3 113 K1
Bousfield Rd NWCR SE14 144 A3
Boutflower Rd BTSEA SW11 140 D6
Boutique Hall LEW SE13 * 145 F5
Bouverie Gdns
KTN/HRWW/WS HA3 61 K3
Bouverie Ms STNW/STAM N16 68 A6
Bouverie Pl BAY/PAD W2 8 B3
Bouverie Rd HRW HA1 60 C3
STNW/STAM N16 68 A6
Bouverie St EMB EC4Y 11 K4
Bouvier Rd PEND EN3 24 E1
Boveney Rd FSTH SE23 164 A2
Bovill Rd FSTH SE23 164 A2
Bovingdon Av WBLY HA9 80 C4
Bovingdon La
CDALE/KGS NW9 45 G4
Bovingdon Rd FUL/PGN SW6 140 A2
Bovington Cl ARCH N19 66 C6
Bow Arrow La DART DA1 171 K1
Bowater Cl BRXS/STRHM SW2 161 K1
CDALE/KGS NW9 63 F2
Bowater Gdns SUN TW16 172 B4
Bowater Pl BKHTH/KID SE3 146 A1
Bowater Rd WBLY HA9 80 D1
WOOL/PLUM SE18 126 C3
Bow Bridge Est BOW E3 105 K2
Bow Churchyard STP EC4M * 12 D4
Bow Common La BOW E3 105 H3
Bowden Cl EBED/NFELT TW14 153 H3
Bowden St LBTH SE11 122 B5
Bowditch DEPT SE8 124 C5
Bowdon Rd WALTH E17 69 J4
Bowen Dr DUL SE21 163 F5
Bowen Rd HRW HA1 60 C4
Bowen St POP/IOD E14 105 K5
Bowens Wd CROY/NA CR0 * 213 H6
Bower Av GNWCH SE10 145 H2
Bower Cl CRW RM5 57 F3
NTHLT UB5 95 G1
Bowerdean St FUL/PGN SW6 140 A2
Bowerman Av NWCR SE14 124 B6
Bower St WCHPL E1 * 105 F5
Bowes Cl BFN/LL DA15 168 C1
Bowes Rd ACT W3 99 G6
BCTR RM8 91 J2
FBAR/BDGN N11 48 B1
PLMGR N13 48 E1
WOT/HER KT12 188 A6
Bowfell Rd HMSMTH W6 119 F6
Bowford Av BXLYHN DA7 149 F2
Bowhill Cl BRXN/ST SW9 142 B1
Bowie Cl CLAP SW4 161 J2
Bowland Rd CLAP SW4 141 J5
WFD IG8 53 G2
Bowland Yd KTBR SW1X * 15 F3
Bow La NFNCH/WDSPK N12 47 G3
STP EC4M 12 D4
Bowl Ct WCHPL E1 7 H7
Bowley Cl NRWD SE19 181 G2
Bowley La NRWD SE19 181 G1
Bowley St POP/IOD E14 105 H6
Bowling Green Cl
PUT/ROE SW15 158 E2
Bowling Green Ct WBLY HA9 62 B6
Bowling Green La
CLKNW EC1R 5 K7
Bowling Green Pl
STHWK SE1 * 18 E2
Bowling Green Rw
WOOL/PLUM SE18 * 126 E4
Bowling Green St LBTH SE11 122 B6
Bowling Green Wk IS N1 7 G4
Bow Locks BOW E3 * 106 A3
Bowls Cl STAN HA7 43 H1
Bowman Av CAN/RD E16 106 E5
Bowman Ms
WAND/EARL SW18 159 J3
Bowmans Cl WEA W13 116 C1
Bowmans Lea FSTH SE23 163 K2
Bowman's Meadow
WLGTN SM6 210 B1
Bowmans Ms WCHPL E1 104 C6
Bowman's Ms HOLWY N7 84 E1
Bowman's Pl HOLWY N7 84 E1
Bowmans Rd DART DA1 170 C2
Bowmead ELTH/MOT SE9 166 E4
Bowmore Wk CAMTN NW1 84 D5
Bowness Cl HACK E8 * 86 B4
Bowness Crs PUT/ROE SW15 176 A1
Bowness Dr HSLWW TW4 134 D5
Bowness Rd BXLYHN DA7 149 J3
CAT SE6 164 E2
Bowness Wy HCH RM12 93 J3
Bowood Rd CLAP SW4 141 F5
PEND EN3 25 F3
Bowring Gn OXHEY WD19 41 G1
Bow Rd BOW E3 105 J2
Bowrons Av ALP/SUD HA0 79 K5
Bowsley Ct FELT TW13 153 K4
Bow St COVGDN WC2E 11 F4
SRTFD E15 88 C3
Bowyer Cl EHAM E6 107 K4
Bowyer Pl CMBW SE5 142 E1
Bowyers Ct TWK TW1 136 C5
Bowyer St CMBW SE5 142 D1
Boxall Rd DUL SE21 163 F1
Boxelder Cl EDGW HA8 44 E3
Boxgrove Rd ABYW SE2 128 C2
Box La BARK IG11 109 H1
Boxley Rd MRDN SM4 194 B1
Boxley St CAN/RD E16 126 A1
Boxmoor Rd CRW RM5 56 E1
KTN/HRWW/WS HA3 61 H1
Boxoll Rd DAGW RM9 92 B2
Boxted Cl BKHH IG9 39 J3
Boxtree La
KTN/HRWW/WS HA3 42 C4
Boxtree Rd
KTN/HRWW/WS HA3 42 D3
Boxwood Cl WDR/YW UB7 112 C2
Boxworth Cl
NFNCH/WDSPK N12 47 H1
Boxworth Gv IS N1 85 F6
Boyard Rd WOOL/PLUM SE18 127 G5
Boyce Wy PLSTW E13 106 E3
Boycroft Av CDALE/KGS NW9 62 E3
Boyd Av STHL UB1 114 E1
Boyd Cl KUTN/CMB KT2 175 H3
Boydell Ct STJWD NW8 83 H5
Boyd Rd WIM/MER SW19 178 C2
Boyd St WCHPL E1 104 C5
Boyfield St STHWK SE1 18 B3
Boyland Rd BMLY BR1 183 J1
Boyle Av STAN HA7 43 G2
Boyle Farm Rd THDIT KT7 190 B3
Boyne Av HDN NW4 64 B1
Boyne Rd DAGE RM10 92 C1
LEW SE13 145 G4
Boyne Terrace Ms NTGHL W11 119 J1
Boyton Cl CEND/HSY/T N8 48 E6
WCHPL E1 105 F3
Boyton Rd CEND/HSY/T N8 48 E6
Brabant Rd WDGN N22 49 F5
Brabazon Av WLGTN SM6 210 E5
Brabazon Rd HEST TW5 134 B1
NTHLT UB5 96 A1
Brabazon St POP/IOD E14 105 K5
Brabourne Cl NRWD SE19 181 F1
Brabourne Crs BXLYHN DA7 129 G6
Brabourne Ri BECK BR3 199 G2
Brabourn Gv PECK SE15 143 K3
Bracewell Av GFD/PVL UB6 79 F3
Bracewell Rd NKENS W10 100 A4
Bracewood Gdns
CROY/NA CR0 212 B1
Bracey St FSBYPK N4 * 66 E6
Bracken Av BAL SW12 161 F1
CROY/NA CR0 213 J1
Brackenbridge Dr RSLP HA4 77 H1
Brackenbury Gdns
HMSMTH W6 118 E3
Brackenbury Rd EFNCH N2 47 G6
HMSMTH W6 118 E3
Bracken Cl EHAM E6 107 K4
WHTN TW2 155 F2
Brackendale WCHMH N21 35 F4
Brackendale Cl HSLW TW3 135 G2
Brackendene RDART DA2 170 B6
Bracken Dr CHIG IG7 54 B2
Bracken End ISLW TW7 135 J6
Bracken Gdns BARN SW13 138 D3
Brackenhill RSLP HA4 * 77 J2
Bracken Hill Cl BMLY BR1 183 J4
Bracken Hill La BMLY BR1 183 J4
Bracken Ms ROMW/RG RM7 74 C3
The Brackens EN EN1 36 A2
ORP BR6 217 G3
The Bracken CHING E4 38 A4
Brackley Av PECK SE15 143 K4
Brackley Cl WLGTN SM6 210 E5
Brackley Rd BECK BR3 182 C3
CHSWK W4 118 B4
Brackley Sq WFD IG8 53 H3
Brackley St BARB EC2Y 12 D1
Brackley Ter CHSWK W4 118 B5
Bracklyn St IS N1 6 E2
Bracknell Cl WDGN N22 49 G4
Bracknell Gdns HAMP NW3 83 F3
Bracknell Wy HAMP NW3 83 F2
Bracondale ESH/CLAY KT10 204 C3
Bracondale Rd ABYW SE2 128 B4
Bracton La RDART DA2 170 C4
Bradbourne Rd BXLY DA5 169 H2
Bradbourne St FUL/PGN SW6 139 K3
Bradbury Cl NWDGN UB2 114 E4
Bradbury St STNW/STAM N16 86 A3
Braddock Cl CRW RM5 56 E2
ISLW TW7 136 A4
Braddon Ct BAR EN5 * 20 C4
Braddon Rd RCH/KEW TW9 137 G4
Braddyll St GNWCH SE10 125 H5
Bradenham Av WELL DA16 148 B5
Bradenham Cl WALW SE17 122 E6
Bradenham Rd
KTN/HRWW/WS HA3 61 H1
YEAD UB4 94 C2
Braden St MV/WKIL W9 101 F3
Bradfield Dr BARK IG11 91 G3
Bradfield Rd CAN/RD E16 125 K2
RSLP HA4 77 J3
Bradford Cl HAYES BR2 200 E5
SYD SE26 163 J6
TOTM N17 50 B2
Bradford Dr HOR/WEW KT19 207 H4
Bradford Rd ACT W3 118 B2
IL IG1 72 D5
Bradfords Cl BKHH IG9 39 H6
Bradgate Rd CAT SE6 164 E1
Brading Crs WAN E11 71 F6
Brading Rd BRXS/STRHM SW2 162 A2
CROY/NA CR0 196 A3
Brading Ter SHB W12 118 D3
Bradiston Rd MV/WKIL W9 100 D2
Bradley Cl HOLWY N7 84 E5
Bradley Gdns WEA W13 97 H5
Bradley Rd NRWD SE19 180 D2
PEND EN3 25 G1
WDGN N22 49 F5
Bradley's Cl IS N1 5 J2
Bradley Stone Rd EHAM E6 107 K5
Bradman Rw EDGW HA8 * 44 E3
Bradmead VX/NE SW8 * 141 G2
Bradmore Park Rd
HMSMTH W6 118 E3
Bradshaw Cl WIM/MER SW19 177 K2
Bradshaw Cots
POP/IOD E14 * 105 G5
Bradshaws Cl SNWD SE25 181 H6
Bradstock Rd EW KT17 207 K3
HOM E9 87 F4
Brad St STHWK SE1 17 K1
Bradwell Av DAGE RM10 74 C6
Bradwell Cl HCH RM12 93 K4
SWFD E18 70 D1
Bradwell Ms UED N18 36 C6
Bradwell Rd BKHH IG9 39 J3
Bradwell St WCHPL E1 105 F2
Brady Dr BMLY BR1 185 F6
Bradymead EHAM E6 108 A5
Brady St WCHPL E1 104 D3
Braemar Av ALP/SUD HA0 79 K5
BXLYHN DA7 149 K5
THHTH CR7 180 B6
WDGN N22 48 E4
WIM/MER SW19 159 K4
WLSDN NW10 81 F1
Braemar Gdns BFN/LL DA15 167 J5
CDALE/KGS NW9 45 F4
WWKM BR4 199 F5
Braemar Rd BTFD TW8 116 E6
PLSTW E13 106 D3
SEVS/STOTM N15 68 A2
WPK KT4 207 K1
Braeside BECK BR3 182 D1
Braeside Av RYNPK SW20 177 H4
Braeside Cl PIN HA5 42 A3
Braeside Crs BXLYHN DA7 149 K5
Braeside Rd
STRHM/NOR SW16 179 H3
Braes St IS N1 85 H5
Braesyde Cl BELV DA17 129 G4
Brafferton Rd CROY/NA CR0 211 J2
Braganza St WALW SE17 122 C5
Bragg Cl BCTR RM8 91 H4
Bragg Rd TEDD TW11 173 K3
Braham St WCHPL E1 13 K4
Braid Av ACT W3 99 G5
Braid Cl FELT TW13 154 E4
Braidwood Rd CAT SE6 165 G3
Braidwood St STHWK SE1 19 G1
Brailsford Cl WIM/MER SW19 178 D3
Brailsford Rd
BRXS/STRHM SW2 162 B1
Brainton Av
EBED/NFELT TW14 154 A2
Braintree Av REDBR IG4 71 J2
Braintree Rd DAGE RM10 92 C1
RSLP HA4 77 F2
Braintree St BETH E2 * 104 E2
Braithwaite Av
ROMW/RG RM7 74 C4
Braithwaite Gdns STAN HA7 43 J4
Braithwaite Rd PEND EN3 25 H4
Bramall Cl SRTFD E15 88 D3
Bramber Ct EA W5 117 F4
Bramber Rd
NFNCH/WDSPK N12 47 J1
WKENS W14 119 J6
Bramble Acres Cl BELMT SM2 208 E5
Bramble Banks CAR SM5 210 A6
Bramblebury Rd
WOOL/PLUM SE18 127 J5
Bramble Cl BECK BR3 199 F2
CROY/NA CR0 213 J2
SEVS/STOTM N15 68 C1
STAN HA7 43 K3
THHTH CR7 180 E4
Bramble Cft ERITH DA8 129 K4
Brambledown Cl WWKM BR4 199 H3
Brambledown Rd CAR SM5 210 A5
SAND/SEL CR2 212 A5
Bramble Gdns SHB W12 99 H6
Bramble La HPTN TW12 172 E2
Brambles Cl ISLW TW7 136 C1
The Brambles CHIG IG7 54 C2
SUT SM1 * 194 C6
WDR/YW UB7 112 A5
WIM/MER SW19 * 177 J1
Bramblewood Cl CAR SM5 194 D5
The Bramblings CHING E4 38 B6
Bramcote Av MTCM CR4 194 E1
Bramcote Gv
BERM/RHTH SE16 123 K5
Bramcote Rd PUT/ROE SW15 138 E5
Bramdean Crs LEE/GVPK SE12 165 K3
Bramdean Gdns
LEE/GVPK SE12 165 K3
Bramerton Rd BECK BR3 182 C6
Bramerton St CHEL SW3 120 D6
Bramfield Rd BTSEA SW11 160 D1
Bramford Rd
WAND/EARL SW18 140 B5
Bramham Ct NTHWD HA6 * 40 C1
Bramham Gdns CHSGTN KT9 * 205 K3
ECT SW5 120 A5
Bramhope La CHARL SE7 126 A6
Bramlands Cl BTSEA SW11 140 D4
Bramley Cl HYS/HAR UB3 94 E6
MLHL NW7 31 G5
ORP BR6 201 G5
PIN HA5 40 D6
SAND/SEL CR2 211 H3
STHGT/OAK N14 22 B6
WALTH E17 51 G5
WFD IG8 53 G3
WHTN TW2 155 H1
Bramley Crs GNTH/NBYPK IG2 72 A3
VX/NE SW8 141 J1
Bramley Gdns OXHEY WD19 41 G2
Bramley Hl SAND/SEL CR2 211 J2
Bramley Hyrst
SAND/SEL CR2 * 211 J3
Bramley Ldg ALP/SUD HA0 79 K2
Bramley Pde
STHGT/OAK N14 22 C5
Bramley Pl DART DA1 150 D5
Bramley Rd BELMT SM2 208 B6
EA W5 116 D3
NKENS W10 100 B6
STHGT/OAK N14 22 B6
SUT SM1 209 H3
Bramley Wy HSLWW TW4 134 E6
WWKM BR4 198 E6
Brampton Cl CLPT E5 68 D6
Brampton Gv HDN NW4 63 K1
KTN/HRWW/WS HA3 61 G1
WBLY HA9 62 C5
Brampton La HDN NW4 64 A1
Brampton Park Rd
WDGN N22 49 G6
Brampton Rd BXLYHN DA7 148 E4
CDALE/KGS NW9 62 C1
CROY/NA CR0 197 G4
EHAM E6 107 H3
OXHEY WD19 26 E5
SEVS/STOTM N15 67 J2
Bramshaw Gdns
OXHEY WD19 41 H1
Bramshaw Ri NWMAL KT3 192 B3
Bramshaw Rd HOM E9 87 F4
Bramshill Gdns KTTN NW5 84 B1
Bramshill Rd WLSDN NW10 99 G1
Bramshot Av CHARL SE7 126 A6
Bramshot Wy OXHEY WD19 26 E4
Bramston Cl BARK/HLT IG6 55 F2
Bramston Rd MTCM CR4 178 E3
WLSDN NW10 99 J1
Bramwell Cl SUN TW16 172 C5
Bramwell Ms IS N1 85 F6
Brancaster Dr MLHL NW7 45 J3
Brancaster Rd
GNTH/NBYPK IG2 72 D3
STRHM/NOR SW16 161 K5
Brancepeth Gdns BKHH IG9 38 E4
Branch Hl HAMP NW3 83 G1
Branch Rd BARK/HLT IG6 55 H1
POP/IOD E14 105 G5
Branch St CMBW SE5 143 F1
Brancker Rd
KTN/HRWW/WS HA3 43 K6
Brancroft Wy PEND EN3 25 G2
Brand Cl FSBYPK N4 67 H5
Brandesbury Sq WFD IG8 54 A3
Brandlehow Rd
PUT/ROE SW15 139 J5
Brandon Est WALW SE17 122 C6
Brandon Ms BARB EC2Y * 12 E1
Brandon Rd DART DA1 171 K2
HOLWY N7 84 E5
NWDGN UB2 114 E5
SUT SM1 209 F2
WALTH E17 70 A1
Brandon St WALW SE17 18 D6
Brandram Ms LEW SE13 * 145 H5
Brandram Rd LEW SE13 145 H4
Brandreth Ct HRW HA1 * 61 F3
Brandreth Rd EHAM E6 107 K5
TOOT SW17 161 G4
The Brandries WLGTN SM6 210 D1
Brand St GNWCH SE10 145 F1
Brandville Gdns BARK/HLT IG6 72 B1
Brandville Rd WDR/YW UB7 112 B2
Brandy Wy BELMT SM2 208 E5
Brangbourne Rd BMLY BR1 183 F1
Brangton Rd LBTH SE11 122 A5
Brangwyn Crs
WIM/MER SW19 178 C4
Branksea St FUL/PGN SW6 139 H1
Branksome Av UED N18 50 B2
Branksome Cl TEDD TW11 155 J6
WOT/HER KT12 188 C6
Branksome Rd
BRXS/STRHM SW2 141 K6
WIM/MER SW19 177 K4
Branksome Wy
KTN/HRWW/WS HA3 62 B3
NWMAL KT3 175 K5
Bransby Rd CHSGTN KT9 206 A5
Branscombe Gdns
WCHMH N21 35 G2
Branscombe St LEW SE13 144 E4
Bransdale Cl
KIL/WHAMP NW6 82 E6
Bransell Cl SWLY BR8 203 J3
Bransgrove Rd EDGW HA8 44 B4
Branston Crs STMC/STPC BR5 201 J5
Branstone Rd RCH/KEW TW9 137 G2
Brants Wk HNWL W7 96 E3
Brantwood Av ERITH DA8 149 K1
ISLW TW7 136 B5
Brantwood Cl WALTH E17 * 51 K6
Brantwood Gdns ENC/FH EN2 22 E5
REDBR IG4 71 J2
Brantwood Rd BXLYHN DA7 149 J3
HNHL SE24 142 D6
SAND/SEL CR2 211 J6
TOTM N17 50 C2
Brantwood Wy
STMC/STPC BR5 186 D6
Brasenose Dr BARN SW13 119 F6
Brasher Cl GFD/PVL UB6 78 D3
Brassey Cl
EBED/NFELT TW14 * 153 K3
Brassey Rd KIL/WHAMP NW6 82 D4
Brassey Sq BTSEA SW11 141 F4
Brassie Av ACT W3 99 G5
Brasted Cl BXLYHS DA6 148 E6
SYD SE26 163 K6
Brasted Rd ERITH DA8 150 B1
Brathway Rd
WAND/EARL SW18 159 K2
Braund Av GFD/PVL UB6 96 B3
Braundton Av BFN/LL DA15 168 A3
Braunston Dr YEAD UB4 95 J3
Bravington Pl MV/WKIL W9 100 D3
Bravington Rd MV/WKIL W9 100 D2
Bravingtons Wk IS N1 5 F3
Braxfield Rd BROCKY SE4 144 B5
Braxted Pk
STRHM/NOR SW16 180 A2
Brayard's Rd PECK SE15 143 J3
Braybourne Dr ISLW TW7 136 A1
Braybrooke Gdns NRWD SE19 181 F3
Braybrook St SHB W12 99 H4
Brayburne Av VX/NE SW8 141 H3
Braycourt Av WOT/HER KT12 188 B4
Bray Crs BERM/RHTH SE16 124 A2
Braydon Rd STNW/STAM N16 68 B5
Bray Dr CAN/RD E16 106 D6
Brayfield Ter IS N1 85 G5
Brayford Sq WCHPL E1 * 104 E5
Bray Pl CHEL SW3 120 E5
Bray Rd MLHL NW7 46 B2
Brayton Gdns ENC/FH EN2 22 D5
Braywood Rd ELTH/MOT SE9 147 J5
Brazier Crs NTHLT UB5 95 K3
Brazil Cl CROY/NA CR0 195 K4
Breach La DAGW RM9 110 C2
Bread St STP EC4M 12 D4
Breakspears Dr
STMC/STPC BR5 186 B4
Breakspears Ms BROCKY SE4 144 D3
Breakspears Rd BROCKY SE4 144 C4
Bream Cl TOTM N17 68 D1
Bream Gdns EHAM E6 108 A2
Breamore Cl PUT/ROE SW15 158 D3
Breamore Rd
GDMY/SEVK IG3 73 F6
Bream's Blds LINN WC2A 11 J3
Bream St BOW E3 87 J5
Breamwater Gdns
RCHPK/HAM TW10 156 C5
Brearley Cl EDGW HA8 44 E3
Breasley Cl PUT/ROE SW15 138 E5
Breasy Pl HDN NW4 * 63 K1
Brechin Pl SKENS SW7 120 B4
Brecknock Rd ARCH N19 84 C2
Brecknock Road Est
ARCH N19 * 84 D3
Brecon Cl MTCM CR4 195 K1
WPK KT4 193 F6
Brecon Gn CDALE/KGS NW9 * 63 G3
Brecon Ms KTTN NW5 84 D4
Brecon Rd HMSMTH W6 119 H6
PEND EN3 24 E5
Brede Cl EHAM E6 108 A2
Bredgar Rd ARCH N19 66 B6
Bredhurst Cl PGE/AN SE20 181 K2
Bredon Rd CROY/NA CR0 197 G4
Breer St FUL/PGN SW6 140 A4
Breezer's Hl WAP E1W * 104 C6
Bremans Rw
WAND/EARL SW18 160 B4

Brember Rd
RYLN/HDSTN HA2 60 C6
Bremer Ms WALTH E17 69 K1
Bremner Rd SKENS SW7 * 120 B3
Brenchley Cl CHST BR7 185 F4
HAYES BR2 199 J2
Brenchley Gdns EDUL SE22 163 K1
Brenchley Rd STMC/STPC BR5 185 K4
Brenda Rd TOOT SW17 160 E4
Brende Gdns
E/WMO/HCT KT8 189 G1
Brendon SCUP DA14 * 168 B6
Brendon Av WLSDN NW10 81 G2
Brendon Cl ERITH DA8 150 B2
ESH/CLAY KT10 204 C4
HYS/HAR UB3 133 F1
Brendon Dr ESH/CLAY KT10 204 C4
Brendon Gdns
RYLN/HDSTN HA2 78 B2
Brendon Gv EFNCH N2 47 G5
Brendon Rd BCTR RM8 74 B5
ELTH/MOT SE9 167 J4
Brendon St MBLAR W1H 8 D3
Brendon Vls WCHMH N21 * 35 J3
Brendon Wy EN EN1 36 A2
Brenley Cl MTCM CR4 179 F6
Brenley Gdns ELTH/MOT SE9 146 C5
Brent Cl BXLY DA5 169 F3
Brentcot Cl WEA W13 97 H3
Brent Crs WLSDN NW10 98 B1
Brent Cross F/O HDN NW4 64 A3
Brentfield WLSDN NW10 80 D5
Brentfield Cl WLSDN NW10 81 F4
Brentfield Gdns CRICK NW2 * 64 B4
Brentfield Rd DART DA1 171 K1
WLSDN NW10 81 F4
Brentford Cl YEAD UB4 95 H3
Brent Gn HDN NW4 64 A2
Brentham Wy EA W5 97 K3
Brenthouse Rd HACK E8 86 D5
Brenthurst Rd WLSDN NW10 81 H4
Brentlands Dr DART DA1 171 K3
Brent La DART DA1 171 J2
Brent Lea BTFD TW8 136 D1
Brentmead Cl HNWL W7 96 E6
Brentmead Gdns
WLSDN NW10 98 B1
Brenton St POP/IOD E14 105 G5
Brent Park Rd
CDALE/KGS NW9 63 J5
HDN NW4 63 K4
Brent Pl BAR EN5 20 D6
Brent River Park Wk
HNWL W7 96 D4
Brent Rd BTFD TW8 116 D6
CAN/RD E16 106 E5
NWDGN UB2 114 B3
SAND/SEL CR2 212 D6
WOOL/PLUM SE18 147 G1
Brentside BTFD TW8 116 D6
Brentside Cl WEA W13 97 F3
Brent St HDN NW4 64 A1
Brent Ter CRICK NW2 64 A6
The Brent DART DA1 171 K2
Brentvale Av ALP/SUD HA0 80 B6
STHL UB1 115 J1
Brent View Rd
CDALE/KGS NW9 63 J5
Brent Wy BTFD TW8 136 E1
FNCH N3 46 E2
WBLY HA9 80 D4
Brentwick Gdns BTFD TW8 117 F4
Brentwood Cl ELTH/MOT SE9 167 H3
Brentwood Rd ROM RM1 75 H3
Brereton Rd TOTM N17 50 B3
Bressay Dr MLHL NW7 45 J3
Bressenden Pl WESTW SW1E 15 K4
Bressey Av EN EN1 24 C2
Bressey Gv SWFD E18 52 D5
Brett Cl NTHLT UB5 95 H2
STNW/STAM N16 68 A6
Brett Crs WLSDN NW10 81 F6
Brettell St WALW SE17 122 E5
Brettenham Av WALTH E17 51 J4
Brettenham Rd UED N18 36 C6
WALTH E17 51 J5
Brett Gdns DAGW RM9 92 A5
Brett Pas HACK E8 86 D3
Brett Rd BAR EN5 20 A6
HACK E8 86 D3
Brett Vls ACT W3 * 99 F4
Brewers Fld RDART DA2 171 F6
Brewer St REGST W1B 10 B5
Brewery Cl ALP/SUD HA0 79 G3
Brewery Rd HAYES BR2 200 D5
HOLWY N7 84 E5
WOOL/PLUM SE18 127 J5
Brewery Sq FSBYE EC1V 6 B7
STHWK SE1 19 J1
Brewhouse La WAP E1W 123 J1
Brewhouse Rd
WOOL/PLUM SE18 126 E4
Brewhouse St PUT/ROE SW15 139 H5
Brewhouse Wk
BERM/RHTH SE16 124 B1
Brewhouse Yd FSBYE EC1V 6 A6
Brewood Rd BCTR RM8 91 H4
Brewster Gdns NKENS W10 100 A4
Brewster Rd LEY E10 69 K5
Brian Cl HCH RM12 93 K2
Brian Rd CHDH RM6 73 J2
Briants Cl PIN HA5 41 J4
Briant St NWCR SE14 144 A2
Briar Av STRHM/NOR SW16 180 A3
Briar Bank CAR SM5 210 A6
Briarbank Rd WEA W13 97 G5
Briar Cl BKHH IG9 39 H4
EFNCH N2 47 G5
HPTN TW12 172 E1
ISLW TW7 136 A6
PLMGR N13 35 J5
Briar Crs NTHLT UB5 78 B4
Briardale Gdns HAMP NW3 82 E1
Briarfield Av EFNCH N2 47 F6
Briarfield Cl BXLYHN DA7 149 H3
Briar Gdns HAYES BR2 199 J5
Briar La CAR SM5 210 A6
CROY/NA CR0 213 K2
Briar Rd BXLY DA5 170 A5
CRICK NW2 82 A2
KTN/HRWW/WS HA3 61 J2
STRHM/NOR SW16 179 K6
WHTN TW2 155 K3
Briarswood Wy ORP BR6 217 F3
Briar Wk EDGW HA8 44 E3
NKENS W10 * 100 C3
PUT/ROE SW15 138 E5
Briar Wy WDR/YW UB7 112 D2
Briarwood Cl
CDALE/KGS NW9 * 62 E3
FELT TW13 153 H5
Briar Wood Cl HAYES BR2 200 D6
Briarwood Ct WPK KT4 * 192 D5
Briarwood Dr NTHWD HA6 40 E5
Briarwood Rd CLAP SW4 141 J6
EW KT17 207 J4
Briary Cl EDGW HA8 44 D5
HAMP NW3 * 83 J5
Briary Ct SCUP DA14 186 C1
Briary Gdns BMLY BR1 184 A1
Briary La ED N9 36 A5
Brickbarn Cl WBPTN SW10 * 140 B1
Brick Ct EMB EC4Y * 11 J4
Brickett Cl RSLP HA4 58 A2
Brick Farm Cl RCH/KEW TW9 137 J2
Brickfield Cl BTFD TW8 136 D1
HOM E9 86 E4
Brickfield Cots
WOOL/PLUM SE18 128 A6
Brickfield Farm Gdns
ORP BR6 216 C2
Brickfield La BAR EN5 31 H1
HYS/HAR UB3 113 G6
Brickfield Rd BOW E3 105 K3
THHTH CR7 180 C4
WIM/MER SW19 160 A6
Brickfields RYLN/HDSTN HA2 60 D6
Brickfields Wy WDR/YW UB7 112 C3
Brickfield Vls CAR SM5 * 209 J1
Brick Kiln Cl OXHEY WD19 27 J1
Brick La BETH E2 7 K5
EN EN1 24 D3
NTHLT UB5 95 K2
PEND EN3 24 E3
STAN HA7 43 K3
WCHPL E1 7 K7
Brick St MYFR/PICC W1J 15 J1
Brickwall La RSLP HA4 58 C5
Brickwood Cl SYD SE26 163 J5
Brickwood Rd CROY/NA CR0 197 F6
Brideale Cl PECK SE15 123 G6
Bride Ct EMB EC4Y 12 A4
Bride La EMB EC4Y 12 A4
Bridel Ms FSBYE EC1V 6 A3
Bride St HOLWY N7 85 F4
Bridewain St STHWK SE1 19 J4
Bridewell Pl BLKFR EC4V 12 A4
WAP E1W 123 J1
Bridford Ms GTPST W1W 9 K1
Bridge Av HMSMTH W6 119 F5
HNWL W7 96 D4
Bridge Cl EN EN1 24 D3
NKENS W10 100 B5
ROMW/RG RM7 75 G3
Bridge Dr PLMGR N13 35 F6
Bridge End WALTH E17 52 A4
Bridge End Cl KUTN/CMB KT2 175 H4
Bridgefield Rd SUT SM1 208 E4
Bridge Gdns E/WMO/HCT KT8 189 J1
STNW/STAM N16 85 K2
Bridge Ga WCHMH N21 35 J2
Bridgehill Cl ALP/SUD HA0 79 K6
Bridge House Quay
POP/IOD E14 125 F1
Bridgeland Rd CAN/RD E16 106 E6
Bridgelands Cl BECK BR3 182 C3
Bridge La BTSEA SW11 140 D2
HDN NW4 64 B1
Bridgeman Rd IS N1 85 F5
TEDD TW11 174 B2
Bridgeman St STJWD NW8 2 C3
Bridge Mdw NWCR SE14 124 A6
Bridgenhall Rd EN EN1 24 B2
Bridgen Rd BXLY DA5 169 F2
Bridge Pde
STRHM/NOR SW16 * 179 K1
WCHMH N21 * 35 J2
Bridge Pl CROY/NA CR0 196 E5
PIM SW1V 15 K6
Bridgepoint Pl HGT N6 66 B5
Bridgeport Pl WAP E1W * 123 H1
Bridge Rd BECK BR3 182 C3
BXLYHN DA7 149 F4
CHSGTN KT9 206 A3
E/WMO/HCT KT8 189 K1
ED N9 36 C5
EHAM E6 89 K5
ERITH DA8 150 C2
HSLW TW3 135 J4
LEY E10 70 B3
NWDGN UB2 114 E2
RAIN RM13 111 J3
SRTFD E15 88 B6
STMC/STPC BR5 202 C3
SUT SM1 209 F4
TWK TW1 156 C1
WALTH E17 69 H4
WBLY HA9 80 C1
WDGN N22 48 E4
WLGTN SM6 210 B3
WLSDN NW10 81 G4
Bridge Rw CROY/NA CR0 * 196 E5
Bridges Ct BTSEA SW11 140 C4
Bridges La CROY/NA CR0 210 E2
Bridges Rd STAN HA7 43 F1
Bridges Road Ms
WIM/MER SW19 178 A2
Bridge St CHSWK W4 118 A4
PIN HA5 41 H6
TWK TW1 156 E1
WHALL SW1A 16 E3
Bridge Ter LEW SE13 * 145 G5
SRTFD E15 88 B5
The Bridge EA W5 * 117 G1
KTN/HRWW/WS HA3 43 F6
Bridgetown Cl NRWD SE19 181 F1
Bridgeview HMSMTH W6 119 F5
Bridge Vls WIM/MER SW19 * 177 K1
Bridgewater Cl
STMC/STPC BR5 185 K5
Bridgewater Gdns EDGW HA8 44 B5
Bridgewater Rd ALP/SUD HA0 79 H4
Bridgewater Sq BARB EC2Y * 12 C1
Bridgewater St BARB EC2Y 12 C1
Bridgewater Wy BUSH WD23 28 B1
Bridgeway ALP/SUD HA0 80 A5
BARK IG11 91 F5
Bridge Wy GLDGN NW11 64 D2
WHTN TW2 155 H2
Bridgeway St CAMTN NW1 4 B3
Bridge Wharf Rd ISLW TW7 136 C4
Bridgewood Cl PGE/AN SE20 181 J3
Bridgewood Rd
STRHM/NOR SW16 179 J3
WPK KT4 207 J2
Bridgford St
WAND/EARL SW18 160 B5
Bridgman Rd CHSWK W4 117 K3
Bridgwater Rd RSLP HA4 76 E2
Bridle Cl HOR/WEW KT19 206 E2
KUT/HW KT1 190 E1
Bridle La SOHO/CST W1F 10 B5
TWK TW1 156 C1
Bridle Pth CROY/NA CR0 210 E1
The Bridle Pth WFD IG8 52 C3
Bridlepath Wy
EBED/NFELT TW14 153 H2
Bridle Rd CROY/NA CR0 213 J2
ESH/CLAY KT10 205 H4
PIN HA5 59 G3
Bridle Wy CROY/NA CR0 213 J3
ORP BR6 216 C2
The Bridle Wy WLGTN SM6 210 C2
Bridlington Rd ED N9 36 D2
OXHEY WD19 27 H5
Bridport Av ROMW/RG RM7 74 D3
Bridport Pl IS N1 7 F1
Bridport Rd GFD/PVL UB6 78 B6
THHTH CR7 180 B6
UED N18 50 A1
Bridstow Pl BAY/PAD W2 100 E5
Brief St BRXN/ST SW9 142 C2
Brierley CROY/NA CR0 213 K4
Brierley Av ED N9 36 E3
Brierley Cl SNWD SE25 197 H1
Brierley Rd BAL SW12 161 H4
WAN E11 88 B2
Brierly Gdns BETH E2 * 104 E1
Brigade Cl RYLN/HDSTN HA2 60 D6
Brigade St BKHTH/KID SE3 * 145 J3
Brigadier Av ENC/FH EN2 23 J2
Brigadier Hl ENC/FH EN2 23 J1
Briggeford Cl CLPT E5 68 C6
Briggs Cl MTCM CR4 179 G4
Bright Cl BELV DA17 128 E4
Brightfield Rd LEE/GVPK SE12 145 H6
Brightling Rd BROCKY SE4 164 C1
Brightlingsea Pl POP/IOD E14 105 H6
Brightman Rd
WAND/EARL SW18 160 C3
Brighton Av WALTH E17 69 H2
Brighton Dr NTHLT UB5 * 78 A4
Brighton Rd BELMT SM2 209 G5
EFNCH N2 47 G5
EHAM E6 108 A2
SAND/SEL CR2 211 J6
STNW/STAM N16 86 A2
SURB KT6 190 D3
Brighton Ter BRXN/ST SW9 142 A5
Brights Av RAIN RM13 111 K3
Brightside Rd LEW SE13 165 G1
The Brightside PEND EN3 25 F2
Bright St POP/IOD E14 105 K5
Brightwell Cl CROY/NA CR0 196 B5
Brightwell Crs TOOT SW17 178 E1
Brightwen Gv STAN HA7 29 G4
Brig Ms DEPT SE8 124 D6
Brigstock Rd BELV DA17 129 J4
THHTH CR7 196 C2
Brill Pl CAMTN NW1 4 D3
Brim Hl EFNCH N2 65 G1
Brimpsfield Cl ABYW SE2 128 C3
Brimsdown Av PEND EN3 25 G2
Brimstone Cl ORP BR6 217 J5
Brindle Ga BFN/LL DA15 167 K3
Brindley Cl ALP/SUD HA0 79 J6
BXLYHN DA7 149 H4
Brindley St BROCKY SE4 144 C2
Brindley Wy BMLY BR1 183 K1
STHL UB1 96 B6
Brindwood Rd CHING E4 37 J5
Brinkburn Cl ABYW SE2 128 B4
EDGW HA8 44 D6
Brinkburn Gdns EDGW HA8 44 C6
Brinkley Rd WPK KT4 192 E6
Brinklow Crs
WOOL/PLUM SE18 147 G1
Brinkworth Rd CLAY IG5 53 J6
Brinkworth Wy HOM E9 87 H4
Brinsdale Rd HDN NW4 46 B6
Brinsley Rd
KTN/HRWW/WS HA3 42 D5
Brinsley St WCHPL E1 * 104 D5
Brinsworth Cl WHTN TW2 155 J4
Brinton Wk STHWK SE1 18 A1
Brion Pl POP/IOD E14 106 A4
Brisbane Av WIM/MER SW19 178 A4
Brisbane Rd IL IG1 72 C4
LEY E10 69 K6
Brisbane St CMBW SE5 142 E1
Briscoe Cl WAN E11 70 D6
Briscoe Rd WIM/MER SW19 178 C2
Briset Rd ELTH/MOT SE9 146 C4
Briset St FARR EC1M 12 A1
Briset Wy HOLWY N7 67 F6
Bristol Cl HSLWW TW4 155 F2
STWL/WRAY TW19 152 B1
WLGTN SM6 210 E6
Bristol Gdns MV/WKIL W9 101 F3
Bristol Ms MV/WKIL W9 101 F3
Bristol Park Rd WALTH E17 * 69 G1
Bristol Rd FSTGT E7 89 G4
GFD/PVL UB6 78 B6
MRDN SM4 194 B2
Briston Gv CEND/HSY/T N8 66 E3
Briston Ms MLHL NW7 45 J3
Bristowe Cl BRXS/STRHM SW2 162 B1
Bristow Rd BXLYHN DA7 149 F2
CROY/NA CR0 210 E2
HSLW TW3 135 G4
NRWD SE19 181 F1
Britannia Cl CLAP SW4 141 J5
ERITH DA8 130 C6
NTHLT UB5 95 H2
Britannia Ga CAN/RD E16 125 K1
Britannia La WHTN TW2 155 H2
Britannia Rd BRYLDS KT5 191 G4
FUL/PGN SW6 140 A1
IL IG1 90 B1
NFNCH/WDSPK N12 33 G5
POP/IOD E14 124 D4
Britannia Rw IS N1 85 H6
Britannia St FSBYW WC1X 5 G4
Britannia Wk IS N1 6 E3
Britannia Wy FUL/PGN SW6 140 A1
STWL/WRAY TW19 152 A2
WLSDN NW10 98 D3
British Est BOW E3 105 H2
British Gv HMSMTH W6 118 C5
British Grove Pas
CHSWK W4 * 118 C5
British Legion Rd CHING E4 38 D4
British St BOW E3 105 H2
Brittage Rd WLSDN NW10 81 G5
Brittain Rd BCTR RM8 92 A1
Britten Cl BORE WD6 29 K1
GLDGN NW11 65 F5
Brittenden Pde ORP BR6 * 217 F4
Britten Dr STHL UB1 96 A5
Britten St CHEL SW3 120 D5
Brittidge Rd WLSDN NW10 * 81 G5
Britton Cl CAT SE6 165 G2
Britton St FARR EC1M 6 A7
Brixham Crs RSLP HA4 58 E5
Brixham Gdns
GDMY/SEVK IG3 90 E3
Brixham Rd WELL DA16 148 E2
Brixham St CAN/RD E16 126 E1
Brixton Hl BRXS/STRHM SW2 162 A1
Brixton Hill Pl
BRXS/STRHM SW2 161 K2
Brixton Rd BRXN/ST SW9 142 B5
LBTH SE11 122 B6
Brixton Station Rd
BRXN/ST SW9 142 B4
Brixton Water La
BRXS/STRHM SW2 142 A6
Broadbent Cl HGT N6 66 B5
Broadbent St
MYFR/PKLN W1K * 9 J5
Broadberry Ct UED N18 50 D1
Broad Bridge Cl
BKHTH/KID SE3 145 K1
Broad Common Est
STNW/STAM N16 * 68 C5
Broadcoombe SAND/SEL CR2 213 F5
Broad Ct COVGDN WC2E * 11 F4
Broadcroft Av STAN HA7 43 K5
Broadcroft Rd
STMC/STPC BR5 201 J4
Broadeaves Cl SAND/SEL CR2 212 A3
Broadfield Cl CRICK NW2 82 A1
ROM RM1 75 H2
Broadfield Ct BUSH WD23 28 E4
Broadfield La CAMTN NW1 84 E5
Broadfield Pde EDGW HA8 * 30 D5
Broadfield Rd CAT SE6 165 H3
Broadfields E/WMO/HCT KT8 189 J3
RYLN/HDSTN HA2 42 B5
Broadfields Av EDGW HA8 30 D5
WCHMH N21 35 G2
Broadfields Hts EDGW HA8 30 D6
Broadfields La OXHEY WD19 27 F3
Broadfield Sq EN EN1 24 D4
Broadfields Wy WLSDN NW10 81 H3
Broadfield Wy BKHH IG9 39 G5
Broadgates Av EBAR EN4 21 F2
Broadgates Rd
WAND/EARL SW18 160 C3
Broad Green Av CROY/NA CR0 196 C4
Broadhead Strd
CDALE/KGS NW9 45 H5
Broadheath Dr CHST BR7 184 E1
Broadhinton Rd CLAP SW4 141 G4
Broadhurst Av EDGW HA8 30 D6
GDMY/SEVK IG3 91 F2
Broadhurst Cl
KIL/WHAMP NW6 83 G4
Broadhurst Gdns
KIL/WHAMP NW6 83 F4
RSLP HA4 59 G6
Broadhusrt Cl
RCHPK/HAM TW10 137 G6
Broadlands FELT TW13 154 E5
Broadlands Av PEND EN3 24 D4
STRHM/NOR SW16 161 K4
Broadlands Cl HGT N6 66 A4
PEND EN3 24 D4
STRHM/NOR SW16 161 K4
Broadlands Rd BMLY BR1 166 A6
HGT N6 65 K4
Broadlands Wy NWMAL KT3 192 C3
Broad La HPTN TW12 172 E3
RDART DA2 170 E6
SEVS/STOTM N15 68 B2
Broad Lawn ELTH/MOT SE9 167 F3
Broadlawns Ct
KTN/HRWW/WS HA3 43 F4
Broadley St STJWD NW8 8 C1
Broadley Ter CAMTN NW1 2 D7
Broadmead CAT SE6 164 D5
Broadmead Av WPK KT4 192 D4
Broadmead Cl HPTN TW12 173 F2
PIN HA5 * 41 J3
Broadmead Rd WFD IG8 52 E2
YEAD UB4 95 J3
Broad Oak WFD IG8 53 F1
Broad Oak Cl CHING E4 51 J1
STMC/STPC BR5 186 B5
Broadoak Rd ERITH DA8 150 A1
Broad Oaks SURB KT6 191 J5
Broad Oaks Wy HAYES BR2 199 J2
Broadstone Pl MHST W1U 9 G2
Broadstone Rd HCH RM12 75 J6
Broad St DAGE RM10 92 C5
TEDD TW11 174 A2
Broad Street Pl LVPST EC2M 13 F2
Broadview CDALE/KGS NW9 62 C3
Broadview Rd
STRHM/NOR SW16 179 J3
Broad Wk WCHMH N21 35 F4
BKHTH/KID SE3 146 B3
HEST TW5 134 C2
ORP BR6 217 K1
RCH/KEW TW9 137 G1
Broadwalk
RYLN/HDSTN HA2 * 60 B2
SWFD E18 52 D6
Broadwalk La GLDGN NW11 64 D4
The Broad Wk KENS W8 120 B2
The Broadwalk NTHWD HA6 40 A5
Broadwall STHWK SE1 11 K7
Broadwater Gdns ORP BR6 216 B2
Broadwater Rd THMD SE28 127 J3
TOOT SW17 160 D6
TOTM N17 50 A5
Broadway BARK IG11 90 C6
BXLYHS DA6 149 F5
GPK RM2 57 J6
HNWL W7 115 K1
RAIN RM13 111 J3
SRTFD E15 88 B5
STJSPK SW1H 16 C3
SURB KT6 191 J5
SWLY BR8 203 K3
WEA W13 116 B1
Broadway Av CROY/NA CR0 196 E2
TWK TW1 156 C1
Broadway Cl WFD IG8 53 F2
Broadway Ct WIM/MER SW19 177 K2
Broadway Gdns MTCM CR4 194 D1
Broadway Market HACK E8 86 D6
Broadway Market Ms
HACK E8 * 86 C6
Broadway Ms PLMGR N13 49 F1
STNW/STAM N16 68 B4
WCHMH N21 35 H3
Broadway Pde CHING E4 * 52 A2
HYS/HAR UB3 * 113 J2
RYLN/HDSTN HA2 * 60 B2
WDR/YW UB7 * 112 B2
The Broadway ACT W3 * 117 H2
BCTR RM8 74 B6
CDALE/KGS NW9 63 H3
CEND/HSY/T N8 66 E3
CHEAM SM3 208 C4
EA W5 97 K6
ED N9 36 C5
FBAR/BDGN N11 * 47 K1
HCH RM12 93 K2
KTN/HRWW/WS HA3 42 E5
MLHL NW7 45 G1
PIN HA5 41 K3
PLSTW E13 106 E1
RYLN/HDSTN HA2 * 60 D6
STAN HA7 43 J1
SUT SM1 209 G2
THDIT KT7 189 K5
WFD IG8 53 F2
WIM/MER SW19 177 J2
Broadwell Pde
KIL/WHAMP NW6 * 83 G4
Broadwick St SOHO/CST W1F 10 B5
Broadwood Av RSLP HA4 58 C3
Broadwood Ter WKENS W14 * 119 J4
Broad Yd FARR EC1M 6 A7
Brocas Cl HAMP NW3 83 J5
Brockdene Dr HAYES BR2 215 H2
Brockdish Av BARK IG11 91 F3
Brockenhurst
E/WMO/HCT KT8 188 E2
Brockenhurst Av WPK KT4 192 B5
Brockenhurst Gdns IL IG1 90 C3
MLHL NW7 45 G1
Brockenhurst Ms UED N18 36 C6
Brockenhurst Rd
CROY/NA CR0 197 J4
Brockenhurst Wy
STRHM/NOR SW16 179 J5
Brocket Wy CHIG IG7 54 E1
Brockham Cl WIM/MER SW19 177 J1
Brockham Crs CROY/NA CR0 214 B5
Brockham Dr
BRXS/STRHM SW2 162 A2
GNTH/NBYPK IG2 72 C3
Brockham St STHWK SE1 18 D4
Brockhurst Cl STAN HA7 43 F2
Brockill Crs BROCKY SE4 144 B5
Brocklebank Rd CHARL SE7 126 A4
WAND/EARL SW18 160 B2
Brocklehurst St NWCR SE14 144 A1
Brocklesby Rd SNWD SE25 197 J1
Brockley Av STAN HA7 30 A5
Brockley Cl STAN HA7 30 A6
Brockley Crs CRW RM5 56 E3
Brockley Cross BROCKY SE4 144 B4
Brockley Gv BROCKY SE4 144 C6
Brockley Hall Rd BROCKY SE4 164 B1
Brockley Hl STAN HA7 29 K4
Brockley Ms BROCKY SE4 144 B6
Brockley Pk FSTH SE23 164 B2
Brockley Ri FSTH SE23 164 B2
Brockley Rd BROCKY SE4 144 C6
FSTH SE23 164 B1
Brockleyside STAN HA7 29 K6
Brockley Vw FSTH SE23 164 B2
Brockley Wy FSTH SE23 144 A6
Brockman Ri BMLY BR1 165 G6
Brock Pl BOW E3 105 K3
Brock Rd PLSTW E13 107 F4
Brocks Dr CHEAM SM3 208 C1
Brockshot Cl BTFD TW8 116 E6
Brock St PECK SE15 * 143 K4
Brockton Cl ROM RM1 75 H1
Brockway Cl WAN E11 70 C6
Brockwell Av BECK BR3 198 E2
Brockwell Cl STMC/STPC BR5 202 A2
Brockwell Park Gdns
HNHL SE24 162 C2
Brockwell Park Rw
BRXS/STRHM SW2 162 B2
Brodia Rd STNW/STAM N16 86 A1
Brodie Rd CHING E4 38 A3
ENC/FH EN2 23 J1
Brodie St STHWK SE1 123 G5
Brodlove La WAP E1W 105 F6
Brodrick Gv ABYW SE2 128 C4
Brodrick Rd TOOT SW17 160 D4
Brograve Gdns BECK BR3 182 E5
Broke Farm Dr ORP BR6 217 J6

Broken Whf BLKFR EC4V 12 C5
Brokesley St BOW E3 105 H3
Broke Wk HACK E8 * 86 C6
Bromar Rd CMBW SE5 143 F4
Bromborough Gn
OXHEY WD19 41 G1
Bromefield STAN HA7 43 J4
Bromehead St WCHPL E1 104 E5
Brome House CHARL SE7 * 146 D1
Bromell's Rd CLAP SW4 141 H5
Brome Rd ELTH/MOT SE9 146 E4
Bromfelde Rd CLAP SW4 141 J4
Bromfield St IS N1 5 K2
Bromhall Rd DAGW RM9 91 H4
Bromhedge ELTH/MOT SE9 166 E5
Bromholm Rd ABYW SE2 128 C3
Bromley Av BMLY BR1 183 H3
Bromley Common HAYES BR2 200 B2
Bromley Ct BMLY BR1 183 H3
Bromley Crs HAYES BR2 183 J6
RSLP HA4 76 D2
Bromley Gdns HAYES BR2 183 J5
Bromley Gv HAYES BR2 183 G5
Bromley Hall Rd POP/IOD E14 106 A4
Bromley High St BOW E3 105 K2
Bromley Hl BMLY BR1 183 G1
Bromley La CHST BR7 185 H3
Bromley Rd BECK BR3 182 D4
CAT SE6 164 E5
CHST BR7 185 G4
HAYES BR2 183 H5
LEY E10 69 K3
TOTM N17 50 B4
UED N18 35 K6
WALTH E17 51 J6
Bromley St WCHPL E1 105 F4
Brompton Ar CHEL SW3 * 14 E3
Brompton Cl HSLWW TW4 134 E6
Brompton Cots
WBPTN SW10 * 120 B6
Brompton Dr ERITH DA8 150 E1
Brompton Gv EFNCH N2 65 J1
Brompton Park Crs
FUL/PGN SW6 120 A6
Brompton Pl CHEL SW3 14 D4
Brompton Rd CHEL SW3 14 C6
Brompton Sq CHEL SW3 14 C4
Brompton Ter
WOOL/PLUM SE18 * 147 F2
Bromwich Av HGT N6 66 A6
Bromyard Av ACT W3 118 B1
Brondesbury Ms
KIL/WHAMP NW6 * 82 E5
Brondesbury Pk
KIL/WHAMP NW6 82 A5
Brondesbury Rd
KIL/WHAMP NW6 100 D1
Brondesbury Vls
KIL/WHAMP NW6 100 D1
Bronhill Ter TOTM N17 * 50 C4
Bronsart Rd FUL/PGN SW6 139 H1
Bronson Rd RYNPK SW20 177 G5
Bronte Cl ERITH DA8 149 J1
FSTGT E7 * 88 E2
GNTH/NBYPK IG2 72 A1
Bronte Gv DART DA1 151 J5
Bronti Cl WALW SE17 122 D5
Bronze Age Wy BELV DA17 129 K3
Bronze St DEPT SE8 144 D1
Brook Av DAGE RM10 92 D5
EDGW HA8 44 D2
WBLY HA9 80 B1
Brookbank Av HNWL W7 96 D4
Brookbank Rd LEW SE13 144 D4
Brook Cl ACT W3 117 H1
GPK RM2 57 H4
HOR/WEW KT19 207 G6
RSLP HA4 58 C4
RYNPK SW20 176 E6
STWL/WRAY TW19 152 C2
TOOT SW17 161 F4
Brook Ct BECK BR3 * 182 C4
Brook Crs CHING E4 37 J6
ED N9 36 D6
Brookdale FBAR/BDGN N11 34 C6
Brookdale Rd BXLY DA5 169 F1
CAT SE6 164 E1
WALTH E17 51 J6
Brookdene Av OXHEY WD19 27 F2
Brookdene Dr NTHWD HA6 40 D3
Brookdene Rd
WOOL/PLUM SE18 127 K4
Brook Dr HRW HA1 60 C1
LBTH SE11 17 K5
RSLP HA4 58 C3
Brooke Av RYLN/HDSTN HA2 78 C1
Brooke Cl BUSH WD23 28 C2
Brookehowse Rd CAT SE6 164 D4
Brookend Rd BFN/LL DA15 167 K3
Brooke Rd STNW/STAM N16 86 C1
WALTH E17 70 A1
Brooke's Market
HCIRC EC1N * 11 J1
Brooke St HCIRC EC1N 11 J2
Brooke Wy BUSH WD23 28 C2
Brookfield Av EA W5 97 K3
MLHL NW7 45 K2
SUT SM1 209 J1
WALTH E17 70 A1
Brookfield Ct MLHL NW7 45 K2
Brookfield Crs
KTN/HRWW/WS HA3 62 A2
MLHL NW7 45 K2
Brookfield Gdns
ESH/CLAY KT10 205 F4
Brookfield Pk KTTN NW5 84 B1
Brookfield Pth WFD IG8 52 B2
Brookfield Rd CHSWK W4 118 A2
ED N9 36 C5
HOM E9 87 G4
Brookfields PEND EN3 25 F5
Brookfields Av MTCM CR4 194 D2
Brook Gdns BARN SW13 138 C4
CHING E4 37 K6
KUTN/CMB KT2 175 K4
Brook Ga MYFR/PKLN W1K 9 F6
Brook Gn HMSMTH W6 119 F3
Brookhill Cl EBAR EN4 21 J6
Brook Hill Cl
WOOL/PLUM SE18 127 G5
Brookhill Rd EBAR EN4 21 H6
WOOL/PLUM SE18 127 G5
Brookhouse Gdns CHING E4 38 C6
Brooking Cl BCTR RM8 91 J1
Brooking Rd FSTGT E7 88 E3
Brookland Cl GLDGN NW11 64 E1
Brookland Garth
GLDGN NW11 64 E1
Brookland Hl GLDGN NW11 64 E1
Brookland Ri GLDGN NW11 64 E1
Brooklands DART DA1 171 H3
Brooklands Ap ROM RM1 75 F1
Brooklands Av BFN/LL DA15 167 J4
WIM/MER SW19 160 A4
Brooklands Cl ROMW/RG RM7 75 F1
Brooklands Ct
KIL/WHAMP NW6 82 D5
WCHMH N21 23 K6
Brooklands Dr GFD/PVL UB6 79 J6
Brooklands La
ROMW/RG RM7 75 F1
Brooklands Pk
BKHTH/KID SE3 145 K4
Brooklands Pl HPTN TW12 173 G1
Brooklands Rd
ROMW/RG RM7 75 F1
THDIT KT7 190 A5
The Brooklands ISLW TW7 * 135 J2
Brook La BKHTH/KID SE3 146 A3
BMLY BR1 183 K2
BXLY DA5 168 E1
Brook La North BTFD TW8 116 E5
Brooklea Cl CDALE/KGS NW9 45 G4
Brooklyn Av SNWD SE25 197 J1
Brooklyn Cl CAR SM5 194 D6
Brooklyn Gv SNWD SE25 197 J1
Brooklyn Rd HAYES BR2 200 C2
SNWD SE25 197 J1
Brooklyn Wy WDR/YW UB7 112 A3
Brookmead CROY/NA CR0 195 H3
Brook Md HOR/WEW KT19 207 G4
Brookmead Av HAYES BR2 200 E2
Brookmead Cl
STMC/STPC BR5 202 C3
Brook Meadow
NFNCH/WDSPK N12 33 F6
Brook Meadow Cl WFD IG8 52 C2
Brookmead Rd CROY/NA CR0 195 H3
Brook Ms North BAY/PAD W2 101 G6
Brookmill Cl OXHEY WD19 * 27 F2
Brookmill Rd DEPT SE8 144 D2
Brook Pk DART DA1 171 K4
Brook Park Cl WCHMH N21 23 H6
Brook Pl BAR EN5 20 E6
Brook Rd BKHH IG9 38 E3
CEND/HSY/T N8 66 E1
CRICK NW2 63 J6
GNTH/NBYPK IG2 72 E3
GPK RM2 57 H5
SURB KT6 191 F6
THHTH CR7 196 D1
TWK TW1 156 B1
WDGN N22 * 49 F5
Brook Rd South BTFD TW8 116 E5
Brooks Av EHAM E6 107 K3
Brooksbank St HOM E9 * 87 F4
Brooksby Ms IS N1 85 G5
Brooksby St IS N1 85 G5
Brooksby's Wk HOM E9 87 F3
Brookscroft CROY/NA CR0 * 213 H6
Brookscroft Rd WALTH E17 51 K4
Brookshill
KTN/HRWW/WS HA3 42 E2
Brookshill Av
KTN/HRWW/WS HA3 42 D1
Brookshill Dr
KTN/HRWW/WS HA3 42 D1
Brookside BARK/HLT IG6 54 C2
CAR SM5 210 A3
EBAR EN4 33 J1
ORP BR6 202 A4
WCHMH N21 35 F1
Brookside Cl BAR EN5 32 B1
FELT TW13 153 K5
KTN/HRWW/WS HA3 61 K2
RSLP HA4 77 J2
Brookside Crs WPK KT4 192 D5
Brookside Rd ARCH N19 66 C6
ED N9 36 D6
GLDGN NW11 64 C3
OXHEY WD19 27 F2
UED N18 36 D6
YEAD UB4 95 G6
Brookside South EBAR EN4 34 A2
Brookside Wy CROY/NA CR0 198 A3
Brooks La CHSWK W4 117 H6
Brook's Ms MYFR/PKLN W1K 9 J5
Brooks Rd CHSWK W4 117 H5
Brook's Rd PLSTW E13 88 E6
Brook St BAY/PAD W2 8 B5
BELV DA17 129 J5
ERITH DA8 149 K1
KUT/HW KT1 175 F5
MYFR/PKLN W1K 9 H5
TOTM N17 50 B5
Brooksville Av
KIL/WHAMP NW6 82 C6
Brookview Rd
STRHM/NOR SW16 179 H1
Brookville Rd FUL/PGN SW6 139 J1
Brook Wk EDGW HA8 45 F2
EFNCH N2 * 47 H4
Brook Water La HDN NW4 * 64 B2
Brookway BKHTH/KID SE3 145 K4
RAIN RM13 111 K4
Brookwood Av BARN SW13 138 C4
Brookwood Cl HAYES BR2 199 J1
Brookwood Rd HSLW TW3 135 G3
WAND/EARL SW18 159 J3
Broom Av STMC/STPC BR5 186 C5
Broom Cl ESH/CLAY KT10 204 B3
HAYES BR2 200 D3
TEDD TW11 174 E3
Broomcroft Av NTHLT UB5 95 G2
Broome Rd HPTN TW12 172 E4
Broome Wy CMBW SE5 142 E1
Broomfield WALTH E17 69 H3
Broomfield Av LOU IG10 39 K1
PLMGR N13 35 F6
Broomfield Cl CRW RM5 57 F2
Broomfield Cots WEA W13 * 116 C1
Broomfield La PLMGR N13 34 E6
Broomfield Pl WEA W13 116 C1
Broomfield Rd BECK BR3 198 B1
BXLYHS DA6 149 H6
CHDH RM6 73 K4
PLMGR N13 48 E1
RCH/KEW TW9 137 G2
SURB KT6 191 G5
TEDD TW11 174 D2
WEA W13 116 C1
Broomfields ESH/CLAY KT10 204 C3
Broomfield St POP/IOD E14 105 J4
Broom Gdns CROY/NA CR0 213 J1
Broomgrove Gdns EDGW HA8 44 C4
Broomgrove Rd
BRXN/ST SW9 142 A3
Broomhall Rd SAND/SEL CR2 211 K6
Broomhill Ri BXLYHS DA6 149 H6
Broomhill Rd DART DA1 170 E1
GDMY/SEVK IG3 73 G6
ORP BR6 202 B4
WAND/EARL SW18 139 K6
WFD IG8 52 E2
Broomhouse La
FUL/PGN SW6 139 K3
Broomhouse Rd
FUL/PGN SW6 139 K3
Broomloan La SUT SM1 193 K6
Broom Lock TEDD TW11 * 174 D1
Broom Md BXLYHS DA6 169 H1
Broom Pk TEDD TW11 174 E3
Broom Rd CROY/NA CR0 213 J1
TEDD TW11 174 C1
Broomsleigh St
KIL/WHAMP NW6 * 82 E3
Broom Water TEDD TW11 174 D1
Broom Water West
TEDD TW11 174 D1
Broomwood Cl BXLY DA5 170 A4
CROY/NA CR0 198 A2
Broomwood Rd BTSEA SW11 160 D1
STMC/STPC BR5 186 C5
Broseley Gv SYD SE26 182 B1
Brosse Wy HAYES BR2 200 D3
Broster Gdns SNWD SE25 181 G6
Brougham Rd ACT W3 98 E5
HACK E8 86 C6
Brougham St BTSEA SW11 140 E3
Brough Cl KUTN/CMB KT2 * 174 E1
VX/NE SW8 141 K1
Broughton Av FNCH N3 46 C6
RCHPK/HAM TW10 156 D6
Broughton Dr BRXN/ST SW9 142 B5
Broughton Gdns HGT N6 66 C3
Broughton Rd FUL/PGN SW6 140 A3
ORP BR6 201 J6
THHTH CR7 196 B3
WEA W13 97 H6
Broughton Road Ap
FUL/PGN SW6 * 140 A3
Broughton St VX/NE SW8 141 F3
Brouncker Rd ACT W3 117 K2
Brow Cl STMC/STPC BR5 202 E4
Brow Crs STMC/STPC BR5 202 D5
Browells La FELT TW13 154 A4
Brown Cl WLGTN SM6 210 D5
Brownfield St POP/IOD E14 105 K5
Browngraves Rd
HYS/HAR UB3 133 F1
Brown Hart Gdns
MYFR/PKLN W1K 9 H5
Brownhill Rd CAT SE6 165 F2
Browning Av HNWL W7 97 F5
SUT SM1 209 J2
WPK KT4 192 E5
Browning Cl HPTN TW12 154 E6
MV/WKIL W9 101 G3
WALTH E17 70 A1
WELL DA16 147 K2
Browning Ms
CAVSQ/HST W1G * 9 H2
Browning Rd DART DA1 151 J5
ENC/FH EN2 23 K1
MNPK E12 89 K4
WAN E11 70 D4
Browning St WALW SE17 122 D5
Browning Wy HEST TW5 134 C2
Brownlea Gdns
GDMY/SEVK IG3 73 G6
Brownlow Cl EBAR EN4 21 H6
Brownlow Ms BMSBY WC1N 5 H6
Brownlow Rd CROY/NA CR0 212 A2
FBAR/BDGN N11 48 E2
FNCH N3 47 F3
FSTGT E7 88 E2
HACK E8 86 B6
WEA W13 * 116 B1
WLSDN NW10 81 G5
Brownlow St HHOL WC1V 11 H2
Brownrigg Rd ASHF TW15 152 D6
Brownspring Dr
ELTH/MOT SE9 167 G5
Brown's Rd BRYLDS KT5 191 G4
WALTH E17 51 J6
Brown St MBLAR W1H 8 E3
Brownswell Rd EFNCH N2 47 H5
Brownswood Rd FSBYPK N4 67 J6
Broxash Rd BTSEA SW11 161 F1
Broxbourne Av SWFD E18 71 F1
Broxbourne House BOW E3 105 K3
Broxbourne Rd FSTGT E7 88 E1
ORP BR6 202 A5
Broxholme Cl SNWD SE25 196 E1
Broxholm Rd WNWD SE27 162 B5
Broxted Rd FSTH SE23 164 C4
Broxwood Wy STJWD NW8 2 D1
Bruce Castle Rd TOTM N17 50 B4
Bruce Cl NKENS W10 100 B4
WELL DA16 148 C2
Bruce Dr SAND/SEL CR2 213 F6
Bruce Gdns TRDG/WHET N20 33 K5
Bruce Gv ORP BR6 202 B5
TOTM N17 50 B5
Bruce Rd BAR EN5 20 C4
BOW E3 105 K2
KTN/HRWW/WS HA3 42 E5
MTCM CR4 179 F3
SNWD SE25 196 E1
WLSDN NW10 81 F5
Bruckner St NKENS W10 100 C2
Brudenell Rd TOOT SW17 160 E5
Bruffs Meadow NTHLT UB5 77 J4
Bruford Ct DEPT SE8 124 D6
Bruges Pl CAMTN NW1 84 C5
Brumfield Rd HOR/WEW KT19 206 E3
Brunel Cl HEST TW5 134 A1
NRWD SE19 181 G2
NTHLT UB5 95 K2
ROM RM1 75 G1
Brunel Ct WLSDN NW10 99 J2
Brunel Est BAY/PAD W2 * 100 E4
Brunel House
WOOL/PLUM SE18 * 146 D1
Brunel Ms NKENS W10 100 B2
Brunel Rd ACT W3 99 G4
BERM/RHTH SE16 123 K2
WALTH E17 69 G3
WFD IG8 53 K1
Brunel St CAN/RD E16 106 D5
Brunel Wk WHTN TW2 155 F2
Brune St WCHPL E1 13 J2
Brunner Cl GLDGN NW11 65 F2
Brunner Rd EA W5 97 K3
WALTH E17 69 H2
Bruno Pl CDALE/KGS NW9 62 E6
Brunswick Av
FBAR/BDGN N11 34 A5
Brunswick Cl BXLYHS DA6 148 E5
PIN HA5 59 J3
THDIT KT7 190 A5
WHTN TW2 155 J5
WOT/HER KT12 188 B6
Brunswick Ct STHWK SE1 19 H3
Brunswick Crs
FBAR/BDGN N11 34 A5
Brunswick Gdns
BARK/HLT IG6 54 C3
EA W5 98 A2
KENS W8 119 K1
Brunswick Gv
FBAR/BDGN N11 34 A5
Brunswick Ms MBLAR W1H 9 F3
STRHM/NOR SW16 179 J2
Brunswick Pk CMBW SE5 142 E2
Brunswick Park Gdns
FBAR/BDGN N11 34 A4
Brunswick Park Rd
FBAR/BDGN N11 34 A5
Brunswick Pl CAMTN NW1 3 H7
IS N1 7 F5
NRWD SE19 181 H3
Brunswick Quay
BERM/RHTH SE16 124 A3
Brunswick Rd BXLYHS DA6 148 E5
EA W5 97 K3
KUTN/CMB KT2 175 H4
LEY E10 70 A5
PEND EN3 25 J1
SEVS/STOTM N15 68 A1
SUT SM1 209 F2
Brunswick Sq BMSBY WC1N 5 F6
TOTM N17 50 B2
Brunswick St WALTH E17 70 A2
Brunswick Vls CMBW SE5 143 F2
Brunswick Wy
FBAR/BDGN N11 34 B6
Brunton Pl POP/IOD E14 105 G5
Brushfield St WCHPL E1 13 H1
Brushwood Cl POP/IOD E14 105 K4
Brussels Rd BTSEA SW11 140 C5
Bruton Cl CHST BR7 184 E3
Bruton La MYFR/PICC W1J 9 K6
Bruton Pl MYFR/PICC W1J 9 K6
Bruton Rd MRDN SM4 194 B1
Bruton St MYFR/PICC W1J 9 K6
Bruton Wy WEA W13 97 G4
Bryan Av WLSDN NW10 81 K5
Bryan Rd BERM/RHTH SE16 124 C2
Bryanston Av WHTN TW2 155 G3
Bryanston Cl NWDGN UB2 114 E4
Bryanstone Rd
CEND/HSY/T N8 66 D2
Bryanston Ms East
MBLAR W1H 8 E2
Bryanston Ms West
MBLAR W1H 8 E2
Bryanston Pl MBLAR W1H 8 E2
Bryanston Sq MBLAR W1H 8 E3
Bryanston St MBLAR W1H 8 E4
Bryant Cl BAR EN5 20 D6
Bryant Rd NTHLT UB5 95 G2
Bryant St SRTFD E15 88 B5
Bryantwood Rd HOLWY N7 85 G3
Brycedale Crs
STHGT/OAK N14 34 D6
Bryce Rd BCTR RM8 91 J2
Bryden Cl SYD SE26 182 B1
Brydges Pl CHCR WC2N 10 E6
Brydges Rd SRTFD E15 88 B3
Brydon Wk IS N1 84 E6
Bryett Rd HOLWY N7 84 E1
Brymay Cl BOW E3 105 J1
Brynmaer Rd BTSEA SW11 140 E2
Bryn-Y-Mawr Rd EN EN1 24 B5
Bryony Rd SHB W12 99 J6
Buchanan Cl WCHMH N21 23 F6
Buchanan Gdns WLSDN NW10 99 K1
Buchan Rd PECK SE15 143 K4
Bucharest Rd
WAND/EARL SW18 160 B2
Buckden Cl LEE/GVPK SE12 165 J1
Buckfast Rd MRDN SM4 194 A1
Buckfast St BETH E2 104 C2
Buckhold Rd
WAND/EARL SW18 159 K1
Buckhurst Av CAR SM5 194 D5
Buckhurst St WCHPL E1 104 D3
Buckhurst Wy BKHH IG9 39 H5
Buckingham Av
E/WMO/HCT KT8 173 G5
EBED/NFELT TW14 154 A1
GFD/PVL UB6 79 G6
THHTH CR7 180 B4
TRDG/WHET N20 33 G2
WELL DA16 147 K5
Buckingham Cl EA W5 97 J4
EN EN1 24 A3
HPTN TW12 172 E1
STMC/STPC BR5 201 K4
Buckingham Ct BELMT SM2 * 208 E6
Buckingham Dr CHST BR7 185 G1
Buckingham Gdns
E/WMO/HCT KT8 173 G5
STAN HA7 44 A3
THHTH CR7 180 B5
Buckingham Ga WESTW SW1E 16 A4
Buckingham La FSTH SE23 164 B2
Buckingham Ms IS N1 86 A4
WESTW SW1E * 16 A4
WLSDN NW10 99 H1
Buckingham Palace Rd
BGVA SW1W 15 J6
Buckingham Pde STAN HA7 * 43 J1
Buckingham Pl WESTW SW1E 16 A4
Buckingham Rd EDGW HA8 44 B3
HPTN TW12 154 E6
HRW HA1 60 D2
IL IG1 72 D6
IS N1 86 A4
KUT/HW KT1 191 G1
LEY E10 87 K1
MTCM CR4 195 K2
RCHPK/HAM TW10 156 E4
SRTFD E15 88 D3
SWFD E18 52 D4
WAN E11 71 F1
WDGN N22 48 E4
WLSDN NW10 99 H1
Buckingham St CHCR WC2N 11 F6
Buckingham Wy WLGTN SM6 210 C6
Buckland Crs HAMP NW3 83 H5
Buckland Ri PIN HA5 41 G4
Buckland Rd CHSGTN KT9 206 B3
LEY E10 70 A6
ORP BR6 216 E2
Bucklands OXHEY WD19 * 27 H5
Bucklands Rd TEDD TW11 174 D2
Buckland St IS N1 7 F3
Bucklands Whf KUT/HW KT1 * 174 E5
Buckland Wk MRDN SM4 194 B1
Buckland Wy WPK KT4 193 F5
Buck La CDALE/KGS NW9 63 F2
Buckleigh Av RYNPK SW20 177 J6
Buckleigh Rd
STRHM/NOR SW16 179 J2
Buckleigh Wy NRWD SE19 181 G4
Bucklersbury MANHO EC4N * 12 E4
Bucklers' Wy CAR SM5 209 K1
Buckle St WCHPL E1 13 K3
Buckley Cl DART DA1 150 C3
FSTH SE23 163 J2
Buckley Rd KIL/WHAMP NW6 82 D5
Buckmaster Rd BTSEA SW11 140 D5
Bucknall St NOXST/BSQ WC1A 10 E3
Bucknall Wy BECK BR3 198 E1
Bucknell Cl BRXS/STRHM SW2 142 A5
Buckner Rd
BRXS/STRHM SW2 142 A5
Buckrell Rd CHING E4 38 B4
Bucks Av OXHEY WD19 27 J2
Buckstone Cl FSTH SE23 163 K1
Buckstone Rd UED N18 50 C2
Buck St CAMTN NW1 84 B6
Buckters Rents
BERM/RHTH SE16 124 B1
Buckthorne Rd BROCKY SE4 164 B1
Budd Cl NFNCH/WDSPK N12 33 F6
Buddings Cir WBLY HA9 80 E1
Bude Cl WALTH E17 69 H2
Budge La MTCM CR4 194 E4
Budge Rw MANHO EC4N 12 E5
Budleigh Crs WELL DA16 148 D2
Budoch Dr GDMY/SEVK IG3 73 G6
Buer Rd FUL/PGN SW6 139 H3
Bugsby's Wy GNWCH SE10 125 K4
Bulganak Rd THHTH CR7 196 D1
Bulinca St WEST SW1P * 16 E7
Bullace Rw CMBW SE5 142 E2
Bullard Rd TEDD TW11 173 K2
Bullards Pl BETH E2 105 F2
Bullbanks Rd BELV DA17 129 K4
Bulleid Wy BGVA SW1W 15 K7
Bullen St BTSEA SW11 140 D3
Buller Cl PECK SE15 143 H1
Buller Rd BARK IG11 90 E5
THHTH CR7 180 E6
TOTM N17 50 C5
WDGN N22 49 G5
WLSDN NW10 100 B2
Bullers Cl SCUP DA14 187 F1
Bullers Wood Dr CHST BR7 184 D4
Bullescroft Rd EDGW HA8 30 C5
Bullivant St POP/IOD E14 106 A6
Bull La CHST BR7 185 J3
DAGE RM10 92 D1
UED N18 50 A1
Bull Rd SRTFD E15 106 D1
Bullrush Cl CAR SM5 194 D6
CROY/NA CR0 197 F3
Bulls Aly MORT/ESHN SW14 * 138 A4
Bull's Br NWDGN UB2 113 K3
Bulls Bridge Rd NWDGN UB2 114 A3
Bullsbrook Rd YEAD UB4 114 B1
Bull's Gdns CHEL SW3 14 D6
Bull Yd PECK SE15 143 H2
Bulmer Gdns
KTN/HRWW/WS HA3 61 K4
Bulstrode Av HSLW TW3 134 E4
Bulstrode Gdns HSLW TW3 135 F4
Bulstrode Pl MHST W1U 9 H2
Bulstrode Rd HSLW TW3 135 F4
Bulstrode St MHST W1U 9 H3
Bulwer Court Rd WAN E11 70 B5
Bulwer Gdns BAR EN5 21 G5
Bulwer Rd BAR EN5 21 F5
UED N18 36 A6
WAN E11 70 B5
Bulwer St SHB W12 119 F1
Bunces La WFD IG8 52 D3
Bungalow Rd SNWD SE25 197 F1
The Bungalows
RYLN/HDSTN HA2 * 77 K1
STRHM/NOR SW16 179 G3
Bunhill Rw STLK EC1Y 6 E6
Bunhouse Pl BGVA SW1W 121 F5
Bunkers Hl GLDGN NW11 65 G4
SCUP DA14 169 G5
Bunker's Hl BELV DA17 129 H4
Bunning Wy HOLWY N7 * 84 E5

Bunn's La MLHL NW7 45 G2
Bunsen St BOW E3 105 G1
Buntingbridge Rd
BARK/HLT IG6 72 D2
Bunting Cl ED N9 37 F3
MTCM CR4 194 E2
Bunton St WOOL/PLUM SE18 127 F3
Bunyan Rd WALTH E17 51 G6
Buonaparte Ms PIM SW1V 121 J5
Burbage Cl HYS/HAR UB3 94 B5
STHWK SE1 18 E5
Burbage Rd HNHL SE24 162 E1
Burberry Cl NWMAL KT3 176 B5
Burbridge Wy TOTM N17 50 C5
Burcham St POP/IOD E14 105 K5
Burcharbro Rd ABYW SE2 128 E6
Burchell Ct BUSH WD23 28 C2
Burchell Rd LEY E10 69 K5
PECK SE15 143 J2
Burcher Gale Gv PECK SE15 143 F1
Burchwall Cl CRW RM5 56 E3
Burcote Rd WAND/EARL SW18 160 C3
Burden Cl BTFD TW8 116 D5
Burdenshott Av
RCHPK/HAM TW10 137 J5
Burden Wy WAN E11 71 F6
Burder Cl IS N1 86 A4
Burder Rd IS N1 86 A4
Burdett Av RYNPK SW20 176 D4
Burdett Cl HNWL W7 * 116 A1
SCUP DA14 187 F1
Burdett Rd BOW E3 105 H3
CROY/NA CR0 196 E3
POP/IOD E14 105 H5
RCH/KEW TW9 137 G3
Burdetts Rd DAGW RM9 92 B6
Burdock Cl CROY/NA CR0 198 A5
Burdock Rd TOTM N17 50 C6
Burdon La BELMT SM2 208 C5
Burdon Pk BELMT SM2 208 D6
Burfield Cl TOOT SW17 160 B6
Burford Cl BARK/HLT IG6 72 C1
BCTR RM8 91 J1
Burford Gdns PLMGR N13 35 F5
Burford Rd BMLY BR1 200 D1
BTFD TW8 117 F5
CAT SE6 164 C4
EHAM E6 107 J2
SRTFD E15 88 B5
SUT SM1 193 K6
WPK KT4 192 D4
Burford Wk FUL/PGN SW6 * 140 A1
Burford Wy CROY/NA CR0 214 A4
Burgate Cl DART DA1 150 C4
Burges Gv BARN SW13 138 E1
Burges Rd EHAM E6 89 K5
Burgess Av CDALE/KGS NW9 63 F3
Burgess Cl FELT TW13 154 D6
Burgess Hl CRICK NW2 82 E2
Burgess Rd SRTFD E15 88 C2
SUT SM1 209 F2
Burgess St POP/IOD E14 105 J4
Burge St STHWK SE1 19 F5
Burghill Rd SYD SE26 164 A6
Burghley Av NWMAL KT3 176 A4
Burghley Hall Cl
WIM/MER SW19 * 159 H3
Burghley Pl MTCM CR4 194 E1
Burghley Rd CEND/HSY/T N8 49 G6
KTTN NW5 84 B2
WAN E11 * 70 C5
WIM/MER SW19 159 G6
Burgh St IS N1 6 B2
Burgon St BLKFR EC4V 12 B4
Burgos Cl CROY/NA CR0 211 G4
Burgos Gv GNWCH SE10 144 E2
Burgoyne Rd BRXN/ST SW9 142 A4
FSBYPK N4 67 H3
SNWD SE25 197 G1
Burham Cl PGE/AN SE20 181 K3
Burhill Gv PIN HA5 41 J5
Burke Cl PUT/ROE SW15 138 B5
Burke St CAN/RD E16 106 D4
Burket Cl NWDGN UB2 114 D4
Burland Rd BTSEA SW11 140 E6
CRW RM5 56 E2
Burleigh Av BFN/LL DA15 148 A6
WLGTN SM6 210 A1
Burleigh Cl ROMW/RG RM7 74 D1
Burleigh Gdns
STHGT/OAK N14 34 C3
Burleigh Pde
STHGT/OAK N14 * 34 D3
Burleigh Pl PUT/ROE SW15 139 G6
Burleigh Rd CHEAM SM3 193 H5
EN EN1 24 A5
Burleigh St COVGDN WC2E 11 F5
Burleigh Wk CAT SE6 165 F3
Burleigh Wy ENC/FH EN2 23 K4
Burley Cl CHING E4 51 J1
STRHM/NOR SW16 179 J5
Burley Rd CAN/RD E16 107 G5
Burlington Ar CONDST W1S 10 A6
Burlington Av RCH/KEW TW9 137 H2
ROMW/RG RM7 74 D3
Burlington Cl
EBED/NFELT TW14 153 G2
EHAM E6 107 J5
MV/WKIL W9 100 E3
ORP BR6 201 G6
PIN HA5 41 F6
Burlington Gdns ACT W3 117 K1
CHDH RM6 74 A4
CHSWK W4 117 K5
CONDST W1S 10 A6
Burlington La CHSWK W4 137 K1
Burlington Ms ACT W3 117 K1
Burlington Pde CRICK NW2 * 82 B2
Burlington Pl FUL/PGN SW6 139 H3
WFD IG8 38 E5
Burlington Ri EBAR EN4 33 J3
Burlington Rd CHSWK W4 * 117 K5
ENC/FH EN2 23 K2
FUL/PGN SW6 139 H3
ISLW TW7 135 J2
MUSWH N10 48 A6
NWMAL KT3 192 C1
THHTH CR7 180 D5
TOTM N17 50 C4
Burma Rd STNW/STAM N16 85 K2
Burma Ter NRWD SE19 * 181 F1
Burmester Rd TOOT SW17 160 B5
Burnaby Crs CHSWK W4 117 J6
Burnaby Gdns CHSWK W4 117 J6
Burnaby St WBPTN SW10 140 B1
Burnbrae Cl
NFNCH/WDSPK N12 47 F2
Burnbury Rd BAL SW12 161 H3
Burncroft Av PEND EN3 24 E3
Burndell Wy YEAD UB4 95 H4
Burnell Av RCHPK/HAM TW10 174 D1
WELL DA16 148 B3
Burnell Gdns STAN HA7 43 K5
Burnell Rd SUT SM1 209 F2
Burnell Wk STHWK SE1 * 123 G5
Burnels Av EHAM E6 108 A2
Burness Cl HOLWY N7 85 F4
Burne St CAMTN NW1 8 C1
Burnet Cl HOM E9 86 E3
Burnett La BARK/HLT IG6 54 B3
Burnett Rd ERITH DA8 131 G6
Burney Av BRYLDS KT5 191 G2
Burney St GNWCH SE10 145 F1
Burnfoot Av FUL/PGN SW6 139 H2
Burnham Av HGDN/ICK UB10 76 A2
Burnham Cl EN EN1 24 A1
KTN/HRWW/WS HA3 61 G1
MLHL NW7 45 J3
STHWK SE1 19 K7
Burnham Crs DART DA1 151 F5
WAN E11 71 G1
Burnham Dr WPK KT4 193 G6
Burnham Gdns CROY/NA CR0 197 G4
HSLWW TW4 134 A2
HYS/HAR UB3 113 G3
Burnham Rd CHING E4 51 H1
DAGW RM9 91 H5
DART DA1 151 G6
MRDN SM4 194 A2
ROMW/RG RM7 56 E6
SCUP DA14 169 F4
Burnham St BETH E2 104 E2
KUTN/CMB KT2 175 H4
Burnham Ter DART DA1 * 151 G6
Burnham Wy SYD SE26 182 C1
WEA W13 116 C4
Burnhill Rd BECK BR3 182 D5
Burnley Cl OXHEY WD19 41 G1
Burnley Rd BRXN/ST SW9 142 A3
WLSDN NW10 81 H3
Burnsall St CHEL SW3 120 D5
Burns Av BFN/LL DA15 168 C1
CHDH RM6 73 J4
EBED/NFELT TW14 153 K1
STHL UB1 96 A6
Burns Cl CAR SM5 210 A6
ERITH DA8 150 C2
WALTH E17 70 A1
WELL DA16 148 A2
WIM/MER SW19 178 C2
YEAD UB4 94 E4
Burnside Av CHING E4 51 H2
Burnside Cl BAR EN5 20 E4
BERM/RHTH SE16 124 A1
TWK TW1 156 B1
Burnside Crs ALP/SUD HA0 79 K6
Burnside Rd BCTR RM8 73 J6
Burns Rd ALP/SUD HA0 98 A1
BTSEA SW11 140 E3
WEA W13 * 116 C2
Burn's Rd WLSDN NW10 81 H6
Burns Wy HEST TW5 134 C2
Burnt Ash Hl LEE/GVPK SE12 165 J1
Burnt Ash La BMLY BR1 183 K2
Burnt Ash Rd LEE/GVPK SE12 145 J6
Burnt House La RDART DA2 171 H6
Burnthwaite Rd
FUL/PGN SW6 139 J1
Burnt Oak Broadway
EDGW HA8 44 D3
Burnt Oak Flds EDGW HA8 44 E4
Burnt Oak La BFN/LL DA15 168 B3
Burntwood Cl
WAND/EARL SW18 * 160 C3
Burntwood Grange Rd
WAND/EARL SW18 160 C3
Burntwood La TOOT SW17 160 C4
Burntwood Vw NRWD SE19 * 181 G1
Buross St WCHPL E1 104 D5
Burpham Cl YEAD UB4 95 H4
Burrage Gv WOOL/PLUM SE18 127 H4
Burrage Pl WOOL/PLUM SE18 127 G5
Burrage Rd WOOL/PLUM SE18 127 H4
Burrard Rd CAN/RD E16 106 E5
KIL/WHAMP NW6 82 E3
Burr Bank Ter RDART DA2 * 171 F6
Burr Cl BXLYHN DA7 149 G4
WAP E1W 123 H1
Burrell Cl CROY/NA CR0 198 B3
EDGW HA8 30 D4
Burrell Rw BECK BR3 182 D5
Burrell St STHWK SE1 12 A7
Burrells Wharf Sq
POP/IOD E14 124 E5
Burrels Whf POP/IOD E14 124 E5
Burrfield Dr STMC/STPC BR5 202 E2
Burritt Rd KUT/HW KT1 175 H5
Burroughs Cots
POP/IOD E14 * 105 G4
Burroughs Gdns HDN NW4 63 K1
The Burroughs HDN NW4 63 K1
Burrow Gn CHIG IG7 55 F1
Burrow Rd CHIG IG7 55 G1
EDUL SE22 143 F5
Burrows Ms STHWK SE1 18 A2
Burrows Rd WLSDN NW10 100 A2
Burr Rd WAND/EARL SW18 159 K3
Bursar St STHWK SE1 * 19 G1
Bursdon Cl BFN/LL DA15 168 A4
Bursland Rd PEND EN3 25 F5
Burslem Av BARK/HLT IG6 55 G2
Burslem St WCHPL E1 * 104 D5
Burstock Rd PUT/ROE SW15 139 H5
Burston Rd PUT/ROE SW15 139 G6
Burstow Rd RYNPK SW20 177 H4
Burtenshaw Rd THDIT KT7 190 B4
Burtley Cl FSBYPK N4 67 J5
Burton Bank IS N1 * 85 K5
Burton Cl CHSGTN KT9 205 K5
THHTH CR7 180 E6
Burton Gdns HEST TW5 134 E2
Burton Gv WALW SE17 122 E5
Burtonhole Cl MLHL NW7 32 B6
Burtonhole La MLHL NW7 32 B6
Burton La BRXN/ST SW9 * 142 B3
Burton Ms BGVA SW1W 15 H7
Burton Pl STPAN WC1H 4 D6
Burton Rd BRXN/ST SW9 142 B3
KIL/WHAMP NW6 82 D5
KUTN/CMB KT2 175 F3
SWFD E18 53 F6
Burtons Ct SRTFD E15 88 B5
Burton's Rd HPTN TW12 155 G6
Burton St STPAN WC1H 4 D6
Burt Rd CAN/RD E16 126 B1
Burtwell La WNWD SE27 162 E6
Burwash Ct STMC/STPC BR5 202 D2
Burwash Rd
WOOL/PLUM SE18 127 J5
Burway Cl SAND/SEL CR2 212 A4
Burwell Av GFD/PVL UB6 78 E4
Burwell Cl WCHPL E1 104 D5
Burwell Rd LEY E10 69 G5
Burwood Av HAYES BR2 200 A6
PIN HA5 59 G2
Burwood Cl SURB KT6 191 H5
Burwood Gdns RAIN RM13 111 H2
Burwood Pl BAY/PAD W2 8 D3
EBAR EN4 21 G2
Bury Av RSLP HA4 58 A3
YEAD UB4 94 C1
Bury Cl BERM/RHTH SE16 124 A1
Bury Ct HDTCH EC3A 13 H3
Bury Gv MRDN SM4 194 A2
Bury Ms ROM RM1 75 H3
Bury Pl NOXST/BSQ WC1A 10 E2
Bury Rd CHING E4 38 C1
DAGE RM10 92 E3
WDGN N22 49 G5
Buryside Cl GNTH/NBYPK IG2 73 F2
Bury St ED N9 36 B2
HDTCH EC3A 13 H4
RSLP HA4 58 B3
STJS SW1Y 10 A7
Bury St West ED N9 36 A2
Bury Wk CHEL SW3 14 C7
Busby Pl KTTN NW5 84 D4
Busch Cl ISLW TW7 136 C2
Bushbaby Cl STHWK SE1 19 G5
Bushberry Rd HOM E9 87 G4
Bush Cl GNTH/NBYPK IG2 72 D2
Bush Cots WAND/EARL SW18 139 K6
Bushell Cl BRXS/STRHM SW2 162 A4
Bushell Gn BUSH WD23 28 D4
Bushell Wy CHST BR7 185 F1
Bush Elms Rd EMPK RM11 75 J4
Bushey Av STMC/STPC BR5 201 J4
SWFD E18 52 D6
Bushey Cl CHING E4 38 A5
Bushey Hill Rd CMBW SE5 143 G2
Bushey La SUT SM1 208 E1
Bushey Lees BFN/LL DA15 * 168 A1
Bushey Rd CROY/NA CR0 198 D6
HYS/HAR UB3 113 H4
PLSTW E13 107 G1
RYNPK SW20 176 E6
SEVS/STOTM N15 68 A3
SUT SM1 208 E2
Bushey Wy BECK BR3 199 G3
Bushfield Cl EDGW HA8 30 D4
Bushfield Crs EDGW HA8 30 D4
Bush Gv CDALE/KGS NW9 62 E4
STAN HA7 43 K3
Bushgrove Rd BCTR RM8 91 K2
Bush Hl WCHMH N21 35 J2
Bush Hill Pde ED N9 * 35 K2
Bush Hill Rd
KTN/HRWW/WS HA3 62 B3
WCHMH N21 35 K1
Bush House
WOOL/PLUM SE18 * 146 D1
Bush La CANST EC4R 12 E5
Bushmead Cl
SEVS/STOTM N15 * 68 B1
Bushmoor Crs
WOOL/PLUM SE18 147 G1
Bushnell Rd TOOT SW17 161 G4
Bush Rd BKHH IG9 39 H6
DEPT SE8 124 A4
HACK E8 86 D6
RCH/KEW TW9 117 G6
WAN E11 70 D4
Bushway BCTR RM8 91 K2
Bushwood WAN E11 70 D5
Bushwood Dr STHWK SE1 19 K7
Bushwood Rd RCH/KEW TW9 117 H6
Bushy Cl CRW RM5 57 F2
Bushy Park Gdns HPTN TW12 173 J1
Bushy Park Rd TEDD TW11 174 C3
Bushy Rd TEDD TW11 173 K2
Butcher Rw WAP E1W 105 F5
Butchers Rd CAN/RD E16 106 E5
Bute Av RCHPK/HAM TW10 157 F4
Bute Gdns HMSMTH W6 119 G4
RCHPK/HAM TW10 * 157 F3
WLGTN SM6 210 C3
Bute Gdns West WLGTN SM6 210 C3
Bute Ms GLDGN NW11 65 F2
Bute Rd BARK/HLT IG6 72 B2
CROY/NA CR0 196 B5
WLGTN SM6 210 C2
Bute St SKENS SW7 14 A6
Bute Wk IS N1 * 85 K4
Butler Av HRW HA1 60 D4
Butler Cl EDGW HA8 44 D5
Butler Rd BCTR RM8 91 H2
HRW HA1 60 C4
WLSDN NW10 81 H5
Butlers Cl HSLWW TW4 134 E5
Butlers & Colonial Whf
STHWK SE1 19 K2
Butlers Farm Cl
RCHPK/HAM TW10 156 E6
Butler St BETH E2 * 104 E2
Buttercup Cl NTHLT UB5 77 K4
Buttercup Sq
STWL/WRAY TW19 * 152 A3
Butterfield Cl
BERM/RHTH SE16 * 123 H2
TOTM N17 49 J2
TWK TW1 156 A1
Butterfield House
CHARL SE7 * 146 D1
Butterfield Ms
WOOL/PLUM SE18 127 G6
Butterfields WALTH E17 70 A2
Butterfield Sq EHAM E6 107 K5
Butterfly Av DART DA1 171 J5
Butterfly La ELTH/MOT SE9 167 G1
Butterfly Wk CMBW SE5 * 142 E2
Butter Hl CAR SM5 210 A1
Butteridges Cl DAGW RM9 92 B6
Butterly Av DART DA1 * 171 J4
Buttermere Cl
EBED/NFELT TW14 153 J3
MRDN SM4 193 G3
SRTFD E15 88 B2
STHWK SE1 19 J7
Buttermere Dr
PUT/ROE SW15 139 H6
Buttermere Rd
STMC/STPC BR5 202 E1
Buttermere Wk HACK E8 86 B4
Butterwick HMSMTH W6 119 F4
Butterworth Gdns WFD IG8 52 E2
Butterworth Ter WALW SE17 * 122 D5
Buttery Ms STHGT/OAK N14 34 E5
Buttesland St IS N1 7 F4
Buttfield Cl DAGE RM10 92 D4
Buttmarsh Cl
WOOL/PLUM SE18 127 G5
Buttsbury Rd IL IG1 90 C3
Butts Crs FELT TW13 155 F5
Buttsmead NTHWD HA6 40 A3
Butts Piece NTHLT UB5 95 F1
Butts Rd BMLY BR1 183 H1
The Butts BTFD TW8 116 E6
Buxhall Crs HOM E9 87 H4
Buxted Rd EDUL SE22 143 F5
HACK E8 86 B5
NFNCH/WDSPK N12 47 J1
Buxton Cl WFD IG8 53 H2
Buxton Crs CHEAM SM3 208 C2
Buxton Dr NWMAL KT3 176 A5
WAN E11 70 C1
Buxton Gdns ACT W3 98 D6
Buxton Ms CLAP SW4 141 J3
Buxton Pth OXHEY WD19 * 27 G5
Buxton Rd ARCH N19 66 D5
CHING E4 38 B2
CRICK NW2 81 K4
EHAM E6 107 J2
ERITH DA8 150 A1
GNTH/NBYPK IG2 72 E3
MORT/ESHN SW14 138 B4
SRTFD E15 88 C3
THHTH CR7 196 C2
WALTH E17 69 G1
Buxton St WCHPL E1 7 K7
Byam St FUL/PGN SW6 140 B3
Byards Cft STRHM/NOR SW16 179 J4
Bychurch End TEDD TW11 * 174 A1
Bycroft Rd STHL UB1 96 A4
Bycroft St PGE/AN SE20 182 A3
Bycullah Av ENC/FH EN2 23 H4
Bycullah Rd ENC/FH EN2 23 H3
Byelands Cl BERM/RHTH SE16 124 A1
The Bye ACT W3 99 G5
Byewaters WATW WD18 26 A1
Bye Ways WHTN TW2 155 G5
The Byeways BRYLDS KT5 191 H2
The Bye Wy
KTN/HRWW/WS HA3 42 E4
The Byeway
MORT/ESHN SW14 137 K4
Byfeld Gdns BARN SW13 138 D2
Byfield Cl BERM/RHTH SE16 124 B2
Byfield Rd ISLW TW7 136 B4
Byford Cl SRTFD E15 88 C5
Bygrove CROY/NA CR0 213 K4
Bygrove Rd WIM/MER SW19 178 C2
Bygrove St POP/IOD E14 105 K5
Byland Cl ABYW SE2 128 C3
CAR SM5 194 B4
STHGT/OAK N14 35 F2
Byne Rd CAR SM5 194 D6
SYD SE26 181 K2
Bynes Rd SAND/SEL CR2 211 K5
Byng Pl GWRST WC1E 4 D7
Byng Rd BAR EN5 20 B4
Byng St POP/IOD E14 124 D2
Bynon Av BXLYHN DA7 149 F4
Byre Rd STHGT/OAK N14 34 A1
Byrne Cl CROY/NA CR0 196 C3
Byrne Rd BAL SW12 161 G3
Byron Av CDALE/KGS NW9 62 D1
HSLWW TW4 134 A3
MNPK E12 89 J4
NWMAL KT3 192 D2
SUT SM1 209 H2
SWFD E18 52 D6
Byron Av East SUT SM1 209 H2
Byron Cl HACK E8 86 C6
HPTN TW12 154 E6
PGE/AN SE20 * 181 J6
SYD SE26 * 164 B6
THMD SE28 128 D1
WOT/HER KT12 188 D5
Byron Ct ENC/FH EN2 23 H3
Byron Dr EFNCH N2 65 H3
ERITH DA8 149 J1
Byron Gdns SUT SM1 209 H2
Byron Hill Rd
RYLN/HDSTN HA2 60 D5
Byron Ms HAMP NW3 83 J3
MV/WKIL W9 100 E3
Byron Rd ALP/SUD HA0 61 J6
CRICK NW2 63 K6
EA W5 117 G1
HRW HA1 60 E3
KTN/HRWW/WS HA3 43 F5
LEY E10 69 K5
MLHL NW7 45 J1
WALTH E17 51 J6
Byron St POP/IOD E14 106 A5
Byron Ter ED N9 * 36 E2
Byron Wy NTHLT UB5 95 J2
WDR/YW UB7 112 C4
YEAD UB4 94 C3
Bysouth Cl CLAY IG5 54 B4
SEVS/STOTM N15 67 K1
By The Wd OXHEY WD19 27 H4
Bythorn St BRXN/ST SW9 142 A4
Byton Rd TOOT SW17 178 E2
Byward Av EBED/NFELT TW14 154 B1
Byward St MON EC3R 13 H6
Bywater Pl BERM/RHTH SE16 124 B1
Bywater St CHEL SW3 120 E5
The Byway BELMT SM2 209 H6
HOR/WEW KT19 207 H2
Bywell Pl GTPST W1W * 10 A2
Bywood Av CROY/NA CR0 197 K3

C

Cabbell St CAMTN NW1 8 C2
Cabinet Wy CHING E4 51 H2
Cable Pl GNWCH SE10 145 F2
Cables Cl ERITH DA8 129 K3
Cable St WCHPL E1 104 C6
Cable Trade Pk CHARL SE7 * 125 K5
Cabot Sq POP/IOD E14 124 D1
Cabot Wy EHAM E6 89 H6
Cabul Rd BTSEA SW11 140 D3
Cactus Cl CMBW SE5 * 143 F3
Cadbury Cl ISLW TW7 136 B2
Cadbury Wy
BERM/RHTH SE16 19 K5
Caddington Cl EBAR EN4 21 J6
Caddington Rd CRICK NW2 82 C1
Caddis Cl STAN HA7 * 43 F3
Cadell Cl BETH E2 7 K3
Cade Rd GNWCH SE10 145 G2
Cader Rd WAND/EARL SW18 160 B1
Cadet Dr STHWK SE1 123 G5
Cadet Pl GNWCH SE10 125 H5
Cadiz Rd DAGE RM10 92 E5
Cadiz St WALW SE17 122 D5
Cadman Cl BRXN/ST SW9 142 C1
Cadmer Cl NWMAL KT3 192 B1
Cadmus Cl CLAP SW4 141 J5
Cadogan Cl HOM E9 * 87 H5
RYLN/HDSTN HA2 78 B2
TEDD TW11 173 K1
Cadogan Ct BELMT SM2 209 F4
Cadogan Gdns CHEL SW3 15 F6
FNCH N3 * 47 F4
SWFD E18 53 F6
WCHMH N21 23 G6
Cadogan Ga KTBR SW1X 15 F6
Cadogan La KTBR SW1X 15 G4
Cadogan Pl KTBR SW1X 15 F4
Cadogan Rd SURB KT6 190 E2
WOOL/PLUM SE18 127 H3
Cadogan Sq KTBR SW1X 14 E5
Cadogan St CHEL SW3 14 E7
KTBR SW1X 15 F6
Cadogan Ter HOM E9 87 H4
Cadoxton Av
SEVS/STOTM N15 68 B3
Cadwallon Rd ELTH/MOT SE9 167 G4
Caedmon Rd HOLWY N7 85 F2
Caerleon Cl ESH/CLAY KT10 205 H5
SCUP DA14 186 D1
Caernarvon Cl MTCM CR4 179 K6
Caernarvon Dr CLAY IG5 54 A4
Caesars Wk MTCM CR4 194 E2
Cahill St STLK EC1Y * 6 D7
Cahir St POP/IOD E14 124 E4
Cain's La EBED/NFELT TW14 133 G6
Caird St NKENS W10 100 C2
Cairn Av EA W5 116 E1
Cairndale Cl BMLY BR1 183 J3
Cairnfield Av CRICK NW2 81 G1
Cairngorm Cl TEDD TW11 174 B1
Cairns Av WFD IG8 53 K2
Cairns Cl DART DA1 151 G6
Cairns Rd BTSEA SW11 140 D6
Cairn Wy STAN HA7 43 F2
Cairo New Rd CROY/NA CR0 196 C6
Cairo Rd WALTH E17 * 69 J1
Caister Ms BAL SW12 161 G2
Caistor Park Rd SRTFD E15 88 D6
Caistor Rd BAL SW12 161 G2
Caithness Gdns
BFN/LL DA15 168 A1
Caithness Rd MTCM CR4 179 G3
WKENS W14 119 G3
Calabria Rd HBRY N5 85 H4
Calais St CMBW SE5 142 C2
Calbourne Av HCH RM12 93 K3
Calbourne Rd BAL SW12 160 E2
Caldbeck Av WPK KT4 192 E6
Caldecote Gdns BUSH WD23 28 E1
Caldecote La BUSH WD23 29 F2
Caldecot Rd CMBW SE5 142 D3
Caldecott Wy CLPT E5 87 F1
Calder Av GFD/PVL UB6 97 F1
Calder Gdns EDGW HA8 44 C6
Calderon Rd WAN E11 88 A2
Calder Rd MRDN SM4 194 B2
Caldervale Rd CLAP SW4 141 J6
Calderwood Pl EBAR EN4 21 F2
Calderwood St
WOOL/PLUM SE18 127 F4
Caldew St CMBW SE5 142 E1
Caldicote Gn
CDALE/KGS NW9 * 63 G3
Caldwell Rd OXHEY WD19 27 H6
Caldwell St BRXN/ST SW9 142 A1
Caldy Rd BELV DA17 129 J3
Caldy Wk IS N1 * 85 J4
Caledonian Cl
GDMY/SEVK IG3 * 73 H5
Caledonian Rd HOLWY N7 85 F3
IS N1 5 G2
Caledonian Sq CAMTN NW1 84 D4
Caledonian Wharf Rd
POP/IOD E14 125 G4
Caledonia Rd
STWL/WRAY TW19 152 B3
Caledonia St IS N1 5 F3
Caledon Rd EHAM E6 89 K6
WLGTN SM6 210 A2
Calendar Ms SURB KT6 190 E3
Cale St CHEL SW3 120 D5

Calidore Cl
BRXS/STRHM SW2 * 162 A1
California La BUSH WD23 28 D3
California Rd NWMAL KT3 191 K1
Callaby Ter IS N1 * 85 K4
Callaghan Cl LEW SE13 145 H5
Callaghan Cots WCHPL E1 * 104 E4
Callander Rd CAT SE6 164 E4
The Callanders BUSH WD23 * 28 E3
Callard Av PLMGR N13 49 H1
Callcott Rd KIL/WHAMP NW6 82 D5
Callcott St KENS W8 119 K1
Callendar Rd SKENS SW7 14 A4
Callingham Cl POP/IOD E14 105 H4
Callis Farm Cl
STWL/WRAY TW19 152 B1
Callisons Pl GNWCH SE10 125 H5
Callis Rd WALTH E17 69 H3
Callow St WBPTN SW10 120 B6
Calmington Rd CMBW SE5 123 F6
Calmont Rd BMLY BR1 183 G2
Calne Av CLAY IG5 54 B4
Calonne Rd WIM/MER SW19 159 G6
Calshot Rd HTHAIR TW6 132 E3
Calshot St IS N1 5 G2
Calshot Wy ENC/FH EN2 23 H4
HTHAIR TW6 132 D3
Calthorpe Gdns EDGW HA8 44 B1
SUT SM1 209 G1
Calthorpe St FSBYW WC1X 5 H6
Calton Av DUL SE21 163 F1
Calton Rd BAR EN5 33 G1
Calverley Cl BECK BR3 182 E2
Calverley Crs DAGE RM10 74 C6
Calverley Gv ARCH N19 66 D5
Calverley Rd EW KT17 207 J4
Calvert Av WCHPL E1 7 H5
Calvert Cl BELV DA17 129 H4
SCUP DA14 187 F2
Calvert Dr RDART DA2 170 A4
Calverton Rd EHAM E6 90 A6
Calvert Rd BAR EN5 20 B3
GNWCH SE10 125 J5
Calvert St CAMTN NW1 84 A6
Calvin Cl STMC/STPC BR5 186 E6
Calvin St WCHPL E1 7 J7
Calydon Rd CHARL SE7 126 A5
Calypso Crs PECK SE15 143 F1
Calypso Wy BERM/RHTH SE16 124 C3
Camac Rd WHTN TW2 155 J3
Camarthen Gn
CDALE/KGS NW9 * 63 G3
Cambalt Rd PUT/ROE SW15 139 G6
Camberley Av EN EN1 24 A5
RYNPK SW20 176 E5
Camberley Cl CHEAM SM3 208 B1
Camberley Rd HTHAIR TW6 132 D4
Cambert Wy BKHTH/KID SE3 146 A5
Camberwell Church St
CMBW SE5 142 E2
Camberwell Glebe CMBW SE5 142 E2
Camberwell Gn CMBW SE5 142 E2
Camberwell Gv CMBW SE5 142 E2
Camberwell New Rd
CMBW SE5 142 C1
Camberwell Rd CMBW SE5 122 D6
Camberwell Station Rd
CMBW SE5 142 D2
Cambeys Rd DAGE RM10 92 E3
Camborne Av WEA W13 116 C2
Camborne Cl HTHAIR TW6 132 D4
Camborne Crs HTHAIR TW6 132 D4
Camborne Ms
WAND/EARL SW18 159 K2
Camborne Rd BELMT SM2 208 E5
CROY/NA CR0 197 H4
RYNPK SW20 193 G2
SCUP DA14 168 D5
WAND/EARL SW18 159 K2
WELL DA16 147 K3
Camborne Wy HEST TW5 135 F2
HTHAIR TW6 132 D4
Cambourne Av ED N9 37 F2
Cambourne Ms NTGHL W11 100 C5
Cambray Rd BAL SW12 161 H3
ORP BR6 202 A4
Cambria Cl BFN/LL DA15 167 J3
HSLW TW3 135 F5
Cambria Ct EBED/NFELT TW14 154 A2
Cambria Gdns
STWL/WRAY TW19 152 B2
Cambrian Av
GNTH/NBYPK IG2 72 E2
Cambrian Cl WNWD SE27 162 C5
Cambrian Gn CDALE/KGS NW9 63 G2
Cambrian Rd LEY E10 69 J4
RCHPK/HAM TW10 157 G1
Cambria Rd CMBW SE5 142 D4
Cambria St FUL/PGN SW6 140 A1
Cambridge Av GFD/PVL UB6 79 F3
KIL/WHAMP NW6 100 E1
NWMAL KT3 176 B5
WELL DA16 148 A5
Cambridge Barracks Rd
WOOL/PLUM SE18 126 E4
Cambridge Circ
SOHO/SHAV W1D 10 D4
Cambridge Cl EBAR EN4 34 A3
HSLWW TW4 134 D5
RYNPK SW20 176 E4
WALTH E17 69 H3
WDGN N22 * 49 G4
WDR/YW UB7 112 A6
WLSDN NW10 80 E1
Cambridge Crs BETH E2 104 D1
TEDD TW11 * 174 B1
Cambridge Dr LEE/GVPK SE12 145 K6
RSLP HA4 59 G6
Cambridge Gdns EN EN1 24 C3
KIL/WHAMP NW6 100 E1
KUT/HW KT1 175 H5
MUSWH N10 48 A4
NKENS W10 100 B5
TOTM N17 49 K3
WCHMH N21 35 K2
Cambridge Ga CAMTN NW1 3 J5
Cambridge Gate Ms
CAMTN NW1 3 K5
Cambridge Gn ELTH/MOT SE9 167 G3
Cambridge Gv HMSMTH W6 118 E4
PGE/AN SE20 * 181 J4
Cambridge Grove Rd
KUT/HW KT1 175 H5
Cambridge Heath Rd
BETH E2 104 D2
Cambridge Pde EN EN1 * 24 C3
Cambridge Pk TWK TW1 156 D2
Cambridge Park Rd WAN E11 70 D4
Cambridge Pas HOM E9 86 E5
Cambridge Pl KENS W8 * 120 A2
Cambridge Rd BARK IG11 90 C5
BARN SW13 138 C3
BMLY BR1 183 K3
BTSEA SW11 140 E2
CAR SM5 209 J4
CHING E4 38 B3
E/WMO/HCT KT8 188 E1
GDMY/SEVK IG3 72 E5
HNWL W7 116 A2
HPTN TW12 172 E3
HSLWW TW4 134 D5
KIL/WHAMP NW6 100 E1
KUT/HW KT1 175 H5
MTCM CR4 179 H6
NWMAL KT3 192 A1
PGE/AN SE20 181 H6
RCH/KEW TW9 137 H1
RYLN/HDSTN HA2 60 A2
RYNPK SW20 176 E4
SCUP DA14 167 K6
STHL UB1 * 114 E1
TEDD TW11 156 B6
TWK TW1 156 E1
WAN E11 70 E3
WOT/HER KT12 188 A3
Cambridge Rd North
CHSWK W4 117 J5
Cambridge Rd South
CHSWK W4 117 J5
Cambridge Rw
WOOL/PLUM SE18 127 G5
Cambridge Sq BAY/PAD W2 8 C3
Cambridge St PIM SW1V 121 G5
Cambridge Ter CAMTN NW1 3 J5
ED N9 * 36 B2
Cambridge Terrace Ms
CAMTN NW1 * 3 K5
Cambridge Yd HNWL W7 * 116 A2
Cambus Cl YEAD UB4 95 J4
Cambus Rd CAN/RD E16 106 E4
Camdale Rd
WOOL/PLUM SE18 148 A1
Camden Av FELT TW13 154 B4
YEAD UB4 95 G6
Camden Cl CHST BR7 185 H4
Camden Gdns CAMTN NW1 * 84 B5
SUT SM1 209 F3
THHTH CR7 180 C6
Camden Gv CHST BR7 185 G2
Camden High St CAMTN NW1 4 A1
Camden Hill Rd NRWD SE19 181 F2
Camdenhurst St POP/IOD E14 105 G5
Camden Lock Pl CAMTN NW1 84 B5
Camden Ms CAMTN NW1 84 D5
Camden Park Rd CAMTN NW1 84 D4
CHST BR7 184 E3
Camden Pas IS N1 6 A2
Camden Rd BXLY DA5 169 G3
CAMTN NW1 * 4 C1
CAMTN NW1 84 B6
CAR SM5 209 K2
SUT SM1 209 F3
WALTH E17 69 H3
WAN E11 71 F3
Camden Rw BKHTH/KID SE3 145 H3
PIN HA5 * 41 G6
Camden Sq CAMTN NW1 84 D4
Camden Ter CAMTN NW1 84 D4
Camden Wk IS N1 6 A1
Camden Wy CHST BR7 184 E3
THHTH CR7 180 C6
Camelford Wk NTGHL W11 * 100 C5
Camel Gv KUTN/CMB KT2 174 E1
Camellia Pl WHTN TW2 155 G2
Camellia St VX/NE SW8 141 K1
Camelot Cl THMD SE28 127 J2
WIM/MER SW19 159 J6
Camel Rd CAN/RD E16 126 C1
Camera Pl WBPTN SW10 120 C6
Cameron Cl BXLY DA5 170 A5
TRDG/WHET N20 33 J4
UED N18 36 D6
Cameron Crs EDGW HA8 44 D4
Cameron Dr DART DA1 151 J3
Cameron Pl
STRHM/NOR SW16 162 B4
Cameron Rd CAT SE6 * 164 C4
CROY/NA CR0 196 C3
GDMY/SEVK IG3 72 E5
HAYES BR2 199 K1
Cameron Sq MTCM CR4 178 D4
Cameron Ter LEE/GVPK SE12 * 166 A5
Camerton Cl HACK E8 86 B4
Camilla Rd BERM/RHTH SE16 123 J4
Camille Cl SNWD SE25 181 H6
Camlan Rd BMLY BR1 165 J6
Camlet St BETH E2 7 J6
Camlet Wy EBAR EN4 20 E3
Camley St KCROSS N1C 4 D1
Camm Gdns KUT/HW KT1 * 175 G5
THDIT KT7 189 K4
Camomile Av MTCM CR4 178 E4
Camomile St HDTCH EC3A 13 H3
OBST EC2N 13 G3
Camomile Rd ROMW/RG RM7 75 F6
Campana Rd FUL/PGN SW6 139 K2
Campbell Av BARK/HLT IG6 54 C4
Campbell Cl ROM RM1 57 G2
RSLP HA4 58 E3
STRHM/NOR SW16 * 179 J1
WHTN TW2 155 J3
WOOL/PLUM SE18 147 F2
Campbell Cots MTCM CR4 * 179 F5
Campbell Cft EDGW HA8 44 C1
Campbell Gordon Wy
CRICK NW2 81 K2
Campbell Rd BOW E3 105 J2
CROY/NA CR0 196 C4
EHAM E6 89 J6
HNWL W7 96 E6
SRTFD E15 88 C2
TOTM N17 50 B4
WALTH E17 69 H1
WHTN TW2 155 J4
Campbell Wk IS N1 84 E6
Campdale Rd HOLWY N7 84 D1
Campden Crs ALP/SUD HA0 79 H1
BCTR RM8 91 J2
Campden Gv KENS W8 119 K2
Campden Hill Gdns KENS W8 119 K1
Campden Hill Ga KENS W8 * 119 K2
Campden Hill Pl NTGHL W11 * 119 J1
Campden Hill Rd KENS W8 119 K1
Campden Hill Sq KENS W8 119 J1
Campden House Cl KENS W8 119 K2
Campden House Ter
KENS W8 * 119 K1
Campden Rd SAND/SEL CR2 212 A3
Campden St KENS W8 119 K1
Campden Ter CHSWK W4 * 118 B5
Campden Wy BCTR RM8 91 H2
Campen Cl WIM/MER SW19 159 H4
Camperdown St WCHPL E1 13 K4
Campfield Rd ELTH/MOT SE9 166 C2
Campion Cl CROY/NA CR0 212 A2
EHAM E6 107 K6
KTN/HRWW/WS HA3 62 B3
ROMW/RG RM7 75 F6
Campion Ct ALP/SUD HA0 * 98 A1
Campion Gdns WFD IG8 52 E1
Campion Pl THMD SE28 128 C1
Campion Rd ISLW TW7 136 A2
LEY E10 69 K4
PUT/ROE SW15 139 F5
Campion Ter CRICK NW2 82 B1
Campion Wy EDGW HA8 30 E6
Camplin Rd
KTN/HRWW/WS HA3 62 A2
Camplin St NWCR SE14 144 A1
Camp Rd WIM/MER SW19 176 E1
Campsbourne Pde
CEND/HSY/T N8 * 66 E1
Campsbourne Rd
CEND/HSY/T N8 48 E6
The Campsbourne
CEND/HSY/T N8 66 E1
Campsey Gdns DAGW RM9 91 H5
Campsey Rd DAGW RM9 91 H5
Campshill Pl LEW SE13 145 F6
Campshill Rd LEW SE13 145 F6
Campus Rd WALTH E17 69 H3
Camp Vw WIM/MER SW19 176 E1
Cam Rd SRTFD E15 88 B6
Camrose Av EDGW HA8 44 B5
ERITH DA8 129 J6
FELT TW13 154 A6
STAN HA7 44 A5
Camrose Cl CROY/NA CR0 198 B4
MRDN SM4 193 K1
Camrose St WOOL/PLUM SE18 128 B5
Canada Av UED N18 49 J2
Canada Crs ACT W3 98 E4
Canada Park Pde
EDGW HA8 * 44 D4
Canada Rd ACT W3 98 E4
ERITH DA8 150 E1
Canada Sq POP/IOD E14 124 E1
Canada St BERM/RHTH SE16 124 A2
Canada Wy SHB W12 99 K6
Canadian Av CAT SE6 164 E3
Canal Ap DEPT SE8 124 B5
Canal Bvd KTTN NW5 84 D4
Canal Cl NKENS W10 100 B3
WCHPL E1 105 G3
Canal Gv PECK SE15 123 H6
Canal Pth BETH E2 7 J1
Canal St CMBW SE5 122 E6
Canal Wk CROY/NA CR0 197 F3
IS N1 85 K6
WLSDN NW10 * 80 E5
Canal Wy NKENS W10 100 B3
Canal Whf GFD/PVL UB6 * 79 G6
Canal Yd NWDGN UB2 * 114 A4
Canberra Cl DAGE RM10 93 F5
HDN NW4 45 J6
Canberra Crs DAGE RM10 93 F5
Canberra Dr NTHLT UB5 95 G2
Canberra Rd HTHAIR TW6 132 D4
ABYW SE2 128 E6
CHARL SE7 126 B6
EHAM E6 89 K6
HTHAIR TW6 132 D4
WEA W13 116 B1
Canbury Av KUTN/CMB KT2 175 G4
Canbury Ms SYD SE26 163 H5
Canbury Park Rd
KUTN/CMB KT2 175 F4
Canbury Pth STMC/STPC BR5 202 B1
Cancell Rd BRXN/ST SW9 142 B2
Candahar Rd BTSEA SW11 140 D3
Candle Gv PECK SE15 143 J4
Candlelight Ct SRTFD E15 88 D4
Candler Ms TWK TW1 156 B2
Candler St SEVS/STOTM N15 * 67 K3
Candover Cl WDR/YW UB7 132 A1
Candover Rd HCH RM12 75 K5
Candover St GTPST W1W * 10 A2
Candy St BOW E3 87 H6
Caney Ms CRICK NW2 64 B6
Canfield Dr RSLP HA4 77 F3
Canfield Gdns
KIL/WHAMP NW6 83 F5
Canfield Pl KIL/WHAMP NW6 83 G4
Canfield Rd RAIN RM13 93 H6
WFD IG8 53 J3
Canford Av NTHLT UB5 77 J6
Canford Cl ENC/FH EN2 23 G3
Canford Gdns NWMAL KT3 192 B3
Canford Pl TEDD TW11 174 D2
Canford Rd CLAP SW4 141 F5
Canham Rd CHSWK W4 118 B2
SNWD SE25 181 F6
Canmore Gdns
STRHM/NOR SW16 179 H3
Cann Hall Rd WAN E11 88 D2
Canning Crs WDGN N22 49 F4
Canning Cross CMBW SE5 143 F3
Canning Pl KENS W8 120 B3
Canning Place Ms KENS W8 * 120 B3
Canning Rd CROY/NA CR0 197 G6
HBRY N5 85 H1
KTN/HRWW/WS HA3 42 E6
SRTFD E15 106 C1
WALTH E17 51 H6
Cannington Rd DAGW RM9 91 J4
Cannizaro Rd WIM/MER SW19 177 F2
Cannonbury Av PIN HA5 59 H3
Cannon Cl HPTN TW12 173 G2
RYNPK SW20 177 F6
Cannon Dr POP/IOD E14 105 J6
Cannon Hl KIL/WHAMP NW6 83 F3
STHGT/OAK N14 34 E5
Cannon Hill La RYNPK SW20 193 G2
Cannon La HAMP NW3 83 H1
PIN HA5 59 J4
Cannon Pl CHARL SE7 126 D5
HAMP NW3 83 G1
Cannon Rd BXLYHN DA7 149 F2
STHGT/OAK N14 34 E5
Cannon St BLKFR EC4V 12 C4
Cannon Street Rd WCHPL E1 104 D5
Cannon Wy E/WMO/HCT KT8 189 F1
Canon Av CHDH RM6 73 J2
Canon Beck Rd
BERM/RHTH SE16 123 K2
Canonbie Rd FSTH SE23 163 K2
Canonbury Crs IS N1 85 J5
Canonbury Gv IS N1 85 J5
Canonbury La IS N1 85 H5
Canonbury Pk North IS N1 85 J4
Canonbury Pk South IS N1 85 J4
Canonbury Rd EN EN1 24 A2
IS N1 85 H5
Canonbury Sq IS N1 85 H5
Canonbury St IS N1 85 J5
Canonbury Vls IS N1 85 H5
Canon Mohan Cl
STHGT/OAK N14 34 A1
Canon Rd BMLY BR1 184 B6
Canon Rw WHALL SW1A 16 E3
Canons Cl EDGW HA8 44 B2
EFNCH N2 65 H4
Canons Cots EDGW HA8 * 44 B2
Canons Ct EDGW HA8 * 44 B2
Canons Dr EDGW HA8 44 B2
Canonsleigh Rd DAGW RM9 91 H5
Canon St IS N1 6 C1
Canon's Wk CROY/NA CR0 213 F1
Canopus Wy NTHWD HA6 26 E6
STWL/WRAY TW19 152 B2
Canrobert St BETH E2 104 D1
Cantelowes Rd CAMTN NW1 84 D4
Canterbury Av BFN/LL DA15 168 D4
IL IG1 71 J4
Canterbury Cl BECK BR3 182 E4
CMBW SE5 * 142 D3
DART DA1 171 K2
EHAM E6 107 K5
GFD/PVL UB6 96 B4
NTHWD HA6 40 D2
Canterbury Crs BRXN/ST SW9 142 B4
Canterbury Gv WNWD SE27 162 B5
Canterbury Pl WALW SE17 18 B7
Canterbury Rd CROY/NA CR0 196 A4
FELT TW13 154 D4
HRW HA1 60 B2
KIL/WHAMP NW6 100 E1
LEY E10 70 A4
MRDN SM4 194 B3
RYLN/HDSTN HA2 60 B2
Canterbury Ter
KIL/WHAMP NW6 100 E1
Cantley Gdns
GNTH/NBYPK IG2 72 C3
NRWD SE19 181 G4
Cantley Rd HNWL W7 116 B3
Canton St POP/IOD E14 105 J5
Cantrell Rd BOW E3 105 J3
Cantwell Rd
WOOL/PLUM SE18 147 G1
Canvey St STHWK SE1 12 C7
Cape Cl BARK IG11 90 B5
Capel Av WLGTN SM6 211 F3
Capel Cl HAYES BR2 200 D5
TRDG/WHET N20 33 G5
Capel Crs STAN HA7 29 G4
Capel Gdns GDMY/SEVK IG3 91 F2
PIN HA5 59 K1
Capella Rd NTHWD HA6 40 D1
Capel Pl RDART DA2 171 F6
Capel Rd EBAR EN4 33 J1
FSTGT E7 89 F2
OXHEY WD19 27 H1
Capeners Cl KTBR SW1X 15 F3
Capener's Cl KTBR SW1X * 15 G3
Capern Rd WAND/EARL SW18 160 B3
Cape Rd TOTM N17 50 C6
Cape Yd WAP E1W 123 H1
Capital Interchange Wy
BTFD TW8 117 H5
Capitol Wy CDALE/KGS NW9 44 E6
Capland St STJWD NW8 2 B6
Caple Pde WLSDN NW10 * 99 H1
Caple Rd WLSDN NW10 99 H1
Caprea Cl YEAD UB4 95 H4
Capri Rd CROY/NA CR0 197 G4
Capstan Cl CHDH RM6 73 H3
Capstan Dr RAIN RM13 111 J4
Capstan Ride ENC/FH EN2 23 G3
Capstan Rd DEPT SE8 124 C4
Capstan Sq POP/IOD E14 125 F2
Capstan Wy
BERM/RHTH SE16 124 B1
Capstone Rd BMLY BR1 165 J6
Capthorne Av
RYLN/HDSTN HA2 59 J5
Capuchin Cl STAN HA7 43 H2
Capulet Ms CAN/RD E16 125 K1
Capworth St LEY E10 69 J5
Caractacus Cottage Vw
WATW WD18 26 E2
Caractacus Gn WATW WD18 26 D1
Caradoc Cl BAY/PAD W2 100 E5
Caradoc Evans Cl
FBAR/BDGN N11 * 48 B1
Caradoc St GNWCH SE10 125 H5
Caradon Ct WAN E11 70 C5
Caradon Wy
SEVS/STOTM N15 * 67 K1
Caravel Cl POP/IOD E14 124 D3
Caravel Ms DEPT SE8 124 D6
Caraway Cl PLSTW E13 107 F4
Caraway Pl WLGTN SM6 210 B1
Carberry Rd NRWD SE19 181 F2
Carbery Av ACT W3 117 G2
Carbis Cl CHING E4 38 B3
Carbis Rd POP/IOD E14 105 H5
Carburton St GTPST W1W 9 K1
Cardale St POP/IOD E14 125 F3
Carden Rd PECK SE15 143 J4
Cardiff Cl CRW RM5 57 F3
Cardiff Rd HNWL W7 116 B3
PEND EN3 24 D5
Cardiff St WOOL/PLUM SE18 147 K1
Cardigan Gdns
GDMY/SEVK IG3 73 G6
Cardigan Pl LEW SE13 * 145 G3
Cardigan Rd BARN SW13 138 D3
BOW E3 105 H1
RCHPK/HAM TW10 157 F1
WIM/MER SW19 178 B2
Cardigan St LBTH SE11 122 B5
Cardigan Wk IS N1 * 85 J5
Cardinal Av KUTN/CMB KT2 175 F1
MRDN SM4 193 H3
Cardinal Bourne St
STHWK SE1 * 19 F5
Cardinal Cl CHST BR7 185 J4
EDGW HA8 44 E3
MRDN SM4 193 H3
WPK KT4 207 J2
Cardinal Crs NWMAL KT3 175 K5
Cardinal Dr BARK/HLT IG6 54 C2
WOT/HER KT12 188 C5
Cardinal Hinsey Cl
WLSDN NW10 99 J1
Cardinal Pl PUT/ROE SW15 139 G5
Cardinal Rd FELT TW13 154 A3
RSLP HA4 59 H5
Cardinal's Wk HPTN TW12 173 H3
Cardinals Wy ARCH N19 66 D5
Cardinal Wy
KTN/HRWW/WS HA3 * 42 E6
Cardine Ms PECK SE15 143 J1
Cardington Sq HSLWW TW4 134 C5
Cardington St CAMTN NW1 4 B4
Cardozo Rd HOLWY N7 84 E3
Cardrew Av
NFNCH/WDSPK N12 47 H1
Cardross St HMSMTH W6 118 E3
Cardwell Rd HOLWY N7 * 84 E2
Cardwell Ter HOLWY N7 * 84 E2
Carew Cl HOLWY N7 67 F6
Carew Rd MTCM CR4 179 F5
NTHWD HA6 40 C2
THHTH CR7 180 C6
TOTM N17 50 C5
WEA W13 116 D2
WLGTN SM6 210 C4
Carew St CMBW SE5 142 D3
Carew Wy OXHEY WD19 27 K5
STMC/STPC BR5 202 D5
Carey Gdns VX/NE SW8 141 H2
Carey La CITYW EC2V 12 C3
Carey Pl PIM SW1V 16 C7
Carey Rd DAGW RM9 92 A2
Carey St LINN WC2A 11 H4
Carey Wy WBLY HA9 80 D2
Carfax Pl CLAP SW4 141 J5
Carfax Rd HCH RM12 93 H2
HYS/HAR UB3 113 K5
The Carfax SYD SE26 * 163 K5
Carfree Cl IS N1 85 G5
Cargill Rd WAND/EARL SW18 160 B3
Cargreen Rd SNWD SE25 197 G1
Carholme Rd FSTH SE23 164 C3
Carisbrook Cl EN EN1 24 B2
Carisbrooke Av BXLY DA5 168 E3
Carisbrooke Cl HSLWW TW4 154 D3
STAN HA7 43 K5
Carisbrooke Ct NTHLT UB5 * 77 K6
Carisbrooke Gdns
PECK SE15 * 143 G1
Carisbrooke Rd HAYES BR2 200 B1
MTCM CR4 195 K1
WALTH E17 * 69 G1
Carker's La ARCH N19 66 D4
KTTN NW5 84 B3
Carleton Av WLGTN SM6 210 D6
Carleton Cl ESH/CLAY KT10 189 J5
Carleton Gdns ARCH N19 * 84 C3
Carleton Rd DART DA1 171 K2
HOLWY N7 84 D2
Carleton Vls KTTN NW5 * 84 C3
Carlile Cl BOW E3 105 H1
Carlina Gdns WFD IG8 53 F1
Carlingford Rd HAMP NW3 83 H2
MRDN SM4 193 G3
SEVS/STOTM N15 49 H6
Carlisle Av ACT W3 99 G5
TWRH EC3N 13 H4
Carlisle Cl KUTN/CMB KT2 175 H4
PIN HA5 59 J4
Carlisle Gdns IL IG1 71 J3
KTN/HRWW/WS HA3 61 K4
Carlisle La STHWK SE1 17 H4
Carlisle Pl FBAR/BDGN N11 34 B6
WEST SW1P 16 A5
Carlisle Rd CDALE/KGS NW9 44 E6
DART DA1 171 K1
FSBYPK N4 67 G5
HPTN TW12 173 G3
KIL/WHAMP NW6 82 C6
LEY E10 69 J5
ROM RM1 75 H2
SUT SM1 208 D4
Carlisle St SOHO/SHAV W1D 10 C4
Carlisle Wk HACK E8 86 B4
Carlisle Wy TOOT SW17 179 F1
Carlos Pl MYFR/PKLN W1K 9 H6
Carlow St CAMTN NW1 4 A2
Carlton Av EBED/NFELT TW14 154 B1
HYS/HAR UB3 113 H4
KTN/HRWW/WS HA3 61 H2
SAND/SEL CR2 211 K5
STHGT/OAK N14 22 D6
Carlton Av East WBLY HA9 61 K6
Carlton Av West
ALP/SUD HA0 61 H6
Carlton Cl CHSGTN KT9 205 K4

EDGW HA8 44 C1
HAMP NW3 64 E6
Carlton Crs CHEAM SM3 208 C2
Carlton Dene EW KT17 * 207 K3
Carlton Dr BARK/HLT IG6 54 D6
PUT/ROE SW15 139 G6
Carlton Gdns EA W5 97 J5
Carlton Ga MV/WKIL W9 100 E4
Carlton Gn SCUP DA14 * 168 A6
Carlton Gv PECK SE15 143 J2
Carlton Hl STJWD NW8 101 G1
Carlton House Ter STJS SW1Y 16 C1
Carlton Ms KIL/WHAMP NW6 * 82 E3
Carlton Pde WBLY HA9 * 62 A5
Carlton Park Av RYNPK SW20 177 F5
Carlton Rd CHSWK W4 118 A2
EA W5 97 J6
ERITH DA8 129 J6
FBAR/BDGN N11 48 A1
FSBYPK N4 67 G4
GPK RM2 75 J2
MNPK E12 89 H2
MORT/ESHN SW14 137 K4
NWMAL KT3 176 B5
SAND/SEL CR2 211 K5
SCUP DA14 186 A1
WALTH E17 51 G4
WAN E11 70 D5
WELL DA16 148 C4
WOT/HER KT12 188 A4
Carlton Sq WCHPL E1 * 105 F3
Carlton St STJS SW1Y 10 C6
Carlton Ter SYD SE26 163 K6
UED N18 * 35 K6
WAN E11 * 71 F2
Carlton Tower Pl KTBR SW1X 15 F4
Carlton V KIL/WHAMP NW6 100 E1
Carlwell St TOOT SW17 178 D1
Carlyle Av BMLY BR1 184 C6
STHL UB1 95 K6
Carlyle Cl E/WMO/HCT KT8 173 G5
EFNCH N2 65 G3
WLSDN NW10 81 F6
Carlyle Ct WBPTN SW10 * 140 B2
Carlyle Gdns STHL UB1 95 K6
Carlyle Pl PUT/ROE SW15 139 G5
Carlyle Rd CROY/NA CR0 197 H6
EA W5 116 D4
MNPK E12 89 J2
THMD SE28 109 H6
Carlyle Sq CHEL SW3 120 C5
Carlyon Av RYLN/HDSTN HA2 77 K2
Carlyon Cl ALP/SUD HA0 80 A6
Carlyon Rd ALP/SUD HA0 98 A1
YEAD UB4 95 G4
Carlys Cl BECK BR3 182 A5
Carmalt Gdns PUT/ROE SW15 139 F5
Carmel Ct KENS W8 * 120 A2
Carmelite Rd
KTN/HRWW/WS HA3 42 C4
Carmelite St EMB EC4Y 11 K5
Carmel Wy RCH/KEW TW9 137 H3
Carmen St POP/IOD E14 105 K5
Carmichael Cl BTSEA SW11 * 140 C4
RSLP HA4 76 E2
Carmichael Ms
WAND/EARL SW18 160 C2
Carmichael Rd SNWD SE25 197 H2
Carminia Rd TOOT SW17 161 G4
Carnaby St SOHO/CST W1F 10 A4
Carnac St WNWD SE27 162 E6
Carnanton Rd WALTH E17 52 B4
Carnarvon Av EN EN1 24 B3
Carnarvon Dr HYS/HAR UB3 113 F3
Carnarvon Rd BAR EN5 20 C4
LEY E10 70 A3
SRTFD E15 88 D4
SWFD E18 52 D4
Carnation Cl ROMW/RG RM7 75 G6
Carnation St ABYW SE2 128 C5
Carnbrook Rd BKHTH/KID SE3 146 C4
Carnecke Gdns
ELTH/MOT SE9 146 D6
Carnegie Cl PEND EN3 25 K1
SURB KT6 191 G6
Carnegie Pl WIM/MER SW19 159 G5
Carnegie St IS N1 5 G1
Carnet Cl DART DA1 170 B2
Carnforth Cl HOR/WEW KT19 206 D4
Carnforth Gdns HCH RM12 93 J3
Carnforth Rd
STRHM/NOR SW16 179 J3
Carnoustie Dr IS N1 85 F5
Carnoustie Cl THMD SE28 109 K5
Carnwath Rd FUL/PGN SW6 139 K4
Carol Cl HDN NW4 64 B1
Carolina Cl SRTFD E15 88 C3
Carolina Rd THHTH CR7 180 C5
Caroline Cl CROY/NA CR0 212 A2
ISLW TW7 135 J1
MUSWH N10 48 B5
STRHM/NOR SW16 162 A5
WDR/YW UB7 112 A2
Caroline Ct STAN HA7 * 43 G2
Caroline Gdns BETH E2 7 H4
PECK SE15 * 143 J1
Caroline Pl BAY/PAD W2 101 F6
BTSEA SW11 141 F3
HYS/HAR UB3 133 H1
OXHEY WD19 27 J1
Caroline Rd WIM/MER SW19 177 J3
Caroline St WCHPL E1 105 F5
Caroline Ter BGVA SW1W 15 G7
Caroline Wk HMSMTH W6 119 H6
Carol St CAMTN NW1 84 C6
Carolyn Dr ORP BR6 217 G1
Carpenders Av OXHEY WD19 27 J5
Carpenter Cl EW KT17 207 H6
Carpenter Gdns WCHMH N21 35 H4
Carpenters Cl BAR EN5 33 F1
Carpenters Ms HOLWY N7 * 84 E3
Carpenter's Pl CLAP SW4 141 J5
Carpenters Rd SRTFD E15 88 A5
Carpenter St
MYFR/PKLN W1K 9 J6
Carrara Ms HACK E8 86 C3
Carr Cl STAN HA7 43 G2
Carre Ms CMBW SE5 142 C2
Carr Gv WOOL/PLUM SE18 126 D4
Carriage Dr East CHEL SW3 121 F6
Carriage Dr North
BTSEA SW11 140 E1
Carriage Dr South
BTSEA SW11 140 E2
Carriage Dr West BTSEA SW11 140 E1
Carriage Ms IL IG1 72 C6
Carrick Cl ISLW TW7 136 B4
Carrick Dr BARK/HLT IG6 54 C4
Carrick Gdns TOTM N17 50 A3
Carrick Ga ESH/CLAY KT10 204 C1
Carrick Ms DEPT SE8 124 D6
Carrill Wy BELV DA17 128 E4
Carrington Av HSLW TW3 135 G6
Carrington Cl CROY/NA CR0 198 B4
Carrington Gdns FSTGT E7 88 E2
Carrington Pl
ESH/CLAY KT10 * 204 B2
Carrington Rd DART DA1 171 J1
RCHPK/HAM TW10 137 H5
Carrington Sq
KTN/HRWW/WS HA3 42 C3
Carrington St MYFR/PICC W1J 15 J1
Carrol Cl KTTN NW5 84 B2
Carroll Cl SRTFD E15 88 D3
Carronade Pl THMD SE28 127 H3
Carron Cl POP/IOD E14 105 K5
Carroun Rd VX/NE SW8 142 A1
Carroway La GFD/PVL UB6 96 D2
Carrow Rd DAGW RM9 91 H5
Carr Rd NTHLT UB5 78 B5
WALTH E17 51 J5
Carrs La WCHMH N21 23 K6
Carr St POP/IOD E14 105 G4
Carshalton Gv SUT SM1 209 H2
Carshalton Park Rd CAR SM5 209 K4
Carshalton Pl CAR SM5 210 A2
Carshalton Rd MTCM CR4 195 F2
SUT SM1 209 G3
Carsington Gdns DART DA1 171 G4
Carslake Rd PUT/ROE SW15 159 F1
Carson Rd CAN/RD E16 106 E4
DUL SE21 162 D4
EBAR EN4 21 K5
Carstairs Rd CAT SE6 165 F5
Carston Cl LEE/GVPK SE12 145 J6
Carswell Cl REDBR IG4 71 H1
Carswell Rd CAT SE6 165 F2
Carter Cl CDALE/KGS NW9 63 F3
CRW RM5 56 D3
WLGTN SM6 210 D5
Carter Dr CRW RM5 56 D2
Carteret St STJSPK SW1H 16 C3
Carteret Wy DEPT SE8 124 B4
Carterhatch La EN EN1 24 B2
Carterhatch Rd PEND EN3 25 G3
Carter La BLKFR EC4V 12 A5
Carter Pl WALW SE17 122 D5
Carter Rd PLSTW E13 89 F6
WIM/MER SW19 178 C2
Carters Cl KTTN NW5 * 84 D4
WPK KT4 193 G6
Carters Hill Cl ELTH/MOT SE9 166 B3
Carter St WALW SE17 122 D6
Carters Yd
WAND/EARL SW18 * 139 K6
Carter's Yd
WAND/EARL SW18 * 139 K6
Carthew Rd HMSMTH W6 118 E3
Carthew Vls HMSMTH W6 118 E3
Carthusian St FARR EC1M 12 C1
Cartier Cir POP/IOD E14 125 F1
Carting La TPL/STR WC2R 11 F6
Cart La CHING E4 38 B3
Cartmel Cl TOTM N17 50 D3
Cartmel Ct NTHLT UB5 77 J4
Cartmel Gdns MRDN SM4 194 B2
Cartmel Rd BXLYHN DA7 149 H2
Cartwright Gdns
STPAN WC1H 4 D5
Cartwright St WCHPL E1 13 K5
Cartwright Wy BARN SW13 138 E1
Carver Cl CHSWK W4 117 K3
Carver Rd HNHL SE24 162 D1
Carville Crs BTFD TW8 117 F4
Cary Rd WAN E11 88 C2
Carysfort Rd CEND/HSY/T N8 66 D2
STNW/STAM N16 85 K1
Cascade Av MUSWH N10 66 C1
Cascade Cl STMC/STPC BR5 186 D6
Cascade Rd BKHH IG9 39 H4
Casella Rd NWCR SE14 144 A1
Casewick Rd WNWD SE27 180 C1
Casey Cl STJWD NW8 2 C5
Casimir Rd CLPT E5 86 D1
Casino Av HNHL SE24 142 D6
Caspian Cl PUR RM19 131 K5
Caspian St CMBW SE5 142 E1
Caspian Wk CAN/RD E16 107 H5
Caspian Wy PUR RM19 131 K5
Cassandra Cl NTHLT UB5 78 D2
Casselden Rd WLSDN NW10 81 F5
Cassidy Rd FUL/PGN SW6 139 K1
Cassilda Rd ABYW SE2 128 B4
Cassilis Rd POP/IOD E14 124 D2
TWK TW1 156 C1
Cassiobury Av
EBED/NFELT TW14 153 J2
Cassiobury Rd WALTH E17 69 F2
Cassland Rd HOM E9 87 F5
THHTH CR7 196 E1
Casslee Rd CAT SE6 164 C2
Casson St WCHPL E1 104 C4
Castellain Rd MV/WKIL W9 101 F3
Castellan Av GPK RM2 57 K6
Castellane Cl STAN HA7 43 F3
Castello Av PUT/ROE SW15 139 F6
Castelnau BARN SW13 138 E1
Casterbridge Rd
BKHTH/KID SE3 145 K4
Casterton St HACK E8 86 D4
Castile Rd WOOL/PLUM SE18 127 F4
Castillon Rd CAT SE6 165 H4
Castlands Rd CAT SE6 164 C4
Castle Av CHING E4 52 B1
EW KT17 207 J6
RAIN RM13 93 G5
Castlebar Hl WEA W13 97 H4
Castlebar Ms EA W5 97 H4
Castlebar Pk EA W5 97 H4
Castlebar Rd WEA W13 97 J5
Castle Baynard St
BLKFR EC4V 12 B5
Castlebrook Cl LBTH SE11 18 A6
Castle Cl ACT W3 117 J2
BUSH WD23 28 B1
HAYES BR2 183 H6
WIM/MER SW19 159 G5
Castlecombe Dr
WIM/MER SW19 159 G2
Castlecombe Rd
ELTH/MOT SE9 184 D1
Castle Ct BANK EC3V * 13 F4
SYD SE26 164 B6
Castledine Rd PGE/AN SE20 181 J3
Castle Dr REDBR IG4 71 J3
Castleford Av ELTH/MOT SE9 167 G3
Castleford Cl TOTM N17 50 B2
Castlegate RCH/KEW TW9 137 G4
Castlehaven Rd CAMTN NW1 84 B5
Castle Hill Av CROY/NA CR0 213 K6
Castle Hill Pde WEA W13 * 97 H6
Castle La WESTW SW1E 16 A4
Castleleigh Ct ENC/FH EN2 23 K6
Castlemaine Av EW KT17 207 K6
SAND/SEL CR2 212 B3
Castlemaine St WCHPL E1 104 D4
Castle Md CMBW SE5 * 142 D1
Castle Ms CAMTN NW1 84 B4
NFNCH/WDSPK N12 47 G1
TOOT SW17 160 D6
Castle Pde EW KT17 * 207 J5
Castle Pl CAMTN NW1 84 B4
Castlereagh St MBLAR W1H 8 E3
Castle Rd CAMTN NW1 84 B4
DAGW RM9 91 H6
ISLW TW7 136 A3
NFNCH/WDSPK N12 47 G1
NTHLT UB5 78 B4
NWDGN UB2 * 114 E3
PEND EN3 25 G2
Castle Rw CHSWK W4 * 118 A5
Castle St EHAM E6 107 G1
KUT/HW KT1 * 175 F5
Castleton Av BXLYHN DA7 150 A2
WBLY HA9 80 A2
Castleton Cl CROY/NA CR0 198 B3
Castleton Gdns WBLY HA9 80 A1
Castleton Rd ELTH/MOT SE9 166 C6
GDMY/SEVK IG3 73 H5
MTCM CR4 195 J1
RSLP HA4 59 H5
WALTH E17 52 B5
Castletown Rd WKENS W14 119 H5
Castleview Cl FSBYPK N4 67 J5
Castleview Gdns IL IG1 71 J3
Castle Vls CRICK NW2 * 81 J4
Castle Wk SUN TW16 * 172 B6
Castle Wy FELT TW13 154 B6
WIM/MER SW19 159 G5
Castlewood Dr ELTH/MOT SE9 146 E3
Castlewood Rd EBAR EN4 21 H4
STNW/STAM N16 68 C3
Castle Yd HGT N6 * 66 A4
RCH/KEW TW9 136 E6
STHWK SE1 * 12 B7
Castor La POP/IOD E14 105 K6
Catalina Rd HTHAIR TW6 132 E4
Catalpa Ct LEW SE13 165 G1
Caterham Av CLAY IG5 54 A5
Caterham Rd LEW SE13 145 F4
Catesby St WALW SE17 19 F7
Catford Broadway CAT SE6 164 E2
Catford Hl CAT SE6 164 C3
Catford Island CAT SE6 * 164 E2
Catford Rd CAT SE6 164 D3
Cathall Rd WAN E11 88 C1
Cathay St BERM/RHTH SE16 123 J2
Cathcart Dr ORP BR6 201 K6
Cathcart Hl ARCH N19 84 C1
Cathcart Rd WBPTN SW10 * 120 A6
Cathcart St KTTN NW5 84 B4
Cathedral St STHWK SE1 12 E7
Catherall Rd HBRY N5 85 J1
Catherine Cl LOU IG10 39 K1
Catherine Ct STHGT/OAK N14 22 C6
Catherine Dr RCH/KEW TW9 137 F5
Catherine Gdns HSLW TW3 135 J5
Catherine Griffiths Ct
CLKNW EC1R 5 K6
Catherine Gv GNWCH SE10 144 E2
Catherine Pl HRW HA1 61 F2
WESTW SW1E 16 A4
Catherine Rd GPK RM2 75 K2
SURB KT6 190 E2
Catherines Cl WDR/YW UB7 * 112 A2
Catherine St HOL/ALD WC2B * 11 G5
Catherine Vls RYNPK SW20 * 176 E3
Catherine Wheel Aly
LVPST EC2M 13 H2
Catherine Wheel Rd
BTFD TW8 136 E1
Catherine Wheel Yd
WHALL SW1A 16 A1
Cat Hl EBAR EN4 33 J1
Cathles Rd BAL SW12 161 G1
Cathnor Rd SHB W12 118 E2
Catling Cl FSTH SE23 163 K5
Catlin's La PIN HA5 41 F6
Catlin St BERM/RHTH SE16 123 H5
Cator La BECK BR3 182 C5
Cato Rd CLAP SW4 141 J4
Cator Rd CAR SM5 209 K3
SYD SE26 182 A2
Cator St PECK SE15 123 G6
Cato St MBLAR W1H 8 D2
Catsey La BUSH WD23 28 C2
Catsey Wd BUSH WD23 28 C2
Catterick Cl FBAR/BDGN N11 48 A2
Cattistock Rd ELTH/MOT SE9 184 D1
Cattley Cl BAR EN5 20 C5
Catton St RSQ WC1B 11 G2
Caudwell Ter
WAND/EARL SW18 * 160 C1
Caulfield Rd CHSWK W4 117 K3
EHAM E6 89 K5
PECK SE15 143 J3
Causeway EBED/NFELT TW14 134 A5
The Causeway BELMT SM2 209 G6
CAR SM5 210 A1
CHSGTN KT9 206 A2
EFNCH N2 65 H1
ESH/CLAY KT10 205 F5
TEDD TW11 174 A2
WAND/EARL SW18 140 A5
WIM/MER SW19 177 F1
Causeyware Rd ED N9 36 D2
Causton Cots POP/IOD E14 * 105 G4
Causton Rd HGT N6 * 66 B4
Causton Sq DAGE RM10 92 C5
Causton St WEST SW1P 16 D7
Cautley Av CLAP SW4 141 H6
Cavalier Cl CHDH RM6 73 J1
Cavalier Gdns HYS/HAR UB3 94 B5
Cavalry Crs HSLWW TW4 134 C5
Cavalry Gdns PUT/ROE SW15 139 H6
Cavan Pl PIN HA5 * 41 K4
Cavaye Pl WBPTN SW10 120 B5
Cavell Crs DART DA1 151 K5
Cavell Dr ENC/FH EN2 23 G3
Cavell Rd TOTM N17 49 K3
Cavell St WCHPL E1 104 D4
Cavendish Av BFN/LL DA15 168 B2
ERITH DA8 129 K6
FNCH N3 46 E5
HCH RM12 93 K4
HRW HA1 78 D2
NWMAL KT3 192 E2
RSLP HA4 77 F3
STJWD NW8 2 B3
WEA W13 97 G4
WELL DA16 148 A4
WFD IG8 53 F3
Cavendish Cl
KIL/WHAMP NW6 82 D4
STJWD NW8 2 B4
UED N18 * 50 D1
YEAD UB4 94 C4
Cavendish Crs HCH RM12 93 K4
Cavendish Dr EDGW HA8 44 B2
ESH/CLAY KT10 204 E3
WAN E11 70 B5
Cavendish Gdns BARK IG11 91 F3
CHDH RM6 74 A2
CLAP SW4 * 161 H1
IL IG1 72 A5
Cavendish Ms SUT SM1 194 B6
Cavendish Ms North
GTPST W1W 9 K1
Cavendish Ms South
GTPST W1W * 9 K2
Cavendish Pde CLAP SW4 * 141 H5
HSLWW TW4 * 134 D3
Cavendish Pl BAL SW12 161 H3
BMLY BR1 184 E6
CAVSQ/HST W1G 9 K3
CRICK NW2 82 B4
Cavendish Rd BAL SW12 161 H2
BAR EN5 20 A4
BELMT SM2 209 G5
CHING E4 52 A2
CHSWK W4 137 K2
CLAP SW4 161 G1
CROY/NA CR0 196 C5
FSBYPK N4 67 H3
KIL/WHAMP NW6 82 C5
NWMAL KT3 192 C2
UED N18 50 D1
WIM/MER SW19 178 D3
Cavendish Sq
CAVSQ/HST W1G 9 K3
Cavendish St IS N1 6 E3
Cavendish Ter BOW E3 * 105 H2
FELT TW13 * 153 K4
Cavendish Wy WWKM BR4 198 E5
Cavenham Gdns IL IG1 90 D1
Caverleigh Wy WPK KT4 192 D5
Caverley Gdns
KTN/HRWW/WS HA3 61 K4
Cave Rd PLSTW E13 107 F1
RCHPK/HAM TW10 156 D6
Caversham Av CHEAM SM3 193 H6
PLMGR N13 35 G5
Caversham Flats CHEL SW3 * 120 E6
Caversham Rd KTTN NW5 84 C4
KUT/HW KT1 175 G5
SEVS/STOTM N15 67 J1
Caversham St CHEL SW3 120 E6
Caverswall St SHB W12 100 A5
Cawdor Crs HNWL W7 116 B4
Cawnpore St NRWD SE19 181 F1
Caxton Gv BOW E3 105 J2
Caxton Ms BTFD TW8 116 D6
Caxton Rd NWDGN UB2 114 C3
SHB W12 119 G1
WDGN N22 49 F5
WIM/MER SW19 178 B1
The Caxtons BRXN/ST SW9 * 142 C1
Caxton St STJSPK SW1H 16 B4
Caxton St North CAN/RD E16 106 D5
Caxton Wy ROM RM1 75 G1
WATW WD18 26 B2
Cayenne Ct STHWK SE1 19 J1
Caygill Cl HAYES BR2 199 J1
Cayley Rd NWDGN UB2 115 G3
Cayton Rd GFD/PVL UB6 96 E1
Cayton St FSBYE EC1V 6 E5
Cazenove Rd
STNW/STAM N16 68 B6
WALTH E17 51 J4
Cecil Av BARK IG11 90 D5
EN EN1 24 B5
WBLY HA9 80 B3
Cecil Cl CHSGTN KT9 205 K2
EA W5 * 97 K4
Cecil Ct BAR EN5 20 B4
CHCR WC2N * 10 E5
LSQ/SEVD WC2H 10 D6
Cecile Pk CEND/HSY/T N8 66 E3
Cecilia Cl EFNCH N2 47 G6
Cecilia Rd HACK E8 86 B3
Cecil Manning Cl
GFD/PVL UB6 79 G6
Cecil Pk PIN HA5 59 J1
Cecil Pl MTCM CR4 194 E2
Cecil Rd ACT W3 98 E4
CDALE/KGS NW9 45 F6
CHDH RM6 73 K4
CROY/NA CR0 195 K3
ENC/FH EN2 23 K5
HSLW TW3 135 H4
IL IG1 90 B2
KTN/HRWW/WS HA3 42 E6
MUSWH N10 48 B5
PLSTW E13 88 E6
STHGT/OAK N14 34 B3
SUT SM1 208 D4
WALTH E17 51 J4
WAN E11 70 C6
WIM/MER SW19 178 A3
WLSDN NW10 81 G6
Cecil Wy HAYES BR2 199 K5
Cedar Av BFN/LL DA15 168 B2
CHDH RM6 74 A2
EBAR EN4 33 J2
HYS/HAR UB3 94 E5
PEND EN3 24 E3
RSLP HA4 77 G3
WDR/YW UB7 * 112 C1
WHTN TW2 155 G1
Cedar Cl BKHH IG9 39 H4
BOW E3 87 H6
CAR SM5 209 K4
DUL SE21 162 D3
HAYES BR2 215 J1
IL IG1 90 D3
KUTN/CMB KT2 158 A6
ROMW/RG RM7 74 E1
SWLY BR8 187 K5
Cedar Copse BMLY BR1 184 E5
Cedar Ct CHARL SE7 * 126 B6
ELTH/MOT SE9 * 166 D1
WIM/MER SW19 159 G5
Cedar Crs HAYES BR2 215 J1
Cedarcroft Rd CHSGTN KT9 206 B2
Cedar Dr EFNCH N2 65 J1
GLDGN NW11 64 E1
PIN HA5 42 A2
Cedar Gdns BELMT SM2 209 G4
Cedar Gv BXLY DA5 168 E1
EA W5 116 E3
STHL UB1 96 A4
Cedar Hts RCHPK/HAM TW10 157 F3
Cedarhurst BMLY BR1 * 183 H3
Cedarhurst Dr ELTH/MOT SE9 146 B6
Cedar Lawn Av BAR EN5 20 C6
Cedar Mt ELTH/MOT SE9 166 C3
Cedarne Rd FUL/PGN SW6 139 K1
Cedar Park Gdns CHDH RM6 73 K4
WIM/MER SW19 176 E1
Cedar Park Rd ENC/FH EN2 23 J1
Cedar Pl CHARL SE7 126 B5
Cedar Ri STHGT/OAK N14 34 A2
Cedar Rd BELMT SM2 209 G4
BMLY BR1 184 B5
CRICK NW2 82 A2
CROY/NA CR0 197 F6
DART DA1 171 G3
E/WMO/HCT KT8 189 K1
EBED/NFELT TW14 153 G3
ENC/FH EN2 23 H1
ERITH DA8 150 D2
HSLWW TW4 134 B3
OXHEY WD19 27 G1
ROMW/RG RM7 74 E1
TEDD TW11 174 B1
TOTM N17 50 B4
Cedars Av MTCM CR4 195 F1
WALTH E17 69 J2
Cedars Cl HDN NW4 46 B6
LEW SE13 145 G4
Cedars Cots PUT/ROE SW15 * 158 D1
Cedars Ct ED N9 36 A4
Cedars Ms CLAP SW4 * 141 G5
Cedars Rd BARN SW13 138 C3
BECK BR3 182 B5
CHSWK W4 117 K6
CLAP SW4 141 G4
CROY/NA CR0 210 E1
ED N9 36 C4
KUT/HW KT1 174 D4
MRDN SM4 193 K1
SRTFD E15 88 C4
WCHMH N21 35 H4
The Cedars BKHH IG9 38 E3
HOM E9 * 87 F5
SRTFD E15 * 88 D6
TEDD TW11 174 A2
Cedar Ter RCH/KEW TW9 137 F5
Cedar Tree Gv WNWD SE27 180 C1
Cedarville Gdns
STRHM/NOR SW16 180 A2
Cedar Wk ESH/CLAY KT10 205 F4
Cedar Wy KCROSS N1C 84 D5
Cedric Av ROM RM1 57 G6
Cedric Rd ELTH/MOT SE9 167 H5
Celadon Cl PEND EN3 25 G4
Celandine Cl POP/IOD E14 105 J4
Celandine Dr HACK E8 86 B5
THMD SE28 128 C1
Celandine Gv STHGT/OAK N14 22 C6
Celandine Wy SRTFD E15 106 C2
Celbridge Ms BAY/PAD W2 * 101 F5
Celestial Gdns LEW SE13 145 G5
Celia Rd ARCH N19 84 C2
Celtic Av HAYES BR2 183 H6
Celtic St POP/IOD E14 105 K4
Cemetery La CHARL SE7 126 D6
Cemetery Rd ABYW SE2 128 C6
FSTGT E7 88 D3
TOTM N17 50 A3
Cenacle Cl HAMP NW3 82 E1
Centaur Ct BTFD TW8 * 117 F5
Centaur St STHWK SE1 17 H4
Centenary Rd PEND EN3 25 H5
Centenary Wk LOU IG10 39 F1
MNPK E12 89 H1
WALTH E17 52 C6
WAN E11 70 C1
WFD IG8 52 C3
Centennial Av BORE WD6 29 H2
Centennial Pk BORE WD6 * 29 J2
Central Ar ASHF TW15 * 152 C6
Central Av E/WMO/HCT KT8 188 E2
ED N9 36 A5
EFNCH N2 47 H5
EN EN1 24 C3
HSLW TW3 135 H5
HYS/HAR UB3 113 J2
MNPK E12 89 H1
PIN HA5 59 K3

WAN E11 70 B6
WELL DA16 148 B3
WLGTN SM6 210 E3
Central Blds EA W5 * 97 K6
Central Circ HDN NW4 63 K2
Central Ct CHIG IG7 54 E1
Central Hall Blds ARCH N19 * 66 C6
Central Hl NRWD SE19 180 D1
Central Pde ACT W3 * 117 H2
BFN/LL DA15 * 168 B5
E/WMO/HCT KT8 * 188 E1
GFD/PVL UB6 * 97 G2
HRW HA1 61 F2
PEND EN3 * 24 E3
PGE/AN SE20 * 182 A3
STRHM/NOR SW16 * 161 K6
SURB KT6 * 191 F3
WALTH E17 * 69 J1
Central Park Av DAGE RM10 92 D1
Central Park Est
HSLWW TW4 * 134 C5
Central Park Rd EHAM E6 107 H1
Central Pl SNWD SE25 * 197 H1
Central Rd ALP/SUD HA0 79 H3
DART DA1 151 H6
MRDN SM4 194 A2
WPK KT4 192 D6
Central Sq E/WMO/HCT KT8 188 E1
GLDGN NW11 64 E3
Central St FSBYE EC1V 6 C4
Central Ter BECK BR3 * 182 A6
Central Wy CAR SM5 209 J5
EBED/NFELT TW14 134 A6
NTHWD HA6 40 C3
THMD SE28 109 G6
WLSDN NW10 98 E2
Centre Av ACT W3 118 A1
Centre Common Rd
CHST BR7 185 H3
Centre Rd DAGE RM10 110 D1
WAN E11 70 E6
Centre St BETH E2 104 D1
Centre Wy ED N9 36 E4
Centric Cl CAMTN NW1 * 84 B6
Centurian Sq
WOOL/PLUM SE18 146 D2
Centurian Wy ERITHM DA18 129 G3
Centurion Cl HOLWY N7 85 F5
Centurion Ct WLGTN SM6 * 195 G6
Centurion La BOW E3 105 H1
Centurion Sq CHARL SE7 * 146 D1
Centurion Wy PUR RM19 131 J4
Century Cl HDN NW4 64 B2
Century Ct WATW WD18 * 26 A2
Century Ms CLPT E5 * 86 E2
HBRY N5 85 H1
Century Rd WALTH E17 51 G6
Cephas Av WCHPL E1 104 E3
Cephas St WCHPL E1 104 E3
Ceres Rd WOOL/PLUM SE18 128 A4
Cerise Rd PECK SE15 143 H2
Cerne Cl YEAD UB4 95 G6
Cerne Rd MRDN SM4 194 B3
Cerney Ms BAY/PAD W2 8 A5
Cervantes Ct BAY/PAD W2 * 101 F5
NTHWD HA6 40 D3
Ceylon Rd WKENS W14 119 G3
Chabot Dr PECK SE15 143 J4
Chadacre Av CLAY IG5 53 K6
Chadacre Rd EW KT17 207 K3
Chadbourn St POP/IOD E14 105 K4
Chad Crs ED N9 36 E5
Chadd Dr BMLY BR1 184 D6
Chadville Gdns CHDH RM6 73 K2
Chadway BCTR RM8 73 J6
Chadwell Av CHDH RM6 73 H4
Chadwell Heath La
CHDH RM6 73 H1
Chadwell La CEND/HSY/T N8 49 F6
Chadwell St CLKNW EC1R 5 K4
Chadwick Av CHING E4 38 B6
WCHMH N21 * 23 F6
WIM/MER SW19 177 K2
Chadwick Cl PUT/ROE SW15 158 C2
TEDD TW11 174 B2
Chadwick Pl SURB KT6 190 D3
Chadwick Rd IL IG1 90 B1
PECK SE15 143 G3
WAN E11 70 C4
WLSDN NW10 81 H6
Chadwick St WEST SW1P 16 C5
Chadwick Wy THMD SE28 109 K6
Chadwin Rd PLSTW E13 107 F4
Chadworth Wy
ESH/CLAY KT10 204 D3
Chaffinch Av CROY/NA CR0 198 A3
Chaffinch Cl CROY/NA CR0 198 A2
ED N9 37 F3
SURB KT6 206 C1
Chaffinch Ct ORP BR6 202 B4
Chaffinch La WATW WD18 26 D2
Chaffinch Rd BECK BR3 182 B4
Chafford Wy CHDH RM6 73 J1
Chagford St CAMTN NW1 2 E7
Chailey Av EN EN1 24 B3
Chailey Cl HEST TW5 134 C2
Chailey St CLPT E5 86 E1
Chalbury Wk IS N1 5 H2
Chalcombe Rd ABYW SE2 128 C3
Chalcot Cl BELMT SM2 208 E5
Chalcot Crs CAMTN NW1 83 K6
Chalcot Gdns HAMP NW3 83 K4
Chalcot Ms STRHM/NOR SW16 161 K5
Chalcot Rd CAMTN NW1 84 A6
Chalcot Sq CAMTN NW1 84 A5
Chalcott Gdns SURB KT6 * 190 D5
Chalcroft Rd LEW SE13 145 H6
Chaldon Rd FUL/PGN SW6 139 H1
Chale Rd BRXS/STRHM SW2 161 K1
Chalet Cl BXLY DA5 170 A6
Chalet Est MLHL NW7 * 31 J6
Chalfont Av WBLY HA9 80 D4
Chalfont Gn ED N9 36 A5
Chalfont Ms
WAND/EARL SW18 159 J3
Chalfont Rd ED N9 36 A5
HYS/HAR UB3 113 K2
SNWD SE25 181 G6
Chalfont Wk PIN HA5 * 41 G5
Chalfont Wy WEA W13 116 C3
Chalford Cl E/WMO/HCT KT8 189 F1
Chalforde Gdns GPK RM2 75 K1
Chalford Rd DUL SE21 162 E6
Chalford Wk WFD IG8 53 H4
Chalgrove Av MRDN SM4 193 K2
Chalgrove Crs CLAY IG5 53 J5
Chalgrove Gdns FNCH N3 46 C6
Chalgrove Rd BELMT SM2 209 H5
HOM E9 86 E4
TOTM N17 50 D4
Chalice Cl WLGTN SM6 210 D4
Chalkenden Cl PGE/AN SE20 181 J3
Chalk Farm Pde HAMP NW3 * 84 A5
Chalk Farm Rd CAMTN NW1 84 A5
Chalk Hl OXHEY WD19 27 J1
Chalk Hill Rd HMSMTH W6 119 G4
Chalkhill Rd WBLY HA9 80 C1
Chalklands WBLY HA9 80 E1
Chalk La EBAR EN4 21 K4
Chalkley Cl MTCM CR4 178 E5
Chalkmill Dr EN EN1 24 D4
Chalk Pit Av STMC/STPC BR5 186 D6
Chalk Pit Rd SUT SM1 209 G3
Chalk Rd PLSTW E13 107 F4
Chalkstone Cl WELL DA16 148 B2
Chalkwell Park Av EN EN1 24 A5
Chalky La CHSGTN KT9 205 K6
Challenge Cl WLSDN NW10 81 G6
Challenge Rd ASHF TW15 153 F5
Challice Wy
BRXS/STRHM SW2 162 A3
Challin St PGE/AN SE20 181 K4
Challis Rd BTFD TW8 116 E5
Challoner Cl EFNCH N2 47 H5
Challoner Crs WKENS W14 119 J5
Challoners Cl
E/WMO/HCT KT8 189 J1
Challoner St WKENS W14 119 J5
Chalmers Rd ASHF TW15 152 E6
Chalmers Rd East ASHF TW15 152 E6
Chalmers Wk WALW SE17 * 122 C6
Chalmers Wy
EBED/NFELT TW14 134 A6
TWK TW1 136 C5
Chalsey Rd BROCKY SE4 144 C5
Chalton Dr EFNCH N2 65 G3
Chalton St CAMTN NW1 4 C2
Chamberlain Cl IL IG1 90 C1
THMD SE28 127 J3
Chamberlain Cots
CMBW SE5 * 142 E2
Chamberlain Crs WWKM BR4 198 E5
Chamberlain Gdns HSLW TW3 135 H2
Chamberlain La PIN HA5 58 E1
Chamberlain Pl WALTH E17 51 G6
Chamberlain Rd EFNCH N2 47 G5
WEA W13 116 B2
Chamberlain St CAMTN NW1 * 83 K5
Chamberlain Wy PIN HA5 41 F6
SURB KT6 191 F4
Chamberlayne Av WBLY HA9 80 A1
Chamberlayne Rd
WLSDN NW10 82 A6
Chamberlens Garages
HMSMTH W6 * 118 E4
Chambers Av SCUP DA14 187 F2
Chambers Gdns EFNCH N2 47 H4
Chambers La WLSDN NW10 81 K5
Chambers Pl SAND/SEL CR2 211 K5
Chambers Rd HOLWY N7 84 E2
Chambers St
BERM/RHTH SE16 123 H2
Chamber St WCHPL E1 13 K5
Chambon Pl HMSMTH W6 118 D4
Chambord St BETH E2 7 K5
Champa Cl TOTM N17 50 B5
Champion Crs SYD SE26 164 B6
Champion Gv CMBW SE5 142 E4
Champion Hl CMBW SE5 142 E4
Champion Pk CMBW SE5 142 E4
Champion Rd SYD SE26 164 B6
Champness Cl WNWD SE27 162 E6
Champness Rd BARK IG11 91 F5
Champneys OXHEY WD19 * 27 J4
Champneys Cl BELMT SM2 208 D5
Chancellor Gdns
SAND/SEL CR2 211 H6
Chancellor Gv DUL SE21 162 D4
Chancellor Pl
CDALE/KGS NW9 45 H5
Chancellor's Rd HMSMTH W6 119 F5
Chancellors St HMSMTH W6 119 F5
Chancellors Whf
HMSMTH W6 119 F6
Chancelot Rd ABYW SE2 128 C4
Chancel St STHWK SE1 12 A7
Chancery La BECK BR3 182 E5
LINN WC2A 11 H2
Chance St BETH E2 7 J6
Chanctonbury Cl
ELTH/MOT SE9 167 G5
Chanctonbury Gdns
BELMT SM2 209 F5
Chanctonbury Wy
NFNCH/WDSPK N12 32 E6
Chandler Av CAN/RD E16 106 E4
Chandler Cl HPTN TW12 172 E4
Chandlers Av GNWCH SE10 125 J3
Chandlers Cl E/WMO/HCT KT8 189 G2
EBED/NFELT TW14 153 J2
Chandlers Ct LEE/GVPK SE12 * 166 A4
Chandlers Dr ERITH DA8 130 A4
Chandlers Ms POP/IOD E14 124 D2
Chandler St WAP E1W 123 J1
Chandlers Wy ROM RM1 75 G2
Chandler Wy PECK SE15 143 G1
Chandos Av EA W5 116 D4
STHGT/OAK N14 34 C5
TRDG/WHET N20 33 H3
WALTH E17 * 51 J5
Chandos Cl BKHH IG9 39 F4
Chandos Ct STAN HA7 43 H2
Chandos Crs EDGW HA8 44 B3
Chandos Pl CHCR WC2N 10 E6
Chandos Rd CRICK NW2 82 A3
EFNCH N2 47 H5
HRW HA1 60 C2
PIN HA5 59 G4
SRTFD E15 88 B3
TOTM N17 50 A5
WLSDN NW10 99 G3
Chandos St CAVSQ/HST W1G 9 K2
Chandos Wy GLDGN NW11 65 F5
Channel Cl HEST TW5 135 F2
Channel Gate Rd NKENS W10 100 A4
WLSDN NW10 99 G2
Channel Islands Est IS N1 85 J4
Channelsea Rd SRTFD E15 88 B6
Chantress Cl DAGE RM10 92 E6
Chantrey Cl SCUP DA14 187 F1
Chantrey Rd BRXN/ST SW9 142 A4
Chantry Cl ABYW SE2 128 D3
ENC/FH EN2 23 J1
KTN/HRWW/WS HA3 62 B2
MLHL NW7 31 H2
MV/WKIL W9 * 100 D3
Chantry Crs WLSDN NW10 81 G3
Chantry La HAYES BR2 200 C2
Chantry Pl
KTN/HRWW/WS HA3 42 B4
Chantry Rd CHSGTN KT9 206 B3
KTN/HRWW/WS HA3 42 B4
Chantry Sq KENS W8 * 120 A3
Chantry St IS N1 6 B1
The Chantry CHING E4 * 38 A3
Chantry Wy MTCM CR4 178 C6
RAIN RM13 111 F1
Chant Sq SRTFD E15 * 88 B5
Chant St SRTFD E15 88 B5
Chapel Av MNPK E12 71 H6
Chapel Cl DART DA1 150 B6
WLSDN NW10 81 H3
Chapel Ct EFNCH N2 47 J6
STHWK SE1 18 E2
WOOL/PLUM SE18 128 A6
Chapel Farm Rd
ELTH/MOT SE9 166 E5
Chapel Hl DART DA1 150 B5
Chapel House St
POP/IOD E14 124 E5
Chapel La CHDH RM6 * 73 K4
PIN HA5 41 H6
Chapel Market IS N1 5 J2
Chapel Mill Rd KUT/HW KT1 175 G6
Chapel Pl CAVSQ/HST W1G 9 J3
IS N1 5 K2
TOTM N17 50 B3
Chapel Rd BXLYHN DA7 149 H5
HSLW TW3 135 G4
IL IG1 90 A1
TWK TW1 156 C2
WEA W13 116 C1
WNWD SE27 162 C6
Chapel Side BAY/PAD W2 101 F6
Chapel St BAY/PAD W2 8 C2
ENC/FH EN2 23 J4
KTBR SW1X 15 H4
Chapel Vw SAND/SEL CR2 212 E5
Chaplemount Rd WFD IG8 * 53 K2
Chaplin Cl ALP/SUD HA0 * 79 K4
STHWK SE1 17 K2
Chaplin Rd ALP/SUD HA0 79 J4
CRICK NW2 81 J4
SRTFD E15 106 C1
TOTM N17 * 50 B6
Chapman Cl WDR/YW UB7 112 C3
Chapman Crs
KTN/HRWW/WS HA3 62 A2
Chapman Rd BELV DA17 129 H5
CROY/NA CR0 196 B5
HOM E9 87 H4
Chapmans Gn WDGN N22 * 49 G4
Chapman's La
STMC/STPC BR5 186 E5
Chapman Sq WIM/MER SW19 159 G4
Chapman St WCHPL E1 104 D6
Chapman Ter WDGN N22 * 49 H4
Chapter Cl CHSWK W4 117 K3
Chapter Rd CRICK NW2 81 J3
WALW SE17 122 C5
Chapter St WEST SW1P 16 C7
Chapter Wy HPTN TW12 155 F6
WIM/MER SW19 178 C4
Chara Pl CHSWK W4 118 A6
Charcroft Gdns PEND EN3 25 F5
Chardin Rd CHSWK W4 * 118 B4
Chardmore Rd
STNW/STAM N16 68 C5
Chardwell Cl EHAM E6 107 J5
Charecroft Wy WKENS W14 119 G2
Charford Rd CAN/RD E16 106 E4
Chargeable La PLSTW E13 106 E3
Chargeable St CAN/RD E16 106 D3
Chargrove Cl
BERM/RHTH SE16 124 A2
Charing Cl ORP BR6 217 F2
Charing Cross CHCR WC2N * 10 E7
Charing Cross Rd
LSQ/SEVD WC2H 10 D5
Chariot Cl BOW E3 87 J6
Charlbert St STJWD NW8 2 C2
Charlbury Av STAN HA7 43 K1
Charlbury Gdns
GDMY/SEVK IG3 73 F6
Charlbury Gv EA W5 97 J5
Charldane Rd ELTH/MOT SE9 167 G5
Charlecote Gv SYD SE26 163 J5
Charlecote Rd BCTR RM8 92 A1
Charlemont Rd EHAM E6 107 K2
Charles Babbage Cl
CHSGTN KT9 205 J5
Charles Barry Cl CLAP SW4 141 H4
Charles Cl SCUP DA14 168 C6
Charles Cobb Gdns
CROY/NA CR0 211 G3
Charles Coveney Rd
CMBW SE5 * 143 G2
Charles Crs HRW HA1 60 D4
Charles Dickens Ter
PGE/AN SE20 * 181 K3
Charlesfield ELTH/MOT SE9 166 B5
Charles Flemwell Ms
CAN/RD E16 * 125 K1
Charles Grinling Wk
WOOL/PLUM SE18 127 F4
Charles Haller St
BRXS/STRHM SW2 162 B2
Charles II Pl CHEL SW3 * 120 E5
Charles II St STJS SW1Y 10 C7
Charles La STJWD NW8 2 C3
Charles Pl CAMTN NW1 * 4 B5
Charles Rd CHDH RM6 73 K4
DAGE RM10 93 F4
FSTGT E7 89 G5
WEA W13 97 G5
WIM/MER SW19 177 K4
Charles Sevright Dr
MLHL NW7 46 B1
Charles Sq IS N1 7 F5
Charles Square Est IS N1 7 F5
Charles St BARN SW13 138 B4
CAN/RD E16 126 B1
CROY/NA CR0 211 J1
EN EN1 24 B6
HSLW TW3 134 E3
MYFR/PICC W1J 9 J7
Charleston Cl FELT TW13 153 K5
Charleston St WALW SE17 18 D7
Charles Whincup Rd
CAN/RD E16 126 A1
Charleville Circ SYD SE26 181 H1
Charleville Rd WKENS W14 119 H5
Charlieville Rd ERITH DA8 149 K1
Charlmont Rd TOOT SW17 178 D2
Charlock Wy WATW WD18 26 D1
Charlotte Cl BXLYHS DA6 149 F6
OXHEY WD19 27 G2
Charlotte Ct ESH/CLAY KT10 204 C3
Charlotte Despard Av
BTSEA SW11 141 G2
Charlotte Gdns CRW RM5 56 D2
Charlotte Ms ESH/CLAY KT10 * 204 B2
FITZ W1T 10 B1
NKENS W10 100 B5
WKENS W14 119 H4
Charlotte Pde FSTH SE23 * 164 B4
Charlotte Park Av BMLY BR1 184 D6
Charlotte Pl FITZ W1T 10 B2
PIM SW1V 16 A7
Charlotte Rd BARN SW13 138 C2
SDTCH EC2A 7 G5
WLGTN SM6 210 C4
Charlotte Rw CLAP SW4 141 H4
Charlotte St FITZ W1T 10 B1
Charlotte Ter IS N1 5 H1
Charlow Cl FUL/PGN SW6 140 B3
Charlton Church La
CHARL SE7 126 B5
Charlton Crs BARK IG11 109 F1
Charlton Dene CHARL SE7 146 B1
Charlton King's Rd KTTN NW5 84 D3
Charlton La CHARL SE7 126 C5
Charlton Park La CHARL SE7 146 C1
Charlton Park Rd CHARL SE7 126 C6
Charlton Pl IS N1 6 A2
Charlton Rd BKHTH/KID SE3 145 K1
CHARL SE7 126 B6
ED N9 37 F3
KTN/HRWW/WS HA3 61 K1
WBLY HA9 62 B5
WLSDN NW10 81 G6
Charlton Wy BKHTH/KID SE3 145 J1
GNWCH SE10 145 H2
Charlwood CROY/NA CR0 213 H6
Charlwood Cl
KTN/HRWW/WS HA3 42 E2
Charlwood Pl PIM SW1V 16 B7
Charlwood Rd PUT/ROE SW15 139 G4
Charlwood St PIM SW1V 16 B7
Charlwood Ter
PUT/ROE SW15 139 G5
Charmian Av STAN HA7 43 K6
Charminster Av
WIM/MER SW19 177 K5
Charminster Rd
ELTH/MOT SE9 166 C6
WPK KT4 193 G5
Charmouth Rd WELL DA16 148 D2
Charnock Rd CLPT E5 86 D1
Charnwood Av
WIM/MER SW19 177 K5
Charnwood Cl NWMAL KT3 192 B1
Charnwood Dr SWFD E18 53 F6
Charnwood Gdns
POP/IOD E14 124 D4
Charnwood Pl
TRDG/WHET N20 33 G5
Charnwood Rd SNWD SE25 196 E2
Charnwood St CLPT E5 * 68 C6
Charnwood Vls SWFD E18 53 F6
Charrington Rd CROY/NA CR0 196 C6
Charrington St CAMTN NW1 4 C2
Charsley Rd CAT SE6 164 E4
Chart Cl CROY/NA CR0 197 K3
HAYES BR2 183 H4
MTCM CR4 194 E1
Charter Av GNTH/NBYPK IG2 72 D5
Charter Crs HSLWW TW4 134 D5
Charter Dr BXLY DA5 169 F2
Charterhouse Av
ALP/SUD HA0 79 J3
Charterhouse Blds
FARR EC1M 6 C7
Charterhouse Ms FARR EC1M 12 B1
Charterhouse Rd HACK E8 86 C2
ORP BR6 217 G1
Charterhouse St FARR EC1M 12 A2
HCIRC EC1N 11 K2
The Charterhouse
FARR EC1M * 6 B7
Charteris Rd FSBYPK N4 67 F5
KIL/WHAMP NW6 82 D6
WFD IG8 53 F2
Charter Rd KUT/HW KT1 175 J6
The Charter Rd WFD IG8 52 C2
Charters Cl NRWD SE19 181 F1
Charter Sq KUT/HW KT1 175 J5
Charter Wy FNCH N3 64 D1
STHGT/OAK N14 34 C1
Chartfield Av PUT/ROE SW15 138 E6
Chartfield Sq
PUT/ROE SW15 * 139 G6
Chartham Gv WNWD SE27 162 B5
Chartham Rd SNWD SE25 181 J6
Chart Hills Cl THMD SE28 110 A5
Chartley Av CRICK NW2 81 G1
STAN HA7 43 F2
Chartley Pde CRICK NW2 * 81 G1
Charton Cl BELV DA17 129 G6
Chartridge OXHEY WD19 * 27 H4
Chartridge Cl BUSH WD23 28 C1
Chart St IS N1 7 F4
Chartwell Cl CROY/NA CR0 196 E5
ELTH/MOT SE9 167 J4
GFD/PVL UB6 78 B6
Chartwell Dr ORP BR6 216 D3
Chartwell Gdns CHEAM SM3 208 C1
Chartwell Pl CHEAM SM3 208 C2
RYLN/HDSTN HA2 60 D6
Chartwell Rd NTHWD HA6 40 D2
Chartwell Wy PGE/AN SE20 181 J4
Charville La HGDN/ICK UB10 94 A2
Charwood STRHM/NOR SW16 162 B6
Chase Ct RYNPK SW20 177 H5
Chase Court Gdns
ENC/FH EN2 23 J4
Chase Cross Rd CRW RM5 56 E3
Chasefield Rd TOOT SW17 160 E6
Chase Gdns CHING E4 37 J6
WHTN TW2 155 J1
Chase Gn ENC/FH EN2 23 J4
Chase Green Av ENC/FH EN2 23 H3
Chase Hl ENC/FH EN2 23 J4
Chase La BARK/HLT IG6 72 D2
Chaseley Ct CHSWK W4 117 J5
Chaseley St POP/IOD E14 * 105 G5
Chasemore Cl MTCM CR4 194 E4
Chasemore Gdns
CROY/NA CR0 211 G3
Chase Ridings ENC/FH EN2 23 G3
Chase Rd ACT W3 99 F3
STHGT/OAK N14 34 D3
Chase Side ENC/FH EN2 23 J3
STHGT/OAK N14 34 A1
Chase Side Av ENC/FH EN2 23 J3
Chaseside Av RYNPK SW20 177 H4
Chaseside Cl ROM RM1 * 57 G2
Chase Side Crs ENC/FH EN2 23 K2
Chase Side Pl ENC/FH EN2 23 J4
The Chase BMLY BR1 184 A6
BXLYHN DA7 149 J4
CLAP SW4 141 G4
EDGW HA8 44 D4
FSTGT E7 89 H2
LOU IG10 39 G2
PIN HA5 59 G3
ROM RM1 57 G6
ROMW/RG RM7 93 F1
STAN HA7 43 G2
STRHM/NOR SW16 180 A3
SUN TW16 172 A4
WLGTN SM6 210 E3
Chaseville Pde WCHMH N21 * 23 F6
Chaseville Park Rd
WCHMH N21 23 F6
Chase Wy STHGT/OAK N14 34 B3
Chasewood Av ENC/FH EN2 23 H3
Chasewood Pk HRW HA1 * 78 E1
Chastilian Rd DART DA1 170 D2
Chatfield Rd BTSEA SW11 140 B4
CROY/NA CR0 196 C5
Chatham Av HAYES BR2 199 J4
Chatham Cl CHEAM SM3 193 J4
GLDGN NW11 64 E2
WOOL/PLUM SE18 127 G3
Chatham Pl HOM E9 86 E4
Chatham Rd BTSEA SW11 160 E1
KUT/HW KT1 175 H5
SWFD E18 52 D5
WALTH E17 51 G6
Chatham St WALW SE17 18 E6
WOOL/PLUM SE18 127 G3
Chatsfield Pl EA W5 98 A5
Chatsworth Av BFN/LL DA15 168 B3
BMLY BR1 184 A1
HDN NW4 46 A5
RYNPK SW20 177 H4
WBLY HA9 80 B3
Chatsworth Cl CHSWK W4 * 117 K6
HDN NW4 46 A5
WWKM BR4 199 J6
Chatsworth Crs HSLW TW3 135 J5
Chatsworth Dr EN EN1 36 C2
Chatsworth Est CLPT E5 * 87 F2
Chatsworth Gdns ACT W3 98 D6
NWMAL KT3 * 192 C2
RYLN/HDSTN HA2 60 B5
Chatsworth Pl MTCM CR4 178 E6
TEDD TW11 156 B6
Chatsworth Ri EA W5 98 B3
Chatsworth Rd CHEAM SM3 208 B2
CHSWK W4 117 K6
CLPT E5 86 E1
CRICK NW2 82 B4
CROY/NA CR0 211 K2
DART DA1 151 F5
EA W5 98 B3
SRTFD E15 88 D3
YEAD UB4 95 F3
Chatsworth Wy WNWD SE27 162 C5
Chattern Hl ASHF TW15 152 E6
Chattern Rd ASHF TW15 153 F6
Chatterton Ms FSBYPK N4 85 H1
Chatterton Rd FSBYPK N4 85 H1
HAYES BR2 200 C2
Chatto Rd BTSEA SW11 140 E6
Chaucer Av HSLWW TW4 134 A3
RCH/KEW TW9 137 H3
YEAD UB4 94 E4
Chaucer Cl FBAR/BDGN N11 48 C1
Chaucer Dr STHWK SE1 19 K7
Chaucer Gdns SUT SM1 208 E1
Chaucer Gn CROY/NA CR0 197 J4
Chaucer Pk DART DA1 171 J2
Chaucer Rd ACT W3 117 K1
ASHF TW15 152 B6
BFN/LL DA15 168 D3
FSTGT E7 88 E4
HARH RM3 57 K3
HNHL SE24 142 B6
SUT SM1 208 E2
WALTH E17 52 A4
WAN E11 70 E3
WELL DA16 148 A2
Chaucer Wy DART DA1 151 K5
WIM/MER SW19 178 C2
Chauncey Cl ED N9 36 C5
Chaundrye Cl ELTH/MOT SE9 166 E1
Chauntler Rd CAN/RD E16 107 F5
Chave Rd RDART DA2 171 H5

Cheam Common Rd WPK KT4 192 E6
Cheam Man CHEAM SM3 * 208 C4
Cheam Park Wy CHEAM SM3 208 B4
Cheam Rd BELMT SM2 208 B6
Cheam St PECK SE15 * 143 J4
Cheapside CITYW EC2V 12 D4
EFNCH N2 * 47 K6
PLMGR N13 35 J6
WDGN N22 * 49 G6
Cheddar Cl FBAR/BDGN N11 47 K2
Cheddar Waye YEAD UB4 95 F5
Cheddington Rd UED N18 35 A6
Cheeseman Cl HPTN TW12 172 D2
Cheesemans Ter
WKENS W14 * 119 J5
Cheethams Rd MNPK E12 89 J1
Chelford Rd BMLY BR1 183 G1
Chelmer Crs BARK IG11 109 H1
Chelmer Rd HOM E9 87 F3
Chelmsford Av CRW RM5 57 F3
Chelmsford Cl BELMT SM2 208 E6
EHAM E6 107 K5
HMSMTH W6 119 G6
Chelmsford Gdns IL IG1 71 J4
Chelmsford Rd
STHGT/OAK N14 34 C2
SWFD E18 52 D4
WALTH E17 69 J3
Chelmsford Sq WLSDN NW10 82 A6
Chelsea Br VX/NE SW8 121 G6
Chelsea Bridge Ga VX/NE SW8 121 F6
Chelsea Bridge Rd
BGVA SW1W 121 F5
Chelsea Cl EDGW HA8 44 C5
HPTN TW12 173 H1
WLSDN NW10 81 F6
WPK KT4 192 D4
Chelsea Crs CRICK NW2 * 82 D4
WBPTN SW10 * 140 B2
Chelsea Emb CHEL SW3 120 E6
Chelsea Gdns BGVA SW1W * 121 F5
CHEAM SM3 208 C2
WEA W13 97 F4
Chelsea Harbour Dr
WBPTN SW10 140 B2
Chelsea Manor Gdns
CHEL SW3 * 120 D6
Chelsea Manor St CHEL SW3 120 D5
Chelsea Ms EMPK RM11 75 K5
Chelsea Park Gdns CHEL SW3 120 C6
Chelsea Sq CAR SM5 209 K6
CHEL SW3 120 C5
Chelsea Towers CHEL SW3 * 120 D6
Chelsea Village
FUL/PGN SW6 * 140 A1
Chelsfield Av ED N9 37 F2
Chelsfield Gdns SYD SE26 163 K5
Chelsfield Hl ORP BR6 217 J6
Chelsfield La ORP BR6 217 K2
STMC/STPC BR5 202 E4
Chelsfield Rd STMC/STPC BR5 202 D3
Chelsham Rd CLAP SW4 141 J4
SAND/SEL CR2 211 K5
Chelston Rd RSLP HA4 58 E6
Chelsworth Dr
WOOL/PLUM SE18 127 J6
Cheltenham Av TWK TW1 156 B2
Cheltenham Cl NTHLT UB5 78 B4
NWMAL KT3 175 K6
Cheltenham Gdns EHAM E6 107 J1
LOU IG10 39 J1
Cheltenham Pl ACT W3 117 K2
KTN/HRWW/WS HA3 62 A1
Cheltenham Rd LEY E10 70 A3
ORP BR6 217 G1
PECK SE15 143 K5
Cheltenham Ter CHEL SW3 120 E5
Chelton Av MLHL NW7 46 B3
Chelverton Rd
PUT/ROE SW15 139 G5
Chelwood Cl CHING E4 37 K1
NTHWD HA6 40 A3
Chelwood Gdns
RCH/KEW TW9 137 H3
Chenappa Cl PLSTW E13 106 E2
Chenduit Wy STAN HA7 43 F1
Cheney Rw WALTH E17 51 H4
Cheneys Rd WAN E11 88 C1
Cheney St PIN HA5 59 C1
Chenies Ms GWRST WC1E 4 C7
Chenies Pl CAMTN NW1 4 D2
Chenies St GWRST WC1E 10 C1
The Chenies ORP BR6 201 K3
RDART DA2 170 B6
Chenies Wy WATW WD18 26 C2
Cheniston Gdns KENS W8 * 120 A3
Chepstow Cl PUT/ROE SW15 139 H6
Chepstow Cnr BAY/PAD W2 * 100 E5
Chepstow Crs
GDMY/SEVK IG3 72 E3
NTGHL W11 100 E6
Chepstow Gdns STHL UB1 95 K5
Chepstow Pl BAY/PAD W2 100 E6
Chepstow Ri CROY/NA CR0 212 A1
Chepstow Rd BAY/PAD W2 100 E5
CROY/NA CR0 212 A1
HNWL W7 116 B3
Chepstow Vls NTGHL W11 100 D6
Chequers BKHH IG9 39 F3
Chequers Cl CDALE/KGS NW9 45 G6
STMC/STPC BR5 202 A1
Chequers La DAGW RM9 110 B3
Chequers Pde PLMGR N13 * 49 J1
The Chequers PIN HA5 * 41 H6
Chequer St STLK EC1Y 6 D7
Chequers Wy PLMGR N13 49 H1
Cherbury Cl THMD SE28 109 K5
Cherbury St IS N1 7 F3
Cherimoya Gdns
E/WMO/HCT KT8 173 G6
Cherington Rd HNWL W7 * 116 A1
Cheriton Av CLAY IG5 54 A5
HAYES BR2 199 J2
Cheriton Cl EA W5 97 J4
EBAR EN4 21 K4
Cheriton Ct WOT/HER KT12 188 B5
Cheriton Dr
WOOL/PLUM SE18 147 J1
Cheriton Sq TOOT SW17 161 F4
Cherry Av STHL UB1 114 C1
Cherry Blossom Cl
PLMGR N13 49 H1
Cherry Cl BRXS/STRHM SW2 * 162 B2
CAR SM5 194 E6
CDALE/KGS NW9 45 H5
EA W5 116 E3
MRDN SM4 193 H1
RSLP HA4 76 D1
Cherrycot Ri ORP BR6 216 C2
Cherry Ct PIN HA5 41 H4
Cherry Crs BTFD TW8 136 C1
Cherry Croft Gdns PIN HA5 * 41 K3
Cherrydown Av CHING E4 37 H5
Cherrydown Cl CHING E4 37 H5
Cherrydown Rd SCUP DA14 168 E4
Cherrydown Wk
ROMW/RG RM7 56 D5
Cherry Gdns DAGW RM9 92 B3
NTHLT UB5 78 B5
Cherry Garden St
BERM/RHTH SE16 123 J2
Cherry Garth BTFD TW8 116 E4
Cherry Gv HYS/HAR UB3 114 A1
UX/CGN UB8 94 A4
Cherry Hl BAR EN5 33 F1
KTN/HRWW/WS HA3 42 E2
Cherry Hill Gdns
CROY/NA CR0 211 F2
Cherry Hills OXHEY WD19 41 J1
Cherrylands Cl
CDALE/KGS NW9 * 62 E6
Cherry La WDR/YW UB7 112 C4
Cherry Orch CHARL SE7 126 B6
WDR/YW UB7 112 B2
Cherry Orchard Cl
STMC/STPC BR5 202 D2
Cherry Orchard Gdns
CROY/NA CR0 196 E5
E/WMO/HCT KT8 172 E6
Cherry Orchard Rd
CROY/NA CR0 196 E5
E/WMO/HCT KT8 173 F6
HAYES BR2 200 D6
Cherry Rd PEND EN3 24 E1
Cherry St ROMW/RG RM7 75 F2
Cherry Tree Cl ALP/SUD HA0 79 G2
HOM E9 86 E6
RAIN RM13 111 J1
Cherry Tree Ct CHARL SE7 * 126 B6
Cherry Tree Dr
STRHM/NOR SW16 161 K5
Cherry Tree Hl EFNCH N2 65 J2
Cherry Tree La RAIN RM13 111 G2
RDART DA2 170 C5
Cherry Tree Ri BKHH IG9 39 G6
Cherry Tree Rd EFNCH N2 65 K1
SRTFD E15 88 C3
Cherry Tree Wk BECK BR3 198 C1
STLK EC1Y 6 D7
WWKM BR4 214 D2
Cherry Tree Wy PLSTW E13 107 H3
STAN HA7 43 H2
Cherry Wk HAYES BR2 199 K5
RAIN RM13 111 H1
Cherry Wy HOR/WEW KT19 207 F4
Cherrywood Cl BOW E3 105 G2
KUTN/CMB KT2 175 H3
Cherrywood Dr
PUT/ROE SW15 139 G6
Cherrywood La RYNPK SW20 193 H1
Chertsey Dr CHEAM SM3 193 H6
Chertsey Rd FELT TW13 153 H6
IL IG1 90 D2
TWK TW1 156 B1
WAN E11 70 B6
WHTN TW2 155 H3
Chertsey St TOOT SW17 179 F1
Chervil Cl FELT TW13 153 K5
Chervil Ms THMD SE28 128 C1
Cherwell Ct HOR/WEW KT19 206 E2
Cherwell Wy RSLP HA4 58 A3
Cheryls Cl FUL/PGN SW6 140 A2
Cheseman St SYD SE26 163 J5
Chesfield Rd KUTN/CMB KT2 175 F3
Chesham Av STMC/STPC BR5 201 G3
Chesham Cl KTBR SW1X * 15 G5
ROMW/RG RM7 75 F1
Chesham Crs PGE/AN SE20 181 K4
Chesham Ms KTBR SW1X 15 G4
Chesham Pl KTBR SW1X 15 G4
Chesham Rd KUT/HW KT1 175 H5
PGE/AN SE20 181 K5
WIM/MER SW19 178 C2
Chesham St KTBR SW1X 15 G5
WLSDN NW10 81 F1
Chesham Ter WEA W13 116 C2
Chesham Wy WATW WD18 26 C1
Cheshire Cl MTCM CR4 179 K6
WALTH E17 51 K4
Cheshire Gdns CHSGTN KT9 205 K4
Cheshire Rd WDGN N22 49 F3
Cheshire St BETH E2 104 C3
Chesholm Rd
STNW/STAM N16 86 A1
Cheshunt Rd BELV DA17 129 H5
FSTGT E7 89 F4
Chesilton Rd FUL/PGN SW6 139 J2
Chesil Wy YEAD UB4 94 D2
Chesley Gdns EHAM E6 107 H1
Chesney Crs CROY/NA CR0 214 A5
Chesney St BTSEA SW11 141 F2
Chesnut Av North WALTH E17 70 A1
Chesnut Gv TOTM N17 50 B6
Chesnut Rd TOTM N17 50 C6
Chesnut Rw FNCH N3 * 46 E3
Chessell Cl THHTH CR7 196 C1
Chessington Av BXLYHN DA7 149 F1
FNCH N3 46 C6
Chessington Cl
HOR/WEW KT19 206 E4
Chessington Ct PIN HA5 59 K1
Chessington Hall Gdns
CHSGTN KT9 205 K5
Chessington Hill Pk
CHSGTN KT9 206 C4
Chessington Pde
CHSGTN KT9 * 205 K3
Chessington Rd CHSGTN KT9 206 C4
HOR/WEW KT19 206 D4
Chessington Wy WWKM BR4 198 E6
Chesson Rd WKENS W14 119 J6
Chesswood Wy PIN HA5 41 H5
Chester Av RCHPK/HAM TW10 157 G1
WHTN TW2 154 E3
Chester Cl BARN SW13 * 138 E4
KTBR SW1X 15 H3
SUT SM1 193 K6
Chester Cl North CAMTN NW1 3 K4
Chester Cl South CAMTN NW1 3 K5
Chester Crs HACK E8 86 B3
Chester Dr RYLN/HDSTN HA2 60 A3
Chesterfield Cl
STMC/STPC BR5 202 E1
Chesterfield Dr DART DA1 150 E6
ESH/CLAY KT10 190 B6
Chesterfield Gdns FSBYPK N4 67 H2
GNWCH SE10 * 145 G1
MYFR/PICC W1J * 9 J7
Chesterfield Gv EDUL SE22 143 G6
Chesterfield Hl
MYFR/PKLN W1K 9 J6
Chesterfield Ms FSBYPK N4 67 H2
Chesterfield Rd BAR EN5 20 B6
CHSWK W4 117 K6
FNCH N3 46 E2
HOR/WEW KT19 207 F5
LEY E10 70 A4
Chesterfield St
MYFR/PICC W1J 9 J7
Chesterfield Wy
HYS/HAR UB3 * 113 K2
PECK SE15 143 K1
Chesterford Gdns HAMP NW3 83 F2
Chesterford Rd MNPK E12 89 K3
Chester Gdns MRDN SM4 194 B2
PEND EN3 36 D1
WEA W13 * 97 H5
Chester Ga CAMTN NW1 3 J5
Chester Ms KTBR SW1X 15 J4
Chester Pl CAMTN NW1 3 J4
NTHWD HA6 * 40 C3
Chester Rd ARCH N19 66 B6
BFN/LL DA15 147 K6
CAMTN NW1 3 H5
CAN/RD E16 106 C3
ED N9 36 D3
FSTGT E7 89 H5
GDMY/SEVK IG3 73 F5
HSLWW TW4 134 A4
HTHAIR TW6 132 D4
NTHWD HA6 40 D3
TOTM N17 49 K6
WALTH E17 69 F2
WAN E11 71 F3
WIM/MER SW19 177 F2
Chester Rw BGVA SW1W 15 G7
Chester Sq BGVA SW1W 15 H6
Chester Square Ms
BGVA SW1W * 15 J5
The Chesters NWMAL KT3 176 B4
Chester St BETH E2 104 C3
KTBR SW1X 15 H4
Chester Ter CAMTN NW1 3 J4
Chesterton Cl GFD/PVL UB6 96 B1
WAND/EARL SW18 139 K6
Chesterton Ct EA W5 * 97 K5
Chesterton Dr
STWL/WRAY TW19 152 C3
Chesterton Rd NKENS W10 100 B4
PLSTW E13 106 E2
Chesterton Sq KENS W8 119 J4
Chesterton Ter KUT/HW KT1 175 H5
PLSTW E13 106 E2
Chester Wy LBTH SE11 17 K7
Chesthunte Rd TOTM N17 49 J4
Chestnut Aly FUL/PGN SW6 * 119 J6
Chestnut Av ALP/SUD HA0 79 H3
BKHH IG9 39 H5
BTFD TW8 116 E5
CEND/HSY/T N8 66 E2
E/WMO/HCT KT8 174 A6
EDGW HA8 44 A2
ESH/CLAY KT10 189 J4
FSTGT E7 89 F2
HCH RM12 75 H6
HOR/WEW KT19 207 G2
HPTN TW12 173 F3
MNPK E12 71 J6
MORT/ESHN SW14 138 A4
NTHWD HA6 40 D5
TEDD TW11 174 A3
WWKM BR4 214 C3
Chestnut Av South
WALTH E17 70 A1
Chestnut Cl ASHF TW15 152 E6
BFN/LL DA15 168 B4
BKHH IG9 39 H5
CAR SM5 194 E5
CAT SE6 165 F6
HYS/HAR UB3 94 C6
HYS/HAR UB3 132 E1
NWCR SE14 144 C2
ORP BR6 217 G3
STHGT/OAK N14 22 C6
STNW/STAM N16 67 K6
STRHM/NOR SW16 162 B6
Chestnut Cots
TRDG/WHET N20 * 32 C3
Chestnut Dr BXLYHN DA7 148 E4
KTN/HRWW/WS HA3 43 F3
PIN HA5 59 H3
WAN E11 70 E3
Chestnut Gln HCH RM12 75 H6
Chestnut Gv ALP/SUD HA0 79 H3
BAL SW12 161 F2
BARK/HLT IG6 54 E2
EA W5 116 E3
EBAR EN4 21 K6
ISLW TW7 136 B5
MTCM CR4 195 J2
NWMAL KT3 176 A6
SAND/SEL CR2 212 D5
Chestnut La TRDG/WHET N20 32 C3
Chestnut Ms WFD IG8 52 E1
Chestnut Pl SYD SE26 163 G6
Chestnut Ri BUSH WD23 28 B2
WOOL/PLUM SE18 127 K5
Chestnut Rd ASHF TW15 152 D6
DART DA1 171 G3
KUTN/CMB KT2 175 F3
RYNPK SW20 177 G5
WHTN TW2 155 K4
WNWD SE27 162 C5
The Chestnuts BECK BR3 * 182 A6
PIN HA5 * 41 K3
Chestnut Ter SUT SM1 * 209 F2
Chestnut Wy FELT TW13 154 A5
Cheston Av CROY/NA CR0 198 B5
Cheswick Cl DART DA1 150 C5
Chesworth Cl ERITH DA8 150 B2
Chettle Cl STHWK SE1 18 E4
Chetwode Rd TOOT SW17 160 E5
Chetwynd Av EBAR EN4 33 K3
Chetwynd Rd KTTN NW5 84 B2
Chetwynd Vls KTTN NW5 * 84 B2
Chevalier Cl STAN HA7 29 K5
Cheval Pl SKENS SW7 14 D4
Cheval St POP/IOD E14 124 D3
Cheveney Wk HAYES BR2 183 K6
Chevening Rd GNWCH SE10 125 J5
KIL/WHAMP NW6 100 B1
NRWD SE19 180 E3
The Chevenings SCUP DA14 168 C5
Cheverton Rd ARCH N19 66 D5
Chevet St HOM E9 87 G3
Chevington CRICK NW2 * 82 D4
Cheviot Cl BELMT SM2 209 H6
BUSH WD23 28 C1
BXLYHN DA7 150 B3
ENC/FH EN2 23 K3
HYS/HAR UB3 133 G1
Cheviot Gdns CRICK NW2 64 B6
Cheviot Rd EMPK RM11 75 J4
WNWD SE27 180 B1
Cheviot Wy GNTH/NBYPK IG2 72 E2
Chevron Cl CAN/RD E16 106 E5
Chevy Rd NWDGN UB2 115 H2
Chewton Rd WALTH E17 69 G1
Cheyne Av SWFD E18 52 D6
WHTN TW2 154 E3
Cheyne Cl HAYES BR2 215 J1
Cheyne Gdns CHEL SW3 120 D6
Cheyne Hl BRYLDS KT5 191 G1
Cheyne Ms CHEL SW3 120 D6
Cheyne Park Dr WWKM BR4 214 A1
Cheyne Pth HNWL W7 97 F4
Cheyne Pl CHEL SW3 * 120 E6
Cheyne Rw CHEL SW3 120 D6
Cheyne Wk CHEL SW3 120 D6
CROY/NA CR0 197 H6
HDN NW4 64 A3
WBPTN SW10 140 C1
WCHMH N21 23 G6
Cheyneys Av EDGW HA8 43 K2
Chichele Gdns CROY/NA CR0 212 A2
Chichele Rd CRICK NW2 82 B3
Chicheley Rd
KTN/HRWW/WS HA3 42 C3
Chicheley St STHWK SE1 17 H2
Chichester Av RSLP HA4 58 B6
Chichester Cl BKHTH/KID SE3 146 B1
EHAM E6 107 J5
HPTN TW12 172 E2
Chichester Ct EW KT17 * 207 H6
STAN HA7 44 A6
Chichester Gdns IL IG1 71 J4
Chichester Rd BAY/PAD W2 * 101 F4
CROY/NA CR0 212 A1
ED N9 36 B3
KIL/WHAMP NW6 100 E1
WAN E11 88 C1
Chichester St PIM SW1V 121 H5
Chichester Wy
EBED/NFELT TW14 154 B2
POP/IOD E14 125 G4
Chichester Whf ERITH DA8 130 B5
Chicksand St WCHPL E1 13 K2
Chiddingfold
NFNCH/WDSPK N12 32 E5
Chiddingstone Av
BXLYHN DA7 149 G1
Chiddingstone St
FUL/PGN SW6 139 K3
Chieftan Dr PUR RM19 131 K4
Chieveley Pde BXLYHN DA7 * 149 J4
Chieveley Rd BXLYHN DA7 149 J5
Chignell Pl WEA W13 116 B1
Chigwell Hl WAP E1W 104 D6
Chigwell Rd SWFD E18 53 F6
WFD IG8 53 K2
Chilcott Cl ALP/SUD HA0 79 J2
Childebert Rd TOOT SW17 161 G4
Childeric Rd NWCR SE14 144 B1
Childerley St FUL/PGN SW6 139 H2
Childers St DEPT SE8 124 B6
The Childers WFD IG8 53 K1
Child La GNWCH SE10 125 J3
Childs Ct HYS/HAR UB3 94 E6
Childs La NRWD SE19 * 181 F2
Child's Ms ECT SW5 * 119 K4
Child's Pl ECT SW5 119 K4
Child's St ECT SW5 119 K4
Child's Wk ECT SW5 * 119 K4
Childs Wy GLDGN NW11 64 D2
Chilham Cl BXLY DA5 169 G2
GFD/PVL UB6 97 G1
Chilham Rd ELTH/MOT SE9 166 D6
Chilham Wy HAYES BR2 199 K4
Chillerton Rd TOOT SW17 179 F1
Chillington Dr BTSEA SW11 140 B5
Chillingworth Gdns
TWK TW1 * 156 A4
Chillingworth Rd HOLWY N7 85 F3
Chilmark Gdns NWMAL KT3 192 C3
Chilmark Rd
STRHM/NOR SW16 179 J5
Chiltern Av BUSH WD23 28 C1
WHTN TW2 155 F3
Chiltern Cl BUSH WD23 28 B1
BXLYHN DA7 150 B2
CROY/NA CR0 212 A1
WPK KT4 193 F6
Chiltern Dene ENC/FH EN2 23 F5
Chiltern Dr BRYLDS KT5 191 J3
Chiltern Gdns CRICK NW2 82 B1
HAYES BR2 199 J1
Chiltern Pl CLPT E5 68 D6
Chiltern Rd BOW E3 105 J3
GNTH/NBYPK IG2 72 E1
PIN HA5 59 G2
The Chilterns BELMT SM2 * 209 F6
Chiltern St MHST W1U 9 F1
Chiltern Wy WFD IG8 38 E5
Chilthorne Cl CAT SE6 164 C2
Chilton Av EA W5 116 E4
Chilton Gv DEPT SE8 124 A4
Chilton Rd EDGW HA8 44 C2
RCH/KEW TW9 137 H4
Chilton St BETH E2 7 K6
Chilvers Cl WHTN TW2 155 K4
Chilver St GNWCH SE10 125 J5
Chilwell Gdns OXHEY WD19 27 G6
Chilworth Gdns SUT SM1 209 G1
Chilworth Ms BAY/PAD W2 101 G5
Chilworth St BAY/PAD W2 101 G5
Chimes Av PLMGR N13 35 G6
China Hall Ms
BERM/RHTH SE16 123 K3
China Ms BRXS/STRHM SW2 162 A2
Chinbrook Crs LEE/GVPK SE12 166 A5
Chinbrook Rd LEE/GVPK SE12 166 A5
Chinchilla Dr HSLWW TW4 134 B3
The Chine ALP/SUD HA0 79 H3
MUSWH N10 66 B1
WCHMH N21 35 H1
Chingdale Rd CHING E4 38 C5
Chingford Av CHING E4 37 J5
Chingford La WFD IG8 38 C6
Chingford Mount Rd
CHING E4 51 J1
Chingford Rd CHING E4 51 J2
WALTH E17 51 K5
Chingley Cl BMLY BR1 183 H2
Ching Wy CHING E4 51 H2
Chinnery Cl EN EN1 24 B1
Chinnor Crs GFD/PVL UB6 96 C1
Chipka St POP/IOD E14 125 F2
Chipley St NWCR SE14 124 B6
Chippendale St CLPT E5 87 F1
Chippenham Cl PIN HA5 * 58 D1
Chippenham Gdns
KIL/WHAMP NW6 100 E2
Chippenham Ms
MV/WKIL W9 * 100 E3
Chippenham Rd MV/WKIL W9 100 E3
Chipperfield Rd
STMC/STPC BR5 186 B5
Chipping Cl BAR EN5 20 C4
Chipstead Av THHTH CR7 196 C1
Chipstead Cl BELMT SM2 209 F6
NRWD SE19 181 G3
Chipstead Gdns CRICK NW2 63 K6
Chipstead Rd ERITH DA8 150 B1
Chipstead St FUL/PGN SW6 139 K2
Chirk Cl YEAD UB4 95 J3
Chisenhale Rd BOW E3 105 G1
Chisholm Rd CROY/NA CR0 197 F6
RCHPK/HAM TW10 157 G1
Chislehurst Av
NFNCH/WDSPK N12 47 G3
Chislehurst High St CHST BR7 185 G2
Chislehurst Rd BMLY BR1 184 D5
ORP BR6 202 A4
RCHPK/HAM TW10 157 F1
SCUP DA14 186 B1
STMC/STPC BR5 201 K1
Chislet Cl BECK BR3 182 D3
Chisley Rd SEVS/STOTM N15 68 A3
Chiswell Sq BKHTH/KID SE3 146 A3
Chiswell St CMBW SE5 * 142 E1
STLK EC1Y 12 E1
Chiswick Br CHSWK W4 137 K3
Chiswick Cl CROY/NA CR0 211 F1
Chiswick Common Rd
CHSWK W4 118 A4
Chiswick High Rd CHSWK W4 117 H5
Chiswick House Grounds
CHSWK W4 * 118 A6
Chiswick La CHSWK W4 118 B5
Chiswick La South CHSWK W4 118 C6
Chiswick Ml CHSWK W4 118 C6
Chiswick Pk CHSWK W4 * 117 K3
Chiswick Pier CHSWK W4 * 138 C1
Chiswick Quay CHSWK W4 137 K2
Chiswick Rd CHSWK W4 117 K4
ED N9 36 C4
Chiswick Sq CHSWK W4 118 B6
Chiswick Staithe CHSWK W4 137 K2
Chiswick Village CHSWK W4 117 H6
Chiswick Whf CHSWK W4 118 C6
Chitterfield Ga WDR/YW UB7 132 D1
Chitty's La BCTR RM8 73 K6
Chitty St FITZ W1T 10 B1
Chivalry Rd BTSEA SW11 140 D6
Chivenor Gv KUTN/CMB KT2 174 E1
Chivers Rd CHING E4 37 K5
Choats Manor Wy DAGW RM9 110 B2
Choats Rd BARK IG11 109 J1
DAGW RM9 110 A2
Chobham Gdns
WIM/MER SW19 159 G4
Chobham Rd SRTFD E15 88 B3
Cholmeley Cl HGT N6 * 66 B4
Cholmeley Crs HGT N6 66 B4
Cholmeley Pk HGT N6 66 B5
Cholmley Gdns
KIL/WHAMP NW6 82 E3
Cholmley Rd THDIT KT7 190 C3
Cholmley Ter THDIT KT7 * 190 C4
Cholmley Vls THDIT KT7 * 190 C4
Cholmondeley Av
WLSDN NW10 99 J1
Chopwell Cl SRTFD E15 * 88 B5
Chorleywood Crs
STMC/STPC BR5 186 A5
Choumert Gv PECK SE15 143 H3
Choumert Ms PECK SE15 143 H3
Choumert Rd PECK SE15 143 G4
Chow Sq HACK E8 86 B3
HACK E8 * 86 B3
Chrislaine Cl
STWL/WRAY TW19 152 A1
Chrisp St POP/IOD E14 105 K4
Christabel Cl ISLW TW7 135 K4
Christchurch Av
ALP/SUD HA0 80 A4
ERITH DA8 130 A6
KIL/WHAMP NW6 82 B6
KTN/HRWW/WS HA3 61 F1
NFNCH/WDSPK N12 47 G2

RAIN RM13 111 H1
TEDD TW11 174 B1
Christchurch Cl *ENC/FH* EN2 23 J3
NFNCH/WDSPK N12 * 47 H3
WIM/MER SW19 178 C3
Christchurch Gdns
KTN/HRWW/WS HA3 61 G1
Christchurch Hl *HAMP* NW3 83 H1
Christ Church La *BAR* EN5 20 C3
Christchurch Ldg *EBAR* EN4 * 21 K5
Christchurch Pk *BELMT* SM2 209 G5
Christ Church Rd *BECK* BR3 * 182 D5
BRYLDS KT5 191 G4
CEND/HSY/T N8 66 E3
Christchurch Rd *BFN/LL* DA15 168 A6
BRXS/STRHM SW2 162 A3
DART DA1 171 F2
IL IG1 72 B5
MORT/ESHN SW14 137 J6
WIM/MER SW19 178 C3
Christchurch Sq *HOM* E9 86 E6
Christchurch St *CHEL* SW3 120 E6
Christchurch Ter *CHEL* SW3 * 120 E6
Christchurch Wy
GNWCH SE10 125 H5
Christian Flds
STRHM/NOR SW16 180 B3
Christian St *WCHPL* E1 104 C5
Christie Dr *CROY/NA* CR0 197 H2
Christie Rd *HOM* E9 87 G4
Christina Sq *FSBYPK* N4 67 H5
Christina St *SDTCH* EC2A 7 G6
Christine Worsley Cl
WCHMH N21 35 H3
Christopher Av *HNWL* W7 116 B3
Christopher Cl
BERM/RHTH SE16 124 A2
BFN/LL DA15 148 A6
Christopher Gdns *DAGW* RM9 91 K3
Christopher Pl *CAMTN* NW1 * 4 D4
Christopher Rd *NWDGN* UB2 114 A4
Christophers Ms *NTGHL* W11 * 119 H1
Christopher St *SDTCH* EC2A 7 F7
Christy Ter *WFD* IG8 53 J3
Chryssell Rd *BRXN/ST* SW9 142 B1
Chubworthy St *NWCR* SE14 124 B6
Chudleigh Crs
GDMY/SEVK IG3 90 E2
Chudleigh Gdns *SUT* SM1 209 G1
Chudleigh Rd *BROCKY* SE4 144 C6
KIL/WHAMP NW6 82 A5
WHTN TW2 155 K1
Chudleigh St *WCHPL* E1 105 F5
Chudleigh Wy *RSLP* HA4 58 E5
Chulsa Rd *SYD* SE26 181 J1
Chumleigh Gdns *CMBW* SE5 * 123 F6
Chumleigh St *CMBW* SE5 123 F6
Chumleigh Wk *BRYLDS* KT5 191 G1
Church Ap *DUL* SE21 162 E5
Church Av *BECK* BR3 182 D4
CAMTN NW1 84 B4
CHING E4 52 B2
MORT/ESHN SW14 138 A5
NTHLT UB5 77 K5
NWDGN UB2 114 D3
PIN HA5 59 J3
RSLP HA4 58 B5
SCUP DA14 186 B1
Churchbury Cl *EN* EN1 24 A3
Churchbury La *EN* EN1 24 A4
Churchbury Rd
ELTH/MOT SE9 166 C2
EN EN1 24 A3
Church Cl *EDGW* HA8 44 E1
HSLW TW3 134 E3
HYS/HAR UB3 94 B4
KENS W8 * 120 A2
NTHWD HA6 40 D3
TRDG/WHET N20 33 J5
WDR/YW UB7 112 B3
Church Crs *FNCH* N3 46 D4
HOM E9 87 F5
MUSWH N10 66 B1
TRDG/WHET N20 33 J5
Churchcroft Cl *BAL* SW12 * 161 F2
Churchdown *BMLY* BR1 165 H6
Church Dr *CDALE/KGS* NW9 63 F5
RYLN/HDSTN HA2 60 A3
WWKM BR4 214 C1
Church Elm La *DAGE* RM10 92 C4
Church End *HDN* NW4 45 K6
WALTH E17 * 69 K1
Church Farm *EBAR* EN4 * 33 K2
Church Farm La *CHEAM* SM3 208 C4
Church Fld *RDART* DA2 171 G4
Churchfield Av
NFNCH/WDSPK N12 47 G2
Churchfield Cl *HYS/HAR* UB3 94 D6
RYLN/HDSTN HA2 60 C1
Churchfield Rd *ACT* W3 117 K1
HNWL W7 115 K2
WEA W13 116 C1
WELL DA16 148 B4
Churchfields *E/WMO/HCT* KT8 173 F6
GNWCH SE10 125 F6
SWFD E18 52 E4
Churchfields Av *FELT* TW13 154 E5
Churchfields Rd *BECK* BR3 182 A5
Churchfield Wy
NFNCH/WDSPK N12 47 G2
Church Gdns *ALP/SUD* HA0 79 G2
EA W5 116 E2
Church Garth *ARCH* N19 * 66 D6
Church Ga *FUL/PGN* SW6 139 H4
Church Gn *BRXN/ST* SW9 * 142 B3
HYS/HAR UB3 94 D5
Church Gv *KUT/HW* KT1 174 D4
LEW SE13 144 E5
Church Hl *CAR* SM5 209 K3
DART DA1 150 B5
HRW HA1 60 E5
ORP BR6 202 B4
RDART DA2 171 G5
WALTH E17 69 J1
WCHMH N21 35 F2
WIM/MER SW19 177 J1
WOOL/PLUM SE18 126 E3
Church Hill Rd *CHEAM* SM3 208 B2
EBAR EN4 33 J1
SURB KT6 191 F2
WALTH E17 69 K1
Church Hill Wd
STMC/STPC BR5 202 A2
Church Hollow *PUR* RM19 131 K5
Church Hyde
WOOL/PLUM SE18 127 K6
Churchill Av
KTN/HRWW/WS HA3 61 H3
Churchill Cl *EBED/NFELT* TW14 153 J3
Churchill Gdns *ACT* W3 98 C5
Churchill Gardens Rd
PIM SW1V 121 G5
Churchill Ms *WFD* IG8 52 D2
Churchill Pl *POP/IOD* E14 124 E1
Churchill Rd *CAN/RD* E16 107 G5
CRICK NW2 81 K4
EDGW HA8 44 B2
KTTN NW5 84 B2
SAND/SEL CR2 211 J6
Churchill Ter *CHING* E4 37 J6
Churchill Wk *HOM* E9 86 E3
Churchill Wy *BMLY* BR1 183 K5
Churchlands Wy *WPK* KT4 193 G6
Church La *CDALE/KGS* NW9 62 E5
CEND/HSY/T N8 67 F1
CHSGTN KT9 206 B4
CHST BR7 185 H4
DAGE RM10 92 D4
EA W5 116 D2
ED N9 36 C4
EFNCH N2 47 H6
ENC/FH EN2 23 K4
HAYES BR2 200 D5
KTN/HRWW/WS HA3 43 F4
PIN HA5 41 J6
PUR RM19 * 131 K5
ROM RM1 75 G1
TEDD TW11 174 A1
THDIT KT7 190 A3
TOOT SW17 178 E1
TOTM N17 50 A4
TWK TW1 156 B3
WALTH E17 69 K1
WAN E11 70 C5
WIM/MER SW19 177 K4
WLGTN SM6 210 D1
Churchley Rd *SYD* SE26 163 J6
Church Manor Wy *ABYW* SE2 128 B3
Church Manorway *ERITH* DA8 130 A3
Church Md *CMBW* SE5 * 142 D1
Churchmead Cl *EBAR* EN4 33 J1
Church Meadow *SURB* KT6 190 D6
Churchmead Rd
WLSDN NW10 81 J4
Churchmore Rd
STRHM/NOR SW16 179 H4
Church Mt *EFNCH* N2 65 H2
Church Paddock Ct
WLGTN SM6 210 D1
Church Pde *ASHF* TW15 * 152 C6
Church Pas *BAR* EN5 * 20 D4
Church Pth *CHSWK* W4 117 K3
MTCM CR4 178 D6
NFNCH/WDSPK N12 * 47 G1
RYNPK SW20 177 J5
WAN E11 70 E2
WIM/MER SW19 177 J5
Church Pl *EA* W5 116 E2
MTCM CR4 178 D6
Church Rd *LEY* E10 69 K6
Church Ri *CHSGTN* KT9 206 B4
FSTH SE23 164 A3
Church Rd *ACT* W3 117 K2
ASHF TW15 152 C6
BARK IG11 90 C4
BARN SW13 138 D3
BKHH IG9 39 F3
BXLYHN DA7 149 G3
CHEAM SM3 208 C4
CROY/NA CR0 * 211 J2
E/WMO/HCT KT8 173 J6
ERITH DA8 129 K5
ESH/CLAY KT10 205 F4
FELT TW13 172 B1
GNTH/NBYPK IG2 72 E3
HAYES BR2 183 H6
HAYES BR2 215 H5
HDN NW4 63 K1
HEST TW5 114 A5
HEST TW5 135 F1
HGT N6 66 A3
HNWL W7 96 E6
HOR/WEW KT19 207 F5
HYS/HAR UB3 94 D5
HYS/HAR UB3 113 J1
IS N1 85 J4
ISLW TW7 135 J2
KUT/HW KT1 175 G5
LEY E10 69 J5
MNPK E12 89 J3
MTCM CR4 178 D6
NRWD SE19 181 F3
NTHLT UB5 77 K5
NTHLT UB5 95 H1
NTHWD HA6 40 D3
NWDGN UB2 114 E3
ORP BR6 216 C3
ORP BR6 217 K4
PEND EN3 36 E1
RCHPK/HAM TW10 137 F6
RCHPK/HAM TW10 157 F6
RCHPK/HAM TW10 175 G1
SCUP DA14 168 B6
STAN HA7 43 H1
SURB KT6 190 D5
TEDD TW11 155 K6
TOTM N17 50 A4
WALTH E17 51 G5
WDR/YW UB7 112 A2
WELL DA16 148 C3
WIM/MER SW19 159 H6
WIM/MER SW19 178 C5
WLGTN SM6 210 C1
WLSDN NW10 81 G4
WPK KT4 192 B5
Church Rw *CHST* BR7 185 H4
FUL/PGN SW6 * 140 A1
HAMP NW3 83 G2
WAND/EARL SW18 140 A6
Church Row Ms *CHST* BR7 185 H3
Church St *BAY/PAD* W2 8 B1
CHSWK W4 118 B6
CROY/NA CR0 211 H1
DAGE RM10 92 D5
ED N9 35 K2
ENC/FH EN2 23 J4
ESH/CLAY KT10 204 B2
EW KT17 207 J6
HPTN TW12 173 H4
HSLW TW3 135 H6
ISLW TW7 136 C4
KUT/HW KT1 174 E5
SRTFD E15 88 C6
TWK TW1 156 B3
Church Street Est
STJWD NW8 2 B7
Church St North *SRTFD* E15 88 C6
Church Ter *BKHTH/KID* SE3 145 H4
FUL/PGN SW6 * 140 A3
HDN NW4 45 K6
RCHPK/HAM TW10 136 E6
Church V *EFNCH* N2 47 K6
FSTH SE23 163 K4
Church Vw *FSTH* SE23 164 A4
Church View Gv *SYD* SE26 182 A2
Churchview Rd *WHTN* TW2 155 J3
Church Wk *BTFD* TW8 116 D6
BUSH WD23 28 A1
CDALE/KGS NW9 63 F6
CRICK NW2 82 D1
HYS/HAR UB3 94 C5
RDART DA2 171 G5
RYNPK SW20 177 F6
STNW/STAM N16 85 K2
STRHM/NOR SW16 179 H5
THDIT KT7 190 A3
Churchway *CAMTN* NW1 4 D4
Church Wy *EBAR* EN4 21 K5
TRDG/WHET N20 33 J5
Churchyard Rw *LBTH* SE11 18 B6
Churston Av *PLSTW* E13 89 F6
Churston Cl
BRXS/STRHM SW2 * 162 C3
Churston Dr *MRDN* SM4 193 G2
Churston Gdns
FBAR/BDGN N11 48 C2
Churton Pl *CHSWK* W4 * 117 J6
PIM SW1V 16 B7
Churton St *PIM* SW1V 16 B7
Chyngton Cl *BFN/LL* DA15 168 A5
Cibber Rd *FSTH* SE23 164 A4
Cicada Rd *WAND/EARL* SW18 160 B1
Cicely Rd *PECK* SE15 143 H2
Cinderford Wy *BMLY* BR1 165 H6
Cinema Pde *EDGW* HA8 * 44 C2
Cinnamon Cl *CROY/NA* CR0 * 195 K4
PECK SE15 143 G1
Cinnamon St *WAP* E1W 123 J1
Cintra Pk *NRWD* SE19 181 G3
Circle Gdns *WIM/MER* SW19 177 K6
The Circle *CRICK* NW2 81 G1
MLHL NW7 45 F2
The Circuits *PIN* HA5 59 G1
Circular Rd *TOTM* N17 50 B6
Circular Wy
WOOL/PLUM SE18 126 E6
Circus Ms *MBLAR* W1H * 8 E1
Circus Pl *LVPST* EC2M * 13 F2
Circus Rd *STJWD* NW8 2 A4
Circus St *GNWCH* SE10 145 F1
Cirencester St *BAY/PAD* W2 101 F4
Cissbury Ring North
NFNCH/WDSPK N12 46 D1
Cissbury Ring South
NFNCH/WDSPK N12 46 D1
Cissbury Rd *SEVS/STOTM* N15 67 K2
Citadel Pl *LBTH* SE11 122 A5
Citizen Rd *HOLWY* N7 85 G1
Citron Ter *PECK* SE15 * 143 J4
City Barracks *SHB* W12 * 119 F1
City Garden Rw *IS* N1 6 B3
City Rd *FSBYE* EC1V 6 A3
STLK EC1Y 7 F7
City Wk *STHWK* SE1 19 G4
Civic Wy *BARK/HLT* IG6 72 C1
RSLP HA4 77 H3
Clabon Ms *KTBR* SW1X 14 E5
Clack St *BERM/RHTH* SE16 123 K2
Clacton Rd *TOTM* N17 * 50 B5
WALTH E17 69 G3
Claire Ct *NFNCH/WDSPK* N12 33 G5
Claire Gdns *STAN* HA7 43 J1
Claire Pl *POP/IOD* E14 124 D3
Clairvale Rd *HEST* TW5 134 C2
Clairview Rd
STRHM/NOR SW16 179 G1
Clairville Gdns *HNWL* W7 115 K1
Clamp Hl *STAN* HA7 42 E1
Clancarty Rd *FUL/PGN* SW6 139 K3
Clandon Cl *ACT* W3 117 J2
EW KT17 207 H4
Clandon Gdns *FNCH* N3 46 E6
Clandon Rd *GDMY/SEVK* IG3 72 E6
Clandon St *DEPT* SE8 144 D3
Clandon Ter *RYNPK* SW20 * 177 G5
Clanricarde Gdns
BAY/PAD W2 100 E6
Clapgate Rd *BUSH* WD23 28 B1
Clapham Common North Side
CLAP SW4 141 F5
Clapham Common South Side
CLAP SW4 141 G6
Clapham Common West Side
BTSEA SW11 140 E5
Clapham Court Ter
CLAP SW4 * 141 K6
Clapham Crs *CLAP* SW4 141 J5
Clapham High St *CLAP* SW4 141 J5
Clapham Manor St *CLAP* SW4 141 H4
Clapham Park Est *CLAP* SW4 * 161 J2
Clapham Park Rd *CLAP* SW4 141 H5
Clapham Park Ter
BRXS/STRHM SW2 * 141 K6
Clapham Rd *BRXN/ST* SW9 141 K3
Claps Gate La *EHAM* E6 108 B3
Clapton Common *CLPT* E5 68 C4
Clapton Sq *CLPT* E5 86 D3
Clapton Ter *CLPT* E5 68 C4
Clapton Wy *CLPT* E5 86 C2
Clara Pl *WOOL/PLUM* SE18 127 F4
Clare Cl *BORE* WD6 30 B1
EFNCH N2 47 G6
Clare Cnr *ELTH/MOT* SE9 167 G2
Clare Ct *NTHWD* HA6 40 C1
Claredale St *BETH* E2 104 C1
Clare Gdns *BARK* IG11 91 F4
FSTGT E7 88 E2
NTGHL W11 * 100 C5
Clare Hl *ESH/CLAY* KT10 204 B3
Clare La *IS* N1 85 J5
Clare Lawn Av
MORT/ESHN SW14 138 A6
Clare Ms *FUL/PGN* SW6 140 A1
Claremont Av
KTN/HRWW/WS HA3 62 A2
NWMAL KT3 192 E2
SUN TW16 172 A4
Claremont Cl
BRXS/STRHM SW2 162 A3
CAN/RD E16 127 F1
IS N1 5 K3
ORP BR6 216 A2
Claremont Crs *DART* DA1 150 B5
Claremont Dr *ESH/CLAY* KT10 204 B5
Claremont End
ESH/CLAY KT10 204 B4
Claremont Gdns
GDMY/SEVK IG3 72 E6
SURB KT6 191 F1
Claremont Gv *CHSWK* W4 138 B1
WFD IG8 53 G2
Claremont House
WATW WD18 * 26 B1
Claremont La *ESH/CLAY* KT10 204 B3
Claremont Pk *FNCH* N3 46 C4
Claremont Park Rd
ESH/CLAY KT10 204 A4
Claremont Rd *BMLY* BR1 200 D1
CRICK NW2 64 A4
CROY/NA CR0 197 H5
EBAR EN4 21 G1
EMPK RM11 75 J3
ESH/CLAY KT10 204 E5
FSTGT E7 89 F3
GLDGN NW11 82 B1
HGT N6 66 B4
KTN/HRWW/WS HA3 42 E5
MV/WKIL W9 100 C1
SURB KT6 191 F2
TEDD TW11 174 A1
TWK TW1 156 C2
WALTH E17 51 G5
WAN E11 88 B1
WEA W13 97 G4
Claremont Sq *IS* N1 5 J3
Claremont St *GNWCH* SE10 124 E6
UED N18 50 C2
Claremont Ter *THDIT* KT7 * 190 C4
Claremont Vls *CMBW* SE5 * 142 E1
KUT/HW KT1 * 175 G5
Claremont Wy *CRICK* NW2 64 A5
Clarence Av *BMLY* BR1 200 D1
CLAP SW4 161 J1
IL IG1 71 K3
NWMAL KT3 175 K5
Clarence Cl *BUSH* WD23 29 F1
EBAR EN4 21 H6
Clarence Ct *MLHL* NW7 45 G1
Clarence Crs *CLAP* SW4 161 J1
SCUP DA14 168 C5
Clarence Gdns *CAMTN* NW1 3 K5
Clarence Ga *CAMTN* NW1 3 F6
CHIG IG7 54 A2
Clarence La *PUT/ROE* SW15 158 C1
Clarence Ms
BERM/RHTH SE16 124 A1
CLPT E5 86 D3
TOOT SW17 160 B5
Clarence Pas *KCROSS* N1C * 4 E3
Clarence Pl *CLPT* E5 86 D3
Clarence Rd *BMLY* BR1 184 D6
BXLYHS DA6 149 F5
CAN/RD E16 106 C3
CHSWK W4 117 H5
CLPT E5 86 D2
CROY/NA CR0 196 E4
DEPT SE8 125 G5
ELTH/MOT SE9 166 D4
KIL/WHAMP NW6 82 D5
MNPK E12 89 G2
PEND EN3 24 E6
RCH/KEW TW9 137 G2
SCUP DA14 168 C5
SEVS/STOTM N15 67 J2
SUT SM1 209 F2
TEDD TW11 174 A2
WALTH E17 51 F5
WDGN N22 48 E3
WIM/MER SW19 178 A2
WLGTN SM6 210 B3
Clarence St *KUT/HW* KT1 174 E5
NWDGN UB2 114 C3
RCH/KEW TW9 137 F5
Clarence Ter *CAMTN* NW1 3 F6
HSLW TW3 135 G5
Clarence Vls *KUT/HW* KT1 * 175 G5
Clarence Wk *CLAP* SW4 141 K3
Clarence Wy *CAMTN* NW1 84 B5
Clarendon Cl *BAY/PAD* W2 * 8 C5
HOM E9 86 E5
STMC/STPC BR5 186 B6
Clarendon Crs *WHTN* TW2 155 J5
Clarendon Cross *NTGHL* W11 100 C6
Clarendon Dr *PUT/ROE* SW15 139 F5
Clarendon Gdns *HDN* NW4 45 J6
IL IG1 71 G3
MV/WKIL W9 101 G3
WBLY HA9 79 K1
Clarendon Ga *BAY/PAD* W2 8 C5
Clarendon Gn
STMC/STPC BR5 186 B6
Clarendon Gv *MTCM* CR4 178 E6
STMC/STPC BR5 202 B1
Clarendon Ms *BAY/PAD* W2 8 C5
Clarendon Pth
STMC/STPC BR5 202 B1
Clarendon Pl *BAY/PAD* W2 8 C5
Clarendon Ri *LEW* SE13 145 F4
Clarendon Rd *ASHF* TW15 152 C6
CEND/HSY/T N8 49 F6
CROY/NA CR0 196 C6
EA W5 98 A2
HRW HA1 60 E3
HYS/HAR UB3 113 J2
NTGHL W11 100 C6
SEVS/STOTM N15 67 H1
SWFD E18 52 E6
UED N18 50 C1
WALTH E17 69 K3
WDGN N22 * 49 F5
WIM/MER SW19 178 D3
WLGTN SM6 210 C3
Clarendon St *PIM* SW1V 121 G5
Clarendon Ter *MV/WKIL* W9 101 G3
Clarendon Wy *CHST* BR7 186 A6
WCHMH N21 35 J2
Clarens St *CAT* SE6 164 C4
Clare Pde *GFD/PVL* UB6 * 78 D4
Clare Rd *GFD/PVL* UB6 78 D4
HSLWW TW4 134 E4
NWCR SE14 144 C3
STWL/WRAY TW19 152 A2
WAN E11 70 B3
WLSDN NW10 81 J5
Clare St *BETH* E2 104 D1
Claret Gdns *SNWD* SE25 197 F1
Clareville Gv *SKENS* SW7 * 120 B4
Clareville Grove Ms
SKENS SW7 * 120 B4
Clareville Rd *STMC/STPC* BR5 201 H6
Clareville St *SKENS* SW7 120 B4
Clare Wy *BXLYHN* DA7 149 F2
Clarges Ms *MYFR/PICC* W1J 9 J7
Clarges St *MYFR/PICC* W1J 9 K7
Claribel Rd *BRXN/ST* SW9 142 C3
Clarice Wy *WLGTN* SM6 210 E6
Claridge Rd *BCTR* RM8 73 K5
Clarissa Rd *CHDH* RM6 73 K3
Clarissa St *HACK* E8 86 B6
Clark Cl *ERITH* DA8 150 D2
Clarke Cl *THHTH* CR7 196 D3
Clarke Ms *ED* N9 36 D5
Clarkes Av *WPK* KT4 193 G5
Clarkes Ms *CAVSQ/HST* W1G 9 H1
Clark Gv *IL* IG1 90 E2
Clarks Md *BUSH* WD23 28 C2
Clarkson Rd *CAN/RD* E16 106 D5
Clarkson Rw *CAMTN* NW1 4 A3
Clarkson St *BETH* E2 * 104 D2
Clark's Rd *IL* IG1 72 D6
Clark St *WCHPL* E1 104 E5
Clark Wy *HEST* TW5 134 C1
Classon Cl *WDR/YW* UB7 112 B2
Claston Cl *DART* DA1 150 B5
Claude Monet Ct *EDUL* SE22 * 143 H6
Claude Rd *LEY* E10 70 A5
PECK SE15 143 J3
PLSTW E13 89 F6
Claude St *POP/IOD* E14 124 D4
Claudia Pl *WIM/MER* SW19 159 H3
Claudius Cl *STAN* HA7 29 K5
Claughton Rd *PLSTW* E13 107 G1
Clauson Av *NTHLT* UB5 78 B3
Clavell St *GNWCH* SE10 125 F6
Claverdale Rd
BRXS/STRHM SW2 162 A2
Clavering Av *BARN* SW13 118 E6
Clavering Cl *TEDD* TW11 156 B6
Clavering Pl *BAL* SW12 161 F1
Clavering Rd *MNPK* E12 71 H5
Claverley Gv *FNCH* N3 46 E4
Claverley Vls *FNCH* N3 47 F3
Claverton St *PIM* SW1V 121 H5
Clave St *WAP* E1W 123 K1
Claxton Gv *HMSMTH* W6 119 G5
Clay Av *MTCM* CR4 179 G5
Claybank Gv *LEW* SE13 144 E4
Claybridge Rd
LEE/GVPK SE12 166 B6
Claybrook Cl *EFNCH* N2 47 H6
Claybrook Rd *HMSMTH* W6 119 G6
Claybury *BUSH* WD23 28 B2
Claybury Rd *WFD* IG8 53 J3
Clay Ct *KTN/HRWW/WS* HA3 61 K1
Claydon Dr *CROY/NA* CR0 210 E2
Claydown Ms
WOOL/PLUM SE18 127 F5
Clayfarm Rd *ELTH/MOT* SE9 167 H4
Claygate Cl *HCH* RM12 93 J2
Claygate Crs *CROY/NA* CR0 214 A4
Claygate La *ESH/CLAY* KT10 205 G1
THDIT KT7 190 B5
Claygate Lodge Cl
ESH/CLAY KT10 204 E5
Claygate Rd *WEA* W13 116 C3
Clayhall Av *CLAY* IG5 53 J5
Clayhill Crs *ELTH/MOT* SE9 166 C6
Claylands Pl *VX/NE* SW8 142 B1
Claylands Rd *VX/NE* SW8 122 A6
Clay La *BUSH* WD23 28 E2
STWL/WRAY TW19 152 C2
Claymore Cl *MRDN* SM4 193 K4
Claypole Dr *HEST* TW5 134 D2
Claypole Rd *SRTFD* E15 * 106 A1
Clayponds Av *BTFD* TW8 117 F4
Clayponds Gdns *EA* W5 116 E4
Clayponds La *BTFD* TW8 117 F5
Clayside *CHIG* IG7 54 C1
Clay St *MHST* W1U 9 F2
Clayton Av *ALP/SUD* HA0 80 A5
Clayton Cl *EHAM* E6 107 K5
Clayton Crs *BTFD* TW8 116 E5
IS N1 5 G1
Clayton Croft Rd *RDART* DA2 170 D4
Clayton Dr *DEPT* SE8 124 B5
Clayton Fld *CDALE/KGS* NW9 45 G4
Clayton Ms *GNWCH* SE10 145 G2
Clayton Rd *CHSGTN* KT9 205 J2
HYS/HAR UB3 113 H2
ISLW TW7 135 K4
PECK SE15 143 H2
ROMW/RG RM7 74 E5
Clayton St *LBTH* SE11 122 B6
Clayton Ter *YEAD* UB4 95 J4
Claytonville Ter *BELV* DA17 * 129 K2
Clay Wood Cl *ORP* BR6 201 K4
Clayworth Cl *BFN/LL* DA15 168 C1
Cleanthus Cl
WOOL/PLUM SE18 147 C2

Cleanthus Rd
WOOL/PLUM SE18 147 G2
Clearbrook Wy WCHPL E1 104 E5
Clearwater Pl SURB KT6 190 D3
Clearwater Ter NTGHL W11 119 G2
Clearwell Dr MV/WKIL W9 101 F3
Cleave Av HYS/HAR UB3 113 H4
ORP BR6 216 E4
Cleaveland Rd SURB KT6 190 E2
Cleaverholme Cl SNWD SE25 197 J3
Cleaver Sq LBTH SE11 122 B5
Cleaver St LBTH SE11 122 B5
Cleeve Ct EBED/NFELT TW14 153 H3
Cleeve Hl FSTH SE23 163 J3
Cleeve Park Gdns SCUP DA14 168 C4
Cleeve Wy PUT/ROE SW15 158 C1
SUT SM1 194 A5
Clegg St PLSTW E13 106 E1
WAP E1W 123 J1
Clematis Cots SHB W12 * 99 J6
Clematis Gdns WFD IG8 52 E1
Clematis St SHB W12 99 H6
Clem Attlee Ct
FUL/PGN SW6 * 119 J6
Clem Attlee Pde
FUL/PGN SW6 * 119 J6
Clemence Rd DAGE RM10 92 E6
Clemence St POP/IOD E14 105 H4
Clement Av CLAP SW4 141 J5
Clement Cl CHSWK W4 118 A4
KIL/WHAMP NW6 82 A5
Clement Gdns HYS/HAR UB3 113 H4
Clementhorpe Rd DAGW RM9 91 J4
Clementina Rd LEY E10 69 H5
Clementine Cl WEA W13 116 C2
Clement Rd BECK BR3 182 A5
WIM/MER SW19 177 H1
Clements Av CAN/RD E16 106 E6
Clements Cl
NFNCH/WDSPK N12 33 F6
Clements La IL IG1 90 B1
Clement's La MANHO EC4N 13 F5
Clements Pl BTFD TW8 116 E5
Clements Rd
BERM/RHTH SE16 * 123 H3
EHAM E6 89 K5
IL IG1 90 B1
WOT/HER KT12 188 A6
Clement's Rd
BERM/RHTH SE16 123 H3
Clendon Wy
WOOL/PLUM SE18 127 J4
Clennam St STHWK SE1 * 18 D2
Clensham Ct SUT SM1 193 K6
Clensham La SUT SM1 193 K6
Clenston Ms MBLAR W1H 8 E3
Cleopatra Cl STAN HA7 29 K5
Clephane Rd IS N1 85 J4
Clere Pl SDTCH EC2A 7 F6
Clere St SDTCH EC2A 7 F6
Clerkenwell Cl CLKNW EC1R 5 K6
Clerkenwell Gn CLKNW EC1R 6 A7
Clerkenwell Rd CLKNW EC1R 5 J7
Clermont Rd HOM E9 86 E6
Clevedon Gdns HEST TW5 134 A3
HYS/HAR UB3 113 G3
Clevedon Rd KUT/HW KT1 175 H5
PGE/AN SE20 182 A4
TWK TW1 156 E1
Cleveland Av CHSWK W4 118 C4
HPTN TW12 172 E3
Cleveland Gdns BARN SW13 138 C3
BAY/PAD W2 101 G5
CRICK NW2 64 B6
SEVS/STOTM N15 67 J2
WPK KT4 192 B6
Cleveland Gv WCHPL E1 104 E3
Cleveland Ms FITZ W1T 10 A1
Cleveland Park Av WALTH E17 69 J1
Cleveland Park Crs
WALTH E17 69 J1
Cleveland Pl STJS SW1Y 10 B7
Cleveland Ri MRDN SM4 193 G4
Cleveland Rd BARN SW13 138 C3
CHSWK W4 117 K3
ED N9 * 36 D2
IL IG1 90 B1
IS N1 85 K5
ISLW TW7 136 B5
NWMAL KT3 192 B1
SWFD E18 52 E6
WEA W13 97 G4
WELL DA16 148 A3
WPK KT4 192 B6
Cleveland Rw WHALL SW1A 16 B1
Cleveland Sq BAY/PAD W2 101 G6
Cleveland St CAMTN NW1 3 K7
Cleveland Ter BAY/PAD W2 101 G5
Cleveland Wy WCHPL E1 104 E3
Cleveley Crs EA W5 98 A1
Cleveleys Rd CLPT E5 86 D1
Clevely Cl CHARL SE7 126 C4
Cleverly Est SHB W12 * 118 D1
Cleve Rd KIL/WHAMP NW6 82 E5
SCUP DA14 168 E5
Cleves Av EW KT17 207 K6
Cleves Cl LOU IG10 39 J1
Cleves Rd EHAM E6 89 H6
RCHPK/HAM TW10 156 D5
Cleves Wk BARK/HLT IG6 54 C3
Cleves Wy HPTN TW12 172 E3
RSLP HA4 59 H5
Clewer Crs
KTN/HRWW/WS HA3 42 D4
Clifden Ms CLPT E5 87 F2
Clifden Rd BTFD TW8 116 E6
CLPT E5 86 E3
TWK TW1 156 A3
Cliffe Rd SAND/SEL CR2 211 K3
Clifford Av CHST BR7 184 E2
CLAY IG5 54 B4
MORT/ESHN SW14 137 K3
RCH/KEW TW9 137 J4
WLGTN SM6 210 C2
Clifford Cl NTHLT UB5 77 J6
PLSTW E13 * 107 F2
Clifford Dr BRXN/ST SW9 142 C5
Clifford Gdns HYS/HAR UB3 113 G4
WLSDN NW10 100 A1
Clifford Gv ASHF TW15 152 D6
Clifford Rd ALP/SUD HA0 79 K6
BAR EN5 21 F4
CAN/RD E16 106 D3
ED N9 36 E1
HSLWW TW4 134 C4
RCHPK/HAM TW10 156 E4
SNWD SE25 197 H1
WALTH E17 52 A5
Clifford St CONDST W1S 10 A6
Clifford Wy WLSDN NW10 81 H2
Cliff Rd CAMTN NW1 84 D4
Cliff Ter DEPT SE8 144 D3
Cliffview Rd LEW SE13 144 D4
Cliff Vls CAMTN NW1 84 D4
Cliff Wk CAN/RD E16 106 D4
Clifton Av FELT TW13 154 B5
FNCH N3 46 D4
KTN/HRWW/WS HA3 43 H5
SHB W12 118 C2
WALTH E17 69 F1
WBLY HA9 80 B4
Clifton Cl ORP BR6 216 C3
Clifton Ct BECK BR3 * 182 E4
Clifton Crs PECK SE15 143 J1
Clifton Gdns CHSWK W4 118 A4
ENC/FH EN2 22 E5
GLDGN NW11 64 D3
MV/WKIL W9 101 G3
SEVS/STOTM N15 68 B3
Clifton Ga WBPTN SW10 * 120 B6
Clifton Gv HACK E8 86 C4
Clifton Hl STJWD NW8 101 G1
Clifton Ms SNWD SE25 197 F1
Clifton Pde FELT TW13 * 154 B6
Clifton Park Av RYNPK SW20 177 F5
Clifton Pl BAY/PAD W2 8 B5
BERM/RHTH SE16 123 K2
KUTN/CMB KT2 * 175 H4
WBPTN SW10 * 120 B6
Clifton Ri NWCR SE14 144 B1
Clifton Rd CAN/RD E16 106 C4
CEND/HSY/T N8 66 D3
EMPK RM11 75 J3
FNCH N3 47 G4
FSTGT E7 89 H4
GFD/PVL UB6 96 C3
GNTH/NBYPK IG2 72 D3
HTHAIR TW6 132 E4
IS N1 85 J4
ISLW TW7 135 K3
KTN/HRWW/WS HA3 62 B2
KUTN/CMB KT2 175 G4
MV/WKIL W9 101 G3
NWDGN UB2 114 D4
SCUP DA14 167 K6
SNWD SE25 197 F1
TEDD TW11 155 K6
WDGN N22 48 C4
WELL DA16 148 D4
WIM/MER SW19 177 G2
WLGTN SM6 210 B3
WLSDN NW10 99 J1
Clifton St SDTCH EC2A 7 G7
Clifton Ter FSBYPK N4 67 G6
Clifton Vls MV/WKIL W9 101 F4
Clifton Wy ALP/SUD HA0 80 A6
PECK SE15 143 K1
Cline Rd FBAR/BDGN N11 48 C2
Clink St STHWK SE1 12 E7
Clinton Av E/WMO/HCT KT8 189 H1
WELL DA16 148 B5
Clinton Crs BARK/HLT IG6 54 E2
Clinton Rd BOW E3 105 G2
FSTGT E7 88 E2
SEVS/STOTM N15 67 K1
Clinton Ter DEPT SE8 * 124 D6
SUT SM1 * 209 G2
Clipper Cl BERM/RHTH SE16 124 A2
Clipper Wy LEW SE13 145 F5
Clippesby Cl CHSGTN KT9 * 206 B4
Clipstone Ms GTPST W1W 10 A1
Clipstone Rd HSLW TW3 135 F4
Clipstone St GTPST W1W 9 K1
Clissold Cl EFNCH N2 47 K6
Clissold Crs STNW/STAM N16 85 K2
Clissold Rd STNW/STAM N16 85 K1
Clitheroe Av
RYLN/HDSTN HA2 60 A5
Clitheroe Gdns OXHEY WD19 27 H5
Clitheroe Rd BRXN/ST SW9 141 K3
CRW RM5 56 E1
Clitherow Av HNWL W7 116 B3
Clitherow Rd BTFD TW8 116 C5
Clitterhouse Crs CRICK NW2 64 A5
Clitterhouse Rd CRICK NW2 64 A5
Clive Av DART DA1 170 C1
UED N18 50 C2
Clive Ct WLSDN NW10 * 81 H5
Cliveden Cl
NFNCH/WDSPK N12 33 G6
Cliveden Pl BGVA SW1W 15 G6
Cliveden Rd WIM/MER SW19 177 J4
Clivedon Ct WEA W13 97 H4
Clivedon Rd CHING E4 52 C1
Clive Rd BELV DA17 129 H4
DUL SE21 162 E5
EBED/NFELT TW14 153 K1
EN EN1 24 C5
ESH/CLAY KT10 204 B2
GPK RM2 75 K2
TWK TW1 156 A6
WIM/MER SW19 178 D2
Clivesdale Dr HYS/HAR UB3 113 K1
Clive Wy EN EN1 24 C5
Cloak La CANST EC4R 12 D5
Clockhouse Av BARK IG11 90 C6
Clockhouse Cl
WIM/MER SW19 159 F5
Clockhouse La ASHF TW15 152 D6
CRW RM5 56 E3
EBED/NFELT TW14 152 E5
Clock House Pde
PLMGR N13 * 49 G1
Clockhouse Pl PUT/ROE SW15 139 H6
Clock House Rd BECK BR3 182 B6
Clock Pde ENC/FH EN2 * 23 K6
Clocktower Ms HNWL W7 * 115 K1
Clock Tower Ms IS N1 6 D1
THMD SE28 109 H6
Clock Tower Pl HOLWY N7 * 84 E4
Clock Tower Rd ISLW TW7 136 A4
Clock View Crs HOLWY N7 84 E4
Cloister Cl RAIN RM13 111 K3
TEDD TW11 174 C1
Cloister Gdns EDGW HA8 44 E1
SNWD SE25 197 J3
Cloister Rd ACT W3 98 E4
CRICK NW2 82 D1
Cloisters Av HAYES BR2 200 E2
Clonard Wy PIN HA5 42 A2
Clonbrock Rd
STNW/STAM N16 86 A2
Cloncurry St FUL/PGN SW6 139 G3
Clonmel Cl RYLN/HDSTN HA2 60 D5
Clonmell Rd TOTM N17 49 K6
Clonmel Rd FUL/PGN SW6 139 J1
TEDD TW11 155 J6
Clonmore St
WAND/EARL SW18 159 J3
Cloonmore Av ORP BR6 217 F3
Clorane Gdns HAMP NW3 82 E1
Closemead Cl NTHWD HA6 40 A2
The Close ALP/SUD HA0 80 A4
BECK BR3 198 B1
BUSH WD23 * 28 A1
BXLY DA5 169 H1
CAR SM5 209 J6
CHDH RM6 74 A3
CHEAM SM3 193 J4
CHING E4 52 A3
EBAR EN4 33 K1
GNTH/NBYPK IG2 72 E3
ISLW TW7 135 J3
MTCM CR4 194 E1
NWMAL KT3 175 K5
PIN HA5 59 G4
RCH/KEW TW9 137 J4
RDART DA2 171 F5
SCUP DA14 186 C1
SNWD SE25 * 197 H3
STHGT/OAK N14 34 D4
STMC/STPC BR5 201 K3
SURB KT6 191 F4
TRDG/WHET N20 32 D4
WBLY HA9 80 E1
Cloth Ct STBT EC1A 12 B2
Cloth Fair STBT EC1A 12 B2
Clothier St HDTCH EC3A 13 H3
Cloth St STBT EC1A 12 C1
Clothworkers Rd
WOOL/PLUM SE18 147 J1
Cloudesdale Rd TOOT SW17 161 G4
Cloudesley Cl SCUP DA14 186 A1
Cloudesley Pl IS N1 5 K1
Cloudesley Rd BXLYHN DA7 149 G2
ERITH DA8 150 C2
IS N1 5 J1
Cloudesley St IS N1 5 K1
Clouston Cl WLGTN SM6 210 E3
Clova Rd FSTGT E7 88 E3
Clove Crs POP/IOD E14 106 A6
Clovelly Av CDALE/KGS NW9 63 H1
HGDN/ICK UB10 76 A2
Clovelly Cl HGDN/ICK UB10 76 A2
PIN HA5 41 F6
Clovelly Gdns EN EN1 36 A2
NRWD SE19 181 G4
ROMW/RG RM7 56 D4
Clovelly Rd BXLYHN DA7 129 F6
CEND/HSY/T N8 66 D1
CHSWK W4 * 118 A2
EA W5 116 D2
HSLW TW3 135 F3
Clovelly Wy ORP BR6 202 A3
RYLN/HDSTN HA2 77 K1
WCHPL E1 104 E5
Clover Cl WAN E11 * 70 B6
Cloverdale Gdns BFN/LL DA15 168 A1
The Clover Fld BUSH WD23 27 K1
Clover Ms CHEL SW3 120 E6
Clover Wy WLGTN SM6 195 F5
Clove St PLSTW E13 106 E3
Clowders Rd CAT SE6 164 C5
Clowser Cl SUT SM1 209 G3
Cloysters Gn WAP E1W * 123 H1
Cloyster Wd EDGW HA8 43 K3
Club Gardens Rd HAYES BR2 199 K4
Club Rw BETH E2 7 J6
The Clumps ASHF TW15 153 G6
Clunbury Av NWDGN UB2 114 E5
Clunbury St IS N1 7 F3
Cluny Est STHWK SE1 19 G4
Cluny Pl STHWK SE1 19 G4
Clutton St POP/IOD E14 105 K4
Clydach Rd EN EN1 24 B5
Clyde Circ SEVS/STOTM N15 68 A1
Clyde Ct CAMTN NW1 4 D2
Clyde Flats FUL/PGN SW6 * 139 J1
Clyde Pl LEY E10 69 K4
Clyde Rd CROY/NA CR0 197 G6
SEVS/STOTM N15 68 A1
STWL/WRAY TW19 152 A3
SUT SM1 208 E3
WDGN N22 48 D4
WLGTN SM6 210 C3
Clydesdale PEND EN3 25 F5
Clydesdale Av STAN HA7 43 K6
Clydesdale Cl ISLW TW7 136 A4
Clydesdale Gdns
RCHPK/HAM TW10 137 J5
Clydesdale Rd EMPK RM11 75 H4
NTGHL W11 100 D5
Clyde St DEPT SE8 124 C6
Clyde Ter FSTH SE23 163 K4
Clyde V FSTH SE23 163 K4
Clyde Wy ROM RM1 57 G4
Clydon Cl ERITH DA8 130 B6
Clyfford Rd RSLP HA4 76 D2
Clymping Dene
EBED/NFELT TW14 154 A2
Clyston Rd WATW WD18 26 D1
Clyston St VX/NE SW8 141 H3
Coach & Horses Yd
CONDST W1S 9 K5
Coach House La HBRY N5 * 85 H2
WIM/MER SW19 159 G6
Coach House Ms FSTH SE23 163 K1
NWCR SE14 * 144 A2
Coach House Yd
WAND/EARL SW18 * 140 A5
Coalecroft Rd PUT/ROE SW15 139 F5
Coal Post Cl ORP BR6 * 217 F5
Coates Av WAND/EARL SW18 160 D1
Coates Cl THHTH CR7 180 D6
Coates Hill Rd BMLY BR1 185 F5
Coates Rd BORE WD6 29 K2
Coate St BETH E2 104 C1
Cobalt Cl BECK BR3 198 A1
Cobbett Rd ELTH/MOT SE9 146 D4
WHTN TW2 155 F3
Cobbetts Av REDBR IG4 71 H2
Cobbett St VX/NE SW8 142 A1
Cobble La IS N1 85 H5
Cobble Ms HBRY N5 85 J1
Cobbler's Wk TEDD TW11 173 K3
Cobblestone Pl CROY/NA CR0 196 D5
Cobbold Ms SHB W12 * 118 C2
Cobbold Rd SHB W12 118 C2
WAN E11 88 D1
WLSDN NW10 81 H4
Cobb's Rd HSLWW TW4 134 E5
Cobb St WCHPL E1 13 J3
Cobden Ms SYD SE26 181 J1
Cobden Rd ORP BR6 216 D2
SNWD SE25 197 H2
WAN E11 88 C1
Cobham Av NWMAL KT3 192 D2
Cobham Cl BFN/LL DA15 168 C1
BTSEA SW11 160 D1
EDGW HA8 44 D5
EN EN1 24 C4
HAYES BR2 200 D4
WLGTN SM6 210 E4
Cobham Ms CAMTN NW1 84 D5
Cobham Pl BXLYHS DA6 148 E6
Cobham Rd GDMY/SEVK IG3 72 E6
HEST TW5 134 B1
KUT/HW KT1 175 H5
WALTH E17 52 A4
Cobland Rd LEE/GVPK SE12 166 B6
Coborn Rd BOW E3 105 H2
Coborn St BOW E3 105 H2
Cobourg Rd CMBW SE5 123 G5
Cobourg St CAMTN NW1 4 B5
Coburg Cl WEST SW1P 16 B6
Coburg Crs BRXS/STRHM SW2 162 A3
Coburg Dwellings
WCHPL E1 * 104 E6
Coburg Gdns CLAY IG5 53 H5
Coburg Rd WDGN N22 49 F5
Cochrane Dr DART DA1 171 G1
Cochrane Ms STJWD NW8 2 B3
Cochrane Rd WIM/MER SW19 177 H3
Cochrane St STJWD NW8 2 B3
Cockcrow Hl SURB KT6 * 190 E5
Cockerell Rd WALTH E17 69 G4
Cockfosters Pde EBAR EN4 * 22 A5
Cockfosters Rd EBAR EN4 21 K4
Cock La STBT EC1A 12 A2
Cockmannings La
STMC/STPC BR5 202 E5
Cockmannings Rd
STMC/STPC BR5 202 E4
Cocks Crs NWMAL KT3 192 C1
Cocksett Av ORP BR6 216 E4
Cockspur Ct STJS SW1Y 10 D7
Cockspur St STJS SW1Y 10 D7
Cocksure La SCUP DA14 169 H6
Code St WCHPL E1 7 K7
Codling Cl WAP E1W 123 H1
Codling Wy ALP/SUD HA0 79 K2
Codrington Hl FSTH SE23 164 B2
Codrington Ms NTGHL W11 100 C5
Cody Cl KTN/HRWW/WS HA3 43 K6
WLGTN SM6 210 D5
Cody Rd CAN/RD E16 106 B3
Coe Av SNWD SE25 197 H3
Coe's Aly BAR EN5 20 C5
Coffey St DEPT SE8 144 D1
Cogan Av WALTH E17 51 G4
Coin St STHWK SE1 11 J7
Coity Rd KTTN NW5 84 A4
Cokers La DUL SE21 162 D3
Coke St WCHPL E1 104 C5
Colas Ms KIL/WHAMP NW6 82 E6
Colbeck Ms SKENS SW7 120 A4
Colbeck Rd HRW HA1 60 C4
Colberg Pl STNW/STAM N16 * 68 B4
Colborne Wy WPK KT4 208 A1
Colbrook Av HYS/HAR UB3 113 G3
Colbrook Cl HYS/HAR UB3 113 G3
Colburn Av PIN HA5 41 J2
Colburn Wy SUT SM1 209 H1
Colby Rd NRWD SE19 181 F1
Colchester Dr PIN HA5 59 H2
Colchester Rd EDGW HA8 44 E3
NTHWD HA6 40 E5
WALTH E17 69 J3
Coldbath Sq CLKNW EC1R 5 J7
Coldbath St LEW SE13 144 E2
Cold Blow Crs BXLY DA5 170 A3
Cold Blow La NWCR SE14 144 A1
Coldershaw Rd WEA W13 116 B2
Coldfall Av MUSWH N10 47 K5
Coldharbour POP/IOD E14 125 F1
Coldharbour Crest
ELTH/MOT SE9 * 167 F5
Coldharbour La
BRXN/ST SW9 142 B5
BUSH WD23 28 B1
HYS/HAR UB3 113 J2
RAIN RM13 130 D1
Coldharbour Pl CMBW SE5 142 D3
Coldharbour Rd
CROY/NA CR0 211 G3
Coldharbour Wy
CROY/NA CR0 211 G3
Coldstream Gdns
WAND/EARL SW18 159 J1
Colebeck Ms IS N1 85 H4
Colebert Av WCHPL E1 104 E3
Colebrook Cl MLHL NW7 46 B3
Colebrooke Av WEA W13 97 H5
Colebrooke Dr WAN E11 71 F4
Colebrooke Pl IS N1 6 B1
Colebrooke Rw IS N1 6 A3
Colebrook Ri HAYES BR2 183 H5
Colebrook Rd
STRHM/NOR SW16 179 K4
Colebrook St ERITH DA8 130 C6
Colebrook Wy
FBAR/BDGN N11 48 B1
Coleby Pth CMBW SE5 * 142 E1
Cole Cl THMD SE28 128 C1
Coledale Dr STAN HA7 43 J4
Coleford Rd
WAND/EARL SW18 140 B6
Cole Gdns HEST TW5 133 K1
Colegrave Rd SRTFD E15 88 B3
Colegrove Rd PECK SE15 123 G6
Coleherne Ms WBPTN SW10 120 A5
Coleherne Rd ECT SW5 120 A5
Colehill Gdns FUL/PGN SW6 * 139 H2
Colehill La FUL/PGN SW6 139 H2
Coleman Cl SNWD SE25 181 H5
Coleman Flds IS N1 85 J6
Coleman Rd BELV DA17 129 H3
CMBW SE5 143 F1
Colemans Heath
ELTH/MOT SE9 167 F5
Coleman St CITYW EC2V 12 E3
Colenso Dr MLHL NW7 45 J3
Colenso Rd CLPT E5 86 E2
GNTH/NBYPK IG2 72 E5
Cole Park Gdns TWK TW1 156 B1
Cole Park Rd TWK TW1 156 B2
Colepits Wood Rd
ELTH/MOT SE9 147 J6
Coleraine Rd BKHTH/KID SE3 125 J6
CEND/HSY/T N8 49 G6
Coleridge Av MNPK E12 89 J4
SUT SM1 209 J2
Coleridge Cl VX/NE SW8 141 G3
Coleridge Dr RSLP HA4 59 F3
Coleridge Gdns
KIL/WHAMP NW6 83 G5
WBPTN SW10 140 B1
Coleridge La CEND/HSY/T N8 66 E3
Coleridge Rd ASHF TW15 152 B6
CEND/HSY/T N8 66 D3
CROY/NA CR0 197 K4
DART DA1 151 K5
FSBYPK N4 67 G6
HARH RM3 57 K3
NFNCH/WDSPK N12 47 G1
WALTH E17 69 H1
Coleridge Sq WEA W13 97 G5
Coleridge Wk GLDGN NW11 64 E1
Coleridge Wy ORP BR6 202 B3
WDR/YW UB7 112 B4
YEAD UB4 94 E5
Cole Rd TWK TW1 156 B1
Colesburg Rd BECK BR3 182 C6
Coles Crs RYLN/HDSTN HA2 60 B6
Coles Gn BUSH WD23 28 C3
Coles Green Rd CRICK NW2 63 J5
Coleshill Rd TEDD TW11 173 K2
Colestown St BTSEA SW11 140 D3
Cole St STHWK SE1 18 D3
Colet Cl PLMGR N13 49 H2
Colet Gdns WKENS W14 119 G5
Coley St FSBYW WC1X 5 H7
Colfe & Hatcliffe Glebe
LEW SE13 * 144 E6
Colfe Rd FSTH SE23 164 B3
Colham Av WDR/YW UB7 112 B1
Colham Mill Rd WDR/YW UB7 112 A1
Colina Ms SEVS/STOTM N15 67 H1
Colina Rd CEND/HSY/T N8 67 H2
Colin Cl CDALE/KGS NW9 63 G1
CROY/NA CR0 213 H1
WWKM BR4 214 D1
Colin Crs CDALE/KGS NW9 63 H2
Colindale Av CDALE/KGS NW9 45 F6
Colindeep Gdns HDN NW4 63 J2
Colindeep La CDALE/KGS NW9 63 H1
Colin Dr CDALE/KGS NW9 63 H2
Colinette Rd PUT/ROE SW15 139 F5
Colin Gdns CDALE/KGS NW9 63 H2
Colin Park Rd
CDALE/KGS NW9 45 G6
Colinton Rd GDMY/SEVK IG3 73 H6
Coliston Rd WAND/EARL SW18 159 K2
Collamore Av
WAND/EARL SW18 160 D3
Collapit Cl HRW HA1 60 B3
Collard Pl CAMTN NW1 84 B5
College Ap GNWCH SE10 125 F6
College Av
KTN/HRWW/WS HA3 42 E4
College Cl
KTN/HRWW/WS HA3 42 E3
UED N18 50 B1
WHTN TW2 155 J3
College Ct EA W5 * 98 A6
College Crs HAMP NW3 83 G4
College Cross IS N1 85 G5
College Dr RSLP HA4 58 E4
THDIT KT7 189 K4
College East WCHPL E1 * 13 K2
College Gdns CHING E4 37 K2
ENC/FH EN2 23 K2
NWMAL KT3 192 C2
REDBR IG4 71 J2
TOOT SW17 160 D4
UED N18 * 50 B1
College Gn NRWD SE19 181 F3
College Gv CAMTN NW1 4 C1
College Hl CANST EC4R * 12 D5
College Hill Rd
KTN/HRWW/WS HA3 42 E3
College Ms IS N1 85 G5
College Pde
KIL/WHAMP NW6 * 82 C6
College Park Cl LEW SE13 145 F5
College Pl WALTH E17 70 C1
WBPTN SW10 * 140 B1
College Rd BMLY BR1 183 K4
CROY/NA CR0 196 E6
DUL SE21 163 F3
ENC/FH EN2 23 K3
HRW HA1 60 E3
ISLW TW7 136 A2
KTN/HRWW/WS HA3 42 E4
NRWD SE19 181 G1
TOTM N17 50 B2
WALTH E17 70 A2
WBLY HA9 61 K5
WCHMH N21 35 G4
WEA W13 97 H5

WIM/MER SW19 178 C2
WLSDN NW10 100 A1
College St CANST EC4R * 12 D5
College Ter FNCH N3 46 D4
College Vw ELTH/MOT SE9 166 C3
College Wy ASHF TW15 152 C6
HYS/HAR UB3 94 E6
NTHWD HA6 40 B2
College Yd KIL/WHAMP NW6 * 82 C6
KTTN NW5 84 B2
Collent St HOM E9 86 E4
Colless Rd SEVS/STOTM N15 68 B2
Collett Rd BERM/RHTH SE16 123 H3
Collett Wy NWDGN UB2 115 G2
Collier Cl EHAM E6 108 B6
HOR/WEW KT19 206 C4
Collier Dr EDGW HA8 44 C5
Collier Row La CRW RM5 56 E4
Collier Row Rd CRW RM5 56 B4
Colliers Shaw HAYES BR2 215 J3
Collier St IS N1 5 G3
Colliers Water La THHTH CR7 196 B3
Collindale Av BFN/LL DA15 168 B3
CDALE/KGS NW9 45 G6
ERITH DA8 129 J6
Collingbourne Rd SHB W12 118 E1
Collingham Gdns ECT SW5 120 A4
Collingham Pl ECT SW5 120 A4
Collingham Rd ECT SW5 120 A4
Collings Cl WDGN N22 49 F2
Collington St GNWCH SE10 * 125 G5
Collingtree Rd SYD SE26 163 K6
Collingwood Av BRYLDS KT5 191 K5
MUSWH N10 48 A6
Colling Wood Cl PGE/AN SE20 181 J4
Collingwood Cl WHTN TW2 155 F2
Collingwood Rd MTCM CR4 178 D5
RAIN RM13 111 H1
SEVS/STOTM N15 68 A1
SUT SM1 208 E2
Collingwood St WCHPL E1 104 D3
Collins Av STAN HA7 44 A5
Collins Dr RSLP HA4 59 G6
Collinson St STHWK SE1 18 C3
Collinson Wk STHWK SE1 18 C3
Collins Rd HBRY N5 85 J2
Collins Sq BKHTH/KID SE3 * 145 J4
Collins St BKHTH/KID SE3 145 H3
Collinwood Av PEND EN3 24 E4
Collinwood Gdns
GNTH/NBYPK IG2 71 K2
Collyer Av CROY/NA CR0 210 E2
Collyer Pl PECK SE15 143 H2
Collyer Rd CROY/NA CR0 210 E2
Colman Pde EN EN1 * 24 A4
Colman Rd CAN/RD E16 107 G4
Colmar Cl WCHPL E1 105 F3
Colmer Pl
KTN/HRWW/WS HA3 42 D3
Colmer Rd STRHM/NOR SW16 179 K3
Colmore Ms PECK SE15 143 J2
Colmore Rd PEND EN3 24 E5
Colnbrook St STHWK SE1 18 A5
Colne Av OXHEY WD19 27 F1
Colne Ct HOR/WEW KT19 206 E2
Colne Rd CLPT E5 87 F2
WCHMH N21 35 K2
WHTN TW2 155 K3
Colne St PLSTW E13 106 E2
Colney Hatch La
FBAR/BDGN N11 47 K2
Colney Rd DART DA1 171 J1
Cologne Rd BTSEA SW11 140 C5
Colombo Rd IL IG1 72 C5
Colombo St STHWK SE1 18 A1
Colomb St GNWCH SE10 125 H5
Colonels Wk ENC/FH EN2 23 H3
Colonial Av WHTN TW2 155 H1
Colonial Dr CHSWK W4 117 K4
Colonial Rd
EBED/NFELT TW14 153 H2
Colonnade BMSBY WC1N 4 E7
The Colonnade DEPT SE8 * 124 C4
Colosseum Ter CAMTN NW1 3 K6
Colson Rd CROY/NA CR0 196 E6
Colson Wy STRHM/NOR SW16 161 H6
Colsterworth Rd
SEVS/STOTM N15 68 B1
Colston Av CAR SM5 209 J2
Colston Rd FSTGT E7 89 H4
MORT/ESHN SW14 137 K5
Colthurst Crs FSBYPK N4 67 H6
Colthurst Dr ED N9 36 D5
Coltness Crs ABYW SE2 128 C5
Colton Gdns TOTM N17 49 J6
Colton Rd HRW HA1 60 E2
Colts Yd WAN E11 * 70 D5
Columbas Dr HAMP NW3 65 H6
Columbia Av EDGW HA8 44 D4
RSLP HA4 59 F5
WPK KT4 192 C4
Columbia Rd BETH E2 7 J4
PLSTW E13 * 106 D3
Columbia Whf PEND EN3 * 25 G6
Columbine Av EHAM E6 107 J4
SAND/SEL CR2 211 H5
Columbine Wy LEW SE13 * 145 F3
Columbus Gdns NTHWD HA6 40 E4
Colvestone Crs HACK E8 86 B3
Colville Est IS N1 7 F1
Colville Gdns NTGHL W11 100 D5
Colville Houses NTGHL W11 100 D5
Colville Ms NTGHL W11 100 D5
Colville Pl FITZ W1T 10 B2
Colville Rd ACT W3 117 J3
ED N9 36 D3
NTGHL W11 100 D5
WALTH E17 51 G5
WAN E11 88 A1
Colville Sq NTGHL W11 * 100 D5
Colville Square Ms
NTGHL W11 * 100 D5
Colville Ter NTGHL W11 100 D5
Colvin Cl SYD SE26 181 K1
Colvin Gdns BARK/HLT IG6 54 C3
CHING E4 38 A5
SWFD E18 71 F1
Colvin Rd EHAM E6 89 J5
THHTH CR7 196 B2
Colwall Gdns WFD IG8 52 E1
Colwell Rd EDUL SE22 143 G6
Colwick Cl HGT N6 66 D4
Colwith Rd HMSMTH W6 119 F6
Colwood Gdns
WIM/MER SW19 178 C3
Colworth Gv WALW SE17 18 D7
Colworth Rd CROY/NA CR0 197 H5
WAN E11 70 C3
Colwyn Av GFD/PVL UB6 97 F1
Colwyn Cl STRHM/NOR SW16 179 H1
Colwyn Crs HSLW TW3 135 H2
Colwyn Gn CDALE/KGS NW9 * 63 G3
Colwyn Rd CRICK NW2 81 K1
Colyer Cl ELTH/MOT SE9 167 G4
Colyers Cl ERITH DA8 150 A2
Colyers La ERITH DA8 149 K2
Colyton Cl ALP/SUD HA0 79 J4
WELL DA16 148 E2
Colyton La STRHM/NOR SW16 180 B1
Colyton Rd EDUL SE22 143 J6
Colyton Wy UED N18 50 C1
Combe Av BKHTH/KID SE3 145 J1
Combedale Rd GNWCH SE10 125 H5
Combemartin Rd
WAND/EARL SW18 159 H2
Comber Cl CRICK NW2 63 J6
Comber Gv CMBW SE5 142 D1
Combermere Rd
BRXN/ST SW9 142 A4
MRDN SM4 194 A3
Combe Rd WATW WD18 26 D1
Comberton Rd CLPT E5 68 D6
Combeside WOOL/PLUM SE18 148 A1
Combes Rd DAGW RM9 92 B5
Combwell Crs ABYW SE2 128 B3
Comely Bank Rd WALTH E17 70 A2
Comeragh Ms WKENS W14 119 H5
Comeragh Rd WKENS W14 119 H5
Comerford Rd BROCKY SE4 144 B5
Comet Cl MNPK E12 89 H2
PUR RM19 131 K4
Comet Pl DEPT SE8 144 D1
Comet Rd STWL/WRAY TW19 152 A2
Comet St DEPT SE8 144 D1
Comfort St PECK SE15 143 F1
Commerce Rd BTFD TW8 116 D6
WDGN N22 49 F4
Commerce Wy CROY/NA CR0 211 F1
Commercial Rd POP/IOD E14 105 G5
UED N18 50 A1
Commercial St WCHPL E1 7 J7
Commercial Wy CMBW SE5 143 G2
WLSDN NW10 98 D1
Commerell Pl GNWCH SE10 125 J5
Commerell St GNWCH SE10 125 H5
Commodore Pde
STRHM/NOR SW16 * 180 A3
Commodore St WCHPL E1 105 F4
Commondale PUT/ROE SW15 139 F3
Common La ESH/CLAY KT10 205 G5
RDART DA2 170 D4
Common Rd BARN SW13 138 D4
ESH/CLAY KT10 205 G4
STAN HA7 28 D5
Commonside HAYES BR2 215 G2
Commonside East MTCM CR4 195 H1
Commonside West
MTCM CR4 179 F6
The Common EA W5 117 F1
NWDGN UB2 114 C4
SRTFD E15 88 D4
STAN HA7 29 F4
Commonwealth Av
HYS/HAR UB3 94 B5
SHB W12 99 K6
Commonwealth Rd
TOTM N17 50 C3
Commonwealth Wy
ABYW SE2 128 C5
Community Cl HEST TW5 134 A2
Community La HOLWY N7 84 D3
Community Rd GFD/PVL UB6 78 C6
SRTFD E15 88 B3
Como Rd FSTH SE23 164 B4
Como St ROMW/RG RM7 75 F2
Compass Cl EDGW HA8 30 B6
Compass Hl
RCHPK/HAM TW10 156 E1
Compayne Gdns
KIL/WHAMP NW6 83 F5
Compton Av ALP/SUD HA0 79 H2
EHAM E6 107 H1
GPK RM2 57 K6
HGT N6 65 J4
IS N1 85 H4
Compton Cl CAMTN NW1 3 K5
EDGW HA8 44 E3
ESH/CLAY KT10 204 D4
GLDGN NW11 82 B1
PECK SE15 143 H1
WEA W13 97 G5
Compton Crs CHSGTN KT9 206 A4
CHSWK W4 117 K6
NTHLT UB5 77 H6
TOTM N17 49 J3
Compton Pas FSBYE EC1V 6 B6
Compton Pl ERITH DA8 130 C6
OXHEY WD19 27 J6
STPAN WC1H 4 E6
Compton Ri PIN HA5 59 J2
Compton Rd CROY/NA CR0 197 J5
HYS/HAR UB3 94 C6
IS N1 85 H4
WCHMH N21 35 H3
WIM/MER SW19 177 J2
WLSDN NW10 100 B2
Compton St FSBYE EC1V 6 A6
Compton Ter IS N1 85 H4
WCHMH N21 * 35 G3
Comreddy Cl ENC/FH EN2 23 H2
Comus Pl WALW SE17 19 G7
Comyn Rd BTSEA SW11 140 D5
Comyns Cl CAN/RD E16 106 D4
Comyns Rd DAGW RM9 92 C5
The Comyns BUSH WD23 28 C3
Conant Ms WCHPL E1 104 C6
Concanon Rd CLAP SW4 142 A5
Concert Hall Ap STHWK SE1 17 H1
Concord Cl NTHLT UB5 95 H2
Concorde Cl HSLW TW3 135 G3
Concorde Dr EHAM E6 107 K4
Concorde Wy
BERM/RHTH SE16 124 A4
Concord Rd ACT W3 98 D3
PEND EN3 24 E6
Concord Wy
BERM/RHTH SE16 * 124 A4
Condell Rd VX/NE SW8 141 H2
Conder St POP/IOD E14 105 G5
Condover Crs
WOOL/PLUM SE18 147 G1
Condray Pl BTSEA SW11 140 D1
Conduit Ct COVGDN WC2E * 10 E5
Conduit La SAND/SEL CR2 212 C3
UED N18 50 E1
Conduit Ms BAY/PAD W2 8 A4
Conduit Pl BAY/PAD W2 8 A4
Conduit Rd WOOL/PLUM SE18 127 G5
Conduit St CONDST W1S 9 K5
Conduit Wy WLSDN NW10 80 E5
Conewood St HBRY N5 85 H1
Coney Burrows CHING E4 38 C4
Coney Hall Pde WWKM BR4 * 214 C1
Coney Hill Rd WWKM BR4 199 H6
Coney Wy VX/NE SW8 122 A6
Conference Cl CHING E4 38 A4
Conference Rd ABYW SE2 128 D4
Congleton Gv
WOOL/PLUM SE18 127 H5
Congo Dr ED N9 36 E5
Congo Rd WOOL/PLUM SE18 127 J5
Congress Rd ABYW SE2 128 D4
Congreve Rd ELTH/MOT SE9 146 E4
Congreve St WALW SE17 19 G7
Conical Cnr ENC/FH EN2 23 J3
Conifer Av CRW RM5 56 D1
Conifer Cl ORP BR6 216 D2
Conifer Gdns EN EN1 35 K1
STRHM/NOR SW16 162 A5
SUT SM1 194 A6
Conifers Cl TEDD TW11 174 C3
Conifer Wy ALP/SUD HA0 79 J1
HYS/HAR UB3 94 E6
SWLY BR8 187 K4
Coniger Rd FUL/PGN SW6 139 K3
Coningham Ms SHB W12 118 D1
Coningham Rd SHB W12 118 E2
Coningsby Av
CDALE/KGS NW9 45 G5
Coningsby Cots EA W5 116 E2
Coningsby Gdns CHING E4 51 K2
Coningsby Rd EA W5 116 D2
FSBYPK N4 67 H4
SAND/SEL CR2 211 J6
Conington Rd LEW SE13 144 E3
Conisbee Ct STHGT/OAK N14 22 C6
Conisborough Crs CAT SE6 165 F5
Coniscliffe Cl CHST BR7 185 F4
Coniscliffe Rd PLMGR N13 35 J5
Coniston Av BARK IG11 90 E5
GFD/PVL UB6 97 H2
WELL DA16 147 K4
Coniston Cl BARN SW13 138 C1
BXLYHN DA7 149 K2
CHSWK W4 137 K2
DART DA1 170 E3
ERITH DA8 150 B1
MRDN SM4 193 G3
Coniston Ct BAY/PAD W2 * 8 D4
Conistone Wy HOLWY N7 84 E5
Coniston Gdns BELMT SM2 * 209 H4
CDALE/KGS NW9 63 F2
ED N9 36 E3
PIN HA5 58 E1
REDBR IG4 71 J1
WBLY HA9 61 J5
Coniston Rd BMLY BR1 183 H2
BXLYHN DA7 149 K2
CROY/NA CR0 197 H4
MUSWH N10 48 B5
TOTM N17 50 C2
WHTN TW2 155 G1
Coniston Wk HOM E9 86 E3
Coniston Wy CHSGTN KT9 206 A1
HCH RM12 93 J3
Conlan St NKENS W10 100 C3
Conley Rd WLSDN NW10 81 G4
Conley St GNWCH SE10 * 125 H5
Connaught Av ASHF TW15 152 B6
CHING E4 38 B2
EBAR EN4 33 K3
EN EN1 24 A3
HSLWW TW4 134 D6
MORT/ESHN SW14 137 K4
Connaught Br CAN/RD E16 107 H6
Connaught Cl BAY/PAD W2 8 C4
EN EN1 24 A3
LEY E10 69 G6
SUT SM1 194 C6
UX/CGN UB8 * 94 A4
Connaught Dr GLDGN NW11 64 E1
Connaught Gdns MRDN SM4 194 B2
MUSWH N10 66 B2
PLMGR N13 35 H6
Connaught La IL IG1 72 C6
Connaught Ms
FUL/PGN SW6 * 139 H2
HAMP NW3 * 83 J3
WOOL/PLUM SE18 127 F5
Connaught Rd BAR EN5 32 B1
CAN/RD E16 126 C1
CHING E4 38 C2
FSBYPK N4 67 G4
IL IG1 72 D6
KTN/HRWW/WS HA3 43 F4
NWMAL KT3 192 B1
RCHPK/HAM TW10 * 137 G6
SUT SM1 194 C6
TEDD TW11 173 J1
WALTH E17 * 69 J2
WAN E11 70 B5
WEA W13 97 H6
WLSDN NW10 99 G1
WOOL/PLUM SE18 127 F5
Connaught Sq BAY/PAD W2 8 D4
Connaught St BAY/PAD W2 8 D4
Connaught Wy PLMGR N13 35 H6
Connect La BARK/HLT IG6 54 C5
Connell Crs EA W5 98 B3
Connemara Cl BORE WD6 * 30 E1
Connington Crs CHING E4 38 B5
Connop Rd PEND EN3 25 F1
Connor Cl BARK/HLT IG6 54 C4
WAN E11 70 C5
Connor Rd DAGW RM9 92 B2
Connor St HOM E9 * 87 F6
Conolly Rd HNWL W7 115 K1
Conrad Dr WPK KT4 193 F5
Conroy Ct SCUP DA14 168 B6
Consfield Av NWMAL KT3 192 D1
Consort Cl FBAR/BDGN N11 47 K1
Consort Ms ISLW TW7 155 J1
Consort Rd PECK SE15 143 J2
Cons St STHWK SE1 * 17 K2
Constable Av CAN/RD E16 126 A1
Constable Cl FBAR/BDGN N11 47 K1
GLDGN NW11 65 F3
YEAD UB4 94 A1
Constable Crs
SEVS/STOTM N15 68 C2
Constable Gdns EDGW HA8 44 C4
ISLW TW7 135 J6
Constable Ms BCTR RM8 91 H3
Constable Wk DUL SE21 163 F5
Constance Crs HAYES BR2 199 J5
Constance Gv DART DA1 171 G1
Constance Rd CROY/NA CR0 196 C4
EN EN1 36 A1
SUT SM1 209 G2
WHTN TW2 155 G2
Constance St CAN/RD E16 126 D1
Constantine Rd HAMP NW3 83 J3
Constitution Hl
MYFR/PICC W1J 15 J2
Constitution Ri
WOOL/PLUM SE18 147 F2
Consul Av DAGW RM9 110 E3
Content St WALW SE17 18 D7
Contessa Cl ORP BR6 216 E3
Control Tower Rd
HTHAIR TW6 132 D4
Convent Cl BAR EN5 20 D3
BECK BR3 183 F3
Convent Gdns EA W5 116 D4
NTGHL W11 100 D5
Convent Hl NRWD SE19 180 D2
Convent Wy NWDGN UB2 114 B4
Conway Cl RAIN RM13 93 J5
STAN HA7 43 G2
Conway Crs CHDH RM6 73 J4
GFD/PVL UB6 96 E1
Conway Dr BELMT SM2 209 F4
HYS/HAR UB3 113 F3
Conway Gdns ENC/FH EN2 24 A1
MTCM CR4 195 J1
WBLY HA9 61 J4
Conway Gv ACT W3 99 F4
Conway Ms FITZ W1T 10 A1
Conway Rd CRICK NW2 64 A6
FELT TW13 172 C1
HSLWW TW4 154 E2
RYNPK SW20 177 F4
SEVS/STOTM N15 67 J2
STHGT/OAK N14 34 E5
WOOL/PLUM SE18 127 J4
Conway St FITZ W1T 4 A7
Conybeare HAMP NW3 83 J5
Conyers Rd
STRHM/NOR SW16 179 J1
Conyer St BOW E3 * 105 G1
Cooden Cl BMLY BR1 184 A3
Cookes Cl WAN E11 70 D6
Cookes La CHEAM SM3 208 C4
Cookham Cl NWDGN UB2 115 G3
Cookham Dene Cl CHST BR7 185 J4
Cookham Rd SCUP DA14 187 H4
Cookhill Rd ABYW SE2 128 C2
Cook's Cl CRW RM5 56 E4
Cooks Ferry Rbt UED N18 51 G1
Cook's Hole Rd ENC/FH EN2 23 H1
Cooks Md BUSH WD23 28 B1
Cookson Gv ERITH DA8 149 J1
Cooks Rd WALW SE17 * 122 C6
Cook's Rd SRTFD E15 105 K1
WALW SE17 122 C6
Coolfin Rd CAN/RD E16 106 E5
Coolgardie Av CHING E4 52 B1
Coolhurst Rd HGT N6 66 D3
Cool Oak Br CDALE/KGS NW9 63 H4
Cool Oak La CDALE/KGS NW9 63 H4
Coomassie Rd MV/WKIL W9 100 D3
Coombe Av CROY/NA CR0 212 A2
Coombe Bank KUTN/CMB KT2 176 B4
Coombe Cl EDGW HA8 44 B5
HSLW TW3 135 F5
Coombe Cnr WCHMH N21 35 H3
Coombe Crs HPTN TW12 172 D3
Coombe Dr RSLP HA4 59 F5
Coombe End KUTN/CMB KT2 176 A3
Coombefield Cl NWMAL KT3 192 B2
Coombe Gdns NWMAL KT3 192 C1
RYNPK SW20 176 D5
Coombe Hill Gld
KUTN/CMB KT2 176 B3
Coombe Hill Rd
KUTN/CMB KT2 176 B3
Coombe House Cha
NWMAL KT3 176 A4
Coombehurst Cl EBAR EN4 21 K3
Coombe La CROY/NA CR0 212 C4
RYNPK SW20 176 C4
Coombe La West
KUTN/CMB KT2 175 K4
Coombe Lea BMLY BR1 184 D6
Coombe Ldg CHARL SE7 126 B6
Coombe Neville
KUTN/CMB KT2 175 K3
Coombe Pk KUTN/CMB KT2 175 K1
Coombe Ridings
KUTN/CMB KT2 175 K1
Coombe Ri KUTN/CMB KT2 175 K4
Coombe Rd BUSH WD23 28 C2
CHSWK W4 118 B5
CROY/NA CR0 211 J2
HPTN TW12 172 E2
KUTN/CMB KT2 175 H4
NWMAL KT3 176 B6
SAND/SEL CR2 212 A2
SYD SE26 163 J6
WDGN N22 49 G5
WEA W13 116 C3
WLSDN NW10 81 F1
Coomber Wy CROY/NA CR0 195 J4
Coombe Vls
WAND/EARL SW18 * 159 K2
Coombewood Dr CHDH RM6 74 B3
Coombe Wood Rd
KUTN/CMB KT2 175 K1
Coombs St IS N1 6 B3
Coomer Ms FUL/PGN SW6 * 119 J6
Coomer Pl FUL/PGN SW6 119 J6
Cooms Wk EDGW HA8 44 D4
Cooperage Cl TOTM N17 50 B2
Cooper Av WALTH E17 51 F4
Cooper Cl STHWK SE1 17 K3
Cooper Crs CAR SM5 209 K1
Cooperdale Cl WFD IG8 53 G3
Cooper Rd CROY/NA CR0 211 G2
HDN NW4 64 B3
WLSDN NW10 81 H3
Coopersale Cl WFD IG8 53 G3
Coopersale Rd HOM E9 87 F3
Coopers Cl DAGE RM10 92 D4
WCHPL E1 104 E3
Coopers Dr RDART DA2 170 B4
Coopers La CAMTN NW1 4 D2
LEE/GVPK SE12 166 A4
Cooper's La LEY E10 69 K5
Coopers Ms BECK BR3 182 D5
Cooper's Rd STHWK SE1 123 G5
Cooper's Rw TWRH EC3N 13 J5
Cooper St CAN/RD E16 106 D4
Coopers Yd IS N1 * 85 H5
Cooper's Yd NRWD SE19 181 F2
Coote Rd BCTR RM8 92 B1
BXLYHN DA7 149 G2
Copeland Rd PECK SE15 143 H3
WALTH E17 69 K2
Copeman Cl SYD SE26 181 K1
Copenhagen Gdns CHEL SW3 120 C5
CHSWK W4 118 A2
Copenhagen Pl POP/IOD E14 105 H5
Copenhagen St IS N1 5 F1
Cope Pl KENS W8 119 K3
Copers Cope Rd BECK BR3 182 C3
Cope St BERM/RHTH SE16 124 A4
Copford Wk IS N1 * 85 J6
Copgate Pth
STRHM/NOR SW16 180 A2
Copland Av ALP/SUD HA0 79 K3
Copland Cl ALP/SUD HA0 79 J3
Copland Ms ALP/SUD HA0 80 A4
Copland Rd ALP/SUD HA0 80 A4
Copleston Rd PECK SE15 143 G4
Copley Cl HNWL W7 97 F5
WALW SE17 122 C6
Copley Dene BMLY BR1 184 C4
Copley Pk STRHM/NOR SW16 180 A2
Copley Rd STAN HA7 43 J1
Copley St WCHPL E1 105 F4
Coppard Gdns CHSGTN KT9 205 J4
Coppelia Rd BKHTH/KID SE3 145 J5
Coppen Rd BCTR RM8 74 B4
Copperas St DEPT SE8 124 E6
Copper Beech Cl CLAY IG5 54 A4
STMC/STPC BR5 202 D2
Copper Cl NRWD SE19 181 G3
TOTM N17 50 D3
Copperdale Rd
HYS/HAR UB3 113 K2
Copperfield CHIG IG7 54 D2
Copperfield Dr
SEVS/STOTM N15 68 B1
Copperfield Rd BOW E3 105 G3
THMD SE28 109 J5
Copperfield St STHWK SE1 18 B2
Copperfield Wy CHST BR7 185 H2
PIN HA5 59 K1
Coppergate Cl BMLY BR1 184 A4
Coppermead Cl CRICK NW2 82 A1
Copper Mill Dr ISLW TW7 136 A3
Copper Mill La TOOT SW17 160 B6
Coppermill La WALTH E17 68 E3
Copper Rw STHWK SE1 19 J1
Coppetts Cl
NFNCH/WDSPK N12 47 K3
Coppetts Rd MUSWH N10 47 K4
Coppice Cl BECK BR3 198 E1
RSLP HA4 * 58 A3
RYNPK SW20 177 F6
STAN HA7 43 F2
Coppice Dr PUT/ROE SW15 158 D1
The Coppice BAR EN5 * 33 F1
BXLY DA5 170 A5
ENC/FH EN2 23 H5
OXHEY WD19 27 G1
Coppice Wk TRDG/WHET N20 32 E5
Coppice Wy SWFD E18 70 D1
Coppies Gv FBAR/BDGN N11 34 B6
Copping Cl CROY/NA CR0 212 A2
The Coppins CROY/NA CR0 213 K4
KTN/HRWW/WS HA3 42 E2
Coppock Cl BTSEA SW11 140 D3
Coppsfield E/WMO/HCT KT8 173 F6
Copse Av WWKM BR4 213 K1
Copse Cl CHARL SE7 126 A6
NTHWD HA6 40 A4
WDR/YW UB7 112 A3
Copse Gld SURB KT6 190 E5
Copse Hl BELMT SM2 209 F5
RYNPK SW20 176 D4
Copsem Dr ESH/CLAY KT10 204 B4
Copsem La ESH/CLAY KT10 204 B4
Copsem Wy ESH/CLAY KT10 204 C4
The Copse CHING E4 38 D3
EFNCH N2 * 47 K6
Copse Vw SAND/SEL CR2 213 F5
Copsewood Cl BFN/LL DA15 167 K1
Copse Wood Wy NTHWD HA6 40 A4
Coptefield Dr BELV DA17 128 E3
Copthall Av LOTH EC2R 13 F3
Copthall Dr MLHL NW7 45 J3
Copthall Gdns MLHL NW7 45 J3
TWK TW1 156 A3
Copthorne Av BAL SW12 161 J2
BARK/HLT IG6 54 B2
HAYES BR2 200 E6
Copthorne Ms HYS/HAR UB3 113 H4
Coptic St NOXST/BSQ WC1A 10 E2
Copton Cl BOW E3 105 J4

Copwood Cl
NFNCH/WDSPK N12 ...33 H6
Coral Cl *CHDH* RM6 ...55 J6
Coraline Cl *STHL* UB1 ...95 K2
Coralline Wk *ABYW* SE2 ...128 D2
Coral Rw *BTSEA* SW11 ...140 B4
Coral St *STHWK* SE1 ...17 K3
Coram St *STPAN* WC1H ...4 E7
Coran Cl *ED* N9 ...37 F2
Corban Rd *HSLW* TW3 ...135 F4
Corbar Cl *EBAR* EN4 ...21 H1
Corbet Cl *WLGTN* SM6 ...195 F5
Corbet Ct *BANK* EC3V ...13 F4
Corbet Pl *WCHPL* E1 ...13 J1
Corbett Gv *FBAR/BDGN* N11 ...48 E3
Corbett Rd *WALTH* E17 ...52 B5
WAN E11 ...71 G3
Corbett's La
BERM/RHTH SE16 ...123 K4
Corbicum *WAN* E11 ...70 C4
Corbiere Ct *WIM/MER* SW19 ...177 G2
Corbin's La *RYLN/HDSTN* HA2 ...78 B1
Corbridge Crs *BETH* E2 ...104 D1
Corbridge Ms *ROM* RM1 ...75 H2
Corby Crs *ENC/FH* EN2 ...22 E5
Corbylands Rd *BFN/LL* DA15 ...167 K2
Corbyn St *FSBYPK* N4 ...66 E5
Corby Rd *WLSDN* NW10 ...98 E1
Cordelia Cl *HNHL* SE24 ...142 C5
Cordelia Gdns
STWL/WRAY TW19 ...152 B2
Cordelia Rd
STWL/WRAY TW19 ...152 B2
Cordelia St *POP/IOD* E14 ...105 K5
Cordingley Rd *RSLP* HA4 ...58 B5
Cording St *POP/IOD* E14 ...105 K4
Cordwell Rd *LEW* SE13 ...145 G6
Corelli Rd *BKHTH/KID* SE3 ...146 D2
Corfe Av *RYLN/HDSTN* HA2 ...78 A2
Corfe Cl *HSLWW* TW4 ...154 D3
YEAD UB4 ...95 G5
Corfield Rd *WCHMH* N21 ...23 F6
Corfield St *BETH* E2 ...104 D3
Corfton Rd *EA* W5 ...98 A5
Coriander Av *POP/IOD* E14 ...106 B5
Cories Cl *BCTR* RM8 ...73 K6
Corinium Cl *WBLY* HA9 ...80 B2
Corinne Rd *ARCH* N19 ...84 C2
Corinthian Manorway
ERITH DA8 ...130 A4
Corinthian Rd *ERITH* DA8 ...130 A4
Corkran Rd *SURB* KT6 ...190 E4
Cork St Ms *CONDST* W1S ...10 A6
Corkscrew Hl *WWKM* BR4 ...199 F6
Cork Sq *WAP* E1W ...123 H1
Cork St *CONDST* W1S ...10 A6
Cork Tree Wy *CHING* E4 ...51 G1
Corlett St *CAMTN* NW1 ...8 C1
Cormont Rd *CMBW* SE5 ...142 C2
Cormorant Cl *WALTH* E17 ...51 F4
Cormorant Rd *FSTGT* E7 ...88 D3
Cornbury Rd *EDGW* HA8 ...43 K3
Cornelia Dr *YEAD* UB4 ...95 G4
Cornelia St *HOLWY* N7 ...85 F4
Cornell Cl *SCUP* DA14 ...187 F2
Cornell Wy *CRW* RM5 ...56 D1
Corner Fielde
BRXS/STRHM SW2 * ...162 A3
Corner Gn *BKHTH/KID* SE3 ...145 K3
Corner Md *CDALE/KGS* NW9 ...45 H3
The Corner *EA* W5 * ...117 F1
Corney Reach Wy *CHSWK* W4 ...138 B1
Corney Rd *CHSWK* W4 ...118 B6
Cornflower La *CROY/NA* CR0 ...198 A5
Cornflower Ter *EDUL* SE22 ...163 J1
Cornford Cl *HAYES* BR2 ...199 K2
Cornford Gv *BAL* SW12 ...161 G4
Cornhill *BANK* EC3V ...13 F4
Cornish Ct *ED* N9 ...36 D2
Cornish Gv *PGE/AN* SE20 ...181 J4
Corn Mill Dr *ORP* BR6 ...202 A4
Cornmill La *LEW* SE13 ...144 E4
Cornmow Dr *WLSDN* NW10 ...81 H3
Cornshaw Rd *BCTR* RM8 ...73 K5
Cornthwaite Rd *CLPT* E5 ...86 E1
Cornwall Av *BETH* E2 ...104 E2
ESH/CLAY KT10 ...205 F5
FNCH N3 ...46 E3
STHL UB1 ...95 K4
WDGN N22 ...48 E4
WELL DA16 ...147 K4
Cornwall Cl *BARK* IG11 ...91 F4
Cornwall Crs *NTGHL* W11 ...100 C6
Cornwall Dr *STMC/STPC* BR5 ...186 D3
Cornwall Gdns *SKENS* SW7 ...120 A3
SNWD SE25 * ...197 G1
WLSDN NW10 ...81 K4
Cornwall Gardens Wk
KENS W8 ...120 A3
Cornwall Gv *CHSWK* W4 ...118 B5
Cornwallis Av *ED* N9 ...36 D4
ELTH/MOT SE9 ...167 J4
Cornwallis Cl *ERITH* DA8 ...130 C6
Cornwallis Gv *ED* N9 ...36 D4
Cornwallis Rd *ARCH* N19 ...66 E6
DAGW RM9 ...92 A2
ED N9 ...36 D4
WALTH E17 ...69 F1
WOOL/PLUM SE18 ...127 H4
Cornwallis Sq *ARCH* N19 ...66 E6
FSBYPK N4 ...67 G6
Cornwallis Wk *ELTH/MOT* SE9 ...146 E4
Cornwall Ms South
SKENS SW7 ...120 B3
Cornwall Ms West
SKENS SW7 * ...120 A3
Cornwall Rd *BELMT* SM2 ...208 D5
CROY/NA CR0 ...196 C6
DART DA1 ...151 J4
FSBYPK N4 ...67 G4
HRW HA1 ...60 C3
PIN HA5 ...41 K3
RSLP HA4 ...58 D6
SEVS/STOTM N15 ...67 K2
STHWK SE1 ...11 J7
TWK TW1 ...156 B2
UED N18 ...50 C1
Cornwall Sq *LBTH* SE11 * ...122 B5
Cornwall St *WCHPL* E1 ...104 D6
Cornwall Ter *CAMTN* NW1 ...3 F7
Cornwall Terrace Ms
CAMTN NW1 ...3 F7
Corn Wy *WAN* E11 ...88 B1
Cornwood Cl *EFNCH* N2 ...65 H2
Cornwood Dr *WCHPL* E1 ...104 E5
Cornworthy Rd *BCTR* RM8 ...91 J3
Corona Rd *LEE/GVPK* SE12 ...165 K2
Coronation Cl *BARK/HLT* IG6 ...72 C1
BXLY DA5 ...168 E1
Coronation Dr *HCH* RM12 ...93 K3
Coronation Rd *HYS/HAR* UB3 ...113 J4
PLSTW E13 ...107 G2
WLSDN NW10 ...98 D3
Coronation Vls
WLSDN NW10 * ...98 D3
Coronet Pde *ALP/SUD* HA0 * ...80 A4
Coronet St *IS* N1 ...7 G5
Corporation Av *HSLWW* TW4 ...134 D5
Corporation Rw *CLKNW* EC1R ...5 K6
Corporation St *HOLWY* N7 ...84 E3
SRTFD E15 ...106 C1
Corrance Rd
BRXS/STRHM SW2 ...141 K5
Corri Av *STHGT/OAK* N14 ...34 D6
Corrib Dr *SUT* SM1 ...209 J3
Corrigan Cl *HDN* NW4 ...46 A6
Corringham Rd *GLDGN* NW11 ...64 E4
WBLY HA9 ...62 C6
Corringway *EA* W5 ...98 B4
GLDGN NW11 ...65 F4
Corris Gn *CDALE/KGS* NW9 * ...63 G3
Corry Dr *BRXN/ST* SW9 ...142 C5
Corsair Cl *STWL/WRAY* TW19 ...152 A2
Corsair Rd *STWL/WRAY* TW19 ...152 B2
Corscombe Cl *KUTN/CMB* KT2 ...175 K1
Corsehill St
STRHM/NOR SW16 ...179 H2
Corsellis Sq *TWK* TW1 ...136 C5
Corsham St *IS* N1 ...7 F5
Corsica St *HBRY* N5 ...85 H4
Cortayne Rd *FUL/PGN* SW6 * ...139 J3
Cortina Dr *DAGW* RM9 ...110 E2
Cortis Rd *PUT/ROE* SW15 ...158 E1
Cortis Ter *PUT/ROE* SW15 ...138 E6
Cortland Cl *DART* DA1 ...170 B1
Corunna Rd *VX/NE* SW8 ...141 H2
Corunna Ter *VX/NE* SW8 ...141 H2
Corwell Gdns *UX/CGN* UB8 ...94 A5
Corwell La *UX/CGN* UB8 ...94 A5
Coryton Pth *MV/WKIL* W9 ...100 D3
Cosbycote Av *HNHL* SE24 ...142 D6
Cosdach Av *WLGTN* SM6 ...210 D5
Cosedge Crs *CROY/NA* CR0 ...211 G3
Cosgrove Cl *WCHMH* N21 ...35 J4
YEAD UB4 ...95 H3
Cosmo Pl *RSQ* WC1B ...11 F1
Cosmur Cl *SHB* W12 ...118 C3
Cossall Wk *PECK* SE15 ...143 J2
Cossar Ms *BRXS/STRHM* SW2 ...162 B1
Cosser St *STHWK* SE1 ...17 J4
Costa St *PECK* SE15 ...143 H3
Costons Av *GFD/PVL* UB6 ...96 D2
Costons La *GFD/PVL* UB6 ...96 D2
Cosway St *CAMTN* NW1 ...8 D1
Cotall St *POP/IOD* E14 ...105 J5
Coteford Cl *PIN* HA5 ...58 E2
Coteford St *TOOT* SW17 ...160 E6
Cotelands *CROY/NA* CR0 ...212 A1
Cotesbach Rd *CLPT* E5 ...86 E1
Cotesmore Gdns *BCTR* RM8 ...91 J2
Cotford Rd *THHTH* CR7 ...196 D1
Cotham St *WALW* SE17 ...18 D7
Cotherstone *HOR/WEW* KT19 ...207 F6
Cotherstone Rd
BRXS/STRHM SW2 ...162 A3
Cotleigh Av *BXLY* DA5 ...168 E4
Cotleigh Rd *KIL/WHAMP* NW6 ...82 E5
ROMW/RG RM7 ...75 F3
Cotman Cl *GLDGN* NW11 ...65 G3
Cotmandene Crs
STMC/STPC BR5 ...186 C5
Cotman Ms *BCTR* RM8 ...91 H3
Cotmans Cl *HYS/HAR* UB3 ...113 K1
Coton Rd *WELL* DA16 ...148 B4
Cotsford Av *NWMAL* KT3 ...191 K2
Cotswold Av *BUSH* WD23 ...28 C1
Cotswold Cl *BXLYHN* DA7 ...150 B2
ESH/CLAY KT10 ...190 A6
KUTN/CMB KT2 ...175 K2
Cotswold Gdns *CRICK* NW2 ...64 B6
EHAM E6 ...107 H2
GNTH/NBYPK IG2 ...72 D4
Cotswold Ga *CRICK* NW2 ...64 C5
Cotswold Gn *ENC/FH* EN2 ...23 F5
Cotswold Ms *BTSEA* SW11 ...140 C2
Cotswold Ri *ORP* BR6 ...202 A3
Cotswold Rd *HPTN* TW12 ...173 F2
Cotswold St *WNWD* SE27 ...162 C6
Cotswold Wy *ENC/FH* EN2 ...23 F4
WPK KT4 ...193 F6
Cottage Av *HAYES* BR2 ...200 D5
Cottage Cl *RSLP* HA4 ...58 B5
RYLN/HDSTN HA2 ...60 D6
Cottage Field Cl *SCUP* DA14 ...168 D3
Cottage Gn *CMBW* SE5 ...142 E1
Cottage Gv *BRXN/ST* SW9 ...141 K4
SURB KT6 ...190 E3
Cottage Pl *CHEL* SW3 ...14 C4
Cottage Rd *HOLWY* N7 ...85 F3
HOR/WEW KT19 ...207 F5
The Cottages *EDGW* HA8 * ...44 D3
Cottage St *POP/IOD* E14 ...105 K6
Cottenham Dr
CDALE/KGS NW9 ...45 H6
RYNPK SW20 ...176 E3
Cottenham Park Rd
RYNPK SW20 ...176 D4
Cottenham Pl *RYNPK* SW20 ...176 E3
Cottenham Rd *WALTH* E17 ...69 H1
Cotterill Rd *SURB* KT6 ...191 G6
Cottesbrook St *NWCR* SE14 ...144 B1
Cottesloe Ms *STHWK* SE1 ...17 K4
Cottesmore Av *CLAY* IG5 ...53 K5
Cottesmore Gdns *KENS* W8 ...120 A3
Cottimore Av *WOT/HER* KT12 ...188 A5
Cottimore Crs *WOT/HER* KT12 ...188 A4
Cottimore La *WOT/HER* KT12 ...188 A4
Cottimore Ter *WOT/HER* KT12 ...188 A4
Cottingham Cha *RSLP* HA4 ...76 E1
Cottingham Rd *PGE/AN* SE20 ...182 A3
VX/NE SW8 ...142 A1
Cottington Rd *FELT* TW13 ...154 C5
Cottington St *LBTH* SE11 ...122 B5
Cotton Av *ACT* W3 ...99 F5
Cotton Cl *DAGW* RM9 ...91 J5
WAN E11 ...70 C6
Cotton Gardens Est
LBTH SE11 ...18 A7
Cottongrass Cl *CROY/NA* CR0 ...198 A5
Cottonham Cl
NFNCH/WDSPK N12 ...47 H1
Cotton Hl *BMLY* BR1 ...165 G6
Cotton Rw *BTSEA* SW11 ...140 C4
Cottons Ap *ROMW/RG* RM7 ...75 F2
Cotton's Gdns *BETH* E2 ...7 H4
Cotton St *POP/IOD* E14 ...106 A6
Couchmore Av *CLAY* IG5 ...53 K5
ESH/CLAY KT10 ...189 K6
Coulgate St *BROCKY* SE4 ...144 B4
Coulson Cl *BCTR* RM8 ...73 J5
Coulson St *CHEL* SW3 ...120 E5
Coulter Cl *YEAD* UB4 ...95 J3
Coulter Rd *HMSMTH* W6 ...118 E3
Councillor St *CMBW* SE5 ...142 D1
Counter St *STHWK* SE1 ...13 G7
Countess Rd *KTTN* NW5 ...84 C3
Countisbury Av *EN* EN1 ...36 B2
Country Wy *FELT* TW13 ...172 B1
County Ga *BAR* EN5 ...33 F1
ELTH/MOT SE9 ...167 H5
County Gv *CMBW* SE5 ...142 D2
County Pde *BTFD* TW8 * ...136 E1
County Rd *EHAM* E6 ...108 B4
THHTH CR7 ...180 C5
County St *STHWK* SE1 ...18 D5
Coupland Pl
WOOL/PLUM SE18 ...127 H5
Courcy Rd *CEND/HSY/T* N8 ...49 G6
Courier Rd *DAGW* RM9 ...110 E3
Courland Gv *VX/NE* SW8 ...141 J2
Courland St *VX/NE* SW8 ...141 J2
The Course *ELTH/MOT* SE9 ...167 F5
Courtauld Rd *ARCH* N19 ...66 D5
Courtaulds Cl *THMD* SE28 ...128 B1
Court Av *BELV* DA17 ...129 G5
Court Cl *KTN/HRWW/WS* HA3 ...43 K6
STJWD NW8 * ...83 H5
WHTN TW2 ...155 G5
WLGTN SM6 ...210 D5
Court Close Av *WHTN* TW2 ...155 G5
Court Crs *CHSGTN* KT9 ...205 K4
Court Downs Rd *BECK* BR3 ...182 E5
Court Dr *CROY/NA* CR0 ...211 F2
STAN HA7 ...30 A6
SUT SM1 ...209 J2
Courtenay Av *BELMT* SM2 ...208 E6
HGT N6 ...65 J4
KTN/HRWW/WS HA3 ...42 B3
Courtenay Dr *BECK* BR3 ...183 G5
Courtenay Ms *WALTH* E17 ...69 G2
Courtenay Pl *WALTH* E17 ...69 G2
Courtenay Rd *PGE/AN* SE20 ...182 A3
WALTH E17 ...69 F2
WAN E11 * ...88 D1
WBLY HA9 * ...79 K1
WPK KT4 ...208 A1
Courtenay Sq *LBTH* SE11 * ...122 B5
Courtenay St *LBTH* SE11 ...122 A5
Courten Ms *STAN* HA7 ...43 J3
Court Farm Av
HOR/WEW KT19 ...207 F3
Court Farm Rd *ELTH/MOT* SE9 ...166 C4
NTHLT UB5 ...78 A5
Courtfield Av *HRW* HA1 * ...61 F2
Courtfield Crs *HRW* HA1 ...61 F2
Courtfield Gdns *ECT* SW5 ...120 A4
RSLP HA4 ...58 D6
WEA W13 ...97 G5
Courtfield Ms *SKENS* SW7 ...120 B4
Courtfield Ri *WWKM* BR4 ...214 B1
Courtfield Rd *ECT* SW5 ...120 B4
Court Gdns *HOLWY* N7 ...85 G4
Courtgate Cl *MLHL* NW7 ...45 H2
Courthill Rd *LEW* SE13 ...145 F5
Courthope Rd *GFD/PVL* UB6 ...96 D1
HAMP NW3 ...83 K2
WIM/MER SW19 ...177 H1
Courthope Vls
WIM/MER SW19 ...177 H3
Courthouse La
STNW/STAM N16 ...86 B2
Court House Rd *FNCH* N3 ...47 F2
Courtland Av *CHING* E4 ...38 D4
IL IG1 ...71 K6
MLHL NW7 ...31 F5
STRHM/NOR SW16 ...180 A3
Courtland Gv *THMD* SE28 ...109 K6
Courtland Rd *EHAM* E6 ...89 J6
Courtlands *CHST* BR7 ...185 G3
RCHPK/HAM TW10 ...137 H6
Courtlands Av *HAYES* BR2 ...199 H5
HPTN TW12 ...172 E2
LEE/GVPK SE12 ...146 A6
RCH/KEW TW9 ...137 J3
Courtlands Cl *RSLP* HA4 ...58 D4
Courtlands Dr
HOR/WEW KT19 ...207 G4
Courtlands Rd *BRYLDS* KT5 ...191 H4
Court La *DUL* SE21 ...163 G2
Court Lane Gdns *DUL* SE21 ...163 F2
Courtleet Dr *BXLYHN* DA7 ...149 J2
Courtleigh Av *EBAR* EN4 ...21 H1
Courtleigh Gdns *GLDGN* NW11 ...64 C1
Courtman Rd *TOTM* N17 ...49 J3
Court Md *NTHLT* UB5 ...95 K2
Courtmead Cl *HNHL* SE24 ...162 D1
Courtnell St *BAY/PAD* W2 ...100 E5
Courtney Cl *NRWD* SE19 ...181 F2
Courtney Crs *CAR* SM5 ...209 K5
Courtney Pl *CROY/NA* CR0 ...211 G1
Courtney Rd *CROY/NA* CR0 ...211 G1
HOLWY N7 ...85 G3
HTHAIR TW6 ...132 D4
WBLY HA9 ...79 K1
WIM/MER SW19 ...178 D3
Courtney Wy *HTHAIR* TW6 ...132 D4
Courtrai Rd *FSTH* SE23 ...164 B1
Court Rd *ELTH/MOT* SE9 ...166 D4
NWDGN UB2 ...114 E4
SNWD SE25 ...181 G5
Court Rd (Orpington By-Pass)
ORP BR6 ...217 H1
Courtside *HGT* N6 ...66 D3
SYD SE26 * ...163 K5
The Courts *STRHM/NOR* SW16 ...179 K3
Courtstreet *BMLY* BR1 ...183 K5
Court St *WCHPL* E1 ...104 D4
The Court *MUSWH* N10 * ...66 C1
RSLP HA4 ...77 J2
Court Vw *HGT* N6 * ...66 B6
Court Wy *ACT* W3 ...98 E4
BARK/HLT IG6 ...54 C6
CDALE/KGS NW9 ...63 G1
WHTN TW2 ...156 A2
The Courtway *OXHEY* WD19 ...27 J4
Court Yd *ELTH/MOT* SE9 ...166 D1
Courtyard Ms *RAIN* RM13 ...93 H6
STMC/STPC BR5 ...186 B3
The Courtyards
WATW WD18 * ...26 B2
The Courtyard *IS* N1 ...85 F5
Cousin La *CANST* EC4R ...12 E5
Couthurst Rd *BKHTH/KID* SE3 ...126 A6
Coutts Av *CHSGTN* KT9 ...206 A3
Coutts Crs *KTTN* NW5 * ...84 A1
Couzins Wk *DART* DA1 ...151 J3
Coval Gdns *MORT/ESHN* SW14 ...137 J5
Coval La *MORT/ESHN* SW14 ...137 J5
Coval Rd *MORT/ESHN* SW14 ...137 K5
Covelees Wall *EHAM* E6 ...108 A5
Covent Gdn *COVGDN* WC2E ...11 F5
Covent Garden Piazza
COVGDN WC2E ...11 F5
Coventry Cl *EHAM* E6 ...107 K5
KIL/WHAMP NW6 ...100 E1
Coventry Cross Est *BOW* E3 ...106 A3
Coventry Rd *BETH* E2 * ...104 D2
IL IG1 ...72 B5
SNWD SE25 ...197 H1
WCHPL E1 ...104 D3
Coventry St *SOHO/SHAV* W1D ...10 C6
Coverack Cl *CROY/NA* CR0 ...198 B4
STHGT/OAK N14 ...34 C1
Coverdale Gdns *CROY/NA* CR0 ...212 B1
Coverdale Rd *CRICK* NW2 ...82 C5
FBAR/BDGN N11 ...48 A2
SHB W12 ...118 E1
The Coverdales *BARK* IG11 ...108 D1
Coverley Cl *WCHPL* E1 * ...104 C4
Coverton Rd *TOOT* SW17 ...160 D6
Covert Rd *BARK/HLT* IG6 ...55 F2
Coverts Rd *ESH/CLAY* KT10 ...205 F5
The Covert *NRWD* SE19 * ...181 G3
NTHWD HA6 ...40 A3
ORP BR6 ...201 K3
Covert Wy *EBAR* EN4 ...21 G3
Covet Wood Cl
STMC/STPC BR5 ...202 A3
Covey Cl *WIM/MER* SW19 ...178 A5
Covey Rd *WPK* KT4 ...193 G6
Covington Gdns
STRHM/NOR SW16 ...180 C3
Covington Wy
STRHM/NOR SW16 ...180 B3
Cowbridge La *BARK* IG11 ...90 B5
Cowbridge Rd
KTN/HRWW/WS HA3 ...62 B1
Cowcross St *FARR* EC1M ...12 A1
Cowdenbeath Pth *IS* N1 ...84 E6
Cowden Rd *ORP* BR6 ...202 A4
Cowden St *CAT* SE6 ...164 D6
Cowdray Rd *HGDN/ICK* UB10 ...76 A6
Cowdray Wy *HCH* RM12 ...93 J2
Cowdrey Cl *EN* EN1 ...24 A3
Cowdrey Ct *DART* DA1 ...170 E2
Cowdrey Rd *WIM/MER* SW19 ...178 A2
Cowen Av *HRW* HA1 ...60 D6
Cowgate Rd *GFD/PVL* UB6 ...96 D2
Cowick Rd *TOOT* SW17 ...160 E6
Cowings Md *NTHLT* UB5 ...77 J5
Cowland Av *PEND* EN3 ...24 E5
Cow La *BUSH* WD23 * ...28 A1
Cow Leaze *EHAM* E6 ...108 A5
Cowleaze Rd *KUTN/CMB* KT2 ...175 F4
Cowley Cl *SAND/SEL* CR2 ...212 E6
Cowley Ct *WAN* E11 * ...88 C1
Cowley La *WAN* E11 * ...88 C1
Cowley Pl *HDN* NW4 ...64 A2
Cowley Rd *ACT* W3 ...118 C1
BRXN/ST SW9 ...142 B2
HARH RM3 ...57 K3
IL IG1 ...71 K4
MORT/ESHN SW14 ...138 B4
WAN E11 ...71 F2
Cowley St *WEST* SW1P ...16 E5
Cowling Cl *NTGHL* W11 ...100 C6
Cowper Av *EHAM* E6 ...89 J5
SUT SM1 ...209 H2
Cowper Cl *HAYES* BR2 ...200 C1
WELL DA16 ...148 B6
Cowper Gdns *STHGT/OAK* N14 ...34 B1
WLGTN SM6 ...210 C4
Cowper Rd *ACT* W3 ...118 A1
BELV DA17 ...129 G4
HAYES BR2 ...200 C1
HNWL W7 ...97 F6
KUTN/CMB KT2 ...175 G1
RAIN RM13 ...111 J3
STHGT/OAK N14 ...34 B3
STNW/STAM N16 ...86 A2
UED N18 ...50 C1
WIM/MER SW19 ...178 B2
Cowper St *STLK* EC1Y ...7 F6
Cowper Ter *NKENS* W10 * ...100 B4
Cowslip Rd *SWFD* E18 ...53 F5
Cowthorpe Rd *VX/NE* SW8 ...141 J2
Coxe Pl *KTN/HRWW/WS* HA3 ...61 G1
Cox La *CHSGTN* KT9 ...206 A2
Coxmount Rd *CHARL* SE7 ...126 C5
Coxson Wy *STHWK* SE1 ...19 J3
Coxwell Rd *NRWD* SE19 ...181 F3
WOOL/PLUM SE18 ...127 J5
Crabbs Croft Cl *ORP* BR6 * ...216 C3
Crab Hl *BECK* BR3 ...183 G3
Crabtree Av *ALP/SUD* HA0 ...98 A1
CHDH RM6 ...73 K1
Crabtree Cl *BETH* E2 ...7 J3
Crabtree La *FUL/PGN* SW6 ...139 G1
Crabtree Manorway North
BELV DA17 ...129 K2
Crabtree Manorway South
BELV DA17 ...129 K2
Crabtree Wk *CROY/NA* CR0 ...197 H5
Craddock Rd *EN* EN1 ...24 B4
Craddock St *KTTN* NW5 * ...84 A4
Cradley Rd *ELTH/MOT* SE9 ...167 J3
Cragie Lea *MUSWH* N10 * ...48 B5
Craigdale Rd *EMPK* RM11 ...75 H3
Craigen Av *CROY/NA* CR0 ...197 J5
Craigerne Rd *BKHTH/KID* SE3 ...146 A1
Craig Gdns *SWFD* E18 ...52 D5
Craigholm *WOOL/PLUM* SE18 ...147 F3
Craigmuir Pk *ALP/SUD* HA0 ...80 B6
Craignair Rd
BRXS/STRHM SW2 ...162 A2
Craignish Av
STRHM/NOR SW16 ...180 A5
Craig Park Rd *UED* N18 ...36 D6
Craig Rd *RCHPK/HAM* TW10 ...156 D6
Craig's Ct *WHALL* SW1A ...10 E7
Craigton Rd *ELTH/MOT* SE9 ...146 E5
Craigweil Cl *STAN* HA7 ...43 K1
Craigweil Dr *STAN* HA7 ...43 K1
Craigwell Av *FELT* TW13 ...153 K5
Crail Rw *WALW* SE17 ...19 F7
Cramer St *MHST* W1U ...9 H2
Crammond Cl *HMSMTH* W6 ...119 H6
Cramond Ct
EBED/NFELT TW14 ...153 G3
Crampton Rd *PGE/AN* SE20 ...181 K2
Cranberry Cl *NTHLT* UB5 ...95 H1
Cranberry La *CAN/RD* E16 ...106 C3
Cranborne Av *NWDGN* UB2 ...115 F4
SURB KT6 ...206 C1
Cranborne Rd *BARK* IG11 ...90 D6
Cranborne Waye *YEAD* UB4 ...95 F5
Cranbourne Av *WAN* E11 ...71 F1
Cranbourne Cl
STRHM/NOR SW16 ...179 K6
Cranbourne Dr *PIN* HA5 ...59 H2
Cranbourne Gdns
BARK/HLT IG6 ...54 C6
GLDGN NW11 ...64 C2
Cranbourne Rd *MNPK* E12 ...89 J3
MUSWH N10 ...48 B5
NTHWD HA6 ...40 D6
SRTFD E15 ...88 A2
Cranbourn St
LSQ/SEVD WC2H ...10 D5
Cranbrook Cl *HAYES* BR2 ...199 K3
Cranbrook Dr *ESH/CLAY* KT10 ...189 H5
GPK RM2 ...75 K1
WHTN TW2 ...155 G3
Cranbrook La
FBAR/BDGN N11 ...34 B6
Cranbrook Ms *WALTH* E17 ...69 H2
Cranbrook Pk *WDGN* N22 ...49 G4
Cranbrook Ri *IL* IG1 ...71 K3
Cranbrook Rd *BARK/HLT* IG6 ...54 C6
BXLYHN DA7 ...149 G2
CHSWK W4 ...118 B5
DEPT SE8 ...144 D2
EBAR EN4 ...33 H1
GNTH/NBYPK IG2 ...72 A3
HSLWW TW4 ...134 E5
IL IG1 ...72 A6
THHTH CR7 ...180 D5
WIM/MER SW19 ...177 H3
Cranbrook St *BETH* E2 ...105 F1
Cranbury Rd *FUL/PGN* SW6 ...140 A3
Crane Av *ACT* W3 ...98 E6
ISLW TW7 ...136 B6
Cranebank Ms *TWK* TW1 * ...136 C6
Cranebrook *WHTN* TW2 ...155 H4
Crane Cl *DAGE* RM10 ...92 C4
Crane Ct *FLST/FETLN* EC4A ...11 K4
MORT/ESHN SW14 * ...137 K5
Craneford Cl *WHTN* TW2 ...156 A2
Craneford Wy *WHTN* TW2 ...155 K2
Crane Gdns *HYS/HAR* UB3 ...113 J4
Crane Gv *HOLWY* N7 ...85 G4
Crane Lodge Rd *HEST* TW5 ...114 A6
Crane Md *BERM/RHTH* SE16 ...124 A4
Crane Park Rd *WHTN* TW2 ...155 G4
Crane Rd *STWL/WRAY* TW19 ...152 D1
WHTN TW2 ...155 K3
Cranesbill Cl *CDALE/KGS* NW9 ...45 F6
STRHM/NOR SW16 ...179 J5
Cranes Dr *BRYLDS* KT5 ...191 F1
Cranes Pk *BRYLDS* KT5 ...191 F1
Cranes Park Av *BRYLDS* KT5 ...191 F1
Cranes Park Crs *BRYLDS* KT5 ...191 G1
Crane St *PECK* SE15 ...143 G2
Craneswater *HYS/HAR* UB3 ...133 J1
Craneswater Pk *NWDGN* UB2 ...114 E5
Crane Wy *WHTN* TW2 ...155 H2
Cranfield Dr *CDALE/KGS* NW9 ...45 G4
Cranfield Rd *BROCKY* SE4 ...144 C4
Cranfield Rd East *CAR* SM5 ...210 A6
Cranfield Rd West *CAR* SM5 * ...209 K6
Cranford Av *PLMGR* N13 ...48 E1
STWL/WRAY TW19 ...152 B2
Cranford Cl *RYNPK* SW20 ...176 E3
STWL/WRAY TW19 ...152 B2
Cranford Cots *WAP* E1W * ...105 F6
Cranford Dr *HYS/HAR* UB3 ...113 J4
Cranford La *HYS/HAR* UB3 ...113 G6
Cranford Ms *HAYES* BR2 ...200 D2
Cranford Park Rd
HYS/HAR UB3 ...113 J4
Cranford Ri *ESH/CLAY* KT10 ...204 C3
Cranford Rd *DART* DA1 ...171 H3
Cranford St *WAP* E1W ...105 F6
Cranford Wy *CEND/HSY/T* N8 ...67 F2
Cranham Rd *EMPK* RM11 ...75 K3
Cranhurst Rd *CRICK* NW2 ...82 A3
Cranleigh Cl *BXLY* DA5 * ...169 J1
ORP BR6 ...217 G1
PGE/AN SE20 ...181 J5
Cranleigh Gdns *BARK* IG11 ...90 D5
KTN/HRWW/WS HA3 ...62 A2
KUTN/CMB KT2 ...175 G2
LOU IG10 ...39 K1
SNWD SE25 ...181 F6
STHL UB1 ...95 K5
SUT SM1 ...194 A6
WCHMH N21 ...23 G6
Cranleigh Ms *BTSEA* SW11 ...140 D3
Cranleigh Rd *ESH/CLAY* KT10 ...189 H5
FELT TW13 ...153 J6

SEVS/STOTM N15 67 J2
WIM/MER SW19 177 K6
Cranleigh St CAMTN NW1 4 B3
Cranley Dr GNTH/NBYPK IG2 72 C4
RSLP HA4 58 D6
Cranley Gdns MUSWH N10 66 B1
PLMGR N13 35 F5
SKENS SW7 120 B5
WLGTN SM6 210 C5
Cranley Ms SKENS SW7 120 B5
Cranley Pl SKENS SW7 14 A7
Cranley Rd GNTH/NBYPK IG2 72 C3
PLSTW E13 107 F4
Cranley Ter HDN NW4 * 46 B5
Cranmer Av WEA W13 116 C3
Cranmer Cl MRDN SM4 193 G3
RSLP HA4 59 H5
STAN HA7 43 J3
Cranmer Ct HPTN TW12 173 G1
KUTN/CMB KT2 156 E6
Cranmer Farm Cl MTCM CR4 194 E1
Cranmer Gdns DAGE RM10 92 E2
Cranmer Rd BRXN/ST SW9 142 B1
CROY/NA CR0 211 H1
EDGW HA8 30 D5
FSTGT E7 89 F2
HPTN TW12 173 G1
HYS/HAR UB3 94 B5
KUTN/CMB KT2 175 F1
MTCM CR4 194 E1
Cranmer Ter TOOT SW17 178 C1
Cranmore Av ISLW TW7 135 H1
Cranmore Rd BMLY BR1 165 H5
CHST BR7 184 E1
Cranmore Wy MUSWH N10 66 C1
Cranston Cl HGDN/ICK UB10 58 B6
HSLW TW3 134 D3
Cranston Est IS N1 7 F2
Cranston Gdns CHING E4 51 K2
Cranston Rd FSTH SE23 164 B3
Cranswick Rd
BERM/RHTH SE16 123 J5
Crantock Rd CAT SE6 165 F4
Cranwell Cl BOW E3 105 K3
Cranwich Av WCHMH N21 35 K2
Cranwich Rd
STNW/STAM N16 68 A4
Cranwood St FSBYE EC1V 7 F5
Cranworth Crs CHING E4 38 B3
Cranworth Gdns
BRXN/ST SW9 142 B2
Craster Rd BRXS/STRHM SW2 162 A2
Crathie Rd LEE/GVPK SE12 166 A1
Cravan Av FELT TW13 153 K4
Craven Av EA W5 97 J6
STHL UB1 95 K4
Craven Cl STNW/STAM N16 * 68 C4
YEAD UB4 94 E5
Craven Gdns BARK IG11 108 E1
BARK/HLT IG6 54 D5
CRW RM5 56 C1
WIM/MER SW19 178 A1
Craven Hill Gdns BAY/PAD W2 101 G6
Craven Ms BTSEA SW11 141 F4
Craven Pk WLSDN NW10 81 F5
Craven Park Ms WLSDN NW10 81 G5
Craven Park Rd
SEVS/STOTM N15 68 B3
WLSDN NW10 81 G6
Craven Pas CHCR WC2N 10 E7
Craven Rd BAY/PAD W2 101 G6
CROY/NA CR0 197 J5
KUTN/CMB KT2 175 G4
ORP BR6 217 K1
WEA W13 97 J6
WLSDN NW10 81 F6
Craven St CHCR WC2N 10 E7
Craven Ter BAY/PAD W2 101 G6
Craven Wk STNW/STAM N16 68 C4
Crawford Av ALP/SUD HA0 79 K3
DART DA1 171 G1
Crawford Cl ISLW TW7 135 K3
Crawford Gdns NTHLT UB5 95 K2
PLMGR N13 35 H5
Crawford Ms MBLAR W1H * 8 E2
Crawford Pas CLKNW EC1R 5 J7
Crawford Pl MBLAR W1H 8 D3
Crawford Rd CMBW SE5 142 D3
Crawford St MBLAR W1H 8 E2
MHST W1U 9 F2
WLSDN NW10 81 F5
Crawley Rd EN EN1 36 A2
LEY E10 69 K5
WDGN N22 49 J5
Crawthew Gv EDUL SE22 143 G5
Cray Av ORP BR6 202 C4
Craybrooke Rd SCUP DA14 168 C6
Craybury End ELTH/MOT SE9 167 H4
Cray Cl DART DA1 150 D6
Craydene Rd ERITH DA8 150 C2
Crayford High St DART DA1 150 B5
Crayford Rd DART DA1 150 C6
HOLWY N7 84 E2
Crayford Wy DART DA1 150 D5
Crayke Hl CHSGTN KT9 206 A5
Craylands STMC/STPC BR5 186 D6
Crayleigh Ter SCUP DA14 * 186 D2
Cray Rd BELV DA17 129 H6
SCUP DA14 186 D2
SWLY BR8 203 K3
Crays Pde STMC/STPC BR5 * 186 D5
Cray Valley Rd
STMC/STPC BR5 202 B2
Cray View Cl STMC/STPC BR5 202 D1
Crealock Gv WFD IG8 52 D1
Crealock St WAND/EARL SW18 160 A1
Creasey Cl EMPK RM11 75 K6
Crebor St EDUL SE22 163 H1
Credenhall Dr HAYES BR2 200 E5
Credenhill St
STRHM/NOR SW16 179 H2
Crediton Hl KIL/WHAMP NW6 83 F3
Crediton Rd CAN/RD E16 106 E5
WLSDN NW10 82 B6
Crediton Wy ESH/CLAY KT10 205 G3
Credon Rd BERM/RHTH SE16 123 J5
PLSTW E13 107 G1
Creechurch La HDTCH EC3A 13 H4
Creechurch Pl HDTCH EC3A * 13 H4
Creed La BLKFR EC4V 12 B4
Creek Cots E/WMO/HCT KT8 * 189 K1
Creek Rd BARK IG11 109 F2
DEPT SE8 124 D6
E/WMO/HCT KT8 189 K1
Creekside DEPT SE8 144 E1
RAIN RM13 111 H3
Creek Wy RAIN RM13 111 G5
Creeland Gv CAT SE6 164 C3
Cree Wy ROM RM1 57 G3
Crefeld Cl HMSMTH W6 119 G6
Creffield Rd EA W5 98 C6
Creighton Av EFNCH N2 47 K5
EHAM E6 107 H1
Creighton Cl SHB W12 99 K6
Creighton Rd EA W5 116 E3
KIL/WHAMP NW6 100 B1
TOTM N17 50 A3
Creigton Av EFNCH N2 47 J6
Cremer St BETH E2 7 J3
Cremorne Est
WBPTN SW10 * 120 C6
Cremorne Gdns
HOR/WEW KT19 207 F6
Cremorne Rd WBPTN SW10 140 B1
Crescent TWRH EC3N 13 J5
Crescent Ar GNWCH SE10 125 F6
Crescent Av HCH RM12 75 H6
Crescent Dr STMC/STPC BR5 201 H3
Crescent East EBAR EN4 21 G1
Crescent Gdns RSLP HA4 59 F4
SWLY BR8 187 K5
WIM/MER SW19 159 K5
Crescent Gv CLAP SW4 141 H5
MTCM CR4 194 D1
Crescent La CLAP SW4 141 J6
Crescent Pl CHEL SW3 14 C6
Crescent Ri EBAR EN4 21 J6
FNCH N3 * 46 D4
WDGN N22 48 D4
Crescent Rd BECK BR3 182 E5
BFN/LL DA15 168 A5
BMLY BR1 183 K3
CEND/HSY/T N8 66 D3
CHING E4 38 C2
DAGE RM10 92 D1
EBAR EN4 33 J1
ED N9 36 C3
EHAM E6 89 G6
ENC/FH EN2 23 H5
ERITH DA8 130 C6
FBAR/BDGN N11 33 K6
FNCH N3 46 D4
KUTN/CMB KT2 175 H3
LEY E10 69 K6
PLSTW E13 88 E6
RYNPK SW20 177 G4
SEVS/STOTM N15 * 49 H6
SWFD E18 53 G5
WDGN N22 48 D4
WOOL/PLUM SE18 127 G5
Crescent Rw STLK EC1Y 6 C7
Crescent St IS N1 * 85 F5
The Crescent ACT W3 99 G5
ALP/SUD HA0 61 H6
BAR EN5 21 F4
BARN SW13 138 C3
BECK BR3 182 D4
BXLY DA5 168 D2
CRICK NW2 81 K1
CROY/NA CR0 196 E3
E/WMO/HCT KT8 188 E1
FBAR/BDGN N11 33 K6
GNTH/NBYPK IG2 72 A3
HYS/HAR UB3 133 F1
LOU IG10 39 H1
NWMAL KT3 175 K5
RYLN/HDSTN HA2 60 C5
SCUP DA14 168 A6
STHL UB1 114 D2
SURB KT6 191 F2
SUT SM1 209 H3
WALTH E17 69 G2
WIM/MER SW19 159 K5
WWKM BR4 199 H3
Crescent Vw LOU IG10 39 H1
Crescent Wy BROCKY SE4 144 D4
Crescentway
NFNCH/WDSPK N12 47 J2
Crescent Wy ORP BR6 216 E3
STRHM/NOR SW16 180 A3
Crescent West EBAR EN4 21 G1
Crescent Wood Rd SYD SE26 163 H5
Cresford Rd FUL/PGN SW6 140 A2
Crespigny Rd HDN NW4 63 K3
Cressage Cl STHL UB1 96 A3
Cresset Rd HOM E9 86 E4
Cresset St CLAP SW4 141 J4
Cressfield Cl KTTN NW5 84 A3
Cressida Rd ARCH N19 66 C5
Cressingham Gv SUT SM1 209 G2
Cressingham Rd EDGW HA8 45 F2
LEW SE13 145 F4
Cressington Cl
STNW/STAM N16 86 A3
Cresswell Pk BKHTH/KID SE3 145 J4
Cresswell Pl WBPTN SW10 120 B5
Cresswell Rd FELT TW13 154 D5
SNWD SE25 197 H1
TWK TW1 156 E1
Cresswell Wy WCHMH N21 35 G2
Cressy Ct HMSMTH W6 118 E3
WCHPL E1 104 E4
Cressy Houses WCHPL E1 * 104 E4
Cressy Pl WCHPL E1 104 E4
Cressy Rd HAMP NW3 83 K2
Cressys Cnr HSLW TW3 * 135 G4
Crestbrook Av PLMGR N13 35 H5
Crestbrook Pl PLMGR N13 * 35 G5
Crest Dr PEND EN3 24 E1
Crestfield St KCROSS N1C 5 F4
Crest Gdns RSLP HA4 77 G1
Creston Wy WPK KT4 193 G5
Crest Rd CRICK NW2 63 J6
HAYES BR2 199 J4
SAND/SEL CR2 212 D5
The Crest BRYLDS KT5 191 H2
HDN NW4 64 A2
HOLWY N7 * 84 D3
PLMGR N13 35 G6
Crest Vw PIN HA5 59 H1
Crest View Dr
STMC/STPC BR5 201 G2
Crestway PUT/ROE SW15 158 D1
Crestwood Wy HSLWW TW4 134 E6
Creswell Dr BECK BR3 198 E2
Creswick Rd ACT W3 98 D6
Creswick Wk GLDGN NW11 64 D1
Creukhorne Rd
WLSDN NW10 * 81 G5
Crewdson Rd BRXN/ST SW9 142 A1
Crewe Pl WLSDN NW10 99 H2
Crews St POP/IOD E14 124 D4
Crewys Rd CRICK NW2 64 D6
PECK SE15 143 J3
Crichton Av WLGTN SM6 210 D3
Crichton Rd CAR SM5 209 K5
Crichton St VX/NE SW8 * 141 H3
Cricketers Arms Rd
ENC/FH EN2 * 23 J3
Cricketers Cl CHSGTN KT9 205 K3
ERITH DA8 130 B5
STHGT/OAK N14 34 C2
Cricketers Ms BAL SW12 161 G2
WAND/EARL SW18 140 A6
Cricketers Wk SYD SE26 181 K1
Cricketfield Rd CLPT E5 86 D2
Cricket Gn MTCM CR4 178 E6
Cricket Ground Rd CHST BR7 185 G4
Cricket La BECK BR3 182 B2
HPTN TW12 173 H1
Cricket Rw EFNCH N2 * 47 H6
Cricklade Av
BRXS/STRHM SW2 161 K4
Cricklewood Broadway
CRICK NW2 82 B2
Cricklewood La CRICK NW2 82 C2
Cridland St SRTFD E15 88 D6
Crieff Ct TEDD TW11 174 D3
Crieff Rd WAND/EARL SW18 160 B1
Criffel Av BRXS/STRHM SW2 161 J4
Crimscott St STHWK SE1 19 H5
Crimsworth Rd VX/NE SW8 141 J1
Crinan St IS N1 5 F2
Cringle St VX/NE SW8 141 H1
Cripplegate St BARB EC2Y * 12 C1
Crispen Rd FELT TW13 154 D6
Crispian Cl WLSDN NW10 81 G2
Crispin Crs CROY/NA CR0 195 J6
Crispin Ms GLDGN NW11 64 D2
Crispin Rd EDGW HA8 44 E2
Crispin St WCHPL E1 13 J2
Crisp Rd HMSMTH W6 119 F5
Cristowe Rd FUL/PGN SW6 * 139 J3
Critchley Av DART DA1 171 G1
Criterion Ms ARCH N19 66 D6
HNHL SE24 142 C6
Crockenhill Hl
STMC/STPC BR5 202 E2
Crockenhill Rd
STMC/STPC BR5 202 E3
Crockerton Rd TOOT SW17 160 E4
Crockham Wy ELTH/MOT SE9 167 F6
Crocus Cl CROY/NA CR0 198 A5
Crocus Fld BAR EN5 32 D1
Croft Av WWKM BR4 199 F5
Croft Cl ABYW SE2 129 G5
CHST BR7 184 E1
HYS/HAR UB3 133 F1
MLHL NW7 31 G5
Croft Ct RSLP HA4 * 58 D5
SUT SM1 * 194 C6
Croftdown Rd KTTN NW5 84 A1
Crofters Cl ISLW TW7 135 J6
Crofters Ct DEPT SE8 124 B4
Crofters Md CROY/NA CR0 213 H6
Crofters Rd NTHWD HA6 26 C6
Crofters Wy CAMTN NW1 84 D6
Croft Gdns HNWL W7 116 B2
RSLP HA4 58 C5
Croft Lodge Cl WFD IG8 53 F2
Croft Ms NFNCH/WDSPK N12 33 G5
Crofton Av BXLY DA5 168 E2
CHSWK W4 137 K1
ORP BR6 201 H6
Crofton Gate Wy BROCKY SE4 144 B6
Crofton Gv CHING E4 38 B6
Crofton La STMC/STPC BR5 201 J5
Crofton Park Rd BROCKY SE4 164 C1
Crofton Rd CMBW SE5 143 F2
ORP BR6 216 A1
PLSTW E13 107 F3
Crofton Ter RCH/KEW TW9 137 G5
Crofton Wy BAR EN5 * 33 F1
ENC/FH EN2 23 G3
Croft Rd BMLY BR1 183 K2
PEND EN3 25 G2
STRHM/NOR SW16 180 B3
SUT SM1 209 H3
WIM/MER SW19 178 B3
Crofts Rd HRW HA1 61 G3
Croft St DEPT SE8 124 B4
WCHPL E1 104 C6
The Croft ALP/SUD HA0 79 J3
BAR EN5 20 C5
CHING E4 38 C4
EA W5 98 A4
HEST TW5 134 D1
PIN HA5 59 K4
RSLP HA4 77 G2
SWLY BR8 187 K6
WLSDN NW10 99 H1
Croft Wy BFN/LL DA15 167 K5
RCHPK/HAM TW10 156 C5
Crogsland Rd CAMTN NW1 84 A5
Croham Cl SAND/SEL CR2 212 A5
Croham Manor Rd
SAND/SEL CR2 212 A5
Croham Mt SAND/SEL CR2 212 A5
Croham Park Av
SAND/SEL CR2 212 B3
Croham Rd SAND/SEL CR2 211 K3
Croham Valley Rd
SAND/SEL CR2 212 C4
Croindene Rd
STRHM/NOR SW16 179 K4
Cromartie Rd ARCH N19 66 D4
Cromarty Rd EDGW HA8 30 D4
Cromarty Vls BAY/PAD W2 * 101 G6
Crombie Cl REDBR IG4 71 K2
Crombie Ms BTSEA SW11 * 140 D3
Crombie Rd BFN/LL DA15 167 J3
Cromer Cl UX/CGN UB8 94 A5
Cromer Hyde MRDN SM4 * 194 A2
Crome Rd WLSDN NW10 81 G4
Cromer Rd BAR EN5 21 G5
CHDH RM6 74 A3
HTHAIR TW6 132 D4
LEY E10 70 B4
ROMW/RG RM7 74 E3
SNWD SE25 181 J6
TOOT SW17 179 F2
TOTM N17 50 C5
Cromer Rd West HTHAIR TW6 132 D4
Cromer St STPAN WC1H 5 F5
Cromer Ter HACK E8 86 C3
Cromer Villas Rd
WAND/EARL SW18 159 J1
Cromford Cl ORP BR6 216 E1
Cromford Rd PUT/ROE SW15 139 J6
Cromford Wy NWMAL KT3 176 A4
Cromlix Cl CHST BR7 185 G5
Crompton Pl PEND EN3 25 J1
Crompton St BAY/PAD W2 2 A7
Cromwell Av HAYES BR2 184 A6
HGT N6 66 B5
HMSMTH W6 118 E5
NWMAL KT3 192 C2
Cromwell Cl CHSWK W4 * 117 J5
EFNCH N2 65 H1
HAYES BR2 200 A1
WOT/HER KT12 188 A5
Cromwell Ct ALP/SUD HA0 98 A1
PEND EN3 25 F6
Cromwell Crs ECT SW5 119 K4
Cromwell Gdns SKENS SW7 14 B6
Cromwell Gv HMSMTH W6 119 F3
Cromwell Ms SKENS SW7 * 14 A6
Cromwell Pde ALP/SUD HA0 * 98 A1
Cromwell Pl ACT W3 117 K1
HGT N6 * 66 B5
MORT/ESHN SW14 137 K4
SKENS SW7 14 B6
Cromwell Rd ALP/SUD HA0 97 K1
BECK BR3 182 B5
BRXN/ST SW9 142 C2
CROY/NA CR0 196 E4
ECT SW5 120 A4
FELT TW13 154 A3
FNCH N3 47 G5
FSTGT E7 89 G5
HSLW TW3 135 F5
HYS/HAR UB3 94 B5
KUTN/CMB KT2 175 F4
MUSWH N10 48 A3
TEDD TW11 174 B2
WALTH E17 70 A2
WIM/MER SW19 177 K1
WOT/HER KT12 188 A6
WPK KT4 207 F1
Cromwell St HSLW TW3 135 F5
Cromwell Ter HSLW TW3 * 135 F5
Crondace Rd FUL/PGN SW6 139 K2
Crondall St IS N1 7 F3
Cronin St PECK SE15 143 G1
Crooked Billet Rbt CHING E4 51 K3
Crooked Usage FNCH N3 46 C6
Crooke Rd DEPT SE8 124 B5
Crookham Rd FUL/PGN SW6 139 J2
Crook Log BXLYHS DA6 148 E4
Crookston Rd ELTH/MOT SE9 147 F4
Croombs Rd CAN/RD E16 107 G4
Croom's Hl GNWCH SE10 145 G1
Croom's Hill Gv GNWCH SE10 145 F1
Cropley St IS N1 6 E2
Croppath Rd DAGE RM10 92 C2
Cropthorne Ct MV/WKIL W9 101 G2
Crosby Cl FELT TW13 154 D6
Crosby Rd DAGE RM10 110 D1
FSTGT E7 88 E4
Crosby Rw STHWK SE1 18 E3
Crosby Sq HDTCH EC3A 13 G4
Crosby Wk HACK E8 86 B4
Crosier Cl BKHTH/KID SE3 146 D2
Crosier Rd HGDN/ICK UB10 76 A2
Crosier Wy RSLP HA4 76 C1
Crosland Pl BTSEA SW11 141 F4
Crossbow Rd CHIG IG7 55 F1
Crossbrook Rd
BKHTH/KID SE3 146 D3
Cross Deep TWK TW1 156 A5
Cross Deep Gdns TWK TW1 156 A4
Crossfield Est DEPT SE8 144 D1
Crossfield Rd HAMP NW3 83 H4
TOTM N17 49 J6
Crossfield St DEPT SE8 144 D1
Crossford St BRXN/ST SW9 142 A3
Crossgate EDGW HA8 30 C5
GFD/PVL UB6 79 H4
Cross Keys Cl ED N9 36 C4
MHST W1U 9 H2
Cross Lances Rd HSLW TW3 135 G5
Crossland Rd THHTH CR7 196 C3
Crosslands Av EA W5 117 G1
NWDGN UB2 114 E5
Crosslands Pde NWDGN UB2 * 115 F5
Crosslands Rd
HOR/WEW KT19 207 F4
Cross La BXLY DA5 169 G2
CEND/HSY/T N8 67 F1
MON EC3R 13 G6
Crosslet St WALW SE17 19 F6
Crosslet V GNWCH SE10 144 E2
Crossley St HOLWY N7 85 G4
Crossmead ELTH/MOT SE9 166 E3
OXHEY WD19 27 F1
Crossmead Av GFD/PVL UB6 96 A2
Crossness Rd BARK IG11 109 F2
Cross Rd CHDH RM6 73 J4
CHING E4 38 B3
CMBW SE5 143 F3
CROY/NA CR0 196 E5
DART DA1 171 F1
EN EN1 24 A5
FBAR/BDGN N11 48 B1
FELT TW13 154 D6
HAYES BR2 200 D6
HRW HA1 60 D1
KTN/HRWW/WS HA3 43 G5
KUTN/CMB KT2 175 G3
OXHEY WD19 27 J1
RDART DA2 171 J6
ROMW/RG RM7 56 C6
RYLN/HDSTN HA2 78 A1
SCUP DA14 168 C6
STMC/STPC BR5 202 C2
SUT SM1 209 H3
WDGN N22 49 G2
WFD IG8 53 K2
WIM/MER SW19 177 K3
Cross St BARN SW13 138 B3
ERITH DA8 130 B6
HPTN TW12 173 H1
IS N1 85 H6
UED N18 50 C1
Crossthwaite Av HNHL SE24 142 E5
Crosswall TWRH EC3N 13 J5
Crossway BCTR RM8 91 J1
CDALE/KGS NW9 63 H1
EN EN1 36 A2
Cross Wy HYS/HAR UB3 113 K2
Crossway NFNCH/WDSPK N12 47 H2
NWMAL KT3 193 F1
PIN HA5 41 F5
RSLP HA4 77 G2
STMC/STPC BR5 201 J1
STNW/STAM N16 86 A3
THMD SE28 109 J5
WEA W13 97 F3
WOT/HER KT12 188 A6
Crossway Pde WDGN N22 * 49 H3
Crossways BELMT SM2 209 H6
GPK RM2 57 K6
SAND/SEL CR2 213 G5
Crossways Rd BECK BR3 198 D1
MTCM CR4 179 G6
Crossways Ter CLPT E5 * 86 E2
The Crossways BRYLDS KT5 * 191 J5
HEST TW5 134 E1
WBLY HA9 62 C6
The Cross Wy
KTN/HRWW/WS HA3 42 E5
The Crossway ELTH/MOT SE9 166 C4
WDGN N22 49 H3
Croston St HACK E8 86 C6
Crosts La WDGN N22 49 G3
Crothall Cl PLMGR N13 35 F5
Crouch Av BARK IG11 109 H1
Crouch Cl BECK BR3 182 D2
Crouch Cft ELTH/MOT SE9 167 F5
Crouch End Hl
CEND/HSY/T N8 66 D4
Crouch Hall Rd
CEND/HSY/T N8 66 D3
Crouch Hl CEND/HSY/T N8 66 E4
Crouchmans Cl SYD SE26 163 G5
Crouch Rd WLSDN NW10 81 F5
Crowborough Pth
OXHEY WD19 27 H6
Crowborough Rd TOOT SW17 179 F1
Crowden Wy THMD SE28 109 J6
Crowder Cl
NFNCH/WDSPK N12 47 G3
Crowder St WCHPL E1 104 D6
Crowfoot Cl HOM E9 87 H3
THMD SE28 127 K1
Crowhurst Cl BRXN/ST SW9 142 B3
Crowhurst Wy
STMC/STPC BR5 202 D2
Crowland Av HYS/HAR UB3 113 H4
Crowland Gdns
STHGT/OAK N14 34 E2
Crowland Rd
SEVS/STOTM N15 68 B2
THHTH CR7 * 196 E1
Crowlands Av ROMW/RG RM7 74 D3
Crowland Ter IS N1 85 K5
Crowland Wk MRDN SM4 194 A3
Crow La ROMW/RG RM7 74 B4
Crowley Crs CROY/NA CR0 211 G3
Crowline Wk IS N1 * 85 J4
Crowmarsh Gdns FSTH SE23 163 K2
Crown Ar KUT/HW KT1 * 174 E5
Crownbourne Ct SUT SM1 * 209 F2
Crown Blds CHING E4 * 38 B3
Crown Cl BOW E3 87 J6
HYS/HAR UB3 113 J2
KIL/WHAMP NW6 83 F4
MLHL NW7 31 H4
ORP BR6 217 G2
WOT/HER KT12 188 B4
Crown Ct HOL/ALD WC2B 11 F4
Crown Dl NRWD SE19 180 D2
Crowndale Rd CAMTN NW1 4 B2
Crownfield Av
GNTH/NBYPK IG2 72 E2
Crownfield Rd SRTFD E15 88 B3
Crown Green Ms WBLY HA9 62 A6
Crown Hl CROY/NA CR0 * 196 D6
Crownhill Rd WFD IG8 53 J3
WLSDN NW10 81 H6
Crown La CHST BR7 185 H4
HAYES BR2 200 C2
MRDN SM4 177 K6
STHGT/OAK N14 34 C3
STRHM/NOR SW16 180 B1
Crown Lane Gdns
STRHM/NOR SW16 * 180 B1
Crown Lane Sp HAYES BR2 200 C3
Crownmead Wy
ROMW/RG RM7 74 D1
Crown Office Rw EMB EC4Y 11 J5
Crown Pde MRDN SM4 * 194 A1
STHGT/OAK N14 * 34 C3
Crown Pas STJS SW1Y 16 B1
Crown Pl KTTN NW5 84 B4
SDTCH EC2A 7 G7
Crown Rd BARK/HLT IG6 72 D1
EN EN1 24 C4
KUTN/CMB KT2 175 K4
MRDN SM4 193 K1
MUSWH N10 48 A3
ORP BR6 217 G3
RSLP HA4 77 H3
SUT SM1 208 E2
TWK TW1 156 C1
Crownstone Rd
BRXS/STRHM SW2 142 B6
Crown St ACT W3 117 J1
CMBW SE5 142 D1
DAGE RM10 92 E4

RYLN/HDSTN HA2 60 D5
Crown Ter CRICK NW2 * 82 B2
RCH/KEW TW9 137 G5
STHGT/OAK N14 * 34 D3
Crowntree Cl ISLW TW7 116 A6
Crown Vls ACT W3 * 117 K2
Crown Wk WBLY HA9 80 B1
Crown Wy WDR/YW UB7 112 C1
Crown Woods La
WOOL/PLUM SE18 147 G3
Crown Woods Wy
ELTH/MOT SE9 147 J6
Crown Yd HSLW TW3 135 H4
Crowshott Av STAN HA7 43 J4
Crows Rd BARK IG11 90 B4
BOW E3 106 B2
Crowther Av BTFD TW8 117 F5
Crowther Cl FUL/PGN SW6 119 J6
Crowther Rd SNWD SE25 197 H1
Crowthorne Cl
WAND/EARL SW18 159 J2
Crowthorne Rd NKENS W10 100 B5
Croxden Cl EDGW HA8 44 C6
Croxden Wk MRDN SM4 194 B3
Croxford Gdns WDGN N22 49 H3
Croxford Wy ROMW/RG RM7 75 F5
Croxley Cl STMC/STPC BR5 186 C5
Croxley Gn STMC/STPC BR5 186 C4
Croxley Rd MV/WKIL W9 100 D2
Croxley Vw WATW WD18 26 C1
Croxted Cl DUL SE21 162 D2
Croxted Ms HNHL SE24 162 D1
Croxted Rd DUL SE21 162 D2
Croyde Av GFD/PVL UB6 96 C2
HYS/HAR UB3 113 H4
Croyde Cl BFN/LL DA15 167 J2
The Croydon F/O
CROY/NA CR0 211 H2
Croydon Gv CROY/NA CR0 196 C5
Croydon Rd BECK BR3 198 A2
CROY/NA CR0 210 E2
HAYES BR2 215 J1
MTCM CR4 195 G2
PGE/AN SE20 181 J5
PLSTW E13 106 D3
WLGTN SM6 210 B2
WWKM BR4 214 C1
Croyland Rd ED N9 36 C3
Croylands Dr SURB KT6 191 F4
Crozier Ter HOM E9 87 F3
Crucible Cl CHDH RM6 73 H3
Crucifix La STHWK SE1 19 G2
Cruden St IS N1 6 B1
Cruickshank St FSBYW WC1X 5 J4
Cruikshank Rd SRTFD E15 88 C2
Crummock Gdns
CDALE/KGS NW9 63 G2
Crumpsall St ABYW SE2 128 D4
Crundale Av CDALE/KGS NW9 62 C2
Crunden Rd SAND/SEL CR2 211 K5
Crusader Cl PUR RM19 131 K4
Crusader Gdns CROY/NA CR0 212 A1
Crusader Wy WATW WD18 26 D1
Crusoe Ms STNW/STAM N16 67 K6
Crusoe Rd ERITH DA8 130 A5
MTCM CR4 178 E3
Crutched Friars TWRH EC3N 13 H5
Crutchfield La WOT/HER KT12 188 A5
Crutchley Rd CAT SE6 165 H4
Crystal Palace NRWD SE19 * 181 H3
Crystal Palace Pde
NRWD SE19 181 G2
Crystal Palace Park Rd
SYD SE26 181 H1
Crystal Palace Rd EDUL SE22 163 G1
Crystal Palace Station Rd
NRWD SE19 181 H2
Crystal Ter NRWD SE19 180 E2
Crystal Wy BCTR RM8 73 J2
HRW HA1 61 F2
Cuba Dr PEND EN3 24 E3
Cuba St POP/IOD E14 124 D2
Cubitt Sq NWDGN UB2 * 115 H1
Cubitt St FSBYW WC1X 5 H5
Cubitt Ter CLAP SW4 141 H4
Cuckmere Wy
STMC/STPC BR5 202 E5
Cuckoo Av HNWL W7 96 E3
Cuckoo Dene HNWL W7 96 D4
Cuckoo Hall La ED N9 36 E3
Cuckoo Hl PIN HA5 41 G6
Cuckoo Hill Dr PIN HA5 41 G6
Cuckoo Hill Rd PIN HA5 59 H1
Cuckoo La HNWL W7 96 E6
Cuda's Cl HOR/WEW KT19 207 H2
Cuddington Av WPK KT4 207 H1
Cudham La North ORP BR6 216 E6
Cudham St CAT SE6 164 E2
Cudworth St WCHPL E1 104 D3
Cuff Crs ELTH/MOT SE9 166 C2
Culford Gdns CHEL SW3 15 F7
Culford Gv IS N1 86 A4
Culford Ms IS N1 85 K4
Culford Rd IS N1 86 A5
Culgaith Gdns ENC/FH EN2 22 E5
Cullera Cl NTHWD HA6 40 D2
Culling Rd BERM/RHTH SE16 123 K3
Cullington Cl
KTN/HRWW/WS HA3 61 G1
Cullingworth Rd
WLSDN NW10 81 K3
Culloden Cl
BERM/RHTH SE16 123 H5
CHARL SE7 126 B6
Culloden Rd ENC/FH EN2 23 H3
Culloden St POP/IOD E14 106 A5
Cullum St FENCHST EC3M 13 G5
Culmington Pde WEA W13 * 97 J6
Culmington Rd SAND/SEL CR2 211 J5
WEA W13 116 D1
Culmore Rd PECK SE15 143 J1
Culmstock Rd BTSEA SW11 141 F6
Culpepper Cl CHIG IG7 54 B2
UED N18 50 D1
Culross Cl SEVS/STOTM N15 67 J1
Culross St MYFR/PKLN W1K 9 G6
Culsac Rd SURB KT6 191 F6
Culverden Rd BAL SW12 161 H5
OXHEY WD19 27 F5
Culver Gv STAN HA7 43 J5
Culverhouse Gdns
STRHM/NOR SW16 162 A6
Culverlands Cl STAN HA7 29 H6
Culverley Rd CAT SE6 164 E3
Culvers Av CAR SM5 194 E6
Culvers Retreat CAR SM5 194 E5
Culverstone Cl HAYES BR2 199 J3
Culvers Wy CAR SM5 194 E6
Culvert Pl BTSEA SW11 141 F3
Culvert Rd BTSEA SW11 140 E3
SEVS/STOTM N15 68 A2
Culworth St STJWD NW8 2 C3
Cumberland Av WELL DA16 147 K4
WLSDN NW10 98 D2
Cumberland Cl BARK/HLT IG6 54 C4
HACK E8 86 B4
RYNPK SW20 177 G3
TWK TW1 156 C1
Cumberland Crs WKENS W14 119 H4
Cumberland Dr BXLYHN DA7 149 F1
CHSGTN KT9 206 A1
DART DA1 171 J2
ESH/CLAY KT10 190 B6
Cumberland Gdns
FSBYW WC1X 5 H4
HDN NW4 * 46 B5
Cumberland Ga BAY/PAD W2 8 E5
CAMTN NW1 3 J4
Cumberland House
KUTN/CMB KT2 175 J3
Cumberland Market
CAMTN NW1 3 K4
Cumberland Ms LBTH SE11 122 B5
Cumberland Pk ACT W3 98 E6
Cumberland Pl CAMTN NW1 3 J4
CAT SE6 165 J3
Cumberland Rd ACT W3 98 E6
ASHF TW15 152 A5
BARN SW13 138 C2
ED N9 36 E3
HAYES BR2 199 H1
HNWL W7 116 A2
HRW HA1 60 B2
MNPK E12 89 H2
PLSTW E13 107 F4
RCH/KEW TW9 137 H2
SNWD SE25 197 J3
STAN HA7 44 B6
WALTH E17 51 G5
WDGN N22 49 F5
Cumberland St PIM SW1V 121 G5
Cumberland Ter CAMTN NW1 3 J3
PGE/AN SE20 * 181 J3
Cumberland Terrace Ms
CAMTN NW1 3 J3
Cumberlow Av SNWD SE25 181 H6
Cumberton Rd TOTM N17 49 K4
Cumbrae Gdns SURB KT6 190 E6
Cumbrian Av BXLYHN DA7 150 B3
Cumbrian Gdns CRICK NW2 64 B6
Cumming St IS N1 5 H3
Cumnor Cl BRXN/ST SW9 * 142 A3
Cumnor Gdns EW KT17 207 J4
Cumnor Rd BELMT SM2 209 G4
Cunard Crs WCHMH N21 35 K1
Cunard Rd WLSDN NW10 99 F2
Cundy Rd CAN/RD E16 107 G5
Cundy St BGVA SW1W 15 H7
Cunliffe Rd HOR/WEW KT19 207 H2
Cunliffe St STRHM/NOR SW16 179 H2
Cunningham Cl CHDH RM6 73 J2
WWKM BR4 198 E6
Cunningham Pk HRW HA1 60 D2
Cunningham Pl STJWD NW8 2 A6
Cunningham Rd
SEVS/STOTM N15 * 68 C1
Cunnington St CHSWK W4 117 K3
Cupar Rd BTSEA SW11 141 F2
Cupola Cl BMLY BR1 184 A1
Curates Wk RDART DA2 171 G5
Cureton St WEST SW1P * 121 J5
Curlew Cl THMD SE28 109 K6
Curlew St STHWK SE1 19 J2
Curlew Wy YEAD UB4 95 H4
Curness St LEW SE13 145 F5
Curnick's La WNWD SE27 162 D6
Curran Av BFN/LL DA15 148 A6
WLGTN SM6 210 A1
Currey Rd NTHLT UB5 78 C4
Curricle St ACT W3 118 B1
Currie Hill Cl WIM/MER SW19 159 J6
Curry Ri MLHL NW7 46 B2
Cursitor St FLST/FETLN EC4A 11 J3
Curtain Pl SDTCH EC2A 7 H5
Curtain Rd FSBYE EC1V 7 H5
SDTCH EC2A 7 G7
Curthwaite Gdns ENC/FH EN2 22 D5
Curtis Dr ACT W3 99 F5
Curtis Field Rd
STRHM/NOR SW16 162 A6
Curtis La ALP/SUD HA0 80 A4
Curtismill Cl STMC/STPC BR5 186 C6
Curtismill Wy STMC/STPC BR5 186 C6
Curtis Rd HOR/WEW KT19 206 E2
HSLWW TW4 154 E2
Curtis St STHWK SE1 19 J6
Curtis Wy STHWK SE1 19 J6
The Curve SHB W12 99 J6
Curwen Av FSTGT E7 89 F2
Curwen Rd SHB W12 118 D2
Curzon Av PEND EN3 25 F6
STAN HA7 43 G4
Curzon Cl ORP BR6 216 D2
Curzon Crs BARK IG11 109 F2
WLSDN NW10 81 G5
Curzon Pl PIN HA5 59 G2
Curzon Rd EA W5 97 H3
MUSWH N10 48 B5
THHTH CR7 196 B3
Curzon St MYFR/PICC W1J 9 J7
MYFR/PKLN W1K 15 H1
Cusack Cl TWK TW1 * 156 A6
Custom House Reach
BERM/RHTH SE16 * 124 C3
Cutcombe Rd CMBW SE5 142 D3
Cuthberga Cl BARK IG11 90 C5
Cuthbert Gdns SNWD SE25 181 F6
Cuthbert Rd CROY/NA CR0 196 C6
UED N18 50 C1
WALTH E17 52 A6
Cuthbert St BAY/PAD W2 2 A7
Cutlers Gardens Ar
LVPST EC2M 13 H3
Cutler St HDTCH EC3A 13 H3
Cutter La GNWCH SE10 125 H2
The Cut STHWK SE1 17 K2
Cuxton Cl BXLYHS DA6 149 F6
Cyclamen Cl HPTN TW12 173 F2
Cyclamen Wy HOR/WEW KT19 206 E3
Cygnet Av EBED/NFELT TW14 154 B2
Cygnet Cl NTHWD HA6 40 A3
WLSDN NW10 81 F3
The Cygnets FELT TW13 154 D6
Cygnet St WCHPL E1 7 K6
Cygnet Wy YEAD UB4 95 H4
Cymbeline Ct HRW HA1 * 61 F3
Cynthia St IS N1 5 H3
Cypress Av WHTN TW2 155 H2
Cypress Cl CLPT E5 68 C6
Cypress Gdns BROCKY SE4 144 B6
Cypress Gv BARK/HLT IG6 54 E2
Cypress Pl FITZ W1T 4 B7
Cypress Rd
KTN/HRWW/WS HA3 42 D5
SNWD SE25 181 F5
Cypress Tree Cl BFN/LL DA15 168 A3
Cyprus Av FNCH N3 46 C5
Cyprus Cl FSBYPK N4 67 G3
Cyprus Gdns FNCH N3 46 C5
Cyprus Pl BETH E2 104 E1
EHAM E6 108 A6
Cyprus Rd ED N9 36 B4
FNCH N3 46 D5
Cyprus St BETH E2 104 E1
Cyrena Rd EDUL SE22 163 G1
Cyril Rd BXLYHN DA7 149 F3
ORP BR6 202 B4
Cyrus St FSBYE EC1V 6 B6
Czar St DEPT SE8 124 D6

D

Dabbling Cl ERITH DA8 * 150 E1
Dabbs Hill La NTHLT UB5 77 K3
D'Abernon Cl ESH/CLAY KT10 204 A2
Dabin Crs GNWCH SE10 145 F2
Dacca St DEPT SE8 124 C6
Dace Rd BOW E3 87 J6
Dacre Av CLAY IG5 54 A5
Dacre Cl GFD/PVL UB6 96 B1
Dacre Gdns LEW SE13 145 H5
Dacre Pk LEW SE13 145 H4
Dacre Pl LEW SE13 145 H4
Dacre Rd CROY/NA CR0 195 K4
PLSTW E13 89 F6
WAN E11 70 D5
Dacres Est FSTH SE23 * 164 A5
Dacres Rd FSTH SE23 164 A5
Dacre St STJSPK SW1H 16 C4
Dade Wy NWDGN UB2 114 E5
Daerwood Cl HAYES BR2 200 E5
Daffodil Cl CROY/NA CR0 198 A5
HPTN TW12 173 F2
Daffodil Gdns IL IG1 90 B3
Daffodil St SHB W12 99 H6
Dafforne Rd TOOT SW17 160 E5
Dagenham Av DAGW RM9 92 A5
Dagenham Rd DAGE RM10 92 E2
LEY E10 69 H5
RAIN RM13 93 F5
ROMW/RG RM7 93 F1
Dagger La BORE WD6 29 G1
Dagmar Av WBLY HA9 80 B2
Dagmar Gdns WLSDN NW10 100 B1
Dagmar Ms NWDGN UB2 114 D3
Dagmar Pas IS N1 85 H6
Dagmar Rd CMBW SE5 143 F2
DAGE RM10 92 E5
FSBYPK N4 67 G4
KUTN/CMB KT2 175 G4
NWDGN UB2 114 D3
SEVS/STOTM N15 67 K1
SNWD SE25 197 F1
WDGN N22 48 D4
Dagmar Ter IS N1 85 H6
Dagnall Pk SNWD SE25 197 F2
Dagnall Rd SNWD SE25 197 F2
Dagnall St BTSEA SW11 140 E3
Dagnan Rd BAL SW12 161 G2
Dagonet Rd BMLY BR1 165 K5
Dahlia Gdns IL IG1 90 B4
MTCM CR4 195 J1
Dahlia Rd ABYW SE2 128 C5
Dahomey Rd
STRHM/NOR SW16 179 H2
Daimler Wy WLGTN SM6 210 E5
Daines Cl MNPK E12 89 K1
Dainford Cl BMLY BR1 183 G1
Daintry Cl
KTN/HRWW/WS HA3 61 G1
Dairsie Rd ELTH/MOT SE9 147 F4
Dairy Cl BMLY BR1 * 184 A3
FUL/PGN SW6 139 J2
THHTH CR7 180 D5
WLSDN NW10 81 J6
Dairy La WOOL/PLUM SE18 126 E4
Dairyman Cl CRICK NW2 82 B1
Dairy Ms EFNCH N2 65 J1
Daisy Cl CDALE/KGS NW9 62 E6
CROY/NA CR0 198 A5
Daisy La FUL/PGN SW6 139 K4
Daisy Rd SWFD E18 53 F5
Dakin Pl WCHPL E1 105 G4
Dakota Cl WLGTN SM6 211 F5
Dalberg Rd BRXS/STRHM SW2 142 B6
Dalberg Wy ABYW SE2 128 E3
Dalby Rd WAND/EARL SW18 140 B5
Dalbys Crs TOTM N17 50 A2
Dalby St KTTN NW5 84 B4
Dalcross Rd HSLWW TW4 134 D3
Dale Av EDGW HA8 44 B4
HSLWW TW4 134 D4
Dalebury Rd TOOT SW17 160 E4
Dale Cl BAR EN5 33 F1
BKHTH/KID SE3 145 K4
DART DA1 170 C1
PIN HA5 41 F4
Dale Dr YEAD UB4 94 D3
Dale Gdns WFD IG8 39 F6
Dale Green Rd
FBAR/BDGN N11 34 B5
Dale Gv NFNCH/WDSPK N12 47 G1
Daleham Gdns HAMP NW3 83 H3
Daleham Ms HAMP NW3 * 83 H4
Dalemain Ms CAN/RD E16 125 K1
Dale Park Av CAR SM5 194 E6
Dale Park Rd NRWD SE19 180 D4
Dale Rd DART DA1 170 C1
KTTN NW5 84 A3
STHL UB1 96 B4
SUT SM1 208 D2
SWLY BR8 187 K6
WALW SE17 122 C6
Dale Rw NTGHL W11 100 C5
Daleside ORP BR6 217 G3
Daleside Cl ORP BR6 217 G4
Daleside Rd HOR/WEW KT19 207 F4
STRHM/NOR SW16 179 G1
Dalestone Ms HARH RM3 57 K2
Dale St CHSWK W4 118 B5
The Dale HAYES BR2 215 H2
Dale Vw BAR EN5 * 20 D4
ERITH DA8 150 D3
Dale View Av CHING E4 38 A4
Dale View Crs CHING E4 38 A5
Dale View Gdns CHING E4 38 B5
Daleview Rd
SEVS/STOTM N15 68 A3
Dalewood Gdns WPK KT4 192 E6
Dale Wood Rd ORP BR6 201 K4
Daley St HOM E9 87 F4
Daley Thompson Wy
VX/NE SW8 141 G3
Dalgarno Gdns NKENS W10 100 A4
Dalgarno Wy NKENS W10 100 A3
Dalkeith Gv STAN HA7 43 K1
Dalkeith Rd DUL SE21 162 D3
IL IG1 90 C1
Dallas Rd CHEAM SM3 208 C4
EA W5 98 B4
HDN NW4 63 J4
SYD SE26 163 J6
Dallas Ter HYS/HAR UB3 113 J3
Dallega Cl HYS/HAR UB3 94 A6
Dallinger Rd LEE/GVPK SE12 165 J1
Dalling Rd HMSMTH W6 118 E4
Dallington Sq FSBYE EC1V 6 B6
Dallington St FSBYE EC1V 6 B6
Dallin Rd BXLYHS DA6 148 E5
WOOL/PLUM SE18 147 G1
Dalmain Rd FSTH SE23 164 A3
Dalmally Rd CROY/NA CR0 197 G4
Dalmeny Av HOLWY N7 84 D2
STRHM/NOR SW16 180 B5
Dalmeny Cl ALP/SUD HA0 79 J4
Dalmeny Crs HSLW TW3 135 J5
Dalmeny Rd ARCH N19 84 D1
BAR EN5 33 G1
CAR SM5 210 A5
ERITH DA8 149 J2
HOLWY N7 84 D2
WPK KT4 207 K1
Dalmeyer Rd WLSDN NW10 81 H4
Dalmore Av ESH/CLAY KT10 205 F4
Dalmore Rd DUL SE21 162 D4
Dalrymple Cl STHGT/OAK N14 34 D1
Dalrymple Rd BROCKY SE4 144 B5
Dalston Gdns STAN HA7 44 A4
Dalston La HACK E8 86 B4
Dalton Av MTCM CR4 178 D5
Dalton Cl ORP BR6 216 E1
YEAD UB4 94 B3
Daltons Rd SWLY BR8 203 K6
Dalton St WNWD SE27 162 C4
Dalwood St CMBW SE5 143 F2
Dalyell Rd BRXN/ST SW9 142 A4
Damask Crs CAN/RD E16 106 C3
Damer Ter WBPTN SW10 140 B1
Dames Rd FSTGT E7 88 E2
Dame St IS N1 6 C2
Damien St WCHPL E1 104 D4
Damon Cl SCUP DA14 168 C5
Damsel Ct BERM/RHTH SE16 * 123 H2
Damson Dr HYS/HAR UB3 94 E6
Damson Wy CAR SM5 209 K6
Damsonwood Rd
NWDGN UB2 115 F3
Danbrook Rd
STRHM/NOR SW16 179 K4
Danbury Cl CHDH RM6 55 K6
Danbury Ms WLGTN SM6 210 B2
Danbury Rd LOU IG10 39 J1
RAIN RM13 93 H6
Danbury St IS N1 6 B2
Danbury Wy WFD IG8 53 G2
Danby St PECK SE15 143 G4
Dancer Rd FUL/PGN SW6 139 J2
RCH/KEW TW9 137 H4
Dandelion Cl ROMW/RG RM7 75 G6
Dando Crs BKHTH/KID SE3 146 A4
Dandridge Cl GNWCH SE10 125 J5
Danebury CROY/NA CR0 213 K4
Danebury Av PUT/ROE SW15 158 C2
Daneby Rd CAT SE6 165 F5
Dane Cl BXLY DA5 169 H2
ORP BR6 216 D3
Danecourt Gdns
CROY/NA CR0 212 B1
Danecroft Rd HNHL SE24 142 D6
Danehurst Gdns REDBR IG4 71 J2
Danehurst St FUL/PGN SW6 139 H2
Daneland EBAR EN4 33 K1
Danemead Gv NTHLT UB5 78 B3
Danemere St PUT/ROE SW15 139 F4
Dane Pl BOW E3 105 G1
Dane Rd IL IG1 90 C3
STHL UB1 95 J6
UED N18 36 E6
WEA W13 97 J6
WIM/MER SW19 178 B4
Danesbury Rd FELT TW13 154 A3
Danescombe LEE/GVPK SE12 165 K3
Danescourt Crs SUT SM1 194 B6
Danescroft Av HDN NW4 * 64 B2
Danescroft Gdns HDN NW4 64 B2
Danesdale Rd HOM E9 87 G4
Danes Ga HRW HA1 42 E6
Danes Rd ROMW/RG RM7 74 E4
Dane St GINN WC1R 11 G2
Daneswood Av CAT SE6 165 F5
Danethorpe Rd ALP/SUD HA0 79 K4
Danetree Cl HOR/WEW KT19 206 E5
Danetree Rd HOR/WEW KT19 206 E5
Danette Gdns DAGE RM10 74 B6
Daneville Rd CMBW SE5 142 E2
Dangan Rd WAN E11 70 E3
Daniel Bolt Cl POP/IOD E14 105 K4
Daniel Cl HSLWW TW4 154 E2
TOOT SW17 178 D2
UED N18 36 E6
Daniel Gdns PECK SE15 143 G1
Daniell Wy CROY/NA CR0 195 K5
Daniel Pl HDN NW4 63 K3
Daniel Rd EA W5 98 B6
Daniel's Rd PECK SE15 143 K4
Dan Leno Wk FUL/PGN SW6 * 140 A1
Dansey Pl SOHO/SHAV W1D 10 C5
Dansington Rd WELL DA16 148 B5
Danson Crs WELL DA16 148 C4
Danson La WELL DA16 148 C5
Danson Md WELL DA16 148 D4
Danson Rd BXLYHS DA6 148 E6
Danson U/P BFN/LL DA15 168 D1
Dante Rd LBTH SE11 18 A6
Danube Cl ED N9 36 E5
Danube St CHEL SW3 120 D5
Danvers Rd CEND/HSY/T N8 66 D1
Danvers St CHEL SW3 120 C6
Daphne Gdns CHING E4 38 A5
Daphne St WAND/EARL SW18 160 B1
Daplyn St WCHPL E1 104 C4
D'Arblay St SOHO/CST W1F 10 B4
Darby Crs SUN TW16 172 B5
Darby Gdns SUN TW16 172 B5
Darcy Av WLGTN SM6 210 C2
Darcy Cl TRDG/WHET N20 33 H4
D'Arcy Dr
KTN/HRWW/WS HA3 61 K1
D'Arcy Gdns DAGW RM9 92 B6
KTN/HRWW/WS HA3 62 A1
D'Arcy Pl HAYES BR2 199 K1
Darcy Rd ISLW TW7 136 B2
STRHM/NOR SW16 179 K5
D'Arcy Rd CHEAM SM3 208 B2
Darell Rd RCH/KEW TW9 137 H4
Darenth Rd DART DA1 171 K4
STNW/STAM N16 68 B4
WELL DA16 148 B2
Darent Valley Pth DART DA1 151 G5
Darfield Rd BROCKY SE4 144 C6
Darfield Wy NKENS W10 100 B6
Darfur St PUT/ROE SW15 139 G4
Dargate Cl NRWD SE19 181 G3
Darien Rd BTSEA SW11 140 C4
Darlands Dr BAR EN5 20 B6
Darlan Rd FUL/PGN SW6 139 J1
Darlaston Rd WIM/MER SW19 177 G3
Darley Cl CROY/NA CR0 198 A3
Darley Dr NWMAL KT3 176 A5
Darley Gdns MRDN SM4 194 A3
Darley Rd BTSEA SW11 160 E1
ED N9 36 B3
Darling Rd BROCKY SE4 144 D4
Darling Rw WCHPL E1 104 D3
Darlington Rd WNWD SE27 180 C1
Darlton Cl DART DA1 150 C3
Darmaine Cl SAND/SEL CR2 211 J5
Darnaway Pl POP/IOD E14 106 A4
Darndale Cl WALTH E17 51 H5
Darnley Rd HACK E8 86 D4
WFD IG8 52 E4
Darnley Ter NTGHL W11 119 G1
Darns Hl SWLY BR8 203 K4
Darrell Rd EDUL SE22 143 H6
Darren Cl FSBYPK N4 67 F4
Darrick Wood Rd ORP BR6 201 J6
Darris Cl YEAD UB4 95 J3
Darsley Dr VX/NE SW8 141 J2
Dartford Av ED N9 36 E1
Dartford Gdns CHDH RM6 73 H2
Dartford Rd BXLY DA5 169 K3
DART DA1 170 D1
Dartford St WALW SE17 122 D6
Dartmoor Wk POP/IOD E14 * 124 D4
Dartmouth Cl NTGHL W11 100 D5
Dartmouth Gv GNWCH SE10 145 F2
Dartmouth Hl GNWCH SE10 145 F2
Dartmouth Park Av
KTTN NW5 84 B1
Dartmouth Park Hl
KTTN NW5 84 B1
Dartmouth Park Rd
KTTN NW5 84 B1
Dartmouth Pl CHSWK W4 118 B6
FSTH SE23 163 K4
Dartmouth Rd CRICK NW2 82 B4
HAYES BR2 199 K4
HDN NW4 63 J3
RSLP HA4 76 E1
SYD SE26 163 J5
Dartmouth Rw GNWCH SE10 145 F3
Dartmouth St STJSPK SW1H 16 C3
Dartmouth Ter GNWCH SE10 145 G2
Dartnell Rd CROY/NA CR0 197 G4
Dartrey Wk WBPTN SW10 * 140 B1
Dart St NKENS W10 100 D2
Darville Rd STNW/STAM N16 86 B1
Darwell Cl EHAM E6 108 A1
Darwin Cl FBAR/BDGN N11 34 B5
ORP BR6 216 D3
Darwin Dr STHL UB1 96 B5
Darwin Gdns OXHEY WD19 41 G1
Darwin Rd EA W5 116 D5
WDGN N22 49 H4
WELL DA16 148 A4
Darwin St WALW SE17 19 F6
Daryngton Dr GFD/PVL UB6 96 D1
Dashwood Cl BXLYHS DA6 149 H6
Dashwood Rd
CEND/HSY/T N8 67 F3
Dassett Rd WNWD SE27 180 C1
Datchelor Pl CMBW SE5 * 142 E2
Datchet Rd CAT SE6 164 C5
Date St WALW SE17 122 D5
Daubeney Gdns TOTM N17 49 J3
Daubeney Rd CLPT E5 87 G2

TOTM N17 49 J3
Dault Rd WAND/EARL SW18 160 B1
Davema Cl CHST BR7 185 F4
Davenant Rd ARCH N19 66 D6
Davenant St WCHPL E1 104 C4
Davenham Av NTHWD HA6 26 D6
Davenport Cl TEDD TW11 * 174 B2
Davenport Rd CAT SE6 164 E1
SCUP DA14 168 E4
Daventer Dr STAN HA7 43 F3
Daventry Av WALTH E17 69 J3
Daventry St CAMTN NW1 8 C1
Davern Cl GNWCH SE10 125 J4
Davey Cl HOLWY N7 85 F4
PLMGR N13 49 F1
Davey Rd HOM E9 87 J5
Davey St PECK SE15 123 G6
David Av GFD/PVL UB6 96 E2
David Cl HYS/HAR UB3 133 G1
Davidge St STHWK SE1 18 A3
David Ms MHST W1U 9 F1
David Rd BCTR RM8 74 A6
Davidson Gdns VX/NE SW8 141 K1
Davidson Rd CROY/NA CR0 197 F5
Davidson Wy ROMW/RG RM7 75 G3
David's Rd FSTH SE23 163 K3
David St SRTFD E15 88 B4
Davids Wy BARK/HLT IG6 54 E3
David Twigg Cl
KUTN/CMB KT2 175 F4
Davies Cl CROY/NA CR0 197 G3
Davies La WAN E11 70 C6
Davies Ms MYFR/PKLN W1K 9 J5
Davies St MYFR/PKLN W1K 9 J5
Davies Wk ISLW TW7 135 J2
Davington Gdns BCTR RM8 91 H3
Davington Rd BCTR RM8 91 H4
Davinia Cl WFD IG8 53 K2
Davis Rd ACT W3 118 C1
CHSGTN KT9 206 C2
Davis St PLSTW E13 107 F1
Davisville Rd SHB W12 118 D2
Davis Wy SCUP DA14 187 F2
Dawes Av ISLW TW7 136 B6
Dawes Ct ESH/CLAY KT10 204 B2
Dawes Rd FUL/PGN SW6 139 J1
Dawes St WALW SE17 122 E5
Dawley Pde HYS/HAR UB3 94 A6
Dawley Rd HYS/HAR UB3 94 B6
Dawlish Av GFD/PVL UB6 97 G1
PLMGR N13 34 E6
WAND/EARL SW18 160 A4
Dawlish Dr GDMY/SEVK IG3 91 F2
PIN HA5 59 J2
RSLP HA4 58 E6
Dawlish Rd CRICK NW2 82 B4
LEY E10 70 A6
TOTM N17 50 C6
Dawnay Gdns
WAND/EARL SW18 160 C4
Dawnay Rd
WAND/EARL SW18 160 B4
Dawn Cl HSLWW TW4 134 D4
Dawn Crs SRTFD E15 88 B6
Dawpool Rd CRICK NW2 63 H6
Daws La MLHL NW7 45 H1
Dawson Av BARK IG11 91 F5
STMC/STPC BR5 186 C5
Dawson Cl HYS/HAR UB3 94 B4
WOOL/PLUM SE18 127 H4
Dawson Dr RAIN RM13 93 K5
Dawson Gdns BARK IG11 91 F5
Dawson Pl BAY/PAD W2 100 E6
Dawson Rd CRICK NW2 82 A3
KUT/HW KT1 175 G6
Dawson St BETH E2 7 K3
Dawson Ter ED N9 * 36 E2
Daybrook Rd WIM/MER SW19 178 A5
Daylesford Av
PUT/ROE SW15 138 D5
Daymer Gdns PIN HA5 59 G1
Daysbrook Rd
BRXS/STRHM SW2 162 A3
Days La BFN/LL DA15 167 K2
Dayton Dr ERITH DA8 131 G6
Dayton Gv PECK SE15 143 K2
Deacon Cl PUR/KEN CR8 210 E6
The Deacon Est CHING E4 * 51 H2
Deacon Ms IS N1 85 K5
Deacon Rd CRICK NW2 81 J4
KUTN/CMB KT2 175 G4
Deacons Cl PIN HA5 41 F5
Deacons Hts BORE WD6 30 C1
Deacons Hl OXHEY WD19 27 G1
Deacons Leas ORP BR6 216 D2
Deacons Ri EFNCH N2 65 H2
Deacons Ter IS N1 * 85 J4
Deacons Wk HPTN TW12 155 F6
Deacon Wy WALW SE17 18 C6
WFD IG8 53 K3
Deakin Cl WATW WD18 26 C2
Deakins Ter ORP BR6 202 B4
Deal Porters Wy
BERM/RHTH SE16 123 K3
Deal Rd TOOT SW17 179 F2
Deals Gtwy LEW SE13 144 E2
Deal St WCHPL E1 104 C4
Dealtry Rd PUT/ROE SW15 139 F5
Deal Wk BRXN/ST SW9 142 B1
Dean Bradley St WEST SW1P 16 E5
Dean Cl BERM/RHTH SE16 124 A1
HOM E9 86 E3
Dean Ct ALP/SUD HA0 79 H1
Deancross St WCHPL E1 104 E5
Dean Dr STAN HA7 44 A5
Deane Av RSLP HA4 77 F3
Deane Ct NTHWD HA6 * 40 C4
Deane Croft Rd PIN HA5 59 G3
Deanery Cl EFNCH N2 65 J1
Deanery Ms
MYFR/PKLN W1K * 9 H7
Deanery Rd SRTFD E15 88 C4
Deanery St MYFR/PKLN W1K 9 H7
Deane Wy RSLP HA4 59 F3
Dean Farrar St STJSPK SW1H 16 D4
Deanfield Gdns
CROY/NA CR0 * 211 K2
Dean Gdns WALTH E17 70 B1
Deanhill Ct
MORT/ESHN SW14 * 137 J5
Deanhill Rd
MORT/ESHN SW14 137 J5
Dean Rd CRICK NW2 82 A4
CROY/NA CR0 211 K2
HPTN TW12 173 F1
HSLW TW3 135 G6
THMD SE28 109 G6
Dean Ryle St WEST SW1P 16 E6
Deansbrook Cl EDGW HA8 44 E3
Deansbrook Rd EDGW HA8 44 D3
Dean's Blds WALW SE17 19 F7
Deans Cl CHSWK W4 117 J6
CROY/NA CR0 212 B1
EDGW HA8 44 E2
Dean's Ct STP EC4M 12 B4
Deanscroft Av
CDALE/KGS NW9 62 E6
Deans Dr PLMGR N13 49 H2
Dean's Dr EDGW HA8 45 F1
Deans Gate Cl FSTH SE23 164 A5
Dean's La EDGW HA8 44 E2
Dean's Ms CAVSQ/HST W1G * 9 K3
Deans Rd SUT SM1 209 F1
Dean's Rd HNWL W7 116 A2
Dean Stanley St WEST SW1P 16 E5
Dean St FSTGT E7 88 E3
SOHO/SHAV W1D 10 C4
Deans Wy EDGW HA8 44 E1
Deansway ED N9 36 A5
EFNCH N2 65 H1
Deans Yd WEST SW1P 16 D4
Dean Trench St WEST SW1P 16 E5
Dean Wy NWDGN UB2 115 G2
Dearne Cl STAN HA7 43 G1
De'Arn Gdns MTCM CR4 178 D6
Dearsley Rd EN EN1 24 C4
Deason St SRTFD E15 * 88 A6
De Barowe Ms HBRY N5 85 H2
Debden Cl CDALE/KGS NW9 45 G4
KUTN/CMB KT2 174 E1
WFD IG8 53 H3
De Beauvoir Crs IS N1 86 A6
De Beauvoir Est IS N1 * 86 A6
De Beauvoir Rd IS N1 86 A5
De Beauvoir Sq IS N1 86 A5
Debnams Rd
BERM/RHTH SE16 123 K4
De Bohun Av STHGT/OAK N14 34 B1
Deborah Cl ISLW TW7 135 K2
Deborah Crs RSLP HA4 58 B4
Debrabant Cl ERITH DA8 130 A6
De Broome Rd FELT TW13 154 B3
Deburgh Rd WIM/MER SW19 178 B3
Decima St STHWK SE1 19 G4
Decimus Cl THHTH CR7 196 E1
Deck Cl BERM/RHTH SE16 124 A1
Decoy Av GLDGN NW11 64 C2
De Crespigny Pk CMBW SE5 142 E3
Deeley Rd VX/NE SW8 141 J2
Deena Cl ACT W3 98 B5
Deepdale WIM/MER SW19 159 G6
Deepdale Av HAYES BR2 199 J1
Deepdale Cl FBAR/BDGN N11 48 A2
Deepdene Av CROY/NA CR0 212 B1
Deepdene Cl WAN E11 70 E1
Deepdene Ct WCHMH N21 35 H1
Deepdene Gdns
BRXS/STRHM SW2 162 A2
Deepdene Rd HNHL SE24 142 D5
WELL DA16 148 B4
Deepwell Cl ISLW TW7 136 B2
Deepwood La GFD/PVL UB6 96 D2
Deerbrook Rd HNHL SE24 162 C3
Deerdale Rd HNHL SE24 142 D5
Deere Av RAIN RM13 93 J4
Deerfield Cl CDALE/KGS NW9 63 H2
Deerhurst Cl FELT TW13 153 K6
Deerhurst Crs HPTN TW12 173 H1
Deerhurst Rd
KIL/WHAMP NW6 82 B5
STRHM/NOR SW16 180 A1
Deerings Dr PIN HA5 58 E2
Deerleap Gv CHING E4 25 K6
Dee Rd RCH/KEW TW9 137 G5
Deer Park Cl KUTN/CMB KT2 175 J3
Deer Park Gdns MTCM CR4 * 194 C1
Deer Park Rd WIM/MER SW19 178 A5
Deer Park Wy WWKM BR4 199 J6
Deeside Rd TOOT SW17 160 C5
Dee St POP/IOD E14 106 A5
Dee Wy ROM RM1 57 G4
Defence Cl THMD SE28 127 K1
Defiant Wy WLGTN SM6 210 E5
Defoe Av RCH/KEW TW9 137 H1
Defoe Cl TOOT SW17 178 D2
Defoe Pl TOOT SW17 160 D4
Defoe Rd BERM/RHTH SE16 124 C2
STNW/STAM N16 68 A6
Defoe Wy CRW RM5 56 C2
De Frene Rd SYD SE26 164 A6
De Gama Pl POP/IOD E14 124 D5
Degema Rd CHST BR7 185 G1
Dehar Crs CDALE/KGS NW9 63 H4
De Haviland Dr
WOOL/PLUM SE18 127 G5
Dehavilland Cl NTHLT UB5 95 H2
De Havilland Ct IL IG1 72 D5
De Havilland Rd EDGW HA8 44 D5
HEST TW5 134 B1
De Havilland Wy
STWL/WRAY TW19 152 A1
Dekker Rd DUL SE21 163 F1
Delacourt Rd BKHTH/KID SE3 146 A1
Delafield Rd CHARL SE7 126 A5
Delaford Rd
BERM/RHTH SE16 123 J5
Delaford St FUL/PGN SW6 139 H1
Delamare Crs CROY/NA CR0 197 K3
Delamere Gdns MLHL NW7 45 F1
Delamere Rd EA W5 117 F1
RYNPK SW20 177 G4
YEAD UB4 95 H6
Delamere St BAY/PAD W2 101 G4
Delamere Ter BAY/PAD W2 101 F4
Delancey Pas CAMTN NW1 3 K1
Delancey St CAMTN NW1 3 K1
De Lapre Cl STMC/STPC BR5 202 E4
De Laune St LBTH SE11 122 C6
Delaware Rd MV/WKIL W9 101 F3
Delawyk Crs HNHL SE24 162 E1
Delcombe Av WPK KT4 193 F5
Delhi Rd EN EN1 36 B2
Delhi St IS N1 5 F1
Delia St WAND/EARL SW18 160 A2
Delisle Rd THMD SE28 127 K1
Delius Cl BORE WD6 29 J1
Delius Gv SRTFD E15 106 A1
Della Pth CLPT E5 86 C1
Dellbow Rd
EBED/NFELT TW14 134 A6
Dell Cl SRTFD E15 88 B6
WFD IG8 39 F5
WLGTN SM6 210 C2
Dell Farm Rd RSLP HA4 58 B2
Dellfield Cl BECK BR3 183 F4
Dell La EW KT17 207 J3
Dellors Cl BAR EN5 20 B6
Dellow Cl GNTH/NBYPK IG2 72 D4
Dellow St WCHPL E1 104 D6
Dell Rd EW KT17 207 J4
PEND EN3 24 E1
WDR/YW UB7 112 C3
Dells Cl CHING E4 37 K2
TEDD TW11 174 A2
Dell's Ms PIM SW1V * 16 B7
The Dell ABYW SE2 128 B5
ALP/SUD HA0 79 H3
BECK BR3 * 182 D3
BTFD TW8 116 D6
BXLY DA5 170 B3
EBED/NFELT TW14 154 A2
NRWD SE19 181 G4
NTHWD HA6 26 C4
PIN HA5 41 H5
WFD IG8 39 F5
Dell Wk NWMAL KT3 176 B5
Dell Wy WEA W13 97 J5
Dellwood Gdns CLAY IG5 54 A6
Delme Crs BKHTH/KID SE3 146 A3
Delmey Cl CROY/NA CR0 212 B1
Deloraine St DEPT SE8 144 D2
Delorme St HMSMTH W6 119 G6
Delta Cl WPK KT4 207 G1
Delta Est BETH E2 * 104 C2
Delta Gain OXHEY WD19 27 H4
Delta Gv NTHLT UB5 95 H2
Delta Rd WPK KT4 207 G1
Delta St BETH E2 * 104 C2
De Luci Rd ERITH DA8 129 K5
De Lucy St ABYW SE2 128 C4
Delvers Md DAGE RM10 92 E2
Delverton Rd WALW SE17 122 C5
Delvino Rd FUL/PGN SW6 139 K2
Demesne Rd WLGTN SM6 210 D2
Demeta Cl WBLY HA9 80 E1
De Montfort Pde
STRHM/NOR SW16 * 161 K5
De Montfort Rd
STRHM/NOR SW16 161 J4
De Morgan Rd
FUL/PGN SW6 140 A4
Dempster Cl SURB KT6 190 D4
Dempster Rd
WAND/EARL SW18 140 B6
Denbar Pde ROMW/RG RM7 * 74 E1
Denberry Dr SCUP DA14 168 C5
Denbigh Cl CHST BR7 184 E2
NTGHL W11 100 D6
STHL UB1 95 K5
SUT SM1 208 D3
Denbigh Dr HYS/HAR UB3 113 F2
Denbigh Gdns
RCHPK/HAM TW10 137 G6
Denbigh Pl PIM SW1V * 121 H5
Denbigh Rd EHAM E6 107 H2
HSLW TW3 135 G3
NTGHL W11 100 D6
STHL UB1 95 K5
WEA W13 97 H6
Denbigh St PIM SW1V 16 A7
Denbigh Ter NTGHL W11 100 D6
Denbridge Rd BMLY BR1 184 E5
Den Cl BECK BR3 199 G1
Dendy St BAL SW12 161 F3
Dene Av BFN/LL DA15 168 C2
HSLW TW3 134 E4
Dene Cl BROCKY SE4 144 B4
HAYES BR2 199 J5
LEY E10 69 K6
RDART DA2 170 B6
WPK KT4 192 C6
Dene Dr ORP BR6 217 H1
Dene Gdns STAN HA7 43 J1
THDIT KT7 190 B6
Denehurst Gdns ACT W3 117 J1
HDN NW4 64 A3
RCHPK/HAM TW10 137 H5
WFD IG8 39 F6
WHTN TW2 155 J2
Dene Rd BKHH IG9 39 J3
DART DA1 171 J2
NTHWD HA6 40 A2
TRDG/WHET N20 33 K3
The Dene CROY/NA CR0 213 F2
E/WMO/HCT KT8 188 E2
WBLY HA9 80 A2
WEA W13 97 H4
Denewood BAR EN5 21 G6
Denewood Rd HGT N6 65 J3
Dengie Wk IS N1 * 85 J6
Denham Cl WELL DA16 148 D4
Denham Crs MTCM CR4 194 E1
Denham Dr GNTH/NBYPK IG2 72 C3
Denham Rd
EBED/NFELT TW14 154 B2
TRDG/WHET N20 33 K4
Denham Wy BARK IG11 90 E6
Denholme Rd MV/WKIL W9 100 D2
Denholme Wk RAIN RM13 93 H4
Denison Cl EFNCH N2 47 G6
Denison Rd EA W5 97 J3
FELT TW13 153 J6
WIM/MER SW19 178 C2
Deniston Av BXLY DA5 168 E3
Denleigh Gdns THDIT KT7 * 189 K3
WCHMH N21 35 G2
Denman Dr ESH/CLAY KT10 205 G3
GLDGN NW11 64 E2
Denman Dr North
GLDGN NW11 64 E2
Denman Dr South
GLDGN NW11 64 E2
Denman Rd PECK SE15 143 G2
Denman St SOHO/SHAV W1D 10 B6
Denmark Av WIM/MER SW19 177 H3
Denmark Ct MRDN SM4 193 K2
Denmark Gdns CAR SM5 209 K1
Denmark Gv IS N1 5 J2
Denmark Hl HNHL SE24 142 E5
Denmark Hill Dr
CDALE/KGS NW9 45 J6
Denmark Rd BMLY BR1 184 A4
CAR SM5 209 K1
CEND/HSY/T N8 67 F1
CMBW SE5 142 D2
KIL/WHAMP NW6 100 D1
KUT/HW KT1 175 F6
SNWD SE25 197 J2
WEA W13 97 H6
WHTN TW2 155 J5
WIM/MER SW19 177 G2
Denmark St LSQ/SEVD WC2H 10 D4
PLSTW E13 107 F4
TOTM N17 50 D4
WAN E11 88 C1
Denmark Ter EFNCH N2 * 47 K6
Denmead Rd CROY/NA CR0 196 C5
Dennan Rd SURB KT6 191 G5
Denner Rd CHING E4 37 J4
Denne Ter HACK E8 7 K1
Dennett Rd CROY/NA CR0 196 B4
Dennett's Gv NWCR SE14 144 A3
Dennett's Rd NWCR SE14 143 K2
Denning Av CROY/NA CR0 211 G3
Denning Cl HPTN TW12 172 E2
STJWD NW8 101 G2
Denning Ms BAL SW12 161 F1
Denning Rd HAMP NW3 83 H2
Dennington Park Rd
KIL/WHAMP NW6 82 E4
The Denningtons WPK KT4 192 B6
Dennis Av WBLY HA9 80 B3
Dennis Gdns STAN HA7 43 J1
Dennis La STAN HA7 29 H6
Dennis Pde STHGT/OAK N14 * 34 D3
Dennis Park Crs RYNPK SW20 177 H4
Dennis Reeve Cl MTCM CR4 178 E4
Dennis Rd E/WMO/HCT KT8 189 H1
Dennis Wy CLAP SW4 141 J4
Denny Crs LBTH SE11 122 B5
Denny Gdns DAGW RM9 91 H5
Denny Rd ED N9 36 D3
Denny St LBTH SE11 122 B5
Den Rd HAYES BR2 183 G6
Densham Rd SRTFD E15 88 C6
Densole Cl BECK BR3 * 182 B4
Densworth Gv ED N9 36 E4
Denton Cl BAR EN5 20 A6
Denton Gv WOT/HER KT12 188 D6
Denton Rd BXLY DA5 170 B3
CEND/HSY/T N8 67 F2
DART DA1 170 B2
TWK TW1 156 E1
UED N18 36 A6
WELL DA16 148 D1
Denton St WAND/EARL SW18 160 A1
Denton Ter BXLY DA5 * 170 B4
Denton Wy CLPT E5 87 F1
Dents Rd BTSEA SW11 160 E1
Denvale Trade Pk MTCM CR4 194 C1
Denver Cl ORP BR6 201 K3
Denver Rd DART DA1 170 D2
STNW/STAM N16 68 A4
Denyer St CHEL SW3 14 D6
Denzil Rd WLSDN NW10 81 H3
Deodar Rd PUT/ROE SW15 139 H5
Deodora Cl TRDG/WHET N20 33 J5
Depot Ap CRICK NW2 82 B2
Depot Rd HSLW TW3 135 J4
SHB W12 100 A6
Depot St CMBW SE5 122 E6
Deptford Br DEPT SE8 144 D2
Deptford Broadway
NWCR SE14 144 D2
Deptford Church St DEPT SE8 124 D6
Deptford Gn DEPT SE8 124 D6
Deptford High St DEPT SE8 124 D6
Deptford Market DEPT SE8 * 144 D1
Deptford Whf DEPT SE8 124 C4
De Quincey Ms CAN/RD E16 125 K1
De Quincey Rd TOTM N17 49 K4
Derby Av KTN/HRWW/WS HA3 42 D4
NFNCH/WDSPK N12 47 G1
ROMW/RG RM7 74 D3
Derby Ga WHALL SW1A 16 E2
Derby Hl FSTH SE23 163 K4
Derby Hill Crs FSTH SE23 163 K4
Derby Rd BRYLDS KT5 191 H5
CROY/NA CR0 196 C6
FSTGT E7 89 H5
GFD/PVL UB6 78 B6
HOM E9 87 F6
HSLW TW3 135 G5
MORT/ESHN SW14 137 J5
PEND EN3 24 D6
SUT SM1 208 D4
SWFD E18 52 D4
UED N18 50 E1
WIM/MER SW19 177 K3
Derbyshire St BETH E2 104 C2
Derby St MYFR/PICC W1J 15 H1
Dereham Pl CRW RM5 56 D2
SDTCH EC2A 7 H6
Dereham Rd BARK IG11 91 F4
Derek Av HOR/WEW KT19 206 C4
WBLY HA9 80 D5
WLGTN SM6 210 B2
Derek Cl HOR/WEW KT19 206 D3
Derek Walcott Cl HNHL SE24 * 142 C6
Deri Av RAIN RM13 111 K3
Dericote St HACK E8 86 C6
Deri Dene Cl
STWL/WRAY TW19 * 152 B1
Derifall Cl EHAM E6 107 K4
Dering Pl CROY/NA CR0 211 J2
Dering Rd CROY/NA CR0 211 J2
Dering St OXSTW W1C 9 J4
Derinton Rd TOOT SW17 161 F6
Derley Rd NWDGN UB2 114 B3
Dermody Gdns LEW SE13 * 145 G6
Dermody Rd LEW SE13 145 G6
Deronda Rd HNHL SE24 162 C3
Deroy Cl CAR SM5 209 K4
Derrick Gdns CHARL SE7 126 B3
Derrick Rd BECK BR3 182 C6
Derry Downs STMC/STPC BR5 202 D3
Derry Rd CROY/NA CR0 210 E1
Derry St KENS W8 120 A2
Dersingham Av MNPK E12 89 K2
Dersingham Rd CRICK NW2 82 C1
Derwent Av CDALE/KGS NW9 63 G2
EBAR EN4 33 K3
MLHL NW7 45 F1
PIN HA5 41 J2
PUT/ROE SW15 158 B6
UED N18 49 K1
Derwent Cl DART DA1 170 E3
EBED/NFELT TW14 153 J3
ESH/CLAY KT10 204 E4
Derwent Crs BXLYHN DA7 149 H3
NFNCH/WDSPK N12 33 G5
STAN HA7 43 J5
Derwent Dr STMC/STPC BR5 201 J4
YEAD UB4 94 C4
Derwent Gdns REDBR IG4 71 J1
WBLY HA9 61 J4
Derwent Gv EDUL SE22 143 G5
Derwent Ri CDALE/KGS NW9 63 G3
Derwent Rd EA W5 116 D3
PGE/AN SE20 181 H5
PLMGR N13 35 F6
RYNPK SW20 193 G3
STHL UB1 95 K5
WHTN TW2 155 G1
Derwent St GNWCH SE10 125 H5
Derwentwater Rd ACT W3 117 K1
Derwent Wy HCH RM12 93 K3
Derwent Yd EA W5 * 116 D3
De Salis Rd HGDN/ICK UB10 94 A3
Desenfans Rd DUL SE21 163 F1
Desford Rd CAN/RD E16 106 C3
Desford Wy ASHF TW15 152 C4
Desmond St NWCR SE14 124 B6
Desmond Tutu Dr FSTH SE23 164 B3
Despard Rd ARCH N19 66 C5
Desvignes Dr LEW SE13 165 G1
Detling Rd BMLY BR1 183 K1
ERITH DA8 150 A1
Detmold Rd CLPT E5 68 D6
Devalls Cl EHAM E6 108 A6
Devana End CAR SM5 209 K1
Devas Rd RYNPK SW20 177 F4
Devas St BOW E3 105 K3
Devenay Rd SRTFD E15 88 D5
Devenish Rd ABYW SE2 128 B2
Deveraux Cl BECK BR3 199 F2
De Vere Cl WLGTN SM6 210 E5
De Vere Gdns IL IG1 71 K5
KENS W8 120 B2
Deverell St STHWK SE1 18 E5
De Vere Ms KENS W8 * 120 B3
Devereux Ct TPL/STR WC2R 11 J5
Devereux La BARN SW13 138 E1
Devereux Rd BTSEA SW11 160 E1
Deveron Wy ROM RM1 57 G4
Devey Cl KUTN/CMB KT2 176 C3
Devizes St IS N1 * 7 F1
Devoke Wy WOT/HER KT12 188 C6
Devon Av WHTN TW2 155 H3
Devon Cl BKHH IG9 39 F4
GFD/PVL UB6 79 J6
TOTM N17 50 B6
Devoncroft Gdns TWK TW1 156 B2
Devon Gdns FSBYPK N4 67 H3
Devonhurst Pl CHSWK W4 * 118 A5
Devonia Gdns UED N18 49 J2
Devonia Rd IS N1 6 B2
Devon Man
KTN/HRWW/WS HA3 * 61 J2
Devonport Gdns IL IG1 71 K3
Devonport Ms SHB W12 * 118 E1
Devonport Rd SHB W12 118 E1
Devonport St WCHPL E1 104 E5
Devon Ri EFNCH N2 65 H1
Devon Rd BARK IG11 90 E6
BELMT SM2 208 C6
Devons Est BOW E3 105 K2
Devonshire Av BELMT SM2 209 G5
DART DA1 170 E1
Devonshire Cl
CAVSQ/HST W1G 9 J1
SRTFD E15 88 C2
Devonshire Ct FELT TW13 * 154 A4
Devonshire Crs MLHL NW7 46 B3
Devonshire Dr GNWCH SE10 144 E2
SURB KT6 190 E5
Devonshire Gdns CHSWK W4 137 K1
TOTM N17 49 J2
WCHMH N21 35 J2
Devonshire Gv PECK SE15 123 J6
Devonshire Hill La TOTM N17 49 J2
Devonshire Ms CHSWK W4 118 B5
Devonshire Ms South
CAVSQ/HST W1G 9 J1
Devonshire Ms West
CAVSQ/HST W1G 3 H7
Devonshire Pl
CAVSQ/HST W1G 3 H7
CRICK NW2 82 E1
KENS W8 120 A3
Devonshire Place Ms
CAVSQ/HST W1G 3 H7
Devonshire Rd BELMT SM2 209 G5
BXLYHS DA6 149 F5
CAN/RD E16 107 F5
CAR SM5 210 A2
CHSWK W4 118 B5
CROY/NA CR0 196 E4
EA W5 116 D3
ED N9 36 E3
ELTH/MOT SE9 166 D4
FELT TW13 154 D5
FSTH SE23 164 A2
GNTH/NBYPK IG2 72 D4
HRW HA1 60 D3
MLHL NW7 46 B3
ORP BR6 202 B4
PIN HA5 59 G3
PLMGR N13 35 F6
STHL UB1 96 A4

TOTM N17 49 J2
WALTH E17 69 J3
WIM/MER SW19 178 D3
Devonshire Rw LVPST EC2M 13 H2
Devonshire Row Ms
GTPST W1W 3 K7
Devonshire Sq HAYES BR2 200 A1
LVPST EC2M 13 H3
Devonshire St
CAVSQ/HST W1G 9 H1
CHSWK W4 118 B5
Devonshire Ter BAY/PAD W2 101 G5
EDUL SE22 * 143 H5
Devonshire Wy CROY/NA CR0 198 C6
YEAD UB4 95 F5
Devons Rd BOW E3 105 J4
Devon St PECK SE15 123 J6
Devon Wy CHSGTN KT9 205 J2
HOR/WEW KT19 206 D3
Devon Waye HEST TW5 134 E1
De Walden St
CAVSQ/HST W1G 9 H2
Dewar St PECK SE15 143 H4
Dewberry Gdns EHAM E6 107 J4
Dewberry St POP/IOD E14 106 A5
Dewey La BRXS/STRHM SW2 162 B1
Dewey Rd DAGE RM10 92 E4
IS N1 5 J2
Dewey St TOOT SW17 178 E1
Dewhurst Rd HMSMTH W6 119 G3
Dewsbury Cl PIN HA5 59 J3
Dewsbury Gdns WPK KT4 207 J1
Dewsbury Rd WLSDN NW10 81 J3
Dexter Rd BAR EN5 32 B1
Deyncourt Rd TOTM N17 49 J4
Deynecourt Gdns WAN E11 71 G1
D'Eynsford Rd CMBW SE5 142 E1
CMBW SE5 142 E2
Diadem Ct SOHO/CST W1F * 10 C3
Diamedes Av
STWL/WRAY TW19 152 A2
Diameter Rd STMC/STPC BR5 201 G4
Diamond Cl BCTR RM8 73 J5
Diamond Rd RSLP HA4 77 H2
Diamond St CMBW SE5 143 F1
WLSDN NW10 81 F5
Diamond Ter GNWCH SE10 145 F1
Diana Cl DEPT SE8 124 C6
SCUP DA14 169 F4
SWFD E18 53 F4
Diana Gdns SURB KT6 191 G6
Diana Rd WALTH E17 51 H6
Dianne Wy EBAR EN4 21 J5
Dianthus Cl ABYW SE2 * 128 C5
Diban Av HCH RM12 93 K2
Dibden St IS N1 85 J6
Dibdin Cl SUT SM1 208 E1
Dibdin Rd SUT SM1 208 E1
Dicey Av CRICK NW2 82 A3
Dickens Av DART DA1 151 K5
FNCH N3 47 G4
Dickens Cl ERITH DA8 149 J1
HYS/HAR UB3 113 H4
RCHPK/HAM TW10 157 F4
Dickens Dr CHST BR7 185 H2
Dickens Est
BERM/RHTH SE16 * 123 H3
Dickens La UED N18 50 A1
Dickens Ms FARR EC1M 6 A7
Dickenson Cl ED N9 36 C3
Dickenson Rd
CEND/HSY/T N8 66 E4
FELT TW13 172 B1
Dickenson's La SNWD SE25 197 H3
Dickenson's Pl SNWD SE25 197 H3
Dickens Rd EHAM E6 107 H1
Dickens Sq STHWK SE1 18 D4
Dickens St VX/NE SW8 141 G3
Dickens Wy ROM RM1 75 G1
Dickens Wood Cl NRWD SE19 180 C3
Dickerage La NWMAL KT3 175 K6
Dickerage Rd NWMAL KT3 175 K5
Dickson Fold PIN HA5 59 H1
Dickson House CHARL SE7 * 146 D1
Dickson Rd ELTH/MOT SE9 146 D4
Dick Turpin Wy
EBED/NFELT TW14 133 J5
Didsbury Cl EHAM E6 89 K6
Digby Crs FSBYPK N4 67 J6
Digby Gdns DAGE RM10 92 C6
Digby Pl CROY/NA CR0 212 B1
Digby Rd BARK IG11 91 F5
HOM E9 87 F4
Digby St BETH E2 104 E2
Diggon St WCHPL E1 105 F4
Dighton Rd WAND/EARL SW18 140 B6
Dignum St IS N1 * 5 J2
Digswell St HOLWY N7 * 85 G4
Dilhorne Cl LEE/GVPK SE12 166 A5
Dilke St CHEL SW3 120 E6
Dillwyn Cl SYD SE26 164 B6
Dilston Cl NTHLT UB5 95 G2
Dilton Gdns PUT/ROE SW15 158 D3
Dimes Pl HMSMTH W6 118 E4
Dimmock Dr GFD/PVL UB6 78 D3
Dimond Cl FSTGT E7 88 E2
Dimsdale Dr CDALE/KGS NW9 62 E5
EN EN1 36 C2
Dimsdale Wk PLSTW E13 88 E6
Dimson Crs BOW E3 105 J3
Dingle Cl BAR EN5 31 H1
Dingle Gdns POP/IOD E14 * 105 J6
Dingley La STRHM/NOR SW16 161 J4
Dingley Pl FSBYE EC1V 6 D5
Dingley Rd FSBYE EC1V 6 C5
Dingwall Av CROY/NA CR0 196 D6
Dingwall Gdns GLDGN NW11 64 E3
Dingwall Rd CAR SM5 209 K6
CROY/NA CR0 196 E6
WAND/EARL SW18 160 B2
Dinmont St BETH E2 104 D1
Dinsdale Gdns BAR EN5 21 F6
SNWD SE25 197 F2
Dinsdale Rd BKHTH/KID SE3 125 J6
Dinsmore Rd BAL SW12 161 G2
Dinton Rd KUTN/CMB KT2 175 G3
WIM/MER SW19 178 C2
Diploma Av EFNCH N2 65 J1
Dirleton Rd SRTFD E15 88 D6
Disbrowe Rd HMSMTH W6 119 H6
Discovery Wk WAP E1W 104 D6
Dishforth La CDALE/KGS NW9 45 G4
Disney Pl STHWK SE1 18 D2
Disney St STHWK SE1 18 D2
Dison Cl PEND EN3 25 F2
Disraeli Cl THMD SE28 128 C1
Disraeli Rd EA W5 116 E1
FSTGT E7 88 E4
PUT/ROE SW15 139 H5
WLSDN NW10 98 E1
Diss St BETH E2 7 J4
Distaff La BLKFR EC4V 12 C5
Distillery La HMSMTH W6 119 F5
Distillery Rd HMSMTH W6 119 F5
Distin St LBTH SE11 17 J7
District Rd ALP/SUD HA0 79 H3
Ditchburn St POP/IOD E14 106 A6
Ditchfield Rd YEAD UB4 95 J3
Dittisham Rd ELTH/MOT SE9 166 D6
Ditton Cl THDIT KT7 190 B4
Dittoncroft Cl CROY/NA CR0 212 A2
Ditton Grange Cl SURB KT6 190 E5
Ditton Grange Dr SURB KT6 190 E5
Ditton Hl SURB KT6 190 D5
Ditton Hill Rd SURB KT6 190 D5
Ditton Lawn THDIT KT7 190 B5
Ditton Pl PGE/AN SE20 * 181 J4
Ditton Reach THDIT KT7 190 C3
Ditton Rd BXLYHS DA6 148 E6
NWDGN UB2 114 E5
SURB KT6 191 F5
Divisional Rd MNPK E12 89 H1
Dixey Cots EFNCH N2 * 65 J2
Dixon Cl EHAM E6 107 K5
Dixon Pl WWKM BR4 198 E5
Dixon Rd NWCR SE14 144 B2
SNWD SE25 181 F6
Dixon Wy WLSDN NW10 81 G5
Dobbin Cl
KTN/HRWW/WS HA3 43 G5
Dobell Rd ELTH/MOT SE9 146 E6
Dobree Av WLSDN NW10 81 K5
Dobson Cl KIL/WHAMP NW6 83 H5
Dockers Tanner Rd
POP/IOD E14 124 D4
Dockhead STHWK SE1 19 K3
Dock Hill Av
BERM/RHTH SE16 124 A2
Dockland St CAN/RD E16 127 F1
Dockley Rd BERM/RHTH SE16 123 H3
Dock Rd BTFD TW8 * 136 E1
CAN/RD E16 106 D6
Dockside Rd CAN/RD E16 107 H6
Dock St WCHPL E1 104 C6
Dockwell Cl
EBED/NFELT TW14 133 K5
Doctors Cl SYD SE26 181 K1
Docwra's Blds IS N1 86 A4
Dodbrooke Rd WNWD SE27 162 B5
Doddington Gv WALW SE17 122 C6
Doddington Pl LBTH SE11 122 C6
Dodsley Pl ED N9 36 E5
Dodson St STHWK SE1 17 K3
Dod St POP/IOD E14 105 J5
Doebury Wk
WOOL/PLUM SE18 128 B6
Doel Cl WIM/MER SW19 178 B3
Doggett Rd CAT SE6 164 D2
Doggetts Ct EBAR EN4 21 J6
Doghurst Av WDR/YW UB7 132 E1
Doghurst Dr WDR/YW UB7 132 E1
Dog Kennel Hl CMBW SE5 143 F4
Dog La WLSDN NW10 81 G2
Dog Rose Ramble NTHLT UB5 77 H6
YEAD UB4 76 E6
Dog Rose Ramble & Hillingdon
Trail YEAD UB4 94 D1
Doherty Rd PLSTW E13 106 E3
Dolben Ct DEPT SE8 * 124 C4
Dolben St STHWK SE1 * 18 B1
Dolby Rd FUL/PGN SW6 139 J3
Dolland St LBTH SE11 122 A5
Dollary Pde KUT/HW KT1 * 175 J6
Dollis Av FNCH N3 46 D4
Dollis Crs RSLP HA4 59 G5
Dollis Hill Av CRICK NW2 81 K1
Dollis Hill Est CRICK NW2 * 81 J1
Dollis Hill La CRICK NW2 81 H2
Dollis Pk FNCH N3 46 D4
Dollis Rd MLHL NW7 46 C4
Dollis Valley Dr BAR EN5 20 D6
Dollis Valley Green Wk
FNCH N3 64 C1
TRDG/WHET N20 33 F5
Dollis Valley Wy EBAR EN4 21 H5
Dolman Cl FNCH N3 47 G5
Dolman Rd CHSWK W4 118 A4
Dolman St CLAP SW4 142 A5
Dolphin Ap ROM RM1 75 H1
Dolphin Cl BERM/RHTH SE16 124 A2
SURB KT6 190 E3
THMD SE28 109 J5
Dolphin La POP/IOD E14 105 K6
Dolphin Rd NTHLT UB5 95 K1
Dolphin Sq CHSWK W4 * 138 B1
PIM SW1V 121 H5
Dolphin St KUT/HW KT1 175 F5
Dombey St BMSBY WC1N 11 G1
Dome Blds RCH/KEW TW9 * 136 E6
Dome Hill Pk SYD SE26 163 G6
Domett Cl CMBW SE5 142 E5
Domingo St FSBYE EC1V 6 C6
Dominica Cl PLSTW E13 107 H2
Dominion Cl HSLW TW3 135 J3
Dominion Dr CRW RM5 56 D2
Dominion Pde HRW HA1 * 61 F2
Dominion Rd CROY/NA CR0 197 G4
NWDGN UB2 114 D3
Dominion St LVPST EC2M 13 F1
Dominion Wy RAIN RM13 111 J2
Domonic Dr ELTH/MOT SE9 167 G5
Domville Cl TRDG/WHET N20 33 H4
Donald Dr CHDH RM6 73 J2
Donald Rd CROY/NA CR0 196 A3
PLSTW E13 89 F6
Donaldson Rd
KIL/WHAMP NW6 82 D6
WOOL/PLUM SE18 147 F2
Donald Woods Gdns
BRYLDS KT5 191 J6
Doncaster Dr NTHLT UB5 77 K3
Doncaster Gdns FSBYPK N4 * 67 J3
NTHLT UB5 77 K3
Doncaster Gn OXHEY WD19 41 G1
Doncaster Rd ED N9 36 D2
Donegal St IS N1 5 H3
Doneraile St FUL/PGN SW6 139 G3
Dongola Rd PLSTW E13 107 F2
TOTM N17 50 A6
WCHPL E1 105 G4
Dongola Rd West PLSTW E13 107 F2
Donington Av BARK/HLT IG6 72 C2
Donkey Aly EDUL SE22 163 H2
Donkey La EN EN1 24 C3
Donnefield Av EDGW HA8 44 A2
Donne Pl CHEL SW3 14 D6
MTCM CR4 195 G1
Donne Rd BCTR RM8 73 J6
Donnington Rd
KTN/HRWW/WS HA3 61 K3
WLSDN NW10 81 K6
WPK KT4 192 D6
Donnybrook Rd
STRHM/NOR SW16 179 H3
Donoghue Cots
POP/IOD E14 * 105 G4
Donovan Av MUSWH N10 48 B5
Donovan Pl WCHMH N21 23 F6
Don Phelan Cl CMBW SE5 142 E2
Don Wy ROM RM1 57 G3
Doone Cl TEDD TW11 174 B2
Doon St STHWK SE1 11 J7
Dorado Gdns ORP BR6 217 K1
Doral Wy CAR SM5 209 K3
Dorando Cl SHB W12 * 99 K6
Doran Gv WOOL/PLUM SE18 147 K1
Dora Rd WIM/MER SW19 177 K1
Dora St POP/IOD E14 105 H5
Dora Wy BRXN/ST SW9 142 B3
Dorchester Av BXLY DA5 168 E3
PLMGR N13 35 J6
RYLN/HDSTN HA2 60 C3
Dorchester Cl DART DA1 171 J2
ESH/CLAY KT10 190 A6
NTHLT UB5 78 B3
STMC/STPC BR5 186 C3
Dorchester Ct CRICK NW2 82 A1
HNHL SE24 142 D6
STHGT/OAK N14 34 B2
Dorchester Dr
EBED/NFELT TW14 153 H1
HNHL SE24 142 D6
Dorchester Gdns CHING E4 37 J6
GLDGN NW11 * 64 E1
Dorchester Gv CHSWK W4 118 B6
Dorchester Ms TWK TW1 156 D1
Dorchester Pde
STRHM/NOR SW16 * 161 K4
Dorchester Rd MRDN SM4 194 A4
NTHLT UB5 78 B3
WPK KT4 193 F5
Dorchester Ter HDN NW4 * 46 B5
Dorchester Wy
KTN/HRWW/WS HA3 62 B2
Dorchester Waye YEAD UB4 95 F5
Dorcis Av BXLYHN DA7 149 F3
Dordrecht Rd ACT W3 118 B1
Dore Av MNPK E12 90 A3
Doreen Av CDALE/KGS NW9 63 F5
Dore Gdns MRDN SM4 194 A4
Dorell Cl STHL UB1 95 K4
Dorian Rd HCH RM12 75 J5
Doria Rd FUL/PGN SW6 139 J3
Doric Wy CAMTN NW1 4 C4
Dorie Ms NFNCH/WDSPK N12 33 F6
Dorien Rd RYNPK SW20 177 G5
Doris Ashby Cl GFD/PVL UB6 79 G6
Doris Av ERITH DA8 149 K2
Doris Rd FSTGT E7 88 E5
Dorking Cl DEPT SE8 124 C6
WPK KT4 193 G6
Dorlcote Rd
WAND/EARL SW18 160 C2
Dorman Pl ED N9 36 C4
Dormans Cl NTHWD HA6 40 B3
Dorman Wy STJWD NW8 83 H6
Dormay St WAND/EARL SW18 140 A6
Dormer Cl BAR EN5 20 B6
SRTFD E15 88 D4
Dormer's Av STHL UB1 96 A5
Dormers Ri STHL UB1 96 B6
Dormer's Wells La STHL UB1 96 A5
Dormywood RSLP HA4 58 D2
Dornberg Cl BKHTH/KID SE3 145 K1
Dornberg Rd
BKHTH/KID SE3 * 146 A1
Dorncliffe Rd FUL/PGN SW6 139 H3
Dorney Ri STMC/STPC BR5 202 A1
Dorney Wy HSLWW TW4 134 D6
Dornfell St KIL/WHAMP NW6 82 D3
Dornton Rd BAL SW12 161 G4
SAND/SEL CR2 212 A3
Dorothy Av ALP/SUD HA0 80 A5
Dorothy Evans Cl
BXLYHN DA7 149 J5
Dorothy Gdns BCTR RM8 91 H2
Dorothy Rd BTSEA SW11 140 E4
Dorrington St HCIRC EC1N 11 J1
Dorrington Wy BECK BR3 199 F2
Dorrit Ms UED N18 36 B6
Dorrit St STHWK SE1 * 18 D2
Dorrit Wy CHST BR7 185 H2
Dors Cl CDALE/KGS NW9 63 F5
Dorset Av NWDGN UB2 115 F4
ROM RM1 57 F6
WELL DA16 148 A5
YEAD UB4 94 C2
Dorset Blds EMB EC4Y * 12 A4
Dorset Cl CAMTN NW1 8 E1
YEAD UB4 * 94 C2
Dorset Dr EDGW HA8 44 B2
Dorset Gdns MTCM CR4 196 A1
Dorset Ms FNCH N3 46 E4
KTBR SW1X 15 J4
Dorset Pl SRTFD E15 88 B4
Dorset Ri EMB EC4Y 12 A4
Dorset Rd ASHF TW15 152 A5
BECK BR3 182 A6
EA W5 116 D3
ELTH/MOT SE9 166 D4
FSTGT E7 89 G5
HRW HA1 60 C3
MTCM CR4 178 D5
SEVS/STOTM N15 67 K1
VX/NE SW8 142 A1
WDGN N22 48 E4
WIM/MER SW19 177 K4
Dorset Sq CAMTN NW1 2 E7
Dorset St MHST W1U 9 F2
Dorset Wy WHTN TW2 155 H3
Dorset Waye HEST TW5 134 E1
Dorton Cl PECK SE15 143 F1
Dorville Crs HMSMTH W6 118 E3
Dorville Rd LEE/GVPK SE12 145 K6
Dothill Rd WOOL/PLUM SE18 147 J1
Douai Gv HPTN TW12 173 H4
Doughty Ms BMSBY WC1N 5 G7
Doughty St BMSBY WC1N 5 G6
Douglas Av ALP/SUD HA0 80 A5
NWMAL KT3 192 E1
WALTH E17 51 J4
Douglas Cl BARK/HLT IG6 54 B3
EBAR EN4 21 H1
STAN HA7 43 G1
WLGTN SM6 210 E4
Douglas Crs YEAD UB4 95 G3
Douglas Dr CROY/NA CR0 213 J1
Douglas Est IS N1 * 85 J4
Douglas Ms CRICK NW2 82 C1
Douglas Pth POP/IOD E14 125 F5
Douglas Pl POP/IOD E14 * 125 F5
Douglas Rd CAN/RD E16 106 E4
CHING E4 38 C2
ESH/CLAY KT10 189 G6
GDMY/SEVK IG3 73 G4
HSLW TW3 135 G4
IS N1 85 J5
KIL/WHAMP NW6 82 D6
KUT/HW KT1 175 J5
ROM RM1 75 H3
STWL/WRAY TW19 152 A1
SURB KT6 191 G6
WDGN N22 49 G4
WELL DA16 148 C2
Douglas Rd North IS N1 85 J4
Douglas Rd South IS N1 * 85 J4
Douglas St WEST SW1P 16 C7
Douglas Ter WALTH E17 51 H4
Douglas Vls KUT/HW KT1 * 175 G5
Douglas Wy NWCR SE14 144 C1
Doulton Ms KIL/WHAMP NW6 83 F4
Dounesforth Gdns
WAND/EARL SW18 160 A3
Douro Pl KENS W8 120 A3
Douro St BOW E3 105 J1
Douthwaite Sq WAP E1W 123 H1
Dove Ap EHAM E6 107 J4
Dove Cl MLHL NW7 45 J3
NTHLT UB5 95 H3
WLGTN SM6 211 F5
Dovecot Cl PIN HA5 59 G2
Dove Ct LOTH EC2R * 12 E4
Dovedale Av CLAY IG5 54 A5
KTN/HRWW/WS HA3 61 J3
Dovedale Cl WELL DA16 148 B2
Dovedale Ri MTCM CR4 178 E3
Dovedale Rd EDUL SE22 143 J6
Dovedon Cl STHGT/OAK N14 34 E4
Dove House Gdns CHING E4 37 J4
Dovehouse Md BARK IG11 108 D1
Dovehouse St CHEL SW3 120 C5
Dove Ms ECT SW5 120 B4
Doveney Cl STMC/STPC BR5 186 D6
Dove Pk PIN HA5 41 K3
Dove Pl ESH/CLAY KT10 205 G6
Dover Cl CRICK NW2 64 B6
CRW RM5 56 E5
Dovercourt Av THHTH CR7 196 B1
Dovercourt Est IS N1 85 K4
Dovercourt Gdns STAN HA7 44 A1
Dovercourt La SUT SM1 209 G1
Dovercourt Rd DUL SE21 163 F1
Doverfield Rd
BRXS/STRHM SW2 161 K1
Dover Gdns CAR SM5 209 K1
Dover House Rd
PUT/ROE SW15 138 D5
Doveridge Gdns PLMGR N13 35 H6
Dove Rd IS N1 85 K4
Dove Rw BETH E2 104 C1
Dover Park Dr PUT/ROE SW15 158 E1
Dover Patrol BKHTH/KID SE3 146 A3
Dover Rd ED N9 36 E4
MNPK E12 71 G6
NRWD SE19 180 E2
WOOL/PLUM SE18 147 G3
Dover St CONDST W1S 9 K6
Dover Ter RCH/KEW TW9 * 137 H3
Dover Yd MYFR/PICC W1J 9 K7
Doves Cl HAYES BR2 200 D6
Doves Yd IS N1 5 J1
Doveton Rd SAND/SEL CR2 211 K3
Doveton St WCHPL E1 104 E3
Dowanhill Rd CAT SE6 165 G3
Dowd Cl FBAR/BDGN N11 34 A4
Dowdeswell Cl
PUT/ROE SW15 138 B5
Dowding Cl HCH RM12 93 K5
Dowding Dr ELTH/MOT SE9 146 B6
Dowding Pl STAN HA7 43 G2
Dowdney Cl KTTN NW5 84 C3
Dower Av WLGTN SM6 210 B6
Dowgate Hl CANST EC4R 12 E5
Dowland St NKENS W10 100 C2
Dowlas St CMBW SE5 143 F1
Dowlerville Rd ORP BR6 217 F4
Dowman Cl WIM/MER SW19 178 A3
Downage HDN NW4 46 A6
Downalong BUSH WD23 28 D3
Downbank Av BXLYHN DA7 150 A2
Down Barns Rd RSLP HA4 77 H2
Down Cl NTHLT UB5 95 F2
Downderry Rd BMLY BR1 165 G5
Downe Cl WELL DA16 148 D1
Downend WOOL/PLUM SE18 147 G1
Downe Rd HAYES BR2 215 J6
MTCM CR4 178 E5
Downes Cl TWK TW1 156 C1
Downes Ct WCHMH N21 35 G3
Downfield WPK KT4 192 C5
Downfield Cl MV/WKIL W9 101 F3
Down Hall Rd KUT/HW KT1 174 E4
Downham Cl CRW RM5 56 C3
Downham La BMLY BR1 183 G1
Downham Rd IS N1 85 K5
Downham Wy BMLY BR1 183 H1
Downhills Av TOTM N17 49 K6
Downhills Park Rd TOTM N17 49 J6
Downhills Wy TOTM N17 49 J5
Downhurst Av MLHL NW7 45 F1
Downing Cl RYLN/HDSTN HA2 42 C6
Downing Dr GFD/PVL UB6 78 E6
Downing Rd DAGW RM9 92 B6
Downings EHAM E6 108 A5
Downing St WHALL SW1A 16 E2
Downland Cl
TRDG/WHET N20 33 G3
Downleys Cl ELTH/MOT SE9 166 D4
Downman Rd ELTH/MOT SE9 146 D4
Down Pl HMSMTH W6 118 E4
Down Rd TEDD TW11 174 C2
Downs Av CHST BR7 184 E1
DART DA1 171 K2
PIN HA5 59 K3
Downs Bridge Rd BECK BR3 183 G4
Downs Court Pde HACK E8 * 86 D3
Downsell Rd SRTFD E15 88 B2
Downsfield Rd WALTH E17 69 G3
Downshall Av GDMY/SEVK IG3 72 E3
Downs Hl BECK BR3 183 G4
Downshire Hl HAMP NW3 83 H2
Downside BECK BR3 * 182 D4
TWK TW1 156 A5
Downside Cl WIM/MER SW19 178 B2
Downside Crs HAMP NW3 83 J3
WEA W13 97 G3
Downside Rd BELMT SM2 209 H4
Downs La CLPT E5 86 D2
Downs Park Rd HACK E8 86 C3
Downs Rd BECK BR3 182 E5
CLPT E5 86 C2
EN EN1 24 A5
THHTH CR7 180 D4
The Downs RYNPK SW20 177 G3
Down St E/WMO/HCT KT8 189 F2
MYFR/PICC W1J 15 J1
Downs Vw ISLW TW7 136 A2
Downsview Gdns NRWD SE19 180 D3
Downsview Rd NRWD SE19 180 D3
Downsway ORP BR6 216 E3
The Downsway BELMT SM2 209 G6
Downton Av
BRXS/STRHM SW2 162 A4
Downtown Rd
BERM/RHTH SE16 124 B2
Downway
NFNCH/WDSPK N12 47 J3
Down Wy NTHLT UB5 95 F2
Dowrey St IS N1 85 G6
Dowsett Rd TOTM N17 50 C5
Dowson Cl CMBW SE5 * 142 E5
Doyce St STHWK SE1 * 18 C2
Doyle Cl ERITH DA8 150 B2
Doyle Gdns WLSDN NW10 81 K6
Doyle Rd SNWD SE25 197 H1
D'Oyley St BGVA SW1W 15 G6
Doynton St ARCH N19 * 66 B6
Draco Ga PUT/ROE SW15 * 139 F4
Draco St WALW SE17 122 D6
Dragmore St CLAP SW4 161 J1
Dragonfly Cl PLSTW E13 107 F2
Dragon Rd LBTH SE11 17 H7
PECK SE15 123 F6
Dragoon Rd DEPT SE8 124 C5
Dragor Rd WLSDN NW10 98 E2
Drake Cl BERM/RHTH SE16 124 A2
Drake Crs THMD SE28 109 J5
Drakefell Rd NWCR SE14 144 A3
Drakefield Rd TOOT SW17 161 F5
Drake Ms HAYES BR2 200 B1
HCH RM12 93 J5
Drake Rd BROCKY SE4 144 D4
CHSGTN KT9 206 C3
CROY/NA CR0 196 A4
MTCM CR4 195 F3
RYLN/HDSTN HA2 59 K6
Drake's Cl ESH/CLAY KT10 204 A3
Drakes Ctyd KIL/WHAMP NW6 82 D5
Drake St ENC/FH EN2 23 K2
FSBYW WC1X 11 G2
Drakewood Rd
STRHM/NOR SW16 179 J3
Draper Cl BELV DA17 129 G4
ISLW TW7 135 J3
Draper Est STHWK SE1 18 B6
Draper Pl IS N1 85 H6
Drapers Rd ENC/FH EN2 23 H3
SRTFD E15 88 A2
TOTM N17 50 B6
Drappers Wy
BERM/RHTH SE16 123 H4
Draven Cl HAYES BR2 199 J4
Drawell Cl WOOL/PLUM SE18 127 K5
Drax Av RYNPK SW20 176 D3
Draxmont WIM/MER SW19 177 H2
Draycot Rd SURB KT6 191 H5
WAN E11 71 F3
Draycott Av CHEL SW3 14 D7
KTN/HRWW/WS HA3 61 H3
Draycott Cl CMBW SE5 142 E1
CRICK NW2 82 B1
KTN/HRWW/WS HA3 61 H3
Draycott Pl CHEL SW3 14 E7
Draycott Ter CHEL SW3 14 E6
Dray Ct ALP/SUD HA0 * 79 J4
Drayford Cl MV/WKIL W9 * 100 D3
Dray Gdns BRXS/STRHM SW2 142 A6
Draymans Ms PECK SE15 143 G3
Draymans Wy ISLW TW7 136 A4
Drayson Ms KENS W8 119 K2
Drayton Av LOU IG10 39 K1
ORP BR6 201 G5
WEA W13 97 G6
Drayton Bridge Rd HNWL W7 97 F6
Drayton Cl HSLWW TW4 134 E6
IL IG1 72 D5
Drayton Ct WDR/YW UB7 * 112 C4
Drayton Court Chambers
WEA W13 * 97 H6
Drayton Gdns WBPTN SW10 120 B5

WCHMH N21 35 H2
WDR/YW UB7 112 A2
WEA W13 97 G6
Drayton Gn WEA W13 97 G6
Drayton Green Rd WEA W13 97 H6
Drayton Gv WEA W13 97 G6
Drayton Pk HBRY N5 85 G3
Drayton Park Ms HOLWY N7 * 85 G3
Drayton Rd CROY/NA CR0 196 C6
TOTM N17 50 A5
WAN E11 70 B5
WEA W13 97 G5
WLSDN NW10 81 H6
Drayton Waye
KTN/HRWW/WS HA3 61 H3
Dreadnought Cl
WIM/MER SW19 178 B5
Dreadnought St GNWCH SE10 125 H3
Drenon Sq HYS/HAR UB3 94 D6
Dresden Cl KIL/WHAMP NW6 83 F4
Dresden Rd ARCH N19 66 C5
Dressington Av BROCKY SE4 164 D1
Drew Av MLHL NW7 46 C2
Drewery Ct BKHTH/KID SE3 * 145 H4
Drew Gdns GFD/PVL UB6 79 F4
Drew Rd CAN/RD E16 126 D1
Drews Cots
STRHM/NOR SW16 * 161 J4
Drewstead La
STRHM/NOR SW16 161 J4
Drewstead Rd
STRHM/NOR SW16 161 J4
Driffield Rd BOW E3 105 G1
The Drift HAYES BR2 215 H1
The Driftway MTCM CR4 179 F4
Drinkwater Rd
RYLN/HDSTN HA2 60 B6
Drive Ct EDGW HA8 * 44 C1
The Drive ACT W3 98 E5
BAR EN5 20 C4
BAR EN5 33 G1
BARK IG11 91 F5
BECK BR3 182 D5
BKHH IG9 39 G2
BXLY DA5 168 D1
CHING E4 38 B2
CHST BR7 186 A3
CHST BR7 186 A6
CRW RM5 57 F4
EBED/NFELT TW14 154 A2
EDGW HA8 44 C1
ENC/FH EN2 23 K2
ERITH DA8 149 J1
ESH/CLAY KT10 189 H5
FBAR/BDGN N11 48 C2
FNCH N3 46 E3
GLDGN NW11 64 C4
HGT N6 65 K2
HOLWY N7 85 F4
HOR/WEW KT19 207 H4
HSLW TW3 135 J3
IL IG1 71 J3
KUTN/CMB KT2 175 K3
MRDN SM4 194 B2
NTHWD HA6 40 C4
ORP BR6 202 A6
RYLN/HDSTN HA2 60 A4
RYNPK SW20 177 F3
SCUP DA14 168 C5
SURB KT6 191 F4
SWFD E18 52 E6
THHTH CR7 196 E1
WALTH E17 51 K6
WBLY HA9 62 E6
WWKM BR4 199 G4
Dr Johnson Av TOOT SW17 161 G5
Droitwich Cl SYD SE26 163 H5
Dromey Gdns
KTN/HRWW/WS HA3 43 F3
Dromore Rd PUT/ROE SW15 159 H1
Dronfield Gdns BCTR RM8 91 J3
Droop St NKENS W10 100 C3
Drovers Pl PECK SE15 143 J1
Drovers Rd SAND/SEL CR2 211 K3
Drovers Wy HOLWY N7 84 E4
Druce Rd DUL SE21 163 F1
Druid St STHWK SE1 19 H2
Druids Wy HAYES BR2 199 G1
Drumaline Rdg WPK KT4 192 B6
Drummond Av
ROMW/RG RM7 75 F1
Drummond Cl ERITH DA8 150 B2
Drummond Crs CAMTN NW1 4 C4
Drummond Dr STAN HA7 43 F3
Drummond Ga PIM SW1V 121 J5
Drummond Rd
BERM/RHTH SE16 123 J3
CROY/NA CR0 196 D6
ROMW/RG RM7 74 E1
WAN E11 71 F3
Drummonds Pl
RCH/KEW TW9 137 F5
Drummond St CAMTN NW1 4 A6
Drury Crs CROY/NA CR0 196 B6
Drury La COVGDN WC2E 11 F4
Drury Rd HRW HA1 60 C4
Drury Wy WLSDN NW10 81 F3
Dryad St PUT/ROE SW15 139 G4
Dryburgh Gdns
CDALE/KGS NW9 44 C6
Dryburgh Rd PUT/ROE SW15 138 E4
Dryden Av HNWL W7 97 F5
Dryden Cl BARK/HLT IG6 55 F2
CLAP SW4 141 J6
Dryden Rd EN EN1 36 A1
KTN/HRWW/WS HA3 43 F4
WELL DA16 148 A2
WIM/MER SW19 178 B2
Dryden St COVGDN WC2E 11 F4
Dryden Wy ORP BR6 202 B5
Dryfield Cl WLSDN NW10 80 E4
Dryfield Rd EDGW HA8 44 E2
Dryhill Rd BELV DA17 129 G6
Dryland Av ORP BR6 217 F2
Drylands Rd CEND/HSY/T N8 66 E3
Drysdale Av CHING E4 37 K1
Drysdale Cl NTHWD HA6 40 C3
Drysdale Dwellings HACK E8 * 86 B3
Drysdale Pl IS N1 7 H4
Drysdale St IS N1 7 H5
Dublin Av HACK E8 86 C6
Du Burstow Ter HNWL W7 115 K2
Ducal St BETH E2 7 K5
Du Cane Cl SHB W12 * 100 A5
Du Cane Rd SHB W12 99 J5
Duchess Cl FBAR/BDGN N11 48 B1
SUT SM1 209 G2
Duchess Gv BKHH IG9 * 39 F4
Duchess Ms CAVSQ/HST W1G 9 K2
Duchess of Bedford's Wk
KENS W8 119 J2
Duchess St REGST W1B 9 K2
Duchy Rd EBAR EN4 21 H1
Duchy St STHWK SE1 11 K7
Ducie St CLAP SW4 141 K5
Duckett Ms FSBYPK N4 67 H3
Duckett Rd FSBYPK N4 67 H3
Ducketts Rd DART DA1 150 C6
Duckett St WCHPL E1 105 F4
Ducking Stool Ct ROM RM1 75 G1
Duck La SOHO/CST W1F 10 C4
Duck Lees La PEND EN3 25 G5
Du Cros Dr STAN HA7 43 K2
Du Cros Rd ACT W3 118 B1
Dudden Hill La WLSDN NW10 81 H2
Dudden Hill Pde
WLSDN NW10 * 81 H2
Duddington Cl ELTH/MOT SE9 166 C6
Dudley Av
KTN/HRWW/WS HA3 43 J6
Dudley Dr MRDN SM4 193 H5
RSLP HA4 77 F3
Dudley Gdns
RYLN/HDSTN HA2 60 D5
WEA W13 116 C2
Dudley Pl HYS/HAR UB3 113 G4
Dudley Rd EBED/NFELT TW14 153 G3
FNCH N3 47 F5
IL IG1 90 B2
KIL/WHAMP NW6 100 C1
KUT/HW KT1 175 G6
NWDGN UB2 114 C2
RCH/KEW TW9 137 G3
RYLN/HDSTN HA2 60 C6
WALTH E17 51 J5
WIM/MER SW19 177 K2
Dudley St BAY/PAD W2 * 8 A2
Dudlington Rd CLPT E5 68 E6
Dudmaston Ms CHEL SW3 120 C5
Dudrich Cl
NFNCH/WDSPK N12 47 K2
Dudrich Ms EDUL SE22 143 G6
Dudsbury Rd DART DA1 170 E1
Dudset La HEST TW5 133 K2
Dufferin Av STLK EC1Y 6 E7
Dufferin St STLK EC1Y 6 D7
Duffield Cl HRW HA1 61 F2
Duffield Dr SEVS/STOTM N15 68 B1
Duff St POP/IOD E14 105 K5
Dufour's Pl SOHO/CST W1F 10 B4
Dugard Wy LBTH SE11 18 A6
Duggan Dr CHST BR7 184 D2
Dugolly Av WBLY HA9 80 D1
Duke Humphrey Rd
BKHTH/KID SE3 145 H2
Duke of Cambridge Cl
WHTN TW2 155 J1
Duke of Edinburgh Rd
SUT SM1 209 H1
The Duke of Wellington Av
WOOL/PLUM SE18 127 G3
Duke of Wellington Pl
KTBR SW1X 15 H3
Duke of York Sq CHEL SW3 120 E5
Duke of York St STJS SW1Y 10 B7
Duke Rd BARK/HLT IG6 72 D1
CHSWK W4 118 A5
Dukes Av EDGW HA8 44 B2
FNCH N3 47 F4
HRW HA1 60 E1
HSLWW TW4 134 D5
MUSWH N10 48 C6
NTHLT UB5 77 J5
NWMAL KT3 176 B6
PIN HA5 59 K3
RCHPK/HAM TW10 156 D6
Duke's Av CHSWK W4 118 A5
Dukes Cl ASHF TW15 153 F6
HPTN TW12 172 E1
Dukes Ga CHSWK W4 * 117 K4
Dukes Green Av
EBED/NFELT TW14 133 K6
Dukes La KENS W8 119 K2
Dukes Lane Chambers
KENS W8 * 120 A2
Dukes Lane Man KENS W8 * 120 A2
Dukes Ms MUSWH N10 48 B6
Duke's Ms MHST W1U 9 H3
Dukes Orch BXLY DA5 169 K3
Duke's Pl HDTCH EC3A 13 J4
Dukes Point HGT N6 66 B5
Dukes Rd ACT W3 98 C3
EHAM E6 90 A6
Duke's Rd CAMTN NW1 4 D5
Dukesthorpe Rd SYD SE26 164 A6
Duke St MHST W1U 9 H3
RCH/KEW TW9 136 E5
SUT SM1 209 H2
Duke Street Hl STHWK SE1 13 F7
Duke Street St James's
MYFR/PICC W1J 10 B7
Dukes Wy WBLY HA9 80 A3
WWKM BR4 214 C1
Duke's Yd MYFR/PKLN W1K 9 H5
Dulas St FSBYPK N4 67 F5
Dulford St NTGHL W11 100 C6
Dulka Rd BTSEA SW11 140 E6
Dulverton Rd ELTH/MOT SE9 167 H4
RSLP HA4 58 E6
Dulwich Common DUL SE21 162 E3
The Dulwich Oaks DUL SE21 * 163 G5
Dulwich Rd HNHL SE24 142 B6
Dulwich Village DUL SE21 162 E1
Dulwich Wood Av NRWD SE19 181 F1
Dulwich Wood Pk
NRWD SE19 163 F6
Dumbarton Rd
BRXS/STRHM SW2 161 K1
Dumbleton Cl KUT/HW KT1 175 J4
Dumbreck Rd ELTH/MOT SE9 147 F5
Dumfries Cl OXHEY WD19 26 E5
Dumont Rd STNW/STAM N16 86 A1
Dumpton Pl CAMTN NW1 84 A5
Dunbar Av BECK BR3 198 B1
DAGE RM10 92 C1
STRHM/NOR SW16 180 B5
Dunbar Cl YEAD UB4 94 E4
Dunbar Gdns DAGE RM10 92 C3
Dunbar Rd FSTGT E7 88 E4
NWMAL KT3 191 K1
WDGN N22 49 G4
Dunbar St WNWD SE27 162 D5
Dunblane Rd ELTH/MOT SE9 146 D4
Dunboyne Rd HAMP NW3 83 K3
Dunbridge St BETH E2 104 C3
Duncan Cl BAR EN5 21 G5
Duncan Gv ACT W3 99 G5
Duncannon St CHCR WC2N 10 E6
Duncan Rd HACK E8 86 D6
RCH/KEW TW9 137 F5
Duncan St IS N1 6 A2
Duncan Ter IS N1 6 A3
Dunch St WCHPL E1 104 D5
Duncombe Hl FSTH SE23 164 B2
Duncombe Rd ARCH N19 66 D5
Duncrievie Rd LEW SE13 165 G1
Duncroft WOOL/PLUM SE18 147 K1
Dundalk Rd BROCKY SE4 144 B4
Dundas Gdns
E/WMO/HCT KT8 173 G6
Dundas Rd PECK SE15 143 K3
Dundee Rd PLSTW E13 107 F1
SNWD SE25 197 J2
Dundee St WAP E1W 123 J1
Dundee Wy PEND EN3 25 G4
Dundee Whf POP/IOD E14 105 H6
Dundela Gdns WPK KT4 207 K2
Dundonald Cl EHAM E6 107 J5
Dundonald Rd
WIM/MER SW19 177 J3
WLSDN NW10 82 B6
Dunedin Rd IL IG1 72 C5
LEY E10 87 K1
RAIN RM13 111 H2
Dunedin Wy YEAD UB4 95 G3
Dunelm St WCHPL E1 105 F5
Dunfield Rd CAT SE6 182 E1
Dunford Rd HOLWY N7 85 F2
Dungarvan Av
PUT/ROE SW15 138 D5
Dunheved Cl THHTH CR7 196 B3
Dunheved Rd North
THHTH CR7 196 B3
Dunheved Rd South
THHTH CR7 196 B3
Dunheved Rd West
THHTH CR7 196 B3
Dunholme Gn ED N9 36 B5
Dunholme La ED N9 36 B5
Dunholme Rd ED N9 36 B5
Dunkeld Rd BCTR RM8 73 H6
SNWD SE25 196 E1
Dunkery Rd ELTH/MOT SE9 166 C6
Dunkin Rd DART DA1 151 K5
Dunkirk St WNWD SE27 * 162 D6
Dunlace Rd CLPT E5 86 E3
Dunleary Cl HSLWW TW4 154 E2
Dunley Dr CROY/NA CR0 214 A4
Dunloe Av TOTM N17 49 K6
Dunloe St BETH E2 7 J3
Dunlop Pl BERM/RHTH SE16 19 K5
Dunmore Rd
KIL/WHAMP NW6 82 C6
RYNPK SW20 177 F4
Dunmow Cl CHDH RM6 73 J2
FELT TW13 * 154 D6
LOU IG10 39 J1
Dunmow Dr RAIN RM13 93 H6
Dunmow Rd SRTFD E15 88 B2
Dunmow Wk IS N1 * 85 J6
Dunnage Crs
BERM/RHTH SE16 124 B4
Dunningford Cl HCH RM12 93 H3
Dunn Md CDALE/KGS NW9 45 H3
Dunnock Cl ED N9 37 F3
Dunnock Rd EHAM E6 107 J5
Dunn St HACK E8 86 B3
Dunollie Pl KTTN NW5 84 C3
Dunollie Rd KTTN NW5 84 C3
Dunoon Gdns FSTH SE23 * 164 A2
Dunoon Rd FSTH SE23 163 K2
Dunraven Dr ENC/FH EN2 23 G3
Dunraven Rd SHB W12 118 D1
Dunraven St MYFR/PKLN W1K 9 F5
Dunsany Rd HMSMTH W6 119 G3
Dunsbury Cl BELMT SM2 209 F6
Dunsfold Wy CROY/NA CR0 213 K5
Dunsford Wy PUT/ROE SW15 158 E2
Dunsmore OXHEY WD19 * 27 H4
Dunsmore Cl BUSH WD23 28 D1
YEAD UB4 95 H3
Dunsmore Rd WOT/HER KT12 188 A2
Dunsmore Wy BUSH WD23 28 C1
Dunsmure Rd
STNW/STAM N16 68 A5
Dunspring La CLAY IG5 54 B5
Dunstable Ms
CAVSQ/HST W1G 9 H1
Dunstable Rd
E/WMO/HCT KT8 188 E1
RCH/KEW TW9 137 F5
Dunstall Rd RYNPK SW20 176 E2
Dunstall Wy E/WMO/HCT KT8 173 G6
Dunstall Welling Est
WELL DA16 * 148 C3
Dunstan Cl EFNCH N2 * 47 G6
Dunstan Gld
STMC/STPC BR5 * 201 J3
Dunstan Houses WCHPL E1 * 104 E4
Dunstan Rd GLDGN NW11 64 D5
Dunstan's Gv EDUL SE22 163 J1
Dunstan's Rd EDUL SE22 163 H2
Dunster Av MRDN SM4 193 G5
Dunster Cl BAR EN5 20 B5
CRW RM5 56 E5
Dunster Ct MON EC3R 13 G5
Dunster Dr CDALE/KGS NW9 62 E5
Dunster Gdns
KIL/WHAMP NW6 82 D5
Dunsterville Wy STHWK SE1 19 F3
Dunster Wy RYLN/HDSTN HA2 77 J1
Dunston Rd BTSEA SW11 141 F3
HACK E8 7 J1
Dunston St HACK E8 86 A6
Dunton Cl SURB KT6 191 F5
Dunton Rd LEY E10 69 K4
ROM RM1 75 G1
STHWK SE1 19 J7
Duntshill Rd
WAND/EARL SW18 160 A3
Dunvegan Cl E/WMO/HCT KT8 189 G1
Dunvegan Rd ELTH/MOT SE9 146 E5
Dunwich Rd BXLYHN DA7 149 G2
Dunworth Ms NTGHL W11 100 D5
Duplex Ride KTBR SW1X 15 F3
Dupont Rd RYNPK SW20 177 G5
Duppas Av CROY/NA CR0 211 H2
Duppas Hill Rd CROY/NA CR0 211 G2
Duppas Hill Ter CROY/NA CR0 211 H1
Duppas Rd CROY/NA CR0 211 G1
Dupree Rd CHARL SE7 126 A5
Dura Den Cl BECK BR3 182 E3
Durand Gdns BRXN/ST SW9 142 A2
Durand Wy WLSDN NW10 80 E5
Durants Park Av PEND EN3 25 F5
Durants Rd PEND EN3 24 E5
Durant St BETH E2 104 C1
Durban Gdns DAGE RM10 92 E5
Durban Rd BECK BR3 182 C5
GNTH/NBYPK IG2 72 E5
SRTFD E15 106 C2
TOTM N17 50 A2
WALTH E17 51 H4
WNWD SE27 162 D6
Durbin Rd CHSGTN KT9 206 A2
Durdans Rd STHL UB1 95 K5
Durell Gdns DAGW RM9 91 K3
Durell Rd DAGW RM9 91 K3
Durfey Pl CMBW SE5 142 E1
Durford Crs PUT/ROE SW15 158 D3
Durham Av HAYES BR2 199 J1
HEST TW5 114 E6
WFD IG8 53 H1
Durham Hl BMLY BR1 165 J6
Durham House St
CHCR WC2N * 11 F6
Durham Pl CHEL SW3 * 120 E5
Durham Ri WOOL/PLUM SE18 127 H5
Durham Rd CAN/RD E16 106 C3
DAGE RM10 92 E3
EA W5 116 E3
EBED/NFELT TW14 154 B2
ED N9 36 C4
EFNCH N2 47 J6
HAYES BR2 199 K1
HOLWY N7 67 F6
HRW HA1 60 B2
MNPK E12 89 H2
RYNPK SW20 176 E4
SCUP DA14 186 C1
Durham Rw WCHPL E1 105 F4
Durham St LBTH SE11 122 A5
Durham Ter BAY/PAD W2 101 F5
PGE/AN SE20 * 181 J3
Durham Wharf Dr BTFD TW8 136 D1
Durham Yd BETH E2 * 104 D2
Duriun Wy ERITH DA8 150 E1
Durley Av PIN HA5 59 J3
Durley Gdns ORP BR6 217 H2
Durley Rd STNW/STAM N16 68 A4
Durlston Rd CLPT E5 68 C6
KUTN/CMB KT2 175 F2
Durnford St SEVS/STOTM N15 68 A2
Durning Rd NRWD SE19 180 E1
Durnsford Av
WIM/MER SW19 159 K4
Durnsford Rd WDGN N22 48 D3
WIM/MER SW19 159 K5
Durrant Wy ORP BR6 216 D3
Durrell Rd FUL/PGN SW6 139 H2
Durrington Av RYNPK SW20 177 F3
Durrington Park Rd
RYNPK SW20 177 F4
Durrington Rd CLPT E5 87 G2
Dursley Cl BKHTH/KID SE3 146 B3
Dursley Gdns BKHTH/KID SE3 146 C2
Dursley Rd BKHTH/KID SE3 146 B3
Durward St WCHPL E1 104 D4
Durweston Ms MHST W1U * 9 F1
Durweston St MBLAR W1H 8 E2
Dury Rd BAR EN5 20 D2
Dutch Barn Cl
STWL/WRAY TW19 152 A1
Dutch Gdns KUTN/CMB KT2 175 J2
Dutch Yd WAND/EARL SW18 139 K6
Duthie St POP/IOD E14 106 A6
Dutton St GNWCH SE10 145 F2
Duxberry Cl HAYES BR2 200 D2
Duxford Cl HCH RM12 93 K4
Dwight Rd WATW WD18 26 B2
Dye House La BOW E3 87 J6
Dyer's Blds FLST/FETLN EC4A 11 J2
Dyers Hall Rd WAN E11 70 B6
Dyer's La PUT/ROE SW15 138 E4
Dyers Wy HARH RM3 57 J3
Dyke Dr STMC/STPC BR5 202 D4
Dykes Wy HAYES BR2 183 J6
Dykewood Cl BXLY DA5 170 A5
Dylan Cl BORE WD6 * 29 K2
Dylan Rd BELV DA17 129 H3
HNHL SE24 142 C5
Dylways CMBW SE5 142 E5
Dymchurch Cl CLAY IG5 54 A6
ORP BR6 216 E2
Dymock St FUL/PGN SW6 140 A4
Dymoke Rd ROM RM1 75 H4
Dyneley Rd LEE/GVPK SE12 166 B6
Dyne Rd KIL/WHAMP NW6 82 D5
Dynevor Rd
RCHPK/HAM TW10 137 F6
STNW/STAM N16 86 A1
Dynham Rd KIL/WHAMP NW6 82 E5
Dyott St LSQ/SEVD WC2H 10 E3
RSQ WC1B 10 D2
Dysart Av KUTN/CMB KT2 174 D1
Dysart St SDTCH EC2A 7 F7
Dyson Ct ALP/SUD HA0 79 G2
Dyson Rd SRTFD E15 88 D4
WAN E11 70 C3
Dyson's Rd UED N18 50 D2

E

Eade Rd FSBYPK N4 67 J4
Eagans Cl EFNCH N2 * 47 H6
Eagle Av CHDH RM6 74 A3
Eagle Cl BERM/RHTH SE16 123 J5
HCH RM12 93 K4
PEND EN3 24 E5
WLGTN SM6 210 E4
Eagle Ct FARR EC1M 12 A1
Eagle Dr CDALE/KGS NW9 45 G5
Eagle Hl NRWD SE19 180 E2
Eagle House Ms CLAP SW4 141 H6
Eagle La WAN E11 70 E1
Eagle Ms IS N1 86 A4
Eagle Pl WBPTN SW10 120 B5
Eagle Rd ALP/SUD HA0 79 K5
HTHAIR TW6 133 J4
Eaglesfield Rd
WOOL/PLUM SE18 147 G2
Eagle St HHOL WC1V 11 G2
Eagle Ter WFD IG8 53 F3
Eagle Wharf Rd IS N1 6 D2
Eagling Cl BOW E3 105 J2
Ealdham Sq ELTH/MOT SE9 146 B5
Ealing Golf Course
GFD/PVL UB6 * 97 G2
Ealing Gn EA W5 116 E1
Ealing Park Gdns EA W5 116 D4
Ealing Rd ALP/SUD HA0 80 A6
ALP/SUD HA0 98 A1
BOW E3 105 K2
EA W5 116 E4
NTHLT UB5 78 A5
Ealing Village EA W5 98 A5
Eamont St STJWD NW8 2 C2
Eardemont Cl DART DA1 150 C5
Eardley Crs ECT SW5 119 K5
Eardley Rd BELV DA17 129 H5
STRHM/NOR SW16 179 H2
Earl Cl FBAR/BDGN N11 48 B1
Earldom Rd PUT/ROE SW15 139 F5
Earle Gdns KUTN/CMB KT2 175 F3
Earlham Gv FSTGT E7 88 D3
WDGN N22 49 F3
Earlham St LSQ/SEVD WC2H 10 D4
Earl Ri WOOL/PLUM SE18 127 J5
Earl Rd MORT/ESHN SW14 137 K5
Earlsbury Gdns EDGW HA8 30 C6
Earls Court Gdns ECT SW5 120 A4
Earl's Court Gdns ECT SW5 * 120 A4
Earls Court Rd KENS W8 * 119 K3
Earl's Court Rd ECT SW5 119 K4
Earl's Court Sq ECT SW5 120 A5
Earls Crs HRW HA1 60 E1
Earlsferry Wy IS N1 84 E5
Earlsfield Rd
WAND/EARL SW18 160 B3
Earlshall Rd ELTH/MOT SE9 146 E5
Earlsmead RYLN/HDSTN HA2 77 K2
Earlsmead Rd
SEVS/STOTM N15 68 B2
WLSDN NW10 100 A2
Earls Ms WAND/EARL SW18 160 B2
Earls Ter KENS W8 119 J3
Earlsthorpe Ms BAL SW12 161 F1
Earlsthorpe Rd SYD SE26 164 A6
Earlstoke Est FSBYE EC1V 6 A4
Earlstoke St FSBYE EC1V 6 A4
Earlston Gv HOM E9 86 D6
Earl St SDTCH EC2A 13 G1
Earls Wk BCTR RM8 91 H2
KENS W8 119 K3
Earlswood Av THHTH CR7 196 B2
Earlswood Gdns CLAY IG5 54 A6
Earlswood St GNWCH SE10 125 H5
Early Ms CAMTN NW1 84 B6
Earnshaw St
NOXST/BSQ WC1A 10 D3
Earsby St WKENS W14 119 H4
Easby Crs MRDN SM4 194 A3
Easebourne Rd BCTR RM8 91 J3
Easedale Dr HCH RM12 93 K3
East Acton Ar ACT W3 * 99 H5
East Acton La ACT W3 118 A1
East Arbour St WCHPL E1 105 F5
East Av EHAM E6 89 J5
HYS/HAR UB3 113 J2
STHL UB1 95 K6
WALTH E17 69 K1
WLGTN SM6 211 F3
East Bank STNW/STAM N16 68 A4
Eastbank Cl WALTH E17 69 K2
Eastbank Rd HPTN TW12 173 H1
East Barnet Rd BAR EN5 21 G5
East Boundary Rd MNPK E12 89 K1
Eastbourne Av ACT W3 99 F5
Eastbourne Gdns
MORT/ESHN SW14 137 K4
Eastbourne Ms BAY/PAD W2 101 G5
Eastbourne Rd BTFD TW8 116 E5
CHSWK W4 117 K6
EHAM E6 108 A2
FELT TW13 154 C4
SEVS/STOTM N15 68 A3
SRTFD E15 88 C6
TOOT SW17 179 F2
Eastbourne Ter BAY/PAD W2 101 G5
Eastbournia Av ED N9 36 D5
Eastbrook Av ED N9 36 E2
Eastbrook Cl DAGE RM10 92 E2
Eastbrook Dr ROMW/RG RM7 93 G1
Eastbrook Rd BKHTH/KID SE3 146 A2
Eastbury Av BARK IG11 90 E6
EN EN1 24 A2
NTHWD HA6 40 C1
Eastbury Ct OXHEY WD19 * 27 G2
Eastbury Gv CHSWK W4 118 B5
Eastbury Rd EHAM E6 108 A3
KUTN/CMB KT2 175 F3
NTHWD HA6 40 C2
OXHEY WD19 27 G2
ROMW/RG RM7 75 F3
STMC/STPC BR5 201 J3
Eastbury Sq BARK IG11 91 F6
Eastbury Ter WCHPL E1 105 F3
Eastcastle St GTPST W1W 10 A3
Eastcheap FENCHST EC3M 13 F5

East Churchfield Rd ACT W3 118 A1
Eastchurch Rd HTHAIR TW6 133 H3
East Cl EA W5 98 C3
EBAR EN4 22 A5
GFD/PVL UB6 96 C1
RAIN RM13 111 K3
Eastcombe Av CHARL SE7 126 A6
Eastcote ORP BR6 202 A5
Eastcote Av E/WMO/HCT KT8 188 E2
GFD/PVL UB6 79 G3
RYLN/HDSTN HA2 60 B6
Eastcote La NTHLT UB5 77 K4
Eastcote La North NTHLT UB5 77 K4
Eastcote Rd PIN HA5 59 H2
RSLP HA4 58 C4
RYLN/HDSTN HA2 78 C1
WELL DA16 147 J3
Eastcote St BRXN/ST SW9 141 K3
Eastcote Vw PIN HA5 59 G1
Eastcott Cl KUTN/CMB KT2 175 K1
East Ct ALP/SUD HA0 61 J6
East Crs EN EN1 24 A6
FBAR/BDGN N11 33 K6
Eastcroft Rd HOR/WEW KT19 207 G5
East Cross Route HOM E9 87 H4
Eastdown Pk LEW SE13 145 G5
East Dr CAR SM5 209 J6
NTHWD HA6 26 C4
STMC/STPC BR5 202 C3
East Duck Lees La PEND EN3 25 G5
East Dulwich Gv EDUL SE22 143 F6
East Dulwich Rd EDUL SE22 143 G5
East End Rd FNCH N3 46 E5
East End Wy PIN HA5 41 J6
East Entrance DAGE RM10 110 D1
Eastern Av CHDH RM6 73 H1
GNTH/NBYPK IG2 72 C3
PIN HA5 59 H4
WAN E11 71 G3
Eastern Av East ROM RM1 57 F6
Eastern Av West CHDH RM6 74 A1
Eastern Gtwy CAN/RD E16 107 G6
Eastern Perimeter Rd
HTHAIR TW6 133 H3
Eastern Rd BROCKY SE4 144 D5
EFNCH N2 47 K6
PLSTW E13 107 F1
ROM RM1 75 G2
WALTH E17 70 A2
WDGN N22 48 E4
Easternville Gdns
GNTH/NBYPK IG2 72 C3
Eastern Wy THMD SE28 128 B2
East Ferry Rd POP/IOD E14 124 E4
Eastfield Gdns DAGE RM10 92 C2
Eastfield Rd CEND/HSY/T N8 48 E6
DAGE RM10 92 C2
PEND EN3 25 F1
WALTH E17 69 J1
Eastfields PIN HA5 59 G2
Eastfields Av
WAND/EARL SW18 139 K5
Eastfields Rd ACT W3 98 E4
MTCM CR4 179 F5
Eastfield St POP/IOD E14 105 G4
East Gdns TOOT SW17 178 D2
Eastgate Cl THMD SE28 109 K5
Eastglade NTHWD HA6 40 C1
PIN HA5 41 K6
East Hall Rd STMC/STPC BR5 203 F4
Eastham Cl BAR EN5 20 C6
East Ham Manor Wy
EHAM E6 108 A5
East Harding St
FLST/FETLN EC4A 11 K3
East Heath Rd HAMP NW3 83 H1
East Hl DART DA1 171 J2
WAND/EARL SW18 140 B6
WBLY HA9 62 C6
East Hill Dr DART DA1 171 J2
Eastholm GLDGN NW11 65 F1
East Holme ERITH DA8 150 A2
Eastholme HYS/HAR UB3 113 K1
East India Dock Rd
POP/IOD E14 105 J6
East India Wy CROY/NA CR0 197 G5
Eastlake Rd CMBW SE5 142 C3
Eastlands Crs EDUL SE22 163 G1
East La ALP/SUD HA0 79 J1
BERM/RHTH SE16 123 H2
KUT/HW KT1 174 E6
Eastlea Ms CAN/RD E16 106 C3
Eastleigh Av
RYLN/HDSTN HA2 60 B6
Eastleigh Cl BELMT SM2 209 F5
CRICK NW2 81 G1
Eastleigh Rd BXLYHN DA7 149 K3
WALTH E17 51 H5
Eastleigh Wy
EBED/NFELT TW14 153 K3
Eastman Rd ACT W3 118 A2
East Md RSLP HA4 77 H1
Eastmead Av GFD/PVL UB6 96 B2
Eastmead Cl BMLY BR1 184 D5
Eastmearn Rd WNWD SE27 162 D4
Eastmont Rd ESH/CLAY KT10 190 A6
Eastmoor Pl CHARL SE7 126 C3
Eastmoor St CHARL SE7 126 C3
WOOL/PLUM SE18 126 C4
East Mount St WCHPL E1 * 104 D4
Eastney Rd CROY/NA CR0 196 C5
Eastney St GNWCH SE10 125 G5
Eastnor Rd ELTH/MOT SE9 167 H3
Easton St FSBYW WC1X 5 J6
East Park Cl CHDH RM6 73 K2
East Parkside GNWCH SE10 125 H2
East Pas STBT EC1A 12 C1
East Pl WNWD SE27 162 D6
East Pole Cots
STHGT/OAK N14 * 22 D5
East Poultry Av FARR EC1M 12 A2
East Rp HTHAIR TW6 132 E2
East Rd CHDH RM6 74 A2
CHEL SW3 121 F5
EBAR EN4 34 A3
EBED/NFELT TW14 153 G2
EDGW HA8 44 D4
IS N1 7 F4
KUTN/CMB KT2 175 F4
PEND EN3 24 E1
ROMW/RG RM7 75 F4
SRTFD E15 88 E6
WDR/YW UB7 112 C4
WELL DA16 148 C3
WIM/MER SW19 178 B2
East Rochester Wy
BFN/LL DA15 147 K6
BFN/LL DA15 168 D1
DART DA1 170 A2
East Rw NKENS W10 100 C3
WAN E11 70 E3
Eastry Av HAYES BR2 199 J3
Eastry Rd ERITH DA8 149 H1
East Sheen Av
MORT/ESHN SW14 138 A5
East Side SHB W12 * 119 F2
Eastside Rd GLDGN NW11 64 D1
East Smithfield WAP E1W 13 K6
East St BARK IG11 90 C5
BMLY BR1 183 K5
BTFD TW8 136 D1
BXLYHN DA7 149 H5
WALW SE17 19 G7
East Surrey Gv PECK SE15 143 G1
East Tenter St WCHPL E1 13 K4
East Ter BFN/LL DA15 * 167 K3
East Towers PIN HA5 59 H3
East V ACT W3 * 118 C1
East Vw BAR EN5 20 D3
CHING E4 52 A1
Eastview Av
WOOL/PLUM SE18 147 K1
Eastville Av GLDGN NW11 64 D2
East Wk EBAR EN4 34 A3
HYS/HAR UB3 113 K2
East Wy CROY/NA CR0 198 B6
HYS/HAR UB3 113 K1
RSLP HA4 58 E5
WAN E11 71 G3
Eastway BOW E3 87 G6
HAYES BR2 199 K4
MRDN SM4 193 G2
WAN E11 71 F2
WLGTN SM6 210 C2
Eastway Crs
RYLN/HDSTN HA2 60 B6
Eastwell Cl BECK BR3 182 B4
Eastwood Cl HOLWY N7 85 G3
SWFD E18 52 E5
TOTM N17 * 50 D3
Eastwood Dr RAIN RM13 111 K5
Eastwood Rd GDMY/SEVK IG3 73 G4
MUSWH N10 48 A5
SWFD E18 52 E5
WDR/YW UB7 112 D2
Eastwood St
STRHM/NOR SW16 179 H2
Eatington Rd LEY E10 70 B2
Eaton Cl BGVA SW1W 15 G6
STAN HA7 29 H6
Eaton Ct EDGW HA8 30 C6
Eaton Dr BRXN/ST SW9 142 C5
CRW RM5 56 D3
KUTN/CMB KT2 175 H3
Eaton Gdns DAGW RM9 92 A5
Eaton Ga BGVA SW1W 15 G6
NTHWD HA6 40 A2
Eaton La BGVA SW1W 15 K5
Eaton Ms North KTBR SW1X 15 H5
Eaton Ms South BGVA SW1W 15 H6
Eaton Ms West BGVA SW1W 15 H6
Eaton Park Rd PLMGR N13 35 G4
Eaton Pl KTBR SW1X 15 G5
Eaton Ri EA W5 97 J4
WAN E11 71 G2
Eaton Rd BELMT SM2 209 H4
EN EN1 24 A4
HDN NW4 64 A2
HSLW TW3 135 J5
SCUP DA14 168 E4
Eaton Rw BGVA SW1W 15 J4
Eatons Md CHING E4 37 J4
Eaton Sq BGVA SW1W 15 H5
Eaton Ter BGVA SW1W 15 G6
BOW E3 * 105 G2
Eaton Terrace Ms BGVA SW1W 15 G6
Eatonville Rd TOOT SW17 160 E4
Eatonville Vls TOOT SW17 160 E4
Ebbisham Dr VX/NE SW8 122 A6
Ebbisham Rd WPK KT4 193 F6
Ebbsfleet Rd CRICK NW2 82 C3
Ebdon Wy BKHTH/KID SE3 146 A4
Ebenezer St IS N1 6 E4
Ebenezer Wk
STRHM/NOR SW16 179 H4
Ebley Cl PECK SE15 123 G6
Ebner St WAND/EARL SW18 140 A6
Ebor St WCHPL E1 7 J6
Ebrington Rd
KTN/HRWW/WS HA3 61 K3
Ebsworth St FSTH SE23 164 A2
Eburne Rd HOLWY N7 84 E1
Ebury Br BGVA SW1W 121 G5
Ebury Bridge Rd BGVA SW1W 121 F5
Ebury Cl HAYES BR2 215 J1
NTHWD HA6 40 A1
Ebury Ms BGVA SW1W 15 H6
Ebury Ms East BGVA SW1W 15 J6
Ebury Sq BGVA SW1W 15 J7
Ebury St BGVA SW1W 15 H7
Ecclesbourne Cl PLMGR N13 49 G1
Ecclesbourne Gdns
PLMGR N13 49 G1
Ecclesbourne Rd IS N1 85 J5
THHTH CR7 196 D2
Eccles Rd BTSEA SW11 140 E5
Eccleston Cl EBAR EN4 21 J6
ORP BR6 * 201 J5
Eccleston Crs CHDH RM6 73 H4
Ecclestone Ct WBLY HA9 80 A3
Ecclestone Ms WBLY HA9 80 A3
Ecclestone Pl WBLY HA9 80 B3
Eccleston Ms KTBR SW1X 15 H5
Eccleston Pl BGVA SW1W 15 J5
Eccleston Rd WEA W13 97 G6
Eccleston Sq PIM SW1V 15 K7
Eccleston Square Ms
PIM SW1V 15 K7
Eccleston St BGVA SW1W 15 H5
Echelforde Dr ASHF TW15 152 D6
Echo Hts CHING E4 * 37 K3
Eckford St IS N1 5 J2
Eckstein Rd BTSEA SW11 140 D5
Eclipse Rd PLSTW E13 107 F4
Ector Rd CAT SE6 165 H4
Edans Ct SHB W12 118 C2
Edbrooke Rd MV/WKIL W9 100 E3
Eddington Cl CROY/NA CR0 214 A4
Eddiscombe Rd FUL/PGN SW6 139 J3
Eddy Cl ROMW/RG RM7 74 D3
Eddystone Rd BROCKY SE4 144 B6
Ede Cl HSLW TW3 134 E4
Edenbridge Cl
BERM/RHTH SE16 * 123 J5
STMC/STPC BR5 202 E1
Edenbridge Rd EN EN1 36 A1
HOM E9 * 87 F5
Eden Cl ALP/SUD HA0 79 K6
BXLY DA5 170 A6
HAMP NW3 64 E6
PEND EN3 25 J1
Edencourt Rd
STRHM/NOR SW16 179 G2
Edendale Rd BXLYHN DA7 150 A2
Edenfield Gdns WPK KT4 207 H1
Eden Gv HOLWY N7 85 F3
WLSDN NW10 81 K4
Edenham Wy NKENS W10 100 D3
Edenhurst Av FUL/PGN SW6 139 J4
Eden Pde BECK BR3 * 198 B1
Eden Park Av BECK BR3 198 C1
Eden Rd BECK BR3 198 B1
BXLY DA5 169 K6
CROY/NA CR0 211 K2
WALTH E17 69 K2
WNWD SE27 180 C1
Edensor Rd CHSWK W4 138 B1
Eden St KUT/HW KT1 174 E5
Edenvale Rd MTCM CR4 179 F3
Edenvale St FUL/PGN SW6 140 A3
Eden Wk KUT/HW KT1 * 175 F5
Eden Wy BECK BR3 198 D2
BOW E3 87 H6
Ederline Av
STRHM/NOR SW16 180 A6
Edgar Kail Wy CMBW SE5 143 F4
Edgarley Ter FUL/PGN SW6 * 139 H2
Edgar Rd BOW E3 105 K2
HSLWW TW4 154 E2
Edgar Wallace Cl PECK SE15 143 F1
Edgbaston Rd OXHEY WD19 27 F5
Edgeborough Wy BMLY BR1 184 C4
Edgebury CHST BR7 167 G6
Edgecombe Cl
KUTN/CMB KT2 176 A3
Edgecoombe SAND/SEL CR2 213 F6
Edgecote Cl ACT W3 117 K1
Edgefield Av BARK IG11 91 F5
Edge Hl WIM/MER SW19 177 G3
WOOL/PLUM SE18 127 G6
Edge Hill Av FNCH N3 64 E1
Edge Hill Ct WIM/MER SW19 177 G3
Edgehill Ct WOT/HER KT12 * 188 B5
Edgehill Gdns DAGE RM10 92 C2
Edgehill Rd CHST BR7 167 H5
MTCM CR4 179 G4
WEA W13 97 J5
Edgeley La CLAP SW4 141 J4
Edgeley Rd CLAP SW4 141 H4
Edgel St WAND/EARL SW18 140 A5
Edge Point Cl
STRHM/NOR SW16 180 C1
Edgepoint Cl WNWD SE27 * 180 C1
Edge St KENS W8 119 K1
Edgewood Dr ORP BR6 217 F3
Edgewood Gn CROY/NA CR0 198 A5
Edgeworth Av HDN NW4 63 J2
Edgeworth Cl HDN NW4 63 J2
Edgeworth Crs HDN NW4 63 J2
Edgeworth Rd EBAR EN4 21 J5
ELTH/MOT SE9 146 B5
Edgington Rd
STRHM/NOR SW16 179 J2
Edgington Wy SCUP DA14 186 D3
Edgwarebury Gdns
EDGW HA8 44 C1
Edgwarebury La EDGW HA8 30 B3
Edgware Rd BAY/PAD W2 2 A7
CDALE/KGS NW9 45 F6
CRICK NW2 64 A6
Edgware Road High St
EDGW HA8 44 C2
Edgware Road The Hyde
CDALE/KGS NW9 63 G1
Edgware Way (Watford
By-Pass) EDGW HA8 30 A4
Edinburgh Cl BETH E2 104 E1
PIN HA5 59 J4
Edinburgh Ct KUT/HW KT1 * 175 F6
Edinburgh Ga KTBR SW1X 14 E2
Edinburgh Rd HNWL W7 116 A2
PLSTW E13 107 F1
SUT SM1 194 B6
UED N18 * 50 C1
WALTH E17 69 J2
Edington Rd ABYW SE2 128 C3
PEND EN3 24 E3
Edison Av HCH RM12 75 H5
Edison Cl HCH RM12 75 H5
WDR/YW UB7 112 C2
Edison Dr STHL UB1 96 B5
WBLY HA9 62 A6
Edison Gv WOOL/PLUM SE18 148 A1
Edison Rd CEND/HSY/T N8 66 D3
HAYES BR2 183 J5
PEND EN3 25 H2
WELL DA16 148 A2
Edis St CAMTN NW1 84 A6
Edith Cavell Wy
WOOL/PLUM SE18 146 D2
Edith Gdns BRYLDS KT5 191 J4
Edith Gv WBPTN SW10 120 B6
Edithna St BRXN/ST SW9 141 K4
Edith Nesbit Wk
ELTH/MOT SE9 146 D5
Edith Neville Cots
CAMTN NW1 4 C4
Edith Rd CHDH RM6 73 K4
EHAM E6 89 H5
FBAR/BDGN N11 48 D3
ORP BR6 217 G3
SNWD SE25 196 E2
SRTFD E15 88 B3
WIM/MER SW19 178 A2
WKENS W14 119 H4
Edith Rw FUL/PGN SW6 140 A2
Edith St BETH E2 7 K2
Edith Ter WBPTN SW10 * 140 B1
Edith Vls WKENS W14 119 J4
Edith Yd WBPTN SW10 140 C1
Edlson Cl WALTH E17 69 J2
Edmansons Cl TOTM N17 50 B5
Edmeston Cl HOM E9 87 G4
Edmund Gv FELT TW13 154 E4
Edmund Halley Wy
GNWCH SE10 125 H2
Edmund Hurst Dr EHAM E6 108 B4
Edmund Rd MTCM CR4 178 D6
RAIN RM13 111 G2
STMC/STPC BR5 202 D3
WELL DA16 148 B4
Edmunds Av STMC/STPC BR5 186 E6
Edmunds Cl YEAD UB4 95 G4
Edmund St CMBW SE5 142 E1
Edmunds Wk EFNCH N2 65 J1
Edna Rd RYNPK SW20 177 G5
Edna St BTSEA SW11 140 D2
Edrick Rd EDGW HA8 44 E2
Edrick Wk EDGW HA8 44 E2
Edric Rd NWCR SE14 144 A1
Edridge Rd CROY/NA CR0 211 J1
Edward Av CHING E4 51 K1
MRDN SM4 194 C2
Edward Cl CRICK NW2 * 82 B2
ED N9 36 B2
HPTN TW12 173 H1
Edward Ct CAN/RD E16 106 E4
Edwardes Pl WKENS W14 119 J3
Edward Gv EBAR EN4 21 H6
Edward Mann Cl East
WCHPL E1 * 105 F5
Edward Mann Cl West
WCHPL E1 * 105 F5
Edward Ms CAMTN NW1 * 3 K4
Edward Pl DEPT SE8 124 C6
Edward Rd BMLY BR1 184 A3
CHDH RM6 74 A3
CHST BR7 185 G1
CROY/NA CR0 197 F4
EBAR EN4 21 H6
EBED/NFELT TW14 133 G6
HPTN TW12 173 H1
NTHLT UB5 95 G1
PGE/AN SE20 182 A3
RYLN/HDSTN HA2 42 C6
WALTH E17 69 F1
Edwards Av RSLP HA4 77 G3
Edwards Cl WPK KT4 193 G6
Edward's Cots IS N1 * 85 H5
Edwards Dr FBAR/BDGN N11 48 D3
Edward's La STNW/STAM N16 67 K6
Edwards Ms IS N1 85 H5
MHST W1U 9 G4
Edwards Pl FBAR/BDGN N11 48 D3
Edward Sq IS N1 5 G1
Edwards Rd BELV DA17 129 H4
Edward St CAN/RD E16 106 E3
NWCR SE14 144 B1
Edward's Wy BROCKY SE4 144 D6
Edward Temme Av
SRTFD E15 88 D5
Edward Tyler Rd
LEE/GVPK SE12 166 A4
Edward Wy ASHF TW15 152 C4
Edwina Gdns REDBR IG4 71 J2
Edwin Av EHAM E6 108 A1
Edwin Cl BXLYHN DA7 129 G6
RAIN RM13 111 H2
Edwin Hall Pl LEW SE13 165 G1
Edwin Pl CROY/NA CR0 196 E5
Edwin Rd EDGW HA8 45 F2
RDART DA2 170 E5
WHTN TW2 155 K3
Edwin's Md HOM E9 87 G2
Edwin St CAN/RD E16 106 E4
WCHPL E1 104 E3
Edwin Ware Ct PIN HA5 * 41 G5
Edwyn Cl BAR EN5 32 A1
Eel Brook Cl FUL/PGN SW6 * 140 A2
Effie Rd FUL/PGN SW6 139 K1
Effingham Cl BELMT SM2 209 F5
Effingham Rd
CEND/HSY/T N8 67 G2
CROY/NA CR0 196 A4
LEE/GVPK SE12 145 H6
SURB KT6 190 C4
Effort St TOOT SW17 178 D1
Effra Pde BRXS/STRHM SW2 142 B6
Effra Rd BRXS/STRHM SW2 142 B6
WIM/MER SW19 178 A2
Egan Wy HYS/HAR UB3 94 C6
Egbert St CAMTN NW1 84 A6
Egerton Cl DART DA1 170 E3
PIN HA5 58 E1
Egerton Crs CHEL SW3 14 D6
Egerton Dr GNWCH SE10 144 E2
Egerton Gdns CHEL SW3 14 C5
GDMY/SEVK IG3 91 F1
HDN NW4 63 K1
WEA W13 97 H5
WLSDN NW10 * 82 A6
Egerton Gardens Ms
CHEL SW3 14 D5
Egerton Pl CHEL SW3 * 14 D5
Egerton Rd ALP/SUD HA0 80 B5
NWMAL KT3 192 C1
SNWD SE25 181 F6
STNW/STAM N16 68 B4
WHTN TW2 155 K2
Egerton Ter CHEL SW3 14 D5
Egerton Wy HYS/HAR UB3 132 E1
Egham Cl CHEAM SM3 193 H6
Egham Crs CHEAM SM3 208 B1
Egham Rd PLSTW E13 107 F4
Eglantine Rd
WAND/EARL SW18 140 B6
Egleston Rd MRDN SM4 194 A3
Eglington Rd CHING E4 38 B2
Eglinton Hl WOOL/PLUM SE18 127 G6
Eglinton Rd
WOOL/PLUM SE18 127 F6
Egliston Ms PUT/ROE SW15 139 F4
Egliston Rd PUT/ROE SW15 139 F4
Eglon Ms CAMTN NW1 83 K5
Egmont Av SURB KT6 191 G5
Egmont Ms HOR/WEW KT19 207 F3
Egmont Rd BELMT SM2 209 G5
NWMAL KT3 192 C1
SURB KT6 191 G5
WOT/HER KT12 188 A4
Egmont St NWCR SE14 144 A1
Egremont Rd WNWD SE27 162 B5
Egret Wy YEAD UB4 95 H5
Eider Cl SRTFD E15 88 D3
Eighteenth Rd MTCM CR4 195 K1
Eighth Av HYS/HAR UB3 113 K1
MNPK E12 89 K2
Eileen Rd SNWD SE25 196 E2
Eindhoven Cl CAR SM5 195 F5
WIM/MER SW19 178 C4
Eisenhower Dr EHAM E6 107 J4
Elaine Gv KTTN NW5 84 A3
Elam Cl CMBW SE5 142 C3
Elam St CMBW SE5 142 C3
Eland Rd BTSEA SW11 140 E4
CROY/NA CR0 211 H1
Elba Pl WALW SE17 * 18 D6
Elberon Av CROY/NA CR0 195 H3
Elbe St FUL/PGN SW6 140 B3
Elborough Rd SNWD SE25 197 H2
Elborough St
WAND/EARL SW18 159 K3
Elbury Dr CAN/RD E16 106 E5
Elcho St BTSEA SW11 140 D1
Elcot Av PECK SE15 143 J1
Elder Av CEND/HSY/T N8 66 E2
Elderberry Cl BARK/HLT IG6 54 B3
Elderberry Rd EA W5 117 F2
Elder Cl BFN/LL DA15 168 A3
TRDG/WHET N20 33 F4
Elder Ct BUSH WD23 28 E4
Elderfield Rd CLPT E5 87 F2
Elderfield Wk WAN E11 71 F2
Elderflower Wy SRTFD E15 88 C5
Elder Oak Cl PGE/AN SE20 181 J4
Elder Rd WNWD SE27 180 D1
Elderslie Cl BECK BR3 198 D3
Elderslie Rd ELTH/MOT SE9 147 F6
Elder St WCHPL E1 13 J1
Elderton Rd SYD SE26 164 B6
Eldertree Pl MTCM CR4 179 H4
Eldertree Wy MTCM CR4 179 G4
Elder Wk IS N1 85 H6
Eldon Av CROY/NA CR0 197 K6
HEST TW5 135 F1
Eldon Gv HAMP NW3 83 H3
Eldon Pde WDGN N22 * 49 H4
Eldon Pk SNWD SE25 197 J1
Eldon Rd ED N9 36 E3
KENS W8 120 A3
WALTH E17 69 H1
WDGN N22 49 H4
Eldon St LVPST EC2M 13 F2
Eldon Wy WLSDN NW10 98 D1
Eldred Dr STMC/STPC BR5 202 E6
Eldrick Ct EBED/NFELT TW14 153 G3
Eldridge Cl EBED/NFELT TW14 153 K3
Eleanora Ter SUT SM1 * 209 G3
Eleanor Cl BERM/RHTH SE16 124 A2
SEVS/STOTM N15 50 B6
Eleanor Crs MLHL NW7 32 B6
Eleanor Gdns BAR EN5 20 B6
Eleanor Gv BARN SW13 138 B4
Eleanor Rd FBAR/BDGN N11 48 E2
HACK E8 86 D4
SRTFD E15 88 D4
Eleanor St BOW E3 105 J2
Electra Av HTHAIR TW6 133 J4
Electric Av BRXN/ST SW9 142 B5
Electric La BRXN/ST SW9 * 142 B5
Electric Pde SURB KT6 190 E3
Elephant & Castle STHWK SE1 18 B6
Elephant La
BERM/RHTH SE16 123 K2
Elephant Rd WALW SE17 18 C6
Elers Rd HYS/HAR UB3 113 F4
WEA W13 116 D2
Eley Rd UED N18 51 F1
Elfindale Rd HNHL SE24 142 D6
Elfin Gv TEDD TW11 174 A1
Elford Cl BKHTH/KID SE3 146 B5
Elfort Rd HBRY N5 85 G2
Elfrida Crs CAT SE6 164 D6
Elf Rw WAP E1W 104 E6
Elfwine Rd HNWL W7 96 E4
Elgal Cl ORP BR6 216 B3
Elgar Av BRYLDS KT5 191 J5
EA W5 117 F2
STRHM/NOR SW16 179 K6
WLSDN NW10 81 F4
Elgar Cl BKHH IG9 39 H4
BORE WD6 29 J2
DEPT SE8 144 D1
PLSTW E13 107 G1
Elgar St BERM/RHTH SE16 124 B2
Elgin Av KTN/HRWW/WS HA3 43 H5
MV/WKIL W9 100 E3
SHB W12 118 D2
Elgin Cl SHB W12 118 E2
Elgin Crs HTHAIR TW6 133 H3
NTGHL W11 100 C6
Elgin Dr NTHWD HA6 40 C3
Elginmeads South
MV/WKIL W9 101 F2
Elgin Ms NTGHL W11 100 C5
Elgin Ms North MV/WKIL W9 101 F2
Elgin Rd CROY/NA CR0 197 G6
GDMY/SEVK IG3 72 E5
SUT SM1 209 G1
WDGN N22 48 C5
WLGTN SM6 210 C4
Elgood Av NTHWD HA6 40 E2
Elgood Cl NTGHL W11 100 C6
Elham Cl BMLY BR1 184 C3
Elia Ms IS N1 6 A3
Elias Pl VX/NE SW8 122 B6
Elia St IS N1 6 A3
Elibank Rd ELTH/MOT SE9 147 F5
Elim St STHWK SE1 19 G4
Elim Wy PLSTW E13 106 D2
Eliot Bank FSTH SE23 163 J4

Eliot Dr RYLN/HDSTN HA2 60 B6
Eliot Gdns PUT/ROE SW15 138 D5
Eliot Hl LEW SE13 145 F3
Eliot Ms STJWD NW8 101 G1
Eliot Pk LEW SE13 145 F3
Eliot Pl BKHTH/KID SE3 145 H3
Eliot Rd DAGW RM9 91 K2
Eliot V BKHTH/KID SE3 145 G3
Elizabethan Wy
STWL/WRAY TW19 152 A2
Elizabeth Av ENC/FH EN2 23 H4
IL IG1 72 D6
IS N1 85 J5
Elizabeth Barnes Ct
FUL/PGN SW6 * 140 A3
Elizabeth Br BGVA SW1W 15 J7
Elizabeth Cl BAR EN5 20 B4
MV/WKIL W9 101 G3
ROMW/RG RM7 56 D4
SUT SM1 208 D2
Elizabeth Clyde Cl
SEVS/STOTM N15 68 A1
Elizabeth Cots RCH/KEW TW9 137 G2
Elizabeth Fry Pl
WOOL/PLUM SE18 146 D2
Elizabeth Fry Rd HACK E8 86 D5
Elizabeth Gdns ACT W3 118 C1
ISLW TW7 136 B5
STAN HA7 43 J2
SUN TW16 172 B6
Elizabeth Ms HAMP NW3 83 J4
Elizabeth Pl SEVS/STOTM N15 67 K1
Elizabeth Ride ED N9 36 D2
Elizabeth Rd EHAM E6 89 H6
RAIN RM13 111 K4
SEVS/STOTM N15 68 A2
Elizabeth Sq
BERM/RHTH SE16 105 G6
Elizabeth St BGVA SW1W 15 H6
Elizabeth Wy FELT TW13 154 B6
NRWD SE19 180 E3
STMC/STPC BR5 202 D2
Elkanette Ms
TRDG/WHET N20 33 G4
Elkington Rd PLSTW E13 107 F3
The Elkins ROM RM1 57 G5
Elkstone Rd NKENS W10 100 D4
Ellaline Rd HMSMTH W6 119 G6
Ella Ms HAMP NW3 83 K2
Ellanby Crs UED N18 50 D1
Elland Cl BAR EN5 21 H6
Elland Rd PECK SE15 143 K5
WOT/HER KT12 188 C6
Ella Rd CEND/HSY/T N8 66 E4
Ellement Cl PIN HA5 59 H2
Ellenborough Pl
PUT/ROE SW15 138 D5
Ellenborough Rd SCUP DA14 186 E2
WDGN N22 49 J4
Ellenbridge Wy
SAND/SEL CR2 212 A6
Ellen Cl BMLY BR1 184 C6
Ellen Ct ED N9 36 E4
Ellen St WCHPL E1 * 104 C5
Ellen Webb Dr
KTN/HRWW/WS HA3 42 E6
Elleray Rd TEDD TW11 174 A2
Ellerby St FUL/PGN SW6 139 G2
Ellerdale Cl HAMP NW3 83 G3
Ellerdale Rd HAMP NW3 83 G3
Ellerdale St LEW SE13 144 E5
Ellerdine Rd HSLW TW3 135 H5
Ellerker Gdns
RCHPK/HAM TW10 157 F1
Ellerman Av WHTN TW2 154 E3
Ellerslie Rd SHB W12 118 E1
Ellerton Gdns DAGW RM9 91 J5
Ellerton Rd BARN SW13 * 138 D2
DAGW RM9 91 J5
RYNPK SW20 176 D3
SURB KT6 191 G6
WAND/EARL SW18 160 C3
Ellery Rd NRWD SE19 180 E3
Ellery St PECK SE15 143 J3
Ellesborough Cl OXHEY WD19 41 G1
Ellesmere Av BECK BR3 182 E5
MLHL NW7 31 F5
Ellesmere Cl RSLP HA4 58 A4
WAN E11 70 D2
Ellesmere Gdns REDBR IG4 71 J2
Ellesmere Gv BAR EN5 20 D6
Ellesmere Rd BOW E3 105 G1
GFD/PVL UB6 96 C3
TWK TW1 156 D1
WLSDN NW10 81 J3
Ellesmere St POP/IOD E14 105 K5
Ellies Ms ASHF TW15 152 B4
Ellingfort Rd HACK E8 86 D5
Ellingham Rd CHSGTN KT9 205 K4
SHB W12 118 D2
SRTFD E15 88 B2
Ellington Rd FELT TW13 153 J6
HSLW TW3 135 G3
MUSWH N10 66 B1
Ellington St HOLWY N7 85 G4
Elliot Cl SRTFD E15 88 C5
WBLY HA9 80 B1
WFD IG8 53 H2
Elliot Rd HDN NW4 63 K3
Elliott Av RSLP HA4 59 F6
Elliott Gdns HARH RM3 57 K4
Elliott Rd BRXN/ST SW9 142 C1
CHSWK W4 118 B4
HAYES BR2 200 C1
STAN HA7 43 G2
THHTH CR7 196 C1
Elliott's Pl IS N1 6 B1
Elliott Sq HAMP NW3 83 J5
Elliott's Rw LBTH SE11 18 B6
Ellis Av RAIN RM13 111 J4
Ellis Cl EDGW HA8 45 G2
ELTH/MOT SE9 167 H4
WLSDN NW10 82 A4
Elliscombe Mt CHARL SE7 * 126 B6
Elliscombe Rd CHARL SE7 126 B5
Ellisfield Dr PUT/ROE SW15 158 C2
Ellison Gdns NWDGN UB2 114 E4
Ellison Rd BARN SW13 138 C3
BFN/LL DA15 167 J3
STRHM/NOR SW16 179 J3
Ellis Rd MTCM CR4 194 E3
NWDGN UB2 115 H1
Ellis St KTBR SW1X 15 F6
Ellis Wy DART DA1 * 171 J4
Ellmore Cl HARH RM3 57 K4
Ellora Rd STRHM/NOR SW16 179 J1
Ellsworth St BETH E2 * 104 D2
Elmar Rd SEVS/STOTM N15 67 K1
Elm Av EA W5 117 F1
OXHEY WD19 27 J2
RSLP HA4 58 E5
Elmbank STHGT/OAK N14 34 E2
Elmbank Av BAR EN5 20 A5
Elmbank Dr BMLY BR1 184 C5
Elm Bank Gdns BARN SW13 138 B3
Elmbank Wy HNWL W7 96 D4
Elmbourne Dr BELV DA17 129 J4
Elmbourne Rd TOOT SW17 161 G5
Elmbridge Av BRYLDS KT5 191 K3
Elmbridge Cl RSLP HA4 58 E3
Elmbridge Dr RSLP HA4 58 E3
Elmbridge Rd BARK/HLT IG6 55 G2
Elmbridge Wk HACK E8 * 86 C5
Elmbrook Cl SUN TW16 172 A4
Elmbrook Gdns
ELTH/MOT SE9 146 D5
Elmbrook Rd SUT SM1 208 D2
Elm Cl BKHH IG9 39 H4
BRYLDS KT5 191 K4
CAR SM5 194 E5
DART DA1 171 F3
HDN NW4 64 B2
HYS/HAR UB3 94 E5
ROMW/RG RM7 56 D4
RYLN/HDSTN HA2 60 B3
RYNPK SW20 193 F1
SAND/SEL CR2 211 K4
STWL/WRAY TW19 152 A3
WAN E11 71 F3
WHTN TW2 155 G4
Elm Cots MTCM CR4 * 178 E5
Elmcourt Rd WNWD SE27 162 C4
Elm Crs EA W5 117 F2
KUTN/CMB KT2 175 F4
Elmcroft CEND/HSY/T N8 67 F2
Elmcroft Av BFN/LL DA15 168 A2
ED N9 36 D1
GLDGN NW11 64 D4
WAN E11 71 F2
Elmcroft Cl CHSGTN KT9 * 206 A1
EA W5 97 K5
EBED/NFELT TW14 153 J1
Elmcroft Crs GLDGN NW11 64 B4
RYLN/HDSTN HA2 42 A6
Elmcroft Dr CHSGTN KT9 206 A1
Elmcroft Gdns
CDALE/KGS NW9 62 C2
Elmcroft Rd ORP BR6 202 B4
Elmcroft St CLPT E5 86 E2
Elmdale Rd PLMGR N13 49 F1
Elmdene BRYLDS KT5 191 K5
Elmdene Cl BECK BR3 198 C2
Elmdene Rd
WOOL/PLUM SE18 127 G5
Elmdon Rd HSLWW TW4 134 C3
HTHAIR TW6 133 J4
Elm Dr RYLN/HDSTN HA2 60 B3
SUN TW16 172 B5
Elmer Cl ENC/FH EN2 23 F4
RAIN RM13 93 J5
Elmer Gdns EDGW HA8 44 D3
ISLW TW7 135 J4
RAIN RM13 93 J5
Elmer Rd CAT SE6 165 F2
Elmer's Dr TEDD TW11 174 C2
Elmers End Rd BECK BR3 181 K6
Elmerside Rd BECK BR3 198 B1
Elmers Rd SNWD SE25 197 H4
Elmfield Av CEND/HSY/T N8 66 E2
MTCM CR4 179 F4
TEDD TW11 174 A1
Elmfield Cl HRW HA1 60 E6
Elmfield Pk BMLY BR1 183 K6
Elmfield Rd BMLY BR1 183 K6
CHING E4 38 A4
EFNCH N2 47 H6
NWDGN UB2 114 D3
TOOT SW17 161 G4
WALTH E17 69 F3
Elmfield Wy MV/WKIL W9 100 E4
SAND/SEL CR2 212 B6
Elm Friars Wk CAMTN NW1 84 D5
Elm Gdns EFNCH N2 47 G6
ENC/FH EN2 23 K1
ESH/CLAY KT10 205 F4
MTCM CR4 195 J1
Elmgate Av FELT TW13 154 A5
Elmgate Gdns EDGW HA8 44 E1
Elm Gn ACT W3 99 G5
Elmgreen Cl SRTFD E15 88 C6
Elm Gv CEND/HSY/T N8 66 E3
CRICK NW2 82 B2
ERITH DA8 150 A1
KUTN/CMB KT2 175 F4
ORP BR6 202 A5
PECK SE15 143 H3
RYLN/HDSTN HA2 60 A4
SUT SM1 209 F2
WIM/MER SW19 177 H3
Elmgrove Crs HRW HA1 61 F2
Elmgrove Gdns HRW HA1 61 G2
Elm Grove Pde CAR SM5 * 210 A1
Elm Grove Rd BARN SW13 138 D3
EA W5 117 F2
Elmgrove Rd CROY/NA CR0 197 J4
HRW HA1 61 F2
Elm Hall Gdns WAN E11 71 F3
Elm Hatch PIN HA5 * 41 K3
Elmhurst BELV DA17 129 F6
Elmhurst Av EFNCH N2 * 47 H6
MTCM CR4 179 F3
Elmhurst Crs EFNCH N2 47 H6
Elmhurst Dr SWFD E18 52 E5
Elmhurst Rd ELTH/MOT SE9 166 D4
FSTGT E7 89 F5
TOTM N17 50 A5
Elmhurst St CLAP SW4 141 J4
Elmhurst Wy LOU IG10 39 K2
Elmington Cl BXLY DA5 169 J2
Elmington Est CMBW SE5 142 D1
Elmington Rd CMBW SE5 142 E2
Elmira St LEW SE13 144 E4
Elm La CAT SE6 164 C4
Elmlee Cl CHST BR7 184 E2
Elmley St WOOL/PLUM SE18 127 J4
Elmore Cl ALP/SUD HA0 98 A1
Elmore Rd PEND EN3 25 F2
WAN E11 88 A1
Elmore St IS N1 85 K5
Elm Pde SCUP DA14 * 168 B6
Elm Pk BRXS/STRHM SW2 162 A1
STAN HA7 43 H1
Elm Park Av HCH RM12 93 J2
SEVS/STOTM N15 68 B2
Elm Park Gdns HDN NW4 64 B2
WBPTN SW10 120 C5
Elm Park La CHEL SW3 120 C5
Elm Park Rd CHEL SW3 120 C6
FNCH N3 46 D3
LEY E10 69 G5
PIN HA5 41 H6
SNWD SE25 181 G6
WCHMH N21 35 J2
Elm Pl SKENS SW7 120 C5
Elm Rd BAR EN5 20 D5
BECK BR3 182 C5
CHSGTN KT9 206 A2
DART DA1 171 G3
EBED/NFELT TW14 153 G3
ERITH DA8 150 D2
ESH/CLAY KT10 205 F4
EW KT17 207 H4
FSTGT E7 88 D4
KUTN/CMB KT2 175 G3
MORT/ESHN SW14 137 K4
NWMAL KT3 176 A6
ORP BR6 217 G5
ROMW/RG RM7 56 D5
SCUP DA14 168 B6
THHTH CR7 196 D1
WALTH E17 70 A2
WBLY HA9 80 A3
WDGN N22 49 H4
WLGTN SM6 195 F5
Elm Rd West CHEAM SM3 193 J4
Elm Rw HAMP NW3 83 G1
Elms Av HDN NW4 64 A2
MUSWH N10 48 B6
Elms Cl EMPK RM11 75 K4
Elmscott Gdns WCHMH N21 35 J1
Elmscott Rd BMLY BR1 183 H1
Elms Ct ALP/SUD HA0 79 F2
Elms Crs CLAP SW4 161 H1
Elmsdale Rd WALTH E17 69 H1
Elmsdene Ms NTHWD HA6 40 A2
Elms Gdns ALP/SUD HA0 79 G2
DAGW RM9 92 B2
Elmshaw Rd PUT/ROE SW15 138 D6
Elmshurst Crs EFNCH N2 65 G1
Elmside CROY/NA CR0 213 K4
Elmside Rd WBLY HA9 80 C1
Elms La ALP/SUD HA0 79 G2
Elmsleigh Av
KTN/HRWW/WS HA3 61 H1
Elmsleigh Rd WHTN TW2 155 J4
Elmslie Cl WFD IG8 53 K2
Elms Ms BAY/PAD W2 8 A5
Elms Park Av ALP/SUD HA0 79 G2
Elms Rd CLAP SW4 141 H6
KTN/HRWW/WS HA3 42 E3
Elmstead Av CHST BR7 184 E1
WBLY HA9 62 A5
Elmstead Cl HOR/WEW KT19 207 G3
TRDG/WHET N20 32 E4
Elmstead Gdns WPK KT4 207 J1
Elmstead Gld CHST BR7 184 E2
Elmstead La CHST BR7 184 D3
Elmstead Rd ERITH DA8 150 B2
GDMY/SEVK IG3 72 E6
Elmsted Crs WELL DA16 128 D6
The Elms BARN SW13 138 C4
ESH/CLAY KT10 * 205 F5
NFNCH/WDSPK N12 * 47 J1
TOOT SW17 * 161 F5
WLGTN SM6 * 210 C2
Elmstone Rd FUL/PGN SW6 139 K2
Elmstone Ter
STMC/STPC BR5 * 202 D1
Elm St FSBYW WC1X 5 H7
Elmsworth Av HSLW TW3 135 G3
Elm Ter CRICK NW2 82 E1
ELTH/MOT SE9 167 F1
KTN/HRWW/WS HA3 42 D3
Elmton Wy CLPT E5 86 C1
Elm Tree Av ESH/CLAY KT10 189 J4
Elm Tree Cl NTHLT UB5 95 K1
STJWD NW8 2 A4
Elm Tree Ct CHARL SE7 * 126 B6
Elm Tree Rd STJWD NW8 2 A4
Elmtree Rd TEDD TW11 173 K1
Elm Vls HNWL W7 * 96 E6
Elm Wk GPK RM2 57 J6
HAMP NW3 64 E6
ORP BR6 215 K1
RYNPK SW20 193 F1
Elm Wy FBAR/BDGN N11 48 A2
HOR/WEW KT19 207 F3
WLSDN NW10 81 G2
WPK KT4 208 A1
Elmwood CHIG IG7 54 D2
Elmwood Av FELT TW13 154 A5
KTN/HRWW/WS HA3 61 G2
PLMGR N13 48 E1
Elmwood Cl EW KT17 207 J5
WLGTN SM6 195 G6
Elmwood Crs
CDALE/KGS NW9 62 E1
Elmwood Dr BXLY DA5 169 F2
EW KT17 207 J5
Elmwood Gdns HNWL W7 96 E5
Elmwood Rd CHSWK W4 117 K6
CROY/NA CR0 196 C4
HNHL SE24 142 E6
MTCM CR4 178 E6
Elmworth Gv DUL SE21 162 E4
Elnathan Ms MV/WKIL W9 101 F3
Elphinstone Rd WALTH E17 51 H5
Elphinstone St HBRY N5 85 H2
Elrick Cl ERITH DA8 130 B6
Elrington Rd HACK E8 86 C4
WFD IG8 52 E1
Elruge Cl WDR/YW UB7 112 A3
Elsa Cots POP/IOD E14 * 105 G4
Elsa Rd WELL DA16 148 D3
Elsa St WCHPL E1 * 105 G4
Elsdale St HOM E9 86 E4
Elsden Ms BETH E2 * 104 E1
Elsden Rd TOTM N17 50 B4
Elsenham Rd MNPK E12 89 K3
Elsenham St
WAND/EARL SW18 159 J3
Elsham Rd WAN E11 88 C1
WKENS W14 119 H2
Elsham Ter WKENS W14 * 119 H2
Elsiedene Rd WCHMH N21 35 J2
Elsiemaud Rd BROCKY SE4 144 C6
Elsie Rd EDUL SE22 143 G5
Elsinore Av
STWL/WRAY TW19 * 152 B2
Elsinore Gdns CRICK NW2 * 82 C1
Elsinore Rd FSTH SE23 164 B3
Elsinore Wy RCH/KEW TW9 137 J4
Elsley Rd BTSEA SW11 140 E4
Elspeth Rd ALP/SUD HA0 80 A3
BTSEA SW11 140 E5
Elsrick Av MRDN SM4 193 K2
Elstan Wy CROY/NA CR0 198 B4
Elsted St WALW SE17 19 F7
Elstow Cl ELTH/MOT SE9 146 E6
RSLP HA4 59 H4
Elstow Gdns DAGW RM9 92 A6
Elstow Rd DAGW RM9 92 A5
Elstree Cl HCH RM12 93 K5
Elstree Gdns BELV DA17 129 F4
ED N9 36 D3
IL IG1 90 C3
Elstree Hl BMLY BR1 183 H3
Elstree Hl South BORE WD6 29 J2
Elstree Pk BORE WD6 * 31 F1
Elstree Rd BORE WD6 29 G1
BUSH WD23 28 D3
Elswick Rd LEW SE13 144 E3
Elswick St FUL/PGN SW6 140 B3
Elsworth Cl
EBED/NFELT TW14 153 H3
Elsworthy THDIT KT7 189 K3
Elsworthy Ri HAMP NW3 83 J5
Elsworthy Rd HAMP NW3 83 J6
Elsworthy Ter HAMP NW3 83 J5
Elsynge Rd WAND/EARL SW18 140 C6
Eltham Gn ELTH/MOT SE9 146 B6
Eltham High St
ELTH/MOT SE9 166 E1
Eltham Hl ELTH/MOT SE9 146 C6
Eltham Palace Rd
ELTH/MOT SE9 166 B1
Eltham Park Gdns
ELTH/MOT SE9 147 F5
Eltham Rd ELTH/MOT SE9 146 B6
LEE/GVPK SE12 145 K6
Elthiron Rd FUL/PGN SW6 139 K2
Elthorne Av HNWL W7 116 A2
Elthorne Ct FELT TW13 154 B3
Elthorne Park Rd HNWL W7 116 A3
Elthorne Rd ARCH N19 66 D6
CDALE/KGS NW9 63 F4
Elthorne Wy CDALE/KGS NW9 63 F3
Elthruda Rd LEW SE13 165 G1
Eltisley Rd IL IG1 90 B2
Elton Av ALP/SUD HA0 79 H3
BAR EN5 20 D6
GFD/PVL UB6 79 F4
Elton Cl KUT/HW KT1 174 D3
Elton Pl STNW/STAM N16 86 A3
Elton Rd KUTN/CMB KT2 175 G4
Eltringham St
WAND/EARL SW18 140 B5
Elvaston Ms SKENS SW7 * 120 B3
Elvaston Pl SKENS SW7 120 B3
Elveden Pl WLSDN NW10 98 C1
Elveden Rd WLSDN NW10 98 C1
Elvedon Rd FELT TW13 153 J5
Elvendon Rd FBAR/BDGN N11 48 C2
Elver Gdns BETH E2 104 C2
Elverson Ms DEPT SE8 * 144 C1
Elverson Rd DEPT SE8 144 E3
Elverton St WEST SW1P 16 C6
Elvington Gn HAYES BR2 199 J2
Elvington La CDALE/KGS NW9 45 G4
Elvino Rd SYD SE26 182 A1
Elvis Rd CRICK NW2 82 A4
Elwill Wy BECK BR3 199 F1
Elwin St BETH E2 104 C2
Elwood Cl BAR EN5 21 G5
Elwood St HBRY N5 85 H1
Elwyn Gdns LEE/GVPK SE12 165 K2
Ely Cl ERITH DA8 150 C3
NWMAL KT3 176 C5
Ely Cots VX/NE SW8 * 142 A1
Ely Gdns DAGE RM10 92 E1
Elyne Rd FSBYPK N4 67 G3
Ely Pl HCIRC EC1N 11 K2
WFD IG8 54 A1
Ely Rd CROY/NA CR0 196 E2
HSLWW TW4 134 B4
HTHAIR TW6 133 J3
LEY E10 70 A3
Elysan Pl SAND/SEL CR2 211 J5
Elysian Av STMC/STPC BR5 201 K3
Elysium Pl FUL/PGN SW6 139 J3
Elysium St FUL/PGN SW6 139 J3
Elystan Cl WLGTN SM6 210 C6
Elystan Pl CHEL SW3 120 D5
Elystan St CHEL SW3 14 C7
Elystan Wk IS N1 5 J1
Emanuel Av ACT W3 98 E5
Embankment PUT/ROE SW15 139 G4
Embankment Gdns CHEL SW3 120 E6
Embankment Pl CHCR WC2N 11 F7
The Embankment TWK TW1 156 B3
Embassy Ct SCUP DA14 168 C5
WLGTN SM6 * 210 B4
Emba St BERM/RHTH SE16 123 H2
Ember Cl STMC/STPC BR5 201 H4
Embercourt Rd THDIT KT7 189 K3
Ember Farm Av
E/WMO/HCT KT8 189 J3
Ember Farm Wy
E/WMO/HCT KT8 189 J2
Ember Gdns THDIT KT7 189 K4
Ember La ESH/CLAY KT10 189 J4
Emblem Ct EDUL SE22 143 H6
Embleton Rd LEW SE13 144 E5
OXHEY WD19 26 E5
Embry Cl STAN HA7 29 G6
Embry Dr STAN HA7 43 G2
Embry Wy STAN HA7 43 G1
Emden Cl WDR/YW UB7 112 D2
Emden St FUL/PGN SW6 140 A2
Emerald Cl CAN/RD E16 107 J5
Emerald Gdns BCTR RM8 74 B5
Emerald Rd WLSDN NW10 81 F6
Emerald Sq NWDGN UB2 114 C3
Emerald St BMSBY WC1N 11 G1
Emerson Gdns
KTN/HRWW/WS HA3 62 B3
Emerson Rd IL IG1 72 A4
Emerson St STHWK SE1 12 C7
Emerton Cl BXLYHS DA6 149 F5
Emery Hill St WEST SW1P 16 B5
Emery St STHWK SE1 17 K4
Emes Rd ERITH DA8 149 K1
Emilia Cl PEND EN3 24 D6
Emily St CAN/RD E16 106 D5
Emlyn Rd SHB W12 118 B2
Emmanuel Rd BAL SW12 161 H3
NTHWD HA6 40 D3
Emma Rd PLSTW E13 106 D1
Emma St BETH E2 104 D1
Emma Ter RYNPK SW20 * 177 F3
Emmaus Wy CHIG IG7 54 A1
Emmott Av BARK/HLT IG6 72 C2
Emmott Cl GLDGN NW11 65 G3
WCHPL E1 105 G3
Emperor's Ga SKENS SW7 120 A3
Empire Av UED N18 49 J2
Empire Ms STRHM/NOR SW16 179 K1
Empire Pde UED N18 * 49 K2
WBLY HA9 * 80 C1
Empire Rd GFD/PVL UB6 79 H6
Empire Sq STHWK SE1 18 E3
Empire Wy WBLY HA9 80 B2
Empire Wharf Rd
POP/IOD E14 125 G4
Empress Av CHING E4 51 K3
IL IG1 72 A6
MNPK E12 71 G6
WFD IG8 52 D3
Empress Dr CHST BR7 185 G2
Empress Pde CHING E4 * 51 J3
Empress Pl FUL/PGN SW6 119 K5
Empress St WALW SE17 122 D6
Empson St BOW E3 105 K3
Emsworth Cl ED N9 36 E3
Emsworth Rd BARK/HLT IG6 54 B5
Emsworth St
BRXS/STRHM SW2 162 A4
Emu Rd VX/NE SW8 141 G3
Ena Rd STRHM/NOR SW16 179 K6
Enbrook St NKENS W10 100 C2
Enclave Ct FSBYE EC1V 6 B6
Endale Cl CAR SM5 194 E6
Endeavour Wy BARK IG11 109 G1
CROY/NA CR0 195 J4
WIM/MER SW19 160 A6
Endell St LSQ/SEVD WC2H 10 E3
Enderby St GNWCH SE10 125 H5
Enderley Rd
KTN/HRWW/WS HA3 42 D4
Endersby Rd BAR EN5 20 A6
Enders Cl ENC/FH EN2 23 G1
Endersleigh Gdns HDN NW4 63 J1
Endlebury Rd CHING E4 38 A4
Endlesham Rd BAL SW12 161 F2
Endsleigh Gdns IL IG1 71 K5
STPAN WC1H 4 C6
SURB KT6 190 D3
Endsleigh Pl STPAN WC1H 4 D6
Endsleigh Rd NWDGN UB2 114 D4
WEA W13 116 B1
Endsleigh St STPAN WC1H 4 D6
Endway BRYLDS KT5 191 H4
Endwell Rd BROCKY SE4 144 B3
Endymion Rd
BRXS/STRHM SW2 162 A1
FSBYPK N4 67 H4
Energen Cl WLSDN NW10 81 G4
Enfield Rd ACT W3 117 J2
BTFD TW8 116 E5
ENC/FH EN2 22 D5
HTHAIR TW6 133 H3
IS N1 86 A5
Enford St CAMTN NW1 8 E1
Engadine Cl CROY/NA CR0 212 B1
Engadine St
WAND/EARL SW18 159 J3
Engate St LEW SE13 145 F5
Engel Pk MLHL NW7 46 A2
Engineer Cl WOOL/PLUM SE18 127 F6
Engineers Wy WBLY HA9 80 C2
England's La HAMP NW3 83 K4
England Wy NWMAL KT3 191 J1
Englefield Cl CROY/NA CR0 196 D3
ENC/FH EN2 23 G3
STMC/STPC BR5 202 A1
Englefield Crs
STMC/STPC BR5 202 B2
Englefield Pth
STMC/STPC BR5 202 B1
Englefield Rd IS N1 85 K5
Engleheart Dr
EBED/NFELT TW14 153 J1
Engleheart Rd CAT SE6 164 E2
Englewood Rd BAL SW12 161 G1
English Grounds STHWK SE1 * 19 G1
English St BOW E3 105 H3
Enid St BERM/RHTH SE16 19 K4
Enmore Av SNWD SE25 197 H2
Enmore Gdns
MORT/ESHN SW14 138 A6
Enmore Rd PUT/ROE SW15 139 F5
SNWD SE25 197 H2
STHL UB1 96 A3
Ennerdale Av HCH RM12 93 J3
STAN HA7 43 J6
Ennerdale Cl
EBED/NFELT TW14 153 J3
SUT SM1 208 D2
Ennerdale Dr
CDALE/KGS NW9 63 G2

Ennerdale Gdns WBLY HA9 61 J5
Ennerdale Rd BXLYHN DA7 149 H2
RCH/KEW TW9 137 G3
Ennersdale Rd LEW SE13 145 G6
Ennismore Av CHSWK W4 118 B4
GFD/PVL UB6 78 E4
Ennismore Gdns SKENS SW7 14 B4
THDIT KT7 189 K3
Ennismore Gardens Ms
SKENS SW7 14 B4
Ennismore Ms SKENS SW7 14 C3
Ennismore St SKENS SW7 14 C4
Ennis Rd FSBYPK N4 67 G5
WOOL/PLUM SE18 127 J6
Ensign Cl HTHAIR TW6 133 H3
STWL/WRAY TW19 152 A3
Ensign Dr PLMGR N13 35 J5
Ensign St WCHPL E1 104 C6
Ensign Wy STWL/WRAY TW19 152 A3
WLGTN SM6 210 E5
Enslin Rd ELTH/MOT SE9 167 F1
Ensor Ms SKENS SW7 120 C5
Enstone Rd PEND EN3 25 G4
Enterprise Cl CROY/NA CR0 196 B5
Enterprise Rw
SEVS/STOTM N15 68 B2
Enterprise Wy TEDD TW11 174 A1
WAND/EARL SW18 139 K5
WLSDN NW10 99 H2
Enterprize Wy DEPT SE8 * 124 C4
Envoy Av HTHAIR TW6 133 J4
Epcot Ms WLSDN NW10 * 100 B2
Epirus Ms FUL/PGN SW6 139 K1
Epirus Rd FUL/PGN SW6 139 J1
Epping Cl POP/IOD E14 124 D4
ROMW/RG RM7 56 D6
Epping Gld CHING E4 38 A1
Epping New Rd BKHH IG9 39 F2
Epping Pl IS N1 85 G4
Epping Wy CHING E4 37 K1
Epple Rd FUL/PGN SW6 139 J2
Epsom Cl BXLYHN DA7 149 J4
NTHLT UB5 77 K3
Epsom Rd CHEAM SM3 * 193 J4
CROY/NA CR0 211 G2
GDMY/SEVK IG3 73 F3
LEY E10 70 A3
MRDN SM4 193 J3
Epstein Rd THMD SE28 128 C1
Epworth Rd ISLW TW7 136 C1
Epworth St SDTCH EC2A 7 F7
Equity Sq BETH E2 7 K5
Erasmus St WEST SW1P 16 D7
Erconwald St SHB W12 99 H5
Erebus Dr THMD SE28 127 H3
Eresby Dr BECK BR3 198 D5
Eresby Pl KIL/WHAMP NW6 82 E5
Erica Gdns CROY/NA CR0 213 K2
Erica St SHB W12 99 J6
Eric Clarke La EHAM E6 108 B3
Ericcson Cl WAND/EARL SW18 139 K6
Eric Est BOW E3 105 H3
Eric Rd CHDH RM6 73 K4
FSTGT E7 88 E2
WLSDN NW10 81 H4
Eric St BOW E3 105 H3
Eridge Green Cl
STMC/STPC BR5 202 D5
Eridge Rd CHSWK W4 118 A3
Erin Cl BMLY BR1 183 H3
FUL/PGN SW6 139 K1
Erindale WOOL/PLUM SE18 127 J6
Erindale Ter
WOOL/PLUM SE18 127 J6
Erin Ms WDGN N22 * 49 H4
Erith Ct PUR RM19 131 K4
Erith Crs CRW RM5 56 E4
Erith High St ERITH DA8 130 B5
Erith Rd BELV DA17 129 J5
BXLYHN DA7 149 J4
Erlanger Rd NWCR SE14 144 A2
Erlesmere Gdns HNWL W7 116 B3
Erlich Cots WCHPL E1 * 104 E4
Ermine Cl HSLWW TW4 134 B3
Ermine Rd LEW SE13 144 E4
SEVS/STOTM N15 68 B3
Ermine Side EN EN1 24 C6
Ermington Rd ELTH/MOT SE9 167 H4
Ernald Av EHAM E6 107 J1
Erncroft Wy TWK TW1 156 A1
Ernest Av WNWD SE27 162 C6
Ernest Cl BECK BR3 198 D2
Ernest Gdns CHSWK W4 117 J6
Ernest Gv BECK BR3 198 C2
Ernest Rd KUT/HW KT1 175 J5
Ernest St WCHPL E1 105 F3
Ernle Rd RYNPK SW20 176 E3
Ernshaw Pl PUT/ROE SW15 139 H6
Erpingham Rd
PUT/ROE SW15 139 F4
Erridge Rd WIM/MER SW19 177 K5
Errington Rd MV/WKIL W9 100 D3
Errol Gdns NWMAL KT3 192 D1
YEAD UB4 95 F3
Erroll Rd ROM RM1 75 H1
Errol St STLK EC1Y 6 D7
Erskine Cl SUT SM1 209 J1
Erskine Crs TOTM N17 68 D1
Erskine Hl GLDGN NW11 64 E1
Erskine Ms HAMP NW3 * 83 K5
Erskine Rd HAMP NW3 83 K5
SUT SM1 209 H2
WALTH E17 69 H1
Erwood Rd CHARL SE7 126 D5
Esam Wy STRHM/NOR SW16 180 B1
Escot Wy BAR EN5 20 A6
Escreet Gv WOOL/PLUM SE18 127 F4
Esher Av CHEAM SM3 208 B1
ROMW/RG RM7 74 E3
WOT/HER KT12 188 A5
Esher Cl BXLY DA5 169 F3
ESH/CLAY KT10 204 B3
Esher Crs HTHAIR TW6 133 J3
Esher Gn ESH/CLAY KT10 204 B2
Esher Green Dr
ESH/CLAY KT10 204 A1
Esher Ms MTCM CR4 179 F6
Esher Park Av ESH/CLAY KT10 204 C3
Esher Place Av
ESH/CLAY KT10 204 A2
Esher Rd E/WMO/HCT KT8 189 J2
GDMY/SEVK IG3 90 E1
Eskdale Av NTHLT UB5 77 K6
Eskdale Cl WBLY HA9 61 K6
Eskdale Rd BXLYHN DA7 149 H3
Eskmont Rdg NRWD SE19 181 F3
Esk Rd PLSTW E13 107 F3
Esk Wy ROM RM1 57 G3
Esmar Crs CDALE/KGS NW9 63 J4
Esmeralda Rd STHWK SE1 123 H4
Esmond Cl RAIN RM13 * 93 K5
Esmond Gdns CHSWK W4 * 118 A4
Esmond Rd CHSWK W4 118 A3
KIL/WHAMP NW6 82 D6
Esmond St PUT/ROE SW15 139 H5
Esparto St WAND/EARL SW18 160 A2
Essenden Rd BELV DA17 129 H5
SAND/SEL CR2 212 A5
Essendine Rd MV/WKIL W9 100 E2
Essex Av ISLW TW7 135 K4
Essex Cl MRDN SM4 193 G4
ROMW/RG RM7 74 D1
RSLP HA4 59 H5
WALTH E17 69 G1
Essex Ct BARN SW13 138 C3
EMB EC4Y * 11 J4
Essex Gdns FSBYPK N4 67 H3
Essex Gv NRWD SE19 180 E2
Essex Pk FNCH N3 47 F2
Essex Park Ms ACT W3 118 B1
Essex Pl CHSWK W4 117 K4
Essex Place Sq CHSWK W4 * 118 A4
Essex Rd ACT W3 98 E6
BARK IG11 90 D5
CHDH RM6 73 J5
CHING E4 38 C3
CHSWK W4 118 A4
DAGE RM10 92 E3
DART DA1 * 171 G1
ENC/FH EN2 23 K5
IS N1 85 H6
LEY E10 70 A3
MNPK E12 89 J3
ROMW/RG RM7 74 D1
SWFD E18 53 F5
WALTH E17 69 G3
WLSDN NW10 81 G5
Essex Rd South WAN E11 70 B4
Essex St FSTGT E7 88 E3
TPL/STR WC2R 11 J4
Essex Vls KENS W8 119 K2
Essex Whf CLPT E5 * 69 F6
Essian St WCHPL E1 105 G4
Essoldo Wy EDGW HA8 44 B6
Estate Wy LEY E10 69 H5
Estcourt Rd FUL/PGN SW6 139 J1
SNWD SE25 197 J3
Estella Av NWMAL KT3 192 E1
Estelle Rd HAMP NW3 83 K2
Esterbrooke St WEST SW1P 16 C7
Este Rd BTSEA SW11 140 D4
Esther Cl WCHMH N21 35 G2
Esther Rd WAN E11 70 C4
Estoria Cl BRXS/STRHM SW2 162 B2
Estreham Rd
STRHM/NOR SW16 179 J2
Estridge Cl HSLW TW3 135 F5
Estuary Cl BARK IG11 109 H2
Eswyn Rd TOOT SW17 160 E6
Etchingham Park Rd
FNCH N3 47 F3
Etchingham Rd SRTFD E15 88 A2
Eternit Wk FUL/PGN SW6 139 F2
Etfield Gv SCUP DA14 186 C1
Ethelbert Gdns REDBR IG4 71 K2
Ethelbert Rd BMLY BR1 183 K6
ERITH DA8 149 K1
RDART DA2 171 H6
RYNPK SW20 177 G4
STMC/STPC BR5 186 E6
Ethelbert St BAL SW12 161 G3
Ethelburga St BTSEA SW11 * 140 D2
Ethelden Av MUSWH N10 66 C1
Ethelden Rd SHB W12 118 E1
Ethelred Est LBTH SE11 17 J7
Ethel Rd CAN/RD E16 107 F6
Ethel St WALW SE17 * 18 D7
Ethel Ter ORP BR6 * 217 J6
Etheridge Rd CRICK NW2 64 A4
Etherley Rd SEVS/STOTM N15 67 J2
Etherow St EDUL SE22 163 H1
Etherstone Rd
STRHM/NOR SW16 162 B6
Ethnard Rd PECK SE15 123 J6
Ethronvi Rd BXLYHN DA7 149 F4
Etloe Rd LEY E10 69 J6
Eton Av ALP/SUD HA0 79 J2
EBAR EN4 33 J1
HAMP NW3 83 J5
HEST TW5 114 E6
NFNCH/WDSPK N12 47 G3
NWMAL KT3 192 A2
Eton Cl WAND/EARL SW18 160 A2
Eton College Rd HAMP NW3 83 K4
Eton Garages HAMP NW3 83 J4
Eton Gv CDALE/KGS NW9 44 C6
LEW SE13 145 H4
Eton Pl HAMP NW3 * 84 A5
Eton Ri HAMP NW3 * 83 K4
Eton Rd HAMP NW3 83 K5
HYS/HAR UB3 133 J1
IL IG1 90 C2
ORP BR6 217 H2
Eton St RCH/KEW TW9 136 E6
Eton Vls HAMP NW3 83 K4
Eton Wy DART DA1 151 F5
Etta St DEPT SE8 124 B6
Etton Rd HSLW TW3 135 H6
Ettrick St POP/IOD E14 106 A5
Etwell Pl BRYLDS KT5 191 G3
Eucalyptus Ms
STRHM/NOR SW16 179 J2
Euesdon Cl ED N9 36 D5
Eugenia Rd BERM/RHTH SE16 123 K5
Eureka Rd KUT/HW KT1 175 H5
Europa Pl FSBYE EC1V 6 C5
Europe Rd WOOL/PLUM SE18 126 E3
Eustace Pl WOOL/PLUM SE18 126 E4
Eustace Rd CHDH RM6 73 K4
EHAM E6 107 J2
FUL/PGN SW6 139 K1
Euston Centre CAMTN NW1 4 A6
Euston Rd CAMTN NW1 4 A6
CROY/NA CR0 196 B5
STPAN WC1H 4 E4
Euston Sq CAMTN NW1 4 C5
Euston St CAMTN NW1 4 B6
Evan Cook Cl PECK SE15 143 K2
Evandale Rd BRXN/ST SW9 142 B3
Evangelist Rd KTTN NW5 84 B2
Evans Cl HACK E8 86 B4
Evansdale RAIN RM13 111 H2
Evans Gv FELT TW13 155 F4
Evans Rd CAT SE6 165 H4
Evanston Av CHING E4 52 A3
Evanston Gdns REDBR IG4 71 J3
Eva Rd CHDH RM6 73 J4
Evelina Rd PECK SE15 143 K4
PGE/AN SE20 181 K3
Eveline Lowe Est
BERM/RHTH SE16 123 H3
Eveline Rd MTCM CR4 178 E4
Evelyn Av CDALE/KGS NW9 63 F1
RSLP HA4 58 D4
Evelyn Cl WHTN TW2 155 G2
Evelyn Denington Rd
EHAM E6 107 J3
Evelyn Dr PIN HA5 41 H3
Evelyn Est DEPT SE8 124 B6
Evelyn Gdns RCH/KEW TW9 137 F5
SKENS SW7 120 B5
Evelyn Gv EA W5 117 G1
STHL UB1 95 K5
Evelyn Rd CAN/RD E16 125 K1
EBAR EN4 21 K5
RCH/KEW TW9 137 F4
RCHPK/HAM TW10 156 D5
WALTH E17 70 A1
WIM/MER SW19 178 A1
Evelyn St DEPT SE8 124 C6
GNWCH SE10 125 F6
Evelyn Ter RCH/KEW TW9 137 F4
Evelyn Wk IS N1 6 E3
Evelyn Wy WLGTN SM6 210 D2
Evensyde WATW WD18 26 A1
Evenwood Cl
PUT/ROE SW15 * 139 H6
Everard Av HAYES BR2 199 K5
Everard Wy WBLY HA9 80 A1
Everatt Cl WAND/EARL SW18 * 159 J1
Everdon Rd BARN SW13 118 D6
Everest Pl POP/IOD E14 106 A4
Everest Rd ELTH/MOT SE9 146 D6
STWL/WRAY TW19 152 A2
Everett Cl BUSH WD23 28 E3
PIN HA5 40 D6
The Everglades HSLW TW3 * 135 H4
Everglade Strd
CDALE/KGS NW9 45 H4
Evergreen Cl PGE/AN SE20 181 K3
Evergreen Ct
STWL/WRAY TW19 * 152 A2
Evergreen Sq HACK E8 86 B5
Evergreen Wy HYS/HAR UB3 94 D6
STWL/WRAY TW19 152 A2
Everilda St IS N1 5 H1
Evering Rd CLPT E5 86 C1
STNW/STAM N16 86 B1
Everington Rd MUSWH N10 47 K5
Everington St HMSMTH W6 119 G6
Everitt Rd WLSDN NW10 99 F2
Everleigh St FSBYPK N4 67 F5
Eve Rd ISLW TW7 136 B5
SRTFD E15 106 C1
TOTM N17 50 A6
WAN E11 88 C2
Eversfield Gdns EDGW HA8 45 G3
Eversfield Rd RCH/KEW TW9 137 G3
Evershed Wk CHSWK W4 117 K3
Eversholt St CAMTN NW1 4 A2
Evershot Rd FSBYPK N4 67 F5
Eversleigh Rd BAR EN5 21 G6
BTSEA SW11 140 E4
EHAM E6 89 H6
FNCH N3 46 D3
Eversley Av BXLYHN DA7 150 B3
WBLY HA9 62 C6
Eversley Cl WCHMH N21 35 F1
Eversley Crs ISLW TW7 135 J2
RSLP HA4 58 C6
WCHMH N21 35 F1
Eversley Cross BXLYHN DA7 150 B3
Eversley Mt WCHMH N21 35 F1
Eversley Pk WIM/MER SW19 176 E1
Eversley Park Rd
WCHMH N21 35 F1
Eversley Rd BRYLDS KT5 191 G1
CHARL SE7 126 A6
NRWD SE19 180 E3
Eversley Wy CROY/NA CR0 213 J1
Everthorpe Rd PECK SE15 143 G4
Everton Blds CAMTN NW1 4 A5
Everton Dr STAN HA7 44 A6
Everton Rd CROY/NA CR0 197 H5
Evesham Av WALTH E17 51 J5
Evesham Cl BELMT SM2 208 E5
GFD/PVL UB6 96 B1
Evesham Gn MRDN SM4 194 A3
Evesham Rd FBAR/BDGN N11 48 C1
MRDN SM4 194 A3
SRTFD E15 88 D5
Evesham St NTGHL W11 100 B6
Evesham Ter SURB KT6 * 190 E3
Evesham Wk BRXN/ST SW9 142 B3
CMBW SE5 142 E3
Evesham Wy BTSEA SW11 141 F4
CLAY IG5 54 A6
Evette Ms CLAY IG5 54 A4
Evry Rd SCUP DA14 186 D2
Ewald Rd FUL/PGN SW6 139 J3
Ewanrigg Ter WFD IG8 53 G1
Ewart Gv WDGN N22 49 G4
Ewart Pl BOW E3 * 105 H1
Ewart Rd FSTH SE23 164 A2
Ewe Cl HOLWY N7 84 E4
Ewell By-Pass EW KT17 207 H4
Ewell Court Av
HOR/WEW KT19 207 G3
Ewellhurst Rd CLAY IG5 53 J5
Ewell Park Gdns EW KT17 207 J5
Ewell Park Wy EW KT17 207 J4
Ewell Rd SURB KT6 191 J5
CHEAM SM3 208 B4
SURB KT6 190 C4
Ewelme Rd FSTH SE23 163 K3
Ewen Crs BRXS/STRHM SW2 162 B2
Ewer St STHWK SE1 18 C1
Ewhurst Av SAND/SEL CR2 212 B6
Ewhurst Cl BELMT SM2 208 A6
WCHPL E1 104 E4
Ewhurst Rd BROCKY SE4 164 C1
Exbury Rd CAT SE6 164 D4
Excel Ct LSQ/SEVD WC2H 10 D6
Excel Marina CAN/RD E16 106 E6
Excelsior Cl KUT/HW KT1 175 H5
Excel Waterfront
CAN/RD E16 107 F6
Exchange Ar LVPST EC2M 13 G2
Exchange Ct COVGDN WC2E * 11 F6
Exchange Sq SDTCH EC2A * 13 H1
Exchange St ROMW/RG RM7 75 G3
Exchange Wk PIN HA5 59 J4
Exeforde Av ASHF TW15 152 D6
Exeter Cl EHAM E6 107 K5
Exeter Gdns IL IG1 71 K5
Exeter Ms FUL/PGN SW6 139 K1
Exeter Pde CRICK NW2 * 82 C4
Exeter Rd CAN/RD E16 106 E4
CRICK NW2 82 C3
CROY/NA CR0 197 F4
DAGE RM10 92 D4
ED N9 36 E4
FELT TW13 154 E5
HTHAIR TW6 133 H4
PEND EN3 25 F4
RYLN/HDSTN HA2 59 J6
STHGT/OAK N14 34 B3
WALTH E17 69 J2
WELL DA16 148 A3
Exeter St COVGDN WC2E 11 F5
Exeter Wy HTHAIR TW6 133 H3
NWCR SE14 144 C1
Exford Gdns LEE/GVPK SE12 166 A3
Exford Rd LEE/GVPK SE12 166 A4
Exhibition Grounds
WBLY HA9 * 80 D2
Exhibition Rd SKENS SW7 14 B5
Exit Rd EFNCH N2 47 H5
Exmoor Cl BARK/HLT IG6 54 C4
Exmoor St NKENS W10 100 B3
Exmouth Market
CLKNW EC1R 5 J6
Exmouth Ms CAMTN NW1 * 4 B5
Exmouth Pl HACK E8 86 D6
Exmouth Rd RSLP HA4 77 G1
WALTH E17 69 H2
WELL DA16 148 D2
YEAD UB4 94 C2
Exmouth St WCHPL E1 104 E5
Exning Rd CAN/RD E16 106 C3
Exon St WALW SE17 19 G7
Explorer Av
STWL/WRAY TW19 152 B3
Explorer Dr WATW WD18 26 D1
Express Dr GDMY/SEVK IG3 73 H5
Exton Cl BCTR RM8 91 J3
Exton Rd WLSDN NW10 80 E5
Exton St STHWK SE1 17 J1
Eyhurst Av HCH RM12 93 J1
Eyhurst Cl CRICK NW2 63 J6
Eylewood Rd WNWD SE27 180 D1
Eynella Rd DUL SE21 163 G2
Eynham Rd SHB W12 100 A5
Eynsford Cl STMC/STPC BR5 201 H4
Eynsford Crs SCUP DA14 168 D3
Eynsford Rd GDMY/SEVK IG3 72 E6
Eynsham Dr ABYW SE2 128 C3
Eynswood Dr SCUP DA14 186 C1
Eyot Gdns HMSMTH W6 118 C5
Eyre Cl GPK RM2 75 K1
Eyre Street Hl CLKNW EC1R 5 J7
Eythorne Rd BRXN/ST SW9 142 B2
Ezra St BETH E2 7 K4

F

Faber Gdns HDN NW4 63 J2
Fabian Rd FUL/PGN SW6 139 J1
Fabian St EHAM E6 107 K3
The Facade FSTH SE23 * 163 K4
Factory La CROY/NA CR0 196 B6
TOTM N17 50 B5
Factory Pl POP/IOD E14 125 F5
Factory Rd CAN/RD E16 126 D1
Factory Yd HNWL W7 115 K1
Faesten Wy BXLY DA5 170 B5
Faggs Rd EBED/NFELT TW14 133 J5
Fairacre ISLW TW7 * 135 J2
NWMAL KT3 176 B6
Fair Acres HAYES BR2 199 K2
Fairacres CROY/NA CR0 213 H6
PUT/ROE SW15 138 C5
RSLP HA4 58 D4
Fairbank Av ORP BR6 201 G6
Fairbank Est IS N1 6 E3
Fairbanks Rd TOTM N17 50 C6
Fairbourne Rd CLAP SW4 161 J1
TOTM N17 50 A6
Fairbridge Rd ARCH N19 66 D6
Fairbrook Cl PLMGR N13 49 G1
Fairby Rd LEE/GVPK SE12 146 A6
Fairchild Cl BTSEA SW11 140 C3
Fairchild Pl SDTCH EC2A * 7 H7
Fairchild St SDTCH EC2A 7 H7
Fair Cl BUSH WD23 28 B2
Fairclough Cl NTHLT UB5 95 K3
Fairclough St WCHPL E1 104 C5
Faircross Av BARK IG11 90 C4
CRW RM5 57 F3
Fairdale Gdns HYS/HAR UB3 113 K2
PUT/ROE SW15 138 E5
Fairey CDALE/KGS NW9 * 45 H5
Fairey Av HYS/HAR UB3 113 J3
Fairfax Av EW KT17 207 K6
Fairfax Cl WOT/HER KT12 188 A5
Fairfax Gdns BKHTH/KID SE3 146 B2
Fairfax Ms CAN/RD E16 126 A1
CEND/HSY/T N8 * 67 H1
PUT/ROE SW15 139 F5
Fairfax Pl KIL/WHAMP NW6 83 G5
WKENS W14 119 H3
Fairfax Rd CEND/HSY/T N8 67 G1
CHSWK W4 118 B3
DART DA1 171 K1
KIL/WHAMP NW6 83 G5
TEDD TW11 174 B3
Fairfax Wy MUSWH N10 48 A3
Fairfield Av EDGW HA8 44 D2
HDN NW4 63 K3
OXHEY WD19 27 G5
RSLP HA4 58 A4
WHTN TW2 155 G3
Fairfield Cl BFN/LL DA15 168 A1
HCH RM12 75 J5
HOR/WEW KT19 207 G3
MTCM CR4 178 D3
NFNCH/WDSPK N12 33 G6
PEND EN3 25 F5
Fairfield Cnr KUT/HW KT1 * 175 G5
Fairfield Ct RSLP HA4 58 B5
Fairfield Crs EDGW HA8 44 D2
Fairfield Dr GFD/PVL UB6 79 J6
RYLN/HDSTN HA2 42 C6
WAND/EARL SW18 140 A6
Fairfield East KUT/HW KT1 175 F5
Fairfield Gdns
CEND/HSY/T N8 66 E2
Fairfield Gv CHARL SE7 126 C6
Fairfield North
KUTN/CMB KT2 175 F5
Fairfield Pth CROY/NA CR0 211 K1
Fairfield Pl KUT/HW KT1 175 F6
Fairfield Rd BECK BR3 182 D5
BMLY BR1 183 K3
BOW E3 105 J1
BXLYHN DA7 149 G3
CEND/HSY/T N8 66 E2
CROY/NA CR0 211 K1
IL IG1 90 B4
KUT/HW KT1 175 F5
STHL UB1 95 K5
STMC/STPC BR5 201 J3
UED N18 36 C6
WALTH E17 51 G5
WDR/YW UB7 112 B1
WFD IG8 52 E2
Fairfields CAT SE6 164 E2
Fairfields Cl CDALE/KGS NW9 62 E2
Fairfields Crs CDALE/KGS NW9 62 E1
Fairfield South KUT/HW KT1 175 F6
Fairfield St WAND/EARL SW18 140 A6
Fairfield Wy BAR EN5 20 E6
HOR/WEW KT19 207 G3
Fairfield West KUT/HW KT1 175 F5
Fairfoot Rd BOW E3 * 105 J3
Fairford Av BXLYHN DA7 149 K2
CROY/NA CR0 198 A2
Fairford Cl CROY/NA CR0 198 A2
Fairford Ct BELMT SM2 * 209 F5
Fairford Gdns WPK KT4 207 H1
Fairgreen EBAR EN4 21 K4
Fairgreen Ct EBAR EN4 * 21 K4
Fairgreen Rd THHTH CR7 196 C2
Fairhaven Av CROY/NA CR0 198 A3
Fairhaven Crs OXHEY WD19 26 E5
Fairhazel Gdns
KIL/WHAMP NW6 83 F4
Fairholme EBED/NFELT TW14 153 G2
Fairholme Av GPK RM2 75 J2
Fairholme Cl FNCH N3 64 C1
Fairholme Ct PIN HA5 * 42 A2
Fairholme Crs YEAD UB4 94 D3
Fairholme Gdns FNCH N3 46 C6
Fairholme Rd CROY/NA CR0 196 B4
HRW HA1 60 E2
IL IG1 71 K4
SUT SM1 208 D4
WKENS W14 119 H5
Fairholt Rd STNW/STAM N16 67 K5
Fairholt St SKENS SW7 14 D4
Fairland Rd SRTFD E15 88 D4
Fairlands Av BKHH IG9 38 E4
SUT SM1 193 K6
THHTH CR7 196 A1
Fairlawn CHARL SE7 146 B1
Fairlawn Av BXLYHN DA7 148 E3
CHSWK W4 117 K4
EFNCH N2 65 J1
Fairlawn Cl ESH/CLAY KT10 205 F4
FELT TW13 154 E6
KUTN/CMB KT2 175 K2
STHGT/OAK N14 34 D1
Fairlawn Ct CHARL SE7 * 146 B1
Fairlawn Dr WFD IG8 52 E3
Fairlawn Gdns STHL UB1 * 95 K6
Fairlawn Gv CHSWK W4 117 K4
Fairlawn Pk SYD SE26 182 B1
Fairlawn Rd WIM/MER SW19 177 J3
Fairlawns PIN HA5 41 G5
TWK TW1 156 D1
Fairlea Pl EA W5 97 J4
Fairlie Gdns FSTH SE23 163 K2
Fairlight Av CHING E4 38 B4
WFD IG8 52 E2
WLSDN NW10 99 G1
Fairlight Cl CHING E4 38 B4
WPK KT4 208 A2
Fairlight Rd TOOT SW17 160 C6
Fairlop Cl HCH RM12 93 K4
Fairlop Gdns BARK/HLT IG6 54 C3
Fairlop Pl STJWD NW8 2 B5
Fairlop Rd BARK/HLT IG6 54 C5
WAN E11 70 B4
Fairmead BMLY BR1 200 E1
BRYLDS KT5 191 J5
Fairmead Cl BMLY BR1 200 E1
HEST TW5 134 C1
NWMAL KT3 176 A6
Fairmead Crs EDGW HA8 30 E6
Fairmead Gdns REDBR IG4 71 H2
Fairmead Rd ARCH N19 84 E1
CROY/NA CR0 196 B4
Fairmile Av
STRHM/NOR SW16 179 J1
Fairmont Av POP/IOD E14 106 B6
Fairmont Cl BELV DA17 129 G5

Fairmount Rd
BRXS/STRHM SW2 162 A1
Fairoak Cl STMC/STPC BR5 201 G4
Fairoak Dr ELTH/MOT SE9 147 J6
Fairoak Gdns ROM RM1 57 G5
Fair Oak Pl BARK/HLT IG6 54 C5
Fairseat Cl BUSH WD23 28 E4
Fairstead Wk IS N1 * 85 J6
Fair St HSLW TW3 135 H4
STHWK SE1 19 H2
Fairthorn Rd CHARL SE7 125 K5
Fairview ERITH DA8 150 C1
Fairview Av ALP/SUD HA0 79 K4
Fairview Cl SYD SE26 182 B1
Fair View Cl WALTH E17 51 G4
Fairview Ct HDN NW4 * 46 B5
Fairview Crs
RYLN/HDSTN HA2 60 A5
Fairview Dr CHIG IG7 54 E1
ORP BR6 216 D2
Fairview Gdns WFD IG8 53 F4
Fairview Pl BRXS/STRHM SW2 162 A2
Fairview Rd ENC/FH EN2 23 G2
SEVS/STOTM N15 68 B3
STRHM/NOR SW16 180 A4
SUT SM1 209 H3
Fairview Vls CHING E4 * 51 J3
Fairview Wy EDGW HA8 30 C6
Fairwater Av WELL DA16 148 B5
Fairway BXLYHS DA6 149 F6
RYNPK SW20 177 F6
STMC/STPC BR5 201 J3
WFD IG8 53 G1
Fairway Av CDALE/KGS NW9 44 D6
Fairway Cl CROY/NA CR0 198 B2
GLDGN NW11 65 G4
HOR/WEW KT19 206 E2
HSLWW TW4 134 B6
Fairway Ct MLHL NW7 * 31 F5
Fairway Dr GFD/PVL UB6 78 B5
THMD SE28 109 K5
Fairway Gdns BECK BR3 199 G3
IL IG1 90 C3
Fairways ISLW TW7 * 135 K2
STAN HA7 44 A5
TEDD TW11 174 E3
WALTH E17 * 70 A1
The Fairway ACT W3 99 G5
ALP/SUD HA0 61 H6
BAR EN5 33 F1
E/WMO/HCT KT8 173 G6
HAYES BR2 200 E2
HNWL W7 * 96 E6
MLHL NW7 31 F5
NTHLT UB5 78 C4
NTHWD HA6 26 C6
NWMAL KT3 176 A4
PLMGR N13 35 J5
RSLP HA4 77 G2
STHGT/OAK N14 34 B1
Fairweather Cl
SEVS/STOTM N15 68 A1
Fairweather Rd
STNW/STAM N16 68 C3
Fairwyn Rd SYD SE26 164 B5
Faithfield BUSH WD23 * 27 J1
Fakenham Cl MLHL NW7 45 J3
NTHLT UB5 78 A4
Fakruddin St WCHPL E1 104 C3
Falaize Av IL IG1 90 B2
Falcon Av BMLY BR1 184 D6
Falconberg Ct
SOHO/SHAV W1D * 10 C3
Falconberg Ms
SOHO/SHAV W1D 10 C3
Falcon Cl CHSWK W4 117 J6
DART DA1 151 J6
NTHWD HA6 40 C3
Falcon Ct IS N1 6 B3
Falcon Crs PEND EN3 25 F6
Falcon Dr STWL/WRAY TW19 152 A1
Falconer Rd BARK/HLT IG6 55 H1
BUSH WD23 28 A1
Falcon Gv BTSEA SW11 140 D4
Falcon La BTSEA SW11 140 D4
Falcon Rd BTSEA SW11 140 D4
HPTN TW12 172 E3
PEND EN3 25 F6
Falcon St PLSTW E13 106 E3
Falcon Ter BTSEA SW11 * 140 D4
Falcon Wy CDALE/KGS NW9 45 G5
KTN/HRWW/WS HA3 62 A2
POP/IOD E14 124 E4
WAN E11 70 E1
Falconwood Av WELL DA16 147 J3
Falconwood Pde WELL DA16 147 K5
Falconwood Rd
CROY/NA CR0 213 H6
Falcourt Cl SUT SM1 209 F3
Falkirk Gdns OXHEY WD19 41 H1
Falkirk St IS N1 7 H3
Falkland Av FBAR/BDGN N11 34 A6
FNCH N3 46 E3
Falkland Park Av SNWD SE25 181 F5
Falkland Pl KTTN NW5 84 C3
Falkland Rd BAR EN5 20 C3
CEND/HSY/T N8 67 G1
KTTN NW5 84 C3
Falloden Wy GLDGN NW11 64 E1
Fallow Cl CHIG IG7 55 F1
Fallow Ct BERM/RHTH SE16 * 123 H5
Fallow Court Av
NFNCH/WDSPK N12 47 G2
Fallowfield STAN HA7 29 G5
Fallowfield Ct STAN HA7 29 G5
Fallow Flds LOU IG10 39 G2
Fallowfields Dr
NFNCH/WDSPK N12 47 J2
Fallows Cl EFNCH N2 47 H5
Fallsbrook Rd
STRHM/NOR SW16 179 G2
Falman Cl ED N9 36 C3
Falmer Rd EN EN1 24 A5
SEVS/STOTM N15 67 J2
WALTH E17 51 K6
Falmouth Av CHING E4 52 B1
Falmouth Cl LEE/GVPK SE12 145 J6
WDGN N22 49 F3
Falmouth Gdns REDBR IG4 71 H1
Falmouth Rd STHWK SE1 18 D5
Falmouth St SRTFD E15 88 B3
Falstaff Cl DART DA1 170 B2
Falstaff Ms HPTN TW12 173 J1
Fambridge Cl SYD SE26 164 C6
Fambridge Rd BCTR RM8 74 C5
Fancourt Ms BMLY BR1 185 F6
Fane St WKENS W14 119 J6
Fanns Ri PUR RM19 131 K4
Fann St FARR EC1M 6 C7
STLK EC1Y 6 C7
Fanshawe Av BARK IG11 90 C4
Fanshawe Crs DAGW RM9 92 A3
Fanshawe Rd
RCHPK/HAM TW10 156 D6
Fanshaw St IS N1 7 G4
Fantail Cl THMD SE28 109 J5
Fanthorpe St PUT/ROE SW15 139 F4
Faraday Av SCUP DA14 168 C4
Faraday Cl HOLWY N7 85 F4
WATW WD18 26 B1
Faraday Pl E/WMO/HCT KT8 189 F1
Faraday Rd ACT W3 98 E6
E/WMO/HCT KT8 189 F1
NKENS W10 100 C4
SRTFD E15 88 D4
STHL UB1 96 B6
WELL DA16 148 B4
WIM/MER SW19 178 A2
Faraday Wy STMC/STPC BR5 202 C1
WOOL/PLUM SE18 126 C3
Fareham Rd
EBED/NFELT TW14 154 B2
Fareham St SOHO/CST W1F * 10 C3
Farewell Pl MTCM CR4 178 C4
Faringdon Av HAYES BR2 201 F4
Faringford Rd SRTFD E15 88 C5
Farjeon Rd BKHTH/KID SE3 146 C2
Farleigh Av HAYES BR2 199 J4
Farleigh Court Rd
CROY/NA CR0 196 A6
Farleigh Pl STNW/STAM N16 86 B2
Farleigh Rd STNW/STAM N16 86 B2
Farley Dr GDMY/SEVK IG3 72 E5
Farley Ms CAT SE6 165 F2
Farley Pl SNWD SE25 197 H1
Farley Rd CAT SE6 165 F2
SAND/SEL CR2 212 C5
Farlow Rd PUT/ROE SW15 139 G4
Farlton Rd WAND/EARL SW18 160 A2
Farman Ter
KTN/HRWW/WS HA3 * 61 K1
Farm Av ALP/SUD HA0 79 J4
CRICK NW2 82 C1
RYLN/HDSTN HA2 60 A4
STRHM/NOR SW16 161 K6
SWLY BR8 187 K6
Farmborough Cl HRW HA1 60 D4
Farm Cl BELMT SM2 209 H5
BKHH IG9 39 G5
DAGE RM10 92 E5
FUL/PGN SW6 * 139 K1
STHL UB1 96 B6
WWKM BR4 214 C1
Farmcote Rd LEE/GVPK SE12 165 K3
Farm Cots E/WMO/HCT KT8 * 190 B1
Farmdale Rd CAR SM5 209 J5
CHARL SE7 125 K5
Farm Dr CROY/NA CR0 198 C6
Farmer Rd LEY E10 69 K5
Farmers Rd CMBW SE5 142 C1
Farmer St KENS W8 * 119 K1
Farmfield Rd BMLY BR1 183 H1
Farmhouse Rd
STRHM/NOR SW16 179 H3
Farmilo Rd WALTH E17 69 J4
Farmington Av SUT SM1 209 H1
Farmlands ENC/FH EN2 23 G2
PIN HA5 58 E1
The Farmlands NTHLT UB5 77 K4
Farmland Wk CHST BR7 185 G1
Farm La CROY/NA CR0 198 C6
FUL/PGN SW6 119 K6
STHGT/OAK N14 34 A1
Farmleigh STHGT/OAK N14 34 C2
Farm Pl DART DA1 150 D5
KENS W8 119 K1
Farm Rd BELMT SM2 209 H5
EDGW HA8 44 E1
ESH/CLAY KT10 189 F5
HSLWW TW4 154 D3
MNPK E12 71 J6
MRDN SM4 194 A2
NTHWD HA6 40 A1
WCHMH N21 35 J3
WLSDN NW10 81 F6
Farmstead Rd CAT SE6 164 E6
KTN/HRWW/WS HA3 42 D4
Farm St MYFR/PICC W1J 9 J6
The Farm WIM/MER SW19 * 159 G2
Farm V BXLY DA5 169 J1
Farm Wk GLDGN NW11 64 D2
Farmway BCTR RM8 91 J2
Farm Wy BKHH IG9 39 G6
HCH RM12 93 K2
NTHWD HA6 26 C6
WPK KT4 208 A1
Farnaby Rd BMLY BR1 183 H4
ELTH/MOT SE9 146 B5
Farnan Av WALTH E17 51 J5
Farnan Rd STRHM/NOR SW16 179 K1
Farnborough Av
SAND/SEL CR2 213 G5
WALTH E17 * 51 G6
Farnborough Cl WBLY HA9 62 D6
Farnborough Common
ORP BR6 216 A2
Farnborough Crs HAYES BR2 199 J5
SAND/SEL CR2 213 G6
Farnborough Hl ORP BR6 216 D3
Farnborough Wy ORP BR6 216 B3
PECK SE15 * 143 F1
Farncombe St
BERM/RHTH SE16 123 H2
Farndale Av PLMGR N13 35 H5
Farndale Crs GFD/PVL UB6 96 C2
Farnell Ms ECT SW5 120 A5
Farnell Pl ACT W3 98 D6
Farnell Rd ISLW TW7 135 J4
Farnham Cl TRDG/WHET N20 33 G2
Farnham Gdns RYNPK SW20 176 E5
Farnham Pl STHWK SE1 18 B1
Farnham Rd GDMY/SEVK IG3 73 F3
WELL DA16 148 D3
Farnham Royal LBTH SE11 122 A5
Farningham Rd TOTM N17 50 C3
Farnley Rd CHING E4 38 C2
SNWD SE25 196 E1
Farnol Rd DART DA1 151 K5
Faro Cl BMLY BR1 185 F5
Faroe Rd WKENS W14 119 G3
Farorna Wk ENC/FH EN2 23 G2
Farquhar Rd NRWD SE19 181 G1
WIM/MER SW19 159 K5
Farquharson Rd
CROY/NA CR0 196 D4
Farrance Rd CHDH RM6 74 A3
Farrance St POP/IOD E14 105 J5
Farrant Av WDGN N22 49 G5
Farrant Cl ORP BR6 217 G5
Farr Av BARK IG11 109 G1
Farren Rd FSTH SE23 164 B4
Farrer Ms CEND/HSY/T N8 66 C1
Farrer Rd CEND/HSY/T N8 66 C1
KTN/HRWW/WS HA3 62 A2
Farrier Cl BMLY BR1 184 C6
Farrier Pl SUT SM1 209 F1
Farrier Rd NTHLT UB5 96 A1
Farrier St CAMTN NW1 84 B5
Farriers Wy BORE WD6 31 F1
Farrier Wk WBPTN SW10 120 B6
Farringdon La CLKNW EC1R 5 K7
Farringdon Rd CLKNW EC1R 5 J6
HCIRC EC1N 12 A2
Farringdon St
FLST/FETLN EC4A 12 A3
Farrington Av
STMC/STPC BR5 186 C6
Farrington Pl CHST BR7 185 J3
Farrins Rents
BERM/RHTH SE16 124 B1
Farrow La NWCR SE14 143 K1
Farrow Pl BERM/RHTH SE16 124 B3
Farr Rd ENC/FH EN2 23 K2
Farthingale Wk SRTFD E15 88 B5
Farthing Aly STHWK SE1 * 123 H2
Farthing Flds WAP E1W 123 J1
Farthings Cl CHING E4 38 C5
PIN HA5 59 F3
The Farthings KUTN/CMB KT2 175 H4
Farthing St HAYES BR2 215 K5
Farwell Rd SCUP DA14 168 C6
Farwig La BMLY BR1 183 K4
Fashion St WCHPL E1 13 J2
Fashoda Rd HAYES BR2 200 C1
Fassett Rd HACK E8 86 C4
KUT/HW KT1 191 F1
Fassett Sq HACK E8 86 C4
Fauconberg Rd CHSWK W4 117 K6
Faulkner Cl BCTR RM8 73 K4
Faulkner St NWCR SE14 143 K2
Fauna Cl CHDH RM6 73 J3
STAN HA7 29 K5
Faunce St WALW SE17 122 C6
Favart Rd FUL/PGN SW6 139 K2
Faversham Av CHING E4 38 C3
EN EN1 35 K1
Faversham Rd BECK BR3 182 C5
CAT SE6 164 C2
MRDN SM4 194 A3
Fawcett Cl BTSEA SW11 140 C3
STRHM/NOR SW16 162 B6
Fawcett Est CLPT E5 * 68 C5
Fawcett Rd CROY/NA CR0 211 H1
WLSDN NW10 81 H5
Fawcett St WBPTN SW10 120 B6
Fawcus Cl ESH/CLAY KT10 204 E4
Fawe Park Rd PUT/ROE SW15 139 J5
Fawe St POP/IOD E14 105 K4
Fawkes Av DART DA1 171 J4
Fawley Rd KIL/WHAMP NW6 83 F3
Fawnbrake Av HNHL SE24 142 C6
Fawn Rd CHIG IG7 55 F1
PLSTW E13 107 G1
Fawns Manor Rd
EBED/NFELT TW14 153 G3
Fawood Av WLSDN NW10 81 F5
Faygate Crs BXLYHS DA6 149 H6
Faygate Rd
BRXS/STRHM SW2 162 A4
Fayland Av
STRHM/NOR SW16 179 H1
Fearnley Crs HPTN TW12 172 D1
Fearon St GNWCH SE10 125 K5
Featherbed La SAND/SEL CR2 213 H5
Feathers Pl GNWCH SE10 125 G6
Featherstone Av FSTH SE23 163 J4
Featherstone Rd MLHL NW7 45 K2
NWDGN UB2 114 D3
Featherstone St STLK EC1Y 6 E6
Featherstone Ter
NWDGN UB2 114 D3
Featley Rd BRXN/ST SW9 142 C4
Federal Rd GFD/PVL UB6 97 J1
Federation Rd ABYW SE2 128 D4
Fee Farm Rd ESH/CLAY KT10 205 F5
Feeny Cl WLSDN NW10 81 H2
Felbridge Av STAN HA7 43 G4
Felbridge Cl BELMT SM2 209 F6
STRHM/NOR SW16 162 B6
Felbrigge Rd GDMY/SEVK IG3 73 F6
Felday Rd LEW SE13 164 E1
Felden Cl PIN HA5 41 J3
Felden St FUL/PGN SW6 139 J2
Feldman Cl STNW/STAM N16 68 C5
Felgate Ms HMSMTH W6 118 E4
Felhampton Rd
ELTH/MOT SE9 167 G5
Felix Av CEND/HSY/T N8 66 E3
Felix Pl BRXS/STRHM SW2 142 B6
Felix Rd WEA W13 97 G6
Felixstowe Rd ABYW SE2 128 C3
ED N9 36 C5
SEVS/STOTM N15 50 B6
WLSDN NW10 99 K2
Felix St BETH E2 * 104 D1
Fellbrigg Rd EDUL SE22 143 G6
Fellbrigg St WCHPL E1 104 D3
Fellbrook RCHPK/HAM TW10 156 C5
Fellmongers Yd
CROY/NA CR0 211 J1
Fellowes Cl YEAD UB4 95 H3
Fellowes Rd CAR SM5 209 J1
Fellows Rd HAMP NW3 83 H5
Fell Rd CROY/NA CR0 211 J1
Felltram Wy CHARL SE7 125 K5
Felmersham Cl CLAP SW4 141 K5
Felmingham Rd PGE/AN SE20 181 K5
Felsberg Rd
BRXS/STRHM SW2 161 K1
Fels Cl DAGE RM10 92 D1
Fels Farm Av DAGE RM10 92 E1
Felsham Ms PUT/ROE SW15 139 G4
Felsham Rd PUT/ROE SW15 139 F4
Felspar Cl WOOL/PLUM SE18 128 A5
Felstead Av CLAY IG5 54 A4
Felstead Rd CRW RM5 56 E2
HOM E9 87 J4
LOU IG10 39 J2
ORP BR6 202 B6
WAN E11 70 E4
Felstead St HOM E9 87 H4
Felsted Rd CAN/RD E16 107 H5
Feltham Av E/WMO/HCT KT8 189 K1
Felthambrook Wy FELT TW13 154 A5
Feltham Rd ASHF TW15 152 E6
MTCM CR4 178 E5
Felton Cl STMC/STPC BR5 201 G3
Felton Lea SCUP DA14 186 A1
Felton Rd BARK IG11 108 E1
WEA W13 116 D2
Felton St IS N1 7 F1
Fencepiece Rd BARK/HLT IG6 54 C2
Fenchurch Av FENCHST EC3M 13 G4
Fenchurch Blds
FENCHST EC3M 13 H4
Fenchurch Pl
FENCHST EC3M * 13 H5
Fenchurch St FENCHST EC3M 13 G5
Fendall Rd HOR/WEW KT19 206 E3
Fendall St STHWK SE1 19 H4
Fendt Cl CAN/RD E16 106 D5
Fendyke Rd BELV DA17 128 E4
Fenelon Pl WKENS W14 119 J4
Fen Gv BFN/LL DA15 168 A1
Fenham Rd PECK SE15 143 H1
Fenman Ct TOTM N17 50 D4
Fenman Gdns
GDMY/SEVK IG3 73 H5
Fenn Cl BMLY BR1 183 K2
Fennel Cl CAN/RD E16 106 C3
CROY/NA CR0 198 A5
Fennells Md HOR/WEW KT19 207 H6
Fennell St WOOL/PLUM SE18 127 F6
Fenner Cl BERM/RHTH SE16 123 J4
Fenner Sq BTSEA SW11 * 140 C4
Fennings Rd CLAP SW4 161 J1
Fenning St STHWK SE1 19 G2
Fenn St HOM E9 87 F3
Fenstanton Av
NFNCH/WDSPK N12 47 H1
Fen St CAN/RD E16 106 D6
Fentiman Rd VX/NE SW8 122 A6
Fentiman Wy
RYLN/HDSTN HA2 60 B6
Fenton Cl BRXN/ST SW9 * 142 A3
CHST BR7 184 E1
HACK E8 86 B4
Fenton Rd TOTM N17 49 J3
Fenton's Av PLSTW E13 107 F2
Fenton St WCHPL E1 104 D5
Fenwick Gv PECK SE15 143 H4
Fenwick Pl BRXN/ST SW9 141 K4
SAND/SEL CR2 211 H5
Fenwick Rd PECK SE15 143 H4
Ferdinand Dr PECK SE15 143 F1
Ferdinand Pl CAMTN NW1 84 A5
Ferdinand St CAMTN NW1 84 A5
Ferguson Av BRYLDS KT5 191 G2
Ferguson Cl BECK BR3 183 F6
Ferguson Dr ACT W3 99 F5
Ferguson's Cl POP/IOD E14 124 D4
Fergus Rd HBRY N5 85 H3
Ferme Park Rd
CEND/HSY/T N8 66 E2
Fermor Rd FSTH SE23 164 B3
Fermoy Rd GFD/PVL UB6 96 B3
MV/WKIL W9 100 D3
Fern Av MTCM CR4 195 J1
Fernbank BKHH IG9 39 F3
Fernbank Av ALP/SUD HA0 79 F2
WOT/HER KT12 188 D4
Fernbank Ms BAL SW12 161 G1
Fernbrook Dr
RYLN/HDSTN HA2 60 B4
Fernbrook Rd LEW SE13 165 H1
Ferncliff Rd HACK E8 86 C3
Fern Cl ERITH DA8 150 E2
IS N1 7 G2
Fern Ct NWCR SE14 144 A3
Ferncroft Av HAMP NW3 82 E1
NFNCH/WDSPK N12 47 J2
RSLP HA4 59 G6
Ferndale BMLY BR1 184 B5
Ferndale Av HSLWW TW4 134 D4
WALTH E17 70 B2
Ferndale Cl BXLYHN DA7 149 F2
Ferndale Rd CLAP SW4 141 K5
CRW RM5 56 E5
FSTGT E7 89 F5
SEVS/STOTM N15 68 B3
SNWD SE25 197 J2
WAN E11 70 D6
Ferndale St EHAM E6 108 B6
Ferndale Ter HRW HA1 61 F1
Ferndale Wy ORP BR6 216 D3
Ferndell Av BXLY DA5 170 A5
Fern Dene WEA W13 97 H4
Ferndene Rd HNHL SE24 142 D5
Fernden Wy ROMW/RG RM7 74 D3
Ferndown NTHWD HA6 40 E5
Ferndown Av ORP BR6 201 J5
Ferndown Cl BELMT SM2 209 H4
PIN HA5 41 J3
Ferndown Rd ELTH/MOT SE9 166 C2
OXHEY WD19 27 G5
Ferney Meade Wy ISLW TW7 136 B3
Ferney Rd EBAR EN4 34 A2
Fern Gv EBED/NFELT TW14 154 A2
Fernhall Dr REDBR IG4 71 H2
Fernham Rd THHTH CR7 180 D6
Fernhead Rd MV/WKIL W9 100 D2
Fernhill Ct WALTH E17 52 B5
Fernhill Gdns KUTN/CMB KT2 174 E1
Fernhill St CAN/RD E16 126 E1
Fernholme Rd PECK SE15 144 A6
Fernhurst Gdns EDGW HA8 44 C2
Fernhurst Rd ASHF TW15 153 F6
CROY/NA CR0 197 H4
FUL/PGN SW6 139 H2
Fern La HEST TW5 114 E5
Fernlea Rd BAL SW12 161 G3
MTCM CR4 179 F5
Fernleigh Cl CROY/NA CR0 211 G2
MV/WKIL W9 100 D2
Fernleigh Ct
RYLN/HDSTN HA2 42 B5
WBLY HA9 62 A5
Fernleigh Rd WCHMH N21 35 G4
Fernley Cl PIN HA5 58 E1
Fernsbury St FSBYW WC1X 5 J5
Fernshaw Cl WBPTN SW10 * 120 B6
Fernshaw Rd WBPTN SW10 120 B6
Fernside BKHH IG9 39 F3
GLDGN NW11 64 E6
THDIT KT7 190 C5
Fernside Av FELT TW13 154 A6
MLHL NW7 31 F5
Fernside Rd BAL SW12 160 E3
Ferns Rd SRTFD E15 88 C4
Fern St BOW E3 105 J3
Fernthorpe Rd
STRHM/NOR SW16 179 H2
Ferntower Rd HBRY N5 85 K3
Fern Wk BERM/RHTH SE16 123 H5
Fernways IL IG1 90 B1
Fernwood Av ALP/SUD HA0 79 J4
STRHM/NOR SW16 161 J6
Fernwood Cl BMLY BR1 184 B5
Fernwood Crs
TRDG/WHET N20 33 K5
Ferny Hl EBAR EN4 21 K1
Ferranti Cl WOOL/PLUM SE18 126 C3
Ferraro Cl HEST TW5 115 F6
Ferrers Av WDR/YW UB7 112 A2
WLGTN SM6 210 D2
Ferrers Rd STRHM/NOR SW16 179 J1
Ferrestone Rd
CEND/HSY/T N8 67 F1
Ferrey Ms BRXN/ST SW9 142 B3
Ferriby Cl IS N1 85 G5
Ferrier St WAND/EARL SW18 140 A5
Ferring Cl RYLN/HDSTN HA2 60 C5
Ferrings DUL SE21 163 F4
Ferris Av CROY/NA CR0 213 H1
Ferris Rd EDUL SE22 143 H5
Ferron Rd CLPT E5 * 86 D1
Ferro Rd RAIN RM13 111 J3
Ferryhills Cl OXHEY WD19 27 G5
Ferry La BARN SW13 118 C6
BTFD TW8 117 F6
RAIN RM13 111 G5
TOTM N17 68 D1
Ferrymead Av GFD/PVL UB6 96 A1
Ferrymead Dr GFD/PVL UB6 96 A2
Ferrymead Gdns
GFD/PVL UB6 96 C1
Ferrymoor RCHPK/HAM TW10 156 C5
Ferry Rd BARN SW13 138 D1
E/WMO/HCT KT8 173 F6
TEDD TW11 174 C1
THDIT KT7 190 C3
TWK TW1 156 C3
Ferry Sq BTFD TW8 117 F6
Ferry St POP/IOD E14 125 F5
Festing Rd PUT/ROE SW15 139 G4
Festival Cl BXLY DA5 168 E3
ERITH DA8 150 C1
Festoon Wy CAN/RD E16 107 H6
Fetter La FLST/FETLN EC4A 11 K3
Ffinch St DEPT SE8 144 D1
Fidgeon Cl BMLY BR1 185 F6
Fidler Pl BUSH WD23 28 B1
Field Cl BKHH IG9 39 G5
BMLY BR1 184 B5
CHING E4 51 K2
CHSGTN KT9 205 J3
CRICK NW2 63 J6
E/WMO/HCT KT8 189 G2
HSLWW TW4 134 A2
HYS/HAR UB3 133 F1
RSLP HA4 58 A5
Fieldcommon La
WOT/HER KT12 188 D5
Field Cots EFNCH N2 * 47 K6
FUL/PGN SW6 * 139 J3
Field Ct GINN WC1R 11 H2
Field End RSLP HA4 77 H4
Fieldend TEDD TW11 156 A6
Field End Cl OXHEY WD19 27 J2
Field End Rd PIN HA5 59 F2
RSLP HA4 77 H1
Fieldend Rd
STRHM/NOR SW16 179 H4
Fielders Cl EN EN1 24 A5
RYLN/HDSTN HA2 60 C5
Fieldfare Rd THMD SE28 109 J6
Fieldgate St WCHPL E1 104 C4
Fieldhouse Cl SWFD E18 53 F4
Fieldhouse Rd BAL SW12 161 H3
Fielding Av WHTN TW2 155 H5
Fielding La HAYES BR2 200 B1
Fielding Rd CHSWK W4 118 A3
WKENS W14 119 G3
The Fieldings FSTH SE23 163 K3
Fielding Ter EA W5 * 98 B6
Field La BTFD TW8 136 D1
TEDD TW11 174 B1
Field Md CDALE/KGS NW9 45 G3
Fieldpark Gdns CROY/NA CR0 198 B5
Field Pl NWMAL KT3 192 C3
Field Rd EBED/NFELT TW14 154 A1
FSTGT E7 88 E2
HMSMTH W6 119 H5
OXHEY WD19 27 J1
TOTM N17 49 K6
Fieldsend Rd CHEAM SM3 208 C3
Fields Est HACK E8 * 86 C5
Fieldside Cl ORP BR6 216 C2
Fieldside Cots
TRDG/WHET N20 * 32 D2

Fieldside Rd BMLY BR1 183 G1
Fields Park Crs CHDH RM6 73 K2
Field St FSBYW WC1X 5 G4
Field Vw FELT TW13 153 G6
Fieldview WAND/EARL SW18 160 C3
Field View Cl ROMW/RG RM7 56 C6
Fieldview Cots
STHGT/OAK N14 * 34 D4
Fieldway STMC/STPC BR5 201 J3
BCTR RM8 91 H2
Field Wy CROY/NA CR0 213 K4
GFD/PVL UB6 78 B6
RSLP HA4 58 A5
WLSDN NW10 80 E5
Fieldway Crs HBRY N5 85 G3
Fiennes Cl BCTR RM8 73 J5
Fiesta Dr RAIN RM13 110 E3
Fife Rd CAN/RD E16 106 E4
KUT/HW KT1 175 F5
MORT/ESHN SW14 137 K6
WDGN N22 49 H3
Fife Ter IS N1 5 H2
Fifield Pth FSTH SE23 164 A5
Fifth Av HYS/HAR UB3 113 J1
MNPK E12 89 K2
NKENS W10 100 C3
Fifth Cross Rd WHTN TW2 155 J4
Fifth Wy WBLY HA9 80 D2
Figge's Rd MTCM CR4 179 F3
Fig Tree Cl WLSDN NW10 81 G6
Filby Rd CHSGTN KT9 206 B4
Filey Av STNW/STAM N16 68 C5
Filey Cl BELMT SM2 209 G5
Filey Waye RSLP HA4 58 E6
Fillebrook Av EN EN1 24 A3
Fillebrook Rd WAN E11 70 B5
Filmer Chambers
FUL/PGN SW6 * 139 J2
Filmer Rd FUL/PGN SW6 139 J2
Filton Cl CDALE/KGS NW9 45 G5
Finborough Rd TOOT SW17 178 E3
WBPTN SW10 120 A6
Finchale Rd ABYW SE2 128 B3
Fincham Cl HGDN/ICK UB10 76 A1
Finch Av WNWD SE27 162 E6
Finch Cl BAR EN5 20 E6
Finch Dr EBED/NFELT TW14 154 C2
Finch Gdns CHING E4 51 J1
Finchingfield Av WFD IG8 53 G3
Finch La BANK EC3V 13 F4
Finchley Cl DART DA1 171 K1
Finchley La HDN NW4 64 B1
Finchley Pk
NFNCH/WDSPK N12 33 G6
Finchley Pl STJWD NW8 2 A2
Finchley Rd GLDGN NW11 64 D2
HAMP NW3 82 E2
STJWD NW8 2 A1
Finchley Vls
NFNCH/WDSPK N12 * 33 H6
Finchley Wy FNCH N3 46 E2
Finch Ms PECK SE15 * 143 G2
Finchs Ct POP/IOD E14 105 K6
Finden Rd FSTGT E7 89 F3
Findhorn Av YEAD UB4 95 F4
Findhorn St POP/IOD E14 106 A5
Findon Cl RYLN/HDSTN HA2 * 78 B1
WAND/EARL SW18 159 K1
Findon Gdns RAIN RM13 111 J4
Findon Rd ED N9 36 D3
SHB W12 118 D2
Fingal St GNWCH SE10 125 J5
Finglesham Cl
STMC/STPC BR5 202 E5
Finland Rd BROCKY SE4 144 B4
Finland St BERM/RHTH SE16 124 B3
Finlays Cl CHSGTN KT9 206 C3
Finlay St FUL/PGN SW6 139 G2
Finney La ISLW TW7 136 B2
Finnis St BETH E2 104 D2
Finnymore Rd DAGW RM9 92 A5
Finsbury Av LVPST EC2M * 13 F2
Finsbury Circ LVPST EC2M 13 F2
Finsbury Cots WDGN N22 48 E3
Finsbury Est CLKNW EC1R 5 K5
Finsbury Market SDTCH EC2A 7 G7
Finsbury Park Av FSBYPK N4 67 J3
Finsbury Park Rd FSBYPK N4 67 H6
Finsbury Pavement
LVPST EC2M 13 F1
Finsbury Rd WDGN N22 49 F3
Finsbury Sq SDTCH EC2A 7 F7
Finsbury St STLK EC1Y 12 E1
Finsbury Wy BXLY DA5 169 G1
Finsen Rd CMBW SE5 142 D5
Finstock Rd NKENS W10 100 B5
Finucane Dr STMC/STPC BR5 202 D4
Finucane Gdns RAIN RM13 93 J4
Finucane Ri BUSH WD23 28 C4
Fiona Ct ENC/FH EN2 * 23 H4
Firbank Cl CAN/RD E16 107 H4
ENC/FH EN2 23 J5
Firbank Dr OXHEY WD19 27 J2
Firbank Rd CRW RM5 56 D1
PECK SE15 143 J3
Fircroft Gdns HRW HA1 78 E1
Fircroft Rd CHSGTN KT9 206 B2
TOOT SW17 160 E5
Firdene BRYLDS KT5 191 K5
Fir Dene ORP BR6 215 K1
Fire Bell Aly SURB KT6 191 F3
Firebell Ms SURB KT6 191 F3
Firecrest Dr HAMP NW3 83 F1
Firefly Cl WLGTN SM6 * 210 E5
Firefly Gdns EHAM E6 107 J3
Firemans Cots EFNCH N2 48 A6
Firethorn Cl EDGW HA8 30 E6
Fir Gv NWMAL KT3 192 C3
Fir Grove Rd BRXN/ST SW9 * 142 B3
Firhill Rd CAT SE6 164 D5
Firle Pl WAND/EARL SW18 160 B2
Firman Cl NWMAL KT3 192 B1
Firmin Rd DART DA1 151 F6
Fir Rd CHEAM SM3 193 J5
FELT TW13 172 C1
Firs Av FBAR/BDGN N11 48 A2
MORT/ESHN SW14 137 K5
MUSWH N10 48 A6
Firsby Av CROY/NA CR0 198 A5
Firsby Rd STNW/STAM N16 68 B5
Firs Cl ESH/CLAY KT10 204 E4
FSTH SE23 164 A2
MTCM CR4 179 G5
Firscroft PLMGR N13 35 J5
Firs Dr HEST TW5 134 A1
Firside Gv BFN/LL DA15 168 A3
Firs La PLMGR N13 35 J5
Firs Park Av WCHMH N21 35 K3
Firs Park Gdns WCHMH N21 35 K3
First Av ACT W3 118 C1
BXLYHN DA7 148 D1
CHDH RM6 73 J2
DAGE RM10 110 D1
E/WMO/HCT KT8 188 E1
EN EN1 24 B6
HDN NW4 64 A1
HOR/WEW KT19 207 G6
HYS/HAR UB3 113 J1
MNPK E12 89 J2
MORT/ESHN SW14 138 B3
NKENS W10 100 D3
PLSTW E13 106 E2
UED N18 36 E6
WALTH E17 69 K2
WBLY HA9 61 K6
WOT/HER KT12 188 A3
First Cl E/WMO/HCT KT8 189 H1
First Cross Rd WHTN TW2 155 K4
First Dr WLSDN NW10 80 E5
The Firs BXLY DA5 170 A3
EA W5 97 K4
EBED/NFELT TW14 * 153 H1
EDGW HA8 * 31 F6
TRDG/WHET N20 33 H3
First St CHEL SW3 14 D6
Firstway RYNPK SW20 177 F5
First Wy WBLY HA9 80 D2
Firs Wk NTHWD HA6 40 B2
WFD IG8 52 E1
Firswood Av HOR/WEW KT19 207 G3
Firth Gdns FUL/PGN SW6 139 H2
Firtree Av MTCM CR4 179 F5
Fir Tree Av WDR/YW UB7 112 D3
Fir Tree Cl EA W5 98 A5
ESH/CLAY KT10 204 C3
HOR/WEW KT19 207 H2
ORP BR6 217 F3
ROM RM1 57 F6
STRHM/NOR SW16 179 H1
Fir Tree Gdns CROY/NA CR0 213 J2
Fir Tree Gv CAR SM5 209 K5
Fir Tree Pl ASHF TW15 * 152 D6
Fir Tree Rd HSLWW TW4 134 D5
Fir Trees Cl BERM/RHTH SE16 124 B1
Fir Tree Wk EN EN1 24 A4
Fir Wk CHEAM SM3 208 B4
Fisher Cl CROY/NA CR0 197 G5
GFD/PVL UB6 96 A2
Fisherdene ESH/CLAY KT10 205 G5
Fisherman Cl
RCHPK/HAM TW10 156 D6
Fishermans Dr
BERM/RHTH SE16 124 A2
Fisher Rd
KTN/HRWW/WS HA3 43 F5
Fishers Cl STRHM/NOR SW16 161 J5
Fishers Ct NWCR SE14 144 A2
Fisher's La CHSWK W4 118 A4
Fisher St CAN/RD E16 106 E4
RSQ WC1B 11 G2
Fisher's Wy BELV DA17 129 K1
Fisherton St STJWD NW8 2 A7
Fishguard Wy CAN/RD E16 127 G1
Fishponds Rd HAYES BR2 215 H3
TOOT SW17 160 D6
Fish Street Hl MON EC3R 13 F6
Fisons Rd CAN/RD E16 125 K1
Fitzalan Rd ESH/CLAY KT10 204 E5
FNCH N3 46 C6
Fitzalan St LBTH SE11 17 H6
Fitzgeorge Av NWMAL KT3 176 A4
WKENS W14 119 H4
Fitzgerald Av
MORT/ESHN SW14 138 B4
Fitzgerald Rd
MORT/ESHN SW14 138 A4
THDIT KT7 190 B3
WAN E11 70 E2
Fitzhardinge St MBLAR W1H 9 G3
Fitzhugh Gv
WAND/EARL SW18 160 C1
Fitzjames Av CROY/NA CR0 197 H6
WKENS W14 119 H4
Fitzjohn Av BAR EN5 20 C6
Fitzjohn's Av HAMP NW3 83 H3
Fitzmaurice Pl
MYFR/PICC W1J * 9 K7
Fitzneal St SHB W12 99 H5
Fitzroy Cl HGT N6 65 K5
Fitzroy Crs CHSWK W4 * 138 A1
Fitzroy Gdns NRWD SE19 181 F3
Fitzroy Ms FITZ W1T 4 A7
Fitzroy Pk HGT N6 65 K5
Fitzroy Rd CAMTN NW1 84 A6
Fitzroy Sq FITZ W1T 4 A7
Fitzroy St FITZ W1T 10 A1
Fitzstephen Rd BCTR RM8 91 H3
Fitzwarren Gdns HGT N6 66 C5
Fitzwilliam Av RCH/KEW TW9 137 G3
Fitzwilliam Cl
TRDG/WHET N20 33 K3
Fitzwilliam Ms CAN/RD E16 106 E6
Fitzwilliam Rd CLAP SW4 141 H4
Fitz Wygram Cl HPTN TW12 173 H1
Five Acre CDALE/KGS NW9 45 H5
Fiveacre Cl CROY/NA CR0 196 B3
Five Elms Rd DAGW RM9 92 B1
HAYES BR2 215 G1
Five Fields Cl OXHEY WD19 27 K4
Five Oaks La CHIG IG7 56 A2
Fiveways Cnr ELTH/MOT SE9 167 G4
Five Ways Jct HDN NW4 45 J4
Fiveways Rd BRXN/ST SW9 142 B3
Fladbury Rd
SEVS/STOTM N15 67 K3
Fladgate Rd WAN E11 70 C3
Flag Cl CROY/NA CR0 198 A5
Flag Wk PIN HA5 58 E3
Flambard Rd HRW HA1 61 G3
Flamborough Rd RSLP HA4 76 E1
Flamborough St
POP/IOD E14 105 G5
Flamborough Wk
POP/IOD E14 * 105 G5
Flamingo Wk HCH RM12 93 J5
Flamstead Gdns DAGW RM9 91 J5
Flamstead Rd DAGW RM9 91 J5
Flamsted Av WBLY HA9 80 C4
Flamsteed Rd CHARL SE7 126 D5
Flanchford Rd SHB W12 118 C3
Flanders Crs TOOT SW17 178 E3
Flanders Rd CHSWK W4 118 B4
EHAM E6 107 K1
Flanders Wy HOM E9 87 F4
Flandrian Cl PEND EN3 25 J2
Flank St WCHPL E1 104 C6
Flask Wk HAMP NW3 83 G2
Flather Cl STRHM/NOR SW16 179 H2
Flavell Ms GNWCH SE10 125 H5
Flaxen Cl CHING E4 37 K5
Flaxen Rd CHING E4 37 K5
Flaxley Rd MRDN SM4 194 A3
Flaxman Rd CMBW SE5 142 C3
Flaxman Ter STPAN WC1H 4 D5
Flaxton Rd WOOL/PLUM SE18 147 J2
Flecker Cl STAN HA7 43 F1
Fleece Dr ED N9 36 C6
Fleece Rd SURB KT6 190 D5
Fleece Wk HOLWY N7 * 84 E4
Fleeming Cl WALTH E17 51 H5
Fleeming Rd WALTH E17 51 H5
Fleet Cl E/WMO/HCT KT8 188 E2
RSLP HA4 58 A3
Fleet Pl FLST/FETLN EC4A 12 A3
Fleet Rd HAMP NW3 83 J3
Fleetside E/WMO/HCT KT8 188 E2
Fleet Sq FSBYW WC1X 5 G5
Fleet St EMB EC4Y 11 J4
Fleet Street Hl WCHPL E1 * 104 C3
Fleet Ter CAT SE6 * 165 F2
Fleetwood Cl CAN/RD E16 107 H4
CHSGTN KT9 205 K5
CROY/NA CR0 212 B1
Fleetwood Rd KUT/HW KT1 175 J6
WLSDN NW10 81 J3
Fleetwood Sq KUT/HW KT1 175 J6
Fleetwood St
STNW/STAM N16 68 A6
Fleetwood Wy OXHEY WD19 27 G6
Fleming Cl MV/WKIL W9 100 E3
WBPTN SW10 * 120 B6
Fleming Ct CROY/NA CR0 211 G3
Fleming Dr WCHMH N21 23 F6
Fleming Md MTCM CR4 178 D3
Fleming Rd STHL UB1 96 B5
WALW SE17 122 C6
Fleming Wk
CDALE/KGS NW9 * 45 G5
Fleming Wy ISLW TW7 136 A4
THMD SE28 109 K6
Flemming Av RSLP HA4 59 F5
Flempton Rd LEY E10 69 G5
Fletcher Cl EHAM E6 108 B6
Fletcher La LEY E10 70 A4
Fletcher Rd CHIG IG7 55 F1
CHSWK W4 117 K3
Fletchers Cl HAYES BR2 200 A1
Fletcher St WCHPL E1 104 C6
Fletching Rd CHARL SE7 126 C6
CLPT E5 86 E1
Fletton Rd FBAR/BDGN N11 48 E3
Fleur De Lis St WCHPL E1 7 H7
Fleur Gates WIM/MER SW19 159 G2
Flexmere Rd TOTM N17 49 K4
Flight Ap CDALE/KGS NW9 * 45 H4
Flimwell Cl BMLY BR1 183 H1
Flint Cl ORP BR6 * 217 F4
SRTFD E15 88 D4
Flint Down Cl
STMC/STPC BR5 * 186 B4
Flintmill Crs BKHTH/KID SE3 146 D3
ELTH/MOT SE9 146 D4
Flinton St WALW SE17 123 F5
Flint St WALW SE17 19 F7
Flitcroft St LSQ/SEVD WC2H 10 D4
Floathaven Cl THMD SE28 128 B1
Flock Mill Pl
WAND/EARL SW18 160 A3
Flockton St BERM/RHTH SE16 123 H2
Flodden Rd CMBW SE5 142 D2
Flood La TWK TW1 * 156 B3
Flood St CHEL SW3 120 D5
Flood Wk CHEL SW3 120 D6
Flora Cl POP/IOD E14 105 K5
STAN HA7 29 K5
Flora Gdns CHDH RM6 73 J3
HMSMTH W6 118 E4
Floral Pl IS N1 85 K3
Floral St COVGDN WC2E 11 F5
Flora St BELV DA17 129 G5
Florence Av ENC/FH EN2 23 J4
MRDN SM4 194 B2
Florence Cl WOT/HER KT12 188 A4
Florence Ct WAN E11 71 F1
Florence Dr ENC/FH EN2 23 J4
Florence Elson Cl MNPK E12 90 A2
Florence Gdns CHSWK W4 117 K6
Florence Rd ABYW SE2 128 D3
BECK BR3 182 A5
BMLY BR1 183 K4
CHSWK W4 118 A3
EA W5 98 A6
EHAM E6 89 G6
FELT TW13 154 A3
FSBYPK N4 67 F4
KUTN/CMB KT2 175 G3
NWCR SE14 144 C2
NWDGN UB2 114 C4
PLSTW E13 106 E1
SAND/SEL CR2 211 K6
WIM/MER SW19 178 A2
WOT/HER KT12 188 A4
Florence St CAN/RD E16 106 D3
HDN NW4 64 A1
IS N1 85 H5
Florence Ter NWCR SE14 144 C2
Florence Vls HGT N6 * 66 B4
Florence Wy BAL SW12 160 E3
Florey Sq WCHMH N21 23 F6
Florfield Rd HACK E8 86 D4
Florian Av SUT SM1 209 H2
Florian Rd PUT/ROE SW15 139 H5
Florida Cl BUSH WD23 28 D4
Florida Rd THHTH CR7 180 C4
Florida St BETH E2 104 C2
Florin Ct UED N18 36 A6
Floris Pl CLAP SW4 141 H4
Floriston Av HGDN/ICK UB10 76 A5
Floriston Cl STAN HA7 43 H4
Floriston Gdns STAN HA7 43 H4
Floss St PUT/ROE SW15 139 F3
Flower & Dean Wk WCHPL E1 13 K2
Flower La MLHL NW7 45 H1
Flower Ms GLDGN NW11 64 C3
Flowerpot Cl
SEVS/STOTM N15 68 B3
Flowers Av RSLP HA4 58 E3
Flowers Cl CRICK NW2 81 J1
Flowers Ms ARCH N19 66 C6
Floyd Rd CHARL SE7 126 B5
Floyer Cl RCHPK/HAM TW10 137 G6
Fludyer St LEW SE13 145 H5
Foley Ms ESH/CLAY KT10 204 E4
Foley Rd ESH/CLAY KT10 204 E5
Foley St GTPST W1W 10 A2
Foley Wd ESH/CLAY KT10 205 F5
Folgate St WCHPL E1 13 H1
Foliot St SHB W12 99 H5
Folkestone Rd EHAM E6 108 A1
UED N18 36 C6
WALTH E17 69 K1
Folkingham La
CDALE/KGS NW9 45 F4
Folkington Cnr
NFNCH/WDSPK N12 46 D1
Follett St POP/IOD E14 106 A5
Folly La WALTH E17 51 G4
Folly Wall POP/IOD E14 125 F2
Fontaine Rd
STRHM/NOR SW16 180 A2
Fontarabia Rd BTSEA SW11 141 F5
Fontayne Av RAIN RM13 93 G5
ROM RM1 57 G5
Fontenoy Rd BAL SW12 161 G4
Fonteyne Gdns WFD IG8 53 H5
Fonthill Ms FSBYPK N4 67 F6
Fonthill Rd FSBYPK N4 67 F6
Font Hills EFNCH N2 47 G5
Fontley Wy PUT/ROE SW15 158 D2
Fontwell Cl
KTN/HRWW/WS HA3 42 E3
NTHLT UB5 78 A4
Fontwell Dr HAYES BR2 201 F2
Footbury Hill Rd ORP BR6 202 B4
The Footpath
PUT/ROE SW15 * 138 D6
Foots Cray High St
SCUP DA14 186 D2
Foots Cray La SCUP DA14 168 D3
Footscray Rd ELTH/MOT SE9 167 G3
Forbes Cl CRICK NW2 81 J1
HCH RM12 75 K5
Forbes St WCHPL E1 104 C5
Forbes Wy RSLP HA4 59 F6
Forburg Rd STNW/STAM N16 68 C5
Ford Cl HRW HA1 60 D4
RAIN RM13 93 H5
THHTH CR7 196 C3
Fordcroft Rd STMC/STPC BR5 202 C2
Forde Av BMLY BR1 184 B6
Fordel Rd CAT SE6 165 G3
Ford End WFD IG8 53 F2
Fordham Cl WPK KT4 192 E5
Fordham Rd EBAR EN4 21 H4
Fordham St WCHPL E1 104 C5
Fordhook Av EA W5 98 B6
Fordingley Rd MV/WKIL W9 100 D2
Fordington Rd HGT N6 65 K1
Ford La RAIN RM13 93 H5
Fordmill Rd CAT SE6 164 D4
Ford Rd ASHF TW15 152 C6
BOW E3 105 G1
DAGW RM9 92 B5
Ford's Gv WCHMH N21 35 J3
Fords Park Rd CAN/RD E16 106 E5
Ford Sq WCHPL E1 104 D4
Ford St BOW E3 87 G6
CAN/RD E16 106 D5
Fordwich Cl ORP BR6 202 A4
Fordwych Rd CRICK NW2 82 C3
Fordyce Rd LEW SE13 165 F1
Fordyke Rd BCTR RM8 74 A6
Foreland Ct HDN NW4 46 C4
Foreland St
WOOL/PLUM SE18 127 J4
Foremark Cl BARK/HLT IG6 55 F2
Foreshore DEPT SE8 124 C5
Forest Ap CHING E4 38 C2
WFD IG8 52 D3
Forest Av CHIG IG7 54 A1
CHING E4 38 C2
Forest Cl CHST BR7 185 F4
KIL/WHAMP NW6 82 C5
WAN E11 70 D2
WFD IG8 39 F6
Forest Ct CHING E4 38 D3
WAN E11 70 C1
Forestdale STHGT/OAK N14 34 D6
Forest Dr HAYES BR2 215 J1
MNPK E12 89 H1
WFD IG8 52 B3
Forest Dr East WAN E11 70 B4
Forest Dr West WAN E11 70 A4
Forest Edge BKHH IG9 39 G5
Forester Rd PECK SE15 143 J5
Foresters Cl WLGTN SM6 210 D5
Foresters Crs BXLYHN DA7 149 J5
Foresters Dr WALTH E17 70 B1
WLGTN SM6 210 D5
Forest Gdns TOTM N17 50 B5
Forest Ga CDALE/KGS NW9 63 G1
Forest Gld CHING E4 52 C1
WAN E11 70 C3
Forest Gv HACK E8 86 B4
Forest Hill Rd EDUL SE22 163 J1
Forestholme Cl FSTH SE23 163 K4
SYD SE26 * 181 K1
Forest La CHIG IG7 54 A1
FSTGT E7 88 E3
Forest Mount Rd WFD IG8 52 B3
Fore St BARB EC2Y 12 E2
ED N9 36 C6
PIN HA5 58 D1
UED N18 50 C1
Forest Rdg BECK BR3 182 D6
HAYES BR2 215 J2
Forest Ri WALTH E17 70 B1
Forest Rd BARK/HLT IG6 54 E4
BARK/HLT IG6 55 G3
CHEAM SM3 193 K5
ED N9 36 D3
ERITH DA8 150 D2
FELT TW13 154 B4
FSTGT E7 88 E2
HACK E8 86 B4
RCH/KEW TW9 137 H1
ROMW/RG RM7 56 D6
TOTM N17 68 E1
WALTH E17 51 J6
WAN E11 70 A4
WFD IG8 38 E5
Forest Side CHING E4 38 D2
FSTGT E7 89 F2
WPK KT4 192 C5
Forest St FSTGT E7 88 E3
The Forest WAN E11 70 C1
Forest Vw CHING E4 38 B1
WAN E11 70 D4
Forest View Av LEY E10 70 B2
Forest View Rd MNPK E12 89 J2
WALTH E17 52 A4
Forest Wy BFN/LL DA15 167 J2
STMC/STPC BR5 202 A2
WFD IG8 39 F6
Forfar Rd BTSEA SW11 141 F2
WDGN N22 49 H4
Forge Cl HAYES BR2 199 K5
HYS/HAR UB3 113 G6
Forge Cots EA W5 * 116 E1
Forge Dr ESH/CLAY KT10 205 G5
Forge La CHEAM SM3 208 C5
FELT TW13 172 D1
NTHWD HA6 40 C3
RCHPK/HAM TW10 157 F3
Forge Ms CROY/NA CR0 213 J3
Forge Pl CAMTN NW1 84 A4
Forman Pl STNW/STAM N16 86 B2
Formby Av
KTN/HRWW/WS HA3 43 J6
Formosa St MV/WKIL W9 101 F3
Formunt Cl CAN/RD E16 106 D4
Forres Gdns GLDGN NW11 64 E3
Forrester Pth SYD SE26 163 K6
Forrest Gdns
STRHM/NOR SW16 180 A6
Forris Av HYS/HAR UB3 113 J1
Forset St MBLAR W1H 8 D3
Forstal Cl HAYES BR2 183 K6
Forster Cl CHING E4 52 B3
Forster Rd BECK BR3 182 B6
BRXS/STRHM SW2 161 K2
TOTM N17 50 B6
WALTH E17 69 G3
Forsters Cl CHDH RM6 74 B3
Forston St IS N1 6 D2
Forsyte Crs NRWD SE19 181 F4
Forsyth Gdns WALW SE17 122 C6
Forsythia Cl IL IG1 90 B3
Forsyth Pl EN EN1 24 A6
Forterie Gdns GDMY/SEVK IG3 91 G1
Fortescue Av WHTN TW2 155 H5
Fortescue Rd EDGW HA8 45 F4
WIM/MER SW19 178 C3
Fortess Gv KTTN NW5 84 C3
Fortess Rd KTTN NW5 84 B3
Fortess Wk KTTN NW5 84 B3
Forthbridge Rd BTSEA SW11 141 F5
Fortis Cl CAN/RD E16 107 G5
Fortis Gn EFNCH N2 47 K6
Fortis Green Av EFNCH N2 48 A6
Fortis Green Rd MUSWH N10 48 A6
Fortismere Av MUSWH N10 48 A6
Fortnam Rd ARCH N19 66 D6
Fortnums Acre STAN HA7 43 F2
Fort Rd NTHLT UB5 78 A5
STHWK SE1 19 K7
Fortrose Cl POP/IOD E14 106 B5
Fortrose Gdns
BRXS/STRHM SW2 161 K3
Fort St CAN/RD E16 126 A1
WCHPL E1 * 13 H2
Fortuna Cl HOLWY N7 * 85 F4
Fortune Av EDGW HA8 44 D4
Fortunegate Rd
WLSDN NW10 81 G6
Fortune Green Rd
KIL/WHAMP NW6 82 E3
Fortune La BORE WD6 29 K1
Fortune Pl STHWK SE1 123 H5
Fortunes Md NTHLT UB5 77 J4
Fortune St STLK EC1Y 6 D7
Fortune Wy WLSDN NW10 99 J2
Forty Acre La CAN/RD E16 106 E4
Forty Av WBLY HA9 80 B1
Forty Cl WBLY HA9 80 B1
Forty La WBLY HA9 62 D6
Forum Cl BOW E3 87 J6
Forum Magnum Sq
STHWK SE1 17 G2
Forumside EDGW HA8 44 C2
The Forum E/WMO/HCT KT8 189 G1
Forval Cl MTCM CR4 194 E2
Forward Dr
KTN/HRWW/WS HA3 61 F1
Fosbury Ms BAY/PAD W2 101 F6
Foscote Ms MV/WKIL W9 100 E3
Foscote Rd HDN NW4 63 K3
Foskett Rd FUL/PGN SW6 139 J3
Foss Av CROY/NA CR0 211 G3
Fossdene Rd CHARL SE7 126 A5
Fossdyke Cl YEAD UB4 95 J4
Fosse Wy WEA W13 97 G4
Fossil Rd LEW SE13 144 D4
Fossington Rd BELV DA17 128 E4
Foss Rd TOOT SW17 160 C6
Fossway BCTR RM8 73 J6
Foster La CITYW EC2V 12 C3
Foster Rd ACT W3 99 G6
CHSWK W4 118 A5
PLSTW E13 106 E3

Fosters Cl CHST BR7 184 E1
SWFD E18 53 F4
Foster St HDN NW4 64 A1
Foster Wk HDN NW4 64 A1
Fothergill Cl PLSTW E13 88 E6
Fothergill Dr WCHMH N21 22 E6
Fotheringham Rd EN EN1 24 B5
Foubert's Pl SOHO/CST W1F 10 A4
Foulden Rd STNW/STAM N16 86 B2
Foulden Ter STNW/STAM N16 86 B2
Foulis Ter SKENS SW7 14 A7
Foulser Rd TOOT SW17 160 E5
Foulsham Rd THHTH CR7 180 D6
Foundation Pl
ELTH/MOT SE9 * 147 F6
Founder Cl EHAM E6 108 B5
Founders Cl NTHLT UB5 95 K2
Founders Gdns NRWD SE19 180 D3
Foundry Cl BERM/RHTH SE16 124 B1
Foundry Ms CAMTN NW1 4 B6
HSLW TW3 135 G5
Foundry Pl
WAND/EARL SW18 * 160 A2
Fountain Cl UX/CGN UB8 94 A4
Fountain Dr CAR SM5 209 K5
NRWD SE19 163 G6
Fountain Green Sq
BERM/RHTH SE16 123 H2
Fountain Ms HAMP NW3 83 K4
Fountain Pl BRXN/ST SW9 142 B2
Fountain Rd THHTH CR7 180 D5
TOOT SW17 178 C1
Fountains Av FELT TW13 154 E5
Fountains Cl FELT TW13 154 E4
Fountains Crs
STHGT/OAK N14 34 E2
Fountayne Rd
SEVS/STOTM N15 68 C1
STNW/STAM N16 68 C6
Fount St VX/NE SW8 141 J1
Fouracres PEND EN3 25 G2
Fourland Wk EDGW HA8 44 E2
Fournier St WCHPL E1 13 J1
Four Seasons Cl BOW E3 105 J1
Four Seasons Crs CHEAM SM3 193 J6
Fourth Av HYS/HAR UB3 113 J1
MNPK E12 89 K2
NKENS W10 100 C3
ROMW/RG RM7 75 G6
Fourth Cross Rd WHTN TW2 155 J4
Fourth Wy WBLY HA9 80 D2
The Four Tubs BUSH WD23 28 D2
The Four Wents CHING E4 38 B4
Fowey Av REDBR IG4 71 H2
Fowey Cl WAP E1W 123 J1
Fowler Cl BTSEA SW11 140 C4
SCUP DA14 187 F1
Fowler Rd BARK/HLT IG6 55 J1
FSTGT E7 88 E2
IS N1 85 H6
Fowler's Wk EA W5 97 K3
Fownes St BTSEA SW11 140 D4
Foxberry Rd BROCKY SE4 144 B5
Foxborough Gdns
BROCKY SE4 164 D1
Foxbourne Rd TOOT SW17 161 F4
Fox Burrow Rd BARK/HLT IG6 55 J1
Foxbury Av CHST BR7 185 J2
Foxbury Cl BMLY BR1 184 A2
ORP BR6 217 G3
Foxbury Dr ORP BR6 217 G4
Foxbury Rd BMLY BR1 184 A2
Fox Cl BORE WD6 29 K1
CAN/RD E16 106 E4
CRW RM5 56 D1
ORP BR6 217 G3
WCHPL E1 104 E3
Foxcombe CROY/NA CR0 213 K4
Foxcroft Rd
WOOL/PLUM SE18 147 G2
Foxdell NTHWD HA6 40 B2
Foxdene Cl SWFD E18 53 F6
Foxearth Sp SAND/SEL CR2 212 E6
Foxes Dl BKHTH/KID SE3 145 K4
HAYES BR2 183 G6
Foxfield Cl NTHWD HA6 40 D2
Foxfield Rd ORP BR6 201 J6
Foxglove Cl BFN/LL DA15 168 B1
ED N9 36 E3
STHL UB1 95 J6
STWL/WRAY TW19 152 A3
Foxglove Gdns WAN E11 71 G1
Foxglove La CHSGTN KT9 206 C2
Foxglove Pth THMD SE28 127 K2
Foxglove Rd ROMW/RG RM7 75 G6
Foxglove St ACT W3 99 H6
Foxglove Wy WLGTN SM6 195 F4
Foxgrove STHGT/OAK N14 34 E5
Fox Gv WOT/HER KT12 188 A4
Foxgrove Av BECK BR3 182 E3
Foxgrove Pth OXHEY WD19 41 H1
Foxgrove Rd BECK BR3 182 E3
Foxham Rd ARCH N19 84 D1
Fox Hl HAYES BR2 215 G3
NRWD SE19 181 G3
Fox Hill Gdns NRWD SE19 181 G3
Foxhole Rd ELTH/MOT SE9 146 D6
Fox Hollow WOT/HER KT12 188 B6
Fox Hollow Cl
WOOL/PLUM SE18 127 K5
Fox Hollow Dr BXLYHN DA7 148 E4
Foxholt Gdns WLSDN NW10 80 E5
Foxhome Cl CHST BR7 185 F2
Fox House Rd BELV DA17 129 J4
Fox & Knot St FARR EC1M * 12 B1
Foxlands Crs DAGE RM10 92 E3
Foxlands Rd DAGE RM10 92 E3
Fox La EA W5 98 A4
HAYES BR2 215 F3
PLMGR N13 35 F5
Foxlees ALP/SUD HA0 79 G2
Foxley Cl HACK E8 86 C3
Foxley Rd CMBW SE5 142 B1
THHTH CR7 196 C1
Foxleys OXHEY WD19 27 J5
Foxley Sq BRXN/ST SW9 * 142 C1
Foxmead Cl ENC/FH EN2 23 F4
Foxmore St BTSEA SW11 140 E2
Fox Rd CAN/RD E16 106 D4
Foxton Gv MTCM CR4 178 C5
Foxwarren ESH/CLAY KT10 205 F6
Foxwell St BROCKY SE4 144 B4
Foxwood Cl FELT TW13 154 A5
MLHL NW7 31 G6
Foxwood Green Cl EN EN1 36 A1
Foxwood Rd BKHTH/KID SE3 145 J5
Foyle Rd BKHTH/KID SE3 125 J6
TOTM N17 50 C4
Framfield Cl
NFNCH/WDSPK N12 32 E6
Framfield Rd HBRY N5 85 H3
HNWL W7 97 F5
MTCM CR4 179 F3
Framlingham Crs
ELTH/MOT SE9 166 D6
Frampton Cl BELMT SM2 208 E5
Frampton Park Rd HOM E9 86 E4
Frampton Rd HSLWW TW4 134 D6
Frampton St STJWD NW8 2 B7
Francemary Rd LEW SE13 144 D6
Frances Rd CHING E4 51 J2
Frances St WOOL/PLUM SE18 126 E4
Franche Court Rd TOOT SW17 160 B5
Francis Av BXLYHN DA7 149 H3
FELT TW13 153 K5
IL IG1 72 D6
Francis Barber Cl
STRHM/NOR SW16 * 162 A6
Francis Bentley Ms CLAP SW4 141 H4
Franciscan Rd TOOT SW17 161 F6
Francis Chichester Wy
BTSEA SW11 * 141 F2
Francis Cl HOR/WEW KT19 207 F2
Francis Gv WIM/MER SW19 177 J3
Francis Ms LEE/GVPK SE12 * 165 J1
Francis Rd CROY/NA CR0 196 C4
DART DA1 151 G6
EFNCH N2 * 65 K1
GFD/PVL UB6 97 J1
HRW HA1 61 G2
HSLWW TW4 134 C3
LEY E10 70 A6
PIN HA5 59 G2
STMC/STPC BR5 186 E6
WLGTN SM6 210 C4
Francis St SRTFD E15 88 C3
WEST SW1P 16 B6
Francis Ter ARCH N19 84 C1
Francis Wk IS N1 85 F6
Francklyn Gdns EDGW HA8 30 C5
Francombe Gdns ROM RM1 75 J3
Franconia Rd CLAP SW4 141 H6
Frank Burton Cl CHARL SE7 126 A5
Frank Dixon Cl DUL SE21 163 F2
Frank Dixon Wy DUL SE21 163 F3
Frankfurt Rd HNHL SE24 142 D6
Frankham St DEPT SE8 144 D1
Frankland Cl
BERM/RHTH SE16 123 J3
WFD IG8 53 G1
Frankland Rd CHING E4 51 J1
SKENS SW7 14 A5
Franklin Av WATW WD18 26 E1
Franklin Cl KUT/HW KT1 175 H6
LEW SE13 144 E2
TRDG/WHET N20 33 G2
WNWD SE27 162 C5
Franklin Crs MTCM CR4 195 H1
Franklin Pl GNWCH SE10 144 E2
Franklin Rd BXLYHN DA7 149 F2
PGE/AN SE20 181 K3
RDART DA2 170 B4
Franklins Ms
RYLN/HDSTN HA2 60 C6
Franklin Sq WKENS W14 119 J5
Franklins Rw CHEL SW3 * 120 E5
Franklin's Rw CHEL SW3 120 E5
Franklin St BOW E3 105 K2
SEVS/STOTM N15 68 A3
Franklin Wy CROY/NA CR0 195 K5
Franklyn Gdns BARK/HLT IG6 54 D2
Franklyn Rd WLSDN NW10 81 H5
WOT/HER KT12 188 A3
Frank Ms STHWK SE1 123 J4
Franks Av NWMAL KT3 191 K1
Franks Wood Av
STMC/STPC BR5 201 G2
Franlaw Crs PLMGR N13 35 J6
Franmil Rd HCH RM12 75 H4
Fransfield Gv SYD SE26 163 J5
Franshams BUSH WD23 * 28 E4
Frant Cl PGE/AN SE20 181 K3
Frant Rd THHTH CR7 196 C2
Fraser Cl BXLY DA5 169 K3
EHAM E6 107 J5
Fraser Rd ED N9 36 D5
ERITH DA8 129 K5
GFD/PVL UB6 79 J6
WALTH E17 69 K2
Fraser St CHSWK W4 118 B5
Frating Crs WFD IG8 52 E2
Frays Av WDR/YW UB7 112 A2
Frays Cl WDR/YW UB7 112 A3
Frazer Av RSLP HA4 77 G3
Frazer Cl ROM RM1 75 H4
Frazier St STHWK SE1 17 J3
Frean St BERM/RHTH SE16 123 H3
Freda Corbett Cl PECK SE15 143 H1
Frederica Rd CHING E4 38 B2
Frederica St HOLWY N7 85 F5
Frederick Cl BAY/PAD W2 8 D5
SUT SM1 208 D2
Frederick Crs BRXN/ST SW9 142 C1
PEND EN3 24 E3
Frederick Gdns CROY/NA CR0 196 C3
SUT SM1 208 D3
Frederick Pl
WOOL/PLUM SE18 127 G5
Frederick Rd RAIN RM13 111 F1
SUT SM1 208 D3
WALW SE17 122 C6
Frederick's Pl LOTH EC2R * 12 E4
NFNCH/WDSPK N12 33 G6
Frederick Sq
BERM/RHTH SE16 105 G6
Frederick's Rw FSBYE EC1V 6 A4
Frederick St FSBYW WC1X 5 G5
Frederick Ter HACK E8 * 86 B5
Frederic Ms KTBR SW1X * 15 G3
Frederic St WALTH E17 69 G2
Fredora Av YEAD UB4 94 D3
Freeborne Gdns RAIN RM13 93 J4
Freedom Cl WALTH E17 69 F1
Freedom Rd TOTM N17 49 K5
Freedom St BTSEA SW11 140 E3
Freegrove Rd HOLWY N7 84 E3
Freeland Pk HDN NW4 46 C5
Freeland Rd EA W5 98 B6
Freelands Av SAND/SEL CR2 213 F6
Freelands Gv BMLY BR1 184 A4
Freelands Rd BMLY BR1 184 A4
Freeland Wy ERITH DA8 150 D2
Freeling St IS N1 85 F5
Freeman Cl NTHLT UB5 77 J5
Freeman Dr E/WMO/HCT KT8 188 E1
Freeman Rd MRDN SM4 194 C2
Freemans La HYS/HAR UB3 94 C6
Freemantle Av PEND EN3 25 F6
Freemantle St WALW SE17 123 F5
Freeman Wk ELTH/MOT SE9 146 B6
Freemasons Rd CAN/RD E16 107 F4
Freemason's Rd
CROY/NA CR0 197 F5
Freesia Cl ORP BR6 217 F3
Freethorpe Cl NRWD SE19 181 F4
Freight La KCROSS N1C 84 E5
Freightmaster Est
RAIN RM13 * 130 D4
Freke Rd BTSEA SW11 141 F4
Fremantle Rd BARK/HLT IG6 54 B5
BELV DA17 129 H4
Fremont St HOM E9 86 D6
French Pl SDTCH EC2A 7 H5
French St SUN TW16 172 B5
Frendsbury Rd BROCKY SE4 144 B5
Frensham Cl STHL UB1 95 K3
Frensham Dr CROY/NA CR0 214 A5
PUT/ROE SW15 158 D4
Frensham Rd ELTH/MOT SE9 167 J4
Frensham St PECK SE15 123 H6
Frere St BTSEA SW11 140 D3
Freshfield Av HACK E8 86 B5
Freshfield Cl LEW SE13 145 G5
Freshfield Dr STHGT/OAK N14 34 B2
Freshfields CROY/NA CR0 198 C4
Freshford St TOOT SW17 160 B5
Fresh Mill La STHL UB1 96 A3
Freshwater Cl TOOT SW17 179 F2
Freshwater Rd BCTR RM8 73 K5
TOOT SW17 179 F2
Freshwell Av CHDH RM6 73 J1
Fresh Wharf Rd BARK IG11 90 B6
Freshwood Cl BECK BR3 182 E4
Freshwood Wy WLGTN SM6 210 C6
Freston Gdns EBAR EN4 22 A6
Freston Pk FNCH N3 46 D5
Freston Rd NKENS W10 100 B6
Freta Rd BXLYHS DA6 149 G6
Frewin Rd WAND/EARL SW18 160 C3
Friar Ms WNWD SE27 162 C5
Friar Rd STMC/STPC BR5 202 B2
YEAD UB4 95 H3
Friars Av PUT/ROE SW15 139 H6
TRDG/WHET N20 33 J5
Friars Cl CHING E4 38 A5
IL IG1 72 D5
NTHLT UB5 95 G2
STHWK SE1 * 12 B7
Friars Gdns ACT W3 99 F5
Friars Gate Cl WFD IG8 38 E6
Friars La RCH/KEW TW9 136 E6
Friars Md POP/IOD E14 125 F3
Friars Ms ELTH/MOT SE9 147 F6
Friars Place La ACT W3 99 F6
Friar's Rd EHAM E6 89 H6
Friars Stile Rd
RCHPK/HAM TW10 157 F1
Friars Wk ABYW SE2 128 E5
STHGT/OAK N14 34 B3
Friars Wy ACT W3 99 F5
Friars Wd CROY/NA CR0 213 G6
Friary Cl NFNCH/WDSPK N12 47 J1
Friary Est PECK SE15 * 143 H1
Friary La WFD IG8 38 E6
Friary Pk
NFNCH/WDSPK N12 * 33 J6
Friary Park Ct ACT W3 * 98 E5
Friary Rd ACT W3 98 E5
NFNCH/WDSPK N12 33 H6
PECK SE15 143 H1
Friary Wy NFNCH/WDSPK N12 33 J6
Friday Hl CHING E4 38 C5
Friday Hl East CHING E4 38 C5
Friday Hl West CHING E4 38 C4
Friday Rd ERITH DA8 130 A5
MTCM CR4 178 E3
Friday St STP EC4M 12 C5
Frideswide Pl KTTN NW5 84 C3
Friendly Pl LEW SE13 144 E2
Friendly St DEPT SE8 144 D2
Friendly Street Ms DEPT SE8 144 D3
Friendship Wy SRTFD E15 * 88 A6
Friends' Rd CROY/NA CR0 211 K1
Friend St FSBYE EC1V 6 A4
Friern Barnet La
TRDG/WHET N20 33 H5
Friern Barnet Rd
FBAR/BDGN N11 48 A1
Friern Mount Dr
TRDG/WHET N20 33 G2
Friern Pk NFNCH/WDSPK N12 47 H1
Friern Rd EDUL SE22 163 H1
Friern Watch Av
NFNCH/WDSPK N12 33 H6
Frigate Ms DEPT SE8 124 D6
Frimley Av WLGTN SM6 210 E3
Frimley Cl CROY/NA CR0 214 A5
WIM/MER SW19 159 H4
Frimley Ct SCUP DA14 186 D1
Frimley Crs CROY/NA CR0 214 A5
Frimley Gdns MTCM CR4 178 D6
Frimley Rd CHSGTN KT9 205 K3
GDMY/SEVK IG3 90 E1
Frimley Wy WCHPL E1 * 105 F3
Frinstead Gv STMC/STPC BR5 202 E1
Frinsted Rd ERITH DA8 150 A1
Frinton Cl OXHEY WD19 27 F4
Frinton Dr WFD IG8 52 B3
Frinton Ms GNTH/NBYPK IG2 72 A3
Frinton Rd CRW RM5 56 C3
EHAM E6 107 H2
SCUP DA14 169 F4
SEVS/STOTM N15 68 A3
TOOT SW17 179 F2
Friston St FUL/PGN SW6 140 A3
Friswell Pl BXLYHN DA7 149 H5
Fritham Cl NWMAL KT3 192 B3
Frith Ct MLHL NW7 46 C3
Frith La MLHL NW7 46 C2
Frith Manor Farm Cots
MLHL NW7 * 46 C1
Frith Rd CROY/NA CR0 196 D6
WAN E11 88 A2
Frith St SOHO/SHAV W1D 10 C4
Frithville Gdns SHB W12 119 F1
Frithwood Av NTHWD HA6 40 D2
Frizlands La DAGE RM10 92 D1
Frobisher Cl BUSH WD23 28 A1
PIN HA5 59 H4
Frobisher Crs BARB EC2Y * 12 D1
STWL/WRAY TW19 152 B2
Frobisher Gdns LEY E10 * 69 K3
Frobisher Ms ENC/FH EN2 23 K5
Frobisher Rd CEND/HSY/T N8 67 G1
EHAM E6 107 K5
ERITH DA8 150 D1
Frog La RAIN RM13 111 F4
Frogley Rd EDUL SE22 143 G5
Frogmore WAND/EARL SW18 139 K6
Frogmore Av YEAD UB4 94 C3
Frogmore Cl CHEAM SM3 208 B1
Frogmore Est HBRY N5 * 85 J2
Frogmore Gdns CHEAM SM3 208 C2
YEAD UB4 94 C3
Frognal HAMP NW3 83 G3
Frognal Av HRW HA1 61 F1
SCUP DA14 186 B2
Frognal Cl HAMP NW3 83 G3
Frognal Gdns HAMP NW3 83 G2
Frognal La HAMP NW3 83 F3
Frognal Man HAMP NW3 * 83 G2
Frognal Pde HAMP NW3 83 G4
Frognal Pl SCUP DA14 186 B2
Frognal Ri HAMP NW3 83 G2
Frognal Wy HAMP NW3 83 G2
Frogwell Cl FSBYPK N4 67 K3
Froissart Rd ELTH/MOT SE9 146 D6
Frome Rd SEVS/STOTM N15 49 H6
Frome St IS N1 6 C2
Fromondes Rd CHEAM SM3 208 C3
Fromows Cnr CHSWK W4 * 117 K5
Frostic Wk WCHPL E1 13 K2
Froude St VX/NE SW8 141 G3
Fruen Rd EBED/NFELT TW14 153 J2
Fryatt Rd TOTM N17 49 K3
Fry Cl CRW RM5 56 C1
Fryday Grove Ms BAL SW12 161 H2
Fryent Cl KTN/HRWW/WS HA3 62 C3
Fryent Crs CDALE/KGS NW9 63 G3
Fryent Flds CDALE/KGS NW9 63 G3
Fryent Gv CDALE/KGS NW9 63 G3
Fryent Wy CDALE/KGS NW9 62 C2
Frying Pan Aly WCHPL E1 13 H2
Fry Rd EHAM E6 89 H5
WLSDN NW10 81 H6
Fryston Av CROY/NA CR0 197 H6
Fuchsia Cl ROMW/RG RM7 75 G6
Fuchsia St ABYW SE2 128 C5
Fulbeck Dr CDALE/KGS NW9 45 G4
Fulbeck Wy RYLN/HDSTN HA2 42 C5
Fulbourne Rd WALTH E17 52 A4
Fulbourne St WCHPL E1 104 D4
Fulbrook Ms ARCH N19 84 C2
Fulbrook Rd ARCH N19 84 C2
Fulford Gv OXHEY WD19 27 F4
Fulford Rd HOR/WEW KT19 207 F5
Fulford St BERM/RHTH SE16 123 J2
Fulham Broadway
FUL/PGN SW6 139 K1
Fulham Cl HGDN/ICK UB10 94 A3
Fulham Est FUL/PGN SW6 119 K6
Fulham High St FUL/PGN SW6 139 H3
Fulham Palace Rd
FUL/PGN SW6 139 G1
Fulham Park Gdns
FUL/PGN SW6 139 J3
Fulham Park Rd
FUL/PGN SW6 139 J3
Fulham Rd FUL/PGN SW6 140 A1
WBPTN SW10 120 C5
Fullbrooks Av WPK KT4 192 C5
Fuller Cl BETH E2 * 104 C3
BUSH WD23 28 D2
ORP BR6 217 F3
Fuller Rd BCTR RM8 91 J1
Fullers Av SURB KT6 191 G6
Fuller's Av SWFD E18 52 D3
Fullers Cl CRW RM5 56 E3
Fuller's Rd SWFD E18 52 D4
Fuller St HDN NW4 64 A1
Fullers Wy North SURB KT6 206 B1
Fullers Wy South CHSGTN KT9 206 A2
Fuller's Wd CROY/NA CR0 213 J3
Fullerton Rd CAR SM5 209 J6
CROY/NA CR0 197 G4
WAND/EARL SW18 140 B6
Fuller Wy HYS/HAR UB3 113 J5
Fullwell Av CLAY IG5 54 A4
Fullwood's Ms IS N1 7 F4
Fulmar Ct BRYLDS KT5 191 G3
Fulmar Rd HCH RM12 93 J5
Fulmead St FUL/PGN SW6 140 A2
Fulmer Cl HPTN TW12 172 D1
Fulmer Rd CAN/RD E16 107 H4
Fulmer Wy WEA W13 116 C3
Fulready Rd LEY E10 70 B2
Fulstone Cl HSLWW TW4 134 E5
Fulthorp Rd BKHTH/KID SE3 145 J3
Fulton Ms BAY/PAD W2 * 101 G6
Fulton Rd WBLY HA9 80 C1
Fulwell Park Av WHTN TW2 155 H4
Fulwell Rd TEDD TW11 155 J6
Fulwich Rd DART DA1 171 J1
Fulwood Av ALP/SUD HA0 98 B1
Fulwood Gdns TWK TW1 156 A1
Fulwood Wk WIM/MER SW19 159 H3
Furber St HMSMTH W6 118 E3
Furham Fld PIN HA5 42 A3
Furley Rd PECK SE15 143 H1
Furlong Cl WLGTN SM6 195 C5
Furlong Rd HOLWY N7 85 G4
The Furlongs ESH/CLAY KT10 204 A1
Furmage St
WAND/EARL SW18 160 A2
Furneaux Av WNWD SE27 180 C1
Furner Cl DART DA1 150 C4
Furness Rd FUL/PGN SW6 140 A3
MRDN SM4 194 A3
RYLN/HDSTN HA2 60 B4
WLSDN NW10 99 J1
Furness Wy HCH RM12 93 J3
Furnival St FLST/FETLN EC4A 11 J3
Furrow La HOM E9 86 E3
The Furrows WOT/HER KT12 188 B6
Fursby Av FNCH N3 46 E2
Further Acre CDALE/KGS NW9 45 H5
Furtherfield Cl CROY/NA CR0 196 B3
Further Green Rd CAT SE6 165 H2
Furze Cl OXHEY WD19 41 G1
Furzedown Dr TOOT SW17 179 G1
Furzedown Rd TOOT SW17 179 G1
Furze Farm Cl CHDH RM6 56 A5
Furzefield Cl CHST BR7 185 G2
Furzefield Rd BKHTH/KID SE3 126 A6
Furzeground Wy STKPK UB11 113 F1
Furzeham Rd WDR/YW UB7 112 B2
Furzehill Sq STMC/STPC BR5 202 C1
Furze Rd THHTH CR7 180 D6
Furze St BOW E3 * 105 J4
Fye Foot La BLKFR EC4V 12 C5
Fyfe Wy BMLY BR1 183 K5
Fyfield Cl HAYES BR2 199 G1
Fyfield Rd BRXN/ST SW9 142 B4
EN EN1 24 A4
RAIN RM13 93 H6
WALTH E17 52 B6
WFD IG8 53 G3
Fynes St WEST SW1P 16 C6

G

Gable Cl DART DA1 150 D6
PIN HA5 42 A3
Gable Ct SYD SE26 163 J6
Gable Ms HAYES BR2 200 D6
Gables Cl CMBW SE5 143 F2
LEE/GVPK SE12 165 K3
The Gables NRWD SE19 * 181 F4
WBLY HA9 80 B1
Gabriel Cl CRW RM5 56 E3
FELT TW13 154 D6
Gabrielle Cl WBLY HA9 80 B1
Gabriel St FSTH SE23 164 A2
Gabriel's Whf STHWK SE1 11 J7
Gad Cl PLSTW E13 107 F2
Gaddesden Av WBLY HA9 80 B4
Gade Cl HYS/HAR UB3 114 A1
Gadesden Rd HOR/WEW KT19 206 E4
Gadsbury Cl CDALE/KGS NW9 63 H3
Gadwall Cl CAN/RD E16 107 F5
Gage Rd CAN/RD E16 106 C4
Gage St BMSBY WC1N 11 F1
Gainford St IS N1 85 G6
Gainsboro Gdns GFD/PVL UB6 78 E3
Gainsborough Av DART DA1 151 F6
MNPK E12 90 A3
Gainsborough Cl BECK BR3 182 D3
ESH/CLAY KT10 * 189 J5
Gainsborough Ct SHB W12 119 F2
Gainsborough Gdns
EDGW HA8 44 B5
GLDGN NW11 64 D4
HAMP NW3 83 H1
HSLW TW3 135 J6
Gainsborough Ms DUL SE21 162 D3
SYD SE26 * 163 J5
Gainsborough Rd BCTR RM8 91 H2
CHSWK W4 118 C4
NFNCH/WDSPK N12 47 F1
NWMAL KT3 192 A3
RAIN RM13 93 J6
RCH/KEW TW9 137 G3
SRTFD E15 106 C2
WAN E11 70 C4
WFD IG8 53 J2
YEAD UB4 94 A1
Gainsborough Sq BXLYHS DA6 148 E4
Gainsborough St HOM E9 87 H4
Gainsborough Ter
BELMT SM2 * 208 D5
Gainsford Rd WALTH E17 69 H1
Gainsford St STHWK SE1 19 J1
Gairloch Rd CMBW SE5 143 F3
Gaisford St KTTN NW5 84 C4
Gaitskell Rd ELTH/MOT SE9 167 H3
Gaitskell Wy STHWK SE1 18 C2
Galahad Rd BMLY BR1 165 K5
ED N9 36 C4
Galata Rd BARN SW13 138 D1
Galatea Sq PECK SE15 143 J4
Galbraith St POP/IOD E14 125 F3
Galdana Av BAR EN5 21 G4
Galeborough Av WFD IG8 52 B3
Gale Cl HPTN TW12 172 D2
MTCM CR4 178 C6
Galena Rd HMSMTH W6 118 E4
Galesbury Rd
WAND/EARL SW18 160 B1
Gales Gdns BETH E2 104 D2
Gale St BOW E3 105 J4
DAGW RM9 91 K5
Gales Wy WFD IG8 53 J3
Galgate Cl WIM/MER SW19 159 G3
Gallants Farm Rd EBAR EN4 33 J2
Galleon Cl BERM/RHTH SE16 123 K2
ERITH DA8 130 A4
Galleons Dr BARK IG11 109 G2
The Galleries IS N1 * 6 A2
Gallery Gdns NTHLT UB5 95 H1
Gallery Rd DUL SE21 162 E3
Galleywall Rd
BERM/RHTH SE16 123 J4
Galleywood Crs CRW RM5 57 F2
Galliard Rd ED N9 36 C2
Gallia Rd HBRY N5 85 H3
Gallions Cl BARK IG11 109 G2

Gallions Rd CAN/RD E16 108 B6
CHARL SE7 126 A4
Gallions View Rd THMD SE28 127 K2
Gallon Cl CHARL SE7 126 B4
The Gallops ESH/CLAY KT10 204 B1
The Gallop BELMT SM2 209 H6
SAND/SEL CR2 212 D5
Gallosson Rd
WOOL/PLUM SE18 127 K4
Galloway Dr DART DA1 170 B2
Galloway Pth CROY/NA CR0 211 K2
Galloway Rd SHB W12 118 D1
Gallus Cl WCHMH N21 35 F1
Gallus Sq BKHTH/KID SE3 146 A4
Galpin's Rd THHTH CR7 195 K1
Galsworthy Av CHDH RM6 73 H4
POP/IOD E14 105 G4
Galsworthy Cl THMD SE28 128 C1
Galsworthy Crs
BKHTH/KID SE3 146 B2
Galsworthy Rd CRICK NW2 82 C2
KUTN/CMB KT2 175 J4
Galton St NKENS W10 100 C3
Galva Cl EBAR EN4 22 A5
Galveston Rd PUT/ROE SW15 139 J6
Galway Cl BERM/RHTH SE16 * 123 J5
Galway St FSBYE EC1V 6 D5
Gambetta St VX/NE SW8 141 G3
Gambia St STHWK SE1 18 B1
Gambole Rd TOOT SW17 160 D6
Games Rd EBAR EN4 21 J4
Gamlen Rd PUT/ROE SW15 139 G5
Gamuel Cl WALTH E17 69 J3
Gander Green Crs HPTN TW12 173 F4
Gander Green La CHEAM SM3 193 H6
SUT SM1 208 D4
Gandhi Cl WALTH E17 69 J3
Gandolfi St CMBW SE5 123 F6
PECK SE15 * 123 F6
Ganton St REGST W1B 10 A5
Ganton Wk OXHEY WD19 * 27 J6
Gantshill Crs GNTH/NBYPK IG2 72 A2
Gap Rd WIM/MER SW19 177 K1
Garage Rd ACT W3 98 C5
Garbrand Wk EW KT17 207 H6
Garbutt Pl MHST W1U * 9 H1
Garden Av BXLYHN DA7 149 G4
MTCM CR4 179 G3
Garden City EDGW HA8 44 C2
Garden Cl BAR EN5 20 A5
CHING E4 51 J1
HPTN TW12 172 E1
LEE/GVPK SE12 166 A5
NTHLT UB5 77 J6
PUT/ROE SW15 158 E2
RSLP HA4 58 C6
WLGTN SM6 210 E3
Garden Ct CHSWK W4 117 K3
EMB EC4Y * 11 J5
HPTN TW12 172 E1
Gardeners Rd CROY/NA CR0 196 C5
Garden Flats HMSMTH W6 * 119 G6
Gardenia Rd BMLY BR1 185 F6
EN EN1 36 A1
Gardenia Wy WFD IG8 52 E2
Garden La BMLY BR1 184 A2
BRXS/STRHM SW2 162 A3
Garden Lodge Ct EFNCH N2 * 47 H6
Garden Pl HACK E8 86 B6
RDART DA2 171 G5
Garden Rd BMLY BR1 184 A3
PGE/AN SE20 181 K4
RCH/KEW TW9 137 H4
STJWD NW8 101 G2
WOT/HER KT12 188 A3
Garden Rw STHWK SE1 18 A5
The Gardens BECK BR3 183 F5
CEND/HSY/T N8 * 66 E1
CLPT E5 * 68 B4
EBED/NFELT TW14 153 G1
EDUL SE22 143 H5
ESH/CLAY KT10 204 A2
HRW HA1 60 C3
PIN HA5 * 59 K3
Garden St WCHPL E1 105 F4
Garden Studios
BAY/PAD W2 * 101 G4
Gardens Wy MNPK E12 89 J1
Garden Ter PIM SW1V * 121 J5
Garden Vls ESH/CLAY KT10 * 205 F5
Garden Wk BECK BR3 182 C4
SDTCH EC2A 7 G6
Garden Wy WLSDN NW10 80 E4
Gardiner Av CRICK NW2 * 82 A3
Gardiner Cl BCTR RM8 91 K2
PEND EN3 37 F1
STMC/STPC BR5 186 D5
Gardiner House CHARL SE7 * 146 D1
Gardner Cl WAN E11 71 F3
Gardner Pl EBED/NFELT TW14 154 A1
Gardner Rd PLSTW E13 107 F3
Gardners Cl FBAR/BDGN N11 34 A4
Gardners La BLKFR EC4V 12 C5
Gardnor Rd HAMP NW3 83 H2
Gard St FSBYE EC1V 6 B4
Garendon Gdns MRDN SM4 194 A4
Garendon Rd MRDN SM4 194 A4
Gareth Cl WPK KT4 193 G6
Gareth Dr ED N9 36 C4
Gareth Gv BMLY BR1 165 K6
Garfield Ms BTSEA SW11 141 G4
Garfield Rd BTSEA SW11 141 F4
CHING E4 38 B3
PEND EN3 24 E5
PLSTW E13 106 D3
TWK TW1 156 B3
WIM/MER SW19 178 B2
Garford St POP/IOD E14 105 J6
Garganey Wk THMD SE28 109 J6
Garibaldi St
WOOL/PLUM SE18 127 K4
Garland Dr HSLW TW3 135 H3
Garland Rd STAN HA7 43 K4
WOOL/PLUM SE18 147 J1
Garlick Hl BLKFR EC4V 12 D5
Garlies Rd FSTH SE23 164 B5
Garlinge Rd CRICK NW2 82 D4
Garman Cl UED N18 49 K1
Garman Rd TOTM N17 50 D3
Garnault Ms CLKNW EC1R 5 K5
Garnault Pl CLKNW EC1R 5 K5
Garnault Rd EN EN1 24 B1
Garner Cl BCTR RM8 73 K5
Garner Rd WALTH E17 52 A4
Garner St BETH E2 104 C1
Garnet Rd THHTH CR7 196 D1
WLSDN NW10 81 G4
Garnet St WAP E1W 104 E6
Garnett Cl ELTH/MOT SE9 146 E4
Garnett Rd HAMP NW3 83 K3
Garnham St STNW/STAM N16 68 B6
Garnies Cl PECK SE15 143 G1
Garrad's Rd
STRHM/NOR SW16 161 J5
Garrard Cl BXLYHN DA7 149 H4
CHST BR7 185 G1
Garrard Wk WLSDN NW10 * 81 G4
Garratt Cl CROY/NA CR0 210 E2
Garratt La TOOT SW17 160 B5
WAND/EARL SW18 160 A2
Garratt Rd EDGW HA8 44 C3
Garratts Rd BUSH WD23 28 C2
Garratt Ter TOOT SW17 160 D6
Garrett Cl ACT W3 99 F4
Garrett St STLK EC1Y 6 C6
Garrick Av GLDGN NW11 64 C3
Garrick Cl EA W5 98 A3
RCH/KEW TW9 136 D6
WAND/EARL SW18 140 B5
Garrick Crs CROY/NA CR0 197 F6
Garrick Dr HDN NW4 46 A5
THMD SE28 127 J3
Garrick Gdns E/WMO/HCT KT8 173 F6
Garrick Pk HDN NW4 46 B5
Garrick Rd CDALE/KGS NW9 63 H3
GFD/PVL UB6 96 B3
RCH/KEW TW9 137 H3
Garrick St COVGDN WC2E 10 E5
Garrick Wy HDN NW4 64 B1
Garrick Yd CHCR WC2N 10 E5
Garrison Cl HSLWW TW4 134 E6
WOOL/PLUM SE18 147 F1
Garrison La CHSGTN KT9 206 A5
Garrison Rd BOW E3 87 J6
Garry Cl ROM RM1 57 G3
Garry Wy ROM RM1 57 G3
Garsdale Ter WKENS W14 * 119 J5
Garside Cl HPTN TW12 173 G3
THMD SE28 127 J3
Garsington Ms BROCKY SE4 144 C4
Garter Wy BERM/RHTH SE16 124 A2
Garth Cl KUTN/CMB KT2 175 G1
MRDN SM4 193 G4
RSLP HA4 59 H5
Garth Ms EA W5 * 98 A3
Garthorne Rd FSTH SE23 164 A2
Garth Rd CHSWK W4 118 A5
CRICK NW2 64 D6
KUTN/CMB KT2 175 G1
MRDN SM4 193 G5
Garthside KUTN/CMB KT2 175 F1
The Garth HPTN TW12 173 G2
KTN/HRWW/WS HA3 62 B3
NFNCH/WDSPK N12 * 47 F1
Garthway
NFNCH/WDSPK N12 47 J2
Gartmoor Gdns
WIM/MER SW19 159 J3
Gartmore Rd GDMY/SEVK IG3 73 F5
Garton Pl WAND/EARL SW18 160 B1
Gartons Cl PEND EN3 24 E6
Gartons Wy BTSEA SW11 140 B4
Garvary Rd CAN/RD E16 107 F5
Garway Rd BAY/PAD W2 101 F5
Gascoigne Cl TOTM N17 50 B4
Gascoigne Gdns WFD IG8 52 A3
Gascoigne Pl BETH E2 7 J4
Gascoigne Rd BARK IG11 90 C6
Gascony Av KIL/WHAMP NW6 82 E5
Gascoyne Dr DART DA1 150 C4
Gascoyne Rd HOM E9 87 F5
Gaselee St POP/IOD E14 106 A6
Gasholder Pl LBTH SE11 122 A5
Gaskarth Rd BAL SW12 161 G1
EDGW HA8 44 E4
Gaskell Rd HGT N6 65 K3
Gaskell St CLAP SW4 141 K3
Gaskin St IS N1 85 H6
Gaspar Ms ECT SW5 120 A4
Gassiot Rd TOOT SW17 160 E6
Gassiot Wy SUT SM1 209 H1
Gastein Rd HMSMTH W6 119 G6
Gaston Bell Cl RCH/KEW TW9 137 G4
Gaston Rd MTCM CR4 179 F6
Gataker St BERM/RHTH SE16 123 J3
Gatcombe Ms EA W5 98 B6
Gatcombe Rd ARCH N19 84 D1
Gatcombe Wy EBAR EN4 21 K4
Gate Cots EDGW HA8 * 30 C4
Gate End NTHWD HA6 40 E3
Gateforth St STJWD NW8 2 C7
Gatehill Rd NTHWD HA6 40 D3
Gatehouse Cl KUTN/CMB KT2 175 K3
Gatehouse Sq STHWK SE1 12 D7
Gateley Rd BRXN/ST SW9 142 A4
Gate Ms SKENS SW7 14 D3
Gater Dr ENC/FH EN2 23 K2
Gates Ct WALW SE17 * 122 D5
Gates Green Rd WWKM BR4 214 E2
Gateside Rd TOOT SW17 160 E5
Gatestone Rd NRWD SE19 181 F2
Gate St LINN WC2A 11 G3
Gateway WALW SE17 122 D6
Gateway Ar IS N1 * 6 A2
Gateway Cl NTHWD HA6 40 A2
Gateway Gdns EHAM E6 107 K2
Gateway Ms FBAR/BDGN N11 48 C2
HACK E8 * 86 B3
The Gateways
RCH/KEW TW9 * 136 E5
Gatfield Gv FELT TW13 155 F4
Gathorne Rd WDGN N22 49 G5
Gathorne St BETH E2 105 F1
Gatley Av HOR/WEW KT19 206 D3
Gatliff Cl BGVA SW1W * 121 F5
Gatliff Rd BGVA SW1W 121 F5
Gatling Rd ABYW SE2 128 B5
Gatonby St PECK SE15 143 G2
Gatton Cl BELMT SM2 * 209 F6
Gatton Rd TOOT SW17 160 D6
Gattons Wy SCUP DA14 169 G6
Gatward Cl WCHMH N21 35 H1
Gatward Gn ED N9 36 A4
Gatwick Rd WAND/EARL SW18 159 J2
Gauden Cl CLAP SW4 141 J4
Gauden Rd CLAP SW4 141 J3
Gaumont Ter SHB W12 * 119 F2
Gauntlet Cl NTHLT UB5 77 J5
Gauntlett Ct ALP/SUD HA0 79 G3
Gauntlett Rd SUT SM1 209 H3
Gaunt St STHWK SE1 18 B4
Gautrey Rd PECK SE15 143 K3
Gavel St WALW SE17 * 19 F6
Gaverick St POP/IOD E14 124 D4
Gavestone Crs
LEE/GVPK SE12 166 A2
Gavestone Rd LEE/GVPK SE12 166 A2
Gavina Cl MRDN SM4 194 D2
Gawain Wk ED N9 36 C5
Gawber St BETH E2 104 E2
Gawsworth Cl SRTFD E15 88 D3
Gawthorne Av MLHL NW7 46 C1
Gay Cl CRICK NW2 81 K3
Gaydon La CDALE/KGS NW9 45 G4
Gayfere Rd CLAY IG5 53 K6
EW KT17 207 J3
Gayfere St WEST SW1P 16 E5
Gayford Rd SHB W12 118 C2
Gay Gdns DAGE RM10 92 E2
Gayhurst Rd HACK E8 86 C5
Gaylor Rd NTHLT UB5 77 K3
Gaynesford Rd CAR SM5 209 K5
FSTH SE23 164 A4
Gaynes Hill Rd WFD IG8 53 J3
Gay Rd SRTFD E15 106 B1
Gaysham Av GNTH/NBYPK IG2 72 A2
Gayton Crs HAMP NW3 83 H2
Gayton Rd HAMP NW3 83 H2
HRW HA1 61 F3
Gayville Rd BTSEA SW11 160 E1
Gaywood Cl
BRXS/STRHM SW2 162 A3
Gaywood Rd WALTH E17 51 J6
Gaywood St STHWK SE1 18 B5
Gaza St WALW SE17 122 C5
Gearlesville Gdns
BARK/HLT IG6 72 B1
Gearing Cl TOOT SW17 161 F6
Geary Rd WLSDN NW10 81 J3
Geary St HOLWY N7 85 F3
Geddes Pl BXLYHS DA6 149 H5
Gedeney Rd TOTM N17 49 J4
Gedling Pl STHWK SE1 19 J4
Geere Rd SRTFD E15 88 D6
Gees Ct MHST W1U 9 H4
Gee St FSBYE EC1V 6 C6
Geffrye Est IS N1 7 H3
Geffrye St BETH E2 7 J2
Geldart Rd PECK SE15 143 J1
Geldeston Rd CLPT E5 68 C6
Gellatly Rd NWCR SE14 143 K3
Gelsthorpe Rd CRW RM5 56 D3
Genas Cl BARK/HLT IG6 54 B4
General Gordon Pl
WOOL/PLUM SE18 127 G3
General Wolfe Rd
GNWCH SE10 145 G2
Genesis Cl STWL/WRAY TW19 152 C3
Genesta Rd WOOL/PLUM SE18 127 G6
Geneva Dr BRXN/ST SW9 142 B5
Geneva Gdns CHDH RM6 74 A2
Geneva Rd KUT/HW KT1 191 F1
THHTH CR7 196 D2
Genever Cl CHING E4 51 J1
Genista Rd UED N18 50 D1
Genoa Av PUT/ROE SW15 139 F6
Genoa Rd PGE/AN SE20 181 K4
Genotin Rd EN EN1 23 K4
Gentleman's Rw ENC/FH EN2 23 J4
Geoffrey Cl CMBW SE5 142 D3
Geoffrey Gdns EHAM E6 107 J1
Geoffrey Rd BROCKY SE4 144 C4
George Beard Rd DEPT SE8 124 C4
George Crs MUSWH N10 48 A3
George Downing Est
STNW/STAM N16 68 B6
George Gange Wy
KTN/HRWW/WS HA3 42 E6
George Groves Rd
PGE/AN SE20 181 H4
George La HAYES BR2 200 A5
LEW SE13 165 F1
SWFD E18 52 E5
George Lowe Ct
BAY/PAD W2 * 101 F4
George Mathers Rd
LBTH SE11 18 A7
George Ms BRXN/ST SW9 142 B3
CAMTN NW1 4 A5
George Rd CHING E4 51 J2
KUTN/CMB KT2 175 K3
NWMAL KT3 192 C1
George Rw BERM/RHTH SE16 123 H2
Georges Md BORE WD6 30 A1
Georges Rd HOLWY N7 85 F4
George's Rd HOLWY N7 85 F3
George St BARK IG11 90 C5
CROY/NA CR0 196 D6
HNWL W7 115 K1
HSLW TW3 134 E3
MBLAR W1H 8 E3
NWDGN UB2 114 D4
RCH/KEW TW9 136 E6
ROM RM1 75 H3
Georgetown Cl NRWD SE19 181 F1
Georgette Pl GNWCH SE10 145 F1
George V Av PIN HA5 60 A1
Georgeville Gdns
BARK/HLT IG6 72 B1
George V Wy GFD/PVL UB6 79 H5
George Wyver Cl
WIM/MER SW19 159 H2
George Yd BANK EC3V 13 F4
MYFR/PKLN W1K 9 H5
Georgiana St CAMTN NW1 84 C6
Georgian Cl HAYES BR2 200 A5
STAN HA7 43 G3
Georgian Ct WBLY HA9 80 C4
Georgian Wy HRW HA1 60 D6
Georgia Rd NWMAL KT3 191 K1
THHTH CR7 180 C4
Georgina Gdns BETH E2 * 7 K4
Geraint Rd BMLY BR1 165 K5
Geraldine Rd CHSWK W4 117 H6
WAND/EARL SW18 140 B6
Geraldine St LBTH SE11 18 A5
Gerald Rd BCTR RM8 74 B6
BGVA SW1W 15 H6
CAN/RD E16 106 D3
Gerard Av HSLWW TW4 155 F2
Gerard Gdns RAIN RM13 111 G1
Gerard Rd BARN SW13 138 C2
HRW HA1 61 G3
Gerards Cl BERM/RHTH SE16 123 K6
Gerda Rd ELTH/MOT SE9 167 G4
Gerdview Dr RDART DA2 171 F6
Germander Wy SRTFD E15 106 C2
Gernon Rd BOW E3 105 G1
Geron Wy CRICK NW2 64 A6
Gerrard Gdns PIN HA5 58 E2
Gerrard Pl SOHO/SHAV W1D * 10 D5
Gerrard Rd IS N1 6 A2
Gerrards Cl STHGT/OAK N14 22 C6
Gerrard St SOHO/SHAV W1D 10 C5
Gerridge St STHWK SE1 17 K3
Gertrude Rd BELV DA17 129 H4
Gertrude St WBPTN SW10 120 B6
Gervase Cl WBLY HA9 80 E1
Gervase Rd EDGW HA8 44 E4
Gervase St PECK SE15 143 J1
Ghent St CAT SE6 164 D4
Ghent Wy HACK E8 86 B4
Giant Arches Rd HNHL SE24 162 D2
Giant Tree Hl BUSH WD23 28 D4
Gibbfield Cl CHDH RM6 56 A6
Gibbins Rd SRTFD E15 88 A5
Gibbon Rd ACT W3 99 G6
KUTN/CMB KT2 175 F4
PECK SE15 143 K3
Gibbons La DART DA1 171 G1
Gibbons Ms GLDGN NW11 64 D2
Gibbons Rd WLSDN NW10 81 F4
Gibbon Wk PUT/ROE SW15 * 138 D5
Gibbs Av NRWD SE19 180 E2
Gibbs Cl NRWD SE19 * 180 E1
Gibbs Couch OXHEY WD19 27 H5
Gibbs Gn EDGW HA8 30 E6
WKENS W14 * 119 J5
Gibbs Green Cl WKENS W14 119 J5
Gibbs Rd UED N18 36 E6
Gibbs Sq NRWD SE19 * 180 E1
Gibraltar Wk BETH E2 7 K5
Gibson Cl CHSGTN KT9 205 J3
ISLW TW7 135 J4
WCHMH N21 35 G1
WCHPL E1 104 E3
Gibson Gdns
STNW/STAM N16 * 68 B6
Gibson Rd BCTR RM8 73 J5
LBTH SE11 17 H7
SUT SM1 209 F3
Gibson's Hl STRHM/NOR SW16 180 B3
Gibson Sq IS N1 85 G6
Gibson St GNWCH SE10 125 H5
Gidea Av GPK RM2 57 J6
Gidea Cl GPK RM2 57 J6
Gideon Cl BELV DA17 129 J4
Gideon Ms EA W5 * 116 E2
Gideon Rd BTSEA SW11 141 F4
Giesbach Rd ARCH N19 66 C6
Giffard Rd UED N18 50 A1
Giffin St DEPT SE8 144 D1
Gifford Gdns HNWL W7 96 D4
Gifford Rd WLSDN NW10 81 G5
Gifford St IS N1 84 E5
Gift La SRTFD E15 88 C6
Giggs Hl STMC/STPC BR5 186 B5
Giggs Hill Gdns THDIT KT7 190 B5
Giggs Hill Rd THDIT KT7 190 B4
Gilbert Cl WIM/MER SW19 * 178 A4
WOOL/PLUM SE18 146 E2
Gilbert Gv EDGW HA8 44 E4
Gilbert Pl NOXST/BSQ WC1A 10 E2
Gilbert Rd BELV DA17 129 H3
BMLY BR1 183 K3
LBTH SE11 17 K6
PIN HA5 59 H1
ROM RM1 75 H1
WIM/MER SW19 178 B3
Gilbert St HSLW TW3 135 H4
MYFR/PKLN W1K 9 H4
SRTFD E15 88 C2
Gilbert White Cl GFD/PVL UB6 79 G6
Gilbey Rd TOOT SW17 160 D6
Gilbeys Yd CAMTN NW1 84 A5
Gilbourne Rd
WOOL/PLUM SE18 128 A6
Gilda Av PEND EN3 25 G6
Gilda Crs STNW/STAM N16 68 C5
Gildea Cl PIN HA5 42 A3
Gildea St GTPST W1W 9 K2
Gilden Crs KTTN NW5 84 A3
Gildersome St
WOOL/PLUM SE18 127 F6
Gilders Rd CHSGTN KT9 206 B4
Giles Coppice NRWD SE19 163 G6
Gilkes Crs DUL SE21 163 F1
Gilkes Pl DUL SE21 163 F1
Gillam Wy RAIN RM13 93 J4
Gillan Gn BUSH WD23 28 C4
Gillards Ms WALTH E17 69 J1
Gillards Wy WALTH E17 69 J1
Gill Av CAN/RD E16 106 E5
Gill Cl WATW WD18 26 A1
Gillender St BOW E3 106 A3
Gillespie Rd HBRY N5 85 G1
Gillett Av EHAM E6 107 J1
Gillett Pl HACK E8 86 A3
Gillett Rd THHTH CR7 196 E1
Gillett St STNW/STAM N16 86 A3
Gillham Ter TOTM N17 50 C2
Gillian Park Rd CHEAM SM3 193 J5
Gillian St LEW SE13 144 E6
Gillian Ter BRYLDS KT5 * 191 G3
Gillies St KTTN NW5 84 A3
Gillingham Rd CRICK NW2 82 C1
Gillingham Rw PIM SW1V 16 A6
Gillingham St PIM SW1V 15 K7
Gillison Wk
BERM/RHTH SE16 * 123 H3
Gillman Dr SRTFD E15 88 C6
Gillmans Rd STMC/STPC BR5 202 C5
Gill St POP/IOD E14 105 H5
Gillum Cl EBAR EN4 33 K3
Gilmore Rd LEW SE13 145 G5
Gilpin Av MORT/ESHN SW14 138 A5
Gilpin Cl MTCM CR4 178 D5
Gilpin Crs UED N18 50 B1
WHTN TW2 155 G2
Gilpin Rd CLPT E5 87 G2
Gilpin Wy HYS/HAR UB3 133 G1
Gilroy Cl RAIN RM13 93 H4
Gilroy Wy STMC/STPC BR5 202 C4
Gilsland Rd THHTH CR7 196 E1
Gilson Pl MUSWH N10 47 K3
Gilstead Rd FUL/PGN SW6 140 A3
Gilston Rd WBPTN SW10 120 B5
Gilton Rd CAT SE6 165 H5
Giltspur St STBT EC1A 12 B3
Gilwell Cl CHING E4 25 K5
Gippeswyck Cl PIN HA5 41 H4
Gipsy Hl NRWD SE19 181 F1
Gipsy La PUT/ROE SW15 138 D4
Gipsy Rd WELL DA16 148 E3
WNWD SE27 162 E6
Gipsy Road Gdns WNWD SE27 162 D6
Giralda Cl CAN/RD E16 107 H4
Giraud St POP/IOD E14 105 K5
Girdlers Rd WKENS W14 119 H3
Girdwood Rd
WAND/EARL SW18 159 H2
Girling Wy EBED/NFELT TW14 133 K4
Gironde Rd FUL/PGN SW6 139 J1
Girton Av CDALE/KGS NW9 44 C6
Girton Cl NTHLT UB5 78 C4
Girton Gdns CROY/NA CR0 213 J1
Girton Rd NTHLT UB5 78 C4
SYD SE26 182 A1
Gisbourne Cl WLGTN SM6 210 D1
Gisburn Rd CEND/HSY/T N8 67 F1
Gissing Wk IS N1 * 85 G5
Gittens Cl BMLY BR1 165 J6
Glacier Wy ALP/SUD HA0 97 K1
Gladbeck Wy ENC/FH EN2 23 H5
Gladding Rd MNPK E12 89 H2
Glade Cl SURB KT6 * 190 E6
Glade Gdns CROY/NA CR0 198 B4
Glade La NWDGN UB2 115 G2
Gladeside CROY/NA CR0 198 A4
WCHMH N21 35 F2
Gladesmore Rd
SEVS/STOTM N15 68 B3
The Glade BELMT SM2 208 C6
BMLY BR1 184 C5
CHARL SE7 146 B1
CLAY IG5 53 K4
CROY/NA CR0 198 B3
ENC/FH EN2 23 G4
EW KT17 207 J4
HACK E8 * 86 B4
NFNCH/WDSPK N12 * 33 H6
SHB W12 118 E2
WCHMH N21 35 F1
WFD IG8 39 F5
WWKM BR4 213 K1
Gladiator St FSTH SE23 164 B1
Glading Ter STNW/STAM N16 86 B1
Gladioli Cl HPTN TW12 173 F2
Gladsdale Dr PIN HA5 58 E1
Gladsmuir Cl WOT/HER KT12 188 B6
Gladsmuir Rd ARCH N19 66 C5
BAR EN5 20 C3
Gladstone Av
EBED/NFELT TW14 153 K1
MNPK E12 89 J5
WDGN N22 49 H5
WHTN TW2 155 J2
Gladstone Gdns HSLW TW3 135 H2
Gladstone Ms
KIL/WHAMP NW6 * 82 D5
PGE/AN SE20 181 K3
WDGN N22 49 G5
Gladstone Pde CRICK NW2 * 82 A1
Gladstone Park Gdns
CRICK NW2 81 K1
Gladstone Pl BAR EN5 * 20 B5
E/WMO/HCT KT8 * 189 K2
Gladstone Rd BKHH IG9 39 G3
CHSWK W4 * 118 A3
CROY/NA CR0 196 E4
DART DA1 171 J1
KUT/HW KT1 175 H6
NWDGN UB2 114 D2
ORP BR6 216 C3
SURB KT6 190 E6
WIM/MER SW19 177 K3
Gladstone St STHWK SE1 18 A4
Gladstone Ter VX/NE SW8 * 141 G2
WNWD SE27 * 162 D6
Gladstone Wy
KTN/HRWW/WS HA3 42 E6
Gladwell Rd BMLY BR1 183 K2
CEND/HSY/T N8 67 F3
Gladwyn Rd PUT/ROE SW15 139 G4
Gladys Rd KIL/WHAMP NW6 82 E5
Glaisher St DEPT SE8 124 D6
Glamis Crs HYS/HAR UB3 113 F3
Glamis Pl WAP E1W 104 E6
Glamis Rd WAP E1W 104 E6
Glamis Wy NTHLT UB5 78 C4
Glamorgan Cl MTCM CR4 179 K6
Glamorgan Rd KUT/HW KT1 174 D3
Glandford Wy CHDH RM6 73 H2
Glanfield Rd BECK BR3 198 C1
Glanleam Rd STAN HA7 29 K6
Glanville Ms STAN HA7 43 G1
Glanville Rd
BRXS/STRHM SW2 141 K6
HAYES BR2 184 A6
Glasbrook Av WHTN TW2 154 E3
Glasbrook Rd ELTH/MOT SE9 166 C2
Glaserton Rd
STNW/STAM N16 68 A4
Glasford St TOOT SW17 178 E2
Glasgow Rd PLSTW E13 107 F1
UED N18 50 D1
Glasgow Ter PIM SW1V 121 H5
Glaskin Ms HOM E9 87 G4
Glasse Cl WEA W13 97 G6
Glasshill St STHWK SE1 18 B2

Glasshouse Flds *WAP* E1W 105 F6
Glasshouse St *REGST* W1B 10 B6
Glasshouse Wk *LBTH* SE11 121 K5
Glasshouse Yd *FARR* EC1M 6 C7
Glasslyn Rd *CEND/HSY/T* N8 66 D2
Glassmill La *HAYES* BR2 183 J5
Glass St *BETH* E2 * 104 D3
Glass Yd *WOOL/PLUM* SE18 127 F3
Glastonbury Av *WFD* IG8 53 H3
Glastonbury Cl
STMC/STPC BR5 202 D5
Glastonbury Pl *WCHPL* E1 104 E5
Glastonbury Rd *ED* N9 36 C3
MRDN SM4 193 K3
Glastonbury St
KIL/WHAMP NW6 82 D3
Glaston Ct *EA* W5 * 116 E1
Glaucus St *BOW* E3 105 K4
Glazbury Rd *WKENS* W14 119 H4
Glazebrook Cl *DUL* SE21 162 E4
Glebe Av *ENC/FH* EN2 23 H4
HGDN/ICK UB10 76 A2
KTN/HRWW/WS HA3 44 A6
MTCM CR4 178 D5
RSLP HA4 77 F4
WFD IG8 52 E2
Glebe Cl *CHSWK* W4 * 118 B5
HGDN/ICK UB10 76 A2
Glebe Ct *BKHTH/KID* SE3 * 145 H4
EA W5 * 116 E1
STAN HA7 43 J1
Glebe Crs *HDN* NW4 64 A1
KTN/HRWW/WS HA3 44 A6
Glebe Gdns *NWMAL* KT3 192 B4
Glebe House Dr *HAYES* BR2 200 A5
Glebelands *DART* DA1 150 C5
E/WMO/HCT KT8 189 G2
ESH/CLAY KT10 205 F6
Glebelands Av
GNTH/NBYPK IG2 72 D4
SWFD E18 52 E5
Glebelands Cl *CMBW* SE5 143 F4
NFNCH/WDSPK N12 47 H4
Glebelands Rd
EBED/NFELT TW14 153 K2
Glebe La *KTN/HRWW/WS* HA3 62 A1
Glebe Pth *MTCM* CR4 178 E6
Glebe Pl *CHEL* SW3 120 D6
Glebe Rd *BARN* SW13 138 D3
BELMT SM2 208 C6
BMLY BR1 183 K4
CAR SM5 209 K4
CEND/HSY/T N8 67 F1
DAGE RM10 92 D4
FNCH N3 47 G4
HACK E8 * 86 B5
RAIN RM13 111 K2
STAN HA7 43 J1
WLSDN NW10 81 J4
Glebe Side *TWK* TW1 156 A1
Glebe Sq *MTCM* CR4 * 178 E6
Glebe St *CHSWK* W4 118 A5
The Glebe *BKHTH/KID* SE3 145 H4
CHST BR7 185 H4
STRHM/NOR SW16 * 161 J6
WDR/YW UB7 112 B4
WPK KT4 192 C5
Glebe Wy *ERITH* DA8 130 B6
FELT TW13 155 F5
Glebeway *WFD* IG8 53 G1
Glebe Wy *WWKM* BR4 199 F6
Gledhow Gdns *ECT* SW5 120 B4
Gledstanes Rd *WKENS* W14 119 H5
Gledwood Av *YEAD* UB4 94 E4
Gledwood Crs *YEAD* UB4 94 D4
Gledwood Dr *YEAD* UB4 94 D4
Gledwood Gdns *YEAD* UB4 94 E4
Gleed Av *BUSH* WD23 28 D4
Gleeson Dr *ORP* BR6 217 F3
Glegg Pl *PUT/ROE* SW15 * 139 G5
Glenaffric Av *POP/IOD* E14 125 F4
Glen Albyn Rd
WIM/MER SW19 159 G4
Glenalla Rd *RSLP* HA4 58 D4
Glenalmond Rd
KTN/HRWW/WS HA3 62 A1
Glenalvon Wy
WOOL/PLUM SE18 126 D4
Glena Mt *SUT* SM1 209 G2
Glenarm Rd *CLPT* E5 86 E2
Glen Av *ASHF* TW15 152 D6
Glenavon Cl *ESH/CLAY* KT10 205 G4
Glenavon Rd *SRTFD* E15 88 C5
Glenbarr Cl *ELTH/MOT* SE9 147 G4
Glenbow Rd *BMLY* BR1 183 H2
Glenbrook North *ENC/FH* EN2 23 F5
Glenbrook Rd
KIL/WHAMP NW6 82 E3
Glenbrook South *ENC/FH* EN2 23 F5
Glenbuck Rd *SURB* KT6 190 E3
Glenburnie Rd *TOOT* SW17 160 E5
Glencairn Dr *EA* W5 97 H3
Glencairne Cl *CAN/RD* E16 107 H4
Glencairn Rd
STRHM/NOR SW16 179 K3
Glencoe Av *GNTH/NBYPK* IG2 72 E4
Glencoe Rd *BUSH* WD23 28 A1
DAGE RM10 92 C2
YEAD UB4 95 H3
Glencorse Gn *OXHEY* WD19 * 27 H6
Glen Crs *WFD* IG8 53 F2
Glendale Av *CHDH* RM6 73 J4
EDGW HA8 30 B6
WDGN N22 49 G3
Glendale Cl *ELTH/MOT* SE9 147 F4
Glendale Dr *WIM/MER* SW19 177 J1
Glendale Gdns *WBLY* HA9 61 K5
Glendale Ms *BECK* BR3 182 E4
Glendale Rd *ERITH* DA8 129 K4
Glendale Wy *THMD* SE28 128 D1
Glendall St *BRXN/ST* SW9 142 A4
Glendarvon St *PUT/ROE* SW15 139 G4
Glendevon Cl *EDGW* HA8 30 D5
Glendish Rd *TOTM* N17 50 C4
Glendor Gdns *MLHL* NW7 31 F6
Glendower Crs *ORP* BR6 202 B3
Glendower Gdns
MORT/ESHN SW14 138 A4
Glendower Pl *SKENS* SW7 14 A6
Glendower Rd *CHING* E4 38 B3
MORT/ESHN SW14 138 A4
Glendown Rd *ABYW* SE2 128 B5
Glendun Rd *ACT* W3 99 G6
Gleneagle Ms
STRHM/NOR SW16 179 J1
Gleneagle Rd
STRHM/NOR SW16 179 J1
Gleneagles *STAN* HA7 43 H2
Gleneagles Cl
BERM/RHTH SE16 * 123 J5
ORP BR6 201 J5
OXHEY WD19 * 41 H1
Gleneldon Ms
STRHM/NOR SW16 179 K1
Gleneldon Rd
STRHM/NOR SW16 161 K6
Glenelg Rd *BRXS/STRHM* SW2 141 K6
Glenesk Rd *ELTH/MOT* SE9 147 F5
Glenfarg Rd *CAT* SE6 165 G3
Glenfield Crs *RSLP* HA4 58 B4
Glenfield Rd *BAL* SW12 161 H3
WEA W13 116 C2
Glenfinlas Wy *CMBW* SE5 142 C1
Glenforth St *GNWCH* SE10 125 J4
Glengall Br *POP/IOD* E14 124 E3
Glengall Gv *POP/IOD* E14 124 E3
Glengall Rd *BXLYHN* DA7 149 F4
EDGW HA8 30 D5
KIL/WHAMP NW6 82 D6
PECK SE15 123 G6
WFD IG8 52 E2
Glengall Ter *PECK* SE15 123 G6
Glen Gdns *CROY/NA* CR0 211 G1
Glengarnock Av *POP/IOD* E14 125 F4
Glengarry Rd *EDUL* SE22 143 F5
Glenham Dr *GNTH/NBYPK* IG2 72 B2
Glenhead Cl *ELTH/MOT* SE9 147 G4
Glenhill Cl *FNCH* N3 46 E5
Glenhouse Rd *ELTH/MOT* SE9 147 F6
Glenhurst Av *BXLY* DA5 169 G3
KTTN NW5 84 A2
RSLP HA4 58 A4
Glenhurst Ri *NRWD* SE19 180 D3
Glenhurst Rd *BTFD* TW8 116 D6
NFNCH/WDSPK N12 33 H6
Glenilla Rd *HAMP* NW3 83 J4
Glenister Park Rd
STRHM/NOR SW16 179 J3
Glenister Rd *GNWCH* SE10 125 J5
Glenlea Rd *ELTH/MOT* SE9 147 F6
Glenloch Rd *HAMP* NW3 83 J4
PEND EN3 24 E3
Glenluge Rd *BKHTH/KID* SE3 125 K6
Glenlyon Rd *ELTH/MOT* SE9 147 F6
Glenmere Av *MLHL* NW7 45 J3
Glenmere Rw *LEE/GVPK* SE12 165 J1
Glen Ms *WALTH* E17 69 H2
Glenmill *HPTN* TW12 172 E1
Glenmore Lawns *WEA* W13 * 97 G5
Glenmore Pde *ALP/SUD* HA0 * 80 A6
Glenmore Rd *HAMP* NW3 83 J4
WELL DA16 148 A2
Glenmore Wy *BARK* IG11 109 G2
Glennie Rd *WNWD* SE27 162 B5
Glenny Rd *BARK* IG11 90 C4
Glenorchy Cl *YEAD* UB4 95 J4
Glenparke Rd *FSTGT* E7 89 F4
Glen Ri *WFD* IG8 53 F2
Glen Rd *CHSGTN* KT9 206 A1
PLSTW E13 107 G3
WALTH E17 69 H2
Glen Road End *WLGTN* SM6 210 B6
Glenrosa St *FUL/PGN* SW6 140 B3
Glenroy St *SHB* W12 100 A5
Glensdale Rd *BROCKY* SE4 144 C4
Glenshiel Rd *ELTH/MOT* SE9 147 F6
Glenside *CHIG* IG7 54 B2
Glentanner Wy *TOOT* SW17 160 C5
Glentham Cots *BARN* SW13 * 118 D6
Glentham Gdns *BARN* SW13 118 E5
Glentham Rd *BARN* SW13 118 D6
The Glen *BELMT* SM2 * 209 G4
CROY/NA CR0 213 F1
ENC/FH EN2 23 H5
HAYES BR2 183 H5
NTHWD HA6 40 B3
NWDGN UB2 114 E5
ORP BR6 215 K1
PIN HA5 59 F2
WBLY HA9 79 K2
Glenthorne Av *CROY/NA* CR0 197 K5
Glenthorne Cl *CHEAM* SM3 193 K5
Glenthorne Gdns
BARK/HLT IG6 54 A6
CHEAM SM3 193 K5
Glenthorne Rd
FBAR/BDGN N11 47 K1
HMSMTH W6 118 E4
KUT/HW KT1 191 G2
WALTH E17 69 G2
Glenthorpe Rd *MRDN* SM4 193 G2
Glenton Cl *ROM* RM1 57 G3
Glenton Rd *LEW* SE13 145 H5
Glenton Wy *ROM* RM1 57 G3
Glentrammon Av *ORP* BR6 217 F4
Glentrammon Cl *ORP* BR6 217 F4
Glentrammon Gdns *ORP* BR6 217 F4
Glentrammon Rd *ORP* BR6 217 F4
Glentworth St *CAMTN* NW1 3 F7
Glenure Rd *ELTH/MOT* SE9 147 F6
Glenview *ABYW* SE2 128 E6
Glen View Rd *BMLY* BR1 184 C5
Glenville Av *ENC/FH* EN2 23 J1
Glenville Gv *DEPT* SE8 144 C1
Glenville Ms
WAND/EARL SW18 160 A2
Glenville Rd *KUTN/CMB* KT2 175 H4
Glenwood Av
CDALE/KGS NW9 63 G5
RAIN RM13 111 J3
Glenwood Cl *HRW* HA1 61 F2
Glenwood Dr *GPK* RM2 75 J2
Glenwood Gdns
GNTH/NBYPK IG2 72 A2
Glenwood Gv
CDALE/KGS NW9 62 E5
Glenwood Rd *CAT* SE6 164 C3
EW KT17 207 J4
HSLW TW3 135 J4
MLHL NW7 31 G5
SEVS/STOTM N15 67 H2
Glenwood Rw *NRWD* SE19 * 181 G4
Glenwood Wy *CROY/NA* CR0 198 A3
Glenworth Av *POP/IOD* E14 125 G4
Gliddon Rd *WKENS* W14 119 H4
Glimpsing Gn *ERITHM* DA18 129 F3
Gload Crs *STMC/STPC* BR5 202 E6
Globe Pond Rd
BERM/RHTH SE16 124 B1
Globe Rd *BETH* E2 104 E2
EMPK RM11 75 J3
SRTFD E15 88 D3
WCHPL E1 104 E2
WFD IG8 53 G2
Globe St *STHWK* SE1 18 E3
Globe Ter *BETH* E2 104 E2
Glossop Rd *SAND/SEL* CR2 211 K6
Gloster Rd *NWMAL* KT3 192 B1
Gloucester Av *BFN/LL* DA15 167 K4
CAMTN NW1 3 H1
WELL DA16 148 A6
Gloucester Circ *GNWCH* SE10 145 F1
Gloucester Cl *THDIT* KT7 * 190 B5
WLSDN NW10 81 F5
Gloucester Ct *MTCM* CR4 * 195 K2
RCH/KEW TW9 * 137 H1
TWRH EC3N * 13 H6
Gloucester Crs *CAMTN* NW1 84 B6
Gloucester Dr *FSBYPK* N4 67 H6
GLDGN NW11 64 E1
Gloucester Gdns
BAY/PAD W2 * 101 G5
EBAR EN4 22 A5
GLDGN NW11 64 D4
IL IG1 71 J4
SUT SM1 194 A6
Gloucester Ga *CAMTN* NW1 3 H2
Gloucester Gate Ms
CAMTN NW1 3 J2
Gloucester Gv *EDGW* HA8 45 F4
Gloucester Ms *BAY/PAD* W2 101 G5
LEY E10 69 J4
Gloucester Ms West
BAY/PAD W2 101 G5
Gloucester Pde
BFN/LL DA15 * 148 B6
HYS/HAR UB3 * 113 F3
Gloucester Pl *CAMTN* NW1 2 E6
MHST W1U 9 F2
Gloucester Place Ms
MHST W1U 9 F3
Gloucester Rd *ACT* W3 117 K2
BAR EN5 21 F6
BELV DA17 129 G5
CROY/NA CR0 196 E4
DART DA1 170 E1
EA W5 116 D2
ENC/FH EN2 23 J1
FELT TW13 154 B3
HPTN TW12 173 G3
HRW HA1 60 B2
HSLWW TW4 134 D5
KUT/HW KT1 175 H5
LEY E10 69 J4
MNPK E12 89 K1
RCH/KEW TW9 137 H1
ROM RM1 75 G3
SKENS SW7 120 B4
TEDD TW11 173 K1
TOTM N17 49 K5
UED N18 50 B1
WALTH E17 51 F5
WAN E11 71 F2
WHTN TW2 155 H3
Gloucester Sq *BAY/PAD* W2 8 B4
BETH E2 86 C6
Gloucester St *PIM* SW1V 121 H5
Gloucester Ter *BAY/PAD* W2 101 F5
STHGT/OAK N14 * 34 D3
Gloucester Wk *KENS* W8 * 119 K2
Gloucester Wy *CLKNW* EC1R 5 K5
Glover Cl *ABYW* SE2 128 D4
Glover Dr *UED* N18 50 E2
Glover Rd *PIN* HA5 59 H3
Glycena Rd *BTSEA* SW11 140 E4
Glyn Av *EBAR* EN4 21 H5
Glyn Cl *EW* KT17 207 J6
SNWD SE25 181 F5
Glyn Ct *STAN* HA7 43 H2
Glyndebourne Pk *ORP* BR6 216 B1
Glynde Ms *CHEL* SW3 14 D5
Glynde Rd *BXLYHN* DA7 148 E4
Glynde St *BROCKY* SE4 164 C1
Glyndon Rd
WOOL/PLUM SE18 127 H4
Glyn Dr *SCUP* DA14 168 C6
Glynfield Rd *WLSDN* NW10 81 G5
Glynne Rd *WDGN* N22 49 G5
Glyn Rd *CLPT* E5 87 F2
PEND EN3 24 E5
WPK KT4 193 G6
Glyn St *LBTH* SE11 122 A5
Glynwood Ct *FSTH* SE23 163 K4
Goat La *EN* EN1 24 B1
Goat Rd *MTCM* CR4 195 F4
Goat Whf *BTFD* TW8 117 F6
Gobions Av *CRW* RM5 57 F3
Godalming Av *WLGTN* SM6 210 E3
Godalming Rd *POP/IOD* E14 105 K4
Godbold Rd *SRTFD* E15 106 C3
Goddard Pl *ARCH* N19 84 C1
Goddard Rd *BECK* BR3 198 A1
Goddards Wy *IL* IG1 72 D5
Goddington Cha *ORP* BR6 217 H2
Goddington La *ORP* BR6 217 G1
Godfrey Av *NTHLT* UB5 77 J6
WHTN TW2 155 J2
Godfrey Hl *WOOL/PLUM* SE18 126 D4
Godfrey Rd *WOOL/PLUM* SE18 126 E4
Godfrey St *CHEL* SW3 120 D5
SRTFD E15 106 A1
Godfrey Wy *HSLWW* TW4 154 D2
Goding St *LBTH* SE11 121 K5
Godley Rd *WAND/EARL* SW18 160 C3
Godliman St *BLKFR* EC4V 12 B4
Godman Rd *PECK* SE15 * 143 J3
Godolphin Cl *PLMGR* N13 49 H2
Godolphin Pl *ACT* W3 99 F6
Godolphin Rd *SHB* W12 118 E1
Godric Crs *CROY/NA* CR0 214 B6
Godson Rd *CROY/NA* CR0 211 G1
Godson St *IS* N1 5 J2
Godstone Rd *SUT* SM1 209 G2
TWK TW1 156 B1
Godstow Rd *ABYW* SE2 128 D2
Godwin Cl *HOR/WEW* KT19 206 E4
IS N1 6 D2
Godwin Rd *FSTGT* E7 89 F2
HAYES BR2 184 B6
Goffers Rd *BKHTH/KID* SE3 145 H2
Goidel Cl *WLGTN* SM6 210 D2
Golborne Gdns *NKENS* W10 * 100 C3
Golborne Ms *NKENS* W10 100 C4
Golborne Rd *NKENS* W10 100 C4
Golda Cl *BAR* EN5 32 B1
Goldbeaters Gv *EDGW* HA8 45 G2
Goldcliff Cl *MRDN* SM4 193 K4
Goldcrest Cl *CAN/RD* E16 107 H4
THMD SE28 109 J6
Goldcrest Ms *EA* W5 * 97 K4
Goldcrest Wy *BUSH* WD23 28 C3
CROY/NA CR0 214 B6
Golden Ct *HSLW* TW3 135 J3
Golden Crs *HYS/HAR* UB3 113 H1
Golden Cross Ms
NTGHL W11 * 100 D5
Golden Hind Pl *DEPT* SE8 * 124 C4
Golden Jubilee Br *STHWK* SE1 11 G7
Golden La *STLK* EC1Y 6 C6
Golden Lane Est *STLK* EC1Y 6 C7
Golden Mnr *HNWL* W7 96 E6
Golden Pde *WALTH* E17 * 52 A6
Golden Plover Cl *CAN/RD* E16 106 E5
Golden Sq *SOHO/CST* W1F 10 B5
Golden Yd *HAMP* NW3 83 G2
Golders Cl *EDGW* HA8 44 D1
Golders Gdns *GLDGN* NW11 64 C4
Golders Green Crs
GLDGN NW11 64 D4
Golders Green Rd
GLDGN NW11 64 C3
Golders Hl *HAMP* NW3 * 65 F6
Goldersslea *GLDGN* NW11 * 64 E5
Golders Manor Dr
GLDGN NW11 64 B3
Golders Park Cl *GLDGN* NW11 64 E5
Golders Ri *HDN* NW4 64 B2
Golders Wy *GLDGN* NW11 64 D4
Goldfinch Cl *ORP* BR6 217 G3
Goldfinch Rd *THMD* SE28 127 J3
Goldhawk Ms *SHB* W12 118 E2
Goldhawk Rd *HMSMTH* W6 118 C4
SHB W12 118 D3
Goldhaze Cl *WFD* IG8 53 G3
Gold Hl *EDGW* HA8 45 F2
Goldhurst Ter
KIL/WHAMP NW6 83 F5
Golding St *WCHPL* E1 104 C5
Goldington Crs *CAMTN* NW1 4 B2
Goldington St *CAMTN* NW1 4 C2
Gold La *EDGW* HA8 45 F2
Goldman Cl *BETH* E2 104 C3
Goldney Rd *MV/WKIL* W9 100 E3
Goldrill Dr *FBAR/BDGN* N11 34 A4
Goldsboro Rd *VX/NE* SW8 141 J2
Goldsborough Crs *CHING* E4 37 K4
Goldsdown Cl *PEND* EN3 25 G3
Goldsdown Rd *PEND* EN3 25 F3
Goldsmid St
WOOL/PLUM SE18 127 K5
Goldsmith Av *ACT* W3 99 F6
CDALE/KGS NW9 63 G2
MNPK E12 89 J4
ROMW/RG RM7 74 C4
Goldsmith Cl
RYLN/HDSTN HA2 60 A5
Goldsmith La *CDALE/KGS* NW9 62 E1
Goldsmith Pl
KIL/WHAMP NW6 * 83 F6
Goldsmith Rd *ACT* W3 118 A1
FBAR/BDGN N11 47 K1
LEY E10 69 K5
PECK SE15 143 H2
WALTH E17 51 F5
Goldsmiths Cl *ACT* W3 * 118 A1
Goldsmith's Rw *BETH* E2 104 C1
Goldsmith St *CITYW* EC2V 12 D3
Goldsworthy Gdns
BERM/RHTH SE16 123 K4
Goldwell Rd *THHTH* CR7 196 A1
Goldwing Cl *CAN/RD* E16 106 E5
Golf Cl *STAN* HA7 43 J3
THHTH CR7 180 B4
Golf Club Dr *KUTN/CMB* KT2 176 A3
Golfe Rd *IL* IG1 90 D1
Golf Rd *BMLY* BR1 185 F6
EA W5 * 98 B5
Golf Side *WHTN* TW2 155 J5
Golf Side Cl *NWMAL* KT3 176 B5
Golfside Cl *TRDG/WHET* N20 33 J5
Gollogly Ter *CHARL* SE7 126 B5
Gomer Gdns *TEDD* TW11 174 B2
Gomer Pl *TEDD* TW11 174 B2
Gomm Rd *BERM/RHTH* SE16 123 K3
Gomshall Av *WLGTN* SM6 210 E3
Gondar Gdns *CRICK* NW2 82 D3
Gonson St *DEPT* SE8 124 E6
Gonston Cl *WIM/MER* SW19 159 H4
Gonville Crs *NTHLT* UB5 78 B4
Gonville Rd *THHTH* CR7 196 A2
Gonville St *FUL/PGN* SW6 139 H4
Goodall Rd *WAN* E11 88 A1
Gooden Ct *HRW* HA1 78 E1
Goodenough Rd
WIM/MER SW19 177 J3
Goodey Rd *BARK* IG11 91 F5
Goodge Pl *FITZ* W1T 10 B2
Goodge St *FITZ* W1T 10 B2
Goodhall Cl *STAN* HA7 43 G2
Goodhall St *WLSDN* NW10 99 G2
Goodhart Wy *WWKM* BR4 199 H3
Goodhew Rd *CROY/NA* CR0 197 H3
Gooding Cl *NWMAL* KT3 191 K1
Goodinge Cl *HOLWY* N7 84 E3
Goodinge Rd *HOLWY* N7 84 E4
Goodman Ct *ALP/SUD* HA0 * 79 K2
Goodman Crs
BRXS/STRHM SW2 161 J4
CROY/NA CR0 196 C3
Goodman Rd *LEY* E10 70 A4
Goodmans Ct *ALP/SUD* HA0 79 K2
Goodman's Yd *TWRH* EC3N 13 J5
Goodmayes Av
GDMY/SEVK IG3 73 G5
Goodmayes La
GDMY/SEVK IG3 91 G2
Goodmayes Rd
GDMY/SEVK IG3 73 G5
Goodmead Rd *ORP* BR6 202 B4
Goodrich Rd *EDUL* SE22 163 G1
Goodson Rd *WLSDN* NW10 81 G5
Goods Wy *KCROSS* N1C 4 E2
Goodway Gdns *POP/IOD* E14 106 B5
Goodwill Dr *RYLN/HDSTN* HA2 60 A5
Goodwin Cl *BERM/RHTH* SE16 19 K5
MTCM CR4 178 C6
Goodwin Dr *SCUP* DA14 168 E4
Goodwin Gdns *CROY/NA* CR0 211 H4
Goodwin Rd *CROY/NA* CR0 211 H3
ED N9 36 E3
SHB W12 118 D2
Goodwins Ct *CHCR* WC2N 10 E5
Goodwin St *FSBYPK* N4 67 G6
Goodwood Cl *MRDN* SM4 193 K1
Goodwood Dr *NTHLT* UB5 78 A4
Goodwood Pde *BECK* BR3 * 198 B1
Goodwood Rd *NWCR* SE14 144 B1
Goodwyn Av *MLHL* NW7 45 G1
Goodwyn's V *MUSWH* N10 48 A4
Goodyers Gdns *HDN* NW4 64 B2
Goosander Wy *THMD* SE28 127 J3
Gooseacre La
KTN/HRWW/WS HA3 61 K2
Goose Green Cl
STMC/STPC BR5 186 B5
Gooseley La *EHAM* E6 108 A2
Goossens Cl *SUT* SM1 209 G3
Gophir La *CANST* EC4R * 12 E5
Gopsall St *IS* N1 7 F1
Gordon Av *CHING* E4 52 C2
HCH RM12 75 H6
MORT/ESHN SW14 138 B5
STAN HA7 43 F2
TWK TW1 136 B6
Gordonbrock Rd *BROCKY* SE4 144 D6
Gordon Cl *WALTH* E17 69 J3
Gordon Cots *KENS* W8 * 119 K2
Gordon Crs *CROY/NA* CR0 197 F5
HYS/HAR UB3 113 K4
Gordondale Rd
WIM/MER SW19 159 K4
Gordon Gdns *EDGW* HA8 44 D5
Gordon Gv *CMBW* SE5 142 C3
Gordon Hl *ENC/FH* EN2 23 J2
Gordon House Rd *KTTN* NW5 84 A2
Gordon Pl *KENS* W8 119 K2
Gordon Rd *ASHF* TW15 152 B5
BARK IG11 90 E6
BECK BR3 182 C6
BELV DA17 129 K4
BFN/LL DA15 147 K6
BRYLDS KT5 191 G4
CAR SM5 209 K4
CHDH RM6 74 B3
CHING E4 38 C2
CHSWK W4 117 J6
DART DA1 171 G2
EA W5 97 J6
ED N9 36 D4
ENC/FH EN2 23 K2
ESH/CLAY KT10 204 E5
FBAR/BDGN N11 48 D3
FNCH N3 46 D3
HSLW TW3 135 H5
IL IG1 90 D1
KTN/HRWW/WS HA3 42 E6
KUTN/CMB KT2 175 G4
NWDGN UB2 114 D4
PECK SE15 143 J3
RCH/KEW TW9 137 G3
SRTFD E15 88 A2
SWFD E18 53 F4
WAN E11 70 E3
Gordon Sq *STPAN* WC1H 4 C6
Gordon St *PLSTW* E13 106 E2
STPAN WC1H 4 C6
Gordon Wy *BAR* EN5 20 D5
BMLY BR1 183 K4
Gorefield Pl *KIL/WHAMP* NW6 100 E1
Gore Rd *HOM* E9 86 E6
RYNPK SW20 177 F5
Goresbrook Rd *DAGW* RM9 91 J6
Gore St *SKENS* SW7 120 B3
Gorham Pl *NTGHL* W11 100 C6
Goring Cl *CRW* RM5 56 E4
Goring Gdns *BCTR* RM8 91 J2
Goring Rd *DAGE* RM10 93 F4
FBAR/BDGN N11 * 48 E2
Goring St *HDTCH* EC3A 13 H3
Goring Wy *GFD/PVL* UB6 96 C1
Gorleston Rd
SEVS/STOTM N15 67 K2
Gorleston St *WKENS* W14 119 H4
Gorman Rd *WOOL/PLUM* SE18 126 E4
Gorringe Park Av *MTCM* CR4 179 F3
Gorse Cl *CAN/RD* E16 106 E5
Gorse Ri *TOOT* SW17 179 F1
Gorse Rd *CROY/NA* CR0 213 J1
STMC/STPC BR5 203 H6
Gorseway *ROMW/RG* RM7 75 G5
Gorst Rd *BTSEA* SW11 160 E1
WLSDN NW10 98 E3
Gorsuch Pl *BETH* E2 7 J4
Gorsuch St *BETH* E2 7 J4
Gosberton Rd *BAL* SW12 160 E3
Gosbury Hl *CHSGTN* KT9 206 A2
Gosfield Rd *BCTR* RM8 74 C5
Gosfield St *GTPST* W1W 9 K1
Gosford Gdns *REDBR* IG4 71 K2
Gosforth La *OXHEY* WD19 26 E5
Gosforth Pth *OXHEY* WD19 26 E5
Goshawk Gdns *YEAD* UB4 94 C2
Goslett Yd *SOHO/SHAV* W1D 10 D3
Gosling Cl *GFD/PVL* UB6 96 A2
Gosling Wy *BRXN/ST* SW9 142 B2
Gospatrick Rd *TOTM* N17 49 J3
Gosport Rd *WALTH* E17 69 H2
Gosport Wy *PECK* SE15 143 G1
Gossage Rd
WOOL/PLUM SE18 127 J5

Gosset St BETH E2 104 C2
Gosshill Rd BMLY BR1 185 F5
Gossington Cl CHST BR7 167 G6
Gosterwood St DEPT SE8 124 B6
Gostling Rd WHTN TW2 155 F3
Goston Gdns THHTH CR7 180 B6
Goswell Pl FSBYE EC1V 6 B5
Goswell Rd FSBYE EC1V 6 B4
Gothic Cl DART DA1 171 G5
Gothic Ct HYS/HAR UB3 113 G6
Gothic Rd WHTN TW2 155 J4
Gottfried Ms KTTN NW5 84 C2
Goudhurst Rd BMLY BR1 183 H1
Gough Rd EN EN1 24 D3
SRTFD E15 88 D2
Gough Sq FLST/FETLN EC4A 11 K3
Gough St FSBYW WC1X 5 H6
Goulding Gdns THHTH CR7 180 D5
Gould Rd EBED/NFELT TW14 153 H2
WHTN TW2 155 K3
Gould Ter HACK E8 86 D3
Goulston St WCHPL E1 13 J3
Goulton Rd CLPT E5 86 D3
Gourley Pl SEVS/STOTM N15 68 A2
Gourley St SEVS/STOTM N15 68 A2
Gourock Rd ELTH/MOT SE9 147 F6
Govan St BETH E2 86 C6
Govier Cl SRTFD E15 88 C5
Gowan Av FUL/PGN SW6 139 H2
Gowan Rd WLSDN NW10 81 K5
Gower Cl CLAP SW4 161 H1
Gower Ms GWRST WC1E 10 D2
Gower Pl GWRST WC1E 4 B6
Gower Rd FSTGT E7 88 E4
ISLW TW7 116 A6
Gower St GWRST WC1E 4 C7
Gower's Wk WCHPL E1 104 C5
Gowland Pl BECK BR3 182 C5
Gowlett Rd PECK SE15 143 H4
Gowlland Cl CROY/NA CR0 197 H4
Gowrie Rd BTSEA SW11 141 F4
Graburn Wy E/WMO/HCT KT8 173 J6
Grace Av BXLYHN DA7 149 G3
Gracechurch St BANK EC3V 13 F5
Grace Cl BARK/HLT IG6 55 F2
EDGW HA8 44 E3
ELTH/MOT SE9 166 C5
Gracedale Rd
STRHM/NOR SW16 179 G1
Gracefield Gdns
STRHM/NOR SW16 161 K5
Grace Jones Cl HACK E8 86 B4
Grace Ms BECK BR3 182 D2
Grace Pl BOW E3 105 K2
Grace Rd CROY/NA CR0 196 D3
Graces Aly WCHPL E1 * 104 C6
Graces Ms STJWD NW8 * 101 G1
Grace's Ms CMBW SE5 142 E3
Grace's Rd CMBW SE5 143 F3
Grace St BOW E3 105 K2
The Gradient SYD SE26 163 H6
Graduate Pl STHWK SE1 19 G4
Graeme Rd EN EN1 24 A3
Graemesdyke Av
MORT/ESHN SW14 137 J4
Grafton Cl HSLWW TW4 154 D3
WEA W13 97 G5
WPK KT4 207 G1
Grafton Ct EBED/NFELT TW14 153 G3
Grafton Crs CAMTN NW1 84 B4
Grafton Gdns BCTR RM8 74 A6
FSBYPK N4 67 J3
Grafton Ms FITZ W1T 4 A7
Grafton Park Rd WPK KT4 192 B6
Grafton Pl CAMTN NW1 4 C5
Grafton Rd ACT W3 98 E6
BCTR RM8 74 A6
CROY/NA CR0 196 B5
ENC/FH EN2 23 F4
HRW HA1 60 C2
KTTN NW5 84 A3
NWMAL KT3 192 B1
WPK KT4 207 F1
Grafton Sq CLAP SW4 141 H4
Grafton St CONDST W1S 9 K6
Grafton Ter HAMP NW3 83 K3
Grafton Wy E/WMO/HCT KT8 188 E1
FITZ W1T 10 A1
Grafton Yd KTTN NW5 84 B4
Graham Av MTCM CR4 179 F4
WEA W13 116 C2
Graham Cl CROY/NA CR0 198 D6
Grahame Park Wy MLHL NW7 45 G3
Graham Gdns SURB KT6 191 F5
Graham Rd BXLYHS DA6 149 G5
CHSWK W4 118 A3
HACK E8 86 C4
HDN NW4 63 K3
HPTN TW12 155 F6
KTN/HRWW/WS HA3 42 E6
MTCM CR4 179 F4
PLSTW E13 106 E3
SEVS/STOTM N15 49 H6
WIM/MER SW19 177 J3
Graham St IS N1 6 B3
Graham Ter BFN/LL DA15 * 168 C1
BGVA SW1W 15 G7
Grainger Cl NTHLT UB5 78 C3
Grainger Rd ISLW TW7 136 A3
WDGN N22 49 J4
Gramer Cl WAN E11 70 B6
Grampian Cl BELMT SM2 209 G5
HYS/HAR UB3 133 G1
ORP BR6 202 A3
Grampian Gdns CRICK NW2 64 C5
Gramsci Wy CAT SE6 164 E5
Granada St TOOT SW17 178 E1
Granard Av PUT/ROE SW15 138 E6
Granard Rd BTSEA SW11 160 E2
Granary Cl ED N9 36 E2
Granary Rd WCHPL E1 104 D3
Granary Sq IS N1 85 G4
Granary St CAMTN NW1 4 C1
Granby Rd ELTH/MOT SE9 146 E3
WOOL/PLUM SE18 127 G3
Granby St BETH E2 7 K6
Granby Ter CAMTN NW1 4 A3
Grand Av BRYLDS KT5 191 J3
FARR EC1M 12 B1
MUSWH N10 66 A1
WBLY HA9 80 C3
Grand Av East WBLY HA9 80 D3
Grand Depot Rd
WOOL/PLUM SE18 127 F5
Grand Dr NWDGN UB2 115 H2
RYNPK SW20 193 F1
Granden Rd
STRHM/NOR SW16 * 179 K5
Grandison Rd BTSEA SW11 140 E6
WPK KT4 193 F6
Grand Junction Whf IS N1 * 6 C3
Grand Pde FSBYPK N4 * 67 H3
MORT/ESHN SW14 * 137 K5
SURB KT6 * 191 H5
WBLY HA9 * 62 D6
Grand Union Canal Wk
BTFD TW8 116 D6
NKENS W10 100 A3
NTHLT UB5 95 K3
WDR/YW UB7 112 E2
WLSDN NW10 98 D1
Grand Union Cl MV/WKIL W9 100 D4
Grand Union Crs HACK E8 * 86 C6
Grand Union Wk
CAMTN NW1 * 84 B5
Grand Wk WCHPL E1 * 105 G3
Granfield St BTSEA SW11 * 140 C2
Grange Av EBAR EN4 33 J3
KTN/HRWW/WS HA3 43 H5
NFNCH/WDSPK N12 47 G1
SNWD SE25 181 F5
TRDG/WHET N20 32 C2
WFD IG8 52 E2
WHTN TW2 155 K4
Grangecliffe Gdns
SNWD SE25 181 F5
Grange Cl BFN/LL DA15 168 B5
E/WMO/HCT KT8 189 G1
HEST TW5 114 E5
HYS/HAR UB3 94 C4
WFD IG8 52 E3
Grange Ct ALP/SUD HA0 * 79 J3
BELMT SM2 * 209 F5
HRW HA1 * 79 F1
NTHLT UB5 95 G1
PIN HA5 * 41 J6
WLGTN SM6 * 210 B1
Grangecourt Rd
STNW/STAM N16 68 A5
Grange Crs CHIG IG7 54 D1
THMD SE28 109 J5
Grangedale Cl NTHWD HA6 40 C4
Grange Dr CHST BR7 184 D2
ORP BR6 217 J6
Grange Farm Cl
RYLN/HDSTN HA2 60 C6
Grange Gdns HAMP NW3 83 F1
PIN HA5 59 K1
SNWD SE25 181 F5
STHGT/OAK N14 34 D3
Grange Gv IS N1 85 J4
Grange Hl EDGW HA8 44 E1
SNWD SE25 181 F5
Grangehill Pl ELTH/MOT SE9 146 E4
Grangehill Rd ELTH/MOT SE9 146 E5
Grange Houses HBRY N5 * 85 J2
Grange La DUL SE21 163 G4
Grange Ms FELT TW13 * 153 G5
Grangemill Rd CAT SE6 164 D5
Grangemill Wy CAT SE6 164 D4
Grange Pk EA W5 117 F1
Grange Park Av WCHMH N21 35 H1
Grange Park Pl RYNPK SW20 176 E3
Grange Park Rd LEY E10 69 K5
THHTH CR7 180 E6
Grange Pl KIL/WHAMP NW6 82 E5
Grange Rd BARN SW13 138 D2
BELMT SM2 208 E5
CHSGTN KT9 206 A2
CHSWK W4 117 J5
E/WMO/HCT KT8 189 G1
EA W5 116 E1
EDGW HA8 45 F2
HARH RM3 57 K2
HGT N6 66 A3
HRW HA1 61 G3
HYS/HAR UB3 94 C5
IL IG1 90 C2
KUT/HW KT1 175 F6
LEY E10 69 J5
ORP BR6 201 H6
PLSTW E13 106 D2
RYLN/HDSTN HA2 60 D6
SNWD SE25 196 E1
STHL UB1 114 D2
STHWK SE1 19 H5
TOTM N17 50 C2
WALTH E17 69 G2
WLSDN NW10 81 K4
Granger Wy ROM RM1 75 J3
Grange St IS N1 7 F1
The Grange ALP/SUD HA0 80 C5
CROY/NA CR0 198 C6
NWMAL KT3 * 192 D2
STHWK SE1 19 J4
WIM/MER SW19 177 G2
WKENS W14 * 119 J4
WOT/HER KT12 188 A6
WPK KT4 207 F2
Grange V BELMT SM2 209 F5
Grangeview Rd
TRDG/WHET N20 33 G3
Grange Wk STHWK SE1 19 H4
Grange Walk Ms STHWK SE1 19 H5
Grange Wy ERITH DA8 150 E1
Grangeway KIL/WHAMP NW6 82 E5
NFNCH/WDSPK N12 33 F6
WFD IG8 39 G6
Grangeway Gdns REDBR IG4 71 J2
The Grangeway WCHMH N21 35 H1
Grangewood BXLY DA5 169 G3
Grangewood Cl PIN HA5 58 E2
Grangewood La BECK BR3 182 C2
Grangewood St EHAM E6 89 H6
Grange Yd STHWK SE1 19 J5
Granham Gdns ED N9 36 B4
Granite St WOOL/PLUM SE18 128 A5
Granleigh Rd WAN E11 70 C6
Gransden Av HACK E8 86 D5
Gransden Rd SHB W12 118 C2
Grantbridge St IS N1 6 B2
Grantchester KUT/HW KT1 * 175 H5
Grantchester Cl HRW HA1 79 F1
Grant Cl STHGT/OAK N14 34 C2
TOTM N17 50 A5
Grantham Cl EDGW HA8 30 A5
Grantham Gdns CHDH RM6 74 B3
Grantham Pl MYFR/PKLN W1K 15 J1
Grantham Rd BRXN/ST SW9 141 K4
CHSWK W4 138 B1
MNPK E12 90 A1
Grantley Pl ESH/CLAY KT10 204 B3
Grantley Rd HSLWW TW4 134 B3
Grantley St WCHPL E1 105 F2
Grantock Rd WALTH E17 52 B4
Granton Rd GDMY/SEVK IG3 73 G5
SCUP DA14 186 C2
STRHM/NOR SW16 179 H4
Grant Pl CROY/NA CR0 197 G5
Grant Rd BTSEA SW11 140 C4
CROY/NA CR0 197 G5
KTN/HRWW/WS HA3 42 E6
Grants Cl MLHL NW7 46 A3
Grant St IS N1 5 J2
PLSTW E13 106 E2
Grant Ter STNW/STAM N16 * 68 C4
Grantully Rd MV/WKIL W9 101 F2
Grant Wy ISLW TW7 116 B6
Granville Ar BRXN/ST SW9 * 142 B5
Granville Av ED N9 36 E5
FELT TW13 153 K4
HSLW TW3 135 F6
Granville Cl CROY/NA CR0 197 F6
Granville Gdns EA W5 117 G1
STRHM/NOR SW16 180 A4
Granville Gv LEW SE13 145 F4
Granville Ms SCUP DA14 168 B6
Granville Pk LEW SE13 145 F4
Granville Pl FUL/PGN SW6 * 140 A1
MBLAR W1H 9 G4
NFNCH/WDSPK N12 * 47 G3
PIN HA5 41 H6
Granville Rd BAR EN5 20 A5
CEND/HSY/T N8 67 F3
CRICK NW2 64 D6
HYS/HAR UB3 113 J4
IL IG1 72 B5
KIL/WHAMP NW6 100 E1
NFNCH/WDSPK N12 47 G3
PLMGR N13 49 F2
SCUP DA14 168 B6
SWFD E18 53 F5
WALTH E17 69 K3
WAND/EARL SW18 159 J2
WDGN N22 49 H4
WELL DA16 148 D4
WIM/MER SW19 177 K3
Granville Sq PECK SE15 * 143 F1
Granville St FSBYW WC1X 5 H5
Grape St LSQ/SEVD WC2H 10 E3
Graphite Sq LBTH SE11 * 122 A5
Grapsome Cl CHSGTN KT9 205 J5
Grasdene Rd
WOOL/PLUM SE18 148 B1
Grasgarth Cl ACT W3 98 E6
Grasmere Av ACT W3 98 E6
HSLW TW3 155 G1
ORP BR6 216 B1
PUT/ROE SW15 158 A6
RSLP HA4 58 A4
WBLY HA9 61 K4
WIM/MER SW19 177 K6
Grasmere Cl
EBED/NFELT TW14 153 J3
Grasmere Ct WDGN N22 49 F2
Grasmere Gdns
KTN/HRWW/WS HA3 43 G5
ORP BR6 216 B1
REDBR IG4 71 J2
Grasmere Rd BMLY BR1 183 J4
BXLYHN DA7 149 K2
MUSWH N10 48 B4
ORP BR6 216 B1
PLSTW E13 106 E1
SNWD SE25 197 J3
STRHM/NOR SW16 180 A1
TOTM N17 50 C2
Grass Banks DART DA1 171 J3
Grasshaven Wy THMD SE28 128 A1
Grassington Cl
FBAR/BDGN N11 48 A2
Grassington Rd SCUP DA14 168 B6
Grassmount FSTH SE23 163 J4
Grass Pk FNCH N3 46 D4
Grassway WLGTN SM6 210 C2
Grasvenor Av BAR EN5 32 E1
Grately Wy PECK SE15 * 143 F1
Gratton Rd WKENS W14 119 H3
Gratton Ter CRICK NW2 82 B1
Gravel Hl BXLYHS DA6 149 J6
CROY/NA CR0 213 F4
FNCH N3 46 D5
Gravel Hill Cl BXLYHS DA6 149 J6
Gravel La WCHPL E1 13 J3
Gravel Pit Wy ORP BR6 202 B6
Gravel Rd HAYES BR2 200 D6
WHTN TW2 155 K3
Gravelwood Cl CHST BR7 167 H5
Gravenel Gdns TOOT SW17 * 178 D1
Graveney Gv PGE/AN SE20 181 K3
Graveney Rd TOOT SW17 160 D6
Gravesend Rd SHB W12 99 J6
Gray Av BCTR RM8 74 B5
Gray Gdns RAIN RM13 93 J4
Grayham Crs NWMAL KT3 192 A1
Grayham Rd NWMAL KT3 192 A1
Grayland Cl BMLY BR1 184 C4
Grayling Cl CAN/RD E16 106 C3
Grayling Ct EA W5 * 116 E1
Grayling Rd STNW/STAM N16 67 K6
Grayling Sq BETH E2 * 104 C2
Grays Cots STMC/STPC BR5 * 186 D4
Grayscroft Rd
STRHM/NOR SW16 179 J3
Grays Farm Rd
STMC/STPC BR5 186 C4
Grayshott Rd BTSEA SW11 141 F4
Gray's Inn Rd FSBYW WC1X 5 F4
Gray's Inn Sq GINN WC1R 11 J1
Grays La ASHF TW15 152 E6
Grayswood Gdns
RYNPK SW20 176 E5
Gray's Yd MHST W1U * 9 H4
Graywood Ct
NFNCH/WDSPK N12 47 G3
Grazebrook Rd
STNW/STAM N16 67 K6
Grazeley Cl BXLYHS DA6 149 K6
Great Amwell La
CEND/HSY/T N8 49 F6
Great Benty WDR/YW UB7 112 B4
Great Brownings DUL SE21 163 G6
Great Bushey Dr
TRDG/WHET N20 33 F3
Great Cambridge Jct
PLMGR N13 49 J1
Great Cambridge Rd ED N9 35 K5
EN EN1 24 C6
UED N18 49 K1
Great Castle St REGST W1B 10 A3
Great Central Av RSLP HA4 77 G3
Great Central St CAMTN NW1 8 E1
Great Central Wy WBLY HA9 80 E3
Great Chapel St
SOHO/SHAV W1D 10 C3
Great Chart St BTSEA SW11 140 B4
Great Chertsey Rd CHSWK W4 138 A2
FELT TW13 154 E5
Great Church La HMSMTH W6 119 G5
Great College St WEST SW1P 16 E4
Great Cross Av GNWCH SE10 145 H1
Great Cullings ROMW/RG RM7 75 G6
Great Cumberland Ms
MBLAR W1H 8 E4
Great Cumberland Pl
MBLAR W1H 8 E3
Great Dover St STHWK SE1 18 E4
Greatdown Rd HNWL W7 97 F4
Great Eastern Rd SRTFD E15 88 B5
Great Eastern St SDTCH EC2A 7 G5
Great Eastern Whf
BTSEA SW11 140 D1
Great Elms Rd HAYES BR2 200 B1
Great Fld CDALE/KGS NW9 45 G4
Greatfield Av EHAM E6 107 K3
Greatfield Cl ARCH N19 84 C2
BROCKY SE4 144 D5
Greatfields Rd BARK IG11 90 D6
Great Galley Cl BARK IG11 109 H2
Great Gardens Rd
EMPK RM11 75 K3
Great Gatton Cl CROY/NA CR0 198 B4
Great George St STJSPK SW1H 16 D3
Great Guildford St
STHWK SE1 18 C1
Great Harry Dr ELTH/MOT SE9 167 F5
Great James St BMSBY WC1N 11 G1
Great Marlborough St
REGST W1B 10 A4
Great Maze Pond STHWK SE1 19 F1
Great New St
FLST/FETLN EC4A * 11 K3
Great North Rd BAR EN5 20 D3
EFNCH N2 65 J1
Great North Way (Barnet
By-Pass) HDN NW4 45 K4
Greatorex St WCHPL E1 104 C4
Great Ormond St
BMSBY WC1N 11 F1
Great Percy St FSBYW WC1X 5 H4
Great Peter St WEST SW1P 16 C5
Great Portland St
GTPST W1W 9 K1
Great Pulteney St
SOHO/CST W1F 10 B5
Great Queen St DART DA1 171 J1
HOL/ALD WC2B 11 F3
Great Russell St RSQ WC1B 10 D3
Great St Thomas Apostle
BLKFR EC4V 12 D5
Great Scotland Yd
WHALL SW1A 16 E1
Great Smith St WEST SW1P 16 D4
Great South-West Rd
EBED/NFELT TW14 153 F2
HSLWW TW4 134 A3
Great Spilmans EDUL SE22 143 F6
Great Strd CDALE/KGS NW9 45 H5
Great Suffolk St STHWK SE1 18 B1
Great Sutton St FSBYE EC1V 6 B7
Great Swan Aly LOTH EC2R 12 E3
Great Thrift STMC/STPC BR5 201 H1
Great Titchfield St
GTPST W1W 9 K1
Great Tower St MON EC3R 13 G5
Great Trinity La BLKFR EC4V 12 D5
Great Turnstile HHOL WC1V * 11 H2
Great Western Rd NTGHL W11 100 D4
Great West Rd BTFD TW8 136 B1
HEST TW5 134 D3
HMSMTH W6 118 E5
ISLW TW7 135 K1
Great West Rd Chiswick
CHSWK W4 118 C5
Great West Road Ellesmere
Rd CHSWK W4 117 K6
Great West Road Hogarth La
CHSWK W4 118 A6
Great Winchester St
OBST EC2N 13 F3
Great Windmill St
SOHO/SHAV W1D 10 C6
Greatwood CHST BR7 185 F3
Greaves Cl BARK IG11 90 D5
Greaves Cots POP/IOD E14 * 105 G4
Greaves Pl TOOT SW17 160 D6
Grebe Av YEAD UB4 95 H5
Grebe Cl BARK IG11 109 G3
FSTGT E7 88 D3
WALTH E17 51 G3
Grebe Ct SUT SM1 208 D3
Grebe Ter KUT/HW KT1 * 175 F6
Grecian Crs NRWD SE19 180 C2
Greek St SOHO/SHAV W1D 10 D4
Greenacre Cl BAR EN5 20 D1
NTHLT UB5 77 K3
Greenacre Gdns WALTH E17 70 A1
Greenacre Pl WLGTN SM6 195 G6
Greenacres BUSH WD23 28 D4
Green Acres CROY/NA CR0 212 B1
Greenacres ELTH/MOT SE9 167 F1
Green Acres SCUP DA14 * 168 A6
Greenacres Cl ORP BR6 216 C2
Greenacres Dr STAN HA7 43 H3
Greenacre Sq
BERM/RHTH SE16 * 124 A2
Greenacre Wk
STHGT/OAK N14 34 D5
Green Arbour Ct STBT EC1A * 12 A3
Green Av MLHL NW7 31 F6
WEA W13 116 C3
Greenaway Av UED N18 * 51 F1
Greenaway Gdns HAMP NW3 83 F2
Green Bank
NFNCH/WDSPK N12 33 F6
WAP E1W 123 J1
Greenbank Av ALP/SUD HA0 79 G3
Greenbank Cl CHING E4 38 A4
Greenbank Crs HDN NW4 64 C1
Greenbanks DART DA1 171 H4
Greenbay Rd CHARL SE7 146 C1
Greenberry St STJWD NW8 2 C3
Greenbrook Av EBAR EN4 21 G2
Green Chain Wk BMLY BR1 183 F1
CHARL SE7 126 C4
ELTH/MOT SE9 166 C4
SYD SE26 182 A2
THMD SE28 128 E1
WELL DA16 148 B2
Green Cl CAR SM5 194 E6
CDALE/KGS NW9 62 E3
FELT TW13 172 D1
GLDGN NW11 65 G4
HAYES BR2 183 H6
Greencoat Pl WEST SW1P 16 B6
Greencoat Rw WEST SW1P 16 B5
Green Court Av CROY/NA CR0 197 J6
Greencourt Av EDGW HA8 44 C4
Green Court Gdns
CROY/NA CR0 197 J6
Greencourt Rd
STMC/STPC BR5 201 K2
Greencroft EDGW HA8 44 E1
Greencroft Av RSLP HA4 59 G6
Greencroft Gdns EN EN1 24 A4
KIL/WHAMP NW6 83 F5
Greencroft Rd HEST TW5 134 E2
Green Dl EDUL SE22 143 F6
Green Dragon La BTFD TW8 117 F5
WCHMH N21 35 H1
Green Dragon Yd WCHPL E1 104 C4
Green Dr STHL UB1 115 F1
Green End CHSGTN KT9 205 K2
WCHMH N21 35 H4
Greenend Rd CHSWK W4 118 B2
Green Farm Cl ORP BR6 217 F3
Greenfell Man DEPT SE8 * 124 C5
Green Ferry Wy WALTH E17 69 F1
Greenfield Av BRYLDS KT5 191 J3
OXHEY WD19 27 J4
Greenfield Ct ELTH/MOT SE9 166 D5
Greenfield Dr BMLY BR1 184 B5
EFNCH N2 65 K1
Greenfield Gdns CRICK NW2 64 C6
DAGW RM9 91 J6
STMC/STPC BR5 201 H4
Greenfield Rd DAGW RM9 91 J6
SEVS/STOTM N15 68 A2
WCHPL E1 104 C4
Greenfields STHL UB1 96 A6
Greenfield Wy
RYLN/HDSTN HA2 42 B6
Greenford Av HNWL W7 96 E5
STHL UB1 95 K6
Greenford Gdns GFD/PVL UB6 96 B2
Greenford Rd STHL UB1 96 C6
SUT SM1 209 F2
Green Gdns ORP BR6 216 C3
Greengate GFD/PVL UB6 79 H4
Greengate St PLSTW E13 107 F1
Greenhalgh Wk EFNCH N2 65 G1
Greenham Cl STHWK SE1 17 J3
Greenham Crs CHING E4 51 H2
Greenham Rd MUSWH N10 48 A5
Greenhaven Dr THMD SE28 109 H5
Greenheys Cl NTHWD HA6 40 C4
Greenheys Dr SWFD E18 52 D6
Greenhill BKHH IG9 39 G3
HAMP NW3 83 H2
SUT SM1 194 B6
WBLY HA9 62 D6
Green Hl WOOL/PLUM SE18 126 E5
Greenhill Ct BAR EN5 * 21 F6
Greenhill Crs WATW WD18 26 C1
Greenhill Gdns NTHLT UB5 95 K1
Greenhill Gv MNPK E12 89 J2
Greenhill Pde BAR EN5 * 21 F6
Greenhill Pk BAR EN5 21 F6
WLSDN NW10 81 G6
Greenhill Rd HRW HA1 60 E3
WLSDN NW10 81 G6
Greenhill's Rents
FARR EC1M * 12 A1
Greenhills Ter IS N1 85 K4
Greenhill Ter NTHLT UB5 * 95 K1
WOOL/PLUM SE18 126 E5
Greenhill Wy HRW HA1 60 E3
WBLY HA9 62 D6
Greenhithe Cl BFN/LL DA15 167 K2
Greenholm Rd ELTH/MOT SE9 147 G6
Green Hundred Rd PECK SE15 123 H6
Greenhurst Rd WNWD SE27 180 B1
Greening St ABYW SE2 128 D4
Greenland Crs NWDGN UB2 114 B3
Greenland Ms DEPT SE8 124 A5
Greenland Pl CAMTN NW1 * 84 B6
Greenland Quay
BERM/RHTH SE16 124 A4
Greenland Rd BAR EN5 32 A1
CAMTN NW1 84 B6
Greenlands HOR/WEW KT19 206 D3
Greenlands La HDN NW4 46 A5
Greenland St CAMTN NW1 * 84 B6
Greenland Wy CROY/NA CR0 195 J4
Green La BCTR RM8 74 A6
CHSGTN KT9 206 A6
E/WMO/HCT KT8 189 G2
EDGW HA8 44 C1
ELTH/MOT SE9 167 F3
FELT TW13 172 D1

GDMY/SEVK IG3 73 G6
HDN NW4 64 B2
HNWL W7 115 K2
HSLWW TW4 134 B6
IL IG1 72 D6
MRDN SM4 193 K3
NTHWD HA6 40 B3
NWMAL KT3 191 K2
OXHEY WD19 27 G3
PGE/AN SE20 182 A3
STAN HA7 29 H6
THHTH CR7 180 C4
UX/CGN UB8 94 A4
WPK KT4 192 D5
Green Lane Cots STAN HA7 * 29 H6
Green Lane Gdns THHTH CR7 180 D5
Green Lanes FSBYPK N4 67 H3
HBRY N5 85 J1
HOR/WEW KT19 207 G6
PLMGR N13 49 F1
SEVS/STOTM N15 67 H1
WCHMH N21 35 J2
Greenlaw Ct EA W5 * 97 K5
Greenlaw Gdns NWMAL KT3 192 C4
Greenlawn La BTFD TW8 116 E4
Green Lawns
NFNCH/WDSPK N12 * 47 F2
RSLP HA4 * 59 G5
Greenlaw St
WOOL/PLUM SE18 127 F3
Green Leaf Av WLGTN SM6 210 D2
Greenleaf Cl
BRXS/STRHM SW2 * 162 B2
Greenleafe Dr BARK/HLT IG6 54 B6
Greenleaf Rd EHAM E6 89 G6
WALTH E17 51 H6
Greenleaf Wy
KTN/HRWW/WS HA3 43 F6
Greenlea Pk
WIM/MER SW19 * 178 D4
Greenleigh Av
STMC/STPC BR5 202 C1
Greenlink Wk RCH/KEW TW9 137 J2
Green Man La
EBED/NFELT TW14 133 K5
WEA W13 97 G6
Greenman St IS N1 85 J5
Greenmead Cl SNWD SE25 197 H2
Green Moor Link WCHMH N21 35 H2
Greenmoor Rd PEND EN3 24 E3
Greenoak Pl EBAR EN4 21 K3
Green Oaks NWDGN UB2 * 114 C4
Greenoak Wy
WIM/MER SW19 159 G6
Greenock Rd ACT W3 117 J3
STRHM/NOR SW16 179 J4
Greenock Wy ROM RM1 57 G3
Green Pde HSLW TW3 * 155 G1
Greenpark Wy GFD/PVL UB6 78 E6
Green Pond Cl WALTH E17 51 G6
Green Pond Rd WALTH E17 51 G6
Green Ride CHING E4 38 E1
Green Rd STHGT/OAK N14 34 B1
TRDG/WHET N20 33 G5
Greenroof Wy GNWCH SE10 125 J3
Greens Ct NTGHL W11 * 119 J1
Green's Ct SOHO/CST W1F 10 C5
Greens End WOOL/PLUM SE18 127 G4
Greenshank Cl WALTH E17 51 G3
Greenside BCTR RM8 73 J6
BXLY DA5 169 F3
Greenside Cl BARK/HLT IG6 54 C3
CAT SE6 165 G4
TRDG/WHET N20 33 H4
Greenside Rd CROY/NA CR0 196 B4
SHB W12 118 D3
Greenslade Rd BARK IG11 90 D5
Greenstead Av WFD IG8 53 G2
Greenstead Gdns
PUT/ROE SW15 138 D6
WFD IG8 53 G2
Greensted Rd LOU IG10 39 J2
Greenstone Ms WAN E11 70 E3
Green St FSTGT E7 89 F3
MYFR/PKLN W1K 9 F5
PEND EN3 24 E3
Greenstreet Hl NWCR SE14 * 144 A4
Greensward BUSH WD23 28 B1
Green Ter CLKNW EC1R 5 K5
The Green ACT W3 99 G5
BKHH IG9 * 39 F3
BXLYHN DA7 149 H2
CAR SM5 * 210 A2
CROY/NA CR0 213 H6
ED N9 36 C4
FELT TW13 154 A4
HAYES BR2 199 K4
HEST TW5 115 F6
HGDN/ICK UB10 58 A6
HRW HA1 61 G6
MRDN SM4 193 H1
NWDGN UB2 114 E2
NWMAL KT3 175 K6
RCH/KEW TW9 136 E6
SCUP DA14 186 B1
SRTFD E15 88 D4
STHGT/OAK N14 34 D4
STMC/STPC BR5 186 C3
SUT SM1 209 F1
TOTM N17 49 J2
WAN E11 71 F3
WCHMH N21 35 G2
WDR/YW UB7 112 A3
WELL DA16 147 K5
WHTN TW2 155 K3
WIM/MER SW19 177 G1
WLGTN SM6 195 F6
Green V BXLYHS DA6 148 E6
EA W5 98 B5
Greenvale Rd ELTH/MOT SE9 146 E5
Green Verges STAN HA7 43 K3
Green Vw CHSGTN KT9 206 B5
Greenview Av BECK BR3 198 B3
CROY/NA CR0 198 B3
Greenview Cl ACT W3 118 B1
Greenview Dr RYNPK SW20 177 F6
Green Wk DART DA1 150 C5
HDN NW4 64 B1
NWDGN UB2 115 F5
RSLP HA4 58 D5
STHWK SE1 19 G5
WFD IG8 53 J2
The Green Wk CHING E4 38 A3
Green Wy ELTH/MOT SE9 146 C6
HAYES BR2 200 D3
Greenway BCTR RM8 73 J6
CHST BR7 185 F1
KTN/HRWW/WS HA3 62 A2
PIN HA5 41 F5
RYNPK SW20 193 F1
STHGT/OAK N14 34 E4
TRDG/WHET N20 32 E4
WLGTN SM6 210 C2
YEAD UB4 95 F3
Greenway Av WALTH E17 70 B1
Greenway Cl
SEVS/STOTM N15 68 B1
CDALE/KGS NW9 45 F5
FBAR/BDGN N11 48 A2
FSBYPK N4 67 J6
TRDG/WHET N20 32 E4
Greenway Ct IL IG1 72 A5
SRTFD E15 106 C1
Greenway Gdns
CDALE/KGS NW9 44 E5
CROY/NA CR0 213 H1
GFD/PVL UB6 96 A2
Green Way Gdns
KTN/HRWW/WS HA3 42 E5
Greenways BECK BR3 182 D5
ESH/CLAY KT10 204 E2
NFNCH/WDSPK N12 * 47 G2
The Greenways TWK TW1 * 156 B1
The Green Wy
KTN/HRWW/WS HA3 42 E4
The Greenway
CDALE/KGS NW9 45 F5
EHAM E6 108 B3
HSLWW TW4 * 134 E5
OLYMPICPK E20 87 K5
PIN HA5 59 K3
SRTFD E15 106 D1
Greenwell St GTPST W1W 3 K7
Greenwich Church St
GNWCH SE10 * 125 F6
Greenwich Crs EHAM E6 107 J4
Greenwich Foot Tnl
GNWCH SE10 125 F5
Greenwich Hts CHARL SE7 * 146 D1
Greenwich High Rd
GNWCH SE10 144 E1
Greenwich House LEW SE13 165 G1
Greenwich Park St
GNWCH SE10 * 125 G6
Greenwich Quay DEPT SE8 * 124 D6
Greenwich South St
GNWCH SE10 144 E2
Greenwich Vw POP/IOD E14 124 E3
Greenwood Av DAGE RM10 92 D2
PEND EN3 25 F2
Greenwood Cl BFN/LL DA15 168 B4
HYS/HAR UB3 113 K1
MRDN SM4 193 H1
STMC/STPC BR5 201 K3
THDIT KT7 190 B5
Greenwood Dr CHING E4 52 A1
Greenwood Gdns
BARK/HLT IG6 54 C3
PLMGR N13 35 H5
Greenwood La HPTN TW12 173 G1
Greenwood Pk
KUTN/CMB KT2 176 B3
Greenwood Pl KTTN NW5 84 B3
Greenwood Rd BXLY DA5 170 A6
CROY/NA CR0 196 C4
HACK E8 86 C3
ISLW TW7 135 K4
MTCM CR4 179 J6
PLSTW E13 106 D1
THDIT KT7 190 B5
Greenwood Ter
WLSDN NW10 * 81 F6
Green Wrythe Crs CAR SM5 194 D5
Green Wrythe La CAR SM5 194 C3
Green Yd FSBYW WC1X 5 H6
Greer Rd KTN/HRWW/WS HA3 42 C4
Greet St STHWK SE1 17 K1
Greg Cl LEY E10 70 A3
Gregor Ms BKHTH/KID SE3 145 K1
Gregory Crs ELTH/MOT SE9 166 C2
Gregory Pl KENS W8 120 A2
Gregory Rd CHDH RM6 73 K1
NWDGN UB2 115 F3
Greig Cl CEND/HSY/T N8 66 E2
Greig Ter WALW SE17 122 C6
Grenaby Av CROY/NA CR0 196 E4
Grenaby Rd CROY/NA CR0 196 E4
Grenada Rd BKHTH/KID SE3 146 B1
Grenade St POP/IOD E14 105 H6
Grenadier St CAN/RD E16 127 F1
Grena Gdns RCH/KEW TW9 137 G5
Grenard Cl PECK SE15 * 143 H1
Grena Rd RCH/KEW TW9 137 G5
Grendon Gdns WBLY HA9 62 C6
Grendon St STJWD NW8 2 C6
Grenfell Av HCH RM12 75 H5
Grenfell Ct MLHL NW7 * 45 K2
Grenfell Gdns
KTN/HRWW/WS HA3 62 A4
Grenfell Rd NTGHL W11 100 B6
TOOT SW17 178 E2
Grennell Cl SUT SM1 194 C6
Grennell Rd SUT SM1 194 B6
Grenoble Gdns PLMGR N13 49 G2
Grenville Cl BRYLDS KT5 191 K5
FNCH N3 46 D4
Grenville Gdns WFD IG8 53 G3
Grenville Ms ARCH N19 66 E5
HPTN TW12 173 G1
Grenville Pl MLHL NW7 45 F1
SKENS SW7 * 120 B3
Grenville Rd ARCH N19 66 E5
CROY/NA CR0 214 A6
Grenville St BMSBY WC1N 5 F7
Gresham Av TRDG/WHET N20 33 K6
Gresham Cl BXLY DA5 169 F1
ENC/FH EN2 23 J4
Gresham Dr CHDH RM6 73 H2
Gresham Gdns GLDGN NW11 64 C5
Gresham Rd BECK BR3 182 B5
BRXN/ST SW9 142 B4
CAN/RD E16 107 F5
EDGW HA8 44 B2
EHAM E6 107 K1
HPTN TW12 173 F2
HSLW TW3 135 H2
SNWD SE25 * 197 H1
WLSDN NW10 81 F3
Gresham St CITYW EC2V 12 C3
Gresham Wy WIM/MER SW19 159 K5
Gresley Cl SEVS/STOTM N15 * 67 K1
WALTH E17 69 G3
Gresley Rd ARCH N19 66 C5
Gressenhall Rd
WAND/EARL SW18 159 J1
Gresse St FITZ W1T 10 C2
Gresswell Cl SCUP DA14 168 B5
Greswell St FUL/PGN SW6 139 G2
Gretton Rd TOTM N17 50 A3
Greville Cl TWK TW1 156 C2
Greville Ms KIL/WHAMP NW6 83 F6
Greville Pl KIL/WHAMP NW6 101 F1
Greville Rd KIL/WHAMP NW6 101 F1
RCHPK/HAM TW10 157 G1
WALTH E17 70 A1
Greville St HCIRC EC1N 11 K2
Grey Cl GLDGN NW11 65 G3
Greycoat Pl WEST SW1P 16 C5
Greycoat St WEST SW1P 16 C5
Greycot Rd BECK BR3 182 D1
Grey Eagle St WCHPL E1 7 K7
Greyfell Cl STAN HA7 43 H1
Greyhound Hl HDN NW4 45 J6
Greyhound La
STRHM/NOR SW16 179 K2
Greyhound Rd HMSMTH W6 119 G6
SUT SM1 209 G3
TOTM N17 50 A6
WLSDN NW10 99 K2
Greyhound Ter
STRHM/NOR SW16 179 H4
Greyhound Wy DART DA1 150 B6
Greyladies Gdns
GNWCH SE10 * 145 F3
Greys Park Cl HAYES BR2 215 G3
Greystead Rd FSTH SE23 163 K2
Greystoke Av PIN HA5 42 A6
Greystoke Cots EA W5 * 98 A3
Greystoke Gdns EA W5 98 A3
ENC/FH EN2 22 D5
Greystone Gdns
BARK/HLT IG6 54 C5
KTN/HRWW/WS HA3 61 J3
Greyswood Av UED N18 * 51 F1
Greyswood St
STRHM/NOR SW16 179 G2
Grierson Rd FSTH SE23 164 B1
Griffin Cl WLSDN NW10 81 K3
Griffin Manor Wy THMD SE28 127 J3
Griffin Rd TOTM N17 50 A5
WOOL/PLUM SE18 127 J5
Griffins Cl WCHMH N21 35 K3
Griffin Wy THMD SE28 127 K3
Griffith Cl CHDH RM6 73 J4
Griffiths Rd WIM/MER SW19 177 K3
Griggs Ap IL IG1 72 C6
Griggs Cl IL IG1 90 E2
Grigg's Pl STHWK SE1 19 H5
Griggs Rd LEY E10 70 A3
Grimsby Gv CAN/RD E16 127 G1
Grimsby St WCHPL E1 7 K7
Grimsdyke Crs BAR EN5 20 A4
Grimsdyke Rd PIN HA5 41 J3
Grimsel Pth CMBW SE5 142 C1
Grimshaw Cl HGT N6 * 66 A4
Grimshaw Wy ROM RM1 75 G2
Grimston Rd FUL/PGN SW6 139 J3
Grimwade Av CROY/NA CR0 212 C1
Grimwade Cl PECK SE15 143 J3
Grimwood Rd TWK TW1 156 A2
Grindall Cl CROY/NA CR0 211 H2
Grindal St STHWK SE1 17 J3
Grindleford Av
FBAR/BDGN N11 34 A4
Grindley Gdns CROY/NA CR0 * 197 G3
Grinling Pl DEPT SE8 124 D6
Grinstead Rd DEPT SE8 124 B5
Grisle Cl ED N9 36 D6
Grittleton Av WBLY HA9 80 D4
Grittleton Rd MV/WKIL W9 100 E3
Grizedale Ter FSTH SE23 163 J4
Grocers' Hall Ct LOTH EC2R * 12 E4
Groombridge Cl WELL DA16 148 B6
Groombridge Rd HOM E9 87 F5
Groom Cl HAYES BR2 200 A1
Groom Crs WAND/EARL SW18 160 C2
Groomfield Cl TOOT SW17 161 F6
Groom Pl KTBR SW1X 15 H4
Grooms Dr PIN HA5 58 E2
Grosmont Rd
WOOL/PLUM SE18 128 A5
Grosse Wy PUT/ROE SW15 158 E1
Grosvenor Av CAR SM5 209 K4
HBRY N5 85 J3
MORT/ESHN SW14 138 B4
RYLN/HDSTN HA2 60 B4
YEAD UB4 94 D1
Grosvenor Br VX/NE SW8 121 G6
Grosvenor Cots KTBR SW1X 15 G6
Grosvenor Crs
CDALE/KGS NW9 62 C1
DART DA1 151 G6
KTBR SW1X 15 H3
Grosvenor Crescent Ms
KTBR SW1X 15 G3
Grosvenor Gdns BGVA SW1W 15 K5
CRICK NW2 82 A4
GLDGN NW11 64 D3
KUTN/CMB KT2 174 E2
MORT/ESHN SW14 138 B4
MUSWH N10 48 C6
STHGT/OAK N14 22 D6
WFD IG8 52 E2
WLGTN SM6 210 C5
Grosvenor Gardens Ms East
BGVA SW1W * 15 K4
Grosvenor Gardens Ms North
BGVA SW1W 15 J5
Grosvenor Ga
MYFR/PKLN W1K 9 F6
Grosvenor Hl
MYFR/PKLN W1K 9 J5
WIM/MER SW19 177 H2
Grosvenor Pde EA W5 * 117 H1
Grosvenor Pk CMBW SE5 142 D1
Grosvenor Park Rd
WALTH E17 69 J2
Grosvenor Pl KTBR SW1X 15 H2
Grosvenor Ri East WALTH E17 69 K2
Grosvenor Rd BCTR RM8 74 B5
BELV DA17 129 G6
BTFD TW8 116 E6
BXLYHS DA6 148 E6
CHSWK W4 117 K5
ED N9 36 D3
EHAM E6 89 H6
FNCH N3 46 D3
FSTGT E7 89 F4
HNWL W7 116 B1
HSLWW TW4 134 E4
IL IG1 90 C1
LEY E10 70 A5
MUSWH N10 48 B4
NTHWD HA6 40 D1
NWDGN UB2 114 E3
PIM SW1V 121 H6
RCHPK/HAM TW10 137 F6
ROMW/RG RM7 75 F4
SNWD SE25 197 H1
STMC/STPC BR5 201 K3
TWK TW1 156 B2
WAN E11 71 F2
WLGTN SM6 210 B4
WWKM BR4 198 E6
Grosvenor Sq
MYFR/PKLN W1K 9 H5
Grosvenor St
MYFR/PKLN W1K 9 H5
Grosvenor Ter CMBW SE5 142 D1
Grosvenor V RSLP HA4 58 D6
Grosvenor Wy TOOT SW17 160 C5
Grosvenor Wharf Rd
POP/IOD E14 125 G4
Grote's Blds BKHTH/KID SE3 145 H3
Grote's Pl BKHTH/KID SE3 145 H3
Groton Rd WAND/EARL SW18 160 A4
Grotto Ct STHWK SE1 * 18 C2
Grotto Pas MHST W1U 9 G1
Grotto Rd TWK TW1 156 A4
Grove Av FNCH N3 46 E3
HNWL W7 96 E5
MUSWH N10 48 C5
PIN HA5 59 J1
SUT SM1 208 E4
TWK TW1 156 A3
Grove Bank OXHEY WD19 * 27 H3
Grovebury Cl ERITH DA8 130 A6
Grovebury Ct STHGT/OAK N14 34 C2
Grovebury Rd ABYW SE2 128 C2
Grove Cl FSTH SE23 164 A3
HAYES BR2 199 K6
KUT/HW KT1 191 G1
STHGT/OAK N14 * 34 B2
Grove Cots CHEL SW3 120 D6
CHSWK W4 * 118 B6
Grove Ct E/WMO/HCT KT8 189 J2
EA W5 * 117 F1
Grove Crs CDALE/KGS NW9 62 E1
FELT TW13 154 D6
KUT/HW KT1 175 F6
SWFD E18 52 D5
WOT/HER KT12 188 A4
Grove Crescent Rd SRTFD E15 88 B4
Grovedale Rd ARCH N19 66 D6
Grove Dwellings WCHPL E1 * 104 E4
Grove End KTTN NW5 84 B2
SWFD E18 52 D5
Grove End La ESH/CLAY KT10 189 J5
Grove End Rd STJWD NW8 2 A3
Grove Farm Pk NTHWD HA6 40 B1
Grove Footpath BRYLDS KT5 191 F1
Grove Gdns HDN NW4 * 63 J2
PEND EN3 25 F2
STJWD NW8 2 D5
TEDD TW11 156 B6
Grove Green Rd WAN E11 88 A1
Groveherst Rd DART DA1 151 J4
Grove Hl HRW HA1 60 E4
SWFD E18 52 D5
Grove Hill Rd CMBW SE5 143 F4
HRW HA1 61 F4
Grove House Rd
CEND/HSY/T N8 66 E1
Groveland Av
STRHM/NOR SW16 180 A3
Groveland Ct STP EC4M 12 D4
Groveland Rd BECK BR3 182 C6
Grovelands E/WMO/HCT KT8 189 F1
Grovelands Cl CMBW SE5 143 F3
RYLN/HDSTN HA2 78 B1
Grovelands Ct
STHGT/OAK N14 34 D2
Grovelands Rd PLMGR N13 35 F6
SEVS/STOTM N15 68 C3
STMC/STPC BR5 186 B3
Groveland Wy NWMAL KT3 191 K2
Grove La CMBW SE5 142 E2
KUT/HW KT1 191 F1
Grove Market Pl
ELTH/MOT SE9 * 166 E1
Grove Ms HMSMTH W6 119 F3
Grove Mill Pl CAR SM5 210 A1
Grove Pk CDALE/KGS NW9 62 E1
CMBW SE5 143 F3
WAN E11 71 F2
Grove Park Av CHING E4 51 K3
Grove Park Br CHSWK W4 137 K1
Grove Park Gdns CHSWK W4 137 J1
Grove Park Rd CHSWK W4 137 J1
ELTH/MOT SE9 166 C5
RAIN RM13 93 J6
SEVS/STOTM N15 68 A1
Grove Park Ter CHSWK W4 137 J1
Grove Pl ACT W3 117 K1
BAL SW12 161 G1
HAMP NW3 83 H1
Grove Rd ACT W3 117 K1
BARN SW13 138 C3
BELV DA17 129 G6
BOW E3 105 G1
BTFD TW8 116 D5
BXLYHN DA7 149 K5
CHDH RM6 73 J4
CHING E4 38 A5
CRICK NW2 82 A4
E/WMO/HCT KT8 189 J1
EA W5 97 K6
EBAR EN4 21 J4
EDGW HA8 44 C2
FBAR/BDGN N11 48 B1
HOM E9 87 F6
HSLW TW3 135 F5
ISLW TW7 135 K2
MTCM CR4 179 G5
NFNCH/WDSPK N12 47 H1
NTHWD HA6 40 B1
PIN HA5 59 K2
RCHPK/HAM TW10 157 G1
SEVS/STOTM N15 68 A2
SURB KT6 190 E2
SUT SM1 208 E4
SWFD E18 52 D5
THHTH CR7 196 B1
WALTH E17 69 K2
WAN E11 70 D4
WHTN TW2 155 J5
WIM/MER SW19 178 B3
Grover Rd OXHEY WD19 27 H1
Groveside Cl ACT W3 98 C5
CAR SM5 194 D6
Groveside Rd CHING E4 38 C5
Grovestile Waye
EBED/NFELT TW14 153 G2
Grove St BERM/RHTH SE16 124 C4
UED N18 50 B1
Grove Ter KTTN NW5 84 A1
STHL UB1 * 96 A6
TEDD TW11 156 B6
Grove Terrace Ms KTTN NW5 84 B1
The Grove BXLYHS DA6 148 E5
CDALE/KGS NW9 63 F2
CEND/HSY/T N8 66 D2
EA W5 116 E1
EDGW HA8 30 D6
ENC/FH EN2 23 G3
FNCH N3 46 E3
FSBYPK N4 67 F4
GFD/PVL UB6 96 C5
GLDGN NW11 64 C4
HGT N6 66 A5
ISLW TW7 135 K2
PLMGR N13 35 G6
SCUP DA14 169 F6
SRTFD E15 88 C5
TEDD TW11 156 B6
WOT/HER KT12 188 A4
WWKM BR4 214 A1
Grove V CHST BR7 185 F2
EDUL SE22 143 F5
Groveway BCTR RM8 91 K2
BRXN/ST SW9 142 A2
Grove Wy ESH/CLAY KT10 189 H4
WBLY HA9 80 E3
Grove Wood Cl BMLY BR1 185 F6
Grovewood Pl WFD IG8 53 K2
Grummant Rd PECK SE15 143 G2
Grundy St POP/IOD E14 105 K5
Gruneisen Rd FNCH N3 47 F3
Guardian Cl EMPK RM11 75 K6
Gubyon Av HNHL SE24 142 C6
Gudden Dr CLPT E5 86 D2
Guernsey Cl HEST TW5 135 F2
Guernsey Gv HNHL SE24 162 D2
Guernsey Rd IS N1 85 J4
LEY E10 70 B5
Guibal Rd LEE/GVPK SE12 165 K2
Guildersfield Rd
STRHM/NOR SW16 179 K3
Guildford Av FELT TW13 153 J4
Guildford Gv GNWCH SE10 144 E2
Guildford Rd CROY/NA CR0 196 E3
EHAM E6 107 J5
GDMY/SEVK IG3 72 E6
VX/NE SW8 141 K2
WALTH E17 52 A4
Guildford Wy WLGTN SM6 210 E3
Guildhall Blds CITYW EC2V 12 D3
Guildhall Yd CITYW EC2V 12 D3
Guildhouse St PIM SW1V 16 A7
Guildown Av
NFNCH/WDSPK N12 33 F6
Guild Rd CHARL SE7 126 C5
ERITH DA8 150 C1
Guildsway WALTH E17 51 H4
Guilford Av BRYLDS KT5 191 G2
Guilford Pl BMSBY WC1N 5 G7
Guilford St BMSBY WC1N 5 G7
Guillemot Pl WDGN N22 * 49 F5
Guinness Cl HOM E9 87 G5
HYS/HAR UB3 113 G3
Guinness Ct CROY/NA CR0 * 197 G6
Guinness Sq STHWK SE1 19 G5
Guinness Trust
STNW/STAM N16 * 68 B5
Guinness Trust Est CHEL SW3 14 E7
SRTFD E15 * 88 D6
Guion Rd FUL/PGN SW6 139 J3
Gulland Wk IS N1 * 85 J4
Gulliver Cl NTHLT UB5 77 K6
Gulliver Rd BFN/LL DA15 167 J4
Gulliver St BERM/RHTH SE16 124 C3
Gumleigh Rd EA W5 116 D4
Gumley Gdns ISLW TW7 136 B4
Gumping Rd STMC/STPC BR5 201 H6
Gundulph Rd HAYES BR2 184 B6
Gunmakers La BOW E3 87 G6
Gunnell Cl CROY/NA CR0 197 G3
SYD SE26 * 163 H6
Gunner La
WOOL/PLUM SE18 127 F5
Gunnersbury Ave ACT W3 117 H3
Gunnersbury Av (North
Circular Rd) EA W5 98 B6
Gunnersbury Cl CHSWK W4 * 117 J5
Gunnersbury Crs ACT W3 117 H2
Gunnersbury Dr EA W5 117 G2
Gunnersbury Gdns ACT W3 117 H2
Gunnersbury La ACT W3 117 H2
Gunnersbury Ms CHSWK W4 117 J5
Gunners Gv CHING E4 38 A5

Gunners Rd
WAND/EARL SW18 160 C4
Gunning St WOOL/PLUM SE18 127 K4
Gunstor Rd
STNW/STAM N16 * 86 A2
Gun St WCHPL E1 13 J2
Gunter Gv EDGW HA8 45 F4
WBPTN SW10 120 B6
Gunterstone Rd WKENS W14 119 H5
Gunthorpe St WCHPL E1 13 K2
Gunton Rd CLPT E5 86 D1
TOOT SW17 179 F2
Gunwhale Cl
BERM/RHTH SE16 124 A1
Gunyard Ms
WOOL/PLUM SE18 * 146 D1
Gurdon Rd CHARL SE7 125 K5
Gurnell Gv WEA W13 97 F3
Gurney Cl BARK IG11 90 B4
SRTFD E15 88 C3
WALTH E17 51 F4
Gurney Crs CROY/NA CR0 196 A5
Gurney Dr EFNCH N2 65 H1
Gurney Rd CAR SM5 210 A2
FUL/PGN SW6 140 B4
NTHLT UB5 95 F2
SRTFD E15 88 C3
Guthrie St CHEL SW3 120 D5
Gutter La CITYW EC2V 12 C3
Guyatt Gdns MTCM CR4 179 F5
Guy Barnett Gv
BKHTH/KID SE3 145 K4
Guy Rd WLGTN SM6 210 D1
Guyscliff Rd LEW SE13 145 F6
Guysfield Cl RAIN RM13 93 J6
Guysfield Dr RAIN RM13 93 J6
Guy St STHWK SE1 19 F2
Gwalior Rd PUT/ROE SW15 139 G5
Gwendolen Av
PUT/ROE SW15 139 G6
Gwendoline Av PLSTW E13 89 F6
Gwendwr Rd WKENS W14 119 H5
Gweneth Cots EDGW HA8 * 44 C2
Gwillim Cl BFN/LL DA15 168 B1
Gwydor Rd BECK BR3 198 A1
Gwydyr Rd HAYES BR2 183 J6
Gwyn Cl FUL/PGN SW6 140 B1
Gwynne Av CROY/NA CR0 198 A4
Gwynne Park Av WFD IG8 53 K2
Gwynne Rd BTSEA SW11 140 C3
Gwynne Whf CHSWK W4 118 C6
Gylcote Cl CMBW SE5 142 E5
Gyles Pk STAN HA7 43 J4
Gyllyngdune Gdns
GDMY/SEVK IG3 91 F1
Gywnne Pl FSBYW WC1X 5 H5

H

Haarlem Rd WKENS W14 119 G3
Haberdasher Pl IS N1 7 F4
Haberdasher St IS N1 7 F4
Habington Cl CMBW SE5 * 142 E1
Habitat Cl PECK SE15 143 J3
Haccombe Rd
WIM/MER SW19 178 B2
Hackbridge Park Gdns
CAR SM5 194 E6
Hackbridge Rd CAR SM5 195 F6
Hackford Rd BRXN/ST SW9 142 A2
Hackford Wk BRXN/ST SW9 142 A2
Hackington Crs BECK BR3 182 D2
Hackney Gv HACK E8 * 86 D4
Hackney Rd BETH E2 7 J4
Hackney Wick HOM E9 87 H4
Hadar Cl TRDG/WHET N20 32 E3
Haddenham Ct
OXHEY WD19 * 27 H5
Hadden Rd THMD SE28 127 K3
Hadden Wy GFD/PVL UB6 78 D4
Haddington Rd BMLY BR1 165 G5
Haddon Cl EN EN1 36 C1
NWMAL KT3 192 C2
Haddon Gv BFN/LL DA15 168 B2
Haddon Rd STMC/STPC BR5 202 D2
SUT SM1 209 F2
Haddo St GNWCH SE10 124 E6
Hadfield Cl STHL UB1 95 K2
Hadfield Rd
STWL/WRAY TW19 152 A1
Hadleigh Cl RYNPK SW20 177 J5
WCHPL E1 104 E3
Hadleigh Dr BELMT SM2 208 E6
Hadleigh Rd ED N9 36 D2
Hadleigh St BETH E2 104 E3
Hadley Cl WCHMH N21 35 G1
Hadley Common BAR EN5 21 G3
Hadley Gdns CHSWK W4 118 A5
NWDGN UB2 114 E5
Hadley Gn BAR EN5 20 D4
Hadley Green Rd BAR EN5 20 D3
Hadley Gn West BAR EN5 20 C3
Hadley Gv BAR EN5 20 C3
Hadley Highstone BAR EN5 20 D1
Hadley Pde BAR EN5 * 20 C4
Hadley Rdg BAR EN5 20 D4
Hadley Rd BAR EN5 21 F4
BELV DA17 129 G4
EBAR EN4 22 A1
ENC/FH EN2 22 E1
MTCM CR4 195 J1
Hadley St KTTN NW5 84 B4
Hadley Wy WCHMH N21 35 G1
Hadley Wood Rd BAR EN5 20 E3
Hadlow Pl NRWD SE19 181 H3
Hadlow Rd SCUP DA14 168 B6
WELL DA16 148 D1
Hadrian Cl BOW E3 87 J6
STWL/WRAY TW19 152 B2
Hadrian Est BETH E2 * 104 C1
Hadrian's Ride EN EN1 24 B6
Hadrian St GNWCH SE10 125 H5
Hadrian Wy
STWL/WRAY TW19 152 A2
Hadyn Park Rd SHB W12 118 D2
Hafer Rd BTSEA SW11 140 E5
Hafton Rd CAT SE6 165 H3
Haggard Rd TWK TW1 156 C2
Hagger Ct WALTH E17 * 52 B6
Haggerston Rd HACK E8 86 B5
Hague St BETH E2 104 C2
Ha-Ha Rd WOOL/PLUM SE18 126 E6
Haig Rd STAN HA7 43 J1
UX/CGN UB8 94 A4
Haig Rd East PLSTW E13 107 G2
Haig Rd West PLSTW E13 107 G2
Haigville Gdns BARK/HLT IG6 72 B1
Hailes Cl CROY/NA CR0 195 J6
WIM/MER SW19 178 B2
Haileybury Av EN EN1 36 B1
Haileybury Rd ORP BR6 217 G2
Hailey Rd ERITHM DA18 129 H2
Hailsham Av
BRXS/STRHM SW2 162 A4
Hailsham Cl SURB KT6 190 E4
Hailsham Dr HRW HA1 42 D6
Hailsham Rd TOOT SW17 179 F2
Hailsham Ter UED N18 * 49 K1
Haimo Rd ELTH/MOT SE9 146 C6
Hainault Blds LEY E10 * 70 A5
Hainault Gore CHDH RM6 74 A2
Hainault Rd CHDH RM6 55 H6
CRW RM5 56 E6
WAN E11 70 A5
Hainault St ELTH/MOT SE9 167 G3
IL IG1 72 B6
Haines Wk MRDN SM4 194 A4
Hainford Cl PECK SE15 144 A5
Haining Cl CHSWK W4 117 H5
Hainthorpe Rd WNWD SE27 162 C5
Hainton Cl WCHPL E1 104 D5
Halberd Ms CLPT E5 68 D6
Halbutt St DAGW RM9 92 B2
Halcomb St IS N1 7 G1
Halcot Av BXLYHS DA6 149 J6
Halcrow St WCHPL E1 * 104 D4
Haldane Cl MUSWH N10 48 B3
PEND EN3 25 K1
Haldane Pl WAND/EARL SW18 160 A3
Haldane Rd EHAM E6 107 H2
FUL/PGN SW6 139 J1
STHL UB1 96 C6
THMD SE28 109 K6
Haldan Rd CHING E4 52 A2
Haldon Rd WAND/EARL SW18 159 J1
Hale Cl CHING E4 38 A5
EDGW HA8 44 E1
ORP BR6 216 C2
Hale Dr MLHL NW7 44 E2
Hale End HARH RM3 57 K2
Hale End Cl RSLP HA4 58 E3
Hale End Rd WALTH E17 52 B5
Halefield Rd TOTM N17 50 C4
Hale Gdns ACT W3 117 H1
TOTM N17 50 C6
Hale Grove Gdns MLHL NW7 45 F1
Hale House
WOOL/PLUM SE18 * 146 D1
Hale La EDGW HA8 44 E1
Hale Rd EHAM E6 107 J3
TOTM N17 50 C6
Halesowen Rd MRDN SM4 194 A4
Hales St DEPT SE8 144 D1
Hale St POP/IOD E14 105 K6
Halesworth Rd LEW SE13 144 E4
The Hale CHING E4 52 B3
TOTM N17 50 C6
Haley Rd HDN NW4 64 A3
Half Acre BTFD TW8 116 E6
Half Acre Ms BTFD TW8 136 E1
Half Acre Rd HNWL W7 115 K1
Half Moon Crs IS N1 5 H2
Half Moon La HNHL SE24 162 D1
Half Moon Pas WCHPL E1 13 K4
Half Moon St MYFR/PICC W1J 9 K7
Halford Cl EDGW HA8 44 D5
Halford Rd FUL/PGN SW6 119 K6
LEY E10 70 B2
RCHPK/HAM TW10 137 F6
Halfway Ct PUR RM19 131 K4
Halfway St BFN/LL DA15 167 K3
Haliburton Rd TWK TW1 136 B6
Haliday Wk IS N1 85 K4
Halifax Cl TEDD TW11 173 K2
Halifax Rd ENC/FH EN2 23 J3
GFD/PVL UB6 78 B6
Halifax St SYD SE26 163 J5
Halifield Dr BELV DA17 129 F3
Haling Gv SAND/SEL CR2 211 J5
Haling Park Gdns
SAND/SEL CR2 211 H4
Haling Park Rd SAND/SEL CR2 211 H4
Haling Rd SAND/SEL CR2 211 K4
Halkin Ar KTBR SW1X 15 G4
Halkin Ms KTBR SW1X * 15 G4
Halkin Pl KTBR SW1X 15 G4
Halkin St KTBR SW1X 15 H3
Hallam Cl CHST BR7 184 E1
Hallam Gdns PIN HA5 41 J3
Hallam Ms GTPST W1W 9 K1
Hallam Rd BARN SW13 138 E4
SEVS/STOTM N15 67 H1
Hallam St GTPST W1W 9 K1
Halland Wy NTHWD HA6 40 B2
Hall Cl EA W5 98 A4
Hall Ct TEDD TW11 174 A1
Hall Dr SYD SE26 181 K1
Halley Gdns LEW SE13 145 G5
Halley Rd FSTGT E7 89 G4
Halley St POP/IOD E14 105 G4
Hall Farm Cl STAN HA7 29 H6
Hall Farm Dr WHTN TW2 155 J2
Hallfield Est BAY/PAD W2 * 101 G5
Hallford Wy DART DA1 171 F1
Hall Gdns CHING E4 37 H6
Halliday Sq NWDGN UB2 115 J1
Halliford St IS N1 85 J5
Halliwell Rd
BRXS/STRHM SW2 162 A1
Halliwick Court Pde
NFNCH/WDSPK N12 * 47 K1
Halliwick Rd MUSWH N10 48 A4
Hall La CHING E4 37 H6
HDN NW4 45 J5
HYS/HAR UB3 133 G1
Hallmead Rd SUT SM1 209 F1
Hall Oak Wk KIL/WHAMP NW6 82 D4
Hallowell Av CROY/NA CR0 210 E2
Hallowell Cl MTCM CR4 179 F6
Hallowell Gdns THHTH CR7 180 D5
Hallowell Rd NTHWD HA6 40 C3
Hallowes Crs OXHEY WD19 26 E5
Hallowfield Wy MTCM CR4 178 C6
Hall Pl BAY/PAD W2 2 A7
Hall Place Crs BXLY DA5 149 K6
Hall Rd CHDH RM6 73 J3
DART DA1 151 J5
EHAM E6 89 K6
GPK RM2 57 K6
ISLW TW7 135 J6
MV/WKIL W9 101 G2
SRTFD E15 88 B2
WLGTN SM6 210 B6
Hallside Rd EN EN1 24 B1
Hall St FSBYE EC1V 6 B4
NFNCH/WDSPK N12 47 G1
Hallsville Rd CAN/RD E16 106 D5
Hallswelle Pde GLDGN NW11 * 64 D2
Hallswelle Rd GLDGN NW11 64 D2
The Hall BKHTH/KID SE3 145 K4
Hall Vw ELTH/MOT SE9 166 C4
Hallywell Crs EHAM E6 107 K4
Halons Rd ELTH/MOT SE9 167 F2
Halpin Pl WALW SE17 19 F7
Halsbrook Rd BKHTH/KID SE3 146 B4
Halsbury Cl STAN HA7 43 H1
Halsbury Rd SHB W12 118 E1
Halsbury Rd East NTHLT UB5 78 C2
Halsbury Rd West NTHLT UB5 78 B3
Halsend HYS/HAR UB3 * 114 A1
Halsey St CHEL SW3 14 E6
Halsham Crs BARK IG11 91 F4
Halsmere Rd CMBW SE5 142 C2
Halstead Cl CROY/NA CR0 211 J1
Halstead Gdns WCHMH N21 35 K3
Halstead Rd EN EN1 24 A5
ERITH DA8 150 B2
WAN E11 71 F2
WCHMH N21 35 K3
Halstow Rd GNWCH SE10 125 K5
WLSDN NW10 100 B2
Halsway HYS/HAR UB3 113 K1
Halton Cl FBAR/BDGN N11 47 K2
Halton Cross St IS N1 * 85 H6
Halton Rd IS N1 85 H5
Halt Pde CDALE/KGS NW9 * 63 F1
Halt Robin Rd BELV DA17 129 H4
Hambalt Rd CLAP SW4 141 H6
Hamble Cl RSLP HA4 58 C6
Hambledon WALW SE17 * 122 E6
Hambledon Ct EA W5 * 98 A6
Hambledon Gdns SNWD SE25 181 G6
Hambledon Pl DUL SE21 163 G3
Hambledon Rd
WAND/EARL SW18 159 J2
Hambledown Rd
BFN/LL DA15 * 167 J2
Hamble St FUL/PGN SW6 140 A4
Hambleton Cl WPK KT4 193 F6
Hambro Av HAYES BR2 199 K5
Hambrook Rd SNWD SE25 181 J6
Hambro Rd
STRHM/NOR SW16 179 J2
Hambrough Rd STHL UB1 114 D1
Ham Common
RCHPK/HAM TW10 156 E5
Ham Croft Cl FELT TW13 153 K5
Hamden Crs DAGE RM10 92 D1
Hamel Cl KTN/HRWW/WS HA3 61 K1
Hameway EHAM E6 108 A3
Ham Farm Rd
RCHPK/HAM TW10 156 E6
Hamfrith Rd SRTFD E15 88 D4
Ham Gate Av
RCHPK/HAM TW10 157 F6
Hamilton Av BARK/HLT IG6 72 B1
CHEAM SM3 193 H6
ED N9 36 C2
ROM RM1 57 F5
SURB KT6 191 H6
Hamilton Cl BERM/RHTH SE16 124 B2
EBAR EN4 21 J5
STJWD NW8 2 A5
TEDD TW11 174 C2
TOTM N17 50 B6
Hamilton Ct EA W5 98 B6
Hamilton Crs HSLW TW3 135 G6
PLMGR N13 35 G6
RYLN/HDSTN HA2 77 K1
Hamilton Gdns STJWD NW8 101 G2
Hamilton La HBRY N5 85 H2
Hamilton Ms MYFR/PICC W1J 15 J2
Hamilton Pde FELT TW13 * 153 K6
Hamilton Pk HBRY N5 85 H2
Hamilton Pk West HBRY N5 85 H2
Hamilton Pl MYFR/PKLN W1K 15 H1
SUN TW16 172 A3
Hamilton Rd BTFD TW8 116 E6
BXLYHN DA7 149 F3
CHSWK W4 118 B3
EA W5 98 A6
EBAR EN4 21 J5
ED N9 36 C2
EFNCH N2 47 G6
FELT TW13 153 J6
GLDGN NW11 64 B4
GPK RM2 75 K2
HRW HA1 60 E2
HYS/HAR UB3 95 F6
IL IG1 90 B2
OXHEY WD19 27 F5
SCUP DA14 168 B6
SRTFD E15 106 C2
STHL UB1 114 E1
THHTH CR7 180 E6
WALTH E17 51 G5
WHTN TW2 155 K3
WIM/MER SW19 178 A3
WLSDN NW10 81 J3
WNWD SE27 162 E6
Hamilton Road Ms
WIM/MER SW19 178 A3
Hamilton Sq
NFNCH/WDSPK N12 * 47 G2
Hamilton St DEPT SE8 124 D6
Hamilton Ter STJWD NW8 101 G2
Hamilton Wy FNCH N3 46 E2
PLMGR N13 35 H6
WLGTN SM6 210 D6
Hamlea Cl LEE/GVPK SE12 145 K6
Hamlet Cl CRW RM5 56 C3
LEW SE13 145 H5
Hamlet Gdns HMSMTH W6 118 D4
Hamlet Rd CRW RM5 56 C3
NRWD SE19 181 G3
Hamlet Sq CRICK NW2 82 C1
Hamlets Wy BOW E3 105 H3
The Hamlet CMBW SE5 142 E4
Hamlet Wy STHWK SE1 19 F3
Hamlin Crs PIN HA5 59 G2
Hamlyn Cl EDGW HA8 30 A5
Hamlyn Gdns NRWD SE19 181 F3
Hammelton Rd BMLY BR1 183 K4
Hammers La MLHL NW7 31 J6
Hammersmith Br
HMSMTH W6 118 E5
Hammersmith Bridge Rd
BARN SW13 118 E5
Hammersmith Broadway
HMSMTH W6 119 F4
Hammersmith Emb
HMSMTH W6 * 119 F6
Hammersmith F/O
HMSMTH W6 119 F5
Hammersmith Gv
HMSMTH W6 * 119 F4
Hammersmith Rd
HMSMTH W6 119 G4
Hammersmith Ter
HMSMTH W6 * 118 D5
Hammerton Cl BXLY DA5 170 B5
Hammet Cl YEAD UB4 95 H4
Hammett St TWRH EC3N 13 J5
Hammond Av MTCM CR4 179 G5
Hammond Cl BAR EN5 20 C6
GFD/PVL UB6 78 D3
HPTN TW12 173 F4
Hammond Rd EN EN1 24 D4
NWDGN UB2 114 D3
Hammonds Cl BCTR RM8 91 J1
Hammond St KTTN NW5 84 C4
Hamond Cl SAND/SEL CR2 211 H6
Hamonde Cl EDGW HA8 30 D4
Hamond Sq IS N1 7 G2
Ham Park Rd SRTFD E15 88 D5
Hampden Av BECK BR3 182 B5
Hampden Cl CAMTN NW1 4 D3
Hampden Gurney St
MBLAR W1H 8 E4
Hampden La TOTM N17 50 B4
Hampden Rd ARCH N19 66 D6
BECK BR3 182 B5
CEND/HSY/T N8 67 G1
KTN/HRWW/WS HA3 42 C4
KUT/HW KT1 175 H6
MUSWH N10 48 A3
TOTM N17 50 C4
Hampden Wy
STHGT/OAK N14 34 B5
Hampermill La OXHEY WD19 26 E3
Hampshire Cl UED N18 50 D1
Hampshire Hog La
HMSMTH W6 * 118 E4
Hampshire Rd WDGN N22 49 F3
Hampshire St KTTN NW5 * 84 D4
Hampson Wy VX/NE SW8 142 A2
Hampstead Av WFD IG8 54 A3
Hampstead Cl THMD SE28 128 C1
Hampstead Gdns
GLDGN NW11 64 E3
Hampstead Ga HAMP NW3 83 G3
Hampstead Gn HAMP NW3 83 J3
Hampstead Gv HAMP NW3 83 G2
Hampstead Hill Gdns
HAMP NW3 83 J2
Hampstead La HGT N6 65 K4
Hampstead Rd CAMTN NW1 4 A5
Hampstead Sq HAMP NW3 83 G1
Hampstead Wy GLDGN NW11 64 E3
Hampton Cl FBAR/BDGN N11 48 A1
KIL/WHAMP NW6 100 E2
RYNPK SW20 * 177 F3
Hampton Ct IS N1 85 H4
Hampton Court Av
E/WMO/HCT KT8 189 J3
Hampton Court Crs
E/WMO/HCT KT8 173 J6
Hampton Court Est
THDIT KT7 * 189 K2
Hampton Court Rd
E/WMO/HCT KT8 174 C6
HPTN TW12 173 J5
Hampton Court Wy
ESH/CLAY KT10 189 K6
Hampton La FELT TW13 154 D6
Hampton Ri
KTN/HRWW/WS HA3 62 A3
Hampton Rd CHING E4 51 H1
CROY/NA CR0 196 D3
FSTGT E7 89 F3
IL IG1 90 C2
TEDD TW11 173 J1
WAN E11 70 B5
WHTN TW2 155 J5
WPK KT4 192 D6
Hampton Rd East FELT TW13 154 E5
Hampton Rd West FELT TW13 154 D4
Hampton St WALW SE17 18 B7
Ham Ridings
RCHPK/HAM TW10 175 G1
Ham Shades Cl BFN/LL DA15 168 A5
Ham St RCHPK/HAM TW10 156 D5
The Ham BTFD TW8 136 D1
Ham Vw CROY/NA CR0 198 B3
Ham Yd SOHO/SHAV W1D * 10 C5
Hanameel St CAN/RD E16 125 K1
Hana Ms CLPT E5 86 D2
Hanbury Cl HDN NW4 46 A6
Hanbury Ct HRW HA1 * 61 F3
Hanbury Dr WAN E11 70 D4
WCHMH N21 23 F5
Hanbury Ms IS N1 6 D1
Hanbury Rd ACT W3 117 J2
TOTM N17 50 D5
Hanbury St WCHPL E1 13 K1
Hancock Rd BOW E3 106 A2
NRWD SE19 180 E2
Handa Wk IS N1 85 J4
Hand Ct HHOL WC1V 11 H2
Handcroft Rd CROY/NA CR0 196 C4
Handel Cl EDGW HA8 44 B2
Handel Pde EDGW HA8 * 44 C2
Handel Pl WLSDN NW10 81 F4
Handel St BMSBY WC1N 4 E6
Handel Wy EDGW HA8 44 C3
Handen Rd LEE/GVPK SE12 145 H6
Handforth Rd BRXN/ST SW9 142 B1
IL IG1 90 B1
Handley Gv CRICK NW2 82 B1
Handley Page Rd WLGTN SM6 211 F5
Handley Rd HOM E9 86 E5
Handowe Cl HDN NW4 63 J1
Handside Cl WPK KT4 193 G5
Handsworth Av CHING E4 52 B2
Handsworth Cl OXHEY WD19 26 E5
Handsworth Rd TOTM N17 49 K6
Handtrough Wy BARK IG11 108 B1
Hanford Cl WAND/EARL SW18 159 K3
Hangar Ruding OXHEY WD19 27 K5
Hanger Gn EA W5 98 C3
Hanger La EA W5 98 A1
Hanger La (North Circular Rd)
EA W5 98 A2
Hanger Vale La EA W5 98 B4
Hanger View Wy ACT W3 98 C5
Hankey Pl STHWK SE1 19 F3
Hankins La MLHL NW7 31 G4
Hanley Gdns FSBYPK N4 67 F5
Hanley Pl BECK BR3 182 D3
Hanley Rd FSBYPK N4 66 E5
Hanmer Wk HOLWY N7 67 F6
Hannah Cl BECK BR3 182 E6
WLSDN NW10 80 E2
Hannah Mary Wy
STHWK SE1 * 123 H4
Hannards Wy BARK/HLT IG6 55 H1
Hannay La ARCH N19 66 D4
Hannell Rd FUL/PGN SW6 139 H1
Hannen Rd WNWD SE27 * 162 C5
Hannibal Rd
STWL/WRAY TW19 152 B2
WCHPL E1 104 E4
Hannibal Wy CROY/NA CR0 211 F3
Hannington Rd CLAP SW4 141 G4
Hanno Cl WLGTN SM6 210 D5
Hanover Av CAN/RD E16 125 K1
FELT TW13 153 K3
Hanover Cir HYS/HAR UB3 94 A5
Hanover Cl CHEAM SM3 208 C2
RCH/KEW TW9 137 H1
Hanover Dr CHST BR7 167 H6
Hanover Gdns BARK/HLT IG6 54 C3
LBTH SE11 122 B6
Hanover Ga STJWD NW8 2 D5
Hanover Pk PECK SE15 143 H2
Hanover Pl COVGDN WC2E 11 F4
Hanover Rd SEVS/STOTM N15 68 B1
WIM/MER SW19 178 B3
WLSDN NW10 82 A5
Hanover Sq CONDST W1S 9 K4
Hanover Steps BAY/PAD W2 * 8 D4
Hanover St CONDST W1S 9 K4
CROY/NA CR0 211 H1
Hanover Ter CAMTN NW1 2 E5
Hanover Terrace Ms
CAMTN NW1 2 D5
Hanover Wy BXLYHS DA6 148 E4
Hanover Yd IS N1 * 6 B2
Hansard Ms WKENS W14 119 G2
Hansart Wy ENC/FH EN2 23 G2
Hans Crs KTBR SW1X 14 E4
Hanselin Cl STAN HA7 43 F1
Hansen Dr WCHMH N21 23 F6
Hanshaw Dr EDGW HA8 45 F4
Hansler Gv E/WMO/HCT KT8 189 J2
Hansler Rd EDUL SE22 143 G6
Hansol Rd BXLYHS DA6 149 F6
Hansom Ter BMLY BR1 * 184 A4
Hanson Cl BAL SW12 161 G2
BECK BR3 * 182 E2
MORT/ESHN SW14 137 K4
WDR/YW UB7 112 C3
Hanson Gdns STHL UB1 114 D2
Hanson St GTPST W1W 10 A1
Hans Pl KTBR SW1X 14 E4
Hans Rd CHEL SW3 14 E4
Hans St KTBR SW1X 15 F5
Hanway Pl FITZ W1T 10 C3
Hanway Rd HNWL W7 96 D5
Hanway St FITZ W1T 10 C3
Hanworth Rd FELT TW13 154 A3
HPTN TW12 154 E6
HPTN TW12 173 F1
HSLW TW3 135 G4
HSLWW TW4 154 E2
Hanworth Ter HSLW TW3 135 G5
Hapgood Cl GFD/PVL UB6 78 D3
Harben Pde HAMP NW3 * 83 H5
Harben Rd KIL/WHAMP NW6 83 G5
Harberson Rd BAL SW12 161 G3
SRTFD E15 88 D6
Harberton Rd ARCH N19 66 C5
Harbet Rd BAY/PAD W2 8 B2
UED N18 51 F1
Harbex Cl BXLY DA5 169 J2
Harbinger Rd POP/IOD E14 124 E4
Harbledown Pl
STMC/STPC BR5 202 D1
Harbledown Rd
FUL/PGN SW6 139 K2
Harbord Cl CMBW SE5 142 E3
Harbord St FUL/PGN SW6 139 G2
Harborne Cl OXHEY WD19 41 G1
Harborough Av BFN/LL DA15 167 K2
Harborough Rd
STRHM/NOR SW16 162 A6
Harbour Av WBPTN SW10 140 B2
Harbour Cl MTCM CR4 179 F4
Harbourer Rd BARK/HLT IG6 55 H1
Harbour Exchange Sq
POP/IOD E14 124 E2
Harbour Rd CMBW SE5 142 D4
Harbour Yd WBPTN SW10 * 140 B2
Harbridge Av PUT/ROE SW15 158 C2
Harbury Rd CAR SM5 209 J6
Harbut Rd BTSEA SW11 140 C5

Harcastle Cl YEAD UB4 95 J3
Harcombe Rd
STNW/STAM N16 86 A1
Harcourt Av BFN/LL DA15 168 D1
EDGW HA8 30 E5
MNPK E12 89 K2
WLGTN SM6 210 B2
Harcourt Blds EMB EC4Y * 11 J5
Harcourt Cl ISLW TW7 136 B4
Harcourt Fld WLGTN SM6 210 B2
Harcourt Ms GPK RM2 75 H2
Harcourt Rd BROCKY SE4 144 C5
BXLYHS DA6 149 F5
SRTFD E15 106 D1
THHTH CR7 196 A3
WDGN N22 48 D4
WIM/MER SW19 177 K3
WLGTN SM6 210 B2
Harcourt St MBLAR W1H 8 D2
Harcourt Ter WBPTN SW10 120 A5
Hardcastle Cl CROY/NA CR0 197 H3
Hardcourts Cl WWKM BR4 213 K2
Hardel Wk BRXS/STRHM SW2 162 B2
Hardens Manorway
WOOL/PLUM SE18 126 C3
Harders Rd PECK SE15 143 J3
Hardess St HNHL SE24 142 D4
Hardie Cl WLSDN NW10 81 F3
Hardie Rd DAGE RM10 92 E1
Harding Cl CROY/NA CR0 212 B1
KUTN/CMB KT2 175 G4
WALW SE17 122 D6
Hardinge Crs
WOOL/PLUM SE18 127 H3
Hardinge Rd UED N18 50 A1
WLSDN NW10 82 A6
Hardinge St WCHPL E1 104 E5
WOOL/PLUM SE18 127 G3
Harding Rd BXLYHN DA7 149 G3
Hardings La PGE/AN SE20 182 A2
Hardman Rd CHARL SE7 126 A5
KUTN/CMB KT2 175 F5
Hardres Ter STMC/STPC BR5 * 202 E6
Hardwick Cl STAN HA7 43 J1
Hardwicke Av HEST TW5 * 135 F2
Hardwicke Ms FSBYW WC1X * 5 H5
Hardwicke Rd CHSWK W4 117 K4
PLMGR N13 48 E1
RCHPK/HAM TW10 156 D6
Hardwicke St BARK IG11 90 C6
Hardwick Gn WEA W13 97 H4
Hardwick Pl
STRHM/NOR SW16 179 H3
Hardwick's Sq
WAND/EARL SW18 139 K6
Hardwick St CLKNW EC1R 5 K5
Hardwidge St STHWK SE1 19 G2
Hardy Av CAN/RD E16 125 K1
DART DA1 171 F2
RSLP HA4 77 F3
Hardy Cl BAR EN5 20 C6
BERM/RHTH SE16 124 A2
PIN HA5 59 H4
Hardy Cots GNWCH SE10 * 125 G6
Hardy Gv DART DA1 151 K5
Hardy Pas WDGN N22 49 F4
Hardy Rd BKHTH/KID SE3 125 J6
CHING E4 51 H2
WIM/MER SW19 178 A3
Hardys Ms E/WMO/HCT KT8 189 K1
Hardy Wy ENC/FH EN2 23 G2
Harebell Dr EHAM E6 108 A4
Hare & Billet Rd
BKHTH/KID SE3 145 G2
Hare Ct EMB EC4Y * 11 J4
Harecourt Rd IS N1 85 J4
Haredale Rd HNHL SE24 142 D5
Haredon Cl FSTH SE23 163 K2
Harefield ESH/CLAY KT10 204 E1
Harefield Av BELMT SM2 208 C6
Harefield Cl ENC/FH EN2 23 G2
Harefield Ms BROCKY SE4 144 C4
Harefield Rd BROCKY SE4 144 C4
CEND/HSY/T N8 66 D2
SCUP DA14 168 E4
STRHM/NOR SW16 180 A3
Hare Hall La GPK RM2 75 K1
Hare La ESH/CLAY KT10 204 D4
Hare Marsh BETH E2 104 C3
Harepit Cl SAND/SEL CR2 211 H5
Hare Rw BETH E2 104 D1
Haresfield Rd DAGE RM10 92 C4
Hare St WOOL/PLUM SE18 127 F3
Hare Wk IS N1 7 H3
Harewood Av CAMTN NW1 2 D7
NTHLT UB5 77 J5
STJWD NW8 2 D6
Harewood Cl NTHLT UB5 77 K5
Harewood Dr CLAY IG5 53 K5
Harewood Pl CONDST W1S 9 K4
Harewood Rd ISLW TW7 136 A1
OXHEY WD19 27 F4
SAND/SEL CR2 212 A4
WIM/MER SW19 178 D2
Harewood Rw CAMTN NW1 8 D1
Harewood Ter NWDGN UB2 114 E4
Harfield Gdns CMBW SE5 * 143 F4
Harfield Rd SUN TW16 172 C5
Harford Cl CHING E4 37 K2
Harford Rd CHING E4 37 K2
Harford St WCHPL E1 105 G3
Harford Wk EFNCH N2 65 H1
Harfst Wy SWLY BR8 187 K4
Harglaze Ter
CDALE/KGS NW9 * 45 G6
Hargood Cl
KTN/HRWW/WS HA3 62 A3
Hargood Rd BKHTH/KID SE3 146 B2
Hargrave Pk ARCH N19 66 C6
Hargrave Pl KTTN NW5 84 D3
Hargrave Rd ARCH N19 66 C6
Hargwyne St BRXN/ST SW9 142 A4
Haringey Pk CEND/HSY/T N8 66 E3
Haringey Rd CEND/HSY/T N8 66 E1
Harington Ter UED N18 * 35 K6
Harkett Cl
KTN/HRWW/WS HA3 43 F5
Harland Av BFN/LL DA15 167 J5
CROY/NA CR0 212 B1
Harland Cl WIM/MER SW19 178 A6
Harland Rd LEE/GVPK SE12 165 K3
Harlands Gv ORP BR6 216 B2
Harlech Gdns HEST TW5 114 B6
PIN HA5 59 H4
Harlech Rd STHGT/OAK N14 34 E5
Harlequin Av BTFD TW8 116 B6
Harlequin Cl ISLW TW7 135 K6
YEAD UB4 95 H4
Harlequin Ct EA W5 * 97 J6
Harlequin Rd TEDD TW11 * 174 C3
Harlescott Rd PECK SE15 144 A5
Harlesden Gdns WLSDN NW10 81 H6
Harlesden Rd WLSDN NW10 81 J6
Harley Cl ALP/SUD HA0 * 79 K4
Harley Crs HRW HA1 60 D1
Harleyford BMLY BR1 184 B4
Harleyford Rd LBTH SE11 122 A6
Harleyford St LBTH SE11 122 B6
Harley Gdns ORP BR6 216 E2
WBPTN SW10 120 B5
Harley Gv BOW E3 105 H2
Harley Pl CAVSQ/HST W1G 9 J2
Harley Rd HAMP NW3 83 H5
HRW HA1 60 D1
WLSDN NW10 99 G1
Harley St CAVSQ/HST W1G 3 J7
Harley Vls WLSDN NW10 * 99 G1
Harlinger St
WOOL/PLUM SE18 126 D3
Harlington Cl HYS/HAR UB3 133 F1
Harlington Rd BXLYHN DA7 149 F4
Harlington Rd East
EBED/NFELT TW14 154 A2
Harlington Rd West
EBED/NFELT TW14 154 A1
Harlow Gdns CRW RM5 56 E2
Harlow Rd PLMGR N13 35 K5
RAIN RM13 93 H6
Harlyn Dr PIN HA5 41 F6
Harman Av WFD IG8 52 D3
Harman Cl CHING E4 38 B6
CRICK NW2 82 C1
STHWK SE1 * 123 H5
Harman Dr BFN/LL DA15 168 A1
CRICK NW2 82 C1
Harman Ri IL IG1 90 E2
Harman Rd EN EN1 24 B6
Harmondsworth La
WDR/YW UB7 112 B6
Harmondsworth Rd
WDR/YW UB7 112 B3
Harmony Cl GLDGN NW11 64 C2
WLGTN SM6 210 E6
Harmony Pl STHWK SE1 123 G5
Harmony Wy BMLY BR1 183 K5
HDN NW4 64 A1
Harmood Gv CAMTN NW1 84 B5
Harmood St CAMTN NW1 84 B4
Harmsworth Ms STHWK SE1 17 K5
Harmsworth St WALW SE17 122 C5
Harmsworth Wy
TRDG/WHET N20 32 D3
Harness Rd THMD SE28 128 B2
Harold Av BELV DA17 129 G5
HYS/HAR UB3 113 J3
Harold Rd CEND/HSY/T N8 67 F2
CHING E4 38 A5
NRWD SE19 180 E3
PLSTW E13 89 F6
RDART DA2 171 J6
SEVS/STOTM N15 68 B2
SUT SM1 209 H2
SWFD E18 52 E4
WAN E11 70 C5
WLSDN NW10 99 F2
Haroldstone Rd WALTH E17 69 F2
Harpenden Rd MNPK E12 71 G6
WNWD SE27 162 C4
Harper Rd EHAM E6 107 K5
STHWK SE1 18 D4
Harpers Yd ISLW TW7 * 136 A3
Harp Island Cl WLSDN NW10 63 F6
Harp La MON EC3R 13 G6
Harpley Sq WCHPL E1 104 E3
Harpour Rd BARK IG11 90 C4
Harp Rd HNWL W7 97 F3
Harpsden St BTSEA SW11 141 F2
Harpur Ms BMSBY WC1N 11 G1
Harpur St BMSBY WC1N 11 G1
Harraden Rd BKHTH/KID SE3 146 B2
Harrier Cl HCH RM12 93 K4
Harrier Ms THMD SE28 127 J2
Harrier Rd CDALE/KGS NW9 45 G5
Harriers Cl EA W5 98 A6
Harrier Wy EHAM E6 107 K4
Harries Rd YEAD UB4 95 G3
Harriet Cl HACK E8 86 C6
Harriet Gdns CROY/NA CR0 197 H6
Harriet Ms WELL DA16 148 C3
Harriet St KTBR SW1X 15 F3
Harriet Tubman Cl
BRXS/STRHM SW2 162 B2
Harriet Wk KTBR SW1X 15 F3
Harriet Wy BUSH WD23 28 D2
Harringay Gdns
CEND/HSY/T N8 67 H1
Harringay Rd
SEVS/STOTM N15 67 H2
Harrington Cl CROY/NA CR0 195 K6
WLSDN NW10 81 F1
Harrington Ct NKENS W10 * 100 D2
Harrington Gdns SKENS SW7 120 A4
Harrington Hl CLPT E5 68 D5
Harrington Rd SKENS SW7 14 A6
SNWD SE25 197 H1
WAN E11 70 C5
Harrington Sq CAMTN NW1 4 A2
Harrington St CAMTN NW1 4 A3
Harrington Wy
WOOL/PLUM SE18 126 C3
Harriott Cl GNWCH SE10 125 J4
Harris Cl ENC/FH EN2 23 H2
HSLW TW3 135 F2
Harrison Cl NTHWD HA6 40 A2
TRDG/WHET N20 33 J3
Harrison Dr BMLY BR1 201 G1
Harrison Rd DAGE RM10 92 D4
WLSDN NW10 81 F6
Harrison's Ri CROY/NA CR0 211 H1
Harrison St STPAN WC1H 5 F5
Harrisons Whf PUR RM19 131 K5
Harris Rd BXLYHN DA7 149 F2
DAGW RM9 92 B3
Harris St CMBW SE5 142 E1
WALTH E17 69 H4
Harrods Gn EDGW HA8 * 44 C1
Harrogate Rd OXHEY WD19 27 G5
Harrold Rd BCTR RM8 91 H3
Harrow Av EN EN1 36 B1
Harroway Rd BTSEA SW11 140 C3
Harrowby St MBLAR W1H 8 D3
Harrow Cl CHSGTN KT9 205 K5
Harrow Crs HARH RM3 57 K3
Harrowdene Cl ALP/SUD HA0 79 K2
Harrowdene Gdns
TEDD TW11 174 B3
Harrowdene Rd ALP/SUD HA0 79 K2
Harrow Dr ED N9 36 B3
Harrowes Meade EDGW HA8 30 C5
Harrow Fields Gdns HRW HA1 78 E1
Harrow Gdns ORP BR6 217 H2
Harrowgate Rd HOM E9 87 G4
Harrow Gn WAN E11 88 C1
Harrow La POP/IOD E14 106 A6
Harrow Manor Wy ABYW SE2 128 D3
Harrow Pk HRW HA1 60 E6
Harrow Pl WCHPL E1 13 H3
Harrow Rd ALP/SUD HA0 79 G2
CAR SM5 209 J4
EBED/NFELT TW14 152 D3
IL IG1 90 C2
MV/WKIL W9 100 E3
WAN E11 88 D1
WBLY HA9 80 C3
WLSDN NW10 99 K2
Harrow Rd F/O BAY/PAD W2 8 B2
Harrow St CAMTN NW1 * 8 D1
Harrow Vw HGDN/ICK UB10 94 A2
HRW HA1 60 D1
HYS/HAR UB3 94 D3
RYLN/HDSTN HA2 42 D6
Harrow View Rd EA W5 97 H3
Harrow Wy OXHEY WD19 27 J5
Harrow Weald Pk
KTN/HRWW/WS HA3 42 D2
Harry Cl THHTH CR7 196 D3
Harry Zeital Wy CLPT E5 68 E6
Harston Dr PEND EN3 25 J1
Hartcliff Cl HNWL W7 * 116 A2
Hart Cl CROY/NA CR0 211 H1
Hart Crs CHIG IG7 55 F1
Hart Dyke Rd STMC/STPC BR5 202 D6
Harte Rd HSLW TW3 134 E3
Hartfield Av NTHLT UB5 95 F1
Hartfield Crs WIM/MER SW19 177 J3
WWKM BR4 214 E1
Hartfield Gv PGE/AN SE20 181 J4
Hartfield Rd CHSGTN KT9 205 K3
WIM/MER SW19 177 J2
WWKM BR4 214 E2
Hartfield Ter BOW E3 105 J1
Hartford Av
KTN/HRWW/WS HA3 43 G6
Hartford Rd BXLY DA5 169 H1
HOR/WEW KT19 206 C4
Hart Gv EA W5 117 H1
STHL UB1 96 A4
Hartham Cl HOLWY N7 84 E3
ISLW TW7 136 B2
Hartham Rd HOLWY N7 84 E3
ISLW TW7 136 A2
TOTM N17 50 B5
Harting Rd ELTH/MOT SE9 166 D6
Hartington Cl HRW HA1 78 E2
ORP BR6 216 C3
Hartington Rd CAN/RD E16 107 F5
CHSWK W4 137 J1
NWDGN UB2 * 114 D3
TWK TW1 156 C2
VX/NE SW8 141 K2
WALTH E17 69 G3
WEA W13 97 H6
Hartismere Rd FUL/PGN SW6 139 J1
Hartlake Rd HOM E9 87 F4
Hartland Cl EDGW HA8 30 C4
WCHMH N21 35 J1
Hartland Dr EDGW HA8 30 C4
RSLP HA4 77 F1
Hartland Rd CAMTN NW1 * 84 B5
FBAR/BDGN N11 47 K1
HCH RM12 75 J6
HPTN TW12 155 G6
ISLW TW7 136 B4
KIL/WHAMP NW6 100 D1
MRDN SM4 193 K4
SRTFD E15 88 D5
Hartland Road Arches
CAMTN NW1 * 84 A5
Hartlands Cl BXLY DA5 169 G1
The Hartlands HEST TW5 114 A6
Hartland Wy CROY/NA CR0 198 B6
MRDN SM4 193 J4
Hartley Av EHAM E6 89 J6
MLHL NW7 45 H1
Hartley Cl BMLY BR1 184 E5
MLHL NW7 45 H1
Hartley Rd CROY/NA CR0 196 D4
WAN E11 70 D5
WELL DA16 148 D1
Hartley St BETH E2 104 E2
Hartmann Rd CAN/RD E16 126 C1
Hartnoll St HOLWY N7 85 F3
Harton Cl BMLY BR1 184 C4
Harton Rd ED N9 36 D4
Harton St DEPT SE8 144 D2
Hartsbourne Av BUSH WD23 28 C4
Hartsbourne Cl BUSH WD23 28 D4
Hartsbourne Rd BUSH WD23 28 D4
Hartscroft CROY/NA CR0 213 G6
Harts Gv WFD IG8 52 E1
Hartshorn Gdns EHAM E6 108 A3
Harts La BARK IG11 90 B5
Hart's La NWCR SE14 144 B1
Hartslock Dr ABYW SE2 128 E2
Hartsmead Rd ELTH/MOT SE9 166 E4
Hart Sq MRDN SM4 * 194 A2
Hart St MON EC3R 13 H5
Hartsway PEND EN3 24 D5
Hartswood Gdns SHB W12 * 118 C3
Hartswood Gn BUSH WD23 28 D4
Hartswood Rd SHB W12 118 C2
Hartsworth Cl PLSTW E13 106 D1
Hartville Rd
WOOL/PLUM SE18 127 K4
Hartwell Cl BRXS/STRHM SW2 162 A3
Hartwell Dr CHING E4 52 A2
Hartwell St HACK E8 86 B4
Harvard Hl CHSWK W4 117 J5
Harvard Rd CHSWK W4 117 J5
ISLW TW7 135 K2
LEW SE13 145 F6
Harvel Cl CHST BR7 186 B6
Harvel Crs ABYW SE2 128 E5
Harvest Bank Rd WWKM BR4 214 E1
Harvesters Cl ISLW TW7 135 J6
Harvest La LOU IG10 39 H2
THDIT KT7 190 B3
Harvest Rd FELT TW13 153 K6
Harvest Wy SWLY BR8 203 K4
Harvey Dr HPTN TW12 173 G4
Harvey Gdns CHARL SE7 126 B5
Harvey Rd CEND/HSY/T N8 67 F2
CMBW SE5 142 E2
HSLWW TW4 154 E2
IL IG1 90 B3
NTHLT UB5 77 G5
WAN E11 70 C5
Harvey's La ROMW/RG RM7 75 F6
Harvey St IS N1 7 F1
Harvill Rd SCUP DA14 186 E1
Harvington Wk HACK E8 * 86 C5
Harvist Rd KIL/WHAMP NW6 100 C1
Harwell Cl RSLP HA4 58 B5
Harwood Av BMLY BR1 184 A5
MTCM CR4 178 D6
Harwood Cl ALP/SUD HA0 79 K2
NFNCH/WDSPK N12 47 J2
Harwood Ms FUL/PGN SW6 * 140 A1
Harwood Rd FUL/PGN SW6 139 K1
Harwood Ter FUL/PGN SW6 140 A2
Hascombe Ter CMBW SE5 * 142 E3
Haselbury Rd UED N18 36 A6
Haseley End FSTH SE23 * 163 K2
Haselrigge Rd CLAP SW4 141 J5
Haseltine Rd SYD SE26 164 C6
Haselwood Dr ENC/FH EN2 23 H5
Haskard Rd DAGW RM9 91 K2
Hasker St CHEL SW3 14 D6
Haslam Av CHEAM SM3 193 H5
Haslam Cl HGDN/ICK UB10 58 A6
IS N1 85 G5
Haslam St PECK SE15 143 G2
Haslemere Av EBAR EN4 33 K3
HDN NW4 64 B3
HEST TW5 134 B3
HNWL W7 116 B3
MTCM CR4 178 C5
WAND/EARL SW18 160 A4
Haslemere Cl HPTN TW12 172 E1
WLGTN SM6 210 E3
Haslemere Gdns FNCH N3 46 D6
Haslemere Heathrow Est
HSLWW TW4 * 134 A3
Haslemere Rd BXLYHN DA7 149 G3
CEND/HSY/T N8 66 E4
GDMY/SEVK IG3 73 F6
THHTH CR7 196 C2
WCHMH N21 35 H4
Hasler Cl THMD SE28 109 H6
Hasluck Gdns BAR EN5 33 G1
Hassard St BETH E2 7 K3
Hassendean Rd
BKHTH/KID SE3 126 A6
Hassett Rd HOM E9 87 F4
Hassocks Cl SYD SE26 163 J5
Hassocks Rd
STRHM/NOR SW16 179 J4
Hassock Wd HAYES BR2 215 H2
Hassop Rd CRICK NW2 82 B2
Hasted Rd CHARL SE7 126 C5
Hastings Av BARK/HLT IG6 72 C1
Hastings Cl ALP/SUD HA0 79 J2
BAR EN5 21 G5
PECK SE15 * 143 H1
Hastings Dr SURB KT6 190 D3
Hastings Pl CROY/NA CR0 197 G5
Hastings Rd CROY/NA CR0 197 G5
FBAR/BDGN N11 48 C1
GPK RM2 75 K2
HAYES BR2 200 D5
TOTM N17 * 49 K6
WEA W13 97 H6
Hastings St STPAN WC1H 4 E5
Hastings Ter
SEVS/STOTM N15 * 67 J2
Hastings St WOOL/PLUM SE18 127 H3
Hastoe Cl YEAD UB4 95 J3
Hatcham Park Ms NWCR SE14 144 A2
Hatcham Park Rd NWCR SE14 144 A2
Hatcham Rd PECK SE15 123 K6
Hatchard Rd ARCH N19 66 D6
Hatchcroft HDN NW4 45 K6
Hatchers Ms STHWK SE1 19 H3
Hatchett Rd
EBED/NFELT TW14 153 F3
Hatch Gv CHDH RM6 74 A1
Hatch La CHING E4 38 B6
WDR/YW UB7 132 A1
Hatch Pl KUTN/CMB KT2 175 G1
Hatch Rd STRHM/NOR SW16 179 K5
Hatch Side CHIG IG7 54 A1
The Hatch PEND EN3 25 F2
Hatchwoods WFD IG8 38 D6
Hatcliffe Cl BKHTH/KID SE3 145 J4
Hatcliffe St GNWCH SE10 125 J5
Hatfield Cl BARK/HLT IG6 54 B6
BELMT SM2 208 E6
MTCM CR4 * 194 C1
Hatfield Ct BKHTH/KID SE3 * 145 K1
Hatfield Rd CHSWK W4 118 A2
HNWL W7 116 B1
SRTFD E15 88 C3
Hatfields STHWK SE1 11 K7
Hathaway Cl CHIG IG7 54 B2
HAYES BR2 200 E5
RSLP HA4 76 D2
STAN HA7 43 G1
Hathaway Crs MNPK E12 89 K4
Hathaway Gdns CHDH RM6 73 K2
WEA W13 97 F4
Hathaway Rd CROY/NA CR0 196 C4
Hatherleigh Cl CHSGTN KT9 205 K3
MLHL NW7 46 B3
MRDN SM4 193 K1
Hatherleigh Rd RSLP HA4 58 E6
Hatherley Crs BFN/LL DA15 168 B4
Hatherley Gdns
CEND/HSY/T N8 66 E3
EHAM E6 107 H2
Hatherley Gv BAY/PAD W2 101 F5
Hatherley Ms WALTH E17 69 J1
Hatherley Rd RCH/KEW TW9 137 G2
SCUP DA14 168 B5
WALTH E17 69 H1
Hatherley St WEST SW1P 16 B7
Hathern Gdns ELTH/MOT SE9 167 F6
Hatherop Rd HPTN TW12 172 E3
Hathorne Cl PECK SE15 143 J3
Hathorne Ter ARCH N19 * 66 D5
Hathway St PECK SE15 143 K3
Hatley Av BARK/HLT IG6 72 C1
Hatley Cl FBAR/BDGN N11 47 K1
Hatley Rd FSBYPK N4 67 F6
Hat & Mitre Ct FARR EC1M 6 B7
Hatteraick St
BERM/RHTH SE16 123 K2
Hattersfield Cl BELV DA17 129 G4
Hatters La WATW WD18 26 B1
Hatton Cl WOOL/PLUM SE18 147 J1
Hatton Cross Est
HTHAIR TW6 * 133 J5
Hatton Gdn HCIRC EC1N 11 K1
Hatton Gdns MTCM CR4 194 E2
Hatton Gn EBED/NFELT TW14 133 K5
Hatton Gv WDR/YW UB7 * 112 A2
Hatton Pl HCIRC EC1N 5 K7
Hatton Rd CROY/NA CR0 196 B5
EBED/NFELT TW14 153 F2
HTHAIR TW6 133 J5
Hatton Rd North HTHAIR TW6 133 G2
Hatton Rw STJWD NW8 * 2 B7
Hatton St STJWD NW8 2 B7
Hatton Wall HCIRC EC1N 11 J1
Haunch of Venison Yd
OXSTW W1C * 9 J4
Havana Cl ROM RM1 75 G2
Havana Rd WIM/MER SW19 159 K4
Havannah St POP/IOD E14 124 D2
Havant Rd WALTH E17 52 A6
Havelock Cl SHB W12 * 99 K6
Havelock Pl HRW HA1 60 E3
Havelock Rd BELV DA17 * 129 G4
CROY/NA CR0 197 G6
DART DA1 170 E2
HAYES BR2 200 B1
KTN/HRWW/WS HA3 42 E6
NWDGN UB2 114 D3
TOTM N17 50 C5
WIM/MER SW19 178 B1
Havelock St IL IG1 72 B6
IS N1 84 E6
Havelock Ter VX/NE SW8 141 G1
Havelock Wk FSTH SE23 163 K3
Haven Cl ELTH/MOT SE9 166 E5
ESH/CLAY KT10 189 K6
SCUP DA14 186 D2
WIM/MER SW19 159 G5
YEAD UB4 94 C4
Haven Ct BRYLDS KT5 * 191 G3
Haven Gn EA W5 97 K5
Havenhurst Ri ENC/FH EN2 23 G3
Haven La EA W5 98 A5
Haven Rd ASHF TW15 152 E6
Havens Ms BOW E3 105 H4
Haven St CAMTN NW1 84 B5
Havenswood Ct
KUTN/CMB KT2 175 J2
The Haven RCH/KEW TW9 137 H4
Havenwood WBLY HA9 80 D1
Haverfield Est BTFD TW8 117 F6
Haverfield Gdns
RCH/KEW TW9 137 H1
Haverfield Rd BOW E3 105 G2
Haverford Wy EDGW HA8 44 B4
Havergal Vls
SEVS/STOTM N15 * 67 H1
Haverhill Rd BAL SW12 161 H3
CHING E4 38 A3
Havering Dr ROM RM1 75 G1
Havering Gdns CHDH RM6 73 J2
Havering Rd ROM RM1 57 F5
Havering St WCHPL E1 105 F5
Havering Wy BARK IG11 109 H2
Haversham Cl TWK TW1 156 E2
Haversham Pl HGT N6 65 K6
Haverstock Hl HAMP NW3 83 J4
Haverstock Pl FSBYE EC1V 5 K3
Haverstock Rd KTTN NW5 84 A3
Haverstock St IS N1 6 B3
Haverthwaite Rd ORP BR6 216 D1
Havil St CMBW SE5 143 F2
Havisham Pl NRWD SE19 180 C2
Hawarden Gv HNHL SE24 162 D2
Hawarden Hl CRICK NW2 81 J1
Hawarden Rd WALTH E17 69 F1
Hawbridge Rd WAN E11 70 B5
Hawes Cl NTHWD HA6 40 D3
Hawes La WWKM BR4 199 F5
Hawes Rd BMLY BR1 184 A4
UED N18 50 D2
Hawes St IS N1 85 H5
Hawfield Bank ORP BR6 217 J1
Hawgood St BOW E3 105 J4
Hawkdene CHING E4 37 K1
Hawke Park Rd WDGN N22 49 H6
Hawke Pl BERM/RHTH SE16 * 124 A2
Hawke Rd NRWD SE19 180 E2
Hawker Pl WALTH E17 52 A5
Hawker Rd CROY/NA CR0 211 F4
Hawkesbury Rd
PUT/ROE SW15 138 E6
Hawkesfield Rd FSTH SE23 164 B4
Hawkesley Cl TWK TW1 156 B6
Hawkes Rd EBED/NFELT TW14 153 K2
MTCM CR4 178 D4
Hawkesworth Cl NTHWD HA6 40 C3
Hawkhurst Gdns CRW RM5 57 F2
Hawkhurst Rd
STRHM/NOR SW16 179 J3
Hawkhurst Wy NWMAL KT3 192 A2

WWKM BR4 198 E6
Hawkins Cl EDGW HA8 45 F1
HRW HA1 60 D4
Hawkins Rd TEDD TW11 174 C2
WLSDN NW10 81 G5
Hawkins Ter CHARL SE7 126 D5
Hawkins Wy CAT SE6 182 D1
Hawkley Gdns WNWD SE27 162 C4
Hawkridge Cl CHDH RM6 73 J3
Hawksbrook La BECK BR3 198 E3
Hawkshaw Cl
BRXS/STRHM SW2 161 K2
Hawkshead Cl BMLY BR1 183 H3
Hawkshead Rd CHSWK W4 118 B3
WLSDN NW10 * 81 H5
Hawkshill Cl ESH/CLAY KT10 204 A4
Hawkshill Pl ESH/CLAY KT10 * 204 A4
Hawkslade Rd PECK SE15 144 A6
Hawksley Rd
STNW/STAM N16 85 K1
Hawks Ms GNWCH SE10 * 145 F1
Hawksmoor Cl EHAM E6 107 J5
WOOL/PLUM SE18 127 K5
Hawksmoor Ms WCHPL E1 104 D6
Hawksmoor St HMSMTH W6 119 G6
Hawksmouth CHING E4 37 K2
Hawks Rd KUT/HW KT1 175 G5
Hawkstone Est
BERM/RHTH SE16 123 K4
Hawkstone Rd
BERM/RHTH SE16 123 K4
Hawkwell Wk IS N1 * 85 J6
Hawkwood Crs CHING E4 37 K1
Hawkwood La CHST BR7 185 H4
Hawkwood Mt CLPT E5 68 D5
Hawlands Dr PIN HA5 59 J4
Hawley Cl HPTN TW12 172 E2
Hawley Crs CAMTN NW1 84 B5
Hawley Ms CAMTN NW1 84 B5
Hawley Rd CAMTN NW1 84 B5
DART DA1 171 H4
UED N18 51 F1
Hawley Ter RDART DA2 * 171 K6
Hawstead Rd CAT SE6 164 E1
Hawsted BKHH IG9 39 F2
Hawthorn Av PLMGR N13 48 E1
RAIN RM13 111 K3
THHTH CR7 180 C4
Hawthorn Centre HRW HA1 61 F1
Hawthorn Cl HEST TW5 134 A1
HPTN TW12 173 F1
STMC/STPC BR5 201 J3
Hawthorn Crs TOOT SW17 179 F1
Hawthornden Cl
NFNCH/WDSPK N12 47 J2
Hawthorndene Cl HAYES BR2 199 J6
Hawthorndene Rd
HAYES BR2 199 K6
Hawthorn Dr
RYLN/HDSTN HA2 60 A3
WWKM BR4 214 C2
Hawthorne Av BOW E3 87 H6
CAR SM5 210 A5
KTN/HRWW/WS HA3 61 G3
MTCM CR4 178 C5
RSLP HA4 59 F3
Hawthorne Cl BMLY BR1 184 E6
IS N1 86 A4
Hawthorne Ct
STWL/WRAY TW19 * 152 A2
Hawthorne Crs WDR/YW UB7 112 C2
Hawthorne Gv
CDALE/KGS NW9 62 E4
Hawthorne Rd BMLY BR1 184 E6
UED N18 50 B2
WALTH E17 51 J6
Hawthorne Wy ED N9 36 B4
STWL/WRAY TW19 152 A2
Hawthorn Farm Av
NTHLT UB5 77 J6
Hawthorn Gdns EA W5 116 E3
Hawthorn Gv ENC/FH EN2 23 K1
PGE/AN SE20 181 J4
Hawthorn Hatch BTFD TW8 136 C1
Hawthorn Ms MLHL NW7 46 C4
Hawthorn Pl ERITH DA8 129 K5
HYS/HAR UB3 * 94 D6
Hawthorn Rd BTFD TW8 136 C1
BXLYHS DA6 * 149 G5
CEND/HSY/T N8 48 D6
DART DA1 171 G3
FELT TW13 153 K3
SUT SM1 209 H3
WFD IG8 39 G6
WLGTN SM6 210 B5
WLSDN NW10 81 J5
Hawthorns WFD IG8 38 E5
The Hawthorns EW KT17 207 H4
Hawthorn Ter BFN/LL DA15 168 A1
Hawthorn Wk NKENS W10 100 C3
Hawtrey Av NTHLT UB5 95 H1
Hawtrey Dr RSLP HA4 58 E4
Hawtrey Rd HAMP NW3 83 J5
Haxted Rd BMLY BR1 184 A4
Hayburn Wy HCH RM12 75 H5
Hay Cl SRTFD E15 88 C5
Haycroft Gdns WLSDN NW10 81 J6
Haycroft Rd
BRXS/STRHM SW2 141 K6
SURB KT6 190 E6
Hay Currie St POP/IOD E14 105 K5
Hayday Rd CAN/RD E16 106 E3
Hayden Dell BUSH WD23 27 K1
Haydens Cl STMC/STPC BR5 202 D4
Hayden's Pl NTGHL W11 100 D5
Hayden Wy CRW RM5 56 E5
Haydock Av NTHLT UB5 78 A4
Haydock Gn NTHLT UB5 78 A4
Haydon Cl CDALE/KGS NW9 62 E1
EN EN1 36 A1
HARH RM3 57 K3
Haydon Dell Farm
BUSH WD23 * 27 K2
Haydon Dr PIN HA5 58 E1
Haydon Park Pas
WIM/MER SW19 178 A1
Haydon Park Rd
WIM/MER SW19 177 K1
Haydon Rd BCTR RM8 73 J6
OXHEY WD19 27 J1
Haydon's Rd WIM/MER SW19 178 A1
Haydon St TWRH EC3N 13 J5
Haydon Wk WCHPL E1 13 J4
Haydon Wy
WAND/EARL SW18 140 B5
Hayes Cha WWKM BR4 199 G3
Hayes Cl HAYES BR2 199 K6
Hayes Crs CHEAM SM3 208 B2
GLDGN NW11 64 D2
Hayes Dr RAIN RM13 93 K5
Hayes End Dr YEAD UB4 94 B4
Hayes End Rd YEAD UB4 94 B3
Hayesford Park Dr
HAYES BR2 199 J2
Hayes Gdn HAYES BR2 199 K6
Hayes Gv EDUL SE22 143 G4
Hayes Hl HAYES BR2 199 H5
Hayes Hill Rd HAYES BR2 199 J5
Hayes La BECK BR3 183 G6
HAYES BR2 199 K3
Hayes Mead Rd HAYES BR2 199 H5
Hayes Pl CAMTN NW1 2 D7
Hayes Rd HAYES BR2 199 K1
NWDGN UB2 114 A4
Hayes St HAYES BR2 200 A5
Hayes Wy BECK BR3 199 F1
Hayes Wood Av HAYES BR2 200 A5
Hayfield Pas WCHPL E1 104 E3
Hayfield Rd STMC/STPC BR5 202 B2
Haygarth Pl WIM/MER SW19 177 G1
Haygreen Cl KUTN/CMB KT2 175 J2
Hay Hl MYFR/PICC W1J 9 K6
Hayland Cl CDALE/KGS NW9 63 F1
Hay La CDALE/KGS NW9 63 F1
Hayles St LBTH SE11 18 A6
Haylett Gdns KUT/HW KT1 * 190 E1
Hayling Av FELT TW13 153 K5
Hayling Cl STNW/STAM N16 86 A3
Hayling Rd OXHEY WD19 26 D5
Hayman Crs YEAD UB4 94 B1
Haymarket STJS SW1Y 10 C6
Haymeads Dr ESH/CLAY KT10 204 C4
Haymer Gdns WPK KT4 207 J1
Haymerle Rd PECK SE15 123 H6
Haymill Cl GFD/PVL UB6 97 F2
Hayne Rd BECK BR3 182 C4
Haynes Cl BKHTH/KID SE3 145 H4
FBAR/BDGN N11 34 A5
TOTM N17 50 D3
Haynes Dr ED N9 36 D5
Haynes La NRWD SE19 181 F2
Haynes Rd ALP/SUD HA0 80 A5
Hayne St STBT EC1A 12 B1
Haynt Wk RYNPK SW20 177 H6
Hay Pl SWLY BR8 * 203 K3
Hay's La STHWK SE1 13 G7
Haysleigh Gdns PGE/AN SE20 181 H5
Hay's Ms MYFR/PICC W1J 9 J6
Haysoms Cl ROM RM1 75 G1
Haystall Cl YEAD UB4 94 C1
Hay St BETH E2 86 C6
Hayter Rd BRXS/STRHM SW2 141 K6
Hayton Cl HACK E8 86 B4
Hayward Cl DART DA1 150 A6
WIM/MER SW19 178 A3
Hayward Dr DART DA1 171 J5
Hayward Gdns
PUT/ROE SW15 159 F1
Hayward Rd THDIT KT7 190 A5
TRDG/WHET N20 33 G4
Haywards Cl CHDH RM6 73 J2
Hayward's Pl CLKNW EC1R * 6 A7
Haywood Cl PIN HA5 41 H5
Haywood Ri ORP BR6 216 E3
Haywood Rd HAYES BR2 200 C1
Hazel Av WDR/YW UB7 112 D3
Hazelbank BRYLDS KT5 191 K5
Hazelbank Rd CAT SE6 165 G4
Hazelbourne Rd BAL SW12 161 G1
Hazelbrouck Gdns
BARK/HLT IG6 54 D3
Hazelbury Cl WIM/MER SW19 177 K5
Hazelbury Gn ED N9 36 A5
Hazelbury La ED N9 36 A5
Hazel Cl BTFD TW8 * 136 C1
CDALE/KGS NW9 45 H5
CROY/NA CR0 198 A4
HCH RM12 93 K1
MTCM CR4 195 J1
PLMGR N13 35 K5
WHTN TW2 155 H2
Hazelcroft PIN HA5 42 A2
Hazeldean Rd WLSDN NW10 81 F5
Hazeldene Dr PIN HA5 41 G6
Hazeldene Gdns
HGDN/ICK UB10 76 A6
Hazeldene Rd
GDMY/SEVK IG3 73 H6
WELL DA16 148 D3
Hazeldon Rd BROCKY SE4 144 B6
Hazel Dr ERITH DA8 150 D2
Hazeleigh Gdns WFD IG8 53 J1
Hazel Gdns EDGW HA8 30 D6
Hazelgreen Cl WCHMH N21 35 H3
Hazel Gv ALP/SUD HA0 80 A6
CHDH RM6 56 A6
EN EN1 * 36 C1
FELT TW13 153 K3
ORP BR6 201 G6
SYD SE26 164 A6
Hazelhurst BECK BR3 183 G4
Hazelhurst Rd TOOT SW17 160 B6
Hazel La BARK/HLT IG6 54 B2
Hazell Crs CRW RM5 56 D4
Hazellville Rd ARCH N19 66 D4
Hazelmere Cl
EBED/NFELT TW14 153 G1
NTHLT UB5 95 K1
Hazelmere Dr NTHLT UB5 95 K1
Hazelmere Gdns EMPK RM11 75 K2
Hazelmere Rd
KIL/WHAMP NW6 82 D6
NTHLT UB5 95 K1
STMC/STPC BR5 201 H1
Hazelmere Wk NTHLT UB5 95 K1
Hazelmere Wy HAYES BR2 199 K3
Hazel Rd DART DA1 171 G4
ERITH DA8 150 D2
SRTFD E15 * 88 C3
WLSDN NW10 99 K2
Hazel Rw
NFNCH/WDSPK N12 * 47 H1
Hazeltree La NTHLT UB5 95 J2
Hazel Wk HAYES BR2 201 F3
Hazel Wy CHING E4 51 H2
STHWK SE1 19 J6
Hazelwood Av MRDN SM4 194 A1
Hazelwood Cl CLPT E5 87 G1
EA W5 117 F2
RYLN/HDSTN HA2 60 B1
Hazelwood Ct SURB KT6 191 F3
Hazelwood Dr PIN HA5 41 F5
Hazelwood La PLMGR N13 35 G6
Hazelwood Park Cl CHIG IG7 54 E1
Hazelwood Rd EN EN1 36 B1
RKW/CH/CXG WD3 26 A1
WALTH E17 69 G2
Hazlebury Rd FUL/PGN SW6 140 A3
Hazledean Rd CROY/NA CR0 196 E6
Hazledene Rd CHSWK W4 117 K6
Hazlemere Gdns WPK KT4 192 D5
Hazlewell Rd PUT/ROE SW15 139 F6
Hazlewood Crs NKENS W10 100 C3
Hazlitt Cl FELT TW13 154 D6
Hazlitt Ms WKENS W14 * 119 H3
Hazlitt Rd WKENS W14 119 H3
Heacham Av HGDN/ICK UB10 76 A1
Headcorn Rd BMLY BR1 183 J1
THHTH CR7 196 A1
TOTM N17 50 B3
Headfort Pl KTBR SW1X 15 H3
Headingley Dr BECK BR3 182 D2
Headington Rd
WAND/EARL SW18 160 B3
Headlam Rd CLAP SW4 161 J1
Headlam St WCHPL E1 104 D3
Headley Ap GNTH/NBYPK IG2 72 A2
Headley Av WLGTN SM6 211 F3
Headley Cl CHSGTN KT9 206 C4
Headley Dr CROY/NA CR0 214 A5
GNTH/NBYPK IG2 72 B3
Heads Ms NTGHL W11 100 E5
Headstone Dr HRW HA1 60 D1
KTN/HRWW/WS HA3 42 E6
Headstone Gdns
RYLN/HDSTN HA2 60 C1
Headstone La
RYLN/HDSTN HA2 42 B5
Headstone Pde HRW HA1 * 60 D1
Headstone Rd HRW HA1 60 E2
Head St WCHPL E1 105 F5
Headway Cl
RCHPK/HAM TW10 156 D6
The Headway EW KT17 207 H6
Heald St NWCR SE14 144 C2
Healey Rd WATW WD18 26 D1
Healey St CAMTN NW1 * 84 B4
Healy Dr ORP BR6 217 F2
Hearne Rd CHSWK W4 117 H5
Hearn Ri NTHLT UB5 77 H6
Hearn Rd ROM RM1 75 H3
Hearn's Blds WALW SE17 19 F7
Hearns Cl STMC/STPC BR5 202 D1
Hearnshaw St POP/IOD E14 105 G5
Hearns Rd STMC/STPC BR5 202 D1
Hearn St SDTCH EC2A 7 H7
Hearnville Rd BAL SW12 161 F3
Heatham Pk WHTN TW2 156 A2
Heath Av BXLYHN DA7 128 E6
Heathbourne Rd BUSH WD23 28 E4
Heath Brow HAMP NW3 83 G1
Heath Cl EA W5 98 B3
GLDGN NW11 65 F4
GPK RM2 57 J6
HYS/HAR UB3 133 G1
SAND/SEL CR2 211 H4
STMC/STPC BR5 202 D3
Heathclose Av DART DA1 170 E2
Heathclose Rd DART DA1 170 D3
Heathcote Av CLAY IG5 53 K5
Heathcote Gv CHING E4 38 A5
Heathcote Rd TWK TW1 156 C1
Heathcote St BMSBY WC1N 5 G6
Heathcote Wy WDR/YW UB7 112 A1
Heathcroft EA W5 98 B3
Heathcroft Gdns WALTH E17 52 B4
Heathdale Av HSLWW TW4 134 D4
Heathdene Dr BELV DA17 129 J4
Heathdene Rd
STRHM/NOR SW16 180 A3
WLGTN SM6 210 B5
Heath Dr BELMT SM2 209 G6
GPK RM2 57 J4
HAMP NW3 83 F2
RYNPK SW20 193 F1
Heathedge SYD SE26 * 163 J4
Heathend Rd BXLY DA5 170 B3
Heather Av ROM RM1 57 F5
Heatherbank CHST BR7 185 F5
ELTH/MOT SE9 146 E3
Heatherbank Cl DART DA1 170 B1
Heather Cl EHAM E6 108 A5
HOLWY N7 85 F1
HPTN TW12 172 E4
ISLW TW7 135 J6
LEW SE13 165 G1
ROM RM1 57 F4
VX/NE SW8 141 G4
Heatherdale Cl
KUTN/CMB KT2 175 H2
Heatherdene Cl MTCM CR4 194 C1
NFNCH/WDSPK N12 47 G4
Heather Dr DART DA1 170 D2
ENC/FH EN2 23 H3
ROM RM1 57 F5
Heatherfold Wy PIN HA5 40 D6
Heather Gdns BELMT SM2 208 E4
GLDGN NW11 64 C3
ROM RM1 57 F5
Heather Gln ROM RM1 57 F5
Heatherlea Gv WPK KT4 193 F5
Heatherley Dr CLAY IG5 53 K6
Heather Park Dr
ALP/SUD HA0 80 C5
Heather Park Pde
ALP/SUD HA0 * 80 B5
Heather Pl ESH/CLAY KT10 204 B2
Heather Rd CHING E4 51 H2
CRICK NW2 63 H6
LEE/GVPK SE12 165 K4
Heatherset Cl ESH/CLAY KT10 204 C3
Heatherset Gdns
STRHM/NOR SW16 180 A3
Heatherside Rd
HOR/WEW KT19 207 F5
SCUP DA14 168 D5
The Heathers
STWL/WRAY TW19 152 C2
Heather Wk EDGW HA8 44 D1
NKENS W10 100 C3
Heather Wy ROM RM1 57 F4
SAND/SEL CR2 213 F6
STAN HA7 43 F2
Heatherwood Cl MNPK E12 71 F6
Heatherwood Dr YEAD UB4 94 B1
Heathfield CHING E4 38 A5
CHST BR7 185 H2
HRW HA1 * 61 F4
Heathfield Av
WAND/EARL SW18 160 C2
Heathfield Cl CAN/RD E16 107 H4
HAYES BR2 215 G3
OXHEY WD19 27 G2
Heathfield Dr MTCM CR4 178 D3
Heathfield Gdns CHSWK W4 117 K5
CROY/NA CR0 * 211 J2
GLDGN NW11 64 B3
WAND/EARL SW18 160 C1
Heathfield La CHST BR7 185 H2
Heathfield North WHTN TW2 155 K2
Heathfield Pk CRICK NW2 82 A4
Heathfield Park Dr
CHDH RM6 73 H2
Heathfield Ri RSLP HA4 58 A4
Heathfield Rd ACT W3 117 J2
BMLY BR1 183 J3
BXLYHS DA6 149 G5
HAYES BR2 215 G3
SAND/SEL CR2 211 K3
WAND/EARL SW18 160 B1
Heathfield South WHTN TW2 156 A2
Heathfield Sq
WAND/EARL SW18 160 C2
Heathfield Ter CHSWK W4 117 K5
WOOL/PLUM SE18 127 K6
Heathfield V SAND/SEL CR2 213 F6
Heath Gdns DART DA1 * 171 F3
TWK TW1 156 A3
Heathgate GLDGN NW11 65 F3
Heathgate Pl HAMP NW3 83 K2
Heath Gv PGE/AN SE20 181 K3
Heath Hurst Rd HAMP NW3 83 J2
Heathhurst Rd SAND/SEL CR2 212 A6
Heathland Rd
STNW/STAM N16 68 A5
Heathlands Cl TWK TW1 156 A4
Heathlands Ct HSLWW TW4 134 D6
Heathlands Ri DART DA1 170 E2
Heathlands Wy HSLWW TW4 134 D6
Heath La BKHTH/KID SE3 145 G3
DART DA1 170 E3
Heathlee Rd BKHTH/KID SE3 145 J5
DART DA1 170 B1
Heathley End CHST BR7 185 H2
Heath Ldg BUSH WD23 * 28 D3
Heathman's Rd FUL/PGN SW6 139 J2
Heath Md WIM/MER SW19 159 G5
Heath Park Dr BMLY BR1 184 D6
Heath Park Rd GPK RM2 75 J2
Heath Ri HAYES BR2 199 K3
PUT/ROE SW15 159 G1
Heath Rd BXLY DA5 169 K3
CHDH RM6 73 K4
DART DA1 170 C1
HGDN/ICK UB10 94 A3
HRW HA1 60 C4
HSLW TW3 135 H5
OXHEY WD19 27 H2
THHTH CR7 180 D6
TWK TW1 156 A3
VX/NE SW8 141 G3
Heath's Cl EN EN1 23 K3
Heathside ESH/CLAY KT10 204 E1
HAMP NW3 83 H2
HSLWW TW4 154 E2
Heath Side STMC/STPC BR5 201 H5
Heathside Av BXLYHN DA7 149 F3
Heathside Cl ESH/CLAY KT10 204 E1
GNTH/NBYPK IG2 72 D2
NTHWD HA6 40 B1
Heathside Rd NTHWD HA6 26 B6
Heathstan Rd SHB W12 99 J5
Heath St DART DA1 171 G2
HAMP NW3 83 G2
The Heath HNWL W7 * 115 K2
Heath Vw EFNCH N2 65 G1
Heathview Av DART DA1 170 B1
Heath View Cl EFNCH N2 65 G1
Heathview Crs DART DA1 170 D2
Heath View Dr ABYW SE2 128 E6
Heathview Gdns
PUT/ROE SW15 159 F2
Heathview Rd THHTH CR7 196 B1
Heath Vls WAND/EARL SW18 * 160 B3
WOOL/PLUM SE18 128 A5
Heathville Rd ARCH N19 66 E4
Heathwall St BTSEA SW11 140 E4
Heath Wy ERITH DA8 149 K2
Heathway BKHTH/KID SE3 145 K1
CROY/NA CR0 213 H1
DAGW RM9 92 B2
NWDGN UB2 * 114 C4
WFD IG8 39 G6
Heathwood Gdns CHARL SE7 126 D4
SWLY BR8 187 K5
Heathwood Pde SWLY BR8 * 187 K5
Heathwood Wk BXLY DA5 170 B3
Heaton Av HARH RM3 57 K3
Heaton Cl CHING E4 38 A5
Heaton Grange Rd GPK RM2 57 H4
Heaton Rd MTCM CR4 179 F3
PECK SE15 143 J4
Heaven Tree Cl IS N1 85 J3
Heaver Rd BTSEA SW11 * 140 C4
Heavitree Cl
WOOL/PLUM SE18 127 J5
Heavitree Rd
WOOL/PLUM SE18 127 J5
Hebden Ter TOTM N17 50 A2
Hebdon Rd TOOT SW17 160 D5
Heber Rd CRICK NW2 82 B3
EDUL SE22 163 G1
Hebron Rd HMSMTH W6 118 E3
Hecham Cl WALTH E17 51 G5
Heckfield Pl FUL/PGN SW6 139 K1
Heckford Cl WATW WD18 26 A1
Heckford St WAP E1W 105 F6
Hector Cl ED N9 36 C4
Hector St WOOL/PLUM SE18 * 127 K4
Heddington Gv HOLWY N7 85 F3
Heddon Cl ISLW TW7 136 B5
Heddon Court Av EBAR EN4 21 K6
Heddon Court Pde
EBAR EN4 * 22 A6
Heddon Rd EBAR EN4 21 K6
Heddon St CONDST W1S 10 A6
Hedge Hl ENC/FH EN2 23 H2
Hedge La PLMGR N13 35 H5
Hedgeley REDBR IG4 71 K1
Hedgemans Rd DAGW RM9 91 K5
Hedgemans Wy DAGW RM9 92 A4
Hedgerley Gdns GFD/PVL UB6 96 C1
Hedger's Gv HOM E9 * 87 G4
Hedger St LBTH SE11 18 A6
Hedgeside Rd NTHWD HA6 40 A1
Hedgewood Gdns CLAY IG5 72 A1
Hedgley Ms LEE/GVPK SE12 145 J6
Hedgley St LEE/GVPK SE12 145 J6
Hedingham Cl IS N1 85 J5
Hedingham Rd BCTR RM8 91 H3
Hedley Rd WHTN TW2 155 F2
Hedley Rw HBRY N5 85 K3
Heenan Cl BARK IG11 90 C4
Heene Rd ENC/FH EN2 23 K3
Heidegger Crs BARN SW13 138 E1
Heigham Rd EHAM E6 89 J5
Heighton Gdns CROY/NA CR0 211 H3
Heights Cl RYNPK SW20 176 E3
The Heights BECK BR3 * 183 F3
CHARL SE7 126 B5
NTHLT UB5 78 A3
Heiron St WALW SE17 122 C6
Helby Rd CLAP SW4 161 J1
Helder Gv LEE/GVPK SE12 165 J2
Helder St SAND/SEL CR2 211 K4
Heldmann Cl HSLW TW3 135 J5
Helegan Cl ORP BR6 217 F2
Helena Pl HACK E8 86 D6
Helena Rd EA W5 97 K4
PLSTW E13 106 D1
WALTH E17 69 J2
WLSDN NW10 81 K3
Helena Sq BERM/RHTH SE16 105 G6
Helen Av EBED/NFELT TW14 154 A2
Helen Cl DART DA1 170 E2
E/WMO/HCT KT8 189 G1
EFNCH N2 47 G6
Helenslea Av GLDGN NW11 64 D5
Helen's Pl BETH E2 104 E2
Helen St WOOL/PLUM SE18 127 G4
Helford Cl RSLP HA4 58 C6
Helios Rd WLGTN SM6 195 F5
Helix Gdns BRXS/STRHM SW2 162 A1
Helix Rd BRXS/STRHM SW2 162 A1
Hellings St WAP E1W 123 H1
Helme Cl WIM/MER SW19 177 J1
Helmet Rw FSBYE EC1V 6 D6
Helmore Rd BARK IG11 91 F5
Helmsdale Cl ROM RM1 57 G3
YEAD UB4 * 95 J3
Helmsdale Rd ROM RM1 57 G3
STRHM/NOR SW16 179 H4
Helmsley Pl HACK E8 86 D5
Helmsley St HACK E8 86 D5
Helperby Rd WLSDN NW10 81 G5
Helsinki Sq BERM/RHTH SE16 124 B3
Helston Cl PIN HA5 41 K3
Helvetia St CAT SE6 164 C4
Hemans St VX/NE SW8 141 J1
Hemery Rd GFD/PVL UB6 78 D3
Hemingford Cl
NFNCH/WDSPK N12 47 H1
Hemingford Rd CHEAM SM3 208 A2
IS N1 85 F6
Heming Rd EDGW HA8 44 D2
Hemington Av
FBAR/BDGN N11 47 K1
Hemlock Cl
STRHM/NOR SW16 179 J5
Hemlock Rd SHB W12 99 H6
Hemmen La HYS/HAR UB3 94 D6
Hemming Cl HPTN TW12 173 F4
Hemmings Cl SCUP DA14 168 C4
Hemmingsmead
HOR/WEW KT19 206 E4
Hemming St WCHPL E1 104 C3
Hemmingway Cl KTTN NW5 84 A2
Hempstead Cl BKHH IG9 38 E4
Hempstead Rd WALTH E17 52 B6
Hemp Wk WALW SE17 19 F6
Hemsby Rd CHSGTN KT9 206 B4
Hemstal Rd KIL/WHAMP NW6 82 E5
Hemsted Rd ERITH DA8 150 B2
Hemswell Dr CDALE/KGS NW9 45 G4
Hemsworth St IS N1 7 G2
Henbury Wy OXHEY WD19 27 H5
Henchman St SHB W12 99 H5
Hendale Av HDN NW4 45 J6
Henderson Cl EMPK RM11 75 K6
WLSDN NW10 80 E4
Henderson Dr DART DA1 151 K5
STJWD NW8 2 A6
Henderson Rd CROY/NA CR0 196 E3
ED N9 36 D3
FSTGT E7 89 G4
WAND/EARL SW18 160 D2
YEAD UB4 94 E2
Hendham Rd TOOT SW17 160 D4
Hendon Av FNCH N3 46 C4
Hendon Gdns CRW RM5 56 E2
Hendon Gv HOR/WEW KT19 206 C6
Hendon Hall Ct HDN NW4 * 46 B6
Hendon La FNCH N3 46 C6
Hendon Park Rw
GLDGN NW11 * 64 D3
Hendon Rd ED N9 36 C4
Hendon Wy CRICK NW2 64 B4
STWL/WRAY TW19 132 A6
Hendon Wood La MLHL NW7 31 J3
Hendren Cl GFD/PVL UB6 78 D3

Hendre Rd STHWK SE1 19 H7
Hendrick Av BAL SW12 160 E1
Heneage St WCHPL E1 13 K1
Henfield Cl ARCH N19 66 C5
BXLY DA5 169 H1
Henfield Rd WIM/MER SW19 177 J4
Hengelo Gdns MTCM CR4 194 C1
Hengest Av ESH/CLAY KT10 205 G1
Hengist Rd ERITH DA8 149 K1
LEE/GVPK SE12 166 A2
Hengist Wy HAYES BR2 199 G1
Hengrave Rd FSTH SE23 163 K2
Hengrove Ct BXLY DA5 169 F3
Hengrove Crs ASHF TW15 152 A5
Henley Av CHEAM SM3 208 C1
Henley Cl BERM/RHTH SE16 * 123 K2
GFD/PVL UB6 * 96 C1
ISLW TW7 136 A2
Henley Dr KUTN/CMB KT2 176 C3
STHWK SE1 19 K6
Henley Gdns CHDH RM6 74 A2
PIN HA5 41 F6
Henley Rd CAN/RD E16 126 E2
IL IG1 90 C2
UED N18 36 A6
WLSDN NW10 82 A6
Henley St BTSEA SW11 141 F3
Henley Wy FELT TW13 172 C1
Henneker Cl CRW RM5 56 E2
Hennel Cl FSTH SE23 163 K5
Hennessy Rd ED N9 36 E4
Henniker Gdns EHAM E6 107 H2
Henniker Ms CHEL SW3 120 C6
Henniker Rd SRTFD E15 88 B3
Henningham Rd TOTM N17 49 K4
Henning St BTSEA SW11 140 D2
Henrietta Cl DEPT SE8 124 D6
Henrietta Ms BMSBY WC1N 5 F6
Henrietta Pl CAVSQ/HST W1G 9 J3
Henrietta St COVGDN WC2E 11 F5
SRTFD E15 88 A3
Henriques St WCHPL E1 104 C5
Henry Addlington Cl
EHAM E6 108 B4
Henry Cl EN EN1 24 A1
Henry Cooper Wy
ELTH/MOT SE9 166 C5
Henry Darlot Dr MLHL NW7 46 B1
Henry Dickens Ct NTGHL W11 100 B6
Henry Doulton Dr TOOT SW17 161 F6
Henry Jackson Rd
PUT/ROE SW15 139 G4
Henry Macaulay Av
KUTN/CMB KT2 174 E4
Henry Peters Dr TEDD TW11 173 K1
Henry Rd EBAR EN4 21 H6
EHAM E6 107 J1
FSBYPK N4 67 J5
Henry's Av WFD IG8 52 D1
Henryson Rd BROCKY SE4 144 D6
Henry St BMLY BR1 184 A4
Henry Tate Ms
STRHM/NOR SW16 180 B1
Hensby Ms OXHEY WD19 27 J1
Henshall St IS N1 85 K4
Henshawe Rd BCTR RM8 91 K1
Henshaw St WALW SE17 18 E6
Henslowe Rd EDUL SE22 143 H6
Henson Av CRICK NW2 82 A3
Henson Cl ORP BR6 201 G6
Henson Pl NTHLT UB5 77 G6
Henstridge Pl STJWD NW8 2 C2
Henty Cl BTSEA SW11 140 D1
Henty Wk PUT/ROE SW15 138 E6
Henville Rd BMLY BR1 184 A4
Henwick Rd ELTH/MOT SE9 146 C4
Henwood Side WFD IG8 53 K2
Hepburn Gdns HAYES BR2 199 J5
Hepple Cl ISLW TW7 136 C3
Hepscott Rd HOM E9 87 J4
Hepworth Gdns BARK IG11 91 G3
Hepworth Rd
STRHM/NOR SW16 179 K3
Herald Gdns WLGTN SM6 210 B1
Heralds Pl LBTH SE11 18 A6
Herald St BETH E2 104 D3
Herbal Hl CLKNW EC1R 5 K7
Herbert Crs KTBR SW1X 15 F4
Herbert Gdns CHDH RM6 73 K4
CHSWK W4 117 J6
WLSDN NW10 99 K1
Herbert Ms BRXS/STRHM SW2 162 B1
Herbert Pl ISLW TW7 135 J3
WOOL/PLUM SE18 127 G6
Herbert Rd BXLYHN DA7 149 F3
CDALE/KGS NW9 63 J3
FBAR/BDGN N11 48 E3
GDMY/SEVK IG3 72 E6
HAYES BR2 200 C2
KUT/HW KT1 175 G6
MNPK E12 89 J2
SEVS/STOTM N15 68 B2
STHL UB1 114 E1
WALTH E17 69 H4
WIM/MER SW19 177 J3
WOOL/PLUM SE18 147 G1
Herbert St KTTN NW5 84 A4
PLSTW E13 106 E1
Herbrand St BMSBY WC1N 4 E7
STPAN WC1H 4 E6
Hercules Pl HOLWY N7 84 E1
Hercules Rd STHWK SE1 17 H5
Hercules St HOLWY N7 84 E1
Hereford Av EBAR EN4 33 K3
Hereford Gdns IL IG1 71 J4
PIN HA5 59 J2
WHTN TW2 * 155 H3
Hereford Ms BAY/PAD W2 * 100 E5
Hereford Pl NWCR SE14 * 144 C1
Hereford Retreat PECK SE15 143 H1
Hereford Rd ACT W3 98 E6
BAY/PAD W2 100 E5
BOW E3 105 H1
EA W5 116 D3
FELT TW13 154 B3
WAN E11 71 F2
Hereford Sq SKENS SW7 120 B4
Hereford St BETH E2 104 C3
Hereford Wy CHSGTN KT9 205 J3
Herent Dr CLAY IG5 53 K6
Heretage Cl BRXN/ST SW9 142 C4
Hereward Gdns PLMGR N13 49 G1
Hereward Rd TOOT SW17 160 D6
Herga Rd
KTN/HRWW/WS HA3 61 F1
Heriot Av CHING E4 37 J4
Heriot Rd HDN NW4 64 A2
Heriots Cl STAN HA7 29 G6
Heritage Av CDALE/KGS NW9 45 H6
Heritage Hl HAYES BR2 215 G3
Heritage Pl
WAND/EARL SW18 * 160 C1
Heritage Vw HRW HA1 79 F1
Herkomer Cl BUSH WD23 28 B1
Herlwyn Av RSLP HA4 76 C1
Herlwyn Gdns TOOT SW17 160 E6
Herm Cl ISLW TW7 135 H1
Hermes Cl MV/WKIL W9 100 E3
Hermes St IS N1 5 J3
Hermes Wy WLGTN SM6 210 D5
Hermiston Av
CEND/HSY/T N8 66 E2
Hermitage Cl ABYW SE2 128 D3
ENC/FH EN2 23 H3
ESH/CLAY KT10 205 G4
RCHPK/HAM TW10 * 136 E6
SWFD E18 70 D1
Hermitage Cots STAN HA7 * 42 E1
Hermitage Gdns CRICK NW2 82 E1
NRWD SE19 180 D3
Hermitage La CRICK NW2 82 E1
CROY/NA CR0 197 G4
STRHM/NOR SW16 180 A3
UED N18 49 K1
Hermitage Rd FSBYPK N4 67 J4
NRWD SE19 180 D3
Hermitage Rw HACK E8 * 86 C3
Hermitage St BAY/PAD W2 8 A2
The Hermitage BARN SW13 * 138 C2
FELT TW13 * 153 J5
FSTH SE23 163 K3
KUT/HW KT1 * 190 E1
LEW SE13 * 145 F3
RCHPK/HAM TW10 137 F6
Hermitage Wk SWFD E18 70 D1
Hermitage Wall WAP E1W 123 H1
Hermitage Wy STAN HA7 43 G4
Hermit Pl KIL/WHAMP NW6 83 F6
Hermit Rd CAN/RD E16 106 D3
Hermit St FSBYE EC1V 6 A4
Hermon Gv HYS/HAR UB3 113 K1
Hermon Hl WAN E11 70 E1
Herndon Rd
WAND/EARL SW18 140 B6
Herne Cl HYS/HAR UB3 94 D5
WLSDN NW10 81 F3
Herne Ct BUSH WD23 * 28 C3
Herne Hl HNHL SE24 142 D6
Herne Hill Rd HNHL SE24 142 D4
Herne Ms UED N18 36 C6
Herne Pl HNHL SE24 162 C1
Herne Rd BUSH WD23 28 B1
SURB KT6 190 E6
Heron Cl BKHH IG9 38 E3
WALTH E17 51 H5
WLSDN NW10 81 G4
Heron Ct HAYES BR2 200 B1
KUT/HW KT1 * 175 F6
Heron Crs SCUP DA14 167 K6
Herondale SAND/SEL CR2 213 F6
Herondale Av
WAND/EARL SW18 160 C3
Heron Dr FSBYPK N4 67 J6
Heron Flight Av HCH RM12 93 J5
Herongate Rd MNPK E12 71 G6
Heron Hl BELV DA17 129 G4
Heron Md PEND EN3 25 J1
Heron Ms IL IG1 72 B6
Heron Pl BERM/RHTH SE16 124 B1
Heron Quays POP/IOD E14 124 D1
Heron Rd CROY/NA CR0 * 197 F5
HNHL SE24 142 D5
TWK TW1 136 B5
Heronsforde WEA W13 97 J5
Heronsgate EDGW HA8 44 C1
Herons Lea HGT N6 * 65 K3
Heronslea Dr STAN HA7 44 A1
Herons Pl ISLW TW7 136 C4
Herons Ri EBAR EN4 21 J5
Heron Wk NTHWD HA6 26 C6
Heron Wy EBED/NFELT TW14 133 K5
Herrick Rd HBRY N5 85 J1
Herrick St WEST SW1P 16 D7
Herries St NKENS W10 100 C1
Herringham Rd CHARL SE7 126 B3
Herrongate Cl EN EN1 24 A3
Hersant Cl WLSDN NW10 81 J6
Herschell Rd FSTH SE23 164 A2
Hersham Cl PUT/ROE SW15 158 D2
Hersham Rd WOT/HER KT12 188 A6
Hershell Ct
MORT/ESHN SW14 * 137 J5
Hertford Av
MORT/ESHN SW14 138 A6
Hertford Cl EBAR EN4 21 H4
Hertford Ct STAN HA7 * 43 K3
Hertford End Ct
NTHWD HA6 * 40 C1
Hertford Pl FITZ W1T 4 A7
Hertford Rd BARK IG11 90 A5
EBAR EN4 21 G4
ED N9 36 D3
EFNCH N2 47 J6
GNTH/NBYPK IG2 72 E3
IS N1 86 A6
PEND EN3 24 E2
PEND EN3 24 E4
Hertford Road High St
PEND EN3 36 E1
Hertford St MYFR/PICC W1J 9 J7
Hertford Wy MTCM CR4 195 K1
Hertslet Rd HOLWY N7 85 F1
Hertsmere Rd POP/IOD E14 105 J6
Hertswood Ct BAR EN5 * 20 C5
Hervey Cl FNCH N3 46 E4
Hervey Park Rd WALTH E17 69 G1
Hesa Rd HYS/HAR UB3 94 E5
Hesewall Cl CLAP SW4 141 H3
Hesketh Pl NTGHL W11 100 C6
Hesketh Rd FSTGT E7 88 E1
Heslop Rd BAL SW12 160 E3
Hesper Ms ECT SW5 120 A5
Hesperus Crs POP/IOD E14 124 E4
Hessel Rd WEA W13 116 B2
Hessel St WCHPL E1 104 D5
Hesselyn Dr RAIN RM13 93 K5
Hestercombe Av
FUL/PGN SW6 139 H3
Hesterman Wy CROY/NA CR0 195 K5
Hester Rd BTSEA SW11 140 D1
UED N18 50 C1
Hester Ter RCH/KEW TW9 137 H4
Heston Av HEST TW5 134 D1
Heston Grange La HEST TW5 114 E6
Heston Rd HEST TW5 135 F1
Heston St NWCR SE14 144 C2
Heswell Gn OXHEY WD19 * 26 E5
Hetherington Rd CLAP SW4 141 K5
Hetley Rd SHB W12 118 E1
Heton Gdns HDN NW4 63 J1
Hevelius Cl GNWCH SE10 125 J5
Hever Cft ELTH/MOT SE9 167 F6
Hever Gdns BMLY BR1 185 F5
Heverham Rd
WOOL/PLUM SE18 127 K4
Heversham Rd BXLYHN DA7 149 H3
Hevingham Dr CHDH RM6 73 J2
Hewens Rd HGDN/ICK UB10 94 A2
Hewer St NKENS W10 100 B4
Hewett Cl STAN HA7 29 H6
Hewett Rd BCTR RM8 91 K3
Hewett St SDTCH EC2A 7 H7
Hewish Rd UED N18 36 A6
Hewison St BOW E3 105 H1
Hewitt Av WDGN N22 49 H5
Hewitt Cl CROY/NA CR0 213 J1
Hewitt Rd CEND/HSY/T N8 67 G2
Hewlett Rd BOW E3 105 G1
The Hexagon HGT N6 65 K5
Hexal Rd CAT SE6 165 H5
Hexham Gdns ISLW TW7 136 B1
NTHLT UB5 77 K3
Hexham Rd BAR EN5 21 F5
MRDN SM4 194 A5
WNWD SE27 162 D4
Heybourne Rd TOTM N17 50 D3
Heybridge Av
STRHM/NOR SW16 180 A2
Heybridge Dr BARK/HLT IG6 54 D6
Heybridge Wy LEY E10 69 G4
Heyford Av RYNPK SW20 177 J6
VX/NE SW8 141 K1
Heyford Rd MTCM CR4 178 D5
Heyford Ter VX/NE SW8 141 K1
Heygate Est WALW SE17 18 D6
Heygate St WALW SE17 18 C7
Heynes Rd BCTR RM8 91 J2
Heysham Dr OXHEY WD19 41 G1
Heysham La HAMP NW3 83 F1
Heysham Rd
SEVS/STOTM N15 67 K3
Heythorp St
WAND/EARL SW18 159 J4
Heywood Av CDALE/KGS NW9 45 G4
Heyworth Rd CLPT E5 86 D2
SRTFD E15 88 D2
Hibbert Rd
KTN/HRWW/WS HA3 43 F5
WALTH E17 69 H4
Hibbert St BTSEA SW11 140 B4
Hibernia Gdns HSLW TW3 135 F6
Hibernia Rd HSLW TW3 135 F5
Hichisson Rd PECK SE15 143 K6
Hicken Rd BRXS/STRHM SW2 142 A6
Hickin Cl CHARL SE7 126 C4
Hickin St POP/IOD E14 125 F3
Hickling Rd IL IG1 90 B3
Hickman Av CHING E4 52 A2
Hickman Cl CAN/RD E16 107 H4
Hickman Rd CHDH RM6 73 J4
Hickory Cl ED N9 36 C2
Hicks Av GFD/PVL UB6 96 D2
Hicks Cl BTSEA SW11 140 D4
Hicks St DEPT SE8 124 B5
Hidcote Gdns RYNPK SW20 176 E6
Hidden Cl E/WMO/HCT KT8 189 H1
Hide Pl WEST SW1P 16 C7
Hide Rd HRW HA1 60 D1
Higham Hill Rd WALTH E17 51 G6
Higham Ms NTHLT UB5 95 K3
Higham Pl WALTH E17 51 G6
Higham Rd TOTM N17 49 K6
WFD IG8 52 E2
Higham Station Av CHING E4 51 K2
The Highams WALTH E17 * 52 A4
Higham St WALTH E17 51 G5
Highbank Pl
WAND/EARL SW18 * 160 A3
Highbanks Cl WELL DA16 148 B1
Highbanks Rd PIN HA5 42 B2
Highbank Wy
CEND/HSY/T N8 67 G3
Highbarrow Rd CROY/NA CR0 197 G5
High Beech SAND/SEL CR2 212 A5
High Beeches ORP BR6 217 G4
SCUP DA14 187 F1
Highbridge Rd BARK IG11 90 B6
Highbrook Rd
BKHTH/KID SE3 146 C4
High Broom Crs WWKM BR4 198 E4
Highbury Av THHTH CR7 180 B5
Highbury Cl NWMAL KT3 191 K1
WWKM BR4 198 E6
Highbury Cnr IS N1 85 H4
Highbury Crs HBRY N5 85 G3
Highbury Est HBRY N5 85 J3
Highbury Gdns
GDMY/SEVK IG3 72 E6
Highbury Gra HBRY N5 85 H2
Highbury Gv HBRY N5 85 H3
Highbury Hl HBRY N5 85 H2
Highbury New Pk HBRY N5 85 H4
Highbury Pk HBRY N5 85 H2
Highbury Pl HBRY N5 85 H4
Highbury Qd HBRY N5 85 J1
Highbury Rd WIM/MER SW19 177 H1
Highbury Station Pde
HBRY N5 * 85 H4
Highbury Station Rd IS N1 * 85 G4
Highbury Ter HBRY N5 85 H3
Highbury Terrace Ms
HBRY N5 85 H3
High Cedar Dr RYNPK SW20 176 E3
Highclere Rd NWMAL KT3 176 A6
Highclere St SYD SE26 164 B6
Highcliffe Dr PUT/ROE SW15 158 C1
Highcliffe Gdns REDBR IG4 71 J2
Highcombe CHARL SE7 126 A6
Highcombe Cl ELTH/MOT SE9 166 C3
High Coombe Pl
KUTN/CMB KT2 176 A3
Highcroft CDALE/KGS NW9 63 G2
Highcroft Av ALP/SUD HA0 80 B5
Highcroft Gdns GLDGN NW11 64 D3
Highcroft Rd ARCH N19 66 E4
High Cross Rd TOTM N17 50 C6
Highcross Wy PUT/ROE SW15 158 D3
Highdaun Dr
STRHM/NOR SW16 196 A1
Highdown WPK KT4 192 B6
Highdown Rd PUT/ROE SW15 158 E1
High Dr NWMAL KT3 175 K4
High Elms WFD IG8 52 E1
High Elms Cl NTHWD HA6 40 A2
High Elms Rd ORP BR6 216 C6
Highfield OXHEY WD19 27 K5
Highfield Av CDALE/KGS NW9 62 E2
ERITH DA8 129 J6
GFD/PVL UB6 78 E3
GLDGN NW11 64 B4
ORP BR6 217 F4
PIN HA5 59 K2
WBLY HA9 80 A1
Highfield Cl CDALE/KGS NW9 62 E2
CRW RM5 56 E2
LEW SE13 165 G1
NTHWD HA6 40 C4
SURB KT6 190 D5
WDGN N22 49 G4
Highfield Ct STHGT/OAK N14 34 C1
Highfield Crs NTHWD HA6 40 C4
Highfield Dr HAYES BR2 199 H1
HOR/WEW KT19 207 H5
WWKM BR4 213 K1
Highfield Gdns GLDGN NW11 64 C3
Highfield Hl NRWD SE19 180 E3
Highfield Link CRW RM5 56 E2
Highfield Rd ACT W3 98 D4
BMLY BR1 200 E1
BRYLDS KT5 191 K4
BXLYHS DA6 149 G6
CHST BR7 186 A6
CRW RM5 56 E2
DART DA1 171 G2
FELT TW13 153 K3
GLDGN NW11 * 64 C3
ISLW TW7 136 A2
NTHWD HA6 40 C4
SUT SM1 209 J3
WCHMH N21 35 H4
WFD IG8 53 J3
Highfield Rd North DART DA1 171 G1
Highfield Rd South DART DA1 171 G2
Highfields Gv HGT N6 66 A5
High Foleys ESH/CLAY KT10 205 H5
High Garth ESH/CLAY KT10 204 C4
Highgate Av HGT N6 66 B4
Highgate Cl HGT N6 66 A4
Highgate Edge EFNCH N2 * 65 J2
Highgate High St HGT N6 66 A5
Highgate Hl ARCH N19 66 B5
Highgate Rd KTTN NW5 84 B2
Highgate Spinney
CEND/HSY/T N8 * 66 D3
Highgate Wk FSTH SE23 163 K4
Highgate West Hl HGT N6 66 A5
High Gv BMLY BR1 184 B4
WOOL/PLUM SE18 147 J1
Highgrove Cl CHST BR7 184 D4
FBAR/BDGN N11 48 A1
Highgrove Ms CAR SM5 209 J1
Highgrove Rd BCTR RM8 91 J3
Highgrove Wy RSLP HA4 58 E3
High Hill Ferry CLPT E5 68 D5
High Holborn HHOL WC1V 11 F3
Highland Av DAGE RM10 92 E1
HNWL W7 96 E5
LOU IG10 39 K1
Highland Cots WLGTN SM6 * 210 B2
Highland Cft BECK BR3 182 E1
Highland Dr BUSH WD23 28 B2
Highland Pk FELT TW13 153 J6
Highland Rd BMLY BR1 183 J4
BXLYHS DA6 149 H5
HAYES BR2 183 J5
NRWD SE19 181 F2
NTHWD HA6 40 E5
Highlands OXHEY WD19 27 G3
Highlands Av ACT W3 98 E6
WCHMH N21 23 F6
Highlands Cl FSBYPK N4 66 E4
HSLW TW3 135 G2
Highlands Gdns IL IG1 71 K5
Highlands Heath
PUT/ROE SW15 159 F2
Highlands Rd BAR EN5 20 E6
STMC/STPC BR5 202 C4
The Highlands BAR EN5 20 E6
EDGW HA8 44 D5
Highland Ter LEW SE13 * 144 E4
High La HNWL W7 96 D5
Highlea Cl CDALE/KGS NW9 45 G4
High Level Dr SYD SE26 163 H6
Highlever Rd NKENS W10 100 A4
High Limes NRWD SE19 * 181 F2
High Md HRW HA1 60 E2
Highmead WOOL/PLUM SE18 148 A1
High Md WWKM BR4 199 G6
Highmead Crs ALP/SUD HA0 80 B5
High Meadow Cl PIN HA5 59 F1
High Meadow Crs
CDALE/KGS NW9 63 F2
High Mdw CHIG IG7 54 D1
High Meads Rd CAN/RD E16 107 H5
Highmore Rd BKHTH/KID SE3 145 H1
High Mt HDN NW4 * 63 J3
High Oaks ENC/FH EN2 23 F1
The High Pde
STRHM/NOR SW16 * 161 K5
High Park Rd RCH/KEW TW9 137 H2
High Pth WIM/MER SW19 178 A4
High Point ELTH/MOT SE9 167 G5
High Rdg MUSWH N10 * 48 B4
Highridge Pl ENC/FH EN2 * 23 F1
High Rd BKHH IG9 * 39 F3
BUSH WD23 28 D3
CHDH RM6 73 K4
EFNCH N2 65 J1
FBAR/BDGN N11 48 B1
FNCH N3 47 H4
GDMY/SEVK IG3 73 G5
IL IG1 90 B1
KTN/HRWW/WS HA3 42 E4
LEY E10 69 K3
LOU IG10 39 G1
NFNCH/WDSPK N12 47 G3
RDART DA2 170 E5
SEVS/STOTM N15 68 B2
TOTM N17 50 B6
TRDG/WHET N20 33 F2
WBLY HA9 80 A3
WDGN N22 49 F3
WDGN N22 49 G6
WLSDN NW10 81 G4
High Rd Eastcote PIN HA5 59 F2
High Rd Leyton LEY E10 69 K6
High Rd Leytonstone
WAN E11 88 C1
High Road Woodford Gn
SWFD E18 52 E4
WFD IG8 38 E6
Highshore Rd PECK SE15 143 G3
Highstead Crs ERITH DA8 150 B2
Highstone Av WAN E11 70 E3
High St ACT W3 117 K1
BAR EN5 20 C4
BARK/HLT IG6 54 C5
BECK BR3 182 D4
BELMT SM2 209 G5
BMLY BR1 183 K5
BTFD TW8 116 E6
BUSH WD23 28 A1
CAR SM5 209 K3
CEND/HSY/T N8 66 E1
CHEAM SM3 208 C4
CROY/NA CR0 211 J1
DART DA1 171 H1
E/WMO/HCT KT8 189 F2
EA W5 97 K6
ESH/CLAY KT10 204 B2
ESH/CLAY KT10 205 F4
EW KT17 207 H6
FBAR/BDGN N11 48 B1
FELT TW13 153 J5
HEST TW5 114 A6
HPTN TW12 173 G4
HRW HA1 60 E5
HSLW TW3 135 G4
HYS/HAR UB3 113 G6
KTN/HRWW/WS HA3 42 E6
KUT/HW KT1 174 D4
MLHL NW7 45 K1
NTHWD HA6 40 D4
NWMAL KT3 192 B1
ORP BR6 202 B5
ORP BR6 216 C3
ORP BR6 217 F3
PGE/AN SE20 181 K3
PIN HA5 41 J6
PLSTW E13 106 E1
PUR RM19 131 K5
ROM RM1 75 G2
RSLP HA4 58 C4
SCUP DA14 168 B6
SNWD SE25 197 G1
SRTFD E15 106 A1
STHGT/OAK N14 34 D3
STMC/STPC BR5 202 D3
STWL/WRAY TW19 152 A1
SUT SM1 209 F4
TEDD TW11 174 B1
THDIT KT7 190 B3
THHTH CR7 196 D1
WALTH E17 69 H1
WAN E11 71 F3
WBLY HA9 80 B2
WDR/YW UB7 112 A6
WHTN TW2 * 155 H2
WIM/MER SW19 177 G1
WWKM BR4 198 E5
High Street Collier's Wd
WIM/MER SW19 178 C3
High Street Harlesden
WLSDN NW10 81 G6
High Street Harlington
HYS/HAR UB3 133 G1
High Street Ms
WIM/MER SW19 177 H1
High St North EHAM E6 89 J6
High St South EHAM E6 107 K1
High Timber St BLKFR EC4V 12 C5
High Tor Cl BMLY BR1 184 A3
High Trees BRXS/STRHM SW2 162 B3
CROY/NA CR0 198 B5
EBAR EN4 21 J6
High Vw PIN HA5 59 G1
WATW WD18 26 D1
Highview Av EDGW HA8 30 E6
High View Av WLGTN SM6 211 F3
High View Cl NRWD SE19 181 G5
Highview Gdns EDGW HA8 44 E1
FBAR/BDGN N11 48 C1
FNCH N3 46 C6
High View Rd NRWD SE19 180 E2
SWFD E18 52 D5
Highview Rd SCUP DA14 168 C6
WEA W13 97 G5
Highview Ter DART DA1 * 151 G6
The Highway BELMT SM2 209 G6
ORP BR6 217 H3
STAN HA7 43 F4
WCHPL E1 104 C6
Highwood Av
NFNCH/WDSPK N12 33 G6
Highwood Cl EDUL SE22 163 H3
ORP BR6 201 H6
Highwood Dr ORP BR6 201 H6
Highwood Gdns CLAY IG5 71 K2
Highwood Gv MLHL NW7 45 F1
Highwood Hl MLHL NW7 31 H4

Highwood Rd ARCH N19 84 E1
High Worple
RYLN/HDSTN HA2 59 J4
Highworth Rd
FBAR/BDGN N11 48 D2
Highworth St CAMTN NW1 * 8 D1
Hilary Av MTCM CR4 179 F6
Hilary Cl ERITH DA8 149 J2
FUL/PGN SW6 * 140 A1
Hilary Rd SHB W12 99 H6
Hilberry Ct BUSH WD23 28 B2
Hilbert Rd CHEAM SM3 208 B2
Hilborough Cl
WIM/MER SW19 178 B3
Hilborough Rd HACK E8 86 B5
Hilborough Wy ORP BR6 216 D3
Hilda Lockert Wk
BRXN/ST SW9 142 C3
Hilda Rd CAN/RD E16 106 C3
EHAM E6 89 H5
Hilda Ter BRXN/ST SW9 * 142 B3
Hilda Vale Rd ORP BR6 216 A2
Hildenborough Gdns
BMLY BR1 183 H2
Hilden Dr ERITH DA8 150 E1
Hildenlea Pl HAYES BR2 183 H5
Hildreth St BAL SW12 161 G3
Hildyard Rd FUL/PGN SW6 119 K6
Hiley Rd WLSDN NW10 100 A2
Hilgrove Rd KIL/WHAMP NW6 83 G5
Hiliary Gdns STAN HA7 43 J5
Hillary Crs WOT/HER KT12 188 B5
Hillary Dr ISLW TW7 136 A5
Hillary Ri BAR EN5 20 E5
Hillary Rd NWDGN UB2 115 F3
Hillbeck Cl PECK SE15 143 K1
Hillbeck Wy GFD/PVL UB6 78 D6
Hillborne Cl HYS/HAR UB3 113 K5
Hillborough Cl
WIM/MER SW19 * 178 B3
Hillbrook Rd TOOT SW17 160 E5
Hill Brow BMLY BR1 184 C4
DART DA1 170 C1
Hillbrow NWMAL KT3 176 C6
Hillbrow Cl BXLY DA5 170 A6
Hillbrow Rd BMLY BR1 183 H3
ESH/CLAY KT10 204 C2
Hillbury Av
KTN/HRWW/WS HA3 61 H2
Hillbury Rd TOOT SW17 161 G5
Hill Cl BAR EN5 20 A6
CHST BR7 185 G1
CRICK NW2 81 K1
GLDGN NW11 64 E3
HRW HA1 78 E1
STAN HA7 29 H6
Hillcote Av STRHM/NOR SW16 180 B3
Hillcourt Av
NFNCH/WDSPK N12 47 F2
Hillcourt Rd EDUL SE22 163 J1
Hill Crs BRYLDS KT5 191 G2
BXLY DA5 169 K3
HRW HA1 61 G2
TRDG/WHET N20 33 F4
WPK KT4 193 F6
Hill Crest SURB KT6 * 191 F4
BFN/LL DA15 168 B2
Hillcrest HGT N6 66 A4
HNHL SE24 * 142 E5
WCHMH N21 35 G2
Hillcrest Av EDGW HA8 30 D6
GLDGN NW11 64 C2
PIN HA5 59 H1
Hillcrest Cl BECK BR3 198 C3
SYD SE26 163 H6
Hill Crest Gdns CRICK NW2 81 J1
Hillcrest Gdns ESH/CLAY KT10 205 F1
FNCH N3 64 C1
Hillcrest Rd ACT W3 117 H1
BMLY BR1 165 K6
DART DA1 170 B2
EA W5 98 A4
EMPK RM11 75 J4
LOU IG10 39 H1
ORP BR6 202 B6
SWFD E18 52 D5
WALTH E17 52 B5
Hillcrest Vw BECK BR3 198 C3
Hillcroft Av PIN HA5 59 K3
Hillcroft Crs EA W5 97 K5
OXHEY WD19 27 F3
RSLP HA4 77 H1
WBLY HA9 80 B2
Hillcroft Rd EHAM E6 108 B4
Hillcroome Rd BELMT SM2 209 H4
Hillcross Av MRDN SM4 193 H3
Hilldale Rd SUT SM1 208 D2
Hilldown Rd HAYES BR2 199 H5
STRHM/NOR SW16 179 K3
Hill Dr CDALE/KGS NW9 62 D5
STRHM/NOR SW16 180 A6
Hilldrop Crs HOLWY N7 84 D3
Hilldrop Est HOLWY N7 84 D3
Hilldrop La HOLWY N7 84 D3
Hilldrop Rd BMLY BR1 183 K2
HOLWY N7 84 D3
Hill End ORP BR6 202 A6
WOOL/PLUM SE18 147 F2
Hillersdon Av BARN SW13 138 D3
EDGW HA8 44 B1
Hillery Cl WALW SE17 19 F7
Hill Farm Rd NKENS W10 100 A4
Hillfield Av ALP/SUD HA0 80 A5
CDALE/KGS NW9 63 G2
CEND/HSY/T N8 67 F1
MRDN SM4 194 D3
Hillfield Cl RYLN/HDSTN HA2 60 C1
Hillfield La South BUSH WD23 28 E1
Hillfield Ms CEND/HSY/T N8 67 F1
Hillfield Pde MRDN SM4 * 194 C3
Hillfield Pk MUSWH N10 48 B6
WCHMH N21 35 G4
Hillfield Park Ms MUSWH N10 66 B1
Hill Field Rd HPTN TW12 172 E3
Hillfield Rd KIL/WHAMP NW6 82 D3
Hillfoot Av CRW RM5 56 E4
Hillfoot Rd CRW RM5 56 E4
Hillgate Pl KENS W8 119 K1
Hillgate St KENS W8 * 119 K1
Hill Gv FELT TW13 154 E4
ROM RM1 57 G6
Hill House Av STAN HA7 43 F3
Hill House Cl WCHMH N21 35 G2
Hill House Dr HPTN TW12 173 F4
Hill House Rd
STRHM/NOR SW16 180 A1
Hilliard Rd NTHWD HA6 40 D4
Hilliard's Ct WAP E1W * 123 K1
Hillier Cl BAR EN5 33 F1
Hillier Gdns CROY/NA CR0 211 G3
Hillier Pl CHSGTN KT9 205 K4
Hillier Rd BTSEA SW11 160 E1
Hillier's La CROY/NA CR0 210 E1
Hillingdon Av
STWL/WRAY TW19 152 B3
Hillingdon Rd BXLYHN DA7 149 K4
Hillingdon St WALW SE17 122 C6
Hillingdon Trail
HGDN/ICK UB10 76 A4
HYS/HAR UB3 113 K5
RSLP HA4 58 A2
Hill La RSLP HA4 58 A5
Hillman Dr NKENS W10 100 A3
Hillman St HACK E8 86 D4
Hillmarton Rd HOLWY N7 84 E3
Hillmarton Ter HOLWY N7 * 84 E3
Hillmead Dr BRXN/ST SW9 142 C5
Hillmont Rd ESH/CLAY KT10 204 E1
Hillmore Gv SYD SE26 182 A1
Hillreach WOOL/PLUM SE18 126 E5
Hill Ri ED N9 36 D1
ESH/CLAY KT10 190 C6
FSTH SE23 163 J3
GFD/PVL UB6 78 C6
GLDGN NW11 65 F1
RCHPK/HAM TW10 136 E6
RSLP HA4 58 A5
Hillrise Rd ARCH N19 66 E4
CRW RM5 56 E2
Hill Rd ALP/SUD HA0 79 H1
CAR SM5 209 J4
HRW HA1 61 G2
MTCM CR4 179 G4
MUSWH N10 47 K4
NTHWD HA6 40 B2
PIN HA5 59 J3
RDART DA2 171 H4
STJWD NW8 101 G1
SUT SM1 209 F3
Hillsboro Rd EDUL SE22 143 F6
Hillsborough Gn
OXHEY WD19 * 26 E5
Hillsgrove Cl WELL DA16 148 D1
Hill Side BAR EN5 21 G6
Hillside CDALE/KGS NW9 63 F1
ESH/CLAY KT10 * 204 B3
WIM/MER SW19 177 G2
WLSDN NW10 81 F6
Hillside Av FBAR/BDGN N11 47 K2
WBLY HA9 80 B2
WFD IG8 53 G1
Hillside Cl MRDN SM4 193 H1
STJWD NW8 101 F1
WFD IG8 53 G1
Hillside Crs ENC/FH EN2 23 K1
NTHWD HA6 40 E4
OXHEY WD19 27 H1
RYLN/HDSTN HA2 60 C6
Hillside Dr EDGW HA8 44 C2
Hillside Gdns BAR EN5 20 C5
BRXS/STRHM SW2 * 162 B4
EDGW HA8 30 B6
FBAR/BDGN N11 * 48 C2
HGT N6 66 A3
KTN/HRWW/WS HA3 62 A4
NTHWD HA6 40 E3
WALTH E17 52 B6
WLGTN SM6 210 C5
Hillside Gv MLHL NW7 45 J3
STHGT/OAK N14 34 D2
Hillside La HAYES BR2 199 K6
Hillside Ri NTHWD HA6 40 E3
Hillside Rd BELMT SM2 208 D5
BRXS/STRHM SW2 162 A4
CROY/NA CR0 211 H3
DART DA1 170 D1
EA W5 98 A4
HAYES BR2 183 J6
NTHWD HA6 40 E3
SEVS/STOTM N15 68 A3
STHL UB1 96 A3
The Hillside ORP BR6 217 H6
Hills La NTHWD HA6 40 C4
Hillsleigh Rd KENS W8 119 J1
Hills Ms EA W5 * 98 A6
Hills Pl SOHO/SHAV W1D 10 A4
Hill's Rd BKHH IG9 39 F3
Hillstowe St CLPT E5 68 E6
Hill St MYFR/PICC W1J 9 J7
RCH/KEW TW9 136 E6
Hill Top CHEAM SM3 193 J4
GLDGN NW11 65 F1
Hilltop WALTH E17 * 51 K6
Hilltop Av WLSDN NW10 80 E5
Hilltop Cots SYD SE26 * 163 J6
Hilltop Gdns DART DA1 151 J6
HDN NW4 45 K5
ORP BR6 201 K6
Hilltop Rd KIL/WHAMP NW6 82 E5
Hill Top Vw WFD IG8 * 53 K2
Hilltop Wy STAN HA7 29 G5
Hillview RYNPK SW20 176 E3
Hillview Av
KTN/HRWW/WS HA3 62 A2
Hillview Cl PIN HA5 41 K2
WBLY HA9 62 B6
Hillview Crs IL IG1 71 K3
ORP BR6 201 K5
Hill View Dr THMD SE28 127 K1
WELL DA16 147 K5
Hill View Gdns
CDALE/KGS NW9 63 F2
Hillview Gdns HDN NW4 64 B1
RYLN/HDSTN HA2 42 A6
Hill View Rd ESH/CLAY KT10 205 G5
ORP BR6 202 A5
TWK TW1 156 B1
Hillview Rd CHST BR7 185 F1
MLHL NW7 32 B6
PIN HA5 41 K3
SUT SM1 209 G1
Hillway CDALE/KGS NW9 63 G5
HGT N6 66 A6
Hillworth BECK BR3 * 182 E5
Hillworth Rd
BRXS/STRHM SW2 162 B2
Hillyard Rd HNWL W7 96 E4
Hillyard St BRXN/ST SW9 142 B2
Hillyfield WALTH E17 51 G5
Hillyfield Cl HOM E9 87 G3
Hilly Flds BROCKY SE4 * 144 D5
Hilly Fields Crs BROCKY SE4 144 D5
Hilsea St CLPT E5 86 E2
Hilton Av NFNCH/WDSPK N12 47 H1
Himalayan Wy WATW WD18 26 D1
Himley Rd TOOT SW17 178 D1
Hinchley Cl ESH/CLAY KT10 205 F1
Hinchley Dr ESH/CLAY KT10 205 F1
Hinchley Wy ESH/CLAY KT10 205 G1
Hinckley Rd PECK SE15 143 H5
Hind Cl CHIG IG7 55 F1
Hind Ct FLST/FETLN EC4A 11 K4
Hind Crs ERITH DA8 149 K1
Hinde Ms MHST W1U * 9 H3
Hindes Rd HRW HA1 60 E2
Hinde St MHST W1U 9 H3
Hind Gv POP/IOD E14 105 J5
Hindhead Gdns NTHLT UB5 77 J6
Hindhead Gn OXHEY WD19 41 G1
Hindhead Wy WLGTN SM6 210 E3
Hindmans Rd EDUL SE22 143 H6
Hindmans Wy DAGW RM9 110 B2
Hindmarsh Cl WCHPL E1 * 104 C6
Hindrey Rd CLPT E5 86 D3
Hindsley's Pl FSTH SE23 163 K4
Hinkler Rd
KTN/HRWW/WS HA3 43 K6
Hinksey Pth ABYW SE2 128 E3
Hinstock Rd
WOOL/PLUM SE18 147 H1
Hinton Av HSLWW TW4 134 C5
Hinton Cl ELTH/MOT SE9 166 D3
Hinton Rd BRXN/ST SW9 142 C4
UED N18 36 A6
WLGTN SM6 210 C4
Hippodrome Pl NTGHL W11 100 C6
Hirst Crs WBLY HA9 80 A1
Hitcham Rd WALTH E17 69 H4
Hitchin La STAN HA7 43 K3
Hithe Gv BERM/RHTH SE16 123 K3
Hitherbroom Rd
HYS/HAR UB3 113 K1
Hither Farm Rd
BKHTH/KID SE3 146 B4
Hitherfield Rd BCTR RM8 74 A6
STRHM/NOR SW16 162 A4
Hither Green La LEW SE13 145 F6
Hitherwell Dr
KTN/HRWW/WS HA3 42 D4
Hitherwood Dr NRWD SE19 163 G6
Hive Cl BUSH WD23 28 D4
Hive Rd BUSH WD23 28 D4
Hoadly Rd STRHM/NOR SW16 161 J5
Hobart Cl TRDG/WHET N20 33 J4
YEAD UB4 95 H3
Hobart Dr YEAD UB4 95 H3
Hobart Gdns THHTH CR7 180 E6
Hobart La YEAD UB4 95 H3
Hobart Pl BGVA SW1W 15 J5
RCHPK/HAM TW10 157 G2
Hobart Rd BARK/HLT IG6 54 C5
DAGW RM9 91 K2
WPK KT4 207 K1
YEAD UB4 95 H3
Hobbayne Rd HNWL W7 96 D5
Hobbes Wk PUT/ROE SW15 138 E6
Hobbs Gn EFNCH N2 47 G6
Hobbs Ms GDMY/SEVK IG3 73 F6
Hobbs Pl IS N1 7 G1
Hobbs Place Est IS N1 7 G2
Hobbs Rd WNWD SE27 162 D6
Hobby St PEND EN3 25 F6
Hobday St POP/IOD E14 105 K5
Hoblands End CHST BR7 185 K2
Hobsons Pl WCHPL E1 * 104 C4
Hobury St WBPTN SW10 120 B6
Hockenden La SWLY BR8 187 H6
Hocker St BETH E2 * 7 J5
Hockley Av EHAM E6 107 J1
Hockley Dr GPK RM2 57 K5
Hockley Ms BARK IG11 108 E1
Hocroft Av CRICK NW2 82 D1
Hocroft Rd CRICK NW2 82 D2
Hocroft Wk CRICK NW2 82 D1
Hodder Dr GFD/PVL UB6 97 F1
Hoddesdon Rd BELV DA17 129 H5
Hodes Rw HAMP NW3 83 K2
Hodford Rd GLDGN NW11 64 D5
Hodges Wy WATW WD18 26 E1
Hodgkins Cl THMD SE28 109 K6
Hodgkins Ms STAN HA7 43 G1
Hodister Cl CMBW SE5 142 D1
Hodnet Gv BERM/RHTH SE16 123 K4
Hodson Cl RYLN/HDSTN HA2 77 K1
Hodson Crs STMC/STPC BR5 202 E3
Hodson Pl PEND EN3 25 J1
Hoe La PEND EN3 24 E1
Hoe St WALTH E17 69 J2
The Hoe OXHEY WD19 27 H4
Hoffmann Gdns
SAND/SEL CR2 212 C4
Hoffman Sq IS N1 * 7 F4
Hofland Rd WKENS W14 119 H3
Hogan Ms BAY/PAD W2 8 A1
Hogarth Cl CAN/RD E16 107 H4
EA W5 98 A4
Hogarth Crs CROY/NA CR0 196 D4
WIM/MER SW19 178 C4
Hogarth Gdns HEST TW5 135 F1
Hogarth Hl GLDGN NW11 64 D1
Hogarth Pl ECT SW5 * 120 A4
Hogarth Rd BCTR RM8 91 H3
ECT SW5 120 A4
EDGW HA8 44 C5
Hogarth Ter CHSWK W4 * 118 B6
Hogarth Wy HPTN TW12 173 H4
Hog Hill Rd CRW RM5 56 B3
Hogshead Pas WAP E1W * 104 D6
Hogsmill La KUT/HW KT1 175 G6
Hogsmill Wy HOR/WEW KT19 206 E3
Holbeach Cl CDALE/KGS NW9 45 G4
Holbeach Gdns BFN/LL DA15 167 K1
Holbeach Rd CAT SE6 164 D2
Holbeck Rw PECK SE15 143 H1
Holbein Ga NTHWD HA6 40 C1
Holbein Ms BGVA SW1W 121 F5
Holbein Pl BGVA SW1W 15 G7
Holberton Gdns WLSDN NW10 99 K2
Holborn GINN WC1R 11 J2
HCIRC EC1N 11 J2
Holborn Circ HCIRC EC1N 11 K2
Holborn Pl HHOL WC1V 11 G2
Holborn Rd PLSTW E13 107 F4
Holborn Viad STBT EC1A 12 A2
Holborn Wy MTCM CR4 178 E5
Holbrook Cl EN EN1 24 B2
Holbrooke Ct HOLWY N7 84 E1
Holbrook La CHST BR7 185 J3
Holbrook Rd SRTFD E15 106 D1
Holbrook Wy HAYES BR2 200 E3
Holburne Cl BKHTH/KID SE3 146 B2
Holburne Gdns
BKHTH/KID SE3 146 C2
Holburne Rd BKHTH/KID SE3 146 B2
Holcombe Hl MLHL NW7 31 J5
Holcombe Rd IL IG1 72 A4
TOTM N17 50 B6
Holcombe St HMSMTH W6 118 E5
Holcote Cl BELV DA17 129 F3
Holcroft Rd HOM E9 86 E5
Holden Av CDALE/KGS NW9 62 E5
NFNCH/WDSPK N12 47 F1
Holdenby Rd BROCKY SE4 144 B6
Holden Cl BCTR RM8 91 H1
Holdenhurst Av FNCH N3 47 F3
Holden Rd
NFNCH/WDSPK N12 33 F6
Holden St BTSEA SW11 141 F3
Holdernesse Rd ISLW TW7 136 B2
TOOT SW17 160 E5
Holderness Wy WNWD SE27 180 C1
Holders Hill Av HDN NW4 46 B5
Holders Hill Crs HDN NW4 46 B5
Holders Hill Dr HDN NW4 46 B5
Holders Hill Gdns HDN NW4 46 B5
Holders Hill Pde MLHL NW7 * 46 C4
Holders Hill Rd HDN NW4 46 B5
Holford Ms FSBYW WC1X * 5 G4
Holford Rd HAMP NW3 83 G1
Holford St FSBYW WC1X 5 J4
Holford Wy PUT/ROE SW15 158 D1
Holford Yd FSBYW WC1X * 5 J3
Holgate Av BTSEA SW11 140 C4
Holgate Rd DAGE RM10 92 C3
Holgate St CHARL SE7 126 C3
Holland Av BELMT SM2 208 E5
RYNPK SW20 176 C4
Holland Cl BAR EN5 33 H2
HAYES BR2 199 J6
ROMW/RG RM7 74 E2
STAN HA7 43 H1
Holland Dr FSTH SE23 164 B5
Holland Gdns BTFD TW8 117 G5
WKENS W14 119 H3
Holland Gv BRXN/ST SW9 142 B1
Holland Pk NTGHL W11 119 J1
Holland Park Av
GDMY/SEVK IG3 72 E3
NTGHL W11 119 H1
Holland Park Gdns
WKENS W14 119 H2
Holland Park Ms NTGHL W11 119 J1
Holland Park Rd WKENS W14 119 J3
Holland Park Ter NTGHL W11 119 H1
Holland Pas IS N1 85 J6
Holland Pl KENS W8 120 A2
Holland Place Chambers
KENS W8 * 120 A2
Holland Rd ALP/SUD HA0 79 K4
EHAM E6 89 K6
SNWD SE25 197 H2
SRTFD E15 106 C2
WKENS W14 119 G2
WLSDN NW10 81 J6
The Hollands WPK KT4 192 C5
Holland St KENS W8 119 K2
STHWK SE1 12 B7
Holland Villas Rd WKENS W14 119 H2
Holland Wk STAN HA7 43 G1
Holland Wy HAYES BR2 199 J6
Hollar Rd STNW/STAM N16 86 B1
Hollen St SOHO/CST W1F 10 B4
Holles Cl HPTN TW12 173 F2
Holles St CAVSQ/HST W1G 9 K3
OXSTW W1C 9 K4
Holley Rd ACT W3 118 B2
Hollickwood Av
NFNCH/WDSPK N12 47 K2
Holliday Sq BTSEA SW11 140 C4
Hollidge Wy DAGE RM10 92 D4
Hollies Av BFN/LL DA15 168 A4
Hollies Cl STRHM/NOR SW16 180 B2
TWK TW1 156 A4
Hollies End MLHL NW7 45 K1
Hollies Rd EA W5 116 D4
The Hollies
KTN/HRWW/WS HA3 61 G1
Hollies Wy BAL SW12 * 161 F2
Holligrave Rd BMLY BR1 183 K4
Hollingbourne Av
BXLYHN DA7 149 G2
Hollingbourne Gdns
WEA W13 97 G4
Hollingbourne Rd HNHL SE24 142 D6
Hollingsworth Rd
CROY/NA CR0 212 D4
Hollington Crs NWMAL KT3 192 C3
Hollington Rd EHAM E6 107 K2
TOTM N17 50 C5
Hollingworth Cl
E/WMO/HCT KT8 188 E1
Hollingworth Rd
STMC/STPC BR5 201 G4
Hollman Gdns
STRHM/NOR SW16 180 C2
Holloway La WDR/YW UB7 112 C5
Holloway Rd ARCH N19 66 D6
EHAM E6 107 K2
HOLWY N7 85 F2
WAN E11 88 B1
Holloway St HSLW TW3 135 G4
The Hollow WFD IG8 38 D6
Holly Av STAN HA7 44 A5
WOT/HER KT12 188 C5
Holly Bank MUSWH N10 * 66 C1
Hollybank Cl HPTN TW12 173 F1
Hollybrake Cl CHST BR7 185 J3
Hollybush Cl
KTN/HRWW/WS HA3 42 E4
OXHEY WD19 27 G2
WAN E11 70 E2
Hollybush Gdns BETH E2 104 D2
Hollybush Hl WAN E11 70 D3
Holly Bush La HPTN TW12 172 E3
Hollybush Pl BETH E2 104 D2
Hollybush Rd KUTN/CMB KT2 175 F1
Hollybush St PLSTW E13 107 F2
Hollybush Ter NRWD SE19 * 181 F2
Holly Bush V HAMP NW3 * 83 G2
Holly Cl BECK BR3 199 F1
BKHH IG9 39 H5
FELT TW13 172 D1
SUN TW16 172 A6
WLGTN SM6 210 B5
WLSDN NW10 81 G5
Holly Crs BECK BR3 198 C2
WFD IG8 52 B3
Hollycroft Av HAMP NW3 82 E1
WBLY HA9 62 A6
Hollycroft Cl SAND/SEL CR2 212 A3
WDR/YW UB7 112 D6
Hollycroft Gdns WDR/YW UB7 112 D6
Hollydale Cl NTHLT UB5 78 B3
Hollydale Dr HAYES BR2 215 K1
Hollydale Rd PECK SE15 143 K3
Hollydown Wy WAN E11 88 B1
Holly Dr CHING E4 37 K2
Holly Farm Rd NWDGN UB2 114 D5
Hollyfield Av FBAR/BDGN N11 47 K1
Hollyfield Rd BRYLDS KT5 191 G4
Holly Gdns BXLYHN DA7 149 K5
WDR/YW UB7 112 C2
Hollygrove BUSH WD23 28 D2
Holly Gv CDALE/KGS NW9 62 E4
PECK SE15 143 G3
PIN HA5 41 J4
Hollygrove Cl HSLW TW3 134 E5
Holly Hedge Ter LEW SE13 145 F6
Holly Hl HAMP NW3 83 G2
WCHMH N21 35 F1
Holly Hill Rd BELV DA17 129 J5
Holly Lodge Gdns HGT N6 66 A6
Hollymead CAR SM5 209 K1
Holly Ms WBPTN SW10 120 B5
Holly Mt HAMP NW3 * 83 G2
Hollymount Cl GNWCH SE10 145 F2
Holly Pk FNCH N3 46 D6
FSBYPK N4 66 E4
Holly Park Gdns FNCH N3 46 E6
Holly Park Rd
FBAR/BDGN N11 48 A1
HNWL W7 116 A1
Holly Rd CHSWK W4 * 118 A4
DART DA1 171 G3
HPTN TW12 173 H2
HSLW TW3 135 G5
ORP BR6 217 G5
TWK TW1 156 B3
WAN E11 70 D4
Holly St HACK E8 86 B5
Hollytree Cl WIM/MER SW19 159 G3
Hollytree Pde SCUP DA14 * 186 D1
Hollyview Cl HDN NW4 63 J3
Holly Vls HMSMTH W6 * 118 E3
Holly Wk HAMP NW3 83 G2
Holly Wy MTCM CR4 195 J1
Hollywell Gv HCH RM12 75 H5
Hollywood Gdns YEAD UB4 95 F5
Hollywood Ms WBPTN SW10 * 120 B6
Hollywood Rd CHING E4 51 G1
WBPTN SW10 120 B6
Hollywoods CROY/NA CR0 213 H6
Hollywood Wy ERITH DA8 150 E1
WFD IG8 52 B3
Holman Ct EW KT17 * 207 J6
Holman Rd BTSEA SW11 140 C3
HOR/WEW KT19 206 E3
Holmbridge Gdns PEND EN3 25 F5
Holmbrook Dr HDN NW4 64 B2
Holmbury Cl BUSH WD23 28 E4
Holmbury Ct WIM/MER SW19 178 D3
Holmbury Gdns HYS/HAR UB3 113 J1
Holmbury Gv CROY/NA CR0 * 213 H5
SAND/SEL CR2 213 H5
Holmbury Mnr SCUP DA14 * 168 B6
Holmbury Pk BMLY BR1 184 D3
Holmbury Vw CLPT E5 68 D5
Holmbush Rd PUT/ROE SW15 159 H1
Holmcote Gdns HBRY N5 85 J3
Holmcroft Wy HAYES BR2 200 E2
Holmdale Gdns HDN NW4 64 B2
Holmdale Rd CHST BR7 185 H1
KIL/WHAMP NW6 82 E3
Holmdale Ter
SEVS/STOTM N15 68 A3
Holmdene Av HNHL SE24 142 D6
MLHL NW7 45 J2
RYLN/HDSTN HA2 42 B6
Holmdene Cl BECK BR3 183 F5
Holmdene Ct BMLY BR1 184 D6
Holmead Rd FUL/PGN SW6 140 A1
Holmebury Cl BUSH WD23 * 28 E4
Holme Ct ISLW TW7 136 B4
Holme Lacey Rd
LEE/GVPK SE12 165 J1
Holme Rd EHAM E6 89 J6
Holmes Av MLHL NW7 46 C1
WALTH E17 51 H6
Holmes Cl EDUL SE22 143 H5
Holmesdale Av
MORT/ESHN SW14 137 J4
Holmesdale Cl SNWD SE25 181 G6
Holmesdale Rd BXLYHN DA7 148 E3
CROY/NA CR0 196 E2
HGT N6 66 B4
RCH/KEW TW9 137 G2
SNWD SE25 197 F1
TEDD TW11 174 D3
Holmesley Rd FSTH SE23 164 B1
Holmes Rd KTTN NW5 84 B3

TWK TW1 156 A4
WIM/MER SW19 178 B3
Holmes Ter STHWK SE1 17 J2
Holme Wy STAN HA7 43 F2
Holmewood Gdns
BRXS/STRHM SW2 162 A2
Holmewood Rd
BRXS/STRHM SW2 161 K2
SNWD SE25 181 F6
Holmfield Av HDN NW4 64 B2
Holmhurst Rd BELV DA17 129 J5
Holmleigh Av DART DA1 151 F5
Holmleigh Rd
STNW/STAM N16 68 A5
Holm Oak Cl PUT/ROE SW15 159 J1
Holmsdale Gv BXLYHN DA7 150 B3
Holmshaw Cl SYD SE26 164 B6
Holmside Ri OXHEY WD19 27 F5
Holmside Rd BAL SW12 161 F1
Holmsley Cl NWMAL KT3 192 C3
Holmstall Av EDGW HA8 44 E5
Holmstall Pde EDGW HA8 * 44 E5
Holmwood Cl BELMT SM2 208 B6
NTHLT UB5 78 B4
RYLN/HDSTN HA2 42 C6
Holmwood Gdns FNCH N3 46 E5
WLGTN SM6 210 B4
Holmwood Gv MLHL NW7 45 F1
Holmwood Rd BELMT SM2 208 A6
CHSGTN KT9 206 A3
GDMY/SEVK IG3 72 E6
Holmwood Vls CHARL SE7 125 K5
Holne Cha EFNCH N2 65 G3
MRDN SM4 193 K3
Holness Rd SRTFD E15 88 D4
Holroyd Rd ESH/CLAY KT10 205 F6
PUT/ROE SW15 139 F5
Holstein Wy ERITHM DA18 128 E3
Holstock Rd IL IG1 72 C6
Holsworth Cl
RYLN/HDSTN HA2 60 C2
Holsworthy Sq FSBYW WC1X 5 H7
Holsworthy Wy CHSGTN KT9 205 J3
Holt Cl CHIG IG7 55 F1
MUSWH N10 66 A1
SCUP DA14 169 F6
THMD SE28 109 H6
Holton St WCHPL E1 105 F3
Holt Rd ALP/SUD HA0 79 H1
CAN/RD E16 126 D1
The Holt BARK/HLT IG6 54 C2
MRDN SM4 * 193 K1
WLGTN SM6 210 C2
Holt Wy CHIG IG7 55 F1
Holtwhite Av ENC/FH EN2 23 J3
Holtwhite's Hl ENC/FH EN2 23 H2
Holwell Pl PIN HA5 59 J1
Holwood Cl WOT/HER KT12 188 B6
Holwood Park Av ORP BR6 215 K2
Holwood Pl CLAP SW4 141 J5
Holybourne Av
PUT/ROE SW15 158 D2
Holyoake Ct
BERM/RHTH SE16 124 B2
Holyoake Wk EA W5 97 J3
EFNCH N2 47 G6
Holyoak Rd LBTH SE11 18 A6
Holyport Rd FUL/PGN SW6 139 F1
Holyrood Av
RYLN/HDSTN HA2 77 J2
Holyrood Gdns EDGW HA8 44 D5
Holyrood Ms CAN/RD E16 125 K1
Holyrood Rd BAR EN5 33 G1
Holyrood St STHWK SE1 19 G1
Holywell Cl
BERM/RHTH SE16 * 123 J5
BKHTH/KID SE3 125 K6
ORP BR6 217 G2
STWL/WRAY TW19 152 B3
Holywell La SDTCH EC2A 7 H6
Holywell Rw SDTCH EC2A 7 G7
Holywell Wy
STWL/WRAY TW19 152 B3
Home Cl CAR SM5 194 E6
NTHLT UB5 95 K2
Home Ct FELT TW13 * 153 K3
SURB KT6 * 190 E2
Homecroft Rd SYD SE26 181 K1
WDGN N22 49 H4
Home Farm Cl ESH/CLAY KT10 204 B4
THDIT KT7 190 A4
Home Farm Gdns
WOT/HER KT12 188 B6
Homefarm Rd HNWL W7 96 E5
Homefield Av
GNTH/NBYPK IG2 72 E2
Homefield Cl STMC/STPC BR5 202 C1
WLSDN NW10 80 E4
YEAD UB4 95 H3
Homefield Gdns EFNCH N2 47 H6
WIM/MER SW19 178 B5
Homefield Ms BECK BR3 * 182 D4
Homefield Pk SUT SM1 209 F4
Homefield Pl CROY/NA CR0 197 G6
Homefield Ri ORP BR6 202 B5
Homefield Rd ALP/SUD HA0 79 G2
BMLY BR1 184 B4
CHSWK W4 118 C4
EDGW HA8 45 F2
WIM/MER SW19 177 H2
WOT/HER KT12 188 E4
Homefield St IS N1 * 7 G3
The Homefield MRDN SM4 * 193 K1
Home Gdns DAGE RM10 92 E1
DART DA1 171 H1
Homeland Dr BELMT SM2 209 F6
Homelands Dr NRWD SE19 181 F3
Home Lea ORP BR6 217 F3
Homeleigh Rd PECK SE15 144 A6
Home Md STAN HA7 43 J4
Homemead Rd CROY/NA CR0 195 H3
HAYES BR2 200 E2
Home Park Ct KUT/HW KT1 * 190 E1
Home Park Rd
WIM/MER SW19 159 J6
Home Park Ter KUT/HW KT1 174 E5
Home Park Wk KUT/HW KT1 190 E1
Homer Cl BXLYHN DA7 149 K2
Homer Dr POP/IOD E14 124 D4
Home Rd BTSEA SW11 140 D3
Homer Rd CROY/NA CR0 198 A3
HOM E9 87 G4
Homer Rw CAMTN NW1 8 D2
Homersham Rd KUT/HW KT1 175 H5
Homer St MBLAR W1H 8 D2
Homerton Gv HOM E9 87 F3
Homerton High St HOM E9 87 F3
Homerton Rd HOM E9 87 H3
Homerton Rw HOM E9 86 E3
Homerton Ter HOM E9 86 E4
Homesdale Cl WAN E11 70 E2
Homesdale Rd HAYES BR2 200 B1
ORP BR6 201 K4
Homesfield GLDGN NW11 64 E2
Homestall Rd EDUL SE22 143 K6
Homestead Gdns
ESH/CLAY KT10 204 E3
Homestead Paddock
STHGT/OAK N14 22 B6
Homestead Pk CRICK NW2 81 H1
Homestead Rd BCTR RM8 74 B6
FUL/PGN SW6 139 J1
ORP BR6 217 H5
The Homestead DART DA1 171 F1
Homewillow Cl WCHMH N21 35 H1
Homewood Cl HPTN TW12 172 E2
Homewood Crs CHST BR7 185 K2
Homewood Gdns
SNWD SE25 * 197 F2
Honduras St FSBYE EC1V 6 C6
Honeybourne Rd
KIL/WHAMP NW6 83 F3
Honeybourne Wy
STMC/STPC BR5 201 H5
Honeybrook Rd BAL SW12 161 H2
Honey Cl DAGE RM10 92 E4
Honeyden Rd SCUP DA14 187 F2
Honeyfield Ms FSTH SE23 164 A5
Honeyman Cl CRICK NW2 82 B5
Honeypot Cl CDALE/KGS NW9 62 B1
Honeypot La CDALE/KGS NW9 62 B1
KTN/HRWW/WS HA3 44 B6
STAN HA7 43 K4
Honeysett Rd TOTM N17 50 B5
Honeysuckle Cl STHL UB1 95 J6
Honeysuckle Gdns
CROY/NA CR0 198 A4
Honeywell Rd BTSEA SW11 160 D1
Honeywood Rd ISLW TW7 * 136 B5
WLSDN NW10 99 H1
Honeywood Wk CAR SM5 209 K2
Honister Cl STAN HA7 43 H4
Honister Gdns STAN HA7 43 H3
Honister Pl STAN HA7 43 H4
Honiton Gdns MLHL NW7 45 J3
PECK SE15 * 143 K3
Honiton Rd KIL/WHAMP NW6 100 D1
ROMW/RG RM7 75 F3
WELL DA16 148 A3
Honley Rd CAT SE6 164 E2
Honnor Gdns ISLW TW7 135 J3
Honor Oak Pk FSTH SE23 163 K1
Honor Oak Ri FSTH SE23 163 K1
Honor Oak Rd FSTH SE23 163 K3
Hood Av MORT/ESHN SW14 137 K6
STHGT/OAK N14 34 B1
STMC/STPC BR5 202 C2
Hood Cl CROY/NA CR0 196 C5
Hoodcote Gdns WCHMH N21 35 H2
Hood Rd RAIN RM13 93 G6
RYNPK SW20 176 C3
Hood Wk ROMW/RG RM7 56 D4
Hooker's Rd WALTH E17 51 F6
Hook Farm Rd HAYES BR2 200 C2
Hook Green La RDART DA2 170 C5
Hooking Gn RYLN/HDSTN HA2 60 B2
Hook La WELL DA16 148 A5
Hook Ri North SURB KT6 206 B1
Hook Ri South CHSGTN KT9 206 B1
Hook Rd CHSGTN KT9 205 K3
HOR/WEW KT19 206 E5
SURB KT6 191 F6
Hooks Hall Dr DAGE RM10 92 E1
Hookstone Wy WFD IG8 53 H3
The Hook BAR EN5 33 H1
Hook Underpass (Kingston
By-Pass) SURB KT6 205 K1
Hook Wk EDGW HA8 44 E2
Hooper Rd CAN/RD E16 106 E5
Hoopers Ms BUSH WD23 28 B3
Hooper's Ms ACT W3 117 K1
Hooper St WCHPL E1 104 C6
Hoop La GLDGN NW11 64 D4
Hop Ct ALP/SUD HA0 * 79 J4
Hope Cl BTFD TW8 117 F5
CHDH RM6 73 K1
IS N1 85 J4
LEE/GVPK SE12 166 A5
SUT SM1 209 G3
Hopedale Rd CHARL SE7 126 A6
Hopefield Av
KIL/WHAMP NW6 100 C1
Hope Gdns ACT W3 117 J2
Hope La ELTH/MOT SE9 167 G5
Hope Pk BMLY BR1 183 J3
Hopes Cl HEST TW5 115 F6
Hope Sq LVPST EC2M 13 G2
Hope St BTSEA SW11 140 C4
Hopetown St WCHPL E1 * 13 K2
Hopewell St CMBW SE5 142 E1
Hopewell Yd CMBW SE5 142 E1
Hop Gdns CHCR WC2N 10 E6
Hopgood St SHB W12 119 F1
Hopkins Cl MUSWH N10 48 A3
Hopkins Ms SRTFD E15 88 D6
Hopkinsons Pl CAMTN NW1 * 83 K6
Hopkins Rd LEY E10 69 K4
Hopkins St SOHO/CST W1F 10 B4
Hoppers Rd WCHMH N21 35 G4
Hoppett Rd CHING E4 38 C5
Hopping La IS N1 * 85 H4
Hoppingwood Av
NWMAL KT3 176 B6
Hoppner Rd YEAD UB4 94 B1
Hop St GNWCH SE10 125 J4
Hopton Gdns NWMAL KT3 192 D3
Hopton Pde
STRHM/NOR SW16 * 179 K1
Hopton Rd STRHM/NOR SW16 179 K1
WOOL/PLUM SE18 127 G3
Hoptons Gdns STHWK SE1 * 12 B7
Hopton St STHWK SE1 12 B6
Hoptree Cl
NFNCH/WDSPK N12 * 33 F6
Hopwood Cl TOOT SW17 160 B5
Hopwood Rd WALW SE17 122 E6
Hopwood Wk HACK E8 * 86 C5
Horace Av ROMW/RG RM7 75 F5
Horace Rd BARK/HLT IG6 54 C6
FSTGT E7 89 F2
KUT/HW KT1 175 G6
Horatio Pl POP/IOD E14 125 F2
Horatio St BETH E2 7 K3
Horatius Wy CROY/NA CR0 211 F4
Horbury Crs NTGHL W11 100 E6
Horbury Ms NTGHL W11 100 D6
Horder Rd FUL/PGN SW6 139 H2
Hordle Prom East PECK SE15 143 G1
Hordle Prom North
PECK SE15 143 G1
Hordle Prom West PECK SE15 143 F1
Horley Cl BXLYHS DA6 149 H6
Horley Rd ELTH/MOT SE9 166 D6
Hormead Rd MV/WKIL W9 100 D3
Hornbeam Cl IL IG1 90 D3
LBTH SE11 17 J6
MLHL NW7 31 H5
NTHLT UB5 77 K3
Hornbeam Crs BTFD TW8 136 C1
Hornbeam Gdns NWMAL KT3 192 D3
Hornbeam Gv CHING E4 38 C5
Hornbeam Rd BKHH IG9 39 H5
YEAD UB4 95 G4
Hornbeam Sq BOW E3 87 H6
Hornbeams Ri
FBAR/BDGN N11 48 A2
Hornbeam Wy HAYES BR2 201 F3
Hornbuckle Cl
RYLN/HDSTN HA2 60 D6
Hornby Cl HAMP NW3 83 H5
Horncastle Cl LEE/GVPK SE12 165 K2
Horncastle Rd LEE/GVPK SE12 165 K2
Hornchurch Cl
KUTN/CMB KT2 174 E1
Hornchurch Rd HCH RM12 75 J5
Horndean Cl PUT/ROE SW15 158 D3
Horndon Cl CRW RM5 56 E4
Horndon Gn CRW RM5 56 E4
Horndon Rd CRW RM5 56 E4
Horne House CHARL SE7 * 146 D1
Horner La MTCM CR4 178 C5
Horne Wy PUT/ROE SW15 139 F3
Hornfair Rd CHARL SE7 126 C6
Hornford Wy ROMW/RG RM7 75 G4
Horniman Dr FSTH SE23 163 J3
Horniman Gdns FSTH SE23 * 163 J3
Horning Cl ELTH/MOT SE9 166 D6
Horn La ACT W3 117 K1
GNWCH SE10 125 K4
WFD IG8 52 E2
Horn Link Wy GNWCH SE10 125 K3
Horn Park Cl LEE/GVPK SE12 146 A6
Horn Park La LEE/GVPK SE12 146 A6
Hornscroft Cl BARK IG11 90 E5
Horns End Pl PIN HA5 59 G1
Hornsey Chambers CLPT E5 * 68 D6
Hornsey La HGT N6 66 C4
Hornsey Lane Est ARCH N19 * 66 D4
Hornsey Lane Gdns HGT N6 66 C4
Hornsey Park Rd
CEND/HSY/T N8 49 F6
Hornsey Ri ARCH N19 66 D4
Hornsey Rise Gdns ARCH N19 66 D4
Hornsey Rd ARCH N19 66 E5
HOLWY N7 85 F1
Hornsey St HOLWY N7 85 F3
Hornshay St PECK SE15 123 K6
Horns Rd BARK/HLT IG6 72 C2
Hornton Pl KENS W8 119 K2
Hornton St KENS W8 119 K2
Horsa Rd ERITH DA8 149 K1
LEE/GVPK SE12 166 B2
Horsebridges Cl DAGW RM9 92 A6
Horsecroft Cl ORP BR6 202 C5
Horsecroft Rd EDGW HA8 45 F3
Horse Fair KUT/HW KT1 174 E5
Horseferry Pl GNWCH SE10 125 F6
Horseferry Rd POP/IOD E14 105 G6
WEST SW1P 16 C5
Horse Guards Av
WHALL SW1A 16 E1
Horse Guards Rd
WHALL SW1A 16 D1
Horse Leaze EHAM E6 108 B5
Horsell Rd HBRY N5 85 G3
STMC/STPC BR5 186 B4
Horselydown La STHWK SE1 19 J2
Horsenden Av GFD/PVL UB6 78 E3
Horsenden Crs GFD/PVL UB6 79 F3
Horsenden La North
GFD/PVL UB6 78 E4
Horsenden La South
GFD/PVL UB6 79 G6
Horseshoe Cl CRICK NW2 63 K6
POP/IOD E14 125 F5
Horse Shoe Crs NTHLT UB5 96 A1
Horseshoe La ENC/FH EN2 23 J4
TRDG/WHET N20 32 B3
Horseshoe Ms
BRXS/STRHM SW2 141 K5
Horse Yd IS N1 85 H6
Horsfeld Gdns ELTH/MOT SE9 146 D6
Horsfeld Rd ELTH/MOT SE9 146 C6
Horsford Rd
BRXS/STRHM SW2 142 A6
Horsham Av
NFNCH/WDSPK N12 47 J1
Horsham Rd BXLYHS DA6 169 G1
EBED/NFELT TW14 153 F1
Horsley Dr CROY/NA CR0 214 A5
KUTN/CMB KT2 174 E1
Horsley Rd BMLY BR1 184 A4
CHING E4 38 A4
Horsley St WALW SE17 122 E6
Horsmans Pl DART DA1 * 171 H2
Horsman St CMBW SE5 122 D6
Horsmonden Cl ORP BR6 201 K4
Horsmonden Rd BROCKY SE4 144 C6
Hortensia Rd WBPTN SW10 120 B6
Horticultural Pl CHSWK W4 118 A5
Horton Av CRICK NW2 82 C2
Horton Bridge Rd
WDR/YW UB7 112 C1
Horton Cl WDR/YW UB7 112 C1
Horton La HOR/WEW KT19 206 D6
Horton Pde WDR/YW UB7 * 112 B1
Horton Rd HACK E8 86 D4
WDR/YW UB7 112 B1
Horton St LEW SE13 144 E4
Horton Wy CROY/NA CR0 198 A2
Hortus Rd NWDGN UB2 114 E2
Hosack Rd TOOT SW17 160 E4
Hoser Av LEE/GVPK SE12 165 K4
Hosier La STBT EC1A 12 A2
Hoskins Cl HYS/HAR UB3 113 J5
Hoskin's Cl CAN/RD E16 107 G5
Hoskins St GNWCH SE10 125 G5
Hospital Bridge Rd
WHTN TW2 155 F2
Hospital Rd HSLW TW3 135 F4
LEY E10 70 B3
Hospital Wy LEW SE13 165 G1
Hotham Cl E/WMO/HCT KT8 173 F6
Hotham Rd PUT/ROE SW15 139 F4
Hotham Road Ms
WIM/MER SW19 178 B3
Hotham St SRTFD E15 88 C6
Hothfield Pl
BERM/RHTH SE16 123 K3
Hotspur Rd NTHLT UB5 96 A1
Hotspur St LBTH SE11 122 B5
Houblon Rd
RCHPK/HAM TW10 137 F6
Houghton Cl HACK E8 * 86 B4
HPTN TW12 172 D2
Houghton Rd
SEVS/STOTM N15 68 B1
Houghton St LINN WC2A * 11 H4
Houlder Crs CROY/NA CR0 211 H3
Houndsden Rd WCHMH N21 35 F1
Houndsditch HDTCH EC3A 13 H3
Houndsfield Rd ED N9 36 D2
Hounslow Av HSLW TW3 135 G6
Hounslow Gdns HSLW TW3 135 G6
Hounslow Rd
EBED/NFELT TW14 154 A2
Houseman Wy CMBW SE5 142 E1
Houston Rd FSTH SE23 164 B4
SURB KT6 190 C3
Hove Av WALTH E17 69 H2
Hoveden Rd CRICK NW2 82 B3
Hove Gdns SUT SM1 194 A5
Hoveton Rd THMD SE28 109 J5
Howard Av BXLY DA5 168 D3
Howard Cl ACT W3 98 D5
BUSH WD23 28 E2
CRICK NW2 * 82 C2
FBAR/BDGN N11 34 A4
HPTN TW12 173 H3
LOU IG10 39 J1
Howard Rd BARK IG11 90 D6
BMLY BR1 183 K3
CRICK NW2 82 B2
DART DA1 171 K1
EHAM E6 107 K1
IL IG1 90 B2
ISLW TW7 136 A4
NWMAL KT3 176 B6
PGE/AN SE20 181 K4
SEVS/STOTM N15 68 A3
SNWD SE25 197 H2
STAN HA7 43 K4
STHL UB1 96 B5
STNW/STAM N16 85 K2
SURB KT6 191 G3
WALTH E17 51 J6
WAN E11 88 C1
Howards Cl PIN HA5 * 41 F5
Howards Crest Cl BECK BR3 183 F5
Howard's La PUT/ROE SW15 139 F5
Howard's Rd PLSTW E13 106 E2
Howard St THDIT KT7 190 C4
Howards Yd
WAND/EARL SW18 160 A2
Howard Wk EFNCH N2 65 G1
Howard Wy BAR EN5 20 B6
Howarth Rd ABYW SE2 128 B5
Howberry Cl EDGW HA8 43 K2
Howberry Rd STAN HA7 43 K2
THHTH CR7 180 E4
Howbury La ERITH DA8 150 D3
Howbury Rd PECK SE15 143 K4
Howcroft Crs FNCH N3 46 E3
Howcroft La GFD/PVL UB6 96 D2
Howden Cl THMD SE28 109 J6
Howden Rd SNWD SE25 181 G5
Howden St PECK SE15 143 H4
Howe Cl ROMW/RG RM7 56 C4
Howell Cl CHDH RM6 73 K2
Howell Wk STHWK SE1 18 B7
Howerd Wy
WOOL/PLUM SE18 146 D2
Howes Cl FNCH N3 46 E6
Howfield Pl TOTM N17 * 50 B6
Howgate Rd
MORT/ESHN SW14 138 A4
Howick Pl WESTW SW1E 16 B5
Howie St BTSEA SW11 140 D1
Howitt Cl HAMP NW3 83 J4
Howitt Rd HAMP NW3 83 J4
Howitts Cl ESH/CLAY KT10 204 A4
Howland Ct PIN HA5 * 42 A2
Howland Ms East FITZ W1T 10 B1
Howland St FITZ W1T 10 B1
Howland Wy
BERM/RHTH SE16 124 B2
Howletts La RSLP HA4 58 A3
Howletts Rd HNHL SE24 162 D1
Howley Pl BAY/PAD W2 101 G4
Howley Rd CROY/NA CR0 211 H1
Howsman Rd BARN SW13 118 D6
Howson Rd BROCKY SE4 144 B5
Howson Ter
RCHPK/HAM TW10 * 157 F1
How's St BETH E2 7 J2
Howton Pl BUSH WD23 28 D3
Hoxton Market IS N1 7 G5
Hoxton Sq IS N1 7 G5
Hoxton St IS N1 7 G1
Hoylake Gdns MTCM CR4 179 H6
OXHEY WD19 27 H6
RSLP HA4 59 F5
Hoylake Rd ACT W3 99 G5
Hoyland Cl PECK SE15 * 143 J1
Hoyle Rd TOOT SW17 178 D1
Hoy St CAN/RD E16 106 D5
Hubbard Dr CHSGTN KT9 205 J4
Hubbard Rd WNWD SE27 162 D6
Hubbard St SRTFD E15 88 C6
Hubert Cl WIM/MER SW19 * 178 B4
Hubert Gv BRXN/ST SW9 141 K4
Hubert Rd EHAM E6 107 H2
RAIN RM13 111 H2
Huddart St BOW E3 105 H4
Huddleston Cl BETH E2 * 104 E1
Huddlestone Rd CRICK NW2 81 K4
FSTGT E7 88 D2
Huddleston Rd HOLWY N7 84 C1
Hudson Cl SHB W12 * 99 K6
Hudson Pl WOOL/PLUM SE18 127 H5
Hudson Rd BXLYHN DA7 149 G3
HYS/HAR UB3 113 G6
Huggins Pl BRXS/STRHM SW2 162 A3
Hughan Rd SRTFD E15 88 B3
Hugh Dalton Av
FUL/PGN SW6 119 J6
Hughenden Av
KTN/HRWW/WS HA3 61 H2
Hughenden Gdns NTHLT UB5 95 G2
Hughenden Rd WPK KT4 192 D4
Hughes Cl
NFNCH/WDSPK N12 47 G1
Hughes Rd HYS/HAR UB3 95 F6
Hughes Ter CAN/RD E16 * 106 D4
Hughes Wk CROY/NA CR0 196 D4
Hugh Gaitskell Cl
FUL/PGN SW6 * 119 J6
Hugh Ms PIM SW1V 15 K7
Hugh Pl WEST SW1P 16 C6
Hugh St PIM SW1V 15 K7
Hugo Gdns RAIN RM13 93 H4
Hugon Rd FUL/PGN SW6 140 A4
Hugo Rd ARCH N19 84 C2
Huguenot Pl
WAND/EARL SW18 140 B6
WCHPL E1 13 K1
Huitt Sq BTSEA SW11 140 C4
Hullbridge Ms IS N1 85 K6
Hull Cl BERM/RHTH SE16 * 124 A1
Hull St FSBYE EC1V 6 C5
Hulme Pl STHWK SE1 18 D3
Hulse Av BARK IG11 90 E4
ROMW/RG RM7 56 D4
Hulsewood Cl RDART DA2 170 E5
Hulverston Cl BELMT SM2 209 F6
Humber Cl WDR/YW UB7 112 A1
Humber Dr NKENS W10 100 B3
Humber Rd BKHTH/KID SE3 125 J6
CRICK NW2 63 K6
DART DA1 151 G6
Humberstone Rd PLSTW E13 107 G2
Humbolt Rd HMSMTH W6 119 H6
Humes Av HNWL W7 116 A3
Hume Wy RSLP HA4 58 E3
Humphrey Cl CLAY IG5 * 53 K4
Humphrey St STHWK SE1 123 G5
Humphries Cl DAGW RM9 92 B2
Hundred Acre
CDALE/KGS NW9 45 H5
Hungerdown CHING E4 38 A3
Hungerford Rd HOLWY N7 84 D4
Hungerford St WCHPL E1 * 104 D5
Hunsdon Cl DAGW RM9 92 A4
Hunsdon Rd NWCR SE14 144 A1
Hunslett St BETH E2 * 104 E1
Hunston Rd MRDN SM4 194 A5
Hunt Cl BKHTH/KID SE3 * 145 K3
NTGHL W11 119 G1
Hunter Cl BAL SW12 161 F3
STHWK SE1 19 F5
WLGTN SM6 210 E5
Hunter Ct CMBW SE5 * 142 E5
Huntercrombe Gdns
OXHEY WD19 41 G1
Hunter Rd RYNPK SW20 177 F4
THHTH CR7 180 E6
Hunters Cl BXLY DA5 170 B5
Hunters Ct RCH/KEW TW9 136 E6
Hunters Gv HYS/HAR UB3 113 K1
KTN/HRWW/WS HA3 61 J1
Hunter's Gv CRW RM5 56 D1
ORP BR6 216 C2
Hunters Hall Rd DAGE RM10 92 C2
Hunters Hl RSLP HA4 77 G1
Hunters Meadow NRWD SE19 163 F6
Hunters Rd CHSGTN KT9 206 A1
IL IG1 90 B3
Hunters Sq DAGE RM10 92 C2
Hunter St BMSBY WC1N 5 F6
Hunters Wy CROY/NA CR0 212 A2
ENC/FH EN2 23 G2
Hunting Cl ESH/CLAY KT10 204 A2
Huntingdon Cl MTCM CR4 195 K1
NTHLT UB5 78 A4
Huntingdon Gdns CHSWK W4 137 K1
WPK KT4 208 A1
Huntingdon Rd ED N9 36 E3
EFNCH N2 47 J6
Huntingdon St CAN/RD E16 106 D5
IS N1 85 F5
Huntingfield CROY/NA CR0 213 H5
Huntingfield Rd
PUT/ROE SW15 158 D1
Hunting Gate Cl ENC/FH EN2 23 G4
Hunting Gate Dr CHSGTN KT9 206 A5
Hunting Gate Ms SUT SM1 209 F1
WHTN TW2 * 155 K3
Huntings Rd DAGE RM10 92 C4
Huntington Cl BXLY DA5 169 J3
Huntland Cl RAIN RM13 111 K4
Huntley Cl STWL/WRAY TW19 152 B2
Huntley St GWRST WC1E 4 B7
Huntley Wy RYNPK SW20 * 176 D5
Huntly Dr FNCH N3 46 E2
Huntly Rd SNWD SE25 181 F6
Hunton St WCHPL E1 104 C4
Hunt Rd NWDGN UB2 115 F3
Hunts Cl BKHTH/KID SE3 145 K3
Hunt's La SRTFD E15 106 A1
Huntsman Cl FELT TW13 154 A6

Huntsman Rd BARK/HLT IG6 55 H2
Huntsman St WALW SE17 19 G7
Hunts Md PEND EN3 25 F4
Hunts Medde Cl CHST BR7 184 D3
Huntsmoor Rd
HOR/WEW KT19 207 F3
Huntspill St TOOT SW17 160 B5
Hunts Slip Rd DUL SE21 163 F4
Huntsworth Ms CAMTN NW1 2 E6
Hurdwick Pl CAMTN NW1 * 4 A2
Hurley Cl WOT/HER KT12 188 A6
Hurley Crs BERM/RHTH SE16 124 A1
Hurley Rd GFD/PVL UB6 96 B4
Hurlfield RDART DA2 171 F5
Hurlingham Gdns
FUL/PGN SW6 139 J4
Hurlingham Pk
FUL/PGN SW6 * 139 J4
Hurlingham Rd BXLYHN DA7 149 G1
FUL/PGN SW6 139 J3
Hurlingham Sq
FUL/PGN SW6 * 139 K4
Hurlock St HBRY N5 85 H1
Hurlstone Rd SNWD SE25 196 E2
Hurn Court Rd HSLWW TW4 134 C3
Huron Cl ORP BR6 216 E4
Huron Rd TOOT SW17 161 F4
Hurren Cl BKHTH/KID SE3 145 H4
Hurricane House
WOOL/PLUM SE18 * 146 D1
Hurricane Rd WLGTN SM6 210 E5
Hurry Cl SRTFD E15 88 C5
Hursley Rd CHIG IG7 55 F1
Hurst Av CHING E4 37 J5
HGT N6 66 C3
Hurstbourne ESH/CLAY KT10 205 F4
Hurstbourne Gdns BARK IG11 90 D4
Hurstbourne Rd FSTH SE23 164 B3
Hurst Cl CHING E4 37 J5
CHSGTN KT9 206 C3
GLDGN NW11 65 F3
HAYES BR2 199 J5
NTHLT UB5 77 K4
Hurstcourt Rd SUT SM1 194 A5
Hurstdene Av HAYES BR2 199 J5
Hurstdene Gdns
SEVS/STOTM N15 68 A4
Hurstfield HAYES BR2 199 K2
Hurstfield Crs YEAD UB4 94 C4
Hurstfield Rd
E/WMO/HCT KT8 173 F6
Hurstlands Dr ORP BR6 217 H1
Hurst La ABYW SE2 128 E5
E/WMO/HCT KT8 189 H1
Hurstleigh Gdns CLAY IG5 53 K4
Hurst Pl ABYW SE2 128 D5
DART DA1 * 171 F1
Hurst Ri BAR EN5 20 E4
Hurst Rd BFN/LL DA15 168 C4
BKHH IG9 39 H3
BXLY DA5 169 F3
CROY/NA CR0 211 K3
E/WMO/HCT KT8 173 F6
ERITH DA8 149 K1
WALTH E17 51 K6
WCHMH N21 35 G3
WOT/HER KT12 188 C1
Hurst Springs BXLY DA5 169 F3
Hurst St HNHL SE24 162 C1
Hurst View Rd SAND/SEL CR2 212 A5
Hurst Wy SAND/SEL CR2 212 A4
Hurstway Rd NTGHL W11 * 100 B6
Hurstway Wk NTGHL W11 * 100 B6
Hurstwood Av BXLY DA5 169 F3
ERITH DA8 150 B2
SWFD E18 71 F1
Hurstwood Dr BMLY BR1 184 E6
Hurstwood Rd GLDGN NW11 64 C1
Hurtwood Rd WOT/HER KT12 188 E4
Huson Cl HAMP NW3 83 J5
Hussain Cl HRW HA1 79 F2
Hussars Cl HSLWW TW4 134 D4
Husseywell Crs HAYES BR2 199 K5
Hutching's St POP/IOD E14 124 D2
Hutchings Wk GLDGN NW11 65 F1
Hutchins Cl SRTFD E15 88 A5
Hutchinson Ter WBLY HA9 79 K1
Hutchins Rd THMD SE28 109 G6
Hutton Cl GFD/PVL UB6 78 D3
WFD IG8 53 F2
Hutton Gv
NFNCH/WDSPK N12 47 F1
Hutton La
KTN/HRWW/WS HA3 42 C3
Hutton Rw EDGW HA8 44 E3
Hutton St EMB EC4Y 11 K4
Hutton Wk
KTN/HRWW/WS HA3 42 C3
Huxbear St BROCKY SE4 144 C6
Huxley UED N18 * 49 K1
Huxley Cl NTHLT UB5 95 J1
Huxley Dr CHDH RM6 73 H4
Huxley Gdns WLSDN NW10 98 B2
Huxley Pde UED N18 * 49 K1
Huxley Pl PLMGR N13 35 H6
Huxley Rd LEY E10 70 A6
UED N18 35 K6
WELL DA16 148 A4
Huxley Sayze UED N18 * 49 K1
Huxley St NKENS W10 100 C2
Hyacinth Cl HPTN TW12 173 F2
IL IG1 90 B4
Hyacinth Rd PUT/ROE SW15 158 D3
Hyde Cl BAR EN5 20 D4
CRW RM5 57 F2
PLSTW E13 106 E1
Hyde Crs CDALE/KGS NW9 63 G2
Hyde Dr STMC/STPC BR5 202 C1
Hyde Estate Rd
CDALE/KGS NW9 63 H2
Hyde Farm Ms BAL SW12 161 J3
Hydefield Cl WCHMH N21 35 K3
Hydefield Ct ED N9 36 A4
Hyde Gv DART DA1 151 J3
Hyde La BTSEA SW11 140 D2
Hyde Park Av WCHMH N21 35 J4
Hyde Park Cnr
MYFR/PICC W1J 15 H2
Hyde Park Crs BAY/PAD W2 8 C4
Hyde Park Gdns BAY/PAD W2 8 B5
WCHMH N21 35 J3
Hyde Park Gardens Ms
BAY/PAD W2 8 B5
Hyde Park Ga SKENS SW7 120 B2
Hyde Park Gate Ms
SKENS SW7 * 120 B2
Hyde Park Pl BAY/PAD W2 8 D5
Hyde Park Sq BAY/PAD W2 8 C4
Hyde Park Square Ms
BAY/PAD W2 8 C4
Hyde Park St BAY/PAD W2 8 C5
Hyderabad Wy SRTFD E15 88 C5
Hyde Rd BXLYHN DA7 149 G3
IS N1 7 F1
RCHPK/HAM TW10 137 G6
Hydeside Gdns ED N9 36 B4
Hyde's Pl IS N1 85 H5
Hyde St DEPT SE8 124 D6
The Hyde CDALE/KGS NW9 * 63 F1
Hydethorpe Av ED N9 36 B4
Hydethorpe Rd BAL SW12 161 H3
Hyde V GNWCH SE10 145 F1
Hyde Wk MRDN SM4 193 K4
Hyde Wy ED N9 36 B4
HYS/HAR UB3 113 J4
Hyland Cl EMPK RM11 75 K4
Hylands Rd WALTH E17 52 B5
Hyland Wy EMPK RM11 75 K4
Hylton St WOOL/PLUM SE18 128 A4
Hyndewood FSTH SE23 * 164 A5
Hyndman St PECK SE15 123 J6
Hynton Rd BCTR RM8 73 J6
Hyperion Pl HOR/WEW KT19 207 F6
Hyrstdene SAND/SEL CR2 211 H2
Hyson Rd BERM/RHTH SE16 123 J5
Hythe Av BXLYHN DA7 149 F1
Hythe Cl STMC/STPC BR5 202 D1
UED N18 36 C6
Hythe Rd THHTH CR7 180 E5
WLSDN NW10 99 H2
Hythe St DART DA1 151 H6
Hyver Hl BAR EN5 31 F1

I

Ibbotson Av CAN/RD E16 106 D5
Ibbott St WCHPL E1 104 E3
Iberian Av WLGTN SM6 210 D2
Ibis La CHSWK W4 137 K2
Ibis Wy YEAD UB4 95 H5
Ibscott Cl DAGE RM10 92 E4
Ibsley Gdns PUT/ROE SW15 158 D3
Ibsley Wy EBAR EN4 21 J6
Iceland Rd BOW E3 87 J6
Ickburgh Est CLPT E5 * 68 D6
Ickburgh Rd CLPT E5 86 D1
Ickenham Cl RSLP HA4 58 B6
Ickenham Rd RSLP HA4 58 B5
Ickleton Rd ELTH/MOT SE9 166 D6
Icknield Dr GNTH/NBYPK IG2 72 B2
Ickworth Park Rd WALTH E17 69 G1
Ida Rd SEVS/STOTM N15 67 K2
Ida St POP/IOD E14 106 A5
Iden Cl HAYES BR2 183 H6
Idlecombe Rd TOOT SW17 179 F2
Idmiston Rd SRTFD E15 88 D3
WNWD SE27 162 D5
WPK KT4 192 C4
Idmiston Sq WPK KT4 192 C4
Idol La MON EC3R 13 G6
Idonia St DEPT SE8 144 C1
Iffley Rd HMSMTH W6 118 E3
Ifield Rd WBPTN SW10 120 A6
Ightham Rd ERITH DA8 149 H1
Ilbert St NKENS W10 100 C2
Ilchester Pl WKENS W14 119 J3
Ilchester Rd BCTR RM8 91 H3
Ildersly Gv DUL SE21 162 E4
Ilderton Rd PECK SE15 123 K6
Ilex Cl SUN TW16 172 B5
Ilex Rd WLSDN NW10 81 H4
Ilex Wy STRHM/NOR SW16 180 B1
Ilford Hl IL IG1 90 A1
MNPK E12 89 K2
Ilford La IL IG1 90 B2
Ilfracombe Gdns CHDH RM6 73 H4
Ilfracombe Rd BMLY BR1 165 J5
Iliffe St WALW SE17 122 C5
Iliffe Yd WALW SE17 122 C5
Ilkley Cl NRWD SE19 * 180 E2
Ilkley Ct FBAR/BDGN N11 48 A2
Ilkley Rd CAN/RD E16 107 G4
OXHEY WD19 41 H1
Illingworth Wy EN EN1 24 A6
Ilmington Rd
KTN/HRWW/WS HA3 61 K3
Ilminster Gdns BTSEA SW11 140 D5
Imber Cl STHGT/OAK N14 34 C2
Imber Cross THDIT KT7 190 A3
Imber Gv ESH/CLAY KT10 189 J4
Imber Park Rd ESH/CLAY KT10 189 J5
Imber St IS N1 6 E1
Imperial Av
STNW/STAM N16 * 86 A2
Imperial Cl CRICK NW2 81 K3
RYLN/HDSTN HA2 60 A3
Imperial College Rd
SKENS SW7 14 A5
Imperial Crs FUL/PGN SW6 140 B3
Imperial Dr RYLN/HDSTN HA2 60 A4
Imperial Gdns MTCM CR4 179 G6
Imperial Ms EHAM E6 107 H1
Imperial Pl CHST BR7 185 F4
Imperial Rd
EBED/NFELT TW14 153 H2
FUL/PGN SW6 140 A2
WDGN N22 48 E4
Imperial Sq FUL/PGN SW6 140 A2
Imperial St BOW E3 106 A2
Imperial Wy CHST BR7 167 H5
CROY/NA CR0 211 F4
KTN/HRWW/WS HA3 62 A3
Imre Cl SHB W12 118 E1
Inca Dr ELTH/MOT SE9 167 G2
Inchmery Rd CAT SE6 164 E4
Inchwood CROY/NA CR0 213 K2
Independent Pl HACK E8 86 B3
Independents Rd
BKHTH/KID SE3 145 J4
Inderwick Rd CEND/HSY/T N8 67 F3
Indescon Ct POP/IOD E14 124 E2
India St TWRH EC3N 13 J4
India Wy SHB W12 99 K6
Indigo Ms POP/IOD E14 * 106 A6
STNW/STAM N16 85 K1
Indus Rd CHARL SE7 146 B1
Infant House
WOOL/PLUM SE18 * 146 D1
Ingal Rd PLSTW E13 106 E3
Ingate Pl VX/NE SW8 141 G2
Ingatestone Rd MNPK E12 71 G5
SNWD SE25 197 J2
WFD IG8 53 F3
Ingelow Rd VX/NE SW8 141 G3
Ingersoll Rd PEND EN3 24 E1
SHB W12 118 E1
Ingestre Pl SOHO/CST W1F 10 B4
Ingestre Rd FSTGT E7 88 E2
KTTN NW5 84 B2
Ingham Cl SAND/SEL CR2 213 F6
Ingham Rd KIL/WHAMP NW6 82 E2
SAND/SEL CR2 212 E6
Inglebert St CLKNW EC1R 5 J4
Ingleborough St
BRXN/ST SW9 142 B3
Ingleby Dr HRW HA1 78 D1
Ingleby Rd DAGE RM10 92 D4
HOLWY N7 84 E1
IL IG1 72 B5
Ingleby Wy CHST BR7 185 F1
WLGTN SM6 210 D6
Ingle Cl PIN HA5 41 K6
Ingledew Rd
WOOL/PLUM SE18 127 J5
Inglefield Sq WAP E1W * 123 J1
Inglehurst Gdns REDBR IG4 71 K2
Inglemere Rd FSTH SE23 164 A5
TOOT SW17 178 E3
Ingleside Cl BECK BR3 182 D3
Ingleside Gv BKHTH/KID SE3 125 J6
Inglethorpe St FUL/PGN SW6 139 G2
Ingleton Av WELL DA16 148 B6
Ingleton Rd CAR SM5 209 J6
UED N18 50 C2
Ingleton St BRXN/ST SW9 142 B3
Ingleway NFNCH/WDSPK N12 47 H2
Inglewood CROY/NA CR0 213 G6
Inglewood Cl BARK/HLT IG6 55 F2
POP/IOD E14 124 D4
Inglewood Copse BMLY BR1 184 D5
Inglewood Ms SURB KT6 191 H5
Inglewood Rd BXLYHN DA7 150 A5
KIL/WHAMP NW6 82 E3
Inglis Rd CROY/NA CR0 197 G5
EA W5 98 B6
Inglis St CMBW SE5 142 C2
Ingram Av GLDGN NW11 65 G4
Ingram Cl LBTH SE11 17 H6
STAN HA7 43 J1
Ingram Rd DART DA1 171 H3
EFNCH N2 65 J1
THHTH CR7 180 D4
Ingram Wy GFD/PVL UB6 78 D6
Ingrave Rd ROM RM1 75 F1
Ingrave St BTSEA SW11 140 C4
Ingrebourne Rd RAIN RM13 111 K3
Ingress St CHSWK W4 118 B5
Inigo Jones Rd CHARL SE7 146 C1
Inkerman Rd KTTN NW5 84 B4
Inks Gn CHING E4 52 A1
Inkwell Cl NFNCH/WDSPK N12 33 G5
Inman Rd WAND/EARL SW18 160 B2
WLSDN NW10 81 G6
Inmans Rw WFD IG8 38 E6
Inner Cir CAMTN NW1 3 G5
Inner Park Rd
WIM/MER SW19 159 G4
Inner Ring East HTHAIR TW6 132 E4
Innes Cl RYNPK SW20 177 H5
Innes Gdns PUT/ROE SW15 158 E1
Innes St PECK SE15 143 F1
Innes Yd CROY/NA CR0 211 J1
Inniskilling Rd PLSTW E13 107 G1
Innovation Cl ALP/SUD HA0 80 A6
Inskip Cl LEY E10 69 K6
Inskip Rd BCTR RM8 73 K5
Institute Pl HACK E8 86 D3
Instone Rd DART DA1 171 G2
Integer Gdns WAN E11 70 B4
International Av HEST TW5 114 B5
Inver Ct BAY/PAD W2 * 101 F5
Inveresk Gdns WPK KT4 207 H1
Inverforth Cl HAMP NW3 65 G6
Inverforth Rd
FBAR/BDGN N11 48 B1
Inverine Rd CHARL SE7 126 A5
Invermore Pl
WOOL/PLUM SE18 127 H4
Inverness Av EN EN1 24 A2
Inverness Dr BARK/HLT IG6 54 E2
Inverness Gdns KENS W8 120 A1
Inverness Pl BAY/PAD W2 * 101 F6
Inverness Rd HSLW TW3 134 E5
NWDGN UB2 114 D4
UED N18 50 D1
WPK KT4 193 G5
Inverness St CAMTN NW1 84 B6
Inverness Ter BAY/PAD W2 * 101 F6
Inverton Rd PECK SE15 144 A5
Invicta Cl CHST BR7 185 F1
EBED/NFELT TW14 153 J3
Invicta Gv NTHLT UB5 95 K2
Invicta Pde SCUP DA14 * 168 C6
Invicta Plaza STHWK SE1 12 A7
Invicta Rd BKHTH/KID SE3 145 K1
Inville Rd WALW SE17 122 E5
Inwood Av HSLW TW3 135 H4
Inwood Cl CROY/NA CR0 198 B6
Inwood Rd HSLW TW3 135 H5
Inworth St BTSEA SW11 140 D3
Inworth Wk IS N1 * 85 J6
Iona Cl CAT SE6 164 D2
MRDN SM4 194 A4
Ion Sq BETH E2 * 104 C1
Ipswich Rd TOOT SW17 179 F2
Ireland Cl EHAM E6 107 K4
Ireland Pl WDGN N22 48 E3
Irene Ms HNWL W7 * 116 A1
Irene Rd FUL/PGN SW6 139 K2
ORP BR6 202 A4
Ireton Cl MUSWH N10 48 A3
Ireton St BOW E3 105 J3
Iris Av BXLY DA5 169 F1
Iris Cl CROY/NA CR0 198 A5
EHAM E6 107 J4
STMC/STPC BR5 202 D2
SURB KT6 * 191 G4
Iris Crs BXLYHN DA7 129 G6
Iris Rd HOR/WEW KT19 206 D3
Iris Wy CHING E4 51 H2
Irkdale Av EN EN1 24 B2
Iron Bridge Cl NWDGN UB2 115 H1
WLSDN NW10 81 G3
Ironbridge Rd STKPK UB11 * 112 D1
Iron Bridge Rd STKPK UB11 * 112 E1
Iron Bridge Rd North
STKPK UB11 112 D1
Iron Bridge Rd South
WDR/YW UB7 112 D2
Iron Mill La DART DA1 150 C5
Iron Mill Pl DART DA1 150 C5
Iron Mill Rd WAND/EARL SW18 160 A1
Ironmonger La CITYW EC2V 12 E4
Ironmonger Rw FSBYE EC1V 6 D5
Ironmongers Pl POP/IOD E14 124 D4
Ironside Cl BERM/RHTH SE16 124 A2
Irons Wy CRW RM5 56 E3
Irvine Av KTN/HRWW/WS HA3 43 G6
Irvine Cl POP/IOD E14 105 K4
TRDG/WHET N20 33 J4
Irvine Wy ORP BR6 202 A4
Irving Av NTHLT UB5 77 H6
Irving Gv BRXN/ST SW9 142 A3
Irving Ms IS N1 85 J4
Irving Rd WKENS W14 119 G3
Irving St LSQ/SEVD WC2H 10 D6
Irving Wy CDALE/KGS NW9 63 H2
Irwell Est BERM/RHTH SE16 * 123 K2
Irwin Av WOOL/PLUM SE18 147 K1
Irwin Gdns WLSDN NW10 81 K6
Isaac Wy STHWK SE1 18 D2
Isabella Cl STHGT/OAK N14 34 C2
Isabella Ct
RCHPK/HAM TW10 * 157 G1
Isabella Dr ORP BR6 216 C2
Isabella Ms IS N1 86 A4
Isabella Pl KUTN/CMB KT2 175 G1
Isabella Rd HOM E9 * 86 E3
Isabella St STHWK SE1 18 A1
Isabel St BRXN/ST SW9 142 A2
Isambard Ms POP/IOD E14 125 F3
Isambard Pl
BERM/RHTH SE16 123 K1
Isham Rd STRHM/NOR SW16 179 K5
Isis Cl PUT/ROE SW15 139 F5
RSLP HA4 58 A3
Isis St WAND/EARL SW18 160 B4
Island Centre Wy PEND EN3 25 J1
Island Farm Av
E/WMO/HCT KT8 188 E2
Island Farm Rd
E/WMO/HCT KT8 188 E2
Island Rd BERM/RHTH SE16 124 A4
MTCM CR4 178 E3
Island Rw POP/IOD E14 105 H5
Isla Rd WOOL/PLUM SE18 127 H6
Islay Gdns HSLWW TW4 134 C6
Islay Wk IS N1 * 85 J4
Islay Whf POP/IOD E14 * 106 A4
Isledon Rd HOLWY N7 85 G1
Islehurst Cl CHST BR7 185 F4
Islington Gn IS N1 6 A1
Islington High St IS N1 6 A2
Islington Park Ms IS N1 85 H5
Islington Park St IS N1 85 G5
Islip Gdns EDGW HA8 45 F2
NTHLT UB5 77 J5
Islip Manor Rd NTHLT UB5 77 J5
Islip St KTTN NW5 84 C3
Ismailia Rd FSTGT E7 89 F5
Isom Cl PLSTW E13 107 F2
Issa Rd HSLW TW3 134 E5
Ivanhoe Dr
KTN/HRWW/WS HA3 43 H5
Ivanhoe Rd CMBW SE5 143 G4
HSLWW TW4 134 C4
Ivatt Pl WKENS W14 119 J5
Ivatt Wy SEVS/STOTM N15 49 H6
Iveagh Av WLSDN NW10 98 C1
Iveagh Cl HOM E9 87 F6
WLSDN NW10 98 C1
Ivedon Rd WELL DA16 148 D3
Ive Farm Cl LEY E10 69 J6
Ive Farm La LEY E10 69 J6
Iveley Rd CLAP SW4 141 H3
Ivere Dr BAR EN5 33 F1
Iverhurst Cl BXLYHS DA6 148 E6
Iverna Ct KENS W8 119 K3
Iverna Gdns
EBED/NFELT TW14 133 G6
KENS W8 119 K3
Iverson Rd KIL/WHAMP NW6 82 D4
Ivers Wy CROY/NA CR0 213 K5
Ives Gdns ROM RM1 75 H1
Ives Rd CAN/RD E16 106 C4
Ives St CHEL SW3 14 D6
Ivimey St BETH E2 * 104 C2
Ivinghoe Cl EN EN1 24 A3
Ivinghoe Rd BCTR RM8 91 H3
BUSH WD23 28 D1
Ivor Gv ELTH/MOT SE9 167 G3
Ivor Pl CAMTN NW1 2 E7
Ivor St CAMTN NW1 84 C5
Ivory Ct FELT TW13 153 K3
Ivorydown BMLY BR1 165 K6
Ivybridge Cl TWK TW1 156 B1
Ivychurch Cl PGE/AN SE20 181 J3
Ivy Church La WALW SE17 * 123 G5
Ivy Cl DART DA1 171 K1
PIN HA5 59 G4
RYLN/HDSTN HA2 77 K2
SUN TW16 172 B5
Ivy Ct BERM/RHTH SE16 * 123 H5
Ivy Crs CHSWK W4 117 K4
Ivydale Rd CAR SM5 194 E6
PECK SE15 144 A6
Ivyday Gv STRHM/NOR SW16 162 A5
Ivydene E/WMO/HCT KT8 188 E2
Ivydene Cl SUT SM1 209 G2
Ivy Gdns CEND/HSY/T N8 66 E3
MTCM CR4 179 J6
Ivyhouse Rd DAGW RM9 91 K4
Ivy La HSLWW TW4 134 E5
Ivymount Rd WNWD SE27 162 B5
Ivy Rd BROCKY SE4 144 C5
CAN/RD E16 106 E5
CRICK NW2 82 A2
HSLW TW3 135 G5
STHGT/OAK N14 34 C2
SURB KT6 * 191 H6
TOOT SW17 178 D1
WALTH E17 69 J3
Ivy St IS N1 7 G2
Ivy Wk DAGW RM9 92 A4
NTHWD HA6 * 40 C4
Ixworth Pl CHEL SW3 14 C7
Izane Rd BXLYHS DA6 149 G5

J

Jacaranda Cl NWMAL KT3 176 B6
Jacaranda Gv HACK E8 86 B5
Jackass La HAYES BR2 215 F4
Jack Clow Rd SRTFD E15 106 C1
Jack Cornwell St MNPK E12 90 A2
Jack Dash Wy EHAM E6 107 J3
Jack Jones Wy DAGW RM9 92 B6
Jackman Ms WLSDN NW10 81 G1
Jackman St HACK E8 86 D6
Jackson Cl HOM E9 87 F5
Jackson Rd BARK IG11 90 D6
EBAR EN4 33 H1
HAYES BR2 200 D6
HOLWY N7 85 F2
Jackson's La HGT N6 66 A4
Jackson's Pl CROY/NA CR0 196 E5
Jackson St WOOL/PLUM SE18 127 F6
Jackson's Wy CROY/NA CR0 213 J1
Jackson Wy HOR/WEW KT19 206 C6
NWDGN UB2 115 G2
Jack Walker Ct HBRY N5 85 H2
Jacobs Cl DAGE RM10 92 D2
Jacob St STHWK SE1 19 K2
Jacob's Well Ms MHST W1U 9 H3
Jacqueline Cl NTHLT UB5 77 J6
Jacqueline Creft Ter HGT N6 * 66 A3
Jacqueline Vls WALTH E17 * 70 A2
Jade Cl BCTR RM8 73 J5
CAN/RD E16 107 H5
CRICK NW2 64 B4
Jade Ter KIL/WHAMP NW6 * 83 G5
Jaffe Rd IL IG1 72 C5
Jaffray Rd HAYES BR2 200 C1
Jaggard Wy BAL SW12 160 E2
Jago Cl WOOL/PLUM SE18 127 H6
Jago Wk CMBW SE5 142 E1
Jamaica Rd BERM/RHTH SE16 123 H3
STHWK SE1 19 K3
THHTH CR7 196 C3
Jamaica St WCHPL E1 104 E4
James Av BCTR RM8 74 B5
CRICK NW2 82 A3
James Bedford Cl PIN HA5 41 G5
James Cl GLDGN NW11 * 64 C3
GPK RM2 75 J2
PLSTW E13 106 E1
James Collins Cl MV/WKIL W9 100 D3
James Gdns TOTM N17 49 J3
James Joyce Wk
BRXN/ST SW9 142 C5
James La WAN E11 70 A4
James Lee Sq PEND EN3 25 J1
Jameson St KENS W8 119 K1
James Pl TOTM N17 50 B3
James Rd DART DA1 170 D2
James St BARK IG11 90 C5
COVGDN WC2E 11 F5
EN EN1 24 B6
HSLW TW3 135 J4
MHST W1U 9 H4
Jamestown Rd CAMTN NW1 84 B6
Jamestown Wy POP/IOD E14 106 B6
James Voller Wy WCHPL E1 104 E5
James Watt Wy ERITH DA8 130 B6
James Wy OXHEY WD19 27 H6
James Yd CHING E4 * 52 B2
Jamuna Cl POP/IOD E14 105 G4
Jane St WCHPL E1 104 D5
Janet St POP/IOD E14 124 D3
Janeway Pl BERM/RHTH SE16 123 J2
Janeway St BERM/RHTH SE16 123 H2
Janson Cl SRTFD E15 88 C3
WLSDN NW10 81 F1
Janson Rd SRTFD E15 88 C3
Jansons Rd SEVS/STOTM N15 50 A6
Japan Crs FSBYPK N4 67 F5
Japan Rd CHDH RM6 73 K3
Jardine Rd WAP E1W 105 F6
Jarrett Cl BRXS/STRHM SW2 162 C3
Jarrow Cl MRDN SM4 194 A2
Jarrow Rd BERM/RHTH SE16 123 K4
CHDH RM6 73 J3
TOTM N17 68 D1
Jarrow Wy HOM E9 87 H2
Jarvis Cl BAR EN5 20 B6
BARK IG11 90 D6
Jarvis Rd EDUL SE22 143 F5
SAND/SEL CR2 211 K4
Jasmin Cl NTHWD HA6 40 D4
Jasmine Cl IL IG1 90 B3
ORP BR6 201 G6
STHL UB1 95 J6
Jasmine Ct LEE/GVPK SE12 165 K1
Jasmine Gdns CROY/NA CR0 213 K1
RYLN/HDSTN HA2 60 A6
Jasmine Gv PGE/AN SE20 181 J4
Jasmine Rd HOR/WEW KT19 206 D4
ROMW/RG RM7 75 G6
Jasmine Ter WDR/YW UB7 112 D2
Jasmin Rd HOR/WEW KT19 206 D3
Jason Wk ELTH/MOT SE9 167 F6

Jasper Cl PEND EN3 24 E1
Jasper Rd CAN/RD E16 107 H5
NRWD SE19 181 G2
Javelin Wy NTHLT UB5 95 H2
Jaycroft ENC/FH EN2 23 G2
Jay Gdns CHST BR7 166 E6
Jay Ms SKENS SW7 120 B2
Jean Batten Cl WLGTN SM6 211 F5
Jebb Av BRXS/STRHM SW2 161 K1
Jebb St BOW E3 105 J1
Jedburgh Rd PLSTW E13 107 G2
Jedburgh St BTSEA SW11 141 F5
Jeddo Ms SHB W12 118 C2
Jeddo Rd SHB W12 118 C2
Jefferson Cl GNTH/NBYPK IG2 72 B2
WEA W13 116 C3
Jeffrey's Pl CAMTN NW1 84 C5
Jeffreys Rd CLAP SW4 141 K3
PEND EN3 25 H5
Jeffrey's St CAMTN NW1 84 B5
Jeffs Cl HPTN TW12 * 173 G2
Jeffs Rd SUT SM1 208 D2
Jeger Av BETH E2 7 J1
Jeken Rd ELTH/MOT SE9 146 B5
Jelf Rd BRXS/STRHM SW2 142 B6
Jellicoe Gdns STAN HA7 43 F2
Jellicoe Rd TOTM N17 49 K3
WATW WD18 26 E1
Jemmett Cl KUTN/CMB KT2 175 J4
Jem Paterson Ct HRW HA1 * 78 E2
Jengar Cl SUT SM1 209 F2
Jenkins La BARK IG11 108 B1
Jenkins Rd PLSTW E13 107 F3
Jenner Av ACT W3 99 F4
Jenner Cl SCUP DA14 168 B6
Jenner Pl BARN SW13 118 E6
Jenner Rd STNW/STAM N16 68 B6
Jenner Wy HOR/WEW KT19 206 C6
Jennett Rd CROY/NA CR0 211 G1
Jennifer Rd BMLY BR1 165 J5
Jennings Cl SURB KT6 190 D4
Jennings Rd EDUL SE22 163 G1
Jennings Wy BAR EN5 20 A4
Jenningtree Rd ERITH DA8 150 E1
Jenningtree Wy BELV DA17 129 K2
Jenny Hammond Cl WAN E11 88 D1
Jenson Wy NRWD SE19 181 G3
Jenton Av BXLYHN DA7 149 F2
Jephson Rd FSTGT E7 89 G5
Jephson St CMBW SE5 142 E2
Jephtha Rd WAND/EARL SW18 159 K1
Jerdan Pl FUL/PGN SW6 139 K1
Jeremiah St POP/IOD E14 105 K5
Jeremy's Gn UED N18 36 D6
Jermyn St STJS SW1Y 10 A7
Jerningham Av CLAY IG5 54 B5
Jerningham Rd NWCR SE14 144 B3
Jerome St WCHPL E1 13 J1
Jerrard St LEW SE13 144 E4
Jerrold St IS N1 * 7 H3
Jersey Av
KTN/HRWW/WS HA3 43 H5
Jersey Dr STMC/STPC BR5 201 J3
Jersey Rd CAN/RD E16 107 G4
HEST TW5 135 G1
HNWL W7 116 B2
HSLW TW3 135 G2
IL IG1 90 B2
ISLW TW7 135 H1
LEY E10 70 B5
RAIN RM13 93 J5
TOOT SW17 179 G3
Jersey St BETH E2 104 D2
Jersey Vls HNWL W7 * 115 K2
Jerusalem Pas CLKNW EC1R 6 A7
Jerviston Gdns
STRHM/NOR SW16 180 B2
Jervois House
WOOL/PLUM SE18 * 146 D1
Jesmond Av WBLY HA9 80 B4
Jesmond Cl MTCM CR4 179 G6
Jesmond Dene HAMP NW3 * 83 G4
Jesmond Rd CROY/NA CR0 197 G4
Jesmond Wy STAN HA7 44 A1
Jessam Av CLPT E5 68 D5
Jessamine Rd HNWL W7 115 K1
Jessamine Ter SWLY BR8 * 187 K4
Jesse Rd LEY E10 70 A5
Jessett Cl ERITH DA8 130 A4
Jessica Rd WAND/EARL SW18 160 B1
Jessop Av NWDGN UB2 114 E4
Jessop Sq POP/IOD E14 * 124 D1
Jessops Wy CROY/NA CR0 195 H3
Jessup Cl WOOL/PLUM SE18 127 H4
Jetstar Wy NTHLT UB5 95 J2
Jevington Wy LEE/GVPK SE12 166 A3
Jewel Rd WALTH E17 51 J6
Jewry St TWRH EC3N 13 J4
Jews Rw WAND/EARL SW18 140 A5
Jews Wk SYD SE26 163 J6
Jeymer Av WLSDN NW10 81 K3
Jeymer Dr GFD/PVL UB6 78 C6
Jeypore Rd WAND/EARL SW18 160 B2
Jillian Cl HPTN TW12 173 F3
Jim Bradley Cl
WOOL/PLUM SE18 127 F4
Jim Veal Dr HOLWY N7 84 E4
Joan Crs ELTH/MOT SE9 166 C2
Joan Gdns BCTR RM8 74 A6
Joan Rd BCTR RM8 74 A6
Joan St STHWK SE1 18 A1
Jocelyn Rd RCH/KEW TW9 137 F4
Jocelyn St PECK SE15 143 H2
Jockey's Flds FSBYW WC1X 11 H1
Jodane St DEPT SE8 124 C4
Jodrell Cl ISLW TW7 136 B2
Jodrell Rd BOW E3 87 H6
Joel St PIN HA5 40 E6
Johanna St STHWK SE1 * 17 J3
John Adam St CHCR WC2N 11 F7
John Aird Ct BAY/PAD W2 101 G4
John Archer Wy
WAND/EARL SW18 160 C1
John Ashby Cl
BRXS/STRHM SW2 161 K1
John Austin Cl
KUTN/CMB KT2 175 G4
John Bradshaw Rd
STHGT/OAK N14 34 D3
John Burns Dr BARK IG11 90 E6
John Campbell Rd
STNW/STAM N16 86 A3
John Carpenter St EMB EC4Y 11 K5
John Felton Rd
BERM/RHTH SE16 * 123 H2
John Fisher St WCHPL E1 104 C6
John Gooch Dr ENC/FH EN2 23 H2
John Goodchild Wy
KUT/HW KT1 175 J6
John Harrison Wy
BERM/RHTH SE16 124 A3
GNWCH SE10 125 J3
John Islip St WEST SW1P 16 E7
John Lamb Ct
KTN/HRWW/WS HA3 42 E4
John Maurice Cl WALW SE17 18 E6
John McKenna Wk
BERM/RHTH SE16 * 123 H3
John Parker Sq BTSEA SW11 * 140 C4
John Penn St LEW SE13 144 E2
John Perrin Pl
KTN/HRWW/WS HA3 62 A4
John Prince's St
CAVSQ/HST W1G 9 K3
John Rennie Wk WAP E1W 104 D6
John Roll Wy
BERM/RHTH SE16 123 H3
John Ruskin St CMBW SE5 142 C1
John's Av HDN NW4 64 A1
John's Cl ASHF TW15 153 F6
John Silkin La DEPT SE8 124 A5
Johns La MRDN SM4 194 B2
John's Ms BMSBY WC1N 5 H7
John Smith Av FUL/PGN SW6 139 J1
John Smith Ms POP/IOD E14 106 B6
Johnson Cl HACK E8 86 C6
Johnson Rd CROY/NA CR0 196 E4
HAYES BR2 200 C2
HEST TW5 134 B1
WLSDN NW10 81 F6
Johnson's Cl CAR SM5 209 K1
Johnson's Ct
FLST/FETLN EC4A 11 K4
Johnsons Dr HPTN TW12 173 H4
Johnson's Pl PIM SW1V 121 H5
Johnson St NWDGN UB2 114 B3
WCHPL E1 104 E5
Johnsons Wy WLSDN NW10 98 D3
John Spencer Sq IS N1 * 85 H4
Johns Pl WCHPL E1 104 D5
John's Ter CROY/NA CR0 197 F5
Johnston Cl BRXN/ST SW9 142 A2
Johnstone Rd EHAM E6 107 K2
Johnstone Ter CRICK NW2 82 B1
Johnston Rd WFD IG8 52 E1
John St BMSBY WC1N 5 H7
EN EN1 24 B6
HSLW TW3 134 D3
SNWD SE25 197 H1
SRTFD E15 88 D6
John Trundle Highwalk
BARB EC2Y * 12 C1
John Watkin Cl
HOR/WEW KT19 206 D6
John Wesley Cl EHAM E6 * 107 K2
John William Cl
KUTN/CMB KT2 * 175 F4
John Williams Cl NWCR SE14 124 A6
John Wilson St
WOOL/PLUM SE18 127 F4
John Wooley Cl LEW SE13 * 145 H5
Joiners Arms Yd CMBW SE5 * 142 E2
Joiner St STHWK SE1 19 F1
Jollys La YEAD UB4 95 H4
Jonathan St LBTH SE11 122 A5
Jones Rd PLSTW E13 107 F3
Jonson Cl MTCM CR4 195 G1
YEAD UB4 94 E4
Jordan Cl RYLN/HDSTN HA2 77 K1
Jordan Rd GFD/PVL UB6 79 H6
Jordans Cl DAGE RM10 92 D2
Jordans Ms WHTN TW2 155 K4
Joseph Av ACT W3 99 F5
Joseph Hardcastle Cl
NWCR SE14 144 A1
Josephine Av
BRXS/STRHM SW2 142 A6
Joseph Locke Wy
ESH/CLAY KT10 189 F6
Joseph Powell Cl BAL SW12 161 H1
Joseph Ray Rd WAN E11 70 C6
Joseph St BOW E3 105 H4
Joseph Trotter Cl
CLKNW EC1R 5 K5
Joshua Cl MUSWH N10 48 B3
SAND/SEL CR2 211 H5
Joshua St POP/IOD E14 106 A5
Joslings Cl SHB W12 99 J6
Joslyn Cl PEND EN3 25 J1
Joubert St BTSEA SW11 140 E3
Jowett St PECK SE15 143 G1
Joyce Av UED N18 50 B1
Joyce Green La ERITH DA8 151 G2
Joyden's Wood Rd BXLY DA5 170 A6
Joydon Dr CHDH RM6 73 H3
Joyners Cl DAGW RM9 92 B2
Jubilee Av CHING E4 52 A2
ROMW/RG RM7 74 E2
WHTN TW2 155 H3
Jubilee Cl CDALE/KGS NW9 63 F3
KUT/HW KT1 174 D4
ROMW/RG RM7 74 D2
WLSDN NW10 99 G1
Jubilee Crs ED N9 36 C3
Jubilee Dr RSLP HA4 77 H2
Jubilee Gdns STHL UB1 96 A4
STHWK SE1 * 17 H1
Jubilee Pl CHEL SW3 120 D5
Jubilee Rd CHEAM SM3 208 B5
GFD/PVL UB6 79 H6
Jubilee St WCHPL E1 104 E5
Jubilee Ter FUL/PGN SW6 * 139 H3
The Jubilee GNWCH SE10 * 144 E1
Jubilee Vls ESH/CLAY KT10 * 189 K5
Jubilee Wy CHSGTN KT9 206 D1
EBED/NFELT TW14 153 K3
SCUP DA14 168 B4
WIM/MER SW19 178 A4
Judd St STPAN WC1H 4 E5
Jude St CAN/RD E16 106 D5
Judge Heath La HYS/HAR UB3 94 A5
Judges' Wk HAMP NW3 83 G1
Judge Wk ESH/CLAY KT10 204 E4
Judith Av CRW RM5 56 D2
Juer St BTSEA SW11 140 D1
Juglans Rd ORP BR6 202 B5
Jules Thorn Av EN EN1 24 C4
Julia Gdns BARK IG11 109 K1
Juliana Cl EFNCH N2 47 G6
Julian Av ACT W3 98 D6
Julian Cl BAR EN5 21 F4
Julian Hl HRW HA1 60 E6
Julian Pl POP/IOD E14 124 E5
Julian Rd ORP BR6 217 G4
Julian Tayler Pth FSTH SE23 * 163 J4
Julien Rd EA W5 116 D3
Juliette Rd PLSTW E13 106 E1
Juliette Wy SOCK/AV RM15 131 J2
Julius Caesar Wy STAN HA7 29 J5
Julius Nyerere Cl IS N1 5 H1
Junction Ap BTSEA SW11 140 D4
Junction Ms BAY/PAD W2 8 C3
Junction Pl BAY/PAD W2 * 8 B3
Junction Rd ARCH N19 84 C1
DART DA1 171 G1
EA W5 116 D4
ED N9 36 C3
HRW HA1 60 D3
PLSTW E13 89 F6
ROM RM1 75 H1
SAND/SEL CR2 211 K4
TOTM N17 50 C6
Junction Rd East CHDH RM6 74 A4
Junction Rd West CHDH RM6 73 K4
Juniper Cl BAR EN5 20 B6
CHSGTN KT9 206 B3
HOR/WEW KT19 207 F6
WBLY HA9 80 B3
Juniper Ct CHDH RM6 73 H3
KTN/HRWW/WS HA3 * 43 F4
NTHWD HA6 * 40 E4
Juniper Crs CAMTN NW1 84 A5
Juniper Dr WAND/EARL SW18 140 B5
Juniper Gdns MTCM CR4 179 H4
Juniper La EHAM E6 107 J4
Juniper Rd IL IG1 90 A2
Juniper St WCHPL E1 * 104 E6
Juniper Wy HYS/HAR UB3 94 B6
Juno Wy NWCR SE14 124 A6
Jupiter Wy HOLWY N7 85 F4
Jupp Rd SRTFD E15 88 B5
Jupp Rd West SRTFD E15 88 B6
Justice Wk CHEL SW3 120 D6
Justin Cl BTFD TW8 136 E1
Justin Rd CHING E4 51 H2
Jute La PEND EN3 25 G3
Jutland Cl ARCH N19 66 E5
Jutland Rd CAT SE6 165 F2
PLSTW E13 106 E3
Jutsums Av ROMW/RG RM7 74 D3
Jutsums La ROMW/RG RM7 74 D3
Juxon Cl KTN/HRWW/WS HA3 42 B4
Juxon St LBTH SE11 17 H6

K

Kaduna Cl PIN HA5 59 F2
Kaine Pl CROY/NA CR0 198 C4
Kale Rd ERITHM DA18 128 E2
Kambala Rd BTSEA SW11 140 C3
Kamrans Pl EDGW HA8 44 B5
Kangley Bridge Rd SYD SE26 182 C1
Kaplan Dr WCHMH N21 23 F6
Kara Wy CRICK NW2 82 B2
Karen Cl RAIN RM13 111 G1
Karen Ct BMLY BR1 183 J4
ELTH/MOT SE9 146 B6
Karenza Ct WBLY HA9 * 61 J4
Karina Cl CHIG IG7 54 E1
Karma Wy RYLN/HDSTN HA2 60 A5
Kashgar Rd
WOOL/PLUM SE18 128 A5
Kashmir Rd CHARL SE7 146 C1
Kassala Rd BTSEA SW11 140 E2
Katharine St CROY/NA CR0 211 J1
Katherine Cl
BERM/RHTH SE16 124 A1
Katherine Gdns BARK/HLT IG6 54 C4
ELTH/MOT SE9 146 C5
Katherine Rd EHAM E6 89 H5
Katherine Sq NTGHL W11 * 119 H1
Kathleen Av ACT W3 98 E4
ALP/SUD HA0 80 A5
Kathleen Rd BTSEA SW11 140 E4
Kayemoor Rd BELMT SM2 209 J5
Kay Rd BRXN/ST SW9 141 K3
Kays Ter SWFD E18 * 52 D5
Kay St BETH E2 104 C1
SRTFD E15 88 B5
WELL DA16 148 C2
Kean St HOL/ALD WC2B 11 G4
Keatley Gn CHING E4 51 H2
Keats Av CAN/RD E16 126 A1
HARH RM3 57 K3
Keats Cl BKHTH/KID SE3 146 B1
CHIG IG7 54 C2
PEND EN3 25 F6
STHWK SE1 19 J7
WAN E11 71 F2
WIM/MER SW19 178 C2
YEAD UB4 94 E4
Keats Est STNW/STAM N16 * 68 B6
Keats Gv HAMP NW3 83 J2
Keats Pde ED N9 36 C4
Keats Rd BELV DA17 129 K3
LEY E10 69 K4
WELL DA16 147 K2
Keats Wy CROY/NA CR0 197 K3
GFD/PVL UB6 96 B4
WDR/YW UB7 112 C4
Keble Cl NTHLT UB5 78 C3
WPK KT4 192 C5
Keble Pl BARN SW13 118 E6
Keble St TOOT SW17 160 B6
Kechill Gdns HAYES BR2 199 K4
Kedleston Dr STMC/STPC BR5 202 A3
Kedleston Wk BETH E2 104 D2
Keeble Cl WOOL/PLUM SE18 * 127 G6
Keedonwood Rd BMLY BR1 165 H6
Keel Cl BARK IG11 109 J1
BERM/RHTH SE16 124 A1
Keeley Rd CROY/NA CR0 196 D6
Keeley St HOL/ALD WC2B 11 G4
Keeling Rd ELTH/MOT SE9 146 C6
Keely Cl EBAR EN4 21 J6
Keemor Cl
WOOL/PLUM SE18 * 147 F1
Keens Cl STRHM/NOR SW16 179 J1
Keen's Rd CROY/NA CR0 211 J2
Keen's Yd IS N1 85 H4
Keepers Ms TEDD TW11 174 D2
The Keep BKHTH/KID SE3 145 K3
KUTN/CMB KT2 175 G2
Keesey St WALW SE17 122 E6
Keeton's Rd
BERM/RHTH SE16 123 J3
Keevil Dr WIM/MER SW19 159 G2
Keighley Cl HOLWY N7 84 E2
Keightley Dr ELTH/MOT SE9 167 H3
Keildon Rd BTSEA SW11 140 E5
Keir Hardie Est CLPT E5 * 68 D5
Keir Hardie Wy BARK IG11 91 G5
YEAD UB4 * 94 E2
Keith Connor Cl VX/NE SW8 141 G4
Keith Gv SHB W12 118 D2
Keith Rd BARK IG11 108 D1
HYS/HAR UB3 113 H3
WALTH E17 51 H4
Kelbrook Rd BKHTH/KID SE3 146 D3
Kelburn Wy RAIN RM13 111 J2
Kelceda Cl CRICK NW2 63 J6
Kelf Gv HYS/HAR UB3 94 D5
Kelfield Gdns NKENS W10 100 B5
Kelfield Ms NKENS W10 100 B4
Kelland Cl CEND/HSY/T N8 * 66 D2
Kelland Rd PLSTW E13 106 E3
Kellaway Rd BKHTH/KID SE3 146 B3
Keller Cresent MNPK E12 89 H2
Kellerton Rd LEW SE13 145 H6
Kellett Rd BRXS/STRHM SW2 142 B5
Kelling Gdns CROY/NA CR0 196 C4
Kellino St TOOT SW17 160 E6
Kellner Rd THMD SE28 128 A3
Kell St STHWK SE1 18 B4
Kelly Av PECK SE15 143 G2
Kelly Cl WLSDN NW10 81 F1
Kelly Ms MV/WKIL W9 * 100 D4
Kelly Rd MLHL NW7 46 C2
Kelly St CAMTN NW1 84 B4
Kelly Wy CHDH RM6 74 A2
Kelman Cl CLAP SW4 141 J3
Kelmore Gv EDUL SE22 143 H5
Kelmscott Cl WALTH E17 51 H4
WATW WD18 26 E1
Kelmscott Gdns SHB W12 118 D3
Kelmscott Rd BTSEA SW11 140 D6
Kelross Rd HBRY N5 85 H2
Kelsall Cl BKHTH/KID SE3 146 A3
Kelsall Ms RCH/KEW TW9 137 J2
Kelsey La BECK BR3 182 D6
Kelsey Park Av BECK BR3 182 E6
Kelsey Park Rd BECK BR3 182 D5
Kelsey Rd STMC/STPC BR5 186 C5
Kelsey Sq BECK BR3 182 D5
Kelsey St BETH E2 104 C3
Kelsey Wy BECK BR3 182 D6
Kelsie Wy BARK/HLT IG6 54 E2
Kelso Pl KENS W8 120 A3
Kelso Rd CAR SM5 194 B4
Kelston Rd BARK/HLT IG6 54 B5
Kelton Vls KUT/HW KT1 * 175 G5
Kelvedon Cl KUTN/CMB KT2 175 H2
Kelvedon Rd FUL/PGN SW6 139 J1
Kelvedon Wy WFD IG8 53 K2
Kelvin Av WDGN N22 49 F2
Kelvinbrook E/WMO/HCT KT8 173 G6
Kelvin Cl HOR/WEW KT19 206 C4
Kelvin Crs
KTN/HRWW/WS HA3 42 E3
Kelvin Dr TWK TW1 156 C1
Kelvin Gdns CROY/NA CR0 195 K4
STHL UB1 96 A5
Kelvin Gv CHSGTN KT9 205 K1
SYD SE26 163 J5
Kelvington Cl CROY/NA CR0 198 B4
Kelvington Rd PECK SE15 144 A6
Kelvin Pde ORP BR6 201 K5
Kelvin Rd HBRY N5 85 H2
WELL DA16 148 B4
Kember St IS N1 85 F5
Kemble Dr HAYES BR2 215 J1
Kemble Rd CROY/NA CR0 211 H1
FSTH SE23 164 A3
TOTM N17 50 C4
Kemble St HOL/ALD WC2B 11 G4
Kemerton Rd BECK BR3 182 E5
CMBW SE5 142 D4
CROY/NA CR0 197 G4
Kemey's St HOM E9 87 G3
Kemnal Rd CHST BR7 185 H2
Kempe Rd KIL/WHAMP NW6 100 B1
Kemp Gdns CROY/NA CR0 196 D3
Kemplay Rd HAMP NW3 83 H2
Kemp Pl BUSH WD23 28 A1
Kemps Dr NTHWD HA6 40 D3
POP/IOD E14 105 J6
Kempsford Gdns ECT SW5 119 K5
Kempsford Rd LBTH SE11 17 K7
Kempshott Rd
STRHM/NOR SW16 179 K3
Kempson Rd FUL/PGN SW6 139 K2
Kempthorne Rd DEPT SE8 124 B4
Kempton Av NTHLT UB5 78 A4
SUN TW16 172 A4
Kempton Cl ERITH DA8 129 K6
HGDN/ICK UB10 76 A2
Kempton Ct SUN TW16 172 A4
Kempton Pk SUN TW16 * 172 B4
Kempton Rd EHAM E6 89 K6
Kempton Wk CROY/NA CR0 198 B3
Kempt St WOOL/PLUM SE18 127 F6
Kemsing Cl BXLY DA5 169 F2
THHTH CR7 * 196 D1
Kemsing Rd GNWCH SE10 125 K5
Kenbury St CMBW SE5 142 D3
Kenchester Cl VX/NE SW8 141 K1
Kencot Wy ERITHM DA18 129 G2
Kendal Av ACT W3 98 C4
BARK IG11 90 E6
UED N18 35 K6
Kendal Cl BRXN/ST SW9 142 C1
EBED/NFELT TW14 153 J3
TRDG/WHET N20 33 J4
WFD IG8 38 D4
YEAD UB4 94 C1
Kendal Ct ACT W3 98 C4
Kendal Cft HCH RM12 93 J3
Kendale Rd BMLY BR1 183 H1
Kendal Gdns SUT SM1 194 B6
UED N18 35 K6
Kendall Av BECK BR3 182 B5
SAND/SEL CR2 211 K6
Kendall Pl MHST W1U 9 G2
Kendall Rd BECK BR3 182 B5
ISLW TW7 136 B3
WOOL/PLUM SE18 146 D2
Kendalmere Cl MUSWH N10 48 B4
Kendal Pde UED N18 35 K6
Kendal Pl PUT/ROE SW15 139 J6
Kendal Rd WLSDN NW10 81 J2
Kendal Steps BAY/PAD W2 * 8 D4
Kendal St BAY/PAD W2 8 D4
Kender St NWCR SE14 143 K1
Kendoa Rd CLAP SW4 141 J5
Kendon Cl WAN E11 71 F2
Kendra Hall Rd SAND/SEL CR2 211 H5
Kendrey Gdns WHTN TW2 155 K1
Kendrick Ms SKENS SW7 14 A6
Kendrick Pl SKENS SW7 * 14 A7
Kenelm Cl HRW HA1 79 G1
Kenerne Dr BAR EN5 20 C6
Kenilford Rd BAL SW12 161 G2
Kenilworth Av
RYLN/HDSTN HA2 77 K2
WALTH E17 51 J5
WIM/MER SW19 177 K1
Kenilworth Crs EN EN1 24 A2
Kenilworth Gdns
GDMY/SEVK IG3 73 F6
LOU IG10 39 K1
OXHEY WD19 41 G1
STHL UB1 * 95 K2
WOOL/PLUM SE18 147 G3
YEAD UB4 94 D4
Kenilworth Rd ASHF TW15 152 A5
BOW E3 105 G1
EA W5 117 F1
EDGW HA8 30 E4
EW KT17 207 J4
KIL/WHAMP NW6 82 D6
PGE/AN SE20 182 A4
STMC/STPC BR5 201 H3
Kenilworth Ter BELMT SM2 * 208 E5
Kenley Av CDALE/KGS NW9 45 G4
Kenley Cl BXLY DA5 169 H2
CHST BR7 185 K6
EBAR EN4 21 J5
Kenley Gdns THHTH CR7 196 C1
Kenley Rd KUT/HW KT1 175 J5
TWK TW1 156 B1
WIM/MER SW19 177 K6
Kenley Wk CHEAM SM3 208 B2
NTGHL W11 * 119 H1
Kenlor Rd TOOT SW17 178 C1
Kenmare Dr MTCM CR4 178 E3
TOTM N17 50 B5
Kenmare Gdns PLMGR N13 35 J6
Kenmare Rd THHTH CR7 196 B3
Kenmere Gdns ALP/SUD HA0 80 C6
Kenmere Rd WELL DA16 148 D3
Kenmont Gdns WLSDN NW10 99 K2
Kenmore Av
KTN/HRWW/WS HA3 61 G2
Kenmore Crs YEAD UB4 94 D2
Kenmore Gdns EDGW HA8 44 D5
Kenmore Rd
KTN/HRWW/WS HA3 43 K6
Kenmure Rd HACK E8 86 D3
Kenmure Yd HACK E8 * 86 D3
Kennacraig Cl CAN/RD E16 126 A1
Kennard Rd FBAR/BDGN N11 47 K1
SRTFD E15 88 B5
Kennard St BTSEA SW11 141 F2
CAN/RD E16 126 E1
Kennedy Av PEND EN3 36 E1
Kennedy Cl MTCM CR4 179 F5
PIN HA5 41 K2
PLSTW E13 106 E1
STMC/STPC BR5 201 J5
Kennedy Rd BARK IG11 90 E6
HNWL W7 96 E4
Kennedy Wk WALW SE17 19 F7
Kennet Cl BTSEA SW11 140 C5
Kennet Dr YEAD UB4 95 J4
Kenneth Av IL IG1 90 B2
Kenneth Crs CRICK NW2 81 K3
Kenneth Gdns STAN HA7 43 G2
Kenneth More Rd IL IG1 90 B1
Kenneth Rd CHDH RM6 74 A4
Kennet Rd DART DA1 150 D4
ISLW TW7 136 A4
MV/WKIL W9 100 D3
Kennet Sq MTCM CR4 178 D4
Kennet St WAP E1W 123 H1
Kennett Wharf La
BLKFR EC4V 12 D5
Kenninghall Rd CLPT E5 86 D1
UED N18 50 D1
Kenning St BERM/RHTH SE16 123 K2
Kennings Wy LBTH SE11 122 B5
Kennington Gdns
KUT/HW KT1 174 E6
Kennington La LBTH SE11 122 A5
Kennington Ov LBTH SE11 122 A6
Kennington Park Gdns
LBTH SE11 122 C6
Kennington Park Pl
LBTH SE11 122 B6
Kennington Park Rd
LBTH SE11 122 B6
Kennington Rd LBTH SE11 17 J5
Kenny Dr CAR SM5 210 A6
Kennylands Rd BARK/HLT IG6 55 G3
Kenrick Pl MHST W1U 9 G1
Kensal Rd NKENS W10 100 C3
Kensal Whf NKENS W10 * 100 C3

Kensington Av MNPK E12 89 J4
THHTH CR7 180 B4
Kensington Church Ct
KENS W8 120 A2
Kensington Church St
KENS W8 119 K1
Kensington Church Wk
KENS W8 120 A2
Kensington Cl
FBAR/BDGN N11 * 48 A1
Kensington Ct KENS W8 120 A2
Kensington Court Gdns
KENS W8 * 120 A3
Kensington Court Ms
KENS W8 * 120 A3
Kensington Court Pl
KENS W8 120 A3
Kensington Dr WFD IG8 53 H5
Kensington Gdns IL IG1 71 K5
Kensington Gardens Sq
BAY/PAD W2 * 101 F5
Kensington Ga KENS W8 120 B3
Kensington Hall Gdns
WKENS W14 * 119 J5
Kensington High St
KENS W8 * 120 A2
WKENS W14 119 H4
Kensington Ml KENS W8 119 K1
Kensington Palace Gdns
KENS W8 120 A2
Kensington Park Gdns
NTGHL W11 100 D6
Kensington Park Ms
NTGHL W11 100 D5
Kensington Park Rd
NTGHL W11 100 D5
Kensington Pl KENS W8 119 K1
Kensington Rd KENS W8 120 A2
NTHLT UB5 96 A1
ROMW/RG RM7 74 E3
Kensington Sq KENS W8 * 120 A2
Kensington Ter
SAND/SEL CR2 211 K5
Kent Av DAGW RM9 110 C3
WEA W13 97 H4
WELL DA16 148 A6
Kent Cl MTCM CR4 195 K1
ORP BR6 216 E4
Kent Ct CDALE/KGS NW9 * 45 G5
Kent Dr EBAR EN4 22 A5
TEDD TW11 173 K1
Kentford Wy NTHLT UB5 77 J6
Kent Gdns RSLP HA4 58 E3
WEA W13 97 H4
Kent Gate Wy CROY/NA CR0 213 H4
Kent House La BECK BR3 182 B2
Kent House Rd BECK BR3 182 A3
SYD SE26 182 B1
Kentish Rd BELV DA17 129 H4
Kentish Town Rd CAMTN NW1 84 B5
Kentish Wy BMLY BR1 184 A5
Kentlea Rd THMD SE28 127 K2
Kentmere Rd
WOOL/PLUM SE18 127 K4
Kenton Av HRW HA1 61 F4
STHL UB1 96 A6
SUN TW16 172 C5
Kenton Gdns
KTN/HRWW/WS HA3 61 J2
Kenton La
KTN/HRWW/WS HA3 43 F3
KTN/HRWW/WS HA3 43 J6
Kenton Park Av
KTN/HRWW/WS HA3 61 K1
Kenton Park Cl
KTN/HRWW/WS HA3 61 J1
Kenton Park Crs
KTN/HRWW/WS HA3 61 K1
Kenton Park Pde
KTN/HRWW/WS HA3 * 61 J2
Kenton Park Rd
KTN/HRWW/WS HA3 61 J1
Kenton Rd HOM E9 87 F4
KTN/HRWW/WS HA3 61 G3
Kenton St STPAN WC1H 4 E6
Kenton Wy YEAD UB4 94 C2
Kent Pas CAMTN NW1 2 E6
Kent Rd CHSWK W4 117 K3
DAGE RM10 92 D3
DART DA1 171 H1
E/WMO/HCT KT8 189 H1
KUT/HW KT1 174 E6
RCH/KEW TW9 137 H1
STMC/STPC BR5 202 C3
WCHMH N21 35 K3
WWKM BR4 198 E5
Kent St BETH E2 7 K2
PLSTW E13 107 F2
Kent Ter CAMTN NW1 2 D5
Kent View Gdns
GDMY/SEVK IG3 72 E6
Kent Wy SURB KT6 206 A1
Kentwell Cl BROCKY SE4 * 144 B5
Kentwode Gn BARN SW13 138 D1
Kent Yd SKENS SW7 14 D3
Kenver Av
NFNCH/WDSPK N12 47 H2
Kenward Rd ELTH/MOT SE9 146 B6
Kenway CRW RM5 56 E5
Ken Wy WBLY HA9 62 E6
Kenway Rd ECT SW5 120 A4
Kenwood Cl HAMP NW3 65 H5
WDR/YW UB7 112 D6
Kenwood Dr BECK BR3 183 F6
Kenwood Gdns CLAY IG5 72 A1
SWFD E18 53 F6
Kenwood Rd ED N9 36 C4
HGT N6 65 K3
Kenworthy Rd HOM E9 87 G3
Kenwyn Dr CRICK NW2 81 G1
Kenwyn Rd CLAP SW4 141 J5
DART DA1 151 G6
RYNPK SW20 177 F4
Kenya Rd CHARL SE7 146 C1
Kenyngton Pl
KTN/HRWW/WS HA3 61 J2
Kenyon St FUL/PGN SW6 139 G2
Keogh Rd SRTFD E15 88 C4
Kepler Rd CLAP SW4 141 K5
Keppel Rd DAGW RM9 92 A2
EHAM E6 89 K5
Keppel St GWRST WC1E 10 D1
Kerbela St BETH E2 104 C3
Kerbey St POP/IOD E14 105 K5
Kerfield Crs CMBW SE5 142 E2
Kerfield Pl CMBW SE5 142 E2
Kerri Cl BAR EN5 20 A5
Kerrison Pl EA W5 116 E1
Kerrison Rd BTSEA SW11 140 D4
EA W5 116 E1
SRTFD E15 88 B6
Kerry Av SOCK/AV RM15 131 J2
STAN HA7 29 J6
Kerry Cl CAN/RD E16 107 F5
PLMGR N13 35 F4
Kerry Ct STAN HA7 29 K6
Kerry Pth NWCR SE14 124 C6
Kerry Rd NWCR SE14 124 C6
Kersfield Rd PUT/ROE SW15 159 G1
WAND/EARL SW18 159 H2
Kershaw Cl WAND/EARL SW18 160 C1
Kershaw Rd DAGE RM10 92 C1
Kersley Ms BTSEA SW11 * 140 E2
Kersley Rd STNW/STAM N16 86 A1
Kersley St BTSEA SW11 140 E3
Kerstin Cl HYS/HAR UB3 94 D6
Kerswell Cl SEVS/STOTM N15 68 A2
Kerwick Cl HOLWY N7 85 F5
Keslake Rd KIL/WHAMP NW6 100 B1
Kessock Cl TOTM N17 68 D2
Kesteven Cl BARK/HLT IG6 55 F2
Keston Av HAYES BR2 215 G3
Keston Cl UED N18 35 K5
WELL DA16 148 D1
Keston Gdns HAYES BR2 215 G2
Keston Park Cl HAYES BR2 215 K2
Keston Rd PECK SE15 143 H4
THHTH CR7 196 A3
TOTM N17 49 K6
Kestrel Av EHAM E6 107 J4
HNHL SE24 142 C6
Kestrel Cl CDALE/KGS NW9 45 G5
HCH RM12 93 K5
KUTN/CMB KT2 156 E6
WLSDN NW10 81 F3
Kestrel Pl NWCR SE14 * 124 B6
Kestrel Wy CROY/NA CR0 214 B6
HYS/HAR UB3 113 G2
Keswick Av PUT/ROE SW15 176 B1
WIM/MER SW19 177 K5
Keswick Cl SUT SM1 209 G2
Keswick Gdns REDBR IG4 71 J2
RSLP HA4 58 B2
WBLY HA9 80 A3
Keswick Ms EA W5 117 F1
Keswick Rd BXLYHN DA7 149 H3
ORP BR6 202 A5
PUT/ROE SW15 139 H6
WHTN TW2 155 H1
WWKM BR4 199 H6
Kettering St
STRHM/NOR SW16 179 G2
Kett Gdns BRXS/STRHM SW2 142 A6
Kettlebaston Rd LEY E10 69 H5
Kettlewell Cl FBAR/BDGN N11 48 A2
Kevelioc Rd TOTM N17 49 J4
Kevin Cl HSLWW TW4 134 C3
Kevington Cl STMC/STPC BR5 202 A1
Kevington Dr CHST BR7 202 A1
Kew Br RCH/KEW TW9 117 H6
Kew Bridge Arches
CHSWK W4 * 117 H6
Kew Bridge Ct BTFD TW8 117 H5
Kew Bridge Rd BTFD TW8 117 G6
Kew Cl CRW RM5 57 G2
Kew Crs CHEAM SM3 208 D1
Kewferry Rd NTHWD HA6 40 A2
Kew Foot Rd RCH/KEW TW9 137 F5
Kew Gardens Rd
RCH/KEW TW9 137 G1
Kew Gn RCH/KEW TW9 117 G6
Kew Meadow Pth
RCH/KEW TW9 137 H2
Kew Riverside Pk
RCH/KEW TW9 137 J1
Kew Rd RCH/KEW TW9 137 F5
Key Cl WCHPL E1 104 D3
Keyes Rd CRICK NW2 82 B3
DART DA1 151 J6
Keymer Rd BRXS/STRHM SW2 162 A4
Keynes Cl EFNCH N2 47 K6
Keynsham Av WFD IG8 38 C6
Keynsham Gdns
ELTH/MOT SE9 146 D6
Keynsham Rd ELTH/MOT SE9 146 D6
MRDN SM4 194 A5
Keysham Av HEST TW5 133 K2
Keystone Crs IS N1 5 F3
Keyworth Cl CLPT E5 87 G2
Keyworth St STHWK SE1 18 B4
Kezia St DEPT SE8 124 B5
Khama Rd TOOT SW17 160 D6
Khartoum Rd IL IG1 90 B3
PLSTW E13 107 F2
TOOT SW17 160 C6
Khyber Rd BTSEA SW11 140 D3
Kibworth St VX/NE SW8 142 A1
Kidbrooke Gdns
BKHTH/KID SE3 145 K3
Kidbrooke Gv BKHTH/KID SE3 145 K2
Kidbrooke La ELTH/MOT SE9 146 D5
Kidbrooke Park Cl
BKHTH/KID SE3 146 A2
Kidbrooke Park Rd
BKHTH/KID SE3 146 A5
Kidbrooke Wy
BKHTH/KID SE3 146 A3
Kidderminster Pl
CROY/NA CR0 196 C5
Kidderminster Rd
CROY/NA CR0 196 C5
Kidderpore Av HAMP NW3 82 E2
Kidderpore Gdns HAMP NW3 82 E2
Kidd Pl CHARL SE7 126 D5
Kielder Cl BARK/HLT IG6 55 F2
Kiffen St SDTCH EC2A 7 F6
Kilberry Cl ISLW TW7 135 J2
Kilburn Br KIL/WHAMP NW6 82 E6
Kilburn High Rd
KIL/WHAMP NW6 82 E5
Kilburn La NKENS W10 100 B2
Kilburn Park Rd
KIL/WHAMP NW6 100 E2
Kilburn Pl KIL/WHAMP NW6 82 E6
Kilburn Priory
KIL/WHAMP NW6 83 F6
Kilburn Sq KIL/WHAMP NW6 82 E6
Kilburn V KIL/WHAMP NW6 82 E6
Kildare Cl RSLP HA4 59 G5
Kildare Rd CAN/RD E16 106 E4
Kildare Ter BAY/PAD W2 100 E5
Kildoran Rd CLAP SW4 141 K6
Kildowan Rd GDMY/SEVK IG3 73 G5
Kilgour Rd FSTH SE23 164 B1
Kilkie St FUL/PGN SW6 140 B3
Killarney Rd
WAND/EARL SW18 160 B1
Killburns Mill Cl WLGTN SM6 195 G6
Killearn Rd CAT SE6 165 G3
Killester Gdns WPK KT4 207 K2
Killewarren Wy
STMC/STPC BR5 202 D4
Killick St IS N1 5 G2
Killieser Av BRXS/STRHM SW2 161 K4
Killip Cl CAN/RD E16 106 D5
Killowen Av NTHLT UB5 78 C3
Killowen Rd HOM E9 * 87 F4
Killyon Rd VX/NE SW8 141 H3
Kilmaine Rd FUL/PGN SW6 139 H1
Kilmarnock Gdns BCTR RM8 91 J1
Kilmarnock Rd OXHEY WD19 27 H6
Kilmarsh Rd HMSMTH W6 119 F4
Kilmartin Av
STRHM/NOR SW16 180 B6
Kilmartin Rd GDMY/SEVK IG3 73 G6
Kilmartin Wy HCH RM12 93 K3
Kilmington Rd BARN SW13 118 D6
Kilmorey Gdns TWK TW1 136 C6
Kilmorey Rd TWK TW1 136 C5
Kilmorie Rd FSTH SE23 164 B3
Kiln Cl HYS/HAR UB3 113 G6
Kilner St POP/IOD E14 105 J4
Kiln Ms TOOT SW17 178 C1
Kiln Pl KTTN NW5 84 A2
Kilnside ESH/CLAY KT10 205 G5
Kiln Wy NTHWD HA6 40 C2
Kiln Wood La ABR/ST RM4 57 F1
Kilpatrick Wy YEAD UB4 95 J4
Kilravock St NKENS W10 100 C2
Kilross Rd EBED/NFELT TW14 153 G3
Kilsha Rd WOT/HER KT12 188 A3
Kilvinton Dr ENC/FH EN2 23 K1
Kimbell Gdns FUL/PGN SW6 139 H2
Kimbell Pl BKHTH/KID SE3 146 B5
Kimberley Av EHAM E6 107 J1
GNTH/NBYPK IG2 72 D4
PECK SE15 143 J3
ROMW/RG RM7 74 D3
Kimberley Ct
KIL/WHAMP NW6 82 C5
Kimberley Dr SCUP DA14 168 E4
Kimberley Gdns EN EN1 24 B4
FSBYPK N4 67 H2
Kimberley Rd BECK BR3 182 A5
BRXN/ST SW9 141 K3
CAN/RD E16 106 D3
CHING E4 38 C3
CROY/NA CR0 196 C3
KIL/WHAMP NW6 82 C6
TOTM N17 50 C5
WALTH E17 51 G4
WAN E11 70 B6
Kimberley Wy CHING E4 38 C3
Kimber Rd WAND/EARL SW18 159 K2
Kimble Cl WATW WD18 * 26 C1
Kimble Crs BUSH WD23 28 C2
Kimble Rd WIM/MER SW19 178 C2
Kimbolton Cl LEE/GVPK SE12 165 J1
Kimmeridge Gdns
ELTH/MOT SE9 166 D6
Kimmeridge Rd
ELTH/MOT SE9 166 D6
Kimpton Park Wy
CHEAM SM3 193 J6
Kimpton Rd CHEAM SM3 193 J6
CHEAM SM3 208 D1
CMBW SE5 142 E2
Kinburn St
BERM/RHTH SE16 * 124 A2
Kincaid Rd PECK SE15 143 J1
Kincardine Gdns
MV/WKIL W9 * 100 E3
Kinch Gv WBLY HA9 62 B4
Kinder Cl THMD SE28 109 J6
Kinder St WCHPL E1 104 D5
Kinderton Cl STHGT/OAK N14 34 C3
Kinfauns Rd
BRXS/STRHM SW2 162 B4
GDMY/SEVK IG3 73 H5
Kingaby Gdns RAIN RM13 93 J5
King Alfred Av CAT SE6 164 D6
King Arthur Cl PECK SE15 143 K1
King Charles Crs BRYLDS KT5 191 G4
King Charles I Island
WHALL SW1A 10 E7
King Charles' Rd BRYLDS KT5 191 G4
King Charles St WHALL SW1A 16 D2
King Charles Ter WAP E1W * 104 D6
King Charles Wk
WIM/MER SW19 * 159 H3
Kingcup Cl CROY/NA CR0 198 A5
King David La WCHPL E1 104 E6
Kingdon Rd KIL/WHAMP NW6 82 E4
King Edward Av DART DA1 171 G1
King Edward Dr CHSGTN KT9 206 A1
King Edward III Ms
BERM/RHTH SE16 123 J2
King Edward Rd BAR EN5 20 E5
LEY E10 70 A5
OXHEY WD19 27 J1
ROM RM1 75 H3
WALTH E17 51 G6
King Edward's Gdns ACT W3 117 H1
King Edward's Gv TEDD TW11 174 C2
King Edwards Pl ACT W3 117 H1
King Edwards Rd RSLP HA4 58 B5
King Edward's Rd BARK IG11 90 D6
ED N9 36 D2
HACK E8 86 D6
HOM E9 86 E6
PEND EN3 25 F5
King Edward St STBT EC1A 12 C3
King Edward Wk STHWK SE1 17 K4
Kingfield Rd EA W5 97 K3
Kingfield St POP/IOD E14 125 F4
Kingfisher Cl
KTN/HRWW/WS HA3 43 F3
STMC/STPC BR5 202 E1
THMD SE28 109 J6
Kingfisher Dr
RCHPK/HAM TW10 156 D6
Kingfisher Ms LEW SE13 144 E6
Kingfisher Pl WDGN N22 * 49 F5
Kingfisher St EHAM E6 107 J4
Kingfisher Wy BECK BR3 198 A2
WLSDN NW10 * 81 F4
King Gdns CROY/NA CR0 211 H3
King Garth Ms FSTH SE23 163 K4
King George Av BUSH WD23 28 B1
CAN/RD E16 107 H5
GNTH/NBYPK IG2 72 D3
WOT/HER KT12 188 C5
King George Cl
ROMW/RG RM7 56 E6
King George Sq
RCHPK/HAM TW10 157 G1
King George St GNWCH SE10 145 F1
King George VI Av MTCM CR4 194 E1
Kingham Cl NTGHL W11 119 H2
WAND/EARL SW18 160 B2
King Harolds Wy BXLYHN DA7 148 E1
King Henry Ms HRW HA1 60 E5
ORP BR6 217 F3
King Henry's Dr CROY/NA CR0 214 A6
King Henry's Reach
HMSMTH W6 119 F6
King Henry's Rd HAMP NW3 83 J5
KUT/HW KT1 175 J6
King Henry St
STNW/STAM N16 86 A3
King Henry's Wk IS N1 86 A4
King Henry's Yd
STNW/STAM N16 86 A3
King Henry Ter WAP E1W * 104 D6
Kinghorn St STBT EC1A 12 C2
King James Ct STHWK SE1 18 B3
King James St STHWK SE1 18 B3
King John Ct SDTCH EC2A 7 H6
King John St WCHPL E1 105 F4
King John's Wk
ELTH/MOT SE9 166 D2
Kinglake Est WALW SE17 * 123 F5
Kinglake St WALW SE17 123 F5
Kinglet Cl FSTGT E7 88 E4
Kingly Ct REGST W1B * 10 B5
Kingly St REGST W1B 10 A4
King & Queen Cl
ELTH/MOT SE9 166 D6
King & Queen St WALW SE17 122 D5
King & Queen Whf
BERM/RHTH SE16 * 124 A1
Kingsand Rd LEE/GVPK SE12 165 K4
King's Arms Yd LOTH EC2R 12 E3
Kingsash Dr YEAD UB4 95 J3
Kings Av BAL SW12 161 J3
BMLY BR1 183 J2
CAR SM5 209 J5
CHDH RM6 74 B3
CLAP SW4 161 K1
EA W5 97 K5
MUSWH N10 48 A6
NWMAL KT3 192 C1
King's Av GFD/PVL UB6 96 B5
HSLW TW3 135 G2
WCHMH N21 35 H3
WFD IG8 53 G1
King's Bench St STHWK SE1 18 B2
Kings Bench Wk EMB EC4Y 11 K4
Kingsbridge Av EA W5 117 G2
Kingsbridge Ct POP/IOD E14 124 D3
Kingsbridge Crs STHL UB1 95 K4
Kingsbridge Dr MLHL NW7 46 B3
Kingsbridge Rd BARK IG11 108 D1
MRDN SM4 193 G4
NKENS W10 100 A5
NWDGN UB2 114 E4
WOT/HER KT12 188 A4
Kingsbury Gn
CDALE/KGS NW9 * 62 E2
Kingsbury Rd
CDALE/KGS NW9 62 C2
IS N1 86 A4
Kingsbury Ter IS N1 86 A4
Kings Cha E/WMO/HCT KT8 173 H6
Kingsclere Cl PUT/ROE SW15 158 D2
Kingsclere Pl ENC/FH EN2 23 J3
Kingscliffe Gdns
WIM/MER SW19 159 J3
Kings Cl DART DA1 150 B5
HDN NW4 64 B1
LEY E10 69 K4
NTHWD HA6 40 D2
THDIT KT7 190 B3
WOT/HER KT12 188 A5
Kings College Rd RSLP HA4 58 D3
King's College Rd
HAMP NW3 * 83 H5
Kingscote Rd CHSWK W4 118 A3
CROY/NA CR0 197 J4
NWMAL KT3 176 A6
Kingscote St BLKFR EC4V 12 A5
Kings Ct PLSTW E13 89 F6
King's Ct STHWK SE1 * 18 B2
Kingscourt Rd
STRHM/NOR SW16 161 J5
King's Crs FSBYPK N4 85 J1
Kingscroft Rd CRICK NW2 82 D4
King's Cross Br IS N1 * 5 F4
King's Cross Rd FSBYW WC1X 5 G4
Kingsdale Gdns NTGHL W11 119 G1
Kingsdale Rd PGE/AN SE20 182 A3
WOOL/PLUM SE18 128 A6
Kingsdown Av ACT W3 99 G6
SAND/SEL CR2 211 J6
WEA W13 116 C2
Kingsdown Cl
BERM/RHTH SE16 * 123 J5
NKENS W10 100 B5
Kingsdowne Ct EA W5 * 98 A6
Kingsdowne Rd SURB KT6 191 F4
Kingsdown Rd ARCH N19 84 E1
CHEAM SM3 208 C3
WAN E11 88 C1
Kingsdown Wy HAYES BR2 199 K3
Kings Dr BRYLDS KT5 191 H4
EDGW HA8 30 B6
WBLY HA9 62 D6
King's Dr THDIT KT7 190 C3
Kingsend RSLP HA4 58 C5
Kingsend Ct RSLP HA4 * 58 C5
Kings Farm WALTH E17 * 51 K4
Kings Farm Av
RCHPK/HAM TW10 137 H5
Kingsfield Av
RYLN/HDSTN HA2 60 B2
Kingsfield Ct OXHEY WD19 27 H1
Kingsfield Rd HRW HA1 * 60 D4
OXHEY WD19 27 H2
Kingsfield Ter DART DA1 * 171 G1
Kingsford St KTTN NW5 83 K3
Kingsford Wy EHAM E6 107 K4
Kings Gdns IL IG1 72 D5
KIL/WHAMP NW6 82 E5
Kingsgate WBLY HA9 80 E1
Kingsgate Av FNCH N3 46 E6
Kingsgate Cl BXLYHN DA7 149 F2
STMC/STPC BR5 186 D6
Kingsgate Est IS N1 * 86 A4
Kings Gate Ms
CEND/HSY/T N8 67 F2
Kingsgate Pl
KIL/WHAMP NW6 82 E5
Kingsgate Rd
KIL/WHAMP NW6 82 E5
KUT/HW KT1 175 F4
Kingsground ELTH/MOT SE9 166 C2
Kings Gv ROM RM1 75 J2
King's Gv PECK SE15 143 J1
Kings Hall Ms LEW SE13 * 145 F4
Kings Hall Rd BECK BR3 182 A3
Kings Head Hl CHING E4 37 K2
King's Hwy WOOL/PLUM SE18 127 K6
Kingshill Av CRW RM5 56 E2
KTN/HRWW/WS HA3 61 H1
NTHLT UB5 95 F2
WPK KT4 192 D4
YEAD UB4 94 C2
Kingshill Cl YEAD UB4 94 E2
Kingshill Ct BAR EN5 * 20 C5
Kingshill Dr
KTN/HRWW/WS HA3 43 H5
Kingshold Rd HOM E9 86 E5
Kingsholm Gdns
ELTH/MOT SE9 146 C5
Kingshurst Rd
LEE/GVPK SE12 165 K2
Kings Keep HAYES BR2 * 183 H6
KUT/HW KT1 * 191 F1
Kingsland Gn
STNW/STAM N16 86 A4
Kingsland High St HACK E8 86 B4
Kingsland Pas HACK E8 86 A4
Kingsland Rd BETH E2 7 H3
HACK E8 86 B5
PLSTW E13 107 G2
King's La SUT SM1 209 H3
Kingslawn Cl PUT/ROE SW15 138 E6
Kingsleigh Cl BTFD TW8 116 E6
Kingsleigh Pl MTCM CR4 178 E6
Kingsley Av DART DA1 151 K6
HSLW TW3 135 H3
STHL UB1 96 A6
SUT SM1 209 H2
WEA W13 97 G5
Kingsley Cl DAGE RM10 92 D2
GLDGN NW11 65 G2
Kingsley Ct EDGW HA8 * 30 D4
GPK RM2 75 K3
Kingsley Dr WPK KT4 192 C6
Kingsley Gdns CHING E4 51 J1
Kingsley Ms CHST BR7 185 G2
IL IG1 72 B6
KENS W8 * 120 A3
SKENS SW7 120 A3
WAP E1W * 104 D6
Kingsley Pl HGT N6 66 A4
Kingsley Rd BARK/HLT IG6 54 C4
CROY/NA CR0 196 B5
FSTGT E7 88 E5
HSLW TW3 135 H3
KIL/WHAMP NW6 82 D6
ORP BR6 217 F4
PIN HA5 59 K1
PLMGR N13 35 G6
RYLN/HDSTN HA2 78 C2
WALTH E17 52 A5
WIM/MER SW19 178 A1
Kingsley St BTSEA SW11 140 E4
Kingsley Wy EFNCH N2 65 G3
GLDGN NW11 65 G3
Kingsley Wood Dr
ELTH/MOT SE9 166 E5
Kingslyn Crs NRWD SE19 181 F4
Kings Ml HMSMTH W6 * 119 F4
Kingsman St
WOOL/PLUM SE18 126 E4
Kingsmead BAR EN5 20 E5
RCHPK/HAM TW10 157 G1
Kingsmead Av
CDALE/KGS NW9 63 F4
ED N9 36 D3
MTCM CR4 179 H6
ROM RM1 75 G3
SUN TW16 172 B6
SURB KT6 191 H6
WPK KT4 207 K1
Kingsmead Cl BFN/LL DA15 168 B4
HOR/WEW KT19 207 F5
TEDD TW11 174 C2
Kingsmead Dr NTHLT UB5 77 K5
Kingsmead Pde NTHLT UB5 * 77 K5
Kings Mead Pk
ESH/CLAY KT10 204 E5
Kingsmead Rd
BRXS/STRHM SW2 162 B4
Kingsmead Wy CLPT E5 87 G2
King's Mead Wy HOM E9 87 G2
Kingsmere Cl PUT/ROE SW15 139 G4
Kingsmere Pk
CDALE/KGS NW9 62 E5

Kingsmere Pl
STNW/STAM N16 * 67 K5
Kingsmere Rd
WIM/MER SW19 159 G4
King's Ms BMSBY WC1N 5 H7
CLAP SW4 141 K6
Kingsmill Gdns DAGW RM9 92 B3
Kingsmill Rd DAGW RM9 92 B3
Kingsmill Ter STJWD NW8 2 B2
Kingsnympton Pk
KUTN/CMB KT2 175 J3
Kings Oak ROMW/RG RM7 56 C6
King's Orch ELTH/MOT SE9 166 D1
King's Paddock HPTN TW12 173 H4
Kings Pde CAR SM5 * 209 J1
SHB W12 * 118 D3
TOTM N17 * 50 B6
WLSDN NW10 * 82 A6
Kingspark Ct SWFD E18 52 E6
Kings Pas WAN E11 * 70 C4
Kings Pl BKHH IG9 39 H4
CHSWK W4 117 K5
LOU IG10 39 H2
King's Pl STHWK SE1 18 C3
King Sq FSBYE EC1V 6 C5
King's Quay WBPTN SW10 * 140 B2
Kings Reach EMB EC4Y * 11 K5
WHALL SW1A 17 F1
Kings Ride Ga
RCHPK/HAM TW10 137 H5
Kingsridge Gdns DART DA1 171 G1
Kings Rd BAR EN5 20 A4
CHEL SW3 * 120 C6
EA W5 97 K4
FELT TW13 154 B3
MTCM CR4 179 F6
ORP BR6 217 F2
RCHPK/HAM TW10 137 G6
RYLN/HDSTN HA2 59 K6
WDGN N22 49 F4
WDR/YW UB7 112 C2
WLSDN NW10 81 K5
WOT/HER KT12 188 A6
King's Rd BARK IG11 90 C5
CHEL SW3 120 C6
CHING E4 38 B3
FUL/PGN SW6 140 A2
KUTN/CMB KT2 175 G3
MORT/ESHN SW14 138 A4
PLSTW E13 89 G6
ROM RM1 75 J2
SNWD SE25 181 H6
SURB KT6 190 D5
TEDD TW11 173 J1
TOTM N17 50 B4
TWK TW1 156 C1
UED N18 * 50 C1
WAN E11 70 C4
WIM/MER SW19 177 K2
King's Scholars' Pas
PIM SW1V 16 A5
King Stairs Cl
BERM/RHTH SE16 123 J2
King's Ter CAMTN NW1 4 A1
Kingsthorpe Rd SYD SE26 164 A6
Kingston Av CHEAM SM3 208 C1
EBED/NFELT TW14 153 H1
Kingston By-Pass
ESH/CLAY KT10 204 E1
RYNPK SW20 176 D5
Kingston Cl CHDH RM6 56 A6
NTHLT UB5 77 K5
TEDD TW11 174 C2
Kingston Crs BECK BR3 182 C4
Kingston Gdns CROY/NA CR0 210 E1
Kingston Ga KUTN/CMB KT2 175 H3
Kingston Hall Rd KUT/HW KT1 174 E6
Kingston Hl KUTN/CMB KT2 175 H4
KUTN/CMB KT2 175 K1
Kingston Hill Av CHDH RM6 56 A6
Kingston Hill Pl
KUTN/CMB KT2 157 K6
Kingston House Est
SURB KT6 * 190 C3
Kingston La TEDD TW11 174 B1
WDR/YW UB7 112 C2
Kingston Ldg NWMAL KT3 192 B1
Kingston Pl
KTN/HRWW/WS HA3 43 F3
Kingston Rd BRYLDS KT5 191 J6
EBAR EN4 21 H6
ED N9 36 C4
HOR/WEW KT19 207 F2
IL IG1 90 C2
KUT/HW KT1 175 J6
NWDGN UB2 114 E2
NWMAL KT3 192 A1
PUT/ROE SW15 158 E3
ROM RM1 75 H1
RYNPK SW20 177 G5
TEDD TW11 174 C2
WIM/MER SW19 177 K3
Kingston Sq NRWD SE19 180 E1
Kingston V PUT/ROE SW15 158 A6
Kingstown St CAMTN NW1 83 K6
King St CITYW EC2V 12 D4
COVGDN WC2E 10 E5
EFNCH N2 47 H6
HMSMTH W6 118 D4
NWDGN UB2 114 D3
PLSTW E13 106 E3
RCH/KEW TW9 136 E6
TOTM N17 50 B4
TWK TW1 156 B3
WHALL SW1A 16 B1
King Street Cloisters
HMSMTH W6 * 118 E4
King Street Pde TWK TW1 * 156 B3
Kingswater Pl BTSEA SW11 * 140 D1
Kings Wy CROY/NA CR0 211 F3
HRW HA1 60 E1
Kingsway HOL/ALD WC2B 11 G4
HYS/HAR UB3 94 A4
MORT/ESHN SW14 137 J4
NFNCH/WDSPK N12 47 G2
NWMAL KT3 193 F1
PEND EN3 24 D6
STMC/STPC BR5 201 J2
STWL/WRAY TW19 152 A3
WBLY HA9 80 A2
WWKM BR4 214 D1
Kingsway Av SAND/SEL CR2 212 E6
Kingsway Crs
RYLN/HDSTN HA2 60 C1
Kingsway Pde
STNW/STAM N16 * 85 K1
Kingsway Pl CLKNW EC1R * 5 K6
Kingsway Rd CHEAM SM3 208 C5
Kingswear Rd KTTN NW5 84 B1
RSLP HA4 58 E6
Kingswood Av BELV DA17 129 G4
HAYES BR2 183 H6
HPTN TW12 173 G2
HSLW TW3 134 E3
KIL/WHAMP NW6 82 C6
THHTH CR7 196 B2
Kingswood Cl ASHF TW15 153 F6
BAR EN5 33 G1
DART DA1 171 F1
EN EN1 24 A6
NWMAL KT3 192 C3
STMC/STPC BR5 201 J4
SURB KT6 191 F4
VX/NE SW8 141 K1
Kingswood Ct LEW SE13 165 G1
Kingswood Dr BELMT SM2 209 F6
CAR SM5 194 E5
DUL SE21 163 F6
Kingswood Pk FNCH N3 46 D5
Kingswood Pl LEW SE13 145 H5
Kingswood Rd
BRXS/STRHM SW2 161 K1
CHSWK W4 117 K3
GDMY/SEVK IG3 73 G5
HAYES BR2 183 H6
PGE/AN SE20 181 K2
WAN E11 70 C4
WBLY HA9 80 C1
WIM/MER SW19 177 J4
Kingswood Ter CHSWK W4 117 K3
Kingswood Wy WLGTN SM6 210 E3
Kingsworth Cl BECK BR3 198 B2
Kingsworthy Cl KUT/HW KT1 175 G5
Kings Yd PUT/ROE SW15 * 139 G5
SRTFD E15 * 87 J4
Kingthorpe Rd WLSDN NW10 81 F5
Kingthorpe Ter
WLSDN NW10 * 81 F5
Kingwell Rd EBAR EN4 21 H1
Kingweston Cl CRICK NW2 82 C1
King William La GNWCH SE10 125 H5
King William St CANST EC4R 13 F5
King William Wk GNWCH SE10 125 F6
Kingwood Rd FUL/PGN SW6 139 H1
Kinlet Rd WOOL/PLUM SE18 147 H1
Kinloch Dr CDALE/KGS NW9 63 G4
Kinloch St HOLWY N7 85 F1
Kinloss Gdns FNCH N3 46 D6
Kinloss Rd CAR SM5 194 B4
Kinnaird Av BMLY BR1 183 J2
CHSWK W4 137 K1
Kinnaird Cl BMLY BR1 183 J2
Kinnaird Wy WFD IG8 53 K2
Kinnear Rd SHB W12 118 C2
Kinnerton Pl North
KTBR SW1X * 15 F3
Kinnerton Pl South
KTBR SW1X * 15 F3
Kinnerton St KTBR SW1X 15 G3
Kinnerton Yd KTBR SW1X * 15 G3
Kinnoul Rd HMSMTH W6 119 H6
Kinross Av WPK KT4 192 D6
Kinross Cl
KTN/HRWW/WS HA3 62 B2
Kinross Ter WALTH E17 51 H5
Kinsale Rd PECK SE15 143 H4
Kinsella Gdns WIM/MER SW19 176 E2
Kintyre Cl STRHM/NOR SW16 180 A3
Kinveachy Gdns CHARL SE7 126 D5
Kinver Rd SYD SE26 163 K6
Kipling Dr WIM/MER SW19 178 C2
Kipling Est STHWK SE1 19 F3
Kipling Rd BXLYHN DA7 149 F2
Kipling St STHWK SE1 19 F3
Kipling Ter ED N9 * 35 K5
Kippington Dr ELTH/MOT SE9 166 C3
Kirby Cl BARK/HLT IG6 54 E2
HOR/WEW KT19 207 H3
LOU IG10 39 J2
NTHWD HA6 40 D2
Kirby Est BERM/RHTH SE16 * 123 J3
Kirby Gv STHWK SE1 19 G2
Kirby St HCIRC EC1N 11 K1
Kirchen Rd WEA W13 97 H6
Kirkcaldy Gn OXHEY WD19 27 G5
Kirkdale SYD SE26 163 J4
Kirkdale Cnr SYD SE26 * 163 K6
Kirkdale Rd WAN E11 70 C5
Kirkfield Cl WEA W13 116 C1
Kirkham Rd EHAM E6 107 J5
Kirkham St WOOL/PLUM SE18 127 K6
Kirkland Av CLAY IG5 54 A5
Kirkland Cl BFN/LL DA15 167 K1
Kirkland Dr ENC/FH EN2 23 J2
Kirkland Ter BECK BR3 182 D2
Kirkland Wk HACK E8 86 B4
Kirk La WOOL/PLUM SE18 127 H6
Kirkleas Rd SURB KT6 191 F5
Kirklees Rd BCTR RM8 91 J3
THHTH CR7 196 B2
Kirkley Rd WIM/MER SW19 177 K4
Kirkly Cl SAND/SEL CR2 212 A6
Kirkmichael Rd POP/IOD E14 106 A5
Kirk Rd WALTH E17 69 H3
Kirkside Rd BKHTH/KID SE3 125 K6
Kirkstall Av TOTM N17 67 K1
Kirkstall Gdns
BRXS/STRHM SW2 161 J3
Kirkstall Rd BRXS/STRHM SW2 161 K3
Kirksted Rd MRDN SM4 194 A5
Kirkstone Wy BMLY BR1 183 H3
Kirkton Rd SEVS/STOTM N15 68 A1
Kirkwall Pl BETH E2 * 104 E2
Kirkwood Rd PECK SE15 143 J3
Kirn Rd WEA W13 97 H6
Kirrane Cl NWMAL KT3 192 C2
Kirtley Rd SYD SE26 164 B6
Kirtling St VX/NE SW8 141 H1
Kirton Cl CHSWK W4 118 A4
Kirton Gdns BETH E2 7 K5
Kirton Ldg
WAND/EARL SW18 * 160 A1
Kirton Rd PLSTW E13 107 G1
Kirton Wk EDGW HA8 44 E3
Kirwyn Wy CMBW SE5 142 D1
Kitcat Ter BOW E3 105 J2
Kitchener Rd EFNCH N2 47 J6
FSTGT E7 89 F4
THHTH CR7 180 E6
TOTM N17 50 A6
WALTH E17 51 K4
Kite Pl BETH E2 * 104 C2
Kite Yd BTSEA SW11 * 140 E2
Kitley Gdns NRWD SE19 181 G4
Kitson Rd BARN SW13 138 D2
CMBW SE5 142 D1
Kittiwake Rd NTHLT UB5 95 H2
Kittiwake Wy YEAD UB4 95 H4
Kitto Rd NWCR SE14 144 A3
Kiver Rd ARCH N19 66 D6
Kiwi Ter EHAM E6 108 A2
Klea Av CLAP SW4 161 H1
Knapdale Cl FSTH SE23 163 J4
Knapmill Rd CAT SE6 164 D4
Knapmill Wy CAT SE6 164 D4
Knapp Cl WLSDN NW10 81 G4
Knapp Rd ASHF TW15 152 C6
BOW E3 105 J3
Knapton Ms TOOT SW17 179 F2
Knaresborough Dr
WAND/EARL SW18 160 A3
Knaresborough Pl ECT SW5 120 A4
Knatchbull Rd CMBW SE5 142 C3
WLSDN NW10 81 F6
Knebworth Av WALTH E17 51 J4
Knebworth Cl BAR EN5 21 F5
Knebworth Rd
STNW/STAM N16 * 86 A2
Knee Hl ABYW SE2 128 D5
Knee Hill Crs ABYW SE2 128 D4
Kneller Gdns ISLW TW7 155 J1
Kneller Rd BROCKY SE4 144 B5
NWMAL KT3 192 B4
WHTN TW2 155 H1
Knevett Ter HSLW TW3 135 F5
Knight Cl BCTR RM8 73 J6
Knighten St WAP E1W 123 J1
Knighthead Point
POP/IOD E14 * 124 D2
Knightland Rd CLPT E5 68 D6
Knighton Cl ROMW/RG RM7 75 F3
SAND/SEL CR2 211 H6
WFD IG8 39 F6
Knighton Dr WFD IG8 39 F6
Knighton La BKHH IG9 39 F4
Knighton Park Rd SYD SE26 182 A1
Knighton Rd FSTGT E7 88 E1
ROMW/RG RM7 74 E3
Knightrider Ct BLKFR EC4V * 12 B5
Knightrider St BLKFR EC4V 12 C5
Knight's Av EA W5 117 F2
Knightsbridge SKENS SW7 14 D3
Knightsbridge Gdns
ROMW/RG RM7 75 F2
Knightsbridge Gn
KTBR SW1X * 14 E3
Knights Chambers ED N9 * 36 C5
Knights Cl E/WMO/HCT KT8 188 E2
Knights Hl WNWD SE27 180 C1
Knight's Hill Sq WNWD SE27 162 C6
Knights Manor Wy DART DA1 171 J1
Knight's Pk KUT/HW KT1 175 F6
Knight's Pl WHTN TW2 155 K3
Knights Rdg ORP BR6 217 H3
Knights Rd CAN/RD E16 125 K1
STAN HA7 29 J6
Knights Wk LBTH SE11 18 A7
Knights Wy BARK/HLT IG6 54 C2
Knightswood Cl EDGW HA8 30 E4
Knightswood Rd RAIN RM13 111 H1
Knightwood Crs NWMAL KT3 192 B3
Knivet Rd FUL/PGN SW6 119 K6
Knockholt Rd ELTH/MOT SE9 146 C6
Knole Cl CROY/NA CR0 * 197 K3
Knole Rd DART DA1 170 D2
The Knole ELTH/MOT SE9 167 F6
Knoll Ct NTHWD HA6 40 C5
Knoll Dr STHGT/OAK N14 34 A2
Knollmead BRYLDS KT5 191 K5
Knoll Ri ORP BR6 202 A5
Knoll Rd BXLY DA5 169 H2
SCUP DA14 186 C1
WAND/EARL SW18 140 A6
Knolls Cl WPK KT4 207 K1
The Knoll BECK BR3 182 E4
EA W5 97 J4
HAYES BR2 199 K6
PIN HA5 * 41 H5
Knollys Cl
STRHM/NOR SW16 * 162 C5
Knolly's Cl STRHM/NOR SW16 162 B5
Knolly's Rd STRHM/NOR SW16 162 B5
Knotley Wy WWKM BR4 198 E6
Knottisford St BETH E2 105 F2
Knotts Green Ms LEY E10 69 K3
Knotts Green Rd LEY E10 69 K3
Knowle Av BXLYHN DA7 149 F1
Knowle Cl BRXN/ST SW9 142 B4
Knowle Rd HAYES BR2 200 D6
WHTN TW2 155 K3
Knowles Cl WDR/YW UB7 112 B1
Knowles Hill Crs LEW SE13 145 G6
Knowlton Gn HAYES BR2 199 J2
Knowsley Av STHL UB1 115 G1
Knowsley Rd BTSEA SW11 140 E3
Knox Rd FSTGT E7 88 E4
Knox St CAMTN NW1 8 E1
Knoyle St NWCR SE14 124 B6
Kohat Rd WIM/MER SW19 178 A1
Koh-I-Noor Av BUSH WD23 28 A1
Kossuth St GNWCH SE10 125 H5
Kramer Ms ECT SW5 * 119 K5
Kreedman Wk HACK E8 * 86 C3
Kuala Gdns
STRHM/NOR SW16 180 A4
Kwesi Ms STRHM/NOR SW16 180 B1
Kydbrook Cl STMC/STPC BR5 201 H4
Kylemore Cl EHAM E6 107 H1
Kylemore Rd
KIL/WHAMP NW6 82 E5
Kymberley Rd HRW HA1 * 60 E3
Kyme Rd ROM RM1 75 H3
Kynance Gdns STAN HA7 43 J4
Kynance Ms SKENS SW7 120 A3
Kynance Pl KENS W8 120 B3
Kynaston Av THHTH CR7 196 D2
Kynaston Cl
KTN/HRWW/WS HA3 42 D3
Kynaston Crs THHTH CR7 196 D2
Kynaston Rd BMLY BR1 183 K1
ENC/FH EN2 23 K2
STMC/STPC BR5 202 C4
STNW/STAM N16 86 A1
THHTH CR7 196 D2
Kynaston Wd
KTN/HRWW/WS HA3 42 D3
Kynnersley Cl CAR SM5 209 K1
Kynoch Rd UED N18 50 E1
Kyrle Rd BTSEA SW11 161 F1
Kyverdale Rd
STNW/STAM N16 68 B4

L

Laburnham Cl BAR EN5 20 D4
Laburnum Av DART DA1 171 F3
ED N9 36 A4
HCH RM12 75 J6
SUT SM1 209 J1
TOTM N17 49 K3
Laburnum Cl ALP/SUD HA0 80 C6
CHING E4 51 H2
PECK SE15 143 K1
Laburnum Ct STAN HA7 29 J6
Laburnum Crs SUN TW16 172 A4
Laburnum Gdns
CROY/NA CR0 198 A4
Laburnum Gv
CDALE/KGS NW9 62 E4
HSLW TW3 134 E5
NWMAL KT3 176 A5
RSLP HA4 58 B3
STHL UB1 95 K3
WCHMH N21 35 J4
Laburnum Pl ELTH/MOT SE9 * 147 F6
Laburnum Rd HYS/HAR UB3 113 J4
MTCM CR4 179 F5
WIM/MER SW19 178 B3
Laburnum St BETH E2 7 J1
Laburnum Wy HAYES BR2 201 F4
STWL/WRAY TW19 152 C3
Lacebark Cl BFN/LL DA15 168 A2
Lacewing Cl PLSTW E13 106 E2
Lacey Cl ED N9 36 C4
Lacey Dr BCTR RM8 91 J1
EDGW HA8 30 A6
HPTN TW12 172 E4
Lacey Ms BOW E3 105 J1
Lackington St SDTCH EC2A 13 F1
Lacock Cl WIM/MER SW19 178 B2
Lacon Rd EDUL SE22 143 H5
Lacrosse Wy
STRHM/NOR SW16 179 J4
Lacy Rd PUT/ROE SW15 139 G5
Ladas Rd WNWD SE27 180 D1
Ladbroke Crs NTGHL W11 100 C5
Ladbroke Gdns NTGHL W11 100 D6
Ladbroke Gv NKENS W10 100 B3
NTGHL W11 100 D6
Ladbroke Ms NTGHL W11 119 H1
Ladbroke Rd EN EN1 36 B1
NTGHL W11 119 J1
Ladbroke Sq NTGHL W11 100 D6
Ladbroke Ter NTGHL W11 100 D6
Ladbroke Wk NTGHL W11 119 J1
Ladbrook Cl BMLY BR1 183 H2
PIN HA5 59 K2
Ladbrooke Crs SCUP DA14 168 E5
Ladbrook Rd SNWD SE25 180 E6
Ladderstile Ride
KUTN/CMB KT2 175 J1
Ladderswood Wy
FBAR/BDGN N11 48 C1
Lady Alesford Av STAN HA7 43 H1
Lady Booth Rd KUT/HW KT1 175 F5
Ladycroft Gdns ORP BR6 216 C3
Ladycroft Rd LEW SE13 144 E4
Ladycroft Wk STAN HA7 43 K4
Ladycroft Wy ORP BR6 216 C3
Lady Forsdyke Wy
HOR/WEW KT19 206 C6
Ladygate La RSLP HA4 58 A3
Ladygrove CROY/NA CR0 213 G6
Lady Harewood Wy
HOR/WEW KT19 206 C6
Lady Hay WPK KT4 192 C6
Lady Margaret Rd KTTN NW5 84 C3
STHL UB1 95 K6
Ladymount WLGTN SM6 210 D2
Ladyship Ter EDUL SE22 * 163 J2
Ladysmith Av EHAM E6 107 J1
GNTH/NBYPK IG2 72 D4
Ladysmith Cl MLHL NW7 45 J3
Ladysmith Rd CAN/RD E16 106 D2
ELTH/MOT SE9 167 F1
EN EN1 24 B3
KTN/HRWW/WS HA3 42 E5
TOTM N17 50 C5
Lady Somerset Rd KTTN NW5 84 B2
Ladywell Cl BROCKY SE4 144 D6
Ladywell Rd LEW SE13 144 D6
Ladywell St SRTFD E15 88 D6
Ladywell Water Tower
BROCKY SE4 * 144 C4
Ladywood Av
STMC/STPC BR5 201 K2
Ladywood Rd SURB KT6 191 H6
Lafone Av FELT TW13 154 B3
Lafone St STHWK SE1 19 J2
Lagado Ms BERM/RHTH SE16 124 A1
Lagonda Av BARK/HLT IG6 55 F2
Lagonda Wy DART DA1 151 F5
Lagoon Rd STMC/STPC BR5 202 C2
Laidlaw Dr WCHMH N21 23 F6
Laing Cl BARK/HLT IG6 54 D2
Laing Dean NTHLT UB5 77 G6
Laings Av MTCM CR4 178 E5
Lainlock Pl HSLW TW3 135 G2
Lainson St WAND/EARL SW18 159 K2
Lairdale Cl DUL SE21 162 D3
Lairs Cl HOLWY N7 * 84 E4
Laitwood Rd BAL SW12 161 G3
Lake Av BMLY BR1 183 K2
Lake Cl BCTR RM8 91 K1
Lakedale Rd
WOOL/PLUM SE18 127 K5
Lake Dr BUSH WD23 28 C4
Lakefield Rd WDGN N22 49 H5
Lake Gdns DAGE RM10 92 C3
RCHPK/HAM TW10 156 C5
WLGTN SM6 210 B1
Lakehall Gdns THHTH CR7 196 C2
Lakehall Rd THHTH CR7 196 C2
Lake House Rd WAN E11 88 E1
Lakehurst Rd HOR/WEW KT19 207 G3
Lakeland Cl
KTN/HRWW/WS HA3 42 D2
Lakenheath STHGT/OAK N14 22 D6
Lake Ri ROM RM1 57 H6
Lake Rd CHDH RM6 73 K1
CROY/NA CR0 198 C6
DAGW RM9 110 D2
LEY E10 69 K4
WIM/MER SW19 177 J1
Lakeside BECK BR3 182 E6
ENC/FH EN2 22 D5
HOR/WEW KT19 207 G4
WEA W13 97 J5
WLGTN SM6 210 B2
Lakeside Av REDBR IG4 71 H1
THMD SE28 128 B1
Lakeside Cl BFN/LL DA15 148 D6
RSLP HA4 58 B1
SNWD SE25 181 H5
Lakeside Crs EBAR EN4 33 K1
Lakeside Dr ESH/CLAY KT10 204 C4
HAYES BR2 215 J1
WLSDN NW10 98 B2
Lakeside Rd PLMGR N13 35 F6
WKENS W14 119 G3
Lakeside Wy WBLY HA9 80 C2
Lakes Rd HAYES BR2 215 G3
Lakeswood Rd
STMC/STPC BR5 201 G3
The Lake BUSH WD23 28 D3
Lake Vw EDGW HA8 44 B1
Lake View Est BOW E3 * 105 F1
Lakeview Rd WELL DA16 148 C5
WNWD SE27 180 B1
Lake View Ter UED N18 * 36 B6
Lakis Cl HAMP NW3 83 G2
Laleham Av MLHL NW7 31 F5
Laleham Ct SUT SM1 * 209 G3
Laleham Rd CAT SE6 165 F2
Lalor St FUL/PGN SW6 139 H3
Lambarde Av ELTH/MOT SE9 167 F6
Lamb Cl NTHLT UB5 95 J2
Lamberhurst Cl
STMC/STPC BR5 202 E5
Lamberhurst Rd BCTR RM8 74 A5
WNWD SE27 162 B6
Lambert Av RCH/KEW TW9 137 H4
Lambert Jones Ms
BARB EC2Y * 12 C1
Lambert Rd
BRXS/STRHM SW2 141 K6
CAN/RD E16 107 F5
NFNCH/WDSPK N12 47 H1
Lambert's Pl CROY/NA CR0 196 E5
Lambert's Rd BRYLDS KT5 191 F2
Lambert St IS N1 85 G5
Lambert Wy
NFNCH/WDSPK N12 47 G1
Lambeth Br WEST SW1P 17 F6
Lambeth High St STHWK SE1 17 G7
Lambeth Hl BLKFR EC4V 12 C5
Lambeth Palace Rd
STHWK SE1 17 G5
Lambeth Rd CROY/NA CR0 196 B5
STHWK SE1 17 J5
Lambeth Wk LBTH SE11 17 H6
PECK SE15 143 G3
Lambkins Ms WALTH E17 70 A1
Lamb La HACK E8 86 D5
Lamble St KTTN NW5 84 A2
Lambley Rd DAGW RM9 91 H4
Lambolle Pl HAMP NW3 83 J4
Lambolle Rd HAMP NW3 83 J4
Lambourn Cl HNWL W7 116 A2
KTTN NW5 * 84 C2
SAND/SEL CR2 211 H6
Lambourne Av
WIM/MER SW19 159 J6
Lambourne Gdns BARK IG11 91 F5
CHING E4 37 J4
EN EN1 24 B3
Lambourne Gv
BERM/RHTH SE16 124 A5
KUT/HW KT1 175 J5
Lambourne Pl BKHTH/KID SE3 146 A2
Lambourne Rd BARK IG11 90 E5
GDMY/SEVK IG3 72 E6
WAN E11 70 A4
Lambourn Rd VX/NE SW8 141 G4
Lambrook Ter FUL/PGN SW6 139 H2
Lambs Cl ED N9 36 C4
Lamb's Conduit Pas
FSBYW WC1X 11 G1
Lamb's Conduit St
BMSBY WC1N 5 G7
Lambscroft Av ELTH/MOT SE9 166 B5
Lambs Meadow WFD IG8 53 H5
Lambs Ms IS N1 6 A1
Lamb's Pas STLK EC1Y 6 E7
Lambs Ter ED N9 * 35 K4
Lamb St WCHPL E1 13 J1
Lambs Wk ENC/FH EN2 23 J3
Lambton Pl NTGHL W11 * 100 D6
Lambton Rd ARCH N19 66 E5
RYNPK SW20 177 F4
Lamb Wk STHWK SE1 19 G3
Lamerock Rd BMLY BR1 165 J6
Lamerton Rd BARK/HLT IG6 54 B5
Lamerton St DEPT SE8 124 D6
Lamford Cl TOTM N17 49 K3
Lamington St HMSMTH W6 118 E4

Lamlash St LBTH SE11 18 A6
Lammas Av MTCM CR4 179 F5
Lammas La ESH/CLAY KT10 204 A2
Lammas Park Gdns EA W5 116 D1
Lammas Rd HOM E9 87 F5
LEY E10 69 G6
RCHPK/HAM TW10 156 H6
Lammermoor Rd BAL SW12 * 161 G2
Lamont Rd WBPTN SW10 120 C6
Lamont Road Pas
WBPTN SW10 * 120 C6
Lamorbey Cl BFN/LL DA15 168 A4
Lamorbey Pk BFN/LL DA15 * 168 C3
Lamorna Cl ORP BR6 202 B4
WALTH E17 52 A5
Lamorna Gv STAN HA7 43 K4
Lampard Gv STNW/STAM N16 68 B5
Lampern Sq BETH E2 * 104 C2
Lampeter Sq HMSMTH W6 119 H6
Lamplighter Cl WCHPL E1 104 E3
Lamplighters Cl DART DA1 171 J1
Lampmead Rd
LEE/GVPK SE12 145 H6
Lamport Cl WOOL/PLUM SE18 126 E4
Lampton Av HSLW TW3 135 F2
Lampton House Cl
WIM/MER SW19 159 G6
Lampton Park Rd HSLW TW3 135 G3
Lampton Rd HSLW TW3 135 G3
Lamson Rd RAIN RM13 111 H3
Lanacre Av CDALE/KGS NW9 45 G4
EDGW HA8 45 F4
Lanadron Cl ISLW TW7 136 A3
Lanark Cl EA W5 97 J4
Lanark Pl MV/WKIL W9 101 G3
Lanark Rd KIL/WHAMP NW6 101 F1
Lanbury Rd PECK SE15 144 A5
Lancashire Ct
MYFR/PKLN W1K 9 J5
Lancaster Av BARK IG11 90 E5
EBAR EN4 21 H1
MTCM CR4 195 K1
WAN E11 71 F1
WIM/MER SW19 177 G1
WNWD SE27 162 C4
Lancaster Cl ASHF TW15 152 B6
CDALE/KGS NW9 45 H3
HAYES BR2 199 J1
STWL/WRAY TW19 152 B1
TOTM N17 * 50 C3
WPK KT4 192 E4
Lancaster Dr HAMP NW3 83 J4
HCH RM12 93 K3
POP/IOD E14 125 F1
Lancaster Garde BMLY BR1 200 D2
Lancaster Gdn
KUTN/CMB KT2 174 E1
Lancaster Gdns
WIM/MER SW19 177 H1
Lancaster Ga BAY/PAD W2 101 G6
Lancaster Gv HAMP NW3 83 J4
Lancaster House
WOOL/PLUM SE18 * 146 D1
Lancaster Ms BAY/PAD W2 * 101 G6
RCHPK/HAM TW10 157 F1
WAND/EARL SW18 * 140 A6
Lancaster Pk
RCHPK/HAM TW10 137 F6
Lancaster Pl TPL/STR WC2R 11 G5
TWK TW1 156 B1
WIM/MER SW19 177 G1
Lancaster Rd EBAR EN4 21 H5
ENC/FH EN2 23 K2
FBAR/BDGN N11 48 D2
FSBYPK N4 67 G4
FSTGT E7 88 E5
NKENS W10 100 B5
NTHLT UB5 78 C4
RYLN/HDSTN HA2 60 A2
SNWD SE25 181 G5
STHL UB1 95 J6
UED N18 50 B1
WALTH E17 51 F5
WAN E11 70 C6
WIM/MER SW19 177 G1
WLSDN NW10 81 H3
Lancaster Stables
HAMP NW3 * 83 J4
Lancaster St STHWK SE1 18 A3
Lancaster Ter BAY/PAD W2 8 A5
Lancaster Wk HYS/HAR UB3 94 A5
Lancaster Wy WPK KT4 193 F4
Lancaster West NTGHL W11 * 100 C5
Lancastrian Rd WLGTN SM6 210 E5
Lancefield St NKENS W10 100 D2
Lancell St STNW/STAM N16 68 A6
Lancelot Av ALP/SUD HA0 79 K2
Lancelot Crs ALP/SUD HA0 79 K2
Lancelot Gdns EBAR EN4 34 A1
Lancelot Pde ALP/SUD HA0 * 80 A3
Lancelot Pl SKENS SW7 14 E3
Lancelot Rd ALP/SUD HA0 79 K2
BARK/HLT IG6 54 E2
WELL DA16 148 B5
Lance Rd HRW HA1 60 C4
Lancer Sq KENS W8 * 120 A2
Lancey Cl CHARL SE7 126 C4
Lanchester Rd HGT N6 65 K2
Lanchester Wy NWCR SE14 143 K2
Lancing Gdns ED N9 36 B3
Lancing Rd CROY/NA CR0 196 A3
FELT TW13 153 J4
GNTH/NBYPK IG2 72 D3
ORP BR6 202 C6
WEA W13 97 H6
Lancing St CAMTN NW1 4 C5
Landale Gdns DART DA1 171 F3
Landau Ter HAYES BR2 215 J2
Landau Wy ERITH DA8 131 G5
Landcroft Rd EDUL SE22 163 G1
Landells Rd EDUL SE22 163 G1
Landford Rd PUT/ROE SW15 139 F4
Landgrove Rd
WIM/MER SW19 177 K1
Landleys Flds HOLWY N7 * 84 D3
Landmann Wy NWCR SE14 124 A6
Landon Pl KTBR SW1X 14 E4
Landons Cl POP/IOD E14 125 F1
Landor Rd BRXN/ST SW9 141 K4
Landor Wk SHB W12 118 D2
Landra Gdns WCHMH N21 35 H1
Landridge Dr EN EN1 24 D1
Landridge Rd FUL/PGN SW6 139 H3
Landrock Rd CEND/HSY/T N8 66 E3
Landscape Rd WFD IG8 53 F3
Landseer Av MNPK E12 90 A3
Landseer Cl EDGW HA8 44 C5
EMPK RM11 75 K5
WIM/MER SW19 178 B4
Landseer Rd ARCH N19 84 E1
EN EN1 24 C6
NWMAL KT3 192 A4
SUT SM1 208 E4
Lands' End BORE WD6 29 K1
Landstead Rd
WOOL/PLUM SE18 147 J1
The Landway STMC/STPC BR5 186 D6
Lane Ap MLHL NW7 * 46 C1
Lane Cl CRICK NW2 82 A1
Lane End BXLYHN DA7 149 J4
Lane Gdns BUSH WD23 28 E3
ESH/CLAY KT10 205 F5
Lane Ms MNPK E12 89 K1
Lanercost Gdns
STHGT/OAK N14 34 E1
Lanercost Rd
BRXS/STRHM SW2 162 B4
Laneside CHST BR7 185 G1
EDGW HA8 44 E1
Laneside Av BCTR RM8 74 B4
The Lane BKHTH/KID SE3 145 K4
STJWD NW8 101 G1
Laneway PUT/ROE SW15 138 E6
Lanfranc Rd BOW E3 105 G1
Lanfrey Pl WKENS W14 119 J5
Langbourne Av HGT N6 66 A6
Langbourne Wy
ESH/CLAY KT10 205 F4
Langbrook Rd BKHTH/KID SE3 146 C4
Langcroft Cl CAR SM5 209 K1
Langdale Av MTCM CR4 178 E6
Langdale Cl BCTR RM8 73 J5
MORT/ESHN SW14 137 J5
ORP BR6 216 B1
Langdale Crs BXLYHN DA7 149 H2
Langdale Dr YEAD UB4 94 C1
Langdale Gdns HCH RM12 93 J3
Langdale Pde MTCM CR4 * 178 E5
Langdale Rd GNWCH SE10 145 F1
THHTH CR7 196 B1
Langdale St WCHPL E1 * 104 D5
Langdon Ct WLSDN NW10 81 G6
Langdon Crs EHAM E6 108 A1
Langdon Dr CDALE/KGS NW9 62 E5
Langdon House
WOOL/PLUM SE18 * 146 D1
Langdon Pk TEDD TW11 174 D3
Langdon Park Rd HGT N6 66 B4
Langdon Pl
MORT/ESHN SW14 137 K4
Langdon Rd EHAM E6 90 A6
HAYES BR2 184 A6
MRDN SM4 194 B2
Langdon Shaw SCUP DA14 186 A1
Langdon Wk MRDN SM4 194 B2
Langdon Wy STHWK SE1 123 H4
Langford Cl HACK E8 86 C3
SEVS/STOTM N15 68 A3
STJWD NW8 101 G1
Langford Crs EBAR EN4 21 K5
Langford Gn CMBW SE5 143 F4
Langford Pl SCUP DA14 168 B5
STJWD NW8 101 G1
Langford Rd EBAR EN4 21 K5
FUL/PGN SW6 140 A3
WFD IG8 53 G2
Langfords BKHH IG9 39 H4
Langham Cl HAYES BR2 200 D6
Langham Ct RSLP HA4 * 77 F3
Langham Dr GDMY/SEVK IG3 73 H3
Langham Gdns ALP/SUD HA0 61 J6
EDGW HA8 44 E3
RCHPK/HAM TW10 156 D6
WCHMH N21 23 G6
WEA W13 97 H6
Langham House Cl
RCHPK/HAM TW10 156 E6
Langham Pde
SEVS/STOTM N15 * 49 H6
Langham Park Pl HAYES BR2 199 J1
Langham Pl CHSWK W4 118 B6
REGST W1B 9 K2
SEVS/STOTM N15 49 H6
Langham Rd EDGW HA8 44 E2
RYNPK SW20 177 F4
SEVS/STOTM N15 49 H6
SEVS/STOTM N15 67 J1
TEDD TW11 174 C1
Langham St GTPST W1W 10 A2
REGST W1B 9 K2
Langhedge Cl UED N18 50 B2
Langhedge La UED N18 50 B1
Langholm Cl BAL SW12 161 J2
Langholme BUSH WD23 28 C3
Langhorn Dr WHTN TW2 155 K2
Langhorne Rd DAGE RM10 92 C5
Langland Ct NTHWD HA6 40 A3
Langland Crs STAN HA7 43 K5
Langland Dr PIN HA5 41 J3
Langland Gdns CROY/NA CR0 198 C6
HAMP NW3 83 F3
Langler Rd WLSDN NW10 100 A1
Langley Av RSLP HA4 59 F6
SURB KT6 190 E5
WPK KT4 193 G6
Langley Ct BECK BR3 * 198 E1
COVGDN WC2E 10 E5
Langley Crs DAGW RM9 91 J5
EDGW HA8 30 E5
HYS/HAR UB3 133 J1
WAN E11 71 F4
Langley Dr ACT W3 117 J2
WAN E11 71 F4
Langley Gdns DAGW RM9 91 K5
STMC/STPC BR5 201 G3
Langley Gv NWMAL KT3 176 A5
Langley La VX/NE SW8 121 K6
Langley Pk MLHL NW7 45 G2
Langley Park Rd BELMT SM2 209 G4
Langley Pl WPK KT4 193 G6
Langley Rd BECK BR3 198 A1
ISLW TW7 136 A3
SAND/SEL CR2 213 F6
SURB KT6 191 F4
WELL DA16 128 D6
WIM/MER SW19 177 J4
Langley Rw BAR EN5 20 D2
Langley St LSQ/SEVD WC2H 10 E4
Langley Wy WWKM BR4 199 G5
Langley Wd BECK BR3 * 199 H2
Langmead Dr BUSH WD23 28 D3
Langmead St WNWD SE27 162 C6
Langport Ct WOT/HER KT12 188 B5
Langridge Ms HPTN TW12 172 E2
Langroyd Rd TOOT SW17 160 E4
Langside Av PUT/ROE SW15 138 D5
Langside Crs STHGT/OAK N14 34 D5
Langstone Wy MLHL NW7 46 B3
Langston Hughes Cl
HNHL SE24 * 142 C5
Lang St WCHPL E1 104 E3
Langthorn Ct LOTH EC2R * 13 F3
Langthorne Rd WAN E11 88 B1
Langthorne St FUL/PGN SW6 139 G2
Langton Av EHAM E6 108 A2
TRDG/WHET N20 33 G2
Langton Cl FSBYW WC1X 5 H5
Langton Gv NTHWD HA6 40 A1
Langton Ri EDUL SE22 163 J2
Langton Rd BRXN/ST SW9 142 C1
CRICK NW2 82 A1
E/WMO/HCT KT8 189 H2
KTN/HRWW/WS HA3 42 C3
Langton St WBPTN SW10 120 B6
Langton Vls TOTM N17 * 50 C4
Langton Wy BKHTH/KID SE3 145 K1
CROY/NA CR0 212 A2
Langtry Rd NTHLT UB5 95 H1
STJWD NW8 83 F6
Langtry Wk STJWD NW8 83 G6
Langwood Cha TEDD TW11 174 D2
Langworth Cl RDART DA2 171 G5
Langworth Dr YEAD UB4 95 F5
Lanhill Rd MV/WKIL W9 100 E3
Lanier Rd LEW SE13 165 F1
Lanigan Dr HSLW TW3 135 G6
Lankaster Gdns EFNCH N2 47 H4
Lankers Dr RYLN/HDSTN HA2 59 K3
Lankton Cl BECK BR3 183 F4
Lannock Rd HYS/HAR UB3 113 J1
Lannoy Rd ELTH/MOT SE9 167 H3
Lanrick Rd POP/IOD E14 106 B4
Lanridge Rd ABYW SE2 128 E3
Lansbury Av BARK IG11 91 G5
CHDH RM6 74 A2
EBED/NFELT TW14 154 A1
UED N18 49 K1
Lansbury Cl WLSDN NW10 80 E3
Lansbury Crs DART DA1 151 K6
Lansbury Dr YEAD UB4 94 D4
Lansbury Gdns
POP/IOD E14 * 106 B5
Lansbury Rd PEND EN3 25 F2
Lansbury Wy UED N18 50 A1
Lanscombe Wk VX/NE SW8 * 141 K1
Lansdell Rd MTCM CR4 179 F5
Lansdown Cl WOT/HER KT12 188 B5
Lansdowne Av BXLYHN DA7 148 D1
ORP BR6 201 G5
Lansdowne Cl BRYLDS KT5 191 J6
TWK TW1 156 A3
Lansdowne Copse WPK KT4 * 192 D6
Lansdowne Ct WPK KT4 192 D6
Lansdowne Crs NTGHL W11 100 C6
Lansdowne Dr HACK E8 86 C5
Lansdowne Gdns VX/NE SW8 141 K2
Lansdowne Gn VX/NE SW8 141 K1
Lansdowne Gv WLSDN NW10 81 G2
Lansdowne Hl WNWD SE27 162 C5
Lansdowne La CHARL SE7 126 C5
Lansdowne Ms CHARL SE7 126 C5
NTGHL W11 119 J1
Lansdowne Pl NRWD SE19 181 G3
STHWK SE1 19 F4
Lansdowne Ri NTGHL W11 100 C6
Lansdowne Rd BMLY BR1 183 K3
CHING E4 37 J4
CROY/NA CR0 196 E5
FNCH N3 46 D3
GDMY/SEVK IG3 73 F5
HACK E8 86 C4
HOR/WEW KT19 206 E5
HSLW TW3 135 G4
MUSWH N10 48 C5
NTGHL W11 100 C6
RYNPK SW20 177 F3
STAN HA7 43 J2
SWFD E18 52 E6
TOTM N17 50 C4
WALTH E17 69 J3
WAN E11 70 D6
Lansdowne Ter BMSBY WC1N 5 F7
Lansdowne Wk NTGHL W11 119 H1
Lansdowne Wy VX/NE SW8 141 K2
Lansdowne Wood Cl
WNWD SE27 162 C5
Lansdown Rd FSTGT E7 89 G5
SCUP DA14 168 C5
Lansfield Av UED N18 36 C6
Lantern Cl ALP/SUD HA0 79 K3
ORP BR6 216 B2
PUT/ROE SW15 138 D5
Lanterns Ct POP/IOD E14 124 D3
Lantern Wy WDR/YW UB7 112 B2
Lant St STHWK SE1 18 C2
Lanvanor Rd PECK SE15 143 K3
Lapford Cl MV/WKIL W9 * 100 D3
Lapse Wood Wk FSTH SE23 163 J3
Lapstone Gdns
KTN/HRWW/WS HA3 61 J3
Lapwing Cl ERITH DA8 * 150 E1
Lapwing Ter FSTGT E7 89 H3
Lapwing Wy YEAD UB4 95 H5
Lapworth Cl ORP BR6 202 D6
Lara Cl CHSGTN KT9 206 A5
LEW SE13 165 F1
Larbert Rd STRHM/NOR SW16 179 H4
Larch Av ACT W3 118 B1
Larch Cl BAL SW12 161 G4
DEPT SE8 124 C6
FBAR/BDGN N11 48 A3
PLSTW E13 107 G3
Larch Crs HOR/WEW KT19 206 D4
YEAD UB4 95 G3
Larch Dene ORP BR6 201 F6
Larch Dr CHSWK W4 * 117 H5
Larches Av MORT/ESHN SW14 138 A5
The Larches PLMGR N13 35 J5
Larch Gv BFN/LL DA15 168 A3
Larch Rd CRICK NW2 82 A2
DART DA1 171 G3
LEY E10 69 J6
Larch Tree Wy CROY/NA CR0 213 J1
Larch Wy HAYES BR2 201 F4
Larchwood Av CRW RM5 56 D2
Larchwood Cl CRW RM5 56 E2
Larchwood Rd ELTH/MOT SE9 167 G4
Larcombe Cl CROY/NA CR0 212 B2
Larcom St WALW SE17 18 D7
Larden Rd ACT W3 118 B2
Largewood Av SURB KT6 191 H6
Larissa St WALW SE17 * 122 E5
Larkbere Rd SYD SE26 164 B6
Larken Cl BUSH WD23 28 C3
Larken Dr BUSH WD23 28 C3
Larkfield Av
KTN/HRWW/WS HA3 43 H6
Larkfield Rd RCH/KEW TW9 137 F5
SCUP DA14 168 A5
Larkhall La CLAP SW4 141 J3
Larkhall Ri CLAP SW4 141 H4
Larkham Cl FELT TW13 153 H5
Larkhill Ter
WOOL/PLUM SE18 * 147 F1
Lark Rw BETH E2 86 E6
Larksfield Gv EN EN1 24 D2
Larks Gv BARK IG11 90 E5
Larkshall Crs CHING E4 38 A6
Larkshall Rd CHING E4 52 A1
Larkspur Cl CDALE/KGS NW9 62 D2
ORP BR6 202 D6
TOTM N17 49 K3
Larkspur Gv EDGW HA8 30 E6
Larkspur Wy HOR/WEW KT19 206 E3
Larkswood Cl ERITH DA8 150 D2
Larkswood Ri PIN HA5 59 G1
Larkswood Rd CHING E4 37 J6
Lark Wy CAR SM5 194 D4
Larkway Cl CDALE/KGS NW9 63 F1
Larnach Rd HMSMTH W6 119 G6
Larne Rd RSLP HA4 58 D4
Larner Rd ERITH DA8 150 B1
Larpent Av PUT/ROE SW15 139 F6
Larwood Cl GFD/PVL UB6 78 D3
Lascelles Av HRW HA1 60 D4
Lascelles Cl WAN E11 70 B6
Lascott's Rd WDGN N22 49 F2
Lassa Rd ELTH/MOT SE9 146 D6
Lassell St GNWCH SE10 125 G5
Lasseter Pl BKHTH/KID SE3 125 H6
Latchett Rd SWFD E18 53 F4
Latchingdon Gdns WFD IG8 53 J2
Latchmere Cl
RCHPK/HAM TW10 175 F1
Latchmere La KUTN/CMB KT2 175 G2
Latchmere Rd BTSEA SW11 140 E3
KUTN/CMB KT2 175 F2
Latchmere St BTSEA SW11 140 E3
Lateward Rd BTFD TW8 116 E6
Latham Cl EHAM E6 107 J5
Latham Rd BXLYHS DA6 149 H6
TWK TW1 156 A2
Latham's Wy CROY/NA CR0 196 A5
Lathkill Cl EN EN1 36 C2
Lathom Rd EHAM E6 89 K5
Latimer Av EHAM E6 89 K6
Latimer Cl PIN HA5 41 G4
WATW WD18 26 C2
WPK KT4 207 K2
Latimer Gdns PIN HA5 41 G4
Latimer Pl NKENS W10 100 A5
Latimer Rd BAR EN5 21 F4
CROY/NA CR0 * 211 H1
FSTGT E7 89 F2
NKENS W10 100 A4
SEVS/STOTM N15 68 A3
TEDD TW11 174 A1
WIM/MER SW19 178 A2
Latona Rd PECK SE15 123 H6
La Tourne Gdns ORP BR6 216 C1
Lattimer Pl CHSWK W4 138 B1
Latton Cl ESH/CLAY KT10 204 B2
WOT/HER KT12 188 E4
Latymer Gdns FNCH N3 * 46 C5
Latymer Rd ED N9 36 B4
Latymer Wy ED N9 35 K4
Laubin Cl TWK TW1 136 C5
Lauder Cl NTHLT UB5 95 H1
Lauderdale Dr
RCHPK/HAM TW10 156 E5
Lauderdale Pde
MV/WKIL W9 * 101 F2
Lauderdale Pl BARB EC2Y * 12 D2
Lauderdale Rd MV/WKIL W9 101 F2
Laud St CROY/NA CR0 211 J1
LBTH SE11 122 A5
Laughton Rd NTHLT UB5 95 H1
Launcelot Rd BMLY BR1 165 K6
Launcelot St STHWK SE1 17 J3
Launceston Gdns
GFD/PVL UB6 79 J6
Launceston Pl KENS W8 120 B3
Launceston Rd GFD/PVL UB6 79 J6
Launch St POP/IOD E14 125 F3
Launders Ga ACT W3 * 117 J2
Laundress La
STNW/STAM N16 86 C1
Laundry Ms FSTH SE23 164 A2
Laundry Rd HMSMTH W6 119 H6
Laura Cl EN EN1 24 A6
WAN E11 71 G2
Lauradale Rd EFNCH N2 65 K1
Laura Pl CLPT E5 86 E2
Laura Ter FSBYPK N4 * 67 H6
Laurel Av TWK TW1 156 A3
Laurel Bank
NFNCH/WDSPK N12 * 33 G6
Laurel Bank Gdns
FUL/PGN SW6 139 J3
Laurel Bank Rd ENC/FH EN2 23 J2
Laurel Cl BARK/HLT IG6 54 C2
BFN/LL DA15 168 B5
DART DA1 171 F3
OXHEY WD19 27 H2
TOOT SW17 178 D1
Laurel Crs CROY/NA CR0 213 J1
ROMW/RG RM7 75 G5
Laurel Dr WCHMH N21 35 G2
Laurel Gdns BMLY BR1 200 D1
CHING E4 37 K2
HNWL W7 115 K1
HSLWW TW4 134 D5
MLHL NW7 31 F5
Laurel Gv PGE/AN SE20 181 J3
SYD SE26 182 A1
Laurel La WDR/YW UB7 112 B4
Laurel Pk
KTN/HRWW/WS HA3 43 F3
Laurel Rd BARN SW13 138 D3
HPTN TW12 173 J1
RYNPK SW20 176 E4
The Laurels BRXN/ST SW9 * 142 C1
BUSH WD23 * 28 E4
RDART DA2 * 171 F5
Laurel St HACK E8 86 B4
Laurel Vw
NFNCH/WDSPK N12 33 F5
TRDG/WHET N20 33 F5
Laurel Vls HNWL W7 * 115 K2
Laurel Wy SWFD E18 70 D1
TRDG/WHET N20 32 E5
Laurence Ms SHB W12 118 D2
Laurence Pountney Hl
CANST EC4R 12 E5
Laurence Pountney La
CANST EC4R 12 E5
Laurie Gv NWCR SE14 144 B2
Laurie Rd HNWL W7 96 E4
Laurier Rd CROY/NA CR0 197 G4
KTTN NW5 84 B1
Laurimel Cl STAN HA7 43 H2
Laurino Pl BUSH WD23 28 C4
Lauriston Rd HOM E9 87 F5
WIM/MER SW19 177 G2
Lausanne Rd CEND/HSY/T N8 67 G1
PECK SE15 143 K2
Lavender Av CDALE/KGS NW9 62 E5
MTCM CR4 178 D4
WPK KT4 208 A1
Lavender Cl CAR SM5 210 A2
CHEL SW3 120 C6
CHING E4 37 J6
HAYES BR2 200 D3
Lavender Ct E/WMO/HCT KT8 173 G6
Lavender Gdns BTSEA SW11 140 E5
ENC/FH EN2 23 H1
KTN/HRWW/WS HA3 42 E2
Lavender Gv HACK E8 86 C5
MTCM CR4 178 D4
Lavender Hl BTSEA SW11 140 E4
ENC/FH EN2 23 G2
Lavender Pl IL IG1 90 B3
Lavender Ri WDR/YW UB7 112 D2
Lavender Rd
BERM/RHTH SE16 124 B1
BTSEA SW11 140 C4
CROY/NA CR0 196 A3
ENC/FH EN2 23 K2
HOR/WEW KT19 206 D3
SUT SM1 209 H2
WLGTN SM6 210 A3
Lavender Sweep BTSEA SW11 140 E5
Lavender Ter BTSEA SW11 * 140 D4
Lavender V WLGTN SM6 210 D4
Lavender Wk BTSEA SW11 140 E5
Lavender Wy CROY/NA CR0 198 A3
Lavengro Rd WNWD SE27 162 D4
Lavenham Rd
WAND/EARL SW18 159 J4
Lavernock Rd BXLYHN DA7 149 H3
Lavers Rd STNW/STAM N16 86 A1
Laverstoke Gdns
PUT/ROE SW15 158 C2
Laverton Ms ECT SW5 120 A4
Laverton Pl ECT SW5 120 A4
Lavidge Rd ELTH/MOT SE9 166 D4
Lavina Gv IS N1 5 G2
Lavington Cl HOM E9 87 H4
Lavington Rd CROY/NA CR0 211 F1
WEA W13 116 C1
Lavington St STHWK SE1 18 B1
Lavinia Rd DART DA1 171 J1
Lawdon Gdns CROY/NA CR0 211 H2
Lawford Gdns DART DA1 151 F6
Lawford Rd CHSWK W4 137 K1
IS N1 86 A5
KTTN NW5 84 C4
Lawless St POP/IOD E14 * 105 K6
Lawley Rd STHGT/OAK N14 34 B2
Lawley St CLPT E5 86 E2
Lawn Cl BMLY BR1 184 A3
EN EN1 36 B2
NWMAL KT3 176 B5
RSLP HA4 76 D1
SWLY BR8 187 K5
Lawn Crs RCH/KEW TW9 137 H3
Lawn Farm Gv CHDH RM6 74 A1
Lawn Gdns HNWL W7 115 K1
Lawn House Cl POP/IOD E14 125 F2
Lawn La VX/NE SW8 121 K6
Lawn Rd BECK BR3 182 C3
HAMP NW3 83 K3
Lawns Ct WBLY HA9 * 62 C6
The Lawns BELMT SM2 208 C5
BKHTH/KID SE3 * 145 J4
CHING E4 51 J1
NRWD SE19 180 E4
PIN HA5 42 B3
SCUP DA14 168 C6
Lawns Wy CRW RM5 56 E3
Lawnswood BAR EN5 * 20 C6
Lawn Ter BKHTH/KID SE3 145 J4
The Lawn NWDGN UB2 115 F5
Lawn V PIN HA5 41 H5
Lawrence Av MLHL NW7 31 G6
MNPK E12 90 A2
NWMAL KT3 192 A3
PLMGR N13 35 H6
WALTH E17 51 F4
WLSDN NW10 81 F6

Lawrence Blds
STNW/STAM N16 86 B1
Lawrence Campe Cl
TRDG/WHET N20 33 H5
Lawrence Cl SEVS/STOTM N15 68 A1
SHB W12 99 K6
Lawrence Ct MLHL NW7 45 G1
OXHEY WD19 * 27 H5
Lawrence Crs DAGE RM10 92 D1
EDGW HA8 44 C5
Lawrence Dr HGDN/ICK UB10 76 A2
Lawrence Gdns MLHL NW7 31 H5
Lawrence Hl CHING E4 37 J4
Lawrence Hill Gdns DART DA1 171 F1
Lawrence Hill Rd DART DA1 171 F1
Lawrence La CITYW EC2V 12 D4
Lawrence Pde ISLW TW7 * 136 C4
Lawrence Pl IS N1 * 84 E6
Lawrence Rd EA W5 116 D4
EHAM E6 89 J6
ERITH DA8 149 J1
GPK RM2 75 K2
HPTN TW12 172 E3
HSLWW TW4 134 B5
PIN HA5 59 H2
PLSTW E13 89 F6
RCHPK/HAM TW10 156 D6
SEVS/STOTM N15 50 A6
SNWD SE25 197 G1
UED N18 36 D6
WWKM BR4 214 E2
YEAD UB4 94 A1
Lawrence St CAN/RD E16 106 D4
CHEL SW3 120 D6
MLHL NW7 31 H6
Lawrence Wy WLSDN NW10 80 E1
Lawrence Yd
SEVS/STOTM N15 68 A1
Lawrie Park Av SYD SE26 181 J1
Lawrie Park Crs SYD SE26 181 J1
Lawrie Park Gdns SYD SE26 181 J1
Lawrie Park Rd SYD SE26 181 K2
Laws Cl SNWD SE25 196 E1
Lawson Cl CAN/RD E16 107 G4
IL IG1 90 D3
WIM/MER SW19 159 G5
Lawson Gdns DART DA1 151 G6
PIN HA5 41 F6
Lawson Rd DART DA1 151 G5
PEND EN3 24 E2
STHL UB1 95 K3
Law St STHWK SE1 19 F4
Lawton Rd BOW E3 105 G2
EBAR EN4 21 H4
LEY E10 70 A5
Laxcon Cl WLSDN NW10 81 F3
Laxey Rd ORP BR6 217 F4
Laxley Cl CMBW SE5 142 C1
Laxton Pl CAMTN NW1 3 K6
Layard Rd BERM/RHTH SE16 123 J4
EN EN1 24 B2
THHTH CR7 180 E5
Layard Sq BERM/RHTH SE16 123 J4
Laycock St IS N1 85 G4
Layer Gdns ACT W3 98 C6
Layfield Cl HDN NW4 63 K4
Layfield Crs HDN NW4 63 K4
Layfield Rd HDN NW4 63 K4
Layhams Rd WWKM BR4 214 C2
Laymarsh Cl BELV DA17 129 G3
Laymead Cl NTHLT UB5 77 J4
Laystall St FSBYW WC1X 5 J7
Layton Crs CROY/NA CR0 211 G3
Layton Pl RCH/KEW TW9 137 H2
Layton Rd BTFD TW8 116 E5
HSLW TW3 135 G5
Layzell Wk ELTH/MOT SE9 166 C3
Lazenby Ct COVGDN WC2E * 10 E5
Leabank Cl HRW HA1 78 E1
Leabank Sq HOM E9 87 J4
Leabank Vw
SEVS/STOTM N15 68 C3
Leabourne Rd
STNW/STAM N16 68 C3
Lea Bridge Rd LEY E10 69 F6
WALTH E17 70 A2
Lea Cl WHTN TW2 154 E2
Lea Cots MTCM CR4 * 179 F5
Lea Crs RSLP HA4 76 D2
Leacroft Av BAL SW12 160 E2
Leacroft Cl WCHMH N21 35 H4
Leadale Av CHING E4 37 J4
Leadale Rd STNW/STAM N16 68 C3
Leadbeaters Cl
FBAR/BDGN N11 47 K1
Leadenhall Pl BANK EC3V 13 G4
Leadenhall St BANK EC3V 13 G4
Leader Av MNPK E12 90 A3
The Leadings WBLY HA9 80 E1
Leaf Cl NTHWD HA6 40 B3
THDIT KT7 189 K2
Leaf Gv WNWD SE27 180 B1
Leafield Cl STRHM/NOR SW16 180 C2
Leafield La SCUP DA14 169 G6
Leafield Rd RYNPK SW20 177 J6
SUT SM1 193 K6
Leafy Gv HAYES BR2 215 G3
Leafy Oak Rd LEE/GVPK SE12 166 B6
Leafy Wy CROY/NA CR0 197 G6
Lea Gdns WBLY HA9 80 B3
Leagrave St CLPT E5 86 E1
Lea Hall Gdns LEY E10 * 69 J5
Lea Hall Rd LEY E10 69 J5
Leahurst Rd LEW SE13 145 G6
Leake St STHWK SE1 17 H2
Lealand Rd SEVS/STOTM N15 68 B3
Leaming Cl MNPK E12 89 J3
Leamington Av BMLY BR1 184 B1
MRDN SM4 193 J1
ORP BR6 216 E2
WALTH E17 69 J2
Leamington Cl BMLY BR1 166 B6
HSLW TW3 135 H6
Leamington Crs
RYLN/HDSTN HA2 77 J1
Leamington Gdns
GDMY/SEVK IG3 73 F6
Leamington Pk ACT W3 99 F4
Leamington Pl YEAD UB4 94 D3
Leamington Rd NWDGN UB2 114 C4
Leamington Road Vls
NTGHL W11 100 D4
Leamore St HMSMTH W6 118 E4
Leamouth Rd EHAM E6 107 J5
POP/IOD E14 106 B5
Leander Rd BRXS/STRHM SW2 162 A1
NTHLT UB5 96 A1
THHTH CR7 196 A1
Learner Dr RYLN/HDSTN HA2 60 A6
Lea Rd BECK BR3 182 D5
ENC/FH EN2 23 K2
NWDGN UB2 114 D4
Learoyd Gdns EHAM E6 108 A6
Leas Cl CHSGTN KT9 206 B5
Leas Dl ELTH/MOT SE9 167 F5
Leas Gn CHST BR7 186 A2
Leaside Av MUSWH N10 48 A6
Leaside Rd CLPT E5 68 E5
Leasowes Rd LEY E10 69 J5
Leathart Cl HCH RM12 93 K5
Leatherbottle Gn
ERITHM DA18 129 G3
Leather Cl MTCM CR4 179 F5
Leatherdale St WCHPL E1 * 105 F2
Leather Gdns SRTFD E15 88 C6
Leatherhead Cl
STNW/STAM N16 68 A5
Leatherhead Rd CHSGTN KT9 205 K5
Leather La CLKNW EC1R 5 J7
HCIRC EC1N 11 J1
Leathermarket Ct STHWK SE1 19 G3
Leathermarket St STHWK SE1 19 G3
Leather Rd
BERM/RHTH SE16 * 124 A4
Leathersellers Cl BAR EN5 * 20 C4
Leather St WAP E1W 105 F6
Leathsale Rd
RYLN/HDSTN HA2 78 B1
Leathwaite Rd BTSEA SW11 140 E5
Leathwell Rd DEPT SE8 144 E3
Lea V DART DA1 150 A5
Lea Valley Rd CHING E4 37 H1
Lea Valley Wk CLPT E5 68 D4
TOTM N17 50 D5
UED N18 37 F6
Leaveland Cl BECK BR3 198 D1
Leaver Gdns GFD/PVL UB6 96 D1
Leavesden Rd STAN HA7 43 G2
Leaway CLPT E5 * 68 E5
Lebanon Av FELT TW13 172 C1
Lebanon Gdns
WAND/EARL SW18 159 K1
Lebanon Pk TWK TW1 156 C2
Lebanon Rd CROY/NA CR0 197 F5
WAND/EARL SW18 139 K6
Lebrun Sq BKHTH/KID SE3 146 A5
Lechmere Ap WFD IG8 53 G5
Lechmere Rd CRICK NW2 81 K4
Leckford Rd
WAND/EARL SW18 160 B4
Leckhampton Pl
BRXS/STRHM SW2 162 B2
Leckwith Av ABYW SE2 129 F6
Lecky St SKENS SW7 120 C5
Leconfield Av BARN SW13 138 C4
Leconfield Rd HBRY N5 85 K2
Leda Av PEND EN3 25 F2
Leda Rd WOOL/PLUM SE18 126 E3
Ledbury Ms North
NTGHL W11 * 100 E6
Ledbury Ms West NTGHL W11 100 E6
Ledbury Rd CROY/NA CR0 211 J2
NTGHL W11 100 D5
Ledbury St PECK SE15 143 H1
Ledrington Rd NRWD SE19 181 G2
Ledway Dr WBLY HA9 62 B4
Lee Av CHDH RM6 74 A3
Leechcroft Av BFN/LL DA15 148 A6
Leechcroft Rd WLGTN SM6 210 A1
Lee Church St LEW SE13 145 H5
Lee Cl WALTH E17 51 F4
Lee Conservancy Rd HOM E9 87 H3
Leecroft Rd BAR EN5 20 C5
Leeds Cl ORP BR6 202 E6
Leeds Rd IL IG1 72 D5
Leeds St UED N18 50 C1
Lee Gn STMC/STPC BR5 202 B2
Lee High Rd LEW SE13 145 G5
Leeke St FSBYW WC1X 5 G4
Leeland Rd WEA W13 116 B1
Leeland Ter WEA W13 116 B1
Leeland Wy WLSDN NW10 81 H2
Leemount Cl HDN NW4 * 64 B1
Lee Pk BKHTH/KID SE3 145 J5
Lee Park Wy ED N9 37 G5
UED N18 51 F1
Lee Rd BKHTH/KID SE3 145 J4
EN EN1 36 C1
GFD/PVL UB6 79 J6
MLHL NW7 46 B3
WIM/MER SW19 178 A4
Lees Av NTHWD HA6 40 D4
Leeside BAR EN5 20 C6
Leeside Crs GLDGN NW11 64 C3
Leeside Rd TOTM N17 50 D2
Leeson Rd HNHL SE24 * 142 B6
Leesons Hl CHST BR7 185 K6
STMC/STPC BR5 186 C6
Leesons Wy STMC/STPC BR5 186 A5
Lees Pl MYFR/PKLN W1K 9 G5
The Lees CROY/NA CR0 198 C6
Lee St HACK E8 86 B6
Lee Ter BKHTH/KID SE3 145 H4
The Lee NTHWD HA6 40 D1
Lee Vw ENC/FH EN2 23 H2
Leeward Gdns
WIM/MER SW19 177 H2
Leeway DEPT SE8 124 C5
Leeway Cl PIN HA5 41 K3
The Leeways CHEAM SM3 * 208 C4
Leewood Cl LEE/GVPK SE12 165 J1
Lefevre Wk BOW E3 87 H6
Leffern Rd SHB W12 118 D2
Lefroy Rd SHB W12 118 C2
Left Side STHGT/OAK N14 * 34 D3
Legard Rd HBRY N5 85 H1
Legatt Rd ELTH/MOT SE9 146 C6
Leggatt Rd SRTFD E15 106 A1
Legge St LEW SE13 145 F6
Leghorn Rd WLSDN NW10 99 J1
WOOL/PLUM SE18 127 J5
Legion Cl IS N1 85 G4
Legion Ct MRDN SM4 193 K3
Legion Ter BOW E3 87 J6
Legion Wy
NFNCH/WDSPK N12 47 J3
Legon Av ROMW/RG RM7 74 E5
Legrace Av HSLWW TW4 134 C3
Leicester Av MTCM CR4 195 K1
Leicester Cl WPK KT4 208 A2
Leicester Gdns
GDMY/SEVK IG3 72 E4
Leicester Pl LSQ/SEVD WC2H * 10 D5
Leicester Rd BAR EN5 21 F6
CROY/NA CR0 197 F4
EFNCH N2 47 J6
WAN E11 71 F2
WLSDN NW10 81 F5
Leicester Sq LSQ/SEVD WC2H 10 D6
Leicester St LSQ/SEVD WC2H 10 D5
Leigham Av
STRHM/NOR SW16 161 K5
Leigham Cl STRHM/NOR SW16 162 B5
Leigham Court Rd
STRHM/NOR SW16 162 A5
Leigham Dr ISLW TW7 135 K1
Leigham Hall Pde
STRHM/NOR SW16 * 161 K5
Leigham V STRHM/NOR SW16 162 B5
Leigh Av REDBR IG4 71 H1
Leigh Cl NWMAL KT3 192 A1
Leigh Ct RYLN/HDSTN HA2 * 60 E5
Leigh Crs CROY/NA CR0 213 K5
Leigh Gdns WLSDN NW10 100 A1
Leigh Hunt Dr
STHGT/OAK N14 34 D3
Leigh Orchard Cl
STRHM/NOR SW16 162 A5
Leigh Pl FELT TW13 154 B3
WELL DA16 148 B3
Leigh Rd EHAM E6 90 A5
HBRY N5 85 H2
HSLW TW3 135 J5
LEY E10 70 A4
Leigh Rodd OXHEY WD19 27 J5
Leigh St STPAN WC1H 4 E6
Leigh Ter STMC/STPC BR5 * 186 C6
The Leigh KUTN/CMB KT2 176 B2
Leighton Av MNPK E12 90 A3
PIN HA5 41 J6
Leighton Cl EDGW HA8 44 C5
Leighton Crs KTTN NW5 84 C3
Leighton Gdns WLSDN NW10 99 K1
Leighton Gv KTTN NW5 84 C3
Leighton Pl KTTN NW5 84 C3
Leighton Rd EN EN1 24 B6
KTN/HRWW/WS HA3 42 D5
KTTN NW5 84 C3
WEA W13 116 B2
Leighton St CROY/NA CR0 196 C5
Leila Parnell Pl CHARL SE7 126 B6
Leinster Av MORT/ESHN SW14 137 K4
Leinster Gdns BAY/PAD W2 101 G5
Leinster Pl BAY/PAD W2 101 G5
Leinster Rd MUSWH N10 66 B1
Leinster Sq BAY/PAD W2 100 E6
Leinster Ter BAY/PAD W2 101 G6
Leisure Wy
NFNCH/WDSPK N12 47 H3
Leith Cl CDALE/KGS NW9 63 F5
Leithcote Gdns
STRHM/NOR SW16 162 A6
Leithcote Pth
STRHM/NOR SW16 162 A5
Leith Hl STMC/STPC BR5 186 B4
Leith Rd WDGN N22 49 H4
Leith Towers BELMT SM2 * 209 F5
Leith Yd KIL/WHAMP NW6 * 82 E6
Lela Av HSLWW TW4 134 B3
Lelitia Cl HACK E8 86 C6
Leman St WCHPL E1 13 K4
Lemark Cl STAN HA7 43 J2
Le May Av LEE/GVPK SE12 166 A5
Lemmon Rd GNWCH SE10 125 H6
Lemna Rd WAN E11 70 C4
Lemonwell Dr ELTH/MOT SE9 147 G6
Lemsford Cl SEVS/STOTM N15 68 C3
Lena Crs ED N9 36 E4
Lena Gdns HMSMTH W6 119 F3
Lena Kennedy Cl CHING E4 52 A2
Lendal Ter CLAP SW4 141 J4
Lenelby Rd SURB KT6 191 H5
Len Freeman Pl
FUL/PGN SW6 119 J6
Lenham Rd BXLYHN DA7 129 G6
LEE/GVPK SE12 145 J5
SUT SM1 209 F2
THHTH CR7 180 E5
Lennard Av WWKM BR4 199 H6
Lennard Cl WWKM BR4 199 H6
Lennard Rd CROY/NA CR0 196 D5
HAYES BR2 200 E5
PGE/AN SE20 182 A2
SYD SE26 181 K2
Lennard Ter PGE/AN SE20 * 182 A2
Lennon Rd CRICK NW2 82 A3
Lennox Cl ROM RM1 75 H3
Lennox Gdns CROY/NA CR0 211 H2
IL IG1 71 K5
KTBR SW1X 14 E5
WLSDN NW10 81 H2
Lennox Gardens Ms
KTBR SW1X 14 E6
Lennox Rd FSBYPK N4 67 F6
WALTH E17 69 H3
Lenor Cl BXLYHS DA6 149 F5
Lensbury Wy ABYW SE2 128 E3
Lens Rd FSTGT E7 89 G5
Lenthall Rd HACK E8 86 B5
Lenthorp Rd GNWCH SE10 125 J4
Lentmead Rd BMLY BR1 165 J5
Lenton Ri RCH/KEW TW9 137 F4
Lenton St WOOL/PLUM SE18 127 J4
Lenton Ter FSBYPK N4 * 67 G6
Leof Crs CAT SE6 182 E1
Leominster Rd MRDN SM4 194 B3
Leominster Wk MRDN SM4 194 B3
Leonard Av MRDN SM4 194 B2
ROMW/RG RM7 75 F5
Leonard Ct KENS W8 119 K3
Leonard Pl HAYES BR2 * 215 J1
STNW/STAM N16 86 A2
Leonard Rd CHING E4 51 J2
ED N9 36 B5
FSTGT E7 88 E2
NWDGN UB2 114 C3
STRHM/NOR SW16 179 H4
Leonard St CAN/RD E16 126 D1
SDTCH EC2A 7 F6
Leonora Tyson Ms DUL SE21 162 E4
Leontine Cl PECK SE15 143 H1
Leopold Av WIM/MER SW19 177 J1
Leopold Ms HOM E9 86 E6
Leopold Rd EA W5 117 G1
EFNCH N2 47 H6
UED N18 50 D1
WALTH E17 69 J2
WIM/MER SW19 159 J6
WLSDN NW10 81 G5
Leopold St BOW E3 105 H4
Leo St PECK SE15 143 J1
Leppoc Rd CLAP SW4 141 J6
Leroy St STHWK SE1 19 G6
Lerry Cl WKENS W14 119 J6
Lescombe Cl FSTH SE23 164 B5
Lescombe Rd FSTH SE23 164 B5
Lesley Cl BXLY DA5 169 J2
Leslie Gdns BELMT SM2 208 E5
Leslie Gv CROY/NA CR0 196 E5
Leslie Grove Pl CROY/NA CR0 197 F5
Leslie Park Rd CROY/NA CR0 197 F5
Leslie Rd CAN/RD E16 107 F5
EFNCH N2 47 H6
WAN E11 88 B2
Lesney Pk ERITH DA8 130 A6
Lesney Park Rd ERITH DA8 130 A6
Lessar Av CLAP SW4 141 H6
Lessingham Av TOOT SW17 160 E6
Lessing St FSTH SE23 164 B2
Lessington Av
ROMW/RG RM7 74 E3
Lessness Av BXLYHN DA7 148 E1
Lessness Pk BELV DA17 129 G5
Lessness Rd MRDN SM4 194 B3
Lester Av SRTFD E15 106 C3
Lestock Cl SNWD SE25 181 H6
Leston Cl RAIN RM13 111 K2
Leswin Pl STNW/STAM N16 86 B1
Leswin Rd STNW/STAM N16 86 B1
Letchford Gdns WLSDN NW10 99 J2
Letchford Ms WLSDN NW10 * 99 J2
Letchford Ter
KTN/HRWW/WS HA3 * 42 B4
Letchworth Av
EBED/NFELT TW14 153 J2
Letchworth Cl HAYES BR2 199 K2
OXHEY WD19 41 H1
Letchworth Dr HAYES BR2 199 K2
Letchworth St TOOT SW17 160 E6
Letterstone Rd FUL/PGN SW6 139 J1
Lettice St FUL/PGN SW6 139 J3
Lett Rd BRXN/ST SW9 142 A2
SRTFD E15 88 B5
Leucha Rd WALTH E17 69 G2
Levana Cl WIM/MER SW19 159 H3
Levehurst Wy CLAP SW4 141 K3
Leven Cl OXHEY WD19 * 41 H1
Levendale Rd FSTH SE23 164 B4
Leven Rd POP/IOD E14 106 A4
Leven Wy HYS/HAR UB3 94 C5
Leverett St CHEL SW3 14 D6
Leverholme Gdns
ELTH/MOT SE9 167 F6
Leverson St
STRHM/NOR SW16 179 H2
Lever St FSBYE EC1V 6 C5
Leverton Pl KTTN NW5 84 C3
Leverton St KTTN NW5 84 C3
Levett Gdns GDMY/SEVK IG3 91 F2
Levett Rd BARK IG11 90 E4
Levine Gdns BARK IG11 109 K1
Lewes Cl NTHLT UB5 78 A4
Lewesdon Cl WIM/MER SW19 159 G3
Lewes Rd BMLY BR1 184 C5
NFNCH/WDSPK N12 47 J1
Leweston Pl STNW/STAM N16 68 B4
Lewgars Av CDALE/KGS NW9 62 E3
Lewing Cl ORP BR6 201 K5
Lewin Rd BXLYHS DA6 149 F5
MORT/ESHN SW14 138 A4
STRHM/NOR SW16 179 J2
Lewin Ter EBED/NFELT TW14 153 G2
Lewis Av WALTH E17 51 J4
Lewis Cl STHGT/OAK N14 34 C2
Lewis Crs WLSDN NW10 81 F3
Lewis Gdns EFNCH N2 47 H5
SEVS/STOTM N15 68 B4
Lewis Gv LEW SE13 145 F5
Lewisham High St LEW SE13 144 E6
Lewisham Hl LEW SE13 145 F3
Lewisham Pk LEW SE13 164 E1
Lewisham Rd LEW SE13 145 F3
Lewisham Wy BROCKY SE4 144 C3
Lewis Pl HACK E8 86 C3
Lewis Rd MTCM CR4 178 D5
RCH/KEW TW9 * 136 E6
SCUP DA14 168 D5
STHL UB1 114 D2
SUT SM1 209 F2
WELL DA16 148 D4
Lewis St CAMTN NW1 84 B5
Lewiston Cl WPK KT4 192 E4
Lewis Wy DAGE RM10 92 D4
Lexden Dr CHDH RM6 73 H3
Lexden Rd ACT W3 98 D6
MTCM CR4 195 J1
Lexham Gdns KENS W8 119 K4
Lexham Ms KENS W8 119 K4
Lexington Pl KUT/HW KT1 174 E4
Lexington St SOHO/CST W1F 10 B4
Lexington Wy BAR EN5 20 B5
Lexton Gdns BAL SW12 161 J3
Leyborne Av WEA W13 116 D2
Leyborne Pk RCH/KEW TW9 137 H2
Leybourne Cl HAYES BR2 199 K2
Leybourne Rd CAMTN NW1 * 84 B5
CDALE/KGS NW9 62 C2
HGDN/ICK UB10 76 A6
WAN E11 70 D5
Leybourne St CAMTN NW1 84 B5
Leyburn Cl WALTH E17 70 A1
Leyburn Gdns CROY/NA CR0 197 F6
Leyburn Gv UED N18 50 C2
Leyburn House CHARL SE7 * 146 D1
Leyburn Rd UED N18 50 C2
Leycroft Gdns ERITH DA8 150 E2
Leyden St WCHPL E1 13 J2
Leydon Cl BERM/RHTH SE16 124 A1
Leyes Rd CAN/RD E16 107 H6
Leyfield WPK KT4 192 B6
Leyland Av PEND EN3 25 G3
Leyland Gdns WFD IG8 53 G1
Leyland Rd LEE/GVPK SE12 145 J6
Leylang Rd NWCR SE14 144 A1
Leys Av DAGE RM10 92 E6
Leys Cl DAGE RM10 92 E5
HRW HA1 60 D1
Leysdown Av BXLYHN DA7 149 K5
Leysdown Rd ELTH/MOT SE9 166 D4
Leysfield Rd SHB W12 118 D2
Leys Gdns EBAR EN4 22 A6
Leyspring Rd WAN E11 70 D5
Leys Rd East PEND EN3 25 G2
The Leys EFNCH N2 65 G1
KTN/HRWW/WS HA3 62 B3
Ley St IL IG1 72 B6
Leyswood Dr
GNTH/NBYPK IG2 72 E2
Leythe Rd ACT W3 117 K2
Leyton Cross Rd RDART DA2 170 C5
Leyton Gra LEY E10 69 J6
Leyton Green Rd LEY E10 70 A3
Leyton Park Rd LEY E10 70 A6
Leyton Rd SRTFD E15 88 A3
WIM/MER SW19 178 B3
Leytonstone Rd SRTFD E15 88 C4
Leywick St SRTFD E15 106 C1
Lezayre Rd ORP BR6 217 F4
Liardet St NWCR SE14 124 B6
Liberia Rd HBRY N5 85 H4
Liberty Av WIM/MER SW19 178 C4
Liberty Cl UED N18 36 B6
WPK KT4 193 F5
Liberty Ms WDGN N22 49 H4
Liberty St BRXN/ST SW9 142 A2
Libra Rd BOW E3 87 H6
PLSTW E13 106 E1
Library Pde WLSDN NW10 * 81 G6
Library St STHWK SE1 18 B3
Library Wy WHTN TW2 155 H2
Lichfield Cl EBAR EN4 21 K4
Lichfield Gdns
RCH/KEW TW9 * 137 F6
Lichfield Gv FNCH N3 46 E4
Lichfield Rd BCTR RM8 91 H2
BOW E3 105 G2
CRICK NW2 82 C2
ED N9 36 C4
EHAM E6 107 H2
HSLWW TW4 134 B4
NTHWD HA6 40 E6
RCH/KEW TW9 137 G2
WFD IG8 38 C6
Lichfield Ter RCH/KEW TW9 * 137 F6
Lidbury Rd MLHL NW7 46 C2
Lidcote Gdns BRXN/ST SW9 * 142 B3
Liddall Wy WDR/YW UB7 112 C1
Liddell Cl KTN/HRWW/WS HA3 43 K6
Liddell Gdns WLSDN NW10 100 A1
Liddell Rd KIL/WHAMP NW6 82 E4
Lidding Rd
KTN/HRWW/WS HA3 61 K2
Liddington Rd SRTFD E15 88 D6
Liddon Rd BMLY BR1 184 B6
PLSTW E13 107 F2
Liden Cl LEY E10 69 H4
Lidfield Rd STNW/STAM N16 85 K2
Lidgate Rd CMBW SE5 * 143 G1
Lidgould Gv RSLP HA4 58 E3
Lidiard Rd WAND/EARL SW18 160 B4
Lidlington Pl CAMTN NW1 4 B3
Lido Sq TOTM N17 49 K5
Lidyard Rd ARCH N19 66 C5
Liffler Rd WOOL/PLUM SE18 127 K5
Lifford St PUT/ROE SW15 139 G5
Lightcliffe Rd PLMGR N13 35 G6
Lighter Cl BERM/RHTH SE16 124 B4
Lighterman Ms WCHPL E1 105 F5
Lighterman's Rd
POP/IOD E14 124 D2
Lightfoot Rd CEND/HSY/T N8 66 E2
Lightley Cl ALP/SUD HA0 80 B6
Ligonier St BETH E2 7 J6
Lilac Cl CHING E4 51 H2
Lilac Gdns CROY/NA CR0 213 J1
EA W5 116 E3
HYS/HAR UB3 94 C5
ROMW/RG RM7 75 G5
Lilac Pl LBTH SE11 17 G7
Lilac St SHB W12 99 J6
Lilah Ms HAYES BR2 183 J5
Lilburne Gdns ELTH/MOT SE9 146 D6
Lilburne Rd ELTH/MOT SE9 146 D6
Lile Crs HNWL W7 96 E4
Lilestone St STJWD NW8 2 C6
Lilford Rd CMBW SE5 142 C3
Lilian Barker Cl
LEE/GVPK SE12 145 K6
Lilian Board Wy GFD/PVL UB6 78 D3
Lilian Gdns WFD IG8 53 F4
Lilian Rd STRHM/NOR SW16 179 H4
Lillechurch Rd BCTR RM8 91 H4
Lilleshall Rd MRDN SM4 194 C2
Lilley Cl WAP E1W 123 H1
Lilley La MLHL NW7 * 45 G1
Lillian Av ACT W3 117 H2
Lillian Rd BARN SW13 118 D6
Lillie Rd FUL/PGN SW6 119 G6
Lillieshall Rd CLAP SW4 141 G4
Lillie Yd FUL/PGN SW6 119 K6
Lillington Gardens Est
PIM SW1V 16 B7
Lilliput Av NTHLT UB5 77 J6
Lilliput Rd ROMW/RG RM7 75 F4
Lily Cl WKENS W14 119 H4
Lily Dr WDR/YW UB7 112 A4
Lily Gdns ALP/SUD HA0 97 J1
Lily Pl FARR EC1M 11 K1
Lily Rd WALTH E17 69 J3
Lilyville Rd FUL/PGN SW6 139 J2

Limbourne Av BCTR RM8 74 B4
Limburg Rd BTSEA SW11 140 D5
Limeburner La STP EC4M 12 A3
Lime Cl BKHH IG9 39 H4
BMLY BR1 200 D1
KTN/HRWW/WS HA3 43 G5
OXHEY WD19 27 H2
PIN HA5 40 D6
ROMW/RG RM7 74 E1
WAP E1W 123 H1
Lime Crs SUN TW16 172 B5
Limecroft Cl HOR/WEW KT19 207 F5
Limedene Cl PIN HA5 41 H4
Lime Gv BARK/HLT IG6 55 F2
BFN/LL DA15 168 A1
CHING E4 51 H2
HYS/HAR UB3 94 B6
NWMAL KT3 176 A6
ORP BR6 201 G6
RSLP HA4 59 F3
SHB W12 119 F2
TRDG/WHET N20 32 C3
TWK TW1 156 A1
Limeharbour POP/IOD E14 124 E3
Limehouse POP/IOD E14 105 J6
Limehouse Cswy
POP/IOD E14 105 H6
Limehouse Link POP/IOD E14 105 G6
Limehouse Link (Tunnel)
POP/IOD E14 105 H6
Lime Kiln Dr CHARL SE7 126 A6
Limekiln Pl NRWD SE19 181 G3
Limerick Cl BAL SW12 161 H2
Limerston St WBPTN SW10 120 B6
Limes Av BARN SW13 138 C3
CAR SM5 194 E5
CHIG IG7 54 C1
CROY/NA CR0 211 F1
GLDGN NW11 64 C4
MLHL NW7 45 G2
MNPK E12 89 J1
NFNCH/WDSPK N12 33 G6
PGE/AN SE20 181 J3
WAN E11 71 F1
The Limes Av
FBAR/BDGN N11 48 B1
Limes Cl CAR SM5 194 E6
FBAR/BDGN N11 * 48 C1
Limesdale Gdns EDGW HA8 44 E5
Limes Field Rd
MORT/ESHN SW14 138 B4
Limesford Rd PECK SE15 144 A5
Limes Gdns WAND/EARL SW18 159 K1
Limes Gv LEW SE13 145 F5
Limes Rd BECK BR3 182 E5
CROY/NA CR0 196 E3
Limes Rw ORP BR6 216 B3
The Limes CMBW SE5 * 143 F4
PUR RM19 131 K5
WAND/EARL SW18 * 159 K1
Limestone Wk ERITHM DA18 128 E2
Lime St FENCHST EC3M 13 G5
WALTH E17 69 G1
Lime Street Pas BANK EC3V * 13 G4
Limes Wk EA W5 116 E2
PECK SE15 * 143 K5
Lime Tree Av ESH/CLAY KT10 189 J5
Limetree Cl BRXS/STRHM SW2 162 A3
Lime Tree Ct PIN HA5 * 42 A3
Lime Tree Gv CROY/NA CR0 213 H1
Limetree Pl MTCM CR4 179 G4
Lime Tree Rd HEST TW5 135 G2
Lime Tree Ter CAT SE6 * 164 C3
Lime Tree Wk BUSH WD23 28 E3
ENC/FH EN2 23 J1
WWKM BR4 214 D2
Lime Wk SRTFD E15 * 88 C6
Limewood Cl BECK BR3 199 F2
WALTH E17 69 H1
WEA W13 97 H5
Limewood Rd ERITH DA8 149 K1
Limpsfield Av THHTH CR7 196 A2
WIM/MER SW19 159 G4
Linacre Cl PECK SE15 143 J4
Linacre Rd CRICK NW2 81 K4
Linchmere Rd LEE/GVPK SE12 165 J2
Lincoln Av ROMW/RG RM7 75 F5
STHGT/OAK N14 34 C5
WHTN TW2 155 H4
WIM/MER SW19 159 G5
Lincoln Cl ERITH DA8 150 C3
GFD/PVL UB6 78 C6
RYLN/HDSTN HA2 59 K2
Lincoln Crs EN EN1 24 A6
Lincoln Dr OXHEY WD19 27 G5
Lincoln Est BOW E3 105 J3
Lincoln Gdns IL IG1 71 J4
Lincoln Green Rd
STMC/STPC BR5 202 A2
Lincoln Ms KIL/WHAMP NW6 82 D6
SEVS/STOTM N15 67 J1
Lincoln Pde EFNCH N2 * 47 J6
Lincoln Rd ALP/SUD HA0 79 K4
EFNCH N2 47 J6
EN EN1 24 A5
ERITH DA8 150 C3
FELT TW13 154 E5
FSTGT E7 89 H4
MTCM CR4 195 K2
NTHWD HA6 40 D6
NWMAL KT3 175 K6
PEND EN3 24 D6
PLSTW E13 107 F3
RYLN/HDSTN HA2 59 K2
SCUP DA14 186 C1
SNWD SE25 181 J6
SWFD E18 52 D4
WPK KT4 192 E5
Lincoln's Inn Flds LINN WC2A 11 G3
The Lincolns MLHL NW7 31 H5
Lincoln St CHEL SW3 14 E7
WAN E11 70 C6
Lincoln Ter BELMT SM2 * 208 E5
Lincoln Wy EN EN1 24 D6
Lincombe Rd BMLY BR1 165 J5
Lindal Crs ENC/FH EN2 22 E6
The Lindales TOTM N17 50 C2
Lindal Rd BROCKY SE4 144 C6
Lindburgh Av WLGTN SM6 210 E6
Linden Av DART DA1 171 F3
EN EN1 24 C2
HSLW TW3 135 G6
RSLP HA4 58 E5
THHTH CR7 196 C1
WBLY HA9 80 B3
WLSDN NW10 100 B1
Linden Cl ORP BR6 217 G3
RSLP HA4 58 E5
STAN HA7 43 H1
STHGT/OAK N14 34 C1
THDIT KT7 190 B4
Linden Cots WIM/MER SW19 * 177 H2
Linden Crs GFD/PVL UB6 79 F4
KUT/HW KT1 175 G5
WFD IG8 53 F2
Lindenfield CHST BR7 185 G5
Linden Gdns BAY/PAD W2 100 E6
CHSWK W4 118 A5
EN EN1 24 C2
Linden Gv NWMAL KT3 176 B6
PECK SE15 143 J4
SYD SE26 181 K2
TEDD TW11 174 A1
Linden Lea EFNCH N2 65 G2
PIN HA5 * 41 K3
Linden Leas WWKM BR4 199 G6
Linden Ms IS N1 85 K3
NTGHL W11 * 100 E6
Linden Pl MTCM CR4 194 D1
Linden Rd FBAR/BDGN N11 33 K4
HPTN TW12 173 F4
MUSWH N10 66 B1
SEVS/STOTM N15 67 J1
The Lindens CHSWK W4 137 K2
CROY/NA CR0 214 A4
NFNCH/WDSPK N12 * 47 H1
WALTH E17 * 69 K1
Linden St ROMW/RG RM7 75 F1
Linden Wk ARCH N19 84 C1
Linden Wy STHGT/OAK N14 34 C1
Lindfield Gdns HAMP NW3 83 G3
Lindfield Rd CROY/NA CR0 197 G3
EA W5 97 J3
Lindfield St POP/IOD E14 105 J5
Lindhill Cl PEND EN3 25 F3
Lindisfarne Md HOM E9 87 G2
Lindisfarne Rd BCTR RM8 91 J1
RYNPK SW20 176 D3
Lindley Est PECK SE15 * 143 H1
Lindley Pl RCH/KEW TW9 137 H2
Lindley Rd LEY E10 69 K6
Lindley St WCHPL E1 104 E4
Lindore Rd BTSEA SW11 140 E5
Lindores Rd CAR SM5 194 B4
Lindo St PECK SE15 143 K3
Lind Rd SUT SM1 209 G3
Lindrop St FUL/PGN SW6 140 B3
Lindsay Cl CHSGTN KT9 206 A5
STWL/WRAY TW19 132 A6
Lindsay Dr
KTN/HRWW/WS HA3 62 A3
Lindsay Rd HPTN TW12 155 G6
WPK KT4 192 E6
Lindsay Sq PIM SW1V 121 J5
Lindsell St GNWCH SE10 145 F2
Lindsey Cl BMLY BR1 184 C6
MTCM CR4 195 K1
Lindsey Gdns
EBED/NFELT TW14 * 153 G2
Lindsey Ms IS N1 85 J5
Lindsey Rd BCTR RM8 91 J1
Lindsey St FARR EC1M 12 B1
Lind St DEPT SE8 144 E3
Lindum Rd TEDD TW11 174 D3
Lindway WNWD SE27 180 C1
Linfield Cl HDN NW4 46 A6
Linford Rd WALTH E17 52 A6
Linford St VX/NE SW8 141 H2
Lingards Rd LEW SE13 145 F5
Lingey Cl BFN/LL DA15 168 A4
Lingfield Av KUT/HW KT1 191 F1
Lingfield Cl EN EN1 36 A1
NTHWD HA6 40 C3
Lingfield Ct NTHLT UB5 * 96 A1
Lingfield Crs ELTH/MOT SE9 147 J5
Lingfield Gdns ED N9 36 D2
Lingfield Rd WIM/MER SW19 177 G1
WPK KT4 208 A1
Lingham St BRXN/ST SW9 141 K3
Lingholm Wy BAR EN5 20 B6
Ling Rd CAN/RD E16 106 E4
ERITH DA8 129 K6
Lingwell Rd TOOT SW17 160 D5
Lingwood Gdns ISLW TW7 135 K1
Lingwood Rd CLPT E5 68 C4
Linhope St CAMTN NW1 2 E6
Linkfield E/WMO/HCT KT8 173 F6
Link Fld HAYES BR2 199 K3
Linkfield Rd ISLW TW7 136 A3
Link La WLGTN SM6 210 D4
Linklea Cl CDALE/KGS NW9 45 G3
Link Rd DAGW RM9 110 D1
EBED/NFELT TW14 153 J2
FBAR/BDGN N11 34 A6
MNPK E12 71 J6
WLGTN SM6 195 F5
Links Av GPK RM2 57 K5
MRDN SM4 193 K1
Links Dr TRDG/WHET N20 32 E3
Links Gdns STRHM/NOR SW16 180 B3
Linkside CHIG IG7 54 C1
NFNCH/WDSPK N12 46 D2
NWMAL KT3 176 B5
Linkside Cl ENC/FH EN2 23 F4
Linkside Gdns ENC/FH EN2 23 F4
Links Rd ACT W3 98 C5
CRICK NW2 63 H6
TOOT SW17 179 F2
WFD IG8 52 E1
WWKM BR4 199 F5
Links Side ENC/FH EN2 23 F4
The Links WALTH E17 69 G1
Link St HOM E9 86 E4
Links Vw DART DA1 171 F3
FNCH N3 46 D3
Links View Cl STAN HA7 43 G2
Linksview Ct HPTN TW12 * 155 J6
Links View Rd CROY/NA CR0 213 J1
HPTN TW12 173 H1
Links Wy BECK BR3 198 D3
NTHWD HA6 40 A4
TOOT SW17 178 E2
Linksway HDN NW4 46 B5
NTHWD HA6 40 B4
Links Yd WCHPL E1 13 K1
The Link ACT W3 98 D5
ALP/SUD HA0 61 J5
CRICK NW2 63 J5
NTHLT UB5 * 77 K3
PEND EN3 25 G2
PIN HA5 59 G3
Link Wy HAYES BR2 200 D4
RCHPK/HAM TW10 156 C4
Linkway BCTR RM8 91 J2
FSBYPK N4 67 J4
NWMAL KT3 192 E1
PIN HA5 41 H4
RYNPK SW20 176 E6
The Linkway BAR EN5 32 E1
BELMT SM2 209 G6
Linkwood Wk CAMTN NW1 84 D5
Linley Crs ROMW/RG RM7 56 D6
Linley Rd TOTM N17 50 A5
Linnell Cl GLDGN NW11 65 F3
Linnell Dr GLDGN NW11 65 F3
Linnell Rd CMBW SE5 143 F3
UED N18 50 C1
Linnet Cl BUSH WD23 28 C3
ED N9 37 F3
THMD SE28 109 J6
Linnet Ms BAL SW12 161 F2
Linnett Cl CHING E4 38 A6
Linom Rd CLAP SW4 141 K5
Linscott Rd CLPT E5 86 E2
Linsdell Rd BARK IG11 90 C6
Linsey St BERM/RHTH SE16 123 H3
Linslade Cl HSLWW TW4 134 D6
PIN HA5 41 F6
Linslade Rd ORP BR6 217 G4
Linstead St KIL/WHAMP NW6 82 E5
Linstead Wy
WAND/EARL SW18 159 H2
Lintaine Cl HMSMTH W6 * 119 H6
Linthorpe Av ALP/SUD HA0 79 J4
Linthorpe Rd EBAR EN4 21 J4
STNW/STAM N16 68 A4
Linton Cl CAR SM5 194 E4
CHARL SE7 126 B5
WELL DA16 148 B2
Linton Ct ROM RM1 57 G5
Linton Gdns EHAM E6 107 J5
Linton Gv WNWD SE27 180 C1
Linton Rd BARK IG11 90 C5
Linton St IS N1 6 D1
Lintott Ct STWL/WRAY TW19 152 A1
Linver Rd FUL/PGN SW6 139 J3
Linwood Cl CMBW SE5 143 G3
Linwood Crs EN EN1 24 C2
Linzee Rd CEND/HSY/T N8 66 E1
Lion Av TWK TW1 156 A3
Lion Cl BROCKY SE4 164 D1
Lionel Gdns ELTH/MOT SE9 146 C6
Lionel Ms NKENS W10 * 100 C4
Lionel Rd ELTH/MOT SE9 146 C6
Lionel Rd North BTFD TW8 117 F3
Lionel Rd South BTFD TW8 117 G5
Lion Gate Gdns
RCH/KEW TW9 137 G4
Lion Gate Ms
WAND/EARL SW18 159 K2
Lion Mills BETH E2 * 104 C1
Lion Park Av CHSGTN KT9 206 C2
Lion Rd BXLYHS DA6 149 F5
CROY/NA CR0 196 D2
ED N9 36 C4
EHAM E6 107 K4
TWK TW1 156 A3
Lions Cl LEE/GVPK SE12 166 B5
Lion Wy BTFD TW8 136 E1
Lion Wharf Rd ISLW TW7 136 C4
Liphook Cl HCH RM12 93 H2
Liphook Crs FSTH SE23 163 K2
Liphook Rd OXHEY WD19 27 H6
Lisbon Av WHTN TW2 155 H4
Lisbon Cl WALTH E17 51 H5
Lisburne Rd HAMP NW3 83 K2
Lisford St PECK SE15 143 G2
Lisgar Ter WKENS W14 119 J4
Liskeard Cl CHST BR7 185 H2
Liskeard Gdns BKHTH/KID SE3 145 K2
Lisle Cl TOOT SW17 161 G6
Lisle St LSQ/SEVD WC2H 10 D5
Lismore WIM/MER SW19 * 177 J1
Lismore Circ KTTN NW5 83 K3
Lismore Cl ISLW TW7 136 B3
Lismore Rd SAND/SEL CR2 212 A4
TOTM N17 49 K6
Lismore Wk IS N1 * 85 J4
Lissant Cl SURB KT6 190 D4
Lissenden Gdns KTTN NW5 84 A2
Lisson Gv CAMTN NW1 2 C7
STJWD NW8 2 B6
Lisson St CAMTN NW1 8 C1
Lister Cl ACT W3 99 F4
MTCM CR4 178 D3
Lister Gdns UED N18 49 J1
Lister Rd WAN E11 70 C5
Liston Rd CLAP SW4 141 H4
TOTM N17 50 C4
Liston Wy WFD IG8 53 G3
Listowel Cl BRXN/ST SW9 142 B1
Listowel Rd DAGE RM10 92 C1
Listria Pk STNW/STAM N16 68 A6
Litchfield Av MRDN SM4 193 J4
SRTFD E15 * 88 C4
Litchfield Gdns WLSDN NW10 81 J4
Litchfield Rd SUT SM1 209 G2
Litchfield St LSQ/SEVD WC2H 10 D5
Litchfield Wy GLDGN NW11 65 G2
Lithgow's Rd HTHAIR TW6 133 H5
Lithos Rd HAMP NW3 83 F4
Litten Cl CRW RM5 56 C2
Little Acre BECK BR3 182 D6
Little Albany St CAMTN NW1 3 K6
Little Argyll St REGST W1B * 10 A4
Little Benty WDR/YW UB7 112 A5
Little Birches BFN/LL DA15 167 K4
The Little Boltons
WBPTN SW10 120 A5
Little Bornes DUL SE21 163 F6
Little Britain STBT EC1A 12 B2
Littlebrook Cl CROY/NA CR0 198 A3
Littlebrook Manor Wy
DART DA1 151 K6
Little Brownings FSTH SE23 163 J4
Littlebury Rd CLAP SW4 * 141 J4
Little Bury St ED N9 36 A2
Little Bushey La BUSH WD23 28 D1
Little Cedars
NFNCH/WDSPK N12 33 G6
Little Chester St KTBR SW1X 15 J4
Little Cloisters WEST SW1P 16 E4
Littlecombe Cl
PUT/ROE SW15 * 159 G1
Little Common STAN HA7 29 G5
Littlecote Cl WIM/MER SW19 159 G2
Littlecote Pl PIN HA5 41 J4
Little Cottage Pl
GNWCH SE10 * 144 E1
Little Ct WWKM BR4 199 H6
Littlecroft ELTH/MOT SE9 147 F4
Littledale ABYW SE2 128 B6
Little Deans Yd WEST SW1P 16 E4
Little Dimocks BAL SW12 161 G4
Little Dorrit Ct STHWK SE1 18 D2
Little Ealing La EA W5 116 D4
Little Edward St
CAMTN NW1 * 3 K4
Little Elms HYS/HAR UB3 133 G1
Little Essex St
TPL/STR WC2R * 11 J5
Little Ferry Rd TWK TW1 * 156 C3
Littlefield Cl ARCH N19 84 C2
KUT/HW KT1 175 F5
Littlefield Rd EDGW HA8 44 E3
Little Friday Rd CHING E4 38 C4
Little Gearies BARK/HLT IG6 72 B1
Little George St WEST SW1P 16 E3
Little Gn RCH/KEW TW9 136 E5
Little Green St KTTN NW5 * 84 B2
Littlegrove EBAR EN4 33 J1
Little Heath CHARL SE7 126 D6
CHDH RM6 73 H1
Little Heath Rd BXLYHN DA7 149 G2
Littleheath Rd SAND/SEL CR2 212 D6
Little Ilford La MNPK E12 89 K2
Littlejohn Rd HNWL W7 97 F5
STMC/STPC BR5 202 B3
Little Marlborough St
REGST W1B * 10 A4
Littlemead ESH/CLAY KT10 204 D2
Littlemede ELTH/MOT SE9 166 E5
Littlemoor Rd IL IG1 90 D1
Littlemore Rd ABYW SE2 128 B2
Little Moss La PIN HA5 41 J5
Little Newport St
LSQ/SEVD WC2H 10 D5
Little New St
FLST/FETLN EC4A 11 K3
Little Orchard Cl PIN HA5 * 41 J5
Little Oxhey La OXHEY WD19 41 J1
Little Park Dr FELT TW13 154 C4
Little Park Gdns ENC/FH EN2 23 J4
Little Pluckett's Wy BKHH IG9 39 H3
Little Portland St REGST W1B 9 K3
Little Potters BUSH WD23 28 D2
Little Queens Rd TEDD TW11 174 A2
Little Queen St DART DA1 171 J2
Little Redlands BMLY BR1 184 D5
Little Rd HYS/HAR UB3 113 J2
Littlers Cl WIM/MER SW19 178 C4
Little Russell St
NOXST/BSQ WC1A 10 E2
Little St James's St
WHALL SW1A 16 A1
Little St Leonards
MORT/ESHN SW14 137 K4
Little Smith St WEST SW1P 16 D4
Little Somerset St
TWRH EC3N 13 J4
Littlestone Cl BECK BR3 182 D2
Little Strd CDALE/KGS NW9 45 H5
Little Stream Cl NTHWD HA6 40 C1
Little Thrift STMC/STPC BR5 201 H1
Little Titchfield St
GTPST W1W 10 A2
Littleton Av CHING E4 38 D3
Littleton Crs HRW HA1 61 F6
Littleton Rd HRW HA1 61 F6
Littleton St WAND/EARL SW18 160 B4
Little Trinity La BLKFR EC4V 12 D5
Little Turnstile HHOL WC1V 11 G2
Littlewood LEW SE13 145 F6
Little Wood Cl
STMC/STPC BR5 186 B4
Littlewood Cl WEA W13 116 C3
Littleworth Av ESH/CLAY KT10 204 D3
Littleworth Common Rd
ESH/CLAY KT10 204 D1
Littleworth La ESH/CLAY KT10 204 D2
Littleworth Pl ESH/CLAY KT10 204 D2
Littleworth Rd
ESH/CLAY KT10 204 D3
Livermere Rd HACK E8 86 B6
Liverpool Gv WALW SE17 122 E5
Liverpool Rd CAN/RD E16 106 C4
EA W5 116 E2
IS N1 5 K1
KUTN/CMB KT2 175 H3
LEY E10 70 A3
THHTH CR7 180 D6
Liverpool St LVPST EC2M 13 G2
Livesey Cl KUT/HW KT1 175 G6
THMD SE28 127 H3
Livesey Pl STHWK SE1 123 H6
Livingstone Rd BTSEA SW11 140 C4
HSLW TW3 135 H5
PLMGR N13 48 E2
STHL UB1 95 H6
THHTH CR7 180 E5
WALTH E17 69 K3
Lizard St FSBYE EC1V 6 D5
Lizban St BKHTH/KID SE3 146 A1
Llanelly Rd CRICK NW2 64 D6
Llanover Rd WBLY HA9 79 K1
WOOL/PLUM SE18 147 F1
Llanthony Rd MRDN SM4 194 C3
Llanvanor Rd CRICK NW2 64 D6
Lloyd Av STRHM/NOR SW16 179 K4
Lloyd Baker St FSBYW WC1X 5 J5
Lloyd Ct PIN HA5 59 H2
Lloyd Ms PEND EN3 25 J1
Lloyd Park Av CROY/NA CR0 212 B2
Lloyd Rd DAGW RM9 92 B4
EHAM E6 89 K6
WALTH E17 69 F1
WPK KT4 208 A1
Lloyd's Av FENCHST EC3M 13 H4
Lloyd's Pl BKHTH/KID SE3 * 145 H3
Lloyd Sq FSBYW WC1X 5 J4
Lloyd's Rw CLKNW EC1R 5 K5
Lloyd St FSBYW WC1X 5 J4
Lloyds Wy BECK BR3 198 B2
Lloyd Thomas Ct WDGN N22 * 49 F3
Lloyd Vls BROCKY SE4 144 D3
Loampit Hl LEW SE13 144 D3
Loampit V LEW SE13 144 E4
Loanda Cl HACK E8 86 B6
Loats Rd BRXS/STRHM SW2 161 K1
Locarno Rd ACT W3 117 K1
GFD/PVL UB6 96 C3
Lochaber Rd LEW SE13 145 H5
Lochaline St HMSMTH W6 119 F6
Lochan Cl YEAD UB4 95 J3
Lochinvar St BAL SW12 161 G2
Lochmere Cl ERITH DA8 129 J6
Lochnagar St POP/IOD E14 106 A4
Lock Cha BKHTH/KID SE3 145 H4
Lock Cl NWDGN UB2 115 H2
Locke Cl RAIN RM13 93 H4
Lockesfield Pl POP/IOD E14 124 E4
Lockesley Dr STMC/STPC BR5 202 A3
Lockesley Sq SURB KT6 * 190 E3
Locket Rd
KTN/HRWW/WS HA3 43 F5
Locket Road Ms
KTN/HRWW/WS HA3 42 E5
Lockfield Av PEND EN3 25 G3
Lockgate Cl HOM E9 87 H3
Lockhart Cl HOLWY N7 85 F4
PEND EN3 24 D6
Lockhart St BOW E3 105 H3
Lockhurst St CLPT E5 87 F2
Lockington Rd VX/NE SW8 141 G2
Lock Keepers Cots
TOTM N17 * 68 D1
Lockmead Rd LEW SE13 145 F4
SEVS/STOTM N15 68 C3
Lock Rd RCHPK/HAM TW10 156 D5
Lock's La MTCM CR4 179 F4
Locksley Est POP/IOD E14 105 H5
Locksley St POP/IOD E14 105 H4
Locksmeade Rd
RCHPK/HAM TW10 156 C6
Lockton St NTGHL W11 * 100 B6
Lockwell Rd DAGE RM10 92 B1
Lockwood Cl EBAR EN4 21 K5
SYD SE26 164 A6
Lockwood Pl CHING E4 51 J2
Lockwood Sq
BERM/RHTH SE16 123 J3
Lockwood Wy CHSGTN KT9 206 C3
WALTH E17 51 F5
Lockyer Cl PEND EN3 25 K1
Lockyer St STHWK SE1 19 F3
Locomotive Dr
EBED/NFELT TW14 153 K2
Locton Gn BOW E3 * 87 H6
Loddiges Rd HOM E9 86 E5
Loder St PECK SE15 143 K1
Lodge Av BCTR RM8 91 H3
CROY/NA CR0 211 F1
DAGW RM9 91 G6
DART DA1 171 F1
GPK RM2 75 J2
KTN/HRWW/WS HA3 62 A1
Lodge Cl EDGW HA8 * 44 B2
ISLW TW7 136 C2
ORP BR6 202 C5
UED N18 49 J1
WLGTN SM6 195 F5
Lodge Ct ALP/SUD HA0 * 80 A3
Lodge Crs ORP BR6 202 C5
Lodge Dr PLMGR N13 35 G6
Lodge Gdns BECK BR3 198 C2
Lodge Hl REDBR IG4 71 J1
WELL DA16 148 C1
Lodgehill Park Cl
RYLN/HDSTN HA2 60 B6
Lodge La BXLY DA5 168 E1
CROY/NA CR0 213 K5
CRW RM5 56 C2
NFNCH/WDSPK N12 47 G1
Lodge Mansions Pde
PLMGR N13 * 35 G6
Lodge Ms HBRY N5 * 85 J2
Lodge Pl SUT SM1 209 F3
Lodge Rd BMLY BR1 184 B3
CROY/NA CR0 196 C3
HDN NW4 64 A1
STJWD NW8 2 B5
SUT SM1 209 F3
WLGTN SM6 210 B3
The Lodge SHB W12 * 119 G2
Lodge Vls WFD IG8 52 D3
Lodge Wy ASHF TW15 152 B4
Lodore Gdns CDALE/KGS NW9 63 G2
Lodore St POP/IOD E14 106 A5
Lofthouse Pl CHSGTN KT9 205 J4
Loftie St BERM/RHTH SE16 123 H2
Lofting Rd IS N1 85 G5
Loftus Rd BARK IG11 90 C4
SHB W12 118 E1
Loftus Vls SHB W12 * 118 E1
Logan Cl HSLWW TW4 134 E4
PEND EN3 25 F2
Logan Ms ECT SW5 119 K4
ROM RM1 75 G2
Logan Pl ECT SW5 119 K4
Logan Rd ED N9 36 D4
WBLY HA9 62 A6
The Logans BAR EN5 * 20 B4
Logs Hl CHST BR7 184 D4
Logs Hill Cl CHST BR7 184 D4
Lolesworth Cl WCHPL E1 13 J2
Lollard St LBTH SE11 17 H6
Loman St STHWK SE1 18 B2
Lomas Cl CROY/NA CR0 214 A5
Lomas Dr HACK E8 * 86 B5
Lombard Av GDMY/SEVK IG3 72 E5

PEND EN3 24 E2
Lombard Ct MANHO EC4N 13 F5
Lombard La EMB EC4Y 11 K4
Lombard Rd BTSEA SW11 140 C3
FBAR/BDGN N11 48 B1
WIM/MER SW19 178 A5
Lombard St BANK EC3V 13 F4
Lombard Vis
FBAR/BDGN N11 * 48 B1
Lombard Wall CHARL SE7 126 A3
Lombardy Cl WFD IG8 54 B3
Lombardy Pl BAY/PAD W2 101 F6
Lomond Cl ALP/SUD HA0 80 B5
SEVS/STOTM N15 68 A1
Lomond Gdns SAND/SEL CR2 213 G5
Lomond Gv CMBW SE5 142 E1
Loncroft Rd CMBW SE5 123 F6
Londesborough Rd
STNW/STAM N16 86 A2
London Br CANST EC4R 13 F6
London Bridge St STHWK SE1 19 F1
London Bridge Wk
STHWK SE1 * 13 F7
Londonderry Pde
ERITH DA8 * 150 A1
London Flds HACK E8 * 86 D5
London Fields East Side
HACK E8 86 D5
London Fields West Side
HACK E8 86 C5
London La BMLY BR1 183 J3
HACK E8 86 D5
London Loop BAR EN5 31 K2
CHING E4 38 B1
ENC/FH EN2 23 J1
HAYES BR2 199 J6
ORP BR6 201 G5
PEND EN3 25 K2
SAND/SEL CR2 212 E5
London Ms BAY/PAD W2 8 B4
London Rd ASHF TW15 152 C4
BARK IG11 90 B5
BMLY BR1 183 J3
BUSH WD23 27 K1
CHEAM SM3 193 G6
CROY/NA CR0 196 C5
DART DA1 150 A6
ENC/FH EN2 23 K5
EW KT17 207 H6
FSTH SE23 163 K3
HRW HA1 60 E6
ISLW TW7 135 K3
KUTN/CMB KT2 175 G5
MRDN SM4 193 K2
MTCM CR4 194 D1
PLSTW E13 106 E1
PUR RM19 131 K5
ROMW/RG RM7 74 C3
SOCK/AV RM15 131 K2
STAN HA7 29 K6
STAN HA7 29 K6
STHWK SE1 18 B4
STRHM/NOR SW16 180 A5
SWLY BR8 187 K5
THHTH CR7 196 B3
TOOT SW17 178 E3
TWK TW1 156 B2
WBLY HA9 80 A3
WLGTN SM6 210 B2
London Stile CHSWK W4 117 H5
London St BAY/PAD W2 8 A3
FENCHST EC3M * 13 H5
London Ter BETH E2 * 104 C1
London Wall CITYW EC2V 12 D2
LVPST EC2M 13 F3
London Wall Blds LVPST EC2M 13 F2
Lonesome Wy MTCM CR4 179 G4
Long Acre CHCR WC2N 10 E5
COVGDN WC2E 10 E4
ORP BR6 202 E6
Long Acre Ct WEA W13 * 97 G4
Longacre Pl CAR SM5 * 210 A4
Longacre Rd WALTH E17 52 B4
Longbeach Rd BTSEA SW11 140 E4
Longboat Rw STHL UB1 95 K5
Longbridge Rd BARK IG11 90 D4
BCTR RM8 91 G2
Longbridge Wy LEW SE13 145 F6
Longbury Cl STMC/STPC BR5 186 C6
Longbury Dr STMC/STPC BR5 186 C6
Longcliffe Pth OXHEY WD19 26 E5
Long Ct PUR RM19 131 K4
Longcroft ELTH/MOT SE9 167 F5
Long Cft OXHEY WD19 27 F2
Longcrofte Rd EDGW HA8 43 K3
Long Deacon Rd CHING E4 38 C3
Longdon Wd HAYES BR2 215 J2
Longdown Rd CAT SE6 164 D6
Long Dr ACT W3 99 G5
GFD/PVL UB6 78 B6
RSLP HA4 77 H2
WDR/YW UB7 * 112 B2
Long Elmes
KTN/HRWW/WS HA3 42 B4
Longfellow Rd WALTH E17 69 H3
WCHPL E1 * 105 G2
WPK KT4 192 D5
Longfellow Wy STHWK SE1 * 19 K7
Longfield BMLY BR1 183 J4
Long Fld CDALE/KGS NW9 45 G3
Longfield Av EA W5 97 J6
EMPK RM11 75 H4
MLHL NW7 45 J3
WALTH E17 69 G1
WBLY HA9 62 A5
WLGTN SM6 195 F5
Longfield Crs SYD SE26 163 K5
Longfield Dr
MORT/ESHN SW14 137 J6
MTCM CR4 178 D4
Longfield Est STHWK SE1 19 K6
Longfield Rd EA W5 97 J5
Longfield St
WAND/EARL SW18 159 K2
Longford Av
EBED/NFELT TW14 153 H1
STHL UB1 96 A6
STWL/WRAY TW19 152 B3
Longford Cl FELT TW13 154 D5
HPTN TW12 155 F6
YEAD UB4 95 H6
Longford Ct HOR/WEW KT19 206 E2
HPTN TW12 173 G2
Longford Gdns SUT SM1 209 G1
YEAD UB4 95 H6
Longford Rd WHTN TW2 155 F3
Longford St CAMTN NW1 3 K6
Longford Wy
STWL/WRAY TW19 152 B3
Longhayes Av CHDH RM6 55 K6
Longheath Gdns
CROY/NA CR0 197 K2
Longhedge St BTSEA SW11 141 F3
Longhill Rd CAT SE6 165 G4
Longhook Gdns NTHLT UB5 94 E1
Longhurst Rd CROY/NA CR0 197 J3
LEW SE13 145 H6
Longland Dr TRDG/WHET N20 33 F5
Longlands Park Crs
BFN/LL DA15 167 K5
Longlands Rd BFN/LL DA15 167 K5
Long La BXLYHN DA7 149 F1
CROY/NA CR0 197 K3
FNCH N3 47 F4
STBT EC1A 12 B1
STHWK SE1 19 F3
STWL/WRAY TW19 152 C3
Longleat Rd EN EN1 24 A6
Longleat Wy
EBED/NFELT TW14 153 F2
Longleigh La ABYW SE2 128 D6
Longley Av ALP/SUD HA0 80 B6
Longley Rd CROY/NA CR0 196 C4
HRW HA1 60 D2
TOOT SW17 178 D2
Long Leys CHING E4 51 K2
Longley St STHWK SE1 123 H4
Longley Wy CRICK NW2 82 A1
Longmans Cl WATW WD18 26 A1
Long Mark Rd CAN/RD E16 107 H5
Longmarsh La THMD SE28 127 K1
Long Md CDALE/KGS NW9 45 H4
Longmead CHST BR7 185 F5
Longmead Dr SCUP DA14 168 E4
Long Meadow KTTN NW5 * 84 D4
Long Meadow Cl WWKM BR4 199 F4
Longmeadow Rd
BFN/LL DA15 167 K3
Longmead Rd HYS/HAR UB3 94 D6
THDIT KT7 189 K4
TOOT SW17 178 E1
Longmoore St PIM SW1V 16 A7
Longmore Av BAR EN5 33 G1
Longnor Rd WCHPL E1 105 F2
Long Pond Rd BKHTH/KID SE3 145 H2
Longport Cl BARK/HLT IG6 55 G2
Long Reach Rd BARK IG11 109 F3
Longreach Rd ERITH DA8 150 E1
Longridge La STHL UB1 96 B6
Longridge Rd ECT SW5 119 K4
Long Rd CLAP SW4 141 H5
Longshaw Rd CHING E4 38 B5
Longshore DEPT SE8 124 C4
Longstaff Crs
WAND/EARL SW18 159 K1
Longstaff Rd
WAND/EARL SW18 159 K1
Longstone Av WLSDN NW10 81 H5
Longstone Rd TOOT SW17 179 G1
Long St BETH E2 7 J3
Longthornton Rd
STRHM/NOR SW16 179 H5
Longton Av SYD SE26 163 H6
Longton Gv SYD SE26 163 J6
Longview Wy CRW RM5 57 F4
Longville Rd LBTH SE11 18 A6
Long Wk NWMAL KT3 175 K6
STHWK SE1 19 H4
WOOL/PLUM SE18 127 G6
Longwalk Rd STKPK UB11 112 E1
Longwood Ct WPK KT4 192 D6
Longwood Dr
PUT/ROE SW15 158 D1
Longwood Gdns CLAY IG5 54 A6
CLAY IG5 71 K1
Longworth Cl THMD SE28 109 K5
Long Yd BMSBY WC1N 5 G7
The Loning CDALE/KGS NW9 63 H1
PEND EN3 24 E1
Lonsdale Av EHAM E6 107 H3
ROMW/RG RM7 74 E3
WBLY HA9 80 A3
Lonsdale Cl EHAM E6 107 J3
ELTH/MOT SE9 166 C5
UX/CGN UB8 94 A5
Lonsdale Crs
GNTH/NBYPK IG2 72 B3
Lonsdale Dr ENC/FH EN2 22 D5
Lonsdale Dr North
ENC/FH EN2 22 E6
Lonsdale Gdns THHTH CR7 196 A1
Lonsdale Ms NTGHL W11 100 D5
RCH/KEW TW9 * 137 H2
Lonsdale Pl IS N1 85 G5
Lonsdale Rd BARN SW13 138 C1
BXLYHN DA7 149 G3
CHSWK W4 118 C4
KIL/WHAMP NW6 82 D6
NTGHL W11 100 D5
NWDGN UB2 114 C3
SNWD SE25 197 J1
WAN E11 70 D4
Lonsdale Sq IS N1 * 85 G5
Loobert Rd SEVS/STOTM N15 50 A6
Looe Gdns BARK/HLT IG6 54 B6
Loop Rd CHST BR7 185 H2
Lopen Rd UED N18 36 A6
Loraine Cl PEND EN3 24 E6
Loraine Cots HOLWY N7 * 85 F2
Loraine Rd CHSWK W4 117 J6
HOLWY N7 85 F2
Lord Av CLAY IG5 71 K1
Lord Chancellor Wk
KUTN/CMB KT2 175 K4
Lordell Pl WIM/MER SW19 177 F2
Lord Hills Rd BAY/PAD W2 101 F4
Lord Holland La
BRXN/ST SW9 * 142 B3
Lord Knyvett Cl
STWL/WRAY TW19 152 A1
Lord Knyvetts Ct
STWL/WRAY TW19 * 152 B1
Lord Napier Pl HMSMTH W6 118 D5
Lord North St WEST SW1P 16 E5
Lord Roberts Ms
FUL/PGN SW6 * 140 A1
Lords Cl DUL SE21 162 D4
FELT TW13 154 D4
Lordship Gv STNW/STAM N16 67 K6
Lordship La EDUL SE22 163 G1
TOTM N17 49 J4
WDGN N22 49 G5
Lordship Pk STNW/STAM N16 67 K6
Lordship Park Ms
STNW/STAM N16 67 J6
Lordship Pl CHEL SW3 120 D6
Lordship Rd NTHLT UB5 77 J5
STNW/STAM N16 67 K5
Lordship Ter STNW/STAM N16 67 K6
Lordsmead Rd TOTM N17 50 A4
Lord St CAN/RD E16 126 D1
Lords Vw STJWD NW8 2 C4
Lord Warwick St
WOOL/PLUM SE18 126 E3
Lorenzo St FSBYW WC1X 5 G4
Loretto Gdns
KTN/HRWW/WS HA3 62 A1
Lorian Cl NFNCH/WDSPK N12 33 F6
Loring Rd ISLW TW7 136 A3
TRDG/WHET N20 33 J4
Loris Rd HMSMTH W6 119 F3
Lorne Av CROY/NA CR0 198 A4
Lorne Cl STJWD NW8 2 D5
Lorne Gdns CROY/NA CR0 198 A4
NTGHL W11 119 G2
WAN E11 71 G1
Lorne Rd FSBYPK N4 67 F5
FSTGT E7 89 F2
KTN/HRWW/WS HA3 43 F5
RCHPK/HAM TW10 137 G6
WALTH E17 69 J2
Lorne Ter FNCH N3 * 46 D5
Lorn Rd BRXN/ST SW9 142 A3
Lorraine Pk
KTN/HRWW/WS HA3 42 E3
Lorrimore Rd WALW SE17 122 C6
Lorrimore Sq WALW SE17 122 C6
Loseberry Rd ESH/CLAY KT10 204 D3
Lothair Rd EA W5 116 E2
Lothair Rd North FSBYPK N4 67 H3
Lothair Rd South FSBYPK N4 67 G4
Lothbury LOTH EC2R 12 E3
Lothian Av YEAD UB4 95 F4
Lothian Cl ALP/SUD HA0 79 G2
Lothian Rd BRXN/ST SW9 142 C1
Lothrop St NKENS W10 100 C2
Lots Rd WBPTN SW10 140 B1
Loubet St TOOT SW17 178 E2
Loudoun Av BARK/HLT IG6 72 B2
Loudoun Rd STJWD NW8 83 G6
Loughborough Pk
BRXN/ST SW9 142 C5
Loughborough Rd
BRXN/ST SW9 142 B3
Loughborough St LBTH SE11 122 A5
Lough Rd HOLWY N7 85 F3
Loughton Wy BKHH IG9 39 H3
Louisa Cl HOM E9 86 E5
Louisa St WCHPL E1 105 F4
Louise Bennett Cl
HNHL SE24 * 142 C5
Louise Gdns RAIN RM13 111 G2
Louise Rd SRTFD E15 88 C4
Louis Gdns CHST BR7 166 E6
Louisville Rd TOOT SW17 161 F5
Louvaine Rd BTSEA SW11 140 C5
Lovage Ap EHAM E6 107 J4
Lovat Cl CRICK NW2 81 H1
Lovat La FENCHST EC3M 13 G5
Lovatt Cl EDGW HA8 44 D2
Loveday Rd WEA W13 116 C1
Lovegrove St STHWK SE1 123 H5
Lovegrove Wk POP/IOD E14 125 F1
Lovekyn Cl KUTN/CMB KT2 175 F5
Lovelace Av HAYES BR2 201 F3
Lovelace Gdns BARK IG11 91 G2
SURB KT6 190 E4
Lovelace Gn ELTH/MOT SE9 146 E4
Lovelace Rd DUL SE21 162 D4
EBAR EN4 33 J2
SURB KT6 190 D4
Lovelace Vls THDIT KT7 * 190 C4
Love La BXLY DA5 169 H1
CHEAM SM3 208 C4
CITYW EC2V 12 D3
MRDN SM4 193 K4
MTCM CR4 178 D6
PIN HA5 41 J6
SNWD SE25 181 J6
SURB KT6 190 E6
TOTM N17 50 B3
WFD IG8 53 K2
WOOL/PLUM SE18 127 F4
Lovel Av WELL DA16 148 B3
Lovelinch Cl PECK SE15 123 K6
Lovell Pl BERM/RHTH SE16 124 B3
Lovell Rd RCHPK/HAM TW10 156 D5
STHL UB1 96 B5
Lovell Wk RAIN RM13 93 J4
Loveridge Ms
KIL/WHAMP NW6 82 D4
Loveridge Rd
KIL/WHAMP NW6 82 D4
Lovett Dr CAR SM5 194 B4
Lovetts Pl WAND/EARL SW18 140 B5
Lovett Wy WLSDN NW10 80 E3
Love Wk CMBW SE5 142 E3
Lovibonds Av ORP BR6 216 B1
Lowbrook Rd IL IG1 90 B2
Lowden Rd ED N9 36 D3
HNHL SE24 142 C5
STHL UB1 95 J6
Lowe Av CAN/RD E16 106 E4
Lowe Cl CHIG IG7 55 G1
Lowell St POP/IOD E14 105 G5
Lowen Rd RAIN RM13 111 F1
Lower Addiscombe Rd
CROY/NA CR0 196 E5
Lower Addison Gdns
WKENS W14 119 H2
Lower Bedfords Rd ROM RM1 57 J2
Lower Belgrave St
BGVA SW1W 15 J5
Lower Broad St DAGE RM10 92 C6
Lower Camden CHST BR7 184 E4
Lower Church St
CROY/NA CR0 * 196 C6
Lower Clapton Rd CLPT E5 86 D2
HACK E8 86 D3
Lower Clarendon Wk
NTGHL W11 100 C5
Lower Common South
PUT/ROE SW15 138 E4
Lower Coombe St
CROY/NA CR0 211 J2
Lower Downs Rd
RYNPK SW20 177 G4
Lower Gravel Rd HAYES BR2 200 D5
Lower Green Gdns WPK KT4 192 D5
Lower Green Rd
ESH/CLAY KT10 189 G6
Lower Gn West MTCM CR4 178 D6
Lower Grosvenor Pl
BGVA SW1W 15 J4
Lower Grove Rd
RCHPK/HAM TW10 157 G1
Lower Hall La CHING E4 51 G1
Lower Hampton Rd
SUN TW16 172 C5
Lower Ham Rd
KUTN/CMB KT2 174 E2
Lower James St
SOHO/CST W1F * 10 B5
Lower John St
SOHO/CST W1F 10 B5
Lower Kenwood Av
ENC/FH EN2 22 E6
Lower Kings Rd
KUTN/CMB KT2 175 F3
Lower Lea Crossing
POP/IOD E14 106 C6
Lower Maidstone Rd
FBAR/BDGN N11 48 C2
Lower Mardyke Av
RAIN RM13 110 E1
Lower Marsh STHWK SE1 17 J3
Lower Marsh La BRYLDS KT5 191 G1
Lower Merton Ri HAMP NW3 83 J5
Lower Morden La MRDN SM4 193 F3
Lower Mortlake Rd
RCH/KEW TW9 137 F5
Lower Paddock Rd
OXHEY WD19 27 J1
Lower Park Rd BELV DA17 129 H3
FBAR/BDGN N11 48 C1
Lower Queen's Rd BKHH IG9 39 J4
Lower Richmond Rd
PUT/ROE SW15 139 F4
RCH/KEW TW9 137 H4
Lower Rd BELV DA17 129 J3
BERM/RHTH SE16 123 K2
ERITH DA8 130 A4
RYLN/HDSTN HA2 60 D6
STMC/STPC BR5 202 C3
SUT SM1 209 H3
Lower Robert St CHCR WC2N 11 F6
Lower Sand Hills SURB KT6 190 D4
Lower Sloane St BGVA SW1W 15 F7
Lower Station Rd DART DA1 170 B1
Lower Strd CDALE/KGS NW9 45 H5
Lower Sunbury Rd
E/WMO/HCT KT8 172 E5
Lower Tail OXHEY WD19 27 J5
Lower Teddington Rd
KUT/HW KT1 174 E4
Lower Ter HAMP NW3 83 G1
Lower Thames St MON EC3R 13 G6
Lower Tub BUSH WD23 28 D2
Lower Wood Rd
ESH/CLAY KT10 205 G4
Loweswater Cl WBLY HA9 61 K6
The Lowe CHIG IG7 55 G1
Lowfield Rd ACT W3 98 E5
KIL/WHAMP NW6 82 E5
Lowfield St DART DA1 171 H2
Low Hall Cl CHING E4 37 J2
Low Hall La WALTH E17 69 G3
Lowick Rd HRW HA1 60 E1
Lowland Gdns
ROMW/RG RM7 74 D3
Lowlands Dr
STWL/WRAY TW19 132 A6
Lowlands Rd HRW HA1 60 E4
PIN HA5 59 G4
Lowman Rd HOLWY N7 85 F2
Lowndes Cl KTBR SW1X 15 H5
Lowndes Ct SOHO/CST W1F * 10 A4
Lowndes Ms
STRHM/NOR SW16 161 K4
Lowndes Pl KTBR SW1X * 15 G5
Lowndes Sq KTBR SW1X 15 F3
Lowndes St KTBR SW1X 15 F4
Lowood St WCHPL E1 104 D6
Lowry Cl ERITH DA8 130 A4
Lowry Crs MTCM CR4 178 D5
Lowry Rd BCTR RM8 91 H3
Lowshoe La CRW RM5 56 D4
Lowson Gv OXHEY WD19 27 J2
Lowswood Cl NTHWD HA6 40 A4
Lowther Dr ENC/FH EN2 22 E5
Lowther Hl FSTH SE23 164 B2
Lowther Man BARN SW13 * 138 D2
Lowther Rd BARN SW13 138 C2
HOLWY N7 * 85 G3
KUTN/CMB KT2 175 G4
STAN HA7 44 B6
WALTH E17 51 G5
Lowth Rd CMBW SE5 142 D3
Loxford Av EHAM E6 107 H1
Loxford La IL IG1 90 C3
Loxford Rd BARK IG11 90 B4
Loxham Rd CHING E4 51 K3
Loxham St STPAN WC1H * 5 F5
Loxley Cl SYD SE26 182 A1
Loxley Rd HPTN TW12 154 E6
WAND/EARL SW18 160 C3
Loxton Rd FSTH SE23 164 A3
Loxwood Cl
EBED/NFELT TW14 153 G3
STMC/STPC BR5 202 E6
Loxwood Rd TOTM N17 50 A6
Lubbock Rd CHST BR7 185 F4
Lubbock St NWCR SE14 143 K1
Lucan Pl CHEL SW3 14 C7
Lucan Rd BAR EN5 20 C4
Lucas Av PLSTW E13 89 F6
RYLN/HDSTN HA2 60 A6
Lucas Gdns EFNCH N2 47 G5
Lucas Rd PGE/AN SE20 181 K2
Lucas Sq GLDGN NW11 64 E3
Lucas St BROCKY SE4 144 D3
Lucerne Cl PLMGR N13 34 E5
Lucerne Gv WALTH E17 70 B1
Lucerne Rd HBRY N5 85 H2
ORP BR6 202 A5
THHTH CR7 196 C2
Lucey Rd BERM/RHTH SE16 123 H3
Lucey Wy BERM/RHTH SE16 123 H3
Lucien Rd TOOT SW17 161 F6
WIM/MER SW19 160 A4
Lucknow St
WOOL/PLUM SE18 147 K1
Lucorn Cl LEE/GVPK SE12 165 J1
Luctons Av BKHH IG9 39 G3
Luddesdon Rd ERITH DA8 149 H1
Ludford Cl CROY/NA CR0 211 H2
Ludgate Broadway
BLKFR EC4V * 12 B4
Ludgate Circ STP EC4M 12 A4
Ludgate Hl STP EC4M 12 A4
Ludgate Sq STP EC4M * 12 B4
Ludham Cl BARK/HLT IG6 54 C4
THMD SE28 109 J5
Ludlow Cl HAYES BR2 * 183 K6
RYLN/HDSTN HA2 77 K2
Ludlow Md OXHEY WD19 27 F5
Ludlow Rd EA W5 97 J3
FELT TW13 153 K5
Ludlow St FSBYE EC1V * 6 C6
Ludlow Wy EFNCH N2 65 G1
Ludovick Wk PUT/ROE SW15 138 B5
Luffield Rd ABYW SE2 128 C3
Luffman Rd LEE/GVPK SE12 166 A5
Lugard Rd PECK SE15 143 J3
Lugg Ap MNPK E12 90 A1
Luke St SDTCH EC2A 7 G6
Lukin Crs CHING E4 38 B5
Lukin St WCHPL E1 104 E5
Lullingstone Cl
STMC/STPC BR5 186 C3
Lullingstone Crs
STMC/STPC BR5 186 B3
Lullingstone La LEW SE13 165 G1
Lullingstone Rd BELV DA17 129 G6
Lullington Garth BMLY BR1 183 H3
NFNCH/WDSPK N12 46 D1
Lullington Rd DAGW RM9 92 A5
PGE/AN SE20 181 H3
Lulot Gdns ARCH N19 66 B6
Lulworth Av HEST TW5 135 G2
WBLY HA9 61 J4
Lulworth Cl RYLN/HDSTN HA2 77 K1
Lulworth Crs MTCM CR4 178 D5
Lulworth Dr CRW RM5 56 D1
PIN HA5 59 H4
Lulworth Gdns
RYLN/HDSTN HA2 59 J6
Lulworth Rd ELTH/MOT SE9 166 D4
PECK SE15 * 143 J3
WELL DA16 148 A3
Lulworth Waye YEAD UB4 95 F5
Lumen Rd WBLY HA9 61 K6
Lumley Cl BELV DA17 129 H6
Lumley Flats BGVA SW1W * 121 F5
Lumley Gdns CHEAM SM3 208 C3
Lumley Rd CHEAM SM3 208 C4
Lumley St OXSTW W1C 9 H4
Luna Rd THHTH CR7 180 D6
Lundin Wk OXHEY WD19 * 27 H6
Lundy Dr HYS/HAR UB3 113 H4
Lundy Wk IS N1 85 J4
Lunham Rd NRWD SE19 181 F2
Lupin Cl BRXS/STRHM SW2 162 C4
CROY/NA CR0 198 A5
ROMW/RG RM7 75 F6
WDR/YW UB7 112 A5
Lupton Cl LEE/GVPK SE12 166 A6
Lupton St KTTN NW5 84 C2
Lupus St PIM SW1V 121 G5
Lurgan Av HMSMTH W6 119 G6
Lurline Gdns BTSEA SW11 141 F2
Luscombe Wy VX/NE SW8 141 K1
Lushington Rd CAT SE6 182 E1
WLSDN NW10 99 K1
Lushington Ter HACK E8 * 86 C3
Luther Cl EDGW HA8 30 E4
Luther King Cl WALTH E17 69 G3
Luther Ms TEDD TW11 174 A1
Luther Rd TEDD TW11 174 A1
Luton Pl GNWCH SE10 145 F1
Luton Rd PLSTW E13 106 E3
SCUP DA14 168 D5
WALTH E17 51 G6
Luton St STJWD NW8 2 B7
Luttrell Av PUT/ROE SW15 138 E6
Lutwyche Rd FSTH SE23 164 C4
Luxborough La CHIG IG7 39 K6
Luxborough St CAMTN NW1 3 G7
MHST W1U 9 G1
Luxembourg Ms SRTFD E15 88 C3
Luxemburg Gdns
HMSMTH W6 119 G4
Luxfield Rd ELTH/MOT SE9 166 D3
Luxford St BERM/RHTH SE16 124 A4
Luxmore St BROCKY SE4 144 C2
Luxor St CMBW SE5 142 D4
Lyall Av DUL SE21 163 F6
Lyall Ms KTBR SW1X 15 G5
Lyall Ms West KTBR SW1X * 15 G5
Lyall St KTBR SW1X 15 G5
Lyal Rd BOW E3 105 G1
Lycett Pl SHB W12 118 D2
Lych Gate Rd ORP BR6 202 B5
Lych Gate Wk HYS/HAR UB3 94 D6
Lyconby Gdns CROY/NA CR0 198 B4
Lydd Cl BFN/LL DA15 167 K5
Lydden Gv WAND/EARL SW18 160 A2
Lydden Rd WAND/EARL SW18 160 A2
Lydd Rd BXLYHN DA7 149 G1
Lydeard Rd EHAM E6 89 K5

Lydford Cl STNW/STAM N16 86 A3
Lydford Rd CRICK NW2 82 B4
MV/WKIL W9 100 D3
SEVS/STOTM N15 67 K2
Lydhurst Av
BRXS/STRHM SW2 162 A4
Lydia Rd ERITH DA8 130 C6
Lydney Cl WIM/MER SW19 159 H4
Lydon Rd CLAP SW4 141 H4
Lydstep Rd CHST BR7 167 F6
Lyford Rd WAND/EARL SW18 160 C2
Lyford St WOOL/PLUM SE18 126 D4
Lygon Pl BGVA SW1W * 15 J5
Lyham Cl BRXS/STRHM SW2 161 K1
Lyham Rd BRXS/STRHM SW2 161 K1
Lyle Cl MTCM CR4 195 F4
Lyme Farm Rd
LEE/GVPK SE12 145 K5
Lyme Gv HOM E9 86 E5
Lymer Av NRWD SE19 181 G1
Lyme Rd WELL DA16 148 C2
Lymescote Gdns SUT SM1 193 K6
Lyme St CAMTN NW1 84 C5
Lyme Ter CAMTN NW1 84 C5
Lyminge Cl SCUP DA14 168 A6
Lyminge Gdns
WAND/EARL SW18 160 D3
Lymington Av WDGN N22 49 G5
Lymington Cl
STRHM/NOR SW16 179 J5
Lymington Dr RSLP HA4 58 B6
Lymington Gdns
HOR/WEW KT19 207 H3
Lymington Rd BCTR RM8 73 K5
KIL/WHAMP NW6 * 83 F4
Lyminster Cl YEAD UB4 95 J4
Lympstone Gdns PECK SE15 143 H1
Lynbridge Gdns PLMGR N13 35 H6
Lynbrook Cl RAIN RM13 111 F1
Lynbrook Gv PECK SE15 143 F1
Lynchen Cl HEST TW5 133 K2
Lyncourt BKHTH/KID SE3 * 145 G3
Lyncroft Av PIN HA5 59 H2
Lyncroft Gdns EW KT17 207 H6
HSLW TW3 135 H6
KIL/WHAMP NW6 82 E3
WEA W13 116 D2
Lyndale CRICK NW2 82 D1
THDIT KT7 * 189 K4
Lyndale Av CRICK NW2 82 D1
Lyndale Cl BKHTH/KID SE3 125 J6
Lyndale Hampton Court Wy
ESH/CLAY KT10 189 K4
Lynden Wy SWLY BR8 187 K6
Lyndhurst Av BRYLDS KT5 191 J5
MLHL NW7 45 G2
NFNCH/WDSPK N12 47 K2
PIN HA5 41 F4
STHL UB1 115 G1
STRHM/NOR SW16 179 J5
WHTN TW2 154 E3
Lyndhurst Cl BXLYHN DA7 149 J4
CROY/NA CR0 212 B1
ORP BR6 216 B2
WLSDN NW10 81 F1
Lyndhurst Ct BELMT SM2 * 208 E5
Lyndhurst Dr LEY E10 70 A4
NWMAL KT3 192 B3
Lyndhurst Gdns BARK IG11 90 E4
EN EN1 24 A5
FNCH N3 46 C4
GNTH/NBYPK IG2 72 D3
HAMP NW3 83 H3
PIN HA5 41 F4
Lyndhurst Gv CMBW SE5 143 F3
Lyndhurst Leys HAYES BR2 * 183 G5
Lyndhurst Prior SNWD SE25 * 181 F6
Lyndhurst Rd BXLYHN DA7 149 J4
CHING E4 52 A3
GFD/PVL UB6 96 B3
HAMP NW3 83 H3
THHTH CR7 196 B1
UED N18 36 C6
WDGN N22 49 G2
Lyndhurst Sq PECK SE15 143 G2
Lyndhurst Ter HAMP NW3 83 H3
Lyndhurst Wy BELMT SM2 208 E6
PECK SE15 143 G2
Lyndon Av BFN/LL DA15 148 A6
PIN HA5 41 J2
WLGTN SM6 210 A1
Lyndon Rd BELV DA17 129 H4
Lyndon Yd TOOT SW17 160 A6
Lyne Crs WALTH E17 51 H4
Lyneham Wk CLPT E5 * 87 G3
Lynette Av CLAP SW4 161 G1
Lynford Cl EDGW HA8 44 E4
Lynford Gdns EDGW HA8 30 D5
GDMY/SEVK IG3 73 F6
Lynford Ter ED N9 * 36 B3
Lynhurst Crs HGDN/ICK UB10 76 A5
Lynhurst Rd HGDN/ICK UB10 76 A5
Lynmere Rd WELL DA16 148 C3
Lyn Ms STNW/STAM N16 * 86 B2
Lynmouth Av EN EN1 36 B1
MRDN SM4 193 G4
Lynmouth Dr RSLP HA4 59 F6
Lynmouth Gdns GFD/PVL UB6 79 H6
HEST TW5 134 C2
Lynmouth Ri STMC/STPC BR5 202 C1
Lynmouth Rd EFNCH N2 47 K6
GFD/PVL UB6 79 H6
STNW/STAM N16 68 B5
WALTH E17 69 G3
Lynn Cl KTN/HRWW/WS HA3 42 D5
Lynne Cl ORP BR6 217 F4
Lynnett Rd BCTR RM8 73 K6
Lynne Wk ESH/CLAY KT10 204 C3
Lynne Wy NTHLT UB5 95 H1
Lynn Ms WAN E11 70 C6
Lynn Rd BAL SW12 161 G2
GNTH/NBYPK IG2 72 D4
WAN E11 70 C6
Lynn St ENC/FH EN2 23 K2
Lynscott Wy SAND/SEL CR2 211 H6
Lynstead Cl BMLY BR1 184 B5
Lynsted Cl BXLYHS DA6 149 J6
Lynsted Ct BECK BR3 182 B5
Lynsted Gdns ELTH/MOT SE9 146 C5
Lynton Av CDALE/KGS NW9 63 H1
NFNCH/WDSPK N12 33 H6
ROMW/RG RM7 56 D4
STMC/STPC BR5 202 C1
WEA W13 97 G5
Lynton Cl CHSGTN KT9 206 A2
ISLW TW7 136 A5
WLSDN NW10 81 G3
Lynton Crs GNTH/NBYPK IG2 72 B3
Lynton Est STHWK SE1 19 K7
Lynton Gdns EN EN1 36 A2
FBAR/BDGN N11 48 D2
Lynton Md TRDG/WHET N20 32 E5
Lynton Rd ACT W3 98 C6
CEND/HSY/T N8 66 D2
CHING E4 51 K1
CROY/NA CR0 196 B3
KIL/WHAMP NW6 82 D6
NWMAL KT3 192 A2
RYLN/HDSTN HA2 59 J6
STHWK SE1 19 K7
Lynton Ter ACT W3 * 98 E5
Lynwood Cl CRW RM5 56 D2
RYLN/HDSTN HA2 77 J1
SWFD E18 53 G4
Lynwood Dr CRW RM5 56 D2
NTHWD HA6 40 C4
WPK KT4 192 D6
Lynwood Gdns CROY/NA CR0 211 F2
STHL UB1 95 K5
Lynwood Gv ORP BR6 201 K4
WCHMH N21 35 G3
Lynwood Rd EA W5 97 K2
THDIT KT7 190 A6
TOOT SW17 160 E5
Lynwood Ter
WIM/MER SW19 * 177 J4
Lyon Meade STAN HA7 43 J4
Lyon Park Av ALP/SUD HA0 80 A4
Lyon Rd HRW HA1 61 F3
ROM RM1 75 H4
WIM/MER SW19 178 B4
WOT/HER KT12 188 D6
Lyonsdown Av BAR EN5 33 H2
Lyonsdown Rd BAR EN5 21 G6
Lyons Pl STJWD NW8 2 A7
Lyon St IS N1 85 F5
Lyons Wk WKENS W14 119 H4
Lyon Wy GFD/PVL UB6 78 E6
Lyoth Rd STMC/STPC BR5 201 H6
Lyric Dr GFD/PVL UB6 96 B3
Lyric Ms SYD SE26 163 K6
Lyric Rd BARN SW13 138 C2
Lysander CDALE/KGS NW9 * 45 H4
Lysander Gdns SURB KT6 191 G3
Lysander Gv ARCH N19 66 D5
Lysander Ms ARCH N19 66 C5
Lysander Rd CROY/NA CR0 211 F4
RSLP HA4 58 B6
Lysander Wy ORP BR6 216 C1
Lysias Rd BAL SW12 161 F1
Lysia St FUL/PGN SW6 139 G1
Lysons Wk PUT/ROE SW15 * 138 D6
Lytchet Rd BMLY BR1 183 K3
Lytchet Wy PEND EN3 24 E2
Lytchgate Cl SAND/SEL CR2 212 A5
Lytcott Dr E/WMO/HCT KT8 172 E6
Lytcott Gv EDUL SE22 143 G6
Lytham Av OXHEY WD19 41 H1
Lytham Cl THMD SE28 110 A5
Lytham St WALW SE17 122 E5
Lyttelton Rd EFNCH N2 65 G2
LEY E10 87 K1
Lyttleton Cl HAMP NW3 83 J5
Lyttleton Rd
CEND/HSY/T N8 * 49 G6
Lytton Av PEND EN3 25 G1
PLMGR N13 35 G4
Lytton Cl EFNCH N2 65 H2
NTHLT UB5 77 K5
Lytton Gdns WLGTN SM6 210 D2
Lytton Gv PUT/ROE SW15 139 G6
Lytton Rd BAR EN5 21 G5
GPK RM2 75 K2
PIN HA5 41 J3
WAN E11 70 C4
Lyveden Rd BKHTH/KID SE3 146 A1
TOOT SW17 178 D2

M

Maberley Crs NRWD SE19 181 H3
Maberley Rd BECK BR3 182 A6
NRWD SE19 181 G4
Mabledon Pl CAMTN NW1 4 D5
Mablethorpe Rd
FUL/PGN SW6 139 H1
Mabley St HOM E9 87 G3
Macaret Cl TRDG/WHET N20 33 F2
Macarthur Cl FSTGT E7 88 E4
WBLY HA9 80 D4
Macarthur Ter CHARL SE7 * 126 C6
Macaulay Av ESH/CLAY KT10 189 K6
Macaulay Rd CLAP SW4 141 G4
EHAM E6 107 H1
Macbean St
WOOL/PLUM SE18 127 F3
Macbeth St HMSMTH W6 118 E5
Macclesfield Br STJWD NW8 2 D2
Macclesfield Rd FSBYE EC1V 6 C4
SNWD SE25 197 J2
Macclesfield St
SOHO/SHAV W1D * 10 D5
Macdonald Av DAGE RM10 92 D1
Macdonald Rd ARCH N19 66 C6
FBAR/BDGN N11 47 K1
FSTGT E7 88 E2
WALTH E17 52 A5
Macduff Rd BTSEA SW11 141 F2
Mace Cl WAP E1W 123 J1
Mace St BETH E2 105 F1
Macfarlane La ISLW TW7 116 A6
Macfarlane Rd SHB W12 119 F1
Mac Farren Pl CAMTN NW1 3 H7
Macgregor Rd CAN/RD E16 107 G4
Machell Rd PECK SE15 143 K4
Mackay Rd VX/NE SW8 141 G4
Mackennal St STJWD NW8 2 D3
Mackenzie Cl SHB W12 99 K6
Mackenzie Rd BECK BR3 182 A5
HOLWY N7 85 F4
Mackeson Rd HAMP NW3 * 83 K2
Mackie Rd BRXS/STRHM SW2 162 B2
Mackintosh La HOM E9 87 F3
Macklin St HOL/ALD WC2B * 11 F3
Macks Rd BERM/RHTH SE16 123 H3
Mackworth St CAMTN NW1 4 A4
Maclean Rd FSTH SE23 164 B1
Macleod House CHARL SE7 * 146 D1
Macleod Rd WCHMH N21 22 E6
Macleod St WALW SE17 122 D5
Maclise Rd WKENS W14 119 H3
Macmillan Wy TOOT SW17 161 G6
Macoma Rd
WOOL/PLUM SE18 127 J6
Macoma Ter
WOOL/PLUM SE18 127 J6
Maconochies Rd
POP/IOD E14 * 124 E5
Macquarie Wy POP/IOD E14 124 E4
Macroom Rd MV/WKIL W9 100 D2
Mada Rd ORP BR6 216 B1
Maddams St BOW E3 105 K3
Maddison Cl EFNCH N2 47 G5
TEDD TW11 174 A2
Maddocks Cl SCUP DA14 186 E2
Maddock Wy WALW SE17 122 C6
Maddox St CONDST W1S 9 K5
Madeira Av BMLY BR1 183 H4
Madeira Gv WFD IG8 53 G2
Madeira Rd MTCM CR4 194 E1
PLMGR N13 35 H6
STRHM/NOR SW16 179 K1
WAN E11 70 B5
Madeleine Ct CHDH RM6 73 J3
CHIG IG7 54 E1
Madeley Rd EA W5 97 K6
Madeline Gv IL IG1 90 D3
Madeline Rd PGE/AN SE20 181 H3
Madge Gill Wy EHAM E6 89 J6
Madge Hl HNWL W7 * 96 E6
Madinah Rd HACK E8 86 C3
Madison Cl BELMT SM2 209 H5
Madison Crs BXLYHN DA7 148 D1
Madison Gdns BXLYHN DA7 148 D1
Madoc Cl CRICK NW2 64 D6
Madras Pl HOLWY N7 85 G4
Madras Rd IL IG1 90 B2
Madrid Rd BARN SW13 138 D2
Madron St WALW SE17 123 F5
Mafeking Av BTFD TW8 117 F6
EHAM E6 107 H1
GNTH/NBYPK IG2 72 D4
Mafeking Rd CAN/RD E16 106 D3
EN EN1 24 B4
TOTM N17 50 C5
Magazine Ga BAY/PAD W2 * 8 D7
Magdala Av ARCH N19 66 C6
Magdala Rd ISLW TW7 136 B4
SAND/SEL CR2 211 K5
Magdalene Gdns EHAM E6 108 A3
Magdalen Rd
WAND/EARL SW18 160 B3
Magdalen St STHWK SE1 19 G1
Magdelan Gv ORP BR6 217 H2
Magee St LBTH SE11 122 B6
Magellan Bvd CAN/RD E16 108 C6
Magellan Pl POP/IOD E14 124 D4
Magnaville Rd BUSH WD23 28 E2
Magnet Rd WBLY HA9 61 K6
Magnin Cl HACK E8 86 C6
Magnolia Cl KUTN/CMB KT2 175 J2
LEY E10 69 J6
Magnolia Ct
KTN/HRWW/WS HA3 62 B4
Magnolia Gdns EDGW HA8 30 E6
Magnolia Pl CLAP SW4 * 141 K6
EA W5 * 97 K4
Magnolia Rd CHSWK W4 117 J6
Magnolia St WDR/YW UB7 112 A4
Magnolia Wy HOR/WEW KT19 206 E3
Magnolia Whf CHSWK W4 * 117 J6
Magpie Cl CDALE/KGS NW9 45 G5
EN EN1 24 C2
FSTGT E7 88 D3
Magpie Hall Cl HAYES BR2 200 D3
Magpie Hall La HAYES BR2 200 D4
Magpie Hall Rd STAN HA7 28 E4
Magpie Pl NWCR SE14 * 124 B6
Magri Wk WCHPL E1 104 E4
Maguire Dr
RCHPK/HAM TW10 156 D6
Maguire St STHWK SE1 19 K2
Mahlon Av RSLP HA4 77 F3
Mahogany Cl
BERM/RHTH SE16 124 B1
Mahon Cl EN EN1 24 B2
Maida Av BAY/PAD W2 101 G4
CHING E4 37 K6
Maida Rd BELV DA17 129 H3
Maida V MV/WKIL W9 101 G2
STJWD NW8 2 A6
Maida Vale Rd DART DA1 150 D6
Maida Wy CHING E4 37 K2
Maiden Erlegh Av BXLY DA5 169 F3
Maiden La CAMTN NW1 84 D5
COVGDN WC2E 11 F5
DART DA1 150 D5
STHWK SE1 18 D1
Maiden Rd SRTFD E15 88 C5
Maidenstone Hl GNWCH SE10 145 F2
Maidstone Av CRW RM5 56 E5
Maidstone Buildings Ms
STHWK SE1 18 D1
Maidstone Rd
FBAR/BDGN N11 48 D2
SCUP DA14 186 E2
SWLY BR8 187 J4
Main Av EN EN1 24 B6
NTHWD HA6 26 A5
Main Barracks
WOOL/PLUM SE18 * 126 E5
Main Dr GFD/PVL UB6 * 97 G2
WBLY HA9 79 K1
Mainridge Rd CHST BR7 167 F6
Main Rd ORP BR6 * 217 J6
ROM RM1 75 H1
SCUP DA14 167 K5
STMC/STPC BR5 186 D4
SWLY BR8 203 K3
Main St FELT TW13 172 C1
Maise Webster Cl
STWL/WRAY TW19 * 152 A2
Maismore St PECK SE15 123 H6
The Maisonettes SUT SM1 * 208 D3
Maitland Cl GNWCH SE10 144 E1
HSLWW TW4 134 E4
WOT/HER KT12 188 D6
Maitland Park Rd HAMP NW3 83 K4
Maitland Park Vls HAMP NW3 83 K4
Maitland Rd PGE/AN SE20 182 A2
SRTFD E15 88 D4
Majendie Rd
WOOL/PLUM SE18 127 J5
Major Cl BRXN/ST SW9 142 C4
Major Draper St
WOOL/PLUM SE18 127 G3
Major Rd BERM/RHTH SE16 * 123 H3
SRTFD E15 88 A3
Makepeace Av HGT N6 66 A6
Makepeace Rd NTHLT UB5 95 J1
WAN E11 70 E1
Makins St CHEL SW3 14 D7
Malabar St POP/IOD E14 124 D2
Malam Gdns POP/IOD E14 105 K6
Malan Sq RAIN RM13 93 K4
Malbrook Rd PUT/ROE SW15 138 E5
Malcolm Cl PGE/AN SE20 * 181 K3
Malcolm Ct STAN HA7 43 J1
Malcolm Crs HDN NW4 63 J2
Malcolm Dr SURB KT6 190 E5
Malcolm Pl BETH E2 104 E3
Malcolm Rd PGE/AN SE20 181 K3
SNWD SE25 197 H3
WCHPL E1 104 E3
WIM/MER SW19 177 H2
Malcolms Wy
STHGT/OAK N14 * 22 C6
Malcolm Wy WAN E11 70 E2
Malden Av GFD/PVL UB6 78 E4
SNWD SE25 197 J1
Malden Green Av WPK KT4 192 C5
Malden Hl NWMAL KT3 192 C1
Malden Hill Gdns NWMAL KT3 176 C6
Malden Pk NWMAL KT3 192 C3
Malden Pl KTTN NW5 84 A3
Malden Rd CHEAM SM3 208 B2
KTTN NW5 83 K3
NWMAL KT3 192 B2
Malden Wy NWMAL KT3 192 A3
Maldon Cl CMBW SE5 * 143 F4
IS N1 85 J6
Maldon Rd ACT W3 98 E6
ED N9 36 B5
ROMW/RG RM7 74 E4
WLGTN SM6 210 B3
Maldon Wk WFD IG8 53 G2
Malet St GWRST WC1E 4 C7
Maley Av WNWD SE27 162 C4
Malford Gv SWFD E18 52 D6
Malfort Rd CMBW SE5 143 F4
Malham Cl FBAR/BDGN N11 48 A2
Malham Rd FSTH SE23 164 A3
Malham Ter UED N18 * 50 D2
Mallams Ms BRXN/ST SW9 142 B4
Mallard Cl BAR EN5 * 33 H1
DART DA1 151 J6
HNWL W7 115 K2
KIL/WHAMP NW6 100 E1
WHTN TW2 155 F2
Mallard Ct WALTH E17 * 52 B6
Mallard Pl TWK TW1 156 B5
WDGN N22 * 49 F5
Mallards Ct OXHEY WD19 27 K5
Mallards Rd BARK IG11 109 G2
WFD IG8 53 F3
Mallard Wk BECK BR3 198 A2
Mallard Wy CDALE/KGS NW9 62 E4
NTHWD HA6 40 A3
WLGTN SM6 210 C6
Mall Chambers KENS W8 * 119 K1
Mallet Dr NTHLT UB5 77 K3
Mallet Rd LEW SE13 165 G1
Malling Cl CROY/NA CR0 * 197 K3
Malling Gdns MRDN SM4 194 B3
Malling Wy HAYES BR2 199 J4
Mallinson Rd BTSEA SW11 140 D6
CROY/NA CR0 210 D1
Mallord St CHEL SW3 120 C6
Mallory Cl BROCKY SE4 144 B5
POP/IOD E14 105 K3
Mallory Ct LEE/GVPK SE12 166 A2
Mallory Gdns EBAR EN4 34 A2
Mallory St STJWD NW8 2 D7
Mallow Cl CROY/NA CR0 198 A5
Mallow Md MLHL NW7 46 C3
Mallow St FSBYE EC1V 6 E6
Mall Rd HMSMTH W6 118 E5
The Mall BTFD TW8 * 116 E6
BXLYHS DA6 * 149 H5
EA W5 98 A6
EMPK RM11 75 K5
KTN/HRWW/WS HA3 62 B3
MORT/ESHN SW14 137 K6
SRTFD E15 * 88 B5
STHGT/OAK N14 34 E5
SURB KT6 190 E2
WHALL SW1A 16 A2
Mall Vls HMSMTH W6 * 118 E5
Malmains Cl BECK BR3 199 G2
Malmains Wy BECK BR3 199 F1
Malmesbury Cl PIN HA5 58 D1
Malmesbury Rd BOW E3 105 H1
CAN/RD E16 106 C4
MRDN SM4 194 B4
SWFD E18 52 D4
Malmesbury Ter CAN/RD E16 106 D4
Malmesbury West Est
BOW E3 105 H2
Malory Cl BECK BR3 182 B5
Malpas Dr PIN HA5 59 H2
Malpas Rd BROCKY SE4 144 C3
DAGW RM9 91 K4
HACK E8 86 D4
Malta Rd LEY E10 69 J5
Malta St FSBYE EC1V 6 A6
Maltby Cl ORP BR6 202 B5
Maltby Dr EN EN1 24 D1
Maltby Rd CHSGTN KT9 206 C4
Maltby St STHWK SE1 19 J3
Malthouse Dr CHSWK W4 118 C6
FELT TW13 172 C1
Maltings Cl BOW E3 106 A2
Maltings Pl FUL/PGN SW6 140 A2
STHWK SE1 19 H2
The Maltings ORP BR6 202 A5
ROM RM1 75 H4
SNWD SE25 * 181 F6
Malting Wy ISLW TW7 136 A4
Malton Ms NKENS W10 * 100 C5
WOOL/PLUM SE18 127 K6
Malton Rd NKENS W10 100 C5
Malton St WOOL/PLUM SE18 127 K6
Maltravers St TPL/STR WC2R 11 H5
Malt St STHWK SE1 123 H6
Malva Cl WAND/EARL SW18 140 A6
Malvern Av BXLYHN DA7 149 F1
CHING E4 52 B3
RYLN/HDSTN HA2 77 J1
Malvern Cl BUSH WD23 28 C1
MTCM CR4 179 H6
NKENS W10 100 D4
SURB KT6 191 F5
Malvern Dr FELT TW13 172 C1
GDMY/SEVK IG3 91 F2
WFD IG8 53 G1
Malvern Gdns CRICK NW2 64 C6
KTN/HRWW/WS HA3 62 A1
LOU IG10 39 K1
Malvern Ms KIL/WHAMP NW6 100 E2
Malvern Pl MV/WKIL W9 * 100 D2
Malvern Rd CEND/HSY/T N8 49 F6
EHAM E6 89 J6
HACK E8 86 C5
HPTN TW12 173 F4
HYS/HAR UB3 133 H1
KIL/WHAMP NW6 100 E2
MV/WKIL W9 * 100 D2
ORP BR6 217 H2
SURB KT6 191 F6
THHTH CR7 196 B1
TOTM N17 50 C6
WAN E11 70 C6
Malvern Ter ED N9 36 B3
IS N1 85 G6
Malvern Wy WEA W13 97 H4
Malwood Rd BAL SW12 161 G1
Malyons Rd LEW SE13 144 E6
Malyons Ter LEW SE13 144 E6
Managers St POP/IOD E14 * 125 F1
Manaton Cl PECK SE15 143 J4
Manaton Crs STHL UB1 96 A5
Manbey Gv SRTFD E15 88 C4
Manbey Park Rd SRTFD E15 88 C4
Manbey Rd SRTFD E15 * 88 C4
Manbey St SRTFD E15 88 C4
Manbre Rd HMSMTH W6 119 F6
Manbrough Av EHAM E6 108 A2
Manchester Ct CAN/RD E16 107 F5
Manchester Dr NKENS W10 * 100 C3
Manchester Gv POP/IOD E14 125 F5
Manchester Ms MHST W1U 9 G2
Manchester Rd POP/IOD E14 125 F5
SEVS/STOTM N15 67 K3
THHTH CR7 180 D6
Manchester Sq MBLAR W1H 9 G3
Manchester St MHST W1U 9 G2
Manchester Wy DAGE RM10 * 92 D2
Manchuria Rd BTSEA SW11 161 F1
Manciple St STHWK SE1 19 F3
Mandalay Rd CLAP SW4 141 H6
Mandarin Wy YEAD UB4 95 H5
Mandela Cl WLSDN NW10 80 E5
Mandela Rd CAN/RD E16 106 E5
Mandela St BRXN/ST SW9 142 B1
CAMTN NW1 84 C6
Mandela Wy STHWK SE1 19 H6
Mandeville Cl WIM/MER SW19 177 H3
Mandeville Ct CHING E4 37 G6
Mandeville Dr SURB KT6 190 E5
Mandeville Pl MHST W1U 9 H3
Mandeville Rd ISLW TW7 136 B3
NTHLT UB5 77 K5
STHGT/OAK N14 34 B4
Mandeville St CLPT E5 87 G1
Mandrake Rd TOOT SW17 160 E5
Mandrake Wy SRTFD E15 * 88 C5
Mandrell Rd
BRXS/STRHM SW2 141 K6
Manette St LSQ/SEVD WC2H 10 D4
Manford Cross CHIG IG7 55 G1
Manford Wy CHIG IG7 54 E1
Manfred Rd PUT/ROE SW15 139 J6
Manger Rd HOLWY N7 84 E4
Mangold Wy ERITHM DA18 128 E3
Manilla St POP/IOD E14 124 D2
Manister Rd ABYW SE2 128 B3
Manley Ct STNW/STAM N16 86 B1
Manley St CAMTN NW1 84 A6
Mann Cl CROY/NA CR0 211 J1
Manningford Cl FSBYE EC1V * 6 A4
Manning Gdns CROY/NA CR0 197 J4
KTN/HRWW/WS HA3 61 K4
Manning Pl
RCHPK/HAM TW10 157 G1
Manning Rd DAGE RM10 92 C4
STMC/STPC BR5 202 E2
WALTH E17 69 G1
Manningtree Cl
WIM/MER SW19 159 H3
Manningtree Rd RSLP HA4 77 F2
Manningtree St WCHPL E1 104 C5
Mannin Rd CHDH RM6 73 H4
Mannock Cl CDALE/KGS NW9 45 F6
Mannock Ms SWFD E18 53 F4
Mannock Rd DART DA1 151 J4
WDGN N22 49 H6
Mann's Cl ISLW TW7 136 A6
Manns Rd EDGW HA8 44 C2
Manoel Rd WHTN TW2 155 H4
Manor Av BROCKY SE4 144 C3
HSLWW TW4 134 C4
NTHLT UB5 77 K5
Manorbrook BKHTH/KID SE3 145 K5
Manor Cl BAR EN5 20 C5
CDALE/KGS NW9 62 D1
DAGE RM10 93 F4

DART DA1 150 A5
MLHL NW7 * 45 F1
RDART DA2 170 D5
ROM RM1 75 J2
RSLP HA4 58 D5
THMD SE28 109 J5
WPK KT4 192 B5
Manor Cots NTHWD HA6 40 D4
Manor Cottages Ap
EFNCH N2 47 G5
Manor Ct ACT W3 * 117 H4
E/WMO/HCT KT8 * 189 F1
HRW HA1 * 61 F3
KUTN/CMB KT2 * 175 H4
WBLY HA9 * 80 A3
Manor Court Rd HNWL W7 96 E6
Manor Crs BRYLDS KT5 191 H3
Manor Cft EDGW HA8 * 44 C2
Manordene Cl THDIT KT7 190 B5
Manordene Rd THMD SE28 109 J5
Manor Dr BRYLDS KT5 191 H3
ESH/CLAY KT10 205 F1
FELT TW13 172 C1
HOR/WEW KT19 207 G4
MLHL NW7 45 F1
STHGT/OAK N14 34 B2
TRDG/WHET N20 33 J5
WBLY HA9 80 B2
Manor Dr North NWMAL KT3 192 A4
The Manor Dr WPK KT4 192 B5
Manor Est BERM/RHTH SE16 123 J4
Manor Farm Cl WPK KT4 192 B5
Manor Farm Dr CHING E4 38 C4
Manor Farm Rd ALP/SUD HA0 97 K1
STRHM/NOR SW16 180 B5
Manorfield Cl ARCH N19 84 C2
Manorfields Cl CHST BR7 186 A6
Manor Gdns ACT W3 117 H4
CLAP SW4 * 141 H3
HOLWY N7 84 E1
HPTN TW12 173 G3
RCH/KEW TW9 137 G5
RSLP HA4 77 G3
RYNPK SW20 177 J5
SAND/SEL CR2 212 B4
Manor Ga NTHLT UB5 77 J5
Manorgate Rd
KUTN/CMB KT2 175 H4
Manor Gv BECK BR3 182 E5
PECK SE15 123 K6
RCH/KEW TW9 137 H5
Manor Hall Av HDN NW4 46 A5
Manor Hall Dr HDN NW4 46 B5
Manor Hall Gdns LEY E10 69 J5
Manor House Dr
KIL/WHAMP NW6 82 B5
Manor House Wy ISLW TW7 136 C4
Manor La FELT TW13 153 K4
HYS/HAR UB3 113 G6
LEE/GVPK SE12 165 H1
LEW SE13 145 H6
SUN TW16 172 A5
SUT SM1 209 G3
Manor Lane Ter LEW SE13 145 H5
Manor Ms BROCKY SE4 144 C3
KIL/WHAMP NW6 100 E1
Manor Mt FSTH SE23 163 K3
Manor Pde HRW HA1 * 61 F3
STNW/STAM N16 * 68 B6
Manor Pk CHST BR7 185 J5
LEW SE13 145 G6
RCH/KEW TW9 137 G5
Manor Park Cl WWKM BR4 198 E5
Manor Park Crs EDGW HA8 44 C2
Manor Park Dr
RYLN/HDSTN HA2 42 B6
Manor Park Gdns EDGW HA8 44 C1
Manor Park Rd CHST BR7 185 H4
EFNCH N2 47 G6
MNPK E12 89 H2
SUT SM1 209 G3
WLSDN NW10 81 G6
WWKM BR4 198 E5
Manor Pl CHST BR7 185 J5
EBED/NFELT TW14 153 K3
MTCM CR4 179 H6
SUT SM1 209 F3
WALW SE17 122 C5
Manor Rd BAR EN5 20 C5
BARK IG11 91 F4
BECK BR3 182 D5
BELMT SM2 208 D5
BFN/LL DA15 168 A5
BXLY DA5 169 J3
CAN/RD E16 106 C4
CHDH RM6 73 K3
CHIG IG7 54 A2
DAGE RM10 92 E4
DART DA1 150 B5
E/WMO/HCT KT8 189 J1
ENC/FH EN2 23 K3
ERITH DA8 130 C6
HRW HA1 61 G3
HYS/HAR UB3 94 E5
LEY E10 69 J4
LOU IG10 39 F1
MTCM CR4 179 H6
RCH/KEW TW9 137 G4
ROM RM1 75 J2
RSLP HA4 58 B5
RYNPK SW20 177 J5
SNWD SE25 197 H1
SRTFD E15 106 C2
STNW/STAM N16 68 A5
TEDD TW11 174 B1
TOTM N17 50 C4
WALTH E17 51 G5
WDGN N22 48 E2
WEA W13 97 G6
WHTN TW2 155 H4
WLGTN SM6 210 B2
WWKM BR4 198 E5
Manor Rd North
ESH/CLAY KT10 205 F1
WLGTN SM6 210 B2
Manor Rd South
ESH/CLAY KT10 204 E2
Manorside BAR EN5 20 C5
Manor Sq BCTR RM8 73 J6
Manor V BTFD TW8 116 D5
Manor Vw FNCH N3 47 F5
Manor Wy BECK BR3 182 D6
BKHTH/KID SE3 145 K5
BXLY DA5 169 H3
BXLYHN DA7 150 A4
CDALE/KGS NW9 63 G1
CHING E4 38 B6
Manorway EN EN1 36 A2
Manor Wy FSTH SE23 163 K2
HAYES BR2 200 D3
MTCM CR4 179 H6
NWDGN UB2 114 C4
RAIN RM13 111 G3
RSLP HA4 58 C4
RYLN/HDSTN HA2 60 B1
SAND/SEL CR2 212 A4
STMC/STPC BR5 201 H1
Manorway WFD IG8 53 G1
Manor Wy WPK KT4 192 B5
The Manor Wy WLGTN SM6 210 B2
Manresa Rd CHEL SW3 120 C5
Mansard Beeches TOOT SW17 179 F1
Mansard Cl HCH RM12 75 J6
PIN HA5 41 H6
Manse Cl HYS/HAR UB3 113 G6
Mansel Gv WALTH E17 51 J4
Mansell Rd ACT W3 118 A1
GFD/PVL UB6 96 B4
Mansell St WCHPL E1 13 K4
Mansel Rd WIM/MER SW19 177 H2
Mansergh Cl CHARL SE7 146 D1
Manse Rd STNW/STAM N16 86 B1
Manser Rd RAIN RM13 111 G2
Mansfield Av EBAR EN4 33 K1
RSLP HA4 59 F5
SEVS/STOTM N15 67 K1
Mansfield Cl ED N9 36 C1
STMC/STPC BR5 202 E4
Mansfield Dr YEAD UB4 94 C3
Mansfield Hl CHING E4 37 K3
Mansfield Ms CAVSQ/HST W1G 9 J2
Mansfield Rd ACT W3 98 D3
CHSGTN KT9 205 J3
HAMP NW3 83 K3
IL IG1 72 A6
SAND/SEL CR2 211 K4
WALTH E17 69 H1
WAN E11 71 F3
Mansfield St CAVSQ/HST W1G 9 J2
Mansford St BETH E2 104 C1
Manship Rd MTCM CR4 179 F4
Mansion Cl BRXN/ST SW9 142 B2
Mansion Gdns HAMP NW3 83 F1
Mansion House Pl
MANHO EC4N * 12 E4
Mansion House St
MANHO EC4N 12 E4
The Mansions ECT SW5 * 120 A5
Manson Ms SKENS SW7 * 120 B4
Manson Pl SKENS SW7 14 A7
Manstead Gdns CHDH RM6 73 J4
RAIN RM13 111 K5
Manston Av NWDGN UB2 115 F4
Manston Cl PGE/AN SE20 181 K4
Manstone Rd CRICK NW2 82 C3
Manston Gv KUTN/CMB KT2 174 E1
Manston Wy HCH RM12 93 K4
Manthorpe Rd
WOOL/PLUM SE18 127 H5
Mantilla Rd TOOT SW17 161 F6
Mantle Rd BROCKY SE4 144 B4
Mantlet Cl STRHM/NOR SW16 179 H3
Mantle Wy SRTFD E15 88 C5
Manton Av HNWL W7 116 A2
Manton Cl HYS/HAR UB3 94 C6
Manton Rd ABYW SE2 128 B4
PEND EN3 25 J1
Mantua St BTSEA SW11 140 C4
Mantus Rd WCHPL E1 104 E3
Manus Wy TRDG/WHET N20 33 G4
Manville Gdns TOOT SW17 161 G4
Manville Rd TOOT SW17 161 F4
Manwood Rd BROCKY SE4 144 C6
Manwood St CAN/RD E16 126 E1
Many Gates BAL SW12 161 G4
Mapesbury Ms
CDALE/KGS NW9 63 J3
Mapesbury Rd CRICK NW2 82 C4
Mapeshill Pl CRICK NW2 82 A4
Mape St BETH E2 104 D3
Maple Av ACT W3 118 B1
CHING E4 51 H2
RYLN/HDSTN HA2 60 B6
Maple Cl BARK/HLT IG6 54 E2
BKHH IG9 39 H5
CLAP SW4 161 J1
FNCH N3 46 E2
HCH RM12 93 K1
HPTN TW12 172 E2
MTCM CR4 179 G4
RSLP HA4 59 F3
STMC/STPC BR5 201 J2
STNW/STAM N16 68 C3
YEAD UB4 95 H2
Maple Ct HACK E8 * 86 C4
NWMAL KT3 176 A6
Maple Crs BFN/LL DA15 168 B1
Maplecroft Cl EHAM E6 107 H5
Mapledale Av CROY/NA CR0 212 D1
Mapledene Est HACK E8 * 86 C5
Mapledene Rd HACK E8 86 B5
Maple Gdns ASHF TW15 152 B4
EDGW HA8 45 G3
Maple Gv BTFD TW8 136 C1
CDALE/KGS NW9 62 E4
EA W5 116 E3
STHL UB1 95 K4
Maplehurst Cl KUT/HW KT1 191 F1
Maple Leaf Dr BFN/LL DA15 168 A3
Mapleleafe Gdns
BARK/HLT IG6 54 B6
Maple Leaf Sq
BERM/RHTH SE16 * 124 A2
Maple Ms KIL/WHAMP NW6 * 101 F1
STRHM/NOR SW16 180 A1
Maple Pl FITZ W1T 10 B1
TOTM N17 50 C3
WDR/YW UB7 112 B1
Maple Rd DART DA1 171 F3
PGE/AN SE20 181 J4
SURB KT6 190 E2
WAN E11 70 C3
YEAD UB4 95 G2
Maples Pl WCHPL E1 * 104 D4
Maplestead Rd
BRXS/STRHM SW2 162 A2
DAGW RM9 91 H6
The Maples ESH/CLAY KT10 * 205 G5
KUT/HW KT1 * 174 D3
Maple St BETH E2 104 C1
FITZ W1T 10 A1
ROMW/RG RM7 74 E1
Maplethorpe Rd THHTH CR7 196 B1
Mapleton Cl HAYES BR2 199 K2
Mapleton Crs PEND EN3 24 E1
WAND/EARL SW18 160 A1
Mapleton Rd CHING E4 38 A5
EN EN1 24 D3
WAND/EARL SW18 159 K1
Maple Tree Pl BKHTH/KID SE3 146 D2
Maple Wk NKENS W10 * 100 B3
Maple Wy FELT TW13 153 K5
Maplin Cl WCHMH N21 35 F1
Maplin Rd CAN/RD E16 106 E5
Maplin St BOW E3 105 H2
Mapperley Dr WFD IG8 52 C3
Marabou Cl MNPK E12 89 J3
Maran Wy ERITHM DA18 128 E3
Marathon Wy THMD SE28 128 A1
Marban Rd MV/WKIL W9 100 D2
Marble Cl ACT W3 117 J1
Marble Dr CRICK NW2 64 B4
Marble Hill Cl TWK TW1 156 C2
Marble Hill Gdns TWK TW1 156 C2
Marble Quay WAP E1W 13 K7
Marbrook Ct LEE/GVPK SE12 166 B5
Marcella Rd BRXN/ST SW9 142 B3
Marcellina Wy ORP BR6 216 E1
Marcet Rd DART DA1 151 F6
Marchant Cl MLHL NW7 45 G2
Marchant Rd WAN E11 70 B6
Marchant St NWCR SE14 124 B6
Marchbank Rd WKENS W14 119 J6
Marchmont Gdns
RCHPK/HAM TW10 137 F6
Marchmont Rd
RCHPK/HAM TW10 137 G6
WLGTN SM6 210 C6
Marchmont St BMSBY WC1N 4 E6
STPAN WC1H 4 E6
March Rd TWK TW1 156 A2
Marchside Cl HEST TW5 134 C2
Marchwood Cl CMBW SE5 143 F1
Marchwood Crs EA W5 97 J5
Marcia Rd STHWK SE1 19 H7
Marcilly Rd WAND/EARL SW18 140 C6
Marconi Pl FBAR/BDGN N11 34 B6
Marconi Rd LEY E10 69 J5
Marconi Wy STHL UB1 96 B5
Marcon Pl HACK E8 86 D4
Marco Rd HMSMTH W6 118 E3
Marcus Garvey Ms EDUL SE22 163 J1
Marcus Garvey Wy
HNHL SE24 142 B5
Marcus Rd DART DA1 170 D2
Marcus St SRTFD E15 88 C6
WAND/EARL SW18 160 A1
Marcus Ter WAND/EARL SW18 160 A1
Mardale Dr CDALE/KGS NW9 63 F2
Mardell Rd CROY/NA CR0 198 A2
Marden Av HAYES BR2 199 K3
Marden Crs BXLY DA5 149 K6
CROY/NA CR0 196 A3
Marden Rd CROY/NA CR0 196 A3
ROM RM1 75 G3
TOTM N17 50 A5
Marden Sq BERM/RHTH SE16 123 J3
Marder Rd WEA W13 116 B2
Mardyke Cl RAIN RM13 110 E1
Marechal Niel Av
BFN/LL DA15 167 J5
Marechal Niel Pde
SCUP DA14 * 167 J5
Maresfield CROY/NA CR0 212 A1
Maresfield Gdns HAMP NW3 83 G3
Mare St HACK E8 86 D6
Marfield Cl WPK KT4 192 D5
Marfleet Cl CAR SM5 194 D6
Margaret Av CHING E4 37 K1
Margaret Bondfield Av
BARK IG11 91 G5
Margaret Cl GPK RM2 75 K2
Margaret Gardner Dr
ELTH/MOT SE9 166 E4
Margaret Ingram Cl
FUL/PGN SW6 * 119 J6
Margaret Lockwood Cl
KUT/HW KT1 * 191 G1
Margaret Rd BXLY DA5 168 E1
EBAR EN4 21 H5
GPK RM2 75 K2
STNW/STAM N16 * 68 B5
WAN E11 70 B3
Margaret Rutherford Pl
BAL SW12 161 H3
Margaret St GTPST W1W 10 A3
REGST W1B 9 K3
Margaretta Ter CHEL SW3 120 D6
Margaretting Rd MNPK E12 71 G6
Margaret Wy REDBR IG4 71 J3
Margate Rd
BRXS/STRHM SW2 141 K6
Margeholes OXHEY WD19 27 J4
Margery Park Rd FSTGT E7 88 E4
Margery Rd BCTR RM8 91 K1
Margery St CLKNW EC1R 5 J5
Margin Dr WIM/MER SW19 177 G1
Margravine Gdns
HMSMTH W6 119 G5
Margravine Rd HMSMTH W6 119 G6
Marguerite Vls RYNPK SW20 * 176 E3
Marham Dr CDALE/KGS NW9 45 G5
Marham Gdns MRDN SM4 194 B3
WAND/EARL SW18 160 D3
Maria Cl STHWK SE1 123 H4
Marian Cl YEAD UB4 95 H3
Marian Pl BETH E2 104 D1
Marian Rd STRHM/NOR SW16 179 H4
Marian St BETH E2 * 104 D1
Marian Wy WLSDN NW10 81 H5
Maria Ter WCHPL E1 105 F4
Maria Theresa Cl NWMAL KT3 192 A2
Maricas Av
KTN/HRWW/WS HA3 42 D4
Marie Curie CMBW SE5 * 143 F2
Marie Lloyd Wk HACK E8 * 86 C4
Mariette Wy WLGTN SM6 210 E6
Marigold Aly STHWK SE1 12 A6
Marigold Cl STHL UB1 95 J6
Marigold Rd TOTM N17 50 E3
Marigold St BERM/RHTH SE16 123 J2
Marigold Wy CROY/NA CR0 198 A5
Marina Ap YEAD UB4 95 J4
Marina Av NWMAL KT3 192 E3
Marina Dr DART DA1 171 K3
WELL DA16 147 K3
Marina Gdns ROMW/RG RM7 74 D2
Marina Pl KUT/HW KT1 174 E5
Marina Wy TEDD TW11 174 E3
Marine Ct PUR RM19 131 J4
Marine Dr BARK IG11 109 G3
WOOL/PLUM SE18 126 E4
Marinefield Rd FUL/PGN SW6 140 A3
Mariner Gdns
RCHPK/HAM TW10 156 C5
Mariner Rd MNPK E12 90 A2
Mariners Ms POP/IOD E14 125 G4
Marine St BERM/RHTH SE16 123 H3
Marion Cl BARK/HLT IG6 54 D3
Marion Crs STMC/STPC BR5 202 C2
Marion Gv WFD IG8 52 C1
Marion Ms DUL SE21 162 E5
Marion Rd MLHL NW7 45 J1
THHTH CR7 196 D2
Marischal Rd LEW SE13 145 G4
Maritime Quay POP/IOD E14 124 D5
Maritime St BOW E3 105 H3
Marius Rd TOOT SW17 161 F4
Marjorie Gv BTSEA SW11 140 E5
Mark Av CHING E4 37 K1
Mark Cl BXLYHN DA7 149 F2
HAYES BR2 215 J2
STHL UB1 115 F1
Markeston Gn OXHEY WD19 27 H6
Market Chambers
ENC/FH EN2 * 23 K4
Market Ct HOLWY N7 84 E4
Market La EDGW HA8 44 E4
SHB W12 * 119 F2
Market Link ROM RM1 75 G1
Market Meadow
STMC/STPC BR5 202 D1
Market Ms MYFR/PICC W1J 15 J1
Market Pde BMLY BR1 * 183 K4
ED N9 * 36 C4
EW KT17 * 207 H6
FELT TW13 * 154 D4
LEY E10 * 69 K3
SCUP DA14 * 168 B6
SNWD SE25 * 197 H1
STNW/STAM N16 * 68 C5
WALTH E17 * 51 H6
Market Pl ACT W3 117 K1
BERM/RHTH SE16 * 123 H4
BTFD TW8 136 D1
BXLYHS DA6 149 H5
DART DA1 171 H2
EFNCH N2 47 H6
GTPST W1W 10 A3
KUT/HW KT1 * 174 E5
ROM RM1 75 G2
Market Rd HOLWY N7 84 E4
RCH/KEW TW9 137 H4
Market Sq ED N9 36 D4
Market St EHAM E6 107 K1
WOOL/PLUM SE18 127 F4
Market Ter BTFD TW8 * 117 F6
The Market CAR SM5 * 194 B5
HNWL W7 * 116 A2
PECK SE15 * 143 H3
RCH/KEW TW9 * 136 E6
SUT SM1 * 194 B5
Market Yard Ms STHWK SE1 19 G4
Markfield Gdns CHING E4 37 K2
Markfield Rd
SEVS/STOTM N15 68 C1
Markham Pl CHEL SW3 120 E5
Markham Sq CHEL SW3 120 E5
Markham St CHEL SW3 120 D5
Markhole Cl HPTN TW12 172 E3
Markhouse Av WALTH E17 69 G3
Markhouse Pas WALTH E17 69 H3
Markhouse Rd WALTH E17 69 H3
Mark La MON EC3R 13 H5
Markmanor Av WALTH E17 69 G4
Mark Rd WDGN N22 49 H5
Marksbury Av
RCH/KEW TW9 137 H4
Marks Rd ROMW/RG RM7 74 E2
Markstone Ter ORP BR6 * 202 B4
Mark St SDTCH EC2A 7 G6
SRTFD E15 88 C5
Mark Ter RYNPK SW20 * 177 F3
Markwade Cl MNPK E12 71 H5
The Markway SUN TW16 172 B5
Markwell Cl SYD SE26 163 J6
Markyate Rd BCTR RM8 91 H3
Marlands Rd CLAY IG5 53 J6
Marlborogh Rd ISLW TW7 136 C2
Marlborough Av EDGW HA8 30 D5
HACK E8 86 C6
RSLP HA4 58 A3
STHGT/OAK N14 34 C5
Marlborough Cl ORP BR6 202 A4
TRDG/WHET N20 33 K5
WALW SE17 18 B7
WIM/MER SW19 178 D2
Marlborough Ct REGST W1B * 10 A5
Marlborough Crs CHSWK W4 118 A3
HYS/HAR UB3 133 G1
Marlborough Dr CLAY IG5 53 J6
Marlborough Gdns
TRDG/WHET N20 33 K5
Marlborough Ga BAY/PAD W2 8 A6
Marlborough Gv STHWK SE1 123 H5
Marlborough Hl HRW HA1 60 E1
STJWD NW8 83 G6
Marlborough La CHARL SE7 126 B6
Marlborough Ms
BRXS/STRHM SW2 142 A5
Marlborough Pde
FSBYPK N4 * 67 J5
Marlborough Park Av
BFN/LL DA15 168 B3
Marlborough Pl STJWD NW8 101 G1
Marlborough Rd ARCH N19 66 E6
BCTR RM8 91 J2
CHING E4 51 K2
CHSWK W4 117 K5
DART DA1 171 F1
EA W5 116 E2
ED N9 36 B3
FELT TW13 154 C4
FSTGT E7 89 G5
HAYES BR2 200 B1
HPTN TW12 173 F2
NWDGN UB2 114 B3
RCHPK/HAM TW10 157 F1
ROMW/RG RM7 74 C1
SAND/SEL CR2 211 J5
SRTFD E15 * 88 C2
SUT SM1 208 E1
SWFD E18 52 E6
WDGN N22 49 F3
WELL DA16 148 E4
WHALL SW1A 16 B1
WIM/MER SW19 178 D2
WOOL/PLUM SE18 127 G3
Marlborough St CHEL SW3 14 C7
Marlborough Yd ARCH N19 66 D6
Marler Rd FSTH SE23 164 C3
Marley Av BXLYHN DA7 128 E6
Marley Cl GFD/PVL UB6 96 A2
SEVS/STOTM N15 67 H1
Marley Rd BERM/RHTH SE16 * 124 A4
Marlingdene Cl HPTN TW12 173 F2
Marlings Cl CHST BR7 201 K1
Marlings Park Av CHST BR7 185 K6
Marlins Cl SUT SM1 * 209 G3
Marlins Meadow WATW WD18 26 B1
The Marlins NTHWD HA6 40 D2
Marloes Cl ALP/SUD HA0 79 K2
Marloes Rd KENS W8 120 A3
Marlow Av PUR RM19 131 K4
Marlow Cl PGE/AN SE20 181 J6
Marlow Ct CDALE/KGS NW9 45 H6
Marlow Crs TWK TW1 156 A1
Marlow Dr CHEAM SM3 208 B1
Marlowe Cl BARK/HLT IG6 54 C4
CHST BR7 185 J2
Marlowe Rd WALTH E17 70 A1
Marlowe Sq MTCM CR4 195 H1
The Marlowes DART DA1 150 A5
STJWD NW8 2 A1
Marlowe Wy CROY/NA CR0 195 K6
Marlow Gdns HYS/HAR UB3 113 G3
Marlow Rd EHAM E6 107 K2
NWDGN UB2 114 E3
PGE/AN SE20 181 J6
Marlow Wy BERM/RHTH SE16 124 A2
Marl Rd WAND/EARL SW18 140 A5
Marlton St GNWCH SE10 125 J5
Marlwood Cl BFN/LL DA15 167 K4
Marlyon Rd BARK/HLT IG6 55 H1
Marmadon Rd
WOOL/PLUM SE18 128 A4
Marmion Ap CHING E4 37 J6
Marmion Av CHING E4 37 H6
Marmion Cl CHING E4 37 H6
Marmion Ms BTSEA SW11 * 141 F4
Marmion Rd BTSEA SW11 141 F5
Marmont Rd PECK SE15 143 H2
Marmora Rd EDUL SE22 163 K1
Marmot Rd HSLWW TW4 134 C4
Marne Av FBAR/BDGN N11 34 B6
WELL DA16 148 B4
Marnell Wy HSLWW TW4 134 C4
Marne St NKENS W10 100 C2
Marney Rd BTSEA SW11 141 F5
Marnfield Crs
BRXS/STRHM SW2 162 A3
Marnham Av CRICK NW2 82 C2
Marnham Crs GFD/PVL UB6 96 B1
Marnock Rd BROCKY SE4 144 C6
Maroon St POP/IOD E14 105 G4
Maroons Wy CAT SE6 182 D1
Marquess Rd IS N1 85 K4
Marquess Rd South IS N1 * 85 J4
Marquis Cl ALP/SUD HA0 80 B5
Marquis Rd CAMTN NW1 84 D4
FSBYPK N4 67 F5
WDGN N22 49 F2
Marrabon Cl BFN/LL DA15 168 B3
Marrick Cl PUT/ROE SW15 138 D5
Married Quarters
EDGW HA8 * 44 D3
Marrilyne Av PEND EN3 25 H1
Marriner Ct HYS/HAR UB3 * 94 C6
Marriot Rd MUSWH N10 47 K4
Marriott Cl EBED/NFELT TW14 153 G1
Marriott Rd BAR EN5 20 B4
DART DA1 171 K2
FSBYPK N4 67 F5
SRTFD E15 88 C6
Marriotts Cl CDALE/KGS NW9 63 H3
Marriotts Yd BAR EN5 * 20 B4
Marryat Cl HSLWW TW4 134 E5
Marryat Pl WIM/MER SW19 159 H6
Marryat Rd WIM/MER SW19 177 G1
Marryfields Wy CAT SE6 164 E2
Marsala Rd LEW SE13 144 E5
Marsden Gdns DART DA1 151 J3
Marsden Rd ED N9 36 D4
PECK SE15 143 G4
Marsden St KTTN NW5 84 A4
Marsden Wy ORP BR6 217 F2
Marshall Cl FBAR/BDGN N11 34 B6
HRW HA1 60 D4
HSLWW TW4 134 E6
WAND/EARL SW18 160 B1
Marshall Dr YEAD UB4 94 D4
Marshall Est MLHL NW7 * 31 J6
Marshall Rd LEY E10 87 K2
TOTM N17 49 K4
Marshalls Dr ROM RM1 57 G6
Marshalls Gv
WOOL/PLUM SE18 126 D4
Marshall's Pl
BERM/RHTH SE16 19 K5
Marshalls Rd ROMW/RG RM7 75 F1

Marshall's Rd *SUT* SM1 ....209 F2
Marshall St *SOHO/CST* W1F 10 B4
Marshalsea Rd *STHWK* SE1 ....18 D2
Marsham Cl *CHST* BR7 * 185 G1
Marsham St *WEST* SW1P 16 D6
Marsh Av *MTCM* CR4 ....178 E5
Marshbrook Cl
BKHTH/KID SE3 ....146 C4
Marsh Cl *MLHL* NW7 ....31 H5
Marsh Dr *CDALE/KGS* NW9 ....63 H3
Marsh Farm Rd *WHTN* TW2 ....156 A3
Marshfield St *POP/IOD* E14 ....125 F3
Marsh Green Rd *DAGE* RM10 ....92 C6
Marsh Hl *HOM* E9 ....87 G3
Marsh La *LEY* E10 ....69 H6
MLHL NW7 ....31 G5
STAN HA7 ....43 J1
TOTM N17 ....50 D3
Marsh Rd *ALP/SUD* HA0 ....97 K2
PIN HA5 ....59 J1
Marshside Cl *ED* N9 ....36 E3
Marsh St *DART* DA1 ....151 K4
POP/IOD E14 * 124 E4
Marsh Ter *STMC/STPC* BR5 * 202 E1
Marsh Wall *POP/IOD* E14 ....124 D2
Marsh Wy *RAIN* RM13 ....111 F5
Marsland Cl *WALW* SE17 ....122 C5
Marston Av *CHSGTN* KT9 ....206 A4
DAGE RM10 ....92 C1
Marston Cl *DAGE* RM10 ....92 C1
KIL/WHAMP NW6 ....83 G5
Marston Ct *WOT/HER* KT12 * 188 B5
Marston Rd *CLAY* IG5 ....53 J5
TEDD TW11 ....174 C1
Marston Wy *NRWD* SE19 ....180 C3
Marsworth Av *PIN* HA5 ....41 H4
Marsworth Cl *WATW* WD18 * 26 C1
YEAD UB4 ....95 J4
Martaban Rd
STNW/STAM N16 ....68 A6
Martara Ms *WALW* SE17 ....122 D5
Martello St *HACK* E8 ....86 D5
Martell Rd *DUL* SE21 ....162 E5
Martel Pl *HACK* E8 ....86 B4
Marten Rd *WALTH* E17 ....51 J5
Martens Av *BXLYHN* DA7 ....149 K5
Martens Cl *BXLYHN* DA7 ....149 K5
Martham Cl *BARK/HLT* IG6 ....54 B4
THMD SE28 ....109 K6
Martha Rd *SRTFD* E15 ....88 C4
Martha's Blds *FSBYE* EC1V 6 E6
Martha St *WCHPL* E1 ....104 E5
Marthorne Crs
KTN/HRWW/WS HA3 ....42 D5
Martin Bowes Rd
ELTH/MOT SE9 ....146 E4
Martin Cl *ED* N9 ....37 F3
Martin Crs *CROY/NA* CR0 ....196 A5
Martindale *MORT/ESHN* SW14 ....137 K6
Martindale Av *CAN/RD* E16 ....106 E6
ORP BR6 ....217 G3
Martindale Rd *BAL* SW12 ....161 G2
HSLWW TW4 ....134 D4
Martin Dene *BXLYHS* DA6 ....149 G6
Martin Dr *NTHLT* UB5 ....77 K3
RAIN RM13 ....111 K3
Martineau Cl *ESH/CLAY* KT10 ....204 D2
Martineau Dr *TWK* TW1 ....136 C5
Martineau Rd *HBRY* N5 ....85 H2
Martingales Cl
RCHPK/HAM TW10 ....156 E5
Martin Gdns *BCTR* RM8 ....91 J2
Martin Gv *MRDN* SM4 ....177 K6
Martin La *CANST* EC4R 13 F5
Martin Ri *BXLYHS* DA6 ....149 G6
Martin Rd *BCTR* RM8 ....91 J2
RDART DA2 ....171 F5
Martins Cl *STMC/STPC* BR5 ....186 E6
WWKM BR4 ....199 G6
Martins Mt *BAR* EN5 ....20 E5
Martins Pl *THMD* SE28 ....127 K1
Martin's Rd *HAYES* BR2 ....183 H5
The Martins *SYD* SE26 ....181 J1
WBLY HA9 * 80 B1
Martin St *THMD* SE28 ....127 K1
Martins Wk *MUSWH* N10 * 48 A4
THMD SE28 ....127 K1
Martin Wy *MRDN* SM4 ....177 H6
Martlet Gv *NTHLT* UB5 ....95 H2
Martlett Ct *HOL/ALD* WC2B 11 F4
Martley Dr *GNTH/NBYPK* IG2 ....72 B2
Martock Cl
KTN/HRWW/WS HA3 ....61 G1
Martock Gdns
FBAR/BDGN N11 ....47 K1
Marton Cl *CAT* SE6 ....164 D5
Marton Rd *STNW/STAM* N16 * 68 A6
Martys Yd *HAMP* NW3 * 83 H2
Marvell Av *YEAD* UB4 ....94 E4
Marvels Cl *LEE/GVPK* SE12 ....166 A4
Marvels La *LEE/GVPK* SE12 ....166 A4
Marville Rd *FUL/PGN* SW6 ....139 J1
Marvin St *HACK* E8 * 86 D4
Marwell Cl *ROM* RM1 ....75 J3
WWKM BR4 ....199 J6
Marwood Cl *WELL* DA16 ....148 C4
Marwood Dr *MLHL* NW7 ....46 B3
Mary Adelaide Cl
PUT/ROE SW15 ....158 B5
Mary Ann Blds *DEPT* SE8 ....124 D6
Maryat Sq *FUL/PGN* SW6 ....139 H2
Maryatt Av *RYLN/HDSTN* HA2 ....60 B6
Marybank *WOOL/PLUM* SE18 ....126 E4
Mary Cl *KTN/HRWW/WS* HA3 ....62 B1
Mary Datchelor Cl
CMBW SE5 ....142 E2
Maryfield Cl *BXLY* DA5 ....170 B5
Mary Gn *STJWD* NW8 * 83 F6
Maryland Pk *SRTFD* E15 ....88 C3
Maryland Rd *MV/WKIL* W9 ....100 E3
SRTFD E15 ....88 B3
THHTH CR7 ....180 C4
WDGN N22 ....49 G2
Maryland Sq *SRTFD* E15 ....88 C3
Marylands Rd *MV/WKIL* W9 ....100 E3
Maryland St *SRTFD* E15 ....88 B3
Maryland Wk *IS* N1 * 85 J6
Mary Lawrencson Pl
BKHTH/KID SE3 ....145 K1
Marylebone F/O *BAY/PAD* W2 ....8 C2
Marylebone High St
CAVSQ/HST W1G 9 H2
Marylebone La *MHST* W1U 9 H3
Marylebone Ms
CAVSQ/HST W1G 9 H2
Marylebone Pas *GTPST* W1W 10 B3
Marylebone Rd *CAMTN* NW1 ....3 F7
MBLAR W1H 8 D1
Marylebone St
CAVSQ/HST W1G 9 H2
Marylee Wy *LBTH* SE11 ....17 H7
Mary Neuner Rd *WDGN* N22 ....49 F6
Maryon Gv *CHARL* SE7 ....126 D4
Maryon Ms *HAMP* NW3 ....83 J2
Maryon Rd *CHARL* SE7 ....126 D4
Mary Peters Dr *GFD/PVL* UB6 ....78 D3
Mary Pl *NTGHL* W11 ....100 C6
Mary Rose Cl *HPTN* TW12 ....173 F4
Maryrose Wy
TRDG/WHET N20 ....33 H3
Mary Seacole Cl *HACK* E8 ....86 B6
Mary's Ter *TWK* TW1 ....156 B2
Mary St *CAN/RD* E16 ....106 D4
IS N1 ....6 D1
Mary Ter *CAMTN* NW1 ....4 A1
Mary Wy *OXHEY* WD19 ....27 G6
Masbro' Rd *WKENS* W14 ....119 G3
Mascalls Rd *CHARL* SE7 ....126 B6
Mascotts Cl *CRICK* NW2 ....81 K1
Masefield Av *STAN* HA7 ....43 F1
STHL UB1 ....96 A6
Masefield Cl *ERITH* DA8 ....150 C2
HARH RM3 ....57 K4
Masefield Crs *STHGT/OAK* N14 ....22 C6
Masefield Gdns *EHAM* E6 ....108 A3
Masefield La *YEAD* UB4 ....95 F3
Masefield Rd *HPTN* TW12 ....154 E6
Masefield Vw *ORP* BR6 ....216 C1
Masefield Wy
STWL/WRAY TW19 ....152 C3
Mashie Rd *ACT* W3 ....99 G5
Mashiters Hl *ROM* RM1 ....57 F4
Mashiters Wk *ROM* RM1 ....57 G6
Maskall Cl *BRXS/STRHM* SW2 * 162 B3
Maskell Rd *TOOT* SW17 ....160 B5
Maskelyne Cl *BTSEA* SW11 ....140 D2
Mason Cl *BERM/RHTH* SE16 ....123 H5
BXLYHN DA7 ....149 J4
CAN/RD E16 ....106 E6
HPTN TW12 ....172 E4
RYNPK SW20 ....177 G4
Mason Ct *WBLY* HA9 * 62 C6
Mason Rd *SUT* SM1 ....209 F3
WFD IG8 ....38 C6
Mason's Arms Ms
CONDST W1S * 9 K4
Masons Av
KTN/HRWW/WS HA3 ....42 E6
Mason's Av *CITYW* EC2V 12 E3
CROY/NA CR0 ....211 J1
Masons Ct *EW* KT17 * 207 J6
Masons Hl *BMLY* BR1 ....183 K6
WOOL/PLUM SE18 ....127 G4
Mason's Pl *FSBYE* EC1V 6 B4
MTCM CR4 ....178 E4
Mason St *WALW* SE17 ....19 F6
Masons Yd *FSBYE* EC1V 6 C6
STJS SW1Y 10 B7
Massey Cl *FBAR/BDGN* N11 ....48 B1
Massie Rd *HACK* E8 ....86 C4
Massingberd Wy *TOOT* SW17 ....161 G6
Massinger St *WALW* SE17 ....19 G7
Massingham St *WCHPL* E1 ....105 F3
Masson Av *RSLP* HA4 ....77 G4
Masterman Rd *EHAM* E6 ....107 J2
Masters Cl *STRHM/NOR* SW16 ....179 H2
Masters Dr *BERM/RHTH* SE16 ....123 J5
Master's St *WCHPL* E1 ....105 F4
Masthouse Ter *POP/IOD* E14 ....124 D4
Mast House Ter
POP/IOD E14 * 124 D4
Mastmaker Rd *POP/IOD* E14 ....124 D2
Mast Quay *WOOL/PLUM* SE18 ....126 E3
Maswell Park Crs *HSLW* TW3 ....135 H5
Maswell Park Rd *HSLW* TW3 ....135 G6
Matcham Rd *WAN* E11 ....88 C1
Matchless Dr
WOOL/PLUM SE18 ....147 F1
Matfield Cl *HAYES* BR2 ....199 K2
Matfield Rd *BELV* DA17 ....129 H6
Matham Gv *EDUL* SE22 ....143 G5
Matham Rd *E/WMO/HCT* KT8 ....189 J2
Matheson Rd *WKENS* W14 ....119 J4
Mathews Av *EHAM* E6 ....108 A1
Mathews Park Av *SRTFD* E15 ....88 D4
Mathews Yd
LSQ/SEVD WC2H * 10 E4
Mathieson Ct *STHWK* SE1 ....18 B3
Matilda Cl *NRWD* SE19 ....180 E3
Matilda Gdns *BOW* E3 ....105 J1
Matilda St *IS* N1 ....5 H1
Matlock Cl *BAR* EN5 ....20 B6
HNHL SE24 ....142 D5
Matlock Crs *CHEAM* SM3 ....208 C2
OXHEY WD19 ....27 G5
Matlock Gdns *CHEAM* SM3 ....208 C2
Matlock Pl *CHEAM* SM3 ....208 C2
Matlock Rd *LEY* E10 ....70 A3
Matlock St *POP/IOD* E14 ....105 G5
Matlock Wy *NWMAL* KT3 ....176 A4
Mattellen Cl *WIM/MER* SW19 ....159 H4
Matthew Cl *NKENS* W10 * 100 B3
Matthew Ct *MTCM* CR4 ....195 J2
Matthews Rd *GFD/PVL* UB6 ....78 D3
Matthews St *BTSEA* SW11 * 140 E3
Matthias Rd *STNW/STAM* N16 ....85 K3
Mattingly Wy *PECK* SE15 ....143 G1
Mattison Rd *FSBYPK* N4 ....67 G3
Mattock La *WEA* W13 ....116 C1
Maud Cashmore Wy
WOOL/PLUM SE18 ....126 E3
Maude Rd *CMBW* SE5 ....143 F3
WALTH E17 ....69 G2
Maudesville Cots *HNWL* W7 ....115 K1
Maude Ter *WALTH* E17 ....69 G1
Maud Gdns *BARK* IG11 ....109 F1
PLSTW E13 ....106 D1
Maudlins Gn *WAP* E1W * 123 H1
Maud Rd *LEY* E10 ....88 A1
PLSTW E13 ....106 D1
Maudslay Rd *ELTH/MOT* SE9 ....146 E4
Maud St *CAN/RD* E16 ....106 D4
Maud Wilkes Cl *KTTN* NW5 ....84 C3
Maugham Wy *ACT* W3 ....117 K3
Mauleverer Rd
BRXS/STRHM SW2 ....141 K6
Maundeby Wk
WLSDN NW10 * 81 G3
Maunder Rd *HNWL* W7 ....115 K1
Maunsel St *WEST* SW1P 16 C6
Maurice Av *WDGN* N22 ....49 H5
Maurice Browne Cl
MLHL NW7 ....46 B1
Maurice St *SHB* W12 ....99 K5
Maurice Wk *GLDGN* NW11 ....65 G1
Maurier Cl *NTHLT* UB5 ....77 G6
Mauritius Rd *GNWCH* SE10 ....125 H4
Maury Rd *STNW/STAM* N16 ....68 C6
Mauveine Gdns *HSLW* TW3 ....135 F5
Mavelstone Rd *BMLY* BR1 ....184 C4
Maverton Rd *BOW* E3 * 87 J6
Mavis Av *HOR/WEW* KT19 ....207 G3
Mavis Cl *HOR/WEW* KT19 ....207 G3
Mawbey Pl *STHWK* SE1 ....123 G5
Mawbey Rd *STHWK* SE1 ....123 G5
Mawbey St *VX/NE* SW8 ....141 K1
Mawney Cl *ROMW/RG* RM7 ....56 D6
Mawney Rd *ROMW/RG* RM7 ....56 D5
ROMW/RG RM7 ....75 F2
Mawson Cl *RYNPK* SW20 ....177 H5
Mawson La *CHSWK* W4 ....118 C6
Maxey Gdns *DAGW* RM9 ....92 A2
Maxey Rd *DAGW* RM9 ....92 A2
WOOL/PLUM SE18 ....127 H4
Maxfield Cl *TRDG/WHET* N20 ....33 G2
Maxilla Wk *NKENS* W10 ....100 B5
Maximfeldt Rd *ERITH* DA8 ....130 B5
Maxim Rd *DART* DA1 ....150 B6
ERITH DA8 ....130 B5
WCHMH N21 ....35 G1
Maxted Pk *HRW* HA1 ....60 E4
Maxted Rd *PECK* SE15 ....143 G4
Maxwell Cl *CROY/NA* CR0 ....195 K5
HYS/HAR UB3 ....94 E6
Maxwell Gdns *ORP* BR6 ....217 F1
Maxwell Ri *OXHEY* WD19 ....27 J2
Maxwell Rd *FUL/PGN* SW6 ....140 A1
NTHWD HA6 ....40 B3
WDR/YW UB7 ....112 B4
WELL DA16 ....148 B5
Maxwelton Av *MLHL* NW7 ....45 F1
Maxwelton Cl *MLHL* NW7 ....45 F1
Maya Cl *PECK* SE15 ....143 J3
Mayall Cl *PEND* EN3 ....25 J1
STHWK SE1 ....18 D1
Mayall Rd *HNHL* SE24 ....142 C6
Maya Pl *FBAR/BDGN* N11 ....48 D3
Maya Rd *EFNCH* N2 ....65 G1
May Av *STMC/STPC* BR5 ....202 C2
Maybank Av *ALP/SUD* HA0 ....79 G3
HCH RM12 ....93 K3
SWFD E18 ....53 F5
Maybank Gdns *PIN* HA5 ....58 E2
Maybank Rd *SWFD* E18 ....53 G4
May Bate Av *KUTN/CMB* KT2 ....174 E4
Mayberry Pl *BRYLDS* KT5 ....191 G4
Maybourne Cl *SYD* SE26 ....181 J1
Maybury Cl *EN* EN1 ....24 D1
STMC/STPC BR5 ....201 G2
Maybury Gdns *WLSDN* NW10 ....81 J5
Maybury Ms *HGT* N6 ....66 C4
Maybury Rd *BARK* IG11 ....109 G1
PLSTW E13 ....107 G3
Maybury St *TOOT* SW17 ....178 D1
Maychurch Cl *STAN* HA7 ....43 K4
May Cl *CHSGTN* KT9 ....206 B4
Maycock Gv *NTHWD* HA6 ....40 D2
Maycroft *PIN* HA5 ....41 F5
Maycross Av *MRDN* SM4 ....193 J1
Mayday Gdns *BKHTH/KID* SE3 ....146 D3
Mayday Rd *THHTH* CR7 ....196 C3
Mayefield Rd *THHTH* CR7 ....196 A1
Mayerne Rd *ELTH/MOT* SE9 ....146 C6
Mayesbrook Rd *BARK* IG11 ....91 F6
GDMY/SEVK IG3 ....91 G1
Mayesford Rd *CHDH* RM6 ....73 J4
Mayes Rd *WDGN* N22 ....49 F5
Mayeswood Rd
LEE/GVPK SE12 ....166 B6
Mayfair Av *BXLYHN* DA7 ....148 E2
CHDH RM6 ....73 K3
IL IG1 ....71 K6
WHTN TW2 ....155 H2
WPK KT4 ....192 D5
Mayfair Cl *BECK* BR3 ....182 E4
SURB KT6 ....191 F5
Mayfair Ct *EDGW* HA8 ....44 B1
Mayfair Gdns *TOTM* N17 ....49 J2
WFD IG8 ....52 E3
Mayfair Ms *CAMTN* NW1 * 83 K5
Mayfair Pl *MYFR/PICC* W1J 9 K7
Mayfair Rd *DART* DA1 ....151 G6
Mayfair Ter *STHGT/OAK* N14 ....34 D2
Mayfield *BXLYHN* DA7 ....149 G4
Mayfield Av *CHSWK* W4 ....118 B4
KTN/HRWW/WS HA3 ....61 H2
NFNCH/WDSPK N12 ....33 G6
ORP BR6 ....202 A5
STHGT/OAK N14 ....34 C4
WEA W13 ....116 C3
WFD IG8 ....52 E2
Mayfield Cl *CLAP* SW4 ....141 J6
HACK E8 ....86 B5
PGE/AN SE20 ....181 J4
THDIT KT7 ....190 C5
Mayfield Crs *ED* N9 ....36 D1
THHTH CR7 ....196 A1
Mayfield Dr *PIN* HA5 ....59 K1
Mayfield Gdns *HDN* NW4 ....64 B3
HNWL W7 ....96 D5
Mayfield Rd *ACT* W3 ....98 D6
BCTR RM8 ....73 J5
BELMT SM2 ....209 H4
BELV DA17 ....129 K4
BMLY BR1 ....200 D2
CEND/HSY/T N8 ....67 F3
CHING E4 ....38 A4
HACK E8 * 86 B5
PEND EN3 ....25 F3
PLSTW E13 ....106 D3
SAND/SEL CR2 ....211 K6
SHB W12 ....118 B2
WALTH E17 ....51 G5
WIM/MER SW19 ....177 J4
Mayfields *WBLY* HA9 ....62 C6
Mayfields Cl *WBLY* HA9 ....62 C6
Mayfield Vls *SCUP* DA14 * 186 D2
Mayflower Cl
BERM/RHTH SE16 ....124 A4
RSLP HA4 ....58 A3
Mayflower Rd *BRXN/ST* SW9 ....141 K4
Mayflower St
BERM/RHTH SE16 ....123 K2
Mayfly Cl *PIN* HA5 ....59 G4
STMC/STPC BR5 ....202 E1
Mayford Cl *BAL* SW12 ....160 E2
BECK BR3 ....182 A6
Mayford Rd *BAL* SW12 ....160 E2
May Gdns *ALP/SUD* HA0 ....97 J2
Maygood St *IS* N1 ....5 H2
Maygreen Crs *EMPK* RM11 ....75 J4
Maygrove Rd
KIL/WHAMP NW6 ....82 D4
Mayhew Cl *CHING* E4 ....37 J5
Mayhill Rd *BAR* EN5 ....20 C6
CHARL SE7 ....126 A6
Maylands Av *HCH* RM12 ....93 K2
Maylands Dr *SCUP* DA14 ....168 E5
Maylands Rd *OXHEY* WD19 ....27 G6
Maynard Cl *ERITH* DA8 ....150 C1
FUL/PGN SW6 ....140 A1
SEVS/STOTM N15 ....68 A2
Maynard Rd *WALTH* E17 ....70 A2
Maynards Quay *WAP* E1W * 104 E6
Maynooth Gdns *CAR* SM5 ....194 E4
Mayola Rd *CLPT* E5 ....86 E2
Mayo Rd *CROY/NA* CR0 ....196 E2
WLSDN NW10 ....81 G4
Mayow Rd *SYD* SE26 ....164 A6
Mayplace Av *DART* DA1 ....150 D5
Mayplace Cl *BXLYHN* DA7 ....149 J4
Mayplace La
WOOL/PLUM SE18 ....127 G6
Mayplace Rd *BXLYHN* DA7 ....149 K4
Mayplace Rd East
BXLYHN DA7 ....149 J4
Mayplace Rd West
BXLYHN DA7 ....149 H5
Maypole Crs *BARK/HLT* IG6 ....54 D3
ERITH DA8 ....131 G6
May Rd *CHING* E4 ....51 J2
PLSTW E13 ....106 E1
RDART DA2 ....171 J6
WHTN TW2 ....155 K3
Mayroyd Av *SURB* KT6 ....191 H6
May's Buildings Ms
GNWCH SE10 ....145 G1
Mays Ct *CHCR* WC2N 10 E6
May's Hill Rd *HAYES* BR2 ....183 H5
May's La *BAR* EN5 ....20 D6
BAR EN5 ....31 K2
Maysoule Rd *BTSEA* SW11 ....140 C5
Mays Rd *TEDD* TW11 ....173 J1
Mayston Ms *BKHTH/KID* SE3 ....125 K5
May St *WKENS* W14 ....119 J5
Mayswood Gdns *DAGE* RM10 ....92 E4
Maythorne Cots *LEW* SE13 ....165 G1
Mayton St *HOLWY* N7 ....85 F1
Maytree Cl *EDGW* HA8 ....30 E5
RAIN RM13 ....111 G1
Maytree Ct *MTCM* CR4 ....179 F6
Maytree La *STAN* HA7 ....43 F2
Maytree Wk
BRXS/STRHM SW2 * 162 B4
Mayville Est
STNW/STAM N16 * 86 A3
Mayville Rd *IL* IG1 ....90 B3
WAN E11 ....70 C6
Maywood Cl *BECK* BR3 ....182 E3
Maze Hl *BKHTH/KID* SE3 ....145 J1
GNWCH SE10 ....125 H6
Mazenod Av
KIL/WHAMP NW6 ....82 E5
Maze Rd *RCH/KEW* TW9 ....137 H1
McAdam Dr *ENC/FH* EN2 ....23 H3
McAuley Cl *ELTH/MOT* SE9 ....147 F6
STHWK SE1 ....17 J4
McCall Cl *CLAP* SW4 ....141 K3
McCall Crs *CHARL* SE7 ....126 D5
McCarthy Rd *FELT* TW13 ....172 C1
McCold Wy *STHWK* SE1 ....18 C3
McCrone Ms *HAMP* NW3 ....83 H4
McCudden Rd *DART* DA1 ....151 J4
McCullum Rd *BOW* E3 ....87 H6
McDermott Cl *BTSEA* SW11 ....140 D3
McDermott Rd *PECK* SE15 ....143 H4
McDonough Cl *CHSGTN* KT9 ....206 A2
McDougall Ct
RCH/KEW TW9 ....137 H3
McDowall Cl *CAN/RD* E16 ....106 E4
McDowall Rd *CMBW* SE5 ....142 D2
McEntee Av *WALTH* E17 ....51 G4
McEwan Wy *SRTFD* E15 * 88 B6
McGrath Rd *SRTFD* E15 ....88 D3
McGregor Rd *NTGHL* W11 ....100 D5
McIntosh Cl *ROM* RM1 ....57 G6
WLGTN SM6 ....210 E5
McIntosh Rd *ROM* RM1 ....57 G6
McKay Rd *RYNPK* SW20 ....176 E3
McKellar Cl *BUSH* WD23 ....28 C4
McKerrell Rd *PECK* SE15 ....143 H2
McKillop Wy *SCUP* DA14 ....186 D3
McLeod Rd *ABYW* SE2 ....128 D4
McLeod's Ms *SKENS* SW7 ....120 A3
McMillan St *DEPT* SE8 ....124 D6
McNair Rd *NWDGN* UB2 ....115 F3
McNeil Rd *CMBW* SE5 ....143 F3
McNicol Dr *WLSDN* NW10 ....98 E1
McRae La *MTCM* CR4 ....194 E4
Mead Cl *CAMTN* NW1 ....84 A5
GPK RM2 ....57 J5
KTN/HRWW/WS HA3 ....42 D4
Mead Ct *CDALE/KGS* NW9 ....62 E2
Mead Crs *CHING* E4 ....38 A6
DART DA1 ....171 G3
SUT SM1 ....209 J2
Meadcroft Rd *LBTH* SE11 ....122 B6
Meade Cl *CHSWK* W4 ....117 H6
Meadfield *EDGW* HA8 ....30 D4
Mead Fld *RYLN/HDSTN* HA2 * 77 K1
Meadfoot Rd
STRHM/NOR SW16 ....179 H4
Meadgate Av *WFD* IG8 ....53 J1
Mead Gv *CHDH* RM6 ....55 K6
Mead House La *YEAD* UB4 ....94 B3
Meadlands Dr
RCHPK/HAM TW10 ....156 E4
Meadow Av *CROY/NA* CR0 ....198 A3
Meadowbank *BKHTH/KID* SE3 ....145 J4
BRYLDS KT5 ....191 G3
HAMP NW3 ....83 K5
OXHEY WD19 ....27 G2
WCHMH N21 ....35 F1
Meadowbank Cl
FUL/PGN SW6 ....139 F1
ISLW TW7 ....135 K2
Meadowbank Gdns
HSLWW TW4 ....133 K3
Meadowbank Rd
CDALE/KGS NW9 ....63 F4
Meadow Cl *BAR* EN5 ....32 D1
BARK IG11 ....91 F5
BXLYHS DA6 ....149 G6
CAT SE6 ....182 D1
CHING E4 ....37 K3
CHST BR7 ....185 G1
ESH/CLAY KT10 ....205 F1
HOM E9 ....87 H3
HSLWW TW4 ....155 F1
NTHLT UB5 ....96 A1
PEND EN3 ....25 G2
RCHPK/HAM TW10 ....157 F3
RSLP HA4 ....58 D3
RYNPK SW20 ....193 F1
Meadowcourt Rd
BKHTH/KID SE3 ....145 J5
Meadow Cft *BMLY* BR1 ....184 E6
Meadowcroft *BUSH* WD23 * 28 B1
Meadowcroft Cl
PLMGR N13 * 35 H4
Meadowcroft Rd *PLMGR* N13 ....35 G4
Meadow Dr *HDN* NW4 ....46 A5
MUSWH N10 ....48 A6
Meadowford Cl *THMD* SE28 ....109 G6
Meadow Gdns *EDGW* HA8 ....44 D2
Meadow Garth *WLSDN* NW10 ....80 E4
Meadow Hl *NWMAL* KT3 ....192 B3
Meadow La *LEE/GVPK* SE12 ....166 B5
Meadowlea Cl *WDR/YW* UB7 ....112 A6
Meadow Ms *VX/NE* SW8 ....122 A6
Meadow Pl *CHSWK* W4 * 138 B1
VX/NE SW8 ....141 K1
Meadow Rd *BARK* IG11 ....91 F5
DAGW RM9 ....92 B4
ESH/CLAY KT10 ....204 E3
FELT TW13 ....154 D4
HAYES BR2 ....183 H4
PIN HA5 ....59 H1
ROMW/RG RM7 ....74 E5
STHL UB1 ....95 K6
SUT SM1 ....209 J2
VX/NE SW8 ....122 A6
WIM/MER SW19 ....178 B3
Meadow Rw *STHWK* SE1 ....18 C5
Meadows Cl *LEY* E10 ....69 J6
Meadowside *BKHTH/KID* SE3 ....146 B5
DART DA1 ....171 H3
TWK TW1 ....156 E2
WOT/HER KT12 ....188 B6
Meadowside Rd *BELMT* SM2 ....208 C6
The Meadows *ORP* BR6 ....217 J4
Meadow Stile *CROY/NA* CR0 ....211 J1
Meadowsweet Cl
CAN/RD E16 ....107 H4
NWMAL KT3 ....193 F2
The Meadow *CHST* BR7 ....185 H2
Meadow Vw *BFN/LL* DA15 ....168 C1
HRW HA1 ....60 E5
STMC/STPC BR5 ....186 D6
Meadowview Rd *BXLY* DA5 ....169 F1
CAT SE6 ....164 D6
HOR/WEW KT19 ....207 G6
Meadow View Rd *THHTH* CR7 ....196 C2
YEAD UB4 ....94 B3
Meadow Wk *DAGW* RM9 ....92 B4
HOR/WEW KT19 ....207 G4
RDART DA2 ....171 F6
SWFD E18 ....70 E1
WLGTN SM6 ....210 B1
Meadow Wy *CDALE/KGS* NW9 ....63 F2
CHSGTN KT9 ....206 A3
ORP BR6 ....216 A1
RSLP HA4 ....59 F3
WBLY HA9 ....79 K2
Meadow Waye *HEST* TW5 ....134 D1
The Meadow Wy
KTN/HRWW/WS HA3 ....42 E4
Mead Pl *CROY/NA* CR0 ....196 C5
HOM E9 ....86 E4
Mead Plat *WLSDN* NW10 ....80 E4
Mead Rd *CHST* BR7 ....185 H2
DART DA1 ....171 G3
EDGW HA8 ....44 C2
RCHPK/HAM TW10 ....156 D5
Mead Rw *STHWK* SE1 ....17 J4
Meadside Cl *BECK* BR3 ....182 B4
Meads La *GDMY/SEVK* IG3 ....73 F4
Meads Rd *PEND* EN3 ....25 G2
WDGN N22 ....49 H5
The Meads *CHEAM* SM3 ....208 B1
EDGW HA8 ....45 F2
MRDN SM4 * 194 D2
The Mead *BECK* BR3 ....183 F5
EFNCH N2 ....47 G5
OXHEY WD19 ....27 J5
WEA W13 ....97 H4
WLGTN SM6 ....210 D4
WWKM BR4 ....199 G5
Meadvale Rd *CROY/NA* CR0 ....197 G4
EA W5 ....97 H3
Mead Wy *CROY/NA* CR0 ....198 B6
HAYES BR2 ....199 J3
RSLP HA4 ....58 B3
Meadway *ASHF* TW15 ....152 D6
BAR EN5 ....20 E5
BECK BR3 ....183 F4
BRYLDS KT5 ....191 K5
ESH/CLAY KT10 ....204 B6
GDMY/SEVK IG3 ....90 E2
GLDGN NW11 ....65 F3

GPK RM2 57 J5
RYNPK SW20 193 F1
STHGT/OAK N14 34 D4
WFD IG8 53 G1
WHTN TW2 155 J3
Meadway Cl BAR EN5 20 E4
GLDGN NW11 65 F3
PIN HA5 42 B2
Meadway Ct EA W5 * 98 B4
Meadway Gdns RSLP HA4 58 B3
The Meadway BKHH IG9 39 H3
BKHTH/KID SE3 145 G3
ORP BR6 217 H3
Meaford Wy PGE/AN SE20 181 J3
Meanley Rd MNPK E12 89 J3
Meard St SOHO/CST W1F 10 C4
Meath Cl STMC/STPC BR5 202 C2
Meath Crs BETH E2 105 F2
Meath Rd IL IG1 90 C1
SRTFD E15 106 D1
Meath St BTSEA SW11 141 G2
Mecklenburgh Pl
BMSBY WC1N 5 G6
Mecklenburgh Sq
BMSBY WC1N 5 G6
Mecklenburgh St
BMSBY WC1N 5 G6
Medburn St CAMTN NW1 4 C2
Medcroft Gdns
MORT/ESHN SW14 137 K5
Medebourne Cl
BKHTH/KID SE3 145 K4
Medesenge Wy PLMGR N13 49 H2
Medfield St PUT/ROE SW15 158 D2
Medhurst Cl BOW E3 105 G1
Medhurst Dr BMLY BR1 183 H1
Median Rd CLPT E5 86 E3
Medici Cl GDMY/SEVK IG3 73 G3
Medina Av ESH/CLAY KT10 204 E1
Medina Rd HOLWY N7 85 G1
Medland Cl WLGTN SM6 195 F5
Medlar Cl NTHLT UB5 95 H1
Medlar St CMBW SE5 142 D2
Medley Rd KIL/WHAMP NW6 82 E4
Medora Rd BRXS/STRHM SW2 162 A1
ROMW/RG RM7 75 F1
Medusa Rd CAT SE6 164 E1
Medway Cl CROY/NA CR0 197 K3
IL IG1 90 C3
Medway Dr GFD/PVL UB6 97 F1
Medway Gdns ALP/SUD HA0 79 G3
Medway Pde GFD/PVL UB6 * 97 F1
Medway Rd BOW E3 105 G1
DART DA1 150 D4
Medway St WEST SW1P 16 C5
Medwin St CLAP SW4 142 A5
Meerbrook Rd
BKHTH/KID SE3 146 B4
Meeson Rd SRTFD E15 88 D5
Meeson St CLPT E5 87 G2
Meesons Whf SRTFD E15 * 106 A1
Meeting Field Pth HOM E9 * 86 E4
Meeting House Aly
WAP E1W * 123 J1
Meeting House La PECK SE15 143 J2
Mehetabel Rd HOM E9 86 E4
Meister Cl IL IG1 72 D5
Melanda Cl CHST BR7 184 E1
Melanie Cl BXLYHN DA7 149 F2
Melbourne Av PIN HA5 42 B6
WDGN N22 49 F2
WEA W13 116 B1
Melbourne Cl ORP BR6 201 K4
WLGTN SM6 210 C3
Melbourne Gdns CHDH RM6 74 A2
Melbourne Gv EDUL SE22 143 F5
Melbourne Ms BRXN/ST SW9 142 B2
CAT SE6 165 F2
Melbourne Pl HOL/ALD WC2B 11 H4
Melbourne Rd BUSH WD23 28 B1
EHAM E6 89 K6
IL IG1 72 B5
LEY E10 69 K4
TEDD TW11 174 D2
WALTH E17 69 G1
WIM/MER SW19 177 K4
WLGTN SM6 210 B3
Melbourne Sq BRXN/ST SW9 142 B2
Melbourne Ter EDUL SE22 * 143 F5
FUL/PGN SW6 * 140 A1
Melbourne Wy EN EN1 36 B1
Melbury Av NWDGN UB2 115 G3
Melbury Cl CHST BR7 184 E2
ESH/CLAY KT10 205 H4
Melbury Ct KENS W8 119 J3
Melbury Dr CMBW SE5 143 F1
Melbury Gdns RYNPK SW20 176 E4
Melbury Rd
KTN/HRWW/WS HA3 62 B2
WKENS W14 119 J3
Melbury Ter CAMTN NW1 2 D7
Melcombe Gdns
KTN/HRWW/WS HA3 62 B3
Melcombe Pl CAMTN NW1 8 E1
Melcombe St CAMTN NW1 3 F7
Meldex Cl MLHL NW7 46 A2
Meldon Cl FUL/PGN SW6 * 140 A2
Meldone Cl BRYLDS KT5 191 J3
Meldrum Cl STMC/STPC BR5 202 D3
Meldrum Rd GDMY/SEVK IG3 73 G6
Melfield Gdns CAT SE6 164 E6
Melford Av BARK IG11 90 D4
Melford Cl CHSGTN KT9 206 B3
Melford Rd EDUL SE22 163 H3
EHAM E6 107 K3
IL IG1 72 D6
WALTH E17 69 G1
WAN E11 70 C6
Melfort Av THHTH CR7 180 C6
Melfort Rd THHTH CR7 180 C6
Melgund Rd HBRY N5 85 G3
Melina Cl HYS/HAR UB3 94 B4
Melina Pl STJWD NW8 2 A5
Melina Rd SHB W12 118 E2
Melior Pl STHWK SE1 * 19 G2
Melior St STHWK SE1 19 F2
Meliot Rd CAT SE6 165 G4
Meller Cl CROY/NA CR0 211 F2
Mellifont Cl MRDN SM4 194 C3
Melling Dr EN EN1 24 C2
Melling St WOOL/PLUM SE18 127 K6
Mellish Gdns WFD IG8 52 E1
Mellish St POP/IOD E14 124 D3
Mellison Rd TOOT SW17 178 D1
Melliss Av RCH/KEW TW9 137 J2
Mellitus St SHB W12 99 H5
Mellor Cl WOT/HER KT12 188 E4
Mellow La East
HGDN/ICK UB10 94 A3
Mellows Rd CLAY IG5 53 K6
WLGTN SM6 210 D3
Mells Crs ELTH/MOT SE9 166 E6
Mell St GNWCH SE10 125 H5
Melody La HBRY N5 85 H3
Melody Rd WAND/EARL SW18 140 B6
Melon Pl KENS W8 119 K2
Melon Rd PECK SE15 143 H2
WAN E11 88 C1
Melrose Av CRICK NW2 82 A3
DART DA1 170 B2
GFD/PVL UB6 96 B1
MTCM CR4 179 G3
STRHM/NOR SW16 180 A6
WDGN N22 49 H4
WHTN TW2 155 G2
WIM/MER SW19 159 J4
Melrose Cl GFD/PVL UB6 96 B1
LEE/GVPK SE12 165 K3
YEAD UB4 94 E4
Melrose Crs ORP BR6 216 D2
Melrose Dr STHL UB1 115 F1
Melrose Gdns EDGW HA8 44 D6
HMSMTH W6 119 F3
NWMAL KT3 176 A6
Melrose Ms NWMAL KT3 176 A6
Melrose Rd BARN SW13 138 C3
PIN HA5 59 K1
WAND/EARL SW18 159 J1
WIM/MER SW19 177 K5
Melrose Ter HMSMTH W6 119 F2
Melrose Vls BECK BR3 * 182 D5
Melsa Rd MRDN SM4 194 B3
Melthorne Dr RSLP HA4 77 G1
Melthorpe Gdns
BKHTH/KID SE3 146 C2
Melton Cl RSLP HA4 59 G5
Melton Flds HOR/WEW KT19 207 F6
Melton Gdns ROM RM1 75 H4
Melton Pl HOR/WEW KT19 207 F6
Melton St CAMTN NW1 4 B5
Melville Av GFD/PVL UB6 79 F3
RYNPK SW20 176 D3
SAND/SEL CR2 212 B3
Melville Cl HGDN/ICK UB10 76 B1
Melville Ct DEPT SE8 124 A4
Melville Gdns PLMGR N13 49 H1
Melville Pl IS N1 85 J5
Melville Rd BARN SW13 138 D2
CRW RM5 56 D3
RAIN RM13 111 J3
SCUP DA14 168 D4
WALTH E17 69 H1
WLSDN NW10 81 F5
Melville Villas Rd ACT W3 * 118 A1
Melvin Rd PGE/AN SE20 181 K4
Memel St STLK EC1Y 6 C7
Memorial Av MNPK E12 71 J6
SRTFD E15 106 C2
Memorial Cl HEST TW5 114 E6
Memorial Sq KUT/HW KT1 174 E5
Mendez Wy PUT/ROE SW15 158 D1
Mendip Cl HYS/HAR UB3 133 G1
SYD SE26 163 K6
WPK KT4 193 F6
Mendip Dr CRICK NW2 64 C6
Mendip Houses BETH E2 * 104 E2
Mendip Rd BTSEA SW11 140 B4
BUSH WD23 28 C1
EMPK RM11 75 J4
ERITH DA8 150 B2
GNTH/NBYPK IG2 72 E2
Mendora Rd FUL/PGN SW6 139 H1
Menelik Rd CRICK NW2 82 C2
Menlo Gdns NRWD SE19 180 E3
Menon Dr ED N9 36 D5
Menotti St BETH E2 * 104 C3
Mentmore Cl
KTN/HRWW/WS HA3 61 J3
Mentmore Ter HACK E8 86 D5
Meon Rd ACT W3 117 K2
Meopham Rd MTCM CR4 179 H4
Mepham Crs
KTN/HRWW/WS HA3 42 C3
Mepham Gdns
KTN/HRWW/WS HA3 42 C3
Mepham St STHWK SE1 17 H1
Mera Dr BXLYHN DA7 149 H5
Merantum Wy
WIM/MER SW19 178 B4
Merbury Cl LEW SE13 145 F6
THMD SE28 127 J1
Merbury Rd THMD SE28 127 J1
Merbury St WOOL/PLUM SE18 127 G3
Mercator Pl POP/IOD E14 124 D5
Mercator Rd LEW SE13 145 G5
Mercer Cl THDIT KT7 190 A4
Merceron Houses BETH E2 * 104 E2
Merceron St WCHPL E1 104 D3
Mercer Pl PIN HA5 41 G5
Mercers Cl GNWCH SE10 125 J4
Mercers Cots WCHPL E1 * 105 G5
Mercers Ms ARCH N19 84 D2
Mercers Pl HMSMTH W6 119 F4
Mercers Rd ARCH N19 84 D1
Mercer St LSQ/SEVD WC2H 10 E4
Merchants Cl SNWD SE25 197 H1
Merchant St BOW E3 105 H2
Merchiston Rd CAT SE6 165 G4
Merchland Rd ELTH/MOT SE9 167 H3
Mercia Gv LEW SE13 145 F4
Mercier Rd PUT/ROE SW15 139 H6
Mercury Gdns ROM RM1 75 G1
Mercury House
HYS/HAR UB3 * 113 J2
Mercury Wy NWCR SE14 124 A6
Mercy Ter LEW SE13 144 E6
Merebank La WLGTN SM6 211 F3
Mere Cl ORP BR6 201 G6
WIM/MER SW19 159 G2
Meredith Av CRICK NW2 82 A3
Meredith Cl PIN HA5 41 H3
Meredith Ms BROCKY SE4 144 C5
Meredith St CLKNW EC1R 6 A5
PLSTW E13 106 E2
Meredyth Rd BARN SW13 138 D3
Mere End CROY/NA CR0 198 A4
Mere Rd ABYW SE2 128 D2
Mereside ORP BR6 201 F6
Mereside Pk ASHF TW15 * 153 F6
Meretone Cl BROCKY SE4 144 B5
Merevale Crs MRDN SM4 194 B3
Mereway Rd WHTN TW2 155 J3
Merewood Cl BMLY BR1 185 F5
Merewood Gdns
CROY/NA CR0 198 A4
Merewood Rd BXLYHN DA7 149 K3
Mereworth Cl HAYES BR2 199 J2
Mereworth Dr
WOOL/PLUM SE18 147 G1
Meriden Cl BARK/HLT IG6 54 C4
BMLY BR1 184 C3
Meridian Cl MLHL NW7 31 F6
Meridian Rd CHARL SE7 146 C1
Meridian Sq SRTFD E15 88 B5
Meridian Wy UED N18 36 E5
UED N18 50 E2
Merifield Rd ELTH/MOT SE9 146 B5
Merino Cl WAN E11 71 G1
Merivale Rd HRW HA1 60 C4
PUT/ROE SW15 139 H5
Merlewood Dr CHST BR7 184 E4
Merley Ct CDALE/KGS NW9 62 E5
Merlin Cl CROY/NA CR0 212 A2
CRW RM5 57 F2
MTCM CR4 178 D6
NTHLT UB5 95 G2
WLGTN SM6 211 F4
Merlin Crs EDGW HA8 44 B4
Merlin Gdns CRW RM5 57 F2
Merling Cl CHSGTN KT9 205 K3
Merlin Gv BARK/HLT IG6 54 B3
BECK BR3 198 C1
Merlin Rd CRW RM5 57 F2
MNPK E12 71 H6
WELL DA16 148 B5
Merlin Rd North WELL DA16 148 B5
Merlins Av RYLN/HDSTN HA2 77 K1
Merlin St FSBYW WC1X 5 J5
Mermagen Dr RAIN RM13 93 K5
Mermaid Ct STHWK SE1 18 E2
Merredene St
BRXS/STRHM SW2 162 A1
Merriam Av HOM E9 87 H4
Merriam Cl CHING E4 52 A1
Merrick Rd NWDGN UB2 114 E4
Merrick Sq STHWK SE1 18 E4
Merridene WCHMH N21 35 H1
Merrielands Crs DAGW RM9 110 B1
Merrilands Rd WPK KT4 193 F5
Merrilees Rd BFN/LL DA15 167 K2
Merrilyn Cl ESH/CLAY KT10 205 G4
Merriman Rd BKHTH/KID SE3 146 B2
Merrington Rd FUL/PGN SW6 119 K6
Merrion Av STAN HA7 43 K1
Merritt Gdns CHSGTN KT9 205 J4
Merritt Rd BROCKY SE4 144 C6
Merrivale STHGT/OAK N14 22 D6
Merrivale Av REDBR IG4 71 H1
Merrivale Ms WDR/YW UB7 * 112 A1
Merrow Rd BELMT SM2 208 B6
Merrows Cl NTHWD HA6 40 A2
Merrow St WALW SE17 122 E5
Merrow Wk WALW SE17 122 E5
Merrow Wy CROY/NA CR0 214 A4
Merrydown Wy CHST BR7 184 D4
Merryfield BKHTH/KID SE3 145 J3
Merryfield Gdns STAN HA7 43 J1
Merryfield Wy CAT SE6 164 E2
Merryhill Cl CHING E4 37 K2
Merry Hill Mt BUSH WD23 28 B3
Merry Hill Rd BUSH WD23 28 A2
Merryhills Dr ENC/FH EN2 22 E5
Merryweather Cl DART DA1 171 J1
Merryweather Ct
NWMAL KT3 * 192 B2
Mersey Rd WALTH E17 51 H6
Mersham Dr CDALE/KGS NW9 62 C2
Mersham Pl PGE/AN SE20 181 J4
THHTH CR7 180 E5
Mersham Rd THHTH CR7 180 E6
Merten Rd CHDH RM6 74 A4
Merthyr Ter BARN SW13 118 E6
Merton Av CHSWK W4 118 C4
NTHLT UB5 78 C3
Merton Gdns STMC/STPC BR5 201 G2
Merton Hall Gdns
RYNPK SW20 177 H4
Merton Hall Rd
WIM/MER SW19 177 H4
Merton High St
WIM/MER SW19 178 B3
Merton La HGT N6 65 K6
Merton Pl WIM/MER SW19 * 178 B4
Merton Ri HAMP NW3 83 J5
Merton Rd BARK IG11 91 F5
ENC/FH EN2 23 K1
GDMY/SEVK IG3 73 F4
RYLN/HDSTN HA2 60 C5
SNWD SE25 197 G2
WALTH E17 70 A2
WAND/EARL SW18 159 K3
WIM/MER SW19 178 A3
Merton Wy E/WMO/HCT KT8 189 H1
Mertoun Ter MBLAR W1H * 8 E3
Merttins Rd PECK SE15 144 A5
Meru Cl KTTN NW5 84 A2
Mervan Rd BRXS/STRHM SW2 142 B5
Mervyn Av ELTH/MOT SE9 167 H5
Mervyn Rd WEA W13 116 B3
Messaline Av ACT W3 98 E5
Messent Rd ELTH/MOT SE9 146 B6
Messeter Pl ELTH/MOT SE9 167 F1
Messina Av KIL/WHAMP NW6 82 E5
Meteor St BTSEA SW11 141 F5
Meteor Wy WLGTN SM6 210 E5
Metford Crs PEND EN3 25 J1
Methley St LBTH SE11 122 B5
Methuen Cl EDGW HA8 44 C3
Methuen Pk MUSWH N10 48 B5
Methuen Rd BELV DA17 129 J4
BXLYHS DA6 149 G5
EDGW HA8 44 C3
Methwold Rd NKENS W10 100 B4
Metropolitan Cl POP/IOD E14 105 J4
Metropolitan Whf WAP E1W * 123 K1
Mews North BGVA SW1W 15 J5
Mews Pl WFD IG8 38 E6
Mews South PIM SW1V 121 H5
Mews St WAP E1W 13 K7
The Mews BECK BR3 182 D4
CEND/HSY/T N8 67 G1
NFNCH/WDSPK N12 * 47 F1
REDBR IG4 71 H2
ROM RM1 75 G1
STRHM/NOR SW16 * 180 A4
TWK TW1 * 156 C1
Mexfield Rd PUT/ROE SW15 139 J6
Meyer Gn EN EN1 24 C1
Meyer Rd ERITH DA8 129 K6
Meymott St STHWK SE1 18 A1
Meynell Crs HOM E9 87 F5
Meynell Gdns HOM E9 87 F5
Meynell Rd HARH RM3 57 K2
HOM E9 87 F5
Meyrick Rd BTSEA SW11 140 C4
WLSDN NW10 81 J4
Mezen Cl NTHWD HA6 40 B1
Miah Ter WAP E1W * 123 H1
Micawber St IS N1 6 C4
Michael Gaynor Cl HNWL W7 116 A1
Michaelmas Cl RYNPK SW20 177 F6
Michael Rd FUL/PGN SW6 140 A2
SNWD SE25 181 F6
WAN E11 70 C5
Michaels Cl LEW SE13 145 H4
Micheldever Rd
LEE/GVPK SE12 165 H1
Michelham Gdns TWK TW1 156 A5
Michelsdale Dr RCH/KEW TW9 137 F5
Michel Wk WOOL/PLUM SE18 127 G5
Michigan Av MNPK E12 89 J2
Michleham Down
NFNCH/WDSPK N12 32 D6
Mickleham Cl STMC/STPC BR5 186 A5
Mickleham Gdns CHEAM SM3 208 C4
Mickleham Rd
STMC/STPC BR5 186 A4
Mickleham Wy CROY/NA CR0 214 B5
Micklethwaite Rd
FUL/PGN SW6 119 K6
Midcroft RSLP HA4 58 C5
Middle Dartrey Wk
WBPTN SW10 * 140 B1
Middle Dene MLHL NW7 31 F5
Middlefield STJWD NW8 83 H6
Middlefielde WEA W13 97 H4
Middlefields CROY/NA CR0 213 G6
WEA W13 97 H4
Middle Green Cl BRYLDS KT5 191 G3
Middleham Gdns UED N18 50 C2
Middleham Rd UED N18 50 C2
Middle La CEND/HSY/T N8 66 E2
TEDD TW11 174 A2
Middle Lane Ms
CEND/HSY/T N8 66 E2
Middle Park Av
ELTH/MOT SE9 166 C1
Middle Rd EBAR EN4 33 J1
PLSTW E13 106 E1
RYLN/HDSTN HA2 60 D6
STRHM/NOR SW16 179 H5
Middle Rw NKENS W10 100 C3
Middlesborough Rd UED N18 50 C2
Middlesex Cl STHL UB1 96 B3
Middlesex Pl HOM E9 86 E4
Middlesex Rd MTCM CR4 195 K2
Middlesex St WCHPL E1 13 H2
Middle St CROY/NA CR0 196 D6
STBT EC1A 12 C1
Middle Temple La EMB EC4Y 11 J4
Middleton Av CHING E4 37 H6
GFD/PVL UB6 96 D1
SCUP DA14 186 D2
Middleton Cl CHING E4 37 H5
Middleton Dr
BERM/RHTH SE16 124 A2
PIN HA5 40 E6
Middleton Gdns
GNTH/NBYPK IG2 72 B3
Middleton Gv HOLWY N7 84 E3
Middleton Ms HOLWY N7 84 E3
Middleton Pl GTPST W1W 10 A2
Middleton Rd CAR SM5 194 D4
GLDGN NW11 64 E4
HACK E8 86 B5
HYS/HAR UB3 94 B4
NWMAL KT3 175 K6
Middleton St BETH E2 104 D2
Middleton Wy LEW SE13 145 G5
Middleway GLDGN NW11 65 F2
Middle Wy STRHM/NOR SW16 179 J5
The Middle Wy
KTN/HRWW/WS HA3 43 F5
Middle Yd STHWK SE1 13 F7
Midfield Av BXLYHN DA7 149 K4
Midfield Wy STMC/STPC BR5 186 C4
Midford Pl FITZ W1T * 4 B7
Midholm GLDGN NW11 65 F1
WBLY HA9 62 C5
Midholm Cl GLDGN NW11 * 65 F1
Midholm Rd CROY/NA CR0 213 G1
Midhope St STPAN WC1H 5 F5
Midhurst Av CROY/NA CR0 196 B4
MUSWH N10 48 A6
Midhurst Cl HCH RM12 93 J2
Midhurst Gdns
HGDN/ICK UB10 76 A5
Midhurst Hl BXLYHS DA6 149 H6
Midhurst Pde MUSWH N10 * 48 A6
Midhurst Rd WEA W13 116 B2
Midhurst Wy CLPT E5 86 C2
Midland Arches CRICK NW2 * 63 K6
Midland Crs HAMP NW3 83 G4
Midland Rd CAMTN NW1 4 D3
LEY E10 70 A4
Midland Ter CRICK NW2 82 B1
WLSDN NW10 99 G3
Midlothian Rd BOW E3 105 H3
Midmoor Rd BAL SW12 161 H3
WIM/MER SW19 177 G4
Midship Cl BERM/RHTH SE16 * 124 A1
Midship Point POP/IOD E14 * 124 D2
Midstrath Rd WLSDN NW10 81 G2
Midsummer Av HSLWW TW4 134 E5
Midway CHEAM SM3 193 J4
WOT/HER KT12 188 A6
Midwinter Cl WELL DA16 148 B4
Midwood Cl CRICK NW2 81 J1
Mighell Av REDBR IG4 71 H2
Milan Rd STHL UB1 114 E2
Milborne Gv WBPTN SW10 120 B5
Milborne St HOM E9 86 E4
Milborough Crs
LEE/GVPK SE12 165 H1
Milbourne La ESH/CLAY KT10 204 C3
Milbrook ESH/CLAY KT10 204 C4
Milcote St STHWK SE1 18 A3
Mildenhall Rd CLPT E5 86 E2
Mildmay Av IS N1 85 K4
Mildmay Gv North IS N1 85 K3
Mildmay Gv South IS N1 85 K3
Mildmay Pk IS N1 85 K3
Mildmay Pl STNW/STAM N16 86 A3
Mildmay Rd IL IG1 90 B1
IS N1 85 K3
ROMW/RG RM7 74 E2
Mildmay St IS N1 85 K4
Mildred Av HYS/HAR UB3 113 G4
NTHLT UB5 78 B3
Mildred Cl DART DA1 171 K1
Mildred Rd ERITH DA8 130 B5
Mile End Pl WCHPL E1 105 F3
Mile End Rd WCHPL E1 104 E4
The Mile End WALTH E17 51 F4
Mile Rd CROY/NA CR0 195 H5
WLGTN SM6 195 F5
Miles Dr THMD SE28 127 K1
Milespit Hl MLHL NW7 45 K1
Miles Pl BRYLDS KT5 * 191 G1
Miles Rd CEND/HSY/T N8 48 E6
MTCM CR4 178 D6
Miles St VX/NE SW8 121 K6
Milestone Cl BELMT SM2 209 H4
ED N9 36 C4
Milestone Rd NRWD SE19 181 G2
Miles Wy TRDG/WHET N20 33 J4
Milfoil St SHB W12 99 J6
Milford Cl ABYW SE2 129 F6
Milford Gdns ALP/SUD HA0 79 K3
CROY/NA CR0 197 K2
EDGW HA8 44 C3
Milford Gv SUT SM1 209 G2
Milford La TPL/STR WC2R 11 J5
Milford Ms STRHM/NOR SW16 162 A5
Milford Rd STHL UB1 96 A6
WEA W13 116 C1
Milk St BMLY BR1 184 A1
CAN/RD E16 127 G1
CITYW EC2V 12 D3
Milkwell Gdns WFD IG8 53 F3
Milkwell Yd CMBW SE5 142 D2
Milkwood Rd HNHL SE24 142 C6
Milk Yd WAP E1W 104 E6
Millais Av MNPK E12 90 A3
Millais Crs HOR/WEW KT19 207 G3
Millais Gdns EDGW HA8 44 C5
Millais Rd EN EN1 24 B6
NWMAL KT3 192 B4
WAN E11 88 A2
Millais Wy HOR/WEW KT19 206 E2
Millard Cl STNW/STAM N16 86 A3
Millard Rd DEPT SE8 124 C5
Millars Meadow
BKHTH/KID SE3 145 J5
Millbank WEST SW1P 16 E6
Millbank Est WEST SW1P 16 D7
Millbank Wy LEE/GVPK SE12 145 K6
Millbourne Rd FELT TW13 154 D6
Mill Br BAR EN5 * 20 D6
Millbrook Av ELTH/MOT SE9 147 J5
Millbrook Gdns CHDH RM6 74 A3
GPK RM2 57 G5
Millbrook Rd BRXN/ST SW9 142 C4
ED N9 36 D3
Mill Brook Rd STMC/STPC BR5 202 D1
Mill Cl CAR SM5 * 195 F6
WDR/YW UB7 112 A3
Mill Cnr BAR EN5 20 D2
Mill Ct WDR/YW UB7 112 A3
Millennium Br STHWK SE1 12 C6
Millennium Cl CAN/RD E16 106 E5
Millennium Dr POP/IOD E14 125 G3
Millennium Pl BETH E2 * 104 D1
Millennium Sq STHWK SE1 19 J2
Millennium Wy GNWCH SE10 125 H2
Millennium Whf POP/IOD E14 125 G4
Miller Av PEND EN3 25 J1
Miller Cl BMLY BR1 183 K1
CRW RM5 56 C3
MTCM CR4 194 E4
Miller Rd CROY/NA CR0 196 A5
WIM/MER SW19 178 C2
Miller's Av HACK E8 86 B3
Millers Cl DART DA1 171 G2
MLHL NW7 31 J6
Miller's Ct CHSWK W4 118 C5
Millers Green Cl ENC/FH EN2 23 H4
Miller's Ter HACK E8 86 B3
Miller St CAMTN NW1 4 A2
Miller's Wy HMSMTH W6 119 F2
Millers Yd FNCH N3 47 F4
Miller Wk STHWK SE1 17 K1
Millet Rd GFD/PVL UB6 96 B2
Mill Farm Cl PIN HA5 41 G5
Mill Farm Crs HSLWW TW4 154 D3
Millfield Av WALTH E17 51 G4
Millfield La HGT N6 65 K6
Millfield Pl HGT N6 66 A6
Millfield Rd EDGW HA8 44 E5
HSLWW TW4 154 D3
Millfields Cl STMC/STPC BR5 202 C1
Millfields Rd CLPT E5 86 E2
Mill Gdns SYD SE26 163 J6
Mill Gn MTCM CR4 195 F4
Mill Green Rd MTCM CR4 195 F4
Millgrove St BTSEA SW11 141 F2
Millharbour POP/IOD E14 124 E3
Millhaven Cl CHDH RM6 73 H3
Mill Hl BARN SW13 138 D4
Mill Hill Gv ACT W3 * 117 J1

Mill Hill Rd ACT W3 117 J2
BARN SW13 138 E4
Mill Hill Ter ACT W3 117 J1
Millhouse Pl WNWD SE27 162 C6
Millicent Gv PLMGR N13 49 H1
Millicent Rd LEY E10 * 69 H5
Milligan St POP/IOD E14 105 H6
Milling Rd EDGW HA8 45 F3
Millington Rd HYS/HAR UB3 113 H3
Mill La CAR SM5 210 A2
CHDH RM6 74 A3
CHING E4 25 K4
CRICK NW2 82 C3
CROY/NA CR0 211 G1
EW KT17 207 H6
KIL/WHAMP NW6 82 E3
WFD IG8 52 D1
WOOL/PLUM SE18 127 F5
Millman Ms BMSBY WC1N * 5 G7
Millman Pl BMSBY WC1N 5 G7
Millman St BMSBY WC1N 5 G7
Millmark Gv NWCR SE14 144 B3
Millmarsh La PEND EN3 25 G3
Mill Mead Rd TOTM N17 50 D6
Mill Pl CHST BR7 185 F4
DART DA1 150 D5
KUT/HW KT1 175 G6
POP/IOD E14 105 G5
Mill Plat ISLW TW7 136 B3
Mill Plat Av ISLW TW7 136 B3
Mill Pond Cl VX/NE SW8 141 J1
Millpond Est
BERM/RHTH SE16 * 123 J2
Mill Pond Rd DART DA1 171 H1
Mill Rdg EDGW HA8 44 B1
Mill Rd CAN/RD E16 126 A1
ERITH DA8 149 K1
ESH/CLAY KT10 189 F6
IL IG1 90 A1
RDART DA2 171 J6
WDR/YW UB7 112 A3
WHTN TW2 155 H4
WIM/MER SW19 178 B3
Mill Rw BXLY DA5 * 169 J2
IS N1 7 H1
Mills Gv HDN NW4 46 B6
POP/IOD E14 106 A4
Millshot Cl FUL/PGN SW6 139 F2
Millshott Cl WHALL SW1A * 10 D7
Millside CAR SM5 194 E6
Millside Pl ISLW TW7 136 C3
Millson Cl TRDG/WHET N20 33 H4
Mills Rw CHSWK W4 118 A4
Millstone Cl SRTFD E15 88 B4
Millstream Cl PLMGR N13 49 G1
Millstream Rd STHWK SE1 19 J3
Mill St CONDST W1S 9 K5
KUT/HW KT1 175 F6
STHWK SE1 19 K3
Mill V HAYES BR2 183 K6
Mill View Cl EW KT17 207 H5
Mill View Gdns CROY/NA CR0 213 F1
Millwall Dock Rd
POP/IOD E14 124 D3
Mill Wy EBED/NFELT TW14 134 A6
MLHL NW7 45 G1
Millway Gdns NTHLT UB5 77 K4
Millwell Crs CHIG IG7 54 D1
Millwood Rd HSLW TW3 135 H6
STMC/STPC BR5 186 D6
Millwood St NKENS W10 100 C4
Mill Yd WCHPL E1 104 C6
Milman Cl PIN HA5 41 H6
Milman Rd KIL/WHAMP NW6 100 B1
Milman's St WBPTN SW10 120 C6
Milne Fld PIN HA5 42 A3
Milne Gdns ELTH/MOT SE9 146 D6
Milner Ct BUSH WD23 28 B1
Milner Dr WHTN TW2 155 J2
Milner Pl IS N1 85 G6
Milner Rd BCTR RM8 73 J6
KUT/HW KT1 174 E6
MRDN SM4 194 C2
SRTFD E15 106 C2
THHTH CR7 180 D6
WIM/MER SW19 178 A4
Milner Sq IS N1 * 85 G5
Milner St CHEL SW3 14 E6
Milnthorpe Rd CHSWK W4 118 A6
Milo Rd EDUL SE22 163 G1
Milroy Wk STHWK SE1 11 K7
Milson Rd WKENS W14 119 H3
Milton Av BAR EN5 20 D6
CDALE/KGS NW9 44 D6
CROY/NA CR0 196 E4
EHAM E6 89 H5
HCH RM12 75 H6
HGT N6 66 C4
SUT SM1 209 H1
WLSDN NW10 81 F6
Milton Cl EFNCH N2 65 G3
STHWK SE1 19 J7
SUT SM1 209 H1
YEAD UB4 94 E5
Milton Ct BARB EC2Y 12 E1
CHDH RM6 73 J4
Milton Court Rd NWCR SE14 124 B6
Milton Crs GNTH/NBYPK IG2 72 C4
Milton Gdns
STWL/WRAY TW19 152 C3
Milton Gv FBAR/BDGN N11 48 C1
STNW/STAM N16 85 K2
Milton Pk HGT N6 66 C4
Milton Rd ACT W3 118 A1
BELV DA17 129 H4
CDALE/KGS NW9 * 63 J4
CROY/NA CR0 196 E4
HGT N6 66 C4
HNHL SE24 142 C6
HNWL W7 97 F6
HPTN TW12 173 F3
HRW HA1 60 E1
MLHL NW7 45 J1
MORT/ESHN SW14 138 A4
MTCM CR4 179 F3
ROM RM1 75 J3
SEVS/STOTM N15 49 H6
SUT SM1 208 E1
WALTH E17 69 J1
WELL DA16 148 A2
WIM/MER SW19 178 B2
WLGTN SM6 210 C4
Milton St BARB EC2Y 12 E1
Milton Wy WDR/YW UB7 112 C4
Milverton Dr HGDN/ICK UB10 76 A2
Milverton Gdns
GDMY/SEVK IG3 73 F6
Milverton Rd
KIL/WHAMP NW6 82 A5
Milverton St LBTH SE11 122 B5
Milverton Wy ELTH/MOT SE9 167 F6
Milward St WCHPL E1 104 D4
Mimosa Cl ORP BR6 202 D6
Mimosa Rd YEAD UB4 95 G4
Mimosa St FUL/PGN SW6 139 J2
Minard Rd CAT SE6 165 H2
Mina Rd STHWK SE1 123 F5
WIM/MER SW19 177 K4
Minchenden Crs
STHGT/OAK N14 34 D5
Mincing La MON EC3R 13 G5
Minden Rd CHEAM SM3 193 H6
PGE/AN SE20 181 J4
Minehead Rd
RYLN/HDSTN HA2 78 A1
STRHM/NOR SW16 180 A1
Mineral Cl BAR EN5 32 A1
Mineral St WOOL/PLUM SE18 127 K4
Minera Ms BGVA SW1W 15 H6
Minerva Cl BRXN/ST SW9 142 B1
SCUP DA14 167 K6
Minerva Rd CHING E4 51 K3
KUT/HW KT1 175 G5
WLSDN NW10 98 E3
Minerva St BETH E2 104 D1
Minet Av WLSDN NW10 99 G1
Minet Dr HYS/HAR UB3 113 K1
Minet Gdns HYS/HAR UB3 114 A1
WLSDN NW10 99 G1
Minet Rd BRXN/ST SW9 142 C3
Minford Gdns WKENS W14 119 G2
Ming St POP/IOD E14 * 105 J6
Minimax Cl EBED/NFELT TW14 153 K1
Ministry Wy ELTH/MOT SE9 166 E4
Mink Ct HSLWW TW4 134 B3
Minniedale BRYLDS KT5 191 G2
Minnow Wk WALW SE17 19 H7
Minories TWRH EC3N 13 J4
Minshull Pl BECK BR3 * 182 D3
Minshull St VX/NE SW8 * 141 J2
Minson Rd HOM E9 87 F6
Minstead Gdns
PUT/ROE SW15 158 C2
Minstead Wy NWMAL KT3 192 B3
Minster Av SUT SM1 193 K6
Minster Ct MON EC3R * 13 G5
Minster Dr CROY/NA CR0 212 A2
Minster Gdns
E/WMO/HCT KT8 188 E1
Minster Rd BMLY BR1 184 A3
CRICK NW2 82 C3
Minster Wk CEND/HSY/T N8 66 E1
Minstrel Gdns BRYLDS KT5 191 G1
Mintern Cl PLMGR N13 35 H5
Minterne Av NWDGN UB2 115 F4
Minterne Rd
KTN/HRWW/WS HA3 62 B2
Minterne Waye YEAD UB4 95 G5
Mintern St IS N1 7 F2
Minton Ms KIL/WHAMP NW6 83 F4
Mint Rd WLGTN SM6 210 B3
Mint St STHWK SE1 18 C2
Mint Wk CROY/NA CR0 211 J1
Mirabel Rd FUL/PGN SW6 139 J1
Miranda Cl WCHPL E1 104 E4
Miranda Rd ARCH N19 66 C5
Mirfield St CHARL SE7 126 C3
Miriam Rd WOOL/PLUM SE18 127 K5
Mirren Cl RYLN/HDSTN HA2 77 K2
Miskin Rd DART DA1 171 F2
Missenden Cl
EBED/NFELT TW14 153 J3
Missenden Gdns MRDN SM4 194 B3
Mission Gv WALTH E17 69 G2
Mission Pl PECK SE15 143 H2
Mistletoe Cl CROY/NA CR0 198 A5
Misty's Fld WOT/HER KT12 188 B5
Mitali Pas WCHPL E1 104 C5
Mitcham La
STRHM/NOR SW16 179 H1
Mitcham Pk MTCM CR4 194 D1
Mitcham Rd CROY/NA CR0 195 K3
EHAM E6 107 J2
GDMY/SEVK IG3 73 F4
TOOT SW17 178 E1
Mitchellbrook Wy
WLSDN NW10 81 F4
Mitchell Cl ABYW SE2 128 D5
BELV DA17 129 K3
DART DA1 171 H4
Mitchell Rd ORP BR6 217 F2
PLMGR N13 49 H1
Mitchell St FSBYE EC1V 6 C6
Mitchell Wy BMLY BR1 183 K4
WLSDN NW10 80 E4
Mitchison Rd IS N1 85 K4
Mitchley Rd TOTM N17 50 C6
Mitford Rd ARCH N19 66 E6
Mitre Cl BELMT SM2 209 G5
Mitre Rd SRTFD E15 106 C1
STHWK SE1 17 K2
Mitre Sq HDTCH EC3A 13 H4
Mitre St HDTCH EC3A 13 H4
The Mitre POP/IOD E14 105 H6
Mitre Wy NKENS W10 99 K4
Moat Cl ORP BR6 217 F4
Moat Ct ELTH/MOT SE9 * 166 E1
Moat Crs FNCH N3 47 F6
Moat Cft WELL DA16 148 D4
Moat Dr HRW HA1 60 C1
PLSTW E13 107 G1
RSLP HA4 58 C4
Moat Farm Rd NTHLT UB5 77 K4
Moat La ERITH DA8 150 D2
Moat Pl ACT W3 98 D5
BRXN/ST SW9 142 A4
Moat Side FELT TW13 154 B6
PEND EN3 24 E5
The Moat NWMAL KT3 176 B4
Moberly Rd CLAP SW4 161 J2
Modbury Gdns KTTN NW5 84 A4
Model Cots MORT/ESHN SW14 137 K4
WEA W13 * 116 C2
Model Farm Cl ELTH/MOT SE9 166 D5
Moelyn Ms HRW HA1 61 G2
Moffat Rd PLMGR N13 48 E2
THHTH CR7 180 D5
TOOT SW17 160 D6
Mogden La ISLW TW7 136 A6
Mohmmad Khan Rd
WAN E11 * 70 D5
Moiety Rd POP/IOD E14 124 D2
Moira Cl TOTM N17 50 A5
Moira Rd ELTH/MOT SE9 146 E5
Moir Cl SAND/SEL CR2 212 C6
Molash Rd STMC/STPC BR5 202 E1
Mole Abbey Gdns
E/WMO/HCT KT8 173 F6
Mole Ct HOR/WEW KT19 206 E2
Molember Ct
E/WMO/HCT KT8 189 K2
Molember Rd
E/WMO/HCT KT8 189 K2
Molescroft ELTH/MOT SE9 167 H5
Molesey Av E/WMO/HCT KT8 188 E1
Molesey Dr CHEAM SM3 193 H6
Molesey Park Av
E/WMO/HCT KT8 189 G2
Molesey Park Cl
E/WMO/HCT KT8 189 H2
Molesey Park Rd
E/WMO/HCT KT8 189 G2
Molesey Rd E/WMO/HCT KT8 188 D2
WOT/HER KT12 188 D5
Molesford Rd FUL/PGN SW6 * 139 K2
Molesham Cl E/WMO/HCT KT8 173 G6
Molesham Wy
E/WMO/HCT KT8 189 G1
Molesworth St LEW SE13 145 F4
Mollison Av PEND EN3 25 G3
Mollison Dr WLGTN SM6 210 E5
Mollison Wy EDGW HA8 44 C5
Molly Huggins Cl BAL SW12 161 H2
Molyneux Dr TOOT SW17 161 G6
Molyneux St MBLAR W1H 8 D2
Monarch Cl
EBED/NFELT TW14 153 H2
RAIN RM13 111 J1
WWKM BR4 214 D2
Monarch Dr CAN/RD E16 107 H4
Monarch Ms
STRHM/NOR SW16 180 B1
Monarch Pde MTCM CR4 * 178 E5
Monarch Pl BKHH IG9 39 G4
Monarch Rd BELV DA17 129 H3
Monarchs Wy RSLP HA4 58 C5
Monarch's Wy RSLP HA4 * 58 B5
Monarch Wy
GNTH/NBYPK IG2 72 D3
Mona Rd PECK SE15 143 K3
Monastery Gdns ENC/FH EN2 23 K3
Mona St CAN/RD E16 106 D4
Monaveen Gdns
E/WMO/HCT KT8 173 G6
Monck's Rw
WAND/EARL SW18 * 159 J1
Monck St WEST SW1P 16 D5
Monclar Rd CMBW SE5 142 E5
Moncorvo Cl SKENS SW7 14 C3
Moncrieff Cl EHAM E6 107 J5
Moncrieff St PECK SE15 143 H3
Monday Aly STNW/STAM N16 86 B1
Mondial Wy HYS/HAR UB3 133 F1
Monega Rd FSTGT E7 89 G4
MNPK E12 89 H4
Money La WDR/YW UB7 112 A3
Monier Rd BOW E3 87 J5
Monivea Rd BECK BR3 182 C3
Monk Dr CAN/RD E16 106 E6
Monkfrith Av STHGT/OAK N14 34 B1
Monkfrith Wy
STHGT/OAK N14 34 B2
Monkham's Av WFD IG8 53 F1
Monkham's Dr WFD IG8 53 F1
Monkham's La WFD IG8 39 F6
Monkleigh Rd MRDN SM4 177 H6
Monks Av BAR EN5 33 G1
E/WMO/HCT KT8 188 E2
Monks Cl ABYW SE2 128 E4
ENC/FH EN2 23 J3
RSLP HA4 77 H2
RYLN/HDSTN HA2 * 60 A6
Monks Crs WOT/HER KT12 188 A5
Monksdene Gdns SUT SM1 209 F1
Monks Dr ACT W3 98 C4
Monks Orch DART DA1 171 F4
Monks Orchard Rd BECK BR3 198 D5
Monks Pk WBLY HA9 80 D4
Monks Park Gdns WBLY HA9 80 D4
Monks Rd ENC/FH EN2 23 H3
Monk St WOOL/PLUM SE18 127 F4
Monks Wy BECK BR3 198 D3
GLDGN NW11 64 D1
STMC/STPC BR5 201 H5
Monkswood Gdns CLAY IG5 54 A6
Monk Ter FSTH SE23 164 C4
Monkton Rd WELL DA16 148 A3
Monkton St LBTH SE11 17 K6
Monkville Av GLDGN NW11 64 D1
Monkville Pde GLDGN NW11 * 64 D1
Monkwell Sq BARB EC2Y 12 D2
Monkwood Cl ROM RM1 75 J2
Monmouth Av KUT/HW KT1 174 D5
SWFD E18 71 F1
Monmouth Cl CHSWK W4 118 A3
MTCM CR4 195 K1
WELL DA16 148 B5
Monmouth Gv BTFD TW8 117 F4
Monmouth Pl BAY/PAD W2 100 E5
Monmouth Rd BAY/PAD W2 100 E5
DAGW RM9 92 B3
ED N9 36 D4
EHAM E6 107 K2
HYS/HAR UB3 113 H4
Monmouth St
LSQ/SEVD WC2H 10 E4
Monnery Rd ARCH N19 84 C1
Monnow Rd STHWK SE1 123 H5
Mono La FELT TW13 154 A4
Monoux Gv WALTH E17 51 H4
Monroe Crs EN EN1 24 D2
Monroe Dr MORT/ESHN SW14 137 J6
Monro Gdns
KTN/HRWW/WS HA3 42 E3
Monro Pl HOR/WEW KT19 206 C6
Monsell Rd FSBYPK N4 85 H1
Monson Rd NWCR SE14 144 A1
WLSDN NW10 99 J1
Mons Wy HAYES BR2 200 D3
Montacute Rd BUSH WD23 28 E2
CAT SE6 164 C2
CROY/NA CR0 214 A6
MRDN SM4 194 C3
Montagu Crs UED N18 36 D5
Montague Av BROCKY SE4 144 C5
HNWL W7 116 A1
Montague Cl BAR EN5 20 D5
STHWK SE1 12 E7
Montague Gdns EA W5 98 C6
Montague Hall Pl BUSH WD23 28 A1
Montague Pl GWRST WC1E 10 D1
Montague Rd
CEND/HSY/T N8 67 F2
CROY/NA CR0 196 C5
HACK E8 86 C3
HNWL W7 116 A2
HSLW TW3 135 G4
NWDGN UB2 114 D4
RCHPK/HAM TW10 157 F1
SEVS/STOTM N15 * 68 C1
WAN E11 70 D6
WEA W13 97 H5
WIM/MER SW19 178 A3
Montague Sq PECK SE15 143 K1
Montague St RSQ WC1B 10 E1
STBT EC1A 12 C2
Montague Ter HAYES BR2 * 199 K1
Montague Waye NWDGN UB2 114 D3
Montagu Gdns UED N18 36 D6
WLGTN SM6 210 C2
Montagu Man MHST W1U 9 F2
Montagu Ms North
MBLAR W1H 9 F2
Montagu Ms South
MBLAR W1H 9 F3
Montagu Ms West
MBLAR W1H 8 E3
Montagu Pl MBLAR W1H 8 E2
Montagu Rd ED N9 36 E5
HDN NW4 63 J3
UED N18 50 D1
Montagu Rw MHST W1U 9 F2
Montagu Sq MBLAR W1H 9 F2
Montagu St MBLAR W1H 9 F3
Montaigne Cl WEST SW1P 16 D7
Montalt Rd WFD IG8 52 D1
Montana Gdns SUT SM1 209 G3
SYD SE26 182 C1
Montana Rd RYNPK SW20 177 F4
TOOT SW17 161 F5
Montbelle Rd ELTH/MOT SE9 167 G5
Montbretia Cl
STMC/STPC BR5 202 D1
Montcalm Cl HAYES BR2 199 K3
YEAD UB4 95 F2
Montcalm Rd CHARL SE7 146 C1
Montclare St BETH E2 7 J5
Monteagle Av BARK IG11 90 C4
Monteagle Wy PECK SE15 143 J4
Montefiore St VX/NE SW8 141 G3
Montem Rd FSTH SE23 164 C2
NWMAL KT3 192 B1
Montem St FSBYPK N4 67 F5
Montenotte Rd
CEND/HSY/T N8 66 C2
Monterey Cl BXLY DA5 169 K4
Montesole Ct PIN HA5 41 G5
Montesquieu Ter
CAN/RD E16 * 106 D5
Montford Pl LBTH SE11 122 B5
Montfort Gdns BARK/HLT IG6 54 C2
Montfort Pl WIM/MER SW19 159 G3
Montgomerie Ms FSTH SE23 163 K2
Montgomery Av
ESH/CLAY KT10 189 K6
Montgomery Cl BFN/LL DA15 147 K6
MTCM CR4 * 195 K1
Montgomery Gdns
BELMT SM2 209 H5
Montgomery Rd CHSWK W4 117 K4
EDGW HA8 44 B2
Montgomery St POP/IOD E14 124 E1
Montholme Rd BTSEA SW11 160 E1
Monthorpe Rd WCHPL E1 104 C4
Montolieu Gdns
PUT/ROE SW15 138 E6
Montpelier Av BXLY DA5 168 E2
EA W5 97 J4
Montpelier Gdns CHDH RM6 73 J4
EHAM E6 107 H2
Montpelier Gv KTTN NW5 84 C3
Montpelier Ms SKENS SW7 14 D4
Montpelier Pl SKENS SW7 14 D4
WCHPL E1 104 E5
Montpelier Ri GLDGN NW11 64 C4
WBLY HA9 61 K5
Montpelier Rd EA W5 97 K4
FNCH N3 47 G4
PECK SE15 143 J2
SUT SM1 209 G2
Montpelier Rw
BKHTH/KID SE3 145 J3
TWK TW1 156 C2
Montpelier Sq SKENS SW7 14 D3
Montpelier St SKENS SW7 14 D3
Montpelier Ter SKENS SW7 14 D3
Montpelier V
BKHTH/KID SE3 * 145 J3
Montpelier Wk SKENS SW7 14 D4
Montpelier Wy GLDGN NW11 64 C4
Montrave Rd PGE/AN SE20 181 K2
Montreal Pl HOL/ALD WC2B 11 G5
Montreal Rd IL IG1 72 C4
Montrell Rd
BRXS/STRHM SW2 161 K3
Montrose Av BFN/LL DA15 168 B2
EDGW HA8 45 F5
KIL/WHAMP NW6 100 C1
WELL DA16 147 J4
WHTN TW2 155 G2
Montrose Cl WELL DA16 148 A4
WFD IG8 38 E6
Montrose Crs ALP/SUD HA0 80 A4
NFNCH/WDSPK N12 47 F2
Montrose Gdns MTCM CR4 178 E6
SUT SM1 194 A6
Montrose Pl KTBR SW1X 15 H3
Montrose Rd
EBED/NFELT TW14 153 G1
KTN/HRWW/WS HA3 42 E5
Montrose Vls HMSMTH W6 * 118 D5
Montrose Wy FSTH SE23 164 A3
Montserrat Av WFD IG8 52 B3
Montserrat Cl NRWD SE19 180 E1
Montserrat Rd
PUT/ROE SW15 139 H5
Monument Wy TOTM N17 50 B6
Monza St WAP E1W 104 E6
Moodkee St
BERM/RHTH SE16 123 K3
Moody St WCHPL E1 105 F2
Moon Ct LEE/GVPK SE12 * 145 K5
Moon La BAR EN5 20 D4
Moon St IS N1 85 H6
Moorcroft EDGW HA8 * 44 D4
Moorcroft Gdns HAYES BR2 200 D2
Moorcroft Rd
STRHM/NOR SW16 161 K5
Moorcroft Wy PIN HA5 59 J2
Moordown WOOL/PLUM SE18 147 F2
Moore Cl MORT/ESHN SW14 137 K4
MTCM CR4 * 179 G5
Moore Crs DAGW RM9 91 H6
Moorefield Rd TOTM N17 50 B6
Mooreland Rd BMLY BR1 183 J3
Moore Park Rd FUL/PGN SW6 140 A1
Moore Rd NRWD SE19 180 D2
Moore St CHEL SW3 14 E6
Moore Wy BELMT SM2 208 E6
Moorey Cl SRTFD E15 88 D6
Moorfield Av EA W5 97 K3
Moorfield Rd CHSGTN KT9 206 A3
ORP BR6 202 B4
PEND EN3 24 E2
Moorfields LVPST EC2M 12 E2
Moorfields Highwalk
BARB EC2Y 12 E2
Moorgate LOTH EC2R 12 E3
LVPST EC2M 12 E2
Moorgate Pl LOTH EC2R * 12 E3
Moorhead Wy BKHTH/KID SE3 146 A4
Moorhen Cl ERITH DA8 150 E6
Moorhouse Rd BAY/PAD W2 100 E5
KTN/HRWW/WS HA3 43 K6
The Moorings CHSWK W4 * 117 H6
Moorland Cl CRW RM5 56 D4
WHTN TW2 155 F2
Moorland Rd BRXN/ST SW9 142 C5
Moorlands Av MLHL NW7 45 K2
Moor La BARB EC2Y 12 E2
CHSGTN KT9 206 B3
Moor Lane Crossing
WATW WD18 26 A2
Moormead Dr
HOR/WEW KT19 207 G3
Moor Mead Rd TWK TW1 156 B1
Moor Park Gdns
KUTN/CMB KT2 176 B3
NTHWD HA6 * 26 A4
Moor Park Rd NTHWD HA6 40 B2
Moorside Rd BMLY BR1 165 H6
Moor St SOHO/SHAV W1D 10 D4
Moortown Rd OXHEY WD19 27 G6
Moor Vw WATW WD18 26 E2
Morant Gdns CRW RM5 56 D1
Morant St POP/IOD E14 105 J6
Mora Rd CRICK NW2 82 A2
Mora St FSBYE EC1V 6 D5
Morat St BRXN/ST SW9 142 A2
Moravian Pl WBPTN SW10 120 C6
Moravian St BETH E2 104 E1
Moray Av HYS/HAR UB3 113 J1
Moray Cl EDGW HA8 * 30 D4
ROM RM1 57 G3
Moray Ms HOLWY N7 67 F6
Moray Rd HOLWY N7 67 F6
Moray Wy ROM RM1 57 F3
Morcambe St WALW SE17 18 D7
Mordaunt Gdns DAGW RM9 92 A5
Mordaunt Rd WLSDN NW10 81 F6
Mordaunt St BRXN/ST SW9 142 A4
Morden Ct MRDN SM4 194 A1
Morden Court Pde
MRDN SM4 * 178 A6
Morden Gdns GFD/PVL UB6 79 F3
MTCM CR4 194 C1
Morden Hall Rd MRDN SM4 178 A6
Morden Hl LEW SE13 145 F3
Morden La LEW SE13 145 F3
Morden Rd BKHTH/KID SE3 145 K3
CHDH RM6 74 A4
MTCM CR4 194 C1
WIM/MER SW19 178 A5
Morden Road Ms
BKHTH/KID SE3 145 K3
Morden St LEW SE13 144 E2
Morden Wy CHEAM SM3 193 K4
Morden Wharf Rd
GNWCH SE10 125 H3
Mordon Rd GDMY/SEVK IG3 73 F4
Mordred Rd CAT SE6 165 H4
Morecambe Cl HCH RM12 93 K3
WCHPL E1 * 105 F4
Morecambe Gdns STAN HA7 29 K6
Morecambe St POP/IOD E14 124 E5
Morecambe Ter UED N18 * 35 K6
More Cl CAN/RD E16 106 D5
WKENS W14 119 G4
Morecoombe Cl
KUTN/CMB KT2 175 J3
Moree Wy UED N18 36 C6
Moreland Cots BOW E3 * 105 J1
Moreland St FSBYE EC1V 6 B4
Moreland Wy CHING E4 37 K5
More La ESH/CLAY KT10 204 B1
Morella Rd BTSEA SW11 160 E2
More London Riverside
STHWK SE1 19 H1
Moremead Rd CAT SE6 164 C6
Morena St CAT SE6 164 E2

Moresby Av BRYLDS KT5 191 J4
Moresby Rd CLPT E5 68 D5
Mores Gdn CHEL SW3 * 120 C6
Moretaine Rd ASHF TW15 152 A5
Moreton Av ISLW TW7 135 J2
Moreton Cl CLPT E5 68 E6
MLHL NW7 46 A2
SEVS/STOTM N15 67 K3
Moreton Ct DART DA1 150 B4
Moreton Gdns WFD IG8 53 J1
Moreton Pl PIM SW1V 121 H5
Moreton Rd SAND/SEL CR2 211 K3
SEVS/STOTM N15 67 K3
WPK KT4 192 D6
Moreton St PIM SW1V 121 J5
Moreton Ter PIM SW1V 121 H5
Moreton Terrace Ms North
PIM SW1V 121 H5
Moreton Terrace Ms South
PIM SW1V * 121 H5
Morford Cl RSLP HA4 59 F4
Morford Wy RSLP HA4 59 F4
Morgan Av WALTH E17 70 B1
Morgan Cl DAGE RM10 92 C5
NTHWD HA6 40 D1
Morgan Rd BMLY BR1 183 K3
HOLWY N7 85 G3
NKENS W10 100 D4
Morgan's La HYS/HAR UB3 94 B4
Morgan St BOW E3 105 G2
CAN/RD E16 106 D4
Morgan Wy WFD IG8 53 J2
Moriarty Cl BMLY BR1 201 G1
Moriatry Cl HOLWY N7 84 E2
Morie St WAND/EARL SW18 140 A5
Morieux Rd LEY E10 69 H5
Moring Rd TOOT SW17 161 F6
Morkyns Wk DUL SE21 * 163 F5
Morland Av CROY/NA CR0 197 F5
DART DA1 150 E6
Morland Cl GLDGN NW11 65 F5
HPTN TW12 172 E1
MTCM CR4 178 D6
Morland Est HACK E8 * 86 C5
Morland Gdns STHL UB1 115 G1
WLSDN NW10 81 F5
Morland Ms IS N1 85 G5
Morland Rd CROY/NA CR0 197 G4
DAGE RM10 92 C5
IL IG1 72 B6
KTN/HRWW/WS HA3 62 A2
PGE/AN SE20 182 A3
SUT SM1 209 G3
WALTH E17 69 F2
Morley Av CHING E4 52 B3
UED N18 36 C6
WDGN N22 49 H4
Morley Cl ORP BR6 201 G6
Morley Crs EDGW HA8 30 E4
RSLP HA4 59 G6
Morley Crs East STAN HA7 43 J6
Morley Crs West STAN HA7 43 J6
Morley Hl ENC/FH EN2 23 K1
Morley Rd BARK IG11 90 D6
CHDH RM6 74 A2
CHEAM SM3 193 J5
CHST BR7 185 H4
LEW SE13 145 F5
LEY E10 70 A5
SRTFD E15 106 D1
TWK TW1 156 E1
Morley St STHWK SE1 17 K3
Morna Rd CMBW SE5 142 D3
Morning La HOM E9 86 E4
Morningside Rd WPK KT4 192 E6
Mornington Av HAYES BR2 184 B6
IL IG1 72 A4
WKENS W14 119 J4
Mornington Ct BXLY DA5 170 A3
Mornington Crs CAMTN NW1 4 A2
HEST TW5 134 A2
Mornington Gv BOW E3 105 J2
Mornington Ms CMBW SE5 142 D2
Mornington Pl CAMTN NW1 3 K2
Mornington Rd CHING E4 38 B2
GFD/PVL UB6 96 B4
NWCR SE14 144 C1
WAN E11 70 D5
WFD IG8 38 D6
Mornington St CAMTN NW1 3 K2
Mornington Ter CAMTN NW1 3 K1
Mornington Wk
RCHPK/HAM TW10 156 D6
Morocco St STHWK SE1 19 G3
Morpeth Gv HOM E9 87 F6
Morpeth Rd HOM E9 86 E6
Morpeth St BETH E2 105 F2
Morpeth Ter WEST SW1P 16 A5
Morpeth Wk TOTM N17 * 50 D3
Morphou Rd MLHL NW7 46 C2
Morrab Gdns GDMY/SEVK IG3 91 F1
Morrel Cl BAR EN5 21 G4
Morrells Yd LBTH SE11 122 B5
Morris Av MNPK E12 89 K3
Morris Bishop Ter HGT N6 * 66 A3
Morris Cl CROY/NA CR0 198 B3
ORP BR6 216 E1
Morris Ct CHING E4 37 K5
Morris Gdns DART DA1 151 K6
WAND/EARL SW18 159 K2
Morrish Rd BRXS/STRHM SW2 161 K2
Morrison Av CHING E4 51 J2
TOTM N17 50 A6
Morrison Rd BARK IG11 110 A1
YEAD UB4 95 F2
Morrison St BTSEA SW11 141 F4
Morris Pl FSBYPK N4 67 G6
Morris Rd BCTR RM8 74 B6
HARH RM3 57 K3
ISLW TW7 136 A4
POP/IOD E14 105 K4
SRTFD E15 88 C2
Morris St WCHPL E1 104 D5
Morriston Cl OXHEY WD19 41 G1
Morse Cl PLSTW E13 106 E2
Morshead Rd MV/WKIL W9 100 E2
Morson Rd PEND EN3 37 G1
Morteyne Rd TOTM N17 49 K4
Mortham St SRTFD E15 88 C6
Mortimer Cl BUSH WD23 28 B1
CRICK NW2 82 D1
STRHM/NOR SW16 161 J4
Mortimer Crs
KIL/WHAMP NW6 83 F6
WPK KT4 207 F1
Mortimer Dr EN EN1 23 K6
Mortimer Pl KIL/WHAMP NW6 83 F6
Mortimer Rd EHAM E6 107 K2
ERITH DA8 130 A6
IS N1 86 A5
MTCM CR4 178 E4
ORP BR6 202 B6
WEA W13 97 J5
WLSDN NW10 100 A2
Mortimer Sq NTGHL W11 100 B6
Mortimer St GTPST W1W 9 K3
Mortimer Ter KTTN NW5 * 84 B2
Mortlake Cl CROY/NA CR0 210 E1
Mortlake Dr MTCM CR4 178 D4
Mortlake High St
MORT/ESHN SW14 138 A4
Mortlake Rd CAN/RD E16 107 F5
IL IG1 90 C2
MORT/ESHN SW14 137 J4
RCH/KEW TW9 137 H1
Morton Cl CLAP SW4 161 J1
WCHPL E1 104 E5
WLGTN SM6 211 F5
Morton Crs STHGT/OAK N14 34 D6
Morton Gdns WLGTN SM6 210 C3
Morton Ms ECT SW5 120 A4
Morton Pl STHWK SE1 17 J5
Morton Rd IS N1 85 J5
MRDN SM4 194 C2
SRTFD E15 88 D5
Morton Wy STHGT/OAK N14 34 C5
Morvale Cl BELV DA17 129 G4
Morval Rd BRXS/STRHM SW2 142 B6
Morven Rd TOOT SW17 160 E5
Morville St BOW E3 105 J1
Morwell St RSQ WC1B 10 C2
Moscow Pl BAY/PAD W2 * 101 F6
Moscow Rd BAY/PAD W2 100 E6
Moselle Av WDGN N22 49 G5
Moselle Cl CEND/HSY/T N8 49 F6
Moselle Pl TOTM N17 50 B3
Moselle St TOTM N17 50 B3
Mossborough Cl
NFNCH/WDSPK N12 47 F2
Mossbury Rd BTSEA SW11 140 D4
Moss Cl PIN HA5 41 K5
WCHPL E1 104 C4
Mossdown Cl BELV DA17 129 H4
Mossford Gn BARK/HLT IG6 54 B6
Mossford La BARK/HLT IG6 54 C5
Mossford St BOW E3 105 H3
Moss Gdns FELT TW13 153 K4
SAND/SEL CR2 213 F5
Moss Hall Crs
NFNCH/WDSPK N12 47 F2
Moss Hall Gv
NFNCH/WDSPK N12 47 F2
Moss La PIN HA5 41 K6
ROM RM1 75 H3
Mosslea Rd HAYES BR2 200 C2
ORP BR6 216 C1
PGE/AN SE20 181 K2
Mossop St CHEL SW3 14 D6
Moss Rd DAGE RM10 92 C5
Mossville Gdns MRDN SM4 177 J6
Moston Cl HYS/HAR UB3 113 J5
Mostyn Av WBLY HA9 80 B3
Mostyn Gdns WLSDN NW10 100 B2
Mostyn Gv BOW E3 105 H1
Mostyn Rd BRXN/ST SW9 142 B2
EDGW HA8 45 F3
WIM/MER SW19 177 J6
Mosul Wy HAYES BR2 200 D3
Mosyer Dr STMC/STPC BR5 202 E6
Motcomb St KTBR SW1X 15 G4
Moth Cl WLGTN SM6 210 E5
The Mothers Sq CLPT E5 * 86 D2
Moth House
WOOL/PLUM SE18 * 146 D1
Motley St VX/NE SW8 141 H3
Motspur Pk NWMAL KT3 192 C3
Mottingham Gdns
ELTH/MOT SE9 166 C3
Mottingham La
LEE/GVPK SE12 166 B3
Mottingham Rd ED N9 37 F1
ELTH/MOT SE9 166 D5
Mottisfont Rd ABYW SE2 128 C3
Moulins Rd HOM E9 86 E5
Moulton Av HSLW TW3 134 D3
Moundfield Rd
STNW/STAM N16 68 C3
Mountacre Cl SYD SE26 163 G6
Mount Adon Pk EDUL SE22 163 H2
Mountague Pl POP/IOD E14 106 A6
Mount Angelus Rd
PUT/ROE SW15 158 C2
Mount Ararat Rd
RCHPK/HAM TW10 137 F6
Mount Ash Rd SYD SE26 163 J5
Mount Av CHING E4 37 J5
EA W5 97 K4
STHL UB1 96 A5
Mountbatten Cl NRWD SE19 181 F1
WOOL/PLUM SE18 127 K6
Mountbatten Ct BKHH IG9 39 H4
Mountbel Rd STAN HA7 * 43 G5
Mount Cl BMLY BR1 184 D4
CAR SM5 210 A6
EA W5 * 97 J4
EBAR EN4 22 A5
Mountcombe Cl SURB KT6 191 F4
Mount Cots BXLYHS DA6 * 149 F5
Mount Ct WWKM BR4 199 H6
Mount Culver Av SCUP DA14 186 E2
Mount Dr RYLN/HDSTN HA2 59 K2
WBLY HA9 62 E6
Mountearl Gdns
STRHM/NOR SW16 162 A5
Mount Echo Av CHING E4 37 K3
Mount Echo Dr CHING E4 37 K3
Mount Ephraim La
STRHM/NOR SW16 161 J5
Mount Ephraim Rd
STRHM/NOR SW16 161 J5
Mountfield Cl CAT SE6 165 G2
Mountfield Rd EA W5 97 K5
EHAM E6 108 A1
FNCH N3 46 E6
Mountfield Ter CAT SE6 165 G2
Mountfield Wy
STMC/STPC BR5 202 D1
Mountfort Crs IS N1 85 G5
Mountfort Ter IS N1 85 G5
Mount Gdns SYD SE26 163 J5
Mount Gv EDGW HA8 30 E5
Mountgrove Rd HBRY N5 85 J1
Mount Holme THDIT KT7 190 C4
Mounthurst Rd HAYES BR2 199 K4
Mountington Park Cl
KTN/HRWW/WS HA3 61 K3
Mountjoy Cl ABYW SE2 128 C2
Mount Ms HPTN TW12 173 G4
Mount Mills FSBYE EC1V 6 B5
Mount Nod Rd
STRHM/NOR SW16 162 A5
Mount Pde EBAR EN4 * 21 J5
Mount Pk CAR SM5 210 A6
Mount Park Av HRW HA1 60 D6
SAND/SEL CR2 211 H6
Mount Park Crs EA W5 97 K5
Mount Park Rd EA W5 97 K4
HRW HA1 60 D6
PIN HA5 58 E2
Mount Pl ACT W3 117 J1
Mount Pleasant ALP/SUD HA0 80 A6
EBAR EN4 21 K5
FSBYW WC1X 5 H7
HRW HA1 * 60 E6
RSLP HA4 77 G1
WNWD SE27 162 D6
Mount Pleasant Crs
FSBYPK N4 * 67 F4
Mount Pleasant Hl CLPT E5 68 D6
Mount Pleasant La CLPT E5 68 D5
Mount Pleasant Pl
WOOL/PLUM SE18 127 J4
Mount Pleasant Rd CRW RM5 57 F2
DART DA1 171 J1
EA W5 97 J3
LEW SE13 165 F1
NWMAL KT3 175 K6
TOTM N17 50 A6
WALTH E17 51 G5
WLSDN NW10 82 A5
Mount Pleasant Vls
FSBYPK N4 67 F4
Mount Ri FSTH SE23 163 K4
Mount Rd BCTR RM8 74 B5
BXLYHS DA6 149 F6
CHSGTN KT9 206 B2
CRICK NW2 81 K1
DART DA1 170 C1
EBAR EN4 21 J6
FELT TW13 154 D5
HDN NW4 63 J3
HYS/HAR UB3 113 K2
MTCM CR4 178 C5
NRWD SE19 * 180 E2
NWMAL KT3 176 A6
WIM/MER SW19 159 K4
Mount Rw MYFR/PKLN W1K 9 J6
Mountside
KTN/HRWW/WS HA3 43 F4
STAN HA7 43 G4
Mounts Pond Rd
BKHTH/KID SE3 145 G3
LEW SE13 145 G3
The Mount Sq HAMP NW3 * 83 G1
Mount Stewart Av
KTN/HRWW/WS HA3 61 K3
Mount St MYFR/PKLN W1K 9 G6
Mount Ter WCHPL E1 104 D4
The Mount BMLY BR1 * 184 D4
BXLYHS DA6 * 149 J6
CLPT E5 * 68 D6
ESH/CLAY KT10 204 A4
EW KT17 207 K2
HAMP NW3 83 G2
NTHLT UB5 * 78 B3
NWMAL KT3 176 C6
TRDG/WHET N20 33 G4
WBLY HA9 62 D6
Mount Vw ENC/FH EN2 23 F1
NWDGN UB2 * 114 C4
Mountview MLHL NW7 31 F5
NTHWD HA6 40 E2
Mountview Cl HAMP NW3 65 G5
Mount View Rd
CDALE/KGS NW9 63 F1
CHING E4 38 A2
ESH/CLAY KT10 205 H5
FSBYPK N4 67 F4
Mountview Rd ORP BR6 202 B4
Mount Vls WNWD SE27 162 C5
Mount Wy CAR SM5 210 A6
Mountwood E/WMO/HCT KT8 173 G6
Movers La BARK IG11 90 D6
Mowatt Cl ARCH N19 66 D5
Mowbray Gdns NTHLT UB5 * 78 A6
Mowbray Rd BAR EN5 21 G5
EDGW HA8 30 C6
KIL/WHAMP NW6 82 C5
NRWD SE19 181 G4
RCHPK/HAM TW10 156 D5
Mowbrays Cl CRW RM5 56 E4
Mowbrays Rd CRW RM5 56 E5
Mowlem St BETH E2 104 D1
Mowll St BRXN/ST SW9 142 B1
Moxon Cl PLSTW E13 106 D1
Moxon St BAR EN5 20 D4
MHST W1U 9 G2
Moye Cl BETH E2 86 C6
Moyers Rd LEY E10 70 A5
Moylan Rd HMSMTH W6 119 H6
Moyne Pl WLSDN NW10 98 C2
Moynihan Dr WCHMH N21 22 E6
Moys Cl CROY/NA CR0 195 K3
Moyser Rd STRHM/NOR SW16 179 G1
Mozart St NKENS W10 100 D2
Muchelney Rd MRDN SM4 194 B3
Muggeridge Cl SAND/SEL CR2 211 K3
Muggeridge Rd DAGE RM10 92 D2
Muirdown Av
MORT/ESHN SW14 137 K5
Muir Dr WAND/EARL SW18 160 C1
Muirfield ACT W3 99 G5
Muirfield Cl
BERM/RHTH SE16 * 123 J5
OXHEY WD19 * 41 G1
Muirfield Crs POP/IOD E14 124 E3
Muirfield Gn OXHEY WD19 27 G6
Muirfield Rd OXHEY WD19 27 F6
Muirkirk Rd CAT SE6 165 F3
Muir Rd CLPT E5 86 C1
Muir St CAN/RD E16 126 E1
Mulberry Av
STWL/WRAY TW19 152 B3
Mulberry Cl CEND/HSY/T N8 66 E2
CHEL SW3 * 120 C6
CHING E4 37 J4
EBAR EN4 21 H5
GPK RM2 75 K1
HDN NW4 46 A6
HOR/WEW KT19 206 E6
NTHLT UB5 95 J1
STRHM/NOR SW16 161 H6
Mulberry Crs BTFD TW8 136 C1
WDR/YW UB7 112 D2
Mulberry Dr PUR RM19 131 J4
Mulberry La CROY/NA CR0 197 G5
Mulberry Ms NWCR SE14 144 C2
Mulberry Pde WDR/YW UB7 112 D3
Mulberry Pl ELTH/MOT SE9 146 C5
HMSMTH W6 118 D5
Mulberry Rd HACK E8 86 B5
Mulberry St WCHPL E1 104 C5
Mulberry Wk CHEL SW3 120 C6
Mulberry Wy BARK/HLT IG6 72 C1
BELV DA17 129 K2
SWFD E18 53 F5
Mulgrave Rd BELMT SM2 209 F4
CROY/NA CR0 211 K1
EA W5 97 K2
HRW HA1 61 G6
WKENS W14 119 J6
WLSDN NW10 81 H2
WOOL/PLUM SE18 126 E4
Mulholland Cl MTCM CR4 179 G5
Mulkern Rd ARCH N19 66 D5
Mullards Cl MTCM CR4 194 E5
Mullet Gdns BETH E2 104 C2
Mullins Pth MORT/ESHN SW14 138 A4
Mullion Cl
KTN/HRWW/WS HA3 42 B4
Mullion Wk OXHEY WD19 27 H6
Mull Wk IS N1 85 J4
Mulready St STJWD NW8 2 C7
Multi Wy ACT W3 118 B2
Multon Rd WAND/EARL SW18 160 C2
Mumford Ct CITYW EC2V 12 D3
Mumford Mills GNWCH SE10 144 D1
Mumford Rd HNHL SE24 142 C6
Muncaster Cl ASHF TW15 152 D6
Muncaster Rd CLAP SW4 140 E5
Muncies Ms CAT SE6 165 F4
Mundania Rd EDUL SE22 163 J1
Munday Rd CAN/RD E16 106 E5
Munden St WKENS W14 119 H4
Mundesly Cl OXHEY WD19 27 G6
Mundford Rd CLPT E5 68 E6
Mundon Gdns IL IG1 72 D5
Mund St WKENS W14 119 J5
Mundy St IS N1 7 G4
Mungo-Park Cl BUSH WD23 * 28 C4
Mungo Park Rd RAIN RM13 93 J4
Mungo Park Wy
STMC/STPC BR5 202 D4
Munnery Wy ORP BR6 216 A1
Munnings Gdns ISLW TW7 135 J6
Munro Dr FBAR/BDGN N11 48 C2
Munroe Ter WBPTN SW10 140 C1
Munro Ms NKENS W10 100 C4
Munro Ter WBPTN SW10 120 C6
Munro Wy CLPT E5 86 C2
Munslow Gdns SUT SM1 209 G2
Munster Av HSLWW TW4 134 D5
Munster Ct FUL/PGN SW6 139 J3
Munster Gdns PLMGR N13 35 J6
Munster Ms FUL/PGN SW6 * 139 J1
Munster Rd FUL/PGN SW6 139 H1
TEDD TW11 174 D2
Munster Sq CAMTN NW1 3 K5
Munton Rd WALW SE17 18 D6
Murchison Av BXLY DA5 168 E3
Murchison Rd LEY E10 70 A6
Murdock Cl CAN/RD E16 106 D5
Murdock St PECK SE15 123 J6
Murfett Cl WIM/MER SW19 159 H4
Muriel St IS N1 5 H1
Murillo Rd LEW SE13 145 G5
Murphy St STHWK SE1 17 J3
Murray Av BMLY BR1 184 A6
HSLW TW3 135 G6
Murray Cl THMD SE28 127 K1
Murray Crs PIN HA5 41 H4
Murray Gv IS N1 6 E3
Murray House
WOOL/PLUM SE18 * 146 D1
Murray Ms CAMTN NW1 84 D5
Murray Rd EA W5 116 D4
NTHWD HA6 40 C4
RCHPK/HAM TW10 156 C4
STMC/STPC BR5 186 C6
WIM/MER SW19 177 G2
Murray Sq CAN/RD E16 106 E5
Murray St CAMTN NW1 84 D5
Murray Ter HAMP NW3 83 G2
Murtwell Dr CHIG IG7 54 C2
Musard Rd HMSMTH W6 119 H6
Musbury St WCHPL E1 104 E5
Muscatel Pl CMBW SE5 143 F2
Muschamp Rd CAR SM5 194 D6
PECK SE15 143 G4
Muscovy St MON EC3R 13 H6
Museum St NOXST/BSQ WC1A 10 E2
Museum Wy ACT W3 117 H2
Musgrave Cl EBAR EN4 21 G2
Musgrave Crs FUL/PGN SW6 139 K1
Musgrave Rd ISLW TW7 136 A2
Musgrove Rd NWCR SE14 144 A2
Musjid Rd BTSEA SW11 140 C3
Musquash Wy HSLWW TW4 134 B3
Muston Rd CLPT E5 68 D6
Muswell Av MUSWH N10 48 B5
Muswell Hl MUSWH N10 48 B6
Muswell Hill Broadway
MUSWH N10 48 B6
Muswell Hill Pl MUSWH N10 66 B1
Muswell Hill Rd HGT N6 66 A3
Muswell Ms MUSWH N10 48 B6
Muswell Rd MUSWH N10 48 B5
Mutrix Rd KIL/WHAMP NW6 82 E6
Mutter Rd CLAP SW4 161 J1
Mutton Pl CAMTN NW1 84 A4
Muybridge Rd NWMAL KT3 175 K5
Myatt Rd BRXN/ST SW9 142 C2
Mycenae Rd BKHTH/KID SE3 125 K6
Myddelton Av EN EN1 24 A1
Myddelton Gdns WCHMH N21 35 J2
Myddelton Pk
TRDG/WHET N20 33 H5
Myddelton Pas CLKNW EC1R 5 K4
Myddelton Rd
CEND/HSY/T N8 48 E6
Myddelton Sq CLKNW EC1R 5 K4
Myddelton St CLKNW EC1R 5 K5
Myddleton Av FSBYPK N4 67 H6
Myddleton Cl STAN HA7 29 G4
Myddleton Rd WDGN N22 48 E3
Myers La NWCR SE14 124 A6
Mylis Cl SYD SE26 163 J6
Mylne Cl HMSMTH W6 * 118 D5
Mylne St IS N1 5 J3
Myra St ABYW SE2 128 B5
Myrdle St WCHPL E1 104 C5
Myrna Cl WIM/MER SW19 178 D3
Myron Pl LEW SE13 145 F4
Myrtle Aly WOOL/PLUM SE18 127 F3
Myrtle Av EBED/NFELT TW14 133 H5
RSLP HA4 58 E4
Myrtleberry Cl HACK E8 * 86 B4
Myrtle Cl EBAR EN4 33 K3
ERITH DA8 150 B1
WDR/YW UB7 112 C4
Myrtledene Rd ABYW SE2 128 B5
Myrtle Gdns HNWL W7 115 K1
Myrtle Gv ENC/FH EN2 23 K1
NWMAL KT3 175 K5
Myrtle Rd ACT W3 117 K1
CROY/NA CR0 213 J1
DART DA1 171 G4
EHAM E6 89 J6
HPTN TW12 173 H2
HSLW TW3 135 H3
IL IG1 72 B6
PLMGR N13 35 J5
SUT SM1 209 G3
WALTH E17 69 G3
Myrtleside Cl NTHWD HA6 40 B3
Myrtle St IS N1 7 G3
Myrtle Wk IS N1 7 G3
Mysore Rd BTSEA SW11 140 E5
Myton Rd DUL SE21 162 E5

N

Nadine St CHARL SE7 126 B5
Nagle Cl WALTH E17 52 B5
Nag's Head La WELL DA16 148 C4
Nags Head Rd PEND EN3 24 E5
Nairne Gv HNHL SE24 142 E6
Nairn Gn OXHEY WD19 26 E5
Nairn Rd RSLP HA4 77 G4
Nairn St POP/IOD E14 106 A4
Nallhead Rd FELT TW13 172 B1
Namba Roy Cl
STRHM/NOR SW16 162 A6
Namton Dr THHTH CR7 196 A1
Nan Clark's La MLHL NW7 31 H4
Nancy Downs OXHEY WD19 27 G2
Nankin St POP/IOD E14 105 J5
Nansen Rd BTSEA SW11 141 F5
Nansen Village
NFNCH/WDSPK N12 * 33 F6
Nantes Cl WAND/EARL SW18 140 B5
Nant Rd CRICK NW2 64 D6
Nant St BETH E2 104 D2
Naoroji St FSBYW WC1X 5 J5
Napier Av FUL/PGN SW6 139 J4
POP/IOD E14 124 D5
Napier Cl DEPT SE8 144 C1
EMPK RM11 75 K5
WDR/YW UB7 112 C3
Napier Ct LEE/GVPK SE12 166 A4
Napier Gv IS N1 6 D3
Napier Pl WKENS W14 119 J3
Napier Rd ALP/SUD HA0 79 K3
BELV DA17 129 G4
EHAM E6 90 A6
HAYES BR2 184 A6
ISLW TW7 136 B5
PEND EN3 25 F6
SAND/SEL CR2 211 K5
SNWD SE25 197 J1
SRTFD E15 106 C1
TOTM N17 50 A6
WAN E11 88 C1
WKENS W14 119 J3
WLSDN NW10 99 K2
Napier Ter IS N1 85 H5
Napoleon Rd CLPT E5 86 D1
TWK TW1 * 156 C2
Napton Cl YEAD UB4 95 J3
Narbonne Av CLAP SW4 141 H6
Narboro Ct ROM RM1 75 J3
Narborough Cl
HGDN/ICK UB10 58 A6
Narborough St FUL/PGN SW6 140 A3
Narcissus Rd
KIL/WHAMP NW6 82 E3
Narford Rd CLPT E5 86 C1
Narrow Boat Cl THMD SE28 127 J2
Narrow St ACT W3 117 J1
POP/IOD E14 105 G6
Narrow Wy HAYES BR2 200 D3
Nascot St SHB W12 100 A5
Naseby Cl ISLW TW7 135 K2
KIL/WHAMP NW6 * 83 G5
Naseby Ct WOT/HER KT12 * 188 B6
Naseby Rd CLAY IG5 53 K4

DAGE RM10 92 C1
NRWD SE19 180 E2
Nash Cl SUT SM1 209 H1
Nash Gn BMLY BR1 183 K3
Nash La HAYES BR2 214 E4
Nash Rd BROCKY SE4 144 B5
CHDH RM6 73 K1
ED N9 36 E4
Nash St CAMTN NW1 3 K4
Nash Wy KTN/HRWW/WS HA3 61 H3
Nasmyth St HMSMTH W6 118 E3
Nassau Rd BARN SW13 138 C2
Nassau St GTPST W1W 10 A2
Nassington Rd HAMP NW3 83 J2
Natalie Cl EBED/NFELT TW14 153 G2
Natalie Ms WHTN TW2 155 J5
Natal Rd FBAR/BDGN N11 48 E1
IL IG1 90 B2
STRHM/NOR SW16 179 J2
THHTH CR7 180 E6
Nathaniel Cl WCHPL E1 13 K2
Nathans Rd ALP/SUD HA0 61 J6
Nathan Wy ABYW SE2 128 B2
THMD SE28 128 A3
National Ter
BERM/RHTH SE16 * 123 J2
Nation Wy CHING E4 38 A3
Naval Rw POP/IOD E14 106 A6
Navarino Gv HACK E8 86 C4
Navarino Rd HACK E8 86 C4
Navarre Gdns CRW RM5 56 D2
Navarre Rd EHAM E6 107 J1
Navarre St BETH E2 7 J6
Navestock Cl CHING E4 * 38 A5
Navestock Crs WFD IG8 53 G4
Navestock Ter WFD IG8 53 G3
Navigator Dr NWDGN UB2 115 H2
Navy St CLAP SW4 141 J4
Nayim Pl HACK E8 86 D4
Naylor Gv PEND EN3 25 F6
Naylor Rd PECK SE15 143 J1
TRDG/WHET N20 33 G4
Nazareth Cl PECK SE15 143 J3
Nazrul St BETH E2 7 J4
Neal Av STHL UB1 95 K3
Neal Cl NTHWD HA6 40 E4
Nealden St BRXN/ST SW9 142 A4
Neale Cl EFNCH N2 47 G6
Neal St LSQ/SEVD WC2H 10 E4
Neal Ter FSTH SE23 * 164 A3
Near Acre CDALE/KGS NW9 45 H4
Neasden Cl WLSDN NW10 81 G3
Neasden La WLSDN NW10 81 G2
Neasham Rd BCTR RM8 91 H3
Neate St CMBW SE5 123 G6
Neath Gdns MRDN SM4 194 B3
Neathouse Pl PIM SW1V 16 A6
Neats Acre RSLP HA4 58 B4
Neatscourt Rd EHAM E6 107 H4
Neckinger BERM/RHTH SE16 19 K4
Neckinger Est
BERM/RHTH SE16 19 K4
Neckinger St STHWK SE1 19 K3
Nectarine Wy LEW SE13 144 E3
Needham Rd BAY/PAD W2 100 E5
Needleman St
BERM/RHTH SE16 124 A2
Neeld Crs HDN NW4 63 K2
WBLY HA9 80 C3
Neils Yd LSQ/SEVD WC2H * 10 E4
Nelgarde Rd CAT SE6 164 D2
Nella Rd HMSMTH W6 119 G6
Nelldale Rd BERM/RHTH SE16 123 J4
Nello James Gdns
WNWD SE27 162 E6
Nelson Cl CROY/NA CR0 196 C5
EBED/NFELT TW14 * 153 J3
KIL/WHAMP NW6 100 E2
ROMW/RG RM7 56 D4
WOT/HER KT12 188 A5
Nelson Gdns BETH E2 104 C2
HSLW TW3 155 F1
Nelson Grove Rd
WIM/MER SW19 178 A4
Nelson Mandela Cl
MUSWH N10 47 K5
Nelson Mandela Rd
BKHTH/KID SE3 146 B4
Nelson Pl IS N1 6 B3
Nelson Rd BELV DA17 129 G5
CEND/HSY/T N8 67 F2
CHING E4 51 K2
DART DA1 171 F1
ED N9 36 D5
GNWCH SE10 125 F6
HAYES BR2 200 B1
HRW HA1 60 D5
HTHAIR TW6 132 C2
NWMAL KT3 192 A2
PEND EN3 37 F1
RAIN RM13 111 H1
SCUP DA14 168 B6
SEVS/STOTM N15 68 A1
STAN HA7 43 J2
WAN E11 70 E1
WHTN TW2 155 F1
WIM/MER SW19 178 A3
Nelson Sq STHWK SE1 18 A2
Nelsons Rw CLAP SW4 141 J5
Nelson St CAN/RD E16 106 D6
EHAM E6 90 A6
WCHPL E1 104 D5
Nelson Ter FSBYE EC1V 6 B3
Nelson Wk HOR/WEW KT19 206 C6
Nemoure Rd ACT W3 98 E6
Nene Gdns FELT TW13 154 E4
Nene Rd HTHAIR TW6 132 E2
Nepaul Rd BTSEA SW11 140 D3
Nepean St PUT/ROE SW15 158 D1
Neptune Cl RAIN RM13 111 H1
Neptune Rd HRW HA1 60 D3
HTHAIR TW6 * 133 F2
Neptune St BERM/RHTH SE16 123 K3
Nesbit Cl BKHTH/KID SE3 145 H4
Nesbit Rd ELTH/MOT SE9 146 C5
Nesbitts Aly BAR EN5 * 20 D4
Nesbitt Sq NRWD SE19 * 181 F3
Nesham St WAP E1W 123 H1
Ness Rd ERITH DA8 131 G6
Ness St BERM/RHTH SE16 123 H3
Nesta Rd WFD IG8 52 D2
Nestle's Av HYS/HAR UB3 113 J3
Nestor Av WCHMH N21 35 H1
Netheravon Rd CHSWK W4 118 C4
HNWL W7 116 A1
Netheravon Rd South
CHSWK W4 118 C6
Netherbury Rd EA W5 116 E3
Netherby Gdns ENC/FH EN2 22 E5
Netherby Rd FSTH SE23 163 K2
Nether Cl FNCH N3 46 E3
Nether Ct MLHL NW7 * 46 D2
Nethercourt Av FNCH N3 46 E2
Netherfield Gdns BARK IG11 90 D4
Netherfield Rd
NFNCH/WDSPK N12 47 F1
TOOT SW17 161 F5
Netherford Rd VX/NE SW8 141 H3
Netherhall Gdns HAMP NW3 83 G3
Netherhall Wy HAMP NW3 83 G3
Netherheys Dr SAND/SEL CR2 211 J5
Netherlands Rd BAR EN5 33 H1
Netherleigh Cl HGT N6 66 B5
Netherpark Dr GPK RM2 57 H5
Nether St FNCH N3 46 E3
Netherton Gv WBPTN SW10 120 B6
Netherton Rd
SEVS/STOTM N15 67 K3
TWK TW1 136 B6
Netherwood Pl
HMSMTH W6 * 119 G3
Netherwood Rd WKENS W14 119 G3
Netherwood St
KIL/WHAMP NW6 82 D5
Netley Cl CHEAM SM3 208 B3
CROY/NA CR0 214 A5
Netley Dr WOT/HER KT12 188 E4
Netley Gdns MRDN SM4 194 B4
Netley Rd BTFD TW8 117 F6
GNTH/NBYPK IG2 72 D2
MRDN SM4 194 B4
WALTH E17 69 H2
Netley St CAMTN NW1 4 A5
Nettlecombe Cl BELMT SM2 209 F6
Nettleden Av WBLY HA9 80 C4
Nettlefold Pl WNWD SE27 162 C5
Nettlestead Cl BECK BR3 182 C3
Nettleton Rd HTHAIR TW6 132 E2
NWCR SE14 144 A1
Nettlewood Rd
STRHM/NOR SW16 179 J3
Neuchatel Rd CAT SE6 164 C4
Nevada Cl NWMAL KT3 191 K1
Nevada St GNWCH SE10 145 F1
Nevern Pl ECT SW5 119 K4
Nevern Rd ECT SW5 119 K4
Nevern Sq ECT SW5 119 K4
Nevil Cl NTHWD HA6 40 B1
Neville Av NWMAL KT3 176 A4
Neville Cl ACT W3 117 K2
BFN/LL DA15 168 A6
CAMTN NW1 4 D3
HSLW TW3 135 F3
KIL/WHAMP NW6 100 D1
PECK SE15 143 H1
WAN E11 88 D1
Neville Dr EFNCH N2 65 G3
Neville Gdns BCTR RM8 91 K1
Neville Gill Cl
WAND/EARL SW18 159 K1
Neville Pl WDGN N22 49 F4
Neville Rd BARK/HLT IG6 54 C4
BCTR RM8 73 K6
CROY/NA CR0 196 E4
EA W5 97 K3
FSTGT E7 88 E5
KIL/WHAMP NW6 * 100 D1
KUT/HW KT1 175 H5
RCHPK/HAM TW10 156 D5
Neville St SKENS SW7 120 C5
Neville Ter SKENS SW7 * 120 C5
Neville Wk CAR SM5 194 D4
Nevill Rd STNW/STAM N16 86 A2
Nevill Wy LOU IG10 39 J1
Nevil Wk CAR SM5 * 194 D4
Nevin Dr CHING E4 37 K3
Nevinson Cl
WAND/EARL SW18 160 C1
Nevis Cl ROM RM1 57 G2
Nevis Rd TOOT SW17 161 F4
New Acres Rd THMD SE28 127 K1
Newall Rd HTHAIR TW6 133 F2
Newark Ct WOT/HER KT12 188 B5
Newark Crs WLSDN NW10 99 F2
Newark Knok EHAM E6 108 A5
Newark Rd SAND/SEL CR2 211 K4
Newark St WCHPL E1 104 D4
Newark Wy HDN NW4 45 J6
New Ash Cl EFNCH N2 47 H6
New Barn Cl WLGTN SM6 211 F4
New Barns Av MTCM CR4 195 J1
New Barn St CAN/RD E16 107 F4
PLSTW E13 106 E3
Newbery Rd ERITH DA8 150 C2
Newbiggin Pth OXHEY WD19 27 G6
Newbold Cots WCHPL E1 * 104 E5
Newbolt Av CHEAM SM3 208 A3
Newbolt Rd STAN HA7 43 F2
New Bond St MYFR/PICC W1J 9 K5
Newborough Gn NWMAL KT3 192 A1
New Brent St HDN NW4 64 A2
New Bridge St EMB EC4Y 12 A4
New Broad St LVPST EC2M 13 F2
New Broadway EA W5 97 J6
Newburgh Rd ACT W3 117 K1
Newburgh St SOHO/CST W1F 10 A4
New Burlington Ms
CONDST W1S 10 A5
New Burlington Pl
CONDST W1S 10 A5
New Burlington St
CONDST W1S 10 A5
Newburn St LBTH SE11 122 A5
Newbury Cl NTHLT UB5 77 K4
Newbury Gdns
HOR/WEW KT19 207 H2
Newbury Ms KTTN NW5 84 A4
Newbury Rd CHING E4 52 A2
GNTH/NBYPK IG2 72 D3
HAYES BR2 183 K6
HTHAIR TW6 132 C2
Newbury St STBT EC1A 12 C2
Newbury Wy NTHLT UB5 77 J4
New Butt La DEPT SE8 * 144 D1
Newby Cl EN EN1 24 A3
Newby Pl POP/IOD E14 106 A6
Newby St VX/NE SW8 141 G4
Newcastle Av BARK/HLT IG6 55 G2
Newcastle Cl
FLST/FETLN EC4A 12 A3
Newcastle Pl BAY/PAD W2 8 B2
Newcastle Rw CLKNW EC1R 5 K7
New Cavendish St
CAVSQ/HST W1G 9 H2
GTPST W1W 10 A1
New Change STP EC4M 12 C4
New Charles St FSBYE EC1V 6 B4
New Church Rd CMBW SE5 142 D1
New City Rd PLSTW E13 107 G2
New Clock Tower Pl
HOLWY N7 84 E4
New Cl FELT TW13 172 D1
WIM/MER SW19 178 B6
New College Ms IS N1 * 85 G5
New College Pde
HAMP NW3 * 83 G4
Newcombe Gdns
HSLWW TW4 134 E5
Newcombe Pk ALP/SUD HA0 80 B6
MLHL NW7 45 G1
Newcombe St KENS W8 * 119 K1
Newcome Gdns
STRHM/NOR SW16 161 K6
Newcomen Rd BTSEA SW11 140 C4
WAN E11 * 88 D1
Newcomen St STHWK SE1 18 E2
New Compton St
LSQ/SEVD WC2H * 10 D4
New Ct EMB EC4Y * 11 J5
NTHLT UB5 78 B3
Newcourt St STJWD NW8 2 C3
New Crane Pl WAP E1W * 123 K1
New Crescent Yd
WLSDN NW10 * 99 H1
New Cross Rd NWCR SE14 143 K1
Newdales Cl ED N9 36 C4
Newdene Av NTHLT UB5 95 H1
Newdigate
STRHM/NOR SW16 * 162 B6
Newell St POP/IOD E14 105 H6
New End HAMP NW3 83 G2
New End Sq HAMP NW3 83 H2
Newent Cl CAR SM5 194 E5
PECK SE15 143 F1
New Era Est IS N1 7 G1
New Farm Av HAYES BR2 199 K1
New Farm La NTHWD HA6 40 C4
New Ferry Ap
WOOL/PLUM SE18 127 F3
New Fetter La
FLST/FETLN EC4A 11 K3
Newfield Cl HPTN TW12 173 F4
Newfield Ri CRICK NW2 81 J1
New Forest La CHIG IG7 54 A2
Newgale Gdns EDGW HA8 44 B4
New Garden Dr WDR/YW UB7 112 B2
Newgate CROY/NA CR0 196 D5
Newgate Cl FELT TW13 154 D4
Newgate St CHING E4 38 C5
STBT EC1A 12 B3
New Globe Wk STHWK SE1 12 C7
New Goulston St WCHPL E1 13 J3
New Green Pl
BRXS/STRHM SW2 162 B2
NRWD SE19 181 F2
Newhall Gdns WOT/HER KT12 188 B6
Newham's Rw STHWK SE1 19 H3
Newham Wy CAN/RD E16 106 D4
EHAM E6 107 J3
PLSTW E13 107 F4
Newhaven Cl HYS/HAR UB3 113 J4
Newhaven Gdns
ELTH/MOT SE9 146 C5
Newhaven La PLSTW E13 106 D4
Newhaven Rd SNWD SE25 196 E2
New Heston Rd HEST TW5 134 E1
Newhouse Av CHDH RM6 55 K6
Newhouse Cl NWMAL KT3 192 B4
Newhouse Wk MRDN SM4 194 B4
Newick Cl BXLY DA5 169 J1
Newick Rd CLPT E5 86 D1
Newing Gn BMLY BR1 184 C3
Newington Barrow Wy
HOLWY N7 85 F1
Newington Butts WALW SE17 18 B7
Newington Cswy STHWK SE1 18 C4
Newington Gn IS N1 85 K3
Newington Green Rd IS N1 85 K3
New Inn Broadway
SDTCH EC2A * 7 H6
New Inn Sq SDTCH EC2A * 7 H6
New Inn St SDTCH EC2A * 7 H6
New Inn Yd SDTCH EC2A 7 H6
New Kelvin Av TEDD TW11 173 K2
New Kent Rd WALW SE17 18 D6
New King's Rd FUL/PGN SW6 139 K2
New King St DEPT SE8 124 D6
Newland Cl PIN HA5 41 J2
Newland Dr EN EN1 24 D2
Newland Gdns WEA W13 116 B2
Newland Rd CEND/HSY/T N8 48 E6
Newlands Av THDIT KT7 189 K5
Newlands Cl ALP/SUD HA0 79 J4
EDGW HA8 30 A5
NWDGN UB2 114 D5
Newlands Pk SYD SE26 181 K2
Newlands Pl BAR EN5 20 B6
Newlands Quay WAP E1W 104 E6
Newlands Rd
STRHM/NOR SW16 179 K5
WFD IG8 38 D4
The Newlands WLGTN SM6 210 C5
Newland St CAN/RD E16 126 D1
Newlands Wy CHSGTN KT9 205 J3
Newlands Woods
CROY/NA CR0 213 H6
Newling Cl EHAM E6 107 K5
Newling Est BETH E2 7 K4
New London St MON EC3R * 13 H5
New Lydenburg St CHARL SE7 126 B3
Newlyn Cl ORP BR6 217 F2
Newlyn Gdns
RYLN/HDSTN HA2 59 K4
Newlyn Rd BAR EN5 20 D5
TOTM N17 50 B4
WELL DA16 148 A3
Newman Ms WDGN N22 49 F3
Newman Rd BMLY BR1 183 K4
CROY/NA CR0 196 A4
HYS/HAR UB3 95 F6
PLSTW E13 107 F2
WALTH E17 69 F2
Newmans La SURB KT6 190 E3
Newman's Rw LINN WC2A 11 H2
Newman St FITZ W1T 10 B2
Newman's Wy EBAR EN4 21 G3
Newmarket Av NTHLT UB5 78 A3
Newmarsh Rd THMD SE28 128 A1
New Mill Rd STMC/STPC BR5 186 D4
Newminster Ct ENC/FH EN2 * 23 H3
Newminster Rd MRDN SM4 194 B3
New Mount St SRTFD E15 88 B5
Newnham Av RSLP HA4 59 G5
Newnham Cl LOU IG10 39 H1
NTHLT UB5 78 C4
THHTH CR7 180 D5
Newnham Gdns NTHLT UB5 78 C4
Newnham Gn WDGN N22 * 49 G4
Newnham Rd WDGN N22 49 F4
Newnhams Cl BMLY BR1 184 E6
Newnham Ter STHWK SE1 17 J4
Newnham Wy
KTN/HRWW/WS HA3 62 A2
New North Pl SDTCH EC2A 7 G6
New North Rd BARK/HLT IG6 54 D3
IS N1 7 F3
New North St BMSBY WC1N 11 G1
Newnton Cl FSBYPK N4 67 K4
New Oak Rd EFNCH N2 47 G5
New Oxford St
NOXST/BSQ WC1A 10 D3
New Pde ASHF TW15 * 152 C6
WDR/YW UB7 * 112 B1
New Park Av PLMGR N13 35 J5
New Park Cl NTHLT UB5 77 J4
New Park Est UED N18 50 E1
New Park Rd
BRXS/STRHM SW2 161 K2
New Place Sq
BERM/RHTH SE16 * 123 J3
New Plaistow Rd SRTFD E15 88 C6
New Pond Pde RSLP HA4 * 76 E1
Newport Av POP/IOD E14 106 B6
Newport Ct LSQ/SEVD WC2H 10 D5
Newport Md OXHEY WD19 * 27 H6
Newport Pl
SOHO/SHAV W1D * 10 D5
Newport Rd HTHAIR TW6 132 D2
ACT W3 117 K2
BARN SW13 138 D2
HTHAIR TW6 132 D2
LEY E10 70 B6
WALTH E17 * 69 G1
YEAD UB4 94 B4
Newport St LBTH SE11 17 G7
Newquay Crs
RYLN/HDSTN HA2 59 J6
Newquay Gdns OXHEY WD19 27 F4
Newquay Rd CAT SE6 164 E4
New Quebec St MBLAR W1H 9 F4
New River Av CEND/HSY/T N8 49 F6
New River Crs PLMGR N13 35 H6
New River Wy FSBYPK N4 67 K4
New Rd ABYW SE2 128 E4
BORE WD6 29 K1
BTFD TW8 * 116 E6
CEND/HSY/T N8 66 D2
CHING E4 37 K6
DAGE RM10 110 C1
E/WMO/HCT KT8 173 F6
EBED/NFELT TW14 153 G1
ED N9 36 D4
ESH/CLAY KT10 204 C2
FELT TW13 172 D1
GDMY/SEVK IG3 72 E6
HRW HA1 79 F2
HSLW TW3 135 G5
HYS/HAR UB3 133 F1
KUTN/CMB KT2 175 H3
MLHL NW7 46 C3
MNPK E12 71 J6
MTCM CR4 195 F5
ORP BR6 202 B4
RAIN RM13 110 E2
RCHPK/HAM TW10 156 D6
TOTM N17 50 B4
UX/CGN UB8 94 A3
WCHPL E1 104 C4
WDGN N22 49 J4
WELL DA16 148 C3
New Road Hl HAYES BR2 215 J6
New Rw CHCR WC2N 10 E5
Newry Rd TWK TW1 136 B5
Newsam Av SEVS/STOTM N15 67 K2
Newsholme Dr WCHMH N21 23 F6
New Spring Gardens Wk
STHWK SE1 * 121 K5
New Sq EBED/NFELT TW14 153 F3
LINN WC2A 11 H3
Newstead Av ORP BR6 216 D1
Newstead Cl
NFNCH/WDSPK N12 47 J2
Newstead Ct NTHLT UB5 * 95 J2
Newstead Rd LEE/GVPK SE12 165 J2
Newstead Wk CAR SM5 194 B4
Newstead Wy
WIM/MER SW19 159 G6
New St LVPST EC2M 13 H2
New Street Hl BMLY BR1 184 A1
New Street Sq
FLST/FETLN EC4A 11 K3
New Tank Hill Rd PUR RM19 131 K3
Newton Av ACT W3 117 K2
MUSWH N10 48 A4
Newton Cl RYLN/HDSTN HA2 60 A6
WALTH E17 69 G3
Newton Gv CHSWK W4 118 B3
Newton Park Pl CHST BR7 184 E3
Newton Pl POP/IOD E14 124 D4
Newton Rd ALP/SUD HA0 80 B5
BAY/PAD W2 101 F5
CRICK NW2 82 A2
HTHAIR TW6 132 B2
ISLW TW7 136 A3
KTN/HRWW/WS HA3 42 E4
SEVS/STOTM N15 68 B2
SRTFD E15 88 B3
WELL DA16 148 B4
WIM/MER SW19 177 H3
Newtons Cl RAIN RM13 93 G5
Newton St HOL/ALD WC2B 11 F3
Newton's Yd
WAND/EARL SW18 139 K6
Newton Ter HAYES BR2 200 C3
Newton Wk EDGW HA8 44 E4
Newton Wy UED N18 49 J1
New Tower Blds WAP E1W * 123 J1
Newtown St BTSEA SW11 141 G2
New Trinity Rd EFNCH N2 47 H6
New Union Cl POP/IOD E14 125 F3
New Union St BARB EC2Y 12 E2
New Vls TOTM N17 * 50 C4
New Wanstead WAN E11 70 E3
New Way Rd CDALE/KGS NW9 63 G1
New Wharf Rd IS N1 5 F2
New Zealand Wy RAIN RM13 111 H2
Niagara Av EA W5 116 D4
Niagara Cl IS N1 6 D2
Nibthwaite Rd HRW HA1 60 E2
Nicholas Cl GFD/PVL UB6 96 B1
Nicholas Gdns EA W5 116 E1
Nicholas La MANHO EC4N 13 F5
Nicholas Rd BCTR RM8 74 B6
BORE WD6 30 B1
CROY/NA CR0 210 E2
WCHPL E1 104 E3
Nicholas Wy NTHWD HA6 40 A4
Nicholay Rd ARCH N19 66 D5
Nichol Cl STHGT/OAK N14 34 D3
Nicholes Rd HSLW TW3 135 F5
Nichol La BMLY BR1 183 K3
Nichollsfield Wk HOLWY N7 84 E3
Nicholl St BETH E2 86 C6
Nichols Cl FSBYPK N4 * 67 G5
Nichols Gn EA W5 98 A4
Nicholson Dr BUSH WD23 28 C3
Nicholson House CHARL SE7 * 146 D1
Nicholson Ms KUT/HW KT1 191 F1
Nicholson Rd CROY/NA CR0 197 G5
Nicholson St STHWK SE1 18 A1
Nickelby Cl THMD SE28 109 J5
Nickols Wk WAND/EARL SW18 140 A5
Nicola Cl KTN/HRWW/WS HA3 42 D5
SAND/SEL CR2 211 J4
Nicola Ms BARK/HLT IG6 54 B3
Nicol Cl TWK TW1 156 C1
Nicoll Pl HDN NW4 63 K3
Nicoll Rd WLSDN NW10 81 G6
Nicolson Rd STMC/STPC BR5 202 D4
Nicosia Rd WAND/EARL SW18 160 D2
Niederwald Rd SYD SE26 164 B6
Nield Rd HYS/HAR UB3 113 J2
Nigel Cl NTHLT UB5 77 J6
Nigel Fisher Wy CHSGTN KT9 205 J5
Nigel Ms IL IG1 90 B2
Nigel Playfair Av
HMSMTH W6 118 E4
Nigel Rd FSTGT E7 89 G3
PECK SE15 143 H4
Nigeria Rd CHARL SE7 146 B1
Nightingale Av CHING E4 52 C1
Nightingale Cl CAR SM5 195 F6
CHING E4 38 C6
CHSWK W4 117 K6
PIN HA5 59 G2
Nightingale Cnr
STMC/STPC BR5 * 202 E1
Nightingale Ct SUT SM1 209 G3
Nightingale Dr
HOR/WEW KT19 206 D4
Nightingale Gv LEW SE13 145 G6
Nightingale La BAL SW12 161 F1
BMLY BR1 184 B5
CEND/HSY/T N8 66 E1
RCHPK/HAM TW10 157 F2
WAN E11 71 F2
Nightingale Ms KUT/HW KT1 * 174 E6
LBTH SE11 17 K6
Nightingale Pl WBPTN SW10 120 B6
WOOL/PLUM SE18 127 F6
Nightingale Rd CAR SM5 209 K1
CLPT E5 86 D1
E/WMO/HCT KT8 189 G2
ED N9 36 E2
HNWL W7 116 A1
HPTN TW12 173 F2
IS N1 85 J4
STMC/STPC BR5 201 H3
WDGN N22 48 E4
WLSDN NW10 99 H1
WOT/HER KT12 * 188 B4
Nightingale Sq BAL SW12 161 F2
The Nightingales
STWL/WRAY TW19 152 C3
Nightingale V
WOOL/PLUM SE18 127 F6
Nightingale Wk BAL SW12 161 G1
Nightingale Wy EHAM E6 107 J4
Nightingale Av HRW HA1 61 H4
Nile Cl STNW/STAM N16 86 B1
Nile Dr ED N9 36 E4
Nile Rd PLSTW E13 107 G1
Nile St IS N1 6 E4
Nile Ter PECK SE15 123 G5
Nimmo Dr BUSH WD23 28 D2
Nimrod Cl NTHLT UB5 95 H2
Nimrod Pas IS N1 86 A4
Nimrod Rd
STRHM/NOR SW16 179 G2
Nina Mackay Cl SRTFD E15 * 88 C6
Nine Acres Cl HYS/HAR UB3 113 F3
MNPK E12 89 J3
Nine Elms Cl
EBED/NFELT TW14 153 J3
Nine Elms La VX/NE SW8 141 H1
Nineteenth Rd MTCM CR4 195 K1
Ninhams Wd ORP BR6 216 A2
Ninth Av HYS/HAR UB3 94 E6
Nipper Aly KUT/HW KT1 175 F5
Nisbett Wk SCUP DA14 168 B6

Nithdale Rd
WOOL/PLUM SE18 147 G1
Nithsdale Gv HGDN/ICK UB10 76 A1
Niton Cl BAR EN5 32 B1
Niton Rd RCH/KEW TW9 * 137 H4
Niton St FUL/PGN SW6 139 G1
No1 St WOOL/PLUM SE18 127 G3
No2 St WOOL/PLUM SE18 127 G3
Noak Hill Rd ABR/ST RM4 57 K1
Nobel Dr HYS/HAR UB3 133 H1
Nobel Rd UED N18 36 E6
Noble Cnr HEST TW5 * 135 F2
Noble St CITYW EC2V 12 C3
Noel Rd ACT W3 98 C5
EHAM E6 107 J3
IS N1 6 A2
Noel St SOHO/CST W1F 10 B4
Nolan Wy CLPT E5 86 C2
Nolton Pl EDGW HA8 44 B4
Nonsuch Cl CHIG IG7 54 B2
Nonsuch Pl CHEAM SM3 * 208 B5
Norbiton Av KUT/HW KT1 175 H5
KUTN/CMB KT2 175 H4
Norbiton Common Rd
KUT/HW KT1 175 J6
Norbiton Rd POP/IOD E14 105 H5
Norbreck Pde EA W5 98 A2
Norbroke St SHB W12 99 H6
Norburn St NKENS W10 100 C4
Norbury Av HSLW TW3 135 J6
STRHM/NOR SW16 180 A4
THHTH CR7 180 B5
Norbury Cl STRHM/NOR SW16 180 B4
Norbury Court Rd
STRHM/NOR SW16 179 K5
Norbury Crs
STRHM/NOR SW16 180 B5
Norbury Cross
STRHM/NOR SW16 179 K6
Norbury Gdns CHDH RM6 73 K2
Norbury Gv MLHL NW7 31 G5
Norbury Hl STRHM/NOR SW16 180 B3
Norbury Ri STRHM/NOR SW16 179 K6
Norbury Rd CHING E4 51 J1
FELT TW13 153 J5
THHTH CR7 180 D5
Norbury Vls KUT/HW KT1 * 175 G5
Norcombe Gdns
KTN/HRWW/WS HA3 61 J3
Norcott Cl YEAD UB4 95 G3
Norcott Rd STNW/STAM N16 68 C6
Norcroft Gdns EDUL SE22 163 H2
Norcutt Rd WHTN TW2 155 K3
Nordenfeldt Rd ERITH DA8 130 A5
Norfield Rd RDART DA2 169 K6
Norfolk Av PLMGR N13 49 H2
SEVS/STOTM N15 68 B3
Norfolk Cl DART DA1 171 K1
EBAR EN4 22 A5
EFNCH N2 47 J6
PLMGR N13 49 H2
TWK TW1 * 156 C1
Norfolk Ct BAR EN5 * 20 C5
Norfolk Crs BAY/PAD W2 8 C3
BFN/LL DA15 167 K2
Norfolk Gdns BXLYHN DA7 149 G2
Norfolk House Rd
STRHM/NOR SW16 161 J5
Norfolk Ms NKENS W10 100 C4
Norfolk Pl BAY/PAD W2 8 B3
WELL DA16 148 B3
Norfolk Rd BAR EN5 20 E4
BARK IG11 90 E5
DAGE RM10 92 D3
EHAM E6 89 K6
ESH/CLAY KT10 204 E3
FELT TW13 154 B3
GDMY/SEVK IG3 72 E5
HRW HA1 60 B2
PEND EN3 24 D6
ROMW/RG RM7 74 E3
STJWD NW8 2 B1
THHTH CR7 180 D6
WALTH E17 51 H6
WIM/MER SW19 178 D3
WLSDN NW10 81 G5
Norfolk Rw STHWK SE1 17 G6
Norfolk Sq BAY/PAD W2 8 B4
Norfolk Square Ms
BAY/PAD W2 8 B4
Norfolk St FSTGT E7 88 E3
Norgrove St BAL SW12 161 F3
Norhyrst Av SNWD SE25 181 G6
Norland Pl NTGHL W11 119 H1
Norland Rd NTGHL W11 119 G1
Norlands Crs CHST BR7 185 G4
Norlands Ga CHST BR7 * 185 G4
Norland Sq NTGHL W11 119 H1
Norley V PUT/ROE SW15 158 D3
Norlington Rd LEY E10 70 A5
Norman Av FELT TW13 154 D4
STHL UB1 95 J6
TWK TW1 156 C2
WDGN N22 49 J4
Normanby Cl PUT/ROE SW15 139 J6
Normanby Rd WLSDN NW10 81 H3
Norman Cl ORP BR6 216 C1
ROMW/RG RM7 56 D5
Norman Crs HEST TW5 134 C1
PIN HA5 41 G4
Normand Gdns WKENS W14 * 119 H6
Normand Ms WKENS W14 119 H6
Normand Rd WKENS W14 119 J6
Normandy Av BAR EN5 20 D6
Normandy Cl SYD SE26 164 B5
Normandy Dr HYS/HAR UB3 94 A5
Normandy Rd BRXN/ST SW9 142 B2
Normandy Ter CAN/RD E16 107 F5
Normandy Wy ERITH DA8 150 B2
Norman Gv BOW E3 105 G1
Normanhurst Av WELL DA16 148 E2
Normanhurst Dr TWK TW1 136 C6
Normanhurst Rd
BRXS/STRHM SW2 162 A4
STMC/STPC BR5 186 C5
WOT/HER KT12 188 C6
Norman Pde SCUP DA14 * 169 F5
Norman Rd BELV DA17 129 J2
DART DA1 171 H3
EHAM E6 107 K3
EMPK RM11 75 J4
GNWCH SE10 144 E1
IL IG1 90 B3
SEVS/STOTM N15 68 B2
SUT SM1 208 E3
THHTH CR7 196 C2
WAN E11 70 C6
WIM/MER SW19 178 B3
Normans Cl WDGN N22 * 49 J4
WLSDN NW10 81 F4
Normansfield Av KUT/HW KT1 174 D3
Normansfield Cl BUSH WD23 28 B2
Normanshire Dr CHING E4 37 J6
Normans Md WLSDN NW10 81 F4
Norman St FSBYE EC1V 6 C5
Norman Ter
KIL/WHAMP NW6 * 82 D3
Normanton Av
WAND/EARL SW18 159 K4
Normanton Pk CHING E4 38 C5
Normanton Rd SAND/SEL CR2 212 A4
Normanton St FSTH SE23 164 A4
Norman Wy ACT W3 98 D4
STHGT/OAK N14 34 E4
Normington Cl
STRHM/NOR SW16 180 B1
Norrice Lea EFNCH N2 65 H2
Norris St STJS SW1Y 10 C6
Norris Wy DART DA1 150 C4
Norroy Rd PUT/ROE SW15 139 G5
Norrys Cl EBAR EN4 21 K6
Norrys Rd EBAR EN4 21 K5
Norseman Cl GDMY/SEVK IG3 73 H5
Norseman Wy GFD/PVL UB6 78 B6
Norstead Pl PUT/ROE SW15 158 D4
North Access Rd WALTH E17 69 F3
North Acre CDALE/KGS NW9 45 G4
North Acton Rd WLSDN NW10 99 F1
Northall Rd BXLYHN DA7 149 K3
Northampton Gv IS N1 85 K3
Northampton Pk IS N1 85 J4
Northampton Rd
CLKNW EC1R 5 K6
CROY/NA CR0 197 H6
PEND EN3 25 G5
Northampton Rw
CLKNW EC1R * 5 K6
Northampton Sq FSBYE EC1V 6 A5
Northampton St IS N1 85 J5
Northanger Rd
STRHM/NOR SW16 179 K2
North Ap NTHWD HA6 26 A4
North Audley St
MYFR/PKLN W1K 9 G5
North Av CAR SM5 210 A5
HYS/HAR UB3 94 E6
RCH/KEW TW9 137 H2
RYLN/HDSTN HA2 60 B3
STHL UB1 95 K6
UED N18 36 C6
WEA W13 97 H5
North Bank STJWD NW8 2 C5
Northbank Rd WALTH E17 52 A5
North Birkbeck Rd WAN E11 88 B1
Northborough Rd
STRHM/NOR SW16 179 K5
North Boundary Rd
MNPK E12 71 H6
Northbourne HAYES BR2 199 K4
Northbourne Rd CLAP SW4 141 J5
Northbrook Dr NTHWD HA6 40 C4
Northbrook Rd BAR EN5 32 C1
CROY/NA CR0 196 E2
IL IG1 72 A6
LEW SE13 145 G6
WDGN N22 48 E2
Northburgh St FSBYE EC1V 6 B7
North Carriage Dr
BAY/PAD W2 8 D5
Northchurch Rd IS N1 85 J5
WBLY HA9 80 C4
Northchurch Ter IS N1 86 A5
North Circular PLMGR N13 49 G1
WALTH E17 51 K4
North Circular Rd BARK IG11 90 A5
CHING E4 * 51 G2
CRICK NW2 81 G1
EFNCH N2 47 G5
GLDGN NW11 64 C3
IL IG1 71 H3
MNPK E12 90 A3
NFNCH/WDSPK N12 47 J3
REDBR IG4 53 G6
WLSDN NW10 98 B1
Northcliffe Cl WPK KT4 207 G1
Northcliffe Dr
TRDG/WHET N20 32 D3
North Cl BAR EN5 20 A6
BXLYHS DA6 148 E5
CHIG IG7 55 G1
DAGE RM10 92 C6
EBED/NFELT TW14 153 G1
MRDN SM4 193 H1
The North Colonnade
POP/IOD E14 124 E1
North Common Rd EA W5 98 A6
Northcote Av BRYLDS KT5 191 H4
EA W5 98 A6
ISLW TW7 136 B6
STHL UB1 95 J6
Northcote Rd BTSEA SW11 140 D5
CROY/NA CR0 196 E3
NWMAL KT3 175 K6
SCUP DA14 167 K6
TWK TW1 136 B6
WALTH E17 69 G1
WLSDN NW10 81 G5
Northcott Av WDGN N22 48 E4
North Countess Rd
WALTH E17 51 H5
Northcourt FITZ W1T 10 B1
North Cray Rd BXLY DA5 169 H4
SCUP DA14 187 F1
North Crs CAN/RD E16 106 B3
FNCH N3 46 D5
GWRST WC1E 10 C1
Northcroft Rd
HOR/WEW KT19 207 G5
WEA W13 116 C2
North Cross Rd BARK/HLT IG6 72 C1
EDUL SE22 143 G6
Northdene CHIG IG7 54 D1
North Dene HSLW TW3 135 G2
MLHL NW7 31 F5
Northdene Gdns
SEVS/STOTM N15 68 A3
Northdown Cl RSLP HA4 76 D1
Northdown Gdns
GNTH/NBYPK IG2 72 E2
Northdown Rd EMPK RM11 75 K4
WELL DA16 148 C3
Northdown St IS N1 5 G3
North Dr BECK BR3 198 E1
HSLW TW3 135 H3
ORP BR6 216 E2
RSLP HA4 58 C4
STRHM/NOR SW16 161 H6
North End BKHH IG9 39 G2
CROY/NA CR0 196 D5
HAMP NW3 65 G6
North End Av HAMP NW3 65 G6
North End Crs WKENS W14 119 J4
North End La ORP BR6 216 B6
Northend Rd ERITH DA8 150 C2
North End Rd FUL/PGN SW6 139 K1
GLDGN NW11 64 E5
WBLY HA9 80 C1
WKENS W14 119 H4
North End Wy HAMP NW3 65 G6
Northern Av ED N9 36 B4
Northernhay Wk MRDN SM4 193 H1
Northern Perimeter Rd
HTHAIR TW6 133 F2
Northern Perimeter Rd (West)
HTHAIR TW6 132 B2
Northern Relief Rd BARK IG11 90 C5
North Eyot Gdns
HMSMTH W6 * 118 C5
Northey St POP/IOD E14 105 G6
North Farm LOU IG10 39 G1
Northfield Av PIN HA5 59 H1
STMC/STPC BR5 202 D3
WEA W13 116 C2
Northfield Cl BMLY BR1 184 D4
HYS/HAR UB3 113 J3
Northfield Crs CHEAM SM3 208 C2
Northfield Pde
HYS/HAR UB3 * 113 J3
Northfield Pk HYS/HAR UB3 113 H3
Northfield Rd DAGW RM9 92 B2
EBAR EN4 21 J4
ED N9 * 24 D6
EHAM E6 89 K4
HEST TW5 114 C6
PEND EN3 36 D1
STNW/STAM N16 68 A4
WEA W13 116 C2
Northfields WAND/EARL SW18 139 K5
Northfields Rd ACT W3 98 E4
North Gdns WIM/MER SW19 178 C3
Northgate NTHWD HA6 40 A3
Northgate Dr
CDALE/KGS NW9 63 G3
North Gower St CAMTN NW1 4 A5
North Gv HGT N6 66 A4
SEVS/STOTM N15 67 K2
North Hl HGT N6 65 K3
North Hill Av HGT N6 65 K3
North Hyde Gdns
HYS/HAR UB3 113 K3
North Hyde La NWDGN UB2 114 D5
North Hyde Rd HYS/HAR UB3 113 H3
North Hyde Whf
NWDGN UB2 * 114 B4
Northiam NFNCH/WDSPK N12 32 E6
Northiam St HACK E8 86 D6
HOM E9 86 E6
Northington St BMSBY WC1N 11 G1
Northlands Av ORP BR6 216 E2
Northlands St CMBW SE5 142 D3
North La TEDD TW11 174 A2
North Lodge Cl
PUT/ROE SW15 * 139 G6
North Ms BMSBY WC1N 5 H7
North Mt TRDG/WHET N20 * 33 G4
Northolm EDGW HA8 31 F6
Northolme Gdns EDGW HA8 44 C4
Northolme Ri ORP BR6 201 K6
Northolme Rd HBRY N5 85 J2
Northolt Av RSLP HA4 77 F3
Northolt Gdns GFD/PVL UB6 79 F3
Northolt Rd HTHAIR TW6 132 B2
RYLN/HDSTN HA2 78 B2
Northover BMLY BR1 165 J6
North Pde CHSGTN KT9 206 B3
EDGW HA8 * 44 C5
STHL UB1 * 96 A5
North Pk ELTH/MOT SE9 166 E1
North Pas WAND/EARL SW18 139 K6
North Peckham Est
PECK SE15 143 G1
North Pl MTCM CR4 178 E3
TEDD TW11 174 A2
Northpoint Cl SUT SM1 209 G1
North Pole La HAYES BR2 214 E4
North Pole Rd SHB W12 100 A5
Northport St IS N1 7 F1
North Ri BAY/PAD W2 * 8 D4
North Rd BELV DA17 129 J3
BMLY BR1 184 A4
BTFD TW8 117 F6
CHDH RM6 74 A2
DART DA1 170 C1
EA W5 116 E3
EBED/NFELT TW14 153 G1
ED N9 36 D3
EDGW HA8 44 D4
GDMY/SEVK IG3 72 E6
HEST TW5 114 B6
HGT N6 66 A4
HOLWY N7 84 E4
HYS/HAR UB3 94 B4
RCH/KEW TW9 137 H3
STHL UB1 96 A6
SURB KT6 190 E3
WDR/YW UB7 112 C3
WIM/MER SW19 178 B2
WOOL/PLUM SE18 127 K4
WWKM BR4 198 E5
Northrop Rd HTHAIR TW6 133 H2
North Rw MYFR/PKLN W1K 9 F5
North Several
BKHTH/KID SE3 * 145 G3
Northside Rd BMLY BR1 183 K4
North Side Wandsworth
Common
WAND/EARL SW18 140 B6
Northspur Rd SUT SM1 208 E1
North Sq ED N9 36 D4
GLDGN NW11 64 E2
Northstead Rd
BRXS/STRHM SW2 162 B4
North St BARK IG11 90 B5
BMLY BR1 183 K4
BXLYHN DA7 149 H5
CAR SM5 209 K2
CLAP SW4 141 G4
DART DA1 171 G2
HDN NW4 64 A2
ISLW TW7 136 B4
PLSTW E13 107 F1
ROM RM1 75 F1
North Tenter St WCHPL E1 13 K4
North Ter SKENS SW7 14 C6
Northumberland Aly
FENCHST EC3M * 13 H4
Northumberland Av
CHCR WC2N 10 E7
EN EN1 24 D1
ISLW TW7 136 A2
MNPK E12 71 G5
WELL DA16 147 K5
Northumberland Cl
ERITH DA8 149 K1
STWL/WRAY TW19 152 B1
Northumberland Crs
EBED/NFELT TW14 153 H1
Northumberland Gdns
BMLY BR1 201 F1
ED N9 36 B5
MTCM CR4 195 J2
Northumberland Gv
TOTM N17 50 D3
Northumberland Pk
ERITH DA8 149 K1
TOTM N17 50 C3
Northumberland Pl
BAY/PAD W2 100 E5
Northumberland Rd BAR EN5 33 G1
EHAM E6 107 J5
RYLN/HDSTN HA2 59 K2
WALTH E17 69 J4
Northumberland St
CHCR WC2N 10 E7
Northumberland Wy
ERITH DA8 149 K2
Northumbria St POP/IOD E14 105 J5
North Verbena Gdns
HMSMTH W6 * 118 D5
North Vw EA W5 97 J3
PIN HA5 59 G4
WIM/MER SW19 176 E1
Northview Crs WLSDN NW10 81 H2
Northview Dr WFD IG8 53 H5
Northview Pde HOLWY N7 * 84 E1
North View Rd
CEND/HSY/T N8 48 D6
North Vls CAMTN NW1 84 D4
North Wk CROY/NA CR0 213 K3
North Wy CDALE/KGS NW9 44 D6
ED N9 36 E4
FBAR/BDGN N11 48 C2
PIN HA5 41 G6
Northway GLDGN NW11 65 F2
MRDN SM4 177 H6
WLGTN SM6 210 C2
Northway Crs MLHL NW7 31 G6
Northway Rd CMBW SE5 142 D4
CROY/NA CR0 197 G3
Northways Pde HAMP NW3 * 83 H5
North Weald Cl HCH RM12 93 K5
North Weald La
KUTN/CMB KT2 174 D1
North Wharf Rd BAY/PAD W2 8 A2
Northwick Av
KTN/HRWW/WS HA3 61 G3
Northwick Cir
KTN/HRWW/WS HA3 61 J3
Northwick Cl STJWD NW8 2 A6
Northwick Park Rd HRW HA1 61 F3
Northwick Rd ALP/SUD HA0 79 K6
OXHEY WD19 27 G6
Northwick Ter STJWD NW8 2 A6
Northwold Dr PIN HA5 41 G6
Northwold Rd
STNW/STAM N16 68 C6
Northwood Av HCH RM12 93 J2
Northwood Gdns CLAY IG5 72 A1
GFD/PVL UB6 79 F3
NFNCH/WDSPK N12 47 H1
Northwood Pl ERITHM DA18 129 G3
Northwood Rd CAR SM5 210 A4
FSTH SE23 164 C3
HGT N6 66 B4
HTHAIR TW6 132 A2
THHTH CR7 180 D5
Northwood Wy NTHWD HA6 40 E3
North Woolwich Rd
CAN/RD E16 125 K1
North Worple Wy
MORT/ESHN SW14 138 A4
Norton Av BRYLDS KT5 191 J4
Norton Cl CHING E4 51 J1
Norton Folgate WCHPL E1 7 H7
Norton Gdns
STRHM/NOR SW16 179 K5
Norton Rd ALP/SUD HA0 79 K4
DAGE RM10 93 F4
LEY E10 69 H5
Norval Gn BRXN/ST SW9 * 142 B3
Norval Rd ALP/SUD HA0 61 H6
Norway Ga BERM/RHTH SE16 124 B3
Norway Pl POP/IOD E14 105 H5
Norway St GNWCH SE10 124 E6
Norwich Crs CHDH RM6 73 H2
Norwich Ms GDMY/SEVK IG3 73 G5
Norwich Rd FSTGT E7 88 E3
GFD/PVL UB6 78 B6
NTHWD HA6 40 D6
THHTH CR7 180 D6
Norwich St FLST/FETLN EC4A 11 J3
Norwich Wk EDGW HA8 44 E3
Norwood Av ALP/SUD HA0 80 B6
ROMW/RG RM7 75 F4
Norwood Cl CRICK NW2 82 C1
NWDGN UB2 115 F4
WHTN TW2 155 J4
Norwood Dr
RYLN/HDSTN HA2 59 K3
Norwood Gdns NWDGN UB2 114 E4
YEAD UB4 95 G3
Norwood Green Rd
NWDGN UB2 115 F4
Norwood High St
WNWD SE27 162 C5
Norwood Park Rd
WNWD SE27 180 D1
Norwood Rd HNHL SE24 162 C3
NWDGN UB2 114 D3
WNWD SE27 162 C4
Notley St CMBW SE5 142 E1
Notson Rd SNWD SE25 197 J1
Notting Barn Rd NKENS W10 100 B3
Nottingdale Sq NTGHL W11 * 119 H1
Nottingham Av CAN/RD E16 107 G4
Nottingham Ct
LSQ/SEVD WC2H 10 E4
Nottingham Pl CAMTN NW1 3 G7
Nottingham Rd ISLW TW7 136 A3
LEY E10 70 A3
SAND/SEL CR2 211 J2
TOOT SW17 160 E3
Nottingham St MHST W1U 9 G1
Nottingham Ter CAMTN NW1 3 G7
Notting Hill Ga KENS W8 119 K1
Nova Ms CHEAM SM3 193 H4
Novar Cl ORP BR6 202 A4
Nova Rd CROY/NA CR0 196 C5
Novar Rd ELTH/MOT SE9 167 H3
Novello St FUL/PGN SW6 139 K2
Nowell Rd BARN SW13 118 D6
Nower Hl PIN HA5 59 K1
Noyna Rd TOOT SW17 160 E5
Nubia Wy BMLY BR1 165 H6
Nuding Cl LEW SE13 144 D4
Nugent Rd ARCH N19 66 E5
SNWD SE25 181 G6
Nugents Ct PIN HA5 * 41 J4
Nugent's Pk PIN HA5 41 J4
Nugent Ter STJWD NW8 101 G1
Nun Ct LOTH EC2R * 12 E3
Nuneaton Rd DAGW RM9 91 K5
Nunhead Crs PECK SE15 143 J4
Nunhead Gv PECK SE15 143 J4
Nunhead La PECK SE15 143 J4
Nunnington Cl ELTH/MOT SE9 166 D5
Nunn's Rd ENC/FH EN2 23 J3
Nupton Dr BAR EN5 32 A1
Nurse Cl EDGW HA8 44 E4
Nursery Av BXLYHN DA7 149 G4
CROY/NA CR0 198 A6
FNCH N3 47 F5
Nursery Cl BROCKY SE4 144 C3
CHDH RM6 73 K3
CROY/NA CR0 198 A6
EBED/NFELT TW14 154 A2
ORP BR6 202 A4
OXHEY WD19 27 F3
PEND EN3 25 F2
PUT/ROE SW15 139 G6
SWLY BR8 187 K5
WFD IG8 53 F1
Nursery Gdns CHST BR7 185 G2
HPTN TW12 154 E6
HSLWW TW4 134 E6
PEND EN3 25 F2
Nursery La BETH E2 7 J1
FSTGT E7 88 E4
NKENS W10 100 A4
Nurserymans Rd
FBAR/BDGN N11 34 A4
Nursery Rd BRXN/ST SW9 142 A5
EFNCH N2 47 H4
HOM E9 86 E4
MNPK E12 71 J6
MTCM CR4 178 D6
PIN HA5 41 G6
STHGT/OAK N14 34 C2
SUT SM1 209 G2
THHTH CR7 196 E1
WIM/MER SW19 177 H3
Nursery Rw BAR EN5 * 20 C4
WALW SE17 18 E7
Nursery St TOTM N17 50 B3
The Nursery ERITH DA8 150 C1
Nursery Wk HDN NW4 45 K6
ROMW/RG RM7 75 F4
Nurstead Rd ERITH DA8 149 H1
Nutbourne St NKENS W10 100 C2
Nutbrook St PECK SE15 143 G4
Nutbrowne Rd DAGW RM9 92 B6
Nutcroft Rd PECK SE15 143 J1
Nutfield Cl CAR SM5 209 J1
UED N18 50 C2
Nutfield Gdns GDMY/SEVK IG3 73 F6
NTHLT UB5 95 G1
Nutfield Rd CRICK NW2 63 J6
EDUL SE22 143 G6
SRTFD E15 88 A2
THHTH CR7 196 C1
Nutfield Wy ORP BR6 201 F6
Nutford Pl MBLAR W1H 8 D3
Nuthatch Cl
STWL/WRAY TW19 152 C3
Nuthatch Gdns THMD SE28 127 J2
Nuthurst Av
BRXS/STRHM SW2 162 A4
Nutley Ter HAMP NW3 83 H4
Nutmead Cl BXLY DA5 169 K3
Nutmeg Cl CAN/RD E16 106 C3
Nutmeg La POP/IOD E14 106 B5
Nuttall St IS N1 7 H2
Nutter La WAN E11 71 G2
Nutt Gv EDGW HA8 29 K4
Nut Tree Cl ORP BR6 217 K1
Nutt St PECK SE15 143 G1
Nutwell St TOOT SW17 178 D1
Nuxley Rd BELV DA17 129 G6
Nyanza St WOOL/PLUM SE18 127 J6
Nylands Av RCH/KEW TW9 137 H3

Nymans Gdns RYNPK SW20 176 E6
Nynehead St NWCR SE14 144 B1
Nyon Gv CAT SE6 164 C4
Nyssa Cl WFD IG8 53 K2
Nyton Cl ARCH N19 66 E5

O

Oak Av CEND/HSY/T N8 66 E1
CROY/NA CR0 198 D6
ENC/FH EN2 23 F2
HEST TW5 134 C1
HPTN TW12 172 D1
MUSWH N10 48 B3
TOTM N17 49 K3
WDR/YW UB7 112 D3
Oakbank CROY/NA CR0 214 A4
Oakbank Av WOT/HER KT12 188 E4
Oakbank Gv HNHL SE24 142 D5
Oakbrook Cl BMLY BR1 166 A6
Oakbury Rd FUL/PGN SW6 140 A3
Oak Cl DART DA1 150 B5
STHGT/OAK N14 34 B2
Oakcombe Cl NWMAL KT3 176 B4
Oak Cottage Cl CAT SE6 165 H3
Oak Cots HNWL W7 * 115 K2
Oak Crs CAN/RD E16 106 C4
Oakcroft Cl PIN HA5 41 F5
Oakcroft Rd CHSGTN KT9 206 B2
LEW SE13 145 G3
Oakcroft Vls CHSGTN KT9 206 B2
Oakdale STHGT/OAK N14 34 B3
Oakdale Av
KTN/HRWW/WS HA3 62 A2
NTHWD HA6 40 E5
Oakdale Cl OXHEY WD19 27 G6
Oakdale Gdns CHING E4 52 A1
Oakdale Rd FSBYPK N4 67 J3
FSTGT E7 89 F5
HOR/WEW KT19 207 F6
OXHEY WD19 27 G5
PECK SE15 143 K4
STRHM/NOR SW16 179 K1
SWFD E18 53 F5
WAN E11 70 B6
Oakdale Wy MTCM CR4 195 F4
Oakdene WEA W13 97 H4
Oakdene Av CHST BR7 185 F1
ERITH DA8 129 K6
THDIT KT7 190 B5
Oak Dene Cl EMPK RM11 75 K3
Oakdene Cl PIN HA5 41 K3
Oakdene Dr BRYLDS KT5 191 K5
Oakdene Ms CHEAM SM3 193 J5
Oakdene Pk FNCH N3 46 D3
Oakdene Rd STMC/STPC BR5 202 B3
Oakden St LBTH SE11 17 K6
Oaken Dr ESH/CLAY KT10 205 F4
Oaken La ESH/CLAY KT10 204 E3
Oakenshaw Cl SURB KT6 191 F4
Oakeshott Av HGT N6 66 A6
Oakey La STHWK SE1 17 J4
Oakfield CHING E4 51 K1
Oakfield Av
KTN/HRWW/WS HA3 43 H6
Oakfield Cl NWMAL KT3 192 C2
RSLP HA4 58 D3
Oakfield Gdns BECK BR3 198 D2
CAR SM5 194 D5
GFD/PVL UB6 96 D3
UED N18 36 A6
Oakfield La DART DA1 171 F4
HAYES BR2 215 G2
RDART DA2 170 B4
Oakfield Park Rd DART DA1 171 G4
Oakfield Pl DART DA1 171 G4
Oakfield Rd ASHF TW15 152 E6
CROY/NA CR0 196 D5
EHAM E6 89 J6
FNCH N3 47 F4
FSBYPK N4 67 G3
IL IG1 90 B1
PGE/AN SE20 181 J3
STHGT/OAK N14 34 E4
WALTH E17 51 G5
WIM/MER SW19 159 G5
Oakfields Rd GLDGN NW11 64 C3
Oakfield St WBPTN SW10 120 B6
Oakford Rd KTTN NW5 84 C2
Oak Gdns CROY/NA CR0 198 D6
EDGW HA8 44 E5
Oak Gv CRICK NW2 82 B2
RSLP HA4 59 F5
SUN TW16 172 A3
WWKM BR4 199 F6
Oak Grove Rd PGE/AN SE20 181 K4
Oak Hall Rd WAN E11 71 F3
Oakham Cl CAT SE6 * 164 C4
Oakham Dr HAYES BR2 199 K1
Oakhampton Rd MLHL NW7 46 B4
Oakhill ESH/CLAY KT10 205 G4
Oak Hl SURB KT6 191 F4
WFD IG8 52 B3
Oakhill Av HAMP NW3 83 F2
PIN HA5 41 J5
Oak Hill Crs SURB KT6 191 F4
WFD IG8 52 C3
Oak Hill Gdns WFD IG8 52 C4
Oak Hill Gv SURB KT6 191 F3
Oak Hill Pk HAMP NW3 83 F2
Oak Hill Park Ms HAMP NW3 83 G2
Oakhill Pl PUT/ROE SW15 139 K6
Oak Hill Rd SURB KT6 * 191 F3
Oakhill Rd BECK BR3 183 F5
ORP BR6 202 A6
PUT/ROE SW15 139 J6
STRHM/NOR SW16 179 K4
SUT SM1 209 F1
Oak Hill Wy HAMP NW3 83 F2
Oakhouse Rd BXLYHS DA6 149 H6
Oakhurst Av BXLYHN DA7 149 F1
EBAR EN4 33 J2
Oakhurst Cl BARK/HLT IG6 54 C4
CHST BR7 184 E4
KUTN/CMB KT2 175 G2
TEDD TW11 173 K1
WALTH E17 70 C1
Oakhurst Gdns BXLYHN DA7 149 F1
CHING E4 38 D3
WALTH E17 70 C1
Oakhurst Gv EDUL SE22 143 H5
Oakhurst Rd HOR/WEW KT19 206 E4
Oakington Av HYS/HAR UB3 113 G4
RYLN/HDSTN HA2 60 A4
WBLY HA9 80 B1
Oakington Cl SUN TW16 172 B5
Oakington Dr SUN TW16 172 B5
Oakington Manor Dr
WBLY HA9 80 C3
Oakington Rd MV/WKIL W9 * 100 E3
Oakington Wy
CEND/HSY/T N8 66 E3
Oakland Pl BKHH IG9 38 E4
Oakland Rd SRTFD E15 88 C2
Oaklands WCHMH N21 35 F4
Oaklands Av BFN/LL DA15 168 A2
ED N9 36 D1
ESH/CLAY KT10 189 J5
ISLW TW7 116 A6
OXHEY WD19 27 F3
ROM RM1 57 G6
THHTH CR7 196 B1
WWKM BR4 213 K1
Oaklands Cl ALP/SUD HA0 79 K3
BXLYHS DA6 149 G6
CHSGTN KT9 205 J2
STMC/STPC BR5 201 K3
Oaklands Dr WHTN TW2 155 H2
Oaklands Ga NTHWD HA6 40 C2
Oaklands Gv SHB W12 118 D1
Oaklands Ms CRICK NW2 82 B2
Oaklands Park Av IL IG1 72 C6
Oaklands Pl CLAP SW4 141 J5
Oaklands Rd BMLY BR1 183 H3
BXLYHS DA6 149 G5
CRICK NW2 82 B2
HNWL W7 116 A2
MORT/ESHN SW14 138 A4
TRDG/WHET N20 32 D2
Oaklands Wy WLGTN SM6 210 C5
Oakland Wy HOR/WEW KT19 207 F4
Oak La EFNCH N2 47 H5
FBAR/BDGN N11 48 D2
ISLW TW7 135 K5
POP/IOD E14 105 H6
TWK TW1 156 B2
WFD IG8 38 D6
Oakleafe Gdns BARK/HLT IG6 54 B6
Oakleigh Av EDGW HA8 44 D5
SURB KT6 191 H5
TRDG/WHET N20 33 H3
Oakleigh Cl TRDG/WHET N20 33 K5
Oakleigh Ct EDGW HA8 * 44 E5
Oakleigh Crs TRDG/WHET N20 33 J5
Oakleigh Dr
RKW/CH/CXG WD3 26 A1
Oakleigh Gdns EDGW HA8 44 B1
ORP BR6 216 E2
TRDG/WHET N20 33 G3
Oakleigh Ms TRDG/WHET N20 33 G4
Oakleigh Park Av CHST BR7 185 F5
Oakleigh Pk North
TRDG/WHET N20 33 H3
Oakleigh Pk South
TRDG/WHET N20 33 J3
Oakleigh Rd HGDN/ICK UB10 76 A5
PIN HA5 41 K2
Oakleigh Rd North
TRDG/WHET N20 33 H4
Oakleigh Rd South
FBAR/BDGN N11 34 A6
Oakleigh Wy MTCM CR4 179 G4
SURB KT6 191 H5
Oakley Av BARK IG11 91 F5
CROY/NA CR0 210 E2
EA W5 98 C6
Oakley Cl CHING E4 38 A5
EHAM E6 107 J5
HNWL W7 96 E6
ISLW TW7 135 J2
Oakley Ct MTCM CR4 195 F4
Oakley Crs FSBYE EC1V * 6 B3
Oakley Dr CAT SE6 165 G1
ELTH/MOT SE9 167 J3
HAYES BR2 215 J1
Oakley Gdns CEND/HSY/T N8 67 F2
CHEL SW3 120 D6
Oakley Pk BXLY DA5 168 D2
Oakley Pl STHWK SE1 123 G5
Oakley Rd HAYES BR2 215 J1
HRW HA1 60 E3
IS N1 85 K5
SNWD SE25 197 J2
Oakley Sq CAMTN NW1 4 B2
Oakley St CHEL SW3 120 D6
Oakley Yd BETH E2 * 7 K6
Oak Lodge Av CHIG IG7 54 D1
Oak Lodge Cl STAN HA7 43 J1
Oak Lodge Dr WWKM BR4 198 E4
Oaklodge Wy MLHL NW7 45 H2
Oakmead Av HAYES BR2 199 K3
Oakmeade PIN HA5 42 A2
Oakmead Gdns EDGW HA8 31 F6
Oakmead Pl MTCM CR4 178 D4
Oakmead Rd BAL SW12 161 G3
CROY/NA CR0 195 J3
Oakmere Rd ABYW SE2 128 B6
Oakmoor Wy CHIG IG7 54 E1
Oakmore Gdns
STMC/STPC BR5 202 D1
Oak Park Gdns
WIM/MER SW19 159 G3
Oakridge Dr EFNCH N2 47 H6
Oakridge Rd BMLY BR1 165 H6
Oak Ri BKHH IG9 39 H5
Oak Rd EA W5 97 K6
ERITH DA8 149 K1
NWMAL KT3 176 A5
ORP BR6 217 G5
Oak Rw MTCM CR4 179 H5
Oaks Av CRW RM5 56 E5
FELT TW13 154 D4
NRWD SE19 181 F1
WPK KT4 207 K2
Oaksford Av SYD SE26 163 J5
Oaks Gv CHING E4 38 C4
Oakshade Rd BMLY BR1 165 G6
Oakshaw Rd
WAND/EARL SW18 160 A2
Oaks La CROY/NA CR0 212 E1
GNTH/NBYPK IG2 72 E1
Oak Sq BRXN/ST SW9 142 A3
Oaks Rd CROY/NA CR0 212 D3
STWL/WRAY TW19 132 A6
The Oaks CHSGTN KT9 205 J1
FELT TW13 * 154 D4
HAYES BR2 * 201 F3
MRDN SM4 * 193 H1
NFNCH/WDSPK N12 33 F6
OXHEY WD19 27 G3
RSLP HA4 58 B4
WFD IG8 52 C3
WOOL/PLUM SE18 127 H5
YEAD UB4 94 A1
Oak St ROMW/RG RM7 74 E2
Oaks Wy CAR SM5 209 K5
SURB KT6 190 E6
Oakthorpe Rd PLMGR N13 49 G1
Oaktree Av PLMGR N13 35 G5
Oak Tree Cl EA W5 * 97 J5
STAN HA7 43 J3
Oak Tree Ct BORE WD6 * 29 K1
Oak Tree Dell
CDALE/KGS NW9 62 E2
Oak Tree Dr TRDG/WHET N20 33 F3
Oak Tree Gdns BMLY BR1 184 A1
Oaktree Gv IL IG1 90 D3
Oak Tree Rd STJWD NW8 2 B5
Oakview Cl OXHEY WD19 27 G1
Oakview Gdns EFNCH N2 65 H1
Oakview Gv CROY/NA CR0 198 B5
Oakview Rd CAT SE6 182 E1
Oak Village HAMP NW3 84 A2
KTTN NW5 84 A2
Oak Vls GLDGN NW11 * 64 D3
Oak Wy ACT W3 118 B1
CROY/NA CR0 198 A3
STHGT/OAK N14 34 A2
EBED/NFELT TW14 153 H3
Oakway HAYES BR2 183 G5
RYNPK SW20 193 F1
Oakway Cl BXLY DA5 169 F1
Oakways ELTH/MOT SE9 167 G1
Oakwood WLGTN SM6 210 B6
Oakwood Av BECK BR3 183 F5
CHSGTN KT9 206 A5
HAYES BR2 184 A6
MTCM CR4 178 C5
STHGT/OAK N14 34 D2
STHL UB1 96 A6
Oakwood Cl CHST BR7 184 E2
LEW SE13 165 G2
STHGT/OAK N14 34 C1
WFD IG8 53 J2
Oakwood Ct WKENS W14 119 J3
Oakwood Crs GFD/PVL UB6 79 G4
WCHMH N21 34 E1
Oakwood Dr BXLYHN DA7 149 K5
EDGW HA8 44 E2
NRWD SE19 180 E2
Oakwood Gdns
GDMY/SEVK IG3 73 F6
ORP BR6 201 H6
SUT SM1 193 K6
Oakwood La WKENS W14 119 J3
Oakwood Pde
STHGT/OAK N14 * 22 C6
Oakwood Park Cots
WCHMH N21 * 35 F1
Oakwood Park Rd
STHGT/OAK N14 34 E1
Oakwood Pl CROY/NA CR0 196 B3
Oakwood Rd CROY/NA CR0 196 B3
GLDGN NW11 64 E2
ORP BR6 201 H6
PIN HA5 41 F5
RYNPK SW20 176 D4
Oakworth Rd NKENS W10 100 A4
Oarsman Pl E/WMO/HCT KT8 189 K1
Oast House Wy
STMC/STPC BR5 202 C1
Oates Cl HAYES BR2 183 G6
Oates Rd CRW RM5 56 D1
Oatfield Rd ORP BR6 202 A5
Oatland Ri WALTH E17 51 G5
Oatlands Rd PEND EN3 24 E2
Oat La CITYW EC2V 12 C3
Oban Cl PLSTW E13 107 G3
Oban Rd PLSTW E13 107 G2
THHTH CR7 196 E1
Oban St POP/IOD E14 106 B5
Oberstein Rd BTSEA SW11 140 C5
Oborne Cl HNHL SE24 142 C6
Observatory Gdns KENS W8 119 K2
Observatory Rd
MORT/ESHN SW14 137 K5
SKENS SW7 14 B4
Occupation La EA W5 116 E4
WOOL/PLUM SE18 147 G2
Occupation Rd WALW SE17 122 D5
WEA W13 116 C2
Ocean Est WCHPL E1 105 F3
Ocean St WCHPL E1 105 F4
Ockendon Ms IS N1 * 85 K4
Ockendon Rd IS N1 85 K4
Ockham Dr GFD/PVL UB6 78 D5
STMC/STPC BR5 186 B3
Ockley Rd CROY/NA CR0 196 A4
STRHM/NOR SW16 161 K6
Octagon Ar LVPST EC2M * 13 G2
Octavia Cl MTCM CR4 194 D2
Octavia Ms CRICK NW2 * 81 K4
Octavia Rd ISLW TW7 136 A4
Octavia St BTSEA SW11 140 D2
Octavius St DEPT SE8 144 D1
October Pl HDN NW4 * 46 B6
Odard Rd E/WMO/HCT KT8 189 F1
Odell Cl BARK IG11 91 F5
Odell Wk LEW SE13 144 E4
Odeon Pde ELTH/MOT SE9 * 146 D5
GFD/PVL UB6 * 79 H4
HOLWY N7 * 84 E1
ISLW TW7 * 135 K3
Odessa Rd FSTGT E7 88 D2
WLSDN NW10 99 J1
Odessa St BERM/RHTH SE16 124 C3
Odger St BTSEA SW11 140 E3
Odhams Wk
LSQ/SEVD WC2H * 10 E4
Odsey Vls FSBYPK N4 * 67 G3
Offa's Md HOM E9 87 G2
Offenham Rd ELTH/MOT SE9 166 E6
Offerton Rd CLAP SW4 141 H4
Offham Slope
NFNCH/WDSPK N12 46 D1
Offley Pl ISLW TW7 135 J3
Offley Rd BRXN/ST SW9 142 B1
Offord Cl TOTM N17 50 C3
Offord Rd IS N1 85 F5
Offord St HOLWY N7 85 F5
Ogilby St WOOL/PLUM SE18 126 E4
Oglander Rd PECK SE15 143 G5
Ogle St GTPST W1W 10 A1
Oglethorpe Rd DAGE RM10 92 B1
Ohio Rd PLSTW E13 106 E3
Oil Mill La HMSMTH W6 118 D5
Okeburn Rd TOOT SW17 179 F1
Okehampton Crs WELL DA16 148 C2
Okehampton Rd
WLSDN NW10 82 A6
Olaf St NTGHL W11 100 B6
Old Bailey STP EC4M 12 B4
Old Barn Cl BELMT SM2 208 C5
Old Barn Wy BXLYHN DA7 150 A5
Old Barrack Yd KTBR SW1X 15 G2
Old Bellgate Whf
POP/IOD E14 124 D3
Oldberry Rd EDGW HA8 45 F2
Old Bethnal Green Rd
BETH E2 104 D2
Old Bexley La BXLY DA5 170 A4
Old Bond St CONDST W1S 10 A6
Oldborough Rd ALP/SUD HA0 61 J6
Old Brewery Ms HAMP NW3 83 H2
Old Bridge Cl NTHLT UB5 96 A1
Old Bridge St KUT/HW KT1 174 E5
Old Broad St OBST EC2N 13 F3
Old Bromley Rd BMLY BR1 183 G1
Old Brompton Rd ECT SW5 120 A5
Old Blds LINN WC2A 11 J3
Old Burlington St
CONDST W1S 10 A5
Oldbury Cl STMC/STPC BR5 202 E1
Oldbury Pl MHST W1U 9 H1
Oldbury Rd EN EN1 24 C3
Old Castle St WCHPL E1 13 J3
Old Cavendish St OXSTW W1C 9 J4
Old Chapel Rd SWLY BR8 203 K4
Old Chestnut Av
ESH/CLAY KT10 204 A4
Old Church Cl ORP BR6 202 C5
Old Church La
CDALE/KGS NW9 62 E6
GFD/PVL UB6 97 G2
STAN HA7 43 H2
Old Church Pth
ESH/CLAY KT10 204 B2
Oldchurch Ri ROMW/RG RM7 75 G3
Old Church Rd CHING E4 37 J5
Oldchurch Rd ROMW/RG RM7 75 F4
Old Church Rd WCHPL E1 * 105 F5
Old Church St CHEL SW3 120 C5
Old Claygate La
ESH/CLAY KT10 205 G4
Old Compton St
SOHO/SHAV W1D 10 C5
Old Cote Dr HEST TW5 115 F6
Old Court Pl KENS W8 120 A2
The Old Ctyd BMLY BR1 184 A4
Old Dairy Ms BAL SW12 161 F3
KTTN NW5 * 84 B4
Old Deer Pk RCH/KEW TW9 * 137 G4
Old Deer Park Gdns
RCH/KEW TW9 137 F4
Old Devonshire Rd BAL SW12 161 G2
Old Dock Cl RCH/KEW TW9 117 H6
Old Dover Rd BKHTH/KID SE3 145 K1
Old Farm Av BFN/LL DA15 167 J3
STHGT/OAK N14 34 C2
Old Farm Cl HSLWW TW4 134 E5
Old Farm Rd EFNCH N2 47 H4
HPTN TW12 172 E2
WDR/YW UB7 112 A2
Old Farm Rd East
BFN/LL DA15 168 B4
Old Farm Rd West
BFN/LL DA15 168 A4
Oldfield Cl BMLY BR1 200 E1
GFD/PVL UB6 78 E3
STAN HA7 43 G1
Oldfield Farm Gdns
GFD/PVL UB6 78 D6
Oldfield Gv BERM/RHTH SE16 124 A4
Oldfield La North
GFD/PVL UB6 78 D6
Oldfield La South
GFD/PVL UB6 96 C2
Oldfield Ms HGT N6 66 C4
Oldfield Rd ACT W3 118 C2
BMLY BR1 200 E1
BXLYHN DA7 149 F3
HPTN TW12 173 F4
STNW/STAM N16 86 A1
WIM/MER SW19 177 H2
WLSDN NW10 81 H5
Oldfields Circ NTHLT UB5 78 C4
Oldfields Rd SUT SM1 193 K6
Old Fish Street Hl
BLKFR EC4V * 12 C5
Old Fleet La FLST/FETLN EC4A 12 A3
Old Fold Cl BAR EN5 * 20 D2
Old Fold La BAR EN5 20 D2
Old Fold Vw BAR EN5 20 A4
Old Ford Lock BOW E3 * 87 J5
Old Ford Rd BETH E2 104 E1
BOW E3 87 G6
Old Forge Cl STAN HA7 29 G6
Old Forge Ms SHB W12 118 E2
Old Forge Rd ARCH N19 66 D6
EN EN1 24 B1
Old Forge Wy SCUP DA14 168 C6
Old Gannon Cl NTHWD HA6 26 A6
Old Gloucester St
BMSBY WC1N 11 F1
Old Hall Cl PIN HA5 41 J4
Old Hall Dr PIN HA5 41 J4
Oldham Ter ACT W3 117 K1
Old Hatch Mnr RSLP HA4 58 D4
Old Hl CHST BR7 185 F4
ORP BR6 216 E4
Oldhill St STNW/STAM N16 68 C5
Old Homesdale Rd HAYES BR2 200 B1
Old Hospital Cl BAL SW12 * 160 E3
Old House Cl WIM/MER SW19 177 H1
Old House Gdns TWK TW1 * 156 D1
Old Howletts La RSLP HA4 58 B3
Old Jamaica Rd
BERM/RHTH SE16 123 H3
Old James St PECK SE15 143 J4
Old Jewry LOTH EC2R * 12 E4
Old Kenton La
CDALE/KGS NW9 62 D2
Old Kent Rd PECK SE15 123 J6
STHWK SE1 19 G6
Old Kingston Rd WPK KT4 206 E1
Old Lodge Wy STAN HA7 43 G1
Old London Rd
KUTN/CMB KT2 175 F5
Old Maidstone Rd SCUP DA14 187 G3
Old Malden La WPK KT4 192 B6
Old Manor Dr ISLW TW7 155 H1
Old Manor Rd NWDGN UB2 114 C4
Old Manor Wy BXLYHN DA7 150 A3
CHST BR7 184 E1
Old Manor Yd ECT SW5 * 120 A4
Old Market Sq BETH E2 7 J4
Old Marylebone Rd
CAMTN NW1 8 D2
Old Mill Ct SWFD E18 53 G6
Old Mill Rd WOOL/PLUM SE18 127 J6
Old Mitre Ct EMB EC4Y * 11 K4
Old Montague St WCHPL E1 104 C4
Old Nichol St BETH E2 7 J6
Old North St FSBYW WC1X * 11 G1
Old Oak Common La
WLSDN NW10 99 G3
Old Oak La WLSDN NW10 99 H2
Old Oak Rd ACT W3 99 H6
Old Orch SUN TW16 172 B5
Old Orchard Cl EBAR EN4 21 H1
The Old Orch HAMP NW3 * 83 K2
Old Palace Rd CROY/NA CR0 211 J1
Old Palace Yd RCH/KEW TW9 136 D6
WHALL SW1A 16 E4
Old Paradise St LBTH SE11 17 G6
Old Park Av BAL SW12 161 F1
ENC/FH EN2 23 J5
Old Park Gv ENC/FH EN2 23 J5
Old Park La MYFR/PKLN W1K 15 H1
Old Park Ms HEST TW5 134 E1
Old Park Ridings WCHMH N21 35 H1
Old Park Rd ABYW SE2 128 B5
ENC/FH EN2 23 H4
PLMGR N13 35 F5
Old Park Rd South
ENC/FH EN2 23 H5
Old Park Vw ENC/FH EN2 23 G4
Old Pearson St GNWCH SE10 144 E1
Old Perry St CHST BR7 185 K3
Old Post Office La
BKHTH/KID SE3 146 A4
Old Pound Cl ISLW TW7 136 B2
Old Pye St WEST SW1P 16 C4
Old Quebec St MBLAR W1H 9 F4
Old Queen St STJSPK SW1H 16 D3
Old Rectory Gdns EDGW HA8 44 C2
Old Redding
KTN/HRWW/WS HA3 42 B1
Oldridge Rd BAL SW12 161 F2
Old Rd DART DA1 150 A5
LEW SE13 145 H5
PEND EN3 24 E2
Old Royal Free Sq IS N1 5 K1
Old Ruislip Rd NTHLT UB5 95 G1
Old's Ap WATW WD18 26 A3
Old School Cl BECK BR3 182 A5
Old School Crs FSTGT E7 88 E4
Old School Pl CROY/NA CR0 211 G2
Old Schools La EW KT17 207 H6
Old School Sq THDIT KT7 190 A3
Old School Ter CHEAM SM3 * 208 B5
Old Seacoal La STP EC4M 12 A4
Old South Cl PIN HA5 41 H4
Old South Lambeth Rd
VX/NE SW8 * 141 K1
Old Sq LINN WC2A 11 H3
Old Stable Ms HBRY N5 85 J1
Old Station Gdns
TEDD TW11 * 174 B2
Old Station Rd HYS/HAR UB3 113 J3
The Old Station Yd
WALTH E17 70 A1
Oldstead Rd BMLY BR1 165 G6
Old St PLSTW E13 107 F1
STLK EC1Y 7 F6
Old Studio Cl CROY/NA CR0 196 E4
Old Swan Yd CAR SM5 209 K2
Old Town CLAP SW4 141 H4
CROY/NA CR0 211 H1
Old Tramyard
WOOL/PLUM SE18 127 K4
Old Woolwich Rd
GNWCH SE10 125 G6
Old York Rd
WAND/EARL SW18 140 A6
Oleander Cl ORP BR6 216 D3
O'Leary Sq WCHPL E1 104 E4
Olga St BOW E3 105 G1
Olinda Rd STNW/STAM N16 68 B3
Oliphant St NKENS W10 100 C2
Olive Gv SEVS/STOTM N15 67 J1
Oliver Av SNWD SE25 181 G6
Oliver Cl CHSWK W4 117 J6
Oliver Gdns EHAM E6 107 J4
Oliver Gv SNWD SE25 197 G1
Oliver Ms PECK SE15 143 H3
Olive Rd CRICK NW2 82 A2
DART DA1 171 G3
EA W5 116 E3
PLSTW E13 107 G2
WIM/MER SW19 * 178 B3
Oliver Rd LEY E10 87 K1
NWMAL KT3 175 K5
RAIN RM13 93 H6
SUT SM1 209 H2
WALTH E17 70 A2

Oliver's Yd STLK EC1Y 7 F6
Olive St ROMW/RG RM7 75 F2
Ollerton Gn BOW E3 87 H6
Ollerton Rd FBAR/BDGN N11 48 D1
Olley Cl WLGTN SM6 210 E5
Ollgar Cl SHB W12 118 C1
Olliffe St POP/IOD E14 125 F3
Olmar St STHWK SE1 123 H6
Olney Rd WALW SE17 122 C6
Olron Crs BXLYHS DA6 148 E6
Olven Rd WOOL/PLUM SE18 147 H1
Olveston Wk CAR SM5 194 C3
Olwen Ms PIN HA5 41 H5
Olyffe Av WELL DA16 148 B3
Olyffe Dr BECK BR3 183 F4
Olympia Wy WKENS W14 119 H3
Olympic Wy GFD/PVL UB6 78 B6
WBLY HA9 80 C1
Olympus Gv WDGN N22 49 G4
Olympus Sq CLPT E5 86 D1
Oman Av CRICK NW2 82 A3
O'Meara St STHWK SE1 18 D1
Omega Pl IS N1 5 F3
Omega St NWCR SE14 144 C2
Ommaney Rd NWCR SE14 144 A2
Omnibus Wy WALTH E17 51 J5
Ondine Rd PECK SE15 143 G5
Onega Ga BERM/RHTH SE16 124 B3
One Tree Cl FSTH SE23 163 K1
Ongar Cl CHDH RM6 73 J2
Ongar Rd FUL/PGN SW6 119 K6
Ongar Wy RAIN RM13 93 G6
Onra Rd WALTH E17 69 J4
Onslow Av RCHPK/HAM TW10 137 F6
Onslow Cl CHING E4 38 B4
NKENS W10 100 D2
Onslow Crs CHST BR7 185 G4
SKENS SW7 14 B7
Onslow Dr SCUP DA14 168 E5
Onslow Gdns MUSWH N10 66 B2
SKENS SW7 14 A7
SWFD E18 53 F6
THDIT KT7 189 K5
WCHMH N21 23 G6
WLGTN SM6 210 C5
Onslow Ms East SKENS SW7 14 A7
Onslow Ms West SKENS SW7 14 A7
Onslow Pde STHGT/OAK N14 * 34 B3
Onslow Rd CROY/NA CR0 196 B4
NWMAL KT3 192 D1
RCHPK/HAM TW10 157 F1
Onslow Sq SKENS SW7 14 A7
Onslow St CLKNW EC1R 5 K7
Onslow Wy THDIT KT7 189 K5
Ontario St STHWK SE1 18 B5
Ontario Wy POP/IOD E14 105 J6
On The Hl OXHEY WD19 27 J4
Onyx Ms SRTFD E15 88 C4
Opal Cl CAN/RD E16 107 H5
Opal Ms KIL/WHAMP NW6 82 D6
Opal St LBTH SE11 18 A7
Openshaw Rd ABYW SE2 128 C4
Openview WAND/EARL SW18 160 B3
Ophir Ter PECK SE15 143 H2
Opossum Wy HSLWW TW4 134 B4
Oppenheim Rd LEW SE13 145 F3
Oppidans Rd HAMP NW3 83 K5
Optima Pk DART DA1 * 150 D4
Orange Court La ORP BR6 216 A6
Orange Gv CHIG IG7 54 C2
WAN E11 88 C1
Orange Hill Rd EDGW HA8 44 E3
Orange Pl BERM/RHTH SE16 123 K3
Orangery La ELTH/MOT SE9 146 E6
The Orangery
RCHPK/HAM TW10 156 D4
Orange St LSQ/SEVD WC2H 10 D6
WAP E1W 123 H1
Orange Tree Hl ABR/ST RM4 57 F1
Oransay Rd IS N1 85 J4
Oratory La CHEL SW3 * 120 C5
Orbain Rd FUL/PGN SW6 139 H1
Orbel St BTSEA SW11 140 D2
Orb St WALW SE17 18 E7
Orchard Av BELV DA17 129 F6
CROY/NA CR0 198 B6
DART DA1 170 E2
EBED/NFELT TW14 133 G6
FNCH N3 46 E6
HEST TW5 134 D1
MTCM CR4 195 F5
NWMAL KT3 176 B5
STHGT/OAK N14 34 C1
STHL UB1 114 D1
THDIT KT7 190 B5
TRDG/WHET N20 33 H4
Orchard Cl ALP/SUD HA0 80 A6
BUSH WD23 28 D3
BXLYHN DA7 149 F2
CHING E4 37 J6
CRICK NW2 81 J1
EDGW HA8 44 A2
FSTH SE23 163 K1
HOR/WEW KT19 * 206 D4
IS N1 85 J5
NKENS W10 100 C4
NTHLT UB5 78 C4
RSLP HA4 58 A4
RYNPK SW20 193 F1
THDIT KT7 190 C5
WOT/HER KT12 188 A4
Orchard Cots HYS/HAR UB3 * 113 H2
KUTN/CMB KT2 * 175 H4
Orchard Ct WLGTN SM6 * 210 B3
WPK KT4 * 192 D5
Orchard Crs EDGW HA8 44 E1
EN EN1 24 B2
Orchard Dr BKHTH/KID SE3 145 H3
EDGW HA8 44 B1
Orchard Gdns CHSGTN KT9 206 A2
Orchard Ga CDALE/KGS NW9 63 G1
ESH/CLAY KT10 189 J5
GFD/PVL UB6 79 H4
Orchard Gn ORP BR6 201 K6
Orchard Gv CROY/NA CR0 198 B4
EDGW HA8 44 C4
KTN/HRWW/WS HA3 62 B2
ORP BR6 202 A6
PGE/AN SE20 181 H3
Orchard Hl DART DA1 150 B6
LEW SE13 144 E2
Orchard La E/WMO/HCT KT8 189 J3
RYNPK SW20 176 E4
WFD IG8 39 G6
Orchardleigh Av PEND EN3 24 E3
Orchardmede WCHMH N21 35 K1
Orchard Ms IS N1 85 K5
TOOT SW17 160 B5
Orchard Pl POP/IOD E14 106 C6
STMC/STPC BR5 * 186 D6
TOTM N17 50 B3
Orchard Ri CROY/NA CR0 198 B5
KUTN/CMB KT2 175 K4
PIN HA5 40 D6
RCHPK/HAM TW10 137 J5
Orchard Ri East BFN/LL DA15 147 K6
Orchard Ri West BFN/LL DA15 147 K6
Orchard Rd BAR EN5 20 C5
BELV DA17 129 H4
BMLY BR1 184 B4
BTFD TW8 116 D6
CHSGTN KT9 206 A2
DAGE RM10 92 C6
FELT TW13 153 K3
HGT N6 66 B4
HPTN TW12 172 E3
HSLWW TW4 134 E6
HYS/HAR UB3 94 E6
KUT/HW KT1 175 F5
ORP BR6 216 B3
ORP BR6 217 J6
PEND EN3 24 E6
RCH/KEW TW9 137 H4
ROMW/RG RM7 56 D5
SCUP DA14 167 K6
SUN TW16 172 A3
SUT SM1 208 E3
TWK TW1 136 B6
WELL DA16 148 C4
Orchardson St STJWD NW8 2 A7
Orchard Sq WKENS W14 * 119 J5
Orchard St DART DA1 171 H1
MBLAR W1H 9 G4
WALTH E17 69 G1
Orchard Ter EN EN1 * 36 C1
WLSDN NW10 * 81 H2
The Orchard BKHTH/KID SE3 145 G3
CHSWK W4 118 A4
EW KT17 207 H5
GLDGN NW11 64 E2
HSLW TW3 135 H3
TRDG/WHET N20 33 F3
WCHMH N21 35 K1
Orchard Vls SCUP DA14 * 186 D2
Orchard Wy ASHF TW15 152 C4
CROY/NA CR0 198 B4
EN EN1 24 A4
ESH/CLAY KT10 204 C4
RDART DA2 171 G5
SUT SM1 209 H2
Orchid Cl CHSGTN KT9 205 J5
EHAM E6 107 J4
LEW SE13 145 G6
STHL UB1 95 J5
Orchid Gdns HSLWW TW4 134 E5
Orchid Rd STHGT/OAK N14 34 C2
Orchid St SHB W12 99 J6
Orde Hall St BMSBY WC1N * 11 G1
Ordell Rd BOW E3 105 H1
Ordnance Cl FELT TW13 153 K4
Ordnance Crs GNWCH SE10 125 G2
Ordnance Hl STJWD NW8 2 B1
Ordnance Ms STJWD NW8 2 B2
Ordnance Rd CAN/RD E16 106 D4
WOOL/PLUM SE18 127 F6
Oregano Dr POP/IOD E14 106 B5
Oregon Av MNPK E12 89 K2
Oregon Cl NWMAL KT3 191 K1
Oregon Sq ORP BR6 201 J5
Orestes Ms KIL/WHAMP NW6 82 E3
Orford Gdns TWK TW1 156 A4
Orford Rd CAT SE6 164 E5
SWFD E18 53 F6
WALTH E17 69 J2
Oriel Cl MTCM CR4 195 J1
Oriel Ct HAMP NW3 83 G2
Oriel Dr BARN SW13 119 F6
Oriel Gdns CLAY IG5 53 K6
Oriel Rd HOM E9 87 F4
Oriel Wy NTHLT UB5 78 B5
Oriental Rd CAN/RD E16 126 C1
Orient St LBTH SE11 18 A6
Orient Wy CLPT E5 87 F1
LEY E10 69 J6
Oriole Wy THMD SE28 109 H6
Orion Rd MUSWH N10 48 A2
Orion Wy NTHWD HA6 26 D6
Orissa Rd WOOL/PLUM SE18 127 K5
Orkney St BTSEA SW11 141 F3
Orlando Rd CLAP SW4 141 H4
Orleans Cl ESH/CLAY KT10 189 J6
Orleans Rd NRWD SE19 180 E2
TWK TW1 156 C2
Orleston Ms HOLWY N7 * 85 G4
Orleston Rd HOLWY N7 85 G4
Orley Farm Rd HRW HA1 78 E1
Ormanton Rd SYD SE26 163 H6
Orme Ct BAY/PAD W2 101 F6
Ormeley Rd BAL SW12 161 G2
Orme Rd KUT/HW KT1 175 J5
SUT SM1 209 F4
Ormerod Gdns MTCM CR4 179 F5
Ormesby Cl THMD SE28 109 K6
Ormesby Wy
KTN/HRWW/WS HA3 62 B3
Orme Sq BAY/PAD W2 101 F6
Orme Square Ga
BAY/PAD W2 101 F6
Ormiston Gv SHB W12 118 D1
Ormiston Rd GNWCH SE10 125 K5
Ormond Av HPTN TW12 173 G4
Ormond Cl BMSBY WC1N 11 F1
Ormond Crs HPTN TW12 173 G3
Ormond Dr HPTN TW12 173 G3
Ormonde Av HOR/WEW KT19 207 F6
ORP BR6 201 H6
Ormonde Ct STJWD NW8 * 2 E1
Ormonde Ga CHEL SW3 * 120 E5
Ormonde Pl BGVA SW1W 15 H7
Ormonde Ri BKHH IG9 39 G3
Ormonde Rd
MORT/ESHN SW14 137 J4
NTHWD HA6 26 B6
Ormonde Ter STJWD NW8 2 E1
Ormond Rd ARCH N19 66 E5
RCHPK/HAM TW10 136 E6
Ormond Yd STJS SW1Y 10 B7
Ormsby BELMT SM2 * 209 F5
Ormsby Gdns GFD/PVL UB6 96 C1
Ormsby Pl STNW/STAM N16 86 B1
Ormsby St BETH E2 7 J2
Ormside St PECK SE15 123 K6
Ormskirk Rd OXHEY WD19 27 H6
Ornan Rd HAMP NW3 83 J3
Oronsay Wk IS N1 * 85 J4
Orpheus St CMBW SE5 142 E2
Orpington By-Pass ORP BR6 217 J2
Orpington Gdns UED N18 36 A5
Orpington Rd CHST BR7 185 K6
WCHMH N21 35 G3
Orpwood Cl HPTN TW12 172 E2
Orsett Ms BAY/PAD W2 101 F5
Orsett St LBTH SE11 122 A5
Orsett Ter BAY/PAD W2 101 F5
WFD IG8 53 G4
Orsman Rd IS N1 7 G1
Orton Gv EN EN1 24 B2
Orton St WAP E1W 123 H1
Orville Rd BTSEA SW11 140 C3
Orwell Cl HYS/HAR UB3 94 C6
Orwell Rd PLSTW E13 107 G1
Osbaldeston Rd
STNW/STAM N16 68 C6
Osberton Rd LEE/GVPK SE12 145 K6
Osbert St WEST SW1P 16 C7
Osborn Cl HACK E8 86 C6
Osborne Av
STWL/WRAY TW19 152 B3
Osborne Cl BECK BR3 198 B1
EBAR EN4 21 K4
EMPK RM11 75 K3
FELT TW13 172 C1
Osborne Ct EA W5 * 98 A4
Osborne Gdns THHTH CR7 180 D5
Osborne Gv WALTH E17 69 H1
Osborne Ms WALTH E17 69 H2
Osborne Rd ACT W3 117 J2
BELV DA17 129 G5
BKHH IG9 39 F3
CRICK NW2 81 K4
EMPK RM11 75 K3
FSBYPK N4 67 G5
FSTGT E7 89 F3
HOM E9 87 H4
HSLW TW3 134 E4
KUTN/CMB KT2 175 F3
LEY E10 87 K1
PEND EN3 25 G3
PLMGR N13 35 G5
STHL UB1 96 C5
THHTH CR7 180 D5
Osborne Sq DAGW RM9 92 B2
Osborne Ter TOOT SW17 * 179 F1
Osborne Wy CHSGTN KT9 206 B3
Osborn Gdns MLHL NW7 46 B3
Osborn La FSTH SE23 164 B2
Osborn St WCHPL E1 13 K2
Osborn Ter BKHTH/KID SE3 145 J5
Osbourne Ct
RYLN/HDSTN HA2 * 60 B1
Oscar Faber Pl IS N1 * 86 A5
Oscar St BROCKY SE4 144 D3
Oseney Crs KTTN NW5 84 C4
Osgood Av ORP BR6 217 F3
Osgood Gdns ORP BR6 217 F3
Osidge La STHGT/OAK N14 34 A3
Osier Crs MUSWH N10 47 K4
Osiers Rd WAND/EARL SW18 139 K5
Osier St WCHPL E1 104 E3
Osier Wy LEY E10 87 K1
MTCM CR4 194 D2
Oslac Rd CAT SE6 182 E1
Osman Cl SEVS/STOTM N15 67 K3
Osman Rd ED N9 36 C5
HMSMTH W6 * 119 F3
Osmond Cl RYLN/HDSTN HA2 60 C6
Osmond Gdns WLGTN SM6 210 C3
Osmund St SHB W12 99 H5
Osnaburgh St CAMTN NW1 3 K6
Osnaburgh Ter CAMTN NW1 3 K6
Osney Wk MRDN SM4 194 C3
Osprey Cl EHAM E6 107 J4
HAYES BR2 200 D5
SUT SM1 208 D3
WALTH E17 51 G3
WAN E11 70 E1
WDR/YW UB7 112 A2
Osprey Est BERM/RHTH SE16 124 A4
Osprey Ms PEND EN3 24 D6
Ospringe Cl PGE/AN SE20 181 K3
Ospringe Rd KTTN NW5 84 C2
Osram Rd WBLY HA9 79 K1
Ossian Rd FSBYPK N4 67 F4
Ossier Ms CHSWK W4 118 C6
Ossington Blds MHST W1U * 9 G1
Ossington Cl BAY/PAD W2 * 100 E6
Ossington St BAY/PAD W2 * 101 F6
Ossory Rd STHWK SE1 123 H5
Ossulston St CAMTN NW1 4 D3
Ossulton Pl EFNCH N2 * 47 G6
Ossulton Wy EFNCH N2 65 G1
Ostade Rd BRXS/STRHM SW2 162 A2
Ostell Crs PEND EN3 25 J1
Osten Ms SKENS SW7 * 120 A3
Osterberg Rd DART DA1 151 J5
Osterley Av ISLW TW7 135 J1
Osterley Cl STMC/STPC BR5 186 B4
Osterley Crs ISLW TW7 135 K2
Osterley Gdns THHTH CR7 180 D5
Osterley La NWDGN UB2 115 G5
Osterley Park Rd NWDGN UB2 114 E3
Osterley Park View Rd
HNWL W7 115 K2
Osterley Rd ISLW TW7 135 K1
STNW/STAM N16 86 A2
Ostliffe Rd PLMGR N13 49 H1
Oswald Rd STHL UB1 114 D1
Oswald's Md HOM E9 87 G2
Oswald St CLPT E5 87 F1
Oswald Ter CRICK NW2 * 82 A1
Osward CROY/NA CR0 213 H6
Osward Pl ED N9 36 C4
Osward Rd BAL SW12 160 E4
Oswin St LBTH SE11 18 B6
Oswyth Rd CMBW SE5 143 F3
Otford Cl BMLY BR1 185 F6
BXLY DA5 169 J1
PGE/AN SE20 181 K4
Otford Crs BROCKY SE4 164 C1
Othello Cl LBTH SE11 122 C5
Otis St BOW E3 106 A2
Otley Ct FBAR/BDGN N11 48 A2
Otley Dr GNTH/NBYPK IG2 72 B3
Otley Rd CAN/RD E16 107 G5
Otley Ter CLPT E5 68 E6
Otley Wy OXHEY WD19 27 G5
Otlinge Rd STMC/STPC BR5 202 E1
Ottawa Gdns DAGE RM10 93 F5
Ottaway St CLPT E5 86 C1
Otterbourne Rd CHING E4 38 B5
CROY/NA CR0 196 D6
Otterburn Gdns ISLW TW7 136 B1
Otterburn St TOOT SW17 178 E2
Otter Cl SRTFD E15 88 A6
Otterden Cl ORP BR6 216 E2
Otterden St CAT SE6 164 D6
Otter Rd GFD/PVL UB6 96 C3
Otters Cl STMC/STPC BR5 202 E1
Otto Cl CAT SE6 164 C5
SYD SE26 163 J4
Otto St WALW SE17 122 C6
Otway Gdns BUSH WD23 28 E2
Oulton Cl THMD SE28 109 J5
Oulton Crs BARK IG11 91 F4
Oulton Rd SEVS/STOTM N15 67 K2
Oulton Wy OXHEY WD19 27 K6
Oundle Av BUSH WD23 28 C1
Ouseley Rd BAL SW12 160 E3
Outer Cir CAMTN NW1 2 D3
Outgate Rd WLSDN NW10 81 H5
Outram Pl IS N1 84 E6
Outram Rd CROY/NA CR0 197 G6
EHAM E6 89 J6
WDGN N22 48 D4
Outwich St HDTCH EC3A * 13 H3
Oval Ct EDGW HA8 * 44 E3
Oval Pl VX/NE SW8 142 A1
Oval Rd CAMTN NW1 84 B6
CROY/NA CR0 196 E6
Oval Rd North DAGE RM10 92 D6
Oval Rd South DAGE RM10 110 D1
The Oval BETH E2 104 D1
BFN/LL DA15 168 B2
Oval Wy LBTH SE11 122 A5
Overbrae BECK BR3 182 D2
Overbrook Wk EDGW HA8 44 C3
Overbury Av BECK BR3 182 E6
Overbury Rd FSBYPK N4 67 K3
Overbury St CLPT E5 87 F2
Overcliff Rd BROCKY SE4 144 D4
Overcourt Cl BFN/LL DA15 168 C1
Overdale Av NWMAL KT3 175 K5
Overdale Rd EA W5 116 D3
Overdown Rd CAT SE6 164 D6
Overhill Cots MTCM CR4 * 179 F5
Overhill Rd EDUL SE22 163 H2
PUR/KEN CR8 211 G6
Overhill Wy BECK BR3 199 G2
Overlea Rd CLPT E5 68 C4
Overmead ELTH/MOT SE9 167 J2
Overstand Cl BECK BR3 198 D2
Overstone Gdns
CROY/NA CR0 198 C4
Overstone Rd HMSMTH W6 119 F4
Overton Cl ISLW TW7 136 A2
WLSDN NW10 80 E4
Overton Dr CHDH RM6 73 J4
WAN E11 71 F4
Overton Rd ABYW SE2 128 D3
BELMT SM2 208 E4
BRXN/ST SW9 142 B3
LEY E10 69 G5
STHGT/OAK N14 22 E6
Overton's Yd CROY/NA CR0 211 J1
Overy Liberty DART DA1 171 H2
Overy St DART DA1 171 J1
Ovesdon Av RYLN/HDSTN HA2 59 K5
Ovett Cl NRWD SE19 181 F2
Ovex Cl POP/IOD E14 125 F3
Ovington Gdns CHEL SW3 14 D5
Ovington Ms CHEL SW3 14 D5
Ovington Sq CHEL SW3 14 D5
Ovington St CHEL SW3 14 D5
Owen Cl CROY/NA CR0 196 E3
CRW RM5 56 C2
NTHLT UB5 77 J4
THMD SE28 128 D1
YEAD UB4 * 95 F2
Owen Gdns WFD IG8 53 J2
Owenite St ABYW SE2 128 C4
Owen Rd PLMGR N13 49 J1
Owens Ms WAN E11 70 C6
Owen's Rw FSBYE EC1V 6 A4
Owen St FSBYE EC1V 5 K3
Owens Wy FSTH SE23 164 B2
Owen Wk PGE/AN SE20 181 H3
Owen Wy WLSDN NW10 80 E4
Owgan Cl CMBW SE5 142 E1
Oxberry Av FUL/PGN SW6 139 H3
Oxenden Wood Rd ORP BR6 217 H4
Oxendon St
SOHO/SHAV W1D * 10 C6
Oxenford St PECK SE15 143 G4
Oxenpark Av WBLY HA9 62 A4
Oxestalls Rd DEPT SE8 124 B5
Oxford Av HEST TW5 115 F5
HYS/HAR UB3 133 J1
RYNPK SW20 177 H5
STHGT/OAK N14 34 C3
Oxford Cl ED N9 36 D4
GPK RM2 75 J2
MTCM CR4 179 H6
NTHWD HA6 26 A6
Oxford Ct MANHO EC4N 12 E5
Oxford Crs NWMAL KT3 192 A3
Oxford Dr RSLP HA4 59 G6
Oxford Gdns CHSWK W4 117 H5
NKENS W10 100 B5
TRDG/WHET N20 33 H3
WCHMH N21 35 J2
Oxford Ga HMSMTH W6 119 G4
Oxford Ms BXLY DA5 169 H3
Oxford Rd CAR SM5 209 J4
EA W5 97 K6
ED N9 36 D4
FSBYPK N4 67 G5
HRW HA1 60 C3
IL IG1 90 C3
KIL/WHAMP NW6 100 E1
KTN/HRWW/WS HA3 43 F6
NRWD SE19 180 E2
PEND EN3 24 D6
PUT/ROE SW15 139 H5
SCUP DA14 186 C1
SRTFD E15 88 B4
TEDD TW11 173 J1
WFD IG8 53 H1
WLGTN SM6 * 210 C3
Oxford Rd North CHSWK W4 117 J5
Oxford Rd South CHSWK W4 117 H5
Oxford Rw SUN TW16 * 172 B6
Oxford Sq BAY/PAD W2 8 C4
Oxford St OXSTW W1C 9 G4
SOHO/SHAV W1D 10 A3
Oxford Wk STHL UB1 114 E1
Oxford Wy FELT TW13 154 C6
Oxgate Court Pde
CRICK NW2 * 63 K6
Oxgate Gdns CRICK NW2 81 K1
Oxgate La CRICK NW2 63 K6
Oxhawth Crs HAYES BR2 201 F2
STMC/STPC BR5 201 G3
Oxhey Av OXHEY WD19 27 H2
Oxhey Dr NTHWD HA6 41 F1
OXHEY WD19 27 G5
Oxhey La OXHEY WD19 27 H2
PIN HA5 42 A1
Oxhey Ridge Cl NTHWD HA6 40 E1
Oxhey Rd OXHEY WD19 27 G2
Oxleas EHAM E6 108 B5
Oxleas Cl WELL DA16 147 J3
Oxleay Rd RYLN/HDSTN HA2 60 A5
Oxleigh Cl NWMAL KT3 192 B2
Oxley Cl STHWK SE1 123 G5
Oxleys Rd CRICK NW2 81 K1
Oxlow La DAGW RM9 92 B2
Oxonian St EDUL SE22 143 G5
Oxted Cl MTCM CR4 178 C6
Oxtoby Wy
STRHM/NOR SW16 179 J4
Oyster Catchers Cl
CAN/RD E16 107 F5
Oyster Rw WCHPL E1 104 E5
Ozolins Wy CAN/RD E16 106 D5

P

Pablo Neruda HNHL SE24 142 C5
Paceheath Cl CRW RM5 57 F2
Pace Pl WCHPL E1 104 D5
Pacific Cl EBED/NFELT TW14 153 J3
Pacific Rd CAN/RD E16 106 E5
Packham Cl ORP BR6 217 J1
Packington Rd ACT W3 117 K3
Packington Sq IS N1 6 C1
Packington St IS N1 6 C1
Packmores Rd ELTH/MOT SE9 147 J6
Padbury Cl EBED/NFELT TW14 153 G3
Padbury Ct BETH E2 7 K5
Padcroft Rd WDR/YW UB7 112 A1
Paddenswick Rd
HMSMTH W6 118 D3
Paddington Cl YEAD UB4 95 H3
Paddington Gn BAY/PAD W2 8 A2
Paddington St MHST W1U 9 G1
Paddock Cl BKHTH/KID SE3 145 K4
NTHLT UB5 96 A1
ORP BR6 216 B2
OXHEY WD19 27 J1
SYD SE26 164 A6
WPK KT4 192 B5
Paddock Gdns NRWD SE19 181 F2
Paddock Rd BXLYHS DA6 149 F5
CRICK NW2 81 J1
RSLP HA4 77 H1
Paddocks Cl
RYLN/HDSTN HA2 78 B2
STMC/STPC BR5 202 E6
The Paddocks EA W5 * 116 E3
EBAR EN4 21 K4
MLHL NW7 * 46 D2
WBLY HA9 62 D6
Paddock Wy CHST BR7 185 J3
PUT/ROE SW15 159 F2
Padelford La STAN HA7 29 G4
Padfield Rd BRXN/ST SW9 142 D4
Padley Cl CHSGTN KT9 206 B3
Padnall Rd CHDH RM6 55 K6
CHDH RM6 74 A1
Padstow Cl ORP BR6 217 F2
Padstow Rd ENC/FH EN2 23 H3
Padstow Wk FELT TW13 153 J4
Padua Rd PGE/AN SE20 181 K4
Pagden St VX/NE SW8 141 G2
Pageant Crs
BERM/RHTH SE16 124 C1
Pageant Wk CROY/NA CR0 212 A1
Page Av WBLY HA9 80 E1
Page Cl DAGW RM9 92 A3
HPTN TW12 172 D2
KTN/HRWW/WS HA3 62 B3
Page Crs CROY/NA CR0 211 H3
ERITH DA8 150 C1
Page Green Rd
SEVS/STOTM N15 * 68 C2
Page Green Ter
SEVS/STOTM N15 68 B2
Page Heath La BMLY BR1 184 C6
Page Heath Vls BMLY BR1 184 C6
Pagehurst Rd CROY/NA CR0 197 H4
Page Meadow MLHL NW7 45 J3
Page Rd EBED/NFELT TW14 153 G1
Page's Hl MUSWH N10 48 A5
Page's La MUSWH N10 48 A5
Page St MLHL NW7 45 J4
WEST SW1P 16 D6

Page's Wk STHWK SE1 19 G6
Pages Yd CHSWK W4 * 118 B6
Page's Yd CHSWK W4 118 C6
Paget Av SUT SM1 209 H1
Paget Cl HPTN TW12 155 J6
Paget Gdns CHST BR7 185 G4
Paget La ISLW TW7 135 J4
Paget Pl KUTN/CMB KT2 * 175 K2
THDIT KT7 190 A5
Paget Ri WOOL/PLUM SE18 147 F1
Paget Rd HGDN/ICK UB10 94 A3
IL IG1 90 B2
STNW/STAM N16 67 K5
Paget St FSBYE EC1V 6 A4
Paget Ter WOOL/PLUM SE18 127 G6
Pagitts Gv EBAR EN4 21 F2
Pagnell St NWCR SE14 144 C1
Pagoda Av RCH/KEW TW9 137 G4
Pagoda Gdns BKHTH/KID SE3 145 G3
Pagoda Gv WNWD SE27 162 D4
Paignton Rd RSLP HA4 76 E1
SEVS/STOTM N15 68 A3
Paines Cl PIN HA5 41 J6
Paine's La PIN HA5 41 J5
Pain's Cl MTCM CR4 179 G5
Painsthorpe Rd
STNW/STAM N16 86 A1
Painters Ms BERM/RHTH SE16 123 H4
Painters Rd GNTH/NBYPK IG2 55 G6
Paisley Rd CAR SM5 194 C5
WDGN N22 49 H4
Paisley Ter CAR SM5 194 C5
Pakeman St HOLWY N7 85 F1
Pakenham Cl BAL SW12 161 F3
Pakenham St FSBYW WC1X 5 H5
Palace Av KENS W8 120 A2
Palace Cl HOM E9 87 H4
Palace Ct BAY/PAD W2 101 F6
KTN/HRWW/WS HA3 62 A3
Palace Court Gdns
MUSWH N10 48 C6
Palace Garden Ms KENS W8 120 A1
Palace Gdns BKHH IG9 39 H3
Palace Gardens Ter KENS W8 119 K1
Palace Ga KENS W8 120 B2
Palace Gates Rd WDGN N22 48 E4
Palace Gn CROY/NA CR0 213 H5
KENS W8 120 A1
Palace Gv BMLY BR1 184 A4
NRWD SE19 181 G3
Palace Ms FUL/PGN SW6 * 139 J1
WALTH E17 69 H1
Palace Pde WALTH E17 * 69 H1
Palace Pl BGVA SW1W 16 A4
Palace Rd BMLY BR1 184 A4
BRXS/STRHM SW2 162 A3
CEND/HSY/T N8 66 D2
E/WMO/HCT KT8 173 H6
FBAR/BDGN N11 48 E3
KUT/HW KT1 190 E1
NRWD SE19 181 G3
RSLP HA4 77 J2
Palace Sq NRWD SE19 181 G3
Palace St WESTW SW1E 15 K4
Palace Vw BMLY BR1 184 A6
CROY/NA CR0 213 H2
LEE/GVPK SE12 165 K4
Palace View Rd CHING E4 51 K1
Palamos Rd LEY E10 69 J5
Palatine Av STNW/STAM N16 86 A2
Palatine Rd STNW/STAM N16 86 A2
Palemead Cl FUL/PGN SW6 139 G2
Palermo Rd WLSDN NW10 99 J1
Palestine Gv WIM/MER SW19 178 C4
Palewell Cl STMC/STPC BR5 186 C5
Palewell Common Dr
MORT/ESHN SW14 138 A6
Palewell Pk
MORT/ESHN SW14 138 A6
Palfrey Pl VX/NE SW8 142 A1
Palgrave Av STHL UB1 96 A6
Palgrave Gdns CAMTN NW1 2 D6
Palgrave Rd SHB W12 118 C3
Palissy St BETH E2 7 J5
Pallant Wy ORP BR6 216 A1
Pallet Wy WOOL/PLUM SE18 146 D2
Palliser Dr RAIN RM13 111 J4
Palliser Rd WKENS W14 119 H5
Pall Ml STJS SW1Y 16 C1
Pall Ml East STJS SW1Y 10 C7
Pall Mall Pl STJS SW1Y 16 B1
Palmar Crs BXLYHN DA7 149 H4
Palmar Rd BXLYHN DA7 149 H3
Palmarsh Rd STMC/STPC BR5 202 E1
Palm Av SCUP DA14 186 E2
Palm Cl LEY E10 87 K1
Palmeira Rd BXLYHN DA7 148 E4
Palmer Av BUSH WD23 28 B1
CHEAM SM3 208 A2
Palmer Cl HEST TW5 135 F2
NTHLT UB5 77 J4
WWKM BR4 199 G6
Palmer Crs KUT/HW KT1 175 F6
Palmer Dr BMLY BR1 201 G1
Palmer Gdns BAR EN5 20 B6
Palmer Pl HOLWY N7 85 G3
Palmer Rd BCTR RM8 73 K5
PLSTW E13 107 F3
Palmers Gv E/WMO/HCT KT8 189 F1
Palmers La PEND EN3 24 E2
Palmers Rd BETH E2 105 F1
MORT/ESHN SW14 137 K4
STRHM/NOR SW16 180 A5
Palmer's Rd FBAR/BDGN N11 48 C1
Palmerston Ct BKHH IG9 39 G4
Palmerston Crs PLMGR N13 49 F1
WOOL/PLUM SE18 127 H6
Palmerston Gv
WIM/MER SW19 177 K3
Palmerston Rd ACT W3 117 K3
BKHH IG9 39 G4
CAR SM5 209 K2
CROY/NA CR0 196 E2
FSTGT E7 89 F3
HSLW TW3 135 H2
KIL/WHAMP NW6 82 D5
KTN/HRWW/WS HA3 43 F6
MORT/ESHN SW14 137 K5
ORP BR6 216 C2
SUT SM1 209 G3
WALTH E17 69 H1
WDGN N22 49 F3
WHTN TW2 155 K1
WIM/MER SW19 177 K3
Palmerston Wy VX/NE SW8 * 141 G1
Palmer St STJSPK SW1H 16 B4
Palmers Whf KUT/HW KT1 * 174 E5
Palm Gv EA W5 117 F3
Palm Rd ROMW/RG RM7 74 E2
Pamela Ct
NFNCH/WDSPK N12 * 47 F2
Pamela Gdns PIN HA5 59 F2
Pampisford Rd SAND/SEL CR2 211 H6
Pams Wy HOR/WEW KT19 207 F3
Pancras La MANHO EC4N 12 D4
Pancras Rd CAMTN NW1 4 C2
KCROSS N1C 4 E3
Pancras Wy BOW E3 105 J1
Pandian Wy KTTN NW5 84 D4
Pandora Rd KIL/WHAMP NW6 82 E4
Panfield Ms GNTH/NBYPK IG2 72 A3
Panfield Rd ABYW SE2 128 B2
Pangbourne Av NKENS W10 * 100 A4
Pangbourne Dr STAN HA7 43 K1
Panhard Pl STHL UB1 96 B6
Pank Av BAR EN5 21 H6
Pankhurst Av CAN/RD E16 * 126 A1
Pankhurst Cl ISLW TW7 136 A4
NWCR SE14 144 A1
Pankhurst Rd WOT/HER KT12 188 B4
Pankridge OXHEY WD19 * 27 H4
Panmuir Rd RYNPK SW20 176 E4
Panmure Cl HBRY N5 85 H2
Panmure Rd SYD SE26 163 J5
Pan Peninsula Sq
POP/IOD E14 124 E2
Pansy Gdns SHB W12 99 J6
Panther Dr WLSDN NW10 81 F3
Pantiles Cl PLMGR N13 49 H1
The Pantiles BMLY BR1 184 D6
BUSH WD23 28 D3
BXLYHN DA7 149 G1
Panton Cl CROY/NA CR0 196 C5
Panton St STJS SW1Y 10 D6
Panyers Gdns DAGE RM10 92 D1
Paper Blds EMB EC4Y * 11 K5
Papermill Cl CAR SM5 210 A2
Papermill La DART DA1 151 G5
Papermill Pl WALTH E17 51 G5
Papillons Wk BKHTH/KID SE3 145 K3
Papworth Gdns HOLWY N7 85 F3
Papworth Wy
BRXS/STRHM SW2 162 B2
Parade Ms BRXS/STRHM SW2 162 C4
Parade Ter CDALE/KGS NW9 * 63 J3
The Parade BROCKY SE4 * 144 C2
BTSEA SW11 * 140 C5
CAR SM5 * 209 K3
CROY/NA CR0 * 195 K3
DART DA1 * 150 C6
EA W5 * 97 K5
EDUL SE22 * 143 F4
ESH/CLAY KT10 204 E4
FSBYPK N4 * 67 G6
GFD/PVL UB6 * 79 H4
KUT/HW KT1 * 175 F5
OXHEY WD19 27 H5
PGE/AN SE20 * 181 K4
RCH/KEW TW9 * 137 H4
SUT SM1 * 208 D1
SYD SE26 * 163 J6
WLGTN SM6 * 211 F3
Paradise Pas HOLWY N7 85 F3
Paradise Rd CLAP SW4 141 K3
RCH/KEW TW9 137 F6
Paradise Rw BETH E2 * 104 D2
Paradise St BERM/RHTH SE16 123 J2
Paradise Wk CHEL SW3 120 E6
Paragon Cl CAN/RD E16 106 E5
Paragon Gv BRYLDS KT5 191 G3
Paragon Ms STHWK SE1 19 F6
Paragon Pl BKHTH/KID SE3 145 J3
Paragon Rd HACK E8 86 D4
The Paragon BKHTH/KID SE3 145 K3
Parbury Ri CHSGTN KT9 206 A4
Parbury Rd FSTH SE23 164 B1
Parchmore Rd THHTH CR7 180 C5
Parchmore Wy THHTH CR7 180 C5
Pardoe Rd LEY E10 69 K4
Pardoner St STHWK SE1 19 F4
Pardon St FSBYE EC1V 6 B6
Parfett St WCHPL E1 104 C4
Parfitt Cl HAMP NW3 65 G5
Parfrey St HMSMTH W6 119 F6
Parham Dr GNTH/NBYPK IG2 72 B3
Paris Gdn STHWK SE1 12 A7
Parish Cl HCH RM12 75 K6
Parish Gate Dr BFN/LL DA15 167 K1
Parish La PGE/AN SE20 182 A2
Parish Whf WOOL/PLUM SE18 126 D4
Park Ap BERM/RHTH SE16 * 123 J3
WELL DA16 148 C5
Park Av BARK IG11 90 C4
BMLY BR1 183 K2
CAR SM5 210 A4
CRICK NW2 81 K4
EHAM E6 90 A6
EN EN1 23 K6
FNCH N3 47 F4
GLDGN NW11 65 F5
HSLW TW3 155 G1
IL IG1 72 A5
MORT/ESHN SW14 138 A5
ORP BR6 200 E6
ORP BR6 217 G1
PLMGR N13 35 G5
RSLP HA4 58 C3
SRTFD E15 88 C4
STHL UB1 114 E2
UED N18 36 C6
WDGN N22 48 E5
WFD IG8 53 F1
WLSDN NW10 98 B2
WWKM BR4 215 F1
Park Av East EW KT17 207 J4
Park Avenue Ms MTCM CR4 179 G3
Park Av North
CEND/HSY/T N8 66 D1
WLSDN NW10 81 K3
Park Avenue Rd TOTM N17 50 D3
Park Av South
CEND/HSY/T N8 66 D1
Park Av West EW KT17 207 J4
Park Bvd GPK RM2 57 H4
Park Cha WBLY HA9 80 B2
Park Cl CAR SM5 209 K4
CRICK NW2 81 J1
HOM E9 86 E6
HPTN TW12 173 H4
HSLW TW3 135 H6
KTN/HRWW/WS HA3 42 E4
KUTN/CMB KT2 175 H4
NFNCH/WDSPK N12 * 33 H6
SKENS SW7 * 14 E3
WKENS W14 119 J3
WLSDN NW10 98 B2
Park Cots FNCH N3 * 46 D5
Park Ct DUL SE21 * 162 E5
NWMAL KT3 192 A1
SYD SE26 * 181 J2
WBLY HA9 80 A3
Park Crs EMPK RM11 75 J4
ENC/FH EN2 23 K5
ERITH DA8 129 K6
FNCH N3 47 F3
KTN/HRWW/WS HA3 42 E4
REGST W1B 3 J7
WHTN TW2 155 J3
Park Crescent Ms East
GTPST W1W 3 K7
Park Crescent Ms West
CAVSQ/HST W1G 3 J7
Park Cft EDGW HA8 44 E4
Parkcroft Rd LEE/GVPK SE12 165 J2
Parkdale Crs WPK KT4 207 F1
Parkdale Rd
WOOL/PLUM SE18 127 K5
Park Dr ACT W3 117 H3
CHARL SE7 126 D5
DAGE RM10 92 E1
GLDGN NW11 65 F5
KTN/HRWW/WS HA3 42 D2
MORT/ESHN SW14 138 A6
ROM RM1 75 F1
RYLN/HDSTN HA2 60 A4
WCHMH N21 35 J1
Park End BMLY BR1 183 J4
HAMP NW3 83 J2
Park End Rd ROM RM1 75 G1
Parker Cl CAN/RD E16 126 D1
CAR SM5 209 K4
Parker Ms HOL/ALD WC2B * 11 F3
Parke Rd BARN SW13 138 D2
Parker Rd CROY/NA CR0 211 J2
Parker's Rw STHWK SE1 19 K3
Parker St CAN/RD E16 126 D1
HOL/ALD WC2B 11 F3
Parker Ter FSTH SE23 164 C4
Parkes Rd CHIG IG7 55 F1
Park Farm Cl EFNCH N2 47 G6
PIN HA5 59 F2
Park Farm Rd BMLY BR1 184 C4
KUTN/CMB KT2 175 F3
Parkfield Av FELT TW13 153 K5
MORT/ESHN SW14 138 B5
NTHLT UB5 95 H1
RYLN/HDSTN HA2 42 C5
Parkfield Cl EDGW HA8 44 D2
NTHLT UB5 95 J1
Parkfield Crs FELT TW13 153 K5
RSLP HA4 59 J6
RYLN/HDSTN HA2 42 C5
Parkfield Dr NTHLT UB5 95 H1
Parkfield Gdns
RYLN/HDSTN HA2 42 B6
Parkfield Pde FELT TW13 * 153 K5
Parkfield Rd CLAP SW4 161 J1
FELT TW13 153 K5
NTHLT UB5 95 J1
NWCR SE14 144 C2
RYLN/HDSTN HA2 78 C1
WLSDN NW10 81 J5
Parkfields CROY/NA CR0 198 C5
PUT/ROE SW15 139 F5
Parkfields Av
CDALE/KGS NW9 63 F5
RYNPK SW20 176 E4
Parkfields Cl CAR SM5 210 A2
Parkfields Rd KUTN/CMB KT2 175 G1
Parkfield St IS N1 5 K2
Parkfield Wy HAYES BR2 200 E3
Park Gdns CDALE/KGS NW9 44 D6
ERITH DA8 130 A4
KUTN/CMB KT2 175 G1
Parkgate BKHTH/KID SE3 145 J4
Park Ga EA W5 97 K4
EFNCH N2 47 H6
WCHMH N21 35 F2
Parkgate Av EBAR EN4 21 G2
Parkgate Cl KUTN/CMB KT2 175 J2
Park Gate Ct HPTN TW12 * 173 H1
Parkgate Crs EBAR EN4 21 G2
Parkgate Gdns
MORT/ESHN SW14 138 A6
Parkgate Ms HGT N6 66 C4
Parkgate Rd BTSEA SW11 140 D1
WLGTN SM6 210 A3
Park Gates
RYLN/HDSTN HA2 * 78 A2
Park Gv BMLY BR1 184 A4
BXLYHN DA7 149 K5
EDGW HA8 44 B1
FBAR/BDGN N11 48 D3
SRTFD E15 88 E6
Park Grove Rd WAN E11 70 C6
Park Hall Rd DUL SE21 162 E4
EFNCH N2 65 J1
Parkham St BTSEA SW11 140 C2
Park Hl BMLY BR1 200 D1
CAR SM5 209 K4
CLAP SW4 141 J6
EA W5 97 K4
FSTH SE23 163 J4
RCHPK/HAM TW10 157 G1
Park Hill Cl CAR SM5 209 J3
Park Hill Ri CROY/NA CR0 197 F6
Park Hill Rd CROY/NA CR0 197 F6
CROY/NA CR0 212 A2
HAYES BR2 183 H5
WLGTN SM6 210 B5
Parkhill Rd BFN/LL DA15 167 K5
BXLY DA5 169 G2
CHING E4 38 A2
HAMP NW3 83 K3
Park Hill Wk HAMP NW3 83 K3
Parkholme Rd HACK E8 86 C4
Park House Gdns TWK TW1 136 D6
Parkhouse St CMBW SE5 142 E1
Parkhurst Gdns BXLY DA5 169 H2
Parkhurst Rd BXLY DA5 169 H2
FBAR/BDGN N11 34 A6
HOLWY N7 84 E2
MNPK E12 90 A2
SUT SM1 209 H3
TOTM N17 50 C5
WALTH E17 * 69 G1
WDGN N22 49 F3
Parkland Av ROM RM1 57 G5
Parkland Gv ASHF TW15 152 D6
ISLW TW7 136 A2
Parkland Md BMLY BR1 185 F6
Parkland Ms CHST BR7 185 J3
Parkland Rd ASHF TW15 152 D6
WDGN N22 49 F5
WFD IG8 53 F3
Parklands BRYLDS KT5 191 G2
BUSH WD23 * 28 C1
HGT N6 66 B4
Parklands Cl EBAR EN4 21 H1
GNTH/NBYPK IG2 72 C4
MORT/ESHN SW14 137 K6
Parklands Dr FNCH N3 46 C6
Parklands Pde HEST TW5 * 134 C3
Parklands Rd
STRHM/NOR SW16 179 G1
Parklands Wy WPK KT4 192 B6
Park La CAR SM5 210 A2
CHDH RM6 73 K3
CHEAM SM3 208 C4
CROY/NA CR0 196 E6
CROY/NA CR0 211 K1
EMPK RM11 75 J4
HCH RM12 93 K4
HEST TW5 133 K1
MYFR/PICC W1J 15 H2
OXSTW W1C 9 F5
RCH/KEW TW9 136 E5
RYLN/HDSTN HA2 78 B1
SRTFD E15 * 88 A6
STAN HA7 29 G5
TEDD TW11 174 A2
TOTM N17 50 B3
UED N18 36 B5
WBLY HA9 80 B2
YEAD UB4 94 C4
Park Lane Cl TOTM N17 50 C3
Parklea Cl CDALE/KGS NW9 45 G4
Parkleigh Rd WIM/MER SW19 178 A4
Parkleys RCHPK/HAM TW10 156 E6
Parkleys Pde
RCHPK/HAM TW10 * 156 E6
Parklodge Av WDR/YW UB7 112 C2
Park Md BFN/LL DA15 148 B6
Parkmead PUT/ROE SW15 158 E1
Park Md RYLN/HDSTN HA2 78 B1
Parkmead Gdns MLHL NW7 45 H2
Park Ms CEND/HSY/T N8 66 E3
GNWCH SE10 125 J5
NKENS W10 100 C1
RAIN RM13 93 J4
STWL/WRAY TW19 152 C2
Park Pde ACT W3 * 117 H3
HYS/HAR UB3 * 94 C5
WLSDN NW10 99 H1
Park Piazza LEW SE13 165 G1
Park Pl ACT W3 117 H4
BMLY BR1 * 184 A4
EA W5 116 E1
HPTN TW12 173 H2
IS N1 85 K6
POP/IOD E14 124 D1
WBLY HA9 80 B2
WHALL SW1A 16 A1
Park Place Vls BAY/PAD W2 101 G4
Park Ridings CEND/HSY/T N8 49 G6
Park Ri KTN/HRWW/WS HA3 42 E4
Park Rise Rd FSTH SE23 164 B3
Park Rd ALP/SUD HA0 80 A4
BAR EN5 20 D5
BECK BR3 182 C3
BMLY BR1 184 A4
BRYLDS KT5 191 G3
BUSH WD23 28 A1
CDALE/KGS NW9 63 F4
CEND/HSY/T N8 66 D2
CHEAM SM3 208 C4
CHST BR7 185 G2
CHSWK W4 118 A6
DART DA1 171 K2
E/WMO/HCT KT8 189 H1
EBAR EN4 21 H5
EFNCH N2 47 H6
ESH/CLAY KT10 204 B2
FBAR/BDGN N11 48 D3
FELT TW13 154 C6
HDN NW4 63 K3
HNWL W7 97 F6
HPTN TW12 173 H1
HSLW TW3 135 H6
IL IG1 90 D1
ISLW TW7 136 C2
KUT/HW KT1 174 D4
KUTN/CMB KT2 175 G1
LEY E10 69 J5
MNPK E12 71 F5
NWMAL KT3 192 A1
PLSTW E13 89 G6
RCHPK/HAM TW10 157 G1
SNWD SE25 197 F1
SRTFD E15 88 E6
STHGT/OAK N14 34 D2
STJWD NW8 2 D5
STMC/STPC BR5 202 D3
SUN TW16 172 A3
TEDD TW11 174 A2
TWK TW1 156 D1
UED N18 36 B6
WALTH E17 69 H2
WIM/MER SW19 178 C2
WLGTN SM6 195 G6
WLGTN SM6 210 B3
WLSDN NW10 * 81 G6
YEAD UB4 94 C4
Park Rd East ACT W3 117 K2
Park Rd North ACT W3 117 J2
CHSWK W4 118 A6
Park Rw GNWCH SE10 125 G6
Park Royal Rd WLSDN NW10 98 E2
Parkshot RCH/KEW TW9 136 E5
Park Side BKHH IG9 39 F4
CRICK NW2 81 J1
HYS/HAR UB3 * 94 C6
Parkside BECK BR3 * 182 E5
BKHTH/KID SE3 * 145 J1
CHEAM SM3 208 C4
FNCH N3 47 F4
HPTN TW12 173 J1
MLHL NW7 45 J2
OXHEY WD19 * 27 G1
SCUP DA14 168 C4
WIM/MER SW19 177 G1
Parkside Av BMLY BR1 200 D1
BXLYHN DA7 150 A3
ROM RM1 57 F5
WIM/MER SW19 177 G1
Parkside Cl PGE/AN SE20 181 K3
Parkside Crs BRYLDS KT5 191 K3
HOLWY N7 85 G1
Parkside Cross BXLYHN DA7 150 B3
Parkside Dr EDGW HA8 30 C5
Parkside Est HOM E9 * 87 F6
Parkside Gdns EBAR EN4 33 K3
WIM/MER SW19 159 G6
Parkside Pde DART DA1 * 150 C3
Parkside Rd BELV DA17 129 J4
HSLW TW3 135 G6
NTHWD HA6 40 D1
Parkside St BTSEA SW11 141 F2
Parkside Ter ORP BR6 * 202 B5
UED N18 * 35 K6
Parkside Wy
RYLN/HDSTN HA2 60 B1
Park Sq East CAMTN NW1 3 J6
Park Square Ms CAMTN NW1 3 J7
Park Sq West CAMTN NW1 3 J6
Parkstead Rd PUT/ROE SW15 138 D6
Park Steps BAY/PAD W2 * 8 D5
Parkstone Av UED N18 50 B1
Parkstone Rd PECK SE15 * 143 H3
WALTH E17 52 A6
Park St CROY/NA CR0 211 J1
MYFR/PKLN W1K 9 G6
STHWK SE1 12 C7
TEDD TW11 173 K2
Park Ter CAR SM5 * 209 J1
PEND EN3 * 25 G1
WPK KT4 192 D5
The Park CAR SM5 209 K3
EA W5 116 E1
GLDGN NW11 65 F5
HGT N6 66 A4
SCUP DA14 186 A1
Parkthorne Cl
RYLN/HDSTN HA2 * 60 B3
Parkthorne Dr
RYLN/HDSTN HA2 60 A3
Parkthorne Rd BAL SW12 161 J2
Park Vw ACT W3 98 E4
NWMAL KT3 176 C6
PIN HA5 41 K4
WBLY HA9 80 D3
WCHMH N21 35 F2
Park View Cl CAR SM5 209 K5
Park View Ct
NFNCH/WDSPK N12 * 33 J6
Park View Crs
FBAR/BDGN N11 34 B6
Parkview Crs WPK KT4 193 F5
Park View Dr MTCM CR4 178 C5
Park View Est HBRY N5 * 85 J2
Parkview Gdns CLAY IG5 71 K1
Park View Gdns HDN NW4 64 A2
WDGN N22 * 49 G4
Parkview Ms RAIN RM13 111 K4
Park View Rd EA W5 98 A4
ELTH/MOT SE9 167 G3
FNCH N3 47 F4
PIN HA5 41 F2
STHL UB1 115 F1
TOTM N17 50 C6
WELL DA16 148 D4
CRICK NW2 81 H2
Parkview Rd CROY/NA CR0 197 H5
Park Village East CAMTN NW1 3 J2
Park Village West
CAMTN NW1 3 J2
Park Vls TOOT SW17 * 178 D1
Parkville Rd FUL/PGN SW6 139 J1
Park Vis GNWCH SE10 125 G6
Park Vista Apartments
CAN/RD E16 106 D2
Park Wk WBPTN SW10 120 B6
Parkwat Crs SRTFD E15 88 B3
Park Wy BXLY DA5 170 C5
E/WMO/HCT KT8 173 G6
EBED/NFELT TW14 154 A2
EDGW HA8 44 D4
ENC/FH EN2 23 G3
GLDGN NW11 64 C2
RSLP HA4 58 E5
TRDG/WHET N20 33 K6
Parkway CAMTN NW1 3 J1
CROY/NA CR0 214 A6
ERITHM DA18 129 F3
GDMY/SEVK IG3 91 F1
GPK RM2 57 H5
RAIN RM13 111 J3
RYNPK SW20 193 G1
STHGT/OAK N14 34 E4
WFD IG8 53 G1
The Parkway HEST TW5 113 K6
NTHLT UB5 95 H2
NWDGN UB2 114 A3
YEAD UB4 95 G6
Park West Pl BAY/PAD W2 8 D3
Parkwood BECK BR3 182 D3
Parkwood Av ESH/CLAY KT10 189 H5
Parkwood Ms HGT N6 66 B3
Parkwood Rd BXLY DA5 169 G2
ISLW TW7 136 A2

WIM/MER SW19 177 J1
Parliament Ct WCHPL E1 * 13 H2
Parliament Hl HAMP NW3 83 J2
Parliament Hill Flds
KTTN NW5 * 84 A1
Parliament Ms
MORT/ESHN SW14 137 K3
Parliament Sq WEST SW1P 16 E3
Parliament St WHALL SW1A 16 E2
Parma Crs BTSEA SW11 140 E5
Parmiter St BETH E2 104 D1
Parnell Cl EDGW HA8 30 D6
SHB W12 118 E3
Parnell Rd BOW E3 87 H6
Parnell Wy
KTN/HRWW/WS HA3 43 H4
Parnham Cl BMLY BR1 185 G6
Parnham St POP/IOD E14 * 105 G5
Parolles Rd ARCH N19 66 C5
Paroma Rd BELV DA17 129 H3
Parr Av EW KT17 207 K6
Parr Cl ED N9 36 D6
Parr Rd EHAM E6 89 H6
STAN HA7 43 K4
Parrs Cl SAND/SEL CR2 211 K6
Parr's Pl HPTN TW12 173 F3
Parr St IS N1 6 E2
Parry Av EHAM E6 107 K5
Parry Cl EW KT17 207 J5
Parry Pl WOOL/PLUM SE18 127 G4
Parry Rd NKENS W10 100 C2
SNWD SE25 181 F6
Parry St VX/NE SW8 121 K6
Parsifal Rd KIL/WHAMP NW6 82 E3
Parsloes Av DAGW RM9 92 A3
Parsonage Cl HYS/HAR UB3 94 D5
Parsonage Gdns ENC/FH EN2 23 J3
Parsonage La ENC/FH EN2 23 K3
SCUP DA14 169 G6
Parsonage Manorway
BELV DA17 129 H6
Parsonage St POP/IOD E14 125 F4
Parsons Crs EDGW HA8 30 C5
Parsons Gn FUL/PGN SW6 139 K2
Parsons Green La
FUL/PGN SW6 139 K2
Parsons Gv EDGW HA8 30 C5
Parsons La RDART DA2 170 E5
Parsons Md E/WMO/HCT KT8 173 H6
Parson's Md CROY/NA CR0 196 C5
Parsons Rd PLSTW E13 107 G1
Parson St HDN NW4 46 A6
Parthenia Rd FUL/PGN SW6 139 K2
Partingdale La MLHL NW7 46 B1
Partington Cl ARCH N19 66 D5
Partridge Cl BAR EN5 32 A1
BUSH WD23 * 28 C3
CAN/RD E16 107 H4
STAN HA7 30 A6
Partridge Dr ORP BR6 216 C1
Partridge Gn ELTH/MOT SE9 167 F5
Partridge Rd HPTN TW12 172 E2
SCUP DA14 167 K5
Partridge Sq EHAM E6 107 J4
Partridge Wy WDGN N22 48 E4
Pasadena Cl HYS/HAR UB3 113 K2
Pascal St VX/NE SW8 141 J1
Pascoe Rd LEW SE13 145 G6
Pasley Cl WALW SE17 122 C5
Pasquier Rd WALTH E17 51 G6
Passey Pl ELTH/MOT SE9 166 E1
Passfield Dr POP/IOD E14 105 K4
Passmore Gdns
FBAR/BDGN N11 48 D2
Passmore St BGVA SW1W 15 G7
Pasteur Cl CDALE/KGS NW9 45 G5
Pasteur Gdns UED N18 49 J1
Paston Cl WLGTN SM6 210 C1
Paston Crs LEE/GVPK SE12 166 A2
Pastor St LBTH SE11 18 B6
Pasture Cl ALP/SUD HA0 79 H1
BUSH WD23 28 C2
Pasture Rd ALP/SUD HA0 61 H6
CAT SE6 165 H3
DAGW RM9 92 B3
Pastures Pth WAN E11 70 C5
The Pastures OXHEY WD19 27 F2
TRDG/WHET N20 32 D3
Patcham Ter VX/NE SW8 141 G2
Patching Wy YEAD UB4 95 J4
Paternoster Sq STP EC4M 12 B4
Pater St KENS W8 119 K3
Pates Manor Dr
EBED/NFELT TW14 153 G2
Pathfield Rd
STRHM/NOR SW16 179 J2
The Path WIM/MER SW19 178 A4
The Pathway OXHEY WD19 27 H3
Patience Rd BTSEA SW11 140 D3
Patio Cl CLAP SW4 161 J1
Patmore St VX/NE SW8 141 H2
Patmore Wy CRW RM5 56 D1
Patmos Rd BRXN/ST SW9 142 C1
Paton Cl BOW E3 105 J2
Patricia Ct WELL DA16 148 C1
Patricia Vls TOTM N17 * 50 D4
Patrick Rd PLSTW E13 107 G2
Patriot Sq BETH E2 104 D1
Patrol Pl CAT SE6 164 E1
Patshull Pl KTTN NW5 84 C4
Patshull Rd KTTN NW5 84 C4
Pattenden Rd CAT SE6 164 C3
Patten Rd WAND/EARL SW18 160 D2
Patterdale Cl BMLY BR1 183 H2
Patterdale Rd PECK SE15 143 K1
Patterson Rd NRWD SE19 181 G2
Pattina Wk BERM/RHTH SE16 124 B1
Pattison Rd CRICK NW2 82 E1
Paul Cl SRTFD E15 88 C5
Paulet Rd CMBW SE5 142 C3
Paulet Wy WLSDN NW10 * 81 G5
Paul Gdns CROY/NA CR0 197 G6
Paulhan Rd
KTN/HRWW/WS HA3 61 K1
Paulin Dr WCHMH N21 35 G2
Pauline Crs WHTN TW2 155 H3
Paulinus Cl STMC/STPC BR5 186 D5
Paul Julius Cl POP/IOD E14 106 B6
Paul Robeson Cl EHAM E6 108 A2
Paul St SDTCH EC2A 7 G6
SRTFD E15 88 C6
Paultons Sq CHEL SW3 120 C6
Paultons St CHEL SW3 120 C6
Pauntley St ARCH N19 66 C5
Paveley Dr BTSEA SW11 140 D1
Paveley St STJWD NW8 2 D5
Pavement Sq CROY/NA CR0 197 H5
The Pavement CLAP SW4 141 H5
EA W5 * 117 F3
TEDD TW11 * 174 C3
WAN E11 * 70 A5
WIM/MER SW19 * 177 J2
WNWD SE27 * 162 D6
Pavet Cl DAGE RM10 92 D4
Pavilion Ldg
RYLN/HDSTN HA2 * 60 D5
Pavilion Ms FNCH N3 46 E5
Pavilion Pde SHB W12 * 100 A5
Pavilion Rd IL IG1 71 K4
KTBR SW1X 15 F3
Pavilion St KTBR SW1X 15 F5
The Pavilion VX/NE SW8 * 141 J1
Pavilion Wy EDGW HA8 44 E3
RSLP HA4 59 G6
Pavillion Sq TOOT SW17 160 D5
Pavillion Ter SHB W12 * 100 A5
Pawleyne Cl PGE/AN SE20 181 K3
Pawsey Cl PLSTW E13 88 E6
Pawson's Rd THHTH CR7 196 D3
Paxford Rd ALP/SUD HA0 61 H6
Paxton Cl RCH/KEW TW9 137 G3
WOT/HER KT12 188 B4
Paxton Pl WNWD SE27 163 F6
Paxton Rd BMLY BR1 183 K3
CHSWK W4 118 B6
FSTH SE23 164 B5
TOTM N17 50 B3
Paxton Ter PIM SW1V 121 G6
Payne Cl BARK IG11 90 E5
Paynell Ct BKHTH/KID SE3 145 H4
Payne Rd BOW E3 105 K1
Paynesfield Av
MORT/ESHN SW14 138 A4
Paynesfield Rd BUSH WD23 29 F2
Payne St DEPT SE8 124 C6
Paynes Wk HMSMTH W6 119 H6
Payzes Gdns WFD IG8 * 52 D2
Peabody Av BGVA SW1W 121 G5
PIM SW1V * 121 G5
Peabody Cl CROY/NA CR0 197 K5
GNWCH SE10 * 144 E2
PIM SW1V 121 G5
Peabody Cots HNHL SE24 * 162 D2
Peabody Est BTSEA SW11 * 140 D5
CHEL SW3 * 120 D6
CLKNW EC1R * 5 K7
CMBW SE5 * 142 E2
FUL/PGN SW6 * 119 K6
HMSMTH W6 * 119 F5
HNHL SE24 162 C2
NKENS W10 * 100 A4
STHWK SE1 * 11 K7
STLK EC1Y * 6 D7
TOTM N17 * 50 A4
Peabody Hl DUL SE21 162 C3
Peabody Sq IS N1 * 85 J6
Peabody Ter CLKNW EC1R * 5 K7
Peace Cl GFD/PVL UB6 78 D6
SNWD SE25 197 F1
STHGT/OAK N14 22 B6
Peace Gv WBLY HA9 80 D1
Peace St WOOL/PLUM SE18 127 F6
Peaches Cl BELMT SM2 208 C5
Peach Gv WAN E11 88 B1
Peach Rd FELT TW13 153 K3
NKENS W10 100 B2
Peachum Rd BKHTH/KID SE3 125 J6
Peachy Cl EDGW HA8 44 C2
Peacock Av
EBED/NFELT TW14 153 G3
Peacock Cl BCTR RM8 73 J5
CHING E4 51 H3
MLHL NW7 46 C1
Peacock St WALW SE17 18 B7
Peacock Yd WALW SE17 18 B7
Peaketon Av REDBR IG4 71 H2
Peak Hl SYD SE26 163 K6
Peak Hill Av SYD SE26 163 K6
Peak Hill Gdns SYD SE26 * 163 K6
The Peak SYD SE26 163 K5
Peal Gdns WEA W13 97 G2
Peall Rd CROY/NA CR0 196 A3
Pearce Cl MTCM CR4 179 F5
Pearcefield Av FSTH SE23 163 K3
Pear Cl CDALE/KGS NW9 63 F1
NWCR SE14 144 B1
Pearcroft Rd WAN E11 70 B6
Peardon St VX/NE SW8 141 G4
Peareswood Gdns STAN HA7 43 K4
Peareswood Rd ERITH DA8 150 C2
Pearfield Rd FSTH SE23 164 B5
Pearing Cl WPK KT4 193 G6
Pearl Cl CRICK NW2 64 B4
EHAM E6 108 A5
Pearl Rd WALTH E17 51 J6
Pearl St WAP E1W 123 J1
Pearman St STHWK SE1 17 K4
Pear Pl STHWK SE1 17 J2
Pear Rd WAN E11 88 B1
Pearscroft Ct FUL/PGN SW6 140 A2
Pearscroft Rd FUL/PGN SW6 140 A3
Pearse St PECK SE15 123 F6
Pearson Cl BAR EN5 21 F4
Pearson's NWCR SE14 144 D2
Pearson's Rd NWCR SE14 * 144 D2
Pearson St BETH E2 7 J2
Pearson Wy DART DA1 171 J4
MTCM CR4 179 F4
Pears Rd HSLW TW3 135 H4
Peartree Av TOOT SW17 178 E2
Pear Tree Cl CHSGTN KT9 206 C3
ERITH DA8 150 A2
MTCM CR4 178 D5
Peartree Cl HAYES BR2 200 C2
Pear Tree Ct CLKNW EC1R 5 K7
Peartree Gdns BCTR RM8 91 H3
ROMW/RG RM7 56 D5
Peartree La WAP E1W * 104 E6
Peartree Rd EN EN1 24 A4
Pear Tree St FSBYE EC1V 6 B6
Peartree Wy GNWCH SE10 125 K4
Pearwood Cots STAN HA7 * 29 J4
Peary Pl BETH E2 104 E2
Pease Cl HCH RM12 93 K5
Peasmead Ter CHING E4 * 38 A6
Peatfield Cl BFN/LL DA15 167 K5
Pebworth Rd HRW HA1 61 G6
Peckarmans Wd SYD SE26 163 H5
Peckett Sq HBRY N5 * 85 J2
Peckford Pl BRXN/ST SW9 142 B3
Peckham Gv PECK SE15 143 F1
Peckham High St PECK SE15 143 H2
Peckham Hill St PECK SE15 143 H1
Peckham Park Rd PECK SE15 143 H1
Peckham Rd CMBW SE5 143 F2
Peckham Rye EDUL SE22 143 H5
Pecks Yd WCHPL E1 * 13 J1
Peckwater St KTTN NW5 84 C3
Pedlars Wk HOLWY N7 * 84 E3
Pedley Rd BCTR RM8 73 J5
Pedley St WCHPL E1 104 C3
Pedro St CLPT E5 87 F1
Peek Crs WIM/MER SW19 177 G1
Peel Cl CHING E4 37 K4
ED N9 36 C5
Peel Dr CDALE/KGS NW9 45 H6
CLAY IG5 53 J6
Peel Gv BETH E2 104 E1
Peel Pas KENS W8 119 K1
Peel Pl CLAY IG5 53 J5
Peel Prec KIL/WHAMP NW6 100 D1
Peel Rd ALP/SUD HA0 79 J1
KIL/WHAMP NW6 100 E2
KTN/HRWW/WS HA3 43 F6
ORP BR6 216 C2
SWFD E18 52 D4
Peel St KENS W8 119 K1
Peerglow Est PEND EN3 * 24 E6
Peerless St FSBYE EC1V 6 E5
Pegamoid Rd UED N18 36 E5
Pegasus Cl STNW/STAM N16 * 85 K2
Pegasus Ct BTFD TW8 117 G5
Pegasus Pl FUL/PGN SW6 * 139 K2
LBTH SE11 * 122 B6
Pegasus Rd CROY/NA CR0 211 G4
Pegasus Wy FBAR/BDGN N11 48 B2
Pegg Rd HEST TW5 134 C1
Pegley Gdns LEE/GVPK SE12 165 K4
Pegwell St WOOL/PLUM SE18 147 K1
Pekin St POP/IOD E14 105 J5
Peldon Wk IS N1 * 85 H6
Pelham Av BARK IG11 91 F6
Pelham Cl CMBW SE5 143 F4
Pelham Cots BXLY DA5 * 169 J3
Pelham Crs SKENS SW7 14 C7
Pelham Pl SKENS SW7 14 C6
Pelham Rd BXLYHN DA7 149 H4
IL IG1 72 D6
PGE/AN SE20 181 K5
SEVS/STOTM N15 68 B1
SWFD E18 53 F6
WDGN N22 49 G5
WIM/MER SW19 177 K3
Pelhams Cl ESH/CLAY KT10 204 A3
Pelham St SKENS SW7 14 B6
Pelhams Wk ESH/CLAY KT10 204 A1
Pelier St WALW SE17 122 D6
Pelinore Rd CAT SE6 165 H4
Pellant Rd FUL/PGN SW6 139 H1
Pellatt Gv WDGN N22 49 G4
Pellatt Rd EDUL SE22 143 G6
WBLY HA9 62 A6
Pellerin Rd STNW/STAM N16 86 A3
Pellings Cl HAYES BR2 183 H6
Pelling St POP/IOD E14 105 H5
Pellipar Cl PLMGR N13 35 G5
Pellipar Rd WOOL/PLUM SE18 126 E5
Pellow Cl BAR EN5 32 D1
Pelly Rd PLSTW E13 106 E1
SRTFD E15 88 E6
Pelter St BETH E2 7 J4
Pelton Rd GNWCH SE10 125 H5
Pembar Av WALTH E17 * 51 G6
Pemberley Cha
HOR/WEW KT19 206 D3
Pemberley Cl HOR/WEW KT19 206 D3
Pember Rd WLSDN NW10 100 B2
Pemberton Av GPK RM2 57 K6
Pemberton Cl
STWL/WRAY TW19 152 B3
Pemberton Gdns ARCH N19 84 C1
CHDH RM6 74 A2
Pemberton Pl ESH/CLAY KT10 204 C1
HACK E8 86 D5
Pemberton Rd
E/WMO/HCT KT8 189 H1
FSBYPK N4 67 H2
Pemberton Rw
FLST/FETLN EC4A 11 K3
Pemberton Ter ARCH N19 84 C1
Pembridge Av WHTN TW2 154 E3
Pembridge Crs NTGHL W11 100 D6
Pembridge Gdns
BAY/PAD W2 * 100 E6
Pembridge Ms NTGHL W11 100 E6
Pembridge Pl NTGHL W11 100 E6
Pembridge Rd NTGHL W11 100 E6
Pembridge Sq BAY/PAD W2 100 E6
Pembridge Vls BAY/PAD W2 100 E6
Pembroke Av BRYLDS KT5 191 J2
EN EN1 24 D2
IS N1 84 E6
KTN/HRWW/WS HA3 43 G6
PIN HA5 59 H5
Pembroke Cl ERITH DA8 129 K4
KTBR SW1X 15 H3
Pembroke Gdns DAGE RM10 92 D1
KENS W8 119 J3
Pembroke Gardens Cl
KENS W8 119 J3
Pembroke Ldg STAN HA7 * 43 J2
Pembroke Ms KENS W8 119 K3
MUSWH N10 48 A4
Pembroke Pde ERITH DA8 * 129 K5
Pembroke Pl EDGW HA8 44 C3
ISLW TW7 135 K3
KENS W8 119 K3
Pembroke Rd BMLY BR1 184 B5
CEND/HSY/T N8 66 E1
EHAM E6 107 K4
ERITH DA8 129 K5
GDMY/SEVK IG3 73 F5
GFD/PVL UB6 96 B3
KENS W8 119 K4
MTCM CR4 179 F5
MUSWH N10 48 A4
NTHWD HA6 26 A5
PLMGR N13 35 J5
RSLP HA4 58 C5
SEVS/STOTM N15 68 B2
SNWD SE25 197 F1
WALTH E17 69 K2
WBLY HA9 79 K1
Pembroke Sq KENS W8 119 K3
Pembroke St IS N1 84 E5
Pembroke Ter STJWD NW8 * 2 A1
Pembroke Vls KENS W8 119 K4
Pembroke Wk KENS W8 119 K4
Pembrook Ms BTSEA SW11 * 140 C5
Pembry Cl BRXN/ST SW9 142 B2
Pembury Av WPK KT4 192 D4
Pembury Cl CLPT E5 * 86 D3
HAYES BR2 199 J4
Pembury Ct HYS/HAR UB3 113 G6
Pembury Crs SCUP DA14 169 F4
Pembury Rd BXLYHN DA7 149 F1
CLPT E5 86 D3
SNWD SE25 197 H1
TOTM N17 50 B4
Pemdevon Rd CROY/NA CR0 196 B4
Pemell Cl WCHPL E1 104 E3
Pemerich Cl HYS/HAR UB3 * 113 J5
Pempath Pl WBLY HA9 61 K6
Penally Pl IS N1 85 K6
Penang St WAP E1W 123 J1
Penard Rd NWDGN UB2 115 F3
Penarth St PECK SE15 123 K6
Penates ESH/CLAY KT10 204 D2
Penberth Rd CAT SE6 165 F3
Penbury Rd NWDGN UB2 114 E5
Pencombe Ms NTGHL W11 100 D6
Pencraig Wy PECK SE15 123 J6
Pencroft Dr DART DA1 171 F2
Pendall Cl EBAR EN4 21 J5
Penda Rd ERITH DA8 149 J1
Pendarves Rd RYNPK SW20 177 F4
Penda's Md HOM E9 87 G2
Pendell Av HYS/HAR UB3 133 J1
Pendennis Rd ORP BR6 202 D6
STRHM/NOR SW16 161 K6
TOTM N17 49 K5
Penderel Rd HSLW TW3 135 F6
Penderry Ri CAT SE6 165 G4
Penderyn Wy HOLWY N7 84 D2
Pendlebury House
CHARL SE7 * 146 D1
Pendle Rd STRHM/NOR SW16 179 G2
Pendlestone Rd WALTH E17 69 K2
Pendlewood Cl EA W5 97 J4
Pendolino Wy ALP/SUD HA0 80 C5
Pendragon Rd BMLY BR1 165 K5
Pendrell Rd NWCR SE14 144 B4
Pendrell St WOOL/PLUM SE18 127 J6
Pendula Dr YEAD UB4 95 H3
Pendulum Ms HACK E8 * 86 B3
Penerley Rd CAT SE6 164 E3
RAIN RM13 111 K4
Penfold Cl CROY/NA CR0 211 G1
Penfold La BXLY DA5 168 E3
Penfold Pl BAY/PAD W2 8 C1
Penfold Rd ED N9 37 F3
Penfold St STJWD NW8 2 B7
Penford Gdns ELTH/MOT SE9 146 C5
Penford St CMBW SE5 142 C3
Pengarth Rd BXLY DA5 148 E6
Penge La PGE/AN SE20 181 K3
Penge Rd PLSTW E13 89 G5
SNWD SE25 181 H6
Penhale Cl ORP BR6 217 G2
Penhall Rd CHARL SE7 126 C4
Penhill Rd BXLY DA5 168 D2
Penhurst Rd BARK/HLT IG6 54 B3
Penifather La GFD/PVL UB6 96 D2
Peninsular Cl
EBED/NFELT TW14 153 G1
Peninsular Park Rd
CHARL SE7 125 K5
Penistone Rd
STRHM/NOR SW16 179 K3
Penketh Dr HRW HA1 78 D1
Penmon Rd ABYW SE2 128 B3
Pennack Rd PECK SE15 123 G6
Pennant Ms KENS W8 120 A4
Pennant Ter WALTH E17 51 H5
Pennard Rd SHB W12 119 F2
The Pennards SUN TW16 172 B6
Penn Cl GFD/PVL UB6 96 B1
KTN/HRWW/WS HA3 61 J1
Penner Cl WIM/MER SW19 159 H4
Penners Gdns SURB KT6 191 F4
Pennethorne Cl HOM E9 86 E6
Pennethorne Rd PECK SE15 143 J1
Penney Cl DART DA1 171 G2
Penn Gdns CHST BR7 185 G5
CRW RM5 56 C3
Pennine Dr CRICK NW2 64 B6
Pennine La CRICK NW2 64 C6
Pennine Pde CRICK NW2 * 64 C6
Pennine Wy BXLYHN DA7 150 B2
HYS/HAR UB3 133 G1
Pennington Cl CRW RM5 56 C2
Pennington Dr WCHMH N21 22 E6
Pennington St WAP E1W 104 D6
Pennington Wy
LEE/GVPK SE12 166 A4
Penniston Cl TOTM N17 49 J5
Penniwell Cl EDGW HA8 30 B6
Penn La BXLY DA5 168 E1
Penn Rd HOLWY N7 84 E3
Penn St IS N1 7 F1
Penny Cl RAIN RM13 111 K2
Pennycroft CROY/NA CR0 213 G6
Pennyfields POP/IOD E14 105 J6
Pennymead Pl
ESH/CLAY KT10 204 A4
Penny Ms WAND/EARL SW18 139 K6
Pennymoor Wk MV/WKIL W9 100 D3
Penny Rd WLSDN NW10 98 D2
Pennyroyal Av EHAM E6 108 A5
Penpoll Rd HACK E8 86 D4
Penpool La WELL DA16 148 C4
Penrhyn Av WALTH E17 51 J4
Penrhyn Crs
MORT/ESHN SW14 137 K5
WALTH E17 51 J4
Penrhyn Gdns KUT/HW KT1 190 E1
Penrhyn Gv WALTH E17 51 J4
Penrhyn Rd KUT/HW KT1 175 F6
Penrith Cl BECK BR3 182 E4
PUT/ROE SW15 139 H6
Penrith Crs HCH RM12 93 J3
Penrith Pl WNWD SE27 162 C4
Penrith Rd BARK/HLT IG6 55 F2
NWMAL KT3 192 A1
SEVS/STOTM N15 67 K2
THHTH CR7 180 D5
Penrith St STRHM/NOR SW16 179 H2
Penrose Av OXHEY WD19 27 J4
Penrose Gv WALW SE17 122 D5
Penrose St WALW SE17 122 D5
Penryn St CAMTN NW1 4 C2
Penry St STHWK SE1 19 H7
Pensbury Pl VX/NE SW8 141 H3
Pensbury St VX/NE SW8 141 H3
Pensford Av RCH/KEW TW9 137 H3
Penshurst Av BFN/LL DA15 168 B1
Penshurst Gdns EDGW HA8 44 D1
Penshurst Gn HAYES BR2 199 J2
Penshurst Rd BXLYHN DA7 149 G2
HOM E9 87 F5
THHTH CR7 196 C2
TOTM N17 50 B3
Penshurst Wy BELMT SM2 208 E5
STMC/STPC BR5 202 D1
Pensilver Cl EBAR EN4 * 21 J5
Penstemon Cl FNCH N3 46 E2
Pentelow Gdns
EBED/NFELT TW14 153 K1
Pentire Rd WALTH E17 52 B4
Pentland Av EDGW HA8 30 D4
Pentland Cl ED N9 36 E4
GLDGN NW11 64 C6
Pentland Pl NTHLT UB5 77 J6
Pentland Rd BUSH WD23 28 C1
KIL/WHAMP NW6 100 E2
Pentlands Cl MTCM CR4 179 G6
Pentland St
WAND/EARL SW18 160 B1
Pentland Wy HGDN/ICK UB10 76 A1
Pentlow St PUT/ROE SW15 139 F3
Pentlow Wy BKHH IG9 39 J2
Pentney Rd BAL SW12 161 H3
CHING E4 38 B3
RYNPK SW20 177 H4
Penton Gv IS N1 5 J3
Penton Pl WALW SE17 18 B7
Penton Ri FSBYW WC1X 5 H4
Penton St IS N1 5 J2
Pentonville Rd IS N1 5 G3
Pentrich Av EN EN1 24 C1
Pentridge St PECK SE15 143 G1
Pentyre Av UED N18 49 K1
Penwerris Av ISLW TW7 135 H1
Penwith Rd
WAND/EARL SW18 160 A4
Penwortham Rd
STRHM/NOR SW16 179 G2
Penylan Pl EDGW HA8 * 44 C4
Penywern Rd ECT SW5 119 K5
Penzance Pl NTGHL W11 119 H1
Penzance St NTGHL W11 119 H1
Peony Gdns SHB W12 99 J6
Pepler Ms CMBW SE5 123 G5
Peploe Rd KIL/WHAMP NW6 100 B1
Peplow Cl WDR/YW UB7 112 A1
Pepper Cl EHAM E6 107 K4
Peppercorn Cl THHTH CR7 180 E5
Peppermead Sq LEW SE13 144 D6
Peppermint Cl CROY/NA CR0 195 K4
Peppermint Pl WAN E11 88 C1
Pepper St POP/IOD E14 124 E3
STHWK SE1 18 C2
Peppie Cl STNW/STAM N16 68 A6
Pepys Crs BAR EN5 20 A6
CAN/RD E16 125 K1
Pepys Est DEPT SE8 124 B4
Pepys Park Est DEPT SE8 124 C4
Pepys Ri ORP BR6 202 A5
Pepys Rd NWCR SE14 144 A3
RYNPK SW20 177 F5
Pepys St TWRH EC3N 13 H5
Perceval Av HAMP NW3 83 J3
Percheron Rd BORE WD6 31 F1
Perch St HACK E8 86 B2
Percival Ct TOTM N17 50 B3
Percival Gdns CHDH RM6 73 J3
Percival Rd EN EN1 24 B5
FELT TW13 153 J4
MORT/ESHN SW14 137 K6
ORP BR6 201 G6
Percival St FSBYE EC1V 6 A6
Percival Wy HOR/WEW KT19 206 E2
Percy Bush Rd WDR/YW UB7 112 C3
Percy Gdns PEND EN3 25 F6
WPK KT4 192 A5
YEAD UB4 94 C2
Percy Ms FITZ W1T 10 C2
Percy Rd BXLYHN DA7 149 F3
CAN/RD E16 106 C4
GDMY/SEVK IG3 73 G4
HPTN TW12 173 F3
ISLW TW7 136 B5
MTCM CR4 195 F4
NFNCH/WDSPK N12 47 G1
PGE/AN SE20 182 A4
ROMW/RG RM7 56 E6
SHB W12 118 D2
SNWD SE25 197 G2
WAN E11 70 C4
WCHMH N21 35 J2
WHTN TW2 155 G3
Percy St FITZ W1T 10 C2
Percy Ter BMLY BR1 185 G6
Percy Wy WHTN TW2 155 H3
Peregrine Cl WLSDN NW10 81 F3
Peregrine Ct WELL DA16 148 A2
Peregrine Gdns
CROY/NA CR0 198 B6
Peregrine Rd BARK/HLT IG6 55 H1
TOTM N17 49 J3

Peregrine Wy
WIM/MER SW19 177 F3
Perham Rd WKENS W14 119 H5
Peridot St EHAM E6 107 J4
Perifield DUL SE21 162 D3
Perimeade Rd GFD/PVL UB6 97 J1
Periton Rd ELTH/MOT SE9 146 C5
Perivale Gdns WEA W13 97 H3
Perivale La GFD/PVL UB6 97 G2
Perivale Village
GFD/PVL UB6 * 97 J2
Periwood Crs GFD/PVL UB6 79 G6
Perkin Cl ALP/SUD HA0 79 H3
HSLW TW3 135 G5
Perkin's Rents WEST SW1P 16 C4
Perkins Rd BARK/HLT IG6 72 D2
Perkins Sq STHWK SE1 12 D7
Perks Cl BKHTH/KID SE3 145 H3
Perpins Rd ELTH/MOT SE9 167 K1
Perran Rd BRXS/STRHM SW2 162 C4
Perrers Rd HMSMTH W6 118 E3
Perrin Rd ALP/SUD HA0 79 G2
Perrin's Ct HAMP NW3 * 83 G2
Perrin's Wk HAMP NW3 83 G2
Perry Av ACT W3 99 F5
Perry Cl GNTH/NBYPK IG2 72 D3
RAIN RM13 111 F1
Perry Ct SEVS/STOTM N15 * 68 A3
Perryfield Wy
CDALE/KGS NW9 63 H3
RCHPK/HAM TW10 156 C4
Perry Gdns ED N9 36 A5
Perry Garth NTHLT UB5 77 G6
Perry Gv DART DA1 151 K5
Perry Hall Cl ORP BR6 202 B4
Perry Hall Rd ORP BR6 202 A3
Perry Hl CAT SE6 164 C4
Perry How WPK KT4 192 C5
Perry Mnr CHST BR7 185 K2
Perrymans Farm Rd
GNTH/NBYPK IG2 72 D3
Perry Md BUSH WD23 28 C1
ENC/FH EN2 23 H3
Perrymead St FUL/PGN SW6 139 K2
Perryn Rd ACT W3 99 F6
BERM/RHTH SE16 123 J3
Perry Ri FSTH SE23 164 B5
Perry Rd DAGW RM9 110 B4
Perry St CHST BR7 185 K2
DART DA1 150 B4
Perry V FSTH SE23 163 K4
Persant Rd CAT SE6 165 H5
Perseverance Pl
BRXN/ST SW9 142 B1
Pershore Cl GNTH/NBYPK IG2 72 B2
Pershore Gv CAR SM5 194 C3
Pert Cl MUSWH N10 48 B3
Perth Av CDALE/KGS NW9 63 F4
YEAD UB4 95 G3
Perth Cl NTHLT UB5 78 A4
NWMAL KT3 176 C5
Perth Rd BARK IG11 108 D1
BECK BR3 183 F5
FSBYPK N4 67 G5
GNTH/NBYPK IG2 72 B3
IL IG1 72 C4
LEY E10 69 G5
PLSTW E13 107 F1
WDGN N22 49 H4
Perth Ter GNTH/NBYPK IG2 72 C4
Perwell Av RYLN/HDSTN HA2 59 K5
Petavel Rd TEDD TW11 173 K2
Peter Av WLSDN NW10 81 K5
Peterboat Cl GNWCH SE10 125 H4
Peterborough Ms
FUL/PGN SW6 139 K3
Peterborough Rd CAR SM5 194 D3
FUL/PGN SW6 139 K3
HRW HA1 60 E5
LEY E10 70 A2
Peterborough Vls
FUL/PGN SW6 140 A2
Petergate BTSEA SW11 140 B5
Peters Cl BCTR RM8 73 K5
STAN HA7 43 K2
WELL DA16 147 K3
Petersfield Cl UED N18 49 J1
Petersfield Ri PUT/ROE SW15 158 E3
Petersfield Rd ACT W3 117 K2
Petersham Cl
RCHPK/HAM TW10 156 E4
SUT SM1 208 D3
Petersham Dr
STMC/STPC BR5 186 A5
Petersham Gdns
STMC/STPC BR5 186 A6
Petersham La SKENS SW7 * 120 B3
Petersham Ms SKENS SW7 120 B3
Petersham Pl SKENS SW7 120 B3
Petersham Rd
RCHPK/HAM TW10 156 E5
Petersham Ter
CROY/NA CR0 * 210 E1
Peter's Hl BLKFR EC4V 12 C5
Peterstone Rd ABYW SE2 128 C2
Peterstow Cl WIM/MER SW19 159 H4
Peter St SOHO/CST W1F 10 C5
Peterwood Wy CROY/NA CR0 196 A6
Petherton Rd HBRY N5 85 J3
Petiver Cl HOM E9 * 86 E5
Petley Rd HMSMTH W6 119 F6
Peto Pl CAMTN NW1 3 K6
Peto St North CAN/RD E16 106 D5
Petrie Cl CRICK NW2 * 82 C4
Petros Gdns
KIL/WHAMP NW6 * 83 F3
Petro St South CAN/RD E16 106 D6
Pettacre Cl THMD SE28 127 H3
Pett Cl EMPK RM11 75 K6
Petten Cl STMC/STPC BR5 202 E5
Petten Gv STMC/STPC BR5 202 D5
Petticoat La WCHPL E1 13 H2
Petticoat Sq WCHPL E1 13 J3
Petticoat Tower WCHPL E1 * 13 J3
Pettits Bvd ROM RM1 57 G5
Pettits Cl ROM RM1 57 G5
Pettits La ROM RM1 57 G5
Pettits La North ROM RM1 57 F4
Pettit's Pl DAGE RM10 92 C3
Pettit's Rd DAGE RM10 92 C3
Pettiward Cl PUT/ROE SW15 139 F5
Pettley Gdns ROMW/RG RM7 75 F2
Pettman Crs THMD SE28 127 J3
Pettsgrove Av ALP/SUD HA0 79 J3
Pett's Hl NTHLT UB5 78 B3
RYLN/HDSTN HA2 78 B2
Pett St WOOL/PLUM SE18 126 D4
Petts Wood Rd
STMC/STPC BR5 201 J2
Petty France WESTW SW1E 16 B4
Petty Wales MON EC3R 13 H6
Petworth Cl NTHLT UB5 77 K5
Petworth Gdns
HGDN/ICK UB10 76 A6
RYNPK SW20 176 E6
Petworth Rd BXLYHS DA6 149 H6
NFNCH/WDSPK N12 47 J1
Petworth St BTSEA SW11 140 D2
Petworth Wy HCH RM12 93 H2
Petyt Pl CHEL SW3 * 120 D6
Petyward CHEL SW3 14 D7
Pevensey Av EN EN1 24 A3
FBAR/BDGN N11 48 D1
Pevensey Cl ISLW TW7 135 H1
Pevensey Rd FELT TW13 154 D3
FSTGT E7 88 E2
TOOT SW17 160 C6
Peverel EHAM E6 108 A5
Peveret Cl FBAR/BDGN N11 * 48 B1
Peveril Dr TEDD TW11 173 J1
Pewsey Cl CHING E4 51 J1
Peyton Pl GNWCH SE10 145 F1
Pharaoh Cl MTCM CR4 194 E4
Pheasant Cl CAN/RD E16 107 F5
Phelp St WALW SE17 122 E6
Phelps Wy HYS/HAR UB3 113 J4
Phene St CHEL SW3 120 D6
Philan Wy CRW RM5 57 F2
Philbeach Gdns ECT SW5 119 K5
Philchurch Pl WCHPL E1 104 C5
Philimore Cl
WOOL/PLUM SE18 127 K5
Philip Av ROMW/RG RM7 75 F5
Philip Gdns CROY/NA CR0 198 C6
Philip La SEVS/STOTM N15 67 K1
Philippa Gdns ELTH/MOT SE9 146 C6
Philip Rd RAIN RM13 111 G2
Philips Cl CAR SM5 195 F5
Philip St PLSTW E13 106 E3
Philip Wk PECK SE15 143 H4
Phillimore Gdns KENS W8 119 K2
WLSDN NW10 82 A6
Phillimore Gardens Cl
KENS W8 119 K3
Phillimore Pl KENS W8 119 K2
Phillimore Ter KENS W8 * 119 K3
Phillimore Wk KENS W8 119 K3
Phillipp St IS N1 7 H1
Phillips Cl DART DA1 170 E1
Philpot La FENCHST EC3M 13 G5
Philpot St WCHPL E1 * 104 D5
Phineas Pett Rd
ELTH/MOT SE9 146 D4
Phipp's Bridge Rd
WIM/MER SW19 178 B5
Phipps Hatch La ENC/FH EN2 23 J1
Phipps Ms BGVA SW1W 15 J5
Phipp St SDTCH EC2A 7 G6
Phoebeth Rd LEW SE13 144 D6
Phoenix Cl HACK E8 * 86 B6
NTHWD HA6 26 D6
WALTH E17 51 H5
WWKM BR4 199 G6
Phoenix Ct BTFD TW8 117 F5
POP/IOD E14 124 D4
Phoenix Dr HAYES BR2 215 H1
Phoenix Pk BTFD TW8 * 116 E5
Phoenix Pl DART DA1 171 G2
FSBYW WC1X 5 H6
Phoenix Rd CAMTN NW1 4 C4
PGE/AN SE20 181 K2
Phoenix St LSQ/SEVD WC2H 10 D4
Phoenix Wy HEST TW5 114 C6
Phoenix Wharf Rd
STHWK SE1 19 K3
Phyllis Av NWMAL KT3 192 E2
Physic Pl CHEL SW3 120 E6
Picardy Manorway
BELV DA17 129 J3
Picardy Rd BELV DA17 129 H5
Picardy St BELV DA17 129 H3
Piccadilly MYFR/PICC W1J 10 A7
Piccadilly Ar STJS SW1Y 10 A7
Piccadilly Circ REGST W1B 10 B6
Pickard Cl STHGT/OAK N14 34 D3
Pickard St FSBYE EC1V 6 B4
Pickering Av EHAM E6 108 A1
Pickering Gdns CROY/NA CR0 197 G3
FBAR/BDGN N11 48 A2
Pickering Ms BAY/PAD W2 101 F5
Pickering Pl WHALL SW1A * 16 B1
Pickering St IS N1 85 H6
Pickets Cl BUSH WD23 28 D3
Pickets St BAL SW12 161 F2
Pickett Cft STAN HA7 43 K4
Pickett's Lock La ED N9 36 E4
Pickford Cl BXLYHN DA7 149 F3
Pickford La BXLYHN DA7 149 F3
Pickford Rd BXLYHN DA7 149 F4
Pickfords Whf IS N1 * 6 C3
Pickhurst Gn HAYES BR2 199 J4
Pickhurst La WWKM BR4 199 H3
Pickhurst Md HAYES BR2 199 J4
Pickhurst Pk HAYES BR2 199 H2
Pickhurst Ri WWKM BR4 199 G5
Pickwick Cl HSLWW TW4 134 D6
Pickwick Ms UED N18 50 A1
Pickwick Pl HRW HA1 60 E4
Pickwick Rd DUL SE21 162 E2
Pickwick St STHWK SE1 18 C3
Pickwick Wy CHST BR7 185 H2
Pickworth Cl VX/NE SW8 * 141 K1
Picton Pl MHST W1U 9 H4
SURB KT6 191 H5
Picton St CMBW SE5 142 E1
Pied Bull Yd IS N1 6 A1
Piedmont Rd
WOOL/PLUM SE18 127 J5
Pier Head WAP E1W * 123 J1
Piermont Pl BMLY BR1 184 C5
Piermont Rd EDUL SE22 143 J6
Pierrepoint Ar IS N1 * 6 A2
Pierrepoint Rd ACT W3 98 D6
Pierrepoint Rw IS N1 6 A2
Pier Rd CAN/RD E16 126 E2
EBED/NFELT TW14 134 A6
ERITH DA8 130 B6
Pier St POP/IOD E14 125 F4
Pier Ter WAND/EARL SW18 140 A5
Pier Wy THMD SE28 127 J3
Pigeon La HPTN TW12 155 F6
Pigott St POP/IOD E14 105 J5
Pike Cl BMLY BR1 184 A1
Pike Rd MLHL NW7 31 F6
Pike's End PIN HA5 59 F1
Pikestone Cl YEAD UB4 * 95 J3
Pilgrimage St STHWK SE1 18 E3
Pilgrim Cl MRDN SM4 194 A4
Pilgrim Hl WNWD SE27 162 D6
Pilgrims Cl NTHLT UB5 78 C3
PLMGR N13 35 F6
Pilgrims Ct DART DA1 151 K6
Pilgrim's La HAMP NW3 83 H2
Pilgrims Ms POP/IOD E14 106 B6
Pilgrims Pl ASHF TW15 * 152 C6
Pilgrim's Ri EBAR EN4 21 J6
Pilgrim St BLKFR EC4V * 12 A4
Pilgrims Wy ARCH N19 66 D5
SAND/SEL CR2 * 212 B3
WBLY HA9 62 D5
Pilgrim's Wy SAND/SEL CR2 212 B4
Pilkington Rd ORP BR6 216 C1
PECK SE15 143 J3
Pilot Cl DEPT SE8 124 C6
Pilsden Cl WIM/MER SW19 * 159 G3
Piltdown Rd OXHEY WD19 27 H6
Pilton Pl WALW SE17 122 D5
Pimlico Rd BGVA SW1W 121 F5
Pinchbeck Rd ORP BR6 217 F4
Pinchin & Johnsons Yd
WCHPL E1 * 104 C6
Pinchin St WCHPL E1 104 C6
Pincott Pl BROCKY SE4 144 A4
Pincott Rd BXLYHS DA6 149 H6
WIM/MER SW19 178 B3
Pindar St SDTCH EC2A 13 G1
Pindock Ms MV/WKIL W9 101 F3
Pine Apple Ct WESTW SW1E * 16 A4
Pine Av SRTFD E15 88 B3
WWKM BR4 198 E5
Pine Cl LEY E10 69 J6
PGE/AN SE20 181 K4
STAN HA7 29 H6
STHGT/OAK N14 34 C2
Pine Coombe CROY/NA CR0 213 F2
Pinecrest Gdns ORP BR6 216 B2
Pinecroft
KTN/HRWW/WS HA3 62 B2
WOOL/PLUM SE18 148 B1
Pinecroft Crs BAR EN5 20 C5
Pinefield Cl POP/IOD E14 * 105 J6
Pine Gdns BRYLDS KT5 191 H3
RSLP HA4 59 F5
Pine Gld ORP BR6 215 K2
Pine Gv FSBYPK N4 66 E6
TRDG/WHET N20 32 D3
WIM/MER SW19 177 J1
Pinelands Cl BKHTH/KID SE3 * 145 J1
Pinelees Ct
MORT/ESHN SW14 * 137 K5
Pinemartin Cl CRICK NW2 82 A1
Pine Rdg CAR SM5 210 A6
Pine Rd CRICK NW2 82 A2
FBAR/BDGN N11 34 A4
Pines Cl NTHWD HA6 40 C2
Pines Rd BMLY BR1 184 D5
The Pines NRWD SE19 * 180 C2
STHGT/OAK N14 22 C6
WFD IG8 38 E6
Pine St CLKNW EC1R 5 J6
Pine Tree Cl HEST TW5 134 A2
Pine Tree Wy LEW SE13 144 E4
Pine Wk BRYLDS KT5 191 H3
Pinewood Av BFN/LL DA15 167 K3
PIN HA5 42 B2
RAIN RM13 111 K3
Pinewood Cl CROY/NA CR0 213 G1
NTHWD HA6 40 E1
ORP BR6 201 J5
PIN HA5 42 B2
Pinewood Dr ORP BR6 216 E3
Pinewood Gv WEA W13 97 G5
Pinewood Ldg BUSH WD23 * 28 D3
Pinewood Ms
STWL/WRAY TW19 152 A1
Pinewood Pl HOR/WEW KT19 207 F2
RDART DA2 170 B4
Pinewood Rd ABYW SE2 128 E6
FELT TW13 154 A5
HAYES BR2 199 K1
Pinfold Rd STRHM/NOR SW16 161 K6
Pinglestone Cl WDR/YW UB7 132 B1
Pinkcoat Cl FELT TW13 154 A5
Pinkwell Av HYS/HAR UB3 113 G4
Pinkwell La HYS/HAR UB3 113 G4
Pinley Gdns DAGW RM9 91 H6
Pinnacle Hl BXLYHN DA7 149 J5
Pinnacle Hl North
BXLYHN DA7 149 J4
Pinnata Cl ENC/FH EN2 23 J2
Pinnell Rd ELTH/MOT SE9 146 C5
Pinner Ct PIN HA5 60 A1
Pinner Gn PIN HA5 41 G5
Pinner Gv PIN HA5 59 J1
Pinner Hl PIN HA5 41 F3
Pinner Hill Rd PIN HA5 41 G4
Pinner Park Av
RYLN/HDSTN HA2 42 C5
Pinner Park Gdns
RYLN/HDSTN HA2 42 C5
Pinner Rd HRW HA1 60 B2
NTHWD HA6 40 D4
OXHEY WD19 27 H1
PIN HA5 59 K1
Pinner Vw HRW HA1 60 C2
Pinn Wy RSLP HA4 58 B4
Pintail Cl EHAM E6 107 J4
Pintail Rd WFD IG8 53 F3
Pintail Wy YEAD UB4 95 H4
Pinto Cl BORE WD6 * 31 F1
Pinto Wy BKHTH/KID SE3 146 A5
Pioneer Cl BOW E3 105 K4
SHB W12 99 K5
Pioneer St PECK SE15 143 H2
Pioneer Wy SHB W12 100 A5
WATW WD18 26 D1
Piper Cl HOLWY N7 85 F4
Piper Rd KUT/HW KT1 175 H6
Pipers Gdns CROY/NA CR0 198 B4
Pipers Gn CDALE/KGS NW9 62 E2
Pipers Green La STAN HA7 30 A5
Piper Wy IL IG1 72 D5
Pipewell Rd CAR SM5 194 D3
Pippin Cl CRICK NW2 81 J1
CROY/NA CR0 198 C5
Pippins Cl WDR/YW UB7 112 A3
Piquet Rd PGE/AN SE20 181 K5
Pirbright Crs CROY/NA CR0 214 A4
Pirbright Rd
WAND/EARL SW18 159 J3
Pirie St CAN/RD E16 126 A1
Pitcairn Cl ROMW/RG RM7 74 C1
Pitcairn Rd MTCM CR4 178 E3
Pitchford St SRTFD E15 88 B5
Pitfield Crs THMD SE28 128 B1
Pitfield St IS N1 7 G4
Pitfield Wy PEND EN3 24 E2
WLSDN NW10 80 E4
Pitfold Rd LEE/GVPK SE12 165 K2
Pitlake CROY/NA CR0 196 C6
Pitman St CMBW SE5 142 D1
Pitsea Pl WCHPL E1 105 F5
Pitsea St WCHPL E1 105 F5
Pitshanger La EA W5 97 H3
Pitt Crs WIM/MER SW19 160 A6
Pittman Gdns IL IG1 90 C3
Pitt Rd ORP BR6 216 C2
RYLN/HDSTN HA2 60 C6
THHTH CR7 196 D2
Pitts Head Ms
MYFR/PICC W1J 15 H1
Pittsmead Av HAYES BR2 199 K4
Pitt St KENS W8 119 K2
Pittville Gdns SNWD SE25 181 H6
Pixley St POP/IOD E14 105 H5
Pixton Wy CROY/NA CR0 213 G6
Place Farm Av ORP BR6 201 J5
Plaistow Gv BMLY BR1 184 A3
SRTFD E15 88 D6
Plaistow La BMLY BR1 183 K3
Plaistow Park Rd PLSTW E13 107 F1
Plaistow Rd SRTFD E15 88 D6
Plane St SYD SE26 163 J5
Plane Tree Crs FELT TW13 154 A5
Plantagenet Cl WPK KT4 207 F2
Plantagenet Gdns CHDH RM6 73 K4
Plantagenet Pl CHDH RM6 73 K4
Plantagenet Rd BAR EN5 21 G5
Plantain Gdns WAN E11 * 88 B1
Plantain Pl STHWK SE1 18 E2
Plantation Dr STMC/STPC BR5 202 E5
Plantation La FENCHST EC3M 13 G5
Plantation Rd ERITH DA8 150 D2
The Plantation
BKHTH/KID SE3 145 K3
Plashet Gv EHAM E6 89 G6
Plashet Rd PLSTW E13 88 E6
Plassy Rd CAT SE6 164 E2
Platina St SDTCH EC2A 7 F6
Platinum Ct ROMW/RG RM7 56 D6
Plato Rd BRXS/STRHM SW2 141 K5
Platt's La HAMP NW3 82 E1
Platts Rd PEND EN3 24 E2
Platt St CAMTN NW1 4 C2
Plawsfield Rd BECK BR3 182 A4
Plaxtol Cl BMLY BR1 184 B4
Plaxtol Rd ERITH DA8 149 H1
Playfair St HMSMTH W6 * 119 F5
Playfield Av CRW RM5 56 E4
Playfield Crs EDUL SE22 143 F6
Playfield Rd EDGW HA8 44 E5
Playford Rd FSBYPK N4 67 F6
Playgreen Wy CAT SE6 164 D6
Playground Cl BECK BR3 182 A5
Playhouse Ct STHWK SE1 18 C2
Playhouse Yd BLKFR EC4V 12 A4
Plaza Pde ALP/SUD HA0 * 80 A4
Plaza Wk CDALE/KGS NW9 44 E6
Pleasance Rd PUT/ROE SW15 138 E6
STMC/STPC BR5 186 C5
The Pleasance
PUT/ROE SW15 138 E5
Pleasant Gv CROY/NA CR0 213 H1
Pleasant Pl IS N1 85 H5
Pleasant Vw ERITH DA8 130 B5
Pleasant View Pl ORP BR6 216 C3
Pleasant Wy ALP/SUD HA0 97 J1
Plender St CAMTN NW1 4 A1
Pleshey Rd ARCH N19 84 D2
Plesman Wy WLGTN SM6 * 210 E6
Plevna Crs SEVS/STOTM N15 68 A3
Plevna Rd ED N9 36 C5
HPTN TW12 173 G4
Plevna St POP/IOD E14 125 F3
Pleydell Av HMSMTH W6 118 C3
NRWD SE19 181 G3
Pleydell Est FSBYE EC1V * 6 D5
Pleydell Gdns NRWD SE19 * 181 G2
Pleydell St EMB EC4Y 11 K4
Plimsoll Cl POP/IOD E14 105 K5
Plimsoll Rd FSBYPK N4 85 H1
Plough Cl WLSDN NW10 99 K2
Plough Farm Cl RSLP HA4 58 B3
Plough La CROY/NA CR0 210 E2
EDUL SE22 163 G1
PUR/KEN CR8 210 E6
TEDD TW11 174 B1
WIM/MER SW19 178 A1
WLGTN SM6 210 E3
Plough Lane Cl WLGTN SM6 210 E3
Ploughmans Cl CAMTN NW1 84 D6
Ploughmans End ISLW TW7 135 J6
Plough Pl FLST/FETLN EC4A 11 K3
Plough Rd BTSEA SW11 140 C4
HOR/WEW KT19 207 F5
Plough St WCHPL E1 * 104 C5
Plough Ter BTSEA SW11 140 C5
Plough Wy BERM/RHTH SE16 124 A4
Plough Yd SDTCH EC2A 7 H7
Plover Wy BERM/RHTH SE16 124 B3
YEAD UB4 95 H5
Plowden Blds EMB EC4Y * 11 J5
Plowman Cl UED N18 49 K1
Plowman Wy BCTR RM8 73 J5
Plumbers Rw WCHPL E1 104 C4
Plumbridge St GNWCH SE10 * 145 F2
Plum Cl FELT TW13 153 K3
Plum Garth BTFD TW8 116 E4
Plum La WOOL/PLUM SE18 147 G1
Plummer La MTCM CR4 178 E4
Plummer Rd CLAP SW4 161 J2
Plumpton Wy CAR SM5 209 J1
Plumstead Common Rd
WOOL/PLUM SE18 127 H6
Plumstead High St
WOOL/PLUM SE18 127 J4
Plumstead Rd
WOOL/PLUM SE18 127 H4
Plumtree Cl DAGE RM10 92 D4
WLGTN SM6 210 D5
Plumtree Ct FLST/FETLN EC4A 11 K3
Plymouth Rd BMLY BR1 184 A4
CAN/RD E16 106 E4
Plymouth Whf POP/IOD E14 125 G4
Plympton Av
KIL/WHAMP NW6 82 D5
Plympton Cl BELV DA17 129 F3
Plympton Pl STJWD NW8 * 2 C7
Plympton Rd
KIL/WHAMP NW6 82 D5
Plympton St STJWD NW8 2 C7
Plymstock Rd WELL DA16 148 D1
Pocklington Cl
CDALE/KGS NW9 45 G5
Pocock Av WDR/YW UB7 112 C3
Pocock St STHWK SE1 18 A2
Podmore Rd
WAND/EARL SW18 140 B5
Poet's Rd HBRY N5 85 K3
Poets Wy HRW HA1 60 E1
Pointalls Cl FNCH N3 47 G5
Point Cl GNWCH SE10 145 F2
Pointer Cl THMD SE28 109 K5
Pointers Cl POP/IOD E14 124 E5
Point Hl GNWCH SE10 145 F2
Point Pl WBLY HA9 80 D5
Point Pleasant
WAND/EARL SW18 139 K5
Point Wharf La BTFD TW8 136 E1
Poland St SOHO/SHAV W1D 10 B3
Polebrook Rd BKHTH/KID SE3 146 B4
Polecroft La CAT SE6 164 C4
Pole Hill Rd CHING E4 38 A2
Polesden Gdns RYNPK SW20 176 E6
Polesworth Rd DAGW RM9 110 B1
Polish War Memorial Rbt
RSLP HA4 77 G4
Pollard Cl CAN/RD E16 106 E6
CHIG IG7 55 G1
HOLWY N7 85 F2
Pollard Rd MRDN SM4 194 C2
TRDG/WHET N20 33 J4
Pollard Rw BETH E2 104 C2
Pollards Crs
STRHM/NOR SW16 179 K6
Pollards Hl East
STRHM/NOR SW16 180 A6
Pollards Hl North
STRHM/NOR SW16 180 A6
Pollards Hl South
STRHM/NOR SW16 179 K6
Pollards Hl West
STRHM/NOR SW16 179 K6
Pollard St BETH E2 * 104 C2
Pollards Wood Rd
STRHM/NOR SW16 179 K5
Pollen St CONDST W1S 9 K4
Pollitt Dr STJWD NW8 2 A6
Polperro Cl ORP BR6 202 A3
Polperro Ms LBTH SE11 17 K6
Polsted Rd CAT SE6 164 C2
Polthorne Gv
WOOL/PLUM SE18 127 H4
Polworth Rd
STRHM/NOR SW16 179 K1
Polygon Rd CAMTN NW1 4 C3
The Polygon CLAP SW4 * 141 H5
Polytechnic St
WOOL/PLUM SE18 127 F4
Pomell Wy WCHPL E1 13 K3
Pomeroy Cl TWK TW1 136 C5
Pomeroy St NWCR SE14 143 K1
Pomfret Rd CMBW SE5 142 C4
Pomoja La ARCH N19 66 E6
Pond Cl BKHTH/KID SE3 145 K3
NFNCH/WDSPK N12 47 J2
Pond Cottage La BECK BR3 198 D5
Pond Cots DUL SE21 163 F3
Ponder St HOLWY N7 * 85 F5
Pond Farm Est CLPT E5 * 86 E1
Pondfield Rd DAGE RM10 92 D3
HAYES BR2 199 H5
ORP BR6 216 B1
Pond Gn RSLP HA4 58 C6
Pond Hill Gdns CHEAM SM3 * 208 C4
Pond Lees Cl DAGE RM10 93 F5
Pond Md DUL SE21 162 E1
Pond Pl CHEL SW3 14 C7
Pond Rd BKHTH/KID SE3 145 J4
SRTFD E15 106 C1
Pondside Av WPK KT4 193 F5
Pondside Cl HYS/HAR UB3 133 G1
Pond St HAMP NW3 83 J3
Pond Wy TEDD TW11 174 D2
Pondwood Ri ORP BR6 201 K4
Ponler St WCHPL E1 104 D5
Ponsard Rd WLSDN NW10 99 K2
Ponsford St HOM E9 86 E4
Ponsonby Pl WEST SW1P 121 J5
Ponsonby Rd PUT/ROE SW15 158 E2
Ponsonby Ter WEST SW1P 121 J5
Pontefract Rd BMLY BR1 183 K1
Ponton Rd VX/NE SW8 141 J1
Pont St KTBR SW1X 14 E5
Pont Street Ms KTBR SW1X 14 E4
Pool Cl BECK BR3 182 D1
E/WMO/HCT KT8 188 E2
Pool Ct CAT SE6 164 D4
Poole Cl RSLP HA4 58 C6
Poole Court Rd HSLWW TW4 134 D3

Poole Rd *HOM* E9 87 F4
HOR/WEW KT19 207 F4
Pooles Blds *FSBYW* WC1X 5 J7
Pooles La *WBPTN* SW10 140 B1
Pooles Pk *FSBYPK* N4 67 G6
Poole St *IS* N1 6 E1
Poole Wy *YEAD* UB4 * 94 C2
Pooley Dr *MORT/ESHN* SW14 137 K4
Poolmans St
BERM/RHTH SE16 124 A2
Pool Rd *E/WMO/HCT* KT8 188 E2
HRW HA1 60 D4
Poolsford Rd
CDALE/KGS NW9 63 G1
Poonah St *WCHPL* E1 104 E5
Pope Cl *EBED/NFELT* TW14 153 J3
WIM/MER SW19 * 178 C2
Pope Rd *HAYES* BR2 200 C2
Pope's Av *WHTN* TW2 155 K4
Popes Dr *FNCH* N3 46 E4
Popes Gv *CROY/NA* CR0 213 H1
Pope's Gv *WHTN* TW2 155 K4
Pope's La *EA* W5 116 E3
Pope's Rd *BRXN/ST* SW9 * 142 B5
Pope St *STHWK* SE1 19 H3
Popham Cl *FELT* TW13 154 D5
Popham Gdns
RCH/KEW TW9 * 137 J4
Popham Rd *IS* N1 85 J6
Popham St *IS* N1 85 J6
Popinjays Rw *CHEAM* SM3 * 208 B3
Poplar Av *MTCM* CR4 178 E4
NWDGN UB2 115 G3
ORP BR6 201 G6
Poplar Bath St *POP/IOD* E14 105 K6
Poplar Cl *HOM* E9 87 H3
PIN HA5 41 H4
Poplar Court Pde *TWK* TW1 * 156 D1
Poplar Crs *HOR/WEW* KT19 206 E4
Poplar Farm Cl
HOR/WEW KT19 206 E4
Poplar Gdns *NWMAL* KT3 176 A5
Poplar Gv *FBAR/BDGN* N11 48 A2
HMSMTH W6 119 F2
NWMAL KT3 176 A6
WBLY HA9 80 E1
Poplar High St *POP/IOD* E14 105 K6
Poplar La *BECK* BR3 198 E2
Poplar Ms *SHB* W12 119 F1
Poplar Mt *BELV* DA17 129 J4
Poplar Pl *BAY/PAD* W2 101 F6
HYS/HAR UB3 94 E6
THMD SE28 109 J6
Poplar Rd *CHEAM* SM3 193 J5
ESH/CLAY KT10 205 G1
HNHL SE24 142 D5
MNPK E12 89 J1
WIM/MER SW19 177 K5
Poplar Rd South
WIM/MER SW19 177 K6
Poplars Cl *RSLP* HA4 58 C5
Poplars Rd *WALTH* E17 69 K3
The Poplars *STHGT/OAK* N14 22 B6
Poplar St *ROMW/RG* RM7 74 E1
Poplar Vw *WBLY* HA9 * 61 K6
Poplar Wk *CROY/NA* CR0 196 D6
HNHL SE24 142 D5
Poplar Wy *BARK/HLT* IG6 72 C1
FELT TW13 153 K5
Poppleton Rd *WAN* E11 70 C3
Poppy Cl *BELV* DA17 129 J3
NTHLT UB5 77 K4
WLGTN SM6 195 F5
Poppy Dr *PEND* EN3 24 D5
Poppy La *CROY/NA* CR0 197 K4
Porchester Gdns
BAY/PAD W2 101 F6
Porchester Gardens Ms
BAY/PAD W2 101 F5
Porchester Ga *BAY/PAD* W2 * 101 G6
Porchester Md *BECK* BR3 182 E2
Porchester Pl *BAY/PAD* W2 8 D4
Porchester Rd *BAY/PAD* W2 101 F5
KUT/HW KT1 175 J5
Porchester Sq *BAY/PAD* W2 101 F5
Porchester Square Ms
BAY/PAD W2 * 101 F5
Porchester Ter *BAY/PAD* W2 101 G6
Porch Wy *TRDG/WHET* N20 33 K5
Porcupine Cl *ELTH/MOT* SE9 166 D4
Porden Rd *BRXS/STRHM* SW2 142 A5
Porlock Av *RYLN/HDSTN* HA2 60 C5
Porlock Rd *EN* EN1 36 B2
Porlock St *STHWK* SE1 19 F2
Porrington Cl *CHST* BR7 184 E4
Portal Cl *RSLP* HA4 76 E2
WNWD SE27 162 B5
Portal Wy *ACT* W3 99 F4
Portbury Cl *PECK* SE15 143 H2
Portchester Cl *HNHL* SE24 142 D5
Portcullis Lodge Rd *EN* EN1 23 K4
Portelet Rd *WCHPL* E1 105 F2
Porten Houses *WKENS* W14 * 119 H3
Porten Rd *WKENS* W14 119 H3
Porter Rd *EHAM* E6 107 K5
Porters Av *DAGW* RM9 91 H4
Porter Sq *ARCH* N19 66 E5
Porter St *MHST* W1U 9 F1
STHWK SE1 12 D7
Porters Wk *WAP* E1W * 104 D6
Porters Wy *WDR/YW* UB7 112 C3
Porteus Rd *BAY/PAD* W2 101 G4
Portgate Cl *MV/WKIL* W9 100 D3
Porthallow Cl *ORP* BR6 217 F2
Porthcawe Rd *SYD* SE26 164 B6
Porthkerry Av *WELL* DA16 148 B5
Portia Wy *BOW* E3 105 H3
The Porticos *CHEL* SW3 * 120 C6
Portinscale Rd
PUT/ROE SW15 139 H6
Portland Av *BFN/LL* DA15 168 B1
NWMAL KT3 192 C4
STNW/STAM N16 68 B5
Portland Cl *CHDH* RM6 74 A2
WPK KT4 192 E4
Portland Cots *CROY/NA* CR0 * 195 J4
Portland Crs *ELTH/MOT* SE9 166 D4
FELT TW13 153 G6
GFD/PVL UB6 96 B3
STAN HA7 43 K5
Portland Crs West *STAN* HA7 43 K6
Portland Dr *EN* EN1 24 A1
Portland Gdns *CHDH* RM6 73 K2
FSBYPK N4 67 H3
Portland Gv *VX/NE* SW8 142 A2
Portland Ms *SOHO/CST* W1F 10 B4
Portland Pl *REGST* W1B 3 J7
SNWD SE25 197 H1
Portland Ri *FSBYPK* N4 67 H5
Portland Rd *ASHF* TW15 152 B5
BMLY BR1 166 B6
ELTH/MOT SE9 166 D4
KUT/HW KT1 175 F6
MTCM CR4 178 D5
NTGHL W11 100 C6
NWDGN UB2 114 E3
SEVS/STOTM N15 68 A1
SNWD SE25 197 H1
YEAD UB4 94 C2
Portland Sq *WAP* E1W 123 J1
Portland St *WALW* SE17 122 E5
Portland Ter *RCH/KEW* TW9 * 136 E5
Portman Av
MORT/ESHN SW14 138 A4
Portman Cl *BXLY* DA5 170 B3
BXLYHS DA6 148 E4
MBLAR W1H 9 G3
Portman Dr *WFD* IG8 53 H5
Portman Gdns
CDALE/KGS NW9 45 F6
Portman Ga *CAMTN* NW1 2 D7
Portman Ms South
MBLAR W1H 9 G4
Portman Pl *BETH* E2 104 E2
Portman Rd *KUT/HW* KT1 175 G5
Portman Sq *MBLAR* W1H 9 F3
Portman St *MBLAR* W1H 9 G4
Portmeadow Wk *ABYW* SE2 128 E2
Portmeers Cl *WALTH* E17 * 69 H3
Portmore Gdns *CRW* RM5 56 C1
Portnall Rd *MV/WKIL* W9 100 D2
Portnoi Cl *ROM* RM1 57 F5
Portobello Ct *NTGHL* W11 * 100 D6
Portobello Ms *NTGHL* W11 100 E6
Portobello Rd *NKENS* W10 100 C4
NTGHL W11 100 D6
Portpool La *FSBYW* WC1X 11 J1
Portree St *POP/IOD* E14 106 B5
Portsdown Av *GLDGN* NW11 64 D3
Portsdown Ms *GLDGN* NW11 64 D3
Portsea Ms *BAY/PAD* W2 8 D4
Portsea Pl *BAY/PAD* W2 8 D4
Portslade Rd *VX/NE* SW8 141 H3
Portsmouth Av *THDIT* KT7 190 B4
Portsmouth Ms *CAN/RD* E16 107 F6
Portsmouth Rd
ESH/CLAY KT10 204 A4
KUT/HW KT1 174 E6
PUT/ROE SW15 158 E2
THDIT KT7 190 C4
Portsmouth St *LINN* WC2A 11 G3
Portsoken St *TWRH* EC3N 13 J5
Portugal Gdns *WHTN* TW2 * 155 H4
Portugal St *LINN* WC2A 11 H4
Portway *RAIN* RM13 93 J6
SRTFD E15 88 E6
Portway Crs *EW* KT17 207 J6
Portway Gdns
WOOL/PLUM SE18 146 C2
Postern Gn *ENC/FH* EN2 23 G3
The Postern *BARB* EC2Y * 12 D2
Post La *WHTN* TW2 155 J3
Postmill Cl *CROY/NA* CR0 212 E1
Post Office Ap *FSTGT* E7 89 F3
Post Office Wy *VX/NE* SW8 141 J1
Post Rd *NWDGN* UB2 115 G3
Postway Ms *IL* IG1 90 B1
Potier St *STHWK* SE1 19 F5
Potter Cl *MTCM* CR4 * 179 G5
The Potteries *BAR* EN5 * 20 E6
Potterne Cl *WIM/MER* SW19 159 G2
Potters Cl *CROY/NA* CR0 198 B5
PECK SE15 * 143 F1
Potters Fld *EN* EN1 * 24 A5
Potters Flds *STHWK* SE1 19 H1
Potters Gv *NWMAL* KT3 191 K1
Potters Heights Cl *PIN* HA5 41 F3
Potter's La *BAR* EN5 20 E5
STRHM/NOR SW16 * 179 J2
Potters Ms *BORE* WD6 29 K1
Potters Rd *FUL/PGN* SW6 140 B3
Potter's Rd *BAR* EN5 21 F5
Potter St *NTHWD* HA6 40 E4
Potter Street Hl *PIN* HA5 41 F2
Pottery Cl *SNWD* SE25 197 J1
Pottery La *NTGHL* W11 119 H1
Pottery Rd *BTFD* TW8 117 F6
BXLY DA5 169 K4
Pottery St
BERM/RHTH SE16 * 123 J2
Pott St *BETH* E2 104 D2
Poulett Gdns *TWK* TW1 156 A4
Poulett Rd *EHAM* E6 107 K1
Poulter Pk *MRDN* SM4 * 194 D3
Poulters Wd *HAYES* BR2 215 H3
Poulton Av *SUT* SM1 209 H1
Poultry *LOTH* EC2R 12 E4
Pound Cl *ORP* BR6 201 J6
SURB KT6 190 D5
Pound Court Dr *ORP* BR6 201 J6
Pound Farm Cl
ESH/CLAY KT10 189 J5
Pound La *WLSDN* NW10 81 J4
Pound Park Rd *CHARL* SE7 126 C4
Pound Pl *ELTH/MOT* SE9 167 F1
Pound St *CAR* SM5 209 K3
Pountney Rd *BTSEA* SW11 141 F4
Poverest Rd *STMC/STPC* BR5 202 A2
Powder Mill La *DART* DA1 171 H4
WHTN TW2 154 E3
Powell Cl *EDGW* HA8 44 B2
Powell Gdns *DAGE* RM10 92 C2
Powell Rd *BKHH* IG9 39 G2
CLPT E5 86 D1
Power Rd *CHSWK* W4 117 H4
Powers Ct *TWK* TW1 156 E2
Powerscroft Rd *CLPT* E5 86 E2
SCUP DA14 186 D2
Powis Ct *BUSH* WD23 * 28 D3
Powis Gdns *GLDGN* NW11 64 D4
NTGHL W11 100 D5
Powis Ms *NTGHL* W11 100 D5
Powis Pl *BMSBY* WC1N 5 F7
Powis Rd *BOW* E3 105 K2
Powis Sq *NTGHL* W11 100 D5
Powis St *WOOL/PLUM* SE18 127 F3
Powis Ter *NTGHL* W11 100 D5
Powlett Pl *CAMTN* NW1 * 84 B5
Pownall Gdns *HSLW* TW3 135 G5
Pownall Rd *HACK* E8 86 C6
HSLW TW3 135 G5
Pownsett Ter *IL* IG1 * 90 C3
Powster Rd *BMLY* BR1 183 K1
Powys Cl *BXLYHN* DA7 128 E6
Powys La *PLMGR* N13 34 E6
Poynders Rd *CLAP* SW4 161 H2
Poynings Cl *ORP* BR6 202 D6
Poynings Rd *ARCH* N19 84 C1
Poynings Wy
NFNCH/WDSPK N12 46 E1
Poyntell Crs *CHST* BR7 185 J4
Poynter Rd *EN* EN1 24 B6
Poynton Rd *TOTM* N17 50 C5
Poyntz Rd *BTSEA* SW11 140 E3
Poyser St *BETH* E2 104 D1
Praed Ms *BAY/PAD* W2 8 B3
Praed St *BAY/PAD* W2 8 B3
Pragel St *PLSTW* E13 107 F1
Pragnell Rd *LEE/GVPK* SE12 166 A4
Prague Pl *BRXS/STRHM* SW2 141 K6
Prah Rd *FSBYPK* N4 67 G6
Prairie St *VX/NE* SW8 141 F3
Pratt Ms *CAMTN* NW1 4 A1
Pratt St *CAMTN* NW1 4 A1
Pratt Wk *LBTH* SE11 17 H6
Prayle Gv *CRICK* NW2 64 B5
Prebend Gdns *HMSMTH* W6 118 C4
Prebend St *IS* N1 6 C1
Precinct Rd *HYS/HAR* UB3 94 E6
The Precinct *IS* N1 * 6 C1
Premiere Pl *POP/IOD* E14 105 J6
Premier Park Rd
WLSDN NW10 98 D1
Prendergast Rd
BKHTH/KID SE3 145 H4
Prentis Rd *STRHM/NOR* SW16 161 J6
Prentiss Ct *CHARL* SE7 126 C4
Presburg Rd *NWMAL* KT3 192 B2
Prescelly Pl *EDGW* HA8 44 B4
Prescot St *WCHPL* E1 13 K5
Prescott Av *STMC/STPC* BR5 201 G3
Prescott Cl *EMPK* RM11 75 K5
Prescott Pl *CLAP* SW4 141 J4
Presentation Ms
BRXS/STRHM SW2 162 A4
Presidents Dr *WAP* E1W 123 J1
President St *FSBYE* EC1V * 6 C4
Prespa Cl *ED* N9 36 E4
Press Rd *WLSDN* NW10 81 F1
Prestage Wy *POP/IOD* E14 106 A6
Prestbury Rd *FSTGT* E7 89 G5
Prestbury Sq *ELTH/MOT* SE9 166 E6
Prested Rd *BTSEA* SW11 140 D5
Preston Av *CHING* E4 52 B2
Preston Cl *STHWK* SE1 19 G6
WHTN TW2 155 K5
Preston Ct *BAR* EN5 21 G5
WOT/HER KT12 188 B5
Preston Dr *BXLYHN* DA7 148 E2
HOR/WEW KT19 207 G4
WAN E11 71 G2
Preston Gdns *IL* IG1 71 J3
WLSDN NW10 * 81 G4
Preston Hl
KTN/HRWW/WS HA3 62 A4
Preston Pl *CRICK* NW2 81 J4
Preston Rd
KTN/HRWW/WS HA3 62 A4
NRWD SE19 180 C2
RYNPK SW20 176 D3
WAN E11 70 C3
WBLY HA9 62 A6
Prestons Rd *WWKM* BR4 214 E1
Preston's Rd *POP/IOD* E14 106 A6
Preston Vls *KUT/HW* KT1 * 175 G5
Preston Waye
KTN/HRWW/WS HA3 62 A5
Prestwich Ter *CLAP* SW4 * 141 J6
Prestwick Cl *NWDGN* UB2 114 D5
Prestwick Rd *OXHEY* WD19 41 G1
Prestwood *OXHEY* WD19 * 27 J4
Prestwood Av
KTN/HRWW/WS HA3 61 H1
Prestwood Cl
KTN/HRWW/WS HA3 61 H1
WOOL/PLUM SE18 148 B1
Prestwood Dr *CRW* RM5 56 E1
Prestwood Gdns
CROY/NA CR0 196 D4
Prestwood St *IS* N1 * 6 D3
Pretoria Av *WALTH* E17 69 G1
Pretoria Crs *CHING* E4 38 A3
Pretoria Pde *BROCKY* SE4 * 144 D3
Pretoria Rd *CAN/RD* E16 106 D2
CHING E4 38 A3
IL IG1 90 B2
LEY E10 70 B5
ROMW/RG RM7 74 E1
STRHM/NOR SW16 179 G2
TOTM N17 50 B2
Pretoria Rd North *UED* N18 50 B2
Prevost Rd *FBAR/BDGN* N11 34 A4
Price Cl *MLHL* NW7 46 C2
TOOT SW17 160 E5
Price Rd *CROY/NA* CR0 211 H3
Price's St *STHWK* SE1 18 B1
Pricklers Hl *BAR* EN5 21 F6
Prickley Wd *HAYES* BR2 199 J5
Priddy's Yd *CROY/NA* CR0 196 D6
Prideaux Pl *ACT* W3 99 F6
FSBYW WC1X 5 H4
Prideaux Rd *BRXN/ST* SW9 141 K4
Pridham Rd *THHTH* CR7 196 E1
Priestfield Rd *FSTH* SE23 164 B5
Priestlands Park Rd
BFN/LL DA15 168 A5
Priestley Cl *STNW/STAM* N16 * 68 B4
Priestley Gdns *CHDH* RM6 73 H3
Priestley Rd *MTCM* CR4 179 F5
Priestley Wy *CRICK* NW2 63 J5
WALTH E17 51 F6
Priest Park Av
RYLN/HDSTN HA2 60 A6
Priests Av *ROM* RM1 57 F5
Priests Br *MORT/ESHN* SW14 138 B4
Prima Rd *BRXN/ST* SW9 142 B1
Primrose Av *ENC/FH* EN2 23 K2
GDMY/SEVK IG3 73 G4
Primrose Cl *BOW* E3 105 J1
CAT SE6 183 F1
FNCH N3 47 F5
RYLN/HDSTN HA2 77 K1
WLGTN SM6 195 G5
Primrose Dr *WDR/YW* UB7 112 A4
Primrose Gdns *BUSH* WD23 28 B2
HAMP NW3 83 J4
RSLP HA4 77 G3
Primrose Hl *EMB* EC4Y 11 K4
Primrose Hill Rd *HAMP* NW3 83 J4
Primrose Hill Studios
CAMTN NW1 84 A6
Primrose La *CROY/NA* CR0 197 K5
Primrose Ms *CAMTN* NW1 * 83 K5
Primrose Pl *ISLW* TW7 136 A3
Primrose Rd *LEY* E10 69 K5
SWFD E18 53 F5
Primrose Sq *HOM* E9 86 E5
Primrose St *SDTCH* EC2A 13 G1
Primrose Wk *EW* KT17 207 H5
NWCR SE14 144 B1
Primrose Wy *ALP/SUD* HA0 97 K1
Primula St *SHB* W12 99 J6
Prince Albert Rd *CAMTN* NW1 3 G1
STJWD NW8 2 C4
Prince Arthur Ms *HAMP* NW3 83 G2
Prince Arthur Rd *HAMP* NW3 83 G2
Prince Charles Dr *HDN* NW4 64 A4
Prince Charles Rd
BKHTH/KID SE3 145 J2
Prince Charles Wy
WLGTN SM6 210 B1
Prince Consort Dr *CHST* BR7 185 J4
Prince Consort Rd
SKENS SW7 14 A4
Princedale Rd *NTGHL* W11 119 H1
Prince Edward Rd *HOM* E9 87 H4
Prince George Av
STHGT/OAK N14 22 C6
STHGT/OAK N14 34 E1
Prince George Rd
STNW/STAM N16 86 A2
Prince George's Av
RYNPK SW20 177 F5
Prince Georges Rd
WIM/MER SW19 178 C4
Prince Henry Rd *CHARL* SE7 146 C1
Prince Imperial Rd *CHST* BR7 185 G3
WOOL/PLUM SE18 146 E2
Prince John Rd
ELTH/MOT SE9 146 D6
Princelet St *WCHPL* E1 13 K1
Prince of Orange La
GNWCH SE10 * 145 F1
Prince of Wales Cl *HDN* NW4 63 K1
Prince of Wales Dr
BTSEA SW11 140 D2
VX/NE SW8 * 141 G1
Prince of Wales Ga
SKENS SW7 14 C2
Prince of Wales Pas
CAMTN NW1 * 4 A5
Prince of Wales Rd
BKHTH/KID SE3 145 J2
CAN/RD E16 107 G5
KTTN NW5 84 A4
Prince of Wales' Rd *SUT* SM1 194 C6
Prince of Wales Ter
CHSWK W4 118 B5
KENS W8 * 120 A2
Prince Regent La *CAN/RD* E16 107 G5
Prince Regent Ms
CAMTN NW1 4 A5
Prince Regent Rd *HSLW* TW3 135 G4
Prince Rd *SNWD* SE25 197 F2
Prince Rupert Rd
ELTH/MOT SE9 146 E5
Princes Ar *MYFR/PICC* W1J 10 B7
Princes Av *ACT* W3 117 H3
CAR SM5 209 K5
CDALE/KGS NW9 62 C1
FNCH N3 47 F4
MUSWH N10 48 A6
PLMGR N13 49 G1
STMC/STPC BR5 201 K2
SURB KT6 191 H6
WDGN N22 48 D4
WFD IG8 39 F6
Prince's Av *GFD/PVL* UB6 96 B5
Princes Cl *CDALE/KGS* NW9 62 C1
EDGW HA8 44 C1
SCUP DA14 168 E5
Prince's Cl *HPTN* TW12 155 J6
Princes Ct *WBLY* HA9 80 A3
Princes Dr *HRW* HA1 42 E6
Princes Gdns *ACT* W3 98 C4
EA W5 97 J3
SKENS SW7 14 B4
Princes Ga *SKENS* SW7 14 B4
Prince's Ga *SKENS* SW7 14 C3
Princes Gate Ct *SKENS* SW7 14 A3
Princes Gate Ms *SKENS* SW7 14 B4
Princes La *MUSWH* N10 48 A6
Princes Ms *HMSMTH* W6 * 118 E5
HSLW TW3 135 F5
Prince's Ms *BAY/PAD* W2 100 E6
Princes Pde *GLDGN* NW11 * 64 C3
Princes Pk *RAIN* RM13 93 J5
Princes Park Av *GLDGN* NW11 64 C3
HYS/HAR UB3 94 B6
Princes Park Cir
HYS/HAR UB3 94 B6
Princes Park Cl *HYS/HAR* UB3 94 B6
Princes Park La *HYS/HAR* UB3 94 B6
Princes Park Pde
HYS/HAR UB3 94 B6
Princes Pl *NTGHL* W11 119 H1
Prince's Pln *HAYES* BR2 200 D4
Princes Ri *LEW* SE13 145 F3
Princes Riverside Rd
BERM/RHTH SE16 124 A1
Princes Rd *BARK/HLT* IG6 72 D1
BKHH IG9 39 G4
DART DA1 170 E2
FELT TW13 153 J5
KUTN/CMB KT2 175 H4
PGE/AN SE20 182 A2
RCH/KEW TW9 137 G2
RCHPK/HAM TW10 137 G6
ROM RM1 75 J2
TEDD TW11 155 J6
UED N18 36 E6
WEA W13 116 C1
Prince's Rd *MORT/ESHN* SW14 138 A4
TEDD TW11 155 J6
WIM/MER SW19 177 K2
Princess Alice Wy *THMD* SE28 127 J2
Princess Av *WBLY* HA9 62 A6
Princess Crs *FSBYPK* N4 67 H6
Princesses Pde *DART* DA1 * 150 C6
Princess La *RSLP* HA4 58 C5
Princess Louise Cl
BAY/PAD W2 8 B1
Princess May Rd
STNW/STAM N16 86 A2
Princess Ms *HAMP* NW3 83 H4
Princess Pde *ORP* BR6 * 216 A1
Prince's Sq *BAY/PAD* W2 100 E6
Princess Rd *CAMTN* NW1 84 A6
CROY/NA CR0 196 D3
KIL/WHAMP NW6 100 E1
Princess St *BXLYHN* DA7 149 G4
STHWK SE1 18 B5
Princes St *REGST* W1B 9 K4
SUT SM1 209 H2
TOTM N17 50 A2
Prince's St *LOTH* EC2R 12 E4
RCH/KEW TW9 137 F5
Prince's Ter *PLSTW* E13 89 F6
Prince St *DEPT* SE8 124 C6
Princes Vw *DART* DA1 171 K3
Princes Wy *BKHH* IG9 39 G4
CROY/NA CR0 211 F3
RSLP HA4 77 J2
WIM/MER SW19 159 H3
WWKM BR4 214 D2
Prince's Yd *IS* N1 5 H1
NTGHL W11 119 H1
Princethorpe Rd *SYD* SE26 164 A6
Princeton St *GINN* WC1R 11 G2
Pringle Gdns
STRHM/NOR SW16 161 H6
Printers Inn Ct
FLST/FETLN EC4A 11 J3
Printinghouse La
HYS/HAR UB3 113 H2
Printing House Yd *BETH* E2 * 7 H5
Priolo Rd *CHARL* SE7 126 B5
Prior Av *BELMT* SM2 209 J5
Prior Bolton St *IS* N1 85 H4
Prioress Rd *WNWD* SE27 162 C5
Prioress St *STHWK* SE1 19 F5
Prior Rd *IL* IG1 90 A1
Priors Cft *WALTH* E17 51 G5
Priors Fld *NTHLT* UB5 77 J4
Priorsford Av *STMC/STPC* BR5 202 B1
Priors Gdns *RSLP* HA4 77 G3
Priors Md *EN* EN1 24 A2
Prior St *GNWCH* SE10 145 F1
Priory Av *ALP/SUD* HA0 79 F2
CEND/HSY/T N8 66 D1
CHEAM SM3 208 B2
CHING E4 37 H5
CHSWK W4 118 B3
STMC/STPC BR5 201 J3
WALTH E17 69 J2
Priory Cl *ALP/SUD* HA0 79 F2
BECK BR3 182 B6
CHING E4 37 H5
CHST BR7 184 E4
DART DA1 151 F6
FNCH N3 46 D4
HPTN TW12 172 E4
HYS/HAR UB3 95 F6
RSLP HA4 58 D5
STAN HA7 29 F5
STHGT/OAK N14 22 B6
SWFD E18 52 E4
TRDG/WHET N20 32 D2
WIM/MER SW19 * 178 A4
Priory Cots *EA* W5 * 98 B4
Priory Ct *BLKFR* EC4V * 12 B4
VX/NE SW8 141 J2
WALTH E17 51 H5
Priory Crs *ALP/SUD* HA0 79 G1
CHEAM SM3 208 B2
NRWD SE19 180 D3
Priory Dr *ABYW* SE2 128 E5
STAN HA7 29 F5
Priory Field Dr *EDGW* HA8 30 D6
Priory Gdns *ALP/SUD* HA0 79 G2
BARN SW13 138 C4
CHSWK W4 * 118 B4
DART DA1 151 G6
HGT N6 66 B3
HPTN TW12 172 E4
SNWD SE25 197 G1
Priory Green Est *IS* N1 5 G2
Priory Gv *VX/NE* SW8 141 K2
Priory Hl *ALP/SUD* HA0 79 G2
DART DA1 171 G1
Priory La *E/WMO/HCT* KT8 189 F1
PUT/ROE SW15 138 C6
Priory Leas *ELTH/MOT* SE9 * 166 D3
Priory Ms *HCH* RM12 75 K5
Priory Pk *BKHTH/KID* SE3 145 J4
Priory Park Rd *ALP/SUD* HA0 79 G2
KIL/WHAMP NW6 82 D6
Priory Pl *DART* DA1 171 G1
Priory Rd *BARK* IG11 90 D5
CEND/HSY/T N8 66 D1
CHEAM SM3 208 B2
CHSGTN KT9 206 A1
CHSWK W4 118 A3
CROY/NA CR0 196 B4
DART DA1 151 G5
EHAM E6 89 H6
HPTN TW12 172 E3
HSLW TW3 135 H6
KIL/WHAMP NW6 83 F5
MUSWH N10 66 C1

RCH/KEW TW9 117 H6
Priory St BOW E3 105 K2
Priory Ter KIL/WHAMP NW6 83 F6
The Priory BKHTH/KID SE3 145 J4
CROY/NA CR0 * 211 G1
ORP BR6 * 202 C4
Priory Vw BUSH WD23 28 E2
Priory Vls FBAR/BDGN N11 * 47 K2
Priory Wk WBPTN SW10 120 B5
Priory Wy NWDGN UB2 114 C3
RYLN/HDSTN HA2 60 B1
WDR/YW UB7 112 B6
Pritchard's Rd BETH E2 104 C1
Priter Rd BERM/RHTH SE16 * 123 H3
Private Rd EN EN1 23 K6
Probert Rd BRXS/STRHM SW2 142 B6
Probyn Rd BRXS/STRHM SW2 162 C4
Procter St GINN WC1R 11 G2
Proctor Cl MTCM CR4 179 F4
Proctors Cl EBED/NFELT TW14 153 K3
Progress Wy CROY/NA CR0 196 A6
EN EN1 24 C6
WDGN N22 49 G4
Promenade Approach Rd
CHSWK W4 138 B1
The Promenade CHSWK W4 138 B2
EDGW HA8 * 44 C1
Prospect Cl BELV DA17 129 H4
BUSH WD23 28 D2
HSLW TW3 134 E2
RSLP HA4 59 H4
SYD SE26 163 J6
Prospect Cots
WAND/EARL SW18 139 K5
Prospect Crs WHTN TW2 155 H1
Prospect Hl WALTH E17 69 K1
Prospect Pl CHSWK W4 118 A5
CRICK NW2 82 D1
CRW RM5 56 E5
EFNCH N2 65 H1
HAYES BR2 184 A6
RYNPK SW20 176 E3
WAP E1W 123 K1
Prospect Ring EFNCH N2 47 H6
Prospect Rd BAR EN5 20 E5
CRICK NW2 82 D1
SURB KT6 190 D3
WFD IG8 53 G1
Prospect St BERM/RHTH SE16 123 J2
Prospect V WOOL/PLUM SE18 126 D4
Prospero Rd ARCH N19 66 D5
Protea Cl CAN/RD E16 106 D3
Prothero Gdns HDN NW4 63 K2
Prothero Rd FUL/PGN SW6 139 H1
Prout Gv WLSDN NW10 81 G2
Prout Rd CLPT E5 86 D1
Provence St IS N1 6 C2
Providence Av
RYLN/HDSTN HA2 60 A5
Providence Cl HOM E9 * 87 F6
Providence Ct
MYFR/PKLN W1K 9 H5
Providence La HYS/HAR UB3 133 G1
Providence Pl CRW RM5 56 B4
IS N1 6 A1
Providence Rd WDR/YW UB7 112 B1
Providence Row Cl BETH E2 104 D2
Providence Sq STHWK SE1 19 G2
Providence Yd BETH E2 * 104 C2
Provincial Ter PGE/AN SE20 * 182 A3
Provost Est IS N1 6 E4
Provost Rd HAMP NW3 83 K5
Provost St FSBYE EC1V 6 E5
IS N1 6 E3
Prowse Av BUSH WD23 28 C4
Prowse Pl CAMTN NW1 84 C5
Prudence La ORP BR6 216 A2
Pruden Cl STHGT/OAK N14 * 34 C4
Prusom St WAP E1W 123 J1
Pucknells Cl SWLY BR8 187 K4
Pudding La MON EC3R 13 F5
Pudding Mill La SRTFD E15 87 K6
Puddle Dock BLKFR EC4V 12 B5
Puffin Cl BARK IG11 109 H2
BECK BR3 198 A2
Pulborough Rd
WAND/EARL SW18 159 J2
Pulborough Wy HSLWW TW4 134 B5
Pulford Rd SEVS/STOTM N15 67 K3
Pulham Av EFNCH N2 65 G1
Puller Rd BAR EN5 20 B3
Pulleyns Av EHAM E6 107 J2
Pullman Gdns PUT/ROE SW15 159 F1
Pullman Ms LEE/GVPK SE12 166 A5
Pullman Pl ELTH/MOT SE9 146 D6
Pulross Rd BRXN/ST SW9 142 A4
Pulteney Cl BOW E3 87 H6
ISLW TW7 136 B4
Pulteney Rd SWFD E18 53 F6
Pulton Pl FUL/PGN SW6 139 K1
Puma Ct WCHPL E1 13 J1
Pump Aly BTFD TW8 136 E1
Pump Cl NTHLT UB5 96 A1
Pump Ct EMB EC4Y * 11 J4
Pump House Cl HAYES BR2 183 J5
Pump House Ms WCHPL E1 * 104 C6
Pumping Station Rd
CHSWK W4 138 B1
Pump La HYS/HAR UB3 113 K2
NWCR SE14 143 K1
Punchard Crs PEND EN3 25 K1
Punderson's Gdns BETH E2 104 D2
Purbeck Av NWMAL KT3 192 C3
Purbeck Dr CRICK NW2 64 B6
Purbeck Rd EMPK RM11 75 J4
Purbrook St STHWK SE1 19 H4
Purcell Crs FUL/PGN SW6 139 G1
Purcell Ms WLSDN NW10 * 81 G5
Purcell Rd GFD/PVL UB6 96 B4
Purcells Ave EDGW HA8 44 C1
Purcell St IS N1 7 G2
Purcers Cross Rd
FUL/PGN SW6 139 J2
Purchese St CAMTN NW1 4 C2
Purdy St BOW E3 105 K3
Purelake Ms LEW SE13 * 145 G4
Purfleet Industrial Access Rd
SOCK/AV RM15 131 K3
Purkis Cl UX/CGN UB8 94 A6
Purland Cl BCTR RM8 74 B5
Purland Rd THMD SE28 128 A3
Purleigh Av WFD IG8 53 J2
Purley Av CRICK NW2 64 C6
Purley Cl CLAY IG5 54 A5
Purley Pl IS N1 85 H5
Purley Rd ED N9 35 K5
SAND/SEL CR2 211 K5
Purley Wy CROY/NA CR0 211 G6
Purneys Rd ELTH/MOT SE9 146 C5
Purrett Rd WOOL/PLUM SE18 128 A5
Pursers Cross Rd
FUL/PGN SW6 * 139 J2
Pursewardens Cl WEA W13 116 D1
Pursley Rd MLHL NW7 45 K3
Purves Rd WLSDN NW10 99 K2
Putney Br PUT/ROE SW15 139 H4
Putney Bridge Ap
FUL/PGN SW6 139 H4
Putney Bridge Rd
PUT/ROE SW15 139 H5
Putney Common
PUT/ROE SW15 139 F4
Putney Ex PUT/ROE SW15 * 139 G5
Putney Heath PUT/ROE SW15 158 E1
Putney Heath La
PUT/ROE SW15 159 G1
Putney High St
PUT/ROE SW15 139 H5
Putney Hl PUT/ROE SW15 159 G1
Putney Park Av
PUT/ROE SW15 138 D5
Putney Park La
PUT/ROE SW15 138 E5
Puttenham Cl OXHEY WD19 27 G5
Pycombe Cnr
NFNCH/WDSPK N12 32 D6
Pycroft Wy ED N9 36 C6
Pylbrook Rd SUT SM1 208 E1
Pylon Wy CROY/NA CR0 195 K5
Pym Cl EBAR EN4 21 H6
Pymers Md DUL SE21 162 D3
Pymmes Brook Trail
EBAR EN4 33 K2
ED N9 36 D5
Pymmes Cl PLMGR N13 49 F1
TOTM N17 50 D4
Pymmes Gdns North ED N9 36 B5
Pymmes Gdns South ED N9 36 B5
Pymmes Green Rd
FBAR/BDGN N11 34 B6
Pymmes Rd PLMGR N13 48 E2
Pymms Brook Dr EBAR EN4 21 J5
Pyne Rd SURB KT6 191 H5
Pynham Cl ABYW SE2 128 B3
Pynnacles Cl STAN HA7 43 H1
Pyrland Rd HBRY N5 85 K3
RCHPK/HAM TW10 157 G1
Pyrmont Gv WNWD SE27 162 C5
Pyrmont Rd CHSWK W4 117 H6
Pytchley Crs NRWD SE19 180 D2
Pytchley Rd EDUL SE22 143 F4

Q

The Quadrangle BAY/PAD W2 8 C3
HNHL SE24 * 142 D6
WBPTN SW10 * 140 B2
Quadrant Ar REGST W1B 10 B6
Quadrant Cl HDN NW4 * 63 K2
Quadrant Gv KTTN NW5 83 K3
Quadrant Rd RCH/KEW TW9 136 E5
THHTH CR7 196 C1
The Quadrant BELMT SM2 209 G4
BXLYHN DA7 148 E1
EDGW HA8 * 44 C2
NKENS W10 * 100 B2
RCH/KEW TW9 136 E6
RYLN/HDSTN HA2 * 42 D6
RYNPK SW20 177 H4
Quad Rd WBLY HA9 * 79 K1
Quaggy Wk BKHTH/KID SE3 145 K5
Quainton St WLSDN NW10 81 F1
Quaker La NWDGN UB2 115 F3
Quakers Course
CDALE/KGS NW9 45 H4
Quakers La ISLW TW7 136 B1
Quakers Pl FSTGT E7 89 H3
Quaker St WCHPL E1 7 J7
Quakers Wk WCHMH N21 35 K1
Quality Ct LINN WC2A 11 J3
Quantock Cl HYS/HAR UB3 133 G1
Quantock Gdns CRICK NW2 * 64 B6
Quantock Ms PECK SE15 143 H3
Quantock Rd BXLYHN DA7 150 B3
Quarles Cl CRW RM5 56 C3
Quarles Park Rd CHDH RM6 73 H3
Quarrendon St FUL/PGN SW6 139 K2
Quarr Rd CAR SM5 194 C3
Quarry Ms PUR RM19 131 K4
Quarry Park Rd SUT SM1 208 D4
Quarry Ri SUT SM1 208 D4
Quarry Rd WAND/EARL SW18 160 B1
Quatre Ports CHING E4 * 52 B1
Quay House POP/IOD E14 * 124 D2
Quebec Ms MBLAR W1H 9 F4
Quebec Rd GNTH/NBYPK IG2 72 C4
YEAD UB4 95 G6
Quebec Wy BERM/RHTH SE16 124 A2
Queen Adelaide Rd
PGE/AN SE20 181 K2
Queen Anne Av HAYES BR2 183 K6
Queen Anne Dr
ESH/CLAY KT10 204 E5
Queen Anne Ga BXLYHN DA7 148 E4
Queen Anne Ms
CAVSQ/HST W1G 9 K2
Queen Anne Rd HOM E9 87 F4
Queen Annes Cl WHTN TW2 155 J5
Queen Anne's Gdns
CHSWK W4 118 B3
EA W5 117 F2
EN EN1 36 A1
MTCM CR4 * 178 E6
Queen Anne's Ga
STJSPK SW1H 16 C3
Queen Anne's Gv CHSWK W4 118 B3
EA W5 117 F2
ED N9 35 K2
EN EN1 36 A1
Queen Anne's Pl EN EN1 36 A1
Queen Annes Sq STHWK SE1 123 H4
Queen Anne St
CAVSQ/HST W1G 9 J2
Queen Anne Ter WAP E1W * 104 D6
Queen Borough Gdns
CHST BR7 185 J2
Queenborough Gdns
GNTH/NBYPK IG2 72 A1
Queen Caroline Est
HMSMTH W6 119 F5
Queen Caroline St
HMSMTH W6 119 F5
Queen Elizabeth Blds
EMB EC4Y * 11 J5
Queen Elizabeth College
GNWCH SE10 * 145 F1
Queen Elizabeth Gdns
MRDN SM4 193 K1
Queen Elizabeth Rd
KUTN/CMB KT2 175 G5
WALTH E17 51 G6
Queen Elizabeth's Cl
STNW/STAM N16 67 K6
Queen Elizabeth's Dr
STHGT/OAK N14 34 E3
Queen Elizabeth St
STHWK SE1 19 H2
Queen Elizabeth's Wk
STNW/STAM N16 67 K5
WLGTN SM6 210 D2
Queen Elizabeth Wk
BARN SW13 138 D2
Queenhithe BLKFR EC4V 12 D6
Queen Isabella Wy STBT EC1A 12 B3
Queen Margaret's Gv IS N1 86 A3
Queen Mary Av RYNPK SW20 193 G2
SWFD E18 52 E4
Queen Mary Cl ROM RM1 75 H3
SURB KT6 206 C1
Queen Mary Rd NRWD SE19 180 C2
Queen Mary's Av CAR SM5 209 K5
Queen Mother Ga
MYFR/PICC W1J 15 H1
Queens Acre CHEAM SM3 208 B5
Queens Av FELT TW13 154 B6
KTN/HRWW/WS HA3 43 H6
MUSWH N10 48 A6
TRDG/WHET N20 33 H4
Queen's Av FNCH N3 47 G3
GFD/PVL UB6 96 B5
WCHMH N21 35 H3
WFD IG8 53 F1
Queensberry Ms West
SKENS SW7 * 14 A6
Queensberry Pl MNPK E12 89 H3
SKENS SW7 14 A6
Queensberry Wy
SKENS SW7 * 14 A6
Queensborough Ms
BAY/PAD W2 * 101 G6
Queensborough Studios
BAY/PAD W2 * 101 F6
Queensborough Ter
BAY/PAD W2 101 F6
Queensbridge Pk ISLW TW7 155 K1
Queensbridge Rd HACK E8 7 K1
Queensbury Rd ALP/SUD HA0 98 B1
CDALE/KGS NW9 63 F4
Queensbury St IS N1 85 J5
Queens Circ VX/NE SW8 141 G1
Queens Cl ESH/CLAY KT10 * 204 B2
Queen's Cl EDGW HA8 44 C1
WLGTN SM6 210 B3
Queens Club Gdns
WKENS W14 * 119 H6
Queen's Club Gdns
WKENS W14 119 H6
Queens Club Ter
WKENS W14 * 119 J6
Queenscourt WBLY HA9 80 A2
Queens Crs
RCHPK/HAM TW10 137 G6
Queen's Crs KTTN NW5 84 A3
Queenscroft Rd
ELTH/MOT SE9 146 C6
Queensdale Crs NTGHL W11 119 G1
Queensdale Pl NTGHL W11 119 H1
Queensdale Rd NTGHL W11 119 G1
Queensdale Wk NTGHL W11 119 H1
Queens Down Rd CLPT E5 86 D2
Queens Dr BRYLDS KT5 191 H4
LEY E10 69 J4
Queen's Dr EA W5 98 B5
FSBYPK N4 67 H6
THDIT KT7 190 B3
Queen's Elm Sq CHEL SW3 * 120 C5
WBPTN SW10 120 C5
Queens Gdns HDN NW4 64 A2
RAIN RM13 111 F1
Queen's Gdns BAY/PAD W2 101 G6
EA W5 97 J4
HEST TW5 134 D2
Queens Garth FSTH SE23 * 163 K4
Queen's Ga SKENS SW7 * 120 B4
Queens Gate Gdns CHST BR7 185 J4
Queensgate Gdns
PUT/ROE SW15 138 E5
Queens Gate Gdns
SKENS SW7 * 120 B3
Queen's Gate Gdns
SKENS SW7 120 B3
Queen's Gate Ms SKENS SW7 120 B3
Queensgate Pl
KIL/WHAMP NW6 82 E5
Queen's Gate Pl SKENS SW7 * 120 B3
Queen's Gate Place Ms
SKENS SW7 * 120 B4
Queen's Gate Ter
SKENS SW7 * 120 B3
Queen's Gv STJWD NW8 2 A1
Queen's Grove Rd CHING E4 38 B3
Queen's Head St IS N1 6 B1
Queens Keep TWK TW1 * 156 D1
Queensland Av UED N18 49 J2
WIM/MER SW19 178 A4
Queensland Cl WALTH E17 51 H5
Queensland Rd HOLWY N7 85 G2
Queens La MUSWH N10 48 B6
Queens Md EDGW HA8 44 B2
Queensmead STJWD NW8 83 H6
Queen's Mead Rd HAYES BR2 183 J5
Queensmere Cl
WIM/MER SW19 159 G4
Queensmere Rd
WIM/MER SW19 159 G4
Queensmill Rd FUL/PGN SW6 139 G1
Queens Pde
CEND/HSY/T N8 * 67 H1
CRICK NW2 * 82 A4
EA W5 * 98 B5
FBAR/BDGN N11 * 47 K1
HDN NW4 * 63 K2
Queens Parade Cl
FBAR/BDGN N11 47 K1
Queens Park Gdns
FELT TW13 * 153 J5
Queen's Pl MRDN SM4 193 K1
Queens Prom KUT/HW KT1 190 E1
Queen Sq BMSBY WC1N 5 F7
Queen's Ride PUT/ROE SW15 138 D5
Queen's Ri RCHPK/HAM TW10 157 G1
Queens Rd BAR EN5 20 B4
ERITH DA8 130 B6
HYS/HAR UB3 94 C5
MRDN SM4 193 K1
WDR/YW UB7 112 C2
Queen's Rd BARK IG11 90 C5
BECK BR3 182 B5
BKHH IG9 39 F4
BMLY BR1 183 K5
CHST BR7 185 G2
CROY/NA CR0 196 C3
EA W5 98 A5
ED N9 36 D4
EN EN1 24 A5
FBAR/BDGN N11 48 E3
FELT TW13 154 A3
FNCH N3 47 G4
HDN NW4 64 A2
HPTN TW12 155 G6
HSLW TW3 135 G4
KUTN/CMB KT2 175 H3
MORT/ESHN SW14 138 A4
MTCM CR4 178 C6
NWDGN UB2 114 C2
NWMAL KT3 192 C1
PECK SE15 143 K2
PLSTW E13 89 F6
RCHPK/HAM TW10 175 H1
TEDD TW11 174 A2
THDIT KT7 190 A2
TWK TW1 156 A3
WALTH E17 69 H3
WAN E11 70 C4
WELL DA16 148 C3
WIM/MER SW19 177 K2
WLGTN SM6 210 B3
Queen's Rd West PLSTW E13 106 E1
Queens Rw WALW SE17 * 122 E6
Queen's Rw WALW SE17 122 E6
Queens Ter ISLW TW7 136 B5
PLSTW E13 89 F6
THDIT KT7 * 190 B3
WCHPL E1 * 104 E3
Queen's Ter ISLW TW7 136 B5
STJWD NW8 2 A1
Queens Terrace Cots
HNWL W7 * 115 K2
Queensthorpe Ms SYD SE26 * 164 A6
Queensthorpe Rd SYD SE26 164 A6
Queenstown Gdns RAIN RM13 111 H2
Queenstown Rd VX/NE SW8 141 G3
Queen St BXLYHN DA7 149 G4
CROY/NA CR0 211 J2
ERITH DA8 * 130 B6
MYFR/PICC W1J 9 J7
ROMW/RG RM7 75 F3
STP EC4M 12 D4
TOTM N17 50 A2
Queen Street Pl CANST EC4R 12 D6
Queensville Rd BAL SW12 161 J2
Queens Wk ASHF TW15 152 A6
CDALE/KGS NW9 62 E6
CHING E4 38 B3
HRW HA1 60 E1
RSLP HA4 77 G1
Queen's Wk EA W5 97 J3
Queens Walk Ter RSLP HA4 * 77 G1
The Queens Wk STHWK SE1 13 H7
Queens Wy FELT TW13 154 B6
HDN NW4 64 A2
Queensway BAY/PAD W2 101 F5
CROY/NA CR0 211 F4
PEND EN3 24 E5
STMC/STPC BR5 201 H2
SUN TW16 172 A5
WWKM BR4 214 E2
Queens Well Av
TRDG/WHET N20 33 J6
Queen's Whf HMSMTH W6 119 F5
Queenswood Av HPTN TW12 173 G2
HSLW TW3 134 E3
THHTH CR7 196 B2
WALTH E17 52 A4
WLGTN SM6 210 D2
Queenswood Gdns WAN E11 70 E5
Queenswood Pk FNCH N3 46 C5
Queenswood Rd
BFN/LL DA15 148 A6
FSTH SE23 164 B5
Queen's Wood Rd HGT N6 66 B3
Queen's Yd FITZ W1T 4 B7
Queen Victoria Av
ALP/SUD HA0 79 K5
Queen Victoria St
BLKFR EC4V 12 A5
MANHO EC4N 12 D4
Queen Victoria Ter
WAP E1W * 104 D6
Quemerford Rd HOLWY N7 85 F3
Quentin Pl LEW SE13 145 H4
Quentin Rd LEW SE13 145 H4
Quernmore Cl BMLY BR1 183 K2
Quernmore Rd BMLY BR1 183 K2
FSBYPK N4 67 G3
Querrin St FUL/PGN SW6 140 B3
Questor DART DA1 * 171 J4
Quex Ms KIL/WHAMP NW6 82 E6
Quex Rd KIL/WHAMP NW6 82 E6
Quick Rd CHSWK W4 118 B5
Quicks Rd WIM/MER SW19 178 A3
Quick St IS N1 6 B3
Quickswood HAMP NW3 83 J5
Quiet Nook HAYES BR2 215 H1
Quill St EA W5 98 A2
FSBYPK N4 85 G1
Quilp St STHWK SE1 18 C2
Quilter Rd STMC/STPC BR5 202 E5
Quilters Pl ELTH/MOT SE9 167 H3
Quilter St BETH E2 104 C2
WOOL/PLUM SE18 128 A5
Quince Rd LEW SE13 144 E3
Quinnel Cl WOOL/PLUM SE18 128 A5
Quinnell Cl WOOL/PLUM SE18 128 A5
Quintin Av RYNPK SW20 177 H4
Quinton Cl BECK BR3 183 F6
HEST TW5 134 A1
WLGTN SM6 210 B2
Quinton Rd THDIT KT7 190 B5
Quinton St WAND/EARL SW18 160 B4
Quixley St POP/IOD E14 106 B6
Quorn Rd EDUL SE22 143 F5

R

Rabbit Rw KENS W8 * 119 K1
Rabbits Rd MNPK E12 89 J2
Rabournmead Dr NTHLT UB5 77 J3
Raby Rd NWMAL KT3 192 A1
Raby St POP/IOD E14 * 105 G5
Raccoon Wy HSLWW TW4 134 B3
Rachel Cl BARK/HLT IG6 72 D1
Rackham Cl WELL DA16 148 C3
Rackham Ms
STRHM/NOR SW16 179 H2
Racton Rd FUL/PGN SW6 119 K6
Radbourne Av EA W5 116 D4
Radbourne Cl CLPT E5 87 F2
Radbourne Ct
KTN/HRWW/WS HA3 * 61 H3
Radbourne Crs WALTH E17 52 B6
Radbourne Rd BAL SW12 161 H2
Radcliffe Av ENC/FH EN2 23 J2
WLSDN NW10 99 J1
Radcliffe Gdns CAR SM5 209 J5
Radcliffe Rd CROY/NA CR0 197 G6
KTN/HRWW/WS HA3 43 G5
STHWK SE1 19 H4
WCHMH N21 35 H3
Radcliffe Sq PUT/ROE SW15 159 G1
Radcliffe Wy NTHLT UB5 95 H2
Radcot St LBTH SE11 122 B5
Raddington Rd NKENS W10 100 C4
Radfield Wy BFN/LL DA15 167 J2
Radford Est WLSDN NW10 * 99 G2
Radford Rd LEW SE13 165 F1
Radford Wy BARK IG11 109 F2
Radipole Rd FUL/PGN SW6 139 J2
Radius Pk
EBED/NFELT TW14 * 133 J5
Radland Rd CAN/RD E16 106 E5
Radlet Av SYD SE26 163 J5
Radlett Cl FSTGT E7 88 D4
Radlett Pl STJWD NW8 2 C1
Radley Av GDMY/SEVK IG3 91 F2
Radley Cl EBED/NFELT TW14 153 J3
Radley Ct BERM/RHTH SE16 124 A2
Radley Gdns
KTN/HRWW/WS HA3 62 A1
Radley Ms KENS W8 119 K3
Radley Rd TOTM N17 50 A5
Radley's La SWFD E18 52 E5
Radleys Md DAGE RM10 92 D4
Radley Sq CLPT E5 * 68 E6
Radley Ter CAN/RD E16 106 D4
Radlix Rd LEY E10 69 J5
Radnor Av HRW HA1 60 E2
WELL DA16 148 C6
Radnor Cl CHST BR7 185 K2
MTCM CR4 195 K2
Radnor Crs REDBR IG4 71 K2
WOOL/PLUM SE18 148 B1
Radnor Gdns EN EN1 24 A2
TWK TW1 156 A4
Radnor Ms BAY/PAD W2 8 B4
Radnor Pl BAY/PAD W2 8 C4
Radnor Rd HRW HA1 60 D2
KIL/WHAMP NW6 82 C6
PECK SE15 143 H1
TWK TW1 156 A3
Radnor St FSBYE EC1V 6 D5
Radnor Ter WKENS W14 119 J4
Radnor Wk CHEL SW3 120 D5
CROY/NA CR0 198 B4
Radnor Wy WLSDN NW10 98 D3
Radstock Av
KTN/HRWW/WS HA3 43 G6
Radstock Cl FBAR/BDGN N11 48 A1
Radstock St BTSEA SW11 * 140 D1
Raeburn Av BRYLDS KT5 191 J4
DART DA1 150 E6
Raeburn Cl GLDGN NW11 65 G3
KUT/HW KT1 174 E3
Raeburn Rd BFN/LL DA15 167 K1
EDGW HA8 44 C5
YEAD UB4 94 B1
Raeburn St BRXS/STRHM SW2 141 K5
Rafford Wy BMLY BR1 184 A5
Raggleswood CHST BR7 185 F4
Raglan Cl HSLWW TW4 134 D6
Raglan Ct SAND/SEL CR2 211 H3
Raglan Gdns OXHEY WD19 27 F3
Raglan Rd BELV DA17 129 G4
EN EN1 36 A2
HAYES BR2 200 B1
WALTH E17 70 A2
WOOL/PLUM SE18 127 H5
Raglan St KTTN NW5 84 B4
Raglan Ter
RYLN/HDSTN HA2 * 78 B2
Raglan Vls WALTH E17 * 70 A2
Raglan Wy NTHLT UB5 78 C4

Ragley Cl ACT W3 117 K2
Raider Cl ROMW/RG RM7 56 D4
Railey Ms KTTN NW5 84 C3
Railshead Rd ISLW TW7 136 C5
Railton Rd HNHL SE24 142 B6
Railway Ap FSBYPK N4 67 G3
HRW HA1 61 F1
STHWK SE1 12 E7
TWK TW1 156 B2
WLGTN SM6 * 210 B4
Railway Ar BRXN/ST SW9 * 142 B5
Railway Av BERM/RHTH SE16 123 K2
Railway Cots HMSMTH W6 * 119 F2
SRTFD E15 * 106 C1
WIM/MER SW19 * 160 A6
Railway Gv NWCR SE14 144 C1
Railway Pl BELV DA17 129 H3
Railway Ri EDUL SE22 143 F5
Railway Rd TEDD TW11 155 K6
Railway Side BARN SW13 138 B4
Railway Station Whf
LEY E10 * 69 G5
Railway St CHDH RM6 73 J5
IS N1 5 F3
Railway Ter FELT TW13 153 K3
LEW SE13 144 E6
WALTH E17 52 A4
Rainborough Cl WBLY HA9 80 E4
Rainbow Av POP/IOD E14 124 E5
Rainbow Ct OXHEY WD19 27 G1
Rainbow Quay
BERM/RHTH SE16 124 B3
Rainbow St CMBW SE5 143 F1
Raine St WAP E1W 123 J1
Rainham Cl BTSEA SW11 160 D1
ELTH/MOT SE9 167 K1
Rainham Rd RAIN RM13 111 J2
WLSDN NW10 100 A2
Rainham Rd North
DAGE RM10 74 D6
Rainham Rd South
DAGE RM10 92 E4
Rainhill Wy BOW E3 105 J2
Rainsborough Av DEPT SE8 124 B4
Rainsford Rd WLSDN NW10 98 C2
Rainsford St BAY/PAD W2 8 C3
Rainsford Wy HCH RM12 75 J5
Rainton Rd CHARL SE7 125 K5
Rainville Rd HMSMTH W6 119 F6
Raisins Hl PIN HA5 41 F6
Raith Av STHGT/OAK N14 34 D5
Raleigh Av WLGTN SM6 210 D2
YEAD UB4 95 F4
Raleigh Cl ERITH DA8 130 C6
HDN NW4 64 A2
PIN HA5 59 H4
RSLP HA4 58 D6
Raleigh Dr BRYLDS KT5 191 K5
ESH/CLAY KT10 204 D3
TRDG/WHET N20 33 J5
Raleigh Gdns
BRXS/STRHM SW2 162 A1
MTCM CR4 178 E5
Raleigh Ms IS N1 6 B1
ORP BR6 217 F3
Raleigh Rd CEND/HSY/T N8 67 G1
ENC/FH EN2 23 K5
FELT TW13 153 J4
NWDGN UB2 114 D5
PGE/AN SE20 182 A3
RCH/KEW TW9 137 G4
Raleigh St IS N1 6 B1
Raleigh Wy FELT TW13 172 B1
STHGT/OAK N14 34 D3
Ralph Perring Ct BECK BR3 198 D1
Ralston St CHEL SW3 120 E5
Ralston Wy OXHEY WD19 27 H4
Rama Cl STRHM/NOR SW16 179 K3
Ramac Wy CHARL SE7 126 A4
Rama La NRWD SE19 181 G3
Rambler Cl STRHM/NOR SW16 161 H6
Rame Cl TOOT SW17 179 F1
Ramilles Cl BRXS/STRHM SW2 161 K1
Ramillies Pl SOHO/CST W1F 10 A4
Ramillies Rd BFN/LL DA15 168 C1
CHSWK W4 118 A3
MLHL NW7 31 G4
Ramillies St SOHO/SHAV W1D 10 A4
Ramones Ter MTCM CR4 * 195 H1
Rampart St WCHPL E1 104 D5
Ram Pas KUT/HW KT1 174 E5
Rampayne St PIM SW1V 121 J5
Rampton Cl CHING E4 37 J5
Ramsay Gdns HARH RM3 57 K4
Ramsay Rd ACT W3 117 K3
FSTGT E7 88 D2
Ramscroft Cl ED N9 36 A2
Ramsdale Rd TOOT SW17 179 F1
Ramsden Cl STMC/STPC BR5 202 D5
Ramsden Dr CRW RM5 56 C3
Ramsden Ga BAL SW12 * 161 G2
Ramsden Rd BAL SW12 161 F2
ERITH DA8 150 A1
FBAR/BDGN N11 47 K1
ORP BR6 202 C4
Ramsey Cl CDALE/KGS NW9 63 H3
GFD/PVL UB6 78 D3
Ramsey Rd THHTH CR7 196 A3
Ramsey St BETH E2 104 C3
Ramsey Wk IS N1 85 K4
Ramsey Wy STHGT/OAK N14 34 C2
Ramsgate Cl CAN/RD E16 126 A1
Ramsgate St HACK E8 * 86 B4
Ramsgill Ap GNTH/NBYPK IG2 73 F1
Ramsgill Dr GNTH/NBYPK IG2 73 F2
Rams Gv CHDH RM6 74 A1
Ramulis Dr YEAD UB4 95 J3
Ramus Wood Av ORP BR6 216 E3
Rancliffe Gdns ELTH/MOT SE9 146 D5
Rancliffe Rd EHAM E6 107 J1
Randall Av CRICK NW2 63 G6
Randall Cl BTSEA SW11 140 D2
ERITH DA8 129 K6
Randall Pl GNWCH SE10 145 F1
Randall Rd LBTH SE11 122 A5
Randall Rw LBTH SE11 17 G7
Randell's Rd IS N1 84 E6
Randisbourne Gdns CAT SE6 * 164 E5
Randle Rd RCHPK/HAM TW10 156 D6
Randlesdown Rd CAT SE6 164 D6
Randolf Rd HAYES BR2 200 E5
Randolph Ap CAN/RD E16 107 G5
Randolph Av MV/WKIL W9 101 F1
Randolph Cl BXLYHN DA7 149 K4
KUTN/CMB KT2 * 175 K1
Randolph Crs MV/WKIL W9 101 G3
Randolph Gdns
KIL/WHAMP NW6 101 F1
Randolph Gv CHDH RM6 73 J2
Randolph Ms MV/WKIL W9 101 G3
Randolph Rd MV/WKIL W9 101 G3
STHL UB1 * 114 E2
WALTH E17 * 69 K2
Randon Cl RYLN/HDSTN HA2 42 B5
Ranelagh Av BARN SW13 138 D3
FUL/PGN SW6 139 J4
Ranelagh Cl EDGW HA8 30 C6
Ranelagh Dr EDGW HA8 30 C6
TWK TW1 136 C5
Ranelagh Gdns CHSWK W4 137 K1
FUL/PGN SW6 139 J4
IL IG1 72 A5
WAN E11 71 G2
Ranelagh Gv BGVA SW1W 121 F5
Ranelagh Pl NWMAL KT3 192 B2
Ranelagh Rd ALP/SUD HA0 79 K3
EA W5 116 E2
EHAM E6 90 A6
PIM SW1V 121 H5
SRTFD E15 88 C6
STHL UB1 114 C1
TOTM N17 50 A6
WAN E11 88 C2
WDGN N22 49 F4
WLSDN NW10 99 H1
Ranfurly Rd SUT SM1 193 K6
Rangefield Rd BMLY BR1 183 H1
Rangemoor Rd
SEVS/STOTM N15 68 B2
Rangers Rd BKHH IG9 38 E2
Rangeworth Pl BFN/LL DA15 168 A5
Rangoon St TWRH EC3N * 13 J4
Rankin Cl CDALE/KGS NW9 45 G6
Ranleigh Gdns BXLYHN DA7 149 G1
Ranmere St BAL SW12 161 G3
Ranmoor Cl HRW HA1 60 D1
Ranmoor Gdns HRW HA1 60 D1
Ranmore Av CROY/NA CR0 212 B1
Ranmore Pth STMC/STPC BR5 202 B1
Ranmore Rd BELMT SM2 208 B6
Rannoch Cl EDGW HA8 30 D4
Rannoch Rd HMSMTH W6 119 F6
Rannock Av CDALE/KGS NW9 63 F4
Ransom Cl OXHEY WD19 27 G2
Ransom Rd CHARL SE7 * 126 B5
Ranston St CAMTN NW1 8 C1
Ranulf Rd CRICK NW2 82 D2
Ranwell Cl BOW E3 * 87 H6
Ranworth Cl ERITH DA8 150 B3
Ranworth Rd ED N9 36 E4
Ranyard Cl CHSGTN KT9 206 B1
Raphael Av ROM RM1 57 H6
Raphael Cl KUT/HW KT1 190 E1
Raphael Dr THDIT KT7 190 A5
Raphael St SKENS SW7 14 E3
Rapier Cl PUR RM19 131 J4
Rasper Rd TRDG/WHET N20 33 G4
Rastell Av BRXS/STRHM SW2 161 J4
Ratcliffe Cl LEE/GVPK SE12 165 K2
Ratcliffe Cross St WCHPL E1 * 105 F5
Ratcliffe La POP/IOD E14 105 G5
Ratcliff Rd FSTGT E7 89 G3
Rathbone Pl FITZ W1T 10 C2
Rathbone Sq CROY/NA CR0 * 211 J2
Rathbone St CAN/RD E16 106 D4
FITZ W1T 10 B2
Rathcoole Av CEND/HSY/T N8 67 F2
Rathcoole Gdns
CEND/HSY/T N8 67 F2
Rathfern Rd CAT SE6 164 C3
Rathgar Av WEA W13 116 C1
Rathgar Cl FNCH N3 46 D5
Rathgar Rd BRXN/ST SW9 142 C4
Rathmell Dr CLAP SW4 161 J1
Rathmore Rd CHARL SE7 126 A5
Rattray Rd BRXS/STRHM SW2 142 B5
Raul Rd PECK SE15 143 H3
Raveley St KTTN NW5 84 C2
Ravencroft Crs
ELTH/MOT SE9 166 E5
Ravenet St BTSEA SW11 141 G2
Ravenfield Rd TOOT SW17 160 E5
Ravenhill Rd PLSTW E13 89 G6
Ravenna Rd PUT/ROE SW15 139 G6
Ravenoak Wy CHIG IG7 54 E1
Ravenor Park Rd
GFD/PVL UB6 96 B2
Raven Rd SWFD E18 53 G5
Raven Rw WCHPL E1 104 D4
Ravens Ait SURB KT6 * 190 E2
Ravensbourne Av HAYES BR2 183 G4
STWL/WRAY TW19 152 B3
Ravensbourne Gdns CLAY IG5 54 A4
WEA W13 97 H4
Ravensbourne Pk CAT SE6 164 D2
Ravensbourne Park Crs
CAT SE6 164 C2
Ravensbourne Pl LEW SE13 144 E3
Ravensbourne Rd BMLY BR1 183 K6
CAT SE6 164 C2
DART DA1 150 D4
TWK TW1 156 D1
Ravensbury Av MRDN SM4 194 B2
Ravensbury Gv MTCM CR4 194 C1
Ravensbury La MTCM CR4 194 C1
Ravensbury Rd
STMC/STPC BR5 202 A1
WAND/EARL SW18 160 A4
Ravensbury Ter
WAND/EARL SW18 160 A4
Ravenscar Rd BMLY BR1 165 H6
SURB KT6 191 G6
Ravens Cl CDALE/KGS NW9 45 H5
EN EN1 24 A3
HAYES BR2 183 J5
SURB KT6 190 E3
Ravenscourt Av HMSMTH W6 118 D4
Ravenscourt Cl DEN/HRF UB9 58 A4
Ravenscourt Gdns
HMSMTH W6 118 C4
Ravenscourt Pk HMSMTH W6 118 D4
Ravenscourt Pl HMSMTH W6 118 E4
Ravenscourt Rd HMSMTH W6 118 E4
STMC/STPC BR5 186 B6
Ravenscourt Sq HMSMTH W6 118 D3
Ravenscraig Rd
FBAR/BDGN N11 34 B6
Ravenscroft Av GLDGN NW11 64 D4
WBLY HA9 62 A5
Ravenscroft Cl CAN/RD E16 106 E4
Ravenscroft Cots BAR EN5 * 32 E1
Ravenscroft Pk BAR EN5 20 B4
Ravenscroft Rd BECK BR3 181 K5
CAN/RD E16 106 E4
CHSWK W4 117 K4
Ravenscroft St BETH E2 7 K3
Ravensdale Av
NFNCH/WDSPK N12 33 G6
Ravensdale Gdns NRWD SE19 180 E3
Ravensdale Rd HSLWW TW4 134 D4
STNW/STAM N16 68 B4
Ravensdon St LBTH SE11 122 B5
Ravensfield DAGW RM9 91 K2
Ravensfield Gdns
HOR/WEW KT19 207 G3
Ravenshaw St
KIL/WHAMP NW6 82 D3
Ravenshill CHST BR7 185 G4
Ravenshurst Av HDN NW4 64 A1
Ravenside Cl UED N18 51 F1
Ravenslea Rd BAL SW12 160 E2
Ravensleigh Gdns BMLY BR1 183 K1
Ravensmead Rd HAYES BR2 183 G3
Ravensmede Wy CHSWK W4 118 C4
Ravens Ms LEE/GVPK SE12 * 145 K6
Ravenstone Rd
CDALE/KGS NW9 * 63 H3
CEND/HSY/T N8 49 F6
Ravenstone St BAL SW12 161 F3
Ravens Wy LEE/GVPK SE12 145 K6
Ravenswood BXLY DA5 169 F3
Ravenswood Av SURB KT6 191 G6
WWKM BR4 199 F5
Ravenswood Cl CRW RM5 56 D1
Ravenswood Ct
KUTN/CMB KT2 * 175 K2
Ravenswood Crs
RYLN/HDSTN HA2 59 K6
WWKM BR4 199 F5
Ravenswood Gdns ISLW TW7 135 K2
Ravenswood Pk NTHWD HA6 40 E2
Ravenswood Rd BAL SW12 161 G2
CROY/NA CR0 211 H1
WALTH E17 70 A1
Ravensworth Rd
ELTH/MOT SE9 166 E6
WLSDN NW10 * 99 K2
Ravey St SDTCH EC2A 7 G6
Ravine Gv WOOL/PLUM SE18 127 K6
Rav Pinter Cl
STNW/STAM N16 68 A4
Rawlings Cl BECK BR3 199 F2
ORP BR6 217 F3
Rawlings Crs WBLY HA9 80 D1
Rawlings St CHEL SW3 14 E6
Rawlins Cl FNCH N3 46 C6
SAND/SEL CR2 213 H5
Rawnsley Av MTCM CR4 194 C2
Rawreth Wk IS N1 * 85 J6
Rawson St BTSEA SW11 141 F2
Rawsthorne Cl CAN/RD E16 126 E1
Rawstorne Pl FSBYE EC1V * 6 A4
Rawstorne St FSBYE EC1V 6 A4
Ray Bell Ct BROCKY SE4 * 144 C3
Raydean Rd BAR EN5 20 E6
Raydons Gdns DAGW RM9 92 A2
Raydons Rd DAGW RM9 92 A3
Raydon St ARCH N19 66 B6
Rayfield Cl HAYES BR2 200 D3
Rayford Av LEE/GVPK SE12 165 J2
Rayford Cl DART DA1 151 F6
Ray Gdns BARK IG11 109 G1
STAN HA7 43 H1
Ray Lamb Wy ERITH DA8 130 E6
Rayleas Cl WOOL/PLUM SE18 147 G2
Rayleigh Av TEDD TW11 173 K2
Rayleigh Cl PLMGR N13 35 K5
Rayleigh Ct KUT/HW KT1 175 H5
Rayleigh Ri SAND/SEL CR2 212 A4
Rayleigh Rd CAN/RD E16 126 A1
PLMGR N13 35 J5
WFD IG8 53 G3
WIM/MER SW19 177 J4
Ray Lodge Rd WFD IG8 53 G2
Raymead Av THHTH CR7 196 B2
Raymere Gdns
WOOL/PLUM SE18 147 J1
Raymond Av SWFD E18 52 D6
WEA W13 116 B3
Raymond Blds GINN WC1R * 11 H1
Raymond Cl SYD SE26 181 K1
Raymond Rd BECK BR3 198 B1
GNTH/NBYPK IG2 72 D4
PLSTW E13 89 G5
WIM/MER SW19 177 H2
Raymond Wy
ESH/CLAY KT10 * 205 G4
Raymouth Rd
BERM/RHTH SE16 123 J4
Rayne Ct SWFD E18 70 D1
Rayners Cl ALP/SUD HA0 79 K3
Rayners Gdns NTHLT UB5 95 F2
Rayners La PIN HA5 59 K4
Rayner's Rd PUT/ROE SW15 139 H6
Raynes Av WAN E11 71 G4
Raynes Pk RYNPK SW20 177 F5
Raynham Av UED N18 50 C2
Raynham Rd HMSMTH W6 118 E4
UED N18 50 C1
Raynham Ter UED N18 50 C1
Raynor Cl STHL UB1 114 E1
Raynor Pl IS N1 85 J6
Raynton Cl RYLN/HDSTN HA2 59 J4
YEAD UB4 94 D3
Raynton Dr YEAD UB4 94 C1
Ray Rd CRW RM5 56 D1
E/WMO/HCT KT8 189 G2
Rays Av UED N18 36 E6
Rays Rd UED N18 36 E6
WWKM BR4 199 F4
Ray St CLKNW EC1R 5 K7
Ray Street Br CLKNW EC1R * 5 K7
Raywood Cl HYS/HAR UB3 133 F1
Reachview Cl CAMTN NW1 84 C5
Read Cl THDIT KT7 190 B4
Reading La HACK E8 86 D4
Reading Rd NTHLT UB5 78 B3
SUT SM1 209 G3
Reading Wy MLHL NW7 46 B1
Reads Cl IL IG1 90 B1
Reapers Cl CAMTN NW1 84 D6
Reapers Wy ISLW TW7 135 J6
Reardon Pth WAP E1W 123 J1
Reardon St WAP E1W 123 J1
Reaston St NWCR SE14 143 K1
Reckitt Rd CHSWK W4 118 B5
Record St PECK SE15 123 K6
Recovery St TOOT SW17 178 D1
Recreation Av
ROMW/RG RM7 74 E2
Recreation Rd HAYES BR2 183 J5
NWDGN UB2 114 D4
SYD SE26 164 A6
Recreation Wy MTCM CR4 179 K6
Rectar Pl ARCH N19 66 B6
Rector St IS N1 6 C1
Rectory Cl CHING E4 37 J5
DART DA1 150 B5
FNCH N3 46 D4
RYNPK SW20 177 F5
SCUP DA14 168 C6
STAN HA7 43 H2
SURB KT6 190 D5
Rectory Field Crs CHARL SE7 146 B1
Rectory Gdns BECK BR3 * 182 D4
CEND/HSY/T N8 66 E1
CHST BR7 * 185 H4
NTHLT UB5 77 K6
Rectory Gn BECK BR3 182 C4
Rectory Gv CLAP SW4 141 H4
CROY/NA CR0 196 C6
HPTN TW12 154 E6
Rectory La BUSH WD23 28 A1
EDGW HA8 44 C2
SCUP DA14 186 D1
STAN HA7 43 H1
SURB KT6 190 D5
TOOT SW17 179 F1
WLGTN SM6 210 C2
Rectory Orch WIM/MER SW19 159 H6
Rectory Park Av NTHLT UB5 95 K2
Rectory Pl CHST BR7 * 185 H4
WOOL/PLUM SE18 127 F4
Rectory Rd BARN SW13 138 D3
BECK BR3 182 D4
DAGE RM10 92 C4
HAYES BR2 215 H5
HSLWW TW4 134 A3
HYS/HAR UB3 94 E5
MNPK E12 89 K3
NWDGN UB2 114 E3
STNW/STAM N16 86 B1
SUT SM1 208 E1
WALTH E17 69 K1
Rectory Sq WCHPL E1 105 F4
Reculver Ms UED N18 36 C6
Reculver Rd
BERM/RHTH SE16 124 A5
Red Anchor Cl CHEL SW3 120 C6
Redan Pl BAY/PAD W2 * 101 F5
Redan St WKENS W14 119 G3
Redan Ter CMBW SE5 142 C3
Red Barracks Rd
WOOL/PLUM SE18 126 E4
Redberry Gv SYD SE26 163 K5
Redbourne Av FNCH N3 46 E4
Redbourne Dr THMD SE28 109 K5
Redbridge Gdns CMBW SE5 143 F1
Redbridge La East REDBR IG4 71 H3
Redbridge La West WAN E11 71 F3
Redburn St CHEL SW3 120 E6
Redbury Cl RAIN RM13 111 K3
Redcar Cl NTHLT UB5 78 B3
Redcar St CMBW SE5 * 142 D1
Redcastle Cl WAP E1W 104 E6
Red Cedars Rd ORP BR6 201 K4
Redchurch St BETH E2 7 J6
WCHPL E1 7 J6
Redcliffe Cl ECT SW5 120 A5
Redcliffe Gdns IL IG1 72 A5
WBPTN SW10 120 A5
Redcliffe Ms WBPTN SW10 120 A5
Redcliffe Pl WBPTN SW10 120 B6
Redcliffe Rd WBPTN SW10 120 B5
Redcliffe Sq WBPTN SW10 120 A5
Redcliffe St WBPTN SW10 * 120 A6
Redclose Av MRDN SM4 193 K2
Redclyffe Rd PLSTW E13 89 G6
Redcroft Rd STHL UB1 96 C6
Redcross Wy STHWK SE1 18 D2
Reddings Cl MLHL NW7 31 H6
The Reddings MLHL NW7 31 H5
Reddington Cl SAND/SEL CR2 211 K6
Reddins Rd PECK SE15 143 H1
Reddons Rd BECK BR3 182 B3
Reddy Rd ERITH DA8 130 C6
Rede Pl BAY/PAD W2 100 E5
Redesdale Gdns ISLW TW7 136 B1
Redesdale St CHEL SW3 120 E6
Redfern Av HSLWW TW4 154 C1
Redfern Rd CAT SE6 165 F2
WLSDN NW10 81 G5
Redfield La ECT SW5 119 K4
Redfield Ms ECT SW5 119 K4
Redford Av THHTH CR7 196 A1
WLGTN SM6 210 E4
Redford Cl FELT TW13 153 J4
Redford Wk IS N1 * 85 H6
Redgate Dr HAYES BR2 200 A6
Redgate Ter PUT/ROE SW15 159 G1
Redgrave Cl CROY/NA CR0 197 G3
Redgrave Rd PUT/ROE SW15 139 G4
Redgrave Ter BETH E2 * 104 C2
Redhall Ter EA W5 * 98 C6
Red Hl CHST BR7 185 F1
Redhill Dr EDGW HA8 44 D5
Redhill St CAMTN NW1 3 K3
Red House La BXLYHS DA6 148 E5
Red House Rd CROY/NA CR0 195 J3
Red House Sq IS N1 85 J5
Redington Gdns HAMP NW3 83 F2
Redington Rd HAMP NW3 83 F1
Redland Gdns
E/WMO/HCT KT8 * 188 E1
Redlands Rd PEND EN3 25 G2
Redlands Wy
BRXS/STRHM SW2 161 K2
Red La ESH/CLAY KT10 205 G4
Redleaf Cl BXLYHN DA7 129 H6
Redlees Cl ISLW TW7 136 B5
Red Lion Cl STMC/STPC BR5 202 D3
WALW SE17 122 E6
Red Lion Ct FLST/FETLN EC4A 11 K3
HSLW TW3 * 135 G4
Red Lion Hl EFNCH N2 47 H5
Red Lion La
WOOL/PLUM SE18 147 F2
Red Lion Pde PIN HA5 * 41 J6
Red Lion Pl
WOOL/PLUM SE18 * 147 F2
Red Lion Rd SURB KT6 191 G6
Red Lion Rw CMBW SE5 122 D6
Red Lion Sq GINN WC1R 11 G2
WAND/EARL SW18 * 139 K6
Red Lion St GINN WC1R 11 G2
RCH/KEW TW9 136 E6
Red Lion Yd
MYFR/PKLN W1K * 9 H7
Red Lodge Crs BXLY DA5 170 A5
Red Lodge Rd BXLY DA5 170 A5
WWKM BR4 199 F5
Redman Cl NTHLT UB5 95 G1
Redman's Rd WCHPL E1 104 E4
Redmead La WAP E1W 123 H1
Redmead Rd HYS/HAR UB3 113 H4
Redmore Rd HMSMTH W6 * 118 E4
Red Oak Cl ORP BR6 201 G6
Red Pl MYFR/PKLN W1K 9 G5
Redpoll Wy ERITHM DA18 128 E3
Red Post Hl HNHL SE24 142 E6
Redriffe Rd PLSTW E13 88 D6
Redriff Rd BERM/RHTH SE16 124 B3
ROMW/RG RM7 56 D5
Redroofs Cl BECK BR3 182 E4
Redruth Cl WDGN N22 49 F3
Redruth Gdns ESH/CLAY KT10 205 F5
Redruth Rd HOM E9 86 E6
Redsan Cl SAND/SEL CR2 211 K5
Redstart Cl EHAM E6 107 J4
NWCR SE14 * 144 B1
Redston Rd CEND/HSY/T N8 66 D1
Redvers Rd WDGN N22 49 G5
Redvers St IS N1 7 H4
Redwald Rd CLPT E5 87 F2
Redway Dr WHTN TW2 155 H2
Redwing Ct ORP BR6 202 B4
Redwing Ms CMBW SE5 142 D3
Redwing Rd WLGTN SM6 210 E5
Redwood Cl
BERM/RHTH SE16 124 B1
BFN/LL DA15 168 B3
BOW E3 105 J1
OXHEY WD19 27 G6
STHGT/OAK N14 34 D2
Redwood Gdns CHIG IG7 55 G1
CHING E4 37 K1
Redwood Gv EA W5 116 D3
Redwood Ms VX/NE SW8 141 G4
Redwood Wy BAR EN5 20 B6
Reece Ms SKENS SW7 14 A6
Reed Av ORP BR6 216 E1
Reed Cl CAN/RD E16 106 E4
LEE/GVPK SE12 145 K6
Reede Rd DAGE RM10 92 C4
Reede Wy DAGE RM10 92 D4
Reedham Cl TOTM N17 68 D1
Reedham St PECK SE15 * 143 H3
Reedholm Vls
STNW/STAM N16 85 K2
Reed Pl BTSEA SW11 140 D5
CLAP SW4 141 J5
Reed Pond Wk GPK RM2 57 H5
Reed Rd TOTM N17 50 B5
Reedsfield Cl ASHF TW15 152 E5
Reedsfield Rd ASHF TW15 152 D6
Reed's Pl CAMTN NW1 84 C5
Reedworth St LBTH SE11 17 K7
Reenglass Rd STAN HA7 * 29 K6
Rees Dr STAN HA7 30 A6
Rees Gdns CROY/NA CR0 197 G3
Reesland Cl MNPK E12 90 A4
Rees St IS N1 6 D1
Reets Farm Cl
CDALE/KGS NW9 63 G3
Reeves Av CDALE/KGS NW9 63 F4
Reeves Cnr CROY/NA CR0 * 196 C6
Reeves Ms MYFR/PKLN W1K 9 G6
Reeves Rd BOW E3 105 K3
WOOL/PLUM SE18 127 G6
Reform Rw TOTM N17 50 B5
Reform St BTSEA SW11 140 E3
Regal Cl EA W5 97 K4
WCHPL E1 104 C4
Regal Ct MTCM CR4 178 E6
UED N18 50 B1
Regal Crs WLGTN SM6 210 B1
Regal Dr FBAR/BDGN N11 48 B1
Regal La CAMTN NW1 3 H1
Regal Rw PECK SE15 143 K2
Regal Wy
KTN/HRWW/WS HA3 62 A3
Regan Wy IS N1 7 G3
Regarder Rd CHIG IG7 55 H1
Regarth Av ROM RM1 75 G3
Regency Cl CHIG IG7 54 C1
EA W5 98 A5
HPTN TW12 172 E1
Regency Ct EN EN1 23 K6
Regency Crs HDN NW4 46 B5
Regency Dr RSLP HA4 58 C5
Regency Gdns WOT/HER KT12 188 C5
Regency Lawn KTTN NW5 * 84 B1
Regency Ms BECK BR3 183 F4
WLSDN NW10 81 J4
Regency Pde HAMP NW3 * 83 H5
Regency Pl WEST SW1P * 16 C6
Regency St WEST SW1P 16 D7
Regency Ter HGT N6 * 65 K3
SEVS/STOTM N15 68 A2
SKENS SW7 * 120 C5

Regency Wk CROY/NA CR0 198 B3
Regency Wy BXLYHS DA6 148 E4
Regeneration Rd
BERM/RHTH SE16 124 A4
Regent Cl HSLWW TW4 134 A2
KTN/HRWW/WS HA3 62 A3
NFNCH/WDSPK N12 47 G1
Regent Gdns GDMY/SEVK IG3 73 G3
Regent Pde BELMT SM2 * 209 G4
STNW/STAM N16 * 68 B4
Regent Pl CROY/NA CR0 197 G5
WIM/MER SW19 178 B1
Regent Rd BRYLDS KT5 191 G2
HNHL SE24 162 C1
Regents Av PLMGR N13 49 G1
Regents Bridge Gdns
VX/NE SW8 121 K6
Regents Cl SAND/SEL CR2 212 A4
YEAD UB4 94 C4
Regents Dr HAYES BR2 215 H3
WFD IG8 54 A2
Regents Ms STJWD NW8 101 G1
Regent's Park Rd
CAMTN NW1 83 K6
FNCH N3 64 D1
Regent's Park Ter
CAMTN NW1 84 B6
Regents Pl LOU IG10 39 H2
Regents Plaza
KIL/WHAMP NW6 * 101 F1
Regent Sq BELV DA17 129 J4
BOW E3 105 K2
STPAN WC1H 5 F5
Regent's Rw BETH E2 86 C6
Regent St CHSWK W4 117 H5
REGST W1B 9 K3
STJS SW1Y 10 C6
WLSDN NW10 100 B2
Regents Whf IS N1 * 5 G2
Reginald Rd DEPT SE8 144 D1
FSTGT E7 88 E5
NTHWD HA6 40 D4
Reginald Sq DEPT SE8 144 D1
Regina Rd FSBYPK N4 67 F5
NWDGN UB2 114 D4
SNWD SE25 181 H6
WEA W13 116 B1
Regina Ter WEA W13 116 B1
Regis Rd KTTN NW5 84 B3
Regnart Blds CAMTN NW1 4 B5
Reid Cl HYS/HAR UB3 94 C5
PIN HA5 40 E6
Reidhaven Rd
WOOL/PLUM SE18 127 K4
Reigate Av SUT SM1 194 A5
Reigate Rd BMLY BR1 165 K4
GDMY/SEVK IG3 73 F6
Reigate Wy WLGTN SM6 210 E3
Reighton Rd CLPT E5 86 C1
Reinckendorf Av
ELTH/MOT SE9 147 H6
Reindeer Cl PLSTW E13 88 E6
Reizel Cl STNW/STAM N16 68 B5
Relay Rd SHB W12 100 A6
Relf Rd PECK SE15 143 H4
Reliance Ar BRXN/ST SW9 * 142 B5
Relton Ms SKENS SW7 14 D4
Rembrandt Cl BGVA SW1W * 121 F5
POP/IOD E14 125 G3
Rembrandt Ct
HOR/WEW KT19 207 H4
Rembrandt Rd EDGW HA8 * 44 C5
LEW SE13 145 H5
Rembrandt Wy
WOT/HER KT12 188 A6
Remington Rd EHAM E6 107 J5
SEVS/STOTM N15 67 K3
Remington St IS N1 6 B3
Remnant St HOL/ALD WC2B 11 G3
Remus Rd BOW E3 87 J5
Renaissance Wk GNWCH SE10 125 J3
Rendle Cl CROY/NA CR0 197 G2
Rendlesham Rd CLPT E5 86 C2
ENC/FH EN2 23 H2
Renforth St BERM/RHTH SE16 123 K2
Renfrew Cl EHAM E6 108 A6
Renfrew Rd HSLWW TW4 134 C3
KUTN/CMB KT2 175 K3
LBTH SE11 18 A6
Renmuir St TOOT SW17 178 E2
Rennell St LEW SE13 145 F4
Renness Rd WALTH E17 51 G6
Rennets Cl ELTH/MOT SE9 147 J6
Rennets Wood Rd
ELTH/MOT SE9 147 J6
Rennie Cl ASHF TW15 152 A5
Rennie Est BERM/RHTH SE16 123 J4
Rennie St STHWK SE1 12 A7
Renown Cl CROY/NA CR0 196 C5
ROMW/RG RM7 56 C4
Rensburg Rd WALTH E17 69 F2
Rensburg Vls WALTH E17 * 69 F2
Renshaw Cl BELV DA17 129 G6
Renters Av HDN NW4 64 A3
Renton Cl BRXS/STRHM SW2 * 162 A1
Renton Dr STMC/STPC BR5 202 E4
Renwick Rd BARK IG11 109 H3
Repens Wy YEAD UB4 95 H3
Rephidim St STHWK SE1 19 F5
Replingham Rd
WAND/EARL SW18 159 J3
Reporton Rd FUL/PGN SW6 139 H2
Repository Rd
WOOL/PLUM SE18 126 E6
Repton Av ALP/SUD HA0 79 J2
GPK RM2 57 J6
HYS/HAR UB3 113 G4
Repton Cl CAR SM5 209 J3
Repton Ct BECK BR3 182 E4
Repton Dr GPK RM2 75 J1
Repton Gdns GPK RM2 57 J6
Repton Gv CLAY IG5 53 K4
Repton Rd
KTN/HRWW/WS HA3 62 B1
ORP BR6 217 G2
Repton St POP/IOD E14 105 G5
Repulse Cl CRW RM5 56 D4
Reservoir Cl THHTH CR7 180 E6
Reservoir Rd BROCKY SE4 144 B3
RSLP HA4 58 A2
STHGT/OAK N14 22 C6
Resham Cl NWDGN UB2 114 B3
Resolution Wy DEPT SE8 144 D1
Restell Cl BKHTH/KID SE3 125 H6
Restmor Wy CAR SM5 195 F6
WLGTN SM6 195 F6
Reston Pl KENS W8 120 B2
Restons Crs ELTH/MOT SE9 167 J2
Reston Wy CAN/RD E16 107 H6
Restormel Cl HSLW TW3 135 F6
Retford St BETH E2 * 7 J4
IS N1 * 7 H3
Retingham Wy CHING E4 37 K4
Retreat Cl
KTN/HRWW/WS HA3 61 J2
Retreat Pl HOM E9 86 E4
Retreat Rd RCH/KEW TW9 136 E6
The Retreat BRYLDS KT5 191 G3
CDALE/KGS NW9 63 F2
MORT/ESHN SW14 138 B4
ORP BR6 217 H4
RYLN/HDSTN HA2 60 A4
THHTH CR7 196 E1
WPK KT4 192 E6
Reunion Rw WAP E1W * 104 D6
Reveley Sq BERM/RHTH SE16 124 B2
Revell Ri WOOL/PLUM SE18 128 A6
Revell Rd KUT/HW KT1 175 J5
SUT SM1 208 D4
Revelon Rd BROCKY SE4 144 B5
Revelstoke Rd
WAND/EARL SW18 159 K4
WIM/MER SW19 159 H6
WIM/MER SW19 178 B2
Reventlow Rd ELTH/MOT SE9 167 H3
Reverdy Rd STHWK SE1 123 H4
Reverend Cl
RYLN/HDSTN HA2 78 B1
Revere Wy HOR/WEW KT19 207 G6
Revesby Rd CAR SM5 194 D3
Review Rd CRICK NW2 63 H6
DAGE RM10 110 D1
Rewell St FUL/PGN SW6 * 140 B1
Rewley Rd CAR SM5 194 C3
Rex Pl MYFR/PKLN W1K 9 H7
Reydon Av WAN E11 71 G3
Reynard Cl BMLY BR1 184 E6
Reynard Dr NRWD SE19 181 G3
Reynard Pl NWCR SE14 * 124 B6
Reynardson Rd TOTM N17 49 J3
Reynolah Gdns CHARL SE7 126 A5
Reynolds Av CHDH RM6 73 J4
CHSGTN KT9 206 A5
MNPK E12 90 A3
Reynolds Cl CAR SM5 194 E5
GLDGN NW11 65 F4
WIM/MER SW19 178 C4
Reynolds Dr EDGW HA8 44 B6
Reynolds Pl BKHTH/KID SE3 146 A1
RCHPK/HAM TW10 157 G1
Reynolds Rd CHSWK W4 117 K3
NWMAL KT3 192 A4
PECK SE15 143 K6
YEAD UB4 95 G3
Reynolds Wy CROY/NA CR0 212 A2
Rheidol Ms IS N1 6 C2
Rheidol Ter IS N1 6 B2
Rheingold Wy WLGTN SM6 210 E6
Rheola Cl TOTM N17 50 B4
Rhoda St BETH E2 7 K6
Rhodes Av WDGN N22 48 C4
Rhodesia Rd BRXN/ST SW9 141 K3
WAN E11 70 B6
Rhodes St HOLWY N7 85 F3
Rhodeswell Rd POP/IOD E14 105 G4
Rhodrons Av CHSGTN KT9 206 A3
Rhondda Gv BOW E3 105 G2
Rhyl Rd GFD/PVL UB6 97 F1
Rhyl St KTTN NW5 84 A4
Rhys Av FBAR/BDGN N11 48 D3
Rialto Rd MTCM CR4 179 F5
Ribble Cl WFD IG8 53 G2
Ribblesdale Av
FBAR/BDGN N11 47 K2
NTHLT UB5 78 B4
Ribblesdale Rd
CEND/HSY/T N8 67 F1
STRHM/NOR SW16 179 G1
Ribbon Dance Ms CMBW SE5 142 E2
Ribchester Av GFD/PVL UB6 97 F2
Ribston Cl HAYES BR2 200 E5
Ricardo St POP/IOD E14 105 K5
Ricards Rd WIM/MER SW19 177 J1
Rice Pde STMC/STPC BR5 * 201 J2
Richard Cl WOOL/PLUM SE18 126 D4
Richard House Dr
CAN/RD E16 107 H5
Richards Av ROMW/RG RM7 74 E2
Richards Cl BUSH WD23 28 D2
HRW HA1 61 G2
HYS/HAR UB3 113 G6
Richards Cots CAR SM5 * 209 K3
Richards Fld HOR/WEW KT19 207 F6
Richardson Cl HACK E8 * 86 B6
Richardson Gdns DAGE RM10 92 D4
Richardson Rd SRTFD E15 * 106 C1
Richardson's Ms FITZ W1T 4 A7
Richards Pl WALTH E17 51 J6
Richard's Pl CHEL SW3 14 D6
Richbell Pl FSBYW WC1X 11 G1
Richborne Ter VX/NE SW8 142 A1
Richborough Cl
STMC/STPC BR5 202 E1
Richborough Rd CRICK NW2 82 B2
Richens Cl HSLW TW3 135 J3
Riches Rd IL IG1 72 C6
Richfield Rd BUSH WD23 28 C2
Richford Ga HMSMTH W6 * 119 F3
Richford Rd SRTFD E15 88 D6
Richford St HMSMTH W6 119 F2
Richill Ldg WHTN TW2 * 155 F1
Richlands Av EW KT17 207 J2
Richmer Rd ERITH DA8 150 D1
Richmond Av CHING E4 52 B1
EBED/NFELT TW14 153 H1
IS N1 85 F6
RYNPK SW20 177 H4
Richmond Br TWK TW1 136 E6
Richmond Blds
SOHO/SHAV W1D 10 C4
Richmond Cl WALTH E17 69 H3
Richmond Crs CHING E4 52 B1
ED N9 36 C3
IS N1 85 F6
Richmond Dr WFD IG8 54 A3
Richmond Gdns HDN NW4 63 J2
KTN/HRWW/WS HA3 43 F3
Richmond Ga KUTN/CMB KT2 175 G2
RCHPK/HAM TW10 157 G2
Richmond Gn CROY/NA CR0 210 E1
Richmond Gv IS N1 85 H5
Richmond Hl
RCHPK/HAM TW10 157 F1
Richmond Ms
SOHO/SHAV W1D 10 C4
Richmond Pde TWK TW1 * 156 D1
Richmond Park Rd
KUTN/CMB KT2 175 F3
MORT/ESHN SW14 137 K6
Richmond Pl
WOOL/PLUM SE18 127 H4
Richmond Rd BAR EN5 21 F6
CHING E4 * 38 B3
CROY/NA CR0 210 E1
EA W5 117 F2
EFNCH N2 * 47 G5
FBAR/BDGN N11 48 E2
FSTGT E7 89 F3
HACK E8 86 B5
IL IG1 90 C1
ISLW TW7 136 B4
KUTN/CMB KT2 174 E1
ROM RM1 75 H3
RYNPK SW20 176 E4
SEVS/STOTM N15 68 A3
THHTH CR7 196 C1
TWK TW1 156 B3
WAN E11 70 B6
Richmond St PLSTW E13 106 E1
Richmond Ter WHALL SW1A 16 E2
Richmond Vls WALTH E17 * 51 K4
Richmond Wy SHB W12 119 G2
WAN E11 70 E6
Richmount Gdns
BKHTH/KID SE3 145 K4
Rich St POP/IOD E14 105 H6
Rickard Cl BRXS/STRHM SW2 162 B3
HDN NW4 63 J1
WDR/YW UB7 112 A3
Rickards Cl SURB KT6 191 F6
Rickett St FUL/PGN SW6 119 K6
Rickman St WCHPL E1 104 E3
Rickmansworth Rd
NTHWD HA6 40 B3
PIN HA5 41 F5
Rick Roberts Wy SRTFD E15 88 B6
Rickthorne Rd ARCH N19 66 E6
Ridding La GFD/PVL UB6 79 F3
Riddons Rd LEE/GVPK SE12 166 B5
Rideout St WOOL/PLUM SE18 126 E4
Rider Cl BFN/LL DA15 167 K1
The Ride BTFD TW8 116 C5
PEND EN3 24 E4
Ridgdale St BOW E3 105 J1
Ridge Av DART DA1 170 C1
WCHMH N21 35 J2
Ridgebrook Rd
BKHTH/KID SE3 146 B5
Ridge Cl CDALE/KGS NW9 63 F1
HDN NW4 46 B5
THMD SE28 127 J2
Ridge Crest ENC/FH EN2 23 F2
Ridgecroft Cl BXLY DA5 169 K3
Ridge Hl GLDGN NW11 64 C5
Ridgemead Cl
STHGT/OAK N14 34 E4
Ridgemont Gdns EDGW HA8 30 E6
Ridgemount Av CROY/NA CR0 198 A6
Ridgemount Cl PGE/AN SE20 181 J3
Ridgemount Gdns
ENC/FH EN2 23 H4
Ridge Rd CEND/HSY/T N8 67 F3
CHEAM SM3 193 J5
CRICK NW2 82 D1
MTCM CR4 179 G3
WCHMH N21 35 K3
Ridges Yd CROY/NA CR0 211 H1
Ridge Ter WCHMH N21 * 35 J2
The Ridge BAR EN5 * 20 D6
BRYLDS KT5 191 H2
BXLY DA5 169 G2
ORP BR6 201 J6
WHTN TW2 155 J2
Ridgeview Cl BAR EN5 32 B1
Ridgeview Rd
TRDG/WHET N20 33 F5
Ridge Wy DART DA1 170 C1
FELT TW13 154 D5
Ridgeway HAYES BR2 199 K6
WFD IG8 39 G6
Ridgeway Av EBAR EN4 33 K1
Ridgeway Crs ORP BR6 216 E1
Ridgeway Crescent Gdns
ORP BR6 201 K6
Ridgeway Dr BMLY BR1 166 A6
Ridgeway East BFN/LL DA15 148 A6
Ridgeway Gdns HGT N6 66 C4
REDBR IG4 71 J2
Ridgeway Rd ISLW TW7 135 K1
Ridgeway Rd North ISLW TW7 135 K1
The Ridgeway ACT W3 117 H3
CDALE/KGS NW9 63 F1
CHING E4 38 A3
CROY/NA CR0 211 F1
ENC/FH EN2 23 G2
FBAR/BDGN N11 33 K6
FNCH N3 47 F3
GLDGN NW11 64 D5
GPK RM2 75 J1
KTN/HRWW/WS HA3 61 J3
MLHL NW7 31 J6
RSLP HA4 58 D4
RYLN/HDSTN HA2 59 K2
STAN HA7 43 J2
STHGT/OAK N14 34 E4
Ridgeway West
BFN/LL DA15 147 K6
Ridgewell Cl DAGE RM10 92 D6
IS N1 85 J6
SYD SE26 164 C6
Ridgmount Gdns
GWRST WC1E 10 C1
Ridgmount Rd
WAND/EARL SW18 140 A6
Ridgmount St GWRST WC1E 10 C1
Ridgway RCHPK/HAM TW10 * 157 F1
WIM/MER SW19 177 F3
Ridgway Gdns
WIM/MER SW19 177 G3
Ridgway Pl WIM/MER SW19 177 H2
Ridgway Rd BRXN/ST SW9 142 C4
The Ridgway BELMT SM2 209 H5
Ridgwell Rd CAN/RD E16 107 G4
Riding House St GTPST W1W 9 K2
Ridings Av WCHMH N21 23 H5
Ridings Cl HGT N6 66 C4
The Ridings BRYLDS KT5 191 H2
EA W5 98 B3
EBAR EN4 * 33 J2
EW KT17 207 H6
The Riding GLDGN NW11 64 D4
Ridler Rd EN EN1 24 A1
Ridley Av WEA W13 116 C3
Ridley Cl BARK IG11 91 F5
HARH RM3 57 K4
Ridley Rd FSTGT E7 89 G2
HACK E8 86 B3
HAYES BR2 183 J6
WELL DA16 148 C2
WIM/MER SW19 178 A3
WLSDN NW10 99 J1
Ridsdale Rd PGE/AN SE20 181 J4
Riefield Rd ELTH/MOT SE9 147 H5
Riesco Dr CROY/NA CR0 212 E4
Riffel Rd CRICK NW2 82 A3
Rifle Pl NTGHL W11 119 G1
Rifle Range La HRW HA1 61 F5
Rifle St POP/IOD E14 105 K4
Rigault Rd FUL/PGN SW6 139 H3
Rigby Cl CROY/NA CR0 211 G1
Rigby La HYS/HAR UB3 113 F2
Rigby Ms IL IG1 72 A6
Rigden St POP/IOD E14 105 K5
Rigeley Rd WLSDN NW10 99 J2
Rigg Ap LEY E10 69 F5
Rigge Pl CLAP SW4 141 J5
Riggindale Rd
STRHM/NOR SW16 179 J1
Right Side STHGT/OAK N14 * 34 D3
Riley Rd PEND EN3 24 E1
STHWK SE1 19 J4
Riley St WBPTN SW10 140 C1
Rinaldo Rd BAL SW12 161 G2
Ring Cl BMLY BR1 184 A3
Ringcroft St HOLWY N7 85 G3
Ringer's Rd BMLY BR1 183 K6
Ringford Rd
WAND/EARL SW18 139 J6
Ringlet Cl CAN/RD E16 107 F4
Ringlewell Cl EN EN1 24 D3
Ringmer Av FUL/PGN SW6 139 H2
Ringmer Pl WCHMH N21 23 K6
Ringmer Wy BMLY BR1 200 E2
Ringmore Ri FSTH SE23 163 J2
Ring Rd SHB W12 119 F1
Ringshall Rd STMC/STPC BR5 186 B6
Ringslade Rd WDGN N22 49 F5
Ringstead Rd CAT SE6 164 E2
SUT SM1 209 H2
Ring Wy FBAR/BDGN N11 48 C2
Ringway NWDGN UB2 114 C5
Ringwold Cl BECK BR3 182 B3
Ringwood Av CROY/NA CR0 195 K4
EFNCH N2 47 K6
Ringwood Cl PIN HA5 * 41 G6
Ringwood Gdns
PUT/ROE SW15 158 D4
Ringwood Rd WALTH E17 69 H3
Ringwood Wy HPTN TW12 155 F6
WCHMH N21 35 H2
Ripley Cl BMLY BR1 200 E2
CROY/NA CR0 214 A4
Ripley Gdns
MORT/ESHN SW14 138 A4
Ripley Ms WAN E11 70 C3
Ripley Rd BELV DA17 129 H4
CAN/RD E16 107 G5
ENC/FH EN2 23 J2
GDMY/SEVK IG3 72 E6
HPTN TW12 173 F3
Ripleys Market DART DA1 * 171 H2
Ripley Vls EA W5 * 97 J5
Ripon Cl NTHLT UB5 78 A3
Ripon Gdns CHSGTN KT9 205 K3
IL IG1 71 J3
Ripon Rd ED N9 36 D2
TOTM N17 49 K6
WOOL/PLUM SE18 127 G6
Rippersley Rd WELL DA16 148 B2
Ripple Rd BARK IG11 90 C5
BARK IG11 91 H6
DAGW RM9 110 A1
Ripplevale Gv IS N1 85 F5
Rippolson Rd
WOOL/PLUM SE18 128 A5
Risborough Cl
MUSWH N10 * 48 B6
Risborough Dr WPK KT4 192 D4
Risborough St STHWK SE1 18 B2
Risdon St BERM/RHTH SE16 123 K2
Risebridge Cha ROM RM1 57 H3
Risebridge Rd GPK RM2 57 H5
Risedale Rd BXLYHN DA7 149 J4
Riseldine Rd FSTH SE23 164 B1
Rise Park Bvd ROM RM1 57 H4
Rise Park Pde ROM RM1 57 G5
The Rise BKHH IG9 39 H3
BXLY DA5 168 D2
DART DA1 150 C5
EDGW HA8 44 D1
GFD/PVL UB6 79 G3
MLHL NW7 45 H2
PLMGR N13 35 G6
SAND/SEL CR2 212 E6
WAN E11 70 E2
WLSDN NW10 81 F1
Rising Hill Cl NTHWD HA6 * 40 A2
Risinghill St IS N1 5 J2
Risingholme Cl BUSH WD23 28 B2
KTN/HRWW/WS HA3 42 E4
Risingholme Rd
KTN/HRWW/WS HA3 42 E5
The Risings WALTH E17 70 B1
Risley Av TOTM N17 49 J4
Rita Rd VX/NE SW8 141 K1
Ritches Rd SEVS/STOTM N15 67 J2
Ritchie Rd CROY/NA CR0 197 J3
Ritchie St IS N1 5 K2
Ritchings Av WALTH E17 69 G1
Ritherdon Rd TOOT SW17 161 F4
Ritson Rd HACK E8 86 B4
Ritter St WOOL/PLUM SE18 127 F6
Rivaz Pl HOM E9 86 E4
Rivenhall Gdns SWFD E18 70 D1
River Av PLMGR N13 35 H5
THDIT KT7 190 B4
Riverbank E/WMO/HCT KT8 173 K6
River Bank THDIT KT7 190 A2
WCHMH N21 35 J2
Riverbank Rd BMLY BR1 165 K5
Riverbank Wy BTFD TW8 116 D6
River Barge Cl POP/IOD E14 125 F2
River Cl NWDGN UB2 115 H2
RAIN RM13 111 K4
RSLP HA4 58 D3
WAN E11 71 G3
River Ct PUR RM19 131 J4
Rivercourt Rd HMSMTH W6 118 E4
River Crane Wy FELT TW13 154 E4
Riverdale Dr
WAND/EARL SW18 160 A3
Riverdale Gdns TWK TW1 136 D6
Riverdale Rd BXLY DA5 169 G2
ERITH DA8 129 J5
FELT TW13 154 D6
TWK TW1 156 D1
WOOL/PLUM SE18 128 A5
Riverdene EDGW HA8 30 E6
Riverdene Rd IL IG1 90 A1
River Front EN EN1 23 K4
River Gdns CAR SM5 195 F6
EBED/NFELT TW14 134 A6
River Grove Pk BECK BR3 182 C4
Riverhead Cl WALTH E17 51 F5
Riverholme Dr
HOR/WEW KT19 207 F6
River La RCHPK/HAM TW10 156 E3
Rivermead E/WMO/HCT KT8 173 H6
KUT/HW KT1 * 190 E2
Rivermead Cl TEDD TW11 174 C1
Rivermead Rd UED N18 * 51 F1
River Meads Av WHTN TW2 155 G5
Rivernook Cl WOT/HER KT12 188 B2
Riverpark Gdns HAYES BR2 183 G3
River Park Rd WDGN N22 49 F5
River Park Vw ORP BR6 202 C4
River Pl IS N1 85 J5
River Reach TEDD TW11 174 D2
River Rd BARK IG11 108 E2
BKHH IG9 39 J3
Riversdale Rd CRW RM5 56 D3
HBRY N5 85 H1
THDIT KT7 190 B2
Riversfield Rd EN EN1 24 A4
Riverside CHARL SE7 126 A3
HDN NW4 63 K4
RCH/KEW TW9 * 117 H6
RCH/KEW TW9 136 E6
SUN TW16 * 172 C5
TWK TW1 156 C3
Riverside Av E/WMO/HCT KT8 189 J2
Riverside Cl CLPT E5 68 E5
HNWL W7 96 E3
KUT/HW KT1 190 E1
ROMW/RG RM7 75 F1
STMC/STPC BR5 186 D5
WLGTN SM6 210 B1
Riverside Ct CHING E4 * 37 K1
Riverside Dr CHSWK W4 138 A1
ESH/CLAY KT10 204 A2
GLDGN NW11 * 64 C3
MTCM CR4 194 D2
RCHPK/HAM TW10 156 C5
Riverside Gdns ALP/SUD HA0 98 A1
ENC/FH EN2 23 J3
HMSMTH W6 118 E5
Riverside Ms CROY/NA CR0 * 210 E1
Riverside Pl
FBAR/BDGN N11 * 34 C5
STWL/WRAY TW19 152 A1
Riverside Rd IL IG1 90 B1
OXHEY WD19 27 F1
SCUP DA14 169 F5
SEVS/STOTM N15 68 C3
SRTFD E15 106 A1
STWL/WRAY TW19 132 A6
TOOT SW17 160 A6
The Riverside
E/WMO/HCT KT8 173 J6
Riverside Vls SURB KT6 * 190 D3
Riverside Wk ISLW TW7 135 K4
KUT/HW KT1 174 E5
Riverside Wy DART DA1 151 H6
Riverside Yd TOOT SW17 160 A5
Riverstone Cl
RYLN/HDSTN HA2 60 D6
River St CLKNW EC1R 5 J4
River Ter HMSMTH W6 119 F5
Riverton Cl MV/WKIL W9 * 100 D2
Riverview Gdns BARN SW13 118 E6
River View Gdns TWK TW1 156 A4
Riverview Gv CHSWK W4 117 J6
Riverview Pk CAT SE6 164 D4
Riverview Rd CHSWK W4 137 J1
HOR/WEW KT19 206 E2
River Wk SUN TW16 172 C5
River Wy GNWCH SE10 125 J3
HOR/WEW KT19 207 F3
Riverway PLMGR N13 49 G1
River Wy WHTN TW2 155 G4
River Whf BELV DA17 * 130 A2
Riverwood La CHST BR7 185 J5
Rivington Av WFD IG8 53 H5
Rivington Crs MLHL NW7 45 G3
Rivington Pl FSBYE EC1V 7 H5
Rivington St SDTCH EC2A 7 H5
Rivington Wk HACK E8 * 86 C6
Rivulet Rd TOTM N17 49 J3
Rixon St HOLWY N7 85 G1
Rixsen Rd MNPK E12 89 J3

Roach Rd BOW E3 87 J5
Roads Pl ARCH N19 66 E6
Roan St GNWCH SE10 125 F6
Robarts Cl PIN HA5 59 F2
Robb Rd STAN HA7 43 G2
Robert Adam St MHST W1U 9 G3
Roberta St BETH E2 104 C2
Robert Cl CHIG IG7 55 F1
MV/WKIL W9 101 G3
Robert Dashwood Wy
WALW SE17 18 C7
Robert Keen Cl PECK SE15 143 H2
Robert Lowe Cl NWCR SE14 144 A1
Roberton Dr BMLY BR1 184 B5
Robertsbridge Rd CAR SM5 194 B4
Roberts Cl CHEAM SM3 208 B5
DAGE RM10 92 C4
ELTH/MOT SE9 167 J3
HARH RM3 57 K4
STMC/STPC BR5 202 D2
THHTH CR7 180 E6
WDR/YW UB7 112 B1
Roberts Ct CHSGTN KT9 205 K3
PGE/AN SE20 181 K4
WLSDN NW10 81 G4
Roberts House
WOOL/PLUM SE18 * 146 D1
Roberts Ms KTBR SW1X * 15 G5
Robertson St VX/NE SW8 141 G3
Robert's Pl CLKNW EC1R * 5 K6
Robert Sq LEW SE13 145 F5
Roberts Rd BELV DA17 129 H5
MLHL NW7 46 C1
WALTH E17 51 K4
Robert St CAMTN NW1 3 K5
CHCR WC2N 11 F6
CROY/NA CR0 211 J1
WOOL/PLUM SE18 127 J4
Robeson St BOW E3 105 H4
Robina Cl BXLYHS DA6 148 E5
NTHWD HA6 40 D5
Robin Cl CRW RM5 57 F3
FELT TW13 172 D1
MLHL NW7 31 G5
Robin Gv BTFD TW8 116 D6
HGT N6 66 A6
KTN/HRWW/WS HA3 62 B3
Robin Hill Dr CHST BR7 184 D2
Robinhood Cl MTCM CR4 195 H1
Robin Hood Dr
KTN/HRWW/WS HA3 43 F3
Robin Hood Gdns
POP/IOD E14 * 106 A6
Robin Hood Gn
STMC/STPC BR5 202 B2
Robin Hood La BXLYHS DA6 149 F6
POP/IOD E14 106 A6
PUT/ROE SW15 158 B5
SUT SM1 208 E3
Robinhood La MTCM CR4 179 H6
Robin Hood Rd
PUT/ROE SW15 158 B6
WIM/MER SW19 176 D1
Robin Hood Wy GFD/PVL UB6 79 F4
PUT/ROE SW15 158 B6
RYNPK SW20 176 C3
Robinia Cl BARK/HLT IG6 54 E2
PGE/AN SE20 181 H4
Robinia Crs LEY E10 69 K6
Robin La HDN NW4 46 B6
Robinscroft Ms GNWCH SE10 145 F2
Robins Gv WWKM BR4 214 E1
Robinson Cl ENC/FH EN2 23 J4
HCH RM12 93 K5
WAN E11 88 C1
Robinson Crs BUSH WD23 28 C3
Robinson Rd BETH E2 104 E1
DAGE RM10 92 C2
TOOT SW17 178 D2
Robinson's Cl WEA W13 97 G4
Robinson St CHEL SW3 120 E6
Robinswood Ms HBRY N5 85 H3
Robin Wy STMC/STPC BR5 186 C6
Robinwood Pl PUT/ROE SW15 158 A6
Rob Pascoe La DAGW RM9 110 A2
Robsart St BRXN/ST SW9 142 A3
Robson Av WLSDN NW10 81 J5
Robson Cl EHAM E6 107 J5
ENC/FH EN2 23 H3
Robson Rd WNWD SE27 162 C5
Rocastle Rd BROCKY SE4 144 B6
Roch Av EDGW HA8 44 B5
Rochdale Rd ABYW SE2 128 C5
WALTH E17 69 J4
Rochdale Wy DEPT SE8 144 D1
Rochelle Cl BTSEA SW11 140 C5
Rochelle St BETH E2 7 J5
Rochemont Wk HACK E8 * 7 K1
Roche Rd STRHM/NOR SW16 179 K4
Rochester Av BMLY BR1 184 A5
FELT TW13 153 J4
PLSTW E13 89 G6
Rochester Cl BFN/LL DA15 168 C1
EN EN1 24 A2
STRHM/NOR SW16 * 179 K3
Rochester Dr BXLY DA5 169 H1
PIN HA5 59 H2
Rochester Gdns
CROY/NA CR0 212 A1
IL IG1 71 K4
Rochester Ms CAMTN NW1 84 C5
EA W5 * 116 D4
Rochester Pde FELT TW13 * 153 K5
Rochester Pl CAMTN NW1 84 C4
Rochester Rd CAMTN NW1 84 C4
CAR SM5 209 K2
DART DA1 171 K2
HCH RM12 93 K5
NTHWD HA6 40 D6
Rochester Rw WEST SW1P 16 B6
Rochester Sq CAMTN NW1 84 C5
Rochester St WEST SW1P 16 C5
Rochester Ter CAMTN NW1 84 C4
Rochester Wk STHWK SE1 * 12 E7
Rochester Wy BKHTH/KID SE3 146 A2
DART DA1 170 B2
ELTH/MOT SE9 146 C4
Rochester Way Relief Rd
ELTH/MOT SE9 146 D6
Roche Wk CAR SM5 194 C3
Rochford Av CHDH RM6 73 J2
Rochford Cl EHAM E6 107 H1
HCH RM12 93 K4
Rochford Wk HACK E8 * 86 C5
Rochford Wy CROY/NA CR0 195 K3
Rock Av MORT/ESHN SW14 138 A4
Rockbourne Rd FSTH SE23 164 A3
Rock Cl MTCM CR4 178 C5
Rockell's Pl EDUL SE22 163 J1
Rockford Av GFD/PVL UB6 97 H1
Rock Grove Wy
BERM/RHTH SE16 123 H4
Rockhall Rd CRICK NW2 82 B2
Rockhampton Rd
SAND/SEL CR2 212 A4
STRHM/NOR SW16 162 B6
Rock Hl DUL SE21 163 G6
Rockingham Av EMPK RM11 75 K3
Rockingham Cl
PUT/ROE SW15 138 C5
Rockingham Ga BUSH WD23 28 C1
Rockingham St STHWK SE1 18 C5
Rockland Rd PUT/ROE SW15 139 H5
Rocklands Dr
KTN/HRWW/WS HA3 43 H5
Rockley Rd SHB W12 119 G2
Rockmount Rd NRWD SE19 180 E2
WOOL/PLUM SE18 128 A5
Rocks La BARN SW13 138 D4
Rock St FSBYPK N4 67 G6
Rockware Av GFD/PVL UB6 78 E6
Rockways BAR EN5 31 H1
Rockwell Gdns NRWD SE19 163 F6
Rockwell Rd DAGE RM10 92 D3
Rocliffe St IS N1 6 B3
Rocombe Crs FSTH SE23 * 163 K2
Rocque La BKHTH/KID SE3 145 J4
Rodborough Rd GLDGN NW11 64 E5
Roden Gdns CROY/NA CR0 197 F3
Rodenhurst Rd CLAP SW4 161 H2
Roden St HOLWY N7 85 F1
IL IG1 90 A1
Rodeo Cl ERITH DA8 150 E2
Roderick Rd HAMP NW3 83 K2
Rodgers Cl BORE WD6 29 K1
Roding Gdns LOU IG10 39 J1
Roding La BKHH IG9 39 J3
Roding La North WFD IG8 53 J5
Roding La South REDBR IG4 71 H1
Roding Ms WAP E1W 123 H1
Roding Rd CLPT E5 87 F2
EHAM E6 108 B4
Rodings Rw BAR EN5 * 20 C5
Roding Vw BKHH IG9 39 H3
Rodmarton St MHST W1U 9 F2
Rodmell Cl YEAD UB4 95 J3
Rodmell Slope
NFNCH/WDSPK N12 46 D1
Rodmere St GNWCH SE10 125 H5
Rodney Cl CROY/NA CR0 196 C5
NWMAL KT3 192 B2
PIN HA5 59 J4
WOT/HER KT12 * 188 B5
Rodney Gdns PIN HA5 59 F2
WWKM BR4 214 E2
Rodney Pl STHWK SE1 18 D6
WALTH E17 51 G5
WIM/MER SW19 178 B4
Rodney Rd MTCM CR4 178 D5
NWMAL KT3 192 B2
WALW SE17 18 D7
WAN E11 71 F1
WHTN TW2 155 F2
WOT/HER KT12 188 A6
Rodney St IS N1 5 H2
Rodney Wy ROMW/RG RM7 56 D4
Rodway Rd BMLY BR1 184 A4
PUT/ROE SW15 158 D2
Rodwell Cl RSLP HA4 * 59 G5
Rodwell Rd EDUL SE22 163 G1
Roebuck Cl FELT TW13 154 A6
Roebuck La BKHH IG9 39 G3
Roebuck Rd BARK/HLT IG6 55 G2
CHSGTN KT9 206 C3
Roedean Av PEND EN3 24 E2
Roedean Cl ORP BR6 217 H2
PEND EN3 24 E2
Roedean Crs PUT/ROE SW15 158 B1
Roe End CDALE/KGS NW9 62 E1
Roe Gn CDALE/KGS NW9 62 E2
Roehampton Cl
PUT/ROE SW15 138 D5
Roehampton Dr CHST BR7 185 H2
Roehampton Ga
PUT/ROE SW15 158 B1
Roehampton High St
PUT/ROE SW15 158 D2
Roehampton La
PUT/ROE SW15 158 E3
Roehampton V
PUT/ROE SW15 158 C5
Roe La CDALE/KGS NW9 62 D1
Roe Rd WLGTN SM6 210 E4
Rofant Rd NTHWD HA6 40 C2
Roffey St POP/IOD E14 125 F2
Rogers Gdns DAGE RM10 92 C3
Rogers Rd CAN/RD E16 106 D5
DAGE RM10 92 C3
TOOT SW17 160 C6
Rogers Ruff NTHWD HA6 40 A4
Roger St BMSBY WC1N 5 H7
Rogers Wk
NFNCH/WDSPK N12 33 F5
Rojack Rd FSTH SE23 164 A3
Rokeby Gdns WFD IG8 52 E4
Rokeby Pl RYNPK SW20 176 E3
Rokeby Rd BROCKY SE4 * 144 C3
Rokeby St SRTFD E15 88 C6
Rokesby Cl WELL DA16 147 J3
Rokesby Pl ALP/SUD HA0 79 K3
Rokesly Av CEND/HSY/T N8 66 E2
Roland Gdns SKENS SW7 120 B5
Roland Ms WCHPL E1 * 105 F4
Roland Rd WALTH E17 70 B1
Roland Wy SKENS SW7 120 B5
WALW SE17 122 E5
WPK KT4 192 C6
Roles Gv CHDH RM6 73 K1
Rolfe Cl EBAR EN4 21 J5
Rolinsden Wy HAYES BR2 215 H2
Rollesby Rd CHSGTN KT9 206 C4
Rollesby Wy THMD SE28 109 J6
Rolleston Av STMC/STPC BR5 201 G3
Rolleston Cl STMC/STPC BR5 201 G4
Rolleston Rd SAND/SEL CR2 211 K5
Roll Gdns GNTH/NBYPK IG2 72 A2
Rollins St PECK SE15 123 K6
Rollit Crs HSLW TW3 135 F6
Rollit St HOLWY N7 85 G3
Rolls Blds FLST/FETLN EC4A 11 J3
Rollscourt Av HNHL SE24 142 D6
Rolls Park Av CHING E4 51 J2
Rolls Park Rd CHING E4 51 K1
Rolls Rd STHWK SE1 123 G5
Rolls Royce Cl WLGTN SM6 210 E5
Rolt St DEPT SE8 124 C6
NWCR SE14 124 B6
Rolvenden Gdns BMLY BR1 184 C4
Rolvenden Pl TOTM N17 50 C4
Roman Cl ACT W3 117 J2
EBED/NFELT TW14 134 B6
RAIN RM13 111 F1
Romanfield Rd
BRXS/STRHM SW2 162 A2
Romanhurst Av HAYES BR2 199 H1
Romanhurst Gdns HAYES BR2 199 H1
Roman Rd BORE WD6 29 K1
CAR SM5 209 K6
Roman Ri NRWD SE19 180 E2
Roman Rd BETH E2 105 F1
BOW E3 87 H6
CHSWK W4 118 B4
CRICK NW2 82 A1
EHAM E6 107 H3
IL IG1 90 B4
MUSWH N10 48 B3
Roman Sq THMD SE28 128 B1
Roman Wy CROY/NA CR0 196 C6
DART DA1 150 B6
EN EN1 24 B6
HOLWY N7 85 F4
Romany Gdns CHEAM SM3 193 K4
Romany Ri STMC/STPC BR5 201 H5
Roma Read Cl PUT/ROE SW15 158 E2
Roma Rd WALTH E17 51 G6
Romberg Rd TOOT SW17 161 F5
Romborough Gdns LEW SE13 145 F6
Romborough Wy LEW SE13 145 F6
Rom Crs ROMW/RG RM7 75 G4
Romeland BORE WD6 29 K1
Romero Cl BRXN/ST SW9 142 A4
Romero Sq BKHTH/KID SE3 146 B5
Romeyn Rd
STRHM/NOR SW16 162 A5
Romford Rd CHIG IG7 55 K2
CRW RM5 56 A3
FSTGT E7 88 E4
MNPK E12 89 K2
SRTFD E15 88 D4
Romford St WCHPL E1 104 C4
Romilly Dr OXHEY WD19 27 J6
Romilly Rd FSBYPK N4 67 H6
Romilly St SOHO/SHAV W1D 10 D5
Rommany Rd WNWD SE27 162 E6
Romney Cl CHSGTN KT9 206 A2
GLDGN NW11 65 G5
NWCR SE14 143 K1
RYLN/HDSTN HA2 60 A4
TOTM N17 50 D4
Romney Dr BMLY BR1 184 C3
RYLN/HDSTN HA2 60 A4
Romney Gdns BXLYHN DA7 149 G2
Romney Rd GNWCH SE10 125 F6
NWMAL KT3 192 A3
WOOL/PLUM SE18 127 H3
YEAD UB4 94 B1
Romney Rw CRICK NW2 * 64 B6
Romney St WEST SW1P 16 D5
Romola Rd HNHL SE24 162 C3
Romsey Cl ORP BR6 216 C2
Romsey Rd DAGW RM9 91 K6
WEA W13 * 97 G6
Romside Pl ROMW/RG RM7 75 F1
Rom Valley Wy
ROMW/RG RM7 75 G3
Ronald Av SRTFD E15 106 C2
Ronald Cl BECK BR3 198 C2
Ronalds Rd BMLY BR1 183 K4
HBRY N5 85 G3
Ronaldstone Rd BFN/LL DA15 167 K1
Rona Rd HAMP NW3 84 A2
Ronart St
KTN/HRWW/WS HA3 43 F6
Rona Wk IS N1 85 K4
Rondu Rd CRICK NW2 82 C3
Ronelean Rd SURB KT6 191 G6
Roneo Cnr ROMW/RG RM7 75 H5
Roneo Link HCH RM12 75 H5
Ronfearn Av STMC/STPC BR5 202 E2
Ron Green Ct ERITH DA8 130 A5
Ron Leighton Wy EHAM E6 89 J6
Ronnie La BCTR RM8 73 J6
Ron Todd Cl DAGE RM10 92 C6
Ronver Rd LEE/GVPK SE12 165 K3
Rood La FENCHST EC3M 13 G5
Rookby Ct WCHMH N21 35 H4
Rook Cl WBLY HA9 80 D1
Rookeries Cl FELT TW13 154 A5
Rookery Dr CHST BR7 185 F4
Rookery Gdns
STMC/STPC BR5 202 D2
Rookery La HAYES BR2 200 C3
Rookery Rd CLAP SW4 141 H5
The Rookery
STRHM/NOR SW16 * 180 A2
Rookery Wy CDALE/KGS NW9 63 H2
Rookesley Rd
STMC/STPC BR5 202 E4
Rookfield Av MUSWH N10 66 C1
Rookfield Cl MUSWH N10 66 C1
Rookley Cl BELMT SM2 209 F6
Rooks Ter WDR/YW UB7 * 112 B2
Rookstone Rd TOOT SW17 178 E1
Rookwood Av NWMAL KT3 192 D1
WLGTN SM6 210 D2
Rookwood Gdns CHING E4 * 38 D4
Rookwood Rd
STNW/STAM N16 68 C4
Roosevelt Wy DAGE RM10 93 F4
Rootes Dr NKENS W10 100 B3
Ropemaker Rd
BERM/RHTH SE16 124 B2
Ropemaker's Flds
POP/IOD E14 * 105 H6
Ropemaker St BARB EC2Y 12 E1
Roper La STHWK SE1 19 H3
Ropers Av CHING E4 52 A1
Ropers Orch CHEL SW3 * 120 D6
Roper St ELTH/MOT SE9 146 E6
Roper Wy MTCM CR4 179 F5
Ropery St BOW E3 105 H3
Rope St BERM/RHTH SE16 124 B3
Ropewalk Gdns WCHPL E1 104 C5
Ropewalk Ms HACK E8 * 86 B5
Ropley St BETH E2 104 C1
Rosa Alba Ms HBRY N5 85 J2
Rosa Av ASHF TW15 152 D6
Rosaline Rd FUL/PGN SW6 139 H1
Rosaline Ter FUL/PGN SW6 * 139 H1
Rosamond St SYD SE26 163 J5
Rosamond Vls
MORT/ESHN SW14 * 138 A5
Rosamund Cl SAND/SEL CR2 211 K2
Rosamun Rd NWDGN UB2 114 D4
Rosary Cl HSLW TW3 134 D3
Rosary Gdns ASHF TW15 152 E6
BUSH WD23 28 E2
SKENS SW7 120 B4
Rosary Ga BTSEA SW11 141 G1
Rosaville Rd FUL/PGN SW6 139 J1
Roscoe St STLK EC1Y 6 D7
Roscoff Cl EDGW HA8 44 D4
Roseacre Cl WEA W13 97 H4
Roseacre Rd WELL DA16 148 C4
Rose Aly STHWK SE1 12 D7
Roseary Cl WDR/YW UB7 112 A4
Rose Av MRDN SM4 194 B2
MTCM CR4 178 E4
SWFD E18 53 F5
Rosebank PGE/AN SE20 181 J3
Rosebank Av ALP/SUD HA0 79 F2
Rose Bank Cl
NFNCH/WDSPK N12 47 J1
Rosebank Cl TEDD TW11 174 B2
Rosebank Est BOW E3 105 H1
Rosebank Gdns ACT W3 * 99 F5
BOW E3 * 105 G1
Rosebank Gv WALTH E17 51 H6
Rosebank Rd HNWL W7 115 K2
WALTH E17 69 J3
Rosebank Wk CAMTN NW1 * 84 D5
Rosebank Wy ACT W3 99 F5
Roseberry Gdns DART DA1 171 F2
FSBYPK N4 67 H3
ORP BR6 216 E1
Roseberry Pl HACK E8 86 B4
Roseberry St
BERM/RHTH SE16 123 J4
Rosebery Av BFN/LL DA15 167 K2
CLKNW EC1R 5 J7
MNPK E12 89 J4
NWMAL KT3 176 C5
RYLN/HDSTN HA2 77 J2
THHTH CR7 180 D5
TOTM N17 50 C5
Rosebery Cl MRDN SM4 193 G3
Rosebery Ct CLKNW EC1R 5 J6
Rosebery Gdns
CEND/HSY/T N8 * 66 E2
SUT SM1 209 F2
WEA W13 97 G5
Rosebery Ms MUSWH N10 48 C5
Rosebery Pde EW KT17 * 207 H5
Rosebery Rd BUSH WD23 28 B3
CLAP SW4 161 K1
HSLW TW3 135 H6
KUT/HW KT1 175 J5
MUSWH N10 48 C5
SUT SM1 208 D4
Rosebine Av WHTN TW2 155 J2
Rosebriars ESH/CLAY KT10 204 C3
Rosebury Rd FUL/PGN SW6 140 A3
Rosebury Sq WFD IG8 54 A3
Rosebury V RSLP HA4 58 E6
Rose Ct WCHPL E1 13 J2
Rosecourt Rd CROY/NA CR0 196 A3
Rosecroft Av HAMP NW3 82 E1
Rosecroft Cl STMC/STPC BR5 202 D3
Rosecroft Ct NTHWD HA6 * 40 A2
Rose Croft Gdns CRICK NW2 81 J1
Rosecroft Gdns WHTN TW2 155 J3
Rosecroft Rd STHL UB1 96 A3
Rosecroft Wk ALP/SUD HA0 79 K3
PIN HA5 59 H2
Rose & Crown Yd STJS SW1Y * 16 B1
Rose Dl ORP BR6 201 G6
Rosedale Av HYS/HAR UB3 94 B4
Rosedale Cl ABYW SE2 128 C3
HNWL W7 116 A2
STAN HA7 43 H2
Rosedale Dr DAGW RM9 91 H6
Rosedale Gdns DAGW RM9 91 H5
Rosedale Pl CROY/NA CR0 198 A4
Rosedale Rd DAGW RM9 91 H5
EW KT17 207 J3
FSTGT E7 89 G3
RCH/KEW TW9 137 F5
ROM RM1 56 E6
Rosedene Av CROY/NA CR0 195 K4
GFD/PVL UB6 96 A2
MRDN SM4 193 K2
STRHM/NOR SW16 162 A5
Rosedene Cl DART DA1 171 F2
Rosedene Gdns
GNTH/NBYPK IG2 72 A1
Rosedene Ter LEY E10 69 K6
Rosedew Rd HMSMTH W6 119 G6
Rose End WPK KT4 193 G5
Rosefield POP/IOD E14 105 J6
Rosefield Cl CAR SM5 209 J3
Rosefield Gdns POP/IOD E14 105 J6
Rose Garden Cl EDGW HA8 44 A2
Rose Gdns EA W5 116 E3
FELT TW13 153 K4
STHL UB1 96 A3
STWL/WRAY TW19 152 A2
Rose Gln CDALE/KGS NW9 63 F1
ROMW/RG RM7 75 G5
Rosehart Ms NTGHL W11 100 E5
Rosehatch Av CHDH RM6 55 K6
Roseheath Rd HSLWW TW4 134 E6
Rosehill ESH/CLAY KT10 205 G4
HPTN TW12 173 F4
Rose Hl SUT SM1 194 A6
Rosehill Av SUT SM1 194 B5
Rosehill Court Pde
MRDN SM4 * 194 B4
Rosehill Gdns GFD/PVL UB6 79 F3
SUT SM1 194 A6
Rose Hill Pk West SUT SM1 194 B5
Rosehill Rd WAND/EARL SW18 160 B1
Rose Joan Ms
KIL/WHAMP NW6 82 E2
Roseland Cl TOTM N17 49 K3
Rose La CHDH RM6 74 A1
Rose Lawn BUSH WD23 28 C3
Roseleigh Av HBRY N5 85 H2
Roseleigh Cl TWK TW1 156 E1
Rosemary Av
E/WMO/HCT KT8 173 F6
ED N9 36 D3
ENC/FH EN2 23 K2
FNCH N3 47 F5
HSLWW TW4 134 C3
ROM RM1 57 H6
Rosemary Cl CROY/NA CR0 195 K4
Rosemary Dr POP/IOD E14 106 B5
REDBR IG4 71 H2
Rosemary Gdns BCTR RM8 74 B5
CHSGTN KT9 206 A2
Rosemary La
MORT/ESHN SW14 137 K4
Rosemary Rd PECK SE15 143 G1
TOOT SW17 160 B5
WELL DA16 148 A2
Rosemary St IS N1 85 K6
Rosemead CDALE/KGS NW9 63 H4
Rosemead Av FELT TW13 153 J4
MTCM CR4 179 H6
WBLY HA9 80 A3
Rosemere Pl HAYES BR2 199 H1
Rose Ms UED N18 36 D6
Rosemont Av
NFNCH/WDSPK N12 47 G2
Rosemont Rd ACT W3 98 D6
HAMP NW3 83 G4
NWMAL KT3 175 K6
RCHPK/HAM TW10 157 F1
Rosemoor St CHEL SW3 14 E7
Rosemount Cl WFD IG8 53 K2
Rosemount Dr BMLY BR1 200 E1
Rosemount Rd ALP/SUD HA0 80 A6
WEA W13 97 G5
Rosenau Crs BTSEA SW11 140 E2
Rosenau Rd BTSEA SW11 140 D2
Rosendale Rd DUL SE21 162 D4
HNHL SE24 162 D2
Roseneath Av WCHMH N21 35 H3
Roseneath Pl
STRHM/NOR SW16 162 B6
Roseneath Rd BTSEA SW11 161 F1
Roseneath Wk EN EN1 24 A5
Rosenheath Cl ORP BR6 217 H5
Rosens Wk EDGW HA8 30 D5
Rosenthal Rd CAT SE6 164 E1
Rosenthorpe Rd PECK SE15 144 A6
Rose Park Cl YEAD UB4 95 G4
Roserton St POP/IOD E14 125 F2
The Rosery CROY/NA CR0 198 A3
Rose Sq CHEL SW3 * 120 C5
The Roses WFD IG8 * 52 D3
Rose St COVGDN WC2E 10 E5
Rosethorn Cl BAL SW12 161 H2
Rosetree Pl HPTN TW12 173 F3
Rosetta Cl VX/NE SW8 141 K1
Roseveare Rd LEE/GVPK SE12 166 B6
Roseville WCHMH N21 35 G3
Roseville Av HSLW TW3 135 F6
Roseville Rd HYS/HAR UB3 113 K5
Rosevine Rd RYNPK SW20 177 F4
Rose Wk BRYLDS KT5 191 J2
WWKM BR4 199 F6
Rose Wy LEE/GVPK SE12 145 K6
Roseway DUL SE21 162 E1
EDGW HA8 30 E6
Rosewell Cl PGE/AN SE20 181 J3
Rosewood RDART DA2 170 B6
Rosewood Av GFD/PVL UB6 79 G3
HCH RM12 93 J3
Rosewood Cl SCUP DA14 168 D5
Rosewood Ct KUTN/CMB KT2 175 H3
Rosewood Gv SUT SM1 194 B6
Rosewood Ter PGE/AN SE20 * 181 K3
Rosher Cl SRTFD E15 88 B5
Rosina St HOM E9 87 F4
Roskell Rd PUT/ROE SW15 139 G4
Roslin Rd ACT W3 117 J3
Roslin Wy BMLY BR1 183 K1
Roslyn Cl MTCM CR4 178 C5
Roslyn Gdns GPK RM2 57 H5
Roslyn Ms SEVS/STOTM N15 * 68 A2
Roslyn Rd SEVS/STOTM N15 67 K2
Rosmead Rd NTGHL W11 100 C6
Rosoman Pl CLKNW EC1R 5 K6
Rosoman St CLKNW EC1R 5 K5
Rossall Cl EMPK RM11 75 J3
Rossall Crs WLSDN NW10 98 B2
Ross Av BCTR RM8 74 B6
Ross Cl HYS/HAR UB3 113 G4
KTN/HRWW/WS HA3 42 C3
NTHLT UB5 78 D2
Rossdale SUT SM1 209 J3
Rossdale Dr CDALE/KGS NW9 62 E5
ED N9 36 E1
Rossdale Rd PUT/ROE SW15 139 F5
Rosse Ms BKHTH/KID SE3 146 A2
Rossendale St CLPT E5 68 D6
Rossendale Wy CAMTN NW1 84 C6
Rossetti Ms STJWD NW8 2 A1
Rossetti Rd BERM/RHTH SE16 123 J5
Ross House CHARL SE7 * 146 D1
Rossignol Gdns CAR SM5 195 F6
Rossindel Rd HSLW TW3 135 F6
Rossington Cl EN EN1 24 D1
Rossington St CLPT E5 68 C6
Rossiter Cl NRWD SE19 180 D3
Rossiter Flds BAR EN5 32 C1
Rossiter Rd BAL SW12 161 G3
Rossland Cl BXLYHS DA6 149 H6
Rosslyn Av BARN SW13 138 B4

BCTR RM8 74 B4
CHING E4 38 D4
EBAR EN4 33 J1
EBED/NFELT TW14 153 K1
Rosslyn Cl HYS/HAR UB3 94 B4
WWKM BR4 214 D1
Rosslyn Crs HRW HA1 61 F1
WBLY HA9 80 A1
Rosslyn Hl HAMP NW3 83 H3
Rosslyn Park Ms HAMP NW3 83 H3
Rosslyn Rd BARK IG11 90 D5
TWK TW1 156 D1
WALTH E17 * 70 A1
Rossmore Cl CAMTN NW1 * 2 D7
PEND EN3 25 F5
Rossmore Rd CAMTN NW1 2 D6
Ross Pde WLGTN SM6 210 B4
Ross Rd DART DA1 170 D1
SNWD SE25 181 F6
WHTN TW2 155 H3
WLGTN SM6 210 C4
Ross Wy ELTH/MOT SE9 146 D4
NTHWD HA6 26 D6
Rosswood Gdns WLGTN SM6 210 B4
Rostella Rd TOOT SW17 160 C6
Rostrever Gdns HYS/HAR UB3 113 H1
Rostrevor Av
SEVS/STOTM N15 68 B3
Rostrevor Gdns NWDGN UB2 114 D5
Rostrevor Rd FUL/PGN SW6 139 J2
WIM/MER SW19 177 K1
Rotary St STHWK SE1 18 A4
Rothbury Av RAIN RM13 111 K4
Rothbury Cots GNWCH SE10 125 H4
Rothbury Gdns ISLW TW7 136 B1
Rothbury Rd HOM E9 87 H5
Rotherfield Rd CAR SM5 210 A2
Rotherfield St IS N1 85 J5
Rotherham Wk STHWK SE1 * 18 B1
Rotherhill Av
STRHM/NOR SW16 179 J2
Rotherhithe New Rd
BERM/RHTH SE16 123 J5
Rotherhithe Old Rd
BERM/RHTH SE16 124 A4
Rotherhithe St
BERM/RHTH SE16 124 B2
Rotherhithe Tnl
BERM/RHTH SE16 123 K2
Rothermere Rd CROY/NA CR0 211 F3
Rotherwick Hl EA W5 98 B3
Rotherwick Rd GLDGN NW11 64 E4
Rotherwood Cl RYNPK SW20 177 H4
Rotherwood Rd
PUT/ROE SW15 139 G4
Rothery St IS N1 85 H6
Rothery Ter BRXN/ST SW9 * 142 C1
Rothesay Av GFD/PVL UB6 78 D4
RCHPK/HAM TW10 137 J5
RYNPK SW20 177 H5
Rothesay Rd SNWD SE25 196 E1
Rothsay Rd FSTGT E7 89 G5
Rothsay St STHWK SE1 19 G4
Rothschild Rd CHSWK W4 117 K4
Rothschild St WNWD SE27 162 C6
Rothwell Gdns DAGW RM9 91 J5
Rothwell Rd DAGW RM9 91 J6
Rothwell St CAMTN NW1 83 K6
Rotterdam Dr POP/IOD E14 125 F3
Rouel Rd BERM/RHTH SE16 123 H3
Rougemont Av MRDN SM4 193 K3
The Roughs NTHWD HA6 26 C5
Roundaway Rd CLAY IG5 53 K5
Roundel Cl BROCKY SE4 144 C5
Round Gv CROY/NA CR0 198 A4
Roundhay Cl FSTH SE23 164 A4
Roundhedge Wy ENC/FH EN2 23 F1
Round Hl SYD SE26 163 J4
Roundhill Dr ENC/FH EN2 23 F5
Roundlyn Gdns
STMC/STPC BR5 202 C1
Roundtable Rd BMLY BR1 165 J5
Roundtree Rd ALP/SUD HA0 79 H3
Roundways RSLP HA4 76 D1
The Roundway
ESH/CLAY KT10 205 F4
TOTM N17 49 J4
WATW WD18 26 D1
Roundwood CHST BR7 185 G5
Roundwood Av STKPK UB11 113 F1
Roundwood Cl RSLP HA4 * 58 B4
Roundwood Pk
WLSDN NW10 * 81 J6
Roundwood Rd WLSDN NW10 81 G4
Roundwood Ter
STNW/STAM N16 68 A4
Rounton Rd BOW E3 105 J3
Roupell Rd BRXS/STRHM SW2 162 A3
Roupell St STHWK SE1 17 K1
Rousden St CAMTN NW1 84 C5
Rouse Gdns DUL SE21 163 F6
Rous Rd BKHH IG9 39 J2
Routemaster Cl PLSTW E13 107 F2
Routh Ct EBED/NFELT TW14 153 G3
Routh Rd WAND/EARL SW18 160 D2
Routh St EHAM E6 107 K4
Rover Av BARK/HLT IG6 55 F2
Rowallan Rd FUL/PGN SW6 139 H1
Rowan Av CHING E4 51 H2
Rowan Cl ALP/SUD HA0 79 G1
ASHF TW15 152 A6
EA W5 117 F2
IL IG1 90 D3
NWMAL KT3 176 B5
STAN HA7 43 F2
STRHM/NOR SW16 179 H4
Rowan Crs DART DA1 171 F3
STRHM/NOR SW16 179 H4
Rowan Dr CDALE/KGS NW9 45 J6
Rowan Gdns CROY/NA CR0 212 B1
Rowan Pl HYS/HAR UB3 94 D6
Rowan Rd BTFD TW8 136 C1
BXLYHN DA7 149 F4
HMSMTH W6 119 G4
STRHM/NOR SW16 179 H5
WDR/YW UB7 112 A4
The Rowans PLMGR N13 35 J5
Rowan Ter HMSMTH W6 119 G4
PGE/AN SE20 * 181 H4
WIM/MER SW19 * 177 H3
Rowantree Cl WCHMH N21 35 K3
Rowantree Ms ENC/FH EN2 23 H3
Rowantree Rd ENC/FH EN2 23 H3
WCHMH N21 35 K3
Rowan Wk EFNCH N2 65 G3
HAYES BR2 215 K1
NKENS W10 * 100 C3
Rowan Wy CHDH RM6 55 J6
Rowanwood Av BFN/LL DA15 168 B3
Rowben Cl TRDG/WHET N20 33 F3
Rowberry Cl FUL/PGN SW6 139 G1
Rowcross St STHWK SE1 123 G5
Rowdell Rd NTHLT UB5 78 A6
Rowden Pde CHING E4 * 51 J2
Rowden Rd BECK BR3 182 B4
CHING E4 51 K2
HOR/WEW KT19 206 E2
Rowditch La BTSEA SW11 141 F3
Rowdon Av WLSDN NW10 81 K5
Rowdown Crs CROY/NA CR0 214 B6
Rowdowns Rd DAGW RM9 92 B6
Rowe Gdns BARK IG11 109 F1
Rowe La HOM E9 86 E3
Rowena Crs BTSEA SW11 140 D3
Rowe Wk RYLN/HDSTN HA2 78 A1
Rowfant Rd TOOT SW17 161 F4
Rowhill Rd CLPT E5 86 D2
RDART DA2 170 D6
Rowington Cl BAY/PAD W2 101 F4
Rowland Av
KTN/HRWW/WS HA3 43 J6
Rowland Gv SYD SE26 163 J5
Rowland Hill Av TOTM N17 49 J3
Rowland Hill St HAMP NW3 83 J3
Rowland Pl NTHWD HA6 * 40 C3
Rowlands Av PIN HA5 42 A2
Rowlands Cl HGT N6 * 66 A3
MLHL NW7 45 J3
Rowlands Rd BCTR RM8 74 B6
Rowland Wy WIM/MER SW19 178 A4
Rowlatt Cl RDART DA2 171 F6
Rowley Av BFN/LL DA15 168 C2
Rowley Cl ALP/SUD HA0 80 B5
OXHEY WD19 27 J1
Rowley Cots WKENS W14 * 119 J4
Rowley Gdns FSBYPK N4 67 J4
Rowley Rd SEVS/STOTM N15 67 J2
Rowley Wy STJWD NW8 83 F6
Rowlheys Pl WDR/YW UB7 112 B3
Rowlls Rd KUT/HW KT1 175 G6
Rowney Gdns DAGW RM9 91 J4
Rowney Rd DAGW RM9 91 H4
Rowntree Clifford Cl
PLSTW E13 107 F3
Rowntree Cl
KIL/WHAMP NW6 * 82 E4
Rowntree Rd WHTN TW2 155 K3
Rowse Cl SRTFD E15 88 A6
Rowsley Av HDN NW4 46 A6
Rowstock Gdns HOLWY N7 84 D4
Rowton Rd WOOL/PLUM SE18 147 H1
Roxborough Av HRW HA1 60 D4
ISLW TW7 136 A1
Roxborough Pk HRW HA1 60 E4
Roxborough Rd HRW HA1 60 D2
Roxbourne Cl NTHLT UB5 77 H4
Roxburgh Rd WNWD SE27 180 C1
Roxburn Wy RSLP HA4 76 D1
Roxby Pl FUL/PGN SW6 119 K6
Roxeth Green Av
RYLN/HDSTN HA2 78 B1
Roxeth Gv RYLN/HDSTN HA2 78 B2
Roxeth Hl RYLN/HDSTN HA2 60 D6
Roxley Rd LEW SE13 164 E1
Roxton Gdns CROY/NA CR0 213 H4
Roxwell Rd BARK IG11 109 G1
SHB W12 118 D2
Roxwell Wy WFD IG8 53 G3
Roxy Av CHDH RM6 73 J4
Royal Albert Wy EHAM E6 107 K6
Royal Ar CONDST W1S 10 A6
Royal Arsenal West
WOOL/PLUM SE18 * 127 F5
Royal Av CHEL SW3 120 E5
WPK KT4 192 B6
Royal Circ WNWD SE27 162 B5
Royal Cl DEPT SE8 124 C6
GDMY/SEVK IG3 73 G4
ORP BR6 216 B2
STNW/STAM N16 68 A5
WIM/MER SW19 159 G4
WPK KT4 192 B6
Royal College St CAMTN NW1 84 C5
Royal Ct BANK EC3V 13 F4
ELTH/MOT SE9 * 166 E3
EN EN1 * 36 A1
Royal Crs GNTH/NBYPK IG2 72 D3
NTGHL W11 119 G2
RSLP HA4 77 J2
Royal Crescent Ms
NTGHL W11 119 G2
Royal Docks Rd EHAM E6 108 B4
Royal Dr FBAR/BDGN N11 48 A1
Royal Herbert Pavilions
WOOL/PLUM SE18 * 146 E2
Royal Hl GNWCH SE10 145 F1
Royal Hospital Rd CHEL SW3 120 E6
Royal Ms BAL SW12 161 G2
Royal Mint Pl WCHPL E1 13 K5
Royal Mint St WCHPL E1 13 K5
Royal Naval Pl NWCR SE14 144 C1
Royal Oak Ms TEDD TW11 174 B1
Royal Oak Pl EDUL SE22 163 J1
Royal Oak Rd BXLYHS DA6 149 G6
HACK E8 86 D4
Royal Oak Yd STHWK SE1 19 G3
Royal Opera Ar STJS SW1Y * 10 C7
Royal Orchard Cl
WAND/EARL SW18 159 H2
Royal Pde BKHTH/KID SE3 145 J3
CHST BR7 185 H3
FUL/PGN SW6 * 139 H1
Royal Pl GNWCH SE10 145 F1
Royal Rd CAN/RD E16 107 H5
LBTH SE11 122 C6
SCUP DA14 168 E5
TEDD TW11 173 J1
Royal Route WBLY HA9 80 B2
Royal St STHWK SE1 17 H4
Royal Victor Pl BOW E3 105 F1
Roycraft Av BARK IG11 109 F1
Roycroft Cl
BRXS/STRHM SW2 * 162 B3
SWFD E18 53 F4
Roydene Rd
WOOL/PLUM SE18 127 K6
Roydon Cl LOU IG10 39 J2
Roy Gdns GNTH/NBYPK IG2 72 E1
Roy Gv HPTN TW12 173 G2
Royle Cl GPK RM2 75 K2
Royle Crs WEA W13 97 G3
Roy Rd NTHWD HA6 40 D3
Roy Sq POP/IOD E14 105 G6
Royston Av CHING E4 51 J1
SUT SM1 209 H1
WLGTN SM6 210 D2
Royston Cl HEST TW5 134 A2
Royston Gdns IL IG1 71 H3
Royston Gv PIN HA5 41 K2
Royston Park Rd PIN HA5 41 K2
Royston Rd DART DA1 170 C1
PGE/AN SE20 182 A4
RCHPK/HAM TW10 137 F6
The Roystons BRYLDS KT5 191 J2
Royston St BETH E2 104 E1
Rozel Rd VX/NE SW8 141 H3
Rubastic Rd NWDGN UB2 114 B3
Rubens Rd NTHLT UB5 95 G1
Rubens St CAT SE6 164 C4
Ruby Cl CLPT E5 87 F1
Ruby Ms WALTH E17 * 51 J6
Ruby Rd WALTH E17 51 J6
Ruby St PECK SE15 123 J6
WLSDN NW10 80 E5
Ruby Triangle PECK SE15 * 123 J6
Ruckholt Cl LEY E10 87 K1
Ruckholt Rd LEY E10 88 A1
Rucklidge Av WLSDN NW10 99 H1
Rudall Crs HAMP NW3 83 H2
Ruddington Cl CLPT E5 87 G2
Ruddock Cl EDGW HA8 44 E3
Ruddstreet Cl
WOOL/PLUM SE18 127 G4
Rudgwick Ter STJWD NW8 * 2 D1
Rudland Rd BXLYHN DA7 149 J4
Rudloe Rd BAL SW12 161 H2
Rudolf Pl VX/NE SW8 121 K6
Rudolph Rd BUSH WD23 28 A1
KIL/WHAMP NW6 100 E1
PLSTW E13 106 D1
Rudyard Gv EDGW HA8 44 E2
Ruffetts Cl SAND/SEL CR2 212 D5
The Ruffetts SAND/SEL CR2 212 D5
Ruffle Cl WDR/YW UB7 112 B2
Rufford Cl
KTN/HRWW/WS HA3 61 G3
Rufford St IS N1 84 E6
Rufford Street Ms IS N1 84 E5
Rufus Cl RSLP HA4 77 H1
Rufus St FSBYE EC1V 7 G5
Rugby Av ALP/SUD HA0 79 J2
ED N9 36 B3
GFD/PVL UB6 78 D4
Rugby Cl HRW HA1 60 E1
Rugby Gdns DAGW RM9 91 J4
Rugby La BELMT SM2 208 B6
Rugby Rd CDALE/KGS NW9 62 C1
CHSWK W4 118 B2
DAGW RM9 91 H5
TWK TW1 155 K1
Rugby St BMSBY WC1N 5 G7
Rugg St POP/IOD E14 105 J6
Ruislip Cl GFD/PVL UB6 96 B3
Ruislip Ct RSLP HA4 * 58 D6
Ruislip Rd GFD/PVL UB6 96 A2
NTHLT UB5 95 J2
Ruislip Rd East GFD/PVL UB6 96 C3
Ruislip St TOOT SW17 160 E6
Rumbold Rd FUL/PGN SW6 140 A1
Rum Cl WAP E1W 104 D6
Rumsey Cl HPTN TW12 172 E2
Rumsey Rd BRXN/ST SW9 142 A4
Runbury Cir CDALE/KGS NW9 63 F6
Runcorn Cl TOTM N17 68 D1
Runcorn Pl NTGHL W11 100 C6
Rundell Crs HDN NW4 63 K2
Runes Cl MTCM CR4 194 C1
Runnelfield HRW HA1 78 E1
Runnymede WIM/MER SW19 178 C4
Runnymede Cl WHTN TW2 155 G1
Runnymede Crs
STRHM/NOR SW16 179 J4
Runnymede Gdns
GFD/PVL UB6 96 D1
HSLW TW3 155 G1
Runnymede Rd WHTN TW2 155 G1
Runway Cl CDALE/KGS NW9 45 H5
The Runway RSLP HA4 77 F3
Rupack St BERM/RHTH SE16 * 123 K2
Rupert Av WBLY HA9 80 A3
Rupert Ct E/WMO/HCT KT8 * 189 F1
SOHO/SHAV W1D 10 C5
Rupert Gdns BRXN/ST SW9 142 C3
Rupert Rd ARCH N19 84 D1
CHSWK W4 118 B3
KIL/WHAMP NW6 100 D1
Rupert St SOHO/SHAV W1D 10 C5
Rural Cl EMPK RM11 75 K5
Rural Wy STRHM/NOR SW16 179 G3
Rusbridge Cl HACK E8 86 C3
Ruscoe Rd CAN/RD E16 106 D5
Ruscombe Wy
EBED/NFELT TW14 153 J2
Rusham Rd BAL SW12 160 E1
Rushbridge Cl CROY/NA CR0 196 D3
Rushbrook Crs WALTH E17 51 H4
Rushbrook Rd ELTH/MOT SE9 167 H4
Rush Common Ms
BRXS/STRHM SW2 161 K2
Rushcroft Rd
BRXS/STRHM SW2 142 B5
CHING E4 51 K3
Rushden Cl NRWD SE19 180 E3
Rushdene ABYW SE2 128 D3
Rushdene Av EBAR EN4 33 J2
Rushdene Cl NTHLT UB5 95 G1
Rushdene Crs NTHLT UB5 95 F1
Rushdene Rd PIN HA5 59 G3
Rushden Gdns CLAY IG5 54 A6
MLHL NW7 46 A2
Rushdon Cl ROM RM1 75 J2
Rushet Rd STMC/STPC BR5 186 B5
Rushett Cl THDIT KT7 190 C5
Rushett Rd THDIT KT7 190 C4
Rushey Cl NWMAL KT3 192 A1
Rushey Gn CAT SE6 164 E2
Rushey Hl ENC/FH EN2 23 F5
Rushey Md BROCKY SE4 144 D6
Rushford Rd BROCKY SE4 164 C1
Rush Green Gdns
ROMW/RG RM7 74 E5
Rush Green Rd
ROMW/RG RM7 74 E5
Rushgrove Av
CDALE/KGS NW9 63 H1
Rushgrove Pde
CDALE/KGS NW9 * 63 H2
Rushgrove St
WOOL/PLUM SE18 126 E4
Rush Hill Ms BTSEA SW11 141 F4
Rush Hill Rd BTSEA SW11 141 F4
Rushley Cl HAYES BR2 215 H2
Rushmead BETH E2 104 D2
RCHPK/HAM TW10 156 C5
Rushmead Cl CROY/NA CR0 212 B2
Rushmere Ct WPK KT4 192 D6
Rushmere Pl WIM/MER SW19 177 G1
Rushmon Pl CHEAM SM3 * 208 C4
Rushmon Vls NWMAL KT3 * 192 C1
Rushmoor Cl PIN HA5 59 F1
Rushmore Cl BMLY BR1 184 D6
Rushmore Ct WATW WD18 * 26 B1
Rushmore Rd CLPT E5 86 E2
Rusholme Av DAGE RM10 92 C1
Rusholme Gv NRWD SE19 181 F1
Rusholme Rd PUT/ROE SW15 159 G1
Rushout Av
KTN/HRWW/WS HA3 61 H3
Rushton St IS N1 7 F2
Rushworth St STHWK SE1 18 B2
Rushy Meadow La CAR SM5 194 D6
Ruskin Av EBED/NFELT TW14 153 J2
MNPK E12 89 J4
RCH/KEW TW9 137 H1
WELL DA16 148 B4
Ruskin Cl GLDGN NW11 65 F3
Ruskin Dr ORP BR6 216 E1
WELL DA16 148 B4
WPK KT4 192 E6
Ruskin Gdns EA W5 97 K3
HARH RM3 57 K4
KTN/HRWW/WS HA3 62 B2
Ruskin Gv DART DA1 151 K6
WELL DA16 148 B3
Ruskin Rd BELV DA17 129 H4
CAR SM5 210 A3
CROY/NA CR0 196 C6
ISLW TW7 136 A4
STHL UB1 95 J6
TOTM N17 50 B4
Ruskin Wk ED N9 36 C4
HAYES BR2 200 D3
HNHL SE24 142 D6
Ruskin Wy WIM/MER SW19 178 C5
Rusland Av ORP BR6 216 D1
Rusland Park Rd HRW HA1 60 E1
Rusper Cl CRICK NW2 82 A1
STAN HA7 29 J6
Rusper Rd DAGW RM9 91 J4
WDGN N22 49 H5
Russel Cl BECK BR3 182 E6
Russell Av WDGN N22 49 H5
Russell Cl BKHTH/KID SE3 146 B1
BXLYHN DA7 149 H5
CHSWK W4 118 C6
DART DA1 150 D4
NTHWD HA6 40 A1
RSLP HA4 59 G6
WLSDN NW10 80 E5
Russell Ct BAR EN5 * 21 G5
WHALL SW1A 16 B1
Russell Dr STWL/WRAY TW19 152 A1
Russell Gdns GLDGN NW11 64 C3
RCHPK/HAM TW10 156 D4
TRDG/WHET N20 33 J4
WDR/YW UB7 112 D5
WKENS W14 * 119 H3
Russell Gardens Ms
WKENS W14 119 H2
Russell Gv BRXN/ST SW9 142 B2
MLHL NW7 45 G1
Russell Kerr Cl CHSWK W4 * 137 K1
Russell La TRDG/WHET N20 33 K4
Russell Pde GLDGN NW11 * 64 C3
Russell Pl HAMP NW3 83 J3
Russell Rd BKHH IG9 39 G3
CAN/RD E16 106 E5
CDALE/KGS NW9 63 H3
CEND/HSY/T N8 66 D3
CHING E4 37 H6
EN EN1 24 B1
MTCM CR4 178 D6
NTHLT UB5 78 C3
NTHWD HA6 26 A5
SEVS/STOTM N15 68 A2
TRDG/WHET N20 33 J4
WALTH E17 69 K3
WDGN N22 49 F2
WHTN TW2 156 A1
WIM/MER SW19 177 K3
WKENS W14 119 H3
Russell Sq RSQ WC1B 10 D1
Russell St HOL/ALD WC2B 11 G4
Russell Wy OXHEY WD19 27 F2
SUT SM1 209 F3
Russet Cl HGDN/ICK UB10 94 A3
Russet Crs HOLWY N7 * 85 F3
Russet Dr CROY/NA CR0 198 B5
Russets Cl CHING E4 38 B6
Russett Cl ORP BR6 217 H3
Russia Dock Rd
BERM/RHTH SE16 * 124 B1
Russia La BETH E2 104 E1
Russia Rw CITYW EC2V 12 D4
Rusthall Av CHSWK W4 118 A3
Rusthall Cl CROY/NA CR0 197 K3
Rustic Av STRHM/NOR SW16 179 G3
Rustic Pl ALP/SUD HA0 79 K2
Rustington Wk CHEAM SM3 193 J4
Ruston Av BRYLDS KT5 191 J4
Ruston Gdns STHGT/OAK N14 34 A1
Ruston Ms NTGHL W11 * 100 C5
Ruston Rd WOOL/PLUM SE18 126 D3
Ruston St BOW E3 87 H6
Rust Sq CMBW SE5 142 E1
Rutford Rd
STRHM/NOR SW16 179 K1
Ruth Cl STAN HA7 62 B1
Rutherford Cl BELMT SM2 209 H4
Rutherford St WEST SW1P 16 C6
Rutherford Wy BUSH WD23 28 D3
WBLY HA9 80 C1
Rutherglen Rd ABYW SE2 128 B6
Rutherwyke Cl EW KT17 207 J4
Ruthin Cl CDALE/KGS NW9 63 G3
Ruthin Rd BKHTH/KID SE3 125 K6
Ruthven St HOM E9 87 F6
Rutland Av BFN/LL DA15 168 B2
Rutland Cl BXLY DA5 168 E3
CHSGTN KT9 206 B4
DART DA1 171 G2
MORT/ESHN SW14 137 J4
WIM/MER SW19 178 D2
Rutland Ct CHST BR7 185 F4
SKENS SW7 14 D3
Rutland Dr MRDN SM4 193 K4
RCHPK/HAM TW10 156 E3
Rutland Gdns BCTR RM8 91 J3
CROY/NA CR0 212 A2
FSBYPK N4 67 H3
SKENS SW7 14 D3
WEA W13 * 97 G4
Rutland Gardens Ms
SKENS SW7 14 D3
Rutland Ga BELV DA17 129 J5
HAYES BR2 199 J1
SKENS SW7 14 C3
Rutland Gate Ms SKENS SW7 * 14 C3
Rutland Gv HMSMTH W6 118 E5
Rutland Ms STJWD NW8 * 83 G6
Rutland Ms South
SKENS SW7 * 14 C4
Rutland Pk CAT SE6 164 C4
CRICK NW2 82 A4
Rutland Pl BUSH WD23 * 28 D3
FARR EC1M * 12 B1
Rutland Rd FSTGT E7 89 H5
HOM E9 87 F6
HRW HA1 60 C3
HYS/HAR UB3 113 G4
IL IG1 90 B2
STHL UB1 96 A3
WALTH E17 69 J3
WAN E11 71 F2
WHTN TW2 155 J4
Rutland St SKENS SW7 14 D4
Rutland Wk CAT SE6 164 C4
Rutland Wy STMC/STPC BR5 202 D3
Rutley Cl WALW SE17 122 C6
Rutlish Rd WIM/MER SW19 177 K4
Rutter Gdns MTCM CR4 194 C1
Rutters Cl WDR/YW UB7 112 D2
Rutt's Ter NWCR SE14 144 A2
The Rutts BUSH WD23 28 D3
Ruvigny Gdns PUT/ROE SW15 139 G4
Ruxley Cl HOR/WEW KT19 206 D3
SCUP DA14 186 E2
Ruxley Crs ESH/CLAY KT10 205 H5
Ruxley La HOR/WEW KT19 206 E3
Ruxley Ms HOR/WEW KT19 206 D3
Ruxley Rdg ESH/CLAY KT10 205 G5
Ruxley Towers
ESH/CLAY KT10 * 205 G5
Ryan Cl BKHTH/KID SE3 146 A5
RSLP HA4 59 F5
Ryan Ct OXHEY WD19 * 27 J2
Ryan Dr BTFD TW8 116 B6
Ryarsh Crs ORP BR6 216 E2
Rycroft Wy TOTM N17 * 50 B6
Ryculff Sq BKHTH/KID SE3 145 J3
Rydal Cl HDN NW4 46 C4
Rydal Crs GFD/PVL UB6 97 H2
Rydal Dr BXLYHN DA7 149 H2
WWKM BR4 199 H6
Rydal Gdns CDALE/KGS NW9 63 G2
HSLW TW3 155 G1
PUT/ROE SW15 176 B1
WBLY HA9 61 J5
Rydal Mt HAYES BR2 * 199 J1
Rydal Rd STRHM/NOR SW16 179 J1
Rydal Wy PEND EN3 36 E1
RSLP HA4 77 G2
Rydens Av WOT/HER KT12 188 B6
Rydens Cl WOT/HER KT12 188 B6
Rydens Pk WOT/HER KT12 188 C6
Rydens Rd WOT/HER KT12 188 B6
Ryde Pl TWK TW1 156 D1
Ryder Av LEY E10 69 K4
Ryder Cl BUSH WD23 28 B1
Ryder Dr BERM/RHTH SE16 123 J5
Ryder Gdns RAIN RM13 93 H4
Ryder St STJS SW1Y 10 B7
Ryder Yd STJS SW1Y 10 B7
Ryde Vale Rd BAL SW12 161 G4
Rydon Ms WIM/MER SW19 177 F3
Rydston Cl HOLWY N7 85 F5
Rye Cl BXLY DA5 169 J1
Ryecotes Md DUL SE21 163 F3
Rye Crs STMC/STPC BR5 202 E5
Ryecroft Av CLAY IG5 54 B5
WHTN TW2 155 G3
Ryecroft Rd LEW SE13 145 F6
STMC/STPC BR5 201 J3
STRHM/NOR SW16 180 B2
Ryecroft St FUL/PGN SW6 140 A2
Ryedale EDUL SE22 163 J1
Ryefield Av HGDN/ICK UB10 76 A6
Ryefield Crs PIN HA5 * 40 E5
Ryefield Pde NTHWD HA6 * 40 E5
Ryefield Rd NRWD SE19 180 D2
Rye Hill Pk PECK SE15 143 K5
Ryelands Crs LEE/GVPK SE12 166 B1
Rye La PECK SE15 143 H3
Rye Rd PECK SE15 144 A5
The Rye STHGT/OAK N14 34 C2
Rye Wk PUT/ROE SW15 139 G6
Rye Wy EDGW HA8 44 B2
Ryfold Rd WIM/MER SW19 159 K5
Ryhope Rd FBAR/BDGN N11 34 B6
Ryland Cl FELT TW13 153 J6

Rylandes Rd CRICK NW2 81 J1
SAND/SEL CR2 212 D6
Ryland Rd KTTN NW5 * 84 B4
Rylett Crs SHB W12 118 C3
Rylett Rd SHB W12 118 C2
Rylston Rd FUL/PGN SW6 119 J6
PLMGR N13 35 K5
Rymer Rd CROY/NA CR0 197 F4
Rymer St HNHL SE24 162 C1
Rymill St CAN/RD E16 127 F1
Rysbrack St CHEL SW3 14 E4
Rythe Cl CHSGTN KT9 205 J5
Rythe Ct THDIT KT7 190 B4
Rythe Rd ESH/CLAY KT10 204 D3
Ryves Cots MTCM CR4 * 179 F5

S

Sabine Rd BTSEA SW11 140 E4
Sable Cl HSLWW TW4 134 B4
Sable St IS N1 85 H5
Sach Rd CLPT E5 68 D6
Sackville Av HAYES BR2 199 K5
Sackville Cl RYLN/HDSTN HA2 78 D1
Sackville Est
STRHM/NOR SW16 161 K5
Sackville Gdns IL IG1 71 K5
Sackville Rd BELMT SM2 208 E5
RDART DA2 171 G4
Sackville St CONDST W1S 10 A6
Saddlers Cl PIN HA5 42 A1
Saddlers Ms KUT/HW KT1 174 D4
Saddlescombe Wy
NFNCH/WDSPK N12 46 E1
Sadler Cl MTCM CR4 178 E5
Sadlers Gate Ms
PUT/ROE SW15 139 F4
Sadlers Ride E/WMO/HCT KT8 173 H5
Saffron Av POP/IOD E14 106 B6
Saffron Cl CROY/NA CR0 195 K3
GLDGN NW11 64 D2
Saffron Hl HCIRC EC1N 11 K1
Saffron Rd CRW RM5 57 F5
Saffron St HCIRC EC1N 11 K1
Saffron Wy SURB KT6 190 E5
Sage Cl EHAM E6 107 K4
Sage Ms EDUL SE22 143 G6
Sage St WCHPL E1 104 E6
Sage Wy FSBYW WC1X 5 G5
Sage Yd SURB KT6 191 G5
Saigasso Cl CAN/RD E16 107 H5
Sail St LBTH SE11 17 H6
Sainfoin Rd TOOT SW17 161 F4
Sainsbury Rd NRWD SE19 181 F1
St Agatha's Gv CAR SM5 194 E5
St Agnes Cl HOM E9 * 86 E6
St Agnes Pl LBTH SE11 122 C6
St Agnes Well STLK EC1Y 7 F6
St Aidan's Rd EDUL SE22 163 J1
WEA W13 116 C2
St Albans Av CHSWK W4 118 A3
FELT TW13 172 C1
St Alban's Av EHAM E6 107 K2
St Albans Crs WDGN N22 49 G4
St Albans Farm
EBED/NFELT TW14 * 134 B6
St Alban's Gdns TEDD TW11 174 B1
St Albans Gv KENS W8 * 120 A3
St Alban's Gv CAR SM5 194 D4
KENS W8 120 A3
St Albans La GLDGN NW11 64 E5
St Alban's Ms BAY/PAD W2 8 B1
St Alban's Pl IS N1 6 A1
St Albans Rd BAR EN5 20 C2
GDMY/SEVK IG3 73 F5
KUTN/CMB KT2 175 F2
SUT SM1 208 D2
St Alban's Rd DART DA1 171 J1
KTTN NW5 84 A1
WFD IG8 52 E3
WLSDN NW10 81 G6
St Alban's St STJS SW1Y 10 C6
St Albans Ter HMSMTH W6 119 H6
St Alfege Pas GNWCH SE10 125 F6
St Alfege Rd CHARL SE7 126 C6
St Alphage Gdns BARB EC2Y 12 D2
St Alphage Highwalk
BARB EC2Y 12 D2
St Alphage Wk EDGW HA8 * 44 E5
St Alphege Rd ED N9 36 E2
St Alphonsus Rd CLAP SW4 141 H5
St Amunds Cl CAT SE6 164 D6
St Andrews Av ALP/SUD HA0 79 G2
HCH RM12 93 H3
St Andrews Cl
BERM/RHTH SE16 * 123 J5
RSLP HA4 59 H6
STAN HA7 * 43 J5
THDIT KT7 190 C5
THMD SE28 109 K5
WIM/MER SW19 178 A2
St Andrew's Cl CRICK NW2 * 81 K1
ISLW TW7 135 J2
NFNCH/WDSPK N12 * 33 G6
St Andrew's Ct
WAND/EARL SW18 160 B4
St Andrews Dr STAN HA7 43 J4
STMC/STPC BR5 202 C3
St Andrew's Gv
STNW/STAM N16 67 K5
St Andrew's Hl BLKFR EC4V 12 B4
St Andrews Ms BAL SW12 161 J3
BKHTH/KID SE3 145 K1
St Andrew's Ms
STNW/STAM N16 68 A5
St Andrew's Pl CAMTN NW1 3 J6
St Andrews Rd CAR SM5 209 J1
CDALE/KGS NW9 63 F5
ED N9 36 E2
MNPK E12 71 J6
ROMW/RG RM7 75 F3
SCUP DA14 168 E5
WKENS W14 * 119 H6
St Andrew's Rd ACT W3 99 G5
CROY/NA CR0 211 J2
EN EN1 23 K4
GLDGN NW11 64 D3
HNWL W7 115 K2
IL IG1 71 K4
PLSTW E13 107 F2
SURB KT6 190 E3
WALTH E17 51 F5
WAN E11 70 C3
WKENS W14 119 H6
WLSDN NW10 81 K4
St Andrew's Sq NTGHL W11 * 100 C5
SURB KT6 190 E3
St Andrews Ter
OXHEY WD19 * 41 G1
St Andrew St HCIRC EC1N 11 K2
St Andrews Wy BOW E3 105 K3
St Anna Rd BAR EN5 * 20 B6
St Anne's Av
STWL/WRAY TW19 152 A2
St Annes Cl OXHEY WD19 27 G6
St Anne's Cl HGT N6 84 A1
St Annes Ct SOHO/CST W1F 10 C4
St Annes Gdns WLSDN NW10 98 B2
St Anne's Pas POP/IOD E14 * 105 H5
St Anne's Rd ALP/SUD HA0 79 K3
LEY E10 70 B6
St Anne's Rw POP/IOD E14 105 H5
St Anne St POP/IOD E14 105 H5
St Ann's BARK IG11 90 C6
St Anns Ct HDN NW4 * 45 K6
St Ann's Crs
WAND/EARL SW18 160 A1
St Ann's Gdns KTTN NW5 84 A4
St Ann's Hl WAND/EARL SW18 140 A6
St Ann's Park Rd
WAND/EARL SW18 160 B1
St Anns Rd BARN SW13 * 138 C3
St Ann's Rd BARK IG11 90 C6
ED N9 36 B4
HRW HA1 60 E3
NTGHL W11 100 B6
SEVS/STOTM N15 67 J2
St Ann's St WEST SW1P 16 D4
St Ann's Ter STJWD NW8 2 B2
St Ann's Vls NTGHL W11 119 G1
St Ann's Wy CROY/NA CR0 211 H4
St Anselms Rd HYS/HAR UB3 113 J2
St Anthony's Av WFD IG8 53 G2
St Anthonys Cl TOOT SW17 160 D4
St Anthony's Cl WAP E1W * 123 H1
St Anthony's Ct ORP BR6 201 G5
St Anthony's Wy
EBED/NFELT TW14 133 J5
St Antony's Rd FSTGT E7 89 F5
St Arvans Cl CROY/NA CR0 212 A1
St Asaph Rd BROCKY SE4 144 A4
St Aubyn's Av HSLW TW3 135 F6
WIM/MER SW19 177 J1
St Aubyns Cl ORP BR6 217 F1
St Aubyns Gdns ORP BR6 202 A6
St Aubyn's Rd NRWD SE19 181 G2
St Audrey Av BXLYHN DA7 149 H3
St Augustine's Av EA W5 98 A1
HAYES BR2 200 D2
SAND/SEL CR2 211 J5
WBLY HA9 80 A1
St Augustine's Rd BELV DA17 129 G4
CAMTN NW1 84 D5
St Austell Cl EDGW HA8 44 B5
St Austell Rd LEW SE13 145 F3
St Awdry's Rd BARK IG11 90 D5
St Barnabas Cl BECK BR3 183 F5
EDUL SE22 143 F5
St Barnabas' Gdns
E/WMO/HCT KT8 189 F2
St Barnabas Ms BGVA SW1W 121 F5
St Barnabas Rd MTCM CR4 179 F3
SUT SM1 209 H3
WALTH E17 69 J3
WFD IG8 53 F4
St Barnabas St BGVA SW1W 121 F5
St Barnabas Ter HOM E9 87 F3
St Barnabas Vls VX/NE SW8 141 K2
St Bartholomew's Cl
SYD SE26 163 K6
St Bartholomew's Rd
EHAM E6 89 J6
St Benets Cl TOOT SW17 160 D4
St Benet's Gv CAR SM5 194 B4
St Benjamins Dr ORP BR6 217 J6
St Bernards CROY/NA CR0 212 A1
St Bernards Cl WNWD SE27 162 E6
St Bernard's Rd EHAM E6 89 H6
St Blaise Av BMLY BR1 184 A5
St Botolph St TWRH EC3N 13 J3
St Bride's Av EDGW HA8 44 B4
St Brides Cl ERITHM DA18 128 E2
St Bride St FLST/FETLN EC4A 12 A3
St Catherines Cl CHSGTN KT9 205 K4
TOOT SW17 * 160 D4
St Catherines Ct FELT TW13 153 K3
St Catherine's Dr NWCR SE14 144 A3
St Catherines Ms CHEL SW3 14 E6
St Catherines Rd CHING E4 37 J4
RSLP HA4 58 A2
St Chads Cl SURB KT6 190 D4
St Chad's Gdns CHDH RM6 74 A4
St Chad's Pl FSBYW WC1X 5 F4
St Chad's Rd CHDH RM6 74 A3
St Chad's St STPAN WC1H 5 F4
St Charles Pl NKENS W10 100 C4
St Charles Sq NKENS W10 100 B4
St Christopher's Cl ISLW TW7 135 K2
St Christophers Dr
HYS/HAR UB3 95 F6
St Christopher's Ms
WLGTN SM6 210 C3
St Christopher's Pl
MHST W1U 9 H4
St Clair Cl CLAY IG5 53 K5
St Clair Dr WPK KT4 207 K1
St Clair Rd PLSTW E13 107 F1
St Clair's Rd CROY/NA CR0 197 F6
St Clare St TWRH EC3N 13 J4
St Clements Ct PUR RM19 131 K4
St Clement's La LINN WC2A 11 H4
St Clements St HOLWY N7 85 G5
St Clements Yd EDUL SE22 * 143 G6
St Cloud Rd WNWD SE27 162 D6
St Crispins Cl HAMP NW3 83 J2
St Crispin's Cl STHL UB1 95 K5
St Cross St HCIRC EC1N 11 K1
St Cuthberts Gdns PIN HA5 * 41 K3
St Cuthberts Rd PLMGR N13 49 G2
St Cuthbert's Rd CRICK NW2 82 D4
St Cyprian's St TOOT SW17 160 E6
St Davids Cl
BERM/RHTH SE16 * 123 J5
WBLY HA9 80 E1
St David's Cl WWKM BR4 198 E4
St David's Dr EDGW HA8 44 B4
St Davids Ms BOW E3 * 105 G2
St David's Pl HDN NW4 63 K4
St Davids Sq POP/IOD E14 124 E5
St Denis Rd WNWD SE27 162 D6
St Dionis Rd FUL/PGN SW6 139 J3
MNPK E12 89 J1
St Donatt's Rd NWCR SE14 144 C2
St Dunstan's Av ACT W3 99 F6
St Dunstans Cl HYS/HAR UB3 113 J4
St Dunstan's Gdns ACT W3 99 F6
St Dunstan's Hl MON EC3R * 13 G6
SUT SM1 208 C4
St Dunstan's La MON EC3R * 13 G6
St Dunstans Rd FSTGT E7 89 F4
St Dunstan's Rd FELT TW13 153 J5
HMSMTH W6 119 G5
HNWL W7 115 K2
HSLWW TW4 134 A3
SNWD SE25 197 G1
St Edmunds Av RSLP HA4 58 B3
St Edmunds Cl ERITHM DA18 128 E2
TOOT SW17 160 D4
St Edmund's Cl STJWD NW8 2 E1
St Edmunds Dr STAN HA7 43 G4
St Edmund's La WHTN TW2 155 G2
St Edmunds Rd DART DA1 151 J5
ED N9 36 C2
St Edmund's Rd IL IG1 71 K3
St Edmunds Sq BARN SW13 119 F6
St Edmund's Ter STJWD NW8 2 D1
St Edward's Cl GLDGN NW11 64 E3
St Edwards Wy ROM RM1 75 F2
St Egberts Wy CHING E4 38 A3
St Elmo Rd SHB W12 118 C2
St Elmos Rd
BERM/RHTH SE16 124 B2
St Erkenwald Ms BARK IG11 90 D6
St Erkenwald Rd BARK IG11 90 D6
St Ervans Rd NKENS W10 100 C4
St Faith's Cl ENC/FH EN2 23 J2
St Faith's Rd DUL SE21 162 C3
St Fidelis' Rd ERITH DA8 130 A4
St Fillans Rd CAT SE6 165 F3
St Francis Cl ORP BR6 201 K3
OXHEY WD19 27 F3
St Francis Rd EDUL SE22 143 F5
St Francis Wy IL IG1 90 D2
St Gabriel's Cl WAN E11 71 F5
St Gabriel's Rd CRICK NW2 82 B3
St George's Av
CDALE/KGS NW9 62 E1
EA W5 116 E2
FSTGT E7 89 F5
HOLWY N7 84 D2
STHL UB1 95 K6
St George's Circ STHWK SE1 18 A3
St Georges Cl HRW HA1 79 G1
THMD SE28 109 K5
VX/NE SW8 141 H2
St George's Cl GLDGN NW11 64 D3
St Georges Dr PIM SW1V * 121 G5
St George's Dr OXHEY WD19 27 J5
PIM SW1V 15 K7
St Georges Flds BAY/PAD W2 8 D5
St George's Gdns SURB KT6 191 J6
St George's Gv TOOT SW17 160 C5
St George's Industrial Est
KUTN/CMB KT2 174 E1
St George's La MON EC3R * 13 F5
St Georges Ms CHSWK W4 * 117 K6
DEPT SE8 124 C4
St George's Ms CAMTN NW1 83 K5
St Georges Pde CAT SE6 * 164 C4
St Georges Rd BMLY BR1 184 E5
CHSWK W4 118 A2
DAGW RM9 92 A3
STMC/STPC BR5 201 J3
St George's Rd BECK BR3 182 E4
EN EN1 24 B1
FELT TW13 154 C6
FSTGT E7 89 F5
GLDGN NW11 64 D3
HNWL W7 116 A1
IL IG1 71 K4
KUTN/CMB KT2 175 G3
LEY E10 88 A1
MTCM CR4 179 G6
PLMGR N13 35 F4
RCH/KEW TW9 137 G4
SCUP DA14 186 E2
STHWK SE1 18 A5
TWK TW1 136 C6
WIM/MER SW19 177 J2
WLGTN SM6 210 B3
St Georges Rd West
BMLY BR1 184 D5
St Georges's Ct STP EC4M * 12 A3
St Georges Sq NWMAL KT3 * 176 B6
PIM SW1V * 121 J5
St George's Sq FSTGT E7 89 F5
PIM SW1V 121 J5
St George's Square Ms
PIM SW1V 121 J5
St Georges Ter PECK SE15 * 143 H1
St George's Ter CAMTN NW1 83 K5
St George St CONDST W1S 9 K5
St George's Wk CROY/NA CR0 196 D6
St Georges Wy PECK SE15 * 123 F6
St George's Wy PECK SE15 123 F6
St Gerards Cl CLAP SW4 141 H6
St German's Pl
BKHTH/KID SE3 145 K2
St German's Rd FSTH SE23 164 B3
St Giles Av DAGE RM10 92 D5
HGDN/ICK UB10 76 A2
St Giles Churchyard
BARB EC2Y * 12 D2
St Giles Circ SOHO/SHAV W1D 10 D3
St Giles Cl DAGE RM10 92 D5
HEST TW5 134 D1
ORP BR6 216 D3
St Giles Ct LSQ/SEVD WC2H 10 D3
St Giles High St
NOXST/BSQ WC1A 10 D3
St Giles Pas LSQ/SEVD WC2H 10 D4
St Giles Rd CMBW SE5 143 F2
St Gothard Rd WNWD SE27 162 E6
St Gregory Cl RSLP HA4 77 G2
St Helena Rd
BERM/RHTH SE16 124 A4
St Helena St FSBYW WC1X * 5 J5
St Helena Ter RCH/KEW TW9 * 136 E6
St Helens THDIT KT7 * 189 K4
St Helens Ct RAIN RM13 111 J3
St Helen's Crs
STRHM/NOR SW16 180 A4
St Helen's Gdns NKENS W10 100 B5
St Helens Pl LEY E10 69 G4
St Helen's Pl HDTCH EC3A 13 G3
St Helens Rd ERITHM DA18 128 E2
St Helen's Rd IL IG1 71 K3
STRHM/NOR SW16 180 A5
WEA W13 116 C1
St Helier Av MRDN SM4 194 B4
St Heliers Av HSLWW TW4 135 F6
St Helier's Rd LEY E10 69 K3
St Hildas Cl
KIL/WHAMP NW6 * 82 B6
TOOT SW17 160 D4
St Hilda's Rd BARN SW13 118 E6
St Hughes Cl TOOT SW17 * 160 D4
St Hugh's Rd PGE/AN SE20 * 181 J4
St Ivians Dr GPK RM2 57 J6
St James Av SUT SM1 208 E3
TRDG/WHET N20 33 J5
St James' Av WEA W13 116 B1
St James Cl EBAR EN4 21 H4
STJWD NW8 2 E2
TRDG/WHET N20 33 J5
St James' Cl NWMAL KT3 192 C2
RSLP HA4 59 G6
St James' Ct WESTW SW1E * 16 B4
St James Gdns CHDH RM6 73 H1
St James' Gdns ALP/SUD HA0 79 K5
St James Ms POP/IOD E14 * 125 F3
St James Pl DART DA1 171 G1
St James Rd CAR SM5 209 J1
St James' Rd ED N9 36 D4
KUT/HW KT1 174 E5
MTCM CR4 179 F3
SRTFD E15 88 D3
SURB KT6 190 E3
SUT SM1 208 E4
St James's NWCR SE14 144 B2
St James's Av BECK BR3 182 B6
BETH E2 104 E1
HPTN TW12 173 H1
St James's Chambers
STJS SW1Y * 10 B7
St James's Cl TOOT SW17 * 160 E4
WOOL/PLUM SE18 127 H5
St James's Cots
RCH/KEW TW9 * 136 E6
St James's Ct KUT/HW KT1 * 175 F6
WESTW SW1E 16 B4
St James's Crs BRXN/ST SW9 142 B4
St James's Dr BAL SW12 160 E3
St James's Gdns
CAMTN NW1 * 4 A5
NTGHL W11 119 G1
St James's Gv BTSEA SW11 140 E3
St James's La MUSWH N10 66 B1
St James's Market
STJS SW1Y * 10 C6
St James's Ms WALTH E17 69 G2
St James's Pk CROY/NA CR0 196 D4
St James's Pl WHALL SW1A 16 A1
St James Sq SURB KT6 190 D4
St James's Rd
BERM/RHTH SE16 123 H5
CROY/NA CR0 196 D4
HPTN TW12 173 G1
St James's Rw CHSGTN KT9 * 205 K4
St James's Sq STJS SW1Y 10 C7
St James's St WALTH E17 69 G2
WHALL SW1A 10 A7
St James's Ter STJWD NW8 2 E1
St James's Terrace Ms
STJWD NW8 2 E1
St James St HMSMTH W6 119 F5
St James Ter BAL SW12 * 161 F3
ORP BR6 * 217 J6
St James Wk CLKNW EC1R 6 A6
St James Wy SCUP DA14 169 F6
St Jerome's Gv UX/CGN UB8 94 A5
St Joan's Rd ED N9 36 B4
St John Cl FUL/PGN SW6 * 139 K1
St John's Av FBAR/BDGN N11 47 K1
PUT/ROE SW15 139 G6
WLSDN NW10 81 H6
St John's Church Rd
HOM E9 * 86 E3
St Johns Cl STHGT/OAK N14 34 C1
St John's Cl FUL/PGN SW6 * 139 K1
RAIN RM13 93 J5
TRDG/WHET N20 * 33 G4
WBLY HA9 80 A3
St Johns Cots PGE/AN SE20 * 181 K3
St Johns Ct BKHH IG9 * 39 F3
St John's Ct BKHH IG9 39 F3
ISLW TW7 136 A3
St John's Crs BRXN/ST SW9 142 B4
St Johns Dr WOT/HER KT12 188 B5
St John's Dr
WAND/EARL SW18 160 A3
St John's Est IS N1 7 F3
STHWK SE1 19 J2
St John's Gdns NTGHL W11 100 C6
St John's Gv ARCH N19 66 C6
BARN SW13 * 138 C3
RCH/KEW TW9 136 E5
St John's Hl BTSEA SW11 140 D5
St John's Hill Gv BTSEA SW11 140 C5
St John's La FARR EC1M 6 A7
St Johns Pde SCUP DA14 * 168 C6
WEA W13 * 116 C1
St John's Pk BKHTH/KID SE3 145 K1
St John's Pl FARR EC1M 6 A7
St Johns Rd CRW RM5 56 E1
GNTH/NBYPK IG2 72 E4
NWMAL KT3 175 K6
STMC/STPC BR5 201 J3
St John's Rd BARK IG11 90 E6
BTSEA SW11 140 D5
CAN/RD E16 106 E5
CAR SM5 209 J1
CHING E4 37 K5
CROY/NA CR0 211 H1
E/WMO/HCT KT8 189 J1
EHAM E6 89 J6
ERITH DA8 130 A5
FELT TW13 154 D6
GLDGN NW11 64 D3
HRW HA1 61 F3
ISLW TW7 136 A3
KUT/HW KT1 174 D5
NWDGN UB2 114 D3
PGE/AN SE20 181 K3
RCH/KEW TW9 137 F5
SCUP DA14 168 C6
SEVS/STOTM N15 68 A3
SUT SM1 193 K6
WALTH E17 51 K5
WBLY HA9 79 K2
WELL DA16 148 C4
WIM/MER SW19 177 H3
St John's Sq FARR EC1M 6 A7
St John's Ter FSTGT E7 89 F4
NKENS W10 100 B3
WOOL/PLUM SE18 127 H6
St John St FSBYE EC1V 5 K3
St John's V BROCKY SE4 144 D3
St Johns Vls KENS W8 * 120 A3
St John's Vls ARCH N19 66 D6
KENS W8 * 120 A3
St John's Wy ARCH N19 66 D5
St John's Wood High St
STJWD NW8 2 B3
St John's Wood Pk
STJWD NW8 2 A1
St John's Wood Rd
STJWD NW8 2 A6
St John's Wood Ter
STJWD NW8 2 C2
St Josephs Cl NKENS W10 100 C4
ORP BR6 217 F2
St Joseph's Dr STHL UB1 114 D1
St Josephs Gv HDN NW4 63 K1
St Joseph's Rd ED N9 36 D2
St Joseph's St VX/NE SW8 * 141 G2
St Joseph's V BKHTH/KID SE3 145 G3
St Jude's Rd BETH E2 104 D1
St Jude St STNW/STAM N16 86 A3
St Julian's Cl
STRHM/NOR SW16 * 162 B6
St Julian's Farm Rd
WNWD SE27 162 B6
St Julian's Rd
KIL/WHAMP NW6 82 D5
St Justin Cl STMC/STPC BR5 186 E6
St Katharine's Prec
CAMTN NW1 * 3 J2
St Katharine's Wy WAP E1W 13 K7
St Katherines Rd
ERITHM DA18 128 E2
St Katherines Wk
NTGHL W11 * 100 B6
St Keverne Rd ELTH/MOT SE9 166 D6
St Kilda Rd ORP BR6 202 A5
WEA W13 116 B2
St Kilda's Rd HRW HA1 60 E3
STNW/STAM N16 67 K5
St Kitts Ter NRWD SE19 181 F1
St Laurence Cl
STMC/STPC BR5 186 E6
St Laurence's Cl
KIL/WHAMP NW6 82 B6
St Lawrence Cl EDGW HA8 44 B3
St Lawrence Cots
POP/IOD E14 * 125 F1
St Lawrence Dr PIN HA5 59 F2
St Lawrence St POP/IOD E14 125 F1
St Lawrence Ter NKENS W10 100 C4
St Lawrence Wy
BRXN/ST SW9 142 B3
St Leonards Av
KTN/HRWW/WS HA3 61 J2
St Leonard's Av CHING E4 52 B2
St Leonards Cl WELL DA16 148 B4
St Leonards Gdns IL IG1 90 C3
St Leonard's Gdns HEST TW5 134 D1
St Leonards Ri ORP BR6 216 E2
St Leonards Rd
MORT/ESHN SW14 137 K4
St Leonard's Rd
CROY/NA CR0 211 H1
ESH/CLAY KT10 205 F4
POP/IOD E14 106 A5
SURB KT6 190 E2
THDIT KT7 190 B3
WEA W13 97 J6
WLSDN NW10 99 F3
St Leonard's Sq KTTN NW5 84 A4
SURB KT6 190 E2
St Leonard's St BOW E3 105 K2
St Leonards Ter CHEL SW3 * 120 E5
St Leonard's Ter CHEL SW3 120 E5
St Leonard's Wk
STRHM/NOR SW16 180 A3
St Leonards Wy EMPK RM11 75 K5
St Loo Av CHEL SW3 120 D6
St Louis Rd WNWD SE27 162 D6
St Loy's Rd TOTM N17 50 A5
St Lucia Dr SRTFD E15 88 D6
St Luke's Av CLAP SW4 141 J5
ENC/FH EN2 23 K1
IL IG1 90 B3
St Luke's Cl SNWD SE25 197 J3
St Luke's Est FSBYE EC1V 6 E5
St Luke's Ms NTGHL W11 100 D5
St Luke's Rd NTGHL W11 100 D4
St Lukes's Cl FSBYE EC1V 6 D6
St Lukes Sq CAN/RD E16 106 D5
St Luke's St CHEL SW3 120 D5
St Lukes Yd MV/WKIL W9 * 100 D1
St Malo Av ED N9 36 E5
St Margarets BARK IG11 90 D6
KUTN/CMB KT2 * 175 K1
St Margarets Av ASHF TW15 152 E6
BFN/LL DA15 167 J5

TRDG/WHET N20 33 G3
St Margaret's Av CHEAM SM3 208 C1
RYLN/HDSTN HA2 78 C1
SEVS/STOTM N15 67 H1
St Margarets Cl ORP BR6 217 H2
St Margarets Ct
PUT/ROE SW15 * 138 E5
St Margaret's Crs
PUT/ROE SW15 * 138 E6
St Margaret's Dr TWK TW1 136 C6
St Margaret's Gv TWK TW1 156 B1
WAN E11 88 D1
WOOL/PLUM SE18 127 H6
St Margarets La KENS W8 * 120 A3
St Margarets Ms
KUTN/CMB KT2 * 175 K1
St Margarets Rd BECK BR3 198 A1
EDGW HA8 44 D1
RSLP HA4 58 B3
St Margaret's Rd BROCKY SE4 144 C5
HNWL W7 115 K2
MNPK E12 71 G6
TOTM N17 50 A6
TWK TW1 136 C5
WLSDN NW10 100 A2
St Margaret's Ter
WOOL/PLUM SE18 127 H5
St Margaret St WEST SW1P 16 E3
St Marks Cl FUL/PGN SW6 139 K2
St Mark's Cl BAR EN5 21 F4
St Mark's Crs CAMTN NW1 * 84 A6
St Marks Ga HOM E9 87 G5
St Mark's Gv WBPTN SW10 * 140 A1
St Mark's Hl SURB KT6 191 F3
St Marks Pl DAGE RM10 92 C4
St Mark's Pl NTGHL W11 100 C5
WIM/MER SW19 * 177 J2
St Mark's Ri HACK E8 86 B3
St Mark's Rd EA W5 117 F1
EN EN1 24 B6
HAYES BR2 184 A6
HNWL W7 115 K2
MTCM CR4 178 E5
NKENS W10 100 B5
NTGHL W11 100 C5
SNWD SE25 197 H1
TEDD TW11 174 C3
St Mark's Sq CAMTN NW1 3 G1
St Mark St WCHPL E1 13 K4
St Marks Vls FSBYPK N4 * 67 F6
St Martin-in-the-Fields
CHCR WC2N * 10 E6
St Martins NTHWD HA6 40 B1
St Martins Ap RSLP HA4 58 C4
St Martin's Av EHAM E6 107 H1
St Martins Cl ERITHM DA18 128 E2
OXHEY WD19 27 G6
St Martin's Cl CAMTN NW1 84 C6
EN EN1 24 D2
St Martins Ct CHCR WC2N 10 E5
St Martin's Ct
LSQ/SEVD WC2H * 10 E5
St Martin's La BECK BR3 198 E2
CHCR WC2N 10 E5
St Martin's le Grand
STBT EC1A 12 C3
St Martin's Pl CHCR WC2N 10 E6
St Martin's Rd BRXN/ST SW9 142 A3
DART DA1 171 J1
ED N9 36 D4
EFNCH N2 47 H4
St Martin's St
LSQ/SEVD WC2H * 10 D6
St Martin's Wy TOOT SW17 160 B5
St Mary Abbots Pl KENS W8 * 119 J3
St Mary Abbot's Pl KENS W8 119 J3
St Mary Abbots Ter
WKENS W14 * 119 J3
St Mary At Hl MON EC3R 13 G6
St Mary Av WLGTN SM6 210 A1
St Mary Axe HDTCH EC3A 13 G4
St Marychurch St
BERM/RHTH SE16 123 K2
St Mary Graces Ct
WCHPL E1 * 13 K6
St Mary Newington Cl
WALW SE17 * 123 F5
St Mary Rd WALTH E17 69 K1
St Marys BARK IG11 108 D1
St Mary's Ap MNPK E12 89 K3
St Marys Av NWDGN UB2 115 F4
St Mary's Av FNCH N3 46 C5
HAYES BR2 183 H6
NTHWD HA6 40 C1
STWL/WRAY TW19 152 A2
TEDD TW11 * 174 A2
WAN E11 71 F3
St Mary's Cl CHSGTN KT9 206 B5
EW KT17 207 H5
STMC/STPC BR5 186 C5
TOTM N17 * 50 C4
St Marys Ct HMSMTH W6 * 118 C3
St Mary's Crs HDN NW4 45 K6
HYS/HAR UB3 94 D6
ISLW TW7 135 J1
STWL/WRAY TW19 152 A2
St Mary's Dr
EBED/NFELT TW14 153 F2
St Marys Est
BERM/RHTH SE16 * 123 K2
St Mary's Gdns LBTH SE11 17 K6
St Marys Ga KENS W8 * 120 A3
St Mary's Ga KENS W8 120 A3
St Mary's Gn EFNCH N2 47 G6
St Mary's Gv BARN SW13 138 E4
CHSWK W4 117 J6
IS N1 85 H4
RCH/KEW TW9 137 G5
St Mary's Man BAY/PAD W2 101 G4
St Mary's Ms
KIL/WHAMP NW6 * 83 F5
St Mary's Pth IS N1 85 H6
WCHPL E1 * 104 C5
St Marys Pl KENS W8 * 120 A3
St Mary's Pl EA W5 116 E2
KENS W8 * 120 A3
St Marys Rd IL IG1 72 C6
St Mary's Rd BXLY DA5 169 K3
CEND/HSY/T N8 66 E1
E/WMO/HCT KT8 189 J2
EA W5 116 E2
EBAR EN4 33 K2
ED N9 36 E3
GLDGN NW11 64 C4
HYS/HAR UB3 94 D6
LEY E10 88 A1
PECK SE15 143 K2
PLSTW E13 107 F1
SNWD SE25 181 F6
SURB KT6 190 D4
WIM/MER SW19 177 H1
WLSDN NW10 81 G6
WPK KT4 192 B6
St Mary's Sq BAY/PAD W2 8 A1
EA W5 * 116 E2
St Marys Ter BORE WD6 * 29 K1
St Mary's Ter BAY/PAD W2 8 A1
St Mary St WOOL/PLUM SE18 126 E4
St Marys Vw
KTN/HRWW/WS HA3 61 J2
St Mary's Wk HYS/HAR UB3 94 D6
LBTH SE11 17 K6
St Marys Wy CHIG IG7 54 A1
St Matthew's Av SURB KT6 191 F5
St Matthews Cl OXHEY WD19 27 H1
St Matthew's Cl RAIN RM13 93 J5
St Matthews Ct SRTFD E15 88 D5
St Matthews Dr BMLY BR1 184 E6
St Matthew's Rd
BRXS/STRHM SW2 142 A6
EA W5 117 F1
St Matthew's Rw BETH E2 104 C2
St Matthew St WEST SW1P 16 C4
St Matthias Cl
CDALE/KGS NW9 63 H2
St Maur Rd FUL/PGN SW6 139 J2
St Meddens CHST BR7 * 185 J3
St Mellion Cl THMD SE28 109 K5
St Merryn Cl
WOOL/PLUM SE18 147 J1
St Michael's Aly BANK EC3V 13 F4
St Michaels Av ED N9 36 E2
St Michael's Av WBLY HA9 80 C4
St Michaels Cl BMLY BR1 184 D6
CAN/RD E16 107 H4
WPK KT4 192 C6
St Michael's Cl ERITHM DA18 * 128 E2
FNCH N3 46 D5
NFNCH/WDSPK N12 47 J1
WOT/HER KT12 188 B6
St Michaels Ct GLDGN NW11 * 64 D4
St Michael's Crs PIN HA5 59 J3
St Michael's Gdns NKENS W10 100 C4
St Michael's Ms BGVA SW1W 15 G7
St Michaels Ri WELL DA16 * 148 C2
St Michael's Rd BRXN/ST SW9 142 A3
CRICK NW2 82 A2
CROY/NA CR0 196 D5
WELL DA16 148 C4
WLGTN SM6 210 C4
St Michael's St BAY/PAD W2 8 B3
St Michaels Ter HGT N6 * 66 A5
St Michael's Ter WDGN N22 48 E4
St Mildred's Ct LOTH EC2R * 12 E4
St Mildreds Rd CAT SE6 165 H2
St Nicholas Av HCH RM12 93 J1
St Nicholas Cl BORE WD6 29 K1
St Nicholas Glebe TOOT SW17 179 F2
St Nicholas Rd SUT SM1 209 F3
THDIT KT7 190 A3
WOOL/PLUM SE18 128 A5
St Nicholas St DEPT SE8 144 C2
St Nicholas Wy SUT SM1 209 F2
St Nicolas La CHST BR7 184 D4
St Ninian's Ct
TRDG/WHET N20 33 K5
St Norbert Rd BROCKY SE4 144 B5
St Olaf's Rd FUL/PGN SW6 139 H1
St Olave's Rd EHAM E6 90 A6
St Olave's Wk
STRHM/NOR SW16 179 H5
St Onge Pde EN EN1 * 23 K4
St Oswalds Pl LBTH SE11 * 122 A5
St Oswald's Pl LBTH SE11 122 A5
St Oswald's Rd
STRHM/NOR SW16 180 C4
St Oswulf St WEST SW1P * 16 D7
St Pancras Gdns
CAMTN NW1 * 4 C2
KCROSS N1C * 4 D1
St Pancras Station Forecourt
KCROSS N1C * 4 E4
St Pancras Wy CAMTN NW1 84 C5
St Paul's Av
BERM/RHTH SE16 * 124 A1
CRICK NW2 81 K4
KTN/HRWW/WS HA3 62 B2
St Paul's Church Yd STP EC4M 12 B4
St Pauls Cl EA W5 117 G2
HYS/HAR UB3 113 G5
St Paul's Cl CAR SM5 194 D4
CHARL SE7 126 C5
CHSGTN KT9 205 K2
EA W5 117 G2
HSLW TW3 134 D3
St Paul's Cray Rd CHST BR7 185 J4
St Pauls Crs CAMTN NW1 84 D4
HDN NW4 * 64 A1
St Paul's Dr SRTFD E15 88 B3
St Pauls Ms CAMTN NW1 84 D5
St Paul's Pl IS N1 85 K4
St Pauls Ri PLMGR N13 49 H2
St Pauls Rd BARK IG11 90 C6
RCH/KEW TW9 137 G4
St Paul's Rd BTFD TW8 116 E6
ERITH DA8 149 K1
IS N1 85 H4
THHTH CR7 180 D6
TOTM N17 50 C3
St Pauls Ter WALW SE17 * 122 C6
St Paul St IS N1 6 C1
St Paul's Wy FNCH N3 47 F3
POP/IOD E14 105 H4
St Paul's Wood Hl
STMC/STPC BR5 185 K5
St Peter's Av BETH E2 104 C1
UED N18 36 C6
WALTH E17 70 C1
St Petersburgh Ms
BAY/PAD W2 * 101 F6
St Petersburgh Pl
BAY/PAD W2 101 F6
St Peters Cl CHST BR7 185 J3
GNTH/NBYPK IG2 72 E1
TOOT SW17 160 D4
St Peter's Cl BETH E2 104 C1
BUSH WD23 28 D3
RSLP HA4 59 H6
St Peters Ct BKHTH/KID SE3 * 145 J6
E/WMO/HCT KT8 189 F1
St Peter's Ct HDN NW4 64 A2
St Peter's Gdns WNWD SE27 162 B5
St Peter's Gv HMSMTH W6 118 D4
St Peters La STMC/STPC BR5 186 B5
St Peters Ms FSBYPK N4 * 67 H2
St Peters Pl MV/WKIL W9 101 F3
St Peters Rd KUT/HW KT1 175 H5
St Peter's Rd CROY/NA CR0 211 K2
E/WMO/HCT KT8 189 F1
ED N9 36 D3
HMSMTH W6 * 118 D5
STHL UB1 96 A4
TWK TW1 136 C6
St Peter's Sq BETH E2 * 104 C1
HMSMTH W6 118 D4
St Peter's St IS N1 6 B1
SAND/SEL CR2 211 K3
St Peter's Ter FUL/PGN SW6 139 H1
St Peter's Vls HMSMTH W6 118 D4
St Peters Wy HYS/HAR UB3 113 G5
St Peter's Wy EA W5 97 K4
IS N1 * 86 A5
St Philip's Av WPK KT4 192 E6
St Philip Sq VX/NE SW8 * 141 G3
St Philip's Rd HACK E8 86 C4
SURB KT6 190 E3
St Philip St VX/NE SW8 141 G3
St Philip's Wy IS N1 85 J6
St Quentin Rd WELL DA16 148 A4
St Quintin Av NKENS W10 100 A4
St Quintin Gdns NKENS W10 100 A4
St Quintin Rd PLSTW E13 107 F2
St Raphael's Wy
WLSDN NW10 80 E3
St Regis Cl MUSWH N10 48 B5
St Ronans Cl EBAR EN4 21 H1
St Ronans Crs WFD IG8 52 E3
St Rowans Vw DART DA1 171 J2
St Rule St VX/NE SW8 141 H3
St Saviours Ct WDGN N22 48 D5
St Saviour's Est STHWK SE1 19 J4
St Saviour's Rd
BRXS/STRHM SW2 142 A6
CROY/NA CR0 196 D3
Saints Cl WNWD SE27 162 C6
Saints Dr FSTGT E7 89 H3
St Silas Pl KTTN NW5 84 A4
St Simon's Av PUT/ROE SW15 139 F6
St Stephen's Av SHB W12 118 E1
WALTH E17 70 A2
WEA W13 97 H5
St Stephens Cl KTTN NW5 * 83 K3
STJWD NW8 2 C1
St Stephen's Cl STHL UB1 96 A4
WALTH E17 69 K2
St Stephen's Crs BAY/PAD W2 100 E5
THHTH CR7 180 B6
St Stephen's Gdns
BAY/PAD W2 100 E5
TWK TW1 156 D1
St Stephen's Gv LEW SE13 145 F4
St Stephen's Ms BAY/PAD W2 100 E4
St Stephens Pde WHALL SW1A 16 E2
St Stephens Rd BAR EN5 20 B6
St Stephen's Rd BOW E3 87 G6
EHAM E6 89 G5
HSLW TW3 155 F1
WALTH E17 69 K2
WDR/YW UB7 112 A1
WEA W13 97 H5
St Stephens Ter VX/NE SW8 * 141 K1
St Stephen's Ter VX/NE SW8 142 A1
St Stephen's Wk SKENS SW7 * 120 B4
St Swithin's La MANHO EC4N 12 E5
St Swithun's Rd LEW SE13 * 145 G6
St Theresas Cl HOM E9 87 J2
St Theresa's Rd
EBED/NFELT TW14 133 J5
St Thomas Cl SURB KT6 191 G5
St Thomas Ct BXLY DA5 169 H2
St Thomas Dr
STMC/STPC BR5 201 H5
St Thomas' Dr PIN HA5 41 J4
STMC/STPC BR5 201 H5
St Thomas Gdns IL IG1 90 C4
St Thomas Rd BELV DA17 129 K2
CAN/RD E16 106 E5
STHGT/OAK N14 34 D2
St Thomas' Rd CHSWK W4 137 K1
St Thomas's Gdns KTTN NW5 84 A4
St Thomas's Pl HOM E9 * 86 E5
St Thomas's Rd FSBYPK N4 67 G6
WLSDN NW10 81 G6
St Thomas's Sq HOM E9 86 D5
St Thomas St STHWK SE1 19 F1
St Thomas's Wy
FUL/PGN SW6 139 J1
St Ursula Gv PIN HA5 59 H2
St Ursula Rd STHL UB1 96 A5
St Vincent Cl WNWD SE27 180 C1
St Vincent Rd WHTN TW2 155 H1
St Vincents Av DART DA1 151 K6
St Vincents La MLHL NW7 31 K6
St Vincents Rd DART DA1 171 K1
St Vincent St MHST W1U 9 H2
St Wilfrid's Cl EBAR EN4 * 21 J6
St Wilfrid's Rd EBAR EN4 21 H6
St Winefride's Av MNPK E12 89 K3
St Winifred's Cl CHIG IG7 54 C1
St Winifred's Rd TEDD TW11 174 C2
Sakura Dr WDGN N22 48 D4
Saladin Dr PUR RM19 131 K4
Salamanca Pl STHWK SE1 17 G7
Salamanca St STHWK SE1 17 G7
Salamander Cl
KUTN/CMB KT2 174 D1
Salamander Quay
KUT/HW KT1 * 174 E4
Salamons Wy RAIN RM13 111 G4
Salcombe Dr CHDH RM6 74 B3
MRDN SM4 193 G5
Salcombe Gdns MLHL NW7 46 A2
Salcombe Rd ASHF TW15 152 B6
STNW/STAM N16 86 B3
WALTH E17 69 H4
Salcombe Wy RSLP HA4 58 E6
Salcott Rd BTSEA SW11 140 D6
CROY/NA CR0 210 E1
Salehurst Cl
KTN/HRWW/WS HA3 62 A2
Salehurst Rd BROCKY SE4 164 C1
Salem Pl CROY/NA CR0 211 J1
Sale Pl BAY/PAD W2 8 C2
Sale St BETH E2 104 C3
Salford Rd BRXS/STRHM SW2 161 J3
Salhouse Cl THMD SE28 109 J5
Salisbury Av BARK IG11 90 D5
FNCH N3 46 D5
SUT SM1 208 D4
Salisbury Cl WALW SE17 18 E6
WPK KT4 207 H1
Salisbury Ct EMB EC4Y 11 K4
Salisbury Gdns
WIM/MER SW19 * 177 H3
Salisbury Pavement
FUL/PGN SW6 * 139 K1
Salisbury Pl BRXN/ST SW9 142 C1
MBLAR W1H 8 E1
Salisbury Prom
CEND/HSY/T N8 * 67 H2
Salisbury Rd BAR EN5 20 C4
BXLY DA5 169 H3
CAR SM5 209 K4
CHING E4 37 J5
DAGE RM10 92 D4
FELT TW13 154 B3
FSBYPK N4 67 H2
FSTGT E7 88 E4
GDMY/SEVK IG3 72 E6
GPK RM2 75 K2
HAYES BR2 200 D2
HRW HA1 60 D2
HSLWW TW4 134 B4
LEY E10 70 A6
MNPK E12 89 H3
NWDGN UB2 * 114 D4
NWMAL KT3 176 A6
PIN HA5 58 E1
RCH/KEW TW9 137 F5
SNWD SE25 197 H3
WALTH E17 70 A2
WDGN N22 49 H5
WEA W13 116 C2
WIM/MER SW19 177 H3
WPK KT4 207 F2
Salisbury Sq EMB EC4Y * 11 K4
Salisbury St ACT W3 117 K2
STJWD NW8 2 B7
Salisbury Ter PECK SE15 143 K4
Salisbury Wk ARCH N19 66 C6
Salix Cl SUN TW16 172 A3
Salix La WFD IG8 53 J4
Sally Murray Cl MNPK E12 90 A2
Salmen Rd PLSTW E13 106 D1
Salmond Cl STAN HA7 43 G2
Salmon La POP/IOD E14 105 G5
Salmon Ms
KIL/WHAMP NW6 * 82 E3
Salmon Rd BELV DA17 129 H5
DART DA1 151 J4
Salmons Rd CHSGTN KT9 206 A4
ED N9 36 C3
Salmon St CDALE/KGS NW9 62 D5
POP/IOD E14 * 105 H5
Salomons Rd PLSTW E13 107 G4
Salop Rd WALTH E17 69 F3
Saltash Cl SUT SM1 208 D2
Saltash Rd BARK/HLT IG6 54 D3
WELL DA16 148 D2
Saltcoats Rd CHSWK W4 118 B2
Saltcote Cl DART DA1 170 B1
Saltcroft Cl WBLY HA9 62 D5
Salter Cl RYLN/HDSTN HA2 77 K1
Salterford Rd TOOT SW17 179 F2
Salter Rd BERM/RHTH SE16 124 A1
Salters' Hall Ct
MANHO EC4N * 12 E5
Salter's Hl NRWD SE19 180 E1
Salters Rd NKENS W10 100 B3
WALTH E17 70 B1
Salters Rw IS N1 * 85 K4
Salter St POP/IOD E14 105 J6
WLSDN NW10 99 J2
Salterton Rd HOLWY N7 84 E1
Saltford Cl ERITH DA8 130 B5
Saltley Cl EHAM E6 107 J5
Saltoun Rd BRXS/STRHM SW2 142 B5
Saltram Cl SEVS/STOTM N15 68 B1
Saltwell St POP/IOD E14 105 J6
Saltwood Cl ORP BR6 217 J2
Saltwood Gv WALW SE17 * 122 E5
Salusbury Rd
KIL/WHAMP NW6 100 D1
Salvador TOOT SW17 178 D1
Salvia Gdns GFD/PVL UB6 97 G1
Salvin Rd PUT/ROE SW15 139 G4
Salway Cl WFD IG8 52 E3
Salway Rd SRTFD E15 88 B4
Samantha Cl WALTH E17 69 H4
Sam Bartram Cl CHARL SE7 126 B5
Sambruck Ms CAT SE6 164 E3
Samels Ct HMSMTH W6 118 D5
Samford St STJWD NW8 2 C7
Samira Cl WALTH E17 69 H3
Samos Rd PGE/AN SE20 181 J5
Sampson Av BAR EN5 20 B6
Sampson Cl BELV DA17 128 E3
Sampson St WAP E1W * 123 H1
Samson St PLSTW E13 107 G1
Samuel Cl HACK E8 86 B6
NWCR SE14 124 A6
STAN HA7 29 G4
WOOL/PLUM SE18 126 D4
Samuel Gray Gdns
KUTN/CMB KT2 174 E4
Samuel Lewis Trust Dwellings
CHEL SW3 * 120 D5
CMBW SE5 * 142 D2
WKENS W14 * 119 H4
Samuel St WOOL/PLUM SE18 126 E4
Sancroft Cl CRICK NW2 81 K1
Sancroft Rd
KTN/HRWW/WS HA3 43 F5
Sancroft St LBTH SE11 122 B5
Sanctuary Cl DART DA1 171 F1
Sanctuary Ms HACK E8 86 B4
Sanctuary Rd HTHAIR TW6 152 D1
Sanctuary St STHWK SE1 18 D3
The Sanctuary BXLY DA5 168 E1
WEST SW1P 16 D4
Sandall Cl EA W5 98 A3
Sandall Rd EA W5 98 A3
KTTN NW5 84 C4
Sandal Rd NWMAL KT3 192 B1
UED N18 50 C1
Sandal St SRTFD E15 88 C6
Sandalwood Cl WCHPL E1 105 G3
Sandalwood Dr RSLP HA4 58 A4
Sandalwood Rd FELT TW13 154 A5
Sandbach Pl
WOOL/PLUM SE18 127 H4
Sandbourne Av
WIM/MER SW19 178 A6
Sandbourne Rd NWCR SE14 144 B3
Sandbrook Cl MLHL NW7 45 F2
Sandbrook Rd
STNW/STAM N16 86 A1
Sandby Gn ELTH/MOT SE9 146 D4
Sandcliff Rd ERITH DA8 130 A4
Sandcroft Cl PLMGR N13 49 H2
Sandell's Av ASHF TW15 153 F6
Sandell St STHWK SE1 17 J2
Sanders Cl HPTN TW12 173 H1
Sanders La MLHL NW7 46 A3
Sanderson Cl KTTN NW5 * 84 B2
Sanders Pde
STRHM/NOR SW16 * 179 K2
Sanderstead Av GLDGN NW11 64 C6
Sanderstead Cl BAL SW12 161 H2
Sanderstead Rd LEY E10 69 G5
SAND/SEL CR2 211 K5
STMC/STPC BR5 202 C3
Sandfield Gdns THHTH CR7 180 C6
Sandfield Pl THHTH CR7 180 D6
Sandfield Rd THHTH CR7 180 C6
Sandford Av WDGN N22 49 H4
Sandford Rd BXLYHS DA6 149 F5
EHAM E6 107 K2
HAYES BR2 199 K1
Sandford Rw WALW SE17 122 E5
Sandford St FUL/PGN SW6 140 A1
Sandgate Cl ROMW/RG RM7 74 E4
Sandgate La
WAND/EARL SW18 160 D3
Sandgate Rd WELL DA16 148 D1
Sandgate St PECK SE15 123 J6
Sandhills WLGTN SM6 210 D2
The Sandhills WBPTN SW10 * 120 B6
Sandhurst Av BRYLDS KT5 191 J4
RYLN/HDSTN HA2 60 B3
Sandhurst Cl SAND/SEL CR2 212 A6
Sandhurst Dr GDMY/SEVK IG3 91 F2
Sandhurst Market CAT SE6 * 165 F3
Sandhurst Pde CAT SE6 * 165 F3
Sandhurst Rd BFN/LL DA15 168 A5
BXLY DA5 148 E6
CAT SE6 165 G3
CDALE/KGS NW9 44 C6
ED N9 36 E1
ORP BR6 217 G1
Sandhurst Wy SAND/SEL CR2 212 A5
Sandifer Dr CRICK NW2 82 B1
Sandiford Rd CHEAM SM3 193 J6
Sandiland Crs HAYES BR2 199 J6
Sandilands CROY/NA CR0 212 C1
Sandilands Rd FUL/PGN SW6 140 A2
Sandison St PECK SE15 143 G4
Sandland St GINN WC1R 11 H2
Sandling Ri ELTH/MOT SE9 167 F5
Sandlings Cl PECK SE15 143 J3
The Sandlings WDGN N22 49 G5
Sandmartin Wy WLGTN SM6 195 F5
Sandmere Rd CLAP SW4 141 K5
Sandon Cl ESH/CLAY KT10 189 J4
Sandow Crs HYS/HAR UB3 113 J3
Sandown Av DAGE RM10 92 E4
ESH/CLAY KT10 204 C3
Sandown Cl HEST TW5 133 K2
Sandown Ct BELMT SM2 * 209 F5
SYD SE26 * 163 J5
Sandown Dr CAR SM5 210 A6
Sandown Ga ESH/CLAY KT10 189 J6
Sandown Rd ESH/CLAY KT10 204 C2
SNWD SE25 197 J2
Sandown Wy NTHLT UB5 77 J4
Sandpiper Cl
BERM/RHTH SE16 124 C2
WALTH E17 51 F3
Sandpiper Dr ERITH DA8 150 E1
Sandpiper Rd SUT SM1 208 D3
Sandpiper Ter CLAY IG5 * 54 B6
Sandpiper Wy
STMC/STPC BR5 202 E1
Sandpit Pl CHARL SE7 126 D5
Sandpit Rd BMLY BR1 183 H1
DART DA1 151 F5
Sandpits Rd CROY/NA CR0 213 F2
RCHPK/HAM TW10 156 E3
Sandra Cl HSLW TW3 135 G6
WDGN N22 49 J4
Sandridge Cl HRW HA1 60 E1
Sandridge St ARCH N19 66 C6
Sandringham Av
RYNPK SW20 177 H4
Sandringham Cl EN EN1 24 A3
WIM/MER SW19 159 G3
Sandringham Crs
RYLN/HDSTN HA2 78 A1
Sandringham Dr ASHF TW15 152 A6
RDART DA2 170 B4
WELL DA16 147 K3
Sandringham Gdns
BARK/HLT IG6 54 C6
CEND/HSY/T N8 66 E3
E/WMO/HCT KT8 189 F1
HEST TW5 133 K2
NFNCH/WDSPK N12 47 H2
Sandringham Ms EA W5 97 K6
HPTN TW12 172 E4
Sandringham Rd BARK IG11 91 F4

BMLY BR1 183 K1
CRICK NW2 81 K3
FSTGT E7 89 G3
GLDGN NW11 64 C4
HACK E8 86 B3
HTHAIR TW6 132 B6
LEY E10 70 B4
NTHLT UB5 78 A5
THHTH CR7 196 D2
WDGN N22 49 J6
WPK KT4 207 J1
Sandrock Pl CROY/NA CR0 213 F2
Sandrock Rd LEW SE13 144 D4
Sands End La FUL/PGN SW6 140 A2
Sandstone La CAN/RD E16 107 F6
Sandstone Pl ARCH N19 66 B6
Sandstone Rd LEE/GVPK SE12 166 A4
Sands Wy WFD IG8 53 K2
Sandtoft Rd CHARL SE7 126 A6
Sandway Rd STMC/STPC BR5 202 D1
Sandwell Crs
KIL/WHAMP NW6 82 E4
Sandwich St STPAN WC1H 4 E5
Sandwick Cl MLHL NW7 45 J3
Sandy Bury ORP BR6 216 D1
Sandycombe Rd
EBED/NFELT TW14 153 K3
RCH/KEW TW9 137 H3
Sandycoombe Rd TWK TW1 156 D1
Sandycroft ABYW SE2 128 B6
Sandy Dr EBED/NFELT TW14 153 H3
Sandy Hill Av
WOOL/PLUM SE18 127 G5
Sandy Hill La
WOOL/PLUM SE18 127 G4
Sandyhill Rd IL IG1 90 B2
Sandy Hill Rd WLGTN SM6 210 C6
WOOL/PLUM SE18 127 G5
Sandy La BELMT SM2 208 C6
KTN/HRWW/WS HA3 62 B3
KUT/HW KT1 174 C4
MTCM CR4 179 F4
NTHWD HA6 40 E1
ORP BR6 202 B4
RCHPK/HAM TW10 156 D4
SCUP DA14 186 E3
STMC/STPC BR5 186 E5
TEDD TW11 174 B3
WOT/HER KT12 188 A3
Sandy La North WLGTN SM6 210 D3
Sandy La South WLGTN SM6 210 C6
Sandy Ldg PIN HA5 * 42 A2
Sandy Lodge Ct NTHWD HA6 * 40 C1
Sandy Lodge La NTHWD HA6 26 B4
Sandy Lodge Wy NTHWD HA6 40 C1
Sandy Md HOR/WEW KT19 206 C6
Sandymount Av STAN HA7 43 J1
Sandy Rdg CHST BR7 185 F2
Sandy's Rw WCHPL E1 13 H2
Sandy Wy CROY/NA CR0 213 H1
Sanford La STNW/STAM N16 68 B6
Sanford St NWCR SE14 124 B6
Sanford Ter STNW/STAM N16 86 B1
Sanger Av CHSGTN KT9 206 B3
Sangley Rd CAT SE6 164 E2
SNWD SE25 197 F1
Sangora Rd BTSEA SW11 140 C5
Sansom Rd WAN E11 * 70 D6
Sansom St CMBW SE5 142 E1
Sans Wk CLKNW EC1R 6 A6
Santley St CLAP SW4 141 K5
Santos Rd WAND/EARL SW18 139 K6
Saperton Wk LBTH SE11 17 H6
Saphora Cl ORP BR6 216 D3
Sapphire Cl BCTR RM8 73 J5
Sapphire Rd DEPT SE8 124 B4
WLSDN NW10 80 E5
Saracen Cl CROY/NA CR0 196 E3
Saracen's Head Yd
FENCHST EC3M 13 H4
Saracen St POP/IOD E14 105 J5
Saratoga Rd CLPT E5 86 E2
Sardinia St HOL/ALD WC2B 11 G4
Sarita Cl KTN/HRWW/WS HA3 42 D5
Sark Cl HEST TW5 135 F1
Sarnesfield Rd ENC/FH EN2 * 23 K3
Sarre Rd CRICK NW2 82 D3
STMC/STPC BR5 202 D2
Sarsen Av HSLW TW3 134 E3
Sarsfeld Rd BAL SW12 160 E3
Sarsfield Rd GFD/PVL UB6 97 H1
Sartor Rd PECK SE15 144 A5
Sarum Ter BOW E3 * 105 H3
Satanita Cl CAN/RD E16 107 H5
Satchell Md CDALE/KGS NW9 45 H4
Satchwell Rd BETH E2 104 C2
Sattar Ms STNW/STAM N16 * 85 K1
Sauls Gn WAN E11 88 C1
Saunders Cl IL IG1 72 D5
POP/IOD E14 * 105 H6
Saunders Ness Rd
POP/IOD E14 125 G4
Saunders Rd
WOOL/PLUM SE18 128 A5
Saunders St LBTH SE11 17 J6
Saunders Wy DART DA1 171 J4
THMD SE28 109 H6
Saunderton Rd ALP/SUD HA0 79 H3
Saunton Av HYS/HAR UB3 133 J1
Saunton Rd HCH RM12 75 J6
Savage Gdns EHAM E6 107 K5
TWRH EC3N 13 H5
Savanah Cl PECK SE15 143 G1
Savera Cl NWDGN UB2 114 B3
Savernake Ct STAN HA7 * 43 J2
Savernake Rd ED N9 36 C1
HAMP NW3 83 K2
Savery Dr SURB KT6 190 C4
Savile Cl NWMAL KT3 192 B2
THDIT KT7 190 A5
Savile Gdns CROY/NA CR0 197 G6
Savile Rw CONDST W1S 10 A5
Saville Rd CAN/RD E16 126 D1
CHDH RM6 74 B3
CHSWK W4 118 A3
TWK TW1 156 A3
Saville Rw HAYES BR2 199 J5
Savill Gdns RYNPK SW20 176 D6
Savill Rw WFD IG8 52 D2
Savona Cl WIM/MER SW19 177 G3
Savona St VX/NE SW8 141 H1
Savoy Av HYS/HAR UB3 113 H5
Savoy Cl EDGW HA8 44 C1
SRTFD E15 88 C6
Savoy Ct TPL/STR WC2R * 11 F6
Savoy Hl TPL/STR WC2R 11 G6
Savoy Ms BRXN/ST SW9 141 K4
Savoy Pde EN EN1 * 24 A4
Savoy Pl CHCR WC2N 11 F6
Savoy Rd DART DA1 151 F6
Savoy Rw TPL/STR WC2R 11 G5
Savoy Steps TPL/STR WC2R * 11 G6
Savoy St TPL/STR WC2R 11 G5
Savoy Wy TPL/STR WC2R 11 G6
Sawbill Cl YEAD UB4 95 H4
Sawkins Cl WIM/MER SW19 159 G4
Sawley Rd SHB W12 118 D1
Saw Mill Wy STNW/STAM N16 68 C3
Sawtry Cl CAR SM5 194 C4
Sawyer Cl ED N9 36 C4
Sawyers Cl DAGE RM10 92 E4
Sawyer's Hl
MORT/ESHN SW14 157 K2
RCHPK/HAM TW10 157 G2
Sawyers Lawn WEA W13 97 G5
Sawyer St STHWK SE1 18 C2
Saxby Rd BRXS/STRHM SW2 161 K2
Saxham Rd BARK IG11 90 E6
Saxlingham Rd CHING E4 38 B5
Saxon Av FELT TW13 154 D4
Saxonbury Av SUN TW16 172 A6
Saxonbury Cl MTCM CR4 178 C6
Saxonbury Gdns SURB KT6 190 D5
Saxon Cha CEND/HSY/T N8 67 F4
Saxon Cl SURB KT6 190 E3
WALTH E17 69 J4
Saxon Dr ACT W3 98 D5
Saxonfield Cl
BRXS/STRHM SW2 162 A2
Saxon Rd BMLY BR1 183 J3
BOW E3 105 H1
EHAM E6 107 K3
IL IG1 90 B4
KUTN/CMB KT2 175 F4
RDART DA2 171 H6
SNWD SE25 196 E2
STHL UB1 95 J6
WBLY HA9 80 E1
WDGN N22 49 H4
Saxon Wy STHGT/OAK N14 34 D1
Saxony Pde HYS/HAR UB3 94 A4
Saxton Cl LEW SE13 145 G4
Saxville Rd STMC/STPC BR5 186 C6
Sayesbury La UED N18 50 C1
Sayes Court Rd
STMC/STPC BR5 186 B6
Sayes Court St DEPT SE8 124 C5
Scadbury Gdns
STMC/STPC BR5 186 B5
Scads Hill Cl ORP BR6 202 A3
Scala St FITZ W1T 10 B1
Scales Rd TOTM N17 50 B6
Scammell Wy WATW WD18 26 D1
Scampton Rd
STWL/WRAY TW19 152 C1
Scandrett St WAP E1W * 123 J1
Scarba Wk IS N1 85 K4
Scarborough Rd ED N9 36 E2
FSBYPK N4 67 G4
HTHAIR TW6 153 F1
WAN E11 70 B5
Scarborough St WCHPL E1 13 K4
Scarbrook Rd CROY/NA CR0 211 J1
Scarle Rd ALP/SUD HA0 79 K4
Scarlet Cl STMC/STPC BR5 202 C1
Scarlet Rd CAT SE6 165 H5
Scarsbrook Rd
BKHTH/KID SE3 146 C4
Scarsdale Pl KENS W8 120 A3
Scarsdale Rd
RYLN/HDSTN HA2 78 C1
Scarsdale Vls KENS W8 119 K3
Scarth Rd BARN SW13 138 C4
Scawen Cl CAR SM5 210 A2
Scawen Rd DEPT SE8 124 B5
Scawfell St BETH E2 7 K3
Scaynes Link
NFNCH/WDSPK N12 32 E6
Sceptre Rd BETH E2 104 E2
Scholars Cl BAR EN5 20 C5
Scholars Rd BAL SW12 161 H3
CHING E4 38 A3
Scholars Wy GPK RM2 75 K2
Scholefield Rd ARCH N19 66 D6
Schonfeld Sq
STNW/STAM N16 67 K6
Schoolbank Rd GNWCH SE10 125 J4
School Crs DART DA1 150 C5
Schoolgate Dr MRDN SM4 194 A2
School House La TEDD TW11 174 C3
Schoolhouse La WAP E1W * 105 F6
School La BUSH WD23 28 B3
KUT/HW KT1 174 D4
PIN HA5 * 59 J1
SURB KT6 191 G5
School Pas KUT/HW KT1 175 G5
STHL UB1 114 E1
School Rd CHST BR7 185 H4
DAGE RM10 92 C6
E/WMO/HCT KT8 189 J1
HPTN TW12 173 H2
HSLW TW3 135 H4
KUT/HW KT1 * 174 D4
MNPK E12 89 K2
WDR/YW UB7 112 A6
WLSDN NW10 99 F3
School Road Av HPTN TW12 173 H2
School Sq GNWCH SE10 125 J3
School Wy BCTR RM8 91 H1
Schoolway
NFNCH/WDSPK N12 47 H2
Schooner Cl BARK IG11 109 H2
BERM/RHTH SE16 124 A2
POP/IOD E14 125 G3
Schubert Rd BORE WD6 29 K1
PUT/ROE SW15 139 J6
Sclater St WCHPL E1 7 J6
Scoble Pl STNW/STAM N16 86 B2
Scoles Crs BRXS/STRHM SW2 162 B3
Scope Wy KUT/HW KT1 191 F1
Scoresby St STHWK SE1 18 A1
Scorton Av GFD/PVL UB6 97 G1
Scotch Common WEA W13 97 G4
Scoter Cl WFD IG8 53 F3
Scot Gv PIN HA5 41 H3
Scotia Rd BRXS/STRHM SW2 162 B2
Scotland Gn TOTM N17 50 B5
Scotland Green Rd PEND EN3 25 F6
Scotland Green Rd North
PEND EN3 25 F5
Scotland Rd BKHH IG9 39 G3
Scotney Cl ORP BR6 216 A2
Scots Cl STWL/WRAY TW19 152 A3
Scotsdale Cl CHEAM SM3 208 C5
STMC/STPC BR5 201 K1
Scotsdale Rd LEE/GVPK SE12 146 A6
Scotswood St CLKNW EC1R * 5 K6
Scotswood Wk TOTM N17 * 50 D3
Scott Av PUT/ROE SW15 159 H1
Scott Cl HOR/WEW KT19 206 E3
STRHM/NOR SW16 180 A4
WDR/YW UB7 112 C4
Scott Crs ERITH DA8 150 C2
RYLN/HDSTN HA2 60 B5
Scott Ellis Gdns STJWD NW8 2 A5
Scottes La BCTR RM8 73 K5
Scott Farm Cl THDIT KT7 190 C5
Scott Gdns HEST TW5 134 C1
Scott Lidgett Crs
BERM/RHTH SE16 123 H2
Scott Rd EDGW HA8 44 D5
Scotts Av HAYES BR2 183 G5
Scotts Dr HPTN TW12 173 G3
Scotts Farm Rd
HOR/WEW KT19 206 E4
Scott's La HAYES BR2 183 G6
Scotts Pas
WOOL/PLUM SE18 * 127 G4
Scotts Rd BMLY BR1 183 K3
NWDGN UB2 114 B3
Scott's Rd LEY E10 70 A5
SHB W12 118 E2
Scott St WCHPL E1 104 D3
Scott's Yd MANHO EC4N 12 E5
Scott Trimmer Wy HSLW TW3 134 D3
Scottwell Dr CDALE/KGS NW9 63 H2
Scoulding Rd CAN/RD E16 106 D5
Scouler St POP/IOD E14 106 B6
Scout Wy MLHL NW7 31 F6
Scovell Crs STHWK SE1 * 18 C3
Scovell Rd STHWK SE1 18 C3
Scrattons Ter BARK IG11 109 K1
Scriven St HACK E8 86 B6
Scrooby St CAT SE6 164 E1
Scrubs La WLSDN NW10 99 J2
Scrutton Cl BAL SW12 161 J2
Scrutton St SDTCH EC2A 7 G7
Scutari Rd EDUL SE22 143 J6
Scylla Crs HTHAIR TW6 152 E2
Scylla Rd HTHAIR TW6 152 E1
PECK SE15 143 J4
Seabright St BETH E2 104 D2
Seabrook Dr WWKM BR4 199 H6
Seabrook Gdns
ROMW/RG RM7 74 C4
Seabrook Rd BCTR RM8 91 K1
Seaburn Cl RAIN RM13 111 G2
Seacole Cl ACT W3 99 F5
Seacourt Rd ABYW SE2 128 E2
Seacroft Gdns OXHEY WD19 27 H5
Seafield Rd FBAR/BDGN N11 34 D6
Seaford Cl RSLP HA4 58 B6
Seaford Rd EN EN1 24 A5
HTHAIR TW6 132 A6
SEVS/STOTM N15 67 K2
WALTH E17 51 K6
WEA W13 116 C1
Seaford St STPAN WC1H 5 F5
Seaforth Av NWMAL KT3 192 E2
Seaforth Cl ROM RM1 57 G3
Seaforth Crs HBRY N5 85 J3
Seaforth Gdns
HOR/WEW KT19 207 H2
WCHMH N21 35 F2
WFD IG8 53 G1
Seaforth Pl WESTW SW1E 16 B4
Seager Blds DEPT SE8 * 144 D2
Seagrave Cl WCHPL E1 * 105 F4
Seagrave Rd FUL/PGN SW6 119 K6
Seagry Rd WAN E11 70 E3
Seagull La CAN/RD E16 106 E6
Sealand Rd HTHAIR TW6 132 D6
Seal St HACK E8 86 B2
Searles Cl BTSEA SW11 140 D1
Searles Dr EHAM E6 108 B4
Searles Rd STHWK SE1 19 F6
Sears St CMBW SE5 142 E1
Seasons Cl HNWL W7 116 A1
Seasprite Cl NTHLT UB5 95 H2
Seaton Av GDMY/SEVK IG3 90 E3
Seaton Cl LBTH SE11 122 C5
PLSTW E13 106 E3
PUT/ROE SW15 158 E2
WHTN TW2 155 J1
Seaton Dr ASHF TW15 152 B4
Seaton Gdns RSLP HA4 76 E1
Seaton Rd ALP/SUD HA0 * 98 A1
DART DA1 170 D2
HYS/HAR UB3 113 G4
MTCM CR4 178 D5
WELL DA16 148 D1
WHTN TW2 155 H1
Seaton St UED N18 50 C1
Sebastian St FSBYE EC1V 6 B5
Sebastopol Rd ED N9 36 C6
Sebbon St IS N1 85 H5
Sebergham Gv MLHL NW7 45 J3
Sebert Rd FSTGT E7 89 F3
Sebright Rd BAR EN5 20 B3
Secker Crs
KTN/HRWW/WS HA3 42 C4
Secker St STHWK SE1 17 J1
Second Av ACT W3 118 C1
CHDH RM6 73 J2
DAGE RM10 110 D1
EN EN1 24 B6
HDN NW4 64 B1
HYS/HAR UB3 113 J1
MNPK E12 89 J2
MORT/ESHN SW14 138 B4
NKENS W10 100 C3
PLSTW E13 106 E2
UED N18 36 E6
WALTH E17 69 J2
WBLY HA9 61 K6
WOT/HER KT12 188 A3
Second Cl E/WMO/HCT KT8 189 G1
Second Cross Rd WHTN TW2 155 J4
Second Wy WBLY HA9 80 D2
Sedan Wy WALW SE17 123 F5
Sedcombe Cl SCUP DA14 168 C6
Sedcote Rd PEND EN3 24 E6
Sedding St KTBR SW1X 15 G6
Seddon Rd MRDN SM4 194 C2
Seddon St FSBYW WC1X 5 G5
Sedgebrook Rd
BKHTH/KID SE3 146 C3
Sedgecombe Av
KTN/HRWW/WS HA3 61 J2
Sedgeford Rd SHB W12 118 C1
Sedgehill Rd CAT SE6 182 D1
Sedgemere Av EFNCH N2 47 G6
Sedgemere Rd ABYW SE2 128 D3
Sedgemoor Dr DAGE RM10 92 C2
Sedge Rd TOTM N17 50 E3
Sedgeway CAT SE6 165 J3
Sedgewood Cl HAYES BR2 199 J4
Sedgmoor Pl CMBW SE5 143 F1
Sedgwick Rd LEY E10 70 A6
Sedgwick St HOM E9 87 F3
Sedleigh Rd
WAND/EARL SW18 159 J1
Sedlescombe Rd
FUL/PGN SW6 119 J6
Sedley Cl EN EN1 24 D1
Sedley Pl OXSTW W1C 9 J4
Sednem Ct PECK SE15 143 H3
Sedum Cl CDALE/KGS NW9 62 D2
Seeley Dr DUL SE21 163 F6
Seelig Av CDALE/KGS NW9 63 J4
Seely Rd TOOT SW17 179 F2
Seething La TWRH EC3N 13 H5
Seething Wells La SURB KT6 190 D3
Sefton Av
KTN/HRWW/WS HA3 42 D4
MLHL NW7 45 F1
Sefton Cl STMC/STPC BR5 202 A1
Sefton Ct ENC/FH EN2 * 23 H3
Sefton Rd CROY/NA CR0 197 H5
STMC/STPC BR5 202 A1
Sefton St PUT/ROE SW15 139 F3
Sekforde St CLKNW EC1R 6 A7
Sekhon Ter FELT TW13 155 F5
Selah Dr SWLY BR8 187 K4
Selan Gdns YEAD UB4 95 F4
Selbie Av WLSDN NW10 81 H3
Selborne Av BXLY DA5 169 F3
MNPK E12 90 A2
WALTH E17 69 H2
Selborne Gdns GFD/PVL UB6 97 G1
HDN NW4 63 J1
Selborne Rd CMBW SE5 142 E3
CROY/NA CR0 212 A1
IL IG1 72 A6
NWMAL KT3 176 B5
SCUP DA14 168 C6
STHGT/OAK N14 34 E5
WALTH E17 69 H2
WDGN N22 49 F4
Selbourne Av SURB KT6 191 G6
Selby Cha RSLP HA4 59 F6
Selby Cl CHSGTN KT9 206 A5
CHST BR7 185 F2
Selby Gdns STHL UB1 96 A3
Selby Gn CAR SM5 194 D4
Selby Rd CAR SM5 194 D4
EA W5 97 H3
PGE/AN SE20 181 H5
PLSTW E13 107 F4
TOTM N17 50 A2
WAN E11 88 C1
Selby St WCHPL E1 104 C3
Selden Rd PECK SE15 143 K3
Selhurst Cl WIM/MER SW19 159 G3
Selhurst New Rd SNWD SE25 197 F3
Selhurst Pl SNWD SE25 197 F3
Selhurst Rd ED N9 35 K5
SNWD SE25 197 F2
Selinas La BCTR RM8 74 A4
Selkirk Dr ERITH DA8 150 B2
Selkirk Rd TOOT SW17 160 D6
WHTN TW2 155 H4
Sellers Hall Cl FNCH N3 46 E3
Sellincourt Rd TOOT SW17 178 D1
Sellindge Cl BECK BR3 182 C3
Sellons Av WLSDN NW10 81 H6
Sellwood Dr BAR EN5 20 B6
Selsdon Av SAND/SEL CR2 211 K4
Selsdon Cl CRW RM5 56 E4
SURB KT6 191 F2
Selsdon Park Rd
CROY/NA CR0 213 G6
Selsdon Rd CRICK NW2 63 H6
PLSTW E13 89 G6
SAND/SEL CR2 211 K4
WAN E11 70 E4
WNWD SE27 162 C5
Selsdon Wy POP/IOD E14 124 E3
Selsea Pl STNW/STAM N16 86 A3
Selsey Crs WELL DA16 148 E2
Selsey St BOW E3 105 J4
Selvage La MLHL NW7 45 F1
Selway Cl PIN HA5 59 F1
Selwood Pl SKENS SW7 120 C5
Selwood Rd CHEAM SM3 193 J5
CHSGTN KT9 205 K2
CROY/NA CR0 197 J6
Selwood Ter SKENS SW7 120 C5
Selworthy Cl WAN E11 70 E2
Selworthy Rd CAT SE6 164 C5
Selwyn Av CHING E4 52 A2
GDMY/SEVK IG3 73 F3
RCH/KEW TW9 137 G4
Selwyn Cl HSLWW TW4 134 D5
Selwyn Ct EDGW HA8 44 D3
Selwyn Crs WELL DA16 148 C4
Selwyn Rd BOW E3 105 H1
NWMAL KT3 192 A2
PLSTW E13 89 F6
WLSDN NW10 81 G5
Semley Pl BGVA SW1W 15 H7
STRHM/NOR SW16 180 A5
Semley Rd STRHM/NOR SW16 179 K5
Senate St PECK SE15 143 K3
Seneca Rd THHTH CR7 196 D1
Senga Rd WLGTN SM6 195 F5
Senhouse Rd CHEAM SM3 208 B1
Senior St BAY/PAD W2 101 F4
Senlac Rd LEE/GVPK SE12 166 A3
Sennen Rd EN EN1 36 B2
Senrab St WCHPL E1 105 F5
Sentamu Cl HNHL SE24 162 C3
Sentinel Cl NTHLT UB5 95 J3
September Wy STAN HA7 43 H2
Sequoia Cl BUSH WD23 28 D3
Sequoia Gdns ORP BR6 202 A4
Sequoia Pk PIN HA5 42 B2
Serbin Cl LEY E10 70 A4
Serenaders Rd BRXN/ST SW9 142 B3
Serjeant's Inn EMB EC4Y * 11 K4
Serle St LINN WC2A 11 H3
Sermon Dr SWLY BR8 187 K6
Sermon La BLKFR EC4V 12 C4
Serpentine Rd SKENS SW7 14 D2
Service Route No 1
SRTFD E15 88 B5
Service Route No 2
SRTFD E15 88 B5
Service Route No 3
SRTFD E15 88 B4
Serviden Dr BMLY BR1 184 C4
Setchell Est STHWK SE1 19 J6
Setchell Rd STHWK SE1 19 J6
Setchell Wy STHWK SE1 19 J6
Seth St BERM/RHTH SE16 123 K2
Seton Gdns DAGW RM9 91 J5
Settles St WCHPL E1 104 C5
Settrington Rd FUL/PGN SW6 140 A3
Seven Acres CAR SM5 194 D6
NTHWD HA6 40 E2
Seven Dials LSQ/SEVD WC2H 10 E4
Sevenex Pde WBLY HA9 * 80 A3
Seven Kings Rd
GDMY/SEVK IG3 72 E5
Seven Kings Wy
KUTN/CMB KT2 174 E4
Sevenoaks Cl BXLYHN DA7 149 K5
Sevenoaks Rd BROCKY SE4 164 C1
ORP BR6 217 F6
Sevenoaks Wy
STMC/STPC BR5 186 C6
Seven Seas Rd HTHAIR TW6 153 F1
Seven Sisters Rd FSBYPK N4 67 H6
HOLWY N7 85 F1
SEVS/STOTM N15 67 K3
Seven Stars Yd WCHPL E1 13 K1
Seventh Av HYS/HAR UB3 113 K1
MNPK E12 89 K2
Severnake Cl POP/IOD E14 124 D4
Severn Av GPK RM2 57 K6
NKENS W10 100 C2
Severn Dr EN EN1 24 C1
ESH/CLAY KT10 190 B6
WOT/HER KT12 188 C6
Severn Wy WLSDN NW10 81 H3
Severus Rd BTSEA SW11 140 D5
Seville Ms IS N1 86 A5
Seville St KTBR SW1X 15 F3
Sevington Rd HDN NW4 63 K3
Sevington St MV/WKIL W9 101 F3
Seward Rd BECK BR3 182 A5
HNWL W7 116 B2
Sewardstone Rd BETH E2 104 E1
CHING E4 25 K5
Seward St FSBYE EC1V 6 B6
Sewdley St CLPT E5 87 F1
Sewell Rd ABYW SE2 128 B2
Sewell St PLSTW E13 106 E2
Sextant Av POP/IOD E14 125 G4
Sexton Cl RAIN RM13 93 H6
Seymer Rd ROM RM1 57 F6
Seymour Av EW KT17 207 K6
MRDN SM4 193 G4
TOTM N17 50 C5
Seymour Cl E/WMO/HCT KT8 189 H2
LOU IG10 39 J1
PIN HA5 41 K4
Seymour Dr HAYES BR2 200 E5
Seymour Gdns BROCKY SE4 144 B4
BRYLDS KT5 191 G2
FELT TW13 154 A6
IL IG1 71 K5
RSLP HA4 59 H5
TWK TW1 156 C2
Seymour Gv OXHEY WD19 27 G2
Seymour Ms MBLAR W1H 9 G3
Seymour Pl MBLAR W1H 8 E2
SNWD SE25 197 J1
Seymour Rd CAR SM5 210 A3
CEND/HSY/T N8 67 H2
CHING E4 37 K3
CHSWK W4 117 K4
E/WMO/HCT KT8 189 H2
ED N9 36 D4
EHAM E6 89 H6
FNCH N3 47 F3
HPTN TW12 173 H1
KUT/HW KT1 174 E4
LEY E10 69 H5
MTCM CR4 195 F4
WAND/EARL SW18 159 J2
WIM/MER SW19 159 G5
Seymour St BAY/PAD W2 8 E4
MBLAR W1H 9 F4
WOOL/PLUM SE18 127 H3
Seymour Ter PGE/AN SE20 181 J4
Seymour Vls PGE/AN SE20 181 J4
Seymour Wk WBPTN SW10 120 B6
Seyssel St POP/IOD E14 125 F4
Shaa Rd ACT W3 99 F6
Shacklegate La TEDD TW11 155 K6
Shackleton Cl FSTH SE23 163 J4
Shackleton Rd STHL UB1 95 K5
Shacklewell La HACK E8 86 B2
Shacklewell Rd
STNW/STAM N16 86 B2
Shacklewell Rw HACK E8 86 B2
Shacklewell St BETH E2 7 K6
Shadbolt Av CHING E4 51 G1
Shadbolt Cl WPK KT4 192 C6

Shad Thames *STHWK* SE1 **19** J1
Shadwell Dr *NTHLT* UB5 **95** K2
Shadwell Gdns *WCHPL* E1 * **104** E6
Shadwell Pierhead *WAP* E1W **104** E6
Shady Bush Cl *BUSH* WD23 **28** C2
Shaef Wy *TEDD* TW11 **174** B3
Shafter Rd *DAGE* RM10 **92** E4
Shaftesbury Av *BAR* EN5 **21** G5
EBED/NFELT TW14 **153** K1
KTN/HRWW/WS HA3 **61** K3
LSQ/SEVD WC2H **10** E3
NWDGN UB2 **115** F4
PEND EN3 **25** F3
RYLN/HDSTN HA2 **60** B5
SOHO/SHAV W1D **10** C5
Shaftesbury Cir
RYLN/HDSTN HA2 * **60** C5
Shaftesbury Gdns
WLSDN NW10 **99** G3
Shaftesbury Ms *CLAP* SW4 **141** H6
KENS W8 **119** K3
Shaftesbury Pde
RYLN/HDSTN HA2 * **60** C5
Shaftesbury Pl *BARB* EC2Y * **12** C2
Shaftesbury Rd *ARCH* N19 **66** E5
BECK BR3 **182** C5
CAR SM5 **194** C4
CHING E4 **38** B3
FSTGT E7 **89** G5
LEY E10 **69** J5
RCH/KEW TW9 **137** F4
ROM RM1 **75** H3
UED N18 **50** A2
WALTH E17 **69** K2
The Shaftesburys *BARK* IG11 **108** C1
Shaftesbury St *IS* N1 **6** D3
Shaftesbury Ter
HMSMTH W6 * **118** C4
Shaftesbury Wy *WHTN* TW2 **155** J5
Shaftesbury Waye *YEAD* UB4 **95** F4
Shafteswood Ct *TOOT* SW17 **160** E5
Shafto Ms *KTBR* SW1X **14** E5
Shafton Ms *HOM* E9 * **87** F6
Shafton Rd *HOM* E9 **87** F6
Shakespeare Av
EBED/NFELT TW14 **153** K1
FBAR/BDGN N11 **48** C1
WLSDN NW10 **80** E6
YEAD UB4 **94** E5
Shakespeare Crs *MNPK* E12 **89** K5
WLSDN NW10 **81** F6
Shakespeare Dr
KTN/HRWW/WS HA3 **62** B3
Shakespeare Gdns *EFNCH* N2 **65** K1
Shakespeare Rd *ACT* W3 **117** K1
BXLYHN DA7 **149** F2
DART DA1 **151** K5
FNCH N3 * **46** E4
HNHL SE24 **142** C6
HNWL W7 **97** F6
MLHL NW7 **31** J6
ROM RM1 **75** H3
WALTH E17 **51** F5
Shakespeare Sq
BARK/HLT IG6 **54** B2
Shakespeare Ter
RCH/KEW TW9 * **137** H4
Shakespeare Wy *FELT* TW13 **154** B6
Shakspeare Ms
STNW/STAM N16 **86** A2
Shakspeare Wk
STNW/STAM N16 **86** A2
Shalbourne Sq *HOM* E9 **87** H4
Shalcomb St *WBPTN* SW10 **120** B6
Shaldon Dr *MRDN* SM4 **193** H2
RSLP HA4 **77** G1
Shaldon Rd *EDGW* HA8 **44** B5
Shalfleet Dr *NKENS* W10 **100** B6
Shalford Cl *ORP* BR6 **216** C2
Shalford Ct *IS* N1 * **6** A2
Shalimar Gdns *ACT* W3 **98** E6
Shalimar Rd *ACT* W3 **98** E6
Shallons Rd *ELTH/MOT* SE9 **167** G6
Shalstone Rd
MORT/ESHN SW14 **137** J4
Shalston Vls *SURB* KT6 **191** G3
Shamrock Rd *CROY/NA* CR0 **196** A3
Shamrock St *CLAP* SW4 **141** J4
Shamrock Wy
STHGT/OAK N14 **34** B3
Shandon Rd *CLAP* SW4 **161** H1
Shand St *STHWK* SE1 **19** H2
Shandy St *WCHPL* E1 **105** F4
Shanklin Gdns *OXHEY* WD19 **27** G6
Shanklin Rd *CEND/HSY/T* N8 **66** D2
SEVS/STOTM N15 **68** C1
Shannon Cl *NWDGN* UB2 **114** C5
Shannon Gv *BRXN/ST* SW9 **142** A5
Shannon Pl *STJWD* NW8 **2** D2
Shannon Wy *BECK* BR3 **182** E2
Shap Crs *CAR* SM5 **194** E5
Shapland Wy *PLMGR* N13 **49** F1
Shapwick Cl *FBAR/BDGN* N11 **47** K1
Shardcroft Av *HNHL* SE24 **142** C6
Shardeloes Rd *BROCKY* SE4 * **144** C6
NWCR SE14 **144** C3
Shard's Sq *PECK* SE15 **123** H6
Sharland Cl *THHTH* CR7 **196** B3
Sharman Ct *SCUP* DA14 **168** B6
Sharnbrooke Cl *WELL* DA16 **148** D4
Sharon Cl *SURB* KT6 **190** D5
Sharon Gdns *HOM* E9 **86** E6
Sharon Rd *CHSWK* W4 **118** A5
PEND EN3 **25** G3
Sharples Hall St *CAMTN* NW1 **83** K5
Sharps La *RSLP* HA4 **58** B4
Sharp Wy *DART* DA1 **151** J4
Sharratt St *PECK* SE15 **123** K6
Sharsted St *WALW* SE17 **122** C5
Sharvel La *YEAD* UB4 **76** E6
Shavers Pl *MYFR/PICC* W1J **10** C6
Shaw Av *BARK* IG11 **110** A1
Shawbrooke Rd
ELTH/MOT SE9 **146** C5
Shawbury Cl *CDALE/KGS* NW9 **45** G4
Shawbury Rd *EDUL* SE22 **143** G6
Shaw Cl *BUSH* WD23 **28** E4
EMPK RM11 **75** K5
THMD SE28 **128** C1
Shaw Crs *POP/IOD* E14 **105** G5
Shaw Dr *WOT/HER* KT12 **188** B4
Shawfield Pk *BMLY* BR1 **184** C5
Shawfield St *CHEL* SW3 **120** D5
Shawford Ct *PUT/ROE* SW15 * **158** D2
Shawford Rd *HOR/WEW* KT19 **207** F4
Shaw Gdns *BARK* IG11 **110** A1
Shaw Rd *BMLY* BR1 **165** J5
EDUL SE22 **143** F5
PEND EN3 **25** F2
Shaws Cots *FSTH* SE23 * **164** B5
Shaw's Cots *FSTH* SE23 **164** B5
Shaw Sq *WALTH* E17 **51** G4
The Shaw *CHST* BR7 * **185** H3
Shaw Wy *WLGTN* SM6 **210** E5
Shaxton Crs *CROY/NA* CR0 **214** A6
Sheaf Cots *THDIT* KT7 * **189** K5
Shearing Dr *CAR* SM5 **194** B4
Shearling Wy *HOLWY* N7 **84** E4
Shearman Rd *BKHTH/KID* SE3 **145** J5
Shears Cl *DART* DA1 **171** F4
Shearwater Cl *BARK* IG11 **109** G2
Shearwater Rd *SUT* SM1 **208** D3
Shearwater Wy *YEAD* UB4 **95** H5
Shearwood Crs *DART* DA1 **150** C4
Sheaths Cots *THDIT* KT7 * **190** C4
Sheaveshill Av
CDALE/KGS NW9 **45** G6
Sheaveshill Pde
CDALE/KGS NW9 * **63** G1
Sheen Common Dr
RCHPK/HAM TW10 **137** H5
Sheen Court Rd
RCHPK/HAM TW10 **137** H5
Sheendale Rd *RCH/KEW* TW9 **137** G5
Sheenewood *SYD* SE26 **181** J1
Sheen Ga *MORT/ESHN* SW14 **157** K1
Sheen Gate Gdns
MORT/ESHN SW14 **137** K5
Sheen Gv *IS* N1 **85** G6
Sheen La *MORT/ESHN* SW14 **137** K5
Sheen Pk *RCH/KEW* TW9 **137** F5
Sheen Rd *RCH/KEW* TW9 **137** F5
STMC/STPC BR5 **202** A1
Sheen Wy *WLGTN* SM6 **211** F3
Sheen Wd *MORT/ESHN* SW14 **137** K6
Sheepcote Cl *HEST* TW5 **133** K1
Sheepcote La *BTSEA* SW11 **140** E3
STMC/STPC BR5 **203** H1
Sheepcote Rd *HRW* HA1 **61** F3
Sheepcotes Rd *CHDH* RM6 **73** K1
Sheephouse Wy *NWMAL* KT3 **192** A5
Sheep La *HACK* E8 **86** D6
Sheep Walk Ms
WIM/MER SW19 **177** G2
Sheerwater Rd *CAN/RD* E16 **107** H4
Sheffield Rd *HTHAIR* TW6 **153** F1
Sheffield St *LINN* WC2A * **11** G4
Sheffield Ter *KENS* W8 **119** K2
Shefton Ri *NTHWD* HA6 **40** E3
Sheila Rd *CRW* RM5 **56** D3
Shelbourne Cl *PIN* HA5 **41** K6
Shelbourne Rd *TOTM* N17 **50** D4
Shelburne Dr *HSLWW* TW4 **155** F1
Shelburne Rd *HOLWY* N7 **85** F2
Shelbury Cl *SCUP* DA14 **168** B5
Shelbury Rd *EDUL* SE22 **143** J6
Sheldon Av *CLAY* IG5 **54** B5
HGT N6 **65** K4
Sheldon Cl *LEE/GVPK* SE12 **146** A6
PGE/AN SE20 **181** J4
Sheldon Pl *BETH* E2 **104** C1
Sheldon Rd *BXLYHN* DA7 **149** G2
CRICK NW2 **82** B2
DAGW RM9 **92** A5
UED N18 **36** A6
Sheldon Sq *BAY/PAD* W2 **101** G4
Sheldon St *CROY/NA* CR0 **211** J1
Sheldrake Cl *CAN/RD* E16 **126** E1
Sheldrake Pl *KENS* W8 **119** J2
Sheldrick Cl *MTCM* CR4 **178** C5
Shelduck Cl *SRTFD* E15 **88** D3
Sheldwich Ter *HAYES* BR2 * **200** D3
Shelford Pl *STNW/STAM* N16 **85** K1
Shelford Ri *NRWD* SE19 **181** F3
Shelford Rd *BAR* EN5 **32** A1
Shelgate Rd *BTSEA* SW11 **140** E6
Shell Cl *HAYES* BR2 **200** D3
Shellduck Cl *CDALE/KGS* NW9 **45** G5
Shelley Av *GFD/PVL* UB6 **96** D2
HCH RM12 **75** H6
MNPK E12 **89** J4
Shelley Cl *EDGW* HA8 **30** C6
GFD/PVL UB6 **96** D2
NTHWD HA6 **40** D1
ORP BR6 **216** E1
PECK SE15 **143** J3
YEAD UB4 **94** E4
Shelley Crs *HEST* TW5 **134** C2
STHL UB1 **95** K5
Shelley Dr *WELL* DA16 **147** K2
Shelley Gdns *ALP/SUD* HA0 **61** J6
Shelley Rd *WLSDN* NW10 **81** F6
Shelley Wy *WIM/MER* SW19 **178** C2
Shellgrove Rd
STNW/STAM N16 * **86** A3
Shellness Rd *CLPT* E5 **86** D3
Shell Rd *LEW* SE13 **144** E4
Shellwood Rd *BTSEA* SW11 **140** E3
Shelmerdine Cl *BOW* E3 **105** J4
Shelson Av *FELT* TW13 **153** J5
Shelson Pde *FELT* TW13 * **153** J5
Shelton Rd *WIM/MER* SW19 **177** K4
Shelton St *LSQ/SEVD* WC2H * **10** E4
Shenfield Rd *WFD* IG8 **53** F3
Shenfield St *IS* N1 **7** H3
Shenley Av *RSLP* HA4 **58** D6
Shenley Rd *CMBW* SE5 **143** F2
DART DA1 **171** K1
HEST TW5 **134** D2
Shenstone Cl *DART* DA1 **150** A6
Shepherd Cl *FELT* TW13 **154** D6
Shepherdess Pl *FSBYE* EC1V **6** D4
Shepherdess Wk *IS* N1 **6** D2
Shepherd Market
MYFR/PICC W1J **15** J1
Shepherd's Bush Gn *SHB* W12 **119** F2
Shepherd's Bush Market
SHB W12 **119** F2
Shepherd's Bush Pl
SHB W12 * **119** G2
Shepherd's Bush Rd
HMSMTH W6 **119** F3
Shepherds Cl *CHDH* RM6 **73** K2
ORP BR6 **217** F1
STAN HA7 **43** G1
Shepherd's Cl *HGT* N6 **66** B3
Shepherds Gn *CHST* BR7 **185** J3
Shepherd's Hl *HGT* N6 **66** B3
Shepherds La *DART* DA1 **170** D3
THMD SE28 **127** K1
Shepherd's La *HOM* E9 **87** F3
Shepherd's Leas
ELTH/MOT SE9 * **147** J5
Shepherds Pl
MYFR/PKLN W1K **9** G5
Shepherd St *MYFR/PICC* W1J **15** J1
Shepherds Wk *BUSH* WD23 **28** D4
CRICK NW2 **63** J6
Shepherd's Wk *HAMP* NW3 **83** H3
Shepherds Wy *SAND/SEL* CR2 **213** F5
Shepiston La *HYS/HAR* UB3 **112** E4
HYS/HAR UB3 **113** G4
Shepley Cl *CAR* SM5 **210** A1
Shepley Ms *PEND* EN3 **25** J1
Sheppard Cl *EN* EN1 **24** D1
KUT/HW KT1 **191** F1
Sheppard Dr
BERM/RHTH SE16 **123** J5
Sheppard St *CAN/RD* E16 **106** D3
Shepperton Rd *IS* N1 **85** K6
STMC/STPC BR5 **201** H3
Sheppey Cl *ERITH* DA8 **150** E1
Sheppey Gdns *DAGW* RM9 **91** J5
Sheppey Rd *DAGW* RM9 **91** H5
Sheppey Wk *IS* N1 * **85** J5
Shepton Houses *BETH* E2 * **104** E2
Sherard Rd *ELTH/MOT* SE9 **146** D6
Sheraton St *SOHO/CST* W1F * **10** C4
Sherborne Av *NWDGN* UB2 **115** F4
PEND EN3 **24** E3
Sherborne Cl *YEAD* UB4 **95** G5
Sherborne Crs *CAR* SM5 **194** D4
Sherborne Gdns
CDALE/KGS NW9 **44** C6
WEA W13 **97** H5
Sherborne La *MANHO* EC4N **12** E5
Sherborne Pl *NTHWD* HA6 **40** B2
Sherborne Rd *CHEAM* SM3 **193** K6
CHSGTN KT9 **206** A3
EBED/NFELT TW14 **153** G2
STMC/STPC BR5 **202** A2
Sherborne St *IS* N1 **85** K6
Sherborne Vls *WEA* W13 * **97** H4
Sherboro Rd
SEVS/STOTM N15 **68** B3
Sherbrooke Cl *BXLYHN* DA7 **149** H5
Sherbrooke Rd *FUL/PGN* SW6 **139** H1
Sherbrooke Ter
FUL/PGN SW6 * **139** H1
Sherbrooke Wy *WPK* KT4 **192** E4
Sherbrook Gdns *WCHMH* N21 **35** H2
Shere Cl *CHSGTN* KT9 **205** K3
Sheredan Rd *CHING* E4 **52** B1
Shere Rd *GNTH/NBYPK* IG2 **72** A2
Sherfield Cl *NWMAL* KT3 **191** J1
Sherfield Gdns
PUT/ROE SW15 **158** C1
Sheridan Cl *HARH* RM3 **57** K3
Sheridan Ct *DART* DA1 **151** K5
HSLWW TW4 **134** D6
Sheridan Crs *CHST* BR7 **185** G5
Sheridan Gdns
KTN/HRWW/WS HA3 **61** K3
Sheridan Ms *WAN* E11 **71** F3
Sheridan Pl *BMLY* BR1 **184** C5
HPTN TW12 **173** G4
Sheridan Rd *BELV* DA17 **129** H4
BXLYHN DA7 **149** F4
FSTGT E7 **88** D1
MNPK E12 **89** J3
OXHEY WD19 **27** H2
RCHPK/HAM TW10 **156** D5
WIM/MER SW19 **177** J4
Sheridan Ter *NTHLT* UB5 * **78** B3
Sheridan Wk *CAR* SM5 **209** K3
GLDGN NW11 **64** E3
Sheridan Wy *BECK* BR3 **182** C4
Sheringham Av *MNPK* E12 **89** K2
ROMW/RG RM7 **74** E3
STHGT/OAK N14 **22** D6
WHTN TW2 **154** E3
Sheringham Dr *BARK* IG11 **91** F3
Sheringham Rd *HOLWY* N7 **85** G4
PGE/AN SE20 **181** J5
Sherington Av *PIN* HA5 **42** A3
Sherington Rd
BKHTH/KID SE3 **126** A6
Sherland Rd *TWK* TW1 **156** A3
Sherlies Av *ORP* BR6 **201** K6
Sherlock Ms *MHST* W1U **9** G1
Shermanbury Cl *ERITH* DA8 **150** C1
Sherman Gdns *CHDH* RM6 **73** J3
Sherman Rd *BMLY* BR1 **183** K4
Shernhall St *WALTH* E17 **70** A2
Sherrard Rd *FSTGT* E7 **89** G4
Sherrards Wy *BAR* EN5 **20** E6
Sherrick Green Rd
WLSDN NW10 **81** K3
Sherriff Cl *ESH/CLAY* KT10 **189** G6
Sherriff Rd *KIL/WHAMP* NW6 **82** E4
Sherringham Av *FELT* TW13 **153** K5
TOTM N17 **50** C5
Sherrock Gdns *HDN* NW4 **63** J1
Sherry Ms *BARK* IG11 **90** D5
Sherwin Rd *NWCR* SE14 **144** A2
Sherwood *SURB* KT6 **190** E6
Sherwood Av *GFD/PVL* UB6 **78** E4
RSLP HA4 **58** C3
STRHM/NOR SW16 **179** J3
SWFD E18 **53** F6
YEAD UB4 **95** F3
Sherwood Cl *BXLY* DA5 **168** D1
WALTH E17 **51** H5
WEA W13 **116** C1
Sherwood Ct *MBLAR* W1H * **8** E2
Sherwood Gdns *BARK* IG11 **90** D5
BERM/RHTH SE16 **123** H5
POP/IOD E14 **124** D4
Sherwood House
RYLN/HDSTN HA2 * **78** C1
Sherwood Park Av
BFN/LL DA15 **168** B2
Sherwood Park Rd
MTCM CR4 **195** H1
SUT SM1 **208** E3
Sherwood Rd *BARK/HLT* IG6 **72** D1
CROY/NA CR0 **197** J4
HDN NW4 **46** A6
HPTN TW12 **173** H1
RYLN/HDSTN HA2 **60** C6
WELL DA16 **147** K4
WIM/MER SW19 **177** J3
Sherwoods Rd *OXHEY* WD19 **27** J2
Sherwood St *SOHO/CST* W1F **10** B5
TRDG/WHET N20 **33** H5
Sherwood Ter
TRDG/WHET N20 **33** H5
Sherwood Wy *WWKM* BR4 **199** F6
Shetland Cl *BORE* WD6 **31** F1
Shetland Rd *BOW* E3 **105** H1
Shield Dr *BTFD* TW8 **116** B6
Shieldhall St *ABYW* SE2 **128** D4
Shield Rd *ASHF* TW15 **153** F6
Shifford Pth *FSTH* SE23 **164** A5
Shillibeer Pl *MBLAR* W1H **8** D2
Shillingford Cl *MLHL* NW7 **46** B3
Shillingford St *IS* N1 **85** H6
Shilling Pl *HNWL* W7 * **116** B1
Shinfield St *SHB* W12 **100** A5
Shinglewell Rd *ERITH* DA8 **149** H1
Shinners Cl *SNWD* SE25 **197** H2
Shipka Rd *BAL* SW12 **161** G3
Ship La *MORT/ESHN* SW14 **137** K4
Shipman Rd *CAN/RD* E16 **107** F5
FSTH SE23 **164** A4
Ship & Mermaid Rw
STHWK SE1 **19** F2
Ship St *DEPT* SE8 **144** D2
Ship Tavern Pas *BANK* EC3V **13** G5
Shipton Cl *BCTR* RM8 **91** K1
Shipton St *BETH* E2 **7** K4
Shipwright Rd
BERM/RHTH SE16 **124** B2
Shipwright Yd *STHWK* SE1 * **19** G1
Shirburn Cl *FSTH* SE23 **163** K2
Shirbutt St *POP/IOD* E14 **105** J6
Shirebrook Rd
BKHTH/KID SE3 **146** C3
Shire Ct *EW* KT17 **207** H5
Shirehall Cl *HDN* NW4 **64** B3
Shirehall Gdns *HDN* NW4 **64** B3
Shirehall La *HDN* NW4 **64** B3
Shirehall Pk *HDN* NW4 **64** B3
Shire Horse Wy *ISLW* TW7 **136** A4
Shire La *ORP* BR6 **215** K5
Shire Ms *WHTN* TW2 **155** H1
The Shires *RCHPK/HAM* TW10 **157** F6
Shirland Ms *MV/WKIL* W9 **100** D2
Shirland Rd *MV/WKIL* W9 **100** E3
Shirley Av *BXLY* DA5 **168** E2
CROY/NA CR0 **197** K5
SUT SM1 **209** J2
Shirley Church Rd
CROY/NA CR0 **213** F1
Shirley Cl *DART* DA1 **151** F5
HSLW TW3 **135** H6
WALTH E17 * **69** K2
Shirley Crs *BECK* BR3 **198** B1
Shirley Dr *HSLW* TW3 **135** H6
Shirley Gdns *BARK* IG11 **90** E4
HNWL W7 **116** A1
Shirley Gv *BTSEA* SW11 **141** F4
ED N9 **36** E2
Shirley Hills Rd *CROY/NA* CR0 **213** F3
Shirley Oaks Rd *CROY/NA* CR0 **198** A5
Shirley Park Rd *CROY/NA* CR0 **197** J5
Shirley Rd *BFN/LL* DA15 **167** K5
CHSWK W4 **118** A2
CROY/NA CR0 **197** J5
ENC/FH EN2 **23** J4
SRTFD E15 **88** C5
WLGTN SM6 **210** C6
Shirley Rw *SNWD* SE25 * **181** H5
Shirley St *CAN/RD* E16 **106** D5
Shirley Wy *CROY/NA* CR0 **213** H1
Shirlock Rd *HAMP* NW3 **83** K2
Shirwell Cl *MLHL* NW7 **46** B3
Shobden Rd *TOTM* N17 **49** K4
Shobroke Cl *CRICK* NW2 **82** A1
Shoebury Rd *EHAM* E6 **89** K5
Shoe La *FLST/FETLN* EC4A **11** K3
HCIRC EC1N **12** A2
Sholden Gdns
STMC/STPC BR5 **202** D2
Shooters Av
KTN/HRWW/WS HA3 **61** J1
Shooters Hill Rd *GNWCH* SE10 **145** H2
Shooters Rd *ENC/FH* EN2 **23** G2
Shoot-Up Hl *CRICK* NW2 **82** C4
Shops *SYD* SE26 * **182** A1
Shore Cl *EBED/NFELT* TW14 **153** K2
HPTN TW12 **172** D1
Shoreditch High St
FSBYE EC1V **7** H5
WCHPL E1 **13** H1
Shore Gv *FELT* TW13 **155** F4
Shoreham Cl *CROY/NA* CR0 **197** K3
WAND/EARL SW18 **140** A6
Shoreham Rd
STMC/STPC BR5 **186** C4
Shoreham Rd (East)
HTHAIR TW6 **132** B6
Shoreham Rd (West)
HTHAIR TW6 **132** B6
Shoreham Wy *HAYES* BR2 **199** K3
Shore Pl *HOM* E9 **86** E5
Shore Rd *HOM* E9 **86** E5
Shore Wy *BRXN/ST* SW9 **142** B3
Shorncliffe Rd *STHWK* SE1 **123** G5
Shorndean St *CAT* SE6 **165** F3
Shorne Cl *BFN/LL* DA15 **168** C1
STMC/STPC BR5 **202** E1
Shornefield Cl *BMLY* BR1 **185** F6
Shorrolds Rd *FUL/PGN* SW6 **139** K1
Shortcroft Rd *EW* KT17 **207** H5
Shortcrofts Rd *DAGW* RM9 **92** B4
Shorter St *TWRH* EC3N **13** J5
Shortgate
NFNCH/WDSPK N12 **32** D6
Shortlands *HMSMTH* W6 **119** G4
HYS/HAR UB3 **113** G6
Shortlands Cl *BELV* DA17 **129** G3
UED N18 **35** K5
Shortlands Gdns *HAYES* BR2 **183** H5
Shortlands Gv *HAYES* BR2 **183** G6
Shortlands Rd *HAYES* BR2 **183** G6
KUTN/CMB KT2 **175** G3
LEY E10 **69** K4
Short La *STWL/WRAY* TW19 **152** C2
Short Rd *CHSWK* W4 **118** B6
WAN E11 **70** C6
Shorts Cft *CDALE/KGS* NW9 **62** D1
Shorts Gdns
LSQ/SEVD WC2H * **10** E4
Shorts Rd *CAR* SM5 **209** J2
Short St *HDN* NW4 **64** A1
STHWK SE1 **17** K2
Shortway *ELTH/MOT* SE9 **146** D4
Short Wy *NFNCH/WDSPK* N12 **47** J2
WHTN TW2 **155** H2
Shotfield *WLGTN* SM6 **210** B4
Shott Cl *SUT* SM1 **209** G3
Shottendane Rd
FUL/PGN SW6 * **139** K2
Shottery Cl *ELTH/MOT* SE9 **166** D5
Shottfield Av
MORT/ESHN SW14 **138** B5
Shoulder of Mutton Aly
POP/IOD E14 **105** G6
Shouldham St *MBLAR* W1H **8** D2
Showers Wy *HYS/HAR* UB3 **113** K1
Shrapnel Cl *WOOL/PLUM* SE18 **146** E1
Shrapnel Rd *ELTH/MOT* SE9 **146** E4
Shrewsbury Av
KTN/HRWW/WS HA3 **62** A1
MORT/ESHN SW14 **137** K5
Shrewsbury Cl *SURB* KT6 **191** F6
Shrewsbury Crs
WLSDN NW10 * **81** F6
Shrewsbury La
WOOL/PLUM SE18 **147** G2
Shrewsbury Ms *BAY/PAD* W2 **100** E5
Shrewsbury Rd *BAY/PAD* W2 **100** E5
BECK BR3 **182** B6
CAR SM5 **194** D4
FBAR/BDGN N11 **48** D2
FSTGT E7 **89** H4
HTHAIR TW6 **153** F1
Shrewsbury St *NKENS* W10 **100** A3
Shrewton Rd *TOOT* SW17 * **178** E3
Shroffold Rd *BMLY* BR1 **165** H6
Shropshire Cl *MTCM* CR4 **195** K1
Shropshire Rd *WDGN* N22 **49** F3
Shroton St *CAMTN* NW1 **8** C1
The Shrubberies *CHIG* IG7 **54** C1
SWFD E18 **52** E5
Shrubbery Gdns *WCHMH* N21 **35** H2
Shrubbery Rd *ED* N9 **36** C5
STHL UB1 **114** E1
STRHM/NOR SW16 **161** K6
The Shrubbery *SURB* KT6 * **191** F5
Shrubland Cl
TRDG/WHET N20 * **33** H4
Shrubland Gv *WPK* KT4 **208** A1
Shrubland Rd *HACK* E8 **86** C6
LEY E10 **69** J4
WALTH E17 **69** J2
Shrublands Av *CROY/NA* CR0 **213** J2
Shrublands Cl *CHIG* IG7 **54** C2
SYD SE26 **163** K5
TRDG/WHET N20 **33** H3
Shrubsall Cl *ELTH/MOT* SE9 **166** D3
Shubbery Cl *IS* N1 **85** J6
Shuna Wk *IS* N1 * **85** K4
Shurland Av *EBAR* EN4 **33** H1
Shurland Gdns *PECK* SE15 * **143** G1
Shurlock Dr *ORP* BR6 **216** C2
Shuters Sq *WKENS* W14 * **119** J5
Shuttle Cl *BFN/LL* DA15 **168** A2
Shuttlemead *BXLY* DA5 **169** G2
Shuttle Rd *DART* DA1 **150** D4
Shuttle St *WCHPL* E1 **104** C3
Shuttleworth Rd *BTSEA* SW11 **140** C3
Sibella Rd *CLAP* SW4 **141** J3
Sibley Cl *BMLY* BR1 **200** D2
BXLYHS DA6 **149** F6
Sibley Ct *UX/CGN* UB8 **94** A4
Sibley Gv *EHAM* E6 **89** J5
MNPK E12 **89** K5
Sibthorpe Rd *LEE/GVPK* SE12 **166** A2
Sibthorp Rd *MTCM* CR4 * **178** E5
Sibton Rd *CAR* SM5 **194** D4
Sicilian Av *NOXST/BSQ* WC1A * **11** F2
Sidbury St *FUL/PGN* SW6 **139** H2
Sidcup By-Pass Rd
SCUP DA14 **186** B2
Sidcup Hl *SCUP* DA14 **186** C1
Sidcup Hill Gdns *SCUP* DA14 * **186** D1
Sidcup Pl *SCUP* DA14 **186** B1
Sidcup Rd *ELTH/MOT* SE9 **166** C3
Siddeley Dr *HSLWW* TW4 **134** D4
Siddons La *CAMTN* NW1 **3** F7
Siddons Rd *CROY/NA* CR0 **211** G1
FSTH SE23 **164** B4
TOTM N17 **50** C4
Side Rd *WALTH* E17 **69** H2
Sidewood Rd *ELTH/MOT* SE9 **167** J3
Sidford Pl *STHWK* SE1 **17** H5
Sidings Ms *HOLWY* N7 **85** G2
The Sidings *LOU* IG10 **39** J1
WAN E11 **70** A5
Sidmouth Av *ISLW* TW7 **135** K3
Sidmouth Cl *OXHEY* WD19 **27** F4
Sidmouth Dr *RSLP* HA4 **76** E1
Sidmouth Ms *STPAN* WC1H **5** G5
Sidmouth Pde *CRICK* NW2 * **82** A5
Sidmouth Rd *CRICK* NW2 **82** A5
LEY E10 **70** A6
PECK SE15 **143** G2
STMC/STPC BR5 **202** C1
WELL DA16 **148** D1
Sidmouth St *STPAN* WC1H **5** F5
Sidney Av *PLMGR* N13 **49** F1
Sidney Elson Wy *EHAM* E6 **108** A1
Sidney Gdns *BTFD* TW8 **116** E6
Sidney Gv *FSBYE* EC1V **6** A3
Sidney Rd *BECK* BR3 **182** B5
BRXN/ST SW9 **142** A3
FSTGT E7 **88** E1
RYLN/HDSTN HA2 **42** C6

SNWD SE25 197 H2
TWK TW1 156 B1
WDGN N22 49 F3
WOT/HER KT12 188 A5
Sidney Sq WCHPL E1 * 104 E4
Sidney St WCHPL E1 104 D4
Sidworth St HACK E8 86 D5
Siebert Rd BKHTH/KID SE3 125 K6
Siemens Rd
WOOL/PLUM SE18 126 C3
Sienna Cl CHSGTN KT9 205 K4
Sienna Ter CRICK NW2 * 63 J6
Sierra Dr DAGE RM10 110 D1
Sigdon Rd HACK E8 86 C3
The Sigers PIN HA5 59 F3
Signmakers Yd CAMTN NW1 * 3 K1
Sigrist Sq KUTN/CMB KT2 175 F4
Silbury Av MTCM CR4 178 D4
Silbury St IS N1 * 6 E4
Silecroft Rd BXLYHN DA7 149 H2
Silesia Blds HACK E8 86 D5
Silex St STHWK SE1 18 B3
Silk Cl LEE/GVPK SE12 145 K6
Silkfield Rd CDALE/KGS NW9 63 G2
Silkin Ms PECK SE15 143 H1
Silk Ms LBTH SE11 122 B5
Silk Mill Rd OXHEY WD19 27 F2
Silk Mills Pth LEW SE13 145 F4
Silkstream Pde EDGW HA8 * 44 E4
Silkstream Rd EDGW HA8 44 E4
Silk St BARB EC2Y 12 D1
Silsoe Rd WDGN N22 49 F6
Silver Birch Av CHING E4 51 H1
Silver Birch Cl CAT SE6 164 C5
FBAR/BDGN N11 48 A2
RDART DA2 170 B6
THMD SE28 128 B1
Silver Birch Ms BARK/HLT IG6 54 C2
Silverbirch Wk HAMP NW3 * 83 K4
Silvercliffe Gdns EBAR EN4 21 J5
Silver Cl KTN/HRWW/WS HA3 42 D3
NWCR SE14 * 144 B1
Silver Crs CHSWK W4 117 J4
Silverdale ENC/FH EN2 22 E5
SYD SE26 163 K6
Silverdale Cl HNWL W7 115 K1
NTHLT UB5 77 K3
SUT SM1 208 D2
Silverdale Dr ELTH/MOT SE9 166 D4
HCH RM12 93 K3
SUN TW16 172 A5
Silverdale Gdns HYS/HAR UB3 113 K2
Silverdale Rd BXLYHN DA7 149 J3
CHING E4 52 B2
HYS/HAR UB3 113 K2
STMC/STPC BR5 201 H1
Silverdene
NFNCH/WDSPK N12 * 47 F2
Silver Dene PUT/ROE SW15 * 139 F6
Silvergate HOR/WEW KT19 206 E3
Silverhall St ISLW TW7 136 B4
Silverholme Cl
KTN/HRWW/WS HA3 62 A4
Silver La WWKM BR4 199 G6
Silverleigh Rd THHTH CR7 196 A1
Silvermere Av CRW RM5 56 D2
Silvermere Dr UED N18 * 51 F1
Silvermere Rd CAT SE6 164 D1
Silvermere Rw SNWD SE25 * 181 H5
Silver Pl SOHO/CST W1F 10 B4
Silver Rd LEW SE13 144 E4
NKENS W10 100 B6
Silver Spring Cl ERITH DA8 129 J6
Silverston Wy STAN HA7 43 J2
Silver St EN EN1 23 K4
UED N18 35 K6
UED N18 50 B1
Silverthorne Rd VX/NE SW8 141 G3
Silverthorn Gdns CHING E4 37 J4
Silverton Rd HMSMTH W6 139 G1
Silvertown Wy CAN/RD E16 106 D6
Silvertree La GFD/PVL UB6 96 D2
Silver Wy ROMW/RG RM7 56 D6
Silverwood Cl BECK BR3 182 D3
CROY/NA CR0 213 H6
NTHWD HA6 40 A4
Silvester Rd EDUL SE22 143 G6
Silvester St STHWK SE1 18 E3
Silwood Estate Regeneration
Area BERM/RHTH SE16 124 A5
Silwood St BERM/RHTH SE16 124 A5
Simmil Rd ESH/CLAY KT10 204 E3
Simmons Cl TRDG/WHET N20 33 J3
Simmons Dr BCTR RM8 92 A1
Simmons Ga ESH/CLAY KT10 204 C3
Simmons La CHING E4 38 B4
Simmons Rd
WOOL/PLUM SE18 127 G5
Simmons' Wy
TRDG/WHET N20 33 J4
Sims Cl CAR SM5 194 D6
Simms Gdns EFNCH N2 47 G5
Simms Rd STHWK SE1 123 H4
Simnel Rd LEE/GVPK SE12 166 A2
Simon Cl NTGHL W11 100 D6
Simonds Rd LEY E10 69 J6
Simone Cl BMLY BR1 184 C4
Simons Wk SRTFD E15 88 B3
Simpson Cl CROY/NA CR0 196 D3
WCHMH N21 23 F6
Simpson Dr ACT W3 99 F5
Simpson Rd HSLWW TW4 154 E1
RAIN RM13 93 H4
RCHPK/HAM TW10 156 D6
Simpson's Rd HAYES BR2 183 K6
POP/IOD E14 105 K6
Simpson St BTSEA SW11 140 D3
Simpsons Wy SURB KT6 190 D3
Simrose Ct WAND/EARL SW18 139 K6
Sims Cl ROM RM1 75 H1
Sinclair Dr BELMT SM2 209 F6
Sinclair Gdns WKENS W14 119 G2
Sinclair Gv GLDGN NW11 64 B3
Sinclair Rd CHING E4 51 H1
WKENS W14 119 H3
Sinclare Cl EN EN1 24 B2
Singapore Rd WEA W13 116 B1
Singer St FSBYE EC1V 7 F5
Singleton Cl CROY/NA CR0 196 D4
HCH RM12 93 H2
TOOT SW17 178 E3
Singleton Rd DAGW RM9 92 B3
Singleton Scarp
NFNCH/WDSPK N12 46 E1
Sinnott Rd WALTH E17 51 F4
Sion Rd TWK TW1 156 C3
Sipson Cl WDR/YW UB7 112 D6
Sipson La WDR/YW UB7 112 E6
Sipson Rd WDR/YW UB7 112 C4
Sipson Wy WDR/YW UB7 132 D1
Sir Abraham Dawes Cots
PUT/ROE SW15 * 139 H5
Sir Alexander Cl ACT W3 118 C1
Sir Cyril Black Wy
WIM/MER SW19 177 J3
Sirdar Rd MTCM CR4 179 F2
NTGHL W11 100 B6
WDGN N22 49 H6
Sir John Kirk Cl CMBW SE5 142 D1
Sir Thomas More Est
CHEL SW3 120 C6
Sirus Rd NTHWD HA6 40 E1
Sise La MANHO EC4N * 12 E4
Sisley Rd BARK IG11 90 E6
Sispara Gdns
WAND/EARL SW18 159 J1
Sissinghurst Cl BMLY BR1 183 H1
Sissinghurst Rd CROY/NA CR0 197 H4
Sister Mabels Wy PECK SE15 * 143 H1
Sisters Av BTSEA SW11 140 E5
Sistova Rd BAL SW12 161 G3
Sisulu Pl BRXN/ST SW9 142 B4
Sittingbourne Av EN EN1 35 K1
Sitwell Gv STAN HA7 43 F1
Siverst Cl NTHLT UB5 78 B4
Siviter Wy DAGE RM10 92 D5
Siward Rd HAYES BR2 184 A6
TOOT SW17 160 B5
TOTM N17 49 K4
Sixth Av HYS/HAR UB3 113 J1
MNPK E12 89 K2
NKENS W10 100 C3
Sixth Cross Rd WHTN TW2 155 H5
Skardu Rd CRICK NW2 82 C3
Skeena Hl WAND/EARL SW18 159 H2
Skeet Hill La STMC/STPC BR5 203 G6
Skeffington Rd EHAM E6 89 K6
Skeffington St
WOOL/PLUM SE18 127 H3
Skelbrook St
WAND/EARL SW18 160 A4
Skelgill Rd PUT/ROE SW15 139 J5
Skelley Rd SRTFD E15 88 D5
Skelton Cl HACK E8 * 86 B4
Skelton Rd FSTGT E7 88 E4
Skelton's La LEY E10 69 K4
Skelwith Rd HMSMTH W6 119 F6
Skerne Rd KUTN/CMB KT2 174 E4
Skerne Wk KUTN/CMB KT2 174 E4
Sketchley Gdns
BERM/RHTH SE16 124 A5
Sketty Rd EN EN1 24 B4
Skiers St SRTFD E15 88 C6
Skiffington Cl
BRXS/STRHM SW2 162 B3
Skinner Pl BGVA SW1W * 15 G7
Skinners La BLKFR EC4V 12 D5
HEST TW5 135 G2
Skinner St CLKNW EC1R 6 A6
FSBYE EC1V 6 A5
Skipsey Av EHAM E6 107 K2
Skipton Cl FBAR/BDGN N11 48 A2
Skipton Dr HYS/HAR UB3 113 F3
Skipworth Rd HOM E9 86 E6
Skylines POP/IOD E14 125 F2
Skylines Village
POP/IOD E14 * 125 F2
Sky Peals Rd WFD IG8 52 B3
Skyport Dr WDR/YW UB7 132 A1
Sladebrook Rd
BKHTH/KID SE3 146 C4
Sladedale Rd
WOOL/PLUM SE18 127 K5
Slade Gdns ERITH DA8 150 C2
Slade Green Rd ERITH DA8 150 C2
Sladen Pl CLPT E5 86 D2
Slades Cl ENC/FH EN2 23 G4
Slades Dr CHST BR7 167 H5
ELTH/MOT SE9 167 H6
Slades Gdns ENC/FH EN2 23 G3
Slades Hl ENC/FH EN2 23 G4
Slades Ri ENC/FH EN2 23 G4
The Slade WOOL/PLUM SE18 127 K6
Slade Wk WALW SE17 122 C6
Slade Wy MTCM CR4 179 F4
Slagrove Pl LEW SE13 144 D6
Slaidburn St WBPTN SW10 120 B6
Slaithwaite Rd LEW SE13 145 F5
Slaney Pl HOLWY N7 85 G3
Slaney Rd ROM RM1 75 G2
Slattery Rd FELT TW13 154 B3
Sleaford Gn OXHEY WD19 27 H5
Sleaford St VX/NE SW8 141 H1
Sledmere Ct
EBED/NFELT TW14 153 H3
Slievemore Cl CLAP SW4 141 J4
Slingsby Pl LSQ/SEVD WC2H 10 E5
Slippers Pl BERM/RHTH SE16 123 J3
Sloane Av CHEL SW3 14 D7
Sloane Ct East CHEL SW3 121 F5
Sloane Ct West CHEL SW3 121 F5
Sloane Gdns BGVA SW1W 15 G7
ORP BR6 216 C1
Sloane Sq BGVA SW1W 15 F7
Sloane St KTBR SW1X 15 F5
Sloane Ter KTBR SW1X 15 F6
Sloane Wk CROY/NA CR0 198 C3
Slocum Cl THMD SE28 109 J6
Slough La CDALE/KGS NW9 62 E3
Sly St WCHPL E1 * 104 D5
Smaldon Cl WDR/YW UB7 112 D3
Smallberry Av ISLW TW7 136 A3
Smallbrook Ms BAY/PAD W2 8 A4
Smalley Cl STNW/STAM N16 86 B1
Smallwood Rd TOOT SW17 160 C6
Smarden Cl BELV DA17 129 H5
Smart Cl HARH RM3 57 K4
Smart's Pl NOXST/BSQ WC1A 11 F3
UED N18 50 C1
Smart St BETH E2 105 F2
Smeaton Rd
WAND/EARL SW18 159 K2
WFD IG8 53 K1
Smeaton St WAP E1W 123 J1
Smedley St VX/NE SW8 141 J3
Smeed Rd BOW E3 87 J5
Smiles Pl LEW SE13 145 F3
Smith Cl BERM/RHTH SE16 124 A1
Smithfield St STBT EC1A 12 A2
Smithies Rd ABYW SE2 128 C4
Smith's Ct SOHO/SHAV W1D * 10 C5
Smithson Rd TOTM N17 49 K4
Smith Sq WEST SW1P 16 E5
Smith St BRYLDS KT5 191 G3
CHEL SW3 120 E5
Smith's Yd CROY/NA CR0 211 J1
Smith Ter CHEL SW3 120 E5
Smithwood Cl
WIM/MER SW19 159 H3
Smithy St WCHPL E1 104 E4
Smugglers Wy
WAND/EARL SW18 140 A5
Smyrks Rd WALW SE17 * 123 F5
Smyrk's Rd WALW SE17 123 F5
Smyrna Rd KIL/WHAMP NW6 82 E5
Smythe Cl ED N9 36 C5
Smythe St POP/IOD E14 105 K6
Snakes La EBAR EN4 22 B4
Snakes La East WFD IG8 53 G2
Snakes La West WFD IG8 52 E2
Snakey La FELT TW13 153 K6
Snaresbrook Dr STAN HA7 29 K6
Snaresbrook Rd WAN E11 70 C1
Snarsgate St NKENS W10 100 A4
Sneath Av GLDGN NW11 64 D4
Snell's Pk UED N18 50 B2
Sneyd Rd CRICK NW2 82 A3
Snipe Cl ERITH DA8 150 E1
Snowberry Cl SRTFD E15 88 B2
Snowbury Rd FUL/PGN SW6 140 A3
Snowden Dr CDALE/KGS NW9 63 G3
Snowdon Crs HYS/HAR UB3 113 F3
Snowdon Rd HTHAIR TW6 153 F1
Snowdown Cl PGE/AN SE20 181 K4
Snowdrop Cl HPTN TW12 173 F2
Snow Hl STBT EC1A 12 A2
Snowsfields STHWK SE1 19 F2
Snowshill Rd MNPK E12 89 J3
Snowy Fielder Waye
ISLW TW7 136 C3
Soames St PECK SE15 143 G4
Soames Wk NWMAL KT3 176 B4
Soane Cl EA W5 116 E2
Soaphouse La BTFD TW8 137 F1
Soho Sq SOHO/SHAV W1D 10 C3
Soho St SOHO/SHAV W1D 10 C3
Sojourner-Truth Cl HACK E8 86 D4
Solander Gdns WCHPL E1 104 D6
Solebay St WCHPL E1 105 G3
Solent Ri PLSTW E13 106 E2
Solent Rd KIL/WHAMP NW6 82 E3
Solna Av PUT/ROE SW15 139 F6
Solna Rd WCHMH N21 35 K3
Solomon Av UED N18 36 C6
Solomon's Pas PECK SE15 143 J5
Solon New Rd CLAP SW4 141 K5
Solon Rd BRXS/STRHM SW2 141 K5
Solway Cl HACK E8 86 B4
HSLWW TW4 134 D4
Solway Rd EDUL SE22 143 H5
WDGN N22 49 H4
Somaford Gv EBAR EN4 33 H1
Somali Rd CRICK NW2 82 D2
Somerby Rd BARK IG11 90 D5
Somercoates Cl EBAR EN4 21 J4
Somerden Rd
STMC/STPC BR5 202 E4
Somerfield Rd FSBYPK N4 67 H6
Somerfield St
BERM/RHTH SE16 124 A5
Somerford Cl PIN HA5 58 E1
Somerford Gv
STNW/STAM N16 86 B2
TOTM N17 50 C3
Somerford St WCHPL E1 * 104 D3
Somerford Wy
BERM/RHTH SE16 124 B2
Somerhill Av BFN/LL DA15 168 C2
Somerhill Rd WELL DA16 148 C3
Somerleyton Rd
BRXN/ST SW9 142 B5
Somersby Gdns REDBR IG4 71 K2
Somers Cl CAMTN NW1 4 C2
Somers Crs BAY/PAD W2 8 C4
Somerset Av CHSGTN KT9 205 K2
RYNPK SW20 176 E5
WELL DA16 148 A6
Somerset Cl CHEAM SM3 208 A1
NWMAL KT3 192 B3
TOTM N17 49 K5
WFD IG8 52 E4
Somerset Gdns HGT N6 66 A4
LEW SE13 144 E3
STRHM/NOR SW16 180 A6
TEDD TW11 173 K1
TOTM N17 * 50 A3
Somerset Rd BAR EN5 21 F6
BTFD TW8 116 D6
CHSWK W4 118 A3
DART DA1 170 E1
HDN NW4 64 A1
HRW HA1 60 C3
KUT/HW KT1 175 G5
ORP BR6 202 B4
PEND EN3 25 J1
STHL UB1 96 A4
TEDD TW11 173 K1
TOTM N17 50 B6
UED N18 50 B1
WALTH E17 69 J2
WEA W13 116 C1
WIM/MER SW19 159 G5
Somerset Sq WKENS W14 * 119 H3
Somerset Waye HEST TW5 114 D6
Somersham Rd BXLYHN DA7 149 F3
Somers Pl BRXS/STRHM SW2 162 A2
Somers Rd BRXS/STRHM SW2 162 A1
WALTH E17 69 H1
Somers Wy BUSH WD23 28 C2
Somerton Av RCH/KEW TW9 137 J4
Somerton Rd CRICK NW2 82 B1
PECK SE15 143 J5
Somertrees Av
LEE/GVPK SE12 166 A4
Somervell Rd
RYLN/HDSTN HA2 77 K3
Somerville Av BARN SW13 119 F6
Somerville Cl BRXN/ST SW9 142 A2
Somerville Rd CHDH RM6 73 J2
DART DA1 171 J1
PGE/AN SE20 182 A3
Sonderburg Rd HOLWY N7 67 F6
Sondes St WALW SE17 122 E6
Songhurst Cl CROY/NA CR0 196 A3
Sonia Cl OXHEY WD19 27 G2
Sonia Gdns HEST TW5 135 F1
NFNCH/WDSPK N12 33 G6
WLSDN NW10 81 H2
Sonning Gdns HPTN TW12 172 D2
Sonning Rd SNWD SE25 197 H3
Soper Cl CHING E4 51 H1
FSTH SE23 164 A3
Soper Ms PEND EN3 25 J1
Sophia Cl HOLWY N7 85 F4
Sophia Rd CAN/RD E16 107 F4
LEY E10 69 K5
Sophia Sq BERM/RHTH SE16 105 G6
Sopwith Av CHSGTN KT9 206 A3
Sopwith Cl KUTN/CMB KT2 175 G1
Sopwith Rd HEST TW5 134 B1
Sopwith Wy KUTN/CMB KT2 175 F4
VX/NE SW8 141 G1
Sorrel Bank CROY/NA CR0 * 213 G6
Sorrel Cl THMD SE28 128 B1
Sorrel Gdns EHAM E6 107 J4
Sorrel La POP/IOD E14 106 B5
Sorrell Cl BRXN/ST SW9 * 142 B3
NWCR SE14 144 B1
Sorrel Wk ROM RM1 57 H6
Sorrento Rd SUT SM1 209 F1
Sotheby Rd HBRY N5 85 J2
Sotheran Cl HACK E8 86 C6
Soudan Rd BTSEA SW11 140 E2
Souldern Rd WKENS W14 * 119 G3
Sounds Ldg SWLY BR8 203 K3
South Access Rd LEY E10 69 F4
South Africa Rd SHB W12 99 K6
Southall Ct STHL UB1 * 95 K6
Southall La HEST TW5 114 A6
Southall Pl STHWK SE1 18 E3
Southampton Blds
LINN WC2A * 11 J2
Southampton Gdns
MTCM CR4 195 K2
Southampton Ms
CAN/RD E16 126 A1
Southampton Pl
NOXST/BSQ WC1A 11 F2
Southampton Rd HAMP NW3 83 K3
Southampton Rd East
HTHAIR TW6 152 C1
Southampton Rd West
HTHAIR TW6 152 C1
Southampton Rw
NOXST/BSQ WC1A 11 F1
RSQ WC1B 10 E1
Southampton St
COVGDN WC2E 11 F5
Southampton Wy CMBW SE5 142 E1
Southam St NKENS W10 100 C3
South Ap NTHWD HA6 26 B5
South Audley St
MYFR/PKLN W1K 9 H6
South Av CAR SM5 210 A5
CHING E4 37 K2
RCH/KEW TW9 * 137 H3
STHL UB1 95 K6
South Avenue Gdns STHL UB1 95 K6
South Bank STHWK SE1 11 K6
SURB KT6 191 F3
Southbank THDIT KT7 190 C4
South Bank Ter SURB KT6 * 191 F3
South Birkbeck Rd WAN E11 88 B1
South Black Lion La
HMSMTH W6 118 D5
South Bolton Gdns
WBPTN SW10 120 A5
Southborough Cl SURB KT6 190 E5
Southborough La HAYES BR2 200 D2
Southborough Rd BMLY BR1 184 D6
HOM E9 86 E6
SURB KT6 191 F5
Southborough Rd (The Lane)
SURB KT6 * 191 F5
South Boundary Rd
MNPK E12 89 K1
Southbourne HAYES BR2 199 K4
Southbourne Av
CDALE/KGS NW9 44 E5
Southbourne Cl PIN HA5 59 J4
Southbourne Crs HDN NW4 64 C1
Southbourne Gdns IL IG1 90 C3
LEE/GVPK SE12 146 A6
RSLP HA4 59 F5
Southbridge Pl CROY/NA CR0 211 J2
Southbridge Rd
CROY/NA CR0 211 J2
Southbridge Wy NWDGN UB2 114 D2
Southbrook Rd
LEE/GVPK SE12 165 H1
STRHM/NOR SW16 179 K4
Southbury Av EN EN1 24 C5
RAIN RM13 111 K4
Southbury Rd EN EN1 24 B5
South Carriage Dr KTBR SW1X 15 F2
SKENS SW7 14 C3
Southchurch Rd EHAM E6 107 K1
South Cl BAR EN5 20 D4
BXLYHS DA6 148 E5
DAGE RM10 92 C6
HGT N6 66 B3
PIN HA5 59 K4
WDR/YW UB7 112 C3
WHTN TW2 155 F5
The South Colonnade
POP/IOD E14 124 D1
Southcombe St WKENS W14 119 H4
Southcote Av BRYLDS KT5 191 J4
FELT TW13 153 J4
Southcote Ri RSLP HA4 58 B4
Southcote Rd ARCH N19 84 C2
SNWD SE25 197 J2
WALTH E17 69 F2
South Countess Rd
WALTH E17 51 H6
South Crs CAN/RD E16 106 B3
Southcroft Av WELL DA16 147 K4
WWKM BR4 199 F6
Southcroft Rd ORP BR6 216 E1
TOOT SW17 179 F2
South Cross Rd BARK/HLT IG6 72 C2
South Croxted Rd DUL SE21 162 E5
Southdale CHIG IG7 54 D2
Southdean Gdns
WIM/MER SW19 159 J4
South Dene MLHL NW7 31 F5
Southdown Av HNWL W7 116 B3
Southdown Crs
GNTH/NBYPK IG2 72 E2
RYLN/HDSTN HA2 60 C5
Southdown Dr RYNPK SW20 177 G3
Southdown Rd CAR SM5 210 A6
EMPK RM11 75 K4
RYNPK SW20 177 G4
Southdown Vls
SEVS/STOTM N15 * 67 H2
South Dr MNPK E12 89 J1
ORP BR6 216 E3
RSLP HA4 58 C5
South Ealing Rd EA W5 116 E2
South Eastern Av ED N9 36 B5
South Eaton Pl BGVA SW1W 15 H6
South Eden Park Rd
BECK BR3 198 E2
South Edwardes Sq KENS W8 119 J3
South End CROY/NA CR0 211 J2
KENS W8 * 120 A3
Southend Cl ELTH/MOT SE9 167 G1
Southend Crs ELTH/MOT SE9 167 F1
Southend La CAT SE6 164 D6
SYD SE26 164 C6
Southend Rd BECK BR3 182 D4
CLAY IG5 53 J6
EHAM E6 89 K5
South End Rd HAMP NW3 83 J2
RAIN RM13 93 J6
Southend Rd (North Circular)
WALTH E17 52 B4
Southend Rd (North Circular
Rd) SWFD E18 52 E5
South End Rw KENS W8 120 A3
Southern Av
EBED/NFELT TW14 153 K3
SNWD SE25 181 G6
Southern Down FELT TW13 * 154 B3
Southern Dr LOU IG10 39 K1
Southerngate Wy NWCR SE14 144 B1
Southern Gv BOW E3 105 H2
Southern Perimeter Rd
HTHAIR TW6 133 F6
STWL/WRAY TW19 152 C1
Southern Rd EFNCH N2 65 K1
PLSTW E13 107 F1
Southern Rw NKENS W10 100 B3
Southern St IS N1 5 G2
Southern Wy GNWCH SE10 125 H4
ROMW/RG RM7 74 C3
Southerton Rd HMSMTH W6 * 119 F4
South Esk Rd FSTGT E7 89 G4
Southey Rd BRXN/ST SW9 142 B2
SEVS/STOTM N15 68 A2
WIM/MER SW19 177 K3
Southey St PGE/AN SE20 182 A3
Southfield BAR EN5 32 B1
Southfield Gdns TWK TW1 156 A6
Southfield Pk
RYLN/HDSTN HA2 60 B1
Southfield Rd CHST BR7 186 A6
CHSWK W4 118 A2
PEND EN3 36 D1
Southfields E/WMO/HCT KT8 189 K3
HDN NW4 45 K6
Southfields Ms
WAND/EARL SW18 * 159 K1
Southfields Rd
WAND/EARL SW18 159 K1
Southfleet Rd ORP BR6 216 E1
South Gdns WBLY HA9 * 62 C6
WIM/MER SW19 178 C3
South Gate Av FELT TW13 153 G6
Southgate Gv IS N1 85 K5
Southgate Rd IS N1 85 K6
MNPK E12 89 H1
South Gipsy Rd WELL DA16 148 E4
South Gv HGT N6 66 A5
SEVS/STOTM N15 67 K2
WALTH E17 69 H2
South Hall Dr RAIN RM13 111 K4
South Hl CHST BR7 184 E2
NTHWD HA6 * 40 C4
South Hill Av
RYLN/HDSTN HA2 78 C1
South Hill Gv HRW HA1 78 E2
South Hill Park Gdns
HAMP NW3 83 J2
South Hill Rd HAYES BR2 183 H6
Southholme Cl NRWD SE19 181 F4
Southill La PIN HA5 58 E1
Southill Rd CHST BR7 184 D3
Southill St POP/IOD E14 105 K5
South Island Pl BRXN/ST SW9 142 A1
South Kensington Station Ar
SKENS SW7 14 B6
South Lambeth Pl
VX/NE SW8 122 A6
South Lambeth Rd
VX/NE SW8 141 K1
Southland Rd
WOOL/PLUM SE18 128 B6
Southlands Av ORP BR6 216 E2
Southlands Dr
WIM/MER SW19 159 G4
Southlands Gv BMLY BR1 184 D6
Southlands Rd HAYES BR2 200 C1
Southland Wy HSLW TW3 135 J6
South La KUT/HW KT1 174 E6
NWMAL KT3 192 A1
South La West NWMAL KT3 192 A1
South Lodge Av MTCM CR4 195 K1
South Lodge Crs ENC/FH EN2 22 D5

South Lodge Dr
STHGT/OAK N14 22 D5
STHGT/OAK N14 22 E6
South Md CDALE/KGS NW9 45 H4
HOR/WEW KT19 207 H5
Southmead Rd
WIM/MER SW19 159 H3
Southmere Dr ABYW SE2 128 D2
South Molton La
MYFR/PKLN W1K 9 J4
South Molton Rd CAN/RD E16 106 E5
South Molton St
MYFR/PKLN W1K 9 J4
Southmont Rd
ESH/CLAY KT10 189 K6
Southmoor Wy HOM E9 87 H4
South Mt TRDG/WHET N20 * 33 G4
South Norwood Hl
SNWD SE25 181 F4
South Oak Rd
STRHM/NOR SW16 162 A6
Southold Ri ELTH/MOT SE9 166 E5
Southolm St BTSEA SW11 141 G2
South Ordnance Rd
PEND EN3 25 J1
Southover BMLY BR1 183 K1
NFNCH/WDSPK N12 32 E6
South Pde CHEL SW3 120 C5
CHSWK W4 118 A4
EDGW HA8 * 44 C5
WLGTN SM6 * 210 C4
South Park Crs CAT SE6 165 H3
IL IG1 90 D1
South Park Dr
GDMY/SEVK IG3 90 E3
South Park Gv NWMAL KT3 191 K1
South Park Hill Rd
SAND/SEL CR2 211 K3
South Park Ms FUL/PGN SW6 140 A4
South Park Rd IL IG1 90 D2
WIM/MER SW19 177 K2
South Park Ter IL IG1 90 D1
South Park Wy RSLP HA4 77 G4
South Pl BRYLDS KT5 191 G4
LVPST EC2M 13 F2
PEND EN3 24 E6
South Place Ms LVPST EC2M 13 F2
Southport Rd
WOOL/PLUM SE18 127 J4
Southridge Pl RYNPK SW20 177 G3
South Ri BAY/PAD W2 * 8 D5
CAR SM5 209 J6
South Rd CHDH RM6 73 J2
EA W5 116 E4
ED N9 36 C3
EDGW HA8 44 D4
ERITH DA8 130 C6
FELT TW13 172 C1
FSTH SE23 164 A4
HPTN TW12 172 D2
STHL UB1 114 E1
WDR/YW UB7 112 D3
WHTN TW2 155 J5
WIM/MER SW19 178 C2
South Rw BKHTH/KID SE3 145 K3
Southsea Rd KUT/HW KT1 191 F1
South Sea St
BERM/RHTH SE16 124 C3
South Side HMSMTH W6 118 C3
SEVS/STOTM N15 * 68 B1
Southside Common
WIM/MER SW19 177 G2
Southspring BFN/LL DA15 167 J2
South Sq GINN WC1R 11 J2
GLDGN NW11 64 E3
South St BMLY BR1 183 K5
EMPK RM11 75 J3
ISLW TW7 136 B4
MYFR/PKLN W1K 9 H7
PEND EN3 25 F6
RAIN RM13 110 E1
ROM RM1 75 G3
South Tenter St WCHPL E1 13 K5
South Ter SKENS SW7 14 C6
SURB KT6 191 F3
WDGN N22 48 E5
South V HRW HA1 78 E2
NRWD SE19 181 F2
Southvale Rd BKHTH/KID SE3 145 H3
South Vale Rd SURB KT6 191 F6
South Vw BMLY BR1 184 B5
Southview Av WLSDN NW10 81 H3
South View Cl BXLY DA5 169 G1
Southview Cl TOOT SW17 179 F1
South View Ct NRWD SE19 * 180 D3
South View Crs
GNTH/NBYPK IG2 72 B3
Southview Dr SWFD E18 53 F6
Southview Gdns WLGTN SM6 210 C5
Southview Rd BMLY BR1 165 G6
South View Rd
CEND/HSY/T N8 48 D6
LOU IG10 39 K1
PIN HA5 41 F2
RDART DA2 171 G5
Southviews SAND/SEL CR2 213 F6
South Vls CAMTN NW1 84 D4
Southville VX/NE SW8 141 J2
Southville Cl
EBED/NFELT TW14 153 H2
HOR/WEW KT19 207 F6
Southville Crs
EBED/NFELT TW14 153 H3
Southville Rd
EBED/NFELT TW14 153 H3
THDIT KT7 190 B4
South Wk WWKM BR4 214 C1
Southwark Br CANST EC4R 12 D6
Southwark Bridge Rd
STHWK SE1 18 B4
Southwark Park Est
BERM/RHTH SE16 * 123 J4
Southwark Park Rd
BERM/RHTH SE16 19 K6
Southwark Pl BMLY BR1 184 E6
Southwark St STHWK SE1 12 B7
Southwater Cl BECK BR3 182 E3
POP/IOD E14 105 H5
South Wy CROY/NA CR0 213 G1
ED N9 36 E4
FBAR/BDGN N11 48 C2
RYLN/HDSTN HA2 60 A1
WBLY HA9 80 C3
Southway GLDGN NW11 65 F3
HAYES BR2 199 K4
RYNPK SW20 193 G1
TRDG/WHET N20 32 E4
WLGTN SM6 210 C2
Southway Cl SHB W12 118 E2
Southwell Av NTHLT UB5 78 A4
Southwell Gdns SKENS SW7 120 B4
Southwell Grove Rd WAN E11 70 C6
Southwell Rd CMBW SE5 142 D4
CROY/NA CR0 196 B3
KTN/HRWW/WS HA3 61 K3
South Western Rd TWK TW1 156 B1
South West India Dock Entrance POP/IOD E14 125 F2
Southwest Rd WAN E11 70 B5
South Wharf Rd BAY/PAD W2 8 A3
Southwick Ms BAY/PAD W2 8 B3
Southwick Pl BAY/PAD W2 8 C4
Southwick St BAY/PAD W2 8 C3
Southwick Yd BAY/PAD W2 * 8 D4
Southwold Dr BARK IG11 91 G3
Southwold Rd BXLY DA5 169 J1
CLPT E5 68 D6
Southwood Av HGT N6 66 B4
KUTN/CMB KT2 175 K4
Southwood Cl BMLY BR1 200 E1
WPK KT4 193 G5
Southwood Dr BRYLDS KT5 191 K4
South Woodford SWFD E18 52 E5
Southwood Gdns
ESH/CLAY KT10 205 G1
GNTH/NBYPK IG2 72 B1
Southwood La HGT N6 66 A4
Southwood Lawn Rd HGT N6 66 A4
Southwood Pk HGT N6 * 66 B4
Southwood Rd
ELTH/MOT SE9 167 G4
THMD SE28 128 C1
South Worple Wy
MORT/ESHN SW14 138 A4
Southy Ms CAN/RD E16 125 K1
Sovereign Cl EA W5 97 J4
RSLP HA4 58 C5
WAP E1W 104 D6
Sovereign Ct
E/WMO/HCT KT8 188 E1
Sovereign Crs
BERM/RHTH SE16 105 G6
Sovereign Gv ALP/SUD HA0 79 K1
Sovereign Ms BETH E2 * 7 J2
EBAR EN4 21 K4
Sovereign Pk WLSDN NW10 * 98 D3
Sovereign Pl HRW HA1 61 F2
Sovereign Rd BARK IG11 109 J2
Sowerby Cl ELTH/MOT SE9 146 E6
Sowrey Av RAIN RM13 93 H4
Space Waye
EBED/NFELT TW14 134 A6
Spafield St CLKNW EC1R 5 J6
Spa Green Est CLKNW EC1R * 5 K4
Spa Hl NRWD SE19 180 E4
Spalding Cl EDGW HA8 45 G3
Spalding Rd HDN NW4 64 A3
TOOT SW17 179 G1
Spanby Rd BOW E3 105 J3
Spaniards Cl GLDGN NW11 65 G5
Spaniards End HAMP NW3 65 G5
Spaniards Rd HAMP NW3 65 G6
Spanish Pl MHST W1U * 9 H3
Spanish Rd WAND/EARL SW18 140 B6
Sparkbridge Rd HRW HA1 60 E1
Sparkes Cl HAYES BR2 200 A1
Sparke Ter CAN/RD E16 * 106 D5
Sparkford Gdns
FBAR/BDGN N11 48 A1
Sparks Cl ACT W3 99 F5
BCTR RM8 73 K6
HPTN TW12 172 D2
Spa Rd BERM/RHTH SE16 19 J5
Sparrow Cl HPTN TW12 172 D2
Sparrow Dr STMC/STPC BR5 201 H5
Sparrow Farm Dr
EBED/NFELT TW14 154 B2
Sparrow Farm Rd EW KT17 207 J2
Sparrow Gn DAGE RM10 92 D1
Sparrows Herne BUSH WD23 28 B2
Sparrows La ELTH/MOT SE9 167 H2
Sparrows Wy BUSH WD23 * 28 C2
Sparrows Wick BUSH WD23 * 28 C3
Sparsholt Rd ARCH N19 67 F5
BARK IG11 90 E6
Spartan Cl WLGTN SM6 210 E5
Sparta St GNWCH SE10 145 F2
Speakers Ct CROY/NA CR0 * 196 E5
Spearman St
WOOL/PLUM SE18 * 127 F6
Spear Ms ECT SW5 119 K4
Spears Rd ARCH N19 66 E5
Speart La HEST TW5 134 D1
Spectrum Pl WALW SE17 122 E5
Spedan Cl HAMP NW3 83 F1
Speedwell St DEPT SE8 144 D1
Speedy Pl STPAN WC1H 4 E5
Speer Rd THDIT KT7 190 A3
Speirs Cl NWMAL KT3 192 C3
Spekehill ELTH/MOT SE9 166 E5
Speke Rd THHTH CR7 180 E5
Speldhurst Cl HAYES BR2 199 J2
Speldhurst Rd CHSWK W4 118 A3
HOM E9 87 F5
Spellbrook Wk IS N1 * 85 J6
Spelman St WCHPL E1 104 C4
Spence Cl BERM/RHTH SE16 124 C2
Spencer Av PLMGR N13 49 F2
YEAD UB4 94 E4
Spencer Cl FNCH N3 46 D5
ORP BR6 201 K6
WFD IG8 53 G1
WLSDN NW10 98 B2
Spencer Dr EFNCH N2 65 G3
Spencer Gdns
MORT/ESHN SW14 137 K6
Spencer Hl WIM/MER SW19 177 H2
Spencer Hill Rd
WIM/MER SW19 177 H3
Spencer House SURB KT6 * 191 F2
Spencer Ms CLAP SW4 141 K2
HMSMTH W6 119 H6
Spencer Pk WAND/EARL SW18 140 C6
Spencer Pl CROY/NA CR0 196 E4
IS N1 85 H5
WEST SW1P 16 B5
Spencer Ri KTTN NW5 84 B2
Spencer Rd ACT W3 117 K1
ALP/SUD HA0 61 J6
BMLY BR1 183 J3
BTSEA SW11 140 C5
CEND/HSY/T N8 67 F2
CHSWK W4 137 K1
E/WMO/HCT KT8 189 H1
EHAM E6 89 H6
FBAR/BDGN N11 34 B6
GDMY/SEVK IG3 73 F5
ISLW TW7 135 J2
KTN/HRWW/WS HA3 42 E5
MTCM CR4 179 F6
MTCM CR4 194 E4
RAIN RM13 111 F2
RYNPK SW20 176 E4
SAND/SEL CR2 212 A3
TOTM N17 50 C4
WALTH E17 52 A5
WHTN TW2 155 K5
Spencer St FSBYE EC1V 6 A5
NWDGN UB2 114 C3
Spencer Wk PUT/ROE SW15 139 G5
Spencer Wy WCHPL E1 104 D5
Spenser Gv STNW/STAM N16 86 A2
Spenser Ms DUL SE21 162 E3
Spenser Rd HNHL SE24 142 C6
Spenser St WESTW SW1E 16 B4
Spensley Wk
STNW/STAM N16 85 K1
Speranza St
WOOL/PLUM SE18 128 A5
Sperling Rd TOTM N17 50 B5
Spert St POP/IOD E14 105 G6
Speyside STHGT/OAK N14 34 C1
Spey St POP/IOD E14 106 A4
Spey Wy ROM RM1 57 G3
Spezia Rd WLSDN NW10 99 J1
Spicer Cl BRXN/ST SW9 142 C3
WOT/HER KT12 188 B3
Spices Yd CROY/NA CR0 211 J2
Spielman Rd DART DA1 151 J5
Spigurnell Rd TOTM N17 49 K4
Spikes Bridge Rd STHL UB1 95 J5
Spindle Cl WOOL/PLUM SE18 126 D3
Spindlewood Gdns
CROY/NA CR0 212 A2
Spindrift Av POP/IOD E14 124 E4
Spinel Cl WOOL/PLUM SE18 128 A5
Spinnaker Cl BARK IG11 109 H2
Spinnells Rd
RYLN/HDSTN HA2 59 K5
Spinney Cl BECK BR3 198 E1
NWMAL KT3 192 B2
RAIN RM13 111 G1
WPK KT4 207 H1
Spinney Dr EBED/NFELT TW14 153 F2
Spinney Gdns DAGW RM9 92 A3
ESH/CLAY KT10 204 B1
NRWD SE19 181 G1
Spinney Oak BMLY BR1 184 D5
The Spinneys BMLY BR1 184 E5
The Spinney ALP/SUD HA0 79 G1
BAR EN5 21 F3
BARN SW13 * 118 E6
CHEAM SM3 208 A2
NFNCH/WDSPK N12 * 47 G3
SCUP DA14 187 F1
STAN HA7 30 A6
STRHM/NOR SW16 161 H5
WCHMH N21 35 G2
The Spires DART DA1 171 G4
Spirit Quay WAP E1W 123 H1
Spital Sq WCHPL E1 13 H1
Spital St DART DA1 171 G1
WCHPL E1 104 C4
Spital Yd WCHPL E1 * 13 H1
Spitfire Est HEST TW5 * 114 B5
Spitfire House
WOOL/PLUM SE18 * 146 D1
Spitfire Rd WLGTN SM6 211 F5
Spitfire Wy HEST TW5 114 B5
Spode Wk KIL/WHAMP NW6 * 83 F3
Spondon Rd
SEVS/STOTM N15 68 C1
Spoonbill Wy YEAD UB4 95 H4
Spooner Wk WLGTN SM6 210 D3
Sportsbank St CAT SE6 165 F2
Sportsman Pl BETH E2 86 C6
Spottons Gv TOTM N17 49 J4
Spout Hl CROY/NA CR0 213 J3
Spratt Hall Rd WAN E11 70 E3
Spray St WOOL/PLUM SE18 127 G4
Spreighton Rd
E/WMO/HCT KT8 189 G1
Sprimont Pl CHEL SW3 120 E5
Springall St PECK SE15 143 J1
Springbank WCHMH N21 35 F1
Springbank Rd LEW SE13 165 H1
Springbank Wk CAMTN NW1 84 D5
Springbourne Ct BECK BR3 183 F4
Spring Bridge Rd EA W5 97 K6
Spring Cl BAR EN5 20 B6
BCTR RM8 73 K4
Springclose La CHEAM SM3 208 C4
Spring Cnr FELT TW13 * 153 K5
Spring Cots SURB KT6 * 190 E2
Spring Court Rd ENC/FH EN2 23 G1
Springcroft Av EFNCH N2 47 K6
Springdale Rd
STNW/STAM N16 85 K2
Spring Dr PIN HA5 58 E3
Springfield BUSH WD23 28 D3
CLPT E5 68 D5
Springfield Av HPTN TW12 173 G2
MUSWH N10 48 C6
RYNPK SW20 177 J6
Springfield Cl
NFNCH/WDSPK N12 47 F1
STAN HA7 29 G5
Springfield Dr
GNTH/NBYPK IG2 72 C2
Springfield Gdns BMLY BR1 200 E1
CDALE/KGS NW9 63 F2
CLPT E5 68 D5
RSLP HA4 59 F5
WFD IG8 53 G3
WWKM BR4 198 E6
Springfield Gv CHARL SE7 126 B6
Springfield La
KIL/WHAMP NW6 83 F6
Springfield Mt
CDALE/KGS NW9 63 G2
Springfield Parade Ms
PLMGR N13 35 G6
Springfield Pl NWMAL KT3 191 K1
Springfield Ri SYD SE26 163 J5
Springfield Rd BMLY BR1 200 E1
BXLYHN DA7 149 J4
CHING E4 38 C3
EHAM E6 89 K5
FBAR/BDGN N11 48 C1
HNWL W7 115 K1
HRW HA1 60 E3
KUT/HW KT1 191 F1
SEVS/STOTM N15 68 C1
SRTFD E15 * 106 C2
STJWD NW8 83 G6
SYD SE26 181 J1
TEDD TW11 174 B1
THHTH CR7 180 D4
WALTH E17 69 H3
WELL DA16 148 C4
WHTN TW2 155 F3
WIM/MER SW19 177 J1
WLGTN SM6 210 B3
YEAD UB4 114 B1
Springfield Wk
KIL/WHAMP NW6 83 F6
Spring Gdns E/WMO/HCT KT8 189 H2
HBRY N5 85 J3
HCH RM12 93 K2
ORP BR6 217 H4
ROMW/RG RM7 74 E2
WFD IG8 53 G3
WHALL SW1A 10 E7
WLGTN SM6 210 C3
Spring Gv CHSWK W4 117 H5
HPTN TW12 173 G4
LOU IG10 39 H1
MTCM CR4 179 F4
Spring Grove Crs HSLW TW3 135 H2
Spring Grove Rd HSLW TW3 135 H2
RCHPK/HAM TW10 137 G6
Springhead Rd ERITH DA8 130 C6
Spring Hl CLPT E5 68 C4
SYD SE26 163 K6
Springhill Cl CMBW SE5 142 E4
Springhurst Cl CROY/NA CR0 213 H2
Spring Lake STAN HA7 29 H6
Spring La CLPT E5 68 D5
MUSWH N10 48 A6
SNWD SE25 197 J3
Spring Ms MHST W1U * 9 F1
Spring Park Av CROY/NA CR0 198 A6
Springpark Dr BECK BR3 183 F6
FSBYPK N4 67 J5
Spring Park Rd CROY/NA CR0 198 A6
Spring Pl BARK IG11 108 C1
KTTN NW5 84 A3
Springpond Rd DAGW RM9 92 A3
Springrice Rd LEW SE13 165 F1
Spring Rd FELT TW13 153 J5
Spring Shaw Rd
STMC/STPC BR5 186 B4
Spring St BAY/PAD W2 8 A4
EW KT17 207 H6
Spring Tide Cl PECK SE15 * 143 H2
Spring V BXLYHN DA7 149 J5
Springvale Av BTFD TW8 116 E5
Spring V North DART DA1 171 G2
Spring V South DART DA1 * 171 G2
Springvale Ter WKENS W14 119 G3
Springvale Wy
STMC/STPC BR5 186 D6
Spring Villa Rd EDGW HA8 44 C3
Spring Vls WEA W13 * 116 C1
Spring Wk WCHPL E1 104 C4
Springwater Cl
WOOL/PLUM SE18 * 147 F2
Springwell Av WLSDN NW10 81 H6
Springwell Rd HEST TW5 134 C2
STRHM/NOR SW16 162 A6
Springwood Cl BOW E3 105 J1
Springwood Crs EDGW HA8 30 E4
Springwood Wy ROM RM1 75 J2
Sprowston Ms FSTGT E7 88 E3
Sprowston Rd FSTGT E7 88 E3
Sprucedale Gdns
CROY/NA CR0 213 F2
WLGTN SM6 210 E6
Spruce Hills Rd WALTH E17 51 K5
Sprules Rd BROCKY SE4 144 B3
Spurfield E/WMO/HCT KT8 173 G6
Spurgeon Av NRWD SE19 180 E4
Spurgeon Rd NRWD SE19 180 E3
Spurgeon St STHWK SE1 18 E5
Spurling Rd DAGW RM9 92 B4
EDUL SE22 * 143 G5
Spurrell Av BXLY DA5 170 A6
Spur Rd BARK IG11 108 C2
EBED/NFELT TW14 134 A6
EDGW HA8 30 A6
ISLW TW7 136 B1
ORP BR6 202 B6
SEVS/STOTM N15 * 67 K1
STHWK SE1 17 J2
WHALL SW1A 16 A3
Spurstowe Rd HACK E8 86 D4
Spurstowe Ter HACK E8 86 C3
The Square CAR SM5 210 A3
HMSMTH W6 119 F5
IL IG1 72 A4
RCH/KEW TW9 137 F6
STKPK UB11 113 G1
WFD IG8 52 E1
Squarey St TOOT SW17 160 B5
Squire Gdns STJWD NW8 2 A5
Squires Ct WIM/MER SW19 159 K6
Squires La FNCH N3 47 F4
Squire's Mt HAMP NW3 83 H1
Squires Wy RDART DA2 170 A6
Squires Wood Dr CHST BR7 * 184 E3
Squirrel Cl HSLWW TW4 134 B4
Squirrel Ms WEA W13 * 97 G6
Squirrels Cl
NFNCH/WDSPK N12 33 G6
Squirrels Gn WPK KT4 192 C6
Squirrel's Heath Av GPK RM2 57 K6
The Squirrels BUSH WD23 28 D1
LEW SE13 145 G4
PIN HA5 41 K6
Squirries St BETH E2 104 C2
Stable Cl KUTN/CMB KT2 175 G2
NTHLT UB5 96 A1
Stable La BXLY DA5 169 J4
Stable Ms TWK TW1 156 A3
WNWD SE27 180 D1
Stables End ORP BR6 216 C1
Stables Wy LBTH SE11 122 B5
Stable Wk EFNCH N2 47 H4
IS N1 5 F2
Stable Wy NKENS W10 100 A5
Stable Yard Rd WHALL SW1A 16 B1
Stacey Av UED N18 36 E6
Stacey Cl LEY E10 70 B2
Stacey St HOLWY N7 85 G1
LSQ/SEVD WC2H 10 D4
Stackhouse St KTBR SW1X 14 E4
Stacy Pth CMBW SE5 * 143 F1
Staddon Cl BECK BR3 198 B1
Staddon Ct BECK BR3 198 B1
Stadium Rd HDN NW4 63 K4
WOOL/PLUM SE18 146 E1
Stadium St WBPTN SW10 140 B1
Stadium Wy DART DA1 170 B1
WBLY HA9 80 B2
Staffa Rd LEY E10 69 G5
Stafford Av CLAY IG5 54 A5
Stafford Cl CHEAM SM3 208 C4
KIL/WHAMP NW6 100 E2
STHGT/OAK N14 22 C6
WALTH E17 69 H3
Stafford Cross CROY/NA CR0 211 F3
Stafford Gdns CROY/NA CR0 211 F3
Stafford Pl RCHPK/HAM TW10 157 G2
WESTW SW1E 16 A4
Stafford Rd BOW E3 105 H1
CROY/NA CR0 211 G2
FSTGT E7 89 G5
KIL/WHAMP NW6 100 E2
KTN/HRWW/WS HA3 42 C3
NWMAL KT3 175 K6
RSLP HA4 76 D2
SCUP DA14 167 K6
WLGTN SM6 210 C4
Staffordshire St PECK SE15 143 H2
Stafford St CONDST W1S 10 A7
Stafford Ter KENS W8 119 K3
Stag Cl EDGW HA8 44 D5
Staggart Gn CHIG IG7 55 F1
Stag La BKHH IG9 39 F4
CDALE/KGS NW9 44 E6
EDGW HA8 44 D5
PUT/ROE SW15 158 C5
Stag Pl WESTW SW1E 16 A4
Stags Wy ISLW TW7 116 A6
Stainbank Rd MTCM CR4 179 G6
Stainby Cl WDR/YW UB7 112 B3
Stainby Rd TOTM N17 50 B6
Stainer St STHWK SE1 19 F1
Staines Av CHEAM SM3 193 G6
Staines Rd EBED/NFELT TW14 134 C6
EBED/NFELT TW14 152 E3
IL IG1 90 D2
WHTN TW2 155 H5
Staines Rd East SUN TW16 172 B4
Stainforth Rd
GNTH/NBYPK IG2 72 D4
WALTH E17 69 J1
Staining La CITYW EC2V 12 D3
Stainmore Cl CHST BR7 185 J4
Stainsbury St BETH E2 104 E1
Stainsby Pl POP/IOD E14 * 105 J5
Stainsby Rd POP/IOD E14 105 J5
Stainton Rd CAT SE6 165 G2
PEND EN3 24 E2
Stalbridge St CAMTN NW1 8 D1
Stalham St BERM/RHTH SE16 123 J3
Stalham Wy BARK/HLT IG6 54 B4
Stambourne Wy NRWD SE19 181 F3
WWKM BR4 214 A1
Stambourne Woodland Wk
NRWD SE19 181 F3
Stamford Brook Av
HMSMTH W6 118 C3
Stamford Brook Gdns
HMSMTH W6 118 C3
Stamford Brook Rd
HMSMTH W6 118 C3
Stamford Cl HAMP NW3 * 83 G1
KTN/HRWW/WS HA3 42 E3
SEVS/STOTM N15 68 C1
STHL UB1 96 A6
Stamford Cots
WBPTN SW10 * 140 A1
Stamford Dr HAYES BR2 199 J1
Stamford Gdns DAGW RM9 91 J5
Stamford Gv East
STNW/STAM N16 68 C5
Stamford Gv West
STNW/STAM N16 68 C5
Stamford Hl STNW/STAM N16 68 B5
Stamford Rd DAGW RM9 91 H5
EHAM E6 89 J6
IS N1 86 A5
SEVS/STOTM N15 68 C2
Stamford St STHWK SE1 11 J7
Stamp Pl BETH E2 7 J3
Stanborough Cl HPTN TW12 172 E2
Stanborough Pas HACK E8 86 B4
Stanborough Rd HSLW TW3 135 J4
Stanbridge Pl WCHMH N21 35 H4
Stanbridge Rd
PUT/ROE SW15 139 F4
Stanbrook Rd ABYW SE2 128 C2
Stanbury Ct HAMP NW3 83 K4
Stanbury Rd PECK SE15 143 J2
Stancroft CDALE/KGS NW9 63 G1
Standale Gv RSLP HA4 58 A2
Standard Pl SDTCH EC2A 7 H5
Standard Rd BELV DA17 129 H5
BXLYHS DA6 149 F5

HSLWW TW4 134 D4
PEND EN3 25 G1
WLSDN NW10 98 E3
Standen Rd
WAND/EARL SW18 159 K2
Standfield Rd DAGE RM10 92 C3
Standish Rd HMSMTH W6 118 D4
Stane Cl WIM/MER SW19 178 A3
Stane Gv VX/NE SW8 141 J3
Stane Wy WOOL/PLUM SE18 146 C1
Stanford Cl HPTN TW12 172 E2
ROMW/RG RM7 74 D3
RSLP HA4 58 A3
WFD IG8 53 J1
Stanford Pl WALW SE17 19 G7
Stanford Rd FBAR/BDGN N11 47 K1
SKENS SW7 120 A3
STRHM/NOR SW16 179 K5
Stanford St PIM SW1V 16 C7
Stanford Wy
STRHM/NOR SW16 179 J5
Stangate Gdns STAN HA7 29 H6
Stanger Rd SNWD SE25 197 H1
Stanham Pl DART DA1 150 D5
Stanham Rd DART DA1 151 F6
Stanhope Av FNCH N3 46 D6
HAYES BR2 199 K5
KTN/HRWW/WS HA3 42 D4
Stanhope Cl
BERM/RHTH SE16 * 124 A2
Stanhope Gdns BCTR RM8 92 B1
FSBYPK N4 67 H3
HGT N6 66 B3
IL IG1 71 K5
MLHL NW7 45 H1
SKENS SW7 120 B4
Stanhope Ga BAY/PAD W2 8 E5
MYFR/PKLN W1K 15 H1
Stanhope Gv BECK BR3 198 C2
Stanhope Ms East SKENS SW7 120 B4
Stanhope Ms South
SKENS SW7 120 B4
Stanhope Ms West
SKENS SW7 120 B4
Stanhope Pde CAMTN NW1 3 K4
Stanhope Park Rd
GFD/PVL UB6 96 C3
Stanhope Pl BAY/PAD W2 8 E4
Stanhope Rd BAR EN5 32 B1
BCTR RM8 74 B6
BFN/LL DA15 168 B6
BXLYHN DA7 149 F3
CAR SM5 210 A5
CROY/NA CR0 212 A1
GFD/PVL UB6 96 C4
HGT N6 66 C3
NFNCH/WDSPK N12 47 G1
RAIN RM13 111 J1
WALTH E17 69 K2
Stanhope Rw
MYFR/PICC W1J * 15 J1
Stanhope St CAMTN NW1 4 A4
Stanhope Ter BAY/PAD W2 8 B5
WHTN TW2 * 156 A2
Stanier Cl WKENS W14 119 J5
Stanlake Rd SHB W12 119 F1
Stanlake Vls SHB W12 119 F1
Stanley Av ALP/SUD HA0 80 A5
BARK IG11 109 F2
BCTR RM8 74 B5
BECK BR3 183 F6
GFD/PVL UB6 78 C6
GPK RM2 75 J1
NWMAL KT3 192 D2
Stanley Cl ALP/SUD HA0 80 A5
ELTH/MOT SE9 167 H3
GPK RM2 75 J1
VX/NE SW8 122 A6
Stanley Crs NTGHL W11 100 D6
Stanleycroft Cl ISLW TW7 135 K2
Stanley Gdns ACT W3 118 B2
CRICK NW2 82 A3
MTCM CR4 * 179 F2
NTGHL W11 100 D6
WLGTN SM6 210 C4
Stanley Gardens Rd
TEDD TW11 173 K1
Stanley Gv CROY/NA CR0 196 B3
VX/NE SW8 141 F3
Stanley Park Dr ALP/SUD HA0 80 B5
Stanley Park Rd CAR SM5 209 K5
WLGTN SM6 210 B5
Stanley Pas KCROSS N1C 4 D3
Stanley Rd ACT W3 117 J3
BELMT SM2 209 F4
CAR SM5 209 K6
CHING E4 38 B3
CROY/NA CR0 196 B4
ED N9 36 B3
EFNCH N2 65 H1
EN EN1 24 A4
FBAR/BDGN N11 48 D2
HAYES BR2 184 B6
HSLW TW3 135 H5
IL IG1 72 D6
MNPK E12 89 J3
MORT/ESHN SW14 137 J5
MRDN SM4 193 K1
MTCM CR4 179 F3
MUSWH N10 48 B3
NTHWD HA6 40 E4
ORP BR6 202 A5
RYLN/HDSTN HA2 60 C6
SCUP DA14 168 B5
SEVS/STOTM N15 67 H1
STHL UB1 95 J6
SWFD E18 52 D4
TEDD TW11 173 K1
WALTH E17 69 K3
WBLY HA9 80 B4
WHTN TW2 155 J5
WIM/MER SW19 177 K3
Stanley Rd North RAIN RM13 93 G6
Stanley Rd South RAIN RM13 111 H1
Stanley Sq CAR SM5 209 K6
Stanley St DEPT SE8 144 C1
Stanley Ter ARCH N19 * 66 E6
BXLYHS DA6 * 149 H5
Stanley Wy STMC/STPC BR5 202 C2
Stanmer St BTSEA SW11 140 D2
Stanmore Gdns
RCH/KEW TW9 137 G4
SUT SM1 209 G1
Stanmore Hl STAN HA7 29 H6
Stanmore Rd BELV DA17 129 K4
RCH/KEW TW9 137 G4
SEVS/STOTM N15 67 H1
WAN E11 70 D5
Stanmore St IS N1 85 F6
Stanmore Ter BECK BR3 182 D5
Stannard Ms HACK E8 * 86 C4
Stannard Rd HACK E8 86 C4
Stannary Pl LBTH SE11 122 B5
Stannary St LBTH SE11 122 B5
Stannet Wy WLGTN SM6 210 C2
Stansbury Sq NKENS W10 100 C2
Stansfeld Rd CAN/RD E16 107 H5
Stansfield Rd BRXN/ST SW9 142 A4
HSLWW TW4 134 A3
Stansgate Rd DAGE RM10 74 C6
Stanstead Cl HAYES BR2 199 J2
Stanstead Gv CAT SE6 164 C3
Stanstead Rd FSTH SE23 164 A3
WAN E11 71 F2
Stansted Cl HCH RM12 93 K4
Stansted Crs BXLY DA5 168 E3
Stanswood Gdns CMBW SE5 143 F1
Stanthorpe Cl
STRHM/NOR SW16 * 179 K1
Stanthorpe Rd
STRHM/NOR SW16 179 K1
Stanton Av TEDD TW11 173 K2
Stanton Cl HOR/WEW KT19 206 D3
STMC/STPC BR5 202 D4
WPK KT4 193 G5
Stanton Rd BARN SW13 138 C3
CROY/NA CR0 196 D4
RYNPK SW20 177 G5
Stanton St PECK SE15 * 143 H2
Stanton Wy SYD SE26 164 C6
Stanway Cl CHIG IG7 54 E1
Stanway Gdns ACT W3 117 H1
EDGW HA8 44 E2
Stanway St IS N1 7 H2
Stanwell Cl STWL/WRAY TW19 152 A1
Stanwell Gdns
STWL/WRAY TW19 152 A1
Stanwell Rd ASHF TW15 152 B6
EBED/NFELT TW14 153 F2
HTHAIR TW6 152 E2
Stanwick Rd WKENS W14 119 J4
Stanworth St STHWK SE1 19 J3
Stanwyck Gdns HARH RM3 57 K1
Stapenhill Rd ALP/SUD HA0 79 H1
Staple Cl BXLY DA5 170 A5
Staplefield Cl
BRXS/STRHM SW2 * 161 K3
PIN HA5 41 J3
Stapleford Av
GNTH/NBYPK IG2 72 E2
Stapleford Cl CHING E4 38 A5
KUT/HW KT1 175 H5
WIM/MER SW19 159 H2
Stapleford Gdns CRW RM5 56 C2
Stapleford Rd ALP/SUD HA0 79 K5
Stapleford Wy BARK IG11 109 H2
Staplehurst Rd CAR SM5 209 J5
LEW SE13 145 G6
Staple Inn HHOL WC1V 11 J2
Staples Cl BERM/RHTH SE16 124 B1
Staple St STHWK SE1 19 F3
Stapleton Crs RAIN RM13 93 J4
Stapleton Gdns CROY/NA CR0 211 G3
Stapleton Hall Rd FSBYPK N4 67 F4
Stapleton Rd BXLYHN DA7 149 G1
ORP BR6 217 F1
TOOT SW17 161 F5
Stapleton Vls
STNW/STAM N16 * 86 A2
Stapley Rd BELV DA17 129 H5
Stapylton Rd BAR EN5 20 C4
Starboard Wy POP/IOD E14 124 D3
Starbuck Cl ELTH/MOT SE9 167 F2
Starch House La
BARK/HLT IG6 54 D5
Star Cl PEND EN3 36 E1
Starcross St CAMTN NW1 4 B5
Starfield Rd SHB W12 118 D2
Star & Garter Hl
RCHPK/HAM TW10 157 F3
Star Hl DART DA1 150 B6
Star La CAN/RD E16 106 C3
STMC/STPC BR5 187 G6
STMC/STPC BR5 202 E1
Starling Cl BKHH IG9 38 E3
PIN HA5 41 G6
Starling Rd CROY/NA CR0 198 B3
Starmans Cl DAGW RM9 92 A6
Star Pl WAP E1W 13 K6
Star Rd HGDN/ICK UB10 94 A3
ISLW TW7 135 J3
WKENS W14 119 J6
Star St BAY/PAD W2 8 B3
Starts Cl ORP BR6 216 A1
Starts Hill Av ORP BR6 216 B3
Starts Hill Rd ORP BR6 216 B1
Starveall Cl WDR/YW UB7 112 C3
Star Yd LINN WC2A 11 J3
State Farm Av ORP BR6 216 B2
Staten Gdns TWK TW1 156 A3
Statham Gv STNW/STAM N16 85 K1
UED N18 50 A1
Station Ap ALP/SUD HA0 79 H4
BAR EN5 21 G5
BECK BR3 182 B4
BELMT SM2 208 C5
BKHH IG9 * 39 H6
BKHTH/KID SE3 146 A4
BXLY DA5 169 H2
BXLYHN DA7 149 F3
BXLYHN DA7 149 K3
CAMTN NW1 * 3 G7
CAR SM5 209 K2
CHING E4 * 38 C2
CHING E4 * 52 B2
CHST BR7 184 D2
CROY/NA CR0 * 196 E6
DART DA1 171 H1
ESH/CLAY KT10 205 F1
FBAR/BDGN N11 48 B1
FSTGT E7 89 F2
FUL/PGN SW6 * 139 H4
GFD/PVL UB6 78 C5
GLDGN NW11 * 64 B4
HAYES BR2 199 K5
HOR/WEW KT19 207 H3
HPTN TW12 173 F4
HYS/HAR UB3 113 J3
KUT/HW KT1 175 H5
NFNCH/WDSPK N12 33 F6
NTHWD HA6 40 C3
ORP BR6 202 A6
ORP BR6 217 H3
OXHEY WD19 27 H5
PIN HA5 41 J6
RCH/KEW TW9 137 H2
RSLP HA4 58 C5
RSLP HA4 77 F3
SAND/SEL CR2 211 K6
STMC/STPC BR5 202 C1
STRHM/NOR SW16 179 J1
SURB KT6 190 E3
SWFD E18 * 53 F5
SYD SE26 182 C1
WALTH E17 69 J2
WAN E11 70 E2
WAN E11 * 88 C2
WDR/YW UB7 112 B1
WELL DA16 148 A3
WFD IG8 53 F2
WLSDN NW10 99 H2
Station Approach Rd
CHSWK W4 137 K1
Station Ar GTPST W1W * 3 K7
Station Av HOR/WEW KT19 207 G6
NWMAL KT3 176 B6
RCH/KEW TW9 137 H2
Station Blds HAYES BR2 * 199 K5
Station Chambers EA W5 * 98 C3
Station Cl HPTN TW12 173 G4
Station Cots WDGN N22 * 48 E5
Station Crs ALP/SUD HA0 79 H4
ASHF TW15 152 A6
BKHTH/KID SE3 125 K5
SEVS/STOTM N15 67 K1
Stationers Hall Ct STP EC4M * 12 B4
Station Est BECK BR3 198 A1
Station Estate Rd
EBED/NFELT TW14 154 A3
Station Garage Ms
STRHM/NOR SW16 * 179 J2
Station Gdns CHSWK W4 137 K1
Station Gv ALP/SUD HA0 80 A4
Station Hl HAYES BR2 199 K6
Station House Ms ED N9 36 C6
Station Pde ACT W3 * 98 C5
BAL SW12 * 161 F3
BARK IG11 90 C5
BECK BR3 * 198 A1
BELMT SM2 * 209 G4
BMLY BR1 * 183 K4
BXLYHN DA7 * 149 F3
CHSWK W4 * 137 K1
CLPT E5 * 86 D1
CRICK NW2 82 A4
EA W5 * 117 G1
EBAR EN4 * 22 A5
EBED/NFELT TW14 * 154 A2
EDGW HA8 * 44 A3
EHAM E6 * 89 J5
HCH RM12 93 K2
KTN/HRWW/WS HA3 * 43 H5
NTHLT UB5 * 78 A5
NTHLT UB5 * 78 B3
PLSTW E13 * 89 G6
RCH/KEW TW9 137 H2
ROM RM1 * 75 G3
RSLP HA4 * 58 A6
RYLN/HDSTN HA2 * 78 B2
STHGT/OAK N14 34 D3
Station Pas PECK SE15 143 K2
SWFD E18 53 F5
Station Pl FSBYPK N4 67 G6
Station Ri WNWD SE27 162 C4
Station Rd ASHF TW15 152 C6
BAR EN5 21 F6
BARK/HLT IG6 54 D6
BARN SW13 138 C3
BCTR RM8 73 K5
BELV DA17 129 H3
BFN/LL DA15 168 B4
BMLY BR1 183 K4
BXLYHN DA7 149 F4
CAR SM5 209 K2
CHING E4 38 B3
CHSGTN KT9 206 A3
CROY/NA CR0 196 D5
DART DA1 170 C1
EA W5 98 B5
EDGW HA8 44 C2
ESH/CLAY KT10 189 J6
ESH/CLAY KT10 204 D3
FBAR/BDGN N11 48 B1
FNCH N3 46 E4
GPK RM2 75 K1
HAYES BR2 183 H5
HDN NW4 63 J3
HNWL W7 115 K1
HOLWY N7 84 C1
HPTN TW12 173 G4
HRW HA1 60 B2
HRW HA1 61 F3
HSLW TW3 135 G5
HYS/HAR UB3 113 H4
IL IG1 90 B1
KUT/HW KT1 174 E4
KUTN/CMB KT2 175 H4
LEW SE13 145 F4
MLHL NW7 45 G2
MNPK E12 89 H2
NWMAL KT3 192 E2
ORP BR6 202 A6
PGE/AN SE20 181 K2
RYLN/HDSTN HA2 60 B2
SCUP DA14 168 B5
SNWD SE25 197 G1
STMC/STPC BR5 202 D1
TEDD TW11 174 B2
THDIT KT7 190 A4
TOTM N17 50 C6
TWK TW1 156 A3
WALTH E17 69 G3
WCHMH N21 35 H3
WDGN N22 48 E5
WDR/YW UB7 112 B2
WIM/MER SW19 178 B4
WLSDN NW10 99 H1
WWKM BR4 199 F5
Station Rd North BELV DA17 129 J3
Station Sq STMC/STPC BR5 201 H2
Station St SRTFD E15 88 B5
Station Ter CMBW SE5 142 D2
WLSDN NW10 100 B1
Station Vw GFD/PVL UB6 78 D6
Station Wy BKHH IG9 39 H6
CHEAM SM3 208 C5
ESH/CLAY KT10 204 E4
Station Yd ASHF TW15 * 152 C6
RSLP HA4 * 58 B6
STHL UB1 * 114 E2
TWK TW1 156 B2
Staunton Rd KUTN/CMB KT2 175 G3
Staunton St DEPT SE8 124 C6
Staveley Cl HOLWY N7 * 84 E2
PECK SE15 143 K2
Staveley Gdns CHSWK W4 138 A2
Staveley Rd CHSWK W4 117 K6
Staverton Rd CRICK NW2 82 A5
Stave Yard Rd
BERM/RHTH SE16 124 B1
Stavordale Rd CAR SM5 194 B4
HBRY N5 85 G2
Stayner's Rd WCHPL E1 105 F3
Stayton Rd SUT SM1 208 E1
Steadfast Rd KUT/HW KT1 174 E4
Stead St WALW SE17 18 E7
Steam Farm La
EBED/NFELT TW14 133 J5
Stean St HACK E8 86 B6
Stebbing Wy BARK IG11 109 G1
Stebondale St POP/IOD E14 125 F5
Stedly SCUP DA14 * 168 B6
Stedman Cl BXLY DA5 170 B5
Steed Cl EMPK RM11 75 K6
Steedman St WALW SE17 18 C7
Steeds Rd MUSWH N10 47 K4
Steel Ap BARK IG11 109 H1
Steele Rd CHSWK W4 117 K3
ISLW TW7 136 B5
TOTM N17 50 A6
WAN E11 88 C2
WLSDN NW10 98 E1
Steele's Ms North
HAMP NW3 * 83 K4
Steele's Ms South HAMP NW3 83 K4
Steele's Rd HAMP NW3 83 K4
Steeles Studios HAMP NW3 * 83 K4
Steel's La WCHPL E1 104 E5
Steep Cl ORP BR6 217 F4
Steep Hl CROY/NA CR0 212 A2
STRHM/NOR SW16 161 J5
Steeplands BUSH WD23 28 B2
Steeple Cl FUL/PGN SW6 139 H4
WIM/MER SW19 159 H6
Steeplestone Cl UED N18 49 J1
Steeple Wk IS N1 * 85 J6
Steerforth St
WAND/EARL SW18 160 A4
Steering Cl ED N9 36 E3
Steers Md MTCM CR4 178 E4
Steers Wy BERM/RHTH SE16 124 B2
Stella Rd TOOT SW17 178 E2
Stelling Rd ERITH DA8 150 A1
Stellman Cl CLPT E5 86 C1
Stembridge Rd PGE/AN SE20 181 J5
Stephan Cl HACK E8 86 C6
Stephen Av RAIN RM13 93 J4
Stephen Cl ORP BR6 217 F1
Stephendale Rd
FUL/PGN SW6 140 A4
Stephen Ms FITZ W1T 10 C2
Stephen Pl CLAP SW4 141 H4
Stephen Rd BXLYHN DA7 149 K4
Stephenson Cl WELL DA16 148 A3
Stephenson Rd HNWL W7 97 F5
WALTH E17 69 G2
WHTN TW2 155 F2
Stephenson St CAN/RD E16 106 C3
WLSDN NW10 99 G2
Stephenson Wy CAMTN NW1 4 B6
Stephen's Rd SRTFD E15 88 C6
Stephen St FITZ W1T 10 C3
Stepney Cswy WCHPL E1 105 F5
Stepney Gn WCHPL E1 104 E4
Stepney High St WCHPL E1 105 F4
Stepney Wy MTCM CR4 179 F4
WCHPL E1 104 D4
Sterling Av EDGW HA8 30 B6
Sterling Cl WLSDN NW10 81 J5
Sterling Gdns NWCR SE14 124 B6
Sterling Pl EA W5 117 F4
Sterling Rd ENC/FH EN2 23 K2
Sterling St SKENS SW7 14 D3
Sterling Way (North Circular)
UED N18 49 K1
Stern Cl BARK IG11 109 J1
Sterndale Rd DART DA1 171 J2
WKENS W14 * 119 G3
Sterne St SHB W12 119 G2
Sternhall La PECK SE15 143 H4
Sternhold Av
BRXS/STRHM SW2 161 J4
Sterry Crs DAGE RM10 92 C3
Sterry Dr HOR/WEW KT19 207 G2
THDIT KT7 189 K3
Sterry Gdns DAGE RM10 92 C4
Sterry Rd BARK IG11 91 F6
DAGE RM10 92 C2
Sterry St STHWK SE1 18 E3
Steucers La FSTH SE23 164 B3
Steve Biko La CAT SE6 164 D6
Steve Biko Rd HOLWY N7 85 G1
Steve Biko Wy HSLW TW3 135 F4
Stevedale Rd WELL DA16 148 D3
Stevedore St WAP E1W 123 J1
Stevenage Rd EHAM E6 90 A4
FUL/PGN SW6 139 G2
Stevens Av HOM E9 86 E4
Stevens Cl BECK BR3 182 D2
BXLY DA5 170 A6
HPTN TW12 172 E2
PIN HA5 59 G2
Stevens Gn BUSH WD23 28 C3
Stevens' La ESH/CLAY KT10 205 G5
Stevenson Cl BAR EN5 33 H1
ERITH DA8 150 E1
Stevenson Crs
BERM/RHTH SE16 123 H5
Stevens Rd BCTR RM8 73 H6
Stevens St STHWK SE1 19 H4
Steventon Rd SHB W12 99 H6
Stewart Cl CDALE/KGS NW9 * 62 E3
CHST BR7 185 G1
HPTN TW12 172 D2
Stewart Quay HYS/HAR UB3 113 H2
Stewart Rd SRTFD E15 88 B2
Stewartsby Cl UED N18 49 J1
Stewarts Gv CHEL SW3 * 120 C5
Stewart's Gv CHEL SW3 120 C5
Stewart's La VX/NE SW8 141 G1
Stewarts Rd VX/NE SW8 141 H1
Stewart's Rd VX/NE SW8 141 H2
Stewart St POP/IOD E14 125 F2
Steyne Rd ACT W3 117 J1
Steyning Gv ELTH/MOT SE9 166 E6
Steynings Wy
NFNCH/WDSPK N12 46 E1
Steyning Wy HSLWW TW4 134 B5
Steynton Av BXLY DA5 169 F4
Stickland Rd BELV DA17 129 H4
Stickleton Cl GFD/PVL UB6 96 B2
Stilecroft Gdns ALP/SUD HA0 79 H1
Stile Hall Gdns CHSWK W4 117 H5
Stiles Cl ERITH DA8 129 J5
HAYES BR2 200 E3
Stillingfleet Rd BARN SW13 138 D1
Stillington St WEST SW1P 16 B6
Stillness Rd FSTH SE23 164 B1
Stipularis Dr YEAD UB4 95 H3
Stirling Av PIN HA5 59 H4
WLGTN SM6 210 E5
Stirling Cl RAIN RM13 111 K2
SCUP DA14 167 K6
STRHM/NOR SW16 179 H4
Stirling Dr ORP BR6 217 H3
Stirling Gv HSLW TW3 135 H3
Stirling Rd ACT W3 117 J3
BRXN/ST SW9 141 K3
HYS/HAR UB3 95 F6
KTN/HRWW/WS HA3 43 F6
PLSTW E13 107 F1
TOTM N17 50 C4
WALTH E17 51 G6
WDGN N22 49 H4
WHTN TW2 155 F2
Stirling Wk BRYLDS KT5 191 J3
Stirling Wy BORE WD6 31 F1
CROY/NA CR0 195 K4
Stiven Crs RYLN/HDSTN HA2 77 K1
Stockbury Rd CROY/NA CR0 197 K3
Stockdale Rd BCTR RM8 74 B6
Stockdove Wy GFD/PVL UB6 97 F2
Stocker Gdns DAGW RM9 91 J5
Stockfield Rd ESH/CLAY KT10 204 E3
STRHM/NOR SW16 162 A5
Stockholm Rd
BERM/RHTH SE16 123 K5
Stockholm Wy WAP E1W 123 H1
Stockhurst Cl PUT/ROE SW15 139 F3
Stockingswater La PEND EN3 25 G4
Stockland Rd ROMW/RG RM7 75 F3
Stock La RDART DA2 171 F6
Stockley Cl WDR/YW UB7 112 E2
Stockley Farm Rd
WDR/YW UB7 112 E3
Stockley Rd WDR/YW UB7 112 E3
Stock Orchard Crs
HOLWY N7 * 85 F2
Stock Orchard St HOLWY N7 85 F3
Stockport Rd
STRHM/NOR SW16 179 J4
Stocksfield Rd WALTH E17 * 52 A6
Stocks Pl POP/IOD E14 105 H6
Stock St PLSTW E13 106 E1
Stockton Cl BAR EN5 21 G5
Stockton Gdns MLHL NW7 31 F5
TOTM N17 49 J3
Stockton Rd TOTM N17 49 J3
UED N18 50 C2
Stockwell Av BRXN/ST SW9 142 A4
Stockwell Cl BMLY BR1 184 A5
Stockwell Gdns BRXN/ST SW9 142 A2
Stockwell Gn BRXN/ST SW9 142 A3
Stockwell La BRXN/ST SW9 142 A3
Stockwell Park Crs
BRXN/ST SW9 142 A3
Stockwell Park Rd
BRXN/ST SW9 142 A2
Stockwell Park Wk
BRXN/ST SW9 142 A4
Stockwell Rd BRXN/ST SW9 142 A3
Stockwell St GNWCH SE10 125 F6
Stockwell Ter BRXN/ST SW9 142 A2
Stodart Rd PGE/AN SE20 181 K4
Stofield Gdns ELTH/MOT SE9 166 C5
Stoford Cl WIM/MER SW19 159 H3
Stoke Av BARK/HLT IG6 55 G2
Stokenchurch St
FUL/PGN SW6 140 A2
Stoke Newington Church St
STNW/STAM N16 85 K1
Stoke Newington Common
STNW/STAM N16 68 B6
Stoke Newington High St
STNW/STAM N16 86 B1
Stoke Newington Rd
HACK E8 86 B3
STNW/STAM N16 86 B2
Stoke Pl WLSDN NW10 99 H2
Stoke Rd KUTN/CMB KT2 175 K3
Stokesby Rd CHSGTN KT9 206 B4
Stokesley St SHB W12 99 H5
Stokes Ms TEDD TW11 174 B1
Stokes Rd CROY/NA CR0 198 A3
EHAM E6 107 J3
Stoll Cl CRICK NW2 82 A1
Stonard Rd BCTR RM8 91 H3
PLMGR N13 35 G5
Stonards Hl LOU IG10 39 K1
Stondon Pk FSTH SE23 164 B1

Stonebridge Ms NRWD SE19 180 D3
Stonebridge Pk WLSDN NW10 81 F5
Stonebridge Rd
SEVS/STOTM N15 68 A2
Stonebridge Wy WBLY HA9 80 D4
Stone Blds LINN WC2A 11 H2
Stonechat Sq EHAM E6 107 J4
Stone Cl BCTR RM8 74 B6
CLAP SW4 141 H3
WDR/YW UB7 112 C1
Stonecot Cl CHEAM SM3 193 H5
Stonecot Hl CHEAM SM3 193 H5
Stone Crs EBED/NFELT TW14 153 J2
Stonecroft Rd ERITH DA8 149 K1
Stonecroft Wy CROY/NA CR0 195 K4
Stonecrop Cl CDALE/KGS NW9 45 F6
Stonecutter St
FLST/FETLN EC4A 12 A3
Stonefield Cl BXLYHN DA7 149 H4
RSLP HA4 77 J3
Stonefield St IS N1 85 G6
Stonefield Wy CHARL SE7 146 C1
RSLP HA4 77 H3
Stonegate Cl STMC/STPC BR5 186 D6
Stone Gv EDGW HA8 30 A6
STAN HA7 30 A6
Stonegrove Gdns EDGW HA8 44 A1
Stonehall Av IL IG1 71 J3
Stone Hall Gdns KENS W8 * 120 A3
Stone Hall Pl KENS W8 * 120 A3
Stone Hall Rd WCHMH N21 35 F2
Stoneham Rd
FBAR/BDGN N11 48 C1
Stonehill Cl MORT/ESHN SW14 138 A6
Stonehill Rd CHSWK W4 117 H5
MORT/ESHN SW14 137 K6
Stonehills Ct DUL SE21 163 F5
Stonehill Woods Pk
SCUP DA14 * 187 J2
Stonehorse Rd PEND EN3 24 E6
Stone House Ct LVPST EC2M 13 H3
Stonehouse La RSEV TN14 217 K6
Stonehouse Rd RSEV TN14 217 K6
Stoneleigh Av EN EN1 24 D1
WPK KT4 207 J1
Stoneleigh Broadway
EW KT17 207 J3
Stoneleigh Crs
HOR/WEW KT19 207 J3
Stoneleigh Park Av
CROY/NA CR0 198 A3
Stoneleigh Park Rd
HOR/WEW KT19 207 H4
Stoneleigh Pl NTGHL W11 100 B6
Stoneleigh Rd BMLY BR1 185 G6
CAR SM5 194 D4
CLAY IG5 53 J6
TOTM N17 50 B5
Stoneleigh St NTGHL W11 100 B6
Stoneleigh Ter ARCH N19 66 B6
Stonell's Rd TOOT SW17 160 B5
Stonemasons Cl
SEVS/STOTM N15 * 67 K1
Stonenest St FSBYPK N4 67 F5
Stone Park Av BECK BR3 198 D1
Stone Pl WPK KT4 192 D6
Stone Rd HAYES BR2 199 J2
Stones Cross Rd SWLY BR8 203 K2
Stones End St STHWK SE1 18 C3
Stonewall EHAM E6 108 A4
Stonewood Rd ERITH DA8 130 B5
Stoney Aly WOOL/PLUM SE18 147 F3
Stoneyard La POP/IOD E14 105 K6
Stoneycroft Cl
LEE/GVPK SE12 165 J2
Stoneycroft Rd WFD IG8 53 J2
Stoneydown WALTH E17 69 G1
Stoneydown Av WALTH E17 69 G1
Stoneyfields Gdns EDGW HA8 30 E6
Stoneyfields La EDGW HA8 44 E1
Stoney La HDTCH EC3A 13 H3
NRWD SE19 181 G2
Stoney St STHWK SE1 12 E7
Stonhouse St CLAP SW4 141 H4
Stonnell's Rd BTSEA SW11 140 E6
Stonor Rd WKENS W14 119 J4
Stonycroft Cl PEND EN3 25 G3
Stopes St PECK SE15 143 G1
Stopford Rd PLSTW E13 88 E6
WALW SE17 122 C5
Store Rd CAN/RD E16 127 F2
Storers Quay POP/IOD E14 125 G4
Store St GWRST WC1E 10 C2
SRTFD E15 88 B3
Storey Rd HGT N6 65 K3
WALTH E17 69 H1
Storey's Ga STJSPK SW1H 16 D3
Stories Ms CMBW SE5 * 143 F3
Stories Rd CMBW SE5 143 F4
Stork Rd FSTGT E7 88 D4
Storksmead Rd EDGW HA8 45 G3
Storks Rd BERM/RHTH SE16 * 123 H3
Stormont Rd BTSEA SW11 141 F5
HGT N6 65 K4
Stormont Wy CHSGTN KT9 205 J3
Stormount Dr HYS/HAR UB3 113 F2
Storrington Rd CROY/NA CR0 197 G5
Story St IS N1 85 F5
Stothard St WCHPL E1 104 E3
Stott Cl WAND/EARL SW18 160 C1
Stoughton Av CHEAM SM3 208 B3
Stoughton Cl LBTH SE11 17 H7
PUT/ROE SW15 158 D3
Stour Av NWDGN UB2 115 F3
Stourcliffe St MBLAR W1H 8 E4
Stour Cl HAYES BR2 215 G2
Stourhead Cl WIM/MER SW19 159 G2
Stourhead Gdns RYNPK SW20 176 D6
Stour Rd BOW E3 87 J5
DAGE RM10 74 C6
DART DA1 150 D4
Stourton Av FELT TW13 154 E6
Stowage DEPT SE8 124 E6
The Stowage DEPT SE8 124 D6
Stow Crs WALTH E17 51 G4
Stowe Gdns ED N9 36 B3
Stowe Pl SEVS/STOTM N15 50 A6
Stowe Rd ORP BR6 217 H2
SHB W12 118 E2
Stowting Rd ORP BR6 216 E2
Stox Md KTN/HRWW/WS HA3 42 D4
Stracey Rd WLSDN NW10 81 F6
Strachan Pl RYNPK SW20 177 F2
Stradbroke Dr CHIG IG7 54 B2
Stradbroke Gv BKHH IG9 39 H3
CLAY IG5 53 J6
Stradbroke Pk CHIG IG7 54 B2
Stradbroke Rd HBRY N5 85 J2
Stradbrook Cl
RYLN/HDSTN HA2 77 K1
Stradella Rd HNHL SE24 162 D1
Strafford Rd ACT W3 117 K2
BAR EN5 20 C4
HSLW TW3 134 E4
TWK TW1 156 B2
Strafford St POP/IOD E14 124 D2
Strahan Rd BOW E3 105 G1
Straight Rd HARH RM3 57 K1
Straightsmouth GNWCH SE10 145 F1
The Straight NWDGN UB2 114 C2
Strait Rd EHAM E6 107 J6
Straker's Rd EDUL SE22 143 J5
Strand CHCR WC2N 11 F6
HOL/ALD WC2B 11 H4
TPL/STR WC2R 11 G5
Strand Dr RCH/KEW TW9 137 H1
Strandfield Cl
WOOL/PLUM SE18 127 K5
Strand-on-the-Green
CHSWK W4 117 H6
Strand Pl UED N18 36 A6
Strangways Ter WKENS W14 119 J3
Stranraer Wy IS N1 84 E5
Strasburg Rd BTSEA SW11 141 F2
Stratfield Park Cl
WCHMH N21 35 H2
Stratford Cl BARK IG11 91 G5
DAGE RM10 92 E5
Stratford Ct NWMAL KT3 192 A1
Stratford Gv PUT/ROE SW15 139 G5
Stratford House Av
BMLY BR1 184 D6
Stratford Pl OXSTW W1C 9 J4
Stratford Rd HTHAIR TW6 152 E1
KENS W8 119 K4
NWDGN UB2 114 D4
PLSTW E13 88 E6
THHTH CR7 196 B1
YEAD UB4 95 F3
Stratford Studios KENS W8 119 K3
Stratford Vls CAMTN NW1 84 C5
Strathan Cl WAND/EARL SW18 159 H1
Strathaven Rd
LEE/GVPK SE12 166 A1
Strathblaine Rd BTSEA SW11 140 C6
Strathbrook Rd
STRHM/NOR SW16 180 A3
Strathcona Rd WBLY HA9 61 K6
Strathdale STRHM/NOR SW16 180 A1
Strathdon Dr TOOT SW17 160 C5
Strathearn Av HYS/HAR UB3 133 J1
WHTN TW2 155 H3
Strathearn Cots
TRDG/WHET N20 * 32 E5
Strathearn Pl BAY/PAD W2 8 C5
Strathearn Rd SUT SM1 208 E3
WIM/MER SW19 177 K1
Stratheden Rd
BKHTH/KID SE3 145 K2
Strathfield Gdns BARK IG11 90 D4
Strathleven Rd
BRXS/STRHM SW2 141 K6
Strathmore Gdns EDGW HA8 44 D5
FNCH N3 47 F4
HCH RM12 75 H5
KENS W8 119 K1
Strathmore Rd CROY/NA CR0 196 D4
TEDD TW11 155 K6
WIM/MER SW19 159 K5
Strathnairn St STHWK SE1 123 H4
Strathray Gdns HAMP NW3 * 83 J4
Strath Ter BTSEA SW11 140 D5
Strathville Rd
WAND/EARL SW18 159 K4
Strathyre Av
STRHM/NOR SW16 180 B6
Stratton Av WLGTN SM6 210 D6
Stratton Cl BXLYHN DA7 149 F4
EDGW HA8 44 B2
HSLW TW3 134 E2
WIM/MER SW19 177 J5
WOT/HER KT12 * 188 B5
Strattondale St POP/IOD E14 125 F3
Stratton Dr BARK IG11 90 E3
Stratton Gdns STHL UB1 95 K5
Stratton Rd BXLYHN DA7 149 F4
WIM/MER SW19 177 K5
Stratton St MYFR/PICC W1J 9 K7
Strauss Rd CHSWK W4 * 118 A2
Strawberry Flds ORP BR6 216 B3
Strawberry Hl CHSGTN KT9 205 K4
Strawberry Hill Rd TWK TW1 156 A5
Strawberry La CAR SM5 209 K1
Strawberry Ter MUSWH N10 * 47 K4
Strawberry V EFNCH N2 47 H4
TWK TW1 156 A5
Streakes Field Rd CRICK NW2 63 J6
Streamdale ABYW SE2 128 C6
Stream La EDGW HA8 44 D2
Streamline Ms EDUL SE22 163 J3
Streamside Cl ED N9 36 B3
HAYES BR2 199 K1
Stream Wy BELV DA17 129 H6
Streatfeild Av EHAM E6 89 K6
Streatfield Rd
KTN/HRWW/WS HA3 43 J6
Streatham Cl
STRHM/NOR SW16 * 161 K4
Streatham Common
STRHM/NOR SW16 * 179 J3
Streatham Common North
STRHM/NOR SW16 180 A1
Streatham Common South
STRHM/NOR SW16 179 K2
Streatham Ct
STRHM/NOR SW16 161 K5
Streatham Gn
STRHM/NOR SW16 * 161 K6
Streatham High Rd
STRHM/NOR SW16 179 K3
Streatham Hl
BRXS/STRHM SW2 161 K3
Streatham Pl
BRXS/STRHM SW2 161 K2
Streatham Rd MTCM CR4 179 F4
Streatham St
NOXST/BSQ WC1A 10 E3
Streatham V
STRHM/NOR SW16 179 H3
Streathbourne Rd
TOOT SW17 161 F4
Streatleigh Pde
STRHM/NOR SW16 * 161 K4
Streatley Pl HAMP NW3 83 H2
Streatley Rd
KIL/WHAMP NW6 82 D5
Streeters La WLGTN SM6 210 D1
Streetfield Ms BKHTH/KID SE3 145 K3
Streimer Rd SRTFD E15 106 A1
Strelley Wy ACT W3 99 G6
Stretton Rd CROY/NA CR0 197 F4
RCHPK/HAM TW10 156 D4
Strickland Av DART DA1 151 J4
Strickland Rw
WAND/EARL SW18 160 C2
Strickland St DEPT SE8 144 D3
Strickland Wy ORP BR6 217 F2
Stride Rd PLSTW E13 106 D1
Strimon Cl ED N9 36 E4
Stripling Wy WATW WD18 26 E1
Strode Cl MUSWH N10 48 A3
Strode Rd FSTGT E7 88 E2
FUL/PGN SW6 139 G1
TOTM N17 50 A5
WLSDN NW10 81 J4
Strond Green Gdns
CROY/NA CR0 197 K4
Strond Green Wy
CROY/NA CR0 197 K4
Strone Rd FSTGT E7 89 G4
MNPK E12 89 H4
Strone Wy YEAD UB4 95 J3
Strongbow Crs
ELTH/MOT SE9 146 E6
Strongbow Rd ELTH/MOT SE9 146 E6
Stronsa Rd SHB W12 118 C2
Strood Av ROMW/RG RM7 75 F5
Stroud Crs PUT/ROE SW15 158 C5
Stroudes Cl WPK KT4 192 C4
Stroud Fld NTHLT UB5 77 J4
Stroud Ga RYLN/HDSTN HA2 78 B2
Stroud Green Rd FSBYPK N4 67 F5
Stroud Green Wy
CROY/NA CR0 197 J4
Stroud Rd SNWD SE25 197 H3
WIM/MER SW19 159 K5
Strouds Cl CHDH RM6 73 H2
Strout's Pl BETH E2 7 J4
Strutton Gnd STJSPK SW1H 16 C4
Strype St WCHPL E1 13 J2
Stuart Av CDALE/KGS NW9 63 J4
EA W5 117 G2
HAYES BR2 199 K5
RYLN/HDSTN HA2 77 K1
WOT/HER KT12 188 B5
Stuart Ct BORE WD6 29 K1
Stuart Crs CROY/NA CR0 213 H1
HYS/HAR UB3 94 A5
WDGN N22 49 F4
Stuart Evans Cl WELL DA16 148 D4
Stuart Gv TEDD TW11 173 K1
Stuart Mantle Wy ERITH DA8 150 A1
Stuart Pl MTCM CR4 178 E4
Stuart Rd ACT W3 117 K1
BARK IG11 91 F6
EBAR EN4 33 J2
KIL/WHAMP NW6 100 E2
KTN/HRWW/WS HA3 43 F6
PECK SE15 143 K5
RCHPK/HAM TW10 156 C4
THHTH CR7 196 D1
WELL DA16 148 C2
WIM/MER SW19 159 K5
Stubbs Cl CDALE/KGS NW9 62 E2
Stubbs Dr BERM/RHTH SE16 123 J5
Stubbs Wy WIM/MER SW19 178 C4
Stucley Pl CAMTN NW1 84 B5
Stucley Rd HEST TW5 135 H1
Studdridge St FUL/PGN SW6 139 K3
Studd St IS N1 85 H6
Studholme Ct HAMP NW3 * 82 E2
Studholme St PECK SE15 143 J1
Studio Ms HDN NW4 64 A1
Studio Pl KTBR SW1X 15 F3
The Studios BUSH WD23 28 A1
Studland Cl BFN/LL DA15 168 A5
Studland Rd HNWL W7 96 D5
KUTN/CMB KT2 175 F2
SYD SE26 182 A1
Studland St HMSMTH W6 118 E4
Studley Av CHING E4 52 B3
Studley Cl CLPT E5 87 G3
Studley Ct SCUP DA14 186 C1
Studley Dr REDBR IG4 71 H3
Studley Grange Rd HNWL W7 115 K3
Studley Rd CLAP SW4 141 K2
DAGW RM9 91 K5
FSTGT E7 89 F4
Stukeley Rd FSTGT E7 89 F5
Stukeley St HOL/ALD WC2B 11 F3
Stumps Hill La BECK BR3 182 D2
Sturdy Rd PECK SE15 143 J3
Sturge Av WALTH E17 51 K4
Sturgeon Rd WALW SE17 122 D5
Sturges Fld CHST BR7 185 J2
Sturgess Av HDN NW4 63 K4
Sturge St STHWK SE1 18 C3
Sturmer Wy HOLWY N7 85 F3
Sturminster Cl YEAD UB4 95 G5
Sturrock Cl SEVS/STOTM N15 67 K1
Sturry St POP/IOD E14 105 K5
Sturt St IS N1 6 D3
Stutfield St WCHPL E1 104 C5
Styles Gdns BRXN/ST SW9 142 C4
Styles Wy BECK BR3 199 F1
Sudbourne Rd
BRXS/STRHM SW2 141 K6
Sudbrooke Rd BAL SW12 160 E1
Sudbrook Gdns
RCHPK/HAM TW10 157 F5
Sudbrook La
RCHPK/HAM TW10 157 F3
Sudbury EHAM E6 108 A5
Sudbury Av ALP/SUD HA0 79 J1
Sudbury Court Dr HRW HA1 79 G1
Sudbury Court Rd HRW HA1 79 G1
Sudbury Crs ALP/SUD HA0 79 H3
BMLY BR1 183 K1
Sudbury Cft ALP/SUD HA0 79 F2
Sudbury Gdns CROY/NA CR0 212 A2
Sudbury Heights Av
GFD/PVL UB6 79 F3
Sudbury Hl HRW HA1 79 F1
Sudbury Hill Cl ALP/SUD HA0 79 F1
Sudbury Rd BARK IG11 91 F3
Sudeley St IS N1 6 B3
Sudlow Rd WAND/EARL SW18 139 K5
Sudrey St STHWK SE1 18 C3
Suez Av GFD/PVL UB6 97 F1
Suez Rd PEND EN3 25 G5
Suffield Rd CHING E4 37 K5
PGE/AN SE20 181 K5
SEVS/STOTM N15 * 68 B2
Suffolk La CANST EC4R 12 E5
Suffolk Park Rd WALTH E17 69 G1
Suffolk Rd BARK IG11 90 D5
BARN SW13 138 C1
DAGE RM10 92 D3
DART DA1 171 H1
GDMY/SEVK IG3 72 E3
PEND EN3 24 D6
PLSTW E13 106 D2
RYLN/HDSTN HA2 59 K3
SCUP DA14 186 D2
SEVS/STOTM N15 67 K3
SNWD SE25 197 G1
WLSDN NW10 81 G5
WPK KT4 192 C6
Suffolk St FSTGT E7 88 E3
STJS SW1Y 10 D7
Suffolk Vls
WAND/EARL SW18 * 159 K2
Sugar House La SRTFD E15 106 A1
Sugar Loaf Wk BETH E2 * 104 E2
Sugden Rd BTSEA SW11 141 F4
THDIT KT7 190 B5
Sugden Wy BARK IG11 109 F1
Sulgrave Gdns HMSMTH W6 119 F2
Sulgrave Rd HMSMTH W6 119 F2
Sulina Rd BRXS/STRHM SW2 161 K2
Sulivan Ct FUL/PGN SW6 139 K3
Sulivan Rd FUL/PGN SW6 139 K4
Sullivan Av CAN/RD E16 107 H4
Sullivan Cl BTSEA SW11 140 D4
DART DA1 170 E1
E/WMO/HCT KT8 173 F6
YEAD UB4 95 G4
Sullivan Rd LBTH SE11 17 K6
Sullivan Wy BORE WD6 29 J1
Sultan Rd WAN E11 71 F1
Sultan St BECK BR3 182 A5
CMBW SE5 142 D1
Sumatra Rd KIL/WHAMP NW6 82 E4
Sumburgh Rd BAL SW12 161 F1
Summer Av E/WMO/HCT KT8 189 K2
Summer Crossing THDIT KT7 190 A2
Summerene Cl
STRHM/NOR SW16 179 H3
Summerfield Av
KIL/WHAMP NW6 100 C1
NFNCH/WDSPK N12 47 J2
Summerfield La SURB KT6 190 E6
Summerfield Rd EA W5 97 H3
LOU IG10 39 H1
Summerfield St
LEE/GVPK SE12 165 J2
Summer Gdns
E/WMO/HCT KT8 189 K2
Summer Gv BORE WD6 29 K1
Summer Hl CHST BR7 185 F5
Summerhill Cl ORP BR6 216 E2
Summerhill Gv EN EN1 36 A1
Summerhill Rd DART DA1 171 G2
SEVS/STOTM N15 67 K1
Summerhill Wy MTCM CR4 179 F4
Summerhouse Av HEST TW5 134 D2
Summerhouse Dr BXLY DA5 170 A6
Summerhouse La
WDR/YW UB7 112 A6
Summerhouse Rd
STNW/STAM N16 68 A6
Summerland Gdns
MUSWH N10 48 B6
Summerlands Av ACT W3 98 E6
Summerlee Av EFNCH N2 65 K1
Summerlee Gdns EFNCH N2 65 K1
Summerley St
WAND/EARL SW18 160 A4
Summer Pl WATW WD18 * 26 D1
Summer Rd E/WMO/HCT KT8 189 J2
THDIT KT7 190 A2
Summersby Rd HGT N6 66 B3
Summers Cl BELMT SM2 208 E5
WBLY HA9 62 D5
Summerskille Cl ED N9 36 D4
Summers La
NFNCH/WDSPK N12 47 H3
Summers Rw
NFNCH/WDSPK N12 47 J2
Summers St CLKNW EC1R 5 J7
Summerstown TOOT SW17 160 B5
Summerton Wy THMD SE28 109 K6
Summer Trees SUN TW16 172 A4
Summerville Gdns SUT SM1 208 D4
Summerwood Rd ISLW TW7 156 A1
TWK TW1 156 A1
Summit Av CDALE/KGS NW9 63 F2
Summit Cl CDALE/KGS NW9 63 F1
EDGW HA8 44 C3
STHGT/OAK N14 34 C4
Summit Dr WFD IG8 53 H5
Summit Est
STNW/STAM N16 * 68 C4
Summit Rd NTHLT UB5 78 A5
WALTH E17 69 K1
Summit Wy NRWD SE19 181 F3
STHGT/OAK N14 34 B4
Sumner Av PECK SE15 * 143 G2
Sumner Cl ORP BR6 216 C2
Sumner Gdns CROY/NA CR0 196 B5
Sumner Pl SKENS SW7 14 B7
Sumner Place Ms SKENS SW7 14 B7
Sumner Rd CROY/NA CR0 196 C5
HRW HA1 60 C4
PECK SE15 143 G2
Sumner Rd South
CROY/NA CR0 196 B5
Sumner St STHWK SE1 12 C7
Sumpter Cl HAMP NW3 83 G4
Sunbeam Crs NKENS W10 100 A3
Sunbeam Rd WLSDN NW10 98 E3
Sunbury Av MLHL NW7 45 F1
MORT/ESHN SW14 138 A5
Sunbury Ct BAR EN5 * 20 C5
SUN TW16 172 C5
Sunbury Court Rd SUN TW16 172 B5
Sunbury Gdns MLHL NW7 45 F1
Sunbury La BTSEA SW11 140 C2
Sunbury Rd CHEAM SM3 208 B1
FELT TW13 153 J5
Sunbury St WOOL/PLUM SE18 126 E3
Sunbury Wy FELT TW13 172 B1
Sun Ct ERITH DA8 150 C3
Suncroft Pl SYD SE26 163 K5
Sunderland Mt FSTH SE23 * 164 A4
Sunderland Rd EA W5 116 E3
FSTH SE23 164 A3
Sunderland Ter
BAY/PAD W2 * 101 F5
Sunderland Wy MNPK E12 71 H6
Sundew Av SHB W12 99 J6
Sundew Ct ALP/SUD HA0 * 98 A1
Sundial Av SNWD SE25 181 G5
Sundial Rd MNPK E12 89 J1
Sundorne Rd CHARL SE7 126 A5
Sundridge Av BMLY BR1 184 C4
WELL DA16 147 J3
Sundridge Cl DART DA1 171 K1
Sundridge Pde BMLY BR1 * 184 A3
Sundridge Pl CROY/NA CR0 197 H5
Sundridge Rd CROY/NA CR0 197 G5
Sunfields Pl BKHTH/KID SE3 146 A1
Sun in Sands Rbt
BKHTH/KID SE3 145 K1
Sunken Rd CROY/NA CR0 212 E3
Sunkist Wy WLGTN SM6 210 E6
Sunland Av BXLYHS DA6 149 F5
Sun La BKHTH/KID SE3 146 A1
Sunleigh Rd ALP/SUD HA0 80 A6
Sunley Gdns GFD/PVL UB6 97 G1
Sunlight Cl WIM/MER SW19 * 178 B2
Sunlight Sq BETH E2 104 D2
Sunna Gdns SUN TW16 172 A5
Sunningdale STHGT/OAK N14 48 D1
Sunningdale Av ACT W3 99 G6
BARK IG11 90 D6
FELT TW13 154 D4
RAIN RM13 111 K3
RSLP HA4 59 G5
Sunningdale Cl
BERM/RHTH SE16 * 123 J5
STAN HA7 43 G3
SURB KT6 191 F6
THMD SE28 110 A5
Sunningdale Gdns
CDALE/KGS NW9 62 E2
KENS W8 * 119 K3
Sunningdale Ldg EDGW HA8 * 44 B1
Sunningdale Rd BMLY BR1 200 D1
RAIN RM13 93 J5
SUT SM1 208 D1
Sunningfield Rd HDN NW4 45 K6
Sunningfields Crs HDN NW4 45 K5
Sunninghill Ct ACT W3 * 117 K2
Sunninghill Rd LEW SE13 144 E3
Sunny Bank SNWD SE25 181 H6
Sunny Crs WLSDN NW10 80 E5
Sunnycroft Rd HSLW TW3 135 G3
SNWD SE25 197 H1
STHL UB1 96 A4
Sunnydale ORP BR6 201 F6
Sunnydale Gdns MLHL NW7 45 F2
Sunnydale Rd LEE/GVPK SE12 146 A6
Sunnydene Av CHING E4 52 B1
RSLP HA4 58 E5
Sunnydene Gdns
ALP/SUD HA0 79 J4
Sunnydene St SYD SE26 164 B6
Sunnyfield MLHL NW7 31 H6
Sunny Gardens Rd HDN NW4 46 A6
Sunny Hl HDN NW4 45 K6
Sunnyhill Cl CLPT E5 87 G2
Sunnyhill Rd
STRHM/NOR SW16 161 K6
Sunnyhurst Cl SUT SM1 208 E1
Sunnymead Av MTCM CR4 179 J6
Sunnymead Rd
CDALE/KGS NW9 63 F4
PUT/ROE SW15 138 E6
Sunnymede Av
HOR/WEW KT19 207 G6
Sunnymede Dr BARK/HLT IG6 72 B1
Sunny Ms CRW RM5 56 E3
Sunny Nook Gdns
SAND/SEL CR2 211 K4
Sunny Pl HDN NW4 64 A1
The Sunny Rd PEND EN3 25 F2
Sunnyside CAT SE6 * 164 C2
CRICK NW2 82 D1
WOT/HER KT12 188 B2
Sunnyside Dr CHING E4 38 A2
Sunnyside Pl WIM/MER SW19 177 H2
Sunnyside Rd ARCH N19 66 D4
EA W5 116 E1
IL IG1 90 C1
LEY E10 69 J5
TEDD TW11 155 J6
Sunnyside Rd East ED N9 36 C5
Sunnyside Rd North ED N9 36 B5
Sunnyside Rd South ED N9 36 B5
Sunny Vw CDALE/KGS NW9 63 F2
Sunny Wy
NFNCH/WDSPK N12 47 J3
Sun Pas BERM/RHTH SE16 123 H3
Sunray Av BRYLDS KT5 191 J6
HAYES BR2 200 D3
HNHL SE24 142 E5
WDR/YW UB7 112 A2
Sunrise Cl FELT TW13 154 E5
Sun Rd WKENS W14 119 J5

Sunset Av CHING E4 37 K3
WFD IG8 52 E1
Sunset Cl ERITH DA8 150 E1
Sunset Dr ABR/ST RM4 57 K1
Sunset Gdns SNWD SE25 181 F5
Sunset Rd HNHL SE24 142 D5
THMD SE28 128 B1
WIM/MER SW19 176 E1
Sunset Vw BAR EN5 20 C3
Sunshine Wy MTCM CR4 178 E5
Sun St SDTCH EC2A 13 F1
Superior Dr ORP BR6 217 F4
Surbiton Ct SURB KT6 190 D3
Surbiton Court Ms SURB KT6 190 E3
Surbiton Crs KUT/HW KT1 191 F1
Surbiton Hall Cl KUT/HW KT1 191 F1
Surbiton Hill Pk BRYLDS KT5 191 G2
Surbiton Hill Rd SURB KT6 191 F1
Surbiton Rd KUT/HW KT1 190 E1
Surlingham Cl THMD SE28 109 K6
Surma Cl WCHPL E1 104 C3
Surmans Cl DAGW RM9 91 J6
Surrendale Pl MV/WKIL W9 100 E3
Surrey Canal Rd PECK SE15 123 K6
Surrey Cl FNCH N3 46 C6
Surrey Crs CHSWK W4 117 H5
Surrey Gdns FSBYPK N4 67 J3
Surrey Gv SUT SM1 209 H1
WALW SE17 123 F5
Surrey La BTSEA SW11 140 D2
Surrey Ms WNWD SE27 163 F6
Surrey Mt FSTH SE23 163 J3
Surrey Quays Rd
BERM/RHTH SE16 123 K3
Surrey Rd BARK IG11 90 E5
DAGE RM10 92 D3
HRW HA1 60 C3
PECK SE15 144 A6
WWKM BR4 198 E5
Surrey Rw STHWK SE1 18 A2
Surrey Sq WALW SE17 123 F5
Surrey St CROY/NA CR0 211 J1
PLSTW E13 107 F2
TPL/STR WC2R 11 H5
Surrey Ter WALW SE17 19 H7
Surrey Water Rd
BERM/RHTH SE16 124 A1
Surridge Gdns NRWD SE19 180 E2
Surr St HOLWY N7 84 E3
Sury Basin KUTN/CMB KT2 175 F4
Susan Cl ROMW/RG RM7 56 E6
Susannah St POP/IOD E14 105 K5
Susan Rd BKHTH/KID SE3 146 A3
Susan Wd CHST BR7 185 F4
Sussex Av ISLW TW7 135 K4
Sussex Cl ARCH N19 * 66 E6
NWMAL KT3 192 B1
REDBR IG4 71 K3
TWK TW1 156 C1
Sussex Crs NTHLT UB5 78 A4
Sussex Gdns BAY/PAD W2 8 B3
CHSGTN KT9 205 K4
FSBYPK N4 67 J2
HGT N6 65 K2
Sussex Ga HGT N6 * 65 K2
Sussex Ms East BAY/PAD W2 * 8 B5
Sussex Ms West BAY/PAD W2 8 B5
Sussex Pl BAY/PAD W2 8 B4
CAMTN NW1 2 E6
HMSMTH W6 119 F5
NWMAL KT3 192 B1
Sussex Ring
NFNCH/WDSPK N12 46 E1
Sussex Rd CAR SM5 209 K4
DART DA1 171 K2
EHAM E6 108 A1
ERITH DA8 149 J1
HGDN/ICK UB10 76 A2
HRW HA1 60 C2
MTCM CR4 * 195 K2
NWDGN UB2 114 C3
NWMAL KT3 192 B1
SAND/SEL CR2 211 K4
SCUP DA14 186 C1
STMC/STPC BR5 202 D3
WWKM BR4 198 E5
Sussex Sq BAY/PAD W2 8 B5
Sussex St PIM SW1V 121 G5
PLSTW E13 107 F2
Sussex Ter PGE/AN SE20 * 181 K3
Sussex Wy ARCH N19 66 D5
EBAR EN4 22 B6
Sutcliffe Cl GLDGN NW11 65 F2
Sutcliffe Rd WELL DA16 148 D3
WOOL/PLUM SE18 127 K6
Sutherland Av HYS/HAR UB3 113 K4
MV/WKIL W9 100 E3
STMC/STPC BR5 202 A3
WEA W13 97 H5
WELL DA16 147 J5
Sutherland Cl BAR EN5 20 C5
Sutherland Ct
CDALE/KGS NW9 62 D1
Sutherland Dr
WIM/MER SW19 178 C4
Sutherland Gdns
MORT/ESHN SW14 138 B4
WPK KT4 192 E5
Sutherland Gv TEDD TW11 173 K1
WAND/EARL SW18 159 J2
Sutherland House
WALTH E17 * 51 G6
Sutherland Pl BAY/PAD W2 100 E5
Sutherland Rd BELV DA17 129 H3
BOW E3 105 H1
CHSWK W4 118 A6
CROY/NA CR0 196 B4
ED N9 36 C3
PEND EN3 37 F1
STHL UB1 95 K5
TOTM N17 50 C3
WALTH E17 51 F5
WEA W13 97 G5
Sutherland Rw PIM SW1V * 121 G5
Sutherland Sq WALW SE17 122 D5
Sutherland St PIM SW1V 121 G5
Sutherland Vls WEA W13 * 97 G6
Sutherland Wk WALW SE17 122 D5
Sutlej Rd CHARL SE7 146 B1
Sutterton St HOLWY N7 85 F4
Sutton Cl BECK BR3 182 E4
CHSWK W4 * 117 K6
LOU IG10 39 J2
PIN HA5 58 E2
Sutton Common Rd
CHEAM SM3 193 J4
Sutton Ct BELMT SM2 209 G5
CHSWK W4 * 117 K6
EA W5 * 117 F1
Sutton Court Rd CHSWK W4 117 K6
PLSTW E13 107 G2
SUT SM1 209 G4
Sutton Crs BAR EN5 20 B6
Sutton Dene HSLW TW3 135 G2
Sutton Dwelling Est
CHEL SW3 120 D5
Sutton Est IS N1 * 85 H5
The Sutton Est IS N1 * 85 H5
Sutton Gdns CROY/NA CR0 197 G2
Sutton Gv SUT SM1 209 H3
Sutton Hall Rd HEST TW5 135 F1
Sutton La FARR EC1M 6 B7
HSLW TW3 134 E3
Sutton La North CHSWK W4 117 K5
Sutton La South CHSWK W4 117 K6
Sutton Park Rd SUT SM1 209 F4
Sutton Pl HOM E9 86 E3
Sutton Rd BARK IG11 108 E1
HEST TW5 135 F2
MUSWH N10 48 A4
PLSTW E13 106 D3
WALTH E17 51 F4
Sutton Rw SOHO/SHAV W1D 10 C3
Sutton Sq HEST TW5 134 E2
HOM E9 * 86 E3
Sutton St WCHPL E1 104 E5
Sutton Wy HEST TW5 134 E2
NKENS W10 100 A4
STLK EC1Y 6 D7
Swaby Rd WAND/EARL SW18 160 B4
Swaffield Rd
WAND/EARL SW18 160 B2
Swain Cl STRHM/NOR SW16 179 G2
Swain Rd THHTH CR7 196 D2
Swains Cl WDR/YW UB7 112 B2
Swain's La HGT N6 84 A1
Swainson Rd ACT W3 118 C2
Swains Rd MTCM CR4 178 E3
Swain St STJWD NW8 2 C6
Swaisland Rd DART DA1 150 E6
Swaislands Dr DART DA1 150 C6
Swaledale Cl FBAR/BDGN N11 48 A2
Swale Rd DART DA1 150 D4
Swallands Rd CAT SE6 164 D5
Swallow Cl BUSH WD23 28 B3
ERITH DA8 150 B2
NWCR SE14 143 K2
Swallow Ct RSLP HA4 * 59 G5
Swallowdale SAND/SEL CR2 213 F6
Swallow Dr NTHLT UB5 96 A1
WLSDN NW10 81 F4
Swallowfield Rd CHARL SE7 126 A5
Swallowfield Wy
HYS/HAR UB3 113 G2
Swallow Gdns
STRHM/NOR SW16 179 J1
Swallow Pl REGST W1B 9 K4
Swallow St EHAM E6 107 J4
REGST W1B 10 B6
Swallowtail Cl
STMC/STPC BR5 202 E1
Swanage Rd CHING E4 52 A3
WAND/EARL SW18 160 B1
Swanage Waye YEAD UB4 95 G5
Swan Ap EHAM E6 107 J4
Swanbridge Rd BXLYHN DA7 149 H2
Swan Cl CROY/NA CR0 * 197 F4
FELT TW13 154 D6
STMC/STPC BR5 186 B6
WALTH E17 51 G4
Swandon Wy
WAND/EARL SW18 140 A5
Swan Dr CDALE/KGS NW9 45 G5
Swanfield St BETH E2 7 J5
Swan Island TWK TW1 * 156 B5
Swan La CANST EC4R 12 E6
DART DA1 170 C2
LOU IG10 39 G2
TRDG/WHET N20 33 G5
Swanley Rd WELL DA16 148 D2
Swan Md STHWK SE1 19 G5
Swan Ms BRXN/ST SW9 142 A3
Swan Pas WCHPL E1 13 K6
Swan & Pike Rd PEND EN3 25 J1
Swan Pl BARN SW13 138 C3
Swan Rd BERM/RHTH SE16 123 K2
FELT TW13 154 D6
STHL UB1 96 B5
WDR/YW UB7 112 A2
WOOL/PLUM SE18 126 C3
Swanscombe Rd CHSWK W4 118 B5
NTGHL W11 119 G1
Swansea Cl CRW RM5 57 F3
Swansea Rd HTHAIR TW6 153 F1
PEND EN3 24 E5
Swanston Pth OXHEY WD19 27 G5
Swan St ISLW TW7 136 C4
STHWK SE1 18 D3
Swanton Gdns
WIM/MER SW19 159 G3
Swanton Rd ERITH DA8 149 H1
Swan Wk CHEL SW3 120 E6
Swan Wy PEND EN3 25 F3
Swanwick Cl PUT/ROE SW15 158 C2
Swan Yd IS N1 85 H4
Sward Rd STMC/STPC BR5 202 B3
Swaton Rd BOW E3 105 J3
Swaylands Rd BELV DA17 129 H6
Swaythling Cl UED N18 36 D6
Swedenbourg Gdns
WCHPL E1 104 C6
Sweden Ga BERM/RHTH SE16 124 B4
Sweeney Crs STHWK SE1 19 K3
Sweeps La STMC/STPC BR5 202 E2
Sweet Briar Gn ED N9 36 B5
Sweet Briar Gv ED N9 36 B5
Sweet Briar Wk UED N18 36 B6
Sweetmans Av PIN HA5 41 H6
Sweets Wy TRDG/WHET N20 33 H4
Swete St PLSTW E13 106 E1
Sweyn Pl BKHTH/KID SE3 145 K3
Swift Cl HYS/HAR UB3 94 D5
RYLN/HDSTN HA2 60 B6
THMD SE28 109 H5
WALTH E17 51 G3
Swift Rd FELT TW13 154 C6
NWDGN UB2 114 E3
Swiftsden Wy BMLY BR1 183 H2
Swift St FUL/PGN SW6 139 H2
Swinbrook Rd NKENS W10 100 C4
Swinburne Crs CROY/NA CR0 197 K3
Swinburne Rd PUT/ROE SW15 138 D5
Swinderby Rd ALP/SUD HA0 80 A4
Swindon Cl GDMY/SEVK IG3 72 E6
Swindon Rd HTHAIR TW6 133 F6
Swindon St SHB W12 * 118 E1
Swinfield Cl FELT TW13 154 D6
Swinford Gdns BRXN/ST SW9 142 C4
Swingate La
WOOL/PLUM SE18 147 K1
Swinnerton St HOM E9 87 G3
Swinton Cl WBLY HA9 62 D5
Swinton Pl FSBYW WC1X 5 G4
Swinton St FSBYW WC1X 5 G4
Swires Shaw HAYES BR2 215 H2
Swithland Gdns
ELTH/MOT SE9 166 E6
Swyncombe Av EA W5 116 C4
Swynford Gdns HDN NW4 63 J1
Sybil Phoenix Cl DEPT SE8 124 A5
Sybourn St WALTH E17 69 H4
Sycamore Av BFN/LL DA15 168 A1
BOW E3 87 H6
EA W5 116 E3
HYS/HAR UB3 94 C6
Sycamore Cl ACT W3 118 B1
CAN/RD E16 106 C3
CAR SM5 209 K2
EBAR EN4 33 H1
ED N9 36 C6
EDGW HA8 30 E6
FELT TW13 153 K5
NTHLT UB5 77 J6
SAND/SEL CR2 212 A3
Sycamore Gdns MTCM CR4 178 C5
SHB W12 118 E2
Sycamore Gv CAT SE6 165 F1
CDALE/KGS NW9 62 E4
GPK RM2 57 J5
NWMAL KT3 176 B6
PGE/AN SE20 181 H4
Sycamore Hl FBAR/BDGN N11 48 A2
Sycamore Ms CLAP SW4 141 H4
ERITH DA8 * 130 A5
Sycamore Rd DART DA1 171 G2
WIM/MER SW19 177 F2
Sycamore St FSBYE EC1V 6 C7
Sycamore Wk NKENS W10 100 C3
Sycamore Wy TEDD TW11 174 D2
Sydcote DUL SE21 * 162 D4
Sydenham Av SYD SE26 181 J1
Sydenham Cl ROM RM1 75 H1
Sydenham Cots
LEE/GVPK SE12 * 166 B4
Sydenham Hl FSTH SE23 163 J4
SYD SE26 163 H5
Sydenham Pk SYD SE26 163 K5
Sydenham Park Rd SYD SE26 163 K5
Sydenham Ri FSTH SE23 163 J4
Sydenham Rd CROY/NA CR0 196 D6
SYD SE26 182 A1
Sydenham Station Ap
SYD SE26 163 K6
Sydmons Ct FSTH SE23 * 163 K2
Sydner Ms STNW/STAM N16 86 B2
Sydner Rd STNW/STAM N16 86 B2
Sydney Chapman Wy
BAR EN5 20 D3
Sydney Cl SKENS SW7 14 B7
Sydney Gv HDN NW4 64 A2
Sydney Ms CHEL SW3 14 B7
Sydney Pl SKENS SW7 14 B7
Sydney Rd ABYW SE2 128 E3
BARK/HLT IG6 54 C5
BXLYHS DA6 148 E5
CEND/HSY/T N8 67 G1
EBED/NFELT TW14 153 K3
ENC/FH EN2 23 K5
MUSWH N10 48 B4
RCH/KEW TW9 137 F5
RYNPK SW20 177 G5
SCUP DA14 167 K6
SUT SM1 208 E2
TEDD TW11 174 A1
WAN E11 71 F3
WEA W13 116 B1
WFD IG8 38 E6
Sydney St CHEL SW3 120 D5
Sydney Ter ESH/CLAY KT10 * 205 F4
Sylvan Av CHDH RM6 74 B3
MLHL NW7 45 G2
WDGN N22 49 G3
Sylvan Gdns SURB KT6 190 E4
Sylvan Gv CRICK NW2 82 B2
PECK SE15 123 J6
Sylvan Hl NRWD SE19 181 F4
Sylvan Rd FSTGT E7 88 E4
IL IG1 72 C6
NRWD SE19 181 G4
WALTH E17 * 69 J2
WAN E11 70 E2
Sylvan Ter PECK SE15 * 143 J1
Sylvan Wk BMLY BR1 184 E6
Sylvan Wy BCTR RM8 91 H1
WWKM BR4 214 C2
Sylverdale Rd CROY/NA CR0 211 H1
Sylvester Av CHST BR7 184 E2
Sylvester Pth HACK E8 * 86 D4
Sylvester Rd ALP/SUD HA0 79 J3
EFNCH N2 47 G5
HACK E8 * 86 D4
WALTH E17 * 69 H4
Sylvia Av PIN HA5 41 K2
Sylvia Gdns WBLY HA9 80 D5
Symes Ms CAMTN NW1 4 A2
Symington Ms HOM E9 87 F3
Symister Ms IS N1 7 G5
Symons Cl PECK SE15 143 K3
Symons St CHEL SW3 15 F7
KTBR SW1X 15 F7
Symphony Cl EDGW HA8 44 D3
Symphony Ms NKENS W10 100 C2
Syon Gate Wy BTFD TW8 136 B1
Syon La ISLW TW7 136 B1
Syon Pk ISLW TW7 * 136 C4
Syon Park Gdns ISLW TW7 136 A1

T

Tabard Garden Est
STHWK SE1 18 E2
Tabard St STHWK SE1 18 E3
Tabernacle Av PLSTW E13 106 E3
Tabernacle St SDTCH EC2A 7 F7
Tableer Av CLAP SW4 141 H6
Tabley Rd HOLWY N7 84 E2
Tabor Gdns CHEAM SM3 208 C4
Tabor Gv WIM/MER SW19 177 H3
Tabor Rd HMSMTH W6 118 E3
Tachbrook Rd
EBED/NFELT TW14 153 J2
NWDGN UB2 114 C4
Tachbrook St PIM SW1V 16 B7
Tack Ms BROCKY SE4 144 D4
Tadema Rd WBPTN SW10 140 B1
Tadmor St SHB W12 119 G1
Tadworth Av NWMAL KT3 192 C1
Tadworth Pde HCH RM12 93 K2
Tadworth Rd CRICK NW2 63 J6
Taeping St POP/IOD E14 124 E4
Taffy's How MTCM CR4 178 D6
Tait Ct BOW E3 87 H6
Tait Rd CROY/NA CR0 197 F4
Tait St WCHPL E1 104 D5
Takeley Cl CRW RM5 57 F5
Talacre Rd KTTN NW5 84 A4
Talbot Av EFNCH N2 47 H6
OXHEY WD19 27 J2
Talbot Cl SEVS/STOTM N15 68 B1
Talbot Ct BANK EC3V 13 F5
Talbot Crs HDN NW4 63 J2
Talbot Gdns GDMY/SEVK IG3 73 G6
Talbot Pl BKHTH/KID SE3 145 H3
Talbot Rd ALP/SUD HA0 79 K3
BAY/PAD W2 100 E5
CAR SM5 210 A3
DAGW RM9 92 B5
EDUL SE22 143 F5
EHAM E6 107 K1
FSTGT E7 88 E2
HGT N6 66 A3
ISLW TW7 136 B5
KTN/HRWW/WS HA3 43 F5
NTGHL W11 100 D5
NWDGN UB2 114 D4
SEVS/STOTM N15 68 B1
THHTH CR7 196 E1
WDGN N22 48 C5
WEA W13 * 97 G6
WHTN TW2 155 K3
Talbot Sq BAY/PAD W2 8 A4
Talbot Wk NTGHL W11 100 C5
WLSDN NW10 81 G4
Talbot Yd STHWK SE1 18 E1
Talcott Pth
BRXS/STRHM SW2 * 162 B3
Talehangers Cl BXLYHS DA6 148 E5
Talfourd Pl PECK SE15 143 G2
Talfourd Rd PECK SE15 143 G2
Talgarth Rd HMSMTH W6 * 119 F5
WKENS W14 119 H5
Talgarth Wk CDALE/KGS NW9 63 G2
Talisman Cl GDMY/SEVK IG3 73 H5
Talisman Sq SYD SE26 163 H6
Talisman Wy WBLY HA9 80 B1
Tallack Cl KTN/HRWW/WS HA3 42 E3
Tallack Rd LEY E10 69 H5
Tall Elms Cl HAYES BR2 199 J2
Tallis Cl CAN/RD E16 107 F5
Tallis Gv CHARL SE7 126 A6
Tallis St EMB EC4Y 11 K5
Tallis Vw WLSDN NW10 81 F4
Tallow Cl DAGW RM9 91 K4
Tallow Rd BTFD TW8 116 D6
Tall Trees STRHM/NOR SW16 180 A6
Talma Gdns WHTN TW2 155 K2
Talmage Cl FSTH SE23 163 K2
Talman Gv STAN HA7 43 K2
Talma Rd BRXS/STRHM SW2 142 B5
Talwin St BOW E3 105 K2
Tamar Cl BOW E3 * 87 H6
Tamarind Yd WAP E1W 123 H1
Tamarisk Sq SHB W12 99 H6
Tamar St CHARL SE7 126 D4
Tamesis Gdns WPK KT4 192 B6
Tamian Wy HSLWW TW4 134 B5
Tamworth Av WFD IG8 52 C2
Tamworth La MTCM CR4 179 G6
Tamworth Pk MTCM CR4 195 G1
Tamworth Pl CROY/NA CR0 * 196 D6
Tamworth Rd CROY/NA CR0 196 D6
Tamworth St FUL/PGN SW6 119 K6
Tancred Rd FSBYPK N4 67 H3
Tandridge Dr ORP BR6 201 J5
Tanfield Av CRICK NW2 81 H2
Tanfield Rd CROY/NA CR0 211 J2
Tangier Rd RCHPK/HAM TW10 137 H5
Tangleberry Cl BMLY BR1 200 E1
Tangle Tree Cl FNCH N3 47 F5
Tanglewood Cl CROY/NA CR0 212 E1
STAN HA7 28 E4
Tanglewood Wy FELT TW13 154 A5
Tangley Gv PUT/ROE SW15 158 C2
Tangley Park Rd HPTN TW12 * 172 E1
Tangmere Crs HCH RM12 93 K4
Tangmere Gdns NTHLT UB5 95 G1
Tangmere Gv KUTN/CMB KT2 174 E1
Tangmere Wy
CDALE/KGS NW9 45 G5
Tanhouse Fld KTTN NW5 * 84 D3
Tankerton Houses
STPAN WC1H * 5 F5
Tankerton Rd SURB KT6 191 G6
Tankerton St STPAN WC1H 5 F5
Tankerton Ter
CROY/NA CR0 * 196 A4
Tankerville Rd
STRHM/NOR SW16 179 J3
Tank Hill Rd PUR RM19 131 K3
Tankridge Rd CRICK NW2 63 K6
The Tanneries WCHPL E1 * 104 E3
Tanners Cl WOT/HER KT12 188 A3
Tanners End La UED N18 36 A6
Tanner's Hl DEPT SE8 144 D2
Tanners La BARK/HLT IG6 54 C6
Tanners Ms DEPT SE8 144 C2
Tanner St BARK IG11 90 C4
STHWK SE1 19 H3
Tannery Cl CROY/NA CR0 198 A2
DAGE RM10 92 D1
Tannington Ter HBRY N5 85 G1
Tannoy Sq WNWD SE27 162 E6
Tannsfeld Rd SYD SE26 182 A1
Tansley Cl HOLWY N7 84 D3
Tanswell St STHWK SE1 * 17 J3
Tansy Cl EHAM E6 108 A5
Tantallon Rd BAL SW12 161 F3
Tant Av CAN/RD E16 106 D5
Tantony Gv CHDH RM6 55 K6
Tanworth Cl NTHWD HA6 40 A2
Tanworth Gdns PIN HA5 41 F5
Tan Yard La BXLY DA5 * 169 H2
Tanza Rd HAMP NW3 83 K2
Tapestry Cl BELMT SM2 209 F5
Taplow Ct MTCM CR4 194 D1
Taplow Rd PLMGR N13 35 J6
Taplow St IS N1 6 D3
Tappesfield Rd PECK SE15 143 K4
Tapping Cl KUTN/CMB KT2 * 175 H3
Tapp St WCHPL E1 104 D3
Tapster St BAR EN5 20 D4
Tara Ms CEND/HSY/T N8 66 E3
Taransay Wk IS N1 85 K4
Tara Ter BROCKY SE4 * 144 B4
Tarbert Rd EDUL SE22 143 F6
Tarbert Wk WCHPL E1 104 E6
Target Cl EBED/NFELT TW14 153 H1
Tariff Rd UED N18 50 C2
Tarleton Gdns FSTH SE23 163 J3
Tarling Cl SCUP DA14 168 C5
Tarling Rd CAN/RD E16 106 D5
EFNCH N2 47 G4
Tarling St WCHPL E1 104 D5
Tarnbank ENC/FH EN2 22 E6
Tarn St STHWK SE1 18 C5
Tarnwood Pk ELTH/MOT SE9 166 E3
Tarragon Cl NWCR SE14 144 B1
Tarragon Gv SYD SE26 182 A2
Tarrant Pl MBLAR W1H 8 E2
Tarriff Crs DEPT SE8 124 C4
Tarrington Cl
STRHM/NOR SW16 161 J6
Tarver Rd WALW SE17 122 C5
Tarves Wy GNWCH SE10 144 E1
Tash Pl FBAR/BDGN N11 * 48 B1
Tasker Cl HYS/HAR UB3 133 F1
Tasker Rd HAMP NW3 83 K3
Tasmania Ter UED N18 49 J2
Tasman Rd BRXN/ST SW9 141 K4
Tasso Rd HMSMTH W6 119 H6
Tate Gdns BUSH WD23 28 E2
Tate Rd CAN/RD E16 126 E1
SUT SM1 208 E3
Tatham Pl STJWD NW8 2 B2
Tatnell Rd FSTH SE23 164 B1
Tattersall Cl ELTH/MOT SE9 146 D6
Tatton Cl CAR SM5 195 F5
Tatton Crs CLPT E5 68 B4
Tatum Rd WLSDN NW10 80 E5
Tatum St WALW SE17 19 F7
Tauheed Cl FSBYPK N4 67 J6
Taunton Av HSLW TW3 135 H3
RYNPK SW20 176 E5
Taunton Cl BARK/HLT IG6 55 F2
BXLYHN DA7 150 A4
CHEAM SM3 193 K5
Taunton Dr EFNCH N2 47 G5
ENC/FH EN2 23 G4
Taunton Ms CAMTN NW1 2 E7
Taunton Pl CAMTN NW1 2 E6
Taunton Rd GFD/PVL UB6 78 B5
LEE/GVPK SE12 145 H6
Taunton Wy STAN HA7 44 A5
Tavern Cl CAR SM5 194 D4
Taverners Cl NTGHL W11 119 H1
Taverner Sq HBRY N5 * 85 J2
Taverners Wy CHING E4 38 C3
Tavistock Av GFD/PVL UB6 97 G1
MLHL NW7 46 B3
WALTH E17 51 F6
Tavistock Cl
STNW/STAM N16 * 86 A3
Tavistock Ct COVGDN WC2E * 11 F5
Tavistock Crs MTCM CR4 195 K1
NTGHL W11 100 D4
Tavistock Gdns
GDMY/SEVK IG3 90 E2
Tavistock Gv CROY/NA CR0 196 E4
Tavistock Ms NTGHL W11 * 100 D5
Tavistock Pl STHGT/OAK N14 * 34 B1
STPAN WC1H 4 D6
Tavistock Rd CAR SM5 194 C5
CROY/NA CR0 196 E5
EDGW HA8 44 B4
FSBYPK N4 67 K3
HAYES BR2 199 K1
HGDN/ICK UB10 76 B3
NTGHL W11 100 D4
SRTFD E15 88 D4
SWFD E18 52 E6
WAN E11 88 D2
WDR/YW UB7 112 A1
WELL DA16 148 D2
WLSDN NW10 99 H1
Tavistock Sq STPAN WC1H 4 D6
Tavistock St COVGDN WC2E 11 F5
HOL/ALD WC2B 11 G5
Tavistock Ter ARCH N19 84 D1
Taviton St STPAN WC1H 4 C6
Tavy Br ABYW SE2 128 D2
Tavy Cl LBTH SE11 122 B5
Tawney Rd THMD SE28 109 H6
Tawny Cl FELT TW13 153 K5
WEA W13 116 C1
Tawny Wy BERM/RHTH SE16 124 A4
Tayben Av WHTN TW2 155 K1

Taybridge Rd BTSEA SW11 141 F4
Tayburn Cl POP/IOD E14 106 A5
Tayfield Cl HGDN/ICK UB10 76 A1
Taylor Av RCH/KEW TW9 137 J3
Taylor Cl CRW RM5 56 C3
DEPT SE8 124 C6
HPTN TW12 173 H1
HSLW TW3 135 H2
ORP BR6 217 F2
TOTM N17 50 C3
Taylor Rd MTCM CR4 178 D3
WLGTN SM6 210 B3
Taylor Rw RDART DA2 171 F5
Taylor's Blds
WOOL/PLUM SE18 127 G4
Taylors Cl SCUP DA14 168 A6
Taylors Ct FELT TW13 153 K4
Taylor's Gn ACT W3 * 99 G5
Taylors La WLSDN NW10 81 G4
Taylor's La BAR EN5 20 D2
SYD SE26 163 J6
WLSDN NW10 81 G5
Taylors Md MLHL NW7 * 45 J1
Taymount Ri FSTH SE23 163 K4
Tayport Cl IS N1 85 F5
Tayside Dr EDGW HA8 30 D5
Tay Wy ROM RM1 57 H4
Taywood Rd NTHLT UB5 95 J3
Teak Cl BERM/RHTH SE16 124 B1
Teal Av STMC/STPC BR5 202 E1
Teal Cl CAN/RD E16 107 H4
Teal Dr NTHWD HA6 40 A3
Teale St BETH E2 104 C1
Tealing Dr HOR/WEW KT19 207 F2
Teal Pl SUT SM1 208 D3
Teal St GNWCH SE10 125 J3
Teasel Cl CROY/NA CR0 198 A5
Teasel Crs THMD SE28 127 K1
Teasel Wy SRTFD E15 106 C2
Tebworth Rd TOTM N17 50 B3
Teck Cl ISLW TW7 136 B3
Tedder Cl CHSGTN KT9 205 J3
RSLP HA4 76 E3
Tedder Rd SAND/SEL CR2 213 F5
Teddington Pk TEDD TW11 174 A1
Teddington Park Rd
TEDD TW11 156 A6
Tedworth Gdns CHEL SW3 120 E5
Tedworth Sq CHEL SW3 * 120 E5
Tees Av GFD/PVL UB6 96 E1
Teesdale Av ISLW TW7 136 B2
Teesdale Cl BETH E2 104 C1
Teesdale Gdns ISLW TW7 136 B2
SNWD SE25 181 F5
Teesdale Rd WAN E11 70 D3
Teesdale St BETH E2 104 D1
Teesdale Yd BETH E2 * 104 D1
The Tee ACT W3 99 G5
Teevan Cl CROY/NA CR0 197 H4
Teevan Rd CROY/NA CR0 197 H4
Teign Ms ELTH/MOT SE9 166 D4
Teignmouth Cl CLAP SW4 141 J5
EDGW HA8 44 B5
Teignmouth Gdns
GFD/PVL UB6 97 G1
Teignmouth Rd CRICK NW2 82 B3
WELL DA16 148 D3
Telcote Wy RSLP HA4 * 59 G4
Telegraph Hl HAMP NW3 83 F1
Telegraph La ESH/CLAY KT10 205 F2
Telegraph Ms GDMY/SEVK IG3 73 F5
Telegraph Pas
BRXS/STRHM SW2 161 K2
Telegraph Pl POP/IOD E14 124 E4
Telegraph Rd PUT/ROE SW15 158 E2
Telegraph St LOTH EC2R 12 E3
Telephone Pl WKENS W14 * 119 J6
Telferscot Rd BAL SW12 161 J3
Telford Av BRXS/STRHM SW2 161 J3
Telford Cl NRWD SE19 181 G2
WALTH E17 69 G4
Telford Dr WOT/HER KT12 188 B4
Telford Rd CDALE/KGS NW9 63 H3
ELTH/MOT SE9 167 J4
NKENS W10 100 C4
STHL UB1 96 B6
WHTN TW2 155 F2
Telford Rd (North Circular Rd)
FBAR/BDGN N11 48 C1
Telfords Yd WAP E1W * 104 C6
Telford Ter PIM SW1V * 121 H6
Telford Wy ACT W3 99 G4
YEAD UB4 95 J4
Telham Rd EHAM E6 108 A1
Tell Gv EDUL SE22 143 G5
Tellisford ESH/CLAY KT10 204 B2
Tellson Av WOOL/PLUM SE18 146 D2
Telscombe Cl ORP BR6 201 K6
Temeraire Pl BTFD TW8 117 G5
Temeraire St
BERM/RHTH SE16 123 K2
Tempelhof Av HDN NW4 64 A4
Temperley Rd BAL SW12 161 F2
Tempest Wy RAIN RM13 93 J4
Templar Dr THMD SE28 109 K5
Templar Pl HPTN TW12 173 F3
Templars Av GLDGN NW11 64 D3
Templars Ct DART DA1 * 151 K6
Templars Crs FNCH N3 46 E5
Templars Dr
KTN/HRWW/WS HA3 * 42 D2
Templar St CMBW SE5 142 C3
Temple Av BCTR RM8 74 C5
CROY/NA CR0 213 H1
EMB EC4Y 11 K5
TRDG/WHET N20 33 H2
Temple Cl FNCH N3 46 D5
THMD SE28 127 H3
WAN E11 70 C4
Templecombe Rd HOM E9 86 E6
Templecombe Wy MRDN SM4 193 H2
Temple Dwellings BETH E2 * 104 D1
Temple Fortune Hl
GLDGN NW11 64 E2
Temple Fortune La
GLDGN NW11 64 D3
Temple Gdns BCTR RM8 91 K1
EMB EC4Y * 11 J5
GLDGN NW11 64 D3
WCHMH N21 * 35 H4
Temple Gv ENC/FH EN2 23 H4
GLDGN NW11 64 E3
Temple Hl DART DA1 151 J6
Temple Hill Sq DART DA1 151 J6
Temple La EMB EC4Y 11 K4
Templeman Rd HNWL W7 97 F4
Templemead Cl ACT W3 99 G5
Temple Mead Cl STAN HA7 43 H2
Temple Mills La SRTFD E15 88 A3
Temple Pde BAR EN5 * 33 H2
Temple Pl TPL/STR WC2R 11 H5
Temple Rd CEND/HSY/T N8 67 F1
CHSWK W4 117 K3
CRICK NW2 82 A2
CROY/NA CR0 211 K2
EA W5 116 E3
EHAM E6 89 J6
HSLW TW3 135 G5
Temple Sheen Rd
MORT/ESHN SW14 137 K5
Temple St BETH E2 104 D1
Temple Ter WDGN N22 * 49 G5
Templeton Av CHING E4 37 J6
Templeton Cl NRWD SE19 180 E4
STNW/STAM N16 * 86 A3
Templeton Pl ECT SW5 119 K4
Templeton Rd FSBYPK N4 67 K3
Temple Wy SUT SM1 209 H1
Templewood WEA W13 97 H4
Templewood Av HAMP NW3 83 F1
Templewood Gdns
HAMP NW3 83 F1
Temple Yd BETH E2 104 C2
Tempsford Cl ENC/FH EN2 23 J4
Temsford Cl RYLN/HDSTN HA2 42 C5
Tenbury Cl FSTGT E7 89 H3
Tenbury Ct BAL SW12 161 J3
Tenby Av KTN/HRWW/WS HA3 43 H5
Tenby Cl CHDH RM6 74 A3
SEVS/STOTM N15 68 B1
Tenby Gdns NTHLT UB5 78 A4
Tenby Rd CHDH RM6 74 A3
EDGW HA8 44 B4
PEND EN3 24 E4
WALTH E17 69 G2
WELL DA16 148 E2
Tench St WAP E1W * 123 J1
Tenda Rd STHWK SE1 123 J4
Tendring Wy CHDH RM6 73 J2
Tenham Av BRXS/STRHM SW2 161 J4
Tenison Wy STHWK SE1 17 J1
Tenniel Cl BAY/PAD W2 101 G5
Tennison Rd SNWD SE25 197 G1
Tennis St STHWK SE1 18 E2
Tenniswood Rd EN EN1 24 A2
Tennyson Av CDALE/KGS NW9 44 E6
MNPK E12 89 J5
NWMAL KT3 192 E2
TWK TW1 156 A3
WAN E11 70 E4
Tennyson Cl
EBED/NFELT TW14 153 K1
PEND EN3 25 F6
WELL DA16 147 K2
Tennyson Rd DART DA1 151 K6
HNWL W7 97 F6
HSLW TW3 135 H3
KIL/WHAMP NW6 82 D6
LEY E10 69 K5
MLHL NW7 45 H1
PGE/AN SE20 182 A3
SRTFD E15 88 C5
WALTH E17 69 H3
WIM/MER SW19 178 B2
Tennyson St VX/NE SW8 141 G3
Tennyson Wy HCH RM12 75 H5
Tensing Rd NWDGN UB2 115 F3
Tentelow La NWDGN UB2 115 G3
Tenterden Cl ELTH/MOT SE9 166 E6
HDN NW4 46 B6
Tenterden Dr HDN NW4 46 B6
Tenterden Gdns
CROY/NA CR0 197 H4
HDN NW4 46 B6
Tenterden Gv HDN NW4 64 A1
Tenterden Rd BCTR RM8 74 B6
CROY/NA CR0 197 H4
TOTM N17 50 B3
Tenterden St CONDST W1S 9 K4
Tenter Gnd WCHPL E1 13 J2
Tent Peg La STMC/STPC BR5 201 H2
Tent St WCHPL E1 104 D3
Teredo St LEW SE13 144 E3
Terling Cl WAN E11 88 D1
Terling Rd BCTR RM8 74 C6
Terling Wk IS N1 * 85 J6
Terminus Pl PIM SW1W 15 K5
Terrace Gdns BARN SW13 138 C3
Terrace Rd HOM E9 87 F5
PLSTW E13 88 E6
WOT/HER KT12 188 A3
The Terrace BARN SW13 138 B3
BETH E2 * 104 E2
CHING E4 * 38 C5
DEPT SE8 * 124 C4
EFNCH N2 * 66 A1
FNCH N3 * 46 D5
FSTH SE23 * 164 B2
KIL/WHAMP NW6 82 E6
Terrace Vls HMSMTH W6 * 118 D5
Terrace Wk DAGW RM9 92 A3
Terrac St RCH/KEW TW9 137 G5
Terrapin Rd TOOT SW17 161 G5
Terretts Pl IS N1 85 H5
Terrick Rd WDGN N22 48 E4
Terrick St SHB W12 99 K5
Terrilands PIN HA5 41 K6
Terront Rd SEVS/STOTM N15 67 J2
Tessa Sanderson Wy
GFD/PVL UB6 78 D3
Testerton Rd NTGHL W11 * 100 B6
Testerton Wk NTGHL W11 * 100 B6
Tetbury Pl IS N1 6 A1
Tetcott Rd WBPTN SW10 140 B1
Tetherdown MUSWH N10 48 A6
Tetty Wy BMLY BR1 183 K5
Teversham La VX/NE SW8 141 K2
Teviot Cl WELL DA16 148 C2
Teviot St POP/IOD E14 106 A4
Tewkesbury Av FSTH SE23 163 J3
PIN HA5 59 J2
Tewkesbury Cl LOU IG10 39 J1
SEVS/STOTM N15 67 K3
Tewkesbury Gdns
CDALE/KGS NW9 44 D6
Tewkesbury Rd CAR SM5 194 C5
SEVS/STOTM N15 67 K4
WEA W13 116 B1
Tewkesbury Ter
FBAR/BDGN N11 48 C2
Tewson Rd WOOL/PLUM SE18 127 K5
Teynham Av EN EN1 35 K1
Teynham Gn HAYES BR2 199 K2
Teynton Ter TOTM N17 49 J4
Thackeray Av TOTM N17 50 C5
Thackeray Cl ISLW TW7 136 B3
WIM/MER SW19 177 G3
Thackeray Dr CHDH RM6 73 H4
Thackeray Ms HACK E8 86 C4
Thackeray Rd EHAM E6 107 H1
VX/NE SW8 141 G3
Thackeray St KENS W8 120 A3
Thakeham Cl SYD SE26 181 J1
Thalia Cl GNWCH SE10 125 G6
Thame Rd BERM/RHTH SE16 124 A2
Thames Av DAGW RM9 110 D3
GFD/PVL UB6 97 F1
WBPTN SW10 140 B2
WPK KT4 193 F5
Thames Bank
MORT/ESHN SW14 137 K3
Thamesbank Pl THMD SE28 109 J5
Thames Cir POP/IOD E14 124 D4
Thames Cl HPTN TW12 173 G5
RAIN RM13 111 K5
Thames Crs CHSWK W4 138 B1
Thames Down Link
BRYLDS KT5 191 K2
HOR/WEW KT19 206 C5
WPK KT4 207 F1
Thames Dr RSLP HA4 58 A3
Thames Eyot TWK TW1 * 156 B4
Thames Ga DART DA1 151 K6
Thamesgate Cl
RCHPK/HAM TW10 156 C6
Thameside TEDD TW11 174 E3
Thames Meadow
E/WMO/HCT KT8 173 F6
Thamesmere Dr THMD SE28 109 G6
Thames Pth BARN SW13 138 C2
BERM/RHTH SE16 124 C3
BOW E3 87 J6
CHEL SW3 121 F6
CLPT E5 87 F1
E/WMO/HCT KT8 190 A1
GNWCH SE10 125 F6
HMSMTH W6 118 E5
HOM E9 87 H3
ISLW TW7 136 C3
KUTN/CMB KT2 174 D1
MORT/ESHN SW14 138 B3
POP/IOD E14 124 D3
PUT/ROE SW15 139 F3
RCH/KEW TW9 136 D6
RCHPK/HAM TW10 156 B5
SRTFD E15 105 K1
STHWK SE1 17 G5
SUN TW16 172 B6
THDIT KT7 190 C3
TPL/STR WC2R 11 H6
TWK TW1 156 B4
TWRH EC3N 13 H7
VX/NE SW8 121 J6
WEST SW1P 17 F5
Thames Pl PUT/ROE SW15 139 G4
Thamespoint TEDD TW11 * 174 E3
Thames Quay WBPTN SW10 * 140 B2
Thames Reach KUT/HW KT1 * 174 E4
Thames Rd BARK IG11 109 G2
CAN/RD E16 126 C1
CHSWK W4 117 H6
DART DA1 150 D4
Thames Side KUT/HW KT1 174 E4
THDIT KT7 190 C3
Thames St GNWCH SE10 124 E6
HPTN TW12 173 G5
KUT/HW KT1 174 E5
SUN TW16 172 A6
Thamesvale Cl HSLW TW3 135 F3
Thames Village CHSWK W4 137 K2
Thamley PUR RM19 131 K4
Thanescroft Gdns
CROY/NA CR0 212 A1
Thanet Dr HAYES BR2 215 H1
Thanet Pl CROY/NA CR0 211 J2
Thanet Rd BXLY DA5 169 H2
ERITH DA8 150 B1
Thanet St STPAN WC1H 4 E5
Thane Vls HOLWY N7 85 F1
Thant Cl LEY E10 87 K1
Tharp Rd WLGTN SM6 210 D3
Thatcham Gdns
TRDG/WHET N20 33 G2
Thatcher Cl WDR/YW UB7 112 B2
Thatchers Wy ISLW TW7 135 J6
Thatches Gv CHDH RM6 56 A6
Thavies Inn FLST/FETLN EC4A 11 K3
Thaxted Pl RYNPK SW20 177 G3
Thaxted Rd BKHH IG9 39 J2
ELTH/MOT SE9 167 H4
Thaxton Rd WKENS W14 119 J6
Thayers Farm Rd BECK BR3 182 B4
Thayer St MHST W1U 9 H3
Theatre Sq SRTFD E15 88 B4
Theatre St BTSEA SW11 140 E4
Theberton St IS N1 85 G6
The Beverly MRDN SM4 193 G3
The Courtyard HAYES BR2 215 J4
Theed St STHWK SE1 17 J1
The Green WIM/MER SW19 177 G1
Thelma Gv TEDD TW11 174 B2
Theobald Crs
KTN/HRWW/WS HA3 42 B4
Theobald Rd CROY/NA CR0 196 C6
WALTH E17 69 H4
Theobald's Rd GINN WC1R 11 G1
Theobald St STHWK SE1 18 E5
Theodora Wy PIN HA5 40 D6
Theodore Rd LEW SE13 165 G1
Therapia La CROY/NA CR0 195 J4
Therapia Rd EDUL SE22 163 K1
Theresa Rd HMSMTH W6 118 D4
Theresa's Wk SAND/SEL CR2 211 K6
Thermopylae Ga
POP/IOD E14 124 E4
Theseus Wk IS N1 6 B3
Thesiger Rd PGE/AN SE20 182 A3
Thessaly Rd VX/NE SW8 141 J2
Thetford Cl PLMGR N13 49 H2
Thetford Rd ASHF TW15 152 B6
DAGW RM9 91 K5
NWMAL KT3 192 A3
Theydon Gdns RAIN RM13 93 G5
Theydon Gv WFD IG8 53 G2
Theydon Rd CLPT E5 68 E6
Theydon St WALTH E17 69 H4
Thicket Crs SUT SM1 209 G2
Thicket Gv DAGW RM9 91 J4
PGE/AN SE20 181 H3
Thicket Rd PGE/AN SE20 181 J3
SUT SM1 209 G2
Thicket Ter PGE/AN SE20 * 181 H3
Third Av ACT W3 118 C1
CHDH RM6 73 J3
DAGE RM10 92 D6
EN EN1 24 B6
HYS/HAR UB3 113 J1
MNPK E12 89 J2
NKENS W10 100 C2
PLSTW E13 106 E2
WALTH E17 69 J2
WBLY HA9 61 K6
Third Cl E/WMO/HCT KT8 189 G1
Third Cross Rd WHTN TW2 155 J4
Thirleby Rd EDGW HA8 45 F4
MLHL NW7 46 C1
WEST SW1P 16 B5
Thirlmere Av GFD/PVL UB6 97 J2
Thirlmere Gdns WBLY HA9 61 J5
Thirlmere Ri BMLY BR1 183 J2
Thirlmere Rd BXLYHN DA7 149 K3
MUSWH N10 48 B4
STRHM/NOR SW16 161 J6
Thirsk Cl NTHLT UB5 78 A4
Thirsk Rd BTSEA SW11 141 F4
MTCM CR4 179 F3
SNWD SE25 196 E1
Thirza Rd DART DA1 171 J1
Thislefield Cl BXLY DA5 168 E3
Thistlebrook ABYW SE2 128 D3
Thistlecroft Gdns STAN HA7 43 K4
Thistledene THDIT KT7 189 K3
Thistledene Av CRW RM5 56 D1
RYLN/HDSTN HA2 77 J1
Thistle Gv WBPTN SW10 * 120 B5
Thistlemead CHST BR7 185 G5
Thistlewaite Rd CLPT E5 86 D1
Thistlewood Cl HOLWY N7 67 F6
Thistleworth Cl ISLW TW7 135 J1
Thistley Cl
NFNCH/WDSPK N12 47 J2
Thomas A Beckett Cl
HRW HA1 79 F2
Thomas Baines Rd
BTSEA SW11 140 C4
Thomas Cribb Ms EHAM E6 107 K5
Thomas Dean Rd SYD SE26 * 164 C6
Thomas Dinwiddy Rd
LEE/GVPK SE12 166 A4
Thomas Doyle St STHWK SE1 18 A4
Thomas Fyre Dr BOW E3 105 J1
Thomas Jacomb Pl
WALTH E17 69 H1
Thomas' La CAT SE6 164 E2
Thomas Moore St WAP E1W 104 C6
Thomas Moore Wy EFNCH N2 47 G6
Thomas More Gdns
ESH/CLAY KT10 189 F6
Thomas More St WAP E1W * 104 C6
Thomas North Ter
CAN/RD E16 * 106 D4
Thomas Pl KENS W8 * 120 A3
Thomas Rd POP/IOD E14 105 H5
Thomas St
WOOL/PLUM SE18 127 F4
Thomas Wall Cl SUT SM1 209 F3
Thompson Av CMBW SE5 142 D1
RCH/KEW TW9 137 J4
Thompson Cl CHEAM SM3 193 K5
IL IG1 72 C6
Thompson Rd DAGW RM9 92 B1
EDUL SE22 163 G1
HSLW TW3 135 G5
Thompson's Av CMBW SE5 * 142 D1
Thomson Crs CROY/NA CR0 196 B5
Thomson Rd
KTN/HRWW/WS HA3 42 E6
Thorburn Sq STHWK SE1 123 H4
Thorburn Wy
WIM/MER SW19 * 178 C4
Thoresby St IS N1 6 D4
Thorkhill Gdns THDIT KT7 190 B5
Thorkhill Rd THDIT KT7 190 C5
Thornaby Gdns UED N18 50 C2
Thorn Av BUSH WD23 28 C3
Thornbury Av ISLW TW7 135 J1
Thornbury Cl
STNW/STAM N16 86 A3
Thornbury Rd CLAP SW4 161 K1
ISLW TW7 135 J3
Thornbury Sq HGT N6 66 C5
Thornby Rd CLPT E5 86 E1
Thorncliffe Rd CLAP SW4 161 J1
NWDGN UB2 114 E5
Thorn Cl HAYES BR2 201 F3
NTHLT UB5 95 K2
Thorncombe Rd EDUL SE22 143 F6
Thorn Ct BELMT SM2 * 209 F5
Thorncroft EMPK RM11 75 K3
Thorncroft Rd SUT SM1 209 F2
Thorncroft St VX/NE SW8 141 K1
Thorndean St
WAND/EARL SW18 160 B4
Thorndene Av
TRDG/WHET N20 34 A3
Thorndike Av NTHLT UB5 77 H6
Thorndike Cl WBPTN SW10 140 B1
Thorndike Rd IS N1 85 K4
Thorndike St PIM SW1V * 16 C7
Thorndon Cl STMC/STPC BR5 186 A5
Thorndon Gdns
HOR/WEW KT19 207 G2
Thorndon Rd STMC/STPC BR5 186 A5
Thorndyke Ct PIN HA5 41 K3
Thorne Cl CAN/RD E16 106 E5
ERITH DA8 129 J6
ESH/CLAY KT10 205 G5
WAN E11 88 C2
Thorneloe Gdns
CROY/NA CR0 211 H3
Thorne Rd VX/NE SW8 141 K1
Thorne's Cl BECK BR3 183 F6
Thorne St BARN SW13 138 B4
Thornet Wood Rd BMLY BR1 185 F6
Thorney Crs BTSEA SW11 * 140 C1
Thorneycroft Cl
WOT/HER KT12 188 B3
Thorneycroft Dr PEND EN3 25 J1
Thorney Hedge Rd
CHSWK W4 117 J4
Thorney St WEST SW1P 16 E6
Thornfield Av MLHL NW7 46 C4
Thornfield Pde MLHL NW7 * 46 C3
Thornfield Rd SHB W12 118 E2
Thornford Rd LEW SE13 145 F6
Thorngate Rd MV/WKIL W9 100 E3
Thorngrove Rd PLSTW E13 89 F6
Thornham Gv SRTFD E15 88 B3
Thornham St GNWCH SE10 124 E6
Thornhaugh St STPAN WC1H 4 D7
Thornhill Av SURB KT6 191 F6
WOOL/PLUM SE18 147 K1
Thornhill Bridge Whf IS N1 5 G1
Thornhill Crs IS N1 85 F5
Thornhill Gdns BARK IG11 90 E5
LEY E10 69 K6
Thornhill Gv IS N1 85 F5
Thornhill Rd CROY/NA CR0 196 D4
IS N1 85 G5
LEY E10 69 K6
NTHWD HA6 26 A6
SURB KT6 191 F6
Thornhill Sq IS N1 85 F6
Thornlaw Rd WNWD SE27 162 B6
Thornley Cl TOTM N17 50 C3
Thornley Dr RYLN/HDSTN HA2 60 B6
Thornsbeach Rd CAT SE6 165 F3
Thornsett Pl PGE/AN SE20 181 J5
Thornsett Rd PGE/AN SE20 181 J5
WAND/EARL SW18 160 A4
Thornsett Ter PGE/AN SE20 * 181 J5
Thornton Av
BRXS/STRHM SW2 161 J3
CHSWK W4 118 B4
CROY/NA CR0 196 A3
WDR/YW UB7 112 C3
Thornton Cl WDR/YW UB7 112 C3
Thornton Dene BECK BR3 182 D5
Thornton Gdns BAL SW12 161 J3
Thornton Gv PIN HA5 42 A2
Thornton Hl WIM/MER SW19 177 H3
Thornton Pl MBLAR W1H 9 F1
Thornton Rd BAL SW12 161 J2
BAR EN5 20 C4
BELV DA17 * 129 J4
BMLY BR1 183 K1
CAR SM5 194 C5
IL IG1 90 B2
MORT/ESHN SW14 138 A4
THHTH CR7 196 B2
UED N18 36 E5
WAN E11 70 B6
WIM/MER SW19 177 G2
Thornton Rw THHTH CR7 196 B2
Thorntons Farm Av
ROMW/RG RM7 74 E6
Thornton St BRXN/ST SW9 142 B3
Thornton Wy GLDGN NW11 65 F2
Thorntree Rd CHARL SE7 126 C5
Thornville Gv MTCM CR4 178 B5
Thornville St DEPT SE8 144 D2
Thornwood Cl SWFD E18 53 F5
Thornwood Rd LEW SE13 145 H6
Thorogood Gdns SRTFD E15 88 C3
Thorogood Wy RAIN RM13 93 G6
Thorold Rd IL IG1 72 B6
WDGN N22 48 E3
Thorparch Rd VX/NE SW8 141 J2
Thorpebank Rd SHB W12 118 D1
Thorpe Cl NKENS W10 100 C5
ORP BR6 201 K6
SYD SE26 * 164 A6
Thorpe Ct TOOT SW17 160 D6
Thorpe Crs OXHEY WD19 27 F2
WALTH E17 51 H5
Thorpedale Gdns
GNTH/NBYPK IG2 72 A1
Thorpedale Rd FSBYPK N4 67 F5
Thorpe Hall Rd WALTH E17 52 A4
Thorpe Rd BARK IG11 90 D5
EHAM E6 89 K6
FSTGT E7 88 E1
KUTN/CMB KT2 175 F3
SEVS/STOTM N15 68 A3
WALTH E17 52 A5
Thorpewood Av SYD SE26 163 J4
Thorpland Av HGDN/ICK UB10 76 A1
Thorsden Wy NRWD SE19 * 181 F1
Thorverton Rd CRICK NW2 82 C1
Thoydon Rd BOW E3 105 G1
Thrale Rd STRHM/NOR SW16 179 H1
Thrale St STHWK SE1 18 D1
Thrasher Cl HACK E8 * 86 B6
Thrawl St WCHPL E1 13 K2
Threadneedle St LOTH EC2R 13 F4
Three Colts La BETH E2 104 D3
Three Colt St POP/IOD E14 * 105 H6
Three Corners BXLYHN DA7 149 J3
Three Kings Yd
MYFR/PKLN W1K 9 J5
Three Meadows Ms
KTN/HRWW/WS HA3 43 F4
Three Mill La BOW E3 106 A2
Three Oak La STHWK SE1 19 J2
Threshers Pl NTGHL W11 100 C6
Thriffwood SYD SE26 163 K5
Thrigby Rd CHSGTN KT9 206 B4
Throckmorten Rd
CAN/RD E16 107 F5
Throgmorton Av OBST EC2N 13 F3

Throgmorton St OBST EC2N.......13 F3
Throwley Cl ABYW SE2..........128 D3
Throwley Rd SUT SM1...........209 F3
Throwley Wy SUT SM1...........209 F2
Thrupp Cl MTCM CR4............179 G5
Thrush Gn RYLN/HDSTN HA2.......60 A1
Thrush St WALW SE17...........122 D5
Thunderer Rd DAGW RM9.........110 A3
Thurbarn Rd CAT SE6...........182 E1
Thurland Rd
BERM/RHTH SE16................123 H3
Thurlby Cl WFD IG8.............53 K1
Thurlby Rd ALP/SUD HA0.........79 K4
WNWD SE27.....................162 B6
Thurleigh Av BAL SW12.........161 F1
Thurleigh Rd BAL SW12.........160 E1
Thurleston Av MRDN SM4........193 H2
Thurlestone Av
GDMY/SEVK IG3..................91 F2
NFNCH/WDSPK N12................47 K2
Thurlestone Rd WNWD SE27......162 B5
Thurloe Cl SKENS SW7...........14 C6
Thurloe Gdns ROM RM1...........75 G3
Thurloe Pl SKENS SW7...........14 B6
Thurloe Place Ms
SKENS SW7 *....................14 B6
Thurloe Sq SKENS SW7...........14 B6
Thurloe St SKENS SW7...........14 B6
Thurlow Cl CHING E4............51 K2
Thurlow Gdns ALP/SUD HA0 *.....79 K3
BARK/HLT IG6...................54 D2
Thurlow Hl DUL SE21...........162 D3
Thurlow Park Rd DUL SE21......162 C4
Thurlow Rd HAMP NW3............83 H3
HNWL W7......................116 B2
Thurlow St WALW SE17..........123 F5
Thurlow Ter KTTN NW5...........83 K3
Thurlow Wk WALW SE17..........123 F5
Thurlston Rd RSLP HA4..........76 E1
Thursland Rd SCUP DA14........187 F1
Thursley Crs CROY/NA CR0......214 B5
Thursley Gdns
WIM/MER SW19..................159 G4
Thursley Rd ELTH/MOT SE9......166 E5
Thurso St TOOT SW17...........160 C6
Thurstan Rd RYNPK SW20........176 E3
Thurston Rd DEPT SE8..........144 E3
STHL UB1.......................95 K5
Thurtle Rd BETH E2..............7 K1
Thwaite Cl ERITH DA8..........129 K6
Thyer Cl ORP BR6..............216 C2
Thyra Gv NFNCH/WDSPK N12.......47 F2
Tibbatt's Rd BOW E3...........105 K3
Tibbenham Pl CAT SE6..........164 D4
Tibberton Sq IS N1 *............85 J5
Tibbets Cl WIM/MER SW19.......159 G3
Tibbet's Ride PUT/ROE SW15....159 G2
Tiber Cl BOW E3.................87 J6
Tiber Gdns IS N1.................5 F1
Ticehurst Cl STMC/STPC BR5....186 B3
Ticehurst Rd FSTH SE23........164 B4
Tickford Cl ABYW SE2..........128 D2
Tidal Basin Rd CAN/RD E16.....106 D6
Tide Cl MTCM CR4..............179 F4
Tidenham Gdns CROY/NA CR0.....212 A1
Tideswell Rd CROY/NA CR0......213 J1
PUT/ROE SW15..................139 F5
Tideway Cl RCHPK/HAM TW10.....156 C6
Tideway Wk VX/NE SW8 *........121 H6
Tidey St BOW E3...............105 J4
Tidford Rd WELL DA16..........148 A3
Tidworth Rd BOW E3............105 J2
Tiepigs La WWKM BR4...........199 H6
Tierney Rd BRXS/STRHM SW2.....161 K3
Tierney Ter
BRXS/STRHM SW2 *..............161 K3
Tiger La HAYES BR2............200 A1
Tiger Wy CLPT E5...............86 D2
Tigres Cl ED N9................36 E4
Tilbrook Rd BKHTH/KID SE3.....146 B4
Tilbury Cl PECK SE15..........143 G1
PIN HA5 *.......................41 K3
STMC/STPC BR5.................186 C5
Tilbury Rd EHAM E6............107 K1
LEY E10.........................70 A4
Tildesley Rd PUT/ROE SW15.....159 F1
Tile Farm Rd ORP BR6..........216 D1
Tilehurst Rd CHEAM SM3........208 C3
WAND/EARL SW18................160 C3
Tile Kiln La BXLY DA5.........169 K4
HGT N6..........................66 B5
PLMGR N13.......................49 J1
Tileyard Rd HOLWY N7...........84 E5
Tilford Av CROY/NA CR0........214 A5
Tilford Gdns WIM/MER SW19.....159 G3
Tilia Cl SUT SM1..............208 D3
Tilia Wk BRXN/ST SW9..........142 C5
Tiller Rd POP/IOD E14.........124 D3
Tillett Cl WLSDN NW10..........80 E4
Tillet Wy BETH E2.............104 C2
Tilley Rd FELT TW13...........153 K3
Tillingbourne Gdns FNCH N3.....46 D6
Tillingbourne Gn
STMC/STPC BR5.................202 B1
Tillingbourne Wy FNCH N3.......64 D1
Tillingham Wy
NFNCH/WDSPK N12................32 E6
Tilling Rd CRICK NW2...........63 K5
Tilling Wy WBLY HA9 *..........79 K1
Tillman St WCHPL E1...........104 D5
Tilloch St IS N1 *..............85 F5
Tillotson Rd ED N9.............36 B4
IL IG1..........................72 A4
KTN/HRWW/WS HA3................42 B3
Tilney Gdns IS N1...............85 K4
Tilney Rd DAGW RM9.............92 B4
NWDGN UB2.....................114 B4
Tilney St MYFR/PKLN W1K.........9 H7
Tilson Cl CMBW SE5............143 F1
Tilson Gdns BRXS/STRHM SW2....161 K2
Tilson Rd TOTM N17.............50 C4
Tilston Cl WAN E11.............88 D1
Tilton St FUL/PGN SW6.........119 H6
The Tiltwood ACT W3............98 E6
Tilt Yard Ap ELTH/MOT SE9.....166 E1
Timber Cl CHST BR7............185 F5
Timbercroft HOR/WEW KT19......207 G2
Timbercroft La
WOOL/PLUM SE18................127 K6
Timberdene Av BARK/HLT IG6.....54 C4
Timberland Cl PECK SE15 *.....143 H1
Timberland Rd WCHPL E1 *......104 D5
Timber Mill Wy CLAP SW4.......141 J4
Timber Pond Rd
BERM/RHTH SE16................124 A2
Timberslip Dr WLGTN SM6.......210 D6
The Timbers CHEAM SM3 *.......208 C4
Timber St FSBYE EC1V *..........6 C6
Timberwharf Rd
SEVS/STOTM N15.................68 C3
Time Sq HACK E8 *...............86 B3
Times Sq SUT SM1 *............209 F3
Timms Cl BMLY BR1.............200 E1
Timothy Cl BXLYHS DA6.........149 F6
Tindal St BRXN/ST SW9.........142 C2
Tine Rd CHIG IG7...............54 E1
Tinniswood Cl HBRY N5..........85 G3
HOLWY N7 *......................85 G3
Tinsley Cl SNWD SE25..........181 J6
Tinsley Rd WCHPL E1...........104 E4
Tintagel Crs EDUL SE22........143 G5
Tintagel Dr STAN HA7...........43 K1
Tintagel Rd ORP BR6...........202 D6
Tintern Av CDALE/KGS NW9.......44 D6
Tintern Cl PUT/ROE SW15.......139 H6
WIM/MER SW19..................178 B3
Tintern Gdns STHGT/OAK N14.....34 E2
Tintern Rd CAR SM5............194 C5
WDGN N22.......................49 J4
Tintern St CLAP SW4...........141 K5
Tintern Wy RYLN/HDSTN HA2......60 B5
Tinto Rd CAN/RD E16...........106 E4
Tinworth St STHWK SE1.........121 K5
Tippetts Cl ENC/FH EN2.........23 J2
Tipthorpe Rd BTSEA SW11.......141 F4
Tipton Dr CROY/NA CR0.........212 A2
Tiptree Cl CHING E4............38 A5
Tiptree Crs CLAY IG5...........54 A5
Tiptree Dr ENC/FH EN2..........23 K5
Tiptree Rd RSLP HA4............77 F2
Tirlemont Rd SAND/SEL CR2.....211 J5
Tirrell Rd CROY/NA CR0........196 D3
Tisbury Rd STRHM/NOR SW16.....179 K5
Tisdall Pl WALW SE17...........19 F7
Titan Ct BTFD TW8.............117 G5
Titchborne Rw BAY/PAD W2.........8 D4
Titchfield Rd CAR SM5.........194 C5
STJWD NW8.......................2 D1
Titchfield Wk CAR SM5.........194 C4
Titchwell Rd
WAND/EARL SW18................160 C2
Tite St CHEL SW3..............120 E6
Tithe Barn Cl KUTN/CMB KT2....175 G4
Tithe Barn Wy NTHLT UB5........95 F1
Tithe Cl MLHL NW7..............45 J4
WOT/HER KT12...................188 A3
YEAD UB4........................94 D4
Tithe Ct HDN NW4 *..............45 J4
Tithe Farm Av
RYLN/HDSTN HA2.................78 A1
Tithe Farm Cl
RYLN/HDSTN HA2.................78 A1
Tithe Wk MLHL NW7..............45 J4
Titian Av BUSH WD23............28 E2
Titley Cl CHING E4..............51 J1
Titmus Cl UX/CGN UB8...........94 A5
Titmuss Av THMD SE28..........109 H6
Titmuss St SHB W12 *...........118 E2
Tiverton Av CLAY IG5............54 A6
Tiverton Cl CROY/NA CR0.......197 G4
Tiverton Rd ALP/SUD HA0........98 A1
EDGW HA8........................44 B5
HSLW TW3.......................135 G3
RSLP HA4........................76 E1
SEVS/STOTM N15..................67 K3
UED N18..........................50 A1
WLSDN NW10......................82 B6
Tiverton St STHWK SE1...........18 C4
Tiverton Wy CHSGTN KT9........205 J3
MLHL NW7.........................46 B3
Tivoli Gdns WOOL/PLUM SE18....126 D4
Tivoli Rd CEND/HSY/T N8.........66 D2
HSLWW TW4.......................134 D5
WNWD SE27.......................180 D1
Toad La HSLWW TW4..............134 E5
Tobago St POP/IOD E14..........124 D2
Tobin Cl HAMP NW3...............83 J5
Toby La WCHPL E1...............105 G3
Toby Wy SURB KT6...............191 J6
Tokenhouse Yd LOTH EC2R.........12 E3
Token Yd PUT/ROE SW15..........139 H5
Tokyngton Av WBLY HA9...........80 C4
Toland Sq PUT/ROE SW15.........138 D6
Tolcarne Dr PIN HA5.............40 E5
Toley Av KTN/HRWW/WS HA3.......62 A4
Tollbridge Cl NKENS W10........100 C3
Tollesbury Gdns
BARK/HLT IG6.....................54 D6
Tollet St WCHPL E1..............105 F3
Tollgate Dr DUL SE21............163 F4
YEAD UB4.........................95 H6
Tollgate Gdns
KIL/WHAMP NW6 *.................100 E1
Tollgate Rd CAN/RD E16.........107 G4
EHAM E6.........................107 J4
Tollhouse La WLGTN SM6.........210 C6
Tollhouse Wy ARCH N19...........66 C6
Tollington Pk FSBYPK N4.........67 F6
Tollington Pl FSBYPK N4.........67 F6
Tollington Rd HOLWY N7..........85 F2
Tollington Wy HOLWY N7..........84 E1
Tolmer's Sq CAMTN NW1............4 B6
Tolpits La WATW WD18.............26 A3
Tolpuddle Av PLSTW E13...........89 G6
Tolpuddle St IS N1................5 J2
Tolsford Rd HACK E8..............86 D3
Tolson Rd ISLW TW7..............136 B4
Tolverne Rd RYNPK SW20..........177 F4
Tolworth Broadway
SURB KT6.........................191 H5
Tolworth Cl SURB KT6............191 J5
Tolworth Gdns CHDH RM6...........73 K2
Tolworth Park Rd SURB KT6.......191 G6
Tolworth Ri North
BRYLDS KT5.......................191 K4
Tolworth Rise North (Kingston By-Pass) BRYLDS KT5.......191 J5
Tolworth Ri South
BRYLDS KT5.......................191 K4
Tolworth Rd SURB KT6............191 F6
Tolworth Underpass
(Kingston By-Pass)
SURB KT6..........................206 C1
Tom Cribb Rd
WOOL/PLUM SE18..................127 H3
Tom Groves Cl SRTFD E15..........88 B3
Tom Hood Cl SRTFD E15............88 B3
Tom Jenkinson Rd
CAN/RD E16.......................125 K1
Tomlin's Gv BOW E3...............105 J2
Tomlinson Cl BETH E2...............7 K5
CHSWK W4.........................117 J5
Tomlins Orch BARK IG11............90 C6
Tomlin's Ter POP/IOD E14.........105 H5
Tom Mann Cl BARK IG11.............90 E6
Tom Nolan Cl SRTFD E15...........106 C1
Tompion St FSBYE EC1V..............6 A5
Tom Smith Cl GNWCH SE10..........125 H6
Tomswood Hl BARK/HLT IG6..........54 B3
Tomswood Rd CHIG IG7..............54 A2
Tonbridge Crs
KTN/HRWW/WS HA3...................62 A1
Tonbridge Rd
E/WMO/HCT KT8....................188 D1
Tonbridge St STPAN WC1H............4 E5
Tonfield Rd CHEAM SM3............193 J5
Tonge Cl BECK BR3................198 D2
Tonsley Hl WAND/EARL SW18........140 A6
Tonsley Pl WAND/EARL SW18........140 A6
Tonsley Rd WAND/EARL SW18........140 A6
Tonsley St WAND/EARL SW18........140 A6
Tonstall Rd MTCM CR4.............179 F5
Tooke Cl PIN HA5..................41 J4
Tookey Cl
KTN/HRWW/WS HA3...................62 B4
Took's Ct FLST/FETLN EC4A.........11 J3
Tooley St STHWK SE1...............13 F7
Toorack Rd
KTN/HRWW/WS HA3...................42 D5
Tooting Bec Gdns
STRHM/NOR SW16...................161 J6
Tooting Bec Rd TOOT SW17.........161 F5
Tooting Gv TOOT SW17.............178 D1
Tooting High St TOOT SW17........178 D2
Tooting Market TOOT SW17 *.......160 E6
Tootswood Rd HAYES BR2...........199 H2
Topcliffe Dr ORP BR6..............216 D2
Topham Sq TOTM N17................49 J4
Topham St CLKNW EC1R *..............5 J6
Top House Ri CHING E4.............38 A2
Topiary Sq RCH/KEW TW9...........137 G4
Topley St ELTH/MOT SE9...........146 B5
Topmast Point POP/IOD E14 *......124 D2
Top Pk BECK BR3...................199 H2
Topsfield Cl CEND/HSY/T N8........66 D2
Topsfield Pde
CEND/HSY/T N8 *....................66 E2
Topsfield Rd CEND/HSY/T N8........66 E2
Topsham Rd TOOT SW17.............160 E5
Torbay Rd KIL/WHAMP NW6...........82 D5
RYLN/HDSTN HA2.....................59 J6
Torbay St CAMTN NW1 *..............84 B5
Torbitt Wy GNTH/NBYPK IG2.........73 F2
Torbridge Cl EDGW HA8.............44 A3
Torcross Dr FSTH SE23............163 K4
Torcross Rd RSLP HA4..............77 F1
Tor Gdns KENS W8.................119 K2
Tor Gv THMD SE28.................127 K1
Tormead Cl SUT SM1...............208 E4
Tormount Rd
WOOL/PLUM SE18....................127 K6
Toronto Av MNPK E12...............89 K2
Toronto Rd IL IG1..................72 B5
Torquay Gdns REDBR IG4............71 H1
Torquay St BAY/PAD W2............101 F4
Torrens Rd BRXS/STRHM SW2........142 A6
SRTFD E15..........................88 D4
Torrens Sq SRTFD E15...............88 D4
Torrens St FSBYE EC1V...............6 A3
Torres Sq POP/IOD E14.............124 D5
Torrey Dr BRXN/ST SW9.............142 B3
Torriano Av KTTN NW5...............84 D3
Torriano Cots KTTN NW5.............84 D3
Torridge Gdns PECK SE15...........143 K5
Torridge Rd THHTH CR7.............196 C2
Torridon Rd CAT SE6...............165 G3
Torrington Av
NFNCH/WDSPK N12....................47 H1
Torrington Cl ESH/CLAY KT10.......204 E4
Torrington Dr
RYLN/HDSTN HA2.....................78 B2
Torrington Gdns
FBAR/BDGN N11......................48 C2
GFD/PVL UB6........................79 J6
Torrington Gv
NFNCH/WDSPK N12....................47 J1
Torrington Pk
NFNCH/WDSPK N12....................33 H6
Torrington Pl FITZ W1T.............10 B1
GWRST WC1E..........................4 C7
WAP E1W............................123 H1
Torrington Rd BCTR RM8.............74 B5
ESH/CLAY KT10......................204 E4
GFD/PVL UB6.........................79 J6
RSLP HA4............................76 E1
Torrington Sq CROY/NA CR0 *.......196 E4
STPAN WC1H...........................4 D7
Torrington Wy MRDN SM4............193 K4
Tor Rd WELL DA16...................148 D2
Torr Rd PGE/AN SE20................182 A3
Torver Rd HRW HA1...................60 E1
Torver Wy ORP BR6..................216 D1
Torwood Rd PUT/ROE SW15............138 D6
Tothill St STJSPK SW1H..............16 C3
Totnes Rd WELL DA16................148 C1
Totnes Vls FBAR/BDGN N11 *..........48 C1
Totnes Wk EFNCH N2..................65 H1
Tottan Ter WCHPL E1 *..............105 F5
Tottenhall Rd PLMGR N13.............49 G2
Tottenham Court Rd
FITZ W1T..............................4 B7
Tottenham Gn East
SEVS/STOTM N15......................68 B1
Tottenham Gn East South
Side SEVS/STOTM N15.................68 B1
Tottenham La
CEND/HSY/T N8.......................66 E2
Tottenham Ms FITZ W1T *.............10 B1
Tottenham Rd IS N1..................86 A4
Tottenham St FITZ W1T...............10 B2
Totterdown St TOOT SW17............160 E6
Totteridge Common
TRDG/WHET N20......................31 J4
Totteridge La
TRDG/WHET N20......................32 E4
Totteridge Village
TRDG/WHET N20......................32 C3
Totternhoe Cl
KTN/HRWW/WS HA3.....................61 J2
Totton Rd THHTH CR7................180 B6
Toucan Cl WLSDN NW10................98 C2
Toulmin St STHWK SE1................18 C3
Toulon St CMBW SE5.................142 D1
Tournay Rd FUL/PGN SW6.............139 J1
Toussaint Wk
BERM/RHTH SE16.....................123 H3
Tovil Cl PGE/AN SE20...............181 H5
Towcester Rd BOW E3................105 K3
Tower Br WAP E1W....................13 J7
Tower Bridge Ap TWRH EC3N...........13 J7
Tower Bridge Ms
ALP/SUD HA0.........................79 F2
Tower Bridge Rd STHWK SE1...........19 G5
Tower Blds WAP E1W *...............123 J1
Tower Cl CHIG IG7...................54 B2
HAMP NW3............................83 H3
ORP BR6.............................202 A6
PGE/AN SE20.........................181 J3
Tower Ct LSQ/SEVD WC2H *.............10 E4
Tower Gdns ESH/CLAY KT10...........205 G5
Tower Gardens Rd TOTM N17...........49 J4
Tower Hamlets Rd FSTGT E7...........88 D2
WALTH E17...........................51 J6
Tower Hl TWRH EC3N..................13 J6
Tower Hill Ter MON EC3R.............13 H6
Tower La WBLY HA9 *.................79 K1
Tower Ms CLPT E5....................87 G2
WALTH E17...........................69 J1
Tower Mill Rd CMBW SE5 *...........143 F1
Tower Park Rd DART DA1.............150 C6
Tower Pl MON EC3R...................13 H6
Tower Ri RCH/KEW TW9...............137 F4
Tower Rd BELV DA17.................129 K4
BXLYHN DA7..........................149 J5
DART DA1............................171 F2
ORP BR6.............................202 A6
TWK TW1.............................156 A5
WLSDN NW10...........................81 J5
Tower Royal MANHO EC4N *.............12 D5
Towers Av HGDN/ICK UB10.............94 A2
Towers Ct HGDN/ICK UB10 *...........94 A2
Towers Pl RCH/KEW TW9..............137 F6
Towers Rd PIN HA5....................41 J4
STHL UB1.............................96 A3
Tower St LSQ/SEVD WC2H...............10 E4
Tower Ter WDGN N22...................49 F5
Tower Vw BUSH WD23...................28 E2
CROY/NA CR0.........................198 B5
Towfield Rd FELT TW13...............154 E4
Towncourt Crs
STMC/STPC BR5.......................201 H2
Towncourt La
STMC/STPC BR5.......................201 J3
Towncourt Pth FSBYPK N4.............67 J5
Town End Pde KUT/HW KT1 *...........174 E6
Towney Md NTHLT UB5.................95 K1
Town Farm Wy
STWL/WRAY TW19 *....................152 A2
Townfield Rd HYS/HAR UB3............113 J1
Townfield Sq HYS/HAR UB3............113 J1
Town Field Wy ISLW TW7..............136 B3
Town Hall Approach Rd
SEVS/STOTM N15.......................68 B1
Townhall Av CHSWK W4................118 A5
Town Hall Pde
BRXS/STRHM SW2 *....................142 A5
Town Hall Rd BTSEA SW11.............140 E4
Townholm Crs HNWL W7................116 A3
Town La STWL/WRAY TW19..............152 A1
Townley Ct SRTFD E15.................88 D4
Townley Rd BXLYHS DA6...............149 G6
EDUL SE22............................143 F6
Townley St WALW SE17 *..............122 E5
Town Meadow BTFD TW8................136 E1
Townmead Rd FUL/PGN SW6..............140 A4
RCH/KEW TW9..........................137 J3
Town Quay BARK IG11...................90 B6
Town Rd ED N9..........................36 D4
Townsend Av STHGT/OAK N14.............34 D6
Townsend La
CDALE/KGS NW9.........................63 F4
Townsend Ms
WAND/EARL SW18......................160 B4
Townsend Rd
SEVS/STOTM N15........................68 B2
STHL UB1..............................114 D1
STJWD NW8...............................2 D2
WOOL/PLUM SE18.......................127 G3
Townsend St WALW SE17..................19 F7
Townsend Wy NTHWD HA6.................40 D3
Townsend Yd HGT N6....................66 A5
Townshend Cl SCUP DA14...............186 C2
Townshend Est STJWD NW8................2 C2
Townshend Rd CHST BR7................185 G1
RCH/KEW TW9...........................137 G5
STJWD NW8...............................2 C1
Townshend Ter
RCH/KEW TW9...........................137 G5
Townson Av NTHLT UB5...................95 F1
Townson Wy NTHLT UB5...................94 E1
Town Whf ISLW TW7 *...................136 C4
Towpath Rd UED N18.....................51 F2
Towpath Wy CROY/NA CR0...............197 G3
Towton Rd WNWD SE27...................162 D4
Toynbec Cl CHST BR7...................167 G6
Toynbee Rd RYNPK SW20.................177 H4
Toynbee St WCHPL E1....................13 J2
Toyne Wy HGT N6........................65 K3
Tracey Av CRICK NW2 *..................82 A3
Trade Cl PLMGR N13.....................35 G6
Trader Rd EHAM E6.....................108 B5
Tradescant Rd VX/NE SW8...............141 K1
Trading Estate Rd
WLSDN NW10 *...........................98 E3
Trafalgar Av PECK SE15................143 G2
TOTM N17...............................50 A2
WPK KT4...............................193 G5
Trafalgar Chambers
CHEL SW3 *............................120 C5
Trafalgar Gdns KENS W8 *..............120 A3
WCHPL E1..............................105 F4
Trafalgar Gv GNWCH SE10...............125 G6
Trafalgar Ms HOM E9 *...................87 H4
Trafalgar Pl UED N18....................50 C1
WAN E11.................................70 E1
Trafalgar Rd DART DA1..................171 H4
GNWCH SE10.............................125 H5
RAIN RM13..............................111 H1
WHTN TW2...............................155 J4
WIM/MER SW19...........................178 A3
Trafalgar Sq STJS SW1Y *................10 D7
Trafalgar St WALW SE17.................122 E5
Trafalgar Wy CROY/NA CR0...............196 A6
POP/IOD E14.............................106 A6
Trafford Cl BARK/HLT IG6................55 F2
Trafford Rd THHTH CR7...................196 A2
Trahorn Cl WCHPL E1.....................104 C3
Tram Cl HNHL SE24.......................142 C4
Tramway Av ED N9.........................36 D2
Tramway Cl PGE/AN SE20.................181 K4
Tramway Pth MTCM CR4....................194 D1
Tranby Ms HOM E9.........................87 F3
Tranley Ms HAMP NW3 *....................83 J2
Tranmere Rd ED N9........................36 B2
WAND/EARL SW18..........................160 B4
WHTN TW2................................155 G2
Tranquil La RYLN/HDSTN HA2..............60 A5
Tranquil Pas BKHTH/KID SE3 *...........145 J3
Tranquil Ri ERITH DA8...................130 B5
Tranquil V BKHTH/KID SE3...............145 H3
Transept St CAMTN NW1.....................8 C2
Transmere Rd
STMC/STPC BR5...........................201 H3
Transom Cl BERM/RHTH SE16..............124 B4
Transom Sq POP/IOD E14..................124 E5
Transport Av BTFD TW8...................116 B5
Tranton Rd BERM/RHTH SE16...............123 J3
Traps La NWMAL KT3......................176 B5
Travellers Wy HSLWW TW4.................134 B3
Travers Cl WALTH E17.....................51 F4
Travers Rd HOLWY N7......................85 G1
Treacy Cl BUSH WD23......................28 C4
Treadgold St NTGHL W11..................100 B6
Treadway St BETH E2.....................104 D1
Treaty St IS N1............................5 G1
Trebeck St MYFR/PICC W1J..................9 J7
Trebovir Rd ECT SW5.....................119 K5
Treby St BOW E3.........................105 H3
Trecastle Wy HOLWY N7....................84 D2
Tredegar Rd BOW E3......................105 H1
FBAR/BDGN N11............................48 D3
RDART DA2...............................170 D5
Tredegar Sq BOW E3......................105 H2
Trederwen Rd HACK E8.....................86 C6
Tredown Rd SYD SE26.....................181 K1
Tredwell Cl BRXS/STRHM SW2..............162 A4
HAYES BR2...............................200 C1
Tredwell Rd WNWD SE27...................162 C6
Tree Cl RCHPK/HAM TW10..................156 E3
Treen Av BARN SW13......................138 B4
Tree Rd CAN/RD E16......................107 G5
Treeside Cl WDR/YW UB7..................112 A4
Tree Top Ms DAGE RM10....................93 F4
Treetops Cl ABYW SE2....................129 F5
NTHWD HA6................................40 B1
Treetops Vw LOU IG10.....................39 H1
Tree View Cl NRWD SE19..................181 F4
Treewall Gdns BMLY BR1..................166 A6
Trefgarne Rd DAGE RM10...................74 C6
Trefoil Rd WAND/EARL SW18...............140 B6
Tregaron Av CEND/HSY/T N8................66 E4
Tregaron Gdns NWMAL KT3..................192 B1
Tregarvon Rd BTSEA SW11..................141 F5
Tregenna Av
RYLN/HDSTN HA2............................78 A2
Tregenna Cl STHGT/OAK N14.................22 C6
Tregony Rd ORP BR6.......................217 F2
Trego Rd HOM E9...........................87 J5
Tregothnan Rd BRXN/ST SW9................141 K4
Tregunter Rd WBPTN SW10..................120 B6
Trehearn Rd BARK/HLT IG6..................54 D3
Treherne Ct BRXN/ST SW9 *.................142 C2
Trehern Rd MORT/ESHN SW14.................138 A4
Trehurst St CLPT E5........................87 G3
Trelawney Est HOM E9 *.....................86 E4
Trelawney Rd BARK/HLT IG6..................54 D3
Trelawn Rd BRXS/STRHM SW2.................142 B6
LEY E10.....................................88 A1
Trelawny Cl WALTH E17......................69 K1
Trellis Sq BOW E3..........................105 H2
Treloar Gdns NRWD SE19....................180 E2
Trelawney Est HOM E9 *.....................86 E4
Tremadoc Rd CLAP SW4......................141 J5
Tremaine Cl BROCKY SE4....................144 D3
Tremaine Rd PGE/AN SE20...................181 J5
Trematon Pl TEDD TW11.....................174 D3
Tremlett Gv ARCH N19.......................84 C1
Tremlett Ms ARCH N19 *.....................84 C1
Trenance Gdns
GDMY/SEVK IG3...............................91 G1
Trenchard Av RSLP HA4......................77 F3
Trenchard Cl CDALE/KGS NW9.................45 G4
STAN HA7....................................43 H2
Trenchard St GNWCH SE10...................125 G5
Trenchold St VX/NE SW8 *..................121 K6
Trenear Cl ORP BR6........................217 G2
Trenholme Rd PGE/AN SE20..................181 J3
Trenholme Ter PGE/AN SE20.................181 J3
Trenmar Gdns WLSDN NW10....................99 K2
Trent Av EA W5.............................116 D3
Trentbridge Cl BARK/HLT IG6................55 F2
Trent Ct WAN E11............................70 E2
Trent Gdns STHGT/OAK N14...................34 B1
Trentham Dr STMC/STPC BR5.................202 B1
Trentham St
WAND/EARL SW18.............................159 K3
Trent Pk EBAR EN4 *.........................22 C3
Trent Rd BKHH IG9...........................39 F3
BRXS/STRHM SW2.............................142 A6
Trent Wy WPK KT4...........................208 A1
YEAD UB4.....................................94 C2
Trentwood Side ENC/FH EN2...................23 F4
Treport St WAND/EARL SW18..................160 A2
Tresco Cl BMLY BR1.........................183 H2
Trescoe Gdns CRW RM5........................56 E1
RYLN/HDSTN HA2...............................59 J4
Tresco Gdns GDMY/SEVK IG3...................73 F6
Tresco Rd PECK SE15........................143 J5
Tresham Crs STJWD NW8........................2 C6
Tresham Rd BARK IG11.........................91 F5

Tresilian Av WCHMH N21 23 F6
Tressell Cl IS N1 85 H5
Tressillian Crs BROCKY SE4 144 D4
Tressillian Rd BROCKY SE4 144 D4
Trestis Cl YEAD UB4 95 H3
Treswell Rd DAGW RM9 92 A6
Tretawn Gdns MLHL NW7 31 G6
Tretawn Pk MLHL NW7 31 G6
Trevanion Rd WKENS W14 * 119 H5
Treve Av HRW HA1 60 C4
Trevelyan Av MNPK E12 89 K2
Trevelyan Cl DART DA1 151 J5
Trevelyan Crs
KTN/HRWW/WS HA3 61 K4
Trevelyan Gdns
WLSDN NW10 * 82 A6
Trevelyan Rd SRTFD E15 88 C2
TOOT SW17 178 E2
Treveris St STHWK SE1 18 B1
Treverton St NKENS W10 100 B3
Treves Cl WCHMH N21 23 F6
Treville St PUT/ROE SW15 158 E2
Treviso Rd FSTH SE23 164 A4
Trevithick Cl
EBED/NFELT TW14 153 J3
Trevithick Dr DART DA1 151 J5
Trevithick St DEPT SE8 124 D6
Trevone Gdns PIN HA5 59 J3
Trevor Cl EBAR EN4 33 H1
HAYES BR2 199 J4
ISLW TW7 136 A6
KTN/HRWW/WS HA3 43 F3
NTHLT UB5 95 G1
Trevor Crs RSLP HA4 76 D2
Trevor Gdns EDGW HA8 45 F4
Trevor Pl SKENS SW7 14 D3
Trevor Rd EDGW HA8 45 F4
HYS/HAR UB3 113 H2
WFD IG8 52 E3
WIM/MER SW19 177 H3
Trevor Sq SKENS SW7 14 D3
Trevor St SKENS SW7 14 D3
Trevose Rd WALTH E17 52 B4
Trevose Wy OXHEY WD19 27 G5
Trewenna Dr CHSGTN KT9 205 K3
Trewince Rd RYNPK SW20 177 F4
Trewint St WAND/EARL SW18 160 B4
Trewsbury Rd SYD SE26 182 A1
Triandra Wy YEAD UB4 95 H4
Triangle Est LBTH SE11 * 122 A5
Triangle Pas EBAR EN4 * 21 G5
Triangle Pl CLAP SW4 141 J5
Triangle Rd HACK E8 86 D6
The Triangle BFN/LL DA15 * 168 B2
HACK E8 86 D6
KUT/HW KT1 175 K5
Triangle Wy ACT W3 117 H3
Trident Pl CHEL SW3 * 120 C6
Trident St BERM/RHTH SE16 124 A4
Trident Wy NWDGN UB2 114 A3
Trigon Rd VX/NE SW8 142 A1
Trilby Rd FSTH SE23 164 A4
Trim St NWCR SE14 124 C6
Trinder Rd ARCH N19 66 E5
BAR EN5 20 A6
Tring Av EA W5 117 G1
STHL UB1 95 K5
WBLY HA9 80 C4
Tring Cl GNTH/NBYPK IG2 72 C2
Trinidad Gdns DAGE RM10 93 F5
Trinidad St POP/IOD E14 105 H6
Trinity Av EFNCH N2 47 H6
EN EN1 36 B1
Trinity Buoy Whf
POP/IOD E14 * 106 B4
Trinity Church Rd BARN SW13 118 E6
Trinity Church Sq STHWK SE1 18 D4
Trinity Cl CLAP SW4 * 141 H5
HACK E8 * 86 B4
HAYES BR2 200 D5
HSLWW TW4 134 D5
LEW SE13 145 G5
NTHWD HA6 40 C2
SAND/SEL CR2 212 A6
WAN E11 70 C6
Trinity Ct ELTH/MOT SE9 167 G1
Trinity Crs TOOT SW17 160 E4
Trinity Dr UX/CGN UB8 94 A5
Trinity Est DEPT SE8 124 C5
Trinity Gdns BRXN/ST SW9 142 A5
CAN/RD E16 106 D4
DART DA1 171 G1
Trinity Gn WCHPL E1 * 104 E4
Trinity Gv GNWCH SE10 145 F2
Trinity Ms PGE/AN SE20 181 J5
Trinity Pde HSLW TW3 * 135 G4
Trinity Pk CHING E4 * 51 H2
Trinity Pl BXLYHS DA6 149 G5
Trinity Ri BRXS/STRHM SW2 162 C2
Trinity Rd BARK/HLT IG6 54 C6
EFNCH N2 47 H6
RCH/KEW TW9 * 137 G4
STHL UB1 114 D1
TOOT SW17 160 E4
WAND/EARL SW18 160 C1
WDGN N22 48 E3
WIM/MER SW19 177 K2
Trinity Sq TWRH EC3N 13 H6
Trinity St CAN/RD E16 106 D4
ENC/FH EN2 23 J3
STHWK SE1 18 D3
Trinity Wy ACT W3 99 G6
CHING E4 51 H2
Trio Pl STHWK SE1 18 D3
Tristan Sq BKHTH/KID SE3 145 H4
Tristram Cl WALTH E17 52 B6
Tristram Dr ED N9 36 B5
Tristram Rd BMLY BR1 165 J6
Triton St CAMTN NW1 3 K6
Tritton Av CROY/NA CR0 210 E2
Tritton Rd DUL SE21 162 E5
Triumph Cl HYS/HAR UB3 133 F2
Triumph Rd EHAM E6 107 K5
Trojan Wy CROY/NA CR0 211 F1
Troon Cl BERM/RHTH SE16 * 123 J5
THMD SE28 109 K5
Troon St WCHPL E1 105 G5
Trosley Rd BELV DA17 129 H6
Trossachs Rd EDUL SE22 143 F6
Trothy Rd STHWK SE1 123 H4
Trott Rd MUSWH N10 48 A3
Trott St BTSEA SW11 140 C2
Trotwood CHIG IG7 54 D1
Troughton Rd CHARL SE7 126 A5
Troutbeck Rd NWCR SE14 144 B2
Trout Rd WDR/YW UB7 112 A1
Trouville Rd CLAP SW4 161 H1
Trowbridge Rd HOM E9 87 H4
Trowlock Av TEDD TW11 174 D2
Trowlock Wy TEDD TW11 174 D2
Troy Ct KENS W8 119 K3
Troy Rd NRWD SE19 180 E2
Troy Town PECK SE15 143 H4
Trubshaw Rd NWDGN UB2 115 F3
Trueman Cl EDGW HA8 * 44 D3
Trulock Rd TOTM N17 50 C3
Truman's Rd STNW/STAM N16 86 A3
Trumpers Wy HNWL W7 116 A3
Trumpington Rd FSTGT E7 88 D2
Trump St CITYW EC2V 12 D4
Trundlers Wy BUSH WD23 28 E3
Trundle St STHWK SE1 18 C2
Trundleys Rd DEPT SE8 124 B6
Trundley's Rd DEPT SE8 124 A5
Trundley's Ter DEPT SE8 124 A4
Truro Gdns IL IG1 71 J4
Truro Rd WALTH E17 69 H1
WDGN N22 48 E3
Truro St KTTN NW5 84 A4
Truro Wy YEAD UB4 94 C2
Trusedale Rd EHAM E6 107 K5
Truslove Rd WNWD SE27 180 B1
Trussley Rd HMSMTH W6 119 F3
Trustons Gdns EMPK RM11 75 J4
Tryfan Cl REDBR IG4 71 H2
Tryon Crs HOM E9 86 E6
Tryon St CHEL SW3 120 E5
Trystings Cl ESH/CLAY KT10 205 G4
Tuam Rd WOOL/PLUM SE18 127 J6
Tubbenden Cl ORP BR6 201 K6
Tubbenden Dr ORP BR6 216 D2
Tubbenden La ORP BR6 216 D2
Tubbenden La South
ORP BR6 216 D3
Tubbs Rd WLSDN NW10 99 H1
Tuck Rd RAIN RM13 93 J4
Tudor Av GPK RM2 57 J6
HPTN TW12 173 F2
WPK KT4 207 K1
Tudor Cl ASHF TW15 152 A6
BRXS/STRHM SW2 * 162 A1
CDALE/KGS NW9 62 E6
CHEAM SM3 208 B3
CHSGTN KT9 206 A3
CHST BR7 184 E4
DART DA1 170 E1
HAMP NW3 83 J3
HGT N6 66 C4
HPTN TW12 173 H1
MLHL NW7 45 J2
PIN HA5 58 E2
WFD IG8 53 F1
WLGTN SM6 210 C5
Tudor Ct ELTH/MOT SE9 * 146 D5
SWLY BR8 203 K4
WALTH E17 69 H4
Tudor Ct North WBLY HA9 80 C3
Tudor Ct South WBLY HA9 80 C3
Tudor Crs BARK/HLT IG6 54 C2
ENC/FH EN2 23 J2
Tudor Dr GPK RM2 75 J1
KUTN/CMB KT2 175 F1
MRDN SM4 193 G3
WOT/HER KT12 188 C5
Tudor Est WLSDN NW10 * 98 D1
Tudor Gdns ACT W3 98 C5
BARN SW13 138 B4
CDALE/KGS NW9 62 E6
GPK RM2 75 J1
TWK TW1 156 A3
WWKM BR4 214 A1
Tudor Gv HOM E9 86 E5
Tudor Ms WLSDN NW10 81 J4
Tudor Pde ELTH/MOT SE9 * 146 D5
Tudor Pl MTCM CR4 178 D3
NRWD SE19 * 181 G3
Tudor Rd BAR EN5 20 E4
BARK IG11 91 F5
BECK BR3 183 F6
CHING E4 51 K2
ED N9 36 D2
HACK E8 86 D6
HPTN TW12 173 F3
HSLW TW3 135 J5
HYS/HAR UB3 94 B5
KTN/HRWW/WS HA3 42 D5
KUTN/CMB KT2 175 H3
NRWD SE19 181 G3
PIN HA5 41 G5
PLSTW E13 88 E6
SNWD SE25 197 J2
STHL UB1 95 J6
Tudor Sq HYS/HAR UB3 94 B4
Tudor St EMB EC4Y 11 K5
Tudor Wy ACT W3 117 H2
STHGT/OAK N14 34 D3
STMC/STPC BR5 201 J3
Tudor Well Cl STAN HA7 43 H1
Tudway Rd BKHTH/KID SE3 146 B5
Tufnail Rd DART DA1 171 J1
Tufnell Park Rd HOLWY N7 84 D2
Tufter Rd CHIG IG7 55 F1
Tufton Gdns E/WMO/HCT KT8 173 G5
Tufton Rd CHING E4 37 J6
Tufton St WEST SW1P 16 E5
Tugboat St THMD SE28 127 K2
Tugela Rd CROY/NA CR0 196 E3
Tugela St CAT SE6 164 C4
Tugmutton Cl ORP BR6 216 B2
Tulip Cl CROY/NA CR0 198 A5
EHAM E6 107 J4
HPTN TW12 172 E2
NWDGN UB2 115 H2
Tulip Gdns CHING E4 * 38 B5
IL IG1 90 B4
Tulip Wy WDR/YW UB7 112 A4
Tull St CAR SM5 194 E4
Tulse Cl BECK BR3 183 F6
Tulse Hl BRXS/STRHM SW2 162 C2
Tulsemere Rd WNWD SE27 162 D4
Tummons Gdns SNWD SE25 181 F5
Tuncombe Rd UED N18 36 A6
Tunis Rd SHB W12 119 F1
Tunley Gn POP/IOD E14 105 H4
Tunley Rd TOOT SW17 161 F4
WLSDN NW10 81 G6
Tunmarsh La PLSTW E13 107 F2
Tunnan Leys EHAM E6 108 A5
Tunnel Av GNWCH SE10 125 G2
Tunnel Gdns FBAR/BDGN N11 48 C3
Tunnel Rd BERM/RHTH SE16 123 K2
Tunnel Rd East WDR/YW UB7 132 E1
Tunnel Rd West WDR/YW UB7 132 D2
Tunstall Av BARK/HLT IG6 55 G2
Tunstall Cl ORP BR6 216 E2
Tunstall Rd BRXN/ST SW9 142 A5
CROY/NA CR0 197 F5
Tunstock Wy BELV DA17 129 F3
Tunworth Cl CDALE/KGS NW9 62 E3
Tunworth Crs PUT/ROE SW15 158 C1
Tupelo Rd LEY E10 69 K6
Tuppy St THMD SE28 127 H3
Turene Cl WAND/EARL SW18 140 B5
Turin Rd ED N9 36 E2
Turin St BETH E2 104 C2
Turkey Oak Cl NRWD SE19 181 F4
Turks Rw CHEL SW3 120 E5
Turle Rd FSBYPK N4 * 67 F6
STRHM/NOR SW16 179 K5
Turlewray Cl FSBYPK N4 67 F5
Turley Cl SRTFD E15 88 C6
Turnagain La
FLST/FETLN EC4A * 12 A3
Turnage Rd BCTR RM8 74 A5
Turnant Rd TOTM N17 49 J4
Turnberry Cl
BERM/RHTH SE16 * 123 J5
HDN NW4 46 B5
Turnberry Ct OXHEY WD19 * 27 G5
Turnberry Wy ORP BR6 201 J5
Turnbury Cl THMD SE28 109 K5
Turnchapel Ms CLAP SW4 141 G4
Turner Av MTCM CR4 178 E4
SEVS/STOTM N15 68 A1
WHTN TW2 155 H5
Turner Cl ALP/SUD HA0 79 K3
BRXN/ST SW9 142 C2
GLDGN NW11 65 F3
Turner Ct CMBW SE5 * 142 E5
DART DA1 151 F6
Turner Crs THHTH CR7 196 D3
Turner Dr GLDGN NW11 65 F3
Turner Ms BELMT SM2 209 F5
Turner Rd EDGW HA8 44 A5
NWMAL KT3 192 A4
WALTH E17 70 A1
Turners Cl TRDG/WHET N20 33 K5
Turners Meadow Wy
BECK BR3 182 C4
Turner's Rd BOW E3 105 H4
Turner St CAN/RD E16 106 D5
WCHPL E1 104 D4
Turners Wy CROY/NA CR0 196 B6
Turner's Wd GLDGN NW11 65 G5
Turneville Rd WKENS W14 119 J6
Turney Rd DUL SE21 162 D2
Turnham Green Ter
CHSWK W4 118 B4
Turnham Rd BROCKY SE4 144 B6
Turnmill St FARR EC1M 5 K7
Turnpike Cl DEPT SE8 144 C1
WELL DA16 148 B4
Turnpike Dr ORP BR6 217 J6
Turnpike La CEND/HSY/T N8 67 G1
SUT SM1 209 G3
Turnpike Link CROY/NA CR0 197 F6
Turnpike Ms
CEND/HSY/T N8 * 49 G6
Turnpike Pde
SEVS/STOTM N15 * 49 H6
Turnpike Wy ISLW TW7 136 B2
Turnstone Cl
CDALE/KGS NW9 * 45 G5
PLSTW E13 106 E2
Turnstone Ter WEA W13 * 97 F3
Turpentine La PIM SW1V 121 G5
Turpin Av CRW RM5 56 C3
Turpin Cl WAP E1W 105 F6
Turpington Cl HAYES BR2 200 D3
Turpington La HAYES BR2 200 D2
Turpin La ERITH DA8 130 D6
Turpin Rd EBED/NFELT TW14 153 J1
Turpin's La WFD IG8 53 K1
Turpins Yd CRICK NW2 * 63 K6
GNWCH SE10 145 F1
Turpin Wy WLGTN SM6 210 B5
Turquand St WALW SE17 18 D7
Turret Gv CLAP SW4 141 H4
Turton Rd ALP/SUD HA0 80 A3
Turville St BETH E2 7 J6
Tuscan Rd WOOL/PLUM SE18 127 J5
Tuskar St GNWCH SE10 125 H5
Tweeddale Gv
HGDN/ICK UB10 76 A1
Tweeddale Rd CAR SM5 194 C5
Tweedmouth Rd PLSTW E13 107 F1
Tweed Wy ROM RM1 57 F3
Tweedy Rd BMLY BR1 183 K4
Twelvetrees Crs BOW E3 106 A3
Twentyman Cl WFD IG8 52 E1
Twickenham Br TWK TW1 136 D6
Twickenham Cl CROY/NA CR0 211 F1
Twickenham Gdns
GFD/PVL UB6 79 G3
KTN/HRWW/WS HA3 42 E3
Twickenham Rd FELT TW13 154 D6
ISLW TW7 136 A5
TEDD TW11 156 B6
WAN E11 70 B6
Twig Folly Cl BETH E2 105 F1
Twig Folly Whf BETH E2 * 105 F1
Twigg Cl ERITH DA8 150 B1
Twilley St WAND/EARL SW18 160 A2
Twine Cl BARK IG11 109 H2
Twine Ct WCHPL E1 104 E6
Twineham Gn
NFNCH/WDSPK N12 32 E6
Twine Ter BOW E3 * 105 H3
Twining Av WHTN TW2 155 H5
Twinn Rd MLHL NW7 46 C2
Twin Tumps Wy THMD SE28 109 G6
Twisden Rd KTTN NW5 84 B2
Twisleton Ct DART DA1 171 G1
Twitten Gv BMLY BR1 184 E6
Twybridge Wy WLSDN NW10 80 E5
Twycross Ms GNWCH SE10 125 H4
Twyford Abbey Rd
WLSDN NW10 98 B2
Twyford Av ACT W3 98 C6
EFNCH N2 47 K6
Twyford Crs ACT W3 117 H1
Twyford Rd CAR SM5 194 C5
IL IG1 90 C3
RYLN/HDSTN HA2 60 B4
Twyford St IS N1 85 F6
Tyas Rd CAN/RD E16 106 D3
Tybenham Rd
WIM/MER SW19 177 K6
Tyberry Rd PEND EN3 24 D4
Tyburn La HRW HA1 60 E4
Tyburn Wy MBLAR W1H 9 F5
Tye La ORP BR6 216 C3
Tyers Ga STHWK SE1 19 G3
Tyers St LBTH SE11 122 A5
Tyers Ter LBTH SE11 122 A5
Tyeshurst Cl ABYW SE2 129 F5
Tylecroft Rd
STRHM/NOR SW16 179 K5
Tylehurst Gdns IL IG1 90 C3
Tyler Cl BETH E2 7 J2
ERITH DA8 149 J1
Tylers Ga KTN/HRWW/WS HA3 62 A3
Tylers Green Rd SWLY BR8 203 K3
Tyler St GNWCH SE10 125 H5
Tylney Av NRWD SE19 181 G1
Tylney Cl CHIG IG7 55 F1
Tylney Rd BMLY BR1 184 C5
FSTGT E7 89 G2
Tynan Cl EBED/NFELT TW14 153 K3
Tyndale La IS N1 85 H5
Tyndale Ter IS N1 85 H5
Tyndall Rd LEY E10 70 A6
WELL DA16 148 A4
Tyneham Cl BTSEA SW11 * 141 F4
Tyneham Rd BTSEA SW11 141 F3
Tynemouth Cl EHAM E6 108 B5
Tynemouth Dr EN EN1 24 C1
Tynemouth Rd MTCM CR4 179 F3
SEVS/STOTM N15 68 B1
WOOL/PLUM SE18 127 K5
Tynemouth St FUL/PGN SW6 140 B3
Tynemouth Ter
SEVS/STOTM N15 * 68 B1
Tyne St WCHPL E1 13 K3
Tynsdale Rd WLSDN NW10 81 G5
Type St BETH E2 105 F1
Tyrawley Rd FUL/PGN SW6 140 A2
Tyre La CDALE/KGS NW9 * 63 G1
Tyrell Cl HRW HA1 78 E2
Tyrone Rd EHAM E6 107 K1
Tyron Wy SCUP DA14 167 K6
Tyrrell Av WELL DA16 148 B6
Tyrrell Rd EDUL SE22 143 H5
Tyrrel Wy CDALE/KGS NW9 63 H4
Tyrwhitt Rd BROCKY SE4 144 D4
Tysoe St CLKNW EC1R 5 K5
FSBYW WC1X 5 J5
Tyson Gdns FSTH SE23 * 163 K2
Tyson Rd FSTH SE23 163 K2
Tyssen Rd STNW/STAM N16 * 86 B1
Tyssen St HACK E8 86 B4
IS N1 7 H2
Tytherton Rd ARCH N19 84 D1

U

Uamvar St POP/IOD E14 105 K4
Uckfield Gv MTCM CR4 179 F4
Udall Gdns CRW RM5 56 C2
Udall St WEST SW1P 16 B7
Udney Park Rd TEDD TW11 174 B1
Uffington Rd WLSDN NW10 81 J6
WNWD SE27 162 B6
Ufford Cl KTN/HRWW/WS HA3 42 B3
Ufford Rd
KTN/HRWW/WS HA3 42 B3
Ufford St STHWK SE1 17 K2
Ufton Rd IS N1 86 A5
Uhura Sq STNW/STAM N16 * 86 A1
Ullathorne Rd
STRHM/NOR SW16 161 H6
Ulleswater Rd
STHGT/OAK N14 34 E6
Ulleswater Vls
STHGT/OAK N14 * 34 E6
Ullin St POP/IOD E14 106 A4
Ullswater Cl BMLY BR1 183 H2
PUT/ROE SW15 * 158 A6
YEAD UB4 94 C1
Ullswater Ct
RYLN/HDSTN HA2 * 60 A4
Ullswater Crs PUT/ROE SW15 158 A6
Ullswater Rd BARN SW13 138 D1
WNWD SE27 162 C5
Ullswater Wy HCH RM12 93 J3
Ulster Gdns PLMGR N13 35 J6
Ulster Pl CAMTN NW1 3 J7
Ulundi Rd BKHTH/KID SE3 125 H6
Ulva Rd PUT/ROE SW15 139 G5
Ulverscroft Rd EDUL SE22 143 H6
Ulverston Rd WALTH E17 52 B5
Ulysses Rd KIL/WHAMP NW6 82 D3
Umberston St WCHPL E1 * 104 C5
Umbria St PUT/ROE SW15 158 D1
Umfreville Rd FSBYPK N4 67 H3
Undercliff Rd LEW SE13 144 D4
Underhill BAR EN5 20 E6
Underhill Ct BAR EN5 * 20 E6
Underhill Rd EDUL SE22 143 H6
Underhill St CAMTN NW1 3 K1
Underne Av STHGT/OAK N14 34 B4
Undershaft HDTCH EC3A 13 G4
Undershaw Rd BMLY BR1 165 H5
Underwood CROY/NA CR0 214 A4
Underwood Rd CHING E4 51 K1
WCHPL E1 104 C3
WFD IG8 53 H3
Underwood Rw IS N1 6 D4
Underwood St IS N1 6 D4
The Underwood
ELTH/MOT SE9 166 E4
Undine Rd POP/IOD E14 124 E4
Undine St TOOT SW17 178 E1
Uneeda Dr GFD/PVL UB6 78 D6
Union Cl WAN E11 88 B2
Union Ct CLAP SW4 141 K3
OBST EC2N 13 G3
Union Dr WCHPL E1 * 105 G3
Union Gv VX/NE SW8 141 J3
Union La ISLW TW7 136 B2
Union Pk GNWCH SE10 125 J5
Union Rd ALP/SUD HA0 80 A4
CLAP SW4 141 J3
CROY/NA CR0 196 D4
FBAR/BDGN N11 48 D2
HAYES BR2 200 C2
NTHLT UB5 96 A1
ROMW/RG RM7 75 F3
VX/NE SW8 141 J3
Union Sq IS N1 6 C1
Union St BAR EN5 20 C5
KUT/HW KT1 174 E5
SRTFD E15 88 B6
STHWK SE1 18 B1
Union Wk BETH E2 7 J4
Unity Cl CROY/NA CR0 213 K6
NRWD SE19 180 D1
WLSDN NW10 81 J4
Unity Ms CAMTN NW1 4 C2
Unity Wy WOOL/PLUM SE18 126 C3
University Cl MLHL NW7 45 H3
University Gdns BXLY DA5 169 G2
University Pl ERITH DA8 149 J1
University Rd
WIM/MER SW19 178 C2
University St FITZ W1T 4 B7
University Wy CAN/RD E16 108 A6
DART DA1 151 J4
Unwin Av EBED/NFELT TW14 133 G6
Unwin Cl PECK SE15 123 H6
Unwin Rd ISLW TW7 135 K4
SKENS SW7 14 B4
Upbrook Ms BAY/PAD W2 101 G5
Upcerne Rd WBPTN SW10 140 B1
Upcroft Av EDGW HA8 44 E1
Updale Rd SCUP DA14 168 A6
Upfield CROY/NA CR0 197 J6
Upfield Rd HNWL W7 97 F3
Uphall Rd IL IG1 90 B3
Upham Park Rd CHSWK W4 118 B4
Uphill Dr CDALE/KGS NW9 62 E2
MLHL NW7 45 G1
Uphill Gv MLHL NW7 31 G6
Uphill Rd MLHL NW7 31 G6
Upland Rd BELMT SM2 209 H5
BXLYHN DA7 149 G4
EDUL SE22 163 H2
PLSTW E13 106 E3
SAND/SEL CR2 211 K3
Uplands BECK BR3 182 D5
Uplands Cl MORT/ESHN SW14 137 J6
WOOL/PLUM SE18 127 G5
Uplands Park Rd ENC/FH EN2 23 G3
Uplands Rd CEND/HSY/T N8 67 F2
CHDH RM6 55 K6
EBAR EN4 34 A3
ORP BR6 202 C5
WFD IG8 53 J3
The Uplands RSLP HA4 58 E5
Uplands Wy WCHMH N21 23 G6
Upminster Rd South
RAIN RM13 111 J3
Upney La BARK IG11 91 F5
Upnor Wy WALW SE17 123 F5
Uppark Dr GNTH/NBYPK IG2 72 C3
Upper Abbey Rd BELV DA17 129 G4
Upper Addison Gdns
WKENS W14 119 H2
Upper Bank St POP/IOD E14 124 E1
Upper Bardsey Wk IS N1 * 85 J4
Upper Belgrave St
KTBR SW1X 15 H4
Upper Berenger Wk
WBPTN SW10 * 140 C1
Upper Berkeley St
MBLAR W1H 8 E4
Upper Beulah Hl NRWD SE19 181 F4
Upper Blantyre Wk
WBPTN SW10 * 140 C1
Upper Brighton Rd SURB KT6 190 E3
Upper Brockley Rd
BROCKY SE4 144 C3
Upper Brook St
MYFR/PKLN W1K 9 G5
Upper Butts BTFD TW8 116 D6
Upper Caldy Wk IS N1 * 85 J4
Upper Camelford Wk
NTGHL W11 * 100 C5
Upper Cavendish Av FNCH N3 46 E6
Upper Cheyne Rw CHEL SW3 120 D6
Upper Clapton Rd CLPT E5 68 D6
Upper Clarendon Wk
NTGHL W11 * 100 C5
Upper Dartrey Wk
WBPTN SW10 * 140 B1
Upper Dengie Wk IS N1 * 85 J6
Upper Elmers End Rd
BECK BR3 198 B1
BECK BR3 198 E3
Upper Farm Rd
E/WMO/HCT KT8 188 E1
Upper Gn East MTCM CR4 178 E5
Upper Gn West MTCM CR4 178 E6
Upper Grosvenor St
MYFR/PKLN W1K 9 G6
Upper Grotto Rd TWK TW1 156 A4
Upper Gnd STHWK SE1 11 J7
Upper Gv SNWD SE25 197 F1
Upper Grove Rd BELV DA17 129 G6
Upper Gulland Wk IS N1 * 85 J4
Upper Ham Rd
RCHPK/HAM TW10 156 E6
Upper Handa Wk IS N1 * 85 K4
Upper Harley St CAMTN NW1 3 H7
Upper Hawkwell Wk IS N1 * 85 J6
Upper Hitch OXHEY WD19 27 J3

Upper Holly Hill Rd
BELV DA17 129 J5
Upper John St SOHO/CST W1F 10 B5
Upper Lismore Wk IS N1 * 85 J4
Upper Ldg KENS W8 * 120 A1
Upper Ml HMSMTH W6 118 D5
Upper Marsh STHWK SE1 17 H4
Upper Montagu St
MBLAR W1H 8 E1
Upper Mulgrave Rd
BELMT SM2 208 C5
Upper North St POP/IOD E14 105 J4
Upper Paddock Rd
OXHEY WD19 27 J1
Upper Park Rd BELV DA17 129 J4
BMLY BR1 184 A4
FBAR/BDGN N11 48 B1
HAMP NW3 83 K4
KUTN/CMB KT2 175 H2
Upper Phillimore Gdns
KENS W8 * 119 K2
Upper Rainham Rd
HCH RM12 93 H2
Upper Rawreth Wk IS N1 * 85 J6
Upper Richmond Rd
PUT/ROE SW15 138 E5
Upper Richmond Rd West
MORT/ESHN SW14 138 A5
RCHPK/HAM TW10 137 H5
Upper Rd PLSTW E13 106 E2
WLGTN SM6 210 D3
Upper St Martin's La
LSQ/SEVD WC2H 10 E4
Upper Selsdon Rd
SAND/SEL CR2 212 B6
Upper Sheppey Wk IS N1 85 J4
Upper Sheridan Rd
BELV DA17 129 H4
Upper Shirley Rd
CROY/NA CR0 212 E1
Upper Sq ISLW TW7 136 B4
Upper St IS N1 5 K2
Upper Sunbury Rd
HPTN TW12 172 E4
Upper Sutton La HEST TW5 135 F2
Upper Tachbrook St
PIM SW1V 16 A6
Upper Tail OXHEY WD19 27 J5
Upper Talbot Wk
NTGHL W11 * 100 C5
Upper Teddington Rd
KUT/HW KT1 174 D4
Upper Ter HAMP NW3 83 G1
Upper Thames St BLKFR EC4V 12 C5
Upper Tollington Pk
FSBYPK N4 67 G5
Upperton Rd SCUP DA14 186 A1
Upperton Rd East PLSTW E13 107 G2
Upperton Rd West
PLSTW E13 107 G2
Upper Tooting Pk TOOT SW17 160 E4
Upper Tooting Rd TOOT SW17 160 E6
Upper Town Rd STHL UB1 96 B3
Upper Tulse Hl
BRXS/STRHM SW2 162 A2
Upper Vernon Rd SUT SM1 209 H3
Upper Walthamstow Rd
WALTH E17 70 B1
Upper Whistler Wk
WBPTN SW10 * 140 B1
Upper Wickham La
WELL DA16 148 C3
Upper Wimpole St
CAVSQ/HST W1G 9 H1
Upper Woburn Pl
CAMTN NW1 4 D5
STPAN WC1H 4 D6
Uppingham Av STAN HA7 43 J6
Upsdell Av PLMGR N13 49 G2
Upstall St CMBW SE5 142 C2
Upton Av FSTGT E7 88 E5
Upton Cl BXLY DA5 169 G1
CRICK NW2 82 C1
Upton Dene BELMT SM2 209 F5
Upton Gdns
KTN/HRWW/WS HA3 61 J3
Upton La FSTGT E7 89 F4
Upton Lodge Cl BUSH WD23 28 C2
Upton Park Rd FSTGT E7 89 F5
Upton Rd BXLYHS DA6 149 F5
HSLW TW3 135 F4
THHTH CR7 180 E5
UED N18 50 C1
WOOL/PLUM SE18 127 H6
Upton Rd South BXLY DA5 169 G1
Upway NFNCH/WDSPK N12 47 J3
Upwood Rd LEE/GVPK SE12 165 K1
STRHM/NOR SW16 179 K4
Urban Ms FSBYPK N4 67 H4
Urlwin St CMBW SE5 122 D6
Urlwin Wk BRXN/ST SW9 142 B2
Urmston Dr WIM/MER SW19 159 H3
Ursula Gould Wy
POP/IOD E14 105 J4
Ursula Ms FSBYPK N4 67 H5
Ursula St BTSEA SW11 140 D2
Urswick Gdns DAGW RM9 92 A5
Urswick Rd CLPT E5 86 E3
DAGW RM9 92 A5
Usborne Ms VX/NE SW8 142 A1
Usher Rd BOW E3 87 H6
Usk Rd BTSEA SW11 140 B5
Usk St BETH E2 105 F2
Uvedale Rd DAGE RM10 92 C1
ENC/FH EN2 23 K6
Uverdale Rd WBPTN SW10 140 B1
Uxbridge Rd EA W5 98 A6
FELT TW13 154 C4
HGDN/ICK UB10 94 A3
HNWL W7 115 K1
HPTN TW12 173 G1
KUT/HW KT1 190 E1
SHB W12 118 D1
STHL UB1 115 F1
WEA W13 116 C1
YEAD UB4 94 E5
Uxbridge Rd (Harrow Weald)
KTN/HRWW/WS HA3 42 C3
Uxbridge Rd (Hatch End)
PIN HA5 41 J4
Uxbridge Road High St
STHL UB1 114 E1
Uxbridge Rd (Pinner) PIN HA5 41 H5
Uxbridge Rd (Stanmore)
STAN HA7 43 F2
Uxbridge Rd The Broadway
YEAD UB4 95 H6
Uxbridge St KENS W8 119 K1
Uxendon Crs WBLY HA9 62 A5
Uxendon Hl WBLY HA9 62 B5

V

Valance Av CHING E4 38 D3
Valan Leas HAYES BR2 183 H6
Vale Cl EFNCH N2 47 K6
MV/WKIL W9 101 G2
ORP BR6 216 A2
TWK TW1 * 156 B5
Vale Cots PUT/ROE SW15 * 158 B5
Vale Ct ACT W3 * 118 C1
Vale Crs PUT/ROE SW15 158 B6
Vale Cft ESH/CLAY KT10 205 F5
PIN HA5 59 J2
Vale Dr BAR EN5 20 D5
Vale End EDUL SE22 143 G5
Vale Gv ACT W3 118 A1
FSBYPK N4 67 J4
Vale La ACT W3 98 C4
Valence Av BCTR RM8 91 K1
Valence Circ BCTR RM8 91 K1
Valence Rd ERITH DA8 150 A1
Valence Wood Rd BCTR RM8 91 K1
Valencia Rd STAN HA7 29 J6
Valency Cl NTHWD HA6 26 D6
Valentia Pl BRXN/ST SW9 142 B5
Valentine Av BXLY DA5 169 F4
Valentine Pl STHWK SE1 18 A2
Valentine Rd HOM E9 * 87 F4
RYLN/HDSTN HA2 78 B1
Valentines Rd IL IG1 72 B5
Valentines Wy
ROMW/RG RM7 75 G6
Vale of Health HAMP NW3 83 G1
Valerian Wy SRTFD E15 106 C2
Vale Ri GLDGN NW11 64 D5
Vale Rd BMLY BR1 185 F5
DART DA1 170 E3
ESH/CLAY KT10 204 E6
FSBYPK N4 67 J4
FSTGT E7 89 F4
HOR/WEW KT19 207 H2
MTCM CR4 179 J6
SUT SM1 209 F2
WPK KT4 207 H1
Vale Rw HBRY N5 85 H1
Vale Royal HOLWY N7 84 E5
Vale St DUL SE21 162 E5
Valeswood Rd BMLY BR1 183 J1
Vale Ter FSBYPK N4 67 J3
The Vale ACT W3 118 A1
CHEL SW3 120 C6
CROY/NA CR0 198 A6
EBED/NFELT TW14 154 A1
GLDGN NW11 82 B1
HEST TW5 114 D6
MUSWH N10 48 A4
RSLP HA4 77 G2
SHB W12 118 C1
STHGT/OAK N14 34 E2
WFD IG8 52 E3
Valetta Gv PLSTW E13 106 E1
Valetta Rd ACT W3 118 B2
Valette St HACK E8 * 86 D4
Valiant Cl NTHLT UB5 95 H2
ROMW/RG RM7 56 C5
Valiant Wy EHAM E6 107 K4
Vallance Rd MUSWH N10 48 C5
WCHPL E1 104 C3
Vallentin Rd WALTH E17 70 A1
Valley Av NFNCH/WDSPK N12 33 H6
Valley Cl DART DA1 170 C1
LOU IG10 39 K1
PIN HA5 41 F5
Valley Dr CDALE/KGS NW9 62 D2
Valleyfield Rd
STRHM/NOR SW16 180 A1
Valley Fields Crs ENC/FH EN2 23 G3
Valley Gdns ALP/SUD HA0 80 B5
WIM/MER SW19 178 C3
Valley Gv CHARL SE7 126 B5
Valley Hl LOU IG10 39 J2
Valley Pk WATW WD18 26 A2
Valley Rd DART DA1 170 C1
ERITH DA8 129 K4
HAYES BR2 183 H5
STMC/STPC BR5 186 C4
STRHM/NOR SW16 162 A6
Valley Side CHING E4 37 J3
Valley Vw BAR EN5 32 C1
Valley Wk CROY/NA CR0 197 K6
Valliere Rd WLSDN NW10 99 J2
Valliers Wood Rd
BFN/LL DA15 167 J3
Vallis Wy CHSGTN KT9 205 K2
WEA W13 97 G4
Valmar Rd CMBW SE5 142 D2
Val McKenzie Av HOLWY N7 85 G1
Valnay St TOOT SW17 178 E1
Valognes Av WALTH E17 51 G4
Valonia Gdns
WAND/EARL SW18 159 J1
Vambery Rd
WOOL/PLUM SE18 127 H6
Vanbrough Crs NTHLT UB5 95 G1
Vanbrugh Dr WOT/HER KT12 188 B4
Vanbrugh Flds
BKHTH/KID SE3 125 J6
Vanbrugh Hl GNWCH SE10 125 H5
Vanbrugh Pk BKHTH/KID SE3 145 J1
Vanbrugh Park Rd
BKHTH/KID SE3 145 J1
Vanbrugh Park Rd West
BKHTH/KID SE3 145 J1
Vanbrugh Rd CHSWK W4 118 A3
Vanbrugh Ter BKHTH/KID SE3 145 J2
Vanburgh Cl CAN/RD E16 107 H4
ORP BR6 201 K5
Vancouver Cl ORP BR6 217 G2
Vancouver Man EDGW HA8 * 44 D4
Vancouver Rd EDGW HA8 44 D4
FSTH SE23 164 B4
RCHPK/HAM TW10 156 D6
YEAD UB4 95 F3
Vanderbilt Rd
WAND/EARL SW18 160 A3
Vanderbilt Vls SHB W12 * 119 G2
Vanderville Gdns EFNCH N2 47 G5
Vandome Cl CAN/RD E16 107 F5
Vandon St STJSPK SW1H 16 B4
Van Dyck Av NWMAL KT3 192 A4
Vandyke Cl PUT/ROE SW15 159 G1
Vandyke Cross ELTH/MOT SE9 146 D6
Vandy St SDTCH EC2A 7 G7
Vane Cl HAMP NW3 83 H3
KTN/HRWW/WS HA3 62 B3
Vanessa Cl BELV DA17 129 H5
Vanessa Wy BXLY DA5 170 A5
Van Gogh Cl ISLW TW7 136 B4
Vanguard CDALE/KGS NW9 * 45 G3
Vanguard Cl CAN/RD E16 106 E4
CROY/NA CR0 196 C5
ROMW/RG RM7 56 D5
Vanguard St DEPT SE8 144 D2
Vanguard Wy CROY/NA CR0 212 B2
HTHAIR TW6 133 H3
SAND/SEL CR2 212 C3
WLGTN SM6 210 E5
Vanneck Sq PUT/ROE SW15 * 138 D6
Vanoc Gdns BMLY BR1 165 K6
Vanquish Cl WHTN TW2 155 F2
Vansittart Rd FSTGT E7 88 E2
Vansittart St NWCR SE14 144 B1
Vanston Pl FUL/PGN SW6 139 K1
Vantage Pl KENS W8 119 K3
Vant Rd TOOT SW17 178 E1
Varcoe Gdns HYS/HAR UB3 94 B5
Varcoe Rd BERM/RHTH SE16 123 J5
Vardens Rd BTSEA SW11 140 C5
Varden St WCHPL E1 104 D5
Vardon Cl ACT W3 99 F5
Varley Dr TWK TW1 136 C5
Varley Rd CAN/RD E16 107 F5
Varley Wy MTCM CR4 178 C5
Varna Rd FUL/PGN SW6 139 H1
HPTN TW12 * 173 G4
Varndell St CAMTN NW1 4 A4
Varsity Dr TWK TW1 135 K6
Varsity Rw MORT/ESHN SW14 137 K3
Vartry Rd SEVS/STOTM N15 68 A3
Vassall Rd BRXN/ST SW9 142 B1
Vauban Est BERM/RHTH SE16 19 K5
Vauban St BERM/RHTH SE16 19 K5
Vaughan Av HDN NW4 63 J2
HMSMTH W6 118 C4
Vaughan Cl DART DA1 171 G2
Vaughan Est BETH E2 * 7 J4
Vaughan Gdns IL IG1 71 K4
Vaughan Rd CMBW SE5 142 D3
HRW HA1 60 C4
SRTFD E15 88 D4
THDIT KT7 190 C4
WELL DA16 148 A3
Vaughan St BERM/RHTH SE16 124 C2
Vaughan Wy WAP E1W 104 C6
Vaughan Williams Cl
DEPT SE8 144 D1
Vauxhall Br VX/NE SW8 121 K5
Vauxhall Bridge Rd PIM SW1V 16 A5
Vauxhall Gdns SAND/SEL CR2 211 J4
Vauxhall Gv VX/NE SW8 122 A6
Vauxhall Pl DART DA1 171 H2
Vauxhall St LBTH SE11 122 A5
Vauxhall Wk LBTH SE11 122 A5
Vawdrey Cl WCHPL E1 104 E3
Veals Md MTCM CR4 178 D4
Vectis Gdns TOOT SW17 179 G2
Vectis Rd TOOT SW17 179 G2
Veda Rd LEW SE13 144 D5
Vega Crs NTHWD HA6 40 D1
Vega Rd BUSH WD23 28 C2
Veitch Cl EBED/NFELT TW14 153 J2
Veldene Wy RYLN/HDSTN HA2 77 K1
Vellum Dr CAR SM5 210 A1
Venables Cl DAGE RM10 92 D2
Venables St STJWD NW8 2 B7
Vencourt Pl HMSMTH W6 118 D4
Venetian Rd CMBW SE5 142 D3
Venetia Rd EA W5 116 E2
FSBYPK N4 67 H3
Venette Cl RAIN RM13 111 K4
Venner Rd SYD SE26 181 K2
Venners Cl BXLYHN DA7 150 B3
Venn St CLAP SW4 141 H5
Ventnor Av STAN HA7 43 H4
Ventnor Dr TRDG/WHET N20 33 F5
Ventnor Gdns BARK IG11 90 E4
Ventnor Rd BELMT SM2 209 F5
NWCR SE14 144 A1
Ventnor Ter
SEVS/STOTM N15 * 68 C1
Venture Cl BXLY DA5 169 F2
Venue St POP/IOD E14 105 K4
Venus Ms MTCM CR4 178 D6
Venus Rd WOOL/PLUM SE18 126 E3
Vera Av WCHMH N21 23 G6
Vera Ct OXHEY WD19 27 H2
Vera Lynn Cl FSTGT E7 88 E2
Vera Rd FUL/PGN SW6 139 H2
Verbena Cl CAN/RD E16 106 C3
Verbena Gdns HMSMTH W6 118 D5
Verdant La CAT SE6 165 H3
Verdayne Av CROY/NA CR0 198 A5
Verderers Rd CHIG IG7 55 G1
Verdun Rd BARN SW13 138 D1
WOOL/PLUM SE18 128 B6
Vereker Rd WKENS W14 * 119 H5
Vere St CAVSQ/HST W1G 9 J4
Vermont Cl ENC/FH EN2 23 H5
Vermont Rd NRWD SE19 180 E2
SUT SM1 209 F1
WAND/EARL SW18 160 A1
Verney Gdns DAGW RM9 92 A2
Verney Rd BERM/RHTH SE16 123 J5
DAGW RM9 92 A2
Verney St WLSDN NW10 81 F1
Verney Wy BERM/RHTH SE16 123 J5
Vernham Rd
WOOL/PLUM SE18 127 H6
Vernon Av MNPK E12 89 K2
RYNPK SW20 177 G5
WFD IG8 53 F2
Vernon Cl HOR/WEW KT19 206 E4
STMC/STPC BR5 186 C6
STWL/WRAY TW19 152 B3
Vernon Crs EBAR EN4 22 A6
Vernon Dr STAN HA7 43 G4
Vernon Pl FSBYW WC1X 11 F2
Vernon Ri FSBYW WC1X 5 H4
GFD/PVL UB6 78 D3
Vernon Rd BOW E3 105 H1
CEND/HSY/T N8 * 49 G6
CRW RM5 56 E1
FELT TW13 153 J4
GDMY/SEVK IG3 73 F5
MORT/ESHN SW14 138 A4
SRTFD E15 88 C5
SUT SM1 209 G3
WALTH E17 69 H1
WAN E11 70 C5
Vernon Sq FSBYW WC1X 5 H4
Vernon St WKENS W14 119 H4
Vernon Yd NTGHL W11 100 D6
Veroan Rd BXLYHN DA7 149 F3
Verona Ct CHSWK W4 118 B5
Verona Dr SURB KT6 191 F6
Veronica Gdns
STRHM/NOR SW16 179 H4
Veronica Rd TOOT SW17 161 G5
Veronique Gdns
BARK/HLT IG6 72 C2
Verran Rd BAL SW12 * 161 G2
Versailles Rd PGE/AN SE20 181 H3
Verulam Av WALTH E17 69 H3
Verulam Ct CDALE/KGS NW9 * 63 J4
Verulam Rd GFD/PVL UB6 96 A3
Verulam St FSBYW WC1X 11 J1
Verwood Dr EBAR EN4 21 K4
Verwood Rd
RYLN/HDSTN HA2 42 C5
Veryan Cl STMC/STPC BR5 202 D1
Vespan Rd SHB W12 118 D2
Vesta Rd BROCKY SE4 144 B3
Vestris Rd FSTH SE23 164 A4
Vestry Ms CMBW SE5 143 F2
Vestry Rd CMBW SE5 143 F2
WALTH E17 69 K2
Vestry St IS N1 6 E4
Vevey St CAT SE6 164 C4
Viaduct Pl BETH E2 104 D2
Viaduct St BETH E2 104 D2
The Viaduct MUSWH N10 * 66 B1
SWFD E18 52 E5
Vian St LEW SE13 144 E4
Vibart Gdns
BRXS/STRHM SW2 162 A2
Vibart Wk IS N1 * 84 E6
Vibia Cl STWL/WRAY TW19 152 A2
Vicarage Cl ERITH DA8 129 K6
NTHLT UB5 77 K6
RSLP HA4 58 B4
WPK KT4 192 B5
Vicarage Ct BECK BR3 * 182 B6
Vicarage Crs BTSEA SW11 140 C3
Vicarage Dr BARK IG11 90 C5
BECK BR3 182 D4
MORT/ESHN SW14 138 A6
Vicarage Farm Rd
HSLWW TW4 134 D3
Vicarage Flds WOT/HER KT12 188 B3
Vicarage Gdns MTCM CR4 178 D6
Vicarage Ga KENS W8 120 A2
Vicarage Gv CMBW SE5 142 E2
Vicarage La EHAM E6 107 K2
IL IG1 72 D5
SRTFD E15 88 C4
Vicarage Ms CHSWK W4 * 118 B6
Vicarage Pde
SEVS/STOTM N15 * 67 J1
Vicarage Pk
WOOL/PLUM SE18 127 H5
Vicarage Rd BXLY DA5 169 J3
CROY/NA CR0 211 G1
DAGE RM10 92 D5
HCH RM12 75 J5
HDN NW4 63 J3
KUT/HW KT1 174 D4
LEY E10 69 K4
MORT/ESHN SW14 137 K6
SRTFD E15 88 D5
SUT SM1 208 E2
TEDD TW11 174 B1
TOTM N17 50 C3
WATW WD18 26 E2
WFD IG8 53 J3
WHTN TW2 155 H1
WOOL/PLUM SE18 127 H5
Vicarage Wk BTSEA SW11 * 140 C2
Vicarage Wy
RYLN/HDSTN HA2 60 A4
WLSDN NW10 81 F1
Vicars Bridge Cl ALP/SUD HA0 98 A1
Vicar's Cl EN EN1 24 A3
HOM E9 86 E6
SRTFD E15 88 E6
Vicars Hl LEW SE13 144 E5
Vicar's Moor La WCHMH N21 35 G2
Vicars Oak Rd NRWD SE19 181 F2
Vicar's Rd KTTN NW5 84 A3
Viceroy Cl EFNCH N2 * 65 J1
Viceroy Pde EFNCH N2 * 65 J1
Viceroy Rd VX/NE SW8 141 K2
Vickers Cl WLGTN SM6 211 F5
Vickers La DART DA1 151 K4
Vickers Rd ERITH DA8 130 A5
Victor Gv ALP/SUD HA0 80 A5
Victoria Ar WESTW SW1E 15 K5
Victoria Av CRW RM5 56 D2
E/WMO/HCT KT8 173 G6
EHAM E6 89 H6
FNCH N3 46 D4
HSLW TW3 135 F6
SURB KT6 190 E3
WBLY HA9 80 D4
WLGTN SM6 210 A1
Victoria Cl E/WMO/HCT KT8 173 F6
EBAR EN4 21 H5
HRW HA1 61 F3
HYS/HAR UB3 94 B5
Victoria Cots RCH/KEW TW9 137 G2
WCHPL E1 * 104 C4
Victoria Ct WBLY HA9 80 C4
Victoria Crs NRWD SE19 181 F2
SEVS/STOTM N15 68 A2
WIM/MER SW19 * 177 J3
Victoria Dock Rd CAN/RD E16 106 D6
Victoria Dr WIM/MER SW19 159 G3
Victoria Emb EMB EC4Y 11 K5
TPL/STR WC2R 11 G6
WHALL SW1A 17 F3
Victoria Embankment Gdns
CHCR WC2N * 11 F6
Victoria Gdns HEST TW5 134 D2
NTGHL W11 119 J1
Victoria Ga BAY/PAD W2 8 B5
Victoria Gv KENS W8 120 B3
NFNCH/WDSPK N12 47 H1
Victoria Grove Ms
BAY/PAD W2 * 101 F6
Victoria La BAR EN5 20 D5
HYS/HAR UB3 113 G5
Victoria Ms KIL/WHAMP NW6 82 E6
WAND/EARL SW18 160 B3
Victorian Gv STNW/STAM N16 86 A1
Victorian Rd STNW/STAM N16 86 A1
Victoria Pde RCH/KEW TW9 * 137 H2
Victoria Park Rd HOM E9 86 E6
Victoria Park Sq BETH E2 104 E2
Victoria Park Studios
HOM E9 * 86 E4
Victoria Pl RCH/KEW TW9 136 E6
Victoria Ri CLAP SW4 141 G4
Victoria Rd ACT W3 99 F4
BARK IG11 90 B4
BFN/LL DA15 168 A5
BKHH IG9 39 H4
BUSH WD23 28 B3
BXLYHS DA6 149 H5
CHING E4 38 C3
CHST BR7 185 F1
DAGE RM10 92 E3
DART DA1 151 G6
EA W5 97 H4
EBAR EN4 21 H5
ED N9 36 B5
ERITH DA8 130 B6
FELT TW13 154 A3
FSBYPK N4 67 F4
HAYES BR2 200 C2
HDN NW4 64 A1
KENS W8 120 B3
KIL/WHAMP NW6 100 D1
KUT/HW KT1 175 G5
MLHL NW7 45 H1
MORT/ESHN SW14 138 A4
MTCM CR4 178 D3
NWDGN UB2 114 E3
PLSTW E13 106 E1
ROM RM1 75 H2
RSLP HA4 58 E5
RSLP HA4 77 F2
SEVS/STOTM N15 * 68 C1
SURB KT6 190 E3
SUT SM1 209 H3
SWFD E18 53 F6
TEDD TW11 174 B2
TWK TW1 156 C2
UED N18 36 B6
WALTH E17 52 A5
WAN E11 88 B2
WDGN N22 48 D4
WIM/MER SW19 178 D3
WLSDN NW10 99 G3
Victoria Sq BGVA SW1W 15 K4
Victoria St BELV DA17 129 G5
SRTFD E15 88 C5
WESTW SW1E 15 K5
Victoria Ter EA W5 * 116 E1
FSBYPK N4 67 G5
HRW HA1 60 E5
Victoria Vls RCH/KEW TW9 137 G4
Victoria Wy CHARL SE7 126 A5
Victoria Works
STMC/STPC BR5 201 H2
Victoria Yd WCHPL E1 * 104 C5
Victor Rd PGE/AN SE20 182 A3
RYLN/HDSTN HA2 42 C6
TEDD TW11 173 K1
WLSDN NW10 99 K2
Victors Dr HPTN TW12 * 172 D2
Victors Wy BAR EN5 20 D4
Victor Vls ED N9 * 35 K5
Victory Av MRDN SM4 194 B2
Victory Cl STWL/WRAY TW19 152 B3
Victory Pk WBLY HA9 * 79 K1
Victory Pl NRWD SE19 * 181 F2
WALW SE17 18 D6
Victory Rd RAIN RM13 111 J1
WAN E11 70 E1
WIM/MER SW19 178 B3
Victory Road Ms
WIM/MER SW19 178 B3
Victory Wy BERM/RHTH SE16 124 B2
HEST TW5 114 B5
ROMW/RG RM7 56 D5
Vienna Cl WFD IG8 53 H5
View Cl CHIG IG7 54 D1
HGT N6 65 K4
HRW HA1 60 D1
View Crs CEND/HSY/T N8 66 D2
Viewfield Cl
KTN/HRWW/WS HA3 62 A4
Viewfield Rd BFN/LL DA15 168 D3
WAND/EARL SW18 159 J1
Viewland Rd
WOOL/PLUM SE18 128 A5
View Rd HGT N6 65 K4
The View ABYW SE2 129 F5
Viga Rd WCHMH N21 35 G1
Vigilant Cl SYD SE26 163 H6
Vignoles Rd ROMW/RG RM7 74 C4
Vigo St CONDST W1S 10 A6
Viking Cl BOW E3 105 G1
Viking Gdns EHAM E6 107 J4
Viking Pl LEY E10 69 H5
Viking Rd STHL UB1 95 J6

Viking Wy ERITH DA8 129 K3
Villacourt Rd
WOOL/PLUM SE18 148 B1
Village Ar CHING E4 * 38 B3
Village Cl CHING E4 52 A1
HAMP NW3 * 83 H3
Village Green Rd DART DA1 150 D5
Village Ms CDALE/KGS NW9 * 63 F6
Village Mt HAMP NW3 * 83 G2
Village Park Cl EN EN1 36 A1
Village Rd EN EN1 24 A6
EN EN1 35 K1
FNCH N3 46 C5
Village Rw BELMT SM2 208 E5
The Village CHARL SE7 126 B6
HAMP NW3 * 65 G6
Village Wy ASHF TW15 152 C6
BARK/HLT IG6 54 C6
BECK BR3 198 D1
DUL SE21 162 E1
PIN HA5 59 J4
WLSDN NW10 81 F2
Village Wy East PIN HA5 59 K4
Villa Rd BRXN/ST SW9 142 B4
Villas Rd WOOL/PLUM SE18 127 H4
Villa St WALW SE17 122 E5
Villiers Av BRYLDS KT5 191 G2
WHTN TW2 154 E3
Villiers Cl BRYLDS KT5 191 G1
LEY E10 69 J6
Villiers Gv BELMT SM2 208 B6
Villiers Rd BECK BR3 182 A5
CRICK NW2 81 J4
ISLW TW7 135 K3
KUT/HW KT1 175 G6
OXHEY WD19 27 J1
STHL UB1 114 E1
Villiers St CHCR WC2N 11 F7
Vimy Cl HSLWW TW4 134 E6
Vimy Dr DART DA1 151 J4
Vincam Cl WHTN TW2 155 F2
Vincennes Est WNWD SE27 * 162 E6
Vincent Av BRYLDS KT5 191 J5
Vincent Cl BAR EN5 20 E4
BARK/HLT IG6 54 C2
BFN/LL DA15 167 K3
ESH/CLAY KT10 204 B1
HAYES BR2 200 A1
WDR/YW UB7 112 D6
Vincent Gdns CRICK NW2 81 H1
Vincent Pde FSBYPK N4 * 66 E5
Vincent Rd ACT W3 117 K3
ALP/SUD HA0 80 B5
CHING E4 52 B2
CROY/NA CR0 197 F4
DAGW RM9 92 A5
HSLWW TW4 134 C4
ISLW TW7 135 J2
KUT/HW KT1 175 H6
SEVS/STOTM N15 67 J1
WDGN N22 49 G5
WOOL/PLUM SE18 127 G4
Vincent Rw HPTN TW12 173 H2
Vincents Cl BERM/RHTH SE16 124 B2
Vincent Sq WDGN N22 * 49 G5
WEST SW1P 16 B6
Vincent St CAN/RD E16 106 E4
WEST SW1P 16 C6
Vincent Ter IS N1 6 A2
Vincent Vls
SEVS/STOTM N15 * 67 J1
Vince St FSBYE EC1V 7 F5
Vine Cl BRYLDS KT5 191 G3
CLPT E5 86 C2
SUT SM1 209 G1
WDR/YW UB7 112 D4
Vine Cots HNWL W7 * 115 K1
WCHPL E1 * 104 E5
Vine Ct KTN/HRWW/WS HA3 62 A3
WCHPL E1 104 C4
Vine Gdns IL IG1 90 C3
Vinegar St WAP E1W 123 J1
Vinegar Yd STHWK SE1 19 G2
Vine Hl CLKNW EC1R 5 J7
Vine La STHWK SE1 19 H1
Vine Pl HSLW TW3 135 G5
Vineries Cl WDR/YW UB7 112 D6
The Vineries CAT SE6 * 164 D3
EN EN1 24 A4
STHGT/OAK N14 34 C1
Vine Rd BARN SW13 138 C4
E/WMO/HCT KT8 189 H1
ORP BR6 217 F4
SRTFD E15 88 D5
Vine Rw RCHPK/HAM TW10 * 137 F6
Viners Cl WOT/HER KT12 188 B3
Vines Av FNCH N3 47 F4
Vine Sq WKENS W14 * 119 J5
Vine St MYFR/PICC W1J 10 B6
ROMW/RG RM7 74 E2
TWRH EC3N 13 J4
Vine Street Br FARR EC1M 5 K7
Vine Yd STHWK SE1 18 D2
Vineyard Av MLHL NW7 46 C3
Vineyard Cl CAT SE6 164 D3
KUT/HW KT1 175 G6
Vineyard Gv FNCH N3 47 F4
Vineyard Hill Rd
WIM/MER SW19 159 K6
Vineyard Ms CLKNW EC1R * 5 J6
Vineyard Pth
MORT/ESHN SW14 138 A4
Vineyard Rd FELT TW13 153 K5
Vineyard Rw KUT/HW KT1 174 D4
The Vineyard
RCHPK/HAM TW10 136 E6
Vineyard Wk CLKNW EC1R 5 J6
Viney Bank CROY/NA CR0 213 H6
Viney Rd LEW SE13 144 E4
Vining St BRXS/STRHM SW2 142 B5
Vinries Bank MLHL NW7 45 K1
Vinson Cl ORP BR6 202 B5
Vintage Ms CHING E4 37 J6
Vintry Ms WALTH E17 69 J1
Viola Av ABYW SE2 128 C4
EBED/NFELT TW14 154 B1
STWL/WRAY TW19 152 B3
Viola Sq SHB W12 99 H6
Violet Av ENC/FH EN2 23 K1
Violet Cl CAN/RD E16 106 C3
CHEAM SM3 193 H5
DEPT SE8 124 C6
WLGTN SM6 195 F5
Violet Gdns CROY/NA CR0 211 H3
Violet Hl STJWD NW8 101 G1
Violet La SAND/SEL CR2 211 H3
Violet Rd BOW E3 105 K3
SWFD E18 53 F5
WALTH E17 69 J3
Violet St BETH E2 104 D3
Virgil St STHWK SE1 17 H4
Virginia Cl CRW RM5 56 E3
HAYES BR2 183 H6
NWMAL KT3 191 K1
Virginia Gdns BARK/HLT IG6 54 D5
Virginia Rd BETH E2 7 J5
THHTH CR7 180 C4
Virginia St WCHPL E1 * 104 C6
Viscount Cl FBAR/BDGN N11 48 B1
Viscount Dr EHAM E6 107 K4
Viscount Gv NTHLT UB5 95 H2
Viscount Rd
STWL/WRAY TW19 152 A2
Viscount St BARB EC2Y 6 C7
Viscount Wy HTHAIR TW6 133 H5
Vista Av PEND EN3 25 F3
Vista Dr REDBR IG4 71 H2
The Vista CHING E4 38 B2
ELTH/MOT SE9 166 C1
Vista Wy KTN/HRWW/WS HA3 62 A3
Viveash Cl HYS/HAR UB3 113 J3
Vivian Av HDN NW4 63 K2
WBLY HA9 80 C4
Vivian Cl OXHEY WD19 26 E4
Vivian Gdns OXHEY WD19 26 E3
WBLY HA9 80 C3
Vivian Rd BOW E3 105 G1
Vivian Sq PECK SE15 143 J4
Vivian Wy EFNCH N2 65 H2
Vivien Cl CHSGTN KT9 206 A5
Vivienne Cl TWK TW1 156 E1
Vixen Ms HACK E8 * 86 B6
Voce Rd WOOL/PLUM SE18 147 J1
Voewood Cl NWMAL KT3 192 C3
Voltaire Rd CLAP SW4 141 J4
Volt Av WLSDN NW10 99 F2
Volta Wy CROY/NA CR0 196 A5
Voluntary Pl WAN E11 70 E3
Vorley Rd ARCH N19 66 C6
Voss Ct STRHM/NOR SW16 179 K2
Voss St BETH E2 104 C2
Voyagers Cl THMD SE28 109 J5
Vulcan Cl EHAM E6 108 A5
Vulcan Ga ENC/FH EN2 23 G3
Vulcan Rd BROCKY SE4 144 C3
Vulcan Ter BROCKY SE4 144 C3
Vulcan Wy HOLWY N7 85 F4
WLGTN SM6 210 E6
Vyner Rd ACT W3 99 F6
Vyner St BETH E2 104 D1
The Vyne BXLYHN DA7 149 J4
Vyse Cl BAR EN5 20 A5

W

Wadbrook St KUT/HW KT1 174 E5
Wadding St WALW SE17 18 E7
Waddington Cl EN EN1 24 A5
Waddington Rd SRTFD E15 88 B3
Waddington St SRTFD E15 88 B4
Waddington Wy NRWD SE19 180 D4
Waddon Cl CROY/NA CR0 211 G1
Waddon Court Rd
CROY/NA CR0 211 G2
Waddon Marsh Wy
CROY/NA CR0 196 A5
Waddon New Rd
CROY/NA CR0 211 H1
Waddon Park Av
CROY/NA CR0 211 G2
Waddon Rd CROY/NA CR0 211 G1
Waddon Wy CROY/NA CR0 211 G4
Wade Av STMC/STPC BR5 202 E4
Wade House STHWK SE1 * 123 H2
Wade's Gv WCHMH N21 35 G2
Wade's Hl WCHMH N21 35 G1
Wade's La TEDD TW11 174 B1
Wadeson St BETH E2 104 D1
Wade's Pl POP/IOD E14 105 K6
Wadeville Av CHDH RM6 74 A3
Wadeville Cl BELV DA17 129 H5
Wadham Av WALTH E17 51 K3
Wadham Gdns GFD/PVL UB6 78 D4
HAMP NW3 83 J5
Wadham Rd CHING E4 52 A4
PUT/ROE SW15 139 H5
WALTH E17 51 K4
Wadhurst Cl PGE/AN SE20 181 J5
Wadhurst Rd CHSWK W4 118 A3
VX/NE SW8 141 H2
Wadley Rd WAN E11 70 C4
Wadsworth Cl GFD/PVL UB6 97 J1
PEND EN3 25 F6
Wadsworth Rd GFD/PVL UB6 97 H1
Wager St BOW E3 105 H3
Waghorn Rd
KTN/HRWW/WS HA3 43 K6
PLSTW E13 89 G6
Waghorn St PECK SE15 143 H4
Wagner St PECK SE15 143 K1
Wagstaff Gdns DAGW RM9 91 J5
Wagtail Cl CDALE/KGS NW9 45 G5
EN EN1 24 D2
Wagtail Wk BECK BR3 199 F2
Wagtail Wy STMC/STPC BR5 202 E1
Waid Cl DART DA1 171 J1
Waights Ct KUTN/CMB KT2 175 F4
Wainfleet Av CRW RM5 56 E5
Wainford Cl WIM/MER SW19 159 G3
Wainwright Gv ISLW TW7 135 J5
Waite Davies Rd
LEE/GVPK SE12 165 J2
Waite St CMBW SE5 123 G6
Wakefield Gdns IL IG1 71 J3
NRWD SE19 181 F3
Wakefield Ms STPAN WC1H 4 E5
Wakefield Rd
FBAR/BDGN N11 48 D1
RCHPK/HAM TW10 136 E6
SEVS/STOTM N15 68 B2
Wakefield St BMSBY WC1N 5 F6
EHAM E6 89 J6
STPAN WC1H 5 F5
UED N18 50 C1
Wakeford Cl CLAP SW4 141 H6
Wakehams Hl PIN HA5 41 K6
Wakeham St IS N1 85 K4
Wakehurst Rd BTSEA SW11 140 D6
Wakeling La ALP/SUD HA0 79 H1
Wakeling Rd HNWL W7 97 F4
Wakeling St WCHPL E1 * 105 G5
Wakelin Rd SRTFD E15 106 C1
Wakeman Rd WLSDN NW10 100 A2
Wakemans Hill Av
CDALE/KGS NW9 63 F2
Wakering Rd BARK IG11 90 C4
Wakerly Cl EHAM E6 107 K5
Wakley St FSBYE EC1V 6 A4
Walberswick St VX/NE SW8 141 K1
Walbrook MANHO EC4N 12 E5
Walburgh St WCHPL E1 104 D5
Walcorde Av WALW SE17 18 D7
Walcot Rd PEND EN3 25 H3
Walcot Sq LBTH SE11 17 K6
Walcott St WEST SW1P * 16 B6
Waldeck Gv WNWD SE27 162 C5
Waldeck Rd CHSWK W4 117 H6
DART DA1 171 J2
MORT/ESHN SW14 137 K4
SEVS/STOTM N15 49 H6
WEA W13 97 H5
Waldegrave Gdns TWK TW1 156 A4
Waldegrave Pk TWK TW1 156 A6
Waldegrave Rd BCTR RM8 73 J6
BMLY BR1 200 D2
CEND/HSY/T N8 * 49 G6
EA W5 98 B6
NRWD SE19 181 G3
TWK TW1 156 A6
Waldegrove CROY/NA CR0 212 B1
Waldemar Av FUL/PGN SW6 139 H2
WEA W13 116 D1
Waldemar Rd
WIM/MER SW19 177 K1
Walden Av CHST BR7 166 E6
PLMGR N13 35 J6
RAIN RM13 111 F1
Walden Cl BELV DA17 129 G5
Walden Gdns THHTH CR7 196 A1
Waldenhurst Rd
STMC/STPC BR5 202 E4
Walden Pde CHST BR7 * 184 E2
Walden Rd CHST BR7 184 E2
TOTM N17 49 K4
Waldens Cl STMC/STPC BR5 202 E4
Waldenshaw Rd FSTH SE23 163 K3
Waldens Rd STMC/STPC BR5 203 F3
Walden St WCHPL E1 * 104 D5
Walden Wy BARK/HLT IG6 54 E3
MLHL NW7 46 B2
Waldo Cl CLAP SW4 141 H6
Waldo Pl MTCM CR4 178 D3
Waldorf Cl SAND/SEL CR2 211 H6
Waldo Rd BMLY BR1 184 B6
WLSDN NW10 99 J2
Waldram Crs FSTH SE23 163 K3
Waldram Park Rd FSTH SE23 164 A3
Waldrist Wy ERITH DA18 129 G2
Waldron Gdns HAYES BR2 183 G6
Waldronhyrst CROY/NA CR0 211 H2
Waldron Ms CHEL SW3 120 C6
Waldron Rd
RYLN/HDSTN HA2 60 E5
WAND/EARL SW18 160 B5
The Waldrons CROY/NA CR0 211 J2
Waldron's Yd
RYLN/HDSTN HA2 60 D6
Waldstock Rd THMD SE28 109 G6
Waleran Cl STAN HA7 43 F2
Walerand Rd LEW SE13 145 F3
Wales Av CAR SM5 209 J3
Wales Cl PECK SE15 143 J1
Wales Farm Rd ACT W3 99 F4
Waleton Acres WLGTN SM6 * 210 C4
Waley St WCHPL E1 * 105 F4
Walfield Av TRDG/WHET N20 33 F2
Walford Rd STNW/STAM N16 86 A2
Walfrey Gdns DAGW RM9 92 A5
Walham Green Ct
FUL/PGN SW6 * 140 A1
Walham Gv FUL/PGN SW6 139 K1
Walham Ri WIM/MER SW19 177 H2
Walham Yd FUL/PGN SW6 139 K1
Walkden Rd CHST BR7 167 F6
Walker Cl CROY/NA CR0 214 A5
DART DA1 150 C4
EBED/NFELT TW14 153 J2
FBAR/BDGN N11 34 C6
HNWL W7 115 K1
HPTN TW12 172 E2
WOOL/PLUM SE18 127 H4
Walker's Ct SOHO/CST W1F 10 C5
Walkerscroft Md CAT SE6 164 E4
DUL SE21 162 D3
Walker's Pl PUT/ROE SW15 139 G5
Walkley Rd DART DA1 150 E6
The Walks EFNCH N2 47 H6
The Walk PLMGR N13 * 35 G5
Wallace Cl THMD SE28 109 K6
Wallace Crs CAR SM5 209 K3
Wallace Rd IS N1 85 J4
Wallace Wy ROM RM1 57 F3
Wallbutton Rd BROCKY SE4 144 B3
Wallcote Av CRICK NW2 64 B5
Walled Garden Cl BECK BR3 198 E1
Wall End Rd EHAM E6 90 A5
Wallenger Av GPK RM2 57 K6
Waller Dr NTHWD HA6 40 E4
Waller Rd NWCR SE14 144 A2
Wallers Cl DAGW RM9 92 A6
WFD IG8 53 K2
Wallflower St SHB W12 99 H6
Wallgrave Rd ECT SW5 120 A4
Wallhouse Rd ERITH DA8 151 F1
Wallingford Av NKENS W10 100 B4
Wallington Cl RSLP HA4 58 A3
Wallington Rd
GDMY/SEVK IG3 73 F4
Wallis Cl BTSEA SW11 140 C4
EMPK RM11 75 K5
RDART DA2 170 D5
Wallis Rd HOM E9 87 H4
STHL UB1 96 B5
Wallman Pl WDGN N22 49 F4
Wallorton Gdns
MORT/ESHN SW14 138 A5
Wallside BARB EC2Y * 12 D2
Wall St IS N1 85 K4
Wallwood Rd WAN E11 70 B4
Wallwood St POP/IOD E14 105 H4
Walmar Cl EBAR EN4 21 H2
Walmer Cl CHING E4 37 K4
ORP BR6 216 D2
ROMW/RG RM7 56 D5
Walmer Gdns WEA W13 116 B2
Walmer Pl MBLAR W1H * 8 E1
Walmer Rd NTGHL W11 100 C6
Walmer Ter WOOL/PLUM SE18 127 H4
Walmgate Rd GFD/PVL UB6 79 H6
Walmington Fold
NFNCH/WDSPK N12 46 E2
Walm La CRICK NW2 82 B3
Walney Wk IS N1 * 85 J4
Walnut Av WDR/YW UB7 112 D3
Walnut Cl BARK/HLT IG6 72 C1
CAR SM5 209 K3
DEPT SE8 124 C6
HYS/HAR UB3 94 C6
Walnut Ct EA W5 * 117 F2
Walnut Gdns SRTFD E15 88 C3
Walnut Gv EN EN1 23 K6
Walnut Ms BELMT SM2 209 G5
Walnut Rd LEY E10 69 J6
Walnuts Rd ORP BR6 202 B5
Walnut Tree Av DART DA1 171 H4
MTCM CR4 * 178 D6
Walnut Tree Cl BARN SW13 138 C2
CHST BR7 185 H4
Walnut Tree Rd BCTR RM8 73 K6
BTFD TW8 117 F6
ERITH DA8 130 B5
GNWCH SE10 * 125 H5
HEST TW5 114 E6
Walnut Tree Wk LBTH SE11 17 J6
Walnut Wy BKHH IG9 39 H5
RSLP HA4 77 G4
Walpole Av RCH/KEW TW9 137 G3
Walpole Cl PIN HA5 42 A2
WEA W13 116 D2
Walpole Crs TEDD TW11 174 A1
Walpole Gdns CHSWK W4 117 K5
WHTN TW2 155 K4
Walpole Ms STJWD NW8 2 A1
Walpole Pl TEDD TW11 174 A1
Walpole Rd CROY/NA CR0 196 E6
EHAM E6 89 G5
HAYES BR2 200 C2
SURB KT6 191 F4
SWFD E18 52 D4
TEDD TW11 174 A1
TOTM N17 49 J5
WALTH E17 69 G1
WHTN TW2 155 K4
WIM/MER SW19 178 C2
Walpole St CHEL SW3 120 E5
Walrond Av WBLY HA9 80 A3
Walsham Cl STNW/STAM N16 68 C5
THMD SE28 109 K6
Walsham Rd
EBED/NFELT TW14 154 A2
NWCR SE14 144 A3
Walsingham Gdns
HOR/WEW KT19 207 G2
Walsingham Pk CHST BR7 185 J5
Walsingham Rd CLAP SW4 161 F1
CLPT E5 86 C1
ENC/FH EN2 23 K5
MTCM CR4 194 E2
STMC/STPC BR5 186 C4
WEA W13 * 116 B1
Walsingham Wk BELV DA17 129 H6
Walter Rodney Cl MNPK E12 89 K4
Walters Cl HYS/HAR UB3 113 J2
Walters Rd PEND EN3 24 E6
Walter's Rd SNWD SE25 197 F1
Walter St BETH E2 105 F2
KUTN/CMB KT2 * 175 F4
Walters Wy FSTH SE23 164 A1
Walters Yd BMLY BR1 183 K5
Walter Ter WCHPL E1 105 F5
Walterton Rd MV/WKIL W9 100 D3
Walter Wk EDGW HA8 44 E2
Waltham Av CDALE/KGS NW9 62 C3
HYS/HAR UB3 113 F3
Waltham Cl DART DA1 170 D1
STMC/STPC BR5 202 E5
Waltham Dr EDGW HA8 44 C5
Waltham Pk WALTH E17 51 J3
Waltham Park Wy CHING E4 * 51 J3
Waltham Rd CAR SM5 194 C5
NWDGN UB2 114 D3
WFD IG8 53 J2
Walthamstow Av CHING E4 51 J3
Walthamstow Av (North
Circular) CHING E4 51 G1
Waltham Wy CHING E4 37 H5
Waltheof Av TOTM N17 49 K4
Waltheof Gdns TOTM N17 49 K4
Walton Av CHEAM SM3 208 D1
NWMAL KT3 192 C1
RYLN/HDSTN HA2 77 K2
WBLY HA9 80 D1
Walton Cl CRICK NW2 63 K6
HRW HA1 60 D1
VX/NE SW8 141 K1
Walton Dr HRW HA1 60 D1
WLSDN NW10 81 F4
Walton Gdns ACT W3 98 D4
FELT TW13 153 J6
WBLY HA9 62 A6
Walton Gn CROY/NA CR0 213 K6
Walton Pk WOT/HER KT12 188 C6
Walton Park La
WOT/HER KT12 188 C6
Walton Pl CHEL SW3 14 E4
Walton Rd CRW RM5 56 B3
E/WMO/HCT KT8 189 F1
HRW HA1 60 D1
MNPK E12 90 A2
PLSTW E13 107 G1
SCUP DA14 168 C5
SEVS/STOTM N15 * 68 B1
WOT/HER KT12 188 C2
Walton St CHEL SW3 14 D6
ENC/FH EN2 23 K2
Walton Vls IS N1 * 86 A5
Walton Wy ACT W3 98 D4
MTCM CR4 195 H1
Walt Whitman Cl HNHL SE24 * 142 C5
Walverns Cl OXHEY WD19 27 G1
Walworth Pl WALW SE17 122 D5
Walworth Rd STHWK SE1 18 C6
Walwyn Av BMLY BR1 184 C6
Wanborough Dr
PUT/ROE SW15 158 E3
Wanderer Dr BARK IG11 109 H2
Wandle Bank CROY/NA CR0 210 E1
WIM/MER SW19 178 C2
Wandle Ct HOR/WEW KT19 206 E2
Wandle Court Gdns
CROY/NA CR0 210 E1
Wandle Rd CROY/NA CR0 210 E1
MRDN SM4 194 C2
TOOT SW17 160 D4
WLGTN SM6 195 G6
Wandle Side CROY/NA CR0 211 F1
WLGTN SM6 210 B1
Wandle Wy MTCM CR4 194 E2
WAND/EARL SW18 160 A3
Wandsworth Br
WAND/EARL SW18 140 B4
Wandsworth Bridge Rd
FUL/PGN SW6 140 A2
Wandsworth Common West
Side WAND/EARL SW18 140 B6
Wandsworth High St
WAND/EARL SW18 139 K6
Wandsworth Rd VX/NE SW8 * 141 J3
Wangey Rd CHDH RM6 73 K4
Wanless Rd HNHL SE24 142 D4
Wanley Rd CMBW SE5 142 E5
Wanlip Rd PLSTW E13 107 F3
Wannock Gdns BARK/HLT IG6 54 B3
Wansbeck Rd HOM E9 87 H5
Wansdown Pl FUL/PGN SW6 140 A1
Wansey St WALW SE17 18 D7
Wansford Rd WFD IG8 53 G4
Wanstead Cl BMLY BR1 184 B5
Wanstead La IL IG1 71 J3
Wanstead Park Av MNPK E12 71 H6
Wanstead Park Rd IL IG1 71 J4
Wanstead Pl WAN E11 70 E3
Wanstead Rd BMLY BR1 184 B5
Wansunt Rd BXLY DA5 169 K3
Wantage Rd LEE/GVPK SE12 145 J6
Wantz La RAIN RM13 111 K3
Wantz Rd DAGE RM10 92 D2
Wapping Dock St WAP E1W * 123 J1
Wapping High St WAP E1W 123 H1
Wapping La WAP E1W 104 D6
Wapping Wall WAP E1W 123 K1
Warbank La KUTN/CMB KT2 176 C3
Warbeck Rd SHB W12 118 E1
Warberry Rd WDGN N22 49 F5
Warboys Ap KUTN/CMB KT2 175 J2
Warboys Crs CHING E4 52 A1
Warboys Rd KUTN/CMB KT2 175 J2
Warburton Cl IS N1 86 A4
KTN/HRWW/WS HA3 42 D2
Warburton Rd HACK E8 86 D6
WHTN TW2 155 G3
Warburton St HACK E8 86 D6
Warburton Ter WALTH E17 51 K5
Wardalls Gv NWCR SE14 * 143 K1
Ward Cl ERITH DA8 130 A6
SAND/SEL CR2 212 A3
Wardell Cl EDGW HA8 45 G3
Wardell Fld CDALE/KGS NW9 45 G4
Warden Av CRW RM5 56 E1
RYLN/HDSTN HA2 59 J5
Warden Rd KTTN NW5 84 A4
Wardens Gv STHWK SE1 18 C1
Wardle St HOM E9 87 F3
Wardley St WAND/EARL SW18 160 A2
Wardo Av FUL/PGN SW6 139 H2
Wardour Ms SOHO/CST W1F 10 B4
Wardour St SOHO/CST W1F 10 B3
Ward Rd ARCH N19 84 C1
SRTFD E15 * 88 B6
Wardrobe Pl BLKFR EC4V * 12 B4
The Wardrobe
RCH/KEW TW9 * 136 E6
Wards Rd GNTH/NBYPK IG2 72 D4
Wards Wharf Ap CAN/RD E16 126 C2
Wareham Cl HSLW TW3 135 F5
Waremead Rd
GNTH/NBYPK IG2 72 B2
Warepoint Dr THMD SE28 127 J2
Warfield Rd
EBED/NFELT TW14 153 H2
HPTN TW12 173 G4
WLSDN NW10 100 B2
Warfield Yd WLSDN NW10 * 100 B2
Wargrave Av
SEVS/STOTM N15 68 B3
Wargrave Rd
RYLN/HDSTN HA2 78 C1
Warham Rd FSBYPK N4 67 G2
KTN/HRWW/WS HA3 43 F5
SAND/SEL CR2 211 J3
Warham St CMBW SE5 142 C1
Waring Cl ORP BR6 217 F4
Waring Dr ORP BR6 217 F4
Waring Rd SCUP DA14 186 D2
Waring St WNWD SE27 162 D6
Warkworth Gdns ISLW TW7 136 B1
Warkworth Rd TOTM N17 49 K3
Warland Rd
WOOL/PLUM SE18 147 J1
Warley Av BCTR RM8 74 B4
YEAD UB4 94 E5
Warley Rd CLAY IG5 54 A4
ED N9 36 E4
WFD IG8 53 F3
YEAD UB4 94 E5
Warley St BETH E2 105 F2

Warlingham Rd THHTH CR7 196 C1
Warlock Rd MV/WKIL W9 100 D3
Warlters Cl HOLWY N7 * 84 E2
Warlters Rd HOLWY N7 84 E2
Warltersville Rd ARCH N19 66 E4
Warming Cl CLPT E5 * 87 F1
Warmington Rd HNHL SE24 162 D1
Warmington St PLSTW E13 106 E3
Warminster Rd SNWD SE25 181 H5
Warminster Sq SNWD SE25 181 H5
Warminster Wy MTCM CR4 179 G4
Warmwell Av
CDALE/KGS NW9 45 G4
Warndon St
BERM/RHTH SE16 123 K4
Warneford Pl OXHEY WD19 27 J1
Warneford Rd
KTN/HRWW/WS HA3 43 K6
Warneford St HOM E9 86 D6
Warne Pl BFN/LL DA15 168 C1
Warner Av CHEAM SM3 193 H6
Warner Cl CDALE/KGS NW9 63 H4
EBAR EN4 21 J1
HPTN TW12 172 E1
HYS/HAR UB3 133 G1
SRTFD E15 88 C3
Warner Pl BETH E2 104 C1
Warner Rd BMLY BR1 183 J3
CEND/HSY/T N8 66 D1
CMBW SE5 142 D2
WALTH E17 69 G1
Warner St CLKNW EC1R 5 J7
Warner Ter POP/IOD E14 * 105 J4
Warner Yd CLKNW EC1R 5 J7
Warnford Rd ORP BR6 217 F3
Warnham Court Rd CAR SM5 209 K5
Warnham Rd
NFNCH/WDSPK N12 47 J1
Warple Ms ACT W3 * 118 B2
Warple Wy ACT W3 118 B2
SHB W12 118 B2
Warren Av BMLY BR1 183 H3
ORP BR6 217 F3
RCHPK/HAM TW10 137 J5
SAND/SEL CR2 213 F5
WAN E11 * 88 B1
Warren Cl BXLYHS DA6 149 H6
ED N9 37 F2
ESH/CLAY KT10 204 C2
WBLY HA9 61 K6
YEAD UB4 95 G4
Warren Ct CHARL SE7 126 B5
Warren Crs ED N9 36 B2
Warren Cutting
KUTN/CMB KT2 176 A3
Warrender Rd ARCH N19 84 C1
Warrender Wy RSLP HA4 58 E4
Warren Dr GFD/PVL UB6 96 B3
HCH RM12 93 J1
ORP BR6 217 H3
RSLP HA4 59 H4
Warren Dr North BRYLDS KT5 191 J5
Warren Dr South BRYLDS KT5 191 K5
The Warren Dr WAN E11 71 G4
Warren Flds STAN HA7 * 29 J6
Warren Gdns ORP BR6 217 G3
Warren La STAN HA7 29 G4
WOOL/PLUM SE18 127 G3
Warren Lane Ga
WOOL/PLUM SE18 127 G3
Warren Ms FITZ W1T 4 A7
Warren Pk KUTN/CMB KT2 175 K2
Warren Park Rd SUT SM1 209 H4
Warren Pond Rd CHING E4 38 D3
Warren Ri KUTN/CMB KT2 176 A4
Warren Rd BARK/HLT IG6 72 D2
BUSH WD23 28 C3
BXLYHS DA6 149 H6
CHING E4 38 A4
CRICK NW2 63 H6
CROY/NA CR0 197 F5
DART DA1 171 H5
HAYES BR2 199 K6
KUTN/CMB KT2 175 K2
LEY E10 88 A1
ORP BR6 217 F3
SCUP DA14 168 D5
WAN E11 71 G3
WHTN TW2 155 J1
WIM/MER SW19 178 D2
Warrens Shawe La EDGW HA8 30 D4
Warren St FITZ W1T 4 A7
The Warren BELMT SM2 209 H6
HEST TW5 134 E1
MNPK E12 89 J2
WPK KT4 207 F2
YEAD UB4 94 E5
Warren Wy EDGW HA8 44 D5
Warren Wood Cl HAYES BR2 199 K6
Warriner Dr ED N9 36 C5
Warriner Gdns BTSEA SW11 140 E2
Warrington Crs MV/WKIL W9 101 G3
Warrington Gdns
MV/WKIL W9 101 G3
Warrington Pl POP/IOD E14 * 125 F1
Warrington Rd BCTR RM8 73 K6
CROY/NA CR0 211 H1
HRW HA1 60 E2
RCHPK/HAM TW10 136 E6
Warrington Sq BCTR RM8 73 K6
Warrior Cl THMD SE28 127 K1
Warrior Sq MNPK E12 90 A2
Warsaw Cl RSLP HA4 77 F4
Warspite Rd
WOOL/PLUM SE18 126 D3
Warton Rd SRTFD E15 88 A6
Warwall EHAM E6 108 B5
Warwick Av EDGW HA8 30 D5
MV/WKIL W9 101 F3
RYLN/HDSTN HA2 77 K2
Warwick Chambers
KENS W8 * 119 K3
Warwick Cl BUSH WD23 28 E2
BXLY DA5 169 G2
EBAR EN4 21 H6
HPTN TW12 173 H3
ORP BR6 217 G1
Warwick Ct HHOL WC1V 11 H2
SURB KT6 191 F6
Warwick Crs BAY/PAD W2 101 G4
YEAD UB4 94 D3
Warwick Dene EA W5 117 F1
Warwick Dr PUT/ROE SW15 138 E4
Warwick Gdns FSBYPK N4 67 J2
IL IG1 72 B5
THDIT KT7 190 A2
THHTH CR7 * 196 B1
WKENS W14 119 J3
Warwick Gv BRYLDS KT5 191 G4
CLPT E5 68 D5
Warwick House St STJS SW1Y 10 D7
Warwick La STP EC4M 12 B3
Warwick Pde
KTN/HRWW/WS HA3 * 43 H5
Warwick Pl EA W5 116 E2
MV/WKIL W9 101 G4
THDIT KT7 * 190 B3
Warwick Pl North PIM SW1V * 16 A7
Warwick Rd BAR EN5 21 F5
CHING E4 51 J1
EA W5 117 F1
FBAR/BDGN N11 48 D2
HSLWW TW4 134 A4
KUT/HW KT1 174 D4
MNPK E12 89 J3
NWDGN UB2 114 E3
NWMAL KT3 175 K6
PGE/AN SE20 181 J6
SCUP DA14 186 C1
SRTFD E15 88 D3
SUT SM1 209 G3
THDIT KT7 190 A2
THHTH CR7 180 B6
UED N18 36 A6
WALTH E17 51 H4
WAN E11 71 F2
WDR/YW UB7 112 B1
WELL DA16 148 D4
WHTN TW2 155 K3
WKENS W14 119 J4
Warwick Rw WESTW SW1E 16 A4
Warwick Sq PIM SW1V 16 A7
STP EC4M * 12 B3
Warwick Square Ms
PIM SW1V 16 A7
Warwick St REGST W1B 10 B5
Warwick Ter WALTH E17 * 70 B2
WOOL/PLUM SE18 127 J6
Warwick Wy DART DA1 171 H4
PIM SW1V 16 A7
Warwick Yd STLK EC1Y * 6 D7
Washington Av MNPK E12 89 J2
Washington Cl BOW E3 105 K2
Washington Rd BARN SW13 138 D1
EHAM E6 89 G5
KUT/HW KT1 175 H5
SWFD E18 52 D5
WPK KT4 192 E6
Wastdale Rd FSTH SE23 164 A3
Watchfield Ct CHSWK W4 * 117 K5
The Watch
NFNCH/WDSPK N12 * 33 G6
Watcombe Rd SNWD SE25 197 J2
Waterbank Rd CAT SE6 164 E5
Waterbeach Rd DAGW RM9 91 J4
Water Brook La HDN NW4 64 A2
Watercress Pl IS N1 86 A5
Waterdale Rd ABYW SE2 128 B6
Waterer Ri WLGTN SM6 210 D4
Waterfall Cots
WIM/MER SW19 178 C2
Waterfall Rd FBAR/BDGN N11 34 B6
WIM/MER SW19 178 C2
Waterfall Ter TOOT SW17 178 D2
Waterfield Cl BELV DA17 129 H3
THMD SE28 128 C1
Waterfield Cots
MORT/ESHN SW14 * 137 J5
Waterfield Gdns SNWD SE25 197 F1
Waterford Rd FUL/PGN SW6 140 A1
Waterford Wy WLSDN NW10 81 K3
The Waterfront BORE WD6 29 H1
Water Gdns STAN HA7 43 H2
The Water Gdns BAY/PAD W2 8 C3
Watergate EMB EC4Y 12 A5
Watergate St DEPT SE8 124 D6
The Watergate OXHEY WD19 27 H4
Waterhall Av CHING E4 38 C6
Waterhall Cl WALTH E17 51 F4
Waterhead Cl ERITH DA8 150 B1
Waterhouse Cl HAMP NW3 83 H3
Wateridge Cl POP/IOD E14 124 D3
Wateringbury Cl
STMC/STPC BR5 186 C6
Water La CAMTN NW1 84 B5
ED N9 36 D3
GDMY/SEVK IG3 91 F1
KUT/HW KT1 174 E4
MON EC3R 13 G6
NWCR SE14 143 K1
PUR RM19 131 K4
SCUP DA14 169 G4
SRTFD E15 88 C4
TWK TW1 156 B3
Water Lily Cl NWDGN UB2 115 H2
Waterloo Br STHWK SE1 11 H6
TPL/STR WC2R 11 G6
Waterloo Cl
EBED/NFELT TW14 153 J3
HOM E9 86 E3
Waterloo Gdns BETH E2 104 E1
ROMW/RG RM7 75 F3
Waterloo Pl CAR SM5 * 209 K1
RCH/KEW TW9 117 H6
STJS SW1Y 10 C7
Waterloo Rd BARK/HLT IG6 54 C5
CRICK NW2 63 J6
EHAM E6 89 G5
FSTGT E7 88 D3
LEY E10 69 J4
ROMW/RG RM7 75 F2
STHWK SE1 11 H7
SUT SM1 209 H3
Waterloo Ter IS N1 85 H5
Waterlow Rd ARCH N19 66 C5
Waterman Cl OXHEY WD19 27 F1
Watermans Cl
KUTN/CMB KT2 * 175 F3
Watermans Ms EA W5 * 98 A6
Waterman Sq PGE/AN SE20 181 K3
Waterman St PUT/ROE SW15 139 G4
Waterman Wy WAP E1W 123 J1
Watermead
EBED/NFELT TW14 153 H3
Watermead La CAR SM5 194 E3
Watermeadow Cl ERITH DA8 150 E1
Watermeadow La
FUL/PGN SW6 140 B3
Watermead Rd CAT SE6 165 F6
Watermead Wy TOTM N17 50 D4
Watermens Sq PGE/AN SE20 * 181 K3
Water Ms PECK SE15 143 K5
Watermill Cl
RCHPK/HAM TW10 156 D5
Watermill La UED N18 50 A1
Water Mill Wy FELT TW13 154 E4
Watermill Wy
WIM/MER SW19 178 B4
Watermint Cl STMC/STPC BR5 202 E1
Watermint Quay
STNW/STAM N16 68 C4
Water Rd ALP/SUD HA0 80 B6
Watersedge HOR/WEW KT19 206 E2
Water's Edge FUL/PGN SW6 * 139 G2
Watersfield Wy EDGW HA8 43 K3
Waterside DART DA1 150 B6
WALTH E17 68 E3
Waterside Av BECK BR3 198 E2
Waterside Cl BARK IG11 91 G2
BERM/RHTH SE16 123 H2
BOW E3 87 H6
NTHLT UB5 95 K2
SURB KT6 191 F6
THMD SE28 128 A1
Waterside Ct LEW SE13 * 145 G5
Waterside Dr WOT/HER KT12 188 A2
Waterside Rd NWDGN UB2 115 F3
Waterside Wy TOOT SW17 160 B6
Watersmeet Wy THMD SE28 109 K5
Waterson St BETH E2 7 H4
Watersplash Cl KUT/HW KT1 175 F6
Watersplash La HEST TW5 114 A5
HYS/HAR UB3 113 K4
Waters Rd CAT SE6 165 H5
KUT/HW KT1 175 J5
Waters Sq KUT/HW KT1 175 J6
Water St TPL/STR WC2R 11 J5
Water Tower Hl CROY/NA CR0 211 K2
Water Tower Pl IS N1 5 K1
Waterway Av LEW SE13 144 E4
Waterworks La CLPT E5 69 F6
Waterworks Rd
BRXS/STRHM SW2 161 K1
Watery La HYS/HAR UB3 113 G5
NTHLT UB5 95 G1
RYNPK SW20 177 J5
STMC/STPC BR5 186 C2
Wates Wy MTCM CR4 194 E3
Wateville Rd TOTM N17 49 J4
Watford Cl BTSEA SW11 140 D2
Watford Heath OXHEY WD19 27 H2
Watford Heath Farm
OXHEY WD19 * 27 H2
Watford Rd BORE WD6 29 J1
CAN/RD E16 106 E4
HRW HA1 79 G1
NTHWD HA6 40 D3
Watford Wy HDN NW4 63 J1
MLHL NW7 31 F6
Watford Way (Barnet
By-Pass) MLHL NW7 45 H1
Watkin Rd WBLY HA9 80 D1
Watkinson Rd HOLWY N7 85 F4
Watling Av EDGW HA8 44 E4
Watling Ct STP EC4M 12 D4
Watling Farm Cl BORE WD6 29 J3
Watlings Cl CROY/NA CR0 198 B3
Watling St BXLYHS DA6 149 K6
PECK SE15 123 F6
STP EC4M 12 C4
Watlington Gv SYD SE26 182 B1
Watney Market WCHPL E1 104 D5
Watney Rd MORT/ESHN SW14 137 K4
Watneys Rd CROY/NA CR0 195 J2
Watney St WCHPL E1 104 D5
Watson Av CHEAM SM3 193 H6
EHAM E6 90 A5
Watson Cl STNW/STAM N16 85 K3
WIM/MER SW19 178 D2
Watson's Ms CAMTN NW1 8 D2
Watsons Rd WDGN N22 49 F4
Watson's St DEPT SE8 144 D1
Wattisfield Rd CLPT E5 86 E1
Watts Cl SEVS/STOTM N15 68 A2
Wattsdown Cl PLSTW E13 88 E6
Watts Gv BOW E3 105 J4
Watt's La CHST BR7 185 G4
TEDD TW11 174 B1
Watts Rd THDIT KT7 190 B4
Watts St PECK SE15 143 G2
WAP E1W 123 J1
Wat Tyler Rd GNWCH SE10 145 F3
Wauthier Cl PLMGR N13 49 H1
Wavell Dr BFN/LL DA15 167 K1
Wavel Ms KIL/WHAMP NW6 83 F5
Wavel Pl SYD SE26 163 G6
Wavendon Av CHSWK W4 118 A5
Waveney Av PECK SE15 143 J5
Waveney Cl WAP E1W 123 H1
Waverley Av BRYLDS KT5 191 J3
CHING E4 37 H6
SUT SM1 194 A6
WALTH E17 52 B6
WBLY HA9 80 B3
WHTN TW2 154 E3
Waverley Cl E/WMO/HCT KT8 189 F2
HAYES BR2 200 C2
HYS/HAR UB3 113 G4
Waverley Crs
WOOL/PLUM SE18 127 J6
Waverley Gdns BARK IG11 108 E1
BARK/HLT IG6 54 C5
EHAM E6 107 J4
NTHWD HA6 40 E4
Waverley Gv FNCH N3 46 B6
Waverley Pl FSBYPK N4 * 67 H5
STJWD NW8 2 A2
Waverley Rd CEND/HSY/T N8 66 D3
ENC/FH EN2 23 H5
EW KT17 207 K3
RAIN RM13 111 K2
RYLN/HDSTN HA2 59 J6
SNWD SE25 197 J1
STHL UB1 96 A6
SWFD E18 53 G4
TOTM N17 50 D3
WALTH E17 52 A6
WOOL/PLUM SE18 127 H5
Waverley Wy CAR SM5 209 J4
Waverton Rd
WAND/EARL SW18 160 B2
Waverton St MYFR/PICC W1J 9 J7
MYFR/PKLN W1K 9 H7
Wavertree Rd
BRXS/STRHM SW2 162 A3
SWFD E18 52 E5
Waxlow Crs STHL UB1 96 A5
Waxlow Rd WLSDN NW10 98 E1
Waxlow Wy NTHLT UB5 95 J3
Waxwell La PIN HA5 41 H6
Wayborne Gv RSLP HA4 58 A3
Waye Av HEST TW5 133 K2
Wayfarer Rd NTHLT UB5 95 J2
Wayford St BTSEA SW11 140 D3
Wayland Av HACK E8 86 C3
Waylands HYS/HAR UB3 94 B4
Waylen Gdns DART DA1 151 J3
Waylett Pl ALP/SUD HA0 * 79 K2
WNWD SE27 162 C5
Wayne Cl ORP BR6 217 F1
Wayneflete Pl ESH/CLAY KT10 204 A1
Wayneflete Tower Av
ESH/CLAY KT10 204 A1
Waynflete Av CROY/NA CR0 211 H1
Waynflete Sq NKENS W10 100 B6
Waynflete St
WAND/EARL SW18 160 B4
Wayside CROY/NA CR0 * 213 K4
GLDGN NW11 64 C5
MORT/ESHN SW14 137 K5
Wayside Av BUSH WD23 28 D1
Wayside Cl ROM RM1 57 H6
STHGT/OAK N14 34 C1
Wayside Ct TWK TW1 156 D1
Wayside Gdns DAGE RM10 92 C3
Wayside Gv ELTH/MOT SE9 166 E6
Wayside Ms GNTH/NBYPK IG2 72 A3
Weald Cl BERM/RHTH SE16 123 J5
HAYES BR2 200 D6
Weald La KTN/HRWW/WS HA3 42 D5
Weald Ri KTN/HRWW/WS HA3 43 F3
Weald Sq CLPT E5 * 68 D6
Wealdstone Rd CHEAM SM3 193 J6
The Weald CHST BR7 184 E2
Weald Wy ROMW/RG RM7 74 D3
YEAD UB4 94 C2
Wealdwood Gdns PIN HA5 42 B2
Weale Rd CHING E4 38 B5
Weardale Gdns ENC/FH EN2 23 K2
Weardale Rd LEW SE13 145 G5
Wearside Rd LEW SE13 144 E5
Weatherley Cl BOW E3 105 H4
Weaver Cl CROY/NA CR0 212 B2
EHAM E6 108 B6
Weavers Cl ISLW TW7 135 K5
Weaver's La STHWK SE1 19 H1
Weavers Ter FUL/PGN SW6 * 119 K6
Weaver St WCHPL E1 104 C3
Weavers Wy CAMTN NW1 84 D6
Weaver Wk WNWD SE27 162 C6
Webb Cl NKENS W10 100 A3
Webber Cl BORE WD6 29 K1
ERITH DA8 150 E1
Webber Rw STHWK SE1 17 K3
Webber St STHWK SE1 17 K2
Webb Est CLPT E5 * 68 C4
Webb Pl WLSDN NW10 99 H2
Webb Rd BKHTH/KID SE3 125 J6
Webbscroft Rd DAGE RM10 92 D2
Webbs Rd YEAD UB4 94 E2
Webb's Rd BTSEA SW11 140 E6
Webb St STHWK SE1 19 G5
Webster Gdns EA W5 116 E1
Webster Rd BERM/RHTH SE16 123 H3
WAN E11 88 A1
Wedderburn Rd BARK IG11 90 D6
HAMP NW3 83 H3
Wedgewood Cl NTHWD HA6 * 40 A3
Wedgwood Wk
KIL/WHAMP NW6 * 83 F3
Wedgwood Wy NRWD SE19 180 D3
Wedlake St NKENS W10 100 C3
Wedmore Av CLAY IG5 54 A4
Wedmore Gdns ARCH N19 66 E6
Wedmore Ms ARCH N19 84 D1
Wedmore Rd GFD/PVL UB6 96 D2
Wedmore St ARCH N19 84 D1
Weech Rd KIL/WHAMP NW6 82 E2
Weedington Rd KTTN NW5 84 A3
Weekley Sq BTSEA SW11 * 140 C4
Weigall Rd LEE/GVPK SE12 145 K5
Weighhouse St
MYFR/PKLN W1K 9 H5
Weighton Rd
KTN/HRWW/WS HA3 42 D4
PGE/AN SE20 181 J5
Weihurst Gdns SUT SM1 209 H3
Weimar St PUT/ROE SW15 139 H4
Weirdale Av TRDG/WHET N20 33 K4
Weir Hall Av UED N18 49 K2
Weir Hall Gdns UED N18 49 K1
Weir Hall Rd UED N18 49 K1
Weir Rd BAL SW12 161 H3
WIM/MER SW19 160 A5
Weirside Gdns WDR/YW UB7 112 A1
Weirs Pas CAMTN NW1 4 D4
Weiss Rd PUT/ROE SW15 139 G4
Welbeck Av BFN/LL DA15 168 B3
BMLY BR1 165 K6
YEAD UB4 95 F3
Welbeck Cl EW KT17 207 J5
NWMAL KT3 192 C2
Welbeck Rd CAR SM5 194 D4
EBAR EN4 33 H1
EHAM E6 107 H2
RYLN/HDSTN HA2 60 B5
SUT SM1 194 C6
Welbeck St CAVSQ/HST W1G 9 H2
Welbeck Vls WCHMH N21 * 35 J3
Welbeck Wy CAVSQ/HST W1G 9 J3
Welby Ct PLSTW E13 107 G1
Welby St CMBW SE5 142 C2
Welch Pl PIN HA5 * 41 G4
Weldon Cl RSLP HA4 77 F4
Weldon Dr E/WMO/HCT KT8 188 E1
Weld Pl FBAR/BDGN N11 48 B1
Welfare Rd SRTFD E15 88 C5
Welford Cl CLPT E5 87 F1
Welford Pl WIM/MER SW19 159 H6
Welham Rd TOOT SW17 179 F1
Welhouse Rd CAR SM5 194 D5
Wellacre Rd
KTN/HRWW/WS HA3 61 H3
Wellan Cl BFN/LL DA15 148 C6
Welland Gdns GFD/PVL UB6 97 F1
Welland Ms WAP E1W 123 H1
Wellands Cl BMLY BR1 184 E5
Welland St GNWCH SE10 125 F6
Well Ap BAR EN5 20 A6
Wellbrook Rd ORP BR6 216 A2
Wellby Cl ED N9 36 C3
Well Cl RSLP HA4 77 J1
STRHM/NOR SW16 162 A6
Wellclose Sq WCHPL E1 104 C6
Wellclose St WCHPL E1 104 C6
Wellcome Av DART DA1 151 H5
Well Cottage Cl WAN E11 71 G4
Well Ct STP EC4M 12 D4
Welldon Crs HRW HA1 60 E3
Weller Ms HAYES BR2 200 A1
Weller St STHWK SE1 18 C2
Wellesley Av HMSMTH W6 118 E3
NTHWD HA6 40 D1
Wellesley Cl CHARL SE7 * 126 B5
Wellesley Ct MV/WKIL W9 101 G2
Wellesley Court Rd
CROY/NA CR0 * 196 E6
Wellesley Crs WHTN TW2 155 K4
Wellesley Gv CROY/NA CR0 196 E6
Wellesley Pde WHTN TW2 * 155 K5
Wellesley Park Ms
ENC/FH EN2 23 H3
Wellesley Pl CAMTN NW1 * 4 C5
KTTN NW5 84 A3
Wellesley Rd BELMT SM2 209 G4
CHSWK W4 117 H5
CROY/NA CR0 196 D5
HRW HA1 60 E2
IL IG1 72 B6
KTTN NW5 84 A3
WALTH E17 69 J3
WAN E11 70 E2
WHTN TW2 155 K5
WOOL/PLUM SE18 147 F1
Wellesley St WCHPL E1 105 F4
Wellesley Ter IS N1 6 D4
Wellfield Av MUSWH N10 48 B6
Wellfield Gdns CAR SM5 209 J6
Wellfield Rd
STRHM/NOR SW16 161 K6
Wellfit St HNHL SE24 142 C4
Wellgarth GFD/PVL UB6 79 H4
Wellgarth Rd GLDGN NW11 65 F5
Well Gv TRDG/WHET N20 33 G3
Well Hall Pde ELTH/MOT SE9 146 E5
Well Hall Rd ELTH/MOT SE9 146 E5
Wellhouse La BAR EN5 20 A5
Wellhouse Rd BECK BR3 198 C1
Wellhurst Cl ORP BR6 217 F5
Welling High St WELL DA16 148 C4
Wellington Av BFN/LL DA15 168 B1
CHING E4 37 J4
ED N9 36 D5
HSLW TW3 135 F6
PIN HA5 41 K4
SEVS/STOTM N15 68 C3
WPK KT4 208 A1
Wellington Cl DAGE RM10 92 E5
NTGHL W11 100 E5
NWCR SE14 144 A2
OXHEY WD19 27 J5
Wellington Crs NWMAL KT3 175 K6
Wellington Dr DAGE RM10 92 E5
Wellington Gdns CHARL SE7 126 B5
WHTN TW2 155 J6
Wellington Gv GNWCH SE10 145 G1
Wellington Ms CHARL SE7 126 B6
EDUL SE22 143 H5
HOLWY N7 85 F4
STRHM/NOR SW16 161 J5
Wellington Pde
BFN/LL DA15 * 148 B6
Wellington Park Est
CRICK NW2 * 63 J6
Wellington Pas WAN E11 70 E2
Wellington Pl EFNCH N2 * 65 J2
STJWD NW8 2 B4
Wellington Rd BELV DA17 129 G5
BXLY DA5 168 E1
CROY/NA CR0 196 C4
DART DA1 171 F1
EA W5 116 D4
EBED/NFELT TW14 133 H6
EHAM E6 89 K6
EN EN1 36 A2
FSTGT E7 88 D2
HAYES BR2 200 B1
HPTN TW12 155 J6
KTN/HRWW/WS HA3 42 E6
LEY E10 69 G5
NKENS W10 * 100 B2
PIN HA5 41 K4
STJWD NW8 2 B3
STMC/STPC BR5 202 C3
WALTH E17 51 G6
WAN E11 70 E2
WIM/MER SW19 159 K4
Wellington Rd North
HSLWW TW4 134 E4
Wellington Rd South
HSLWW TW4 134 E5
Wellington Rw BETH E2 7 K4
Wellington Sq CHEL SW3 120 E5
IS N1 * 84 E6
Wellington St COVGDN WC2E 11 F5
WOOL/PLUM SE18 127 F4
Wellington Ter BAY/PAD W2 * 100 E6
CEND/HSY/T N8 * 49 G6
HRW HA1 60 D5
WAP E1W * 123 J1

Wellington Wy BOW E3 105 J2
Welling Wy ELTH/MOT SE9 147 J4
WELL DA16 147 K4
Well La MORT/ESHN SW14 137 K6
Wellmeadow Rd CAT SE6 165 H3
HNWL W7 116 B4
LEW SE13 165 H1
Well Rd BAR EN5 20 A6
HAMP NW3 83 H1
Wells Cl NTHLT UB5 95 G2
SAND/SEL CR2 212 A3
Wells Dr CDALE/KGS NW9 63 F5
Wells Gdns IL IG1 71 J4
RAIN RM13 93 H4
Wells House Rd WLSDN NW10 99 G4
Wellside Cl BAR EN5 20 A5
Wellside Gdns
MORT/ESHN SW14 137 K5
Wells Ms FITZ W1T * 10 B2
Wellsmoor Gdns BMLY BR1 185 F6
Wells Park Rd SYD SE26 163 H5
Wells Pl CMBW SE5 143 F1
WAND/EARL SW18 160 B2
Wellspring Crs WBLY HA9 62 D6
Wellspring Ms SYD SE26 163 J5
Wells Ri STJWD NW8 2 E1
Wells Rd BMLY BR1 184 E5
SHB W12 119 F2
Wells Sq FSBYW WC1X 5 G5
Wells St FITZ W1T 10 B3
GTPST W1W 10 A2
Wellstead Av ED N9 36 E2
Wellstead Rd EHAM E6 108 A1
Wells Ter FSBYPK N4 67 G6
The Wells STHGT/OAK N14 34 D2
Well St HOM E9 86 E5
SRTFD E15 88 C4
Wells Wy SKENS SW7 14 A4
WALW SE17 122 E6
Well Wk HAMP NW3 83 H1
Wellwood Rd GDMY/SEVK IG3 73 G5
Welsford St STHWK SE1 123 H5
Welsh Cl PLSTW E13 106 E2
Welshpool St HACK E8 * 86 C6
Welshside CDALE/KGS NW9 * 63 G2
Welstead Wy CHSWK W4 118 C3
Weltje Rd HMSMTH W6 118 D5
Welton Rd WOOL/PLUM SE18 147 K1
Welwyn Av EBED/NFELT TW14 153 J1
Welwyn St BETH E2 104 E2
Welwyn Wy YEAD UB4 94 C3
Wembley Hill Rd WBLY HA9 80 B3
Wembley Park Dr WBLY HA9 80 B2
Wembley Rd HPTN TW12 173 F4
Wembley Wy WBLY HA9 80 D4
Wemborough Rd STAN HA7 43 H4
Wembury Ms HGT N6 66 B4
Wembury Rd HGT N6 66 B4
Wemyss Rd BKHTH/KID SE3 145 J3
Wendela Ct HRW HA1 78 E1
Wendell Rd SHB W12 118 C2
Wendling Rd SUT SM1 194 C5
Wendon St BOW E3 87 H6
Wendover Cl YEAD UB4 95 H3
Wendover Dr NWMAL KT3 192 C3
Wendover Rd ELTH/MOT SE9 146 C4
HAYES BR2 200 A1
WLSDN NW10 99 H1
Wendover Wy BUSH WD23 28 C1
ORP BR6 202 B3
WELL DA16 148 B6
Wendy Cl EN EN1 36 B1
Wendy Wy ALP/SUD HA0 80 A6
Wenlock Gdns HDN NW4 * 63 J1
Wenlock Rd EDGW HA8 44 D2
IS N1 6 C3
Wenlock St IS N1 6 D3
Wennington Rd BOW E3 105 F1
RAIN RM13 111 K4
Wensley Av WFD IG8 52 E3
Wensley Cl CRW RM5 56 C1
ELTH/MOT SE9 166 E1
FBAR/BDGN N11 48 A2
Wensleydale Av CLAY IG5 53 J5
Wensleydale Gdns
HPTN TW12 173 G3
Wensleydale Rd HPTN TW12 173 F4
Wensley Rd UED N18 50 D2
Wentland Cl CAT SE6 165 G4
Wentland Rd CAT SE6 165 G4
Wentworth Av FNCH N3 46 E3
Wentworth Cl ASHF TW15 152 E6
FNCH N3 47 F3
HAYES BR2 * 199 K6
MRDN SM4 193 K4
ORP BR6 216 E3
SURB KT6 190 E6
THMD SE28 109 K5
Wentworth Crs HYS/HAR UB3 113 G3
PECK SE15 143 H1
Wentworth Dr DART DA1 170 D2
OXHEY WD19 41 H1
PIN HA5 58 E2
Wentworth Gdns PLMGR N13 35 H5
Wentworth Hl WBLY HA9 62 B5
Wentworth Ms BOW E3 105 G3
Wentworth Pk FNCH N3 47 F3
Wentworth Pl STAN HA7 * 43 H2
Wentworth Rd BAR EN5 20 B3
CROY/NA CR0 196 B4
GLDGN NW11 64 D3
MNPK E12 89 H2
NWDGN UB2 114 B4
Wentworth St WCHPL E1 13 J3
Wentworth Wy PIN HA5 59 H1
RAIN RM13 111 K2
Wenvoe Av BXLYHN DA7 149 J3
Wepham Cl YEAD UB4 95 H4
Wernbrook St
WOOL/PLUM SE18 127 H6
Werndee Rd SNWD SE25 197 H1
Werneth Hall Rd CLAY IG5 53 K6
Werrington St CAMTN NW1 4 B3
Werter Rd PUT/ROE SW15 139 H5
Wesleyan Pl KTTN NW5 84 B2
Wesley Av CAN/RD E16 125 K1
HSLW TW3 134 D3
WLSDN NW10 99 F2
Wesley Cl HOLWY N7 67 F6
LBTH SE11 122 C5
RYLN/HDSTN HA2 60 C6
STMC/STPC BR5 186 D6
WALW SE17 18 B7
Wesley Rd HYS/HAR UB3 94 E6
LEY E10 70 A4
WLSDN NW10 80 E6
Wesley Sq NTGHL W11 100 B5
Wesley St CAVSQ/HST W1G 9 H2
Wessex Av WIM/MER SW19 177 K5
Wessex Cl GDMY/SEVK IG3 72 E3
KUT/HW KT1 175 J4
THDIT KT7 190 A6
Wessex Ct BECK BR3 * 182 B4
Wessex Dr ERITH DA8 150 B3
PIN HA5 41 J3
Wessex Gdns GLDGN NW11 64 C5
Wessex La GFD/PVL UB6 96 D1
Wessex St BETH E2 104 E2
Wessex Ter MTCM CR4 * 194 D2
Wessex Wk RDART DA2 170 A4
Wessex Wy GLDGN NW11 64 C4
Wesson Md CMBW SE5 * 142 D1
Westacott YEAD UB4 94 C4
Westacott Cl ARCH N19 66 D5
West Ap STMC/STPC BR5 201 H2
West Arbour St WCHPL E1 104 E5
West Av FNCH N3 46 E2
HDN NW4 64 B2
HYS/HAR UB3 94 D6
PIN HA5 59 K3
STHL UB1 95 K6
WALTH E17 69 K2
WLGTN SM6 210 E3
West Avenue Rd WALTH E17 69 J1
West Bank BARK IG11 90 B6
ENC/FH EN2 23 J4
STNW/STAM N16 68 A4
Westbank Rd HPTN TW12 173 H2
West Barnes La NWMAL KT3 192 D2
RYNPK SW20 176 E6
Westbeech Rd WDGN N22 49 G6
Westbere Dr STAN HA7 43 K1
Westbere Rd CRICK NW2 82 C2
Westbourne Av ACT W3 99 F5
CHEAM SM3 193 H6
Westbourne Cl YEAD UB4 95 G3
Westbourne Crs BAY/PAD W2 8 A5
Westbourne Crescent Ms
BAY/PAD W2 8 A5
Westbourne Dr FSTH SE23 164 A3
Westbourne Gdns
BAY/PAD W2 101 F5
Westbourne Ga BAY/PAD W2 8 B5
Westbourne Gv BAY/PAD W2 100 E5
NTGHL W11 100 E5
Westbourne Grove Ms
NTGHL W11 * 100 E5
Westbourne Grove Ter
BAY/PAD W2 101 F5
Westbourne Park Rd
BAY/PAD W2 100 E5
Westbourne Pl ED N9 36 D5
Westbourne Rd BXLYHN DA7 148 E1
CROY/NA CR0 197 G3
FELT TW13 153 J5
HOLWY N7 85 F4
SYD SE26 182 A2
Westbourne St BAY/PAD W2 8 A5
Westbourne Ter BAY/PAD W2 101 G4
Westbourne Terrace Ms
BAY/PAD W2 101 G5
Westbourne Terrace Rd
BAY/PAD W2 101 G4
Westbridge Cl SHB W12 118 D1
Westbridge Rd BTSEA SW11 140 C2
Westbrook Av HPTN TW12 172 E3
Westbrook Cl EBAR EN4 21 H4
Westbrook Crs EBAR EN4 21 H4
Westbrook Dr
STMC/STPC BR5 202 E5
Westbrooke Crs WELL DA16 148 D4
Westbrooke Rd BFN/LL DA15 167 J4
WELL DA16 148 D4
Westbrook Rd
BKHTH/KID SE3 145 K2
HEST TW5 134 E1
THHTH CR7 180 E4
Westbury Ar WDGN N22 * 49 H6
Westbury Av ALP/SUD HA0 80 A5
ESH/CLAY KT10 205 F4
SEVS/STOTM N15 49 H6
STHL UB1 96 A3
WDGN N22 49 H5
Westbury Cl RSLP HA4 58 E4
Westbury Gv
NFNCH/WDSPK N12 46 E2
Westbury La BKHH IG9 39 G4
Westbury Lodge Cl PIN HA5 41 H6
Westbury Pl BTFD TW8 116 E6
Westbury Rd ALP/SUD HA0 80 A5
BARK IG11 90 D6
BECK BR3 182 B6
BKHH IG9 39 G3
BMLY BR1 184 C4
CROY/NA CR0 196 E3
EA W5 98 A5
FBAR/BDGN N11 48 E2
FELT TW13 154 C3
FSTGT E7 89 F3
IL IG1 72 A6
NFNCH/WDSPK N12 46 E2
NTHWD HA6 26 C6
NWMAL KT3 192 A1
PGE/AN SE20 182 A4
WALTH E17 69 J1
Westbury Ter FSTGT E7 89 F4
West Carriage Dr
BAY/PAD W2 14 B1
West Central St
LSQ/SEVD WC2H 10 E3
West Chantry
KTN/HRWW/WS HA3 42 B4
Westchester Dr HDN NW4 46 B6
Westcliffe Vls KUT/HW KT1 * 175 G5
West Cl ASHF TW15 152 B6
EBAR EN4 22 A5
ED N9 36 B5
GFD/PVL UB6 96 C1
RAIN RM13 111 K3
WBLY HA9 62 B5
Westcombe Av CROY/NA CR0 195 K3
Westcombe Dr BAR EN5 20 E6
Westcombe Hl
BKHTH/KID SE3 125 K6
Westcombe Lodge Dr
YEAD UB4 94 B4
Westcombe Park Rd
BKHTH/KID SE3 125 H6
West Common Rd HAYES BR2 199 K6
HAYES BR2 215 F2
Westcoombe Av RYNPK SW20 176 C4
Westcote Ri RSLP HA4 58 A4
Westcote Rd
STRHM/NOR SW16 179 H1
Westcott Cl BMLY BR1 200 D2
CROY/NA CR0 213 K6
SEVS/STOTM N15 68 B3
Westcott Crs HNWL W7 96 E4
Westcott House
POP/IOD E14 * 105 J6
Westcott Rd WALW SE17 122 C6
West Ct ALP/SUD HA0 61 J6
Westcroft Cl CRICK NW2 82 C2
PEND EN3 24 E1
Westcroft Gdns MRDN SM4 177 J6
Westcroft Ms HMSMTH W6 * 118 D4
Westcroft Rd CAR SM5 210 A2
Westcroft Sq HMSMTH W6 118 D4
Westcroft Wy CRICK NW2 82 C2
West Cromwell Rd ECT SW5 119 K4
West Cross Route NTGHL W11 119 G1
West Cross Wy BTFD TW8 116 C6
Westdale Rd
WOOL/PLUM SE18 127 G6
Westdean Av LEE/GVPK SE12 166 A3
Westdean Cl
WAND/EARL SW18 160 A1
Westdown Rd CAT SE6 164 D2
SRTFD E15 88 A2
West Drayton Park Av
WDR/YW UB7 112 B3
West Drayton Rd
UX/CGN UB8 94 A4
UX/CGN UB8 94 A4
West Dr BELMT SM2 208 B6
KTN/HRWW/WS HA3 42 D2
STRHM/NOR SW16 161 G6
West Drive Gdns
KTN/HRWW/WS HA3 42 D2
West Eaton Pl BGVA SW1W 15 G6
West Eaton Place Ms
KTBR SW1X 15 G6
West Ella Rd WLSDN NW10 81 G5
West End Av LEY E10 70 A2
PIN HA5 59 H1
West End Cl WLSDN NW10 80 E5
West End Ct PIN HA5 * 59 H1
West End Gdns NTHLT UB5 95 G1
West End La BAR EN5 20 B5
HYS/HAR UB3 133 F1
KIL/WHAMP NW6 82 E6
PIN HA5 59 H1
West End Rd NTHLT UB5 77 G5
RSLP HA4 76 D1
STHL UB1 114 D1
Westerdale Rd GNWCH SE10 125 K5
Westerfield Rd
SEVS/STOTM N15 * 68 B2
Westergate Rd ABYW SE2 129 F6
Westerham Av ED N9 35 K5
UED N18 35 K5
Westerham Dr BFN/LL DA15 168 D1
Westerham Rd HAYES BR2 215 H4
LEY E10 69 K3
Westerley Crs SYD SE26 * 182 C1
Western Av ACT W3 98 C3
DAGE RM10 92 E4
EA W5 98 A2
GFD/PVL UB6 78 A6
GFD/PVL UB6 97 F2
GLDGN NW11 64 B3
RSLP HA4 77 F5
Western Ct FNCH N3 * 46 E2
Western Gdns EA W5 98 C6
Western Gtwy CAN/RD E16 106 E6
Western La BAL SW12 161 F2
Western Man BAR EN5 * 21 F6
Western Ms MV/WKIL W9 100 D3
Western Pde BAR EN5 20 E6
Western Pl BERM/RHTH SE16 123 K2
Western Rd BRXN/ST SW9 142 B4
EA W5 97 K6
EFNCH N2 47 K6
MTCM CR4 178 D4
NWDGN UB2 114 B4
PLSTW E13 89 F6
ROM RM1 75 G2
SUT SM1 208 E3
WALTH E17 70 A2
WDGN N22 49 F5
WLSDN NW10 98 E3
Western Ter HMSMTH W6 * 118 D5
Western Vw HYS/HAR UB3 113 J2
Westernville Gdns
GNTH/NBYPK IG2 72 C4
Western Wy BAR EN5 32 E1
THMD SE28 127 J3
Westferry Circ POP/IOD E14 124 D1
Westferry Rd POP/IOD E14 124 D3
Westfield Cl CDALE/KGS NW9 44 E6
FUL/PGN SW6 * 140 B1
PEND EN3 25 G4
SUT SM1 208 D2
WBPTN SW10 140 B1
Westfield Dr
KTN/HRWW/WS HA3 61 K2
Westfield Gdns CHDH RM6 73 J3
KTN/HRWW/WS HA3 61 K1
Westfield Pk PIN HA5 41 K3
Westfield Park Dr WFD IG8 53 J2
Westfield Rd BECK BR3 182 C5
BXLYHN DA7 149 K4
CROY/NA CR0 196 C6
DAGW RM9 92 A2
MLHL NW7 31 F5
MTCM CR4 178 D5
SURB KT6 190 E2
SUT SM1 208 D2
WEA W13 116 B1
WOT/HER KT12 188 D4
Westfields BARN SW13 138 C4
Westfields Av BARN SW13 138 B4
Westfields Rd ACT W3 98 D4
Westfield St
WOOL/PLUM SE18 126 C3
Westfield Wy RSLP HA4 76 C1
WCHPL E1 105 G2
West Gdns TOOT SW17 178 D2
WAP E1W 104 D6
West Ga EA W5 98 A2
Westgate Est
EBED/NFELT TW14 * 152 E3
Westgate Rd BECK BR3 183 F4
DART DA1 171 G1
SNWD SE25 197 J1
Westgate St HACK E8 86 D6
Westgate Ter WBPTN SW10 120 A5
Westglade Ct
KTN/HRWW/WS HA3 61 K2
West Green Pl GFD/PVL UB6 78 D6
West Green Rd
SEVS/STOTM N15 67 H1
West Gv GNWCH SE10 145 F2
WFD IG8 53 G2
Westgrove La GNWCH SE10 145 F2
West Halkin St KTBR SW1X 15 G4
West Hallowes ELTH/MOT SE9 166 C3
West Ham La SRTFD E15 88 B5
West Hampstead Ms
KIL/WHAMP NW6 83 F4
West Harding St
FLST/FETLN EC4A * 11 K3
West Hatch Mnr RSLP HA4 58 D5
Westhay Gdns
MORT/ESHN SW14 137 J6
West Heath Av GLDGN NW11 64 E5
West Heath Cl DART DA1 * 170 C1
HAMP NW3 82 E1
West Heath Dr GLDGN NW11 64 E5
West Heath Gdns HAMP NW3 64 E6
West Heath Rd ABYW SE2 128 E6
DART DA1 170 C1
HAMP NW3 64 E6
HAMP NW3 83 G1
West Hl DART DA1 171 G1
PUT/ROE SW15 159 H1
RYLN/HDSTN HA2 60 E6
SAND/SEL CR2 212 A6
WAND/EARL SW18 139 K6
WBLY HA9 62 B5
WIM/MER SW19 159 G2
West Hill Dr DART DA1 171 F1
Westhill Pk HGT N6 65 K6
West Hill Ri DART DA1 171 G1
West Hill Rd
WAND/EARL SW18 159 J1
West Hill Wy TRDG/WHET N20 33 F3
Westholm GLDGN NW11 65 F1
West Holme ERITH DA8 149 K2
Westholme ORP BR6 201 K4
Westholme Gdns RSLP HA4 58 E5
Westhorne Av ELTH/MOT SE9 166 B1
LEE/GVPK SE12 165 K2
Westhorpe Gdns HDN NW4 46 A6
Westhorpe Rd
PUT/ROE SW15 139 F4
West House Cl
WIM/MER SW19 159 H3
Westhurst Dr CHST BR7 185 G1
West India Av POP/IOD E14 124 D1
West India Dock Rd
POP/IOD E14 105 K6
Westlake Cl PLMGR N13 35 G5
YEAD UB4 95 J3
Westland Cl
STWL/WRAY TW19 * 152 B1
Westland Dr HAYES BR2 199 J6
Westland Pl FSBYE EC1V 6 E4
Westlands Cl HYS/HAR UB3 113 K4
Westlands Ter BAL SW12 161 H1
Westlea Rd HNWL W7 116 B3
Westleigh Av PUT/ROE SW15 139 F6
Westleigh Dr BMLY BR1 184 D5
Westleigh Gdns EDGW HA8 44 C4
West Links ALP/SUD HA0 97 K2
Westlinton Cl MLHL NW7 46 C2
West Lodge Av ACT W3 117 H1
West Lodge Ct ACT W3 * 117 H1
Westmacott Dr
EBED/NFELT TW14 153 J2
West Ml KENS W8 * 119 K1
West Malling Wy HCH RM12 93 K3
West Md HOR/WEW KT19 207 G4
Westmead PUT/ROE SW15 158 E2
West Md RSLP HA4 77 G2
Westmead Rd SUT SM1 209 H2
Westmede BARK/HLT IG6 54 C2
Westmere Dr MLHL NW7 31 F5
West Mersea Cl CAN/RD E16 126 A1
West Ms PIM SW1V 15 K7
TOTM N17 * 50 D3
Westminster Av THHTH CR7 180 C5
Westminster Br WHALL SW1A 17 F3
Westminster Bridge Rd
WHALL SW1A 17 F3
Westminster Cl
EBED/NFELT TW14 153 K3
TEDD TW11 174 B1
Westminster Dr PLMGR N13 48 E1
Westminster Gdns BARK IG11 108 E1
BARK/HLT IG6 54 D5
CHING E4 38 C3
Westminster Rd ED N9 36 D3
HNWL W7 115 K1
SUT SM1 194 C6
Westmoat Cl BECK BR3 183 F3
Westmont Rd ESH/CLAY KT10 189 K6
Westmoor Gdns PEND EN3 25 F3
Westmoor Rd PEND EN3 25 F3
Westmoor St CHARL SE7 126 C4
Westmoreland Av WELL DA16 147 K4
Westmoreland Dr BELMT SM2 209 F6
Westmoreland Pl BMLY BR1 * 183 K6
EA W5 * 97 K4
PIM SW1V * 121 G5
Westmoreland Rd
BARN SW13 138 C2
HAYES BR2 199 H2
KTN/HRWW/WS HA3 62 B1
WALW SE17 122 E6
WWKM BR4 199 H2
Westmoreland St
CAVSQ/HST W1G 9 H2
Westmoreland Ter
PGE/AN SE20 * 181 J3
PIM SW1V 121 G5
Westmorland Cl MNPK E12 71 H6
TWK TW1 156 C1
Westmorland Rd HRW HA1 60 B2
WALTH E17 69 J3
Westmorland Wy MTCM CR4 195 J1
Westmount Cl WPK KT4 193 F5
Westmount Ct EA W5 * 98 B4
Westmount Rd
ELTH/MOT SE9 146 E4
West Oak BECK BR3 183 G4
Westoe Rd ED N9 36 D4
Weston Av E/WMO/HCT KT8 188 D1
THDIT KT7 189 K4
Weston Dr STAN HA7 43 H4
Weston Gdns ISLW TW7 135 J2
Weston Gn DAGW RM9 92 A2
THDIT KT7 189 K6
Weston Green Rd
ESH/CLAY KT10 189 J5
Weston Gv BMLY BR1 183 J3
Weston Pk CEND/HSY/T N8 66 E3
KUT/HW KT1 175 F5
THDIT KT7 189 K5
Weston Park Cl THDIT KT7 * 189 K5
Weston Ri FSBYW WC1X 5 H4
Weston Rd BMLY BR1 183 J4
CHSWK W4 117 K3
DAGW RM9 92 A2
ENC/FH EN2 23 K3
THDIT KT7 189 K5
Weston St STHWK SE1 19 F4
Weston Wk HACK E8 86 D5
Westover Cl BELMT SM2 209 F6
Westover Hl HAMP NW3 64 E6
Westover Rd
WAND/EARL SW18 160 B1
Westow Hl NRWD SE19 181 F2
Westow St NRWD SE19 181 F2
West Pk ELTH/MOT SE9 166 D4
West Park Av RCH/KEW TW9 137 H2
West Park Cl CHDH RM6 73 K2
HEST TW5 114 E6
West Park Rd NWDGN UB2 115 H1
RCH/KEW TW9 137 H2
West Parkside GNWCH SE10 125 H2
West Pl NWDGN UB2 * 115 G4
WIM/MER SW19 177 F1
Westpole Av EBAR EN4 22 B5
Westport Rd PLSTW E13 107 F3
Westport St WCHPL E1 105 F5
West Poultry Av FARR EC1M 12 A2
West Quarters SHB W12 99 J5
West Quay Dr YEAD UB4 95 J4
West Ridge Gdns
GFD/PVL UB6 96 C1
West Ri BAY/PAD W2 * 8 D5
West Rd CHDH RM6 74 A3
CHEL SW3 120 E6
CLAP SW4 141 J6
EA W5 98 A4
EBAR EN4 34 A3
EBED/NFELT TW14 153 G2
KUTN/CMB KT2 175 K4
ROMW/RG RM7 75 F4
SRTFD E15 88 D6
TOTM N17 50 D2
WDR/YW UB7 112 C3
West Rw NKENS W10 100 C3
Westrow Dr BARK IG11 91 G3
Westrow Gdns
GDMY/SEVK IG3 73 F6
West Sheen V RCH/KEW TW9 137 G5
Westside HDN NW4 45 K5
West Side Common
WIM/MER SW19 177 F1
West Smithfield STBT EC1A 12 A2
West Sq LBTH SE11 18 A5
West St BETH E2 104 D1
BMLY BR1 183 K4
BXLYHN DA7 149 G5
CAR SM5 209 K1
CROY/NA CR0 211 J2
ERITH DA8 130 A4
HRW HA1 60 D5
LSQ/SEVD WC2H 10 D4
SUT SM1 209 F3
WALTH E17 69 K2
WAN E11 88 C1
West Street La CAR SM5 209 K2
West Street Pl
CROY/NA CR0 * 211 J2
West Temple Sheen
MORT/ESHN SW14 137 J6
West Tenter St WCHPL E1 13 K4
West Ter BFN/LL DA15 * 167 K3
West Towers PIN HA5 59 H3
West Vw EBED/NFELT TW14 153 F3
Westview HNWL W7 96 E5
Westview Cl NKENS W10 100 A5
WLSDN NW10 81 H3
Westview Ct BORE WD6 29 K1
Westview Crs ED N9 36 A2
Westview Dr WFD IG8 53 H5
West View Gdns BORE WD6 29 K1
West View Rd DART DA1 171 J1
Westville Rd SHB W12 118 D2
THDIT KT7 190 B4
West Wk EBAR EN4 34 A3
HYS/HAR UB3 113 K1
Westward Rd CHING E4 51 H1
Westward Wy
KTN/HRWW/WS HA3 62 A3
West Warwick Pl PIM SW1V * 16 A7
West Wy CROY/NA CR0 198 B6
EDGW HA8 44 D2
HEST TW5 134 E2
PIN HA5 41 H6
RSLP HA4 58 D5
STMC/STPC BR5 201 J2
UED N18 35 K6
WLSDN NW10 81 F2
WWKM BR4 199 G3
Westway NKENS W10 100 D4

RYNPK SW20 192 E1
SHB W12 99 J6
Westway Cl RYNPK SW20 176 E6
West Way Gdns CROY/NA CR0 198 A6
Westways HOR/WEW KT19 207 H2
Westwell Cl STMC/STPC BR5 202 E5
Westwell Rd
STRHM/NOR SW16 179 K2
Westwell Road Ap
STRHM/NOR SW16 179 K2
Westwick Gdns HMSMTH W6 119 G2
HSLWW TW4 134 A3
Westwood Av NRWD SE19 180 D4
RYLN/HDSTN HA2 78 B2
Westwood Cl BMLY BR1 184 C6
ESH/CLAY KT10 204 C1
Westwood Gdns BARN SW13 138 C4
Westwood Hl SYD SE26 181 H1
Westwood La WELL DA16 148 B5
Westwood Pk FSTH SE23 163 J2
Westwood Pl SYD SE26 * 181 H1
Westwood Rd BARN SW13 138 C4
GDMY/SEVK IG3 73 F5
West Woodside BXLY DA5 169 F3
Wetheral Dr STAN HA7 43 H4
Wetherby Cl NTHLT UB5 78 B4
Wetherby Gdns ECT SW5 120 B4
Wetherby Ms ECT SW5 120 A5
Wetherby Pl ECT SW5 120 B4
Wetherby Rd ENC/FH EN2 23 J2
Wetherby Wy CHSGTN KT9 206 A5
Wetherden St WALTH E17 69 H4
Wetherell Rd HOM E9 87 F6
Wetherill Rd MUSWH N10 48 A4
Wexford Rd BAL SW12 160 E2
Weybourne St
WAND/EARL SW18 160 B4
Weybridge Ct
BERM/RHTH SE16 * 123 J5
Weybridge Rd THHTH CR7 196 B1
Wey Ct HOR/WEW KT19 206 E2
Weydown Cl WIM/MER SW19 159 H3
Weyhill Rd WCHPL E1 * 104 C5
Weylond Rd BCTR RM8 92 B1
Weyman Rd BKHTH/KID SE3 146 B2
Weymouth Av EA W5 116 D3
MLHL NW7 45 G1
Weymouth Cl EHAM E6 108 B5
Weymouth Ct BELMT SM2 * 209 F5
Weymouth Ms
CAVSQ/HST W1G 9 J1
Weymouth Rd YEAD UB4 94 C2
Weymouth St
CAVSQ/HST W1G 9 H1
Weymouth Ter BETH E2 7 K2
Weymouth Vls FSBYPK N4 * 67 F6
Weymouth Wk STAN HA7 43 G2
Whadcoat St FSBYPK N4 67 G6
Whalebone Av CHDH RM6 74 B3
Whalebone Gv CHDH RM6 74 B3
Whalebone La North
CHDH RM6 74 A1
CRW RM5 56 A3
Whalebone La South
BCTR RM8 74 B4
Whales Yd SRTFD E15 * 88 C5
Wharfdale Cl FBAR/BDGN N11 48 A2
Wharfdale Rd IS N1 5 F2
Wharfedale Gdns THHTH CR7 196 A1
Wharfedale St WBPTN SW10 120 A5
Wharf La POP/IOD E14 105 H5
TWK TW1 156 B3
Wharf Pl BETH E2 86 C6
Wharf Rd IS N1 6 C3
KCROSS N1C 4 D1
PEND EN3 37 G1
SRTFD E15 88 B6
Wharfside Cl ERITH DA8 130 C5
Wharfside Rd POP/IOD E14 106 C5
Wharf St CAN/RD E16 106 C4
Wharf Ter PUT/ROE SW15 139 H4
Wharncliffe Dr STHL UB1 115 J1
Wharncliffe Gdns SNWD SE25 181 F5
Wharncliffe Rd SNWD SE25 180 E5
Wharton Cl WLSDN NW10 81 G4
Wharton Cots FSBYW WC1X * 5 H5
Wharton Rd BMLY BR1 184 A4
Wharton St FSBYW WC1X 5 H5
Whateley Rd EDUL SE22 143 G6
PGE/AN SE20 182 A3
Whatley Av RYNPK SW20 177 G6
Whatman Rd FSTH SE23 164 A2
Wheastone Rd NKENS W10 * 100 C4
Wheatfields PEND EN3 25 G2
Wheatfield Wy KUT/HW KT1 175 F5
Wheathill Rd PGE/AN SE20 181 J5
Wheatlands HEST TW5 115 F6
Wheatlands Rd TOOT SW17 161 F5
Wheatley Cl HDN NW4 45 J5
Wheatley Crs HYS/HAR UB3 94 E6
Wheatley Gdns ED N9 36 A4
Wheatley Rd ISLW TW7 136 A4
Wheatley St CAVSQ/HST W1G 9 H2
Wheatley Terrace Rd
ERITH DA8 130 C6
Wheatsheaf Cl NTHLT UB5 77 J3
Wheat Sheaf Cl POP/IOD E14 124 D4
Wheatsheaf La FUL/PGN SW6 139 F1
VX/NE SW8 141 K1
Wheatsheaf Rd ROM RM1 75 H3
Wheatsheaf Ter
FUL/PGN SW6 * 139 J1
Wheatstone Cl
WIM/MER SW19 178 C4
Wheatstone Rd NKENS W10 100 C4
Wheeler Gdns IS N1 84 E6
Wheeler La WCHPL E1 13 J1
Wheeler Pl HAYES BR2 200 A1
Wheelers Cross BARK IG11 108 D1
Wheelers Dr RSLP HA4 58 A3
Wheel Farm Dr DAGE RM10 92 E1
Wheelock Cl ERITH DA8 149 J1
Wheelright Cl BUSH WD23 28 B1
Wheelwright St HOLWY N7 85 F5
Whelan Wy WLGTN SM6 210 D1
Wheler St WCHPL E1 7 J7
Whellock Rd CHSWK W4 118 B3
Whenman Av BXLY DA5 169 K4
Whetstone Cl
TRDG/WHET N20 33 H4
Whetstone Pk LINN WC2A 11 G3
Whetstone Rd
BKHTH/KID SE3 146 B3
Whewell Rd ARCH N19 66 E6
Whichcote St STHWK SE1 * 17 J1
Whidborne Cl DEPT SE8 144 D3
Whidborne St STPAN WC1H 5 F5
Whimbrel Wy YEAD UB4 95 H5
Whinchat Rd THMD SE28 127 J3
Whinfell Cl STRHM/NOR SW16 179 J1
Whinyates Rd ELTH/MOT SE9 146 D4
Whippendell Cl
STMC/STPC BR5 186 C4
Whippendell Wy
STMC/STPC BR5 186 C4
Whipps Cross Rd WAN E11 70 C2
Whiskin St CLKNW EC1R 6 A5
Whistler Gdns EDGW HA8 44 B5
Whistler Ms PECK SE15 143 G1
Whistlers Av BTSEA SW11 * 140 C1
Whistler St HBRY N5 85 H2
Whistler Wk WBPTN SW10 * 140 B1
Whiston Rd BETH E2 7 J2
Whitbread Cl TOTM N17 50 C4
Whitbread Rd BROCKY SE4 144 B5
Whitburn Rd LEW SE13 144 E6
Whitby Av WLSDN NW10 98 D2
Whitby Gdns CDALE/KGS NW9 44 C6
SUT SM1 194 C6
Whitby Pde RSLP HA4 * 59 G6
Whitby Rd RSLP HA4 77 F1
RYLN/HDSTN HA2 78 C1
SUT SM1 194 C6
WOOL/PLUM SE18 126 E4
Whitby St WCHPL E1 7 J6
Whitcher Cl NWCR SE14 124 B6
Whitcher Pl CAMTN NW1 84 C4
Whitchurch Av EDGW HA8 44 B3
Whitchurch Cl EDGW HA8 44 B2
Whitchurch Gdns EDGW HA8 44 B2
Whitchurch La EDGW HA8 44 A3
Whitchurch Pde EDGW HA8 * 44 C3
Whitchurch Rd NKENS W10 100 B6
Whitcomb St
SOHO/SHAV W1D 10 C5
Whitcome Ms RCH/KEW TW9 137 J2
Whiteadder Wy POP/IOD E14 124 E4
Whitear Wk SRTFD E15 88 B4
Whitebarn La DAGE RM10 92 C6
Whitebeam Av HAYES BR2 201 F4
Whitebeam Cl VX/NE SW8 * 142 A1
White Bear Pl HAMP NW3 * 83 H2
White Bear Yd CLKNW EC1R * 5 J7
White Bridge Av MTCM CR4 194 C1
White Bridge Cl
EBED/NFELT TW14 153 J1
White Butts Rd RSLP HA4 77 H1
Whitechapel High St
TWRH EC3N 13 K3
Whitechapel Rd WCHPL E1 104 C5
White Church La WCHPL E1 104 C5
White City Cl SHB W12 100 A6
White City Rd SHB W12 99 K6
White Conduit St IS N1 5 K2
Whitecote Rd STHL UB1 96 C5
White Craig Cl PIN HA5 42 A1
Whitecroft Cl BECK BR3 199 G1
Whitecroft Wy BECK BR3 199 F1
Whitecross St STLK EC1Y 6 D6
Whitefield Av CRICK NW2 64 A4
Whitefield Cl PUT/ROE SW15 159 H1
STMC/STPC BR5 186 D6
Whitefoot La BMLY BR1 165 G6
Whitefoot Ter BMLY BR1 165 J5
Whitefriars Av
KTN/HRWW/WS HA3 42 E5
Whitefriars Dr
KTN/HRWW/WS HA3 42 E5
Whitefriars St EMB EC4Y 11 K4
White Gdns DAGE RM10 92 C4
White Gate Gdns
KTN/HRWW/WS HA3 42 E3
White Gates THDIT KT7 190 B4
Whitehall WHALL SW1A 16 E1
Whitehall Ct WHALL SW1A 16 E1
Whitehall Crs CHSGTN KT9 205 K3
Whitehall Gdns ACT W3 117 H1
CHING E4 38 B3
CHSWK W4 117 J6
WHALL SW1A 16 E1
Whitehall La BKHH IG9 38 E4
ERITH DA8 150 C3
Whitehall Pk ARCH N19 66 C5
Whitehall Park Rd CHSWK W4 117 J6
Whitehall Pl WHALL SW1A 16 E1
WLGTN SM6 210 B2
Whitehall Rd CHING E4 38 C4
HAYES BR2 200 C2
HNWL W7 116 B2
HRW HA1 60 E4
THHTH CR7 196 B2
WFD IG8 38 E5
Whitehall St TOTM N17 50 B3
White Hart Av
WOOL/PLUM SE18 128 A3
White Hart La BARN SW13 138 B3
ROMW/RG RM7 56 C4
TOTM N17 49 J3
White Hart Rd ORP BR6 202 B4
WOOL/PLUM SE18 127 K4
White Hart St LBTH SE11 122 B5
White Hart Ter TOTM N17 * 50 B3
White Hart Yd STHWK SE1 18 E1
Whitehaven Cl HAYES BR2 199 K1
Whitehaven St STJWD NW8 2 C7
Whitehead Cl RDART DA2 171 F5
UED N18 49 K1
WAND/EARL SW18 160 B2
Whiteheads Gv CHEL SW3 14 D7
Whitehead's Gv CHEL SW3 120 D5
White Heart Av UX/CGN UB8 94 A4
Whiteheath Av RSLP HA4 58 A4
White Heron Ms TEDD TW11 * 174 A2
Whitehill Rd DART DA1 150 D6
Whitehorn Pl WDR/YW UB7 112 C1
White Horse Hl CHST BR7 167 F6
Whitehorse La SNWD SE25 197 F1
White Horse La WCHPL E1 105 F3
White Horse Ms PEND EN3 25 F3
White Horse Rd EHAM E6 107 K2
WCHPL E1 105 G5
Whitehorse Rd CROY/NA CR0 196 D4
WCHPL E1 105 G4
White Horse St
MYFR/PICC W1J 15 K1
White Horse Yd LOTH EC2R 12 E3
White House Dr STAN HA7 29 J6
White House La ENC/FH EN2 23 J2
Whitehouse Wy
STHGT/OAK N14 34 B4
Whitehurst Dr UED N18 * 51 F1
White Kennett St
HDTCH EC3A 13 H3
Whitelands Crs
WAND/EARL SW18 159 H2
White Ledges WEA W13 97 J5
Whitelegg Rd PLSTW E13 106 D1
Whiteley Rd NRWD SE19 180 E1
Whiteleys Wy FELT TW13 155 F5
White Lion Ct LOTH EC2R 13 G4
PECK SE15 * 123 K6
White Lion Hl BLKFR EC4V 12 B5
White Lion St IS N1 5 J3
White Ldg NRWD SE19 180 C3
White Lodge Cl BELMT SM2 209 G5
EFNCH N2 65 H3
ISLW TW7 136 B3
The White Ldg BAR EN5 * 20 C4
White Lyon Ct STBT EC1A 12 C1
White Oak Dr BECK BR3 183 F5
White Oak Gdns BFN/LL DA15 168 A2
Whiteoaks La GFD/PVL UB6 96 D1
White Orchards STAN HA7 43 G1
TRDG/WHET N20 32 D2
White Post La HOM E9 87 H5
White Post St NWCR SE14 143 K1
White Rd SRTFD E15 88 C5
Whites Av GNTH/NBYPK IG2 72 E3
White's Grounds STHWK SE1 19 H2
Whites Grounds Est
STHWK SE1 19 H2
Whites Meadow BMLY BR1 * 201 F1
White's Rw WCHPL E1 13 J2
White's Sq CLAP SW4 141 J5
Whitestile Rd BTFD TW8 116 D5
Whitestone La HAMP NW3 83 G1
Whitestone Wk HAMP NW3 83 G1
Whitestone Wy CROY/NA CR0 211 G1
White St STHL UB1 114 C2
Whitethorn Gdns
CROY/NA CR0 197 J6
ENC/FH EN2 23 K6
Whitethorn St BOW E3 105 J3
White Tower Wy WCHPL E1 105 G4
Whitewebbs Wy
STMC/STPC BR5 186 A4
Whitfield Ct RYNPK SW20 177 G5
Whitfield Pl FITZ W1T 4 A7
Whitfield Rd BXLYHN DA7 149 G1
EHAM E6 89 G5
GNWCH SE10 145 G2
Whitfield St FITZ W1T 10 B1
Whitford Gdns MTCM CR4 178 E6
Whitgift Av SAND/SEL CR2 211 J3
Whitgift St CROY/NA CR0 211 J1
STHWK SE1 17 G6
Whitings Rd BAR EN5 20 A6
Whitings Wy EHAM E6 108 A4
Whitland Rd CAR SM5 194 C5
Whitley Cl STWL/WRAY TW19 152 B1
Whitley Rd TOTM N17 50 A5
Whitlock Dr WIM/MER SW19 159 H2
Whitman Rd WCHPL E1 105 G3
Whitmead Cl SAND/SEL CR2 211 K4
Whitmore Cl FBAR/BDGN N11 48 B1
Whitmore Est IS N1 7 H1
Whitmore Gdns WLSDN NW10 100 A1
Whitmore Rd BECK BR3 182 C6
HRW HA1 60 C4
IS N1 7 G1
Whitnell Wy PUT/ROE SW15 * 139 H6
Whitney Av REDBR IG4 71 H1
Whitney Rd LEY E10 69 J4
Whitney Wk SCUP DA14 187 F2
Whitstable Cl BECK BR3 182 C4
Whitstable Pl CROY/NA CR0 211 J2
Whitstone La BECK BR3 198 E2
Whittaker Av RCH/KEW TW9 * 136 E6
Whittaker Rd CHEAM SM3 208 D1
EHAM E6 89 G5
Whittaker St BGVA SW1W 15 G7
Whitta Rd MNPK E12 89 H2
Whittell Gdns SYD SE26 163 K5
Whittingstall Rd
FUL/PGN SW6 139 J2
Whittington Av BANK EC3V 13 G4
YEAD UB4 94 D4
Whittington Ms
NFNCH/WDSPK N12 33 G6
Whittington Rd WDGN N22 48 E3
Whittington Wy PIN HA5 59 J2
Whittlebury Cl CAR SM5 209 K5
Whittle Cl STHL UB1 96 B5
WALTH E17 69 G3
Whittle Rd HEST TW5 134 B1
NWDGN UB2 115 G2
Whittlesea Rd
KTN/HRWW/WS HA3 42 C3
Whittlesey St STHWK SE1 17 K1
Whitton Av East
GFD/PVL UB6 79 F3
Whitton Av West NTHLT UB5 78 B3
Whitton Cl GFD/PVL UB6 79 H4
Whitton Dene HSLW TW3 135 G6
ISLW TW7 135 J6
WHTN TW2 155 J1
Whitton Dr GFD/PVL UB6 79 G4
Whitton Manor Rd
WHTN TW2 155 H1
Whitton Rd HSLW TW3 135 G6
WHTN TW2 155 K1
Whitton Waye HSLW TW3 155 F1
Whitwell Rd PLSTW E13 106 E2
Whitworth Rd SNWD SE25 181 F6
WOOL/PLUM SE18 147 F1
Whitworth St GNWCH SE10 125 H5
Whorlton Rd PECK SE15 143 H4
Whybridge Cl RAIN RM13 93 G6
Whymark Av WDGN N22 49 G6
Whytecroft HEST TW5 134 C1
Whyteville Rd FSTGT E7 89 F4
Wichling Cl STMC/STPC BR5 202 E5
Wickersley Rd BTSEA SW11 141 F3
Wickers Oake NRWD SE19 163 G6
Wicker St WCHPL E1 * 104 C5
Wicket Rd GFD/PVL UB6 97 G2
Wickets Cl STMC/STPC BR5 202 D2
The Wickets ASHF TW15 152 B6
Wickets Wy BARK/HLT IG6 55 F2
The Wicket CROY/NA CR0 213 J3
Wickford St WCHPL E1 104 E3
Wickford Wy WALTH E17 69 F1
Wickham Av CHEAM SM3 208 A3
CROY/NA CR0 198 B6
Wickham Cha WWKM BR4 199 G4
Wickham Cl NWMAL KT3 192 C2
PEND EN3 24 D4
WCHPL E1 104 E4
Wickham Ct WWKM BR4 * 214 B2
Wickham Court Rd
WWKM BR4 199 F6
Wickham Crs WWKM BR4 199 F6
Wickham Gdns BROCKY SE4 144 C4
Wickham La ABYW SE2 128 B6
Wickham Ms BROCKY SE4 144 C3
Wickham Rd BECK BR3 182 E6
BROCKY SE4 144 C4
CHING E4 52 A3
CROY/NA CR0 197 K6
KTN/HRWW/WS HA3 42 D5
Wickham St LBTH SE11 122 A5
WELL DA16 147 K3
WELL DA16 148 B2
Wickham Wy BECK BR3 199 F2
Wick La BOW E3 105 J1
Wickliffe Av FNCH N3 46 C5
Wickliffe Gdns WBLY HA9 62 C6
Wicklow St FSBYW WC1X 5 G4
Wick Rd HOM E9 87 F4
TEDD TW11 174 C3
Wicks Cl LEE/GVPK SE12 166 C6
Wicksteed Cl BXLY DA5 170 A5
Wickwood St CMBW SE5 142 C3
Widdenham Rd HOLWY N7 85 F2
Widdicombe Av
RYLN/HDSTN HA2 59 J6
Widdin St SRTFD E15 88 C5
Widecombe Gdns REDBR IG4 71 J1
Widecombe Rd
ELTH/MOT SE9 166 D5
Widecombe Wy EFNCH N2 65 H2
Widegate St WCHPL E1 13 H2
Widenham Cl PIN HA5 59 G2
Wide Wy MTCM CR4 179 J6
Widgeon Cl CAN/RD E16 107 F5
Widgeon Rd ERITH DA8 150 E1
Widley Rd MV/WKIL W9 100 E2
Widmore Lodge Rd BMLY BR1 184 C5
Widmore Rd BMLY BR1 184 A5
Wieland Rd NTHWD HA6 40 E3
Wigeon Wy YEAD UB4 95 H5
Wiggins La RCHPK/HAM TW10 156 D4
Wiggins Md CDALE/KGS NW9 45 H3
Wigginton Av WBLY HA9 80 C4
Wightman Rd
CEND/HSY/T N8 67 G1
Wigley Rd FELT TW13 154 C3
Wigmore Pl MHST W1U * 9 J3
Wigmore Rd CAR SM5 194 C6
Wigmore St MHST W1U 9 H3
Wigram Rd WAN E11 71 G3
Wigram Sq WALTH E17 52 A6
Wigston Cl UED N18 50 A1
Wigston Rd PLSTW E13 107 F3
Wigton Gdns STAN HA7 44 A4
Wigton Pl LBTH SE11 122 B5
Wigton Rd WALTH E17 51 H4
Wilberforce Ms CLAP SW4 141 J5
Wilberforce Rd
CDALE/KGS NW9 63 J3
FSBYPK N4 67 H6
Wilberforce Wk SRTFD E15 88 C3
Wilberforce Wy
WIM/MER SW19 177 G2
Wilbraham Pl KTBR SW1X 15 G6
Wilbury Wy UED N18 49 K1
Wilby Ms NTGHL W11 100 D6
Wilcot Av OXHEY WD19 27 J2
Wilcot Cl OXHEY WD19 27 J2
Wilcox Cl VX/NE SW8 141 K1
Wilcox Rd SUT SM1 * 209 F2
TEDD TW11 155 J6
VX/NE SW8 141 K1
Wildacres NTHWD HA6 26 D6
Wild Ct HOL/ALD WC2B 11 G3
Wildcroft Gdns STAN HA7 43 K2
Wildcroft Rd PUT/ROE SW15 159 F2
Wilde Cl HACK E8 86 C6
Wilde Pl PLMGR N13 49 H2
WAND/EARL SW18 160 C2
Wilder Cl RSLP HA4 59 F5
Wilderness Ms CLAP SW4 141 G5
Wilderness Rd CHST BR7 185 G3
The Wilderness
E/WMO/HCT KT8 189 H2
HPTN TW12 * 155 G6
Wilde Rd ERITH DA8 149 J1
Wilderton Rd
STNW/STAM N16 68 A4
Wildfell Rd CAT SE6 164 E2
Wild Goose Dr NWCR SE14 143 K2
Wild Hatch GLDGN NW11 64 E3
Wild Oaks Cl NTHWD HA6 40 D2
Wild's Rents STHWK SE1 19 G4
Wild St HOL/ALD WC2B 11 F4
Wildwood NTHWD HA6 40 B2
Wildwood Cl LEE/GVPK SE12 165 J2
Wildwood Gv HAMP NW3 65 G5
Wildwood Ri GLDGN NW11 65 G5
Wildwood Rd GLDGN NW11 65 F3
Wildwood Ter HAMP NW3 65 G5
Wilford Cl ENC/FH EN2 * 23 K4
NTHWD HA6 40 B3
Wilfred Av RAIN RM13 111 J4
Wilfred Owen Cl
WIM/MER SW19 178 B2
Wilfred St WESTW SW1E 16 A4
Wilfrid Gdns ACT W3 98 E4
Wilkes Rd BTFD TW8 117 F6
Wilkes St WCHPL E1 13 K1
Wilkins Cl HYS/HAR UB3 113 J5
MTCM CR4 178 D4
Wilkinson Gdns SNWD SE25 181 F4
Wilkinson Rd CAN/RD E16 107 G5
Wilkinson St VX/NE SW8 142 A1
Wilkinson Wy CHSWK W4 118 A2
Wilkin St KTTN NW5 84 A4
Wilkin Street Ms KTTN NW5 84 A4
Wilks Av DART DA1 171 J4
Wilks Gdns CROY/NA CR0 198 B5
Wilks Pl IS N1 7 H3
Willan Rd TOTM N17 49 K5
Willan Wall CAN/RD E16 106 D6
Willard St VX/NE SW8 141 G4
Willcocks Cl CHSGTN KT9 206 A1
Willcott Rd ACT W3 117 J1
Will Crooks Gdns
ELTH/MOT SE9 146 C5
Willenfield Rd WLSDN NW10 98 D1
Willenhall Av BAR EN5 33 G1
Willenhall Dr HYS/HAR UB3 94 C6
Willenhall Rd
WOOL/PLUM SE18 127 G5
Willerfield Rd WLSDN NW10 98 E2
Willersley Av BFN/LL DA15 168 A3
ORP BR6 216 D1
Willersley Cl BFN/LL DA15 168 A3
Willesden La
KIL/WHAMP NW6 82 B5
Willes Rd KTTN NW5 84 B4
Willett Cl NTHLT UB5 95 G2
STMC/STPC BR5 201 K3
Willett Rd THHTH CR7 196 B2
Willett Wy STMC/STPC BR5 201 J2
William Ash Cl DAGW RM9 91 H4
William Barefoot Dr
ELTH/MOT SE9 167 F6
William Booth Rd
PGE/AN SE20 181 H4
William Carey Wy HRW HA1 60 E3
William Cl CRW RM5 56 E4
EFNCH N2 47 H5
LEW SE13 145 F4
NWDGN UB2 115 H2
William Covell Cl
ENC/FH EN2 * 23 F1
William Dr STAN HA7 43 G2
William Ellis Wy
BERM/RHTH SE16 * 123 H3
William Foster La WELL DA16 148 B3
William Gdns PUT/ROE SW15 138 E6
William Guy Gdns BOW E3 105 K2
William IV St CHCR WC2N 10 E6
William Margrie Cl
PECK SE15 * 143 H3
William Ms KTBR SW1X 15 F3
William Morley Cl EHAM E6 89 H6
William Morris Cl WALTH E17 51 H6
William Morris Wy
FUL/PGN SW6 140 B4
William Petty Wy
STMC/STPC BR5 202 D5
William Rd CAMTN NW1 4 A5
SUT SM1 209 G3
WIM/MER SW19 177 H3
Williams Av WALTH E17 51 H4
William's Blds WCHPL E1 * 104 E3
Williams Cl CEND/HSY/T N8 * 66 D3
FUL/PGN SW6 139 H1
Williams Dr HSLW TW3 135 F5
Williams Gv SURB KT6 190 D3
WDGN N22 49 G4
Williams La MORT/ESHN SW14 137 K3
MRDN SM4 194 B3
Williamson Cl GNWCH SE10 125 J5
Williamson Rd FSBYPK N4 67 H3
Williamson St HOLWY N7 * 84 E2
William Sq BERM/RHTH SE16 124 B1
Williams Rd NWDGN UB2 114 D4
William's Rd WEA W13 * 116 B1
Williams Ter CROY/NA CR0 211 G4
William St BARK IG11 90 C5
CAR SM5 209 J1
KTBR SW1X 15 F3
LEY E10 69 K3
TOTM N17 50 B3
Williams Wy RDART DA2 170 A4
Willifield Wy GLDGN NW11 64 E2
Willingdon Rd WDGN N22 49 H5
Willingham Cl KTTN NW5 84 C3
Willingham Ter KTTN NW5 * 84 C3
Willingham Wy KUT/HW KT1 175 H5
Willington Rd BRXN/ST SW9 141 K4
Willis Av BELMT SM2 209 J4
Willis Rd CROY/NA CR0 196 D4
ERITH DA8 129 K4
SRTFD E15 88 D6
Willis St POP/IOD E14 105 K5
Willmore End
WIM/MER SW19 178 A4
Willoughby Av CROY/NA CR0 211 F2
Willoughby Dr RAIN RM13 93 G5
Willoughby Gv TOTM N17 50 D3
Willoughby La BMLY BR1 184 B3
TOTM N17 50 D3
Willoughby Ms TOTM N17 50 D3
Willoughby Park Rd
TOTM N17 50 D3
Willoughby Rd
CEND/HSY/T N8 49 G6
HAMP NW3 83 H2
KUTN/CMB KT2 175 G4
TWK TW1 136 D6
Willoughby Wy CHARL SE7 126 A4
Willow Av BARN SW13 138 C3
BFN/LL DA15 168 B1
Willow Bank
RCHPK/HAM TW10 156 C5
Willowbay Cl BAR EN5 32 B1
Willow Bridge Rd IS N1 85 J4
Willowbrook HPTN TW12 173 G1
Willowbrook Est PECK SE15 * 143 G1
Willowbrook Rd NWDGN UB2 114 E3
PECK SE15 123 G6
STWL/WRAY TW19 152 B3
The Willow Centre MTCM CR4 194 E2
Willow Cl BKHH IG9 39 H5
BTFD TW8 116 D6
BXLY DA5 169 G1
CAT SE6 165 J3

HAYES BR2 200 E2
HCH RM12 93 K1
STMC/STPC BR5 202 C3
Willow Ct STAN HA7 * 43 K3
Willowcourt Av
KTN/HRWW/WS HA3 61 H2
Willow Dean PIN HA5 * 41 H5
Willow Dene BUSH WD23 28 E2
PIN HA5 41 H5
Willowdene HGT N6 * 65 K4
Willowdene Cl WHTN TW2 155 H2
Willow Dr BAR EN5 20 C5
Willow End NTHWD HA6 40 E2
SURB KT6 191 F5
TRDG/WHET N20 32 E4
Willowfields Cl
WOOL/PLUM SE18 127 K5
Willow Gdns HSLW TW3 * 135 F2
RSLP HA4 58 D6
Willow Gv CHST BR7 185 F2
RSLP HA4 58 D6
Willowhayne Dr
WOT/HER KT12 188 A4
Willowhayne Gdns WPK KT4 208 A2
Willow La MTCM CR4 194 E2
WOOL/PLUM SE18 126 E4
Willowmead Cl EA W5 97 K4
Willowmere ESH/CLAY KT10 204 C2
Willow Mt CROY/NA CR0 212 A2
Willow Pl WEST SW1P 16 B6
Willow Rd CHDH RM6 74 A3
DART DA1 171 F3
EA W5 117 F2
EN EN1 24 A3
ERITH DA8 150 D2
HAMP NW3 83 H2
MNPK E12 89 K1
NWMAL KT3 191 K1
WLGTN SM6 210 B5
Willows Av MRDN SM4 194 A2
Willows Cl PIN HA5 41 G5
Willows Ter WLSDN NW10 * 99 H1
The Willows BECK BR3 * 182 D4
EBAR EN4 * 33 J1
ESH/CLAY KT10 204 E4
OXHEY WD19 27 F2
Willow St CHING E4 38 B2
ROMW/RG RM7 74 E1
SDTCH EC2A 7 G6
Willow Ter PGE/AN SE20 * 181 J4
Willow Tree Cl BOW E3 87 G6
NTHLT UB5 77 J4
WAND/EARL SW18 160 A3
YEAD UB4 95 G3
Willowtree Cl HGDN/ICK UB10 76 A1
Willow Tree La YEAD UB4 95 G3
Willow Tree Wk BMLY BR1 184 A4
Willowtree Wy THHTH CR7 180 B4
Willow V CHST BR7 185 F2
SHB W12 118 D1
Willow Vw WIM/MER SW19 178 C4
Willow Wk CHEAM SM3 208 D1
DART DA1 * 151 H6
ORP BR6 216 B1
SEVS/STOTM N15 67 H1
STHWK SE1 19 H6
WALTH E17 69 H2
WCHMH N21 35 F1
Willow Wy ALP/SUD HA0 * 79 G1
FNCH N3 47 F3
HOR/WEW KT19 207 F4
NTGHL W11 100 B6
SYD SE26 163 J5
WHTN TW2 155 G4
Willow Wood Crs SNWD SE25 197 F3
Willow Wren Whf
NWDGN UB2 * 114 A4
Will Rd KTTN NW5 84 B4
Willrose Crs ABYW SE2 128 C5
Wills Crs HSLW TW3 155 G1
Wills Gv MLHL NW7 45 J1
Wilman Gv HACK E8 86 C5
Wilmar Cl YEAD UB4 94 B3
Wilmar Gdns WWKM BR4 198 E5
Wilmer Cl KUTN/CMB KT2 175 G1
Wilmer Crs KUTN/CMB KT2 175 G1
Wilmer Gdns IS N1 7 G1
Wilmer Lea Cl SRTFD E15 88 A5
Wilmer Pl STNW/STAM N16 68 B6
Wilmer Wy FBAR/BDGN N11 48 D1
Wilmington Av CHSWK W4 138 A1
ORP BR6 202 D6
Wilmington Court Rd
RDART DA2 170 D5
Wilmington Gdns BARK IG11 90 D5
Wilmington Sq FSBYW WC1X 5 J5
Wilmington St FSBYW WC1X 5 J5
Wilmot Cl PECK SE15 * 143 H1
Wilmot Pl CAMTN NW1 84 C5
HNWL W7 115 K1
Wilmot Rd CAR SM5 * 209 K3
DART DA1 150 E6
LEY E10 69 K6
TOTM N17 49 K6
Wilmot St BETH E2 104 D3
Wilmount St
WOOL/PLUM SE18 127 G4
Wilna Rd WAND/EARL SW18 160 B2
Wilsham St NTGHL W11 119 G1
Wilshaw Cl HDN NW4 45 J6
Wilshaw St NWCR SE14 144 D2
Wilsmere Dr
KTN/HRWW/WS HA3 42 E3
NTHLT UB5 77 J4
Wilson Av MTCM CR4 178 D3
Wilson Cl SAND/SEL CR2 211 K3
WBLY HA9 62 B4
Wilson Dr WBLY HA9 62 B4
Wilson Gdns HRW HA1 60 C4
Wilson Gv BERM/RHTH SE16 123 J2
Wilson Rd CHSGTN KT9 206 B4
CMBW SE5 142 E2
IL IG1 71 K4
PLSTW E13 107 H2
Wilson's Av TOTM N17 50 B5
Wilson's Pl POP/IOD E14 105 H5
Wilson's Rd HMSMTH W6 119 G5
Wilson St LVPST EC2M 13 F1
WALTH E17 70 A2
WCHMH N21 35 G2
Wilson Wk CHSWK W4 * 118 C4
Wilstone Cl YEAD UB4 95 J3
Wilthorne Gdns DAGE RM10 92 D5
Wilton Av CHSWK W4 118 B5
Wilton Cl WDR/YW UB7 112 A6
Wilton Crs KTBR SW1X 15 G3
WIM/MER SW19 177 J4
Wilton Dr CRW RM5 56 E3
Wilton Est HACK E8 * 86 C4
Wilton Gdns E/WMO/HCT KT8 173 F6
WOT/HER KT12 188 C5
Wilton Gv NWMAL KT3 192 C3
WIM/MER SW19 177 J3
Wilton Ms HACK E8 * 86 D4
KTBR SW1X 15 H4
Wilton Pl KTBR SW1X 15 G2
Wilton Rd ABYW SE2 128 D3
EBAR EN4 21 K5
HSLWW TW4 134 C4
MUSWH N10 48 A5
PIM SW1V 15 K5
WIM/MER SW19 178 D3
Wilton Rw KTBR SW1X 15 G3
Wilton Sq IS N1 85 K6
Wilton St KTBR SW1X 15 J4
Wilton Ter KTBR SW1X 15 G4
Wilton Vls IS N1 6 E1
Wilton Wk FELT TW13 * 154 A4
Wilton Wy HACK E8 86 C4
Wiltshire Cl CHEL SW3 14 D7
MLHL NW7 * 45 H1
Wiltshire Gdns FSBYPK N4 67 J3
WHTN TW2 155 H3
Wiltshire La PIN HA5 58 E1
Wiltshire Rd BRXN/ST SW9 142 B4
ORP BR6 202 B4
THHTH CR7 180 B6
Wiltshire Rw IS N1 6 E1
Wilverley Crs NWMAL KT3 192 B3
Wimbart Rd
BRXS/STRHM SW2 * 162 A2
Wimbledon Br
WIM/MER SW19 177 J2
Wimbledon Hill Rd
WIM/MER SW19 177 H2
Wimbledon Park Rd
WAND/EARL SW18 159 J3
WIM/MER SW19 159 H5
Wimbledon Park Side
PUT/ROE SW15 158 E3
WIM/MER SW19 159 G4
Wimbledon Rd TOOT SW17 160 B6
Wimbolt St BETH E2 104 C2
Wimborne Av NWDGN UB2 115 F4
STMC/STPC BR5 186 A6
YEAD UB4 95 F5
Wimborne Cl BKHH IG9 39 G4
LEE/GVPK SE12 145 J6
WPK KT4 193 F5
Wimborne Dr EDGW HA8 44 C6
PIN HA5 59 H4
Wimborne Gdns WEA W13 97 H5
Wimborne Rd ED N9 36 C4
TOTM N17 50 A5
Wimborne Wy BECK BR3 182 A6
Wimbourne St IS N1 6 E2
Wimpole Cl HAYES BR2 200 B1
KUT/HW KT1 175 G5
Wimpole Ms CAVSQ/HST W1G 9 J1
Wimpole Rd WDR/YW UB7 112 A1
Wimpole St CAVSQ/HST W1G 9 J2
Wimshurst Cl CROY/NA CR0 195 K5
Winans Wk BRXN/ST SW9 142 B3
Wincanton Crs NTHLT UB5 78 A3
Wincanton Gdns
BARK/HLT IG6 54 B6
Wincanton Rd
WAND/EARL SW18 159 J2
Winchcombe Rd CAR SM5 194 C6
Winchcomb Gdns
ELTH/MOT SE9 146 C4
Winchelsea Av BXLYHN DA7 149 G1
Winchelsea Cl PUT/ROE SW15 139 G6
Winchelsea Rd FSTGT E7 88 E2
TOTM N17 50 A6
WLSDN NW10 81 F6
Winchelsey Ri SAND/SEL CR2 212 B4
Winchendon Rd
FUL/PGN SW6 139 J1
TEDD TW11 155 J6
Winchester Av
CDALE/KGS NW9 44 B6
HEST TW5 114 E6
KIL/WHAMP NW6 82 C5
Winchester Cl EN EN1 * 24 A6
ESH/CLAY KT10 204 A2
HAYES BR2 183 J6
KUTN/CMB KT2 175 J3
LBTH SE11 * 18 B7
Winchester Dr PIN HA5 59 H2
Winchester Ms WPK KT4 193 G6
Winchester Pk HAYES BR2 183 J6
Winchester Pl HACK E8 86 B3
HGT N6 66 B5
Winchester Rd BXLYHN DA7 148 E3
CHING E4 52 A3
ED N9 36 B3
FELT TW13 154 E5
HAMP NW3 83 H5
HAYES BR2 183 J6
HGT N6 66 B5
HYS/HAR UB3 133 H1
IL IG1 90 D1
KTN/HRWW/WS HA3 62 A1
ORP BR6 217 J2
TWK TW1 156 C1
Winchester Sq STHWK SE1 12 E7
Winchester St ACT W3 117 K1
PIM SW1V 121 G5
Winchester Wk STHWK SE1 12 E7
Winchfield Cl
KTN/HRWW/WS HA3 61 J3
Winchfield Rd SYD SE26 182 B1
Winchilsea Crs
E/WMO/HCT KT8 173 H5
Winchmore Hill Rd
STHGT/OAK N14 34 D3
Winchmore Vls WCHMH N21 * 35 F2
Winckley Cl
KTN/HRWW/WS HA3 62 B2
Wincott St LBTH SE11 17 K6
Wincrofts Dr ELTH/MOT SE9 147 J5
Windall Cl NRWD SE19 181 H4
Windborough Rd CAR SM5 210 A5
Windermere Av FNCH N3 46 E5
HCH RM12 93 J3
KIL/WHAMP NW6 82 C6
RSLP HA4 59 G4
WBLY HA9 61 J5
WIM/MER SW19 178 A6
Windermere Cl DART DA1 170 E3
EBED/NFELT TW14 153 H3
ORP BR6 216 B1
STWL/WRAY TW19 152 A4
Windermere Gdns REDBR IG4 71 J2
Windermere Gv WBLY HA9 61 J5
Windermere Hall EDGW HA8 * 44 B1
Windermere Rd ARCH N19 * 66 C6
BXLYHN DA7 149 K3
CROY/NA CR0 197 G5
EA W5 116 D3
MUSWH N10 48 B4
PUT/ROE SW15 158 B6
STHL UB1 95 K4
STRHM/NOR SW16 179 H4
WWKM BR4 199 H6
Windermere Wy
WDR/YW UB7 112 B1
Winders Rd BTSEA SW11 140 D3
Windfield Cl SYD SE26 164 A6
Windham Rd RCH/KEW TW9 137 G4
Winding Wy BCTR RM8 91 J1
Windlass Pl DEPT SE8 124 B4
Windlesham Gv
WIM/MER SW19 159 G3
Windley Cl FSTH SE23 163 K4
Windmill Cl LEW SE13 * 145 F3
STHWK SE1 * 123 H4
SURB KT6 190 D5
Windmill Dr CLAP SW4 141 G6
CRICK NW2 82 C1
Windmill Gdns ENC/FH EN2 23 G3
Windmill Gv CROY/NA CR0 196 D4
Windmill Hl ENC/FH EN2 23 H4
HAMP NW3 * 83 G1
RSLP HA4 58 D4
Windmill La BAR EN5 31 H1
BUSH WD23 28 E3
GFD/PVL UB6 96 C4
HAYES BR2 215 G2
ISLW TW7 115 K4
NWDGN UB2 115 H2
SRTFD E15 88 B4
SURB KT6 190 C4
Windmill Pas CHSWK W4 * 118 B4
Windmill Ri KUTN/CMB KT2 175 J3
Windmill Rd CHSWK W4 118 B4
CROY/NA CR0 196 D4
EA W5 116 D4
HPTN TW12 173 G1
MTCM CR4 195 H2
UED N18 35 K6
WAND/EARL SW18 160 C1
WIM/MER SW19 176 E1
Windmill Rw LBTH SE11 * 122 B5
Windmill St BUSH WD23 28 E3
FITZ W1T 10 C2
Windmill Wk STHWK SE1 * 17 K1
Windmill Wy RSLP HA4 58 D5
Windover Av CDALE/KGS NW9 63 F1
Windrose Cl
BERM/RHTH SE16 124 A2
Windrush NWMAL KT3 191 J1
Windrush Cl BTSEA SW11 * 140 C5
CHSWK W4 * 137 K1
HACK E8 86 C5
TOTM N17 50 A4
Windrush La FSTH SE23 164 A5
Windrush Rd WLSDN NW10 81 F6
Windsor Av CHEAM SM3 208 C1
E/WMO/HCT KT8 173 F6
EDGW HA8 30 D6
NWMAL KT3 191 K2
WALTH E17 51 G5
WIM/MER SW19 178 B4
Windsor Cl CHST BR7 185 G1
FNCH N3 46 C5
NTHWD HA6 40 E5
RYLN/HDSTN HA2 78 A1
WNWD SE27 162 D6
Windsor Ct PIN HA5 * 41 H6
STHGT/OAK N14 34 C2
Windsor Crs
RYLN/HDSTN HA2 78 A1
WBLY HA9 80 C1
Windsor Dr ASHF TW15 152 A6
DART DA1 170 D1
EBAR EN4 33 K1
ORP BR6 217 G4
Windsor Gdns CROY/NA CR0 210 E1
HYS/HAR UB3 113 G3
MV/WKIL W9 100 E4
Windsor Gv WNWD SE27 162 D6
Windsor Ms CAT SE6 165 F3
Windsor Park Rd
HYS/HAR UB3 133 J1
Windsor Rd BAR EN5 32 B1
BCTR RM8 92 A1
BXLYHS DA6 149 F5
CHING E4 37 K6
CRICK NW2 81 K4
EA W5 98 A6
FNCH N3 46 C5
FSTGT E7 89 F3
HOLWY N7 84 E1
HSLWW TW4 134 A3
IL IG1 90 C2
KTN/HRWW/WS HA3 42 C4
KUTN/CMB KT2 175 F3
LEY E10 69 K6
NWDGN UB2 114 E3
PLMGR N13 35 G5
RCH/KEW TW9 137 G3
TEDD TW11 173 J1
THHTH CR7 180 C5
TOTM N17 50 C5
WAN E11 70 E5
WPK KT4 192 D6
The Windsors BKHH IG9 39 J4
Windsor St IS N1 85 H6
Windsor Ter IS N1 6 D4
Windsor Wk CMBW SE5 142 E3
Windsor Wy WKENS W14 119 G4
Windspoint Dr PECK SE15 123 J6
Windstock Cl
BERM/RHTH SE16 124 C3
Windus Rd STNW/STAM N16 68 B5
Windy Rdg BMLY BR1 184 D4
Windy Ridge Cl
WIM/MER SW19 177 G1
Wine Cl WAP E1W 104 E6
Wine Office Ct
FLST/FETLN EC4A 11 K3
Winery La KUT/HW KT1 175 G6
Winey Cl CHSGTN KT9 205 J5
Winforton St GNWCH SE10 145 F2
Winfrith Rd
WAND/EARL SW18 160 B2
Wingate Crs CROY/NA CR0 195 K3
Wingate Rd HMSMTH W6 118 E3
IL IG1 90 B3
SCUP DA14 186 D1
Wingate Sq CLAP SW4 141 H5
Wingfield Ct WATW WD18 * 26 B1
Wingfield Ms PECK SE15 143 H4
Wingfield Rd KUTN/CMB KT2 175 G2
SRTFD E15 88 C3
WALTH E17 69 K2
Wingfield St PECK SE15 143 H4
Wingfield Wy RSLP HA4 77 F4
Wingford Rd
BRXS/STRHM SW2 161 K1
Wingmore Rd HNHL SE24 142 D4
Wingrave Rd HMSMTH W6 119 F6
Wingrove Rd CAT SE6 165 H4
Wings Cl SUT SM1 208 E2
Winifred Cl BAR EN5 31 H1
Winifred Pl
NFNCH/WDSPK N12 47 G1
Winifred Rd BCTR RM8 74 A6
DART DA1 150 E6
ERITH DA8 130 B5
HPTN TW12 155 F6
WIM/MER SW19 177 K4
Winifred St CAN/RD E16 126 E1
Winifred Ter EN EN1 36 B2
PLSTW E13 106 E1
Winkfield Rd WDGN N22 49 G4
Winkley St BETH E2 104 D1
Winkworth Cots WCHPL E1 * 104 E3
Winlaton Rd BMLY BR1 165 G6
Winmill Rd BCTR RM8 92 B1
Winn Common Rd
WOOL/PLUM SE18 127 K6
Winnett St SOHO/SHAV W1D 10 C5
Winnington Cl EFNCH N2 65 H3
Winnington Rd EFNCH N2 65 H4
PEND EN3 24 E1
Winnipeg Dr ORP BR6 217 F4
Winnock Rd WDR/YW UB7 112 A1
Winn Rd LEE/GVPK SE12 165 K3
Winns Av WALTH E17 51 H6
Winns Ms SEVS/STOTM N15 68 A1
Winns Ter WALTH E17 51 J5
Winsbeach WALTH E17 52 B6
Winscombe Crs EA W5 97 K3
Winscombe St KTTN NW5 84 B1
Winscombe Wy STAN HA7 43 G1
Winsford Rd CAT SE6 164 C5
Winsford Ter UED N18 * 49 K1
Winsham Gv BTSEA SW11 141 F6
Winslade Rd
BRXS/STRHM SW2 141 K6
Winsland Ms BAY/PAD W2 8 A3
Winsland St BAY/PAD W2 8 A3
Winsley St GTPST W1W 10 A3
Winslow Cl PIN HA5 59 F3
WLSDN NW10 81 G1
Winslow Gv CHING E4 38 C4
Winslow Rd HMSMTH W6 119 F6
Winslow Wy FELT TW13 154 C5
Winsor Ter EHAM E6 108 A4
Winstanley Rd BTSEA SW11 140 C4
Winstead Gdns DAGE RM10 92 E3
Winston Av CDALE/KGS NW9 63 G4
Winston Cl
KTN/HRWW/WS HA3 43 F2
ROMW/RG RM7 74 D1
Winston Ct
KTN/HRWW/WS HA3 42 B3
Winston House SURB KT6 * 191 F2
Winston Rd STNW/STAM N16 85 K2
Winston Wy IL IG1 90 B1
Winter Av EHAM E6 89 J6
Winterbourne Av ORP BR6 216 D1
Winterbourne Rd BCTR RM8 73 J6
CAT SE6 164 C3
THHTH CR7 196 B1
Winter Box Wk
RCHPK/HAM TW10 137 G6
Winterbrook Rd HNHL SE24 162 D1
Winterburn Cl
FBAR/BDGN N11 48 A2
Winterfold Cl WIM/MER SW19 159 H4
Winters Rd THDIT KT7 190 C4
Winterstoke Rd FSTH SE23 164 C3
Winterton Pl WBPTN SW10 120 B6
Winterwell Rd
BRXS/STRHM SW2 141 K6
Winthorpe Rd PUT/ROE SW15 139 H5
Winthorpe St WCHPL E1 104 D4
Winthrop St WCHPL E1 * 104 D4
Winton Av FBAR/BDGN N11 48 C3
Winton Cl ED N9 37 F2
Winton Gdns EDGW HA8 44 B3
Winton Rd ORP BR6 216 B2
The Wintons BUSH WD23 * 28 D3
Winton Wy
STRHM/NOR SW16 180 B1
Wirral Wood Cl CHST BR7 185 F2
Wisbeach Rd CROY/NA CR0 196 E2
Wisborough Rd
SAND/SEL CR2 212 B6
Wisdons Cl DAGE RM10 74 D5
Wise La MLHL NW7 45 J2
WDR/YW UB7 112 A4
Wiseman Rd LEY E10 * 69 J6
Wise Rd SRTFD E15 88 A6
Wiseton Rd TOOT SW17 160 D3
Wishart Rd BKHTH/KID SE3 146 C2
Wishaw Wk FBAR/BDGN N11 48 E2
Wisley Rd BTSEA SW11 140 E6
STMC/STPC BR5 186 B3
Wistaria Cl ORP BR6 201 G6
Wisteria Cl IL IG1 90 B3
MLHL NW7 45 H2
Wisteria Rd LEW SE13 145 G5
Witanhurst La HGT N6 66 A5
Witan St BETH E2 104 D2
Witham Cl LOU IG10 39 J1
Witham Rd DAGE RM10 92 C3
GPK RM2 75 K2
ISLW TW7 135 J2
PGE/AN SE20 181 K6
WEA W13 116 B1
Withens Cl STMC/STPC BR5 * 202 D1
Witherby Cl CROY/NA CR0 212 A3
Witherington Rd HBRY N5 * 85 G3
Withers Md CDALE/KGS NW9 45 H4
Witherston Wy
ELTH/MOT SE9 167 F4
Withycombe Rd
WIM/MER SW19 159 G2
Withy La RSLP HA4 58 A2
Withy Md CHING E4 38 B5
Witley Crs CROY/NA CR0 214 A4
Witley Gdns NWDGN UB2 114 E4
Witley Rd ARCH N19 66 C6
Witney Cl PIN HA5 41 K2
Witney Pth FSTH SE23 164 A5
Wittenham Wy CHING E4 38 B5
Wittering Cl KUTN/CMB KT2 174 E1
Wittersham Rd BMLY BR1 183 J1
Wivenhoe Cl PECK SE15 143 H4
Wivenhoe Ct HSLW TW3 134 E5
Wivenhoe Rd BARK IG11 109 G1
Wiverton Rd SYD SE26 181 K2
Wix Rd DAGW RM9 91 K6
Wix's La CLAP SW4 141 G5
Woburn WEA W13 * 97 H4
Woburn Av HCH RM12 93 J2
Woburn Cl BUSH WD23 28 C1
THMD SE28 109 K5
WIM/MER SW19 178 B2
Woburn Pl STPAN WC1H 4 E6
Woburn Rd CAR SM5 194 D5
CROY/NA CR0 196 D5
Woburn Sq STPAN WC1H 4 D7
Woburn Wk STPAN WC1H * 4 D5
Wodeham Gdns WCHPL E1 104 C4
Wodehouse Av CMBW SE5 143 G2
Wodehouse Rd DART DA1 151 K5
Woffington Cl TEDD TW11 174 D3
Woking Cl PUT/ROE SW15 138 C5
Woldham Pl HAYES BR2 200 B1
Woldham Rd HAYES BR2 200 B1
Wolds Dr ORP BR6 216 A2
Wolfe Cl HAYES BR2 199 K3
YEAD UB4 95 F2
Wolfe Crs CHARL SE7 126 C5
Wolferton Rd MNPK E12 89 K2
Wolfington Rd WNWD SE27 162 C6
Wolfram Cl LEW SE13 145 H6
Wolftencroft Cl BTSEA SW11 140 D4
Wollaston Cl STHWK SE1 18 B6
Wolmer Cl EDGW HA8 30 C6
Wolmer Gdns EDGW HA8 30 C5
Wolseley Av
WAND/EARL SW18 159 K4
Wolseley Gdns CHSWK W4 117 J6
Wolseley Rd CEND/HSY/T N8 66 D3
CHSWK W4 117 K4
FSTGT E7 89 F5
KTN/HRWW/WS HA3 42 E6
MTCM CR4 195 F4
ROMW/RG RM7 75 F4
WDGN N22 49 F4
Wolseley St STHWK SE1 19 K3
Wolsey Av EHAM E6 108 A2
THDIT KT7 190 A2
WALTH E17 51 H6
Wolsey Cl HSLW TW3 135 H5
KUTN/CMB KT2 175 J4
NWDGN UB2 115 H3
RYNPK SW20 176 E3
WPK KT4 207 J2
Wolsey Ct ELTH/MOT SE9 * 166 E1
Wolsey Crs CROY/NA CR0 214 A6
MRDN SM4 193 J4
Wolsey Dr KUTN/CMB KT2 175 F1
WOT/HER KT12 188 C5
Wolsey Gdns BARK/HLT IG6 54 B2
Wolsey Gv EDGW HA8 45 F3
ESH/CLAY KT10 204 B2
Wolsey Ms KTTN NW5 84 C4
ORP BR6 217 F3
Wolsey Rd ASHF TW15 152 B6
E/WMO/HCT KT8 189 J1
EN EN1 24 D3
ESH/CLAY KT10 204 B2
HPTN TW12 173 G2
IS N1 85 K3
NTHWD HA6 26 A4
Wolsey St WCHPL E1 104 E4
Wolsey Wy CHSGTN KT9 206 C3
Wolsley Cl DART DA1 150 B6
Wolstonbury
NFNCH/WDSPK N12 46 E1
Wolvercote Rd ABYW SE2 128 E2
Wolverley St BETH E2 * 104 D2
Wolverton Av KUTN/CMB KT2 175 H4
Wolverton Gdns EA W5 98 B6
HMSMTH W6 119 G4
Wolverton Rd STAN HA7 43 H2
Wolverton Wy
STHGT/OAK N14 22 C6
Wolves La WDGN N22 49 G3
Womersley Rd
CEND/HSY/T N8 67 F3
Wonersh Wy BELMT SM2 208 B6
Wonford Cl KUTN/CMB KT2 176 B4
Wontner Cl IS N1 85 J5
Wontner Rd BAL SW12 160 E4
Woodall Cl CHSGTN KT9 205 J5
Woodall Rd PEND EN3 25 F6
Woodbank Rd BMLY BR1 165 J5
Woodbastwick Rd SYD SE26 182 A2
Woodberry Av
RYLN/HDSTN HA2 60 C1
WCHMH N21 35 G4

Woodberry Cl MLHL NW7 46 B3
Woodberry Crs MUSWH N10 48 B6
Woodberry Down FSBYPK N4 67 J5
Woodberry Gdns
NFNCH/WDSPK N12 47 G2
Woodberry Gv BXLY DA5 170 A5
FSBYPK N4 67 J4
NFNCH/WDSPK N12 47 G2
Woodberry Wy CHING E4 38 A2
NFNCH/WDSPK N12 47 G2
Woodbine Cl WHTN TW2 155 J4
Woodbine Gv ENC/FH EN2 23 K1
PGE/AN SE20 181 J3
Woodbine La WPK KT4 207 K1
Woodbine Pl WAN E11 70 E3
Woodbine Rd BFN/LL DA15 167 K3
Woodbines Av KUT/HW KT1 174 E6
Woodbine Ter HOM E9 86 E4
Woodborough Rd
PUT/ROE SW15 138 E5
Woodbourne Av
STRHM/NOR SW16 161 J5
Woodbourne Dr
ESH/CLAY KT10 205 F4
Woodbourne Gdns
WLGTN SM6 210 B5
Woodbridge Cl HOLWY N7 67 F6
Woodbridge Rd BARK IG11 91 F3
Woodbridge St CLKNW EC1R 6 A6
Woodbrook Rd ABYW SE2 128 B6
Woodburn Cl HDN NW4 64 B2
Woodbury Cl CROY/NA CR0 197 G6
WAN E11 71 F1
Woodbury Gdns
LEE/GVPK SE12 166 A5
Woodbury Park Rd WEA W13 97 H3
Woodbury Rd WALTH E17 69 K1
Woodbury St TOOT SW17 178 D1
Woodchester Sq BAY/PAD W2 101 F4
Woodchurch Cl SCUP DA14 167 J5
Woodchurch Dr BMLY BR1 184 C5
Woodchurch Rd
KIL/WHAMP NW6 82 E5
Wood Cl BETH E2 104 C3
BXLY DA5 170 B5
CDALE/KGS NW9 63 F4
HRW HA1 60 D4
Woodclyffe Dr CHST BR7 185 F5
Woodcock Dell Av
KTN/HRWW/WS HA3 61 J4
Woodcock Hl
KTN/HRWW/WS HA3 61 J3
Woodcocks CAN/RD E16 107 G4
Woodcombe Crs FSTH SE23 163 K3
Woodcot Cl PEND EN3 36 E1
Woodcote Av HCH RM12 93 J2
MLHL NW7 46 A2
THHTH CR7 196 C1
WLGTN SM6 210 B6
Woodcote Cl KUTN/CMB KT2 175 G1
Woodcote Dr ORP BR6 201 J4
Woodcote Gn WLGTN SM6 210 C6
Woodcote Ms LOU IG10 39 H2
WLGTN SM6 210 B4
Woodcote Pl WNWD SE27 * 180 C1
Woodcote Rd WAN E11 70 E4
WLGTN SM6 210 B4
Wood Crest BELMT SM2 * 209 G5
Woodcroft ELTH/MOT SE9 166 E5
GFD/PVL UB6 79 G4
WCHMH N21 35 F3
Woodcroft Av MLHL NW7 45 G3
STAN HA7 43 G4
Woodcroft Ms DEPT SE8 124 B4
Woodcroft Rd THHTH CR7 196 C2
Wood Dene PECK SE15 * 143 J2
Wood Dr CHST BR7 184 D2
Woodedge Cl CHING E4 38 D3
Wooden Bridge Ter
WNWD SE27 * 162 C5
Wood End HYS/HAR UB3 94 C5
SWLY BR8 203 K1
Woodend ESH/CLAY KT10 189 H6
NRWD SE19 180 D2
SUT SM1 194 B6
Wood End Av
RYLN/HDSTN HA2 78 B2
Wood End Cl NTHLT UB5 78 D3
Woodend Gdns ENC/FH EN2 22 E5
Wood End Gdns NTHLT UB5 78 C3
Wood End Gn YEAD UB4 94 D4
Wood End Green Rd
HYS/HAR UB3 * 94 A5
Wood End La NTHLT UB5 78 B4
Wood End Rd HRW HA1 78 D2
Woodend Rd WALTH E17 52 A5
The Wood End WLGTN SM6 210 B6
Wood End Wy NTHLT UB5 78 C3
Wooder Gdns FSTGT E7 88 D2
Wooderson Cl SNWD SE25 197 F1
Woodfall Av BAR EN5 20 D6
Woodfall Dr DART DA1 150 C5
Woodfall Rd FSBYPK N4 67 G5
Woodfall St CHEL SW3 120 E5
Woodfarrs CMBW SE5 142 E5
Wood Fld HAMP NW3 * 83 K3
Woodfield Av ALP/SUD HA0 79 J1
CAR SM5 210 A4
CDALE/KGS NW9 63 G1
EA W5 97 J3
NTHWD HA6 26 C6
STRHM/NOR SW16 161 J5
Woodfield Cl EN EN1 24 A5
NRWD SE19 180 D3
Woodfield Crs EA W5 97 K3
Woodfield Dr EBAR EN4 34 A3
GPK RM2 75 J1
Woodfield Gdns NWMAL KT3 192 C2
Woodfield Gv
STRHM/NOR SW16 161 J5
Woodfield La
STRHM/NOR SW16 161 J5
Woodfield Pl MV/WKIL W9 100 D4
Woodfield Ri BUSH WD23 28 D2
Woodfield Rd EA W5 97 J3
HSLWW TW4 134 A3
MV/WKIL W9 100 D4
THDIT KT7 190 A6
Woodfield Wy
FBAR/BDGN N11 48 D3
Woodford Av
GNTH/NBYPK IG2 71 K2
Woodford Bridge Rd
REDBR IG4 53 H6
Woodford Crs PIN HA5 41 F5
Woodford New Rd
WALTH E17 52 C6
Woodford Pl WBLY HA9 62 A5
Woodford Rd FSTGT E7 89 F2
SWFD E18 70 E1
Woodgate Av CHSGTN KT9 205 K3
Woodgate Crs NTHWD HA6 40 E2
Woodgate Dr
STRHM/NOR SW16 179 J3
Woodger Rd SHB W12 119 F2
Woodget Cl EHAM E6 107 J5
Woodgrange Av EA W5 117 G1
EN EN1 36 C1
KTN/HRWW/WS HA3 61 J2
NFNCH/WDSPK N12 47 H2
Woodgrange Cl
KTN/HRWW/WS HA3 61 K2
Woodgrange Gdns EN EN1 36 C1
Woodgrange Rd FSTGT E7 88 E3
Woodgrange Ter EN EN1 * 36 C1
Woodhall Av DUL SE21 163 G5
PIN HA5 41 J4
Woodhall Dr DUL SE21 163 G5
PIN HA5 41 H4
Woodhall Ga PIN HA5 41 H3
Woodhall La OXHEY WD19 27 H5
Woodham Ct SWFD E18 70 D1
Woodham Rd CAT SE6 165 F5
Woodhatch Cl EHAM E6 107 J4
Woodhaven Gdns
BARK/HLT IG6 72 C1
Woodhayes Rd
WIM/MER SW19 177 F2
Woodhead Dr ORP BR6 216 E1
Woodheyes Rd WLSDN NW10 81 G3
Woodhill WOOL/PLUM SE18 126 D4
Woodhill Crs
KTN/HRWW/WS HA3 61 K3
Woodhouse Av GFD/PVL UB6 97 F1
Woodhouse Cl EDUL SE22 143 H5
GFD/PVL UB6 97 F1
HYS/HAR UB3 113 H3
Woodhouse Eaves
NTHWD HA6 40 E1
Woodhouse Gv FSTGT E7 89 J4
Woodhouse Rd
NFNCH/WDSPK N12 47 G2
WAN E11 88 D1
Woodhurst Av
STMC/STPC BR5 201 H3
Woodhurst Rd ABYW SE2 128 B5
ACT W3 117 K1
Woodies La NWMAL KT3 192 A3
Woodington Cl
ELTH/MOT SE9 167 F1
Woodknoll Dr CHST BR7 184 E4
Woodland Ap GFD/PVL UB6 79 G4
Woodland Av MNPK E12 89 J1
Woodland Cl CDALE/KGS NW9 62 E3
HOR/WEW KT19 * 207 G4
NRWD SE19 181 F2
WFD IG8 39 F5
Woodland Ct GLDGN NW11 * 64 C2
Woodland Crs
BERM/RHTH SE16 124 A2
GNWCH SE10 125 H6
Woodland Gdns ISLW TW7 135 K4
MUSWH N10 66 B2
Woodland Gv CROY/NA CR0 211 G5
GNWCH SE10 125 H5
Woodland Hl NRWD SE19 181 F2
Woodland Ms
STRHM/NOR SW16 161 K5
Woodland Ri GFD/PVL UB6 79 G4
MUSWH N10 66 B1
Woodland Rd CHING E4 38 A3
FBAR/BDGN N11 48 B1
NRWD SE19 181 F1
THHTH CR7 196 B1
Woodlands BXLYHS DA6 149 J6
GLDGN NW11 64 C2
RYLN/HDSTN HA2 60 A1
RYNPK SW20 193 F1
Woodlands Av ACT W3 117 J1
BFN/LL DA15 167 K3
CHDH RM6 74 A3
FNCH N3 47 G3
NWMAL KT3 176 A4
RSLP HA4 59 G5
WAN E11 71 F5
WPK KT4 192 C6
Woodlands Cl BMLY BR1 184 E5
ESH/CLAY KT10 205 F5
GLDGN NW11 64 C2
Woodlands Dr STAN HA7 43 F2
SUN TW16 172 B5
Woodlands Gdns
WALTH E17 * 70 C1
Woodlands Gv ISLW TW7 135 K3
Woodlands Pk BXLY DA5 169 K6
Woodlands Park Rd
GNWCH SE10 125 H6
SEVS/STOTM N15 67 J2
Woodlands Rd BARN SW13 138 C4
BMLY BR1 184 E5
BXLYHN DA7 149 F4
ED N9 36 E3
ENC/FH EN2 23 K1
HRW HA1 61 F2
IL IG1 90 C1
ISLW TW7 135 K4
ORP BR6 217 G4
ROM RM1 57 H6
STHL UB1 114 C1
SURB KT6 190 E4
WALTH E17 52 A6
WAN E11 70 C6
Woodlands St LEW SE13 165 G2
Woodlands Ter SWLY BR8 * 203 K3
The Woodlands
BRXN/ST SW9 * 142 C1
ESH/CLAY KT10 189 H6
HRW HA1 * 60 E6
ISLW TW7 136 A3
LEW SE13 165 G2
NRWD SE19 180 D3
ORP BR6 217 H4
STAN HA7 * 43 H1
STHGT/OAK N14 34 B3
WLGTN SM6 210 B6
Woodland St HACK E8 * 86 B4
Woodlands Wy
PUT/ROE SW15 139 J6
Woodland Ter CHARL SE7 126 D4
Woodland Wk HAMP NW3 83 J3
HOR/WEW KT19 206 C4
Woodland Wy ABYW SE2 128 E4
BRYLDS KT5 191 J6
CROY/NA CR0 198 B5
MLHL NW7 45 G2
MRDN SM4 193 J1
MTCM CR4 179 F3
STMC/STPC BR5 201 H1
WCHMH N21 35 G4
WFD IG8 39 F5
WWKM BR4 214 A1
Wood La BCTR RM8 74 C6
CDALE/KGS NW9 63 F4
DAGW RM9 92 A1
HCH RM12 93 J3
HGT N6 66 B3
ISLW TW7 115 K6
ISLW TW7 136 A1
MUSWH N10 66 C2
RSLP HA4 58 B6
SHB W12 100 A6
STAN HA7 29 H5
WFD IG8 52 D1
Woodlawn Cl PUT/ROE SW15 139 J6
Woodlawn Crs WHTN TW2 155 G4
Woodlawn Dr FELT TW13 154 C4
Woodlawn Rd FUL/PGN SW6 139 G1
Woodlea Dr HAYES BR2 199 H2
Woodlea Gv NTHWD HA6 40 A2
Woodlea Rd STNW/STAM N16 86 A1
Woodleigh Av
NFNCH/WDSPK N12 47 J2
Woodleigh Gdns
STRHM/NOR SW16 161 K5
Woodley Cl TOOT SW17 178 E3
Woodley La SUT SM1 209 J1
Woodley Rd ORP BR6 202 D6
Wood Lodge Gdns BMLY BR1 184 D3
Wood Lodge La WWKM BR4 214 A1
Woodman Ms RCH/KEW TW9 137 J2
Woodman Pth BARK/HLT IG6 54 E1
Woodman Rd BARK/HLT IG6 54 E2
Woodmans Gv WLSDN NW10 81 H3
Woodmansterne Rd CAR SM5 209 J6
STRHM/NOR SW16 179 H3
Woodman St CAN/RD E16 127 F1
Wood Md TOTM N17 * 50 C2
Woodmere ELTH/MOT SE9 166 E2
Woodmere Av CROY/NA CR0 198 A4
Woodmere Cl BTSEA SW11 141 F4
CROY/NA CR0 198 A4
Woodmere Gdns
CROY/NA CR0 198 A4
Woodmere Wy BECK BR3 199 G2
Woodmill Rd CLPT E5 68 E6
Woodnook Rd
STRHM/NOR SW16 179 G1
Woodpecker Cl BUSH WD23 28 C3
ED N9 36 D1
KTN/HRWW/WS HA3 43 F4
Woodpecker Ms LEW SE13 145 G5
Woodpecker Mt
CROY/NA CR0 213 G6
Woodpecker Rd THMD SE28 109 J6
Woodquest Av HNHL SE24 142 C6
Wood Ride EBAR EN4 21 H2
STMC/STPC BR5 201 J1
Woodridge Cl ENC/FH EN2 * 23 G2
Woodridge Wy NTHWD HA6 40 C2
Woodridings Av PIN HA5 41 K4
Woodridings Cl PIN HA5 41 K3
Woodriffe Rd WAN E11 70 B4
Wood Ri PIN HA5 58 E2
Wood Rd WLSDN NW10 80 E5
Woodrow WOOL/PLUM SE18 126 D4
Woodrow Av YEAD UB4 94 D4
Woodrow Cl GFD/PVL UB6 79 H5
Woodrow Ct TOTM N17 50 D3
Woodrush Cl NWCR SE14 144 B1
Woodrush Wy CHDH RM6 73 K1
Woodseer St WCHPL E1 13 K1
Woodsford Sq WKENS W14 119 H2
Woodshire Rd DAGE RM10 92 D1
Woodside BKHH IG9 39 G4
GLDGN NW11 64 E2
ORP BR6 217 G3
WIM/MER SW19 177 J1
Woodside Av ALP/SUD HA0 80 A6
CHST BR7 185 H1
ESH/CLAY KT10 189 K4
HGT N6 65 K2
NFNCH/WDSPK N12 33 G6
SNWD SE25 197 J3
Woodside Cl ALP/SUD HA0 80 A6
BRYLDS KT5 191 K4
BXLYHN DA7 150 A5
RSLP HA4 58 B3
STAN HA7 43 G1
Woodside Ct EA W5 * 117 F1
Woodside Court Rd
CROY/NA CR0 197 H4
Woodside Crs BFN/LL DA15 167 K5
Woodside Dr RDART DA2 170 B6
Woodside End ALP/SUD HA0 80 A6
Woodside Gdns CHING E4 51 K1
TOTM N17 50 B5
Woodside Grange Rd
NFNCH/WDSPK N12 33 F6
Woodside Gn SNWD SE25 197 H3
Woodside Gv
NFNCH/WDSPK N12 33 G5
Woodside La BXLY DA5 168 E1
TRDG/WHET N20 33 F5
Woodside Pde BFN/LL DA15 * 167 K5
Woodside Pk SNWD SE25 197 H3
Woodside Park Av WALTH E17 70 B1
Woodside Park Rd
NFNCH/WDSPK N12 33 F6
Woodside Pl ALP/SUD HA0 80 A6
Woodside Rd BFN/LL DA15 167 K5
BMLY BR1 200 D2
BXLYHN DA7 150 A5
KUTN/CMB KT2 175 F3
NTHWD HA6 40 D3
NWMAL KT3 176 A5
PLSTW E13 107 G3
SNWD SE25 197 J3
SUT SM1 209 G1
WDGN N22 49 G3
WFD IG8 38 E6
Woodside Wy CROY/NA CR0 197 K3
MTCM CR4 179 G4
Wood's Ms MYFR/PKLN W1K 9 F5
Woodsome Rd KTTN NW5 84 A1
Wood's Pl STHWK SE1 19 H5
Woodspring Rd
WIM/MER SW19 159 H4
Wood's Rd PECK SE15 143 J2
Woodstead Gv EDGW HA8 44 A2
The Woods NTHWD HA6 40 E1
Woodstock Av CHEAM SM3 193 J4
GLDGN NW11 64 C4
ISLW TW7 136 B6
STHL UB1 95 K2
WEA W13 116 B3
Woodstock Cl BXLY DA5 169 G3
STAN HA7 44 A5
Woodstock Crs ED N9 36 D1
Woodstock Gdns BECK BR3 182 E4
GDMY/SEVK IG3 73 G6
YEAD UB4 94 D4
Woodstock Gra EA W5 * 117 F1
Woodstock Gv SHB W12 119 G2
Woodstock La North
SURB KT6 190 D6
Woodstock La South
ESH/CLAY KT10 205 H3
Woodstock Ms
CAVSQ/HST W1G 9 H2
Woodstock Ri CHEAM SM3 193 J5
Woodstock Rd ALP/SUD HA0 80 B5
BUSH WD23 28 E2
CAR SM5 210 A3
CHSWK W4 118 B4
CROY/NA CR0 211 K1
FSBYPK N4 67 G5
FSTGT E7 89 G5
GLDGN NW11 64 D4
WALTH E17 52 B5
Woodstock St CAN/RD E16 106 D5
OXSTW W1C 9 J4
Woodstock Ter POP/IOD E14 105 K6
Woodstock Wy MTCM CR4 179 H5
Woodstone Av EW KT17 207 J3
Wood St BAR EN5 20 A5
BARB EC2Y 12 D2
CAN/RD E16 107 F6
CHSWK W4 118 B5
CITYW EC2V 12 D3
KUT/HW KT1 174 E4
MTCM CR4 195 F4
WALTH E17 52 A6
Woodsyre SYD SE26 163 G6
Wood Ter CRICK NW2 * 63 H6
Woodthorpe Rd ASHF TW15 152 B6
PUT/ROE SW15 138 E5
Woodtree Cl HDN NW4 46 A5
Wood V FSTH SE23 163 J3
MUSWH N10 66 C2
Woodvale Av SNWD SE25 181 G6
Woodvale Wy GLDGN NW11 82 B1
Woodview Av CHING E4 38 A6
Woodview Cl ORP BR6 201 H6
PUT/ROE SW15 158 A6
Woodview Rd SWLY BR8 187 K5
Woodville Cl LEE/GVPK SE12 145 K6
TEDD TW11 156 B6
Woodville Gdns BARK/HLT IG6 54 B6
EA W5 98 A5
RSLP HA4 58 A4
SURB KT6 * 190 E4
Woodville Gv WELL DA16 * 148 B4
Woodville Rd BAR EN5 21 F4
EA W5 98 A5
GLDGN NW11 64 C4
KIL/WHAMP NW6 * 100 D1
MRDN SM4 193 K1
RCHPK/HAM TW10 156 C5
STNW/STAM N16 86 A3
SWFD E18 53 F5
THHTH CR7 180 E6
WALTH E17 69 G1
WAN E11 70 D5
Woodville St
WOOL/PLUM SE18 126 D4
Woodward Av HDN NW4 63 J2
Woodward Cl ESH/CLAY KT10 205 F4
Woodwarde Rd EDUL SE22 163 F1
Woodward Gdns DAGW RM9 91 J5
STAN HA7 43 F3
Woodward Rd DAGW RM9 91 H5
Wood Wy ORP BR6 201 F6
Woodway Crs HRW HA1 61 G3
Woodwaye OXHEY WD19 27 G2
Woodwell St
WAND/EARL SW18 140 B6
Wood Whf GNWCH SE10 124 E6
Woodyard Cl KTTN NW5 84 A3
Woodyard La DUL SE21 163 F2
Woodyates Rd
LEE/GVPK SE12 165 K1
Woolacombe Rd
BKHTH/KID SE3 146 B3
Woolacombe Wy
HYS/HAR UB3 113 H4
Woolbrook Rd DART DA1 170 B1
Wooler St WALW SE17 122 E5
Woolf Cl THMD SE28 128 C1
Woolf Ms STPAN WC1H 4 E6
Woollaston Rd FSBYPK N4 67 H3
Woollett Cl DART DA1 150 D5
Woolmead Av
CDALE/KGS NW9 63 J4
Woolmer Gdns UED N18 50 C1
Woolmer Rd UED N18 50 C1
Woolmore St POP/IOD E14 106 A6
Woolneigh St FUL/PGN SW6 140 A4
Woolridge Cl
EBED/NFELT TW14 153 F3
Woolridge Wy HOM E9 * 86 E5
Wool Rd RYNPK SW20 176 E2
Woolstaplers Wy
BERM/RHTH SE16 123 H3
Woolston Cl WALTH E17 51 F5
Woolstone Rd FSTH SE23 164 B4
Woolwich Church St
WOOL/PLUM SE18 126 D3
Woolwich Common
WOOL/PLUM SE18 127 F6
Woolwich Foot Tnl
CAN/RD E16 127 F2
Woolwich High St
WOOL/PLUM SE18 127 F3
Woolwich Manorway
CAN/RD E16 127 G2
Woolwich Manor Wy
CAN/RD E16 127 G1
EHAM E6 107 K3
Woolwich New Rd
WOOL/PLUM SE18 127 F5
Woolwich Rd ABYW SE2 128 E6
BXLYHN DA7 149 H4
CHARL SE7 126 B4
GNWCH SE10 125 K5
Wooster Gdns POP/IOD E14 106 B5
Wootton Gv FNCH N3 46 E4
Wootton St STHWK SE1 17 K2
Worbeck Rd PGE/AN SE20 181 J5
Worcester Av TOTM N17 50 C3
Worcester Cl CRICK NW2 81 J1
CROY/NA CR0 198 C6
MTCM CR4 179 F5
Worcester Ct WOT/HER KT12 188 B6
Worcester Crs MLHL NW7 31 G5
WFD IG8 39 G6
Worcester Dr CHSWK W4 118 B3
Worcester Gdns GFD/PVL UB6 78 C4
IL IG1 71 J4
WPK KT4 207 G1
Worcester Ms
KIL/WHAMP NW6 83 F4
Worcester Park Rd WPK KT4 206 E1
Worcester Rd BELMT SM2 208 E5
MNPK E12 89 K1
WALTH E17 51 F5
WIM/MER SW19 177 J1
Worcesters Av EN EN1 24 C1
Wordsworth Av GFD/PVL UB6 96 D1
MNPK E12 89 J5
SWFD E18 52 D6
Wordsworth Dr CHEAM SM3 208 A2
Wordsworth Pde
CEND/HSY/T N8 * 67 H1
Wordsworth Pl HAMP NW3 83 K3
Wordsworth Rd HPTN TW12 154 E6
PGE/AN SE20 182 A3
STHWK SE1 19 J7
STNW/STAM N16 86 A2
WELL DA16 147 K2
WLGTN SM6 210 C4
Wordsworth Wk
GLDGN NW11 64 D1
Wordsworth Wy DART DA1 151 K5
WDR/YW UB7 112 B4
Worfield St BTSEA SW11 140 D1
Worgan St BERM/RHTH SE16 124 A3
LBTH SE11 122 A5
Worland Rd SRTFD E15 88 C5
Worlds End Est
WBPTN SW10 * 140 C1
Worlds End La ORP BR6 217 G5
World's End La WCHMH N21 23 F6
Worlds End Pas
WBPTN SW10 * 140 C1
Worleys Dr ORP BR6 216 D2
Worlidge St HMSMTH W6 119 F5
Worlingham Rd EDUL SE22 143 G5
Wormholt Rd SHB W12 118 D1
Wormholt Ter SHB W12 * 118 D1
Wormwood St OBST EC2N 13 G3
Wornington Rd NKENS W10 100 C4
Woronzow Rd STJWD NW8 2 B1
Worple Av ISLW TW7 136 B6
WIM/MER SW19 177 G3
Worple Cl RYLN/HDSTN HA2 59 K5
Worple Rd ISLW TW7 136 B5
RYNPK SW20 177 F5
WIM/MER SW19 177 H3
Worple Road Ms
WIM/MER SW19 177 J2
Worple St MORT/ESHN SW14 138 A4
Worple Wy RCHPK/HAM TW10 137 F6
RYLN/HDSTN HA2 59 K5
Worship St SDTCH EC2A 7 F7
Worslade Rd TOOT SW17 160 C6
Worsley Bridge Rd SYD SE26 182 C1
Worsley Gv CLPT E5 86 C2
Worsley Rd WAN E11 88 C2
Worsopp Dr CLAP SW4 141 H6
Worth Cl ORP BR6 216 E2
Worthfield Cl HOR/WEW KT19 207 F5
Worth Gv WALW SE17 * 122 E5
Worthing Cl SRTFD E15 88 C6
Worthing Rd HEST TW5 114 E6
Worthington Cl MTCM CR4 195 G1
Worthington Rd SURB KT6 191 G5
Wortley Rd CROY/NA CR0 196 B4
EHAM E6 89 H5
Worton Gdns ISLW TW7 135 J3
Worton Rd ISLW TW7 136 A4
Worton Wy ISLW TW7 135 J3
Wotton Gn STMC/STPC BR5 202 E1
Wotton Rd CRICK NW2 82 A2
DEPT SE8 124 C6
Wouldham Rd CAN/RD E16 106 D5
Wouldham Ter
STMC/STPC BR5 * 186 C6
Wragby Rd WAN E11 * 88 C1
Wrampling Pl ED N9 36 C3
Wray Av CLAY IG5 54 A6
Wray Crs FSBYPK N4 66 E6
Wrayfield Rd CHEAM SM3 208 B1
Wray Rd BELMT SM2 208 D6
Wraysbury Cl HSLWW TW4 134 D6
Wrays Wy YEAD UB4 94 C4
Wrekin Rd WOOL/PLUM SE18 147 H1
Wren Av CRICK NW2 82 A2
NWDGN UB2 114 E4
Wren Cl CAN/RD E16 106 D5
ED N9 37 F3

STMC/STPC BR5 186 E6
Wren Crs BUSH WD23 28 C3
Wren Dr WDR/YW UB7 112 A2
Wren Gdns DAGW RM9 91 K3
HCH RM12 75 H5
Wren La RSLP HA4 59 F3
Wren Ms LEW SE13 * 145 H5
Wren Rd CMBW SE5 142 E2
DAGW RM9 91 K3
SCUP DA14 168 D5
Wren St FSBYW WC1X 5 H6
Wrentham Av WLSDN NW10 100 B1
Wrenthorpe Rd BMLY BR1 165 H6
Wrenwood Wy PIN HA5 59 F1
Wrexham Rd BOW E3 105 J1
Wricklemarsh Rd
BKHTH/KID SE3 146 A3
Wrigglesworth St NWCR SE14 144 A1
Wright Cl LEW SE13 145 G5
Wright Rd HEST TW5 134 B1
Wrights Cl DAGE RM10 92 D2
Wrights La KENS W8 * 119 K3
Wright's La KENS W8 119 K2
Wrights Pl WLSDN NW10 * 80 E4
Wrights Rd SNWD SE25 181 F6
Wright's Rd BOW E3 105 H1
Wright's Rw WLGTN SM6 210 B2
Wrigley Cl CHING E4 * 52 B1
Wrotham Rd BAR EN5 20 C3
CAMTN NW1 * 84 C5
WEA W13 116 D1
WELL DA16 148 D2
Wrottesley Rd WLSDN NW10 99 J1
WOOL/PLUM SE18 127 H6
Wroughton Rd BTSEA SW11 160 E1
Wroughton Ter HDN NW4 * 63 K1
Wroxall Rd DAGW RM9 91 J4
Wroxham Gdns
FBAR/BDGN N11 48 C3
Wroxham Rd THMD SE28 109 K6
Wroxham Wy BARK/HLT IG6 54 B4
Wroxton Rd PECK SE15 143 J3
Wrythe Gn CAR SM5 209 K1
Wrythe Green Rd CAR SM5 209 K1
Wrythe La CAR SM5 194 C5
Wulfstan St SHB W12 99 H5
Wyatt Cl BUSH WD23 28 E2
FELT TW13 154 C3
YEAD UB4 94 E4
Wyatt Dr BARN SW13 118 E6
Wyatt Park Rd
BRXS/STRHM SW2 162 A4
Wyatt Rd DART DA1 150 C4
FSTGT E7 88 E4
HBRY N5 85 J1
Wyatt's La WALTH E17 52 A6
Wybert St CAMTN NW1 3 K6
Wyborne Wy WLSDN NW10 80 E5
Wyburn Av BAR EN5 20 D4
Wychcombe Studios
HAMP NW3 * 83 K4
Wyche Gv SAND/SEL CR2 211 J5
Wych Elm Cl KUTN/CMB KT2 175 G3
Wycherley Cl BKHTH/KID SE3 145 J1
Wycherley Crs BAR EN5 33 F1
Wychwood Av EDGW HA8 43 K2
THHTH CR7 180 C6
Wychwood Cl EDGW HA8 43 K2
Wychwood End HGT N6 66 C4
Wychwood Gdns CLAY IG5 71 K1
Wychwood Wy NTHWD HA6 40 D3
Wycliffe Cl WELL DA16 148 A2
Wycliffe Rd BTSEA SW11 141 F3
WIM/MER SW19 178 A2
Wyclif St FSBYE EC1V 6 A5
Wycombe Gdns GLDGN NW11 64 D6
Wycombe Pl
WAND/EARL SW18 160 B1
Wycombe Rd ALP/SUD HA0 80 C6
GNTH/NBYPK IG2 71 K2
TOTM N17 50 C4
Wydell Cl MRDN SM4 193 F3
Wydenhurst Rd CROY/NA CR0 197 H4
Wydeville Manor Rd
LEE/GVPK SE12 166 A6
Wye Cl ASHF TW15 152 E6
ORP BR6 202 A4
RSLP HA4 58 A3
Wyemead Crs CHING E4 38 C4
Wye St BTSEA SW11 140 C4
Wyevale Cl NTHWD HA6 40 E6
Wyfields CLAY IG5 54 B4
Wyfold Rd FUL/PGN SW6 139 H2
Wyke Cl ISLW TW7 116 A6
Wyke Gdns HNWL W7 116 A3
Wykeham Av DAGW RM9 91 J4
Wykeham Cl WDR/YW UB7 112 D6
Wykeham Gn DAGW RM9 91 J4
Wykeham Hl WBLY HA9 62 B5
Wykeham Ri TRDG/WHET N20 32 C3
Wykeham Rd HDN NW4 64 A2
KTN/HRWW/WS HA3 61 H1
Wyke Rd BOW E3 87 J5
RYNPK SW20 177 F5
Wylchin Cl PIN HA5 58 D1
Wyldes Cl GLDGN NW11 65 G5
Wyldfield Gdns ED N9 36 B4
Wyld Wy WBLY HA9 80 D4
Wyleu St FSTH SE23 164 B2
Wylie Rd NWDGN UB2 115 F3
Wyllen Cl WCHPL E1 104 E3
Wylo Dr BAR EN5 31 H1
Wymark Cl RAIN RM13 111 H1
Wymering Rd MV/WKIL W9 100 E2
Wymond St PUT/ROE SW15 139 F4
Wynan Rd POP/IOD E14 124 E5
Wynaud Ct WDGN N22 49 F2
Wyncham Av BFN/LL DA15 167 K3
Wynchgate
KTN/HRWW/WS HA3 42 E3
STHGT/OAK N14 34 E2
Wyncote Wy SAND/SEL CR2 213 F6
Wyncroft Cl BMLY BR1 184 E6
Wyndale Av CDALE/KGS NW9 62 C3
Wyndcliff Rd CHARL SE7 126 A6
Wyndcroft Cl ENC/FH EN2 23 H4
Wyndham Cl BELMT SM2 208 E5
ORP BR6 201 H5
Wyndham Crs HSLWW TW4 154 E1
KTTN NW5 84 C1
Wyndham Est CMBW SE5 142 D1
Wyndham Ms MBLAR W1H 8 E2
Wyndham Pl MBLAR W1H 8 E2
Wyndham Rd CMBW SE5 142 D1
EBAR EN4 33 K3
EHAM E6 89 H5
KUTN/CMB KT2 175 G3
WEA W13 116 C3
Wyndham St CAMTN NW1 8 E1
Wyndham Yd MBLAR W1H * 8 E2
Wyndhurst Cl SAND/SEL CR2 211 H5
Wyneham Rd HNHL SE24 142 E6
Wynell Rd FSTH SE23 164 A5
Wynford Gv STMC/STPC BR5 186 C6
Wynford Pl BELV DA17 129 H6
Wynford Rd IS N1 5 G2
Wynford Wy ELTH/MOT SE9 166 E5
Wynlie Gdns PIN HA5 41 F5
Wynn Bridge Cl WFD IG8 53 H4
Wynndale Rd SWFD E18 53 F4
Wynne Rd BRXN/ST SW9 142 B3
Wynn's Av BFN/LL DA15 148 B6
Wynnstay Gdns KENS W8 * 119 K3
Wynter St BTSEA SW11 140 B5
Wynton Gdns SNWD SE25 197 F2
Wynton Pl ACT W3 98 D5
Wynyard Ter LBTH SE11 * 122 A5
Wynyatt St FSBYE EC1V 6 A4
Wyre Gv EDGW HA8 30 D5
HYS/HAR UB3 113 K4
Wyresdale Crs GFD/PVL UB6 97 F2
Wyteleaf Cl RSLP HA4 58 A3
Wythburn Pl MBLAR W1H 8 E4
Wythenshawe Rd DAGE RM10 92 C1
Wythes Cl BMLY BR1 184 E5
Wythes Rd CAN/RD E16 126 D1
Wythfield Rd ELTH/MOT SE9 166 E1
Wyvenhoe Rd
RYLN/HDSTN HA2 78 C1
Wyvern Cl DART DA1 171 F2
ORP BR6 217 H1
Wyvern Est NWMAL KT3 * 176 D6
Wyvil Rd VX/NE SW8 141 K1
Wyvis St POP/IOD E14 105 K4

Y

Yabsley St POP/IOD E14 125 F1
Yalding Gv STMC/STPC BR5 202 E1
Yalding Rd BERM/RHTH SE16 123 H3
Yale Cl HSLWW TW4 134 E6
Yale Wy HCH RM12 93 J2
Yarborough Rd
WIM/MER SW19 178 C4
Yardley Cl CHING E4 25 K6
Yardley La CHING E4 25 K6
Yardley St FSBYW WC1X 5 J5
Yarmouth Crs TOTM N17 68 D2
Yarmouth Pl MYFR/PICC W1J 15 J1
Yarnton Wy ABYW SE2 128 D2
ERITHM DA18 129 F2
Yarrow Crs EHAM E6 107 J4
Yateley St WOOL/PLUM SE18 126 C3
Yeading Av RYLN/HDSTN HA2 59 J6
Yeading Fk YEAD UB4 95 G4
Yeading Gdns YEAD UB4 95 F4
Yeading La YEAD UB4 95 F5
Yeames Cl WEA W13 97 G5
Yeate St IS N1 85 K5
Yeatman Rd HGT N6 65 K3
Yeats Cl HNWL W7 97 F6
LEW SE13 * 145 G3
WLSDN NW10 81 G4
Ye Cnr OXHEY WD19 27 H1
Yeend Cl E/WMO/HCT KT8 189 F1
Yeldham Rd HMSMTH W6 119 G5
Yeldham Vls HMSMTH W6 * 119 G5
Yelverton Rd BTSEA SW11 140 C3
Yenston Cl MRDN SM4 193 K3
Yeoman Cl EHAM E6 108 B6
Yeoman Dr STWL/WRAY TW19 152 B3
Yeoman Rd NTHLT UB5 77 J5
Yeomans Acre RSLP HA4 58 E3
Yeoman's Rw CHEL SW3 14 D5
Yeoman St BERM/RHTH SE16 124 B4
Yeomans Wy PEND EN3 * 24 D3
Yeoman's Yd WCHPL E1 13 K5
Yeomen Wy BARK/HLT IG6 54 C2
Yeo St BOW E3 105 K4
Yeovil Cl ORP BR6 201 K6
Yeovilton Pl KUTN/CMB KT2 174 E1
Yerbury Rd ARCH N19 84 D1
Yester Dr CHST BR7 184 D3
Yester Pk CHST BR7 184 E3
Yester Rd CHST BR7 184 E3
Yew Cl BKHH IG9 39 H4
Yewdale Cl BMLY BR1 183 H2
Yewfield Rd WLSDN NW10 81 H4
Yew Gv CRICK NW2 82 B2
The Yews ASHF TW15 * 152 E6
Yew Tree Cl LEW SE13 145 F4
Yewtree Cl MUSWH N10 48 C4
RYLN/HDSTN HA2 60 B1
Yew Tree Cl WCHMH N21 35 G2
WELL DA16 148 B2
WPK KT4 192 B5
Yew Tree Ct BORE WD6 29 K1
Yew Tree Gdns CHDH RM6 74 A2
ROMW/RG RM7 75 F2
Yew Tree Rd BECK BR3 182 C6
SHB W12 99 H6
Yew Tree Wk HSLWW TW4 134 E6
Yew Wk HRW HA1 60 E5
Yoakley Rd STNW/STAM N16 68 A6
Yoke Cl HOLWY N7 84 E4
Yolande Gdns ELTH/MOT SE9 146 D6
Yonge Pk HOLWY N7 85 G1
York Av BFN/LL DA15 167 K4
HNWL W7 115 K1
HYS/HAR UB3 94 A5
MORT/ESHN SW14 137 K6
STAN HA7 43 H4
York Br CAMTN NW1 3 G6
York Blds CHCR WC2N 11 F6
York Cl CMBW SE5 * 142 D3
EHAM E6 107 K5
HNWL W7 115 K1
MRDN SM4 194 A1
York Gdns WOT/HER KT12 188 C6
York Ga CAMTN NW1 3 H7
STHGT/OAK N14 34 E2
York Gv PECK SE15 143 K2
York Hl WNWD SE27 162 C5
York House Pl KENS W8 120 A2
Yorkland Av WELL DA16 148 A5
York Ms IL IG1 72 A6
KTTN NW5 84 B3
York Pde BTFD TW8 * 116 E5
CDALE/KGS NW9 * 63 J3
York Pl BTSEA SW11 140 B4
IL IG1 72 A6
York Ri KTTN NW5 84 B1
ORP BR6 201 K5
York Rd ACT W3 98 E5
BAR EN5 21 G6
BELMT SM2 208 E6
BTFD TW8 116 E5
BTSEA SW11 140 B5
CHING E4 51 J1
CROY/NA CR0 196 B4
DART DA1 171 J2
EA W5 116 D3
FBAR/BDGN N11 48 D2
FSTGT E7 88 E4
HSLW TW3 135 G4
IL IG1 90 A1
KUTN/CMB KT2 175 G3
LEY E10 88 A1
NTHWD HA6 40 E5
RAIN RM13 93 F5
RCHPK/HAM TW10 137 G6
STHWK SE1 17 H2
TEDD TW11 155 K6
UED N18 50 D1
WALTH E17 69 F2
WCHMH N21 35 K2
WIM/MER SW19 178 A2
Yorkshire Cl STNW/STAM N16 86 A1
Yorkshire Gdns UED N18 50 D1
Yorkshire Grey Yd
GINN WC1R * 11 G2
Yorkshire Rd MTCM CR4 195 K2
POP/IOD E14 105 G5
York Sq POP/IOD E14 105 G5
York St MBLAR W1H 8 E2
MHST W1U 9 F1
MTCM CR4 195 F4
York Street Chambers
MHST W1U * 9 F1
York Ter ENC/FH EN2 23 J1
ERITH DA8 149 K2
York Ter East CAMTN NW1 3 H7
York Ter West CAMTN NW1 3 G7
Yorkton St BETH E2 104 C1
York Wy CHSGTN KT9 205 K5
FELT TW13 154 E5
HOLWY N7 84 D4
IS N1 5 F1
KCROSS N1C 5 F2
TRDG/WHET N20 33 K5
York Way Ct IS N1 5 F1
York Way Est HOLWY N7 84 E4
Youngmans Cl ENC/FH EN2 23 J2
Young Rd CAN/RD E16 107 G5
Youngs Rd GNTH/NBYPK IG2 72 D2
Young St KENS W8 120 A2
Yoxley Ap GNTH/NBYPK IG2 72 C3
Yoxley Dr GNTH/NBYPK IG2 72 C3
Yukon Rd BAL SW12 161 G2
Yunus Khan Cl WALTH E17 69 J2

Z

Zambezie Dr ED N9 36 E5
Zampa Rd BERM/RHTH SE16 123 K5
Zander Ct BETH E2 104 C2
Zangwill Rd BKHTH/KID SE3 146 C2
Zealand Av WDR/YW UB7 132 A1
Zealand Rd BOW E3 105 G1
Zelah Rd STMC/STPC BR5 202 C4
Zennor Rd BAL SW12 161 H3
Zenoria St EDUL SE22 143 G5
Zermatt Rd THHTH CR7 196 D1
Zetland St POP/IOD E14 106 A4
Zion Pl THHTH CR7 196 E1
Zion Rd THHTH CR7 196 E1
Zoar St STHWK SE1 12 C7
Zoffany St ARCH N19 66 D6

Index - featured places

O_2 Centre
HAMP NW3 83 G4
2 Willow Road (NT)
HAMP NW3 83 J2
30 St Mary Axe
HDTCH EC3A 13 H4
41 Hotel
BGVA SW1W 15 K4
7/7 Memorial
MYFR/PKLN W1K 15 G1
Aarotya Medical Centre
SEVS/STOTM N15 67 J1
Abbey Business Centre
VX/NE SW8 141 H2
Abbey Christian School for the English Language
STJWD NW8 101 G1
The Abbey Clinic
BELV DA17 129 G5
Abbey College London
BAY/PAD W2 100 E5
Abbey Industrial Estate
ALP/SUD HA0 80 B6
MTCM CR4 194 E2
Abbey Lane Commercial Estate
SRTFD E15 106 B1
Abbey Medical Centre
STJWD NW8 83 F6
Abbey Mills
WIM/MER SW19 178 B4
Abbey Park Industrial Estate
BARK IG11 108 B1
Abbey Primary School
ABYW SE2 128 D3
MRDN SM4 193 K4
Abbey Road ⊖
SRTFD E15 106 B1
Abbey Road Health Centre
SRTFD E15 88 C6
Abbey Road Studios
STJWD NW8 101 G1
Abbey Sports Centre
BARK IG11 90 C6
Abbey Trading Estate
SYD SE26 182 B1
Abbey Wharf Industrial Estate
BARK IG11 108 D2
Abbey Wood ⇌
ABYW SE2 128 D3
Abbotsbury Primary School
MRDN SM4 193 K2
Abbs Cross School & Arts College
HCH RM12 93 K1
ABC Cinema
PUT/ROE SW15 139 H4
Abercorn Place School
CAMTN NW1 8 D1
Abercorn School
MBLAR W1H 8 E2
Aberdeen Wharf
WAP E1W 123 J1
Aberglen Industrial Estate
HYS/HAR UB3 113 G2
Abingdon House School
KENS W8 119 K3
Abney Park Cemetery
STNW/STAM N16 68 A6
Acacia Business Centre
WAN E11 88 C1
Academic College of London
WBLY HA9 79 K1
The Academy School
HAMP NW3 83 H2
Acland Burghley School
KTTN NW5 84 B2
Acorn Industrial Park
DART DA1 150 D6
Acorn Medical Centre
TWK TW1 156 B3
Acorns Independent College
STHL UB1 115 F1
Acre Road Health Clinic
KUTN/CMB KT2 175 G3
Acton Business Centre
WLSDN NW10 99 F3
Acton Central ⊖
ACT W3 118 A1
Acton Central Industrial Estate
ACT W3 98 D6
Acton Health Centre
ACT W3 117 K1
Acton High School
ACT W3 117 H2
Acton Hospital
ACT W3 117 H2
Acton Lane Medical Centre
CHSWK W4 117 K2
Acton Main Line ⇌
ACT W3 98 E5
Acton Park Industrial Estate
ACT W3 118 A2
Acton Superbowl
ACT W3 98 C4
Acton Swimming Baths
ACT W3 117 K1
Acton Town ⊖
ACT W3 117 H2
Acton & West London College
ACT W3 117 J1
Acumen (Anglo School)
NRWD SE19 181 F4
Adams Bridge Business Centre
WBLY HA9 80 D3
Adamsrill Primary School
SYD SE26 164 B5
Adath Yisroel Cemetery
EN EN1 24 B2
Ad-Dean Primary School
IL IG1 90 C2
Addey & Stanhope School
NWCR SE14 144 C2
Addington Court Golf Club
CROY/NA CR0 213 H6
Addington Golf Club
CROY/NA CR0 213 H2
Addington Palace Golf Club
CROY/NA CR0 213 G4
Addington Village ⊖
CROY/NA CR0 213 J4
Addiscombe ⊖
CROY/NA CR0 197 H5
Addiscombe CC
CROY/NA CR0 212 C1
Addison Primary School
WKENS W14 119 G3
Adelphi Theatre
COVGDN WC2E 11 F6
Adler Industrial Estate
HYS/HAR UB3 113 G2
Admiral Hyson Industrial Estate
STHWK SE1 123 J4
Admiralty Arch
STJS SW1Y 10 D7
The Adult College of Barking & Dagenham
BARK IG11 90 E4
The Aerodrome School
CROY/NA CR0 211 H3
Africa Centre
COVGDN WC2E 11 F5
Aga Khan University
CAN/RD E16 106 D4
RSQ WC1B 10 D2
Agnew's
CONDST W1S 10 A7
Agora Shopping Centre
PECK SE15 143 H3
AHA International London Centre
BMSBY WC1N 11 H1
Ainslie Wood Primary School
CHING E4 51 K1
Airbase Unity Elementary School
RSLP HA4 58 A6
Airbus Coach Station
HTHAIR TW6 132 C4
Air Call Business Centre
CDALE/KGS NW9 45 F6
Airedale Physiotherapy Clinic
CHSWK W4 118 C5
Airlinks Golf Club
NWDGN UB2 114 B4
Air Links Industrial Estate
HEST TW5 114 B5
Airport Gate Business Centre
WDR/YW UB7 132 C1
Akiva School
FNCH N3 46 E5
Aksaray Sports Club
STNW/STAM N16 85 K2
Al-Azhar Primary School
WCHPL E1 104 C5
Albany Centre & Theatre
DEPT SE8 144 C1
Albany Clinic
BFN/LL DA15 168 B6
WIM/MER SW19 178 A3
Albany Park ⇌
SCUP DA14 168 E4
Albany Park Canoe & Sailing Centre
KUTN/CMB KT2 174 E2
The Albany School
HCH RM12 75 K6
Albemarle College
BAY/PAD W2 101 F6
Albemarle Primary School
WIM/MER SW19 159 H4
Albert Memorial
SKENS SW7 14 A2
Albion College
RSQ WC1B 10 E2
Albion Health Centre
WCHPL E1 104 D4
Albion Primary School
BERM/RHTH SE16 123 K2
Albion Street Health Centre
BERM/RHTH SE16 123 K2
Albright Industrial Estate
RAIN RM13 111 H4
Alchemea College of Audio Engineering
IS N1 85 H6
The Alchemy Gallery
CLKNW EC1R 5 J6
Alderbrook Primary School
BAL SW12 161 G2
Aldersbrook County Secondary School
MNPK E12 71 G5
Aldersbrook Primary School
MNPK E12 71 F5
Alderwood Primary School
ELTH/MOT SE9 167 J1
Aldgate ⊖
TWRH EC3N 13 J4
Aldgate Bus Station
HDTCH EC3A 13 J3
Aldgate East ⊖
WCHPL E1 13 K3
Aldwych Theatre
HOL/ALD WC2B 11 G4
Alexander McLeod Primary School
ABYW SE2 128 C5
Alexandra Avenue Clinic
RYLN/HDSTN HA2 59 K6

Alexandra Business Centre
PEND EN3 25 F5
Alexandra Infant School
KUTN/CMB KT2 175 H3
PGE/AN SE20 182 A3
Alexandra Junior School
HSLW TW3 135 G3
SYD SE26 182 A2
Alexandra Palace
WDGN N22 48 D6
Alexandra Palace Ice Rink
WDGN N22 48 D5
Alexandra Park School
FBAR/BDGN N11 48 C3
Alexandra Primary School
WDGN N22 49 F5
Alexandra School
RYLN/HDSTN HA2 59 K6
Al Falah Boys School
CLPT E5 86 D1
Al Falah Primary School
CLPT E5 86 D1
Alfred Salter Primary School
BERM/RHTH SE16 124 A2
Alfreds Way Industrial Estate
BARK IG11 91 G6
Al-Khair Primary & Secondary School
CROY/NA CR0 196 E5
Allenby Primary School
STHL UB1 96 A5
Allen Edwards Primary School
CLAP SW4 141 K2
The All England Lawn Tennis & Croquet Club
WIM/MER SW19 159 G5
Alleyns Junior School
EDUL SE22 143 F6
Allfarthing JMI School
WAND/EARL SW18 160 B1
All Saints ⊖
POP/IOD E14 106 A5
All Saints Benhilton CE Primary
SUT SM1 209 F1
All Saints Catholic School
BCTR RM8 74 C5
All Saints CE Primary School
BKHTH/KID SE3 145 H3
CAR SM5 210 A3
CRICK NW2 82 D1
FUL/PGN SW6 139 H3
PUT/ROE SW15 139 F4
TRDG/WHET N20 33 H4
WIM/MER SW19 178 B3
All Saints J & I School
NRWD SE19 181 F4
All Souls CE Primary School
GTPST W1W 10 A2
Allum Medical Centre
WAN E11 70 B4
Alma Primary School
BERM/RHTH SE16 123 H4
PEND EN3 25 G6
Almeida Theatre
IS N1 85 H5
Al-Noor Primary School
GDMY/SEVK IG3 73 H5
Alperton ⊖
ALP/SUD HA0 79 K6
Alperton Cemetery
ALP/SUD HA0 79 K6
Alperton Community School
ALP/SUD HA0 79 K5
Alperton Sports Ground
ALP/SUD HA0 97 K1
Alpha Business Centre
WALTH E17 69 H2
Alpha Preparatory School
HRW HA1 60 E2
Alpine Business Centre
EHAM E6 108 A4
Al-Risaala School
BAL SW12 161 G3
Al-Sadiq Boys & Al-Zahra Girls Schools
KIL/WHAMP NW6 82 C6
Alscot Road Industrial Estate
STHWK SE1 19 K6
Altmore Infant School
EHAM E6 89 K5
The Alton School
PUT/ROE SW15 158 C2
Ambler Primary School
FSBYPK N4 85 H1
Ambleside Junior School
WOT/HER KT12 188 B5
AMC Business Centre
WLSDN NW10 98 D2
American Intercontinental University
MHST W1U 9 H2
The American School in London
STJWD NW8 101 G1
AMF Bowling
LEW SE13 145 F4
Amida Golf
FELT TW13 155 F5
Ampere Way ⊖
CROY/NA CR0 196 A5
Ampthill Square Medical Centre
CAMTN NW1 4 B3
Anchorage Point Industrial Estate
CHARL SE7 126 B3
Anchor Bay Industrial Estate
ERITH DA8 150 C1
Anchor Retail Park
WCHPL E1 104 E3
The Anchor School
SUT SM1 194 A6
ANdAZ Hotel
LVPST EC2M 13 G2
Andover Medical Centre
HOLWY N7 85 F1
The Andrew Ewing Primary School
HEST TW5 134 E1
Anerley ⇌ ⊖
PGE/AN SE20 181 H4
Anerley School
NRWD SE19 181 H4
Angel ⊖
IS N1 6 A2
Angel Centre
DART DA1 171 H1
Angel Road ⇌
UED N18 50 E1
Angerstein Business Park
GNWCH SE10 125 K4
Anglian Industrial Estate
BARK IG11 109 F3
Animal Cemetery
REDBR IG4 53 H6
Annemount School
EFNCH N2 65 G3
Annunciation RC Infant School
EDGW HA8 45 F4
The Annunciation RC Junior School
MLHL NW7 45 F2
Anson Primary School
CRICK NW2 82 B3
Apex Hotel
MON EC3R 13 H5
Apex Industrial Estate
WLSDN NW10 99 H3
Apex Primary School
IL IG1 72 A5
Apex Retail Park
FELT TW13 154 E5
Apollo Theatre
SOHO/CST W1F 10 C5
Apollo Victoria Theatre
PIM SW1V 16 A5
Apostolic Nuncio
WIM/MER SW19 159 F5
Applegarth Primary School
CROY/NA CR0 213 K4
Apsley House, The Wellington Museum
KTBR SW1X 15 G2
Aquarius Business Park
CRICK NW2 63 J5
Aquarius Golf Club
EDUL SE22 143 K6
Aquatics Centre
OLYMPICPK E20 88 A5
Aragon Primary School
MRDN SM4 193 H4
Arcadia Shopping Centre
EA W5 97 K6
Arcadia University
BAY/PAD W2 101 F6
Archbishop Sumners CE Primary School
LBTH SE11 17 K7
Archbishop Tenisons CE School
CROY/NA CR0 212 B1
Archbishop Tenison's School
VX/NE SW8 122 A6
Archdale Business Centre
RYLN/HDSTN HA2 60 C6
Archdeacon Cambridge's CE Primary School
WHTN TW2 155 K4
Arches Business Centre
NWDGN UB2 114 E2
Arches Leisure Centre
GNWCH SE10 125 G6
Archgate Business Centre
NFNCH/WDSPK N12 33 G6
Architectural Association School of Architecture
RSQ WC1B 10 C2
Archway ⊖
ARCH N19 66 C6
Archway Business Centre
ARCH N19 84 D1
Archway Leisure Centre
ARCH N19 66 C6
Arena ⊖
SNWD SE25 197 K2
Arena Estate
FSBYPK N4 67 H3
Argent Centre Industrial Estate
HYS/HAR UB3 113 K2
Argyle Primary School
STPAN WC1H 5 F5
Ark Academy
WBLY HA9 62 C6
Ark Atwood Primary Academy
HOL/ALD WC2B 11 G3
Arklow Trading Estate
NWCR SE14 124 B6
Armourers & Braziers' Hall
LOTH EC2R 12 E2
Arndale Health Centre
WAND/EARL SW18 159 K1
Arnhem Wharf Primary School
POP/IOD E14 124 C3
Arnold House School
STJWD NW8 2 A2
Arnos Grove ⊖
FBAR/BDGN N11 34 C6
Arnos Pool
FBAR/BDGN N11 48 D1
Arrivals
HTHAIR TW6 132 C4
Arsenal ⊖
HBRY N5 85 G1
Arsenal FC (Emirates Stadium)
HOLWY N7 85 G2
Artsdepot
NFNCH/WDSPK N12 47 G1
The Arts Educational School
CHSWK W4 118 B4
Arts Theatre
LSQ/SEVD WC2H 10 D5
Ashbourne College
KENS W8 120 A2
Ashburnham Primary School
WBPTN SW10 140 C1
Ashby Mill
BRXS/STRHM SW2 161 K1
Ashby Mill School
CLAP SW4 141 K6
Ashcroft Technology Academy
PUT/ROE SW15 139 J6
Ashfield Junior School
BUSH WD23 28 B2
Ashford ⇌
ASHF TW15 152 C5
Ashford Cemetery
STWL/WRAY TW19 152 C4
Ashford Clinic
ASHF TW15 152 B5
Ashford Hospital
STWL/WRAY TW19 152 B4
Ashford Industrial Estate
ASHF TW15 153 F6
Ashford Sports Club
ASHF TW15 152 A6
STWL/WRAY TW19 152 C3
Ashgrove College
WALTH E17 51 J6
Ashgrove School
BMLY BR1 184 A5
Ashgrove Trading Estate
BMLY BR1 183 G2
Ashleigh Commercial Estate
CHARL SE7 126 B4
Ashmead Primary School
BROCKY SE4 144 D3
Ashmole Academy
STHGT/OAK N14 34 C3
Ashmole Centre
STHGT/OAK N14 34 C3
Ashmole Primary School
VX/NE SW8 122 A6
Ashmount Primary School
ARCH N19 66 D4
Ashton House School
ISLW TW7 135 J2
Ashton Playing Fields Track
WFD IG8 53 J2
Aspen House School
LBTH SE11 122 C6
Aspen House Secondary & Primary School
BRXS/STRHM SW2 161 K3
Asquith Court School
HPTN TW12 173 G4
KTN/HRWW/WS HA3 61 H3
Asquith School
PEND EN3 24 E5
Associated Newspapers Offices
BERM/RHTH SE16 124 A3
Assunah School
TOTM N17 50 B5
Aston Clinic
NWMAL KT3 192 B1
Aston House School
EA W5 97 K5
Asylum Medical Centre
CEND/HSY/T N8 49 G6
Athelney Primary School
CAT SE6 164 D5
Athelstan House School
HPTN TW12 173 F4
Athenaeum Hotel
MYFR/PICC W1J 15 J1
Athena Medical Centre
CLPT E5 86 E2
Atherton Leisure Centre
SRTFD E15 88 D4
Athletes Village
OLYMPICPK E20 88 A3
Athlone House Hospital
HGT N6 65 K5
Athlon Industrial Estate
ALP/SUD HA0 97 K1
Atkinson Morley Hospital
RYNPK SW20 176 E3
Atlantic House (Richmond American International University)
KENS W8 120 A3
Atlas Business Centre
CRICK NW2 63 K6
Atlas Transport Estate
BTSEA SW11 140 B3
Attlee Youth & Community Centre
WCHPL E1 13 K2
Auriol Junior School
HOR/WEW KT19 207 H2
Australia House
HOL/ALD WC2B 11 H4
Avenue House Museum
FNCH N3 46 D5
Avenue House School
WEA W13 97 H5
Avenue Industrial Estate
CHING E4 51 H2
Avenue Pre-Preparatory School
HGT N6 66 B4
Avenue Primary School
MNPK E12 89 J2
Avenue Road ⊖
BECK BR3 182 A5
Avery Hill Park
ELTH/MOT SE9 167 H1
Avondale Park Primary School
NTGHL W11 100 B6
Avon House School
WFD IG8 38 E6
Avon Trading Estate
WKENS W14 119 J4
Ayesha Community School
HDN NW4 63 J3
The Aylesham Centre
PECK SE15 143 H2
Aylward Academy
UED N18 35 K6
Aylward Primary School
STAN HA7 43 K1
Azhar Academy
FSTGT E7 88 E4
BAA Heathrow Visitor Centre
HTHAIR TW6 132 E2
Babington House School
CHST BR7 184 E2
BackCare Clinic
WPK KT4 192 D5
Bacon's College
BERM/RHTH SE16 124 B1
Baden Powell House
SKENS SW7 120 B4
Baglioni Hotel
KENS W8 120 B2
Bakers Hall
MON EC3R 13 H6
Baker Street ⊖
CAMTN NW1 3 F7
Balaam Leisure Centre
PLSTW E13 106 E3
Bales College
NKENS W10 100 B2
Balfour Business Centre
NWDGN UB2 114 C3
Balgowan Primary School
BECK BR3 182 B5
Balham ⇌ ⊖
BAL SW12 161 G3
Balham Girls Preparatory Secondary School
TOOT SW17 160 E5
Balham Health Centre
BAL SW12 161 G4
Balham Leisure Centre
TOOT SW17 161 F4
Balmoral Trading Estate
BARK IG11 109 F3
Baltic Exchange
HDTCH EC3A 13 H3
Bancrofts School
WFD IG8 38 E5
Bandon Hill Cemetery
WLGTN SM6 210 D3
Bandon Hill Primary School
WLGTN SM6 210 D4
Bangabandhu Primary School
BETH E2 104 E2
Bank ⊖ ⊖
LOTH EC2R 12 E4
Bank of England Extension
CITYW EC2V 12 C4
Bank of England (& Museum)
LOTH EC2R 12 E4
Bankside Gallery
STHWK SE1 12 B6
Bankside Jetty
STHWK SE1 12 C6
Bankside Park Industrial Estate
BARK IG11 109 G2
Bannister Stadium
KTN/HRWW/WS HA3 42 C2
Bannockburn Primary School
WOOL/PLUM SE18 128 A4
The Banqueting House, Whitehall
WHALL SW1A 16 E1
Barbara Speake Theatre School
ACT W3 99 G6
Barber Surgeons' Hall
BARB EC2Y 12 D2
Barbican ⊖
FARR EC1M 12 B1
Barbican Cinema
BARB EC2Y 12 C1
Barbican Exhibition Halls
BARB EC2Y 12 D1
The Barbican
BARB EC2Y 12 C1
Barbican Theatre
BARB EC2Y 12 D1
Barclay Primary School
LEY E10 70 B3
Barham Primary School
ALP/SUD HA0 79 J4
Baring Primary School
LEE/GVPK SE12 165 K2
Baring Road Medical Centre
BMLY BR1 165 K4
Barkantine Clinic
POP/IOD E14 124 D2
Barking ⇌ ⊖ ⊖
BARK IG11 90 C5
Barking Abbey Comprehensive School (Lower)
IL IG1 90 D3
Barking Abbey Comprehensive School (Upper)
BARK IG11 91 F4
Barking Abbey Industrial Estate
BARK IG11 90 B6
Barking Abbey Leisure Centre
BARK IG11 91 G4
Barking Abbey School
BARK IG11 91 F4
Barking & Dagenham College
ROMW/RG RM7 75 F6
Barking FC
BCTR RM8 91 H3
Barking Hospital
BARK IG11 91 F5
Barking Industrial Park
BARK IG11 91 F6
Barking RUFC
DAGW RM9 91 K6
Barkingside ⊖
BARK/HLT IG6 72 D1
Barkingside Cemetery
BARK/HLT IG6 54 B6
Barkingside FC
BARK/HLT IG6 72 D1
Barlby Primary School
NKENS W10 100 B3
Barley Lane Primary School
GDMY/SEVK IG3 73 G4
Barnabas Medical Centre
NTHLT UB5 78 C4
Barn Croft Primary School
WALTH E17 69 G3
Barnehurst ⇌
BXLYHN DA7 149 K3
Barnehurst Primary School
ERITH DA8 149 K2
Barnehurst Public Golf Club
BXLYHN DA7 150 A4
Barn Elms Athletics Track
BARN SW13 138 E3
Barn Elms Sports Centre
BARN SW13 139 F2
Barn Elms Water Sports Centre
PUT/ROE SW15 139 F3
Barnes ⇌
BARN SW13 138 D4
Barnes Bridge ⇌
BARN SW13 138 B3
Barnes Hospital
MORT/ESHN SW14 138 B4
Barnes Primary School
BARN SW13 138 B4
Barnes Sports Club
BARN SW13 138 C2
Barnet College
BAR EN5 20 D5
CDALE/KGS NW9 45 H4
EBAR EN4 33 K3
FBAR/BDGN N11 33 K5
NFNCH/WDSPK N12 47 G1
Barnet Copthall Pool
HDN NW4 45 K3
Barnet Copthall Stadium
HDN NW4 46 A4
Barnet County Court
FNCH N3 46 E4
Barnet FC (Underhill)
BAR EN5 20 E6
Barnet General Hospital
BAR EN5 20 B5
Barnet Health Centre
BAR EN5 20 E6
Barnet Hospital Chest Clinic
BAR EN5 20 B5
Barnet Magistrates Court
BAR EN5 20 D5
Barnet Museum
BAR EN5 20 C5
Barnet Trading Estate
BAR EN5 20 D4
Barnfield Primary School
EDGW HA8 44 E4
Barnhill Community High School
YEAD UB4 95 F2
Barn Hotel
RSLP HA4 58 C6
Barnsbury Complex
HOLWY N7 85 G5
Barnsbury School for Girls
IS N1 85 G4
Barons Court ⊖
HMSMTH W6 119 G5
Barons Court Theatre
WKENS W14 119 H5
Barratt Industrial Park
BOW E3 106 A3
Barrett Industrial Park
STHL UB1 115 F1
Barrett Way Industrial Estate
RYLN/HDSTN HA2 42 D6
Barrington Primary School
WELL DA16 148 E3
Barrow Hedges Primary School
CAR SM5 209 J5
Barrow Hill Junior School
STJWD NW8 2 C3
Barton House Health Centre
STNW/STAM N16 85 K1
Barwell Business Park
CHSGTN KT9 205 K5
Basketball Arena
OLYMPICPK E20 87 K3
Bassett House School
NKENS W10 100 B5
Baston House School
HAYES BR2 200 A6
Bath Factory Estate
HNHL SE24 162 D1
Battersea Arts Centre (BAC)
BTSEA SW11 140 E4
Battersea Business Centre
BTSEA SW11 141 F4
Battersea Dogs' Home
VX/NE SW8 141 G1
Battersea Park ⇌
BTSEA SW11 141 G1
Battersea Park School
BTSEA SW11 140 E2
Battersea Power Station (disused)
VX/NE SW8 121 G6
Battersea Sports Centre
BTSEA SW11 140 C4
Battersea Tutorial College
TOOT SW17 161 F4
Bayswater ⊖
BAY/PAD W2 101 F6
BBC Broadcasting House
REGST W1B 9 K2
BBC Media Village
SHB W12 100 A6
BBC Studios
MV/WKIL W9 101 F3
BBC Television Centre
SHB W12 100 A6
BBC Worldwide
SHB W12 100 A5
Beal High School
REDBR IG4 53 J6
Beam Primary School
DAGE RM10 110 E1
Beatrice Tate School
BETH E2 104 D2
Beatrix Potter Primary School
WAND/EARL SW18 160 B3
Beauclerc Infant School
SUN TW16 172 B6
The Beaufort Hotel
CHEL SW3 14 E5
Beaumont Primary School
LEY E10 69 K4
Beaver College
BAY/PAD W2 100 E6

The Beavers Community Primary School *HSLWW* TW4 134 B4
Beaverwood School for Girls *CHST* BR7 185 K2
Beckenham Business Centre *BECK* BR3 182 B2
Beckenham Crematorium *BECK* BR3 181 K6
Beckenham CC *BECK* BR3 182 E3
Beckenham Hill ⇌ *CAT* SE6 183 F1
Beckenham Hospital *BECK* BR3 182 C5
Beckenham Junction ⇌ ⊖ *BECK* BR3 182 D4
Beckenham Leisure Centre *BECK* BR3 182 B4
Beckenham RFC *BECK* BR3 198 B1
Beckenham Road ⊖ *BECK* BR3 182 A4
Beckenham School of Art *BECK* BR3 198 B2
Beckenham Theatre Centre *BECK* BR3 182 E5
Beckenham Town FC *BECK* BR3 198 D2
Becket Sports Centre *DART* DA1 171 F1
Beckford Primary School *KIL/WHAMP* NW6 82 D3
Beckmead School *BECK* BR3 198 D5
The Beck Theatre *HYS/HAR* UB3 94 D5
Beckton ⊖ *EHAM* E6 108 A4
Beckton Park ⊖ *EHAM* E6 107 K6
Beckton Ski Centre *EHAM* E6 108 A3
Beckton Triangle Retail Park *EHAM* E6 108 B2
Becontree ⊖ *DAGW* RM9 91 J4
Becontree Day Hospital *BCTR* RM8 74 A6
Becontree Primary School *BCTR* RM8 91 H1
Bective House Clinic *PUT/ROE* SW15 139 J5
Beddington Infant School *WLGTN* SM6 210 C1
Beddington Lane ⊖ *CROY/NA* CR0 195 H3
Beddington Medical Centre *CROY/NA* CR0 210 E2
Beddington Park Primary School *CROY/NA* CR0 210 D1
Beddington Trading Estate *CROY/NA* CR0 195 K5
Bedelsford School *KUT/HW* KT1 175 F6
Bedensfield Clinic *SCUP* DA14 187 F1
Bedfont Cemetery *EBED/NFELT* TW14 153 F3
Bedfont Health Clinic *EBED/NFELT* TW14 153 H2
Bedfont Industrial Park *ASHF* TW15 153 G5
Bedfont Lakes Country Park *EBED/NFELT* TW14 153 F4
Bedfont Lakes Office Park *EBED/NFELT* TW14 153 F3
Bedfont Primary School *EBED/NFELT* TW14 153 H1
Bedford Hotel *RSQ* WC1B 10 E1
Bedonwell Clinic *ABYW* SE2 129 F6
Bedonwell Medical Centre *BELV* DA17 129 G5
Bedonwell Primary School *BXLYHN* DA7 129 F6
Beecholme Primary School *MTCM* CR4 179 G4
Beechwood School *STRHM/NOR* SW16 161 K5
Beehive Preparatory School *REDBR* IG4 71 K1
The Beehive School *ARCH* N19 66 D4
Beis Chinuch Lebonos Girls School *FSBYPK* N4 67 J4
Beis Malka Girls School *STNW/STAM* N16 68 B5
Beis Rochel d'Satmar Girls School *STNW/STAM* N16 68 A4
Beis Trana Girls School *STNW/STAM* N16 68 C5
Beis Yaakov Primary School *CDALE/KGS* NW9 45 F6
Belgrave Walk ⊖ *MTCM* CR4 194 C1
Bellamy's Wharf *BERM/RHTH* SE16 124 A1
Bellenden Primary School *PECK* SE15 143 H4
Bellenden Road Business Centre *PECK* SE15 143 G3
Bellenden Road Retail Park *PECK* SE15 143 G2
Bellerbys College *DEPT* SE8 124 E6
Belleville Primary School *BTSEA* SW11 140 E6
Belle Vue Cinema *WLSDN* NW10 81 K5
Bell Industrial Estate *CHSWK* W4 117 K4
Bellingham ⇌ *CAT* SE6 164 E5
Bellingham Trading Estate *CAT* SE6 164 E5
Belmont Bowling Club *STRHM/NOR* SW16 161 K5
Belmont Infant School *TOTM* N17 49 J6
Belmont Mill Hill Preparatory School *MLHL* NW7 31 J5
Belmont Park School *LEY* E10 70 A3
Belmont Primary School *CHSWK* W4 118 A4
ERITH DA8 149 H1
Belmont School *KTN/HRWW/WS* HA3 43 F5
Belmore Primary School *YEAD* UB4 95 F2
Belsize Park ⊖ *HAMP* NW3 83 J3
Belvedere ⇌ *BELV* DA17 129 J3
Belvedere Day Hospital *WLSDN* NW10 81 J6
Belvedere Industrial Estate *BELV* DA17 130 A1
Belvedere Link Business Park *ERITH* DA8 129 K3
Belvedere Primary School *BELV* DA17 129 J4
Belvue Business Centre *NTHLT* UB5 78 B5
Belvue School *NTHLT* UB5 78 A6
Benedict House Preparatory School *BFN/LL* DA15 168 A6
Benedict Primary School *MTCM* CR4 178 C6
Benjamin Franklin House *CHCR* WC2N 10 E7
Ben Jonson Primary School *WCHPL* E1 105 G3
Bensham Manor School *THHTH* CR7 196 D2
Benson Primary School *CROY/NA* CR0 213 G1
The Bentall Centre *KUT/HW* KT1 174 E5
Benthal Primary School *STNW/STAM* N16 86 C1
The Bentley Hotel *SKENS* SW7 120 B4
Bentley Wood Girls School *STAN* HA7 43 F1
Bentworth Primary School *SHB* W12 99 K5
Ben Uri Gallery, London Jewish Museum of Art *STJWD* NW8 83 F6
Beormund School *STHWK* SE1 18 E3
Beresford Square Outdoor Market *WOOL/PLUM* SE18 127 G4
Berger Primary School *HOM* E9 87 F4
The Berkeley Hotel *KTBR* SW1X 15 G2
Berkeley Primary School *HEST* TW5 114 C6
Berlitz School of Languages *HHOL* WC1V 11 H2
Bermondsey ⊖ ⊖ *BERM/RHTH* SE16 123 H3
Bermondsey Town Hall *STHWK* SE1 19 J5
Bermondsey Trading Estate *BERM/RHTH* SE16 123 K5
Berrylands ⇌ *BRYLDS* KT5 191 J1
Berrymede Infant School *ACT* W3 117 J2
Berrymede Junior School *ACT* W3 117 J2
Bertram House School *TOOT* SW17 161 F4
Bessemer Grange J & I School *HNHL* SE24 142 E6
Bessemer Park Industrial Estate *BRXN/ST* SW9 142 C5
Best Western Bromley Court Hotel *BMLY* BR1 183 H2
Best Western Cumberland Hotel *HRW* HA1 61 F3
Best Western Lodge Hotel *PUT/ROE* SW15 139 J6
Best Western Mostyn Hotel *MBLAR* W1H 9 F4
Beth Jacob Grammar School *HDN* NW4 64 B1
Bethlem Royal Hospital *BECK* BR3 198 D4
Bethnal Green ⊖ *BETH* E2 104 E2
WCHPL E1 104 D3
Bethnal Green Technology College *BETH* E2 7 K5
Beths Grammar School for Boys *BXLY* DA5 169 H1
The Betty Layward School *STNW/STAM* N16 85 K1
Beulah Infant School *THHTH* CR7 180 D5
Beverley School *NWMAL* KT3 192 D2
Beverley Trading Estate *MRDN* SM4 193 G4
Bevington Primary School *NKENS* W10 100 C4
Bexley ⇌ *BXLY* DA5 169 H3
Bexley College *BELV* DA17 129 K4
Bexley CC *BXLY* DA5 169 H3
Bexley Grammar School *WELL* DA16 148 C5
Bexleyheath ⇌ *BXLYHN* DA7 149 F3
Bexleyheath Cemetery *BXLYHN* DA7 149 G4
Bexleyheath Centre *BXLYHS* DA6 149 F5
Bexleyheath Golf Club *BXLYHS* DA6 149 F6
Bexleyheath Marriott Hotel *BXLYHS* DA6 149 J5
Bexleyheath School *BXLYHN* DA7 149 G4
Bexleyheath Superbowl *BXLYHS* DA6 149 G5
Bexley RFC *BXLY* DA5 169 H2
BFI *STHWK* SE1 11 H7
BFI London IMAX Cinema *STHWK* SE1 17 H1
Bickenhall College of Computing *CAMTN* NW1 9 F1
Bickerly School of Dance *HAYES* BR2 200 D2
Bickley ⇌ *BMLY* BR1 184 D6
Bickley Park CC *BMLY* BR1 184 D5
Bickley Park Pre-Preparatory School *BMLY* BR1 184 D6
Bickley Park Preparatory School *BMLY* BR1 184 C6
Big Ben *WHALL* SW1A 17 F3
Bigland Green Primary School *WCHPL* E1 104 D5
Billingsgate Fish Market *POP/IOD* E14 124 E1
Bingham Hotel *TWK* TW1 156 E1
Birchmere Business Park *THMD* SE28 128 B2
Birchwood Park Golf Club *RDART* DA2 187 K3
Bird College *SCUP* DA14 168 B5
Birkbeck ⇌ ⊖ *BECK* BR3 181 K5
Birkbeck College *GWRST* WC1E 4 D7
RSQ WC1B 10 D2
Birkbeck Primary School *SCUP* DA14 168 C5
Birkenhall College of Computing *MBLAR* W14 9 F1
Bishop Challoner Catholic Collegiate School *WCHPL* E1 104 E6
Bishop Challoner Girls School *WCHPL* E1 104 C6
Bishop Challoner School *HAYES* BR2 183 G5
Bishop Douglass RC School *EFNCH* N2 47 G5
Bishop Gilpin Primary School *WIM/MER* SW19 177 J1
Bishop John Robinson CE Primary School *THMD* SE28 109 J6
Bishop Justus CE (Secondary) School *HAYES* BR2 200 D4
Bishop Perrin CE Primary School *WHTN* TW2 155 G2
Bishop Ramsey CE School *RSLP* HA4 58 D4
Bishopsgate Institute *LVPST* EC2M 13 H2
Bishop Thomas Grant School *STRHM/NOR* SW16 180 A1
Bishop Winnington Ingram CE Primary School *RSLP* HA4 58 B4
Bittacy Business Centre *MLHL* NW7 46 C2
Blackburn Trading Estate *STWL/WRAY* TW19 152 C1
Blackfen Medical Centre *BFN/LL* DA15 148 A6
Blackfen School for Girls *BFN/LL* DA15 168 C1
Blackfriars ⇌ ⊖ *BLKFR* EC4V 12 A5
Blackfriars Millennium Pier *EMB* EC4Y 11 K5
Blackfriars Pier *BLKFR* EC4V 12 B6
Blackheath ⇌ *BKHTH/KID* SE3 145 J4
Blackheath Bluecoat School *BKHTH/KID* SE3 146 A1
Blackheath Business Estate *GNWCH* SE10 145 F2
The Blackheath Clinic *BKHTH/KID* SE3 145 K5
Blackheath High School GDST *BKHTH/KID* SE3 145 J3
Blackheath High Senior School *BKHTH/KID* SE3 145 K1
Blackheath Hospital *BKHTH/KID* SE3 145 J4
Blackheath Preparatory School *BKHTH/KID* SE3 145 K2
Blackheath RFC (The Rectory Field) *BKHTH/KID* SE3 146 A1
Blackhorse ⊖ *CROY/NA* CR0 197 H4
Blackhorse Road ⊖ ⊖ *WALTH* E17 69 F1
Blackwall ⊖ *POP/IOD* E14 106 A6
Blackwall Trading Estate *POP/IOD* E14 106 B4
Blair Peach Primary School *STHL* UB1 114 C1
Blake College *GTPST* W1W 10 A1
Blanche Nevile School *HGT* N6 65 K3
MUSWH N10 48 A6
Blenheim Business Centre *MTCM* CR4 178 E4
Blenheim Primary School *ORP* BR6 202 E6
Blenheim Shopping Centre *PGE/AN* SE20 181 K3
Blessed Dominic RC Primary School *CDALE/KGS* NW9 45 G5
Blessed Sacrament RC Primary School *IS* N1 5 F1
Bloo House School *ESH/CLAY* KT10 204 A3
Bloomfield Clinic Guys *STHWK* SE1 19 F2
Bloomsbury International *NOXST/BSQ* WC1A 11 F2
Bloomsbury Theatre *GWRST* WC1E 4 C6
Blossom House School *RYNPK* SW20 177 F3
Blossoms Inn Medical Centre *BLKFR* EC4V 12 D5
Blue Gate Fields Infant School *WCHPL* E1 104 E6
The Blue School *ISLW* TW7 136 B4
Blyth's Wharf *POP/IOD* E14 105 G6
BMI Medical Centre *CAVSQ/HST* W1G 9 H2
BMX Track *OLYMPICPK* E20 87 K3
Bnois Jerusalem Girls School *STNW/STAM* N16 67 K4
Bnos Beis Yaakov Primary School *CDALE/KGS* NW9 62 E2
The Bob Hope Theatre *ELTH/MOT* SE9 166 E1
Bobov Foundation School *STNW/STAM* N16 68 B4
The Bobov Foundation School for Girls *CLPT* E5 68 B4
Bodywise Natural Health Centre *BETH* E2 104 E2
Boleyn Cinema *EHAM* E6 107 H1
Bolingbroke Hospital *BTSEA* SW11 140 D6
Bolingbroke Primary School *BTSEA* SW11 140 C2
Bond First School *MTCM* CR4 178 E5
Bond Primary School *MTCM* CR4 178 E5
Bond Street ⊖ *OXSTW* W1C 9 H4
Bonner Primary School *BETH* E2 105 F1
Bonneville Primary School *CLAP* SW4 161 H1
Bonus Pastor Catholic College *BMLY* BR1 165 G6
Boomes Industrial Estate *RAIN* RM13 111 H3
Booster Cushion Theatre *WDGN* N22 49 F5
Borough ⊖ *STHWK* SE1 18 D3
Borough Cemetery *HSLWW* TW4 155 F2
Borough Market *STHWK* SE1 12 E7
Borthwick Wharf *DEPT* SE8 124 D5
Boston Business Park *HNWL* W7 115 K3
Boston Manor ⊖ *HNWL* W7 116 B4
Boston University *SKENS* SW7 120 B4
Botwell House Catholic Primary School *HYS/HAR* UB3 113 J2
Boundary Business Park *MTCM* CR4 178 C5
Bounds Green ⊖ *FBAR/BDGN* N11 48 D3
Bounds Green Health Centre *FBAR/BDGN* N11 48 D3
Bounds Green Industrial Estate *FBAR/BDGN* N11 48 B2
Bounds Green Infant School *FBAR/BDGN* N11 48 D3
Bourne CP School *RSLP* HA4 77 G3
Bourne Hall Health Centre *EW* KT17 207 H6
Bourne Hall Museum *EW* KT17 207 H6
Bourne Road Industrial Park *DART* DA1 150 A6
Bourneside Sports Club *STHGT/OAK* N14 34 E3
Bousfield Primary School *WBPTN* SW10 120 B5
Boutcher CE Primary School *STHWK* SE1 19 J5
Bowater House *SKENS* SW7 14 E3
Bow Church ⊖ *BOW* E3 105 J2
Bow County Court *SRTFD* E15 88 C4
Bowden House Clinic *HRW* HA1 60 E6
Bower Park School *ROM* RM1 57 G2
Bowes Park ⇌ *WDGN* N22 48 E3
Bowes Primary School *FBAR/BDGN* N11 48 D1
Bowes Road Clinic *FBAR/BDGN* N11 48 C1
Bow Junior & Youth Centre *BOW* E3 105 H4
Bowman Trading Estate *CDALE/KGS* NW9 44 C6
Bow Road ⊖ *BOW* E3 105 J2
Bow Secondary School *BOW* E3 105 J1
Bow Triangle Business Centre *BOW* E3 105 J3
Boxgrove Primary School *ABYW* SE2 128 D3
BPP Law School *HHOL* WC1V 11 G2
Brackenbury Health Centre *HMSMTH* W6 118 E3
Brackenbury Primary School *HMSMTH* W6 118 E3
Bracken Industrial Estate *BARK/HLT* IG6 55 F3
Bracton Centre *RDART* DA2 170 C4
Brady Recreation Centre *WCHPL* E1 104 C4
Braeside Senior School *BKHH* IG9 39 F3
Braincroft Primary School *CRICK* NW2 81 H1
Braintree Road Industrial Estate *RSLP* HA4 77 F2
Bramah's Tea & Coffee Museum *STHWK* SE1 18 D1
Brampton College *HDN* NW4 64 A1
Brampton Manor School *EHAM* E6 107 H3
Brampton Primary School *BXLYHN* DA7 148 E3
EHAM E6 107 J2
Brandlehow Primary School *PUT/ROE* SW15 139 J5
Branollys Health Centre *PLSTW* E13 106 E3
Breakspear Crematorium *RSLP* HA4 58 A2
Breaside Preparatory School *BMLY* BR1 184 B4
Brecknock Primary School *HOLWY* N7 84 D4
Bredinghurst School *PECK* SE15 143 K5
Brent Adult College *WLSDN* NW10 81 F6
Brent Arts Council *CRICK* NW2 81 J1
Brent Child & Family Clinic *WLSDN* NW10 81 H3
Brent Cross ⊖ *GLDGN* NW11 64 B4
Brent Cross Shopping Centre *HDN* NW4 64 A4
Brentfield Medical Centre *WLSDN* NW10 81 F4
Brentfield Primary School *WLSDN* NW10 81 F4
Brentford ⇌ *BTFD* TW8 116 E6
Brentford Business Centre *BTFD* TW8 136 D1
Brentford County Court *BTFD* TW8 136 E1
Brentford FC (Griffin Park) *BTFD* TW8 116 E6
Brentford Fountain Leisure Centre *BTFD* TW8 117 G5
Brentford Health Centre *BTFD* TW8 116 D6
Brentford School for Girls *BTFD* TW8 116 E6
Brent Knoll School *FSTH* SE23 164 A5
Brent Magistrates Court House *WLSDN* NW10 81 G4
Brent Park Industrial Estate *NWDGN* UB2 114 A3
Brentside First School *HNWL* W7 96 E4
Brentside High School *HNWL* W7 96 E3
Brentside Primary School *HNWL* W7 96 E3
Brent Trading Estate *WLSDN* NW10 81 G3
Brentwaters Business Park *BTFD* TW8 136 D1
Brettenham Primary School *ED* N9 36 C6
Brewers' Hall *CITYW* EC2V 12 D2
Brewery Industrial Estate *IS* N1 6 C3
Brewery Mews Business Centre *ISLW* TW7 136 A4
The Brewery *ROMW/RG* RM7 75 G3
Brick Lane Music Hall *CAN/RD* E16 126 C1
Brick Lane Music House *WCHPL* E1 7 K7
Bricklayer Arms Industrial Estate *STHWK* SE1 19 J7
The Bridewell Theatre *EMB* EC4Y 12 A4

The Bridge Academy
BETH E2 ... 7 J1
The Bridge Business Centre
NWDGN UB2 ... 115 F2
Bridge Lane Theatre
BTSEA SW11 ... 140 D2
The Bridge Leisure Centre
SYD SE26 ... 182 C1
Bridge Park Business & Leisure Centre
WLSDN NW10 ... 80 D5
The Bridge School
ARCH N19 ... 66 C6
HOLWY N7 ... 84 D4
Brigham Young University
BAY/PAD W2 ... 100 E6
Bright Sparks Montessori School
WKENS W14 ... 119 G2
Brigstock Medical Centre
THHTH CR7 ... 196 C2
Brimsdown ⇌
PEND EN3 ... 25 G3
Brimsdown Industrial Estate
PEND EN3 ... 24 E3
Brimsdown Primary School
PEND EN3 ... 25 F4
Brindishe Green School
LEW SE13 ... 165 G1
Brindishe Lee School
LEE/GVPK SE12 ... 145 J6
Britain & London Visitor Centre
STJS SW1Y ... 10 C7
Britannia Business Centre
CRICK NW2 ... 82 B2
Britannia College of Excellence
IS N1 ... 7 F5
Britannia Leisure Centre
IS N1 ... 7 F1
Britannia Sports Ground
WALTH E17 ... 51 J3
Britannia Village Primary School
CAN/RD E16 ... 126 A1
British Airways Museum
HTHAIR TW6 ... 133 H5
The British American Drama Academy
CAMTN NW1 ... 3 H1
British Cartoon Centre
BMSBY WC1N ... 5 F7
British College of Osteopathy
HAMP NW3 ... 83 G4
British Dental Association
CAVSQ/HST W1G ... 9 J2
The British Hernia Centre
HDN NW4 ... 63 K2
British Library
CAMTN NW1 ... 4 D4
British Library Newspaper Library
CDALE/KGS NW9 ... 45 G6
British Medical Association
STPAN WC1H ... 4 D6
British Museum
RSQ WC1B ... 10 E2
British Telecom Tower
GTPST W1W ... 10 A1
The BRIT School
SNWD SE25 ... 196 E3
Brittons School Technology College
RAIN RM13 ... 93 H5
Brixton ⇌ ⊖
BRXN/ST SW9 ... 142 B5
Brixton Academy
BRXN/ST SW9 ... 142 B4
Brixton Recreation Centre
BRXN/ST SW9 ... 142 B4
Broadfields Primary School
EDGW HA8 ... 30 C4
Broadgate
LVPST EC2M ... 13 F1
STRHM/NOR SW16 ... 161 J5
Broadgate Ice Arena
LVPST EC2M ... 13 F2
Broadhurst School
KIL/WHAMP NW6 ... 83 G5
Broadmead Primary School
CROY/NA CR0 ... 196 E3
Broadreach College
THMD SE28 ... 128 A3
Broadwalk Shopping Centre
EDGW HA8 ... 44 C2
Broadwater Farm Primary School
TOTM N17 ... 49 K5
Broadwater Primary School
TOOT SW17 ... 160 C6
Broadway Clinic
EDGW HA8 ... 44 D4
Broadway Retail Park
CRICK NW2 ... 82 B2
Broadway Shopping Centre
BXLYHS DA6 ... 149 H5
HMSMTH W6 ... 119 F5
Broadway Squash & Fitness Centre
HMSMTH W6 ... 119 G4
Brocklebank Health Centre
WAND/EARL SW18 ... 160 A2
Brocklebank Industrial Estate
GNWCH SE10 ... 125 K4
Brockley ⇌ ⊖
BROCKY SE4 ... 144 C4
Brockley Cross Business Centre
BROCKY SE4 ... 144 B4
Brockley Primary School
BROCKY SE4 ... 144 C6
Brockwell Lido
HNHL SE24 ... 162 C1
Bromet Primary School
OXHEY WD19 ... 27 H2
Bromley by Bow ⊖
BOW E3 ... 105 K2
Bromley Cemetery
BMLY BR1 ... 183 J3
Bromley Civic Centre
BMLY BR1 ... 184 A5
Bromley College of Further & Higher Education
BMLY BR1 ... 183 K4
HAYES BR2 ... 200 C3
Bromley County Court
BMLY BR1 ... 183 K4
Bromley FC
HAYES BR2 ... 200 A2
Bromley High School GDST
BMLY BR1 ... 201 F1
Bromley Industrial Centre
BMLY BR1 ... 184 C6
Bromley Mall Indoor Market
BMLY BR1 ... 183 K5
Bromley Museum
ORP BR6 ... 202 C4
Bromley North ⇌
BMLY BR1 ... 183 K4
Bromley Road Infant School
BECK BR3 ... 182 E4
Bromley Road Retail Park
CAT SE6 ... 164 E4
Bromley Ski Centre
STMC/STPC BR5 ... 186 E4
Bromley South ⇌
BMLY BR1 ... 184 A6
Bromley Tennis Centre
ORP BR6 ... 216 D1
Bromley Wendover Lawn Tennis Club
HAYES BR2 ... 200 A1
Brompton Cemetery
WBPTN SW10 ... 120 A6
Brompton Medical Centre
ECT SW5 ... 120 A5
Brompton Oratory
SKENS SW7 ... 14 C5
Bromyard Leisure Centre
ACT W3 ... 118 B1
Brondesbury ⊖
KIL/WHAMP NW6 ... 82 D5
Brondesbury College for Boys
KIL/WHAMP NW6 ... 82 B5
Brondesbury Park ⊖
KIL/WHAMP NW6 ... 82 C6
Brook Community Primary School
HACK E8 ... 86 C3
Brooke Trading Estate
ROM RM1 ... 75 H4
Brookfield House School
WFD IG8 ... 52 C2
Brookfield Primary School
CHEAM SM3 ... 193 H5
HGT N6 ... 66 B6
Brook House FC
YEAD UB4 ... 94 D2
Brook Industrial Estate
YEAD UB4 ... 114 C1
Brook Industrial Park
STMC/STPC BR5 ... 202 D1
Brookland Junior School
GLDGN NW11 ... 65 F1
Brooklands Primary School
BKHTH/KID SE3 ... 145 K4
Brook Lane Business Centre
BTFD TW8 ... 116 E5
Brookmarsh Trading Estate
DEPT SE8 ... 144 E1
Brookmead Industrial Estate
CROY/NA CR0 ... 195 H3
Brookside Primary School
YEAD UB4 ... 95 G2
Broomfield House School
RCH/KEW TW9 ... 137 G2
Broomfield School
FBAR/BDGN N11 ... 48 D1
Broomsleigh Business Park
SYD SE26 ... 182 C1
Broomwood Hall Lower School
BAL SW12 ... 160 E1
Brownlow Medical Centre
FBAR/BDGN N11 ... 48 E1
Brown's Hotel
MYFR/PICC W1J ... 9 K6
Bruce Castle Museum
TOTM N17 ... 50 A4
Bruce Grove ⇌
TOTM N17 ... 50 B5
Bruce Grove Primary School
TOTM N17 ... 50 B5
Brunei Gallery
STPAN WC1H ... 4 D7
Brunel Engine House
BERM/RHTH SE16 ... 123 K2
Brunel University
GLDGN NW11 ... 64 B3
ISLW TW7 ... 135 K1
TWK TW1 ... 136 C5
Brunel University (Osterley Campus) Track
ISLW TW7 ... 135 K1
Brunswick Health Centre
FBAR/BDGN N11 ... 34 A4
Brunswick Housing & Shopping Centre
BMSBY WC1N ... 5 F6
Brunswick Industrial Park
FBAR/BDGN N11 ... 34 B6
Brunswick Medical Centre
BMSBY WC1N ... 4 E6
Brunswick Park JMI School
STHGT/OAK N14 ... 34 A3
Brunswick Park Primary School
CMBW SE5 ... 142 E1
B Six Sixth Form College
CLPT E5 ... 86 D1
BT Centre
STBT EC1A ... 12 C3
Buckhurst Hill ⊖
BKHH IG9 ... 39 H4
Buckhurst Hill FC
BKHH IG9 ... 39 J3
Buckhurst Hill Primary School
BKHH IG9 ... 39 J4
Buckingham College Preparatory School
PIN HA5 ... 59 K4
Buckingham Palace
WHALL SW1A ... 16 A3
Buckingham Primary School
HPTN TW12 ... 172 E1
Buckingham Road Cemetery
IL IG1 ... 72 D6
The Building Centre
GWRST WC1E ... 10 C2
Building Crafts College
SRTFD E15 ... 88 B5
Bullers Wood School
CHST BR7 ... 184 E4
Bullsbridge Industrial Estate
NWDGN UB2 ... 114 A4
The Bull Theatre
BAR EN5 ... 20 D5
BUPA Roding Hospital
REDBR IG4 ... 53 H6
Burbage School
IS N1 ... 7 G2
Burdett Coutts CE Primary School
WEST SW1P ... 16 C5
Burgess Business Park
CMBW SE5 ... 142 E1
Burgess Park Tennis Centre
CMBW SE5 ... 122 D6
Burlington College Independent Sixth Form
EDGW HA8 ... 44 B6
Burlington Danes School
SHB W12 ... 99 K5
Burlington Infant School
NWMAL KT3 ... 192 C1
Burney Street Clinic
GNWCH SE10 ... 145 F1
Burnham Trading Estate
DART DA1 ... 151 G5
Burnhill Business Centre
BECK BR3 ... 182 D5
Burnley Road Clinic
WLSDN NW10 ... 81 J3
Burns Hotel
ECT SW5 ... 120 A4
Burnside Industrial Estate
BARK/HLT IG6 ... 55 H1
Burnt Ash Primary School
BMLY BR1 ... 183 K1
Burnt Oak ⊖
EDGW HA8 ... 44 E4
Burnt Oak Junior School
BFN/LL DA15 ... 168 B3
Burntwood School
TOOT SW17 ... 160 C4
Bursted Wood Primary School
BXLYHN DA7 ... 149 J3
Burwell Industrial Estate
LEY E10 ... 69 G5
Burwood School
ORP BR6 ... 202 E6
Bushey ⇌ ⊖
OXHEY WD19 ... 27 H1
Bushey Academy
BUSH WD23 ... 27 K1
Bushey Golf & Country Club
BUSH WD23 ... 28 A1
Bushey Health Centre
BUSH WD23 ... 27 K1
Bushey Heath Primary School
BUSH WD23 ... 28 D3
Bushey Museum & Art Gallery
BUSH WD23 ... 28 A1
Bush Hill Park ⇌
EN EN1 ... 36 B1
Bush Hill Park Golf Club
WCHMH N21 ... 23 J6
Bush Hill Park Medical Centre
EN EN1 ... 36 B1
Bush Hill Park Primary School
EN EN1 ... 24 C6
Bush House (BBC)
HOL/ALD WC2B ... 11 G4
Bush Industrial Estate
ARCH N19 ... 84 C1
WLSDN NW10 ... 99 F3
The Business Academy Bexley
ERITHM DA18 ... 129 F2
The Business Centre
CEND/HSY/T N8 ... 48 E5
The Business Design Centre
IS N1 ... 5 K1
Business Training & Solutions
CDALE/KGS NW9 ... 45 H4
Bute House Preparatory School for Girls
HMSMTH W6 ... 119 F4
Butlers Wharf
STHWK SE1 ... 19 K1
Butler's Wharf Business Centre
STHWK SE1 ... 19 K2
Butler's Wharf Pier
STHWK SE1 ... 19 K1
Butterfly Sports Club
ELTH/MOT SE9 ... 167 G1
Buxlow Preparatory School
WBLY HA9 ... 80 A1
Buxton School
WAN E11 ... 88 D1
Buzzard Creek Industrial Estate
BARK IG11 ... 109 F4
Byam Shaw School of Art
ARCH N19 ... 66 C6
Byfleet Industrial Estate
WATW WD18 ... 26 A3
Bygrove Primary School
POP/IOD E14 ... 105 K5
Byron Court Primary School
ALP/SUD HA0 ... 61 J6
Cable Car
CAN/RD E16 ... 125 J1
Cabot Place
POP/IOD E14 ... 124 D1
Cadogan Hall
CHEL SW3 ... 15 F6
The Cadogan Hotel
KTBR SW1X ... 15 F5
Cadogan Pier
CHEL SW3 ... 120 D6
Caledonian Market
STHWK SE1 ... 19 H4
Caledonian Road ⊖
HOLWY N7 ... 84 E3
Caledonian Road & Barnsbury ⊖
HOLWY N7 ... 85 F5
Cally Pool
IS N1 ... 85 F6
Calverton Primary School
CAN/RD E16 ... 107 H5
Cambell Primary School
DAGW RM9 ... 91 K5
Camberwell Business Centre
CMBW SE5 ... 142 E1
Camberwell College of Arts
CMBW SE5 ... 143 F2
Camberwell Leisure Centre
CMBW SE5 ... 142 E2
Camberwell New Cemetery
PECK SE15 ... 164 A1
Camberwell Trading Estate
CMBW SE5 ... 142 C3
Cambodian Embassy
CRICK NW2 ... 82 A5
Cambridge Heath ⇌
BETH E2 ... 104 D1
Cambridge Heath Sixth Form
BETH E2 ... 104 E2
Cambridge Park Bowling & Sports Club
TWK TW1 ... 156 D1
Cambridge School
HMSMTH W6 ... 118 E4
Cambridge Theatre
LSQ/SEVD WC2H ... 10 E4
Camden Arts Centre
HAMP NW3 ... 83 F3
Camden House Clinic
BKHTH/KID SE3 ... 145 H3
Camden Junior School
CAR SM5 ... 209 K2
Camden Market
CAMTN NW1 ... 84 A5
Camden Mews Day Hospital
CAMTN NW1 ... 84 C5
Camden People's Theatre
CAMTN NW1 ... 4 A5
Camden Road ⊖
CAMTN NW1 ... 84 C5
Camden School for Girls
KTTN NW5 ... 84 C4
Camden Theatre
CAMTN NW1 ... 4 A2
Camden Town ⊖
CAMTN NW1 ... 84 B6
Camden Town Hall & St Pancras Library
CAMTN NW1 ... 4 E4
Camelot Primary School
PECK SE15 ... 143 J1
Cameron House School
CHEL SW3 ... 120 C6
Camperdown House
WCHPL E1 ... 13 K4
Campion House College
ISLW TW7 ... 135 J1
Campsbourne School
CEND/HSY/T N8 ... 48 E6
Camrose Primary School
EDGW HA8 ... 44 B4
Canada House
STJS SW1Y ... 10 D7
Canada House Business Centre
RSLP HA4 ... 59 G5
Canada Place
POP/IOD E14 ... 124 D1
Canada Square
POP/IOD E14 ... 124 E1
Canada Water ⇌ ⊖
BERM/RHTH SE16 ... 123 K3
Canada Water Retail Park
BERM/RHTH SE16 ... 124 A3
Canada Wharf Museum
BERM/RHTH SE16 ... 124 C1
Canal Cafe Theatre
BAY/PAD W2 ... 101 G4
Canary Riverside
BERM/RHTH SE16 ... 124 C1
Canary Wharf ⊖
POP/IOD E14 ... 124 D1
Canary Wharf Pier
POP/IOD E14 ... 124 C1
Canberra Primary School
SHB W12 ... 99 K6
Canbury 2000 Business Park
KUTN/CMB KT2 ... 175 F4
Canbury Business Centre
KUTN/CMB KT2 ... 175 F4
Canbury Medical Centre
KUTN/CMB KT2 ... 175 G4
Canbury School
KUTN/CMB KT2 ... 175 J2
Cann Hall Primary School
WAN E11 ... 88 D1
Canning Town ⊖
POP/IOD E14 ... 106 C5
Cannizaro House Hotel
WIM/MER SW19 ... 177 F2
Cannon Hill Clinic
STHGT/OAK N14 ... 34 E5
Cannon Lane Junior School
PIN HA5 ... 59 H3
Cannon Sports Club
CANST EC4R ... 12 D5
Cannon Street ⇌ ⊖
CANST EC4R ... 12 E6
Cannon Trading Estate
WBLY HA9 ... 80 D2
Cannon Wharf Business Centre
DEPT SE8 ... 124 B4
Canon Barnett Primary School
WCHPL E1 ... 13 K3
Canonbury ⇌ ⊖
IS N1 ... 85 J4
Canonbury Business Centre
IS N1 ... 85 J6
Canonbury Primary School
IS N1 ... 85 H4
Canon Palmer RC High School
IL IG1 ... 72 E5
Canons High School
EDGW HA8 ... 44 B5
The Canons Leisure Centre
MTCM CR4 ... 194 E1
Canons Park ⊖
EDGW HA8 ... 44 A3
Canterbury Industrial Estate
NWCR SE14 ... 124 A6
Cantium Retail Park
STHWK SE1 ... 123 H6
Capital Business Centre
ALP/SUD HA0 ... 97 K1
MTCM CR4 ... 194 E2
SAND/SEL CR2 ... 211 K4
Capital City Academy
WLSDN NW10 ... 81 K6
The Capital Hotel
CHEL SW3 ... 14 E3
Capital Industrial Estate
BELV DA17 ... 129 K1
Capital Radio
LSQ/SEVD WC2H ... 10 D6
Capital Wharf
WAP E1W ... 123 H1
Capitol Industrial Park
CDALE/KGS NW9 ... 44 E6
Caplan Estate
MTCM CR4 ... 179 H4
Cardiff Road Industrial Estate
WATW WD18 ... 27 F1
Cardinal Pole RC School
HOM E9 ... 87 G4
Cardinal Pole RC School (Lower)
HOM E9 ... 87 F5
Cardinal Road Infant School
FELT TW13 ... 154 A3
The Cardinal Vaughan Memorial
WKENS W14 ... 119 H2
Cardinal Wiseman RC School (Technology & Art College)
GFD/PVL UB6 ... 96 C4
Cardwell Primary School
WOOL/PLUM SE18 ... 126 E4
Carew Manor School
WLGTN SM6 ... 210 D1
Carlisle Infant School
HPTN TW12 ... 173 G2
Carlton House
STJS SW1Y ... 16 C1
The Carlton Mitre Hotel
E/WMO/HCT KT8 ... 173 K6
Carlton Primary School
KTTN NW5 ... 84 A3
Carlton Vale Infant School
MV/WKIL W9 ... 100 D2
Carlyle's House (NT)
CHEL SW3 ... 120 D6
Carnwath Road Industrial Estate
FUL/PGN SW6 ... 140 A4
Carpenders Park ⊖
OXHEY WD19 ... 27 H5
Carpenders Park Cemetery
OXHEY WD19 ... 27 K6
Carpenters' Hall
OBST EC2N ... 13 F2
Carpenters Primary School
SRTFD E15 ... 88 A6
Carshalton ⇌
CAR SM5 ... 209 J2
Carshalton AFC
SUT SM1 ... 209 J1
Carshalton Beeches ⇌
CAR SM5 ... 209 K4
Carshalton Boys Sports College
CAR SM5 ... 194 C6
Carshalton College
CAR SM5 ... 209 K1
Carshalton High School for Girls
CAR SM5 ... 209 J1
Carshalton War Memorial Hospital
CAR SM5 ... 209 K3
Carterhatch Infant School
EN EN1 ... 24 D2
The Cartoon Museum
RSQ WC1B ... 10 E2
Caryl Thomas Clinic
HRW HA1 ... 60 E1
Cass Business School
STLK EC1Y ... 6 E7
The Cassel Hospital
RCHPK/HAM TW10 ... 156 E6
Cassidy Medical Centre
FUL/PGN SW6 ... 139 K1
Castilion Primary School
THMD SE28 ... 109 J5
Castle Bar Park ⇌
HNWL W7 ... 97 F4
Castlebar School
HNWL W7 ... 97 F4
Castlebar Special School
WEA W13 ... 97 G4
Castlecombe Primary School
ELTH/MOT SE9 ... 184 D1
Castle Hill Primary School
CROY/NA CR0 ... 214 A4
Castle Industrial Estate
WALW SE17 ... 18 C6
Casualty Plus Clinic
BTFD TW8 ... 116 D5
Caterham High School
CLAY IG5 ... 53 K5
Catford ⇌
CAT SE6 ... 164 D2
Catford Bridge ⇌
CAT SE6 ... 164 D2
Catford Cricket & Sports Club
CAT SE6 ... 164 E3
Catford Cyphers CC
CAT SE6 ... 164 C4

Catford Trading Estate *CAT* SE6 164 E4
Catford Wanderers Sports Club *CAT* SE6 165 F6
Cathall Leisure Centre *WAN* E11 88 B1
Cathedral School of St Saviour & St Mary Overy *STHWK* SE1 18 D2
Cator Park School for Girls *BECK* BR3 182 B3
Cavendish College *FITZ* W1T 10 C1
Cavendish Hotel *STJS* SW1Y 10 B7
Cavendish Primary School *CHSWK* W4 138 B1
Cavendish School *BERM/RHTH* SE16 123 K4
The Cavendish School *CAMTN* NW1 84 B6
Cavendish Special School *HNWL* W7 97 F5
Caxton Hall *STJSPK* SW1H 16 C4
Caxton Trading Estate *HYS/HAR* UB3 113 H2
Cayley Primary School *WCHPL* E1 105 G4
Cecil Park Clinic *PIN* HA5 59 J1
The Cedar School *FSTGT* E7 89 G4
Cedars Manor School *KTN/HRWW/WS* HA3 42 C4
The Cedars Primary School *HEST* TW5 133 K1
Cedar Way Industrial Estate *CAMTN* NW1 84 D5
Cenotaph *WHALL* SW1A 16 E2
Centaurs Business Centre *ISLW* TW7 116 B6
Centaurs RFC *ISLW* TW7 116 A6
Central Business Centre *WLSDN* NW10 81 G3
The Central College of London *WCHPL* E1 13 K2
Central Criminal Court *STP* EC4M 12 A3
Centrale ⊖ *CROY/NA* CR0 196 D6
Centrale Shopping Centre *CROY/NA* CR0 196 D6
Central Foundation Boys School *SDTCH* EC2A 7 F6
Central Foundation Girls School (Lower) *BOW* E3 105 G2
Central Foundation Girls School (Upper) *BOW* E3 105 H2
Central Hall *STJSPK* SW1H 16 D3
Central Hendon Clinic *HDN* NW4 63 K1
Central London County Court *CAVSQ/HST* W1G 3 J7
Central London Golf Club *TOOT* SW17 160 C4
Central London Markets *STBT* EC1A 12 A2
Central Medical Centre *MRDN* SM4 194 B1
Central Middlesex Hospital *WLSDN* NW10 98 E2
Central Park Arena *DART* DA1 171 H3
Central Park Primary School *EHAM* E6 107 H1
Central St Martins College of Art & Design *RSQ* WC1B 11 G2
Central School of Ballet *CLKNW* EC1R 5 K7
Central School of Fashion *GTPST* W1W 10 A2
Central School of Speech & Drama *HAMP* NW3 83 H5
Central Square Shopping Centre *WBLY* HA9 80 A4
Central YMCA *ELTH/MOT* SE9 166 C4
Centre Court Shopping Centre *WIM/MER* SW19 177 J2
The Centre Performing Arts College *CHARL* SE7 126 C3
Centre Point *LSQ/SEVD* WC2H 10 D3
Chace Community School *EN* EN1 24 A2
Chadwell Heath ≠ *CHDH* RM6 73 K4
Chadwell Heath Academy *CHDH* RM6 73 H3
Chadwell Heath Industrial Park *BCTR* RM8 74 A5
Chadwell Heath Leisure Centre *CHDH* RM6 73 K3
Chadwell Infant & Primary School *CHDH* RM6 73 J4
Chaffinch Business Park *BECK* BR3 182 A6
Chailey Industrial Estate *HYS/HAR* UB3 113 K2
Chalcot School *CAMTN* NW1 84 B4
Chalgrove Primary School *FNCH* N3 46 C6
Chalk Farm ⊖ *HAMP* NW3 84 A5
Chalkhill Primary School *WBLY* HA9 80 D1
The Chamberlain Hotel *TWRH* EC3N 13 J5
Chambers Business Park *WDR/YW* UB7 112 D6
Chambers Wharf *BERM/RHTH* SE16 123 H2
Chancery Court Hotel *HHOL* WC1V 11 G2
Chancery Lane ⊖ *FSBYW* WC1X 11 J2
Chandlers Field Primary School *E/WMO/HCT* KT8 189 F2
Chandos Business Centre *WLGTN* SM6 210 C4
Channelsea Business Centre *SRTFD* E15 106 B1
Channing School *HGT* N6 66 B5
Chapel End Infant School *WALTH* E17 51 K5
Chapel End Junior School *WALTH* E17 51 K4
Chapman Park Industrial Estate *WLSDN* NW10 81 H4
Charing Cross ≠ *CHCR* WC2N 10 E7
Charing Cross Hospital *HMSMTH* W6 119 G6
Charing Cross Hotel *CHCR* WC2N 10 E6
The Charles Dickens Museum *BMSBY* WC1N 5 G7
Charles Dickens Primary School *STHWK* SE1 18 C3
Charles Edward Brooke School (Lower School) *CMBW* SE5 142 C2
Charles Edward Brooke School (Upper School) *BRXN/ST* SW9 142 C2
Charlotte Sharman Primary School *LBTH* SE11 18 A5
Charlton ≠ *CHARL* SE7 126 B5
Charlton Athletic FC (The Valley) *CHARL* SE7 126 B5
Charlton Cemetery *CHARL* SE7 126 D6
Charlton Health & Fitness Centre *CHARL* SE7 126 B5
Charlton House *CHARL* SE7 126 C6
Charlton Manor Junior School *CHARL* SE7 146 C1
Charlton RFC *ELTH/MOT* SE9 167 G2
Charlton School *CHARL* SE7 126 D6
Charrington Bowl *SURB* KT6 191 J6
Charrville Primary School *YEAD* UB4 94 C1
Charter Clinic *CHEL* SW3 120 E5
Charterhouse *FARR* EC1M 6 B7
Charteris Road Sports Centre
HAMP NW3 83 J3
KIL/WHAMP NW6 82 D6
Charter Nightingale Hospital & Counselling Centre *CAMTN* NW1 8 D1
The Charter School *HNHL* SE24 142 E6
Chartwell Business Centre *BMLY* BR1 184 C6
Chase Bridge Primary School *WHTN* TW2 155 K1
Chase Farm Hospital *ENC/FH* EN2 23 G1
Chase Lane Primary School *CHING* E4 37 H6
Chase Road Trading Estate *WLSDN* NW10 99 F3
Chase Side Primary School *ENC/FH* EN2 23 J3
Chaseville Clinic *WCHMH* N21 35 F1
Chatsworth Infant School *BFN/LL* DA15 168 B3
Chatsworth Primary School *HSLW* TW3 135 H5
Chaucer Clinic *NWDGN* UB2 115 J2
Cheam ≠ *BELMT* SM2 208 D5
Cheam Common J & I School *WPK* KT4 192 E6
Cheam Fields Primary School *CHEAM* SM3 208 C3
Cheam High School *CHEAM* SM3 208 C2
Cheam Leisure Centre *CHEAM* SM3 208 B2
Cheam Park Farm Junior School *CHEAM* SM3 208 C1
Cheam Sports Club *CHEAM* SM3 208 C5
Chelsea Bridge Business Centre *VX/NE* SW8 141 G1
Chelsea Centre & Theatre *WBPTN* SW10 140 B1
Chelsea Cinema *CHEL* SW3 120 D5
The Chelsea Club Leisure Centre *FUL/PGN* SW6 120 A6
Chelsea College of Art & Design
CHEL SW3 120 D5
FUL/PGN SW6 140 B3
SHB W12 118 E2
WEST SW1P 121 K5
Chelsea FC (Stamford Bridge) *FUL/PGN* SW6 140 A1
Chelsea Fields Industrial Estate *WIM/MER* SW19 178 C4
Chelsea Group of Children *WBPTN* SW10 140 B1
Chelsea Independent College *FUL/PGN* SW6 140 A1
Chelsea Leisure Centre *CHEL* SW3 120 D5
Chelsea Old Town Hall *CHEL* SW3 120 D5
Chelsea Physic Garden *CHEL* SW3 120 E6
Chelsea & Westminster Hospital *WBPTN* SW10 120 B6
Chelsea Wharf *WBPTN* SW10 140 C1
Chelsfield ≠ *ORP* BR6 217 H3
Chennestone Community School *SUN* TW16 172 A5
Cherington House Health Centre *HNWL* W7 116 A1
Cherry Garden Pier *BERM/RHTH* SE16 123 J2
Cherry Garden School *BERM/RHTH* SE16 123 H4
Cherry Lane Primary School *WDR/YW* UB7 112 C4
Cherry Orchard Primary School *CHARL* SE7 146 B1
The Cherry Trees *BOW* E3 105 J2
Chessington Community College *CHSGTN* KT9 205 K5
Chessington CC *CHSGTN* KT9 205 J5
Chessington Golf Club *CHSGTN* KT9 205 K5
Chessington North ≠ *CHSGTN* KT9 206 A3
Chessington South ≠ *CHSGTN* KT9 205 K5
The Chesterfield Mayfair Hotel *MYFR/PICC* W1J 9 J7
Chesterton Primary School *BTSEA* SW11 141 F2
Chestnut Grove School *BAL* SW12 161 F3
Chestnuts Primary School *SEVS/STOTM* N15 67 J2
Cheyne Centre *CHEL* SW3 120 C6
Chicken Shed Theatre *STHGT/OAK* N14 22 A6
Chigwell Golf Club *CHIG* IG7 54 A1
Childeric Primary School *NWCR* SE14 144 B1
Childrens House Upper School *IS* N1 86 A3
Childs Hill Clinic *CRICK* NW2 64 D6
Childs Hill Primary School *CRICK* NW2 82 C1
Childs Welfare Clinic *BCTR* RM8 91 J3
Chiltonian Industrial Estate *LEE/GVPK* SE12 165 J1
Chimnocks Wharf *POP/IOD* E14 105 G6
Chingford ≠ *CHING* E4 38 C2
Chingford CE Infant School *CHING* E4 38 B3
Chingford CE Junior School *CHING* E4 38 B3
Chingford Foundation School *CHING* E4 37 K3
Chingford Hall Primary School *CHING* E4 51 H2
Chingford Health Centre *CHING* E4 37 J6
Chingford Industrial Centre *CHING* E4 51 G1
Chingford Mount Cemetery *CHING* E4 37 K5
Chingford RFC *CHING* E4 37 J3
Chisenhale Primary School *BOW* E3 105 G1
Chislehurst ≠ *BMLY* BR1 185 F5
Chislehurst Caves *CHST* BR7 185 F4
Chislehurst Cemetery *CHST* BR7 185 K1
Chislehurst Golf Club *CHST* BR7 185 G3
Chislehurst Natural Health Centre *CHST* BR7 185 G2
Chislehurst & Sidcup Grammar School *BFN/LL* DA15 168 C4
Chiswick ≠ *CHSWK* W4 137 K1
Chiswick & Bedford Park Preparatory School *CHSWK* W4 118 B4
Chiswick Business Park *CHSWK* W4 117 J4
Chiswick Community School *CHSWK* W4 138 A1
Chiswick House *CHSWK* W4 118 A6
Chiswick Moran Hotel *CHSWK* W4 117 J5
Chiswick Park ⊖ *CHSWK* W4 117 K4
Chrisp Street Health Centre *POP/IOD* E14 105 K5
Christ Church Bentinck CE Primary School *CAMTN* NW1 8 C1
Christ Church Brondesbury CE J & I School *KIL/WHAMP* NW6 82 D6
Christ Church CE Junior School *EA* W5 97 K6
Christ Church CE Primary School
BAR EN5 20 B3
BRXN/ST SW9 142 B2
BRYLDS KT5 191 H3
BTSEA SW11 140 D4
CHEL SW3 120 E6
FSTH SE23 164 A4
WOOL/PLUM SE18 147 F2
Christchurch CE Primary School
HAMP NW3 83 H1
WCHPL E1 13 K2
Christ Church CE VA Primary School *ERITH* DA8 130 A6
Christchurch Industrial Centre *STHWK* SE1 12 A7
Christ Church New Malden CE Primary School *NWMAL* KT3 176 B6
Christchurch Primary School *IL* IG1 72 B5
Christ Church Primary School *NWMAL* KT3 176 A6
Christ Church School *CAMTN* NW1 3 K3
Christian Meeting Hall *BECK* BR3 182 D4
Christopher Hatton Primary School *FSBYW* WC1X 5 J7
Christs College Finchley *FNCH* N3 47 F6
Christs College School *EFNCH* N2 47 F6
Christs School *RCHPK/HAM* TW10 137 G6
Christ the King RC Primary School *FSBYPK* N4 67 F5
Christ the King Sixth Form College *LEW* SE13 145 G4
Chrysalis Theatre *BAL* SW12 161 F3
Chrysanthemum Clinic *CHSWK* W4 137 K1
Chrysolyte Independent Christian School *STHWK* SE1 19 F4
Church Down Adult School *LEE/GVPK* SE12 165 K4
Church End Medical Centre *WLSDN* NW10 81 G4
Church Farm House Museum *HDN* NW4 45 K6
Church Farm Swimming Pool *EBAR* EN4 33 K3
Churchfield Primary School *ED* N9 36 B3
Churchfields J & I School *SWFD* E18 52 E4
Churchfields Primary School *BECK* BR3 182 A6
Church House *WEST* SW1P 16 D4
Churchill Clinic *STHWK* SE1 17 K4
Churchill College *RYNPK* SW20 177 F5
Churchill Gardens Primary School *PIM* SW1V 121 H5
Churchill Theatre *BMLY* BR1 183 K5
Churchill War Rooms *STJSPK* SW1H 16 D2
Church Stairs *BERM/RHTH* SE16 123 J2
Church Street ⊖ *CROY/NA* CR0 196 D6
Church Trading Estate *ERITH* DA8 150 D1
Cineworld
CHEL SW3 120 C6
CRICK NW2 63 K5
EA W5 97 K6
EN EN1 24 C5
FELT TW13 154 A4
HMSMTH W6 118 E4
SOHO/SHAV W1D 10 C6
WBPTN SW10 120 C5
BXLYHS DA6 149 J5
WDGN N22 49 G5
Citigroup Tower *POP/IOD* E14 124 E1
The City Academy Hackney *HOM* E9 86 E3
City Banking College *STHWK* SE1 19 G2
City Business Centre *BERM/RHTH* SE16 123 K2
City Business College *FSBYE* EC1V 6 B5
City Central Estate *FSBYE* EC1V 6 C5
City College of Higher Education *IS* N1 7 F4
City & Guilds of London Art School *LBTH* SE11 122 B5
City Health Centre *FSBYE* EC1V 6 E6
City & Islington College
FSBYE EC1V 6 D5
FSBYPK N4 67 H6
HBRY N5 85 G4
HOLWY N7 84 E2
HOLWY N7 85 F1
IS N1 85 J6
City & Islington Sixth Form College *FSBYE* EC1V 6 A3
City Literary College *HHOL* WC1V 11 F3
City of London Academy *STHWK* SE1 123 H5
The City of London Academy Islington *IS* N1 6 C1
The City of London Academy *EDUL* SE22 143 H6
City of London Business College
SEVS/STOTM N15 68 A2
SEVS/STOTM N15 68 C2
City of London Cemetery *MNPK* E12 71 J6
City of London Club *OBST* EC2N 13 G3
City of London College *WCHPL* E1 104 C5
City of London Crematorium *MNPK* E12 89 J1
City of London Magistrates Court *LOTH* EC2R 12 E4
City of London School for Girls *BARB* EC2Y 12 C1
City of London School Sports Ground *LEE/GVPK* SE12 166 B4
City of Westminster Cemetery *HNWL* W7 116 A1
City of Westminster College
BAY/PAD W2 8 A1
MV/WKIL W9 100 D2
MV/WKIL W9 101 F3
City of Westminster Vehicle Pound *MYFR/PKLN* W1K 9 F6
City Thameslink ≠ *FLST/FETLN* EC4A 12 A3
City University
CLKNW EC1R 6 A5
IS N1 6 C3
STBT EC1A 12 C2
WCHPL E1 104 D4
City University Business School *BARB* EC2Y 12 D1
Civic Medical Centre *HRW* HA1 60 E2
Civil Service Sports Ground
CHSWK W4 138 B2
LEE/GVPK SE12 166 B1
Clapham Common ⊖ *CLAP* SW4 141 H5
Clapham Common Clinic *CLAP* SW4 141 J5
Clapham High Street ≠ ⊖ *CLAP* SW4 141 J4
Clapham Junction ≠ ⊖ *BTSEA* SW11 140 D5
Clapham Manor Primary School *CLAP* SW4 141 H4
Clapham Manor Street Public Baths *CLAP* SW4 141 J4
Clapham North ⊖ *CLAP* SW4 141 J4
Clapham North Business Centre *CLAP* SW4 141 J4
Clapham Picture House *CLAP* SW4 141 H5
Clapham South ⊖ *CLAP* SW4 161 G1
Clapton ≠ *CLPT* E5 68 D6
Clapton Girls Technology College *CLPT* E5 86 E2
Clara Grant Primary School *BOW* E3 105 J3
Clare House Primary School *BECK* BR3 183 F5
Claremont Clinic *FSTGT* E7 89 G3
Claremont Fan Court School *ESH/CLAY* KT10 204 B4
Claremont High School Academy Trust *KTN/HRWW/WS* HA3 62 A2
Claremont Landscape Garden (NT) *ESH/CLAY* KT10 204 A5
Claremont Primary School *CRICK* NW2 64 B6
Claremont Way Industrial Estate *CRICK* NW2 64 A5
Clarence House *WHALL* SW1A 16 B2
Clarendon Primary School *ASHF* TW15 152 C5
Clarendon Special School *HPTN* TW12 173 G2
Claridge's Hotel *MYFR/PKLN* W1K 9 J5
Claverings Industrial Estate *ED* N9 36 E4
Claygate ≠ *ESH/CLAY* KT10 204 D4
Claygate Primary School *ESH/CLAY* KT10 204 E5
Clayhall Clinic *CLAY* IG5 53 J6
Claypoints Hospital *BTFD* TW8 117 F4
Cleeve Park School *SCUP* DA14 168 D5
Clementine Churchill Hospital *HRW* HA1 78 E1
Cleopatra's Needle *CHCR* WC2N 11 G7

Clerkenwell County Court *IS* N1 6 A2
Clerkenwell Heritage Centre *FARR* EC1M 6 A7
Clerkenwell Parochial CE Primary School *CLKNW* EC1R 5 J5
Cleveland Primary School *IL* IG1 90 B2
Cleves Primary School *EHAM* E6 89 H6
C & L Golf & Country Club *NTHLT* UB5 77 F5
Clifton Lodge School *EA* W5 97 J6
Clifton Primary School *NWDGN* UB2 114 D4
Clink Exhibition *STHWK* SE1 12 E7
Clissold Leisure Centre *STNW/STAM* N16 85 K1
Clissold Park Natural Health Centre *STNW/STAM* N16 68 A6
C & L Leisure Centre *RSLP* HA4 77 F5
Clock House ⇌ *BECK* BR3 182 B5
Clockhouse Industrial Estate *EBED/NFELT* TW14 152 E3
Clockhouse Primary School *CRW* RM5 56 D2
Clock Mill *POP/IOD* E14 106 A2
Clock Museum *CITYW* EC2V 12 D3
Cloisters Business Centre *VX/NE* SW8 141 G1
Clore Gallery *WEST* SW1P 16 E7
Clore Tikva School *BARK/HLT* IG6 54 C5
Clothworkers' Hall *FENCHST* EC3M 13 H5
Clouster's Green *WAP* E1W 123 H1
Cobbold Estate *WLSDN* NW10 81 H4
Cobourg Primary School *CMBW* SE5 123 G6
Cochrane Theatre *GINN* WC1R 11 G2
Cockfosters ⊖ *EBAR* EN4 22 A5
Cockfosters Sports Ground *EBAR* EN4 21 K4
The Cockpit Theatre *STJWD* NW8 2 C7
Coldharbour Industrial Estate *CMBW* SE5 142 D3
Coldharbour Leisure Centre *ELTH/MOT* SE9 166 E4
Coldharbour Sports Ground *ELTH/MOT* SE9 167 F4
Colebrooke Primary School *IS* N1 6 A2
Colegrave School *SRTFD* E15 88 B3
Coleraine Park Primary School *TOTM* N17 50 D4
Coleridge Primary School *HGT* N6 66 D4
Colfes Pre-Preparatory School *LEE/GVPK* SE12 166 A1
Colfe's Preparatory School *LEE/GVPK* SE12 165 K1
Colindale ⊖ *CDALE/KGS* NW9 45 G6
Colindale Business Park *CDALE/KGS* NW9 44 E6
Colindale Hospital *CDALE/KGS* NW9 45 G6
Colindale Primary School *CDALE/KGS* NW9 63 H1
Coliseum Theatre *CHCR* WC2N 10 E6
College Fields Business Centre *WIM/MER* SW19 178 D4
College of Arms *BLKFR* EC4V 12 C4
College of Central London *SDTCH* EC2A 7 G6
College of Fuel Technology *HGT* N6 66 A3
College of Haringey, Enfield & North East London
PEND EN3 24 E4
SEVS/STOTM N15 68 B1
The College of Law
FITZ W1T 10 C2
LINN WC2A 11 J3
College of North East London
CEND/HSY/T N8 67 G1
WDGN N22 48 C4
College of North West London
KIL/WHAMP NW6 82 E6
WBLY HA9 80 C1
WLSDN NW10 81 H3
College of Organists *FLST/FETLN* EC4A 11 K2
College Park School *BAY/PAD* W2 101 F5
Collier Row Clinic *CRW* RM5 56 D4
Collier Row FC *CRW* RM5 56 B4
Collier's Wood ⊖ *WIM/MER* SW19 178 C3
Collingwood Business Centre *ARCH* N19 84 E1
Collingwood School *WLGTN* SM6 210 B3
Collins Method School *CRICK* NW2 82 A4
Collis Primary School *TEDD* TW11 174 C2
Colnbrook School *OXHEY* WD19 27 G4
Colonnades Leisure Park *CROY/NA* CR0 211 G4
The Colonnades Shopping Centre *BGVA* SW1W 15 J6
Colours Sports Club *SUT* SM1 209 G3
Columbia Primary School *BETH* E2 7 K4
Colvestone Primary School *HACK* E8 86 B3
Colville Primary School *NTGHL* W11 100 D5
Colyers Lane Medical Centre *ERITH* DA8 150 A2
Comber Grove Primary School *CMBW* SE5 142 D1
Comedy Theatre *STJS* SW1Y 10 C6
Comelle House Trading Estate *DEPT* SE8 124 B5
Comfort Hotel *ENC/FH* EN2 23 H3
Comfort Inn *HYS/HAR* UB3 113 H5
Commonwealth Institute *WKENS* W14 119 J3
Community Arts Centre *GNWCH* SE10 144 E1
Community Care Centre *ENC/FH* EN2 23 K2
Community Centre (Island History Trust) *POP/IOD* E14 125 F4
Community College & School *GNWCH* SE10 145 F1
The Community College *HACK* E8 86 D6
Compass Theatre *HGDN/ICK* UB10 76 A1
Complementary Health Centre *LEE/GVPK* SE12 165 H1
The Compton School *NFNCH/WDSPK* N12 47 J2
Compton Sports Centre *NFNCH/WDSPK* N12 47 J2
Concord Business Centre *ACT* W3 98 D4
Conduit House *GNWCH* SE10 145 G1
Coney Hill School *HAYES* BR2 199 J6
Conisborough College *CAT* SE6 165 G5
Connaught Business Centre
CDALE/KGS NW9 63 H2
CROY/NA CR0 211 F4
MTCM CR4 194 E2
The Connaught Hotel *MYFR/PKLN* W1K 9 H6
Connaught House School *BAY/PAD* W2 8 D4
Connaught School for Girls *WAN* E11 70 C5
Consort Clinic *PECK* SE15 143 J4
Consulate General of Monaco *SKENS* SW7 14 A6
Consulate of Burkina Faso *BTSEA* SW11 140 B4
Consulate of Chile *CAVSQ/HST* W1G 3 J7
Consulate of Colombia *GTPST* W1W 10 A3
Consulate of Eritrea *IS* N1 5 K2
Consulate of Guinea *MYFR/PKLN* W1K 9 G6
Consulate of Panama *MYFR/PICC* W1J 15 J1
The Continental Hotel *HSLW* TW3 135 F4
Convent of Jesus & Mary Infant School *CRICK* NW2 82 A4
Convent of Jesus & Mary Language College *WLSDN* NW10 81 H6
Convoy's Wharf *DEPT* SE8 124 C5
Conway Medical Centre *WOOL/PLUM* SE18 127 J5
Conway Primary School *WOOL/PLUM* SE18 127 K4
Coombe Girls School *NWMAL* KT3 176 A5
Coombe Hill Golf Club *KUTN/CMB* KT2 176 A3
Coombe Hill J & I School *NWMAL* KT3 176 A4
Coombe Lane ⊖ *CROY/NA* CR0 212 E3
Coombe Wood Golf Club *KUTN/CMB* KT2 175 J3
Coopers' Hall *LVPST* EC2M 13 H2
Coopers Lane Primary School *LEE/GVPK* SE12 165 K4
Coopers Technology College *CHST* BR7 185 H4
Copenhagen Primary School *IS* N1 5 F1
Copland Specialist Science College *WBLY* HA9 80 B3
Coppermill Primary School *WALTH* E17 69 F2
Coppetts Wood Hospital *MUSWH* N10 47 K4
Coppetts Wood Primary School *MUSWH* N10 48 A4
Coppice Primary School *CHIG* IG7 55 G1
Copthall School *MLHL* NW7 45 K3
Copthorne Tara Hotel *KENS* W8 120 A3
Cordwainers College *HACK* E8 86 E5
Corinthian Casuals FC *SURB* KT6 206 C1
Coronet Cinema
KENS W8 119 K1
SEVS/STOTM N15 49 H6
Corpus Christi RC Primary School *BRXS/STRHM* SW2 142 A6
Cosmopolitan College *IS* N1 5 G3
Coston Primary School *GFD/PVL* UB6 96 C2
Coteford Infant School *PIN* HA5 58 E2
County Council Offices *BUSH* WD23 28 D2
Courtauld Institute Gallery *TPL/STR* WC2R 11 G5
Courtauld Institute of Art *TPL/STR* WC2R 11 H5
Court Farm Industrial Estate *STWL/WRAY* TW19 152 C1
Courtfield Medical Centre *ECT* SW5 120 A4
Courtland JMI School *MLHL* NW7 31 G4
Covent Garden ⊖ *COVGDN* WC2E 10 E5
Covent Garden Flower Market *VX/NE* SW8 121 J6
Covent Garden Medical Centre *LSQ/SEVD* WC2H 10 E4
Crafts Council *IS* N1 5 K3
Crampton Primary School *WALW* SE17 18 B7
Cranbrook College *IL* IG1 72 A6
Cranbrook Primary School *IL* IG1 71 K4
Crane Park Island Nature Reserve *FELT* TW13 154 E4
Cranford Community College *HEST* TW5 114 A6
Cranford Infant School *HSLWW* TW4 133 K3
Cranford Junior School *HSLWW* TW4 134 A3
Cranford Park Junior School *HYS/HAR* UB3 113 J4
Cranford Park Primary School *HYS/HAR* UB3 113 J2
Cranleigh Gardens Industrial Estate *STHL* UB1 95 K4
The Cranley Hotel *ECT* SW5 120 B5
Cranmer Primary School *MTCM* CR4 194 E1
The Craven Clinic *HMSMTH* W6 118 E4
Craven Park Health Centre *WLSDN* NW10 81 F6
Craven Park Medical Centre *WLSDN* NW10 81 F6
Crawford Primary School *CMBW* SE5 142 D2
Crayfield Industrial Park *STMC/STPC* BR5 186 D5
Crayfields Business Park *STMC/STPC* BR5 186 D4
Crayford ⇌ *DART* DA1 170 B1
Crayford Commercial Centre *DART* DA1 150 B6
Crayford Industrial Estate *DART* DA1 150 C6
Crayford Leisure Centre & Greyhound Stadium *DART* DA1 170 B1
Crayford Medical Centre *DART* DA1 150 C6
Crayside Industrial Estate *DART* DA1 150 D4
Creekmouth Industrial Estate *BARK* IG11 109 F3
Creek Road Health Centre *DEPT* SE8 124 D6
Creek Road Industrial Estate *DEPT* SE8 124 E6
The Crest Boys Academy *CRICK* NW2 81 H1
Crewe House *MYFR/PICC* W1J 9 J7
Cricket Green School *MTCM* CR4 178 D6
Cricklefield Stadium *IL* IG1 72 E6
Cricklewood ⇌ *CRICK* NW2 82 B1
Cricklewood Trading Estate *CRICK* NW2 82 C1
Crispin Industrial Centre *UED* N18 50 E1
Criterion Theatre *MYFR/PICC* W1J 10 B6
Crockenhill Primary School *SWLY* BR8 203 K3
Crofton Leisure Centre *BROCKY* SE4 164 D1
Crofton Park ⇌ *BROCKY* SE4 144 C6
Croham Hurst Golf Club *SAND/SEL* CR2 212 B4
Cromer Road Primary School *BAR* EN5 21 F4
Cromwell Business Centre *BARK* IG11 108 E2
Cromwell Hospital *KENS* W8 120 A4
Crook Log Primary School *BXLYHS* DA6 148 E5
Crook Log Sports Centre *WELL* DA16 148 E4
Crossharbour ⊖ *POP/IOD* E14 124 E3
Crossways Sixth Form *BROCKY* SE4 144 B3
Crouch End Art School *CEND/HSY/T* N8 66 E2
Crouch End Health Centre *CEND/HSY/T* N8 66 E2
Crouch Hill ⊖ *FSBYPK* N4 67 F4
Crouch Hill Recreation Centre *CEND/HSY/T* N8 66 E4
Crowland Primary School *SEVS/STOTM* N15 68 C2
Crowlands Primary School *ROMW/RG* RM7 74 E3
Crown Business Centre *WDR/YW* UB7 112 C1
Crown Close Business Centre *BOW* E3 87 J6
Crown Court at The Borough *STHWK* SE1 18 B2
Crowndale Health Centre *CAMTN* NW1 4 B2
Crowne Plaza
EA W5 98 A2
WDR/YW UB7 112 D4
Crowne Plaza Hotel
BETH E2 7 J5
CAN/RD E16 106 E6
EMB EC4Y 12 A5
SKENS SW7 120 B4
Crownfield Primary School *ROMW/RG* RM7 56 C5
Crown Lane Clinic *STHGT/OAK* N14 34 C3
Crown Lane Primary School *WNWD* SE27 162 D6
Crown Moran Hotel *CRICK* NW2 82 B2
Crown Trading Centre *HYS/HAR* UB3 113 H2
Crown Woods School *ELTH/MOT* SE9 147 H6
Croydon Airport Industrial Estate *CROY/NA* CR0 211 G5
Croydon Bowling Club *SAND/SEL* CR2 211 J3
Croydon Cemetery *CROY/NA* CR0 196 A2
Croydon Clocktower Cinema *CROY/NA* CR0 211 J1
Croydon College *CROY/NA* CR0 211 K1
Croydon Combined Courts *CROY/NA* CR0 211 K1
Croydon Crematorium *THHTH* CR7 195 K2
Croydon Fairfield Halls Cinema *CROY/NA* CR0 211 K1
Croydon FC *SNWD* SE25 197 K2
Croydon Road Industrial Estate *BECK* BR3 197 K1
Croydon Sports Arena *SNWD* SE25 197 K2
Crusader Industrial Estate *FSBYPK* N4 67 J3
Crystal Palace ⇌ ⊖ *PGE/AN* SE20 181 H2
Crystal Palace FC (Selhurst Park) *SNWD* SE25 197 F1
Crystal Palace FC Soccer & Sports Centre *BRXN/ST* SW9 142 A4
Crystal Palace Museum *NRWD* SE19 181 G2
Cuaco Sports Ground *BECK* BR3 182 D2
Cubitt Town Infant School *POP/IOD* E14 125 F3
Cuckoo Hall Academy *ED* N9 36 E2
Cuddington Cemetery *WPK* KT4 192 E6
Cuddington CP School *WPK* KT4 207 H1
Cuddington Croft Primary School *BELMT* SM2 208 B6
Culloden Primary School *POP/IOD* E14 106 B5
Culvers House Primary School *MTCM* CR4 195 F5
Cumberland Business Park *WLSDN* NW10 98 D2
The Cumberland Hotel
FITZ W1T 10 C3
MBLAR W1H 9 F4
Cumberland Park Industrial Estate *WLSDN* NW10 99 J2
The Cumming Museum *WALW* SE17 18 C7
Cumnor House School *SAND/SEL* CR2 211 H6
Curwen Primary School *PLSTW* E13 106 E1
Curzon Mayfair Cinema *MYFR/PICC* W1J 15 J1
Curzon Soho Cinema *SOHO/SHAV* W1D 10 D5
Custom House *MON* EC3R 13 G6
Custom House for ExCeL ⊖ *CAN/RD* E16 107 F6
Custom House Hotel *CAN/RD* E16 107 F6
Cutlers' Hall *STP* EC4M 12 B3
Cutty Sark ⊖ *GNWCH* SE10 125 F6
Cutty Sark Clipper Ship *GNWCH* SE10 125 F6
Cygnet Clinic Beckton *EHAM* E6 108 B4
Cygnus Business Centre *WLSDN* NW10 81 H3
Cypress Infant School *SNWD* SE25 181 F5
Cypress Junior School *SNWD* SE25 181 F5
Cyprus ⊖ *CAN/RD* E16 108 A6
Cyprus College of Art *WNWD* SE27 162 C6
Cyril Jackson Primary School *POP/IOD* E14 105 H6
Dagenham Chest Clinic *BCTR* RM8 92 B1
Dagenham Civic Centre *DAGE* RM10 74 D6
Dagenham Dock ⇌ *DAGW* RM9 110 B1
Dagenham East ⊖ *DAGE* RM10 92 E4
Dagenham Heathway ⊖ *DAGW* RM9 92 B4
Dagenham Park CE School *DAGE* RM10 92 D5
Dagenham & Redbridge FC *DAGE* RM10 92 D3
Dagenham Superbowl *DAGE* RM10 110 D1
Dagenham Swimming Pool *DAGE* RM10 74 C6
Daiglen School *BKHH* IG9 39 G3
Daily Telegraph Newspaper Offices *POP/IOD* E14 124 D3
Dairy Meadow Primary School *NWDGN* UB2 114 E3
D'Albiac House *HTHAIR* TW6 132 D3
Dali Universe *STHWK* SE1 17 G2
Dallington School *FSBYE* EC1V 6 B6
Dalmain Primary School *FSTH* SE23 164 B3
Dalston Junction ⊖ *HACK* E8 86 B4
Dalston Kingsland ⊖ *IS* N1 86 A4
Damilola Taylor Centre *PECK* SE15 143 G1
Danegrove Primary School *EBAR* EN4 33 J1
Danesfield Manor School *WOT/HER* KT12 188 A6
Danetree School *HOR/WEW* KT19 206 E5
Danson House *BXLYHS* DA6 148 D5
Danson Primary School *WELL* DA16 148 C5
Danson Watersports Centre *BXLYHS* DA6 148 D6
Darell Primary School *RCH/KEW* TW9 137 H4
Darent Industrial Park *ERITH* DA8 131 G5
Darrick Wood Primary School *ORP* BR6 216 B2
Darrick Wood School *ORP* BR6 216 B1
Darrick Wood Sports Centre *ORP* BR6 216 C1
Darrick Wood Swimming Pool *ORP* BR6 216 B1
Dartford ⇌ *DART* DA1 151 H6
Dartford Adult Education Centre *DART* DA1 171 F2
Dartford Bridge Community Primary School *DART* DA1 151 J3
Dartford County Court *DART* DA1 171 H1
Dartford Golf Club *DART* DA1 170 E4
Dartford Grammar School for Boys *DART* DA1 171 F1
Dartford Grammar School for Girls *DART* DA1 171 F2
Dartford Magistrates Court *DART* DA1 171 G1
Dartford Museum & Library *DART* DA1 171 H2
Dartford Natural Health Centre *DART* DA1 171 H2
Dartford Technology College *DART* DA1 171 F2
Dartford West Health Centre *DART* DA1 171 F1
Darwin Centre *SKENS* SW7 14 A5
Datapoint Business Centre *BOW* E3 106 B3
Date Valley School *MTCM* CR4 178 E6
Daubeney Primary School *CLPT* E5 87 G2
David Ives (Erith) Stadium *ERITH* DA8 130 B6
David Livingstone Primary School *THHTH* CR7 180 D4
David Lloyd Leisure
BKHH IG9 39 K3
NFNCH/WDSPK N12 47 H3
David Lloyd Leisure Centre *KENS* W8 120 A4
David Lloyd Sports Centre *EN* EN1 24 C3
David Lloyd Tennis Centre *SCUP* DA14 186 D1
Davidson Primary School *CROY/NA* CR0 197 G4
Davies Laing & Dick College *BAY/PAD* W2 100 E6
Davies Lane Primary School *WAN* E11 70 D6
Davies's College *STHWK* SE1 18 E2
Dawlish Primary School *LEY* E10 70 A5

Days Hotel
BETH E2 104 D1
HSLW TW3 135 G4
MLHL NW7 30 E4
RSLP HA4 77 G3
STHWK SE1 17 J5
Days Hotel London South Ruislip
RSLP HA4 77 G2
Days Inn
BAY/PAD W2 8 B4
PIM SW1V 121 H5
Days Lane Primary School
BFN/LL DA15 168 A1
Dean College of London
HOLWY N7 85 F1
Deanesfield Primary School
RSLP HA4 77 H2
Deansbrook Infant School
MLHL NW7 44 E2
Deansfield Primary School
ELTH/MOT SE9 147 F4
De Bohun Primary School
STHGT/OAK N14 22 B6
Delta Wharf
GNWCH SE10 125 G2
Denmark Hill ≈ ⊖
CMBW SE5 142 E4
Denmead School
HPTN TW12 173 F3
Denvale Trade Centre
STMC/STPC BR5 202 C2
Denver Industrial Estate
RAIN RM13 111 H5
Department for Environment, Food & Rural Affairs
CHCR WC2N 10 E7
Department for Transport
WEST SW1P 16 D6
Department of Art & Design (London Metropolitan University)
WCHPL E1 13 K3
Department of Economics (London Metropolitan University)
TWRH EC3N 13 J4
Department of Education
STJSPK SW1H 16 D3
Department of Health
WHALL SW1A 16 E2
Department of Trade & Industry
STJSPK SW1H 16 D4
Deptford ≈
DEPT SE8 144 D1
Deptford Bridge ⊖
DEPT SE8 144 D2
Deptford Business Centre
NWCR SE14 124 A5
Deptford Green School
NWCR SE14 144 C1
Deptford Park Business Centre
DEPT SE8 124 B5
Deptford Park Primary School
DEPT SE8 124 B5
Deptford Trading Estate
DEPT SE8 124 B5
Dersingham Primary School
MNPK E12 89 K3
Derwentwater Primary School
ACT W3 117 K1
Design Centre
FUL/PGN SW6 140 B2
Design Museum
STHWK SE1 19 K1
Deutsche Schule
RCHPK/HAM TW10 156 E3
Devonshire Hospital
MHST W1U 9 H1
Devonshire House School
HAMP NW3 83 G3
Devonshire Primary School
BELMT SM2 209 G5
Devons Road ⊖
BOW E3 105 K3
Diamond College
SOHO/SHAV W1D 10 D3
Diana Fountain
E/WMO/HCT KT8 174 A5
Diana Princess of Wales Memorial Fountain
BAY/PAD W2 14 B1
Diane Matthews Clinic
ROMW/RG RM7 75 F1
Dilloway Industrial Estate
NWDGN UB2 114 D2
Discovery Business Park
BERM/RHTH SE16 123 H3
Discovery Primary School
THMD SE28 128 A1
Docklands Medical Centre
POP/IOD E14 124 D4
Docklands Sailing & Watersports Centre
POP/IOD E14 124 D3
Dockwell's Industrial Estate
EBED/NFELT TW14 134 A6
Dockyard Industrial Estate
WOOL/PLUM SE18 126 D3
Dog Kennel Hill Primary School
EDUL SE22 143 F4
Dokal Industrial Estate
NWDGN UB2 114 D2
Dollis Hill ⊖
WLSDN NW10 81 J3
Dollis Infant School
MLHL NW7 46 A3
The Dolphin Leisure Centre
ROM RM1 75 H1
Dolphin School
BTSEA SW11 140 D6
The Dominie
BTSEA SW11 140 E2
Dominion Business Park
ED N9 37 F4
Dominion Theatre
RSQ WC1B 10 D3
Donhead School
WIM/MER SW19 177 G3
Donmar Warehouse Theatre
LSQ/SEVD WC2H 10 E4
Donnington Primary School
WLSDN NW10 81 K5
The Dorchester Hotel
MYFR/PKLN W1K 9 H7
Dorchester Primary School
WPK KT4 193 F5
Dorma Trading Park
LEY E10 69 F5
Dormers Wells High School
STHL UB1 96 A5
Dormers Wells Junior School
STHL UB1 96 B6
Dormers Wells Leisure Centre
STHL UB1 96 B5
Dormers Wells Medical Centre
STHL UB1 96 A5
Dorothy Barley Primary School
BCTR RM8 91 H3
Dorset Road Infant School
ELTH/MOT SE9 166 D4
Douglas Bader Foundation
PUT/ROE SW15 158 D1
Dovers Corner Industrial Estate
RAIN RM13 111 H2
Downderry Primary School
BMLY BR1 165 H6
Downe Manor Primary School
NTHLT UB5 95 F2
Downham Health Centre
BMLY BR1 165 H6
Downhills Primary School
TOTM N17 67 K1
Downsell Primary School
SRTFD E15 88 B2
Downshall Primary School
GNTH/NBYPK IG2 72 E4
Downsview Primary School
NRWD SE19 180 D3
Downsview School
CLPT E5 86 D2
Drama Centre London
KTTN NW5 84 A4
Drapers Hall
LOTH EC2R 13 F3
The Draycott Hotel
CHEL SW3 15 F6
Drayton Green ≈
HNWL W7 97 F6
Drayton Green Primary School
WEA W13 97 G6
Drayton Manor High School
HNWL W7 97 F6
Drayton Park ≈
HOLWY N7 85 G3
Drayton Park Primary School
HBRY N5 85 G3
DRCA Business Centre
BTSEA SW11 141 F2
Drew Primary School
CAN/RD E16 126 D1
The Drill Hall
GWRST WC1E 10 C1
The Drizen School
EDGW HA8 44 C3
Dr Johnson's House
FLST/FETLN EC4A 11 K3
Dr Tripletts CE J & I School
HYS/HAR UB3 94 D5
Drury Way Industrial Estate
WLSDN NW10 81 F2
Duchess Theatre
COVGDN WC2E 11 G5
Duff Miller College
SKENS SW7 120 B3
Duke of York Column
STJS SW1Y 16 D1
Duke of York Theatre
CHCR WC2N 10 E6
Dukes Hotel
WHALL SW1A 16 A1
Dulverton Primary School
ELTH/MOT SE9 167 J4
Dulwich College
DUL SE21 163 F3
Dulwich College Pre-Preparatory School
DUL SE21 163 F5
Dulwich College Track
DUL SE21 163 F4
Dulwich Hamlet FC
EDUL SE22 143 F5
Dulwich Hamlet Junior School
HNHL SE24 162 E1
Dulwich Hospital
EDUL SE22 143 F5
Dulwich Leisure Centre
EDUL SE22 143 H5
Dulwich Medical Centre
EDUL SE22 143 H6
Dulwich Picture Gallery
DUL SE21 163 F2
Dulwich & Sydenham Hill Golf Club
DUL SE21 163 H4
Dulwich Village CE Infant School
DUL SE21 163 F1
Dunbar Wharf
POP/IOD E14 105 H6
Duncombe Primary School
ARCH N19 66 E5
Dundee Wharf
POP/IOD E14 105 H6
Dundonald Primary School
WIM/MER SW19 177 J3
Dundonald Road ⊖
WIM/MER SW19 177 J3
Dunraven Lower School
STRHM/NOR SW16 162 A5
Dunraven School Upper
STRHM/NOR SW16 162 A5
Durand Primary School
BRXN/ST SW9 142 A2
Durands Wharf
BERM/RHTH SE16 124 C2
Durants School
PEND EN3 24 E2
Durdans Park Primary School
STHL UB1 95 K4
Durston House School
EA W5 97 K5
Dysart School
KUTN/CMB KT2 156 E6
SURB KT6 191 F4
Dyslexia Teaching Centre
ECT SW5 120 A5
Eaglesfield School
WOOL/PLUM SE18 147 F2
Eagle Trading Estate
MTCM CR4 194 E3
Ealdham Primary School
ELTH/MOT SE9 146 B5
Ealing Abbey
EA W5 97 J5
Ealing Abbey Scriptorium
WEA W13 97 J5
Ealing Broadway ≈ ⊖
EA W5 97 K6
The Ealing Broadway Centre
EA W5 97 K6
Ealing Central Sports Ground
GFD/PVL UB6 97 G1
Ealing Civic Centre
EA W5 97 J6
Ealing College Upper School
WEA W13 97 H5
Ealing Common ⊖
EA W5 117 G1
Ealing Conservative Bowling Club
EA W5 97 J6
Ealing CC
EA W5 98 A5
Ealing Film Studios
EA W5 116 D1
Ealing Golf Club
GFD/PVL UB6 97 H2
Ealing Hammersmith & West London College
WKENS W14 119 G4
Ealing Hospital
NWDGN UB2 115 J2
Ealing Independent College
EA W5 97 J6
Ealing Northern Sports Centre
GFD/PVL UB6 78 D2
Ealing Park Health Centre
EA W5 116 E4
Ealing Road Trading Estate
BTFD TW8 116 E5
Ealing Snooker Club
WEA W13 116 C1
Ealing Sports Centre
EA W5 98 A6
Ealing & West London College
EA W5 116 D1
Eardley Primary School
STRHM/NOR SW16 179 H2
Earlham Primary School
FSTGT E7 88 D3
WDGN N22 49 F3
Earl's Court ⊖
ECT SW5 119 K4
Earl's Court Exhibition Centre
FUL/PGN SW6 119 K5
Earlsfield ≈
WAND/EARL SW18 160 B3
Earlsfield Primary School
WAND/EARL SW18 160 B4
Earlsmead Primary School
RYLN/HDSTN HA2 77 K2
SEVS/STOTM N15 68 B1
Earth Galleries
SKENS SW7 14 B5
East Acton ⊖
SHB W12 99 H5
East Acton Primary School
ACT W3 99 G6
East Barking Centre
BCTR RM8 91 J3
East Barnet Health Centre
EBAR EN4 21 H6
East Barnet School
EBAR EN4 33 K1
East Beckton District Centre
EHAM E6 107 K5
Eastbrook Comprehensive School
DAGE RM10 92 E2
Eastbrook End Cemetery
ROMW/RG RM7 93 G1
Eastbrookend Country Park
ROMW/RG RM7 93 F2
Eastbury Comprehensive School
BARK IG11 91 F6
Eastbury Farm JMI School
NTHWD HA6 26 D6
Eastbury Primary School
BARK IG11 91 F5
Eastcote ⊖
RSLP HA4 59 G4
Eastcote CC
PIN HA5 59 F2
Eastcote Health Centre
PIN HA5 59 G4
Eastcote Industrial Estate
RSLP HA4 59 G4
Eastcote Lane Cemetery
RYLN/HDSTN HA2 78 B1
Eastcote Primary School
WELL DA16 147 J4
Eastcourt Independent School
GDMY/SEVK IG3 73 G5
East Croydon ≈ ⊖
CROY/NA CR0 196 E6
East Dulwich ≈
EDUL SE22 143 F5
East End Computing & Business College
WCHPL E1 104 D5
Eastern Business Park
HTHAIR TW6 133 J3
Eastfield Primary School
PEND EN3 25 F1
East Finchley ⊖
EFNCH N2 65 J1
East Finchley Cemetery
EFNCH N2 47 F6
East Finchley Medical Centre
EFNCH N2 65 J1
East Finchley School of English
EFNCH N2 47 J6
Eastgate Business Park
LEY E10 69 G5
East Greenwich Christ Church CE Primary School
GNWCH SE10 125 H4
East Ham ⊖
EHAM E6 89 J5
East Ham Industrial Estate
EHAM E6 107 H4
East Ham Jewish Cemetery
EHAM E6 107 J2
East Ham Leisure Centre
EHAM E6 89 K6
East Ham Memorial Hospital
EHAM E6 89 H5
East Ham Nature Reserve
EHAM E6 107 K3
East Hill Cemetery
DART DA1 171 K2
East India ⊖
POP/IOD E14 106 B6
Eastlea Community Centre
CAN/RD E16 106 D3
Eastlea Community School
CAN/RD E16 106 C3
East London Business College
WAN E11 70 C5
East London Cemetery
PLSTW E13 106 D2
East London Christian Choir School
IS N1 86 A5
East London Crematorium
SRTFD E15 106 D2
East London RFC
EHAM E6 107 K4
East London RUFC
SRTFD E15 106 D1
Eastman Dental Hospital
FSBYW WC1X 5 G6
East Molesey CC
E/WMO/HCT KT8 173 H6
East Putney ⊖
PUT/ROE SW15 139 H6
East Sheen Cemetery
RCHPK/HAM TW10 137 H6
East Sheen Primary School
MORT/ESHN SW14 138 B5
East Thamesmead Business Park
ERITHM DA18 129 G2
East Wickham Primary School
WELL DA16 148 A2
Eaton Manor RFC
WAN E11 71 G2
Eaton Square Pre-Preparatory School
BGVA SW1W 15 J6
Eaton Square School
PIM SW1V 16 A7
Ebrahim Community College
WCHPL E1 104 C4
Ecclesbourne Primary School
THHTH CR7 196 D2
Eden College
STHWK SE1 18 B4
Edenham High School
CROY/NA CR0 198 B4
Eden High School
FUL/PGN SW6 139 J2
Eden Medical Centre
WKENS W14 119 J4
Eden Park ≈
BECK BR3 198 D2
Edenvale Child Health Clinic
MTCM CR4 179 F3
Eden Walk Shopping Centre
KUT/HW KT1 175 F5
Edes Business Park
WLGTN SM6 195 F6
Edgebury Primary School
CHST BR7 167 H6
Edge Business Centre
CRICK NW2 63 K6
Edgware ⊖
EDGW HA8 44 D2
Edgware Blood Transfusion Centre
EDGW HA8 44 D3
Edgwarebury Cemetery
EDGW HA8 30 C4
Edgware Clinic
EDGW HA8 44 C2
Edgware College
KIL/WHAMP NW6 83 G4
Edgware Community Hospital
EDGW HA8 44 D3
Edgware FC & Wealdstone FC
EDGW HA8 44 C3
Edgware Infant School
EDGW HA8 44 C2
Edgware Jewish Girls-Beis Chinuch
EDGW HA8 44 C2
Edgware Jewish Primary School
EDGW HA8 44 D1
Edgware Junior School
EDGW HA8 44 D2
Edgware Road ⊖
BAY/PAD W2 8 B2
Edinburgh Primary School
WALTH E17 69 H2
Edith Neville Primary School
CAMTN NW1 4 C3
Edmonton Cemetery
WCHMH N21 35 K4
Edmonton County Court
UED N18 50 C1
Edmonton County Lower School
ED N9 36 A3
Edmonton Green ≈
ED N9 36 C4
Edmonton Green Shopping Centre
ED N9 36 D4
Edmonton Leisure Centre
ED N9 36 C5
Edmonton Upper School
EN EN1 36 B2
Edmund Waller Primary School
NWCR SE14 144 A3
Education Centre
WOOL/PLUM SE18 127 G5
Edward Betham CE Primary School
GFD/PVL UB6 96 D2
Edward Pauling School
FELT TW13 153 H4
Edward Wilson Primary School
BAY/PAD W2 101 F4
Edwin Lambert School
EMPK RM11 75 J3
Effra Road Retail Park
BRXS/STRHM SW2 142 B6
The Egerton House Hotel
CHEL SW3 14 D5
Eglinton Junior School
WOOL/PLUM SE18 127 F6
Eglinton Primary School
WOOL/PLUM SE18 147 F1
Elbourne Trading Estate
BELV DA17 129 J3
Eldenwall Industrial Estate
BCTR RM8 74 A5
Eldon Infant School
ED N9 36 D3
Eldon Junior School
ED N9 36 E3
Eleanor Palmer Primary School
KTTN NW5 84 C2
Eleanor Smith School
CAN/RD E16 107 G5
Eleanor Smith Special School & Primary Support Service
PLSTW E13 106 E1
Electrical Trades Union College
ESH/CLAY KT10 204 A2
Electric Cinema
NTGHL W11 100 D5
Electron Trade Centre
STMC/STPC BR5 202 C1
Elephant & Castle ≈ ⊖
STHWK SE1 18 B5
Elephant & Castle Leisure Centre
LBTH SE11 18 B6
Elephant & Castle Shopping Centre
STHWK SE1 18 B5
Elers Clinic
HYS/HAR UB3 113 G4
Elfrida Primary School
CAT SE6 164 E6
Eliot Bank Primary School
FSTH SE23 163 J4
Elizabeth Garrett Anderson Hospital
CAMTN NW1 4 D5
Elizabeth Garrett Anderson Language College
IS N1 5 H2
Elizabeth Selby Infant School
BETH E2 104 C2
Elizabeth Trading Estate
NWCR SE14 124 A6
Ellen Wilkinson Primary School
CAN/RD E16 107 H4
Ellen Wilkinson School for Girls
ACT W3 98 B5
Ellern Mede School
TRDG/WHET N20 32 B3
Ellerslie Square Industrial Estate
BRXS/STRHM SW2 141 K5
Ellingham Primary School
CHSGTN KT9 205 K5
Elliott School
PUT/ROE SW15 159 F1
Elmbridge Leisure Centre
WOT/HER KT12 188 A2
Elm Court School
WNWD SE27 162 C4
Elmers End ≈ ⊖
BECK BR3 198 A1
The Elmgreen School
WNWD SE27 162 C4
Elmgrove Junior School
KTN/HRWW/WS HA3 61 G1
Elmhurst Primary School
FSTGT E7 89 F5
Elmhurst School
SAND/SEL CR2 211 K3
Elm Lea Trading Estate
TOTM N17 50 C3
Elm Park ⊖
HCH RM12 93 J2
Elm Park Primary
HCH RM12 93 H3
The Elms Football & Tennis Club
STAN HA7 43 H1
Elmstead Woods ≈
CHST BR7 184 D2
Elmwood J & I School
CROY/NA CR0 196 C4
Elm Wood Primary School
DUL SE21 162 E5
Elsdale Street Health Centre
HOM E9 86 E5
Elsley Primary School
WBLY HA9 80 B4
Elsley School
BTSEA SW11 141 F4

Eltham ⇌ ELTH/MOT SE9 146 E5
Eltham Bus Station ELTH/MOT SE9 146 E6
Eltham CE Primary School ELTH/MOT SE9 146 E6
Eltham College Junior School ELTH/MOT SE9 166 C3
Eltham College Senior School ELTH/MOT SE9 166 C4
Eltham Crematorium ELTH/MOT SE9 147 J5
The Eltham Foundation School ELTH/MOT SE9 166 C1
Eltham Health Clinic ELTH/MOT SE9 146 D6
Eltham Health & Fitness Centre ELTH/MOT SE9 167 F1
Eltham Hill Technology College ELTH/MOT SE9 166 D1
Eltham Palace ELTH/MOT SE9 166 D2
Eltham Pools ELTH/MOT SE9 146 D6
Eltham Warren Golf Club ELTH/MOT SE9 147 G6
Elthorne Park High School HNWL W7 116 A3
Elthorne Sports Centre HNWL W7 116 A3
Elverson Road ⊖ LEW SE13 144 E3
Elystan Business Centre YEAD UB4 95 G6
Emanuel School BTSEA SW11 140 C6
Embankment ⊖ CHCR WC2N 11 F7
Embankment Pier CHCR WC2N 11 G7
Embassy of Afghanistan SKENS SW7 14 A3
Embassy of Albania BGVA SW1W 15 K5
Embassy of Algeria NTGHL W11 119 H1
Embassy of Angola MYFR/PKLN W1K 9 G6
Embassy of Argentina MYFR/PKLN W1K 9 J5
Embassy of Armenia KENS W8 120 A3
Embassy of Austria KTBR SW1X 15 G4
Embassy of Bahrain SKENS SW7 120 B3
Embassy of Belarus KENS W8 120 A2
Embassy of Belgium KTBR SW1X 15 H5
Embassy of Bolivia BGVA SW1W 15 H5
Embassy of Bosnia-Herzegovina CAVSQ/HST W1G 9 K3
Embassy of Brazil MYFR/PKLN W1K 9 G5
Embassy of Bulgaria SKENS SW7 120 B3
Embassy of Cameroon NTGHL W11 119 H1
Embassy of China CAVSQ/HST W1G 9 J1
Embassy of Costa Rica BAY/PAD W2 101 G6
Embassy of Cote d'Ivoire KTBR SW1X 15 H4
Embassy of Croatia GTPST W1W 3 K7
Embassy of Cuba LSQ/SEVD WC2H 10 E3
Embassy of Democratic Republic of The Congo KTBR SW1X 15 F5
Embassy of Denmark KTBR SW1X 14 E4
Embassy of Dominican Republic BAY/PAD W2 101 F5
Embassy of Ecuador KTBR SW1X 14 E4
Embassy of Egypt MYFR/PICC W1J 9 J7
Embassy of Estonia SKENS SW7 120 B2
Embassy of Ethiopia SKENS SW7 14 B3
Embassy of Finland KTBR SW1X 15 G4
Embassy of France KTBR SW1X 15 F2
Embassy of Georgia KENS W8 120 A2
Embassy of Germany KTBR SW1X 15 G4
Embassy of Ghana HGT N6 66 B5
Embassy of Greece NTGHL W11 119 J1
Embassy of Guatemala WBPTN SW10 120 A6
Embassy of Honduras MBLAR W1H 8 E1
Embassy of Hungary KTBR SW1X 15 H5
Embassy of Iceland KTBR SW1X 15 G6
Embassy of Indonesia MYFR/PKLN W1K 9 H6
Embassy of Iran SKENS SW7 14 B3
Embassy of Iraq SKENS SW7 120 B3
Embassy of Ireland KTBR SW1X 15 J3
Embassy of Israel KENS W8 120 A2
Embassy of Italy MYFR/PKLN W1K 9 H5
Embassy of Japan MYFR/PICC W1J 15 K1
Embassy of Jordan KENS W8 119 K2
Embassy of Korea WESTW SW1E 16 B4
Embassy of Krygyzstan MBLAR W1H 8 E2
Embassy of Kuwait KTBR SW1X 15 F2
Embassy of Latvia CAMTN NW1 3 G7
Embassy of Lebanon KENS W8 120 A1
Embassy of Liberia BAY/PAD W2 100 E6
Embassy of Lithuania MBLAR W1H 8 E2
Embassy of Luxembourg KTBR SW1X 15 G3
Embassy of Mexico MYFR/PICC W1J 15 J1
Embassy of Mongolia KENS W8 120 A2
Embassy of Morocco SKENS SW7 120 B4
Embassy of Mozambique FITZ W1T 4 A7
Embassy of Myanmar MYFR/PICC W1J 9 J7
Embassy of Nepal KENS W8 120 A1
Embassy of Netherlands SKENS SW7 120 B2
Embassy of Norway KTBR SW1X 15 H4
Embassy of Paraguay SKENS SW7 120 A3
Embassy of Peru KTBR SW1X 15 F4
Embassy of Philippines KENS W8 120 A1
Embassy of Poland CAVSQ/HST W1G 9 J1
Embassy of Portugal KTBR SW1X 15 G3
Embassy of Qatar MYFR/PKLN W1K 15 H1
Embassy of Romania KENS W8 120 A2
Embassy of Russian Federation KENS W8 120 A1
Embassy of Saudi Arabia MYFR/PICC W1J 9 J7
Embassy of Senegal CRICK NW2 82 A5
Embassy of Slovak Republic KENS W8 120 A1
Embassy of Slovenia MHST W1U 9 J3
Embassy of Spain KTBR SW1X 15 H4
Embassy of Sudan WHALL SW1A 16 A1
Embassy of Sweden MBLAR W1H 8 E2
Embassy of Switzerland MBLAR W1H 8 E2
Embassy of Syria KTBR SW1X 15 G3
Embassy of Thailand SKENS SW7 120 B3
Embassy of The Holy See WIM/MER SW19 159 F5
Embassy of The Republic of Gabon SKENS SW7 120 B3
Embassy of The US MYFR/PKLN W1K 9 G5
Embassy of Tunisia SKENS SW7 14 B3
Embassy of Turkey KTBR SW1X 15 H3
Embassy of Turkmenistan FITZ W1T 10 B2
Embassy of Ukraine NTGHL W11 119 H1
Embassy of United Arab Emirates BAY/PAD W2 14 B2
Embassy of Uruguay SKENS SW7 14 D4
Embassy of Uzbekistan NTGHL W11 119 J1
Embassy of Venezuela SKENS SW7 14 B5
Embassy of Yemen SKENS SW7 14 A6
Emberhurst School ESH/CLAY KT10 189 J4
Ember Sports Club ESH/CLAY KT10 189 H5
Embroidery World Business Centre WFD IG8 53 H5
Emd Walthamstow Cinema WALTH E17 69 J1
Emery Theatre POP/IOD E14 105 K5
Emirates Air Line CAN/RD E16 125 H1
Emmanuel CE Primary School KIL/WHAMP NW6 82 E3
Empire Cinema LSQ/SEVD WC2H 10 D5
Endsleigh Industrial Estate NWDGN UB2 114 D4
Enfield Business Centre PEND EN3 24 E3
Enfield CC EN EN1 24 A5
Enfield Chase ⇌ ENC/FH EN2 23 J4
Enfield County School ENC/FH EN2 23 K4
ENC/FH EN2 24 A1
Enfield FC ED N9 36 E4
Enfield Golf Club ENC/FH EN2 23 H5
Enfield Grammar School Lower EN EN1 23 K3
Enfield Grammar School Upper ENC/FH EN2 23 K4
Enfield Town ⇌ EN EN1 23 K5
English Martyrs RC Primary School WALW SE17 18 E7
WCHPL E1 13 K4
Ensham Secondary School TOOT SW17 178 E1
Enterprise Business Park POP/IOD E14 124 E2
Enterprise Industrial Estate BERM/RHTH SE16 123 K5
Epsom & Ewell High School HOR/WEW KT19 206 E4
Eric Liddell Sports Centre ELTH/MOT SE9 166 C4
Eridge House Preparatory School FUL/PGN SW6 139 J3
Erith ⇌ ERITH DA8 130 A5
Erith & District Hospital ERITH DA8 130 A6
Erith Health Centre ERITH DA8 130 B6
Erith Leisure Centre ERITH DA8 130 B6
Erith Library & Museum ERITH DA8 130 B5
Erith Playhouse ERITH DA8 130 C5
Erith School ERITH DA8 149 K1
Erith School Community Sports Centre ERITH DA8 149 K1
Erith Small Business Centre ERITH DA8 130 C6
Ernest Bevin College TOOT SW17 160 D5
Eros MYFR/PICC W1J 10 C6
Esher ⇌ ESH/CLAY KT10 189 J6
Esher CE High School ESH/CLAY KT10 204 A1
Esher Church Primary School ESH/CLAY KT10 204 C4
Esher College THDIT KT7 189 K4
Esher RFC WOT/HER KT12 188 D6
Essendine Primary School MV/WKIL W9 100 E2
Essex Primary School MNPK E12 89 J4
Essex Road ⇌ IS N1 85 J5
Ethames Graduate School POP/IOD E14 124 E2
Ethelburga GM School BTSEA SW11 140 D2
Eton Manor OLYMPICPK E20 87 K2
Euro Business Centre SRTFD E15 88 D6
Euro Freightliner Terminal ⇌ WLSDN NW10 99 G2
Eurolink Business Centre BRXS/STRHM SW2 142 B5
Europa Trading Estate ERITH DA8 130 A5
European Business Centre CDALE/KGS NW9 45 F6
European Business School London CAMTN NW1 3 G6
European School of Economics KTBR SW1X 15 H3
European Vocational College HDTCH EC3A 13 H4
Euro Way School CEND/HSY/T N8 49 G6
Euro Way School London FSBYPK N4 67 H4
Euston ⇌ ⊖ ⊖ CAMTN NW1 4 C5
Euston Centre University of Westminster CAMTN NW1 3 K6
Euston Square ⊖ CAMTN NW1 4 B6
Euston Tower CAMTN NW1 4 A6
Evans Business Centre CRICK NW2 81 J1
Eveline Day School TOOT SW17 160 E4
Evelyn Grace Academy BRXN/ST SW9 142 C5
Evendine College SOHO/SHAV W1D 10 C3
Eversley Medical Centre CROY/NA CR0 196 B3
Eversley Primary School WCHMH N21 22 E6
Everyman Baker Street MHST W1U 9 F1
Everyman Belsize Park HAMP NW3 83 J3
Everyman Cinema HAMP NW3 83 G2
Everyman Screen on the Green IS N1 6 A1
Evolution House, Kew Gardens RCH/KEW TW9 137 F3
Ewell Athletics Track HOR/WEW KT19 207 F4
Ewell Castle Junior School EW KT17 207 H6
Ewell Castle School EW KT17 207 J6
Ewell Grove Infant School EW KT17 207 H6
Ewell West ⇌ HOR/WEW KT19 207 G6
ExCeL Exhibition Centre CAN/RD E16 107 F6
Excellence Christian School BETH E2 86 E6
Excelsior College UED N18 50 A2
Exchange Square SDTCH EC2A 13 G1
The Exchange IL IG1 72 B6
Executive Medical & Occupational Health Centre CROY/NA CR0 211 K1
Exhibition Halls WBLY HA9 80 C2
Express by Holiday Inn CAN/RD E16 106 D5
CHING E4 51 J3
CROY/NA CR0 196 D6
FNCH N3 64 D1
FUL/PGN SW6 119 J6
GNTH/NBYPK IG2 72 D3
SDTCH EC2A 7 G5
STHWK SE1 12 B7
WAP E1W 105 F6
WIM/MER SW19 178 C3
The Eye Clinic NOXST/BSQ WC1A 10 D3
Faculty of Engineering & Science (University of Westminster) FITZ W1T 10 B1
Faircharm Trading Estate DEPT SE8 144 E1
IS N1 6 C2
The Faircross Complementary Medical Centre BARK IG11 90 E4
Fairfield Clinic BKHH IG9 39 F3
Fairfield Pool & Leisure Centre DART DA1 171 H2
Fairfield Trade Park KUT/HW KT1 175 G6
Fairholme Primary School EBED/NFELT TW14 153 G3
Fairlawn Primary School FSTH SE23 163 K2
Fairley House Junior School STHWK SE1 17 G5
Fairley House School PIM SW1V 16 C7
Fairlop ⊖ BARK/HLT IG6 54 E4
Fairlop Primary School BARK/HLT IG6 54 C4
Fairview Industrial Centre RAIN RM13 111 F5
Fairview Industrial Estate HYS/HAR UB3 113 J2
Fairview Medical Centre STRHM/NOR SW16 179 K4
Fairway Primary School MLHL NW7 31 F4
Fairways Business Park LEY E10 69 G6
Falconbrook Primary School BTSEA SW11 140 C3
Falcon Business Centre BTSEA SW11 140 D5
Falcon Park Industrial Estate WLSDN NW10 81 G3
The Falcon Preparatory School for Boys RCH/KEW TW9 136 E4
The Falcons Preparatory School CHSWK W4 117 J6
The Falcons School for Girls EA W5 117 G1
Falconwood ⇌ ELTH/MOT SE9 147 J4
Falkner House School SKENS SW7 120 B5
Family Records Centre FSBYW WC1X 5 J5
Fanmakers' Hall LVPST EC2M 13 G2
The Fan Museum GNWCH SE10 145 F1
Faraday Building BLKFR EC4V 12 B4
Faraday School POP/IOD E14 106 C6
Farm Lane Trading Estate FUL/PGN SW6 119 K6
Farnborough Primary School ORP BR6 216 D3
Farnell House Medical Centre HSLW TW3 135 G2
Farnham Green Primary School GDMY/SEVK IG3 73 G3
Farringdon ⇌ ⊖ FARR EC1M 11 K1
Farrington & Stratford House School CHST BR7 185 J3
Fashion Retail Academy FITZ W1T 10 C3
Featherstone Industrial Estate NWDGN UB2 114 D2
Featherstone Primary School NWDGN UB2 114 C4
Featherstone Road Health Clinic NWDGN UB2 114 D3
Federation of St Elpheges RC School WLGTN SM6 210 E4
Felnex Trading Estate WLGTN SM6 195 F6
Feltham ⇌ FELT TW13 154 A3
Feltham Airparcs Leisure Centre FELT TW13 154 C4
Feltham Athletics Arena EBED/NFELT TW14 153 K2
Felthambrook Industrial Estate FELT TW13 154 A5
Feltham Cemetery FELT TW13 153 J5
Feltham Community College FELT TW13 154 B4
Feltham Hill Infant School FELT TW13 153 J5
Feltham Hill Junior School FELT TW13 153 J5
Feltham & Hounslow Borough FC EBED/NFELT TW14 153 K2
Feltham Superbowl FELT TW13 154 A4
Fenchurch Street ⇌ FENCHST EC3M 13 H5
Fenstanton J & I School BRXS/STRHM SW2 162 B3
Fenton House (NT) HAMP NW3 83 G1
Fern Hill Primary School KUTN/CMB KT2 175 F2
Ferrier Industrial Estate WAND/EARL SW18 140 A5
Ferry Island Retail Park TOTM N17 50 B6
Ferry Lane Industrial Estate RAIN RM13 111 J4
WALTH E17 50 E6
Ferry Lane Primary School TOTM N17 68 D1
Festival Pier STHWK SE1 11 H7
Field End J & I Schools RSLP HA4 59 H6
Fielding Primary School WEA W13 116 C3
Fieldway ⊖ CROY/NA CR0 213 K5
Film House Cinema RCH/KEW TW9 136 E6
Financial Times STHWK SE1 12 D7
Financial Times Newspaper Offices POP/IOD E14 106 A5
Finchley Catholic High School NFNCH/WDSPK N12 33 G5
Finchley Central ⊖ FNCH N3 46 E4
Finchley CC FNCH N3 47 F5
Finchley Golf Club MLHL NW7 46 D2
Finchley Industrial Centre NFNCH/WDSPK N12 33 G6
Finchley Lawn Tennis Club FNCH N3 46 D2
Finchley Lido Leisure Centre NFNCH/WDSPK N12 47 H3
Finchley Memorial Hospital NFNCH/WDSPK N12 47 G3
Finchley Road ⊖ KIL/WHAMP NW6 83 G4
Finchley Road & Frognal ⊖ KIL/WHAMP NW6 83 F3
Finchley Youth Theatre EFNCH N2 47 J6
Finsbury Circus Medical Centre LVPST EC2M 13 F2
Finsbury Health Centre CLKNW EC1R 5 J6
Finsbury Leisure Centre FSBYE EC1V 6 D5
Finsbury Park ⇌ ⊖ FSBYPK N4 67 G6
Finsbury Park Track FSBYPK N4 67 H4
Finton House School TOOT SW17 160 E4
Fircroft Primary School TOOT SW17 160 E4
Fire Brigade HQ STHWK SE1 17 G6
Fire Brigade Museum STHWK SE1 18 C2
Firepower Royal Artillery Museum WOOL/PLUM SE18 127 G3
Firs Farm Primary School PLMGR N13 35 K5
Fisher Athletic FC BERM/RHTH SE16 124 A1
Fishmonger's Hall CANST EC4R 12 E6
Fitness Unlimited Leisure Centre BOW E3 105 J1
Fitzrovia Medical Centre FITZ W1T 4 A7
Fitzroy Nuffield Hospital MBLAR W1H 8 E3
Five Bridges School LBTH SE11 122 A5
Five Elms Primary School DAGW RM9 92 B1
Five Ways Business Centre FELT TW13 154 A5
Flamsteed House Museum GNWCH SE10 145 G1
Flaxman Sports Centre CMBW SE5 142 D3
Fleecefield Primary School ED N9 36 C6
Fleet Primary School HAMP NW3 83 K3
Fleetway Business Park GFD/PVL UB6 97 H1
Fleming Lab Museum BAY/PAD W2 8 B3
Flora Gardens Primary School HMSMTH W6 118 E4

Flutters Leisure Centre
FUL/PGN SW6 **139** K1
Follys End Christian High School
SNWD SE25 **197** F3
Follys End Christian School
SAND/SEL CR2 **212** A2
The Foot Clinic
WIM/MER SW19 **177** H2
Fordbridge Medical Centre
ASHF TW15 **152** C6
The Ford College
CONDST W1S **9** K4
Fordgate Business Park
BELV DA17 **129** K2
Ford Industrial Park
DAGW RM9 **110** D2
Fordview Industrial Estate
RAIN RM13 **111** F2
Foreign & Commonwealth Office
WHALL SW1A **16** D2
Foreland Medical Centre
NTGHL W11 **100** C6
Forest Business Park
LEY E10 **69** F4
Forestdale Primary School
CROY/NA CR0 **213** G6
Foresters Primary School
WLGTN SM6 **210** D4
Forest Gate ⇌
FSTGT E7 **88** E3
Forest Gate Community School
FSTGT E7 **88** E3
Forest Hill ⇌ ⊖
FSTH SE23 **163** K4
Forest Hill Business Centre
FSTH SE23 **163** K4
Forest Hill Industrial Estate
FSTH SE23 **163** K4
Forest Hill Pools
SYD SE26 **163** K4
Forest Hill School
FSTH SE23 **164** A5
Forest House Business Centre
WAN E11 **70** D4
Forest Industrial Park
BARK/HLT IG6 **54** E3
Forest Park Cemetery & Crematorium
BARK/HLT IG6 **55** J1
Forest Pathway College
WALTH E17 **69** K1
Forest Road Medical Centre
WALTH E17 **51** H6
Forest Trading Estate
WALTH E17 **51** F6
Forge Close Clinic
HAYES BR2 **199** K5
Forge Lane Primary School
FELT TW13 **172** D2
The Former Health Centre
CHARL SE7 **126** C4
Forster Park Primary School
CAT SE6 **165** H5
Fortis Green Health Clinic
EFNCH N2 **48** A6
Fortismere School
EFNCH N2 **47** K5
Fortune Theatre
HOL/ALD WC2B **11** F4
The Forum
EDGW HA8 **44** C2
Fossdene Primary School
CHARL SE7 **126** A5
Foster's Primary School
WELL DA16 **148** D4
Foulds School
BAR EN5 **20** B4
The Foundling Museum
BMSBY WC1N **5** F6
The Fountain Studios
WBLY HA9 **80** C1
Fountayne Business Centre
SEVS/STOTM N15 **68** C1
Fountayne Road Health Centre
STNW/STAM N16 **68** C6
Four Seasons Hotel
BERM/RHTH SE16 **124** C1
MYFR/PKLN W1K **15** J2
Foxfield Primary School
WOOL/PLUM SE18 **127** H5
Fox Primary School
KENS W8 **119** K1
Frances Bardsley School for Girls
ROM RM1 **75** J3
Franciscan Primary School
TOOT SW17 **161** F6
Francis Holland School
BGVA SW1W **15** H7
CAMTN NW1 **2** E7
Frank Barnes Primary School
STJWD NW8 **83** H5
Franklin Industrial Estate
PGE/AN SE20 **181** K4
Frederick Bremer Secondary School
WALTH E17 **52** A5
Frederick Hugh House
CHEL SW3 **120** D6
Freehold Industrial Centre
HSLWW TW4 **134** B6
Free Trade Wharf
WAP E1W **105** F6
The French Institute
SKENS SW7 **14** A6
Fresh Wharf Estate
BARK IG11 **90** B6
Freuchen Medical Centre
WLSDN NW10 **99** H1
Freud Museum
HAMP NW3 **83** H4
Friars Primary Foundation School
STHWK SE1 **18** A2
Friends House
CAMTN NW1 **4** C5
Friern Barnet School
FBAR/BDGN N11 **47** K1
Friern Bridge Retail Park
FBAR/BDGN N11 **48** B2
Frithwood Primary School
NTHWD HA6 **40** D2
Frogmore Industrial Estate
HBRY N5 **85** J2
HYS/HAR UB3 **113** H2
WLSDN NW10 **98** E2
Fryent Country Park
KTN/HRWW/WS HA3 **62** C4
Fryent Medical Centre
CDALE/KGS NW9 **62** E4
Fryent Primary School
CDALE/KGS NW9 **62** E4
Fulham Broadway ⊖
FUL/PGN SW6 **139** K1
Fulham Cemetery
FUL/PGN SW6 **139** G1
Fulham & Chelsea College
FUL/PGN SW6 **139** H3
Fulham Clinic
HMSMTH W6 **119** H6
Fulham Cross Girls School
FUL/PGN SW6 **139** G1
Fulham FC (Craven Cottage)
PUT/ROE SW15 **139** F2
Fulham Medical Centre
FUL/PGN SW6 **140** A1
Fulham Palace
FUL/PGN SW6 **139** G3
Fulham Pools
FUL/PGN SW6 **119** J6
Fulham Preparatory School
WKENS W14 **119** H6
Fulham Pre-Preparatory School
FUL/PGN SW6 **139** H3
Fulham Primary School
FUL/PGN SW6 **119** K6
Fuller Smith & Turner Sports Club
CHSWK W4 **138** B2
Fullwell Cross Health Centre
BARK/HLT IG6 **54** C5
Fullwell Cross Swimming Pool & Recreation Centre
BARK/HLT IG6 **54** C5
Fullwood Primary School
BARK/HLT IG6 **72** C1
Fulwell ⇌
WHTN TW2 **155** J6
Fulwell Golf Club
HPTN TW12 **155** J6
Furness Primary School
WLSDN NW10 **99** J1
Furzedown Primary School
TOOT SW17 **179** G2
Furze Infant School
CHDH RM6 **74** A3
Future Business College
CONDST W1S **9** K4
Gainsborough Clinic
PLMGR N13 **35** F6
Gainsborough Primary School
HOM E9 **87** H4
SRTFD E15 **106** C2
Galliard Primary School
ED N9 **36** C1
Gallions Mount Primary School
WOOL/PLUM SE18 **128** A5
Gallions Primary School
EHAM E6 **108** B5
Gallions Reach ⊖
EHAM E6 **108** B6
Gallions Reach Shopping Park
EHAM E6 **108** B4
Gants Hill ⊖
GNTH/NBYPK IG2 **72** A3
Gants Hill Medical Centre
GNTH/NBYPK IG2 **72** A3
Gardener Industrial Estate
SYD SE26 **182** B1
Garden House School
BGVA SW1W **121** F5
The Garden Museum
STHWK SE1 **17** F5
Garden Primary School
MTCM CR4 **179** J6
Garden Suburb Infant School
GLDGN NW11 **64** D2
Garfield Primary School
FBAR/BDGN N11 **48** B1
WIM/MER SW19 **178** B2
Garratt Park Secondary Special School
WAND/EARL SW18 **160** B5
Garrick Industrial Centre
CDALE/KGS NW9 **63** H2
Garrick Theatre
LSQ/SEVD WC2H **10** E6
Garth Primary School
MRDN SM4 **194** C2
The Garth Road Industrial Centre
MRDN SM4 **193** F4
Gascoigne Primary School
BARK IG11 **90** C6
Gate Cinema
KENS W8 **119** K1
Gatehouse School
BETH E2 **105** F1
The Gatehouse Theatre
HGT N6 **66** A4
Gate Theatre
NTGHL W11 **119** K1
Gateway Retail Park
EHAM E6 **108** B3
Gateway Business Centre
SYD SE26 **182** B2
Gateway Industrial Estate
WLSDN NW10 **99** H2
Gateway Primary School
STJWD NW8 **2** B6
Gatton School
TOOT SW17 **160** D6
Gayhurst Primary School
HACK E8 **86** C5
Gearies Infant School
GNTH/NBYPK IG2 **72** A2
Gearies Junior School
GNTH/NBYPK IG2 **72** B2
Geffrye Museum
BETH E2 **7** H3
Gem Hampshire School
SKENS SW7 **14** C3
Gemini Business Estate
NWCR SE14 **124** A5
General Medical Clinics
WCHPL E1 **13** J1
Genesis Cinema
WCHPL E1 **104** E3
The Geoffrey Lloyd Foulkes Clinic
IL IG1 **72** A6
Geoffrey Whitworth Theatre
DART DA1 **150** D5
George Eliot Community Primary School
STJWD NW8 **83** G6
George Greens School
POP/IOD E14 **125** F5
George Mitchell Primary School
LEY E10 **69** K5
George Spicer Primary School
EN EN1 **24** B4
George Street ⊖
CROY/NA CR0 **196** D6
George Tomlinson Primary School
WAN E11 **70** C5
Germal College
FSBYPK N4 **67** G5
Getters Talmud Torah School
SEVS/STOTM N15 **67** K3
Gibbs Green Special School
WKENS W14 **119** J5
Gibson Business Centre
TOTM N17 **50** B2
Gidea Park ⇌
GPK RM2 **75** K1
Gidea Park College
GPK RM2 **57** J6
Gidea Park Primary School
GPK RM2 **75** H1
Gidea Park Tennis Club
GPK RM2 **57** J6
The Gielgud Theatre
SOHO/CST W1F **10** C5
Giffin Business Centre
DEPT SE8 **144** D1
Gifford Primary School
NTHLT UB5 **95** K1
Gilbert Collection
TPL/STR WC2R **11** H5
Gilbert Colvin Primary School
CLAY IG5 **54** A4
Gilbert Scott Primary School
SAND/SEL CR2 **213** G5
Gillespie Primary School
HBRY N5 **85** H1
Gipsy Hill ⇌
NRWD SE19 **181** F1
Girdlers' Hall
CITYW EC2V **12** D2
Glade Primary School
CLAY IG5 **53** K4
The Glades Shopping Centre
BMLY BR1 **183** K5
Gladstone Medical Centre
CRICK NW2 **81** H2
Gladstone Park Primary School
WLSDN NW10 **81** J3
Glaziers/Scientific Instrument Makers Hall
STHWK SE1 **12** E7
Glebe Primary School
HGDN/ICK UB10 **76** B2
KTN/HRWW/WS HA3 **61** K1
Glebe School
WWKM BR4 **199** G5
Gleen Lecky Health Centre
PUT/ROE SW15 **139** G5
Glenbrook Primary School
CLAP SW4 **161** J1
Glencairn Sports Club
FBAR/BDGN N11 **48** C3
Glendower Preparatory School
SKENS SW7 **120** B4
Glenham College
IL IG1 **72** B6
Glenlyn Medical Centre
E/WMO/HCT KT8 **189** H2
Glenthorne High Specialist Arts College
CHEAM SM3 **193** K5
Globe Academy Lower School
STHWK SE1 **18** E5
Globe Primary School
BETH E2 **104** E2
Globe Wharf
BERM/RHTH SE16 **105** F6
Gloucester House
HAMP NW3 **83** H3
Gloucester Primary School
PECK SE15 **143** F1
Gloucester Road ⊖
SKENS SW7 **120** B4
Godolphin & Latymer School
HMSMTH W6 **118** E4
Godwin Junior School
FSTGT E7 **89** F2
Godwin Primary School
DAGW RM9 **92** A5
Goethe Institute
SKENS SW7 **14** B4
Golborne Medical Centre
NKENS W10 **100** D3
Goldbeaters Primary School
EDGW HA8 **45** F4
Golden Hinde Educational Trust
STHWK SE1 **12** E6
Golden Lane Campus
STLK EC1Y **6** D7
Golders Green ⊖
GLDGN NW11 **64** E4
Golders Green Crematorium
GLDGN NW11 **64** E4
Golders Green Health Centre
GLDGN NW11 **65** F5
Golders Hill Health Centre
GLDGN NW11 **65** G3
Golders Hill School
GLDGN NW11 **64** E4
Goldhawk Industrial Estate
SHB W12 **118** E3
Goldhawk Road ⊖
SHB W12 **119** F2
Goldsmiths College Sports Ground
SCUP DA14 **169** G5
Goldsmiths Hall
STBT EC1A **12** C3
Goldsmiths University of London
BROCKY SE4 **144** C4
DEPT SE8 **124** D6
LEW SE13 **145** H5
NWCR SE14 **144** B2
Gonville Academy
THHTH CR7 **196** A2
Goodge St ⊖
FITZ W1T **10** B1
Goodinge Health Centre
HOLWY N7 **84** E4
Goodmayes ⇌
GDMY/SEVK IG3 **73** G5
Goodmayes Retail Park
CHDH RM6 **73** H4
Goodrich J & I School
EDUL SE22 **163** H1
Good Shepherd RC Primary School
BMLY BR1 **165** J6
CROY/NA CR0 **213** K5
The Good Shepherd RC Primary School
SHB W12 **118** C2
Goodwyn School
MLHL NW7 **45** J1
Goose Green Primary School
EDUL SE22 **143** G5
Goose Green Trading Estate
EDUL SE22 **143** H5
Gordonbrock Primary School
BROCKY SE4 **144** D6
Gordon Hill ⇌
ENC/FH EN2 **23** H2
Gordon Hospital
WEST SW1P **16** C7
Gordon House Health Centre
WEA W13 **116** C1
Gordon Infant School
IL IG1 **90** D1
Gordon Primary School
ELTH/MOT SE9 **146** E5
Goresbrook Leisure Centre
DAGW RM9 **91** K6
Goresbrook Sports Centre
DAGW RM9 **91** K6
The Goring Hotel
BGVA SW1W **15** K4
Gorringe Park Primary School
MTCM CR4 **179** F4
Gosai Cinema
WEA W13 **116** C1
Gosbury Hill Health Centre
CHSGTN KT9 **206** A2
Gosford Primary School
REDBR IG4 **71** K2
Gospel Oak ⊖
KTTN NW5 **84** A2
Gospel Oak Primary School
HAMP NW3 **84** A2
Gove Farm Retail Park
CHDH RM6 **73** J4
Government Offices
WHALL SW1A **10** E7
Gower House School
CDALE/KGS NW9 **62** E6
The Gower School
IS N1 **5** H3
Grace Business Centre
MTCM CR4 **194** E3
Grace Theatre at The Latchmere
BTSEA SW11 **140** E3
Graduate School of Management
TOTM N17 **50** B4
Grafton Primary School
BCTR RM8 **74** A6
HOLWY N7 **84** E1
Grahame Park Health Centre
CDALE/KGS NW9 **45** G4
Grahame Park J & I School
CDALE/KGS NW9 **45** G4
Granard Business Centre
MLHL NW7 **45** G2
Granard Primary School
PUT/ROE SW15 **158** E1
Granby Sports Club
CHST BR7 **184** D1
Grand Avenue Primary School
BRYLDS KT5 **191** K3
Grande Vitesse Industrial Centre
STHWK SE1 **18** B1
Grand Union Industrial Estate
WLSDN NW10 **98** D1
The Grange City Hotel
TWRH EC3N **13** J5
Grange J & I School
RYLN/HDSTN HA2 **60** B5
The Grange Museum
CRICK NW2 **81** H2
Grange Park ⇌
WCHMH N21 **23** H6
Grange Park Clinic
YEAD UB4 **94** D3
Grange Park Junior School
YEAD UB4 **94** D3
Grange Park Preparatory School
WCHMH N21 **35** H1
Grange Park Primary School
WCHMH N21 **23** G5
Grange Primary School
CAN/RD E16 **106** D3
EA W5 **116** E2
STHWK SE1 **19** G5
Grange Whitehall Hotel
RSQ WC1B **10** E2
Grangewood Independent School
FSTGT E7 **89** H5
Grangewood School
PIN HA5 **58** E2
Granton Primary School
STRHM/NOR SW16 **179** H3
Granville Road Industrial Estate
CRICK NW2 **64** D6
Grasmere Primary School
STNW/STAM N16 **85** K2
Grasshoppers RFC
ISLW TW7 **116** A6
Grassroots School
HPTN TW12 **173** F4
Grasvenor Avenue Infant School
BAR EN5 **32** E1
Gravel Hill ⊖
CROY/NA CR0 **213** G5
Gravel Hill Primary School
BXLYHS DA6 **149** J6
Graveney School
TOOT SW17 **179** G2
Graves Yard Industrial Estate
WELL DA16 **148** B3
Grays Farm Primary School
STMC/STPC BR5 **186** C4
Grazebrook Primary School
STNW/STAM N16 **68** A6
Great Cambridge Industrial Estate
EN EN1 **24** D6
Great Chapel Street Medical Centre
SOHO/SHAV W1D **10** C3
Greater London Authority Headquarters (City Hall)
STHWK SE1 **19** H1
Great Jubilee Wharf
WAP E1W **123** K1
Great Ormond Street Hospital for Children
BMSBY WC1N **5** F7
Great Portland Street ⊖
GTPST W1W **3** K7
Great Scotland Yard
WHALL SW1A **10** E7
Great Western Industrial Park
NWDGN UB2 **115** G2
Great West London College
GFD/PVL UB6 **78** D6
Great West Trading Estate
BTFD TW8 **116** C6
Greek School of London
ACT W3 **98** D6
Greenacres Primary School
ELTH/MOT SE9 **167** F4
The Green CE Primary School
TOTM N17 **50** B6
Green Dragon Primary School
BTFD TW8 **117** F5
Greenfield Medical Centre
CRICK NW2 **82** C1
Greenfields Junior School
SHB W12 **99** H6
Greenfields Primary School
OXHEY WD19 **41** G1
Greenfields Special School
MUSWH N10 **47** K4
Greenford ⇌ ⊖
GFD/PVL UB6 **78** D6
Greenford Avenue Medical Centre
HNWL W7 **96** E4
Greenford Green Clinic
GFD/PVL UB6 **78** E3
Greenford High School
STHL UB1 **96** A2
Greenford Industrial Estate
GFD/PVL UB6 **78** B6
Greenford Park Cemetery
GFD/PVL UB6 **96** B4
Greenford Road Medical Centre
GFD/PVL UB6 **96** D1
Greenford Sports Centre
STHL UB1 **96** A2
Greengate Medical Centre
PLSTW E13 **107** F2
Greengrove College
STHGT/OAK N14 **34** E4
Greenheath Business Centre
BETH E2 **104** D2
Greenhill College
HRW HA1 **61** F2
Greenhill Park Medical Centre
WLSDN NW10 **81** G6
Greenland Pier
BERM/RHTH SE16 **124** C3
Green Lane Business Park
ELTH/MOT SE9 **167** F4
Green Lane Primary School
WPK KT4 **192** E4
Greenleaf Primary School
WALTH E17 **51** H6
Greenmead Primary School
PUT/ROE SW15 **138** E6
Green Park ⊖
MYFR/PICC W1J **10** A7
The Green School
ISLW TW7 **136** B1
Greenshaw High School
SUT SM1 **194** B6
Greenshields Industrial Estate
CAN/RD E16 **125** K1
Greenside Primary School
SHB W12 **118** D2

Greenslade Primary School
WOOL/PLUM SE18 127 J6
Green Street Green Primary School
ORP BR6 217 F4
Greenvale School
FSTH SE23 164 B5
Greenwich ⇌ ⊖
GNWCH SE10 144 E1
Greenwich Centre Business Park
DEPT SE8 144 E1
Greenwich Cinema
GNWCH SE10 145 F1
Greenwich Community College
WOOL/PLUM SE18 127 G4
WOOL/PLUM SE18 127 J6
Greenwich Industrial Estate
CHARL SE7 126 A4
GNWCH SE10 144 E1
Greenwich Natural Health Centre
GNWCH SE10 145 F1
Greenwich Odeon Cinema
GNWCH SE10 125 J4
Greenwich Park
GNWCH SE10 145 H1
Greenwich Pier
GNWCH SE10 125 F5
Greenwich School of Management
GNWCH SE10 145 F1
Greenwich Steiner School
BKHTH/KID SE3 125 K6
Greenwich Theatre & Art Gallery
GNWCH SE10 145 G1
Greenwood Primary School
NTHLT UB5 78 C3
Greenwood Theatre
STHWK SE1 19 F2
Green Wrythe Primary School
CAR SM5 194 C3
Gresham Way Industrial Estate
WIM/MER SW19 160 A5
Grey Coat Hospital CE School for Girls
WEST SW1P 16 C5
Grey Coat Hospital St Michaels
WEST SW1P 16 C7
Grey Court School
RCHPK/HAM TW10 156 E5
Griffen Manor School
WOOL/PLUM SE18 147 K2
Grimsdell Mill Hill Pre-Preparatory School
MLHL NW7 45 K1
Grims Dyke Golf Club
PIN HA5 42 A1
Grim's Dyke Hotel
KTN/HRWW/WS HA3 28 C6
Grimsdyke School
PIN HA5 41 K2
Grinling Gibbons Primary School
DEPT SE8 124 C6
Grist Memorial Sports Club
E/WMO/HCT KT8 189 K2
Grocers' Hall
CITYW EC2V 12 E4
The Grosvenor Hotel
BGVA SW1W 15 K5
Grosvenor House Hotel
MYFR/PKLN W1K 9 G6
The Grove Health Centre
SHB W12 118 E2
Grove House (Froebel College)
PUT/ROE SW15 158 C1
Grove House Primary School for Deaf Children
WNWD SE27 162 C4
Grovelands Priory Hospital
STHGT/OAK N14 34 E3
Grovelands School
WOT/HER KT12 188 A3
Grove Medical Centre
DEPT SE8 124 B4
The Grove Medical Centre
ARCH N19 66 D6
Grove Park ⇌
BMLY BR1 165 K5
Grove Park Cemetery
LEE/GVPK SE12 166 C6
Grove Park Industrial Estate
CDALE/KGS NW9 63 F1
Grove Park Primary School
CHSWK W4 117 K6
Grove Primary School
CHDH RM6 73 H2
Grove Road Primary School
HSLW TW3 135 F5
The Groves Medical Centre
NWMAL KT3 176 B6
Grove Village Medical Centre
EBED/NFELT TW14 153 H3
Guardian Angels RC Primary School
BOW E3 105 G3
Guardian Newspapers
POP/IOD E14 124 E2
Guards' Chapel & Museum
STJSPK SW1H 16 B3
Gumley House Convent School
ISLW TW7 136 B4
Gunnersbury ⊖ ⊖
CHSWK W4 117 J5
Gunnersbury Catholic School
BTFD TW8 116 D5
Gunnersbury Cemetery
BTFD TW8 117 H4
Gunnersbury Park Museum
ACT W3 117 H3
Gurnell Leisure Centre
WEA W13 97 F2
Guru Gobind Singh Khalsa College
CHIG IG7 39 K3
Guru Nanak Medical Centre
STHL UB1 114 C1
Guru Nanak Sikh Academy
YEAD UB4 114 B1
Guy's Hospital
STHWK SE1 19 F1
Guys Kings & Thomas Medical School (Kings College London)
STHWK SE1 12 C7
Gwyn Jones Primary School
WAN E11 70 B4
GX Superbowl
EHAM E6 108 A4
Gypsy Moth IV
GNWCH SE10 125 F6
Haberdashers Askes Crayford Academy
DART DA1 150 D5
Haberdashers Askes Hatcham College
NWCR SE14 144 A3
Haberdashers Askes Knights Academy
BMLY BR1 165 K6
Haberdashers' Hall
STBT EC1A 12 A2
Hackbridge ⇌
WLGTN SM6 195 G6
Hackbridge Primary School
WLGTN SM6 195 F5
Hackney Business Centre
HACK E8 86 D4
Hackney Central ⊖
HACK E8 86 D4
Hackney City Farm
BETH E2 104 C1
Hackney Community College
IS N1 7 G3
Hackney Downs ⇌
HACK E8 86 C3
Hackney Empire Variety Theatre
HACK E8 86 D4
Hackney Free & Parochial CE School
HOM E9 86 E4
Hackney Marshes Centre
HOM E9 87 J2
The Hackney Museum
HACK E8 86 D4
Hackney Wick ⊖
HOM E9 87 J4
Hadley Wood ⇌
EBAR EN4 21 G1
Hadley Wood Golf Club
EBAR EN4 21 J2
Hadley Wood Primary School
EBAR EN4 21 G1
The Haelan Clinic
CEND/HSY/T N8 66 E3
Haggerston ⊖
HACK E8 86 A5
Haggerston School
BETH E2 7 K2
Haggerston Swimming Pool
BETH E2 7 K1
Hague Primary School
BETH E2 104 D3
Hailey Road Business Park
ERITHM DA18 129 H2
Haimo Primary School
ELTH/MOT SE9 146 C6
Hainault ⊖
BARK/HLT IG6 54 D3
Hainault Business Park
BARK/HLT IG6 55 J1
Hainault Forest Golf Complex
CHIG IG7 55 K2
Hainault Forest High School & The Learning Centre
BARK/HLT IG6 55 G1
Hakim Qureshi Clinic
NWDGN UB2 114 D3
The Hale Clinic
CAMTN NW1 3 K7
Half Moon Theatre
WCHPL E1 105 F3
The Halkin Hotel
KTBR SW1X 15 H3
Halley Primary School
POP/IOD E14 105 G4
Hallfield Clinic
BAY/PAD W2 101 G5
Hallfield Primary School
BAY/PAD W2 101 F5
Hallmark Trading Estate
WBLY HA9 80 E2
Hall Place & Gardens
BXLY DA5 169 K1
The Hall Pre-Preparatory School
NTHWD HA6 40 B2
Halls Business Centre
HYS/HAR UB3 113 K3
The Hall School
HAMP NW3 83 H4
Hall School Wimbledon
RYNPK SW20 177 G4
Hall School Wimbledon Junior Department
PUT/ROE SW15 158 D5
Hallsville Primary School
CAN/RD E16 106 E5
Halstow Primary School
GNWCH SE10 125 J5
Hambledon Clinic
CMBW SE5 142 E4
Hambrough Primary School
STHL UB1 114 D1
Hamer Indoor Market
BOW E3 105 H1
Ham Health Clinic
RCHPK/HAM TW10 156 D5
Ham House & Garden (NT)
RCHPK/HAM TW10 156 D3
Hamilton Road Industrial Estate
WNWD SE27 162 E6
Ham Lands Nature Reserve
RCHPK/HAM TW10 156 C6
Hamlet International Industrial Estate
ERITH DA8 130 A5
Hammersmith ⊖
HMSMTH W6 119 F4
Hammersmith Apollo
HMSMTH W6 119 F5
Hammersmith Cemetery
HMSMTH W6 119 G5
Hammersmith Hospital
SHB W12 99 J5
Hammersmith Industrial Estate
HMSMTH W6 119 F6
Hammersmith New Cemetery
RCH/KEW TW9 137 J3
Hammersmith Physio & Sports Injury Clinic
HMSMTH W6 119 F4
Hammersmith & West London College
WKENS W14 119 H4
Hampden Gurney School
MBLAR W1H 8 D3
Ham & Petersham CC
RCHPK/HAM TW10 156 E6
Hampstead ⊖
HAMP NW3 83 G2
Hampstead Cemetery
CRICK NW2 82 D2
Hampstead College of Fine Arts
HAMP NW3 83 J4
Hampstead CC
KIL/WHAMP NW6 83 F4
Hampstead Golf Club
GLDGN NW11 65 G4
Hampstead Heath ⊖
HAMP NW3 83 J2
Hampstead Medical Centre
HAMP NW3 83 G2
Hampstead Parochial CE School
HAMP NW3 83 G2
Hampstead School
CRICK NW2 82 C2
The Hampstead School of Art
HAMP NW3 82 E2
Hampstead School of English
KIL/WHAMP NW6 82 E2
Hampstead Theatre
HAMP NW3 83 H5
Hampton ⇌
HPTN TW12 173 F4
Hampton Academy
HPTN TW12 173 F1
Hampton Cemetery
HPTN TW12 173 F3
Hampton Court ⇌
E/WMO/HCT KT8 189 K1
Hampton Court House School
E/WMO/HCT KT8 173 K5
Hampton Court Palace
E/WMO/HCT KT8 174 A6
Hampton Court Palace Golf Club
SURB KT6 190 D2
Hampton Farm Industrial Estate
FELT TW13 154 D5
Hampton FC
HPTN TW12 173 G4
Hampton Hill Junior School
HPTN TW12 173 H1
Hampton Infant School
HPTN TW12 172 E3
Hampton Junior School
HPTN TW12 173 F4
The Hampton Medical Centre
HPTN TW12 173 F3
Hampton Open Air Pool
HPTN TW12 173 H3
Hampton Road Industrial Park
CROY/NA CR0 196 D3
Hampton School
HPTN TW12 173 F1
Hampton Wick ⇌
KUT/HW KT1 174 E4
Hampton Wick Infant School
TEDD TW11 174 D3
Handball Arena
OLYMPICPK E20 87 J4
Handel's House
MYFR/PKLN W1K 9 J5
Handsworth Health Clinic
CHING E4 52 B2
Hanger Lane ⊖
EA W5 98 B2
Hanover Primary School
IS N1 6 B2
Hanover Trading Estate
HOLWY N7 84 E3
Hanover West Industrial Estate
WLSDN NW10 98 E2
Hanwell ⇌
HNWL W7 96 E6
Hanworth Trading Estate
FELT TW13 154 D5
Harbinger Primary School
POP/IOD E14 124 D4
Harenc School
SCUP DA14 186 D1
Hargrave Park Primary School
ARCH N19 66 C6
Haringey Arts Council
ED N9 36 C4
Haringey Community Health Clinic
SEVS/STOTM N15 68 B1
Haringey Magistrates Court
HGT N6 66 A3
Haringey Sixth Form Centre
TOTM N17 50 B3
Harlequins RFC & Harlequins RL (The Stoop)
WHTN TW2 155 K2
Harlesden ⊖ ⊖
WLSDN NW10 99 F1
Harlesden Primary School
WLSDN NW10 99 G1
Harley Medical Centre
CAVSQ/HST W1G 9 K3
The Harley Medical Centre
CANST EC4R 12 D5
Harley Street Clinic
CAVSQ/HST W1G 9 J2
The Harley Street Clinic
CAVSQ/HST W1G 9 J1
Harlington Community School
HYS/HAR UB3 113 G4
Harlyn Primary School
PIN HA5 41 F6
The Harold Macmillan Medical Centre
HRW HA1 60 D4
Harp Business Centre
CRICK NW2 63 J6
Harringay ⇌
FSBYPK N4 67 G3
Harringay Green Lanes ⊖
FSBYPK N4 67 H3
Harrington Hall Hotel
SKENS SW7 120 B4
Harrington Hill Primary School
CLPT E5 68 D5
Harrington Road ⊖
SNWD SE25 181 K6
Harris Academy at Peckham
PECK SE15 143 G2
Harris Academy Bermondsey
STHWK SE1 19 K6
Harris Academy Falconwood
WELL DA16 147 J5
Harris Academy Merton
STRHM/NOR SW16 179 J6
Harris Academy South Norwood
SNWD SE25 181 G6
Harris Boys Academy East Dulwich
EDUL SE22 143 J6
Harris City Academy Crystal Palace
NRWD SE19 181 G4
Harris Girls Academy
EDUL SE22 143 K6
Harrodian School
BARN SW13 138 C1
Harrods Store
CHEL SW3 14 E4
Harrovian Business Village
HRW HA1 60 D4
Harrow Arts Centre
PIN HA5 42 A3
Harrow Borough FC
RYLN/HDSTN HA2 78 A2
Harrow Cemetery
HRW HA1 60 D3
Harrow College
HRW HA1 60 E4
KTN/HRWW/WS HA3 42 E2
Harrow CC
HRW HA1 78 E2
Harrow Crown Courts
HRW HA1 42 D6
Harrow Driving Cycling & Road Safety Centre
KTN/HRWW/WS HA3 43 G6
Harrow Heritage Museum
RYLN/HDSTN HA2 42 C6
Harrow High School
HRW HA1 61 G3
Harrow Leisure Centre
KTN/HRWW/WS HA3 43 F6
Harrow Magistrates Court
HRW HA1 61 F1
Harrow-on-the-Hill ⇌ ⊖
HRW HA1 60 E3
Harrow RFC
STAN HA7 29 H5
Harrow Road Health Centre
BAY/PAD W2 100 E4
Harrow School
RYLN/HDSTN HA2 60 E6
Harrow Town CC
RYLN/HDSTN HA2 60 A5
Harrow Weald Cemetery
KTN/HRWW/WS HA3 42 E2
Harrow & Wealdstone ⇌ ⊖ ⊖
HRW HA1 60 E1
Harry Gosling Primary School
WCHPL E1 104 C5
Hartley Primary School
EHAM E6 89 J6
Hartsbourne Primary School
BUSH WD23 28 D4
Harvington School
EA W5 97 J5
Haseltine Primary School
SYD SE26 164 C6
Haslemere Business Centre
EN EN1 24 D5
Haslemere Industrial Estate
EBED/NFELT TW14 133 K6
WAND/EARL SW18 160 A4
Haslemere Primary School
MTCM CR4 178 C5
Hasmonean High School Boys Site
HDN NW4 46 B5
Hasmonean High School Girls Site
MLHL NW7 45 J4
Hasmonean Primary School
HDN NW4 64 B2
Haste Hill Golf Club
NTHWD HA6 40 C5
Hastings Clinic
BRXS/STRHM SW2 142 A6
Hastingwood Trading Estate
UED N18 51 G2
Hatcham Mews Business Centre
NWCR SE14 144 A1
Hatch End ⊖
PIN HA5 42 A3
Hatch End High School
KTN/HRWW/WS HA3 42 B3
Hatch End Swimming Pool
PIN HA5 42 A3
Hatfield Primary School
MRDN SM4 193 H3
Hatton Cross ⊖
HTHAIR TW6 133 J5
Hatton School
WFD IG8 53 H6
Havelock Primary School
NWDGN UB2 114 E3
Haven Green Clinic
EA W5 97 K5
Havering College of Further & Higher Education
EMPK RM11 75 K4
Havering Magistrates Court
ROM RM1 75 G1
Haverstock School
HAMP NW3 84 A4
Hawes Down Clinic
WWKM BR4 199 G6
Hawes Down Primary School
WWKM BR4 199 G5
The Hawker Centre
KUTN/CMB KT2 174 E1
Hawkesdown House School
KENS W8 119 K1
Hawkins Clinic
PUT/ROE SW15 139 G5
RYNPK SW20 176 C4
Hawksmoor Primary School
THMD SE28 109 H6
Hawley Infant School
CAMTN NW1 84 B5
Haydon School
PIN HA5 40 E6
Haydons Road ⇌
WIM/MER SW19 178 B1
Hayes ⇌
HAYES BR2 199 J5
Hayes Bridge Middle School
STHL UB1 114 D2
Hayes Bridge Retail Park
YEAD UB4 95 G6
Hayes CC
HYS/HAR UB3 94 D5
Hayes FC
HYS/HAR UB3 94 D6
Hayes Grove Priory Hospital
HAYES BR2 199 K6
Hayes & Harlington ⇌
HYS/HAR UB3 113 J3
The Hayes Manor School
HYS/HAR UB3 94 B5
Hayes Park J & I School
YEAD UB4 94 D3
Hayes Pool
HYS/HAR UB3 113 J1
Hayes Primary School
HAYES BR2 200 A5
Hayes School
HAYES BR2 200 A6
Hayes Social & Sports Club
HYS/HAR UB3 94 D6
Hayes Stadium Sports Centre
HYS/HAR UB3 94 B5
Hay Lane School
CDALE/KGS NW9 62 E1
Haymerle School
PECK SE15 123 H6
Hays Galleria
STHWK SE1 13 G7
Hayward Gallery
STHWK SE1 17 H1
Hazelbury Junior School
ED N9 36 A5
Hazeldene Medical Centre
WBLY HA9 80 D4
Hazelwood Schools
PLMGR N13 35 G6
Headstart Montessori School
TOOT SW17 160 B5
Headstone Lane ⊖
RYLN/HDSTN HA2 42 B4
Health & Vitality Osteopathic Clinic
HOR/WEW KT19 207 F3
Healy Medical Centre
CLPT E5 68 D5
The Heart Hospital
CAVSQ/HST W1G 9 H2
Heartlands High School
WDGN N22 49 F5
The Heart of Greenwich Development
GNWCH SE10 125 J5
Heathbrook Primary School
VX/NE SW8 141 H3
Heath Business Centre
HSLW TW3 135 H5
Heathcote School
CHING E4 38 C4
The Heatherley School of Fine Art
FUL/PGN SW6 140 B1
Heathfield College
HAYES BR2 215 G4
Heathfield House School
CHSWK W4 117 K5
Heathfield Primary School
WHTN TW2 155 F3
Heathfield School
PIN HA5 59 H4
Heath House Preparatory School
BKHTH/KID SE3 145 J3
Heathland School
RYLN/HDSTN HA2 78 A1
The Heathland School
HSLWW TW4 154 E1
Heathmere Primary School
PUT/ROE SW15 158 D3
Heathrow Airport Central Bus & Coach Station
HTHAIR TW6 132 D4
Heathrow Airport Terminal 4
HTHAIR TW6 132 E6

Heathrow Airport (Terminals 1, 2, 3) *HTHAIR* TW6 132 E3
Heathrow Air Traffic Control Tower *HTHAIR* TW6 132 E4
Heathrow International Trading Estate *HSLWW* TW4 134 A4
Heathrow Medical Centre *HYS/HAR* UB3 113 G5
Heathrow Primary School *WDR/YW* UB7 112 C6
Heathrow Terminal 4 *HTHAIR* TW6 153 F1
Heathrow Terminals 1 & 3 *HTHAIR* TW6 132 E4
Heathrow Viewing Area *HTHAIR* TW6 132 E4
Heathrow World Cargo Centre *HTHAIR* TW6 132 C6
Heathside Preparatory School *HAMP* NW3 83 G2
Heathside Preparatory School (Upper) *HAMP* NW3 83 G2
Heathway Industrial Estate *DAGE* RM10 92 D2
Heathway Medical Centre *DAGW* RM9 92 B2
Heavers Farm Primary School *SNWD* SE25 197 G2
Heber Primary School *EDUL* SE22 163 G1
Heckford Street Business Centre *WAP* E1W 105 F6
Hedges & Butler Estate *SRTFD* E15 106 A1
Hedgewood School *YEAD* UB4 94 C2
Helena Road Clinic *WLSDN* NW10 81 K2
Heliport Industrial Estate *BTSEA* SW11 140 C3
Helston Court Business Centre *WIM/MER* SW19 176 E1
Henderson Hospital *BELMT* SM2 208 E6
Hendon *HDN* NW4 63 J3
Hendon Cemetery *MLHL* NW7 46 B4
Hendon Central *HDN* NW4 63 K2
Hendon Crematorium *MLHL* NW7 46 B3
Hendon FC *CRICK* NW2 64 B6
Hendon Golf Club *MLHL* NW7 46 A3
Hendon Hall Hotel *HDN* NW4 46 A6
Hendon Preparatory School *HDN* NW4 46 B6
Hendon School *HDN* NW4 64 B2
Hendon Secretarial College *HDN* NW4 63 K2
Hendon Youth Sports Centre *CRICK* NW2 64 B4
Henrietta Barnett School *GLDGN* NW11 65 F2
Henry Cavendish Primary School *BAL* SW12 161 H3
Henry Compton School *FUL/PGN* SW6 139 G2
Henry Fawcett Primary School *LBTH* SE11 122 B6
Henry Green Primary School *BCTR* RM8 73 K5
Henwick Primary School *ELTH/MOT* SE9 146 C4
Herbert Morrison Primary School *VX/NE* SW8 141 K1
Hereward House School *HAMP* NW3 83 J4
Her Majestys' Theatre *STJS* SW1Y 10 D7
Hermitage Primary School *WAP* E1W 123 H1
Herne Hill *HNHL* SE24 142 C6
Herne Hill School *HNHL* SE24 142 D6
Herne Hill Stadium (Cycle Centre) *HNHL* SE24 162 E1
Heron Industrial Estate *SRTFD* E15 105 K1
Heron Quays *POP/IOD* E14 124 D1
Heronsgate Primary School *THMD* SE28 127 J3
Heron Trading Estate *ACT* W3 98 D4
Hersham Trading Estate *WOT/HER* KT12 188 D6
Heston Community School *HEST* TW5 135 F1
Heston Community Sports Hall *HEST* TW5 135 F1
Heston Industrial Mall *HEST* TW5 134 E1
Heston Infant School *HEST* TW5 135 F1
Heston Junior School *HEST* TW5 135 F1
Heston Park CC *HEST* TW5 114 E6
Heston Swimming Baths *HEST* TW5 114 E6
Higgs Industrial Estate *HNHL* SE24 142 C4
Highams Lodge Business Centre *WALTH* E17 51 F6
Highams Park *CHING* E4 52 A2
Highams Park Primary School *CHING* E4 52 B2
High Barnet *BAR* EN5 20 E5
Highbury Corner Magistrates Court *HOLWY* N7 85 G4
Highbury Fields School *HBRY* N5 85 H2
Highbury Grove School *HBRY* N5 85 J3
Highbury & Islington *IS* N1 85 G4
Highbury Park Clinic *HBRY* N5 85 H1
Highbury Pool *HBRY* N5 85 H4
Highbury Quadrant Primary School *HBRY* N5 85 J2
Highbury Square Development *HBRY* N5 85 H1
High Commission of Angola *MHST* W1U 9 F2
High Commission of Antigua & Barbuda *MHST* W1U 9 G3
High Commission of Bahamas *MYFR/PICC* W1J 9 H7
High Commission of Bangladesh *SKENS* SW7 120 B3
High Commission of Barbados *FITZ* W1T 10 C3
High Commission of Belize *CAVSQ/HST* W1G 9 K3
High Commission of Botswana *OXSTW* W1C 9 J4
High Commission of Brunei *KTBR* SW1X 15 G4
High Commission of Canada *MYFR/PKLN* W1K 9 H5
High Commission of Cyprus *MYFR/PKLN* W1K 9 G5
High Commission of Dominica *ECT* SW5 120 A4
High Commission of Fiji *SKENS* SW7 120 B2
High Commission of Grenada *ECT* SW5 120 A5
High Commission of Guyana *BAY/PAD* W2 101 F6
High Commission of Jamaica *SKENS* SW7 14 A3
High Commission of Kenya *CAVSQ/HST* W1G 9 J1
High Commission of Lesotho *KTBR* SW1X 15 G4
High Commission of Malawi *MYFR/PKLN* W1K 9 J5
High Commission of Malaysia *KTBR* SW1X 15 H3
High Commission of Maldives *MHST* W1U 9 G1
High Commission of Malta *CONDST* W1S 10 B6
High Commission of Namibia *CAVSQ/HST* W1G 9 K2
High Commission of New Zealand *STJS* SW1Y 10 C7
High Commission of Nigeria *CHCR* WC2N 10 E7; *EMB* EC4Y 11 K4
High Commission of Pakistan *KTBR* SW1X 15 F4
High Commission of Papua New Guinea *STJS* SW1Y 10 B7
High Commission of St Lucia *KENS* W8 120 A2
High Commission of Seychelles *MHST* W1U 9 F1
High Commission of Sierra Leone *REGST* W1B 10 A3
High Commission of Singapore *KTBR* SW1X 15 F3; *KTBR* SW1X 15 G5
High Commission of South Africa *CHCR* WC2N 10 E7
High Commission of Sri Lanka *BAY/PAD* W2 8 B5
High Commission of Swaziland *WESTW* SW1E 16 A4
High Commission of The Gambia *KENS* W8 120 A2
High Commission of Tonga *MBLAR* W1H 8 D2
High Commission of Trinidad & Tobago *KTBR* SW1X 15 G4
High Commission of Uganda *CHCR* WC2N 10 D7
High Commission of Zambia *SKENS* SW7 120 B2
High Commission of Zimbabwe *CHCR* WC2N 10 E6
High Cross Centre *SEVS/STOTM* N15 68 C1
High Elms Country Park *ORP* BR6 216 C5
Highfield Infant School *HAYES* BR2 199 J1
Highfield Junior School *HAYES* BR2 199 H1
Highfield Primary School *WCHMH* N21 35 H3
Highfield School *WAND/EARL* SW18 160 D2
Highgate *HGT* N6 66 B3
Highgate Cemetery *HGT* N6 66 A5
Highgate Golf Club *EFNCH* N2 65 J3
Highgate Junior School *HGT* N6 65 K4
Highgate Private Hospital *HGT* N6 65 K3
Highgate School *HGT* N6 65 K4
Highgate Wood School *MUSWH* N10 66 C2
Highgrove Pool *RSLP* HA4 58 E4
Highlands J & I School *IL* IG1 71 K5
Highlands Primary School *IL* IG1 71 J5
Highshore School *PECK* SE15 143 G2
High Street Kensington *KENS* W8 120 A3
High View Primary School *BTSEA* SW11 140 C5
Highview Primary School *WLGTN* SM6 210 E3
The Highway Primary School *ORP* BR6 217 J3
The Highway Trading Centre *WAP* E1W 105 F6
Hillbrook Primary School *TOOT* SW17 160 E6
Hillcroft College *SURB* KT6 191 F3
Hillcrost Primary School *MRDN* SM4 193 J1
Hill House International Junior School *KTBR* SW1X 15 F5
Hill House Preparatory School *CHEL* SW3 120 D6
Hill House School *KTBR* SW1X 14 E5
Hill Mead Infant School *BRXN/ST* SW9 142 C5
Hillmead Primary School *BRXN/ST* SW9 142 C5
Hills Grove Primary School *WELL* DA16 148 D1
Hillside Infant School *NTHWD* HA6 40 E3
Hillside Primary School *STMC/STPC* BR5 202 D4
Hillyfield Primary School *WALTH* E17 51 G6
Hilly Fields Medical Centre *BROCKY* SE4 144 D6
Hilton Docklands Pier *BERM/RHTH* SE16 124 C1
The Hiltongrove Business Centre *WALTH* E17 69 J1
Hinchley Wood *ESH/CLAY* KT10 205 F1
Hinchley Wood Primary School *ESH/CLAY* KT10 190 B6
Hinchley Wood School & Sixth Form Centre *ESH/CLAY* KT10 190 B6
Hinley Clinic *LBTH* SE11 17 K7
Hispaniola *WHALL* SW1A 17 F1
Hitherfield Primary School *STRHM/NOR* SW16 162 B4
Hither Green *LEW* SE13 165 H1
Hither Green Cemetery *CAT* SE6 165 J4
HM Customs & Excise *HTHAIR* TW6 132 E2
HM Prison *BRXS/STRHM* SW2 161 K1; *HOLWY* N7 84 E2; *SHB* W12 99 J5; *THMD* SE28 127 K3; *WAND/EARL* SW18 160 C2
HMS Belfast *STHWK* SE1 13 H7
HMS President *EMB* EC4Y 11 K5
HM Young Offenders Institution *FELT* TW13 153 G5
Hobbayne First & Middle School *HNWL* W7 97 F5
Hobbayne Primary School *HNWL* W7 96 E5
Hockey Centre *OLYMPICPK* E20 87 J3
Hogarth Business Park *CHSWK* W4 118 B6
Hogarth Industrial Estate *WLSDN* NW10 99 J3
Hogarth's House *CHSWK* W4 118 A6
Holbeach Primary School *CAT* SE6 164 D2
Holborn *HHOL* WC1V 11 F3
Holborn College *WOOL/PLUM* SE18 126 C4
Holborn College Independent School *HMSMTH* W6 119 F5
Holborn Medical Centre *BMSBY* WC1N 5 G7
Holborn Town Hall *HHOL* WC1V 11 F3
Holiday Inn *BMSBY* WC1N 4 E7; *BTFD* TW8 136 D1; *BXLY* DA5 169 J1; *CAMTN* NW1 84 B5; *CHSGTN* KT9 205 J6; *CRICK* NW2 64 A5; *FSBYW* WC1X 5 H5; *GTPST* W1W 3 K7; *HYS/HAR* UB3 133 G2; *MYFR/PICC* W1J 9 K6; *SKENS* SW7 120 B4; *SURB* KT6 190 C3; *SUT* SM1 209 F3; *WDR/YW* UB7 112 D5; *WDR/YW* UB7 132 D2
Holiday Inn Express *ACT* W3 99 F4; *HMSMTH* W6 118 E4; *PIM* SW1V 121 H5; *WAND/EARL* SW18 140 A5
Holland House *WKENS* W14 119 J2
Holland House School *EDGW* HA8 30 C6
Holland Park *NTGHL* W11 119 J1
Holland Park Pre-Preparatory School *WKENS* W14 119 J3
Holland Park School *KENS* W8 119 J2
Holland Park Theatre *WKENS* W14 119 J2
Holland Street Clinic *KENS* W8 119 K2
Hollickwood JMI School *MUSWH* N10 48 B3
Holloway Road *HOLWY* N7 85 F3
Holloway School *HOLWY* N7 84 D3
Hollydale Primary School *PECK* SE15 143 K3
The Hollyfield School *SURB* KT6 191 F2
Holly House Private Hospital *BKHH* IG9 39 F4
Hollymount Primary School *RYNPK* SW20 177 F4
Holly Park JMI School *FBAR/BDGN* N11 48 A1
Holly Park Montessori School *FSBYPK* N4 66 E4
Hollywood Bowl *BERM/RHTH* SE16 124 A3
The Holme *CAMTN* NW1 3 F5
The Holmewood School London *NFNCH/WDSPK* N12 33 F6
Holmleigh Primary School *STNW/STAM* N16 68 B5
Holocaust Memorial Garden *KTBR* SW1X 15 F2
The Holy Cross Catholic Girls School *NWMAL* KT3 192 A1
Holy Cross Preparatory School *KUTN/CMB* KT2 175 K3
Holy Cross Primary School *FUL/PGN* SW6 139 K2
Holy Cross RC Primary School *CAT* SE6 165 F3
Holy Family RC Primary School *BKHTH/KID* SE3 146 A5; *POP/IOD* E14 105 J6
Holy Family Technology College *WALTH* E17 52 A6; *WALTH* E17 69 K1
Holy Ghost RC Primary School *BAL* SW12 160 E2
Holy Innocents Catholic Primary School *ORP* BR6 217 F1
Holy Trinity CE Junior School *WLGTN* SM6 210 C2
Holy Trinity CE Primary School *BRXS/STRHM* SW2 162 A2; *DART* DA1 151 F6; *EFNCH* N2 47 H6; *KIL/WHAMP* NW6 83 G4; *KTBR* SW1X 15 G6; *NTHWD* HA6 40 A2; *RCHPK/HAM* TW10 137 H5; *SYD* SE26 163 K4
Holy Trinity College *BMLY* BR1 184 B4
Holy Trinity in St Silas *CAMTN* NW1 84 B5
Holy Trinity Lamorbey CE Primary School *BFN/LL* DA15 168 B3
Holy Trinity Primary School *HACK* E8 86 B4; *WIM/MER* SW19 177 K2
Holy Trinity School *CHEL* SW3 15 F6
Holywell School *WATW* WD18 26 D1
Homefield Preparatory School *SUT* SM1 208 E3
Home Office *WEST* SW1P 16 D5
Homerton *HOM* E9 87 F4
Homerton University Hospital *HOM* E9 87 F3
Homoeopathic Health Centre *PLSTW* E13 106 E3
The Homoeopathic Health Centre *MLHL* NW7 45 H1
Honeypot Business Centre *STAN* HA7 44 A4
Honeypot Lane Centre *STAN* HA7 43 K4
Honeypot Medical Centre *STAN* HA7 44 A5
Honeywell Primary School *BTSEA* SW11 160 E1
Honor Oak Crematorium *FSTH* SE23 144 A6
Honor Oak Gallery *FSTH* SE23 164 A1
Honor Oak Health Centre *BROCKY* SE4 144 B5
Honor Oak Park *FSTH* SE23 164 A1
Honourable Artillery Company HQ *STLK* EC1Y 6 E7
Hook Lane Primary School *WELL* DA16 148 B4
Hook Rise South Industrial Park *CHSGTN* KT9 206 B1
Hopewell School *BARK* IG11 90 D4
Horizon Business Centre *ED* N9 37 F4
Horizon Industrial Estate *PECK* SE15 123 H6
Horizon School *STNW/STAM* N16 86 A2
The Horniman Museum & Gardens *FSTH* SE23 163 J3
Horniman Primary School *FSTH* SE23 163 J3
Horn Park Primary School *LEE/GVPK* SE12 166 A2
Hornsby House School *BAL* SW12 161 F3
Hornsey *CEND/HSY/T* N8 67 F1
Hornsey Central Hospital *CEND/HSY/T* N8 66 C2
Hornsey Coroners Court & Public Mortuary *CEND/HSY/T* N8 66 E1
Hornsey Rise Health Centre *ARCH* N19 66 D4
Hornsey Secondary School for Girls *CEND/HSY/T* N8 67 F2
Horn Stairs *BERM/RHTH* SE16 124 C1
Horseferry Road Magistrates Court *WEST* SW1P 16 D5
Horse Guards Parade *WHALL* SW1A 16 D1
Horsenden Hill Golf Club *GFD/PVL* UB6 79 H4
Horsenden Primary School *GFD/PVL* UB6 78 E4
Horton Country Park *HOR/WEW* KT19 206 C6
Horton Industrial Park *WDR/YW* UB7 112 C1
Horton Park Golf & Country Club *HOR/WEW* KT19 206 E5
Hortus Cemetery *NWDGN* UB2 114 E2
Hospital of St John & St Elizabeth *STJWD* NW8 2 A3
Hotel Indigo *BAY/PAD* W2 8 B4
Hotel Russell *RSQ* WC1B 4 E7
Hotel Verta *BTSEA* SW11 140 C3
Hotham Primary School *PUT/ROE* SW15 139 G5
Hotspur Industrial Estate *TOTM* N17 50 D2
Houndsfield Primary School *ED* N9 36 C2
Hounslow *HSLW* TW3 135 H5
Hounslow Business Park *HSLW* TW3 135 F5
Hounslow CC *HSLW* TW3 134 E3
Hounslow Cemetery *HSLWW* TW4 154 E2
Hounslow Central *HSLW* TW3 135 G3
Hounslow East *HSLW* TW3 135 H3
Hounslow Heath Infant School *HSLWW* TW4 134 D4
Hounslow Heath Junior School *HSLWW* TW4 134 D4
Hounslow Manor School *HSLW* TW3 135 G4
Hounslow Manor Sports Hall *HSLW* TW3 135 G4
Hounslow Town Primary School *HSLW* TW3 135 H4
Hounslow West *HSLWW* TW4 134 D3
The Household Cavalry Museum *WHALL* SW1A 16 E1
House Mill *POP/IOD* E14 106 A2
House of Detention *CLKNW* EC1R 5 K6
House of St Barnabus *SOHO/SHAV* W1D 10 C4
Houses of Parliament *WHALL* SW1A 17 F3
Houston Business Park *YEAD* UB4 114 B1
Howard Primary School *SAND/SEL* CR2 211 J2
Howbury Centre *ERITH* DA8 150 D1
Howland Quay *BERM/RHTH* SE16 124 A3
Hoxton *BETH* E2 7 J3
Hoxton Hall Community Theatre *IS* N1 7 G2
HQS Wellington (Master Mariners) *TPL/STR* WC2R 11 J6
HSBC Sports Club *BECK* BR3 182 B2
HSBC Tower *POP/IOD* E14 124 E1

Hubbinet Industrial Estate ROMW/RG RM7 56 E6
Hugh Myddelton Primary School CLKNW EC1R 5 K5
The Humana Wellington Hospital STJWD NW8 2 B4
Humber Trading Estate CRICK NW2 63 K6
Hunterian Museum LINN WC2A 11 H3
Hunters Hall Primary School DAGE RM10 92 D3
Hunter Street Health Centre STPAN WC1H 4 E6
Huntsman Sports Club BKHTH/KID SE3 145 K5
Hurlingham Business Park FUL/PGN SW6 139 K4
Hurlingham & Chelsea Secondary School FUL/PGN SW6 139 K4
Hurlingham House FUL/PGN SW6 139 K4
Hurlingham Private School PUT/ROE SW15 139 J5
Huron University RSQ WC1B 10 E1
Hurricane Trading Centre CDALE/KGS NW9 45 H4
Hurstmere School BFN/LL DA15 168 C3
Hurst Park Primary School E/WMO/HCT KT8 173 F6
Hurst Primary School BXLY DA5 168 E3
Hyatt Carlton Tower Hotel KTBR SW1X 15 F5
Hyatt Regency-The Churchill MBLAR W1H 9 F3
The Hyde Industrial Estate CDALE/KGS NW9 63 H2
Hyde Park BAY/PAD W2 8 E7
Hyde Park Corner KTBR SW1X 15 G2
The Hyde School CDALE/KGS NW9 63 H2
Hyland House School WALTH E17 52 B5
Hylands Primary School EMPK RM11 75 J3
Hyleford Leavers Unit School BARK/HLT IG6 54 D5
Hythe Road Industrial Estate WLSDN NW10 99 J3
Ian Mikardo High School BOW E3 105 K2; POP/IOD E14 105 K6
Ibis Hotel BARK IG11 90 B6; CAMTN NW1 4 B5; CAN/RD E16 107 F6; FUL/PGN SW6 119 K6; GNWCH SE10 125 F6; HYS/HAR UB3 133 H2; POP/IOD E14 106 A6; SRTFD E15 88 C4; WBLY HA9 80 C3; WCHPL E1 13 K3
Ibstock Place School PUT/ROE SW15 158 B1
ICA Cinema STJS SW1Y 10 D7
ICC London CAN/RD E16 107 G6
Ickburgh School CLPT E5 86 D1
Ickenham HGDN/ICK UB10 76 A2
Ickenham Clinic HGDN/ICK UB10 76 A1
Icon College of Technology & Management WCHPL E1 104 C5
Ihlara Sport FC HBRY N5 85 J2
Ilderton Primary School PECK SE15 123 K6
Ilford IL IG1 90 A1
Ilford County High School BARK/HLT IG6 54 C5
Ilford Golf Club IL IG1 71 K5
Ilford Jewish Primary School BARK/HLT IG6 54 D6
Ilford Medical Centre IL IG1 90 B1
Ilford Preparatory School GDMY/SEVK IG3 73 F5
Ilford Retail Park IL IG1 72 C6
Ilford Swimming Pool IL IG1 72 D6
Ilford Ursuline High School IL IG1 72 A6
Ilford Ursuline Preparatory School IL IG1 72 B6
Iman Zakaria Academy FSTGT E7 89 F3
Imber Court Trading Estate E/WMO/HCT KT8 189 J3
Immanuel CE Primary School STRHM/NOR SW16 179 K2
Immanuel College BUSH WD23 28 E2
Immanuel School ROM RM1 57 G2
Imperial College PUT/ROE SW15 139 G3; SKENS SW7 14 A4; WEST SW1P 120 C5
Imperial College Athletic Ground HYS/HAR UB3 113 F6
Imperial College of London SKENS SW7 14 A3
Imperial College of Science FUL/PGN SW6 119 K6
Imperial College of Science & Technology SKENS SW7 14 B3
Imperial College School of Medicine PIM SW1V 16 C7; PIM SW1V 121 J5
Imperial War Museum STHWK SE1 17 K5
Imperial War Museum Annexe LBTH SE11 17 K5
Imperial Wharf FUL/PGN SW6 140 B2
Inchbald School of Design BGVA SW1W 15 G6
Independent Industrial Estate WDR/YW UB7 112 C1
India House HOL/ALD WC2B 11 G5
Inner London Sessions House (Crown Court) STHWK SE1 18 C4
Innholders Hall CANST EC4R 12 E5
Innkeeper's Lodge CHEAM SM3 193 K5; NTHLT UB5 78 A4; SAND/SEL CR2 211 J6
Inns of Court & Chancery TPL/STR WC2R 11 J4
Inns of Court Law School GINN WC1R 11 H1
Insight Independent School WEA W13 97 H6
The Institute Hampstead Garden Suburb EFNCH N2 65 J1
Institute of Education University of London RSQ WC1B 4 D7
Institute of European Studies RSQ WC1B 11 F1
Instituto Espanol Canada Blanch NKENS W10 100 C4
International Broadcast Centre OLYMPICPK E20 87 J3
International Business Park SRTFD E15 88 B6
International Community School BAY/PAD W2 8 C3
International Community School Primary CAMTN NW1 3 G7
International School of Business Studies PIN HA5 60 A4
International School of London ACT W3 117 H4
International Trading Estate NWDGN UB2 114 A3
Invicta Industrial Estate SRTFD E15 106 A2
Invicta Primary School BKHTH/KID SE3 125 K6
Invicta Sports Club DART DA1 151 G6
Inwood Business Centre HSLW TW3 135 G5
Ironmonger Row Baths FSBYE EC1V 6 C5
Ironmongers Hall STBT EC1A 12 C2
Islamia Girls School KIL/WHAMP NW6 82 C6
Islamic College for Advanced Studies WLSDN NW10 81 K5
The Islamic Grammar School WAND/EARL SW18 159 J2
Islamic Shaksiyah Foundation School WALTH E17 69 G2
Island Clinic POP/IOD E14 125 F2
Island Gardens POP/IOD E14 125 F4
Isleworth ISLW TW7 136 A3
Isleworth Cemetery ISLW TW7 136 B3
Isleworth Recreation Centre ISLW TW7 136 A5
Isleworth Crown Court ISLW TW7 135 K2
Isleworth & Syon School for Boys ISLW TW7 135 K1
Isleworth Town Primary School ISLW TW7 136 A3
Islington Arts & Media School FSBYPK N4 67 F5
Islington Business Centre IS N1 85 J6
Islington Crematorium MUSWH N10 47 K4
Islington Green Medical Centre IS N1 85 H6
Islington Tennis Centre HOLWY N7 84 E4
Islington Town Hall IS N1 85 H5
Ismaili Centre SKENS SW7 14 B6
Italia Conti Academy of Theatre Arts BRXN/ST SW9 141 K4; FARR EC1M 6 C7
Italian Hospital PIM SW1V 16 A6
Ithaca College SKENS SW7 120 B4
Ivybridge Primary School TWK TW1 156 A1
Ivybridge Retail Park ISLW TW7 136 A6
Ivydale Primary School PECK SE15 144 A5
Jack & Jill School HPTN TW12 173 F2
Jack Taylor School STJWD NW8 83 G6
Jack Tizard School FUL/PGN SW6 139 G2; SHB W12 100 A6
Jacques Prevert School HMSMTH W6 119 G4
James Allens Preparatory Girls School HNHL SE24 142 E6
James Dixon Primary School PGE/AN SE20 181 H4
Jamestown Mental Health Centre HAMP NW3 83 K5
James Wolfe Primary School GNWCH SE10 144 E1
Jamiah Madaniyah Primary School FSTGT E7 89 H4
Jamiatul Ummah School WCHPL E1 104 D5
Janet Adegoke Leisure Centre SHB W12 99 J6
The Japanese School ACT W3 98 C6
Japan Green Medical Centre ACT W3 117 J1
Jenner Health Centre FSTH SE23 164 B3
Jenny Hammond Primary School WAN E11 88 C2
Jermyn Street Theatre MYFR/PICC W1J 10 B6
Jessop Primary School HNHL SE24 142 C5
Jewel Tower WEST SW1P 16 E4
Jewish Cemetery GLDGN NW11 64 E3
Jewish Community Theatre HNHL SE24 142 E4
Jewish Free School KTN/HRWW/WS HA3 62 C3; KTTN NW5 84 D4
The Jewish Museum CAMTN NW1 3 J1; FNCH N3 47 F5
Johanna Primary School STHWK SE1 17 J3
John Ball Primary School BKHTH/KID SE3 145 H3
John Betts Primary School HMSMTH W6 118 D3
John Bramston Primary School BARK/HLT IG6 55 G2
John Burns Primary School BTSEA SW11 141 F3
John Chilton School NTHLT UB5 77 J5
John Dixon Clinic BERM/RHTH SE16 123 J3
John Donne Primary School PECK SE15 143 J2
John F Kennedy School CAN/RD E16 107 H4
John F Kennedy Special School SRTFD E15 88 C6
John Keble Anglican Church Primary School WLSDN NW10 99 H1
The John Loughborough School TOTM N17 50 B5
John Lyon School RYLN/HDSTN HA2 60 D5
John Nightingale School E/WMO/HCT KT8 172 E6
John Orwell Sports Centre WAP E1W 123 H1
John Paul II RC School WIM/MER SW19 159 G2
John Perryn Primary School ACT W3 99 G5
John Perry Primary School DAGE RM10 93 F4
John Roan School BKHTH/KID SE3 145 H1
John Ruskin College SAND/SEL CR2 213 G5
John Ruskin Primary School WALW SE17 122 D6
John Scott Health Centre FSBYPK N4 67 J5
John Scurr Primary School WCHPL E1 104 E3
John Smith House WALW SE17 18 C7
Johnsons Industrial Estate HYS/HAR UB3 113 K3
John Stainer Primary School BROCKY SE4 144 B4
The Jo Richardson Community School DAGW RM9 91 K6
Joseph Clarke Special School CHING E4 52 B2
Joseph Hood Primary School RYNPK SW20 177 H5
Joydens Wood Infant School RDART DA2 170 B6
Joydens Wood Junior School BXLY DA5 170 B6
Jubilee Country Park BMLY BR1 201 G1
Jubilee Market COVGDN WC2E 11 F5
Jubilee Primary School BRXS/STRHM SW2 162 B1; THMD SE28 109 J6
Jubilee Sports Ground CHING E4 38 B6
Julians Primary School STRHM/NOR SW16 162 B6
Jumeirah Carlton Tower Hotel KTBR SW1X 15 F4
Jumeirah Lowndes Hotel KTBR SW1X 15 F4
Juno Way Industrial Estate NWCR SE14 124 A6
Jurys Inn Chelsea FUL/PGN SW6 140 B2
Jurys Inn Hotel HTHAIR TW6 133 J4
JVC Business Park CRICK NW2 63 J5
Kaizen Primary School PLSTW E13 107 F3
Kangley Business Centre SYD SE26 182 C1
Katella Trading Estate BARK IG11 108 E2
Katherine Road Medical Centre FSTGT E7 89 G4
Keats House HAMP NW3 83 H2
Keble Preparatory School WCHMH N21 35 G2
Keen Students Supplementary School WCHPL E1 104 C4
Keir Hardie Primary School CAN/RD E16 106 E4
Keith Davis Cue Sports Club DAGW RM9 91 K5
Kelmscott Community Centre WALTH E17 69 H3
Kelmscott Leisure Centre WALTH E17 69 H3
Kelmscott School WALTH E17 69 H3
Kelsey Park Sports College BECK BR3 182 D6
Kelvin Industrial Estate GFD/PVL UB6 78 B6
Kemnal Technology College STMC/STPC BR5 186 C3
Kempton Park SUN TW16 172 A3
Kempton Park Racecourse SUN TW16 172 A3
Ken Barrington Centre LBTH SE11 122 A6
Kender Primary School NWCR SE14 143 K2
Kenmont Primary School WLSDN NW10 99 J2
Kenmore Park Infant School KTN/HRWW/WS HA3 43 K6
Kenneth More Theatre IL IG1 90 C1
Kennington LBTH SE11 122 C5
Kensal Green WLSDN NW10 100 A2
Kensal Green Cemetery WLSDN NW10 99 K2
Kensal Rise WLSDN NW10 100 A1
Kensal Rise Primary School KIL/WHAMP NW6 100 B1
Kensington & Chelsea College NKENS W10 100 C3
Kensington Avenue Primary School THHTH CR7 180 B4
Kensington Business Centre SKENS SW7 14 D4
Kensington & Chelsea College NTGHL W11 119 J2; WBPTN SW10 140 B1
Kensington & Chelsea Town Hall KENS W8 119 K2
Kensington College of Business HOL/ALD WC2B 11 G3
The Kensington Dyslexia Teaching Centre KENS W8 120 A3
Kensington Leisure Centre NTGHL W11 100 B6
Kensington Market KENS W8 120 A2
Kensington (Olympia) WKENS W14 119 H3
Kensington Palace State Apartments & Royal Ceremonial Dress Collection KENS W8 120 A2
Kensington Park School REGST W1B 9 K1
Kensington Preparatory School FUL/PGN SW6 139 J2
Kensington Primary School MNPK E12 89 K4
Kensington School of Business HCIRC EC1N 11 K1
Kensington Wharf WBPTN SW10 140 C1
Kensit Memorial College FNCH N3 46 C5
Kent House BECK BR3 182 B4
Kentish Town KTTN NW5 84 C3
Kentish Town CE Primary School KTTN NW5 84 C3
Kentish Town Health Centre KTTN NW5 84 C4
Kentish Town Industrial Estate KTTN NW5 84 B3
Kentish Town Sports Centre KTTN NW5 84 A4
Kentish Town West KTTN NW5 84 B4
Kenton KTN/HRWW/WS HA3 61 H3
Kenton CC KTN/HRWW/WS HA3 61 J1
Kenton Clinic KTN/HRWW/WS HA3 62 A2
Kent Park Industrial Estate PECK SE15 123 J6
Kenwood House HAMP NW3 65 J5
The Kerem School EFNCH N2 65 H2
Keston CE Primary School HAYES BR2 215 H3
Kestrel House School CEND/HSY/T N8 66 E3
Kew Bridge BTFD TW8 117 G5
Kew Bridge Steam Museum BTFD TW8 117 G5
Kew College RCH/KEW TW9 137 H1
Kew Gardens RCH/KEW TW9 137 H2
Kew Palace RCH/KEW TW9 137 F1
Kew Retail Park RCH/KEW TW9 137 J2
Kew Riverside Primary School RCH/KEW TW9 137 J3
Keyplan & Roxburghe College FITZ W1T 4 B7
Keys Meadow Primary School PEND EN3 25 J1
Keyworth Primary School WALW SE17 122 C5
Khalsa College London HRW HA1 61 F3
Khalsa VA Primary School NWDGN UB2 115 F4
Kidbrooke BKHTH/KID SE3 146 B4
Kidbrooke Park Primary School BKHTH/KID SE3 146 B3
Kidbrooke School BKHTH/KID SE3 146 C3
Kilburn CRICK NW2 82 C4
Kilburn High Road KIL/WHAMP NW6 83 F6
Kilburn Park KIL/WHAMP NW6 100 E1
Kilburn Park Junior School KIL/WHAMP NW6 100 D2
Killick Street Medical Centre IS N1 5 G2
Kilmorie Primary School FSTH SE23 164 B4
Kimberley Industrial Estate WALTH E17 51 H3
Kimpton Industrial Estate CHEAM SM3 193 J6
King Alfred School GLDGN NW11 65 F5
King Athelstan Primary School KUT/HW KT1 175 G6
Kingdom Hall of Jehovah's Witnesses ORP BR6 202 A6
King Edwards Road Clinic RSLP HA4 58 B5
King Edward VII Hospital for Officers MHST W1U 9 H1
King Fahad Academy ACT W3 99 G6
King Fahad Academy (Girls Upper School) EA W5 116 D4
The Kingfisher Medical Centre DEPT SE8 124 C6
The Kingfisher Sports Centre KUT/HW KT1 175 F5
King George Hospital GNTH/NBYPK IG2 73 G2
King George V CAN/RD E16 127 F1
King George VI Youth Hostel KENS W8 119 J2
Kingham Industrial Estate WLSDN NW10 99 F2
King Henry's Drive CROY/NA CR0 213 K6
King Henry VIII Mound RCHPK/HAM TW10 157 F3
King & Queen Wharf BERM/RHTH SE16 105 F6
Kings Avenue Medical Centre STHL UB1 96 C5
Kings Avenue School CLAP SW4 141 K6
Kingsbury CDALE/KGS NW9 62 C2
Kingsbury Green Primary School CDALE/KGS NW9 62 D2
Kingsbury High School CDALE/KGS NW9 62 E1
Kingsbury High Upper School CDALE/KGS NW9 62 D1
Kingsbury Hospital CDALE/KGS NW9 62 C1
Kingsbury Trading Estate CDALE/KGS NW9 62 E3
Kings College (Hampstead Campus) HAMP NW3 82 E2
King's College Hospital CMBW SE5 142 D4
Kings College London CMBW SE5 142 E3; HOL/ALD WC2B 11 F4; KENS W8 119 K2; STHWK SE1 12 A7; STHWK SE1 18 D1; WEST SW1P 16 B6
Kings College London - Humanities TPL/STR WC2R 11 G5

Kings College London - Law
TPL/STR WC2R 11 H5
Kings College London (Waterloo Campus)
STHWK SE1 17 J1
Kings College School
WIM/MER SW19 177 F2
Kings College School of Medicine & Dentistry
DUL SE21 162 E1
Kings College Sports Ground
RSLP HA4 58 C3
King's Cross
KCROSS N1C 4 E3
King's Cross St Pancras
CAMTN NW1 4 E4
Kingsdale School
DUL SE21 163 F5
Kings Estate
HCH RM12 93 J2
Kingsford Community School
PLSTW E13 107 G3
Kingsgate Business Centre
KUTN/CMB KT2 175 F4
Kingsgate Primary School
KIL/WHAMP NW6 82 E5
Kings Hall Leisure Centre
CLPT E5 86 E3
Kings Head Theatre
IS N1 85 G6
Kings House School
RCHPK/HAM TW10 137 G6
Kingsland College of Business Studies
SRTFD E15 106 B1
Kingsland Health Centre
HACK E8 86 B5
Kingsland Shopping Centre
HACK E8 86 B4
Kings Langley College of Management
NWCR SE14 144 B1
The Kingsley Hotel
NOXST/BSQ WC1A 10 E2
Kingsley Primary School
CROY/NA CR0 196 A5
Kings Mall Shopping Centre
HMSMTH W6 119 F4
Kingsmeadow Athletics Centre
KUT/HW KT1 175 H6
Kingsmead Primary School
CLPT E5 87 G2
Kingsmead School
EN EN1 24 C4
Kings Oak Primary School
NWMAL KT3 175 J6
The Kings Oak Private Hospital
ENC/FH EN2 23 G1
King Solomon Academy
CAMTN NW1 8 C1
King Solomon High School
BARK/HLT IG6 54 D5
Kings Place
IS N1 5 F2
Kings Private Clinic
GDMY/SEVK IG3 73 F5
MHST W1U 9 G1
Kings School of English
BECK BR3 182 C5
Kings Stairs
BERM/RHTH SE16 123 J2
Kingston
KUTN/CMB KT2 175 F4
Kingston Business Centre
CHSGTN KT9 206 A1
Kingston Cemetery
KUT/HW KT1 175 G6
Kingston College
KUT/HW KT1 175 F6
Kingston College Theatre
KUT/HW KT1 174 E6
Kingston Crematorium
KUT/HW KT1 175 H6
Kingston Crown Court
KUT/HW KT1 174 E6
Kingston Grammar School
KUT/HW KT1 175 G5
Kingston Hospital
KUTN/CMB KT2 175 H4
Kingstonian FC
NWMAL KT3 175 J6
Kingston University
KUT/HW KT1 175 F6
KUT/HW KT1 191 F1
KUTN/CMB KT2 176 A1
KUTN/CMB KT2 176 A3
PUT/ROE SW15 158 C4
King Street College
HMSMTH W6 119 F4
Kingsway Business Park
HPTN TW12 172 E4
Kingsway College
CAMTN NW1 4 A6
KTTN NW5 84 B4
STPAN WC1H 5 G5
Kingswood Primary School
WNWD SE27 162 E6
Kisharon School
GLDGN NW11 64 D3
Kisimul School
SURB KT6 190 D6
K+K Hotel George
ECT SW5 119 K4
KLC School of Design
WBPTN SW10 140 B2
Knightsbridge
CHEL SW3 14 D4
Knightsbridge Barracks
SKENS SW7 14 D3
Knightsbridge Medical Centre
KTBR SW1X 15 F4
Knightsbridge School
KTBR SW1X 14 E5
The Knightsbridge Under School
SKENS SW7 120 B4
Knollmead Primary School
BRYLDS KT5 191 K6
Knowledge Point School
HOLWY N7 85 F4
KP Estate
RAIN RM13 111 G6
Krishna-Avanti Primary School
EDGW HA8 44 C4
Kubrick Business Estate
FSTGT E7 89 F2
K West Hotel
SHB W12 119 G2
Laban Centre for Movement & Dance
DEPT SE8 144 E1
Laburnum Health Centre
DAGE RM10 74 C6
Ladbroke Grove
NKENS W10 100 C5
Lady Bankes Junior School
RSLP HA4 58 E6
The Lady Eleanor Holles School
HPTN TW12 173 G1
Lady Margaret Primary School
STHL UB1 95 K4
Lady Margaret School
FUL/PGN SW6 139 K2
Ladywell
LEW SE13 144 E6
Ladywell Arena
LEW SE13 164 E1
Ladywell Cemetery
BROCKY SE4 144 C6
Ladywell Leisure Centre
LEW SE13 145 F6
Lake Business Centre
TOTM N17 50 C2
Laker Industrial Estate
BECK BR3 182 C1
Lambeth Academy
CLAP SW4 141 H6
Lambeth Cemetery
TOOT SW17 178 B1
Lambeth College
CLAP SW4 141 H6
STHWK SE1 19 H1
STRHM/NOR SW16 161 K4
VX/NE SW8 141 J2
Lambeth County Court
LBTH SE11 122 B5
Lambeth Crematorium
TOOT SW17 160 B6
Lambeth Hospital
BRXN/ST SW9 141 K4
Lambeth North
STHWK SE1 17 J4
Lambeth Palace
STHWK SE1 17 G5
Lambs Court
POP/IOD E14 105 G6
Lammas School
LEY E10 69 H5
Lamont Business Centre
CROY/NA CR0 195 K4
Lamorbey Swimming Centre
BFN/LL DA15 168 B4
Lampton School
HSLW TW3 135 F2
The Lanark Medical Centre
MV/WKIL W9 101 F2
Lancaster Gate
BAY/PAD W2 8 A5
Lancaster Hotel
BAY/PAD W2 8 A5
Lancaster House
WHALL SW1A 16 A2
Lancasterian Primary School
TOTM N17 50 A4
Lancaster Road Industrial Estate
EBAR EN4 21 H6
Lancelot Medical Centre
ALP/SUD HA0 79 K3
The Landmark Hotel
CAMTN NW1 8 E1
The Lanesborough Hotel
KTBR SW1X 15 G2
Lanford Obesity Clinic
ED N9 36 D2
Langbourne Primary School
DUL SE21 163 F5
Langdon Down Centre
TEDD TW11 174 D3
Langdon Park
POP/IOD E14 105 K4
Langdon Park School
POP/IOD E14 105 K5
Langdon School
EHAM E6 108 B1
Langford Primary School
FUL/PGN SW6 140 A3
The Langham Hotel
REGST W1B 9 K2
Langhedge Lane Industrial Estate
UED N18 50 B2
Langley Park Girls School & Sports Centre
BECK BR3 198 E2
Langley Park Golf Club
BECK BR3 199 G3
Langley Park School for Boys
BECK BR3 198 E3
Langthorne Health Centre
WAN E11 88 B1
Langthorne Hospital
WAN E11 88 B2
Lansbury Lawrence Primary School
POP/IOD E14 105 K5
Lansdowne College
BAY/PAD W2 101 F6
Lansdowne School
BRXN/ST SW9 142 A4
Lantern of Knowledge Boys
LEY E10 70 A6
La Retraite RC Girls School
BAL SW12 161 H2
Lark Hall Primary School
CLAP SW4 141 J3
Larkshall Business Centre
CHING E4 38 B4
Larkswood Primary School
CHING E4 37 K6
Larmenier & Sacred Catholic Primary School
HMSMTH W6 119 G4
La Sainte Union Catholic Secondary School
HGT N6 84 A1
La Sainte Union Convent School
KTTN NW5 84 B1
La Salette RC Primary School
RAIN RM13 111 J2
Latchmere Leisure Centre
BTSEA SW11 140 E3
Latchmere Primary School
KUTN/CMB KT2 175 G2
Lathom Junior School
EHAM E6 89 J5
Latimer Road
NTGHL W11 100 B6
Latymer All Saints CE Primary School
ED N9 36 B4
The Latymer Preparatory School
HMSMTH W6 118 D5
The Latymer School
ED N9 36 A4
Latymer Upper School
HMSMTH W6 118 D4
Launcelot Primary School
BMLY BR1 165 K6
Laurance Haines Primary School
WATW WD18 26 E1
Laurel Clinic
EA W5 116 D4
Laurel Lane Primary
WDR/YW UB7 112 A4
Lauriston Primary School
HOM E9 87 F6
Lavender Primary School
ENC/FH EN2 23 K1
Lawdale Junior School
BETH E2 104 C2
Lawrence Trading Estate
GNWCH SE10 125 H4
Lawrence Wharf
BERM/RHTH SE16 124 C1
Laycock Primary School
IS N1 85 G4
Lazards Sports Club
SUN TW16 172 A4
Leadenhall Market
BANK EC3V 13 G4
Lea Park Trading Estate
LEY E10 69 H4
Leaside Business Centre
PEND EN3 25 H3
Leathermarket Gardens
STHWK SE1 19 G3
Leathersellers Sports Ground
LEE/GVPK SE12 166 B2
Leathers Hall
HDTCH EC3A 13 G3
Lea Valley Primary School
TOTM N17 50 C3
Lea Valley Trading Estate
UED N18 36 E6
UED N18 51 F2
Lebanon Road
CROY/NA CR0 197 F6
L'Ecole de Battersea
BTSEA SW11 140 C2
L'Ecole des Petits
FUL/PGN SW6 140 A3
Lee
LEE/GVPK SE12 165 K1
Lee Manor Primary School
LEW SE13 165 H1
Leeside Court
BERM/RHTH SE16 124 A1
Leeside Trading Estate
TOTM N17 50 E3
Leesons Primary School
STMC/STPC BR5 186 B6
Lee Valley Camping & Caravan Park
ED N9 37 G3
Lee Valley Campsite
CHING E4 25 K3
Lee Valley Ice Centre
LEY E10 69 F6
Lee Valley Leisure Complex, Athletics Centre & Golf Club
ED N9 37 G2
Lee Valley Watersports Centre
CHING E4 51 G2
Leicester Square
LSQ/SEVD WC2H 10 D5
Leigh Close Industrial Estate
NWMAL KT3 192 A1
Leigh Technology Academy
DART DA1 171 K3
Leighton House Museum
WKENS W14 119 J3
Le Meridien Hotel
REGST W1B 10 B6
Lena Gardens Primary School
HMSMTH W6 119 F3
Leopold Primary School
WLSDN NW10 81 H5
Leopold Street Clinic
BOW E3 105 H4
Lesnes Abbey
BELV DA17 128 E4
Lessness Heath Primary School
BELV DA17 129 H5
The Levin Hotel
KTBR SW1X 14 E4
Lewin Mead Community Mental Health Centre
STRHM/NOR SW16 179 J2
Lewis Clinic
CAR SM5 210 A2
Lewisham
DEPT SE8 144 E3
Lewisham Bridge Primary School
LEW SE13 144 E4
Lewisham Business Centre
NWCR SE14 124 A6
Lewisham Centre
LEW SE13 145 F5
Lewisham College
BROCKY SE4 144 D3
Lewisham Crematorium
CAT SE6 165 J4
Lewisham Lions Centre
BERM/RHTH SE16 123 K5
Lexi Cinema
WLSDN NW10 82 A6
The Leys Primary School
DAGE RM10 92 E5
Leyton
LEY E10 88 A1
Leyton Business Centre
LEY E10 69 H6
Leyton Cross
RDART DA2 170 D4
Leyton FC
LEY E10 69 H5
Leyton Industrial Village
LEY E10 69 F4
Leyton Leisure Centre
LEY E10 69 K4
Leyton Midland Road
LEY E10 70 A5
Leyton Mills Retail Park
LEY E10 88 A1
Leyton Orient FC (Matchroom Stadium)
LEY E10 87 K1
Leyton Sixth Form College
LEY E10 70 B3
Leytonstone
WAN E11 70 C5
Leytonstone Business & Enterprise Specialist School
WAN E11 70 C3
Leytonstone High Road
WAN E11 70 C6
Leyton Youth Sports Ground
LEY E10 69 K5
The Liberty City Clinic
SDTCH EC2A 7 G6
Liberty II Centre
ROM RM1 75 G1
Liberty Middle School
MTCM CR4 178 D5
The Liberty
ROM RM1 75 G2
Library & Community Centre
BTSEA SW11 140 C4
The Lighthouse Group (TLG) Centre
LBTH SE11 122 B6
L'Ile Aux Enfants
KTTN NW5 84 A3
Lilian Baylis Technology School
LBTH SE11 122 A5
Lillian Baylis School
LBTH SE11 17 H7
VX/NE SW8 121 K6
Lillian Baylis Theatre
CLKNW EC1R 6 A4
Lillian Bishop School of English
SKENS SW7 14 A6
Limehouse
WCHPL E1 105 G5
Limehouse Hole Stairs
BERM/RHTH SE16 124 C1
Limes Farm Primary School
CHIG IG7 54 D2
Lime Trees Park Golf Club
NTHLT UB5 77 G6
Lincoln Road Clinic
EN EN1 24 C6
Lincoln's Inn
LINN WC2A 11 H3
Linden Bridge School
WPK KT4 207 G1
Linden Lodge School
WIM/MER SW19 159 H3
Lindon Bennett School
FELT TW13 172 C1
Linford Christie Stadium
SHB W12 99 J4
The Link Day Primary School
CROY/NA CR0 210 E2
The Link Secondary School
CROY/NA CR0 211 F2
Links Primary School
TOOT SW17 179 F2
Linley House School
BRYLDS KT5 191 G3
Linley Sambourne House
WKENS W14 119 J2
Linnet House Clinic
STJWD NW8 2 C3
Linton Mead Primary School
THMD SE28 109 H6
Lionel Road Primary School
BTFD TW8 117 F4
Lion House School
PUT/ROE SW15 139 G5
Lismarrine Industrial Park
BORE WD6 29 H1
Lisson Grove Health Centre
STJWD NW8 2 C6
Lister Community School
PLSTW E13 107 F1
The Lister Hospital
BGVA SW1W 121 G5
Lister House Clinic
CAVSQ/HST W1G 9 J3
Little Danson Welfare Clinic
WELL DA16 148 B5
Little Davids School
CROY/NA CR0 213 K4
Little Hands Theatre
HDN NW4 64 A1
Little Heath School
CHDH RM6 73 H1
Little Ilford School
MNPK E12 89 K3
Little St Helens School
NTHWD HA6 40 C2
Little Wandsworth School
TOOT SW17 161 F4
Liverpool Street
LVPST EC2M 13 G1
Livesey Museum for Children
PECK SE15 123 J6
Livingstone Hospital
DART DA1 171 J2
Livingstone Primary School
EBAR EN4 21 H4
The Livity School
BRXS/STRHM SW2 141 K6
Lloyd Park
CROY/NA CR0 212 B2
Lloyd Park Centre
WALTH E17 51 J5
Lloyd's of London
HDTCH EC3A 13 G4
Lloyds Register CC
DUL SE21 162 E3
Lloyd Williamson School
NKENS W10 100 C4
Locks View Court
POP/IOD E14 105 G6
Lockwood Industrial Park
TOTM N17 50 D6
Lombard Business Centre
BTSEA SW11 140 C3
Lombard Business Park
CROY/NA CR0 196 A4
WAND/EARL SW18 160 C1
WIM/MER SW19 178 B5
Lombard Trading Estate
CHARL SE7 126 A4
Lombardy Retail Park
HYS/HAR UB3 95 F6
London 2012 Games Venues:
Aquatics Centre
OLYMPICPK E20 88 A5
Basketball Arena
OLYMPICPK E20 87 K3
BMX Track
OLYMPICPK E20 87 K3
Earl's Court
ECT SW5 119 K5
Eton Manor
OLYMPICPK E20 87 K2
ExCeL
CAN/RD E16 107 F6
Greenwich Park
GNWCH SE10 145 H1
Hampton Court Palace
E/WMO/HCT KT8 174 A6
Handball Arena
OLYMPICPK E20 87 J4
Hockey Centre
OLYMPICPK E20 87 J3
Horse Guards Parade
WHALL SW1A 16 D1
Hyde Park
BAY/PAD W2 8 E7
Lord's Cricket Ground
STJWD NW8 2 B4
The Mall
WHALL SW1A 16 A2
North Greenwich Arena
POP/IOD E14 125 H1
Olympic Stadium
OLYMPICPK E20 87 K5
The Royal Artillery Barracks
WOOL/PLUM SE18 126 E6
Velodrome
OLYMPICPK E20 87 K3
Water Polo Arena
OLYMPICPK E20 87 K5
Wembley Arena
WBLY HA9 80 C2
Wembley Stadium
WBLY HA9 80 C2
Wimbledon
WIM/MER SW19 159 H6
London Academy
EDGW HA8 30 B6
London Academy of Music & Dramatic Art
KENS W8 119 K4
London Allergy Clinic
CAVSQ/HST W1G 9 J2
London Ambassador College
WCHPL E1 104 C4
London Bridge
STHWK SE1 19 F1
London Bridge City Pier
STHWK SE1 13 G7
London Bridge Hospital
STHWK SE1 13 F7
London Bridge Hotel
STHWK SE1 18 E1
London Bridge Sports Centre
CANST EC4R 12 E6
London Brookes College
HDN NW4 63 K1
London Business School
CAMTN NW1 2 E6
London Butterfly House
BTFD TW8 136 D2
The London Canal Museum
IS N1 5 F2
London Capital College
CAMTN NW1 84 B6
The London Centre for Children with Cerebral Palsy
MUSWH N10 48 B6
London Centre of Contemporary Music
STHWK SE1 18 D1
London Chest Hospital
BETH E2 104 E1
London Chinese Dance School
CAN/RD E16 106 B4
REGST W1B 9 K1
London Christian Learning Centre
MNPK E12 89 H2

London Christian School STHWK SE1 18 E3
London City Airport CAN/RD E16 126 D1
London City Airport ⊖ CAN/RD E16 126 D1
London City College (English Language Institute) & Schiller International University STHWK SE1 17 H1
London City Mission STHWK SE1 19 H2
The London Clinic CAVSQ/HST W1G 3 H7
London College of Business & Computer Studies CLAP SW4 141 J5
London College of Business & Computing BETH E2 104 D1
London College of Communication LBTH SE11 18 B5
London College of Fashion CAVSQ/HST W1G 9 K3; MHST W1U 9 H3; SDTCH EC2A 7 H6
London College of Further Education LBTH SE11 18 A7
London College of Higher Education CLAP SW4 141 G4
London College of International Business Studies HHOL WC1V 11 F2
The London College KENS W8 119 K1
London Commodity Exchange WAP E1W 13 K6
London Contemporary Dance School PLSTW E13 106 D2
London Contemporary Dance School at The Place STPAN WC1H 4 D5
London Cornish RFC PUT/ROE SW15 158 C5
The London Dungeon STHWK SE1 19 F1
London Electronics College ECT SW5 119 K5
London Esthetique POP/IOD E14 106 C5
London Eye STHWK SE1 17 G2
London Eye Clinic CAVSQ/HST W1G 9 J2
London Eye Millennium Pier STHWK SE1 17 G2
London Fields ⇌ HACK E8 86 D5
London Fields Lido HACK E8 86 D5
London Fields Primary School HACK E8 86 D6
London Film Academy FUL/PGN SW6 139 K1
London Film School LSQ/SEVD WC2H 10 E4
London Financial Training College FSBYPK N4 67 H2
London Foot Hospital FITZ W1T 4 A7
London Gender Clinic HDN NW4 63 K3
London Group Business Park CRICK NW2 63 H5
London Heart Clinic CAVSQ/HST W1G 9 J2
The London Industrial Estate EHAM E6 108 A4
London Industrial Park EHAM E6 108 B4
London International College POP/IOD E14 106 C5; SOHO/SHAV W1D 10 B3
The London Irish Youth Theatre HGT N6 66 B5
London Islamic School WCHPL E1 104 D5
London Jewish Girls High School HDN NW4 64 A2
London Ladies & Girls FC CAT SE6 182 E1
London Lane Clinic BMLY BR1 183 J3
London Lighthouse NTGHL W11 100 C5
London Living Theatre SYD SE26 164 A6
The London Make-Up Academy UED N18 50 D1
London Marriott Hotel HAMP NW3 83 J5; MYFR/PKLN W1K 9 H5; OXSTW W1C 9 F5; POP/IOD E14 105 J6; STHWK SE1 17 G2; WHTN TW2 155 K1
London Metrocity College BOW E3 105 J2
London Metropolitan University HBRY N5 85 J3; HOLWY N7 85 F2; LVPST EC2M 13 F2; WCHPL E1 13 J3; WCHPL E1 104 C5
London Natural Therapy School POP/IOD E14 106 C6; SOHO/CST W1F 10 B5
London Nautical School STHWK SE1 11 K7
London Open College FSBYE EC1V 6 B4
London Oratory School FUL/PGN SW6 139 K1
London Road Medical Centre CROY/NA CR0 196 B3
London School of Business & Finance HCIRC EC1N 11 J2
London School of Economics CLKNW EC1R 5 K5; HHOL WC1V 10 E3; STHWK SE1 12 C7
London School of Economics & Political Science HOL/ALD WC2B 11 G4
London School of Hygiene & Tropical Medicine GWRST WC1E 10 D1
London School of Jewish Studies HDN NW4 64 B1
London School of Theology NTHWD HA6 40 B2
London Scottish Golf Club WIM/MER SW19 158 E5
London Silver Vaults LINN WC2A 11 J2
London Soccerdome GNWCH SE10 125 J2
London South Bank University STHWK SE1 18 B4
London Stock Exchange STBT EC1A 12 B3
The London Television Centre STHWK SE1 11 J7
London Tourist Board & Convention Centre BGVA SW1W 15 J4
London Toy & Model Museum BAY/PAD W2 101 G6
London Transport Bus Depot BXLYHN DA7 149 J4
London Transport Museum HOL/ALD WC2B 11 F5
London Underwriting Centre MON EC3R 13 G5
London Wall BARB EC2Y 12 C2
London Weather Centre HCIRC EC1N 11 J1
The London Welbeck Hospital CAVSQ/HST W1G 9 H2
London Welsh FC RCH/KEW TW9 137 F4
London West Crematorium WLSDN NW10 99 K3
Lonesome Primary School MTCM CR4 179 G5
Long Ditton Cemetery SURB KT6 190 D6
Long Ditton County Infant School SURB KT6 190 D5
Long Ditton St Marys CE Junior School THDIT KT7 190 C5
Longfield J & I School RYLN/HDSTN HA2 60 A3
Longford Community School EBED/NFELT TW14 153 J2
Longford Industrial Estate HPTN TW12 173 G2
Longlands Primary School BFN/LL DA15 167 K5
Long Lane AFC BKHTH/KID SE3 146 B3
Longshaw Primary School CHING E4 38 B5
Lord Chancellors Department WEST SW1P 16 D5
Lord's Cricket Ground STJWD NW8 2 B4
Lord Lister Health Centre FSTGT E7 88 E2
Lordship Lane Clinic TOTM N17 50 A5
Lordship Lane Primary School WDGN N22 49 J4
Lord's Tour & MCC Museum STJWD NW8 2 A5
Lorimar Business Centre RAIN RM13 111 G5
Loughborough Junction ⇌ CMBW SE5 142 C3
Loughborough Primary School CMBW SE5 142 C3
Lovelace Primary School CHSGTN KT9 205 J3
Lovell's Wharf GNWCH SE10 125 G5
Lower Clapton Health Centre CLPT E5 86 E3
Lower Place Business Centre WLSDN NW10 98 E1
Lower Sydenham ⇌ SYD SE26 182 C1
Lower Sydenham Industrial Estate SYD SE26 182 C1
Lowfield Medical Centre DART DA1 171 H2
Low Hall Sports Ground LEY E10 69 F3
Lowther Primary School BARN SW13 118 D6
Loxford School of Science & Technology IL IG1 90 D3
Loyola Preparatory School BKHH IG9 39 G3
LPR Sports Club BARK/HLT IG6 55 F4
LSE Sports Club NWMAL KT3 192 A3
Lubavitch Boys Primary School CLPT E5 68 B4
Lubavitch House School (Senior Girls) STNW/STAM N16 68 A4
Lucas Vale Primary School DEPT SE8 144 D2
Lutomer House Business Centre POP/IOD E14 124 E1
Lux Cinema IS N1 7 G5
Lycee Francais SKENS SW7 14 A6
Lycee Francais Charles De Gaulle BTSEA SW11 141 G5
Lyceum Independent School SDTCH EC2A 7 G7
The Lyceum Theatre COVGDN WC2E 11 G5
Lyndean Industrial Estate ABYW SE2 128 D3
Lyndhurst House Preparatory School HAMP NW3 83 H3
Lyndhurst Primary School CMBW SE5 142 E3
Lyon Business Park BARK IG11 108 E1
Lyon Park Infant School ALP/SUD HA0 80 B5
Lyonsdown School BAR EN5 21 G6
Lyric Theatre SOHO/SHAV W1D 10 C5
Lyric Theatre Hammersmith HMSMTH W6 119 F4
Mabwin Supplementary School ED N9 36 D4
Macaulay CE Primary School CLAP SW4 141 G4
Madame Tussauds CAMTN NW1 3 G7
Madeira Grove Clinic WFD IG8 53 F1
Madison Bowl NTHWD HA6 40 C3
Madni Girls School WCHPL E1 104 D5
Madrasah-E-Darue Qirat Majidiah School WCHPL E1 104 D6
Mahatma Gandhi Industrial Estate BRXN/ST SW9 142 C4
Maida Vale ⊖ MV/WKIL W9 101 F2
Maida Vale Medical Centre MV/WKIL W9 101 F2
Malcolm Primary School PGE/AN SE20 181 K3
The Malden Centre NWMAL KT3 192 C1
Malden Golf Club NWMAL KT3 176 B5
Malden Manor ⇌ NWMAL KT3 192 B4
Malden Manor Primary School NWMAL KT3 192 B4
Malden Parochial Primary School WPK KT4 192 B5
Malden Road Baths CHEAM SM3 208 B2
Malham Road Industrial Estate FSTH SE23 164 A3
The Mall WHALL SW1A 16 A2
The Mall Bexleyheath BXLYHS DA6 149 H5
Mall Galleries STJS SW1Y 10 D7
The Mall School WHTN TW2 155 J5
Malmaison Charterhouse Square Hotel FARR EC1M 12 B1
Malmesbury Primary School BOW E3 105 H2; MRDN SM4 194 B4
Malorees Junior School KIL/WHAMP NW6 82 B5
Mandarin Oriental Hotel KTBR SW1X 15 F2
The Mandeville Hotel MHST W1U 9 H3
Mandeville Primary School CLPT E5 87 G1
Mandeville Special School NTHLT UB5 77 K4
Manford Industrial Estate ERITH DA8 130 E6
Manford Primary School CHIG IG7 55 F1
Manford Way Health Centre BARK/HLT IG6 55 F2
Manor Brook Medical Centre BKHTH/KID SE3 146 A3
Manor Drive Health Centre WPK KT4 192 C5
Manorfield Primary School POP/IOD E14 105 K4
Manor House ⊖ FSBYPK N4 67 J5
Manor Infant School BARK IG11 91 F4
Manor Oak Primary School STMC/STPC BR5 202 E2
Manor Park ⇌ MNPK E12 89 H2
Manor Park Cemetery FSTGT E7 89 H2
Manor Park Crematorium FSTGT E7 89 G2
Manor Park Methodist School MNPK E12 89 J2
Manor Park Primary School SUT SM1 209 G3
Manor Primary School SRTFD E15 106 C1
Manorside Primary School FNCH N3 47 F4
Manor Special School WLSDN NW10 100 B1
Manor Way Business Centre RAIN RM13 111 F4
Mansfield Infant College IL IG1 72 A6
Mansion House ⊖ STP EC4M 12 D4
Mapledown School CRICK NW2 64 B4
Maple Grove Business Centre HSLWW TW4 134 B5
Maple House Independant Montessori School THHTH CR7 180 D6
Maple Industrial Estate FELT TW13 153 K4
Maples Business Centre IS N1 85 G5
Maple Walk School WLSDN NW10 81 H6
Marble Arch MBLAR W1H 9 F5
Marble Arch ⊖ OXSTW W1C 9 F5
Marble Hill House TWK TW1 156 D2
Maria Fidelis Convent School CAMTN NW1 4 B5
Maria Montessori Childrens House HAMP NW3 83 H3
Mariner Business Centre CROY/NA CR0 211 F3
Marion Richardson Primary School WCHPL E1 105 F5
Marion Vian Primary School BECK BR3 198 A2
Maritime Greenwich College DEPT SE8 144 D1
Maritime Industrial Estate CHARL SE7 126 A4
Maritime Museum GNWCH SE10 125 H4
Marjorie McClure School CHST BR7 185 H4
The Marjory Kinnon School EBED/NFELT TW14 133 H6
Market Trading Estate NWDGN UB2 114 A4
Marks Gate Clinic CHDH RM6 56 A6
Marks Gate Junior School CHDH RM6 56 A6
Marlborough College of Business & Technology FSTGT E7 88 E3
Marlborough CC DUL SE21 163 H3
Marlborough Day Hospital STJWD NW8 101 G1
Marlborough House STJS SW1Y 16 B1
Marlborough Primary School CHEL SW3 14 D7; HRW HA1 60 E1; ISLW TW7 136 B2
Marlborough School BFN/LL DA15 168 B3
Marlborough Trading Estate RCH/KEW TW9 137 J2
Marlowe Business Centre NWCR SE14 144 B1
Marner Primary School BOW E3 105 K3
Marriott Hotel ECT SW5 120 A4; HYS/HAR UB3 133 G1; KIL/WHAMP NW6 101 F1; MBLAR W1H 8 D3
Marshalls Park School ROM RM1 57 G5
Marsh Gate Business Centre SRTFD E15 106 A1
Marshgate Primary School RCHPK/HAM TW10 137 G6
Marsh Green School DAGW RM9 110 C1
Martan College HOL/ALD WC2B 11 F3
Martinbridge Industrial Estate EN EN1 24 C6
Martindale Industrial Estate EN EN1 24 A6
Martin Primary School EFNCH N2 65 J1
Marvels Lane Primary School LEE/GVPK SE12 166 B6
Maryland ⇌ SRTFD E15 88 C3
Maryland Industrial Estate SRTFD E15 88 C3
Maryland Primary School SRTFD E15 88 C3
Marylebone ⇌ ⊖ CAMTN NW1 2 D7
Marylebone Health Centre CAMTN NW1 3 H7
Marylebone Magistrates Court CAMTN NW1 8 D1
Marymount International School KUTN/CMB KT2 175 K3
Mary Wallace Theatre TWK TW1 156 B3
Maswell Park Health Centre HSLW TW3 135 H6
Mathilda Marks Kennedy Primary School MLHL NW7 45 F1
Matrix Business Centre DART DA1 151 H6
Maudlin's Green WAP E1W 13 K7
The Maudsley Hospital CMBW SE5 142 E3
Maughan Library (Kings College) LINN WC2A 11 J3
Mawbrey Brough Health Centre VX/NE SW8 141 K1
The Mawney School ROMW/RG RM7 75 F2
Mayday University Hospital THHTH CR7 196 C3
Mayesbrook Park Arena BARK IG11 91 G3
Mayespark Primary School GDMY/SEVK IG3 91 G1
Mayfield Primary School HNWL W7 96 D5
Mayfield School BCTR RM8 73 J5; PIN HA5 41 J6
Mayflower Primary School POP/IOD E14 105 J5
Mayplace Primary School BXLYHN DA7 150 A5
Maypole Primary School RDART DA2 170 B5
Maytime School IL IG1 90 A1
Mayville Junior & Primary School WAN E11 88 C1
Maze Hill ⇌ GNWCH SE10 125 H6
McKay Trading Estate NKENS W10 100 C3
McMillan Clinic HYS/HAR UB3 94 A6
MDQ Majidiah School WCHPL E1 104 D6
The Mead Infant School WPK KT4 207 H1
Meadlands Primary School RCHPK/HAM TW10 156 D6
Meadowgate School BROCKY SE4 144 A4
Meadowside Leisure Centre BKHTH/KID SE3 146 B5
The Meadow Special School STMC/STPC BR5 186 B3
Mead Road Infant School CHST BR7 185 H2
Medical Centres CROY/NA CR0 198 B6
The Medical Centre WAND/EARL SW18 160 A1
Medical Express Clinic CAVSQ/HST W1G 9 J1
Mednurs Clinic STNW/STAM N16 67 K4
Megabowl KUTN/CMB KT2 175 F5
Melcombe Primary School HMSMTH W6 119 G6
Melia White House Hotel CAMTN NW1 3 K6
Mellish Industrial Estate WOOL/PLUM SE18 126 C3
Mellow Lane School HGDN/ICK UB10 94 A3
Melrose Special School MTCM CR4 178 D6
Memorial Hospital WOOL/PLUM SE18 147 F3
Menorah Grammar School EDGW HA8 44 E3; GLDGN NW11 64 C4
Menorah High School for Girls CRICK NW2 81 H1
Menorah Primary School GLDGN NW11 64 C4
MERC Education WOOL/PLUM SE18 127 G3
Mercers' Hall LOTH EC2R 12 E4
The Merchant Taylors Hall BANK EC3V 13 F4
Merchant Taylors School NTHWD HA6 26 C3
Mercure London City Bankside Hotel STHWK SE1 18 C1
Meridian Clinic BRXN/ST SW9 142 A4
Meridian Locality Mental Health Centre CHARL SE7 126 B6
Meridian Primary School GNWCH SE10 125 G5
Meridian Sports Club CHARL SE7 146 D1
Meridian Trading Estate CHARL SE7 126 A4
Merlin Primary School BMLY BR1 165 K5
Merlin School PUT/ROE SW15 139 G6
Mermaid Theatre BLKFR EC4V 12 B5
Merrielands Retail Park DAGW RM9 92 B6
Merry Hill Infant School BUSH WD23 28 B2
Merryhills Clinic ENC/FH EN2 23 F4
Merryhills Primary School ENC/FH EN2 23 F5
Merton Abbey Primary School WIM/MER SW19 178 A4
Merton Adult College RYNPK SW20 177 H6
Merton College MRDN SM4 193 J3
Merton Court Preparatory School SCUP DA14 168 D6

Merton Industrial Park *WIM/MER* SW19 178 B4
Merton Park ⊖ *WIM/MER* SW19 177 K4
Merton Park Primary School *WIM/MER* SW19 177 J5
Merton Road Industrial Estate *WAND/EARL* SW18 159 K2
The Method Studio *FSBYW* WC1X 11 G1
Metro Business Centre *SYD* SE26 182 C2
The Metro Golf Centre *HDN* NW4 46 A4
Metro Industrial Centre *ISLW* TW7 135 K3
Metropolitan Business Centre *IS* N1 86 A5
Metropolitan Hospital *STHWK* SE1 17 K4
Metropolitan London Hotel *MYFR/PKLN* W1K 15 J1
Metropolitan Police FC *E/WMO/HCT* KT8 189 J3
Metropolitan Police Hayes Sports Club *HAYES* BR2 199 J6
Metropolitan Police (Hendon) Track *CDALE/KGS* NW9 45 H6
Metropolitan Police Training School, Hendon *CDALE/KGS* NW9 45 H6
Metropolitan Tabernacle *STHWK* SE1 18 B6
Metro Trading Centre *WBLY* HA9 80 D2
Michael Faraday Primary School *WALW* SE17 122 E5
Michael Manley Industrial Estate *VX/NE* SW8 141 H2
Michael Sobell Sinai School *KTN/HRWW/WS* HA3 62 C3
The Michael Tippett School *LBTH* SE11 17 K7
Midas Business Centre *DAGE* RM10 92 C2
Midas Industrial Estate *DAGE* RM10 92 C2
Middle Park Primary School *ELTH/MOT* SE9 166 C2
Middle Row Primary School *NKENS* W10 100 C3
Middlesex Business Centre *NWDGN* UB2 115 F2
Middlesex CCC (Lord's Cricket Ground) *STJWD* NW8 2 B4
Middlesex Hospital Medical School *FITZ* W1T 10 B1
Middlesex Hospital Nurses Home *GTPST* W1W 10 A1
Middlesex Hospital School of Physiotherapy *FITZ* W1T 10 B1
Middlesex Hospital Sports Ground *CHST* BR7 186 A1
Middlesex School of Complementary Medicine *STAN* HA7 44 A4
Middlesex University *ARCH* N19 66 C5
GLDGN NW11 65 F5
PEND EN3 25 F6
WDGN N22 48 E5
Middlesex University (Cat Hill Campus) *EBAR* EN4 34 A1
Middlesex University (Enfield Campus) *PEND* EN3 24 D6
Middlesex University (Hendon Campus) *HDN* NW4 63 K1
Middlesex University (Trent Park Campus) *EBAR* EN4 22 C3
Midfield Primary School *STMC/STPC* BR5 186 B3
Midway Mission Hospital *BETH* E2 7 J5
Milbourne Lodge School *ESH/CLAY* KT10 204 D4
Mile End ⊖ *BOW* E3 105 H3
Mile End & Bow Business Centre *WCHPL* E1 104 D4
Mile End Hospital *WCHPL* E1 105 F2
Mile End Stadium *POP/IOD* E14 105 H4
Milehams Industrial Estate *PUR* RM19 131 K3
Miles Coverdale Primary School *SHB* W12 119 F2
Milestone Hotel *KENS* W8 120 A2
Military Barracks *WOOL/PLUM* SE18 127 F5
Millbank Millennium Pier *WEST* SW1P 16 E7
Millbank Primary School *WEST* SW1P 16 D7
Millbank Tower *WEST* SW1P 16 E7
Millennium Arena *BTSEA* SW11 141 F1
Millennium Bailey's Hotel *SKENS* SW7 120 B4
Millennium Balloon *STHWK* SE1 19 H1
Millennium & Copthorne Hotels at Chelsea FC *FUL/PGN* SW6 140 A1
Millennium Dance 2000 Theatre School *HAMP* NW3 83 J3
Millennium Gloucester Hotel *ECT* SW5 120 A4
Millennium Harbour *POP/IOD* E14 124 C2
Millennium Hotel *KTBR* SW1X 15 F3
Millennium Hotel London Mayfair *MYFR/PKLN* W1K 9 H6
Millennium Primary School *GNWCH* SE10 125 J3
Millennium Quay *DEPT* SE8 124 E6
Millennium Wharf *POP/IOD* E14 125 G3
Mill Farm Business Park *HSLWW* TW4 154 D2
Millfields Primary School *CLPT* E5 86 E2
Millfield Theatre *UED* N18 35 K6
Mill Green Business Park *MTCM* CR4 194 E4
Mill Hill Broadway ⇌ *MLHL* NW7 45 G2
Mill Hill Cemetery *MLHL* NW7 46 A2
Mill Hill County High School *EBAR* EN4 33 K2
MLHL NW7 31 G4
The Mill Hill CC *MLHL* NW7 32 A5
Mill Hill East ⊖ *MLHL* NW7 46 B3
Mill Hill Golf Club *MLHL* NW7 31 G4
Mill Hill Industrial Estate *MLHL* NW7 45 H2
Mill Hill School *MLHL* NW7 31 K6
Mill Lane Medical Centre *KIL/WHAMP* NW6 82 E3
Mill Lane Trading Estate *CROY/NA* CR0 211 F1
Mill River Trading Estate *PEND* EN3 25 G5
Millside Industrial Estate *DART* DA1 151 G5
Mill Street Clinic *STHWK* SE1 19 K2
Mill Trading Estate *WLSDN* NW10 98 D1
The Mill Trading Estate *WLSDN* NW10 98 E2
Millwall FC (The New Den) *BERM/RHTH* SE16 123 K5
Milmead Industrial Centre *TOTM* N17 50 D5
Milton Natural Health Centre *HGT* N6 66 C4
Minet Clinic *HYS/HAR* UB3 113 K1
Minet J & I Schools *HYS/HAR* UB3 114 A1
Ministry of Defence *WHALL* SW1A 16 E1
Mint Business Park *CAN/RD* E16 106 E4
Mint Hotel *WEST* SW1P 16 E6
Mirravale Trading Estate *CHDH* RM6 74 A4
Mission Grove Primary School *WALTH* E17 69 H2
Mitcham ⊖ *MTCM* CR4 194 D1
Mitcham CC *MTCM* CR4 194 D1
Mitcham Eastfields ⇌ *MTCM* CR4 179 F5
Mitcham Golf Club *MTCM* CR4 195 F2
Mitcham Industrial Estate *MTCM* CR4 179 F4
Mitcham Junction ⇌ ⊖ *MTCM* CR4 195 F2
Mitcham Vale High School *STRHM/NOR* SW16 179 H5
Mitchell Brook Primary School *WLSDN* NW10 81 F4
Mitre Bridge Industrial Park *NKENS* W10 99 K3
Mitre House Hotel *BAY/PAD* W2 8 A4
Moatbridge School *ELTH/MOT* SE9 166 C1
The Moat School *FUL/PGN* SW6 139 H3
Moberly Sports & Education Centre *WLSDN* NW10 100 B2
Molesey Cemetery *E/WMO/HCT* KT8 173 F6
Molesey Hospital *E/WMO/HCT* KT8 189 F2
Mollison Drive Health Centre *WLGTN* SM6 210 E5
Monega Primary School *MNPK* E12 89 H3
Monken Hadley CE Primary School *BAR* EN5 20 E2
Monkfrith Primary School *EBAR* EN4 34 A2
Monks Hill Sports Centre *SAND/SEL* CR2 213 F5
Monks Orchard Primary School *CROY/NA* CR0 198 A2
The Montague on The Gardens Hotel *RSQ* WC1B 10 E1
Montbelle Primary School *ELTH/MOT* SE9 167 F6
The Montcalm Hotel *MBLAR* W1H 9 F4
Monteagle Primary School *DAGW* RM9 91 H6
Montem Primary School *HOLWY* N7 85 F1
Montpelier Primary School *EA* W5 97 K4
Monument ⊖ *MANHO* EC4N 13 F5
The Monument *CANST* EC4R 13 F5
Moore Place Golf Club *ESH/CLAY* KT10 204 A3
Moorfields Eye Hospital *FSBYE* EC1V 6 E5
Moorgate ⇌ ⊖ *BARB* EC2Y 12 E2
Moor Lane Junior School *CHSGTN* KT9 206 B3
Moor Park ⊖ *NTHWD* HA6 26 B5
Moor Park Industrial Estate *WATW* WD18 26 A2
Mora Primary School *CRICK* NW2 82 A2
Morasha Jewish Primary School *FNCH* N3 47 F2
Morden ⊖ *WIM/MER* SW19 178 A6
Morden Cemetery *MRDN* SM4 193 F3
Morden College Homes *BKHTH/KID* SE3 145 K3
Morden First School *MRDN* SM4 193 K2
Morden Hall Medical Centre *WIM/MER* SW19 178 A6
Morden Hall Park (NT) *MRDN* SM4 194 B1
Morden Mount Primary School *LEW* SE13 144 E3
Morden Park Pool *MRDN* SM4 193 J2
Morden Road ⊖ *WIM/MER* SW19 178 A5
Morden Road Clinic *WIM/MER* SW19 178 A6
Morden South ⇌ *MRDN* SM4 193 K2
Moreland Primary School *FSBYE* EC1V 6 B4
Moriah Jewish Day School *PIN* HA5 59 J5
Morley College *STHWK* SE1 17 K4
Morningside Primary School *HOM* E9 86 E4
Mornington Crescent ⊖ *CAMTN* NW1 4 A2
Mornington Sports & Fitness Centre *CAMTN* NW1 84 B6
Morpeth School *BETH* E2 104 E2
Mortimer Road Clinic *WLSDN* NW10 100 A2
Mortimer School *STRHM/NOR* SW16 161 J4
Mortlake ⇌ *MORT/ESHN* SW14 137 K4
Mortlake Cemetery *MORT/ESHN* SW14 138 B4
Mortlake Crematorium *RCH/KEW* TW9 137 J3
Moselle School *TOTM* N17 50 A5
Moselle Special School *TOTM* N17 49 K5
Mosiah Foundation Supplementary School *STNW/STAM* N16 68 A5
Mossbourne Community Academy *HACK* E8 86 C2
Mossford Green Primary School *BARK/HLT* IG6 54 C5
The Mother & Baby Clinic *HOM* E9 86 E4
Motspur Park ⇌ *NWMAL* KT3 192 E2
Mottingham ⇌ *ELTH/MOT* SE9 166 E3
Mottingham Community Health Clinic *ELTH/MOT* SE9 166 D6
Mottingham Primary School *ELTH/MOT* SE9 166 E5
Mount Carmel RC Primary School *EA* W5 116 D3
Mount Carmel RC Technical College for Girls *ARCH* N19 66 D5
Mount Medical Centre *FELT* TW13 154 D4
Mount School *MLHL* NW7 45 K1
Mount Stewart Infant School *KTN/HRWW/WS* HA3 61 K3
The Movieum of London *STHWK* SE1 17 G2
Mowlem Primary School *BETH* E2 104 E1
Mowlem Trading Estate *TOTM* N17 50 E3
MPR Eurotots School *KIL/WHAMP* NW6 82 B5
MS Business Centre *PIN* HA5 41 H6
MSP Business Centre *WBLY* HA9 80 D2
Mudchute ⊖ *POP/IOD* E14 124 E4
Mudchute City Farm *POP/IOD* E14 125 F4
Mudlands Estate *RAIN* RM13 111 G2
Mulberry Business Centre *BERM/RHTH* SE16 124 A2
Mulberry House School *CRICK* NW2 82 C3
Mulberry Primary School *TOTM* N17 50 B5
Mulberry School for Girls *WCHPL* E1 104 D5
Mulgrave Primary School *WOOL/PLUM* SE18 127 F4
Munroe Centre *STHWK* SE1 19 F2
Murky Puddle Theatre *NWMAL* KT3 176 C6
Murray Business Centre *STMC/STPC* BR5 186 C6
Muschamp Primary School *CAR* SM5 194 D6
Museum of Brands, Packaging & Advertising *NTGHL* W11 100 D5
Museum of Domestic Design & Architecture *EBAR* EN4 21 K6
Museum of Fulham Palace *FUL/PGN* SW6 139 G3
Museum of London *BARB* EC2Y 12 C2
Museum of London Archaeology *IS* N1 6 D1
Museum of London Docklands *POP/IOD* E14 105 J6
Museum of Richmond *TWK* TW1 136 E6
Museum of The Artillery in The Rotunda *CHARL* SE7 126 D5
Museum of The Order of St John *FARR* EC1M 6 B7
Musical Museum *BTFD* TW8 117 F6
Mustard School *IS* N1 7 H2
Muswell Hill Bowling Club *MUSWH* N10 48 A6
Muswell Hill Golf Club *MUSWH* N10 48 B4
Muswell Hill Primary School *MUSWH* N10 48 B6
Myatt Garden Primary School *BROCKY* SE4 144 C3
Myatts Field Clinic *BRXN/ST* SW9 142 C2
N1 Shopping Centre *IS* N1 5 K2
Nagi Business Centre *ALP/SUD* HA0 97 K1
Nags Head Shopping Centre *HOLWY* N7 84 E1
Naima Jewish Preparatory School *KIL/WHAMP* NW6 101 F1
Nancy Reuben Primary School *HDN* NW4 64 B1
Nash College of Further Education *WWKM* BR4 214 D1
The National Archives *RCH/KEW* TW9 137 H1
National Army Museum *CHEL* SW3 120 E6
National Gallery *LSQ/SEVD* WC2H 10 D6
National Hospital for Neurology & Neurosurgery *RSQ* WC1B 4 E7
National Maritime Museum *GNWCH* SE10 125 G6
National Physical Laboratory *TEDD* TW11 173 K2
National Portrait Gallery *LSQ/SEVD* WC2H 10 D6
National Sports Centre *NRWD* SE19 181 H2
National Temperance Hospital *CAMTN* NW1 4 A4
National Tennis Centre *PUT/ROE* SW15 138 B6
National Youth Theatre Great Britain *HOLWY* N7 84 E1
The Natural History Museum *SKENS* SW7 14 A5
Natural Therapy Clinic *TOOT* SW17 179 G1
Natwest Sports Club *BECK* BR3 182 C2
Neasden ⊖ *WLSDN* NW10 81 G3
Negus Sixth Form Centre *WOOL/PLUM* SE18 127 J6
Nelson Dock Museum *BERM/RHTH* SE16 124 C1
Nelson Hospital *RYNPK* SW20 177 J5
Nelson Primary School *EHAM* E6 108 A1
WHTN TW2 155 G1
Nelson's Column *STJS* SW1Y 10 D7
Nelson Trading Estate *WIM/MER* SW19 178 A4
Neo Clinic *PIM* SW1V 16 A6
The New Ambassadors Theatre *LSQ/SEVD* WC2H 10 D4
New Atlas Wharf *POP/IOD* E14 124 C3
The New Aylesbury Medical Centre *WALW* SE17 122 E5
New Barnet ⇌ *BAR* EN5 21 G6
New Beckenham ⇌ *BECK* BR3 182 B3
New Brentford Cemetery *HSLW* TW3 134 E3
Newbridge School *CHDH* RM6 73 H2
IL IG1 90 E2
Newbury Park ⊖ *GNTH/NBYPK* IG2 72 D3
Newbury Park Health Centre *GNTH/NBYPK* IG2 72 D3
The New Business Centre *WLSDN* NW10 99 H2
New Caledonian Wharf *BERM/RHTH* SE16 124 C3
New Chiswick Pool *CHSWK* W4 138 B1
New City Primary School *PLSTW* E13 107 G2
New Connaught Rooms *HOL/ALD* WC2B 11 F4
New Covent Garden Market *VX/NE* SW8 141 J1
New Crane Wharf *WAP* E1W 123 K1
New Cross ⇌ ⊖ *NWCR* SE14 144 C1
New Cross Gate ⇌ ⊖ *NWCR* SE14 144 B1
New Cross Sports Arena *NWCR* SE14 144 B1
New Eltham ⇌ *ELTH/MOT* SE9 167 G3
New End Primary School *HAMP* NW3 83 G2
New End Theatre *HAMP* NW3 83 G1
New England Industrial Estate *BARK* IG11 108 C1
Newfield Primary School *WLSDN* NW10 81 H5
Newham College of Further Education *EHAM* E6 107 K1
SRTFD E15 88 C5
Newham General Hospital *PLSTW* E13 107 G3
Newham Leisure Centre *PLSTW* E13 107 G4
Newham Medical Centre *PLSTW* E13 107 G1
Newham Sixth Form College *PLSTW* E13 107 F3
Newham Training & Education Centre *SRTFD* E15 88 C4
New Health Centre *TOTM* N17 50 A4
New Hope Christian School *EDUL* SE22 143 G5
New Horizons Computer Learning Centre *FSBYE* EC1V 6 E5
Newington Court Business Centre *STHWK* SE1 18 C5
Newington Green Primary School *STNW/STAM* N16 86 A3
Newington Industrial Estate *WALW* SE17 18 B7
New Kings Primary School *FUL/PGN* SW6 139 J3
Newland House School *TWK* TW1 156 A6
New London Theatre *LSQ/SEVD* WC2H 11 F3
New Malden ⇌ *NWMAL* KT3 176 B6
Newman Catholic College *WLSDN* NW10 81 J6
Newnham Junior School *RSLP* HA4 59 G5
New North Community School *IS* N1 85 J5
Newport School *LEY* E10 70 A6
New River College *ARCH* N19 66 D6
New River Sports Centre *WDGN* N22 49 H3
New River Village *CEND/HSY/T* N8 49 F6
New Rush Hall School *IL* IG1 72 C6
New School *FUL/PGN* SW6 139 J2
New Scotland Yard *STJSPK* SW1H 16 C4
News International *WAP* E1W 104 D6
New Southgate ⇌ *FBAR/BDGN* N11 48 A1
New Southgate Cemetery *FBAR/BDGN* N11 34 B5
New Southgate Crematorium *FBAR/BDGN* N11 34 B5
New Southgate Industrial Estate *FBAR/BDGN* N11 48 C1
New Southgate Pain Clinic & Medical Centre *FBAR/BDGN* N11 48 C1
New Spitalfields Market *LEY* E10 87 J2
Newstead Wood School for Girls *ORP* BR6 216 D1
Newton Farm J & I School *RYLN/HDSTN* HA2 59 K6
Newton Industrial Estate *CHDH* RM6 73 K1
Newton Medical Centre *BAY/PAD* W2 101 F5
Newton Preparatory School *VX/NE* SW8 141 G1
Newtons Primary School *RAIN* RM13 111 F1
New Victoria Hospital *KUTN/CMB* KT2 176 B4
New Woodlands School *BMLY* BR1 165 H6

Nightingale Academy
ED N9 36 E2
Nightingale Clinic
PLSTW E13 107 G1
Nightingale Primary School
CLPT E5 86 C1
SWFD E18 71 G1
WDGN N22 49 F4
WOOL/PLUM SE18 127 G6
Nightingale School
TOOT SW17 160 D4
No1 Poultry
MANHO EC4N 12 D4
Noel Coward Theatre
CHCR WC2N 10 E5
Noel Park Primary School
WDGN N22 49 H5
Nonsuch High School for Girls
CHEAM SM3 208 B5
Nonsuch Primary School
EW KT17 207 K3
Noor Ul Islam Primary School
LEY E10 70 A6
Norbiton ⇌
KUTN/CMB KT2 175 H4
Norbury ⇌
STRHM/NOR SW16 180 A4
Norbury Complementary Therapy Clinic
STRHM/NOR SW16 180 A4
Norbury First & Middle School
HRW HA1 60 E2
Norbury Health Centre
STRHM/NOR SW16 180 A5
Norbury Manor Business & Enterprise College for Girls
STRHM/NOR SW16 180 B4
Norbury Manor Primary School
STRHM/NOR SW16 179 K4
Norbury Trading Estate
STRHM/NOR SW16 180 A5
Norfolk House School
MUSWH N10 48 B5
Norland Place School
NTGHL W11 119 H1
Norlington School
LEY E10 70 B5
Normanby College
CMBW SE5 142 D3
Normand Croft Community School
WKENS W14 119 J6
Normandy Primary School
BXLYHN DA7 150 A2
Normanhurst School
CHING E4 38 B2
Norman Park Athletics Track
HAYES BR2 200 A3
Norman Shaw Building (MP's Offices)
WHALL SW1A 16 E2
North Acton ⊖
WLSDN NW10 99 F3
North Acton Business Park
ACT W3 99 F5
North Beckton Primary School
EHAM E6 107 K3
North Bridge House Junior School
HAMP NW3 83 G4
North Bridge House Preparatory School
CAMTN NW1 3 J1
North Bridge House School
HAMP NW3 83 H4
Northbury Primary School
BARK IG11 90 B4
North Clinic
BMLY BR1 183 K4
Northcote Lodge School
BTSEA SW11 160 E1
North Croydon Medical Centre
THHTH CR7 196 C3
North Dulwich ⇌
HNHL SE24 142 E6
North Ealing ⊖
ACT W3 98 B5
North Ealing Primary School
WEA W13 97 H3
North East Surrey Crematorium
NWMAL KT3 193 F3
North End Trading Estate
ERITH DA8 150 B1
Northern Spectator Transport Mall
OLYMPICPK E20 87 J2
North Feltham Trading Estate
EBED/NFELT TW14 134 A5
Northfields ⊖
WEA W13 116 D3
Northfields Industrial Estate
ALP/SUD HA0 80 C6
Northfields Prospect Business Centre
PUT/ROE SW15 139 J5
Northgate Business Centre
EN EN1 24 D4
Northgate Clinic
CDALE/KGS NW9 63 G3
Northgate Industrial Park
CRW RM5 56 B5
North Greenwich ⊖
GNWCH SE10 125 H2
North Greenwich Arena
GNWCH E14 125 H1
North Greenwich Pier
GNWCH E14 125 J1
North Harringay Primary School
CEND/HSY/T N8 67 G1
North Harrow ⊖
RYLN/HDSTN HA2 60 A2
North Havering College of Adult Education
ROM RM1 75 G1
North Kensington Video-Drama Project
NKENS W10 100 C5
North London College
SEVS/STOTM N15 50 B6
North London Collegiate School
EDGW HA8 44 A2
The North London Hospice
NFNCH/WDSPK N12 33 F5
North London International School
FBAR/BDGN N11 47 K1
NFNCH/WDSPK N12 47 F1
North London International School (Diploma Centre)
NFNCH/WDSPK N12 47 J1
North London International School (Lower School)
NFNCH/WDSPK N12 33 F5
North London Nuffield Hospital
ENC/FH EN2 23 G3
North London School of Physiotherapy
ARCH N19 66 C5
North London Tutorial College
HDN NW4 64 A3
North Middlesex Golf Club
NFNCH/WDSPK N12 33 H5
North Middlesex Hospital
UED N18 50 A1
Northolt ⊖
NTHLT UB5 78 A5
Northolt Aerodrome
RSLP HA4 76 E4
Northolt High School
NTHLT UB5 77 K4
Northolt Park ⇌
RYLN/HDSTN HA2 78 B2
Northolt Road Clinic
RYLN/HDSTN HA2 78 C1
Northolt Swimarama
NTHLT UB5 78 A4
North Pole Depot
WLSDN NW10 99 H3
North Primary School
STHL UB1 95 K6
North Sheen ⇌
RCH/KEW TW9 137 H5
Northside Primary School
NFNCH/WDSPK N12 47 G1
The North Street Health Centre
CLAP SW4 141 H4
Northumberland Heath Medical Centre
ERITH DA8 150 A1
Northumberland Heath Primary
ERITH DA8 149 J1
Northumberland Park ⇌
TOTM N17 50 D4
Northumberland Park Community School
TOTM N17 50 C3
Northumberland Park Industrial Estate
TOTM N17 50 D2
Northview Primary School
WLSDN NW10 81 G2
Northway School
MLHL NW7 31 F4
North Wembley ⊖ ⊖
ALP/SUD HA0 79 K1
North West Kent Behaviour Service
RDART DA2 171 F5
North West Kent College
RDART DA2 170 E4
North West London Jewish Day School
CRICK NW2 82 C5
North West London Medical Centre
MV/WKIL W9 101 G2
North Westminster Community Secondary School
MV/WKIL W9 100 E3
North Weylands Industrial Estate
WOT/HER KT12 188 D6
Northwick Park ⊖
KTN/HRWW/WS HA3 61 H4
Northwick Park Hospital & Clinical Research Centre
HRW HA1 61 H4
Northwold Primary School
CLPT E5 68 C6
Northwood ⊖
NTHWD HA6 40 C3
Northwood Cemetery
NTHWD HA6 40 D5
Northwood College
NTHWD HA6 40 B3
Northwood FC
NTHWD HA6 40 D5
Northwood Golf Club
NTHWD HA6 40 B3
Northwood Hills ⊖
NTHWD HA6 40 E5
Northwood & Pinner Community Hospital
NTHWD HA6 40 E4
Northwood Preparatory School
RKW/CH/CXG WD3 26 A4
Northwood Primary School
ERITHM DA18 129 F3
Northwood School
NTHWD HA6 41 F4
Northwood Sports Centre
NTHWD HA6 41 F4
Norwegian/British Monument
BAY/PAD W2 8 C7
The Norwegian School
WIM/MER SW19 177 F3
Norwood Green Infant School
NWDGN UB2 114 D5
Norwood Green Junior School
NWDGN UB2 114 D5
Norwood Heights Shopping Centre
NRWD SE19 181 F2
Norwood Junction ⇌ ⊖
SNWD SE25 197 H1
Norwood School
NRWD SE19 180 D1
Notre Dame RC Girls School
STHWK SE1 18 A4
Notre Dame RC Primary School
WOOL/PLUM SE18 127 G6
Notre Dame University
LSQ/SEVD WC2H 10 D6
Notting Hill & Ealing High School
WEA W13 97 H4
Notting Hill Gate ⊖
BAY/PAD W2 119 K1
Novello Theatre
HOL/ALD WC2B 11 G5
Novotel
BAY/PAD W2 101 G4
CAMTN NW1 4 D4
CAN/RD E16 107 F6
GNWCH SE10 144 E1
STHWK SE1 17 G6
WDR/YW UB7 112 D4
Novotel London West
HMSMTH W6 119 G5
Nower Hill High School
PIN HA5 60 A1
NTGB Sports Ground
EHAM E6 90 A4
Nugent Shopping Park
STMC/STPC BR5 202 C1
Number 10 Bowling
ROM RM1 75 G2
Nunhead ⇌
PECK SE15 143 K4
Nutrilife Clinic
MHST W1U 9 G1
The O_2
POP/IOD E14 125 G1
Oakdale Infant School
SWFD E18 53 F5
Oakdale Junior School
SWFD E18 53 G5
Oakfield Community Primary School
DART DA1 171 G4
Oakfield Preparatory School
DUL SE21 162 E4
Oakfield Road Industrial Estate
PGE/AN SE20 181 J3
Oak Heights Independent School
HSLW TW3 135 G4
Oak Hill Health Centre
SURB KT6 191 F3
Oak Hill Theological College
STHGT/OAK N14 34 A1
Oakington Manor School
WBLY HA9 80 D3
Oakland CP School
EBAR EN4 33 K1
Oaklands Primary School
HNWL W7 116 A2
Oaklands School
ISLW TW7 135 J4
Oaklands Secondary School
BETH E2 104 C2
Oak Lane Cemetery
TWK TW1 156 B2
Oak Lane Medical Centre
TWK TW1 156 C2
Oak Lee Montessori School
PIN HA5 41 H6
Oakleigh Park ⇌
TRDG/WHET N20 33 H2
Oakleigh School
TRDG/WHET N20 33 J5
Oak Lodge JMI School
WWKM BR4 198 E4
Oak Lodge Medical Centre
EDGW HA8 44 D3
Oak Lodge School
BAL SW12 160 E2
EFNCH N2 47 G6
Oaks Park High School
GNTH/NBYPK IG2 72 D2
Oakthorpe Primary School
UED N18 49 J1
Oak Tree Medical Centre
GDMY/SEVK IG3 72 E6
Oakwood ⊖
STHGT/OAK N14 22 C5
Oakwood Business Park
WLSDN NW10 99 F2
Oakwood Medical Centre
STHGT/OAK N14 22 C6
Oakwood School
BXLYHN DA7 150 A5
Oasis Academy Hadley
PEND EN3 25 F1
Oasis Academy Shirley Park
CROY/NA CR0 197 J3
Oasis Sports Centre
LSQ/SEVD WC2H 10 E3
Odeon
KENS W8 119 K3
Odeon Cinema
BAR EN5 20 E6
BAY/PAD W2 8 E4
BECK BR3 182 D5
BERM/RHTH SE16 124 A3
CAMTN NW1 84 B6
ED N9 37 F2
ELTH/MOT SE9 146 D5
ESH/CLAY KT10 204 B2
FITZ W1T 10 C2
HAMP NW3 83 H5
HAYES BR2 183 K5
HOLWY N7 84 E1
KUT/HW KT1 175 F5
MUSWH N10 66 A1
RCH/KEW TW9 136 E6
ROM RM1 75 H2
STJS SW1Y 10 C6
STRHM/NOR SW16 161 K5
SWFD E18 52 E5
WIM/MER SW19 177 K3
Odeon Covent Garden Cinema
LSQ/SEVD WC2H 10 D4
Odeon Wardour Street Cinema
SOHO/SHAV W1D 10 C5
Odessa Infant School
FSTGT E7 88 E3
Odyssey Business Park
RSLP HA4 77 F3
Old Abbotstonians RFC
YEAD UB4 94 B1
Old Actonians Sports Club
EA W5 117 G2
Old Admiralty
STJS SW1Y 16 D1
Old Bancroftians FC
BKHH IG9 39 H6
Old Barnes Cemetery
BARN SW13 138 E3
Old Beckenhamian RFC
WWKM BR4 214 B1
Old Bellgate Wharf
POP/IOD E14 124 C3
Old Bexley Business Park
BXLY DA5 169 J2
Old Bexley CE Primary School
BXLY DA5 169 G3
Old Brockleians Sports Ground
LEE/GVPK SE12 166 B1
Old Bromlians CC
HAYES BR2 200 A2
Old Cemetery
EDUL SE22 163 J1
Old Colfeian Sports Club
LEE/GVPK SE12 145 K6
Old Curiosity Shop
LINN WC2A 11 G3
Old Elthamians Sports Club
CHST BR7 185 K2
Oldfield House Special School
HPTN TW12 172 E4
Oldfield Primary School
GFD/PVL UB6 96 D1
Oldfields Trading Estate
SUT SM1 208 E1
Old Fold Manor Golf Club
BAR EN5 20 C2
Old Ford Primary School
BOW E3 105 H1
Oldhill Medical Centre
STNW/STAM N16 68 B5
Old Jamaica Business Estate
BERM/RHTH SE16 19 K4
Old Lyonian Sports Ground
RYLN/HDSTN HA2 60 C2
Old Millhillians Sports Ground
RYLN/HDSTN HA2 42 A4
Old Oak Primary School
SHB W12 99 H5
Old Operating Theatre & Herb Garret Museum
STHWK SE1 18 E1
Old Owens Sports Ground
TRDG/WHET N20 33 H3
Old Palace Primary School
BOW E3 105 K2
Old Palace School
CROY/NA CR0 211 H1
Old Palace School of John Whitgift Junior Site
SAND/SEL CR2 212 B4
Old Royal Naval College
GNWCH SE10 125 G5
Old Royal Observatory Greenwich
GNWCH SE10 145 G1
Old Spitalfields Market Hall
WCHPL E1 13 J1
Old Street ⇌ ⊖
FSBYE EC1V 6 E5
Old Sun Wharf
POP/IOD E14 105 G6
Old Tiffinians Sports Ground
E/WMO/HCT KT8 189 K2
Old Treasury
WHALL SW1A 16 E2
Old Vicarage School
RCHPK/HAM TW10 157 F1
Old Vic Theatre
STHWK SE1 17 K2
Old War Office
WHALL SW1A 16 E1
Old Wilsonians Sports Club
WWKM BR4 199 H5
Olga Primary School
BOW E3 105 G1
Oliver Business Park
WLSDN NW10 98 E1
Oliver Goldsmith Primary School
CDALE/KGS NW9 63 F2
CMBW SE5 143 G2
Oliver House Preparatory School
CLAP SW4 161 G1
Olympia
WKENS W14 119 H3
Olympia Industrial Estate
WDGN N22 49 F5
Olympic Industrial Estate
WBLY HA9 80 D2
Olympic Park
OLYMPICPK E20 87 J5
Olympic Retail Park
WBLY HA9 80 C2
Olympic Stadium
OLYMPICPK E20 87 K5
Olympic Trading Estate
WBLY HA9 80 D2
One Aldwych Hotel
COVGDN WC2E 11 G5
One New Change
CITYW EC2V 12 C4
The One Stanley Medical Centre
ALP/SUD HA0 80 A5
On Sai Clinic
ECT SW5 120 A4
The Open University
FSBYW WC1X 5 G4
HAMP NW3 82 E2
Ophaboom Theatre
WLSDN NW10 99 K1
Optimax Laser Eye Clinic
HAMP NW3 83 G4
Orange Tree Theatre
RCH/KEW TW9 137 F5
Oratory RC Primary School
CHEL SW3 120 D5
The Orbit Tower
OLYMPICPK E20 87 K5
Orchard Business Centre
BECK BR3 182 C1
The Orchard Health Centre
BARK IG11 108 C1
Orchard Hill College
WLGTN SM6 210 B4
Orchard House School
CHSWK W4 118 A4
Orchard J & I School
HOM E9 86 E5
The Orchard Junior School
HSLWW TW4 135 F5
Orchard Primary School
SCUP DA14 186 C1
The Orchard School
BRXS/STRHM SW2 162 A3
E/WMO/HCT KT8 189 J2
Orchard Shopping Centre
DART DA1 171 H1
The Orchard Theatre
DART DA1 171 H1
Orchard Way Primary School
CROY/NA CR0 198 B4
Oriel Primary School
FELT TW13 154 D5
Orient Industrial Park
LEY E10 69 J6
Orion Business Centre
NWCR SE14 124 A5
The Orion Primary School
CDALE/KGS NW9 45 G4
Orleans House Gallery
TWK TW1 156 C3
Orleans Infant School
TWK TW1 156 C2
Orley Farm School
HRW HA1 78 D1
Orpington ⇌
ORP BR6 201 K6
Orpington College of Further Education
ORP BR6 202 B5
The Orpington Halls
ORP BR6 202 B6
Orpington Hospital
ORP BR6 217 F2
Orpington Mental Health Centre
ORP BR6 217 F1
Orpington Priory
ORP BR6 202 C4
Orpington Retail Park
STMC/STPC BR5 202 D1
Orpington Superbowl
ORP BR6 202 B5
Orpington Trade Centre
STMC/STPC BR5 186 C6
Osidge JMI School
STHGT/OAK N14 34 C3
Osier Industrial Estate
WAND/EARL SW18 139 K5
Osmani Primary School
WCHPL E1 104 C4
Osterley ⊖
ISLW TW7 135 J1
Osterley Park & House (NT)
ISLW TW7 115 H6
Osterley RFC
NWDGN UB2 115 G3
Our Lady Immaculate RC Primary School
BRYLDS KT5 191 J5
Our Lady of Dolours RC Primary School
BAY/PAD W2 101 F4
Our Lady of Grace RC Junior School
CRICK NW2 81 K1
Our Lady of Grace RC Primary School
CHARL SE7 126 A6
Our Lady of Lourdes RC Primary
FBAR/BDGN N11 48 B1
NFNCH/WDSPK N12 47 G3
Our Lady of Lourdes RC Primary School
WAN E11 70 D3
WLSDN NW10 80 E6
Our Lady of Muswell RC Primary
MUSWH N10 48 A5
Our Lady of The Rosary RC Primary School
ELTH/MOT SE9 167 K1
Our Lady of The Sacred Heart School
HOLWY N7 85 F3
Our Lady of The Visitation RC Combined Primary School
GFD/PVL UB6 96 C3
Our Lady of Victories RC Primary School
PUT/ROE SW15 139 G5
SKENS SW7 120 B4
Our Lady Queen of Heaven RC Primary School
PUT/ROE SW15 159 G2
Our Lady RC Primary School
POP/IOD E14 105 H5
Our Lady & St Georges Catholic Primary School
WALTH E17 51 K6

WALTH E17 ... 70 A1
Our Lady & St Johns RC Primary School
BTFD TW8 ... 116 D5
Our Lady & St Joseph Primary School
IS N1 ... 86 A4
Our Lady & St Philip Neri RC Infant School
FSTH SE23 ... 164 A5
Our Lady & St Philip Neri RC Primary School
SYD SE26 ... 164 B6
Our Ladys Catholic Primary School
DART DA1 ... 171 G1
Our Ladys Convent High School
CLPT E5 ... 68 D5
Our Ladys RC Primary School
CAMTN NW1 ... 84 C6
Oval ⊖
LBTH SE11 ... 122 B6
Oval Business Centre
LBTH SE11 ... 122 A5
Oval House Theatre
LBTH SE11 ... 122 B6
Oval Primary School
CROY/NA CR0 ... 197 F5
Overton Grange School
BELMT SM2 ... 209 F6
Oxford Circus ⊖
REGST W1B ... 9 K3
Oxford Gardens Primary School
NKENS W10 ... 100 B5
Oxford House College
SOHO/SHAV W1D ... 10 C3
Oxhey Park Golf Centre
OXHEY WD19 ... 27 H3
Oxhey Wood Primary School
OXHEY WD19 ... 27 G6
Oxo Tower Wharf
STHWK SE1 ... 11 K6
Paddington ⇌ ⊖
BAY/PAD W2 ... 8 A3
Paddington Academy
MV/WKIL W9 ... 100 E3
Paddington Bowling & Sports Club
MV/WKIL W9 ... 101 F3
Paddington Green Primary School
BAY/PAD W2 ... 2 A7
Paddington Recreation Ground Athletics Track
MV/WKIL W9 ... 100 E2
Paddock Primary School
BTSEA SW11 ... 141 F5
Paddock School
PUT/ROE SW15 ... 138 C5
Paines Lane Cemetery
PIN HA5 ... 41 J6
Pain Relief Clinic
HDN NW4 ... 63 K3
Paint Pots Montessori School
WBPTN SW10 ... 120 B6
Pakeman Primary School
HOLWY N7 ... 85 F1
Palace Gardens Shopping Centre
ENC/FH EN2 ... 23 K4
Palace of Westminster
WHALL SW1A ... 17 F3
Palace Theatre
SOHO/SHAV W1D ... 10 D5
Palladium Theatre
SOHO/CST W1F ... 10 A4
Palmers Green ⇌
PLMGR N13 ... 35 F6
Palmers Green High School
WCHMH N21 ... 35 G4
Palmerston Business Centre
SUT SM1 ... 209 G3
Palm House, Kew Gardens
RCH/KEW TW9 ... 137 G2
Panorama Pier
STHWK SE1 ... 12 C6
Paradise Swimming Pools
MLHL NW7 ... 45 G1
Paragon Christian Academy
CLPT E5 ... 87 F2
Paray House School
FUL/PGN SW6 ... 139 J3
Parayhouse School
WBPTN SW10 ... 140 B1
Parchmore Medical Centre
THHTH CR7 ... 180 D6
Pardes House & Beis Yaakov School
FNCH N3 ... 46 D5
Parent Infant Clinic
HAMP NW3 ... 83 G3
Parish CE Primary School
BMLY BR1 ... 183 K3
Park Business Centre
MV/WKIL W9 ... 100 E2
Parkfield Industrial Estate
BTSEA SW11 ... 141 F3
Parkfield JMI School
HDN NW4 ... 63 K4
Parkgate House School
CLAP SW4 ... 141 F5
Park Hall Trading Estate
WNWD SE27 ... 162 D5
Park High School
STAN HA7 ... 43 K5
Park Hill Junior School
CROY/NA CR0 ... 211 K1
Parkhill Primary School
CLAY IG5 ... 53 K6
Park Hill School
KUTN/CMB KT2 ... 175 H3
Park House Medical Centre
KIL/WHAMP NW6 ... 100 C1
Park House RFC
HAYES BR2 ... 200 B6
Park Inn
WDR/YW UB7 ... 132 E1
Parklands Primary School
ROM RM1 ... 57 F6
Park Lane Primary School
WBLY HA9 ... 80 A2
Park Medical Centre
BERM/RHTH SE16 ... 124 A4
Park Mews Small Business Centre
HNHL SE24 ... 162 D1
Park Plaza Hotel
PIM SW1V ... 16 A6
STHWK SE1 ... 17 G7
STHWK SE1 ... 17 H2
Park Primary School
SRTFD E15 ... 88 D5
Park Road Clinic
CEND/HSY/T N8 ... 66 D2
Park Road Swimming Centre
CEND/HSY/T N8 ... 66 D2
Park Royal ⊖
EA W5 ... 98 C3
Park Royal Business Centre
WLSDN NW10 ... 99 F3
Park School for Girls
IL IG1 ... 72 A6
Parkside Business Estate
DEPT SE8 ... 124 C6
Parkside Clinic
NTGHL W11 ... 100 C5
Parkside Health
NTGHL W11 ... 100 C5
Parkside Hospital
WIM/MER SW19 ... 159 G5
Park View School
SEVS/STOTM N15 ... 67 J1
Park Walk Primary School
WBPTN SW10 ... 120 C6
Parkway Primary School
ERITHM DA18 ... 129 F3
Parkway Trading Estate
HEST TW5 ... 114 B6
Parkwood Primary School
FSBYPK N4 ... 67 H6
Parliament Hill Fields Athletics Track
HAMP NW3 ... 83 K2
Parliament Hill Lido
HAMP NW3 ... 84 A2
Parliament Hill School
KTTN NW5 ... 84 A2
Parmiter Industrial Centre
BETH E2 ... 104 D1
Parnells Sports Ground
KTN/HRWW/WS HA3 ... 62 B3
Parsloes Primary School
DAGW RM9 ... 92 B4
Parsons Green ⊖
FUL/PGN SW6 ... 139 K2
Parsons Green Health Clinic
FUL/PGN SW6 ... 139 K2
Pascals College
BECK BR3 ... 182 D5
Passport Language Schools
BMLY BR1 ... 184 A4
Pastoria Hotel
LSQ/SEVD WC2H ... 10 D6
Patent Office
FLST/FETLN EC4A ... 11 J2
The Patrick Doody Clinic & Health Centre
WIM/MER SW19 ... 177 K3
Pattinson Clinic
RCH/KEW TW9 ... 136 E6
The Paul Robeson Theatre
HSLW TW3 ... 135 G4
Pavilion Barclays Sports Ground
EA W5 ... 98 A4
The Pavilion Leisure Centre
BMLY BR1 ... 183 K5
Pavilion Restaurant
RCH/KEW TW9 ... 137 F3
Paxton Primary School
NRWD SE19 ... 181 G2
PCMS London
SRTFD E15 ... 106 B1
PDSA Hospital
REDBR IG4 ... 53 H6
Peace Pagoda
CHEL SW3 ... 140 E1
Peacock Estate
TOTM N17 ... 50 B2
Peacock Industrial Estate
TOTM N17 ... 50 B3
The Peacock Theatre
HOL/ALD WC2B ... 11 G4
Peall Road Industrial Estate
CROY/NA CR0 ... 196 A3
Peareswood Primary School
ERITH DA8 ... 150 C2
Peckham Park Primary School
PECK SE15 ... 143 H1
The Peckham Pulse Health & Leisure Centre
PECK SE15 ... 143 H2
Peckham Rye ⇌ ⊖
PECK SE15 ... 143 H3
Pelham Primary School
BXLYHN DA7 ... 149 H4
WIM/MER SW19 ... 177 K3
Pembridge Hall Preparatory School for Girls
BAY/PAD W2 ... 100 E6
Pendragon School
BMLY BR1 ... 165 K5
Penge East ⇌
SYD SE26 ... 181 K2
Penge West ⇌ ⊖
PGE/AN SE20 ... 181 J3
Pentavia Retail Park
MLHL NW7 ... 45 H3
Penwortham Primary School
STRHM/NOR SW16 ... 179 G2
Percival David Foundation of Chinese Art
STPAN WC1H ... 4 D6
Perivale ⊖
GFD/PVL UB6 ... 97 G1
Perivale Industrial Park
GFD/PVL UB6 ... 79 G6
GFD/PVL UB6 ... 97 G1
Perivale New Business Centre
GFD/PVL UB6 ... 97 J1
Perivale Park Athletics Track
GFD/PVL UB6 ... 96 E2
Perivale Park Golf Course
GFD/PVL UB6 ... 96 E2
Perrin Road Clinic
ALP/SUD HA0 ... 79 H2
Perry Hall Primary School
ORP BR6 ... 202 A3
Perrymount Primary School
FSTH SE23 ... 164 A4
The Petchy Academy
HACK E8 ... 86 B3
Peterborough & St Margarets High School
STAN HA7 ... 28 E5
Peter Hills School
BERM/RHTH SE16 ... 124 A1
Peter James Business Centre
HYS/HAR UB3 ... 113 K2
Peterley Business Centre
BETH E2 ... 104 D1
Peter Pan Statue
BAY/PAD W2 ... 8 A7
The Petersham Hotel
RCHPK/HAM TW10 ... 157 F2
Petrie Museum of Egyptian Archaeology
FITZ W1T ... 4 B7
Petts Hill Primary School
NTHLT UB5 ... 78 B3
Petts Wood ⇌
STMC/STPC BR5 ... 201 H2
Pewterers' Hall
CITYW EC2V ... 12 D2
Pheasantry Welcome Centre
TEDD TW11 ... 174 A4
Phipps Bridge ⊖
WIM/MER SW19 ... 178 B6
Phoenix Academy
ED N9 ... 36 D3
Phoenix Business Centre
POP/IOD E14 ... 105 J4
Phoenix Cinema
EFNCH N2 ... 65 J1
Phoenix College
MRDN SM4 ... 194 A2
Phoenix High School
SHB W12 ... 99 J6
Phoenix Industrial Estate
HRW HA1 ... 61 F1
Phoenix Leisure Centre
CAT SE6 ... 164 E2
Phoenix Primary School
STHWK SE1 ... 123 H5
Phoenix School
HAMP NW3 ... 83 H4
Phoenix Secondary & Primary School
BOW E3 ... 105 H2
Phoenix Theatre
LSQ/SEVD WC2H ... 10 D4
Phoenix Trading Estate
GFD/PVL UB6 ... 79 J6
Physical Energy Statue
BAY/PAD W2 ... 14 A1
Piccadilly Circus ⊖
MYFR/PICC W1J ... 10 C6
Piccadilly Theatre
SOHO/SHAV W1D ... 10 C5
Pickford Lane Medical Centre
BXLYHN DA7 ... 149 F2
Pickhurst Infant School
WWKM BR4 ... 199 H3
Pickhurst Junior School
WWKM BR4 ... 199 J3
Picture House Cinema
SRTFD E15 ... 88 B4
Pilgrims Way J & I School
PECK SE15 ... 123 K6
Pilot Industrial Centre
WLSDN NW10 ... 99 G3
Pilton Estate
CROY/NA CR0 ... 196 C6
Pimlico ⊖
PIM SW1V ... 121 J5
Pimlico Academy
PIM SW1V ... 121 H5
Pinewood Primary School
CRW RM5 ... 56 D1
Pinkwell Primary School
HYS/HAR UB3 ... 113 F4
Pinnacles Cricket & Squash Club
SUT SM1 ... 208 E4
Pinner ⊖
PIN HA5 ... 59 J1
Pinner Hill Golf Club
PIN HA5 ... 41 F2
Pinner Medical Centre
PIN HA5 ... 59 J1
Pinner New Cemetery
PIN HA5 ... 42 A6
Pinner Park Infant School
PIN HA5 ... 42 B6
Pinner Park Junior School
RYLN/HDSTN HA2 ... 42 B6
Pinner View Medical Centre
HRW HA1 ... 60 C2
Pinner Wood School
PIN HA5 ... 41 G4
Pioneers Industrial Park
CROY/NA CR0 ... 195 K5
Pippins School
ASHF TW15 ... 152 C6
Pitshanger Manor Museum
EA W5 ... 116 D1
Plaisterers Hall
STBT EC1A ... 12 C2
Plaistow ⊖
SRTFD E15 ... 106 D1
Plaistow Hospital
PLSTW E13 ... 107 F1
Plaistow Jamia Islamia School
PLSTW E13 ... 107 F2
Plaistow Primary School
PLSTW E13 ... 89 G6
PLSTW E13 ... 107 F1
Plantation House Medical Centre
LOTH EC2R ... 13 F3
Plashet Jewish Cemetery
MNPK E12 ... 89 H4
Plashet Road Medical Centre
FSTGT E7 ... 89 F5
Plashet School
EHAM E6 ... 89 J5
Players Theatre
CHCR WC2N ... 11 F7
Playgolf Northwick Park
HRW HA1 ... 61 G5
The Playhouse
CHCR WC2N ... 11 F7
Plaza Business Centre
PEND EN3 ... 25 H3
Plaza on the River Hotel
STHWK SE1 ... 17 G7
Pleasance Theatre
HOLWY N7 ... 84 E4
Plumcroft Primary School
WOOL/PLUM SE18 ... 127 H6
Plumstead ⇌
WOOL/PLUM SE18 ... 127 J4
Plumstead Cemetery
ABYW SE2 ... 148 C1
Plumstead Leisure Centre
WOOL/PLUM SE18 ... 128 A5
Plumstead Manor School
WOOL/PLUM SE18 ... 127 J5
The Pointer School
BKHTH/KID SE3 ... 145 K2
Police Cadet School
WAN E11 ... 70 E5
The Polish Institute & Sikorski Museum
SKENS SW7 ... 14 B3
Polish War Memorial
RSLP HA4 ... 77 F4
Polka Theatre for Children
WIM/MER SW19 ... 178 A2
Ponders End ⇌
PEND EN3 ... 25 G6
Ponders End Industrial Estate
PEND EN3 ... 25 H5
Pontoon Dock ⊖
CAN/RD E16 ... 126 B1
Pooles Park Primary School
FSBYPK N4 ... 67 F6
Pools on the Park
RCH/KEW TW9 ... 136 E5
Pope John Primary School
SHB W12 ... 99 K6
Pop In Business Centre
WBLY HA9 ... 80 D3
Poplar ⊖
POP/IOD E14 ... 105 K6
Poplar Business Park
POP/IOD E14 ... 124 D2
Poplar Coroners Court
POP/IOD E14 ... 105 K6
Poplar Primary School
WIM/MER SW19 ... 177 K6
Pop Up Theatre
CLKNW EC1R ... 5 K3
Porchester Leisure Centre
BAY/PAD W2 ... 101 F5
Portcullis House
WHALL SW1A ... 17 F3
Portico City Learning Centre
CLPT E5 ... 86 E2
The Portland Hospital
REGST W1B ... 3 K7
Portland House Medical Centre
GFD/PVL UB6 ... 96 B3
Portland Medical Centre
SNWD SE25 ... 197 J2
Portland Place School
REGST W1B ... 9 K1
The Portman Clinic
HAMP NW3 ... 83 H4
Portobello Market
NKENS W10 ... 100 C4
Portobello Medical Centre
NTGHL W11 ... 100 C5
Portway Primary School
SRTFD E15 ... 88 E6
The Pountney Clinic
HSLW TW3 ... 135 F4
Poverest Primary School Tillingbourne Green
STMC/STPC BR5 ... 202 B2
Powergate Business Park
WLSDN NW10 ... 99 F2
Power Industrial Estate
ERITH DA8 ... 150 C2
Premier Cinema
PECK SE15 ... 143 H3
Premier Inn
BARK IG11 ... 90 B6
Prendergast Hilly Fields College
BROCKY SE4 ... 144 D5
Prendergast Ladywell Fields College
BROCKY SE4 ... 164 D1
Preston Manor School
WBLY HA9 ... 62 B6
Preston Medical Centre
WBLY HA9 ... 80 A1
Preston Park Primary School
WBLY HA9 ... 61 K5
Preston Road ⊖
WBLY HA9 ... 62 A5
Priestmead Primary School
KTN/HRWW/WS HA3 ... 43 H6
Primrose Hill School
CAMTN NW1 ... 84 A6
Primrose Montessori School
HBRY N5 ... 85 J1
Prince Charles Cinema
LSQ/SEVD WC2H ... 10 D5
Prince Edward Theatre
SOHO/SHAV W1D ... 10 C4
Prince of Wales Theatre
STJS SW1Y ... 10 C6
Prince Regent ⊖
CAN/RD E16 ... 107 G6
Princes College
NOXST/BSQ WC1A ... 10 E3
Princes Court Business Centre
WAP E1W ... 104 D6
Princes Park Stadium
DART DA1 ... 171 K3
Princes Plain Primary School
HAYES BR2 ... 200 D4
Princess Avenue School
MUSWH N10 ... 48 B6
Princess Frederica CE J & I School
WLSDN NW10 ... 99 K1
Princess Grace Hospital
MHST W1U ... 3 G7
Princess Louise Hospital
NKENS W10 ... 100 A4
Princess May Primary School
STNW/STAM N16 ... 86 A3
Princess of Wales Conservatory
RCH/KEW TW9 ... 137 G1
The Princess Royal Distribution Centre
WLSDN NW10 ... 80 D6
The Princess Royal University Hospital
ORP BR6 ... 216 A1
Priory CE Primary School
WIM/MER SW19 ... 178 A1
The Priory Leisure Centre
STMC/STPC BR5 ... 202 D5
Priory Retail Park
WIM/MER SW19 ... 178 C3
Priory School
STMC/STPC BR5 ... 202 D5
Priory Shopping Centre
DART DA1 ... 171 G1
Priory Special School
SNWD SE25 ... 197 G1
Privy Council
STJS SW1Y ... 16 C1
Privy Council Office
WHALL SW1A ... 16 E1
Progress Business Park
CROY/NA CR0 ... 196 A6
Promised Land Academy
PLSTW E13 ... 106 E3
Pronto Trading Estate
YEAD UB4 ... 94 C4
Prospect House School
PUT/ROE SW15 ... 159 G2
Proteus School
KIL/WHAMP NW6 ... 83 F5
Proud Gallery
CHCR WC2N ... 10 E6
Providence Road School
WDR/YW UB7 ... 112 B1
Provident Industrial Estate
HYS/HAR UB3 ... 113 K2
PS Tattershall Castle
WHALL SW1A ... 17 F1
Pudding Mill Lane ⊖
SRTFD E15 ... 87 K6
Pumphouse Educational Museum
BERM/RHTH SE16 ... 124 B1
Pump Lane Industrial Estate
HYS/HAR UB3 ... 114 A2
The Purcell School
HRW HA1 ... 78 D1
Purdy Hicks Gallery
STHWK SE1 ... 12 A7
Purfleet ⇌
PUR RM19 ... 131 K5
Purfleet Industrial Park
SOCK/AV RM15 ... 131 J2
Purfleet Primary School
PUR RM19 ... 131 K4
Purley Oaks ⇌
SAND/SEL CR2 ... 211 K6
Purley Oaks Primary School
SAND/SEL CR2 ... 211 K5
Pursuit Centre
WAP E1W ... 104 E6
Putney ⇌
PUT/ROE SW15 ... 139 G5
Putney Animal Hospital
PUT/ROE SW15 ... 139 G5
Putney Arts Theatre
PUT/ROE SW15 ... 139 G5
Putney Bridge ⊖
FUL/PGN SW6 ... 139 J4
Putney Exchange Shopping Centre
PUT/ROE SW15 ... 139 G5
Putney High School
PUT/ROE SW15 ... 139 G6
Putney Leisure Centre
PUT/ROE SW15 ... 139 F5
Putney Lower Common Cemetery
BARN SW13 ... 138 E3
Putneymead Medical Centre
PUT/ROE SW15 ... 139 F5
Putney Park School
PUT/ROE SW15 ... 138 E5
Putney School of Art & Design
PUT/ROE SW15 ... 139 H5
Putney Town Social & Bowls Club
PUT/ROE SW15 ... 139 F3
Putney Vale Cemetery
PUT/ROE SW15 ... 158 D4
Putney Vale Crematorium
PUT/ROE SW15 ... 158 D4
Pylon Trading Estate
CAN/RD E16 ... 106 B3
Quadrant Business Park
KIL/WHAMP NW6 ... 82 C6
Quality Hotel
WBLY HA9 ... 80 C2
Quebec Industrial Estate
BERM/RHTH SE16 ... 124 B2
Queen Charlotte's & Chelsea Hospital
SHB W12 ... 99 K5

Queen Charlotte's Cottage, Kew Gardens RCH/KEW TW9 136 E3
Queen Elizabeth Conference Centre WEST SW1P 16 D3
Queen Elizabeth Hall STHWK SE1 11 G7
Queen Elizabeth Hospital WOOL/PLUM SE18 126 E6
Queen Elizabeth II School MV/WKIL W9 100 D3
Queen Elizabeth Leisure Centre BAR EN5 20 D5
Queen Elizabeth Museum CHING E4 38 D2
Queen Elizabeths Boys School BAR EN5 20 B4
Queen Elizabeths Girls School BAR EN5 20 D5
Queen Elizabeth Stadium EN EN1 24 B3
Queenhithe Stairs BLKFR EC4V 12 C6
Queen Mary College WCHPL E1 105 F3
Queen Marys Hospital SCUP DA14 186 B1
Queen Mary's Hospital HAMP NW3 83 G1
Queen Mary's Hospital for Children SUT SM1 194 B5
Queen Mary's University Hospital PUT/ROE SW15 158 D1
Queen Mary & Westfield College SWFD E18 52 E4
Queen Mother Sports Centre PIM SW1V 16 A6
Queensbridge Primary School HACK E8 86 B5
Queensbridge Sports Centre HACK E8 86 B5
Queen's Building HTHAIR TW6 132 E4
Queensbury ⊖ STAN HA7 44 B6
Queens Business & Secretarial College SKENS SW7 14 A6
The Queens CE Primary School RCH/KEW TW9 137 G1
Queen's Club WKENS W14 119 H5
Queens College London CAVSQ/HST W1G 9 J2
Queens College Preparatory School CAVSQ/HST W1G 9 J1
The Queen's Gallery BGVA SW1W 15 K3
Queens Gate School SKENS SW7 14 A6
SKENS SW7 120 B4
Queens Hospital ROMW/RG RM7 75 G4
The Queens House GNWCH SE10 125 G6
Queens Ice Rink & Bowl BAY/PAD W2 101 F6
Queensland College London - London Campus ACT W3 117 J1
Queens Manor Primary School FUL/PGN SW6 139 F1
Queensmead School RSLP HA4 77 H2
Queensmead Sports Centre RSLP HA4 77 H3
Queens Medical Centre RCHPK/HAM TW10 137 G6
Queensmill School FUL/PGN SW6 139 K3
Queens Park ⊖ ⊖ KIL/WHAMP NW6 100 D1
Queens Park Community School WLSDN NW10 82 A6
Queens Park Health Centre NKENS W10 100 C2
Queens Park Primary School NKENS W10 100 C2
Queens Park Rangers FC (Loftus Road Stadium) SHB W12 118 E1
Queen's Road Cemetery CROY/NA CR0 196 D3
Queen's Road Peckham ⇌ ⊖ PECK SE15 143 J2
Queens Theatre SOHO/SHAV W1D 10 C5
Queenstown Road Battersea ⇌ VX/NE SW8 141 G2
Queensway ⊖ BAY/PAD W2 101 F6
Queensway Business Centre PEND EN3 24 E5
Queenswell Infant School TRDG/WHET N20 33 H4
Queen Victoria Memorial WHALL SW1A 16 A3
The Quest Academy SAND/SEL CR2 213 F5
Quest Business Training ECT SW5 120 A4
The Questors Theatre EA W5 97 J6
Quwwat UL Islam Girl's School FSTGT E7 88 E4
Radcliffe College SOHO/SHAV W1D 10 A4
Radisson Edwardian Hotel POP/IOD E14 106 A6
Radisson Blu Hotel MBLAR W1H 9 F3
Radisson Edwardian Berkshire Hotel OXSTW W1C 9 J4
Radisson Edwardian Grafton Hotel CAMTN NW1 4 A6
Radisson Edwardian Hotel HYS/HAR UB3 133 F1
RSQ WC1B 10 D2
Radisson Edwardian Marlborough Hotel NOXST/BSQ WC1A 10 D3
Radisson Edwardian Mayfair Hotel MYFR/PICC W1J 9 K6
Radisson Edwardian Mountbatten Hotel LSQ/SEVD WC2H 10 E4
Radisson Edwardian Vanderbilt Hotel SKENS SW7 120 B4
Radnor House TWK TW1 156 B4
RAF West Ruislip (University of Maryland) HGDN/ICK UB10 58 A6
Raglan Infant School EN EN1 36 A1
Raglan Junior School EN EN1 36 A2
Raglan Primary School HAYES BR2 200 B1
Railton Road Clinic HNHL SE24 142 C6
Rainbow Clinic BAY/PAD W2 2 B7
Rainbow Industrial Estate RYNPK SW20 176 E5
Rainbow Montessori School KIL/WHAMP NW6 83 F5
Rainbow Quay BERM/RHTH SE16 124 B3
Rainbow School for Autistic Children WAND/EARL SW18 160 B4
Raines Foundation School BETH E2 104 D2
Rainham ⇌ RAIN RM13 111 H3
Rainham Hall (NT) RAIN RM13 111 J3
Rainham Marshes RSPB Reserve RAIN RM13 111 K6
Rainham Trading Estate RAIN RM13 111 G2
Rainham Village Primary School RAIN RM13 111 J3
Ramac Industrial Estate CHARL SE7 125 K5
Ramada Encore Hotel ACT W3 99 F4
Ramada Hotel BAY/PAD W2 101 F6
Ramada Hotel & Suites CAN/RD E16 107 H6
Ramada London Heathrow HEST TW5 133 K2
Rambert School of Ballet & Contemporary Dance TWK TW1 136 C6
Randal Cremer Primary School BETH E2 7 J2
Ranelagh Gardens (site of Chelsea Flower Show) CHEL SW3 121 F5
Ranelagh Primary School SRTFD E15 106 C1
Rangefield Primary School BMLY BR1 183 H1
Ransomes Dock Business Centre BTSEA SW11 140 D1
The Rathbone Education Centre CAN/RD E16 106 D4
Rathfern Primary School FSTH SE23 164 C3
Ravenor Primary School GFD/PVL UB6 96 A2
Ravensbourne ⇌ BECK BR3 183 F3
Ravensbourne GNWCH SE10 125 H2
The Ravensbourne School HAYES BR2 200 A1
Ravenscourt Park ⊖ HMSMTH W6 118 D4
Ravenscourt Park Preparatory School HMSMTH W6 118 D4
Ravenscroft Medical Centre GLDGN NW11 64 D4
Ravenscroft Primary School CAN/RD E16 106 E3
Ravenscroft School TRDG/WHET N20 32 D2
Ravenside Retail Park UED N18 51 F2
Ravens Lawn Tennis Club NFNCH/WDSPK N12 33 H6
Ravensquay Business Centre STMC/STPC BR5 202 C2
Ravenstone Preparatory School SKENS SW7 120 B3
Ravenstone Primary School BAL SW12 161 F3
Ravenswood Industrial Estate WALTH E17 70 A1
Ravens Wood School HAYES BR2 215 H1
Rayat London College HEST TW5 134 E1
Ray Lodge Primary School WFD IG8 53 H2
Rayners Lane ⊖ RYLN/HDSTN HA2 59 K5
Raynes Park ⇌ RYNPK SW20 177 F5
Raynes Park High School RYNPK SW20 176 E6
Raynes Park Sports Ground RYNPK SW20 176 D5
Raynes Park Vale FC RYNPK SW20 193 G2
Raynham Primary School UED N18 50 C1
RCA SKENS SW7 120 B3
RCA Sculpture School BTSEA SW11 140 D1
Reay Primary School BRXN/ST SW9 142 B1
Records Office CLKNW EC1R 5 K6
Rectory Business Centre SCUP DA14 168 C6
Rectory Road ⇌ STNW/STAM N16 86 C1
Red Balloon Learner Centre HRW HA1 61 F4
Redbridge ⊖ REDBR IG4 71 H3
Redbridge College CHDH RM6 73 H2
Redbridge Drama Centre SWFD E18 52 E4
Redbridge Museum IL IG1 90 B1
Redbridge Primary School REDBR IG4 71 J2
Redbridge Sports Centre BARK/HLT IG6 54 D4
Redburn Industrial Estate PEND EN3 37 F1
Redcliffe School WBPTN SW10 120 B6
Reddiford School PIN HA5 59 J1
Redford Lodge Psychiatric Hospital ED N9 36 C4
Red Gates School CROY/NA CR0 211 G3
Redhill Primary School CHST BR7 185 G2
Red House (NT) BXLYHS DA6 149 F5
Redlands Primary School WCHPL E1 104 E4
Red Lion Business Park SURB KT6 191 G6
Redriff Primary School BERM/RHTH SE16 124 B2
Red Rose Trading Estate EBAR EN4 21 H6
Reeves Corner ⊖ CROY/NA CR0 196 C6
Regal International College ALP/SUD HA0 80 A3
Regent Business Centre HYS/HAR UB3 114 A2
Regent Clinic CAVSQ/HST W1G 9 J2
Regent College London PIN HA5 59 K4
Regent's Park ⊖ CAMTN NW1 3 J7
Regent's Park Barracks CAMTN NW1 3 J3
Regent's Park Clinic CAMTN NW1 2 E6
Regent's Park Medical Centre CAMTN NW1 3 K4
Regent's Park Open Air Theatre CAMTN NW1 3 G5
Regent's Park Track STJWD NW8 2 E2
Regina Coeli RC Primary School SAND/SEL CR2 211 H5
Renaissance Hotel HTHAIR TW6 132 E2
Renoir Cinema BMSBY WC1N 5 F6
Renwick Industrial Estate BARK IG11 109 H1
Rewards Centre HSLW TW3 135 H4
Reynard Mills Trading Estate BTFD TW8 116 D5
Reynolds Health & Fitness RDART DA2 170 B4
Reynolds Sports Centre ACT W3 117 H2
Rhodes Avenue Primary School WDGN N22 48 C4
Rhodes Farm Clinic MLHL NW7 32 A6
Rhyl Primary School KTTN NW5 84 A4
RIBA Library Drawings & Manuscript Collection MBLAR W1H 9 F3
Ricards Lodge High School WIM/MER SW19 159 J6
Richard Alibon Primary School DAGE RM10 92 C3
Richard Atkins Primary School BRXS/STRHM SW2 161 K2
Richard Cloudesley School STLK EC1Y 6 C7
Richard Cobden Primary School CAMTN NW1 4 B1
Richdales Institute ALP/SUD HA0 79 K6
Rich Industrial Estate PECK SE15 123 J6
STHWK SE1 19 H5
Richmond ⇌ ⊖ ⊖ RCH/KEW TW9 137 F5
Richmond Adult & Community College RCH/KEW TW9 136 E5
Richmond American International University in London RCHPK/HAM TW10 157 F1
The Richmond Clinic RCH/KEW TW9 137 G5
Richmond Community College TWK TW1 156 A3
Richmond FC RCH/KEW TW9 136 E5
The Richmond Gate Hotel RCHPK/HAM TW10 157 F2
The Richmond Golf Club RCHPK/HAM TW10 157 F4
The Richmond Green Medical Centre RCH/KEW TW9 136 E6
The Richmond Hill Hotel RCHPK/HAM TW10 157 F2
Richmond House School HPTN TW12 172 E1
Richmond Magistrates Court RCH/KEW TW9 136 E5
Richmond Park Academy MORT/ESHN SW14 138 B5
Richmond Park Golf Club PUT/ROE SW15 158 B2
Richmond Park National Nature Reserve RCHPK/HAM TW10 158 B4
Richmond Road Medical Centre KUTN/CMB KT2 175 F3
Richmond Theatre RCH/KEW TW9 136 E5
Richmond upon Thames College WHTN TW2 155 K2
Ridge House Clinic WCHMH N21 35 K2
Ridgeway Primary School SAND/SEL CR2 212 A6
Rio Cinema HACK E8 86 B3
Ripley Arts Centre BMLY BR1 184 C4
Ripple Primary School BARK IG11 90 E6
Rippleside Cemetery BARK IG11 91 G6
Risebridge Golf Club ROM RM1 57 H3
Rise Park Junior School ROM RM1 57 F4
Risley Avenue Primary School TOTM N17 50 A4
The Ritz Hotel WHALL SW1A 10 A7
Ritzy Cinema BRXN/ST SW9 142 B5
River Brent Business Park HNWL W7 115 K3
River Gardens Business Centre EBED/NFELT TW14 134 A5
River House Montessori School POP/IOD E14 124 D1
Riverley Primary School LEY E10 69 J5
River Mole Business Park ESH/CLAY KT10 189 F5
River Place Health Centre IS N1 85 J5
River Road Business Park BARK IG11 108 E2
Riversdale Primary School WAND/EARL SW18 159 K3
Riverside Business Centre WAND/EARL SW18 160 A3
Riverside Business Park WIM/MER SW19 178 B4
Riverside Community Health Care WKENS W14 119 G3
Riverside Golf Club THMD SE28 110 A5
Riverside Industrial Estate BARK IG11 109 G2
DART DA1 151 H6
Riverside Primary School BERM/RHTH SE16 123 H2
Riverside Quarter WAND/EARL SW18 139 K5
Riverside School STMC/STPC BR5 186 D5
Riverside Studios Cinema HMSMTH W6 119 F5
Riverside Wandle Trading Estate MTCM CR4 194 E4
Riverston School LEE/GVPK SE12 145 K6
Riverview CE Primary School HOR/WEW KT19 206 E2
The RJ Mitchell Primary School HCH RM12 93 K4
RNLI Lifeboat Station TWRH EC3N 13 H7
Roan Industrial Estate MTCM CR4 178 D4
Robert Blair Primary School HOLWY N7 84 E4
Robert Browning Primary School WALW SE17 122 E5
Robert Clack School BCTR RM8 74 B6
Robin Hood Infant School SUT SM1 208 E3
Robin Hood Junior School SUT SM1 209 F3
Robin Hood Lane Health Centre SUT SM1 208 E3
Robin Hood Primary School KUTN/CMB KT2 176 A1
Robinsfield Infant School STJWD NW8 2 B2
The Roche School WAND/EARL SW18 139 K6
Rockliffe Manor Primary School WOOL/PLUM SE18 128 A6
Rockmount Primary School NRWD SE19 180 D2
Rockware Business Centre GFD/PVL UB6 78 D6
Roding Lane Cemetery WFD IG8 53 J4
Roding Primary School BCTR RM8 91 J2
WFD IG8 53 J3
Roding Valley ⊖ BKHH IG9 39 H6
Roebuck Road Trading Estate BARK/HLT IG6 55 H2
Roe Green Junior School CDALE/KGS NW9 62 D1
Roehampton Church School PUT/ROE SW15 158 E2
The Roehampton Priory Hospital PUT/ROE SW15 138 C5
Roehampton Recreation Centre PUT/ROE SW15 158 C2
Roehampton University (Digby Stuart College) PUT/ROE SW15 138 C6
Roehampton University (Froebel College) PUT/ROE SW15 158 C1
Roehampton University (Southlands College) PUT/ROE SW15 138 C6
Roehampton University (Whitelands College) PUT/ROE SW15 158 C2
Roger Ascham Primary School WALTH E17 51 H4
Roger Bannister Sports Ground KTN/HRWW/WS HA3 42 C2
Rokeby School KUTN/CMB KT2 175 K3
SRTFD E15 88 B5
Rokesly Junior School CEND/HSY/T N8 66 E2
Roman Bath TPL/STR WC2R 11 H5
Roman Industrial Estate CROY/NA CR0 197 F4
Roman Road Primary School EHAM E6 107 H3
Romford ⇌ ROM RM1 75 G3
Romford Cemetery ROMW/RG RM7 74 E4
Romford Clinic ROM RM1 75 H1
Romford County Court ROM RM1 75 H1
Romford Golf Club GPK RM2 57 J6
Romford Ice Arena ROMW/RG RM7 75 G4
Romford IT Learning Centre ROM RM1 75 G2
Romford Shopping Hall ROM RM1 75 G1
Ronald Rose Primary School PUT/ROE SW15 159 G2
Rood Lane Medical Centre FENCHST EC3M 13 G5
Rooks Heath College Business & Enterprise RYLN/HDSTN HA2 78 A1
Roosevelt Memorial MYFR/PKLN W1K 9 H5
Ropery Business Park CHARL SE7 126 B4
Rosary Priory High School BUSH WD23 28 E1
Rosary RC Infant School HEST TW5 114 E6
Rosary RC Primary School HAMP NW3 83 J3
Rosebery Industrial Park TOTM N17 50 D5
Rose Bruford College BFN/LL DA15 168 C3
Rosedale College HYS/HAR UB3 94 B5
Roselands Clinic NWMAL KT3 191 K1
Rose McAndrew Clinic BRXN/ST SW9 142 A3
Rosemary Works School IS N1 85 K6
Rosemead Preparatory School DUL SE21 162 D4
Rosendale Primary School DUL SE21 162 D2
Rose of Kingston (Kingston Theatre) KUT/HW KT1 174 E5
Rose Theatre Exhibition STHWK SE1 12 C7
Rosetta Primary School CAN/RD E16 107 F4
Rosewood Medical Centre HCH RM12 93 K3
Rosh Pinah Primary School EDGW HA8 30 D4
Rosslyn Park RFC PUT/ROE SW15 138 C5
Rotherfield Primary School IS N1 85 J6
Rotherhithe ⊖ BERM/RHTH SE16 123 K2
Rotherhithe Civic Centre BERM/RHTH SE16 123 K2
Rotherhithe Primary School BERM/RHTH SE16 123 K4
The Rotunda KUT/HW KT1 175 F5
The Roundhouse Theatre CAMTN NW1 84 A5
Roundshaw J & I School WLGTN SM6 210 E5

Rowan Preparatory School
ESH/CLAY KT10 205 F5
Rowans School
RYNPK SW20 176 D3
Rowhill School
RDART DA2 171 F6
Rowley Industrial Park
ACT W3 117 J3
Roxbourne Junior School
RYLN/HDSTN HA2 59 H6
Roxbourne Medical Centre
RYLN/HDSTN HA2 60 B6
Roxeth Mead School
RYLN/HDSTN HA2 60 D6
Roxeth Primary School
RYLN/HDSTN HA2 60 D6
Roxwell Trading Park
LEY E10 69 G4
Royal Academy of Arts
MYFR/PICC W1J 10 A6
Royal Academy of Dramatic Art
GWRST WC1E 10 C1
Royal Academy of Music
CAMTN NW1 3 H7
Royal Air Force Museum London
CDALE/KGS NW9 45 J5
Royal Albert ⊖
CAN/RD E16 107 J6
Royal Albert Hall
SKENS SW7 14 A3
Royal Arsenal
WOOL/PLUM SE18 127 G3
The Royal Artillery Barracks
WOOL/PLUM SE18 126 E6
The Royal Ballet School (White Lodge)
RCHPK/HAM TW10 158 A3
Royal Ballet Upper School
COVGDN WC2E 11 F4
Royal Blackheath Golf Club
ELTH/MOT SE9 166 E2
Royal Botanic Gardens, Kew
BTFD TW8 137 F1
Royal Botanic Gardens Kew School
RCH/KEW TW9 137 G1
Royal Brompton Hospital
CHEL SW3 120 C5
Royal Chace Hotel
ENC/FH EN2 23 F1
Royal College of Anaesthetists
RSQ WC1B 10 E1
Royal College of Art
SKENS SW7 120 B2
Royal College of Music
SHB W12 118 D3
SKENS SW7 14 A4
Royal College of Nursing
CAMTN NW1 4 B6
IS N1 6 A1
Royal College of Obstetricians & Gynaecologists
CAMTN NW1 2 E6
Royal College of Ophthalmologists
CAMTN NW1 3 G7
Royal College of Paediatrics & Child Health
GTPST W1W 9 K1
The Royal College of Pathology
STJS SW1Y 16 C1
Royal College of Physicians
CAMTN NW1 3 J6
Royal College of Surgeons
LINN WC2A 11 H3
Royal College of Veterinary Surgeons
WEST SW1P 16 E6
Royal Courts of Justice
LINN WC2A 11 H4
Royal Court Theatre
BGVA SW1W 15 G7
Royal Court Young Peoples Theatre
NKENS W10 100 C4
The Royal Docks Community School
CAN/RD E16 107 G5
Royal Docks Medical Centre
EHAM E6 108 A5
Royal Epping Forest Golf Club
CHING E4 38 C2
Royal Exchange
BANK EC3V 13 F4
Royal Festival Hall
STHWK SE1 17 G1
Royal Free Hospital School of Medicine
HAMP NW3 83 J3
Royal Garden Hotel
KENS W8 120 A2
Royal Geographical Society
SKENS SW7 14 A3
The Royal Horseguards Hotel
WHALL SW1A 17 F1
Royal Horticultural Society New Hall
WEST SW1P 16 C5
Royal Horticultural Society Old Hall
WEST SW1P 16 C6
Royal Hospital
RCH/KEW TW9 137 F4
Royal Hospital Chelsea
CHEL SW3 120 E5
Royal Hospital for Neuro-disability
PUT/ROE SW15 159 H1
Royal Hospital & Home
PUT/ROE SW15 158 E2
Royal Hospital Museum
CHEL SW3 121 F5
Royal Institute of British Architects
REGST W1B 9 K1
Royal Institution's Faraday Museum
CONDST W1S 10 A6
The Royal London Estate
TOTM N17 50 D3
Royal London Homeopathic Hospital
BMSBY WC1N 11 F1
Royal Marsden Hospital
CHEL SW3 120 C5
The Royal Mews
BGVA SW1W 15 K4
Royal Mid-Surrey Golf Club
RCH/KEW TW9 136 E4
Royal Military School of Music
WHTN TW2 155 J1
Royal Mint Court
TWRH EC3N 13 K6
Royal National Orthopaedic Hospital
GTPST W1W 3 K7
STAN HA7 29 H3
Royal National Theatre
STHWK SE1 11 J7
Royal National Throat Nose & Ear Hospital
FSBYW WC1X 5 G4
Royal Oak ⊖
BAY/PAD W2 101 F4
Royal Opera House
COVGDN WC2E 11 F4
Royal Park Primary School
SCUP DA14 169 F5
The Royal School
HAMP NW3 83 H2
Royal Society of Arts
CHCR WC2N 11 F6
Royal Society of Medicine
CAVSQ/HST W1G 9 J3
The Royal Trafalgar Hotel
LSQ/SEVD WC2H 10 D6
Royal Veterinary College
CAMTN NW1 4 C1
Royal Victoria ⊖
CAN/RD E16 106 E6
Royal Victoria Docks Watersports Centre
CAN/RD E16 106 E6
Royal Wimbledon Golf Club
WIM/MER SW19 176 E1
Royston Primary School
PGE/AN SE20 182 A4
RSPCA Animal Hospital
FSBYPK N4 67 F6
Rudolph Steiner Hall
CAMTN NW1 2 E6
Rufus Business Centre
WIM/MER SW19 160 A4
Ruislip ⊖
RSLP HA4 58 C6
Ruislip Gardens ⊖
RSLP HA4 76 E2
Ruislip Gardens Primary School
RSLP HA4 76 C2
Ruislip Golf Club
HGDN/ICK UB10 58 A6
Ruislip High School
RSLP HA4 76 E1
Ruislip Manor ⊖
RSLP HA4 58 E5
Ruislip Manor FC
RSLP HA4 58 D6
Ruislip RFC
RSLP HA4 58 C6
Ruislip Woods National Nature Reserve
NTHWD HA6 40 A6
RSLP HA4 58 C2
Rushcroft School
CHING E4 51 K3
Rushey Green Primary School
CAT SE6 164 E3
Rush Green Primary School
ROMW/RG RM7 75 F5
Rushmore Primary School
CLPT E5 86 E2
Ruskin House School
HNHL SE24 142 D6
The Russell School
RCHPK/HAM TW10 156 E3
Russell Square ⊖
STPAN WC1H 4 E7
Russet House School
EN EN1 24 D2
Rutlish School
RYNPK SW20 177 J5
Ruxley Corner Industrial Estate
SCUP DA14 186 E2
Ruxley Park Golf Centre
STMC/STPC BR5 186 E4
Ryefield Primary School
HGDN/ICK UB10 76 B6
Ryelands Primary School
SNWD SE25 197 J2
Rye Oak Primary School
PECK SE15 143 J4
Sacred Heart Catholic Primary School
PUT/ROE SW15 138 D6
Sacred Heart High School
HMSMTH W6 119 F4
Sacred Heart Language College
KTN/HRWW/WS HA3 42 E5
Sacred Heart RC Infant School
BTSEA SW11 140 D3
Sacred Heart RC JMI School
TRDG/WHET N20 33 J4
Sacred Heart RC Primary School
NWMAL KT3 192 D1
OXHEY WD19 27 K1
RSLP HA4 58 C6
TEDD TW11 174 C3
Sacred Heart RC School
CMBW SE5 142 D2
Sacred Heart School
HOLWY N7 85 F3
Saddlers Hall
CITYW EC2V 12 D3
Sadler's Wells Theatre
CLKNW EC1R 5 K4
SAE Institute
HOLWY N7 84 E3
Safari Cinema
CROY/NA CR0 196 C5
Safari Cinema & Bingo
HRW HA1 61 F2
Sai Medical Centre
POP/IOD E14 106 A6
St Agathas RC Primary School
KUTN/CMB KT2 175 G2
St Agnes RC Primary School
BOW E3 105 J2
CRICK NW2 82 C1
St Aidans Primary School
FSBYPK N4 67 G4
St Aidans RC Primary School
IL IG1 72 D5
St Albans CE Primary School
HCIRC EC1N 11 J1
St Albans Health Clinic
HGT N6 84 A1
St Albans RC Aided Primary School
E/WMO/HCT KT8 189 G2
St Albans RC Church & School Presbytery
HCH RM12 93 J3
St Albans RC JMI School
HCH RM12 93 K5
St Albans Road Infant School
DART DA1 171 J1
St Alfege with St Peter CE Primary School
GNWCH SE10 125 F6
St Aloysius RC College
HGT N6 66 C5
St Aloysius RC Infant School
CAMTN NW1 4 C4
St Aloysius RC Junior School
CAMTN NW1 4 B3
St Andrew & St Francis CE JMI School
CRICK NW2 81 J4
St Andrews CE High School
CROY/NA CR0 211 H1
St Andrews CE JMI School
TRDG/WHET N20 32 D4
St Andrews CE Primary School
EN EN1 23 K3
STHGT/OAK N14 34 C2
St Andrews Greek School
CAMTN NW1 84 B4
St Andrews Primary School
BRXN/ST SW9 142 A3
IS N1 85 F6
St Andrews & St Marks CE Junior School
SURB KT6 190 E2
St Andrews School
RYLN/HDSTN HA2 60 B2
WLSDN NW10 81 K5
St Angela's & St Bonaventures Sixth Form Centre
FSTGT E7 89 F4
St Angela's Ursuline School
FSTGT E7 89 F4
St Annes Catholic High School for Girls
ENC/FH EN2 24 A5
PLMGR N13 35 G6
St Annes CE Primary School
WAND/EARL SW18 140 A6
St Annes RC Primary School
LBTH SE11 122 A6
St Anne's Special School
MRDN SM4 193 K2
St Anne's Trading Estate
POP/IOD E14 105 H5
St Anns CE Primary School
SEVS/STOTM N15 67 K2
St Ann's General Hospital
FSBYPK N4 67 J2
St Anns School
HNWL W7 115 K1
St Ann's Shopping Centre
HRW HA1 60 E3
St Anselms RC Primary School
DART DA1 151 J6
HRW HA1 60 E4
NWDGN UB2 114 E3
St Anslems RC Primary School
TOOT SW17 161 F5
St Anthonys Hospital
WPK KT4 193 G5
St Anthonys RC Primary School
EDUL SE22 163 H1
PGE/AN SE20 181 J4
St Anthony's School (Junior House)
HAMP NW3 83 H3
St Anthony's School (Senior House)
HAMP NW3 83 G3
St Antonys RC Primary School
FSTGT E7 88 E5
WFD IG8 38 E6
St Aubyns School
WFD IG8 52 D3
St Augustines CE High School
KIL/WHAMP NW6 100 E1
St Augustines Primary School
BELV DA17 129 G3
KIL/WHAMP NW6 101 F1
St Augustines Priory School
EA W5 98 A4
St Augustines RC Infant School
GNTH/NBYPK IG2 72 B2
St Augustines RC Primary School
CAT SE6 182 E1
GNTH/NBYPK IG2 72 B2
WKENS W14 119 H6
St Barnabas & St Philip's CE Primary School
KENS W8 119 K3
St Bartholomews CE Primary School
SYD SE26 163 K6
St Bartholomews Hospital
STBT EC1A 12 B2
St Bartholomews Medical School
FARR EC1M 6 B7
St Bartholomews & Royal London School of Medicine
FARR EC1M 12 C1
St Bartholomew's the Great
STBT EC1A 12 B2
St Bartholomews & The Royal London Hospital
WCHPL E1 104 D4
St Barts Hospital Sports Ground
CHST BR7 185 J2
St Bedes RC Infant School
BAL SW12 161 J3
St Bedes RC Primary School
CHDH RM6 73 J2
St Benedicts Junior School
EA W5 97 J4
St Benedicts School
EA W5 97 K4
St Bernadette Catholic Junior School
BAL SW12 161 H2
St Bernadettes RC First & Middle School
KTN/HRWW/WS HA3 62 A1
St Bonaventures School
FSTGT E7 88 E5
St Boniface RC Primary School
TOOT SW17 178 E1
St Catherines RC Girls School
BXLYHS DA6 149 J6
St Catherines RC J & I School
WDR/YW UB7 112 A2
St Catherines RC School
BAR EN5 20 D5
St Catherines School
TWK TW1 156 A4
St Cecilias CE School
WAND/EARL SW18 159 J2
St Cecilias RC Primary School
WPK KT4 193 G6
St Chads RC Primary School
SNWD SE25 197 F2
St Charles Hospital
NKENS W10 100 B4
St Charles Primary School
NKENS W10 100 B4
St Christinas RC Preparatory School
STJWD NW8 2 D2
St Christophers School
BECK BR3 183 F5
HAMP NW3 83 H3
WBLY HA9 80 B1
St Clare Business Park
HPTN TW12 173 H2
St Clement Danes CE Primary School
HOL/ALD WC2B 11 G4
St Clement & St James CE Primary School
NTGHL W11 119 G1
St Clements Hospital
BOW E3 105 H2
St Clements Primary School
EW KT17 207 H6
St Columbas RC Boys School
BXLYHS DA6 149 J6
St Cuthbert with St Matthias CE Primary School
ECT SW5 119 K5
St Cyprians Greek Orthodox Primary School
THHTH CR7 180 D5
St Davids College
WWKM BR4 198 E4
St Davids Health Centre
STWL/WRAY TW19 152 A2
St Dominics RC Primary School
HAMP NW3 83 K3
HOM E9 87 G4
St Dominics Sixth Form College
HRW HA1 60 E6
St Dunstans CE Primary School
CHEAM SM3 208 C4
St Dunstans College
CAT SE6 164 C3
St Ebba's Hospital
HOR/WEW KT19 206 E6
St Edmunds RC Primary School
ED N9 36 D3
POP/IOD E14 124 D4
WHTN TW2 155 G2
St Edwards CE Comprehensive School
CHDH RM6 74 C3
St Edwards CE Primary School
ROM RM1 75 F1
St Edwards RC JMI School
STJWD NW8 2 C7
St Elizabeths RC Primary School
BETH E2 104 E1
RCHPK/HAM TW10 157 G1
St Eugene de Mazenod RC Primary School
KIL/WHAMP NW6 82 E5
St Faiths CE Primary School
WAND/EARL SW18 140 A6
St Fidelis Catholic Primary School
ERITH DA8 129 K6
St Francesca Cabrini Primary School
FSTH SE23 163 K1
St Francis de Sales RC J & I School
TOTM N17 50 B3
St Francis of Assisi Primary School
NKENS W10 100 B6
St Francis RC Primary School
PECK SE15 123 H6
SRTFD E15 88 C3
St Francis Xavier College
BAL SW12 161 G1
St Gabriels CE Primary School
PIM SW1V 121 H5
St George's Cathedral
STHWK SE1 17 K4
St Georges CE Primary School
BMLY BR1 184 B5
CMBW SE5 143 F1
VX/NE SW8 141 H1
St Georges College
HOLWY N7 85 G1
St Georges Elizabethan Theatre
HOLWY N7 84 D2
St Georges Hanover Square CE Primary School
MYFR/PKLN W1K 9 H6
St Georges Hospital
TOOT SW17 178 D1
St Georges Industrial Estate
KUTN/CMB KT2 174 E1
PLMGR N13 49 H3
St Georges Medical Centre
HDN NW4 45 K6
St Georges RC Primary School
ENC/FH EN2 23 K3
HRW HA1 79 F1
St Georges RC School
MV/WKIL W9 101 F1
St Georges Shopping Centre & Cinema
HRW HA1 60 D3
St Georges University of London
TOOT SW17 178 C1
St George the Martyr CE Primary School
BMSBY WC1N 5 G7
St George Wharf
VX/NE SW8 121 K6
St Gildas RC Junior School
CEND/HSY/T N8 66 E4
St Giles College London Central
RSQ WC1B 11 F1
St Giles School
SAND/SEL CR2 211 H4
St Gregorys High School
KTN/HRWW/WS HA3 61 K2
St Gregorys RC Primary School
EA W5 97 J3
St Helens Catholic Infant School
WALTH E17 70 A2
St Helens RC Primary School
BRXN/ST SW9 142 B4
CAN/RD E16 106 D3
St Helens School
NTHWD HA6 40 C2
St Helier ⇌
MRDN SM4 193 K3
St Helier Hospital
CAR SM5 194 B5
St Hildas School
BUSH WD23 28 B2
St Ignatius RC Primary School
SEVS/STOTM N15 68 A3
St James CE J & I School
BERM/RHTH SE16 123 H3
St James CE Primary School
MUSWH N10 66 A1
PEND EN3 24 E3
St James CE Junior School
FSTGT E7 88 D3
St James Hatcham CE School
NWCR SE14 144 B2
St James Junior School
WKENS W14 119 H4
St James Medical Centre
CROY/NA CR0 196 E4
St James RC Primary School
HAYES BR2 201 G2
WHTN TW2 155 K5
St James & St Michaels CE Primary School
BAY/PAD W2 101 G6
St James Senior Girls School
WKENS W14 119 H4
St James's Health Centre
WALTH E17 69 G2
St James's Hotel & Club
WHALL SW1A 10 A7
St James's Palace
WHALL SW1A 16 B1
St James's Park ⊖
STJSPK SW1H 16 C4
St James Street ⇌
WALTH E17 69 G2
St James the Great RC Primary School
PECK SE15 143 G2
THHTH CR7 180 C5
St Joachims RC Primary School
CAN/RD E16 107 G5
St Joan of Arc RC Primary School
HBRY N5 85 H2
St John Fisher RC Primary School
ERITHM DA18 129 F3
GFD/PVL UB6 97 J2
PIN HA5 60 A1
RYNPK SW20 193 F2
St John of Jerusalem CE Primary School
HOM E9 86 E5
St Johns ⇌
DEPT SE8 144 D3
St Johns Ambulance Station
WEA W13 116 C1
St Johns & St James CE School
UED N18 50 B1
St Johns Angell Town CE Primary School
BRXN/ST SW9 142 B3

St Johns CE Primary School
BETH E2 **104** E1
BKHH IG9 **39** F3
CROY/NA CR0 **213** F1
FBAR/BDGN N11 **33** K6
KUT/HW KT1 **175** F6
PGE/AN SE20 **181** K3
TRDG/WHET N20 **33** G4
St Johns CE School
CDALE/KGS NW9 **63** G2
St John's CE Walham Green Primary School
FUL/PGN SW6 **139** H2
St Johns Church of England School
STAN HA7 **29** G6
St John's Concert Hall
WEST SW1P **16** E5
St Johns Highbury Vale CE Primary School
HBRY N5 **85** H2
St John's Hospital Day Centre
BTSEA SW11 **140** C5
St John's Lodge
CAMTN NW1 **3** G4
St Johns Primary School
WEA W13 **97** G6
St Johns RC Primary School
BERM/RHTH SE16 **124** B2
St Johns RC Special School
WFD IG8 **54** A1
St Johns & St Clements CE J & I School
PECK SE15 **143** H4
St Johns School
NTHWD HA6 **41** F2
St Johns Senior School
ENC/FH EN2 **23** G2
St Johns Upper Holloway CE Primary School
ARCH N19 **66** C6
St Johns Walworth CE Primary School
WALW SE17 **18** C7
St Johns Way Medical Centre
ARCH N19 **66** D5
St John's Wood ⊖
STJWD NW8 **2** A2
St Johns Wood Pre-Preparatory School
STJWD NW8 **2** C4
St John the Baptist CE Junior School
KUT/HW KT1 **174** E3
St John the Baptist CE Primary School
BMLY BR1 **165** F6
St John the Baptist VA CE Primary School
IS N1 **7** G3
St John the Divine CE Primary School
CMBW SE5 **142** C1
St John the Evangelist RC Primary School
IS N1 **6** A2
St John Vianney RC Primary School
SEVS/STOTM N15 **67** H1
St Joseph's Annexe
ABYW SE2 **128** D6
St Josephs Catholic Infant School
LEY E10 **69** H5
St Josephs Catholic Junior School
CMBW SE5 **142** D1
St Josephs Catholic Primary School
BMLY BR1 **184** B3
DAGW RM9 **92** B2
KUT/HW KT1 **175** G5
St Josephs College
STRHM/NOR SW16 **180** C2
St Josephs Convent School
WAN E11 **70** E3
St Josephs Primary School
WAND/EARL SW18 **139** K6
St Joseph's RC College
MLHL NW7 **31** H6
St Josephs RC First & Middle School
KTN/HRWW/WS HA3 **43** G5
St Josephs RC Infant School
NRWD SE19 **180** D2
St Josephs RC J & I School
HDN NW4 **63** K1
WBLY HA9 **80** B3
St Josephs RC Junior School
LEY E10 **69** J5
NRWD SE19 **180** D2
St Josephs RC Primary School
ARCH N19 **66** B5
BARK IG11 **90** C6
BERM/RHTH SE16 **123** K3
CHEL SW3 **14** E7
DART DA1 **150** A5
DEPT SE8 **144** D1
GNWCH SE10 **125** H5
HNWL W7 **115** K1
HOL/ALD WC2B **11** F3
OXHEY WD19 **27** F5
STHWK SE1 **18** D2
STHWK SE1 **123** H2
WLSDN NW10 **81** G5
St Joseph's RC Primary School
MV/WKIL W9 **101** G2
St Judes CE Primary School
HNHL SE24 **162** C1
STHWK SE1 **18** A5
St Judes & St Pauls CE Primary School
IS N1 **86** A3
St Katharine Pier
WAP E1W **13** K7
St Katherine
TPL/STR WC2R **11** H6
St Lawrence Business Centre
FELT TW13 **154** A4
St Lawrence Catholic School
FELT TW13 **154** A4
St Lawrence Junior School
E/WMO/HCT KT8 **173** J6
St Lawrence University
BMSBY WC1N **5** H7
St Leonards CE Primary School
STRHM/NOR SW16 **179** J1
St Leonards Hospital
IS N1 **7** H2
St Luke's Catholic Sixth Form College
SCUP DA14 **186** A1
St Lukes Cemetery
HAYES BR2 **200** E3
St Lukes CE Primary School
CAN/RD E16 **106** D5
FSBYE EC1V **6** D5
KUTN/CMB KT2 **175** G4
MV/WKIL W9 **100** D1
POP/IOD E14 **125** G4
WNWD SE27 **180** D1
St Luke's Health Centre
CAN/RD E16 **106** D5
St Lukes Hospital for The Clergy
FITZ W1T **4** A7
St Lukes School
THHTH CR7 **196** B1
St Lukes Woodside Hospital
MUSWH N10 **66** A1
St Margaret Clitherow RC Primary School
THMD SE28 **128** C1
St Margaret Lee CE Primary School
LEW SE13 **145** H5
St Margaret's ⇌
TWK TW1 **156** C1
St Margarets Business Centre
TWK TW1 **156** B2
St Margarets CE Primary School
WOOL/PLUM SE18 **127** H6
St Margarets Clitherow RC Primary School
WBLY HA9 **80** E1
St Margarets Primary School
BARK IG11 **90** B6
St Margarets School
BUSH WD23 **28** A2
HAMP NW3 **83** F2
St Marks Catholic School
HSLW TW3 **134** E4
St Marks CE Academy
MTCM CR4 **179** G5
St Marks CE Primary School
ARCH N19 **66** E6
HAYES BR2 **183** K6
LBTH SE11 **122** A6
SNWD SE25 **197** H1
St Marks Industrial Estate
CAN/RD E16 **126** C1
St Marks Primary School
HNWL W7 **115** K2
MTCM CR4 **178** E5
St Marthas Senior School
EBAR EN4 **20** E2
St Martin-in-the-Fields
CHCR WC2N **10** E6
St Martin in the Fields High School
BRXS/STRHM SW2 **162** C3
St Martin of Porres Primary School
FBAR/BDGN N11 **48** C2
St Martins Hospital
MYFR/PKLN W1K **9** G5
St Martins Medical Centre
RSLP HA4 **58** C4
St Martins School
MLHL NW7 **45** G1
St Martins School of Art
SOHO/SHAV W1D **10** D4
St Martins Theatre
LSQ/SEVD WC2H **10** D5
St Mary Abbots CE Primary School
KENS W8 **120** A2
St Mary & St Pancras CE Primary School
CAMTN NW1 **4** C3
St Mary Cray ⇌
STMC/STPC BR5 **202** B1
St Mary Cray Cemetery
STMC/STPC BR5 **202** E1
The St Marylebone CE School
MHST W1U **9** H1
St Marylebone Crematorium
FNCH N3 **47** F6
St Mary Magdalene Academy
HOLWY N7 **85** G4
St Mary Magdalene CE Primary School
MV/WKIL W9 **101** F4
WOOL/PLUM SE18 **126** E4
St Mary Magdalen RC Junior School
CRICK NW2 **81** K4
St Mary Magdalens Catholic Primary School
MORT/ESHN SW14 **138** A4
St Mary of The Angels RC Primary School
NTGHL W11 **100** E5
St Marys Abbey
MLHL NW7 **31** J5
St Mary & St Michael Primary School
WCHPL E1 **104** E5
St Mary & St Peters CE Primary School
TEDD TW11 **173** K1
St Marys Bryanston Square CE Primary School
MBLAR W1H **8** D1
St Marys Catholic Primary School
CHING E4 **38** B3
HCH RM12 **75** J5
St Marys CE High School
HDN NW4 **45** K6
St Marys CE Infant School
CEND/HSY/T N8 **67** F1
St Marys CE Junior School
CEND/HSY/T N8 **66** E1
STWL/WRAY TW19 **152** B1
St Mary's Cemetery
BTSEA SW11 **140** D6
St Marys CE Primary School
CHSGTN KT9 **206** A4
EBAR EN4 **33** J1
FNCH N3 **46** D4
IS N1 **85** H5
LEW SE13 **144** E6
STNW/STAM N16 **67** K6
TWK TW1 **156** B2
WALTH E17 **69** K1
WLSDN NW10 **81** G4
St Mary's CE Primary School
PUT/ROE SW15 **139** G4
St Mary's CE School
HDN NW4 **45** K6
St Marys College
TWK TW1 **156** A5
St Marys Greek Cathedral
WDGN N22 **49** F4
St Marys High School
CROY/NA CR0 **196** D5
St Marys Hospital
BAY/PAD W2 **8** B3
St Marys Hospital Medical School
BAY/PAD W2 **8** B3
St Marys Infant School
CAR SM5 **209** J2
St Marys Kilburn Primary School
KIL/WHAMP NW6 **82** E6
St Marys Magdalens Catholic Primary School
BROCKY SE4 **144** B5
St Marys Primary School
WKENS W14 **119** G3
St Marys RC Infant School
CAR SM5 **209** K3
St Marys RC J & I School
CROY/NA CR0 **196** E5
St Marys RC Junior School
FSBYPK N4 **67** K2
St Marys RC Primary School
BECK BR3 **183** F3
CLAP SW4 **141** H6
ELTH/MOT SE9 **147** F6
ISLW TW7 **136** B4
KIL/WHAMP NW6 **100** E1
NKENS W10 **100** C3
PEND EN3 **25** F5
VX/NE SW8 **141** G2
WIM/MER SW19 **177** K3
St Mary's RC Primary School
CHSWK W4 **118** B5
St Marys & St Johns CE Primary School
HDN NW4 **63** K2
St Marys School
CEND/HSY/T N8 **67** F2
HAMP NW3 **83** G3
St Mary's Western Eye Hospital
MBLAR W1H **8** E1
St Matthew Academy
LEW SE13 **145** G4
St Matthews CE Primary School
PEND EN3 **24** E6
RYNPK SW20 **176** D4
SURB KT6 **191** F4
WDR/YW UB7 **112** B1
St Matthias CE Primary School
BETH E2 **7** K6
STNW/STAM N16 **86** A3
St Meryl JMI School
OXHEY WD19 **27** J5
St Michael & All Angels CE Academy
CMBW SE5 **142** C1
St Michael At Bowes CE Junior School
PLMGR N13 **49** G2
St Michaels & St Martins RC Primary School
HSLWW TW4 **134** E4
St Michaels Catholic College
BERM/RHTH SE16 **123** H2
St Michaels Catholic Grammar School
NFNCH/WDSPK N12 **47** F1
St Michaels CE Primary School
ENC/FH EN2 **23** J2
HGT N6 **66** A4
WAND/EARL SW18 **159** J2
WDGN N22 **49** F4
WELL DA16 **148** D2
St Michaels RC Primary School
EHAM E6 **107** K1
St Michaels Sydenham CE Primary School
SYD SE26 **164** B6
The St Michael Steiner School
WAND/EARL SW18 **139** K6
St Monicas RC Primary School
STHGT/OAK N14 **34** E5
St Monica's RC Primary School
IS N1 **7** G4
St Nicholas Centre
SUT SM1 **209** F3
St Nicholas Preparatory School
SKENS SW7 **14** B3
St Nicholas School
BORE WD6 **30** A1
CDALE/KGS NW9 **62** E6
CHST BR7 **185** H3
St Olaves Grammar School
ORP BR6 **217** H1
St Olaves Preparatory School
ELTH/MOT SE9 **167** G4
St Pancras Hospital
CAMTN NW1 **4** C1
St Pancras International ⇌ ⊖
KCROSS N1C **4** E3
St Pancras International Youth Hostel
CAMTN NW1 **4** D4
St Pancras & Islington Cemetery
EFNCH N2 **47** J4
St Pancras Renaissance Hotel
CAMTN NW1 **4** D4
St Patricks Church School
STHWK SE1 **17** J1
St Patricks Infant School
WAP E1W **123** J1
St Patricks International School
SOHO/SHAV W1D **10** B3
St Patricks Primary School
KTTN NW5 **84** B4
St Patricks RC JMI School
ROMW/RG RM7 **56** D4
St Patricks RC Primary School
WALTH E17 **69** G1
WOOL/PLUM SE18 **127** J4
St Paulinus CE Primary School
DART DA1 **150** B5
St Paul's ⊖
STP EC4M **12** C3
St Pauls & All Hallows Junior School
TOTM N17 **50** C3
St Pauls & All Hallows CE Infant School
TOTM N17 **50** C3
St Paul's Cathedral
STP EC4M **12** C4
St Pauls CE Primary School
BTFD TW8 **116** E6
CHSGTN KT9 **206** A2
FBAR/BDGN N11 **48** A1
HAMP NW3 **83** J5
MLHL NW7 **31** K6
WALW SE17 **122** C5
WCHMH N21 **35** H2
St Pauls CE Junior School
KUTN/CMB KT2 **175** H3
St Pauls Cray CE Primary School
STMC/STPC BR5 **186** D6
St Pauls Cray Health Clinic
STMC/STPC BR5 **186** B5
St Pauls Girls School
HMSMTH W6 **119** G4
St Paul's Primary School
HMSMTH W6 **119** F5
St Pauls RC Primary School
THDIT KT7 **189** K4
WDGN N22 **49** F5
St Pauls RC School
ABYW SE2 **128** B6
St Pauls Road Medical Centre
IS N1 **85** H4
St Pauls School
BARN SW13 **118** E5
St Pauls Steiner School
IS N1 **85** K4
St Pauls Trust School
BOW E3 **105** J4
St Pauls with St Lukes CE Primary School
BOW E3 **105** H4
St Pauls with St Michaels CE Primary School
HACK E8 **86** C6
St Peter Chanel RC Primary School
SCUP DA14 **186** D1
St Peter in Chains RC Infant School
CEND/HSY/T N8 **66** E3
St Peter & St Paul RC Primary School
MTCM CR4 **194** E1
STMC/STPC BR5 **185** K5
St Peter & St Pauls Primary School
FSBYE EC1V **6** A6
St Peters Catholic Primary School
ROM RM1 **57** F6
St Peters CE Primary School
HMSMTH W6 **118** D5
MV/WKIL W9 **100** E3
WALW SE17 **122** E5
WAP E1W **123** K1
St Peter's Church
KTBR SW1X **15** J4
St Peters Eaton Square CE Primary School
BGVA SW1W **15** J5
St Peter's Hospital
COVGDN WC2E **11** F5
St Peters Primary School
SAND/SEL CR2 **211** K4
St Peters RC Primary School
DAGW RM9 **92** B6
WOOL/PLUM SE18 **127** G5
St Philips School
CHSGTN KT9 **205** K4
SKENS SW7 **120** B4
St Phillips Infant School
SYD SE26 **163** J6
St Philomenas Catholic High School
CAR SM5 **209** J3
St Philomenas CP Primary School
STMC/STPC BR5 **202** D4
St Quintins Health Centre
NKENS W10 **100** A4
St Raphaels Hospice
WPK KT4 **193** G6
St Raphaels RC Primary School
NTHLT UB5 **95** F1
St Raphaels Way Medical Centre
WLSDN NW10 **80** E3
St Richards with St Andrews CE Primary School
RCHPK/HAM TW10 **156** C5
St Robert Southwell RC Primary School
CDALE/KGS NW9 **62** E3
St Saviour & St Olaves School
STHWK SE1 **19** F5
St Saviours CE Primary School
HNHL SE24 **142** D4
MV/WKIL W9 **101** F3
POP/IOD E14 **105** K4
St Saviour's CE Primary School
WALTH E17 **69** H4
St Saviours CE Infant School
EA W5 **116** E1
St Saviours RC Primary School
LEW SE13 **145** F5
St Scholasticas RC Primary School
CLPT E5 **86** C1
St Stephens CE Junior School
TWK TW1 **156** B1
St Stephens CE Primary School
BAY/PAD W2 **100** E4
DEPT SE8 **144** D3
SHB W12 **118** E1
St Stephens CE School
VX/NE SW8 **141** K1
St Stephens RC Primary School
WELL DA16 **148** B4
St Stephens School & Childrens Centre
EHAM E6 **89** G5
St Swithun Wells Catholic Primary School
RSLP HA4 **77** G1
The St Teresa Catholic Primary School
BCTR RM8 **91** J2
St Teresa RC First & Middle School
KTN/HRWW/WS HA3 **42** C4
St Teresa's Catholic Primary School
KTN/HRWW/WS HA3 **42** B4
St Theresas RC Primary School
FNCH N3 **46** E6
St Thomas a' Becket RC Primary School
ABYW SE2 **128** B3
St Thomas Becket RC Primary School
SNWD SE25 **197** H3
St Thomas CE Primary School
NKENS W10 **100** C3
St Thomas' Hospital
STHWK SE1 **17** G4
St Thomas More Language College
CHEL SW3 **14** E7
St Thomas More RC Primary School
BXLYHN DA7 **149** G3
ELTH/MOT SE9 **146** D4
St Thomas More RC School
ELTH/MOT SE9 **167** F1
WDGN N22 **49** G3
St Thomas of Canterbury Catholic Primary School
FUL/PGN SW6 **139** J1
MTCM CR4 **179** F6
St Thomas the Apostle College
PECK SE15 **143** K2
St Ursulas Catholic Infant School
HARH RM3 **57** K2
St Ursulas Convent School
GNWCH SE10 **145** G1
St Vincent de Paul RC Primary School
WEST SW1P **16** A5
St Vincents Catholic Primary School
ELTH/MOT SE9 **166** D6
St Vincents Hospital
PIN HA5 **40** C6
St Vincents RC Primary School
BCTR RM8 **73** J6
MLHL NW7 **31** K6
St Vincent's RC Primary School
MHST W1U **9** G2
St Walter & St John Sports Ground
TOOT SW17 **160** D3
St William of York Primary School
FSTH SE23 **164** B3
St Winefrides Catholic Primary School
MNPK E12 **89** K3
St Winifreds Catholic Junior School
LEE/GVPK SE12 **165** J1
St Winifreds RC Infant School
LEW SE13 **145** H6
Salcombe Preparatory Lower School
STHGT/OAK N14 **34** D2
Salcombe Preparatory School (Infants)
STHGT/OAK N14 **34** B1
Salcombe Preparatory School (Juniors)
STHGT/OAK N14 **34** B2
Salesian College
BTSEA SW11 **140** D2
Salisbury Primary School
MNPK E12 **89** H3
Salisbury School
ED N9 **36** E3
Salters' Hall
BARB EC2Y **12** D2
Salusbury Primary School
KIL/WHAMP NW6 **82** C6
Salvatorian College
KTN/HRWW/WS HA3 **42** D5
Samuel Jones Industrial Estate
PECK SE15 **143** F1

Samuel Rhodes School *IS* N1 85 G6
Sanderstead ⇌ *SAND/SEL* CR2 211 K6
Sanderstead Junior School *SAND/SEL* CR2 211 K6
Sandgate Trading Estate *BERM/RHTH* SE16 123 J5
Sandhurst Primary School *CAT* SE6 165 H2
Sandilands ⊖ *CROY/NA* CR0 197 G6
Sandown Grandstand & Exhibition Centre *ESH/CLAY* KT10 204 B1
Sandown Industrial Park *ESH/CLAY* KT10 189 F6
Sandown Park Racecourse *ESH/CLAY* KT10 204 B1
Sandown Sports Club & Dry Ski Slope *ESH/CLAY* KT10 204 B1
Sandringham Primary School *FSTGT* E7 89 G4
Sandy Lodge Golf Club *NTHWD* HA6 26 B4
Sapcote Trading Centre *WLSDN* NW10 81 H3
Sarah Bonnell School *SRTFD* E15 88 C4
Sarum Hall School *HAMP* NW3 83 J5
Satmer Trust School *STNW/STAM* N16 68 C6
Savoy Pier *TPL/STR* WC2R 11 G6
The Savoy *TPL/STR* WC2R 11 F6
Savoy Theatre *TPL/STR* WC2R 11 G6
Saxon Business Centre *WIM/MER* SW19 178 B5
Sayer Clinic *CROY/NA* CR0 211 F2
Sayer Clinics *MBLAR* W1H 9 F4
Scargill Infant School *RAIN* RM13 93 J5
Scargill Junior School *RAIN* RM13 93 J4
Schomberg House *STJS* SW1Y 16 B1
School of English *GLDGN* NW11 64 E5
School of Oriental & African Studies *GWRST* WC1E 4 D7
The School of Pharmacy *BMSBY* WC1N 5 F6
The School of St David & St Katharine *CEND/HSY/T* N8 66 E1
The School of The Islamic Republic *KIL/WHAMP* NW6 100 E1
Science Museum *SKENS* SW7 14 B5
Science Museum IMAX Cinema *SKENS* SW7 14 A5
The Science Museum Library *SKENS* SW7 14 A4
Scotts Park Primary School *BMLY* BR1 184 B4
Sealife London Aquarium *WHALL* SW1A 17 G3
Sebright Primary School *BETH* E2 104 C1
Secombe Centre *SUT* SM1 209 F4
Sedgehill School *CAT* SE6 182 E1
Sedgewick Centre *WCHPL* E1 13 K3
Selborne Primary School *GFD/PVL* UB6 97 F1
Selhurst ⇌ *SNWD* SE25 197 F2
The Selhurst Medical Centre *SNWD* SE25 197 F3
Sellincourt School *TOOT* SW17 178 D2
Selsdon Primary School *SAND/SEL* CR2 212 E6
Selsdon Road Industrial Estate *SAND/SEL* CR2 211 K5
Selwyn Primary School *CHING* E4 52 A3
PLSTW E13 88 E6
Sergeant Industrial Estate *WAND/EARL* SW18 160 A1
Serpentine Gallery *BAY/PAD* W2 14 B1
Serpentine Lido & Cafe *SKENS* SW7 14 C2
Servite RC Primary School *WBPTN* SW10 120 B6
Seven Islands Leisure Centre *BERM/RHTH* SE16 123 K3
Seven Kings ⇌ *GDMY/SEVK* IG3 72 E5
Seven Kings Health Centre *GDMY/SEVK* IG3 72 E5
Seven Kings High School *GNTH/NBYPK* IG2 72 D4
Seven Mills Primary School *POP/IOD* E14 124 D2
Sevenoaks Way Industrial Estate *STMC/STPC* BR5 186 D6
Seven Sisters ⇌ ⊖ *SEVS/STOTM* N15 68 A2
Seven Sisters Primary School *SEVS/STOTM* N15 67 K2
Seymour Gardens Medical Centre *IL* IG1 71 K5
Seymour Leisure Centre *MBLAR* W1H 8 E2
Shaare Zedek Medical Centre *GLDGN* NW11 64 D3
Shacklewell Primary School *HACK* E8 86 B2
Shadwell ⊖ *WCHPL* E1 104 D5
Shadwell Dock Stairs *WAP* E1W 105 F6
Shaftesbury Hospital *LSQ/SEVD* WC2H 10 E4
Shaftesbury Medical Centre *RYLN/HDSTN* HA2 60 C5
Shaftesbury Park Primary School *BTSEA* SW11 141 F4
Shaftesbury Primary School *FSTGT* E7 89 G5
Shaftesbury Theatre *LSQ/SEVD* WC2H 10 E3
Shahjalal Medical Centre *WCHPL* E1 104 C5
Shakespeare Business Centre *BRXN/ST* SW9 142 C4
Shakespeare's Globe Exhibition & Theatre Tour *STHWK* SE1 12 C7
The Shamrock Sports Club *ACT* W3 98 E5
Shannon Corner Retail Park *NWMAL* KT3 192 D1
Shapla Primary School *WCHPL* E1 104 C6
Sharp Sports Centre *EDGW* HA8 44 C2
Shawcroft School *STMC/STPC* BR5 203 F2
Sheen Lane Health Centre *MORT/ESHN* SW14 137 K4
Sheen Lawn Tennis & Squash Club *MORT/ESHN* SW14 137 K6
Sheen Mount Primary School *RCHPK/HAM* TW10 137 J6
Sheen Sports Centre *MORT/ESHN* SW14 138 B5
Shell Centre *STHWK* SE1 17 H1
Shelley School *CLAP* SW4 141 H4
Shenstone School *DART* DA1 150 A6
Shepherd's Bush ⇌ ⊖ ⊖ *SHB* W12 119 G2
Shepherd's Bush CC *ACT* W3 99 G6
Shepherd's Bush Empire *SHB* W12 119 F2
Shepherd's Bush Market ⊖ *SHB* W12 119 F1
Sheraton Business Centre *GFD/PVL* UB6 97 J1
Sheraton Park Tower Hotel *KTBR* SW1X 15 F2
Sheraton Skyline Hotel *HYS/HAR* UB3 133 G1
Sheringdale Primary School *WAND/EARL* SW18 159 J3
Sheringham Junior School *MNPK* E12 89 K2
Sherington Primary School *CHARL* SE7 126 A6
Sherlock Holmes Hotel *MHST* W1U 9 F1
Sherlock Holmes Museum *CAMTN* NW1 3 F7
Sherwood Park Primary School *BFN/LL* DA15 168 C1
Sherwood Park School *WLGTN* SM6 210 D1
Sherwood School *MTCM* CR4 195 H1
The Shire London *BAR* EN5 20 A1
Shirley Clinic *CROY/NA* CR0 197 K5
Shirley High School *CROY/NA* CR0 213 F1
Shirley Oaks Hospital *CROY/NA* CR0 197 K4
Shirley Park Golf Club *CROY/NA* CR0 197 J6
Shirley Wanderers RFC *WWKM* BR4 214 A2
Shirley Windmill *CROY/NA* CR0 212 E1
Shooters Hill Golf Club *WOOL/PLUM* SE18 147 H2
Shooters Hill Post 16 Campus *WOOL/PLUM* SE18 147 F1
Shooting Star House (Childrens Hospice) *HPTN* TW12 172 E2
Shopping City *WDGN* N22 49 F5
The Shopping Hall *EHAM* E6 89 J6
Shopping Mall *SWFD* E18 52 E5
Shore Business Centre *HOM* E9 86 E5
Shoreditch Comprehensive School *IS* N1 7 H3
Shoreditch County Court *STLK* EC1Y 7 F6
Shoreditch High Street ⊖ *WCHPL* E1 7 J7
Shortlands ⇌ *HAYES* BR2 183 H5
Shotfield Health Clinic *WLGTN* SM6 210 B4
Showcase Cinema *WDGN* N22 49 G5
Showcase Newham Cinema *BARK* IG11 108 C2
Shrewsbury House School *SURB* KT6 190 E6
Shrewsbury Lodge School *ESH/CLAY* KT10 204 C3
Shrewsbury Road Health Centre *FSTGT* E7 89 H5
Sidcup ⇌ *BFN/LL* DA15 168 B4
Sidcup Cemetery *BXLY* DA5 168 E4
Sidcup Golf Club *BFN/LL* DA15 168 B4
Sidcup Health Centre *SCUP* DA14 168 B5
Sidcup Sports Club *SCUP* DA14 168 A6
Sidney Russell School *DAGW* RM9 92 A2
Silicon Business Centre *GFD/PVL* UB6 97 J1
Silverdale Industrial Estate *HYS/HAR* UB3 113 K2
Silver Industrial Estate *TOTM* N17 50 B5
Silver Street ⇌ *UED* N18 36 B6
Silver Street Medical Centre *UED* N18 36 A6
Silver Wing Industrial Estate *CROY/NA* CR0 211 F4
Simon Marks Jewish Primary School *STNW/STAM* N16 68 B5
Singlegate Primary School *WIM/MER* SW19 178 C3
Sion College *EMB* EC4Y 11 K5
Sion Manning RC Girls School *NKENS* W10 100 B4
Sir Francis Drake Primary School *DEPT* SE8 124 B5
Sir George Monoux College *WALTH* E17 51 K5
Sir James Altham Swimming Pool *OXHEY* WD19 41 J1
Sir James Barrie School *VX/NE* SW8 141 H2
Sir John Cass Foundation & Redcoat CE Secondary School *WCHPL* E1 105 F4
Sir John Heron Primary School *MNPK* E12 89 K2
Sir John Lillie Primary School *HMSMTH* W6 119 H6
Sir John Soane's Museum *LINN* WC2A 11 G3
Sir Thomas Abney Primary School *STNW/STAM* N16 67 K4
Sir Thomas Lipton Memorial Hospital *STHGT/OAK* N14 34 B2
Sir William Burrough Primary School *POP/IOD* E14 105 G5
Six Bridges Trading Estate *STHWK* SE1 123 H5
Skillion Business Park *BARK* IG11 109 F2
Skinners Academy Hackney *STNW/STAM* N16 68 A4
Slade Green ⇌ *ERITH* DA8 150 D2
Slade Green FC *ERITH* DA8 150 E2
Slade Green Primary School *ERITH* DA8 150 D1
Slade School of Fine Art *STPAN* WC1H 4 D5
Sleaford Industrial Estate *VX/NE* SW8 141 H1
Sloane Hospital *BECK* BR3 183 G4
Sloane Square ⊖ *BGVA* SW1W 15 G7
Smallberry Green Primary School *ISLW* TW7 136 B3
Smallwood Primary School *TOOT* SW17 160 C6
SMA Medical Centre *LEY* E10 69 K4
Smithy Street School *WCHPL* E1 104 E4
Snaresbrook ⊖ *WAN* E11 70 E2
Snaresbrook College Preparatory School *SWFD* E18 52 E5
Snaresbrook Crown Court *WAN* E11 70 D2
Snaresbrook Primary School *SWFD* E18 70 E1
Snowflake School for Children with Autism *ECT* SW5 119 K4
Snowsfields Primary School *STHWK* SE1 19 G2
Sobell Leisure Centre *HOLWY* N7 85 F1
Sobell Medical Centre *HOLWY* N7 85 G2
Sofitel Hotel *STJS* SW1Y 10 C7
Soho Parish CE Primary School *SOHO/CST* W1F 10 C5
Solent Road Health Centre *KIL/WHAMP* NW6 82 E4
Somerset House *COVGDN* WC2E 11 G5
Somers Town Community Sports Centre *CAMTN* NW1 4 B3
Sorsby Health Centre *CLPT* E5 87 F2
South Acton ⊖ *ACT* W3 117 K3
Southall ⇌ *STHL* UB1 114 E2
Southall & West London College *STHL* UB1 114 D2
South Bank Business Centre *VX/NE* SW8 121 J6
Southbank International School Hampstead *HAMP* NW3 83 G4
Southbank International School Kensington *NTGHL* W11 100 D6
South Bank University *STHWK* SE1 18 A4
South Bermondsey ⇌ *BERM/RHTH* SE16 123 K5
Southborough High School *SURB* KT6 206 A1
Southborough Primary School *HAYES* BR2 201 F2
Southbury ⇌ *EN* EN1 24 D5
Southbury Primary School *PEND* EN3 24 D5
South Camden Community School *CAMTN* NW1 4 B2
South Chelsea College *BRXN/ST* SW9 142 A5
South Croydon ⇌ *SAND/SEL* CR2 211 K3
South Croydon Medical Centre *SAND/SEL* CR2 211 J5
South Croydon Sports Club *CROY/NA* CR0 212 A3
South Ealing ⊖ *EA* W5 116 E3
South Ealing Cemetery *EA* W5 116 E4
South Eastern University *HOLWY* N7 85 F1
Southern Road Primary School *PLSTW* E13 107 F1
Southern Spectator Transport Mall *SRTFD* E15 88 A6
Southfield First & Middle School *CHSWK* W4 118 B2
Southfield Medical Centre *CHSWK* W4 118 A2
Southfields ⊖ *WAND/EARL* SW18 159 J3
The Southfields Clinic *WAND/EARL* SW18 159 K1
Southfields Community College *WAND/EARL* SW18 159 K3
Southgate ⊖ *STHGT/OAK* N14 34 D3
Southgate Cemetery *STHGT/OAK* N14 34 C4
Southgate College *STHGT/OAK* N14 34 C4
Southgate Compton CC *EBAR* EN4 21 K5
Southgate Leisure Centre *STHGT/OAK* N14 34 D2
Southgate Road Medical Centre *IS* N1 85 K5
Southgate School *EBAR* EN4 22 B6
South Greenford ⇌ *GFD/PVL* UB6 96 E2
South Grove Primary School *WALTH* E17 69 G3
South Hampstead ⊖ *STJWD* NW8 83 G5
South Hampstead CC *CRICK* NW2 82 A5
South Hampstead High School *HAMP* NW3 83 G4
South Harringay Junior School *FSBYPK* N4 67 H2
South Harrow ⊖ *RYLN/HDSTN* HA2 78 C1
South Herts Golf Club *TRDG/WHET* N20 32 E3
South Kensington ⊖ *SKENS* SW7 14 B6
South Kenton ⊖ ⊖ *ALP/SUD* HA0 61 J5
Southlake Primary School *ABYW* SE2 128 E2
South Lewisham Health Centre *CAT* SE6 165 F6
South London Crematorium *MTCM* CR4 179 H5
South London Gallery *CMBW* SE5 143 F2
The South London Natural Health Centre *CLAP* SW4 141 H5
South London Tamil School *CROY/NA* CR0 196 D4
South London Theatre *WNWD* SE27 162 D5
Southmead Primary School *WIM/MER* SW19 159 H3
South Merton ⇌ *RYNPK* SW20 177 J6
South Norwood Country Park *SNWD* SE25 197 K1
South Norwood Hill Medical Centre *SNWD* SE25 181 F5
South Norwood Medical Centre *SNWD* SE25 197 F1
South Norwood Pools & Fitness Centre *SNWD* SE25 197 H2
South Norwood Primary School *SNWD* SE25 197 H2
South Park Business Centre *IL* IG1 72 E6
South Park Hotel *SAND/SEL* CR2 212 A2
South Park Primary School *GDMY/SEVK* IG3 90 E1
South Quay ⊖ *POP/IOD* E14 124 E2
South Quay Plaza *POP/IOD* E14 124 E2
South Rise Primary School *WOOL/PLUM* SE18 127 J5
South Ruislip ⇌ ⊖ *RSLP* HA4 77 G2
Southside Industrial Estate *VX/NE* SW8 141 H1
Southside Shopping Centre *WAND/EARL* SW18 160 A1
South Thames College *MRDN* SM4 193 J2
PUT/ROE SW15 139 G6
PUT/ROE SW15 158 C1
TOOT SW17 178 D1
WAND/EARL SW18 140 A6
South Tottenham ⊖ *SEVS/STOTM* N15 68 B2
Southville Infant School *EBED/NFELT* TW14 153 J3
Southwark ⊖ *STHWK* SE1 18 A1
Southwark Bridge Stairs *BLKFR* EC4V 12 C6
Southwark Cathedral *STHWK* SE1 12 E7
Southwark College *BERM/RHTH* SE16 123 J3
CMBW SE5 143 F1
STHWK SE1 17 K2
STHWK SE1 19 H4
Southwark Coroners Court *STHWK* SE1 18 E2
Southwark Crown Court *STHWK* SE1 13 G7
Southwark Park Primary School *BERM/RHTH* SE16 123 J3
Southwark Park Sports Centre *BERM/RHTH* SE16 123 K4
Southwark Rose Hotel *STHWK* SE1 18 D1
Southwark Sports Ground *DUL* SE21 163 G3
South West Middlesex Crematorium *FELT* TW13 154 D3
South Wimbledon ⊖ *WIM/MER* SW19 178 A3
Southwold Primary School *CLPT* E5 68 E6
South Woodford ⊖ *SWFD* E18 52 E5
South Woodford Health Centre *SWFD* E18 52 E4
Southwood Hospital *HGT* N6 66 A4
Southwood Primary School *DAGW* RM9 92 A2
Sovereign Business Centre *PEND* EN3 25 H4
The Space Arts Centre Cinema *DEPT* SE8 124 C4
Sparrow Farm Infant School *EBED/NFELT* TW14 154 B2
Sparrow Farm Junior School *EBED/NFELT* TW14 154 B2
Spa School *STHWK* SE1 123 H4
Speakers Corner *BAY/PAD* W2 9 F5
The Speech & Language Hearing Centre *CAMTN* NW1 4 D5
Speedway Industrial Estate *HYS/HAR* UB3 113 G2
Speke's Monument *BAY/PAD* W2 101 G6
Spencer House *WHALL* SW1A 16 A1
The Spires Shopping Centre *BAR* EN5 20 C4
Spitalfields Community Farm *WCHPL* E1 104 C3
Spitalfields Health Centre *WCHPL* E1 13 K2
Spitfire Business Park *CROY/NA* CR0 211 G4
Splashworld Swimming Centre *BXLYHS* DA6 148 D5
Springfield Christian School *CAT* SE6 164 C5
Springfield Community Primary School *SEVS/STOTM* N15 68 C3
Springfield Hospital *TOOT* SW17 160 D5
Springfield Primary School *VX/NE* SW8 141 J1
Spring Grove Primary School *ISLW* TW7 135 J3
Springhallow School *HNWL* W7 97 F5
Spring Park Primary School *CROY/NA* CR0 213 J1
Springvale Retail Park *STMC/STPC* BR5 186 D6
Springwell Infant School *HEST* TW5 134 D1
Springwell Junior School *HEST* TW5 134 D1
Spurgeons College *SNWD* SE25 181 F5
Squirrels Heath Infant School *GPK* RM2 75 K2
Squirrels Heath Junior School *GPK* RM2 75 K2
Squirrels Trading Estate *HYS/HAR* UB3 113 J3
SS Peter & Pauls Catholic Primary School *IL* IG1 90 D1
St Johns Health Centre *TWK* TW1 156 B2

The Stables Gallery & Art Centre CRICK NW2 81 J2
Stadium Business Centre WBLY HA9 80 D1
Stadium Industrial Estate WBLY HA9 80 D3
Stadium Retail Park WBLY HA9 80 C1
Stafford Cross Business Park CROY/NA CR0 211 F3
The Stafford London Hotel WHALL SW1A 15 K1
Stag Lane J & I School EDGW HA8 44 C5
Stag Lane Medical Centre CDALE/KGS NW9 44 E6
Stamford Brook ⊖ CHSWK W4 118 C4
Stamford Clinic HMSMTH W6 118 D3
Stamford Hill ⇌ SEVS/STOTM N15 68 A3
Stamford Hill Primary School SEVS/STOTM N15 67 K3
Stanburn First School STAN HA7 43 J3
Stanburn Junior School STAN HA7 43 J3
Standard Industrial Estate CAN/RD E16 126 C2
Stanford Primary School STRHM/NOR SW16 179 J4
Stanhope Primary School GFD/PVL UB6 96 C3
Stanley Park High School CAR SM5 210 A4
Stanley Park Primary School CAR SM5 209 K5
Stanley Primary School TEDD TW11 155 K6
Stanmore ⊖ STAN HA7 29 K6
Stanmore College STAN HA7 43 H2
Stanmore Golf Club STAN HA7 43 H3
Stanmore Medical Centre STAN HA7 43 G2
Stanton School of English BAY/PAD W2 101 F5
Stanton Square Industrial Estate SYD SE26 164 C6
Stanwell Fields CE School STWL/WRAY TW19 152 B2
Staple Inn Buildings HHOL WC1V 11 J2
Staples Corner Business Park CRICK NW2 63 J5
Star Business Centre RAIN RM13 111 F4
Starksfield Primary School ED N9 36 A3
Star Lane ⊖ CAN/RD E16 106 C3
Star Primary School CAN/RD E16 106 C3
Stationers Hall STP EC4M 12 B4
Stationery Office HOL/ALD WC2B 11 G3
Stebon Primary School POP/IOD E14 105 H4
Stephen Hawking Primary Special School POP/IOD E14 105 G5
Stepney Day Hospital WCHPL E1 104 E5
Stepney Green ⊖ WCHPL E1 105 F3
Stepney Greencoat CE Primary School POP/IOD E14 105 H5
Stepney Green Maths & Computing College WCHPL E1 105 F4
Sterling Industrial Estate DAGE RM10 92 D2
Sterling Way Clinic UED N18 50 B1
Stewart Fleming Primary School PGE/AN SE20 181 K6
Stewart Headlam Primary School WCHPL E1 104 D3
Stillness Primary School FSTH SE23 164 B1
Stirling Retail Park BORE WD6 31 F1
Stirling Way Industrial Estates CROY/NA CR0 195 K4
Stockley Park Business Centre STKPK UB11 113 F1
Stockley Park Golf Club STKPK UB11 94 A6
Stockwell ⊖ CLAP SW4 141 K3
Stockwell Park School BRXN/ST SW9 142 A2
Stockwell Primary School BRXN/ST SW9 142 A4
Stoke Newington ⇌ STNW/STAM N16 68 B6
Stoke Newington School & Sixth Form STNW/STAM N16 85 K1
Stonebridge Park ⊖ ⊖ ALP/SUD HA0 80 C5
The Stonebridge Primary School (London Welsh School) WLSDN NW10 80 E6
Stonebridge Shopping Centre WLSDN NW10 81 F6
Stonehill Business Centre UED N18 51 F2
Stonehill Business Park UED N18 51 F1
Stone Lake Retail Park CHARL SE7 126 B4
Stoneleigh ⇌ HOR/WEW KT19 207 H3
Stoneleigh First School EW KT17 207 K2
Stoneydown Park Primary School WALTH E17 69 G1
Strand on the Green J & I School CHSWK W4 117 H6
Strand Palace Hotel COVGDN WC2E 11 F5
Stratford College SRTFD E15 88 C5
Stratford High Street ⊖ SRTFD E15 88 B6
Stratford International ⇌ ⊖ OLYMPICPK E20 88 A4
Stratford Magistrates Court SRTFD E15 88 B5
Stratford ⇌ ⊖ ⊖ ⊖ OLYMPICPK E20 88 A4
Stratford School FSTGT E7 88 E5
Stratford Shopping Centre SRTFD E15 88 B5
Strathmore School RCHPK/HAM TW10 156 E3
Strawberry Fields School NTGHL W11 100 E5
Strawberry Hill ⇌ WHTN TW2 155 K5
Strawberry Hill Golf Club WHTN TW2 155 K5
Streatham ⇌ STRHM/NOR SW16 179 J1
Streatham Cemetery TOOT SW17 160 D5
Streatham & Clapham High School STRHM/NOR SW16 161 H5
BRXS/STRHM SW2 162 A3
Streatham Common ⇌ STRHM/NOR SW16 179 J2
Streatham & Croydon RFC THHTH CR7 196 B2
Streatham Hill ⇌ STRHM/NOR SW16 161 K4
Streatham Ice Rink STRHM/NOR SW16 179 K1
Streatham Leisure Centre STRHM/NOR SW16 161 K4
Streatham Modern School STRHM/NOR SW16 179 K2
Streatham Park Cemetery MTCM CR4 179 H5
Streatham Swimming Pool STRHM/NOR SW16 179 K1
Streatham Vale Sports Club STRHM/NOR SW16 179 H3
Streatham Wells Primary School BRXS/STRHM SW2 162 A4
Stroud Green Primary School FSBYPK N4 67 G5
Studholme Medical Centre ASHF TW15 152 C6
The Study Preparatory School WIM/MER SW19 177 G1
The Study School NWMAL KT3 192 B2
Sudbourne Primary School BRXS/STRHM SW2 142 A6
Sudbury Court Sports Club ALP/SUD HA0 79 J1
Sudbury Golf Club GFD/PVL UB6 79 J4
Sudbury & Harrow Road ⇌ ALP/SUD HA0 79 H3
Sudbury Hill ⊖ HRW HA1 78 E2
Sudbury Primary School ALP/SUD HA0 79 H2
Sudbury Town ⊖ GFD/PVL UB6 79 H4
Suffolks Primary School EN EN1 24 D3
Sulivan Primary School FUL/PGN SW6 139 K3
Summerside JMI School NFNCH/WDSPK N12 47 H2
Sunbury Court SUN TW16 172 C5
Sundridge Park ⇌ BMLY BR1 184 A3
Sundridge Park Golf Club BMLY BR1 184 B2
Sun Life Trading Estate EBED/NFELT TW14 133 K4
Sunnyfields Primary School HDN NW4 45 K6
Sunnyhill Primary School STRHM/NOR SW16 162 A6
Sunrise School TOTM N17 50 C2
Sunshine House School NTHWD HA6 40 B2
Surbiton ⇌ SURB KT6 191 F3
Surbiton Assembly Rooms SURB KT6 191 F1
Surbiton Business Centre SURB KT6 190 E3
Surbiton Cemetery KUT/HW KT1 191 H1
Surbiton Golf Club CHSGTN KT9 205 H2
Surbiton High School KUT/HW KT1 191 F1
Surbiton Hospital SURB KT6 191 F3
Surbiton Natural Health Centre SURB KT6 191 F3
Surrey CCC (The Oval) LBTH SE11 122 A6
Surrey Docks Farm BERM/RHTH SE16 124 C2
Surrey Docks Health Centre BERM/RHTH SE16 124 B2
Surrey Docks Watersports Centre BERM/RHTH SE16 124 B3
Surrey Quays ⊖ BERM/RHTH SE16 124 A4
Surrey Quays Leisure Park BERM/RHTH SE16 124 A3
Surrey Quays Shopping Centre BERM/RHTH SE16 124 A3
Surrey Square Primary School WALW SE17 123 F5
Susi Earnshaw Theatre School BAR EN5 20 D4
Sussex Hotel OXSTW W1C 9 G4
Sussex House School KTBR SW1X 14 E6
Sutcliffe Park Athletics Track LEE/GVPK SE12 146 A6
Sutton ⇌ SUT SM1 209 G4
Sutton Alternative Health Centre SUT SM1 209 F3
Sutton Arena CAR SM5 194 C4
Sutton Bowling Club BELMT SM2 208 E6
Sutton Cemetery CHEAM SM3 193 J6
Sutton Civic Centre SUT SM1 209 F3
Sutton College of Learning for Adults SUT SM1 209 F3
Sutton Common ⇌ SUT SM1 193 K6
Sutton Grammar School SUT SM1 209 G3
Sutton High Junior School SUT SM1 209 F4
Sutton High School for Girls GDST SUT SM1 208 E4
Sutton House HACK E8 86 E3
Suttons Business Park RAIN RM13 111 F2
Sutton Superbowl SUT SM1 209 F3
Sutton United FC SUT SM1 208 E2
Sutton West Centre SUT SM1 208 E3
Swaffield Primary School WAND/EARL SW18 160 B1
Swaminarayan School WLSDN NW10 81 F4
Swan Business Centre CHSWK W4 118 A4
Swan Business Park DART DA1 151 G5
Swan Lane Pier CANST EC4R 12 E6
Swanlea School WCHPL E1 104 D3
Swansmere School WOT/HER KT12 188 B5
Swedish School BARN SW13 118 D6
Swiss Cottage ⊖ KIL/WHAMP NW6 83 H5
Swiss Cottage Leisure Centre HAMP NW3 83 H5
Swiss Cottage School STJWD NW8 83 H6
Sybil Elgar School EA W5 98 A6
The Sybil Elgar School NWDGN UB2 114 E3
Sybourn Infant School LEY E10 69 G5
The Sybourn Junior School WALTH E17 69 H4
Sybourn Primary School WALTH E17 69 H4
Sydenham ⇌ ⊖ SYD SE26 181 K1
Sydenham Girls School SYD SE26 163 J5
Sydenham High School SYD SE26 163 J6
Sydenham High School Sports Ground CAT SE6 182 D1
Sydenham High Senior School SYD SE26 181 J1
Sydenham Hill ⇌ DUL SE21 163 F5
The Sydney Russell School DAGW RM9 91 K3
Syon House BTFD TW8 136 D2
Syon Lane ⇌ ISLW TW7 136 B1
Syon Park BTFD TW8 136 D3
Syracuse University NTGHL W11 100 D6
Tabard Theatre CHSWK W4 118 B4
Tabernacle School NTGHL W11 119 G1
Taberner House CROY/NA CR0 211 J1
TA Centre EDGW HA8 44 D3
HRW HA1 61 F2
NFNCH/WDSPK N12 47 H4
Tait Road Industrial Estate CROY/NA CR0 197 F3
Taj Suites & Residences Hotel WESTW SW1E 16 B4
Talmud Torah Machzikei Hadass School STNW/STAM N16 68 C4
Tamian Industrial Estate HSLWW TW4 134 B5
Tandem Centre WIM/MER SW19 178 C4
Tashbar of Edgware Primary School EDGW HA8 30 C6
Tate Britain WEST SW1P 16 E7
Tate Modern STHWK SE1 12 B7
Tavistock Clinic HAMP NW3 83 H4
TAVR Centre KUT/HW KT1 190 E1
Tavy Clinic ABYW SE2 128 D2
Tawhid Boys School STNW/STAM N16 68 B6
Tayyibah Girls School STNW/STAM N16 68 C5
Teddington ⇌ TEDD TW11 174 B2
Teddington Business Park TEDD TW11 174 A1
Teddington Cemetery TEDD TW11 155 K6
Teddington Clinic TEDD TW11 173 K2
Teddington Memorial Hospital TEDD TW11 173 K2
Teddington Pool & Fitness Centre TEDD TW11 174 B1
Teddington School TEDD TW11 174 E2
The Teddington Theatre Club E/WMO/HCT KT8 189 J2
Telferscot Primary School BAL SW12 161 H3
Temperate House, Kew Gardens RCH/KEW TW9 137 G3
Temple Hill Primary School DART DA1 151 K6
Temple of Bacchus CMBW SE5 142 D3
Temple of Mithras MANHO EC4N 12 E4
Tenby Road Clinic EDGW HA8 44 B5
Tenterden Sports Ground KTN/HRWW/WS HA3 62 A4
Terence McMillan Stadium PLSTW E13 107 G3
Tetherdown Primary School MUSWH N10 66 A1
Thames Barrier CAN/RD E16 126 C2
Thames Barrier Information & Learning Centre CHARL SE7 126 C3
Thames Christian College BTSEA SW11 140 C4
Thames College of Technology WOOL/PLUM SE18 127 F4
Thames Ditton ⇌ THDIT KT7 189 K4
Thames Ditton & Esher Golf Club ESH/CLAY KT10 189 J6
Thames Ditton Infant School THDIT KT7 190 A3
Thames Ditton Junior School THDIT KT7 190 A4
Thames Gateway Park DAGW RM9 110 B2
Thames House WEST SW1P 16 E6
Thameside Industrial Estate CAN/RD E16 126 C1
Thames Magistrates Court BOW E3 105 J2
Thamesmead Leisure Centre THMD SE28 109 H6
Thamesmead Shopping Centre THMD SE28 109 G6
Thamesview Business Centre RAIN RM13 111 G4
Thames View Clinic BARK IG11 109 F1
Thames View J & I School BARK IG11 109 G1
Thames Water Tower NTGHL W11 119 G2
Theatre de l'Ange Fou International School of Corporeal Mime ARCH N19 66 E5
Theatre for Mankind FSBYPK N4 67 F5
Theatre Museum Library & Archive COVGDN WC2E 11 F5
Theatre of The Dispossessed WIM/MER SW19 159 G3
Theatre Royal HOL/ALD WC2B 11 F4
SRTFD E15 88 B4
Theatre Royal Haymarket STJS SW1Y 10 D6
Theodore McLeary Primary School EDUL SE22 143 G5
Therapia Lane ⊖ CROY/NA CR0 195 K4
Therapia Trading Estate CROY/NA CR0 195 J4
Thistlebrook Industrial Estate ABYW SE2 128 D3
Thistle Hotel BAY/PAD W2 101 G6
CAMTN NW1 4 B5
FITZ W1T 10 B3
FSBYE EC1V 6 C5
WESTW SW1E 15 K5
Thistle Hyde Park Hotel BAY/PAD W2 101 G6
Thistle Marble Arch Hotel MBLAR W1H 9 F4
Thistle Piccadilly Hotel SOHO/SHAV W1D 10 D6
Thomas Arnold Primary School DAGW RM9 92 B5
Thomas Buxton Infant School WCHPL E1 104 C3
Thomas Fairchild Primary School IS N1 6 E2
Thomas Francis Academy BRXN/ST SW9 142 C5
Thomas Gamuel Primary School WALTH E17 69 J3
Thomas Jones Primary School NTGHL W11 100 C5
Thomas Knyvett College ASHF TW15 152 B5
Thomas London Independent Day School KENS W8 120 A3
Thomas Road Industrial Estate POP/IOD E14 105 J4
Thomas's Clapham Primary School BTSEA SW11 140 E6
Thomas's Fulham FUL/PGN SW6 140 A4
Thomas's London Day Schools KENS W8 120 B3
Thomas's Preparatory School BTSEA SW11 140 C2
Thomas Tallis School BKHTH/KID SE3 146 A4
Thornhill Primary School IS N1 85 G5
Thornton Heath ⇌ THHTH CR7 196 D1
Thornton Heath Health Centre THHTH CR7 196 D1
Thornton Heath Pools & Fitness Centre THHTH CR7 196 D1
Thornton Road Industrial Estate CROY/NA CR0 195 K3
Thorntree Primary School CHARL SE7 126 C5
Thorpe Hall Primary School WALTH E17 52 A4
Three Bridges Business Centre NWDGN UB2 115 H2
Three Bridges Primary School NWDGN UB2 115 G3
Three Mills Heritage Centre BOW E3 106 A2
Thurston Industrial Estate LEW SE13 144 E4
Tibetan Buddhist Centre WALW SE17 122 D5
Tidemill Primary School DEPT SE8 144 D1
Tideway Industrial Estate VX/NE SW8 121 H6
Tiffin Girls School KUTN/CMB KT2 175 F2
Tiffin School & Sports Centre KUTN/CMB KT2 175 G5
Tiller Centre (Swimming Baths) POP/IOD E14 124 D3
Tiller Leisure Centre POP/IOD E14 124 D3
Timbercroft Primary School WOOL/PLUM SE18 147 K1
Timbers Clinic KTN/HRWW/WS HA3 42 D2
Timebridge Youth & Community Centre CROY/NA CR0 213 K3
Times Square Shopping Centre SUT SM1 209 F3
Tiverton Primary School SEVS/STOTM N15 67 K3
Tobacco Dock WAP E1W 104 D6
Tokyngton Community Centre WBLY HA9 80 D3
Toldos School STNW/STAM N16 67 K5
Tollgate DUL SE21 163 F4
Tollgate Primary School PLSTW E13 107 G3
Tolworth ⇌ BRYLDS KT5 191 J6
Tolworth CP School SURB KT6 191 G5
Tolworth Girls School SURB KT6 206 B1
Tolworth Recreation Centre SURB KT6 206 B1
Tooting ⇌ TOOT SW17 178 E2
Tooting Bec ⊖ TOOT SW17 161 F5
Tooting Bec Athletics Track TOOT SW17 161 G6
Tooting Broadway ⊖ TOOT SW17 178 D1
Tooting Leisure Centre TOOT SW17 160 C6
Tooting & Mitcham United FC MTCM CR4 179 F4
Torah Temimah Primary School CRICK NW2 81 K2
Torah Vodaas GLDGN NW11 64 D6
Torat Emet Primary School HDN NW4 64 B2
Torriano Junior School KTTN NW5 84 C3
Torridon Primary School CAT SE6 165 G4

Torrington Clinic
NFNCH/WDSPK N12 47 G1
Torrington Park Health Centre
NFNCH/WDSPK N12 33 G6
Total Health Clinic
SHB W12 118 E2
Tottenham Cemetery
TOTM N17 50 A3
Tottenham Court Road ⊖
SOHO/SHAV W1D 10 C3
Tottenham Green Leisure Centre
SEVS/STOTM N15 68 A1
Tottenham Hale ⇌ ⊖
TOTM N17 50 D6
Tottenham Hale Retail Park
SEVS/STOTM N15 68 C1
Tottenham Hotspur FC (White Hart Lane)
TOTM N17 50 B3
Tottenham Park Cemetery
ED N9 36 D5
Tottenham Sports Centre
TOTM N17 50 B4
Totteridge CC
TRDG/WHET N20 32 E4
Totteridge & Whetstone ⊖
TRDG/WHET N20 33 F4
Tower 42
OBST EC2N 13 G3
The Tower Bridge Exhibition
STHWK SE1 19 J1
Tower Bridge Primary School
STHWK SE1 19 J2
Tower Bridge Wharf
WAP E1W 123 H1
Tower Gateway ⊖
TWRH EC3N 13 J5
Tower Hamlets College
POP/IOD E14 105 K6
WCHPL E1 104 E4
Tower Hill ⊖
TWRH EC3N 13 J6
The Tower Hotel
WAP E1W 13 K7
Tower House School
MORT/ESHN SW14 137 K5
Tower Industrial Estate
SNWD SE25 197 H1
Tower Medical Centre
WCHPL E1 104 C5
Tower Millennium Pier
TWRH EC3N 13 H7
Tower of London
TWRH EC3N 13 J6
Tower Retail Park
DART DA1 150 C6
Towers Business Park
WBLY HA9 80 D2
Tower Stairs
MON EC3R 13 G6
Town Farm Primary School
STWL/WRAY TW19 152 A2
Townley Grammar School for Girls
BXLYHS DA6 169 G1
Townmead Business Centre
FUL/PGN SW6 140 B3
Townsend Industrial Estate
WLSDN NW10 80 E6
Townsend Primary School
WALW SE17 19 F6
Toynbee Hall & Curtain Theatre
WCHPL E1 13 J2
Trade Union Congress
NOXST/BSQ WC1A 10 D3
Trafalgar Business Centre
BARK IG11 109 F3
Trafalgar Infant School
WHTN TW2 155 J3
Trafalgar Junior School
WHTN TW2 155 J4
Trafalgar Square
STJS SW1Y 10 D7
Trafalgar Trading Estate
PEND EN3 25 H5
Tramshed Theatre
WOOL/PLUM SE18 127 G4
Trans Atlantic College
BETH E2 7 H2
Transport for London Lost Property Office
CAMTN NW1 3 F7
Transport House
WEST SW1P 16 E5
Travelodge
CAN/RD E16 126 C1
FELT TW13 153 K3
FSBYW WC1X 5 H5
HEST TW5 114 B6
IL IG1 90 B1
SURB KT6 191 J5
Treasury
WHALL SW1A 16 E3
The Treaty Centre
HSLW TW3 135 G4
Treehouse School
MUSWH N10 66 A1
The Treehouse School
BMSBY WC1N 5 G6
Trent CE Primary School
EBAR EN4 21 K5
Trent Country Park
EBAR EN4 22 A3
Trent Park Cemetery
EBAR EN4 22 A4
Trent Park Golf Club
STHGT/OAK N14 22 C5
Trevor Roberts School
HAMP NW3 83 H5
Tricycle Theatre
KIL/WHAMP NW6 82 D5
Trident Business Centre
TOOT SW17 178 E1
Trinity Business Centre
BERM/RHTH SE16 124 C2
Trinity Catholic High School
WFD IG8 38 E6
Trinity College Centre
PECK SE15 143 F1
Trinity College London
STHWK SE1 121 K5
Trinity College of Music
GNWCH SE10 125 F6
MHST W1U 9 H2
Trinity Hospital
GNWCH SE10 125 G5
Trinity House
TWRH EC3N 13 H5
Trinity RC High School Upper
WFD IG8 38 E6
Trinity St Marys Primary School
BAL SW12 161 F3
Trinity School
DAGE RM10 92 C1
LEE/GVPK SE12 145 H6
Trinity School Belvedere
BELV DA17 129 K4
Trinity Trading Estate
HYS/HAR UB3 113 K3
Tripcock Point Development Site
THMD SE28 109 F6
Triumph Trading Estate
TOTM N17 50 C2
Trocadero
SOHO/SHAV W1D 10 C6
Trojan Business Centre
WLSDN NW10 81 H4
Troy Industrial Estate
HRW HA1 61 F2
True Buddha School
IS N1 5 G1
TS Queen Mary
TPL/STR WC2R 11 G6
Tubbenden J & I Schools
ORP BR6 216 D2
Tudor Enterprise Park
KTN/HRWW/WS HA3 42 D6
Tudor Lodge Health Centre
WIM/MER SW19 159 G3
Tudor Lodge Hotel
PIN HA5 59 F3
Tudor Primary School
FNCH N3 47 G4
STHL UB1 95 J6
Tufnell Park ⊖
KTTN NW5 84 B2
Tufnell Park Primary School
HOLWY N7 84 D2
Tuke School
PECK SE15 143 J2
Tulse Hill ⇌
WNWD SE27 162 C4
Tunnel Avenue Trading Estate
GNWCH SE10 125 G2
Turney School
DUL SE21 162 D2
Turnham Green ⊖
CHSWK W4 118 B4
Turnham Primary School
BROCKY SE4 144 B5
Turnpike Lane ⊖
SEVS/STOTM N15 49 H6
Turtle Key Arts Centre
FUL/PGN SW6 119 K6
Tweeddale Primary School
CAR SM5 194 C4
Twenty Nevern Square Hotel
ECT SW5 119 K4
Twickenham ⇌
TWK TW1 156 B2
Twickenham Academy
WHTN TW2 155 G4
Twickenham Cemetery
WHTN TW2 155 G3
Twickenham Park Health Centre
TWK TW1 156 D1
Twickenham Preparatory School
HPTN TW12 173 G4
Twickenham Stadium
ISLW TW7 155 K1
Twickenham Trading Estate
TWK TW1 156 A1
Two Bridges Business Park
SAND/SEL CR2 211 K4
Twyford CE High School
ACT W3 117 H1
Twyford Sports Centre
ACT W3 117 J1
Tyburn Infant School
STJWD NW8 2 B6
Tynemouth Road Health Centre
SEVS/STOTM N15 68 B1
The Type Museum
BRXN/ST SW9 142 A2
Tyssen Primary School
STNW/STAM N16 68 C5
UCI Cinema
SUT SM1 209 F3
UCI Empire Cinema
LSQ/SEVD WC2H 10 D6
UK Passport Office
PIM SW1V 15 K6
Underhill Infant School
BAR EN5 20 C6
Unicorn Primary School
BECK BR3 198 E2
Unicorn School
RCH/KEW TW9 137 G2
Unicorn Theatre
STHWK SE1 19 H2
United Medical & Dental Schools
STHWK SE1 17 G4
Unity Trading Estate
WFD IG8 53 H6
University Church of Christ the King
STPAN WC1H 4 C7
University College Hospital
CAMTN NW1 4 B6
HAMP NW3 83 H4
University College London
FITZ W1T 10 B1
STPAN WC1H 4 C6
University College London, Astor College
FITZ W1T 10 B1
University College London C/O The Chorley Institute
GWRST WC1E 4 C7
University College London Medical School
FITZ W1T 10 A1
University College London Obstetrics Hospital
GWRST WC1E 4 B7
University College School
HAMP NW3 83 G3
University Hospital Lewisham
LEW SE13 144 E6
University of California
WHALL SW1A 16 A1
University of East London
BARK IG11 91 G2
CAN/RD E16 108 A6
PLSTW E13 107 F2
SRTFD E15 88 B6
SRTFD E15 106 D1
University of Greenwich
DART DA1 171 J4
GNWCH SE10 125 G5
WOOL/PLUM SE18 127 F3
University of Greenwich (Mansion Site)
ELTH/MOT SE9 167 H1
University of Greenwich (Southwood Site)
ELTH/MOT SE9 167 H2
University of Greenwich Sports Ground
ELTH/MOT SE9 146 D5
ELTH/MOT SE9 167 H2
University of London
BAY/PAD W2 8 A4
BMSBY WC1N 5 F7
CLKNW EC1R 5 K6
GWRST WC1E 10 D1
MBLAR W1H 8 D3
STHWK SE1 18 E1
STPAN WC1H 4 D6
University of London Athletics Ground
NWMAL KT3 192 D2
University of West London
EA W5 97 J6
EA W5 116 D1
University of Westminster
CAMTN NW1 4 A6
CAVSQ/HST W1G 9 K3
CHSWK W4 137 K2
GTPST W1W 9 K1
HRW HA1 61 G4
University of Westminster - Environment
MHST W1U 9 G1
Uphall Primary School
IL IG1 90 B3
Upland Primary School
BXLYHN DA7 149 G4
Uplands Business Park
WALTH E17 51 F5
Upney ⊖
BARK IG11 91 F5
Upper Holloway ⊖
ARCH N19 66 D6
Upper Montagu Street Clinic
CAMTN NW1 8 E1
Upper Tooting Independent High School
TOOT SW17 160 D4
Upton Cross Primary School
PLSTW E13 89 F6
Upton Day Hospital
BXLYHS DA6 149 F5
Upton Lane Medical Centre
FSTGT E7 89 F4
Upton Park ⊖
PLSTW E13 89 G6
Upton Primary School
BXLY DA5 149 F6
Upton Road School
BXLYHS DA6 149 F6
The Urdang Academy
FSBYW WC1X 5 J5
LSQ/SEVD WC2H 10 E4
Ursuline High School
RYNPK SW20 177 G3
Ursuline Preparatory School
RYNPK SW20 177 G3
Uxbridge College
HYS/HAR UB3 94 E6
Uxbridge County Court
HYS/HAR UB3 94 C4
Uxendon Manor JMI School
KTN/HRWW/WS HA3 62 A2
Vale Farm Sports Centre
ALP/SUD HA0 79 H2
Vale Industrial Estate
WATW WD18 26 A3
The Vale Medical Centre
FSTH SE23 164 B4
Valence House Museum & Library
BCTR RM8 73 K6
Valence Primary School
BCTR RM8 73 K6
Valentine High School
GNTH/NBYPK IG2 72 A3
Valentines High Lower School
GNTH/NBYPK IG2 72 B2
Vale Park Industrial
ACT W3 118 B2
The Vale School
SKENS SW7 120 B3
Valley Link Business centre
PEND EN3 37 G1
Valley Link Business Estate
PEND EN3 37 G1
Valley Primary School
HAYES BR2 183 J5
Valmar Trading Estate
CMBW SE5 142 D2
V & A Museum of Childhood
BETH E2 104 E2
Vanbrugh Theatre
GWRST WC1E 4 C7
Vaudeville Theatre
COVGDN WC2E 11 F5
Vaughan Primary School
RYLN/HDSTN HA2 60 C3
Vauxhall ⇌ ⊖
VX/NE SW8 121 K6
Vauxhall Primary School
LBTH SE11 122 A5
Velodrome
OLYMPICPK E20 87 K3
Vernon House Special School
WLSDN NW10 80 E3
Vestry Hall
MTCM CR4 178 E6
Vestry House Museum
WALTH E17 69 K1
Vicarage Fields Health Clinic
BARK IG11 90 C5
The Vicarage Field Shopping Centre
BARK IG11 90 C5
Vicarage Primary School
EHAM E6 107 K2
Vicars Green Primary School
GFD/PVL UB6 97 J1
V I Components Industrial Park
ERITH DA8 130 B5
Victoria ⇌ ⊖
PIM SW1V 15 K6
Victoria & Albert Museum
SKENS SW7 14 B5
Victoria Business Centre
WELL DA16 148 B3
Victoria Bus Station
PIM SW1V 15 K5
Victoria Chiropractic Clinic
SKENS SW7 14 E3
Victoria Coach Station
BGVA SW1W 15 J7
Victoria Hall
FNCH N3 46 D4
Victoria Industrial Estate
ACT W3 99 F4
Victoria Industrial Park
DART DA1 151 G6
Victoria Junior School
FELT TW13 154 A3
Victoria Medical Centre
PIM SW1V 16 B7
Victoria Palace Theatre
BGVA SW1W 15 K5
Victoria Park Industrial Centre
HOM E9 87 H5
Victoria Place Shopping Centre
BGVA SW1W 15 K6
Victoria Rail/Air Terminal
PIM SW1V 15 K6
Victoria Retail Park
RSLP HA4 77 H3
Victoria Wharf
POP/IOD E14 105 G6
Victoria Wharf Industrial Estate
DEPT SE8 124 B5
Victor Seymour Infant School
CAR SM5 209 K1
Victory Business Centre
ISLW TW7 136 A5
Victory Day School
THHTH CR7 196 D1
Victory Primary School
WALW SE17 18 D6
Viking Business Centre
ROMW/RG RM7 74 E4
Viking Primary School
NTHLT UB5 95 H2
Village Infant School
DAGE RM10 92 C5
Village Operations Support Centre
SRTFD E15 88 A2
The Village School
CDALE/KGS NW9 62 E1
HAMP NW3 83 K4
Villiers High School
STHL UB1 115 F1
The Vine Clinic
KUTN/CMB KT2 175 F2
Vine Medical Centre
E/WMO/HCT KT8 173 H6
The Vines School
BTSEA SW11 141 F5
The Vineyard Primary School
RCHPK/HAM TW10 157 F1
Vinopolis, City of Wine
STHWK SE1 12 D7
Vinters' Hall
BLKFR EC4V 12 D5
VIP Trading Estate
CHARL SE7 126 B4
Virginia Primary School
BETH E2 7 J5
Virgo Fidelis Convent Schools
NRWD SE19 180 D2
Visage School of Hair & Beauty
ELTH/MOT SE9 167 F1
Vision College of Technology
HOM E9 87 J4
Vita et Pax School
STHGT/OAK N14 22 B6
Vittoria Primary School
IS N1 5 J1
Voyager Business Estate
BERM/RHTH SE16 123 H3
Vue Cinema
ACT W3 98 C3
CROY/NA CR0 196 A6
DAGW RM9 92 A6
FUL/PGN SW6 139 K1
HAMP NW3 83 G4
HRW HA1 60 E3
LSQ/SEVD WC2H 10 D5
NFNCH/WDSPK N12 47 H3
ROMW/RG RM7 75 G2
SHB W12 119 G2
Vulcan Business Centre
CROY/NA CR0 214 C6
Waddon ⇌
CROY/NA CR0 211 G2
Waddon Clinic
CROY/NA CR0 211 G3
Waddon Marsh ⊖
CROY/NA CR0 196 B6
Wadham Lodge Sports Centre
WALTH E17 51 K4
Wadsworth Business Centre
GFD/PVL UB6 97 J1
The Waldegrave Clinic
TEDD TW11 174 A1
Waldegrave Girls School
WHTN TW2 155 J5
Waldo Industrial Estate
BMLY BR1 184 B6
Waldorf School of SW London
BAL SW12 161 H4
Waldron Health Centre & Surgery
NWCR SE14 144 C1
Walker Primary School
STHGT/OAK N14 34 D4
The Wallace Centre
DEPT SE8 124 E6
The Wallace Collection
MHST W1U 9 G3
Wallbrook Business Centre
HSLWW TW4 134 A4
Wall Hotel
LOTH EC2R 12 E3
Wallington ⇌
WLGTN SM6 210 B4
Wallington County Grammar School
WLGTN SM6 210 B1
Wallington High School for Girls
WLGTN SM6 210 B6
Walmer Road Clinic
NTGHL W11 100 C6
Walm Lane Clinic
CRICK NW2 82 B3
Walnuts Leisure Centre
ORP BR6 202 B5
Walnuts Shopping Centre
ORP BR6 202 B5
Walnut Tree Walk Primary School
LBTH SE11 17 J6
Waltham Forest College
WALTH E17 50 E6
WALTH E17 51 K6
Waltham Forest Magistrates Court
WALTH E17 51 K6
Waltham Forest Pool & Track
WALTH E17 51 K5
Waltham Forest Theatre
WALTH E17 51 H6
Walthamstow Academy
WALTH E17 51 H4
Walthamstow Business Centre
WALTH E17 52 A5
Walthamstow Central ⇌ ⊖
WALTH E17 69 J2
Walthamstow Marsh Nature Reserve
CLPT E5 68 D4
Walthamstow Queens Road ⊖
WALTH E17 69 J2
Walthamstow School for Girls
WALTH E17 69 K1
Walton Business Centre
WOT/HER KT12 188 A4
Walton Casuals FC
WOT/HER KT12 188 A2
Walton Community Hospital
WOT/HER KT12 188 A6
Walton Swimming Pool
WOT/HER KT12 188 A5
Walworth Lower Secondary School
WALW SE17 122 E5
Walworth Town Hall
WALW SE17 18 C7
Wandle Park ⊖
CROY/NA CR0 196 B6
Wandle Recreation Centre
WAND/EARL SW18 160 A1
Wandle Trading Estate
MTCM CR4 194 E4
Wandle Valley School Sutton Parent Partnership
CAR SM5 194 D4
Wandsworth Adult College
BTSEA SW11 141 F2
TOOT SW17 160 D4
Wandsworth Cemetery
WAND/EARL SW18 160 B3
Wandsworth Common ⇌
TOOT SW17 160 D2
Wandsworth County Court
PUT/ROE SW15 139 H6
Wandsworth Road ⇌ ⊖
VX/NE SW8 141 H3
Wandsworth Town ⇌
WAND/EARL SW18 140 A5
Wandsworth Trading Estate
WAND/EARL SW18 160 A2
Wanstead ⊖
WAN E11 71 F3
Wanstead CC
WAN E11 71 F4
Wanstead CE Primary School
WAN E11 70 E2
Wanstead Golf Club
WAN E11 71 G4
Wanstead High School
WAN E11 71 G3
Wanstead Hospital
WAN E11 71 F1
Wanstead Leisure Centre
WAN E11 71 G3